2017 Edition for 2016 Returns

PREPARING YOUR INCOME TAX RETURNS

D1308319

WITHDRAWN

Wolters Kluwer Canada Limited
300-90 Sheppard Avenue East
Toronto Ontario
M2N 6X1
1 800 268 4522
www.wolterskluwer.ca

Published by Wolters Kluwer Canada Limited

Important Disclaimer: This publication is sold with the understanding that (1) the authors and editors are not responsible for the results of any actions taken on the basis of information in this work, nor for any errors or omissions; and (2) the publisher is not engaged in rendering legal, accounting or other professional services. The publisher, and the authors and editors, expressly disclaim all and any liability to any person, whether a purchaser of this publication or not, in respect of anything and of the consequences of anything done or omitted to be done by any such person in reliance, whether whole or partial, upon the whole or any part of the contents of this publication. If legal advice or other expert assistance is required, the services of a competent professional person should be sought.

Library and Archives Canada has catalogued this publication as follows:

1. Income tax — Canada — Popular works. 2. Tax returns — Canada — Popular works.

I. Wolters Kluwer Canada Limited. II. Title: Preparing your income tax returns, Canada and provinces.

HJ4661 343.7105'2 C75-032880-0

ISBN 978-1-55496-912-8

© 2016, Wolters Kluwer Canada Limited

All rights reserved. No part of this work covered by the publisher's copyright may be reproduced or copied in any form or by any means (graphic, electronic or mechanical, including photocopying, recording, taping, or information and retrieval systems) without the written permission of the publisher.

A licence, however, is hereby given by the publisher:

(a) to a lawyer to make a copy of any part of this publication to give to a judge or other presiding officer or to other parties in making legal submissions in judicial proceedings;

(b) to a judge or other presiding officer to reproduce any part of this publication in any decision in judicial proceedings; or

(c) to anyone to reproduce any part of this publication for the purposes of parliamentary proceedings.

"Judicial proceedings" includes proceedings before any court, tribunal or person having authority to decide any matter affecting a person's legal rights or liabilities.

Typeset by Wolters Kluwer Canada Limited.

Printed in the United States.

Foreword

The principal objective of this book is to provide a reasonably complete, easy-to-understand, practical guide for those who prepare T1 individual tax returns.

It is Wolters Kluwer's goal to provide a high standard of practical and accessible guidance to T1 return preparation. To this end, we have assembled a team of experts, listed below, who contribute their specialized knowledge to the content of this book in order to provide tax professionals with the excellent return preparation support that they have come to expect from Wolters Kluwer.

Wolters Kluwer also acknowledges the assistance and co-operation of officials in the Canada Revenue Agency, the Department of Finance, and the provincial and territorial authorities. Their knowledge and assistance is greatly appreciated.

Because of the complexity of the Canadian *Income Tax Act* and the fact that relatively few of its provisions have been interpreted by the courts or by the CRA, it is not possible to provide answers to all of the questions that may arise. Also, some of the interpretations suggested in this book may not be in accordance with those eventually adopted by the tax authorities. However, it is hoped that the book will answer all of the common questions which arise. It is not, nor could any book of this kind be, a substitute for expert professional accounting or legal advice in appropriate circumstances.

CONTRIBUTORS

Dentons

MNP LLP

Lori Adams, M.B.A., J.D.

Robert Boucher, CPA, CA

Jennifer Corris, B.Math

Lisa Feil Payne, CPA, CGA

Joseph Frankovic, LL.B., LL.M., Ph.D., CFA

Harry Hoogkamp, CPA, CMA, CBV

Cameron Mancell, CFP®

Roderick McBey, LL.B., T.E.P.

John Nicoletti, CPA, CA

Jacques Roberge, B.Comm.

Peter Tomlinson, LL.B.

December 2016

Wolters Kluwer Canada Limited

Table of Contents

How to Use Preparing Your Income Tax Returns

This book on personal income tax has been written as a manual to provide straightforward answers to your questions.

It is not necessary to read this book from cover to cover.

At the front of this book, you will find a Table of Contents showing a breakdown of topical chapters. Detailed tables of contents also appear at the beginning of each chapter.

A summary of Recent Tax Changes can be found in the front matter to this publication, providing an overview of new tax developments since the last edition. Specific information on recent changes can also be found at the beginning of each topical chapter.

Quick reference charts at the front of the book show key tax rates and amounts for the current taxation year. This is followed by a convenient Client Organizer template.

As well, at the end of this publication, a comprehensive Topical Index has been provided to make it easy for you to find the specific information you need, quickly.

The rates, credits and exemptions set out in the current commentary are those applicable to the 2016 tax year. In some instances we provide five years of historical information where amounts have changed from year to year. This book does not provide any 2017 rates, as these were not available at the time of publication.

PARAGRAPH NUMBER REFERENCES

References in the Topical Index, Table of Contents in each chapter and cross-references in the text are to *paragraph numbers* (¶). The first one or two digits of the paragraph number indicate the chapter in which that paragraph is located; for example, ¶330 is in Chapter 3, Employment Income and Deductions, and ¶1106 is in Chapter 11, Personal Tax Amount Credits. This referencing system should help you to go directly to the particular examples or commentary you are looking for. The gaps in the numbering of paragraphs are provided for use in other years' editions and do not represent any missing material in your copy of this book.

DETAILED INFORMATION, EXAMPLES, AND RECENT CHANGES

Detailed information is contained in each chapter, including numerous illustrative examples. At the beginning of most of the chapters, immediately following the detailed Table of Contents is a box listing the lines of the T1 Personal Tax Return, CRA Forms and Guides, and other CRA interpretive materials related to topics that are covered in that chapter. In addition, each chapter begins with a "What You Should Know" feature detailing recent changes in the topical area. "Specific Questions and Answers" are provided at the conclusion of some chapters. Key forms are no longer reproduced at the end of each chapter. Instead, key forms can be found on the CRA website at: http://www.cra-arc.gc.ca/formspubs/menu-eng.html

PROPOSED LEGISLATION

This edition features proposed commentary due to changes to the Act relating to legislative amendments and outstanding bills not yet enacted as at November 30, 2016. The proposed commentary is highlighted in a shaded, boxed format, consistent with how we publish proposed amendments in our other publications, and the commentary reflects the changes of that legislation when enacted.

Example:

Commentary on Bill C-29 Measures (Oct. 25, 2016)

Note: When Bill C-29, October 25, 2016, achieves Royal Assent, the commentary will be modified to read:

Effective January 1, 2017, the eligible capital property rules have been repealed and replaced by a new Class 14.1 of depreciable property. Property that previously was eligible capital property is now depreciable capital property, and expenditures and receipts that previously were accounted for under the eligible capital property rules are now accounted for under the rules for depreciable property and capital property.

A NOTE ON BILL C-2

Although Bill C-2, December 9, 2015, has not been enacted as at the date of writing of this publication (November 30, 2016), it is expected that this bill will ultimately pass as originally presented. Therefore, we have shown the measures proposed by it as being in effect as at January 1, 2016. The Canada Revenue Agency has accepted all the rate changes proposed by this bill as being in effect as at January 1, 2016.

SOURCE REFERENCES

Interested readers will find, at the end of all paragraphs which include information based directly on official sources, source references for the material discussed in that paragraph. Among other sources, these include references to the following:

ITA — The federal *Income Tax Act*

ITR — The federal *Income Tax Regulations*

ITAR — The federal *Income Tax Application Rules, 1971*

IT — Interpretation Bulletin (federal). Note that Interpretation Bulletins are gradually being replaced by the CRA with Income Tax Folios. As this publication was written, the CRA has added an "Archived Content" notice to all IT Bulletins on its website. However, this CRA notice states that the archive classification has no effect on the status or reliability of IT Bulletins, until each bulletin is cancelled and replaced by an Income Tax Folio. Although the content of IT Bulletins is no longer being updated by the CRA, these publications are current to the effective date shown in each publication. As IT Bulletins are replaced by Folios, the references in this text are being updated.

IC — Information Circular (federal)

ITTN — *Income Tax Technical News*. Note that ITTNs are gradually being replaced by the CRA with Income Tax Folios. As this publication was written, the CRA has added an "Archived Content" notice to all ITTNs on its website. However, this notice states that the archive classification has no effect on the status or reliability of ITTNs, which are current to the effective date stated in each publication. As ITTNs are replaced by Folios, references in this text are being updated.

CPP — The *Canada Pension Plan*

DTC — *Dominion Tax Cases*, published by Wolters Kluwer Limited.

ETA — *Excise Tax Act*

Income Tax Folio — Income Tax Folios

I.R.S. Code — The *Internal Revenue Code* (U.S.)

Window on Canadian Tax — *Window on Canadian Tax*, a service published by Wolters Kluwer Limited that provides commentary on CRA Documents (see below)

CRA Documents — The Canada Revenue Agency's technical opinions, rulings, and interpretations. They are published in Wolters Kluwer *Tax Window Files*, an electronic product produced by Wolters Kluwer Limited. The number references are to numbers assigned by the CRA and they can be searched by this number in any database of these official opinions.

CTF Round Table — Canadian Tax Foundation Annual Conference Reports

AITA — Alberta *Income Tax Act*

APITA — Alberta *Personal Income Tax Act*

BCITA — British Columbia *Income Tax Act*

MITA — The Manitoba *Income Tax Act*

NBITA — New Brunswick *Income Tax Act*

NITA — Newfoundland and Labrador *Income Tax Act, 2000*

NSITA — Nova Scotia *Income Tax Act*

NUITA — Nunavut *Income Tax Act*

NWTITA — Northwest Territories *Income Tax Act*

OITA — Ontario *Income Tax Act* (for years prior to 2009)

OTA — Ontario *Taxation Act, 2007*

OTAR — Ontario *Taxation Act Regulations*

OITAR — Ontario *Income Tax Regulations* (for years prior to 2009)

QTA — Quebec *Taxation Act*

QTAR — Quebec *Taxation Act Regulations*

IMP — Interprétation Revenu Québec (Impôts)

PEIITA — Prince Edward Island *Income Tax Act*

SITA — The *Income Tax Act, 2000* (Saskatchewan)

YITA — Yukon *Income Tax Act*

Recent Tax Changes

The tax changes announced since the last edition of the book are summarized on a chapter-by-chapter basis at the beginning of each chapter. If you have only a few specific areas of concern, please turn to the beginning of the chapters which cover the subject matter that is most relevant to you. In this space, we provide a general overview of the significant personal income tax developments that relate to the 2016 tax year.

2016 FEDERAL BUDGET

Personal Income Tax Credits

Budget 2016 replaced the former Canada Child Tax Benefit with the new Canada Child Benefit. The new benefit is designed to increase the amount that the average Canadian family receives. The first payment of the new benefit amount occurred on July 20, 2016. See ¶1498.

Effective for 2016 and subsequent taxation years, qualifying teachers may claim a new refundable school supplies tax credit of up to $150 per year with respect to eligible school supplies expenses. See ¶1360b.

The Budget also repealed a number of personal tax credits. These include the children's arts and fitness credits (¶1356a and ¶1356), the family tax cut (¶1317), and the education and textbook credits (¶1337).

Budget 2016 restored the labour-sponsored venture capital corporation (LSVCC) tax credit to 15% for share purchases of provincially registered LSVCCs for 2016 and subsequent tax years. The tax credit for federally registered LSVCCs remains at 5% for 2016 and will be eliminated in 2017. See ¶1466.

Business Measures

The small business deduction rate for Canadian-controlled private corporations is maintained at 17.5% for 2016 and subsequent years (the 2015 Budget had proposed the rate be 18% for 2017, 18.5% for 2018 and 19% after 2018). The federal rate for eligible small business income is therefore 10.5% (28% rate minus the 17.5% deduction). See ¶404.22.

The government followed-through on its prior promise to transition the eligible capital property regime to the capital cost allowance rules. The changes are scheduled to take effect as of January 1, 2017. See ¶770a.

Budget 2016 again expanded CCA Classes 43.1 and 43.2, this time to allow for accelerated CCA rates for electric vehicle charging stations and electrical energy storage property. See ¶889.05.

The Budget introduced new rules to clarify the tax treatment of emissions allowances, which affects businesses that are required to obtain allowances for their CO2 emissions. See ¶758.25 and ¶766.40.

Budget 2016 announced amendments to ensure that the back-to-back rules that apply to cross-border interest payments for Part XIII withholding tax purposes will apply to arrangements that involve multiple intermediaries. See ¶2080.01. The Budget also extended the back-to-back rules to cross-border rent and royalty payments, and certain "character substitution" arrangements. See ¶2080.05.

Investments, Insurance, and Tax-Deferred Plans

Budget 2016 introduced a rule which ensures that the interest accrued upon a sale of a "linked note" is included in the vendor's income as interest rather than as a capital gain. The measure will apply to sales of linked notes after 2016. See ¶440.

The Budget also introduced rules regarding the taxation of "switch fund" mutual fund corporations. Under the former rules, investors were able to exchange shares of one class of the mutual fund corporation for shares of another class, and could rely on section 51 to deem the switch not to be a disposition for income tax purposes. After 2016, switches within such a fund will trigger a deemed disposition. See ¶588.

The Budget introduced a new rule applicable to dispositions of interests in life insurance policies after March 21, 2016 to non-arm's length persons. See ¶981.

The TFSA annual contribution limit for 2016 was reduced to $5,500 (from $10,000 for 2015). See ¶478.

The Budget announced rules that will ensure that derivative instruments are not considered inventory for income tax purposes and further rules relating to the taxation of derivatives. See ¶758.20.

OTHER CHANGES

Applicable as of July 1, 2015, Bill C-15 enacted a set of tax rules that apply to farmers with ownership in the reorganized Canadian Wheat Board. The new tax rules applicable to farmers' ownership in the Wheat Board are explained at ¶1788.

On October 3, 2016, the Department of Finance announced tax measures that narrow the circumstances under which taxpayers are eligible for principal residence exemption. Amendments apply to non-residents, taxpayers who were non-resident when they acquired their property, and trusts. Moreover, the CRA now requires that a tax-free disposition of a principal residence be reported on Schedule 3. See ¶553 and ¶2040 under "Principal Residence Exemption".

On September 16, 2016, the Department of Finance released a series of draft technical changes, many of which are considered "housekeeping" amendments. Several of these proposed changes are reflected throughout the book.

Applicable to payments made after 2015 and originally announced by Budget 2015, a new withholding tax exemption process applies to non-resident individuals earning employment income in Canada who are employed by a non-resident employer. See ¶2020.10 and ¶2080b.

Provincial Tax Changes

Since last year's edition, many personal tax changes have been announced at the provincial/territorial level. New Brunswick eliminated its highest personal tax rate and reduced its second-highest rate. In contrast, Newfoundland and Labrador has increased its personal tax rates for all income brackets. Many of the provinces have added, removed, or changed their personal tax credits. See the beginning of Chapter 15 (Chapter 16 for Quebec) for the pertinent changes to provincial/territorial income tax.

Administrative Changes

The CRA has continued cancelling interpretation bulletins and replacing its tax positions with the new income tax folios. Since last year's publication, the following new folios have been released:

- S1-F3-C4, *Moving Expenses*
- S2-F3-C2, *Benefits and Allowances Received from Employment*
- S3-F10-C1, *Qualified Investments — RRSPs, RESPs, RRIFs, RDSPs and TFSAs*
- S3-F10-C2, *Prohibited Investments — RRSPs, RRIFs and TFSAs*
- S4-F15-C1, *Manufacturing and Processing*
- S5-F4-C1, *Income Tax Reporting Currency*

As of February 15, 2016, individuals and their tax representatives may use the new Auto-fill functionality to complete parts of a tax return. Auto-fill will pull existing information that is in the CRA's files such as a T3 or T4 receipt, saving the preparer time that was previously spent locating receipts and inputting the boxes.

Beginning in February 2016, the CRA simplified the Notice of Assessment (NOA) in order to make it easier to understand for individual taxpayers.

Tables of Rates and Credits

[¶50] PERSONAL INCOME TAX RATES — 2016 (INCLUDING SURTAXES)

(See ¶62–¶64 for the federal rates for 2015–2017.)

		Basic Tax		Surtax
		Rates	Brackets	
Federal[1]		15.00%	$0	
		20.50%	$45,282	
		26.00%	$90,563	
		29.00%	$140,388	
		33.00%	$200,000	
Provincial or Territorial[2]	Alberta	10.00%	$0	
		12.00%	$125,000	
		13.00%	$150,000	
		14.00%	$200,000	
		15.00%	$300,000	
	British Columbia	5.06%	$0	
		7.70%	$38,210	
		10.50%	$76,421	
		12.29%	$87,741	
		14.70%	$106,543	
	Manitoba	10.80%	$0	
		12.75%	$31,000	
		17.40%	$67,000	
	New Brunswick	9.68%	$0	
		14.82%	$40,492	
		16.52%	$80,985	No surtax
		17.84%	$131,664	
		20.30%	$150,000	
	Newfoundland and Labrador	8.20%	$0	
		13.50%	$35,148	
		14.55%	$70,295	
		15.80%	$125,500	
		16.80%	$175,700	
	Northwest Territories	5.90%	$0	
		8.60%	$41,011	
		12.20%	$82,024	
		14.05%	$133,353	
	Nova Scotia	8.79%	$0	
		14.95%	$29,590	
		16.67%	$59,180	
		17.50%	$93,000	
		21.00%	$150,000	
	Nunavut	4.00%	$0	
		7.00%	$43,176	
		9.00%	$86,351	
		11.50%	$140,388	
	Ontario	5.05%	$0	
		9.15%	$41,536	
		11.16%	$83,075	20% of tax above $4,484 + 36% of tax above $5,739
		12.16%	$150,000	
		13.16%	$220,000	
	Prince Edward Island	9.80%	$0	
		13.80%	$31,984	10% of tax above $12,500
		16.70%	$63,969	
	Quebec[1]	16.00%	$0	
		20.00%	$42,390	
		24.00%	$84,780	
		25.75%	$103,150	
	Saskatchewan	11.00%	$0	
		13.00%	$44,601	No surtax
		15.00%	$127,430	
	Yukon	6.40%	$0	
		9.00%	$45,282	
		10.90%	$90,563	
		12.80%	$140,388	
		15.00%	$500,000	
Non-residents[3]		7.20%	$0	
		9.84%	$45,282	
		12.48%	$90,563	No surtax
		13.92%	$140,388	
		15.84%	$200,000	

Notes:

1. In Quebec, federal tax is reduced by 16.5% for Quebec's abatement of basic federal tax.
2. Individuals may also be subject to provincial health levies or other personal tax levies (i.e., Newfoundland and Labrador temporary deficit reduction levy). See **Provincial Health Care Premiums and Personal Tax Levies – 2016**.
3. Instead of provincial or territorial tax, non-residents pay an additional 48% of basic federal tax on income taxable in Canada that is not earned in a province or territory. Non-residents are subject to provincial or territorial rates (in this table) on employment income earned, and business income connected with a permanent establishment, in the respective province or territory. Different rates may apply to non-residents in other circumstances.

[¶52] PERSONAL TAX CREDITS — 2016

(See ¶65 for the federal personal amounts from 2012–2016.)

The two tables below contain information concerning select non-refundable personal tax credits. The first contains the federal and provincial/territorial rates used in the calculation of personal tax credits. The second shows the value of the credits. Provinces and territories use their own prescribed amounts to determine their personal tax credits.

		Personal tax credit rates (See table below for some limitations)													
		Federal	**Alt.**	**B.C.**	**Man.**	**N.B.**	**Nfld. & Lab.**	**N.W.T.**	**N.S.**	**Nun.**	**Ont.**	**P.E.I.**	**Que.**[1]	**Sask.**	**Yukon**
General factor[2] / **Charitable donations**	First $200	15%[4]	10%	5.06%	10.8%	9.68%	8.2%	5.9%	8.79%	4%	5.05%	9.8%	20%	11%	6.4%
Charitable donations	Amount over $200	29% or 33%[4]	21%	14.7%	17.4%	17.95%	16.8%	14.05%	21%	11.5%	11.16%	16.7%	24%[1]	15%	12.8%
Dividend tax credit[3] (on grossed-up amount)	Eligible	15.0198%	10%	10%	8%	13.5%	5.4%	11.5%	8.85%	5.51%	10%	10.5%	11.9%	11%	15%
	Non-eligible	10.5217%	3.08%	2.47%	0.7835%	3.625%	4.1% or 3.5%[5]	6%	3.33%	2.91%	4.2863%	3.05%	7.05%	3.367%	3.14%

		Federal amounts	Maximum value (before surtaxes) of credits that are based on prescribed amounts													
			Federal[9]	**Alt.**	**B.C.**	**Man.**	**N.B.**	**Nfld. & Lab.**	**N.W.T.**	**N.S.**	**Nun.**	**Ont.**	**P.E.I.**	**Que.**[1]	**Sask.**	**Yukon**
Basic		$11,474[6]	$1,721[6]	$1,845	$507	$986	$945	$722	$831	$745	$518	$506	$784	$2,310[1]	$1,743	$734[6]
Spouse					$434		$802	$590				$429	$666	N/A		
Equivalent to spouse																
Age 65		$7,125	$1,069	$514	$228	$403	$461	$461	$406	$364	$388	$247	$369	$497[1]	$531[12]	$456
Disability	Basic	$8,001	$1,200	$1,423	$381	$667	$765	$487	$674	$645	$518	$408	$675	$525		$512
	Under 18 supplement	$4,667	$700							$303			$394			$299
Infirm dependant (18 or over)		$6,788[6]	$1,018[6]	$1,068	$222	$389	$446	$229	$275	$246	$187	$238	$240	N/A[1]	$1,027	$434[6]
Caregiver		$4,667[6]	$700[6]							$431						$299[6]
Pension income		$2,000	$300	$142	$51	$108	$97	$82	$59	$103	$80	$70	$98	$442[1]	$110	$128
Adoption		$15,453	$2,318	$1,262	$782	$1,080	N/A	$974	N/A			$617	N/A	N/A[1]	N/A	$989
Children's fitness		N/A[7]	N/A[7]	N/A	$25[10]	$54	N/A					N/A[11]	N/A	N/A[1]	N/A[11]	N/A[7]
Children's arts		$250[7]	$38[7]													$32[7]
Canada Pension Plan (CPP)		$2,544	$382	$254	$129	$275	$246	$209	$150	$224	$102	$128	$249	N/A	$280	$163
Quebec Pension Plan (QPP)		$2,737[1]	$411	N/A										N/A[1]	N/A	
Employment Insurance (EI)	not in Quebec	$955	$143	$96	$48	$103	$92	$78	$56	$84	$38	$48	$94	N/A	$105	$61
	in Quebec	$772[1]	$116	N/A										N/A[1]	N/A	
Canada Employment		$1,161	$174	N/A												$74
Education (per month)	Full-time	$400[8]	$60	$72	$10	$43	$39	$16	$24	$18	$16	$27[8]	$39	$426[1]	$44	$26[8]
	Part-time	$120[8]	$18	$22	$3	$13	$12	$5	$7	$5	$5	$8[8]	$12	N/A	$13	$8[8]
Textbook (per month)	Full-time	$65[8]	$10	N/A							$3	N/A				$4[8]
	Part-time	$20[8]	$3								$1					$1[8]
												× 1.2 or × 1.56	*× 1.1*			

Factors at bottom of table increase value of credits to reflect surtaxes.[13]

Notes:

1. See below for Quebec's special credits and rules.
2. The general factor, multiplied by the federal (or provincial/territorial) amount, yields the value of the federal (or provincial/territorial) credit.
3. Eligible dividends are designated as such by the payor. They are grossed up by 38% and include dividends paid by:
   - public corporations or other corporations that are not Canadian-controlled private corporations (CCPCs), are resident in Canada and are subject to the federal general corporate income tax rate (i.e., 15% in 2016); or
   - CCPCs, to the extent that the CCPC's income is:
     - not investment income (other than eligible dividends from public corporations); and
     - subject to the federal general corporate income tax rate (i.e., the income is active business income not subject to the federal small business rate).

   Non-eligible dividends are grossed up by 17% and include dividends paid out of either income eligible for the federal small business rate or a CCPC's investment income (other than eligible dividends received from public corporations).
4. A temporary First-time Donor's Super Credit (FDSC) can be claimed by first-time donors only once after 2012 and before 2018. The FDSC is an additional 25% tax credit (on top of claiming the Charitable Donations Tax Credit) on up to $1,000 of donations made after March 20, 2013.

   For charitable donations exceeding $200, the tax credit rate is:
   - 33% for donations made after 2015, to the extent the individual has income that is subject to the federal 33% personal income tax rate; and
   - 29% for all other donations
5. For Newfoundland and Labrador, the non-eligible dividend tax credit rate is:
   - 4.1% for dividends received before July 1, 2016; and
   - 3.5% for dividends received after June 30, 2016.

6. Caregivers of dependants with a mental or physical infirmity can claim the Family Caregiver Tax Credit. This credit, which is valued at $318 (i.e., $2,121 x 15%), is:
   - already included in the infirm dependant (18 or over) tax credit;
   - increases the spouse/equivalent to spouse or caregiver tax credit; or
   - claimed for infirm children under 18 as the family caregiver for infirm children under 18 tax credit.

   Only one Family Caregiver Tax Credit can be claimed for each infirm dependant. The Yukon has paralleled this credit, with an increase of $136 (i.e., $2,121 x 6.4%).
7. A federal (and Yukon) refundable tax credit is available for children's fitness, providing up to $75 ($64 in the Yukon) per year for children under 17, and up to $150 ($96 in the Yukon) per year for children under 19 who qualify for the disability tax credit. The federal children's fitness and children's arts tax credits will be eliminated after December 31, 2016. However, the Yukon will retain these credits and not mirror the federal elimination of these credits.
8. The federal (and Yukon) education and textbook tax credits will be eliminated after December 31, 2016, but unused credits can be carried forward for use after 2016. The Ontario education tax credit will also be eliminated (the Ontario credit can be claimed in respect of months of study before September 2017 and unused credits can be carried forward after 2017 if the taxpayer remains resident in Ontario).
9. In Quebec, federal values are reduced by 16.5%.
10. In British Columbia, parents can claim a children's fitness equipment tax credit that equals 50% of the BC children's fitness credit amount claimed.
11. A refundable tax credit for children is available in Ontario for fitness and certain non-fitness activities; it will be eliminated as of January 1, 2017. Saskatchewan's credit for cultural, recreational and sports activity fees was eliminated, retroactive to January 1, 2016.
12. In Saskatchewan, an additional credit of $140 is available to individuals who are 65 or older, regardless of their income.
13. For taxpayers in Ontario or Prince Edward Island affected by provincial surtaxes, the value of the credits shown will be higher by the factors indicated. For example, for a taxpayer in Ontario's top bracket, the $506 shown for the basic Ontario credit would be worth $789 (i.e., $506 × 1.56).

[¶53] QUEBEC'S SPECIAL CREDITS AND RULES — 2016

The following special rules apply to Quebec's non-refundable tax credits:

- the minimum basic personal credit, the Quebec Pension Plan (QPP), Employment Insurance (EI), Health Services Fund and Quebec Parental Insurance Plan (QPIP) credits are combined into a single basic personal credit of $11,550 (value of $2,310);
- employees, employers and the self-employed must contribute to the QPIP, from which maternity, adoption and parental leave benefits are paid. As a result, federal EI premiums are lower for Quebec employees than for other employees ($772 instead of $955). A federal credit is available to individuals for QPIP premiums;
- an adult student can transfer the unused portion of the basic personal credit to a parent, but if this transfer is made, the other dependant (18 or over) credit of $3,100 (value of $620) cannot be claimed for that student;
- most non-refundable credits, such as the basic personal credit and the age credit, can be transferred to a spouse, if not used by the taxpayer;
- the age, pension and living alone credits are reduced if net family income exceeds $33,505;
- the age to qualify for the age credit will increase gradually from age 66 in 2016 to age 70 in 2020
- a person that lives alone or with a dependant can claim a credit of $1,355 (value of $271);
- a person that qualifies for the living alone credit and lives with an eligible student is eligible for an additional $1,675 (value of $335) credit;
- the maximum education credit of $2,130 (value of $426) per term (maximum two terms per year) can be claimed by a supporting Quebec parent (but is not transferable) for a child under 18 who attends post-secondary school full-time (part-time for infirm dependants);
- a student can transfer the unused portion of the tuition and examination tax credits to a parent or grandparent;
- the medical expense credit is based on the amount by which qualifying expenses exceed 3% of net family income (see below for details on the refundable medical expense credit); and
- effective 2017 taxation years, the charitable donation tax credit rate will increase to 25.75%, but only to the extent the individual has income subject to the top 25.75% tax rate.

Select Quebec refundable tax credits are listed in the table below.

	Details
Adoption	50% of eligible adoption expenses (maximum credit of $10,000)
Child care	26% to 75% of qualifying child care expenses (limits apply)
Youth activities[1]	Maximum credit is $80 for children age five to under 17; $160 for children with a disability, age five to under 19; available to families with incomes of $134,095 or less
Seniors' activities	Maximum credit is $40 for seniors age 70 or older with incomes of $40,865 or less
Caregivers[2]	Basic credit of $642[2] plus supplement of $525; the supplement is reduced if the dependant's income exceeds $23,330
Respite expenses for informal caregivers	30% of eligible respite expenses paid for the care of a person who resides with the caregiver and has a significant disability; maximum credit of $1,560 is reduced if family income exceeds $56,515
Informal caregivers	Maximum credit of $500 for each care recipient can be allocated to a volunteer who provides home respite to informal caregivers of the care recipient
Home support for seniors[3]	34% of eligible expenses; maximum credit of $6,630 for independent seniors (reduced if family income exceeds $56,515) and $8,670 for dependent seniors, age 70 and over; expenses eligible for this credit will not qualify for the medical expense credit
Medical	25% of medical expenses eligible for the non-refundable credit and 25% of amount deducted for impairment support products and services; maximum credit of $1,166 is reduced if family income exceeds $22,560

Notes:

1. The youth activities credit will increase in 2017 to up to $100 per child age five to under 17, and up to $200 per child with a disability age five to under 19.
2. The caregivers credit has three components:
   i. caregivers who house, in the strict sense of the term, an eligible relative – see table for details of the credit;
   ii. caregivers who cohabit with an eligible relative unable to live alone – see table for details of the credit; and
   iii. caregivers caring for an elderly spouse – these caregivers qualify only for a basic credit, which is higher than the basic credit for the first two components; and is $1,000 in 2016 (indexed thereafter).
3. For the home support for seniors credit, the tax credit rate and maximum credits will increase in 2017, to 35% (maximum credit of $6,825 for independent seniors and $8,925 for dependent seniors).

[¶54] CREDITS: FEDERAL LIMITATIONS AND OTHER INFORMATION — 2016

This table presents additional information related to federal credits. Other restrictions may also apply. The provinces/territories may have comparable thresholds and rules.

	Limitations	To whom the credit may be transferred	Carry-forward
Tuition	Credit is available only if at least $100 is paid in fees to an institution	Spouse, parent or grandparent (Maximum combined tuition, education and textbook credits transferable is $750)	Indefinite
Education	Credit is $60/month for full-time students and certain disabled part-time students; $18/month for other part-time students		
Textbook	Credit is $10/month for full-time students and certain disabled part-time students; $3/month for other part-time students		
Medical	Credit is based on amount by which qualifying medical expenses exceed the lesser of $2,237 and 3% of net income (generally, expenses for any twelve-month period ending in the year can be claimed)	Either spouse may claim	
CPP/QPP and EI	For employees, maximum credit is $525 (in Quebec, $440[1]); self-employed persons deduct 50% of CPP/QPP premiums paid for their own coverage (maximum deduction of $2,544; in Quebec $2,737) and claim a credit for the non-deductible half of premiums paid (maximum credit $382; in Quebec $343[1]); self-employed persons are not required to pay EI premiums, but may opt to do so	N/A	
Canada Employment	Credit is based on employment income		
Transit pass	Public transit passes (monthly or longer) and certain weekly and electronic payment cards for travel are eligible	Spouse or parent	
Student loan interest	Interest must be paid on qualifying student loans	N/A	5 years
Charitable donations	Eligible donations are limited to 75% of net income	Either spouse may claim	
Spousal and equivalent to spouse	Reduced by any net income of the spouse or qualifying dependant	N/A	
Infirm dependant	Reduced if dependant's income exceeds $6,807		
Caregiver	For providers of in-home care for an adult relative (reduced if relative's income exceeds $15,940)		
Age	Reduced if income exceeds $35,927	Spouse	
Pension	Credit is not available for CPP, QPP, Old Age Security or Guaranteed Income Supplement payments		
Adoption	Must be claimed in the year the adoption period ends	Either parent may claim	
Children's fitness	The credit is refundable. For more details, see note 7 under **Non-Refundable Personal Tax Credits**.		
Children's arts	Maximum credit is $38 for children under 17; $113 for children under 19 who qualify for the disability tax credit		
Disability — Basic	For individuals with severe and prolonged impairment	Spouse, parent, grandparent, child, grandchild, sibling, aunt, uncle, niece or nephew	
Disability — Under 18 supplement	Reduced if child care expenses and attendant care expenses (claimed as a medical expense for child) exceed $2,734		

Notes:

1. In Quebec, federal values are reduced by 16.5%. The amounts shown reflect this reduction.

[¶56] 2016 COMBINED MARGINAL TAX RATES

Individual Marginal Rates for 2016

(Prepared from information available as of June 15, 2016)

These tables show combined federal and provincial (or federal and territorial) marginal tax rates – the percentage of tax paid on the last dollar of income, or on additional income.

	Taxable income $11,474 to $45,282					Taxable income $45,282 to $90,563				
	Brackets	Ordinary income & interest	Capital gains	Canadian dividends		Brackets	Ordinary income & interest	Capital gains	Canadian dividends	
				Eligible[2]	Non-eligible[2]				Eligible[2]	Non-eligible
Federal only	$11,474	15.00%	7.50%	(0.03%) to 0%	5.24%	$45,282	20.50%	10.25%	7.56%	11.67%
Alberta	$18,451	25.00%	12.50%	(0.03%) to 0%	13.34%	$45,282	30.50%	15.25%	7.56%	19.77%
	$11,474	15.00%	7.50%	(0.03%) to 0%	5.24%					
British Columbia[1]	$38,210	22.70%	11.35%	(3.20%) to 0%	11.36%	$87,741	32.79%	16.40%	10.72%	23.16%
	$11,474	20.06%	10.03%	(6.84%) to 0%	8.27%	$76,421	31.00%	15.50%	8.25%	21.07%
						$45,282	28.20%	14.10%	4.39% to 7.56%	17.79%
Manitoba[1]	$31,000	27.75%	13.88%	6.53% to 6.56%	19.24%	$67,000	37.90%	18.95%	20.53%	31.12%
	$11,474	25.80%	12.90%	3.84% to 3.86%	16.96%	$45,282	33.25%	16.63%	14.12%	25.68%
New Brunswick[1]	$40,492	29.82%	14.91%	1.79% to 1.82%	18.34%	$80,985	37.02%	18.51%	11.73%	26.76%
	$11,474	24.68%	12.34%	(5.30%) to 0%	12.32%	$45,282	35.32%	17.66%	9.38%	24.77%
Newfoundland and	$35,148	28.50%	14.25%	11.15% to 11.18%	16.94%[5]	$70,295	35.05%	17.53%	20.19%	24.60%[5]
Labrador[1]	$11,474	23.20%	11.60%	3.84% to 3.86%	10.74%[5]	$45,282	34.00%	17.00%	18.74%	23.37%[5]
Non-resident[3]	$11,474	22.20%	11.10%	(0.04%) to 0%	7.75%	$45,282	30.34%	15.17%	11.19%	17.28%
Northwest Territories	$41,011	23.60%	11.80%	(4.03%) to 0%	8.28%	$82,024	32.70%	16.35%	8.53%	18.93%
	$14,081	20.90%	10.45%	(7.76%) to 0%	5.12% to 5.24%	$45,282	29.10%	14.55%	3.56% to 7.56%	14.72%
	$11,474	15.00%	7.50%	(0.03%) to 0%	5.24%					
Nova Scotia[1]	$29,590	29.95%	14.98%	8.39% to 8.42%	18.84%	$59,180	37.17%	18.59%	18.35%	27.28%
	$11,474	23.79%	11.90%	(0.11%) to 0%	11.63%	$45,282	35.45%	17.73%	15.98%	25.27%
Nunavut	$43,176	22.00%	11.00%	2.03% to 2.06%	10.02%	$86,351	29.50%	14.75%	12.38%	18.80%
	$12,947	19.00%	9.50%	(2.11%) to 0%	6.51%	$45,282	27.50%	13.75%	9.62%	16.46%
	$11,474	15.00%	7.50%	(0.03%) to 0%	5.24%					
Ontario[1]	$41,536	24.15%	12.08%	(1.20%) to 0%	10.93%	$86,177[4]	37.91%	18.95%	17.79%	27.03%
	$11,474	20.05%	10.03%	(6.86%) to 0%	6.13%	$83,075	33.89%	16.95%	12.24%	22.33%
						$73,142[4]	31.48%	15.74%	8.92%	19.51%
						$45,282	29.65%	14.83%	6.39% to 7.56%	17.37%
Prince Edward Island[1]	$31,984	28.80%	14.40%	4.53% to 4.55%	17.82%	$63,969	37.20%	18.60%	16.12%	27.65%
	$11,474	24.80%	12.40%	(0.99%) to 0%	13.14%	$45,282	34.30%	17.15%	12.12%	24.25%
Quebec	$42,390	32.53%	16.26%	11.16% to 11.18%	19.53%	$84,780	41.12%	20.56%	23.01%	29.58%
	$14,438	28.53%	14.26%	5.64% to 5.66%	14.85%	$45,282	37.12%	18.56%	17.49%	24.90%
	$11,474	12.53%	6.26%	(0.02%) to 0%	4.38%					
Saskatchewan	$44,601	28.00%	14.00%	2.73% to 2.76%	16.51%	$45,282	33.50%	16.75%	10.32%	22.95%
	$15,843	26.00%	13.00%	(0.03%) to 0%	14.17%					
	$11,474	15.00%	7.50%	(0.03%) to 0%	5.24%					
Yukon	$11,474	21.40%	10.70%	(11.90%) to 0%	9.05%	$45,282	29.50%	14.75%	(0.72%) to 7.56%	18.53%

2016 COMBINED MARGINAL TAX RATES (continued)

Taxable income $90,563 to $140,388

	Brackets	Ordinary income & interest	Capital gains	Canadian dividends	
				Eligible[2]	Non-eligible
Federal only	$90,563	26.00%	13.00%	15.15%	18.11%
Alberta	$125,000	38.00%	19.00%	17.91%	28.55%
	$90,563	36.00%	18.00%	15.15%	26.21%
British Columbia	$106,543	40.70%	20.35%	21.64%	32.42%
	$90,563	38.29%	19.15%	18.31%	29.60%
Manitoba	$90,563	43.40%	21.70%	28.12%	37.55%
New Brunswick	$131,664	43.84%	21.92%	21.14%	34.74%
	$90,563	42.52%	21.26%	19.32%	33.20%
Newfoundland and Labrador	$125,500	41.80%	20.90%	29.50%	32.50%[5]
	$90,563	40.55%	20.28%	27.78%	31.04%[5]
Non-resident[3]	$90,563	38.48%	19.24%	22.43%	26.80%
Northwest Territories	$133,353	40.05%	20.03%	18.67%	27.53%
	$90,563	38.20%	19.10%	16.12%	25.36%
Nova Scotia	$93,000	43.50%	21.75%	27.09%	34.69%
	$90,563	42.67%	21.34%	25.94%	33.72%
Nunavut	$90,563	35.00%	17.50%	19.97%	25.23%
Ontario	$90,563	43.41%	21.70%	25.38%	33.46%
Prince Edward Island	$98,314[4]	44.37%	22.19%	24.56%	35.68%
	$90,563	42.70%	21.35%	23.71%	34.08%
Quebec	$103,150	47.46%	23.73%	31.77%	37.00%
	$90,563	45.71%	22.86%	29.35%	34.95%
Saskatchewan	$127,430	41.00%	20.50%	20.67%	31.72%
	$90,563	39.00%	19.50%	17.91%	29.38%
Yukon	$90,563	36.90%	18.45%	9.49% to 15.15%	27.19%

Taxable income $140,388 to $200,000

	Brackets	Ordinary income & interest	Capital gains	Canadian dividends	
				Eligible[2]	Non-eligible
Federal only	$140,388	29.00%	14.50%	19.29%	21.62%
Alberta	$150,000	42.00%	21.00%	23.43%	33.23%
	$140,388	41.00%	20.50%	22.05%	32.06%
British Columbia	$140,388	43.70%	21.85%	25.78%	35.93%
Manitoba	$140,388	46.40%	23.20%	32.26%	41.06%
New Brunswick	$150,000	49.30%	24.65%	28.68%	41.13%
	$140,388	46.84%	23.42%	25.28%	38.25%
Newfoundland and Labrador	$175,700	45.80%	22.90%	35.02%	37.18%[5]
	$140,388	44.80%	22.40%	33.64%	36.01%[5]
Non-resident[3]	$140,388	42.92%	21.46%	28.55%	32.00%
Northwest Territories	$140,388	43.05%	21.53%	22.81%	31.04%
Nova Scotia	$150,000	50.00%	25.00%	36.06%	42.29%
	$140,388	46.50%	23.25%	31.23%	38.20%
Nunavut	$140,388	40.50%	20.25%	27.56%	31.67%
Ontario	$150,000	47.97%	23.98%	31.67%	38.80%
	$140,388	46.41%	23.20%	29.52%	36.97%
Prince Edward Island	$140,388	47.37%	23.69%	28.70%	39.19%
Quebec	$140,388	49.97%	24.98%	35.22%	39.93%
Saskatchewan	$140,388	44.00%	22.00%	24.81%	35.23%
Yukon	$140,388	41.80%	20.90%	16.26% to 19.29%	32.92%

Taxable income over $200,000

	Brackets	Ordinary income & interest	Capital gains	Canadian dividends	
				Eligible[2]	Non-eligible
Federal only	$200,000	33.00%	16.50%	24.81%	26.30%
Alberta	$300,000	48.00%	24.00%	31.71%	40.25%
	$200,000	47.00%	23.50%	30.33%	39.08%
British Columbia	$200,000	47.70%	23.85%	31.30%	40.61%
Manitoba	$200,000	50.40%	25.20%	37.78%	45.74%
New Brunswick	$200,000	53.30%	26.65%	34.20%	45.81%
Newfoundland and Labrador	$200,000	49.80%	24.90%	40.54%	41.86%[5]
Non-resident[3]	$200,000	48.84%	24.42%	36.72%	38.92%
Northwest Territories	$200,000	47.05%	23.53%	28.33%	35.72%
Nova Scotia	$200,000	54.00%	27.00%	41.58%	46.97%
Nunavut	$200,000	44.50%	22.25%	33.08%	36.35%
Ontario	$220,000	53.53%	26.76%	39.34%	45.30%
	$200,000	51.97%	25.98%	37.19%	43.48%
Prince Edward Island	$200,000	51.37%	25.69%	34.22%	43.87%
Quebec	$200,000	53.31%	26.65%	39.83%	43.84%
Saskatchewan	$200,000	48.00%	24.00%	30.33%	39.91%
Yukon	$500,000	48.00%	24.00%	24.81%	40.18%
	$200,000	45.80%	22.90%	21.78% to 24.81%	37.60%

(1) The table does not take into account the low-income tax reductions in British Columbia, New Brunswick, Newfoundland and Labrador, Nova Scotia, Ontario and Prince Edward Island, or the Manitoba Family Tax Benefit (for low-income taxpayers), which may affect the rates shown.

(2) When two dividend rates are indicated, the lower rate has a negative federal and/or provincial/territorial component. A negative federal component shelters other income from federal tax and a negative provincial/territorial component shelters other income from provincial/territorial tax. As a result, the combined federal and provincial/territorial rate that applies depends on the level of the taxpayer's other income, with the higher rate applying if the taxpayer has no other income.

(3) A non-resident can claim the personal basic credit only if all or substantially all (i.e., 90% or more) of the non-resident's worldwide income is included in his or her taxable income earned in Canada for the year.

Non-resident rates for interest and dividends apply only in limited circumstances. Generally, interest (other than most interest paid to arm's length non-residents) and dividends paid to non-residents are subject to Part XIII withholding tax.)

(4) The bracket relates to surtaxes levied by Ontario or Prince Edward Island, and assumes that only the basic personal credit is available.

(5) For Newfoundland and Labrador, the non-eligible dividend rates shown are for dividends received after June 30, 2016. The rates before July 1, 2016 are 0.70% lower.

[¶57] FEDERAL AND PROVINCIAL INCOME TAXES PAYABLE BY INDIVIDUALS AT VARIOUS LEVELS OF TAXABLE INCOME — 2016

This table shows the combined federal and provincial (or territorial) income taxes payable, including surtaxes, assuming only the basic personal tax credit is claimed (except for non-residents — see footnote 2, below), and that all income is either interest or ordinary income (such as salary). When income includes at least $1,161 of salary, the Canada Employment Credit, described under **Non-Refundable Personal Tax Credits — 2016** (see table), will reduce the results shown by $174 ($145 in Quebec). The amounts do not take into account employee payroll taxes, provincial health levies or other personal tax levies (see **Provincial Health Care Premiums and Personal Tax Levies — 2016**). Depending on the types of income and deductions, the alternative minimum tax (AMT) may apply.

2016	Alberta	British Columbia[1]	Manitoba[1]	New Brunswick[1]	Newfoundland and Labrador[1]	Non-resident[2]	Northwest Territories	Nova Scotia[1]	Nunavut	Ontario[1]	Prince Edward Island[1]	Quebec[5]	Saskatchewan	Yukon
$1,000,000	$447,751	$447,802	$477,889	$501,765	$469,947	$459,269	$441,738	$508,988	$416,546	$499,107	$486,735	$505,976	$453,412	$441,296
$500,000	$207,751	$209,302	$225,889	$235,265	$220,947	$215,069	$206,488	$238,988	$194,046	$231,459	$229,885	$239,451	$213,412	$201,296
$400,000	$159,751	$161,602	$175,489	$181,965	$171,147	$166,229	$159,438	$184,988	$149,546	$177,929	$178,515	$186,146	$165,412	$155,496
$300,000	$111,751	$113,902	$125,089	$128,665	$121,347	$117,389	$112,388	$130,988	$105,046	$124,400	$127,145	$132,841	$117,412	$109,696
$250,000	$88,251	$90,052	$99,889	$102,015	$96,447	$92,969	$88,863	$103,988	$82,796	$97,635	$101,460	$106,188	$93,412	$86,796
$200,000	$64,751	$66,202	$74,689	$75,365	$71,547	$68,549	$65,338	$76,988	$60,546	$71,182	$75,775	$79,536	$69,412	$63,896
$150,000	$43,751	$44,352	$51,489	$50,715	$48,904	$47,089	$43,813	$51,988	$40,296	$47,197	$52,090	$54,553	$47,412	$42,996
$100,000	$24,962	$23,871	$29,501	$28,925	$28,035	$27,422	$24,116	$29,949	$22,267	$25,204	$29,617	$30,637	$27,173	$24,075
$90,000	$21,393	$20,073	$25,192	$24,704	$24,011	$23,620	$20,327	$25,655	$18,798	$20,894	$25,350	$26,092	$23,304	$20,427
$80,000	$18,343	$16,932	$21,402	$21,019	$20,506	$20,586	$17,130	$21,938	$15,975	$17,425	$21,630	$22,172	$19,954	$17,477
$70,000	$15,293	$14,012	$17,612	$17,487	$17,004	$17,552	$14,220	$18,221	$13,225	$14,335	$17,910	$18,460	$16,604	$14,527
$60,000	$12,243	$11,192	$14,147	$13,955	$13,604	$14,518	$11,310	$14,504	$10,475	$11,370	$14,305	$14,748	$13,254	$11,577
$50,000	$9,193	$8,372	$10,822	$10,423	$10,204	$11,484	$8,400	$10,945	$7,725	$8,405	$10,875	$11,036	$9,904	$8,627
$40,000	$6,434	$5,843	$7,788	$7,206	$7,094	$8,880	$5,808	$7,691	$5,361	$5,793	$7,736	$7,663	$6,936	$6,105
$30,000	$3,934	$3,790	$5,032	$4,738	$4,517	$6,660	$3,718	$4,696	$3,461	$3,788	$4,935	$4,810	$4,336	$3,965
$20,000	$1,434	$1,784	$2,452	$2,270	$2,197	$4,440	$1,628	$2,291	$1,561	$1,783	$2,455	$1,958	$1,736	$1,825
Top marginal rates:														
Canadian dividends														
(eligible)	31.71%	31.30%	37.78%	34.20%	40.54%	36.72%[3]	28.33%	41.58%	33.08%	39.34%	34.22%	39.83%	30.33%	24.81%
(non-eligible)	40.25%	40.61%	45.74%	45.81%	41.86%[6]	38.92%[3]	35.72%	46.97%	36.35%	45.30%	43.87%	43.84%	39.91%	40.18%
Capital gains	24.00%	23.85%	25.20%	26.65%	24.90%	24.42%	23.53%	27.00%	22.25%	26.76%	25.69%	26.65%	24.00%	24.00%
Other income	48.00%	47.70%	50.40%	53.30%	49.80%	48.84%[3]	47.05%	54.00%	44.50%	53.53%	51.37%	53.31%	48.00%	48.00%
Maximum value:[4]														
Dividend tax credit:														
(eligible)	25.02%	25.02%	23.02%	28.52%	20.42%	22.23%	26.52%	23.87%	20.53%	25.02%	26.57%	24.44%	26.02%	30.02%
(non-eligible)	13.60%	12.99%	11.31%	14.15%	14.02%[6]	15.57%	16.52%	13.85%	13.43%	14.81%	13.88%	15.84%	13.89%	13.66%
Other tax credits	25.00%	20.06%	25.80%	24.68%	23.20%	22.20%	20.90%	23.79%	19.00%	22.88%	25.78%	32.53%	26.00%	21.40%

1 These provinces have low-income tax reductions, which may decrease some amounts shown.

2 This table assumes the non-resident will not qualify for the federal basic personal tax credit of $11,474. Non-residents can claim this credit only if all or substantially all (i.e., 90% or more) of the non-resident's worldwide income is included in his or her taxable income earned in Canada for the year. The non-resident amounts apply to income taxable in Canada that is not earned in a province or territory.

3 Non-resident rates for interest and dividends apply only in limited circumstances. Generally, interest (other than most interest paid to arm's length non-residents) and dividends paid to non-residents are subject to Part XIII withholding tax.

4 When personal tax credits in addition to the basic personal tax credit are available, the results in this table are too high. The maximum value of the dividend tax credit is determined by multiplying the dividend tax credit rate by the amount of eligible dividends (grossed up by 38%) or of non-eligible dividends (grossed up by 17%). The maximum value of other personal tax credits is determined by multiplying the other tax credit rate by the amount of those other personal tax credits. The maximum values reflect the surtax rates levied by Ontario (except for dividend tax credit rates, which are calculated before surtaxes in Ontario) and Prince Edward Island. Charitable donations over $200 have a higher maximum value, as do those that benefit from the First-time Donor's Super Credit.

5 Taxable income may differ for federal and Quebec purposes, in which case the amounts shown in the table may require adjustment.

6 For Newfoundland and Labrador, the non-eligible dividend rates shown are for dividends received after June 30, 2016. The rates before July 1, 2016 are: (i) top marginal non-eligible dividend tax rate: 41.16%; and (ii) maximum non-eligible dividend tax credit value: 14.62%.

[¶58] TOP MARGINAL RATES — A 17-YEAR HISTORY

<table>
<tr><th colspan="2"></th><th>2000</th><th>2001</th><th>2002</th><th>2003</th><th>2004</th><th>2005</th><th>2006</th><th>2007</th><th>2008</th><th>2009</th><th>2010</th><th>2011</th><th>2012</th><th>2013</th><th>2014</th><th>2015</th><th>2016</th></tr>
<tr><td colspan="2">Federal rates (including surtaxes)</td><td>30.45</td><td colspan="15">29.00</td><td>33.00</td></tr>
<tr><td rowspan="15">Combined rates (%) (including surtaxes and flat taxes)</td><td>Alberta</td><td>43.71</td><td colspan="14">39.00</td><td>40.25 (1)</td><td>48.00 (1)</td></tr>
<tr><td>British Columbia</td><td>51.26</td><td>45.70</td><td colspan="12">43.70</td><td colspan="2">45.80</td><td>47.70</td></tr>
<tr><td>Manitoba</td><td>48.08</td><td colspan="15">46.40</td><td>50.40</td></tr>
<tr><td>New Brunswick</td><td>48.77</td><td colspan="6">46.84</td><td colspan="2">46.95</td><td>46.00</td><td colspan="3">43.30</td><td>45.07</td><td>46.84</td><td>54.75 (2)</td><td>53.30</td></tr>
<tr><td>Newfoundland and Labrador</td><td>51.31</td><td colspan="6">48.64</td><td>47.04</td><td>45.00</td><td colspan="2">43.40</td><td colspan="4">42.30</td><td>43.30</td><td>49.80</td></tr>
<tr><td>Non-resident</td><td>44.37</td><td colspan="15">42.92</td><td>48.84</td></tr>
<tr><td>Northwest Territories</td><td>43.50</td><td colspan="3">42.05</td><td>42.55</td><td colspan="11">43.05</td><td>47.05</td></tr>
<tr><td>Nova Scotia</td><td>48.79</td><td colspan="3">47.34</td><td colspan="6">48.25</td><td colspan="6">50.00</td><td>54.00</td></tr>
<tr><td>Nunavut</td><td>43.50</td><td>42.05</td><td colspan="14">40.50</td><td>44.50</td></tr>
<tr><td>Ontario</td><td>47.86</td><td colspan="11">46.41</td><td>47.97 (3)</td><td colspan="3">49.53 (3)</td><td>53.53 (3)</td></tr>
<tr><td>Prince Edward Island</td><td>48.79</td><td colspan="15">47.37</td><td>51.37</td></tr>
<tr><td>Quebec</td><td>50.67</td><td>48.72</td><td colspan="11">48.22</td><td colspan="3">49.97</td><td>53.31</td></tr>
<tr><td>Saskatchewan</td><td>49.73</td><td>45.00</td><td>44.50</td><td colspan="13">44.00</td><td>48.00</td></tr>
<tr><td>Yukon</td><td>45.37</td><td>43.01</td><td colspan="13">42.40</td><td>44.00 (4)</td><td>48.00 (4)</td></tr>
</table>

(1) For Alberta, in 2015 and 2016, the top combined federal/Alberta marginal rate applies to incomes over $300,000. The rate is 40.00% in 2015 and 47.00% in 2016, if the individual's income is $300,000 or less, but over $200,000.

(2) For New Brunswick, in 2015, the top combined federal/New Brunswick marginal rate applies to incomes over $250,000. The rate is 50.00%, if the individual's income is $250,000 or less, but over $150,000.

(3) For Ontario, the top combined federal/Ontario marginal rate applies to incomes over $500,000 in 2012, $509,000 in 2013 and $220,000 in 2014, 2015 and 2016. The rate is: (i) 46.41%, if the individual's income is $500,000 or less, but over $132,406 in 2012 or $509,000 or less, but over $135,054 in 2013; (ii) 47.97%, if the individual's income is $220,000 or less, but over $150,000 in 2014 and 2015; and (iii) 51.97%, if the individual's income is $220,000 or less, but over $200,000 in 2016.

(4) For the Yukon, in 2015 and 2016, the top combined federal/Yukon marginal rate applies to incomes over $500,000. The rate is: (i) 41.80%, if the individual's income is $500,000 or less, but over $138,586 in 2015; and (ii) 45.80%, if the individual's income is $500,000 or less, but over $200,000 in 2016.

[¶62] 2016 FEDERAL INCOME TAX RATES

The federal tax brackets are indexed each year. This means that the brackets are reset every year based on the year over year change in the Consumer Price index as of the preceding September 30.

Taxable income	*Tax*
$45,282 or less	15%
In excess of	
$45,282	$6,792 + 20.5% on next $45,281
$90,563	$16,075 + 26% on next $49,825
$140,388	$29,030 + 29% on next $59,612
$200,000	$46,317 + 33% on remainder

[¶63] 2015 FEDERAL INCOME TAX RATES

The federal tax brackets are indexed each year. This means that the brackets are reset every year based on the year over year change in the Consumer Price index as of the preceding September 30.

Taxable income	*Tax*
$44,701 or less	15%
In excess of	
$44,701	$6,705 + 22% on next $44,700
$89,401	$16,539 + 26% on next $49,185
$138,586	$29,327 + 29% on remainder

[¶64] ANTICIPATED 2017 FEDERAL INCOME TAX RATES

The four federal tax brackets are indexed each year. This means that the brackets are reset every year based on the year over year change in the Consumer Price index as of the preceding September 30.

2017 rates are not available at date of print, but will be included in the online and DVD versions of *Preparing Your Income Tax Returns*.

Tables of rates going back before 2015 can be found at ¶1415.

[¶65] PERSONAL AMOUNTS

"Personal amounts" are aggregated and converted to tax credits by multiplying by the lowest personal tax rate from the tax table for the year (found at ¶1415 or above), i.e., for 2011 and later years, 15%. The effect is to give the equivalent of a deduction to taxpayers in the lowest bracket, but a tax benefit of more limited value to taxpayers in higher brackets. Although tax rates are usually fixed for several years, tax brackets, personal amounts, and the income amounts that reduce personal amounts for certain dependants are all indexed annually. That is, they are increased from year to year by the amount of the Consumer Price Index increase for 12 months to September 30 of the preceding year. On occasion, amounts are reset by statute over and above the amounts that would be achieved by indexing. It is the actual amounts (not the credits) for a year that are shown in the following table.

	2012	*2013*	*2014*	*2015*	*2016*
Indexing factor	2.8%	2.0%	0.9%	1.7%	1.3%
Basic personal amount	$10,822	$11,038	$11,138	$11,327	$11,474
Spouse or common-law partner amount	10,822[1]	11,038[1]	11,138[1]	11,327[1]	11,474[1]
Amount for an eligible dependant	10,822[1]	11,038[1]	11,138[1]	11,327[1]	11,474[1]
Age amount	6,720	6,854	6,916	7,033	7,125
Net income threshold	33,884	34,562	34,873	35,466	35,927
Amount for children under age 18	2,191[1]	2,234[1]	2,255[1]	N/A[3]	N/A[3]
Canada employment amount	1,095	1,117	1,127	1,146	1,161
Disability amount	7,546	7,697	7,766	7,899	8,001
Supplement for children with disabilities	4,402	4,490	4,530	4,607	4,667
Threshold relating to allowable child care and attendant care expenses	2,578	2,630	2,654	2,699	2,734
Infirm dependant amount	6,402[2]	6,530[2]	6,589[2]	6,700[2]	6,788[2]
Net income threshold	6,420	6,548	6,607	6,720	6,807
Caregiver amount	4,402[1]	4,490[1]	4,530[1]	4,608[1]	4,667[1]
Net income threshold	15,033	15,334	15,472	15,735	15,940
Adoption expenses	11,440	11,669	15,000	15,255	15,453
Medical expense tax credit, 3% of net income ceiling	2,109	2,152	2,171	2,208	2,237
Refundable medical expense supplement amounts:					
Maximum supplement	1,119	1,142	1,152	1,172	1,187
Family net income threshold	24,783	25,278	25,506	25,939	26,277
Minimum earnings threshold	3,268	3,333	3,363	3,421	3,465
Threshold income above which reduction or clawback tax applies to:					
GST credit	33,884	34,561	34,872	35,465	35,926
Old Age Security benefit received	69,562	70,954	71,592	72,809	73,756

[1] There is an additional family caregiver amount in respect of an eligible infirm dependant of $2,000 for 2012, $2,040 for 2013, $2,058 for 2014, $2,093 for 2015, and $2,121 for 2016.

[2] Includes the family caregiver amount of an additional $2,000 for 2012, $2,040 for 2013, $2,058 for 2014, $2,093 for 2015, and $2,121 for 2016.

[3] The child tax credit is repealed for 2015 and following years.

The net income thresholds are the amounts that may be earned by the person for whom you are making the claim (yourself in the case of the age credit) before claims are eroded by the person's income. Thus, in 2016, a disabled dependent child 18 years of age or older can earn $6,807 and be eligible for a full $6,788 claim, but every dollar earned by the dependant in excess of $6,807 will reduce the claim by $1. See Chapter 11.

[¶70] ALLOWANCES FOR TEAM MEMBERS

(See ¶390.15.)

Year	2012	2013	2014	2015	2016
Maximum Monthly Allowance	$329	$335	$338	$344	$348

[¶72] ALLOWANCES FOR TRADESPERSONS' TOOLS

(See ¶373b.)

Year	2012	2013	2014	2015	2016
Maximum Monthly Allowance	$1,095	$1,117	$1,127	$1,146	$1,161

[¶80] PRESCRIBED INTEREST RATES (2000–2016)

- Deemed interest on employee and shareholder loans and effective July 1, 2010, rate also applies to overpaid taxes for corporate taxpayers
- Rate for overpaid taxes for all taxpayers prior to July 1, 2010 and for non-corporate taxpayers after June 30, 2010
- Late or deficient income tax payments and unremitted withholdings

	Jan. 1 - Mar. 31			Apr. 1 - June 30			July 1 - Sept. 30			Oct. 1 - Dec. 31		
2000	5	7	9	6	8	10	6	8	10	6	8	10
2001	6	8	10	6	8	10	5	7	9	5	7	9
2002	3	5	7	2	4	6	3	5	7	3	5	7
2003	3	5	7	3	5	7	4	6	8	3	5	7
2004	3	5	7	3	5	7	2	4	6	3	5	7
2005	3	5	7	3	5	7	3	5	7	3	5	7
2006	3	5	7	4	6	8	4	6	8	5	7	9
2007	5	7	9	5	7	9	5	7	9	5	7	9
2008	4	6	8	4	6	8	3	5	7	3	5	7
2009	2	4	6	1	3	5	1	3	5	1	3	5
2010	1	3	5	1	3	5	1	3	5	1	3	5
2011	1	3	5	1	3	5	1	3	5	1	3	5
2012	1	3	5	1	3	5	1	3	5	1	3	5
2013	1	3	5	1	3	5	1	3	5	2	4	6
2014	1	3	5	1	3	5	1	3	5	1	3	5
2015	1	3	5	1	3	5	1	3	5	1	3	5
2016	1	3	5	1	3	5	1	3	5	1	3	5

[¶82] DEFERRED INCOME PLAN CONTRIBUTIONS LIMITS

The maximum annual deductible RRSP, DPSP and money purchase RPP contribution limits for 2014 to 2018 are as shown:

Dollar Limits:	2014	2015	2016	2017	2018
RRSP	$24,270	$24,930	$25,370	$26,010	$26,230
DPSP	$12,465	$12,685	$13,005	$13,115	Indexed[1]
Money Purchase RPP	$24,930	$25,370	$26,010	$26,230	Indexed[1]

[1] Increased for increases in the Average Wage.

[¶83] CPP CONTRIBUTIONS

The following data for the current year is discussed in ¶1305.

Year	2013	2014	2015	2016	2017
Maximum Pensionable Earnings	$51,100	$52,500	$53,600	$54,900	$55,300
Basic Exemption	$3,500	$3,500	$3,500	$3,500	$3,500
Subject to Contribution	$47,600	$49,000	$50,100	$51,400	$51,800
Employee Contribution Rate	4.95%	4.95%	4.95%	4.95%	4.95%
Self-Employed Contribution Rate	9.9%	9.9%	9.9%	9.9%	9.9%
Maximum Employee Contribution	$2,356.20	$2,425.50	$2,479.95	$2,544.30	$2,564.10
Maximum Self-Employed Contribution	$4,712.40	$4,851.00	$4,959.90	$5,088.60	$5,128.20

[¶83c] QPP CONTRIBUTIONS

The following data for the current year is discussed in ¶1650d.

Year	2013	2014	2015	2016	2017
Maximum Pensionable Earnings	$51,100	$52,500	$53,600	$54,900	$55,300
Basic Exemption	$3,500	$3,500	$3,500	$3,500	$3,500
Subject to Contribution	$47,600	$49,000	$50,100	$51,400	$51,800
Employee Contribution Rate	5.10%	5.175%	5.25%	5.325%	5.40%
Self-Employed Contribution Rate	10.20%	10.35%	10.50%	10.65%	10.80%
Maximum Employee Contribution	$2,427.60	$2,535.75	$2,630.25	$2,737.05	$2,797.20
Maximum Self-Employed Contribution	$4,855.20	$5,071.50	$5,260.50	$5,474.10	$5,594.40

[¶84] EI CONTRIBUTIONS

The following data for the current year is discussed in ¶1307.

General Information

Year	2013	2014	2015	2016	2017
Maximum Insurable Earnings	$47,400	$48,600	$49,500	$50,800	$51,300
Rate per $100 of Earnings: Employees outside Quebec	1.88	1.88	1.88	1.88	1.63
Rate per $100 of Earnings: Employers outside Quebec, 1.4 times employee contribution					

Year	2013	2014	2015	2016	2017
Maximum Employee Contribution	$891.12	$913.68	$930.60	$955.04	$836.19
Maximum Employer Contribution	$1,247.57	$1,279.15	$1,302.84	$1,339.06	$1,170.67
Rate per $100 of Earnings: Quebec Employees	1.52	1.53	1.54	1.52	1.27
Rate per $100 of Earnings: Quebec Employers, 1.4 times employee contribution					

Year	2013	2014	2015	2016	2017
Maximum Quebec Employee Contribution	$720.48	$743.58	$762.30	$772.16	$651.51
Maximum Quebec Employer Contribution	$1,008.67	$1,041.10	$1,067.22	$1,081.02	$912.11

[¶84c] QUEBEC PARENTAL INSURANCE PLAN (QPIP) CONTRIBUTIONS

The following data for the current year is discussed in ¶1307 and ¶1650d.10.

Year	2013	2014	2015	2016	2017
Maximum Insurable Earnings	$67,500	$69,000	$70,000	$71,500	$72,500
Rate per $100 of Earnings: Employees	0.559	0.559	0.559	0.548	0.548
Rate per $100 of Earnings: Employers	0.782	0.782	0.782	0.767	0.767
Maximum employee contribution	$377.33	$385.71	$391.30	$391.82	$397.30
Maximum employer contribution	$527.85	$539.58	$547.40	$548.41	$556.08
Rate per $100 of self-employment income earnings	0.993	0.993	0.993	0.993	0.973
Maximum QPIP self-employment contribution employee contribution	$670.28	$685.17	$695.10	$710	$705.43

[¶86] AUTOMOBILE RATES AND LIMITS

The following rates and limits are prescribed in sections 7305.1 to 7307 of the *Income Tax Regulations*. In recent years, the Department of Finance has been adjusting the amounts by News Release issued at the end of the calendar year.

See the definitions of "automobile" and "passenger vehicle" in subsection 248(1) of the *Income Tax Act*

	Jan. 1/06-Dec. 31/07	Jan. 1/08-Dec. 31/11	Jan. 1/12-Dec. 31/12	Jan. 1/13-Dec. 31/13	Jan. 1/14-Dec. 31/14	Jan. 1/15-Dec. 31/15	Jan. 1/16-Dec. 31/16
Operating expense benefit - per kilometre [1]							
Employees	22¢	24¢	26¢	27¢	27¢	27¢	26¢
Employees employed principally in selling or leasing automobiles	19¢	21¢	23¢	24¢	24¢	24¢	23¢

	Jan. 1/06-Dec. 31/07	Jan. 1/08-Dec. 31/11	Jan. 1/12-Dec. 31/12	Jan. 1/13-Dec. 31/13	Jan. 1/14-Dec. 31/14	Jan. 1/15-Dec. 31/15	Jan. 1/16-Dec. 31/16
Reasonable allowance per kilometre [2]							
Deductible by employer where tax-free allowance paid to employee:							
All Provinces*	50¢/44¢	52¢/46¢	53¢/47¢	54¢/48¢	54¢/48¢	55¢/49¢	54¢/48¢
Nunavut, Yukon and Northwest Territories*	54¢/48¢	56¢/50¢	57¢/51¢	58¢/52¢	58¢/52¢	59¢/53¢	58¢/52¢

	Jan. 1/06-Dec. 31/07	Jan. 1/08-Dec. 31/11	Jan. 1/12-Dec. 31/12	Jan. 1/13-Dec. 31/13	Jan. 1/14-Dec. 31/14	Jan. 1/15-Dec. 31/15	Jan. 1/16-Dec. 31/16
Cost of passenger vehicle [3]	$30,000**	$30,000**	$30,000**	$30,000**	$30,000**	$30,000**	$30,000**
Prescribed monthly interest [4]	$300	$300	$300	$300	$300	$300	$300
Monthly lease amount [5]	$800**	$800**	$800**	$800**	$800**	$800**	$800**

* First number applies to the first 5,000 kilometres driven in the year. The second number applies to subsequent kilometres driven in the year.

** Applicable federal and provincial sales taxes are added to these figures to calculate the ceiling amount.

[1] Reg. 7305.1; prescribed for s. 6(1)(*k*).

[2] Reg. 7306; prescribed for s. 18(1)(*r*).

[3] Reg. 7307(1); prescribed for ss. 13(2), 13(7)(*g*), 13(7)(*h*)(iii), 20(4), 20(16.1), the description of B in s. 67.3(*d*), ai

[4] Reg. 7307(2); prescribed for the description of A in s. 67.2.

[5] Reg. 7307(3); prescribed for the description of A in s. 67.3(*c*).

2017 rates are not available at date of print, but will be included in the online and DVD versions of *Preparing Your Income Tax Returns*.

[¶87] MILEAGE RATES AND MEAL ALLOWANCES

Certain amounts for travel are allowed in connection with northern residents' deductions (¶361a), moving expenses (¶1039), and transportation to obtain medical services (¶1205). Generally speaking, travel expenses for these purposes may include any of the following amounts:

- air, train, and bus fares;
- vehicle expenses;
- meals;
- hotel and motel accommodations, and camping fees; and
- other incidental expenses, such as taxis and road or ferry tolls.

Where actual vehicle and meal expenses are claimed, they should be supported by receipts. However, the CRA does permit a simplified alternative calculation for these items.

Mileage

In limited situations, the CRA will permit mileage deductions to be calculated on an arbitrary cents per kilometre basis, rather than as a proration of actual annual expenditures prorated by mileage. This option is available in calculating northern residents' deductions (¶361a), moving expenses (¶1039), and transportation to obtain medical services (¶1205). This option is not available for employees claiming deduction of auto expenses in the course of employment (¶370).

Where the option is permitted, the acceptable mileage rates are:

Province or Territory	*Cents per kilometre for taxation year*				
	2011	2012	2013	2014	2015
Alberta	53.0	50.0	51.5	45.5	44.5
British Columbia	52.0	49.5	51.0	49.5	48.5
Manitoba	49.0	47.0	47.5	48.5	47.0
New Brunswick	52.0	49.0	49.5	51.0	49.0
Newfoundland and Labrador	55.0	52.0	53.0	53.5	52.0
Northwest Territories	61.5	58.0	58.5	63.0	61.5
Nova Scotia	53.0	50.5	51.0	51.5	49.5
Nunavut	61.5	58.0	58.5	61.0	61.0
Ontario	57.0	55.0	55.0	57.5	55.0
Prince Edward Island	52.0	49.5	50.5	50.5	48.5
Quebec	59.0	57.0	57.0	52.0	50.5
Saskatchewan	47.5	45.0	45.5	47.5	46.5
Yukon	63.5	61.5	63.5	64.0	60.5

For travel from one province to another, or for travel from Canada to outside Canada, use the per kilometre rate for the province or territory where travel began. For travel from outside Canada into Canada, use the per kilometre rate for the province or territory of final destination. For travel between countries outside Canada, the actual expense method should be used.

Flat Rate Meal Allowances

Similarly, in calculating northern residents' deductions (¶361a), moving expenses (¶1039), and transportation to obtain medical services (¶1205), the CRA will allow flat rate meal allowances for the travel period in lieu of actual "reasonable" expenses. The rates for 2011–2015 are $17 per meal to a maximum of $51 per day.

Actual expenses must be supported by receipts; flat rate allowances need not be.

2017 rates are not available at date of print, but will be included in the online and DVD versions of *Preparing Your Income Tax Returns.*

[¶90] 2015 MONTHLY AVERAGE CONVERSION RATES FOR U.S. DOLLAR, U.K. POUND, AND EUROPEAN EURO TRANSACTIONS

Monthly average noon exchange rates for U.S. dollars, U.K. pounds, and European euros are taken from an extensive list of monthly averages which, at the time of writing, appeared on the Bank of Canada website at http://www.bankofcanada.ca/rates/exchange/. Readers in search of monthly average rates for other countries should consult that website. Daily rates can also be found on that website.

Complete 2016 rates are not available at date of print, but will be included in the online and DVD versions of *Preparing Your Income Tax Returns*.

Where you have a major transaction involving a foreign currency (such as the sale of a U.S. property), you should use the currency value on the actual date of the transaction. This can be obtained from the Bank of Canada website (http://www.bankofcanada.ca/rates/exchange/), or possibly from your Tax Services Office (¶287). Where a sale is followed by a currency conversion, there may be a separate gain or loss on the conversion date. Where you receive periodic income from the U.S., or have a series of relatively small transactions, the CRA will normally accept the reporting of all transactions converted at (i.e., multiplied by) the average rate for the year (see ¶95).

To determine the value of Canadian dollars in U.S. terms (e.g., for reporting Canadian income on U.S. returns), use 1 divided by the rate shown above. For example, if the average monthly exchange rate for U.S. dollars is US$1 = C$1.21231429, then C$1 = US$1 / 1.21231429 = US$0.82486861.

[¶95] YEARLY AVERAGE CONVERSION RATES FOR MAJOR CURRENCIES (2012–2015)

For a complete list of monthly and annual conversion rate averages, see the "Exchange Rates" page on the Bank of Canada website at http://www.bankofcanada.ca/rates/exchange/.

2016 rates are not available at date of print, but will be included in the online and DVD versions of *Preparing Your Income Tax Returns*.

All Canadian tax returns (except for those of certain corporations which may operate primarily in a foreign currency and elect to use foreign currency reporting) must report income in Canadian dollars. Where you have a major transaction where you received proceeds (or acquired capital or depreciable property) in a foreign currency, you should use the currency value on the actual date of the transaction. This can be obtained from the Bank of Canada website (http://www.bankofcanada.ca/rates/exchange/). Where a sale is followed by a currency conversion, there may be a separate gain or loss on the conversion date. Where you receive periodic income in a foreign currency, or have a series of relatively small transactions, the CRA will normally accept the reporting of all transactions converted at (i.e., multiplied by) the average rate for the year. A table of average rates for several currencies is posted on the Bank of Canada website (http://www.bankofcanada.ca/rates/exchange/).

Where you receive income reported to you in foreign currency, multiply by the rate above to report in Canadian dollars. For example, if you received 2015 income reported to you as US$100 (100 U.S. dollars), you must report Canadian income of $100 × 1.27871080 = CDN$127.87 (127.87 Canadian dollars). If you were reporting Canadian dollar receipts to a foreign government, you would divide the Canadian dollars by the number shown. For example, if you have to report CDN$100 (100 Canadian dollars) on a U.S. tax return, you would report CDN$100 / 1.27871080 = US$78.20.

[¶96] RATES OF WITHHOLDING TAX UNDER INCOME TAX AGREEMENTS SIGNED BY CANADA

This chart is intended for use only as a quick reference guide for the rates of withholding tax for selected types of payments under the income tax agreements Canada has signed with various countries. The rates listed in the chart are the maximum rates that Canada and the other country may withhold for the type of payment noted. Many of the treaties have unique exceptions and qualifications on withholding tax which cannot be listed in a chart such as this. Therefore, the specific treaty should be consulted when determining whether or not there is a tax liability exigible on a payment.

Countries	*Date*	*Interest*	*Dividends — % of Ownership*	*Regular Dividends*	*Royalties*	*Pension and Annuity*	*From Estate or Trust*
Algeria . . .	1999	15%[3]	15%	15%	15%, royalties for use of computer software and patents exempt.	15%[9,14,16]	—
Argentina	1993	12.5%[3]	10%[5]	15%	15% generally 3%, 5%, 10% for specific items	15%[9,14,16]	—
Armenia . .	2004	10%[3]	5%[5]for investment >US $100,000.	15%	10%	pen. 15%[9,14,16]	15%
Australia . .	1980[2]	10%	5%[4,6]	15%	10%	15%[10,17]	15% (Can)
Austria . . .	1976[2]	10%[3]	5%[4,6]	15%	10%[8]	[9,11]	15% (Can)
Azerbaijan	2004	10%[3]	10%[4]	15%	5% on computer software, patents, industrial, commercial or scientific experience royalties; 10% on other royalties	—	15%
Bangladesh	1982	15%[3]	15%	15%	10%	15%[9]	—
Barbados . .	1980[2]	15%[3]	15%	15%	10%[7]	15%[9,14,16]	15% (Can)
Belgium . .	2002[2]	10%[3]	5%[4]	15%	10%[8]	[9,11] [13] for certain pensions	15%
Brazil . . .	1984	15%[3] 10% Brazil in certain circumstances	15%[4]	[11]	15% 25% on trademarks	[15] [9] unless over $4,000	—
Bulgaria . .	1999	10%[3]	10%[4,6]	15%	10%[7]	pen. 15% ann. 10%[9]	15% (Can)
Cameroon	1982	15% (Can) 20% (Cam)	15% (Can) 20% (Cam)	15% (Can) 20% (Cam)	15% (Can) 20% (Cam)	[11]	—
Chile	1998	15%	10%[5]	15%	15%	pen.[13] ann. 15%[9]	15% (Can)
China . . .	1986	10%[3]	10%[4]	15%	10%	[11]	—
Colombia	2008	10%[3]	5%[4]	15%	10%	15%[9,14,16]	15% (Can)
Croatia . . .	1997	10%	5%[4,5,6]	15%	10%	pen. 15%[15] ann. 10%[9]	15%
Cyprus . . .	1984	15%[3]	15%	15%	10%[7]	15%[9] [13,] for certain pensions[15,16]	15%
Czech Republic . .	2001	10%[3]	5%[4]	15%	10%	15%[9]	15%

Countries	Date	Interest	Dividends — % of Ownership	Regular Dividends	Royalties	Pension and Annuity	From Estate or Trust
Denmark	1997	10%[3]	5%[5](if owned by a company) 10% if paid by Cdn. NRO invest. corp.	15%	10%[8]	[9,13]	15%
Dominican Republic . .	1976	18%[3]	18%	18%	18%[7]	18%[9,16]	18%
Ecuador . .	2001	10%[3]	5%[5]	15%	10% on use of industrial, commercial, or scientific equipment; 15% on other	pen. 15%[14,15,16] ann. 15%[9]	15%
Egypt . . .	1983	15%[3]	15%	15% (20% if paid to an individual resident in Canada)	15%	[11]	15%
Estonia . .	1995	10%[3]	5%[5,6]	15%	10%	15%[16] ann. 10%[9]	15%
Finland . .	2006	10%[3]	5%[4]	15%	10%[8]	pen. 20%[14] ann. 15%[9]	15%
France . . .	1975[2]	10%[3]	5%[4] 10% if paid by Cdn. NRO invest. corp.	15%	10%[8]	pen.[13,14] ann.[9,11]	15%
Gabon . . .	2002	10%[3]	15%	15%	10%	pen.[11] ann.[11]	—
Germany . .	2001	10%[3]	5%[4]	15%	10%[8]	pen.[11] ann.[9,11]	—
Greece . . .	2009	10%[3]	5%[5]	15%	10%[7]	15%[9,14,15,16]	15%
Guyana . .	1985	15% (Can)[3] 25% (Guy)[3]	15%	15%	10%	[9,11,14]	—
Hong Kong (PRC) . . .	2012	10%[3]	5%[4]	15%	10%	pen.[11]	—
Hungary . .	1992[2]	10%[3]	5%[5] 10% if paid by Cdn. NRO invest. corp.	15%	10%[7]	pen. 15%[14,16] ann. 10%[9]	15%
Iceland . .	1997	10%[3]	5%[4,6]	15%	10%[8]	pen. 15%[14,16] ann. 15%[9]	15%
India	1996	15%[3]	15%[4]	25%	10% 15% 20%	[13]	15%
Indonesia	1979[2]	10%[3]	10%[5]	15%	10%	15%[9,14]	—
Ireland . . .	2003	10%[3]	5%[4,6]	15%	10%[8]	pen. 15%[14,16] ann. 15%	15%
Israel	1975	15%[3]	15%	15%	15%[7]	15%[9,14,17]	15%
Israel	2016[1]	10%[3]	5%[5]	15%	10%[7]	pen. 15%[14,16] ann. 15%[9]	15%
Italy	2002	10%[3]	5%[4,6]	15%	5%[7], on computer software, patents, industrial, commercial or scientific experience royalties, 10% on other royalties[7]	pen. 15%[14,15,16]	15%

Countries	*Date*	*Interest*	*Dividends — % of Ownership*	*Regular Dividends*	*Royalties*	*Pension and Annuity*	*From Estate or Trust*
Ivory Coast	1983	15%[3]	15% 18% on certain divs. from Ivory Coast	15% 18% on certain divs. from Ivory Coast	10%	15%	—
Jamaica . .	1978	15%[3]	15% 22.5% (Jam)[4]	15%	10%	pen.[11,14,16] ann. 15%[9]	15% (Can)
Japan . . .	1986[2]	10%[3]	5%[5]	15%	10%	[11]	—
Jordan . . .	1999	10%[3]	10%[4,6]	15%	10%	[13]	—
Kazakhstan	1996	10%[3]	5%[4,6]	15%	10%	pen. 15%[9] [13] for certain pensions	—
Kenya . . .	1983	15%[3]	15%[4]	25%	15%	15%	—
Korea . . .	2006	10%[3]	5%[5]	15%	10%	pen. 15%[9,16] ann. 10%	—
Kuwait . . .	2002	10%[3]	5%[4,5,6]	15%	10%	15%	—
Kyrgyzstan	1998	15%[3]	15%	15%	10%[8]	15%[9,14,16]	15%
Latvia . . .	1995	10%[3]	5%[5,6]	15%	10%	pen. 15%[16] ann. 10%[9]	15%
Lebanon . .	1998[1]	10%[3]	5%[4,6]	15%	5% on cultural, computer software, industrial, commercial or scientific "know-how" royalties, 10% on other royalties	pen. 15%[9,14]	—
Lithuania	1996	10%[3]	5%[5,6]	15%	10%	pen. 15%[16] ann. 10%[9]	15%
Luxembourg . . .	1999[2]	10%[3]	5%[4](if owned by a company) 10% if paid by Cdn. NRO invest. corp.	15%	10%[8]	[9,11,14] [13] for certain pensions	15%
Malaysia . .	1976	15%[3]	15%	15%	15% certain royalties excluded	15%[14,16]	15% (Can)
Malta . . .	1986	15%[3]	15% (Can) not to exceed tax on profits (Malta)	15% (Can) not to exceed tax on profits (Malta)	10%[7]	15%[9,14,16]	15%
Mexico . . .	2006	10%[3]	5%[4]	15%	10%[7]	pen. 15%[9,14,16] ann. 15%	15%
Moldova . .	2002	10%[3]	5%[5]	15%	10%	15%[14]	15%
Mongolia	2002	10%[3]	5%[4]	15%	5% on cultural, computer software, patent, industrial, commercial or scientific experience royalties, 10% on other royalties	pen. 15%[14,16] ann. 15%[9]	15%
Morocco . .	1975	15%[3]	15%	15%	10% 5% on cultural royalties	[11]	—
Namibia . .	2010[1]	10%[3]	5%[5]	15%	10%[7]	pen.[12]	15%
Netherlands	1986[2]	10%[3]	5%[4,5](if owned by a company) 10% if paid by Cdn. NRO invest. corp.	15%	10%[8]	15%[9]	15% (Can)

Countries	*Date*	*Interest*	*Dividends — % of Ownership*	*Regular Dividends*	*Royalties*	*Pension and Annuity*	*From Estate or Trust*
New Zealand . .	2012	10%[3]	5%[4]	15%	5% on cultural, computer software, industrial, commercial or scientific info; 10% on other royalties	pen. 15%[14,16] ann. 15%[9]	15% (Can)
Nigeria . . .	1992	12.5%[3]	12.5%[4]	15%	12.5%	[14,11]	—
Norway . .	2002	10%[3]	5%[4,6]	15%	10%[8]	15[9,14]	15%
Oman . . .	2004	10%[3]	5%[4]	15%	10%[8]	pen. 15%[14,16] ann. 15%[9]	15%
Pakistan . .	1976	15% (Can)[3] 25% (Pak)[3]	15% (Can) 15% (Pak)[5]	15% (Can) 20% (Pak)	15% (Can)[7] 20% (Pak)[7]copyright, trademark equipment, films 15% (Pak) technical know-how	[13] Canada may withhold 15% on alimony	15% (Can)
Papua New Guinea . . .	1987	10%[3]	15% (Can) 25% (PNG)	15% (Can) 25% (PNG)	10%	15%[10,14,16]	—
Peru	2001	15%	10%[4]	15%	15%	15%[9,14]	15%
Philippines	1976	15%[3]	15% (Can) 15% (Phil)[4]	15% (Can) 25% (Phil)	10% (Can) 25% (Phil)	[13]	—
Poland . . .	2012	10%[3]	5%[4]	15%	5% on cultural, industrial, commercial, or scientific info; 10% on other royalties	pen. 15%[14,16] ann. 15%[9]	15%
Portugal . .	1999	10%[3]	10%[5,6]	15%	10%	15%[9,14,16]	15%
Romania . .	2004	10%[3]	5%[4]	15%	10% 5% on cultural, software, industrial, commercial, scientific info.	pen. 15%	—
Russia . . .	1995	10%[3]	10%[4]	15%	10%[8]	[13]	—
Senegal . .	2001	15% (Can)[3] 20% (Sen)[3] 16% (Sen)[3]	15% (Can) 16% (Sen)	15% (Can) 16% (Sen)	15%	15%[9,14]	15%
Serbia . . .	2012	10%[3]	5%[5]	15%	10%	pen. 15%	15%
Singapore	1976[2]	15%[3]	15% 0% (Sing) depending on domestic law	15% 0% (Sing) depending on domestic law	15%	[13] Canada may withhold 15% on alimony	15% (Can)
Slovak Republic . .	2001	10%[3]	5%[4]	15%	10%[7]	pen. 15%[14,16] ann. 15%	15%
Slovenia . .	2000	10%[3]	5% (Can)[4,6] 5% (Slo)[5]	15%	10%	pen. 15%[16] (Can) (Slo)[13,] ann. 10%[9]	15%
South Africa . . .	1995	10%[3]	5%[4,6]	15%	10% 6% on cultural, software, industrial, commercial, scientific info.	[11]	15%
Spain . . .	1976	10%[3]	5%[4]	15%	10%[7]	15%[9,14,16]	—

Countries	*Date*	*Interest*	*Dividends — % of Ownership*	*Regular Dividends*	*Royalties*	*Pension and Annuity*	*From Estate or Trust*
Sri Lanka	1982	15%[3]	15%	15%	10%[7]	15%[9,14,16]	15% (Can)
Sweden . .	1996	10%[3]	5%[5] 10% if paid by Cdn. NRO invest corp.	15%	10%[8]	[9,11,14]	15% (Can)
Switzerland	1997[2]	10%[3]	5%[4]	15%	10%[8]	15%[9,14]	—
Taiwan . . .	2016[1]	10%[3]	10%[5]	15%	10%	pen. 15%[16], ann. 15%[9]	15%
Tanzania . .	1995	15%[3]	20%[5]	25%	20%	15%[9,14] [16] (Can)	—
Thailand . .	1984	15% (Can) 10% (Thai) if to fin. instit. 25% (Thai) otherwise[3]	15% (Can) 15% (Thai) in certain cases 20%[5] (Thai)	15% (Can) taxed under laws of Thailand	15% 5% on cultural	[13]	15% (Can)
Trinidad and Tobago . .	1995	10%[3]	5%[4,6]	15%	10%[7]	pen. 15%[9,14]	—
Tunisia . . .	1982	15%[3]	15%	15%	20%[7] on patents, trademarks, films, videos, industrial, commercial, scientific or harbour equip.; 15% on other	[11]	15%
Turkey . . .	2009	15%[3]	15%[4]	20%	10%	15%[9,14,15,16]	—
Ukraine . .	1996	10%[3]	5%[5,6]	15%	10% computer software exempt	[13]	15%
United Arab Emirates . .	2002	10%[3]	5%[4] 10% if paid by Cdn. NRO invest. corp.	15%	10%[8]	[11]	15%
United Kingdom . .	1978[2]	10%[3]	5%[4]	15%	10%[8]	pen.[12] ann. 10%[9]	15% (Can)
U.S.A. . . .	1980[2]	0%[3,18]	5%[4]	15%	10%[8]	15%[9,14]	15%
Uzbekistan	1999	10%[3]	5%[4]	15%	5% on cultural, computer software, industrial, commercial or scientific "know-how" royalties, 10% on other royalties	[13]	—
Venezuela	2001	10%[3]	10%[5]	15%	5% on cultural, computer software, industrial, commercial or scientific experience royalties, 10% on other royalties	[11,14]	—
Socialist Republic of Vietnam . .	1997	10%[3]	5% (if 70% controlled by corporate owner) 10% (if 25%–69% controlled by corporate owner)	15%	10%	pen. 15% ann.[9,11]	15%

Countries	*Date*	*Interest*	*Dividends — % of Ownership*	*Regular Dividends*	*Royalties*	*Pension and Annuity*	*From Estate or Trust*
Zambia . .	1984	15%[3]	15%	15%	15%	15%[14]	15% (Can)
Zimbabwe	1992	15%[3]	10%[5]	15% (Can) 20% (Zim)	10%	15%[9,14,16]	15% (Can)

[1] Not yet ratified.

[2] Revised by subsequent Protocol.

[3] No withholding tax under the treaty on certain types of interest. After 2007, the Canadian *Income Tax Act* exempts interest payments to non-residents from withholding tax, except for certain interest paid or payable to a non-arms length person or participating debt interest. See paragraph 212(1)*(b)*.

[4] If recipient company owns at least 10% of capital or voting stock or has 10% of voting power of stock on which dividends are paid (see specific treaty).

[5] If recipient company owns a specified percentage of capital or voting power of stock on which dividends are paid (see specific treaty for level of ownership specified).

[6] Does not apply to dividends from a non-resident-owned investment corporation resident in Canada.

[7] Cultural royalties are exempt from withholding tax. These include copyright royalties for production or reproduction of literary, dramatic, musical or artistic work. They usually do not include royalties on films or videotapes.

[8] Cultural royalties, computer software, industrial, commercial or scientific "know-how" royalties are exempt.

[9] Alimony and child support taxed only in the country of person receiving the payment.

[10] Alimony and child support taxed only in the paying country.

[11] May be taxed in source country — No treaty rate.

[12] Exempt from tax in source country.

[13] Taxed only in source country.

[14] Certain pensions exempt from tax in both countries.

[15] Tax withheld only if payment over a certain amount.

[16] For pensions, tax withheld is not to exceed the amount that would be payable if the recipient were resident in the source country.

[17] For pensions and annuities, tax withheld is not to exceed the amount that would be payable if the recipient were resident in the source country.

[18] Under the Canada–U.S. Treaty, the Fifth Protocol provides that withholding tax on interest will be completely eliminated for interest paid or credited after December 31, 2009. The maximum rate for withholding on interest paid or credited between January 1, 2008 and December 31, 2008 is 7%, and 4% on interest paid or credited between January 1, 2009 and December 31, 2009.

[¶100] CLIENT ORGANIZER

PERSONAL TAX ORGANIZER
For the year ___________

Please complete this T1 Organizer before your appointment. Please attach all applicable slips, receipts, lists, and other supplemental information.

1. Personal Information

	Name	SIN	Date of Birth (dd/mm/yy)	Phone Office	Ext.
Taxpayer					
Spouse					
Address				Home	
				Mobile	
Email					

Marital Status: ☐ Married ☐ Single ☐ Common-law ☐ Separated ☐ Divorced ☐ Widowed

If married or common-law, should your return be filed jointly with your spouse's return? ☐ Yes ☐ No

If marital status changed during the year, provide date of change (dd/mm/yy): ___________

2. Residence

Province or territory of residence on December 31: ___________

Did the taxpayer immigrate to Canada or emigrate from Canada during the year? ☐ Yes ☐ No

If yes, provide date of entry into Canada ___________ or date of departure ___________

3. Elections Canada

Is the taxpayer a Canadian citizen? ☐ Yes ☐ No

If yes, the taxpayer authorizes the CRA to provide his/her name, address, and date of birth to Elections Canada to update his/her information on the National Register of Electors. ☐ Yes ☐ No

4. Foreign Reporting—T1135

Did the taxpayer own or hold foreign property with a total cost of between CDN $100,000 and $250,000 at any time during the year? ☐ Yes ☐ No

Did the taxpayer own or hold foreign property with a total cost of more than CDN $250,000 at any time during the year? ☐ Yes ☐ No

If yes, please provide list and relevant details.

5. Change in Personal or Financial Situation during the Year

Date the taxpayer declared bankruptcy during the year. ___________

Date the taxpayer refinanced a business with new or revised debt. ___________

Date the taxpayer closed a bank account or investment account. ___________

CLIENT ORGANIZER (continued)

6. Dependants

Name	Relationship	Date of Birth	SIN	Physically or Mentally Infirmed?	Income	Child Care Expenses

Universal child care benefit (UCCB)—Is RC62 slip attached? ☐ Yes ☐ No

If the taxpayer is a single parent, is the UCCB designated to a dependant? ☐ Yes ☐ No

7. General Income/Deductions

T4 slips—Employment income? ☐ Yes ☐ No

T4A—Commission and self-employment? ☐ Yes ☐ No

T4E—Employment insurance? ☐ Yes ☐ No

T5007—Social assistance? ☐ Yes ☐ No

Employment income or taxable benefits not shown on the T4 slip? ____________

Amount paid for union and professional dues and organization names? ____________

List of child care expenses, with receipts, for each child? ☐ Yes ☐ No

List of moving expenses paid? Yes ☐ No ☐

List of spousal support payments made or received? ☐ Yes ☐ No

List of deductible employment expenses? ☐ Yes ☐ No

Is a signed form T2200 attached? ☐ Yes ☐ No

8. Pension Income

T4A—Pension, retirement, and annuity income? ☐ Yes ☐ No

T4AP—Canada pension plan benefits? ☐ Yes ☐ No

T4A(OAS)—Old age security pension slip/foreign pensions? ☐ Yes ☐ No

T4A(RCA)—Retirement compensation arrangements? ☐ Yes ☐ No

T4RSP—Registered retirement savings plan income? ☐ Yes ☐ No

T4RIF—Registered retirement income fund income? ☐ Yes ☐ No

Does the taxpayer elect to split eligible pension income with his/her spouse or common-law partner? ☐ Yes ☐ No

CLIENT ORGANIZER (continued)

9. Investment Income/Deductions

T3—Income from trust allocations?	☐ Yes	☐ No
T5—Investment income?	☐ Yes	☐ No
T4PS—Income from profit sharing plans?	☐ Yes	☐ No
T5013/T5013(A) —Partnership income?	☐ Yes	☐ No
T5008—Income from securities transactions?	☐ Yes	☐ No

Did the taxpayer dispose of property or investments during the year, including a principal residence? If so, provide the following details in a separate list:

Description of Property and Quantity	Date Acquired	Date Disposed of	Sales Proceeds	Cost	Expenses for Disposal

Interest paid to earn investment income ______ Management fees ______ Accounting/ legal fees ______

10. Self-Employment/Business Income

Financial statement(s)/ schedule of revenue and expenses attached?	☐ Yes	☐ No
Has the taxpayer registered to be eligible for Employment Insurance special benefits?	☐ Yes	☐ No
If an owner/manager, did the taxpayer have a shareholder loan outstanding during the year?	☐ Yes	☐ No

If yes, provide details of borrowings, repayments, and year-end balance if owner/manager owes the company money:

______

If the taxpayer used a vehicle for business, are the vehicle expenses and both total and business mileage attached?	☐ Yes	☐ No
If the taxpayer used a portion of his/her home for business, are the home expenses and both total and business square footage attached?	☐ Yes	☐ No
Is a list of all asset additions and disposals (including cars, equipment, etc.) attached?	☐ Yes	☐ No

11. Rental Income

If the taxpayer owned rental property, is a statement of rental income attached?	☐ Yes	☐ No
Does the taxpayer also live in the rental property (in which case no CCA should be claimed)?	☐ Yes	☐ No

12. RRSP/PRPP Contributions

T-slip for contributions made attached?	☐ Yes	☐ No
Were any amounts repaid during the year to a home buyers' plan or a lifelong learning plan?	☐ Yes	☐ No

13. Other Credits

T2202—Tuition/education amount for taxpayer?	☐ Yes	☐ No
T2202—Tuition/education amount claimed on transfer from dependant?	☐ Yes	☐ No
Receipt or amount for taxpayer's student loan interest?	☐ Yes	☐ No
Receipts/listing of all medical expenses paid in the year for taxpayer, spouse, and dependants?	☐ Yes	☐ No
First time making charitable donations?	☐ Yes	☐ No

CLIENT ORGANIZER (continued)

Receipts for charitable donations or donations made by way of gifting an item in kind?	☐ Yes	☐ No
Were any loans associated with the charitable donations?	☐ Yes	☐ No
Receipts for political contributions?	☐ Yes	☐ No
List of eligible teaching supplies purchased (for teachers and early childhood educators only)?	☐ Yes	☐ No
Public transit passes (receipts/details)?	☐ Yes	☐ No
Receipts/listing for fitness and arts activity amounts paid for each child?	☐ Yes	☐ No
Information pertaining to new home purchase to claim the first-time home buyers' amount?	☐ Yes	☐ No
Amount of property taxes/rent paid in the year and the name of the landlord/municipality?	☐ Yes	☐ No

14. Prior Year Tax Return Information/Correspondence

Is a copy of the Notice of Assessment for last year's tax return attached?	☐ Yes	☐ No
If new to the firm, are tax returns (and corresponding Notices of Assessment) for the last three years attached?	☐ Yes	☐ No
If taxpayer claimed a loss carryback in any of the preceding three years, are the Notices of Reassessment for those years attached?	☐ Yes	☐ No
Is a copy of any other correspondence from the Canada Revenue Agency attached?	☐ Yes	☐ No
If you would like your tax refund deposited directly into your account and if you have not already registered for direct deposit, is a void cheque attached?	☐ Yes	☐ No
Is your statement of instalments paid for the year attached?	☐ Yes	☐ No

Chapter 1

The Basic Rules of Residency and Canadian Income Taxation

THESE POINTS ARE COVERED IN THIS CHAPTER

CRA REFERENCES RELATING TO THIS CHAPTER

CRA Guides

5000-G, "General Income Tax and Benefit Guide"; **5013-G**, "General Income Tax and Benefit Guide for Non-Residents and Deemed Residents of Canada"; **T4055**, "Newcomers to Canada"; **T4058**, "Non-residents and Income Tax"; **T4144**, "Income Tax Guide for Electing Under Section 216" **T4145** "Electing Under Section 217 of the Income Tax Act"

CRA Forms

5013-R, "T1 General — Income Tax and Benefit Return for Non-Residents and Deemed Residents of Canada"; **NR73**, "Determination of Residency Status (Leaving Canada)"; **NR74**, "Determination of Residency Status (Entering Canada)"; **T1234**, "Schedule B, Allowable Amount of Non-Refundable Tax Credits"; **T1248**, "Schedule D, Information About Your Residency Status"

Income Tax Folios

S5-F2-C1, "Determining an Individual's Residence Status"

Interpretation Bulletins

IT-106R3, "Crown Corporation Employees Abroad"

Information Circulars

IC 77-16R4, "Non-Resident Income Tax"

Income Tax Technical News

No. 35, February 26, 2007, "Treaty Residence — Resident of Convenience"

[¶103] INTRODUCTION

The federal Government of Canada and the provincial governments impose a tax on the income of residents of Canada and on the income of non-residents derived from Canadian sources. This introductory chapter summarizes the distinction between residents and non-residents, as well as the general reporting requirements for non-residents and deemed residents.

[¶105] CANADIAN RESIDENTS

Filing Requirements

If you are a factual resident of Canada (¶115) or a deemed resident of Canada (¶117), you must report all of your income regardless of whether the income is from sources inside or outside of Canada. If you are a factual resident, you must use the T1 Form and General Tax Guide for the province or territory in which you resided at the end of the year. If you are a deemed resident, you may be required to file the special T1 return "Income Tax and Benefit Return for Non-residents and Deemed Residents in Canada", as described at ¶110 below.

If you are taxed on income earned or sourced in another country, foreign tax credits or tax treaty relief will generally ensure that you are not subject to double taxation (see ¶1450 and ¶2005).

In certain situations, such as where you have no tax payable, you may not be required to file the T1 return (see ¶200 for details).

(ITA: 2(1), (2), (3))

[¶110] NON-RESIDENTS

Filing Requirements

If you are not a resident of Canada, you are liable to tax in Canada only on income from Canadian sources. The income tax rules and requirements applicable to non-residents are discussed in more detail in Chapter 20. If you are a Canadian resident for part of the year and a non-resident for another part of the year, you are subject to special rules described in Chapter 21.

Generally speaking, if you are a factual or deemed non-resident under the rules discussed at ¶115 or ¶116 and earned Part I Canadian-sourced income under the Act, you will use either a special T1 return and package for non-residents, or the usual T1 return and package applicable to the province or territory where you earned the income. Both requirements and packages are described below.

If you only received Canadian-sourced income that was subject to Part XIII non-resident withholding tax (see ¶2080), you do not have to file a Part I return unless you elect to have some of that income subject to Part I tax (such as under sections 216, 216.1, or 217, discussed below).

If you are a factual or deemed non-resident and are reporting only Part I income from employment in Canada, from a business or partnership with a permanent establishment in Canada, including a non-resident actor electing to file a return under section 216.1 (see ¶2078), use the tax package for the province or territory where you earned the income. In this case, you should also use the Canada Revenue Agency ("CRA") guide T4058, "Non-Residents and Income Tax". If you are also reporting other types of Canadian-source income such as research grants or capital gains from disposing of taxable Canadian property, or if you carried on business in more than one province, you will need the CRA form T2203, "Provincial and Territorial Taxes — Multiple Jurisdictions".

On the other hand, the CRA provides that if you are a non-resident and are reporting only Part I Canadian-source income **other** than from employment in Canada, a business with a permanent establishment in Canada, rental income from real property located in Canada, or timber royalties on a timber resource property or a timber limit in Canada, you should use the special T1 return for non-residents form 5013-R, "Income Tax and Benefit Return for Non-residents and Deemed Residents in Canada". This return is accompanied by the guide 5013-G, General Income Tax and Benefit Guide for Non-Residents and Deemed Residents of Canada. Typically, this special return and guide are used if you are reporting **only** Canadian-source income from taxable scholarships, fellowships, bursaries, research grants, capital gains from disposing of taxable Canadian property, or a business with no permanent establishment in Canada. A non-resident who elects under section 217 to pay Part I tax on certain types of benefits, or under section 216.1 on amounts received for acting services, should also use this special return and guide (see ¶2086). Non-residents using this return and guide should also consult the general guide T4058, Non-Residents and Income Tax.

If you are a deemed resident of Canada under the rules discussed at ¶117, you should also use the 5013-R return and 5013-G guide unless you are reporting **only** income from a business with a permanent establishment in a province or territory, in which case you use that province's or territory's tax package.

If you were a non-resident and received rental income from real property located in Canada or timber royalties on a timber resource property or a timber limit in Canada, and you elect under section 216 to have such income taxed under Part I of the Act (rather than being subject to Part XIII withholding tax), you should use guide T4144, "Income Tax Guide for Electing Under Section 216". The section 216 election is discussed at ¶2080.05.

(ITA: 2; 114; 115; 116; ITR: 2602 Non-Residents; 5013-G, "General Income Tax and Benefit Guide for Non-Residents and Deemed Residents of Canada")

[¶115] MEANING OF CANADIAN RESIDENCE

The usual tension in disputes over residence has been between individuals who wanted to claim non-resident status to avoid tax on world income while living abroad, and the CRA, which wanted to continue taxing the individual on world income if at all possible. The rules discussed below have evolved from disputes in which the taxpayer sought non-resident status and the CRA resisted. The impact of departure tax — a deemed disposition of assets at fair market value upon becoming non-resident — shifts the nature of the argument in some cases, with the CRA being happy to impose immediate tax on the assets of the departing Canadian individual (especially the departing Canadian who has substantial assets to tax), and the Canadian individual resisting classification as a non-resident.

In other cases the argument will be resolved or shifted to new ground by the deemed non-resident rules (discussed at ¶116), which will force the application of treaty rules if the Canadian moves to a country with which Canada has a tax treaty.

As noted, the departure tax rules add new importance to advance determinations of residence status, which the CRA will provide as discussed under the fourth subheading below. Even the most casually departing Canadian should now be concerned with establishing the consequences of their departure in advance.

[¶115.05] *Residence in Fact (Common-Law Residence)*

The CRA distinguishes between a "factual resident" and a "deemed resident". You will be a "factual resident" if you are in fact resident in Canada under the tests discussed here and are not deemed to be a non-resident under the rules at ¶116. If you do not meet the tests for residence described here, you may nevertheless be a deemed resident under the rules at ¶117. However, the factual rules take precedence over the rules at ¶117; that is, if you are a factual resident you cannot be a deemed resident at the same time, although you may be a deemed resident at some other time in the same year.

Factual residence is a question of fact based on Canadian tax case law. The law does not define a factual resident under a bright-line test, but provides only general guidelines. In general, you are a resident of Canada if you live primarily or have your major residential ties in Canada. Because the determination of factual residence is based on judge-made law rather than bright-line statutory rules, a factual resident is sometimes referred to as a "common-law resident".

You may be also considered a factual Canadian resident if you reside for most of the year in another country but maintain a home or family in Canada (subject to the rules at ¶116). If you had Canadian residence at one time but have since moved to another country, you may be considered to have retained your Canadian residence if you still have sufficient residential ties here. In Income Tax Folio S5-F1-C1: Determining an Individual's Residence Status, the CRA distinguishes between "significant residential ties" and "secondary residential ties". While acknowledging, as case law requires, that the residence status of an individual can only be determined on a case-by-case basis after taking into consideration all of the relevant facts, the CRA nevertheless sets out as a general policy that unless an individual severs all significant residential ties with Canada upon leaving Canada, the individual will continue to be a factual resident of Canada and subject to Canadian tax on his or her worldwide income (again, subject to the rules at ¶116).

Significant Residential Ties

In Income Tax Folio S5-F1-C1, the CRA states that the residential ties of an individual that will almost always be significant residential ties for the purpose of determining residence status are the individual's:

(1) dwelling place (or places),

(2) spouse or common-law partner, and

(3) dependants.

Where an individual who leaves Canada keeps a dwelling place in Canada (whether owned or leased) available for his or her occupation, that dwelling place will be considered to be a significant residential tie with Canada during the individual's stay abroad. However, if an individual leases a dwelling place located in Canada to a third party on arm's length terms and conditions, the CRA will take into account all of the circumstances of the situation (including the relationship between the individual and the third party, the real estate market at the time of the individual's departure from Canada, and the purpose of the stay abroad) and may not consider the dwelling place to be a significant residential tie with Canada except when taken together with other residential ties.

If an individual who is married or cohabiting with a common-law partner leaves Canada but his or her spouse or common-law partner remains in Canada, then that spouse or common-law partner will usually be a significant residential tie with Canada during the individual's absence. Similarly, if an individual with dependants leaves Canada but his or her dependants remain behind, then those dependants will usually be considered to be a significant residential tie with Canada while the individual is abroad. Where an individual was living separate and apart from his or her spouse or common-law partner prior to leaving Canada, by reason of a breakdown of their marriage or common-law partnership, that spouse or common-law partner will not be considered to be a significant tie with Canada.

Secondary Residential Ties

Where your residence cannot be determined solely by reference to significant residential ties, the CRA will look to secondary residential ties. Unlike significant ties, where any one test may be determinative, the CRA concedes that secondary residential ties must be looked at collectively in order to evaluate the significance of any one such tie. Therefore, it would be unusual for a single secondary residential tie with Canada to be sufficient in and by itself to lead to a determination that an individual is factually resident in Canada while abroad.

Secondary residential ties that will be taken into account in determining the residence status of an individual while outside Canada are:

(1) personal property in Canada (such as furniture, clothing, automobiles, and recreational vehicles),

(2) social ties with Canada (such as memberships in Canadian recreational and religious organizations),

(3) economic ties with Canada (such as employment with a Canadian employer and active involvement in a Canadian business, and Canadian bank accounts, retirement savings plans, credit cards, and securities accounts),

(4) landed immigrant status or appropriate work permits in Canada,

(5) hospitalization and medical insurance coverage from a province or territory of Canada,

(6) a driver's license from a province or territory of Canada,

(7) a vehicle registered in a province or territory of Canada,

(8) a seasonal dwelling place in Canada or dwelling place the individual has leased to a third party, as discussed above,

(9) a Canadian passport, and

(10) memberships in Canadian unions or professional organizations.

The courts have enumerated other residential ties that may be relevant in determining the residence status of an individual while outside Canada. These other ties include the retention of a Canadian mailing address, post office box, or safety deposit box; personal stationery (including business cards) showing a Canadian address, telephone listings in Canada; and local (Canadian) newspaper and magazine subscriptions. These residential ties are generally of limited importance except when taken together with other residential ties, or with other factors such as those described immediately below.

"Ordinarily Resident"

Where an individual has not severed all of his or her residential ties with Canada but is physically absent from Canada for a considerable period of time (that is, for a period of time extending over several months or years), the courts have at times focused on the term "ordinarily resident" in determining the individual's residence status while abroad. In this regard, subsection 250(3) of the Act provides that a person resident in Canada includes a person who is at the relevant time ordinarily resident in Canada. The CRA has concluded from its reading of court cases that, in general, a temporary absence from Canada, even on an extended basis, is insufficient to avoid Canadian residence for tax purposes. Accordingly, where an individual maintains residential ties with Canada while abroad, the following factors will be taken into account in evaluating the significance of those ties:

- evidence of intention to permanently sever residential ties with Canada,
- regularity and length of visits to Canada, and
- residential ties outside Canada.

It would appear that no one element in this list is determinative by itself. In any event, the CRA has said that it does not consider that intention to return to Canada, in and of itself and in the absence of any residential ties, is a factor whose presence is sufficient to lead to a determination that an individual is resident in Canada while abroad. The comments above are largely drawn from Income Tax Folio S5-F1-C1. They are not, however, a complete summary, and affected taxpayers should consider the folio in full.

Date of Becoming Non-Resident

If it is determined that you have become a non-resident, the CRA considers that the date on which you ceased to be resident is generally the latest of

(1) the date you left Canada,

(2) the date your spouse and/or dependants left Canada, or

(3) the date you became a resident of the country to which you immigrated.

An exception applies where you were previously resident in another country and are leaving Canada to re-establish residence in that country. In this case, you will generally become a non-resident on the date you leave Canada, even if your spouse remains temporarily behind in Canada (e.g., to dispose of your home in Canada) or your dependants temporarily remain in Canada (e.g., to complete a school year already in progress).

If you leave Canada but remain a factual resident, you will be liable for Canadian tax on your world income (subject to the rules in ¶116 if you move to a treaty country), with credit given for taxes paid to foreign jurisdictions on business and employment income that are sourced there and certain other income. A special tax credit may be available to certain employees working abroad who are considered residents of Canada under the rules above (see ¶1458). On the other hand, if you are considered to have become a non-resident of Canada, you may face special taxes and reporting requirements if you own any substantial assets at the time of departure. These are considered in detail in ¶2153.

If you are a factual resident of Canada, you will be a resident of a province or territory and will file returns for the province in which you resided (under these rules) on December 31. Quebec is the only province which makes an independent determination of residence, and in theory Quebec is more restrictive in acknowledging that an individual has given up Quebec residence upon leaving the country (see ¶1605).

[¶115.10] *Temporary Residence in Canada*

The remarks above are directed primarily to Canadians who leave the country. Essentially the same considerations, however, apply to residents of other countries who enter Canada and spend some time in the country. They must determine whether they have become residents in fact by using the residential ties discussed above. In other words, the CRA will apply essentially the same criteria described above to the determination of whether the potential resident has brought his or her family and established substantial ties here. Even if you are not a factual resident of Canada, however, you may be a deemed resident under the rules at ¶117.

[¶115.15] *Dual Residence and Treaty Protection*

Under Canadian law, you can be a resident in two countries at once. In theory, this could lead to taxation in both countries. Most countries, including Canada, have elaborate domestic rules to prevent double taxation. As well, Canada has tax treaties with many countries, and these treaties provide for a determination of residence for tax purposes and rules to determine which country has the jurisdiction to tax various sources of income in order to avoid double taxation. This is discussed further in Chapter 20; see especially ¶2005. The rules in a treaty may override the rules above and determine your residence status, as discussed at ¶116.

[¶115.20] *Official Determination of Residency*

CRA Determination of Residency

In general, the CRA has centralized determination of residency questions in its International Tax Services Office in Ottawa (see listing at ¶287), established centralized procedures to determine in advance whether you will become a non-resident if you present the facts of your case to them, and issued new forms to assist in making this determination. You are not required to obtain this prior determination, but you may do so if you want your residency status for tax purposes clarified in advance. Form NR73 is the general form for individuals leaving Canada, and form NR74 is provided for individuals entering Canada. There are also special forms for deemed residents described in ¶117, below.

You can contact the International Tax Services Office at 1-800-959-8281 (toll free in Canada and the United States), or 613-940-8495 (for service in English), or 613-940-8496 (for service in French). Written inquiries should be addressed to:

International Tax Services Office
Post Office Box 9769, Station T
Ottawa ON K1G 3Y4
CANADA

You can obtain forms NR73 or NR74 and Income Tax Folio S5-F1-C1 from the CRA's website and usually from any of the Tax Services Offices listed at ¶287, as well as the International Tax Services Office.

In most cases, the International Tax Services Office will be able to provide an opinion regarding a taxpayer's residence status from the information recorded on the completed form. This opinion is based entirely on the facts provided by the taxpayer to the CRA in form NR73 or NR74, as applicable. Therefore, it is critical that the taxpayer provide all of the details concerning his or her residential ties with Canada and abroad. This opinion is not binding on the CRA and may be subject to a more detailed review at a later date. Supporting documentation may be required at that time.

Income Tax Ruling

Where certainty is required in respect of the tax consequences of the proposed departure from or arrival in Canada of a particular individual taxpayer, the Income Tax Rulings Directorate may issue a binding advance income tax ruling with respect to the residency status of that taxpayer. Generally, such a ruling will only be available where all of the facts of the situation can be ascertained in advance of the proposed departure from or arrival in Canada of the taxpayer. The procedures for obtaining an advance ruling are discussed at ¶284, and more detailed information is provided in Information Circular 70-6R7. The CRA's advance income tax rulings are not binding on Revenu Québec, although they are binding on all other provincial authorities.

Competent Authorities

In limited situations, it may be necessary for a taxpayer to request the assistance of Competent Authority Services in order to resolve residency issues with Canada and a treaty country (e.g., where an individual may be resident under the domestic law of both Canada and the treaty country). In this circumstance, you should use the current version of Information Circular 71-17R5, Guidance on Competent Authority Assistance Under Canada's Tax Conventions.

[¶115.25] *Special Situations*

The CRA publishes guides and pamphlets covering several special situations, as follows:

- Newcomers to Canada (Immigrants — T4055)
- Non-Residents and Income Tax (T4058).

All of these guides are available without charge from the CRA's website, most Tax Services Offices (listed at ¶287), and from any Canadian embassy or consulate abroad.

(Income Tax Folio: S5-F1-C1 Determining an Individual's Residence Status)

[¶116] DEEMED NON-RESIDENTS

Since a resident is liable for tax on world income while a non-resident is taxable only on Canadian-source income, it is usually the taxpayer who argues for non-resident status. The opposite may be true, however, where the taxpayer faces departure tax on ceasing to be a resident (see ¶2153). Where a Canadian resident takes up residence in a country with which Canada has a tax treaty, the taxpayer could try to seek the best of both worlds by claiming Canadian residence in fact (in effect claiming dual residence), thus escaping departure tax, and invoking tax treaty protection on foreign-source income. However, the Act forbids this alternative by effectively compelling a dual resident of Canada and a country with which Canada has a tax treaty to determine residence for all Canadian tax purposes under the terms of that treaty. Most treaties have "tie-breaker rules" to determine residence for treaty purposes; by way of example, see the description of the Canada–U.S. treaty rules at ¶2174.60. The rules of the treaty (if any) with the particular other country in which you could claim residence status must be examined to determine Canadian residence. A list of treaty countries can be found on the CRA website in the International and non-resident section.

More particularly, the deeming rule under subsection 250(5) provides that, where a person who would otherwise be resident in Canada at a time for the purposes of the Act is, under a tax treaty with another country, resident in the other country and not resident in Canada, the person is deemed to be not resident in Canada at that time for the purposes of the Act. This rule applies to individuals who took up residence in a treaty country after February 23, 1998, such that individuals already resident in a treaty country on or before that date will not be subject to this rule until the individual next becomes resident under a treaty in a treaty country.

The deemed non-residence rule can apply whether or not you claim treaty protection. Simply having residence status in a treaty country under the treaty with that country is sufficient to make you a non-resident of Canada. The operation of the deeming provision appears to apply at the time the tie-breaker rules under the relevant treaty would have first operated, had the treaty been invoked. The treaties themselves generally do not address the question of when in a year this might occur. The intention appears to be that you are deemed a non-resident at the time your ties with the foreign country become such that the treaty would operate to make you a resident there.

It would seem that if you are a dual resident of Canada and a foreign country:

- with which Canada has no treaty, or
- with which Canada has a treaty under which you are not considered resident in the foreign country,

and Canada signs a new or revised treaty under which you are considered a resident in the foreign country, you cease to be a Canadian resident when the new treaty provisions become effective. See ¶2005 for further information respecting tax treaties.

[¶116.05] *Deemed Non-Resident Trumps Deemed Resident*

The deemed non-resident rule discussed above overrides the sojourner and deemed resident rule at ¶117. In theory it also overrides the rules at ¶117 for Canadians employed abroad in an official or quasi-official capacity, but as a practical matter such employees are not usually taxed in the foreign state and therefore are usually not considered resident there under the treaty.

(ITA: 250(5); Income Tax Folio: S5-F1-C1 Determining an Individual's Residence Status)

[¶117] DEEMED RESIDENTS

Under subsection 250(1) of the Act, certain persons are deemed to be residents of Canada and therefore are liable to pay Canadian tax on their world income, although they are not factual residents or common-law residents under the rules in ¶115. However, as noted at ¶116, if such a deemed resident is otherwise determined to be resident in another country under a tax treaty with that country, the latter rule prevails such that the individual will be considered a non-resident under the Canadian Act.

[¶117.05] *Sojourners in Canada*

The most common deemed residents of Canada are sojourners. If you sojourn in Canada (i.e., visit Canada temporarily) for periods totaling 183 days or more in a year, you are deemed to be resident in Canada for the whole year, unless you are deemed to be a non-resident under the rules at ¶116. This rule applies only if you are not otherwise a factual resident of Canada, and this status may change from year to year without any substantial change in your way of life.

For example, a resident of New York state might visit Canada for 200 days in Year 1 and 150 days in Year 2 in connection with his employment as an engineer. While in Canada, he lives in various hotels. For Year 1, he will be considered a Canadian resident and be taxable in Canada on his income from all sources. For Year 2, he is considered a non-resident of Canada and is taxable in Canada only on his income from Canadian sources. This type of individual must be distinguished from one who actually takes up factual residence in Canada during the year whether or not he is present for more than 183 days in that year. An individual who actually takes up residence in Canada (or leaves Canada) during the year will be taxed as a "part-time" resident as described in Chapter 21. You could also be a deemed resident for the year, however, if you contrived to sojourn in Canada for 183 days or more before taking up or after giving up factual residence.

On the CRA website ("Individuals — International and non-resident taxes"/"Deemed residents"), the CRA indicates that the 183 days sojourning in Canada include the days you attended a Canadian university or college, the days you worked in Canada, and the days you spent on vacation in Canada including on weekend trips. If you lived in the United States and commuted to work in Canada, you do **not** include commuting days in the calculation.

Foreign students in Canada are often sojourners under this rule, and are therefore subject to Canadian tax. Foreign students who are deemed resident could in the first instance be taxable in Canada on grants or other formal assistance (but not on support from parents or guardians) from their home country as well as Canadian-source assistance; however, such formal assistance may be protected by the tax treaty between

Canada and the country from which the student has come. See the general discussion of treaties at ¶2005.

If you reside in the United States (or another country) and commute to work in Canada, the commuting is not considered "sojourning" in Canada for the purposes of the 183-day rule.

Although a sojourner is deemed a resident of Canada under the 183-day rule, only Quebec has a special rule which deems a non-resident of Canada sojourning in the province for 183 days to be a resident of the province. The result is that a non-resident who has been in Canada but not in Quebec for 183 days is treated as a resident of Canada but not a province, and accordingly files the T1 General for Non-Residents and Deemed Residents. He or she will file no provincial forms with the T1 return but will pay a federal surtax (¶1445) in lieu of provincial tax (¶1504). Such deemed residents are, in general, not eligible for provincial tax credits.

As discussed at ¶110, there is an exception for deemed residents who carry on business through a permanent establishment in Canada at any time during the year. These individuals are not deemed to be resident in a province but are required to allocate income to the province for provincial tax purposes and, accordingly, must file a return for the province or territory in which the permanent establishment was located (see ¶110). Certain provincial tax credits may be applicable for such individuals (see Chapter 15).

Sojourners in Quebec are deemed residents of both Quebec and Canada, and file returns as Quebec residents. Since federal law does not actually provide for this situation, the federal government provides for this situation by way of a periodic remission order under authority of the *Financial Administration Act*. In addition, on the CRA website ("Individuals — International and non-resident taxes"/"Deemed residents"), the CRA provides as follows: "To avoid double taxation (surtax for non-residents and deemed residents of Canada **plus** Quebec provincial income tax), attach a note to your federal return telling us that you are subject to Quebec provincial income tax, you are filing a Quebec provincial return, and that you are asking for relief from the non-resident and deemed resident of Canada surtax. For more information, contact the Canada Revenue Agency".

(ITA: 250(1)(a), (3); QTA: 8(a); IT-106R3 Crown Corporation Employees Abroad; Income Tax Folio: S5-F1-C1 Determining an Individual's Residence Status; Other Publications: Income Earned in Quebec Income Tax Remission Order)

[¶117.10] Canadians Employed Abroad in Official or Quasi-Official Capacity

You are deemed to be a resident of Canada throughout a taxation year if:

(1) You are, at any time in the year, a member of the Canadian Armed Forces;

(2) You are, at any time in the year, an ambassador, minister, high commissioner, officer or servant of Canada, or an agent-general, officer or servant of a province, who was resident in Canada or deemed to be resident in Canada immediately prior to appointment or employment or received representation allowances in respect of the year. The terms "officer or servant of Canada" and "officer or servant of a province" have been interpreted by the CRA as including any officer or employee of a federal or provincial Crown corporation or agency if, in the statute under which it is organized or established, its officers and employees are given the status of servants to Her Majesty or are designated as being part of the public service of Canada or the province. If the corporation or agency is designated as an agent of Her Majesty without specific mention being made as to the status of its officers and employees, they will be assumed to be officers or servants of Canada or a province. An officer or employee of a Crown corporation or agency who is required to perform the duties of his office or employment outside Canada for an extended period of time should ask his employer whether or not he is an officer or servant of Canada or of a province, and whether or not he will be taxed as a deemed resident of Canada;

(3) You performed services, at any time in the year, in a foreign country under an international development assistance program of the Canadian International Development Agency (CIDA) that is financed out of external affairs appropriations (specified in Regulation 3400), if you were resident in Canada at any time in the three-month period preceding the day services commenced; if you fall into the classification of employment under such a prescribed international development assistance program, CIDA will usually inform you of this;

(4) You are, at any time in the year, a member of the overseas Canadian Armed Forces school staff and have filed your income tax return for the year on the basis you were resident in Canada throughout the period that you are a member;

(5) You are, at any time in the year, a dependent child of a person described in (1), (2), (3), or (4) above, and your income does not exceed the basic personal amount for individuals at ¶1106 or line 300 of the T1 return. Accordingly, the dependent child is deemed be a resident of Canada for 2012 where the child's income does not exceed $10,822. This amount is indexed annually (see ¶65). Where the deeming rule does not operate because income is exceeded, residence will be a question of fact under ¶115 or of the deeming rule at ¶116. "Dependent" means dependent for support at any time in the year on the parent who is a deemed resident. "Child" has a broader definition than might be expected, as discussed at ¶1122.15. "Dependent", on the other hand, has no specific definition; it is a question of fact in each case; or

(6) You are, at any time in the year, entitled to an exemption from tax in a country other than Canada by virtue of a provision of a treaty between Canada and that country or an international agreement (such as the *Visiting Forces Act*) because you are related to or a member of the family of an individual resident in Canada (usually but not necessarily a deemed resident). However, this deeming rule does not apply if the treaty or agreement in question does not exempt you from tax on all or substantially all of your income for the year from all sources. The CRA usually takes "all or substantially all" to mean 90%, while admitting that this is a rule of thumb and not a rule of law.

A special overriding rule (subsection 250(2)) provides that, if at any time in a taxation year you cease to be a person described in items (1) through (4) above, you are deemed to be resident in Canada throughout the part of the taxation year preceding that time (i.e., you are not deemed to be resident throughout the entire taxation year as per the regular deeming rules). Similarly, if your spouse or child would otherwise be deemed resident under item (5) or (6) above, they are deemed to be resident in Canada throughout the part of the taxation year preceding that time.

[¶117.15] General Rules for Deemed Residents

Deemed residents may deduct some foreign payments normally allowed only for payments made within Canada, including payments for moving expenses (¶1039), child care expenses (¶1051), and attendant care expenses for the infirm.

Deemed residents are particularly likely to receive representation or other special allowances which are specifically exempt from employment income; see ¶341 and ¶344. Deemed residents are eligible to claim foreign tax credits in respect of foreign income or profits taxes paid on income received from outside Canada and reported for Canadian tax purposes (see ¶1450).

Deemed residents (as opposed to factual residents, discussed at ¶115) are, except for deemed residents of Quebec described below, not deemed to be residents of a province, and therefore should obtain and file the 5013R T1 general form for Non-residents and Deemed Residents (see ¶110, above). Government agency employees posted abroad or dependants of such employees may also file form NR73 to obtain a determination of residence status if their residence is in doubt. The forms may be obtained from the CRA's website, any Tax Services Office, or from the International Tax Services Office (see ¶287). They are also typically available from Canadian consulates and embassies abroad. If you are a deemed resident at the end of the taxation year and you are reporting only income from a business with a permanent establishment in a province or territory of Canada, you should use the tax package for that province or territory.

As discussed above, although non-Quebec deemed residents are not deemed resident in a province, deemed residents who carry on business through a permanent establishment in Canada at any time during the year are nevertheless required to allocate income to the province for provincial tax purposes and accordingly must file a return for the province or territory in which the permanent establishment was located (see ¶110).

Quebec alone has parallel rules deeming its employees (and their families) abroad who were resident in Quebec immediately prior to their employment to be resident in Quebec as well as Canada. Quebec also claims jurisdiction over CIDA employees (see (3), above) who were resident in Quebec at any time in the six months (not three months) preceding the day on which CIDA-sponsored services commenced. Since the rules for Quebec (¶1605) and the federal government do not harmonize entirely, the filing of returns is easily confused, and contradictory information has been given in some guides in the past. All deemed residents of Canada should file the non-resident version of the T1 return (unless they have business income from a permanent establishment in Quebec, in which case they use the Quebec package) regardless of whether they are also deemed residents of Quebec. Those who are deemed residents of Quebec as well are expected to verify this with Quebec authorities and, of course, to file a Quebec return. If you are filing both a Canadian non-resident/deemed resident T1 return and a Quebec resident return, you should enclose a note with the federal T1 return explaining that you are a deemed resident of Quebec filing a Quebec return. You should not include any federal surtax in lieu of provincial tax on the federal non-resident T1 return at line 404; this tax should be waived by the federal government by virtue of a federal Remission Order since you will be paying Quebec tax instead. Of course, if you can regard yourself as a factual resident (¶115) your life may be easier, in that you simply file a federal Quebec T1 return and the same Quebec return. It is probably only where you want to assert your non-resident status because you will not be returning directly to Canada after your foreign service that it is worthwhile asserting the deemed resident position.

Members of the overseas Canadian forces staff school are in an especially peculiar position, since they are not automatically deemed resident in Canada. If they have ceased to be factual residents, they may opt to be deemed residents under the rule in (4), above, by filing appropriate Canadian returns. Since certain foreign service allowances are tax-free, opting for deemed residence may be beneficial as an alternative to suffering the deemed disposition rules on emigration (¶2153).

(ITA: 250; ITR: 2601 Residents of Canada; QTA: 8; IT-106R3 Crown Corporation Employees Abroad; Income Tax Folio: S5-F1-C1 Determining an Individual's Residence Status; Other Publications: Income Earned in Quebec Income Tax Remission Order)

[¶120] RESIDENTS NOT TAXABLE

[¶120.05] *Officials of Foreign Governments*

Under paragraph 149(1)(*a*) of the Act, an officer or servant of the government of a country other than Canada whose duties require him or her to reside in Canada is not taxable in Canada if:

(1) immediately before assuming such duties he or she resided outside Canada;

(2) that country grants similar privileges to an officer or servant of Canada of the same class;

(3) he or she was not at any time engaged in a business or employment in Canada other than his or her government position; and

(4) he or she was not, during the period, a Canadian citizen.

Under paragraph 149(1)(*b*), a member of the family of a person described above who resides with him or her, or a servant employed by him or her, will also be exempt from Canadian tax if:

(1) the foreign country grants similar privileges to family members and servants of Canadian officials abroad who are of the same class;

(2) in the case of a family member, he or she was not at any time lawfully admitted to Canada for permanent residence;

(3) in the case of a servant, immediately before his or her duties as servant of the person described above, he resided outside Canada;

(4) he or she has not, at any time in the period, engaged in business or been otherwise employed in Canada; and

(5) he or she was not, during the period, a Canadian citizen.

Only officers or servants of the government of another country qualify. Any other employee of a state, country, or other political subdivision of a country would not be exempt from tax under the above rule.

(ITA: 149(1)(*a*), (*b*))

[¶120.10] *Other Special Cases*

Under the terms of a few of Canada's tax agreements (¶2005), certain residents of Canada are exempt from Canadian taxation. For example, visiting foreign teachers and professors are sometimes exempt from Canadian taxation on their teaching income.

Similarly, students who are temporary residents of Canada (deemed or otherwise) solely for educational purposes but were resident in a treaty country immediately before coming to Canada may be exempt from Canadian tax on foreign maintenance or education payments (see ¶2024).

[¶123] VISITING FORCES

The *Visiting Forces Act* exempts visiting members of the armed forces of specified countries, as well as accompanying civilian personnel (from some but not all of those countries) from Canadian taxation on their service pay. The exemption does not apply to Canadian citizens. The sojourn of a member of a visiting force is deemed not to be a period of residence for tax purposes and not to create a change of residence or domicile.

Canada's tax treaties with other countries (¶2005) may also provide special treatment for visiting forces from that country whether or not it is listed in the *Visiting Forces Act*.

The listed countries specified in the *Visiting Forces Act* or in supplementary executive orders are listed in Chapter 20 at ¶2028.

[¶125] INCOME TAXABLE

If you are a Canadian resident, you are taxed on your income from your office or employment, your business, on income or taxable capital gains from any property you may own, and on certain other items of income as described in Chapter 9. You are not taxed on gifts you receive and certain miscellaneous types of income listed at ¶991.

(ITA: 3)

[¶130] EXEMPTIONS AND DEDUCTIONS

In recognition of the fact that some individuals have family responsibilities, personal disabilities, or low income levels which make them less able to afford the payment of tax than other individuals, certain basic credits are allowed against tax. These are discussed in chapters 11 to 13.

All persons, except some part-time residents or non-residents, may earn at least the basic personal credit amount without paying any federal tax (provinces vary this number, and for several provinces the basic exemption is lower, while for others it is higher). A variety of special deductions and credits will increase the exempt amount for low income earners with dependants (Chapter 11 for federal amounts, Chapter 15 for provincial amounts, Chapter 16 for Quebec amounts), so that a married couple with two children under 18 and one earned income would begin to pay federal tax at an income level of around $25,000 or more (usually somewhat higher depending on amounts already paid for such things as Canada Pension Plan and Employment Insurance). Such a family would also be eligible for several refundable tax credits (Chapter 14), which are now generally paid out periodically by the government based on prior years' returns.

Of course, not all income is treated equally. Only $^1/_2$ of capital gains are included in income (Chapter 5), whereas 118% or 138% of most Canadian source dividends are included in income (although dividend credits offset this result and actually reduce the tax payable on the dividends; see ¶404).

Some special taxes, notably Canada Pension Plan contributions, have a lower income threshold. The CPP threshold for self-employment earnings is $3,500. Accordingly, self-employed individuals with self-employment earnings of more than $3,500 should file a return even if total income is less than the basic personal credit amount.

Low income individuals who are resident in Canada may be eligible for what are in effect social safety net benefits obtained by filing a tax return. These include an annual GST benefit (¶1496) and a rather more substantial per child amount paid to low income parents (¶1498). Provincial benefits may supplement these amounts (see Chapter 15). The upshot is that it may be beneficial to file a tax return even if your income is below taxable levels.

(ITA: 117; 117.1; 118; 248)

[¶135] RATES OF TAX

For several years, federal income tax rates have varied from 15% to 29% of taxable income with the rates increasing as income increases (¶1415). Effective for 2016, the federal income tax rates vary from 15% to 33% of taxable income.

In addition, provincial income taxes are imposed by the province or territory in which you reside or carry on business (¶1504). All provinces and territories impose a graduated income tax on taxable income as measured for federal purposes (Alberta used to have a flat tax, but a graduated tax was introduced effective as of October 1, 2015). These provincial taxes, other than those from Quebec, are collected on behalf of the provinces by the federal government as part of the federal tax return process. They are all discussed in detail in Chapter 15.

Residents of Quebec or persons carrying on business in Quebec are allowed a 16.5% abatement from the federal tax (¶1435) and must file a separate Quebec income tax return. The rates of tax in Quebec vary from 16% to 25.75% of Quebec taxable income. See Chapter 16 for details.

The combined federal and provincial rates of tax for individuals vary depending on the province of residence and the level of income. The combined tax rates and brackets for each province are reproduced in tables preceding this chapter (see ¶56 and ¶57).

In certain cases, residents or non-residents must pay a special federal surtax of 48% of basic federal tax in respect of their income that is not considered income earned in a province. This surtax is described in the commentary at ¶1445.

(ITA: 117; 117.1; 180.1; QTA: 750)

[¶140] SELF-REPORTING

By April 30 of each year, you are required to make your own calculation of your income and the tax thereon for the preceding year, and report this information on an income tax return (¶200). It is also your responsibility to pay the required tax by April 30. The period for which the calculations are made is the calendar year; that is, the period from January 1 to December 31.

There is an exception to the April 30 filing requirement for an individual who earns income from a business during the year and for the spouse or common-law partner of such an individual. The exception defers the required filing deadline to June 15, although payment of tax is still required by April 30. A business for these purposes can include a partnership business but not a tax shelter investment (see ¶705).

(ITA: 150)

[¶145] ADMINISTRATION

The CRA administers and enforces the federal income tax laws. Prior to 2004, this agency was called the Canada Customs and Revenue Agency (CCRA). Prior to November 1999, the CRA's functions were carried out by the Department of National Revenue, which for many years had been referring to itself as Revenue Canada, Taxation. As with the 2004 change, the 1999 change had virtually no effect on taxpayers (apart perhaps from some confusion about the name), as the offices and staff remained essentially the same.

On the other hand, the Department of Finance drafts the income tax laws. The Department makes annual changes to the Act pursuant to the annual Federal Budget, and the Department frequently makes technical and other amendments to the Act.

In the case of federal income tax disputes that make their way to the courts, the Department of Justice represents the federal government and defends the relevant CRA assessments on behalf of the Crown.

Chapter 2

Income Tax Returns and Administrative Matters

THESE POINTS ARE COVERED IN THIS CHAPTER

CRA REFERENCES RELATING TO THIS CHAPTER

T1 Lines and Schedules

- Line 130 — Other income
- Line 420 — Net federal tax
- Line 422 — Social benefits repayment
- Line 428 — Provincial or territorial tax
- Line 437 — Total income tax deducted
- Line 456 — Part XII.2 trust tax credit
- Line 476 — Tax paid by instalments
- Line 479 — Provincial or territorial credits
- Line 484 — Refund
- Line 485 — Balance owing
- Line 486 — Amount enclosed
- Schedule 1, Federal Tax
- Schedule 2, Federal Amounts Transferred From Your Spouse or Common-Law Partner
- Schedule 3, Capital Gains (or Losses)
- Schedule 4, Statement of Investment Income
- Schedule 5, Amounts for Spouse or Common-Law Partner and Dependants
- Schedule 6, Working Income Tax Benefit
- Schedule 7, RRSP and PRPP Unused Contributions, Transfers, and HBP or LLP Activities
- Schedule 8, CPP Contributions on Self-Employment and Other Earnings
- Schedule 9, Donations and Gifts
- Schedule 11, Tuition, Education, and Textbook Amounts
- Schedule 13, Employment Insurance Premiums on Self-Employment and Other Eligible Earnings
- Schedule A, Statement of World Income
- Schedule B, Allowable Amount of Non-Refundable Tax Credits (includes Schedule D, Information About your Residency Status)
- Schedule C, Electing Under Section 217 of the Income Tax Act

CRA Guides

5000-G, "General Income Tax and Benefit Guide"; **P110**, "Paying Your Income Tax by Instalments"; **P148**, "Resolving Your Dispute: Objection and Appeal Rights Under the Income Tax Act"; **RC4157**, "Deducting Income Tax on Pension and Other Income, and Filing the T4A Slip and Summary"; **RC4445**, "T4A-NR — Payments to Non-Residents for Services Provided in Canada"; **T4001**, "Employers' Guide — Payroll Deductions and Remittances"; **T4044**, "Employment Expenses — Includes Forms T777, TL2, T2200, and GST370"; **T4061**, "NR4 — Non-Resident Tax Withholding, Remitting and Reporting"; **T4155**, "Old Age Security Return of Income Guide for Non-Residents"

CRA Forms

5000-R, "T1 General — Income Tax and Benefit Return"; **5011-C1**, "YT 432 — Yukon First Nations Tax — T1 General"; **DC905**, "Bankruptcy Identification Form"; **INNS1**, "Instalment Reminder"; **INNS2**, "Instalment Payment Summary"; **NR4**, "Statement of Amounts Paid or Credited to Non-Residents of Canada"; **NR4(OAS)**, "Statement of Old Age Security Pension Paid or Credited to Non-Residents of Canada"; **RC71**, "Statement of Discounting Transaction"; **T1-ADJ**, "T1 Adjustment Request"; **T3**, "Statement of Trust Income Allocations and Designations"; **T4**, "Statement of Remuneration Paid"; **T5**, "Statement of Investment Income"; **T183**, "Information Return for Electronic Filing of an Individual's Income Tax and Benefit Return"; **T400A**, "Objection — Income Tax Act"; **T777**, "Statement of Employment Expenses"; **T778**, "Child Care Expenses Deduction"; **T1013**, "Authorizing or Cancelling a Representative"; **T1132**, "Alternative Address Authorization"; **T1135**, "Foreign Income Verification Statement"; **T1136**, "Old Age Security Return of Income"; **T1161**, "List of Properties by an Emigrant of Canada"; **T1162A-1**, "Pre-Authorized Payment Plan (Personal Quarterly Instalment Payments)"; **T1198**, "Statement of Qualifying Retroactive Lump-Sum Payment"; **T2029**, "Waiver in Respect of the Normal Reassessment Period or Extended Reassessment Period"; **T2200**, "Declaration of Conditions of Employment"; **T2201**, "Disability Tax Credit Certificate"; **TD1**, "Personal Tax Credits Return"; **TD3F**, "Fisher's Election for Tax Deductions at Source"

Information Circulars

00-1R3, "Voluntary Disclosures Program"; **01-1**, "Third-Party Civil Penalties"; **07-1**, "Taxpayer Relief Provisions"; **75-7R3**, "Reassessment of a Return of Income"; **77-9R**, "Books, Records and Other Requirements for Taxpayers Having Foreign Affiliates"; **78-10R5**, "Books and Records Retention/ Destruction"; **84-1**, "Revision of Capital Cost Allowance Claims and Other Permissive Deductions"; **88-2**, "General Anti-Avoidance Rule — Section 245 of the Income Tax Act"; **88-2S1**, "General Anti-Avoidance Rule"; **97-2R16**, "Customized Forms"; **98-1R4**, "Tax Collections Policies"

Income Tax Technical News

[Income Tax Technical News (ITTN) is gradually being replaced by Income Tax Folios. All previously archived ITTNs were removed from the Canada Revenue Agency (the CRA) website effective

September 30, 2012. The following ITTNs have not yet been replaced but are shown as "Archived Content" on the CRA website. The CRA has indicated that the ITTNs will be cancelled as the updated information is published in the new Income Tax Folios.]

No. 22, January 11, 2002, "General Anti-Avoidance Rule (GAAR)"; **No. 27**, April 17, 2003, "Archived Interpretation Bulletins" and "Income Tax Publications Subscriber List"; **No. 29**, July 14, 2003, "Income Tax Rulings Directorate New Automated Telephone System"; **No. 32**, July 15, 2005, "Revocation of Previously Issued Rulings" and "Taxpayer's Opportunities to Respond to Assessments"; **No. 34**, April 27, 2006, "Review of Advance Rulings Process" and "GAAR and Audit Issues/Concerns"; **No. 44**, April 14, 2011, "Filings Based on Proposed Changes to Law"

WHAT YOU SHOULD KNOW ABOUT INCOME TAX RETURNS AND ADMINISTRATIVE MATTERS

RECENT CHANGES

Bill C-15

As of July 2016, the Canada child benefit (CCB) has replaced the Canada child tax benefit (CCTB), the national child benefit supplement (NCBS), and the universal child care benefit (UCCB) (see ¶1498).

The basic and additional residency amounts used to calculate the northern residency deduction have both increased for 2016 to $11 per day. See ¶361a.20.

The maximum eligible fees per child (excluding the supplement for children with disabilities) for the children's fitness tax credit has been reduced to $500. This credit, including the disability supplement, is eliminated for 2017 and later tax years. See ¶1356.

The maximum eligible fees per child (excluding the supplement for children with disabilities) for the children's arts amount has been reduced to $250. This credit, including the disability supplement, is eliminated for 2017 and later years. See ¶1356a.

For 2016 and subsequent taxation years, you can claim the home accessibility tax credit to a maximum of $10,000 for eligible home accessibility expenses incurred for work done or goods acquired for an eligible dwelling (see ¶1358).

The family tax cut has been eliminated for 2016 and later years (see ¶1317).

If you were an eligible educator, you can claim up to $1,000 for eligible teaching supplies expenses (the eligible educator school supply tax credit — see ¶1360b).

The rate that applies to "other than eligible dividends" has changed for 2016 and later tax years. If you received "other than eligible dividends," the federal dividend tax credit is 10.5217% of your taxable amount of dividends reported on line 180 of your return. See ¶1425.

Eligibility for the mineral exploration tax credit has been extended to flow-through share agreements entered into before April 2017 (see ¶1463).

The tax credit for the purchase of shares of provincially or territorially registered labour-sponsored venture capital corporations has been restored to 15% for 2016 and later tax years. The tax credit for the purchase of shares of federally registered labour-sponsored venture capital corporations has decreased to 5% and will be eliminated for 2017 and later tax years. See ¶2522.

Bill C-2

The amount you can contribute to your tax-free savings account (TFSA) for 2016 has been reduced to $5,500 (see ¶2532c.05) and will be indexed thereafter.

The personal income tax rates and income levels have changed.

The donations and gifts tax credit calculation has also changed. See ¶1263.

The tax rate for split income of a child under 18 has increased to 33% (see ¶2529).

Legislative Proposals, October 3, 2016

The sale of a principal residence will need to be reported, along with any principal residence designation, on Schedule 3. Under the proposed changes the CRA will be able to accept a late designation in certain circumstances, but a penalty may apply. Refer to cra.gc.ca/gncy/bdgt/2016/qa11-eng.html, question 7. See ¶554.

For tax years that end after October 2, 2016, the CRA may at any time reassess your income tax return if you fail to report a sale or other disposition of real estate. See ¶267.

Other Changes

For 2016 and subsequent taxation years, you can claim the home accessibility tax credit to a maximum of $10,000 for eligible home accessibility expenses incurred for work done or goods acquired for an eligible dwelling (see ¶1358).

MyBenefits CRA is a new mobile application that lets you securely view your benefits information. You can see your personalized benefit amounts and dates, including related provincial and territorial programs, or the status of your application for child benefits. For more details, see ¶220.07.

If you would like to get your CRA mail online, see ¶202.

Tax Returns

Changes to the T1 form itself are discussed at ¶202.

[¶200] WHO MUST FILE AN INCOME TAX RETURN

[¶200.01] *Overview*

You must file an income tax return for a taxation year if any of the following circumstances apply:

(1) You have tax payable for the year (in excess of amounts already withheld on your behalf);

(2) You have earnings of $3,500 or more in the year and so must make CPP contributions, even if your income is otherwise below taxable levels;

(3) Either you or your spouse or common-law partner are entitled to receive the Canada Child Benefit; that is, if either of you is entitled to receive Canada Child Benefit, both of you must file returns to continue receiving it (if separated, only the parent receiving benefits need file for this purpose; see ¶1498);

(4) You applied for and received advance payments in 2016 of your Working Income Tax Benefit (¶1495); or you wish to obtain advance payments of your 2017 benefit;

(5) You disposed of a capital property in the year (regardless of whether you had gain or loss on the property, and regardless of whether you claimed an exemption (¶502) for it) or you realized a taxable capital gain in the year;

(6) You had a taxable capital gain in the year (as you would, for example, if you claimed a capital gain reserve in the preceding year) even if the application of losses, exemptions or a new capital gain reserve results in no tax owing;

(7) You have to repay all or part of your Old Age Security (OAS) (because your overall income exceeded the OAS "clawback tax" income threshold — see ¶1419);

(8) You have to repay all or part of your Employment Insurance benefits (because you received benefits in the current year and your overall income exceeded the relevant income threshold — see ¶1419);

(9) You have not repaid all amounts you withdrew from your RRSP under the Home Buyers' Plan (¶2625.05) or the Lifelong Learning Plan (¶2626a);

(10) You ceased to be a Canadian resident during the year and had, at that time capital property; you are deemed to dispose of very nearly all capital property on emigration, and that deemed disposition will bring you under the rule in (5), above. A separate rule (¶201, below) requires disclosure if the value of all your property (capital or otherwise) exceeded $25,000; in general, see ¶2153 regarding departure tax;

(11) You have received a demand from the CRA to file a return;

(12) You and your spouse or common-law partner have elected to split pension income; or

(13) You are paying Employment Insurance (EI) premiums on self-employment and other eligible earnings, where you have entered into an agreement with the Canada Employment Insurance Commission through Service Canada in 2012 or later to participate in the EI measure for self-employed people; see Schedule 13 and the discussion at ¶1307.

If you are not required to file a return under the rules above, you are still entitled to file a return. You might want to do this for the following reasons:

(1) If no tax is payable but tax has been withheld or otherwise paid to the government, you must file in order to obtain a refund of tax. In general, a return must be filed within three calendar years of the year for which tax is overpaid, or the refund will be denied, although legislation permits an individual to obtain a refund at the discretion of the Minister of National Revenue where returns have not been filed within the three-year limit (see ¶239);

(2) You want to claim federal and provincial credits to which you may be entitled. For example, you may be eligible for a Canada Child Benefit (paid monthly over the following year), a Goods and Services Tax/Harmonized Sales Tax credit (paid in instalments over the following year), advance payment of the Working Income Tax Benefit credit, or any of several refundable provincial tax credits. These credits are a form of income supplement for low-income taxpayers, especially families with children; they are paid to you in cash if they exceed your tax payable (or if you have no tax payable). Refundable federal credits are discussed in Chapter 14, starting at ¶1496; provincial credits are discussed by province in Chapter 15;

(3) You had a non-capital loss in the year which you want to record so that it can be carried forward or back to reduce income of other years (see ¶1097);

(4) You were a student in the taxation year and have excess tuition/education/textbook/amounts (the education and textbook credits were repealed effective January 1, 2017) to be carried forward (¶1319);

(5) You had income eligible for RRSP and/or pooled registered pension plan ("PRPP") contributions in the year; even if you make no such contributions currently, filing a return will enable the CRA to maintain a record of income eligible for RRSP and PRPP contributions; and this income carries forward to enable you to make additional contributions in future (¶2610.15);

(6) You have investment tax credits (¶1463) either from your own operation of a business, your investment in flow-through shares, or flowed through to you from a trust, partnership, etc. Where the credits are not earned directly by you through a business or partnership and reduce your tax below taxable levels, you do not necessarily need to file, but filing will ensure your eligibility for the credits and allow you to claim carryforwards where they exceed your income; or

(7) You are receiving Guaranteed Income Supplement or Allowance benefits under the Old Age Security program. Filing a return by April 30 will usually renew your benefit. Otherwise, you will need to complete a renewal application form.

Failure to report a capital gain on the disposition of qualified farm and fishing property (¶502f), or shares of a small business corporation (¶502i) may deny you a later claim for the capital gains exemption (¶502) on that gain, and failure to file a return claiming capital gains exemption within one year of the due date for a return may also deny you a claim for the exemption.

Residents of Quebec, persons with a business establishment in Quebec, or non-residents of Canada employed in Quebec or disposing of taxable Quebec property are also required to file a Quebec return and should see Chapter 16.

Non-residents of Canada who receive income from Canada may be required to file returns and should refer to Chapter 20.

(ITA: 110.6(6); 150(1), (2); 164)

[¶200.05] *Elections Canada Option*

On the front page of the T1 return there is a question which, if answered yes, authorizes the CRA to disclose your name, address, date of birth, and Canadian citizenship status (but no other information) to Elections Canada. The information would be used by Elections Canada to update its National Register of Electors, which it is authorized to maintain on a permanent basis, and becomes the basis for lists of eligible electors for every federal election and referendum.

Every year, millions of Canadians move; few of them notify Elections Canada. The provision of this limited information from the CRA is intended to help automate the process of maintaining the electoral registry and thus reduce its overall cost to Canadians generally.

Note that checking the yes box does not add your name to the register, and checking the no box does not remove it. However, where yes is checked and you have turned 18, Elections Canada will apparently send a letter asking if they want to be added to the register.

Additional information is available from Elections Canada: call (800) 463-6868, or online at www.elections.ca.

[¶201] OTHER FILING REQUIREMENTS

Partnerships may have filing obligations, as discussed at ¶1880.

Non-residents of Canada are subject to special filing requirements discussed in Chapters 20 and 21. For non-resident recipients of Old Age Security payments, see also ¶225.

If during the year you became a non-resident of Canada in fact (¶115) or a deemed non-resident (¶116), and at the time you ceased resident status your property was worth more than $25,000, you must disclose all your property holdings to the CRA (on form T1161), whether or not you are subject to the departure tax. There is an exception for personal-use property (clothing, household goods, etc.) with a value of less than $10,000. Filing is required by your filing-due date (¶218) for the calendar year in which you ceased to be a Canadian resident. See ¶2153. Becoming a non-resident is closely defined and is more than simply travelling abroad for an extended period; see the discussion in Chapter 1.

If you loan or transfer funds to a foreign trust, or receive distributions (even of capital) from a foreign trust, you must fill out separate reporting forms disclosing the transactions whether or not you think they are subject to Canadian tax, and whether or not you must file a T1 income tax return. These rules may be retroactive in some cases. See ¶496.

If you have, individually or with other Canadian residents, a 10% or more interest in a foreign company or trust, extensive reporting requirements apply as discussed at ¶495.

If as a Canadian resident you had at any time in the year foreign assets (not counting assets used by you in the course of carrying on an active business nor foreign assets held primarily for personal use and enjoyment) with a value of more than $100,000 (expressed in Canadian dollars), you must file form T1135 regardless of whether you must otherwise file a T1 return for the year; see ¶496.

Individuals, trusts and partnerships who do more than $1 million of business with related non-residents in the year will be required to file returns disclosing the transactions and in particular to maintain contemporaneous documentation disclosing how the prices used in the transactions are arrived at; see ¶796.

INCOME TAX RETURN FILING REQUIREMENTS

[¶202] FORM T1 GENERAL

2016 GENERAL TAX RETURN CHANGES

Based on draft returns available as this was written in late-2016, there were minimal changes to the 2016 returns.

Provincial changes are summarized in Chapter 15.

The 2016 Individual Income Tax Return (form T1 General 2016) is a four-page form and is supplemented by a package of, except for Quebec, 14 schedules (numbered 1 to 9, 11, and 13, and A to C) and a three-page set of federal worksheets. The Quebec T1 package and the Non-Residents and Deemed Residents T1 package both include a Schedule 10 to account for Quebec Parental Insurance Plan contributions.

The supplementary package also includes any forms necessary for calculating provincial income taxes and tax credits (except for Quebec, which requires its residents or taxpayers to file a completely separate form).

Several versions of the T1 General are available for individuals ordinarily resident in Canada, differentiated slightly as follows:

- a general return for residents of Alberta, Manitoba, New Brunswick and Nunavut;
- a return for Ontario residents, which adds a box on page 4 encouraging you to make a gift of your tax refund to the province;
- a return for Quebec residents, which adds (i) lines 438 and 439 on page 4, permitting transfers of non-Quebec withholdings to Quebec for Quebec residents and (ii) line 223 (for deductions of provincial parental insurance plan ("PPIP") premiums paid by the self-employed);
- a return for B.C. residents which adds a box on page 1 indicating residence within Nisga'a Lands on December 31;
- residents of Saskatchewan, Nova Scotia, and Prince Edward Island each have their own return;
- a return for Newfoundland and Labrador residents, which adds a box on page 1 for identifying residents of Labrador Inuit lands or an Inuit community (see ¶1545.75);
- a return for Yukon residents, distinguished by (i) the provision on page 1 of an area indicating residence on December 31 in one of the several Yukon First Nation settlement lands, including the name and code number found on form YT432 which accompanies Yukon

returns, and (ii) the provision on page 4 of line 432 for the Yukon First Nations tax (which is paid in place of 75% of federal and 95% of Yukon tax payable for residents of First Nation settlements — see ¶1596f) and line 441 for the abatement of federal tax for residents of First Nation settlements (offsetting federal share of Yukon First Nations tax); and

- a return for residents of the Northwest Territories, distinguished by a box on page 1 that asks if the taxpayer resided in Tâîchô lands or in a Tâîchô community at the end of the year (see ¶1550b).

The returns above, other than the general return, can be identified by a two-letter (postal) code above the top box on the right hand side of page 1 of the T1.

A separate version of the T1 General, the T1 General Return for Non-Residents, is available for non-residents who are subject to tax in Canada (see Chapter 20) and deemed residents (¶117), although non-residents who earn employment income in a province or territory, or have business income from a business with a permanent establishment in a province or territory should file a resident return; see ¶110. In addition to numbered schedules, this version of the T1 carries three extra schedules, A, B, and C, reproduced with Chapter 20, to assist in the complex calculation of tax credits available to non-residents. It has no provincial schedules. There may be circumstances in which a non-resident or deemed resident will file an ordinary federal/provincial return, and in this case, form T1234 and T1248, which include non-resident Schedule B and a Schedule D, should be filed.

Although there are only ten versions of the T1 General, there remains, due to provincial differences, a distinct package of supplementary forms for residents of each different province, the Northwest Territories, Nunavut, and the Yukon Territory, as well as for non-residents who are subject to tax in Canada. The supplementary forms differ in terms of provincial tax rates and provincial tax credits, as discussed in Chapter 15.

You should use the forms package for the province or territory in which you resided on December 31 of the relevant taxation year; if you ceased Canadian residence during the year (see ¶115 and Chapter 21), use the form for the province in which you resided immediately before your departure. If you left Canada on assignment for the Canadian Forces or a government department or agency, you may be a deemed resident and the CRA directs you to file a non-resident form; see ¶117 and ¶1445.

At one time, the CRA specified a detailed order of attachments to the T1 return. Information Circular 97-2R14 provided (in paragraph 37) the following advice; however the revised version, IC 97-2R16, does not include any specifics regarding the ordering of attachments for paper-filed returns. We have reproduced the list from IC 97-2R14 as follows:

> A cheque or money order should be attached to page 1 of the return if applicable. All other applicable enclosures should be attached to the top left-hand corner of page 3 (of the 4-page return), of page 4 (of the 5-page return), or page 3 (of the 3-page return):
>
> (a) T1-KFS (the keying field summary form generated with the *T1 General — Condensed* return);
>
> (b) Form T1244, *Election Under Subsection 220(4.5) of the Income Tax Act, to Defer the Payment of Tax on Income relating to the Deemed Disposition of Property*;
>
> (c) T1163 Statement A & T1164 Statement B — AgriStability & AgriInvest Programs/CAIS forms;
>
> (d) T1273 Statement A & T1274 Statement B — Harmonized AgriStability and AgriInvest Programs Information and Statement of Farming Activities for Individuals/Additional Farming Operations;
>
> (e) Form RC71, *Statement of Discounting Transaction* [if your return has been prepared by a tax discounter who paid your refund immediately at less than its face amount];
>
> (f) Form DC905, *Bankruptcy Identification Form*;
>
> (g) Form CCA-2736, *Statement of Lending Transaction* (Industry Canada);
>
> (h) Form T1-DD — *Direct Deposit Request — Individuals*;
>
> (i) Form T1132, *Alternative Address Authorization*;
>
> (j) T1A — *Request for Loss Carry-Back*;
>
> (k) Federal keying schedules in any order;
>
> (l) Provincial territorial keying schedules in any order;
>
> (m) Form T2201, *Disability Tax Credit Certificate*;
>
> (n) ON-BEN — *Application for the 2012 Ontario Trillium Benefit and the Ontario Senior Homeowners' Property Tax Grant*;
>
> (o) ON-BEN — *Application for the 2011 Ontario Senior Homeowners' Property Tax Grant, the 2011 Ontario Energy and Property Tax Credit, and the 2011 Northern Ontario Energy Credit*;
>
> (p) Form T2203, *Provincial and Territorial Taxes Multiple Jurisdictions*;
>
> (q) Form RC359, *Tax on Excess Employees Profit Sharing Plan Amounts*;
>
> (r) Form RC360, *SK Graduate Retention Program*;
>
> (s) Form T1198, *Statement of Qualifying Retroactive Lump-Sum Payment*;
>
> (t) Form RC381, *Inter-provincial calculation for CPP and QPP contributions and overpayments*;
>
> (u) All other CRA forms with keying fields in any order;
>
> (v) Information slips — T4, then all others in any order (NR4, T3, T5, etc.);
>
> (w) RRSP contribution receipts;
>
> (x) All other schedules, forms, and receipts in any order.

Prior IC's used to say that unused schedules should not be filed, which is still good advice. Similarly, elections should be prominently noted in relevant schedules or by separate attachments.

Of the schedules provided with the return, some must be filed with the return if they are applicable, while others are provided merely as a convenience to taxpayers who have the option of using the schedules or furnishing the necessary information on their own stationery.

The following schedules must be filed if applicable:

- Schedule 1 — Federal Tax
- Schedule 2 — Federal Amounts Transferred from Your Spouse or Common-Law Partner
- Schedule 3 — Capital Gains (or Losses)
- Schedule 5 — Details of Dependant
- Schedule 6 — Working Income Tax Benefit
- Schedule 7 — RRSP and PRPP Unused Contributions, Transfers, and HBP or LLP Activities
- Schedule 8 — Calculating Canada Pension Plan (Quebec Pension Plan with Quebec returns) Contributions on Self-Employment and Other Earnings
- Schedule 9 — Donations and Gifts
- Schedule 10 — EI and PPIP Premiums (Quebec and Non-Residents Only)
- Schedule 11 — Federal Tuition and Education Amounts
- Schedule 13 — EI Premiums on Self-Employment Earnings
- Schedule A — (only with T1 General for Non-Residents) Statement of World Income
- Schedule B — (only with T1 General for Non-Residents) Allowable Amount of Non-Refundable Tax Credits
- Schedule C — (only with T1 General for Non-Residents) Electing Under Section 217 of the *Income Tax Act*

Notes:

Schedules 1, 2, 8, and 11 are issued in two versions: a general version and a special Quebec and non-resident version. Schedule 10 is issued only with Quebec and non-resident returns. All the differences are accounted for by references to the Quebec Provincial Parental Insurance Plan (PPIP), under which the federal government has ceded to Quebec a portion of the taxing room under the federal Employment Insurance Program. This requires special allocations on Schedule 10 for Quebec residents, and additional lines on Quebec Schedule 1 to accommodate the Schedule 10 adjustments. Changes to Quebec Schedules 2, 8, and 11 differ from the general version in line references due to the different Schedule 1. Schedule 9 also appears in a Quebec version, but that appears to be merely because it shares a page with Schedule 8; the content appears to be identical to the general version.

In addition to the general version of Schedule 6, there is a separate version for each of Alberta, British Columbia, Quebec, and Nunavut, those provinces having reached agreements with the federal government to modify payment formulae.

In certain situations described in the Guide for the T1 for Non-Residents, a non-resident or deemed resident may file an ordinary federal/provincial return. In these cases, you also file a form T1248, which includes a modified version of Schedule B (designated T1234) and a Schedule D (designated T1248). These Schedules are designed to capture information which is generally captured by the standard T1 for Non-Residents and Deemed residents.

Use of the following schedule is optional, in that you may present the information in any suitable format:

- Schedule 4 — Statement of Investment Income

File all charitable donation receipts related to the year, even if some relate to carryover amounts (see ¶1270 and ¶1272). Be sure to keep copies for yourself.

If you would like to get your CRA mail online, read and agree to the terms and conditions (see page 17 of the General Income Tax and Benefit Guide 2016) and enter your email address on page 1. You can also register for online mail using My Account at cra.gc.ca/myaccount and selecting the "Manage online mail" service.

[¶203] FORMS T1 SPECIAL

Previously the CRA provided certain preselected taxpayers with alternative forms of the general tax return tailored to certain specific circumstances. A notice posted on the CRA's website on May 21, 2013 states "[a]s the CRA is no longer producing abbreviated forms and guides, all taxpayers must now use the General Income Tax and Benefit Guide and forms".

[¶204] MISSING INFORMATION SLIPS

Employers and most other issuers of information slips are required to forward these slips to the last known address of the recipient on or before the last day of February in the year subsequent to the payment. Perhaps a change of address notice may be all you require to ensure the issuers send you your information slips. If your employer has your current address and you have not received the information slip by mid-March, you should follow up promptly with the employer.

After all reasonable attempts have been made to obtain an information slip, your income and related deductions (such as Canada Pension Plan contributions and Employment Insurance premiums) should be estimated on the T1 form. Attach a letter to your form stating that you were unable to obtain an information slip and outline the estimated amounts. Unless you are filing electronically, you should file any documentary support (such as periodic pay slips) on which your estimates are based. The CRA asks you to give the payer's name and address, the type of income involved, and what you are doing to obtain the slip.

You should always file your return by the due date even if you know information is missing, and you should attach a statement explaining what is missing, including estimated amounts. See also ¶221.

If your T5 (investment income) slips are missing, contact the institutions that issued them. A T5 slip might not be issued to you if the interest you received was less than $50. You are nevertheless required to report this income. If you cannot obtain a T5 slip, attach a letter estimating the income and giving the name and address of the organization that paid you.

Foreign income and related taxes and expenses must be reported in Canadian dollars although the slips reporting the income to you (if any) will typically be denominated in foreign currency (unless these are amounts being reported through a Canadian payer on a T3 or T5 slip). A table of U.S. and selected other currency conversion rates precedes Chapter 1 at ¶90 and ¶95. In theory, you should use the conversion rate for the day of receipt, although where there are many receipts during the year (or there are no very large receipts) you are usually permitted to use an average rate for the year as shown at ¶95; for rates not shown, contact any CRA office (¶287).

(T1 Guide)

[¶205] MISSING RECEIPTS

Receipts for certain deductions such as charitable donations, medical expenses, and RRSP contributions must be attached to your T1 form if you are paper filing. The processing of your return will be delayed if such receipts are missing. If you are missing such receipts, you should contact the person or organization who is responsible for issuing them prior to mailing your form. If a receipt cannot be obtained before April 30, you should file your return and forward the missing receipt to the CRA (in the manner described in ¶221) when you obtain it.

There are sundry other receipts which the CRA does not require you to file with your return, but which you are instructed to keep on hand for possible review by the CRA. This is especially true of electronically filed returns, where the instruction not to file receipts but keep them on hand is a much more general one. One must expect that in due course the CRA will develop programs (if it has not already) to check for receipts on some kind of selective basis. One could further surmise that any pattern of missing receipts will be met with regular demands in future, and in extreme cases with an effort to establish criminal evasion.

[¶206] RESIDENTS OF QUEBEC

Individuals resident in the Province of Quebec must file a Quebec Income Tax Return in addition to filing a federal form T1 (see Chapter 16).

[¶209] HOW TO OBTAIN FORMS

Individuals will no longer receive the required blank forms in the mail from the CRA prior to the filing deadline. The CRA discontinued the mailing of the forms in 2013 for 2012 returns. If you still want to manually prepare your tax return, blank forms can be obtained from the CRA website at www.cra-arc.gc.ca/formspubs/t1gnrl/menu-eng.html, at your local postal outlet, or Service Canada office (www.servicecanada.gc.ca). You can also call 1-800-959-8281 to request that the forms be mailed to you.

You may require certain forms in addition to the T1; for example, form T778 to claim deductions for child care expenses, or T2201 to claim disability deduction. Most forms and guides may be viewed on and downloaded from the CRA website (www.cra-arc.gc.ca). Copies of these and other forms as well as guides for specific topics may also be obtained by mail (by telephone or mail request).

[¶212] PREPRINTED IDENTIFICATION DATA

The CRA ceased mailing preprinted labels to taxpayers in 2014. The CRA's emphasis now is for tax returns to be filed online.

[¶213] IDENTIFYING YOUR SPOUSE OR PARTNER

Page 1 of the T1 return asks for your marital status and for information about your spouse or common-law partner. The T1 Guide provides a brief description of the information the CRA requires. An extensive discussion of the definition of "common-law spouse or partner" is found in ¶1113.

The T1 Guide discussion is adequate for most taxpayers, but you should know that there are situations which it does not cover.

First, for some purposes you may have more than one spouse or common-law partner. Most commonly this occurs if you still have a legal spouse but you are separated and living with someone else. Essentially, the CRA wants the details of your current partner. For some esoteric purposes, such as the transfer of property between spouses at cost (¶531), you may claim the benefit of the rule for transfers to either spouse or partner. To the extent you have to deal with these items on a T1 return, for example, where you want to elect not to have the spousal transfer rule apply on a transfer to someone other than your current partner, you can only do so by a note attached to the return which explains the circumstances. You should always identify your current partner as of December 31 of the taxation year on page 1 of the T1. If you have more than one current partner at that time, it is a nice but undecided question whether either or both relationships constitute a "conjugal relationship" for tax purposes, as the definition of common-law partner requires.

Another situation in which there can be uncertainty is if you were separated on December 31 of the taxation year but reconciled within a 90-day period after the separation commenced. For example, you commenced to live separate and apart from your common-law partner "because of a breakdown in your conjugal relationship" on December 1 but commenced to live together again on February 2. For purposes of the T1 return, the CRA apparently wants you to report yourself as separated on December 31, so long as the separation was on account of breakdown of the relationship. (The mere fact that you were living apart for other reasons, such as working in different cities, does not by itself amount to a separation. In *Lawin v. The Queen*, 2006 DTC 2768 (T.C.C.), the Court ruled that a separation occurring because one spouse was confined to a long-term medical care facility did not constitute separation on account of marriage breakdown.) The CRA will take account of the separation in calculating various personal amounts, as discussed in Chapter 11. On the other hand, a separation which proves in retrospect not to have lasted for 90 days is not regarded as a separation for purposes of the GST credit (¶1496) or the federal or provincial Canada Child Benefit (¶1498). For those purposes you are instructed to wait out the 90-day period and then report a change of status to the CRA, typically by using the toll-free number provided for that purpose. The CRA will make any necessary retroactive adjustments to the GST and child benefit credits (which will usually be favourable) based on that information.

There are situations which the T1 technically cannot cover. For example, the Nova Scotia low income tax reduction is claimed on the T1, so presumably on the basis of a separation at December 31, even though the provincial definition is tied to the Canada Child Benefit definition, so that in the case of a separation which in fact lasted less than 90 days you are not entitled to the credit as calculated for persons separated on December 31. There appears to be nothing you can do about this. Once you have declared yourself separated on December 31, you should carry through the T1 on that basis, and let the CRA pick up the pieces if they can find them.

When a person becomes or ceases to be an eligible individual's cohabiting spouse or common-law partner, the Minister is to be notified before the end of the month following the month in which the event occurs. This requirement is in relation to eligibility for the Canada Child Benefit (CCB) and is meant to make taxpayers more accountable in providing spousal information to the CRA. This measure in respect of the CCB mirrors the existing rules relating to the GST/HST credit found in subsection 122.5(6.1) of the *Income Tax Act*.

(CRA Document No.: Meaning of Spouse-Separation, *January 18, 2002*, CRA Document No. 2001-0114117)

[¶213.20] *Spouse or Partner's Income and Universal Child Care Benefits (UCCB) Repayments*

A box on the right hand side of Page 1 of the T1 return asks you to enter the income of your spouse or common law partner (as identified above) for the taxation year. Essentially, the box is trying to arrive at net family income for GST/HST credit purposes (¶1496), although it is also used for some other purposes, such as net family income for the refundable medical expense credit (¶1237). If your spouse or common-law partner is not required to complete a return under the rules at ¶200, the income box on your return is the only source the CRA has for this information, and failure to complete the box is likely to delay your GST/HST credit. The income of your spouse or common-law partner should be declared even if it is nil. The amount is the amount that appears on line 236 of your spouse/partner's return, or would so appear if the spouse/partner actually filed a return.

The spouse/partner income box includes UCCB (¶935) from line 117 of your spouse's or common-law partner's actual or putative T1 return, and repayments of such benefits on line 213 of that return. These adjustments are made because such payments are not included in the net family income calculation, and so again provide the CRA with sufficient data to make the appropriate calculation. Rarer adjustments, such as spousal/partner income from registered disability savings plans (¶2529), which are similarly excluded, are not accounted for in the T1 box.

[¶215] SOCIAL INSURANCE NUMBERS

You must enter your Social Insurance Number in the space provided on page 1 of the T1 General. There is a separate penalty for not providing a Social Insurance Number.

Every individual who lived or worked in Canada in a year and is required to file an income tax return must make application for a Social Insurance Number if the person does not already have one. You should do this by completing form NAS2120 "Social Insurance Number Application", which can be obtained from any Service Canada Centre. These centres are usually listed in your local telephone book. The form should be filed in timely fashion so the SIN can be issued in time for use on your return.

If you are married, your spouse's Social Insurance Number should be entered on the right-hand side of Page 1 of your return. If your spouse does not have a Social Insurance Number, it may not be necessary to apply for one at this time, unless your spouse is applying for the Canada Child Benefit.

Note that a spouse includes a common-law spouse or partner as defined in ¶1113, and the law requires you to provide the Social Insurance Number of your common-law spouse. Information on your common-law spouse is necessary to correctly calculate such items as Canada Child Benefit, goods and services tax credit, and a variety of other tax credits, and failure to provide information on a common-law spouse may amount to filing a false return.

It is possible that for tax purposes you will have more than one spouse. For example, if you left your legal spouse more than a year ago to live with your common-law spouse or partner, but are not divorced, both spouses are spouses for tax purposes although a number of claims can only be made for one. In general, you should list the Social Insurance Number of the spouse you will be dealing with on your return. If you or the spouse you are living with will be claiming the Canada Child Benefit (¶1498), you should use that spouse's Social Insurance Number. If some claims (such as medical expenses or RRSP spousal plan contributions) are to be made for both spouses, you should probably list the Social Insurance Number of the spouse you are living with on your return and provide a note with the return showing the Social Insurance Number of the other spouse and the claims to which it is relevant. See ¶1113.

(ITA: 237; ITR: 3800 [Prescribed form])

[¶218] TIME AND PLACE FOR FILING

If you choose to mail your return, you need to send it to the appropriate Tax Centre listed below.

In general, your return will be processed in one of the following Tax Centres. The addresses given below are where you are to send your T1 return. Tax Centres have slightly different addresses for other correspondence; these addresses can be found on the CRA website (www.cra-arc.gc.ca).

You may also deliver returns by hand to local Tax Services Offices (listed at ¶287.15), where drop boxes are available. Note that all the TSOs have removed their self-serve stamping machines, so you will no longer have the option to keep proof of delivery by bringing a photocopy of your document(s) to be stamped. In any event, the CRA would prefer that couriered returns go to Tax Centres.

Send your T1 return to one of the following Tax Centres:

Send your return to the following:	*For individuals served by Tax Services Offices in:*
Canada Revenue Agency Tax Centre 9755 King George Boulevard Surrey BC V3T 5E1	British Columbia, Yukon, and Regina
Canada Revenue Agency Tax Centre 66 Stapon Road Winnipeg MB R3C 3M2	Alberta, Manitoba, Northwest Territories, London, Saskatoon, Thunder Bay, and Windsor
Canada Revenue Agency Tax Centre P.O. Box 20000, Station A Sudbury ON P3A 5C1	Toronto Centre, Toronto East, Toronto North, Toronto West, Barrie, and Sudbury (the area of Sudbury/Nickel Belt only[1])
Canada Revenue Agency Tax Centre 4695 Shawinigan-Sud Boulevard Shawinigan QC G9P 5H9	Laval, Montréal, Nunavut, Ottawa, Rouyn-Noranda, Sherbrooke, and Sudbury (other than the area of Sudbury/Nickel Belt[1])
Canada Revenue Agency Tax Centre 2251 René Lévesque Boulevard Jonquière QC G7S 5J2	Chicoutimi, Montérégie-Rive-Sud, Outaouais, Québec, Rimouski, and Trois-Rivières
Canada Revenue Agency Tax Centre P.O. Box 12071, Station A St. John's NL A1B 3Z1	New Brunswick, Newfoundland and Labrador, Nova Scotia, Kingston, Peterborough, and St. Catharines

[1] Sudbury/Nickel Belt areas include all postal codes beginning with P3A, P3B, P3C, P3E, P3G, P3L, P3N, P3P, P3Y, and all postal codes beginning with P0M and ending with 1A0, 1B0, 1E0, 1H0, 1J0, 1K0, 1L0, 1M0, 1N0, 1P0, 1R0, 1S0, 1T0, 1W0, 1Y0, 2C0, 2E0, 2M0, 2R0, 2S0, 2X0, 2Y0, 3A0, 3B0, 3C0, 3E0, and 3H0.

Send your return to the following:	*For individuals served by Tax Services Offices in:*
Canada Revenue Agency Tax Centre 275 Pope Road Summerside PE C1N 6A2	Prince Edward Island, Belleville, Hamilton, and Kitchener/Waterloo
Winnipeg Tax Centre 66 Stapon Road Winnipeg MB R3C 3M2	Persons participating in the AgriStability (¶1770.10) and AgriInvest (¶1770.15) programs
International Tax Office PO Box 9769 Station T Ottawa ON K1G 3Y4	Non-resident individuals

It is important that you keep with your tax records the address of the Tax Centre to which you send your return, in case you have to send additional information later (as discussed in ¶221).

If you are seeking information about filing or indeed about other tax matters, you would normally call your local TSO in the first instance. A list of offices is provided at ¶287.

[¶218.05] *Filing-Due Date*

The "filing-due date" for a taxation year means, as you might expect, the date on which your ordinary income tax return for that taxation year is due. The term filing-due date is used throughout the income tax rules and CRA publications as a deadline for other requirements as well (information returns such as T1135, for example). It must not be confused with the "balance-due day" (¶229), the date on which amounts owing to the government are due. The two are often but not always the same, and penalties for failure to file (¶242) differ from costs for failure to pay (¶248).

The *Income Tax Act* specifies that anything sent by "first class mail or its equivalent" is considered to be received by the person to whom it was sent on the day it was mailed. Courier service is understood to be the "equivalent" of first class mail. There is an exception for remittance of amounts withheld on behalf of another, and for corporate payments, which are received only when received, but that is not relevant to the general taxpayer. The point is, a tax return must be sent by first class mail or courier (or hand delivered to a TSO) no later than the filing-due date to be timely.

Individuals, deceased individuals, trusts, and corporations all have different filing-due dates. For an individual, the following filing-due dates are possible:

(1) General Filing-Due Date

Unless you fall under (2) or (3), below, your filing-due date is April 30 of the year following the taxation year for which it is filed. That is, your 2016 taxation year return must be completed and filed on or before April 30, 2017, by you or, if you are unable for any reason, by your guardian, curator, tutor, committee, or other legal representative. Your tax is also payable at that time (¶229).

(2) Filing Deadline for Self-Employed Taxpayer and Spouse

Notwithstanding the general April 30 deadline, if you carry on a business in the taxation year you are given until June 15 of the following year to file a return. Your spouse (including a common-law spouse or partner (¶1113)) is similarly granted an extended filing deadline of June 15 if you are carrying on a business. However, where your spouse/partner is living separate and apart at December 31 of the taxation year by reason of a breakdown of the marriage and for a period of at least 90 days which includes December 31, the spouse does not qualify for the June 15 deadline and must file by April 30. Where both you and your spouse/partner carried on a business in the taxation year, you are each granted a June 15 deadline regardless of whether you are living together.

The extended June 15 filing deadline does not extend the balance-due day (¶229) for actually paying taxes owing for the preceding year, which remains April 30 for all living taxpayers. The extension is related to the fact that all individuals carrying on business are now required to have a December 31 year end (or to pay tax as though they did), as discussed at ¶705.

Example

Joe and Edna Parsons are both regularly employed. Edna also runs a small business from a stand in the flea market on Saturdays. Some years the business makes money and some years it loses a bit; Edna always reports the income or deducts the losses, as the case may be. For 2016, there was a loss. Joe and Edna are nevertheless both entitled to delay filing their returns until June 15, 2017, although their tax must be paid in full by April 30. Since, in fact, in this example they would be likely to have refunds, nothing is accomplished by the delay, but they are entitled to use it.

A more common and practical example is a dentist who carries on business through a partnership with two other dentists. The partnership will have to have a fiscal year end of December 31 (¶705), but by the time its books and records are finalized and partnership profit for the year is established and reported to the partners, it is March, and by the time the partners argue about the allocations and settle them, it is April. The partners each have until June 15 to file their returns, but each must pay his or her full estimated tax liability by April 30 to avoid interest charges. Filing the returns by June 15 will avoid late-filing penalties (¶242), but if the returns show amounts still owing, interest will be charged on those amounts from April 30 (¶229, ¶248).

The extension does not apply where the only business carried on is a tax shelter investment. More specifically, the extension does not apply if the expenditures made in the course of carrying on the business are primarily, or are primarily the cost or capital cost of, tax shelter investments; tax shelter investments for this purpose are limited partnership interests or registered tax shelters as defined in ¶2521.

The extension for the spouse of the person carrying on business is granted to facilitate compliance with the Canada Child Benefit provisions requiring filings by both spouses. Accordingly, the issue of whether spouses (including but not limited to common-law spouses) are living together is determined under the Canada Child Benefit rules (¶1498). However, the extension applies regardless of whether the spouse actually receives the Canada Child Benefit; for example, it applies even if there are no children.

As with the April 30 rule, where a person is unable to file, the guardian, etc., must file on the person's behalf.

(3) Filing Deadline for Deceased Taxpayers

If a taxpayer dies in the period commencing November 1 of a year and ending either April 30 of the following year, or if the deceased would have qualified for the extension for the self-employed and their spouses, June 15 of the following year, a return for the year of death must be filed by the later of the ordinary due-date for the deceased taxpayer for that year or six months after the date of death. If the taxpayer had already filed a return prior to death, the legal representative may refile the return within this deadline. If the taxpayer dies after the filing deadline in a year and before November 1, the legal representative must file a return for the year of death by the normal due-date for the deceased taxpayer.

For more information on year-of-death returns, see Chapter 19.

(4) Trusts

Tax returns for trusts, which are technically individuals although subject to special computation and filing rules, are due 90 days after the year end of the trust (which may not in all cases be a calendar year end). Tax owing is due at the same time.

(5) Filing by Designated Person

If the required return is not filed, the CRA may require you or any other person to file the return and may specify the time within which the return must be filed.

(ITA: 248(1) "balance-due day", "filing-due date", (7); 150(1)(*d*)(i); 143.2(1) "tax shelter investment"; 150(1)(*d*)(ii); 150(1)(*b*), (*d*); 150(1)(*c*); 150(1)(*e*))

[¶219] EFILE (ELECTRONIC FILING OF RETURNS)

EFILE is a system of filing returns directly by electronic transmission, with no paper return required. The EFILE system is designed for use by tax return preparation services, and not for use by individual filers. (As an individual, you can prepare your own return on authorized software and file it via the Internet under the procedures at ¶220). Professional users of the system must register with the CRA and comply with the CRA's specifications as to timing, computer software, transmission procedures, and the like. Application must now be made on the Internet, by logging on to the CRA website and searching out the EFILE program. Preparers must update their EFILE registration annually, also on the Internet.

For individuals who have their returns prepared for them, this offers the option of using a preparer who participates in the EFILE program. The EFILE return preparer must have the taxpayer sign form T183, authorizing electronic filing. The advantages of EFILE are in the speed of assessment and refund (if you are entitled to a refund), since it bypasses the CRA's manual input of data from your return into its computer. This may save days or weeks of processing time. There may be offsetting disadvantages for individuals who prefer to deal with the CRA themselves on the basis of a paper return common to the CRA and the taxpayer.

Tax preparers who accept payment to prepare more than 10 tax returns for individuals (or more than 10 tax returns for corporations) are required to file the returns electronically. This requirement is effective for 2012 and subsequent year returns that were filed in 2013 or later. The preparer is subject to a penalty if the returns are not filed electronically as required.

If you use an EFILE service you should review the return as prepared by the preparer as it is you, and not the preparer, who takes responsibility for its completeness and accuracy. If you use an EFILE service and therefore sign form T183, note that it authorizes the preparer to make adjustments in the refund or balance owing of up to $300 without referring back to you. This is a function of the mechanics of the EFILE system, where an EFILEd return is scanned by the CRA prior to acceptance and rejected for errors or inconsistencies. The preparer is expected to correct these and re-EFILE promptly where the correction is within the $300 margin of error.

Returns which are properly filed on a timely basis by EFILE registrants will be accepted as timely by the CRA.

There are certain returns which the EFILE system is not equipped to accept. These include returns involving non-resident status, bankruptcy status, and income tax payable in more than one province. Filers in these (and perhaps a few other) situations must file paper returns. The CRA estimates that 95% of personal returns should be eligible for EFILE procedures.

(ITA: 150.1(2.3))

[¶220] NETFILE (INTERNET FILING), MYBENEFITS CRA, AND TELEFILE (TELEPHONE FILING DISCONTINUED)

[¶220.05] *NETFILE (Internet Filing)*

The CRA has a program that permits most taxpayers to file their T1 tax returns directly via the Internet, rather than going through commercial EFILE preparers. It has dubbed this program "NETFILE". In 2013, effective for filing 2012 and future returns, the CRA eliminated the need for eligible filers to use an access code to NETFILE their returns. Instead of an access code to transmit the return, at the time of filing, the CRA will request the taxpayer's Social Insurance Number and date of birth.

The NETFILE system should be operating to accommodate the filing of 2016 returns from February 2017.

Use of the NETFILE system requires you to use T1 preparation software certified by the CRA for current year returns. You should be able to access a list of certified software, as it becomes available and is approved, on the CRA's dedicated NETFILE website, www.netfile.gc.ca. You will also find there a list of the restrictions on use of NETFILE. The list is extensive and you should check it carefully. Speaking generally, it limits NETFILE to actual (not deemed or part-year) Canadian residents. You cannot use NETFILE in conjunction with a number of specified claims, such as employment income earned from an international organization credit, or foreign tax credit in respect of more than three countries. This is only a partial list, and, again, you should verify your eligibility against the full list of restrictions at www.netfile.gc.ca.

[¶220.07] *MyBenefits CRA*

You can use MyBenefits CRA mobile app to securely access your benefit information. You can see your personalized benefit amounts and dates, including related provincial and territorial programs, or the status of your application for child benefits. To get more details on the MyBenefits CRA mobile app, go to cra.gc.ca/mobileapps.

[¶220.10] *TELEFILE (Telephone Filing Discontinued)*

The CRA had a system which permitted simple returns to be filed by touch-tone telephone. In a News Release dated June 27, 2012, the CRA announced the TeleFile service would be discontinued.

[¶221] AMENDING RETURNS

After filing a return, you may discover that an error or omission was made which either increases or decreases the tax payable. The CRA prefers that you do not file an amended income tax return in these circumstances. Instead, you have two options for amending/changing your return. The first option is to write to the Tax Centre where you filed your return (see ¶218), with an explanation and any additional material such as T4 slips, T5 slips and receipts. The CRA would prefer that you also include form T1-ADJ (available online at www.cra-arc.gc.ca) to organize the presentation of your adjustment request in a convenient fashion. All written requests for adjustment should be sent to your Tax Centre. The second option is to file the adjustment online through the "My Account" service (¶287.06) offered by the CRA. If you have signed up for this service, it offers a convenient option to change your return for the current year and for the last 10 years.

Correspondence with the CRA should include your Social Insurance Number or Identification Number. If you want to discuss your return or assessment in person you must book an appointment in advance and bring your own copy of the return and assessment to your TSO (¶287). However, if you think it is necessary to actually paper-file the return, you should get in touch with your TSO to arrange for them to obtain the file from the Tax Centre. In some cases this may take considerable time and you may want to check with them to be sure that they have the file.

If you receive a Notice of Assessment and do not formally object to it within 90 days of its mailing date, or within one year of the due date of the T1 return to which the assessment relates, whichever is later, you are technically bound by it. See ¶266. Notwithstanding the time limitations on a formal objection, the CRA normally will reassess for errors or omissions which are brought to its attention, including errors which are in the taxpayer's favour; see ¶268. (An exception is that the CRA will not reassess where you change your mind about optional deductions, such as capital cost allowance.) However, if you discovered an error in your favour and reported it to the CRA, but the 90-day/one-year time limit will expire before a reassessment is received, you may wish to file a Notice of Objection (see ¶266) to protect your statutory right to the tax recovery.

(ITA: 60.021; 152; 165(1); IC 75-7R3 Reassessment of a return of income; IC 84-1 Revision of capital cost allowance claims and other permissive deductions)

[¶222] FILING BASED ON PENDING LEGISLATION

It frequently happens that tax changes are not enacted by the time returns are due based on those changes. This occasionally happens with budget measures, but more often with technical amendments, which can be published and republished with slight variations for years before being enacted. In some cases, usually those unfavourable to the taxpayer, a provision is made in the legislation itself for filing to be deferred until some stated time after the rules are finally enacted. These extensions are typically reported in this book when pending legislation is described.

The CRA has a stated policy (in *Income Tax Technical News* No. 44, under the heading "Filings Based on Proposed Changes to Law"):

> It is the CRA's longstanding practice to ask taxpayers to file on the basis of proposed legislation. This practice eases both the compliance burden on taxpayers and the administrative burden on the CRA. However, where proposed legislation results in an increase in benefits (e.g. Canada Child Benefit) to the taxpayer or a significant amount of rebate or refund is at stake, generally, the CRA's past practice has been to wait until the measure has been enacted.

Presumably, the restriction on rebates or refunds means that the CRA wants you to file the return in accordance with pending legislation, but may withhold assessment, and therefore payment, of a "significant" refund.

In some cases, pending legislation is effectively abandoned or postponed. The CRA addressed this issue at the 2010 Canadian Tax Foundation Round Table, saying (as set out in *Income Tax Technical News* No. 44),

> In the event that the government announces that it will not proceed with a particular amendment, any taxpayers who have filed on the basis of the proposed amendment are expected to take immediate steps to put their affairs in order and, if applicable, pay any taxes owing. Where taxpayers acted reasonably in the circumstances, took immediate steps to put their affairs in order, and paid any taxes owing, the CRA will waive penalties and/or interest as appropriate.

According to CRA policy (in *Income Tax Technical News* No. 44), the CRA will request a waiver or assess based on legislation if a waiver is refused, with regard to statute-barred years.

PAYMENT OF TAX

[¶224] WITHHOLDING TAX ON EMPLOYMENT INCOME

If you are an employee, all or most of the tax that relates to your salary or wages will have been withheld from your salary or wages by your employer and remitted to the government on your account. On or before the last day of February of the year following the year for which you are filing an income tax return, you should receive from your employer two copies of form T4 (Statement of Remuneration Paid) which will state the salary or wages and other taxable amounts paid to you for the year and the amount of tax, Employment Insurance premiums and Canada or Quebec Pension Plan payments withheld. An employer who pays you less than $500 in a year and has withheld no tax, Employment Insurance or Canada Pension Plan contributions, is not required to prepare a T4 form but you are still taxable on such amounts.

If the federal and provincial taxes owing on line 485 of your return after accounting for amounts withheld from salary or wages or other remuneration (or other items) does not exceed $3,000 for the year (or for residents of Quebec, if your federal tax only owing does not exceed $1,800), you need only indicate the withheld tax on your return as a payment, calculate any balance of tax owing and remit this balance by cheque or money order when filing your return, or if filing electronically, go to www.cra.gc.ca/mypayment. Any overpayment should be shown on the return as refundable. Where your tax owing exceeds $3,000 ($1,800 for Quebec residents), see ¶227.

If you are employed, you are required to sign and file with their employer a declaration on form TD1 (Employee's Personal Tax Credit Return). This form shows the personal amount tax credits to which you are entitled (see Chapter 11) and is used by your employer in calculating amounts of tax to be withheld from your remuneration. If your personal amount tax credits will exceed the amount of the basic personal credit for the year it is to your advantage to file this form, since otherwise your employer is required to withhold tax on the assumption that you are a single person entitled to only the minimum credit.

If you certify on form TD1 that your total earnings received and receivable during the calendar year from all sources will not exceed the personal amount value of your personal tax credits, no tax need be withheld by your employer.

[¶224.05] *Additional Voluntary Withholding*

When you file your income tax return you may find that you owe a considerable amount of tax because you received income from which tax deductions at source were not required to be made or were insufficient. In some cases, instalment payments may be required. If you expect that you will continue to have substantial tax to pay when you file your next return, you may find it convenient to request your employer (or pension payer) to make additional withholdings from your employment or other (T4A) income to offset the liabilities on other income. You may do this on your TD1 form, either when you file it originally or by filing a revised TD1 with your employer. Although the penalties for misestimating your income on TD1 may not be great, if you consistently do so to the degree that instalment payments should have been made, you may face very high interest and penalty charges on the deficient instalments. See ¶227.

[¶224.10] *Requesting Reduced Withholding*

In situations where regular withholdings will exceed your expected tax liability for the year and the withholdings are an undue hardship to you, you may apply to the Minister of National Revenue to authorize your employer to reduce the amount of tax withheld from your salaries and wages. To apply for reduced withholding, complete form T1213, *Request to Reduce Tax Deductions at Source for Year* and send with supporting documents to the Taxpayer Services Division of your local TSO (¶287). For example, if you are making deductible support payments, you would include a copy of the order or agreement under which you make the payments and of form T1158, *Registration of Family Support Payments*. If you make regular RRSP contributions, you should provide documents to show the amounts you contribute.

Form T1213 seems to be designed primarily to be filed early in the year to accommodate regular items known at the time, such as recurring support payments. Where you are filing late in the year, and want alleviation of irregular deductions, you should at least supplement form T1213 with a detailed explanation of your request. The form is helpful in suggesting required documentation.

Typically, if you have deductible support payments to make, or have made RRSP contributions or purchased resource tax shelters or incurred substantial deductible interest expense, your TSO (¶287) will provide a letter to your employer authorizing reduced withholdings. If you are making a request late in the year, you should take account of withholding payments already made in asking for a reduced withholding so that total withholdings will approximate your actual tax liability for the year.

Another common situation arises where you have substantial non-cash benefits, for example, on the exercise of a stock option. The CRA has historically taken the position that full withholding is required from any accompanying remuneration, but will usually grant a waiver where it can be shown that your ultimate tax liability warrants it. For more detail, see ¶2565. For employee stock option benefits, the Act specifically provides that employee stock option benefits will be subject to regular withholding as if the benefit was a cash bonus payment. (But the withholding does not apply to a benefit in respect of the acquisition of a security of a Canadian-controlled private corporation where the benefit is deferred.) The Act also provides that the CRA cannot reduce the withholding at source upon the taxpayer's request solely because the amount of withholding arose from a non-cash benefit (e.g., the benefit arising on the acquisition of the securities pursuant to the option). However, the amount subject to withholding will be reduced by one half if the one-half deduction in computing taxable income under paragraph 110(1)(*d*) is available to the employee. See ¶330.56.

If your employer is making payments which clearly have a non-taxable result, such as paying a retiring allowance directly to an RRSP, withholding may not be required, nor does the employer have to have a letter of authorization you have received from Source Deductions sections. Details are provided in the *Employers' Guide — Payroll Deductions and Remittances* (T4001 — Chapter 5, subheading "Reducing Remuneration Subject to Income Tax") and the guide "Deducting Income Tax on Pension and Other Income, and Filing the T4A Slip and Summary" (RC4157).

[¶224.15] *Income Not Subject to Withholding*

If you have income from sources other than from employment such as dividends, interest, business income, rent, taxable capital gains, etc., tax will not have been withheld on this income and you must remit any tax resulting from this income yourself. This income may also trigger instalment liability, as discussed below.

(ITA: 153(1), (1.1), (1.2), (1.3), (2); 227(2); ITR: 205 Date Returns to be Filed)

[¶225] WITHHOLDING FOR CLAWBACK TAX ON OLD AGE SECURITY PAYMENTS

Income tax is not normally deducted from OAS payments under the general rules, since the OAS amounts by themselves are below normal withholding limits. The T4A (OAS) slip does provide for withholding, which can occur if the taxpayer requests it.

However, the government does withhold from OAS payments amounts on account of the clawback tax on individuals with net income in excess of (for 2016) $73,756 (¶1419). Withholding for the period January–June is to be calculated on the basis of second prior year returns, and for July–December on prior year returns.

Where there has been no return filed for the base year of a resident and no demand for a return for that year has been made by the CRA, no withholding is to be made from current OAS. This leaves unsettled the issue that arises where a return has been filed but is late-filed or simply has not been processed by the CRA in time to withhold. This is especially likely in view of the June 15 filing deadline granted to the self-employed. It is understood that in these circumstances the CRA will probably determine withholding on the basis of the most recently processed return until the system provides revised information; however, once revised information becomes available, withholding will be based on that number from that time on. No effort is expected to try to compensate for earlier misinformation within a six-month period. True-ups will of course occur on the T1 return.

If no return has been filed for a relevant base year and the CRA has formally demanded one, the government may withhold the entire OAS payment (less any non-resident tax currently being withheld on the same payment).

[¶225.05] *Non-Residents*

The OAS clawback (¶1419) applies to non-residents (since it is not a Part I tax), and a "return" for purposes of OAS clawback tax includes a T1 return where the individual was resident in Canada throughout the year, and a T1136 return in any other case.

Where no return has been filed for a relevant base year but you were non-resident at any time in that year, the government may withhold the full amount of the OAS payment less any non-resident withholding tax currently being withheld on the same payment.

It is evident that this system requires non-residents to file a return of world income in order to qualify for OAS payments. That return is designated as T1136, *Old Age Security Return of Income*. Form T1136 has not always been available from the CRA offices; in some years only a personalized version was sent, together with a guide to these rules (*Old Age Security Return of Income Guide for Non-Residents*, T4155), to OAS recipients known to the CRA to be non-residents. More recently, the form has at least appeared on the CRA website, from which it can be downloaded. Non-resident recipients of OAS who, for whatever reason, cannot access form T1136 are required to file the T1 General for Non-Residents instead. This could be the case for the year you become a non-resident, unless you have confirmed your non-resident status with the CRA before departure. Where OAS payments have ceased under these rules but your world income is below the level at which they are obliterated altogether by the rules at ¶1419, you can recover back payments by filing form T1136 or a T1 General for Non-Residents, for the base years in issue.

As with ordinary salary withholding, OAS clawback withholding, although based on the prior year's experience, is on account of current year liability, and so the amount withheld may be more or less than final liability where your income (stated in Canadian dollars) in the base year has changed in the current year. The T1136 return for the current year will true up your actual liability against the amounts withheld and result in a refund or additional tax owing, as well as providing a base year calculation for future withholding.

The OAS authorities should send you an NR4-OAS either with your December payment or early in the following year showing your OAS income and two differing withholding tax amounts: box 27 for use on the T1136 return, and box 17 if you also choose to file a "section 217 election". The section 217 election, discussed at ¶2086, may benefit you if your marginal Canadian tax rate if you were a Canadian resident would be less than the non-resident withholding rate applied to your Canadian source income.

Several Canadian tax treaties (¶2005) limit the amount of tax that Canada can impose on OAS payments made to residents of the other treaty country, and these rules override the 100% withholding requirement and thus (perhaps) the requirement to file form T1136. The CRA's "Old Age Security Return of Income Guide for Non-Residents" (T4155) lists (for 2015) 40 countries whose residents are protected from the OAS clawback tax, although not necessarily from ordinary withholding tax. Those countries include (among others) Australia, Ireland, Israel, Mexico, Poland, and the United Kingdom, as well as the United States, which is discussed in Chapter 20. The CRA also says in the Guide that it will forgo its (questionable) right to insist on the filing of form T1136 for residents of countries where the treaty exempts them from clawback.

The actual T1136 may be confusing, especially to those accustomed to the ordinary T1 return. It stresses retirement income, using the same line numbers as the T1 return. It also provides for interest and investment income, capital gains, rental income and RRSP income. However, it lumps together almost all omitted lines from the T1 return at line 130, with the annotation "see line 130 in the guide". The Guide referred to is the *Old Age Security Return of Income* guide (T4155), not the T1 Guide. Thus employment income, taxable support payments received, and the like are to be reported at line 130. Support payments are income only to the extent they would be income in Canada under the rules in Chapter 23.

(ITA: 180.2)

[¶227] INSTALMENT TAX ON INCOME FROM SOURCES OTHER THAN EMPLOYMENT

The rules which determine whether you must pay instalments of tax for the current year look back to either of the two preceding years as well as the current year in determining current year liability. This harmonizes the threshold system with the instalment notice system, so that it should in theory not be possible for instalment liability to arise without receiving instalment liability notices. At least, this should be true so long as timely returns have been filed regularly and the CRA assesses with even some semblance of promptness.

A problem can arise with instalment notices based on prior years' liability which need not be paid because no current liability is anticipated.

[¶227.05] *Calculating Instalments: (1) Are They Required?*

If you have recurring income which is not subject to the withholding system, that is, income from which no deductions have been taken by the payer and remitted to the CRA on your behalf, you may be required to pay instalments on account of tax payable for the current year. Generally speaking, if the extra income is a one-time occurrence, such as the income that would arise on the sale of a cottage in 2015, no instalment is required for 2015 or 2016. However, where you regularly have income not subject to adequate withholding, so that you regularly owe the CRA more than $3,000 on your federal tax return ($1,800 for residents of Quebec), you will be required to make instalment payments of tax. Thus, if your tax balance owing (on line 485 of the T1 return, but not counting any instalments on line 476) exceeded $3,000 in either of the two preceding years, and you will have a similar excess in the current year, you must make instalment payments for the current year on March 15, June 15, September 15, and December 15.

Even if you are not required to make instalment payments for the current year because you did not meet the threshold tests in either of the preceding two years, you may want to consider making payments periodically under the rules described under the heading "Calculating Instalments: (3)" at ¶227.15, below, if you have a source of income not subject to withholding for 2016. You would do this to avoid the significant lump-sum tax payment which will otherwise face you on April 30 of the next year.

The technical rules for determining whether you must make instalment payments, and the various methods of calculating those payments, are discussed below.

General Rule (except Quebec): To determine whether instalments are due for the current year, the key question is whether your tax liability for the current year and either one of the two preceding years minus all amounts withheld on account of that year exceeds $3,000. If this "net tax owing" for the current year, or for both of the two preceding years, is $3,000 or less, you are not liable for instalment payments for the current year. If the net tax owing for both the current year and either of the two preceding years is over $3,000, instalments are required for the current year. Net tax owing includes federal tax and federal surtax, OAS (but not EI) clawback tax (¶1419), and all provincial and First Nations tax collected under various income tax agreements (i.e., all federal tax from line 420, all provincial tax from line 428, and all Yukon First Nations tax on line 432 of the return for the year in question, but only the amount from line 422 that represents OAS clawback); from this is deducted all amounts withheld for the year (line 437) and all income tax credits other than those paid out over time by the government (i.e., other than GST credit and Canada Child Benefit). In short, net tax owing is the sum of lines 420, 422 (OAS clawback), and 428 from the T1 minus all the credits on lines 437, 452, 453, 454, 456, and 479. Canada Pension Plan and Employment Insurance credits do not enter into the calculation because strictly speaking they are not income tax items, although once liability is established under the test, Canada Pension Plan liability will be relevant to determine instalments. Once it is established under this test that instalment liability exists for the year, the calculation of that liability may be carried out by the methods in either of the two subheadings on that subject below. Liability must be determined on a current year basis; carrybacks of losses or credits from future years cannot affect it, nor can any credits (such as GST credit) which become payable after the balance-due date. Certain reassessments which carry back revisions to flow-through share deductions similarly will not retroactively trigger instalment liability (¶248a).

General Rule (Quebec residents only): Since the federal government does not collect tax on behalf of Quebec, and gives an abatement to Quebec residents in recognition of the taxes collected by the Quebec government, both the threshold amount and the calculation of net tax owing must be modified for Quebec residents. For any particular year (i.e., the current year or either of the past two years) in which you were resident in Quebec on December 31, the threshold amount becomes $1,800 (to recognize that it does not include provincial tax), and the "net tax owing" is limited to all federal tax, federal surtax and OAS (but not EI) clawback tax, minus the total of the Quebec abatement, all amounts withheld for the year on account of federal tax, and all federal tax, credits other than those paid out over time by the government (i.e., other than GST credit and Canada Child Benefit). Thus for continuing Quebec residents, if the net (federal) tax owing for both the current year and either of the two preceding years is over $1,800, instalments are required for the current year. If you were resident in Quebec in 2014, elsewhere in 2015, and Quebec again in 2016, you must determine liability for 2016 instalments using the threshold under the Quebec rule for 2014 and 2016, but under the general rule for 2015. As above, once liability is established under this test, instalments are calculated as described below. As with the general rule for other provinces, liability must be determined on a current year basis; carrybacks of losses or credits from future years cannot affect it, nor can any credits (such as GST credit) which become payable after the balance-due date. Certain reassessments which carry back revisions to flow-through share deductions similarly will not retroactively trigger instalment liability by increasing either federal tax or Quebec abatement (¶248a). Quebec residents who are liable for federal instalment payments under these rules may have a second parallel set of instalments to pay to Quebec under its very similar rules. Quebec also has its own system of instalment notices, similar to the federal reminders described under the next subheading, and provides form TP-1026-V for calculating Quebec instalments under the various options it provides. Quebec instalments are, of course, based on income as it appears on Quebec rather than federal returns.

(ITA: 153(2); 156.1)

[¶227.10] *Calculating Instalments: (2) CRA Instalment Reminders*

If you had an instalment liability for either of the two preceding taxation years, the CRA should send you instalment reminders for each quarter of the current year. The CRA uses a system of sending the reminders twice a year, so that in February you receive an instalment notice for each of the March 15 and June 15 payments, and in August you receive notices for the September 15 and December 15 payments. The first two instalments will be based on your tax return for the second preceding year and each should be equal to one fourth of your second preceding year instalment liability (excluding any revisions to that liability arising from carrybacks of losses, investment tax credits, and similar retroactive adjustments). The second two instalments will be based on your tax return for the first preceding year and will each represent one half of your instalment liability for that year (exclusive of carryback revisions) in excess of the total of the first two payments. Note that these amounts are fixed and are not adjusted for instalment payments actually made. On the other hand, if you have made partial payments or overpayments prior to receiving your instalment reminder, you need only pay the amount (if any) which will bring your payments for the period up to the amount shown on the notice.

The system of sending a notice covering two instalments at once is intended to reduce processing costs for the CRA.

The great advantage of paying the amounts on the instalment reminders is that they represent an absolute safe haven for instalment payers. If you pay the amounts shown on the notices by the due dates, you will have no liability for interest or penalty for instalment deficiencies even if the notices are in error or another method of calculation would have required higher instalments.

There may, however, be serious drawbacks to paying instalment reminder amounts in several common situations. One such situation will occur where you are aware that your income is falling below levels of prior years. This commonly affects individuals living on investment income; if investment income has fallen sharply since the two preceding years, instalment notices would be unrealistically high. (Investment income often falls with declining interest rates, but may have fallen for other reasons.) The alternative to paying instalment notices likely to be excessive is doing a self-calculation as described below. To the extent the self-calculation is based on the preceding year's income, however, it may be difficult for all but the most organized to meet the March 15 instalment date. There are several alternatives. Perhaps the easiest is to make both March 15 and June 15 payments together on April 30. By April 30 you will be able to calculate proper instalments based entirely on the preceding year's tax, and if you make this combined payment by April 30 the interest on the late payment for March 15 should be substantially offset by the interest credit on the prepayment for June 15 (see the discussion of "Interest on Instalments", below). Alternatively, if you can manage to make the March 15 payment, you can reduce the June 15 payment by the amount overpaid in March when you do calculate your own instalments. Although these alternatives do not provide the same safe haven, they may provide a better result than making substantial overpayments which can only be recovered when you file your return for the year.

Another common problem area will arise for people who are coming into the instalment system for the first time.

Example

> Janine retired in Year 1 and in addition to tax withheld before retirement of $10,000, she had an additional $10,000 of tax to pay. She had never before had to pay instalments. In fact she paid the additional $10,000 when filing her return on April 30, Year 2. Had she thought about the additional liability in Year 1, she might have preferred to pay at least some payments periodically, even though these were not technically required. However, since she had been

fully withheld prior to Year 1, she has no penalty or interest for instalment shortfalls for Year 1. As well, for Year 2, she will have no instalment liability until September 15. Her first Instalment Notice will direct her to pay $5,000 by September 15. Her second will direct her to pay $5,000 by December 15. She has now been required to pay $20,000 between April 30 and December 15, Year 2. You can see why she might have preferred prepayments. Even in Year 2, with the inevitable $10,000 payment in April, she may prefer to pay $2,500 per quarter rather than larger amounts later. She is entitled to do this. If she pays $2,500 in March and again in June, she will only have to pay $2,500 in September and December rather than the $5,000 demanded. If Janine does not notice her instalment liability until her tax return is prepared in April Year 2, she can make a $5,000 instalment on April 30 (covering March and June both) and successive $2,500 instalments in September and December. This should incur no interest since there would be no instalment notices for the first two periods.

A similar problem may arise where you are already in the instalment system but your income not subject to withholding increases in the year. If, for example, the CRA does not succeed in processing your return in time to issue an instalment notice for September 2016, it appears that the September (and probably the December) installment will simply continue based on 2014. This is simply a variation on the problem that if you rely on the notices when your income not subject to withholding is increasing, you will be faced with a large tax payment down the road. The notices can give you a false sense of security if you don't keep track of your own potential tax liability.

More complex situations will arise where income fluctuates from year to year because of, for example, occasional capital gains. Where instalment notices are based on extraordinarily high income unlikely to recur in the present year, it may be desirable to base your instalments on estimated income as described below, although this always involves some risk.

(ITA: 156; 161(4.01))

[¶227.15] *Calculating Instalments: (3) Calculating Your Own Instalments*

There are three options for calculating your current year instalments. The first is to use the same method used by the CRA in issuing its instalment reminders described above. There seems to be little point to this if you are receiving the CRA notices, since you are merely replicating what they have already done. Still, if you are not receiving the reminders but believe you have a current instalment liability, you can calculate it, for each of the first two current year instalments based on one fourth of the total second preceding year instalments and, for each of the second current year payments based on one half of the amount by which total preceding year instalments exceed one half of the second preceding year instalments. The calculation for each of the two preceding years can be done (separately) on copies of the Calculation Chart which appear in the CRA pamphlet "Paying Your Income Tax by Instalments" (P110).

Second, you may choose to use only your preceding year income to calculate your current year instalments. That is, you take the total preceding year tax liability after all credits and withholding (except instalments), divide by four, and pay the result quarterly by the 15th of March, June, September, and December of the current year. Again, you can work out the instalments on the Calculation Chart in the CRA pamphlet "Paying Your Income Tax by Instalments" (P110), which is designed for this purpose.

Third, you may choose to estimate your total federal and provincial tax payable, plus Canada Pension Plan payments and minus amounts otherwise remitted during the year, and make quarterly payments of the balance divided by four. The drawback to this estimated tax payment is that if it turns out your actual tax is higher than the estimate, you may be liable for very substantial interest and penalties, as described below.

In general, no interest or penalty will arise for any quarter except to the extent your actual payment is less than the least amount required under the three options above and also less than the actual amount shown on your CRA instalment reminders. It follows that if you commence making instalment payments under any particular option above and discover in the course of the year that this will result in an overpayment, you can in effect shift at any time in the year to another option and make reduced payments for the balance of the year, taking account of earlier overpayments as reductions of later payments due. See also the discussion of interest below.

The technically minded will want to know that the descriptions above represent CRA policy, as understood, and do not literally reflect Regulation 5300. The regulation requires instalments calculated by reference to earlier years to be based on actual total tax liability for those years, making no allowance for amounts withheld (e.g., on employment income) or tax credits. The CRA, however, appears quite sensibly to use actual instalment liabilities rather than entire tax liabilities of preceding years in its calculations. It is understood that the regulation may be corrected eventually.

References to federal tax above include alternative minimum tax (AMT — see Chapter 24). Where previously paid AMT may be drawn down to reduce your tax in the current year, this may be taken into account in estimating your liability (at your own risk).

(ITA: 156; 161(4.01); ITR: 5300 Individuals)

[¶227.20] *Paying Your Instalments*

You should receive instalment remittance forms (designated INNS3) with your instalment reminders, if you are receiving them, or you can obtain the forms from TSOs (¶287, call 1-800-959-8281). Payments should always be accompanied by a remittance form.

The remittance forms are not available for download from the CRA website, apparently because of the Magnetic Ink Character Recognition technology they require.

You may make your instalment payment by cheque or money order, payable to the Receiver General (write your Social Insurance Number on the back), and send it (with a remittance form) to the Canada Revenue Agency, 875 Heron Road, Ottawa, ON, K1A 1B1. Alternatively, you may make your payment in person at any branch of a Canadian chartered bank, caisse populaire, credit union affiliated with CUNA International, Alberta Treasury Branch office, or Ontario Provincial Savings Branch office. The CRA does not accept payments at CRA TSOs. Their focus is to encourage taxpayers to make their required instalment payments online.

As an alternative to going into the bank (or using its online or telephone banking features), you can have your instalment payments debited from your bank account. To do this, complete form T1162A-1, Pre-Authorized Payment Plan (Personal Quarterly Instalment Payments), and follow the directions on the form for sending it to the CRA.

Payments made in person at financial institutions are generally considered received by the government when made, as evidenced by the date stamp provided by the institution on your receipt.

Note that, in the case of individuals, payments sent by mail are considered received on the day they are mailed provided they are sent by "first class mail or its equivalent". "Equivalent" is understood to mean courier service. Payments mailed in any other fashion are considered received when received by the Receiver General of Canada.

Taxpayers and businesses are able to send payments, including instalments payments, to the CRA directly from their accounts at participating financial institutions using the "My Payment" service. My Payment is accessed using a portal on the CRA website. The service lets individuals and businesses send payments electronically through a secure link with Canadian financial institutions who offer Interac® Online or Visa® debit payment service (credit cards are not accepted). Currently, those institutions include the following:

- bank access cards with the Interac Online logo only:
  - BMO Bank of Montreal (personal accounts only),
  - RBC Royal Bank,
  - Scotiabank,
  - TD Canada Trust,
  - First Nations Bank of Canada,
  - Acadian Credit Union,
  - Accent Credit Union,
  - Access Credit Union,
  - Assiniboine Credit Union,
  - Beaubear Credit Union,
  - Caisse Populaire de Clare,
  - Coastal Financial
  - Columbia Valley Credit Union,
  - Community First Credit Union,
  - Copperfin Credit Union,
  - Credit Union Atlantic,
  - East Coast Credit Union,
  - Eagle River Credit Union,
  - Envision Financial,
  - Évangéline-Central Credit
  - Goodsoil Credit Union
  - iNova Credit Union,
  - Interior Savings Credit Union,
  - Kindred Credit Union,
  - Kingston Community Credit Union,
  - Libro Credit Union,
  - Limestone Credit Union,
  - Mennonite Savings and Credit Union,
  - Morell Credit Union,
  - NBTA Credit Union,
  - OPPA Credit Union,
  - OMISTA Credit Union,
  - PenFinancial Credit Union,
  - Progressive Credit Union Limited,
  - Public Service Credit Union,
  - Provincial Credit Union,
  - Reddy Kilowatt Credit Union,
  - Souris Credit Union,
  - Sydney Credit Union,
  - Tandia Financial Credit Union,
  - The Police Credit Union,
  - Tignish Credit Union,
  - Toronto Municipal Employees' Credit Union,
  - Valley Credit Union,
  - Venture Credit Union,
  - Windsor Family Credit Union, and
  - Your Credit Union; and
- bank access cards with the Visa Debit logo (if your card has both a Visa Debit logo and an *Interac* logo, use the Visa Debit option to pay):
  - CIBC,
  - RBC Royal Bank,
  - Scotiabank, and
  - TD Canada Trust.

Transactions completed through My Payment can contain several payments for a combination of both individual and business accounts at the CRA. Payments can be made from a personal or a corporate bank account at a participating financial institution. For a list of the types of remittances that can be made using My Payment, please visit the CRA website at www.cra-arc.gc.ca

The CRA does not provide regular acknowledgements of each payment (so you should keep receipts and cancelled cheques), but does show amounts it has credited to your account on form INNS1 (Instalment Reminder) or INNS2 (Instalment Payment Summary), usually issued in August and/or February.

Be sure to account for the amounts you have already paid for the year on line 476 of your return for the year.

(ITA: 248(7))

[¶227.25] *Interest on Instalments*

Failure to pay instalments will incur interest (¶248) from the time the instalments are due. Where you have paid amounts other than interest or penalty in full, but there is interest or penalty of $25 or less outstanding, the CRA has discretion to waive the interest or penalty. One assumes that this discretion would generally be exercised and will continue to be built into computerized assessments.

An interest offset method is used in the calculation of interest charged on late or deficient tax instalment payments. Under this method, you can reduce or eliminate interest charges on a deficient tax instalment by overpaying other instalments or paying other instalments before their due date. This interest offset only operates to reduce a potential interest liability on instalment payments for the taxation year as a whole; it cannot create an obligation on the government to pay interest on excess instalments. For example, under this rule, 2016 instalment interest for the period commencing January 1, 2016 and ending April 30, 2017, cannot exceed:

(1) total interest for the period on your instalment liability calculated as if no instalments had been paid

minus

(2) interest that would be paid by the government on a refund of your instalments for 2016 made in the period if there were no tax owing for 2016 and no April 30, 2017 final payment, and the refund were calculated on your instalments from the later of January 1, 2016 or the day the overpayment arose.

Interest is charged on funds you owe to the government at a rate that is two points higher than the interest rate on funds the government owes you. This differential does not apply to the contra-interest rules, which specifically require that the same (higher) interest rate is applied for all purposes in contra-interest calculations.

The intention of these rules is that instalment interest is calculated by first computing a debit interest charge from the due date of each instalment to the due date the final instalment is due (the "balance due date"). A credit offset ("offset interest") is allowed on each instalment payment at the instalment interest rate from the payment date to the balance due date. Interest will be chargeable only to the extent that the debit instalment interest charge exceeds the offset interest.

Essentially, this means that if you have forgotten to make an instalment payment when it was due, you can cure the defect by an early payment of a subsequent instalment (allowing for quarterly interest rate changes) or by an overpayment of the deficient instalment calculated to accrue sufficient interest on a daily basis (compounded daily) for the period of deficiency.

Apart from the "contra-interest" provisions, there is no provision for interest to the taxpayer on instalment overpayments. Tax overpaid for a year will receive interest from the time that is the later of 30 days after the balance-due day of April 30 (i.e., May 31 of the following year) or 30 days after the return for the year is filed.

(ITA: 161(2)–(2.2); 164(3); 248(11); ITR: 4301 Prescribed Rate of Interest)

[¶227.30] *Penalty Interest on Instalments*

In addition to the interest described above on late or deficient instalment payments, a penalty is applicable to individuals with excessive instalment shortfalls. This penalty is 50% of:

(1) interest payable on instalment shortfalls for the year (offset by contra-interest if applicable)

minus the greater of:

(2) $1,000, and

(3) 25% of the interest you would have had to pay for instalment shortfalls if you had made no instalment payments at all in the year.

Thus this penalty can only apply where the interest on instalment shortfalls reaches a threshold of $1,000, after the application of the contra-interest calculation. In general, this implies an instalment requirement of at least $10,000 for the year.

(ITA: 163.1)

[¶227.35] *Instalments and Flow-Through Shares*

Flow-through shares are discussed in ¶2521.50. Briefly, they are permitted tax shelters through which investors can participate in (receive a flow-out of) resource expenditures described in Chapter 22, with the hope of eventual profit if, so to speak, the well comes in. The flow-through share rules permit companies to flow out expenditures as year one deductions although the expenditures will not actually be incurred until year two. It follows that the expenditures may not in fact be incurred, and the system will deal with this by forcing revision of amounts previously flowed out. Where this occurs, the investor will have a retroactive tax burden imposed. The system intends that while the burden of a lower deduction will fall on the investor, the concomitant costs of retroactive interest, both in general and for inadequate instalments, will in effect be borne by a special tax on the issuing company. Accordingly, the investor who is issued a notice reducing a prior flow-through share allocation of Canadian exploration expenses and Canadian development expenses *in these circumstances* is in effect given a grace period until April 30 of the calendar year following the year in which the flow-through deduction was originally claimed to ante up the difference without having to pay interest. See also ¶248a.

(ITA: 66(12.66), (12.73); 161(6.2); 163(2.1), (2.2))

[¶227.40] *Transfer of Instalments to Another Year or Account*

Subsection 221.2(1) allows the CRA to transfer payments received from one income tax account to another (including CPP and EI accounts) and from one year to another. Where this is done, the transfer is deemed to be effective at the time the original payment was made (and not to be effective *vis-à-vis* the original account from the same time). The amounts need not be instalment payments, but include any amounts that are or may become payable by the taxpayer.

A further provision allows transfer of amounts between the *Income Tax Act*, the *Air Travellers Security Charge Act*, the *Excise Act*, and the *Excise Tax Act*. The most common use of this authority for the average individual would be transfers between income tax accounts of a proprietor and GST/HST accounts of the business.

(ITA: 221.2)

[¶227.45] *Refund of Instalments: Undue Hardship*

From June 26, 2013, the CRA is allowed to refund excessive instalment amounts.

In order for such a refund to be made, all the following conditions must be met:

(1) you must have paid one or more instalments of tax under the rules above;

(2) it must be reasonable to conclude that the total amount of the instalments you have paid exceeds the total amount of taxes payable for the year; and

(3) the Minister must be satisfied that the payment of the instalments has caused or will cause you undue hardship.

The refund is completely at the discretion of the CRA. Similarly, the amount of any instalment refund is to be decided by the Minister; the Minister may refund all or any part of an excessive instalment. For the purposes of computing interest and penalties, if you receive an instalment refund you are treated as not having paid the instalment to that extent.

(ITA: 164(1.51)–(1.53))

[¶229] TIMELY PAYMENT

[¶229.05] *Balance-Due Day*

You are required to pay any tax owing by your "balance-due day". In general, this is April 30 of the year following the taxation year. The balance-due day is April 30 regardless of whether your return is due April 30, as is generally the case, or

June 15, as is the case for self-employed individuals and their spouses (see ¶218).

Where a taxpayer has died after October 31 of the taxation year and before May 1 of the following year, tax is payable six months after the date of death (notwithstanding that the return may be due somewhat later under the rules at ¶218).

Tax returns for trusts, which are technically considered individuals, are due 90 days after the year end of the trust, and payment of tax is due at that time.

If you file a return on a timely basis but the tax owing is not paid, you will be liable for interest on the unpaid amounts (¶248) but not for penalties (¶242). However, the CRA will undoubtedly commence collection proceedings shortly (see ¶233).

[¶229.10] *When Amounts are Considered Paid*

The *Income Tax Act* specifies that anything sent by "first class mail or its equivalent" is considered to be received by the person to whom it was sent on the day it was mailed. Courier service is understood to be the "equivalent" of first class mail. There is an exception for the remittance of amounts withheld on behalf of another, which are received only when received, but that is not relevant to the general taxpayer. The point is, a remittance of tax (or instalments) must be sent by first class mail or courier to be timely.

The law does not require that payments (or returns) be sent by registered mail, although many taxpayers consider that the registration receipt affords them at least some measure of proof of timely filing or payment, especially where the item is mailed close to a deadline.

Remittances may also be paid either in person or through online/telephone banking through chartered banks, and usually through caisse populaire, credit unions, Alberta Treasury Branch offices, or Ontario Provincial Savings Branch offices. Although not specifically provided for in the Act, it appears that these remittances by or on behalf of individuals are considered received by the government on the date of the teller's stamp affixed by the bank, or the confirmation date if paid through online/telephone banking.

Taxpayers and businesses are also able to send payments, including instalments payments, to the CRA directly from their accounts at participating financial institutions using the "My Payment" service. My Payment is accessed using a portal on the CRA website. The service lets individuals and businesses send payments electronically through a secure link with Canadian financial institutions who offer Interac® or Visa® debit Online payment service (credit cards are not accepted). Those institutions are listed at ¶227.20. Transactions completed through My Payment can contain several payments for a combination of both individual and business accounts at the CRA. Payments can be made from a personal or a corporate bank account at a participating financial institution. For a list of the types of remittances that can be made using My Payment, please visit the CRA website at www.cra-arc.gc.ca.

(ITA: 156.1(4); 248(1) "balance-due day"; 248(7))

[¶230] INSTALMENTS FOR FARMERS AND FISHERS

Farmers and fishers are required to make instalment payments of tax, but on a different basis. See Chapter 17.

(ITA: 155)

[¶233] COLLECTION POLICY

If you are unable or, for some reason, unwilling to pay an amount of income tax, non-resident tax or Canada Pension Plan contributions specified in a Notice of Assessment, you should contact your local Tax Services Office and inform them of your reasons for non-payment. This will enable the appropriate officers of the CRA to deal with any points in dispute and to give consideration to requests for extension of time for payment.

The CRA recognizes that there may be circumstances where payment cannot be made within the time limit set out in the *Income Tax Act* and, in such circumstances, the CRA may accept security for the unpaid balance and may allow the amount owing to be paid in regular payments in the shortest possible time, consistent with the taxpayer's earning capacity and ability to pay.

The CRA cannot normally commence formal collection proceedings (except for failure to remit withholdings) until 90 days after the date of the assessment or reassessment. Exceptions to this rule permit immediate collection where (i) reassessments have been issued pursuant to the CRA's discretion to waive the usual three-year time limit at the taxpayer's request (¶268); (ii) reassessments have been issued giving effect to the CRA's discretionary authority to waive interest and penalties (¶249); and (iii) reassessments are issued under an agreement consented to by the taxpayer to settle issues where judicial appeal is pending (¶269 and ¶272).

Although it cannot commence collection procedures for 90 days, the CRA can immediately set off amounts it believes it is owed from any amount owed by Canada to the taxpayer. A useful discussion of the CRA's undertaking (in Information Circular 98-1R4, "Legal Action to Collect") to use the right of set-off only where eventual recovery of the debt seems to be at risk, and of the alternative right to demand repayment of amounts in issue once an objection or appeal is launched (¶239.14), is found in the Wolters Kluwer Newsletter *Tax Topics* No. 1901, dated August 14, 2008.

If you file a Notice of Objection (¶266) within the normal 90-day period preceding collection proceedings, the CRA will not require the payment of taxes or the posting of security until 90 days after the objection has been dealt with by the CRA by formal confirmation or variation.

Where a Notice of Objection is filed after the 90-day time limit but within the alternative one-year limit, the CRA will typically have begun its collection procedures after the original 90 days; at the very least they will have begun issuing nasty demand letters, and may have taken further steps. Once a timely Notice of Objection is filed, it is understood to be CRA policy that such collection procedures will normally be suspended until 90 days after the Notice of Objection is dealt with by formal confirmation or variation.

Once the Minister has dealt with an objection by formal confirmation or variation, if you appeal further within the next 90 days either to the Tax Court of Canada or directly to the Federal Court, the CRA must again defer collection until the first court appeal is decided. If you appeal the decision of the court further, you may be required either to pay the disputed taxes plus applicable interest or to post the appropriate security.

The CRA's internal communications processes tend to be slow, and you may find that a collection notice is issued even though a timely Notice of Objection (¶266) has been filed. Typically, this occurs because the Collections Division of your TSO has not been apprised of the objection by the Appeals Division, or has not processed it. In this situation, you should write to the Collections Division pointing out that a Notice of Objection has been filed and that section 225.1 should operate to prevent demands for collection. A copy of the letter to the TSO Director might also be considered.

Although these procedures limit the CRA's right to collect amounts in dispute, the CRA's assessments are payable when issued, and interest will run from the date returns were due to the extent the CRA eventually prevails. You may elect to pay disputed amounts to avoid non-deductible interest costs should the CRA succeed. To the extent you succeed, you will recover disputed amounts that you have paid, plus interest thereon. The interest will be taxable.

Where you have already paid the taxes under dispute you may request a refund. This request may be made at the point you appeal the CRA's assessment or reassessment to a court. If the Notice of Objection remains outstanding and has not been dealt with after 120 days, you are equally entitled to request a refund.

If the collection of taxes could be reasonably regarded as being placed in jeopardy by stalling collection procedures or by refunding taxes, the CRA can commence immediate collection proceedings or refuse to refund disputed taxes. Special appeals to the courts on the collection issue are possible. It is also open to the CRA to accept security for amounts subject to collection. Also, where the courts determine that the basis of an appeal against a tax assessment is groundless and that one of the main purposes of the appeal is to delay the payment of assessed taxes, a 10% penalty may be imposed. If you do not voluntarily pay amounts the CRA is entitled to collect, it will collect the unpaid amount through a form of garnishment or seizure and sale of assets with the costs payable by you.

The interest rate for amounts owed to you or by you is prescribed and is set quarterly based on the average interest rate on 90-day treasury bills during the first month of the preceding quarter. For amounts owing by you, 4% is added to this rate. For amounts owing by the CRA to you, 2% is added to this rate.

The prescribed interest rates applicable to 2016, including the additional 4% applicable to late or underpayments of instalments or other liabilities by a taxpayer, are:

January – March	5%
April – June	5%
July – September	5%
October – December	5%

A table of interest rates over the past several years is found in ¶80 in the information material preceding Chapter 1.

A refund of tax claimed by you as a result of overpayment is checked against prior year debts and where amounts are found to be owing, the overpayment is applied against the debts plus accrued interest and only the remainder, if any, refunded.

Where in the opinion of the CRA you are attempting to avoid payment of tax, the CRA may demand immediate payment of all taxes, penalties and interest. The CRA may collect delinquent taxes by means of garnishment of wages, other income or bank deposits or by seizure and sale of assets. Where the CRA investigates and proves that you are wilfully evading the payment of tax assessed, the policy of the CRA is to recommend prosecuting by indictment to the Department of Justice, the penalties for which include imprisonment for a term ranging from two months to five years.

When a person dies owing income taxes, collection notices setting out the amount owing and requesting payment are sent to the executor or administrator of the deceased person's estate and the CRA looks to him or her for payment. If he or she does not respond to the notices, all of the legal options outlined above are available to the CRA and are used if necessary to collect the debt.

If there has been a transfer of the deceased's assets to beneficiaries and there is an income tax debt outstanding or tax of more than the remaining value of the estate is later assessed, the CRA will hold the person who made the distribution personally liable for unpaid taxes to the extent of the assets he or she has transferred to beneficiaries, unless he or she had asked for and received a certificate from the CRA stating that no taxes are owing as of the date of the certificate.

(ITA: 158; 159; 164; 223; 224; 225; 225.1; 225.2; IC 98-1R4 Tax Collection Policies)

[¶233.15] *Statutory Limitation on Collections*

Sometimes (albeit rarely) it happens that the CRA overlooks its own collection procedures. This is not necessarily a good thing for the taxpayer. In *Queen v. Markevich*, 2003 DTC 5185 (S.C.C.), the taxpayer had been assessed in 1986 for $234,136 in respect of earlier years. The balance was neither challenged nor paid by the taxpayer, and the CRA did not attempt to collect it or reflect the liability in subsequent statements of account sent to the taxpayer from 1987 through 1997. However, in 1998, the CRA presented a bill for $770,583, being the 1986 liability plus interest. The Supreme Court ruled that the federal *Crown Liability and Proceedings Act* (CLPA) applied to limit the CRA's ability to begin collection proceedings more than six years after the issuance of the original assessment. The government responded by enacting a 10-year time limit in which it can initiate collection procedures in respect of income tax assessments. The 10-year period commences 90 days after a Notice of Assessment is mailed to or served on the taxpayer. Moreover, if a liability was outstanding on March 4, 2004, or would have been outstanding but for another statute (the CLPA), the 10-year period commences March 4, 2004. The validity of this rule was upheld in *Collins v. The Queen*, 2005 DTC 5679 (T.C.C.).

(ITA: 222)

[¶236] BLOCKED CURRENCIES

Even though you may be prohibited from repatriating income from certain countries because of foreign exchange restrictions, if you account for your income on a cash basis you (income of a farmer or fisher, employment income and dividend income), you must include income received in the foreign country by an agent.

Accrual basis taxpayers must include in income all revenue made regardless of how or when payment is to be made.

If the payment of tax on such income will impose extreme hardship, the Minister has the discretion to postpone payment of the tax for a period to be determined by the Minister.

(ITA: 161(6))

[¶239] REFUNDS

[¶239.05] *Refunds on Returns Filed When Due*

If the tax withheld from your income, plus any tax you have remitted yourself, exceeds the tax payable for the year, you are entitled to a refund.

In most cases, the refund payment will be made to you at the time a Notice of Assessment is mailed for the year with no further application being necessary. The CRA may, instead of refunding the amount, apply it against any other tax liability you may have or you can request that this be done.

If the refund is not made at the time the Notice of Assessment is mailed, you may apply in writing for the refund which should then be paid to you.

(ITA: 164; 248(11))

[¶239.10] *Refunds on Late-Filed Returns*

In order to have a right to obtain a refund, you are required to file a tax return for the year within three years after the end of the year, i.e., by December 31 of the third year following the year for which refund is sought. Thus, to obtain a refund for 2013, you must have filed a return by December 31, 2016, subject to the discretion described below. Of course, your liability for tax unpaid continues until a return is filed and the return has become statute-barred as described at ¶268.

Subsection 164(1.5) gives the Minister of National Revenue the discretion to permit a refund to an individual (or a graduated rate estate) all or part of an overpayment in a year if the tax return is filed within 10 calendar years after the end of the taxation year. That is, you have 10 calendar years after the end of the taxation year in issue to seek a refund. Thus, in calendar year 2016, for example, the CRA will only accept applications to apply these rules to 2006 and later taxation years. In the case of a partnership, the period is 10 years after the end of the partnership's fiscal period.

Information Circular 07-1, "Taxpayer Relief Provisions", sets out in some detail specific guidelines on when such refunds will be permitted. The objective of these guidelines seems to be to permit refunds so long as an adequate record of the payments made to the CRA for a particular year and the taxes owing for that year can be reconstructed. The CRA will assist to the extent its own records permit, but of course the CRA itself will not keep its records forever. Application for late-filed refunds should be made to the TSO for your area (¶287). The CRA is not required to honour these late refund requests if you do not provide adequate documentation of your claim. See also ¶249 and ¶268.

(ITA: 152(4.2); 164(1.5))

[¶239.12] *Refunds Blocked until all Returns Filed*

The CRA is not permitted to make refunds (or to repay or apply to other debts or set-off against obligations of the taxpayer) until all returns "of which the Minister has knowledge" which the taxpayer is required to file under the *Air Travellers Security Charge Act*, the *Excise Act*, and the *Excise Tax Act* have in fact been filed. For individuals, this is likely to mean GST/HST returns which a self-employed individual is required to file. There appears to be no provision to earn refund interest accruing during these delays.

(ITA: 164(2.01))

[¶239.14] *Refunds of Amounts in Dispute*

As discussed in ¶233, there are restrictions on the ability of the CRA to institute collection proceedings of amounts in dispute. In addition, you have a right to demand repayment of amounts in dispute where you have filed a Notice of Objection which has had no official response within 120 days, or where you have appealed an assessment to the Tax Court. This right does not operate where the CRA has obtained a judicial order declaring the amount in jeopardy.

The demand for refund is not something you should undertake automatically. If you lose the dispute, you will owe the amount plus the substantial interest that will accrue during the resolution.

Some discussion of the collection and refund provisions is found in the Wolters Kluwer Newsletter *Tax Topics* No. 1901, dated August 14, 2008.

(ITA: 164(1.1), (1.2))

[¶239.15] *Interest on Current Year Returns*

The CRA will pay you interest on tax overpayments from the date that is the latest of (1) the day that is 30 days after the balance-due day (i.e., May 30 for an individual), (2) the date that is 30 days after the return was filed, or (3) the date the overpayment arose, until the overpayment is refunded to you or applied to another debt or instalment owing to the CRA.

Interest is paid on overpayments at the rates prescribed by the CRA. Prescribed interest rates change quarterly, and are always two points less than the rates the government itself charges on unpaid amounts (see ¶248). A table of interest rates for recent years is found at ¶80 preceding Chapter 1. As with interest on amounts owing to the government, interest on refunds owing to the taxpayer is compounded daily.

Interest you receive on overpayments (called "refund interest") is subject to tax in the taxation year received, subject to the comments below.

(ITA: 152(4.2); 164; 248(11))

[¶239.20] *Interest Where Amounts Carried Back to Earlier Years*

Certain amounts, such as losses and investment tax credits which arise in a particular year and exceed the income or tax for that year, may be carried back to earlier years, usually to the three preceding years. (Items eligible for this treatment are listed under subheading "Six-Year Rule for Carrybacks" at ¶268, which discussed the six year statutory period for which earlier years stay open to apply the carrybacks.)

Where an amount arising in a particular year is carried back to an earlier year, giving rise to a refund for the earlier year, interest on that refund will be payable from the day that is 30 days after the latest of:

(1) the first day following the particular year;

(2) the day on which the return for the particular year is filed;

(3) if an amended return or prescribed form amending the return for the earlier year is filed, the day that return or form is filed; and

(4) where a written request is made to the CRA to reassess the earlier year, the day on which that request was made.

Interest under this rule is paid at the prescribed rate, which is two points less than the rate the government charges on unpaid amounts (see ¶248). A table of interest rates for recent years is found at ¶80 preceding Chapter 1. As with interest on amounts owing to the government, interest on refunds is compounded daily.

Interest you receive from the government is subject to tax in the year received, subject to the comments below.

(ITA: 161(7)(*b*); 164(5))

[¶239.25] *Offset of Interest on Underpayments and Overpayments*

It is possible that interest in respect of different taxation years may be accruing for you (refund interest) and against you (arrears interest) at the same time. The refund interest will not only be accruing at two points less than the arrears interest, but it will be taxable whereas the arrears interest is not deductible. In its 2000 Budget, the government announced that it had come to the view that "this can produce inappropriate results in situations where an individual who owes interest on unpaid tax from one taxation year is concurrently owed interest on a tax overpayment from another taxation year. In this circumstance, the cost of the non-deductible interest payable by the individual exceeds the after-tax value of the taxable interest receivable by the individual".

However, the proposal was abandoned in an announcement dated December 21, 2000. Finance News Release 00-101 stated that Finance and the CRA "are working to develop a mechanism under which this proposal can be given effect, for implementation at the earliest opportunity". One assumes that Finance could not draft legislation which the CRA considered workable; the issue may or may not be resolved between them in the foreseeable future, if it ever is.

(Other Publications: 2000 Federal Budget, Resolution 23; Finance News Release 00-101)

[¶239.30] *Refund Interest Repaid*

If you have been paid refund interest which was included in your income in the current year or an earlier year, and you are reassessed and required to repay some of that interest, you may deduct repayments made in the year of repayment (at line 121 of your T1 return) to the extent of the previous income inclusion.

(ITA: 20(1)(*ll*))

[¶239.35] *Refunds of Instalment Payments*

See subheading "Refund of Instalments: Undue Hardship" in ¶227.45.

[¶240] AMOUNTS YOU MAY HAVE TO WITHHOLD FOR OTHERS

Just as your employer is required to withhold amounts on account of your taxes, there are circumstances in which you may have to withhold and remit to the government amounts on account of the tax on amounts you pay to, or in some cases amounts you owe to or receive on behalf of, others.

Obviously, if you are yourself an employer, you must withhold from employee remuneration amounts on account of income tax, Canada or Quebec Pension Plan, and Employment Insurance. This is described in the CRA's booklet "Employer's Guide to Payroll Deductions" (T4001).

If you purchase "taxable Canadian property" from a non-resident, you have to withhold on account of the vendor's Canadian tax liability, as described in ¶2040–¶2042. This most often arises when you purchase Canadian real estate owned by a non-resident of Canada, but the category of taxable Canadian property is broader than just real estate.

If you receive on behalf of a non-resident any of the amounts described in ¶2080, you may be obliged to withhold amounts on account of the non-resident's tax, regardless of whether you actually pay the amounts to the non-resident in the year. The CRA publishes a "Non-Resident Withholding Tax" guide (T4061) to discuss these situations.

If at the end of your taxation year you owe interest, dividends or proceeds of disposition to a person unknown to you, you must remit amounts on account of the potential tax within 60 days of year end. If and when the amounts are eventually claimed, the claimant is credited with the tax paid, and can usually obtain a refund, if due, by filing a tax return. This provision most commonly applies to brokers and dealers in securities who receive such amounts on behalf of unnamed accounts, but in theory could apply to anyone who has a blind obligation to pay interest or proceeds of disposition to an unknown party.

Taxpayers resident in Quebec should note that Quebec imposes parallel rules in all these cases except the ¶2080 non-resident withholdings. Thus, if you acquire Quebec taxable property from a non-resident, for example, you must comply with Quebec as well as federal rules. See Chapter 16, especially ¶1608.

PENALTIES

[¶242] FAILURE TO FILE RETURN

An individual who fails to file a T1 income tax return when required is liable to a penalty of 5% of the tax unpaid at the time the return was due. A further penalty of 1% of such unpaid tax times the number of months the return is not filed to a maximum of 12% is also levied.

A "second occurrence" penalty provides a penalty of 10% of the unpaid amount plus an additional 2% per month to a maximum of 20 months if a penalty under the first occurrence rule was assessed for a failure to file a return for any of the three preceding taxation years. The second occurrence penalty is imposed only if the taxpayer has failed to file for the year and a formal demand for filing has been issued by the Minister.

These penalties for failure to file a return are not reduced for carrybacks to the year for which the return was not filed on a timely basis.

An individual who administers another person's property, and is required to file an income tax return for that other person, and who fails to do so, may be liable to a penalty of $10 for each day of default (maximum $50).

An individual who fails to file a required return may also be convicted of an offence, and on summary conviction is liable to an additional fine of not less than $1,000 or more than $25,000, and up to 12 months' imprisonment.

These penalties are in addition to interest and penalties on unpaid amounts described at ¶248.

(ITA: 162(1)–(3), (11); 238)

[¶245] FAILURE TO COMPLETE INFORMATION

An individual who fails to complete the required information on a return is liable to a penalty of $100 for every failure. However, if the information could only be obtained from a third party and was not obtained despite reasonable effort, this penalty is excused.

(ITA: 162(5))

[¶246] REPEATED FAILURE TO REPORT INCOME

Prior to 2015, this penalty applied if you failed to report an amount that was required to be included in your income and you failed to report an amount in a return of any of the three preceding taxation years. The penalty was 10% of the unreported amount, but it did not apply where the penalty discussed at ¶251 applied to that amount.

Applicable to 2015 and subsequent years, the penalty will only apply if you fail to report at least $500 of income and you failed to report at least $500 of income in a return of any of the three preceding taxation years. Therefore, the penalty does not apply when relatively small amounts have gone unreported. It also continues not to apply where the you are liable for the penalty discussed at ¶251. For 2015 and subsequent years, the repeated failure to file penalty is the lesser of:

(a) 10% of the unreported amount;

(b) ½ the amount that would otherwise be the penalty described at ¶251.

(ITA: 163(1), (1.1))

[¶248] FAILURE TO PAY TAX — INTEREST

Late or deficient payments of tax are subject to interest at a rate which is set quarterly based on the average interest rate on 90-day treasury bills (T-bill) during the first month of the preceding quarter (see ¶233 for rates). The interest rate is the average rate on 90-day T-bills as determined above plus 4% (i.e., a prior quarter T-bill rate of 1% would mean the taxpayer would be liable for 5% interest).

Note that interest on amounts owing by the government to the taxpayer is paid at a lower rate, as discussed at ¶239.

For information concerning the 50%-of-interest penalty on late and deficient tax instalments, see ¶227.

A table of interest rates by quarter to the end of last year is found in the information material immediately preceding Chapter 1.

Interest, whether owed to or by the taxpayer, is compounded on a daily basis. Thus, actual interest is slightly higher than stated interest. For example, 10% interest on $100 compounded daily for one year would be $10.51 (simple interest i.e., not compounded — would of course be $10). The interest at 10% on $100 compounded daily over five years would be $64.86, compared to $50 simple interest.

Interest applies not only to taxes and instalments unpaid, from the time they were due, but also to penalties. Penalties for late-filed returns and false returns (¶242) are subject to interest from the time a correct return should have been filed. The 50% additional interest penalty on underpaid instalments incurs interest from April 30 of the following year, i.e., the date final payment is due. Other penalties — on an employer for failure to withhold, for example — incur interest from the date of the assessment of the penalty.

There is some alleviation of the interest due on underpayments of instalments if compensatory overpayments are made; see ¶227.

Special rules mitigate interest liability on some reassessments of flow-through share deductions; see ¶248a.

Where you have paid all amounts other than interest and penalty in full, and there is interest or penalty of $25 or less outstanding, the CRA has discretion to waive the interest or penalty.

(ITA: 161; 161.3; 248(11))

[¶248a] INTEREST AND FLOW-THROUGH SHARES

Flow-through shares are discussed in ¶2521.50. Briefly, they are permitted tax shelters through which investors can participate in (receive a flow-out of) resource expenditures described in Chapter 22, with the hope of eventual profit if, so to speak, the well comes in. The flow-through share rules permit companies to flow out expenditures as Year 1 deductions although the expenditures will not actually be incurred until Year 2. It follows that the expenditures may not in fact be incurred, and the system will deal with this by forcing revision of amounts previously flowed out. Where this occurs, the investor will have a retroactive tax burden imposed. The system intends that while the burden of a lower deduction will fall on the investor, the concomitant costs of retroactive interest, both in general and for inadequate instalments, will in effect be borne by a special tax on the issuing company.

Accordingly, the investor who is issued a notice reducing a prior flow-through share allocation of Canadian exploration expenses and Canadian development expenses *in these circumstances*, is in effect given a grace period until April 30 of the calendar year following the year in which the flow-through deduction was originally claimed to ante up the difference without interest or penalty. Technically, the provision operates by deeming, for all interest purposes, that the additional tax required is deemed to have been paid on the balance-due day for the original taxation year and to have been refunded on April 30 of the following year. As well, the trigger mechanism for instalment tax payments (¶227) will not be set off by retroactive reassessments in the circumstances described.

There are special penalties where a person has knowingly or in circumstances amounting to gross negligence acquiesced in the making of false statements or omissions under these rules, but in most cases these would apply to the issuing company rather than the investor.

Although there has long been a rule permitting reassessment of the flow-through shareholder who received an excessive flow-through of deductions for any reason, the reassessment period for such a reassessment has been extended to six years for 1996 and later reassessments (¶268). This is only partially consequential on the revised flow-through deduction rules. The six-year carryback rule is effective for all excessive flow-through reassessments issued in and after 1996, which seems to make it retroactive by opening Years 4, 5 and 6 following the year of redetermination, to a 1996 assessment, even if they previously seemed statute-barred. This extended reassessment period may also be further lengthened where a taxpayer files a waiver within the three-year period following the normal reassessment period.

(ITA: 66(12.66), (12.73); 152(4)(b)(v); 152(4)(c); 161(6.2); 163(2.1), (2.2); 248(1) "specified future tax consequence")

[¶249] MINISTER'S DISCRETION TO WAIVE PENALTIES AND INTEREST (TAXPAYER RELIEF PROVISIONS)

Under the taxpayer relief provisions, the CRA may at any time waive or cancel all or any portion of any penalty or interest assessable under the *Income Tax Act*. (The taxpayer relief concept also includes: the discretion to give refunds in statute-barred years (¶268.25); the discretion to permit specified late-filed elections (¶268.35); and the discretion to permit refunds where returns have not been filed within the required three-year period (¶239.10).)

You have 10 calendar years after the end of the taxation year in issue to seek to have the taxpayer relief provisions apply. Thus, in calendar 2016, for example, the CRA will only accept applications to apply these rules to 2006 and later taxation years. In the case of a partnership, the period is 10 years after the end of the partnership's fiscal period.

However, the 10-year rule has been modified due to the recent decision of *Bozzer v. The Queen*, 2011 DTC 5106. In *Bozzer*, the Federal Court of Appeal ruled that the taxpayer's interest incurred during the 10-year period could be waived by the Minister, regardless of when the debt was incurred. The Federal Court of Appeal's rationale was that nowhere in the legislation was there a reference to the year of the assessment. Therefore, interest could be waived in any taxation year in the 10-year period preceding an application for a waiver of interest. Taxpayers seeking interest relief under the taxpayer relief provisions, where the debt was incurred more than 10 years prior to an application, can now cite *Bozzer* to request interest relief for the 10-year period preceding an application. The CRA has stated that they will administer the 10-year time limit in accordance with the *Bozzer* decision.

An application for waiver must be made in writing, giving the reasons justifying the waiver in your particular case.

The government has indicated that situations in which it will consider the exercise of discretion to waive penalty or interest fall into three broad categories:

(1) extraordinary circumstances

(2) actions of the CRA (for example, publishing information which misleads the taxpayer)

(3) inability to pay or financial hardship

Extraordinary circumstances include:

- serious illness or accident;
- serious emotional or mental distress, such as death in the immediate family;
- natural or human-made disasters, such as flood or fire; and
- civil disturbance or disruption in services, such as a postal strike.

Guidelines to the exercise of this discretion by the CRA are set out in Information Circular IC 07-1, "Taxpayer Relief Provisions" and form RC4288. Anyone seeking a waiver should obtain Information Circular IC 07-1 (by phone from 1-800-959-2221, from the web at www.cra.gc.ca, or from TSOs listed at ¶287) and make a written request indicating, if at all possible, how you fall within the guidelines. If all else fails, however, note the provision in item 6 of the circular that "these are only guidelines" and "they are not intended to be exhaustive, and are not meant to restrict the spirit or intent of the legislation".

The law is quite clear that the CRA's exercise of discretion to waive penalties and interest which it is entitled to enforce is solely within its judgment. Although taxpayers have argued in the courts that the CRA should exercise its discretion in their particular circumstances, the courts have not given much overall encouragement to judicial review of this discretion. In the case of *Barron v. M.N.R.*, 96 DTC 6262 (F.C.T.D.), the Federal Court–Trial Division ruled that under similar discretionary provisions relating to reassessing statute-barred years (¶268), the CRA had at least certain duties to taxpayers when applying such discretionary provisions. The Court decision turns on the CRA's own internal procedures for applying discretion in so-called "fairness package" cases (which, as noted above, include, under separate provisions, waivers of both penalty/interest and statute-barred rules, and which would now be called the "taxpayer relief provisions"). The CRA's Tax Services Offices typically establish an internal "fairness committee" to review taxpayer applications for waiver of statute-barred or penalty rules. The Court found that the CRA had a duty to taxpayers who made fairness applications to both make them aware of the factors the fairness committee would consider and to afford them an opportunity to make representations to the committee. The Court ruled that the taxpayers had a right to participate in the proceedings and to confront the case against them. The Court also ruled that the committee had to abide by the CRA's own guidelines, and determined that in the particular case before it that had not been done. The Court apparently felt that it had no authority to exercise the CRA's discretion itself and issue a judgment on the applications; rather, its remedy was to set aside the decision of the original fairness committee and to order the CRA to set up a freshly constituted fairness committee to reconsider the applications, inform the taxpayers of the factors to be considered and provide an opportunity to make representations.

A similar decision, in *Bilida v. M.N.R.*, 97 DTC 5041 (F.C.T.D.), required the CRA to reconsider its refusal to waive penalties and interest. There the Federal Court–Trial Division simply said that the CRA had not paid sufficient attention to its own guidelines (at that time laid down in Information Circular IC 92-2), and referred the case back for reconsideration. This indicates that the Federal Court–Trial Division can review the exercise of ministerial discretion under any of the several situations in which it is applicable.

Shortly after the *Bilida* decision, the *Barron* case was reversed by the Federal Court of Appeal (97 DTC 5121), which found that the trial judge had erred in finding as fact that the Minister had failed to inform the taxpayers of the factors to be considered and failed to provide an opportunity to make representations. Those findings were contrary to the evidence. While they were not given an opportunity for an oral hearing before the fairness committee, "the law is clear that, save in exceptional cases, fairness does not require an oral hearing". The Federal Court of Appeal set out the following policy where appeals are taken from the exercise of ministerial discretion:

> ... the reviewing court is not called upon to exercise the discretion conferred on the person who made the decision. The court may intervene and set aside the discretionary decision under review only if that decision was made in bad faith, if its author clearly ignored some relevant facts or took into consideration irrelevant facts or if the decision is contrary to law.

The Appellate Court also implied that where a court finds a decision was contrary to law, it must state clearly the ministerial error in law, so that this can be reviewed on appeal. Even after the Federal Court of Appeal decision, the case seems to stand for the proposition that while the courts will not review the CRA's discretionary decisions as such, they will review cases to ensure that the CRA follows certain basic principles of administrative fairness, which at a minimum include the taxpayer's right to be informed of the principles governing the application of discretion (presumably set out in information circulars and perhaps other internal policies) and to make representations to the decision-makers in light of those principles. However, it also seems that a ministerial discretion can be set aside only if it is so flagrantly egregious as to constitute bad faith; it is not sufficient that the reviewing court find the CRA's decision uncongenial. A showing of bad faith is a very high standard to set.

Leave to appeal the *Barron* decision to the Supreme Court was refused; it therefore remains the leading decision on scope of judicial review of the CRA's decisions under the "fairness provisions" (and so under the "taxpayer relief provisions", which are after all the same provisions under a new name). Accordingly, it is difficult for the taxpayer can get another kick at the cat by having the courts review the CRA's discretionary decisions, however appalling, so long as the CRA made its appalling decisions in good faith.

Even after *Barron*, however, a court is sometimes sufficiently outraged by CRA behaviour as to at least refer an issue back to the CRA for further consideration. In *Robertson v. M.N.R.*, 2001 DTC 5465 (F.C.T.D.), the Federal Court–Trial Division referred a case back to the CRA for reconsideration in accordance with its own procedures. In that case a second "independent" review panel within the CRA had included one of the members of the first review panel, contrary to CRA policy. The Court concluded, on the basis of *Barron*, that the failure did not amount to bad faith permitting the Court to substitute its own judgment. However, the CRA's failure to follow its own public policy regarding fairness was sufficient for the Court to order the CRA to set up a new and genuinely independent second review. Similarly, in *Miller v. CCRA*, 2004 DTC 6057 (F.C.T.D.), the Court found that the CRA had (in the words of the *Barron* decision) "ignored some relevant facts". These included evidence of timely filing of a return never acknowledged to have been received by the CRA, an excellent compliance history for 27 years, and distress to the taxpayer caused by the death from cancer of her brother and then her mother. The Court rather neatly stood *Barron* on its head, saying: "While it is not open to me to substitute my opinion for that of the ministerial delegate, neither is it my function to speculate on what the ultimate decision might have been had all the relevant factors been considered". Accordingly, the case was referred back to the CRA for reconsideration. While it is true the CRA could then uphold its original decision, it would at least have had to defend it in a detailed opinion it might well have found not easy to write.

In yet another line of cases referring adverse fairness decisions back for reconsideration, the Federal Court has criticized the CRA for imposing non-statutory standards or failing to analyze whether its written standards were supported by case law. This has led one commentator to suggest that taxpayers making applications for judicial review of ministerial fairness decisions should review any applicable guidelines being relied upon by the CRA decision-maker. If these are found to have no statutory or common law basis, the argument must be that such reliance by the Minister is misplaced, and will be struck down on judicial review. See *Chisholm v. CCRA*, 2005 DTC 5159 (F.C.), and *Dorothea Knitting Mills Ltd. v. M.N.R. et al.*, 2005 DTC 5177 (F.C.), and the case comment at the end of the Wolters Kluwer Newsletter *Dominion Tax Cases* No. 113, March 25, 2005.

In *Lanno v. CCRA*, 2005 DTC 5245 (F.C.A.), the Federal Court of Appeal addressed the interesting question of whether the CRA must allow a fairness appeal based on a court ruling involving another taxpayer. It has always been the CRA's position that it will not allow a fairness appeal in such a case where normal appeal procedures have not been followed. That is, a taxpayer is not entitled to a fairness decision reversing a statute-barred year (or merely a year for which the time for a proper appeal has expired) simply because a subsequent court decision would have changed the result if the taxpayer had been the appellant. The taxpayer must follow the procedures in ¶266a to benefit from the decision in another case. In *Lanno*, the Court specifically approved that general position, but went on to refer the case back to the CRA based on its specific facts. These included the fact that

(1) the CRA's discretion did allow for the possibility of such a reversal of assessment notwithstanding the general (and permissible) policy against it, which the CRA appeared not to recognize in the decision under review;

(2) the taxpayer had demonstrably intended to join the normal judicial appeal launched by a group of taxpayers similarly situated, but that intention had been frustrated by misunderstandings with the other taxpayers' joint representative; and

(3) apparently other taxpayers in that group similarly situated had had fairness appeals allowed; the CRA had not recognized the basis of the taxpayer's appeal, simply relying on the general policy, and had not addressed the issue of why the taxpayer was treated differently from others in the same group involving the same project and issues.

The Court also distinguished the *Barron* case, which, it said, addressed the grounds for judicial review of fairness appeals but not the standard to be applied by the courts in such cases. Acknowledging that earlier cases were divided on the standards issue, the Court said the correct standard was whether the Court found the CRA decision reasonable, not whether it was patently unreasonable. Although this may sound like an arcane legal point, it does put the taxpayer in a somewhat better position in general. Oddly, the *Lanno* case was before the Federal Court of Appeal again (2006 DTC 6462). The CRA's new determination, pursuant to the earlier Court order, essentially reaffirmed its original one, to the extent of telling the Court it was wrong. The taxpayer appealed again to the Federal Court of Appeal, which simply said that at that stage it was the wrong venue, and the taxpayer should first pursue his remedy in the (trial division of) the Federal Court.

The upshot appears to be that judicial review of the substance of these CRA decisions (that is, where the Court simply reviews and reverses the CRA decision and grants the taxpayer's request) will be rare indeed under the *Barron* decision, but one can at least compel the CRA to be rigorous in establishing and following procedures which demonstrate its commitment to fairness.

(ITA: 152(4.2); 220(3.1); IC 07-1 Taxpayer Relief Provisions; Form RC4288; *Bilida v. M.N.R.*, 97 DTC 5041 (F.C.T.D.); *The Queen v. Barron*, 97 DTC 5121 (F.C.A.), reversing; *Barron v. M.N.R.*, 96 DTC 6262 (F.C.T.D.); *Robertson v. M.N.R.*, 2001 DTC 5465 (F.C.T.D.); *Miller v. CCRA*, 2004 DTC 6057 (F.C.T.D.))

[¶249.03] *Where the CRA Reneges*

In *M.N.R. v. Liddar*, 2008 GTC 1053 (F.C.A.), reversing in part 2006 GTC 1304 (F.C.), the individual taxpayer had paid an amount of GST on behalf of his corporation on the understanding that the associated penalties and interest would be waived once all outstanding balances had been paid in full. For whatever reason, the CRA declined to honour its commitment (which was not in writing). The trial court accepted that such a commitment had been given, in part because the CRA's own records indicated that it had (although the CRA characterized this as a "misunderstanding"). The taxpayer applied to the Federal Court for judicial review of the Minister's decision to refuse the waiver.

The Federal Court seemed more than prepared to oblige, and ordered the CRA to repay the amounts to the individual. The CRA appealed to the Federal Court of Appeal, which agreed that there was no authority in the statute for the CRA to refund the corporation's money to the taxpayer. However, the case was referred back to the CRA to reconsider its decision not to refund the penalties and interest to the corporation, which could settle up with the taxpayer. The CRA could not review the question of whether it had made the commitment, as that issue had already been litigated.

The case seems to indicate that the courts are prepared to lean heavily on the CRA to carry out commitments it has given. Obviously, the taxpayer's chances are much better if commitments are obtained in writing as part of the agreement process.

[¶249.05] *Interest on Amounts Waived*

Where a waiver is granted and a consequent overpayment is refunded or applied to another liability of the taxpayer, interest is payable from 30 days after the CRA received a "satisfactory" request until the amount is refunded or applied. The notion of a satisfactory request is apparently intended to ensure that no specific form is required to trigger the waiver, but on the other hand to ensure that a request is sufficiently clear to describe relief sought and the reasons for it.

(ITA: 164(3.2))

[¶249.10] *Disaster Waivers*

From time to time, the CRA will make a general announcement, by way of press release, that it will apply the fairness provisions (now called "taxpayer relief provisions") for a class of taxpayers facing a particular disaster, such as a flood or wildfire. (This rather light class of relief must be distinguished from the more substantial waivers of tax liability itself described at ¶345d. It should also be distinguished from the exercise of the CRA's authority to extend filing deadlines for a class of taxpayers.) The extended date becomes the new filing date, and penalties apply from that new date.

The most recent announcement was made on May 6, 2016 with respect to taxpayers affected by wildfires in north-east Alberta. The announcement provides that any affected individual or business unable to meet their tax obligations due to a natural disaster should contact the CRA to apply for taxpayer relief. Requests are considered by the CRA on a case-by-case basis. In addition to taking requests for taxpayer relief, the CRA has taken the following steps:

- ceasing all collections, audit related activities, and administrative correspondence;
- cancelling all penalties/ interests for impacted individuals who are unable to file their tax return or pay amounts owing; and
- making designated telephone agents available to provide assistance to callers affected by the wildfires (individuals can contact the CRA at 1-800-959-8281 and business callers can call 1-800-959-5525).

The announcements are usuallyno more than a reminder that the CRA has discretion to take account of such situations, but that it lies with the taxpayer to make specific application for relief.

(ITA: 220(3), (3.1); Form RC4288)

[¶249.15] *Voluntary Disclosures Program*

Another method of seeking relief under the Taxpayer Relief Provisions is through the Voluntary Disclosures Program ("VDP"). This program is available to taxpayers to correct inaccurate or incomplete information or to file information not previously reported. The definition of "taxpayer" includes corporations.

The purpose of the VDP as stated by the CRA is to promote compliance with Canada's tax laws by encouraging taxpayers to voluntarily come forward to correct omissions in their dealings with the CRA. It is not intended to act as a means for a taxpayer to intentionally avoid their legal obligations under Acts administered by the CRA.

Taxpayers who make a valid disclosure will have to pay any taxes owing plus interest. However, where a valid disclosure is made, the taxpayer will not be charged penalties or prosecuted with respect to the disclosure. In addition to penalty and prosecution relief, there may be partial interest relief granted in respect of the years or reporting periods preceding the three most recent years of returns required to be filed. For example, where a taxpayer has not filed tax returns from 2009 to 2015 and makes a valid voluntary disclosure in 2016, there may be partial interest relief granted for the years from 2009 to 2012. The years 2013 to 2015 are the three most recent years preceding the application; therefore, they are not eligible for interest relief.

As with other taxpayer relief applications, the Minister's ability to grant relief is limited to the previous 10 years before the calendar year in which the application is made. For example, where a voluntary disclosure application is made in 2016 for the taxation years spanning from 2003 to 2012, the Minister can only grant interest relief for the period from 2006 to 2012.

To qualify as a valid voluntary disclosure, the four following conditions must be met.

(1) Disclosure must be voluntary. For example, this would mean that the taxpayer had no knowledge or was not aware of any audit, investigation, or enforcement action to be conducted by the CRA.

(2) The disclosure must be complete, meaning the taxpayer must provide full and accurate facts and documentation for all taxation years or reporting periods where there was inaccurate, incomplete, or unreported information.

(3) The disclosure must involve the potential application of a penalty. The penalty type may be a late-filing penalty, a failure to remit penalty, an instalment penalty, or a discretionary penalty such as a gross negligence penalty. If a penalty does not apply to the disclosure, then the taxpayer should still submit the information and it will be handled through the CRA's normal processing procedures.

(4) The disclosure must include information that is at least one year past due.

Voluntary disclosure applications must be made in writing to the Voluntary Disclosure Program, Individual and Returns Compliance Division of the Tax Centre that has jurisdiction over the area where the taxpayer resides. Form RC199 or IC 00-1R4 list the two Tax Centres that handle all voluntary disclosures.

Form RC199, "Taxpayer Agreement", can be used, or the taxpayer can provide written submissions that provide similar information to that requested by form RC199.

If a taxpayer's voluntary disclosure application is denied and the taxpayer believes that the Minister has not exercised discretion in a fair and reasonable manner, then the taxpayer may request in writing that the Director of the TSO where the original decision was issued conduct a second administrative review. If the second review is also negative, then the taxpayer can file a notice of application with the Federal Court of Canada within 30 days of the date of notification of the decision. Typically, a taxpayer will apply for a second administrative review before filing a notice of application with the Federal Court.

Guidelines to this program are set out in Information Circular 00-1R4, "Voluntary Disclosures Program". IC 00-1R4 and further information on the Voluntary Disclosures Program can be found on the CRA website.

(ITA: 220(3.1); IC 00-1R4 Voluntary Disclosures Program)

[¶250] DISHONOURED CHEQUES

The CRA is authorized (perhaps required) to impose a penalty for dealing with cheques drawn by you on a financial institution which does not honour them. That is to say, there is a fee for bounced cheques. Payment is generally considered made when presented or mailed by first class mail (see ¶229). This "fee" is presumably in addition to interest and other possible penalties which might arise from failure to make timely payment.

(ITA: 220(3.8))

[¶251] FALSE STATEMENTS, NEGLIGENT OMISSIONS, WILFUL EVASION OF TAX, AND FALSE CREDIT CLAIMS

[¶251.05] *False Statement and Negligent Omissions*

Every person who, knowingly or in circumstances amounting to gross negligence, has made, participated in, assented to or acquiesced in the making of a false statement or omission in a return, form, certificate, statement or answer filed or made under the *Income Tax Act* in respect of a taxation year can be penalized by a fine of 50% of the tax avoided or benefit improperly claimed for that year due to the false statement or omission. The fine cannot be less than $100.

The test of gross negligence implies more than just oversight; it stands somewhere between simple inadvertence and intentional wrong. Its use here means that the government doesn't have to prove intent to deceive to apply the penalty. As you can imagine, the standard is fluid. A cynic might say a grossly negligent omission is one the judge cannot imagine having made himself or herself. Perhaps more charitably, it is one the judge cannot imagine even the idiot before him or her having made inadvertently.

Note that there is a lesser penalty for repeated but inadvertent omissions; see ¶246.

Every taxation year stands on its own with respect to penalties for the return, etc. for that year, although of course it is open to the CRA to infer wilful misconduct from a pattern of behaviour over several years.

The penalty is measured as 50% of the difference between the tax payable as reported and the tax that would have been payable but for the false statement or omission. Erroneous benefit claims (such as the Canada Child Benefit) are essentially the same. Since the penalty turns on the amount of tax avoided (or benefit claimed) by the false statement, the question arises of how subsequent tax adjustments such as carrybacks affect the penalty. Generally speaking, penalties for false statements or omissions will not be reduced where specified carrybacks reduce tax liability as it appeared at the time of the failure to report income.

(ITA: 163(2), (2.1), (4))

[¶251.10] *Criminal Penalties*

In addition to the penalties above, deliberate evasions of tax, or deliberate abuse of the refundable credit provisions (such as false child tax credit or false Canada Child Benefit claims), including the making of false statements, destruction of records and similar actions, can be penalized by criminal charges leading to a fine of 50% to 200% of the tax sought to be evaded and imprisonment for up to five years.

(ITA: 239(1), (2))

[¶253] TAX ADVISER/PREPARER PENALTIES

[¶253.05] *Failure to File in Appropriate Manner — Tax Preparer*

A penalty to tax preparers (individual or firm) was introduced effective January 1, 2013 for 2012 and later returns filed on or after 2013. A tax preparer who fails to file an individual's tax return electronically as required by subsection 150.1(2.3) (i.e., where the tax preparer accepts payment for filing more than 10 tax returns, see ¶219) is subject to a penalty of $25 for each such failure. The penalty is $100 for each failure to file a corporate return in electronic format.

[¶253.10] *Misrepresentation of a Tax Matter by a Third Party*

In its 1999 Budget, the federal government introduced a very contentious proposal to impose civil penalties on tax advisers and preparers for knowingly or in circumstances amounting to gross negligence making false statements or omissions in respect of another person's tax matters. In the view of the Department of Finance, this was simply an effort to find a less drastic (but therefore much more usable) weapon than the law of criminal conspiracy to deal with tax advisers collaborating in schemes which they knew or ought to have known were not permissible. In the view of the accounting and legal professions, the proposals denominated tax advisers rather than the CRA as the policemen of the tax system. In particular, they were concerned that any advice about areas (of which there are many) in which the law is unclear, unsettled or subject to policy changes by the CRA could result in automatic penalties for the adviser if the taxpayer's position should not be sustained, even after litigation in which different courts expressed different opinions, and even if the advice was accurate at the time and carefully explained (as would be customary) the aggressive nature of a particular position.

At a less sophisticated level, there was concern that a tax return preparer, including the internal preparer of a corporation, could be liable for such matters as failing to demand and verify all receipts for expenses claimed.

There was also concern that penalties against preparers could be automatic whenever gross negligence penalties were assessed against a client.

It is fair to say that the Department of Finance made at least some effort to cope with the concerns of tax advisers. On September 10, 1999, it tabled draft legislation explaining its revised position. The draft legislation was again revised in Parliament. The final version was enacted in 2000 and is effective for statements (and omissions) made after June 29, 2000.

Notwithstanding these changes, there has been a great deal of concern expressed in the accounting and legal professions that the sins of clients will be visited on their advisers even where professional standards would insist that the advice was sound and properly hedged. The CRA has gone some way to meeting these concerns. It has formed a head office committee in Ottawa which will be the final arbiter of these penalty assessments. That is, an assessor who believes a penalty assessment is warranted under these provisions must refer the issue to Ottawa, which must in turn review each situation and authorize a penalty if it seems warranted. The intention is both to provide uniformity and prevent assessors from using the penalty as a bargaining chip. This system will be familiar to tax practitioners from the general anti-avoidance rule (GAAR — see ¶285), which operates on the same system. It is probably fair to say that that system has restrained any tendency to an overzealous use of GAAR, and it is not unreasonable to hope that it will have the same result here. On the other hand, it means that the CRA has picked its GAAR cases carefully, and it was only in the 1999–2001 period that significant GAAR cases began working their way up the court system, a good 10 years after implementation.

The CRA also issued Information Circular 01-1 on *Third Party Civil Penalties*, which every tax practitioner will find useful if not always reassuring.

For its part, the CRA has said (in *Income Tax Technical News* No. 32): "The CRA intends to strictly control the application of the penalties. To this end, the CRA established a Headquarters review committee". The committee is, apparently, composed of representatives from the CRA's Compliance Programs Branch and Policy and Legislation Branch as well as from the Departments of Finance and Justice. It is said to be charged with ensuring that the tax adviser/preparer penalties are assessed in a fair and consistent manner, and only when clearly justified in the most egregious situations. At the annual conference of the Canadian Tax Foundation, in September 2005, the CRA provided an update on its Third-Party Penalty Review Committee. The Committee had up to that time considered 13 cases, of which five had not been approved for penalties and two had been approved for penalties under either income or GST provisions. Both of these cases involved situations where the CRA believed that tax returns were filed relying on information known by the tax practitioner to be fictitious. Another six cases were currently under audit.

The rules as enacted impose a penalty in two situations:

(1) Misrepresentations in Tax Planning Arrangements ("Planner Penalty")

This penalty applies where the adviser (or any person) makes or furnishes a statement (or causes someone else to) which the adviser knew or would be expected but for circumstances amounting to "culpable conduct" to know was a false statement that could be used by an "other person" for *Income Tax Act* purposes. A false statement includes a statement that is misleading because of an omission.

If the false statement is in connection with a planning or valuation activity, the penalty is the greater of $1,000 and the adviser's "gross entitlements"; otherwise the penalty is $1,000. A planning activity includes organizing or creating an arrangement, entity, plan or scheme, or assisting therein; or participating directly or indirectly in the selling of an interest in or the promotion of an arrangement, entity, plan, property or scheme. A valuation activity is anything done in determining the value of a property or service. Gross entitlements are essentially all amounts received or receivable in connection with a tax planning or valuation activity.

This penalty is aimed first at tax advisers and valuators, and then at promoters of commercial tax shelters. In particular, statements as to the value of a property or service can be presumed culpable unless within a prescribed range of fair market value.

The "other person" would typically be the client of the tax adviser or valuator or the purchaser of a tax shelter scheme.

Where there is no planning or valuation issue involved, merely making a statement ("I think this might be deductible") one knew or should but for culpable conduct should have known was false can incur the $1,000 penalty.

Along with the tax advisers' concerns discussed above and below, there would also seem to be freedom of speech issues in that the $1,000 penalty would seem to apply to an individual who as a political position advocated that, for example, federal policy in some matter was unconscionable and as a protest income tax or a portion thereof should not be paid.

(2) Participating in a Misrepresentation ("Preparer Penalty")

This penalty is imposed where a preparer (or any person) makes, participates in, assents to or acquiesces in the making of a statement to, by or on behalf of the "other person" that the preparer, etc. knows or would be expected to know but for circumstances amounting to culpable conduct is a false statement that could be used by or on behalf of the other person for a purpose of the *Income Tax Act*. The penalty is the greater of $1,000 and the actual false statement or omission penalty (¶251) imposed on the "other person" (generally but not necessarily the client). However, where this penalty is based on the penalty assessed on the other person, it may not exceed the total of $100,000 plus the gross compensation up to the time of the penalty assessment on the other person in respect of the false statement. As above, a false statement includes a statement that is misleading because of an omission, and gross entitlements are essentially all amounts received or receivable in connection with the false statement.

This penalty is aimed at the tax return preparer who knowingly or in circumstances amounting to culpable conduct accedes to a false statement by the client, although it is certainly broad enough to cover general tax advice relied on in the preparation of a return. The omissions penalty on the other person (the actual taxpayer) applies where that person knowingly or in circumstances amounting to gross negligence has made or acquiesced in a false statement or omission in a tax return, form, statement or answer. That penalty (described at ¶251, above) is the greater of $100 and 50% of the tax payable by that taxpayer which was presumably to be avoided by the omission or false statement.

[¶253.15] *Culpable Conduct*

The penalties do not apply to false statements unless the adviser/preparer, etc. knew them to be false (often hard to prove) or unless "culpable conduct" is shown. Culpable conduct is defined as:

> conduct, whether an act or a failure to act, that
>
> (i) is tantamount to intentional conduct;
>
> (ii) shows an indifference as to whether [the *Income Tax Act*] is complied with; or
>
> (iii) shows a wilful, reckless or wanton disregard for the law.

[¶253.20] *Mitigating Factors*

It is evident that the sweep of these provisions is very broad. The culpable conduct standard is said by the CRA to be intended to give some comfort that the penalty will not be applied in cases of honest error of judgment or honest difference of opinion. How much comfort it in fact provides is probably one of those matters on which there can be honest difference of opinion. (For the alarmist view, see Wolters Kluwer *Tax Topics* Nos. 1437 and 1438; however, the same authors confess themselves a bit more optimistic in *Tax Topics* 1531, based in part on the practical availability of insurance.)

A further comfort provision allows that the penalties will not apply to a person who acts on behalf of an "other person" (e.g., an adviser or preparer who acts on behalf of a client) solely because the actor relied, *in good faith*, on information provided by the other person or, because of such reliance, failed to verify, investigate or correct the information. This exception will generally protect a preparer, for example, who relies on statements made by a client. The exception will only apply where the preparer is not involved in promoting, selling or accepting consideration for a tax shelter.

The preparer's comfort may be somewhat undermined by a statement from the Department of Finance that an EFILE preparer may stand on different ground from a preparer of paper returns, in that the EFILE preparer may be expected to verify receipts (charitable donation receipts were the example used) where the paper preparer could rely on a representation (unless the amounts were disproportionate to the return). Presumably this addresses the situation where receipts would normally be filed with a return and are not filed because of the EFILE system; the EFILE preparer has an obligation to verify the existence of receipts which would otherwise be filed. (This argument was advanced in the context of the personal EFILE system, since the corporate system was not in effect at the time.) In any event, the CRA clearly intends to stress the good faith requirement. An adviser is not acting in good faith in accepting a representation the adviser knows to be wrong or false, or should have so known within the scope of the work assignment.

Another comfort provision is an assurance from both Department of Finance and the CRA that penalties under this provision will not be issued without prior head office review; this is supposed to ensure that they will at least not be automatic when the client is penalized. Moreover, "private sector tax professionals" will be consulted by the CRA in the development of guidelines for the administration of the penalty rules and periodically on the CRA's ongoing experience with the penalty provisions.

A final comfort provision shifts the burden of establishing the facts justifying the assessment of the penalty to the Minister where there is an appeal of the penalty assessment. The Minister cannot rely on the usual rule that the taxpayer must demonstrate any errors of fact.

[¶253.25] *Valuators*

Valuators are subject to a special liability, in that if their valuations prove to be outside a permissible range of error (to be established by regulation after "consultations on the appropriate percentages"), the valuation is presumed to be a false statement, subject to rebuttal by the valuator, who is entitled to show that the statement was reasonable in the circumstances and made in good faith. That is, the onus of proof remains on the valuator; the Minister's assessment is assumed in the first instance to be correct.

[¶253.30] *Bookkeepers, Controllers, and the Public at Large*

There is a provision to exclude secretarial and clerical staff (other than bookkeepers) from liability under these rules, which perhaps only indicates how sweeping they are.

Although it is the professional community which has most strenuously objected to these provisions, it should be noted that the penalties are not limited to tax professionals. Writers in Wolters Kluwer *Tax Topics* (Nos. 1437 and 1438), cited above, have been particularly alarmist about the implications. They suggest, for example, that the penalty for participating in a misrepresentation could apply to a bookkeeper or controller told by his or her boss (the president and sole shareholder) to process as company expenses travel or other items which the bookkeeper might know, or reasonably assume, to be personal. He or she must choose between his or her job now and a civil penalty if the president is reassessed. The penalty might similarly arise where a payment is made to a contractor who did work on the president's home and was told to invoice the company. Moreover, since the penalty is based on the president's tax rates, and the bookkeeper makes rather less than the president, 50% of the tax avoided would be disproportionately damaging, perhaps destroying the retirement income of the bookkeeper while only an annoyance to the president.

The government responded to these concerns in two ways. First, it created the $100,000 cap on the preparer's penalty, as noted above. Second, it created an exception for an employee of the "other person" (typically the tax plan client or person (or company) for whom a return is prepared). In general, the penalty does not apply to an employee of the "other person" to the extent that the false statement could be used by or on behalf of that employer, and the conduct of the employee is deemed to be that of the employer. However, this rule does not apply to "specified employees" (generally employees who have a 10% shareholding in or do not deal at arm's length with the employer), and does not apply to employees engaged in or selling a tax planning arrangement.

This is fine as far as the employee goes, but does not seem to protect, say, the contractor in the *Tax Topics* example above.

(ITA: 162(7.3); 163(3); 163.2; Tax Topics: Nos. 1437; 1438; 1476; 1491; 1531; IC 01-1 Third-Party Civil Penalties; Other Publications: Department of Finance News Release 99-076)

ASSESSMENTS, OBJECTIONS, APPEALS

[¶254] REVIEW BY THE CANADA REVENUE AGENCY

After you have filed your income tax return for the year, depending on how you filed your return usually determines how long you may have to wait before receiving any word from the CRA. For returns filed electronically, the CRA indicates in their service standards that the processing time is usually two weeks. For returns that are paper-filed, you may have to wait several months before receiving any word from the CRA. For paper-filed returns, the information on the return is either being entered manually on the CRA's records or scanned using the bar code format on page 1 of the return and then the return is reviewed.

[¶257] RETURN ASSESSED AS FILED

If the review indicates no errors, and further information is not required, you will be mailed a Notice of Assessment indicating that your tax has been assessed in accordance with the return you filed. In most cases you will not need to concern yourself any further with that year's taxes. However, the issuance of a Notice of Assessment does not bind the government and should they subsequently find that your return was in error they are entitled to assess additional tax. A reassessment can be issued at any time within three years of the date of mailing of the original Notice of Assessment, or at any later time if you sign a waiver (see ¶277) of the three-year limit or if the CRA can prove fraud or misrepresentation in the return you filed. "Misrepresentation" can include neglect or carelessness as well as wilful default.

In some cases, you may have six years rather than three to seek reassessment; see ¶268. Where other years are in dispute and the dispute is resolved after an undisputed year is statute-barred but the resolution affects tax balances relevant to the undisputed year, it may be reassessed. See ¶268.

The date of mailing of the original Notice of Assessment can also be important should you find you have filed an incorrect return and overpaid tax. You have the later of one year after the filing-due date of the return or 90 days from the sending of the Notice of Assessment to file a Notice of Objection. See ¶266.

(ITA: 152(4), (4.1)–(4.3); 165(1))

[¶260] REQUESTS FOR FURTHER INFORMATION

The first word you will hear from the CRA may be a request for further information. Such requests should be answered fully and promptly. The CRA has the power to enforce such requests if satisfactory replies are not given.

Such requests do not necessarily indicate that the CRA will ask for additional tax.

Although co-operation with the CRA and its information demands is generally the best policy, it has its limitations. The CRA's authority to demand and compel the production of information and documents for the purposes of assessing tax against the taxpayer on whom the demand is made is very broad indeed, but they are more limited in other situations. There may come a point in a tax audit at which the CRA is contemplating criminal tax evasion penalties. At that point, it can no longer rely on its general powers to compel information and must seek court warrants for further information, and there may be protections or at least additional processes protecting the taxpayer from disclosure. Identifying that point is at best difficult. The taxpayer who fears it is being approached should seek professional advice from lawyers accustomed to dealing with CRA investigations. See *Jarvis v. The Queen*, 2002 DTC 7547 (S.C.C.), and subsequent cases which rely on *Jarvis*.

Demands for information concerning third parties are another situation in which the CRA's powers can be limited. Again, case law limits the reach of the CRA's power to compel such information indiscriminately. See *Richardson v. The Queen*, 84 DTC 6325 (S.C.C.); *Redeemer Foundation v. The Queen*, 2005 DTC 5617 (F.C.T.D.). Where a taxpayer is concerned about the CRA's demands for third party information, consultation with an experienced tax lawyer is pretty well the only form of resistance open to the average individual.

[¶263] TAX LIABILITY

If the CRA feels there are errors of arithmetic, in reporting of items on T4 or other information slips submitted, or of interpretation of tax rules in the return you submitted, it will normally issue a Notice of Assessment (often with your refund or statement of balance owing) with an explanation of any changes it has made. In some cases this may be preceded by a letter outlining proposed changes, but usually a letter will be issued only if the changes are very substantial indeed.

If the CRA feels that its original assessment was in error, and especially if it has informed you that it is "auditing" your return, you may receive a letter describing the proposed changes and you will be given a specified time within which to consider the changes and notify the CRA of your acceptance or rejection of the changes. In some cases an assessment (or reassessment) notice changing your tax liability may be sent to you without a prior letter.

The CRA is not always correct, and you should consider carefully the proposed or assessed changes to the return you filed or to any later assessment.

If you believe that the assessment or letter is incorrect you should draw the matter to the CRA's attention at once. You may do this in writing by sending your inquiry to the Tax Centre to which you sent your return (¶218). However, your first point of contact should now be the general inquiries line (see ¶287.10). If an agent cannot resolve your inquiry, they can refer you to a senior agent or, in certain circumstances, arrange for you to meet with an agent at your TSO. You can no longer just show up to a TSO and expect that someone will be available to deal with your inquiry. For the purposes of identification, you should state your full name, address, and identification number or Social Insurance Number; as well, state the amount owing according to the notice and the reason for believing the assessment or stated position of the CRA is not correct.

If the CRA is not convinced you are correct, it will advise you that it will not change the Notice of Assessment if one was issued, or if it previously sent you a letter, a Notice of Assessment will be issued incorporating the changes and requesting additional tax and possibly interest.

In some cases you may simply receive a Notice of Assessment for more tax without a previous form letter and with a minimal computer printed explanation. If you disagree with the revision you should contact the CRA; however, you are still technically bound to pay the assessment within 90 days from the mailing date of the assessment unless you file an objection as described at ¶266 and choose to avail yourself of the right to defer collection as described at ¶233.

Once a Notice of Assessment is received, collection procedures may commence after 90 days from the mailing date on the Notice unless you file a Notice of Objection (¶266). The collection procedures should stop if a later timely Notice of Objection is filed under the one-year rule if that is possible. Although you should pursue the discussions with the CRA outlined above, you should not allow the 90-day/one-year deadlines to pass without considering whether to file a Notice of Objection. If the amount in dispute is substantial, you may want to seek professional advice well within the 90-day limit.

(ITA: 165(1); 225.1)

[¶266] NOTICE OF OBJECTION

After you have discussed a proposed adjustment to your return with the CRA, and if you feel that the CRA has improperly assessed taxes, you should then consider whether or not to file a Notice of Objection. You have until *the later of*:

(1) one year from the due date of the return for the taxation year in issue, or

(2) 90 days from the date printed on your Notice of Assessment,

to file a Notice of Objection.

Thus, for example, you can file a Notice of Objection to an assessment of your 2015 return, assuming it was due April 30, 2016, up to the later of April 30, 2017, or 90 days from the mailing date on your Notice of Assessment (or Reassessment) for taxation year 2015.

The additional period for filing a Notice of Objection (up to one year following the return due date) only applies to ordinary income tax, surtax, and clawback taxes on Old Age Security payments. The additional period applies only for individuals and, after 2015, graduated rate estates, and not for corporations and other trusts. Prior to 2016, it also applied to testamentary trusts in general.

If you do not file the Notice of Objection on time, you can apply to the CRA within one year of the filing deadline described above to extend the time for filing the Notice. You must demonstrate that before the filing deadline you were unable to act or to instruct another to act in your name, or you had a *bona fide* intention to object to the assessment; that it would be just and equitable to grant your application; and your application was made as soon as circumstances permitted. If the CRA refuses your application, you can apply further to the Tax Court of Canada.

A Notice of Objection must be in writing and must outline your reasons for objecting to the CRA's assessment; it must also adequately identify you (through your Social Insurance Number) and the assessment (particularly as to taxation year) to which you object. The CRA makes available form T400A to assist you in organizing your objection; although its use is not mandatory, it is advisable. Your objection, whether or not on form T400A, need not be sent by registered mail; it will be sufficient if the Notice of Objection is addressed to the Chief of Appeals in a TSO or a Tax Centre of the CRA and delivered or mailed to that office. Although the law does not specify which Tax Services Office, the Notice of Assessment to which you are objecting should specify the Tax Services Office which issued the Notice and to which you should send the Notice of Objection. If you cannot locate this information on the Notice of Assessment, send your Notice of Objection to the TSO which serves you (¶287) or the Tax Centre to which you sent your return (¶218). In its effort to provide more online services for taxpayers, the CRA allows taxpayers to file their objection online through the "My Account" service, using the option "Register my formal dispute". An online submission through the "My Account" service provides you with an automatic confirmation number of receipt.

Although form T400A is no longer mandatory, an optional version is available on the CRA website at www.cra-arc.gc.ca using the search feature "T400A" for filing a formal Notice of Objection. The use of form T400A is recommended because it makes it clear that you are initiating the formal procedure for a review which stays the CRA's collection proceedings and moves the review of your claims to a separate set of CRA officials from those who issue the assessment or reassessment. Since this does involve a second independent review of all issues, you may want to be sure that you have reached an impasse at the ordinary assessment level before proceeding. On the other hand, a timely Notice of Objection is essential to preserve your rights to this second review as well as to later judicial review. If you are sure you want to initiate this proceeding, you should either use form T400A or put at the top of your objection letter the heading "Notice of Objection", so that there can be no mistake about your intentions.

After filing your Notice of Objection, you will typically be obliged to wait several months while your notice works its way up the queue. Generally, you will be sent an acknowledgement that your Notice of Objection has been received. If an acknowledgement is not received, you can, armed with your Social Insurance Number, birth date, and the Notice of Assessment itself, telephone the Appeals Division of your TSO and verify that your Notice of Objection has been received. In the circumstances, even though registered mail is not required, the comfort level of the taxpayer may be improved if registered mail is used and a follow-up telephone call (within the objection period if possible) is documented.

After filing your Notice of Objection, you will (eventually) be contacted by the TSO Appeals Officer conducting the review. If necessary, you will be invited to make representations either in writing or at a meeting.

As described in the CRA's pamphlet P148, discussed in ¶266.03, the CRA will make all relevant documents available to taxpayers at the outset of the objection stage. As well, taxpayers are to be informed of discussions between the CRA's appeals officers and its audit officers regarding the assessment.

In due course, the appeals officer will make recommendations which, together with all the relevant facts, will then be reviewed by the District Chief of Appeals, who may decide to settle the objections based on a mutual agreement with you. (In practice, an agreement may be worked out by you with the appeals officer, but it must be sanctioned by the Chief of Appeals.)

If no agreement is reached with you, the Chief of Appeals will either confirm the assessment or vary it. Where an assessment is confirmed you will receive a formal notification by registered mail. If the decision is to vary the assessment, you will receive a Notice of Reassessment by registered mail. If the reply is unsatisfactory to you, or if you receive no reply within 90 days after you have filed the Notice of Objection, you may appeal the assessment to the Tax Court of Canada (¶269).

(ITA: 165; 169)

[¶266.03] *CRA Publication*

The CRA offers a pamphlet with a detailed discussion of your objection and appeal rights. See "Resolving Your Dispute: Objection and Appeal Rights Under the Income Tax Act", P148, available from the CRA.

[¶266.05] *Collection of Amounts in Dispute*

Filing a Notice of Objection within 90 days of an assessment will in most cases prevent the CRA from instituting collection procedures for amounts in dispute. This may or may not be desirable, depending on how confident you are of your case. If you hold the money during the dispute, interest will be charged at very high rates if you lose. If you pay before filing your Notice of Objection and let the CRA hold the money, you will earn interest if you win. See the more detailed discussion at ¶233.

Where a Notice of Objection is filed after the 90-day time limit but within the alternative one-year limit, the CRA will typically have begun its collection procedures after the original 90 days; at the very least they will have begun issuing nasty demand letters, and may have taken further steps. Once a timely Notice of Objection is filed, it is understood to be a written internal CRA policy that such collection procedures should be suspended until 90 days after the Objection is dealt with.

(ITA: 222–225; 225.1)

[¶266.10] *Objections to Reassessments*

As noted above, where a Notice of Objection is confirmed or varied by the CRA, the next stage is an appeal to the Tax Court. However, where the CRA reassesses in other circumstances, typically to give effect to new information volunteered by the taxpayer or discovered on a review of your return as filed (called an "audit"), or to give effect to a carryback of losses or tax credits (¶268), you may file Notice of Objection to this assessment or reassessment provided you do so within 90 days of its date as stated on the Notice of Assessment. However, this right to file an objection to what is typically a reassessment changing an original assessment is limited in certain circumstances.

For example, where a reassessment is issued:

- to give effect to a carryback of losses or credits listed in ¶268,
- to give effect to a court decision on a previous appeal,
- disallowing expenses because they are criminal in nature,
- giving effect to a late-filed election, or
- involving a change to a tax-avoidance transaction assessment,

a Notice of Objection to this reassessment must be limited to issues which "may reasonably be regarded as relating to a matter that gave rise to the assessment" in issue. That is, it now seems to be intended that you can file a Notice of Objection to a reassessment described in the list above within 90 days of its date, but you cannot raise new issues in that objection. By contrast, a timely objection to an original assessment or to any reassessment not covered in the list above (for example, a reassessment arising out of a tax audit) can raise any issue involving the return for which the assessment/reassessment was issued.

(ITA: 165(1.1); 169)

[¶266.15] *No Objection Allowed on Consent or Discretionary Reassessments*

Where the CRA exercises its discretion to reassess after a return would normally become statute-barred to give effect to a refund request or reduction in tax, no objection may be filed in respect of that discretionary adjustment. This restriction should not apply where a timely request for readjustment has been made and, if necessary, a waiver of time limit (¶277) has been filed.

Similarly, no objection will be permitted where the CRA exercises its discretion to waive penalties and interest which it is entitled to enforce (¶249), or where an assessment is issued with the concurrence of the taxpayer to resolve issues under judicial appeal (¶269 and ¶272).

(ITA: 165(1.2))

[¶266a] OBJECTIONS BASED ON CASES UNDER APPEAL

It sometimes happens that a taxpayer will win a decision in court reversing a long-established CRA policy or interpretation. The facts in that case may be similar or identical to a situation of your own. For example, in *Symes v. The Queen*, 89 DTC 5243, the Federal Court–Trial Division ruled that a female lawyer could deduct the cost of a nanny's salary as a cost of doing business, rather than being limited by the child care expense rules in ¶1049 *et seq.* Where did this leave other taxpayers earning business income who had to provide care for their children in order to take the time to earn income?

First, you had to decide if the Court's decision would apply to the facts of your own situation. This was clear enough if you were a female lawyer with a career and a nanny. Suppose your facts were slightly different. Did it matter if you were a man (part of the argument in the case was that women traditionally bore special responsibility for child-rearing)? Did it matter if you were the higher wage earner (not really addressed in the case)? Could you create a business loss against other (say employment) income with such deductions? All these questions might require professional advice, although if you brought an intelligent judgment to the facts you could in many cases work out the answer for yourself.

If you decide that the facts of your case are covered, or are probably covered, by a favourable court decision, you may file your own tax return on that basis for the current year, and also go back and refile earlier year returns to the extent they are not statute-barred (¶268), since the implications of a court decision are normally that the court is providing a correct interpretation of the way the law has always been (this may not always be so in constitutional cases).

Normally, when the CRA loses a case of this kind, it will appeal to a higher court (as it did in the *Symes* case). This means that it will, as a matter of policy, refuse to reassess in accordance with the court decision until a final decision is reached by a higher court (which can take years). At this stage you are well advised to file a Notice of Objection to preserve your rights, at least for the years for which this procedure is still available (see ¶266). Local CRA officials may sometimes advise you that this step is not necessary, since the CRA will be governed by the final decision. Nevertheless, you should always file a clearly labelled Notice of Objection if you think your situation is governed by a case currently in dispute. First, this will preserve your claims from becoming statute-barred if the pending litigation takes several years. Second, if the CRA finally loses, the government may legislate a result it finds more favourable, and will sometimes make that legislation retroactive except for claims which have already been the subject of a Notice of Objection.

When you file a return based on a case under litigation, and you expect to file a Notice of Objection if necessary, you have to make a decision as to whether or not you will pay the tax in issue. As discussed in ¶266, you can refuse to pay an amount in dispute until the issues are resolved by the courts. If the CRA agrees that the facts of your case will be governed by other litigation in progress (i.e., by someone else's case under appeal), it will, generally speaking, not attempt to collect your amount in dispute until that case is finally settled. However, if the CRA does finally win its case, it will collect not only the amount you have withheld but compound interest thereon (¶233). On the other hand, if you pay the amount in dispute but file a Notice of Objection which the CRA agrees will be governed by another case in litigation, and the taxpayer wins that case, the CRA will refund your money with interest (¶239). Given the uncertainties of litigation, you may well decide that the possibility of a future windfall is preferable to a sudden large debt.

When the case in litigation is decided, that may not be the end of the issue. In the *Symes* case, the original court decision was reversed by the Federal Court of Appeal (91 DTC 5397) and the taxpayer appealed further to the Supreme Court of Canada. The CRA did not seek to assess outstanding Notices of Objection finally until the Supreme Court finally ruled on the case (against the taxpayer, 94 DTC 6001). This is normal procedure: the CRA will not normally assess outstanding objections based on a particular test case until the time for appeal of the most recent decision has expired or, if the case has gone to Supreme Court, that Court has issued its judgment.

It is always possible that the CRA will not agree that your case is necessarily governed by another case under litigation and force you to the next stage of appeal. This does not usually occur where the facts seem similar. It is also possible that the final court decision will be decided in such a way that the CRA believes your case, although similar, is not governed by the final decision. In this case, you will have to decide whether you want to pursue litigation yourself on your facts.

[¶267] REASSESSMENTS MADE AFTER THREE-YEAR LIMIT

If you file a valid Notice of Objection on a timely basis, the Minister must reconsider the assessment and vacate, confirm or vary it or reassess, whether or not the three-year (or six-year) limit described in ¶268 has expired. Once the relevant time limit has expired, and provided you have not made a misrepresentation attributable to neglect, carelessness or wilful default and have not committed fraud, the Minister cannot include an amount (revenue or expense) in computing the income of the year being reassessed that was not included in an assessment made before the limit expired. The Minister can, however, include an amount (revenue or expense) that relates to the subject matter of the Notice of Objection such as:

(1) personal exemptions where a disallowance of support payments is the subject matter; and

(2) capital cost allowance where a disallowance of repairs is the subject matter.

The CRA is not enamoured of situations in which it can reassess down but not up, and will normally request a waiver if the three-year period is about to expire; see the discussion at ¶277.

Commentary on Legislative Proposals (Oct. 3, 2016)

Note: When the Notice of Ways and Means Motion, October 3, 2016, achieves Royal Assent, the commentary will be modified to read:

Effective for taxation years ending after October 2, 2016, taxpayers having failed to report the disposition of their principal residence in their income tax return could be reassessed by the CRA beyond their normal reassessment period in respect of such unreported disposition. For a mutual fund trust or corporation other than a Canadian-controlled private corporation, the normal reassessment period ends four years after the lesser of: (1) sending date of original assessment notice; and (2) sending date of original notification that no tax was payable. For any other taxpayer, the normal reassessment period is three years after the lesser of those two dates.

(ITA: 152(4), (5), (6); 165(3), (5); IC 75-7R3 Reassessment of a return of income)

[¶267a] CRA NOTICES SENT ELECTRONICALLY

The Act permits the electronic issuance of certain notices by the CRA (e.g., notice of assessment, notice of objection). However, notices that are specifically required to be served personally or by registered or certified mail are not eligible to be transmitted electronically.

A section on page 1 allows you to include your email address. By completing this section you are registering for online mail and authorizing the CRA to send you email notifications when you have mail to view in My Account.

These measures, found in subsections 244(14) and (14.1), provide the CRA with the authority to issue electronic notices if authorized by a taxpayer, which will be made available on the CRA's existing secure online account for that taxpayer (either the "My Account" or "My Business Account" platform, which can be accessed through the CRA website). The CRA is allowed to send the electronic message to the taxpayer, indicating that the notice or other document is available in the secure electronic account. The date that the message is sent will be presumed to be the date on which the notice or other document is sent. Taxpayers who give authority for the electronic issuance can revoke that authority, which takes effect the day after the revocation.

As a result of the measures, provisions in the Act that refer to the "mailing" of the relevant notices by the CRA have been amended to read the "sending" of such notices.

[¶268] RETURNS THAT ARE STATUTE-BARRED

[¶268.05] *General Three-Year Rule (Normal Reassessment Period)*

As discussed in the preceding paragraphs, you generally have three years from the date of an original Notice of Assessment (the "assessment date") to raise an issue with the Minister and ask for a reassessment. Although the government is not bound to reassess at your request unless you file a Notice of Objection (¶266) by the later of (i) 90 days after the date on that original assessment, or (ii) one year from the due date of the return for the year, it will normally reassess within the three-year period at your request unless you are changing an "optional deduction" such as capital cost allowance or capital gains reserve, where the amount you may deduct is any amount up to the specified limit for the year. Changes of optional amounts within a return which do not change the overall amount taxable may also be accepted. (These policies are discussed in the CRA's Information Circular IC 84-1.)

The CRA also typically has a three-year time frame within which to reassess, commencing with the date of the original Notice of Assessment.

The three-year limit, after which returns are referred to as "statute-barred", may be waived as discussed at ¶277.

The *Income Tax Act*, and a number of CRA publications, refer to the "Normal Reassessment Period". This is a defined term, meaning (for individuals) the period that ends three years after the earlier of the day of sending an original assessment and the day of sending an original notification that no tax is payable for the year. Thus it is always the first (usually *pro forma*) notice that starts the period running.

(ITA: 152(3), (3.1), (4); 165(3), (5); IC 75-7R3 Reassessment of a return of income; IC 84-1 Revision of capital cost allowance claims and other permissive deductions)

[¶268.10] *Six-Year Rule for Carrybacks*

Where you have a statutory right to carry an amount back to a return, that return stays open for six years from the original assessment date rather than three. For example, if you incurred a loss in 2016 which could be carried back to 2013, your 2013 return can be reassessed at any time within six years from its original assessment date. The contingencies which give rise to a six-year assessment period for individuals are subsequent losses (¶1083); subsequent investment tax credits (¶1463); subsequent business foreign tax credits (¶1455(3)(A)); subsequent reductions of amounts determined to have been renounced under flow-through share rules (¶248a); and, death giving rise to potential carrybacks of capital losses against other income (¶578), carrybacks of certain charitable donations (¶1931), deduction of outstanding pension contributions for buy-backs of pre-1990 service (¶1913c), and an election to treat certain estate losses [graduated rate estate losses for 2016 and subsequent taxation years] as those of the individual (¶1946). If your return is affected by the reassessment of another taxpayer, for example, because that taxpayer is carrying back losses, it will stay open for six years, although this is very rare in the case of individuals.

Certain other contingencies can keep a return open for six years. First, you may be reassessed on transactions with related non-residents at any time within a six-year period. Second, where you have received from or paid to a foreign government income or profits tax, your return will stay open for six years for possible reassessment in connection with those taxes. As well, the normal reassessment period is extended by three years where the assessment or reassessment is made to give effect to the application of sections 94, 94.1, and 94.2 (having to do with non-resident trusts and offshore investment funds).

Where a six-year period applies, you can request a change within that period (which the CRA need not grant) or the CRA can reassess on its own initiative.

The 2013 Budget provided that the normal reassessment is extended by three years if the prescribed information return for a tax shelter (see ¶2521) or a reportable transaction (see ¶285a) is not filed on time. As well, applicable to 2013 and subsequent taxation years, the normal reassessment period is extended by three years if the taxpayer fails to report income from a specified foreign property on the tax return and form T1135, *Foreign Income Verification Statement* is not filed on time or the required information is not provided on the T1135 (see ¶496.10). In Document No. 2013-0485761C6, dated June 10, 2013, the CRA confirmed that the extension of the normal reassessment period in this circumstance applies for all purposes and not just to income from the unreported foreign assets.

This extended reassessment period may also be further lengthened where a taxpayer files a waiver within the three-year period following the normal three-year reassessment period.

(ITA: 152(3.1)–(6); IC 75-7R3 Reassessment of a return of income; IC 84-1 Revision of capital cost allowance claims and other permissive deductions)

[¶268.15] *Taxpayer Migration Credit Carrybacks*

The taxpayer migration rules discussed at ¶2153 involve several situations in which tax credits can be carried back, typically to the year of departure from Canada. The statute-barred rules permit these carrybacks to the extent provided for in the taxpayer migration rules themselves. In this regard, section 119 of the Act provides a tax credit in certain circumstances to an individual who ceased to be resident in

Canada in a particular year, where the stop-loss rule in subsection 40(3.7) applied on the disposition of taxable Canadian property in a subsequent year. An assessment to take into account the credit is allowed provided that the taxpayer has filed a return for the particular year and then files a form amending the return for the particular year by the filing-due date for the subsequent year. For taxation years ending before June 26, 2013, the filing deadline is the filing-due date for the 2013 year.

(ITA: 152(6)(*f*))

[¶268.20] *Special Rule for Consequential Changes*

Under subsection 152(4.3), either the CRA or the taxpayer can require a reassessment of a statute-barred year notwithstanding the general limitations if the tax balances for that particular year are altered by a "settlement" of balances for another year. A settlement may arise from an assessment (where issues have been in dispute with the CRA and an agreement is reached) or from a court decision. A "balance" means income, taxable income, taxable income earned in Canada, loss, or any tax or other amount payable or refundable or deemed paid. The reassessment of the statute-barred year must be made by the CRA or demanded by the taxpayer within one year after all rights of objection and appeal have expired for the year for which the settlement was reached. Revisions to the statute-barred year can only be made to the extent the changes can reasonably be considered to relate to the changed balances for the settlement year.

Legislation originally released on November 5, 2010, passed June 26, 2013 to amend subsection 152(4.3) to also allow, under the same conditions, the modification of a refund or other amount payable by a taxpayer for the other year. This amendment applies to reassessments, redeterminations, and modifications in respect of taxation years that relate to changes in balances for other taxation years as a result of an assessment made, or a decision on appeal rendered, after November 5, 2010.

In *Sherway Centre Limited v. The Queen*, 2003 DTC 5082 (F.C.A.), the Federal Court of Appeal took a restrictive view of the consequential change provision. In that case, the taxpayer had won an appeal for Years 1 and 2 as a result of which its income for those years was reduced. Its losses previously applied to reduce Year 1 and 2 income were consequently also reduced, and its loss carryforwards from those years consequently enhanced. The CRA applied the consequential change provision to apply those loss carryforwards in Years 3 and 4. The taxpayer objected that the principles which reduced income for Years 1 and 2 were also applicable to Years 3 and 4, although it had not filed objections or waivers for those years. The taxpayer argued that the CRA should apply the same income principles as in Years 1 and 2, reducing income for Years 3 and 4 and postponing loss carryforwards still further. The Court dismissed the taxpayer's argument. The CRA had correctly adjusted the balances for Years 3 and 4 based on the changes to Years 1 and 2. The CRA was not obliged — indeed, was not empowered — by the consequential change rule to go behind the consequential changes and re-examine the underlying assessment logic of statute-barred years.

(ITA: 152(4.3), (4.4))

[¶268.25] *Requests for Revision or Refund after Statute-Barred Period (Taxpayer Relief Provision)*

The CRA has discretion to reassess at a taxpayer's request to give effect to a reduction in tax originally assessed or to a late refund request for any of the 10 preceding taxation years. That is, in 2016, the CRA will consider requests in respect of 2006 and later taxation years. It appears to be intended that under this rule the CRA will give effect to written requests for such adjustments where it is satisfied that the request for adjustment would have been processed if it had been made within the normal reassessment period. Guidelines are available to clarify the circumstances in which such late requests will be honoured; see ¶249. Although the courts will not review the CRA's exercise of discretion as such, they may review the CRA's administrative procedures to ensure fairness and compliance with its own policies; see ¶249.

(ITA: 152(4.2); 164(1.5)(*a*); IC 07-1 Taxpayer Relief Provisions; *Barron v. M.N.R.*, 97 DTC 5121 (F.C.A.), reversing 96 DTC 6262 (F.C.T.D.))

[¶268.26] *Refunds under Regulation 105 or Section 116*

In Bill C-47, which received Royal Assent on December 15, 2010, the Department of Finance corrected a "unique problem" affecting non-residents in respect of whom an amount of tax was withheld pursuant to regulation 105 (services rendered in Canada) or section 116 (disposition of taxable Canadian property and similar property). That is, there was no deadline for the CRA to assess the person required to withhold such amounts, in respect of the failure to withhold the taxes, such that there could be cases where the non-resident could not claim a refund under the regular refund limitation periods. As a result, the taxpayer relief provisions of subsection 164(1.5) were amended. For an overpayment in respect of which an application for a refund is made by a taxpayer after March 4, 2010, paragraph 164(1.5)(*c*) allows the CRA to make the refund to the extent that the overpayment for the relevant taxation year relates to another assessment of another taxpayer under subsection 227(10) or (10.1) (failure to withhold or remit taxes, etc.). The taxpayer's tax return for the taxation year must be filed on or before the day that is two years after the date of the other assessment of the other taxpayer. The other assessment must relate to, in the case of an amount assessed under subsection 227(10), a payment to the taxpayer of a fee, commission, or other amount in respect of services rendered in Canada by a non-resident person or partnership (i.e., tax withheld under regulation 105). In the case of an amount assessed under subsection 227(10.1), the other assessment must relate to an amount payable under subsection 116(5) or (5.3) in respect of a disposition of property by the taxpayer (generally, amounts withheld on account of a non-resident's tax for dispositions of taxable Canadian property and other similar properties).

[¶268.27] *Nil Assessments*

An assessment indicating that no tax is payable is referred to as a "nil assessment". Typically, this will arise in a loss year, although it may (rarely) occur in other cases, perhaps where a non-resident is treaty-protected. Long-standing case law suggests that a nil assessment is not an assessment, because no amount of tax is in issue. It follows that no appeal can be taken from a nil assessment, even though by explicit statutory provision the three-year (or other applicable) time limit on reassessments will apply from the date of a notice "that no tax is payable", i.e., from a nil assessment. This can create hardship where a taxpayer wants certainty as to the treatment of issues arising in that year. Where a nil assessment arises due to losses, provision is made to allow the taxpayer to ask the Minister for a "determination of losses". In theory, the CRA will then audit the loss year and issue a "determination", which is subject to objection and appeal as if it were an "assessment". This process may work to the taxpayer's advantage in certain circumstances, in that there appears to be no statutory time limit on the right to ask for a determination in respect of a loss year. (This is confirmed by the CRA in Wolters Kluwer's *Window on Canadian Tax* at 3779, and Wolters Kluwer's *Tax Window Files* at No. 9518017.)

In practice, however, it lies with the CRA to simply confirm the return as filed. In the absence of a taxpayer's request for a determination, the mere confirmation of a taxpayer's return as filed does not bring the determination process into operation, and the nil assessment problem remains. The Tax Court upheld this result in *Inco Limited v. The Queen*, 2004 DTC 2847 (T.C.C.), aff'd 2005 DTC 5110 (F.C.A.). Where losses are in issue, the CRA may contest its own confirmation (as opposed to determination) in the year to which the losses are applied. This will be so even if there is a pattern of losses, so that the argument over the losses of a particular year may arise 15 or 20 years later, since the original year never became statute-barred.

Special problems can arise where federal tax is nil but provincial income tax is assessed on a return. The CRA has successfully argued in court that in this situation there can be no appeal to the federal courts (*Lornex Mining Corporation Ltd. v. M.N.R.*, 88 DTC 6399 (F.C.T.D.)). Where the CRA issues an assessment which shows a particular amount of provincial tax but nil federal tax, it would appear that the CRA must act on a Notice of Objection to the assessment, but no appeal lies beyond the CRA to the Tax Court of Canada or Federal Court. Since these cases typically arise from the application of federal investment tax credits and not the application of losses, there may also be no opportunity to demand a determination of loss and invoke an appeal on that basis. One would reasonably expect that if there is no appeal to the federal courts, it must be possible to appeal to provincial courts. In the case of Quebec, which of course assesses its own tax, appeals lie from a Quebec assessment to the Quebec courts. In other provinces, however, it may be that the taxpayer has no recourse to the courts whatever. If recourse to provincial courts is possible, filing limitations will depend on provincial law. Given the complexity, not to say absurdity, of the problem, it would be well to consider the appeal problem before a confirmation of assessment is issued on a Notice of Objection in these circumstances.

As noted above, generally, the Tax Court does not have the jurisdiction to hear appeals on nil assessments, however, many individuals who may otherwise qualify for the disability tax credit ("DTC") may have no income for a taxation year in which they hope to qualify for the DTC. A negative determination by the Minister in these circumstances would leave these individuals with no right to appeal the determination. This point was noted in the Tax Court decision of *Tozzi v. The Queen*, 2010 DTC 1374 (T.C.C.).

In response to the *Tozzi* decision, subsection 152(1.01) was enacted through Bill C-3, which received Royal Assent on June 26, 2011. Subsection 152(1.01) provides that the Minister of National Revenue shall make a determination of eligibility for the DTC under section 118.3 if an individual makes a request for a determination by prescribed form. Subsection 152(1.01) allows an individual to make a request from the Minister of National Revenue for a determination of DTC eligibility. Thus, a nil assessment will not preclude the individual from appealing a negative determination by the Minister in respect of DTC eligibility as was the case in *Tozzi*.

Subsection 152(1.01) is applicable after the 2009 taxation year in respect of forms filed for the DTC with the Minister of National Revenue after June 26, 2011. However, for forms filed for the DTC with the Minister of National Revenue after the 2007 taxation year and before the date of Royal Assent on June 26, 2011, and where the Minister has issued a notice that no tax is payable, the Minister is deemed to have issued a notice of determination on the latter of the date of Royal Assent (June 26, 2011) or the actual day the notice of no tax payable was issued. The determination may be objected to within 180 days of the date of the deemed notice.

(ITA: 152(1.1); 152(1.01))

[¶268.30] *In General*

The CRA can always reassess if it can prove fraud or misrepresentation in the return you filed. "Misrepresentation" can include neglect or carelessness as well as wilful default. There is no statute-bar period in cases of fraud or misrepresentation. A review of some of the case law on misrepresentation can be found in *Ridge Run Developments Inc. v. The Queen*, 2007 DTC 734 (T.C.C.). On the same subject, see also *McKellar v. The Queen*, 2007 DTC 1007 (T.C.C.), which, on the whole, cites cases more favourable to the taxpayer.

Different time limits will apply to corporations in a variety of circumstances.

(ITA: 152(4), (6); IC 75-7R3 Reassessment of a return of income; IC 84-1 Revision of capital cost allowance claims and other permissive deductions)

[¶268.35] *Late-Filed Elections*

A number of provisions of the *Income Tax Act* permit special tax treatment where the taxpayer files a formal election to have these rules apply. For example, transfers of property between spouses normally occur at cost, so that no capital gain is realized. However, it is possible to elect to have the transfer occur at fair market value, and this could be beneficial in some cases. Often these elections must be filed in a timely return, and cannot be late filed at all, and of course certainly not if they are statute-barred.

Notwithstanding the general rules for filing elections at a specified time, the CRA has discretion to accept certain specified late-filed elections. Where the taxpayer has elected to its disadvantage, the CRA also has discretion to permit the taxpayer to amend or revoke these elections retroactively. The application for a late-filed election, amendment or revocation under these rules must be made within 10 calendar years of the end of the taxation year (or for a partnership, the fiscal period) in which the election was originally to have been made.

Tax penalties and interest can be waived retroactively where these elections or revocations are permitted under the "taxpayer relief provisions" discussed at ¶249. One would normally apply for all applicable waivers for a particular incidence in the same application.

Application of these rules is discretionary. The CRA discusses the circumstances in which it is prepared to consider a revised, revoked or late-filed election in Information Circular 07-1, available on the CRA website (¶287). In general, the CRA will accept such elections where there are unintended consequences (for example, a *bona fide* valuation must be revised); where there is a suitable reason beyond the control of the taxpayer (such as fire, flood, strike, illness, death in the family); where the taxpayer acted on incorrect information provided by the CRA; where a purely mechanical error was made in setting out an elected amount in a previous election; where subsequent accounting indicates all parties intended the election to be made; or where the taxpayer was unaware of the election despite reasonable efforts to comply with the law. The CRA is not prepared to accept late-filed elections where the intention is to accomplish retroactive tax planning; where adequate records do not exist; or where the original failure was negligent or careless oversight.

For the limitations on the CRA's discretion, see ¶249.

The elections which may be late-filed or revoked are specified in the regulations. They are:

- capitalization of the cost of borrowed money (¶1073);
- election to defer recapture or capital gain where capital property replaced (¶523–¶525);
- election to transfer depreciable property among classes (¶870);
- election for property to pass to spouse on death at fair market value (¶1922);

- proceeds of disposition of certain farm property transferred on death (¶1923);
- election to claim certain reserves where property passes to spouse on death (¶1918);
- transfers between spouses elected to occur at fair market value (¶531); and
- preferred beneficiary election (¶452).

The following elections were added to the list of eligible elections effective December 15, 1993; as with the originally prescribed elections, the CRA has discretion to reassess statute-barred years to give effect to elections or revocations under the following provisions:

- election to have dividends included in spouse's income (¶408);
- election to reduce capital cost of depreciable property on which inducement payments have been received instead of including the inducement in income (¶729);
- election to ignore change of use to income earning purpose (this continues an existing policy; see ¶555 and ¶819);
- election to ignore change of use from income earning purpose to principal residence (¶555);
- election to deem property to be taxable Canadian property on emigration (under 1992 rules; see next list below for comparable current rules) (¶2153);
- election to deem property not to be taxable Canadian property on emigration (under 1992 rules; see next list below for comparable current rules) (¶2153); and
- election by representative of a deceased taxpayer to deem losses of estate to be those of the taxpayer (¶1946).

The following elections were added to the list of eligible elections in July 1995; as with the originally prescribed elections, the CRA has discretion to reassess statute-barred years to give effect to elections or revocations under the following provisions:

- election to have a deemed disposition of a worthless share (¶564);
- election to deem property to be taxable Canadian property on emigration (under rules for 1993 [but terminated after October 1, 1996]);
- election to deem property not to be taxable Canadian property or continuing inventory on emigration (under rules for 1993 [but a similar rule is applicable to the replacement provision after October 1, 1996]);
- election to reduce adjusted cost base of capital property on which inducement payments have been received, instead of including the inducement in income (¶729); and
- election to transfer RRSP Home Buyers' Plan repayment liability from the deceased taxpayer to the surviving spouse (¶2625c).

The following elections have been added effective after October 1, 1996, in consequence of the 1996 taxpayer migration rules, which themselves were only enacted (with retroactive effect) in 2001. These elections were actually added to the list in May 2005 and then inadvertently withdrawn in June 2005 as additional elections were added. In 2006, they were enacted yet again. Presumably they are retroactive to the enactment of the sections to which they refer (October 2, 1996), although the regulations specify no effective date:

- elections by a returning individual to reverse departure tax (this can entail three separate elections, for taxable Canadian property, other property, and trust property acquired by a beneficiary; ¶2153); and
- election by an emigrating individual to be deemed to have disposed of property on emigration which would otherwise not be subject to the deemed disposition on emigration rule (generally used to trigger a loss to offset gains which must be recognized on emigration; ¶2153).

The following elections were added to the list of eligible elections in February 1996; as with the originally prescribed elections, the CRA has discretion to reassess statute-barred years to give effect to elections or revocations under the following provisions:

- election by a holder of foreign affiliate (¶495) with respect to assets received by foreign affiliate on expropriation and received in turn by the holder as dividend or benefit;
- election by a trust to defer 21-year deemed disposition [this election is no longer available as it was repealed in 2013] (Chapter 4); and
- election by a corporation under debt-parking rules on wind-up of a subsidiary.

The following election was added to the list of eligible elections on October 27, 1997; as with the originally prescribed elections, the CRA has discretion to reassess statute-barred years to give effect to elections or revocations under the following provisions:

- election to have a deemed disposition of a bad debt (¶563); note that the election to have deemed disposition of a worthless share was included in the 1995 additions.

The following election was added to the list of eligible elections on June 14, 2001, specifically applicable to 1998 and later years:

- election by a communal organization (usually a religious community) to be treated as a trust (¶1081).

The following election was added to the list of eligible elections on April 11, 2002, applicable on and from that date:

- election to obtain rollover treatment under foreign spin-off rules (typically used by a Canadian shareholder of a U.S. corporation undergoing a divisive reorganization under U.S. rules (see ¶536c)).

The following elections were added to the list of eligible elections on May 18, 2005, effective June 29, 2005, and later re-enacted August 29, 2006, effective June 1, 2005:

- long-term project election to accelerate availability for use of property for capital cost allowance purposes (see ¶804b);
- election by estate to recognize loss on stock options held at death (see ¶1925); and
- election to reduce cost of property in place of income inclusion for government assistance (see ¶729).

The following election was added, as an afterthought, along with the 2006 amendments in respect of taxpayer migration rules. The election is not a taxpayer migration election, but is consequential on trust rule amendments enacted effective October 2, 1996. Presumably the addition is retroactive to the enactment of the section to which it refers (October 2, 1996), although the regulations specify no effective date:

- election by a trust to opt out of rollover rules in respect of distribution of capital interest.

The following election was added to the list of eligible elections on August 29, 2006, retroactive to January 1, 2001:

- election to transfer reserve related to future undertaking assumed by new party (see ¶732.10).

The election available on the death of an individual who participated in a Lifelong Learning Plan in subsection 146.02(7), under which the surviving spouse or common-law partner takes over the repayment obligations, was added, in force on May 12, 2010.

The election available to trusts as proposed in the 2013 federal Budget to have the deeming rule not apply to a loss restriction event is effective March 21, 2013 when this Bill received Royal Assent.

It is evident that the tax authorities have been willing to expand this list of elections whenever it seems equitable to do so. Accordingly, if you will benefit from making or revoking an election not on the list, you should make your case to the CRA and attempt to see that it is at least considered at head office level.

Taxpayers filing corporate returns should note that in addition to the returns prescribed in Regulation 600, the CRA has indicated that it will accept late-filed returns pertaining to subsections 80(3), 83(2), 184(3), and 256(9) of the *Income Tax Act*, and subsection 5907(2.1) of the *Income Tax Regulations*.

(ITA: 220; ITR: 600 [Prescribed provisions for late, amended or revoked elections]; IC 07-1 Taxpayer Relief Provisions)

[¶269] TAX COURT OF CANADA

To appeal to the Tax Court of Canada you must have filed a timely Notice of Objection (¶266) to your assessment; after that, you may file your appeal either:

(1) after 90 days have passed since you filed your Notice of Objection if no confirmation of assessment or reassessment has been issued; or

(2) within 90 days from the date of mailing of confirmation of assessment or reassessment in response to your Notice of Objection.

Taxpayers who have for each taxation year in dispute, a maximum of $25,000 in tax and penalty or $50,000 in loss determination in dispute, may elect to appeal under "Informal Procedure Rules" which allow representation by agents other than lawyers under less formal rules than would otherwise apply. These dollar amounts were increased from $12,000 and $24,000, respectively for appeals filed after June 26, 2013. Strict time limits are set for the Minister to reply to an appeal, for the hearing date, and the decision date. Decisions under these accelerated procedures are not to have value as judicial precedent, and an appeal may be taken only on issues of law, jurisdiction, and gross error. There is no filing fee. It appears that if you have somewhat more than the $25,000/$50,000 limits in dispute but not enough more to bear the extra burden of a general procedure appeal, you can elect to waive amounts in excess of the limits and proceed with an informal appeal for the limited amounts.

As an alternative to the informal procedures described above, ordinary appeals may be taken to the Tax Court of Canada under more formal rules, and appeals of the Tax Court of Canada decisions under this option may be taken as of right to the Federal Court of Appeal on issues of fact and law. Appeals under the formal procedure are usually handled by a lawyer.

Note that appeals to the Federal Court of Appeal must be filed within 30 days of the Tax Court judgment or order.

Appeals to the Tax Court must (in most cases) be taken within the 90-day time limits set out at the beginning of this commentary (¶269).

Appeals to the Tax Court of Canada are instituted by either sending a written appeal to:

The Registrar of the Tax Court of Canada
200 Kent Street
Ottawa, ON
K1A 0M1

or any Tax Court of Canada office, by fax, or through the Tax Court of Canada's Electronic Filing Service available on their website at www.tcc-cci.gc.ca.

Appeals under the Informal Procedure Rules "may be brought" in the form set out in Schedule 4 of the *Tax Court of Canada Informal Procedure Rules*. That form includes an informal procedure election. It appears that if the format of Schedule 4 is followed, it may not be necessary to use a government-provided form. A letter should be sufficient, but it must be filed in triplicate and must specify:

- your full name, your mailing address, telephone number and fax number (if available), and those of your lawyer or agent (if applicable);
- the taxation year(s) under appeal or the assessment number; the date of the reassessment or confirmation (if applicable, attach a copy);
- the grounds for the appeal;
- a statement that you are appealing under the Informal Procedure;
- if applicable (in an income tax appeal), a statement that you are limiting the amount of your appeal to $25,000 for each year under appeal; and
- the date of your appeal and your signature.

Appeals under the formal procedure are generally filed in the format described as form 21(1)(*a*) of the *Tax Court of Canada General Procedure Rules*. Forms for instituting appeals and information about them are available from the Registrar of the Tax Court. In addition to the address above, the Registrar maintains offices in Montreal, Toronto and Vancouver. There is a Canada-wide 800 number for contacting the Office of the Registrar: 1-800-927-5499, and each office has local phone and fax numbers.

The right to re-appeal an assessment based on a court order will be limited to the issues raised in the original appeal if ordinary time limits for appeal of new issues have passed.

(*Tax Court Act; Federal Court Act*: 27; ITA: 165, 167, 169, 171, 172; Other Publications: CRA Pamphlet *Resolving Your Dispute: Objection and Appeal Rights under the Income Tax Act*, P148)

[¶269.10] *Frivolity Penalty*

Where the CRA feels that an appeal to the Tax Court, or some issue or element of the appeal, is not only wholly unwarranted but is merely to defer the payment of tax, it can apply to the Tax Court for a special penalty of 10% of the amount of tax in controversy on which the appeal was unwarranted. The Tax Court has complete discretion with respect to the CRA's application, but cannot impose the penalty on its own initiative in the absence of such an application.

(ITA: 179.1)

[¶272] FEDERAL COURT AND SUPREME COURT

An adverse decision of the Tax Court of Canada can be appealed to the Federal Court of Appeal. Judgments of the Federal Court of Appeal can be appealed to the Supreme Court of Canada only with the consent of the Supreme Court. It is necessary to retain legal counsel if an appeal to the Federal Court or Supreme Court is undertaken.

(ITA: 171(4); 175; 180)

[¶273] REFUND PENDING FURTHER APPEAL

Where a court has ordered the Minister to reassess, he shall with all due dispatch make the reassessment and refund any resulting overpayment, notwithstanding his intention to appeal the decision of the court. Also, the Minister may similarly repay the taxes of any other taxpayer who appealed or objected where the reasons given on the successful appeal are such that it is just and equitable to do so.

(ITA: 164(2), (4.1))

[¶275] NOTICE OF REASSESSMENT

When tax for a year is first assessed, a Notice of Assessment is issued. If the tax liability is subsequently changed a Notice of Reassessment will be issued. It has the same effect as a Notice of Assessment and may be objected to, or appealed, in the same manner. Where a reassessment has been issued after a Notice of Objection has been filed or after appeal to the courts has been launched, the taxpayer may appeal to the Tax Court or continue his appeal from the original assessment without filing a new Notice of Objection.

(ITA: 152(4); 165(7))

[¶277] WAIVERS

Where you foresee any event which may cause a refund for a particular taxation year and it appears that the event will not be settled or consummated until after three years from the mailing date of your original Notice of Assessment for that particular year, you should file a waiver with respect to the items reported on your T1 return for that year which are expected to change. You should be careful to limit the waiver to those items which you expect to change in your favour.

To be valid, a waiver must be filed on form T2029 and filed within the three-year period commencing with the date of mailing of your original Notice of Assessment for the taxation year in question.

As a practical matter, a waiver is usually filed where there is a continuing dispute with the CRA about a particular year and the three-year time limit is about to expire. If the CRA is proposing to reassess more tax, they will often ask you to file a waiver and threaten to assess the full amount in dispute if you do not agree to the waiver. Although these requests could be more civil than they often are, the CRA does have a very reasonable point in insisting on the waiver. In its absence they may not be able to enforce an assessment about which they are now negotiating with you in good faith. You are being given a choice of continuing the negotiation or moving it to the Appeals Division of the CRA by accepting a reassessment and filing a Notice of Objection (¶266).

On the other side, if you are asking the CRA to revise your tax liability downward and the three-year limit is approaching, you may well want to file a waiver on your own initiative. Although the CRA now has the authority to reassess in your favour past the three-year limit, you can lose the right to appeal such an assessment (should it be issued) by failing to file a waiver (¶266). (Note that if you are disputing a matter pursuant to a Notice of Objection you have filed, it is not necessary for you to initiate a waiver, although the CRA is likely to do so; see ¶267.)

You can revoke a waiver on six months' notice after which no further assessments can be made under it (with the usual exceptions for fraud and misrepresentation). A revocation of waiver should be made on form T652.

Budget 2013 has extended these rules to include participants in tax shelters who have not filed an information return (¶2521) or where a taxpayer has failed to report foreign property and has not filed a form T1135 on time (¶496).

A different kind of waiver may be agreed with the CRA as part of a settlement of issues raised in an audit or assessment dispute. Here the taxpayer waives the right to appeal to the Tax Court of Canada (¶269) the assessment or reassessment issued pursuant to the agreement. Recent legislation gives legal authority to these waivers by withdrawing the right of appeal on any specific issue for which the right of objection or appeal has been waived in writing by the taxpayer. This rule is retroactive in that it applies after June 22, 1995 to waivers signed at any time. Clearly, the taxpayer must be confident of the substance of the agreement of issues before signing such a waiver.

(ITA: 152(4), (4.1), (4.01); 169(2.2))

[¶279] NET WORTH ASSESSMENT

If your records are inadequate to determine your tax liability properly, the CRA may assess you on a "net worth" basis. This is done by determining your assets and liabilities (i.e., net worth) at the end of the taxation year and at the end of the last previous year for which your tax could be determined, and assuming that your income for the intervening period was equal to the increase in your net worth in the period plus the estimated amount spent for personal and living expenses.

No allowance will be made for the possibility that part of the increase in your net worth results from gifts and other non-taxable items, unless you can produce satisfactory evidence that you received such amounts.

(ITA: 152(7))

OTHER CONSIDERATIONS

[¶281] GENERAL CONSIDERATIONS

When preparing your return, and conducting any subsequent correspondence or discussions with the CRA, the following general comments should be kept in mind:

(1) The CRA attempts to cooperate with taxpayers and will in most cases be fair and reasonable in assessing tax. However, their primary responsibility is to ensure that all taxes required to be paid are paid. Consequently, it is up to the taxpayer to ensure that he or she does not overpay tax.

(2) A tax liability is governed by the rules of law, even where the law may seem unfair, and the CRA is bound to follow the law. Consequently, a taxpayer will gain nothing by claiming that income is not taxable or expenses are deductible because this produces a fair result. Such claims must be supportable in law.

(3) Where there is a dispute between a taxpayer and the CRA, the CRA's statement of the facts on which its assessment is based is, at least in most circumstances, considered to be correct unless the taxpayer can produce evidence to refute that statement. That is, it is generally said that the onus is on the taxpayer to refute the facts alleged by the CRA. Although the foregoing states the traditional view (and certainly the CRA's view), some authorities have suggested it overstates the case, and that the burden of proof may perhaps be shifted to the CRA more easily than supposed; see the paper by Joel Nitikman presented at the 1997 Canadian Tax Foundation Annual Conference. The thesis that the taxpayer's burden of proof is merely an evidentiary rule to be applied where the taxpayer is in fact the party with the best access to the facts of a transaction finds support in the case of *Redash Trading Incorporated v. The Queen*, 2004 GTC 386 (T.C.C.), which in turn is subject to commentary in the 2005 *Canadian Tax Journal*, Vol. 53, No. 1, at page 214. An attempt to place the onus on the CRA where new assumptions are pleaded at trial failed in *The Queen v. Anchor Pointe Energy Ltd.*, 2007 DTC 5379 (F.C.A.), reversing 2006 DTC 2695 (T.C.C.). The *Anchor Pointe* decision is criticized in the Canadian Tax Foundation's *Canadian Tax Highlights*, Vol. 15, No. 7, July 2007. In *Forest v. The Queen*, 2008 DTC 6506 (F.C.A.), reversing 2007 DTC 632 (T.C.C.), the Court ruled that in apportioning a payment between damages and taxable compensation, the taxpayer had met the burden of proof by introducing evidence from which the apportionment could be deduced by the Court. The taxpayer should in any event ensure that he or she retains all possible evidence to support his or her case. Regardless of who has the onus of leading evidence to determine tax liability in particular circumstances, the CRA always has the onus to prove charges of misrepresentation or fraud.

(4) The CRA has issued a policy document that they call a Taxpayer Bill of Rights. This document, which of itself is not legally binding on the CRA, outlines certain "rights" that all taxpayers should enjoy. They include a right to service in both official languages, information, courtesy and consideration, presumption of honesty, privacy and confidentiality, consistent application of the law, independent review, an impartial review before payment, and to every benefit allowed by the law. As you might expect, an organization the size of the CRA cannot invariably honour these objectives in practice, especially such subjective matters as impartiality, courtesy and consideration. Nevertheless, one must recognize that an honest effort has been made recently to fulfill these goals. The CRA has even gone so far as to establish a "Problem Resolution Program" in each TSO which seems intended in part to monitor internal compliance with the Declaration. This may be worth trying, although you should not neglect the formal argument and objection procedures available to you. Other useful devices to use in your disputes with the CRA are the *Canadian Charter of Rights and Freedoms*, the *Constitution Act, 1982*, and the *Freedom of Information Act*. Discussions of these pieces of legislation are beyond the scope of this book. However, you should seek professional advice whenever it appears that such assistance may be required in a dispute.

(5) A taxpayer may file returns and appeal assessments as far as the Tax Court of Canada without retaining professional advice, provided the amount in issue is below specified limits and the taxpayer is prepared to choose the "fast track" procedures discussed at ¶269. However, it is generally advisable to obtain professional assistance prior to filing a Notice of Objection, if not earlier, to ensure that you have correctly raised all relevant issues.

[¶281.10] *Foreign Currency Income and Loss*

Individuals must report income (and losses and expenses) in Canadian dollars. Where the income, etc., arises on a particular transaction on a particular day, for example on a disposition of foreign property, the exchange rate for that day should be used. Where items arise from time to time in the course of a year, for example where a business incurs travelling expenses in various foreign currencies, the CRA will normally accept the annual average conversion rate for the year, although the taxpayer who takes the time to record conversion rates for particular currency transactions should be able to use them. A table of annual conversion rates for various currencies is found at ¶95; monthly rates for the U.S. dollar and U.K. pound are at ¶90. The Bank of Canada website provides an excellent history of daily, as well as annual, rates for most foreign currencies.

Corporations which deal primarily in a foreign currency and present their financial statements in that currency can, in specified circumstances, report income in that currency.

(ITA: 261)

[¶281.20] *Calculation of Days Between Events*

There are many instances in which a time measurement is called for by tax laws. For example, appeals must be taken within specified time limits, and very often elections under new rules must be made within a certain number of days after Royal Assent. The best solution, of course, is to be well within the time limits. Where there is an intention to leave the event until the last possible moment, the calculation of that moment must be done with care. A useful analysis of the relevant laws is found in an article in the Wolters Kluwer Newsletter *Tax Topics* No. 1912, dated October 30, 2008.

[¶282] BOOKS AND RECORDS

If you are carrying on a business or if you are required to pay tax, you must keep records and books of account. As a minimum you must keep your books and records for six years. In addition, you may need permission from other federal, provincial or municipal authorities to dispose of these records. See ¶796.

(ITA: 230(1), (4); IC 78-10R5 Books and Records Retention/Destruction; IC 05-1R1 Electronic Record Keeping)

[¶283] CRA PUBLICATIONS

In addition to tax forms themselves, the CRA offers a wide range of publications — literally hundreds — to assist taxpayers. These include:

Guides and Pamphlets

These tend to be organized for particular taxpayers: employees with deductible expenses; employers trying to fill out T4 slips for employees, and so on. The most commonly used are updated annually, and so are frequently the most up-to-date sources of information.

Information Circulars (ICs)

Usually fairly short (several pages) documents explaining CRA procedures in particular areas. For example, there are circulars to explain the CRA's "taxpayer relief" procedures, that is, the circumstances in which it will exercise its discretion to waive penalties and interest. These tend to be stable from year to year. Occasionally they are updated or withdrawn. The archiving procedures described below for interpretation bulletins apply to information circulars as well. That is, the

CRA maintains on its website versions of the circulars that have been withdrawn or replaced.

Interpretation Bulletins (ITs)

These are documents of varying length, from very few to quite a few pages, in which the CRA examines particular aspects of the *Income Tax Act* and attempts to forewarn tax practitioners of its policies in regard to specific tax provisions.

In 2013, all Interpretation Bulletins were classified as "Archived Content". In CRA's notice of this fact, they state that archiving does not affect "the status or reliability of the ITs. They are current up to the effective date stated in each publication." However, Interpretation Bulletins are no longer updated to reflect either changes in the law or the CRA's administrative positions and each is to be withdrawn as it is replaced by an Income Tax Folio.

Income Tax Folios

In March 2013, the CRA launched its new set of publications called Income Tax Folios. These publications are organized into seven series within which are several folios which are further divided into chapters. They are replacing the Interpretation Bulletins and are to be phased in over a period of years.

Technical Opinions and Rulings

A series of responses to very specific taxpayer inquiries, these are published with excisions to avoid identifying the taxpayers in question. They are often a useful source of particular information, but as there are thousands of them, they must generally be searched through a database such as Wolters Kluwer's *Tax Window Files*.

Income Tax Technical News

A series of short bulletins in which the CRA announces procedural or policy changes. These are most commonly used to announce supplements to or changes in CRA positions published as ITs. As with ITs, the CRA has now cancelled all archived issues (all issues before 2002) of *Income Tax Technical News* effective September 30, 2012. The CRA has indicated on their website that the *Income Tax Technical News* will be cancelled as the updated information is published in the new Income Tax Folios. Even more than with the ITs, it is not clear that archiving means a change in any particular policy.

In General

Virtually all CRA publications are available on its website, www.cra-arc.gc.ca, or in some instances may be requested by phone (¶287). They are a rich source of useful information, and we have drawn upon them freely in compiling this book. CRA publications related to subjects discussed in this book are, insofar as possible, always cited either in the text or in reference lines at the end of each section.

[¶284] ADVANCE INCOME TAX RULINGS

In complex transactions involving large sums, it is often thought desirable not only to anticipate the tax consequences but to seek assurances from the CRA that they will agree on the consequences.

The CRA will issue advance income tax rulings subject to certain limitations and qualifications. These advance rulings will be given only in respect of proposed transactions which are seriously contemplated. The advance income tax ruling will be legally binding only on the taxpayer, or a specific group of taxpayers, requesting the ruling. It will be regarded as legally binding on the CRA provided that (1) the taxpayer has made no material omission or misrepresentation in his or her statement of facts or disclosure of purpose, (2) the law involved is not subsequently altered or its interpretation changed by court decision, and (3) the proposed transactions are substantially completed within the time limit specified in the ruling. Extensions of the time period for completion of transactions ruled upon may be granted by the CRA. Rulings found to be in error may be revoked before a series of transactions is completed, but will not be revoked with respect to completed transactions.

Where a ruling has been obtained, it is essential that the tax returns report the consequences of the transaction as agreed.

In addition, as part of its rulings service, the CRA provides consultations in advance of a ruling request (pre-ruling consultations) from the Income Tax Rulings Directorate. This allows taxpayers and/or their authorized representatives to discuss any unique, new technical issue that is critical to the structuring of a definite transaction or transactions that a taxpayer is contemplating in advance of submitting a ruling request. At the conclusion of the consultation, the Rulings Directorate will inform the taxpayer whether it will consider the issue further in the context of a ruling request. Within five business days of receipt of a request for a consultation, the Rulings Directorate will contact the taxpayer to indicate whether the request is accepted. The directorate's goal is to schedule a teleconference within three weeks of receipt of a complete request. The consultation will generally be via teleconference, although a meeting may be arranged. Any comments provided by the Rulings Directorate during the teleconference or meeting will not be binding on the CRA. The Rulings Directorate will not provide any written comments in connection with a pre-ruling consultation.

The CRA will charge a fee for advance rulings and pre-ruling consultations computed at a rate set by Order in Council (and thus subject to change upon published notice). At last notice, this was $100 (plus GST/HST) per hour for each of the first 10 hours or part of an hour, and $155 (plus GST/HST) for each subsequent hour or part thereof spent on the ruling request or pre-ruling consultation. A deposit of $2,500 is required in advance, which is applied against the fee charged. Requests for advance rulings or pre-ruling consultation should be submitted, together with all relevant documents, accompanied by the $2,500 deposit, to the Income Tax Rulings Directorate, Canada Revenue Agency, 11th Floor, Tower B, Place de Ville, 112 Kent Street, Ottawa, ON K1A 0L5. Requests must contain a clear statement of the question, a statement of the relevant facts, a frank disclosure of the purposes of the transaction, an indication of the provisions of the Act involved, and the taxpayer's interpretation of those provisions with the reasons and authorities which support his interpretation (pre-ruling consultation requests must also use Appendix G, "Pre-ruling Consultation request and undertaking"). Requests may be made by fax or email provided the taxpayer assumes responsibility for failure of confidentiality arising from fax transmissions.

The CRA may refuse to give rulings under a number of circumstances. All general policies related to advance rulings and pre-ruling consultations are set out in Information Circular IC 70-6R7, available from TSOs (¶287) and from the CRA website, which should be obtained by anyone contemplating this procedure.

Because of the complex rules relating to formal advance rulings, it would seem that any taxpayer considering such a request for ruling should seek professional tax advice.

In addition to the formal advance ruling system outlined above, there are two other systems for obtaining CRA opinions. First, the Rulings Directorate will respond to specific written requests with quasi-official technical interpretations, so long as the matter is general in nature rather than a request for a ruling on a specific set of facts. Since these opinions are free, they tend to be down the list of Directorate business, and may take months or years. They are assembled and published (electronically) in several private databases, including one offered by Wolters Kluwer Limited. In the alternative, local and sometimes head office officials of the CRA will give opinions or advice as to tax matters on an informal basis. These informal opinions are usually restricted to routine or simple matters, and are not generally given in writing. Technical interpretations, even if from the Rulings Directorate in writing, are not legally binding, although of course Rulings Directorate opinions in writing carry more weight with other officials than informal opinions.

(IC 70-6R7 Advance Income Tax Rulings and Technical Interpretations)

[¶285] GENERAL ANTI-AVOIDANCE RULE (GAAR)

In 1988 the federal government introduced a variation of the *bona fide* business test into Canadian law. Roughly speaking, it provides that where a transaction or series of transactions achieves a reduction, avoidance or deferral of tax and is not primarily for *bona fide* purposes other than to obtain the tax benefit, the government may invalidate the tax consequences of the transaction(s). An avoidance transaction must involve a misuse or abuse of the provisions of the *Income Tax Act*. The rule applies to all taxes imposed under the Act, and therefore would extend to both income tax and the various penalty taxes imposed by the *Income Tax Act*.

The federal anti-avoidance rule is titled the general anti-avoidance rule, and is widely known by the acronym GAAR. In general, it may be said to be intended to apply to complex transactions with a tax avoidance motive. It is common to seek advance rulings from the CRA in advance of transactions complex enough to be fraught with uncertainty, and to seek assurances in addition to those anticipated under law that GAAR will not be applied.

The scope of GAAR has been getting a significant testing by the courts. The earliest judgments in that series were in favour of the taxpayer, and taken together seemed to put significant limitations on the use of GAAR; see for example *Canadian Pacific v. The Queen*, 2000 DTC 2428 (T.C.C.), *Geranski v. The Queen*, 2001 DTC 243 (T.C.C.). Essentially, these cases held that where there was a *bona fide* purpose to a series of transactions, the fact that the series was structured to achieve an enhanced tax result was not sufficient to invoke GAAR. This pro-taxpayer line of cases came to a screeching halt with the September 11, 2001 Federal Court of Appeal decision in *OSFC Holdings Ltd. v. The Queen*, 2001 DTC 5471 (F.C.A.), which essentially holds that if GAAR means anything it must mean that a series of steps which are technically correct in themselves and may be in furtherance of a genuine business transaction may nevertheless violate GAAR where they violate a clear and unambiguous overriding policy of the *Income Tax Act*. This case seems to put the issue as squarely as it can be put. The Supreme Court of Canada has declined to accept an appeal of the *OSFC* case, so for a time it was the definitive judgment on the scope of GAAR.

The GAAR rules finally reached the Supreme Court in 2005. In two decisions, *The Queen v. Canada Trustco Mortgage Company*, 2005 DTC 5523, and *Mathew v. The Queen* (*sub nom. Kaulius v. The Queen*), 2005 DTC 5538, the Court basically adhered to the doctrines of *OSFC Holdings Ltd.* and subsequent cases (although Brian Arnold seems to dispute this in his *Canadian Tax Journal* article cited below), while varying the details. Essentially, the Crown must show that a tax planning scheme violated a basic policy tenet of the *Income Tax Act* in order to be found in violation of GAAR. The doctrine of economic substance (essentially, that a transaction has no economic purpose except to obtain a tax benefit) is not by itself sufficient to invoke GAAR. The Supreme Court decisions will doubtless be the subject of severe and prolonged analysis. Initial efforts are found in Wolters Kluwer Newsletters *Tax Topics* Nos. 1756, dated November 3, 2005, and 1757, dated November 10, 2005. Of particular interest is a highly critical article by Brian Arnold, putative drafter of GAAR, in 2006 *Canadian Tax Journal* Vol. 54, No. 1, p. 167. The same edition of the Journal contains another useful analysis of the Supreme Court decisions.

A review of case law subsequent to the Supreme Court decisions, pointing out that apparently similar cases can yield differing results, is found in *Tax Topics* No. 1782, dated May 4, 2006. That discussion includes a review of Judge Bowman's decision in *Lipson v. The Queen*, 2006 DTC 2687 (T.C.C.), holding that a plan to render mortgage interest deductible violated GAAR, saying incidentally that: "Generally speaking, interest on borrowed money is deductible when the money is used for a commercial purpose. It is not deductible when the money is used for an ineligible (i.e., non-commercial or personal) purpose." Judge Bowman found several factual issues in the case inadequately explained, which may have contributed to the result, but it certainly should give pause to those reading the Supreme Court decision in *Singleton* (¶1063.10) as giving *carte blanche* to such planning. The *Lipson* decision was upheld by the Federal Court of Appeal (2007 DTC 5172). A further appeal was heard by the Supreme Court on April 23, 2008. On January 8, 2009, the Supreme Court of Canada released its divided decision against the taxpayer, with four justices in the majority and three justices in dissent. A more thorough review of the Supreme Court decisions and other cases on GAAR can be found in the commentary to section 245 in the Wolters Kluwer *Canadian Tax Reporter*.

A lengthy list of issues in which the CRA considers that "GAAR is a concern" is found in *Income Tax Technical News* No. 34, dated April 27, 2006. Heading the list is the "artificial" creation of capital losses.

(ITA: 245; IC 88-2)

[¶285a] REPORTING FOR AVOIDANCE TRANSACTIONS

In the 2010 federal Budget, the Department of Finance announced proposals to require the reporting of certain tax avoidance transactions. The reporting requirements, which received Royal Assent on June 26, 2013, are intended to provide the CRA with sufficient notice of tax avoidance transactions so that it can determine whether to apply the general anti-avoidance rule (GAAR) of section 245 or more specific anti-avoidance rules under the Act.

The legislation provides that an information return must be filed in respect of a "reportable transaction". This term is defined as an "avoidance transaction" entered into for the benefit of a person (including a trust), or a transaction that is part of a series of transactions that includes such an avoidance transaction, where **any two** of the following conditions apply in respect of the avoidance transaction or the series:

(1) an adviser or a promoter (or a non-arm's length party to such person) has an entitlement to a fee that is based on the amount of a tax benefit that results from the avoidance transaction or series, or is contingent upon the obtaining of a tax benefit that results from the avoidance transaction or series, or is attributable to the number of persons who participate in the avoidance transaction or series or who have been provided access to advice or an opinion given by the adviser or promoter regarding the tax consequences from the avoidance transaction or series;

(2) an adviser or promoter (or a non-arm's length party) obtains or obtained "confidential protection" in respect of the avoidance transaction or series. In the case of an adviser, from a person the adviser provided any assistance or advice with respect to the avoidance transaction or series under the terms of an engagement of the adviser; and in the case of a promoter from a person as described in the definition of "promoter"; or

(3) either the person obtaining the benefit or another person who entered into the avoidance transaction (or a non-arm's length party to either such person) has or had "contractual protection" in respect of the avoidance transaction or series, or the adviser or promoter (or a non-arm's length party) has or had contractual protection otherwise than as a result of a fee described in item (1) above.

For these purposes, an "avoidance transaction" has the same meaning as under subsection 245(3) for the rules relating to the GAAR. Accordingly it is a single transaction or a transaction that is part of a series of transactions, where the single transaction or the series results in a tax benefit (e.g., a reduction in tax, refund of tax, deferral of tax), unless the transaction was undertaken for *bona fide* purposes other than to obtain the tax benefit. In addition to forming the basis of a reportable transaction, an avoidance transaction is potentially subject to the GAAR, and if so, the tax benefit is denied.

Note that if a tax avoidance transaction is "saved" by subsection 245(4), that is, where the transaction does not result in a misuse of abuse of the Act, the GAAR will not apply, but the transaction can still be considered a "reportable transaction" for the purposes of the new reporting rules. In this regard, the reporting of the transaction is expressly not considered to be an admission that the GAAR should apply or that the transaction is a part of a series of transactions.

"Confidential protection" in respect of a transaction or series of transactions means anything that prohibits the disclosure to any person, including the CRA, of the details or structure of the transaction or series of transactions under which the tax benefit results.

"Contractual protection" includes insurance (other than standard professional liability insurance) or any similar protection, including an indemnity, compensation, or a guarantee that protects the person in respect of the denial or failure of the tax benefit or amounts that may be incurred as a result of a dispute (e.g., with the CRA) over the tax benefit, and any undertaking provided by a promoter (or non-arm's length person to the promoter) that provides assistance in the course of a dispute in respect of the tax benefit.

"Solicitor-client privilege" has the meaning assigned by subsection 232(1). For greater certainty, a lawyer who is an adviser in respect of a reportable transaction is not required to disclose any information in an information return with respect to the transaction or series which the lawyer believes is subject to solicitor-client privilege.

A reportable transaction does not include a transaction that is an acquisition of a tax shelter or the issuance of a flow-through share, although such transactions are subject to existing reporting requirements for tax shelters and flow-through shares.

The filing requirement applies to the person for whom the tax benefit results from the reportable transaction, anyone who entered into the transaction for the benefit of that person, and generally an adviser or promoter who is entitled to a fee in respect of the transaction or series. However, as long as one of these persons properly files the information return in respect of a reportable transaction, the others do not have to file the return for that transaction.

The information return must be filed by June 30 of the calendar year following the calendar year in which the avoidance transaction first became a reportable transaction. If the return is not filed properly on time, a late-filing penalty is payable, generally equal to the total fees to which an adviser or promoter (or a non-arm's length party) is entitled (including any such fee that is in respect of the contractual protection as described above). The CRA may make such assessments, determinations, and redeterminations as are necessary to impose the penalty, without regard to the usual time limitation periods in subsections 152(4) through (5). Furthermore, if the late-filing penalty or interest thereon is not paid and the filing does not occur, the tax benefit resulting from the transaction is denied — the same result that occurs if the GAAR actually applies to a transaction.

A "due diligence" exception is available, and if it applies, the late-filing penalty does not apply to the person exhibiting the due diligence. This exception applies if the relevant person has exercised the degree of care, diligence, and skill to prevent the failure to file that a reasonably prudent person would have exercised in comparable circumstances.

The new reporting requirements apply in respect of avoidance transactions that are entered into after 2010 or that are part of a series of transactions that began before 2011 and is completed after 2010, except that, in its application to an avoidance transaction that is part of a series that began before 2011, the definition "confidential protection" in subsection 237.3(1) of the Act, as enacted by subsection (1), is to be read as follows:

> "confidential protection", in respect of a transaction or series of transactions, means anything that prohibits the disclosure to any person or to the Minister of the details or structure of the transaction or series under which a tax benefit results, or would result but for section 245, but does not include a prohibition on disclosure that relates to an agreement entered into before March 4, 2010 between an adviser and his or her client for the provision of accounting, legal or similar tax advisory services, and for greater certainty, the disclaiming or restricting of an adviser's liability shall not be considered confidential protection if it does not prohibit the disclosure of the details or structure of the transaction or series.

If the filing of an information return under section 237.3 of the Act, as enacted by subsection 237.3(1), would be required before July 1, 2012, the information return is deemed to be filed before that day if it is filed before the day that is 120 days after the day on which this Act receives Royal Assent, in other words, October 24, 2013.

(ITA: 237.3)

[¶286] BANKRUPTCY RETURNS

If you declared bankruptcy in the year, your income (or loss) may be divided among three separate tax returns.

When you declare bankruptcy, a trustee takes over the administration of your property. From a tax point of view, however, the trustee is administering your affairs on your behalf, as an agent. For the period between the declaration of bankruptcy and the discharge from bankruptcy (which should be no longer than one year) the trustee will be responsible for tax returns concerning income arising from the trustee's dealings in your property or business. However, you are also responsible for filing certain tax returns for the periods involved.

In the year you declare bankruptcy, three returns are usually involved, as follows:

(1) First, you are deemed to have a year end the day before your declaration of bankruptcy, and you must file a return covering that period (as if it were a whole year) by April 30 of the following year. In this return, you report all income and loss and all normal deductions for the period covered. Note that certain claims, such as capital cost allowance, may by their terms be prorated for short taxation years. The personal amount credits must be apportioned between this return and the return described in (3), below. The apportionment

will work as follows: personal amount credits, age credit, disability credit, and transfers of credits from other individuals (such as a spouse or child) will be prorated by days in the taxation year before the bankruptcy over days in the calendar year, and claimed on this return. A similar calculation for days commencing with the day of bankruptcy will apply to determine credits under the return in (3), below. Pension credits, CPP/EI premium contribution credits, medical expense credit, tuition and education credits (the education and textbook tax credits were repealed effective January 1, 2017), and student loan interest credit are based on related income or expenditure of each period. Charitable donations credit for gifts made before the bankruptcy is claimed on the return for that period, but credit for gifts or donations made in the year on or after the day of bankruptcy are claimed on the trustee's return described in (2), below. It would appear that if you accumulate any carryforward of unused education/tuition credits in the return terminating just before bankruptcy, those credits (and any earlier balance carried forward) can be used only in the trustee's return. All these credits are discussed in Chapters 11, 12, and 13. In no case can any particular credit allocated or apportioned between returns be greater than the amount that could be claimed if there were a single return filed for the year. The allocation rules are modelled on those for part-year residents, which are discussed in detail at ¶2107.

(2) Second, the trustee must file a return covering the trustee's dealings with your property and business during the period of your bankruptcy in the year. The trustee's return, having calculated net income (loss) for the trustee's dealings on your account, may then apply only loss carryovers in arriving at taxable income. The trustee's return may not include any personal amount credits whatsoever except as described in (b), below. The trustee's return must be filed by the end of March of the following year. For bankruptcies that occur after April 26, 1995, the following changes are made:

(a) The trustee's return should also claim any deductions offsetting related income in the trustee's return in respect of employee stock options (¶330), prospectors' shares (¶776), deferred profit sharing plan (DPSP) shares received in lump-sum settlement, and capital gains eligible for the qualified farm or fishing property or qualified small business corporation share exemption (¶502).

(b) The trustee's return may claim charitable donation credit for any gifts made by the bankrupt individual on or after the day of bankruptcy. This applies to ordinary and cultural gifts, gifts to governments, and any other gifts generating charitable donation credit (Chapter 12). The trustee's return may also claim the bankrupt's carryforwards of unused education/tuition credit. Finally, there seems to be no prohibition against the trustee's use of the bankrupt's CPP/EI credits during the bankruptcy period, although the credit rules themselves suggest these would go with the bankrupt's employment earnings for that period.

(c) The trustee's return continues to apply loss carryovers, but no losses may be carried back to those returns for taxation years after the bankrupt has received an absolute discharge.

(d) In computing ordinary income, the trustee's return may not deduct any carrybacks of investment tax credit arising from expenditures incurred, or property acquired by, the individual after the date of absolute discharge.

(e) The trustee's return may claim any alternative minimum tax carryover (¶2481).

(3) Third, you must file a second return for the year, covering the period from the date of bankruptcy to December 31 (whether or not you received your discharge). This return also treats the portion of the year it covers as if it were a whole year, and must be filed by April 30 of the following year. This return covers any income or other transactions not included in the trustee's return. It might therefore typically include your employment income for the period. On this return you may not claim any carryovers of losses of any kind; these are available only to the trustee. The personal amount credits must be apportioned between this return and the return in (1), above, as discussed there. A number of deductions or credits cannot be claimed on this return and are claimed on the trustee's return in (2), above; these items may not be claimed on the individual's second return even if the trustee does not in fact make the claim.

Special rules govern RRSP contributions for bankruptcies. Under these rules, notwithstanding the general division of the year into two taxation years, you will treat the two taxation years as one year for the purposes of determining all the amounts required to calculate present and future RRSP deduction eligibility, such as earned income, RRSP deduction limit, unused RRSP room, and so on. You then compute your RRSP deduction on your first return, using the aggregate earnings and so on from the two returns, for contributions made to your own or a spousal plan during the period covered by the return or 60 days thereafter. Your deductions on the second return will be for contributions made in the period of that return or 60 days thereafter, and your "deduction limit" will be reduced by amounts deducted on the first return.

Income from both returns of the individual for the year of bankruptcy (returns (1) and (3), above) will be included in calculating income for purposes of determining GST credit and Canada Child Benefit. Previously, only the income from the second of these returns (the post-bankruptcy return of the individual) was counted. These provisions will apply equally where the spouse becomes bankrupt.

In a technical opinion (CRA Document No. 2004-0092961E5), the CRA says that:

> Where an individual becomes a bankrupt in a calendar year and resides in different provinces at the end of each taxation year ending in that calendar year, the individual can claim a portion of these credits allowed in the province of residence at the end of each taxation year as can reasonably be considered applicable to that taxation year. In our view, that portion must be calculated on a *pro rata* basis, based on the number of days in the period for which the applicable pre-bankruptcy or post-bankruptcy return is filed.

[¶286.05] *Discharge from Bankruptcy*

In the year you receive your discharge from bankruptcy, if it follows the calendar year in which you declared bankruptcy, there will be two returns. The trustee will file a return for the period during which the trustee administered your affairs, and you must file an ordinary return for the year, excluding any items dealt with by the trustee in the trustee's return.

When you receive your discharge from bankruptcy, it may discharge (cancel) all your debts up to the time of your declaration of bankruptcy, including your debts to the CRA up to that time. This is called an absolute discharge. However, you may receive a conditional discharge, which could require you to pay further amounts to creditors, including the CRA. If you have received an absolute discharge, cancelling all your prior debts, you may not carry forward any tax losses of any kind which arose in any year prior to the year in which the absolute discharge is granted and apply them in the year of discharge or any later year. For bankruptcies occurring after April 26, 1995, a number of other carryforwards are limited for taxation years ending after an absolute discharge from bankruptcy. These are:

(1) You may not deduct any minimum tax carryover (¶2481) from alternative minimum tax arising from taxation years ending before the absolute discharge.

(2) You may not claim any charitable donation credits (Chapter 12) for gifts made in taxation years ending before the absolute discharge. This includes ordinary and cultural gifts, gifts to governments, and any other gifts generating charitable donation credit.

(3) You may not claim any investment tax credits for expenditures you incurred or property you acquired in taxation years ending before the absolute discharge.

(4) You may not claim any carryforward of unused textbook/education/tuition amounts (Chapter 13; the education and textbook credits were repealed effective January 1, 2017) from taxation years ending before the absolute discharge.

If for any reason the trustee deals with any of your affairs after an order of discharge (i.e., where there is a conditional and not an absolute discharge), the general rules covering a trustee's return will operate as if you were bankrupt in that year.

Where an individual withdraws funds from an RRSP under the Home Buyers' Plan (Chapter 26) and subsequently becomes bankrupt, the CRA is of the view that the bankruptcy does not affect the obligation of the individual to repay the withdrawn funds to an RRSP. Only the tax liability of the individual for the period of bankruptcy would be affected to the extent of income inclusion in that period. Presumably, this is because the repayment liability arises annually as a matter of law and therefore does not become a debt until the year it arises.

(ITA: 118.95; 120.2(4); 122.5(7); 122.61(3.1); 128; Window on Canadian Tax: 2666)

[¶287] CANADA REVENUE AGENCY OFFICES

The Canada Revenue Agency (CRA) is the federal government ministry charged with collecting federal income and sales (GST) taxes. It also collects provincial income taxes for all provinces except Quebec, and provincial sales taxes (HST) for participating provinces. The CRA administers tax programs, and delivers some economic and social benefits.

According to the CRA's website, "The Minister of National Revenue is accountable to Parliament for all the CRA's activities, including the administration and enforcement of the *Income Tax Act* and the *Excise Tax Act*", and 16 other acts.

(Other Publications: CRA website: www.cra-arc.gc.ca)

[¶287.05] *The CRA Website*

The CRA maintains an excellent website, from which virtually all its publications and forms can be downloaded, along with other materials such as press releases. The URL for the CRA website is: www.cra-arc.gc.ca.

[¶287.06] *My Account*

The CRA introduced the "My Account" service in its efforts to provide taxpayers with online access to certain elements of their tax accounts in order to reduce the telephone/in-person inquiries. The information that you can see if you sign up for My Account is:

- your tax refund or balance owing;
- direct deposit information that is on file;
- your RRSP deduction limit, prior year deduction limits and calculations, unused contributions available to deduct, prior year contribution history, Home Buyers' Plan, and Lifelong Learning Plan;
- Tax-Free Savings Account contribution room limit, transaction summary, and details of excess contributions;
- the tax returns filed for the current and 10 prior years and the status of each (not received, received, assessed, reassessment in progress, reassessed) and the date processed;
- any carryover amounts (capital gain/loss, non-capital losses, investment tax credit, allowable business investment loss, capital gains deduction, tuition, education, and textbook date history; the education and textbook credits were repealed effective January 1, 2017);
- tax information slips — T4, T4A, T4A(P), T4A(OAS), and T4E;
- disability tax credit entitlement information for you, your spouse and/or dependants;
- current account balance and payments on filing;
- instalments paid and instalment reminder notices;
- Canada Child Benefit and related provincial and territorial programs payments, account balance, and statement of account;
- GST/HST credit and related provincial programs payments, account balance, and statement of account;
- Universal Child Care Benefit payments, account balance, statement of account, and RC62;
- children for which you are the primary caregiver;
- Working Income Tax Benefit advanced payments and RC210;
- pre-authorized payment plan;
- if you have authorized a representative;
- your current address and telephone numbers; and
- your current marital status.

In addition, you can also manage your information by:

- changing your return(s) (i.e., filing a T1-Adjustment);
- changing your address or telephone numbers;
- applying for child benefits;
- ending care of a child;
- arranging your direct deposit;

- authorizing your representative;
- setting up a pre-authorized payment plan;
- formally disputing your assessment or determination;
- changing your marital status;
- ordering remittance voucher(s); and
- submitting documents as requested by the CRA.

There are two ways to sign up for the My Account service, using a CRA login or a sign-in partner.

To use the CRA login, you must first register with the CRA for a CRA user ID and password. For the initial sign up procedure, you need to have your Social Insurance Number; date of birth; current postal code; and a copy of your most recent income tax return. You will create a CRA user ID and password and security questions and answers. Once these have been set up and submitted, this will generate the CRA sending you a CRA security code in the mail within 5–10 business days. Once you receive the code, the first time you use your CRA login, you will be asked to enter the security code. After the initial login, you no longer need the CRA security code.

The sign-in partner login service, called SecureKey Concierge, allows you to log in using your online banking information if you have an account with one of the participating sign-in partners (BMO Financial Group, Choice Rewards Mastercard, Desjardins Group, RBC Royal Bank, Scotiabank, Tangerine, TD Canada Trust, Caisses Populaires Acadiennes, or Caisses Populaires). The benefit of using this service is that you don't have to remember another user ID and login. However, it is only available with specific sign-in partners. Note that the information you enter and the identity of the financial institution are not shared with the CRA and, conversely, no information about the government service being accessed is shared with the user's bank.

The process for accessing the sign-in partner for the first time is similar to the CRA login set-up. You will need to have your Social Insurance Number; date of birth; current postal code; and a copy of your most recent income tax return. Instead of creating a CRA user ID and password, you select your financial institution. You will then be routed to the login page where you will enter your banking login information. You will receive the CRA security code in the mail within 5–10 business days. For your first login, you enter the CRA security code, and then for future logins, you just enter your online banking login information.

For additional assistance, the CRA has an e-Services Helpdesk for individuals at 1-800-714-7257.

[¶287.10] *Contacting the CRA by Phone*

The CRA has introduced a system of toll-free national telephone numbers for all inquiries which would usually be directed to your local TSO. These are:

General (personal) Inquiries, including forms and publications: 1-800-959-8281

Business (including T2) Inquiries, including forms and publications: 1-800-959-5525

The locations reached by these numbers may be in any particular TSO or none. Increasingly, the CRA is separating its inquiry numbers from the physical location of its offices. Thus, several Toronto-area offices share a common phone number which is actually in a location separate from all of them. Computerization of tax return data allows the CRA to access data on your return from pretty well anywhere.

This system is, among other things, supposed to reduce waiting times by automatically shifting calls to lines which are free or have the least waiting times, even if the call is thus routed out of your area altogether.

Note that questions concerning tax return requirements for non-residents are centralized in the International TSO, which does have its own phone numbers, listed below.

[¶287.15] *Canada Revenue Agency (CRA) Offices*

The central offices of the CRA are located in Ottawa, Ontario.

There are Tax Centres in Newfoundland, Prince Edward Island, Quebec, Ontario, Manitoba, and British Columbia (see ¶218). Non-resident returns are processed in the International TSO, a separate location in Ottawa.

General inquiries and requests for forms must now be made online or by telephone. The TSO — formerly called a District Taxation Office no longer provides payment or inquiry counter service. Matters relating to audits and assessments are normally dealt with through the TSO that is responsible for the area in which you reside. The CRA assigns TSOs to taxpayers based on the taxpayers' postal codes. This system relates the TSO boundaries to a surrounding geographical area. However, there is no longer any accessible geographical map of these boundaries; there is merely a very long list of postal codes and corresponding TSOs.

In the "Contact us" section of the CRA website, you can determine the location of the TSO associated with any given postal code.

If you receive any correspondence from the CRA, it should indicate the TSO serving you, and perhaps other information service numbers as well.

In recent years, the CRA has been cutting back on the services available at TSOs, relying primarily on its 800 phone number to receive taxpayer contacts.

You can arrange appointments (by telephone to the central 800 number, 1-800-959-8281) at most (but not all) TSOs, but you can no longer walk in off the street and get service related to your particular tax account. Nor can you drop off a return or other communication at a staffed counter and receive a receipt, although secure drop boxes are provided at all TSOs. As of October 2013, the CRA closed all payment and inquiry counter services. They also removed the self-serve stamping machines installed in April 2009 that provided taxpayers with a proof of delivery receipt. An external drop box is the only service available for correspondence and payments. The CRA website indicates that the drop boxes are "typically emptied of their contents twice daily". In addition, the contents are stamped by their mail operations the same day. However, there is no mechanism to provide the taxpayer with proof of delivery or payment for their records. This move coincides with the CRA's initiative to move more services online; however, for the returns/elections/payments that cannot be made online, it seems registered mail or courier are the options to provide taxpayers with peace of mind that their filings were made on time.

Federal TSOs are as follows:

INTERNATIONAL TAX SERVICES OFFICE

Office address:
2204 Walkley Road
Ottawa ON K1A 1A8
Mailing address:
P.O. Box 9769, Station T
Ottawa ON K1G 3Y4
Calls from Canada and U.S.: 1-855-959-8281
Calls from outside Canada and U.S. (collect calls

accepted): 1-613-940-8495
The CRA has centralized its non-resident filing and information centres here. Inquiries concerning non-residents, immigrants, and emigrants should be directed to this office.

ALBERTA

Calgary (Southern Alberta)
Office/mailing address:
220 4th Avenue South East
Calgary AB T2G 0L1

Edmonton
Office address:
Main Floor, 9700 Jasper Avenue
Edmonton AB T5J 4C8
Mailing address:
9700 Jasper Avenue, Suite 10
Edmonton AB T5J 4C8

Lethbridge (Southern Alberta)
Office address:
200-419 7th Street South
Lethbridge AB T1J 4A9
Mailing address:
P.O. Box 3009 Station Main
Lethbridge AB T1J 4A9

Red Deer (Southern Alberta)
Office/mailing address:
4996 49th Avenue
Red Deer AB T4N 6X2

BRITISH COLUMBIA

Surrey (Fraser Valley and Northern)
Office address:
9737 King George Boulevard
Surrey BC V3T 5W6
Mailing address:
9755 King George Boulevard
Surrey BC V3T 5E1

Prince George (Fraser Valley and Northern)
Office address:
280 Victoria Street
Prince George BC V2L 4X3
Mailing address:
9755 King George Boulevard
Surrey BC V3T 5E1

Kelowna (Southern Interior B.C.)
Office address:
200-471 Queensway Avenue
Kelowna BC V1Y 6S5
Mailing address:
9755 King George Boulevard
Surrey BC V3T 5E1

Penticton (Southern Interior B.C.)
Office address:
277 Winnipeg Street
Penticton BC V2A 1N6
Mailing address:
9755 King George Boulevard
Surrey BC V3T 5E1

Vancouver
Office address:
1166 West Pender Street
Vancouver BC V6E 3H8
Mailing address:
9755 King George Boulevard
Surrey BC V3T 5E1

Victoria (Vancouver Island)
Office address:
1415 Vancouver Street
Victoria BC V8V 3W4
Mailing address:
9755 King George Boulevard
Surrey BC V3T 5E1

MANITOBA

Brandon
Office/mailing address:
210-153 11th Street
Brandon MB R7A 7K6

Winnipeg
Office/mailing address:
325 Broadway
Winnipeg MB R3C 4T4

NEW BRUNSWICK

Bathurst
Office/mailing address:
201 St. George Street
Bathurst NB E2A 1B8

Moncton
Office/mailing address:
Assumption Place
217–770 Main Street
Moncton NB E1C 1E7

Saint John
Office address:
65 Canterbury Street
Saint John NB E2L 2C7
Mailing address:
P.O. Box 6300
Retail Postal Outlet Brunswick Square
Saint John NB E2L 4H9

NEWFOUNDLAND AND LABRADOR

Newfoundland and Labrador
Office address:
Sir Humphrey Gilbert Building
165 Duckworth Street
St. John's NL A1B 1G4
Mailing address:
P.O. Box 12075, Station A
St. John's NL A1B 4R5

NORTHWEST TERRITORIES

(Administered by Edmonton TSO. See above.)

NOVA SCOTIA

Halifax
Office address:
100-145 Hobsons Lake Drive
Halifax NS B3S 0J1
Mailing address:
P.O. Box 638
Halifax NS B3J 2T5
Box 638, Station Central
Halifax NS B3J 2T5

Sydney
Office address:
47 Dorchester Street
Sydney NS B1P 7H5
Mailing address:

P.O. Box 1300, Station A
Sydney NS B1P 6K3

NUNAVUT

(Administered by Ottawa TSO. See below.)

ONTARIO

Barrie (Toronto North-Barrie)
Office/mailing address:
81 Mulcaster Street
Barrie ON L4M 6T7

Belleville (East Central Ontario)
Office/mailing address:
11 Station Street
Belleville ON K8N 2S3

Hamilton (Hamilton-Niagara)
Office/mailing address:
55 Bay Street North
Hamilton ON L8R 3P7

Kingston (East Central Ontario)
Office address:
1475 John Counter Boulevard
Kingston ON K7M 0E6
Mailing address:
102-1475 John Counter Boulevard
Kingston ON K7M 0E6

Kitchener/Waterloo
Office/mailing address:
166 Frederick Street
Kitchener ON N2H 0A9

London (London-Windsor)
Office/mailing address:
451 Talbot Street
London ON N6A 5E5

Mississauga (Toronto West-Thunder Bay)
Office/mailing address:
5800 Hurontario Street
Mississauga ON L5R 4B4

Ottawa (International and Ottawa)
Office/mailing address:
333 Laurier Avenue West
Ottawa ON K1A 0L9

Ottawa (Technology Centre)
Office/mailing address:
Ottawa Technology Centre
875 Heron Road
Ottawa ON K1A 1A2

Peterborough (East Central Ontario)
Office/mailing address:
1161 Crawford Drive
Peterborough ON K9J 6X6

St. Catharines (Hamilton-Niagara)
Office/mailing address:
32 Church Street
St. Catharines ON L2R 3B9

Sudbury
Office/mailing address:
1050 Notre Dame Avenue
Sudbury ON P3A 5C1

Thunder Bay (Toronto West-Thunder Bay)
Office/mailing address:
130 South Syndicate Avenue
Thunder Bay ON P7E 1C7

Toronto Centre
Office/mailing address:
1 Front Street West
Toronto ON M5J 2X6

Toronto East
Office/mailing address:
200 Town Centre Court
Toronto ON M1P 4Y3

Toronto North (Toronto North-Barrie)
Office/mailing address:
5001 Yonge Street
Toronto ON M2N 6R9

Windsor (London-Windsor)
Office/mailing address:
185 Ouellette Avenue
Windsor ON N9A 4H7

PRINCE EDWARD ISLAND

Charlottetown
Office address:
1-30 Brackley Point Road
Charlottetown PE C1A 6X9
Mailing address:
P.O. Box 8500, Station Central
Charlottetown PE C1A 8L3

QUEBEC

Brossard (Central and Southern Quebec)
Office/mailing address:
3250 Lapinière Boulevard
Brossard QC J4Z 3T8

Chicoutimi (Eastern Quebec)
Office Address:
100 La Fontaine Street
Chicoutimi QC G7H 6X2
Mailing address:
PO Box 1660 Station Bureau-chef
Jonquière QC G7S 4L3

Gatineau (Western Quebec)
Office/mailing address:
85 Chemin de la Savane
Gatineau QC K1A 1L4

Laval (Western Quebec)
Office/mailing address:
3400 Jean-Béraud Avenue
Laval QC H7T 2Z2

Montreal
Office/mailing address:
305 René-Lévesque Boulevard West
Montreal QC H2Z 1A6

Quebec (Eastern Quebec)
Office/mailing address:
2575 Ste Anne Boulevard
Québec QC G1J 1Y5

Rimouski (Eastern Quebec)
Office/mailing address:
180 de la Cathédrale Avenue, Suite 101
Rimouski QC G5L 5H9

Rouyn-Noranda (Western Quebec)
Office/mailing address:
44 du Lac Avenue
Rouyn-Noranda QC J9X 6Z9

Sherbrooke (Central and Southern Quebec)
Office/mailing address:
50 Place de la Cité
PO Box 1300
Sherbrooke QC J1H 5L8

Trois-Rivières (Central and Southern Quebec)
Office/mailing address:
2250 St. Oliver Street
Trois-Rivières QC G9A 4E9

SASKATCHEWAN

Regina
Office/mailing address:
1955 Smith Street
Regina SK S4P 2N9

Saskatoon
Office/mailing address:
340 3rd Avenue North
Saskatoon SK S7K 0A8

YUKON

(Administered by Prince George TSO. See above.)

[¶288] INQUIRIES

Should you wish to obtain further information regarding the preparation of your tax return, you may telephone the central inquiry number for individuals, as discussed in ¶287.

Inquiries by mail on how to prepare your return should be made to your TSO and *not* to the Taxation Data Centre. Inquiries about assessments should be directed as indicated at ¶263.

[¶288.10] *Taxpayer Disputes; Taxpayer Complaints; Taxpayer Ombudsman*

The CRA has a number of internal mechanisms for dealing with taxpayers who disagree with its assessments. In general, it prefers that you go through these procedures before going on to the more formal objection procedures discussed at ¶266 *et seq.* Be sure to not let your rights to formal objections and appeals, which are governed by strict time limits, slip by while you go through these less formal procedures.

In addition to its procedures for dealing with disagreements about assessments, the CRA has a separate institutionalized complaints mechanism for taxpayers who are not satisfied with its service. In general, these are complaints about the quality and timeliness of the work performed by the CRA. Service-related complaints would include: mistakes, which could refer to misunderstandings, omissions or oversights; undue delays; poor or misleading information; and/or staff behaviour. The CRA publishes a pamphlet, RC4420, *Information on CRA — Service Complaints*, describing this process.

The Minister of National Revenue has appointed a Taxpayer Ombudsman to supervise this process and ensure its independence. The CRA website includes information about these services. The Ombudsman's office publishes its own guide, which is available from Canada Service Centres (as opposed to TSOs), the Ombudsman's website, www.taxpayersrights.gc.ca or from the Ombudsman's toll-free phone number, 1-866-586-3839.

Chapter 3

Employment Income and Deductions

THESE POINTS ARE COVERED IN THIS CHAPTER

CRA REFERENCES RELATING TO THIS CHAPTER

T1 Lines

- Line 101 — Employment income (box 14 on T4 slips) [¶308.01]
- Line 102 — Commissions included on Line 101 (box 42 on T4 slips) [¶304.05]
- Line 104 — Other employment income [¶363.35] [¶379.20]
- Line 130 — Other income [¶373c.10]
- Line 144 — Workers' compensation benefits [¶358]
- Line 207 — Registered pension plan deduction [¶365] [¶365a]
- Line 212 — Annual union, professional, or like dues (box 44 on T4 slips and receipts) [¶372]
- Line 229 — Other employment expenses [¶358] [¶362.15] [¶370] [¶372] [¶373b] [¶373c]
- Line 231 — Clergy residence deduction [¶376]
- Line 244 — Canadian Forces personnel and police deduction (box 43 on all T4 slips) [¶385.10]
- Line 248 — Employee home relocation loan deduction (box 37 on T4 slips) [¶353.05]
- Line 249 — Security options deductions [¶330.25] [¶330.50] [¶330.65]
- Line 250 — Other payments deduction [¶358]
- Line 255 — Northern residents deduction [¶361a]
- Line 437 — Total income tax deducted
- Line 457 — Employee and partner GST/HST rebate [¶363.10]

CRA Guides

5000-G, "General Income Tax and Benefit Guide"; **RC4110**, "Employee or Self-Employed?"; **RC4120**, "Employers' Guide — Filing the **T4** Slip and

Summary"; **T4001**, "Employer's Guide — Payroll Deductions and Remittances"; **T4002**, "Business and Professional Income — Includes Form T2125"; **T4040**, "RRSPs and Other Registered Plans for Retirement"; **T4041**, "Retirement Compensation Arrangements Guide"; **T4044**, "Employment Expenses — Includes Forms T777, TL2, T2200, and GST 370"; **T4115**, "T5007 Guide — Return of Benefits"; **T4130**, "Employers' Guide — Taxable Benefits and Allowances"

CRA Forms

GST370, "Employee and Partner GST/HST Rebate Application"; **T4**, "Statement of Remuneration Paid"; **T4PS**, "Statement of Employee Profit-Sharing Plan Allocations and Payments"; **T777**, "Statement of Employment Expenses"; **T1198**; "Statement of Qualifying Retroactive Lump-Sum Payment"; **T1223**; "Clergy Residence Deduction"; **T2200**, "Declaration of Conditions of Employment"; **T2222**, "Northern Residents Deductions"; **T5007**, "Statement of Benefits"; **TL2**; "Claim for Meals and Lodging Expenses"

Income Tax Folios

S1-F2-C2, "Tuition Tax Credit"; **S1-F2-C3**, "Scholarships, Research Grants and Other Education Assistance"; **S2-F1-C1**, "Health and Welfare Trusts"; **S2-F3-C1**, "Payments from Employer to Employee"; **S2-F3-C2**, "Benefits and Allowances Received from Employment"; **S3-F9-C1**, "Lottery Winnings, Miscellaneous Receipts, and Income (and Losses) from Crime"

Interpretation Bulletins

IT-63R5, "Benefits, Including Standby Charge for an Automobile, from the Personal Use of a Motor Vehicle Supplied by an Employer — After 1992" [Archived]; **IT-91R4**, "Employment at Special Work Sites or Remote Work Locations" [Archived]; **IT-99R5 (Consolidated)**, "Legal and Accounting Fees" [Archived]; **IT-103R**, "Dues Paid to a Union or to a Parity or Advisory Committee" [Archived]; **IT-113R4**, "Benefits to Employees — Stock Options" [Archived]; **IT-141R (Consolidated)**, "Clergy Residence Deduction" [Archived]; **IT-158R2**, "Employees' Professional Membership Dues" [Archived]; **IT-167R6**, "Registered Pension Funds or Plans — Employee's Contributions" [Archived]; **IT-168R3**, "Athletes and Players Employed by Football, Hockey and Similar Clubs" [Archived]; **IT-202R2**, "Employees' or Workers' Compensation" [Archived]; **IT-257R**, "Canada Council Grants" [Archived]; **IT-280R**, "Employees Profit Sharing Plans — Payments Computed by Reference to Profits" [Archived]; **IT-292**, "Taxation of Elected Officers of Incorporated Municipalities, School Boards, Municipal Commissions and Similar Bodies" [Archived]; **IT-352R2**, "Employee's Expenses, Including Work Space in Home Expenses" [Archived]; **IT-365R2**, "Damages, Settlements, and Similar Receipts" [Archived]; **IT-379R**, "Employees Profit Sharing Plans — Allocations to Beneficiaries" [Archived]; **IT-421R2**, "Benefits to Individuals, Corporations and Shareholders from Loans or Debt" [Archived]; **IT-428**, "Wage Loss Replacement Plans" [Archived]; **IT-502**, "Employee Benefit Plans and Employee Trusts" [Archived]; **IT-504R2 (Consolidated)**, "Visual Artists and Writers" [Archived]; **IT-522R**, "Vehicle, Travel and Sales Expenses of Employees" [Archived]; **IT-525R (Consolidated)**, "Performing Artists" [Archived]; **IT-529**, "Flexible Employee Benefit Programs" [Archived]

Income Tax Technical News

No. **38**, September 22, 2008, "Employee Stock Option Deduction"

WHAT YOU SHOULD KNOW ABOUT EMPLOYMENT INCOME AND ALLOWABLE EXPENSES

RECENT CHANGES

2016 New Income Tax Folios

In 2016, the CRA released the following income tax folios:

- S2-F3-C2, "Benefits and Allowances Received from Employment", issued July 7, 2016 (New)

Regulatory Changes: Mileage Rates

2016 Mileage and Deduction Rates

Limits/ Deductions	Amount	Discussed in
Limits on deduction for capital cost allowance on automobile and interest and leasing costs	unchanged	¶370.05, ¶810a
Limits on deduction of tax-exempt allowances paid by employers to employees using their personal vehicle for business purposes	• Yukon, Northwest Territories, and Nunavut: $0.58 per kilometre for the first 5,000 kilometres driven and $0.52 for each additional kilometre • Excluding Yukon, Northwest Territories, and Nunavut: $0.54 per kilometre for the first 5,000 kilometres driven and $0.48 for each additional kilometre	¶738.55, ¶86
Prescribed rate used generally to determine the taxable benefit relating to the personal portion of automobile operating expenses paid by employers	For taxpayers employed principally in selling or leasing automobiles: $0.23 per kilometre • All taxpayers except the above: $0.26 per kilometre	¶324.15, ¶738.60

[¶304] EMPLOYEE OR SELF-EMPLOYED?

This chapter discusses the taxation of an employee on employment income. Income from self-employment is business or professional income, which is discussed in Chapter 7.

It is sometimes difficult to distinguish between employment and self-employment. At the one extreme, if you work regularly providing your services to one person or company whether on commission or for a fixed amount computed hourly, weekly, monthly, or annually, you are an employee. At the other extreme, if you provide services to a series of different payers at essentially the same time, determining the nature or degree of service and prioritizing the demands of your clients on your own, you are probably operating a business.

The issue more commonly arises in Canada Pension Plan ("CPP") and Employment Insurance ("EI") assessments. The CRA will often classify all the workers of a particular enterprise as employees, while the employer (and very often the employees as well) resist this classification. Self-employed workers will have to pay the CPP contributions themselves in any event, but EI contributions, which do not apply to a self-employed worker, are seen as an unnecessary cost by those who do not anticipate claiming benefits.

Although administered by the CRA, CPP/EI is handled by a different division and its judgments do not prevent a separate appeal on income tax issues. On the other hand, since a CPP/EI ruling of employment will result in the issuance of T4 slips, it does create a presumption of employment income on the income tax return.

Each case is judged from the point of view of the person offering services (i.e., the potential employee) and not the employer. The courts have cited with approval the principle that "the fundamental test to be applied is this: Is the person who has engaged himself to perform these services performing them as a person in business on his own account?" If the answer is yes, the person is self-employed.

The CRA has attempted to analyze the criteria for separating employees from the self-employed in guide RC4110, "Employee or Self-Employed?", which is available only in electronic format on their website. It lays out the lines of argument to which the CRA will look in the first instance, and it is a reasonable starting point for the argument.

The CRA guide also points out that employment status in Quebec is determined under somewhat different rules under the Civil Code of Quebec, which sets out statutory rules for the determination of employment. There is a useful discussion of how the CRA endeavours to apply Quebec criteria.

See also the discussion at ¶700, and, for those in the arts, ¶789.

Planning Opportunities

Although whether you are employed or self-employed is ultimately a question of fact, it is open to you and the person to whom you provide services to structure your arrangement to support a conclusion one way or the other. If you are in doubt, you can write to the CRA, summarizing the terms of your arrangement, and the CRA will provide an opinion on your status.

Relevant Case Law

Employed or Self-Employed

The leading case is *Wiebe Door Services Ltd. v. M.N.R.*, 87 DTC 5025 (FCA) in which four tests were identified:

(1) whether the worker was subject to the control of the payer as to the use of time and the way in which services were to be performed,

(2) whether the worker provided his or her own tools,

(3) whether the worker had an opportunity for profit or a risk of loss from his enterprise, and

(4) whether the services performed were integral to the business or accessory to it.

In more recent decisions, the courts have also taken the intention of the parties into account, particularly where the *Wiebe Door* tests do not yield a clear answer.

In *Lang v. The Queen*, 2007 DTC 1754 (TCC), Chief Justice Bowman of the Tax Court gave an extensive review of case law. He concluded that the *Wiebe Door* tests remain significant, but the tests have been reduced to "guidelines relevant and helpful in ascertaining the intent of the parties". On the other hand, whether intent is always determinative remains unclear at best. In short, the issue remains one that will be decided on a case-by-case basis.

(RC4110, "Employee or Self-Employed?"; *Wiebe Door Services Ltd. v. M.N.R.*, 87 DTC 5025 (FCA); A valuable summary of subsequent case law is found in *Lang v. The Queen*, 2007 DTC 1754 (TCC))

[¶304.05] *Commission Salespersons — Line 102*

The general principles outlined in ¶304 apply equally to commission salespersons. It is not unusual for a commission salesperson to be subject to less direct control than are employees in other positions, but usually the amount of control is discussed at the beginning of your relationship with your company and is made clear by the terms and conditions under which your services are to be performed.

For example, as a commission salesperson, you are probably an employee if the business whose product you handle:

- trains you, pays you a basic salary, has the right to discharge you;
- requires you to sell from their premises and follow established hours;
- restricts you to their own products and expects you to maintain a quota;
- directs you as to what territory to cover, what clients to approach, and when and how to do so;
- supplies the vehicle you use, pays your expenses or provides you with an allowance; or
- expects you to collect on a regular basis and make regular reports.

The CRA has historically considered three main factors in determining the relationship between a salesperson and a business. The presence of all following three factors at once indicates self-employment status:

- You are not restricted to the business's products but are free to sell others whether or not they are competitive.
- You are not required to perform the services personally. The business is interested in the results of the work and not the methods.
- You are given no instructions about what territory to cover, what clients to approach, or when and how to carry out the services.

Should one of these factors be missing in the relationship, then the factors listed earlier must be considered.

If you are an employed commission salesperson, you are entitled to deduct expenses that are not allowed for other employees. See ¶368. Of course, if you are self-employed, there is even a broader range of deductible expenses.

[¶305] PERSONAL SERVICE BUSINESS (THE INCORPORATED EMPLOYEE)

A personal services business is defined as a business carried on by a corporation where a specified shareholder of the corporation or a related party (the "incorporated employee") provides services to an entity, and in the absence of the corporation, the incorporated employee could reasonably be regarded as an officer or employee of the entity.

A "specified shareholder" is a person owning 10% or more of the corporation's shares of any class and, for these purposes, all shares owned by non-arm's length parties are taken into account. A business is not a personal services business, though, if the services are provided to an associated corporation — i.e., to one under common control with the service provider.

The intent of the personal services business rules is to eliminate any tax reduction or deferral by converting personal income into corporate income by interposing a corporation between an employee and an employer.

Deductions in computing income from a personal services business are restricted to: (i) the salary, wages or other remuneration paid to the incorporated employee, (ii) the cost of benefits or allowances provided to him or her, (iii) amounts expended in connection with the selling of property or negotiating of contracts if these amounts would otherwise be deductible by the incorporated employee if he or she were an employee, and (iv) legal expenses incurred in collecting amounts owing for the services rendered.

The disadvantages of having a business covered by these rules fall almost entirely on the corporation. (See ¶785). For taxation years that begin after October 31, 2011, a corporation's income from a personal services business is not eligible for the general corporate rate reduction, so that it is taxed at a significantly higher rate than regular corporate income. There is therefore no tax saving or deferral where what would otherwise be employment income is taxed in a corporation. This is discussed at ¶2550.

Example

Janet owns all the shares of Familyco. Her husband, Jim, is employed by Acme Tool. In an attempt to divert some of his income to Janet, Jim arranges for Acme Tool to enter into a service contract with Familyco and his salary is paid to the company. The after-tax income is to be paid as a dividend to Janet.

Familyco is carrying on a personal services business and can only deduct the cost of wages and benefits that are taxable to Jim, and the other limited deductions outlined above. More importantly, Familyco cannot claim either the small business deduction or the general rate reduction, and therefore pays tax at a high rate.

Planning Opportunities

A corporation can apply non-capital losses against personal services business income. Where the corporation cannot otherwise use the losses, it may be possible to apply them against what would otherwise be employment income. If, for example, Familyco in the example above had non-capital losses carried forward, it could deduct them against the fee income from Acme Tool. It might therefore be possible to put a personal services business in place temporarily, and wind it up once all the losses have been used.

(ITA: 18(1)(p); 248(1) "personal services business")

[¶306] HOW YOUR PAY IS TAXED

Your income from an office or employment includes all amounts received and benefits enjoyed by you in the year — that is, employment income is generally taxed on a cash basis. You may also have to include in your employment income certain deferred salary amounts described at ¶307.

Only certain specified deductions are permitted and these are reviewed in detail in this chapter. You should keep in mind the important distinction between computing income from a business or property and computing income from an office or employment. Income from a business or property is computed after deducting any reasonable expenditure which is deductible under ordinary commercial accounting practices, unless the deduction is specifically prohibited under the *Income Tax Act*. In computing your income from an office or employment you may deduct only those amounts specifically allowed.

Form T4 is used by your employer to report your employment income for the year. The T4 should report the full amount of your pay before any deductions for income tax withheld at source, medical or hospital insurance, pension deductions, Canada savings bonds purchases, union dues, or any other deductions from your salary.

If you have a question on any amount reported on your T4 slip, contact the employer who issued the slip. The employer is in a position to provide you with full particulars of the amounts shown since the slip is prepared by the employer. For example, the employer would know the nature of any taxable allowances and benefits which may be included in your T4 slip.

Your employment income is included in calculating your total income at line 150, and any employment related deductions you may claim are deducted, usually at lines 207, 212 and 229, in computing net income. Tax withheld from your wages, which is also reported on your T4, is included in line 437.

(ITA: 5(1); 8(1); 8(2))

[¶307] SALARY DEFERRAL ARRANGEMENTS

You may be taxed on employment income earned but not received in the year. In particular, "deferred amounts" under a "salary deferral arrangement" are taxed in the year they arise and not the year of receipt.

[¶307.05] *Taxation of Deferred Amounts*

A salary deferral arrangement is an arrangement between an employer and employee under which the employee postpones the receipt of remuneration beyond the end of a year in which it is earned, where it is reasonable to consider that one of the main purposes for the postponement is to defer the tax payable by the employee. The remuneration that is postponed under a salary deferral arrangement is referred to as a "deferred amount".

If you participate in a deferral arrangement, the deferred amount is considered to be a benefit received in the year. It is therefore included in your income for the year, to the extent you have not already reported it.

Interest or other returns credited with respect to a deferred amount are similarly included in your income as they arise and not when they are paid. Salary deferral arrangements are excluded from the definition of an "investment contract" so that income accruing on deferred amounts is taken into income as employment income, and not as investment income under the rules described at ¶432. However, interest earned by a trust governed by a salary deferral arrangement is not included in employment income, presumably because it will be taxed at personal rates in the trust or taxed as regular income if paid to you by the trust.

You must report as employment income amounts you receive in the year under a salary deferral arrangement to the extent they exceed the aggregate of: (1) deferred amounts included in your income in preceding years, plus (2) deferred amounts deducted by you in the year or preceding years under the forfeiture rules discussed at ¶307.40. This mopping-up provision does not apply to amounts received by you from a trusteed salary deferral arrangement, as the normal rules which tax only amounts paid or payable from a trust will apply to such plans.

[¶307.15] *Exceptions — Temporary Residents*

The salary deferral rules contain an exception for employees temporarily transferred to Canada. The exception is limited to deferred amounts arising under a salary deferral arrangement established primarily for the benefit of non-resident employees for services rendered outside Canada. Deferred amounts relating to services rendered in Canada by an employee who becomes a Canadian resident for up to three years are not subject to the salary deferral arrangement rules, as long as the arrangement applied to the employee before becoming a resident of Canada.

[¶307.20] *Exclusions — Statutory Plans*

A number of plans given special treatment under the *Income Tax Act* are specifically excluded from the salary deferral arrangement rules, as these plans have their own rules. These excluded plans are:

(1) a registered pension fund or plan;

(2) a disability or income maintenance plan under a policy with an insurance company;

(3) a deferred profit sharing plan;

(4) an employee profit sharing plan;

(5) an employee trust;

(6) a group sickness or accident insurance plan;

(7) a supplemental unemployment benefit plan;

(8) a vacation pay trust as defined in the *Income Tax Act*;

(9) a plan or arrangement the sole purpose of which is to provide education or training for employees to improve their work or work-related skills and abilities;

(10) a plan or arrangement established for the purpose of deferring the salary or wages of a professional athlete for his services as such with a team that participates in a league having regularly scheduled games;

(11) a plan or arrangement under which a taxpayer has a right to receive a bonus or similar payment in respect of services rendered by him in a taxation year to be paid within three years following the end of the year; and

(12) a prescribed plan (see ¶307.25).

[¶307.25] *Exclusions — Prescribed Plans*

The following plans, described in the regulations, are not subject to the salary deferral arrangement rules.

Leave of absence/Sabbatical plans. The salary deferral rules do not apply to self-funded leave of absence arrangements — typically found, for example, in school and university settings. Plans are excluded if they provide for deferrals for not more than six years of not more than 1/3 of your salary, to provide for a leave of absence of at least six months (three months where the leave is to permit full-time attendance at an educational institution described in ¶1323 or ¶1335). The leave of absence must start no later than the seventh year following the first deferral. The plan must provide for you to return to work for a period at least as long as the leave, and must pay out the deferred amounts in the seventh year regardless of whether leave is taken. Interest or other returns accruing on deferred amounts are taxable currently as they arise. Finally, the plan must not allow a doubling-up of deferred salary plus normal salary for the year of leave. The CRA has given an opinion (CRA Document No. 9907105) that in determining whether you have returned to work (or presumably the period of a return to work), banked vacation leave, banked overtime, or banked sick leave do not count as a return to work.

Hockey officials. An exclusion is provided for a plan established for deferring the salary of a professional on-ice official with the National Hockey League. If the official is resident in Canada, the trust or custodian of the plan must also be resident in Canada.

Plans based on stock values. The salary deferral rules do not apply to a plan which provides for payments to you on retirement or death based on the value of shares of the employer corporation, or of a related corporation. The payments must be made by the end of the calendar year following the year of death or retirement. The plan cannot guarantee market value.

[¶307.35] *Deferred Amounts Subject to a Contingency*

The courts have generally held that an amount is not considered "earned" if it is subject to a contingency: for example, if it would not be paid to you if you left your employment before the age of 65. Until your right to receive a contingent amount is absolute, it is not income. The salary deferral arrangement rules anticipate the possible abuse of the contingency concept by providing that where a deferred amount is subject to one or more conditions, these conditions are ignored unless there is a "substantial risk" that the conditions will not be satisfied. "Substantial risk" is a term without a precise meaning which will have to be interpreted by the courts based on the facts.

Amounts which escape the salary deferral arrangement rules, presumably because deferral of income is not a main purpose of the arrangement, may be taxed under the Retirement Compensation Arrangement or Employee Benefit Plan provisions. See ¶359.

[¶307.40] *Deductions for Forfeited Amounts*

Recognizing that under the contingency rules described above, deferred amounts may be included in income even though they are subject to a contingency, and that the contingency may come into play so that the amounts are never received, provision is made for a deduction in a year for deferred amounts that have been included in your income as a benefit under a salary deferral arrangement in a preceding year and which are forfeited in the year.

This provision applies where your right to receive the deferred amount under the arrangement is subject to a condition that is not met and your entitlement thereto is extinguished. A deduction is permitted if the forfeited amount was included in your income for a preceding year. In addition, a deduction is allowed if you have no further rights under the arrangement and did not receive all the deferred amounts previously included in income. This may occur, for example, where the deferred amount previously included in income is based on the value of a share and this value subsequently declines, reducing the deferred amounts that are ultimately paid.

(ITA: 6(1)(*a*); (*i*); (11)-(14); 8(1)(*o*); 18(1)(*o.1*); 20(1)(*pp*); 248(1) "salary deferral arrangement"; ITR: 6801 [Prescribed plan or arrangement – salary deferral arrangement])

WHAT IS INCLUDED IN EMPLOYMENT INCOME

[¶308] EMPLOYMENT INCOME

[¶308.01] *General — Line 101*

Your income from an office or employment includes all amounts received in the year as:

- Salary
- Wages
- Commissions
- Director's fees
- Bonuses
- Tips
- Gratuities
- Honoraria
- Certain GST and QST rebates.

In addition, certain amounts earned but not received may be included in income as described at ¶307.

The total of the above items is included in box 14 of your T4 slip and is reported at line 101 of your T1 return. Box 14 will include your commission income as an employed salesperson (¶304.05), which is entered again on line 102. Any employment income which you received but was not reported on a T4 slip is to be reported by you on line 104 of your T1 return — tips are a common example.

Pension and retirement benefits (line 115), including retiring allowances (line 130), Employment Insurance benefits (line 119) and death benefits (line 130) are not income from an office or employment. They are described in Chapter 9.

(ITA: 5(1); 6(1); (3); 56(1); Income Tax Folio: S2-F3-C1 Payments from Employer to Employee)

[¶308.05] *Foreign Pension (401k) Contributions Deducted*

Contributions you have made to a foreign pension plan are not generally deductible; see ¶365a. There may be limited exceptions for Canadian-administered plans; see ¶359.

If you are reporting foreign salary or wages under Canadian rules, and have only the foreign reporting slips, the income they show may have been reduced by contributions (typically withheld by the employer from the foreign income) to a foreign pension plan. The most common example will be U.S. wages reported on a U.S. W-2 slip; these wages may be reduced by contributions to a 401(k), 457 or 403(b) plan, US Medicare, and *Federal Insurance Contributions Act* ("FICA"). These reductions must be added back so they are included in your employment income on line 104.

(5000-G, "General Income Tax and Benefit Guide" (T1 Guide), Line 104)

[¶308.10] *Income Related to Other Years*

If you receive an amount that represents several employment income payments lumped together, some of which you were actually entitled to in other taxation years, you may be able to spread the applicable tax calculation over those years. Income related to other years must exceed $3,000 for the rule to apply and the eligible amount is reduced by any related deductions taken. Eligible amounts should be reported to you on form T1198, and the CRA will average the income over the years to which it applies automatically, if you deal with form T1198.

(ITA: 110.2; 120.31)

[¶308.15] *Amounts Receivable Under a Covenant*

Amounts in respect of a restrictive covenant — for example, where you agree not to compete with your employer after leaving the employment — are normally included in your income in the year of receipt. If the covenant amount is receivable at the end of a taxation year but is not yet received, it is included in income if the covenant was agreed to more than 36 months before the end of the year. The 36-month test effectively allows some deferral of covenant payments agreed to but not received.

However, payments which fall under the Salary Deferral Arrangement Rules at ¶307 are taxed as they are earned, not when they are received. It will be a question of fact whether the payment relates to a covenant or represents a deferral of income earned in the year.

Where you are taxed currently on a covenant payment not yet received, you are not taxed again when you receive it. A deduction is provided in a later year if a covenant amount you have previously taken into income becomes a bad debt, which will be a question of fact.

If a covenant payment bad debt deducted is later recovered, you must include it in income in the year of receipt.

For a more detailed summary of the taxation of covenant payments, see ¶929.

(ITA: 6(3.1); 56(1)(*m*); 56.4; 60(*f*); 248(28); IT-442R [Archived], para. 6)

[¶308.20] *Doctor's Income Under Provincial Remote Areas Program*

The government of Quebec offers "installation bonuses" to physicians to assist them in establishing a practice in a remote area. The CRA has given an opinion (in French) that these payments are taxable. If you are a salaried physician, include these amounts in your employment income. If you are self-employed, include the amounts in your business income under the rules at ¶729 as government assistance, not subject to any specified exceptions.

(Tax Topics: No. 1778, dated April 6, 2006; CRA Document No.: Primes d'Installation Médecins, *February 17, 2006*, CRA Document No. 2005-0153931E5)

[¶309] OTHER PAYMENTS FROM AN EMPLOYER

Fees you receive in respect of, in the course of, or by virtue of an office or employment are included in your employment income. These include director's fees and executor's fees, where they are not received in the course of carrying on a business of acting as an executor, but do not include juror's fees.

Juror's Fees not Employment Income

Juror's fees are not employment, business, or property income. Accordingly, the income from such fees, which the CRA characterizes as fees for services, is reduced by related expenses without regard to the deduction limitations governing employment income. Deductible expenses are reduced by related allowances (e.g., travel expenses are reduced by any travel allowance received). Net income from juror's fees is reported at line 130 of the T1 return.

Employment Income Includes Amounts Related to Becoming or Ceasing to be Employed

Your income from an office or employment includes both amounts received while employed and amounts received under an agreement made either immediately before, during, or immediately after the employment, if paid to you for accepting an office or employment, or as consideration for a covenant controlling your actions before or after termination of the employment. For example, payments to induce you to leave one employer for another are taxable as income from employment. Payments for agreeing not to work for someone else are covenant payments, discussed at ¶308.15.

Relevant Case Law

Director's Fees not Business Income

In *The Queen v. Nisker*, 2008 DTC 6102 (FCA), reversing 2007 DTC 230 (TCC), discussed at ¶719.15, a corporate director was denied a deduction for damages related to actions in bad faith. He had claimed the deduction on the argument that he was in the business of being a director.

(CRA Document No.: CTF Ontario Conference- Trust payment to Minor, *October 30, 2012*, CRA Document No. 2012-0462931C6; Income Tax Folio: S2-F3-C2 Benefits and Allowances Received from Employment)

[¶309.05] *Termination Payments and Damages*

All amounts you receive in respect of termination of your employment are fully taxable, whether or not they are on account of damages.

If the terminated employment commenced before 1996, a portion of such damages may qualify for contribution to a registered retirement savings plan, over and above your normal contribution limit (see ¶2612.05). The contribution must be made within 60 days following the end of the year in which the damages were received. Technically, such damages are included in the definition of retiring allowance (see ¶923), and your former employer should issue a T4A form reporting tax withheld from the damage award. The T4A is to show (in a footnote) the portion of the award not eligible for contribution to an RRSP. You should be able to make the necessary calculation yourself based on the information in ¶2612.05. You must file Schedule 7 with your return if you make this special RRSP contribution.

If you receive employment income or damages for loss of office under the order of a court or other competent tribunal, under an arbitration award, or under a contract terminating a legal proceeding (i.e., an out-of-court settlement), and part or all of the amount relates to other years, you may be eligible for averaging as discussed at ¶308.10.

(ITA: 6(1)(*c*); (3); 8(1); 56(1)(*a*); 110.2; 120.31; IT-365R2 [Archived]; Income Tax Folio: S2-F3-C1 Payments from Employer to Employee)

[¶310] TUITION FEES AND TRAINING EXPENSES

[¶310.01] *Overview*

If your employer pays tuition fees on your behalf, or reimburses you for tuition fees you paid, for a course which is merely of personal interest to you or provides technical skills which are not related to your employer's business, the payment is included in your employment income in the year of receipt.

Payments for courses taken for maintaining or upgrading of employment-related skills, when it is reasonable to assume that you will resume your employment for a reasonable period of time after completion of the courses, are considered primarily to benefit your employer and therefore are not taxable.

Other business-related courses, although not directly related to your employer's business, will generally be considered non-taxable. Examples include courses dealing with stress management, employment equity, first-aid and language skills. Normally, in-house training is not considered to create a taxable benefit.

The CRA will not necessarily follow these rules if you and your employer do not deal at arm's length (¶812), or in specific cases where it appears the courses are for your benefit. Their concern seems to relate to situations in which you accept a lower income and obtain what would otherwise be taxable remuneration in the form of training costs.

Generally speaking, your employer will make the initial determination of taxability in filling out your T4 slip.

If you are required to include tuition fees in your income, you may be entitled to a related tuition or education amount tax credit (see ¶1319; the education and textbook credits are repealed effective January 1, 2017). If your employer pays your tuition fees, directly or by reimbursing you, and the amount is not included in your income, you are not able to claim either tuition credit or education amounts as you have not incurred a net cost (see ¶1337).

A non-taxable allowance from your employer for your child's education in an official language (see ¶344), reduces the amount on which tuition tax credits can be claimed (Chapter 13).

(ITA: 6(1)(*a*); 118.5; 118.6; Income Tax Folio: S1-F2-C3 Scholarships, Research Grants and Other Education Assistance; S2-F3-C2 Benefits and Allowances Received from Employment)

[¶310.05] *Employer-Provided Scholarships for Employees' Family Members*

Scholarships are governed by the rules at ¶953. At one time, the CRA held that an employer's payment of tuition or similar amounts for an employee's children or other dependants resulted in a taxable employment benefit. The courts disagreed and the judicial decisions are now incorporated in the law.

Such payments, made after October 30, 2011, for the benefit of persons other than you as an employee, such as your family members, are not taxable where you and the employer deal at arm's length and the amount is not a substitute for your salary or other remuneration.

Payments made prior to that date were found by the courts similarly not to create a taxable benefit.

Relevant Case Law

Payment of Tuition did not Create a Taxable Benefit

In *The Queen v. DiMaria*, 2009 DTC 5019 (FCA), the court confirmed that an employer's post-secondary tuition program for the children of employees did not constitute a taxable benefit to the employee even though, in the CRA's view, it provided an unlimited number of scholarships and did not impose standards that were any higher than those any post-secondary student was likely to meet. The Court found that as the scholarship was paid to the student, it did not enrich the parent.

(CRA Document No.: Employer-Provided Scholarship Program, *September 1, 2009*, CRA Document No. 2009-0312451E5; Income Tax Folio: S1-F2-C3 Scholarships, Research Grants and Other Education Assistance)

[¶310.10] *Employer-Provided Educational Allowances for Employees' Children*

The CRA takes the view that if you receive an allowance for the education of your child, the allowance is taxable to you. Presumably, this is based on the fact that the Act provides that all allowances are taxable except those specifically itemized, and educational allowances are not listed.

An exception is made if you and your family have to live in a specific location away from home and the schools in the area do not meet the educational needs of the your children. Then, an educational allowance will not be taxable if all of the following conditions are met:

(1) The education provided is in the official language of Canada primarily used by you.

(2) The school is the closest suitable one available in that official language.

(3) Your child is in full-time attendance at the school.

(4) The allowance you receive is reasonable.

Planning Opportunity

If your employer is prepared to contribute to the cost of educating your family members, it is better to have the employer reimburse some or all of the direct cost of tuition rather than to pay you an allowance. The reimbursement is not taxable to you; the allowance is. You will be taxable on the reimbursement, however, if you do not deal at arm's length with the employer or if the education contribution is found to be a substitute for wages you would otherwise earn.

(ITA: 6(1)(*b*)(ix))

[¶311] BOARD AND LODGING

Where your employer furnishes your board and lodging, you are considered to receive a taxable benefit equal to the fair market value of the accommodation less any amount paid by you. The value of the benefit is determined on the same basis as that for subsidized meals, as the cost to your employer, net of any amounts you paid for the board and lodging (see ¶350).

Board and lodging benefits may not be taxable if they relate to a "special work site" (see ¶360). As well, you may be entitled to a special deduction if you live in a remote community (see ¶361a).

(ITA: 6(1)(*a*); Income Tax Folio: S2-F3-C2 Benefits and Allowances Received from Employment)

[¶312] RENT-FREE AND LOW-RENT HOUSING

Where your employer provides you with living accommodation, the difference between what is charged and the fair market rent for equivalent accommodation is a taxable benefit.

As with board and lodging, there are special rules for remote work sites (see ¶360) or if you live in a remote area (see ¶361a).

(ITA: 6(1)(*a*); Income Tax Folio: S2-F3-C2 Benefits and Allowances Received from Employment)

[¶313] ASSETS PURCHASED

[¶313.05] *Assets Purchased from Employer*

If your employer sells assets, e.g., an automobile, furniture, etc., to you at a bargain price, and it is not a standard practice extended to all employees, the difference between the price charged and fair market value is a taxable benefit. This rule applies in principle to computers as well, but in some circumstances your employer may provide you with a computer without creating a taxable benefit (see ¶355c).

(ITA: 6(1)(*a*); Income Tax Folio: S2-F3-C2 Benefits and Allowances Received from Employment)

[¶313.10] *Purchase of Customer Lists by One Salesperson from Another*

See ¶368.05.

(ITA: 6(1)(*a*); Income Tax Folio: S2-F3-C2 Benefits and Allowances Received from Employment)

[¶313.15] *Worker's Tools*

If your employer pays you to offset the cost of tools you purchase and which are required for your work, the payments are employment income.

While you are not generally allowed to claim a deduction for the cost of tools you purchase, deductions are permitted under the following very specific rules:

(1) capital cost allowance on automobiles and aircraft (see ¶370);

(2) capital cost allowance on musical instruments (see ¶379.10);

(3) supplies and power saws (see ¶372);

(4) tools purchased by a tradesperson (see ¶373b); and

(5) tools purchased by an apprentice mechanic (see ¶373c).

[¶314] VACATIONS WITH PAY

Vacation pay is income subject to tax.

(ITA: 5(1))

[¶315] GIFTS FROM EMPLOYER, INCLUDING SUGGESTION AWARDS

All gifts and awards, whether in cash or in kind, and including suggestion awards made to you by your employer, are income in your hands. However, as a matter of policy, the CRA will make certain concessions, as outlined below.

[¶315.07] *Policy for Gifts and Awards*

The CRA has an administrative policy dealing with non-cash gifts and awards. The policy does not apply to cash or near-cash gifts or awards. Gift certificates or other items that can readily be converted to cash or used as cash do not fall under the exemption, and always give rise to a taxable benefit. If a taxable benefit arises, your employer should include this in your income as reported on your T4 form.

Right to Choose a Non-Monetary Gift

The CRA's policy is that if you receive a right to choose your non-monetary gift — from a catalogue or inventory of gifts made available by your employer — the right is effectively cash, and does not fall under the policy dealing with non-monetary gifts.

Where this policy applies, the CRA will accept that no benefit is to be taken into your income. The policy is summarized as follows:

- Non-cash gifts and non-cash awards, regardless of number, are not taxable if the total value is less than $500 annually. The value in excess of $500 annually is taxable.
- A separate non-cash long service/anniversary award may also qualify for non-taxable status if its total value is $500 or less. The value in excess of $500 is taxable. In order to qualify, the anniversary award cannot be for less than five years of service or be awarded less than five years since the last long service award to the employee. The annual gifts and awards threshold and the long service/anniversary awards threshold are separate and a shortfall under one policy cannot be used to offset an excess under the other.
- The employer gift and award policy does not apply if you do not deal at arm's length with your employer (e.g., if you are a relative of a proprietor, or of the shareholders of a closely held corporation) or if you are related to a non-arm's length employee.
- Items of nominal value, such as coffee, tea, T-shirts with employer logos, mugs, plaques, trophies, etc., are not be considered to create a taxable benefit. There is no defined monetary threshold that determines an immaterial amount. Factors that may be taken into account include the value, frequency, and administrative practicability of accounting for nominal benefits.

Example — Taken from Income Tax Technical News, No. 40

Jeffrey's employer has given him the following gifts and awards:

Gifts & Awards	Value
T-shirt with employer logo	$15 (cost)
Birthday gift (monetary gift certificate)	$75
Reward for meeting sales performance target (weekend holiday)	$400
10-year anniversary award (art print). The last anniversary award received was for his 5-year anniversary with the employer	$275
Wedding gift (crystal vase)	$300
Innovation and excellence award (tickets to a sporting event)	$250
Holiday season gift (watch)	$150

Tax consequences:

The T-shirt has no tax consequences as it is of a nominal value.

The gift certificate is not eligible for the gift and award policy as it is a near-cash gift.

The weekend holiday given for meeting the sales performance target is not eligible for the gift and award policy. It is considered to be a form of remuneration.

The 10-year anniversary award is eligible under the long service/anniversary award policy. No taxable benefit arises for this award as Jeffrey has not received an anniversary award for the past five years of service and the total value of the gift was not in excess of $500.

The total value of the remaining gifts and awards (wedding, innovation and excellence and holiday season) amounts to $700. Jeffrey is considered to have received a taxable benefit in the amount of $200 ($700 - $500).

Although the 10-year service/anniversary award was $225 less than the allowable $500 threshold, this shortfall **cannot** be applied to offset the taxable benefit arising as a result of the excess value of the annual gifts and awards over $500.

For the CRA policy regarding Christmas parties, see ¶355b. For other fringe benefits, see ¶346 *et seq.*

(T4130 "Employers' Guide — Taxable Benefits and Allowances")

[¶316] PREMIUMS UNDER PROVINCIAL HOSPITALIZATION OR MEDICAL SERVICES PROGRAMS

Premiums paid by your employer on your behalf under any provincial hospitalization or medical services plan are a taxable benefit if, under the provincial plan, you are required to pay the premium personally. This would include contributions such as the Quebec Health Services Fund contribution (¶1663.10) or the Ontario Health Premium (¶1564.20). Those premiums are borne by individuals, employees or otherwise, so that if your employer contributes to your premium, the contribution is a taxable benefit.

On the other hand, certain health-related levies are imposed directly on employers and you are not taxed on a benefit when you employer makes the payment. In Ontario and Manitoba, for example, a tax referred to as a health care contribution is imposed on employers, so its payment does not constitute a benefit to the payer's employees. In Quebec, medicare is partially funded by a contribution required from employers; since this is the employer's liability, this portion of the premiums is similarly not a taxable benefit.

Premiums paid by your employer under a private health services plan, or a group sickness or accident insurance plan, are not taxable benefits. Also, benefits paid under a hospital or medical insurance plan are not taxable. However, these should not be confused with income-maintenance plans as discussed at ¶328, under which benefits may be taxable.

(ITA: 6(1)(*a*); Income Tax Folio: S2-F3-C2 Benefits and Allowances Received from Employment)

[¶317] PREMIUMS ON GROUP TERM LIFE INSURANCE COVERAGE

If your employer pays all or part of the premiums on a group term life insurance policy, the prescribed portion of the employer's payment relating to your coverage is a taxable benefit to you. The benefit is reported on line 104 of the T4A slip.

Premiums paid by your employer with respect to group life insurance which is not term insurance also give rise to a taxable benefit.

(ITA: 6(1); (4); ITR: 2700 Definitions & Interpretation; 2705 Prescribed Premium and Insurance)

[¶317c] DEMUTUALIZATION BENEFITS

As discussed at ¶420, a mutual life insurance company is permitted to "demutualize", i.e., to replace ownership by policyholders with ownership by shareholders. Shares are received on the conversion without tax, but any other benefits are taxable as dividends to the recipient. Where an employer holds a policy for the benefit of employees, the rules contemplate that the employer can flow the benefits received out to the employees, who will in turn receive them, under the rules in ¶420, as exchanged shares or dividends and not as employment income.

In some cases, demutualization benefits to which you are entitled may be used by an employer to purchase additional coverage under an employee-paid disability insurance plan. This does not represent a contribution to the plan by your employer (see ¶328.15).

(ITA: 139.1(16); (17))

[¶318] PERSONAL OR LIVING EXPENSE ALLOWANCES

With very few and very specific exceptions, all allowances and advances you receive from your employer for personal or living expenses are taxable benefits. For the exceptions, see ¶335 to ¶344.

In certain cases, if you are in receipt of a taxable allowance, you may be able to deduct the actual expenses you incurred.

Allowance vs. Reimbursement

An allowance is an amount you receive without the requirement that you account for how you spent it. A reimbursement is an amount you receive for which you have to account, usually by submitting an expense report and supporting invoices and other documentation. If you are reimbursed for a personal expense — a haircut, say — the reimbursement is taxable. As there is no employment-related purpose to the outlay, you receive a benefit when your employer reimburses you for what would otherwise be a personal outlay.

A reimbursement of an expense you incur for the benefit of your employer is never taxable. Thus, if you purchase photocopy paper for your office, submit the related bill and are reimbursed for the cost, you have received no benefit and you report no income. If, in the alternative, your employer gives you an allowance from which you are to pay for supplies you purchase, with no subsequent accounting, the allowance is taken into your income.

An expense advance for which you must account to your employer is not a taxable allowance.

(ITA: 6(1)(*b*); 8(1))

[¶319] TRAVELLING EXPENSES OF YOUR SPOUSE

If your spouse accompanies you on a business trip and your spouse's travelling expenses are paid or reimbursed to you by your employer, they must be included in your income unless your spouse engaged primarily in business activities on behalf of your employer during the trip. This will always be a question of fact, turning on the nature of the activities undertaken on the trip and whether or not your spouse's attendance was required.

Relevant CRA Documents

Spouse Accompanying Employee on a Business Trip

The cost of a spouse accompanying an employee on a week-long trip was a taxable benefit to the employee, unless "it can be proven that the spouse's attendance was needed for business reasons". (CRA Document No. 2013-0477911E5)

(CRA Document No.: Expenses to host employees and spouses at a resort, *March 1, 2013*, CRA Document No. 2013-0477911E5; Income Tax Folio: S2-F3-C2 Benefits and Allowances Received from Employment)

[¶320] REMUNERATION RECEIVED AS AN EMPLOYEE OF YOUR SPOUSE

Employment income paid to you by your spouse or a partnership in which your spouse is a partner is taxable as received under the regular rules. The salary will be a deductible business expense to the employer to the extent that it is reasonable (see ¶368.25, ¶741, ¶1808).

(ITA: 5(1))

[¶321] PRIZES FROM EMPLOYER — PROMOTED CONTESTS

The fair market value of a prize or a sales or work incentive award from your employer is included in your employment income. This includes amounts received for exceeding sales targets, success in examinations, suggestion awards, and payments for exceptional service. However, as outlined at ¶315.07, the CRA has an administrative policy regarding the non-taxability of the first $500 of annual non-cash gifts and awards and certain long-service awards.

After 2013, if you are a seller of lottery tickets and you win a prize in respect of tickets you have sold, the prize is taxable to you.

Historical Information

Prior to 2014, the CRA's policy was to treat lottery prizes awarded to the vendor of the winning ticket as non-taxable.

(ITA: 6(1)(*a*); CRA Document No.: Lottery Commissions, *April 23, 2014*, CRA Document No. 2014-0522731M4; Income Tax Folio: S3-F9-C1 Lottery Winnings, Miscellaneous Receipts, and Income (and Losses) from Crime)

[¶322] PERSONAL USE OF EMPLOYER'S AUTOMOBILE

Where your employer makes an automobile available to you, you must include in income both a standby charge (¶326) and an operating cost benefit (¶324). The standby charge includes a benefit in your income for the fact that the automobile is available for your use, whether you actually use it or not. The operating cost benefit includes in your income a benefit attributable to the cost of operating the automobile for the distance you drove it personally.

Where these rules apply, the standby charge and operating cost benefit are calculated using fixed formulas.

If your employer provides a vehicle that is not an automobile, you are required to include a taxable benefit in your income if you use it personally, but there are no fixed rules on how that benefit is calculated (see ¶322.05).

What is an Automobile?

An automobile for these purposes is a defined term. It includes any motor vehicle with a seating capacity for the driver and up to eight passengers (a larger capacity vehicle is excluded).

The following are excluded from the definition and are not automobiles:

(1) an ambulance,

(2) a vehicle acquired for use primarily (i.e., more than 50%) as a taxi or as a bus used in the business of transporting passengers (even if limited to eight passengers or fewer),

(3) a hearse used primarily in a business of arranging or managing funerals, and

(4) a clearly marked emergency response vehicle used in connection with or in the course of an individual's office or employment with a fire department, the police, or an emergency medical response or ambulance service.

Pickup Trucks

A van, pickup truck, or similar vehicle is an automobile unless it is both:

(1) designed or adapted to carry not more than the driver and two passengers, and

(2) in the year it is acquired or leased is used primarily for transportation of goods or equipment in the course of gaining or producing income.

A van, pickup truck, or similar vehicle, regardless of its seating capacity, is not an automobile if, in the year it is acquired, it is used 90% or more for the transportation of goods, equipment, or passengers in the course of gaining or producing income.

The CRA has said that a Hummer all-terrain vehicle is considered a "similar vehicle".

There is a further exclusion from the definition of automobile for a pickup truck regardless of capacity (i.e., an extended cab pickup) that is used, in the taxation year in which it is acquired or leased, primarily for the transportation of goods, equipment, or passengers in the course of earning or producing income (for the employer) at one or more locations in Canada that are both:

(1) a special or remote work site (as described in ¶360), and

(2) at least 30 kilometres from the nearest boundary of the nearest urban area with a population of at least 40,000 (as determined in the last Statistics Canada census published before the taxation year for which the determination is being made).

Vehicles acquired, sold, or leased in the course of a business of selling, renting or leasing them, and funeral vehicles other than hearses above, are excluded from the definition of automobile for most purposes but not for purposes of the standby charge/operating benefit rules. That is, the standby rules apply to these vehicles even though they are not considered automobiles for some other purposes.

In most cases, the value of both the operating benefits and the standby charge will be included on your T4 slip.

Example 1

Joe's family farm corporation purchases a pickup truck on November 15, 20XX. Joe keeps a detailed log and in 20XX 75% of the mileage on the vehicle relates directly to use on the farm. Because the truck is used primarily for business purposes in the year of acquisition, it is never an automobile and the standard formulas do not apply in calculating any benefit conferred on an employee who uses it.

Example 2

Elise is the manager of a drilling operation in the Northwest Territories. Her employer provides her with a pickup truck which she uses to drive back and forth from the bunkhouse to the drilling site and, on weekends, to the nearest community which is 100 kilometres away. Because she is working at a remote work site that is more than 30 kilometres from the nearest urban centre, the pickup truck is not an automobile. Elise has a taxable benefit for her personal use, but there are no fixed rules on how to calculate the benefit.

(ITA: 6(1)(*a*); (*e*); (*k*); (*l*); 6(2); 6(2.2); 248(1) "automobile"; IT-63R5 [Archived]; CRA Document No.: Motor Vehicle Benefits, *April 29, 2004*, CRA Document No. 2004-0059511E5)

[¶322.05] *If Not an Automobile*

As discussed at ¶322, a motor vehicle must meet certain definitions to be classified as an automobile subject to the statutory standby charge and operating benefit calculations. Where the motor vehicle is not an automobile, there are no fixed rules on how to calculate the value of a benefit you enjoy where your employer makes the vehicle available for your personal use.

The CRA considered a situation where an employer provided a motor vehicle to an employee and required the employee to take the vehicle home for business reasons, while also prohibiting any other personal use of the vehicle. The CRA noted that where the motor vehicle is not an "automobile", the employment benefit for the personal use of the vehicle "is determined by the reasonable economic benefit derived by the employee from the personal use". The CRA generally accepts the rates prescribed in section 7306 of the Regulations for this purpose. See "2016 Mileage and Deduction Rates" at the beginning of this chapter.

However, the CRA goes on to provide that, in the circumstances described above, the employee might still have to incur the costs of acquiring a vehicle for personal purposes. In this case, the economic benefit received by the employee for the use of the employer's vehicle is only the variable costs of the commute. It would be more reasonable to calculate this benefit based on the operating benefit rate that applies to automobiles (¶324.15), which is lower than the Regulation 7306 rate. The CRA will accept that this lower rate represents a reasonable benefit where all of the following conditions are met:

(1) The terms under which the motor vehicle is provided prohibit any personal use of the motor vehicle other than commuting between home and work and the vehicle has in fact not been used for any other personal use.

(2) The employer has bona fide business reasons for requiring the employee to take the motor vehicle home, such as: there are reasonable security concerns with respect to the employer's tools and equipment being left at the work site or overnight at the employer's premises, or the employee is on-call to respond to emergencies and the motor vehicle is provided to improve response to emergencies. The CRA will generally consider an emergency to be an event directed towards the health and safety of the general population, or significant disruption to the employer's operations.

(3) The motor vehicle is specifically designed, or suited for, the employer's business or trade and is essential in a fundamental way for the performance of the employment duties. The mere transportation of the employee does not meet the condition of "performance of employment duties".

Examples

The CRA provides the following examples in its Payroll Guide:

Example 1: Delivery Van

ABC Restaurant Inc. uses a van that has been specially modified so it can be used more efficiently to transport and deliver food orders. The employer has asked the manager, Leslie, to take the van home at night in case she needs to respond to an emergency at the restaurant, such as an after hour alarm or to fill in on busy nights. Leslie is not allowed to use the van for any other personal use. Since she is the manager, her employment duties do not include delivering food orders, even on a busy night.

ABC Restaurant cannot use the lower rate when calculating Leslie's taxable benefit. These circumstances do not meet all of the conditions of the administrative policy. Although the vehicle has been modified for business needs, Leslie does not need the van to perform her employment duties, so she does not have to bring it home for valid business reasons.

Example 2: Emergency Vehicle

Mary works for a gas utility company and has to be on-call two weekends out of every month. On these weekends, she has to be able to respond to emergencies directly from her home. The van, which the employer provides Mary for these weekends, displays the company's name, has a light on the roof, and has been permanently modified to carry specialized equipment to the scene of the emergencies. The company has a written policy prohibiting any other personal use of these vehicles, other than driving between the work site and home. Mary has not used the vehicle for any other personal driving.

Since this situation meets all of the conditions of the administrative policy, Mary's employer may calculate the personal use of the vehicle using the reduced rate applicable to the operating cost benefit calculation rather than the higher rate which limits the employer's deduction.

Relevant Case Law

No Benefit where Emergency Vehicle Made Available

In *Anderson et al. v. The Queen*, 2002 DTC 1876 (TCC), the taxpayers were assigned pickup trucks or vans by their employer which did not meet the definition of automobile and were specially outfitted for repair duty. The employees were essentially always on call to deal with emergencies, and were required to take the vehicles home with them. The Court found there was little personal use and no benefit to the employees as vehicles were always under the direction of the employer.

[¶323] WHAT IS MEANT BY "MADE AVAILABLE" AND "PERSONAL USE"

A motor vehicle is considered to be available to you whenever your employer gives you custody and control over it, whether you actually use it personally or not.

If you use your employer's motor vehicle to travel between your place of work and your home, you are considered to be using it for personal purposes. However, if your employer requires you to proceed directly from your home to a point of call, other than your normal place of work (e.g., a salesperson visiting customers), you are considered to be on your employer's business from the time you leave your home and you are also considered to be on your employer's business until you return home from your last call.

Where privately-owned motor vehicles are prohibited from entering a restricted area where your employment duties are performed, and the distances to be travelled within the restricted area are such that a motor vehicle is necessary, the use of your employer's motor vehicle in the restricted area is not considered to be for personal use.

Employers and employees are expected to maintain logs of personal and business kilometres driven to support allocations.

(ITA: 6(1); (2); (2.2); IT-63R5 [Archived])

[¶323.05] *Partial-Use Lease*

In *The Queen v. Adams*, 98 DTC 6266 (FCA), employees of a car dealership leased the employer's automobiles from the employer for evenings and weekends at less than full rates. The court confirmed the CRA's assessment of the standby charge as the difference between the statutory charge computed under ¶326 and the amounts paid under the lease.

[¶324] OPERATING COSTS BENEFIT AND STANDBY CHARGES

A standby charge includes in your income the benefit that arises because an automobile is available for your use. In addition to this, a benefit arises for operating costs paid by your employer which relate to your personal use.

[¶324.05] *What is an Operating Cost?*

The CRA view is that virtually all expenses associated with an automobile are operating costs. These would include the cost of gasoline, oil, other lubricants, tires, maintenance, and repairs (net of insurance proceeds).

Parking charges are not operating costs. No benefit arises to the extent parking charges paid or reimbursed by your employer relate to use of the vehicle in the course of employment. However, any parking charges paid or reimbursed on personal account are taxable benefits. If you receive an allowance for automobile expenses, which might include the cost of parking, it would fall under the rules at ¶337. See also ¶352c.

(ITA: 6(1.1))

[¶324.10] *Where No Standby Charge*

The standby charge only applies where your employer provides you with the automobile. If you use your own automobile for employment purposes, there can be no standby charge.

[¶324.15] *How are Operating Costs Paid by Employer Taxed to Employee Subject to Standby Charge?*

The operating cost benefit applies where your employer pays the operating costs related to an automobile that is made available to you — i.e., one for which you are taxed on a standby charge. There are two ways in which the operating cost benefit can be calculated.

The general rule is that the benefit is calculated by applying a prescribed rate to the number of personal kilometres you drive in the year. A lower rate is provided if your principal source of employment income is selling or leasing automobiles. The benefit so computed is reduced by all amounts you pay to the person who pays the operating charges (typically your employer) within 45 days of the end of the calendar year to which the costs relate.

These prescribed per-kilometre amounts are subject to adjustment annually and are set out in "2016 Mileage and Deduction Rates" at the beginning of this chapter, and in the table reproduced at ¶86 which includes historic information.

An alternative calculation is available if you use the automobile primarily (i.e., more than 50%) in the performance of your employment duties. If this test is met, the operating cost benefit may be calculated as simply one-half the standby charge for the year. If you wish to use this alternative method, you must notify your employer in writing by December 31 of the year for which the benefit is to be calculated. As with the general rule, the benefit computed under this rule will be reduced by all amounts you pay to the person who pays the operating charges (typically the employer) within 45 days of the end of the calendar year to which the costs relate.

Examples of the calculation of the standby charge and the availability of the alternative method are provided at ¶326.

[¶324.17] *Where No Operating Benefit Received*

If you use your own vehicle in earning employment income and your employer does not contribute towards the operating costs, or provides an unreasonable allowance towards such costs, you may be allowed to deduct the employment-related costs of operating the vehicle. The requirements you must meet to claim the deduction are discussed in ¶369.

[¶324.25] *Form Available*

The CRA has created a worksheet, RC18, for the calculation of the standby charge and operating cost benefit. The worksheet is updated annually as per-kilometre and other limitations change, so be sure you are using the one, as labelled at the top, as relating to the applicable taxation year. The form can be downloaded from the CRA website.

The CRA website also offers an "Automobile Benefits Online Calculator" as an alternative to form RC18. The calculator calculates the standby charge and operating benefit together.

(ITA: 6(1)(*a*); (*k*); (*l*); 6(1.1); ITR: 7305.1 [Prescribed amount – automobile operating expense benefit]; IT-63R5 [Archived]; T4130, "Employer's Guide — Taxable Benefits and Allowances")

[¶326] WHAT IS A "REASONABLE STANDBY CHARGE"?

The automobile standby charge calculation varies with whether your employer leases or owns the automobile.

The standby charge is 2% per month of the capital cost or 2/3 of the lease cost of the automobile. The calculation is summarized as follows:

A × B/(1,667 × number of months made available)

where

A =

(i) *If the employer owns the car*, 2% per month × number of months made available while owned × the cost of car

OR

(ii) *If the employer leases the car*, 2/3 of lease payments for number of months made available less insurance portion

B = Lesser of:

(i) personal use kilometres (aggregate km driven otherwise than in performance of duties), and

(ii) 1,667 × number of months made available

Strictly speaking, the "number of months made available" is the number of days in the taxation year during which the automobile was made available to you, divided by 30. Where a fraction results, it is rounded to the nearest whole number; where the fraction is exactly one-half, it is rounded down.

The proration in the second part of the formula reduces the standby charge where personal use is less than 1,667 kilometres per 30-day period (20,004 kilometres annually). This proration is only available to you on two conditions:

(1) your use of the automobile, as measured by distance travelled, is primarily (i.e., more than 50%) for business purposes and not for personal use (as discussed at ¶323); and

(2) you are required by your employer to use the automobile in the course of your employment.

It is up to you to establish that you meet the over 50% test, and unless it is clear that you never use your employer's automobile for personal purposes, the best proof will be a detailed kilometre log of your personal and business use to substantiate your claim.

No matter which method is appropriate, the capital cost of an owned automobile and the lease payment on a leased automobile include both GST/HST and provincial sales tax, regardless of whether exemptions from these taxes are available or whether any of the taxes were rebated or otherwise recovered by your employer. As well, lease cost includes any associated costs paid under the lease, such as maintenance contracts, excess mileage charges, and terminal charges less terminal credits. As noted above, insurance costs are excluded from the lease payment used to calculate the standby charge.

Example

(1) Sam Smith had a company automobile made available to him for an entire year. Sam drove the car 5,000 kilometres for personal use and drove 15,000 kilometres for employment purposes. His employer paid all the operating expenses for the year, which came to $2,400. Sam includes in income as an operating cost benefit (¶324) 26¢ per kilometre × 5,000 kilometres, or $1,300. Alternatively, as Sam used the automobile more than 50% in the course of his employment, the operating cost benefit can be calculated as one-half of the standby charge. Sam should choose this option, since under this alternative, the operating benefit would be:

- if owned: $2,372.53 (from (2), below) × 50% = $1,186.27
- if leased: $2,259.55 (from (3), below) × 50% = $1,129.77

Sam is required to notify his employer in writing before the end of the taxation year that he wishes to use the alternative method. His employer is then required to use it (even if it results in a higher benefit) in preparing Sam's T4 slip.

(2) Assuming the automobile made available to Sam was owned by his employer and the cost of the automobile was $39,550 ($35,000 plus 8% provincial sales tax (PST) and 5% GST), Sam includes in his income $2,372.53 as a standby charge. The benefit is prorated because Sam's personal use is less than 20,004 kilometres and more than 50% of his use is employment related.

5,000 / 20,004 × 2% × 12 months × $39,550 = $2,372.53

(3) Assuming the automobile was leased by his employer for $1,130 per month ($1,000 plus 8% provincial sales tax (PST) and 5% GST), Sam includes in his income as a standby charge:

5,000 / 20,004 × 2/3 × 12 months × $1,130 = $2,259.55

[¶326.05] *Standby Benefits from Car Pools*

Administratively, the CRA provides special rules for computing the standby charge if an automobile is made available to you on a pooling or similar basis. These rules allow an averaging of the cost of the automobiles in the pool where they are used interchangeably and not by a specific employee for an extended period. In theory, at least, the employer and employees must agree on this alternate treatment.

For a complete explanation of the pooling rules, consult Interpretation Bulletin IT-63R5 (paragraphs 19–21). This Bulletin is archived and its description of the treatment of operating costs no longer reflects the law, which bases the operating cost benefit solely on personal kilometres driven. It is understood that its description of the calculation of the standby charge still reflects the CRA's policy.

[¶326.10] *Special Rules for Automobile Salespersons*

If you are employed primarily in leasing or selling new or used automobiles, your standby charge is calculated as 1.5% of the average cost of the automobile inventory acquired by the employer in the year for each 30-day period automobiles are made available for your use. No exception to using the average cost of the entire fleet acquired in the year is permitted, even where expensive automobiles are not made available to employees. (CRA Document No. 2006-0177111E5)

If you are such an employee, your prescribed operating cost benefit, based on personal kilometres driven, is 3¢ per kilometre less than the general rate (see "2016 Mileage and Deduction Rates" at the beginning of this chapter and historical information in the table at ¶86).

If you are an automobile salesperson and lease a vehicle from your employer at a rate not available to the general public, you may be subject to standby charge (see ¶323).

(ITA: 6(2.1); ITR: 7305.1 [Prescribed amount – automobile operating expense benefit]; CRA Document No.: Auto Standby Benefit Calculation, *July 17, 2006*, CRA Document No. 2006-0177111E5)

[¶326.15] *Cost of Automobile or Lease Charge*

The cost of an automobile on which the standby charge is calculated is the actual cost to your employer and not the limited amount on which capital cost allowance can be claimed (described at ¶810a). Cost includes provincial sales tax as well as GST/HST, even if such taxes were not payable or were recovered, in whole or in part, as a rebate or input tax credit. The cost of the automobile does not, however, include the cost of equipment (such as radio equipment) required for business operating purposes.

Where the automobile is leased, the lease payment includes all amounts that may reasonably be regarded as having been payable by your employer to the lessor for the purpose of leasing the automobile for the relevant period. Leasing payments will therefore include (i) kilometre charges, (ii) charges for repairs and maintenance, (iii) provincial sales tax and GST/HST, whether or not payable or recovered, and (iv) terminal charges less terminal credits (amounts credited at the end of a lease term). Lease payments are not limited to amounts deductible by the employer, which may be restricted (see ¶738). Insurance is considered by the CRA to give rise to an operating cost benefit and is not included in the lease payment.

[¶326.20] *GST/HST Included in Benefit*

Whether the automobile is owned by the employer or leased, the standby charge is calculated on an amount that includes both provincial sales tax and GST/HST, so that the standby charge includes the employer's sales tax cost. These taxes are included whether or not the employer paid them and whether or not any portion of the tax was recovered by the employer. The result is that the standby charge is the same regardless of the employer's status under sales tax legislation.

(ITA: 6(7))

[¶326.25] *Employer/Employee Responsibilities*

The standby charge and operating cost benefit are calculated by your employer for inclusion in your T4 slip. The best official source of information on the calculation is found in T4130, "Employer's Guide — Taxable Benefits and Allowances". Since your standby charge will be less if your annual personal use is less than 20,004 kilometres and your business use is more than 50%, you should ensure that you can document these conditions for your employer if they apply.

If you think your employer has over-calculated your standby charge and the employer will not correct it, you can report what you believe to be the correct amount rather than your T4 amount. However, you will almost certainly be reassessed by the CRA for the T4 amount and have to make your case directly to the CRA (see ¶221 and ¶266).

The best source for determining the appropriate income inclusions is a well-maintained logbook of personal and business use of a vehicle. Ultimately it is the employee who must maintain this. However, the CRA has opined that an employer is obligated to ensure that an employee maintains a logbook in respect of the personal use of an employer-provided motor vehicle in order for the employer to comply with its reporting requirements. Presumably, if faced with a recalcitrant employee, the employer's recourse is to treat all the employee's use of a vehicle as personal use.

In 2011 the CRA published an administrative policy which may make it easier to maintain a log book.

(CRA Document No.: Mv Benefits-Employer's Record Keeping Require., *March 14, 2005,* CRA Document No. 2005-0119451E5; Other Publications: Documenting the Use of a Vehicle http://www.cra-arc.gc.ca/whtsnw/lgbkeng.html)

[¶327] PERSONAL USE OF AIRCRAFT

There are no specific rules in the *Income Tax Act* which govern the valuation of a benefit you enjoy from the use of an aircraft owned by your employer. The general rule will apply: the value of a benefit is the fair market value of the use of the aircraft. This could be represented by the cost of an equivalent commercial airfare.

Relevant CRA Documents

Valuation of Benefit from Use of Aircraft

At one time, the CRA had developed an extensive policy on the valuation of the benefit from the use of an aircraft, but the related interpretation bulletin has been withdrawn. The benefit should be based on what would be paid to an independent provider of similar air transportation services, and not on the cost of the aircraft to the employer. (CRA Document No. 2014-0528841I7)

(CRA Document No.: , CRA Document No. 2014-0528841I7)

[¶328] SICKNESS, ACCIDENT, OR DISABILITY PAYMENTS

Contributions by your employer to a group sickness or accident insurance plan which provides only for periodic payments to you do not constitute a benefit and therefore are not included in your income. However, where the employer contribution is made after 2013, the contribution is a taxable benefit to the extent the related coverage can be paid to you in a lump sum.

Periodic payments you receive in respect of a loss of your employment income under a sickness, accident, disability or income maintenance insurance plan are included in your income if your employer contributed to the plan. This is true whether the plan is formal or informal, and whether the amount you receive is paid to you by your employer, a former employer, or an insurer.

The amount included in your income is the total of periodic payments received less the total of the contributions you made to the plan since the last year you included in income amounts received under the plan. That is, if you and your employer both contribute to the plan, your contributions are returned to you first tax-free, and all remaining receipts are taxable.

Such benefits are not included in your income if your employer made no contributions to the plan, nor are lump-sum payments taxable whether your employer contributed to the plan or not.

There is therefore a trade-off in arranging for coverage under such plans. If your employer funds any part of the premium for periodic benefit coverage, you are not taxed on the employer's contribution but you are taxed on periodic benefits under the plan (other than a return of you own premiums).

If your employer funds any part of the premium for lump sum coverage, the contribution is a taxable benefit to you but the lump sums received under the plan are not taxable.

If your employer does not fund any portion of the premium, the entire premium is borne by you as the employee but none of the benefits received under the plan are taxable, whether paid periodically or in a lump sum. Any premium you pay to such a plan is not deductible.

[¶328.10] *Top-Up Payments Where Insurer Insolvent*

A top-up payment is one the employer or former employer makes either to an insurer to maintain payments which would otherwise be discontinued or reduced due to an insurer's insolvency, or makes directly to you to replace all or part of disability insurance payments no longer being made on account of the insolvency. If the payment is made to you, there must be an undertaking requiring you to reimburse the employer to the extent that periodic payments covered by the top-up payments are later reimbursed by an insurer.

Payments made under these provisions are subject to taxation in your hands in exactly the same manner as if they had been paid under the original plan by the insurer, as described at ¶328.

[¶328.15] *Top-Up Payments on Demutualization*

As discussed at ¶420, mutual life insurance companies are allowed to "demutualize", i.e., replace ownership by policyholders with ownership by shareholders. Shares issued on the conversion are received tax free, but any other benefits are treated as taxable dividends to the recipient.

Where the policyholder is an employer holding a group employee-paid policy on behalf of employees, which typically provides disability or other benefits which are tax free to the employee as long as the employer has not contributed to the premiums, the demutualization rules contemplate that the employer can apply demutualization benefits towards benefit enhancements without tainting the policy, so that periodic benefits remain tax free.

[¶328.25] *Disability Plans and Workers' Compensation*

The treatment of disability payments may be complicated where the disability is subject to workers' compensation awards. For payments to which workers' compensation awards may apply, whether or not they have been paid in the year, see ¶358.

[¶328.30] *Continuing Salary during Disability and Repayments to Employer*

Salary and wages paid to you by your employer, during periods when you were away from work because of illness or an accident, are included in your employment income as received. Where you receive disability payments from your employer, and you are required to repay your employer for wages previously paid, whether from insurance proceeds, from damages received from third parties, or otherwise, the repayments are deductible in the year you pay them, up to the amount received by you during the period of disability and which you included in your employment income.

Your employer may advance money to you to tide you over until insurance or damages proceeds are available. If it is established that such payments are a loan and are not deducted by the employer, they will not be taxable to you, although there may be an imputed interest benefit (see ¶353).

[¶328.35] *Averaging of Taxable Payments*

If you receive an amount that represents several periodic payments under a taxable wage loss replacement plan lumped together, some of which would ordinarily have been received in other taxation years, you may be eligible for a form of income averaging which spreads the applicable tax calculation over those years (see ¶308.10).

(ITA: 6(1)(*a*); (*e*.1); (*f*); 6(17); 6(18); 8(1)(*n*); (*n*.1); 110.2; 120.31; 139.1(15); ITAR: 19; IT-428 [Archived])

[¶328a] EMPLOYEE LIFE AND HEALTH TRUSTS

An employee life and health trust ("ELHT") is a trust to which an employer contributes to fund "designated employee benefits" for its employees, their spouses or common-law partners, and related members of their households. "Designated employee benefits" are benefits from a group sickness or accident insurance plan, a group term life insurance policy, or a private health services plan.

You are not taxed on a benefit from your employer's contributions to an ELHT. Generally, designated employee benefits from the trust are subject to tax as if you had received them directly without the trust. Thus, private health services benefits received through a private health services plan in the trust (e.g., health or dental services) are generally tax-free. Payments from a group sickness or accident insurance plan held by the trust are subject to taxation as described at ¶328. If employer contributions to the ELHT are used to purchase group term life insurance, the prescribed value of the group term life insurance coverage is a taxable employment benefit during each year of coverage under the plan; see ¶317. Payments you receive from an ELHT that are not covered by a specific exclusion are taxable.

You can make an employee contribution to an ELHT, and the trust can identify the designated employee benefits to which your contributions relate, so that they keep their character in determining the taxation of benefits you receive.

(ITA: 144.1)

[¶329] ADVANCES FROM EMPLOYER

If you receive an advance from your employer on account of future salary or wages or employment commissions, you include the advance in your income when it is received.

Where you have included an advance in income and subsequently repay part or all of it, the amount repaid ordinarily is deductible from your income in the year of repayment. If the amount repaid exceeds your income from employment for the year of repayment, you may deduct this excess from the preceding year's income.

An advance on account of future earnings, on the other hand, is generally a payment for salary, wages or commissions that you are expected to earn through your future services. Normally, you are not required to repay a payroll advance other than by an offset against future earnings.

Advance or Loan?

These rules do not apply if you receive a loan rather than an advance, although you may be subject to an imputed interest benefit on a loan (see ¶353).

Whether an amount you receive is a loan or an advance is a question of fact. The usual characteristics of a *bona fide* loan include:

(1) a signed note or acknowledgement of the debt;

(2) an agreement that interest will be paid;

(3) an arrangement for repayment within a reasonable time;

(4) the receipt of one substantial amount rather than smaller amounts received more or less regularly throughout the year; and

(5) the employer's intention to collect the entire loan, and reasonable efforts to do so.

Expense Advances

While these rules apply to advances against earnings, they do not apply to advances against expenses. Where your employer advances you $1,000 against business expenses on an impending trip, for example, and you must account for your expenses and refund any excess (or be reimbursed any additional charges), the advance is not income.

(ITA: 5(1))

[¶330] STOCK OPTION BENEFITS

[¶330.05] *Taxable Event*

There are special rules where a "qualifying person" (a corporation or Canadian mutual fund) agrees to sell or issue shares of its stock or units of its mutual funds to an employee or to an employee of a non-arm's length qualifying person. Such an agreement is referred to as a "stock option".

You are generally not taxed on a stock option benefit at the time the option is granted. Rather, any benefit you enjoy under the option, as a result of being able to buy the optioned securities at a price lower than their market price, is taken into your income at the time you exercise the option.

There is a key exception. The benefit relating to a stock option on shares of Canadian-controlled private corporations ("CCPCs") is generally not taken into income until you actually sell the optioned shares. See ¶330.65.

Historical Information

An election to defer the recognition of a stock option benefit relating to publicly traded shares was available where the option was exercised prior to 4 p.m. EST on March 4, 2010. Where the election could be made, the stock option benefit was taxed when the optioned securities were sold, not when they were acquired. See ¶330.35.

[¶330.10] *General Rule*

The general rule is that you are deemed to have received a benefit at the time you acquire shares under a stock option agreement. The benefit is the amount, if any, by which the fair value of the securities exceeds the total of the option price and any amount you paid to acquire the option. The adjusted cost base of the shares is the sum of the benefit, the amount you paid on exercising the option and the amount, if any, you paid to acquire the option.

Example

Sally's employer is a public corporation. In 20X1 Sally is granted an option to purchase 1,000 shares of her employer at $10 a share. At the time the option is granted, the shares are trading at $8. In 20X5, the shares are trading at $15 and Sally exercises the option. She has a stock option benefit of $5,000, as she paid only $10,000 to buy shares worth $15,000, and this is included in her employment income. The adjusted cost base of the shares to Sally is the sum of what she paid ($10,000) and the stock option benefit ($5,000), for a total of $15,000. The value of the shares at the date the option was granted in year 1 does not enter into the determination of Sally's stock option benefit or the adjusted cost base of the shares, but it will be important in determining her taxable income. This is discussed at ¶330.25.

If you transfer an option to someone with whom you do not deal at arm's length, and the transferee exercises the option, the stock option benefit is included in your income. If a transferor employee is deceased when the option is exercised, the transferee takes the stock option benefit into income.

If you dispose of an option to an arm's length person, you recognize employment income equal to the excess of the proceeds of disposition over the amount, if any, you paid to acquire the option. Non-arm's length dispositions are discussed at ¶330.85.

[¶330.15] *Units of Mutual Fund Trusts*

If you are an employee of a Canadian mutual fund trust, options to acquire units of the mutual fund receive the same treatment as options on shares of a public corporation.

[¶330.20] *If Employee Option Rules Do Not Apply*

If the general rule does not apply (because the issuer was not a corporation or mutual fund), the tax consequences of an option granted to an employee are not specified in the *Income Tax Act*.

In principle, the fair market value of an option granted to you (less any amount you paid for it) is a taxable benefit when the option is granted, albeit a difficult one to value. An option that is acquired is treated as capital property for tax purposes.

The sum of this benefit and any amount you paid to acquire the option should become the adjusted cost base of the option, and the rules at ¶561 should roll over that cost base into the cost base of the securities or other property you acquire if the option is exercised.

Relevant CRA Documents

Options Granted by a Partner

Where an employee of a partnership was granted stock options by a partner, the CRA opined that, although the transaction was not covered by the employee stock option rules, there would nevertheless be a taxable employment benefit on the exercise of the option equal to the value of the share acquired on the date of acquisition less the amount paid therefor by the employee. This amount would be added to the cost base of the share. (CRA Document No. 9324345)

(CRA Document No.: Stock Option Plan of Partnership, *October 29, 1993*, CRA Document No. 9324345)

[¶330.25] *One-Half Deduction Under the General Rule — Line 249*

Where the general rule applies and you have an income inclusion on the exercise or disposition of an option, you are allowed a deduction in computing taxable income equal to one half of the option benefit. The deduction is intended to reduce the net benefit subject to tax to what it would have been if you had had a capital gain.

A stock option or mutual fund unit will qualify for this offsetting deduction from taxable income if all the following conditions are met:

(1) **Issuer.** The seller or issuer of the shares or units is the employer corporation or a corporation not at arm's length from the employer (see ¶330.05).

(2) **Share/Unit Attributes.** The shares acquired qualify (under Regulation 6204) at the time of their acquisition. The qualification rules are extensive, but generally speaking they define the characteristics of common shares, with no minimum or maximum dividend rates or liquidation values, although the shares need not have voting rights. The rules also provide that neither the corporation issuing or selling the shares nor a related person can reasonably be expected to redeem, acquire, or cancel the shares in whole or in part or reduce their paid-up capital within two years of the exercise of the option. The issuer of shares need not be a Canadian corporation. In the case of mutual fund units, there are no prescribed rules as such but the units must be of a widely held class of units which conforms to the regulations which permit the issuer to meet the definition of "mutual fund trust".

(3) **Option Exercise Price.** The option's exercise price must be at least equal to the excess of the fair market value of the shares or units at the time the option was granted over any amount you paid to acquire the option. The option price must be determined without reference to any foreign exchange (currency) fluctuations which occur after the option is given. However, the fair market value option price requirement can be waived where the stock price has fallen; see ¶330.30.

(4) **Arm's Length.** Immediately after the option was granted, you dealt at arm's length with: the particular qualifying person granting the option; each other qualifying person that, at the time, was your employer and was not dealing at arm's length with the grantor; and the qualifying person whose security you acquired under the option.

Commentary on Legislative Proposals (Sept. 16, 2016)

Note: When Legislative Proposals, September 16, 2016, achieves Royal Assent, the commentary will be modified to read:

(5) **Taxpayer Death.** If a taxpayer dies owning an unexercised employee stock option, and the option is exercised and the shares are acquired within the first taxation year of the deceased's graduated rate estate by the graduated rate estate, a beneficiary of the graduated

rate estate, or a person in whom the option has vested as a result of the death. For taxation years ending before 2016, "graduated rate estate" is to be read as "estate".

As discussed at ¶330.65, where the option relates to shares in a Canadian-controlled private corporation, an alternative deduction of one-half the stock option benefit is allowed if the shares are held for at least two years.

Options received in exchange for qualifying options in consequence of certain corporate restructurings will themselves qualify, as long as no current economic gain has been derived from the exchange.

The stock option deduction does not affect the calculation of the adjusted cost base of the shares or units acquired.

Example (see ¶330.10)

When Sally exercised her option, she included $5,000 in her employment income as a stock option benefit. As the option price of $10 was greater than the fair value of the optioned shares when the option was granted, $8, she can claim the stock option deduction in computing her taxable income (on the assumption that the shares meet the tests outlined above, and that she deals at arm's length with her employer). Thus, her taxable income is increased by $2,500 overall — a $5,000 employment income inclusion and a $2,500 deduction in computing taxable income. The adjusted cost base of $15,000 is not affected by the stock option deduction.

Cashing Out a Stock Option

A stock option is "cashed out" when you surrender the option in return for a cash payment. The stock option deduction is not allowed on a cash out unless you actually acquire the optioned securities.

An exception is made, and the stock option deduction can be claimed even where the securities are not acquired, if the qualifying person elects that neither it nor any non-arm's length person will deduct any amount for a payment made to you on cashing out the option. The employer must provide you with written evidence that the election has been made and you must file the evidence with your return.

Example (see ¶330.10)

Sally's option agreement provides that rather than buying shares of her employer, the employer will cash out the option for 90% of the fair value of the stock. This feature is provided so that Sally does not have to open a brokerage account and pay commissions on selling the shares. Sally triggers this cash out when the employer shares are trading at $14, and she receives $2,600 (90% of the fair value of the shares, less the $10,000 she would have paid to exercise the option). The full amount is included in her employment income and she is not entitled to the stock option deduction. Alternatively, her employer can elect not to deduct any of the amount it paid her and, on providing her with proof of the election which she files with her tax return, she can claim a $1,300 stock option deduction.

[¶330.30] *Offsetting Deduction Where Shares Have Lost Value*

Condition (3) in ¶330.25 requires that the option price cannot be less than the fair market value of the shares at the time the option was granted less the amount, if any, you paid to acquire the option. An exception of sorts permits the issuer to exchange options or, where the option agreement permits it, to re-price the existing options as long as there is no economic benefit in doing so, i.e., so long as the newly acquired/re-priced options do not exceed the value of the options given up. Where the share price has fallen after the option was issued and before it was exercised, this exception permits your employer to substitute options at a lower price. If the price subsequently rises and the new options are exercised, condition (3) does not bar the offsetting deduction because of the exception for exchanges.

Example (see ¶330.10)

Sally's employer has not fared well, and the stock price has dropped to $3. Sally's option agreement does not provide for re-pricing the options, so the employer offers to allow her to exchange her existing option, which permits her to buy shares at $10 a share, for one that permits her to buy the shares at $5 a share. Sally receives no economic benefit — both options have no value — so she will still be eligible for the stock option deduction when she exercises the new option.

[¶330.35] *Options on Publicly Listed Shares and Mutual Fund Trusts Exercised before 4 p.m. EST March 4, 2010*

An election was available to defer the recognition of some or all of a stock option benefit where a public company option was exercised after February 27, 2000 and before 4 p.m. EST on March 4, 2010. Although this election is no longer available, if it was made it could affect the taxation of the related income to the end of 2014, as discussed at ¶330.36.

There was a $100,000 annual limit on the options eligible for deferral of the benefit; for options above that limit, the general rules applied.

Where the election was made, the related stock option benefit and stock option deduction were accounted for in the year the optioned securities were sold.

[¶330.36] *Elimination of Deferral for Publicly Listed Shares and Mutual Fund Units*

As discussed at ¶330.35, the election to defer the taxation of a stock option benefit on public company shares was eliminated for options exercised after 4 p.m. EST on March 4, 2010.

If you had elected that the deferral apply before that time, and you disposed of the securities before 2015, an election was available that had the effect of eliminating the stock option benefit entirely and replacing it with a capital gain equal to the lesser of the stock option benefit deduction you could claim and the capital loss otherwise incurred on the disposition of the securities. The resulting allowable capital loss can be used to offset the resulting taxable capital gain.

However, you were still liable to pay a federal tax for the year of the disposition equal to your proceeds of disposition (2/3 of the amount for Quebec residents).

This election was designed to provide relief where the stock option benefit deferred under the original election had been eroded by a decline in the value of the optioned security from the time of the deferral until the security was sold.

Example (see ¶330.10)

Assume that Sally exercised her options before 2010 and elected to defer the stock option benefit of $5,000. In 2014, she still owned the stock but the price had declined to $1 a share. If she sells the shares in 2014, she recognizes employment income equal to the deferred stock option benefit of $5,000 and can claim the stock option deduction of $2,500. She has a capital loss of $14,000 on the sale, half of which is allowable but can only be claimed against taxable capital gains.

In the alternative, she can elect not to recognize the stock option benefit or the stock option deduction. As a result, she is deemed to have a capital gain equal to the lesser of 1) the stock option benefit deduction of $2,500 and 2) the capital loss otherwise realized on the disposition ($1,000 - $15,000) = $14,000. She also has an actual capital loss of $14,000. Sally will therefore report a net capital loss of $11,500 ($5,750 of which is allowable) but she must pay tax equal to the entire proceeds of disposition ($1,000) as the price of electing.

[¶330.50] Offsetting Deduction Where Shares Donated—Line 249

Where you exercise an option to acquire shares listed on a Canadian or foreign stock exchange or to acquire mutual fund units, and donate the securities to a qualified donee within 30 days of acquisition and within the same taxation year, the taxable benefit is reduced to nil. The reduction is accomplished by providing an additional deduction from taxable income on top of the regular stock option deduction, all reported at line 249.

A qualified donee is a registered charity (other than a private foundation) or other donee as described in ¶1265, gifts to which normally entitle you to a charitable donation tax credit.

If the security declines in value during the 30-day period between acquisition and gift, your supplementary deduction is based on the lesser value. If the value increases, the increase is a capital gain to which the rules at ¶1290d on the donation of qualified securities will apply.

The rules contemplate that when you exercise options you can request your employer to dispose of the shares or units and donate all or a portion of the proceeds to a qualified charity. The consequences are the same as if you had exercised the option and donated either the shares or that *pro rata* portion of the shares which represents the donated proceeds. This gives the charity cash instead of shares but preserves the extra deduction. It also eliminates the problem of gain or loss in the interim between exercise and donation.

These provisions are intended to offer treatment comparable to the capital gain treatment on share donations discussed at ¶1290d.

(ITA: 110(1)(d.01))

[¶330.56] Withholding Requirements for Stock Option Benefits

Stock option benefits are subject to withholding at source under the general rules in section 153. The CRA has historically waived this requirement in certain cases where there were insufficient funds from which the employer could withhold.

However, the Act specifically provides that employee stock option benefits are subject to regular withholding as if the benefit were a cash bonus payment. The CRA cannot reduce the withholding at source upon the taxpayer's request (under the "undue hardship" provision in subsection 153(1.1)) solely because the withholding arises from a non-cash benefit. The amount subject to withholding is reduced by one half if the stock option deduction is available (see ¶330.25). The withholding does not apply to a benefit in respect of the acquisition of a security of a Canadian-controlled private corporation where the benefit is deferred (¶330.65).

Historical Information

The formal requirement to withhold tax on a stock option benefit does not apply to options granted before 2011, if the stock option agreement was entered into before 4:00 p.m. EST on March 4, 2010 and contained a written condition that restricts the employee from disposing of the securities for a period of time after exercise,

[¶330.65] Canadian-Controlled Private Corporation Shares Acquired on Exercise of Option—Line 249

If you are granted an employee stock option by a Canadian-controlled private corporation (CCPC), you are not required to recognize a taxable benefit at the time you exercise the option; the benefit is recognized when you sell the shares. To qualify, the option must be for shares of a CCPC that is your employer or of a CCPC related to your employer, and, at the time immediately after the option is granted, you must deal at arm's length with the corporation whose shares are to be acquired.

You account for the proceeds of an eventual disposition of the shares in the following fashion:

(1) You recognize as employment income the difference between the fair value of the shares at the time you acquire them and the total of what you paid to acquire the shares and the amount, if any, that you paid to acquire the option. This difference is added to the adjusted cost base of the shares.

(2) You may claim a deduction of 50% of the employment income inclusion (claimed on line 249 of your return) provided that (a) the share was not disposed of or exchanged, other than as a consequence of death, within two years after its acquisition, and (b) no claim has been made for a deduction that is generally available for stock option benefits. This deduction does not reduce the adjusted cost base of the share.

(3) The difference, if any, between the adjusted cost base for the shares and your proceeds of disposition is a capital gain or loss. If you realize a capital gain, it may be eligible for the lifetime capital gains exemption for qualifying small business corporation shares (see ¶502i).

Identical shares are deemed to be disposed of in the order of acquisition.

Shares of a CCPC do not have to meet the qualifying share rules described in (2) or (3) at ¶330.25 to be eligible for this treatment. That is, among other things, the shares do not have to have the attributes of common shares. On the other hand, the arm's length rules in (1) and (4) are applicable.

If a deduction is not available under these rules, typically because the two-year qualifying period is not met, you can then look to the qualifying share rules to see if that deduction will apply. Thus, where you exercise a CCPC option in Year 1, say, and dispose of the shares in Year 2, so that the two-year holding period is not met, the income inclusion is nevertheless in Year 2, and if the shares are also qualifying shares an offsetting deduction may be claimed in Year 2 under the general rules applicable to options for public company shares.

[¶330.70] *Option Date Determines CCPC Tax Treatment*

If a corporation is a CCPC at the time it grants the options, the CCPC rules apply even if it has ceased to be a CCPC prior to the exercise of the options.

[¶330.75] *Cost Base Issues: Ordering of Share (Unit) Dispositions*

The general rule is that where identical properties are acquired at various times, the adjusted cost base is determined by averaging their costs. However, where a stock option is exercised and the related employment benefit is deferred under the CCPC rules, the identical share rule does not apply. Thus, each security acquired on a particular exercise of a stock option has a particular identifiable adjusted cost base. Generally, you are deemed to dispose of tax deferred stock option securities only after having disposed of non-deferred securities, and then to dispose of tax deferred securities in the order in which you acquired them.

Where you exercise options and dispose of the shares acquired within 30 days, you can designate those shares as the ones disposed of, thereby avoiding a presumption that older shares were disposed of first. This designation is not limited to shares acquired under an option where the employment benefit was deferred under the CCPC rules. There are several conditions to making this designation, as follows:

(1) the particular security must have been acquired under an employee stock option agreement;

(2) the disposition must occur no later than 30 days after you acquire the particular security;

(3) there must be no other acquisitions or dispositions of identical securities in the intervening period. This does not preclude you from acquiring other identical securities at the same time as the optioned security is acquired, or from disposing of other identical securities at the same time as the disposition in respect of which the designation is being made;

(4) you must make the designation in your return for the year in which the disposition occurs; and

(5) you must not have designated the optioned security in connection with the disposition of any other security.

Example

On May 1, 20X0, Joseph acquires 750 shares of his corporate employer on the open market. On May 1, 20X1, he acquires another 750 shares on the open market. On May 1, 20X2, he acquires an additional 1,000 shares under a stock option. Within 30 days of exercising the option, he sells 1,500 shares. In his return of income for 20X2, he designates the 1,000 stock option shares as constituting part of the shares that were sold. The 1,500 shares sold are deemed to comprise the 1,000 stock option shares and 500 of the 1,500 shares that Joseph acquired on the open market in 20X0 and 20X1.

[¶330.80] *Where Rights Cease To Be Exercisable*

Specific rules deal with your rights under an option agreement ceasing to be exercisable, where the cessation is not otherwise considered to be a disposition of those rights.

If you receive an amount in respect of such a cessation, you are deemed, for the purposes of the employment benefit and offsetting deduction rules only, to have disposed of the rights for proceeds equal to that amount. Accordingly, you have an employment income benefit equal to the amount so received less the amount, if any, you paid to acquire the rights. If the conditions for the offsetting deduction are satisfied, you can deduct half the benefit in computing taxable income.

Generally, the amount you deduct against the employment income benefit will be the actual amount you paid, if any, to acquire the rights in question. However, if you receive payments relating to the cessation on more than one occasion, the amount you are deemed to have paid to acquire the rights will, for each disposition after the initial deemed disposition, be reduced by the total of all the amounts previously received in respect of the cessation. This ensures you do not get credit for more than the actual amount paid.

[¶330.85] *Stock Options Transferred Not at Arm's Length*

If you transfer your employee stock options in a non-arm's length transaction, e.g., to a spouse or relative or to a company you own, you will nevertheless be taxed when the options are exercised (see ¶330.10). If the options are exercised after your death, the transferee will be taxed when the options are exercised (see ¶1925).

[¶330.90] *Exchange of Stock Options or Shares*

As described at ¶330.30, a stock option can be re-priced or exchanged for another so long as you are not made better off as a result. These provisions also apply where options are exchanged in the course of a reorganization. They deem a disposition not to have occurred and deem the new option to be the same as, and a continuation of, the original option.

[¶330.100] *Redemption of Shares (as Opposed to Sale)*

Where a company redeems or purchases and cancels its own shares, the shareholder is normally deemed to receive both a dividend equal to the amount received in excess of the paid-up capital of the shares, and proceeds of disposition equal to the amount received less the portion thereof deemed to be a dividend. It is the CRA's view that if a corporation redeems shares you acquired under an option on which the gain has been deferred using the CCPC rules, the amount received is accounted for as follows:

(1) the stock option benefit is the amount received less the amount you paid to acquire the option. The stock option deduction is available under the normal rules;

(2) you are deemed to receive a dividend equal to the excess of the amount received over the paid-up capital of the shares; and

(3) you are deemed to receive proceeds of disposition equal to the amount received in excess of the portion deemed to be a dividend. As the adjusted cost base of the shares will include the stock option benefit amount, this will normally result in a capital loss.

(CRA Document No.: Employee Stock Option Deemend Dividend, *March 26, 2003,* CRA Document No. 2002-0179145)

[¶330.105] *Stock Options and Non-Residents*

There are no tax consequences relating to stock options you hold at the time you cease to be a resident of Canada, but you will be taxed on an employment benefit when you exercise the option (see ¶2021).

On the other hand, at the time you cease to be a Canadian resident, you are deemed to dispose of CCPC shares acquired under a stock option on which recognition of the employment income gain has been deferred (see ¶2153).

The rules apply slightly differently depending on whether the shares were acquired after February 27, 2000 or before February 28, 2000. In the former case, the adjusted cost base of the shares is increased by the amount that would have been added as the stock option benefit had the shares actually been disposed of. If the shares were acquired before February 28, 2000, the same result is achieved by reducing the proceeds of disposition on ceasing residency by the amount that would have been the adjusted cost base addition.

(ITA: 7(1.6); 53(1)(*j*); 128.1(4)(*d*.1))

[¶330.115] *Stock Options Held at Death*

See ¶1925.

[¶330.120] *Phantom Stock Option Plans*

See ¶359.

(ITA: 7; 53(1)(*j*); 110(1)(*d*); (*d*.1); 132(6); ITR: 6204 Prescribed Shares; IT-113R4 [Archived])

[¶331] PERSONAL COUNSELLING FEES

You are not taxable on a benefit where your employer provides counselling services in respect of:

(1) Your physical or mental health or that of a person related to you (including counselling services for tobacco, drug, or alcohol abuse, or for stress management). This exclusion does not apply to the costs of recreational, sporting, or other facilities where your employer is denied a deduction under the rules at ¶731; or

(2) Your re-employment or retirement.

Where your employer provides counselling other than that specifically excluded, the value will generally be taxable.

In-house Counselling

The rules would appear to encompass benefits that derive from counselling services (other than those that are excluded), even if your employer arranges for these to be provided in-house. However, the CRA employer's guide to taxable benefits (T4130) refers to "fees [the employer] pay[s]" for such services, which appears to imply that there is no requirement to allocate in-house costs to value a counselling benefit.

(ITA: 6(1)(*a*)(iv); Income Tax Folio: S2-F3-C2 Benefits and Allowances Received from Employment)

[¶332] BENEFITS RECEIVED FROM AN EMPLOYEES' PROFIT SHARING PLAN

[¶332.05] *Allocation by Trustee to Employees*

Your employer may pay amounts to a trustee of an employees' profit sharing plan ("EPSP"). The trustee is required to allocate the following amounts to the individual employees:

(1) amounts received in the year from the employer or a corporation with which the employer does not deal at arm's length;

(2) income of the trust for the year;

(3) capital gains realized and capital losses sustained by the trust in the year; and

(4) amounts originally allocated to other employees who have, after 1971 and in the current year, lost their right thereto.

[¶332.10] *Taxation of Employees*

If you are a beneficiary of an EPSP, you are taxed on allocations made by the trustee and not generally on payments you receive. You cannot deduct contributions you make to the plan.

You will be notified annually of the amounts allocated to you under the plan. You are required to include in your income each year the total of the amounts referred to in (1), (2), (3), and (4), above allocated to you. If foreign taxes were paid on any of the income allocated to you, you may also be eligible for a foreign tax credit (see ¶1450). You are entitled to a dividend tax credit in respect of dividends from taxable Canadian corporations which are allocated to you (see ¶1425).

Capital gains or losses allocated to you are treated as if you had realized them personally (see ¶519).

Where an EPSP makes a distribution to you in kind, e.g., shares or other securities, you are deemed to receive the property at an amount equal to its adjusted cost base to the plan. This rule will generally result in the distribution being non-taxable.

Exempt Gains Balance

A special rule applies where the capital gains exemption election was made by a beneficiary on his or her interest in the plan, thereby creating an "exempt gains balance" with respect to the plan. Since capital property is distributed from the plan at its adjusted cost base, the beneficiary is allowed to elect to increase the adjusted cost base of the property so distributed by the exempt gains balance. Although exempt gains balances generally ceased to exist after 2004, the concept is maintained indefinitely where the balance relates to an employees' profit sharing plan.

[¶332.15] *Where Employee Leaves Plan and Forfeits Payments*

If you cease to be a beneficiary of an employee profit sharing plan during the year, and do not rejoin the plan during the year, you may deduct an amount in computing your employment income. The deduction relates only to amounts that have been allocated contingently — i.e., which were included in your income but which you will not now receive. If the allocation has vested or has been received, no deduction is permitted.

The contingent amounts which are forfeited are computed as follows:

(1) where dividends from taxable Canadian corporations have been allocated to you, the dividend gross-up (see ¶404) is ignored and only the actual amount of the dividend is deducted. The deduction is further reduced by an arbitrary 25% of all dividends, to reflect the fact that you will have been entitled to a dividend tax credit on the original contingent allocation;

(2) capital gain or loss allocations are not included in the amount deductible; and

(3) amounts actually received or receivable and which were included in income (as opposed to taxable allocations) are not included in the amount deductible.

The provision dealing with deduction implies that the deduction is optional, and to the extent you choose not to claim it, carries forward for claim in the future.

If you rejoin a plan in the year of forfeiture, no deduction is permitted. Where you rejoin a plan in a year subsequent to the year of forfeiture, any carryforward amounts on hand cease to be available for deduction. It would appear, and seems to be the official view, that any carryforwards remaining on hand are simply lost from the year of rejoining forward, even if you leave the plan again. This matter is not, however, completely clear.

The forfeiture deduction does not come into play when an individual dies. If forfeiture occurs after death, the estate or heir is entitled to the deduction.

[¶332.20] *Penalty Tax for Excess EPSP Amounts — Line 418 (Schedule 1)*

You may be subject to a special tax on EPSP contributions made after March 28, 2012. The tax addresses concerns that EPSPs have been used by business owners to direct profits to members of their families to reduce or defer payment of income tax on these profits.

Part XI.4 tax applies to a specified employee's "excess EPSP amount". The latter is defined as the employer's contributions in a year to the EPSP that are allocated to the specified employee in excess of 20% of that employee's gross income from employment (not including regular EPSP allocated amounts included in income or stock option benefits). A "specified employee", defined in subsection 248(1), generally includes an employee who does not deal at arm's length with the employer or who owns at least 10% of the shares of any class of a corporate employer. The penalty tax is payable by the specified employee.

The tax on the excess EPSP amount equals the top federal rate of 33% (prior to 2016, 29%) plus the top provincial rate for the province of the employee's residence (not including Quebec). If the employee is not resident in a province, the second rate is 14%. Income which is subject to this tax is not subject to regular Part I income tax. The CRA may waive or cancel part or all of the tax if it considers it just and equitable to do so.

To prevent double taxation, the excess EPSP amount is deducted in computing your income.

If you are subject to this tax, you must complete form RC359 and report the tax on Line 418 on Schedule 1. The excess EPSP amount is deducted at line 229 of your return so that it is not subject to regular tax.

Louis is employed by Opco which is wholly owned by his parents. His income for the year is his regular employment income from Opco of $25,000 and an allocation of $18,000 under Opco's EPSP. His excess EPSP amount is $13,000, the amount by which his EPSP allocation exceeds 20% of his regular salary. Louis reports $30,000 as his income subject to Part I tax: $25,000 of salary plus the $18,000 EPSP allocation, less the $13,000 excess EPSP amount. He pays tax at the top rate (33% after 2015, 29% before 2016), using form RC359, on the $13,000 excess amount and is taxed at regular graduated rates on the other $30,000.

(ITA: 8(1)(o.1); 144; IT-280R [Archived]; IT-379R [Archived])

[¶333] CONVENTIONS

Where your employer requires that you attend a convention as part of your employment, and reimburses you for reasonable costs incurred in so doing, the reimbursement is not normally income to you. On the other hand, if your employer gives you a non-accountable allowance to cover the cost of attending such a convention, you are required to include the allowance in income. In either case, you are not entitled to deduct any of the costs of attending a convention in computing your income.

If you attend a convention and go on to take a holiday, any costs borne by your employer over and above the costs of attending the convention are a taxable benefit (see also ¶319).

(Income Tax Folio: S2-F3-C2 Benefits and Allowances Received from Employment)

[¶334] TRANSPORTATION PASSES

There are no statutory rules dealing with the taxation of a benefit you may receive where your employer provides you with subsidized transportation passes, but the CRA has developed administrative policies which provide some relief. The CRA will not seek to tax a benefit if you are an employee of a bus, rail or ferry company and you are provided with free or subsidized transportation. The policy does not extend to the transportation of your vehicle or equipment you own.

Airline passes available to airline employees create a taxable benefit only if you travel on a space-confirmed basis and you pay less than 50% of the economy fare available for that trip. If you travel on a standby basis or pay 50% or more of the economy fare for a confirmed space, no taxable benefit arises.

Retired employees of transportation companies are not taxed on pass benefits under any circumstances (they are no longer employed and cannot, therefore, enjoy an employment benefit).

(CRA Document No.: Taxable benefit arising from ferry passes, *October 21, 2009*, CRA Document No. 2008-0298021E5; Income Tax Folio: S2-F3-C2 Benefits and Allowances Received from Employment)

RECEIPTS WHICH ARE NOT TAXABLE

[¶335] REASONABLE TRAVELLING EXPENSE ALLOWANCES OF A SALESPERSON

If you are employed as a salesperson, reasonable travel allowances you receive are not taxable. If the allowance is unreasonably high, the excess over a reasonable allowance is a taxable benefit.

If the allowance is unreasonably low, you may add the whole of the allowance to your income and deduct the actual expenses you incurred (see ¶368).

Motor Vehicle Allowances

If you receive a travel allowance that relates to a motor vehicle, specific rules govern whether the allowance is reasonable or not. A motor vehicle allowance is deemed to be unreasonable unless two conditions are met:

(1) The allowance is based solely on kilometres driven in the course of your employment. It follows that you must keep a log to support your per-kilometre allowance claim, and that the log will differentiate personal and employment use. As to what constitutes personal use, see ¶323.

(2) No reimbursement for motor vehicle use is provided in addition to your per-kilometre motor vehicle allowance, other than reimbursement in respect of supplementary business insurance or parking, toll, or ferry charges.

If your motor vehicle allowance fails to meet either of these tests, the whole allowance is considered to be unreasonable and must be added to your income. You may then deduct motor vehicle expenses as discussed at ¶370.

Even if your allowance does meet these tests, if it is otherwise considered unreasonably high or low, it is to be included in income and you can deduct your related expenses.

Examples

(1) Jim receives a fixed automobile allowance of $500 a month. As this is not based solely on kilometres driven, it is deemed to be unreasonable and Jim must include it in his income. He may then be able to claim the automobile expenses he incurs that relate to his employment travel.

(2) Sue receives an advance of $400 a month for her automobile costs. Periodically, she submits a report to her employer and the advance is reconciled to the 35¢ a kilometre she is entitled to. As the allowance is based solely on kilometres driven, it is not deemed to be unreasonable and is not taxable.

(3) Andrew receives 50¢ a kilometre as an allowance for the use of his automobile. His employer also reimburses the additional cost of business insurance he must pay for to cover the fact that his vehicle is not used solely for personal use. Although an otherwise reasonable allowance is rendered unreasonable, and therefore taxable, where it is accompanied by a reimbursement of expenses, a reimbursement of insurance as Andrew receives is permitted. Andrew's allowance is therefore not deemed to be unreasonable and remains non-taxable.

(ITA: 6(1)(*b*); IT-522R [Archived])

[¶336] REASONABLE TRANSPORTATION ALLOWANCES RECEIVED BY A CLERGY PERSON

Reasonable allowances received by you as a minister or clergy person in charge of or ministering to a diocese, parish or congregation for transportation expenses incurred in the discharge of your duties are not taxable. If the allowance received is unreasonably high, the excess over a reasonable allowance is a taxable benefit.

If the allowance is unreasonably low, you may add the whole of it to your income and deduct your actual expenses incurred under the rules at ¶369.

Where the allowance is in respect of a motor vehicle, the two limitations as to kilometres and lack of other reimbursement apply as described at ¶335. Where the allowance is found to be unreasonable under these rules, it must, of course, be included in income, but actual expenses may be deducted subject to the limitations at ¶369 and ¶370.

See also ¶376.

(ITA: 6(1)(*b*)(vi); IT-522R [Archived])

[¶337] REASONABLE ALLOWANCES FOR TRAVELLING AND AUTOMOBILE EXPENSES OF AN EMPLOYEE

[¶337.05] *Travel Allowances*

If you are neither a salesperson (¶335) nor a member of the clergy (¶336), separate rules govern the taxation of allowances for the use of a motor vehicle and other travel allowances.

Reasonable allowances for your travelling expenses (other than motor vehicle allowances) are not taxable if (i) they relate to employment travel out of the municipality or metropolitan area where you usually work or report, or (ii) you are employed in connection with the selling of property or the negotiating of contracts for the employer. If the allowance received is unreasonably high, the excess over a reasonable allowance is a taxable benefit to you. If the allowance is unreasonably low, you may add it to income and deduct the allowable expenses incurred to the extent permitted by ¶369.

An allowance for these purposes is a flat amount, for which you are not required to account to your employer, to cover various expenses of travelling, usually such items as laundry, meals, etc. This is not the same thing as a reimbursement of specific expenses which you submit to your employer. A reimbursement is not an allowance and is not taxable.

The CRA has stated that travel allowances paid for travel within the municipality or metropolitan area may be excluded from income if the allowance is paid primarily for the benefit of the employer. That is, an allowance may be excluded from income when its principal objective is to ensure that your employment duties are undertaken in a more efficient manner even where the travel is within the municipality or metropolitan area (Income Tax Folio S2-F3-C2).

[¶337.10] *Tax-Free Motor Vehicle Allowances*

Reasonable motor vehicle allowances are covered under a separate rule. Any employee (not just a salesperson or member of the clergy) may receive a tax-free allowance for the use of a motor vehicle for travel in the performance of his duties if the two conditions governing its reasonableness outlined at ¶335 are met. The motor vehicle allowance provision is a general one and does not apply only to travel away from your municipality or metropolitan area.

As with a salesperson, if your motor vehicle allowance fails to meet either of the two tests, the whole allowance is considered unreasonable and is added to your income. In that case, you may deduct your related expenses as discussed at ¶369 and ¶370. If your motor vehicle allowance meets these tests, but is otherwise considered unreasonably high, the difference will be a taxable benefit. Similarly, if your automobile allowance meets the tests but is otherwise unreasonably low, you may add it to income and claim the deduction as discussed at ¶369.

If your employer pays a per-kilometre motor vehicle allowance (one which meets the above tests), the amount that the employer can deduct is limited by regulation — see the table at ¶86. Where a per-kilometre allowance does not exceed these limits, the CRA generally accepts that it is reasonable. Where the allowance exceeds the prescribed amount, the CRA may question whether it is reasonable and you may have to substantiate that a larger allowance you receive is reasonable in the circumstances.

Flat and Per-kilometre Allowances

At one time, the CRA had a relieving administrative policy which dealt with an employee receiving both a reasonable per-kilometre allowance and a flat allowance. This permitted the employee to take into income only the flat allowance. However, this policy was withdrawn (in 1991) so that now the receipt of a flat allowance renders the per-kilometre allowance taxable, and both must be taken into income.

Relevant Case Law

Ceiling on Allowance

In *Melville Motors Ltd. v. The Queen*, 2004 UDTC 174 (TCC), the Tax Court ruled that an allowance based on kilometres but subject to a ceiling was a reasonable allowance in fact, even though the allowance hit the ceiling in every case.

[¶337.15] *Part-Time Employees Travelling over 80 Kilometres*

If you are a part-time employee, you may receive a non-taxable travelling allowance. The exemption will apply where (i) you perform your part-time employment services for an arm's length employer during a period when you have other employment or you are carrying on a business, and (ii) in connection with the part-time employment you are required to travel a distance which is at least 80 kilometres away from both your residence and principal work location.

The CRA is silent on how the 80 kilometres is measured, but presumably the principles of the Giannakopoulos case, discussed at ¶1039, should be persuasive — i.e., using the shortest direct route and not "as the crow flies".

(ITA: 81(3.1))

[¶337.20] *Part-Time Teachers and Professors Travelling over 80 Kilometres*

A variation on the rule immediately above waives the requirement that the part-time employee must have another business or employment in order to claim the exemption, if you are a part-time professor or teacher who travels 80 kilometres or more to work at a designated educational institution. A "designated educational institution" is a Canadian post-secondary institution and certified Canadian vocational institution, as described at ¶1323. Furthermore, the place of residence is the only criterion for measuring distance, as there is no other place or employment or business.

(ITA: 6(1)(*b*); 81(3.1); IT-522R [Archived])

[¶338] VOLUNTEER EMERGENCY WORKERS

A special rule applies if you are employed or "otherwise engaged" in a volunteer capacity by a government, municipality, or public authority, as an ambulance technician, a firefighter, or a person who assists in the search for or rescue of individuals in emergency situations. You may benefit from this special rule if you receive amounts that relate to these services, provided that the payer is willing to certify, if the Minister demands:

(1) that you are such a volunteer; and

(2) that during the year in question you were not employed or otherwise engaged by that employer in connection with any of the duties described (or any similar duties) other than as a volunteer.

Where these conditions are met, the first $1,000 you receive is exempt from tax. The amount should not appear on your T4, and should not be reported on your T1 return, although you may add the actual amounts received to earned income for child care expense deduction purposes.

If you serve as a volunteer for more than one such employer (for example, as a volunteer firefighter for two different municipalities), the $1,000 exemption will apply against the income from each.

Example

> Robert served as a volunteer firefighter in two neighbouring municipalities. He received $700 from the first and $1,200 from the second in the year. He needs not include in income the $700 in respect of the first municipality (because the lesser of $1,000 and the amount received is exempt), but should include $200 from the second.

The exemption is denied if you were employed in the year, other than as a volunteer, by that employer. Thus, for example, if you were employed by a municipality as a regular ambulance driver, and served as a volunteer firefighter for the same municipality, you cannot claim the $1,000 exemption at all. If you served as a volunteer firefighter in a neighbouring municipality you can claim the exemption on income from that municipality.

There are also tax credits for volunteer firefighters and for volunteer search and rescue personnel. If you claim either of these credits you are not eligible for the exemption and must include all amounts you receive for your volunteer services in income. See ¶1360 and ¶1360a.

(ITA: 81(4); 118.06; 118.07)

[¶339] GOVERNMENT TRAVELLING OR PERSONAL EXPENSE ALLOWANCES

Travelling, personal, or living expense allowances fixed by an Act of the Parliament of Canada are not taxable. Such amounts include certain per diem travelling allowances for judges and Tax Court of Canada members, and expense, travelling, motor vehicle and residence allowances paid to Members of Parliament, Ministers of the Crown, the Leader of the Opposition, the Speakers of each House, etc. Similarly, allowances paid by the federal Treasury Board to commissioners or employees of commissions appointed under the federal *Inquiries Act* are explicitly exempt from tax provided they are paid in respect of official duties.

(ITA: 6(1)(*b*)(i))

[¶341] REPRESENTATION OR OTHER SPECIAL ALLOWANCES OF AMBASSADORS, MINISTERS

Representation or other special allowances are not taxable when received by an ambassador, minister, high commissioner, officer, or servant of Canada, or a member of the Canadian Armed Forces, or an agent-general, officer, or servant of a province, in respect of a period of absence from Canada. Representation or other special allowances received by an agent-general of a province in respect to the period while he or she was in Ottawa as the agent-general of the province are also not taxable. Similarly, representation or other special allowances received by persons working in foreign countries under international development assistance programs of the Canadian International Development Agency that are financed out of the Special Account established by External Affairs are not taxable.

(ITA: 6(1)(*b*)(iii); (iv))

[¶342] ALLOWANCES OF ELECTED OFFICIALS

An allowance is not taxable when you receive it as an appointed member of a school board, or an elected member of a provincial legislature, an incorporated municipality, a school board or school district, a municipal utilities board, commission or corporation, or any other similar body, for expenses incidental to the discharge of your duties, except to the extent it exceeds one-half of your salary or other remuneration for that position.

You are not entitled to claim home office expenses (see ¶373) if you have been reimbursed or are entitled to be reimbursed for such expenses. It is the CRA's view that if you receive a tax-free allowance for expenses incidental to the discharge of your duties, you have in effect been reimbursed for your home office expenses and cannot claim them. The CRA opinion seems to have been given in the context of municipal council members, but presumably is of general application.

It is not clear whether the same rule applies to the rather differently worded deductions for travel and motor vehicle expenses in ¶369. Although there is no statutory provision dealing with this question, the CRA's views were set out in Interpretation Bulletins which have subsequently been archived: where a tax-free elected officials allowance was received, the related motor vehicle costs could not be deducted. With the archiving of the Bulletins, the motor vehicle deduction issue is perhaps less certain, but it likely remains the CRA assessing position.

(ITA: 81(2); (3); IT-292 [Archived]; CRA Document No.: When to Issue T2200, *June 16, 2005,* CRA Document No. 2005-0131691E5)

[¶344] SUBSIDIZED SCHOOL SERVICES

You are not taxable on a reasonable allowance from your employer to allow your children who live away from home to attend school because there is no suitable school where you are required to live by virtue of your employment. The school must be the closest one with suitable boarding facilities and in which the language primarily used for instruction is an official language of Canada, and that language is primarily used by you.

See ¶310 for the treatment of tuition fees where your employer pays the cost of the tuition of your children.

Where employment is in a remote or unorganized area, employers frequently assume responsibility for essential community services of a kind normally borne by a municipal organization. Free or subsidized school services provided in such a situation are not a taxable benefit.

(ITA: 6(1)(*b*)(ix); Income Tax Folio: S2-F3-C2 Benefits and Allowances Received from Employment)

[¶344d] CHILD CARE EXPENSES

Child care provided by your employer is not taxable if all of the following conditions are met:

(1) the services are provided at the employer's place of business;

(2) the services are managed directly by the employer;

(3) the services are provided to all of the employees at minimal or no cost; and

(4) the services are not available to the general public, only employees.

If these conditions are not met, you are taxable on a benefit. If your employer subsidizes a facility operated by a third party in exchange for subsidized rates for its employees, or if it makes facilities available to non-employees for a higher rate than it charges you and its other employees, the difference is a taxable benefit to you.

(CRA Document No.: Child Care Expenses, *May 5, 2005,* CRA Document No. 2005-0124661E5)

[¶345] STRIKE PAY

The Supreme Court has confirmed that strike pay is not taxable (*Wally Fries v. The Queen*, 90 DTC 6662 (SCC)). Payments for services performed during a strike are taxable if you are an employee of the union.

(Income Tax Folio: S3-F9-C1, ¶1.10; *Wally Fries v. The Queen,* 90 DTC 6662 (SCC))

[¶345b] GIFTS FROM UNION

In a technical opinion, the CRA said that, following the *Fries* case referred to in ¶345, it is of the view that a retirement gift provided by a union from union funds to a member of the union is not income from a source and is consequently not taxable. The opinion was premised on the understanding that the amount of the gifts was relatively insignificant (somewhere between $300 and $600 in the request under consideration).

In a subsequent interpretation, the CRA was of the view that while the value of gift certificates distributed by a union to its members was not taxable, the equivalent amount of union dues were not deductible in computing employment income (see ¶372.05).

(CRA Document No.: Cash Retirement Gift From a Union, *March 15, 2005,* CRA Document No. 2005-011406117; Distribution of Gift Certificates to Union Members, *December 16, 2008,* CRA Document No. 2007-0261121E5)

[¶345d] DISASTER RELIEF PAYMENTS AND LOANS

In general, you are not taxed on government disaster relief payments to cover personal losses, or to replace or repair rental or business properties. Your personal expenses or losses occasioned by disaster are not deductible. Damage or destruction of property may bring into play capital gain or loss rules, including the rules denying losses on personal use property (see ¶525 and ¶545).

In some cases of natural disaster, the government will provide tax relief, usually by issuing a "remission order", for relief payments made by employers over and above normal salary. (This form of relief should not be confused with the more common custom of waiving late payments of tax where a natural disaster results in taxpayers being unable to remit payments, usually tax instalments, on a timely basis. See "Disaster Waivers" at ¶249.10).

The CRA has a standardized press release for announcing this type of remission; it is somewhat more detailed than the actual orders. It specifies that the payments must have been made under the following conditions:

- the assistance must be in addition to your regular salary, paid even when you were unable to report to work because of the specified disaster;
- the assistance must be reasonable in the circumstances;
- the assistance must be based on an employer–employee relationship and not on the fact that you own shares in the business;
- the employer must have granted the assistance on a voluntary basis;
- the employer must have made the payment without regard to your work performance, length of service, or any other work-related factor;
- the employer cannot have granted financial assistance in exchange for past or future services;
- the employer cannot have used the amount of assistance to compensate you for your loss of employment income.

Typically, employers are directed not to complete a T4 for these benefits, since they do not have the quality of income in the first place. The payments are nevertheless deductible to the employer, unless the assistance is advanced by way of a loan.

(Other Publications: 1998 Ice Storm: Remission Order, P.C. 1998-2047)

FRINGE BENEFITS FROM YOUR EMPLOYER

[¶346] GENERAL

The value of benefits of any kind whatever, received or enjoyed by you in the year in respect of, in the course of, or by virtue of an office or employment are included in your employment income, subject to the exceptions itemized in the law and noted in this chapter.

While this statement seems broad enough at face value to cover most contingencies, its application turns on first determining whether an economic advantage has accrued to you, the employee, and then whether that advantage is primarily for your benefit or the benefit of your employer. This question is subject to periodic review in the courts. Based on various court decisions, Income Tax Folio S2-F3-C2 concludes that there only needs to be a small connection between a benefit and the employment for the benefit to be included in the employee's income.

Similarly, although the law specifies that employer-provided allowances are generally taxable, the determination of whether an "allowance" confers an employee benefit has been held to depend on whether the primary benefit accrues to the employee, at least in cases involving free parking for employees (¶352c), meal allowances, and transportation to and from the job of employees working overtime (¶352f). The CRA has to some extent accepted this doctrine there and elsewhere (employer-provided courses and computers, for example; see ¶310 and ¶355c) and incorporated its solutions as administrative policies. Nevertheless, it is not yet clear that the doctrine of "no benefit, no income" has the stability to be applied in other situations.

An extensive review of the case law and underlying principles by Chief Justice Bowman of the Tax Court, in which he acknowledged that the cases come down on all sides of the issue, led him to extract at least one general principle:

> I think the principle that can be extracted from these cases — Canada, United Kingdom and United States — is that a "benefit" is not included in an employee's income if it is primarily for the need or convenience of the employer. ... this is so even where it represents a material acquisition or something of value.

(ITA: 6(1)(*a*); *Rachfalowski v. The Queen*, 2008 DTC 3626 (TCC))

[¶346.05] *Timing of Benefits*

An employer provided a system of award credits for such things as suggestions to improve the business, demonstrating extraordinary customer service, outstanding job performance, etc. The credits could be accumulated and redeemed for gift certificates, merchandise, travel, etc. The CRA opined that the awards were taxable benefits but the benefits only arose at the time the awards were redeemed, not when they were earned.

(CRA Document No.: Employee Award Program, *March 23, 1999,* CRA Document No. 9906905)

[¶346.10] *Employment Benefits Received by Relatives*

Any taxable employment benefit received by a person not dealing at arm's length with the employee is included in the employee's, not the recipient's, income. Any benefit received in respect of motor vehicle operating expenses attributable to personal use by an employee's relative is also included in the employee's income.

An amount received by virtue of employment from an employee benefit plan, or from the disposition of an interest in such a plan, by a person not dealing at arm's length with the employee, is included in the employee's, not the recipient's, income provided the employee is alive at the time the amount was received.

Any benefit received by an individual other than the employee under an employer's program designed to help the individual further his or her education is excluded from the employee's income if the employee deals at arm's length with the employer and if the benefit is not a disguised form of remuneration (see ¶310.05).

(ITA: 6(1)(*a*); 6(1)(*g*); 6(1)(*l*); 6(1.2))

[¶346c] LOYALTY AND FREQUENT FLYER PROGRAMS

These programs allow you to accumulate credits which may be exchanged for air travel or other benefits. The CRA historically took the position that if you accumulate such credits while travelling on employer-paid business trips and use them to obtain air travel or other benefits for your personal use, or for personal use of a relative, the fair market value of the air travel or other benefit is to be included in your income. This policy has now been relaxed somewhat.

Where the employer controls your use of accumulated points (for example, where the points accumulate and credits can only be claimed on a company credit card), the employer is expected to T4 the benefit.

Where the employer does not control the use of accumulated points, the CRA administratively does not require an employment benefit to be included in your income, so long as:

(1) the points are not converted to cash,

(2) the plan or arrangement is not indicative of an alternate form of remuneration, and

(3) the plan or arrangement is not for tax avoidance purposes.

In its Income Tax Technical News No. 40, the CRA provides the following examples:

Example — Personal Credit Card

Pauline's employer has allowed her to use her personal credit cards whenever possible to pay for business expenses, which the employer subsequently reimburses. To maximize the points earned, Pauline used her personal credit cards to pay for various employer business costs, including travel expenses of other employees.

The CRA would not consider such an arrangement to qualify as a non-taxable amount under the administrative policy. The arrangement is indicative of having been made in order to provide a benefit to the employee as an alternate form of remuneration. In this case, Pauline must determine and include the value of benefits received or enjoyed in income on her personal income tax return.

Example — Company Credit Card Points as Benefit to the Employee

Jennifer's employer has a company credit card, under which loyalty points are earned. The employer is billed and pays the credit card charges. The employer allows Jennifer to redeem the points for her personal use. In such circumstances, the fair market value of the goods or services received by Jennifer will represent a taxable employment benefit. The employer must include and report the value of the benefit on the employee's T4 slip.

(Income Tax Folio: S2-F3-C2 Benefits and Allowances Received from Employment; *Mommersteeg et al. v. The Queen*, 96 DTC 1011 (TCC))

[¶348] MERCHANDISE DISCOUNTS

The CRA's previous policy was to not tax employees on a benefit where their employer allowed them to buy merchandise at a discount, provided that the policy applied equally to all employees and the purchase price was not less than the employer's cost. Income Tax Folio S2-F3-C2 states that effective July 7, 2016, the value of the discount is generally included in the employee's income, regardless of the purchase price. The discount may be provided by the employer or by a third-party. The value of the benefit is equal to the fair market value of the merchandise purchased, less the amount paid by the employee. However, no amount is included in the employee's income if the discount is also available to the general public or to specific public groups.

A commission received by you as a salesperson on merchandise acquired for your personal use is not taxable. Similarly, where a life insurance salesperson acquires a life insurance policy, a commission received by that person on that policy is not taxable provided the salesperson owns the policy and is obliged to make the required premium payments.

The CRA has confirmed its view that if you receive a cash rebate in the form of a cheque from your manufacturer employer for buying its products for personal use, you should include the rebate in your income unless the price after rebate is the same as the one paid by the general public. Although rebates are to be afforded the same general treatment as price discounts, the details of the rebate program have to be examined carefully to determine if they trigger a taxable benefit.

(CRA Document No.: Commission Income on Life Insurance Policies, *May 8, 2012*, CRA Document No. 2012-0436141C6; Deductibility of employee rebate, *November 23, 2011*, CRA Document No. 2011-0399661E5; Income Tax Folio: S2-F3-C2 Benefits and Allowances Received from Employment)

[¶350] SUBSIDIZED MEALS

Subsidized meals provided by your employer are not considered to be a taxable benefit if you are required to pay a reasonable charge. A reasonable charge is generally defined as one that covers the cost of food, its preparation, and service. Where less than a reasonable charge is imposed, the value of the benefit is the employer's cost less any payment you make.

(Income Tax Folio: S2-F3-C2 Benefits and Allowances Received from Employment)

[¶351] UNIFORMS AND SPECIAL CLOTHING

Where your employer supplies uniforms and special clothing which you are required to wear, or the employer pays for your laundry or dry cleaning costs for the uniforms or special clothing, no taxable benefit is considered to arise.

(Income Tax Folio: S2-F3-C2 Benefits and Allowances Received from Employment)

[¶352] TRANSPORTATION TO THE JOB

You are not considered to enjoy a taxable benefit where your employer provides transportation from pickup points to a location of employment at which, for security or other reasons, public or private vehicles are not welcome or not practical. However, a reimbursement or allowance paid to you for transportation to and from the location of employment is included in income (subject to the rules on remote work sites at ¶360).

(Income Tax Folio: S2-F3-C2 Benefits and Allowances Received from Employment)

[¶352a] TRANSIT EMPLOYEES

If you are employed in the operation of buses, streetcars, subways, commuter trains, and ferry services your employer may provide free or discounted transit passes. The CRA has historically treated these passes as non-taxable when provided to the transit employees and their families (see ¶334).

(Income Tax Folio: S2-F3-C2 Benefits and Allowances Received from Employment)

[¶352c] PARKING

Employer-provided parking generally constitutes a taxable benefit to you, whether or not the employer owns the parking lot. The benefit is the fair market value of the parking minus any payment you make to use the space.

The CRA has an administrative policy not to impute a benefit to employer-provided parking where:

- a business operates from a shopping centre or industrial park, where parking is available to both employees and non-employees;
- your employer provides scramble parking (i.e., there are fewer spaces than there are employees who require

parking, and the spaces are available on a first-come, first-served basis); or

- your employer requires that you have a vehicle available and it is used regularly in providing employment services.

Scramble Parking

The following factors are considered in deciding if there is scramble parking:

- the number of employees who use the parking lot at any given time, taking into account shift work or absences due to vacation, sick days, or other reasons;
- whether the parking lot is full at various times during the day;
- whether, on an average day, most employees get a parking spot; and
- whether the workplace is in a downtown area with alternative parking.

With respect to the exclusion of a benefit where a vehicle is required to be available, the CRA made the following comments:

> In our view, if an employee is required to use his or her vehicle 3 or more days on a weekly basis for employment-related travel and requires the parking space for this purpose, the parking space would be considered to be used regularly for employment-related reasons. Therefore, the employee would not be in receipt of taxable benefit.
>
> Where it is determined that the employee is not regularly required to use a vehicle for employment-related purposes, but needs the use of a parking space on occasions when he or she is required to use the vehicle to travel away from the office during the day for employment-related business reasons, then the employment benefit otherwise determined may be reduced on a reasonable basis to account for such use. For example, the parking benefit could be prorated on the basis of the number of days in the calendar year when the employee was required to use the vehicle during the workday, and therefore required the parking space for business reasons.

If you have a disability, in particular a severe and prolonged mobility impairment which markedly restricts your ability to perform a basic activity of daily living, the parking benefit is generally not taxable (see ¶361d). For more about this disability criterion, see ¶1209.

(T4130, "Employer's Guide — Taxable Benefits and Allowances"; Income Tax Folio: S2-F3-C2 Benefits and Allowances Received from Employment)

[¶352f] OVERTIME MEAL AND TRAVEL ALLOWANCES

[¶352f.05] *Meal Allowances*

As a matter of policy, the CRA allows your employer to reimburse you for overtime meals, or give you a reasonable allowance for overtime meals, without insisting on a taxable benefit to the employee, in the following circumstances:

- you work two or more hours of overtime right after your scheduled hours of work; and
- the overtime is infrequent and occasional in nature (less than three times a week).

If overtime occurs more frequently, the CRA considers that an overtime meal reimbursement or allowance starts to take on the character of additional remuneration and constitutes a taxable benefit.

What is a Reasonable Allowance?

The CRA considers a reimbursement or allowance to be reasonable if it does not exceed $17 per meal.

However, in *Morissette v. The Queen*, 2012 DTC 1090 (TCC), the Tax Court of Canada concluded that a meal allowance of $20 per meal paid to an employee who worked more than two hours of overtime away from his regular workplace and not having access to the place where he normally ate was reasonable and not taxable.

The employer's deduction is limited by the 50% rule at ¶734 where you are not subject to a taxable benefit. Where there is a taxable benefit, it should be included in box 14 and under code 40 on your T4 slip, and would count as income for CPP contributions and EI premiums as well as income tax. Exception (4) at ¶734 will then apply to permit a full deduction to the employer.

Special rules apply to rail and transport employees; see ¶374.

(T4130, "Employer's Guide — Taxable Benefits and Allowances"; *Morissette v. The Queen*, 2012 DTC 1090 (TCC))

[¶352f.10] *Travel Allowances*

Travel allowances are generally governed by the strict rules at ¶335 to ¶337. In particular, travel from home to work and back is considered a personal or living expense so that a reimbursement of this cost, or an allowance to cover it, is always taxable. However, the CRA has carved out a narrow exception, similar to the overtime meal allowance, where an employer provides you with a mileage allowance or reimbursement if you are required to work overtime. The reimbursement or allowance for travel home is not treated as a taxable benefit where:

(1) you are required to work at least three hours in addition to and immediately subsequent to the regular hours of work;

(2) public transportation is not available or your physical safety is at risk at the time of travel; and

(3) such overtime occurs only occasionally.

There is also an exception if you are blind or eligible for the disability tax credit. See ¶361d.

This policy does not apply to travel as a result of a call to return to work. A reimbursement of such travelling expenses is included in your income in the same manner as reimbursements for regularly scheduled trips to the workplace.

This exception is not referred to in T4130, "Employer's Guide — Taxable Benefits and Allowances".

(CRA Document No.: Taxable Benefits - Shuttle home to work, *February 2, 2011*, CRA Document No. 2010-0385881E5; Overtime Meal Allowance and Taxi Fare Home, *March 11, 1993*, CRA Document No. 9301105)

[¶353] INTEREST-FREE OR LOW-INTEREST LOANS; FORGIVEN LOANS

A loan from your employer which bears interest at less than the prescribed rate may result in the inclusion of a benefit in your income. If the loan is advanced to someone with whom you do not deal at arm's length, the benefit is included in your income, and not the borrower's. Similar benefit rules apply where a loan is made by a corporation to a shareholder.

A taxable benefit arises on any type of indebtedness, not only a formal loan arrangement. This would therefore include an advance you received (other than an advance otherwise required to be included in your income — see ¶329) and other debts you owe to your employer. The benefit is the difference between the interest for the year if it were calculated at the prescribed rates in effect from time to time during the year and the amount of interest you pay in the year or within 30 days after the end of the year.

You can become liable for this imputed interest benefit where the loan or debt is incurred as a consequence of current, intended, or previous employment. Where the personal services business rules apply (¶305), the corporation with the business/employment relationship is required to include the imputed interest in income, rather than the individual who actually provides the services.

Interest Rate is Capped on Certain Loans

A special rule applies if you receive either a home purchase loan or a home relocation loan by virtue of your employment. For these, the prescribed rate of interest will not exceed the rate in effect at the time the loan was received. A home purchase loan is deemed to be a new loan on each fifth anniversary of the day the loan was received, so that a new prescribed rate ceiling applies for the computation of the taxable benefit every five years.

A "home purchase loan" is one you receive from your employer to acquire a dwelling in which you or someone related to you lives, or to repay or replace a similar loan. A "home relocation loan" is one you receive to assist you in acquiring a home as a result of an employment-related move, and is discussed at ¶353.05.

The imputed interest benefit on other loans will reflect fluctuations in the prescribed rates used to calculate it. Prescribed interest rates for the past several years are set out in a table in the information material immediately preceding Chapter 1.

The imputed interest benefit under these provisions may be subject to an offsetting deduction in certain circumstances. See ¶409.

(ITA: 80.4(7) "home purchase loan"; 248(1) "home relocation loan"; T4130, "Employer's Guide — Taxable Benefits and Allowances")

[¶353.05] *Home Relocation Loan — Line 248*

If you move and receive a low-interest loan in connection with a change of work location, whether to take up a new job or as a result of a transfer, you are entitled to claim an offsetting deduction against any imputed interest benefit included in your income. To qualify for the deduction, the distance between your old residence and your new work location must be at least 40 kilometres greater than the distance between your new residence and the new work location. Your new residence must be in Canada, the loan must have been used to acquire the new residence, the residence must be for your habitation, and the loan must have been received by virtue of employment. Finally, you must designate the loan as a home relocation loan in your return, and you may have only one such loan for a particular move and only one loan outstanding at a time.

If you meet all these criteria, you may deduct the lesser of the taxable benefit on the loan and the amount of the benefit that represents the interest inclusion on a $25,000 loan. The loan is considered to have been extinguished five years after the day it is made (unless it was actually extinguished earlier), so that the imputed interest on the first $25,000 of a home relocation loan is tax free for up to five years.

Your T4 slip should include the full amount of the loan benefit and the amount deductible in the "Other Information" area under Codes 36 and 37, respectively. The amount in Box 14 of your T4 will include the loan benefit; you should deduct the deductible amount at line 248. Although you are technically required to designate a particular loan as the home relocation loan, the CRA considers that you have done so if you claim the deduction.

Example

Angela was relocated from Toronto to Calgary by her employer. She had rented an apartment in Toronto, but in Calgary she bought a home. Her employer advanced $30,000, interest free, to allow her to buy her home, at a time when the prescribed rate for the imputed interest benefit was 2%. For the first five years, Angela's employer must add not more than $600 a year to her income as the imputed interest benefit. This amount does not vary if the prescribed rate increases, but will be reduced if the prescribed rate decreases. The benefit relating to the first $25,000 of the loan ($500 if the prescribed rate does not decease) is deductible by Angela in computing her taxable income. On the fifth anniversary of the loan, the prescribed interest ceiling is reset at the prescribed rate at that time. From that time Angela is no longer entitled to the home relocation loan deduction.

(ITA: 80.4; 110(1)(*j*); 248(1) "home relocation loan"; ITR: 4300 [Interpretation]; IT-421R2 [Archived])

[¶353.15] *Forgiveness of Loan*

If your employer forgives some or all of a loan made to you, the forgiven amount is a taxable benefit.

The forgiven amount is defined by reference to the definition of "forgiven amount" at ¶565 except that:

(1) The debt needs not be a "commercial obligation". That is, although the general rules governing forgiven debts only apply if interest on such debts is or would be deductible, the employment income benefit arises whether interest would be deductible or not.

(2) The forgiven amount is not reduced for amounts otherwise included in income (if it were, the definition would be circular since the amount included in employment income here would reduce the amount included in employment income!)

(3) The forgiven amount is not reduced by the amount taken into account in determining the proceeds of disposition of property subject to foreclosure or repossession under the rules at ¶518.

(4) Interest payable on the principal amount is not included in the forgiven amount. There is no employment income inclusion if accrued interest on a debt is forgiven, although there may be tax consequences under ¶518 or ¶565 if the obligation was a commercial obligation.

It is intended that where a debt is forgiven, there is an ordering of tax consequences under which the unpaid amount rules at ¶746 operate first, then the employment income rules here, then the shareholder rules at ¶409, then the ordinary business income rules, then the foreclosure rules at ¶518, and finally the rules at ¶565.

Where the debt is a commercial obligation, the rules at ¶565 concerning debt parking and deemed settlement when statutory rights to recovery expire could apply. It would appear that debt included in income under the employee rules is simply included in income; there is no reduction of tax attributes as with a debt included under the rules at ¶565.

(ITA: 6(1)(*a*); (15); (15.1); 79; 80; 80.01)

[¶354] RECREATIONAL FACILITIES

You are not taxed on a benefit where recreational facilities are provided for your use or enjoyment, whether the employer owns the facilities or contracts with another organization to provide them, provided they are made available to all employees (see ¶355).

(Income Tax Folio: S2-F3-C2 Benefits and Allowances Received from Employment)

[¶354c] WEIGHT LOSS PROGRAM

The CRA has opined that a benefit arises where an employer-provided weight loss program is made available. The benefit is the cost of the program to the employer less any recovery from an employee who participates in the program.

(CRA Document No.: Taxable Benefit-Weight Loss Program, *March 4, 2005*, CRA Document No. 2005-0109731E5)

[¶355] SOCIAL OR ATHLETIC CLUB FEES

If your employer pays your fees for membership in a social or athletic club, you are not considered to receive a taxable benefit if your membership is to your employer's business advantage. There will be a taxable benefit if it is merely a fringe benefit. Presumably, where membership is made available to all employees equally, as discussed at ¶354, it is easier for your employer to argue that membership is provided as a matter of employee health and morale, especially in the case of athletic facilities, and therefore creates a business advantage.

Relevant Case Law

No Benefit where Facilities Not Wanted or Used

In *Rachfalowski v. The Queen*, 2008 DTC 3626 (TCC), an employee was given a golf club membership, which he did not want and did not much use. The employer insisted on his accepting the membership as being consistent with his position. The Court found that there was no taxable benefit.

(Income Tax Folio: S2-F3-C2 Benefits and Allowances Received from Employment)

[¶355b] CHRISTMAS PARTIES AND OTHER SOCIAL EVENTS

It is the CRA's policy that if your employer provides a free party or other social event to all its employees, at a cost of $100 per person or less, no taxable benefit arises. The $100 limit does not include the cost of overnight accommodation or transportation home, the cost of which can increase the limit without rendering the benefit taxable. However, if the cost of the event exceeds the $100 limit, the benefit (including the cost of overnight accommodation, transportation home, and taxi fares) is taxable.

Relevant Case Law

Christmas Party Benefit was Taxable

In *Dunlap v. The Queen*, 98 DTC 2053 (TCC), the Court upheld the CRA's assessment as a taxable benefit of a Christmas party at which the taxpayer, presumably among other employees, was put up overnight at the Westin Hotel in Ottawa. The taxpayer was assessed a benefit of about $200 in connection with the party and another $100 for room charges. This appears to be the first time the CRA assessed a Christmas party as a fringe benefit.

(T4130, "Employer's Guide — Taxable Benefits and Allowances")

[¶355c] COMPUTERS, CELLPHONES, INTERNET PROVIDED TO EMPLOYEES

[¶355c.05] *Computers*

There are no rules in the *Income Tax Act* which deal specifically with whether a benefit arises where your employer makes a computer, cellphone, or internet access available to you. The CRA has issued numerous interpretations in which it confirms that the general principles apply: if you enjoy a benefit, the value of the benefit is taxable. These rulings also acknowledge, however, that employers often make such equipment and services available, or contribute to their cost, primarily for the employer's benefit. In those cases, the CRA will not seek to tax you on a personal benefit which arises because of incidental use, but will tax a benefit if your employer contributes to the cost of buying a device which you own.

Relevant CRA Documents

Ultimately, the issue is always a question of fact. A sample of the various interpretations that the CRA has issued on this question follows below.

Bring your own Device

Where an employer provides a fixed contribution towards an employee's purchase of a computer, the employee is taxable on a benefit unless ownership of the device transfers to the employer. If it does, incidental use by the employee will not be viewed as creating a taxable benefit. (CRA Document No. 2011-0425801C6)

Subsidized Software

Employees purchasing upgraded computer software previously purchased by their employer at a significant discount (2% of retail price) were taxable on the difference between the retail price and the discount price. (CRA Document No. 2011-0409721E5)

Cellphone Use Charges

An employer reimbursed a percentage of the employee's monthly cellphone charges, to a fixed dollar maximum, on submission by the employee of a copy of the bill and proof of payment. The employer did not assist with the purchase of the phone, nor did it contribute towards enhanced plans or roaming charges unless these were incurred in connection with business use. The CRA's view was that the reimbursement of cellphone costs does not result in a taxable benefit to the employee. (CRA Document No. 2014-0553481I7)

(CRA Document No.: Taxable benefit - employee computer equipment, *November 29, 2011*, CRA Document No. 2011-0425801C6; Employee taxable benefits, *January 24, 2012*, CRA Document No. 2011-0409721E5; Taxable benefit – cell phones, *March 6, 2015*, CRA Document No. 2014-0553481I7)

[¶355c.10] *Internet Connections*

If your employer provides you with internet service at home, you are not taxable on a benefit as long as your employer is the primary beneficiary of the service. If a portion of the use is personal, that use creates a taxable benefit valued at the fair market value of the service less any amount you reimburse to your employer. However, the CRA accepts that no personal benefit arises if all of the following conditions are met:

(1) The plan's cost is reasonable.

(2) The plan is a basic plan with a fixed cost.

(3) Your personal use does not result in charges in addition to the basic cost.

(T4130, "Employers Guide — Taxable Benefits and Allowances")

[¶355c.15] *Cellphones*

The CRA's policies on internet connections at ¶355c.10 extend to your employer's contribution to your cellphone plan, and no benefit arises to the extent all of the conditions outlined there are met. As discussed at ¶355c.05, the benefit is taxed to the extent your employer contributes to the cost of purchasing a cellphone.

(T4130, "Employers Guide — Taxable Benefits and Allowances")

[¶355d] DIRECTORS' INSURANCE

Directors and officers of corporations are permitted generally under corporate law to be insured against liabilities incurred in those capacities, so long as they act honestly and in good faith.

The CRA's view is that a taxable benefit is not conferred where the corporation pays the premiums on such insurance or where there is a settlement from the insurance company for risks that were inherent and normal occurrences in carrying out your duties as a director or officer. The CRA also indicated that a taxable benefit does not arise where the corporation assumes your liability as a director or officer, provided the indemnification does not exceed that provided for under corporate law.

The cost to the corporation of providing such insurance would normally be a deductible business expense.

(CRA Document No.: Indemnification of Directors Directly or by Insurance, *December 15, 1992,* CRA Document No. 9231905)

[¶355f] PROFESSIONAL DUES

It is the CRA's view that if your employer pays your professional dues you are not taxable on a benefit if your employer is the primary beneficiary. Where the professional association is related to your duties, and membership is a requirement of employment, the CRA accepts that the employer is the primary beneficiary. If membership is not a condition of employment, your employer will normally make this determination in assessing whether a benefit is to be included in your income.

If you pay your professional dues, you may be able to deduct them under the rules at ¶372 to the extent they are not reimbursed by your employer.

(T4130, "Employers Guide — Taxable Benefits and Allowances"; Income Tax Folio: S2-F3-C2 Benefits and Allowances Received from Employment)

[¶356] MOVING EXPENSES

Where you are reimbursed by your employer for the cost of moving your family and household effects, you are not viewed as receiving a taxable benefit if the move occurs either as the result of your transfer from one business establishment of the employer to another, or where you have accepted new employment at a place other than where your former home was located. The rule is not tied to the deduction for unreimbursed moving expenses discussed at ¶1039 to ¶1047. Accordingly there is no 40-kilometre test under this rule, and the list of reimbursable expenses differs. For example, the CRA permits your employer to pay for your house-hunting expeditions without creating a taxable benefit, which is clearly not included in the deductible expenses at ¶1045.

If you are reimbursed for only part of the costs of moving, the balance will be deductible by you subject to the regular rules at ¶1039 et seq. Your deduction for unreimbursed costs is subject to the tests at ¶1045.

T4130, "Employer's Guide — Taxable Benefits and Allowances", contains a summary of CRA's views on the moving expenses your employer can cover without creating a taxable benefit.

[¶356.05] *Reimbursement of Housing Costs Associated with a Move*

Any amount paid or assistance provided to you by anyone in the course of or because of your employment in respect of the acquisition or use of, or right to use, a residence is a taxable benefit. Exceptions to this general rule may be found in:

(1) the loss reimbursement rules, discussed below;

(2) the home relocation loan rules at ¶353.05; and

(3) the special work site or remote location rules at ¶360.

"Residence" is not a defined term, but it appears the rule will not deny a tax-free reimbursement of such things as your hotel expenses while travelling on company business or interfere with the various deductions permitted for travel allowances, the Northern residents deduction, etc., discussed in this chapter.

(ITA: 6(23))

[¶356.10] *Reimbursement of Housing Losses*

You are not taxed on a limited reimbursement of an eligible housing loss, which is one incurred in respect of an eligible relocation of you or someone with whom you do not deal at arm's length (typically a spouse or family member — see ¶812). You must designate the residence on which the loss is incurred and no more than one residence may be so designated in respect of an eligible relocation. A reimbursement of a loss that is not an eligible housing loss is fully taxable.

The definition of an "eligible relocation" is used for several different purposes, including the moving expenses deduction at ¶1047. It therefore incorporates several elements not usually relevant to the reimbursement of housing losses. An eligible relocation is one where:

(1) the relocation occurs to enable you to be employed at a location in Canada (or carry on a business in Canada or be a student in full-time attendance enrolled in a post-secondary program at the location of an educational institution);

(2) both the old residence and the new one are in Canada, except that if you have been absent from Canada but nevertheless taxed in Canada as a resident (see ¶115 to ¶117), the "in Canada" requirement here and in (1), above, does not apply; and

(3) the distance between your old designated residence and your new work location is not less than 40 kilometres greater than the distance between your new residence and your new work location.

The first $15,000 of eligible housing loss is not taxable and half the excess is. The rule contemplates that the loss may be reimbursed over a number of years, so that you take into income the taxable portion of the eligible housing loss reimbursement as you receive it.

You do not actually have to have realized an eligible housing loss in order to apply these rules to reimbursement. The loss can be measured "at any time" as the amount by which:

(1) the greater of (i) the adjusted cost base at that time, or (ii) the highest fair market value in a six-month period ending at that time exceeds

(2) if the residence has been disposed of before the end of the first taxation year that begins after that time, the lesser of (i) proceeds of disposition, and (ii) fair market value at that time; and

(3) in any other case, the fair market value at that time.

Thus, if you receive a reimbursement in a year for a residence you still own at the end of that year, the loss is the amount by which its adjusted cost base (or highest fair market value over the preceding six months, if determinable) exceeds its fair market value at the time of the reimbursement.

Example (Updated from the Department of Finance Technical Notes)

Paul purchases a home for $100,000 and begins work at a national corporation. Two years later, the land bordering his home is rezoned to permit the development of an industrial park. A few years later, in Year 1, Paul is offered a promotion on the condition that he relocate to a new community (1,000 kilometres from his home town) by March of Year 1. Paul has trouble selling his home because of the heavy industry that now surrounds the property; however, he eventually accepts an offer of $60,000 and completes the sale in August of Year 1. His employer has agreed to compensate him for any loss he incurs on the sale of his property. Because of the size of the loss the employer pays out the compensation as two payments of $20,000 each. Paul receives $20,000 in Year 1 and $20,000 in Year 2. The amount of Paul's employment benefit in Year 1 is $2,500 (one-half of the amount by which $20,000 exceeds $15,000). In Year 2, the benefit is $10,000, calculated as follows: 1/2 × ($40,000 - $15,000) (the total of all amounts received in the year or a preceding year in excess of $15,000) - $2,500 (the amount included in income under this rule in a prior year) = $10,000.

The CRA has issued an opinion that an eligible relocation

> … refers to a relocation which occurred to enable the taxpayer to be employed at a new work location. In our view, an employee may meet this criterion even though he or she starts work at the new location prior to actually relocating. However, the longer the time between the commencement of work at the new location and the relocation, the less likely the relocation will have occurred to enable the taxpayer to be employed at the new location.

(ITA: 6(19)–6(23); Tax Topics: No. 1787, dated June 8, 2006 (provides English summary of CRA Document No. 2005-0131231E5); T4130, "Employer's Guide — Taxable Benefits and Allowances"; CRA Document No.: 9903205; 2005-0131231E5 (French); Income Tax Folio: S2-F3-C2 Benefits and Allowances Received from Employment)

[¶356.25] *Visas*

The CRA has indicated its view that the reimbursement of work permit charges and visa fees to a new employee immigrating to Canada does not result in a taxable benefit. The exception does not apply to the cost of a permanent residence visa, which is considered a personal expense.

(CRA Document No.: , CRA Document No. 2002-013774; Reimbursement of Permanent Resident, *January 29, 2003*, CRA Document No. 2003-0183825)

[¶357] EMPLOYER'S CONTRIBUTIONS TO PENSION PLANS, ETC.

You are not taxable on a benefit derived from your employer's contributions to or under a registered pension fund or plan, a group sickness or accident insurance plan, a pooled registered pension plan, a private health services plan, a supplementary unemployment benefit plan, or a deferred profit sharing plan. See ¶317 with respect to group term life insurance coverage and see ¶316 with respect to premiums paid by an employer under provincial hospitalization plans or provincial medical services plans. Employer contributions to an unregistered or non-resident pension plan may create a variety of tax consequences; see ¶307, ¶332 and ¶359.

(ITA: 6(1)(*a*)(i); IT-502 [Archived]; T4130, "Employer's Guide — Taxable Benefits and Allowances")

[¶358] WORKERS' COMPENSATION — LINES 144, 229, 250

Compensation you receive under an employees' or workers' compensation law in respect of an injury, disability, or death is included in your income, but is deductible in computing your taxable income (¶1000). You therefore pay no tax on the amount received, but it may reduce your entitlement to other deductions or credits available to you or others for whom you qualify as a dependant which are based on net income, such as the personal credit your spouse or common-law partner may claim for you on line 303 of Schedule 1 (see ¶1103). You report such benefits received on line 144 and deduct the same amount on line 250.

Workers' compensation benefits are reported on form T5007 prepared by the relevant workers' compensation authority (here, referred to as "the Board"), and include all amounts paid to you, whether directly from the Board or indirectly from a self-insured or a private insurer which is then reimbursed by the Board. If your claim is filed in Year 1 but not accepted by the Board until Year 2, the slip will be issued in Year 2.

If your employer continues to pay your wages until your claim is accepted, those wages will be subject to normal withholdings and will be reported on your T4 slip. If, in the same year or a later year, your employer receives a Board award, your employer should show that award in the "other information" area of your T4, using code 77. You are permitted to deduct the amount on line 229 of your T1 (see ¶362). If the award is received in a year after the wages were paid, the deduction may create a loss for that year. This will be a non-capital loss (¶1085) which may be carried forward or back, as discussed at ¶1087.

If your employer advances you funds against the anticipated award, the advance is not employment income and is not subject to withholding. If your employer advances an amount in addition to the anticipated claim, that additional amount is employment income and is subject to withholding. If the Board denies the claim, the advance is employment income in the year the claim is denied. If the claim is denied, and your employer utilizes your sick leave credits to repay the advance, the repayment constitutes employment income and is subject to withholding.

Similarly, an insurer may pay you an amount equivalent to your regular salary and will issue a T4A slip. If you or the Board subsequently repays the insurance company, the insurance company will issue a receipt or a letter to you. This will allow you to claim a deduction for the repayment. The T5007 amount will be reported and deducted in the usual fashion.

"Top-up" amounts are sometimes paid by your employer in addition to (and after notice of) a Board award. These amounts are employment income but not insurable earnings; accordingly withholdings will be slightly different.

The T4001 Employer's Guide contains examples of how the employer should report its payments to employees in various workers' compensation situations, and the tax consequences for the employee.

(ITA: 56(1)(v); 110(1)(*f*); IT-202R2 Employees' or workers' compensation; T4001, "Employer's Guide — Payroll Deductions and Remittances"; T4115, "T5007 Guide — Return of Benefits")

[¶359] DEFERRED COMPENSATION, "PHANTOM STOCK" PLANS, UNREGISTERED PENSION PLANS

An employer may establish a scheme which provides that some of your compensation is deferred to a future year, usually after retirement, when your tax rate may be lower. The future compensation may be linked to the value of the employer company's stock, to your earnings, or to other criteria. These deferral arrangements are generally governed by the salary deferral rules discussed at ¶307, although some plans are not salary deferral arrangements, either because of contingencies (see ¶307) or because the purpose is incentive rather than deferral. Typically, your employer will obtain the necessary professional tax advice.

If your employer pays amounts on your behalf to a plan under which you will enjoy future benefits, and the plan is not a registered pension plan (¶357) and is not covered by the salary deferral rules (¶307), the plan will almost certainly be either a Retirement Compensation Arrangement or an Employee Benefit Plan, or, less commonly, a foreign pension plan which is not a Retirement Compensation Arrangement.

[¶359.05] *Retirement Compensation Arrangements*

A Retirement Compensation Arrangement ("RCA") is an unregistered pension plan. An RCA is funded by your employer to provide benefits on retirement or termination of employment, or on a substantial change in the nature of the services you render to your employer. Your employer's contributions to an RCA have no immediate tax consequences to you, but the plan is subject to a special refundable tax, to ensure that the contributions cannot be invested on a pre-tax basis. Payments out of the plan to you will be taxable when received.

Certain government pension plans may be or may choose to be treated as RCAs.

You may be able to deduct certain contributions to an RCA (¶365a) and may, in the case of some foreign plans, defer taxable returns of previously undeducted contributions (¶919).

RCA contributions may limit the amount you can contribute to an RRSP (see Chapter 26).

[¶359.10] *Employee Benefit Plans*

A plan to which your employer has contributed for your benefit which is neither a salary deferral arrangement nor an RCA is probably an Employee Benefit Plan ("EBP"). Amounts contributed by your employer to an EBP are not immediately taxable, but amounts you receive either from the EBP or from disposing of an interest in an EBP are included in your employment income. However, the following amounts are not taxable when received from an EBP:

(1) a death benefit (i.e., the whole amount of the benefit paid on death in recognition of employment services, not only the amount given special non-taxable treatment described at ¶925);

(2) a return of amounts contributed to the plan by you or by a deceased employee of whom you are an heir or the legal representative, to the extent that the amount was not deducted by you or the deceased employee in any taxation year;

(3) a superannuation or pension benefit attributable to your services in a period during which you were not resident in Canada; and

(4) an amount that would be a "designated benefit" if it were paid from an Employee Life and Health Trust. These benefits are taxed under the rules applicable to such plans (see ¶328a).

It is possible that an arrangement might constitute both an employee benefit plan and a salary deferral arrangement. Where a salary deferral arrangement is part of a combination plan providing other benefits, it will be treated as a separate arrangement that is not an employee benefit plan. An ordering rule provides that payments out of a combination plan are generally treated as having been received out of the salary deferral arrangement first, to the extent of prior deferred amounts under that arrangement.

Where your employer has established an employee trust, amounts allocated to you for the year by the trustee are included in your income from an office or employment for the year.

[¶359.15] *Foreign Pension Plans*

See ¶365a.

[¶359.20] *Phantom Plans*

There may be plans which are not subject to any of the rules outlined elsewhere. Typically, these are unfunded plans such as "phantom stock option plans", under which your employer undertakes to pay you a bonus the amount of which depends on the value or change in value of the employer's shares. Provided that the conditions set out at ¶328 are met, so that the plan is not a salary deferral arrangement, you will be taxed on these payments when they are received by you and not at any earlier time.

(ITA: 6(1)(*g*); (*h*); 6(14); 56(1)(*x*)–(*z*); 56(10); 56(11); 207.5–207.7; 212(1)(*j*); IT-502 Employee Benefit Plans and Employee Trusts)

[¶359.25] *Employee Trusts*

An employee trust is an arrangement that meets all of the following conditions:

(1) Payments are made by an employer to a trustee in trust for the sole benefit of employees (or former employees) of the employer or of a person who does not deal at arm's length with the employer.

(2) The right to the benefit vests in the beneficiaries at time of each payment.

(3) The value of the benefit is not dependent on the beneficiary's performance, position, or compensation as an employee.

(4) The trustee allocates annually to the beneficiaries, in a reasonable manner, the total of: (a) the employer's or non-arm's length person's contributions for the year and (b) the annual income of the trust computed without reference to subsection 104(6) — that is, computed without taking into account the deduction a trust can claim for income paid or payable to its beneficiaries. The trust cannot allocate losses to beneficiaries and these cannot be applied to other years' income.

(5) The trustee elects in the T3 Trust Income Tax and Information Return filed within 90 days of the first taxation year of the trust for the trust to be an employee trust.

You are taxed on the amounts allocated to you from an employee trust as employment income, regardless of their nature (interest, capital gains, etc.). Payments to you or for your benefit from the trust are not taxable and your employer can deduct contributions as made.

Employee profit sharing plans and deferred profit sharing plans are not employee trusts.

(ITA: 6(1)(*h*); 248(1) "employee trust"; IT-502 Employee Benefit Plans and Employee Trusts)

[¶360] REASONABLE ALLOWANCES FOR BOARD, LODGING, AND TRANSPORTATION FOR EMPLOYMENT AT A SPECIAL WORK SITE OR REMOTE WORK LOCATION

You are not taxable on board and lodging or a reasonable allowance for board and lodging, if:

(1) you are required to work temporarily at a special work site, which was too far away from your ordinary residence to commute to daily; and

(2) you are required to be away from your ordinary residence, or to be at the location, for a period of at least 36 hours;

OR

(3) you were required to work at a location at which, by virtue of its remoteness from any established community (see ¶361), you could not reasonably be expected to establish and maintain a self-contained domestic establishment (see ¶1122.10); and

(4) you were required to be away from your ordinary residence, or to be at the location, for a period of at least 36 hours.

The requirements of (1) and (2) are referred to as the "special work site" rules, and the requirements of (3) and (4) are the "remote work location" rules. Although the result is the same, so long as one or the other applies, the distinction can be important, as other tax provisions apply in one situation but not the other. This is true for Northern residents deduction limitations, for example, and for an employer's ability to deduct 100% of meal costs.

To meet the requirements (1) of the special work site rules, you must in fact have a "self-contained domestic establishment" at which you are ordinarily resident (see ¶1122.10), that is available for your use, that is not rented out to anyone else, and that is beyond commuting distance from the special work site.

You are also not subject to tax on any allowance or reimbursement received in respect of transportation between your ordinary residence and the special work site as described in (1) and (2), or between your ordinary residence in Canada or country in which you are employed and the remote work site as described in (3) and (4). This applies where the transportation expenses are incurred with respect to the period when you were required to work at that special or remote work site and during which period you received board and lodging, or a reasonable allowance in respect of board and lodging, from your employer.

If all the requirements in (1) and (2) are met, you should confirm this by completing form TD4 and providing it to you employer. The allowances are then not included on your T4 slip.

Where the requirements in (3) and (4) are met you are not required to complete form TD4.

Relevant CRA Documents

Transportation Provided by Someone Other than the Employer

The CRA confirmed that non-taxable transportation need not be provided by the employer. No benefit arises where the transportation to the special work site was provided by the employer's customer. (CRA Document No. 2014-0563801E5)

(ITA: 6(6); IT-91R4 [Archived]; CRA Document No.: Transportation allowance - remote work location, *May 13, 2015*, CRA Document No. 2014-0563801E5)

[¶361] WHAT IS MEANT BY "REMOTENESS", "ESTABLISHED COMMUNITY", AND "TEMPORARILY"?

These terms are not defined in the Act, so the CRA has developed policies on how it will interpret them.

Factors considered in judging remoteness are:

(1) the availability of transportation;

(2) the distance from an established community; and

(3) the time required to travel that distance.

A work location is generally considered by the CRA to be remote if the nearest established community with a population of 1,000 or more is no closer than 80 kilometres by the most direct route normally travelled.

The CRA considers "established community" to mean a body of people who reside in the same locality and who are permanently settled in that location. A location will not be an established community if it lacks essential services or such services are not available within a reasonable commuting distance. Essential services include a basic food store, a basic clothing store with merchandise in stock (not a mail-order outlet), and access to certain medical assistance and educational facilities.

Whether you are working temporarily at a special work site depends on the duties you perform and not on the expected duration of the project as a whole. The following factors are considered in determining if the work is temporary in nature:

(1) the nature of the work you are to perform;

(2) the overall time estimated for a project, or the particular phase of a project on which you will work; and

(3) the agreed period of time stated in the employment contract or other terms of the engagement.

(IT-91R4 [Archived])

[¶361a] NORTHERN RESIDENTS — LINE 255

[¶361a.05] *General Requirements*

There are two special deductions available for residents of northern areas:

(1) an employee may claim a travel benefit deduction for certain travel benefits provided by an employer (the "travel benefits deduction"); and

(2) all individuals, whether or not employees, may claim a deduction simply for residing in a prescribed northern area and, in some cases, their housing costs (the "residence deduction").

You are only eligible to claim these special deductions if you resided in one or more prescribed areas throughout a six-month period commencing or ending in the taxation year for which a return is being filed.

Two different northern areas are prescribed: the "intermediate zone" and the "northern zone". If you reside in the intermediate zone, you may only claim one-half of the amounts that would be calculated if you lived in the northern zone.

The zone in which you reside, generally speaking, is determined under the rules in ¶1504.

If you move from place to place or from zone to zone in the north, you will qualify for the deductions as long as you meet the overall six-month test. In such a case, your travel benefits deduction is calculated by reference to the zone in which you were employed at the time of the travel; the northern residence deduction is calculated based on the number of days you resided in each zone.

You calculate the deductions using form T2222 and enter the deductions on line 255. If your return is paper-filed, the form should accompany it. Otherwise, simply retain it and produce it should the CRA request it. Both deductions are frequently audited by the CRA. The form includes a useful information sheet, "Northern Residents Deductions".

[¶361a.10] *Geographical Areas*

There are two geographical areas which entitle residents to these special deductions.

Residents of the "northern zone" are entitled to the full deductions described below. Residents of the "intermediate zone" are entitled to half the deduction otherwise calculated.

The northern zone includes all of Labrador, the Yukon, Nunavut and Northwest Territories, and certain areas of each province except Nova Scotia, Newfoundland (except for Labrador), New Brunswick and Prince Edward Island. There are similarly intermediate zones in each province except the four Atlantic provinces (saving Sable Island in Nova Scotia, which is an intermediate zone). The CRA website contains a voluminous list of place names which are in either zone.

[¶361a.15] *Travel Benefits Deduction*

If you are employed in a prescribed zone, you may claim a deduction in computing your taxable income in respect of certain taxable travel benefits provided to you or your family.

Two types of taxable travel benefits qualify for the deduction:

(1) All trips made by you or a member of your household for the purpose of obtaining necessary medical services not available locally. The CRA's policy is that if it is necessary for the patient to have an attendant, another member of the household may accompany the patient and the employer-paid cost of this will also qualify for the deduction.

(2) Not more than two trips made for any other purpose in a calendar year by you and each member of your household.

For each trip, the deduction is the least of three amounts:

(1) the cost of the return economy airfare to the designated city nearest to your place of residence at the time of travel. The designated cities are Vancouver, Edmonton, Calgary, Saskatoon, Winnipeg, North Bay, Toronto, Ottawa, Montreal, Quebec City, Moncton, Halifax and St. John's;

(2) the actual cost of the trip to you; and

(3) the benefit included in your income for the employer's contribution to the cost of your travel.

Although airfares fix a maximum allowable deduction under these rules, you are not obliged to travel by air. If you use some other form of transportation, the actual costs you incur in making the trip will be relevant (item (2), above) and may limit your deduction.

In theory, deductions based on travel in your personal motor vehicle are calculated by recording the annual costs of operating and maintaining the vehicle (gas, insurance, maintenance, taxes, financing costs) and prorating these by the kilometres driven on the deductible trip. Administratively, the CRA allows you to determine the cost of using your vehicle using a fixed per kilometre amount. These are shown in the table at ¶87.

Similarly, if you are not travelling by air, you may include your meal expenses in the cost of travel. You have the choice of recording your actual expenses (which must be reasonable) supported by receipts, or you may use the flat rate meal allowance fixed by the CRA, also shown in the table at ¶87. If you opt for the allowance system, receipts are not required.

You cannot claim a deduction for travel expenses to the extent that you or any member of your household received, or was entitled to receive, non-taxable amounts as travel assistance, a travel allowance, or as a reimbursement for those expenses, or if someone else has already claimed the deduction for travel expenses for the trip. You may not claim expenses to the extent medical expense credit is claimed for them.

To claim the travel benefits deductions, you must receive the taxable travel benefits in the same year you have the travel expenses. Thus, if a trip straddles a year end, the deduction must be claimed for the year in which employment benefits in respect of the trip are taxable (presumably the year the benefits are received).

[¶361a.20] *Northern Residence Deduction*

If you meet the six-month residency requirements discussed in ¶361a.05 you may claim a deduction in respect of being resident in the north and a further deduction (one per household) in respect of a self-contained domestic establishment which you maintained and in which you resided. This deduction can be claimed whether you are employed or not and, if you are employed, may be claimed in addition to the travel benefits deduction.

If you lived in the prescribed northern zone in a taxation year, you may deduct the lesser of

(1) 20% of your income for the taxation year, and

(2) the total of:

- $11 per day for the number of days in your residency period in the zone; plus
- $11 per day for the number of days in your residency period in the zone in which you maintained and lived in a self-contained domestic establishment. Only one person may claim the deduction for maintaining a self-contained domestic establishment in respect of any particular day. You may share the deduction among qualifying residents of the household as long as no two persons claim the deduction in respect of the same day.

If you lived in the intermediate zone, you may deduct the lesser of (i) 20% of your income for the taxation year, and (ii) one-half of the per diem amounts calculated for a northern zone.

A "self-contained domestic establishment" is a dwelling-house, apartment, or other similar place of residence in which a person as a general rule eats or sleeps (see ¶1122.10). The CRA comments that, generally,

> this is a complete and separate living unit with a kitchen, bathroom, sleeping facilities, and its own private access. It includes a house, apartment, mobile home, or other similar place of residence in which a person usually sleeps and eats. It does not include a bunkhouse, dormitory, hotel room, or room in a boarding house.

The residence deduction is further limited if:

(1) you normally reside outside a prescribed area and have been employed at a special work site in a prescribed area; and

(2) you have received benefits which would normally be taxable as employment income but are excluded from your income by virtue of the reduction for board and lodging at a special work site described at ¶360 condition (1) (but not a remote work site at ¶360 condition (3)). The impact of these exclusions on your Northern residence claim is discussed at ¶361a.25.

Example

Joe lived in the northern zone throughout the year, which was not a leap year. Initially, he lived in a hotel room but he moved into an apartment on July 1 with his friend Elise, with whom he shared the unit. Joe can claim $4,015 (365 days at $11 per day) as the basic claim for his residency period. Elise is entitled to a similar claim for the number of days she lived in northern zone. An additional amount of $11 per day can be claimed for the 184 days that Joe and Elise shared the apartment. Either Elise or Joe can make the claim for any particular day so long as their total claim does not exceed $2,024 (184 days at $11 per day). Each must limit the deduction to 20% of his or her income.

(ITA: 110.7; 248(1) "self-contained domestic establishment"; ITR: 7303.1 [Prescribed northern and intermediate zones]; 7304 [Prescribed amount – northern residents deduction])

[¶361a.25] *Special and Remote Work Sites and Northern Residents Deductions*

If you are employed at a special work site (see ¶360), your entitlement to receive a non-taxable allowance for board and lodging and your entitlement to the northern residence deduction are coordinated.

Employment at a Special Work Site

If you qualify to receive non-taxable board and lodging benefits under the special work site exclusion (see ¶360 conditions (1) and (2)) you must generally reduce the northern residence deduction you are otherwise entitled to by non-taxable benefits, provided that the benefits relate to a period for which you qualify for the deduction. The reduction does not apply, however, if the special work site is at least 30 kilometres outside the nearest population centre of at least 40,000 people. (This is the same test which allows a deduction of 100% of the cost of meals at such a work site; see ¶734).

Example

Joe in the example at ¶361a.20 worked for two weeks at a special work site, which was 20 kilometres outside Edmonton. His employer provided bunkhouse accommodation on the site. The employer calculated that the value of the housing benefit Joe received was $1,200.

During the two weeks at the special site, Joe did not reside in a northern zone and he cannot claim the $11 per diem basic residency amount.

If Joe worked at the site prior to July 1, the benefit is taxable because prior to that date he did not maintain a home — he was living in a hotel.

If he worked at the site after June 30, the benefit is not taxable, because he maintained an apartment, but the $1,200 non-taxable benefit reduces the northern residence deduction to which he is entitled. In fact, the $1,200 benefit completely eliminates the $11 per diem deduction he could otherwise claim. Presumably, though, Elise can claim the additional residency amount for those two weeks.

If the special work site had been 30 kilometres or more from the nearest community of 40,000 or more, the post-June 30 non-taxable board and lodging benefit would not reduce his northern residence deduction.

Employment at a Remote Work Site

If you are employed at a remote work site (see ¶360 conditions (3) and (4)) and receive non-taxable board and lodging benefits, these benefits do not reduce the northern residence deduction to which you are otherwise entitled.

(IT-91R4 [Archived]; T4130, "Employer's Guide — Taxable Benefits and Allowances")

[¶361d] DISABILITY-RELATED EMPLOYMENT BENEFITS

If you are blind or have been certified as disabled on form T2201 (see ¶1209) by reason of a mobility impairment, you are not taxable on either the amount paid by your employer or a reasonable allowance given to you for transportation to and from work, including parking costs.

If you have been certified as disabled (on form T2201) for any reason, you are not taxable on the amount paid by your employer, or a reasonable allowance given to you, for an attendant to assist you in performing your employment duties.

(ITA: 6(16))

DEDUCTIONS FROM EMPLOYMENT INCOME

[¶362] WHAT YOU CAN DEDUCT FROM EMPLOYMENT INCOME

You are entitled to claim only very limited types of expenses you incur in earning your employment income.

Documentation Requirements

Specific supporting documentation is required for many employment-related deductions or credits:

(1) Pension plan contributions — T4 slip

(2) Automobile, travel, office, and supplies expenses — form T2200

(3) Trade union, professional, or like dues — official receipt from union or society, or T4 slip

(4) Employment insurance premiums and Canada Pension Plan or Quebec Pension Plan contributions — T4 slip

(5) Transport employees' board and lodging — TL2

You should always be prepared to support your claim for all deductions. For expenses other than those itemized above, and as described in the following sections, you should be careful to retain the related invoices, receipts, cancelled cheques and other documents for review by the CRA should they request them.

If your return is filed electronically, you are not required to submit any of the supporting documentation unless you are asked to do so by the CRA. If you paper-file your return, you should include with it a copy of your T4 slip and the receipts supporting your claim for professional memberships and union dues, if the latter are not reported on your T4. If you claim automobile expenses, the CRA asks that you submit form T777 with your paper-filed return, as it supports your calculation of the amount you can deduct.

If you incur a specific deductible expense, such as a professional membership fee, and you are reimbursed by your employer in full or in part, you can only deduct the portion that is not reimbursed.

If you are entitled to deduct expenses, the amount you deduct should always include any GST/HST that you paid. You may be able to recover a portion of the tax, as described at ¶363.10.

(5000-G, "General Income Tax and Benefit Guide" (T1 Guide), line 229; T4044, "Employment Expenses")

[¶362.10] *Deductions Offset by Reimbursements*

A specific rule requires that you take into your employment income amounts received as awards or reimbursements of amounts otherwise deductible from employment income. The award or reimbursement need not be made by your employer; any recovery of an amount deductible from employment income is to be treated as employment income. The rule does not apply if you have reduced the amount you deducted by the award or reimbursement. Although it is worded generally, this provision is aimed primarily at your deduction for legal expenses where you are awarded costs.

(ITA: 6(1)(*j*))

[¶362.15] *Repayment of Salary or Wages — Line 229*

You may deduct an amount you pay, or that is paid on your behalf, under an arrangement requiring you to reimburse employment income you were paid for a period in which you did not perform your duties of employment. Your deduction cannot exceed the employment income you received for the period of non-performance of employment duties.

The repayment is included in your calculation of other employment expenses on form 777, and carries up to line 229.

It is quite possible that the income inclusion will occur in one year and the repayment and corresponding deduction in a later year. If the repayment exceeds your other income for the year the excess is a non-capital loss, which can be carried back three years or carried forward for twenty years (see ¶1085).

The same treatment is available if you reside in Quebec, but you have the option of claiming a refundable tax credit instead. See ¶1676d.

(ITA: 8(1)(*n*))

[¶363] EMPLOYMENT INCOME AND GST/HST

The federal Goods and Services Tax ("GST") is a broad-based consumption tax that applies at 5% to most goods and services supplied in Canada. The harmonized sales tax ("HST") is an extension of the GST, administered under the same legislation, but levied at a higher and varying rate in harmonized (or "participating") provinces of New Brunswick, Nova Scotia, and Newfoundland and Labrador from 1997, Ontario from 2010, and Prince Edward Island from 2013. The combined tax is referred to as GST/HST.

Quebec, which already had a sales tax regime similar to the GST, further harmonized its QST with the GST on January 1, 2013. However, Quebec is not a participating province under the GST/HST, and the QST remains a separate provincial sales tax, even though it is substantially equivalent to the GST.

These taxes have several income tax implications. The impact on employment income is considered here.

[¶363.05] *GST/HST on Taxable Benefits*

If you receive a benefit from your employer and the cost of the related property or service is used in determining the benefit amount that is taxable to you, the cost must include GST/HST (and provincial sales tax, if applicable). This is true even if your employer recovers the GST/HST it pays as an input tax credit or a rebate or if your employer is exempt from paying either GST/HST or provincial sales tax. The benefit your employer includes in your income and reports on your T4 will therefore be calculated as though the taxes were paid. However, no GST/HST is included on benefits which are exempt from GST/HST by their nature.

Example

Sandra's employer pays for her coverage under a group life insurance policy and also provides her with an automobile. In calculating her taxable benefits, the cost of the insurance is simply the premium paid, as insurance is exempt from GST/HST. The purchase of the automobile is a taxable supply and her employer pays GST/HST, which it recovers as an input tax credit. Sandra's standby charge benefit is, however, calculated on the cost including GST/HST. If Sandra lives in a non-participating province that has a retail sales tax, the automobile's cost for purposes of calculating her benefit also includes that tax.

Employer Remits GST/HST on Taxable Benefits

Although it does not affect you as the employee directly, your employer is required to remit GST/HST on the value of any benefit taxed under paragraphs 6(1)(*a*) (general benefits — but only to the extent the underlying goods and services are not zero-rated or exempt by nature), (*e*) (automobile standby charge), and (*k*) and (*l*) (automobile operating cost benefits). The remittance is calculated by applying a prescribed factor to the total value of the taxable benefits, as follows:

Province/Territory (effective 2016)	Non-Auto Taxable Benefit	Auto Standby Taxable Benefit	Auto Operating Cost Benefit
British Columbia	4/104	4/104	3%
Alberta	4/104	4/104	3%
Saskatchewan	4/104	4/104	3%
Manitoba	4/104	4/104	3%
Ontario (non-large enterprise)	12/112	12/112	9%
Ontario (large enterprise)[1]	12/112	4/104	7.2%
Quebec[2]	4/104	4/104	3%
New Brunswick	14/114[3]	14/114[1]	10%[4]
Nova Scotia	14/114	14/114	11%
Prince Edward (non-large enterprise)	14/114[5]	14/114[3]	10.25%[6]
Prince Edward Island (large enterprise)	14/114[3]	4/104	6.5%
Newfoundland and Labrador	14/114[1]	14/114[1]	10%[2]
Northwest Territories	4/104	4/104	3%
Nunavut	4/104	4/104	3%
Yukon Territory	4/104	4/104	3%

[1] The different rates for auto operating costs and auto standby benefits are for large enterprises, subject to the recapture of input tax credits on the supplied vehicles.

[2] The ratios in the chart depict only the GST rates.

[3] 14/114 factor effective July 1, 2016, prior factor is 12/112.

[4] This is a blended factor taking into account the increase of the HST rate of July 1; in 2017 the factor is 11%.

[5] This is the factor effective October 1, 2016; prior to October the factor is 13/113.

[6] This is a blended factor taking into account the HST increase of October 1. In 2017, the factor is 11%.

(ITA: 6(7))

[¶363.10] *GST/HST Rebate on Employment Income Deductions — Line 457*

If you are employed by a GST registrant other than a listed financial institution, and you deduct employment expenses, you are entitled to recover the GST/HST included in the amounts you deduct. The recovery is claimed as a rebate on your income tax return. The rebate is calculated using a ratio which is intended to measure the GST/HST included in your deductible expenses. The ratio varies with the GST/HST rate that applies in the province where you acquired the goods and services, which is not necessarily the province in which you live and pay provincial taxes. The rebate is calculated on the amount you deduct and will therefore be reduced to the extent your employer covered a portion of your expenses, either by reimbursement or allowance.

Your GST/HST rebate claim must be filed within four years of the end of the year to which it relates.

If you are employed in a non-participating province your rebate is calculated as:

$$A \times (B - C)$$

where

- A is the GST ratio (currently 5/105),
- B is the amount deducted from income or claimed as capital cost allowance, and
- C is the total of all reimbursements you received, or are entitled to receive, from your employer in respect of the amount deducted.

In participating provinces, the HST rate substitutes the GST rate, as follows:

Employee Rebate Ratios (2016)

	Employee Rebate
Ontario	13/113
Quebec — GST	5/105
N.S.	15/115
N.B., Nfld. and Lab. (expenses incurred up to June 30, 2016)	13/113
N.B., Nfld. and Lab. (expenses incurred from July 1, 2016 on).	15/115
P.E.I. (expenses incurred prior to October 1, 2016)	14/114
P.E.I. (expenses incurred from October 1, 2016 on)	15/115
B.C., Alta., Sask., Man.	5/105

Employee Rebate Ratios (2015, 2014)

	Employee Rebate
P.E.I.	14/114
Ontario	13/113
Quebec — GST	5/105
N.S.	15/115
N.B., Nfld. and Lab.	13/113
B.C., Alta., Sask., Man.	5/105

Employee Rebate Ratios (2013)

	Employee Rebate
B.C.	6.75/106.75
Ontario	13/113
Quebec — GST	5/105
N.S.	15/115
N.B., Nfld. and Lab.	13/113
P.E.I. (expenses incurred prior to April 1, 2013)	5/105
P.E.I. (expenses incurred after April 1, 2013)	14/114
Alta., Sask., Man.	5/105

As with all items you claim, you must maintain records to support the rebate. If you incur deductible employment expenses in both participating and non-participating provinces (for example, where you travel on business during the year), your records must separate expenses that include only GST from those that include HST.

GST/HST Rebate and Allowances — Employer Certification

The rebate is only available on expenses you can deduct in computing your income. It follows that if you are in receipt of allowance related to your employment, and the allowance is not taxable, you will not be entitled to a rebate for the costs the allowance is designed to cover as you cannot deduct these expenses. Although it does not affect you directly, your employer is allowed a recovery of the GST/HST that is deemed to be included in such a non-taxable allowance.

A problem can arise if your employer pays you an allowance which is considered to be reasonable at the time but which you ultimately determine is too low and, therefore, both unreasonable and taxable to you. As you will now be required to take the allowance into income, you can claim your related expenses and the GST/HST rebate on the costs you deduct. However, your employer will also have recovered GST/HST on the allowance as it was paid to you.

To deal with this potential conflict, your employer is required to certify on your form GST370 that you were not in receipt of a non-taxable reasonable allowance with respect to the costs on which you are claiming the rebate. Presumably, on giving this certification, your employer will repay any GST/HST it previously recovered on the allowance.

[¶363.20] *Which Employees are Eligible for GST/HST Rebates*

You are entitled to claim the GST/HST employee rebate if your employer is registered for GST/HST purposes, unless your employer is a "listed financial institution", such as a bank, investment dealer, trust company, insurance company, credit union, or a business whose principal activity is lending money. Financial institutions are typically registered but do not generally collect GST/HST on their revenues; accordingly, their employees may not claim the rebate.

Most provincial and federal government departments are registered, from which it follows that if you are employed by a provincial government or the federal government, you are entitled to claim the rebate if you deduct employment expenses.

(ETA: 174; 253)

[¶363.30] *CRA Form and Guides*

Claim your GST/HST rebate by completing form GST370, "Employee and Partner GST/HST Rebate Application". As noted above, your employer is required to certify it. The rebate itself is claimed at line 457 of your income tax return, and is treated effectively as though it were an income tax instalment payment.

[¶363.35] *GST/HST Rebate Taxable in Following Year — Line 104*

Your GST/HST rebate is a recovery of an amount you deducted for income tax purposes, so the rebate is included in your income when you receive it. The rebate is received when your return on which the rebate is claimed is assessed, as the rebate will either be paid to you as part of your refund or applied against tax owing. In your return for the year in which the assessment is issued (typically the year following the rebate claim), you must include the rebate on line 104 of your federal return, "Other Employment Income".

If you reside in Quebec, and have received a QST rebate under similar Quebec rules, you must also include the Quebec rebate on the federal return. Likewise, both federal and Quebec rebates are included in your income for Quebec purposes on line 107 of the Quebec return.

A special rule applies where your GST/HST rebate is calculated on your capital cost allowance deduction (see ¶370 and ¶379). This portion of your rebate is not added to your income directly but reduces the capital cost of the asset on which the capital cost allowance was claimed.

[¶363.40] *Value of Rebate*

Many employees find that their rebate is not a material amount, and you will want to consider whether the rebate you will receive justifies the additional accounting and record keeping needed to support it.

Example 1: Purchased Automobile

Brian purchased a car in a non-participating province. The car cost $23,000 and he paid $1,840 provincial sales tax ("PST") and $1,150 GST so that the capital cost of the car is $25,990. Brian also paid $4,000 in operating expenses in the year, all of which were subject to GST/HST. The car is used 25% for employment purposes. Brian can deduct capital cost allowance ("CCA") of (25% × $25,990 × 15% (CCA rate for year of acquisition)) = $975, plus the operating expenses of $1,000, for a total of $1,975.

Brian's GST rebate is 5/105 × $975 = $46.43 on the capital cost allowance and 5/105 × $1,000 = $47.62 on the $1,000 operating expenses, for a total of $94.05.

The rebate is based on Brian's capital cost allowance deduction and therefore it is prorated for his employment use. Similarly, if the maximum capital cost were limited under the rules at ¶370, that limit is reflected in the amount on which he can claim the rebate. On the other hand, Brian's capital cost includes the provincial sales tax he paid, and the rebate calculation does not attempt to adjust for this.

Brian will include $47.62 in his income and will reduce the undepreciated capital cost of his car by $46.43, both in the year his return is assessed.

Example 2: Expenses Subject to Varying Rates of GST/HST

Paula is a commissioned salesperson and she qualifies to deduct the related expenses she incurs. In the current year, her deductible expenses, including all taxes, are $5,000, none of which relates to capital cost allowance. $4,000 of these were incurred in her home province, where the GST/HST rate is 13%. The other $1,000 were incurred on a trip she made to call on a major client in a province where the GST/HST rate is 15%.

Her rebate is 13/113 × $4,000 = $460.18 plus 15/115 × $1,000 = $130.43, or $590.61. She records the rebate as employment income in the year her return is assessed.

(ETA: 123; 165(1); 253; ITA: 6(1)(e.1); 6(7); 6(8))

[¶363.45] *Quebec QST Rebate*

The Quebec sales tax ("QST") follows the GST model in many respects; accordingly, it allows employees to claim QST rebates on deductible employment expenses (¶1624). The GST/HST and QST are separate taxes with separate rates, so you must also claim the rebates separately. As discussed at ¶363.35, your QST rebate is accounted for in the same manner as the federal rebate: the rebate relating to capital cost allowance reduces the undepreciated capital cost of the asset; the rebate relating to other expenses is taken into income, both in the year the rebate is received.

(ITA: 6(1)(j); 12(1)(x); 13(7.1); 13(7.4))

[¶365] REGISTERED PENSION PLAN CONTRIBUTIONS — LINE 207

If you participate in a registered pension plan, your contributions to the plan are deductible at line 207. These contributions are reported in Box 20 of your T4 slip.

Your employer's contribution to the plan, if any, is not a taxable benefit to you.

The total benefits that accrue to you under a registered pension plan are coordinated with the amounts you are able to contribute to other deferred income plans, specifically Deferred Profit Sharing Plans or Registered Retirement Savings Plans. This coordination is reflected in a "pension adjustment" which your employer calculates and reports to you in Box 52 of your T4 slip and which limits your ability to make contributions to these other plans. Enter your pension adjustment at Line 206 on your return. The amount is not taxable; it must simply be reported.

Contributions to your pension plan are governed by the plan itself and, as the plan must be registered, are limited by the rules administered by the CRA. These rules permit a deduction for current contributions to your pension plan to reflect the purchase of coverage for prior years or to reflect enhancements to the plan, all subject to strict limits. These rules are summarized at ¶2645 *et seq.*

(ITR: 8300(1) "individual pension plan"; 8304(10) Individual Pension Plans)

[¶365.05] *Past Service Contributions: The Interest Factor in Buying Past Service Pension*

If you borrow to make contributions to a registered pension plan, the interest is not deductible.

If you elect to pay a past service contribution in a year, you will likely be required to pay accrued interest in addition to the basic contribution for the past services. If the past service contribution, including accrued interest, is to be paid in instalments, it is probable that further interest will have to be paid in respect of each instalment.

The CRA's position is that such interest is simply included in your past-service contribution and is deductible to the extent the contribution is, if you elected to make past service contributions after 1981. This policy is set out in Chapter 1 of CRA Guide T4040.

[¶365.10] *Contributions to Certain U.S. Plans*

If you contribute under the *Railroad Retirement Tax Act* of the United States, your contributions are considered to have been made to an Employee Benefit Plan and are not deductible (see ¶359.10). You are not taxed on a withdrawal of your contributions to the plan.

Relevant CRA Documents

No Foreign Tax Credit

Payments of U.S. Social Security tax ("FICA" tax) are not deductible, but may, in some circumstances, be claimed as the payment of foreign tax. See ¶367 and ¶1450. (CRA Document No. 2004-0103871E5)

[¶365.15] *Other Pension Issues*

The taxation of pension benefits you receive is discussed at ¶911. Rollovers of pension benefits are discussed at ¶1021. The treatment of retirement income of various kinds is covered at ¶903–¶925. Planning issues are considered at ¶2555.

(ITA: 8(1)(m); 18(10); 18(11); 248(1) "additional voluntary contribution"; T4040, "RRSPs and Other Registered Plans for Retirement")

[¶365a] FOREIGN AND UNREGISTERED PENSION PLANS — LINE 207

An unregistered Canadian pension plan is typically a Retirement Compensation Arrangement ("RCA"). Contributions you make under an RCA are deductible, as discussed at ¶359. As a general rule, contributions you make to a foreign pension plan are not deductible.

Exception — U.S. Short-term Assignment in Canada

The Canada–U.S. income tax treaty addresses the case of a short-term assignment where you participate in a "qualifying retirement plan" ("QRP") in one state (the "home state") and you perform your services as an employee for a limited period of time, generally up to five years, in the other state (the "host state"). Thus, if your home state is the United States and you work temporarily in Canada, your contributions to a U.S. QRP are covered by this treaty provision and may be deductible.

In order for the contributions to be deductible, the following criteria must be met:

(1) you must perform your employment services in the host state (that is, Canada) and your remuneration for such services must be taxable in Canada;

(2) you must have been participating in the QRP (or a similar substituted plan) before you began performing your employment services in Canada;

(3) you must not have been a resident of Canada immediately before you began to perform those services;

(4) you are limited in performing your services to no more than 60 of the 120 months preceding the current year;

(5) the contributions to, and the benefits from, the QRP are attributable to the services performed in Canada and are made or accrued during the time you perform the services; and

(6) you generally do not participate in any other QRP during the taxation year.

Your deduction in Canada is limited to the amount that would have been deductible in the United States if the services had been rendered there.

If you qualify for this deduction, complete form RC267 to substantiate the deduction you claim. This form also requires that you compute the pension adjustment that arises from your contributions to the QRP. As discussed at ¶365, your pension adjustment limits your ability to contribute to other registered deferred income plans.

Transfer of Lump Sum Amounts from a Foreign Pension Plan

There is a provision for the contribution of lump-sum payments received out of foreign plans to Canadian RRSPs or registered pension plans; see ¶1021. This treatment is explicitly extended to U.S. IRAs; see ¶919. Contributions to foreign government pension plans may be regulated by tax or social security treaties; see ¶367 and ¶2080.04.

(ITA: 6(1)(*g*); 8(1)(*m*.2); 60(*j*); 248(1) "retirement compensation arrangement"; IT-502 Employee Benefit Plans and Employee Trusts)

[¶367] U.S. SOCIAL SECURITY

If you are or will be employed in the United States as well as in Canada, you may find you are required to make both Canada Pension Plan and U.S. Social Security contributions. There is an agreement in place between Canada and the United States, the "Totalization Agreement", under which problems that arise as a result can be resolved in advance. See ¶2111.

If you have had U.S. Social Security ("FICA") payments withheld, you may claim a Canadian foreign tax credit to the extent you report U.S.-source income (see ¶1450). However, under the Totalization Agreement, if you are a U.S. citizen on a permanent assignment to Canada (greater than 60 months) FICA payments you make are not creditable in Canada as foreign taxes.

See ¶921 for the income inclusion rules relating to U.S. Social Security benefits.

[¶368] COMMISSION SALESPERSONS' EXPENSES

If you are employed as a salesperson and are paid, in whole or in part, by commissions, you are entitled to deduct all expenses incurred in earning your commissions, provided:

(1) you are required to pay your own expenses;

(2) you do not receive a non-taxable travel allowance (see ¶337);

(3) you ordinarily perform you duties away from your employer's office; and

(4) your employer confirms your conditions of employment using form T2200.

Your expense deduction cannot exceed the commissions you received during the year, and your claim is subject to the overriding limitation that only 50% of food, beverage, and entertainment expenses are deductible (¶734).

You must meet all of the conditions above to claim under this provision. If you do not, you may be able to claim some expenses under the other provisions applicable to employees generally.

Travelling Allowances

The rules governing travelling allowances are discussed at ¶337. A per-kilometre allowance that is reasonable in amount is not taxable so that, if you receive such an allowance, you cannot deduct your expenses as a salesperson.

If you receive travelling allowances which are non-taxable as they relate to non-motor vehicle items but taxable as they relate to motor vehicles (¶335), you can include both allowances in income and claim actual expenses as deductions to the extent of commission income. You also have the alternative of excluding the non-taxable allowance, including the taxable motor vehicle allowance and claiming the motor vehicle expenses under ¶369, which is not limited to commission income.

Expenses are Limited by Commissions Earned

While expenses claimed under this provision are generally limited by your commission income for the year, an exception is made for interest or capital cost allowance on a motor vehicle or an aircraft used to earn employment income. If these deductions cause your expenses to exceed your commission income, the excess continues to be deductible. One result is that you can claim capital cost allowance on a motor vehicle in excess of your commission income, but not the cost of leasing a motor vehicle.

Even if you otherwise qualify, you are not required to deduct your employment expenses under this provision. Where your expenses will exceed your commissions, and will therefore be limited, you may be better off claiming your expenses under the other rules that are available, and where the commission-limitation does not apply:

(1) office rent, salaries, and supplies (see ¶372);

(2) office-in-home expenses (these are limited by your employment income) (see ¶373);

(3) motor vehicle and other travel expenses (see ¶369).

A claim for motor vehicle and other travelling expenses (¶369) cannot be made if you make a claim under the rules that apply to a commission salesperson, but you are allowed to claim office rent and office-in-home expenses even if you make a commission salesperson claim. You may benefit by claiming other expenses up to the amount of your commissions, and making the office rent and office-in-home claims against the balance of your employment income (base salary, for example), if any.

General Limitations on Expenses

The limitations which generally apply to the deduction of outlays and expenses must be taken into account when you calculate your commission salesperson deductions.

Meals and Entertainment. You may only deduct 50% of the cost of these items, in accordance with the rules discussed at ¶734. In addition, the cost of your own meals can only be deducted if they are consumed during periods of at least 12 hours during which you were required by your duties:

(1) to be away from the municipality of the employer's establishment to which you normally report, and

(2) to be away from the metropolitan area (if any) in which that establishment is located.

It is only your own meals that are subject to this limitation so that if you take a client or prospective client to lunch locally, you may deduct the cost to you of the client's meal (subject to the overriding 50% limitation) but not your own.

Purchased Motor Vehicles. The amount on which you can claim capital cost allowance is restricted as discussed at ¶810a. Similarly, your interest expense on a vehicle loan is limited to the amount shown in the "Daily interest limit" column in the table at ¶370.05.

Leased Motor Vehicles. If you lease your vehicle, your deductible leasing payments are limited as discussed at ¶738.

Other Expenses. You are entitled to deduct all legitimate business expenses which will include trade association fees, telephone charges, payment to lease cell phones, computers and other equipment (but not capital cost allowance if you purchase these items), home office expenses (subject to specific rules), secretary's wages, entertainment, commissions paid for sales leads, advertising and promotion, licensing fees, insurance and bonding premiums, and so on.

Although you may claim the employment-related portion of capital cost allowance on your motor vehicle or aircraft, you may not claim a terminal loss on their disposal. You cannot claim any deductions for maintenance of recreational facilities, or for club dues.

As with tax reporting in general, you are required to maintain documentation to support all amounts you deduct, should the CRA ask for it.

Relevant Case Law

Away from your Employer's Office

In *Verrier v. The Queen*, 90 DTC 6202 (FCA), the Court ruled that an automobile salesperson was entitled to claim under this provision although there was no explicit contract specifying where he performed his duties. The evidence was that the salesperson spent much time away from the showroom visiting customers and potential customers, meeting them with demonstrator cars, socializing with them, and so on. In *McKee v. The Queen*, 90 DTC 6205 (FCA), the same result was reached where the employee was required to spend six hours a day in the showroom.

(ITA: 8(1)(*f*); 8(1)(*j*); 8(4); 8(10); 220(2.1); T4044, "Employment Expenses", Chapter 2; IT-522R [Archived], para. 37)

[¶368.05] *Payment for Client List*

In *Gifford v. The Queen*, 2004 DTC 6120 (SCC), the Court confirmed the denial of a deduction claimed under the commission salesperson provisions for a $100,000 payment made by a securities salesman to access a departing salesman's client list. The Court found that the $100,000 payment was on capital account and therefore not deductible.

[¶368.20] *More than One Employer*

It is the CRA's view that the deduction limitation operates on an employer-by-employer basis.

Where an employee changed employers in the year and had expenses in excess of income in the year from Employer A, he could not claim the excess against income from Employer B.

(CRA Document No.: Repayment of Salary, *March 6, 2006*, CRA Document No. 2004-0103391E5)

[¶368.25] *Employment of Assistant*

In *Longtin v. The Queen*, 2006 DTC 3254 (TCC), the Court allowed a commission salesman to deduct the cost of his wife as an employee under either the deduction for salespersons' expenses at ¶368 or the deduction for an assistant at ¶372.03. There was no specific requirement in the salesman's contract that he employ an assistant, and the employer did not assert (on form T2200) that one was required. The Court nevertheless accepted that the facts overrode the T2200 requirement, to infer that the employment of a subordinate was required.

In *Alvin Burlando v. Her Majesty the Queen*, 2014 DTC 1105 (TCC), a commission car sales manager was denied an employment expense deduction for payments he made to his wife who worked at home as his assistant in selling cars. Burlando failed to produce documentation to prove that his wife worked for him and assisted him in the selling of vehicles.

[¶369] AUTOMOBILE OR OTHER TRAVELLING EXPENSES OF EMPLOYEES

You may deduct your travelling expenses provided:

(1) you are ordinarily required to work away from your employer's place of business or in different places;

(2) you are required by your employer to pay your own travelling expenses; and

(3) you do not receive a non-taxable allowance for travelling expenses from your employer by virtue of exemptions for allowances of salespersons (¶335), clergy persons (¶336), or other employees (¶337).

The rules separate motor vehicle allowances from other travel allowances under rule (3), so that a tax-free travel allowance for other than motor vehicle use will not deny a deduction for motor vehicle expenses and a tax-free motor vehicle allowance will not disqualify the deduction of other travel expenses, if you meet the other conditions above.

If you are entitled to deduct your motor vehicle expenses, your deduction will be limited by the rules in ¶370 below.

As with any claim for employment expenses, your employer must certify your conditions of employment using form T2200.

Reasonable Allowances

There is no fixed rule for determining whether an allowance for travelling expenses other than for the use of a motor vehicle is reasonable. This will always be a question of fact. As noted at ¶335, however, an allowance for the use of a motor vehicle can be unreasonable in fact (either too low or too high) or it will be deemed to be unreasonable if it is calculated on anything other than business-related kilometres drive or if it is accompanied by an expense reimbursement.

If you receive a non-taxable allowance which is less than your deductible expenses would be, either in the travel expense or motor vehicle category, the question arises as to whether you can add the allowance to income and deduct the expenses.

In *The Queen v. Mina*, 88 DTC 6245 (FCTD), the Court said that an allowance which is "woefully inadequate" is unreasonable, and this phrase runs through subsequent case law as a test, although the statutory test is merely "unreasonable". In any event, it is clear that an allowance is not unreasonable merely because it does not cover your actual costs; you must be able to demonstrate that it falls far short in your particular circumstances.

Conversely, of course, if you receive an unreasonably high allowance, the CRA will add it to your income and insist that you justify your actual expenses.

While there is no objective test that can be applied in determining if the per-kilometre allowance you receive is reasonable in amount, the CRA will normally accept as reasonable the prescribed allowances set out in the "Automobile Rates and Limits" at ¶86. These amounts are, however, prescribed solely for the purposes of limiting the deduction of the payment of the allowance to your employer, and it is open to you to argue that they are not reasonable when applied to your particular circumstance and, therefore, taxable as unreasonably high or, more likely, unreasonably low.

You can claim as a travelling expense the cost of meals if you are away from the municipality or metropolitan area in which your employer's establishment is located for a period of at least 12 hours. The general limitation applies so that only 50% of the cost of a meal is deductible; see ¶734.

Transport employees who qualify to deduct their meals under this rule, but not using the rules specific to transport employees as described at ¶374, are nonetheless allowed to use the simplified method of calculating meal costs described there. The CRA's position is that only transport employees are entitled to this option; it is not available to other employees claiming meal deductions under these rules. See the discussion at ¶374.40.

The deductions for motor vehicle expenses and travelling expenses are not limited to your employment income. However, you cannot claim the travelling expense deduction (i.e., for expenses other than motor vehicle expenses) if you claim a deduction as:

(1) a commission salesperson (¶368),

(2) a railway employee (¶374.50), or

(3) a transport employee (¶374).

The motor vehicle expense deduction may not be claimed if you have chosen to take any deduction as a commission salesperson (¶368).

As with all expense claims, you must be able to support any deduction you claim for travelling expenses, including those related to your use of your motor vehicle. As noted at the table reproduced at ¶87, the CRA does not permit you to estimate your motor vehicle travel costs using the per-kilometre amounts it accepts for the purposes of claiming the northern residents deduction, moving expenses, and transportation to obtain medical services. You must be prepared to substantiate your actual costs.

(ITA: 6(1)(*b*)(vii); (viii); 8(1)(*h*); (*h*.1); 8(4); 220(2.1); IT-522R [Archived]; *Rozen v. The Queen*, 85 DTC 5611 (FCTD))

[¶369.03] *Travelling from Home*

The CRA generally takes the position that travelling from home to work is a personal expense and the related costs are therefore not deductible. There are cases which demonstrate that this is a rule of thumb and not an inflexible principle.

Relevant Case Law

Travel Expenses

In *Homsy v. The Queen*, 2004 DTC 2390 (TCC), the Court ruled on the case of a tax assessor who typically went from home to the premises of the audit subject, and only occasionally to the employer's office. The distance to the subject premises was, as it happened, typically less than to the employer's, so that going to the employer first and then the subject premises would have been pointless. The Court ruled that the travel to the audit subject was not personal and the related costs were deductible.

In *Toutov v. The Queen*, 2006 DTC 2928 (TCC), the taxpayer was employed as a computer programmer performing most of his work at his home in Kingston, Ontario. His employer occasionally required the taxpayer to travel at his own expense to the employer's offices in Ottawa and to other destinations to meet with clients. The Court found that the taxpayer's home office in Kingston was an extension of his employer's place of business and his principal place of employment, and that the travel expenses as he incurred were deductible.

In *Cook v. The Queen*, 2007 DTC 1140 (TCC), the taxpayer leased a truck in connection with his work as a sheet metal worker. He regularly kept his tools in the truck. There was no personal use of the truck, except that the taxpayer kept it at home and drove each day either to the employer's warehouse, where he would pick up ductwork material, or to a job site as designated by the employer. The CRA took the position that the expenses were primarily incurred in travelling from the taxpayer's home to his employer's place of business, and so no deduction was warranted. The Court found that the truck was used in the course of employment for driving to various job sites, and arbitrarily assigned half of the expenses to that function. Although it is not mentioned, it is evident the taxpayer did not maintain a log of work versus commuting distance or time, which is likely why the assessment was issued in the first place.

[¶369.05] *Member of the Legislative Assembly ("MLA")*

Under the now cancelled Interpretation Bulletin IT-266, the CRA took the position that members of provincial legislatures do not qualify for the travel expense deduction, nor presumably for automobile expenses at ¶370. It is doubtful that the cancellation of this bulletin represents a change in policy.

In any event, an MLA can receive a non-taxable allowance, so long as it does not exceed 50% of taxable MLA remuneration and relates to expenses incidental to the discharge of the MLA's duties (see ¶342). In addition an MLA can be reimbursed for travel costs. See CRA Document No. 2000-0048324 for further information on municipal officers' allowance.

(ITA: 81(2); CRA Document No.: Municipal Officers Allowance, *October 16, 2000*, CRA Document No. 2000-0048324)

[¶370] AUTOMOBILE AND AIRCRAFT EXPENSES — LINE 229

If you are an employee entitled to deduct motor vehicle (or aircraft) expenses from your employment income under the rules at ¶368 or ¶369, you should keep a record of your expenses supported by the relevant invoices or receipts.

In most cases, your vehicle will have been used both personally and for business purposes, so that it is necessary to apportion the relevant expenses between these uses. You should therefore keep a record of total kilometres travelled during the year, divided between business (i.e., employment) mileage and personal mileage. Travelling between your home and your business is personal mileage. See ¶738.70 for a discussion of the latest CRA policy on logbook and record-keeping requirements.

Motor vehicle expenses are recorded using form T777, showing separately fuel, maintenance and repairs, insurance, licence, and registration, lease payments, interest on borrowed money to acquire the motor vehicle, other expenses and capital cost allowance. See ¶822 for particulars on the calculation of capital cost allowance. Your employer must complete form T2200, "Declaration of Conditions of Employment", in order for you to be able to claim these expenses.

[¶370.05] *Limitations on Amounts Eligible for Proration*

Where you acquired or leased an automobile and use it in the course of your employment, there are limitations on the amount you may claim for capital cost allowance and financing charges if you purchased the automobile, and for leasing costs if you leased the automobile. These limits apply before you prorate your costs between personal and employment-related use. The restrictions are intended to limit you to the amounts that you can claim on a mid-price vehicle. They are subject to annual adjustment but have not changed since 2001. See the chart at ¶738.25.

These restrictions apply only to motor vehicles which are "automobiles" as defined in ¶738 and ¶810a.

Purchased Automobile

Where you purchased an automobile which you use in the course of your employment, your capital cost allowance ("CCA") is calculated on the cost shown in the "Cost limit" column. For more detail, see ¶810a.

Interest Expense

If you borrowed money to purchase an automobile which you use in the course of your employment, the amount of interest you can deduct is limited to the amount shown under "Daily interest limit" times the number of days for which you paid interest.

Additional Limitation — Leased Automobile

If you leased an automobile which you use in the course of your employment, and if:

(1) the manufacturer's list price for the automobile exceeds the "MSLP limit";

(2) the monthly leasing payments are more than the "Monthly lease limit"; or

(3) you made special deposits or prepayments on the lease,

the amount you may use in calculating your employment portion of expense may be limited as discussed at ¶738. The CRA provides a detailed calculation of the leasing cost formula in its Employment Expenses guide (T4044); see also ¶738.

(ITA: 8(1)(*j*); ITR: 7307 [Prescribed amount – automobile deduction limits]; IT-522R [Archived])

[¶370.15] *Employee's Aircraft Expenses*

If you meet the requirements for claiming deductions in ¶368 or ¶369 you can deduct capital cost allowance and interest expense relating to an aircraft you own, and you can deduct the cost of renting an aircraft, provided the aircraft is used to earn employment income. These deductions cannot exceed an amount that is reasonable in the circumstances, having regard to the relative cost and availability of other modes of transportation.

(ITA: 8(1)(*j*); IT-522R [Archived])

[¶370g] MOTOR VEHICLE AND OTHER EMPLOYMENT EXPENSES — EXAMPLE

Malcolm Whyte was employed as a commission salesman in a non-participating province by HighTech Co.. Malcolm's employer requires he use his automobile in the performance of his duties (his employer will so certify on form T2200) and he is required to pay his own expenses. During the year, Malcolm earned a base salary of $35,000, plus $41,000 in commissions, and received $500 per month as a motor vehicle allowance. The allowance is taxable (it is not based solely on kilometres driven) and was included in his employment income on his T4. In year 4, he incurred the following expenses:

— Motor vehicle expenses (80% business use):
- Gas: .... $3,400[1]
- Insurance $1,430/year
- Maintenance .... $1,400[1]
- Licence $75/year
- Lease .... $810/month[2]
- Parking .... $1,266[1]

— Entertainment expenses .... $4,915[1]
— Meals .... $910[1]
— Lodging .... $1,403[1]
— Supplies .... $304[1]

[1] These costs include the GST of 5%.

[2] Malcolm paid 8% PST and 5% GST on this monthly lease cost, in addition to the $810 lease cost shown.

Malcolm entered into the lease for his automobile on January 1, Year 1. At that time, the automobile's manufacturer's list price excluding GST and provincial sales tax was $37,341 (the limit for that year was $30,000 plus applicable taxes).

Malcolm claimed a total of $32,950.80 of leasing costs in the prior years ($10,983.60 for each of the first three years of the lease). The applicable cost limit, pursuant to the schedule in ¶370.05, including taxes is $33,900.

All the claimable expenses are reported in the "Expenses" section of form T777. The motor vehicle expenses at line 1 of the T777 are taken from the calculation on that form. The deductible leasing expenses are not calculated on form T777 but are computed using the chart in the T4044 Employment Expenses Guide. The leasing expense rules are discussed in detail in ¶738.

Based on the above facts, the total expenses Malcolm can claim on form T777 is $19,716.38, computed as follows:

Expenses		
Allowable motor vehicle expenses (see Schedule 1 below)		$13,830.88
Food, beverages, and entertainment expenses	(50% × $5,825)	2,912.50
Lodging		1,403.00
Parking (100% business related)		1,266.00
Supplies		304.00
Total expenses		$19,716.38

Schedule 1 — Motor Vehicle Expenses		
Gas	$3,400.00	
Insurance	1,430.00	
Maintenance	1,400.00	
Licence	75.00	
Lease (see Schedule 2)	10,983.60	
Total		$17,288.60
Allowable amount (80%)		$13,830.88

Schedule 2 — Employment Deduction — Car Lease (see ¶738)

Least of:

A. (904[1] × 1,461[2]) / 30 - $32,950.80	$11,074.00
B. ($33,900 × $10,983.60[3]) / (.85 × greater of (i) 37,341[4] or (ii) $39,882.35[5])	$10,983.60

[1] $800 limit plus tax.

[2] Number of days: 365 in Year 1 + 365 in Year 2 + 365 in Year 3 + 366 in Year 4 = 1,461 total.

[3] The actual lease cost for the year including 5% GST and 8% PST. $810 × 1.13 × 12 = $915.30 × 12 = $10,983.60.

[4] Manufacturer's suggested list price.

[5] 100/85 × the car limit of $30,000 plus 5% GST and 8% PST.

Because the MSLP is less than 100/85 of the applicable cost limit of $33,900, the formula in B, and therefore the deductible lease cost, will always be equivalent to the actual lease charges. See ¶738.30.

Leasing Costs and Related Taxes

The regulations which impose the limits on deductible lease payments specifically require that the dollar limits referred to are to be increased by GST/HST and provincial sales taxes that those lease payments attract. The CRA's discussion of the limits in the Employment Expenses guide (T4044) states, rather confusingly:

> Most leases do not include items such as insurance, maintenance and taxes. You have to pay these amounts separately. Therefore, list these expenses separately on form T777. Do not include them in your calculation of eligible leasing costs.

The paragraph immediately following goes on to say:

> If the lease agreement for your passenger vehicle does include items such as insurance, maintenance, and taxes, include them as part of the lease charges in your calculation.

These comments seem to imply that if your lease agreement does not specifically include sales taxes in the lease payment, you can exclude them from the lease limitation calculation and claim them separately. The better view is that you should claim insurance and maintenance separately, if they are not included in the lease payment, but that GST/HST and provincial sales taxes are included in, and subject to the limitations on, your deductible lease payments. This view is supported by the Business and Professional Income guide (T4002), which states:

> Generally, leases include taxes (GST and PST, or HST/QST), but not items such as insurance and maintenance. You have to pay these amounts separately. Include the taxes on line 1 when you complete Chart C, and list the items such as insurance and maintenance on the appropriate lines of "Chart A — Motor vehicle expenses".

[¶371] LEGAL EXPENSES

You may deduct legal expenses you pay to collect salary or wages owed to you by an employer or former employer and tfo establish a right to salary or wages. In either case, the deduction is limited to the amounts you pay in the year and is reduced by any amount you receive pursuant to an award for costs made by a court.

The deduction is available for collecting or establishing a right to any amount to be included in your employment income. Thus, if the legal fees relate, for example, to collecting an amount owed to you by an insurer under an employer-provided benefit program, the fees are deductible if the receipt from the insurer is included in your employment income.

The rules permit the deduction of amounts to establish a right, and it has been widely suggested that you should be able deduct the expenses of trying to establish a right whether or not you succeed.

This view has been supported by the courts. The Court has concluded that a taxpayer need not win his or her action to deduct the expenses (see *Fortin v. The Queen*, 2001 DTC 3754 (TCC), and *Rogers v. The Queen*, 2007 DTC 570 (TCC)). More significantly, in *Loo v. The Queen*, 2004 DTC 6540 (FCA), the Court specifically allowed legal expense deductions where a taxpayer sued claiming higher wages were owed for the work performed, although the taxpayer lost the case.

Legal expenses you incur in the year to collect or establish a right to a pension benefit, termination payment or retiring allowance (as described at ¶923) stand on different ground, as these amounts do not constitute employment income, and are deductible under specific rules discussed at ¶924 and ¶2612.05.

Relevant CRA Documents

Legal Fees Where Employment not Terminated

An employee was given a termination notice and hired a lawyer to negotiate a settlement. The employee continued working during the negotiations and ultimately continued working for the same employer, but with reduced benefits. The CRA found the employee's legal expenses to be non-deductible, as his salary was never terminated and so the payments were not made to establish a right or collect an amount. (CRA Document No. 2005-0113991E5)

Legal Fees need not be Paid to a Lawyer

The CRA has commented that where fees are paid to a party other than a legal firm to negotiate a termination payment, the amount is considered to be deductible, so long as they pertained to a matter of law. (CRA Document No. 9424305)

(ITA: 6(1)(*j*); 8(1)(*b*); 56(1)(*l*); (*l*.1); 60(*o*.1); IT-99R5 [Archived]; CRA Document No.: Legal Expenses of Employee, *June 1, 2005*, CRA Document No. 2005-0113991E5; Legal Fees, *March 24, 1995*, CRA Document No. 9424305)

[¶372] OFFICE RENT AND SALARIES PAID, SUPPLIES CONSUMED, TRADE UNION OR PROFESSIONAL MEMBERSHIP DUES, AND OTHER UNREIMBURSED EXPENSES OF EMPLOYEES — LINES 212 AND 229

You may deduct any of the following amounts you pay, to the extent you are not reimbursed for them, or to the extent someone else pays them but the amount is included in your employment income.

[¶372.01] Annual Professional Membership Dues

You may deduct annual professional membership dues required to maintain a professional status recognized by statute. For example, annual dues paid by a professional accountant, lawyer, doctor, or engineer to a professional association or society are deductible under this provision.

Annual dues you pay that are not directly related to the ordinary membership in the association are not deductible, i.e., if they are paid under a superannuation fund or plan, or for or under a fund or plan for annuities, insurance (other than malpractice insurance required to maintain membership), or similar benefits. Dues you pay as a student before becoming a member of a professional organization are not deductible, but might qualify as tuition fees. See ¶1319.

Recognized by Statute

The condition that the professional status be "recognized by statute" means that the profession be acknowledged in a statute, even if it is not regulated (*Montgomery v. the Queen*, 99 DTC 5186 (FCA)). Thus, a member of the Appraisal Institute of Canada ("AIC") was entitled to deduct membership fees because certain provincial statutes provide that only certain members of the AIC are entitled to make appraisals recognized by statute. The fact that the AIC was not a self-regulating profession recognized by statute was not a bar to the deduction.

Relevant CRA Documents

Profession Not Recognized

However, the CRA declined to authorize the deduction of membership fees for the Corporation des officers municipaux du Québec ("COMAQ"). COMAQ legislation regulates municipal officers working in Quebec municipalities. The officers must pay annual dues to the corporation to keep their membership and to be entitled to use the "certified municipal officer" designation. The CRA opinion took the position that while the status of the association may be recognized by a Quebec statute, the professional status of the municipal officers was not. (CRA Document No. 2005-0112871E5)

(ITA: 8(1)(*i*); 8(5); IT-158R2 [Archived]; CRA Document No.: Cotisation Professionnelle, *August 2, 2005*, CRA Document No. 2005-0112871E5)

[¶372.02] *Dues to a Professions Board, Parity or Advisory Committee*

Your dues to a Professions Board, Parity or Advisory Committee are deductible if payment is required under the laws of a province. If the payment relates to a parity or advisory committee, the payment must be required by provincial law "in respect of the employment for the year".

Payments that are not solely for membership are not deductible, i.e., if they are paid for or under a superannuation fund or plan, or for or under a fund or plan for annuities, insurance (other than required malpractice insurance), or similar benefits.

(ITA: 8(1)(*i*); 8(5); IT-158R2 [Archived])

[¶372.03] *Office Rent, or Salary to an Assistant or Substitute*

If the terms of your employment require that you maintain an office or an assistant or substitute, office rent and the salary to an assistant or substitute are deductible. You may also deduct the employer contributions you make to Employment Insurance, the Canada Pension Plan or the Quebec Pension Plan and under the Quebec Parental Insurance Plan ("QPIP") relating to the assistant or substitute. You must have your employer certify on form T2200 that you are required to incur these expenses in the course of your employment and that you are not reimbursed for them.

See ¶368.25 for a discussion of the courts' views on employment of a spouse as an assistant.

(ITA: 8(1)(*i*); IT-352R2 [Archived])

[¶372.04] *Cost of Supplies Consumed*

You may deduct the cost of supplies consumed in your employment and which were required to be supplied by you by the terms of your employment, as certified by your employer on form T2200.

The CRA interprets "supplies" to be limited to materials that are consumed directly in the performance of your employment duties and thereafter are unfit for further use. This will include gasoline and oil used in the operation of power saws used in forestry operations, dynamite used by miners, bandages and medicines used by salaried doctors, and various stationery items (other than books) such as pens, pencils, paper clips, charts, etc., used by teachers. It will not include the monthly basic service charge for a telephone line, amounts paid to connect or license a cellular phone, special clothing customarily worn or required to be worn for the performance of your duties, and any types of tools which generally fall into the category of equipment. See also ¶373.

(ITA: 8(1)(*i*); IT-352R2 [Archived])

[¶372.05] *Taxpayers Employed in Forestry Operations*

If you are employed in forestry operations and are required to supply your own power saw, you can deduct your related expenses as well as the cost (net of trade-ins) of any saw purchased during the year. This deduction is allowed on the CRA's understanding that power saws have a limited life and are effectively consumed in their use. The CRA therefore treats such saws as supplies. Your employer must certify on form T2200 that you are required to incur the expenses in the course of your employment and are not reimbursed for them.

(ITA: 8(1)(*i*); IT-352R2 [Archived]; T4044, "Employment Expenses")

[¶372.06] *Annual Dues To Maintain Membership in a Trade Union or an Association of Public Servants*

Annual dues you pay to maintain membership in a trade union or an association of public servants are deductible. You may deduct annual dues which are withheld by your employer from your salary or wages pursuant to the provisions of a collective agreement, even if you are not a member.

Such dues are deductible only to the extent that they relate to membership in the union or association and they are not deductible if they are levied for or under a superannuation fund or plan, or for or under a fund or plan for annuities, insurance, or similar benefits.

However, where a portion of your trade union dues is being paid into a registered superannuation fund, such amounts may still be deducted as pension fund contributions. See ¶365.

Any portion of regular union dues which is for the purpose of providing a fund for current or anticipated costs of prosecuting legal strikes of the union is, if reasonable in the circumstances, deductible for tax purposes. However, special assessments for strike funds are not deductible.

Trade union dues levied for the creation or maintenance of a building fund or a fund for the payment of funeral expenses are not deductible.

(ITA: 8(1)(*i*); 8(5); IT-103R [Archived])

[¶373] EMPLOYEE'S HOME OFFICE EXPENSES

If you maintain an office in part of your house or in an apartment you rent, a portion of your occupancy costs is deductible, provided your employer certifies on form T2200 that you are required to maintain the office and you are not reimbursed or entitled to be reimbursed for your costs.

In computing the occupancy costs of a home you own, you may deduct a reasonable portion of expenses incurred for the maintenance of the premises, such as fuel, electricity, light bulbs, cleaning materials, and minor repairs but capital cost allowance, taxes, insurance, and mortgage interest are not allowed.

If you are a commission salesperson, in addition to the expenses listed above, you may deduct an appropriate portion of taxes and insurance paid on your home, but not mortgage interest and capital cost allowance. No deduction can be made to cover the rental value of premises set aside and used as an office in your own home. That is, one cannot say "I could receive, or would have to pay, $100 per month for this room of my house as office space, and therefore I can deduct that amount".

[¶373.05] *Overriding Restrictions*

Your deduction for home office expenses is subject to two conditions.

Use of Space

To make the claim for a "work space" in a "self-contained domestic establishment" in which you live, the space must meet at least one of two tests:

(1) the work space is where you principally perform the duties of your employment; or

(2) the work space is both used exclusively during the period to which the deductible expenses relate for the purpose of earning income from your employment and is used on a regular and continuous basis for meeting customers or other persons in the ordinary course of performing the duties of your employment.

A "self-contained domestic establishment" is a dwelling house, apartment or other similar place of residence in which, as a general rule, you eat and sleep.

Under rule (1) you do not have to set aside part of the home exclusively for employment use so long as it is the work space where you principally perform your employment duties. Your expenses in respect of the space, however, should be prorated both for square footage and time allocated to employment. For example, if you use 10% of your floor space as a work space, and it is used 60% of the time for that purpose, your employment expenses would be 60% of 10% of your related occupancy costs.

If you qualify under rule (2), the criterion that the work-space must be used for meeting clients, customers, or patients on a regular and continuous basis is the same as for the similar limitations on business income in ¶742. Accordingly, case law and CRA opinions under both rules should be consulted in interpreting this provision.

Income Limitation

The amount you may otherwise deduct is limited to your income from the employment before claiming any deductions for the work space in your home. That is, you cannot use deductions for office-in-home expenses to create or increase a loss from the employment to which the expenses are related.

Expenses which would create or increase a loss may be carried forward and are treated as having been incurred in the immediately subsequent year.

(ITA: 8(1)(*i*); 8(13); IT-352R2 [Archived])

[¶373a] DEDUCTING THE COST OF TOOLS

Employees are generally not allowed to deduct the cost of equipment which they must supply themselves. Exceptions are made for capital cost allowance on motor vehicles and aircraft (¶370), and on musical instruments (¶379.10), and the cost of supplies and power saws (¶372). However, if you are employed as a tradesperson or as an apprentice mechanic, two separate but related provisions may allow you to deduct a portion of the cost of tools you acquire in the year.

The first provision — the tradespersons' tools deduction — is available to anyone employed in a trade. The second provision — the apprentice mechanics' tools deduction — can only be claimed if you are employed as an apprentice mechanic.

The deductions available to an apprentice and to a tradesperson are not mutually exclusive. If you are an apprentice mechanic you are also, clearly, a tradesperson, and can therefore claim both deductions provided you meet the conditions set out below. You cannot deduct an amount under either provision, however, to the extent the cost has already been deducted elsewhere. This allows you to claim, say, 60% of the cost of a tool under one provision and 40% under the other, and the provisions clearly contemplate this.

No matter which provision you claim a deduction under, the mechanism for claiming the GST/HST rebate and the way in which you account for a disposition of a tool on which you have claimed a deduction are the same. The GST/HST rebate is discussed at ¶373c.05; the treatment of a disposition is discussed at ¶373c.10.

[¶373b] TRADESPERSONS' TOOLS DEDUCTION — LINE 229

Amount for 2016: $1,161

[¶373b.01] *Calculating the Deduction*

If you are employed as a tradesperson, you can deduct the amount by which the lesser of

(1) the cost of eligible tools you acquired in the year, and

(2) your income for the year from employment as a tradesperson, after other deductions specific to that employment income (generally, ¶365 to ¶379 inclusive) but before this deduction, plus any grants received under the federal apprenticeship incentive program and included in your income in the year (net of any such grants you had to refund and could deduct in the year),

exceeds

(3) the amount for the year (this is an indexed amount).

The deduction cannot exceed $500. There is no provision for carrying forward undeducted tool costs (as there is under the apprenticeship deduction at ¶373c), but nothing prevents you from acquiring your tools over a period of years if that is compatible with your employment.

Example — Modified from the Employment Expense Guide

Karsten is employed as an electrician with ABC Company, and he needs to purchase additional tools for his job. He paid $2,500 for the tools he needed, and he earned $45,000 in employment income in the year as an electrician.

He calculates his maximum deduction for eligible tools as the lesser of:

(1) 500; and

(2) the amount, if any, determined by the formula

A - $1,161

where

A = the lesser of:

(i) $2,500; and

(ii) $45,000

Karsten's maximum deduction is the lesser of $500 and $1,339 ($2,500 - $1,161). Karsten claims a deduction of $500 on line 229.

History

The indexed threshold was $1,065 for 2011, $1,095 for 2012, $1,117 for 2013, $1,127 for 2014, and $1,146 for 2015.

[¶373b.02] *Who is a "Tradesperson"?*

The term "tradesperson" is not defined in the *Income Tax Act*. It is the CRA's view that the term should be interpreted using its ordinary or everyday meaning, saying:

> ... it is our view that any person engaged in an occupation that demands a certain level of skill may be considered a tradesperson for purposes of the deduction, whether the person is registered or not.

(CRA Document No.: Meaning of "tradesperson", *February 19, 2007*, CRA Document No. 2006-0216591I7)

[¶373b.04] *What is an "Eligible Tool"?*

An eligible tool is one that:

(1) you acquire for use in connection with your employment as a tradesperson;

(2) has not been used for any purpose before you acquired it;

(3) is certified in prescribed form by your employer to be required to be provided by you as a condition of, and for use in, your employment as a tradesperson; and

(4) is not an electronic communication device or electronic data processing equipment, unless the device or equipment can be used only for the purpose of measuring, locating, or calculating.

You are obliged to provide a list of tools purchased to your employer, which your employer certifies as necessary and returns to you.

[¶373b.07] *Cost of Tools*

The cost of your tools includes the related GST/HST and provincial sales taxes, including the QST. The cost of the tools is used to calculate your GST/HST/QST rebates, as illustrated for apprenticeship tools in ¶373c.05. The cost is also used in accounting for a disposition of your tools, as discussed at ¶373c.10. An example of how the cost of tools is calculated under either the tradesperson's tool deduction or the apprentice mechanic's tool deduction is given at ¶373c.07.

(ITA: 8(1)(s); 8(6.1); 8(7); 56(1)(k))

[¶373c] APPRENTICE MECHANICS' TOOLS DEDUCTION — LINE 229

If you are employed as an apprentice mechanic, you are typically required to provide your own tools for the on-the-job component of the apprenticeship. In addition to and in parallel with the deduction for a tradesperson's tools (see ¶373b), a deduction is allowed for the cost of tools you purchase as an apprentice mechanic.

To qualify for this deduction, you must be an "eligible apprentice mechanic", which is to say you must have been both (i) registered in a provincial or territorial or federal program leading to designation as a mechanic licensed to repair automobiles, aircraft, or any other self-propelled motorized vehicles, and (ii) employed as an apprentice mechanic in the same taxation year.

[¶373c.01] *Calculating the Deduction*

The apprentice mechanic's tool deduction is:

(1) the total cost of eligible tools you acquired in the taxation year and, if you first became employed as an eligible apprentice mechanic in the taxation year, the cost of eligible tools acquired in the last three months of the preceding year, minus

(2) the greater of

(a) $500 plus the amount eligible for your employment tax credit at ¶1351 (the amount you claim at box 363 (line 10) on schedule 1 of your return). This cannot exceed $1,161 for 2016, although it can be less if your employment income is less than $1,161; and

(b) 5% of the sum of (i) your apprenticeship income for the year, after other deductions specific to that employment income (generally, ¶365 to ¶379 inclusive) but before this deduction, plus (ii) any grants received under the federal apprenticeship incentive program and included in your income in the year net of any such grants you had to refund and could deduct in the year.

The maximum amount you can claim as your employment tax credit is indexed annually. The indexed amounts are the same as the limit for the tradespersons' tool credit, described at ¶373b.01.

The deduction cannot exceed your income for the taxation year and cannot, therefore, be claimed to create or increase a loss. Any part of the deduction that is not taken in the year it first becomes available, whether because it exceeds your income or because you choose to defer part of the claim, is carried forward and can be deducted in any subsequent taxation year to the extent you choose.

The apprentice mechanics' tool deduction has a considerably higher cost threshold than the companion deduction for tradespersons' tools at ¶373b, so where you qualify for both in the year, you may be able to claim under that provision where you cannot claim under this one. On the other hand, there is no carry-forward of undeducted amounts under the tradespersons' deduction comparable to the carryforward of undeducted apprenticeship amounts.

The deduction is available annually, as long as you continue to be employed as an apprentice mechanic and you purchase eligible tools in more than one taxation year. Each year provides a new limitation and its carryover. It is only the practical need to acquire the tools to carry out your apprenticeship that will limit the multiplication of the limits in this way.

Example — Modified from the Employment Expense Guide

The Motor Company hired Bill as a second-year eligible apprentice mechanic on November 1, 20X1. Based on the tools he bought during 20X1, Bill calculated his maximum deduction for eligible tools in 20X1 to be $3,500. He only claimed $1,500 of this amount on his 20X1 return. In 20X2, Bill received $18,000 in income from his job as an eligible apprentice mechanic. In 20X2, he received $1,000 under the *Apprenticeship Incentive Grant* program, and he also received income of $4,000 from other sources.

During 20X2, Bill bought two eligible tools for $4,500. He already calculated and claimed a tradesperson's tools deduction of $500 and claimed a Canada employment amount of $1,161 for 20X2. Bill calculates his maximum deduction for eligible tools in 20X2 as follows:

Maximum deduction for eligible tools = (A - B) + C

where

A = $4,500

B = the lesser of:

(i) $4,500 (the cost of tools acquired in 20X2); and

(ii) the greater of:

- $1,661 ($500 + $1,161 (the Canada employment amount)); and
- $925 (5% of [$18,000 + $1,000 - $500 (the tradesperson's tool deduction)])

C = $2,000 (the apprentice mechanic's deduction carried forward)

Therefore, Bill's maximum deduction in 20X2 is $4,839 ([$4,500 - $1,661] + $2,000). Bill's claim for the year cannot be more than his net income of $22,500 ([$18,000 + $1,000 - $500] + $4,000). Bill claims his deduction on line 229 of his return.

[¶373c.04] *Eligible Tools*

Eligible tools include any tool (including ancillary equipment, which is apparently meant to cover such things as tool boxes) which:

- you acquire for use in connection with your employment as an eligible apprentice mechanic;
- is new;
- is certified in prescribed form by your employer; and
- is not an electronic communication device or electronic data processing equipment, unless the device or equipment can be used only for the purpose of measuring, locating, or calculating. This prohibits the deduction for such things as computers, pagers, and cell phones, but permits it for such things as automotive diagnostic equipment, used for example to locate faults and problems.

Each year that you are employed as an apprentice mechanic, you should produce a list of the tools purchased. Your employer is to certify on form T2200 that the tools on the list were acquired in connection with your employment, and that the employment is pursuant to a provincially registered apprenticeship program.

You are not required to submit the form to the CRA, unless they ask for it. As with all tax-related deductions, you should keep the T2200, the signed list, and the invoices for the purchase of the tools.

[¶373c.05] *GST/HST/QST Rebate*

If you are entitled to a deduction for the cost of tools as either a tradesperson or an apprentice mechanic, you will also be entitled to claim the GST/HST rebate and, in Quebec, the QST rebate. The rebates are calculated using the normal rules, described at ¶363.10 and ¶363.45.

The rebates are calculated on the deduction you claim on the return. If, for example, you choose to claim only a portion of the apprentice mechanics' deduction to which you are entitled and to carry the balance forward, the current year's rebate is calculated on the amount you deduct and the rebate on the deduction carried forward will be claimed in the year you deduct the balance carried forward.

As is normally the case, rebates claimed in one year are taken into income in the following year.

[¶373c.07] *Cost of Tools*

The cost of the tools you acquire for purposes of calculating both the tradesperson's deduction and the apprentice mechanic's deduction, and for calculating your GST/HST and QST rebate, is the actual cost to you, including all sales taxes.

You are, however, required to keep track of an adjusted amount which constitutes the cost of the tool for purposes of calculating your income, should you sell the tool. For these purposes, your cost is reduced by the amount of the tradespersons' tool deduction and/or the apprentice mechanic's tool deduction you are entitled to deduct, whether you actually deduct the amount or not. Thus, if you choose to claim less than the full apprentice mechanics' tool deduction in the year, and carry the balance forward, the cost of the related tool is reduced by both the amount you deduct and the amount you carry forward. A deduction of the carried forward amount in a subsequent year does not affect the cost of the tool.

If you acquire more than one tool which qualifies for either deduction, the deductions to which you are entitled reduce the cost of the tools *pro rata*.

Example

The two tools acquired by Bill in the example at ¶373c.01 had costs of $3,000 and $1,500, determined under the normal rules. Of the $4,839 apprentice mechanic's deduction to which he was otherwise entitled, $2,000 represents an amount carried forward and reduced the cost of the tools acquired in the earlier year in which it arose. Only $2,839 (the deduction arising in the current year) reduces the cost of tools acquired in the year.

Bill calculates the cost of the tools he acquired in the year as follows:

First tool: $3,000 – ($2,839 × $3,000/$4,500) = $1,107.

Second tool: $1,500 – ($2,839 × $1,500/$4,500) = $554.

[¶373c.10] *Disposition of Tools — Line 130*

If you sell a tool on which you claimed either the tradespersons' tools deduction or the apprentice mechanics' tool deduction for more than its cost, as adjusted as described at ¶373c.07, the difference is income. Unlike capital property generally, there is no rule which allows any amount you realize on a sale in excess of the gross (original) cost to be treated as a capital gain. Presumably, this reflects an assumption that tools can only depreciate, which is usually true.

If you sell a tool and are paid the purchase price over two or more years, you recognize income only when the cumulative amount you have received exceeds the adjusted cost.

Example

Bill in ¶373c.07 sells the tool with an adjusted cost of $549 for $750. He agrees to accept $250 a year over three years. In the first and second years, he has no income to report as the cumulative amounts he has received, $250 and $500, respectively, do not exceed his adjusted cost. In year three he takes $201 into income, reporting it as "Other Income" on Line 130.

Sale by Someone Other than the Tradesperson or Mechanic

If the tools are sold by someone other than the tradesperson or apprentice who claimed the deduction, and the vendor does not deal at arm's length with the tradesperson or apprentice, it is the vendor that reports the income. It is not clear how the non-arm's length person is supposed to have acquired the tools. If by gift or sale, the non-arm's length transfer rules (¶530) should have applied to cause the original owner to account for fair value proceeds and to give the new owner cost base in a similar amount, unless the transfer was between spouses and occurred at adjusted cost base (¶531). In any event, the provisions track through the income arising on the disposition of the tool to the ultimate non-arm's length vendor.

If the proceeds on the sale of the tools are received by an arm's length person, the provision does not apply. In that case, any income inclusion would have been taxed in the hands of the person who originally claimed the deduction, based on the proceeds he or she received on transferring the tools to the arm's length person.

The income inclusion rule does not apply to a disposition by a corporation which acquired the property in a rollover transaction (under subsection 85(5.1)) or on a disposition by a partnership which acquired the property under a subsection 97(5) rollover. These exceptions permit you to transfer the tools to an incorporated business or partnership without passing the obligation to report income on the sale of the tools to the corporation or partnership.

(ITA: 8(1)(r); 8(6); 8(7); 56(1)(k); T4044, "Employment Expenses", Chapter 7)

SPECIAL STATUS EMPLOYEES

[¶374] TRANSPORTATION INDUSTRY EMPLOYEES

If you are employed in the transportation industry, you may be able to deduct amounts you pay for meals and lodging while away from home. Separate rules apply to employees of railway companies (see ¶374.50) and employees of other transportation businesses (see ¶374.10–¶374.40). Although some of the conditions that apply if you work for a railway differ from those that apply if you work for a business engaged in another form of transportation, other conditions are common to both deductions and these are described below.

If you are not employed by either a railway or another transportation company, you may still be able to claim travel expenses (see ¶374.20 and ¶374.30).

[¶374.05] *General Conditions for Claiming Lodging and Meals*

Certain general conditions govern the deduction of expenses if you are employed in the transportation industry. These conditions are relevant whether you make your claim as an employee of a railway or of a business engaged in another form of transportation.

Simplified Method for Meals

As with all tax deductions you claim, you must generally keep records of your actual costs of meals and lodging. As an alternative to keeping detailed records of the cost of each meal you enjoy while travelling, if you are claiming meals as an employee of either a railway or another transportation business, the CRA permits you to claim a flat $8.50 per meal (50% of $17), to a maximum of $25.50 (50% of $51) per day. You are still required to maintain a time and travel log to support your claim. If your employment travel is in the United States, the dollar amounts are to be read in U.S. dollars, and translated into Canadian dollars when you claim the deduction.

Where a crew of workers, such as a crew on a work train, is provided with cooking facilities, and purchases groceries and prepare meals either collectively or separately, the CRA will accept claims without supporting vouchers for $17 (50% of $34) per person per day.

Expenses Incurred in U.S. Dollars

When making a claim in U.S. dollars, the CRA instructs you to accumulate your U.S. dollar claims for meals and lodging and convert the result to Canadian dollars by multiplying the total by the average conversion rate for the U.S. dollar for the year (see ¶95, preceding Chapter 1). If you use the simplified method for accounting for meals, which is an administrative concession, you probably have to follow this direction, even where it would be more beneficial to use a conversion rate that applies to the date the cost was incurred.

Form TL2

Whichever method you use to calculate your meals expense, if claiming meals and lodging as a transportation employee you are required to obtain form TL2, "Claim for Meals and Lodging Expenses", complete it, and have it certified by your employer. Do not file it with your return; simply retain it for examination should the CRA request it.

Travel Away from a Metropolitan Area

With certain exceptions, meals and lodging can only be claimed where you are required to travel away from your metropolitan area, if there is one. It is the CRA's view that you may claim one meal after every four hours that you are away to a maximum of three per day. If you do not leave the municipality or metropolitan area directly on a particular trip, your time away commences when your trip leaves the last stop in the municipality or metropolitan area.

A metropolitan area, in the CRA's view, is the surrounding metropolitan area integrated with a municipality (a major urban centre and its environs). This is not particularly helpful. For example, it is not clear if metropolitan Toronto stops at the west side of Mississauga, or goes on all the way to Hamilton.

Alternative Claim

Although specific rules are provided for railway employees and employees of general transportation businesses, it is possible that, if you qualify under either of these, you may also qualify under the general provisions that apply to all employees who are required to travel, under the rules at ¶369. This may or may not be to your benefit, as the conditions for making a claim under the general provision are more onerous than the ones here. If you make a claim under the general rule, you will require a form T2200 from your employer.

[¶374.10] *Transport Employees in General*

Where you are an employee of an airline, railway, bus company, short-haul trucking company, or other employer whose principal business is the transportation of passengers and/or goods, and you are regularly required to travel away from the municipality and, if there is one, the metropolitan area (see ¶374.05) in which your home terminal is located, on vehicles used by your employer to transport the goods or passengers, you are entitled to deduct your cost of lodging and 50% of your cost of meals incurred while away.

Your deduction is reduced to the extent you are or will be reimbursed, and may not exceed a reasonable amount. You must keep detailed records of expenses incurred. However, in calculating your deduction for meals, you are allowed to use the simplified method described at ¶374.05. If costs are incurred in U.S. dollars, the comments at ¶374.05 on translating them into Canadian dollars apply. You are required to obtain form TL2 from your employer if you deduct expenses as a transport employee, as discussed at ¶374.05.

Lodging Includes the Cost of Showers

In guide T4044, "Employment Expenses", the CRA states:

> The costs of showers are also considered to be deductible as part of lodging expenses for transportation employees who may have slept in the cab of their

truck rather than at a hotel. You need to keep your receipts to support the amount you deduct.

Meals but no Lodging

In *Renko et al. v. The Queen*, 2003 DTC 5417 (FCA), the Court confirmed that the deduction was not available to ferry workers who returned to their home port each night, because the statute requires that expenses be for meals *and* lodging, and the ferry workers incurred no lodging expense.

No doubt as a consequence, the CRA has said (in IC 73-21R9) that it will allow an employee to claim the cost of meals even when not obliged to incur lodging:

> However, the CRA is prepared to allow a deduction for meals only, even though no disbursement has been made for lodging, provided the duties of employment required the employee to stay away overnight and the employee can demonstrate that, rather than paying for lodging, he or she used other facilities. This may be the case where a transport employee uses a truck equipped with a sleeper cab.
>
> A deduction for meals only may also be allowed (to the extent of a reasonable number of meals) where a transport employee, although regularly required to travel away on journeys of substantial distance and duration so as to require disbursements for both meals and lodging, occasionally travels, as part of the employment, on journeys of shorter distance and duration not requiring him or her to stay away from home overnight. Where the shorter journey is scheduled for 10 hours or less, the CRA would expect the transport employee to eat breakfast and dinner meals at home, as is the case with most other employees. Accordingly, only one meal per day, namely lunch, will be permitted in these circumstances, ...

[¶374.20] *Messengers and Rickshaw Drivers*

As discussed in ¶777c, if you are a self-employed foot and bicycle messenger or rickshaw driver you are allowed to deduct meal expenses subject to the dollar limits applied to transport employees above. If you are an employee of such a business you are not eligible for the deduction, either under the transport rules above or the general deduction for travelling expenses at ¶369, since both require that you are required to travel away from the municipality in which you normally work.

[¶374.30] *Long-Haul Truck Drivers*

If you are employed as a long-haul truck driver, you are entitled to deduct 80% of the cost of your meals consumed during an eligible travel period, rather than 50%, provided you meet the other conditions that generally apply to an employee of a transportation business. You are eligible to use the simplified method for accounting for your meals, if you qualify for this enhanced deduction.

A "long-haul truck driver" is an individual whose principal business or principal duty of employment is driving a long-haul truck that transports goods. A "long-haul truck" is defined to be a truck or a tractor that is designed for hauling freight, and that has a gross vehicle weight rating of more than 11,788 kilograms.

An "eligible period" is a period of at least 24 continuous hours during which you are away from the municipality or metropolitan area in which the establishment of your employer to which you normally report is located. Finally, your absence must be for the purpose of driving a long-haul truck that transports goods to, or from, a location that is beyond a radius of 160 kilometres from that location.

[¶374.40] *Other Transport Employees*

Guide T4044, "Employment Expenses", contains the following passage:

> Even if you do not meet all of the conditions listed in the section called "Employees of a transport business" on this page, you may still be able to claim the cost of meals you incur in the year. For example, you may be an employee whose main duty of employment is transporting goods, but your employer's main business is not transporting goods or passengers.
>
> If you satisfy the conditions listed under the section called "Travelling expenses", you will still qualify to use the simplified method of meal reporting ...

It is understood that this means that the CRA will accept the simplified method of accounting for meals if you are employed in transporting goods or passengers, but the transportation service is not your employer's principal business. The CRA has confirmed informally that the simplified method is not available to you if you claim your expenses under the general rule for travel costs described at ¶369.

(ITA: 8(1)(*g*); 67.1(1); 67.1(1.1); 67.1(5))

[¶374.50] *Certain Railway Employees*

If you are employed as a station agent, or as a railway maintenance and repair worker, you can claim the actual cost of lodging and 50% of your actual cost of meals incurred while away from your ordinary place of residence.

If you are employed by a railway in any other capacity, such as an engineer, these deductions are available only if you are employed away from home and away from the municipality or metropolitan area where your home terminal is located (see ¶374.05).

In either case, the deduction is limited to costs which are reasonable and which are not reimbursed or to be reimbursed by your employer. You are allowed to use the simplified method for accounting for meals, described at ¶374.05. If costs are incurred in U.S. dollars, the comments at ¶374.05 on translating them into Canadian dollars apply. You are required to obtain form TL2 from your employer if you deduct expenses as a transport employee, as discussed at ¶374.05.

(ITA: 8(1)(*e*))

[¶376] RESIDENCES OF CLERGY — LINE 231

You can claim a clergy residence deduction if:

(1) you are a member of the clergy or of a religious order, or a regular minister of a religious denomination; and

(2) you are:

(a) in charge of a diocese, parish or congregation,

(b) ministering to a diocese, parish or congregation, or

(c) engaged exclusively in full-time administrative service by appointment of a religious order or denomination.

If you meet these conditions and your living accommodation is supplied by your employer, you can deduct the value of such accommodation (including the value of utilities) to the extent that it is included in your income as a benefit.

If you meet these conditions but you rent or own your living accommodation, you are entitled to deduct the least of:

(1) rent and utilities you paid for your principal place of residence which you ordinarily occupy during the year, or, where you or your spouse or common-law partner own such a residence or accommodation, its fair rental value (including utilities);

(2) your remuneration for the year from the office or employment;

(3) the greater of:

- 1/3 of your total remuneration from your employment as a member of the clergy for the year, and
- $1,000 for each month (to a maximum of 10) in the year during which you meet the conditions set out above; and

(4) the rent paid or, if the accommodation is owned by you or your spouse, fair rental value of the residence, reduced by the total of all other amounts deducted in computing any individual's income from a business or from an office or employment in connection with the same accommodation and that can be considered to relate to the same period. This condition is relevant where, for example, two spouses who are members of the clergy occupy the same accommodation.

T1223 Form Required

You are required to obtain form T1223 from your employer to confirm your eligibility for this deduction. Do not file the form with your return, but retain in case the CRA asks to see it.

Status Test — Who Is a Member of the Clergy?

Interpretation Bulletin IT-141R contains the CRA's views on what it means to be a "member of the clergy" or a "regular minister".

The CRA considers you to be a member of the clergy if you are set apart from the congregation or religious order as a spiritual leader. It is not necessary for your appointment to be referred to as an ordination or that the appointment be made by someone higher up in the ecclesiastical hierarchy; it may be done by the congregation itself.

A regular minister, in the CRA's view, is a person who:

(1) is authorized or empowered to perform spiritual duties, conduct religious services, administer sacraments and carry out similar religious functions;

(2) is appointed or recognized by a body or person with the legitimate authority to appoint or ordain ministers on behalf of or within the denomination; and

(3) is in a position or appointment of some permanence.

Function Test

In addition to holding the office of a member of the clergy or as a regular minister, the deduction is only available if you are engaged in the functions listed in item (2) at ¶376.

Relevant CRA Documents

Not a Member of the Clergy

In CRA Document No. 2012-0436101E5, the CRA confirmed that an executive pastor could not claim the clergy residence deduction. Although he was a member of the clergy, his ministerial duties were incidental and not an integral part of his job and he therefore did not meet the function test.

(ITA: 8(1)(c); 8(10); 220(2.1); IT-141R [Archived]; CRA Document No.: Clergy Residence Deduction, *April 2, 2012*, CRA Document No. 2012-0436101E5)

[¶377] TEACHERS' EXCHANGE FUND CONTRIBUTION

If you are a teacher, you may deduct up to $250 contributed to a fund established by the Canadian Education Association for the benefit of exchange teachers who come to Canada from Commonwealth countries.

(ITA: 8(1)(d))

[¶378] EMPLOYMENT OUTSIDE CANADA

If you are employed outside Canada in a limited number of occupations, you may be entitled to a tax credit which effectively eliminates the Canadian tax on a portion of the related income. This credit is being phased out and will no longer be available after 2015. See ¶1458.

(ITA: 122.3)

[¶379] ARTISTS' EMPLOYMENT EXPENSES

You may be able to deduct artists' employment expenses if you are employed as an artist, and your artistic activities consist of:

(1) the creation of (but not the reproduction of) paintings, prints, etchings, drawings, sculptures, or similar works of art;

(2) the composition of a dramatic, musical, or literary work;

(3) the performance of a dramatic or musical work as an actor, dancer, singer, or musician; or

(4) activities as a member of a professional artists' association that is certified by the Minister of Canadian Heritage.

No information is available on what associations might be certified by the Minister of Canadian Heritage and very little guidance has been published by the CRA on what types of activities it views as falling under these rules.

Relevant CRA Documents

Who is an Artist?

The CRA was asked whether film editors, film directors, sound editors, animators, directors of photography, art directors, costume designers, and sound mixers would be viewed as "artists". It was their view that only an animator could potentially be viewed as an artist. (CRA Document No. 92207453)

(IT-525R [Archived])

[¶379.05] *Artists' Employment Expenses: General Deduction*

If you qualify for the deduction under the conditions described at ¶379, you can deduct the lesser of:

(1) any related expenses actually paid in the year; and

(2) the amount, if any, by which:

(a) the lesser of $1,000 and 20% of your employment income from the activities described at ¶379, before claiming the artists' expense deduction,

exceeds

(b) the total of the deductions you claim for interest and capital cost allowance on a motor vehicle or aircraft (see ¶370) and the cost of musical instruments (see ¶379.10).

Expenses you cannot deduct in the current year because of the 20%/$1,000 limitation (and which cannot be deducted in the year under any other provision) carry forward from year to year until sufficient artistic income is generated to absorb them.

Other employment expenses you may incur, such as gasoline as a travelling expense, do not reduce the claim under this provision, although of course the same expense may not be counted twice. In general, it seems that expenses which may be deducted from employment income under other provisions operate independently of the artists' expense rules and may be claimed under their own rules without affecting your claim for artists' expenses.

There are no specific limitations on the types of expenses you can deduct under this provision, so any outlay that you incur that relates to earning qualifying income should be deductible. However, you cannot claim capital cost allowance under the artists' expense rule.

The following chart demonstrates how the deductions that may be available to you tie together:

Income from all artistic employment:	______(A)
Limitation:	
20% of (A) (maximum: $1,000)	______(i)
MINUS	
(a) Current year deduction for automobile (and airplane) interest and CCA related to artistic use	______(ii)
(b) Current year deduction for musical instruments	______(iii)
Maximum artists' expense deduction ((i) - ((ii) + (iii)))	______(B)
Expense calculation:	
All current year eligible artistic expenses:	______(iv)
PLUS	
Carryforward from preceding year	______(v)
Total artists' expenses ((iv) + (v))	______(C)
Allowable artists' deduction:	
(lesser of (B) and (C))	______(D)

If (C) is greater than (B) (i.e., if expenses exceed the limitation), the difference ((C) - (B)) carries forward for future deduction at (v).

[¶379.10] *Employee's Musical Instruments*

If you are employed as a musician and are required to provide a musical instrument as a condition of your employment, you may deduct the cost of maintenance, rental, and insurance for the instrument, and, where you own the instrument, capital cost allowance of 20% per year of the undepreciated capital cost of the instrument.

Your musical instrument deduction is calculated and claimed separately from the more general deduction available to an artist, discussed at ¶379.05, and is not subject to the limitations that apply to that claim. However, you cannot deduct costs related to your musical instrument under this provision if the deduction exceeds your income from employment as a musician. As noted at ¶379.05, however, your deduction for musical instruments reduces the amount on which the general artist's deduction can be claimed.

Example

Andrew had a $1,200 deduction available for insurance, rental, and maintenance costs related to his musical instrument, and another $300 available under the general artists' rule. He can deduct the $1,200 (provided he had income from his employment as a musician in at least this amount), but he cannot claim the additional $300, since the $1,000 general artists' expense limit is reduced by the $1,200 he deducted as a musician.

This deduction and its limitation only apply if you are employed as a musician. If you are self-employed, see ¶789.

(ITA: 8(1)(*p*); (*q*); IT-504R2 [Archived])

[¶379.20] *Canada Council (and other Arts) Grants — Line 104*

If you are employed and receive a grant or award from the Canada Council or some other granting body related to your employment activities, you should include the amount in your employment income. If it was not included in your T4, enter it at line 104 of your return.

Certain awards and prizes, such as the Governor General's Literary Awards, are entirely exempt from tax, as described at ¶960. It would be very unusual for such a prize to be awarded to you in your capacity as an employee.

(IT-257R [Archived]; CRA Document No.: Canada Council Awards, *March 20, 2000*, CRA Document No. 2000-0002565; Indian Status Income, *June 29, 1998*, CRA Document No. 9805875; Canada Council Grants A & B Presribed Prize, *March 31, 1993*, CRA Document No. 9305045; Grants and Prizes to 24(1) Artists, *August 20, 1992*, CRA Document No. 9220935)

[¶385] CANADIAN FORCES PERSONNEL AND POLICE

[¶385.10] *Pay and Danger Pay — Line 244*

If you are a member of the Canadian Forces or a police officer, you are subject to tax on your basic pay, no matter where you are deployed when you earn it. However, special allowances for high-risk missions are, generally speaking, non-taxable.

If you serve on a "deployed operational mission" you may be entitled to deduct the income earned while serving on the mission, to the extent that income does not exceed the maximum rate of pay earned by a non-commissioned member of the Canadian Forces. The deduction is available where the risk allowance of the mission, as determined by the Department of National Defense, exceeds a certain amount and, in lower-risk missions, where the mission has been certified by the Minister of Finance.

Your employer will calculate the deduction to which you are entitled and report it in Box 43 of your T4. Deduct the amount at line 244.

(ITA: 6(1)(*b*)(*ii*); 110(1)(*f*))

[¶385.20] *Canadian Forces and Veterans Awards and Benefits*

The Minister of Veterans Affairs may provide awards, benefits, and other forms of assistance (such as job placement assistance) to Canadian Forces and veterans. If you are in receipt of such benefits, they will have been reported to you on a T4 or T4A slip.

Income replacement benefits, supplementary retirement benefits, or permanent impairment allowances (effective April 1, 2017, "permanent impairment allowances" is replaced with "career impact allowance") are included in your employment income on line 104. The income is generally reported to you in box 28 of a T4A slip.

Income support benefits and most critical injury, disability, death, clothing allowance, and detention benefits, as well as family caregiver relief benefits, are not taxable.

Counselling services in respect of re-employment or retirement are not specifically covered in the enabling legislation, presumably because they are not considered taxable benefits under general principles (see ¶331).

(ITA: 6(1)(*a*)(iv); 6(1)(*f.*1); 81(1)(*d.*1); Income Tax Folio: S2-F3-C2 Benefits and Allowances Received from Employment)

[¶385.30] *Armed Forces Travelling and Separation Allowances*

Travelling and separation allowances you receive under service regulations as a member of the Canadian Armed Forces are not taxable.

(ITA: 6(1)(*b*)(ii))

[¶390] PROFESSIONAL ATHLETES

If you are employed as a player or other officer of a football, hockey, or similar club, your employment income includes:

(1) salaries, including income from personal service contracts;

(2) bonuses, whether for good performance, all-star rating, signing contracts, etc.;

(3) scouting, refereeing, or special coaching fees;

(4) living and travelling allowances during and after the training and tryout periods, other than accommodation provided or expenses reimbursed during that period as explained below;

(5) honoraria;

(6) payments for time lost from other employment;

(7) commuting expenses;

(8) free or subsidized use of automobiles;

(9) awards, whether in cash or in kind;

(10) payments on your behalf that would otherwise be a non-deductible expense to you, such as agent's fees, legal fees, income taxes, fines; and

(11) other benefits under the rules that apply generally to employees.

Expense Allowances and Travel Expenses

If you receive an allowance, even if it is paid during a training and tryout period and before you sign a contract, the allowance is generally to be included in your employment income. A reasonable allowance for travelling expenses (see ¶337) or in respect of board and lodging for employment at a special work site (see ¶360), is not taxable provided you meet the conditions that generally apply to employees receiving such allowances.

If you receive an allowance for travel expenses which is included in your income, you may be able to deduct your related travel costs, as described at ¶369.

Where the club provides a dining room or dormitories, the value during the training and tryout period is not regarded as income, provided the facilities are reasonable in the circumstances.

If you live in the general location of the training and tryout camp, and for personal reasons commute from your home, any allowance for travelling, meals, etc., is taxable. Where such an allowance is included in income, the deduction described at ¶369 is not available, as the cost of travel from your home to your place of employment is considered to be a personal outlay.

You are not taxable on a reimbursement by the club for the cost of travelling on *bona fide* club business away from the club's home base. However, amounts reimbursed for personal travel are taxable.

Deferred Compensation

Your contract may provide that part of your remuneration is to be deferred.

Generally, under the salary deferral arrangement rules described at ¶307, your income is taxed in the year it is earned and not when it is received. As noted at ¶307.20, however, an exception is made if you play in a league with regularly scheduled games, in which case your deferred compensation is taxed when you receive it. If you are not resident in Canada at the time the deferred remuneration is received, the rules outlined in ¶2020 would apply.

Deductions

As an employed player, you are limited to the deductions from employment income that are specifically available to employees (see ¶362–¶377). For example, legal fees incurred in the negotiation of your contract are not deductible, since to be deductible the fees must be incurred in collecting salary or wages owed to you. Fines are also not deductible.

Incorporation/Endorsement Income

If you arrange to have what would otherwise be your employment income paid to a corporation, you will be subject to the personal services business rules described at ¶305. The corporation will pay tax at a high rate and will be limited in what it can deduct.

Although you are likely an employee of the club you play for, you will normally be viewed as self-employed with respect to income from personal endorsements and public appearances, if you earn them directly rather than through the team. You can therefore deduct related expenses using the rules that apply generally to the determination of business income. The CRA takes the reasonable position that such endorsement and appearance income, when earned through a corporation, is not personal services business income.

(IT-168R3 [Archived])

[¶390.05] *Amateur Athletes*

If you are an athlete who must maintain amateur status under international competition rules, you may be able to benefit from a trust established to receive certain payments on your behalf; see ¶777.

[¶390.15] *Team Members Under 21: Allowances from Charities or Non-Profits*

If you are employed by a registered charity or a non-profit organization in connection with its operation of a sports team or recreation program for persons under 21 years of age, and you are a registered member or participant of the team, you are not taxable on an allowance of up $348 per month for board and lodging. The allowance must be attributable to the cost to you of living away from the place where, but for your employment with the team, you would usually reside.

Your employer must be a registered charity or a non-profit organization exempt from income tax under the exclusion for clubs, societies, or associations operated exclusively for social welfare, civic improvement, pleasure, recreation, etc., and all participants or members of the team must be under 21. The provision is intended generally to apply to members of junior hockey clubs, but is available to any team member that meets the qualifying criteria. Only allowances related to team membership or participation qualify. Allowances attributable to your services as a coach, instructor, trainer, referee, administrator, or other similar function are taxable under the normal rules

History

The maximum monthly allowance not subject to tax under this provision was $344 in 2015, $338 in 2014, $335 in 2013, $329 in 2012 and $320 in 2011.

(ITA: 6(1)(*b*)(v.1); 117.1; 149(1)(*l*))

HOW TO REPORT INCOME FROM EMPLOYMENT AND CLAIM ALLOWABLE EXPENSES

[¶392] INCOME FROM EMPLOYMENT

Report your gross income from employment on page 2 of the Individual Income Tax Return. Ordinary employment income (from box 14 of T4 slips) is reported at line 101. If the T4 shows a note that a benefit for a clergy residence allowance (¶376) is included in box 14, deduct the benefit from the amount in box 14 before reporting the income on line 101, and report the benefit on line 104. If you are entitled to the clergy residence deduction, claim it at line 231.

Commissions received in your capacity as an employee (see ¶304) are entered on line 102. Typically, these are reported to you in box 42 of a T4 slip. Line 102 is for reference only, identifying amounts eligible for particular deductions (¶368); amounts included on line 102 are also included in the amount reported on line 101, and should not be added again when totalling income at line 150.

If you are an independent (self-employed) commission salesperson, your commissions should be reported on a T4A slip. Your commission income is then reported as business income and does not affect the reporting of your employment income (see Chapter 7).

Tips, gratuities, and any other employment income (including foreign income) not reported on a T4 slip are entered on line 104. A GST/HST/QST tax rebate claimed last year under the rules at ¶363 and ¶363.45 and reported as paid to you on your notice of assessment for that year is also included on line 104.

The CRA also asks, either in the T1 Guide or elsewhere, for several other items to be included on line 104 which are not, technically speaking, employment income. These include royalties from a work or invention, research grants (net of expenses, ¶961), amounts received from a supplementary unemployment benefit plan, the taxable element (as shown on a T4A slip at box 28) of an income maintenance insurance plan, and veterans' benefits (box 127 of a T4A). Note that royalties (¶787) or net research grants may be business rather than employment income, and if so you should report them at line 135 rather than line 104.

[¶393] ALLOWABLE EXPENSES

Your deductions against your employment income are all claimed on page 3 of the T1. Some of these deductions have specific lines provided for them, such as registered pension plan contributions (line 207), union or professional dues (line 212) and the clergy residence deduction (line 231). Other expenses, such as automobile or office costs which you are required to pay in the course of your employment and for which you are not reimbursed, are entered on line 229. Form T777 is useful in summarizing the deductible expenses that are generally available to employees, and can be used to accumulate the total deductions to which you are entitled for entry at line 229.

Some deductions in arriving at taxable income (line 260) are also specific to employees. A complete list of these references is at ¶1077. Finally, some costs of earning income generate tax credits rather than deductions. These include Canada or Quebec Pension Plan contributions, Employment Insurance, and Quebec Parental Insurance Plan premiums. These items are listed in Schedule 1 of the Return at lines 308, 310, 312, and 317 and discussed in Chapter 13.

SPECIFIC QUESTIONS AND ANSWERS

[¶395] SPECIFIC QUESTIONS AND ANSWERS

Commissions Earned in Year 1 — Received in Year 2

I am a commission salesperson and my commissions are calculated on a monthly basis. During Year 1, I earned commissions totalling $36,000 for the months of January to November, and by December 31 I had received all $36,000 from my employer. My sales for December were very good and I earned $6,000 on that month's sales. However, I did not receive the $6,000 until January 25, Year 2. In fact, it was not until the company's books were closed and the necessary calculations were made in the first week of January that either the company or myself were aware of how much my commission would be. Do I have to include the $6,000 in my Year 1 income?

No. You should include only those amounts actually received by you or credited unconditionally to your account in Year 1. The other $6,000 should be included in Year 2. Your employer should prepare your T4 slip on that basis. The salary deferral rules (¶307) should not apply to you as it seems unlikely your situation constitutes a plan to defer tax.

Cash Advances Against Commissions

My company gives me cash advances of $1,500 per month against my commission earnings. My earned commissions are calculated annually and I receive a cheque in February of the following year for the excess of my earnings over these advances. In Year 1, my earned commissions totalled only $15,500 while my advances were $18,000. I was not asked to repay the $2,500 difference immediately but this debit balance was carried over in my account for Year 2. Do I have to pay tax on this $2,500 in Year 1?

Yes. The $2,500 advance must be included in your Year 1 income as your employment income must be reported in the year in which you receive it. See ¶329. It would be difficult for you to argue successfully that the advance constitutes a loan — in which case it is not taken into income as it is advanced, but only when it is offset by earnings or forgiven — as there are no specific terms of repayment, you are not apparently required to sign a note, interest in not charged, etc.

Cash Advances Repaid

I left the company for which I had worked as a commission salesperson for the past three years. At that time I had a $300 debit balance in my earnings advance account and I repaid this amount to the company. I have always paid tax as reported by the company on my T4 slip — on all advances I received rather than on my commission earned. Can I deduct the $300 I repaid?

In general, yes, assuming your income from that company in the year exceeds the advance you repay. It has traditionally been the CRA's position that if the advance repayment exceeds current year's income, you should carry back the excess to deduct in the prior year. See ¶329. It is not entirely clear why the excess cannot be treated as an employment loss in the year it occurs (¶1085).

Note that this treatment applies to an advance against income. If you are a commission salesperson repaying an advance against your expenses, and those expenses exceed your income for the year from that employer, it is the CRA's view that no deduction from other income is available. In these circumstances, technically speaking, it appears that no loss arises against other income. See ¶368.

Can an Employee Receive "Fees" from an Employer

I am employed as treasurer of a manufacturing company. In addition to my regular salary, I receive a fee for preparing and presenting training programs to company employees. I do the preparation and conduct the sessions in the evenings on Saturdays and received four fees of $500 each for this work. May I claim expenses, such as travelling to the office for such sessions, from my $2,000 in fees?

No. Because of your master–servant relationship with your employer, and because you received the fees by virtue of your employment as treasurer, it is not possible for you to act as an independent contractor on receipt of "fees". As an employee, you are entitled to deduct travelling expenses only under certain specific conditions. One of these is that you were ordinarily required to carry on the duties of your employment away from your employer's place of business.

Executor's Fees

During the year, I received $2,000 in executor's fees in connection with my deceased brother's estate. I incurred some expenses which were necessary to earn this income, particularly, wages paid to a part-time secretary of $600. Can I deduct the $600?

The CRA's view is that unless you carry on a business of acting as an executor, executor's fees are income from employment. Salaries paid to an assistant are only deductible if they are required to be paid by the contract of employment. However, you might have some grounds for arguing that you were implicitly required to utilize necessary services; the case of *Rozen v. The Queen*, 85 DTC 5611 (FCTD), although not directly on point, may support this view. See ¶309 and ¶372.03.

Earnings Directed to be Paid to Sister

I earned a bonus of $6,000 during the year, and directed my employer to pay the money to my widowed sister. Do I have to pay tax on this $6,000 that I never actually received?

Yes. The only offset you may be entitled to is the personal exemption credit for your sister if you meet the conditions at ¶1126.

Salesperson's Travelling Expenses

I am a salesperson who travels overseas and I receive an allowance from my employer for travelling expenses. Can I claim a deduction for additional expenses which I pay out of my own pocket?

If you are engaged in selling property or negotiating contracts for your employer, you may add the allowance to your income and claim your actual expenses if you can demonstrate that it is unreasonable — presumably, here, unreasonably low. Your employer will have to certify on form T2200 that the expenses were incurred to earn income and that you were not in receipt of a reasonable allowance. See ¶368, ¶369.

Employee's Travelling Expenses

I am a salaried employee and am away from my employer's place of business for short periods of approximately 20% of my working time. This is done on a regular basis — about one day a week. Can I deduct expenses I incurred?

Yes. You must be ordinarily required to conduct your duties away from your employer's place of business. "Ordinarily" has been interpreted by the CRA to mean "customarily" or "habitually" rather than "continually". There should be some degree of regularity in your travelling, and occasional absences from your place of employment will not qualify. However, you must obtain form T2200, signed by your employer, to support your claim.

Employees' Discount Purchases

My employer, a large retail store, permits its employees to purchase electrical goods at a 25% discount off retail selling price. During the year, I purchased an air conditioner for $300, the retail price being $400. Do I need to add the $100 to my income as a benefit received from employment?

Prior to July 7, 2016, where it was the practice of an employer to sell merchandise to employees at a discount, the benefits that an employee may have derived from exercising such a privilege was not normally regarded as taxable benefits, unless the policy permitted employees to purchase merchandise at less than the employer's cost. As of July 7, 2016, the value of the discount is generally included in the employee's income, regardless of the purchase price. See ¶348.

Board and Lodging of Hotel Employees

I am an employee of a large hotel. In addition to my salary of $600 per week, I receive free room and board valued at $200 per week. The cost of board and lodging to my employer is $160 per week. On which amount am I taxable?

The CRA says you are taxable on the "approximate" fair market value of the room and board, $200 per week. There is some case law which suggests that the fair market value to you may be less than what a third-party person would pay for it. Very possibly your employer has in fact used a cost-plus calculation for your T4. It is possible, if the hotel is isolated, it may qualify as a special work site (¶360).

If I contributed $140 per week towards my room and board, on what amount would I pay tax?

You would again pay tax on your salary, of course, plus the fair market value of your room and board minus your contribution, i.e., $600 + $200 - $140 = $660 per week. See ¶311.

House Provided Rent-Free by Employer

Throughout the year, my employer provided me with a house rent-free. A fair rent for a similar house would be $550 per month. Am I taxable on any portion of the $550 per month?

Yes, on all of it. Your employer should include $550 × 12 = $6,600 in your T4 slip. However, the tax liability is yours and the income should be reported regardless of whether your employer has prepared the T4 properly. See ¶312.

Vacation Expenses Paid by Employer

Our company sends employees on an extended vacation to Europe for six months as a token of appreciation for 40 years' faithful service. All expenses, which amounted to $25,000, were paid by the company. Are they taxable on this amount?

Yes. The sum of $25,000 must be added to their income as a taxable benefit.

Would it make any difference if they had received an automobile worth $25,000 instead of the vacation?

It makes no difference. Prizes and holidays in return for extended or meritorious service are all considered to be taxable benefits and must be included in the taxpayer's income. See ¶315 for the CRA's policies on not taxing certain employer-provided awards.

IMPORTANT POINTS TO REMEMBER

[¶398] IMPORTANT POINTS TO REMEMBER

- Attach copies of your T4 and other slips to your return (if paper filed). For returns that are electronically filed, retain these slips on hand in case the CRA requests them.
- You must include in your income such items as tips and income from part-time jobs, whether they are reported to you on a T4 or other slip or not.
- If you are claiming expenses for the use of your own motor vehicle, or for supplies and office space which you are required to provide in the course of your employment, you must have your employer certify on form T2200 that these are requirements of employment. Although you need not file the T2200 with your return, you must have it on hand if requested by the CRA.

Chapter 4

Investment Income

THESE POINTS ARE COVERED IN THIS CHAPTER

CRA REFERENCES RELATING TO THIS CHAPTER

T1 Lines and Schedule

- Line 120 — Taxable amount of dividends (eligible and other than eligible) from taxable Canadian corporations
- Line 121 — Interest and other investment income
- Line 221 — Carrying charges and interest expenses
- Schedule 4, Statement of Investment Income

CRA Guides

5000-G, "General Income Tax and Benefit Guide"; **RC4169**, "Tax Treatment of Mutual Funds for Individuals"; **RC4466**, "Tax-Free Savings Account — Information Sheet"; **T4011**, "Preparing Returns for Deceased Persons"; **T4013**, "T3 — Trust Guide"; **T4015**, "T5 Guide — Return of Investment Income"

CRA Forms

T3, "Statement of Trust Income Allocations and Designations"; **T5**, "Statement of Investment Income"; **T1135**, "Foreign Income Verification Statement"; **T1141**, "Information Return in Respect of Transfers or Loans to a Non-Resident Trust"; **T1142**, "Information Return in Respect of Transfers or Loans to a Non-Resident Trust"; **T2036**, "Provincial or Territorial Foreign Tax Credit"; **T2209**, "Federal Foreign Tax Credits"

Income Tax Folios

S1-F5-C1, "Related Persons and Dealing at Arm's Length"; **S3-F6-C1**, "Interest Deductibility"; **S5-F2-C1**, "Foreign Tax Credit"; **S6-F2-C1**, "Disposition of an Income Interest in a Trust";

Interpretation Bulletins

IT-66R6, "Capital Dividends"; **IT-67R3**, "Taxable Dividends from Corporations Resident in Canada"; **IT-87R2**, "Policyholders' Income from Life Insurance Policies"; **IT-88R2**, "Stock Dividends"; **IT-95R**, "Foreign Exchange Gains and Losses"; **IT-99R5 (Consolidated)**, "Legal and Accounting Fees"; **IT-119R4**, "Debts of Shareholders and Certain Persons Connected With Shareholders"; **IT-126R2**, "Meaning of "Winding-up""; **IT-201R2**, "Foreign Tax Credit — Trusts and Beneficiaries"; **IT-238R2**, "Fees Paid to Investment Counsel"; **IT-295R4**, "Taxable Dividends Received After 1987 by a Spouse"; **IT-342R**, "Trusts — Income Payable to Beneficiaries"; **IT-346R**, "Commodity Futures and Certain Commodities"; **IT-362R**, "Patronage Dividends"; **IT-394R2**, "Preferred Beneficiary Election"; **IT-396R**, "Interest Income"; **IT-421R2**, "Benefits to Individuals, Corporations and Shareholders from Loans or Debt"; **IT-432R2**, "Benefits Conferred on Shareholders"; **IT-440R2**, "Transfer of Rights to Income"; **IT-462**, "Payments Based on Production or Use"; **IT-465R**, "Non-Resident Beneficiaries of Trusts"; **IT-510**, "Transfers and Loans of Property Made after May 22, 1985 to a Related Minor"; **IT-511R**; "Interspousal and Certain Other Transfers and Loans of Property"; **IT-527**, "Distress Preferred Shares"

Information Circulars	**Income Tax Technical News**
93-3R1, "Registered Education Savings Plan"	**No. 31R2**, May 16, 2006, "Social Security Taxes and the Foreign Tax Credit"; **No. 38**, September 22, 2008, "SIFT Rules — Transitional Normal Growth; SIFT Entities — Definition of 'Real Estate Investment Trust' in Section 122.1"

WHAT YOU SHOULD KNOW ABOUT INVESTMENT INCOME

RECENT CHANGES

2016 Changes

Bill C-29 introduced a new rule which ensures that the interest accrued upon a sale of a "linked note" is included in the vendor's income as interest rather than as a capital gain. The rule was originally scheduled to apply to transfers occurring after September 2016; however, the measure will only apply to sales of linked notes after 2016. See ¶440.

Bill C-29 also proposed to extend back-to-back loan provisions to the existing shareholder loan rules. See ¶409.06.

The TFSA annual contribution limit for 2016 was reduced from the $10,000 amount for 2015 to $5,500. The limit is indexed to inflation and adjusted upward to the nearest $500 increment. See ¶478.

Draft legislation released on September 16, 2016, proposes some changes to the "character conversion" rules. See ¶443 under "Application".

2015 Federal Budget and Other Changes

The 2015 Federal Budget increased the small business deduction for Canadian-controlled private corporations for taxation years after 2015. As a result, the gross-up rates and dividend tax credit amounts for ineligible dividends have been amended for years after 2015. See ¶404.20 for these changes.

The Budget increased the annual TFSA contribution limit to $10,000, beginning in 2015. However, as noted above, for 2016 and subsequent years the limit has been reduced back to $5,500 (the limit for 2013 and 2014). See ¶478.

The Budget also extended the tax deferral that applies to patronage dividends paid to members by an eligible agricultural cooperative in the form of eligible shares. Originally applicable to shares issued before 2016, the deferral applies to shares issued before 2021. See ¶413.

[¶400] INVESTMENT INCOME AND LIFETIME RECORD MAY BE REQUIRED

An individual's "investment income" is not defined for the purposes of the Act (except for purposes of the capital gains exemption, as noted below), although it is understood to mean the individual's income from property as reported on Schedule 4 and issued T3 and T5 slips. As such, the investment income discussed in this chapter generally includes income you receive as a result of your ownership of corporation shares, bank deposits, bonds, debentures, mortgages, notes, annuity contracts, beneficial interests in an estate or trust, patents and in general, any other property with the exception of real estate. You should report real estate rentals on the Statement of Real Estate Rentals (see Chapter 6). Schedule 4 also includes a line (22) for net income or loss from a partnership if you were a limited partner or not actively involved in the partnership; limited partnerships are discussed in Chapter 18. Capital gains and losses, although perhaps colloquially considered investment income or losses, are not reported on Schedule 4, but rather Schedule 3, and are discussed in Chapter 5.

Tracking Investment Income for Computation of CNIL

If you dispose of qualified farm or fishing property (¶502f) or qualified small business corporation shares (¶502i), you should maintain an account of lifetime investment income and loss called the cumulative net investment loss (CNIL) account. The CNIL account is not otherwise relevant for investment purposes, but it is relevant in determining your capital gains exemption In a nutshell, if your lifetime investment expenses, such as interest, exceed your lifetime investment income, these specialized capital gains exemptions (should you ever claim them) will be reduced. As a practical matter, the CRA's computers keep track of this account from year to year. If your investment income invariably exceeds your associated investment expenses, you need not bother with the calculation yourself.

In general, the CNIL account is only of concern to investors who borrow heavily to finance their investments, or who invest in tax shelters. Details of the CNIL account are discussed at ¶502q in the context of capital gains. If you choose to keep track of the CNIL account yourself, you may use form T936 for this purpose. You need not file form T936 if you claim no capital gains exemption for the year; if you do claim exemption, you can obtain details of your account from your local CRA office (¶287) for the purpose of completing form T936. If you consider it at all likely that your investment costs will exceed your investment income, you should complete a T936 every year and ask the CRA for a statement of their determination of the account balance for comparison, so that differences can be reconciled while the issues are fresh.

Quebec's Investment Loss Limitation

Quebec has adopted a similar concept to limit the deduction of specified investment expenses (most notably interest) to specified investment income for the year. Quebec's objective, however, is to deny a deduction for current investment losses against other income. Excess expenses may be carried back three years and forward indefinitely against investment income (net of investment expenses) of those other years. Neither business nor rental income will be subject to this limitation. See ¶1635.

[¶401] DEEMED INCOME ON TRANSFERRED RIGHTS OR PROPERTY

Attribution Rules With Respect to Non-Arm's Length Individuals

If you have transferred or assigned a right to income to a person with whom you are not dealing at arm's length, subsection 56(4) of the Act provides that the income received by that person will be deemed to be your income, unless you have also transferred or assigned the property which gives rise to that income. If you have transferred the property, the attribution rules summarized below may apply.

Another attribution rule requires that you include the income arising from any property you have loaned directly or indirectly to any individual with whom you do not deal at arm's length if it can reasonably be considered that one of the main reasons for the loan is to reduce tax by causing the income to be reported in the hands of the non-arm's length individual. The rule applies to any indebtedness owing to you from a non-arm's length individual in respect of property acquired by the individual. The rule is aimed primarily at loans to and indebtedness incurred by non-arm's length adults, although it is not invoked as readily as the other attribution rules owing to the "main reason" test that must be met. The rule does not apply to loans to or indebtedness incurred by nieces or nephews.

Attribution Rules With Respect to Spouses, Common-law Partners, and Minors

Under the income attribution rules of section 74.1, any income or loss from property (e.g., investment income or loss) loaned or transferred to your spouse or common-law partner (or a person who has since become your spouse or common-law partner) is included as income or loss in your hands as long as you are resident in Canada. This rule also applies to any income from a property substituted for the property transferred. However, if you become divorced or you are separated and are living apart from your spouse or common-law partner by reason of a breakdown in your marriage or relationship, the income is no longer taxable in your hands. There is a similar attribution rule in respect of capital gains or losses in respect of property transferred to your spouse or common-law partner.

Similarly, any income or loss from property loaned or transferred to a non-arm's length person or niece or nephew under the age of 18 (a minor) is included in your income or loss if you are resident in Canada and the minor has not attained the age of 18 before the end of the relevant taxation year. Again, the rule also applies to any income from a property substituted for the property transferred. This attribution rule does not apply to capital gains or losses.

If you have attributed investment income, you should report it in the applicable line and schedule for that type of investment income (e.g. line 120 for dividends, line 121 for interest). These lines and schedules are discussed below under the type of income.

There are various exceptions to the income attribution rules. One exception provides that income from loaned property (or property acquired with a loan) will not be included in your income if interest on the loan was charged at the lesser of commercial rates or prescribed rates. There is also an exception for transfers made for fair market value consideration.

See ¶977 and ¶2529 for more details.

(ITA: 56(4); (4.1); 74.1–74.5; 75; IT-440R2 Transfer of Rights to Income; IT-510 Transfers and loans of property made after May 22, 1985 to related minor; IT-511R Interspousal and certain other transfers and loans of property; Income Tax Folio: S1-F5-C1 Related Persons and Dealing at Arm's Length)

DIVIDEND INCOME

[¶402] MEANING OF "DIVIDEND"

For income tax purposes, the word "dividend" generally means a share of the profits of a corporation distributed to its shareholders. While the term is also used to describe such things as a share of earnings allocated to the holders of participating insurance policies or a proportional payment to the creditors of a bankrupt corporation, such payments are not dividends in an income tax sense.

In most cases, you will have little difficulty in determining whether you have received a dividend. Canadian corporations are required to supply shareholders who have received dividends totaling $50 or more during the year with a T5 tax receipt, which indicates the total amount of dividends paid by the corporation to the shareholder in the year. You are required to file one copy of this form with your annual income tax return. The form is a valuable aid, since it shows not only the actual amount of dividends, but also the "taxable amount" and the amount of "Federal Dividend Tax Credit" available.

You may receive a dividend but not receive a T5. In this case, you should determine whether the dividend you receive is taxable. It may be that the dividend is not taxable or that the dividend was less than $50 and the company paying the dividend is not required to issue a T5 to you. If it is a non-taxable dividend, see ¶415. If it is a taxable dividend, you should record it as income. See ¶404 and ¶407.

(ITR: 201 Investment Income; T4015 T5 Guide — Return of Investment Income — 2015; IT-67R3 Taxable Dividends from Corporations Resident in Canada)

[¶403] WHEN DIVIDENDS ARE TAXABLE

Dividends are included in income in the year they are received. For income tax purposes, amounts are considered received on the day they are sent by first class mail or the equivalent. You cannot defer a dividend to next year because the payment was delayed (or lost) in the mail.

(ITA: 82; 90; 248(7))

[¶404] DIVIDENDS FROM CANADIAN CORPORATIONS

Taxable dividends received from taxable Canadian corporations receive special tax treatment. An individual (including a trust or estate) receiving a dividend from a taxable Canadian corporation includes in his or her investment income an amount called the "Taxable Amount" in respect of that dividend. This amount includes the dividend itself, plus a specified percentage of the dividend called the "gross-up". An offsetting "dividend tax credit" is then allowed (on Schedule 1, ¶1425) which, when applied, reduces the actual tax on the dividend income to less than it would have been if the dividend had merely been taxed as ordinary income. These amounts are discussed in the commentary below.

[¶404.05] *Purpose of Dividend Gross-up and Tax Credit*

The purpose of the gross-up and credit mechanism is to give an individual receiving dividends from a Canadian corporation recognition for the corporate income tax the corporation has presumably paid on the income from which it paid the dividend. In theory, the gross-up restores the dividend to the amount the corporation would have paid you if it had not had to pay corporate income tax which reduced the amount available for dividends. Generally speaking, the dividend tax credit represents the corporate income tax paid. Thus, at the end of the day, you pay tax at your personal marginal rate on the notional income the corporation could have paid you but for corporate income tax, but you have received a refund (through the dividend tax credit) of the notional corporate tax paid on that income. The result should be as if the corporation had never paid corporate tax, but merely passed its income on to you for you to pay tax on.

All provinces (and territories) similarly tax grossed-up dividends and offer dividend tax credits which are meant to offset the provincial corporate income tax.

Although this system does not always work perfectly, since it works off notional rather than actual corporate tax paid, it usually provides a result that is close to the theoretical norm.

There are two types of taxable dividends you can receive from Canadian corporations. An eligible dividend is generally a dividend paid out of a corporation's income that was subject to the general corporate tax rate (15% federal rate in 2016). A non-eligible dividend is generally a dividend received out of a corporation's income that was subject to the small business deduction and therefore subject to a lower rate of tax (10.5% federal rate in 2016). There are various exceptions and modifications to these rules.

Although tracing the income and paying dividends out of the correct "pot" will often be a complex task for the corporation, the matter is a simple one for you. Your T3 or T5 slip will show which dividends are eligible dividends and which are other dividends, and any penalties for faulty designation of dividends as eligible will be the liability of the corporation and not the dividend recipient.

Although you can rely on your reporting slip, where a corporation designates an eligible dividend in excess of the amount it was properly entitled to pay as an eligible dividend, it may ask you to accept a change to that reporting and report some or all of the eligible dividend as an other dividend, to relieve it of the penalty tax on the excess. The corporation cannot impose this change unless it obtains the concurrence of all shareholders who received, or were entitled to receive, the dividend and whose addresses are known to it. This would seem, as a practical matter, to limit relief of the corporate penalty to the case of closely held corporations. In the case of a large public corporation, the concurrence requirement would seem an insuperable barrier.

[¶404.10] *Eligible Dividends*

If you received a dividend designated as an "eligible dividend" on your T3 or T5 slip, you must report as income on line 120 of your return the taxable amount of the dividend, obtained by increasing the actual dividend received by 38%. This addition to the actual dividend amount is referred to as the "gross-up". The taxable amount is also reported on line 5 of Schedule 4.

If you have received an eligible dividend from a taxable Canadian corporation, you will be entitled to claim a credit against your federal tax equal to $^{6}/_{11}$ of the "gross-up" amount. This is equivalent to 15.0198% of the taxable amount of the dividend.

As a practical matter, your actual dividend, grossed up dividend, and dividend tax credit are calculated by each payer corporation on the T5 (or T3 if the dividend has passed through a trust) slip it provides to you. You merely have to add up the taxable dividends from various slips and report them on line 120, and add up the dividend tax credits and report them on line 425 on page 2 of Schedule 1. If you have both eligible and other dividends, using Schedule 4 should make the procedure clear, especially the inclusion of the grossed-up taxable amounts of both eligible and other dividends in line 120.

Until recently, corporations could not designate part of a dividend as an eligible dividend. This rule was changed in the 2012 Federal Budget. Thus, if you receive a dividend in 2015, a portion of which is designated as an eligible dividend, that portion is eligible for the gross-up and dividend tax credit mechanism discussed above.

As discussed further at ¶491.10, if a trust is a SIFT trust and is not otherwise exempt from the SIFT rules, distributions of the trust entity are treated as eligible dividends. Under the SIFT rules, the trust is treated similarly to a corporation in respect of certain non-portfolio earnings such that distributions of such amounts are generally treated as eligible dividends in the hands of the unitholders.

[¶404.13] *Changing Eligible Dividend Rates (2010 and Later)*

Since the purpose of the eligible dividend rules is to compensate shareholders for (notional) tax paid at the corporate level, it follows that the gross-up and credit machinery should be adjusted in tandem with changes in corporate tax rates. The general corporate tax rate has been reduced in recent years, and the gross-up and credit rates on *eligible* dividends, which compensate for the general corporate tax rate, have also changed, as follows:

Year	*Gross-up*	*Credit on gross-up*	*Credit on grossed-up dividend*
2010	44%	$^{10}/_{17}$	17.9739%
2011	41%	$^{13}/_{23}$	16.4354%
2012 and later	38%	$^{6}/_{11}$	15.0198%

[¶404.20] *Other Canadian "Non-Eligible" Dividends*

If you received a dividend designated as an "other dividend" on your T3 or T5 slip, you must include, for each such dividend, the total of other dividends on line 180 and in the total taxable amount of dividends on line 120, the amount obtained by increasing the actual dividend received by 17%. This addition to the actual dividend amount is referred to as the "gross-up". If you have more than one dividend altogether (eligible and other), using Schedule 4 should make the procedure clear, especially the inclusion of the grossed-up taxable amounts of both eligible and other dividends in line 120 of your tax return. As noted earlier, non-eligible dividends are generally those paid out of CCPC business income subject to the small business rate of tax.

If you have received such a dividend from a taxable Canadian corporation, you will be entitled to claim a credit against your federal tax equal to $^{21}/_{29}$ of the gross-up. The credit is therefore approximately 10.5% of the grossed-up amount of the non-eligible dividend.

Gross-up Rates for "Non-Eligible" Dividends

The non-eligible dividend gross-up rate was amended to correlate with the increases to the small business deduction. A year-by-year breakdown of the gross-up rates and corresponding dividend tax credit for non-eligible dividends is provided below:

Year	Gross-Up Amount	Dividend Tax Credit	Credit on Grossed-Up Dividend
After 2015	17%	$^{21}/_{29}$	10.5%
2015	18%	$^{13}/_{18}$	11%
2014	18%	$^{13}/_{18}$	11%

Example

Lucille Petersen received two dividends of $100 from taxable Canadian corporations. The first was reported to her as an "eligible dividend", the second as an "other dividend".

In respect of the eligible dividend, Lucille must include in her income the amount of $100 plus the gross-up of 38% × $100 = $38, for a total taxable amount of $138. When calculating her tax, Lucille may claim a dividend tax credit of $^{6}/_{11}$ of $38, or $20.73.

In respect of the other dividend, Lucille must include in her income the amount of $100 plus the gross-up of 17%, for a total taxable amount of $117. When calculating her tax, Lucille may claim a federal dividend tax credit of $^{21}/_{29}$ of $17, or $12.31.

When calculating her tax, Lucille must report as income $138 for the eligible dividend, plus $117 for the other dividend, and may claim a combined federal dividend tax credit of $20.73 + $12.31 = $33.04.

Historical Information

For 2014 and 2015, the gross-up for non-eligible dividends was 18% and the federal dividend tax credit was $^{13}/_{18}$ of the gross-up. Prior to 2014, the gross-up for non-eligible dividends was 25% and the federal dividend tax credit was $^{2}/_{3}$ of the gross-up.

[¶404.25] *Certain capital gains may be treated as dividends for purposes of "kiddie tax"*

The tax on split income of minor children, sometimes referred to as the "kiddie tax", applies to dividends received from corporations whose shares are not listed on a designated stock exchange. In addition, capital gains realized by a minor from a disposition of shares of a corporation to a non-arm's length person are treated as dividends, if taxable dividends on such shares would have been subject to the tax on split income. In other words, these capital gains are deemed to be dividends and will not benefit from the one-half inclusion rate applicable to capital gains or the lifetime capital gain exemption. This rule applies to capital gains realized on or after March 22, 2011. See Chapter 14 at ¶1490 for a detailed discussion of the tax on split income of a minor.

[¶404.30] *In General*

In most cases, T5 information forms are provided to each shareholder receiving a dividend and these will indicate whether or not the subject dividends are from taxable Canadian corporations and, if so, whether they are eligible or other dividends. The T5 form also indicates the taxable amount of each type of dividend and the amount of dividend tax credit for that dividend. Where dividends from taxable Canadian companies received by a trust have been allocated to a beneficiary, the same rules apply as if the beneficiary had received the dividends directly; the aggregate amounts of each type of dividend which passed through the trust are reported on a T3 slip rather than a T5 slip.

(ITA: 82; 84; 121; IT-67R3 Taxable Dividends from Corporations Resident in Canada; Other Publications: Department of Finance Press Release 2006-028)

[¶404.35] *Provincial Dividend Tax Credit*

The provinces are entitled to base their tax on federal taxable income (which means it includes the dividend gross-up) but to levy their own tax rates and credits. These credits, including the provincial dividend tax credits, are discussed in Chapter 15. Quebec continues to collect its own provincial tax; it accepts the federal gross-up rate and offers its own dividend tax credit, discussed at ¶1666.

[¶406] STOCK DIVIDENDS

If you receive a stock dividend from a private corporation or from a public or non-resident corporation, you are deemed to have received a dividend equal to your share of the increase in the paid-up capital of the corporation resulting from the payment of the stock dividend. The T5 information slip will show the deemed actual amount and the taxable amount of the stock dividend. The taxable amount must be included in your income for the year.

A stock split is not taxable. It is not always easy, however, to distinguish between a stock dividend and a stock split. For example an 11 for 10 stock split may result in the same amount of shares as a 10% stock dividend. If you are not sure what you have received, you should contact the paying corporation or its disbursing agent.

(ITA: 52; 248(1) "stock dividend"; IT-67R3 Taxable Dividends from Corporations Resident in Canada; IT-88R2 Stock Dividends)

[¶407] DIVIDENDS RECEIVED FROM NON-RESIDENT CORPORATIONS

If you receive dividends from a non-resident corporation, you must include them in income. Dividends from non-resident corporations are not subject to the gross-up nor are they eligible for the dividend tax credit. The actual amount of the dividends should be entered as foreign source income on Part II of Schedule 4 and on line 121 of your tax return.

Dividends from foreign corporations should be included in your income in Canadian dollars. Generally, the amount received will be converted to Canadian dollars when received. You should note the Canadian dollar equivalent at that time for reference when preparing your income tax return. Where foreign tax has been withheld from such dividends, the gross amounts (i.e., before withholding is deducted) should be shown as income and a foreign tax credit claimed (see ¶1450). Foreign dividends receive the same treatment as foreign interest (see ¶435).

Some foreign companies may pay a special dividend which is not taxable under the laws of that foreign country. For example, a U.S. corporation may pay a "capital gain dividend" which receives special treatment under the U.S. tax laws. However, the U.S. tax status has no effect on the taxability of the amount in Canada; if you receive a dividend in cash or kind, it will be taxed as dividend income and not as a capital gain.

The income tax law contains rules which require certain Canadian resident shareholders of a foreign company or Canadian resident beneficiaries of a foreign trust to report and pay tax on their share of investment income received by the foreign company or trust. This income will be reportable by the Canadian resident even though it is not distributed to him by the foreign company or trust. See ¶493 for more details.

Foreign source dividends implies ownership of shares in foreign companies. Where the cost amount of foreign investment assets (including but not limited to shares) exceeds $100,000, special reporting of those assets is required regardless of whether they generate income; see ¶496. Where alone or together with other Canadians you hold 10% or more of the shares of any class of a foreign company, you may be required to report under the rules at ¶495 as well as or instead of ¶496. If you have a 10% or more beneficial interest in a non-resident trust, you may be required to report under ¶495.

(ITA: 82; 90; 91; 94; 104; 121; 126; IT-67R3 Taxable Dividends from Corporations Resident in Canada)

[¶407.05] *Recovering Foreign Taxes Withheld*

When you receive dividends from foreign (non-Canadian) corporations, the country in which the corporation is resident will typically withhold tax. Canada provides a credit for this tax so long as it does not exceed 15% of the dividend. You record the entire dividend (including the amount withheld which you did not in fact receive) as income, and claim foreign tax credit on Schedule 1 as discussed at ¶1450 *et seq.* To the extent withholding exceeds 15% of the dividend, it is deductible rather than creditable as discussed in ¶1455(3)(B).

Canada's extensive system of tax treaties (listed at ¶2005) in general limits withholding by the foreign country to 15% for individuals. This must be verified against the appropriate treaty; the CRA (¶287) will give you the rate for a particular country. Also see the chart at ¶96.

It often happens that the foreign country will want verification that you are a Canadian taxpayer before lowering its actual withholding to the (usually 15%) rate specified in the treaty. Each country has its own practices, and often the same country is not consistent with regard to different sources within that country.

Example — U.S.-Sourced Dividends

Where the foreign country is the U.S., you may receive a form from the payer which simply requires you to affirm that you are a "non-resident alien" of the U.S. and return the form to the payer. For some U.S.-source payments, you may receive a U.S. form from the U.S. Internal Revenue Service which must be countersigned by the CRA and returned to the U.S. Any CRA service office can do this for you; you take (or, if you're brave, send) the form in and the CRA will verify that you filed a return for the most recent period and stamp the U.S. form. If you are a Canadian resident but not a Canadian taxpayer, you will have to explain and justify this to the CRA (see also ¶2546). You should study the tax documentation you receive from foreign (especially U.S.) sources to ensure that only correct amounts have been withheld.

[¶408] ELECTION ON DIVIDENDS RECEIVED BY YOUR SPOUSE

You may elect to include in your income taxable dividends received by your spouse or common-law partner from taxable Canadian corporations. This election may only be made where your spousal tax credit (line 303 on your return, ¶1114) would be created or increased if *all* of your spouse's taxable dividends from corporations resident in Canada were excluded from your spouse's income.

The test of whether this election can be made refers to all taxable dividends from corporations resident in Canada; the election itself is in respect of only taxable dividends from taxable Canadian corporations (i.e., those eligible for the 17% gross-up and the dividend tax credit or 38% as described at ¶404.10 and ¶404.20). Situations where a corporation is resident in Canada but is not a taxable Canadian corporation will be rare, but can occur. The election must be made for all of your spouse's dividends from taxable Canadian corporations; you may not make a partial election. If your spouse has unused pension income deductions or other amounts which may be transferred to you on Schedule 2, the election on dividends will reduce your spouse's taxable income on Schedule 2.

This election would normally be made where your spousal credit (see ¶1114) is reduced as a result of the receipt of dividends by your spouse and where your spouse does not have any income taxes to pay. The election has the effect of deleting the dividends from your spouse's income, including them in your income, and entitling you to claim the dividend tax credit. On the other hand, if you are 65 or over, the transfer may impair your age credit if it brings your net income above the dollar threshold at which the age credit begins to erode (¶1108). The personal amount for a spouse is worth more than the age amount, but where the spouse amount will be impaired by income to some extent even after the transfer, you must weigh the value of the transfer carefully. If your income before the transfer is already high enough that the age credit is lost in any event, this consideration may be irrelevant.

This election is only available for dividends received by your spouse or common-law partner; it does not apply to dividends received by another dependent, even if you are claiming the spousal equivalent exemption. Also note that this election must be made in respect of all taxable dividends received by your spouse from taxable Canadian corporations and that you are not allowed to deduct any interest or other charges paid by your spouse to earn the taxable dividends.

(ITA: 82(3); 118.8; IT-295R4 Taxable dividends received after 1987 by a spouse)

[¶409] LOANS TO SHAREHOLDERS OR EMPLOYEES

[¶409.05] *Inclusion of Shareholder Loans in Income*

Under subsection 15(2) of the Act, if you are a shareholder, directly or through a partnership or trust, or if you are non-arm's length with a shareholder (see ¶812) of a corporation and you have obtained a loan from or otherwise incurred a debt to that particular corporation or a corporation related to it, or from a partnership of which either the particular corporation or the related corporation is a member, the loan or debt is treated as income received by you in the year of the loan or debt. This rule also applies if you (or a partnership) receive such a loan or incur indebtedness and you (or the partnership) are affiliated with a shareholder of the corporation (see ¶852 for a discussion of the concept of "affiliated persons"). Loans which meet the initial criteria for inclusion in income are referred to as "shareholder loans". A shareholder loan which is deemed to be income under this rule is not considered to be a dividend, and, therefore, is not subject to the "gross-up" and is not eligible for the dividend tax credit.

The term "incurred a debt" includes all forms of indebtedness owed by the shareholder (or a person related to the shareholder) or owed by any person by virtue of his or someone else's employment. Indebtedness could include the unpaid purchase price of property purchased from the company and notes payable.

> **Commentary on Bill C-29 Measures (Oct. 25, 2016)**
>
> Note: When Bill C-29, October 25, 2016, achieves Royal Assent, the commentary will be modified to read:
>
> Furthermore, there are new rules under which certain back-to-back loans or debt can be subject to the shareholder loan rules. See ¶409.06 below.

Fortunately, there are several exceptions to the shareholder loan inclusion rule, outlined below. However, where they do not apply, the imputed interest rules discussed at ¶409.15 may apply if the loan or debt carries no interest or a rate of interest below the prescribed rate of interest.

If the shareholder loan inclusion rule applies, there is an offsetting deduction in the year in which you repay the loan or debt (paragraph 20(1)(*j*)). In Interpretation Bulletin IT-119R4, the CRA says that, in general, repayments are considered to apply first to the oldest loan or debt outstanding (first-in, first-out basis) "unless the facts clearly indicate otherwise".

Exceptions

As noted, there are various exceptions where a shareholder loan or debt is not included in income. They are summarized below.

Loan from money-lender

An exception applies where the loan was made in the ordinary course of business of a corporation whose business is the lending of money or the debt arose in the ordinary course of the creditor's business, provided however that bona fide arrangements for repayment within a reasonable time were made at the time the loan or debt arose.

Repayment within one year after year of loan

The rule does not apply if the loan or debt is repaid within one year from the end of the corporation's taxation year in which it was made, This exception does not apply where the loan is part of a series of loans and repayments. The CRA takes the position (in its publication Technical News, No. 3, confirmed in Interpretation Bulletin IT-119R4, para. 29) that *bona fide* repayments of shareholder loans which are the result of the declaration of dividends, salaries or bonuses should not be considered part of a series of loans or other transactions. The focus of taxation in these circumstances will presumably shift to the imputed interest rules described under ¶409.15.

Loans between non-residents

The rule does not apply to the indebtedness between non-resident persons.

Loans to certain employees

Loans or debts to employee shareholders are excluded from the shareholder loan rule provided two initial conditions are both met at the time the loan or debt is incurred. These initial conditions are:

(1) *bona fide* arrangements have been made to repay the loan within a reasonable time; and

(2) it is reasonable to conclude that the employee received the loan or became indebted because of the employment relationship and not because of any person's shareholdings.

In its interpretation bulletin IT-119R4, the CRA comments on this condition: "Whether or not a loan made by a corporation to an individual is considered to have been received by that individual in his or her capacity as an employee or as a shareholder involves a finding of fact in each particular case. When a public corporation makes a loan to a shareholder on the same terms and conditions as to other employees who are not shareholders, the loan is normally considered to be a loan received by virtue of that individual's office or employment rather than his or her shareholdings. However, when the opportunity to borrow funds is only made available to shareholders or when the terms and conditions attached to loans to employee-shareholders are more favourable than those attached to loans to other employees, the loan will be considered to have been made to the employee-shareholder in his or her capacity as a shareholder unless the facts clearly indicate otherwise."

If the employee is not a specified employee of the lender or creditor, the above exception applies if the two criteria are met. A specified employee is essentially one who owns directly or indirectly at any time in the year 10% or more of any class of shares of the corporation or a related corporation. The actual definition is far more elaborate and specific so that, for example, a taxpayer is deemed to own each share owned by a non-arm's length (¶812) person and a person who does not deal at arm's length with a specified employee is also a specified employee.

If the loan is made in respect of an employee who is a specified employee, one of the following criteria must also be met:

(1) it is in respect of an employee (or the employee's spouse) of the lender/creditor to help the employee acquire a dwelling house (including a country house, a summer cottage, or a suite in an apartment block or unit in a duplex) which is for the employee's habitation;

(2) it is in respect of an employee of a particular lender/creditor corporation (or a corporation related to the particular corporation) to enable or assist an employee to buy fully paid treasury (previously unissued) shares from the lender/creditor corporation or from a corporation related to the lender/creditor corporation to be held for the employee's own benefit; or

(3) it is in respect of an employee of the lender/creditor to enable or assist the employee to acquire a motor vehicle to be used by the employee in the performance of the employee's duties.

(ITA: 15(2)–(2.6), (7), (8); 248(1) "specified employee", "specified shareholder"; IT-119R4 Debts of Shareholders and Certain Persons Connected with Shareholders; *The Queen v. Silden*, 93 DTC 5362 (F.C.A.); *Attis v. M.N.R.*, 92 DTC 1128 (T.C.C.); Other Publications: 1986 Revenue Canada Round Table, Q. 63)

[¶409.06] *Back-to-Back Shareholder Loans*

> **Commentary on Bill C-29 Measures (Oct. 25, 2016)**
>
> Note: When Bill C-29, October 25, 2016, achieves Royal Assent, the commentary will be modified to read:

In the 2016 Federal Budget, the government expressed the need to issue new provisions to catch back-to-back loans:

"In situations where the shareholder loan rules would otherwise apply in respect of a debt owing by a shareholder to a corporation, there is an incentive to use a back-to-back arrangement to avoid their application by interposing a third party (that is not connected to the shareholder) between the corporation and its shareholder, in order to avoid the income inclusion or withholding tax. To address the use of back-to-back arrangements to circumvent the shareholder loan rules, Budget 2016 proposes to amend the shareholder loan rules to include rules that are similar to the existing back-to-back loans rules, except that the proposed rules will apply to debts owing to Canadian-resident corporations rather than debts owing by Canadian-resident taxpayers."

In general terms, this applies where an intermediary person or partnership that is not connected with the shareholder is owed an amount by the shareholder or certain parties connected to the shareholder (the "shareholder debt") and either:

(1) the intermediary owes an amount to the corporation (the "intermediary debt"), where either (a) recourse in respect of the intermediary debt is limited to the amount that the intermediary recovers on the shareholder debt or (b) it can reasonably be concluded that the shareholder debt became owing or was permitted to remain owing because the intermediary debt was, or was anticipated to be, entered into; or

(2) the intermediary has a "specified right" in respect of a property (such as a right to mortgage, hypothecate, assign, pledge or in any way encumber the property to secure payment of an obligation) that was granted to the Canadian-resident corporation and either (a) the existence of the specified right is required under the terms of the shareholder debt or (b) it can reasonably be concluded that the shareholder debt became owing or was permitted to remain owing because the specified right was, or was anticipated to be, granted.

If a back-to-back shareholder loan arrangement is found to exist, then the shareholder will be deemed to be indebted to the Canadian corporation in an amount equal to the lesser of (a) the shareholder debt and (b) the aggregate of the intermediary debt and the fair market value of the property over which the intermediary has a specified right. As a result, the indebtedness would be subject to subsection 15(2) in the case of a Canadian resident shareholder or Part XIII in the case of a non-resident. There are additional provisions dealing with subsequent changes in the amount of the indebtedness.

This applies to back-to-back shareholder loans and indebtedness received or incurred after March 21, 2016, and also to the portion of any previous loans or debt still outstanding as of March 22, 2016.

[¶409.10] *Forgiven Loans*

Any loan or other debt of a shareholder to a company which is forgiven by the company or retired for less than its face or outstanding amount is a taxable benefit to the extent it exceeds amounts already included in the shareholder's income under the above rules and amounts repaid by the shareholder.

More specifically, the forgiven amount of the loan or debt is defined by reference to the definition of "forgiven amount" in the more general loan forgiveness rules at ¶565 (which can apply to any forgiven loan used for income earning purposes) except that:

(1) the debt need not be a "commercial obligation", that is, need not have been incurred by the shareholder to earn income; the forgiveness rules at ¶565 operate only on commercial obligations which are defined to be those on which interest paid would be deductible;

(2) the forgiven amount at ¶565 is not reduced for amounts otherwise included in income (which might give a circular definition, since the amount included in income here would reduce the amount to be included in income here; ordering rules are provided for income inclusions);

(3) the forgiven amount is not reduced to reflect the extent to which the obligation is taken into account in determining proceeds of disposition of property subject to foreclosure or repossession under the rules at ¶518; and

(4) interest payable on the principal amount is not included in the forgiven amount here. In the event that an obligation with respect to interest payable on the debt is settled, there is no employment income inclusion, although there may be tax consequences under ¶518 or ¶565 if the obligation was a commercial obligation (see (1)).

Where a debt is forgiven, there is an ordering of tax consequences under which the unpaid amount rules at ¶746 operate first, then the employment income rules at ¶353, then the shareholder rules here, then the ordinary business income rules, then the foreclosure rules at ¶518, and finally the rules at ¶565.

Where the debt is a commercial obligation, the rules at ¶565 concerning debt parking and deemed settlement when statutory rights to recovery expire could apply. However, when applied to a debt which will be included in income under the shareholder rules, they will apply to the forgiven amount under the rules described above. It appears that debt included in income under the shareholder forgiveness rules is simply included in income; there is no grind of tax attributes as with a debt included under the rules at ¶565.

(ITA: 15(1), (1.2), (1.21))

[¶409.15] *Imputed Interest on Shareholder and Employee Loans*

Employee loans

In addition to the above rules, if you or someone related to you receives a low-interest or interest-free loan or otherwise incurs a debt as a result of your past, present or contemplated future office or employment, you will be deemed to have received a taxable benefit.

The benefit deemed received will be equal to the excess of:

(1) the interest calculated on the loan or debt at prescribed rates for the period of the year during which it was outstanding in that year; and

(2) any interest paid or payable by:

(a) your employer or intended employer, or

(b) someone related to your employer

over

(3) interest on the loan for the year paid either by you or those persons discussed in (2), above, within 30 days after the end of the year.

Prescribed interest rates change quarterly; a table of rates by quarter is found in the information material immediately preceding Chapter 1.

The CRA's bulletin on this subject (IT-421R2) is rather vague on some details of the interest calculation. Presumably, the interest is prorated, where the loan is outstanding for only part of a quarter, by days in the quarter during which the loan was outstanding over the total number of days in the quarter. If the loan balance changes during a quarter, again one presumes there is proration for the balance outstanding on a daily basis. However, there seems to be no official confirmation of these policies.

Shareholder loans

If you are a shareholder of a corporation, connected with (essentially, not at arm's length with or affiliated with) a shareholder of a corporation, or a beneficiary of a trust that was a shareholder of a corporation, and received a loan or incurred other forms of debt by virtue of the shareholding from the corporation or a related corporation, you will be deemed to have received a taxable benefit, computing similarly to that noted above for employee loans. The benefit will be the difference between the interest on the loan or debt computed at the prescribed rate and the interest for the year actually paid within 30 days of the end of the year.

There is no deemed interest benefit for shareholders or employees where the interest rate on the loan is equal to or greater than the interest rate that would have been negotiated between arm's length parties at the time the loan was made, having regard to all the circumstances, including the terms and conditions of the loan. The portion of any loan or debt that has been included in your income, such as a shareholder loan (¶409.05), is also excluded from the deemed benefit rules.

Both employee and shareholder

Where you are both a shareholder and an employee of the same company (or related companies), and you receive a loan, it is important to determine whether the loan is received in your capacity as shareholder or employee. This is a question of fact in each case, and will depend on such things as whether others who are not both shareholders and employees can receive such loans as one or the other. If your loan is received as a shareholder, it may be subject to income inclusion if outstanding over two year ends (as discussed above) and may in any case be subject to the imputed interest rules if interest is charged at less than prescribed rates (as discussed above). If the loan is received as an employee, it may escape inclusion in income if it meets the exceptions described above; in addition, if it is a home purchase loan, the inclusion of imputed interest may be alleviated as described below.

Special rules for employee home purchase loans

Where a loan is received by virtue of employment and is used to purchase or refinance a dwelling for an employee or relative of an employee, or a loan is received by a personal services company (see ¶785) by virtue of the services of a specified shareholder or a relative of a specified shareholder, any interest benefit computed under the rules above by reference to the prescribed rate in effect at any time during the year may not exceed the benefit computed as if the prescribed rate for the particular period was the prescribed rate that was in effect at the time the home purchase loan was made. Thus any increase in the prescribed rate of interest that occurs after the date the home purchase loan was received will not increase the amount of the benefit, whereas any decrease in the prescribed rate from the prescribed rate in effect at the time the loan was made will reduce the amount of the benefit. However, where a home purchase loan has a term of repayment in excess of five years, it is treated as a new loan every five years. This means that the benefit on a home purchase loan is determined for the first five-year period by reference to the prescribed rate when the loan was made. At the expiry of one five-year period, the benefit for the next five-year period will be measured in relation to the prescribed rate in effect at that time.

An exception allows an employee who has commenced employment at a new work location and by reason thereof has moved to a residence which is at least 40 kilometres closer to his new work location in Canada than was his previous residence, to reduce his taxable benefit relating to interest on a housing loan received from his employer in connection with the move. The benefit is to be reduced for a five-year period by an amount equal to the benefit of a $25,000 interest-free loan outstanding for a period of five years from the date on which the loan was made. This effectively allows an employee to have a $25,000 interest-free loan for five years provided that he has moved to a new residence as a result of his employment. There has been some case law which suggests that relocation loans generally may not give rise to an income benefit; see ¶353.

Where your spouse or another person has received a low-interest or interest-free loan by virtue of your employment you will be required to include the interest benefit in your income and not that of your spouse. By contrast, it appears that the taxable benefit of a loan received by someone else by virtue of your shareholding is in the first instance taxed to the actual recipient, although rules exist to allow the CRA to redirect the benefit to you.

Possible offsetting deduction for imputed interest expense

If you are required to include in your income a taxable imputed interest benefit in respect of a loan or debt, and the loan or debt has been used for the purpose of earning income from a business or property or to acquire certain annuities (see ¶432), you will be entitled to an offsetting deduction equal to the amount of the benefit. However, where the loan or debt is deemed to have been received or incurred by another person you will be denied the deduction.

For example, if your spouse receives an interest-free loan from your employer to purchase shares, you will be deemed to have received a taxable benefit, however, you are not entitled to the deduction as the loan was not used by you. It appears, however, that your spouse may be entitled to the interest deduction.

If you are required to include in your income a taxable benefit as a result of receiving an interest-free or low-interest loan, by virtue of your employment, for the purpose of purchasing an automobile or an aircraft, and you are eligible to deduct expenses under either the salesman's or travel expense provisions, you will be entitled to an offsetting deduction. See ¶368 and ¶369.

(ITA: 8; 15(9); 56(2); 80.4; 80.5; 110(1)(*j*); IT-421R2 Benefits to Individuals, Corporations and Shareholders from Loans or Debt)

[¶409a] OTHER SHAREHOLDER BENEFITS

Shareholder benefit included in income

In addition to the special rules on loans to shareholders, subsection 15(1) provides that any benefit conferred on a shareholder will be taxable to the shareholder. The rule is intended primarily to deal with situations where private corporations confer benefits on their shareholders: buying them cars, for instance, or simply giving them money. However, the rules are very broad, and more severe than the shareholders rules, in that the benefit conferred is taxable to the shareholder and not deductible to the company, and the situation cannot be reversed by repaying the benefit, whereas a shareholder loan included in shareholder income can be reversed by way of a deduction (in the year of repayment) by repaying the loan.

Subsection 15(1) applies to a benefit conferred by a corporation on a member of a partnership that is a shareholder in the corporation. Furthermore, where a benefit is conferred upon an individual — other than a trust in which no individual (other than a trust) is a beneficiary — who does not deal at arm's length with or is affiliated with a shareholder, the benefit is included in the shareholder's income.

Certain benefits are specifically exempted from the shareholder benefit rule. Dividends are not subject to the rule since there is a separate system for determining their taxability. Returns of capital are generally not considered benefits, again since there is a system of rules to determine their taxability. The issuance of rights to all common shareholders to acquire additional shares of the company is not a benefit, provided the rights are identical for all common shareholders.

In a technical interpretation, the CRA held that a corporation's payment of tuition and living expenses to an 18-year-old individual (who was not an employee of the corporation) related to a shareholder of the corporation was a shareholder benefit included in the shareholder's income; see CRA Document No. 2013-0502151E5. This position is in contrast to the CRA's position that such a payment would generally be considered a non-taxable scholarship if paid by an employer to a child or other dependant of an employee; see ¶953.

Value of Benefit

Where shareholder benefits are proven, there remains a problem of measuring the "value" of the benefit. This was illustrated in the case of *The Queen v. Fingold*, 96 DTC 1305 (T.C.C.), rev'd 97 DTC 5449 (F.C.A.). A corporation owned a Florida condominium costing some $4 million which was used by its chief executive, who was also a controlling shareholder. The Federal Court of Appeal held that the corporation made available a luxury home for the shareholder's use, and the benefit was to be calculated on the "equity rate of return", i.e., the amount, that would have been earned by the company had it invested the $4 million dollars at a reasonable rate of return, which the CRA estimated for the year in question to be $445,675. The Court overturned the finding of the Tax Court, which held that the condo was acquired and held for business purposes, and in such circumstances the value of the benefit was the fair rental value for the year.

(ITA: 15(1); IT-432R2 Benefits Conferred on Shareholders)

[¶409a.05] *Single-Purpose Corporations*

Individuals owning single-purpose corporations that hold property for their benefit, such as U.S. real estate, may be assessed a shareholder benefit under subsection 15(1) if the individuals enjoy the use of the property without adequate consideration. For example, in *Youngman* (90 DTC 6322), the taxpayer and his family moved into a home that had been paid for by a company owned by him, his wife and his children. The taxpayer was assessed a shareholder benefit arising from the use of the house. However, the amount of the benefit was reduced by the imputed interest on an interest-free loan of $100,000 that the taxpayer had made to the company to finance the construction of the house.

In Interpretation Bulletin IT-432R2, the CRA confirmed its support for the rationale in the *Youngman* decision (and the position was again confirmed in a recent technical interpretation — CRA Document No. 2008-0267401E5):

> If the fair market rent is not an appropriate measure, or if it does not exist or cannot be determined, the amount or value of the benefit would then usually be determined by multiplying a normal rate of return times the greater of the cost or fair market value of the property and adding the operating costs related to the property. The total of these two amounts is often referred to as the "imputed rent".
>
> Any consideration paid to the corporation by the shareholder for the use of the property is then subtracted from the imputed rent. In applying this formula, the amount representing the greater of the cost or fair market value of the property may first be reduced by any outstanding interest-free loans or advances to the corporation made by the shareholder (in circumstances that are essentially the same as in the Youngman case) to enable the corporation to acquire the property, before multiplying by the normal rate of return.

Grandfathering Transitional Relief for Corporations Owned Before 2005

At one time the CRA had an administrative position (old policy) under which it would not assess a taxable benefit to shareholders of a single-purpose corporation established to hold U.S.-based real property. However, this policy was abandoned as of January 1, 2005, with some grandfathering relief as follows.

Income Tax Technical News No. 31R2 states that, subject to the transitional relief described below, after December 31, 2004 the old policy with regard to single-purpose corporations will no longer apply for:

- any new property acquired by a single-purpose corporation; or
- a person who acquires shares of a single-purpose corporation unless such share acquisition is the result of the death of the individual's spouse or common-law partner.

However, the old policy will continue to apply to those arrangements in place as of January 1, 2005, until the earlier of:

- the disposition of the particular U.S.-based real estate by the single-purpose corporation; or
- a disposition of the shares of the single-purpose corporation, other than a transfer of such shares to the shareholder's spouse or common-law partner (or, per a technical opinion in CRA Document No. 2005-0136421E5, to a spousal trust as defined) as a result of the death of the shareholder.

In a grandfathering position not found in the original version, the CRA now says its old policy toward the shareholders of single-purpose corporations will continue to apply to any renovation or addition to a dwelling which was acquired before January 1, 2005, and to a dwelling which was under construction on December 31, 2004. For greater certainty, a dwelling will be considered to be under construction where the foundation or other support has been put in place. However, transitional relief will not be provided where vacant land has been acquired but the foundation or other support has not been put in place. Similarly, transitional relief will not be provided where land with an existing building has been acquired before January 1, 2005, but it is the intention of the taxpayer to demolish the existing building and construct a new dwelling on the land. Similar comments are made in Income Tax Technical News No. 32, dated July 15, 2005.

See also CRA Document No. 2010-0360001E5, February 11, 2001, in which the CRA restated its position and indicated that it could apply the same reasoning to a single-purpose corporation that owned an airplane for the sole use and enjoyment of its shareholder.

(Tax Topics: No. 1700, dated October 7, 2004. A more formal but rather less forthcoming version of the 2004 Round Table discussion is found in *Income Tax Technical News* No. 32; ITTN: No. 31R2)

[¶410] DIVIDEND STRIPPING

Corporate income is taxed at corporate rates as earned by the corporation and the balance is taxed again in the hands of individual shareholders when distributed as dividends. As discussed above, partial relief from double taxation is given to Canadian resident individuals through the dividend tax credit. (See ¶404.) At one time, the *Income Tax Act* left open a variety of methods by which the shareholders of a closely held corporation were able to avoid paying tax on corporate earnings distributed to them. This type of tax avoidance is known as "surplus stripping" or "dividend stripping".

Attempts at surplus stripping may be subject to the general anti-avoidance rule (GAAR) which purports to reverse any reduction, avoidance or deferral of tax which results from a "misuse or abuse" of technical tax rules. Several Tax Court decisions have applied GAAR in so-called dividend stripping transactions. In *McNichol v. The Queen*, 97 DTC 111, *RMM Canadian Enterprises*, 97 DTC 302, and *Nadeau v. The Queen*, 99 DTC 324, the GAAR was found to be applicable to such transactions. The Tax Court essentially held that the provisions of the Act read as a whole contemplated that distributions to shareholders should be included in income. Transactions that were structured to defeat this treatment were regarded as conferring a tax benefit and, assuming they had no primary commercial or non-tax objective, were viewed as abusive of the provisions of the Act read as a whole.

In addition to the general anti-avoidance rule, harsh penalty taxes remain for corporations which attempt to distribute surplus in the form of capital gain, although these rules have now been limited to corporations with publicly traded shares.

Non-residents disposing of shares of one Canadian corporation to another corporation may similarly be able to convert surplus into capital gain free of Canadian tax, and there are explicit rules to deem dividends paid (and subject to withholding tax) where transactions occur which create the potential for this kind of surplus strip.

No prospective transaction involving the purchase or sale of shares of a closely held corporation, the issue or redemption of preferred shares or the reorganization of the capital structure of a corporation, should be entered into without first giving these provisions of the *Income Tax Act* very careful consideration and taking professional tax advice.

(ITA: 82; 183.1; 245)

[¶412] INCOME BONDS OR DEBENTURES

[¶412.10] *Income Bonds or Debentures*

An income bond or debenture is an obligation of a corporation where interest is payable only if the corporation makes a profit. They are in effect a variation of the small business development bonds described above. Since 1978, these bonds may be issued only by corporations in bankruptcy or receivership, or in circumstances of financial difficulty (as defined) to replace obligations likely to be in default. There are restrictions on the use of the proceeds to the issuer.

Any income that you receive from a Canadian resident corporation on an income bond or debenture that was issued before November 17, 1978 is treated as a dividend subject to the "gross-up" and dividend tax credit rules (¶404), so long as the payer corporation is not entitled to deduct the amount from its income.

Income bonds or debentures issued before 1980 under an agreement entered into before November 17, 1978 could be used in a much broader variety of financing situations, and those old bonds retain their income bond tax characteristics if not materially altered.

Interpretation Bulletins IT-52R4, "Income Bonds and Debentures", and IT-388, "Income Bonds Issued by Foreign Corporations", were cancelled (¶283) by the CRA in 2004, and IT-507R, "Small Business Development Bonds and Small Business Bonds", in 2005. No reason was given, and it is not clear that any particular policies set out there have been rethought.

[¶412.15] *Distress Financing Shares Generally*

The income tax rules offer three distinct versions of what is essentially the same scheme of financing corporations in financial difficulty by issuing debt obligations (typically in exchange for existing debt) on which the interest payments are treated as taxable dividends to the recipient but are not deductible to the payer. The result is to make the yield more attractive to the recipient, as it is taxed at favourable (dividend) rates (which can be nil for corporations), at a negligible cost to the payer since it cannot make use of the interest deduction in any event, having hypothetically no taxable income in its distressed circumstances. Two of these schemes, the small business development bonds and the income bonds or debentures, are set out above. The third scheme, "distress preferred shares", exists as an exception to anti-avoidance rules. Differences among these alternatives in terms of feasibility to the parties and difficulty of complying with the CRA restrictions are discussed by the CRA in Interpretation Bulletin IT-527.

(ITA: 15; 15.1; 15.2; 18(1)(*g*); 82; 248; IT-527 Distress preferred shares)

[¶413] PATRONAGE DIVIDENDS

A patronage payment is a payment to a customer computed at a rate in proportion to patronage (i.e., the amount of business done with a company in a year). Usually, these are offered by cooperative corporations, but they can be offered by others. If you have received a patronage dividend, you must include this amount in your taxable income unless the payment was in respect of consumer goods or services the cost of which you cannot deduct in computing income. You should receive a T4A for such payments which will show (in box 30) the amounts received for consumer goods or services and other amounts. The amount is reported on line 130 the T1 return.

The payer of the patronage dividend is normally obliged to withhold 15% of the amount of the dividend in excess of $100 on account of your tax for the year. However, members of an agricultural cooperative may receive patronage dividends in the form of shares which are not taxable until disposition. This exception is discussed under the next subheading below.

In general, all amounts except those in respect of undeducted consumer goods or services must be included in your tax return as other income. Such payments are not to be reported as dividends and are not eligible for the dividend tax credit. A patronage dividend or allocation which is merely a refund or cost reduction on the cost of consumer goods you could not deduct from income should not be reported as income, even though you received a T4A showing the amount in box 30.

(ITA: 135; IT-362R Patronage dividends)

[¶413.05] *Patronage Dividends from Agricultural Cooperatives*

Deferral of taxation

Where an agricultural cooperative (co-op) pays patronage dividends to eligible members in the form of "tax deferred cooperative shares", there is no immediate income inclusion and no withholding of tax. Rather, tax is deferred until the eligible member disposes of the shares. The deferral was originally applicable only to shares issued after 2005 and before 2016, but the 2015 Federal Budget extended the deferral to shares issued before 2021.

Essentially, in the first instance, your income inclusion for tax deferred co-op shares (TDCS) received as an eligible member is nil, although you can elect to have a higher income inclusion, up to the value of the patronage dividend the shares represent. This is in effect a tax averaging measure, allowing you to prepay tax in a year of low income, thereby reducing the eventual tax on disposition of the shares. If you elect to have an income inclusion in respect of patronage dividend shares received in the year, the elected amount is added to your "tax-paid balance" for the year. Your tax-paid balance at the end of a particular year is the sum of your balance at the end of the prior year plus your current year elected amounts, in excess of proceeds of disposition of TDCS during the year.

To the nil or elected value of your income inclusion for a particular year must be added the proceeds of disposition TDCS disposed of in the year in excess of the sum of your "tax-paid balance" at the end of the preceding year plus your elected income inclusion for the current year.

Disposition of Share

A disposition may be an actual disposition, typically by way of redemption of TDCS by the co-op. As well, you are deemed to have disposed of TDCS when the paid-up capital of the shares is reduced other than by redemption, or when you pledge, assign or in any way alienate the share as security for indebtedness. If you have a deemed disposition of particular shares, you are deemed to have proceeds of disposition equal to the original dividend value of those shares, and you are also deemed to have reacquired them immediately afterward at the same value.

If the TDCS is redeemed, acquired, or cancelled by the co-op corporation, it must withhold 15% from the amount payable to the shareholder. However, withholding is not required if the shareholder is a trust governed by an RRSP or RRIF. Also, there is no income inclusion and withholding is not required if the redemption, acquisition or cancellation results from a re-organization of capital of the co-op corporation, generally if the shareholder receives as consideration only new TDCS of the corporation, and the paid-up capital of, and the amount that the shareholder can receive on the redemption, acquisition of cancellation of, the new TDCS, is the same as that for the old TDCS.

Eligible Member of Agricultural Co-op

An agricultural co-op for these rules is one the principal business of which is an agricultural business as defined below, and/or has a membership 75% of which are either themselves agricultural co-ops or are members whose principal business is farming (in the sense discussed in Chapter 17, as distinct from carrying on an agricultural business as defined below).

To be an eligible member of an agricultural co-op, you must carry on an agricultural business in Canada. An eligible member may be an individual resident in Canada, an agricultural co-op, a corporation resident in Canada that carries on the business of farming in Canada, or a partnership that carries on the business of farming in Canada, all of the members of which are eligible members.

An agricultural business, for these purposes, is a business carried on in Canada that consists of (i) farming (including, if the person carrying on the business is a cooperative corporation, the production, processing, storing and wholesale marketing, of the products of its members' farming activities), or (ii) the provision of goods or services (other than financial services) that are required for farming. An example of the provision of goods required for farming is the sale of livestock feed and supplements. An example of the provision of a service required for farming is grain marketing services.

This program appears to be a response to the similar Quebec program described at ¶1642a.20. Tax deferred preferred shares are called preferred units in Quebec tax parlance. One assumes, perhaps without complete confidence, that a Quebec preferred unit would achieve more or less the same results federally and in Quebec.

(ITA: 135.1)

[¶414] DIVIDENDS IN KIND

If a corporation pays you a taxable dividend in the form of non-cash property, you include income the fair market value at the date of receipt of property received as the amount of the dividend. The gross-up and credit rules as discussed at ¶404 also apply to dividends of this type.

A stock dividend is not a dividend in kind. A stock dividend (see ¶406) is measured by the increase in paid-up capital of the issuing company and not by fair market value. A distribution of assets on the winding-up of a company may give rise to dividends, but special rules of calculation will apply (see ¶417).

(ITA: 52; 89)

[¶415] NON-TAXABLE DIVIDENDS

[¶415.05] *Capital Dividends*

A private corporation may elect to pay a "capital dividend" out of a surplus account called its "Capital Dividend Account". Generally, its capital dividend account consists of the non-taxable portion (¶500) of capital gains realized by the company since 1971, but the category includes several other items, notably, the proceeds of life insurance policies of which the company is a beneficiary. This type of dividend is not taxable and should not be reported on your income tax return. However, capital dividends paid to non-residents are subject to Part XIII withholding tax (see ¶2080).

You might not receive a T5 information slip showing these non-taxable capital dividends, but you will likely receive notification from the company which paid the dividends explaining the special nature of them. Receipt of a capital dividend will not require any adjustment to the adjusted cost base of your shares (unlike certain other non-taxable dividends now essentially defunct). However, capital dividends may reduce capital losses on the eventual disposition of the shares on which the dividends have been received; see ¶580d.

A capital dividend must not be confused with a "Capital Gains Dividend" which is a distribution of capital gains earned by a mutual fund or investment corporation and reported on box 18 of the T5 information slip (see ¶418).

(ITA: 53(1)(*a*); 83; 89; 131; 212; IT-66R6 Capital Dividends)

[¶415.10] *Other Non-Taxable Dividends*

Stock splits (¶406) and liquidation dividends (¶417) may in certain circumstances be non-taxable, as described in the paragraphs referred to.

(ITA: 53(2)(*a*); 83(6); 89; 131; 212; ITR: 2107 Tax-deferred Preferred Series)

[¶416] DEEMED DIVIDENDS

You may be deemed to have received a dividend if a Canadian resident corporation in which you own shares has undertaken certain transactions which include:

(1) a reorganization which increased paid-up capital;

(2) a distribution of funds and/or property on liquidation;

(3) a reduction of paid-up capital; or

(4) a share redemption or cancellation or repurchase (see ¶417).

An exception permits the capital gains treatment rather than the deemed dividend treatment on share redemptions after May 23, 1985, of prescribed shares held by an arm's length (¶812) individual who resides in Canada. Only Class I Special Shares of Reed Stenhouse Companies Limited issued before January 1, 1986, are presently prescribed under this exception. Redemption of these shares will give rise to proceeds of disposition (¶528) and capital gain rather than deemed dividend. See ¶538.

If you receive a deemed dividend from a corporation, it should issue you a T5 information slip reporting the amount of the dividend.

(ITA: 84; ITR: 6206 Prescribed Shares)

[¶417] CORPORATE LIQUIDATIONS

Deemed Dividend Treatment

Under subsection 84(2) of the Act, where funds and/or other property of a corporation are distributed to you as a shareholder on the winding-up, discontinuance, or reorganization of its business, you are deemed to have received a dividend equal to the amount by which the funds and/or the fair market value of property received by you exceeds the corporation's paid-up capital attributable to your shares that is reduced on the distribution.

Similarly, under subsection 84(3), where a corporation resident in Canada redeems, acquires, or cancels your shares in the corporation, the amount paid to you on the redemption, acquisition, or cancellation in excess of the paid-up capital in respect of your shares is deemed to be a dividend.

In either of the above instances, the amount of the deemed dividend is excluded from the proceeds of disposition of the shares for capital gains purposes.

The T5 information form will indicate the amount of the distribution or payment which is considered to be a dividend.

Rare Case: Pre-1972 Capital Surplus on Hand Account

Where a Canadian corporation that has a pre-1972 Capital Surplus on Hand Account is wound up and distributes all or substantially all of its property on the winding, any dividends that you receive out of the pre-1972 Capital Surplus on Hand of a corporation on winding-up are not considered to be dividends for tax purposes and should not be reported on your income tax return. The amount of the dividends, however, is considered to be proceeds of disposition of the shares and may therefore give rise to capital gains.

(ITA: 84; 88; IT-126R2 Meaning of "Winding-up")

[¶418] CAPITAL GAINS DISTRIBUTIONS

For a discussion of income (as opposed to capital distributions) from mutual funds, see ¶491.

[¶418.05] *From a Mutual Fund Corporation, Investment Corporation, or Mortgage Investment Corporation*

A capital gains dividend is a dividend paid during the year by a mutual fund corporation, an investment corporation or a mortgage investment corporation which the corporation has elected to treat as a distribution out of its pool of realized capital gains. The amount on which it has elected is called a capital gains dividend, and is deemed to be a capital gain distribution to you. (See Chapter 5.) A capital gains dividend (reported to you on a T5 slip) should not be reported as investment income on Schedule 4. Rather, you should report it on Schedule 3 of your income tax return. No dividend tax credit (¶404) can be claimed for this dividend.

(ITA: 130.1(4); 131(1))

[¶418.10] *From a Mutual Fund or Other Trust*

Capital gain distributions from a mutual fund *trust* are not actually dividends, and operate under slightly different rules. They are reported to you on T3 slips (in box 21), not T5 slips, but, like capital gains dividends, are reported by you on Schedule 3 of your T1 return.

Trusts other than mutual fund trusts also have the ability to flow out current capital gains to trust beneficiaries with their capital gain characteristics intact, and these are also reported to you in box 21 of your T3 slip from the trust.

Box 21 of your T3 slip should include the full amount of the capital gain or loss allocated to you by the trust, including any amounts eligible for the capital gains deduction (exemption) for qualified small business corporation shares or farming or fishing property, as indicated in box 30. Box 30 amounts must be subtracted from box 21, as they are reported separately in the qualified small business shares or qualified farm property sections of Schedule 3. Any remaining box 21 amounts must be carried to Schedule 3 of your T1 return.

Personal trusts may also allocate capital gains to beneficiaries, some of which may represent eligible proceeds from disposition of qualified small business shares and farming property. However, there is no exempt capital gains balance in respect of a personal trust. See ¶465.

[¶420] DEMUTUALIZATION BENEFITS

Mutual life insurance companies are permitted to convert to stock companies — i.e., those with issued share capital. In these conversions, policyholders give up rights in exchange for shares of the insurer (or a holding company), and/or other benefits. The shares received (or ownership rights in a mutual holding company) are capital assets received on a tax-free rollover basis with a cost to the policyholder of nil, so that no capital gain arises on the demutualization but eventual capital gain will arise on disposition of shares or rights received on the demutualization.

Any benefits received on demutualization other than (i) shares or rights to shares in the insurance company or a holding company thereof, or (ii) ownership rights in a mutual insurance holding company of the insurer are "taxable conversion benefits". These may include cash payments, policy dividends or parts thereof received in connection with the demutualization, enhanced policy benefits, a new insurance policy, and a reduction in future premiums. In general, the proposals to policyholders setting out the terms on which they may accede to the conversion should set out the various benefits received in exchange. Taxable conversion benefits are treated as taxable dividends from a Canadian corporation, and therefore are eligible for the gross-up and credit machinery discussed at ¶404.

Employer-Held Policies

Where an employer holds a policy for the benefit of employees, the rules contemplate that the employer can flow out the benefits received to the individuals, who in turn receive them under these rules as exchanged shares or dividends as the case may be (and not as employment income). Although this rule contemplates employer–employee situations, it is broad enough to cover any situation in which a policyholder transfers demutualization receipts to an individual who has rights or benefits under the policy and had borne part of the cost of the policy.

Where the policyholder is an employer holding a group employee-paid policy on behalf of employees, which typically provides disability or other benefits which are tax free to the employee so long as the employer has not contributed to premiums, the demutualization rules contemplate that the employer can apply demutualization benefits it receives toward benefit enhancements under such policies without tainting the policy, so that benefits remain tax free. See ¶368.

The following companies have already been demutualized:

- Mutual Life Assurance Company of Canada (now Clarica Life Insurance Company)
- Manufacturers Life Insurance Company
- Canada Life Assurance Company
- Sun Life Assurance Company of Canada

(ITA: 139.1; Other Publications: Notice of Ways and Means Motions and Dept. of Finance Technical Notes of December 7, 1999; CRA website entry on "Demutualization"; Office of Superintendent of Financial Institutions website)

[¶422] SECURITIES LENDING ARRANGEMENTS

Meaning of Securities Lending Arrangement

A securities lending arrangement is a transaction in which the borrower acquires securities on a temporary basis from the lender, and eventually returns not necessarily the exact share certificates, but identical securities. The borrower typically requires the shares to honour a commitment, typically on a short sale (a sale of securities the borrower did not own). The lender typically gets the use of cash or other liquid collateral and a fee for the use of the shares.

The income tax system attempts to deal with these transactions from two points of view. First, it facilitates them by ensuring that specified transactions will in fact be treated as loans and not dispositions. Second it seeks to ensure that the transactions are not designed to facilitate revenue leakage; that is, that the parties cannot use the transactions to avoid tax.

A "securities lending arrangement" for tax purposes is defined to be an arrangement under which:

(1) a person (lender) lends a qualifying security to another person (borrower);

(2) it may reasonably be expected that the borrower will transfer or return to the lender a security that is identical to the security so transferred or lent;

(3) the borrower is obligated to pay to the lender amounts equal to and as compensation for all amounts paid on the security after the security is transferred to the borrower and prior to such security being returned to the lender;

(4) the lender's risk of loss or opportunity for gain or profit is not changed in any material respect; and

(5) if the lender and the borrower do not deal with each other at arm's length, it is not intended that the arrangement, nor any series of securities lending arrangements, loans or other transactions of which the arrangement is a part, be in effect for more than 270 days.

The definition also contains an anti-avoidance provision which excludes from the definition of a securities lending arrangement any arrangement, one of the main purposes of which may reasonably be considered to be to avoid or defer the inclusion in income of any gain or profit with respect to the security. The effect of the anti-avoidance rule is to deny the non-disposition treatment generally provided where the purpose of the arrangement is simply to defer the inclusion in income of any gain by a holder of capital property or profit by a person holding the securities as inventory.

These rules apply only to:

(1) shares of corporations listed on Canadian or foreign stock exchanges;

(2) shares of a class of stock which, although unlisted, allows or requires a company to be considered a Canadian "public" company;

(3) bonds, debentures, notes or similar obligations of companies in (1) or (2) or of companies controlled by them;

(4) warrants, rights, options or similar instruments with respect to shares described in (1) or (2); Canadian corporate shares, bonds, options, or the like, or Canadian mutual fund trust units, traded on a recognized Canadian or foreign stock exchange, although they do extend to shares, bonds, options, etc. of Canadian "public" corporations which may not be listed; and

(5) units of Canadian mutual fund trusts listed on a Canadian or foreign stock exchange.

Tax Treatment

Essentially, the rules provide that securities lending arrangements of qualified securities are not dispositions, and that the securities returned are considered to be the ones lent. Where it is reasonable to consider that the lender would have received proceeds of disposition while the securities are lent, the proceeds are indeed considered proceeds of disposition at that time.

Similarly, to the extent the compensation payment from the borrower to the lender represents a dividend distribution from a Canadian public corporation, it maintains those dividend characteristics in the hands of the lender. Thus, to the extent the payment compensated for a Canadian dividend distributed while the shares were in the hands of the borrower, the lender (if an individual) would be entitled to the dividend gross-up and tax credit. If the underlying payment is a trust distribution with dividend or other specific characteristics designated by the trust, or a distribution of property from the trust, the distribution maintains those characteristics in the hands of the lender. If a distribution does not fall into any of the preceding characterizations, it is deemed to be interest.

Several anti-avoidance rules attach to the compensation rule. It does not apply where a main reason for the transaction is to enable the lender to receive a deductible distribution in any year (typically applicable to corporations which can deduct dividends received) or to receive any distribution not included in income. Essentially, this rule is added to deal with non-taxable trust distributions. That is, the purpose of the transaction cannot be to shift tax to another year. As well, the compensation rule does not apply to amounts received under a securities lending arrangement from a non-resident unless the non-resident carries on business through a permanent establishment in Canada. (This limitation does not apply to amounts received by a registered Canadian securities dealer in the ordinary course of business.)

The borrower who pays the compensation amount has several alternative treatments of the payment. If the payment is made by a registered securities dealer, to the extent it is a dividend compensation payment, the dealer may deduct two-thirds of it. Any borrower (including but not limited to registered securities dealers) may make a deduction in respect of compensation amounts that are not dividend compensation payments. The amount of this deduction is computed differently depending on the actions of the taxpayer in question (the one who made the payment and seeks to deduct it). If the taxpayer has disposed of the borrowed security and has included any resulting gain or loss in computing business income, the compensation amount is fully deductible. In any other case, the taxpayer is allowed a deduction to the extent of the lesser of (i) the compensation amount and (ii) the amount included in the taxable income of the taxpayer or persons related to the taxpayer.

(ITA: 82(1)(*b*); 89(1) "public corporation"; 260)

[¶422.05] *Partnerships*

For purposes of the securities lending arrangement rules, a partnership is deemed to be a person, and if all partners are registered securities dealers, it is also deemed to be a registered securities dealer. Each partner is considered to receive its *pro rata* share of compensation payments received. In the case of individuals, each partner who is an individual is considered to have paid his or her *pro rata* share of compensation payments paid by the partnership, and to the *pro rata* extent they compensated the lender for dividends, may deduct them from the individual's taxable dividends received.

Transitional rule

Partnerships became eligible to participate in securities lending arrangements as of December 21, 2002. However, an election made by all parties to the dividend lending arrangement allows these rules to be retroactive to arrangements made after November 2, 1998 under the securities lending provisions as they read at that time. The election must have been made within 90 days of Royal Assent to relevant legislation embodying the amendments: Royal Assent was received on June 26, 2013.

(ITA: 82(1)(*b*); 89(1) "public corporation"; 248(1) "specified proportion"; 260)

[¶423] DIVIDEND RENTAL ARRANGEMENTS

Meaning

A "dividend rental arrangement" is generally, although perhaps not invariably, a subset of the securities lending arrangements discussed above. It is an arrangement entered into by a person where it may reasonably be considered that the main reason is to enable the person to receive a dividend on a share of a corporation in circumstances where someone other than that person bears the risk of loss or opportunity for gain with respect to the share. The 2015 Federal Budget extended the meaning of "dividend rental arrangement" to include "synthetic equity arrangements", which, in very general terms, are certain derivative arrangements that might otherwise escape the definition of a dividend rental arrangement.

In a typical dividend rental arrangement, the borrower of the share expects to benefit from the preferential tax treatment accorded to dividends, whereas the lender of the share is a non-taxable entity and therefore indifferent as to the receipt of a dividend or receipt of another type of income. The borrower holds the share until a dividend is declared and received, after which the share is returned to the vendor for the original purchase price plus a negotiated fee. The tax consequences in such an arrangement would, but for the dividend rental rules, be favourable for the borrower. If the borrower was an individual, the taxable dividends would be subject to the gross-up and the corresponding dividend tax credit, as described in ¶404. If the borrower was a corporation, it would be allowed to deduct an amount equal to the taxable dividend received under intercorporate dividend rules.

Tax Treatment

If the transaction is considered a dividend rental arrangement, an individual is denied the gross-up with respect to taxable dividends received in the arrangement, and is therefore denied the dividend tax credit. (A corporation is denied a deduction from income for taxable dividends received in a dividend rental arrangement.) The overall effect of these arrangements is that the borrower is taxed at "normal" marginal tax rates and is denied the otherwise preferential treatment accorded to dividends.

Where a dividend rental arrangement is also a securities lending arrangement, the corporate taxpayer who borrows the shares can obtain a deduction for compensation paid, to the extent deemed a dividend to the lender. The individual gets similar relief, to the extent discussed in ¶422.

Generally speaking, it is probably normal for a dividend rental arrangement to be a securities lending arrangement as well. In both cases there is a temporary transfer of a share. A private company share will not qualify for the securities arrangement rules, so that is one instance where they diverge. Under the rental rule, the intent is for the borrower to receive the dividend, so the anti-avoidance aspects of the securities rules generally would not come into play. So the two sets of rules, although not wholly congruent, will frequently overlap.

[¶423.05] *Partnerships*

As with the securities lending rules at ¶422 the dividend rental rules were made applicable to partnerships as of December 20, 2002. All parties to an arrangement could jointly elect to have the rules apply to transactions after November 2, 1998. The election must have been made within

90 days of Royal Assent to relevant legislation, which occurred on June 26, 2013.

(ITA: 112(2.3); 248(1) "dividend rental arrangement"; 260(6.1))

INTEREST INCOME

[¶430] MEANING OF "INTEREST"

Interest is compensation paid for the use of borrowed funds and is fully included in income. The timing of the inclusion is discussed at ¶432. The usual sources of interest income include savings bank accounts, government, municipal and corporate bonds and loans to other persons.

Although all interest income is fully taxable, if the interest income is part of your pension income a tax credit is available to offset tax on the first $2,000 of the pension income. You should consider whether any income you receive may qualify for that deduction. Generally speaking, certain annuity or pension payments from life insurance companies are most likely to qualify for this choice. These payments are discussed at ¶480. Also, amounts of interest income paid out of your RRSP or RRIF may qualify as pension income eligible for the credit. See ¶1311.

Discounts as Interest

Special problems arise where part of the compensation for the use of money is received in the form of a higher price on redemption of a security than was paid for it. The most common example is treasury bills, where the obligation is simply issued at a discount — for example, where you pay $97 today for the government to repay you $100 in 90 days. There is not much doubt that the $3 received on maturity is interest received at the time of maturity; see ¶437.

More complicated considerations arise where bonds are issued for a longer period and bear some interest but are also issued at a discount. By statute, discounts on obligations issued by governments, tax-exempt persons or non-residents not carrying on business in Canada are wholly taxable as interest if they raise the effective yield to more than $^4/_3$ of the stipulated interest (¶438). A number of other special obligations, such as strip bonds, may give rise to interest calculated under special rules. Professional advice as to the tax consequences of holding such investments may be desirable; often they are suitable only for holding through tax-exempt entities such as RRSPs.

Discounts implicit in the original issue price of a bond (primary discount) must be distinguished from discounts which arise from the purchase of a bond in the open market which trades for less than its face value because interest rates have risen since the bond was issued (secondary discount). In the case of a secondary discount, the regular (below-market) interest received on the bond is reported as such, but the difference between face value and purchase price may be a capital gain or loss at maturity, provided the bond has been held as a capital asset and not, for example, as an adventure in the nature of trade (see ¶500). Even T-Bills sold before maturity might give rise to a capital gain or loss as well as an interest element depending on the shift in interest rates between acquisition and sale.

Some imaginative taxpayers have taken the position that the Canadian securities election described at ¶501 can convert discounts into capital gains. Professional tax advisers in general took a dim view of this possibility, knowing that the intention of the election was merely to ensure consistent capital treatment for regular investors in securities. The issue finally worked its way to the Federal Court of Appeal, which ruled flatly that the discount on T-Bills held is interest, regardless of whether the guaranteed capital gains election is made (*Satinder v. The Queen*, 95 DTC 5340 (F.C.A.)). See also the technical discussion at ¶501.

See also ¶436 to ¶442 below on special situations. Also, ¶432 deals with the complex rules on when you must report accrued but unpaid interest, and ¶433 deals with Canada Savings Bonds.

(ITA: 12; 16; IT-396R Interest Income; *O'Neil v. M.N.R.*, 91 DTC 692 (T.C.C.); *Gestion Guy Menard Inc. v. M.N.R.*, 93 DTC 1058 (T.C.C.) the most thorough review of technical interest rules is found in Ulmer, Taxation of Interest Income)

[¶431] INFORMATION RETURNS AND SLIPS

Banks and certain other persons who, as principal or agent, have paid a resident of Canada interest of more than $50 in a year, are required to furnish the payee with a T5 Supplementary slip for inclusion with his T1 return.

However, if you receive interest income but do not receive an information slip, either because the amount is less than $50 or for any other reason, you must still report the interest on your income tax return. The interest is reported on Part II of Schedule 4 and line 121 of the T1 tax return.

Normally, investment information slips such as T5 slips are made out by the payer (e.g., a bank) in the names in which the account is held. For income tax purposes, the income should be divided and reported in the same ratio as the contribution to the account. The following rules will determine how the income is to be reported for spouses:

(1) In the case of a joint bank account in which all money was deposited from one spouse's earnings, or from money the spouse gave to the other spouse, the interest must all be reported by the spouse whose earnings/money were deposited.

(2) Should the money in the account originate from both spouses, the interest could then be divided between them in the same proportion as their contributions to the account. In such cases, the information slip may be filed with either return.

If interest was paid through a trust and then paid or deemed paid to you, it should be reported on a T3 rather than a T5. Payments through a trust generally maintain their character in the hands of the ultimate recipient.

You should receive a T-BD slip if you have had treasury bills mature during the year; see ¶437 for the implications of these.

If you earned income from bearer interest coupons or dividend warrants or accrued interest on the sale of securities during the year you should receive either a T600 or T600B from the encashing agent or financial company and these amounts should also be reported in your return. As between spouses or common-law partners, the income should be divided and reported in the same ratio as the contribution to the bonds or other securities.

If the payer withheld tax when you cashed in your bonds, the withholdings should be shown on page 4 of your return as part of your total tax credits. See ¶1494.

In all cases where bonds, treasury bills, or other debt instruments are cashed in, you must be careful not to double count income reported to you. In many cases, some accrued interest income will have already been reported for tax purposes (see ¶432). You must determine what amount of the money you received on cashing a bond is a return of capital (i.e., the return to you of the money you originally invested) and what amount represents interest. You must then determine whether any of the interest has already been reported for tax purposes in earlier years. Finally, you must check to see whether current year interest is being reported twice in any fashion; for example, once on a T5 slip and again in the proceeds of disposition of a treasury bill. Although T5 slip reporting is generally reliable, you should have sufficient grasp of your investment income to ensure that you are not reporting the same income twice.

(ITA: 12; 74.1; 234; ITR: 201 Investment Income; T4015 T5 Guide — Return of Investment Income — 2015; IT-511R Interspousal and certain other transfers and loans of property)

[¶432] TIMING OF INCOME RECOGNITION

Under paragraph 12(1)(*c*) of the Act, and subject to the accrual rules discussed below, you include interest income in the year in which you receive it or it becomes receivable by you, depending on the method you regularly follow. In other words, the cash or receivable method may be employed, but your use of the method be regularly followed from year to year.

Notwithstanding paragraph 12(1)(*c*), subsection 12(4) mandates a modified accrual method of including interest income if you hold an "investment contract". Typically, this will be a debt obligation for which you do not report the interest on the debt at least annually; see ¶432.05 below. On the other hand, if you report interest on a debt at periodical intervals not exceeding a year, in respect of the interest accrued during each such interval, the modified accrual rules do not apply, and the regular rule in paragraph 12(1)(*c*) applies. The modified accrual rule typically applies when the interest on a debt obligation is paid upon redemption of the debt or in a year subsequent to the year in question, rather than on an annual basis.

[¶432.05] *Current Accrual Rule (Debt Investments Made after 1989)*

As noted, investment contracts may be subject to an annual accrual rule. Interest must be included in income every year even if it is not received, for example, because it is interest on a compound bond or long-term investment certificate. This rule typically applies to investments which do not in fact pay the full amount of accrued interest for the year on an annual basis.

The annual accrual requirement requires reporting of investments on an investment year basis, so that amounts should be accrued on a daily basis from the date of issue of the investment to the immediately preceding day of the following year, and so on from year to year (each "anniversary day"). In the year of disposition the accrual stops on the disposition date, which is also considered an "anniversary day".

Under the annual accrual rule, interest on a long-term investment certificate must be reported annually at the stated long-term rate (including compound interest) even if a lower rate might apply if the certificate is cashed early. If a lower rate in fact applies because you cash the certificate early, you will be able to deduct in the year of disposition any amount by which total interest reported over the life of the certificate exceeds total interest received. Generally speaking, compound or bonus features must be included in the annual accrual, with an offsetting deduction where at redemption or disposition interest reported exceeds interest received in fact. These rules will be generally unchanged from those discussed under the heading "Compound Interest, Long-Term Certificates, Bonuses, etc." below.

In its T1 guide, the CRA provides the following advice with respect to term deposits, guaranteed investment certificates (GICs), and other similar investments that do not pay interest until maturity:

> On these investments, interest builds up over a period of time, usually longer than one year. Generally, you do not receive the interest until the investment matures or you cash it in.
>
> The income you report is based on the interest you earned during each complete investment year. For example, if you made a long-term investment on July 1, 2013, report on your return for 2014 the interest that accumulated to the end of June 2014, even if you do not receive a T5 slip. Report the interest from July 2014 to June 2015 on your 2015 return.
>
> Note
>
> If your investment agreement specified a different interest rate each year, report the amount on your T5 slips, even if it is different from what the agreement specifies or what you received. The issuer of your investment can tell you how this amount was calculated.

You may still report interest on a "received or receivable" basis under paragraph 12(1)(*c*) to the extent you are not overtaken by the annual accrual rules. If you have an obligation which pays you full interest at least once a year commencing within a year of issue, you simply report the interest received. This, of course, assumes there is no compound or bonus interest accrued but unpaid on your investment in addition to regular interest. The receivable method generally related to coupon bonds, and permitted you to report interest as coupons became payable, even if you didn't cash them. Since these bonds, should any still be being issued, typically have a bonus for not cashing coupons currently, they would generally be overtaken by the annual accrual requirements discussed below under "Compound Interest, Long-Term Certificates, Bonuses, etc.".

There should be no double-up of accruals with actual interest, since only the interest not otherwise included in your income is to be included under the accrual rules.

[¶432.10] *Grandfathering Rule: Interest on Investments Made in 1989 or Earlier Years*

For debt investments made prior to 1990, and subject to the "three-year accrual requirements" discussed below at ¶432.15 for debt obligations acquired after November 12, 1981, you have the option of reporting your interest income as it is received (cash), as it becomes receivable, or as it accrues. Under the accrual method, interest is recognized as being earned on a daily basis, regardless of the date that the interest debt becomes receivable or is received. If you receive several types of interest income, for example, interest on coupon bonds and interest on non-coupon bonds, it is possible to report each type on either the received, receivable or accrual basis provided the method followed in each case is used consistently. The CRA takes the position that interest from the same payer on the same type of property must be reported using the same method.

You are permitted to change from the cash to the receivable or the accrual basis, and prior to 1988 you might have done so to take advantage of the $1,000 interest and dividend deduction. Remember that once you have changed to the receivable or accrual method you will not be permitted to change back to the cash method of recording interest income, but on the other hand you are only bound by your choice on each type of interest income, as discussed in the first paragraph above.

When you elect to use the accrual method, you must, in the year of election, report all previously accrued but unreported income to December 31 of the election year on the obligation on which you elect.

An election to use the accrual method is to be made (for obligations other than insurance or annuity contracts described below) in the taxpayer's return. Since there is no prescribed form, *a letter or statement with the return specifying the obligation(s) elected upon is necessary to make the election.*

If a creditor adds unpaid interest to the principal of a debt and calculates interest on the total, the amount added to the principal is not considered to be interest received until it is actually paid. However, where interest is due and payable, but is unpaid, and the debtor issues the creditor a new security such as a bond, debenture or promissory note, the creditor will be deemed to have received interest income equal to the lesser of the value of the new security, and the income debt which was due and payable before that time.

Where interest is reported on the received basis, you will be considered to have received the interest when you have effective use of the funds (e.g., credited to your savings bank account) or when you receive a cheque in payment, regardless of when it is cashed or deposited.

Any payment which discharges or reduces an interest obligation whether it is paid in money or with other forms of property is includible as interest income of the creditor.

[¶432.15] *Grandfathering Rule: Three-Year Accrual Requirement on Investments Made in 1989 or Earlier Years*

For these investments, you are required to include in your income interest that has accrued after December 31, 1981, in respect of an "investment contract". "Investment contracts" are defined to include *any debt obligation* except an income bond or debenture, a small business development bond or a small business bond (see ¶412). Regulations exclude RRSPs, RHOSPs, and RRIFs, other than such plans where a trust is a party, where the annuitant or beneficiary of the plan is alive.

Interest that accrued on these obligations after December 31, 1981 must be reported by the lender where he holds the obligation on the "third anniversary date" of the contract to the extent he has not previously included it in income.

For the purposes of the three-year accrual rule, the third anniversary of an investment contract is three years after December 31 of the year in which the contract is issued and every third December 31 thereafter. For example, the third anniversary of an investment contract issued at any time in 1982 will first occur on December 31, 1985, next on December 31, 1988, and so on. On a contract acquired before 1982, its issue date was deemed to be December 31, 1988, provided it has been held continuously since 1982. Thus, the first interest accrual on pre-1982 contracts occurred in 1991.

Investments made prior to November 13, 1981 will not be subject to these rules where you are "locked into" the investment — that is, where you cannot require at any time after November 12, 1981 its repayment, acquisition, cancellation or conversion (otherwise than by reason of default) under the terms thereof. This protection will be lost if the maturity date is extended or the terms or conditions relating to payments are changed after November 12, 1981.

As the investor (contract holder), you may elect to be taxed annually on any particular pre-1990 contract which does not pay full annual interest by so stating in your return and reporting the income, as discussed under the preceding heading above. It is possible, if you have informed the issuer you want to be on an accrual basis, that you will receive a T5 slip on an accrual basis. It is more likely, however, that you will have T5 interest on deferred interest investments reported on a three-year accrual basis; that is, no interest in Years 1 and 2 and three years' interest in Year 3, since this is the CRA's instruction to T5 preparers. You should be sure whether and how your interest income is being reported on T5 slips, and maintain adequate records to reconcile your tax reporting to the T5 where you have chosen annual reporting on an investment which does not pay annual interest. The CRA provides form T1 CSB for Canada Savings Bond holders who made the election for 1990.

[¶432a] ANNUITY CONTRACTS AND LIFE INSURANCE

Interest Acquired after 1989

Annuity contracts and insurance policies issued after 1989 which are not exempt polices or prescribed annuity contracts are subject to annual accrual inclusion rules under section 12.2 of the Act. Most life insurance policies currently issued are in fact exempt; it is the issuer who is responsible for meeting the tests and reporting income accordingly. Policies issued before 1990 and not materially altered after 1989 continue to be subject to the rules and exceptions set out below. For annuities issued before 1990, the portion of the annuity fixed before 1990 is subject to triennial or (for grandfathered annuities under the old rules) deferred reporting, but any portion which becomes fixed after 1989 is subject to annual reporting.

Interest Acquired After December 1, 1982 and Before 1990

If you acquired an interest in this time period, you are required to report accrued but unreceived income every three years — that is, at the end of each year in which a third anniversary of the contract or policy occurs. This applies only to income accrued after 1982. These accrual rules also apply to annuity contracts acquired after December 19, 1980 and before December 2, 1982 if annuity payments had not been made before that latter date. Exception from the triennial recognition rule is also provided for certain "locked-in" deferred annuities acquired before December 1, 1982.

The first "third anniversary" of an annuity acquired before December 2, 1982 and on which annuity payments had not commenced before that date was December 31, 1987. No change was made in this date to parallel the additional deferral for debt obligations described above. Income on pre-December 2, 1982 annuities had to be reported in 1987, unless the annuities were exempt as described below.

Exceptions

Certain life insurance policies and annuities are exempt from both the one-year and the three-year accrual requirement. These include exempt policies, prescribed annuity contracts and annuity contracts which derive from life insurance policies acquired before December 2, 1982.

In general terms, an exempt policy is a life insurance policy where the savings component does not exceed accumulating funds in respect of certain exemption test policies. Certain technical amendments to the exemption tests will apply to policies issued after 2016, with grandfathering provisions for existing policies (generally in regulation 306).

A "prescribed annuity contract" includes an annuity under most deferred income plans such as RRSPs and DPSPs. It also generally includes an annuity that has begun making annuity payments, and the holder is an individual or a certain type of trust (regulation 304). Certain technical amendments to the definition were made that are applicable to annuities issued after 2015.

See also ¶981 concerning the proceeds of disposition of insurance policies.

(ITA: 12; 12.2; 20(21); 76; ITR: 304 Prescribed Annuity Contracts; 306 Exempt Policies; 7000 Prescribed Debt Obligations; IT-396R Interest Income; IT-87R2 Policyholders' Income from Life Insurance Policies)

[¶432a.05] *Leveraged Insurance Annuities (LIAs)*

Changes first announced in the 2013 Federal Budget target the "unintended tax benefits" in respect of arrangements known as "LIA policies". Prior to these changes, income earned on the invested capital was generally not taxed under the accrual rules described above because most life insurance policies were exempt policies. Interest expense on the borrowed funds was deductible, and a deduction was allowed for part of the policy premium. Under the new rules, a life insurance policy issued on the life of an individual is an LIA policy if:

- a person or partnership becomes obligated on or after Budget Day to repay an amount to another person or partnership (the lender) at a time determined by reference to the death of the individual; and
- an annuity contract, the terms of which provide that payments are to continue for the life of the individual, and the policy are assigned to the lender.

Under the new rules, an LIA will no longer be an exempt policy, such that it will be subject to the annual accrual rules described above. Premiums paid on the policy will not be deductible. The new rules generally apply to taxation years that end on or after March 21, 2013.

[¶433] CANADA SAVINGS BONDS

Canada Savings Bonds (CSBs) come in two kinds. "R" bonds pay full interest annually; that is, you actually receive the interest money every year and must pay tax on that interest. "C" bonds are compound interest bonds; that is, you do not actually receive the interest until the bond is cashed. Because the government continues to hold the interest money, the rate of interest paid is slightly higher. However, even though you don't receive the interest on C bonds currently, you must pay tax annually on series 45 and later bonds.

In general, for Series 45 and later bonds (issued in or after 1990), all reporting is done on the T5 slips from the Bank of Canada. This is apparently so whether you cash the bonds early or not, and whether they are C or R bonds. As with other T5 slips, there is no requirement that they be issued for amounts less than $50, but you are still required to report the interest income. Interest from Canada Savings Bonds is reported on line 121 of the return along with other interest and investment income.

Historical Information

For the rules in place on Series 44 and earlier bonds (which matured before 2002), see the 2008 and earlier editions of this book.

(ITA: 12(1)(c), (4)–(11); T1 Guide; IT-396R Interest Income)

[¶435] FOREIGN SOURCE INTEREST

Inclusion in Canadian Dollars

Interest from foreign bonds or other obligations, (e.g., U.S. Government bonds), should be included in income in Canadian dollars. In theory, conversion of foreign currency income amounts should be recorded at the date the income is received. You can usually obtain the conversion rate for a particular currency for a particular day from the Bank of Canada website. In general, for income receipts that occur throughout the year, the CRA will not object if conversions are made at an average rate for the year, so long as you are consistent from year to year in your method. A table of conversion rates precedes Chapter 1.

The amount is reported on Schedule 4 and line 121 of the T1 return.

When foreign tax has been withheld from such interest, the full interest (including the amount withheld) should be included and a foreign tax credit claimed (see ¶1450).

Foreign Tax Credit or Deduction

Generally, the maximum foreign tax credit allowed on such income is 15% of the amount. If the foreign tax withheld on foreign source income (including interest) from property other than real estate is in excess of 15% of the income you may deduct the excess tax withheld from that income. The claim for the deduction should be shown on Schedule 4 in the category marked "Other" carrying charges. You may only use the reduced income and a maximum of 15% foreign tax withheld in the calculation of the foreign tax credit.

Alternatively, you need not claim any credit for foreign taxes paid. Instead, you can deduct a part or all of the foreign taxes paid directly from the foreign source interest and include the lesser amount of interest in your income. This may be beneficial if you cannot fully utilize the foreign tax credit available to you. As well, certain foreign taxes are required to be used as a deduction from income for Canadian purposes and not as a foreign tax credit. This will apply where the foreign country refunds the taxes to someone other than yourself. Such refund schemes are not common.

You may also be required to report and pay tax on your share of interest and other investment income earned by a foreign company of which you are a Canadian resident shareholder, or by a foreign trust of which you are a Canadian resident beneficiary. This is discussed in more detail at ¶493.

Possible Accrual Method

Foreign source interest not paid on a regular basis, or that includes bonus or discount features, is normally subject to the annual accrual reporting requirements at ¶432.05. This can create foreign tax credit problems, since eligibility for credit only arises when amounts are actually paid and foreign tax withheld. It appears that the CRA will allow waivers (¶277) to keep open the years in which unpaid interest is reported, and allow the related credit when tax is eventually withheld.

(ITA: 20; 94; 95; 126; IT-95R Foreign Exchange Gains and Losses; Income Tax Folio: S5-F2-C1 Foreign Tax Credit)

[¶436] INTEREST AND PRINCIPAL COMBINED

If a loan is made without interest or at a low rate of interest and the borrower has agreed to repay a greater principal sum than was lent, the extra principal amount or some part of it may be regarded as interest income of the creditor when received. However, where the rate of interest charged on the loan is not abnormally low in the circumstance, any extra principal amount received by the creditor will usually be treated as a capital gain. See also ¶430.

Similarly, a blended payment is an amount made up partly of capital and partly of interest (subsection 16(1) of the Act). It is not always easy to identify the interest component and the payer is typically not obligated to issue a T5 slip to you. In any event, the CRA notes that you must treat as interest on a debt obligation the part that can be reasonably considered to be interest. Report this amount in the same way you would report any other interest.

The interest accrual rules at ¶432 may apply to force recognition of significant principal or interest premiums before they are realized. In general, Part LXX of the Income Tax Regulations may be said to attempt to apply accounting principles to accrued bonuses or premiums on an annual basis on defined obligations.

Interpretation Bulletin IT-265R3, "Payments of Income and Capital Combined", has been cancelled (¶283), meaning it can no longer be relied on as policy. Nevertheless, used with caution, it still presents a reasonable overview of the issues.

See also ¶442 on indexed securities.

(ITA: 12(9); 16; ITR: 7000 Prescribed Debt Obligations)

[¶437] TREASURY BILLS

Interest upon Redemption

The discount on treasury bills is interest income and any amount you received on maturity of a treasury bill over the cost is fully taxable as interest income.

You should receive a T5008 slip or similar statement that records the proceeds of disposition of treasury bills which have matured in the year. Unlike other information slips, such as the T5, the slip does not report the taxable amount. Rather, it reports proceeds received on the bills. From the proceeds you must subtract the cost to arrive at income. The income should be reported on Part II of Schedule 4 as interest, domestic or foreign, as the case may be, and then on line 121 of the return.

Treasury bills are usually thought of as short-term paper, e.g., 90 days. Where the term is not more than a year, income should be reported in the year proceeds are received. If you hold such obligations, i.e., obligations acquired on issue with no stated interest and an original issue discount, and these obligations have a holding period of more than one year, you will be subject to the annual accrual interest rules at ¶432.05.

Brokerage Costs

Brokerage costs on the handling of T-Bills should reduce income reported from them. That is, they should reduce your costs on acquisition, as they would be with a capital investment, so that they reduce interest finally computed on disposition. Any brokerage costs on disposition should therefore match the timing of interest reporting.

Possible Capital Gain or Loss

If you did not hold your treasury bills to maturity, you may have an element of capital gain or loss on disposition if interest rates changed between the time you acquired the bills and the time you disposed of them. As well, your interest will be prorated for the shortened period for which you held the T-Bill. The CRA's *Capital Gains* guide (T4037) has on occasion included a useful example of the calculation of interest and gain or loss in these circumstances, on which the following example is based:

Example

Tom purchased a T-Bill on May 1 for $49,500. The T-Bill's term is 91 days and its maturity value on August 1 is $50,000. Accordingly, the effective yield rate at the time of purchase can be established as 4.05%. However, Tom sold the T-Bill on June 13 for $49,750. Interest and capital gain are calculated as follows:

Purchase price × Effective yield rate	x	Number of days T-Bill held / Number of days in year sold	= interest
$49,500 × 4.05%	x	44 / 365	= $241.67

Proceeds of disposition	$49,750.00
Minus: Interest	$ 241.67
Minus: Adjusted cost base	$49,500.00
Equals: Capital gain	$ 8.33

(T1 Guide; Other Publications: 1988 Revenue Canada Round Table at 1988 CTF Conference Reports 53:17)

[¶438] BONDS ISSUED AT A DISCOUNT

Subsection 16(3) provides special rules for certain debt instruments issued at a discount. In particular, for bonds, debentures, notes, mortgages or any similar obligations issued after June 18, 1971, by tax-exempt persons, non-residents not carrying on business in Canada, or a government, municipality or other public body performing a function of government, if the debt obligation is issued for an amount that is less than its principal amount, and the effective yield on the debt (under any circumstances in which it may be called) exceeds 4/3 of the stipulated rate, the excess of the principal amount over the actual issue amount must be included in income of the first taxable Canadian resident to acquire the debt as a capital property in the year it is acquired by that person.

See also the special rules at ¶442 for indexed debt obligations, which may take precedence over these rules.

(ITA: 16)

[¶439] PURCHASE OF CANADA SAVINGS BONDS THROUGH PAYROLL DEDUCTION

If you purchase Canada Savings Bonds through a payroll deduction plan, in effect, your employer's bank lends you the money to buy the bond, and allows you to repay the principal, *with interest*, by payroll deductions over a one-year period. You are entitled to claim the interest portion of the loan repayment as a carrying charge, that is, a deductible interest expense payment. See ¶445.

(ITA: 20)

[¶440] PURCHASE OR SALE OF BONDS

At the time a bond or other interest bearing security is bought or sold there may be interest accrued to the date of purchase or sale. Under subsection 20(14), the interest accrued to the date of sale is included in the income to the seller (except to the extent it was otherwise included). The purchaser may deduct interest accrued at the purchase date from interest income subsequently received.

See ¶432 for a discussion of accrued interest income. See ¶433 if you cashed Canada Savings Bonds.

Possible Capital Gain or Loss

Where interest rates fluctuate, and you sell a bond (which was capital property to you, see ¶500) prior to maturity, you may have a capital gain or loss on the difference between face value and selling price. Similarly, when you buy a bond for more or less than its face value and hold it to maturity, you may have a capital gain or loss at maturity. See also ¶511 and ¶512.

Example

You own a $100,000 bond that carries 4% annual interest, payable each December 31. You sell it halfway through the year for $102,500. Ignoring compounding, you would include $2,000 accrued interest income and the remaining $500 proceeds would constitute a capital gain.

See ¶432 for a discussion of accrued interest income. See ¶433 if you cashed Canada Savings Bonds.

Commentary on Bill C-29 Measures (Oct. 25, 2016)

Note: When Bill C-29, October 25, 2016, achieves Royal Assent, the commentary will be modified to read:

Sale of "Linked Note"

A linked note is a debt obligation that pays "interest" based on some reference point such as the future value of a stock market index, commodity index, or similar index or asset. The interest is typically paid upon the maturity of the note. For example, a five-year note may pay the principal and all returns in five years upon maturity, with the "interest" being computed with reference to the value of a stock index at the time of maturity relative to its value at the time of the issuance of the note.

It is often difficult, if not impossible, to apply the interest accrual rules of subsection 20(14) (discussed above) to linked notes when they are transferred prior to maturity. As a result, some taxpayers have taken the position that any accrued gain on the transfer should be considered to be a capital gain rather than interest income.

Effective for transfers after 2016, subsection 20(14.2), generally provides that the pre-transfer accrued gain on a transfer of a linked note (or similar debt obligation described in Regulation 7100(1)(*d*)) will be deemed to be interest. The deemed interest will be subject to the accrual rules of subsection 20(14), which add the interest to the transferor's income and provide a deduction in computing the transferee's income. Generally, the deemed interest will equal the transfer price paid for the note minus the original issue price of the note, without regard to any portions of the gain that result from foreign currency fluctuations. Any portion of the accrued gain that is attributable to an increase in the value of fixed-interest payments because of a decrease in market interest rates, will be excluded from the deemed interest rule under subsection 20(14.2), and will be treated as a capital gain.

(ITA: 20(14); 20(14.2); *Antosko et al. v. The Queen*, 94 DTC 6314 (S.C.C.))

[¶442] INDEXED DEBT OBLIGATIONS

Specific overriding rules deal with the taxation of defined inflation-linked debt securities. Such a debt obligation is called an "indexed debt obligation". An indexed debt obligation is one which by its terms provides for an adjustment to the amount payable in respect of the debt for the period it is outstanding determined by reference to a change in the purchasing power of money. The change, in principle, could be an increase in purchasing power (deflation) or a decrease in purchasing power (inflation).

What the government visualizes is a security issued at less than market rates but carrying a condition that at maturity the investor will be paid a special amount in addition to interest and principal representing, for example, loss of purchasing power as represented by a change in the Consumer Price Index. However, the definition is broad enough to permit a variety of such special conditions.

Where such an indexed security is issued, interest must be reported annually as taxable income (whether or not received). Complex regulations will provide for the determination of interest taking into account the shifts in potential interest represented by the indexing features of the debt. (The same rules will apply to the issuer of the security to determine its deduction position.) The amount should be reported on a T5 slip issued to you.

It appears that if interest is paid annually at a stated rate with an final adjustment to come later, the adjustment must be accounted for under the annual accrual rules (¶432) each year as an amount of interest paid to the debt holder if there is inflation or as deductible interest paid by the debt holder to the issuer if there is deflation. It follows that these adjustments would also be included in CNIL adjustments (¶400).

(ITA: 16(6); 248(1); ITR: 7001 Indexed Debt Obligations)

CHARACTER CONVERSION TRANSACTIONS

[¶443] CHARACTER CONVERSION TRANSACTIONS

In its 2013 Federal Budget, the government announced new rules meant to prevent the conversion of ordinary income to capital gains through the use of certain derivative contracts. The rules are aimed at certain "character conversion transactions", described by the Department of Finance as follows: "A character conversion transaction typically involves an agreement (called a forward agreement) to buy or sell a capital property at a specified future date. The purchase or sale price of the capital property under a derivative forward agreement is not based on the performance of the capital property between the date of the agreement and the future date — instead, the price is determined, in whole or in part, by reference to some other measure, often the performance of a portfolio of investments. The reference portfolio typically contains investments that generally produce fully taxable ordinary income." The character conversion transactions subject to these rules are those that involve property subject to a "derivate forward agreement", as defined under the subheading below.

Tax Treatment

The rules generally treat the increase in the sale price of the property owing to the forward agreement as ordinary income. In particular, if a taxpayer disposes of a property under a "derivative forward agreement", the amount by which the sale price of the property exceeds the fair market value of the property at the time the agreement is entered into by the taxpayer is included in the taxpayer's income (subparagraph 12(1)(z.7)(ii)). A loss will arise if the fair market value of the property at the time the agreement is entered into exceeds the amount paid for the property (paragraph 20(1)(xx)).

If a taxpayer acquires a property under a derivative forward agreement, the amount by which the fair market value of the property at the time it is acquired exceeds the cost to the taxpayer of the property is included in the taxpayer's income (subparagraph 12(1)(z.7)(i)). A loss will arise if the amount paid for the property exceeds the fair market value of the property at the time it is acquired by the taxpayer (paragraph 20(1)(xx)).

The income (loss) for the taxpayer is added to (deducted from) the adjusted cost base of the property (for capital gains purposes) that is subject to the agreement.

Commentary on Legislative Proposals (Sept. 16, 2016)

Note: When Legislative Proposals, September 16, 2016, achieves Royal Assent, the commentary will be modified to read:

The rules generally treat the increase in the sale price of the property owing to the forward agreement as ordinary income. In particular, if a taxpayer disposes of a property under a "derivative forward agreement", the amount by which the sale price of the property exceeds the fair market value of the property at the time the agreement is entered into by the taxpayer that is attributable to an underlying interest other than an underlying interest that is specifically excluded in the definition of a "derivative forward agreement" (discussed below) is included in the taxpayer's income (subparagraph 12(1)(z.7)(ii)). A loss will arise if the fair market value of the property at the time the agreement is entered into exceeds the amount paid for the property (paragraph 20(1)(xx)).

If a taxpayer acquires a property under a derivative forward agreement, the amount by which the fair market value of the property at the time it is acquired exceeds the cost to the taxpayer of the property that is attributable to an underlying interest other than an underlying interest that is specifically excluded in the definition of a "derivative forward agreement" (discussed below) is included in the taxpayer's income (subparagraph 12(1)(z.7)(i)). A loss will arise if the amount paid for the property exceeds the fair market value of the property at the time it is acquired by the taxpayer (paragraph 20(1)(xx)).

The income (loss) for the taxpayer is added to (deducted from) the adjusted cost base of the property (for capital gains purposes) that is subject to the agreement.

Meaning of Derivative Forward Agreement

For these purposes, a derivative forward agreement (subsection 248(1)) is one under which the taxpayer agrees to purchase or sell a capital property, where

- the term of the agreement exceeds 180 days, or the agreement is part of a series of agreements with a term that exceeds 180 days;
- generally, in the case of a purchase agreement, the difference between the fair market value of the property upon acquisition and its purchase price is unrelated to the property itself, in that it is attributable to something other than revenue or cash flow from, or changes in the value of, the property, or any similar criteria in respect of the property. For these purposes, if the purchase price is denominated in a foreign currency, changes in the value of the Canadian currency relative to the foreign currency do not itself make the agreement a derivative forward agreement (see also "Application", discussed below);
- in the case of a sale agreement, the difference between the sale price of the property and its fair market value at the time the agreement is entered into by the taxpayer is attributable to something other than revenue or cash flow from, or changes in the value of, the property, or any similar criteria in respect of the property. Again, if the sale price is denominated in a foreign currency, changes in the value of the Canadian currency relative to the foreign currency does not itself make the agreement a derivative forward agreement. Furthermore, the agreement must be part of an arrangement that has the effect "of eliminating a majority of the taxpayer's risk of loss and opportunity for gain or profit in respect of the property for a period of more than 180 days". The Department's explanatory notes to the provision explain that this latter requirement ensures that the derivative forward agreement rules will not apply where the taxpayer's economic exposure is still based primarily on the property being

sold, even if there is a derivative component to the sale agreement.

Example

The Department of Finance provided the following example of how the rules work (the example involves a mutual fund, but the same calculations would apply in respect of an individual).

Forward Sale

A mutual fund trust purchases a portfolio of non-dividend paying Canadian securities worth $100 million. These are capital properties to the trust. The trust then enters into an agreement to sell the portfolio of Canadian securities to a counterparty in five years for a price determined by reference to the performance of a bond fund (i.e., the price is equivalent to what a $100 million investment in the bond fund would be worth after five years).

At the end of the five-year term of the forward sale agreement, the portfolio of Canadian securities is worth $110 million and the notional investment in the bond fund would be worth $125 million. The portfolio of Canadian securities would therefore be sold for $125 million (irrespective of the fair market value of the Canadian securities portfolio at the end of the five-year term).

The sale agreement would be a derivative forward agreement. It has a term in excess of 180 days. The difference between the fair market value of the property sold at the time of entering into the agreement ($100 million) and the sale price ($125 million) is determined by reference to an underlying interest (i.e., the notional investment in the bond fund) that is unrelated to the property sold. Lastly, the sale agreement has the effect of eliminating a majority of the trust's opportunity for gain or profit and risk of loss in respect of the Canadian securities portfolio.

The mutual fund trust would be required to include $25 million in computing its income for the year of the sale under paragraph 12(1)(*z.7*), being the difference between the fair market value of the property at the time the agreement is entered into ($100 million) and its sale price ($125 million). The total adjusted cost base of the Canadian securities would be increased by $25 million under paragraph 53(1)(*t*) so that there would be no capital gain or loss on the disposition of the Canadian securities for $125 million.

Application

The character conversion rules generally apply to acquisitions and dispositions of property that occur after March 20, 2013, in respect of agreements entered into after that date, with limited grandfathering rules. Furthermore, for agreements entered into before March 21, 2013, the new rules will apply if the term of the agreement is extended beyond 2014, or if the notional amount of the agreement is increased by a certain amount any time after March 20, 2013. The full transitional rules are described on the Department of Finance website, at http://www.fin.gc.ca/drleg-apl/ita-lir0913-n-eng.asp, being the explanatory notes to paragraph 12(1)(z.7).

Commentary on Legislative Proposals (Sept. 16, 2016)

Note: When Legislative Proposals, September 16, 2016, achieves Royal Assent, the commentary will be modified to read:

Furthermore, effective March 21, 2013, a purchase or sale agreement is not considered to be a derivative forward agreement if the underlying interest relates to a purchase of currency, and if it can reasonably be considered that the purchase is agreed to by the taxpayer in order to reduce the risk of fluctuations in the value of the currency in which a purchase or sale by the taxpayer of a capital property is denominated, in which an obligation that is a capital property of the taxpayer is denominated, or from which a capital property of the taxpayer derives its value.

DEDUCTIONS IN COMPUTING INVESTMENT INCOME

[¶445] "CARRYING CHARGES" DEFINED

Most reasonable expenses relating to the earnings of investment income are deductible. Such charges will include, for example, interest on money borrowed to purchase investments, fees for the management of investments, and accounting and bookkeeping fees for keeping records of investments.

Fees (other than commissions) paid to a professional investment counsellor for managing or for advice on buying or selling specific shares or securities of the taxpayer are deductible. A professional investment counsellor is one whose principal business is providing such management services or advice. Fees and commissions to stockbrokers are not *per se* deductible under this rule, but where the stockbroker provides management services and charges a separate fee for them, the fee is deductible.

Carrying charges are reported on Part III of Schedule 4 and deducted at line 221 of the T1 return.

In some cases, the total interest paid and carrying charges may exceed the amount of investment income received. Even so, the excess is generally deductible. However, the deduction may add to your CNIL account and therefore impair the ability to claim the capital gains exemption for qualified farm or fishing property (¶502f) and qualified small business shares (¶502i); see ¶502q.

Where investments include corporation shares, it is not necessary to deduct the carrying charges relating to those shares from the dividend income for purposes of computing the dividend tax credit. However, it is necessary to allocate carrying charges to foreign investment income for purposes of calculating the foreign tax credit. (See ¶1450.) Accordingly, carrying charges related to foreign income should be separately identified on Schedule 4 (or its equivalent list), even though the schedule does not provide for this distinction.

Costs incurred in the actual purchase (or sale) of securities held as capital property form part of the cost of (or proceeds from) the security and are not deductible as an expense. This would include such costs as a broker's commission on the purchase (or sale). These non-deductible costs form part of the adjusted cost base of the property, against which capital gain or loss is measured on disposition; see ¶506.

Restrictions and Other Rules

Although carrying charges are generally deductible, there are a number of exceptions; in general, these relate to costs associated with the acquisition of tax shelters. See the discussion of limited recourse financing at ¶1064 and ¶2521, limited partnership losses at ¶1818, and alternative minimum tax at Chapter 24. Carrying costs are also a component of the CNIL account, which limits the capital gains exemption on qualifying farming and fishing property and small business shares; see ¶400.

See also ¶446 below for a discussion of other scenarios under which interest may not be deductible — for example, where the money is borrowed to earn income in an RRSP, RRIF or similar tax-deferred plan.

Deduction of interest charges is also discussed in somewhat broader context at ¶1063.

(ITA: 18(1)(*a*), (*u*), (11); 20(1)(*c*); IT-67R3 Taxable Dividends from Corporations Resident in Canada; IT-238R2 Fees paid to investment counsel)

[¶446] NON-DEDUCTIBLE INTEREST

In general, interest is not deductible if the borrowed money:

(1) is loaned interest free;

(2) is loaned under circumstances where the terms of payment of interest are not clearly established;

(3) is not used to earn income from your business or from a property acquired with that borrowed money; or

(4) is used to fund certain deferred income plans, such as RRSP, RPP, or TFSA contributions (see ¶1064).

If you sell your home and receive a mortgage as part payment, and purchase another home on which there is a mortgage payable, interest received on the first mortgage will be taxable but interest paid on the mortgage on your new home will not be deductible because it is considered as a personal or living expense (but see ¶1065 and ¶2543).

If you borrow money to purchase undeveloped land, the interest will not be deductible but will be added to the cost of the land. See ¶665.

If you borrow money to purchase an income-producing asset and then sell the asset and use the money for some purpose other than producing income, the interest will cease to be deductible as of the time of the sale. Similarly, if the asset becomes clearly worthless, even though you have not disposed of it, you will lose the right to deduct the interest (although, where this occurs, part of the interest may remain deductible; see ¶1067).

A more detailed discussion of interest deductibility is found at ¶1063–¶1075.

[¶447] CONTINGENT AMOUNTS

Section 143.3 provides that a taxpayer's expenditure is a "contingent amount" and, therefore, reduced to the extent that the taxpayer has a right to reduce or eliminate the amount that is required to be paid in respect of the expenditure. The provision was introduced by the Department of Finance in response to the decision in *Collins v. The Queen* (2010 DTC 5028). In *Collins*, the Federal Court of Appeal allowed the taxpayers to deduct the full face amount of expenses in the years in which they accrued, even though the taxpayers had the right to subsequently reduce the amounts of those expenses.

The rules apply to an otherwise unconditional expenditure in respect of which there is a contingent amount. Subsection 143.4(1) defines the "contingent amount" of a taxpayer at any time (other than a time at which the taxpayer is a bankrupt) to include an amount to the extent that the taxpayer, or another taxpayer that does not deal at arm's length with the taxpayer, has a right to reduce the amount at that time. An "expenditure" of a taxpayer means an expense, expenditure, or outlay made or incurred by the taxpayer, or a cost or capital cost of property acquired by the taxpayer. The "right to reduce" an amount of expenditure means a right to reduce or eliminate the amount, including a right that is contingent upon the occurrence of an event, or in any other way, but only if it is reasonable to conclude having regard to all the circumstances, that the right will become exercisable.

Subsection 143.4(2) will reduce the amount of a taxpayer's expenditure incurred in a taxation year by the amount of the contingent amount in respect of the expenditure net of any amount paid by the taxpayer to obtain the right to reduce the amount of the expenditure. Under subsection 143.4(3), if the taxpayer pays the contingent amount in a subsequent year, the amount is deemed to have been incurred in and become payable in respect of that subsequent year. The amount paid is deemed to have been incurred for the same purpose and to have the same character as the expenditure that was reduced.

Subsection 143.4(4) applies where the taxpayer, or a person not dealing at arm's length with the taxpayer, has at any time in a taxation year after the year in which the expenditure was incurred, a right to reduce the amount of the expenditure (where the right would have reduced the expenditure under subsection 143.4(2), had it been in existence in the year of expenditure). The taxpayer is deemed to receive a "subsequent contingent amount" in respect of the "prior expenditure" in the course of earning income from a business or property under paragraph 12(1)(*x*), and the amount is deemed to be a refund, reimbursement, or similar amount in respect of the expenditure, as described in subparagraph 12(1)(*x*)(iv). The subsequent contingent amount is, therefore, included in the taxpayer's income. The amount of the subsequent contingent amount is the maximum amount of the prior expenditure that may be reduced under the right to reduce net of any amount paid to obtain the right to reduce.

However, subsection 143.4(4) does not apply if it is reasonable to conclude, having regard to all the circumstances, that one of the purposes for having a right to reduce an amount in respect of an expenditure after the end of the taxation year in which the expenditure occurred was to avoid a reduction under subsection 143.4(2) in respect of the expenditure. In such case, subsection 143.4(6) provides that the taxpayer is deemed to have the right to reduce in the year in which the expenditure occurred, effectively subjecting the expenditure to the reduction under subsection 143.4(2) in the year in which the expenditure occurred.

Section 143.4 applies in respect of taxation years that end on or after March 16, 2011.

(ITA: 18(1)(*a*), (*h*), (2), (11); 20(1)(*c*); Income Tax Folio: S3-F6-C1 Interest Deductibility)

INCOME FROM TRUSTS OR ESTATES

[¶450] GENERAL RULES PERTAINING TO BENEFICIARIES OF TRUSTS

This section primarily discusses trusts which arise on the death of an individual (testamentary trusts) or are set up during life by an individual (*inter-vivos* trusts) to provide for the maintenance of assets for the benefit of family members. Typically these trusts are resident in Canada and flow through the income characteristics of their earnings to beneficiaries, reporting these to the beneficiary on form T3 (¶455).

Certain types of trust income paid out or allocated to beneficiaries retain their form and the amounts reported on the T3 slip are reported on the applicable Schedule or line of the T1 return. For example, the taxable portion of eligible or non-eligible dividends flowed out to you are reported in boxes 50 and 32 of the T3 slip, and are then reported on line 121 of the return. Other reporting requirements are noted in the commentary below.

Family trusts may also have been set up in other countries for the benefit of Canadians, and the income of these trusts is taxable to Canadian beneficiaries when they can enforce payment according to the rules below. However, where any Canadian resident can be identified as a contributor to a non-resident trust, very stringent rules may tax the trust and the contributor, as discussed at ¶470. For the beneficiary of a non-resident trust, the income will typically be foreign source income to be reported on Part II of Schedule 4 (¶458). Receipt by a beneficiary of income from a non-resident trust may also trigger additional filing requirements on form T1142, discussed at ¶496.

In addition to the family trusts discussed here, there are commercial investment trusts and some commercial business trusts. If Canadian, these trusts should also report your income to you on a T3 or on a form describing its tax character. If non-resident, the income will generally be simply foreign source income. Commercial trusts are discussed in greater detail at ¶491; capital gains distributions from mutual fund trusts in particular are discussed at ¶418. Foreign trusts are taxed under complex rules discussed at ¶470. Other foreign investment vehicles may be taxed in accordance with the rules at ¶492.

In general, if you are a beneficiary of a trust or estate, you are taxable upon your share of the income of the trust or estate for the year *unless* this income is not allocated to you and you have no legal right to enforce payment and you did not make a preferred beneficiary election. (See ¶452.) Where the right to income has vested in a minor, and it was not paid solely because the beneficiary was a minor, the income is deemed to be the income of the minor for the year; see ¶454.

The portion of the income of the trust or estate which is income to you in a year is the portion of the income of the trust or estate that was paid to you, plus the following:

- The unpaid portion of the income of the trust or estate that was payable to you, i.e., you were entitled to enforce payment in the year.
- The value of all benefits to you during the year from or under the trust or estate.
- A reasonable portion of the amount of any payments during the year out of income of the trust or estate for the upkeep, maintenance and taxes of the property that is required to be maintained for your use.

(ITA: 104; 105)

[¶451] INCOME INTEREST IN TRUST

Under rules found in section 106 of the Act, if you are an income beneficiary of a trust and have sold your income interest, the amount you received on the sale must be included in your income.

If you have bought an income interest in a trust, you may deduct the price you paid to purchase the income interest against the income you have received from the trust.

This deduction may not exceed the income received from the trust or the amount received on the sale of the income interest and, to the extent that you have not deducted the cost of the income interest, you may carry this forward to future years.

The cost to you of an income interest in a trust acquired is nil unless the interest was acquired from a person who was the beneficiary in respect of the interest immediately before you acquired it.

If you have sold an income interest in a trust which you had previously purchased, you may deduct any unclaimed balance of the price you paid to purchase the income interest against the amount you received on the sale of the income interest.

Example

Mina Payne is an income beneficiary of her late father's estate. In June, she sold her income interest to her friend Mary Barclay for $20,000. On December 31, Mary received $16,000 from the estate as a distribution of income.

Mina must include $20,000 in her investment income for the year.

Mary's income will be calculated as follows:

Income received from estate	$16,000
Less — cost of income interest	20,000
	—

Mary will not include in her income for the year any income received from the estate since her cost exceeds the income distributed to her.

Mary can carry forward $4,000 as a deduction to be applied against future income she receives from the estate.

(ITA: 106; Income Tax Folio: S6-F2-C1 Disposition of an Income Interest in a Trust)

[¶452] SPECIAL ELECTION BY PREFERRED BENEFICIARIES

Election to Tax Beneficiary on Income Retained in Trust

If you are a preferred beneficiary of a trust, you may elect jointly with the trustees to be treated as having received each year all or any part of your share of the trust's accumulating income. Accumulating income means income of the trust that is not payable to the beneficiary in the year.

A preferred beneficiary of a trust is an individual resident in Canada who is a beneficiary under the trust and is:

(1) the settlor of the trust;

(2) the spouse or former spouse of the settlor of the trust; or

(3) a child, grandchild or great-grandchild of the settlor of the trust, or the spouse of any such person,

and, for trust taxation years commencing after 1996, is

(4) an individual who is suffering from severe and prolonged physical impairment (as described in ¶1209) and has filed a medical certificate to that effect (it does not matter whether attendant care medical credits at ¶1207 or the special allowance at ¶1255 is also claimed for the beneficiary),

or

(5) an individual who attained the age of 18 before the end of the year, was a dependent of someone else (per ¶1122) for the year due to physical or mental infirmity, and whose income for the year (before preferred beneficiary allocations) did not exceed the basic personal amount; as discussed in ¶1209, the infirmity standard under this provision is lower than the disability standard under (4), above.

You should consider making this election if you qualify as a preferred beneficiary and if your tax rate is lower than the tax rate of the trust. Professional advice should be sought in this area as the rules are complex.

Filing of Election

This election must be made within 90 days of year end of the trust and should be made by filing the following documents:

(1) a signed statement by the preferred beneficiary (or legal guardian, usually a parent) and a trustee which designates that part of the accumulating income in respect of which the election is being made. A statement is required for each year in which an election is made;

(2) a statement signed by the beneficiary indicating the beneficiary's Social Insurance Number, relationship to the settlor of the trust, and whether:

- the beneficiary is claiming a disability amount (¶1255),
- a supporting individual is claiming the disability amount (¶1255) for that beneficiary, and if so, the name, address and Social Insurance Number of the supporting individual, or
- the beneficiary is 18 years or older, and in the beneficiary's taxation year which ends in the trust's taxation year another individual can claim in respect of the beneficiary a personal amount for an infirm dependant age 18 or older (¶1122), or could claim such an amount but for the beneficiary's income allocated under the election; if this is the case, provide a statement from the doctor, etc., confirming the infirmity in the first year the claim is made.

(ITA: 104(6), (14)–(14.02), (18); 108(1); ITR: 2800 [Election filing requirements]; IT-394R2 Preferred Beneficiary Election)

[¶453] PAYMENTS OUT OF CAPITAL

If you receive payments out of the capital of a trust or estate they should not be reported as income on your income tax return.

(ITA: 107)

[¶454] INFANTS AND MINORS

As a general rule, income of a trust payable to a beneficiary in the year is taxed to the beneficiary and not the trust.

However, if the income of a trust or estate is not paid or payable to a beneficiary, but instead is held in trust for an individual who did not reach 21 years of age before the end of the trust year, the income will be considered to have been payable to the individual in the year if the following conditions are met:

(1) the right to the income vested at or before the end of the trust year otherwise than because of the exercise of or failure to exercise any discretionary power; and

(2) the right to the income is not subject to any future condition (other than a condition that the individual survive to an age not exceeding 40 years).

Where the rule operates, an income tax return may have to be filed by or for the minor for the year and its interest in the trust income reported as its income.

(ITA: 104(6), (18))

[¶455] STATEMENT OF TRUST INCOME ALLOCATION (T3 SLIP)

In most cases, if you are a beneficiary, you will receive from the trustee of the estate or trust multiple copies of a T3 slip. The T3 slip will indicate the amount of income to be reported in your income tax return for the year.

The T3 slip indicates your portion of the trust's income representing dividends received by the estate or trust from taxable Canadian corporations, the taxable amount of those dividends (see ¶404), and the federal dividend tax credit; your portion of capital gains to be included on your T1Schedule 3; your portion of capital gains eligible for the capital gains exemption (¶465 and ¶502); your portion of RRSP allocations eligible for rollover to your own tax-deferred savings plan (box 22, see also ¶1021) and of pension income eligible for the non-refundable pension income credit (¶1311); your portion of foreign business and non-business income and the amount of any foreign taxes paid on this foreign income (¶458); your portion of interest and other general income; your portion of farming or fishing income (see Chapter 17); death benefits allocated to you and eligible for special deduction (¶925); and your portion of the amount invested in qualified property and of the federal or provincial (except Quebec) tax credit thereon. All of these amounts have significance to you for your income tax return. The T3 slip indicates the line of your tax return on which these amounts should be reported.

Income that is not specifically flowed out to you as noted above, such as interest income from the trust, is reported as other income on line 130 of the return.

Special rules ensure the consistency of treatment for trusts which have both resident and non-resident beneficiaries and have capital gains on the sale of "taxable Canadian property" (¶2040) or income from real property (i.e., rental income), timber resources, Canadian oil and gas property, and business carried on by the trust. This situation will result in a special tax in the trust, which is allocated to Canadian resident beneficiaries as income together with an offsetting tax credit for the same amount. The result for the Canadian beneficiary is the same as if the trust had not paid the special tax and allocated all the special income to Canadians for tax in their hands. See ¶460.

The form T3 must be mailed by the trustee or executor of the trust or estate within 90 days after the end of the taxation year of the trust or estate.

(ITA: 53(1)(*h*); 104; 210.2; ITR: 204 Estates and Trusts)

[¶455.05] *Stop-Loss Rule for Non-Taxable Dividends*

Non-taxable dividends (¶415) allocated to a beneficiary by a trust which then or later become payable to the beneficiary may reduce any capital loss of the beneficiary from an eventual disposition by the beneficiary of its capital interest in the trust. See ¶580d.

(ITA: 104(20); 107(1)(*c*); 112(3))

[¶457] DIVIDENDS FROM TAXABLE CANADIAN CORPORATIONS

If you receive dividends directly from taxable Canadian corporations you are obliged to add 17% to "other" dividends or 38% to "eligible" dividends to arrive at the taxable amount included in income. However, you are entitled to deduct as a dividend tax credit $^{21}/_{29}$ or $^{6}/_{11}$, respectively, of the "gross-up" (the difference between the taxable amount and actual amount of dividends) from your federal tax otherwise payable. The details and logic of this system are discussed at ¶404. This principle is also applied in connection with income from estates or trusts.

If you are an income beneficiary of an estate or trust, the trust may designate to you a share of the other or eligible dividends it has received in its taxation year. The shares of such dividends designated to you retain their characteristics in your hands; that is, they are treated exactly as if you received the dividends directly from a Canadian corporation. Accordingly, you must gross them up by type, and claim the associated dividend tax credit. In such a case, the T3 slip which you receive will show the "actual amount" and the "taxable amount" (being the dividend plus the "gross-up" as described at ¶404) for each type of dividend. Report the "taxable amount" on Schedule 4 under "Taxable Amount of Dividends from Taxable Canadian Corporations", along with any other taxable dividend amounts from other sources. Total taxable amounts are carried to line 120 of the T1 return. Dividend tax credits (along with those from other sources) are reported on line 425 of Schedule 1.

(ITA: 82; 104)

[¶458] FOREIGN INCOME

Subject to certain limits, if you receive income from foreign sources, and have paid foreign taxes thereon, you are entitled to deduct the foreign taxes paid from your Canadian tax otherwise payable (see ¶1450 and ¶1455). This principle also applies to income from trusts or estates, where a portion of this income represents foreign income earned by the trust or estate.

The trust is permitted to allocate to its beneficiaries the foreign taxes it has paid. This will permit the beneficiaries to utilize the foreign taxes as a credit against their Canadian taxes. However, where the trust has claimed the foreign taxes paid as a deduction in computing its income the foreign taxes may not also be allocated to the trust's beneficiaries.

The amount of "foreign source income" and foreign tax paid thereon are indicated in boxes 24, 25, 33 and 34 on form T3 supplementary. The amounts in these boxes should be used to calculate the foreign tax credit when computing your income taxes on Schedule 1.

If the foreign tax withheld on the foreign source income from property other than real property is in excess of 15% of the gross amount of that foreign source income, you may deduct the excess tax withheld from the gross amount. This will also affect the calculation of your foreign tax credit. The foreign source income should be reduced by the excess tax withheld and a maximum of 15% foreign tax withheld should be used in the foreign tax credit calculation.

You need not deduct the foreign taxes paid from your Canadian tax otherwise payable. Instead, you may deduct a part or all of the foreign taxes paid directly from the foreign source income. This may be beneficial to the extent that you cannot fully utilize the foreign tax credit available to you. See ¶1450 and ¶1455.

If you have received foreign source income reported to you in a foreign currency, you must report it in Canadian dollars. You should convert the amounts at the exchange rate effective for the day you received the funds, although in general, especially if no major amounts are involved, the CRA will accept conversions of all amounts in a particular foreign currency at the average exchange rate for that currency for the year. A table of U.S. dollar exchange rates precedes Chapter 1.

(ITA: 20; 104; 126; IT-95R Foreign Exchange Gains and Losses; IT-201R2 Foreign Tax Credit — Trust and Beneficiaries)

[¶459] CAPITAL COST ALLOWANCES AND INVESTMENT TAX CREDIT

If a trust or estate owns depreciable property (¶803) or a resource property, it is entitled to claim the capital cost allowances (CCA, or tax deprecation). The deductions cannot be claimed by beneficiaries of the trust.

A trust is also entitled to the investment tax credit (¶1463) and certain other tax credits. Some (but not all) trusts are allowed to allocate these credits to beneficiaries. This information will be shown on boxes 40, 41 and 42 of the T3 information slip. See explanations on the T3 slip.

The investment tax credit may be designated by the trustee among the beneficiaries in a reasonable manner.

(ITA: 13; 104; 127(7))

[¶460] NON-RESIDENT BENEFICIARIES

Part XIII Withholding Tax

Generally, amounts paid or credited by a trust or estate resident in Canada to a non-resident beneficiary are subject to a 25% withholding tax under Part XIII. This would be the only Canadian tax payable on this income by such beneficiaries.

In some cases this rate will not apply because of the existence of an agreement between Canada and the country in which the beneficiary resides (see ¶2020; withholding rates are set out in Information Circular 76-12R6). For example, payments made by a Canadian trust or estate out of income from sources inside Canada to a resident of the United States are subject to a 15% withholding tax. However, payments made by a Canadian trust or estate *out of income from sources outside Canada* are not subject to the 15% tax if the beneficiary is a resident of the U.S. The tax will also not apply in situations where the trust has already been taxed on the income.

Part XII.2 Tax

Where a non-resident is a beneficiary of a trust other than a "graduated rate estate" (generally a deceased's estate for up to 36 months after the death), the trust will be subject to a special "Part XII.2 Tax" of 40% on certain types of income allocations to all beneficiaries (prior to 2106, the rate was 36%). To the extent a trust has net income from real properties situated in Canada, timber resource properties, Canadian resource properties, businesses carried on by it in Canada or net capital gains from the disposition of taxable Canadian property (as defined at ¶2040), and has non-resident beneficiaries, it will be liable for this tax. When income net of tax is allocated to beneficiaries, resident Canadian beneficiaries will include in income their *pro rata* share of the tax paid (presumably in box 26 or 36, and will receive full tax credit for that tax (box 38 of T3 slip). Non-resident beneficiaries will receive their *pro rata* share of the income remaining after tax, subject to 25% or less non-resident withholding tax, and will receive no credit for the tax paid in the trust (unless they are subject to ordinary Canadian income tax as discussed in Chapter 1). This special tax system is said to be designed both to ensure that income of this kind is taxed at full personal tax rates, and to prevent Canadian resident beneficiaries from bearing an undue share of the tax.

The dividend gross-up and credit machinery (¶404) is denied to dividends received by a trust in the year if the dividends can reasonably be considered as having been included in the income of a non-resident beneficiary.

Part XIII.2 Tax

Recently enacted Part XIII.2 provides that a distribution in respect of a unit or share of a mutual fund trust or corporation held by a "non-resident investor" (a non-resident person or a partnership other than a Canadian partnership) that is not otherwise subject to tax under Part I or Part XIII will be a gain from the deemed disposition of taxable Canadian property, if the unit or share is listed on a designated stock exchange and more than 50% of the value of the unit or share is attributable to real property in Canada, Canadian resource property, or timber resource property. A 15% withholding tax will generally apply to the gain. Part XIII.2 is discussed at ¶2083.05.

(ITA: 104(13), (30), (31); 210–210.3; 212; IT-465R Non-Resident Beneficiaries of Trusts)

[¶460.05] *Property Distributions to Non-Residents*

Where a trust distributes property to a non-resident beneficiary in respect of part or all of the beneficiary's capital interest in the trust, there is a deemed disposition by the trust of the property at its fair market value (subsections 107(2.1) and (5) of the Act). The deemed disposition may generate gains or losses at the time of distribution. There are exceptions to the rule for real property located in Canada, property in a business carried on in Canada through a permanent establishment, and certain "excluded rights or interests". Security may be provided by or on behalf of the trust in respect of any resulting tax payable on the deemed disposition of property that is taxable Canadian property (subsection 220(4.6)). Canadian trusts which themselves become non-resident suffer a similar deemed disposition. Trusts which become non-resident are subject to special reporting rules as well (¶2153).

[¶461] ESTATES OR TRUSTS ARISING ON DEATH

[¶461.05] *Taxation of Beneficiary*

Generally, if you are a beneficiary of a trust you are taxable on benefits received from the trust or estate in the calendar year in which you received them (or in which you are entitled to receive them if that is earlier). However, this is not necessarily the case where the trust or estate arose on the death of another person.

A graduated rate estate (generally, an estate for up to 36 months after the deceased's death) may have a taxation year of its own which does not coincide with the calendar year. (Prior to 2016, this rule applied to any testamentary trust.) A beneficiary of such an estate or trust is taxable for a particular calendar year only on benefits derived from the trust or estate during the taxation year of the trust or estate ending in that calendar year. Thus, benefits received after the end of the taxation year of the trust or estate, but before the end of the calendar year, are not taxable until the following calendar year.

Beginning in 2016, any other testamentary trust must have a taxation year which coincides with the calendar year. Thus, the taxation year of the trust will coincide with that of an individual beneficiary. An estate can have an off-calendar year-end for up to 36 months. Similarly, a qualified disability trust can have an off-calendar year-end. This inclusion rule for the beneficiary as stated above remains the same.

It is possible for the beneficiary of a deceased person's estate to become subject to income tax on the value of property owned by the deceased at the time of his death.

(ITA: 104)

[¶461.10] *Taxation of Deceased*

When a person dies, the general rule under subsection 70(1) is that he is taxable on all income received or accrued to the time of death. His estate, or the beneficiary of his estate, is taxable on income earned after that date.

In addition, under subsection 70(2), the income taxable to the deceased includes the value of "rights or things" owned at the time of death which would have been included in his income if realized or disposed of (see ¶1908).

If rights or things are transferred or distributed to a beneficiary of the estate within a specified time, the beneficiary will be taxable on the amounts realized from such rights or things, when he receives these amounts. The deceased person or his estate will then not be taxed on these amounts.

Additionally, under subsection 70(5) there is a deemed disposition at the time of death of capital properties and certain other properties at their fair market value. An exception is made to property left to a spouse or common-law partner.

Losses on capital and depreciable property of a testamentary trust, as well as certain losses implicit in stock options, may be transferred to the return of the deceased beneficiary at the election of the legal representative.

The tax treatment of deceased taxpayers is discussed in detail in Chapter 19.

(ITA: 70; 164(6), (6.1); T4013 T3 Trust Guide 2015)

[¶465] CAPITAL GAINS OF A TRUST

The net capital gains of a Canadian resident trust, being its taxable capital gains for the year net of its allowable capital losses for the year and its capital loss carryovers deducted in the year, may be allocated to trust beneficiaries, who may claim ordinary capital gains treatment on this allocation. As a practical matter, the trust must calculate net taxable capital gain, being the taxable portion of the full gain (¶502 and ¶2429) net of losses, plus applicable loss carryovers, but then must multiply this value by two and report the full net gain on your T3 slip so that it flows through your Schedule 3 correctly (see Chapter 5).

Lifetime Capital Gains Exemption

For the amount of lifetime capital gains from farming and fishing property and small business shares eligible for capital gains exemption, see ¶502. Capital gains of a trust eligible for the lifetime capital gains exemption are not merely the capital gains allocated to you for ordinary capital gains purposes. The trust must apply annual and cumulative capital gain limitations at the trust level to determine allocations to beneficiaries. This does not mean that the relevant limitation is applied at the trust level, but rather that capital losses and particularly allowable business investment losses of the trust are taken into account before allocation of amounts eligible for capital gains exemption in your hands. The net eligible capital gains must be allocated in the same proportion among beneficiaries as the capital gains allocation for other purposes. The trust must allocate ordinary capital losses, farm capital losses, fishing capital losses, and small business capital losses separately, applying the allocation rules in each case. Again as a practical matter, the trust operates on a net (i.e., "taxable capital gain") basis, but reports the gain eligible for exemption on a gross basis on your T3 slip.

Tax Reporting

There are practical aspects of reporting the general and eligible taxable capital gains reported to you on a T3 slip. The important thing is not to double count, since capital gains eligible for the exemption are included in both box 21 and box 30 and the box 30 amounts must be subtracted in reporting the box 21 amount. If amounts are reported in box 30 you will need to complete form T657 as well as Schedule 3. The information from boxes 21 and 30 is also required on form T936 to calculate CNIL carryforwards (¶400).

A personal (non-commercial) trust can claim the principal residence exemption on the distribution of property to beneficiaries, although the rule of one principal residence per family unit remains.

(ITA: 104(21)–(21.3); 107(2.01); T4013 T3 Trust Guide 2015)

[¶470] NON-RESIDENT TRUSTS

Contributors to non-resident trusts usually face formidable reporting requirements on form T1141. Beneficiaries of such trusts face somewhat less onerous reporting requirements using form T1135. The filing requirements for these forms are discussed in detail at ¶496.

Taxation of Trust and Liability of Beneficiary

Subsection 94(3) of the Act provides that whenever a Canadian resident has "contributed" (generally, loaned or transferred) property to a non-resident trust, or the non-resident trust had a resident beneficiary and a "connected contributor" (e.g., certain former residents), the trust is deemed to be resident in Canada for various purposes and subject to tax in Canada on its worldwide income (other than certain income from its "non-resident portion" of property, as noted below). The rules can capture certain non-resident trusts where contributions have been made within five years of immigration or emigration by the contributor. The contributor and certain specified Canadian beneficiaries will be jointly and severally liable for the tax (thus, the tax liability could be passed on to the Canadian contributor if the tax cannot be collected from the trust itself), although there is a limit that generally applies to certain beneficiaries and some contributors to the extent of their "recovery limit".

However, an alternative tax liability can apply to an "electing contributor", effective for taxation years that end after March 4, 2010. Under this alternative, instead of being jointly and severally liable for all of the trust's tax obligations, the electing contributor will include a portion of the trust's income: the trust income included in the contributor's income will generally be based on the proportion of the fair market value of the contributor's contributions to the trust to the fair market value of all contributions received by the trust from resident or "connected" contributors.

The rules in section 94 further provide that trust property of a non-resident trust subject to the rules be divided into a "resident portion" and a "non-resident portion". Generally speaking, the resident portion will consist of property acquired from residents and certain former residents (connected contributors), while the non-resident portion will consist of everything that is not part of the resident portion. Assuming the trust makes the appropriate election, the trust is subject to tax on its worldwide income from property of the resident portion as noted above. However, income earned on the non-resident portion that would not otherwise be subject to Canadian tax because it is not Canadian-source income will not be included in the trust's income.

The definition of "contribution" under these rules is made to bear a great deal of weight. A contribution is basically any transfer or loan of property other than an arm's length transfer. The arm's length transfer exception is specifically defined for this purpose. One of the requirements for the arm's length transfer exception is that it be a transfer where it is reasonable to conclude that none of the reasons for the transfer is the acquisition at any time by any entity of any interest as a beneficiary under any non-resident trust. There are a number of further details for the genuine payment of interest, dividends, or other returns on investment, and so on. There are elaborate provisions to ensure that indirect contributions are caught. The purpose here is to provide an exception for arm's length transactions with foreign entities that happen to be trusts, such as when a foreign trust invests in a Canadian company's shares, or makes a genuine arm's length loan to a Canadian business.

Exceptions

Certain foreign trusts are exempt from the reach of these rules, so that contributions to them do not put the Canadian contributors (or beneficiaries) at risk. These include foreign trusts controlling prescribed foreign universities, operating foreign pension or employee benefit plans primarily for the benefit of non-resident individuals, foreign charities, and a very few essentially personal foreign trusts for the benefit of infirm foreign dependants or of non-resident children of a broken marriage.

There is also a special exception intended to exempt investments in certain widely held foreign mutual funds and other commercial trusts. This exception, according to the Department of Finance explanatory notes, is intended to apply to non-resident investment trusts that are "truly commercial". The trust under this exception must have only beneficiaries whose rights to receive the trust income or capital are "specified fixed interests" in the trust (generally meaning, where distribution of the income or capital is not subject to a discretionary power), and the trust must also exhibit one of a list of characteristics, such as having at least 150 beneficiaries each of whose specified fixed interests have a value of at least $500, having all the specified fixed interests listed on a designated stock exchange, among others; the full list is found in paragraph (*h*) of the definition of "exempt foreign trust" in subsection 94(1).

Although this type of trust, if it falls within the exception, is not subject to the rules discussed above, an investor in the trust may be subject to modified accrual rules in section 94.2, if the investor is a resident beneficiary who, together with any person not dealing at arm's length with the beneficiary, holds 10% or more of all specified fixed interests in the trust determined by fair market value. The modified accrual rules can also apply to a person who contributes "restricted property" (defined in subsection 94(1)) to the trust. The modified accrual rules are similar to former paragraph 94(1)(*d*), in that they generally treat the trust as a controlled foreign affiliate of the investor such that the foreign accrual property income (FAPI) rules may apply to the investor (FAPI is discussed at ¶493). The investor's share of the FAPI of the trust is based on the fair market value of the investor's specified fixed interests of the trust relative to the fair market value of all specified fixed interests in the trust (a *de minimis* exception provides that the inclusion is nil if the trust's FAPI for the year is $5,000 or less).

Lastly, if the type of commercial trust described in the above paragraph is an exempt foreign trust and also not caught by section 94.2 (e.g., if the investor and non-arm's length persons own less than 10% of the specified fixed interests in the trust), the investor may nonetheless be subject to the offshore investment property rules in section 94.1 of the Act; see ¶492.

For several years, there was an exemption from the non-resident trust rules for the first 60 months of foreign trusts set up by individuals immigrating to Canada. The rule effectively allowed recent immigrants to avoid the non-resident trust rules for up to five years. Unexpectedly, the 2014 Federal Budget eliminated this exemption for trust taxation years that end on or after February 11, 2014, although it is eliminated only for taxation years ending after 2014 if, at any time that is after 2013 and before February 11, 2014, the 60-month exemption applied in respect of the trust and no contributions were made to the trust on or after February 11, 2014 and before 2015.

Historical Information

The rules discussed above generally apply after 2006, and are far more-reaching than the previous non-resident trust rules. The rules here were first proposed in the 1999 Federal Budget. The original proposal called for a consultation period with new rules to be in place for taxation years commencing after 2000. Draft rules were published June 22, 2000. The new proposals aroused serious concerns, in part because of the FIE rules (see ¶492) to which they were linked, and in part because of their retrospective effect on existing non-resident trusts. On September 7, 2000, the government announced that further consultations would be allowed, that revised proposals would be tabled in 2001, and that implementation would be deferred to taxation years commencing after 2001. A 2001 version of the draft legislation was published August 2, 2001, and was originally set for implementation for trust taxation years that commence after 2001. However, in an announcement dated December 17, 2001, the Department of Finance acknowledged receipt of further representations it was willing to study, and deferred implementation of the rules until taxation years that commence after 2002. Further draft revisions were published October 11, 2002, October 30, 2003, July 18, 2005, November 9, 2006, and August 27, 2010. More recently, the non-resident trust proposals were reintroduced in draft legislation dated November 21, 2012, which contains most of the previous proposals along with some amendments first announced in the March 2010 Federal Budget. Although most of the rules apply to taxation years that end after 2006 (except as otherwise noted), a trust can elect that the rules apply to its taxation years ending after 2000 and before 2007. Finally, the non-resident trust proposals received Royal Assent on June 26, 2013.

(ITA: 94; for mutual fund exceptions, see especially 94(2)(*h*) and existing; ITR: 4801.1 [Exempt foreign trust]; Other Publications: Department of Finance News Releases 2000-050; 2000-064; 2001-067; 2001-120; 2002-84)

[¶475] INCOME AND MUTUAL FUND TRUSTS; AFFILIATED TRUST RULES

As discussed in ¶450, the information in the preceding paragraphs (starting at ¶450 is primarily devoted to trusts which arise on the death of an individual or are set up by an individual during life to provide for the maintenance of assets for family members. Trusts of a more commercial nature are discussed elsewhere in this chapter, as indicated below.

Income from investments in mutual fund trusts is reported on the T3 slip. Capital gain distributions from mutual fund trusts are discussed in some detail in ¶418. Other income distributions from a mutual fund trust are discussed in ¶491.

Income trusts are a subspecies of Canadian mutual fund trusts which are designed to allow investors to invest in a particular business controlled by the trust, rather than a broad range of investments made by the trust. These are discussed under the heading "Income Trusts" in ¶491.

Transactions between trusts or between trusts and their beneficiaries where the parties are considered to have a common economic interest (as, for example, being subject to common control) may be subject to special rules, commonly denying loss recognition. These "affiliated person" rules are discussed in ¶852.

TAX-FREE SAVINGS ACCOUNTS

[¶478] TAX-FREE SAVINGS ACCOUNTS ("TFSAS")

The TFSA has been in place since 2009. The annual TFSA contribution limit is indexed to inflation and adjusted upward to the nearest $500. For 2016, the limit is $5,500; for previous years, see below.

To the extent you have accumulated contribution room, you can contribute to a TFSA, which is rather like an RRSP in that it is a trust account administered by a bank, trust company, credit union, or annuities issuer (typically a life insurance company). Contributions are not deductible, but investment earnings accumulate tax-free in your account, and can be withdrawn without penalty at any time. Any withdrawals in a year add to the contribution room for the next year, in addition to the regular annual contribution limit.

Contribution limits for previous years were:

- 2009 through 2012: $5,000
- 2013 and 2014: $5,500
- 2015: $10,000 (this increase applied only for one year; the limit for 2016 was reduced back to $5,500).

Details of TFSAs are discussed in Chapter 25 at ¶2532c.

(ITA: 12(11) "investment contract"; 18(1)(*u*), (11); 146.2; 149(1), 207.01–207.07)

ANNUITIES

[¶480] ANNUITIES

Amounts which you receive as annuities may be reported in different ways. The identifiable interest paid in connection with ordinary annuity contracts reported to you as interest in box 13 or box 19 of T5 slips should be treated as interest on Schedule 4 and line 121 of your T1 return. However, if you are 65 years or older, the income element of a "mixed annuity payment" (a fixed annuity payment in which the income and capital elements are prescribed by regulations (¶483)) as well as certain interest accruals will be eligible for the pension deduction (¶1311), should be reported as pension income on line 115. This is also true if you are under 65 and receiving these amounts by virtue of the death of a spouse. Although the CRA has said that it has directed insurance companies and other T5 issuers to report the interest portion of blended or accrued annuity payments as annuity income in box 19 and not box 13, so that it can readily be identified as eligible pension income, the guide for T5 issuers is far from clear insofar as mixed annuities are concerned, and it is really the expertise of the company which issues the annuity (and the T5 slip) that you are relying on to ensure that the correct amounts are in the correct box.

Annuity and/or periodic DPSP income reported to you in box 24, 133, or 194 on a T4A slip, and RRIF income from box 16 or 20 of the T4RIF slip should ordinarily be reported on line 130. However, if you are 65 years of age or older in the year for which tax is calculated, this income is generally eligible for the pension credit (¶1311) and should be reported on line 115. Where you are not yet 65 but such annuity income is received by you in consequence of the death of your spouse, it can qualify for the pension income deduction and should be reported on line 115. If you receive Saskatchewan Pension Plan payments shown in box 016 of your T4A slip, they should be reported on line 115.

All amounts paid out of an RRSP should be reported on line 129; however, the portion of an RRSP payment which represents annuity payments out of a "mature" RRSP (reported in box 16 of the T4 RSP) is eligible for the pension income credit (¶1311).

However, amounts received out of or under an annuity contract issued or effected as a TFSA, which are excluded from income inclusion as per subparagraph 56(1)(*d*)(iii), which applies to 2009 and subsequent years.

(ITA: 56(1)(*d*); 60(*a*); 118(3), (7), (8); T1 Guide)

[¶480.05] *Annuities and Pensions*

Although annuity income may qualify for pension credit treatment, it does not follow that pension income qualifies for annuity treatment. A "superannuation or pension benefit" is generally taxable in full (although pension income credit will offset some of the tax). That is, pension income does not qualify for the deduction of capital element discussed at ¶483. See ¶911.

(ITA: 248(1) "superannuation or pension benefit"; *Cooper v. M.N.R.,* 81 DTC 40 (T.R.B.))

[¶481] DEDUCTIONS ALLOWED

The amount of the annuity payments to be reported as income can be reduced by the portion representing a return of capital. The calculation of the capital element is described in the sections of the commentary below.

Annuities under superannuation or pension plans, registered retirement savings plans, deferred profit sharing plans, registered retirement income funds, "non-exempt" deferred income annuities (see ¶432), and annuities purchased with an RRSP refund of premiums where the purchase price was deducted from income (¶903) do not qualify for any of these capital deductions. However they may qualify for the pension credit on up to $2,000 of pension income.

(ITA: 16; 58; 60(*a*))

[¶482] CALCULATION OF THE CAPITAL ELEMENT OF AN ANNUITY UNDER A WILL OR TRUST

The part of an annuity payment made under a will or trust which can be deducted as the capital element is that part which the recipient can establish as not having been paid *out of income* of the trust or estate. It is up to you to prove that you have properly determined this amount.

Such factors as the terms of the will or trust, determinations by the trustee or executor as to the source of the payment, the total income of the trust or estate, and the amount of payments made to other beneficiaries in the year must be considered. For example, a will might state that all annuities are to be paid out of capital, in which case the entire annuity would be non-taxable. If the trustee or executor has been given discretion to make annuity payments out of either income or capital, the amount determined to have been out of capital will be accepted as the capital element of the annuity. Of course, if the income of the trust or estate is less than the annuity payments, at least part of the payments must be out of capital.

(ITA: 60(*a*))

[¶483] CALCULATION OF THE CAPITAL ELEMENT OF AN ANNUITY NOT UNDER A WILL OR TRUST

Regulations under the Act determine the capital element of annuity payments not made under a will or trust. The capital element is normally calculated as of the date when annuity payments commence.

Regulation 300 provides that the capital elements of an annuity contract that is a prescribed annuity contract (see ¶432) will be determined as at the later of January 31, 1983 and the commencement of the date of the payment. Where the annuity contract is not a prescribed annuity contract, the capital element will be determined immediately before the commencement of payments.

In general, the rules result in the capital portion of annuity payments being calculated as the proportion of the payments which the cost of the annuity bears to the total of payments to be made or expected to be made under the annuity contract.

The cost of the annuity contract for the purpose of the calculation is usually the sum of the premiums paid to acquire the annuity. However, for most annuity contracts entered into before 1970, the value of the annuity contract as of its second anniversary date after October 22, 1968 plus premiums paid since that date will be used in the place of cost in applying this formula if this value results in a greater capital element. In addition, special rules exist for annuity contracts that commence on the death of a person, or commence after the expiration of a term of years and which are paid under a life annuity contract entered into prior to October 23, 1968 or are paid under any other annuity contract entered into before January 4, 1968.

Where annuity payments depend on the length of life of an individual, mortality tables are used to estimate the payments expected to be made under the annuity. Recent technical amendments to the regulations provide reference to update mortality tables, generally for annuities issued after 2016 (paragraph 300(2)(*a*) of the regulations).

In most cases, the payer of the annuity will notify the recipient of the amount of the payment representing the capital element. Your T4A slip, however, may only indicate the taxable portion (in box 24). See ¶486.

(ITA: 60(*a*); ITR: 300 Capital Element of Annuity Payments)

[¶486] INFORMATION RETURNS

If you receive an initial annuity payment you should receive from the payer, by the end of February in the next calendar year, a form T4A supplementary, indicating the taxable portion of annuities paid to you (i.e., the portion not paid out of capital).

You should keep one copy on file and report the taxable amount as income for each year in which you receive the annuity.

[¶488] CANCELLATION OF ANNUITY CONTRACTS

If you are the holder of a life or fixed term annuity contract and you receive a lump-sum payment in full satisfaction of your rights under the contract, the amount of the lump-sum payment which may reasonably be regarded as interest income (¶480) (the difference between the amount received and the cost of the annuity or the aggregate of premiums paid) must be included in income. The balance is a non-taxable receipt.

If you are the holder of an income-averaging annuity contract and you receive a lump-sum payment in full satisfaction of your rights under the contract, the entire amount received must be included in income.

(ITA: 56)

OTHER INVESTMENT INCOME

[¶490] ROYALTIES AND PAYMENTS BASED ON PRODUCTION OR USE

Depending on the circumstances, income from royalties may be either investment income or business income. Where royalties are reported in box 17 of a T5 slip, the CRA says on the back of the slip that they should be reported as miscellaneous employment income on line 104 of the T1 return if from a work or invention (¶308), as business income on line 135 if the royalties have expenses associated with them or as investment income on line 121 if otherwise. The reporting of royalties from a work or invention on line 104 may be appropriate for continuing royalties where there are no associated expenses which have not been written off, but in many circumstances these royalties should be reported as business income instead; see ¶787 and ¶789.

For example, if you are an author and you have a book published, royalties you collect may be considered to be business income (¶789). If you purchase a patent as an investment, however, the royalties received from licensing the patent would be considered to be investment income.

"Investment income" royalties represent amounts paid to you for the use of property you own, such as a copyright, trademark, or patent. However, payments received for the use, by others, of real estate which you own should be reported as real estate rentals. See Chapter 6.

Proceeds received in instalments from the disposition of property may constitute royalty income if the amount of the proceeds is dependent upon use of or production from the property sold.

(ITA: 12(1)(*g*); IT-462 Payments Based on Production or Use)

[¶491] CANADIAN MUTUAL FUND INCOME

[¶491.05] *Investment Funds*

Canadian mutual funds are Canadian corporations or trusts formed to pool the money of investors. Investors in these vehicles purchase shares, if the mutual fund is incorporated, or units if the mutual fund is a trust. The fund in turn invests the money. Most mutual funds invest in stocks and/or bonds, but these may have a wide array of built-in preferences. Some funds are oriented to general investments, some to investments in "small cap" companies which may offer higher growth but entail higher risk, some to investments sensitive to the price of precious metals, and so on. There are mutual funds called mortgage investment corporations (MICs) which invest primarily in mortgages, and there are similar investment vehicles, called real estate investment trusts (REITs), which invest in real estate. Many funds restrict themselves to investments eligible for Canadian RRSPs, so that they in turn are eligible RRSP investments. Other funds invest in foreign investments to such a degree as to be ineligible for RRSP or TFSA investment, or invest in other items making them ineligible. Normally, a fund will tell you if it is a qualified RRSP or TFSA investment.

In theory, the advantage of investing through a mutual fund rather than directly is that the large number of investors can acquire a much broader range of investments than an individual. In practice, investors in mutual funds are typically relying on the investment skills of the fund managers to make sound investment decisions, rather than trying to make such decisions themselves.

Canadian mutual funds which comply with Canadian tax rules (as most do) can flow out to their investors the underlying characteristics of their investments. Thus, where the fund receives Canadian dividends eligible for dividend tax credit, it can assign a portion of the dividends and credits to each investor in the fund. Similarly, capital gains realized by the fund can be flowed out to investors and taxed as capital gains of the investor (for more detail on capital gain distributions, see ¶418). Mutual fund income is reported to you on T5 slips (if the fund is a corporation) or T3 slips (if a trust), which show the dividend, dividend tax credit, foreign income, foreign tax credit, capital gain, and general income components of the annual fund distributions to you. (The rules governing distributions from Canadian mutual fund trusts are essentially the same as for trusts generally, with minor variations for tax exempt dividends received by the trust.)

Investments in mutual fund shares or units are normally capital investments. You typically get out of the fund by having it redeem your shares or units, and the funds you receive on redemption will be proceeds of disposition, giving rise to capital gain or loss depending on the amount compared to the cost of the investment. Many funds provide for automatic reinvestment of annual distributions to you. In this case, you are taxable on the distribution and the amount reinvested adds to the cost base of your investment. The fund will typically keep track of this data for you.

Qualified funds held by RRSPs essentially operate under the same rules, but the RRSP is not taxable on the current fund income, and all income realized in the RRSP is fully taxable when RRSP distributions are made to you, regardless of its character as dividend, capital gain, etc.

(ITA: 104(6), (20); 108(2); 130; 130.1; 131; 132)

[¶491.10] *Income Trusts/Specified Investment Flow-Through Trusts (SIFTs)*

As discussed above, Canadian mutual fund trusts have traditionally been used by investors seeking to achieve a balanced investment portfolio by pooling their resources in a trust which in turn invested in underlying portfolio investments, typically bonds and shares of a variety of companies. There have, however, long been on the market specialized trusts which invested in one primary asset, usually an oil or gas production facility, which provided a stream of ordinary income.

More recently, Canadian mutual fund trusts have, in addition to their traditional uses, been adopted to serve as so-called "Income Trusts", where the trust acquires a business as a going concern. Income trusts, known as specified investment flow-through trusts or SIFT trusts, are essentially taxed as corporations. Distributions from SIFT trusts are treated as eligible dividends and are subject to the gross-up and dividend tax credit mechanism and reported in the manner discussed at ¶404. The trust should issue you a T3 slip with the required information.

A real estate investment trust or "REIT" is not considered a SIFT trust. Distributions from a REIT are treated in the same manner as other commercial *inter vivos* trusts, and allocations and flow-through of trust income is reported on the T3 slip issued to the unitholder.

Historical Information

Since income trusts were previously taxed as trusts and thus avoided the corporate level of tax, investments in the trust were taxed preferentially relative to shares in corporations. The government's first response to this issue was to enhance the dividend tax credit mechanism for shares in public corporations (see ¶404), in order to integrate the corporate and individual taxes payable on dividends, which would approximate the tax paid on distributions from income trusts. However, since the foregoing would provide a solution only in respect of fully taxable investors (and not, for example, tax-exempt investors and non-residents), in 2006 the federal government proposed a corporate-type tax on income trusts, or, as they became known, "specified investment flow-through trusts" (SIFTs). As noted above, distributions out of the trust are treated as eligible dividends in the hands of the investors.

Although these changes were effective as of October 31, 2006, income trusts which were already being publicly traded before November 2006 were not subject to the new rules before taxation years ending in 2011 (unless the trust exceeded "normal growth" guidelines issued by the Department of Finance), allowing time for the impact of the new rules to be absorbed. However, any new income trusts which entered the market after October 31, 2006, would be subject to the new rules immediately. There is also an exception for "real estate investment trusts" (REITs). An article summarizing the proposals and rules is found in the Wolters Kluwer Newsletter *Tax Topics* No. 1809, dated November 9, 2006, with updates following in No. 1835 on real estate investment trusts (May 10, 2007) and in No. 1847 (August 2, 2007).

Once a trust falls under the new SIFT regime, either because it is newly formed after October 31, 2006 (unlikely), because it has fallen offside under transitional rules (possible), or because 2011 has arrived (inevitable), distributions from the trust are treated as eligible dividends (¶404). This is appropriate, since the SIFT is taxed at public corporation rates.

(ITA: 104, esp. 104(20); 122.1; 132; Other Publications: Department of Finance Press Release 2005-082)

[¶491.15] *Cost Base Adjustments*

Mutual fund units (or shares) are identical properties; that is, each property in the group is the same as all the others. You may buy and sell several identical properties at different prices over a period of time. The average cost per unit or share (and therefore its adjusted cost base, or ACB) of your mutual fund investment increases or decreases when you purchase new units or shares, or reinvest your distributions, depending on the price when the transaction occurred. With investment trusts you traditionally cashed out your investment with the trust, which kept track of your cost base, so this was not in practice much of a problem.

With the spread of income trusts, however, the problems multiply. First, these trusts are more likely than traditional investment trusts to, for example, make a return of capital or suffer recapture of capital cost allowance, which are things that affect the unitholder's adjusted cost base (ACB) of the trust units. Moreover, with income trusts you may trade units in the open market, so you are more likely to have to keep track of your cost base yourself.

In any event, the CRA has added Box 42 to the T3 reporting slip to report to you changes in the capital balance in the mutual fund trust identified on the slip. A positive amount in box 42 will result in a reduction to your ACB while a negative amount will result in an increase to your ACB. The CRA also offers an information sheet, *Tax Treatment of Mutual Funds for Individuals* (RC4169) to assist you in accounting for mutual fund distributions and tracking cost base adjustments.

(ITA: 47(1); 53(1)(*d*.2), (2)(*h*))

[¶491.20] *Affiliated Trust Rules*

Transactions between trusts or between trusts and their beneficiaries where the parties are considered to have a common economic interest (as, for example, being subject to common control) may be subject to special rules, commonly denying loss recognition. Probably in consequence of the rise of income trusts, these "affiliated person" rules being extended to specific trust situations. The affiliated person rules are discussed in ¶852.

[¶491.25] *Non-Resident Investors*

Non-residents receiving income distributions from Canadian resident trusts including mutual fund trusts are subject to Part XIII withholding tax at the rate of 25%. The rate is often reduced under an income tax treaty.

Special Tax on Capital Gains from Taxable Canadian Property

By virtue of subsection 131(5.1), non-residents investing in Canadian mutual funds will be subject to withholding tax at dividend rates on capital gains distributions from the funds in respect of gains realized from dispositions of taxable Canadian properties. The rule applies only where more than 5% of a dividend paid is received by or for non-residents. The rate is often reduced by treaty.

Special Tax on Assessable Dividends

Part XIII.2 of the Act applies a 15% withholding tax as a tax on certain distributions to non-residents that are not otherwise subject to tax under Part I or Part XIII (paid or credited by certain mutual funds to their non-resident investors). Such distributions are called "assessable distributions".

The tax generally applies to non-resident investors in Canadian mutual funds which both derive their value primarily from Canadian real estate and are listed on a designated stock exchange. Certain losses can be used to offset the tax.

These taxes are discussed in more detail in the Chapter 20 on Non-Residents, at ¶2083.

(ITA: 131(5.1), (5.2), (6); 132(4), (5.1), (5.2); 218.3)

[¶492] FOREIGN MUTUAL FUNDS/OFFSHORE INVESTMENT FUND PROPERTY

[¶492.05] *Foreign Mutual Funds: General*

Canadian taxpayers who invest in foreign mutual funds (or for that matter in Canadian investment vehicles which contrive not to qualify for the flow-through rules) simply receive all distributions from a foreign mutual fund as dividends if the foreign mutual fund is a corporation, or as property income if the foreign mutual fund is a trust. The fact that the fund may report some of the income as dividends or capital gains for purposes of taxation of residents of its home country does not give them that character for Canadian tax purposes. If the foreign mutual fund is a corporation, its distributions would be dividends from a foreign corporation and not from a Canadian company and therefore not eligible for dividend tax credit.

If the country of residence of the foreign fund withholds tax on the distribution, the gross amount (before tax withheld) is Canadian income and the amount withheld is eligible for foreign tax credit (¶1450).

By contrast, where the foreign mutual fund flows out foreign taxes paid, it would seem that these have no utility to the Canadian investor, although the matter is perhaps not entirely clear.

Where a foreign mutual fund contrives to operate as a partnership, there may be more scope to argue that the underlying income (and foreign tax) retains its characteristics in the hands of the investor.

(ITA: 94.1; ITR: 6900 [Prescribed offshore investment fund property]; Window on Canadian Tax: 2767; CRA Document No.: Capital gain distributions from a U.S. corporation, *November 10, 1995*, CRA Document No. 9523875; Capital Gains Distribution — Foreign Mutual Funds, *October 29, 1993*, CRA Document No. 9311645)

[¶492.10] *Offshore Investment Fund Property*

Although the above comments generally apply to foreign mutual funds, section 94.1 of the Act can apply to certain offshore funds where one of the main reasons for the investment is to defer or reduce Part 1 tax and the taxpayer and non-arm's length persons have a less than 10% interest in the fund (if the investment is 10% or more, the FAPI rules may apply; see ¶470.10). In general terms, the rule can apply in a taxation year where you have an interest in a "non-resident entity" (e.g., a non-resident corporation, trust, partnership, or organization) that may reasonably be considered to derive its value, directly or indirectly, primarily from portfolio investments of that or any other non-resident entity; and one of the main reasons for acquiring, holding, or having the interest is to derive a benefit from portfolio investments in such a manner that the taxes on the income from such assets in the year are less than what would have been payable had you earned the income directly.

Where the rule applies, a notional amount of income is included annually in computing your income equal to the "designated cost" of such property multiplied by the prevailing prescribed interest rate (applicable to items such as interest-free employee loans) plus 2%. The calculation is done monthly based on the designated cost of the property at the end of the month.

Historical Information

The Federal Budget of February 16, 1999 proposed new rules to govern Canadian investments in foreign-based investment funds. The original 1999 rules would have subjected Canadian taxpayers to annual tax on their *pro rata* share of all undistributed income of such funds, subject to a foreign tax credit for the funds' tax liabilities on that income.

Tax advisers identified numerous problems with these rules (see, for example, Wolters Kluwer *Tax Topics* No. 1480). On September 7, 2000, the government announced that further consultations would be allowed, that revised proposals would be tabled in 2001, and that implementation would be deferred to taxation years commencing after 2001.

Several versions of the rules were drafted. The last version was found in Bill C-10 in 2008. Eventually, in the 2010 Federal Budget, the Department of Finance announced that it was abandoning these proposals, and essentially sticking with the existing offshore investment fund property rules, with an additional 2% being added to the annual income charge under those rules. These are the current rules described above.

If you, along with any non-arm's length persons, own 10% or more of the value of interests in an offshore fund, you are not normally be subject to the offshore investment fund property rules, but rather the potentially more onerous FAPI rules, by virtue of section 94.2 or paragraph 94(1)(*d*); see ¶470.10.

[¶493] FOREIGN ACCRUAL PROPERTY INCOME (FAPI)

General Rules

In general terms, a "controlled foreign affiliate" means a foreign affiliate of the taxpayer under the rules at ¶495 which is controlled by the taxpayer, or would be controlled by the taxpayer if the taxpayer owned all of the shares of the foreign affiliate owned by:

(1) the taxpayer;

(2) not more than four persons resident in Canada other than the taxpayer;

(3) a person or persons with whom the taxpayer does not deal at arm's length (¶812); and

(4) a person or persons with whom one of the four residents noted above does not deal at arm's length.

If you have a controlled foreign affiliate (which can include certain trusts), you are required to include in your income your participating percentage share of that foreign affiliate's foreign accrual property income (FAPI) whether or not such income is actually remitted to you. You are allowed a deduction from that income for your participating percentage share of the underlying foreign taxes paid by the foreign affiliate on that income.

Commentary on Legislative Proposals (Sept. 16, 2016)

Note: When Legislative Proposals, September 16, 2016, achieves Royal Assent, the commentary will be modified to read:

> Effective July 12, 2013, "stub period" FAPI is included in the income of a taxpayer for the taxation year in which the taxpayer disposes of, or reduces in certain circumstances, its interest in a foreign affiliate.

Meaning of FAPI

FAPI consists primarily of income from property (e.g., interest, dividends), income from non-active business (and generally including income of active financial intermediaries), and realized taxable capital gains net of allowable capital losses (on disposition of a property not used in the corporation's business). Specified types of losses are deductible from FAPI within prescribed limits and FAPI may be reduced by expenses of the foreign affiliate which are reasonably applicable to that income. If the foreign affiliate's FAPI is less than $5,000, you need not include in your income nor pay tax on any portion of it not received by you in the year.

The FAPI provisions also apply to Canadian resident beneficiaries of certain foreign trusts, as discussed in ¶470 under the heading "Exceptions".

Dividends Received

Any dividends you receive from the foreign affiliate must be included in your income. However, you are entitled to a deduction for any portion of the dividend which represents previously taxed FAPI.

FAPI is a highly complex area of taxation. If you think you are subject to these rules, you should obtain advice from your professional tax adviser.

Historical Information

Numerous glitches remained in the complex and cumbersome foreign affiliate rules, which are something of a tax specialty unto themselves. The Department of Finance issued a number of "comfort letters", primarily in 2000 and 2001, which essentially said the rules will be fixed, eventually, with something like retroactive effect. More specifically, Department of Finance officials have let it be known that a package of technical amendments would be tabled in due course which in all probability would be prospective on their face but carry an election to have them apply to taxation years of foreign affiliates that begin after 1994. The amendments finally surfaced in draft legislation published, with extensive technical notes, on December 20, 2002. Those amendments, somewhat revised, were republished as a separate section of the omnibus draft technical amendments issued February 27, 2004.

Many of the revised new proposals were finally incorporated into the government's Bill C-28 implementing the 2007 Budget, which received Royal Assent on December 14, 2007. Subsequently, on December 18, 2009, the Department of Finance released draft legislation and regulations that, among other things, are "relevant in determining whether or not to make any of the retroactive elections provided for in Bill C-28". Those proposals then formed part of draft legislation released August 27, 2010, which also contains some proposals from the 2010 Budget along with several previously announced tax measures. The remaining foreign affiliate proposals from the February 27, 2004 draft legislation were re-released, with some changes, in draft legislation dated August 19, 2011. The changes were then consolidated and re-released on October 24, 2012 and subsequently as Bill C-48, which received Royal Assent on June 26, 2013.

(ITA: 91; 94; 95; ITR: 5903 Deductible Loss; 5904 Participating Percentage; ITTN: No. 36, May 16, 2006)

FOREIGN INVESTMENT AND INCOME REPORTING REQUIREMENTS

[¶495] FOREIGN AFFILIATE REPORTING GENERALLY

In addition to the controlled foreign affiliate rules at ¶493, Canadian residents who individually or as a group have a 10% or more interest in a foreign company must consider that company a foreign affiliate. In some cases, as discussed below, a foreign trust may also be a foreign affiliate. Beginning with taxation years that commence in 1996, an individual (or a corporation or trust) with a foreign affiliate is subject to reporting requirements which must be met whether or not the foreign affiliate has income taxable in Canada. For controlled foreign affiliates, these rules will be in addition to the FAPI reporting rules discussed at ¶493.

[¶495.05] *Foreign Affiliate Defined*

Strictly speaking, a foreign affiliate is a non-resident corporation in which both (a) the Canadian resident taxpayer's equity percentage is not less than 1% *and* (b) the total of the equity percentages of the taxpayer and each related person is not less than 10%.

"Equity percentage" is the sum of "direct equity percentage" and "indirect equity percentage", generally defined as follows:

(1) "direct equity percentage" is the highest percentage of any class of shares of a foreign company held directly by the Canadian taxpayer; and

(2) "indirect equity percentage" is the sum of all percentages each of which is the product of the Canadian taxpayer's direct and indirect equity percentage in any other "intermediate" corporation (whether resident or non-resident) multiplied by the intermediate's direct equity percentage shares in the foreign corporation.

In calculating indirect equity percentage for purposes of the filing requirement, however, the reference to any other intermediate corporation is read as only applying to non-resident corporations. In computing the indirect equity percentages to arrive at the 10%, the equity percentages of any person in the taxpayer (if incorporated) or a related person are to be ignored.

Any type of share, whether voting or otherwise, qualifies as a shareholding for the equity percentage calculation.

A "non-resident-owned investment corporation" is excluded from the definition of foreign affiliate. Essentially, this was a Canadian corporation which served as an investment vehicle for non-residents of Canada.

[¶495.10] *Non-Resident Non-Discretionary Trusts as Foreign Affiliates*

As discussed at ¶470.10, certain non-resident non-discretionary trusts are deemed to be non-resident corporations controlled by the beneficiary with respect to beneficiaries who have a 10% or more beneficial interest in the trust. With respect to such deemed corporations, each beneficiary is deemed to own shares in proportion to the fair market value of its beneficial interest in the trust. The purpose of these rules is to subject 10%-or-more beneficiaries to both the controlled foreign affiliate rules (¶493) and the reporting rules described below.

A non-resident discretionary trust, on the other hand, may itself be deemed resident in Canada if a person resident in Canada was directly or indirectly beneficially interested in the trust and the trust had directly or indirectly acquired property from a person resident in Canada who was related to or did not deal at arm's length with the beneficiary. (The actual rules are complex and there are exceptions.) (See ¶470.) Discretionary trusts subject to this rule, although deemed resident taxpayers for certain purposes, remain non-resident trusts for purposes of these reporting rules, so that reporting forms with respect to them must be filed as applicable. At the same time, these trusts are deemed to be resident for the purpose of the *obligation* to file the foreign affiliate return, meaning that they must file the return in respect of their foreign affiliates, if any.

(ITA: 94(1))

[¶495.15] *Foreign Affiliate Reporting (Form T1134)*

Note that form T1134 is rarely filed by individuals, and is not included in this book. It is available from any CRA office (¶287).

Reporting Requirements

Under subsection 233.4(4), where a corporation or trust is a foreign affiliate of a Canadian resident individual or partnership (or corporation or trust), subject to a slightly limited definition of foreign affiliate to exclude resident intermediate corporations from the indirect equity rule, the taxpayer must file an annual information return in respect of the foreign affiliate. The limited definition was originally designed to ensure that (for purposes of filing form T1134 only) a non-resident would be a foreign affiliate of only the lowest tier corporation in a group of Canadian corporations; later revisions, however, require that form T1134 must also be filed by each member of a Canadian partnership which has a "direct equity percentage" (defined above) in the foreign affiliate or controlled foreign affiliate. Revisions also provide an exception for dormant or inactive foreign affiliates. Although this exception is not apparent in the legislation, the forms themselves permit the exception for a dormant or inactive foreign affiliate, which is said to be one that both (i) had gross receipts (including proceeds from the disposition of property) of less than $25,000 in the year, and (ii) at no time in the year has assets with a total fair market value of more than C$1 million. No filing is required by a new Canadian individual resident for its first year of residence.

The filing deadline for either version of form T1134 is 15 months after the end of the taxation year for which it is filed; it need not (and indeed should not) be filed with the T1 return. Form T1134 is required for each taxation year *commencing after* 1995; however, for 1996, 1997, and 1998 taxation years, no return was required before the later of the reporting entity's T1134 due date and June 30, 1998.

Penalties

The whole rationale of this reporting system is to force taxpayers to disclose underlying information on potential income which they have interpreted as non-taxable. The system therefore imposes severe penalties for non-compliance in addition to the basic penalty for simple failure to file a return. Where a return is not filed, or a filing demand issued by the CRA is not complied with, knowingly or in circumstances amounting to gross negligence, the penalty is increased to $500 per month (including the month of failure and the month of compliance) to a maximum of $12,000, doubled to $1,000/$24,000 where the CRA has demanded a return which is not forthcoming. After 24 months, there is an additional penalty which (if greater) raises the total penalty to 5% of the filer's highest cost amount in the course of the year of shares or indebtedness of the foreign affiliate.

False statements or omissions in T1134 made knowingly or in circumstances amounting to gross negligence are subject to penalties of the greater of $24,000 and 5% of the filer's highest cost in the year of shares or debt of the foreign affiliate.

Cost of shares or debt can flow up a chain of controlled foreign affiliates for purposes of determining penalties.

The government recognized that the information it is demanding concerning foreign affiliates will in some cases be beyond the powers of the filer to obtain. Accordingly, a provision has been added whereby a person or partnership will be exempted from reporting information, provided the following conditions are met:

- there is reasonable disclosure in the return of the unavailability of the information;
- the taxpayer has prior to the filing date exercised due diligence in attempting to obtain the required information;
- if the return is in respect of a controlled foreign affiliate, it was reasonable to expect at the time of each transaction entered into after March 5, 1996 that gives rise to a filing requirement that sufficient information would be available to comply with the filing requirement; and
- if the information subsequently becomes available to the filer, it is filed no more than 90 days after it becomes available.

Note also the filing requirements for offshore investments, transfers, etc., at ¶496.

(ITA: 162(10)–(10.4); 163(2.4)–(2.91); 233(2); 233.4; 233.5; 233.7)

[¶496] FOREIGN INVESTMENTS, OFFSHORE TRANSFERS, AND FOREIGN RECEIPTS

The reporting requirements discussed below apply to foreign investments, transfers, and income. These rules as finally enacted impose extensive reporting requirements and substantial penalties for failure to comply. In general, it might be said that the thrust of these rules is to compel the taxpayer to choose between disclosure of offshore tax planning methods and deliberate violation of reporting requirements. The rules concern foreign property holdings (Form T1135), transfers and loan to foreign trusts (T1141), and distributions from foreign trusts (Form T1142).

[¶496.05] *Penalties*

There is a general penalty for failure to file information returns that depends on the number of returns and the number of days that the failure continues (subsection 162(7) or 162(7.01)). Additionally, if a T1135 or T1141 return is not filed, or a filing demand issued by the CRA for one of these forms is not complied with, knowingly or in circumstances amounting to gross negligence, there is a further penalty of $500 per month (including the month of failure and the month of compliance) to a maximum of $12,000, doubled to $1,000/$24,000 where the CRA has demanded a return which is not forthcoming. After 24 months, there is an additional penalty which (if greater) raises the total penalty to 5% of the unreported amounts.

False statements or omissions in T1135 or T1141 made knowingly or in circumstances amounting to gross negligence are subject to penalties of the greater of $24,000 and 5% of all the amounts which should have been reported on the return.

For failure to report trust distributions and debt obligations on form T1142, the penalty is $25 per day to a maximum of $2,500. For deliberate or grossly negligent omissions or false statements, the penalty is the greater of $2,500 and 5% of all misrepresented distributions plus 5% of the greatest unpaid principal amount of the misrepresented debt owning to the trust by the filer in the year for which the return is due.

Under subsection 162(7.01), there is a general penalty for failure to file on time. The penalty is based on the number of prescribed information returns of a particular type that are late-filed and the number of days that they are late. In addition, for returns required to be filed after 2009, there is also a penalty for failing to file a prescribed information return required by the Income Tax Regulations in the appropriate manner, as per new subsection 162(7.02).

(ITA: 162(7), (7.01), (7.02), (10)–(10.4); 163(2.4) –(2.9))

[¶496.10] *Foreign Property Holdings (Form T1135)*

Filing Requirement

Under section 233.3, every Canadian resident individuals and trusts (and most corporations) which hold "specified foreign property" with a cost amount more than $100,000 at any time in a year are required to file form T1135. For individuals, the form is due at the same time as the T1 return (April 30 or, for persons in business and their spouses, June 15). Individuals who do not file a paper return (because they EFILE, NETFILE, etc. — see ¶219 and ¶220) must send form T1135 to the taxation centre to which they would have sent a paper return (see ¶218; although in a pinch any taxation centre will do).

For the purposes of the $100,000 threshold, cost amount is a defined term which has a specific definition for nearly every type of property. Generally speaking, the cost amount of capital property is its adjusted cost base (¶506–¶508); of inventory, its inventory value for tax purposes (¶757–¶760); of depreciable property, its undepreciated capital cost (¶801).

On its website, the CRA states that it "has implemented changes to Form T1135 for the 2014 and later tax years. The changes will allow taxpayers to report aggregate amounts for specified foreign property held in accounts with registered securities dealers and Canadian trust companies rather than providing the detail of each such property. This reporting method requires taxpayers to provide the aggregate fair market value of the property in these accounts by country. In addition the T3/T5 reporting exception has been eliminated".

Furthermore, the 2015 Federal Budget proposed a simplified reporting process, stated as follows: "Under the revised form being developed by the Canada Revenue Agency, if the total cost of a taxpayer's specified foreign property is less than $250,000 throughout the year, the taxpayer will be able to report these assets to the Canada Revenue Agency under a new simplified foreign asset reporting system. The current reporting requirements will continue to apply to taxpayers with specified foreign property that has a total cost at any time during the year of $250,000 or more." In this regard, on its website, the CRA provides as follows:

> The Form T1135 has been redesigned to implement a two-tier information reporting structure for specified foreign property. Part A is a new simplified reporting method for taxpayers who held specified foreign property with a total cost of more than $100,000, but less than $250,000, throughout the year. This reporting method allows taxpayers to check the box for each type of property they held during the year rather than providing the details of each property. Part B, the current detailed reporting method, will continue to apply to those taxpayers who, at any time during a year, held specified foreign property with a total cost of $250,000 or more.

Partnerships are also reporting entities unless 90% or more of their income or loss for the fiscal period would be attributable to non-residents. Partnerships holding the requisite foreign property must file by the return due-date for form T5013, as discussed at ¶1880, whether or not the partnership is actually required to file form T5013.

Meaning of specified foreign property

"Specified foreign property" is broadly defined, but is subject to overriding exceptions for personal use property and foreign business property.

Specified foreign property includes:

- deposits or intangible property situated, deposited or held outside Canada; for example, foreign bank accounts or shares of Canadian companies deposited with a foreign broker;
- tangible property located outside Canada;
- any interest in or right to a non-resident entity (e.g., shares in a foreign company) other than a foreign affiliate subject to reporting at ¶495;
- debts owed by non-resident persons (e.g., bonds issued by foreign entities or simply loans to non-residents);
- interests in partnerships unless 90% or more of their income or loss for the fiscal period ending in the taxpayer's taxation year would be attributable to non-residents;
- interests in non-resident trusts except: trusts not acquired for consideration by the reporting person or a related person; trusts which are foreign affiliates of the reporting person (and so subject to reporting at ¶495, [but this exception should disappear after 2006 as the new foreign trust rules at ¶470 supersede the foreign affiliate rules for foreign trusts]); and trusts which are foreign pension funds or foreign retirement arrangements (IRAs);
- interests in non-resident trusts deemed resident under whichever set of rules at ¶470 is in force for the taxation year, if the interest was not acquired for consideration;
- any interest or right, immediately or in future, absolute or contingent, in specified foreign property; and
- any property which by its terms is convertible to or exchangeable for specified foreign property.

Exceptions

The two major overriding exceptions are that specified foreign property will not include: (1) property that is used or held exclusively in the course of carrying on an active business of the reporting person or partnership; and (2) personal-use property (as defined at ¶545) of the reporting person or partnership. Personal use property is property you own primarily for your own personal use or enjoyment, or that of someone related to you.

There are other exceptions. An interest in a foreign trust need not be reported unless you or a person related to you acquired the interest for consideration (i.e., you bought an interest in the trust rather than having it settled on you). An interest in a foreign trust which is an exempt trust for purposes of form T1141, discussed below, need not be reported except in the case of foreign mutual fund investments, which must be reported on form T1135. You need not report a partnership interest if the partnership itself is required to file form T1135 for the year. Property which is subject to reporting requirements on form T1134 (i.e., shares or debt of a foreign affiliate) is not subject also to form T1135 reporting. Finally, an interest in or a right to acquire property excluded from the reporting requirement is in turn excluded.

You do not have to file Form T1135 in the year in which you first become a resident of Canada. Certain corporations and trusts are generally exempt from requirement to file form T1135. The exempt trusts would be the same ones discussed in the context of form T1142 below.

Reassessment Period

The normal reassessment period for a taxation year of a taxpayer is extended by three years if (i) Form T1135 was not filed on time, or a specified foreign property was not identified, or was improperly identified, on Form T1135, and (ii) you failed to report income from a specified foreign property on your annual income tax return.

(ITA: 233.3)

[¶496.20] *Transfers and Loans to Foreign Trusts (Form T1141)*

Generally speaking, under section 233.2 of the Act,, a person (including an individual, a trust, or, for that matter, a corporation) must file form T1141 for the person's taxation year in which a trust's taxation year ends if:

(i) the trust was a non-resident at the end of that taxation year (regardless of whether it has been deemed resident under the rules at ¶470);

(ii) the person made a contribution to the trust at any time during the trust's taxation year *or a preceding taxation year* of the trust; and

(iii) the contributor was resident in Canada at the end of the trust's taxation year. (There is a long list of exceptions for entities such as Canadian mutual funds, exempt entities, and special purpose trusts such as employee benefit trusts.)

Partnerships are also subject to this reporting regime, now under the foreign trust rules which specify that a contribution by a partnership is considered to have been made jointly by the partnership and each partner, except for certain limited partners.

The filing requirement under these rules turns largely on the definition of "contribution" in the foreign trust rules. A contribution is any transfer or loan of property other than an arm's length transfer. The arm's length transfer exception is specifically defined for this purpose. Essentially it is a transfer where it is reasonable to conclude that none of the reasons for the transfer is the acquisition at any time by any entity of any interest as a beneficiary under any non-resident trust. There are a number of further detailed exceptions for the genuine payment of interest, dividends, or other returns on investment, and so on. There are elaborate provisions to ensure that indirect contributions are caught.

Under an extended rule, any non-arm's length loan or transfer (i.e. any loan or transfer not excused by the non-arm's length standard for foreign trusts) which is subsequently held under any arrangement governed by foreign law, or by a foreign entity, must be reported unless it was made solely in exchange for specified foreign property (as defined for purposes of form T1135 reporting as discussed above, but with none of the exceptions mentioned). This extended reporting requirement does not apply to contributions to entities protected under specific exceptions for such things as "exempt trusts" as previously defined (essentially, (i) foreign pension or retirement fund trusts which are exempt under local income tax laws and are either primarily for the benefit of non-residents of Canada or are governed by an employees' profit sharing plan, and (ii) foreign retirement arrangements (i.e., U.S. IRAs, see ¶919)), nor to contributions to "exempt foreign trusts" as defined under the revised ¶470 foreign trust rules.

(ITA: 233.2; 233.5)

[¶496.25] *Distributions Received from and Debts Owing to Foreign Trusts (Form T1142)*

Canadian resident individuals, trusts and partnerships (and most corporations) must file form T1142 if they both:

(1) received distributions of property from or were indebted to a non-resident trust in the taxation year; and

(2) had a beneficial interest at any time in the taxation year.

Form T1142 requires disclosure of any such distributions and/or debt. It would seem that in the case of debt the requirement continues for each year in which the same debt is outstanding.

Form T1142 is due by the filer's T1 filing deadline (whether or not a T1 is required).

Exceptions

Reporting (on form T1142) is required on distributions from or debts owing to non-resident trusts, not merely specified foreign trusts, with the following exceptions:

- estate trusts arising on and in consequence of the death of an individual;
- trusts which are foreign pension plan trusts that are tax exempt in their country of residence (which must impose an income tax in the first place) or are "foreign retirement arrangements" (e.g., United States Individual Retirement Accounts (IRAs) — ¶919);
- trusts which are foreign affiliates of the reporting person or partnership (and so subject to reporting at ¶495);
- trusts reported as foreign property on form T1135 strictly speaking, this exemption applies even if T1135 turns out retroactively not to be required; however, the Department of Finance is likely to correct this when it enacts the T1135 deferral, and it would be a brave or foolhardy taxpayer who relies on this to excuse filing; and
- trusts in respect of which the reporting entity is required to file form T1141 for the year or period, disclosing loans or transfers to the trust.

New residents of Canada are exempt from filing form T1142 in their first year of residence. Certain corporations and trusts are generally exempt from requirement to file form T1142. The information sheets which accompany the form are reasonably clear about exemptions. The reference to trusts exempt under subsection 108(1) definition covers amateur athlete trusts, segregated fund (life insurance) trusts, religious organizations, retirement compensation arrangements, funeral arrangement trusts, and certain subtrusts of those trusts. The exception for registered investment trusts covers certain investment vehicles for RRSPs and similar deferred income plans.

(ITA: 233.6)

[¶496a] INVESTMENTS IN U.S. LIMITED LIABILITY COMPANIES

A U.S. limited liability company (US LLC) may be treated as a partnership or corporation for U.S. tax purposes. However, the CRA has historically considered the US LLC to be a corporation for Canadian tax purposes. Their position has been regularly stated as follows or in similar terms (CRA Document No. 2011-0428781E5, October 17, 2012):

> ... Canadian owners will be taxed in Canada on any distributions from USLLC and may be eligible to claim a FTC [foreign tax credit] or make a deduction from income pursuant to subsections 20(11) or 20(12). Where a distribution is considered a dividend and the recipient is considered a qualifying person pursuant to Article XXIX-A of the [Canada-US] Treaty, Article X, if applicable, should limit the US tax withheld on the distribution to 15%.

New section 93.2 of the Act is meant to "clarify" that these entities are considered corporations for Canadian tax purposes. The provision deems interests in US LLCs to be shares in a corporation but it does not explicitly deal with the tax treatment of distributions from US LLCs.

WHERE TO REPORT INVESTMENT INCOME

[¶497] REPORT INVESTMENT INCOME

Report your investment income on Schedule 4 of your return.

SPECIFIC QUESTIONS AND ANSWERS

[¶498] SPECIFIC QUESTIONS AND ANSWERS

Dividend Declared in One Year and Paid in Another Year

I have held common shares in a public company for several years. A dividend was declared on this stock on December 28, Year 1, payable January 15, Year 2, to shareholders of record as of January 11, Year 2. When is it taxable to me?

The dividend was not paid until Year 2. Therefore, it is included in income in the Year 2 taxation year.

Stock Purchased "Cum Dividend"

On October 25, I purchased 10 shares of common stock "cum dividend". Who pays tax on the dividend, which had been declared but not paid?

The dividend will be included in your income in the year received.

Life Insurance "Dividend"

I received a notice from a life insurance company that I had been credited with a dividend of $75 on my life insurance policy. Is it taxable? What if I use the dividend to pay a portion of my premium?

Dividends from life insurance policies, even if used to reduce premiums, are taxable only to the extent that they exceed the "adjusted cost basis" of the policy. See ¶981.

Stock Dividend

I was notified in November, by a company whose stock I hold, that I had been given a stock dividend of 10 shares of the company's common stock. I received no cash — only share certificates. What is my tax position?

You are taxable to the extent that the stock dividend represents an increase of the company's paid-up capital. If you have not received a T5, contact the company's secretary or transfer agent to determine the amount you should include in income. The dividend will be subject to the ordinary dividend "gross-up and credit" rules at ¶404. Note that if this was a stock split rather than a true dividend, so that the total paid-up capital of all your shares did not increase, there is no tax consequence.

Dividend in Liquidation

I inherited 500 shares of common stock in a company from my father. This stock never paid any dividend, but last year I received a cheque for $1,000 which the company said was a dividend in liquidation. Am I taxable on the $1,000?

Yes — to the extent that the dividend does not represent a return of capital or a dividend payment out of the capital dividend (¶415) or pre-1972 capital surplus (¶417) accounts, that amount will be included in income as a normal dividend. You should have received a T5 supplementary form showing the taxable amount. If not, contact the company's secretary or transfer agent to determine the amount taxable, if any. This transaction may also result in a capital gain or loss and you should refer to Chapter 5 for further details. See ¶416.

Patronage Dividend

We buy most of our groceries from a cooperative store. Last year we received a patronage dividend of $75 which was allocated on the basis of consumer goods and services we had purchased. Should I include the $75 in income?

No. Such payments are not taxable but are regarded as being in effect a reduction of the cost to the customer of the goods or services. However, note that patronage dividends *not* in respect of consumer goods and services are fully taxable. Amounts are *not* taxable only if they relate to goods and services which are not deductible purchases of the consumer. Where the dividends do relate to deductible goods and services, they are included in income, since the full cost of the items has presumably been deducted. See ¶413.

Loan to Take a Trip

I am not a shareholder in a private company controlled by my son. Two years ago the company loaned me $3,000 to take a trip to visit my relatives in the U.K. No arrangements were made for repayment — my son told me the company didn't need the *money and I could take my time about repaying. Are there any tax implications in this situation?*

Yes. Because you are connected to a shareholder, and the loan has not been repaid within one year from the end of the taxation year of the corporation in which it was made, the full amount of the $3,000 loan is taxable as income in the year it was received by you and no dividend tax credit is available to you. Should you repay the loan it will be deductible in computing your income in the year of repayment. See ¶409.

As the loan is included in your income in the year it is received, there is no deemed interest benefit to be included in your income. See ¶409.

Loan to Buy a Home

I am the secretary-treasurer of a small private company and the holder of a nominal amount of common stock (10 shares out of 1,000 issued). I borrowed $20,000 from the company to use as a down payment on a house for me and my family. I agreed to repay the loan over a 10-year period at 0.75% interest. At the time I received the loan, the market interest rate was 3%. As a shareholder, I am concerned that the unpaid balance of this loan may be treated as income. What is my position?

The most difficult question is whether the loan was received in your capacity as shareholder or employee, because the results are different. In your case, given your position as a key employee and your nominal shareholding, it seems likely that your loan was received in your capacity as employee. Given this determination, your loan will not be considered income since *bona fide* arrangements were made for repayment and because the purpose of the loan, received by virtue of your employment, was to assist you in purchasing a dwelling house for your own occupation. The same result would have been obtained if you had borrowed the money to buy stock from the company or to buy an automobile to be used in the performance of your duties.

However, as the interest rate on the loan is 0.75%, which was below the prescribed rates for each of the four quarters of 2014 (rates were 1%, 1%, 1%, and 1%), you will be taxed as if you had earned income at the rate of 1% for the first quarter and and 0.25% for each of the last three quarters on the outstanding balance of the loan for those quarters. A table of prescribed interest rates for several years past is found at ¶80 preceding Chapter 1.

Note that an employee who has commenced employment at a new work location and by reason thereof has moved to a residence which is at least 40 kilometres closer to his new work location in Canada than was his previous residence can reduce his taxable benefit relating to interest on a housing loan from his employer for a period of five years by an amount equal to the benefit on a $25,000 interest-free loan outstanding for a period of five years from the date on which the loan was made. Therefore, if you had moved to a new location as a result of your employment you would not be taxed on any imputed interest benefit on your housing loan, since it did not exceed the $25,000 maximum. See ¶353.

Interest-Free Loan to Shareholder

On January 15, Year 1, I borrowed $10,000 from a corporation of which I am a shareholder to meet personal medical expenses. By December 15, Year 1, I was able to repay the loan although I paid no interest. The corporation has a calendar taxation year. Am I taxable in any way?

The loan was repaid within one year and therefore will not be taxed to you as income. However, as this was not an excluded loan (see ¶409) you will be deemed to have received imputed interest as a taxable benefit. As you did not pay any interest on the loan, the taxable benefit to be included in your Year 1 income will be the interest on the loan calculated at the prescribed rates. Interest for the first quarter and the last quarter will be prorated for days in the period that the loan was outstanding. See ¶409, and especially ¶409.15.

Stock Split

I held 100 common shares of a company which split its stock 10 for 1 during the year. As a result I now hold 1,000 shares which have a market value $500 higher than my former holdings. Should I report this in my return?

No. Stock splits do not attract tax.

Dividends on Shares Gifted to Wife

During the year I gave my wife 200 shares of common stock of a public company. I understand that the dividends she received will be deemed to have been received by me. Will the dividend tax credit be available to me?

Yes. Since you must include such dividends in your income, a specific provision entitles you to the dividend tax credit if the dividend is subject to either the "eligible" or "other" gross-up described at ¶404.

Dividends from U.S. Corporation

I hold stock in a large U.S. corporation which pays regular dividends. What special rules apply to such dividends?

Such dividends are included in income. However, you should note the following:

- You should include the gross amount of the dividends (actual cash received plus tax withheld) in income, which is reported in Canadian dollars.
- Foreign tax withheld in excess of 15% of the gross amount of the dividend may be deducted on Part IV of Schedule 4 as carrying charges.
- Tax withheld at source (up to 15% of gross dividend) should be converted to Canadian funds in making your foreign tax credit claim. See ¶1450. You may deduct the amount of foreign tax paid from your income instead of claiming a foreign tax credit.
- The dividend tax credit is not available.
- The gross-up rules for Canadian dividends (¶404) do not apply.

Chapter 5

Capital Gains and Losses

THESE POINTS ARE COVERED IN THIS CHAPTER

CRA REFERENCES RELATING TO THIS CHAPTER

T1 Lines and Schedule

- Line 127 — Taxable capital gains
- Line 217 — Business investment loss (Allowable deduction)
- Line 228 — Business investment loss (Gross)
- Line 254 — Capital gains deduction
- Schedule 3 — Capital Gains (or Losses)

CRA Guides

5000-G, "General Income Tax and Benefit Guide"; **RC4169**, "Tax Treatment of Mutual Funds for Individuals"; **T4013**, "T3 — Trust Guide"; **T4036**, "Rental Income — Includes Form T776"; **T4037**, "Capital Gains";

T4091, "T5008 Guide — Return of Securities Transactions"

CRA Forms

T1A, "Request for Loss Carryback"; **T3**, "Statement of Trust Income Allocations and Designations"; **T657**, "Calculation of Capital Gains Deduction"; **T936**, "Calculation of Cumulative Net Investment Loss (CNIL)"; **T1170**, "Capital Gains on Gifts of Certain Capital Property"; **T2017**, "Summary of Reserves on Dispositions of Capital Property"; **T2059**, "Election on Disposition of Property by a Taxpayer to a Canadian Partnership"; **T5008**, "Statement of Securities Transactions"

Income Tax Folios

S1-F3-C2, "Principal Residence"

Interpretation Bulletins

IT-88R2, "Stock Dividends"; **IT-95R**, "Foreign Exchange Gains and Losses"; **IT-96R6**, "Options Granted by Corporations to Acquire Shares, Bonds or Debentures and by Trusts to Acquire Trust Units"; **IT-113R4**, "Benefits to Employees — Stock Options"; **IT-159R3**, "Capital Debts Established to be Bad Debts"; **IT-209R**, "Inter Vivos Gifts of Capital Property to Individuals Directly or Through Trusts"; **IT-218R**, "Profits, Capital Gains and Losses from the Sale of Real Estate, Including Farmland and Inherited Land and Conversion of Real Estate from Capital Property to Inventory and Vice Versa"; **IT-232R3**, "Losses — Their Deductibility in the Loss Year or in Other Years"; **IT-259R4**, "Exchanges of Property"; **IT-264R**, "Part Dispositions"; **IT-293R**, "Debtor's Gain on Settlement of Debt"; **IT-325R2**, "Property Transfers After Divorce and Annulment"; **IT-346R**, "Commodity Futures and Certain Commodities"; **IT-365R2**, "Damages, Settlements and Similar Receipts"; **IT-379R**, "Employees Profit Sharing Plans — Allocations to Beneficiaries"; **IT-387R2 (Consolidated)**, "Meaning of "Identical Properties"; **IT-407R4 (Consolidated)**, "Dispositions of Cultural Property to Designated Canadian Institutions"; **IT-413R**, "Election by Members of a Partnership Under Subsection 97(2)"; **IT-448**, "Dispositions — Changes in Terms of Securities"; **IT-456R**, "Capital Property — Some Adjustments to Cost Base"; **IT-460**, "Dispositions — Absence of Consideration"; **IT-479R**, "Transactions in Securities"; **IT-484R2**, "Business Investment Losses"; **IT-491**, "Former Business Property"; **IT-511R**, "Interspousal and Certain Other Transfers and Loans of Property";

Information Circulars

72-17R6, "Procedures Concerning the Disposition of Taxable Canadian Property by Non-Residents of Canada — Section 116"; **07-1**, "Taxpayer Relief Provisions"

Income Tax Technical News

No. 39, December 4, 2008, "Settlement of a Shareholder Class Action Suit — Compensation by Way of Cash and Shares"

WHAT YOU SHOULD KNOW ABOUT CAPITAL GAINS AND LOSSES

RECENT CHANGES

Proposed Legislation, October 3, 2016

Principle Residence Exemption

Individuals having sold their principal residence after October 2, 2016 may only use the one-plus rule to calculate the principal residence exemption if they resided in Canada in the year of acquisition of the residence. If this is not the case, they cannot use that year to calculate the exemption. Therefore, taxpayers residing outside Canada during the whole period of ownership of the residence cannot claim the exemption on any portion of the capital gain realized on the sale of the residence.

Personal trusts designating a property as their principal residence for taxation years beginning after 2016 must meet additional eligibility criteria. Those criteria will better align the eligibility of the trusts to the principal residence exemption with situations where the residence is held directly by an individual. Eligible trusts are spousal or common-law partner trusts, alter ego trusts, qualifying disability trusts, or trusts for the benefit of a minor child of deceased parents.

CRA Announcement, October 3, 2016

Effective for 2016, taxpayers disposing of a residence during a particular taxation year in respect of which they claimed the principal residence exemption must report the disposition in Schedule 3 of their income tax return for that year plus basic information such as acquisition date, disposition proceeds, and property description even if they are eligible for the principal residence exemption on the total amount of capital gain. Those failing to provide such information may still qualify for a late designation but could be subject to a late designation penalty (of the lesser of $8,000 and $100 times the number of complete months between the due date of their return and the date when they applied to the CRA for the late designation).

Effective for 2016, if a residence was their principal residence for all the years they owned it, taxpayers must also make the designation of their residence as their principal residence on Schedule 3 of their income tax return. It is designated on Forms T2091 or T1255 if this was not the case.

Effective for taxation years ending after October 2, 2016, taxpayers having disposed of real or immovable property during a taxation year but not having reported the related disposition in their income tax return for the year could be reassessed by the CRA for disposition beyond the normal reassessment period (i.e., four years for mutual fund trust or corporation other than a Canadian-controlled private corporation and three years for other taxpayers).

Bill C-29 (Introduced October 25, 2016)

Bill C-29 introduced new rules regarding the taxation of "switch funds" of mutual fund corporations. Under the former rules, investors were able to exchange shares of one class of the mutual fund corporation for shares of another class, and could rely on section 51 to deem the switch not to be a disposition for income tax purposes (or in some cases, another rollover provision would apply). The new rules, generally applicable after 2016, will provide a deemed disposition of the shares in this situation. See ¶588.

Effective January 1, 2017, the eligible capital property rules have been repealed and replaced by a new Class 14.1 of depreciable property. Property that previously was eligible capital property is now depreciable capital property, and expenditures and receipts that previously were accounted for under the eligible capital property rules are now accounted for under the rules for depreciable property and capital property.

[¶500] WHAT IS A CAPITAL GAIN OR LOSS?

Capital gains and capital losses are subject to special treatment. In particular, one-half of capital gains are included in income as taxable capital gains and one-half of capital losses are allowable capital losses that can be deducted against taxable capital gains. However, you must first determine whether the amount you are dealing with is actually a capital gain or capital loss as opposed to ordinary income or loss

Some gains and losses will appear to be capital in nature and subject to the capital gain or loss treatment described in this chapter, but are not actually treated as capital gains or losses because of specific exceptions in the law. These types of gains and losses will be discussed later in this chapter. One special category is "eligible capital property", which is usually an intangible such as goodwill, or a right under a patent or quota. These are treated as partial business expenses (see ¶766), and proceeds of disposition are treated in part as business income. (See ¶766 to ¶770.) There is an exception for proceeds of disposition in excess of original cost of certain eligible capital property which is farm property; within limits this may be characterized as capital gain eligible for capital gains exemption; see at ¶502f.

Commentary on Bill C-29 Measures (Oct. 25, 2016)

Note: When Bill C-29, October 25, 2016, achieves Royal Assent, the commentary will be modified to read:

Some gains and losses will appear to be capital in nature and subject to the capital gain or loss treatment described in this chapter, but are not actually treated as capital gains or losses because of specific exceptions in the law. These types of gains and losses will be discussed later in this chapter. One special category is "eligible capital property", which is usually an intangible such as goodwill, or a right under a patent or quota. These are treated as partial business expenses (see ¶766), and proceeds of disposition are treated in part as business income. (See ¶766 to ¶770.) There is an exception for proceeds of disposition in excess of original cost of certain eligible capital property which is farm property; within limits this may be characterized as capital gain eligible for capital gains exemption; see at ¶502f. Note that the eligible capital property rules have been repealed starting in 2017 and property that was previously eligible capital property is now considered depreciable capital property and included in Class 14.1.

Meaning of Capital Gain or Loss

The law does not give a precise definition of capital gains or losses. In some cases it may be very difficult to decide whether a gain is a capital gain, or a loss a capital loss, or whether the gain or loss in fact falls within some other category. However, in most cases some general rules can be applied to determine whether or not you have a capital gain or capital loss.

First, to be a capital gain or loss, the gain or loss must result from a disposition of property (or a deemed disposition as discussed at ¶528 to ¶539). In general, a disposition of property occurs when there is a transaction which entitles you to receive proceeds, or, in some cases, when there is a deemed disposition.

Although a disposition of property is required before you can have a capital gain or loss, such a disposition does not necessarily produce a capital gain or loss. To produce a capital gain or loss the property involved must be a capital property.

The question of whether a property is or is not a capital property depends on both the nature of the property and the manner in which the property is dealt with by the owner. If it is the owner's intention to trade or to realize a profit from the property rather than to hold it for the income it produces, the gain or loss realized will be treated as an ordinary income gain or loss rather than a capital gain or loss.

General principles from the courts

In deciding whether the gain from a particular transaction is of a capital or an income nature, the courts in the past have developed some guidelines to be considered.

(1) The period of ownership — Normally, property held only a short time will be considered to have been purchased for the purposes of resale and the profits will be treated as income, while property that has been held a long time is more likely to be considered as an investment, thus giving rise to a capital gain.

(2) The frequency of similar transactions — A history of extensive buying and selling of similar properties or of quick turnovers of properties may be taken as evidence indicating that a taxpayer is carrying on a business. Obviously, if you are carrying on a business, it is assumed that any assets forming part of the inventory of the business were purchased for the purpose of resale, and gains or losses on sale of these assets will not be of a capital nature.

(3) Improvement and development work — When an organized effort is made to put property into a more marketable condition it may indicate a business of selling properties.

(4) Reasons for and nature of sale — If a sale of property is the result of an active campaign to sell it rather than the result of something unanticipated at the time of purchase (e.g., expropriation, sudden need of money, frustration of original intentions), the profits will be considered business income.

(5) The relationship of the transaction to the taxpayer's ordinary business (e.g., sale of land by persons ordinarily active in the real estate business).

Where an isolated property (most commonly undeveloped real estate) is found to be held on income rather than capital account, it may be considered inventory of an "adventure in the nature of trade" rather than a business; in this case special rules apply to it. See ¶758.

Also, a subsidiary or secondary intention at the time of purchase is relevant in determining how a gain from a disposition is to be treated. For example, if you have an alternate or secondary intention to resell at a profit if your original investment intention is frustrated or thwarted, then the gain may be taxed as income rather than as a capital gain.

Real estate

Real estate transactions probably produce the majority of disputes as to whether a gain or loss is capital in nature or should be treated as ordinary income or loss. As mentioned previously, intention is an important factor, but this is not always easy to determine. Your personal residence will almost always be a capital property, but if you frequently renovate your residences and sell them at a profit, the CRA may consider you to be in the business of home renovation. Real estate which you rent to others may be a capital property if your rental return is reasonable in relation to your investment and carrying costs and you hold it for an extended period. However, these are only two of the facts which may be relevant, and you should be prepared to substantiate your investment intentions by as many facts as possible if you are claiming that your profit on resale is a capital gain. For an article discussing two cases involving the capital versus income determination, see Wolters Kluwer *Tax Topics* No. 2027, January 13, 2011.

With regard to the taxation of real estate profits, it is the CRA's policy to treat passive members of a joint venture or syndicate similarly to the active members. The actions and intention of the active members will be imputed to the passive members.

For partnerships, capital gains are calculated at the partnership level and flow through to the members (see ¶1801).

(ITA: 39; 54; 248(1) "disposition"; IT-218R [Archived]; IT-460 [Archived])

[¶500.05] *Are Shares Always on Capital Account?*

In contrast to its position on raw land, the CRA is generally prepared to accept that share dispositions are on capital account. Note that shares acquired by employees under stock option plans are subject to special rules at ¶330, and that there is an election to permit a taxpayer other than a trader or dealer in securities to insist on capital treatment on dispositions of Canadian securities (see ¶501).

Professional securities dealers or traders can generally be identified as such by the nature of their employment or business, and their securities dealings will generally be held to be income rather than capital transactions. Most cases arise where a taxpayer not obviously engaged in the profession of securities dealing claims losses on securities transactions to be on income account. There have been cases in which a taxpayer has succeeded in persuading the courts that he or she was a trader by virtue of having specialized knowledge of the market for a particular company's shares (typically because he or she was an employee or insider). See *Howard v. The Queen*, 2008 DTC 2788 (T.C.C.). Of course, the argument can work both ways; in *Kane v. The Queen*, 94 DTC 6671 (F.C.T.D.), a taxpayer was found to be a trader on similar grounds, and was denied capital gains treatment.

In *Hawa v. The Queen*, 2007 DTC 28 (T.C.C.), the taxpayer engaged in 151 share purchases in 16 companies in a year, generally holding shares for only a brief period, and sustaining considerable losses. Chief Justice Bowman of the Tax Court had no difficulty in finding that the volume of trades and short holding periods made the activity on income and not capital account. Indeed, the income was probably on business account and not an adventure in the nature of trade.

In *Richer v. The Queen*, 2009 DTC 1007 (T.C.C.), an investment adviser reported his income from trading flow-through shares as capital gains, and his losses from trading other securities as business losses. However, his gains were recharacterized as business income. Although he claimed that his primary motivation in trading the flow-through shares was to generate a tax benefit, he had a secondary intention of generating a profit.

A summary of litigation on this use and the case to be made for ordinary loss treatment appears in Wolters Kluwer's *Wealth Management Times*, issue No. 47, dated April 2008.

[¶500a] INCLUSION RATE: WHAT IS "TAXABLE CAPITAL GAIN" AND "ALLOWABLE CAPITAL LOSS"?

Only a specified portion, currently 50%, of your capital gains for the current year net of your capital losses for the year (if any) are taxable. This "inclusion portion" of the net gains is technically called your "taxable capital gain" for the year; it is calculated as the last item on your Schedule 3 and carried to line 127 of your T1.

Similarly, if your overall capital losses for the current year exceed your overall capital gains for the year (if any), only a portion, currently 50%, of the loss becomes a net capital loss. Generally speaking, a net capital loss is not deductible from income, but goes into a carryover pool which may be applied to capital gains of the preceding three years or any following year. (For treatment of net capital losses on hand at the year of death, see ¶1933.) For this reason, the capital gain and loss inclusion rates for preceding years remain relevant (summarized below; see also ¶1093.10).

However, capital losses arising on dispositions (or deemed dispositions) of certain types of property may yield different results. These are summarized at ¶575. In particular, the inclusion portion of capital losses which qualify as "business investment losses" (¶580) may be deducted from other income of the current year and, to the extent not so deducted, go into the non-capital loss pool described at ¶1085.

[¶500a.02] *Importance of Inclusion Rate for Loss Carryovers*

If your capital losses for the current year (other than losses from listed personal property, described at ¶548) exceed your gains for the year, you may not deduct any portion of these losses from ordinary income. Rather, the inclusion portion of the net loss (the "allowable capital loss"), reduced by the inclusion portion of business investment losses ("allowable business investment losses"), goes into a carryover pool called "net capital loss" for deduction against past and future taxable capital gains (¶1093). Here it is important to know your applicable inclusion rate for taxable capital gains of each preceding year to which a loss may carried, and your applicable inclusion rate for the allowable capital loss of each year included in the net capital loss pool. The tax system intends that net capital gains (before adjustment to arrive at the taxable portion) of, say, $100 in any year may be set off by a net capital loss (before adjustment) of $100 from any prior year (or from any of the next three years). To achieve this result, the inclusion rates for losses in the allowable capital loss pool are adjusted when the losses are claimed in a particular year. This is discussed at ¶1093.

Capital losses which qualify as business investment losses (¶580) are first pooled with other general capital losses to determine the applicable inclusion rate under the rules above, but are then separated from general capital losses. Both are subject to the same inclusion rate for the year, but the business investment losses times the applicable inclusion rate become allowable business investment losses. These are not netted against taxable capital gains, but (unlike other capital losses) may be deducted from other income of the current year and, to the extent not so deducted, go into the non-capital loss pool described at ¶1085.

[¶500a.05] Inclusion Rate: 2001 and Later Years (Relevant for Carryforwards)

For 2001 and later taxation years, the inclusion rate for capital gains recognized in the year is 50%. (Technically, the rule is that the inclusion portion (or inclusion rate) is 50% ($^1/_2$1/2) for taxation years which commence after October 17, 2000, but for individuals, capital gains inclusion rates apply on a calendar year basis.)

[¶500a.10] Inclusion Rate: 2000 Taxation Year (Relevant for Carryforwards)

For 2000, the inclusion portion (or inclusion rate) moved in the other direction: it was 75% before February 28, 2000, 66$^2/_3$% in the interim period February 28 to October 17, 2000, inclusive, and 50% after October 17, 2000 (and is simply 50% for taxation years after 2000). For an individual (other than a trust), capital gains must be calculated on a calendar-year basis, and where there were gains and/or losses in more than one period in 2000, the inclusion rate had to be calculated according to a decision tree which could yield an inclusion rate of 75%, 66$^2/_3$%, 50%, or some blended number between 50% and 75%.

[¶500a.15] Inclusion Rate: 1999 and Earlier Years (Relevant for Carryforwards)

Unfortunately, at least from the point of view of simplicity, the portion of a capital gain or loss which qualifies as taxable capital gain or allowable capital loss is a movable feast. From 1972 to 1987 it was 50%; for 1988 and 1989, 66$^2/_3$; and from 1990 through February 27, 2000, 75%.

[¶500a.20] Importance of Remembering Previous Inclusion Rates

For reasons discussed above, once the inclusion rate for a taxation year is determined, it is essential to keep it prominently on file, since carryovers of losses to or from that year will have to be adjusted by that inclusion rate. (Actually, the inclusion rate is expressed for taxation years ending before February 28, 2000, in the period February 28 to October 17, 2000, or after October 17, 2000, but for individuals other than trusts, capital gains will be calculated on a calendar-year basis so that the distinction is irrelevant. For partners in non-calendar year partnerships, it may be significant in theory although probably not in practice.)

[¶500a.30] Inclusion Rate for Charitable and Ecological Donations

The taxable portion of capital gains arising on charitable donations of certain publicly traded securities (described at ¶1290d) to qualified donees is zero, even though their full fair market value may qualify for the donations credit. Similarly, capital gains from donations of ecological property and Canadian Cultural Property are exempt if made to certain qualified donees.

The full amount of actual losses on charitable donations of qualifying securities and ecological property are pooled with other general capital losses of the applicable period to determine the inclusion rate for the year, and are subjected to the full applicable inclusion rate with no special qualifications.

[¶500a.35] Default Inclusion Rate

A number of provisions of the *Income Tax Act* (the "Act") operate with reference to your inclusion rate for the year, even for a year in which you have no capital gains or losses. For example, the debt forgiveness rules at ¶565 can require an income inclusion at your personal inclusion rate for the year, and the partnership allocation rules immediately below can require you to use your personal inclusion rate for a year in which you have no gains or losses other than those from the partnership.

The structure of the inclusion rate changes appears to provide, in effect, that if there are no gains or losses in the year to vary the result under the rules above, your default inclusion rate for the year is 75% for taxation years ending before February 28, 2000, 66$^2/_3$% for taxation years ending after February 27, 2000 and before October 18, 2000, and 50% for taxation years ending after October 17, 2000.

Accordingly, for an individual other than a trust with no capital gains or losses (or business investment losses) in the year, the inclusion rate is 75% for 1990 through 1999 inclusive and 50% for 2000 and later years.

[¶500a.40] Inclusion Rate for Partnership Gain/Loss Allocations

In the absence of a special provision, the taxable capital gains, allowable capital losses, and allowable business investment losses of a partnership are computed at the partnership level according to the inclusion rate calculated for the partnership's fiscal period, and the results so calculated flow out to the each partner in its taxation year which includes the end of the partnership's fiscal period. This is fine as far as it goes, but it obviously results in a mismatch of inclusion rates for a partner as its own gains and losses are subjected to carryovers computed at a potentially different inclusion rate.

Subsection 96(1.7) of the Act requires each partner to apply the following calculation to the taxable capital gain, allowable capital loss, and allowable business investment loss flowed out from each partnership to which the partner belongs:

$$A \times B/C$$

where

A = is the taxable capital gain, allowable capital loss, and allowable business investment loss flowed out from the partnership for the taxation year;

B = is the partner's inclusion rate for the taxation year; and

C = is the inclusion rate used by the partnership for the fiscal period ending in the partner's taxation year.

The easy way to do this, of course, is to calculate whole capital gain net of whole loss (or whole loss net of whole gain), back out business investment loss, and subject the result to the partner's inclusion rate instead of the partnership's. The same would apply to the business investment loss.

Example (loss occurred in 2000, where rate changed twice)

Jo has a calendar 2000 taxation year which includes capital gains and losses which produce an inclusion rate of 58%, applied to a capital gain of $1,000, for a taxable capital gain of $580. She is a one-third partner in partnership Z, which for its fiscal period ending in 2000 has capital gains and losses which give it an inclusion rate of 75%, applied to a capital loss of $6,000, resulting in an allowable capital loss of $4,500, one-third of which ($1,500) is allocated to Jo.

Jo performs the magic rites, and determines that her allowable capital loss from Z is $1,500 × .58/.75 = $1,160. Remarkably, this is also 58% of her one-third share of the $6,000 whole capital loss (58% × $2,000 = $1,160). Accordingly, her allowable capital loss for the year is $1,160 - $580 = $580, and this amount is available to carry back or forward against taxable capital gains.

Again, the simple way to look at this is to say that Jo had a whole gain of $1,000 and a whole loss (from the partnership) of $2,000, and the net whole loss of $1,000 goes into her loss carryover pool at her 58% inclusion rate.

If you assume that Z had flowed out an allowable business investment loss of $1,500, the same conversion would transform it to Jo's loss of $1,160, reducing 2000 income by that amount.

If the partner is allocated a taxable capital gain or allowable capital loss with no indication of the partnership inclusion rate, the rate is deemed to be 75% for fiscal periods beginning before February 28, 2000, 66⅔% for fiscal periods beginning after February 27 and before October 18, 2000, and 50% for fiscal periods beginning after October 17, 2000.

In theory, this conversion is required for all taxation years ending after February 27, 2000. However, once inclusion rates have settled down to a constant number (50%) (i.e., where both the partnership fiscal period and the partner's taxation year commence after October 17, 2000), the calculation will be irrelevant, since if both partners and partnership have the same inclusion rate, the applicable fraction will be 1.

As discussed under the subheading "Default Inclusion Rate", above, where the partner has no capital gains or losses to determine an inclusion rate of its own, the partner's default inclusion rate will be the lowest rate it could have for a taxation year. Thus, for taxation years ending before February 28, 2000, the partner's default inclusion rate will be 75%, for taxation years ending after February 27, 2000 and before October 18, 2000, the default inclusion rate will be 66⅔%, and for taxation years ending after October 17, 2000, the default inclusion rate of the partner will be 50%. For individuals (other than trusts), the default rate is 75% for 1999 and earlier years, and 50% for 2000 and later years.

(ITA: 3(*b*); 38)

[¶501] CANADIAN SECURITIES — ELECTION

You may elect, in your return for the year of disposition, to have gains and losses from dispositions of Canadian securities treated as capital gains or losses provided you are neither a trader or dealer in securities nor a non-resident. You need not be a professional trader as such to be ineligible to make this election. It may be sufficient that you have specialized knowledge of the market for the shares in which you have traded. See *Kane v. The Queen*, 94 DTC 6671 (F.C.T.D.) and the discussion at ¶500.05.

Form T123 is to be used for this election and it is available in electronic format on the CRA website.

The effect of this election is that Canadian securities owned by you in the election year or subsequent taxation years will be treated as capital property, and dispositions of these securities by you will be dispositions of capital property. Accordingly, you should assess your situation carefully to ensure that treatment of transactions as capital gains or losses in future years will be advantageous to you. The election cannot be reversed.

A Canadian security for the purposes of this election is defined as a security (other than a prescribed security described below) that is a share of the capital stock of a corporation resident in Canada, a unit of a mutual fund trust or a bond, debenture, bill, note, mortgage, hypothec or similar obligation issued by a person resident in Canada.

A prescribed security not qualifying for the Canadian securities election is:

(1) a share of the capital stock of a corporation, other than a public corporation, having a value at the time of disposition that is primarily attributable to real property, an interest in or option on real property, Canadian or foreign resource property or property that would have been Canadian or foreign resource property, if acquired after 1971;

(2) a security issued by a corporation, other than a public corporation, if at any time prior to the disposition of the security you did not deal at arm's length (¶812) with the corporation issuing the security;

(3) a security acquired by you from another party with whom you do not deal at arm's length or acquired by you from a corporation at a value elected under special provisions of the tax laws (¶585);

(4) a share acquired by you as consideration for your incurring Canadian exploration expenses ("CEE"), Canadian development expenses ("CDE"), and Canadian oil and gas property expenses ("COGPE"); or

(5) a security acquired by you as proceeds of disposition for, or in exchange or substitution for, a security that is any of the securities listed in items (1) through (4).

If you disposed of a non-qualifying security, the gain or loss may still be a capital gain or loss, but this must be determined under the rules in ¶500 and not by an election.

Many professional tax advisers advise against making this election except in very unusual circumstances. They feel that in most situations which can be covered by an election, the securities transactions are likely to give rise to capital gain in any event, and by not electing you may preserve the option of arguing that certain losses may be on income account. In general, you might want to obtain professional tax advice before making this election.

(ITA: 39(4)–(6); ITR: 6200 Prescribed Securities; IT-479R [Archived]; *The Queen v. Vancouver Art Metal Works Limited*, 93 DTC 5116 (FCA); rev'g 91 DTC 5643 (FCTD); *Kane v. The Queen*, 94 DTC 6671 (FCTD))

[¶501.05] *Election on Debts with No Stated Rate of Interest*

Some adventurous taxpayers have attempted to apply the guaranteed capital gains election to securities issued at a discount, such as treasury bills, in an effort to convert into capital gains amounts which under case law and conventional experience are undoubtedly interest income. It is certainly true that a Canadian Treasury Bill would be a Canadian security, and it would seem that when the face amount of the bill is paid there is a disposition so that the basic conditions for the election are met.

The CRA very clearly takes the position (in Interpretation Bulletin IT-479R, paragraph 21) that where the proceeds on a discount obligation are clearly interest, whether under case law or statutory provisions, those provisions override the capital gains election. The CRA's view is, in the abstract, the correct one. It has now been confirmed by the Federal Court of Appeal, which has ruled that the discount on T-Bills held is interest, regardless of whether the guaranteed capital gains election is made (*Satinder v. The Queen*, 95 DTC 5340 (F.C.A.)).

(ITA: 16(3); 39(4)–(6); IT-479R [Archived])

INDIVIDUAL CAPITAL GAINS EXEMPTION

[¶502] LIFETIME CAPITAL GAINS EXEMPTION

[¶502.03] *Lifetime and Enhanced Exemption*

Effective as of the 2014 taxation year, the lifetime capital gains exemption was increased to $800,000, up from the previous $750,000 amount. After 2014, the $800,000 is indexed to inflation, so that the limit has increased to $813,600 for 2015 and $824,176 for 2016.

Where a capital gain is realized after April 20, 2015 on qualified farm or fishing property, an enhanced exemption can be claimed. The enhanced exemption increases the lifetime claim to the greater of $1 million, which is not indexed, and the general indexed limit described above. Thus, the additional exemption will be available until indexing increases the general limit to $1 million or more. See ¶502f.

The exemption applies to dispositions of shares of a qualified small business corporation or of qualified farm or fishing property. A claim of the exemption in any particular year in which you have eligible gains is optional, but unless you have offsetting losses or confidence of future eligible gains, it is usually beneficial. (See ¶2525 for a discussion of planning considerations where there may be concurrent losses.) Note that the lifetime limit is expressed above in actual or whole gains; this is much easier to conceptualize than is the actual formula for calculating the deduction (discussed below), which operates in the taxable capital gain mode, necessitating, among other confusions, cumulative corrections every time the capital gain inclusion rate changes. The exemption is discussed in detail at ¶502f (farming or fishing property) and ¶502i (small business corporation shares), with additional comment on the concepts and limitations of these calculations in ¶502m to ¶502q.

The exemption is actually a deduction in computing taxable income under section 110.6 of the Act. The exemption is computed on form T657.

The exemption may be claimed only by individuals resident in Canada throughout the year. However, a part-year resident will be deemed resident throughout the year for this purpose if he is resident throughout the preceding or following year.

A trust may not claim the capital gains exemption, but it can allocate gains eligible for the exemption to beneficiaries. If you have capital gains allocated from a trust on a T3 slip, the allocation for exemption purposes may be different from the allocation for general purposes. See ¶465.

[¶502.05] *Historical Information: $500,000 Exemption on Dispositions before March 19, 2007*

For dispositions prior to March 19, 2007, you could claim an exemption of up to $500,000 of the capital gains when you disposed of shares of a qualified small business corporation or of qualified farm property (or, for dispositions after May 1, 2006, qualified fishing property). For dispositions after March 18, 2007 and before 2014, the $500,000 lifetime limit was increased to $750,000, as discussed above. (The $500,000 is expressed in actual or whole gains and has not changed since it was introduced in 1985, as discussed above.)

(ITA: 110.6(1)–(5))

[¶502.07] *Historical Information: Transition from $500,000 Exemption to $750,000 Exemption in 2007 and 2008*

As explained in ¶502.03, the capital gains exemption is usually referred to in terms of the whole gain that may be sheltered ($500,000 or $750,000), whereas the technical rules deal with only the taxable portion of the gain (currently one-half, so $250,000 or $375,000). The change to the higher exemption level was effective, as a practical matter, for dispositions on or after March 19, 2007. However, technically speaking, the change was effective in the first instance only for taxation years which begin on or after March 19, 2007. Since an individual's taxation year is in general the calendar year, the change was effective (except in some cases of bankruptcy — see ¶286 — or, perhaps, birth) only for 2008 calendar years, and 2007 is governed by a special transitional rule.

For the typical 2007 taxation year of an individual, the capital gains exemption was, in the first instance, calculated using the $250,000 amount in the calculation in ¶502f.05, above. Technically, the "transition year" is the year which includes March 19, 2007, and, barring birth, death, or bankruptcy, that was, for individuals, the 2007 calendar year. For 2007 dispositions of eligible farm or fishing property or small business corporation shares occurring in the transition year on or after March 19, 2007, you could deduct an additional amount not exceeding the least of:

(1) $125,000;

(2) the cumulative gains limit at the end of the transition year (¶502o), less the total of all amounts already deducted in the year for all types of eligible property under the $250,000 taxable gain limit;

(3) the annual gains limit (¶502m) at the end of the transition year less the total of all amounts already deducted in the year for all types of eligible property under the $250,000 taxable gain limit; and

(4) net capital gains from the disposition of all types of eligible property in the transition year.

The transition year rule applies only to individuals and not to trusts. Trusts cannot themselves, in any event, generally utilize the exemption, but they can flow out ("designate") the characteristics of dispositions of qualifying property to beneficiaries (see ¶465). For a trust's taxation year that ends in a beneficiary's taxation year that includes March 19, 2007 (so typically for a trust with a taxation year that ended after March 18, 2007 and before January 1, 2008), the law directs it to designate, in addition to eligible gains from each type of eligible property (farming, fishing, etc.), gains from each type of property realized in the taxation year from dispositions on or after March 19, 2007. (What it actually must designate is the beneficiary's share of the whole eligible gain on each type of property prorated by post-March 18 dispositions over all dispositions in the trust's year from each type of qualified property.) These were eligible for the transition year deduction in the hands of the beneficiary. It is possible that a trust could have pre-March 19, 2007 dispositions of eligible property in its 2008 taxation year. These would show up in the 2008 taxation year of the individual beneficiary and not in the transition year. There is a specific rule which denies the individual any excess realized on dispositions before March 19, 2007 over the exemption that would have been calculated before that date.

As explained above, there is a general rule to ensure that no gain in excess of the $500,000 lifetime limitation can be sheltered in respect of dispositions before March 19, 2007. Technically, the rule only applies to taxation years beginning after March 19, 2007, which is not consistent with the transition year machinery, in that it does not cover March 19 itself. Since as an individual your taxation year will normally begin on January 1, this may be an error without a consequence. The rule will generally apply to your 2008 and later taxation years, and prevent recognition of excess gains deferred through capital gain reserve claims.

No transition rule was required for the change in the exemption limit from $750,000 to $800,000, as the change took effect for the 2014 taxation year, and the limit is thereafter indexed annually.

[¶502f] QUALIFIED FARM OR FISHING PROPERTY

Note the general comments at ¶502.03. More details are provided below.

[¶502f.05] *Calculating the Deduction*

Basic Deduction

The qualified farm or fishing property deduction is calculated on form T657. The gains or losses from dispositions of the property are recorded on line 2 of Schedule 3.

Prior to the introduction in 2014 of the definition of "qualified farm or fishing property", separate calculations were provided for the deduction with respect to gains on qualified farm property and qualified fishing property. These calculations have been merged, and the permitted lifetime capital gains deduction for a year in respect of qualified farm or fishing property (defined below) is equal to the least of four amounts (subsection 110.6(2)):

(1) The individual's unused lifetime exemption for the year. This is calculated in the "taxable capital gain" mode, such that it changes every time the capital gains inclusion rate changes to compensate for different inclusion rates in different years. For 2014 and subsequent years, the amount is indexed to inflation. For the 2016 taxation year, the regular unused exemption is the amount by which $412,088 exceeds the total of:

(a) all capital gains deductions claimed in 1985, 1986, and 1987 or after October 17, 2000; plus

(b) $^3/_4$ of all capital gains deductions claimed in 1988 and 1989 on property other than deductions of account of eligible capital property (¶768) claimed in those years; plus

(c) $^2/_3$ of all capital gains deductions claimed in 1990 through 1999 inclusive, plus $^2/_3$ of amounts deducted in 1988 and 1989 in respect of eligible capital property (¶768); plus

(d) for capital gains deductions in the 2000 taxation year, the 2000 capitals gains deduction times the reciprocal of the multiplier used to determine the lifetime limit for 2000, or, looked at another way, your capital gain inclusion rate for 2000 (determined under ¶500a) multiplied by one-half instead of two.

(2) The individual's cumulative gains limit at the end of the year, as described in ¶502o, below.

(3) The individual's annual gains limit for the year, as described in ¶502m, below.

(4) The individual's net taxable capital gains for the year from the disposition of qualified farm or fishing property. This amount would include taxable gains from previous years included in income in the current year under the capital gains reserve mechanism provided such reserve relates to a disposition of qualified farm or fishing property.

Additional Deduction for Dispositions after April 20, 2015

As noted at ¶502.03, an additional capital gains deduction limit is provided where a gain is realized on qualified farm or fishing property after April 20, 2015. The additional deduction effectively increases the lifetime limit from the regular amount of $412,088 (2016 amount), which is indexed, to $500,000, which is not indexed. Thus, the additional deduction will be available until the indexed regular amount increases to $500,000, after which only the regular amount will apply.

The increased limit is implemented by providing a separate capital gains deduction under subsection 110.6(2.2), which can only be claimed against qualified farming or fishing property gains realized after April 20, 2015.

Historical Information

The maximum exemption amount was increased to $400,000 in 2014, to be indexed to inflation in future years. For taxation years commencing on or after March 19, 2007 and ending before 2014 (so, for the 2008 to 2013 taxation years of most individuals), the maximum amount was $375,000. For taxation years commencing in 2001 and before March 19, 2007, the amount was $250,000 (subject to an additional amount that was potentially available in that year).

[¶502f.08] *Values in (1) to (4): Accounting for Differing Inclusion Rates Before 2001*

The values in (1) to (4) in ¶502f.05 trace the values in terms of the taxable portion of claims made at the differing capital gains inclusion rates in effect over the history of the capital gains exemption (¶500a). Generally speaking, the only difficulty to be encountered is with the value in (4), since the inclusion rate for 2000 was a variable number, as the rate changed twice in that year (from $^3/_4$ to $^2/_3$ and then $^1/_2$). For examples relating to the 2000 year, please consult prior versions of this book. The rate since 2001 has remained $^1/_2$.

The historical inclusion rates are provided in Chart 3 of the Form T657.

[¶502f.10] *Qualified Farm or Fishing Property Defined*

Real Property or Fishing Vessel

The definitions of "qualified farm property" and "qualified fishing property" were merged for 2014 and subsequent years into the definition of "qualified farm or fishing property" in subsection 110.6(1). The new definition includes real property or a fishing vessel owned by an individual or his or her spouse or common-law partner or a family fishing partnership in which the taxpayer or spouse or common-law partner has an interest, which was used by

(1) the taxpayer,

(2) his or her spouse or common-law partner, or any of his or her children or parents,

(3) a personal trust beneficiary entitled to receive directly trust income or capital, or

(4) a family fishing corporation or a family fishing partnership in which anyone listed in (1) to (3) has a share or interest,

in the course of carrying on the business of farming or fishing in Canada. The property need not actually be used in carrying on a farming or fishing business at the time of its disposition if it meets all the other tests set out here.

The new definition of "qualified farm and fishing property" is also relieving in nature, in that tests in the definitions that require that property be principally used in the business will now be met where they are used principally in both farming and fishing or either (for example, previously if property was used 30% in farming and 30% in fishing, it did not meet the "principally used" test).

There are two separate rules for determining whether property is considered to be "used in the course of carrying on the business of farming or fishing in Canada" (subsection 110.6(1.3)).

The general rule (regardless of when the property was acquired) is that a two-part test must be met to determine if the property is considered used in a farming business in Canada at any particular time:

(1) the property must have been held or substituted for a property held for 24 months prior to the time by one of the permitted users described above; and

(2) in any two years of ownership by a family member or personal trust who is a permitted user described above, the gross revenue of the said user (or trust beneficiary) from the farming or fishing business in which the property was principally used must have exceeded income from all other sources, or, where the permitted user is a family farm corporation or partnership, an individual who was a permitted user (or trust beneficiary) was for at least 24 months actively engaged on a regular and continuous basis in the farming or fishing business in which the property was used.

Transitional Rule

For property acquired before June 18, 1987, or after that date pursuant to an agreement entered into before the date, a vendor who fails to meet the tests above may nevertheless qualify if the property has been used principally in a farming business in Canada in the year of its disposition or in at least five years during which time it was owned by any of the related users described above. Note, however, that a trust is a qualified user only in respect of proceeds recognized in and after 1988.

Shares or Interests in Family Farm or Fishing Corporation or Partnership

In addition to land and vessels, shares in a family farm or fishing corporation or an interest in a family farm or fishing partnership will qualify for the capital gains exemption. A corporation or partnership for purposes of the exemption is, in general terms, one in which an individual who is a permitted user in relation to the shareholder/partner has used 50% or more of the corporation/partnership assets (measured by fair market value) to carry on the business of farming in Canada and the property throughout any 24-month period prior to disposition. In addition to the 50%/24-month test, 90% of the fair market value of the underlying assets must be used in the course of carrying on the business of farming in Canada at the time of the disposition.

Similar to the amendment above relating to qualified farm or fishing property, starting in 2014 and subsequent years, the 50% and 90% use tests refer to the assets being used in the course of carrying on the business of farming or fishing or both.

Assets typically include interests in qualifying corporations or partnerships, so that holding companies, or farming or fishing companies held by partnerships, will (by and large) qualify. Technical amendments seem to be made to these rules almost continuously; by and large they are relieving provisions intended to carry out the broad intent of the rules as stated. In all but the simplest situations, professional advice is likely to be required prior to sale to assure qualification.

[¶502f.15] *Eligible Capital Farm or Fishing Property*

Qualified farm or fishing property includes eligible capital property (such as milk or fishing quotas, etc. — see ¶1717) used by a permitted user in the course of carrying on the business of farming in Canada. Beginning in 2014, the relevant definition refers to eligible capital property being used in a farming or fishing business in Canada (consistent with changes described above at ¶502f.10).

Eligible capital property which is farming or fishing property only gives rise to capital gain rather than recapture characterized as business income to the extent it is eligible for the capital gains exemption (subsection 14(1.1)). This in turn is measured by the lesser of:

(1) the business income inclusion from disposition of the eligible capital property otherwise measured, and

(2) the excess of the taxable amount of cumulative net gains for taxation years commencing after 1987 from the dispositions of eligible capital property that is farm property over the amount of such taxable net gains as have already received taxable capital gains treatment.

To the extent eligible capital property dispositions give rise to capital gain under this rule, the same amount is of course backed out of the normal recapture of business income which arises on the disposition of eligible capital property (¶768).

Eligible capital property that passes on death to someone other than a spouse or common-law partner (typically a child) who does not carry on the business of the deceased may become capital property to the beneficiary (¶1909); a similar rule applies to transfers to children under the rules at ¶1759 value (a). The property can nevertheless qualify as eligible capital farm property under these rules where other conditions are met.

Commentary on Bill C-29 Measures (Oct. 25, 2016)

Note: When Bill C-29, October 25, 2016, achieves Royal Assent, the commentary will be modified to read:

Effective January 1, 2017, the eligible capital property rules have been repealed and replaced by a new Class 14.1 of depreciable property. Property that previously was eligible capital property is now depreciable capital property, and expenditures and receipts that previously were accounted for under the eligible capital property rules are now accounted for under the rules for depreciable property and capital property.

[¶502f.20] *Transfers to Children*

In addition to the capital gains exemption, farm or fishing property may be transferred to children at cost, and that it is possible to combine use of the exemption with the rollover to children; see ¶1759. Note that the definition of family farm or fishing corporation or partnership is similar but not exactly the same for the rollover as for the exemption.

(ITA: 14(1), (1.1); 110.6(1), (2), (2.2), (2.3), (4), (31), (32))

[¶502i] SMALL BUSINESS CORPORATION SHARES

Note the general comments at ¶502.03.

[¶502i.05] *Calculating the Deduction*

The qualified small business shares deduction must be calculated on form T657. The gains or losses from the dispositions of the shares are recorded on line 1 of Schedule 3.

The permitted lifetime capital gains deduction for a year in respect of qualified small business corporation shares (defined below) is equal to the least of four amounts:

(1) The individual's unused lifetime exemption for the year in respect of post-June 17, 1987 net taxable capital gains on qualified small business corporation shares. Unfortunately this is calculated in the "taxable capital gain" mode, and so changes every time the capital gains inclusion rate changes to compensate for different inclusion rates in different years. For 2014 and subsequent years, the amount is indexed to inflation. For the 2016 taxation year, the regular unused exemption is the amount by which $412,088:

exceeds the total of:

(a) all capital gains deductions claimed in 1985, 1986, and 1987, and after October 17, 2000; plus

(b) ³/₄ of all capital gains deductions claimed in 1988 and 1989 on property other than deductions of account of eligible capital property (¶768) claimed in those years; plus

(c) ²/₃ of all capital gains deductions claimed in 1990 through 1999 inclusive, plus ²/₃ of amounts deducted in 1988 and 1989 in respect of eligible capital property (¶768); plus

(d) for capital gains deductions in the 2000 taxation year, the 2000 capitals gains deduction times the reciprocal of the multiplier used to determine the lifetime limit for 2000; or, looked at another way, your capital gain inclusion rate for 2000 (determined under ¶500a) multiplied by ¹/₂ instead of 2.

(2) The individual's cumulative gains limit at the end of the year, as described in ¶502o, below, in excess of amounts deducted in the current year on account of the qualified farm property rules at ¶502f (the rules essentially provide an order of applying farm property claims, then small business share claims, then fishing property claims, in determining this limit for the year).

(3) The individual's "annual gains limit" for the year, as described in ¶502m, below, in excess of amounts deducted in the current year on account of the qualified farm property rules at ¶502f (the rules essentially provide an order of applying farm property claims, then small business share claims, then fishing property claims, in determining this limit for the year).

(4) The individual's net taxable capital gains recognized for the year from dispositions of qualified small business corporation shares after June 17, 1987, less any amounts included under the comparable rule for qualified farm property dispositions and qualified fishing property dispositions. In general, this amount would include taxable gains from dispositions in previous years (but after June 17, 1987) included in income under the capital gains reserve mechanism.

Historical Information

The maximum exemption amount was increased to $400,000 in 2014, to be indexed to inflation in future years. As noted, for 2016 the amount is $412,088. For taxation years commencing on or after March 19, 2007 and ending before 2014 (so, for the 2008 to 2013 taxation years of most individuals), the maximum amount was $375,000. For taxation years commencing in 2001 and before March 19, 2007 (so, in general, for 2007 and earlier taxation years), the amount was $250,000.

[¶502i.08] *Values in (1) to (4): Accounting for Differing Inclusion Rates Before 2001*

The values in (1) to (4) in ¶502i.05 trace the values in terms of the taxable portion of claims made at the differing capital gains inclusion rates in effect over the history of the capital gains exemption (¶500a). Generally speaking, the only difficulty to be encountered is with the value in (4), since the inclusion rate for 2000 was a variable number as the rate changed twice in that year (from ³/₄ to ²/₃ and then ¹/₂). For examples relating to the 2000 year, please consult prior versions of this book. The rate since 2001 has remained ¹/₂.

The historical inclusion rates are also provided in Chart 3 of the Form T657.

[¶502i.10] *What Are Qualified Small Business Corporation Shares?*

The definition of "qualified small business corporation shares" (subsection 110.6(1)) is complex. In general, the major criteria are:

(1) The shares must be shares of a Canadian-controlled small business corporation (as defined at ¶580) which, at the time of disposition, uses 90% or more of its assets either directly in an active business carried on in Canada or as a holding company for such a corporation. The 90% measurement is based on the fair market value of all assets at the time of disposition.

(2) The shares must be owned by the taxpayer, the taxpayer's spouse or common-law partner, or a partnership related to the taxpayer. Presumably, this qualifies some gains attributed to the taxpayer under the attribution rules (¶531).

(3) The shares must not have been owned by anyone other than the taxpayer or a related person during the 24 months preceding disposition. Although this rule seems straightforward, it has complex implications. It appears that a person can incorporate his or her personal proprietorship and sell it immediately, since the shares will not have been held by an unrelated person. It further appears that shares issued on a rollover to a holding company for common shares will qualify, or at least not be automatically disqualified. On the other hand, newly issued treasury shares are disqualified. The death of a taxpayer does not mitigate the

24-month requirement. Clearly the ramifications of this rule require professional advice in all but clear-cut situations.

(4) Throughout the 24-month holding period, at least 50% of the assets of the corporation must have been used principally in an active business, or to finance a "connected" active business. However, where shares of a holding company are involved and the company's investments failed to meet the 50% test, a substitute 90% test appears to apply for the subsidiary connected companies.

These tests generally pose little problem where they are readily met. At the margins, however, substantial problems can arise. The 90% asset test in (1), above, for example, in many cases requires continual monitoring to ensure that it is met. This is especially true since the taxpayer may be hit by a bus and deemed to dispose of his or her shares at virtually any moment. It may be possible to structure transactions which "purify" a company; this entails professional tax planning advice. Similarly, the implications of the holding period requirement and related party tests can create complex problems requiring professional advice. In general, taxpayers with large accrued gains on small business company shares must weigh the costs of such advice against potential tax savings under these rules.

The 90% test is the CRA's interpretation of the statutory phrase "all or substantially all". The Tax Court of Canada, in interpreting the same phrase for GST purposes, was satisfied with an 80% test. See *McKay v. The Queen*, 2001 GTC 208 (T.C.C.), and *Ruhl v. The Queen*, 1998 GTC 2055 (T.C.C.). Thus, while it is always desirable to arrange matters to meet the 90% test, a marginal failure to meet the 90% rule may not be catastrophic.

Technical amendments seem to be made to these rules almost continually. Often they are technical relieving provisions intended to carry out the broad intent of the rules as stated; occasionally they are new restrictions designed to counter (sometimes retroactively) an earlier failure by the drafters to achieve technical perfection. The technical complexity of these rules is such that, in all but the simplest situations, professional advice is necessary to ensure that a corporation's shares are eligible for the enhanced exemption.

(ITA: 110.6(1), (2.1), (2.3), (4), (31), (32))

[¶502i.15] *Where a Company Becomes Public (or Ceases To Be Private by Operation of Law)*

Individuals who own shares of a qualified small business corporation which become disqualified by virtue of being listed on a Canadian stock exchange can use the capital gains exemption by electing to create a notional disposition and reacquisition of the shares immediately before the time of disqualification. This general rule allows the utilization of the capital gains exemption by pre-existing shareholders when a qualified small business corporation goes public, as often happens if the small business is very successful (or very popular).

Where a qualified small business corporation ceases to be such because a class of its shares is listed on a prescribed stock exchange and an individual who is a shareholder at the time of the change so elects for the taxation year of the change, there is a deemed disposition and reacquisition at the time at a value which must be the greater of (a) the adjusted cost base ("ACB") of the share, and (b) an elected value chosen by the shareholder, which may not however exceed the fair market value of the share. In principle, the election appears to be made on a share-by-share basis, but in practice the identical property rules at ¶512 mean the election will normally be made on all shares at a value (up to fair market value) which maximizes but does not exceed the gain available for whatever lifetime exemption remains to you. In effect, the elected amount is added to the cost base of the shares, so the exemption is locked in ("capitalized") until some or all shares are later disposed of.

The election (on form T2101) is normally required by the individual's filing-due date (¶218) for the calendar year in which the change of status of the corporation occurs.

(ITA: 48.1; 125(7))

[¶502i.20] *Sale of Shares to Public or Non-Resident Company*

Historical Information

It has traditionally been thought that where shares of a qualifying Canadian-controlled private corporation (CCPC) are sold, the identity of the purchaser is irrelevant to the application of the capital gains exemption to the transferor. In *La Survivance v. The Queen*, 2008 DTC 2334 (T.C.C.), the Court ruled that, because of certain timing provisions in the Act (subsection 256(9)), control was deemed to change at the beginning of the day of the transfer but prior to the transfer itself, so that the company was no longer a CCPC when the actual transfer occurred. In a 2008 technical opinion (2006-0214781E5), the CRA confirmed this result.

As a result of this anomaly, remedial legislation was introduced in the 2009 Federal Budget to exclude a small business corporation or a CCPC from the application of subsection 256(9). Control is no longer deemed to change at the beginning of the day, so the status of the corporation remains as a CCPC or small business corporation when the actual transfer occurs.

[¶502m] DEFINITION OF "ANNUAL GAINS LIMIT"

The annual gains limit of an individual for a taxation year represents the extent to which his or her net taxable capital gains for the year might qualify for the exemption. This is used as one of the limiting factors for the purposes of calculating the individual's permitted deductions, as noted at ¶502f.05 (farm and fishing property) and ¶502i.05 (small business corporation shares).

[¶502m.05] *Annual Gains Limit*

Beginning with 1996, the annual gains limit has been considerably simplified because it is only relevant for the capital gains exemption applicable to qualified farming and (since 2006) fishing property and small business shares. (Previously it had been complicated by the requirements of the $100,000 exemption for other capital property.)

The annual gains limit is defined in subsection 110.6(1). It equals:

the lesser of:

(1) net taxable capital gain (if any) for the year as calculated on Schedule 3; therefore it is full capital gains net of full current capital losses after all reserve calculations are accounted for, reduced to the taxable portion, and, prior to 2017, includes deemed taxable capital gains on eligible capital property which is qualified farming or fishing property (¶768.25) (if the net position for a year is a loss position, the annual gains limit is nil); and

(2) the amount in (1), above, recalculated as if the only gains and losses in the year had been from qualified farm property and qualified small business shares disposed of in the year, and from recognition of capital gain reserves on qualified farm property disposed of

after 1984, qualified small business shares disposed of after June 17, 1987, and qualified fishing property disposed of after May 1, 2006;

minus the total of:

(3) net capital loss carryovers applied in the current year in excess of the amount (if any) by which actual taxable capital gains for the year exceed the gain eligible for exemption (lesser of (1) and (2), above); and

(4) all allowable business investment losses (¶580) of the current year.

Reporting the Limit

The annual gains limit is computed on Part 1 of Form T657. Lines 1 through 10 are relevant for items 1 and 2 above, lines 11 and 12 apply to items 3 and 4.

(ITA: 110.6(1) "annual gains limit")

[¶502o] DEFINITION OF "CUMULATIVE GAINS LIMIT"

General

The cumulative gains limit of an individual at the end of a taxation year represents the extent to which his cumulative net gains after 1984 might qualify for the lifetime capital gains exemption and is used as one of the limiting factors for the purposes of calculating the individual's permitted deductions. In concept, the cumulative gains limit measures the taxable portion of net economic gain since 1985 which should be eligible for exemption. Accordingly, it backs out prior gains on which exemption has already been claimed, and is also used to apply the "cumulative net investment loss" rules which are intended to reduce net economic gain eligible for exemption by net investment losses in and after 1988. Both accounts represent running lifetime calculations, the cumulative gains limit commencing in 1985 and the cumulative net investment loss account commencing in 1988.

Computation and Recording of Limit

The cumulative gains limit is defined in subsection 110.6(1).

It is computed by first determining the taxpayer's cumulative net taxable capital gains since 1984, that is, the aggregate of all amounts determined as inclusions in the definition of "annual gains limit" for the year and all prior years ending after 1984. Since the annual limit includes the taxable portion of gains in any year, no true-up was required as the inclusion rate shifted upwards in 1988 and again in 1990. These amounts are recorded in Part 2 of Form T657 (lines 15 through 22).

The taxable capital gain total arrived at above is then reduced by several items. First, the aggregate of all net capital loss carryovers deducted in the year (whether deducted from capital gains or other income) and in prior years after 1984 and all allowable business investment losses realized in the year and all prior years after 1984 is deducted. This subtraction item is simply the aggregate of all amounts determined as reductions in the definition of "annual gains limit" for the year and all prior years ending after 1984. The amounts are reported on lines 25 through 27 of Part 2 of T657. Line 24 makes specific provision for the 1985 allowable capital loss because of the peculiarities of that transitional year; see ¶576.

Since all allowable business investment losses ("ABILs") are deducted as they arise, whether or not deducted in the year, there is no necessity to track their carryovers through the ordinary loss pool. However, if unused as ordinary losses these ABILs resurface after 10 years as capital losses. They are then deducted a second time when applied. Despite much tinkering with all these rules over the years, it appears that this problem remains, although it could not arise before 1993.

Second, the aggregate of all capital gains exemptions claimed in previous years is deducted from the cumulative limit (line 29 of Part 2)

Third, the running total of the "cumulative net investment loss (CNIL)" account is deducted from the cumulative limit (line 28 of Part 2). This account is defined below.

(ITA: 110.6(1))

[¶502q] DEFINITION OF "CUMULATIVE NET INVESTMENT LOSS" (CNIL) ACCOUNT

General

The cumulative net investment loss ("CNIL") deducted from the cumulative gains account above is intended to measure lifetime losses from passive investments to the extent they exceed lifetime income, commencing in 1988. The concept is that if, for example, you borrow money to buy a rental building or shares, and the interest and other costs of your investment exceed the income from it, thereby creating a deduction from tax, you should not then be allowed to sell the property for a tax-free capital gain. Accordingly, the CNIL account limits the capital gains exemption to the extent you have deducted your passive investment losses. Passive investments are, in general, investments in assets you acquire neither as trading inventory nor for use in carrying on a business. However, the actual definition is more explicit, and actually favours a few tax shelter incentives by excluding them from the CNIL pool.

The cumulative net investment loss is generally abbreviated as CNIL, and generally pronounced by tax practitioners as "senile".

Components of CNIL Account

CNIL is defined in subsection 110.6(1).

Investment Expense

Basically, your CNIL account consists, on the "positive" or limiting side, of "investment expense", defined as the aggregate of the following amounts:

(1) All amounts deducted by you in a year in computing your income from property. The most common item here will be interest costs and carrying charges. However, the CRA has also identified repayments of shareholder loans and of inducements, deductions (as opposed to credits) for foreign taxes paid, and several other items, such as property income expenses. The related income is an offset on the income side. Deductions for natural resource exploration and development expenses are specifically excluded here, as they are subject to the special rules given below. Since this item is technically broad enough to include most expenses specifically mentioned below, it is provided that there will be no double-counting and deductions are not included here if expensed in the following items. As well, there is no double-counting where deductions under other provisions reduce reported income, and non-deductible interest incurred on funds borrowed to contribute to income-averaging annuity contract ("IAACs"), registered retirement savings plans ("RRSPs"), and registered pension plans ("RPPs") is not included in investment expense. Finally, both shareholder loans included in income (¶409) and deduc-

tions by virtue of the repayment of those loans are to be excluded from CNIL calculations. (However, a grandfathering rule allowed taxpayers with shareholder loans included in taxable income to include them in CNIL investment income (in (7), below) for 1988 and 1989 if an election to do this was made by notifying the Minister of National Revenue in writing before January 1, 1993. Amounts so included in investment income should be included here in investment expense when repaid.)

(2) All losses for the year from property owned by you or a partnership of which you are a member (except to the extent partnership losses are deducted below). This explicitly includes losses from renting or leasing a building, including a multiple unit residential building, and including a leasehold interest in a building, owned by you jointly or otherwise and used in the year the loss arises principally for the purpose of producing rent. That is to say, a rental building will generally produce investment expense (or income) which goes into the CNIL account even if you can argue that this is a business rather than a property investment.

(3) All deductions for expenses incurred to finance your acquisition of a partnership interest if you are a limited or passive partner. You are a limited partner if you meet the description in ¶1818, and you are a passive partner unless (i) you are actively engaged in the activities of the partnership business other than financing activities, or (ii) you carry on a similar business outside the partnership. These include primarily interest and other financing costs, but also specifically include certain fees (other than commissions) for advice or management of your interest. Essentially this picks up financing outside the partnership which may escape limited partner restrictions. Also, certain current financing deductions permitted where a partnership has ceased to exist will be included in investment expense.

(4) All losses other than allowable capital losses allocated to you by a partnership if you are a limited or passive partner as described above. In the case of limited partners, this includes your limited partnership loss carryover only in the year it is claimed as a deduction.

(5) Only 50% of your Canadian exploration expenses, Canadian development expenses, Canadian oil and gas property expenses, foreign exploration and development expenses, and cumulative foreign resource expenses claimed in the year (see Chapter 22) go into the CNIL expense pool.

(6) For 1992 and later years, the investment expense side of the CNIL calculation includes capital loss carryovers applied in the current year in excess of the inclusion amounts eligible for the annual gains limit (amounts (1) and (2) of the 1992 and later annual gains limit definition at ¶502m). This inclusion only makes sense as the flip side of the interest income (CNIL reduction) in (12), below, since the net effect of these items is a potential reduction in CNIL for the ineligible portion of capital gains.

Investment Income

The offsetting side of the CNIL calculation, which reduces or cancels the limitation imposed by the above expenses, is called investment income. It is, as you might expect, the flip side of the additions above. In computing the CNIL account, you subtract all income for 1988 and subsequent years which is:

(7) All income from property, including recapture of capital cost allowance, but not double-counting any income included below.

(8) All income from property, including real estate specifically mentioned in (2), above.

(9) All income allocations other than taxable capital gains from membership in a partnership as a limited or passive partner (see (3) above), including amounts arising as recapture of capital cost allowance in the partnership.

(10) 50% of natural resource income (see Chapter 22).

(11) Taxable annuity income (i.e., net of the return of capital component) other than income from an IAAC (see ¶480) or an annuity purchased pursuant to a deferred profit sharing plan.

(12) For 1992 and later years, taxable capital gains for the year in excess of the eligible portion of non-qualified real estate taxable capital gains and of the taxable capital gain on pre-1985 reserves recognized in the year. This CNIL reduction will always offset and sometimes more than offset the CNIL additions in (6), above. The net effect of (6) and (7) is to provide that certain amounts ineligible for capital gains exemption are added to investment income, which reduces the CNIL account. These items are the taxable 75% of (i) capital gains realized before 1985 but deferred for tax purposes under the reserve rules and now brought into income, and (ii) the ineligible portion of capital gains arising on real estate sold after February 29, 1992. Where net capital losses of other years are applied in the year to these two ineligible items, those net capital losses become "investment expenses" (in (6)), which increase the CNIL account. The result of these changes seems to be that dispositions of property ineligible for the capital gains exemption will reduce the CNIL account to the extent they are not offset by net capital losses of other years. The taxable capital gain on a deemed disposition of non-qualified real property is reduced for the ineligible portion of the gain. Accordingly, the non-qualified portion of the taxable capital gain is not effectively realized on the deemed disposition, and therefore never gets included in the definition of investment income or in this calculation.

Income or loss as it is used in all the items above except (6) and (12) means items included on income account, that is, it does not include capital gains and losses.

The CNIL account is in theory an essential calculation for every year commencing with 1988 if you ever want to claim the capital gains exemption in future. It is not enough to calculate it only when the capital gains exemption arises. It may be that if you virtually never have passive investment losses, the CRA will treat the calculation as immaterial, although you may lose the benefit of the income calculations if you should have losses.

Reporting CNIL

The CNIL account is calculated on form T936. The CRA does appear to keep a running total in its computers. In theory, you should do the T936 calculation each year even if you are not claiming capital gains exemption in the year, and then compare the running total with the one the CRA will give you after the assessment for the year if you ask them.

(ITA: 110.6(1); ITR: 1100(14) Rental Properties)

[¶503] NET CAPITAL LOSS RULES

Ordinary capital losses that are realized in a particular year are now only deductible to the extent of realized capital gains. (Up to $2,000 a year of capital losses incurred prior to 1985 can be deducted against income from other sources, including pre-1986 losses carried forward.)

The net capital gain available in a particular year for the lifetime exemption will also be reduced by your allowable business investment losses realized in that year; by your capital losses of other years applied against capital gains of the current year; and by "pre-1986" capital losses applied against other income of the current year. For years after 1984, business investment losses will be deductible against other income only to the extent that the loss exceeds the total capital gains exemption claimed in previous years.

Historical Rate Changes

The inclusion portion of losses shifted upwards from $^1/_2$ in 1987 to 2/3 in 1988 and 1989 and to $^3/_4$ in 1990, and down again to $^2/_3$ after February 27, 2000 and $^1/_2$ after October 17, 2000 (¶500a), making it necessary to adjust the allowable portion of losses applied to a particular year to ensure that it represents the same actual loss in the year the carryover is incurred as in the year it is applied. This is done by multiplying the loss in the year it is applied by the inclusion rate for the year of application divided by the inclusion rate for the year of loss. This concept is further discussed and illustrated in ¶1093.

(ITA: 110.6; 111)

CALCULATION OF GAIN OR LOSS

[¶505] HOW TO CALCULATE A CAPITAL GAIN OR CAPITAL LOSS: GENERAL RULES

The general rule (subsection 40(1)) is that a capital gain or capital loss is the difference between (1) the amount received as proceeds of disposition of the property in question, and (2) the property's ACB plus any costs of disposing of the property.

In some cases, the proceeds of disposition will be deemed for tax purposes to be something other than the actual proceeds. For example, if you receive proceeds on the redemption of shares in a corporation in excess of the amount that the shares were originally issued for by the corporation (the paid-up capital) you may be deemed to have received proceeds equal to the paid-up capital in computing your capital gain or loss. If your actual proceeds are in excess of the deemed proceeds, the difference is treated as a deemed dividend (see ¶416). For a discussion of deemed proceeds on transfers of property to a related person see ¶510. Also, when a building and the land upon which it stands are sold together, the proceeds may be allocated to each in such a way as to reduce any "terminal loss" on the building (see ¶851 and ¶859).

In most cases, the ACB of the property is the actual amount you paid to acquire the property, but for certain kinds of property there are adjustments which must be made to this original cost amount to arrive at the ACB of the property. These are discussed in detail at ¶507 and ¶508. In other cases, you may be deemed to have acquired a property at a certain cost.

Costs of disposing of a property may include such things as an agent's or broker's commission, legal costs of drawing up sale documents, advertising costs, a bonus paid to discharge a mortgage on real property prior to maturity, and any other expenses directly caused by the disposition. If the property disposed of includes depreciable property, you may allocate a reasonable portion of the selling costs to the depreciables. This allocation to depreciables would reduce recapture of capital cost allowance (see ¶557 to ¶559 and Chapter 8).

Example

In Year 1, you paid $1,000 to acquire 100 common shares of A Company, and the brokerage charge was $50. The shares were sold five years later for $2,000, and the brokerage charge on sale was $100.

Your disposition would be reported on Schedule 3 of your return, in section 3, Publicly traded shares. You would report 100 shares of A Company, purchased in Year 1, proceeds of disposition of $2,000, adjusted cost base of $1,050, and outlays and expenses of $100 for a gain of $850.

(ITA: 40(1); 53; 54)

[¶506] CALCULATION OF ADJUSTED COST BASE

The ACB of the property (subsection 54(1)) is deducted from the proceeds of disposition in determining the capital gain or loss.

The starting point for determining ACB is the cost of the property or its deemed cost. For property acquired after 1971 the cost is generally the actual purchase price, although see ¶510, ¶514, ¶516, and ¶519 for situations where another amount may be relevant. For property owned on December 31, 1971, the cost of the property is determined by special rules described at ¶589 to ¶597.

Cost generally includes all costs associated with the acquisition, such as brokerage fees, non-deductible legal fees, etc.

After determining the cost or deemed cost of the property it may be necessary to increase or decrease this amount to arrive at the ACB. See ¶507 and ¶508, below. See also the CRA interpretation bulletin IT-456 Capital Property — Some Adjustments to Cost Base (now archived).

There are forms required to be filed on certain rollover transactions where there may not be a capital gain or loss (see ¶585). These include:

T2057 — Section 85 election on property exchanged for shares

T2058 — Section 85 election on partnership interest exchanged for shares

T2059 — Section 97 election on roll-in to partnership

T2060 — Section 98 election on partnership wind-up.

Finally, certain forms are required in various circumstances, including:

T2091 — Designation of a principal residence (see ¶553).

(ITA: 53; 54)

[¶507] DEDUCTIONS IN COMPUTING ADJUSTED COST BASE

The deductions which must be made from cost in arriving at the ACB of a property include the following (subsection 53(2)):

(1) Shares: Certain distributions such as tax-free dividends (excluding capital dividends and the short-lived life insurance capital dividends where a suitable election was made) received from a corporation with respect to its shares owned by you will result in a reduction of the ACB of those shares. Dividends of this kind were common before 1979 but thereafter were limited to dividends paid before October 2, 1991 on shares prescribed under Regulation 2107 (the first five share issues referred to in ¶538). Corporations which made distributions of this kind presumably notified you at the time of the dividend of the amount to be deducted from the ACB, and you should have retained adequate documentation to determine the cost base on your disposition of the shares.

If a shareholder receives compensation as a result of a shareholder class action suit, the shareholder's ACB of shares owned at the time of the receipt of the compensation may be reduced; see ¶573.

Capital dividends (¶415) do not reduce your ACB but may cause related problems, as discussed at ¶580d.

The cost base of shares may also be reduced by a return of paid-up capital, either as such or on winding-up, to the extent the amount is not considered a dividend. Cost base reduction may also occur as part of a deferral of capital gain, as where shares of a small business corporation are sold and the proceeds reinvested in other small business corporations. See ¶572.

(2) As discussed in Chapter 18, the ACB of an interest in a partnership must be reduced by your share of certain partnership losses, and drawings, and by certain other amounts.

(3) Where you dispose of a portion of a property, your ACB of the remaining part must be reduced, as described at ¶520.

(4) As described at ¶565, the cancellation or reduction of a debt may require the reduction of the ACB of capital property owned by you.

(5) Certain debt obligations where the return (interest or bonus) is variable and linked to the rate of inflation or deflation have specific cost base adjustments to reflect adjustments under these rules; see ¶442.

(6) Certain distributions from trusts will reduce the ACB of your interest in the trust. Presumably the executor of the trust will notify you of the amount of the reduction. (See Chapter 4 at ¶453.) In particular, mutual fund trusts may make certain tax-free distributions which will reduce the cost base of your trust unit. The trust should advise you of these adjustments.

(7) Grants, subsidies or other assistance received from a government, municipality or other public authority will require a reduction in your ACB of the related property. There are certain exceptions for provincial assistance provided on shares of "prescribed" venture capital corporations, labour-sponsored venture capital corporations, and stock savings plans (see commentary on provincial tax credits in Chapter 14; also ¶2522).

(8) Certain amounts included in income with respect to foreign affiliates (¶407 and ¶493).

(9) In general, any part of the cost of property, except depreciable property (see ¶509), that is deductible in computing income under a specific provision of the law must be deducted from the ACB for purposes of calculating your capital gain or capital loss.

(10) Share-purchase tax credits (see ¶1466) and any scientific research tax credits to which you are entitled will require a reduction to the ACB of the shares.

(11) Where you receive certain inducements or reimbursements in the course of carrying on business, these may be included in income unless an election is made to reduce the cost of related assets (see ¶729 and ¶826).

(12) Adjustments to the cost base of employee stock options held at death may be required to avoid double-counting. See ¶1925.

(ITA: 53(2); 127.2(8); 127.3(6); ITR: 6700 [Prescribed venture capital corporations]; 6701 [Prescribed labour-sponsored venture capital corporation]; IT-456R [Archived])

[¶508] ADDITIONS TO ADJUSTED COST BASE

The additions which must be made to cost in arriving at the ACB of property include the following (subsection 53(1)):

(1) In general, contributions of capital to a corporation, other than by way of loan, should be added to the ACB of any shares you hold in the corporation.

(2) Certain dividends deemed to be received from corporations may be added to the ACB of shares of that corporation that you hold. Presumably the amounts to be added to the ACB will be indicated by the corporation involved.

(3) A "superficial loss" as described at ¶579 should be added to the ACB of the property.

(4) Where a bond, debenture, bill, note, mortgage, hypothec, or similar obligation has been issued for an amount less than the principal amount indicated on the obligation, the difference may be required to be included in computing your income, as outlined at ¶438. If this is the case, the amount included in income should also be added to your ACB of the obligation.

(5) Certain debt obligations where the return (interest or bonus) is variable and linked to the rate of inflation or deflation have specific cost base adjustments to reflect notional interest accrued under these rules; see ¶442.

(6) As described at ¶665, interest and property taxes may, in some circumstances, be added to the ACB of land held by you if they have not been allowed as a deduction in computing income for tax purposes.

(7) As described at ¶1750, that portion of a farming loss created or increased by the payment of interest or property taxes may be added to the ACB of the land used in a farming business.

(8) In some cases, the deduction of amounts from the ACB of a property will result in a negative ACB amount. If this happens, the negative amount must be treated as a capital gain realized in the year the negative balance arises, as discussed at ¶535. The negative

amount may then be added to the ACB of the property for purposes of determining your subsequent capital gains or capital losses. However, if the ACB of an interest in a partnership is negative, no capital gain will arise. See ¶1842.

(9) Certain amounts not received but included in income with respect to foreign affiliates (¶493).

(10) Where you or a non-arm's length person (¶812) own a share acquired under an employee stock option plan or a mutual fund unit acquired under a similar plan, the amount by which the actual cost of the share (or unit) under the option is less than the fair market value of the share (or unit) on its date of acquisition is added to the ACB of the share (or unit) to the extent that the amount is included in your income as a stock option benefit (see ¶330). The entire amount included in your income (either in the year of acquisition or year of disposition of the security — see ¶330) is added to ACB, typically bringing ACB up to fair market value at the date of acquisition, even though part of the stock option benefit included (or to be included) in your income may be entitled to a partially offsetting one-half deduction in computing taxable income.

For shares acquired before 1972 under a stock option plan, see the special rule discussed in ¶591 with respect to the treatment of the difference between actual cost and fair market value on the date of acquisition.

(11) Certain amounts with respect to an interest in a partnership. See Chapter 18.

(12) The amount of a loss which has been denied under the rules at ¶585 either on a transfer of property to an affiliated corporation or, under earlier rules, on a transfer of property to a corporation controlled by you or your spouse or common-law partner is not deductible but is added to the ACB of the shares of the corporation.

(13) In general, if you have received capital property under circumstances in which the value of the property or a portion thereof has been included in your income under other provisions of this law, the amount of the benefit included in your income is added to the ACB of the property received.

(14) The costs of surveying or valuing property incurred by you for the purpose of acquiring or disposing of the property are added to the ACB of the property.

(15) Certain designations from a mutual fund trust may create income for you without corresponding cash proceeds, and these should increase the cost base of your trust units. The trust should advise you of these adjustments. See also ¶526.

(16) In certain circumstances a holder of real estate may divide his or her interest in the property into a "life interest" and a "remainder interest"; special rules govern these transactions and consequent cost base adjustments (see ¶541).

(17) Dispositions to a controlled corporation or partnership may result in a loss denied and added to the ACB of the shares or partnership interest (¶565); also, "debt parking" transactions may involve cost base adjustments (¶565).

(18) Where an election was made on a flow-through entity to create a continuing capital gain exemption balance against the annual gains flowed out to the elector, any remaining unused balance after 2004 is wound up and added to the ACB of the entity to the elector. Similarly, where the property on which the election was made is disposed of before 2005 and a related capital gain exemption balance remains unused, that balance will be added to the ACB of the property immediately before the disposition; typically this will allow recognition of a loss accrued since February 22, 1994.

(19) Payments made on shares received under the rollover rules in the course of demutualization of life insurance companies which are transferred to (typically, but not always) employees, as described at ¶741, are added to the cost base of the shares as described at ¶741.

(ITA: 40(3); 52(1); 53(1); IT-456R [Archived])

[¶509] ADJUSTED COST BASE OF DEPRECIABLE PROPERTY

The adjustments to the ACB of a property mentioned above do not apply where the property is "depreciable property" (section 54 "adjusted cost base"). For depreciable property, your ACB is normally the "capital cost" of the depreciable property and is not subject to the ordinary cost base adjustments described in this chapter. This said, it should be noted that adjustments to "capital cost" frequently parallel the adjustments to ACB where similar adjustments are involved, e.g., receipt of government grants (see Chapter 8 at ¶811 *et seq.*). Also, some adjustments to capital cost apply by their own terms for purposes of the depreciation rules but not for purposes of the capital gain rules, so that there can be a spread, albeit in unusual circumstances, between cost base for capital cost allowance/recapture purposes and cost base for capital gain purposes (see, for example, ¶813 and ¶814). Some of the adjustments which must be made to capital cost are reversed again on death (see ¶1920).

(ITA: 13; 54 "proceeds of disposition" (a))

[¶510] PROPERTY ACQUIRED FROM RELATED PERSONS

Generally, when property is acquired for an amount in excess of its fair market value from a related person, or from any other person with whom you are not dealing at arm's length, you will be deemed to have acquired the property for its fair market value (paragraph 69(1)(*a*)). The actual price paid for the property may therefore be irrelevant for purposes of determining the cost to you. Similarly, when you dispose of property in a non-arm's length transaction for less than its fair market value, you are deemed to have received proceeds equal to its fair market value for calculating your capital gain or loss (paragraph 69(1)(*b*)).

See ¶812 for a discussion of what constitutes a "related person" and the meaning of "arm's length". The CRA discusses the issue in its Tax Folio S1-F5-C1, "Related persons and dealing at arm's length".

See ¶594 for rules relating to property acquired from a related person who owned the property on June 18, 1971.

Special rules apply in the case of gifts, bequests or sales to a spouse or common-law partner, or bequests of depreciable property. (See ¶531 and ¶532.) Special rules may also apply in the case of transfers involving a corporation, partnership or trust, but since such transfers will normally require professional advice, they are not dealt with in detail in this book. Special rules may also apply to transfers of farm property or family farm corporations to your children (¶1759).

(ITA: 69; 70; 73; 26(5); Income Tax Folio: S1-F5-C1 Related Persons and Dealing at Arm's Length)

[¶511] OBLIGATIONS TRANSFERRED BETWEEN INTEREST DATES

If you sell an interest-bearing obligation between interest dates, the accrued interest to the date of sale is your income and thus reduces the interest income reported later by the person acquiring the obligation and ultimately receiving the entire interest payment (subsection 20(14); see also ¶440).

The proceeds of disposition of the obligation should be reduced by the amount of the accrued interest (which will be reported as interest income).

The ACB of the obligation to the purchaser does not include the accrued interest (paragraph 53(2)(*l*)).

(ITA: 20(14); 53(2)(i))

[¶512] IDENTICAL PROPERTIES

General Rule

Where you hold two or more properties of the same kind, a capital gain or loss may arise upon the disposition of any one of the identical properties. You are not permitted to wait until disposing of all the identical items before reporting your gain or loss.

For purposes of calculating the ACB of identical properties, the ACB of each of the properties held at any particular time will be considered to be the same. In other words, the ACB of each property is calculated by adding together the cost base of all such properties and dividing by the number of such identical properties to arrive at an average cost, which will then be the ACB for each property (subsection 47(1)).

Where some identical properties were acquired before 1972, and some after 1971, one ACB is calculated for all properties acquired before 1972 and a separate ACB for those acquired after 1971. See ¶593 for details.

Debt Instruments

In the case of bonds, debentures, bills, notes or other similar obligations, issued by the same debtor, these obligations will be considered to be identical properties if all rights attached to them, with the exception of the principal amounts thereof, are identical.

To calculate the ACB of identical debt instruments, it is necessary to first determine a notional number of properties held to be used in the averaging process described above. This notional number of properties held is computed by dividing the total principal amount of all the identical debt obligations held, by the principal amount of the particular obligation for which it is necessary to calculate an ACB (subsection 47(2)).

Example

You acquired three bonds of F Company at a total cost of $2,400. The bonds are identical in all respects except that two have a principal value of $1,000 each and one has a principal value of $500. The ACB of each of the $1,000 bonds would be:

Notional number of identical properties	2,500/1000 =	2.5
Total cost		$2,400
ACB	$2,400 ÷ 2.5 =	$960

The ACB of the $500 bond would be:

Notional number of identical properties	2,500/500 =	5
Total cost		$2,400
ACB	$2,400 ÷ 5 =	$ 480

Otherwise identical shares or units of a mutual fund trust may be treated differently if acquired by an employee of the issuing company under a stock (or unit) option plan. See ¶330.

(ITA: 18(13); 47; 26(8); IT-387R2 (Consolidated) [Archived])

[¶513] DIVIDED USE

Divided Use since Acquisition

It is possible for a capital asset to be used for more than one purpose at the same time.

Where a property has a divided use, and one of the uses is for the purpose of gaining or producing income, and the other use is for some other purpose, the cost of acquisition should be divided between the portions of the property in relation to the use of the property.

Should the property be disposed of, the proceeds of disposition should also be divided between the parts of the property used for different purposes, in a ratio determined by the relative uses of the property in question (paragraph 45(1)(*b*)).

Change in Use

Where there is a change of use of a property, and where one of the uses is for the purpose of gaining or producing income, and the other use is for some other purpose, you are deemed to have disposed of all or a part of the property at the time the use of the property changes (paragraph 45(1)(*a*)).

This deemed disposition is treated as a disposition for capital gain or loss purposes, and therefore a capital gain or a capital loss may arise as a result of a change of use of property even where no sale or other actual disposition of property has occurred. This would occur, for example, if you move out of your house and rent it out or if you buy an apartment to rent out and later begin using it as a residence. (Note that where property consisting of land and building changes from income to personal-use and there is a loss at that time, the loss must be divided into terminal loss on the building (¶859) and a capital loss on the land.)

The proceeds of such a deemed disposition of property is determined by the fair market value of the property at the time the change of use occurs. If there is a partial change of use of the property, only the related portion of the property is deemed to have been disposed of, at a price equal to that portion of the fair market value of the entire property. The ACB of the property deemed to have been disposed of is calculated in the normal manner, except that only a portion of the ACB can be deducted where only a portion of the property is subject to the deemed disposition rule.

Where you have been deemed to dispose of all or part of a property at fair market value, you are then deemed to have immediately reacquired it for the same value, so that you carry your new ACB forward for future calculations.

(Income Tax Folio: S1-F3-C2 Principal Residence)

[¶513.05] *Partial Change in Use*

It is possible that the relative uses of a property with a divided use may change from time to time. For example, a property with a 40% business use could change to 70% business use. The rules governing this are complex, and as a practical matter where small amounts are involved it is often ignored. Situations where it might be important would most often involve real estate. The concepts and details are discussed at ¶823. This case must be distinguished from a complete change of use, discussed below and at ¶819.

[¶513.10] *Complete Change in Use*

Election to Ignore Change in Use

Where the use of a property has changed from a non-income producing purpose to an income producing purpose, you may elect under subsection 45(2) of the Act to continue to treat the property as a non-income producing one. If this election is made in respect of depreciable property, you will not be permitted to claim capital cost allowances related to the property as long as the election remains outstanding. This election is discussed at ¶555 and applies to capital property of any kind.

If in a subsequent year, the election is rescinded, the property will be deemed to have changed its use on the first day of that subsequent year, possibly resulting in capital gain or capital loss determined on the basis of the fair market value of the property at that later date. This may be more or less advantageous than if the change of use and deemed disposition had been considered to have occurred in the first year, if no election had been made. This should be considered when deciding whether or not to make the election referred to above. The disadvantage of not being able to claim capital cost allowances during the years in which the election remains outstanding should also be kept in mind before deciding to file the election.

Remember that the rules in this chapter apply primarily for the purpose of determining cost for capital gain or loss purposes; cost for capital cost allowance and recapture purposes may be determined under different rules discussed in Chapter 8. See ¶819 and ¶855.

An election is also allowed to ignore the change in use when a property that was an income-producing property and is converted into a principal residence; see ¶555.

(ITA: 45)

[¶514] PROPERTY ACQUIRED BY WAY OF DIVIDEND

Where, as a shareholder, you receive a dividend in kind (that is, in some form other than cash) the fair market value of capital property received from the corporation at that time is deemed to be your cost of that property (subsection 52(2)). See ¶414.

On the other hand, stock dividends are considered to have a cost equal to the amount by which the corporation's paid-up capital has increased as a result of the dividend (subsection 52(3)).

Stock dividends are treated as ordinary dividends for income tax purposes. This will result in tax being paid on dividend income when the stock is received rather than tax being paid on a capital gain when the shares are sold. The amount of the dividend is typically measured by the *pro rata* increase in the corporation's paid-up capital, and this amount also becomes the cost of the shares for determining subsequent capital gain or loss. An anti-avoidance rule provides that where the purpose of a stock dividend is to alter the value of an interest of a 10% or more shareholder, the benefit may be included as taxable income, and if it is, then the cost basis of the shares is increased accordingly. See also ¶406.

Historical Information

Shares received from a corporation by a shareholder (except non-resident parties owning more than 10% of the corporation) as a stock dividend from a public corporation after March 31, 1977 and before May 24, 1985 or from a non-resident corporation after 1976 and before May 24, 1985 were not taxable dividends. They were considered capital property with an ACB of nil; hence, a capital gain on disposition of these stock dividends will be realized to the extent that proceeds on disposition exceed the appropriate ACB (see also ¶512 re identical properties — averaging).

(ITA: 15(1.1); 52(2), (3); 248(1); IT-88R2 [Archived])

[¶516] DEEMED COST OF PROPERTY FOR IMMIGRANTS TO CANADA

If you have immigrated to Canada after 1971, any capital property you held at the time of immigration, except for taxable Canadian property as defined in ¶2040, is deemed to have been acquired by you at the date of immigration to Canada, at a cost equal to its fair market value at that time (paragraph 128.1(1)(c)).

The deemed cost will be used in calculating your capital gain or loss with respect to this property when it is actually sold or otherwise disposed of after your arrival in Canada, or when it is deemed to be disposed of on your subsequent departure. See Chapter 21.

However, this is not necessarily the cost from which you may claim capital cost allowance. See ¶811.

Because of this rule, you should prepare a list of such property and retain any information you may have with respect to its fair market value at the date of immigration, so that this information will be readily available for use in future Canadian income tax returns.

[¶516.05] *Property Other Than Capital Property*

The rule requiring a deemed valuation on immigration is not limited to capital property. In fact, all property you own at the time of becoming a Canadian resident is subject to a notional disposition and reacquisition at fair market value, with the following exceptions:

(1) taxable Canadian property (see ¶2040);

(2) inventory and eligible capital property (¶766) of a business carried on in Canada immediately prior to becoming a Canadian resident;

Commentary on Bill C-29 Measures (Oct. 25, 2016)

Note: When Bill C-29, October 25, 2016, achieves Royal Assent, the commentary will be modified to read:

(2) inventory and, prior to 2017, eligible capital property and after 2016 property included in Class 14.1 (¶766) of a business carried on in Canada immediately prior to becoming a Canadian resident;

(3) an "excluded right or interest". This is a subcategory of property which would not be subject to departure tax for emigrants from Canada, defined in ¶2153. It includes such things as rights to benefits or payments under pension, RRSP, and other benefit plans — many of which are employee-sponsored benefits plans — and interests in certain trusts and insurance contracts. However, the exclusion does not extend to an interest in a non-resident trust that was never acquired for consideration, and such an interest is subject to revaluation on immigration.

See also Chapter 21, especially ¶2117.

(ITA: 48(3) (repealed); 128.1(1)(*b*), (9))

[¶517] WARRANTY COSTS AND RESTRICTIVE COVENANTS

In some cases, a capital property may be sold subject to a warranty provided by the vendor. Any portion of the proceeds on the disposition of a property which relates to consideration for the warranty is treated as proceeds in determining the capital gain or loss on the sale of the property.

[¶517.10] *Dispositions Subject to a Warranty*

Under paragraph 42(1)(*a*) of the Act, an amount received or receivable by you as consideration for a warranty, a covenant or another conditional or contingent obligation given or incurred by you in respect of a property you disposed of, at any time, is:

- if the amount is received or becomes receivable on or before your filing-due date for the taxation year in which your disposed of the property, to be included in computing your proceeds of disposition of the property in that taxation year; and
- if the amount is received or becomes receivable after that filing-due date, deemed to be a capital gain from the disposition that occurs at the time when the amount is received or becomes receivable.

In short, amounts received or receivable for the warranty, etc., before the filing-due date for the year of disposition are rolled into proceeds of disposition for that year. Amounts received or receivable subsequently are proceeds of disposition giving rise to capital gain in the taxation year they first become received or receivable.

Note that there is an implicit assumption that the warranty proceeds can be separately identified.

A mirror image rule under paragraph 42(1)(*b*) provides that an outlay or expense paid or payable by you in a taxation year under a warranty, covenant or another conditional or contingent obligation given or incurred by you in respect of property disposed of is:

- to be deducted in computing your proceeds of disposition of the property if the amount is paid or becomes payable on or before your filing-due date for the taxation year in which you disposed of the property, and
- deemed to be a capital loss from the disposition that occurs at the time when the amount is paid or becomes payable if the amount is paid or becomes payable after that filing–due date.

The restrictive covenant rules discussed below specifically override these rules. That is, the warranty rules above do not apply to amounts received or receivable as consideration for a restrictive covenant. Note that the override only applies to amounts received or receivable by the vendor. Presumably the warranty rules remain applicable to amounts paid by the vendor, which continue to be treated as capital losses.

(ITA: 42)

[¶517.15] *Non-Competition Clause/Restrictive Covenant*

One of the most common agreements given by the vendor of a business will be a covenant not to enter into competition with the business being sold, either for a period of years or forever, in consideration for a non-competition payment.

The general rules dealing with restrictive covenants (section 56.4) require payments under a "restrictive covenant" as defined to be treated as ordinary income. However, there are exceptions — for example, on the sale of shares or a partnership interest, if there is a joint agreement with the purchaser under which both purchaser and vendor treat the amounts as proceeds of the disposition of shares or, in the case of a sole proprietorship, there is a joint agreement to treat the amount as eligible capital property. Where there is no joint agreement, the amounts will be ordinary income to the vendor who receives the payments and, presumably, eligible capital expenditures to the purchaser, who may amortize them under the rules at ¶767. See ¶929 for a detailed discussion on the restrictive covenant rules.

Commentary on Bill C-29 Measures (Oct. 25, 2016)

Note: When Bill C-29, October 25, 2016, achieves Royal Assent, the commentary will be modified to read:

The general rules dealing with restrictive covenants (section 56.4) require payments under a "restrictive covenant" as defined to be treated as ordinary income. However, there are exceptions — for example, on the sale of shares or a partnership interest, if there is a joint agreement with the purchaser under which both purchaser and vendor treat the amounts as proceeds of the disposition of shares or, in the case of a sole proprietorship, there is a joint agreement to treat the amount as eligible capital property. Where there is no joint agreement, the amounts will be ordinary income to the vendor who receives the payments and, presumably, eligible capital expenditures to the purchaser, who may amortize them under the rules at ¶767. See ¶929 for a detailed discussion on the restrictive covenant rules. Effective January 1, 2017, the eligible capital property rules have been repealed and replaced by a new Class 14.1 of depreciable property. Property that previously was eligible capital property is now depreciable capital property and expenditures and receipts that previously were accounted for under the eligible capital property rules are now accounted for under the rules for depreciable property and capital property.

(ITA: 68(c))

[¶518] MORTGAGE FORECLOSURES AND CONDITIONAL SALE REPOSSESSIONS

Sections 79 and 79.1 of the Act apply where property subject to a mortgage or conditional sales agreement is acquired or reacquired by the vendor upon failure to pay all or part of the related debt. Section 79 applies to the debtor;

section 79.1 to the creditor. Any gain or loss is reported on lines 154 and 155 of Schedule 3.

Debtor's Position

The debtor whose property is acquired by a creditor is deemed to have surrendered the property for proceeds of disposition equal to total unpaid principal and interest at the time of surrender. Where several properties are surrendered in consequence of one debt, proceeds are allocated on the basis of fair market values of the properties. Presumably, the consequences of proceeds of disposition will depend on the nature of the property (capital, inventory, etc.). As before, where the debtor makes further payments following surrender, these are deemed to be losses on the disposition of property. The statute now makes it clear that the treatment of these losses also follows the nature of the property to which the debt related.

Creditor's Position

Property acquired or reacquired in consequence of default of debt is deemed to have a cost to the creditor equal to the cost base of the debt, adjusted for capital property for non-arm's length transactions, plus otherwise unaccounted expenses of the creditor to protect the creditor's interest. Where several properties are covered by the debt, cost base of the debt is allocated among them in proportion to their fair market values. As before, reserves need not be added back but rather reduce the deemed cost of the (re)acquired property to the creditor. However, where this reduction reduced the cost base below zero, reserves must be recognized to bring the cost base back to nil. Where property is reacquired by a creditor in the same year it was sold to the debtor so that no reserve has been available to the creditor, the new rules permit a reduction of the creditor's original proceeds of disposition by the unpaid portion of those proceeds at the time of seizure.

(ITA: 79; 79.1)

[¶519] PROPERTY RECEIVED FROM EMPLOYEES' PROFIT SHARING PLAN

If you are a beneficiary under an employees' profit sharing plan and you receive an amount from the trust in a form other than cash, there is a rollover to you. For example, if the trust were to distribute a share on which there was an accrued but unrealized capital gain, the gain would not be taxed on distribution to you, but would be taxed when you dispose of the share.

The cost of the property to you is, in effect, the amount which has been attributed to you and included in your income or is otherwise exempt from inclusion. You should obtain details of your cost of the property from the administrator of the plan.

If you made a 1994 capital gains exemption election on the plan, you may be carrying forward an eligible capital gains balance which you can use to increase the cost base (and so reduce any future gain) on property distributed to you in this fashion. See ¶332.

(ITA: 144(7.1); IT-379R [Archived])

[¶520] PARTIAL DISPOSITIONS

When only part of a capital property has been sold or otherwise disposed of, you may not wait until all of the property has been disposed of before reporting a capital gain or capital loss. A disposition of any part of a capital property will be a disposal for tax purposes and must be reported.

When a partial disposition occurs, you deduct from your proceeds of disposal the portion of your ACB for the property which can reasonably be attributed to the part of the property that has been sold (subsection 43(1)). The remaining ACB for the property which you retain will be determined by deducting from your ACB for the entire property the portion of the ACB which you deducted in determining your gain or loss at the time of the partial disposition.

Example

You own a summer cottage which has an ACB of $10,000, and which does not qualify as a "principal residence" (see ¶554). You sell a half-interest in the cottage to a friend for $6,000.

The capital gain to be reported would be $1,000, being the proceeds of disposition of $6,000 less $^{1}/_{2}$ the ACB of the cottage, $5,000. The half-interest in the cottage which you retained would have an ACB of $5,000 for purposes of subsequent capital gain or capital loss calculations.

See also interpretation bulletin IT-264, Part Dispositions, and its Special Release (archived).

The rules in this chapter apply primarily for the purpose of determining cost for capital gain or loss purposes; cost of depreciable property for capital cost allowance and recapture purposes may be determined under different rules discussed in Chapter 8, especially ¶813 and ¶860.

(ITA: 43; 53(2)(*d*); IT-264R [Archived])

[¶522] COMMODITIES AND COMMODITY FUTURES TRANSACTIONS

CRA Positions

The CRA has stated that you must report gains and losses from trading in commodities or commodity futures as ordinary income or loss if you:

(1) take commodity future positions as part of a business activity or on commodities grown, traded, or connected with your business; or

(2) are an officer or employee of a business that is concerned with the particular commodity, and you have access to information about the commodity which you use to your benefit in the futures transactions.

See generally IT346R Commodity futures and certain commodities (archived).

Transactions not related to the above, which will generally include all speculative transactions, may be reported at your option as either income transactions or as capital transactions, but once you have adopted one of these methods you must use it consistently for all future transactions in commodities or commodity futures.

If you are a speculator and you prefer to use the income treatment in reporting your gains and losses in commodity futures or commodities, you may do so provided this reporting practice is followed consistently from year to year. If you choose income treatment, the CRA will normally not permit you to change your method of reporting.

It is possible for you to have commodity or futures trading activities in a commodity which is not connected with your business, as well as a commodity which is connected with your business. In this situation the part associated with your business would be afforded income treatment whereas the remainder could be, if so desired, treated as capital in nature.

If you finance your transactions in futures or commodities through borrowings and such transactions are given income treatment, the interest on the borrowed funds is a deductible expense provided the normal tests of reasonableness, legal liability, etc., are met. See ¶1063.

To the extent that your borrowings are used to finance futures or commodity transactions that are given capital treatment, interest in respect thereof is not deductible in computing either your income or your capital gains or losses.

Straddles and Other Transactions

Some taxpayers have tried to use these rules to their benefit through so-called commodity straddles. This consists of taking both buy and sell positions in the same future. As year-end approaches, the losing position is closed out and a business loss is elected. Early in the new year, the gain position is closed out to offset the actual loss incurred. The result is that the loss is claimed to reduce income in Year 1, although of course the gain must be recognized in Year 2. There are two problems with this strategy. First, it can lead to pyramiding if the pattern is continued to shelter Year 2 income. Second, the CRA has indicated that it will consider both close-outs part of the same transaction — that is, that the Year 1 transaction would be ineffective for tax purposes. It is worth noting that in its one effort at litigation on this issue (*A.D. Friedberg v. The Queen*, 89 DTC 5115 (F.C.T.D.); affirmed on this issue, 92 DTC 6031 (F.C.A.), 93 DTC 5507 (S.C.C.)), the CRA lost decisively. It may be relevant, however, that the taxpayer in that case was a professional commodity trader, so the same result might not follow where the straddle transaction was unique or, perhaps, was one of an annual pattern of deferral transactions. In any event, the commodity straddle transaction should probably be undertaken only with professional advice and with a full appreciation of the tax (and market) risks involved.

The case of *Schultz v. The Queen*, 95 DTC 5657 (F.C.A.), indicates that the CRA continues to pursue its attack on commodity straddles and similar tax planning techniques. In the *Schultz* case, a husband and wife took opposite positions on long and short sales of publicly traded shares, and closed them out in such a fashion that the husband achieved losses reducing his high income and the wife increased her low income. The Federal Court of Appeal found they were in partnership and each spouse had an equal interest in the gains and losses achieved. The CRA was entitled to assess on the basis that the transaction did not close until both sides were closed out.

(IT-346R [Archived])

[¶523] DISPOSITION OF BUSINESS PROPERTY

If you are carrying on business as a sole proprietor, and you dispose of a capital property used in the business, you should report any capital gain or loss on the property in the calendar year of the disposition, not in the fiscal period of the business (see ¶706).

However, any recapture of capital cost allowance (¶843) or terminal loss on the disposition must be reported in the fiscal period of the business, for both proprietors and partners.

Election to Defer Gain

If you have voluntarily disposed of real property (land or land and building) used by you or a person related to you (such as a corporation you control) for the purpose of earning income from a business, and you have acquired a replacement property described below within a specified time frame, you may elect to defer a capital gain which would otherwise arise to the extent you have invested the amount of the proceeds in the replacement property (subsection 44(1)).

The specified time frame requires that the replacement property be acquired before the later of:

- the end of the first taxation year following the taxation year in which the original property is deemed to be disposed of; and
- 12 months after the end of the taxation year in which the disposition occurred.

This election is to be made in your return for the year in which you acquired the replacement property. Form T1030 is used for the election.

The election cannot be made if the property disposed of was used principally for the purpose of producing rental income in the taxation year that it was disposed of or if it was not capital property (e.g., inventory). A different election is to be used if any capital property was disposed of *involuntarily*, (i.e. as a result of fire or flood, etc., see ¶525.) The replacement property must be acquired for the same or a similar use as that of the former property, and for use in the same or a similar business.

A replacement property must meet several specific tests (see subsection 44(5)), which can be described as follows:

(1) it is reasonable to conclude that the property was acquired by the taxpayer to replace the former property;

(2) it must be property acquired by the taxpayer and used by the taxpayer or a person related to the taxpayer for a use that is the same as or similar to the use to which the taxpayer or a person related to the taxpayer put the former property (but note that an election to change the wording of this condition is possible in circumstances outlined below);

(3) where the former property was used in a business (rather than merely to produce income — i.e., rental property) by the taxpayer or by a related person, the replacement property must be acquired for use in the same or a similar business or by a person related to the taxpayer for such a purpose;

(4) where the former property was taxable Canadian property as defined in ¶2040, the replacement property must also be taxable Canadian property; and

(5) if the former property was taxable Canadian property which was not "treaty-protected property", the replacement property must similarly be taxable Canadian property which is not treaty-protected property. Treaty-protected property is essentially property from which the gain (if any) would be exempt from Canadian income tax under a Canadian tax treaty if disposed of at the time in question (see Chapter 20).

The point of the rule in (4) appears to be to prevent the capital gain deferral from operating where a property used or situated in Canada is replaced with a property used or situated outside Canada. However, it appears that a Canadian resident can use the replacement rules to replace a former foreign property with a new similar property.

The tests in (3) and (4) are conditional; that is, if the conditions do not apply, the tests need not be met.

The replacement property may be acquired before or after the former property is disposed of, but if acquired before, it must still be owned at the time of the former property's disposition.

To obtain the full benefit of this rule, the replacement property must have a cost equal to or greater than the amount of the proceeds received for the former property. If the proceeds exceed the cost of the replacement property, this excess must be reported as a capital gain in the year the former property is disposed of to the extent that a capital gain arose on the disposition. If a portion of the proceeds from the disposition is not due until after the end of the year in which the disposition takes place, the capital gain may be further deferred by claiming a reserve for proceeds not due (as discussed at ¶581) calculated against undeferred proceeds only. This reserve, like the general capital gains reserve, must be claimed in prescribed form filed with the return for the year it is claimed.

The cost of the replacement property is reduced by the amount of the capital gain on the former property which would otherwise be determined minus any portion of that gain which must be reported in your income tax return. The cost of the replacement property should be reduced at the later of the time when it was acquired or the time when the former property is disposed of.

If the original property was a depreciable asset, and the replacement property was acquired before the original property is deemed to have been disposed of, the actual cost of the replacement property will qualify for capital cost allowance until the year of the original property's deemed disposition. See ¶845. At that time, the undepreciated capital cost of the class in which the replacement property was placed must be reduced by the amount of the capital gain on the original property which is subject to this special rule (¶846). If this reduction is greater than the undepreciated capital cost of the class, all of the excess must be reported in the year when the original property is considered to have been disposed of (which is not necessarily the year in which the deferred capital gain is otherwise applied to reduce undepreciated capital cost), as proceeds of disposal of a depreciable properly of the class to which the replacement property belongs. Thus, it may not be beneficial to make this election in all circumstances, especially if an instalment reserve is available to reduce proceeds of disposition (see ¶581).

Where the former property was depreciable property, an election for purposes of capital gain deferral applies also for purposes of recaptured depreciation (see ¶843) and vice versa.

Example

Dave Skire sold his small plant (land and building) in Don Mills, Ontario, during the year for $175,000 (cost: $130,000) and purchased a replacement property in Mississauga for $225,000. He may elect to defer capital gain as follows:

Don Mills land and building — replaced:

	Land	Building
Proceeds of disposition	$50,000	$125,000
ACB/capital cost	$30,000	$100,000
Replacement property cost — Mississauga	$75,000	$150,000

Computation of capital gain:

Lesser of:		
(a) Proceeds of disposition	$ 50,000	$125,000
Less: ACB/capital cost	(30,000)	(100,000)
Capital gain otherwise determined	$ 20,000	$ 25,000
(b) Proceeds of disposition	$ 50,000	$125,000
Lesser of:		
Less: Cost of replacement property	(75,000)	(150,000)
Proceeds not re-invested	Nil	Nil
Capital gain recognized	Nil	Nil

The capital gain deferred equals $20,000 on the land and $25,000 on the building.

Computation of the cost of the Mississauga replacement property:

	Land	Building
Actual cost	$ 75,000	$150,000
Less: Capital gain deferred	(20,000)	(25,000)
Deemed cost of replacement property	$ 55,000	$125,000

If any gain remains after using this rollover because full proceeds of disposition were not reinvested in the replacement property, a special reserve provision allows the deferral of the remaining gain *pro rata* to unreceived proceeds, but this reserve must be recognized over five years in a manner identical to the general reserve provision at ¶581. (The recognition period is extended to 10 years for real or immovable property used in a farming or fishing business where the gain arose on a rollover to children to which the rules in ¶1759 item (a) or ¶1785 item (a) applied.) However, the reserve must be claimed on form T1030 rather than form T2017 as with the general reserve. The reserve is not available on a transfer to a corporation which is *de facto* controlled by the transferor.

Deferral of Recapture

If recapture of capital cost allowance would arise on the disposition of the property replaced, a related election will defer the recapture to the extent the proceeds of depreciable property are reinvested in replacement depreciable property (subsection 13(4)). To invoke the capital gain deferral is automatically to invoke the depreciable property deferral, and vice versa. This means that if there seems to be a recapture and a section 44 election is made, the recapture calculation will be governed (and usually deferred) under the replacement property rules for depreciable property. This is discussed at ¶846.

(ITA: 13(4), (4.1); 44(1), (4), (5), (7); IT-259R4 [Archived]; IT-491 [Archived])

[¶524] REALLOCATION OF PROCEEDS OF BUSINESS PROPERTY

Where real property is disposed of in circumstances where the election described in ¶523 will be made, and where the property disposed of is a property used in a business consisting of a building and land (or an interest therein), and the land is either subjacent to or immediately contiguous to and necessary for the use of the building, the taxpayer can further elect in the year the replacement property was purchased to change the allocation of the proceeds between land and building for the purposes of calculating and deferring any capital gain (subsection 44(6)). It would normally be desirable to make this further election where the proceeds of disposition otherwise determined on one component (e.g., land) exceed the cost of the replacement property for that component.

Example

Fran Chan sold her hotel (land and building) in Calgary, Alberta for $400,000 (cost = $200,000) and purchased a replacement property in Banff for $480,000. She may elect to defer the capital gain as follows:

Calgary land and building — replaced:

	Land	Building
Proceeds of disposition	$100,000	$300,000
ACB/capital cost	$ 50,000	$150,000
Replacement property cost — Banff	$ 80,000	$400,000

Computation of capital gain:

Lesser of:			
(a)	Proceeds of disposition	$100,000	$300,000
	Less: ACB/capital cost	(50,000)	(150,000)
	Capital gain otherwise determined	$ 50,000	$150,000
(b)	Proceeds of disposition	$100,000	$300,000
	Less: Cost of replacement property	(80,000)	(400,000)
	Proceeds not re-invested	$ 20,000	Nil

The proceeds not re-invested are a capital gain.

However, Ms. Chan may elect to reduce the proceeds of disposition of the land by $20,000 so that the proceeds of disposition otherwise determined will be $80,000 for purposes of the rollover rule in ¶523. The reduction in the proceeds of disposition of the land would be added to the proceeds of disposition of the building.

This election to shift the allocation of proceeds between land and building must be made in the return for the year the replacement property is acquired.

(ITA: 44(1)(e)(i)(A), (6); IT-259R4 [Archived])

[¶524.05] *Business Expansion*

In 2002, the CRA announced a modification of its policies concerning the replacement property rules in the context of a business expansion. The change is discussed in detail in the context of capital cost allowance under "Business Expansion" at ¶846.25, but those comments apply equally to the capital gain aspect of the replacement property rules discussed here.

[¶525] INVOLUNTARY DISPOSITIONS

Special rules may apply to proceeds received for capital property that has been disposed of involuntarily (paragraph 44(1)(*a*)). These rules apply to:

- Insurance proceeds for capital property which was lost or destroyed;
- Other compensation for capital property which was destroyed;
- Compensation for capital property which was stolen; and
- Compensation for property taken under statutory authority (typically by expropriation, but bankruptcy or corporate squeeze-out under the authority of a *Corporations Act* are also possibilities), or the sale price of property sold to a person who has given notice of an intention to take the property under statutory authority. The property does not include shares of a corporation.

The first rule is that the date of disposition of the property and the date the proceeds for it are considered to be receivable will be the earliest of:

(1) the date that you agree with the settlement;

(2) the date on which the compensation is finally determined by a court or tribunal; or

(3) two years after the expropriation, loss or destruction if no claim, suit or appeal is launched by that date.

See subsection 44(2).

If you emigrate from Canada or die between the time the property is actually lost, taken, or destroyed and the time it would be considered to have been disposed of under the above rule, the property will be deemed to have been disposed of at the time of emigration or death, presumably for proceeds based on the amount of any compensation received to that date plus the fair market value of your uncollected rights to or claim for compensation at that time.

In a technical opinion (CRA Document No. 2007-0227601E5), the CRA examined a case where a taxpayer's property had been inadvertently destroyed by a contractor working on it. The contractor signed over the proceeds of insurance to the taxpayer, who then sued the contractor for the additional value of the property. The issue was whether the insurance proceeds were reported separately when received or only when the suit was settled. It was the CRA's opinion that there can be only one time of disposition, and that in the circumstances this would be on final settlement (assuming the suit had been filed in good faith).

Election to Defer Gain

The second rule is that if a replacement capital property is acquired within a specified time frame, part or all of any capital gain which would otherwise be determined may be excluded in calculating your income and instead will be applied to reduce the cost of the replacement property (subsection 44(1)). The second rule is also met where you are given replacement property within the specified time by an expropriating authority as compensation for the expropriated property.

The specified time frame requires that the replacement property be acquired before the later of:

- the end of the second taxation year following the taxation year in which the original property is deemed to be disposed of; and
- 24 months after the end of the taxation year in which the disposition occurred.

A replacement property must meet several specific tests:

(1) it is reasonable to conclude that the property was acquired by the taxpayer to replace the former property;

(2) it must be property acquired by the taxpayer and used by the taxpayer or a person related to the taxpayer for a use that is the same as or similar to the use to which the taxpayer or a person related to the taxpayer put the former property (but note that an election to change the wording of this condition is possible in circumstances outlined below);

(3) where the former property was used in a business (rather than merely to produce income — i.e., rental

property) by the taxpayer or by a related person, the replacement property must be acquired for use in the same or a similar business or by a person related to the taxpayer for such a purpose;

(4) where the former property was taxable Canadian property as defined in ¶2040, the replacement property must also be taxable Canadian property. Taxable Canadian property is essentially Canadian real property or any capital property used in carrying on business in Canada. It also includes, as a practical matter, Canadian resource and timber resource properties, and a number of other items listed at ¶2040 which, however, are intangible and would not normally seem subject to involuntary disposition; and

(5) if the former property was taxable Canadian property which was not treaty-protected property, the replacement property must similarly be taxable Canadian property which is not treaty-protected property. Treaty-protected property is essentially property from which the gain (if any) would be exempt from Canadian income tax under a Canadian tax treaty if disposed of at the time in question (see Chapter 20).

The point of the rule in (4) appears to be to prevent the capital gain deferral from operating where a property used or situated in Canada is replaced with a property used or situated outside Canada. However, it appears that a Canadian resident can use the replacement rules to replace a former foreign property with a new similar property.

The tests in (3) and (4) are conditional; that is, if the conditions do not apply the tests need not be met.

Unlike the comparable rule for voluntary replacements at ¶523, the involuntary disposition rule can apply whether or not the former property was used in a business, or indeed whether or not it earned income. This appears to be true notwithstanding rule (4), since that rule is conditional on a property being taxable Canadian property in the first place. If it were not, the rule would not apply at all. Thus, if an insured bracelet were lost and replaced by using the insurance proceeds, the election would appear to be available. The CRA has confirmed this in the context of a vacation property. It does draw the line, however, at replacements of vacant land, taking the position that a non-use of property cannot be brought within the concept of the same or a similar use. See Wolters Kluwer Window on Canadian Tax, ¶2682.

The replacement property may be acquired before or after the original property is considered to be disposed of, but if acquired before, it must still be owned at the date of the original property's deemed disposition in order for the special rule to apply.

To obtain the full benefit of this rule, the replacement property must have a cost equal to or greater than the amount of the compensation received. If the compensation proceeds exceed the cost of the replacement property, this excess must be reported as a capital gain in the year the original property is considered to be disposed of to the extent that a capital gain arose on the disposition. If a portion of the proceeds from the disposition is not due until after the end of the year in which the disposition takes place, the capital gain may be further deferred by claiming a reserve for proceeds not due as discussed at ¶581. This reserve, like the general capital gains reserve, must be claimed in prescribed form filed with the return for the year it is claimed.

If the special rule applies, the cost of the replacement property is reduced at the later of the time when it is acquired or the time when the original property is deemed to be disposed of, by the amount of the capital gain on the original property which would otherwise be determined minus any portion of that gain which is required to be reported in your income tax return.

If the original property was a depreciable asset, and the replacement property was acquired before the original property is deemed to have been disposed of, the actual cost of the replacement property will qualify for capital cost allowance until the year of the original property's deemed disposition (see ¶845). At that time, the undepreciated capital cost of the class in which the replacement property was placed must be reduced by the amount of the capital gain on the original property which is subject to this special rule. If this reduction is greater than the undepreciated capital cost of the class, all of the excess must be reported in the year that the original property is considered to have been disposed of (which is not necessarily the year in which the deferred capital gain is otherwise applied to reduce undepreciated capital cost), as proceeds of disposal of a depreciable property of the class to which the replacement property belongs. Thus it may not be beneficial to make this election in all circumstances, especially if an instalment reserve is available to reduce proceeds of disposition (see ¶581).

Where under the first special rule, a disposition is considered to occur, the second rule (capital gain deferral) will be applied only if you file an election with your return for the year in which you acquired the replacement property. The CRA has not advised how this election is to be made. Presumably, a note and supporting calculation attached to your return will suffice. If the replacement property is acquired in the first or second year following the involuntary disposition, you could file an amended return for the previous years and claim an appropriate refund.

Note that where the former property was depreciable property, an election for purposes of capital gain deferral applies also for purposes of recaptured depreciation (see Chapter 8) and *vice versa*. See ¶845 for similar rules relating to the recapture. See ¶523 for an example of a similar replacement calculation.

Former interpretation bulletin IT-271R, "Expropriations — Time and proceeds of disposition", was archived (¶283) in 2004, meaning it can no longer be relied on as policy. Nevertheless, used with caution, it still presents a reasonable overview of the issues.

(ITA: 13(4), (4.1); 44(1), (2), (4); IT-259R4 [Archived])

[¶526] DISPOSITIONS TO TRUSTS

If you transfer property to a trust, the general rule is that you are deemed to have disposed of the property at fair market value (paragraph 69(1)(*b*)). However, there are some exceptions where a partial or full "rollover" may apply, in which case you will recognize no gain or a partial gain.

Possible Rollovers

If you transfer property to a spousal or common-law trust, joint spousal or common-law partner trust, alter ego trust, or self-benefit trust where the transfer of the property to the trust did not result in a change in the beneficial ownership of the property, you are deemed to dispose of the property at its cost (subsection 73(1)). However, you can elect out of this rollover, in which case you will have a deemed disposition at fair market value.

Similarly, if you transfer a property to a trust under a "qualifying disposition" (section 107.4), you can elect to have a full rollover, or partial rollover (proceeds between your cost and fair market value). A qualifying disposition by a natural individual is a disposition to a trust that does not result in any change in the beneficial ownership of the property, and that meets the following conditions:

- the proceeds would not be determined under any other provision of the Act if it were read without reference to sections 69 and 73;
- the trust is resident in Canada;
- immediately after the disposition, there is no absolute or contingent right of a person as a beneficiary (determined with reference to subsection 104(1.1)) other than the contributor;
- for natural individuals, the disposition cannot be to a trust described in any of paragraphs (*a*) to (*e*.1) of the definition "trust" in subsection 108(1) (RRSPs and other deferred income plans governed by trusts);
- the disposition is not part of a series of transactions or events that includes either the subsequent acquisition of a capital or income interest in a personal trust for consideration given to the trust, or the disposition of a capital or income interest in a personal trust other than a disposition solely as a consequence of a distribution from the trust in satisfaction of all or part of that interest;
- the disposition is not part of a series of transactions or events that begins after June 5, 2000 and includes the transfer to the trust, as consideration for the acquisition of a capital interest therein, of property intended to fund a distribution (other than a distribution in satisfaction of a capital interest in the trust);
- the contributor receives no consideration for the transfer other than an interest as beneficiary of the trust or the assumption of debt by the trust that is secured by the transferred property; and
- subsection 73(1) does not apply to the disposition, and would not apply to the disposition if no election had been made under that subsection and section 73 were read without reference to subsection 73(1.02) — therefore, for example, a qualifying disposition cannot be made to a trust that would otherwise qualify as an alter ego trust but for the fact that the contributor had not reached the age of 65.

[¶526.05] *Dispositions of Mutual Fund Trust Units*

In general, where you are dealing with a mutual fund trust as an investor, the ordinary rules at ¶491 should continue to apply. The Department of Finance technical notes offer the following examples of the rules:

Example

Joseph buys 1,000 units of XYZ Mutual Fund on December 23, 2000 for $10,000. XYZ has not made an election under subsection 132.11(1) to have a December 15 year end. XYZ makes $400 of its income for its 2000 taxation year payable to Joseph on December 31, 2000. However, without making any cash distribution of the income, XYZ issues 42 additional units on that date in satisfaction of the $400 of income payable. In November 2001, Joseph disposes of his 1,042 units for $10,700.

Results:

(1) Under the trust rules (subsection 104(13)), Joseph is required to include $400 in computing his income for the 2000 taxation year.

(2) The right to enforce the payment of the distribution is treated as part of Joseph's capital interest in the trust. However, under the revised definition of disposition, there is no disposition of that part of the capital interest on the satisfaction of the right through the issuing of shares.

(3) No part of the ACB of the original interest is allocated to the right to the income payable when the right is satisfied (subsection 43(3)). Without taking into account the identical properties rule in ¶512 this ensures that the ACB of Joseph's original 1,000 units will remain $10,000 once the right to income is satisfied, notwithstanding that Joseph acquired the units late in the 2000 taxation year.

(4) The 42 additional units issued in satisfaction of the right to income are acquired at a cost of $400 because the rules (subsection 248(25.3)) ensure that the cost of the units issued directly in satisfaction of the income payable is equal to that amount. Consequently, the total ACB of the 1,042 units at the time of the disposition is $10,400.

(5) Consequently, the capital gain realized on the subsequent disposition of all of the units is $300.

Note that this is pretty much what you might expect in the abstract: Joseph bought units for $10,000 and sold them for $10,700, of which $400 had already been taxed. The remaining $300 is capital gain on disposition.

Suppose Joseph sold to a third party half his interest in trust after the declaration of his right to $400 income but before the issuance of shares in satisfaction. The selling price is $5,700, and in effect he sells 5,000 units plus the right to payment of $400. The results are:

(6) As before, Joseph must include $400 in computing his income for the 2000 taxation year.

(7) The right to enforce payment of the $400 amount by the trust is treated as part of his capital interest in the trust (under subsection 108(1)). Per (2), above, a payment by the trust in satisfaction of the right would not be a disposition. However, the sale of the 500 units in the trust is a disposition of part of the capital interest that includes a part of her right to enforce payment from the trust.

(8) As the ACB of the right disposed of is nil, Joseph realizes a gain of $200 (i.e., 1/2 of the total amount to which the right to enforce relates) upon its sale to the third party. Specific rules (subsection 248(25.4)) should apply in these circumstances to provide a $200 bump in the ACB of the capital interest in the trust otherwise determined immediately before the disposition. Consequently, the total ACB of the 500 units sold is $5,200 (i.e., $5,000 + $200). Note that the bump appears to attach to the capital interest sold and not to the whole capital interest; the Department of Finance example is essential to make this point, since it is perhaps not self-evident in the statute.

(9) The capital gain realized on the disposition of the 500 units is $500 ($5,700 - $5,200). In effect, in this case has retained $200 of the $400 distribution but been taxed on $400. The $200 adds to the cost base of the units sold (it might more logically have been attributed to the right being sold, but never mind). Presumably the $5,000 ACB of the units Joseph retains is increased by the $200 he will receive in satisfaction of the right he didn't sell when that right is satisfied.

(ITA: 43(3); 54 "disposition", "proceeds of disposition"; 104; 107; 108; 248(1) "disposition"; 248(25.1)–248(25.4); ITR: 6754)

[¶526.10] *Deferred Income Trusts*

Where you are dealing with a retirement trust such as an RRSP or RRIF, or with a trust which is a tax-free savings account (TFSA), transfers of property to the trust should continue to be dispositions (¶2627.65) and transfers from the trust are acquired at fair market value, subject to various rollover provisions (¶1021). Note, however, that a stop-loss rule prevents recognition of capital losses on property transferred from an individual to an RRSP, RRIF, or TFSA.

Transfers from one deferred income trust to another, such as from an RRSP to another RRSP or a RRIF, will not normally involve dispositions unless the annuitant changes, although it may be possible to elect to have a taxable event rather than a non-taxable one. Transfers between one TFSA and another will not normally involve dispositions.

(ITA: 40(2)(*c*), (*g*); 69(1)(*b*)(iii); 248(1) "disposition" (*f*)(vi))

[¶526.15] *In General*

Dealings with personal trusts, and especially non-resident trusts, generally involve tax planning considerations beyond the scope of this book, although some comments will be found in chapters 4 and 25.

See also the comments on trusts at ¶526.

[¶527] TIMING: WHEN DO YOU HAVE A DISPOSITION OF PROPERTY?

As previously mentioned in ¶500, a disposition of property normally occurs for tax purposes when you are entitled to receive proceeds of disposition.

Except in special circumstances for dispositions of certain business properties (¶523), involuntary dispositions (¶525) and deemed dispositions discussed below, a disposition normally will take place when title to property passes from the vendor to the purchaser.

The disposition date for stock and bond transactions through a stock market is considered to be the "settlement date". The settlement date is usually three business days after the "trade date" (the day your broker executed your sell order). This means if you sell a security at least three business days before the last business day of the year, the transaction will be reported in that taxation year. Thus, taxes on gains may be deferred one year by delaying a sell order for a few days so that the settlement date falls within the subsequent taxation year. On the other hand, if you are selling to realize capital losses to offset prior gains in the year, you must be careful, in view of the holidays preceding December 31, to leave sufficient business days for settlement to ensure that you have a current year loss.

(ITA: 54 "proceeds of disposition"; 248(1) "disposition"; IT-460 [Archived])

DEEMED DISPOSITIONS

[¶528] DEEMED DISPOSITION OF PROPERTY

As previously mentioned, to have a capital gain or capital loss, you must first have a disposition of property. As a general rule, any transfer of ownership of a property will constitute a disposition, although some exceptions exist.

Deemed Dispositions

Obviously, if you have sold a property, you have a disposition. Other events which are deemed to result in a disposition of property, even though there may have been no actual sale, include the following (subsection 248(1) "disposition"):

- An election to have a deemed disposition of property owned on February 22, 1994, to take advantage of the capital gains exemption; note that the election could be made up to April 30, 1997 for individuals.
- A redemption, cancellation, or acquisition of a share, bond, debenture, note, certificate, mortgage, hypothec, agreement of sale or similar property, or an interest therein.
- The settlement or cancellation of a debt or other amount owing to you (see ¶563).
- The expiry of an option held by you to acquire or dispose of property (see ¶561).
- The conversion of a share to another share in a corporation because of an amalgamation or a merger of corporations (see ¶536).
- The making of a gift (see ¶530).
- The death of a taxpayer (see ¶530 and ¶1920).
- Emigration from Canada (see ¶534).
- A change of use of an asset (see ¶513).
- An expropriation, theft or destruction of an asset (see ¶525).
- Negative ACB (see ¶535).
- The repurchase of an outstanding bond or debenture of the taxpayer.
- Property contributed to an RRSP, deferred profit sharing plan, employees profit sharing plan, registered retirement income fund or a registered home ownership savings plan. If a loss has arisen, see ¶579.
- A share of the capital stock of a corporation which has become bankrupt (see ¶564 and ¶580).
- Share-for-share exchange (see ¶537).

- In some situations, where the terms of a security have been changed (see ¶539).

- A number of transactions with respect to a life insurance policy, including taking out policy loans, may constitute a disposition, but the proceeds are treated as investment income rather than capital gains; see ¶981.

Where there is a deemed disposition of property there is no sale price which can be used to determine what the proceeds of disposition are. Therefore special rules are required to establish the amount which you are deemed to have received in these situations. These rules are explained in ¶530 to ¶538.

(ITA: 248(1) "disposition")

[¶529] TRANSACTIONS NOT REGARDED AS DISPOSITIONS OF PROPERTY

There are certain transactions which are not considered to be dispositions of property, although there may appear to have been a legal disposition of the property in question. These include the following (subsection 248(1) "disposition"):

- A transfer of legal ownership for the purpose only of securing a debt or a loan, or for the purpose of returning property that has been used as security for a debt or loan.

- A change of legal ownership of a property where there is no change in beneficial ownership, except where the transfer is to a trust for the benefit of the transferor. However, where you have transferred property to an RRSP, deferred profit sharing plan or similar plan under which you are a beneficiary, there is a disposition, but no loss may be recognized (¶579).

See also ¶526 regarding transfers to trusts.

(ITA: 248(1) "disposition")

[¶530] GIFTS AND BEQUESTS

General Rule

A gift or bequest of capital property is deemed to be a disposition of the property resulting in a realization of capital gain or capital loss by the person who has made the gift or died and left the bequest.

The proceeds of disposition are deemed to be the fair market value of the property at the time of the gift or bequest. The recipient is deemed to have acquired the property at its fair market value.

Exceptions

However, there are various exceptions to this general rule, which include the following:

(1) A gift or bequest to a spouse or common-law partner (see ¶531).

(2) A bequest of depreciable property (see ¶532).

(3) A gift of certain types of property to charity (see ¶533).

(4) A transfer of farm or fishing property or depreciable property on the death of a farmer to his or her child, grandchild or great grandchild (see ¶1923). For the purpose of calculating any subsequent capital gain on a sale by the child, the child will be deemed to have owned the property on December 31, 1971 if the transferor owned the property on December 31, 1971.

(5) A transfer of farm land or depreciable property by a farmer to his or her child, grandchild or great grandchild by sale or gift during his or her lifetime. Rules similar to those outlined in ¶1923 apply. However, where the transfer is to a child under 18 and the child sells the property before reaching 18 and while the transferor is still alive any resulting gain or loss will be treated as that of the transferor, not of the child (see ¶1759).

A gift of farm or fishing property or small business shares may be eligible for the capital gains exemption (¶502) to the extent the property qualifies in the hands of the donor and the donor has unused exemption available.

In any of the cases above, the recipient of a gift or bequest should have no immediate tax consequence; the only issue raised for the recipient is what his or her cost base will be when he or she disposes of the item in turn. At present, no province levies a provincial tax on gifts and bequests apart from the provincial share of taxes arising from the individual making the gift or bequest. That is, there is no separate inheritance or gift tax in addition to the taxes imposed under the rules above.

(ITA: 69(1); 70(5), (6), (9); 73(1), (3), (4), (5); 1(6)–(9))

[¶531] TRANSFERS TO A SPOUSE OR COMMON-LAW PARTNER

Rollover

Generally, in the case of a gift to your spouse or common-law partner (¶1113), the transfer is deemed to be a disposition of property, but the proceeds of disposition and the cost to your spouse or common-law partner are deemed to be equal to the ACB of the property to you (subsection 73(1)). This means that no capital gain or capital loss will arise at the time of the gift. (Where the property is depreciable property however, that is, property on which you claim capital cost allowance, you must see the special rules at ¶532.)

Any capital gain or capital loss will not be recognized until your spouse or common-law partner subsequently disposes of the property. At that time, any gain or loss must be reported for tax purposes.

A gift is also subject to these rules if it was made to a "spouse trust" created by you under the terms of which (1) your spouse or common-law partner will receive all income of the trust during his or her lifetime, or (2) no one other than your spouse or common-law partner can obtain any income or capital of the trust during your spouse's or common-law partner's lifetime. In addition, you and the trust must be resident in Canada at the time of the transfer.

A gift is also subject to these rules (disposition at ACB and a rollover of that cost base to the recipient) if the gift is made to a trust created after 1999 by an individual at least 65 years old at the time the trust is established, provided the trust is for the exclusive benefit of the individual (an alter ego trust) or is for the joint benefit of the individual and the individual's spouse or common-law partner. In the case of an alter ego trust, the rollover does not operate if the trust has elected to have a 21-year deemed disposition rule apply rather than having a deemed disposition at death, which is normal for such an alter ego trust.

Election out of Rollover

You may elect, by attaching a note to your tax return, not to have the provision apply which allows the property to be transferred at the ACB; if you make this election the proceeds of disposition to you and the cost to your spouse or common-law partner (or trust as described above) will be equal to the fair market value. Normally, any loss will be denied under the superficial loss rules (¶579), unless the transfer occurs as a result of your death.

Similar rules apply on death (see ¶1922).

[¶531.05] *Attribution Rules*

Attribution of Future Capital Gains or Losses

If you have loaned or transferred (directly or indirectly) to your spouse or common-law partner, or to a person who has since become your spouse or common-law partner, and your spouse or common-law partner later disposes of the property, subsection 74.2 of the Act provides that any taxable capital gains on such property for the year (net of allowable capital losses on such property for the year) are included in your income (i.e., attributed to you). If losses so calculated for a year exceed gains, the loss is similarly attributed to you. The same rules apply to net listed personal property gains on loaned or transferred property.

Exceptions to Attribution and Related Rules

There are important exceptions. The attribution rules do not apply to transfers made where fair market value consideration is received for the transfer and you have elected out of the rollover that would otherwise occur. Similarly, the rules do not apply to loans (whenever made) if the lesser of market or prescribed rates of interest are paid on the loan. (Prescribed rates change quarterly, and the rate in force when the loan was made is crucial. Accordingly, a record of the applicable rate should be kept with the records of the transaction. Prescribed rates are set out in a table at ¶80, preceding Chapter 1. Note that the prescribed rate for this purpose does not include the 4% added to interest rates on amounts owing to the government.) Interest must be paid at least annually within 30 days of year-end to qualify the loan for this exception.

The attribution rules do not apply to gains or losses attributable to a period

(1) following the death of the transferor or transferee;

(2) throughout which the transferor is not resident in Canada; or

(3) after the transferee ceases to be the transferor's spouse or common-law partner.

Where the transferee has not (yet) ceased to be a spouse or common-law partner, but the couple is living separate and apart by reason of marriage (partnership) breakdown, the attribution rules do not apply if the couple jointly elect not to have them apply. The election may be filed in any year after the separation and will apply for that year and later years.

If the recipient spouse or common-law partner emigrates from Canada while holding the property, there would in the normal course of events be a deemed disposition on emigration (¶2153), with attribution of the resulting gain or loss. There is a special rule to say that on an actual subsequent disposition, the spouses/partners can jointly elect to have the attribution rules apply to the actual rather than the deemed disposition. There is authority to reassess statute-barred years to give effect to this election (without affecting interest owing to or from the taxpayers for the interim period). The purpose is apparently to facilitate the operation of the post-emigration loss rules.

Note that there is no attribution of capital gain or loss on property transferred to minors, except where the farm property has been transferred to a child on a rollover basis as described at ¶1759 item (a). In that case, the entire gain on a disposition by the child before the year the child reaches the age of 18 will be taxed to the transferor. Transfers to a trust for a related minor (child, grandchild, niece or nephew) are allocated to the minor for purposes of the attribution rules, but capital gain or loss is not then attributed to the transferor.

For income considerations on transferred property, see ¶977. Capital gains attributed to the transferor may be eligible for the capital gains exemption of the transferor only.

(ITA: 70(6); 73(1); 74.2; 74.3; 74.5; IT-209R [Archived]; IT-325R2 [Archived]; IT-511R [Archived])

[¶532] TRANSFERS OF DEPRECIABLE PROPERTY

Depreciable property (property used to earn income and on which you may claim capital cost allowance as described in Chapter 8) transferred to a spouse or common-law partner or spouse trust (¶531) by way of a gift during your life (and not by bequest) is deemed to be transferred at your "undepreciated capital cost" (UCC). You may elect jointly with your spouse/common-law partner not to have this rule apply, in which case the transfer is considered to occur at fair market value. Where the transfer occurs at an undepreciated capital cost, cost and depreciation are also deemed transferred. In either case, attribution rules will apply as described above.

Example

> John acquired a computer for use in his business for $400. He claimed depreciation of $144 and later gave the typewriter to his wife Mary. No election was filed. John is deemed to have proceeds of disposition of $256 and so has no immediate gain or recapture. Mary is deemed to have acquired a computer with an undepreciated capital cost of $256 and a cost of $400. If Mary sells the computer for $450, it appears that the $144 recapture and $50 capital gain are attributed to John. If Mary first uses the computer in her business and claims a further $50 depreciation, that should not be attributed to John on Mary's disposition on the assumption that the recapture is business income, which does not attribute. If John and Mary elected, the transfer would be deemed to occur at $400 and John would have immediate recapture of $144.

"Undepreciated capital cost" is a term explained in Chapter 8 (¶801). If you make a gift and retain other property of a similar kind, which is included in the same "capital cost class" (see ¶866), the undepreciated capital cost of the transferred property is to be determined by calculating the ratio of the fair market value of the transferred property to the fair market value of all the property in the class immediately before the transfer, and applying this ratio to the total undepreciated capital cost of the class immediately before the transfer.

The effect of deeming the transfer price to be undepreciated capital cost is that no tax will be imposed at the time of a gift to your spouse or common-law partner. Any gain or loss will be recognized upon a subsequent disposition by your spouse or common-law partner, subject to the rules at ¶531.

A gift of depreciable property to someone other than your spouse or common-law partner is considered to be a disposition at the fair market value of the property at that time. Therefore, a capital gain can arise and there may also be a recapture of capital cost allowances as discussed at ¶843. The recipient of the gifted property is considered to have a cost of the property equal to its fair market value unless you are not at arm's length in which case the recipient's cost for capital cost allowance purposes is limited as described at ¶813.

Transfers of depreciable property on death are subject to similar but somewhat more elaborate rules; these are discussed at ¶1920 and ¶1922.

(ITA: 69(1); 70(5), (6); 72(2); 73(1), (2); IT-209R [Archived]; IT-511R [Archived])

[¶533] GIFTS TO CHARITIES

General Rule

In general, when you make a gift of property to charity, you are deemed to dispose of the property at its fair market value (paragraph 69(1)(*b*)), and you must recognize any gain or loss which arises on the deemed disposition.

If you donate capital property to a charity, in certain circumstances you can choose to value the donated property for purposes of calculating your capital gain at any amount between its ACB to you and its fair market value at the time the donation is made. See ¶1290.

The donation rules are discussed in detail in Chapter 12.

Donations Exempt from Capital Gains Taxation

Gifts of publicly traded securities to charities incur zero taxable capital gains on the disposition of the security (see ¶1290d.05 and paragraph 38(*a*.1) of the Act).

Similarly, there is no tax on gains on the exchange of securities where the securities received are qualified publicly traded securities, provided (i) the exchange occurs pursuant to an exchange feature of the shares given up, (ii) no consideration is received on the exchange except the exchanged shares, and (iii) the publicly traded securities received are donated to a qualified donee not more than 30 days after the exchange. A similar rule will apply where partnership interests are exchanged for publicly traded shares, subject to rules intended to limit the capital gains exemption to gains that reflect economic appreciation of the partnership interest and not gains arising from ACB reductions to the partnership interest. See ¶1290d.07. On the other hand, gifts made of non-qualified securities issued by persons (typically corporations) with which you do not deal at arm's length may yield capital gains but no tax credit for the gift; the gain in these circumstances can be deferred for up to five years. See ¶1290d.

Gifts of ecologically sensitive land are generally exempt from tax on any capital gain realized on the gift. See ¶1268d and paragraph 38(*a*.2) of the Act.

Similarly, if you have transferred Canadian cultural property to a Canadian museum, art gallery or other institution, a resultant gain will generally not be taxable. See ¶547, ¶1268, and subparagraph 39(1)(*a*)(i.1)).

Flow-through Shares

Gifts of publicly listed flow-through shares are generally subject to taxable capital gains treatment by virtue of subsection 40(12). More particularly, if a flow-through share is acquired pursuant to an agreement issued on or after March 22, 2011 and the flow-through share is subsequently donated to a qualified donee so that subparagraph 38(a.1)(i) or (iii) (described above) would apply to exempt the capital gain realized on the donation of the shares, the donor will be deemed to have a capital gain from a disposition of another capital property at that time. The capital gain will be equal to the lesser of

- the amount of the taxpayer's "exemption threshold" (generally, a pool of the actual cost to the taxpayer of flow-through shares acquired after the later of March 22, 2011 or the taxpayers fresh-start date, less prior capital gains from the disposition of the shares or identical properties); or
- the total capital gains from the disposition of the actual property.

The effect of this rule is that the capital gains exemption on donations of publicly listed flow-through shares will only be permitted to the extent that the realized capital gain from the donation exceeds the actual cost paid for the flow-through share as opposed to the determined nil cost base of the flow-through share.

Historical Information

Subsection 40(12) applies to dispositions made after March 22, 2011.

Other Miscellaneous Rules

If you are an artist donating works you have created to charity, see ¶1291.

If you are donating items which are not capital property but inventory, see ¶1290g.

(ITA: 39(1)(*a*)(i.1); 38(*a*.1), (*a*.2); 110(2.1); 1(6))

[¶534] EFFECT OF EMIGRATION

If you emigrate from Canada to take up residence elsewhere, you may be deemed to have disposed of certain capital property which you owned at the date of departure, whether or not you have actually disposed of this property. Details are provided in Chapter 21.

(ITA: 128.1(4))

[¶535] NEGATIVE ADJUSTED COST BASE

As discussed at ¶506 the ACB of a property is its original cost (or deemed cost) plus or minus various possible adjustments. It is possible for deductions from the original cost to produce a negative ACB.

If the result of any event during the year is to produce a negative ACB, this negative amount will constitute a capital gain (**unless**, in some cases, the property involved is a partnership interest; see ¶1842).

The resulting capital gain must be reported as such on that year's tax return, but is added to the ACB of the property so that it will reduce any subsequent gain or increase any subsequent loss.

Example

You acquired shares of F Company in 1988 for $1,000 and over the following years you have received a series of tax-free dividends which the company indicated would reduce the ACB of your shares. At the end of last year, you had received $1,000 of such dividends, so your adjusted cost was exactly nil. This year you receive another such distribution in the amount of $200. You are required to report a capital gain as follows:

Cost of shares	$1,000
All prior year reductions	1,000
Closing prior year ACB	Nil
Less: Current year reduction of cost base	$200
Capital gain	$(200)

The $200 is in determining your ACB so that for purposes of calculating any subsequent capital gain or loss your ACB will be "nil". The taxable portion of your capital gain would be eligible for the capital gains exemption (¶502) on the same basis as any other gain.

A capital gain is required to be reported and included in income even though events later in the year may increase the ACB of the property so that the base would again be a positive amount.

(ITA: 40(3); 53(1)(*a*))

[¶536] SHARE CONVERSIONS ON AMALGAMATIONS OR REORGANIZATIONS

When two or more corporations amalgamate or merge, their shareholders convert their shares in the predecessor companies to shares in the amalgamated or merged company. On a reorganization of capital, shareholders usually receive new securities in exchange for those previously held.

In the absence of special rules, this exchange of shares would be treated in the same way as a sale of shares at their fair market value, followed by an acquisition of different shares, also at their fair market value. Some share conversions resulting from amalgamations, mergers, or reorganizations will, in fact, have this result.

However, there are some special rules applicable to such share conversions, which in some cases will deem no disposition or acquisition of shares to have taken place, and in other cases will deem the disposition and acquisition to have taken place at the ACB of the original shares to the shareholder (generally under subsection 87(4))

The special rules are too complex to explain in a book of this scope and presumably the tax consequences to shareholders will be explained to them by the amalgamating, merging or reorganizing corporations. If you are a shareholder in an amalgamating, merging or reorganizing corporation, you should look to the corporation involved for such an explanation.

[¶536.05] *Foreign Mergers*

Where the rules permitting a tax-deferred exchange (rollover) of shares you held in predecessor corporations for shares in the merged or amalgamated corporations do apply, they can apply if all the predecessor corporations are Canadian corporations or if all the predecessor corporations are residents of the same foreign jurisdiction. Subsection 87(8) extends this rollover to mergers of corporations in different foreign jurisdictions.

(ITA: 54 "adjusted cost base" (*b*); 86; 87)

[¶536c] FOREIGN SPIN-OFFS

In general terms, section 86.1 allows a tax deferral, generally on an elective basis, on certain foreign distributions of spin-off shares by a foreign corporation that are received by Canadian resident shareholders of the foreign corporation.

A spin-off is a divisive reorganization under U.S. tax rules in which you receive shares in a newly created (spun-off) company based on your original shareholding. There is no precise equivalent in Canadian tax law.

The foreign spin-off rules permit you to exclude from income an amount in respect of an eligible distribution of spin-off shares. The cost base of the new (spun-off) shares to you is not their fair market value as otherwise provided; rather, the cost of the original share which generated the distribution of the spin-off share will be allocated between the surviving and new shares.

Eligible Distribution

A distribution of spin-off shares to a taxpayer is an eligible distribution only if a number of conditions are met:

First, the distribution to the taxpayer must be because the taxpayer owns common shares in the distributing corporation (i.e., the "original shares").

Second, the distribution to the taxpayer must consist solely of common shares of the capital stock of another corporation owned by the distributing corporation (i.e., the "spin-off shares"); the distribution to the taxpayer must not include non-share consideration.

Third, in the case of a distribution made by a corporation in the United States:

(1) both the distributing corporation and the spun-off corporation (the issued shares of which are being spun-off) must be residents of the United States at the time of the distribution and must never have been resident in Canada;

(2) the taxpayer's original shares must be included in a class of stock that is widely held and actively traded on a prescribed stock exchange (section 3201 of the *Canadian Income Tax Regulations* — see ¶2618) in the United States at the time of the distribution or are required to be and in fact have been registered with the SEC under U.S. securities law; and

(3) the shareholders of the distributing corporation that are resident in the United States must not be taxable in respect of the distribution under the United States *Internal Revenue Code.*

Fourth, in the case of a distribution that is not made in the United States and that is prescribed by regulation 5600,

- both the distributing corporation and the spun-off corporation (the issued shares of which are being spun off) must be residents of the same foreign country, other than the United States, with which Canada has a tax treaty and those corporations must never have been resident in Canada;
- the taxpayer's original shares must be included in a class of stock that is widely held and actively traded on a prescribed stock exchange (section 3201 of the *Canadian Income Tax Regulations* — see ¶2618) at the time of the distribution;
- under the law of the country in which the distributing corporation is resident, the shareholders of the distributing corporation must not be taxable in respect of the distribution; and
- such terms and conditions as are considered appropriate in the circumstances with respect to the prescription must be met.

Fifth, the distributing corporation must provide to the CRA, before the later of the end of the sixth month following the day of distribution evidence satisfactory to it of certain matters including the type and fair market value of each property distributed to residents of Canada and the name and address of each resident of Canada that received property because of the distribution. Property that is distributed to residents of Canada includes, for example, property that is distributed to investment dealers resident in Canada as well as individual and corporate shareholders. The CRA maintains a section of its website called "Foreign spin-offs" (most recently found at www.cra-arc.gc.ca/tx/bsnss/tpcs/frgn-eng.html) which, among other things, lists spin-offs that have been approved by the CRA; however, the posted list includes only those distributing corporations that consent to have their transaction made public. It is the responsibility of the Canadian resident shareholder to contact the corporation that distributed the spin-off shares, either directly or through a broker, to determine if the shares meet the eligibility criteria for the tax deferral election.

Sixth, the taxpayer acquiring the spin-off shares must elect in writing with his or her tax return for the year in which distribution occurs (subject to the extensions and late-filing considerations discussed below) to have section 86.1 apply to the distribution, and must provide evidence satisfactory to the Minister of National Revenue on certain matters relating to the distribution and to the taxpayer. The late-filed election regulations (discussed under the subheading "Late-Filed Elections" at ¶268) apply to this election, permitting the CRA to exercise discretion to accept a late-filed election.

The information submitted by the taxpayer must establish, for example, the number, cost amount and fair market value of the taxpayer's original shares immediately before the distribution, and the number and the fair market value of the spin-off shares immediately after the distribution.

These rules provide for an amount to be both deducted from the cost amount of each original share and set as the cost of the corresponding spin-off share. That amount is determined by the formula:

$$A \times (B/C)$$

where

A is the cost amount to the taxpayer of the original share (determined without reference to these rules),

B is the fair market value of the spin-off share immediately after its distribution to the taxpayer,

C is the total of:

- the fair market value of the original share immediately after the distribution of the spin-off share to the taxpayer, and
- the fair market value of spin-off share immediately after its distribution to the taxpayer.

Example

John owns one original common share of DC Ltd. (resident in the United States), which distributes one spin-off share of SO Ltd. (also resident in the United States) on a per share basis to holders of common shares of DC Ltd. The cost amount of John's original share of DC Ltd. is $10 immediately before the distribution and its fair market value immediately after the distribution is $70. The fair market value of the SO Ltd. spin-off share is $30 immediately after the distribution.

The cost of the spin-off share and the reduction to cost of the original share is:

$$A \times (B/C)$$

where

A = $10

B = $30

C = $100 ($70 + $30).

Accordingly, the cost of the spin-off share in SO Ltd. is ($10 × (30/100)) = $3, and the $10 cost of the original share is reduced by $3 to $7.

(ITA: 86.1; ITR: 600(c); CRA Income Tax Technical News No. 28; Other Publications: CRA website at www.cra-arc.gc.ca/tx/bsnss/tpcs/frgn-eng.html; Department of Finance comfort letter re foreign spin-offs, reproduced in Wolters Kluwer Canadian Income Tax Act with Regulations in association with section 86.1)

[¶537] SHARE FOR SHARE EXCHANGE

If you receive treasury shares issued to you by a Canadian corporation in exchange for shares of another corporation that you are holding as capital property, and:

(1) you receive no consideration except for shares of one class of the Canadian corporation;

(2) before the exchange, you were dealing at arm's length with the Canadian corporation;

(3) after the exchange, you and/or persons with whom you do not deal at arm's length do not control the Canadian corporation nor own shares of the Canadian corporation representing more than 50% of the fair market value of all its issued shares; and

(4) an election is not filed under the rules relating to the transfer of property to a corporation ¶585),

a rollover provision (subsection 85.1(1)) may apply under which you are deemed to have disposed of the exchanged shares for proceeds equal to their ACB prior to the exchange and acquired the shares received in the exchange at the same amount. Any capital gain or loss will be deferred until the new shares are disposed of.

If the shares given up in the exchange were taxable Canadian property (¶2040), the shares received on the exchange will also be taxable Canadian property. This appears to be true whether or not you elect to defer the current capital gain.

You are not required to use this rollover provision if you do not wish to do so. If you do not, you will compute your capital gain or loss from the disposition of the exchanged shares by considering the proceeds of their disposition as being equal to their fair market value immediately before the exchange.

If you are a non-resident and the shares disposed of in the exchange are taxable Canadian property, the shares you receive in the exchange will be deemed to be taxable Canadian property to you.

(ITA: 85.1(1), (2); Income Tax Folio: S4-F5-C1 Share for Share Exchange)

[¶537.05] *Share Exchanges of Shares in Foreign Corporations*

Where a Canadian taxpayer holds shares in a foreign corporation which are exchanged for shares issued by another foreign company to the taxpayer, rollover rules in subsection 85.1(6) apply which are identical to the rules above where both companies are Canadian. As with the domestic share election, the rollover is automatic, unless you choose to include the resulting gain or loss in income.

(ITA: 85.1(5), (6))

[¶537.11] *Historical Information: Unit for Share Exchange (SIFTs) Before 2013*

Where a Canadian taxpayer disposes of a unit in a specified investment flow-through, ("SIFT") wind-up entity to a corporation in exchange for a share in the corporation, rollover rules apply if certain conditions are met (subsections 85.1(7) and (8)). The taxpayer must receive only shares as consideration; the shares issued to all unitholders must be of a single class; the corporation must be a taxable Canadian corporation; the disposition must occur within a specified 60-day period; subsections 85(1)or (2) do not apply to the disposition; and the disposition must occur before 2013.

If the above conditions apply to the transaction, there is a tax-deferred rollover of the SIFT unit for the exchanged share.

If the unit given up in the exchange was taxable Canadian property (¶2040), the share received on the exchange is deemed to be taxable Canadian property.

If the fair market value of the exchanged share exceeds the fair market value of the SIFT unit at the time of disposition, the excess is deemed to be an income inclusion as a shareholder benefit under section 15.

The rollover is applicable to dispositions that occur on or after July 14, 2008, and before 2013. For dispositions on or after December 20, 2007, and before July 14, 2008, an election can be filed by the corporation with the Minister to elect that the rollover on SIFT unit rules apply to a disposition, although the election must be made jointly with the taxpayer if the taxpayer and corporation had originally validly elected that subsections 85(1) or (2) apply to the disposition.

This rollover provision does not apply to a taxpayer who makes a joint election with the corporation under subsections 85(1) or (2) (discussed at ¶585), in which case a full or partial rollover can occur on the disposition of the unit to the corporation. Note also that a similar rollover applies where a SIFT trust distributes its shares in a taxable Canadian corporation to its beneficiaries on the redemption of the beneficiaries' units or interests in the trust (new subsection 107(3.1)).

(ITA: 15; 85.1(7), (8); 107(3), (3.1))

[¶537.15] *Other Share Exchange Provisions*

Shares received on a merger or amalgamation may receive rollover treatment under the rules at ¶536. For share exchanges of convertible securities, see ¶560. Shares can also be transferred to a corporation under the section 85 provisions discussed at ¶585.

[¶537d] DEMUTUALIZATION

Effective December 15, 1998, mutual life insurance companies are permitted to convert to stock companies. As discussed at ¶420, four companies did so, and it appears that virtually all transactions occurred in 1999.

Essentially, policyholders gave up rights in exchange for shares of the insurer (or a holding company) and/or other benefits. It is understood that in most cases the policyholder could choose between shares and other benefits, but this must be confirmed against the actual proposals made to the policyholders.

In any event, shares (or ownership rights in a mutual holding company) received in the course of a demutualization are capital assets received on a tax-free rollover basis with a cost to the policyholder of nil (subsection 139.1(4)) so that no capital gain will arise on the demutualization but eventual capital gain will arise on disposition of shares or rights received on the demutualization. In this case, the CRA has said there is no reportable transaction until the shares received are themselves disposed of, giving rise to capital gain.

Any benefits received on demutualization, other than (i) shares or rights to shares in the insurance company or a holding company thereof, or (ii) ownership rights in a mutual insurance holding company of the insurer, are "taxable conversion benefits" and are treated as dividends received, as discussed at ¶420. You should receive a T5 slip from the insurance company which should provide all necessary information for reporting these benefits.

Where your employer holds a policy for the benefit of employees, you may receive demutualization shares or other benefits through your employer rather than directly from the insurer; see ¶741.

(ITA: 139.1)

[¶538] SHARES ENTITLING SHAREHOLDER TO SPECIAL DIVIDENDS

Stock dividends are treated as dividends whether or not they are issued by a public company (see ¶406). However, shares received as stock dividends declared before May 24, 1985, but redeemed after May 23, 1985, will be treated as dividends on redemption (see ¶416).

Historical Information and Exceptions

There are five share issues outstanding where the dividends received before October 2, 1992 were not included in your income when received, but instead reduced the ACB of the shares. Capital gains treatment will occur when the shares are sold or the ACB of the shares becomes negative (see ¶535).

The five share issues outstanding are:

- The Algoma Steel Corporation, Limited, 8% Tax Deferred Preference Shares Series A;
- Aluminum Company of Canada, Limited, $2.00 Tax Deferred Retractable Preferred Shares;
- Brascan Limited, 81/2% Tax Deferred Preferred Shares Series A;
- Canada Permanent Mortgage Corporation, 63/4% Tax Deferred Convertible Preference Shares Series A; and
- Cominco Ltd., $2.00 Tax Deferred Exchangeable Preferred Shares Series A.

Under another set of rules, this time protecting transactions in process on May 23, 1985, the following shares give rise to capital gain rather than deemed dividend when redeemed (see ¶416):

- Reed Stenhouse Companies Limited, Class I Special Shares issued before January 1, 1986.

(ITA: 40(3); 51; 83(6); 84; 248; ITR: 2107 Tax-deferred Preferred Series; 6206 Prescribed Shares)

[¶539] CHANGE IN TERMS OF A SECURITY

A disposition resulting in a capital gain or loss may be considered to occur where the terms of a security have been altered to effect significant change in the nature of the security. There are no rules which have universal application to determine whether a change in terms is significant enough to be considered as a disposition.

However, the CRA has established a set of guidelines to help determine whether or not a disposition has occurred. Generally, an exchange of old share certificates for new certificates with no change in terms is not a disposition. Alternatively, a change in terms need not be accompanied by new certificates to be considered a disposition.

The following changes in the terms of debt securities normally result in a disposition:

- Change from interest bearing to non-interest bearing or *vice versa*;
- Change in maturity date or repayment schedule;
- An increase or decrease in the principal amount;
- Addition, alteration, or elimination of a premium payable upon retirement;
- A change in the debtor; and
- Conversion of a fixed interest bond to a bond in respect of which interest is payable only to the extent that the debtor has made a profit or *vice versa*.

Addition of a conversion feature or a change in the security underlying a debt do not in themselves result in a disposition.

The following changes in the terms of shares normally result in a disposition:

- A change in voting rights that results in a change in voting control of the corporation;
- A change in entitlement of preferred shares to share in assets upon dissolution (e.g., change in par value);
- Addition or deletion of a right to dividends beyond a fixed rate or amount; and
- A change from cumulative to non-cumulative rights to dividends or vice versa.

If the terms of the original share issue provided for amendments to the shares, there is generally no disposition because the possibility of a change was inherent in the issue.

This is not a complete list of changes in terms of securities that will result in dispositions. Moreover, the validity of the CRA's interpretation that a disposition occurs at all in these circumstances has been challenged by some tax experts. If you are in doubt as to whether a particular change has resulted in a disposition, the corporation issuing the security should be able to advise you of the tax implications. Alternatively, you should consult a tax specialist.

(ITA: 248(1) "disposition"; Tax Profile February 2008 - Tax Consequences of Debt Restructuring and Workouts in Canada; IT-448 [Archived])

[¶540] PAYMENTS FOLLOWING DISPOSITION

It may happen that after non-depreciable capital property has been disposed of, the former owner is called upon to make a repayment of assistance received in acquiring the property which assistance had originally reduced the ACB (¶507), resulting in an increased capital gain on the disposition. Under subsection 39(13), the repayments subsequent to disposition give rise to a deemed capital loss in the year of repayment. For purposes of calculating annual and cumulative limits under the lifetime capital gains exemption (¶502), the loss is deemed to arise from a disposition of property in the year of repayment.

(ITA: 39(13))

[¶540g] PARTITION OF PROPERTY

Special rules in subsection 248(20) deal with situations in which property owned jointly by two or more persons is re-divided in some fashion. Typically a partition of property occurs when real estate owned by two or more persons jointly or as tenants in common is divided into distinct parcels with each parcel held separately by one of the former joint owners. At its simplest, suppose Mr. A and Mr. B are joint owners of single land parcel XY. The land is partitioned into lot X and lot Y; Mr. A becomes sole owner of lot X and Mr. B of lot Y.

Partitions of property often occur on separation or divorce; the rules here do not apply to those situations; rather, there are special rules described at ¶2327.

Partitions (even in commercial rather than matrimonial situations) are often achieved by court order. These orders may, from a technical legal point of view, declare that they are completely retroactive, i.e., that Mr. A and Mr. B always owned lots X and Y respectively and were never joint owners. The income tax rules purport to override this legal fiction and impose a disposition or acquisition for tax purposes at fair market values at the time of the partition.

Thus, where the fair market value of an interest in a particular property is reduced following a partition, there is considered to be a disposition by the person at the time of partition of an interest representing that reduction. The converse is true where the value of an interest increases. Often these transactions represent trades of properties, and consequences must be considered separately for each property.

Example

Assume that A has a 50% share, as a co-owner, of property 1, which has a fair market value of $200,000, and of property 2, which has a fair market value of $250,000.

Following the partition of the properties, A becomes sole owner of property 1 in exchange for his interest in property 2. In addition, A receives $25,000 in consideration for the difference in the fair market value of the two properties.

Under the partition rules, A shall be deemed not to have disposed of the part of his interests in property 1 and 2 that corresponds to the following proportions and to have disposed of the other part:

	Property 1		Property 2	
Fair market value of his interest after partition	$200,000	= 200%	$0	= 0%
Fair market value of his interest before partition	$100,000		$125,000	

A will therefore be deemed not to have disposed of any part of his interest in property 1 and to have disposed of all of his interest in property 2.

A will further be deemed not to have acquired the part of his interest in property 1 that corresponds to the following proportion, and to have acquired the other part:

	Property 1	
Fair market value of his interest before partition	$100,000	= 50%
Fair market value of his interest after partition	$200,000	

A will therefore be deemed to have acquired a 50% interest in property 1.

The proceeds of disposition of A's interest in property 2 are equivalent to what he received upon the disposition, i.e., an interest in property 1 worth $100,000 plus $25,000. The cost of the interest that A acquired in property 1 is the value of the interest in property 2 that he gave in exchange, i.e., $100,000.

The rules do provide an exception where a property is subdivided and distributed (in whole or in part) in such a way that each owner preserves an undiminished share of the fair market value of the property (subsection 248(21)). The exception is expected to apply most commonly to the subdivision of land and buildings between joint owners.

(ITA: 248(20), (21))

[¶541] DIVIDED REAL ESTATE INTERESTS

An owner of real estate may create different interests in the property, and each interest would constitute a separate property. Section 43.1 of the Act deals with one such case. This is where the property is divided into a "life estate", which is the right to occupy, use and deal with the property during the lifetime of a particular individual, and a remainder estate, which is the right to full ownership of the whole property after the death of the individual by whose life the life estate is measured. (Where the individual whose life is the measure is not the same individual granted the use of the estate during that life, the interest is referred to as an estate *pur autre vie*, but the rules here are the same for a life estate measured by the life of the person granted use of the property and an estate *pur autre vie.*)

Holder of Life Estate

Where a person retains a life estate but disposes of a remainder estate (for example, by gifting the remainder to children) the rules make clear that for capital gains purposes the taxpayer is deemed to have disposed of the life interest at the time for proceeds of disposition equal to the fair market value of the life interest, and to have reacquired the life interest at the time for a cost of the fair market value of the life interest. The consequence is that the whole capital gain is realized at the time of the carve-out of the life interest, since the taxpayer is actually disposing of the remainder interest and is deemed to dispose of the life interest. The alternative prior to this rule seems to have been the deferral of recognition of capital gain on the life interest until eventual disposition of the melded remainder interest. That is, although there might have been recognition of a typically low-value remainder interest at the time of division, the life interest would have virtually no value just before death, and the CRA would not see any tax until the melded remainder interest was disposed of.

These rules do not apply if the remainder interest is disposed of to any of the charitable organizations described in ¶1265. The rules also do not apply to the transfer of a remainder interest in a farm property to a child if the special rollover rules (at ¶1759 item (a)) governing the transfer of farm property to a child during the life of the farmer transferor otherwise apply to the transfer.

To round out the rules, at the death of the measuring life (that is, when the life interest ceases and the holder of the remainder interest becomes entitled to the whole property, the life interest holder is deemed to have a disposition immediately before the death of the life interest for a value equal to its ACB. Accordingly, there will be no capital gain or loss to the life interest holder when the interest expires.

Holder of Remainder Interest

The remainder interest holder presumably acquires the remainder at its fair market value at the time of the carve-out. If the remainder holder is at arm's length from the life estate holder, there is no further adjustment to that cost base on the termination of the life estate. If, however, the remainder holder did not deal at arm's length with the life estate holder immediately before the death, then there is an addition to the ACB of the remainder holder at the termination of the life estate equal to the lesser of the ACB of the life estate immediately before termination and the amount by which the fair market value of the whole property exceeds the ACB of the remainder interest at that time.

(ITA: 43.1; 53(1)(o))

[¶542] TRANSITIONAL RULE: DEEMED CAPITAL GAIN ON TAX-DEFERRAL ELECTION FOR EMPLOYEE STOCK OPTIONS

At one time it was possible to elect to defer the taxation of a stock option benefit on a portion of the income arising on the exercise of the option. This is no longer possible. See ¶330.36.

[¶542a] SYNTHETIC DISPOSITIONS

Rules have been introduced to combat certain transactions in which taxpayers effectively disposed of or eliminated the economic risks associated with the ownership of property while retaining legal ownership of the property. Where the rules apply, the taxpayer will be deemed to dispose of the property for fair market proceeds and to reacquire it for the same amount. According to the Department:

> Certain financial arrangements (synthetic disposition transactions) seek to defer tax or obtain other tax benefits by allowing a taxpayer to economically dispose of a property while continuing to own it for income tax purposes.
>
> A synthetic disposition transaction typically involves a taxpayer entering into an arrangement under which the taxpayer eliminates their future risk of loss and opportunity for gain or profit in respect of a property and acquires another property (or a right to acquire another property) the value of which approximates what the taxpayer would have received as proceeds from disposing of the property. A taxpayer may enter into a synthetic disposition transaction to defer the tax associated with a sale or to obtain tax benefits associated with the continued ownership of a property (e.g., to avoid the application of the stop-loss rules in section 112 of the Income Tax Act).

Synthetic Disposition Arrangement

Under subsection 80.6(1), if a taxpayer enters into a "synthetic disposition arrangement" in respect of a property owned by the taxpayer and the "synthetic disposition period" is one year or more, the taxpayer is deemed

- to have disposed of the property immediately before the beginning of the synthetic disposition period for proceeds equal to its fair market value at the beginning of the synthetic disposition period; and
- to have reacquired the property at the beginning of the synthetic disposition period at a cost equal to that fair market value.

A "synthetic disposition arrangement" (definition in subsection 248(1)), in respect of a property owned by a taxpayer, is one or more agreements or other arrangements entered into by the taxpayer (or a non-arm's length person or partnership) that have the effect of eliminating all or substantially all the taxpayer's risk of loss and opportunity for gain or profit in respect of the property for a definite or indefinite period of time. For an agreement or arrangement entered into by a person or partnership that does not deal at arm's length with the taxpayer, it falls within the definition only if it can reasonably be considered to have been entered into, in whole or in part, with the purpose of obtaining the effect of eliminating the risk of loss or gain. According to the Budget papers, this means that the definition will not apply if it is reasonable to conclude that the non-arm's length person did this without knowledge of the taxpayer's ownership of the property.

The "synthetic disposition period" of a synthetic disposition arrangement is essentially the definite or indefinite period of time during which the synthetic disposition arrangement has the effect of eliminating the taxpayer's risk or loss and opportunity for gain (definition in subsection 248(1)).

In its explanatory notes to section 80.6, the Department of Finance provides the following example, illustrating the effect of the provision:

Example

John owns shares of ABC Co. that have an ACB of $1 million and a fair market value of $10 million. If John sold the shares outright, he would realize a $9 million capital gain. John, however, wants to sell the shares without any immediate tax consequences. In order to effectively sell the shares while deferring tax on the accrued capital gain, John enters into a synthetic disposition arrangement.

John receives a five-year loan for $10 million from a purchaser (with interest of $2 million payable in five years). Under the arrangement, John obtains a right to settle the loan (including accrued interest) in five years by transferring the ABC Co. shares to the purchaser, and the purchaser obtains a right to acquire the shares from John in five years for $12 million. As a result, John has eliminated his risk of loss and opportunity for gain or profit in respect of the ABC Co. shares. If the value of the shares is less than $12 million in five years, John would settle the loan by transferring ownership of the shares to the purchaser. If the value of the shares is greater than $12 million in five years, the purchaser would exercise the right to acquire the shares for $12 million.

Under section 80.6, John will be deemed to have disposed of the ABC Co. shares at their fair market value of $10 million when he enters into the arrangement and will be deemed to have immediately reacquired the shares at a cost of $10 million. As a result, John will have an immediate capital gain of $9 million.

In five years, John will dispose of the shares for proceeds of $12 million (either to settle the $12 million debt or to settle the purchaser's right to acquire the shares for $12 million), which will exceed the $10 million ACB of the ABC Co. shares to John at that time. As a result of the application of new paragraph 12(1)(z.7), John will have a $2 million income inclusion and no additional capital gain will result from the final disposition.

In terms of the definition of "synthetic disposition arrangement", the Department provides the following examples:

Examples — Put-Call Arrangement

Example 1 (synthetic disposition arrangement) — A taxpayer owns a non-income producing property with a value of $85. The taxpayer acquires a right to sell the property for $100 in five years (a put) and grants a right to buy the property for $100 in five years (a call). The taxpayer has eliminated all or substantially all of both the taxpayer's risk of loss and opportunity for gain or profit in respect of the property. At the end of five years, if the property is worth $115, the call option holder will exercise the right and purchase the property for $100. If, instead, the property is worth $85 at the end of five years, the taxpayer would exercise the put right and sell the property for $100.

Example 2 (not a synthetic disposition arrangement) — A taxpayer owns a property with a value of $100. The taxpayer buys (for $1) a right to sell the property for $50 in five years and sells (for $1) a right to buy the property for $150 in five years. In this example, the taxpayer would retain a significant economic exposure to the property and would generally not be considered to have eliminated all or substantially all of either of the taxpayer's risk of loss or opportunity for gain or profit.

Example 3 (synthetic disposition arrangement) — A taxpayer owns shares of a publicly traded company with a value of $100 and the company is not expected to pay dividends in the foreseeable future. The taxpayer buys (for $4) a right to sell the property for $100 in two years and sells (for $4) a right to buy the property for $102 in two years. The taxpayer would have entered into a synthetic disposition arrangement because the taxpayer has eliminated substantially all their risk of loss and opportunity for gain or profit in respect of the property. The taxpayer would also be considered to have entered into a synthetic disposition arrangement if the taxpayer sold (for $99) a right to buy the property for $2 in two years, as it would be reasonable to expect the option holder to exercise the option.

Examples — Secured Loan

Example 1 (synthetic disposition arrangement) — A taxpayer owns a property with a value of $100. As part of an arrangement, the taxpayer receives a loan of $100 and receives a right to settle the loan by transferring the property to the lender. Also as part of the arrangement, the lender obtains the right to acquire the property for $100. The taxpayer has eliminated substantially all of both the taxpayer's risk of loss and opportunity for gain or profit in respect of the property. If the property's value exceeds $100 at the end of the term of the loan, the lender would exercise its right to acquire the property for $100. If the property's value is less than $100 at the end of the term of the loan, the taxpayer would use the property to settle the loan.

Example 2 (not a synthetic disposition arrangement) — A taxpayer owns a property with a value of $100. A taxpayer receives a loan of $100 that is secured by the property. The taxpayer would generally not be considered to have eliminated substantially all of either of the taxpayer's risk of loss or opportunity for gain or profit. Even if the taxpayer received a right to settle the debt with the property, the taxpayer would not generally be considered to have entered into a synthetic disposition arrangement since the taxpayer would not have eliminated all or substantially all of the taxpayer's opportunity for gain or profit in respect of the property.

Lastly, where the deemed disposition and reacquisition applies, the taxpayer will be considered to not own the property for the purposes of meeting meets the holding period tests in the stop-loss rules in section 112 (generally 365 days before the disposition) and the foreign tax credit rules in subsection 126(4.2) (more than one year before the disposition).

Application / Historical Information

The synthetic disposition rules apply to agreements and arrangements entered into after March 20, 2013, and to an agreement or arrangement entered into before March 21, 2013, the term of which is extended after March 20, 2013, as if the agreement or arrangement were entered into at the time of the extension.

[¶542b] CHARACTER CONVERSION TRANSACTIONS

Rules have been introduced that apply to so-called character conversion transactions, under which a sale of capital property coupled with a forward derivative contract ostensibly changes the character of any gain or profit from ordinary income to a capital gain. Under the new rules, the gain is considered ordinary income. These rules are discussed at ¶443.

SPECIAL CATEGORIES OF PROPERTY

[¶543] LIST OF SPECIAL TYPES OF PROPERTY

As stated at ¶505, the general rule is that a capital gain or loss is calculated by deducting the ACB of the property and any costs of disposal from the proceeds of disposition.

However, there are special rules for calculating capital gain or loss in the case of the following categories of property:

(1) Personal-use property (see ¶545),

(2) Principal residences (see ¶553),

(3) Foreign currencies (see ¶556),

(4) Depreciable property (see ¶557),

(5) Convertible securities (see ¶560),

(6) Options (see ¶561),

(7) Debts (see ¶565),

(8) Goodwill and other intangible properties (see ¶566),

(9) Resource properties (see ¶567),

(10) Lottery winnings and other prizes (see ¶568),

(11) Life insurance (see ¶569),

(12) Property acquired with personal injury awards (see ¶570),

(13) Timber resources (see ¶571),

(14) Shares of small business corporations transferred to child before 1987 (see ¶572),

(15) Farm property transferred to child (see ¶1759).

[¶545] PERSONAL-USE PROPERTY

Capital property may be acquired as an investment, with the intention of keeping it to produce income, such as in the case of a share or bond or rental property. On the other hand, a capital asset may be acquired with no intention of having it produce income, but merely with the intention of owning it for personal use or enjoyment.

Where property is owned primarily for personal use or enjoyment by yourself or by someone related to you, the tax law terms this property "personal-use property".

Personal-use property normally includes such things as a car, a boat, or a cottage primarily held for personal-use and not rental income. As a matter of definition, it is the primary use to which you put the property, and not the nature of the property, that determines whether it is personal-use property. On the other hand, you will not succeed in arguing that an income-producing property such as a bond or stock certificate is personal-use property because you spend a lot of time admiring the engraving on the certificate!

The category of "personal-use property" is in turn divided into two sub-categories. One of these sub-categories is called "listed personal property" and the other sub-category is simply called "personal-use property" and includes all personal-use property which is not "listed personal property". The difference between properties in these subcategories lies in the treatment of losses which arise on dispositions of them. In terms of calculating capital gains (¶547), both are personal-use property. Gains or losses from personal-use property are reported on line 7 of Schedule 3, while those from listed personal property are reported on line 8.

Former interpretation bulletin IT-332R, "Personal-use property", has been archived (¶283), presumably because of the legislative changes discussed in ¶547. Accordingly, it can no longer be relied on as policy. Nevertheless, used with caution, it still presents a reasonable overview of the general rules.

(ITA: 54 "personal-use property")

[¶546] DEFINITION OF "LISTED PERSONAL PROPERTY"

"Listed personal property" (section 54) is defined as being any personal-use property that is one of the following:

(1) a print, etching, drawing, painting, sculpture, or other similar work of art;

(2) jewellery;

(3) a rare folio, rare manuscript, or rare book;

(4) a stamp; or

(5) a coin.

An asset acquired for personal-use which is not described in this list is not listed personal property; therefore, an asset such as a car, boat, furniture, camera, etc., is personal-use property.

(ITA: 54 "listed personal property")

[¶547] CAPITAL GAINS FROM PERSONAL-USE PROPERTY

The capital gain from a disposition of personal-use property is calculated in the same way whether the asset is listed personal property or another kind of personal-use property. Any capital gains from personal-use property are taxed in the same way as other capital gains, but there is a special rule which applies to the calculation of the adjusted cost base and proceeds of an item of personal-use property.

The special rule is that both the adjusted cost base and the proceeds of disposition of an item of personal-use property are each deemed always to be at least $1,000 (subsection 46(1)). This means that a disposal of personal-use property will never produce a capital gain and be subject to tax unless the proceeds of disposal exceed $1,000.

Example

A camera is purchased for $500, and subsequently sold for $700. There would be no tax on the gain, since the ACB and proceeds would both be deemed to be $1,000, resulting in no gain or loss when the ACB was subtracted from the proceeds of disposal.

[¶547.05] *Canadian Cultural Property*

If you disposed of certain cultural property to an institution designated by the Canadian Cultural Export Review Board, no capital gain will result. The donee institution will advise whether your property qualifies for this treatment. You should obtain a certificate from the Canadian Cultural Export Review Board stating that your property qualifies for capital gains exemption. The Board is also required to determine and certify the fair market value of the property. It should provide you with the Form T871, *Cultural Property Income Tax Certificate*. These certifications should be filed with your return. If the property was donated, you may also qualify for a charitable donation credit; see ¶1268.

(ITA: 39(1)(a)(i.1); 46(1); IT-407R4 [Archived])

[¶547.10] *Works of Art Donated to Charity*

Background

For several years, there was a tax scam (as the CRA saw it) which provided taxpayers with a series of works of art for, say, $250 each, which were then disposed of as a charitable donation to a qualified donee (such as a charity or university) at an appraised value of, usually, $1,000 each. There was no capital gain on the disposition (deemed to have proceeds and an ACB of $1,000) under the personal-use property rule, and the taxpayer acquired a tax credit worth about $500 for a cost of $250. The CRA has very specifically warned that it would reassess these donations as a scam, and Finance had enacted potential penalties against the promoters, but apparently both feared that they might not win in court and that in any event the scheme was getting out of hand.

Anti-avoidance Rules

The next step in attempting to stop these schemes (subsection 46(5)) provides that the $1,000 deemed cost base and proceeds for personal-use property will not apply to property acquired under an arrangement where "it is reasonable to conclude that the acquisition of the property relates to an arrangement, plan or scheme that is promoted by another person or partnership and under which it is reasonable to conclude that the property will be the subject of a gift" to which the charitable donation tax credit rules apply. In other words, if you work this out by yourself and find your own personal-use property to contribute, the scheme will still work. It is the commercialization that the government finds objectionable.

Apparently these measures were inadequate to stop the gifting transactions in question, and eventually Finance brought in a further set of rules (subsection 248(35)). Under these rules, the value of a gift is the lesser of its fair market value and its cost (or ACB, but that is essentially the same thing) if the gift is made:

- as part of a gifting arrangement, as defined; or
- unless the gift is made in consequence of death (which most people consider carries tax planning too far)
  - within three years of the acquisition of the property, OR
  - within 10 years of the acquisition, if it is reasonable to conclude that at the time the taxpayer acquired the property the taxpayer expected to make a gift of it.

There are exceptions for gifts of inventory, Canadian real property, ecological property, publicly traded shares, and certified cultural property.

It is generally conceded that this is at long last likely to put a stop to these types of transactions. Further detail is provided in ¶2521 and in chapter 12 dealing with charitable donations.

Historical Information

Valuation cases on gifts of art only made their way through the courts in the period 2004 through 2006, and the taxpayers seem to have lost absolutely, thus rendering superfluous (but not cancelling) the intervening legislation. In *Klotz v. The Queen*, 2004 DTC 2236 (T.C.C.), the Tax Court ruled that, while the works of art in question were personal-use property even though the taxpayer had never seen them, the fair market value of the gifts was what the purchaser who made the gifts paid for them, and not the higher donation value allegedly established by the promoter of the scheme. The Tax Court decision was affirmed (2005 DTC 5279 (F.C.A.)) on the ground that fair market value was a question of fact for the trial judge. A contrary result was reached by a different Tax Court judge in three related cases, *Nash v. The Queen*, 2004 DTC 3391 (T.C.C.), *Tolley v. The Queen*, 2004 DTC 3360 (T.C.C.), and *Quinn v. The Queen*, 2004 DTC 3328 (T.C.C.). In those cases, the Tax Court reviewed at length extensive valuation evidence, and valuation principles in arriving at fair market value, and found the spread between acquisition and donation values to be justified. In a later decision, the *Nash* cases were reversed by Federal Court of Appeal, 2005 DTC 5696. The F.C.A. found that the works of art were purchased in bulk on the wholesale market, whereas the Tax Court had accepted a valuation which ignored the wholesale market and assumed the standard of comparison was the retail market for the works individually. This was, as a matter of law, not the correct comparison in the circumstances. The F.C.A. quoted with approval the Tax Court's decision in *Klotz*, noting that there was "no credible explanation" for the increase in value from the purchase price. The finding with respect to a requirement for a "credible explanation" bodes ill for taxpayers in future cases along these lines, and may cast doubt on future tax schemes depending on sudden increases in value. In what may be *obiter dicta*, given the main holding, the F.C.A. appeared to dismiss out of hand the notion that a group of prints purchased wholesale could be personal use property. Leave to appeal the *Klotz* and *Nash* decisions to the Supreme Court was denied in 2006. In the most recent charitable donation case, *Maréchaux v. The Queen*, 2010 DTC 5174, the Federal Court of Appeal ruled against the taxpayer by finding that no gift was made and that the taxpayer had received a significant benefit from the donation. Leave to appeal the *Maréchaux* decision to the Supreme Court was denied in 2011.

(ITA: 46(1), (2), (5); 248(35)–(37))

[¶548] CAPITAL LOSSES FROM PERSONAL-USE PROPERTY

Capital losses denied except for Listed Personal Property

A capital loss resulting from the disposal of personal-use property (¶545) which is not listed personal property is not deductible in any circumstances, even against gains from other dispositions of personal-use property.

Capital losses resulting from the disposition of listed personal property are deductible, but only within very limited restrictions. First, to have a capital loss from the disposition of listed personal property, the asset must have an actual cost in excess of $1,000. This is because the proceeds of disposal of an item of listed personal property are always deemed to be at least $1,000. (No capital gain will result from the application of this rule because the adjusted cost base will also be deemed to be at least $1,000, as is the case for all personal-use property.)

If a listed personal property has an adjusted cost base of more than $1,000, and is sold for less than its adjusted cost base, a capital loss will result. However, capital losses with respect to listed personal property can only be deducted against capital gains arising from disposal of listed personal property, which severely restricts the utilization of this deduction.

Carryover of Listed Personal Property losses

If a capital loss does arise from a disposition of listed personal property, and there are insufficient capital gains in the same year from disposals of such property, the loss which cannot be used in the year of disposition can be applied against gains from dispositions of listed personal property arising in the three taxation years immediately preceding the current year, or any of the seven following years.

Where the loss is carried back to a preceding year, form T1A must be filed with your return. Oddly, it is the whole loss which is carried over against whole net listed personal property gains, and then the inclusion rate is applied to determine taxable capital gain from listed personal property for the carryover year. It is therefore never necessary to convert listed personal property losses into fractions, as with ordinary allowable capital losses.

The CRA provides the following example in its T4037 Guide:

Example

Nathan bought some jewellery in 1997 for $5,800. In 2014, he sold it for $6,000. He ended up with a gain of $200. He also sold a coin collection for $2,000 in 2014. Nathan had originally bought this collection in 1999 for $1,700. He ended up with a gain of $300 when he sold the coin collection. In addition, he sold a painting in 2014 for $8,000. However, Nathan bought the painting in 2000 for $12,000. Therefore, he had a loss of $4,000. He had no outlays and expenses for these three transactions.

Nathan's loss from selling listed personal property in 2014 was more than his gain: his loss was $4,000; his total gain was $500 ($200 + $300). As a result, his net loss was $3,500 ($4,000 - $500). Nathan cannot use the difference to offset his capital gain on the sale of a property other than on listed personal property in the year. In addition, he cannot offset any income he had from other sources. However, he can apply his listed personal property loss against his gains from dispositions of listed personal property in any of the three preceding years or the seven years following 2014.

Nathan should not complete Schedule 3 for 2014. However, he should keep a record of his listed personal property loss in case he wants to apply the loss against listed personal property gains in another year.

A capital loss can also arise from dispositions of certified cultural property (see ¶1268). The type of capital loss will depend on the nature of the property.

(ITA: 40(2)(g)(iii); 41(2), (3); 46(1); IT-407R4)

[¶549] PARTIAL DISPOSITIONS OF PERSONAL-USE PROPERTY

Where only part of a personal-use property is disposed of, the rule that the ACB or the proceeds of disposal must be at least $1,000 is modified.

As described at ¶520, when there is a partial disposition of property, its ACB must be prorated to determine the ACB of the part which has been disposed of. The same ratio is applied to the $1,000 minimum discussed at ¶547 and ¶548 to determine the minimum ACB or proceeds applicable to the part disposition.

(ITA: 46(2))

[¶550] SETS OF ITEMS OF PERSONAL-USE PROPERTY

Some items of personal-use property may constitute parts of a set of similar items. For income tax purposes, a personal-use property will be considered part of a set of items if it would "ordinarily be disposed of in one disposition as a set".

The term "set" is not defined in the Act and therefore carries its ordinary meaning in the context in which it is used. The CRA considers that a set for these purposes is a number of properties belonging together and relating to each other, which were produced and issued simultaneously or over a short period of time. The fact that the value of a number of properties, if sold together, exceeds the aggregate of their values, if sold individually, may indicate the existence of a set. However, this is not in itself a decisive factor.

Since capital gains from personal-use property cannot arise unless the proceeds of disposition exceed $1,000, taxpayers would obviously avoid tax if they could sell each item in a set individually and assume a $1,000 cost base for each item.

To prevent this, the law provides that, in specified circumstances, all items of a set will be considered a single personal-use property.

This rule (subsection 46(3)) applies only where:

(1) the set had a fair market value before the first disposition of more than $1,000; and

(2) all of the items in the set have been acquired either by one person, or by a group of persons who did not deal with each other at arm's length.

(ITA: 46(3))

[¶551] PERSONAL-USE PROPERTY OWNED BY A CORPORATION, PARTNERSHIP, OR TRUST

Personal-use property may be owned by a corporation, a partnership, or a trust. As a result, increases or decreases in the value of such personal-use property will affect the value of the corporation's shares, a partner's interest in the partnership, or a beneficiary's interest in the trust.

Since shares, partnership interests, and interests in trusts are normally treated as capital property, a disposition will produce a capital gain or capital loss. In the absence of a special rule, changes in value of the personal-use property owned by any of these entities would affect the amount of the capital gain or loss.

As explained at ¶548, losses arising from dispositions of personal-use property are not allowed as deductions against other income. To prevent a taxpayer from indirectly obtaining such a deduction, a capital gain or loss resulting from the disposition of a share, a partnership interest, or an interest in a trust must be calculated ignoring any decrease in value caused by a decrease in value of personal-use property owned by the corporation, partnership, or trust.

(ITA: 46(4))

[¶552] DEALERS IN PERSONAL-USE PROPERTY

The types of assets constituting listed personal property, or personal-use property of another kind, will not be treated as such for tax purposes if you are a dealer in such property. In this case, the assets will form part of your inventory, and transactions in these assets will be regarded as part of your business operations, and will be taxed as described in Chapter 7.

[¶553] PRINCIPAL RESIDENCES

[¶553.10] *General Rule: Where No Election Made to Have Deemed Disposition on February 22, 1994*

A special exemption is provided in the case of a capital gain realized upon the disposition of a property which constitutes your "principal residence", or has qualified as such at any time after 1971. See ¶554a and ¶2541 for tax planning points related to a principal residence.

The general effect of this special exemption (paragraph 40(2)(*b*)) is that you will not be taxed on a gain from the sale of your residence if it qualifies as your principal residence for each year you have owned it since 1971. However, you may be taxable if the residence does not qualify as a principal residence for each such year. It is very important to determine whether the property does in fact qualify as a principal residence for each year you have owned it since 1971, and the requirements for qualification are discussed in ¶554.

The period of ownership used to determine the numerator and denominator in the exemption formulae below is restricted to the period after you last acquired or reacquired the property.

The calculation of the portion of your gain on the sale of your house which is exempt depends upon whether or not you owned your house at the end of 1981 and continuously thereafter until sold.

Formula for Exemption

Commentary on Legislative Proposals (Oct. 3, 2016)

Note: When the Notice of Ways and Means Motion, October 3, 2016, achieves Royal Assent, the commentary will be modified to read:

Effective for sales of residences after October 2, 2016, only taxpayers residing in Canada in the year of acquisition of the residence may use the one-plus rule described below to calculate their principal residence exemption. Those who did not reside in Canada in that year cannot use it to calculate their exemption. Taxpayers who did not reside in Canada at any time during the period of ownership of the residence cannot claim the exemption for any portion of the capital gain realized on the disposition of the residence.

If you did not own your house at the end of 1981 and your residence meets the requirements of a "principal-residence" for your years of ownership (or all but one year), as outlined in ¶554, you should first calculate your capital gain (you cannot have a capital loss from personal-use property — see ¶548) in the normal way by reference to the proceeds of sale and the ACB of the house or apartment. The portion of your gain which is exempt is then calculated by the following formula:

$$\frac{\text{One plus the number of taxation years ending after the acquisition date (post-1971) for which the property was your principal residence and during which you were resident in Canada.}}{\text{The number of taxation years ending after the acquisition date (post-1971) during which you owned the property.}} \times \text{Capital Gain} = \text{Exempt Gain}$$

After calculating the exempt portion of the gain, as above, deduct it from your actual capital gain.

In the numerator above, both the year of acquisition (where after 1971) and the year of disposition can be included if the property qualified as a principal residence in the year. Similarly, the denominator will always include both the year of acquisition (if after 1971) and the year of disposition.

Example

On January 1, Year 1, you purchased a house which you determine under the normal rules to have an ACB of $100,000. For Years 1 through 4, the house meets all the requirements of a principal residence, and in Year 4 you sell the house for $120,000.

Your gain on the sale of the home in Year 4 will be exempt under the formula, provided you designate the house as having been your principal residence for Years 1 through 3.

Note that it would not be necessary to designate the house as a principal residence for Years 1 through 4 because of the "bonus" year allowed in the formula. If you designate the house as your principal residence for Years 1 through 3 (or for any three of the four years) the exempt gain would be calculated as:

$$\frac{1 + 3}{4} \times \text{Gain (\$20,000)} = \text{Exempt gain (\$20,000)}$$

The fraction you use to multiply the capital gain cannot be larger than one, so any designation producing a larger fraction is wasted. The purpose of the bonus year is to deal with overlaps in the acquisition of a new residence and the disposition of an old one.

Where you and your family own only one residence, and the entire gain is clearly exempt because it has always been your principal residence and you, your spouse or common-law partner or a minor child have not owned another residence during the period it has been your residence, you can claim the exemption by the simple expedient of not reporting the disposition on Schedule 3. Where, however, matters are more complex, you should obtain form T2091 or T1255 to designate years and calculate any taxable gain.

Taxpayers disposing of their principal residence after 2015 must make the principal residence designation in Schedule 3 of their income tax return if the residence has been their principal residence for every year they owned it. If this was not the case, the designation must be made on Form T2091 if the taxpayer making the designation is still alive and on Form T1255 if the designation is made by the legal representative of the deceased. Taxpayers must also report the disposition of the residence and basic information like its acquisition date, disposition proceeds, and property description in Schedule 3 of their return.

Commentary on Legislative Proposals (Oct. 3, 2016)

Note: When the Notice of Ways and Means Motion, October 3, 2016, achieves Royal Assent, the commentary will be modified to read:

Taxpayers having failed to designate their residence as their principal residence on Schedule 3 of their tax return can still qualify for a late designation by applying to the CRA to amend their tax return but could be subject to a late designation penalty for the lesser of $8,000 and $100 times the number of complete months between the due date of their return and the date of application to the CRA.

Taxpayers not reporting the disposition of their principal residence and basic information on Schedule 3 of their return can be reassessed beyond the normal reassessment period in respect of that disposition.

History — Previous Rule for Families

Prior to 1982, each member of a family unit could own a principal residence and claim the exemption on it. Thus a husband could own a cottage and his wife a home in town and both would be exempt. This rule was changed so that after 1981 only one residence of a family unit (taxpayer, spouse, and unmarried children under 18 — see ¶554) could qualify as a principal residence in any given year. The meaning of "spouse" for this purpose has changed over time, as discussed at ¶1113. Where you become subject to this rule by virtue of a change in the rules at ¶1113, see also the discussion at ¶2541.

[¶553.15] *Special Rule for Homes Owned on December 31, 1981*

When the rule was introduced at the beginning of 1982 to prevent families from designating more than one home as a principal residence for any year of ownership, a transitional rule was added to protect the gain accrued on property which could have been designated under the old rule but would not be designated under the new rule.

Technically, the rule applies to any principal residence owned on December 31, 1981 and continuously thereafter until the rule is invoked on disposition. The rule creates a notional disposition on December 31, 1981, and recognizes the capital gain to that date and permits designation of the gain to December 31, 1981 on final disposition under the old rules, where each family member could designate a property. The property is notionally reacquired on January 1, 1982, at its fair market value at that time, and a separate computation of capital gain is made for the period from that date to the date of actual disposition. An election may also be made to designate the property as a principal residence for any number of years in this period, but this election will be subject to the limitation that only one family member may elect in respect of any particular year in the period and that the "one-plus" rule in the usual formula will not apply. Only the actual years of principal residence may be claimed in the numerator.

The objective of this provision is to create a valuation day on January 1, 1982 for purposes of the new family unit rule, so that all properties held before that time are protected under the old rules on value accrued to that time. Because of this change, owners were advised to obtain valuations at the end of 1981. If you do not have such a valuation from that time, you may still be able to get a reasonable approximation of value from a valuator or real estate agent who has been operating in the area since 1981.

If the value of the property on December 31, 1981 was actually higher than the actual proceeds of disposition on eventual sale, the difference may be deducted from the gain recognized after applying the exemption formula to the period before 1982. In this case you would not want to designate more years than necessary to achieve a complete offset.

Example

In 1977 you acquired a cottage for $40,000. It was valued at December 31, 1981, at $90,000. You sold it in 2004 for $125,000. Your spouse has owned your city house throughout this period.

You may designate the cottage as a principal residence to December 31, 1981, without impairing your spouse's principal residence claim on the city house. Suppose you want to do this, because of the greater potential gain on the city house, and your ability to claim capital gains exemption on the remaining taxable gain. Accordingly, you designate the period to December 31, 1981 (on form T2091).

Under the ordinary principal residence rule, your gain would be:

Proceeds of disposition	$125,000
Less: Adjusted cost base	40,000
Capital gain	$ 85,000

Minus principal residence exemption:

$$\frac{1 + \text{years designated (1977 to 1981)}}{\text{Taxation years of ownership}} \times \text{capital gain}$$

$$\frac{1 + 5}{28} \times \$85{,}000 = \$18{,}214$$

Capital gain subject to tax: $85,000 - $18,214 = $66,786

Under the special transitional rule, your capital gain will be limited to:

Step 1: Gain to December 31, 1981

Proceeds of notional disposition (fair market value at Dec. 31, 1981)	$ 90,000
Cost	40,000
Notional gain	$ 50,000

Designate years to 1981 and apply principal residence exemption:

$$\frac{1 + 5}{5} \times \$50{,}000 = \$50{,}000 \text{ (cannot exceed gain)}$$

Taxable gain: $50,000 - $50,000 = nil

Step 2: Gain after December 31, 1981

Actual proceeds of disposition	$125,000
Fair market value at Jan. 1, 1982	90,000
Notional gain	$ 35,000

Designate any years since 1981 and apply principal residence exemption:

$0/23 \times \$35{,}000 = \text{nil}$

Notional gain: $35,000 - nil = $35,000

Step 3: Gain under transitional rule

Gain from Step 1 (nil) plus gain from Step 2 ($35,000) equals gain recognized: $35,000.

There are several points to be noted from this example:

(1) In Step 1, you would not normally designate more years than needed to reduce your gain for the period to nil.

(2) If you elected in 1994 to utilize any or all of your remaining 1994 $100,000 capital gains exemption on the cottage, there will be a further step to reduce the $35,000 gain, as discussed above. Remember that this election could be late-filed, normally up to April 30, 1997. If you had disposed of the property before February 23, 1994, the $35,000 gain under Step 2 would have been eligible for capital gains exemption (¶502) provided you made the claim on a 1994 return filed no more than a year late.

(3) If the accrued value since January 1, 1982 exceeds the value accrued before that date, the transitional rule calculation will yield a higher value than the ordinary calculation. In this case, the ordinary calculation will prevail. The transitional rule provides a limitation only; it cannot set a higher capital gain than the general rule.

(4) If the value of the property declined between January 1, 1982, and the date of sale, that decrease would be subtracted from the sum of the gains recognized in Steps 1 and 2.

(5) If your spouse had disposed of your city house in, say, 1986, you would want to claim an additional designation on the cottage for that and subsequent years. You must always weigh the alternatives, however, where more than one family member (spouse or child under 18 years of age) owns a principal residence in a year.

Where a partial designation is made on the disposition of a principal residence, form T2091 should be filed. This need not be done if all the years of ownership are being designated.

The definition of spouse, or of common-law partner, has changed over time, as discussed at ¶1113. However, once you have a disposition in a year to which the expanded definition applies, you use that definition when looking back at prior years.

If you and your spouse or common-law partner jointly own both a home and a cottage, and have jointly owned at least one of them since 1981 or earlier, there may be some benefit in transferring ownership before an arm's length sale to utilize the pre-1982 transitional rules. This is discussed at ¶554a, below.

[¶553.20] *Filing Requirements*

Current Rules

Taxpayers disposing of their principal residence after 2015 must make the principal residence designation in Schedule 3 of their income tax return if the residence has been their principal residence for every year they owned it. If this was not the case, the designation must be made on Form T2091 if the taxpayer making the designation is still alive and on Form T1255 if the designation is made by the legal representative of the deceased. Taxpayers must also report the disposition of the residence and basic information like its acquisition date, disposition proceeds, and property description in Schedule 3 of their return.

> **Commentary on Legislative Proposals (Oct. 3, 2016)**
>
> Note: When the Notice of Ways and Means Motion, October 3, 2016, achieves Royal Assent, the commentary will be modified to read:
>
> Taxpayers having failed to designate their residence as their principal residence on Schedule 3 of their tax return can still qualify for a late designation by applying to the CRA to amend their tax return, but could be subject to a late designation penalty for the lesser of $8,000 and $100 times the number of complete months between the due date of their return and the date of application to the CRA.
>
> Taxpayers not reporting the disposition of their principal residence and basic information on Schedule 3 of their return can be reassessed beyond the normal reassessment period in respect of that disposition.

History

Strictly speaking, the law requires you to file form T2091 with your T1 return for the year in which you sell (or grant an option on) your principal residence to designate the years you are using in the exemption calculation and calculate any gain which remains (section 54 "principal residence"). However, it is the CRA's policy (stated in the Capital Gains Guide and Income Tax Folio S1-F3-C2, Principal Residence) that in general you need not complete and file form T2091 unless a taxable capital gain on the disposition remains after using the principal residence exemption. There is an exception, however, where you made the 1994 election to utilize part of your then-remaining $100,000 capital gains exemption on a house you sell (or are deemed to dispose of) in the current year which was your principal residence in 1994 or which you are designating as your principal residence in the current year. In this latter situation, you must also file a form T2091 and use form T2091(IND)-WS to calculate the reduction due to the 1994 election

Where you use the principal residence exemption to eliminate a gain on the disposition of a property and so are not required to complete and file form T2091, a designation of the property is considered to have been made by you for the years necessary to eliminate the gain.

Thus in the common case where you sell your house and it is the only one owned by you and your immediate family, and you have used it as a principal residence for at least some time during all the years you owned it, you in effect need not report the disposition. Where any of the issues raised in these paragraphs may indicate that the principal residence exemption may not cover the full capital gain on the house, you should file form T2091. Where you or your family own two or more properties and you clearly intend to use the full exemption on the property you sold in the year, you need not file T2091 but you should keep a record of the years designated on the property sold so that you do not use them again on another property.

Form T1255 must be used for a principal residence designation by the legal representative of the deceased.

[¶553.25] *Principal Residence of Farmer*

If you are a farmer, and you dispose of land used in your farming business which includes your principal residence, you may elect to reduce your gain on sale of this land by $1,000 plus $1,000 for each year after the acquisition date (post 1971) for which the property was your principal residence and during which you were resident in Canada, instead of using the general principal residence formula described above (paragraph 40(2)(c)).

If you choose not to make this election you must allocate the proceeds of disposition and the ACB on a reasonable basis between (i) the principal residence and adjoining land which may reasonably be regarded as contributing to your use and enjoyment of the residence and (ii) the remaining land which is used in the farming business. The CRA usually regards one-half hectare as being the maximum portion of land which can be reasonably regarded as contributing to your use and enjoyment of the principal residence.

In the case of a disposition of land used in a farming business, which includes a principal residence, the election mentioned previously should be made by attaching a letter to the tax return for the year in which the disposition occurred. This letter should:

(1) be signed by you;

(2) state that an election is being made under subparagraph 40(2)(c)(ii) of the Act;

(3) state the number of taxation years after the acquisition date (post-1971) for which the property was your principal residence and during which you were resident in Canada; and

(4) give a description of the property sufficient to identify it with the property designated as the principal residence.

If your return is filed electronically, you should send the letter to the data centre for your area.

The CRA describes the alternatives open to farmers in detail in sections 2.39 – 2.46 of Income Tax Folio S1-F3-C2.

(ITA: 40(2)(*b*), (*c*), (6); 54 "principal residence"; ITR: 2300 [Election]; Income Tax Folio: S1-F3-C2 Principal Residence)

[¶554] MEANING OF "PRINCIPAL RESIDENCE"

General Rules

As mentioned above, the exemption is dependent upon the number of years after 1971 for which the residence is considered to be your "principal residence". To be considered a principal residence for a year, a residence must meet the following conditions (section 54):

(1) The property involved must be a housing unit, a leasehold interest therein, or a share of the capital stock of a cooperative housing corporation.

(2) The housing unit, leasehold interest or share of capital stock, must have been owned in the year by you, although this ownership may be joint ownership with some other person.

(3) If a housing unit, either it must have been ordinarily inhabited in the year by you, your spouse or common-law partner or former spouse or common-law partner, or your child, or it must have been subject for the year to an election described at ¶555. The definition of "child" includes any natural child of you or your spouse or common-law partner; your adopted child; a person wholly dependent on you for support and of whom you have or had custody and control immediately before the person reached 19 years old.

(4) If a share of a cooperative housing corporation, the share must have been acquired for the sole purpose of acquiring the right to inhabit a housing unit owned by the corporation that was ordinarily inhabited by you, your spouse or common-law partner or former spouse or common-law partner, or your child in the year, or was the subject of an election for the year as described at ¶555. The definitions of child and the changes thereto are identical to those described at (3), above.

(5) If a housing unit, the property qualifying for the exemption is limited to the building itself, and land, including immediately surrounding land that may reasonably be regarded as contributing to your use and enjoyment of the housing unit as a residence. However, that land may not be included to the extent that it exceeds 1/2 hectare in size, unless you can establish that this excess land was necessary for use and enjoyment of the housing unit. In a press release dated April 9, 1987, the CRA announced that it would follow the decision for the Federal Court of Appeal in *The Queen v. Yates*, 86 DTC 6296, and allow land to qualify as part of your principal residence even if it exceeds 1/2 hectare to the extent the land was a required residential lot size under a zoning by-law in force at the time of purchase, and was not readily severable under zoning by-laws in force at the time of disposition. In the more recent decision of *Cassidy v. The Queen*, 2011 DTC 5160 (F.C.A.), the taxpayer sold his home, which stood on 2.43 hectares of land, and claimed the principal residence on the capital gain realized on the whole property. He had owned and lived on the property from 1994 until the sale in November 2003. Until 2003, the land could not be legally subdivided. The Court held that the principal residence designation is done on an annual basis, and during each year of ownership the taxpayer was precluded from having a small lot of land for his principal residence. As a result, the entire gain was exempt under the principal residence exemption.

(6) The housing unit or share must have been "designated" by you as your principal residence for the year. As noted above, the designation is not required if the exemption fully exempts your gain from taxation.

(7) No other housing unit or share can have been "designated" as a principal residence by you for the same year.

(8) Only one housing unit or share per family may be "designated" as a principal residence in 1982 and subsequent years. A "family" includes you, your spouse or common-law partner (unless you and your spouse or common-law partner were separated throughout the year pursuant to a court order or written agreement) and your unmarried children who were under 18 at any time in year. If you were not during the year a married person and were under 18, then a "family" includes you, your mother and father and your brothers and sisters who were not during the year married or over 18.

(9) A "personal trust" may also own a home which can qualify as a principal residence. A personal trust is one established on death or, if established during life, one in which the beneficiaries' interests were acquired for no consideration to the trust or its contributors. Further conditions apply specifically to trusts with respect to determining whether a property is considered its principal residence. For dispositions of principal residences by a trust, the residence can qualify as a principal residence if it was ordinarily inhabited by a specified beneficiary. Specified beneficiaries are trust beneficiaries, their spouses or common-law partners, former spouses or common-law partners, children, and grandchildren.

A housing unit might include a house, apartment in a duplex or apartment building or condominium, cottage, mobile home, trailer, or houseboat, and the land upon which the housing unit stands (including any adjoining land that contributes to the use and enjoyment of the housing unit).

It is necessary to own and inhabit the housing unit at some time during a year, but not necessarily throughout the entire year, to be able to designate the housing unit or share as a principal residence for that year (unless you have made the election discussed at ¶555 for the year). However, you may only designate one property as a principal residence each year, even if you own and inhabit more than one residence during the year.

Since joint ownership qualifies as ownership, it is possible for the same property to be the principal residence of more than one person in the same year. For example, a house owned jointly by a husband and wife could be the principal residence of each of them in the same year.

Only Part Qualifies as Principal Residence

A property may have more than one use; for example, part of a house may be used as a personal residence and another part rented to tenants. In this case, the divided-use rules described at ¶513 will apply, and only that portion of the property used as your personal residence will qualify for exemption. The land related to the building should be pro-rated between the "principal residence" and the part of the property used for other purposes, in the same ratio as the building is pro-rated. See paragraphs 2.37 and 2.38 of Income Tax Folio S1-F3-C2 for an example of this rule.

In some cases, the business or rental use of a principal residence will be ancillary to the main use of the residence, such as the rental of one or two rooms to boarders, the use of a room for the care of children or for an office or a work area, etc. In these cases, provided that you have set aside and used a certain area of your principal residence solely for the purpose of earning income, you may claim a deduction for a reasonable portion of expenditures for maintenance of the residence. In the event that you do not claim capital cost allowance on any portion of the residence, it is the CRA's view that a change in use of the property has **not** occurred (as discussed in ¶555) and that the entire residence maintains its nature as a principal residence provided it so qualifies otherwise.

If you would qualify, except that you claimed capital cost allowance on part of your residence prior to 1972 you may claim the entire residence as a principal residence for 1972 and subsequent years as long as it meets all other tests. Any recapture of capital cost allowance claimed prior to 1972 must be accounted for when the residence is disposed of, or is deemed to be disposed of, after 1971.

Designation

Taxpayers disposing of their principal residence after 2015 must make the principal residence designation in Schedule 3 of their income tax return if the residence has been their principal residence for every year they owned it. If this was not the case, the designation must be made on Form T2091 if the taxpayer making the designation is still alive and on Form T1255 if the designation is made by the legal representative of the deceased. They must also report the sale of the residence and basic information such as its acquisition date, disposition proceeds, and property description on Schedule 3.

Taxpayers having failed to designate their residence as their principal residence on Schedule 3 of their tax return can still qualify for a late designation by applying to the CRA to amend their tax return but could be subject to a late designation penalty for the lesser of $8,000 and $100 times the number of complete months between the due date of their return and the date of application to the CRA.

Commentary on Legislative Proposals (Oct. 3, 2016)

Note: When the Notice of Ways and Means Motion, October 3, 2016, achieves Royal Assent, the commentary will be modified to read:

Taxpayers not reporting the disposition of their principal residence and basic information on Schedule 3 of their return can be reassessed beyond the normal reassessment period in respect of that disposition.

Although you are required to designate a property as your principal residence for any year in which you wish to treat it as such, it is not necessary to make this designation in tax returns for every year. Instead, only in the year where a disposition of the property occurs (or is deemed to occur) will it be necessary to indicate whether the property is being designated as your principal residence for the year or preceding years. The designation must also be made in the tax return for any year in which you have granted someone an option to acquire the property. Where it is necessary to file the designation with the CRA, it may be made on form T2091 or T1255, which are available from the CRA website.

Two or More Residences

If you only owned one residence in a particular year, obviously this residence will be designated as your principal residence for that year, if the necessity arises on a sale of that property. However, if two or more residences are owned in a year, or are likely to be owned in some future year, the choice of which property to designate as your principal residence for a year requires consideration. In these situations, you should consider the potential capital gain which might arise upon the disposition of each of the properties owned in that year, since it will normally be more advantageous to designate as your principal residence for the year the property with the largest potential capital gain. However, this will not always be the case, as you may not anticipate disposing of that property for many years, if ever, and it may be more advantageous to use the available exemption for the property which has been sold. Remember that there will be a deemed disposition of all capital properties at the time of death and therefore the disposition or deemed disposition of a property cannot be postponed indefinitely. See ¶1920. Remember also that, for property owned on December 31, 1971, the capital gain may be measured from the value of the property on Valuation Day (see special rules for capital property owned on December 31, 1971 at the end of the chapter) and therefore the property with the largest potential capital gain for tax purposes will not necessarily be the property which has appreciated the most in value since its acquisition.

The formula provided for calculating your exempt gain, as outlined in ¶553, above, grants you a "bonus" of one year in calculating the numerator of one of the fractions. As a result, it will usually be to your advantage, where you were, or are likely to be, the owner of two or more residences in the same year, not to designate the residence you have sold as a principal residence for its last year of ownership. Upon sale of the other property at some later date, you will then be able to designate the property subsequently sold as a principal residence for this year, and, in effect, save the bonus year for future use.

Commentary on Legislative Proposals (Oct. 3, 2016)

Note: When the Notice of Ways and Means Motion, October 3, 2016, achieves Royal Assent, the commentary will be modified to read:

The formula provided for calculating your exempt gain, as outlined in ¶553, grants you a "bonus" of one year in calculating the numerator of one of the fractions. Note that, for dispositions of principal residences after October 2, 2016, the one-year bonus is only available to taxpayers residing in Canada during the year of acquisition of the residence. As a result, it will usually be to your advantage, where you were, or are likely to be, the owner of two or more residences in the same year, not to designate the residence you have sold as a principal residence for its last year of ownership. Upon sale of the other property at some later date, you will then be able to designate the property subsequently sold as a principal residence for this year, and, in effect, save the bonus year for future use.

(ITA: 40(4); 54 "principal residence"; ITR: 2300 [Election]; 2301 [Designation]; Income Tax Folio: S1-F3-C2 Principal Residence)

[¶554a] TRANSFER OF PRINCIPAL RESIDENCE TO SPOUSE OR SPOUSAL TRUST

As discussed in ¶510 and ¶531, it is possible for a person to transfer capital property to his or her spouse or common-law partner without recognition of capital gain or loss at that time. This also applies to a transfer of capital property to a trust for the benefit of a spouse or common-law partner, provided the trust meets the conditions outlined for a spouse trust, and to transfers to an alter ego trust created after 1999, as both as described in ¶531.

Where the property so transferred is a residence, special rules apply. The rules differ somewhat depending upon whether the transfer was a sale or gift during the lifetime of the transferor, or was a transfer resulting from a bequest upon death of the previous owner.

Although a trust other than a spouse trust may claim principal residence exemption (¶554(9)), the special transfer rules described here only operate where the transfer is to a spouse trust, and not merely any personal trust.

Deemed Ownership and Principal Residence Rules

In the case of any transfer of a residence to a spouse or common-law partner, whether during the lifetime of the transferor or upon his or her death, the spouse or common-law partner receiving the property is deemed to have owned the property throughout the period during which the transferring spouse, etc., owned the property (subsection 40(4)). In other words, in applying the exemption formula to a subsequent disposition of the residence, the period of ownership includes all years in which either the spouse or common-law partner originally owning the property or the spouse or common-law partner or trust to which the property was transferred owned the property. This means that to qualify for a complete exemption when the property is eventually disposed of, it will be necessary for the spouse or common-law partner or trust owning the property at that time to designate the residence as a principal residence for all of those years of ownership, including years of ownership by the other spouse or common-law partner. This necessitates another special rule, since in the absence of such a special rule the spouse, common-law partner or trust to whom the residence was transferred would not be able to designate the residence as a principal residence for those years prior to the transfer, since they did not own the residence in those years, which is one of the requirements mentioned previously. This special rule does not apply if the spouse, etc., has elected to transfer the residence at fair market value.

Where the transfer to the spouse or common-law partner or trust has occurred as a result of the death of the other spouse, etc., the spouse, common-law partner or trust receiving the property becomes entitled to designate the residence as a principal residence for any year in which the deceased spouse would have been entitled to designate the residence as a principal residence. In addition, of course, the spouse, common-law partner, or trust can designate the property as a principal residence for each year in which it actually owned the property, assuming it meets the other requirements for a principal residence. Note that, if the deceased spouse could not have designated the property as a principal residence for one or more of the years of ownership, then the spouse, common-law partner ,or trust which has received the property cannot do so either. In effect, the spouse, common-law partner, or trust receiving the property on the death of the other spouse is placed in the same position with respect to the residence as the deceased spouse would have been in if he or she had not died and had retained the property.

The situation with respect to a residence transferred to a spouse, common-law partner or trust during the lifetime of the transferor is somewhat different, and the difference may be important. In this case, the residence is deemed to be a principal residence of the spouse, common-law partner, or trust only for those years in which the property was actually a principal residence of the spouse who formerly owned the property. (Of course, the spouse or trust to whom the property was transferred can designate the residence as a principal residence for any year in which the spouse, common-law partner, or trust actually owned the property.) Since the residence will only be a principal residence of the former spouse or common-law partner for any of his or her years of ownership if he or she has designated it as such, it appears that the spouse or trust receiving the property should attempt to ensure that the former owner has actually made this designation if a full exemption on subsequent sale is desired. It appears that the transferor spouse or common-law partner could make this designation at any time before or after the transfer to the spouse, common-law partner, or the trust, but events such as his or her death, divorce, etc., could make obtaining this designation at a later date impractical or impossible. It might, therefore, be advisable for the spouse who originally owned the property to designate the property as his or her principal residence for prior years at the time the transfer to the spouse, partner, or trust occurs, to prevent possible future difficulties in obtaining exemption. The definition of "spouse or common-law partner" has changed over time as discussed at ¶1113.

The rules also provide that a property held by a spouse trust is to all intents and purposes part of a family unit and no double-up principal residence exemption can be achieved by this device. See also ¶465 concerning capital gain exemption and principal residence designations by a trust.

One of the requirements for claiming the exemption is that the taxpayer must have been resident in Canada for each year in which he or she is claiming a property to be a principal residence. If you transfer a residence to a trust, the trust is deemed to have been a Canadian resident for every year during which you were a Canadian resident.

Where the residence is transferred to a trust, the requirement that the residence must be "inhabited" by the individual in the year in order to be a principal residence will be satisfied provided that the spouse or common-law partner for whose benefit the trust has been established has ordinarily inhabited the residence during the year.

A trust cannot be considered to have a principal residence unless the residence in question was acquired from a spouse or common-law partner of the person for whose benefit the trust has been established, and unless it is subject to the special rules described above. Consequently, if the trust acquires a residence from the other spouse, and subsequently disposes of this residence and replaces it with a different residence, the new residence cannot qualify as a principal residence. The same result will arise where a trust uses other assets to acquire a residence for the trust beneficiary from someone other than the other spouse or common-law partner. Therefore, it may be disadvantageous from a tax point of view to hold a residence in a trust, where it cannot qualify for the special rules discussed above, since any gain on subsequent sale of such a residence may be ineligible for the principal residence exemption.

(ITA: 40(4); 54 "principal residence"; ITR: 2300 [Election]; 2301 [Designation]; Income Tax Folio: S1-F3-C2 Principal Residence)

[¶554a.05] *Transfer of Home and Cottage to Utilize Pre-1981 Rules*

As discussed at ¶553, special rules apply where both you and other family members owned more than one principal residence prior to 1982. The typical case is where you own both a house and a cottage, although any situation where you and a spouse or common-law partner or minor child owned more than one residence is covered. Those rules offer some protection against capital gains realized after 1981 on residences owned before that time, and it may still be possible to rearrange your affairs to utilize this protection before you sell one of the residences.

Suppose, for example, that a husband and wife jointly own a home and a cottage acquired before 1971 (when the capital gain rules first commenced). They now plan to dispose of the home and move into the cottage. It is anticipated that the gain on the cottage will not exceed the gain about to be realized on the sale of the home.

If the home is sold while it is jointly owned, it will have to be designated as the principal residence of both the husband and wife for the years from 1971 to the year before sale (owing to the "plus one" formula discussed at ¶553). On a subsequent disposition of the cottage, the years designated to the home will not be available to reduce the capital gain on the cottage when applying the ¶553 formula.

Commentary on Legislative Proposals (Oct. 3, 2016)

Note: When the Notice of Ways and Means Motion, October 3, 2016, achieves Royal Assent, the commentary will be modified to read:

Effective for dispositions of principal residences after October 2, 2016, the one-plus rule cannot be used to calculate the principal residence exemption if the taxpayer did not reside in Canada in the year of acquisition of the residence. More specifically, no principal residence exemption can be claimed for any year (including the year of acquisition of the residence) during which the taxpayer did not reside in Canada.

If the ownerships are rearranged prior to the first sale, so that the home is owned by, say, the husband, and the cottage by the wife, an additional principal residence exemption may be claimed in respect of the cottage for the period 1971 to 1981. Note that the transfers may be accomplished free of income tax consequences under the rules discussed at the beginning of ¶554a. Land transfer tax should be considered, although it may not apply on spousal transfers in your province. You should verify this for the province in which the residences are situated.

Under the rules above, where you dispose of a property to your spouse at cost, your spouse is considered to have owned the property throughout the period during which you owned it, and the property is considered to have been your spouse's principal residence throughout the period for which you designated it. Thus, in the example above, the husband will be considered to have owned his wife's interest in the house from 1971 and will be able to designate it for the entire period to the year of sale. It appears that the wife's designation of her interest for that period is not necessary, since the husband is deemed to own it throughout and it was in fact his principal residence. Similarly, the wife will be considered to own the cottage since 1971. When the cottage is eventually sold, she will be able to claim principal residence exemption from 1971 to 1981, under the transitional rules at ¶553, and again for the period following the sale of the home.

Problems may arise under the attribution rules in these situations. For example, if the husband and wife in fact each contributed 50% to the cost of the home, 50% of any income earned by the husband on the proceeds of the home would be attributed to the wife. Similarly, if the husband actually contributed 50% to the cost of the cottage, half the capital gain recognized on the eventual sale (because of the missing years from 1982 to the sale of home in the exemption formula) would be attributed to him. See ¶977. It appears that the principal residence exemption reduces capital gain before attribution so that only the residual gain is attributed *pro rata* to the original investment. On the other hand, each spouse may claim lifetime capital gain exemption on any gain recognized in his or her hands after principal residence exemption (¶502). The lifetime exemption operates after attribution is measured.

A spouse in this discussion includes a spouse or common-law partner under the rules applicable for the year of disposition, as discussed at ¶1113. Once you have a disposition in a year to which the expanded definition applies, you use that definition when looking back at prior years.

(ITA: 40(2)(b), (4)–(6); 73(1); 74.1(1); 74.2; Income Tax Folio: S1-F3-C2 Principal Residence)

[¶555] CONVERSION TO AND FROM A PRINCIPAL RESIDENCE

[¶555.05] Conversion of Principal Residence to Income Use

Deemed Disposition

A property may be acquired originally for use as a principal residence, but may later be converted to an income-producing property, such as where the residence is rented to other persons.

As described at ¶513, a change of use of a capital property from a non-income-producing use to an income-producing use is considered to be a disposition of the property at fair market value (subsection 45(1)), which can result in a capital gain to the owner of the property.

Election out of Deemed Disposition

However, in the tax return for the year in which the change of use occurs, subsection 45(2) allows you to make a special election which deems the change of use not to have occurred. The election is made by attaching to your return a letter (or sending it to the CRA, where your return is electronically filed), signed by you, describing the property in respect of which the election is being made and stating that you are making the election. Where the property qualified as a principal residence (as described at ¶554) immediately prior to the change of use, the election will allow the principal residence characterization to continue. The CRA states Income Tax Folio S1-F3-C2, Principal Residence that while it has the authority to accept a late-filed election under certain conditions (¶268), one of its conditions is "that no CCA [capital cost allowance] has been claimed on the property since the change in use has occurred and during the period in which the election is to remain in force". If capital cost allowance is claimed on the property, the CRA considers that the election is rescinded on the first day of the year in which that claim is made.

One effect of making this election is that no capital gain will be considered to have been realized in the year the use of the property actually changed.

Once the election has been made, it will remain in effect for subsequent years, until rescinded by you in a later return. This means that the property can be designated as your principal residence for later years, as well as the initial year the change of use occurred.

Once an election is rescinded for a year, either in writing with a return or by claiming CCA in a return, the CRA considers that there is a deemed disposition and reacquisition on the first day of that year.

Continued Status as Principal Residence

The ability to designate the residence as a principal residence as a result of filing this election is available for four years. After the four years have expired, you can only designate the residence as your principal residence for subsequent years if you actually inhabit the residence in those later years (but see "Special Rule for Employees Moving to New Work Location", below). However, the election continues to be effective to prevent a deemed capital gain arising on the change of use.

Another important consequence of filing this election is that you will not be able to claim capital cost allowance with respect to the property against your income from the property for those years in which the election remains in effect.

It is not necessary that you formally designate a residence as your principal residence for those years in which the election discussed above is in effect. Whether or not you wish to do so will depend on whether you own another qualifying residence. As a practical matter, you need not decide until the first sale of a qualifying residence occurs.

It will not necessarily be to your advantage to make the election and you should consider carefully the possible effects of the election before making your decision. In effect, if you expect the change of use to be permanent, you must weigh the value of extending the principal residence exemption (assuming you will not use the designation of another property for those years) plus the deferral of tax on the capital gain now against the cash value of capital cost allowance. In computing the capital cost allowance, special rules will apply to determine capital cost (see ¶819).

If the reason you have ceased to inhabit the property is that you have moved to another country, there will be no advantage to filing the election merely for the purpose of continuing to treat the property as a principal residence, since the exemption for principal residences does not apply with respect to years in which you are a non-resident of Canada. The election will, however, defer application of the deemed disposition rule indefinitely so long as you do not claim capital cost allowance, and it may well be worthwhile for that reason.

Example (from Income Tax Folio S1-F3-C2)

> Mr. A and his family lived in a house for a number of years until September 30, 2003. From October 1, 2003 until March 31, 2008 they lived elsewhere and Mr. A rented the house to a third party. On April 1, 2008, they moved back into the house and lived in it until it was sold in 2011. When he filed his 2011 income tax return, Mr. A designated the house as his principal residence for the 2004 to 2007 tax years inclusive (that is, the maximum four years) by virtue of a subsection 45(2) election (which he had already filed with his 2003 income tax return) having been in force for those years. (He was able to make this designation because no other property had been designated as a principal residence by him or a member of his family unit for those years.) He designated the house as his principal residence for all the other years in which he owned it by virtue of his having ordinarily inhabited it during those years, including the 2003 and 2008 years. Having been resident in Canada at all times, Mr. A's gain otherwise determined on the disposition of the house in 2011 was, therefore, completely eliminated by the principal residence exemption.

[¶555.10] *Special Rule for Employees Moving to New Work Location*

If you cease to inhabit your principal residence due to the relocation of the place of employment of you or your spouse or common-law partner and the place to which you move is at least 40 kilometres closer to the new place of employment than was your old principal residence, then you may make the above-mentioned election and the four-year limitation will not apply (section 54.1)). In order to claim the property as a principal residence for more than four years, you or your spouse or common-law partner, as the case may be, must resume ordinary habitation in the residence while still employed or in the year immediately following the year of termination of employment with that employer, unless you or your spouse or common-law partner die during the term of your employment. Note that to preserve your principal residence status of your original residence during your absence, every subsequent residence must be 40 kilometres closer to the workplace than your original residence. Also, the employer must deal with you and your spouse at arm's length (¶812).

[¶555.15] *Converting Income Property to Principal Residence*

If you acquire your property to gain or produce income but later cease to use it for that purpose and it becomes your principal residence, you may elect under subsection 45(3) not to have a deemed disposition at the time of change provided you have not claimed capital cost allowance on the property for any year after 1984. If you make the election, the principal residence rules can apply to pro-rate your gain on eventual disposition for the number of years of principal residence, plus up to four years preceding the year you come to ordinarily inhabit it.

Example (from Income Tax Folio S1-F3-C2)

> Mr. X bought a house in 2003 and rented it to a third party until mid-2009. Mr. X and his family then lived in the house until it was sold in 2011. Mr. X has been resident in Canada at all times. When he filed his 2011 income tax return, Mr. X designated the house as his principal residence for the 2009 to 2011 tax years inclusive, by virtue of his having ordinarily inhabited it during those years. He also designated the house as his principal residence for the 2005 to 2008 years inclusive (that is, the maximum 4 years) by virtue of a subsection 45(3) election, which he filed with his 2011 income tax return (he was able to make this designation because (i) no other property had been designated by him or a member of his family unit for those years, and (ii) he did not claim any CCA when reporting the net income from the property before the change in use). However, his gain otherwise determined on the disposition of the house in 2011 could not be fully eliminated by the principal residence exemption formula because he could not designate the house as his principal residence for the 2003 and 2004 years.

The election must be made on or before the earlier of two days — the day that is 90 days after the CRA demands the election and your filing-due date for the year in which the property is actually disposed of. Typically this will be April 30 of the following year, although it can in some cases be June 15, and could differ for a trust; see ¶218.05.

[¶555.20] *Partial Conversions*

The elections above do not apply to partial conversions; when you commence to rent out part of your house, for example, or when you move into part of a house and continue renting out the rest of it. Technically, upon a partial change in use, you are subject to the deemed disposition rules described at ¶513 and ¶513.10.

However, where you commence to rent out part of your personal residence, the CRA will not apply the partial disposition rules so long as the income use is ancillary to the main use as a principal residence, there is no structural change to the property, and no capital cost allowance is claimed. This will allow you to claim the full principal residence exemption on disposition (provided you otherwise qualify). In particular, in its guide T4036, the CRA indicates that, when changing part of your residence to a rental property, there will be no deemed change in use if:

- the part you use for rental purposes is small in relation to the whole property;
- you do not make any structural changes to the property to make it more suitable for rental purposes; and
- you do not deduct any CCA on the part you are using for rental purposes.

The CRA goes on to confirm: "If you meet all the above conditions, the whole property may qualify as your principal residence even though you are using part of it for rental purposes". See also Income Tax Folio S1-F3-C2, Principal Residence, at paragraphs 2.57 through 2.60.

[¶555.25] *Non-Residents*

Commentary on Legislative Proposals (Oct. 3, 2016)

Note: When the Notice of Ways and Means Motion, October 3, 2016, achieves Royal Assent, the commentary will be modified to read:

Effective for dispositions of principal residences after October 2, 2016, taxpayers not residing in Canada in the year of acquisition of the residence cannot use that year to calculate their principal residence exemption. In other words, a non-resident who never resided in Canada during the period of ownership of a residence cannot claim the exemption against any portion of the capital gain realized on the sale of the residence.

A principal residence, or indeed any Canadian real estate, is taxable Canadian property (¶2040) subject to the compliance procedures at ¶2042 on disposition. A conversion of use may also trigger these procedures. The CRA comments on this in CRA Document No. 2005-0113981E5.

(ITA: 45(2), (3), (4); 54 "principal residence"; 54.1; Income Tax Folio: S1-F3-C2 Principal Residence)

[¶556] FOREIGN CURRENCIES

Currency may in certain circumstances be considered a capital property, and holdings of currency other than Canadian currency can result in a capital gain or capital loss from fluctuations in foreign exchange rates.

Dispositions of Foreign Currency

Under subsection 39(1.1), these capital gains or capital losses are calculated and treated in the same way as any other capital gain or capital loss, except that there is a $200 per year exemption in the case of a capital gain of this nature. A capital loss from foreign exchange holdings will result only to the extent that the loss exceeds $200 for the year.

Before deducting the $200 amount from the capital gain or loss otherwise determined, all capital gains and losses for the year from foreign currency must be netted, and the $200 deduction is then applied against the net foreign exchange gain or loss for the year.

Dispositions of Other Property or Repayment of Foreign Debt

The $200 threshold applies only with respect to foreign exchange gains and losses incurred on the disposition of foreign currency, generally applicable to gains and losses incurred after August 19, 2011. The full amount of gains and losses incurred on the disposition of other assets or the repayment of an obligation is determined under regular rules regarding capital gains and losses (subsection 39(1) will apply to dispositions of assets, while subsection 39(2) will apply to repayment or settlement of obligations). The changes in the rules address concerns arising from the Supreme Court of Canada decision in the *Imperial Oil/Inco* decision (2006 DTC 6639), in which the Court appeared to hold that the repayment of a foreign debt obligation could not, in itself, generate a gain or loss; see the Tax Topics article no. 1826, March 8, 2007, for a discussion of the relevant concerns.

Weak Currency Debt

In *Shell Canada Limited v. The Queen*, 99 DTC 5669 (S.C.C.), the Supreme Court of Canada ruled in favour of a transaction in which the taxpayer borrowed in a weak currency (which carried a high rate of interest) and hedged the transaction at its inception so that the extra borrowing cost was offset by a locked-in capital gain. The Court found the interest deductible and the offsetting gain to be on capital account and so not accountable for tax until the eventual disposition of the major business asset so funded. The government, not surprisingly, found this result unfair, and enacted section 20.3, which generally provides that the interest on weak currency borrowings pursuant to such plans will not be deductible to the extent it exceeds interest that would be paid on a direct borrowing of the target currency, and foreign exchange gain or loss on both the foreign currency transactions and any associated hedge would be on income account. These rules are largely of interest to large corporate borrowers in foreign currencies, and apply only to borrowings in excess of C$500,000. The matter is discussed in greater detail at ¶1064.

(ITA: 393; 39(2); 261(3); IT-95R [Archived])

[¶557] DEPRECIABLE PROPERTY

The term "depreciable property" refers to a capital asset for which capital cost allowances have been claimed (or could have been claimed) by the taxpayer owning the asset. A complete discussion of capital cost allowances and depreciable property is contained in Chapter 8.

Property is not depreciable merely because it is a kind of property which actually does depreciate in use, since not all such property is eligible for capital cost allowance claims. For example, an automobile used only personally will depreciate, but is not depreciable property for tax purposes.

Some special rules apply to the determination of a capital gain or capital loss arising from the disposition of a depreciable property.

[¶558] LOSSES FROM DEPRECIABLE PROPERTY

A capital loss cannot arise on the disposition of depreciable property. This is due to the fact that the cost of a depreciable property can be deducted for income tax purposes by other means. During the period the asset is held, capital cost allowances may be deducted in computing income. If the entire cost has not been deducted through capital cost allowances by the time the asset is disposed of, the remaining cost may be deducted either through capital cost allowance claims in the future or by means of a terminal loss deduction. These deductions are explained fully in Chapter 8.

Property disposed of may consist of both non-depreciable and depreciable elements; this is commonly the case with land and building, such as a rental property. In that case, the loss must be computed separately on the land (which is not depreciable property) under capital gain/loss rules in this chapter, and the building (which is depreciable if used for income purposes) under the capital cost allowance/terminal loss rules at ¶859.

(ITA: 39(1)(b)(i))

[¶559] GAINS FROM DEPRECIABLE PROPERTY

Capital gains on depreciable property are calculated and taxed in the same way as other capital gains described in this chapter, by reference to the proceeds of disposition, ACB and costs of disposal, with one exception. The exception is that the ACB of such depreciable property will (almost) always be its "capital cost" so that the adjustments made to it are those described in Chapter 8 rather than those described at ¶507 or ¶508. There can be circumstances, however, in which specific overriding provisions of the law may cause a difference between the capital cost of a depreciable property and its ACB; see ¶509.

(ITA: 54 "adjusted cost base" (a))

[¶560] CONVERTIBLE SECURITIES

Where the terms of a share, bond, debenture or note of a corporation permit the security to be exchanged for shares of the capital stock of the corporation, the exchange of the security for shares will not be considered to be a disposition of the original security held (subsection 51(1)).

Instead, the ACB of the original security will merely be transferred to the shares of the corporation acquired on conversion and no capital gain or loss will arise until these shares are eventually disposed of.

The right to convert the security need not have been conferred upon the security holder at the time the security was issued and the exchange will be permitted even though the terms and conditions of the shares given up did not permit a right of exchange or conversion.

You may receive shares of more than one class of capital stock on the conversion without causing a deemed disposition. The cost of the converted property must be allocated among the classes of shares received on the conversion in proportion to their respective fair market values immediately after the exchange.

There are several other rules under which share exchanges may also occur on a tax-deferred basis; see ¶537 and ¶585.

(ITA: 51)

[¶560c] BOND EXCHANGES

If you own a bond, debenture or note which is capital property, and you exchange the bond for another bond, debenture or note of the same debtor, section 51.1 provides you with a mandatory "rollover" of the obligation. That is, you will be considered to have disposed of the old obligation at its ACB (so there is no gain or loss) and to have acquired the new obligation at the old ACB. These provisions apply only where:

(1) the bond, note or debenture given up in exchange contained in its issue terms a provision conferring upon holders the right to make the exchange; and

(2) the principal amount is the same for both new and old obligations.

(ITA: 51.1)

[¶561] OPTIONS AND WARRANTS YOU PURCHASE

If you pay another person for granting to you or selling to you an option which gives you the right to acquire capital property, the amount you pay to acquire the option is not deductible as long as the option is outstanding and owned by you.

If you exercise your option, and acquire the capital property, the amount you paid for the option itself will simply be treated as part of the cost of the capital property you subsequently acquired under the option (subsection 49(3)).

However, if the option subsequently expires without being exercised, you will have a capital loss in the year of expiry equal to the ACB of the option.

Payments made for extending or renewing an option are subject to the same treatment as the consideration for the original option. That is, the option cost is rolled into the eventual property cost if the option is exercised (subsection 49(5)). If the option is not exercised, loss is recognized on the final termination of the last extension or renewal, and not for each stage of the option.

(ITA: 49; IT-96R6 [Archived])

[¶561.05] *Employee Stock/Mutual Fund Options*

Where you acquire options under an agreement with your employer, the tax consequences are governed by the rules at ¶330 rather than the rules immediately above.

[¶562] PAYMENTS RECEIVED FOR GRANTING OPTIONS

If you have received money or other consideration in exchange for granting an option to someone else with respect to capital property, you are considered to have disposed of a capital property at the time the option is granted (subsection 49(1)).

The entire amount received for granting the option is treated as a capital gain. This rule does not apply where the option relates to your principal residence.

If the option is actually exercised in the same year it is granted, the above-mentioned rule does not apply and the consideration received for the option is treated as part of the proceeds of disposition of the capital property disposed of under the option agreement.

If the option is exercised in a year subsequent to the year in which it was granted, the consideration for granting the option will be treated as part of the proceeds of disposition of the capital property in the subsequent year for purposes of calculating capital gain or capital loss in that year. The capital gain reported in the year in which the option was granted may be reversed by filing an amended tax return for the original year (subsection 49(4)).

Proceeds received for extending or renewing an option are subject to the same rules as applied to the original receipts.

(ITA: 49; IT-96R6 [Archived])

[¶563] BAD DEBT RECEIVABLES

If someone owes you money, and the debt becomes uncollectible, the loss may be treated as a capital loss for tax purposes, but only if it qualifies under the deemed disposition rules discussed below, and if it meets certain other conditions. A debt which is on capital account and which is actually disposed of will give rise to a capital gain or a capital loss, under general rules at ¶505, subject to the stop-loss rules discussed below. A debt settled for less than its face value will have consequences for the debtor and, in some related party cases, the creditor (¶565).

Uncollectible trade (income) debts are fully deductible but are not capital losses and therefore are not a subject for this chapter. They are discussed in Chapter 7 (see ¶733). Similarly, there are special rules for bad debts arising on the sale of depreciable property (¶847) or eligible capital property (¶768).

[¶563.05] *Deemed Disposition of Debt*

When a debt owing to you is established to be a bad debt (not merely overdue or doubtful of collection) and you elect to have a deemed disposition of the debt in your return of income for the year, the debt is deemed to have been disposed of at the end of your taxation year for nil proceeds of disposition, and to have been reacquired immediately after the end of that year at a nil cost (subsection 50(1)). The election requirement is intended to allow you to defer the occurrence of tax consequences in a related debtor company triggered by your bad debt claim against the company. Normally, the deemed disposition rules do not by themselves trigger the forgiveness of debt rules, but this can happen under the complex rules intended to deal with debt parking (¶565.60). The election requirement is intended to allow you to choose to defer your own deductions and avoid the tax consequences of a forgiveness of debt in the debtor company.

The election requirement appears to have no direct bearing on the capital loss rules (or the allowable business investment loss at ¶580) for a creditor, except that the election is mandatory in order to claim a capital or allowable capital loss where the debt has not actually been disposed of.

No form has been prescribed for this election. The CRA's Capital Gains Guide (T4037) provides that you make the election by attaching to your return a letter signed by you stating that you want subsection 50(1) of the Act to apply to the particular debt (or sending it to the CRA where your return is filed electronically). Where this is overlooked, it can be argued that filing a return as if the election had been made (i.e., claiming the capital or allowable business investment loss) is tantamount to making an election. The CRA has been disposed to accept this kind of inferred election with some other elective provisions, but is not known to have commented on its position in this context.

To provide for the situation where the debt, or part of it, is subsequently collected, if you elect to have a disposition of a debt (and so claim a capital or allowable capital loss), you are deemed to have reacquired the debt at a cost equal to nil, and therefore any subsequent collection will result in a capital gain to you in the year of collection (since the debt, or some portion of it, is disposed of for proceeds in excess of its nil cost base).

(ITA: 50(1); 248(1) "disposition"; IT-159R3 [Archived])

[¶563.10] *Additional Limitations on Capital Loss Claims on Debt (Stop-Loss Rules)*

A capital loss can arise on the actual or deemed disposition of debt only if the debt was acquired for the purpose of gaining or producing income, or if the debt was consideration for a disposition of capital property in an arm's length transaction.

A capital loss cannot arise on the disposition of debt arising on a sale of personal-use property (see ¶545) other than listed personal property (¶546) except in the circumstances described below. Subject to these stop-loss rules, a capital loss arising on a disposition or deemed disposition can be treated as a capital loss for the year.

(ITA: 40(2)(g)(ii), (iii); IT-159R3 Capital debts established to be bad debts)

[¶563.15] *Low-Interest Loans and Guarantees*

As stated above, loans arising on capital property dispositions apart, a loss arising on the disposition of a debt is a capital loss only where the debt was acquired by you for the purpose of earning income from a property or business. Accordingly, it is the CRA's stated view, in interpretation bulletin IT-533, paragraph 33 (now archived), that where providing guarantees is part of a taxpayer's business (i.e., for a fee), interest expense on borrowed money to honour the guarantee would generally meet the requirements for deductibility. Where providing guarantees is not part of a taxpayer's business, the direct use of borrowed money to honour a guarantee is generally not for an income-earning purpose and such interest would not be deductible (citing *74712 Alberta Ltd. v. The Queen*, 97 DTC 5126 (F.C.A.)). However, where interest is charged to the defaulting party, the purpose test could be met.

The Bulletin goes on to say:

> In certain situations there could be exceptions to the direct use rule. Where the taxpayer can show that the guarantee was given for the purpose of increasing its income-earning capacity and must subsequently borrow money to honour the guarantee, the borrowed money may be considered to be used for the purpose of earning income. For example, there may be circumstances where the guarantor had access to the proceeds of the loan that was guaranteed. In this situation, the interest is deductible on the amount of the borrowing to honour the guarantee that can be traced to the funds that were used by the taxpayer for the purpose of earning income. There may be other situations where the taxpayer can demonstrate that the indirect use test is met. Such would be the case where a parent company guaranteed the debts of its wholly owned subsidiary (or in cases of multiple shareholders, where shareholders guarantee a loan in proportion to their shareholdings) and can show that it reasonably expected to earn income from the transaction, such as in the form of potential increased dividends to be received. A deduction for interest in other situations involving borrowings to honour a guarantee may also be warranted, such as in *Lewisporte v. The Queen*, 99 DTC 253 (T.C.C.), where the Court concluded that the purpose of the borrowing to honour the guarantee was to obtain complete control over all the assets of two subsidiaries for the purpose of gaining or producing income from these assets.

The CRA position above was carried through to S3-F6-C1: Interest Deductibility, at paragraphs 1.78 to 1.80.

In *The Queen v. Byram*, 99 DTC 5117 (F.C.A.), the taxpayer made interest-free loans both directly and through an intermediary company to a U.S. company from which, directly or indirectly, he expected profits which would be returned to him as dividends. When the U.S. company failed, the taxpayer sold the debt for $1 and claimed a capital loss. The Federal Court of Appeal ruled that while the interest deductibility rules require examination of both the use of borrowed money and the purpose behind the use, the capital gain stop-loss rule looks only at the purpose of the debt. The analogy to interest deductibility rules put forward by the CRA was therefore inappropriate, since the correct rule for determining whether a capital loss is recognized is only the purpose of the debt.

In a forum at the 1999 Annual Canadian Tax Foundation Conference, the CRA announced (as reported in Wolters Kluwer Tax Topics No. 1440) that it accepted the *Byram* decision and would eventually revise IT-293R2 to reflect it. Eventually, IT-293R2 was withdrawn and the comments in IT-533 substituted. Those comments are clearer in light of the *Byram* case:

> If you guarantee a debt, you are considered to have acquired a debt at the time you are required to fulfill your guarantee obligation. You may be allowed a deduction for a bad debt if you establish that the debt acquired is a bad debt and your guarantee was given for the purpose of earning income (and not preserving an income source). It has in the past been the CRA's policy to allow a loss deduction to the guarantor where a corporation, whose loan was guaranteed, agrees to have the rules for debt forgiveness (¶565) apply to it, although the source for this is no longer apparent.

Special rules apply if the debt was receivable from a CCPC (see ¶580).

(ITA: 40(2)(g)(ii); Income Tax Folio: S3-F6-C1 Interest Deductibility)

[¶563.20] *Special Rules for Debt on Personal-Use Property*

Where an arm's length debt arises on an arm's length disposition of personal-use property and the debt proves uncollectible, special rules apply. First, subsection 50(2) provides that the loss arises when the debt is established to be a bad debt. No election is required (or permitted) to create a deemed disposition. It would seem that actual disposition of the debt cannot give rise to a capital loss by virtue of the stop-loss rules above, but a deemed disposition can. The CRA has not commented on this anomaly, although it may reflect the likelihood that it would be virtually impossible to dispose of an uncollectible debt owed on the sale of personal-use property. The taxpayer is deemed to have disposed of the debt at the end of the year and reacquired it immediately after the end of the year, so that subsequent gain will be recognized, as under the regular deemed disposition rules. Second, any capital loss on the debt is limited to any capital gain recognized on the disposition of the property. That is, proceeds of disposition on the uncollectible debt are deemed to be the ACB of the debt immediately before the end of the year minus the gain from the disposition of the underlying personal-use property.

(ITA: 40(2)(g)(iii); 50(2); IT-159R3 Capital debts established to be bad debts)

[¶564] SHARES OF BANKRUPT OR INSOLVENT CORPORATION

Election

If you own a share of the capital stock of a corporation which has become a bankrupt (as defined in the *Bankruptcy Act* or the *Winding-up Act*) during the year you can elect under subsection 50(1) to have disposed of that share at the end of the year for no proceeds. You may then report a capital loss on the share in the year the corporation becomes bankrupt. If the share is subsequently sold you must report any proceeds on the sale as a capital gain.

In addition to situations of formal bankruptcy or insolvency, there are useful rules in place to alleviate the problem of recognizing a loss where the corporation is clearly defunct but not formally in bankruptcy proceedings.

You can elect to have a disposition of shares occur where at the end of your taxation year (i.e., the end of the shareholder's taxation year and not the corporation's year):

(1) the issuing corporation is insolvent in fact;

(2) neither the corporation nor a corporation controlled by it carries on business;

(3) the fair market value of the share is nil; and

(4) it is reasonable to expect that the issuing corporation will be dissolved or wound up and will not commence to carry on business.

Where a deemed disposition occurs at the end of a taxation year under any of the rules above, you are deemed to reacquire the shares at nil cost at the beginning of the immediately following taxation year. It follows that any actual disposition for more than nil proceeds will result in a capital gain.

No form is prescribed for this election. The CRA's Capital Gains Guide (T4037), in its section on allowable business investment losses, says that you make the election by attaching to your return a letter (or mailing it in, where the return is electronically filed), signed by you, stating that you want subsection 50(1) of the Act to apply to the particular shares in question.

Purpose of Election

The rule permitting you to elect before the corporation becomes bankrupt under the *Bankruptcy Act* or insolvent under section 6 of the *Insolvency Act* is intended to let you claim a capital or allowable business investment loss when shares are obviously worthless but no one wants the bother of formally winding-up the company. In the absence of this rule it would be necessary to find an arm's length person willing to buy the shares for, typically, $1, to trigger the loss (and at one time this indeed was necessary). The reason for making these rules elective where the corporation was already bankrupt under the *Bankruptcy Act* or insolvent under section 6 of the *Insolvency Act* at the time of the election is to allow you to defer the occurrence of tax consequences in a related debtor company triggered by the company's insolvency and your bad debt claim against the company. Normally, the deemed disposition rules do not by themselves trigger the forgiveness of debt rules, but this can happen under the complex rules intended to deal with debt parking (¶565.60). The election requirement in these circumstances is intended to allow you to choose to defer your own deductions and avoid the tax consequences of a forgiveness of debt in the insolvent company.

Business Re-starts

To deal with the situation where an apparently defunct corporation is somehow revived, subsection 50(1.1) provides that if: (i) a shareholder has elected to have the rules apply, and (ii) during the 24 months following the deemed disposition the corporation or a corporation controlled by it carries on business, and (iii) either the shareholder or a person with whom the shareholder does not deal at arm's length holds the shares subject to the election at the time the corporation carries on business within the 24-month period, there is a further deemed disposition and reacquisition at the earliest time the business was carried on and, accordingly, a capital gain on the shares arises in the hands of the shareholder or non-arm's length person, as the case may be, at that time. This rule does not apply where the corporation was already bankrupt under the *Bankruptcy Act* or insolvent under section 6 of the *Insolvency Act* at the time of the election.

(ITA: 50(1)(b), (1.1))

[¶565] GAIN ON SETTLEMENT OF A DEBT ("SECTION 80" GAIN)

Debts of an exclusively personal or non-commercial nature are not affected by the debt forgiveness provisions. The actual test is that the rules can apply where interest on the forgiven debt or obligation is or would be deductible. Under the general rules in the Act, interest is deductible only where the borrowings are made to earn income from business or property — generally, debts incurred in a commercial situation.

Interest-free debt will be subject to the debt forgiveness rules where interest, if paid or payable, would have been deductible. Debts for which an interest deduction was denied under the thin capitalization provisions will also be caught. Where a commercial debt is forgiven, the "forgiven amount" is the figure used in calculating the tax consequences to the debtor. That amount is defined by the new rules as the lesser of the principal amount and the amount for which the debt was issued, minus a number of adjustments, including any payments made in satisfaction of the principal amount. The use of the lesser of those two amounts effectively means that neither discounts allowed nor premiums paid when the debt was originally issued will have to be taken into account when calculating the forgiven amount.

[¶565.25] *Amount of Forgiven Debt*

The rules commence by defining the forgiven amount (subsection 80(1)), which is the principal amount reduced by:

(1) any amount paid at the time of settlement in satisfaction of the principal amount;

(2) amounts included in the income of an employee (under ¶353) or shareholder (¶409) on the forgiveness of a debt owed in that capacity; also, in the case of a shareholder, loans already included in the shareholder's income under ¶409;

(3) amounts included in income under the prepaid interest rules at ¶1074;

(4) amounts recognized as deemed capital gains on the repurchase of a debt issued by the taxpayer (typically this applies only to bonds, debentures and similar obligations issued by an corporation and traded in an open market);

(5) any portion of the principal amount related to resource deductions renounced by a corporation to other corporations under specified provisions;

(6) amounts accounted for as proceeds of disposition under the foreclosure rules (¶518);

(7) amounts previously accounted for under the debt parking rules (see below);

(8) amounts representing accrued interest added to the principal which have been included in the income of an employee (or a personal service corporation which is essentially an incorporated employee as discussed at ¶305) or shareholder as imputed interest under the loan rules at ¶409;

(9) where the taxpayer is bankrupt at the time, the entire principal amount is cancelled, so there is no forgiven amount;

(10) the principal amount of a loan which has been recognized as assistance for income tax purposes under the rules at ¶729, or would have been so recognized if not for the prescribed exclusions or allocation to cost bases allowed there; or of a loan which has been recognized as assistance from a government, municipality or public authority reducing the cost base of a depreciable asset under subsection 13(7.1) of the Act (¶825; also in part ¶827 and ¶828);

(11) a loan issued by the debtor which has been included back in income under the unpaid amount rules (¶746);

(12) amounts of principal included in the debtor's income by virtue of any other provisions of the Act (typically this might be certain trade payables); and

(13) consideration previously given by the debtor to another person for the assumption by the other person of the obligation.

The forgiven amount is in effect nullified in the event that a debtor is an "active" member of a partnership and the obligation has always been payable to an active member of the partnership. An active member is one actively engaged, on a regular, continuous and substantial basis, in partnership activities other than the financing of the business.

Assuming that there is a forgiven amount after all the determinations above, the new rules then expand on the old to provide that the forgiven amount may be applied in the following order.

[¶565.30] *Application of Forgiven Debt*

The forgiven amount is applied first to reduce carryover losses of the debtor, then to reduce the capital cost of certain depreciable property and the ACB of certain capital property. Finally, any remaining amounts is included in the income of the debtor in the manner described more fully below.

Loss Reduction

The rules will first require the reduction of the following amounts, in order:

(1) unapplied non-capital losses of preceding years, excluding allowable business investment losses (see ¶1087), starting with the oldest losses;

(2) farm losses of preceding years (oldest first, ¶1087);

(3) restricted farm losses of preceding years (oldest first, ¶1089);

(4) allowable business investment losses of preceding years (oldest first), allowing for adjustments from full to allowable loss (i.e., forgiveness of $100 debt will be consumed to eliminate $50 of ABIL; see ¶580); and

(5) net capital losses of preceding years (oldest first), allowing for adjustments from full to net loss (i.e., forgiveness of $100 debt will be consumed to eliminate $50 of net capital loss; see ¶1093).

Carryover losses for an earlier taxation year must be reduced before carryover losses incurred in a subsequent year. In addition, carryover losses in each category must be exhausted before moving on to the next category.

Reductions in Cost Base

Amounts remaining after loss carryforwards are eliminated may be applied, at the option of the debtor, to reduce the following, in order:

(6) capital cost of depreciable property (¶811); and

(7) undepreciated capital cost of depreciable property of a prescribed class (but the balance cannot be reduced below nil; that is, it cannot create a negative undepreciated capital cost for the class).

Although the order in which the forgiven amount is to be applied is prescribed by the rules, the taxpayer is entitled to determine, within each category, the particular property or properties which will be affected.

Other Reductions

Where forgiven amounts remain after the optional deductions above, they may be applied, at the option of the debtor, to reduce:

(8) prior to 2017, cumulative eligible capital, allowing for adjustments from full to allowable loss (i.e., forgiveness of $100 debt will be consumed to eliminate $75 of CEC; see ¶766);

(9) any resource account balances for successor pools (corporations only), CEE (¶2213), CDE (¶2217), COGPE (¶2223), and for Canadian residents only, for-

eign E&D expenses and foreign resource expenses (¶2225);

(10) ACB of non-depreciable capital property with certain exceptions, principally for shares and debt where the debtor is a specified shareholder (a 10% shareholder, counting in the related person's shares), and non-taxable Canadian property of non-residents;

(11) ACB of shares or debt of unrelated companies in which the taxpayer is a specified shareholder, subject to complex limitations;

(12) to the extent designated by the taxpayer, the ACB of shares or debt of related companies, subject to complex considerations; and

(13) current year capital losses, including those arising on wind-up of a 90%-owned subsidiary.

In order to be eligible for the reduction in cost base in items (6), (7), (8), (9), and (10), property must be owned by the debtor "immediately" after the time of settlement. This is presumably intended to prevent the debtor from acquiring property before the end of the tax year in which the settlement occurred, in order to "soak up" any unapplied forgiven amounts, thereby avoiding further tax consequences.

(ITA: 80)

[¶565.35] *Income Inclusion*

If the debtor chooses not to utilize all the reductions outlined above, or where a forgiven amount remains after all possible reductions have been made, one-half of any outstanding amounts will be included in the income of the debtor for the year from the same source in connection with which the original obligation was issued.

Where Reductions Optional

It would appear that the forgiven amount must be applied first to loss carryovers, but then will be optional as between items (6) to (10), inclusive. If the forgiven amount is applied to losses insofar as possible, and to items (6) to (10) as "designated" (i.e., at the option of the taxpayer), and no application is made under items (11) to (13), inclusive, then the specified fraction (your capital gain/loss inclusion rate for the year from ¶500a) of any amount remaining will be income. The taxpayer is free to choose income treatment rather than reductions to items (6) to (10) (although this would be a rare choice). On the other hand, the forgiven amount must be applied to items (6) to (10) to the maximum extent possible before any application to items (11) to (13) can be made.

(ITA: 80(13); 80(10), (11), (12))

[¶565.40] *Reserve Against Income Inclusion*

Some relief is provided to the debtor who brings forgiven amounts into income. The debtor may spread the recognition of that income out over several years by claiming a reserve.

However, there is a risk for taxpayers who have opted not to reduce the tax attributes of property as outlined above to the maximum extent possible, and who then claim a reserve in respect of an income inclusion. In some circumstances, the Minister has the ability to make those reductions to the extent that the debtor would have been able to — in effect, override the taxpayer's elections with respect to the forgiven amount.

Under the reserve mechanism found in subsection 61.2(1), a Canadian resident individual who has been subjected to an income inclusion by reason of a forgiveness of debt under these rules may claim an annual deduction equal to:

(1) the total of all such income inclusions for the year (including the individual's share of such income inclusions as a member of a partnership for fiscal periods that end in the year); minus the total of:

(2) deductions claimed in respect of income inclusions from a partnership under these rules by virtue of rules designed to provide relief to the partners for undeducted loss carryforwards and resource expenditure pools attributable to partnership activity; and

(3) if the individual's income for the year exceeds $40,000, 20% of the excess.

The amount deducted as a reserve is added back in the following year (section 56.2) and a new reserve calculated. As a result, the income inclusion is effectively deferred until a taxation year in which the taxpayer has, in effect, over $40,000 of other income. Other income is calculated before the income inclusion itself, the deduction of clawback tax on Old Age Security payments, and the inclusion of prior year reserves under these rules.

(ITA: 56.2; 61.2)

[¶565.45] *Exceptions*

The rules do not apply if interest on the debt would not have been deductible for income tax purposes, if the debtor is bankrupt at the time the debt is settled, if the reduction in the debt is required to be included in income under some other rule, if the reduction will reduce the cost base of some other asset by virtue of some other rule, or (for individuals) if the debt is forgiven by will. However, if interest was not deductible only because it was capitalized or required to be capitalized, the rules do apply.

Special overriding rules apply where a mortgage has been foreclosed or there has been a repossession; see ¶518.

[¶565.50] *Limitation Periods*

A creditor has a specified amount of time (the length of which varies, depending on the provincial jurisdiction and the type of the debt) to institute legal action to recover on a debt. Once that limitation period has expired, no legal action for recovery can take place. Although the creditor is then statute-barred from obtaining a judgment, the debt still exists and the CRA does not consider that the old debt forgiveness rules would apply.

Subsection 80.01(9) of the Act provides that where a debt becomes unenforceable by reason of the expiry of a statutory limitation period, the debt forgiveness rules will apply as if the debt were settled for no payment — in other words, as if the entire amount of the debt were forgiven.

(ITA: 80.01(9))

[¶565.55] *Conversion of Debt into Equity*

Corporations in financial difficulty may restructure debt by issuing shares in exchange for outstanding debt obligations, such as corporate bonds or debentures. The rules provide that where such shares are issued, the exchanged debt will be deemed to be settled for an amount equal to the aggregate of the fair market value of the shares at the time of issuance and the increase, as a result of the settlement, in the value of other shares of the corporation owned by the debt-holder. Therefore, a forgiven amount will be created to the extent that the shares' fair market value and any increase in the value of the debt-holder's shares is less than the value of the exchanged debt. Some exceptions from this rule are provided for, generally involving certain grandfathered debt obligations or distress preferred shares.

(ITA: 80(2)(*g*))

[¶565.60] *Debt Parking*

In order to avoid the application of the forgiveness of debt rules, creditors and debtors at one time resorted to the practice of debt parking. Essentially, a lender holding a loan which was unlikely to be repaid in whole or in part would, rather than simply writing it off, sell the loan (at a substantial discount) to a person who was a non-arm's length person to the debtor. The new creditor would leave the debt outstanding, since any settlement or forgiveness of the debt would trigger the application of section 80, to the detriment of the related debtor.

The rules limit the usefulness of such arrangements by treating debt sold for less than 80% of its principal amount to a party who is not arm's length from the individual debtor as having been settled for the amount of its cost to the non-arm's length party. In other words, a discount of more than 20% on the debt will become a forgiven amount, and the debtor will be required to apply it in the manner outlined above.

Example

Debtco owes $16,000 to a financial institution. That debt is acquired by a person who is not at arm's length from Debtco for $12,000. At that time, the debt will be considered settled and Debtco will be required to treat $4,000 ($16,000 - $12,000) as a forgiven amount. Note that had the debt been sold for $12,800 (80% of $16,000) or more, the *de minimis* rule would apply, and there would be no immediate tax consequences to Debtco.

The remaining debt now held by the related party will not be subject to the debt forgiveness rules unless and until the new creditor attempts to treat it as a bad debt — in other words, to claim a loss as allowed by the Act. Once that happens, the entire balance of the debt will be treated as if it were settled without payment, and treated as a forgiveness of debt to the debtor.

(ITA: 80.01(6)-(8))

[¶565.65] *Repayment of Forgiven or Parked Debt*

Some relief is provided for taxpayers who ultimately pay off forgiven or parked debt, in whole or in part, in that they will be entitled to deduct from income a portion of that payment in the year in which it is made.

(ITA: 80.01(10))

[¶565.70] *Distress Preferred Shares*

One of the results of the recession has been the development of financing instruments used by companies in financial difficulty — among them distress preferred shares. Typically, a company in financial difficulty would issue such shares to existing holders of its debt obligations as a replacement for those obligations. In a number of instances, the CRA was prepared to assist in this regard by granting tax rulings confirming favourable tax treatment to dividends received by holders of such shares.

Subsection 80.02(2) provides that where distress preferred shares are issued in substitution for a company's debt obligation, that obligation is deemed to have been settled for the lesser of its principal amount and the increase in the paid-up capital of shares of that class attributable to the issuance of the distress preferred shares. Any difference between the principal amount and the deemed settlement amount will then be treated as a forgiveness of debt.

(ITA: 80.02)

[¶565.75] *Transfers of Forgiven Amounts*

A debtor will be able, under the rules, to transfer forgiven amounts to certain related corporations or partnerships. In most cases, this ability would be utilized where the debtor has exhausted all of the mechanisms available to "use up" the forgiven amount, and may be required to include amounts in income.

While the ability to transfer a forgiven amount and thereby access the carryover losses, cost bases, etc., of a related taxpayer is attractive, there are significant risks and potential costs to the debtor with respect to the tax liability of the transferee in subsequent years. Any such plan should be undertaken only after an assessment of the relative benefits and risks is carried out in conjunction with professional tax advisers.

(ITA: 80.04)

[¶565.80] *Caution*

It seems advisable to repeat here the caution given at the outset: these rules are so complex that the above discussion must be regarded as superficial. Professional advice is warranted.

(ITA: 20(1)(n.1); 61.2; 79; 79.1; 80; 80.01; 80.02; 80.03; 80.04)

[¶566] GOODWILL AND OTHER INTANGIBLE PROPERTY

The goodwill of a business may have a measurable value, and the same comment applies to other forms of intangible business property, such as franchises, trademarks, and various other types of contractual rights. However, such intangible assets are not considered to be capital property, unless they are eligible for capital cost allowances, as described in Chapter 8, in which case they are treated as depreciable property as discussed at ¶557. Patents, franchises, licences and the like with a fixed term are depreciable property (¶880), but those with an unlimited life are not.

Unless such intangible property qualifies as depreciable property it will not be treated as an asset subject to the capital gain and capital loss rules, but instead will be treated as eligible capital property. The special tax treatment of eligible capital property is outlined in Chapter 7 at ¶766 to ¶770. Chapter 7 also contains a more complete description of the types of property which will be treated as eligible capital property. Commencing in 1988, dispositions of eligible capital property by individuals can give rise to capital gains eligible for capital gains exemption, but the taxable gain is determined under the eligible capital property rules and not under the ordinary capital gain rules. See ¶768.

Commentary on Bill C-29 Measures (Oct. 25, 2016)

Note: When Bill C-29, October 25, 2016, achieves Royal Assent, the commentary will be modified to read:

Unless such intangible property qualifies as depreciable property it will not be treated as an asset subject to the capital gain and capital loss rules, but instead will be treated as eligible capital property. The special tax treatment of eligible capital property is outlined in Chapter 7 at ¶766 to ¶770. Chapter 7 also contains a more complete description of the types of property which will be treated as eligible capital property. Commencing in 1988, dispositions of eligible capital property by individuals can give rise to capital gains eligible for capital gains exemption, but the taxable gain is determined under the eligible capital property rules and not under the ordinary capital gain rules. See ¶768. Effective January 1, 2017, the eligible capital property rules have been repealed and replaced by a new Class 14.1 of depreciable property. Property that previously was eligible capital property is now depreciable capital property, and expenditures and receipts that previously were accounted for under the eligible capital property rules are now accounted for under the rules for depreciable property and capital property.

[¶567] RESOURCE PROPERTIES

Resource properties are, in general, properties related to oil and gas and mining activities, and are defined and discussed in detail in Chapter 22.

Such properties are subject to the special tax treatment outlined in Chapter 22 and are not subject to the capital gain and loss rules.

[¶568] LOTTERIES AND OTHER PRIZE WINNINGS

Lottery winnings, along with other gains resulting from gambling, prizes, etc., where chance is the determining factor, are not considered capital gains and are therefore not subject to tax. This exemption also applies to the gain arising from a sale or other disposition of a ticket or other right to win a prize.

Keep in mind that this tax exemption does not extend to scholarships, as discussed in Chapter 9, or to prizes related to employment, where services are rendered in exchange for the award, or to other activities which are carried on extensively enough to be considered a business.

Where a capital property has been won as a prize, the cost is deemed to be the fair market value at the time the prize was awarded for purposes of calculating an ACB.

For gambling proceeds generally, and other windfall profits, see ¶991.10.

(ITA: 40(2)(*f*); 52(4); Income Tax Folio: S3-F9-C1 Lottery Winnings, Miscellaneous Receipts, and Income (and Losses) from Crime)

[¶569] LIFE INSURANCE

Death benefits received under life insurance policies are not taxable, since they are specifically exempted under the law.

However, gains arising at the time of maturity of a life insurance policy, or upon cancellation or transfer of the policy before maturity, are taxable as discussed at ¶981. Such gains are on income account and are not capital gains.

[¶570] GAINS ON PERSONAL INJURY AWARDS PROPERTY

If you are under 21 years old and have received an award for damages for physical or mental injury, any capital gain on the disposition of property purchased with the award, or on property substituted therefor, is not included in the determination of your income if the gain arose before or during the year you became 21 years old.

In addition, any income earned on the award or substituted property is not included in your income for years prior to or in which you become 21 years old (see ¶991). These exemptions also apply to gains or income arising on damage awards or substituted property held by someone else for the benefit of the injured person.

(ITA: 81(1)(*g.1*), (*g.2*); IT-365R2 [Archived])

[¶571] TIMBER RESOURCE PROPERTY

A gain from the sale of timber resource property is not a capital gain but is on income account. You cannot have a capital loss on disposition of a timber resource property, since this is a depreciable property. See ¶881.

(ITA: 39(1)(*a*)(*iv*))

[¶572] SMALL BUSINESS CORPORATIONS

Several sets of rules benefit the holders of shares and/or debt of small Canadian-controlled business corporations who dispose of their interest and realize a capital gain or loss. These rules include:

- The capital gains exemption for capital gains realized during your lifetime (or at death) on qualified small business corporation shares, as defined at ¶502i;
- Deduction of allowable capital losses on small business corporation shares or debt (as defined at ¶580) from ordinary income rather than from capital gains only, as discussed at ¶580; and
- Deferral of capital gain recognition on dispositions of small business corporation shares where gains are reinvested in other small businesses, as discussed below.

Small CCPCs enjoy or confer on their investors many special benefits in areas other than capital gains. Employees of such CCPCs can enjoy especially favourable treatment on stock options (¶330). Arm's length investments can, generally speaking, be made through an RRSP. Other benefits are discussed at ¶2501.

[¶572.05] *Deferral of Capital Gains Reinvested in Eligible Small Business Corporations*

Under subsection 44(2) of the Act, where an individual disposes of shares of a small business corporation (the "old" corporation) and realizes a capital gain, that gain can be deferred for tax purposes to the extent the proceeds of disposition of the old corporation shares are reinvested in one or more qualifying small business corporations (the "new" corporation(s)).

The cost base of the new investment will be reduced by the capital gain deferred in respect of the initial investment. Accordingly, the gain is deferred until the disposition of the new investment (unless the rollover is invoked again on those proceeds).

Qualifying Dispositions

Only an individual can obtain this capital gain deferral, and only in respect of a gain arising on a qualifying disposition. A qualifying disposition is a disposition of common shares of the capital stock of a corporation where each such share was:

- a common share issued to you (i.e., a treasury share) by a corporation which was an eligible small business corporation at the time you acquired the share;
- a common share of the capital stock of an active business corporation throughout the time you owned it; and
- owned by you throughout the 185-day period that ended immediately before the disposition.

An eligible small business corporation is a CCPC all or substantially all of the assets of which (measured by fair market value at the time of your acquisition of the shares) are used principally in an active business carried on primarily in Canada, or are shares or debt of related eligible small business corporations, or any combination thereof. The total carrying value of the assets of the corporation and its related corporations must not exceed $50 million immediately before and immediately after the investment. There are look-through rules to account for assets held by the corporation through partnerships and trusts. An eligible small business corporation does not include: a professional corporation; a specified financial institution; a corporation whose principal business is the leasing, rental, development, or sale of real property owned by it; or a corporation more than 50% of the fair market value of the property of which (net of debts incurred to acquire it) is attributable to real property.

An active business corporation for these purposes is a taxable Canadian corporation all or substantially all of the assets of which (measured by fair market value) are used in an active business, or are shares or debt of other related eligible active business corporations (or any combination thereof). The active business of the corporation referred has to be carried on primarily in Canada at all times in the period that began when the individual last acquired the share and ended when the disposition occurred (the "ownership period"), if that period is less than 730 days. In any other case, that active business has to be carried on primarily in Canada for at least 730 days during the ownership period. The same exclusions for professional corporations, etc., that apply to an eligible small business corporation apply to an active business corporation.

There are rules in place to permit or require shares acquired on certain statutory rollovers in exchange for shares of another corporation to be deemed to carry forward cost and eligibility characteristics of the old shares provided specified criteria are met. In effect, in specified circumstances, eligibility can be rolled over to the new shares.

The purpose of having the eligible corporation and active business rules is that the corporation must be a relatively small CCPC engaged primarily in an active business in Canada when the original investment is made, but can become a large and/or public corporation with its primary business outside Canada (subject to the 730-day rule) before the disposition without impairing the tax-deferred reinvestment quality of the shares.

The statutory phrase "all or substantially all" is usually interpreted by the CRA as meaning 90%, although it will acknowledge that this is a rule of thumb rather than a rule of law. The Tax Court of Canada, in interpreting the same phrase for GST purposes, has been satisfied with an 80% test. *See McKay v. The Queen*, 2001 GTC 208 (T.C.C.), and *Ruhl v. The Queen*, 1998 GTC 2055 (T.C.C.). Thus, while the corporation should always arrange matters to meet the 90% test, a marginal failure to reach 90% may not be catastrophic.

Eligible Small Business Investment Reinvestment

An eligible small business reinvestment (the "replacement shares") must have all the following characteristics:

- the investment is in ordinary common shares issued from treasury of the new corporation to the investor;
- the new corporation is, at the time the shares are issued, an eligible small business corporation; the definition is the same as for "Qualifying Dispositions", above;
- the replacement investment must be purchased in the year of the qualifying disposition or within 120 days after the year; and
- a designation of the replacement shares in respect of each qualifying disposition must be made in your income tax return for the year of the qualifying disposition.

Eligible Investor

The small business rollover is available only to individuals. An individual who acquires shares from a related individual on a rollover basis currently provided under the Act (e.g., on death or marriage breakdown) will be considered for the purpose of this measure to have acquired the shares at the time and under the same circumstances that they were acquired by that related individual.

The measure will also be available to individuals in respect of their capital gains on eligible small business investments that are held through an eligible pooling arrangement. It is contemplated that such an arrangement will permit an investment manager to identify eligible investments and pool eligible investments for those investors, while treating each investor as having his or her own share portfolio within the vehicle.

Calculation of Capital Gain Deferral

The capital gain that can be deferred ("permitted deferral") in respect of the qualifying portion of a qualifying disposition from the disposition of an eligible small business investment is determined by the following formula:

$$(G / H) \times I$$

where:

G = the total cost of all replacement eligible small business investments (not exceeding H);

H = the qualifying portion of the proceeds of disposition from an eligible disposition; and

I = the capital gain arising from the qualifying disposition.

ACB Adjustment

The final formula in this process assigns an ACB to the replacement shares. The actual cost of each replacement share is reduced by the permitted deferral pro-rated by the actual cost of the share over the cost of all replacement shares associated with the qualifying disposition.

The Department of Finance provided the following example in the Technical Notes to section 44.1.

Example

Facts

An individual makes a qualifying disposition of shares of corporation A with an ACB of $3 million for proceeds of disposition of $4.5 million. The individual purchases replacement shares in corporation B for $3 million.

Determinations

The capital gain of the individual otherwise determined is $1,500,000 ($4,500,000 - $3,000,000).

The permitted deferral of the individual in respect of the disposition is determined to be $1,000,000 by the formula (G/H) × I, here $3,000,000/$4,500,000 × $1,500,000 = $1,000,000.

The capital gain from the disposition after deducting the permitted deferral in respect of the disposition is determined as $1,500,000 - $1,000,000 = $500,000.

Anti-Avoidance Rule

An anti-avoidance rule specific to the reinvestment rollover applies where an individual or persons related to the individual dispose of shares of a particular corporation (which would normally result in the use of the corporate reorganization rules or a return of paid-up capital of shares of the corporation) and acquire new shares of the particular corporation or a corporation that does not deal at arm's length with the particular corporation principally for the purpose of increasing the total amount of permitted deferrals with respect to qualifying dispositions of the individual and the related persons. Where the rule applies, the permitted deferral with respect to qualifying dispositions of the new shares is deemed to be nil. The rule is extended to apply to the following circumstances:

- when the new shares are issued by a corporation that, at or immediately after the time of issue of the new shares, was a corporation that was not dealing at arm's length with the individual; and
- when the new shares are issued, by a corporation that acquired the old shares (or by another corporation related to that corporation), as part of the transaction or event or series of transactions or events that included that acquisition of the old shares.

(ITA: 44.1)

[¶573] SHAREHOLDER CLASS ACTION SUIT — COMPENSATION BY WAY OF CASH AND SHARES

The CRA published a bulletin, Income Tax Technical News No. 39, in December 2008, to provide guidance on how to treat compensation by way of cash and shares as a result of a shareholder class action suit. Where shares are held outside an RRSP or RRIF and the taxpayer still owns all or part of the shares when the cash settlement is received, the cash settlement payment is an adjustment to the ACB of the shares. Where the shares are held outside an RRSP or RRIF and the taxpayer no longer holds the shares at the time of receipt of the settlement, the cash settlement payment is reported as a capital gain if the shares were held on account of capital, and business income if the shares had been held on account of income. For details regarding how to account for the settlement payment if the shares are held inside an RRSP or RRIF, see ¶2612.35. The following examples, taken from Income Tax Technical News No. 39, illustrates how to account for the settlement payment when the taxpayer still owns all the original shares:

Example 1

You own 10 Original Shares of the corporation with an adjusted cost base of $1,200 or $120 per share. You receive a Settlement Payment consisting of $100 in cash plus 1 share. Your adjusted cost base for your 11 shares is now $1,100 ($1,200 - $100), or $100 per share.

Modifying the above example to illustrate the calculation if the taxpayer no longer owns any of the original shares:

Example 2

You no longer own any shares of the corporation. You receive a Settlement Payment consisting of $100 cash plus 1 share that has a fair market value of $50. If you held the original shares on account of capital, you will have a taxable capital gain of $75 in the current year and the adjusted cost base of the share received is $50. If you held the shares on account of income, you will have $150 business income for the year and the share received is held as inventory with a cost of $50.

(ITA: 39(1)(a); Income Tax Technical News No. 39)

LOSSES

[¶575] TYPES OF CAPITAL LOSSES

After deducting the ACB of a capital property and any costs of disposal from proceeds of disposition the result may be a capital loss. The deductibility of such losses will be determined in part by the nature of the property involved. The kinds of property which are relevant in this connection are:

- Personal-use property, other than listed personal property (see ¶545);
- Listed personal property (see ¶546);
- Shares or debt of a CCPC (see ¶580); and
- Other capital properties.

[¶576] APPLICATION OF LOSSES IN CURRENT YEAR

General Rule

Losses on capital property other than personal-use property may be deducted from capital gains resulting from dispositions in the year of other capital properties, including personal-use properties and listed personal properties.

Ordinary capital property losses incurred in the current year are applied in the year against ordinary capital gains to produce either a net gain or loss. It is this net number which is reduced to a "taxable portion" which can be carried over to another year, as described at ¶577.

If you have an allowable business investment loss, see ¶580.

Personal-use Property

Losses arising from dispositions of personal-use property are not deductible, not even against gains from dispositions of other personal-use property. For this reason it is not necessary to report on your tax return dispositions of such personal-use property where a loss is involved (see ¶548).

Losses arising from dispositions of listed personal property may be deducted, but only against gains arising from listed personal property. Even if there are no gains from such property in the year, or insufficient gains to offset the losses, all listed personal property losses should be reported. This is because the excess losses may be deductible in other years, as described at ¶577.

As discussed at ¶558 and ¶566, losses from depreciable property and, prior to 2017, eligible capital property are not capital losses for tax purposes. Deductions for these types of property, to the extent they are permitted, operate under special rules as deductions from ordinary income.

[¶576.05] *Capital Losses and the $2,000 Rule*

Prior to 1985, excess capital losses could be deducted from up to $2,000 of other income. This rule is now restricted to carryforwards of so-called "pre-1986 losses" as described below and at ¶577.

The $2,000 deduction for capital losses can still be relevant in terms of carry-forwards:

(1) Net allowable capital losses from years prior to 1985 and for the stub period prior to May 23, 1985 (to the extent that stub period losses were reflected in final net capital losses), continue to be deductible to the extent of $2,000 per year to the extent the unused pool of such losses exceeds all prior claims of cumulative capital gains exemption. These claims against other income also reduce the annual and cumulative gains limits for purposes of calculating the capital gains exemption at ¶502.

(2) In general, net capital losses arising after 1984 are not available for carryback to 1984 and earlier years for use against $2,000 of other income. There was an exception for 1985 stub period losses in excess of $2,000 to the extent of 1985 capital losses for the year as a whole.

For an example of the treatment of losses incurred before May 23, 1985, see "Chart 5" of the CRA guide T4037.

Where claims against other income are made out of the pre-1986 loss pool, they should be claimed together with any capital loss carryovers that may be applicable at line 253 of the T1 return.

(ITA: 3(*b*), (*e*); 40(2)(*a*)(iii); 41(2); 111(3), (8) "pre-1986 capital loss balance")

[¶577] APPLICATION OF CURRENT YEAR LOSSES IN OTHER YEARS – LINE 253

Carryover of Losses

Allowable capital losses in a year in excess of taxable capital gains give rise to a net capital loss, which can be carried back three years or forward indefinitely. Given the changes in the taxable portion factor (currently one-half), it is necessary to adjust a capital loss carryover in the year it is applied to match the inclusion factor for that year. The formula is that the taxable (or "allowable") portion of a capital loss of a particular year is multiplied, when claimed in another year, by the inclusion rate for the year of application divided by the inclusion rate for the year the loss arose. This is illustrated in the discussion of capital losses at ¶1093.

As discussed at ¶576 capital losses arising from other capital properties before May 23, 1985 may be deducted against capital gains of the year and one-half of any excess loss may be deducted against other income to a maximum of $2,000.

Net capital losses may be carried back against taxable capital gains of the three preceding years. This should be done by filing form T1A with your return by April 30 of the calendar year following the loss year. Failure to file a timely carryback request may result in forfeiture of the right to apply losses to prior years (see ¶1097). If you have no prior years' gains to absorb the loss, or if you choose not to carry back losses (although you would want to do this only in very limited circumstances), capital losses may be carried forward indefinitely to be applied against future gains. (See ¶1093.) Also see ¶503 for discussion of the interplay of capital loss carryovers and capital gains exemption.

Prior years' net capital losses can be deducted in the current year to the extent of taxable capital gains. This is reported in computing taxable income on line 253 of your T1 return.

Listed Personal Property

If you have listed personal property losses in the year in excess of listed personal property gains you may file form T1A to deduct your excess listed personal property loss against listed personal property gains in the three preceding taxation years.

In the event you had no listed personal property gains in the three immediately preceding years, or insufficient gains to offset the available loss, the unused listed personal property loss may be deducted in any of the seven years following the year the loss was incurred. Listed personal property losses need not be carried back first and then forward year by year. They may be deducted in any open year. However, losses incurred first must be deducted first in any given year.

Listed personal property losses are carried forward or back as the whole amount of the loss, and netted against the whole listed personal property gains on Schedule 3, unlike ordinary capital losses which carry over at taxable portion rates and are claimed at line 253 of the T1.

Allowable Business Investment Losses

An allowable business investment loss (ABIL; see ¶580) not utilized in the year receives the same treatment as a non-capital loss, except that if the allowable carryover period for application of these losses as non-capital losses was expired, they survive as net capital losses. See the discussion of non-capital losses at ¶1085.

(ITA: 41(2); 111(1)(*b*), (1.1), (8)(*b*))

[¶578] CAPITAL LOSS DEDUCTIONS FOR DECEASED TAXPAYERS

As discussed at ¶1920, deceased persons are considered to have disposed of each of their capital properties as of the date of death. The deemed dispositions are deemed to occur at fair market value at the date of death, subject to the rollover provisions discussed in Chapter 19. These deemed dispositions, together with any actual dispositions made in the year of but preceding death, produce taxable capital gains (at your inclusion rate for the year) and allowable capital losses (at your inclusion rate for the year) which net out in the usual fashion for the year to a final amount of taxable capital gain or allowable capital loss.

Net gain in Year of Death

If the final result is a taxable capital gain for the year, it can be offset by any accumulated but unused allowable capital losses (called "net capital losses") carried forward from earlier years. In applying net capital losses from earlier years, the adjustments described in ¶1093 (and calculated on a chart in the CRA's free booklet Capital Gains Tax Guide) must be made to allow for the lower inclusion rates of those years. To the extent net capital losses of prior years exceed amounts used to offset taxable capital gains of the year of death, the excess (minus total capital gains exemptions (¶502) claimed in all years) can be deducted against other taxable income of the year of death and the year immediately preceding death, in whatever amounts the taxpayer's representative chooses.

Net Loss in Year of Death

If the final capital gain/loss tally for the year of death produces an overall allowable capital loss for the year, the loss becomes a net capital loss. From here there are essentially two options. The net capital loss can be carried back to the extent chosen to any of the three preceding years, as discussed in ¶1087, under normal rules. However, to the extent the taxpayer's representative chooses not to do this, the capital loss joins other accumulated net capital losses accumulated but unused from other years and the total (minus total capital gains exemptions claimed in all years) can be applied to the extent chosen against any taxable income of the year of death and the year preceding death.

The taxpayer's representative appears to have complete flexibility in utilizing various amounts of net capital losses for carryback or against current or prior year taxable income as described above. Where losses cannot be fully utilized in any combination, it may be advantageous to forgo rollovers described in Chapter 19 and step up cost base to the recipient, and also to forgo the optional special returns in Chapter 19 (¶1901) and include additional income in the year of death return.

Form T1A is used to carry losses back to other years. Losses carried forward can be calculated on a chart in the CRA's Capital Gains Tax Guide (T4037). Both are available without charge from CRA offices (¶287) or from the CRA website.

These special rules with respect to the deductibility of capital losses for deceased persons do not apply to excess listed personal property losses, for which the normal rules described at ¶548 remain applicable.

Example 1: Capital Losses Arising in Year of Death

Ms. Jordan died in 2009. Her income for 2009 was $42,841, not including her deemed capital losses in excess of gains of $15,000. Her 2008 income was $38,707, plus a capital gain of $6,000, and so she had a 2008 taxable capital gain of $3,000.

Her 2009 net capital loss available for carryover is 50% of $15,000 = $7,500. Ms. Jordan's representative decides to apply $2,115 to reduce ordinary income for 2009 to $40,726, eliminating all income above the lowest rate bracket, and leaving $5,385 of net capital loss to apply.

The representative then looks at 2008. The first step is to use $3,000 to eliminate the 2008 taxable capital gain of $3,000. (There is no adjustment required for inclusion rates, since the 50% inclusion rate applies to both 2009 and 2008.) The next step is to apply enough of the remaining $2,385 to lower 2008 income to $37,885, which requires $822. Both 2008 and 2009 incomes taxed above the lowest bracket have now been eliminated, and $1,563 of loss remains to be used. Since the applicable federal tax rate on this income is the same for both years, this is not a governing consideration. Changes in provincial tax rates, where applicable, should be borne in mind as an advantage or disadvantage, as the case may be, in carrying losses back. In general, there are a number of other beneficial rules for the year of death which might lower that income, which may, in some circumstances, make a carryback preferable.

Example 2: Capital Losses Carried Forward to Year of Death

Mr. Unlucky had a 1988 capital gain of $15,000 (taxable capital gain of $10,000) against which he claimed capital gains exemption of $10,000. In 1995 he had a capital loss of $10,000 (allowable capital loss and net capital loss carryover of $7,500 at the then applicable 75% inclusion rate). The loss is still on hand in its entirety. In 2008 he had ordinary income of $40,000 and a capital loss of $28,000. His capital gain inclusion rate for 2008 was (of course) 50%, so this became an allowable capital loss of 50% = $14,000 available for carryover. In 2009, he had income of $38,000 prior to his death in the year, and $6,000 of capital gain ($3,000 of taxable capital gain). He had no other capital gains or losses after 1972.

The ordering provisions presumably apply to require use of the 1995 net capital loss before the 2008 loss in 2009. As discussed at ¶1093, the 1995 net capital loss of $7,500 must be stepped down (by 50%/75%, or 2/3) to $5,000 when carried to 2009 to account for the change in inclusion rates. Accordingly, $3,000 of the $5,000 available taxable capital loss is used to offset the 2009 taxable capital gain; the $2,000 balance is stepped back up (by 3/2) to $3,000, which is the remaining 1995 net capital loss carryforward. (This calculation can be made in the chart in the CRA's Capital Gains Tax Guide.) Looked at another way, to achieve a target loss of $3,000 to offset the 2009 gain with 1995 loss requires 75%/50% or 3/2 of $3,000, or $4,500 of the $7,500 1995 net capital loss, leaving a $3,000 balance. The remaining $14,000 of 2008 net capital loss and $3,000 of 1995 net capital loss must be reduced by the $10,000 capital gains exemption claimed in 1988, and the remainder ($14,000 + $3,000 - $10,000 = $7,000) can be used against ordinary income of 2009 and/or 2008, as seems most beneficial.

(ITA: 70(5); 111(1.1), (2); IT-232R3 para. 30 [Archived])

[¶579] SUPERFICIAL LOSSES

No recognition of a loss on disposition of property is permitted where the loss is a superficial loss. Instead, the cost base of the substituted property is increased by the amount of the loss denied.

[¶579.05] *Meaning of Superficial Loss for Individuals*

A superficial loss (section 54) is the loss from the disposition by an individual of a property where:

(1) during the period that begins 30 days before the disposition and ends 30 days after the disposition, the disposing taxpayer or a person affiliated with the disposing taxpayer acquired or had a right to acquire the same property or an identical property; and

(2) at the end of the 60-day period, the disposing taxpayer or a person affiliated with the disposing taxpayer owned or had a right to acquire the same property or an "identical property". The concept of an affiliated person is discussed at ¶852.There are a number of exceptions to the superficial loss rules. These are:

(3) a deemed disposition arising because the taxpayer ceases to be a resident of Canada, as discussed at ¶534;

(4) a deemed disposition arising because of the taxpayer's death, as discussed at ¶1920;

(5) a deemed disposition arising from the expiry of an option, as discussed at ¶561;

(6) a deemed disposition on a change of use of property, discussed at ¶513;

(7) a deemed disposition of a bad debt (¶563) or of shares of an insolvent corporation (¶564);

(8) where a loss is already denied under certain other rules (this rule was slightly modified on December 8, 1997);

(9) certain dispositions deemed to have been made by trusts; a number of corporate transactions by mutual funds, insurers, financial institutions and securities dealers; a change in corporate status to or from an exempt corporation; and, a number of corporate or partnership dispositions governed by more specific rules similar to those in ¶585 or ¶851;

(10) where there is a change of control of the disposing corporation within 30 days after the disposition; and

(11) where there is a change of exempt status of the disposing corporation within 30 days after the disposition.

[¶579.15] *Application of the Rules*

For purposes of the superficial loss rule, "identical property" will include certain bonds, debentures, bills, notes or other similar obligations as discussed at ¶512. However, there is also an explicit provision in the superficial loss rules that a right to acquire property (such as an exchange or conversion right attached to shares) is deemed to be a property identical to the property which is the subject of the right. This rule does not apply to security rights derived from a mortgage, hypothec, agreement for sale, or similar obligation.

Where the rule applies to disallow a capital loss deduction to you, the loss denied to you at that time may be added to the ACB of the property obtained in substitution. As a result, the loss will eventually become deductible when the substituted property is disposed of.

The apparent purpose of this denial of a loss deduction where the same or identical property is reacquired is to prevent taxpayers from realizing deductible capital loss without any real intention to rid themselves of the property occasioning the loss.

A loss from the disposition of property by you to a trust governed by an RRSP, a deferred profit sharing plan, an employees profit sharing plan, a registered disability savings plan, a registered retirement income fund, a registered home ownership savings plan, or a tax-free savings account under which you are a beneficiary or immediately after the disposition you become a beneficiary is deemed to be nil. The loss is also nil where property is disposed of to a trust governed by an RRSP under which your spouse or common-law partner (¶1113) is an annuitant or became, within 60 days after the end of the taxation year in which the disposition occurs, an annuitant. In these situations the loss denied to you cannot be added to the ACB of the property obtained in substitution since it is not a superficial loss.

(ITA: 40(2)(*g*)(i), (iv); 53(1)(*f*); 54 "superficial loss"; IT-387R2 (Consolidated) [Archived])

[¶580] BUSINESS INVESTMENT LOSS

BILS and ABILs

If you disposed of a share or a debt owed you by a small business corporation (defined below)

- to a person with whom you deal at arm's length (see ¶812), or
  - (in the case of shares) because the corporation has become formally bankrupt or effectively insolvent under the rules at ¶564, or
  - (in the case of debt) because the debt is uncollectible and the deemed disposition rules at ¶563 apply,

and as a result you incurred a capital loss, the loss is considered a business investment loss, or BIL (paragraph 39(1)(*c*)). The BIL is reported on line 228 of your T1 return.

One-half of the BIL is an allowable business investment loss (ABIL), which you may deduct from your income for the year from any source on line 217 of your T1 return. The carryforward period for unused ABILs (as for non-capital losses) arising in taxation years is 10 years.

Conversion of ABIL in Future Years to Net Capital Loss

If a loss arising in a taxation year ending cannot be fully utilized against income by the end of the carryforward period, it then becomes a net capital loss in that year. Thus, for example, an allowable business investment loss incurred in 2005, to the extent it was not used in a prior or subsequent year up to and including 2015, becomes a net capital loss carryover (¶1093) originating in 2016. The loss is available for carryforward, but only against taxable capital gains. In theory, of course, it remains available for carryback as well, but in practice it should have already been used to the extent desired in prior years.

Determining that a share is eligible for the loss claim in a particular year because of insolvency is assisted by the rules at ¶564, but you must ensure that you do make a claim as soon as the conditions there appear to be met. Determining when a debt was uncollectible may be more difficult. The case of *Earl v. M.N.R.*, 89 DTC 221 (T.C.C.), suggests that the taxpayer's subjective determination will carry considerable weight.

[¶580.10] *Definition of Small Business Corporation*

A "small business corporation" (subsection 248(1)) is defined as a CCPC all or substantially all of whose assets are:

(1) used by the corporation or a related corporation primarily in carrying on an active business in Canada (an active business is any business carried on by the corporation other than a specified investment business or a personal service business. A specified investment business is a business (one not having five or more full-time employees) the principal purpose of which is to earn income from property. A personal service business is one where, except for the existence of the corporation, the shareholder would reasonably be regarded as officer or employee of the entity to which

the corporation is providing service ("incorporated employee"), see ¶785;

(2) shares or debt obligations of other small business corporations "connected with" the corporation (a corporation is "connected with" a second corporation if it controls the second corporation in law or if it owns shares of the second corporation which represent more than 10% of the voting rights and more than 10% of the fair market value of all issued shares of the second corporation); or

(3) a combination of assets all of which are described in either (1) or (2).

The intent of these rules is to include corporations which devote 90% or more of their assets to active business operations or are holding companies for such corporations. The 90% test must be measured by the fair market value of the assets at the time the realization of loss occurs.

Since the assets of a company whose shares are being sold or whose debt is uncollectible may no longer be in use, a special rule provides that an allowable business loss may arise on the shares or debt of a corporation that met the definition of a small business corporation at any time in 12 months preceding the disposition of the shares or bankruptcy or establishment of uncollectibility of the debt.

A further special rule deals with the situation of a business investment loss that arises on disposition of debts of a corporation that was a small business corporation at the time of bankruptcy or insolvency but had ceased to be so when the debts are disposed of. Provided the corporation was a small business corporation as defined above at the time of a bankruptcy as defined in the federal *Bankruptcy Act* or at the time of a winding-up order under the *Winding-up Act*, the losses incurred by individuals on debt owed by the corporation will qualify as business investment losses.

There are special relieving rules dealing with a life insurance policy on the life of a shareholder of that corporation, or of any connected corporation or any corporation connected to a connected corporation, as well as certain anomalies which can arise in a chain of corporations.

[¶580.15] *Business Investment Loss Arising on Guarantee*

In the case of a payment made by a taxpayer under a guarantee in respect of a corporation's liabilities, a debt does not arise between the corporation and the guarantor until the guarantee payment is made. This may not occur within the 12-month period following cessation of business normally allowed within the definition of "small business corporation" described above. Subsection 39(12) effectively allows a payment under an arm's length guarantee to be treated as a debt owing by a small business corporation where the corporation was a small business corporation both (1) at the time the debt in respect of which the guarantee payment is made was incurred, and (2) at any time in the 12 months before the time an amount first became payable under the guarantee. Thus the debt need not actually be disposed of or become bad within 12 months of cessation of business, as long as the guarantee is called and becomes payable within 12 months. This may still be a less than generous time frame if the guarantee is contested.

[¶580.20] *Adjustments to Business Investment Loss*

Reduced by Capital Gains Exemption Claimed

The utilization of the business investment loss provisions is affected by capital gains exemption claims (¶502). A business investment loss of an individual (other than a trust) is reduced in a taxation year where he or she has claimed a capital gains exemption in a previous taxation year. The reduction in the individual's business investment loss (subsection 39(9)) is the lesser of:

- the individual's business investment loss for the year otherwise determined; and
- each amount deducted as a lifetime capital gains exemption (¶502) in computing his or her taxable income for each previous taxation year, multiplied by the reciprocal of the capital gains inclusion portion applicable in that year, except to the extent that any other business investment loss was reduced in the current or a previous year under this provision; thus, the amount here is the total of
  - all capital gains exemptions claimed before 1988 or (for calendar taxation years) after 2000 times 2,
  - all exemptions claimed in 1988 and 1989 times $^3/_2$,
  - all exemptions claimed after 1989 and before 2000 times $^4/_3$, and
  - exemptions claimed for 2000 (calendar taxation years) by the reciprocal of your inclusion rate for 2000 (except to the extent that any other business investment loss was reduced in the current or a previous year under this provision).

The objective of this provision is to ensure that the capital gains exemption applies only to net cumulative economic gains. If a subsequent capital loss is deducted against other income, in the form of a business investment loss, the exemption is considered to have been over-applied. Hence, the business investment loss (before it is reduced for carryover purposes — see ¶500) is in effect reduced by a previous capital gain which was reduced and offset by capital gains exemption (¶502).

Any reduction in an individual's business investment loss by virtue of this provision will be treated as a capital loss for the year in which it arose.

The CRA provides a useful and accurate chart (Chart 6) for calculating the business loss reduction for capital gains exemptions in its T4037 Capital Gains Tax Guide. The chart accompanies the discussion of allowable business investment losses in the Guide.

As for trusts, the rules provide for a reduction of a business investment loss of a trust where in a previous taxation year the trust has designated a capital gain allocated to a beneficiary of the trust to be eligible for the capital gains exemption. The reduction in the trust's business investment loss (subsection 39(10)) will be equal to the lesser of:

(1) the trust's business investment loss for the year otherwise determined; and

(2) the reciprocal of the relevant capital gains inclusion portion of the amounts designated by the trust in respect of beneficiaries for previous taxation years except to the extent that any other business investment loss of the year or of a previous year was reduced under this provision.

Any reduction in a trust's business investment loss in a taxation year under this provision will be considered to be a capital loss of the trust in the year in which it arose.

Other Reductions

If the business investment loss arises on a share issued before 1972, or a share substituted therefor, the loss must be reduced by any dividends received by you or related persons, in respect of the share, or a substituted share. This rule does not apply if the share was acquired after 1971 from a person with whom you were dealing at arm's length. A business investment loss may also arise if the shares are redeemed or purchased for cancellation. Shares are deemed to have been disposed of at the time they are redeemed or cancelled and thus, any deemed dividend on a redemption or cancellation of a pre-1972 share reduces the business investment loss.

Certain additions to the cost of the shares of a CCPC must reduce the business investment loss, but the loss would still be a capital loss, see item 11, ¶508.

(ITA: 39(1)(c), (9), (10); 110.6(15); 111(8)(b); 248(1); IT-484R2 [Archived])

[¶580d] STOP-LOSS RULE ON SHARES WITH CAPITAL DIVIDENDS

Capital Dividends

Capital dividends can only be paid by private corporations. They are a mechanism for flowing out certain items, such as the non-taxable portion of capital gains and life insurance proceeds, free of tax to the shareholders, thus putting them in the same position as if they had received these normally tax-free amounts directly. Capital dividends must not be confused with capital gains dividends, which may be distributed by flow-through entities (typically mutual funds), represent distributions out of the whole capital gains realized in the fund, and are taxed as capital gains realized by the investor (see ¶418).

Private Corporation

Private corporations for tax purposes are essentially Canadian corporations which are not publicly traded or are not controlled by publicly traded corporations other than venture capital corporations. In a few cases, corporations which might seem private may elect for tax purposes to be considered public corporations. Where a private corporation which paid capital dividends has later become a public corporation, the stop-loss rules below remain in effect, but will not operate to the extent the dividends were treated as taxable dividends in the hands of the shareholder, which can happen under anti-avoidance rules where the main purpose of a transaction is to receive a particular capital dividend.

Stop-Loss Rule

A capital loss of an individual otherwise calculated on the disposition of a share must be reduced by the lesser of (subsection 112(3)):

(1) any capital dividends (¶415.05) received by the taxpayer on the shares; and

(2) the loss itself without backing out capital dividends minus any taxable dividends received by the taxpayer on the shares.

The overall intent of the rule is to reduce the loss by capital dividends received; the intent of the rule in (2) is to ensure that the loss is not reduced to the extent it is attributable to taxable dividends.

The capital loss reduction for capital dividends received (in (1), above) will not apply to a person who meets both the following tests:

(3) the capital dividends were received at a time when the taxpayer (together with any non-arm's length persons; see ¶812) did not own more than 5% of the issued shares of any class of the corporation's stock; and

(4) the capital dividends were received on a share that the taxpayer owned throughout the 365-day period that ended immediately before the disposition.

Similar rules apply where the shares are held by a partnership or a trust.

(ITA: 112(3)–(3.2))

[¶580d.05] *Losses on Trust Interest*

Essentially, the stop-loss rules for capital dividends are replicated where the dividend flows through a trust to the beneficiary. The rules appear to be somewhat different, in that all non-taxable dividends (¶415.05) and not merely capital dividends reduce the loss on the disposition of a capital interest in the trust (paragraph 107(1)(*c*)).

(ITA: 104(20); 107(1)(c))

MISCELLANEOUS RULES

[¶581] RESERVE FOR PROCEEDS NOT DUE

If the proceeds of disposition from a sale of capital property are not all receivable in the year of sale, realization of a portion of the capital gain may be deferred, within specified limits, until the year in which the proceeds become receivable.

You must file form T2017 to claim a capital gain reserve. Reserves, or reductions of reserves, calculated on T2017 are carried to Schedule 3 of your T1.

Calculation of Reserve

The maximum reserve that may be claimed in a year is the lesser of two amounts or limits (subparagraph 40(1)(*a*)(iii)).

First Limit

The portion of the gain which may be deferred for tax purposes under the first limit is required to be a "reasonable" portion of the gain. This is normally determined by calculating the ratio of the capital gain to the total proceeds of disposition, and applying this ratio to the amount not payable until after the end of the year.

That is, a reasonable reserve would be:

$$\frac{\text{profit (i.e., capital gain)}}{\text{selling price (i.e., proceeds of disposition)}} \times \text{amount payable after the end of the taxation year} = \text{reserve}$$

The CRA has indicated that it will accept reserves computed in this manner. However, in certain circumstances (such as inadequate security), a greater reserve may be appropriate.

Interpretation bulletin IT-236R4, dealing with reserves on dispositions of capital property, was archived (¶283) in late 2004, meaning it can no longer be relied on as policy. Nevertheless, used with caution, it still presents a reasonable overview of the issues. In the absence of the IT, official guidance is limited to the information in the CRA Capital Gains Guide (T4037) and on form T2017.

The formula refers to amounts payable after the relevant year rather than due after the year. This is intended to avoid penalizing creditors who exercise acceleration clauses pursuant to an agreement under which the creditor sold property and received, as part of the consideration, a note payable by the purchaser. The acceleration is typically exercised only if the purchaser is in default.

Second Limit

An additional limitation normally restricts the reserve to a maximum of five years, and requires a minimum recognition of 20% of the capital gain in the year of disposition and an additional 20% in each succeeding year. Note that this is 20% of the whole gain and not 20% of the reserve otherwise calculated.

More precisely, you may claim as a reserve the lesser of:

(1) a reasonable amount of the gain as calculated above; and

(2) 1/5 of the total capital gain (i.e., proceeds net of adjusted cost base and costs of disposition) x (4 minus the number of preceding taxation years ending after disposition)

("Preceding year ending after disposition" in (2) will not include the year of disposition itself.)

One result of the above rule requiring 20% annual recognition of gain that often causes confusion is that if you receive a large payment on account of proceeds of disposition on closing, with the balance spread over or deferred for several years, you may find that the 20% rule does not operate in the early years. For example, suppose you purchased property for $10,000 and sold it for $60,000. Your capital gain is $50,000. You received $30,000 at the time of sale with the remaining $30,000 to be paid only after five years. In the year of sale your reserve under general rules would be $25,000 (half your capital gain). Your reserve under the restriction, however, would be $40,000 (1/5 of your capital gain times 4). You would claim the smaller reserve of $25,000. In each succeeding year before final payment your reserve under the general rule would remain at $25,000, since there is no change in proceeds not due, the only variable factor in the general formula. However, your reserve calculated under the restriction would be $30,000 in Year 2 and $20,000 in Year 3. In Year 3 the restriction reserve would be less than the general reserve and you would have additional capital gain included in income for the first time since the year of disposition. Looked at from the point of view of capital gain reported rather than deduction claimed, although the restriction required 20% recognition in each year, the general rule required 50% recognition in the first year. The general rule then required no further recognition until further proceeds were due, but the restriction required 40% recognition in Year 2 (but since 50% was already recognized this had no effect) and 60% in Year 3, at which point it became the effective rule.

10-Year Limit

The five-year rule discussed above is extended to 10 years in certain cases under subsection 40(1.1). Where you transfer to your child, grandchild, or great-grandchild who is resident in Canada at the time, property which immediately before the transfer was:

(1) land or depreciable property in Canada that was used by you or your spouse or common-law partner or your child or parent in a farming business carried on in Canada;

(2) a share in the capital stock of a family farm corporation (as defined for purposes of the intergenerational rollover at ¶1923, and not the somewhat more restrictive capital gains exemption rules at ¶502);

(3) an interest in a family farm partnership (as defined for purposes of the intergenerational rollover at ¶1923, and not the somewhat more restrictive capital gains exemption rules at ¶502); or

(4) a share in the capital stock of a small business corporation (as defined in ¶502i.10 for earlier dispositions),

or, after May 1, 2006, you transfer to your child, grandchild or great-grandchild who is resident in Canada at the time, property which immediately before the transfer was:

(5) land or depreciable property in Canada that was used by you or your spouse or common-law partner or your child or parent in a fishing business carried on in Canada;

(6) a share in the capital stock of a family fishing corporation (as defined for purposes of the intergenerational rollover at ¶1923d, and not the somewhat more restrictive capital gains exemption rules at ¶502); or

(7) an interest in a family fishing partnership (as defined for purposes of the intergenerational rollover at ¶1923d, and not the somewhat more restrictive capital gains exemption rules at ¶502);

you may claim as a reserve the lesser of:

(1) a reasonable amount of the gain as calculated above; and

(2) 1/10 of the total capital gain x (9 minus the number of preceding taxation years ending after the transfer).

"Child" or "parent" for purposes of the 10-year rule have the extended meanings discussed in ¶1122.

Reserve Brought Back into Income

A reserve claimed at the end of one year must be brought back into income in the following year and reported on Schedule 3. If not all the proceeds are due in that following year, a new reserve may be claimed then. This practice should be followed each year until all proceeds have been collected. However, the amount of the reserve claimed in a year may not exceed the amount claimed in respect of that property in the immediately preceding year.

Reserve for Donations of Non-qualified Securities

If you donate a non-qualifying security to a qualified donee and have a capital gain, you may be able to claim a reserve in order to defer the capital gain. See ¶1290d.15.

[¶581.05] Reserve Denied in Some Cases

Under paragraph 40(2)(*a*), the reserve will not be permitted where the acquiror was a corporation which immediately after the acquisition of the property was controlled directly or indirectly by you. Similarly, the reserve is not permitted where the acquiror was a partnership in which immediately after the acquisition of the property you were a majority interest partner.

The reserve is also denied in circumstances where at the end of the year in respect of which the reserve is claimed or at any time in the immediately following year, you were not resident in Canada.

These reserve denials apply to both the general capital gains reserve claimed under these rules and the virtually identical reserve claimed where a replacement property is acquired and gain deferred under the rules at ¶523 or ¶525.

[¶581.15] *Reserves and Capital Gains Exemption*

Where a reserve has been claimed on a capital gain in a prior year, the amount eligible for capital gains exemption is reduced accordingly, and the later inclusion of this reserve in income will qualify for the capital gains exemption on farming or fishing property or small business shares.

(ITA: 40(1)(*a*)(iii), (1.1), (2)(*a*); 70(10)(*a*); 110.6(1); IT-236R4 [Archived])

[¶582] RESERVE ON SALE OF MORTGAGED PROPERTY

If you sell a property which at the time of the sale is subject to an existing mortgage, the CRA will allow you to use an alternate calculation in determining the amount of the reasonable portion of the reserve discussed at ¶581. The reserve is calculated by substituting the amount of your equity in the property for proceeds of disposition. Your equity in such a property is the amount by which the proceeds of the sale exceed the amount of the debt attached to that property. The debt which may be used to reduce proceeds of disposition is limited to the amount of any existing mortgage assumed by the new purchaser which you had given to a third party either at the time of your purchase of the land or to finance improvements to the land (such as construction or improvement of a building). It does not apply to a mortgage you put on the property when borrowing funds for any other reason (e.g., to purchase securities).

Example

A capital property with an ACB of $7,000 was sold for $10,000. The existing mortgage of $2,000 was assumed by the purchaser and the vendor agreed to carry a second mortgage for $6,000. The vendor's equity in the property is $8,000 ($10,000 - $2,000) and his capital gain is $3,000 ($10,000 - $7,000).

You may claim a reserve of $2,250 against the capital gain in the year of disposition calculated as follows:

$$\$3,000 / \$8,000 \times \$6,000 = \$2,250$$

Using this alternate calculation, the amount of reserve is increased and a larger deferral of the tax payable on your capital gain is achieved. (If the reserve limitation described at ¶581 applied, the denominator would be proceeds of disposition of $10,000 and the limitation would be $1,800.)

The per-year reserve limitation described at ¶581 does apply, but in the example above it would be 80% of the $3,000 gain, or $2,400, and would not be a limiting factor.

Much of the information above was originally supported by interpretation bulletin IT-236R4, dealing with reserves on dispositions of capital property, which was archived (¶283) in late 2004, meaning it can no longer be relied on as policy. Nevertheless, there is no particular reason to suppose the policies outlined here have changed. In the absence of the Bulletin, official guidance is limited to the information in the CRA Capital Gains Guide (T4037) and form T2017, neither of which ever referred to the mortgage issue before 2004, nor do they now.

[¶583] INSTALMENT PAYMENTS OF TAX ARISING ON DEATH OR EMIGRATION

If capital gains are deemed to result because of the death of a taxpayer, the taxpayer's legal representative can elect (on form T2075) to pay the tax on those gains in up to 10 equal annual instalments (subsection 159(5)). Interest will be charged the rate prescribed by the government (presumably the rate for amounts owing to the Receiver General, so the prescribed rate plus 4%) and security will be required. See ¶1926.

Where capital gains are deemed to arise because of the emigration of an individual, tax payments may be deferred without penalty or interest provided adequate security is posted to cover the deemed gains (subsection 220(4.5)). Tax on up to $100,000 of gains can be deferred without posting security. See ¶2153.

(ITA: 70; 128.1; 159(4), (5), (7); 220(4.5); 220(4.54); ITR: 4301 Prescribed Rate of Interest)

[¶584] INCOME AVERAGING NOT APPLICABLE TO CAPITAL GAINS

Since capital gains do not represent a regularly recurring source of income, and since, unless they are subject to the instalment sale rules described at ¶581 and ¶582, they must be taken into income in the year the capital gain is realized, they can result in income for the year in which the capital gain is realized significantly higher than a normal level of income for the taxpayer.

Capital gains may also give rise to alternative minimum tax, which may be viewed as a compulsory form of averaging. See Chapter 24.

[¶585] TRANSFERS OF CAPITAL PROPERTY TO OR FROM CORPORATIONS OR PARTNERSHIPS

There are special rules which may apply where capital properties are transferred to and from corporations, partnerships or trusts. Some of these rules (called "rollovers") are permissive, allowing property to be contributed to a corporation or partnership without current realization of capital gain. Other rules (called "stop-loss rules") are prohibitive, preventing realization of losses on transfers where the transferor may be thought to still have an effective interest or control over the property.

The rules involved in this area are very technical in nature. It is inadvisable to make transfers (other than normal arm's length dispositions) of capital property to corporations, trusts, and partnerships without the advice of competent tax advisers.

[¶585.05] *Section 85 Rollover*

This is a tax provision which allows you to transfer properties with accrued gains to a corporation and not be taxed on the accrued gain immediately. You must take back shares of the corporation in exchange, and you may also take back cash or other property up to the cost base of the property you transfer to the corporation. The cost base of the shares you receive in exchange will in effect represent the difference (if any) between the cost base of the property transferred and any cash or other non-share property taken back in exchange. You may select a higher value than cost (up to fair market value) for the disposition value of the transferred property, and realize a gain on the difference, and increase the cost base of shares or property taken in exchange. This election is not limited to capital property; depreciable property, certain inventory, and other items may also be transferred in this way.

Because the gain inherent in the property transferred in effect reduces the cost base of the shares taken back (from fair market value of the property transferred), taxation of the gain is theoretically deferred until the shares are sold or otherwise disposed of; notionally this need not occur until the later of the death of the transferor or the transferor's spouse or common-law partner.

This election is usually used by individuals who operate a business and want to incorporate it, or who have an incorporated business and wish to contribute additional assets to it, but the rules may apply in a much wider variety of situations.

The rules and limitations are very complex, and you should not undertake such a transaction without professional advice.

(ITA: 85; IT-291R3 [Archived]; T2057 Election on Disposition of Property by a Taxpayer to a Taxable Canadian Corporation)

[¶585.10] *Section 97 Rollover*

Rules similar to those for a section 85 election allow you to contribute property to a partnership on a tax-deferred basis.

(ITA: 97; IT-413R [Archived]; T2059 Election on Disposition of Property by a Taxpayer to a Canadian Partnership)

[¶585.15] *Other Rollovers*

See ¶523, ¶531, ¶532, ¶536, ¶536c, and ¶537.

[¶585.20] *Stop-Loss Rules*

Where you dispose of capital property to an "affiliated person", as defined in ¶852, the superficial loss rules may apply as described at ¶579. Where you receive capital property from an affiliated corporation or partnership, specific rules may apply which will have much the same result of denying final recognition of the loss by the transferor until there is a final non-affiliated disposition. See the similar rules on dispositions of depreciable property at ¶851.

(ITA: 40(2)(*d*), (3.3), (3.5); 53(1)(*f*.1); 85(4))

[¶586] ACQUISITIONS OF CAPITAL PROPERTY FROM NON-RESIDENTS

It is important to be aware that you may be required to withhold 25% of the purchase price if you purchase real property situated in Canada, capital property used in carrying on a business in Canada, a share of a private Canadian corporation, a partnership interest, or an interest in a trust from a non-resident vendor.

Because a non-resident of Canada may be subject to Canadian tax on a capital gain arising from a disposition of taxable Canadian property and may be outside the jurisdiction of Canadian tax authorities, a purchaser of such property is required to withhold tax from a non-resident vendor and remit this tax to the Canadian tax authorities. The tax to be withheld is 25% of the purchase price of the property. "Taxable Canadian property" is defined in greater detail at ¶2040.

The liability to withhold tax can only be avoided by obtaining a certificate indicating an amount approved by the CRA as not being subject to the 25% withholding tax. Unless the certificate is obtained, the purchaser is liable for the withholding tax, whether or not the non-resident is actually taxable upon his disposition of property. This certificate will be issued, in appropriate circumstances and upon application by the non-resident, to both the non-resident vendor and the purchaser.

If you are a purchaser of taxable Canadian property and you are not sure of the place of residence of the vendor, you are required to make "reasonable inquiries" before assuming you are not dealing with a non-resident.

The CRA takes the view that reasonable inquiry requires that you at least inquire of the vendor's solicitors or agent as to his or her place of residence and, failing to get a definite answer, that you get a letter from the vendor stating that he or she is a Canadian resident.

The withholding rate is 50% if you buy from a non-resident a Canadian resource property, a timber resource property, real property that is not capital property, depreciable property that is taxable Canadian property, or a life insurance policy originally issued to a Canadian resident.

This matter is discussed in more detail at ¶2042.

Residents of Quebec purchasing Quebec real property from non-residents of Canada face a parallel set of rules imposed by Quebec. See ¶1608.

(ITA: 116(1), (5), (5.2), (5.3))

[¶587] ARTIFICIAL TRANSACTIONS

There is a rule relating to capital gains and losses designed to prevent you from unduly or artificially gaining a tax advantage through a transaction which technically results in a capital gain or capital loss.

The rule permits the CRA to recalculate a capital gain or capital loss your report if the CRA can reasonably consider the reported gain or loss to have been artificially or unduly understated or overstated.

A similar rule — one among many — provides that a series of transactions designed to convert income into exempt capital gains will not qualify the income for exemption.

(ITA: 55(1); 110.6; 245)

[¶588] TAXATION OF SWITCH FUNDS

Commentary on Bill C-29 Measures (Oct. 25, 2016)

Note: When Bill C-29, October 25, 2016, achieves Royal Assent, the commentary will be modified to read:

Canadian mutual funds can be structured as a trust or a corporation. If a mutual fund is structured as a corporation it may be organized as a "switch fund". Switch funds use separate share classes in the same corporation to hold the assets for each fund. Prior to legislative changes in 2016, investors were able to exchange shares of one class of the mutual fund corporation for shares of another class and rely on section 51 of the *Income Tax Act* to deem the switch not to be a disposition for income tax purposes.

For transactions occurring after 2016, an exchange of shares ("old shares") of a mutual fund corporation or investment corporation for other shares ("new shares") in a mutual fund corporation will be considered to be a disposition for tax purposes. Section 51 and the various other rollover provisions will not apply, such that the proceeds of disposition of the old shares will presumably equal the fair market value of the new shares received as consideration.

These rules do not apply to certain transactions where the old shares and new shares derive their

> value from the same properties or portfolios and in the same proportions.

(ITA: 131(4.1))

SPECIAL RULES FOR CAPITAL PROPERTY OWNED ON DECEMBER 31, 1971

[¶589] ASSETS OWNED ON DECEMBER 31, 1971

Only the increase in value of assets after 1971 results in capital gains subject to tax, and only reductions in the value of assets occurring after 1971 will be allowed to be deducted as capital losses.

For assets owned on December 31, 1971, special rules are necessary so that gains and losses accruing up to that date will be excluded from tax calculations.

When calculating the capital gain or capital loss from disposal of an asset which was owned on December 31, 1971, it may be necessary to substitute another amount for the actual original cost of the asset when calculating the asset's ACB. There are two permissible ways of determining the amount which should be substituted for the actual original cost of the asset, discussed respectively at ¶590 and ¶591 below.

(ITA: 26(1), (3))

[¶590] USE OF VALUATION DAY VALUE

One method is to substitute for the actual original cost of all capital assets owned on December 31, 1971, the value of the assets on a date which is termed "Valuation Day". Valuation Day is December 31, 1971, for all capital assets except for publicly-traded Canadian securities indicated on a list published by the CRA. This list may be obtained at no cost from your Tax Services Office. For the publicly-traded securities on the list, Valuation Day is December 22, 1971.

If the Valuation Day value method is chosen, you must elect this method for the first year in which you have disposed of one of the assets owned on December 31, 1971 (see below). If you do not elect this method for the year the first disposal occurs, you will not be able to use the Valuation Day method in calculating capital gain or loss for that year or any subsequent year. On the other hand, if you do indicate choice of this method you will be required to use it for all capital assets owned on December 31, 1971, whenever disposed of, and therefore you should be sure this is the most advantageous choice before completing your tax return.

There is an exception to the rule requiring the election to be made with the tax return for the first year in which any of the capital property owned on December 31, 1971, is disposed of. If the only property disposed of since December 31, 1971, which was owned on that date is of the following kinds it will not be necessary to make the election to use Valuation Day values in the return for the year in which the disposition occurs:

- personal-use property (see ¶545) that was not listed personal property (see ¶546) or real property;
- listed personal property if proceeds were less than $1,000;
- principal residence (see ¶554);
- personal-use property that was real property if proceeds of disposition are less than $1,000; or
- property for which proceeds equal Valuation Day value (e.g., Canada Savings Bonds).

If the taxation year for which you are reporting capital gain or loss is the first year in which you disposed of capital property which was owned by you on December 31, 1971, you may elect to establish the cost of all such capital property as being its fair market value on Valuation Day and ignore the tax-free zone rule (see ¶591). The election to be valid must be made not later than the day on or before which you are required to file the income tax return for the taxation year in which a disposition occurred (i.e., April 30, or June 15 if self-employed). To make such an election, complete and attach form T2076 to your income tax return. Form T2076 may be obtained from your Tax Services Office or on the CRA website.

Except for publicly-traded Canadian securities shown on the list referred to above, there are no specific rules provided in the law for determining values of assets on Valuation Day. These values will therefore be a question of fact subject to possible negotiation with the tax authorities.

The Toronto Bond Traders' Association has issued a booklet showing prices for a number of bonds on Valuation Day (December 31, 1971). The CRA has stated that it will ordinarily accept the prices shown as Valuation Day values for bonds, although neither the CRA nor taxpayers are necessarily bound to use these prices.

A list of net asset values of mutual fund shares prepared by the Canadian Mutual Funds Association has been stated by the CRA to be acceptable as a basis for determining Valuation Day values of mutual fund shares.

For other assets, if there was a quoted market value on December 31, 1971, this would probably be acceptable. In the case of real estate it may be necessary to obtain an appraisal.

The CRA has established Business Equity Valuation Groups in Halifax, Quebec, Montreal, Ottawa, Toronto, Hamilton, Kitchener, London, Winnipeg, Calgary, Edmonton, and Vancouver. Taxpayers may discuss valuations relating to securities, partnerships, proprietorships, copyrights, patents and similar business assets with these groups. In addition, the CRA has assembled information relating to real estate known as the Real Estate Data Bank. Taxpayers will be able to obtain certain information contained in the Bank.

(ITA: 24; 26(7); IT-139R [Archived])

[¶591] TAX-FREE ZONE VALUATION

If you do not elect to use of Valuation Day value as a substitute for actual cost for all assets owned on December 31, 1971, then an alternative method, known as the "tax-free zone" method (or "median amount" method) must be used. This alternative method requires you to determine three amounts with respect to each asset owned on December 31, 1971, and disposed of after that date, as follows:

(1) Proceeds of disposal;

(2) Value on Valuation Day; and

(3) Actual original cost.

Your cost of the asset is deemed to be the amount which is neither the largest nor the smallest of the three amounts (i.e., the median number). If two or more of the three amounts are identical, you use that amount as your cost.

Example 1

If on December 31, 1971, you owned a share of a public Canadian company which you had purchased in 1965 for $10, which was valued at $20 on December 22, 1971 (the Valuation Day for publicly traded Canadian shares) and which was sold in the current year for $25, you would substitute for the actual original cost of the share the value on Valuation Day of $20 (the amount which is neither the largest nor the smallest of the three relevant figures).

The capital gain to be reported on your current tax return would therefore be:

Proceeds of disposition	$25
Deemed cost	20
Capital gain	$5

You will note that this has the effect of eliminating the $10 gain accruing between 1965 and 1971 from your calculation.

Example 2

To illustrate the effect of this calculation on a loss in value, if the value of the share in the above example had been $25 when purchased in 1965, $20 on Valuation Day and $10 when sold in the current year, the amount substituted for your actual cost would still be the $20 Valuation Day value, and your capital loss realized would be:

Deemed cost	$20
Proceeds of disposition	10
Capital loss	$10

It is important to note that in applying the "tax-free zone" method the amount of "proceeds of disposal" will be the gross selling price before deduction of any costs of sale. This will have the effect of producing a capital loss in any situation where there are costs of sale, and the actual gross proceeds fall in the "tax-free zone" between actual original cost and Valuation Day value.

Example 3

You acquired a share of stock before 1972 for $50, the share was valued at $100 on Valuation Day, and you sold the share in the current year for $75, incurring a brokerage fee of $5.

Under the tax-free zone rule your deemed cost of the share is $75, equal to the gross sale proceeds, and therefore $75 is your "cost for the share.

Your capital loss will be $5 calculated as follows (see ¶505):

ACB	$75
Cost of disposal	5
	$80
Proceeds of disposition	75
Capital loss	$5

In certain cases you may have to calculate a deemed cost without having disposed of the asset (see ¶533 or ¶534). Where this is the case, the same rules apply substituting "current fair market value" for "proceeds" in the formula.

A discussion of the considerations involved in determining which method to select of the two methods of determining "cost" described above is contained at ¶2527.

A different rule is also provided for purposes of determining the cost of an interest in a partnership owned on December 31, 1971, and is discussed at ¶1848.

Transactions may occur after 1971 which increase or decrease the ACB of an asset, as described at ¶507 and ¶508. If the property was owned on December 31, 1971, and the tax-free zone method is adopted, such transactions require an adjustment to the amount used as "proceeds of disposition" in applying the special rule. Amounts which reduce the ACB will increase the proceeds amount used. Amounts which increase the ACB will reduce the proceeds amount.

Example 4

You owned shares of D Company on December 31, 1971, acquired at an actual cost of $1,000. Their value on Valuation Day was $1,500 and they were sold in the current year for $1,400. In 1975, a $200 tax-free dividend was received and the Company indicated this dividend would reduce the cost base of the shares. Your deemed cost under the tax-free zone rule would be:

Actual cost	$1,000	(1)
Valuation Day value	$1,500	(2)
Proceeds of disposition	$1,400	
Add: tax-free dividend	200	
Adjusted proceeds	$1,600	(3)
Deemed cost (the median amount of (1), (2), or (3))	$1,500	

Your ACB for the shares would be:

Deemed cost	$1,500
Deduct: tax-free dividend	200
ACB	$1,300

Your capital gain would be:

Actual proceeds of disposition	$1,400
ACB	1,300
Capital gain	$100

A special rule will apply to determine the actual cost to you of shares owned on December 31, 1971, and acquired as a result of the conversion of shares into new shares of a corporation at the time of an amalgamation of two or more corporations. If you own such shares in an amalgamated corporation, their actual cost should be determined by applying to the actual cost of the original shares owned by you and converted at the time of the amalgamation the ratio of the fair market value of the shares of the new corporation received in exchange for the old shares to the fair market value of all of the shares of the new corporation acquired by you as a result of the amalgamation.

Example 5

In 1965, you acquired 100 shares of Corporation G at a cost of $1,000. In 1968, Corporation G amalgamated with Corporation H, and in exchange for your original shares of Corporation G you received Class A shares of the amalgamated Corporation I valued at $600 and Class B shares of Corporation I valued at $1,400. You still owned these shares at December 31, 1971.

For purposes of calculations under the tax-free zone method you would determine the actual cost of your Class A and Class B shares as follows:

Actual cost of Class A shares = $ 600/$2,000 × $1,000 =	$ 300
Actual cost of Class B shares = $1,400/$2,000 × $1,000 =	700
Total actual cost	$1,000

The actual cost of shares of capital stock owned by you on December 31, 1971, and acquired pursuant to a stock option plan, will be the greater of (1) the actual amount paid by you with respect to the acquisition of the share, and (2) the fair market value of the share at the time you acquired it.

If you received capital property before 1972 from a pension fund or plan, employees' profit sharing plan, retirement savings plan, supplementary unemployment benefit plan or deferred profit sharing plan, and owned the property thereafter without interruption until after 1971, the actual cost of the property is deemed to be its fair market value at the time the property was received.

[¶591.05] *Intervening Transactions*

A number of special provisions ensure that if you owned shares, options or certain debt obligations on December 31, 1971, and have received substitute investments in the course of a corporate reorganization (such as an amalgamation) that was carried out under specific tax deferral provisions, your tax-free zone calculations apply to the substitute property on your eventual disposition of it. In general, you will have to obtain this deferral information from the corporation in the year of substitution (or else you will report capital gain at that time). The year of substitution is probably the time to ensure that the tax-free zone also flows through the corporate reorganization; you must then carry this information forward yourself to the year of disposition.

(ITA: 26(3); (4); (21)–(28); 87(4); IT-84 [Archived]; IT-107 [Archived])

[¶592] BONDS AND MORTGAGES OWNED ON DECEMBER 31, 1971

A special rule is provided for bonds and mortgages and similar obligations (debentures, bills, notes, hypothecs or agreements of sale) owned on December 31, 1971. Instead of using the original cost of the asset, in applying the tax-free zone rule the amount to be used as the "cost" is the "amortized cost".

The amortized cost of the obligation will be an amount determined as follows:

(1) If the actual cost to you of the obligation was between 95% and 100% of the principal amount and the obligation was issued before November 8, 1969, the amortized cost is that principal amount.

(2) If the actual cost of the obligation to you was between 100% and 105% of the principal amount, the amortized cost will be your actual cost.

(3) In any other case, to determine the amortized cost you increase your actual cost (where you purchased at a discount) or decrease your actual cost (where you purchased at a premium) by the proportion of the discount or premium that applies to the period between the date of acquisition and Valuation Day. This proportion is determined by calculating the fraction resulting from using as a numerator the number of full months between the day of acquisition and Valuation Day, and using as a denominator the number of full months between the day of acquisition and the maturity date of the obligation.

Example

You acquired a bond with a principal value of $100 in April 1970, for $85. The bond matures April 30, 1985. Your deemed cost is:

Number of full months between date of acquisition and Valuation Day	$20
Number of full months between date of acquisition and maturity date	$180
Discount: $100 - $85 =	$15
Amount to be added to actual cost— 20/180 × $15 =	$2
Amortized cost: $85 + $2 =	$87

If the bond had a quoted market value on December 31, 1971, of $96, and was sold by you in February 1985, for $85 your capital gain or loss using the tax-free zone rule would be:

(1) Proceeds of disposition	$85
(2) Amortized cost	$87
(3) Valuation Day value	$96
Deemed cost (neither the largest nor the smallest of (1), (2) and (3))	$87
Proceeds of disposition	85
Capital loss	$2

(ITA: 26(3)(*a*); IT-319 [Archived])

[¶593] IDENTICAL PROPERTIES

As discussed in ¶512 where you hold two or more properties of the same kind, they may be treated for income tax purposes as being identical properties.

For purposes of calculating the ACB of identical properties purchased prior to December 31, 1971, the ACB of each property is determined by adding together the cost base of all such property and dividing by the number of such identical properties.

Where some identical properties were acquired before 1972, and some after December 31, 1971, a separate ACB is calculated for all properties acquired before 1972 and a separate ACB for those acquired after 1971.

If there was a series of purchases and sales prior to 1972, the properties owned on December 31, 1971 are considered to be those most recently purchased before that date, in determining their ACB; and of course the special rules discussed at ¶590 and ¶591 for determining the cost of assets owned on December 31, 1971, are applicable. When dispositions of some of the identical properties occur after 1971, the first disposals are deemed to be out of the group owned on December 31, 1971.

Example

You acquired shares of E Company as follows:		Cost
January 1971 — 100 shares @ $3	$ 300	
June 1971 — 50 shares @ $6	300	$ 600
February 1972 — 300 shares @ $15	$4,500	
March 1972 — 300 shares @ $25	7,500	12,000
		$12,600

The Valuation Day value of the shares was $14 each. In the current year, you sold 500 shares for proceeds of $15,000. If you use the tax-free zone method, your capital gain would be calculated as follows:

(1) Calculate the average cost of the shares acquired before 1972.

$600 / 150 =	$ 4	per share

(2) Calculate the deemed cost of shares owned on December 31, 1971 (see ¶512).

Actual cost (average cost)	$ 4	
Valuation Day value	$14	
Proceeds of disposition ($15,000 / 500)	$30	
Deemed cost	$14	per share (I)

(3) Calculate the average cost of the shares acquired after 1971.

$12,000 / 600 =	$20	per share (II)

(4) Calculate your capital gain.

Proceeds of disposition		$15,000
Adjusted cost base of 500 shares:		
150 shares acquired before 1972 @ $14 (I) =	$2,100	
350 shares acquired in 1972 @ $20 (II) =	$7,000	$9,100
Capital gain		$5,900

(ITA: 26(8); IT-78 [Archived])

[¶594] PROPERTY ACQUIRED FROM RELATED PERSONS

If you owned property on June 18, 1971 that has been transferred to a related person (¶812), generally the actual cost or amortized cost (see ¶592) to the subsequent owner will be deemed to be the same as your actual or amortized cost and the subsequent owner will be deemed to have owned the property without interruption since June 18, 1971. There are the following exceptions to this rule:

(1) The rule does not apply where the property is depreciable property (see ¶813) or a partnership interest.

(2) The rule does not apply where the property was owned by you on December 31, 1971 and you have elected to use the Valuation Day method (¶590) of calculating your cost of the property upon its disposition after 1971.

(3) Where the property was acquired by its subsequent owner after 1971, his or her ACB may be increased by the amount of any capital gain reported by you; or must be decreased by the amount of any capital loss reported by you. Certain stop-loss transactions (¶585 and ¶851) are excepted from this rule.

Where significant amounts are involved you should consider obtaining professional advice on the application of these rules.

One effect of the above rules is to deny a potential tax benefit which might otherwise have arisen from a transfer of property between related persons after June 18, 1971 (when the new laws were announced in detail) and before 1972. This benefit would have resulted where an asset had been sold to a related person at a price higher than its actual cost to the original owner, so that the cost to the purchaser would be inflated for subsequent calculations under the tax-free zone method of determining a cost base, potentially creating or increasing a deductible capital loss.

Another effect of the rules is that any property acquired after 1971 from a related person who owned it on June 18, 1971 must be treated as an asset owned on December 31, 1971. However, the Valuation Day Method (¶590) cannot be used for that asset even though the Valuation Day election may have been made. The tax-free zone method (¶591) of determining its cost must be used. Any disposition of the property may require consideration of the election described at ¶590.

For a discussion of the possible consequences of a transfer of a residence to a spouse. See also ¶554a.

(ITA: 26(5); IT-132R2 [Archived])

[¶595] IDENTICAL PROPERTY ACQUIRED FROM RELATED PERSONS

As explained in ¶593 there is a separate ACB for identical properties acquired before 1972 and a separate ACB for identical properties acquired after 1971.

If you acquire property from a related person and the related person owned the property on June 18, 1971, you are deemed to have owned the property since June 18, 1971 (see ¶594). If this property is identical to other property which you own, then you will have a third group of identical properties for which you must compute their individual cost base as discussed in ¶593.

When calculating capital gains and losses, you are deemed to dispose of the identical property acquired before 1972 and property acquired from related persons before identical properties acquired after 1971. Only when all of these properties are disposed of will you be deemed to have disposed of identical property acquired after 1971.

If you dispose of only a portion of the identical properties acquired before 1972 and those acquired from related persons, you may allocate which of the identical properties disposed of were from the group acquired before 1972 and which identical properties were from the group acquired from related persons.

(IT-199 [Archived])

[¶596] GAINS FROM DEPRECIABLE PROPERTY OWNED ON DECEMBER 31, 1971

If depreciable property was owned on December 31, 1971, and is disposed of at a later date, a special rule is required to calculate the capital gain arising from the disposition. This special rule is required because it is necessary to allocate any gain on disposal between the capital gain portion, and the portion which represents a recapture of capital cost allowances claimed in previous years. This special calculation is described in detail at ¶844.

[¶597] PROPERTY DISPOSED OF BETWEEN JUNE 18, 1971 AND 1972 AND REACQUIRED

There is a special rule for capital property which was owned on June 18, 1971, and disposed of after that date but before 1972, where the same or substantially identical property was reacquired or acquired within 30 days following the disposition.

The effect is to treat the disposition as if it had not occurred for purposes of calculating capital gain or loss on the reacquired or substantially identical property.

(ITA: 26(6))

HOW TO REPORT CAPITAL GAINS AND LOSSES

[¶598] CAPITAL GAINS AND LOSSES

Capital gains and losses from actual dispositions in the current year, from prior years' dispositions where you claimed a capital gain reserve, or from flow-through entities such as mutual fund corporations or trusts, must be reported on Schedule 3 provided with the T1 General Individual Income Tax Return. Hence, you must use the T1 General return and not an alternate. If the space on this schedule is not sufficient you should prepare and attach your own list, using the same headings as on the schedule.

If your capital gains recognized in the current year exceed your capital losses for the year, your taxable capital gain (the amount you actually include in income) is one-half of that excess; that is, the "inclusion rate" is 50% of actual (whole) gains in excess of the actual losses.

A nil inclusion rate applies to the capital gain arising on gifts of certain publicly traded securities, cultural gifts, and gifts of ecologically sensitive property. This special calculation requires form T1170, "Capital Gains on Gifts of Certain Capital Property".

If you have capital gains from dispositions of farming or fishing property (¶502f), and/or qualified small business shares (¶502i), you may be able to claim the capital gains exemption on form T657 (see ¶502). Form T657 in turn requires form T936 to complete the cumulative net investment loss (CNIL) account calculation.

If you have capital gains in the year from the disposition of shares in what was originally an eligible small business corporation (which is not quite the same thing as a qualified small business corporation) and you reinvest the proceeds in similarly eligible small business corporations, you may defer some or all of the capital gain (the deferral reduces the cost base of the new shares). To do this, you report the entire gain on Schedule 3 (in either section 1 or section 3, as applicable) and deduct the deferral on line 161 of Schedule 3. See ¶572.05.

You may defer the amount of gain to be reported in respect of proceeds of disposition not payable in the year (see ¶581 and ¶582); these deferrals (reserves) must be accounted for in subsequent years. Use form T2017 for the calculation of capital gain reserves.

If your capital losses recognized in the year exceed your gains, one-half of the net loss (all capital losses for the year in excess of all capital gains) becomes your "net capital loss" for the year. The net capital loss for a year is not immediately deductible. (There is an exception for allowable business investment losses, see ¶580.) The net capital loss for a year may be carried back three years and forward indefinitely, but may only be claimed against the taxable portion of capital gains of those other years. If the amount calculated on Schedule 3 is negative — an allowable capital loss — you should apply it against any capital gains taxed in the preceding three years by filling out form T1A and filing it with your tax return by April 30 (or June 15 if you are eligible for that filing date; see ¶558). The T1A is described in ¶1093 and reproduced at the end of Chapter 10. If no prior capital gains are available, you should note the loss for use against future capital gains. See ¶575–579.

Application of prior years' losses against this year's income is claimed on line 253 of page 3 of the T1. See ¶1093.

You cannot have a loss on Schedule 3 on depreciable property; such losses are dealt with through the capital cost allowance system (¶558).

The tax system recognizes gains but not losses from dispositions of personal-use property (see ¶548), other than listed personal property, and therefore, "Gain only" should be reported for this kind of property.

Losses from listed personal property may only be applied against gains from the same kind of property. You may not deduct a net loss from listed personal property from other gains or income; therefore only a net gain is reported for this kind of property. If your capital losses from dispositions of listed personal property exceed capital gains for the year from such property, see ¶577 for details of how you may be able to deduct this excess loss in returns for other years.

Prior to 2017, special rules provided for capital gains arising on the disposition of eligible capital property such as goodwill, farm quotas and government rights, and other miscellaneous items. See ¶768.

The transactions and sections on Schedule 3 and special adjustments which may be required in determining your capital gains or losses are discussed in this chapter. The CRA issues an annual Capital Gains Tax Guide (T4037) which provides both useful information and most of the commonly used forms you may need in addition to Schedule 3.

Historical Information

If you had accrued but unrealized capital gains for the period preceding February 23, 1994, you could preserve the tax-free status of up to $100,000 of capital gain ($75,000 of taxable capital gain) by making a 1994 election. The tax-free gain thus preserved is usually reflected in a higher cost base resulting from the election, so a lower gain on actual subsequent disposition. If you elected on flow-through properties, such as shares or units of a mutual fund, or a partnership interest, the election had a current benefit in that it created a notional pool which could, for the 1994 through 2004 taxation years, eliminate current tax on capital gains that flowed out to you from the flow-through entity. Any balance remaining after 2004 increases the cost base of the investment on which the election was made, if still on hand. You must keep track of any cost base and/or pool adjustments to correctly report your (reduced) capital gains.

Chapter 6

Rental Income and Undeveloped Land

THESE POINTS ARE COVERED IN THIS CHAPTER

CRA REFERENCES RELATING TO THIS CHAPTER

T1 Lines

- Line 126 — Rental income (Net)
- Line 160 — Rental income (Gross)

CRA Guides

5000-G, "General Income Tax and Benefit Guide"; **T4036**, "Rental Income — Includes Form T776"

CRA Forms

T776, "Statement of Real Estate Rentals"

Income Tax Folios

S1-F3-C2, "Principal Residence"; **S3-F6-C1**, "Interest Deductibility"

Interpretation Bulletins [Archived]

IT-95R, "Foreign Exchange Gains and Losses"; **IT-99R5 (Consolidated)**, "Legal and Accounting Fees"; **IT-128R**, "Capital Cost Allowance — Depreciable Property"; **IT-153R3**, "Land Developers — Subdivision and Development Costs and Carrying Charges on Land"; **IT-195R4**, "Rental Property — Capital Cost Allowance Restrictions"; **IT-261R**,

"Prepayment of Rents"; **IT-274R**, "Rental Properties — Capital Cost of $50,000 or More"; **IT-304R2**, "Condominiums"; **IT-359R2**, "Premiums and Other Amounts With Respect to Leases"; **IT-403R**, "Options on Real Estate"; **IT-434RSR**, "Rental of Real Property by Individual"; **IT-443**, "Leasing Property — Capital Cost Allowance Restrictions"

WHAT YOU SHOULD KNOW ABOUT RENTAL INCOME

[¶600] RENTAL OF REAL PROPERTY

The subject of this chapter is primarily income from real estate rental property and the deduction of expenses from undeveloped land. The chapter is concerned with income and expenses related to land and buildings, and with related assets such as furnishings in rental apartments. Income from renting other assets, such as machinery, equipment, cars, etc., is touched on briefly at ¶655; such income is subject to special restrictions considered at ¶655 and in Chapter 8 at ¶873 and ¶873a.

Depending on the circumstances, rental income from real estate will be either income from a business or income from property. This distinction may be important as income from a business is sometimes subject to different tax treatment than income from property. However, it is often difficult to determine the distinction between income from a business and income from property as the *Income Tax Act* does not specifically define the terms "business income" or "property income". This chapter deals with property income. Chapter 7 deals with business income.

If you delegate the management and supervision of real property, this in itself will not alter the nature of the rental income. If the renting of the property would have constituted a business if you had run it yourself, then it will still be a business when undertaken by an agent.

Where the renting of real property to others is incidental to your business, the renting will likely be regarded as a business operation and any rental income or loss will form part of your business income or loss. For example, the renting of temporarily unused space in your factory or warehouse and the renting of land held for future expansion will form part of your business income.

Where the renting of real property is not part of, or incidental to, an existing business, the renting is not in itself indicative of a business operation. It will be regarded as a business operation only where the services that you make available to your tenants are such that the rental operation has gone beyond the mere rental of real property. The number and kinds of services you provide to your tenants will be the determining factors. However, the size and extent of rental properties, your time required for management and supervision, and the degree of furnishings provided with the rental property are not factors in determining if the operation is a business.

For example, where you rent an office building *en bloc* and you provide the basic types of maintenance such as heat and air conditioning, the rental is likely of property and does not constitute the carrying on of a business.

If you rent suites in an apartment block and provide the customary services of elevator service, heat, water, parking spaces, laundry facilities, and maintenance of the building itself, the income is likely income from property and not income from a business.

However, if the services provided go beyond the customary services, you may be carrying on a business. Generally, the more services you provide, the greater the likelihood that you are earning income from a business. For example, the services supplied in an office building may include the basic services mentioned above and also include office cleaning and protective services. These latter services could be the decisive factor in determining that you are carrying on a business. In the case of an apartment block it is the extent to which basic and additional services are supplied to your tenants that will determine if the income is income from a business. These additional services may include having a restaurant or lounge on the premises, maid service for tenants, supplying fresh linens, etc.

The operation of a hotel or motel is a business. Even the operation of a rooming or lodging-house where you rent rooms is likely to be a business because of the supplying of cleaning and maid service.

Where two or more individuals participate in a rental operation, the question of whether it is a business still must be determined according to the principles outlined above. The fact that a rental operation is carried on by what appears or purports to be a partnership does not, in itself, justify an assumption that the operation is a business.

There are certain situations where it will be significant to determine whether the income from the rental of real property by an individual constitutes business or property income.

- Whether the income from your rental operation is characterized as business income or as property income may determine the manner and the extent to which rent prepayments are to be included in income (see ¶625).
- Any income or loss arising from property that you transferred to your spouse or common-law partner (or to a person who has since become your spouse or common-law partner) or to a minor is deemed to be your income or loss. This attribution applies when the transferred property produces property income. However, no income or loss will attribute back to you if the income is from a business. See ¶977 for a discussion on attribution on the transfer of property and rights to income.
- Rental income from real property, whether business or property income, constitutes "earned income" for purposes of calculating the deduction allowable for registered retirement savings plan premiums paid. In addition, if your rental income constitutes income from a business, it will qualify as "earned income" for purposes of calculating the child care expense deduction (see ¶1055).
- If you receive rental income that constitutes income from property, that income is deemed to be income earned in the province or territory in which you reside on the last day of the taxation year. However, if the rental income constitutes income from a business, the rental income must be allocated to the provinces in which it was considered to have been earned and thereby subject to the rate of tax applied by those particular provinces.

- Where a non-resident receives rental income from real property situated in Canada and the income constitutes income from a business, the non-resident is required to file a return in Canada and calculate his or her taxable income from that business, and is eligible for deductions in the normal manner (see ¶2030). However, if a non-resident's rental income is income from a property, he or she may instead be subject to withholding tax (see ¶2080).
- Whether you have income from a business or income from property will also determine whether you are allowed to deduct certain expenses from income. See ¶602 and ¶730.
- You are allowed to deduct capital cost allowance on assets used in a business and assets held to earn income from property. However, the deduction allowed may be different for the first year of operation in computing income from a business than the deduction for computing income from property. In addition to the "half-year" rule applicable to the year property is acquired, which applies for both business and property purposes, a business with a short fiscal year must prorate its capital cost allowance for that year. An individual holding rental rather than business property computes capital cost allowance on a calendar year basis.
- Rental income or loss (as opposed to business income or loss) must be included in the cumulative net investment loss (CNIL) account described at ¶502q. This requires a lifetime record of investment income and loss in order to claim the capital gains exemption on *any* qualified farm property or small business shares. You may use form T936 if you choose to keep track of the CNIL account yourself. See the general comments at ¶400.

The profit or gain (or loss) that you realize upon the sale of rental property is normally regarded as on capital account, such that one-half of the gain will be a taxable capital gain and one-half of any loss will be an allowable capital loss. However, if you are found to be in the business of buying and selling properties, the whole amount will be included as business income or loss, as the case may be.

Assuming your rental income is income from property, use form T776, Statement of Real Estate Rentals, to report your rental income and expenses for the year. See also guide T4036, Rental Income, which includes the form T776. If you earned the income through a partnership, include your T5013 slips or a copy of the partnership's financial statement. If your rental income is from a business, use guide T4002, Business and Professional Income, and form T2125.

See also archived Interpretation Bulletins IT-434R and IT-434RSR, which provide a summary of the CRA's views on whether rental income is income from property or business.

(IT-434R Rental of real property by individual; IT-434RSR (Special Release, July 7, 1989))

[¶601] WHAT IS REAL PROPERTY?

"Real property" is not defined in the *Income Tax Act*. The traditional common law definition is that it includes land, any interest in land (except a mortgage interest), and anything attached to the land (buildings and crops still attached to the land are included, but once crops are severed for sale they seem to cease being real property). Real property normally includes land and the buildings on it, and where these are sold together there is no question that the entire sale is one of real property. The matter might be less clear where a building is sold and, as it were, carted away. The more probable view is that the building remains real property to the vendor, and therefore gives rise to a real property gain or loss. It is less certain (not that it was certain to begin with) whether it remains real property until it is settled in some new and relatively permanent fashion.

A motor home would probably not be real property while mobile, but might become real property if attached to land in some relatively permanent way.

Leases are an interest in real property, and if you sold a lease you might well realize a capital gain on it (see ¶879). This would seem to be a real property gain, although again there is no formal pronouncement on this point. In any event, the gain would be a capital gain unless you were found to be in the business of buying and selling leases.

Where land and building are sold and the building is torn down immediately before or after sale, issues may arise as to the allocation of proceeds between the land and building (see ¶859). However, once the allocation is determined, the separate question remains as to whether the entire transaction is one in real property. Almost certainly it is.

CALCULATION OF RENTAL INCOME

[¶602] RENTAL INCOME

The net rental income reported for tax purposes will be the sum of rental revenues, less expenses incurred in earning these revenues, and less capital cost allowance.

[¶602a] DEDUCTIBLE EXPENSES

The following types of expenditures will usually be deductible from rental revenue in the year they are incurred:

- Property taxes (but there are restrictions if the property is vacant land (¶665), or while a building is undergoing construction, renovation or alteration (¶771));
- Insurance on the rental property (but if a policy covers more than one year, you must deduct in each year only the portion of the premium relating to that year);
- Maintenance and repairs (but not capital expense renovations; see ¶805);
- Heat, light and water (to the extent paid by you and not the tenant);
- Advertising;
- Interest on money borrowed to purchase or improve the rental property; see ¶771 for a discussion of restrictions on the deductibility of costs relating to real estate development, and note that certain ordinarily deductible "soft costs" such as interest may not be deductible during a period of construction, renovation or alteration; see ¶690 where interest expenses exceed related rental income. See ¶1063–¶1065 for more details on interest deductibility generally; see ¶1067 where interest continues on property sold at a loss; finally,

interest deductions on some rental properties may trigger alternative minimum tax where the deduction is restricted (¶2405 and ¶2420);

- In addition to interest itself, certain costs of arranging a mortgage, mortgage guarantee fees, and the like may be wholly or partially deductible as discussed at ¶764;
- Salaries and wages paid to superintendents, maintenance people, and other persons employed in the operation or supervision of the property;
- Accounting expenses;
- Legal expenses (but not in connection with the purchase of the property — these must be capitalized);
- Commissions paid to obtain tenants or to collection agents;
- Landscaping of grounds around a building or other structure;
- Certain automobile expenses. See ¶605;
- Office supplies.

Note that all expenditures on a particular property, except for landscaping, capital cost allowance, and modifications to assist the disabled, may be restricted while a building is undergoing construction, renovation or alteration. See ¶771.

(ITA: 18; 20; *Rental Income Tax Guide* (T4036))

[¶603] LEASE CANCELLATION PAYMENTS

[¶603.03] *Payments Made by Landlord*

You are not allowed a full deduction for lease cancellation payments you make as a landlord to the person that leased the property from you in the year you incur the expense. Rather you must amortize the payment you make and deduct it in equal amounts over the term of the lease remaining immediately before the lease was cancelled, including renewal periods up to a maximum of 40 years.

If the property in respect of which the lease cancellation payment was made is disposed of at arm's length (¶812) before all possible annual deductions are claimed, you may deduct a final amount in respect of the remaining undeducted balance. That amount is tied to the capital gain inclusion rate, which is currently 50%.

If the property on which the lease cancellation payments were made was inventory rather than capital property, then the entire remaining balance is deductible when the building is sold.

(ITA: 20(1)(z); 20(1)(z.1))

[¶603.10] *Payments Made to Landlord*

Where, as a landlord, you receive payment from a tenant on the cancellation of a lease, the payment is considered to be on income account to the extent it represents rental income lost; but it may be on capital account to the extent it can be shown to be compensation for impairment of the capital value of the building. This seems to be the result of *Spezzano v. The Queen*, 2007 DTC 5580 (F.C.A.), aff'g 2006 DTC 3047 (T.C.C.), which, on the facts, held that lease cancellation payments received were income (notwithstanding evidence that the building had a lower capital value after the cancellation). The taxpayer landlord had argued that a lease cancellation payment was on capital account because the building had a lower capital value after the cancellation. Despite the result in that particular case, there are grounds in the opinions of both Courts to infer that it need not always be true that the whole amount of all cancellation payments received by the landlord will always be on income account.

Although the opinions do not say this, general principles suggest that a well-drafted agreement between landlord and tenant making reasonable assignments of lease cancellation payments to rent foregone and capital impairment (if that can be substantiated) might at least have a fighting chance of success. One may assume that some landlords, especially the litigious, will be inclined to attempt to structure cancellation payments, and indeed leases themselves, to contemplate at least a part of any cancellation payment to be on capital account.

[¶603.20] *Payments Made by Tenant*

Ordinary rental payments made by a business tenant are generally deductible under the rules in Chapter 7, subject to the prepaid expense rules at ¶608. Lease cancellation payments made by the business tenant are generally deductible, provided the rent was deductible.

However, an amount a tenant pays to obtain or extend a lease or sublease or to permit a sublease is a capital expenditure to acquire property that is a leasehold interest. Consequently, the tenant may be entitled to claim capital cost allowance on the payments under the rules at ¶879.

Where a tenant or prospective tenant reimburses a landlord for some or all amounts spent by the landlord to increase, alter, improve, etc., the leased premises, the reimbursement may qualify as an eligible capital expenditure (¶766) unless ownership of the new property vests in the tenant, in which case, the reimbursement is the cost of acquiring a capital property on which capital cost allowance may be allowable.

If a tenant prepays the lease payments in respect of future years, the deduction of the payments is deferred until those years. See ¶608 below.

Where a tenant is subject to a lease with an escalating rent clause — that is, future years' rent will increase by an amount determined under the lease — financial accounting principles may allow an averaging for the purposes of a current deduction of the rent to take into account those increases. However, for income tax purposes, it appears that the future increases cannot be recognized before the years in which the increases actually occur; see CRA document nos. 2008-0272771I7 — Straight-Line Amortization or Averaging of Rent, May 26, 2008 and 2012-043524117 — Prepaid Rent and Escalating Rent Payments, February 14, 2012.

(IT-359R2 [Archived])

[¶605] NON-DEDUCTIBLE EXPENSES

You may not claim a deduction of any kind for the cost of land, or repayments of the principal portion of borrowed money. Also, personal or living expenses are not deductible. Generally, expenses for travelling between your home and rental property are considered personal expenses and are not deductible. However, if your rental income is income from a business (see ¶600) reasonable travelling expenses will be deductible. The CRA will allow you to deduct travelling expenses in certain other circumstances even where your rental income is not considered business income.

For example, if you own only one rental building and you perform repairs or maintenance for the building, you can deduct travelling expenses you incur in transporting tools and material. However, if you use your automobile to get to a locality, city or town outside the general area of your home, the expenses in travelling between the two localities will not be deductible even if you transport tools and material.

On the other hand, if you own more than one rental building, the CRA will allow you to deduct reasonable automobile expenses incurred by you for the purpose of collecting rents, supervising repairs and generally providing management services for the properties. In this case you can even deduct expenses of travelling between two localities, cities or towns, if they are reasonable. However, for your motor vehicle expenses to be deductible, your rental properties have to be located in at least two sites that are different from the site of your principal residence.

See also CRA Guide T4036, at the descriptions for lines 9200 and 9281.

The apparent reason for the difference in the CRA policy between the one-rental property scenario and the more-than-one rental scenario is the CRA's view that the ownership of one rental property does not normally constitute the carrying on of a business. As such, the restriction of paragraph 18(1)(*h*) applies, disallowing the deduction of motor vehicle expenses because they are "personal or living expenses of the taxpayer, other than travel expenses incurred by the taxpayer while away from home in the course of carrying on the taxpayer's business". If the rental properties constitute a business, the restriction in paragraph 18(1)(*h*) does not apply. See CRA document No. 2006-0191571I7, August 10, 2006.

(ITA: 18; *Rental Income Tax Guide* (T4036))

[¶608] PREPAID EXPENSES

If you prepay an amount in respect of interest, taxes, rents, royalties, insurance or services to be rendered after the end of the year, the deduction may be taken only in the year to which these items relate.

Prepaid Expenses

Prepayment of building maintenance for December Year 1 and January and February Year 2.

Amount of payment	$900
Date of payment — December 1, Year 1	
Fiscal year end — December 31	
Amount deductible in Year 1	$300
Amount deductible in Year 2	$600

Presumably this apportionment should be made on a daily accrual basis.

The general rule regarding the allocation of prepaid expenses to the period to which they relate was apparently considered inadequate to deal with fees or other amounts paid to obtain a reduction of an interest rate, or with penalty or bonus payments made on the cancellation of a debt. Accordingly, a specific provision ensures that a payment to reduce an interest rate (as opposed to a prepayment of interest) must be deducted over the period the interest is payable, and a penalty or bonus on cancellation of a debt must be deducted over the period for which the debt would otherwise have remained outstanding. This is discussed at ¶1074. The provision does successfully ensure that the recipient of such payments must treat them as interest income on receipt. Note also that trusts, corporations, and partnerships that prepay interest are subject to a somewhat different amortization deduction than individuals; see ¶3670 of the Wolters Kluwer publication *Preparing Your Corporate Tax Returns*.

(ITA: 18(9), (9.1))

[¶610] CAPITAL EXPENDITURES

Certain types of expenditures are considered to be of a capital nature and may be deducted from income only through capital cost allowances, including of course the rental building itself (see ¶805).

- Purchase price of the rental property (but not land — see ¶605);
- Legal and other costs in connection with the purchase of the property (excluding the amount allocable to land — see ¶605);
- Purchase price of equipment rented with the property (such as apartment refrigerators, stoves, furniture in a furnished apartment, etc.) and replacements;
- Major repairs which extend the useful life of the property (such as replacement of a roof, a new elevator in an apartment building, etc., but usually not including periodic painting, glass replacement and other "routine" repairs). Separating routine maintenance, such as periodic re-roofing, from substantial betterment, such as re-roofing with an improved type of roof, can be a vexing problem; some further guidance is provided at ¶805.

(ITA: 18; IT-99R5 (Consolidated) [Archived]; IT-128R, para. 4 [Archived]; *Rental Income Tax Guide* (T4036))

[¶610.05] *Capital Expenditures to Assist the Disabled*

You may deduct amounts paid in the year for "prescribed" renovations or alterations to an income-producing (as opposed to personal-use) building made to enable individuals who have a mobility impairment to gain access to the building or to be mobile within it. This rule applies to allow such expenses to be deducted by the owner of a building who has paid them. The rule also allows such expenses to be deducted by any person who has paid them and who uses the building primarily to gain or produce income from the building or from a business. Prescribed modifications include the installation of interior and exterior ramps and hand-activated electric door openers, the widening of doorways and modifications to bathrooms, elevators or doorways to accommodate use by a person in a wheelchair.

A further rule allows a current deduction from business or property income for any expenses paid in the year for any prescribed disability-specific device or equipment. Prescribed devices in this category include elevator car position indicators (such as Braille or audio signal) for individuals having a sight impairment, visual fire alarm indicators, listening devices for group meetings or telephone devices for individuals having a hearing impairment, and a disability-specific computer software or hardware attachment.

Some of the items which are prescribed might normally be paid for by businesses for their employees or customers; some (elevator car position indicators and visual fire alarm indicators) might more commonly be paid for by landlords. Regardless of whether the landlord or business pays, however, the amounts paid should be deductible from business or property income of the payer.

It would appear that any expenses which are deductible from income under these rules *must* be deducted from current income rather than depreciated under the capital cost allowance system. This is because the CCA regulations specifically exclude from CCA classes any property the cost of which is "deductible" in computing the taxpayer's income (¶810), whether or not the deduction from income is claimed.

(ITA: 20(1)(*qq*), (*rr*); ITR: 1102(1)(a); 8800 [Prescribed renovations and alterations]; 8801 [Prescribed devices and equipment])

[¶612] LEASEHOLD INDUCEMENTS

The treatment of leasehold inducements has long been a question for both landlords and tenants. On the tenant's side, the issues have generated much litigation and legislation; see ¶826.

On the landlord's side it has usually been argued that the inducement is a running expense deductible when incurred. See *The Queen v. Oxford Shopping Centres Ltd.*, 79 DTC 5458 (F.C.T.D.), aff'd 81 DTC 5065 (F.C.A.), and *Baker Lovick Limited v. M.N.R.*, 91 DTC 1041 (T.C.C.). This argument was rejected by the Federal Court of Appeal in *The Queen v. Canderel Limited*, 95 DTC 5101 (F.C.A.), which ruled that tenant inducement payments made by a property management company must be amortized over the lifetime of the lease rather than deducted in a lump sum when incurred. The *Canderel* decision was reversed by the Supreme Court of Canada (98 DTC 6100), which held the expenses to be running expenses deductible on a current basis. The Supreme Court is thus the current state of the law, although the tax treatment in any particular situation will depend on the facts.

(Tax Topics: No. 1392, p. 3)

[¶615] CASH OR ACCRUAL METHOD

You are generally required to report all rental income, whether from a business or property, on an accrual basis (see ¶714), but subject to the reserve described at ¶620. This means that you would report rent receivable by you whether or not received (subject to a reserve for bad or doubtful debts, ¶733), and deduct expenses as incurred whether or not actually paid. However, the CRA acknowledges that individuals may operate on a cash basis where the result is substantially the same. See the discussion in ¶713 and ¶714.

(ITA: 9; *Rental Income Tax Guide* (T4036))

[¶620] ADVANCE RECEIPTS OF RENTS

If you receive rent in advance you may exclude that portion that relates to future years from your income, taking the excluded portion into income in the year or years to which it relates (through a reserve mechanism in subsection 20(1)(*m*)). This point is discussed below at ¶625.

(ITA: 20(1)(m)(iii); IT-261R [Archived])

[¶625] LUMP-SUM PAYMENTS

The treatment of a lump-sum payment received by you from a tenant may differ depending on whether income is reported as income from property or income from a business (see ¶600).

Where a lease calls for a payment of a premium that is actually a prepayment of rent, the prepayment is income. Distinguishing between a premium and a prepayment can be difficult. A prepayment generally involves no subsequent rent or a lower subsequent rent than would otherwise occur in the absence of the prepayment (i.e., the subsequent rent is less than fair market value). If as a landlord you receive a prepayment of rent and your rental income is considered income from a business, the prepayment is expressly included in income in the year received but eligible for offsetting reserve for future years (¶732). A prepayment of rent which is income from property should, in theory, arrive at the same result on the basis of accrual accounting (¶615, ¶620), although if you generally report property income on a cash basis, and the CRA accepts this, the prepayment would be income in the year received. However, for accrual basis taxpayers, the CRA generally allows the recognition of prepaid rent that is property income to be deferred to the year to which it relates, so that the net result is the same as that seen in the case of prepaid rent received by a rental business where the reserve applies (CRA Document No. 2004-0105461R3, June 1, 2005; see also paragraph 10 of Interpretation Bulletin IT-261R [now archived]).

A premium which is not a prepayment of rent would appear to be income when received if the rental operation amounts to a business. In general, this would also seem to be true if the rental operation yields income from property. On the other hand, Interpretation Bulletin IT-359R2 [now archived] suggests (in paragraph 5) that there may be circumstances in which an amount received for granting or extending a lease or permitting a sublease is not income (especially in the case of property income), and in those (rather obscure) cases the amount received would be proceeds of disposition of rights which would reduce the cost base of the property.

If you receive a payment from a tenant for cancelling a lease or sublease, the payment will normally constitute income to you.

(IT-261R [Archived]; IT-359R2 [Archived])

INCOME FROM RENTAL BUILDINGS

[¶630] CAPITAL COST ALLOWANCE RESTRICTION

If you receive rental income from real estate, you will generally be allowed to claim capital cost allowance on any buildings on the rented property (see Chapter 8). However, you will not be allowed to create or increase a rental loss by claiming capital cost allowance on buildings. If you own more than one rental building, all of the rental income from the buildings must be combined to determine the total income or loss for the year for the purposes of the capital cost allowance restriction. Capital cost allowance can only be claimed on the buildings to the extent of any net income from the rental of those properties before claiming the allowance.

When determining the net income from rental buildings for the purpose of the allowable capital cost allowance, you must include any recapture of capital cost allowance on other rental buildings (see ¶843). Similarly, if you have a terminal loss from the disposition of a rental building (see ¶851), the terminal loss must be deducted in calculating your net income or loss before capital cost allowance from rental buildings.

A terminal loss is not subject to the general capital cost allowance restriction on rental buildings and must be deducted in the year it arises, even if this creates a loss. However, the amount of a terminal loss may itself be limited on dispositions of buildings; see ¶851, ¶859 and ¶872.

Furthermore, for rental buildings costing more than $50,000, each property must be placed in a separate class of depreciable property; see ¶640 below.

If you are a member of a partnership, refer to ¶1812.

Example — Rental Income

John Bull owns one duplex from which he collected rents of $4,800 in Year 1. John incurred deductible expenses of $1,800. John cannot claim capital cost allowance on this duplex for Year 1 in excess of $3,000:

Rental income	$4,800
Expenses before capital cost allowance	1,800
Rental income before capital cost allowance	$3,000

Example — Rental Loss

George Piper owns a building from which he collected $7,200 in rent during Year 1. He incurred $7,500 of allowable expenses. George will not be allowed to claim any capital cost allowance on this building for Year 1 as he cannot increase his rental loss by capital cost allowance:

Rental income	$7,200
Expenses other than capital cost allowance	7,500
Rental loss before claiming capital cost allowance	$(300)

He may, however, claim his $300 loss as a deduction from his other income.

Example — Two Rental Properties

Mary Hubbard owns two apartment buildings. A summary of her Year 1 rental operation is as follows:

	Building A	*Building B*
Rent	$17,000	$15,000
Allowable expenses other than capital cost allowance	15,200	16,000
Net rental income (loss) before claiming capital cost allowance	$ 1,800	$(1,000)

Mary can only claim $800 of capital cost allowance for the year because she must combine her rental income on Building A with her rental loss on Building B to determine the net income available for reduction by capital cost allowance.

If the two buildings are in separate capital cost allowance classes, Mary may choose to claim the capital cost allowance under either of those classes (subject of course to the normal limitations). For example, if Building B is for sale and may be sold in Year 2, the capital cost allowance claimed on it currently may be recaptured (see ¶843). Mary should therefore claim the $800 of capital cost allowance for Year 1 on the class which includes building A.

Capital cost allowance which may be claimed on a building or other property *in the year it is acquired* is limited to one-half of the amount normally applicable. See ¶802.

In addition to the capital cost allowance restrictions on rental properties, rental losses created by carrying costs (usually interest) may be restricted by the alternative minimum tax rules if your income before these deductions exceeds $40,000. See Chapter 24.

(ITA: 13; 20; ITR: 1100(11)–(14.2); Sch. II; IT-195R4 [Archived])

[¶630.05] *Terminal Losses on Restricted Property*

It is the CRA's view (in CRA Document No. 2002-0177677) that property on which capital cost allowance has never been claimed because of the restrictions above, is nevertheless depreciable property. (There was some argument to the contrary in earlier opinions, but this now seems to be the prevailing view.) Accordingly, a terminal loss may be claimed on such property subject to the applicability of the "reasonable expectation of profit test" where the property has a personal-use element, or, if that test should be legislated back into life (as now seems unlikely), in other cases. See the discussion at ¶690.

[¶640] RENTAL BUILDINGS COSTING $50,000 OR MORE

Each rental building acquired after 1971 at a cost of $50,000 or more is included in a separate capital cost allowance class. The separate class means that when the building is disposed of, any recaptured capital cost allowance will be brought into income or any terminal loss will be deductible in the year of disposition. This rule is discussed in detail at ¶872.

If you acquired a rental building after 1971 under a tenancy in common and your share of the cost of the building (as distinguished from land or equipment) is less than $50,000 you are not required to create a separate capital cost allowance class unless there is a partnership and the rental property is a partnership property (¶872). Therefore, if you have two or more properties under tenancy in common and the aggregate cost of each is under $50,000 they are all in the same capital cost allowance class. This treatment could be beneficial if one of the buildings were sold. If the proceeds of sale are less than the undepreciated capital cost of all the buildings in that class there would be no recaptured capital cost allowance.

If you acquire two or more condominiums in the same building or in the same row-housing structure, the condominiums will be considered as one building. If their aggregate cost allocable to buildings (as distinguished from land or equipment) is $50,000 or more, a separate capital cost allowance class is required. See ¶876.

(ITR: 1101 Businesses and Properties; IT-274R [Archived])

[¶642] RENTAL PROPERTY IN THE UNITED STATES

If you own rental property in the United States, any rental income that you receive must be included in your income. To the extent U.S. income tax is paid on the rent, typically through the withholding system (i.e., the tenant pays a portion of your rent to the government on account of tax), you should be eligible for foreign tax credit (¶1450).

For Canadian tax purposes, the rules concerning rental loss restrictions (see ¶630) and rental buildings costing $50,000 or more (see ¶640) will apply. Generally you may claim capital cost allowance as a deduction. As an alternative, you may be able to classify the rental property as a principal residence (see ¶553, ¶554, and ¶645).

All transactions conducted in the United States must be expressed in Canadian dollars. You should convert the purchase or sale price of a capital asset in U.S. dollars to the equivalent Canadian dollars at the time of the transaction. Transactions of an income nature should be converted to Canadian dollars by using the rate of exchange at the transaction date. The Bank of Canada exchange rate is used for these purposes. The CRA has in the past accepted the use of the average exchange rate for the year for income transactions where, for instance, there are a series of transactions in U.S. currency. To be accepted, this alternative must be used consistently. Where you are reporting on an accrual basis (see ¶714) rather than a cash basis (see ¶713), more complicated alternatives are described in Interpretation Bulletin IT-95R, available from the CRA.

Fluctuations of exchange rates give rise to foreign exchange gains or losses. The nature of the transactions giving rise to the foreign exchange gain or loss will determine how the gain or loss is to be treated in your income. If the transaction is of an income nature, such as the collection of rents in U.S. dollars, the gain or loss is reflected in your income for the year. If, however, your gain or loss arises from a transaction of a capital nature, such as the monthly payment on the principal of a mortgage, the gain or loss will be treated as a capital gain or capital loss (see ¶556).

Example — Foreign Exchange Gain and Loss on Capital Transactions

John Langley purchased a small office building in Houston, Texas for US$300,000 in December Year 1. John paid US$60,000 down and mortgaged the balance of US$240,000 repayable at US$1,000 per month on account of principal. John sold the building for US$350,000 in December Year 2. He repaid the balance of US$228,000 outstanding on the mortgage. The U.S.–Canadian exchange rates were:

	Canadian equivalent of US$1.00
December Year 1	$1.18
December Year 2	$1.19
Average for Year 2	$1.20

	U.S. $	*Translation Rate*	*Cdn. $*
Gain on disposal of building:			
Proceeds from sale	$350,000	1.19	$416,500
Less cost of building	300,000	1.18	354,000
Gain	$ 50,000		$ 62,500
Loss on retirement of mortgage:			
December Year 2 payout	$228,000	1.19	$271,320
Year 2 instalments	12,000	1.20	14,400
Total payments	$240,000		$285,720
Less initial mortgage	240,000	1.18	283,200
Loss			$ 2,520

John's gain for Year 2 will be:	
Gain on disposal of building	$ 62,500
Less loss on mortgage retirement	(2,520)
Foreign exchange loss exclusion (see ¶556) ..	200
Total gain	$ 60,180

You should note that the gain on the building above is not a foreign exchange gain, since it does not pertain to a debt obligation. The CRA takes the position that only debt obligations give rise to exchange gain or loss subject to the $200 exclusion.

If John did not sell his property in Year 2, his loss on foreign exchange, on the mortgage repayment, would be calculated as follows:

Mortgage payments US$12,000 @ $1.20	$14,400
Mortgage principal retired US$12,000 @ 1.18	14,160
Loss on foreign exchange	$ 240
Foreign exchange loss exclusion	200
Loss on foreign exchange	$ 40

Example — Rental Property in Florida

Barry Day purchased a condominium in Florida for cash in December Year 1. Barry paid US$90,000 of which $85,000 was for the building and $5,000 for the land. Barry uses the condominium in December but rents it out for the other 11 months of the year. Barry received US$6,600 in rental payments during Year 2. He incurred US$2,600 in operating expenses during the 11 months he rented the condominium.

The U.S.–Canadian exchange rates were:

	Canadian equivalent of US$1.00
December Year 1	$1.18
December Year 2	$1.19
Average for Year 2	$1.20

Barry's rental income will be reported on his Year 2 Canadian tax return as follows:

	U.S. $	*Translation Rate*	*Cdn. $*
Rental revenue	$6,600	1.20	$7,920
Operating expense	2,600	1.20	3,120
Rental income before CCA	$4,000		$4,800

Capital Cost Allowance:

Capital cost of condominium in U.S. $	$ 85,000	
Translation rate at date of purchase	× 1.18	
Capital cost of condominium in Cdn. $	$ 100,300	
Proportion used for rental purposes (see ¶513)	× $^{11}/_{12}$	
Cost of rental property for CCA purposes	$ 91,942	
CCA rate (see ¶898)	× 5%	4,597
Net rental income		$ 203

In addition to reporting your U.S. income on your Canadian tax return, you will be subject to U.S. tax. Tax will initially be withheld from rental payments made to you. You have the option of filing a U.S. tax return and paying tax on your net income, as determined under U.S. rules. If you so elect, your tenant is no longer required to withhold tax from rent paid to you and any tax previously withheld is treated as an instalment payment. Some relief from this double taxation may be available to you through foreign tax credits and the Canada–U.S. Tax Convention (see ¶1450, ¶1455, and ¶1506). You should seek professional counsel on the mechanics of the Canada–U.S. Tax Convention as the rules are very complex and beyond the scope of this book.

(ITA: 9; 20; 39; 54; ITR: Schedule II Capital Cost Allowances ; IT-95R [Archived])

[¶643] REPORTING FOR FOREIGN INVESTMENT PROPERTY

If you are resident in Canada and own foreign investment property, including real estate, at any time in a taxation year with a cost of more than $100,000 (in Canadian dollars), you are required to file the prescribed form T1135 "Information Return Relating to Foreign Property". The return is due on the filing due date for the relevant taxation year. The return is not required if the property is personal-use property, that is, property which is used primarily for your personal use or enjoyment or that of a related person. The reporting requirement is discussed in Chapter 20. As discussed therein, the form has been modified to introduce a simplified reporting method for individuals who own specified foreign property with a total cost of less than $250,000.

[¶645] RENTAL OF RESIDENCE OF OWNER

A property, whether located in Canada or elsewhere, can qualify as your principal residence (see ¶554) if you have ordinarily inhabited it during a taxation year. In some cases, even if the residence is not ordinarily inhabited in a given year, the property may still qualify as a principal residence (see ¶555). Designation of the property as your principal residence for each year you owned it will eliminate taxes on capital gains when you dispose it, but precludes you from claiming capital cost allowance on it. For example, if you occupy a vacation home for only a short period of time during a taxation year it is the CRA's view that you have ordinarily inhabited that residence, provided the main reason for owning the property was not for the purpose of gaining or producing income from it. If you receive an incidental amount of rental income from such a seasonal residence the property is not considered to be owned for the purpose of gaining or producing income.

If the above paragraph applies to you, you must decide whether the most beneficial tax treatment will result from treating the property as a rental property or as a principal residence. If you plan on selling the property in the foreseeable future and expect to realize a substantial gain, significant Canadian tax savings may be expected if you can classify the property as a principal residence. Your decision to treat the property as a rental property or a principal residence should be made at the time you file your first income tax return which includes rental income from the property.

For capital gains accruing after 1981, only one residence of an individual, his or her spouse or common-law partner and his or her unmarried, minor children will qualify as a principal residence. See ¶554.

If you rent part of the building in which you live to others, you must include the rent received in the year in your income and you may claim as deductions therefrom expenses incurred to earn those rentals. Any expenses which relate specifically to the rented part of the building may be claimed in full, but those which relate to the whole property, e.g., taxes and insurance, must be apportioned between the rented part of the property and that which is being used as a residence by yourself. Such apportionment would usually be made on the basis of square feet or number of rooms rented. Capital cost allowance may be claimed only on that part of the property which is rented to others. See ¶513 and ¶821. However, claiming capital cost allowance on a portion of your residence may impair your principal residence exemption — for details see ¶553 and ¶554.

(ITA: 9; 18; 40; 54; ITR: 1102 Property Not Included; IT-434R [Archived]; Income Tax Folio: S1-F3-C2 Principal Residence)

[¶650] "RENTALS" TO FAMILY MEMBERS

Remember that expenses are only deductible if they are incurred for the purpose of earning income. It is very common for sons, daughters, and other relatives to pay amounts to the family head on account of upkeep of the family residence. These amounts may be nominal, in which case their receipt would generally not entitle the householder to claim a rental loss, since he or she would have no profit motive or commercial activity and no source of income.

(ITA: 18)

OTHER RENTAL PROPERTIES

[¶655] RENTAL INCOME FROM PROPERTIES OTHER THAN BUILDINGS

Income from renting out property other than real estate is, in tax terminology, not usually considered "rental income" but is likely to be "leasing income". If you have only one or a few such properties, the income is probably investment income and should be considered subject to the rules in Chapter 4. This would be the case if, for example, you hold a taxi licence, but have retired as a driver and lease the licence to someone else. The income from renting out your licence would appear to be investment income. On the other hand, if you regularly rent out items to different customers, the income from those rentals is probably business income, subject to the rules in Chapter 7. This would usually be the case if you rent out cars, machinery, equipment, etc.

If you are a partner in a partnership which leases out property other than real estate, it is likely the partnership is in business and you as a partner are considered to have business income from that partnership, although a number of restrictions may apply to your allocations. See ¶1812–¶1821.

If your non-real estate rental income is considered investment income, it will not qualify as earned income for RRSP purposes, and there may be minor variations in the deductibility of expenses; travelling expenses in particular might not be deductible. If the income is business income, related expenses are deductible and the income will qualify as earned for RRSP purposes. If the income is from a partnership, deductions may be limited by the special rules in Chapter 18 referred to above, and the income will only be RRSP earned income if you are "actively engaged" in the partnership activities.

Regardless of whether your leasing income is business, investment or partnership income, it is in principle subject to special restrictions on capital cost allowance unless it derives from property acquired before May 26, 1976, or property substituted therefor under the involuntary disposition rules at ¶846.

[¶655.05] *Acquired before May 26, 1976*

If you receive income from rental properties other than rental buildings (e.g., equipment), you will be allowed to claim maximum capital cost allowance on the rented property even though this claim will create a loss to offset income from other sources.

[¶655.10] *Acquired after May 25, 1976*

You will not be allowed to create or increase a rental loss by claiming capital cost allowance on any such property that you acquired after May 25, 1976. Rental assets other than buildings which are acquired after May 25, 1976 are referred to as "leasing properties".

Example — Leasing Income

Jean-Guy Morin purchased a truck on June 1 which he leased out for the remainder of the year for $3,100. Jean-Guy incurred deductible expenses of $1,900. Jean-Guy cannot claim capital cost allowance on this truck in excess of $1,200.

Leasing income	$3,100
Expenses before capital cost allowance	1,900
Leasing income before capital cost allowance	$1,200

If you rent more than one property, all of the rental income from these properties must be combined to determine your total income or loss for the year before claiming capital cost allowance. Capital cost allowance may only be claimed on leasing properties to the extent of any net income from the rental of these properties or similar properties acquired after May 25, 1976.

Leasing properties will be put into different capital cost allowance classes than properties acquired before May 26, 1976 even though the leasing property is of the same nature and is subject to the same capital cost allowance rate as property acquired before that date.

If the properties you rent out are in different capital cost allowance classes, you may choose to claim the capital cost allowance under any one, or combination, of those classes (subject, of course, to the normal limitations).

The restrictions on the capital cost allowance claims for leasing property do not apply to:

- certified feature films (see ¶874); and
- rental property, which is subject to its own restrictions.

In addition to capital cost allowance, leasing properties may be eligible for an investment tax credit as detailed in ¶1463.

In some cases, it may be argued that a substantial part of the revenue related to a leasing property is actually business income from related services and is not really leasing income as such. Effective for property acquired after May 22, 1985, this income is to be included as leasing income if you are not continuously active in the business throughout the year in which it is carried on. Partnerships will not be subject to this rule if 2/3 of their income/loss allocation is to active members and corporations.

[¶655.15] *"Specified Leasing Property"*

Further limitations apply to capital cost allowance on tangible property other than real estate. These specified leasing property rules limit capital cost allowance to the amount that would be repayments of capital on a fully financed sale; they apply only to specified leasing property costing in excess of $25,000 per item. For leases entered into after 4:00 p.m. Eastern Standard Time March 4, 2010, the specified leasing property rules will apply to otherwise exempt property that is the subject of a lease to a government or other tax-exempt entity, or to a non-resident. However, such a lease will continue to be exempt if the total value of the property that is the subject of the lease is less than $1 million. See ¶873a.

(ITA: 18(1); 127; ITR: 1100(15)–(20); 1101; IT-443 [Archived])

[¶660] FURNISHED SUITES

[¶660.05] *Furnishings Acquired after May 25, 1976*

Where furnishings acquired prior to May 26, 1976, are still on hand, capital cost allowance on them can be used to create a loss against other income as outlined below. In effect you must keep a segregated record of such property for each class in which it exists. Furnishings acquired after May 25, 1976, are simply subject to the same overall restrictions as the buildings which they furnish. It would seem that where you have some net rental income, you would want to (and be entitled to) claim capital cost allowance from building classes first to reduce total net rental income to nil. Where building CCA is insufficient, furnishing CCA may be used. The point is that when income permits, higher rate classes may be depreciated more rapidly than low rate classes. Nothing is achieved, however, by segregating rental income into portions relating to building rent and furnishings rent, since no loss can be created on either.

[¶660.10] *Furnishings Acquired before May 26, 1976*

If you own a rental building in Class 3, 6, or 13, and part of the capital cost has been allocated to other classes (e.g., furnishings included in Class 8, or a fence included in Class 6) which you purchased prior to May 26, 1976, you may claim capital cost allowance on these other classes to create or increase a rental loss even though capital cost allowance on the building may be restricted.

However, where a significant portion of the rent is attributable to the furniture, the capital cost allowance on the furniture must first be used to offset the rent attributable to the furniture. Any remaining available capital cost allowance from the furniture may then be used as a deduction against income from other sources. Capital cost allowance on the building will be calculated on the rental income attributable to the building and will be subject to the restrictions described in ¶630.

Normally this procedure need not be followed unless:

- there is a separate and significant rental charge for the use of property other than the building in the lease or rental agreement;
- the rent charged to tenants using the property other than the building is markedly higher than that charged to other tenants not using such property; or
- the capital cost of the property other than the building is significant in relation to the capital cost of the building.

Generally an allocation of income is not necessary for a tenant's use of kitchen appliances included in all units of a rental property, other appliances or facilities provided for the common use of all tenants, or indoor or outdoor parking areas.

Example — Furnished Suites

Frank Leschenko owns a triplex which he purchased in 1972 and has rented all three units as furnished suites. Frank received rentals during the year of $8,000 and incurred cash expenses of $6,000. His maximum capital cost allowance available is $3,000 on the Class 6 building and $1,000 on the Class 8 furnishings.

Frank should apportion his rental income between the amount received for the basic suites and the amount received for the furnishings if he receives significant additional rent due to furnishing the suites in his building. If Frank receives an extra $20 per month for each suite because the suites are furnished, his tax position will be calculated as follows:

	Furnishings	*Building*
Rental income	$ 720	$ 7,280
Expenses (including $50 for refrigerator repairs)	50	5,950
	$ 670	$ 1,330
Capital cost allowance claim	1,000	1,330
Loss for tax purposes	$ (330)	$ —

Example — Furnished Suites

Harry Neumann acquired an apartment building after May 26, 1976 which he is renting as furnished apartments. The building is a Class 32 property so capital cost allowance on this building is not restricted. Harry received rentals during the year of $23,000 and incurred cash expenses of $22,000. His maximum capital cost allowance available on the building is $7,000, and $2,000 on the Class 8 furnishings, both of which are not restricted to rental income.

Harry should apportion his rental income between the amount received for the basic apartments and the amount received for the furnishings if a significant portion of the rent is attributable to the furnishings. Harry receives an extra $250 per month for the apartments because the apartments are furnished. His tax position will be calculated as follows:

	Furnishings	*Building*
Rental income	$3,000	$20,000
Expenses (including cleaning and repair furnishings)	1,980	20,020
	$1,020	$(20)
Capital cost allowance claim	2,000	7,000
Loss for tax purposes	$ (980)	$(7,020)

Example — Unfurnished Building

Ann Gordon owns a duplex which she inherited in 1973 (i.e., before May 26, 1976 — see ¶655). She rents out both unfurnished suites. Included in the suites are refrigerators, stoves and drapes. During the year, Ann receives net rental income of $1,500 before capital cost allowance. The maximum capital cost allowance available to Ann in the year is $500 on Class 8 fixtures and $1,700 on the Class 6 building.

Rental income before capital cost allowance	$ 1,500
Maximum capital cost allowance allowable on Class 6 building	(1,500)
Maximum capital cost allowance on Class 8 fixtures	(500)
Loss for tax purposes	$ (500)

(ITR: 1100 [Capital cost allowance – deductions allowed]; IT-443 [Archived])

UNDEVELOPED LAND

[¶665] RESTRICTION ON PROPERTY TAXES AND INTEREST ON UNDEVELOPED LAND

If you own undeveloped land, you may be restricted in the amount of interest or property taxes in respect of the land that you can deduct when computing income for tax purposes.

You are only allowed to deduct interest and property taxes on undeveloped land to the extent that any rental or other income from the land exceeds other allowable expenses relating to the land. The result of this restriction is that you are prevented from creating or increasing a rental loss by deducting interest or property taxes.

However, the above restriction does not apply if you used the land in the course of a business carried on in the particular year (other than a business in the ordinary course of which land is held *primarily* for the purpose of resale or development), or if it was held primarily for the purpose of gaining or producing income from the land (i.e., rent) for the particular year. In either such case, the interest expense and property taxes incurred in the year are generally deductible in full under the regular rules governing their deductibility. See, however, ¶690 regarding the reasonable expectation of profit concept.

If the land is capital property, you may add interest and property taxes to the adjusted cost base of the land, to the extent they cannot be deducted because of the above restriction. This will affect any computation of capital gain or loss when the land is sold. See ¶508.

If the land is inventory (see ¶667), you may similarly add interest and property taxes, to the extent they cannot be deducted, to the inventory cost of the land so that it will reduce the profit (or increase the loss) on its final disposition.

Unlike the capital cost allowance restriction on rental buildings, the restriction on property taxes and interest is determined separately for each parcel of land. You may be precluded from deducting interest and property taxes on one piece of undeveloped land even though you have net rental income on other undeveloped land. The restriction applies to interest on money borrowed to purchase land or on amounts payable for land, and to property taxes on the land which are paid or payable to a province or Canadian municipality. If the land is outside Canada, the property tax restriction does not apply.

This restriction does not apply to land that is underneath or adjacent to a building to the extent that it can reasonably be considered to be used in connection with the building, such as a parking lot or yard used by tenants of an apartment building.

Example

(1) Ronald Spector owns a piece of undeveloped land which he holds as an investment. He receives no rent from the land and therefore cannot deduct any interest or property taxes.

(2) Charles Stevens owns two parcels of undeveloped land and had the following transactions:

	Parcel 1	*Parcel 2*
Rent received from allowing storage on the land	$ 1,200	$ 3,000
Liability insurance premiums paid	200	500
Mortgage interest paid	5,000	1,500
Property taxes paid	1,000	400

For Parcel 1, Charles will be able to deduct $1,000 of property taxes and interest, since his net rental income before these items is $1,200 - $200 or $1,000. The remaining $5,000 will be added to his adjusted cost base of the property. For Parcel 2, Charles may deduct all the interest and property taxes since his net rental income exceeds these items.

The rule disallowing interest in excess of revenue also applies if you borrow money and use it to assist a non-arm's length person to acquire property, unless the assistance is by way of a loan at reasonable rates. It applies equally if you use the money to assist a corporation in which you are a "specified" shareholder or a partnership in which you have a 10% or greater interest. A specified shareholder generally means a person who has, or is related to a person who has, a 10% or greater interest in the corporation. Deductions disallowed under this rule add to the adjusted cost base or inventory costs of the land itself, in the hands of whoever may actually hold title.

See ¶771 for a discussion of the deductibility of interest and property taxes (and other "soft costs") incurred during the construction, renovation or alteration of buildings.

(ITA: 18(2), (3); 53; IT-153R3 [Archived])

[¶667] SALE OF UNDEVELOPED LAND

Unless undeveloped land is held with an intention to develop it which is somehow frustrated, gains or losses on disposition are often treated as ordinary income or loss rather than capital gain or loss (see ¶500). The holding of land with an intention to sell it at a profit rather than to develop it is not exactly a business, but is referred to as an "adventure in the nature of trade". Historically, this raised questions about whether the land so held was subject to the regular inventory rules that allowed a write-down for income tax purposes when the value of the property decreased. In *Friesen v. The Queen*, 95 DTC 5551, the Supreme Court of Canada ruled that such property was inventory and was indeed subject to write-down in years prior to disposition. The government responded by amending the rules (on December 20, 1995) such that the regular inventory rules that apply to the valuation of business inventory on an annual basis do not apply to property held as an adventure in the nature of trade. Income or loss from the sale of such property is now recognized only on disposition. Where you claimed an inventory write-down for property held as an adventure in the nature of trade for a taxation year ending before December 21, 1995, the amount reported as fair market value (or reassessed as such) will be considered the cost for determining gain or loss on disposition, except that the additions to cost base permitted for interest and taxes denied current deduction under ¶665 after December 20, 1995 may be made. These issues, which include complex transitional rules, are discussed further at ¶758.

(ITA: 10, esp. 10(1.01))

SPECIAL RULES

[¶670] OPTIONS TO PURCHASE

If you are the owner of property and you give the lessee an option to purchase the property with rentals paid to be applied against the purchase price if the option is exercised, the rentals paid do not become a part of the sale price insofar as you are concerned but are regarded as rental income. However, if the contract is really an agreement for sale rather than an option agreement, even though certain payments may be called rent, they will be treated as a part of the sale price. See ¶833.

(IT-403R [Archived])

[¶675] NON-RESIDENT PROPERTY OWNERS

If you are a non-resident receiving rental income from property in Canada, you have a choice of two methods of paying tax. One method involves a flat withholding tax on the gross amount of rent received; the other involves filing a Part 1 return and paying regular Part 1 tax (at graduated rates) on the net amount of rent income. See ¶2165 for details.

RENTAL LOSSES

[¶690] RENTAL LOSSES AND THE EXPECTATION OF PROFIT

There are a number of provisions to restrict losses arising on real estate rentals; see, for example, the restrictions at ¶665 and the capital cost allowance restrictions at ¶630. As well, real estate deductions may be disallowed in determining income for alternative minimum tax purposes (¶2420).

Above and beyond these statutory rules, one of the main weapons of the CRA arsenal to deny real estate operating losses (usually arising primarily from mortgage interest deductions in excess of rental revenue) has historically been the stringent application of the judicial doctrine that you must have a reasonable expectation of profit (REOP) from a property to be entitled to deduct any expenses at all. In particular, the CRA was likely to challenge all rental losses where you invested in a property with the intention of making a speculative gain on the price of the property rather than an economic profit on rent (and incidentally supported the cost of carrying the rental property out of tax reductions obtained by deducting operating losses). The theory on which the loss was denied in this situation was that if you had no reasonable expectation of rental income (in excess of expense), you did not have a source of rental income from which to deduct rental losses (the "REOP" test). See, for example, the Federal Court of Appeal decision in *Stewart v. The Queen*, 98 DTC 1600 (T.C.C.), aff'd 2000 DTC 6163 (F.C.A.) (but later reversed, as discussed below).

In *Stewart v. The Queen*, 2002 DTC 6969 (S.C.C.), the Supreme Court reversed the Federal Court of Appeal and ruled that *where there is no element of personal use* of the real property, the investment in it is intrinsically commercial and there is a source the loss from which can be used against other income. "... whether or not a taxpayer has a source of income from a particular activity is determined by considering whether the taxpayer intends to carry on the activity for profit, and whether there is evidence to support that intention. As well, where an activity is clearly commercial and lacks any personal element, there is no need to search further. Such activities are sources of income." It does not matter that the venture will never run at an annual *profit*; the test is not periodic profit but the intention to profit, in the general sense of that word, in the long run, whether from ultimate capital gain or otherwise. If there is no personal element, and so no personal or living expense to be denied, there is no basis on which to second-guess the taxpayer's decision to make the investment, misguided though it may prove to have been. The Supreme Court made similar findings in the case of *The Queen v. Walls and Buvyer*, 2002 DTC 6960 (S.C.C.), a decision rendered concurrently with the *Stewart* decision. The *Walls* case similarly involved a highly leveraged real estate rental investment that carried significant interest expense.

In both the *Stewart* and *Walls* decisions, the Supreme Court clearly rejected the application of a REOP test to commercial rental activities that have no personal element. The Court held that, where the nature of a taxpayer's activity is clearly commercial, the pursuit of profit is established and there is no need to further analyze the taxpayer's business decisions or its REOP. The Court relegated REOP to a secondary role to be applied only to activities with a personal element. The Court held that REOP is only one of many factors to be considered in the personal element cases, in the determination of whether the activity in question is carried on in a sufficiently commercial manner, and therefore, whether it constitutes a source of income. In *Stewart*, the Supreme Court also rejected the Crown's argument that the taxpayer's anticipated capital gain on the disposition of its rental properties (the investments at issue) was irrelevant in the determination of whether the taxpayer had a source of income. In contrast, the Court held that a taxpayer's anticipation of a capital gain could, in the personal element cases, be a factor in the assessment of whether the taxpayer had a source of income. In summary, the Supreme Court decisions in *Stewart* and *Walls* relegated REOP to a secondary role to be applied only in the personal element cases, as one of several factors that can apply to determine whether sufficient commerciality exists in those cases.

Where current losses are not deductible but there is an expectation of capital gain, the taxpayer might look to *McPherson v. The Queen*, 98 DTC 1062 (T.C.C.). There, although annual rental losses were denied because there was no reasonable expectation of profit, the taxpayer was allowed a business loss on disposition in a falling market. However, there was no element of personal use in that case. The Court accepted that the taxpayer's true intention was to sell at a profit and not utilize rental losses as a tax shelter, and treated the project, in effect, as an adventure in the nature of trade with losses recognized as a full deduction (and not a capital loss) in the year of disposition. Compare the discussion of adventure in the nature of trade losses at ¶758.

In *Lanno v. CCRA*, 2005 DTC 5245 (F.C.A.), the Court referred a fairness decision back to the CRA in a case in which one taxpayer in a particular group appealing a reasonable expectation of profit case under the *Stewart* decision was denied the benefit of the *Stewart* case while others were apparently given a favourable reassessment. The case is discussed at ¶249.

In *Burnett v. The Queen*, 2009 DTC 1283 (T.C.C.), the taxpayer's appeal to the Tax Court of Canada was allowed in part. In reassessing the taxpayer for 2003 and 2004, the Minister disallowed the deduction of rental losses claimed with respect to three residential properties ("Black Walnut Trail", "Allcroft Trail", and "Beechnut Row"). On appeal to the Tax Court of Canada, the taxpayer abandoned his rental loss deduction claim for Black Walnut Trail. The Court ruled that there was a significant personal element involved in the taxpayer's activities with respect to one of his rental activities relating to Allcroft Trail. The taxpayer did not approach his rental activities relating to Allcroft Trail in a sufficiently commercial manner to constitute that property as a source of income. The Minister conceded, however, that the taxpayer's rental activities relating to Beechnut Row constituted a business. The Minister was, therefore, ordered to reassess on the basis that no rental loss deductions should be permitted with respect to Allcroft Trail, but that a rental expense deduction of $400 in excess of the amounts permitted by the Minister should be allowed with respect to Beechnut Row.

(S3-F6-C1 Interest Deductibility)

HOW TO REPORT YOUR RENTAL INCOME

[¶692] RENTAL INCOME

Details of the address of the property, gross rentals, expenses incurred, and capital cost allowance claimed should be entered on form T776, "Statement of Real Estate Rentals" provided with the *Rental Income Tax Guide* (T4036) available from CRA Tax Services Offices (¶287). Note especially the Adjustment Schedule reproduced in Chapter 8. Gross rental income is reported on line 160 and net rental income on line 176 of the T1 return.

Chapter 7

Business and Professional Income

THESE POINTS ARE COVERED IN THIS CHAPTER

CRA REFERENCES RELATING TO THIS CHAPTER

T1 Lines and Schedule

- Line 135 — Business income (Net)
- Line 137 — Professional income (Net)
- Line 139 — Commission income (Net)
- Line 162 — Business income (Gross)
- Line 164 — Professional income (Gross)
- Line 166 — Commission income (Gross)
- Schedule 8 — CPP Contributions on Self-Employment and Other Earnings

CRA Guides

5000-G, "General Income Tax and Benefit Guide"; **P134**, "Using your Home for Day Care"; **RC4015**, "Reconciliation of Business Income for Tax Purposes"; **RC4070**, "Guide for Canadian Small Businesses"; **RC4110**, "Employee or Self-Employed?"; **RC4120**, "Employers' Guide — Filing the T4 Slip and Summary"; **T4001**, "Employers' Guide — Payroll Deductions and Remittances"; **T4002**, "Business and Professional Income — Includes Form T2125"; **T4088**, "Guide to Form T661 — Scientific Research and Experimental Development (SR&ED) Expenditures Claim"; **T4130**, "Employers' Guide — Taxable Benefits and Allowances"

CRA Forms

CPT1, "Request for a Ruling as to the Status of a Worker Under the Canada Pension Plan or Employment Insurance Act"; **T1A**, "Request for Loss Carryback"; **T1-ADJ**, "T1 Adjustment Request"; **T106**, "Information Return of Non-Arm's Length Transactions with Non-Residents"; **T661**, "Scientific Research and Experimental Development (SR&ED) Expenditures Claim"; **T1139**, "Reconciliation of Business Income for Tax Purposes"; **T1204**, "Government Service Contract Payments"; **T2022**, "Election in Respect of the Sale of Debts Receivable"; **T2038(IND)**, "Investment Tax Credit (Individuals)"; **T2047**, "Agreement in Respect of Unpaid Amounts"; **T2125**, "Statement of Business or Professional Activities"; **T5013**, "Statement of Partnership Income"; **T5013-INST**, "Statement of Partnership Income — Instructions for Recipient"; **T5018**, "Statement of Contract Payments"

Income Tax Folios

S1-F2-C3, "Scholarships, Research Grants and Other Education Assistance"; **S1-F3-C2**, "Principal Residence"; **S3-F9-C1**, "Lottery Winnings, Miscellaneous Receipts, and Income (and Losses) from Crime"; **S5-F2-C1**, "Foreign Tax Credit";

S4-F2-C1, "Deductibility of Fines and Penalties"; **S3-F6-C1**, "Interest Deductibility"

Interpretation Bulletins [All Archived]

IT-92R2, "Income of Contractors"; **IT-99R5 (Consolidated)**, "Legal and Accounting Fees"; **IT-109R2**, "Unpaid Amounts"; **IT-123R6**, "Transactions Involving Eligible Capital Property"; **IT-129R**, "Lawyers' Trust Accounts and Disbursements"; **IT-131R2**, "Convention Expenses"; **IT-143R3**, "Meaning of Eligible Capital Expenditure"; **IT-148R3**, "Recreational Properties and Club Dues"; **IT-152R3**, "Special Reserves — Sale of Land"; **IT-153R3**, "Land Developers — Subdivision and Development Costs and Carrying Charges on Land"; **IT-154R**, "Special Reserves"; **IT-187**, "Customer Lists and Ledger Accounts"; **IT-188R**, "Sale of Accounts Receivable"; **IT-206R**, "Separate Businesses"; **IT-218R**, "Profits, Capital Gains and Losses from the Sale of Real Estate, Including Farmland and Inherited Land and Conversion of Real Estate from Capital Property to Inventory and Vice Versa"; **IT-259R4**, "Exchanges of Property"; **IT-261R**, "Prepayment of Rents"; **IT-273R2**, "Government Assistance — General Comments"; **IT-287R2**, "Sale of Inventory"; **IT-291R3**, "Transfer of Property to a Corporation Under Subsection 85(1)"; **IT-309R2**, "Premium on Life Insurance Used as Collateral"; **IT-313R2**, "Eligible Capital Property — Rules Where a Taxpayer Has Ceased Carrying on a Business or Has Died"; **IT-341R4**, "Expenses of Issuing or Selling Shares, Units in a Trust, Interests in a Partnership or Syndicate and Expenses of Borrowing Money"; **IT-346R**, "Commodity Futures and Certain Commodities"; **IT-350R**, "Investigation of Site"; **IT-357R2**, "Expenses of Training"; **IT-365R2**, "Damages, Settlements, and Similar Receipts"; **IT-386R**, "Eligible Capital Amounts"; **IT-417R2**, "Prepaid Expenses and Deferred Charges"; **IT-426R**, "Shares Sold Subject to an Earnout Agreement"; **IT-442R**, "Bad Debts and Reserves for Doubtful Debts"; **IT-457R**, "Election by Professionals to Exclude Work in Progress From Income"; **IT-459**, "Adventure or Concern in the Nature of Trade"; **IT-467R2**, "Damages, Settlements and Similar Payments"; **IT-473R**, "Inventory Valuation"; **IT-475**, "Expenditures on Research and for Business Expansion"; **IT-478R2**, "Capital Cost Allowance — Recapture and Terminal Loss"; **IT-485**, "Cost of Clearing or Levelling Land"; **IT-490**, "Barter Transactions"; **IT-504R2 (Consolidated)**, "Visual Artists and Writers"; **IT-514**, "Work Space in Home Expenses"; **IT-518R**, "Food, Beverages and Entertainment Expenses"; **IT-521R**, "Motor Vehicle Expenses Claimed by Self-Employed Individuals"; **IT-522R**, "Vehicle, Travel and Sales Expenses of Employees"; **IT-525R (Consolidated)**, "Performing Artists"

Information Circulars

05-1R1, "Electronic Record Keeping"; **72-5R2**, "Registered Supplementary Unemployment Benefit Plans"; **77-1R5**, "Deferred Profit Sharing Plans"; **78-10R5**, "Books and Records Retention/ Destruction"; **87-2R**, " International Transfer Pricing"

Income Tax Technical News

No. 12, February 11, 1998, "Meals and Beverages at Golf Clubs" (Archived by the CRA); **No. 29**, July 14, 2003, "Application of paragraph 12(1)(*x*)"

WHAT YOU SHOULD KNOW ABOUT INCOME FROM A BUSINESS

RECENT CHANGES

2016 Changes

Bill C-29 (Introduced October 25, 2016)

In the 2016 Federal Budget, the government confirmed that the eligible capital property regime will transition to the capital cost allowance rules, as previously suggested in the 2014 and 2015 federal Budgets. The rules are proposed in Bill C-29 at the time of writing. The changes are scheduled to take effect as of January 1, 2017. Further details of the 2017 rules will be provided in next year's edition of this book. See ¶770a.

Bill C-29 introduced rules that ensure that derivative instruments are not considered inventory for income tax purposes and further rules relating to the taxation of derivatives. See ¶758.20.

Legislative Proposals, September 16, 2016

On September 16, 2016, the Department of Finance introduced draft legislation that proposed a minor change to the reporting for SR&ED expenditures, to take effect on Royal Assent. See ¶740.15. The draft legislation also proposes minor changes to the tax treatment of restrictive covenants; see ¶929.

Regulatory Changes: Mileage Rates

2016 Mileage Rates and Other Automobile Rates

The Department of Finance announced that the limitations on deduction of automobile capital cost, interest, and leasing costs would be constant for 2016 at the rates prescribed for several years now. See ¶738.25 for leasing costs, and ¶738.45 for interest. Capital cost allowance limits are discussed at ¶810a.

The limit on the deduction of tax-exempt allowances paid by employers to employees using their personal vehicle for business purposes for 2016 is 54¢ per kilometre for the first 5,000 kilometres driven and 48¢ for each additional kilometre. For the Yukon, Northwest Territories and Nunavut, deduction of tax-exempt allowances is 58¢ for the first 5,000 kilometres driven and 52¢ for each additional kilometre. See the subheading "Disallowance to Employer of Employee Allowances" at ¶738.55 and the "Table of Per Kilometre Limitations" at ¶738.65.

The general prescribed rate used to determine the taxable benefit relating to the personal portion of automobile operating expenses paid by employers for 2016 is 26¢ per kilometre. For taxpayers employed principally in selling or leasing automobiles, the prescribed rate is 23¢ per kilometre. See ¶738.60 and the "Automobile Rates and Limits" at ¶86.

Capital Cost Allowance

See the changes proposed to capital cost allowance rules in the "Recent Changes" section at the beginning of Chapter 8.

[¶700] WHAT IS A "BUSINESS"?

A business is defined by the *Income Tax Act* to include a profession, calling, trade, manufacture or undertaking of any kind whatever. It also includes an adventure or concern in the nature of trade but does not include an office or employment.

A "business" may be thought of as an activity involving the purchase or production of goods or services with the intention of selling such goods or services at a profit. If you are an employee, you are not in business even though your activities may be similar to those of someone in business. If you are an investor, you are not in business because you did not buy the investment property for the purpose of resale. Instead, an investor holds the property and derives his profit from the interest, dividends or other income which the property produces.

These are general rules and may be difficult to apply in specific instances. For example, you may buy and sell on the stock market frequently but may not be considered to be in the "business of dealing in stocks" unless a substantial portion of your time and energy is devoted to your stock market transactions. See ¶500.05. On the other hand, if you buy real property (or any speculative commodity) and sell it at a profit within a short space of time, the tax authorities may consider the transaction to be an adventure in the nature of trade and consequently any profit from the transaction will be treated as business income. For more on an adventure in the nature of trade, see ¶758.05.

A hobby may constitute a business if it produces income and is carried on entirely or partially with a profit motive. See ¶704.

You may have more than one business, in which case the profits of each must be calculated separately. See ¶702.

The distinction between income from a business and income from employment, investments, or other sources can be very important. An individual in business is, in general, permitted to claim deductions for many expenses not deductible by an employee and perhaps not allowed to investors. On the other hand, a profit on sale of property will be fully taxable to a person in the business of trading in such properties, but taxable as a capital gain (see Chapter 5) to an investor.

The distinction between employment and self-employment (business) is discussed in greater detail in ¶304, and in a Guide called *Employee or Self-Employed?* (RC4110), available from on the CRA website. If you are in doubt as to whether you are considered an employee or a self-employed person, you may request a ruling from the CRA for the purposes of the *Canada Pension Plan* Act by filing form CPT1.

(ITA: 248; IT-218R [Archived]; IT-459 [Archived])

[¶700.50] *Selling Self-Generated Power Back to the Power Grid*

In two opinions issued in 2008, the CRA considered various Ontario programs under which an individual invests in environmentally friendly power generating equipment, typically solar panels, for a personal residence. The power produced offsets power costs of the individual and perhaps, under at least one program, can generate net revenue. The first program, net metering, seems to be accepted as not involving a taxable transaction. The second, in which the power company buys power at a fixed rate, may be taxed as a business with no offset for the individual's reduced power costs.

In CRA Document No. 2008-0287671E5, the CRA stated:

> It is our understanding that the Ontario Power Authority ("OPA") and the Ontario Energy Board have developed a Renewable Energy Standard Offer Program for the Province of Ontario (the "Program") designed to encourage and promote greater use of renewable energy sources, including solar, from smaller generating projects that would be connected to an electricity distribution system in Ontario. Under the Program, an applicant would enter into a contract with the OPA, pursuant to which the applicant will deliver electricity to a local electricity distribution system in Ontario for a 20-year period and receive $0.42 per kWh of production. This Program is to be distinguished from "net metering". Where an Ontario customer generates electricity primarily for their own use from a renewable source (such as solar power) using equipment of maximum cumulative output up to 500 kilowatts in size, they are eligible for net metering. With net metering all of the regulated charges apply only to net consumption and where the customer supplies more than they consume, they will receive a credit that can be carried forward for 12 months. If you require further information on the Program see www.powerauthority.on.ca.

The opinion then seems to go on to accept that net metering does not involve a taxable transaction. (What the opinion actually says is that equipment acquired for purposes of a net metering transaction is not acquired for the purposes of earning income, from which one must infer that any benefits obtained under the program are not taxable. In fairness, the transactions the CRA was asked to comment on involved the purchase program and not the net metering program.) The opinion then goes on to say that on the facts it was given, i.e., the acquisition of solar panels for personal use only for a "summer retreat" under the Renewable Energy Standard Offer Program, the individual would be in the business of selling energy to the OPA.

In a second opinion, the CRA apparently deals only with the Renewable Energy Standard Offer Program (as opposed, presumably, to the net metering program). In this opinion (CRA Document No. 2008-0275351E5), the CRA seems to say that the income from the Standard Offer Program is probably taxable income from a business, even if, for the most part, it reduces your power costs, rather than actually creating income as most people would think of it.

In the case the CRA reviewed, an individual entered into an agreement under the Program. The individual was required to, and did, incur considerable expense to install solar panels on his house. After that, the facts become a bit murky. It appears that the credits for power generated would rarely exceed the individual's personal power consumption, so in effect it would reduce his hydro costs rather than generating positive income.

Apparently the CRA will take the following position: "Based on our understanding of the terms of the Program, the participant's sale of electricity to the grid is a separate transaction from the participant's personal consumption of electricity". This seems to say that the sale of power to the grid creates business income, whereas the consumption of power by the individual is a personal expense, so the expense does not offset the income. It seems to be implicit (but not explicit) in the opinion that the individual consumer expects that, in the long run, increasing power costs will render the program an income generator.

While this is perhaps a tenable position from a technical point of view, one may be permitted to doubt that it is necessarily tenable from a political point of view. It surely vitiates the point of the Ontario program, in that it must discourage individuals from incurring the very substantial expense of buying into it. On the other hand, the very existence of the non-taxable net metering program does cast the Standard Offer Program in a more commercial light. Nevertheless, one might expect Ontario to protest, and to find support for that protest in the renewable energy movement, which may find support in a minority Parliament. In short, without any insult intended to the CRA, it seems likely that this opinion will be subject to further judicial and/or political consideration.

The opinion is hedged somewhat, stating: "Accordingly, income from such an arrangement would generally be income from a source that is a business ... provided there is a reasonable expectation of profit". This seems to recognize (without saying so) that the courts might well distinguish between an investment made for a personal home and a more obviously commercial investment, depending on the facts of the case.

The opinion goes on to say that the investment in equipment would probably be Class 43.2 property for capital cost allowance purposes (¶889) *if it is* acquired for the purpose of earning income from a business or property. However, capital cost allowance would probably be constrained by the specified energy property restrictions (¶889.25) to the income from the business.

The opinion considers the impact of Program on the principal residence exemption. In general, it says that there will probably be no effect provided that the income-producing use is ancillary to the main use of the property as a residence, there is no structural change to the property, and no CCA is claimed on the property. This, too, is rather murky. Can one claim CCA on the solar panels but not the house without impairing the principal residence claim? How much structural change is permitted to accommodate the solar panel installation?

At best, the opinion may mean very little, since the Courts might well (as the opinion seems to admit) conclude in any particular case that the overall transaction was not entered into for profit. At worst, however, it may indicate the CRA's intent to fight all cases under the program, contending that the reduction of the taxpayer's normal power cost must always be treated as income, with no offset for capital cost allowance without impairing the principal residence exemption. There may perhaps be a middle ground, permitting CCA on the solar equipment alone to zero out power income without impairing the principal residence exemption, although this does not seem to be a result contemplated in the CRA opinion. No doubt there will eventually be further word to come.

[¶700.80] *Starting a New Business?*

If you are starting a new business, especially for the first time, you should know that the CRA puts out a very useful and extensive guide on the tax implications. You can obtain the *Guide for Canadian Small Businesses* (RC4070) by making a telephone request to 1-800-959-2221 (toll free) or by download from the CRA website, www.cra-arc.gc.ca.

[¶701] REAL ESTATE

If you sell real estate, other than your principal residence, any profit on the sale may be taxed either as income from a business or as a capital gain. See ¶500 for a discussion of the points to be considered in deciding whether the profit will be treated as income or as a capital gain.

If you invest in real estate for rental income, the income may be income from a business or from property, as discussed at ¶600. For losses on rental property, see ¶690.

(IT-218R [Archived])

[¶702] SEPARATE BUSINESSES

The question of whether you are conducting one business or more than one business in a taxation year can arise when more than one business operation is being carried on simultaneously or successively. It can be of importance, for example, where:

(1) you have disposed of a property and will recapture capital cost allowance if that and other similar property that you own are in separate classes because they are used in separate businesses (¶870);

(2) you are computing your cumulative eligible capital and eligible capital amounts for each of your separate businesses (¶766); or

(3) you are allocating the income of each separate business to the provinces where it was earned (¶1440).

Where you are carrying on two or more business operations simultaneously, the CRA's interpretation of whether this constitutes a single business depends on the degree of interconnection, or interdependence of the business operations. The fact that your business operations are of a different nature, such as manufacturing and selling, does not preclude them from being the same business if there is sufficient interconnection or interdependence between the operations.

If you become bankrupt or your business is taken over by an interim receiver, the trustee or receiver, as the case may be, is considered to carry on the same business that you formerly carried on.

(Window on Canadian Tax: 9639; IT-206R [Archived])

[¶703] PARTNERSHIPS

If you are a member of a partnership, you should refer to Chapter 18 for a discussion of the special rules affecting you. These rules generally provide that partnership income is computed separately from your personal income, even if it is from the same type of business. Losses from partnerships may be subject to special restrictions.

As a partner, you may still, however, claim as business expenses those expenses related to your income from the partnership incurred personally and not by the partnership. These additional deductions include capital cost allowances on business assets owned by you and not by the partnership and other business expenses that you paid personally.

[¶704] HOBBIES AND SIDELINE BUSINESSES

You may be regularly employed or regularly engaged in business and also have some other activity which you carry on. Examples of these activities include photography, dog-raising, gambling, gardening, etc. If these activities produce income or result in expenses, the question arises as to whether this income is taxable or these expenses are deductible.

If the activity is not a business, the income from it is not subject to tax and the expenses are not deductible. However, if you sell a personal-use property produced in such activity for proceeds of more than $1,000, any gain you receive may be subject to income tax as a capital gain from a personal-use property. See ¶545.

A hobby may constitute a business if it is carried on with the intention of earning profit and there is a reasonable expectation of profit. Intention is indicated by conduct and by the nature of activity. A reasonable expectation of profit is determined by the performance of the activity over a period of years and also the status, capacity, experience and interest of the persons involved. Some activities are not likely ever to be profitable. Similarly, a person may be pursuing a hobby as a commercial enterprise but with little or no intention to earn profits therefrom. In such cases, the activities would not be regarded as a business. The expenses incurred would therefore be non-deductible personal and living expenses.

However, the Supreme Court, in *The Queen v. Jack Walls and Rupert Buvyer*, 2002 DTC 6960 (S.C.C.), ruled that where an endeavour was clearly commercial in nature and had no personal element (i.e., no hobby aspect), there is clearly a source of income and loss for income tax purposes. It is only where there is a personal element that the issue arises as to whether there is a source at all. The CRA may still question whether a particular expense is reasonable in the circumstances. Presumably, although the Court did not comment on it, there are some activities (gardening, etc., as discussed above) in which a personal element is intrinsically more probable, and the question of source would still arise. (In *Walls*, a storage park operation was structured so that there were bound to be losses for tax purposes. The Court clearly could not imagine — nor did the CRA argue — that anyone went into the storage park business as a hobby.) See also the *Stewart* case, discussed at ¶690.

All the facts must be considered to determine whether an activity is a business or a hobby. Important factors in this determination are the amount of time spent on the activity and the extent of efforts made to sell its products.

As the *Walls* case makes clear, the fact that an activity does not produce profits is not conclusive. As long as the *intention* was to earn profits and there was a serious commercial aspect to the endeavour, there is a business. Only if there is a personal or hobby element does one examine the issue of reasonable expectation of profit as one aspect of whether there was a commercial endeavour. A tax shelter motive does not affect the result, provided the transactions are structured to avoid the numerous restrictions discussed at ¶2521.

Draft legislation introduced October 31, 2003, would have overturned the effect of *Walls* and reintroduced the reasonable expectation of profit test as a condition for deducting losses for taxation years that begin in or after 2005. The draft legislation remained outstanding for several years as the government heard submissions from the private sector. Eventually, the draft legislation was withdrawn via a press release dated November 17, 2014 (it was excluded from the "List of outstanding specific legislative proposals for listed tax laws announced prior to April 1, 2013"). Accordingly, the Supreme Court decisions in *Stewart* and *Walls* remain the authoritative law on point.

Where farming is involved, see ¶1750.

Where artistic activity is involved, see ¶789.

(ITA: 18, 46; IT-459 [Archived]; Income Tax Folio: S1-F3-C2 Principal Residence)

[¶704d] GAMBLING AS A BUSINESS

Generally speaking, gambling winnings qualify as windfall gain (¶991.10) and are not taxable income. This may not be true where there is an indication of systematic pursuit of gain to the extent that the activity constitutes a business. The flip side, of course, is that where there is a business, losses will be deductible. A thorough review of gambling cases is found in *Leblanc et al. v. The Queen*, 2007 DTC 307 (T.C.C.); see especially paragraph 37, as follows:

> [37] The gambling cases fall into three broad categories:
>
> (a) There are cases involving the gamblers for whom gambling is a pleasurable pursuit. They are not taxable even though they do it regularly, even compulsively and with some sort of organization or system. *Graham v. Green*, *Balanko*, *Markowitz v. M.N.R.*, 64 DTC 397, *Walker v. M.N.R.*, 52 DTC 1001, and *Beaudin* and *Epel v. The Queen*, 2003 DTC 1361, are examples.
>
> (b) Gambling gains have been held to be taxable where the gambling was an adjunct or incident of a business carried on, for example by a casino owner who gambles in his own casino or an owner of horses who trains and races horses and who bets on the races; (*Down* or *Badame v. M.N.R.*, 51 DTC 29).
>
> (c) Gambling gains have also been held to be taxable where a person uses his own expertise and skill to earn a livelihood in a gambling game in which skill is a significant component (for example the pool player who, in cold sobriety, challenges inebriated pool players to a game of pool). Another more flamboyant example is the professional riverboat gambler.

The *Leblanc* case itself dealt with lottery winnings. The taxpayers spent truly massive amounts of money on a more or less daily basis making high-risk bets on various (legal) lottery games. Over time, their winnings apparently exceeded their losses by about $5 million (gains of $55 million and losses of $50 million). The CRA contended that, in effect, the activities were sufficiently organized to constitute a business. The taxpayers contended that the gains were capital in nature and exempt by virtue of the statutory rule that exempts gambling gains from capital gains, and indeed by virtue of that rule could never be business earnings, and that in the alternative the activity of the taxpayers did not amount to an organized business. The Tax Court clearly viewed the case with a certain relish due to its odd facts, but nevertheless produced a very detailed opinion that summarized much of the relevant law on the issue of gambling generally and lotteries in particular. The Court was clearly impressed with expert testimony about the odds against any organized system beating lottery odds, and while it did not hold that such winnings could never constitute business income, it will be very difficult for the CRA to make such a contention again in the face of the decision. In any event, on the facts of the case, there was no business, despite the degree of activity involved.

In *Cohen v The Queen* (2011 DTC 1195), the taxpayer had been a lawyer in a large Toronto law firm. After learning that he had been passed up for partnership, he decided to leave the practice of law and take up poker playing on a full-time basis for the 2006 taxation year. However, he did not resign from the firm, but instead decided to turn down work and pass on files to other lawyers, with the expectation that he would be terminated and paid a severance. He was in fact terminated and paid a severance, at which point the taxpayer claimed that he started a gambling business. He claimed gambling losses of approximately $122,000 in 2006, which he deducted against his law employment income. The CRA denied the losses on the basis that the gambling activities were personal in nature and lack sufficient commerciality to constitute a business. Upon the taxpayer's appeal, the Tax Court upheld the CRA's decision and denied the losses.

The Tax Court specifically looked at the following factors in reaching its decision: the taxpayer's profit and loss experience in past years; the taxpayer's training; his intended course of action; the capability of the venture to show a profit; and other factors such as the taxpayer's skill level, his management of risk, his discipline, and the frequency of his play. Applying the various factors, the Court found that the taxpayer did not have sufficient training or expertise in gambling, his planning documents were a "loose compilation of notes from reading materials" that did not constitute a business plan, he did not take sufficient steps to minimize risk and in fact increased his risk by switching from low stakes games to higher stakes games with more experienced players, and more generally, that the taxpayer failed to provide credible evidence that his gambling activities had the capacity to show a profit. As a result, the Court concluded that the taxpayer did not carry on a gambling business.

BUSINESS YEAR ENDS

[¶705] GENERAL

[¶705.20] *General Rule*

Under fiscal period rules, where an individual conducts a business which has a fiscal period which does not coincide with the calendar year, income of the business is calculated for that fiscal period as if it were a taxation year. This can be important in calculating the income, especially where new rules come into force with transitional provisions which make special provision for non-calendar taxation years. For example, the capital cost allowance rate changes are sometimes prorated for non-calendar fiscal periods according to the days in each rate period in a fiscal year (see ¶878). Similarly, the automobile rules apply to fiscal periods (see ¶738). Recapture of capital cost allowance and terminal loss rules operate on a fiscal period basis, since these are adjustments to business income. On the other hand, capital gain or loss from dispositions of capital property other than eligible capital property are always considered dispositions by the individual, even if the property is used in a business, and the capital gain element of dispositions must be reported by individuals in the calendar year in which they occur regardless of fiscal periods (but see ¶706).

(ITA: 11; IT-478R2, para. 12 [Archived])

[¶705.25] *Fiscal Period of Business and Calendar Year*

Businesses must either adopt a calendar taxation year as the fiscal period or make a special election that allows an off-calendar year fiscal period. Generally speaking, adopting the calendar year is the easiest approach. Making the election is appropriate if the business is seasonal and December 31 falls in the middle of the season, so that it does not represent a fair or easily ascertainable picture of profit, or where an individual is joining an existing non-calendar business (usually a partnership). Mechanics of the election are discussed in detail under the subheading "Election to have a Non-Calendar Year End" at ¶705.30. The election defers the proprietor's (or partner's) income for the opening year but requires a double income inclusion in the following year, a result which can be avoided by choosing to include an amount in income in the opening year and so averaging the two. This is discussed under the subheading "New Businesses: Election to Have Additional Business Income" at ¶705.35, below.

The fiscal period of an individual, an *inter vivos* trust (and, after 2015, a testamentary trust that is not a graduated rate estate), or a partnership which includes any individuals as partners (or meets certain other conditions described at ¶1804) must end at the end of the calendar year in which it began. An exception to this general rule is permitted for a business operated by an individual or, under certain circumstances a partnership, provided an election is made as described below. There are also exceptions to the general rule for a business which is not carried on in Canada or a prescribed business. The prescribed business seems to be a safety valve; no official indication has been given that there will be any prescribed businesses. There is also an exemption for tax-exempt persons, which would seem to apply primarily to tax-exempt trusts.

Rules for the election to maintain a non-calendar fiscal period are discussed below; partnerships are considered at ¶1804.

[¶705.30] *Election to Have a Non-Calendar Year End ("The Alternative Method" — Form T1139)*

A business carried on by an individual, either directly or as a partner in a partnership of individuals which is not itself a member of another partnership (see also ¶1804), may elect to opt out of the calendar year fiscal period requirement for the business. The election (referred to on the election form T1139 as "the alternative method") must be filed with the individual's return of income for the taxation year that includes the first day of the first fiscal period of the business, and that return must be filed by the individual's filing due date (which can be June 15 of the following year; see ¶218). Thus, *for a new business commencing in Year 1, the election must be made by June 15 of Year 2 even if the fiscal period is to end after that time.*

The requirement that the election must be made by the filing deadline for the year in which the fiscal period commences can be something of a trap. An election is required for that year even if no income is to be reported from the business (or at all). The penalty for late filing the election is, presumably, that the non-calendar year election is denied and the December 31 fiscal period adopted, with no possibility of change except by appealing to the discretion of the CRA, which does have the authority to permit a change of fiscal period if it chooses. There is no late-filing provision, a point emphasized in a CRA tax opinion reported at CRA Document No. 9711417.

Once made, the election continues until it is revoked. An election to revoke will apply to a fiscal period commencing in the year if it is made with a timely return of income for the year. Revocation will create two fiscal periods ending in that year, with no special transitional reserve (but no special additional income inclusion under the following rules).

The CRA provides form T1139 for making (or revoking) the election, and for maintaining the annual tax calculations necessary once you have made the election. It also provides a *Reconciliation of Business Income for Tax Purposes* tax guide (RC4015), which offers valuable assistance in preparing form T1139.

A partnership must make the election (or revocation) at the partnership level; it then becomes mandatory for each partner who is an individual (other than a testamentary trust before 2016 or a graduated rate estate for 2016 and subsequent years) to make an additional business income computation under these rules.

When the election to have a non-calendar taxation year is made, a special income inclusion must be made to approximate the stub period income for the fiscal period which commenced in the year but did not end in the year due to the election. After the first year, a continuing inclusion is required based on income for the fiscal period that did end in the year. (Technically, the inclusion is required for the first year as well; as there is no base for calculation, it always turns out to be zero.) The inclusion is not required for the taxation year in which an individual dies, ceases to carry on the business, or becomes bankrupt.

The special income inclusion, or "additional business income" (ABI), is income for all fiscal periods of the business which did end in the year (but not including deemed taxable capital gains from dispositions of eligible capital property included in income but deducted again under the capital gains exemption rules) prorated by:

$$\frac{\text{days the individual carried on business in the year in the fiscal period that commenced but did not end in the year}}{\text{days the individual carried on the business in fiscal periods that did end in the year}}$$

ABI added to the income of an individual in Year 1 is deducted in Year 2, when a new computation of ABI is required.

Example

Helen commenced a business on February 1, Year 1. She elected to have a January 31, Year 2 year end. The business earned $140,000 in that fiscal period. If Helen makes the election to have a non-calendar year end but makes no election to report income in Year 1 from that business (under the rules at ¶705.35, below), she will have no Year 1 business income, but will have to report Year 2 income of $140,000 plus $128,110 additional income. The additional income is, for Year 2, $140,000 prorated by days in calendar Year 2 after January 31 (334) over days in the fiscal period ending in Year 2 (365 days), so $140,000 × $^{334}/_{365}$ = $128,110. Thus, Year 2 income will be $268,110.

In Year 3, Helen will have an income inclusion calculated for additional income, but will deduct the Year 2 inclusion of $128,110. Thus tax on the deferral which the government finds inherent in the non-calendar year is always (after the year in which the business commences) pre-paid.

[¶705.35] *New Businesses: Election to Have Additional Business Income*

It is evident (after a while) that the above formula for ABI will yield zero in the first taxation year of a new business where an election is made to have a non-calendar year end. The deferral thus achieved for the first few months of the business will be paid for in the following year, when both income from the actual fiscal period and ABI must be reported.

The rules solve this problem by permitting the individual faced with it to elect to have a Year 1 income inclusion of any amount of income from the opening non-calendar fiscal period (ending in Year 2) up to the income for that period (minus the eligible capital property gains deducted under the capital gains exemption, see ¶768.25, item (3)) prorated by:

$$\frac{\text{days the individual carried on business that are in the calendar year and in the fiscal period that commenced but did not end in the year}}{\text{days the individual carried on the business in the first fiscal periods that end after the year}}$$

Amounts added to the income of an individual under the election in Year 1 is deducted in Year 2, when a new computation of ABI is required.

Example

Rather than accepting the result of her non-calendar year election in Year 2 in the example above, Helen may elect to report Year 1 income of $140,000 prorated by days in calendar Year 1 that are in the fiscal period which begins in Year 1 and ends in Year 2 (334 for Year 1) over days in the fiscal period ending in Year 2 (365 days), so, $140,000 × $^{334}/_{365}$ = $128,110. (Actually, she may report such amount as she designates up to a maximum of $128,110.) This income will be reported a year early, but (assuming no other Year 1 income) will be taxed (below the maximum rate threshold for Year 1) at lower rates and with a full set of personal amount credits. In Year 2, Helen will report $140,000 of income plus $128,110 ABI minus $128,110 reported in Year 1. (There will be a slight discrepancy between income reported in the first year and the deduction for the subsequent year when there is a leap year.) After the first year of the business, ABI calculations based on income of the fiscal period(s) ending in the year (as discussed above) become mandatory until the business elects to move to a calendar year basis.

Note that this system assumes Helen can make a reasonable guess about Year 2 fiscal period income when she files her Year 1 return. (As a business person she has until June 15, Year 2, to file her Year 1 return, but only until April 30, Year 2, to make an estimated tax payment.) The election must be made by the filing-due date for the return for the individual for the taxation (calendar) year that includes the first day of the fiscal period (Year 1 in the example). There was initially some waffling over the issue of whether there could be a late-filed election, and eventually provision was made by regulation for late filed elections up to January 31, 1998. Now that the grace period has expired, however, the CRA seems to take the view (in a tax opinion, CRA Document No. 9711417) that no late-filed election is possible.

[¶705.50] *CRA Guide and Form T1139*

Form T1139 allows you (if you qualify) to elect to maintain a non-calendar year for a new business, or to revoke such an election previously made and move to a calendar year basis.

The CRA publishes a *Reconciliation of Business Income for Tax Purposes* tax guide (RC4015), which includes form T1139 and has a detailed discussion of its contents.

(ITA: 5; 11; 34.1; 34.2; 38; 96(3); 248(1) "fiscal period"; 249; 249.1; ITR: 1104(1); IT-179R [Archived]; IT-478R2, para. 12, 13 [Archived])

[¶706] YEAR OF CAPITAL GAIN RECOGNITION

As stated in ¶705, it has always been the position of the CRA that the capital gains of an individual (other than deemed capital gains from eligible capital property) are recognized on a calendar year basis, as part of the gains of the individual for the individual's taxation year, rather than on a business fiscal period basis. This is true whether or not the gain is on assets used in the course of a proprietorship with a non-calendar fiscal period. This can create anomalous results where recapture and capital gain occur on the disposition of assets used in a business, and must be reported in different years on the same disposition, but in practice the rules have not been difficult to apply.

[¶707] YEAR END WHERE BUSINESS DISPOSED OF (OR PARTNERSHIP CEASES)

For several years, the value of the off year-end election has been truncated by the rules at ¶705, which in effect put nearly all unincorporated businesses on a calendar year basis. Nevertheless, the option remains for calendar year businesses to elect to have a December 31 year end in the year a proprietorship is disposed of or a partnership ceases, rather than the actual date of disposition/cessation. As before, the elector must be resident in Canada at the time of the elected year end.

In the case of a partnership which has been wound up, it is not necessary for all partners to make the election as to the year end. Each partner can make his own choice.

Businesses which have used the alternative election at ¶705 to continue on a non-calendar year basis are not eligible for this election, and accordingly will be considered to have a final fiscal period ending when a proprietorship is disposed of or a partnership ceases. In this case, there can be two fiscal periods ending in the calendar year, with a potential double-up of income. Note, however, that an individual who has elected the alternative method need not include "additional business income" in that year, as generally required, but will be entitled to deduct the previous year inclusion.

Ceasing to carry on business involves additional considerations concerning purchased goodwill or other items the business may be depreciating as eligible capital expenditures. See ¶770.

(ITA: 11; 25; 34.1(8); 99; IT-478R2, para. 13 [Archived])

CALCULATION OF NET INCOME

[¶711] CALCULATION OF NET INCOME

There are two basic methods of accounting used in determining income from a business; the cash method and the accrual method. As a general rule all taxpayers should use the accrual method of accounting unless the *Income Tax Act* provides otherwise in respect of specific items of income or expense. Farmers and fishers may however elect to use the cash method of accounting. The CRA states (in the *Business and Professional Income* guide) that a self-employed commission sales agent may use the cash method "as long as it accurately shows your income for the year". This would generally be the case unless you actually carried a large inventory of goods for sale. See ¶713, below.

(ITA: 28)

[¶713] THE CASH METHOD OF COMPUTING INCOME

The cash method of computing income is, strictly speaking, what its name suggests: income (or loss) for a fiscal period is computed by measuring cash (or current cheques) received and expenses actually paid. It is a commonplace to say that except for the specific provisions mentioned below, the cash method of accounting cannot be used in computing income from a business. This may somewhat overstate the case. If your business is such that you regularly have virtually no amounts receivable but uncollected and no major expenses incurred but unpaid at the end of your fiscal period, and have no inventory of goods to sell and no costs of your services partially performed to carry forward into a new fiscal period, you probably are to all intents and purposes a cash-basis taxpayer. Although the rules at ¶716, for example, still technically apply to you, it is doubtful that any serious distortion of your income will occur from computing it in practice on a cash basis. However, this is true in only the simplest of cases, where there is no appreciable difference between the result of the cash method and the result of strict adherence to the rules discussed in this chapter.

A special statutory "cash method" of computing income is available to farmers and fishers; this is discussed at ¶1705.

A special method of computing income is available to specified professionals, who are defined to include accountants, dentists, lawyers, Quebec notaries, medical doctors, veterinarians, and chiropractors. The details of this method are described at ¶778–¶781.

[¶714] THE ACCRUAL METHOD OF COMPUTING INCOME

Under the accrual method of accounting, income is generally computed for the period during which it has been earned, i.e., at the time goods are delivered or services are rendered even though accounts receivable for such goods or services may not have been collected. In computing income on the accrual basis, expenses incurred to earn the income of the period are deducted whether or not they have been paid. As with the cash method, transactions which give rise to capital receipts or expenditures will have no effect on the profit from a business except to the extent that capital cost allowance may be deductible on depreciable assets.

The accrual method requires inventory or stock of goods on hand at the beginning and end of each year to be taken into account in the determination of income. Bad and doubtful accounts receivable may be deducted in the computation of business profit (¶733).

(ITA: 12; 18; 20)

INCLUSIONS IN COMPUTING BUSINESS INCOME

[¶716] AMOUNTS RECEIVED OR RECEIVABLE

You are generally required to include in income every amount received in the year in the course of the business:

(1) relating to goods to be delivered or services to be rendered after the end of the fiscal year;

(2) that for any reason is not regarded as having been earned in the year, e.g., rent received in advance; and

(3) relating to returnable containers in which goods were delivered.

You are also required to include in income every amount legally owing to you as of the year end with respect to goods sold or services rendered in the course of your business in the current year. These amounts must be included in income even though not collectible until some future date. (However, see ¶732 for reserves deductible from income in respect of these amounts.)

(ITA: 12)

[¶717] INCOME FROM BARTERING

If you are involved in a bartering transaction, amounts could be deemed to be received by you as proceeds from a business operation. A barter transaction is effected when any two persons agree to a reciprocal exchange of goods and services, and carry out that exchange without using money. If you are in a business or profession that provides services which are offered in a barter transaction in exchange for goods or services, the value of those services provided by you must be included in your income.

Examples would include situations where you are a lawyer or the owner of a service station who agrees to provide legal advice or automobile parts (respectively) in return for services or property provided by the other party. Where you are in an employment situation, e.g., an electrician, occasional help given to a friend or neighbour in exchange for something would not be taxable unless you made a regular habit of providing such services for cash or barter.

In the case of goods bartered by you for either goods or services, the value of those goods must similarly be brought into your income if they are business-related. In addition, other goods bartered may give rise to a capital gain (Chapter 5). Such would be the case if capital property in the form of a valuable sculpture, a yacht or land is bartered for goods and services.

In arm's length transactions, where an amount must be brought into your income or treated as proceeds of disposition of capital property, that amount is the price which you would normally have charged a stranger for your services or for which you would normally have sold your goods or property to a stranger. The cost of the services, goods or properties received by him is the same amount as the total value of the goods, property or services given up, plus any cash given by him as part of the barter, and minus any cash received by him as part of the barter. The transactions contemplated above would be considered to take place at fair market value in non-arm's length situations.

Where the goods or services given up cannot be readily valued but the goods or services received can, the CRA will normally accept the value of the latter as being the price at which the transaction took place if the parties were dealing at arm's length.

(IT-490 [Archived])

[¶718] REPOSSESSIONS

If your business includes the selling of property under conditional sales contracts and if you have repossessed any of this property you should refer to ¶518 to determine the effect on your tax position as a result of the repossession.

(ITA: 79)

[¶719] DAMAGES — BREACH OF CONTRACT

[¶719.05] *Damages Received*

If you are carrying on business and receive damages for the breach of a business contract, you must include such damages in your income. Depending on the facts, the amount received by you may be either an income or a capital receipt. However, damages relating to depreciable property may result in the recapture of capital cost allowances and in a capital gain (¶843). Damages relating to other capital assets may result in a capital gain or loss.

Where the amount of compensation is of a capital nature but it does not relate to a particular asset, the amount will be considered as compensation for the destruction of, or as damages to, the whole profit-making apparatus of your business. Such compensation may result in an "eligible capital amount". See ¶768.

The views above reflect the position of the CRA that damages must have some impact for tax purposes. In *Westcoast Energy Inc. v. The Queen*, 91 DTC 5334, the Federal Court–Trial Division held that damages related to the making good of the position of the purchaser of a defective pipeline were neither income nor reduction of capital cost. The Court did not consider the eligible capital amount alternative (which apparently the CRA did not advance) and left the impression that the damages were a nothing for tax purposes. An appeal to the Federal Court of Appeal was dismissed without comment (92 DTC 6253). See ¶729.

The damages issue reappeared in *Ipsco Inc. v. The Queen*, 2002 DTC 1421 (T.C.C.). In that case, the taxpayer had a plant constructed for it which did not perform as specified. The taxpayer incurred about $7 million in additional costs to make the plant usable, if perhaps still not as specified, and of course added that amount to the capital cost of the plant. It sued the company which built the plant under a number of headings (loss of profit, special and general damages, etc.), but eventually settled for $4.8 million under an agreement which recited that the payment was for the plaintiff taxpayer's additional construction and installation costs, and that all other claims and counterclaims were to be discontinued. The CRA assessed on the basis that the damages reduced the capital cost of the plant, per IT-365R2. The Tax Court found that the damages did not reduce capital cost. They did not constitute a reimbursement under ¶729, per the *Westcoast* case above, nor could they be characterized as proceeds of disposition reducing capital cost, the specific language of the provision which governs reductions of capital cost. The damages were not for the disposition of property because there was no disposition of the property capitalized. The exchange of releases from further litigation did not constitute property for purposes of the disposition rules. The specific rules reducing capital cost by amounts received as compensation for property damaged or injuriously affected did not apply. The taxpayer's property had not been damaged by the company which built the plant and paid the damages; rather, the plant had failed to live up to specifications, which is not the same thing. The "injuriously affected" provision relates to expropriation matters, and had no bearing on this case. In short, the payment was neither a taxable reimbursement nor a reduction of cost under the specific capital cost allowance rules, notwithstanding IT-365R2 to the contrary.

(ITA: 13(21) "proceeds of disposition"; IT-365R2 [Archived])

[¶719.10] *Damages Paid*

The deductibility of damages you are required to pay is governed by the same general rules as other deductions: the outlay must be to gain or produce income, not be on account of capital (in which case it might be part of capital cost or perhaps an eligible capital property), not be a personal or living expense, must be reasonable, and so on. In the past, the CRA has associated the payment of damages with fines and penalties, and denied deductions for damages payable as a result of illegal acts or wrongful conduct (see paragraph 5 of IT-467R, now withdrawn). In *Robert McNeill v. The Queen*, 2000 DTC 6211 (F.C.A.), the Court ruled that this policy had in effect been overruled by the Supreme Court decision in *65302 British Columbia Ltd. v. The Queen*, 99 DTC 5799, discussed at length in ¶763. The CRA announced its acceptance of this position in IT-467R2, which, while it restates the general rules for the deductibility of any expense, says that, in establishing whether damages have been laid out to earn income, the taxpayer need not have attempted to prevent the act or omission which resulted in the damages, and need only establish that there was an income-earning purpose for the act or omission, regardless of whether that purpose was actually achieved. It would appear that the legislation to reverse *65302 British Columbia Ltd.* (¶763.05) does not necessarily reverse *McNeill* as well, since the revised rules appear to be limited to fines and penalties imposed by duly constituted political authorities, and thus may not extend to, say, civil damages. It remains to be seen whether the CRA will revisit these policies in the light of that legislation.

Where damages are determined by a court, they are considered to be intrinsically reasonable. Where damages are determined in a settlement, however, the CRA says it will look to the facts to determine reasonableness.

(ITA: 18(1)(*a*), (*b*), (*c*), (*h*), 67; IT-467R2 [Archived])

[¶719.15] *Damages Paid by Director*

In *The Queen v. Nisker*, 2008 DTC 6102 (F.C.A.), rev'g 2007 DTC 230 (T.C.C.), a corporate director who had been found to be acting in bad faith, and therefore liable for damages caused by the corporation, was not permitted to deduct the damages as a business loss. The director was not in the business of acting as a director; nor could it be said that the fact that he had been found personally liable meant that he, and not the corporation, was carrying on the corporation's business. The Court distinguished a U.S. case in which a director of numerous arm's length corporations was found to be in the business of being a corporate director.

For deductibility of directors' insurance costs, see ¶355d.

[¶720] GAINS ON SETTLEMENT OF DEBTS

If a debt owing by you was cancelled or settled for less than face value you should refer to ¶565 to determine the effect on your tax position.

(ITA: 80)

[¶721] STANDING TIMBER SALES

Any profits from the sale of standing timber computed on a stumpage basis must be included in your income. See ¶1707. In British Columbia and Quebec you also may be liable for provincial logging tax. You should obtain professional advice if you are in this category.

(ITA: 9)

[¶722] COMPENSATION FOR LOSSES

Certain compensation receipts for loss of property or income may have to be included in your income. Amounts received from a relief fund to provide aid for some disaster (e.g., flood) are not income, as they are generally voluntary payments by the relief fund, to which you have no legal right. However, this may not be true where you receive compensation from a not-for-profit organization which is in turn funded by a government organization; in this case the reimbursement may come under the indirect government assistance rule in ¶729.

However, where you have a right to compensation for a property or income loss because of contract, statute law, etc., the compensation for loss or destruction of inventory or for loss of profits is considered income from the business. Compensation for loss or destruction of capital property is deemed to be proceeds of disposition of the property and thus may result in a recapture of capital cost allowances (¶843) and/or a capital gain or loss (Chapter 5).

(ITA: 12(1)(*x*); IT-273R2 [Archived])

[¶723] SERVICE CONTRACT FEES

Fees charged for entering into service contracts must be included in the income of the service business except where such amounts are deposits which must be returned eventually to the customer.

(Income Tax Folio: S3-F9-C1 Lottery Winnings, Miscellaneous Receipts, and Income (and Losses) from Crime)

[¶724] PRIZES WON BY MERCHANTS

If the winning of a prize is determined on the basis of the quality or value of your business' merchandise purchased or sold, or of services rendered by you within a certain time or territory, the value of the prize must be included in your income.

However, if you have participated in a draw or other chance method of determining a winner, any prize will not be income. See ¶568.

A prize for achievement may be eligible for an exemption (¶953 and ¶955). However, a prize received in the course of a business is not eligible for an exemption, so it is not likely to apply to the kind of prizes discussed here.

(Income Tax Folio: S1-F2-C3 Scholarships, Research Grants and Other Education Assistance)

[¶725] INSURANCE TO COVER FIXED COSTS OR LOSS OF INCOME

The following information is based on former Interpretation Bulletin IT-233R, which was archived in 2004 is now cancelled. No reason was given for archiving the Bulletin, and this is often done where the CRA believes the information is available elsewhere. However, this particular information is not obvious elsewhere, and so may be suspect, although there is no obvious reason to think the policy has changed.

Two types of insurance may be obtained to cover the fixed costs of and income from your business, in the event of your business being interrupted because of illness or accident. Premiums paid for insurance to reimburse fixed overhead costs and loss of income are treated differently.

(1) Overhead expense insurance — This will normally provide reimbursement of the actual amount of the overhead expenses incurred. The premium for this type of insurance will be deductible. The amount reimbursed less the actual overhead expenses incurred will be included in your income.

(2) Income insurance — This will provide compensation for your lost income earning capacity. The premium is regarded as a personal expense and is therefore not

deductible. Any benefits you receive are not considered to be income.

If your policy provides life insurance as well as the benefits described above, only the premium applicable to the overhead expense insurance will be allowable as a deduction.

(ITA: 18)

[¶727] COMMODITIES AND COMMODITY FUTURE TRANSACTIONS

In certain instances profit from trading in commodities or commodity futures may be included in business income. For a detailed discussion see ¶522.

(IT-346R [Archived])

[¶728] INVESTMENT TAX CREDIT

If you deducted any investment tax credits (¶1463) from your federal tax payable for the *preceding* year, you must reduce the undepreciated capital cost of your depreciable property (¶827) or reduce the deduction for scientific research (¶740). Any investment tax credits you have deducted against federal tax of the preceding year that cannot be applied as outlined above must be included in your business income for the current year.

(ITA: 12(1)(*t*); 13(7.1); 37)

[¶729] INDUCEMENTS OR REIMBURSEMENTS, INCLUDING GOVERNMENT ASSISTANCE AND GST/HST CREDITS

[¶729.05] *Government Grants or Loans*

If you receive amounts from the government, the treatment depends on the reason for the assistance. Amounts received as subsidies for the purchase of assets are treated as reductions to the cost of those assets. In this manner they would be recognized as reductions in the base on which capital cost allowance is claimed.

Amounts received to reimburse current expenses would be recognized as reductions in expenses and therefore are effectively included in income. Where you receive government assistance in advance for future expenses the assistance is credited to current expenses. However, you may claim a reserve for the amount of the expenses relating to future years.

In some cases, the government may provide assistance by way of a loan to cover certain specified expenditures, and that loan may be considered income under these rules. Where an amount included in income under these rules is repaid pursuant to a legal obligation, the repayment may be deducted from income in the year made.

The above is a very general summary of rules codified and discussed in more detail below.

(ITA: 13(7.1), (7.2); 20(1)(*hh*); 53(2)(*k*); IT-273R2 [Archived])

[¶729.15] *Statutory Rules: Inducements, Reimbursements or Government Assistance*

Where you receive an amount in the course of earning income from a business or property (but not, presumably, as business profit in the ordinary sense) as an inducement or reimbursement from a payer who pays it in the course of earning income from a business or property or to achieve a benefit, or who is a government, municipality or other authority, the amount received is income to the extent it has not reduced the capital cost of depreciable property (¶825 and ¶826) or the cost base of other capital property (¶506 and ¶507). Elections to reduce costs are provided where this might not happen automatically, as with tenant inducements. See ¶826.

In addition, these amounts are not included in income under these rules if the inducements relate to an acquisition by the payer of an interest in the taxpayer, his business or property. Such payments could of course be proceeds of disposition of capital or eligible capital property to the recipient. Amounts are not included in income under these rules if they are taxed as ordinary "other" income under the restrictive covenant rules in ¶929.

The rules specify that inducements or reimbursements may include "a grant, subsidy, forgivable loan, deduction from tax, allowance or any other form" of inducement or assistance. Note that the concept of a deduction from tax would include a tax credit but not necessarily a deduction from income for provincial purposes, which is the form of many Quebec incentives. It is not clear whether an amount deemed to be a prepayment of provincial tax would be a "deduction from tax". Remember that these rules apply to amounts received in the course of earning income from a business, so that personal tax credits, for example, are not covered.

The rules also apply to a receipt in the circumstances above of any refund, reimbursement, contribution, allowance, or assistance (whether as grant, subsidy, forgivable loan, deduction from tax, etc.) given in respect of an outlay or expense or in respect of an amount included in or deducted as the cost of property. This commonly picks up government tax incentives. The reference to "refund", a 1995 addition retroactive to 1990, is intended to reverse the decision in the case of *The Queen v. Johnson & Johnson Inc.*, 94 DTC 6125 (F.C.A.). In that case a refund of the old federal sales tax related to a taxation year that was statute barred by the time it was paid by government; the Court held that it could not be included in income in the year it was received. Such a refund would now, if not included in earlier year's income, be included in income in the year of receipt. In CRA Document No. 2002-0164407, the CRA opined that the income inclusion for a refund operates regardless of whether the amount refunded was deductible in the first place. In that instance, the company had to include in income the refund of an overpaid Crown royalty which had not been deductible in the first place. The opinion noted that the election to reduce a related expense instead (discussed below) might apply. If the election were not available, one might think that the policy against double taxation in subsection 248(28) could apply. The rather terse opinion did not discuss this possibility.

Loans included in income under these provisions are deductible when repaid.

(ITA: 12(1)(*x*), (2.1); 13(7.4); 20(1)(*hh*); 53(2)(*s*), (2.1); *The Queen v. Canadian Pacific Limited*, 77 DTC 5383 (F.C.A.); *The Queen v. Consumers Gas Company Ltd.*, 84 DTC 6058 (F.C.A.))

[¶729.20] *Timing of Assistance*

Where amounts are received which are taxed as income under these provisions (i.e., do not reduce capital cost, are not subject to an election to reduce associated cost as discussed below, and are not taxed under other provisions of the *Income Tax Act*), they are normally taxable when received. A special regime for input tax credits under the *Goods and Services Tax* is discussed below. Tax credits and deductions are also discussed separately below.

Forgivable loans and payments by government organization guarantors if included in income under these rules are taxable at the time the loan is granted or the guarantor makes a payment to the creditor. If repayments prove to be less than the amount taxed, the difference is deductible when the lesser repayment is made. Similarly, if the taxpayer is required to repay a guarantee payment to the guarantor or an amount previously included in income, the repayment is deductible when made. The fact that a loan carries no or low interest does not give rise to tax under these particular provisions.

(IT-273R2, para. 16 [Archived])

[¶729.25] *Tax Credits and Deductions*

Prior to July 14, 2003, the CRA's view of the timing of receipt of tax credits or deductions included in income under these provisions (i.e., amounts which do not reduce capital cost, are not subject to an election to reduce associated cost as discussed below, are not taxed under other provisions of the *Income Tax Act*) was stated to be:

> A tax credit or deduction from tax is considered to be received (and therefore included in income if it is an inducement or assistance in respect of the cost of property or an expense) at the earliest of when it is applied:
>
> - to reduce a taxpayer's tax instalment payable, and
> - to create or increase a tax refund or to reduce tax liability for a taxation year.

In *Technical News* No. 29, dated July 14, 2003, the CRA announced that it had re-examined its position in relation to provincial tax credits and come to somewhat different conclusions:

> The word "received" is not defined in the Act. Its interpretation is determined using the ordinary meaning of the word as established by the courts. In this regard, the jurisprudence indicates that it is not necessary that an amount be effectively paid. For example, an amount can be constructively received when a fiscal authority credits an amount to the taxpayer's account.
>
> Moreover, the jurisprudence indicates that a tax reduction is also considered as an amount received when the tax is reduced (see the decision of the Tax Court of Canada in *Tioxide Canada Inc. v. Her Majesty the Queen*, 93 DTC 1499, ... confirmed by the Federal Court of Appeal, 96 DTC 6296 ...
>
> We are now of the opinion that a tax credit or a reduction in the tax calculation is considered to be received at the earliest of:
>
> (a) when the amount is applied as a reduction of instalment payments to be paid by the taxpayer, if it is credited to his instalment account by the fiscal authorities; or
>
> (b) when all the conditions for its receipt are met, at the earliest of:
>
> - when it reduces the tax payable for a taxation year, or
> - when it is paid, if it allows for or increases a tax refund.
>
> Paragraph 17 of Interpretation Bulletin IT-273R2 will be amended to take our revised position into account.

Technical News No. 29 is silent on the timing of the change in policy. One would generally assume that it would be effective on publication. That is, it would be expected to be effective for assessments and reassessments made after July 14, 2003, but the CRA would not normally go back and reopen assessments on the issue, although it might be within its rights to do so.

[¶729.30] *Indirect Government Assistance*

Apparently there have been situations in which taxpayers have received funding from not-for-profit entities which in turn have been funded by government or another payer in circumstances in which the funds would have been caught by the inducement rules above had the funds been received directly. The government included such indirect funding in the ambit of the rules.

Amounts received in circumstances where "it is reasonable to conclude" that the payer would not have paid the amount but for the receipt by the payer of amounts from another payer described in the inducement rules above, will be included in the recipient's income to the extent they would have been if received directly.

(ITA: 12(1)(x)(i)(C))

[¶729.35] *Election to Reduce Related Expense*

The *Income Tax Act* normally provides (in subsection 13(7.1) and paragraph 53(1)(*k*)) that government assistance which the taxpayer has received or is entitled to receive in respect of or for the acquisition of capital property reduces the capital cost of depreciable property or the adjusted cost base of other capital property, as the case may be. Where this rule operates (as for example it typically does in the case of GST rebates on amounts paid for capital property, discussed below), it trumps the income inclusion rule, so that the amounts which reduce cost do not come into income under that rule.

Where inducements other than government assistance are brought into income under these rules, the subsection 13(7.1) and paragraph 53(1)(*k*) rules on their face do not apply, so in the first instance all such inducements are income. However, where the inducement can be considered to be in respect of a particular property, an election can be made to treat the assistance as a reduction of cost of that property rather than an item of income.

The election to reduce a related outlay or expense must be made by the due date of the return for the year the assistance is considered to be received, or, if the related outlay or expense is not made until the following year, by the due date for that following year. Although the election must be made by the due date for the year in which the assistance is an income item (or perhaps the following year), it can be made if the related expense has been made in *any* prior year. Interpretation Bulletin IT-273R2 (paragraph 10) discusses the formalities of the election without giving any examples of the circumstances which might give rise to it. The bulletin requires that the election be made by a letter attached to the return which specifies the subsection under which the election is made; the elected amount; the amount of assistance and when received; the date the property was acquired; and the ACB or capital cost of the property before the election. The election need not be for the full amount of the assistance or cost, but may not exceed the least of the cost of the property otherwise determined, the assistance received, and nil if the property was disposed of before the assistance was received.

(ITA: 12(1)(*x*), (2.1), (2.2); 13(7.1), (7.4); 20(1)(*hh*); 53(1)(*k*), (2.1); IT-273R2 [Archived])

[¶729.40] *Damages not Reimbursement*

The Federal Court–Trial Division has ruled that damages are not necessarily a "reimbursement" required to be included in income under these rules. In the case decided, *Westcoast*

Energy Inc. v. The Queen, 91 DTC 5334, the taxpayer had a gas pipeline built for it at a cost of $6 million. The pipeline proved deficient and the taxpayer constructed a replacement for it at a cost of about $22 million. The taxpayer sued the original contractor for this amount and eventually settled for about $20 million. The new pipeline was treated as a depreciable asset for tax purposes, but the $20 million was not treated as a reduction of cost but rather as non-taxable damages for breach of contract. The Federal Court ruled that this treatment was correct. The rules requiring a reimbursement of cost to be included in income if not treated as a reduction of cost did not apply in this case because the settlement was received as damages for breach of contract and negligence and not as reimbursement. The Court concluded that "reimbursement does not include damage awards". An appeal to the Federal Court of Appeal was dismissed without comment (92 DTC 6253). See also the discussion at ¶719, for the proposition that such a payment would not reduce capital cost under the definitions in the capital cost allowance recapture provisions.

[¶729.45] *GST/HST Credits and Rebates as Government Assistance*

A business may pay GST/HST on expenditures for goods and services, and recover the amount paid as either an input tax credit or rebate of GST/HST. The *Income Tax Act* treats these credits or rebates as "government assistance" by definition. Where the expenditure is for capital property, the credit or rebate would automatically reduce the capital cost or adjusted cost base, as the case may be; see ¶506, ¶825, and ¶828. Similarly, GST/HST credits or rebates in respect of scientific expenditures would reduce that expenditure pool rather than being treated as income under this provision.

Where an expenditure has no associated capital property or associated scientific research expenditure, the GST/HST credit or rebate will be income. This would generally be the case with expenditures for services. However, a special provision will permit an election to reduce the related outlay or expense (other than a property expense) rather than treat the credit/rebate as income, although in many cases the result would be the same.

Timing Rules

The rules governing the time at which GST/HST credits or rebates must be recognized (provided in subsections 248(16)–(18) of the *Income Tax Act*) provide the following three alternatives:

(1) *General rule for big business:* This rule applies to GST-registered businesses which exceed the $500,000 GST/HST threshold of taxable supplies (as determined under subsection 249(1) of the *Excise Tax Act*). Under this rule, an input tax credit is considered to be received, for income tax purposes, when the GST/HST was originally paid (or payable) on the expenditure. Hence, GST/HST paid in one reporting period results in the income tax inclusion (or netting) at the same time, even though the input tax credit will be claimed later, following the end of the GST/HST reporting period. However, this rule applies only if the input tax credit is claimed before the year in which the income inclusion becomes statute-barred for income tax purposes (in fact at least 120 days before that year). This requires businesses to write down cost (or recognize income) for input tax credits immediately after the expenditure generating the potential credit. The rule does not function where the input tax credit claim has been deferred for years; presumably these are circumstances where input tax credits have been overlooked or miscalculated.

(2) *General rule for small businesses:* An input tax credit is considered to be received at the end of the reporting period in which it is claimed if the GST/HST threshold amount (as determined under subsection 249(1) of the *Excise Tax Act*) is less than $500,000 for the year GST/HST was paid or became payable.

(3) *Fallback rule:* This rule applies if neither of the first two rules apply. The input tax credit is considered received for income inclusion in the taxation year that is the earliest of (1) the year after the GST/HST was paid, and (2) the year when the input tax credit inclusion would become statute-barred for income tax purposes.

In accordance with the general rule considering input tax credits to be "government assistance", where the recapture of input tax credits rules apply, the amount recaptured is considered "assistance repaid" at the time the amount is recaptured.

The regime for employees and partners claiming GST/HST input tax credits as described at ¶363 remains essentially unchanged.

Election

The election to reduce a related outlay or expense must be made by the due date of the return for the year the GST/HST "assistance" is considered to be received, or if the related outlay or expense is not made until the following year, by the due date for that following year. Although the election must be made by the due date for the year the assistance is an income item (or perhaps the following year), it can be made, if the related expense has been made in any prior year, in the year the election is made, or the year following the year the GST/HST input tax credit appears as assistance. The taxpayer may elect on any amount up to the GST/HST credit/rebate, but cannot reduce the related outlay or expense to less than nil.

This election seems to be intended to apply only to those cases where the set-off of an expense or outlay does not otherwise occur, e.g., where there is no related property cost to reduce and, because of timing considerations governing deduction of the expenditure, there is not an immediate match of GST/HST expense and credit. In most cases, the election simplifies accounting procedures by allowing a business to operate as if GST/HST were simply not included in its income tax deductible expenditures, rather than deducting the GST/HST and then tracking the related GST/HST input tax credit on each expenditure to ensure proper income tax inclusions. However, the election is phrased in general terms; that is, it is not on its face limited to GST/HST credit/rebate situations. Accordingly, it would appear to apply to any inducement or assistance where there is no other write-down of property or research pool.

(ITA: 12(1)(x), (2.1), (2.2); 13(7.4); 53(2.1); 248(15)–(18))

[¶729.50] *Quebec Sales Tax (QST) Refunds and Rebates*

Although Quebec further harmonized its QST regime to the GST/HST on January 1, 2013, the two separate taxes remain, with the GST rate at 5% and the QST rate at 9. 975%. Hence, the QST issue discussed herein remains.

Quebec sales tax input tax refunds (the term for QST, as opposed to input tax credits, the term for GST/HST) or QST rebates present a similar issue for income inclusion. Where there are no input tax refunds, sales tax paid on expenditures is simply part of the cost for income tax purposes, as with any other provincial sales tax. Where there are Quebec input tax refunds claimed, these refunds fall into the definition of "government assistance" to be included in income, thus offsetting the deduction claimed for the tax-included expenditure. Hence, the treatment is similar to that for GST/HST credits and rebates. There are no federal deeming provisions to take the claim back to match the date QST becomes paid or payable, as there is for federal GST/HST. Where input tax refunds are repaid, they are deemed to be government assistance repaid in accordance with section 248(18.1).

However, if the QST input tax refunds are government assistance, they would be eligible for the election to reduce a related expense discussed above, since the election is of general application.

For taxation years commencing after February 27, 2004, the federal Act provides that the new timing rules which commence for GST/HST purposes after December 20, 2002 as described above will apply equally to QST rules for purposes of determining the federal income tax adjustments. The $500,000 threshold amount for these federal purposes is the amount determined under section 462 of the Quebec *Sales Tax Act*, rather than subsection 249(1) of the federal *Excise Tax Act*.

(ITA: 12(1)(x), (2.1), (2.2); 248(15)–(18))

[¶729a] RESTRICTIVE COVENANTS

On the sale of a business or in certain other circumstances, a person may agree not to compete or provide goods or services, and receive a payment in consideration therefore, sometimes referred to as a "non-competition payment". After two court decisions that held that some of these payments were not taxable, the Department of Finance introduced rules on October 7, 2003 that included such amounts received under "restrictive covenants" in the income of the recipient, with certain exceptions. The new rules are found primarily in new section 56.4 and are discussed in detail in Chapter 9 at ¶929.

DEDUCTIONS IN DETERMINING BUSINESS INCOME

[¶730] GENERAL RULES

As a general rule, all reasonable expenses which you have incurred in connection with the earning or producing of income from your business will be deductible in determining the net income from the business.

Although interest to finance the business will normally be a deductible expense, special rules apply to financing obtained to help businesses in financial difficulty (see ¶412). Interest expenses are discussed in detail in Chapter 10, commencing at ¶1063.

No deduction is permitted with respect to capital expenditures except as specifically permitted under the Act. Common expenditures that may be deducted include capital cost allowances (depreciation) on capital assets specified by law (see Chapter 8), exploration and development expenses (see ¶2210–¶2230), depletion allowed on income from oil and gas wells and certain mines or amortization of eligible capital expenditures (see ¶767).

No deduction is permitted for an amount which is provided as a reserve for contingencies or for any other purpose except for so-called reserves which are expressly permitted by law such as a reserve for doubtful accounts receivable, undelivered goods and services, rent received in advance, etc. (see ¶732). A reserve for warranties is regarded as contingent and is not allowable. Expenditures incurred in honouring warranties are deductible only as incurred.

No deduction is permitted from business income for your personal or living expenses except for travelling expenses (including lodging but only 50% of the cost of meals — see ¶734) incurred while on business away from home.

No deduction is permitted for dues paid to clubs whose main function is to provide recreational, dining or sporting facilities for its members. However, 50% (see ¶734) of the charges for meals paid at such clubs may be deductible if they are incurred for business purposes; special problems arise for dining at golf clubs, as discussed at ¶731.

If you are self-employed, you are operating a business and you cannot be an employee of your own (unincorporated) business. If you take a regular draw from the business which you view as "salary", you may not deduct this amount in determining profit or loss from the business. Compare the treatment of partnership allocations at ¶1802. In general, the same would be true of fringe benefits you provide to yourself, but see the special rules for private health plan insurance premiums at ¶741.

(ITA: 18; 20; 67; IT-148R3 [Archived])

[¶730.05] *Timing of Expense Deductions*

It is commonplace to say that expenses are deductible when incurred, which in general means that an expense can be deducted in the taxation year (fiscal period) incurred. This generality contains a multitude of exceptions. Business expenses are typically deductible when incurred even if they remain unpaid in the fiscal period; this is true for taxpayers on the accrual method (¶714), which includes most businesses other than exceptionally simple ones or farming and fishing businesses discussed in Chapter 17. Farmers, fishers, and other "cash basis" taxpayers (if any) generally deduct expenses when paid rather than when incurred. Prepaid expenses (prepaid rent, for example) are generally subject to limitations matching them to the period to which they relate, as discussed in ¶753, again with (limited) exceptions for farmers and fishers.

Certain expenses are general exceptions to the rule that expenses are deducted when incurred. Inventory expenses (the cost of goods sold) are calculated in determining gross profit from sales. This in effect defers deductions and matches them to the revenue from the sale of goods (see ¶757). Capital expenses are not deductible as such, but are recognized through the capital cost allowance system (Chapter 8), the eligible capital property system (¶766–¶768), or by adding the expense to the cost base of the property to which it relates, so that it is recognized only on disposition (¶505). Certain expenditures typically associated with tax shelters must be deferred to match the income under a plethora of overlapping rules: see ¶1818, ¶1842, and ¶2521.

In some relatively rare cases, there will be expenditures which do not fit neatly into the category of ordinary expenses, inventory, or capital expense. Once it is established that an expense is not on capital account (see ¶805), the question may remain as to whether the expense may be deducted in full when incurred or may or must be deferred in whole or in part. Deferral may be permitted or required if it is determined that the expense must be matched to income items either as inventory or through some other form of amortization over a period of years. In these cases, the courts will look at the accounting treatment of the item, although the Supreme Court of Canada has made it clear (in *Canderel Limited v. The*

Queen, 98 DTC 6100) that accounting treatment is suggestive rather than definitive. The CRA has indicated that it understands the *Canderel* case to mean in part that it cannot compel taxpayers to amortize expenses where they can show a significant current benefit. Perhaps a more important element of the *Canderel* case is the holding that once the taxpayer has justified a particular method of calculating income as presenting a reasonable picture of profit, the onus shifts to the CRA to show that its contrasting method presents a more accurate picture. For an application of *Canderel* principles, see ¶612. For further discussion on the importance of accounting principles, see ¶805.

[¶730.10] *Contingent Amounts*

As a general rule, an expense or the cost of property incurred for the purpose of earning income from a business is not recognized if it is contingent or conditional (paragraph 18(1)(*e*)).

An expense that is incurred and not otherwise contingent, but which may be reduced or eliminated upon the occurrence or non-occurrence of a future event (sometimes called a "condition subsequent"), is nonetheless, as a general rule, recognized when incurred. However, this state of affairs changes for certain expenditures. An expenditure will be a "contingent amount" and, therefore, reduced to the extent that you have a right to reduce or eliminate the amount that is required to be paid in respect of the expenditure. A contingent amount at any time includes an amount to the extent that you, or another taxpayer that does not deal at arm's length with you, has a right to reduce the amount at that time. The contingent amount of the expenditure is not recognized, even if it would otherwise be deductible in computing income from a business or form the cost of property. However, if you pay the contingent amount in a subsequent year, the amount will be recognized in that subsequent year. These rules are discussed at ¶447.

[¶731] CLUBS, YACHTS, CAMPS, LODGES, AND GOLF COURSES; AIRCRAFT

[¶731.05] *Club Fees or Dues*

No deduction is allowed for any expense incurred in respect of membership fees or dues (whether initiation fees or otherwise) which entitles you or your employees (or anyone else) to use the facilities of any club, the main purposes of which is to provide dining, recreational or sporting facilities to its members. Note that it is only initiation and membership fees or dues which are prohibited; the expenses of entertaining at your club may be deductible if the entertainment has a business purpose, subject to the limitations at ¶734 and the discussion below.

[¶731.10] *Use of Yacht, Camp, Lodge, or Golf Course*

No deduction is permitted for an outlay or expense made for the use or maintenance of a yacht, camp, lodge or golf course unless you are actually in the business of providing such facilities for hire or for a fee.

The CRA considers that a lodge includes an inn or resort hotel, particularly one that is a centre for recreational activities. Lodge also includes a dwelling occupied on a seasonal basis in connection with activities such as hunting or fishing, but does not include a small cottage or similar dwelling designed for the use of a single family. Thus a self-employed individual may claim cottage expenses within the scope of the office-in-home rules (¶742).

Although the costs of using or maintaining a yacht, lodge, golf course or facility and the capital cost allowance on such properties may be restricted, normal business entertainment expenses incurred in connection with these facilities are deductible (but remember the 50% disallowance rule at ¶734). The distinction can be a subtle one. The CRA takes the view that if a resort hotel or lodge is used for a genuine business purpose which does not include the entertainment or recreation of clients, suppliers, shareholders or employees, the related expenses are not restricted by this rule (although the deduction may be limited to 50%, see ¶734), but where there are some business meetings but the main activity is recreation or entertainment, the entire expense is denied.

In 1997, the CRA announced an even more restrictive rule for golf clubs. In revised IT-148R3 (dated July 21, 1997), it stated that the cost of food and beverages in conjunction with a game of golf or other recreational activity at the club would not be deductible, although food and beverages would be deductible (subject to the 50% rule) provided there was a genuine business purpose and the expenses were not incurred "in conjunction with a game of golf or other recreational activity at the golf club". This rather tortuous rule seemed to say that you could lunch at one golf club and go on to another for a game, but could not lunch and play at the same club and still deduct the lunch. This interpretation was rescinded in *Income Tax Technical News* No. 12, dated February 11, 1998, which ruled that the dining rooms, banquet halls, conference rooms, beverage rooms and lounges of a golf course would be treated in the same way as other eating and drinking establishments. Nevertheless, meal and beverage expenses incurred at a golf club must be itemized; an inclusive charge will be denied altogether.

This kind of nit-picking has, not surprisingly, been the subject of litigation. In *The Queen v. Jaddco Anderson Limited*, 84 DTC 6135, the Federal Court of Appeal held that the expense of renting a fishing lodge to entertain clients was not deductible. In *Sie-Mac Pipeline Contractors Ltd. v. M.N.R.*, 89 DTC 230, the Tax Court of Canada attempted to distinguish a case in which the taxpayer paid the expenses of its clients at "educational sessions" held at a lodge. The Court found that since the payments were not for an *exclusive* right to use the lodge (i.e., there could have been other members of the public staying there) and were in large part for services of the kind a hotel would provide (as indicated in the detailed billing presented to the taxpayer) they were not payments for "rent or use" of the lodge. The Federal Court–Trial Division affirmed the *Sie-Mac* decision (90 DTC 6344), stressing that "... the evil contemplated by this subsection is not the commercial use of country properties or fishing lodges instead of downtown hotels, but is related to property which is somehow in the possession of the taxpayer at which people are being entertained ... where it was thought the company was using it to entertain guests occasionally and writing off expense which should have been its own expense ...". The *Sie-Mac* decision was reversed by the Federal Court of Appeal (92 DTC 6461), which explicitly reaffirmed the *Jaddco* decision. The Court of Appeal said that the payments were clearly for "use" of the lodge; it went on to say, "The anomaly of allowing deductions for entertainment of customers in restaurants or hotels, but not on yachts or in lodges is obvious, but it is within the authority of Parliament to make these distinctions if it so chooses".

The CRA was asked to comment on the *Sie-Mac* decision at the 1993 Revenue Canada Round Table of the Canadian Tax Foundation. It said that provisionally (subject to an internal review and now confirmed) it will disallow expenses related to the use of facilities of camps, lodges, yachts and golf courses whether for long or short term. However, it will also abide by its comment at the 1984 Round Table that:

> In this regard, the CRA considers the word "lodge", for this purpose, to mean an inn or a resort hotel, particularly one that is a centre for recreational activities, such as hunting or fishing.
>
> When, however, a resort property is used for genuine business purposes, which purposes do not

include the entertainment or recreation of clients, suppliers, shareholders, or employees, the CRA will not consider that the related expenses, provided they are reasonable in the circumstances, fall within the provisions of paragraph 18(1)(*l*) of the Act. [That is, the CRA will not deny a deduction in these circumstances.]

The CRA confirmed the above position in a 1994 memorandum (Wolters Kluwer *Tax Window Files*, document 9406688), summarizing its position by saying that "expenses incurred at a resort hotel or lodge are presumed to be non-deductible unless the facts establish that they were laid out for genuine business purposes, which purposes do not include the entertainment or recreation of clients, suppliers, shareholders or employees". This position is reaffirmed in the 1997 version of Interpretation Bulletin IT-148R3, now archived.

Whether a vessel is a "yacht" will, in the CRA's view, depend on the use to which it is put; a vessel will be considered a yacht where the primary purpose is for the entertainment or recreation of clients, suppliers, shareholders or employees. In *The Queen v. C.I.P. Inc.*, 88 DTC 6005 (F.C.T.D.), the expense of chartering a boat to entertain clients was allowed because the boat itself was a tugboat converted to a residence for its owners and was rented out only occasionally; accordingly, it could not be said to be generally used for pleasurable purposes and was not therefore a "yacht". The CRA notes that expenses in connection with a yacht are not denied if they are essential to the business operations and substantially all (90% or more) for business purposes. Business purposes do not include the entertainment or recreation of clients, suppliers, shareholders or employees.

There are also restrictions on capital cost allowance on inactive participants in businesses leasing property and offering related services; these were said by the Department of Finance to be aimed at such businesses as those which offer services in combination with the use of yachts, recreational vehicles, and hotels. See ¶873.

(ITA: 18(1)(*l*); ITR: 1102 Property Not Included; Window on Canadian Tax: 2982; IT-148R3 [Archived])

[¶731.15] *Use of Aircraft*

Reasonable costs incurred in providing air travel are deductible to the extent that they are laid out to earn income from a business or property. Generally, an employer may deduct reasonable costs incurred in providing air transportation to an employee, whether for business or personal purposes (although flights for personal purposes will involve a taxable benefit to the employee, see ¶318, ¶327, and ¶333). In calculating the income of an unincorporated taxpayer who uses an aircraft in carrying on business, no deduction will be allowed for any costs associated with the taxpayer's personal use of the aircraft. (The same is true for corporations' expenses for personal aircraft use by shareholders.) The personal portion should be apportioned on a reasonable basis, such as the percentage of personal use in a period or a breakdown of costs on a flight-by-flight basis. Capital cost allowance on aircraft must also be apportioned between business and personal use, as with automobiles.

Some of the information in the preceding paragraph was supported by Interpretation Bulletin IT-160R3, "Personal Use of Aircraft", now cancelled, meaning it can no longer be relied on as policy. Nevertheless, used with caution, it still presents a reasonable overview of the issues.

(IT-160R3 [Archived])

[¶732] "RESERVES" WHICH MAY BE DEDUCTED

[¶732.05] *Reserve for Goods or Services to be Provided after Year End*

Where you have been required to include amounts in income merely because they were received by the end of the year, although not yet earned (¶716), you are entitled to deduct from your income a reasonable amount as a reserve. If you are using the cash method of computing income, you may not claim such reserves.

A reasonable reserve would be any amount up to the amount included in income, in the year or in a prior year, for which goods are to be delivered or services are to be rendered after the end of the year. Note that special exceptions apply to reserves in respect of a manufacturer's warranty, and in respect of food and drink and transportation services, discussed under separate subheadings below.

Where trading stamps or special cash register tapes are issued that are redeemable for merchandise, a reasonable reserve will be allowed for the cost of merchandise that will have to be delivered to redeem stamps or tapes issued and not redeemed at the end of the fiscal year.

Reserves claimed in Year 1 must be added back to income in Year 2, and a new reserve calculated as applicable.

This general reserve provision came under scrutiny in 2003 in circumstances indicating that the CRA is of the view that it is not always applicable. A certain amount of technical background is necessary to grasp its view. Essentially, there are two provisions of the *Income Tax Act* which might sweep in arguably unearned income. Section 9 simply includes " profit" in income without specifying how it is to be calculated. The courts have indicated that profit is profit in a legal sense, so that accounting rules may be indicative but not controlling (see "Impact of Accounting Treatment" at ¶805.10). Paragraph 12(1)(*a*) is at first blush broader, sweeping in *amounts received* for services not rendered, goods not delivered, or other income unearned in the year. Paragraph 20(1)(*m*) then allows the reserve described above against amounts included under 12(1)(*a*), but not against amounts included under section 9. At the 2003 Annual Conference of the Canadian Tax Foundation (CTF), the CRA discussed this view. An unofficial transcript appearing in Wolters Kluwer *Tax Topics* No. 1648, issued October 9, 2003, contains the following summary:

> The CRA's current position on the taxation of prepaid income is that an amount will be included in income under subsection 9(1) rather than under paragraph 12(1)(*a*) where the inclusion under subsection 9(1) gives a more accurate picture of income. This would be the case where there has been a substantial performance of services at the time of the payment and there are no restrictions on the taxpayer keeping the payment if future services are not provided.

The remarks were later published in somewhat more loquacious form in *Income Tax Technical News* No. 30, but the Wolters Kluwer summary is essentially accurate.

In *Ellis Vision Incorporated v. The Queen*, 2004 DTC 2024 (T.C.C.), the CRA argued its position and lost. The Tax Court expressly rejected the Crown's argument, saying (in paragraph 47):

> I do not agree with the respondent's position that if a taxpayer's income from a business is its profits from that business pursuant to subsection 9(1), one is foreclosed from considering

amounts described in subsection 12(1)(*a*). Amounts included in income for purposes of subsection 9(1) may be described in paragraph 12(1)(*a*): services not rendered or goods not delivered before the end of the year or rent or other amounts for possession or use of chattels, for example, paid in advance are amounts described in paragraph 12(1)(*a*). Paragraph 20(1)(*m*) permits a reasonable reserve when amounts that are "described" in paragraph 12(1)(*a*) have been included in computing the taxpayer's income from a business for the year, or previous year, and rents or other amounts have been paid in advance, or services may reasonably be anticipated to be rendered in a future year. I agree with appellant's counsel: the word "described" in paragraph 20(1)(*m*) means just what it says it does. The word in the French version of the Act is "*visées*", which, in the context of paragraph 20(1)(*m*), is analogous to the words "referred to", or "directed at" in English. The "amounts described in paragraph 12(1)(*a*)" do not mean only amounts that were included in income "by virtue of" paragraph 12(1)(*a*); the amounts may be included in income by virtue of paragraph 12(1)(*a*) and the amounts may also be included in income as profit from a business in accordance with subsection 9(1).

In the Tax Court decision of *Doteasy Technology Inc. v. The Queen*, 2009 DTC 1187, the *Ellis Vision* decision on this point was confirmed: "In *Ellis Vision*, Justice Rip, as he then was, found that the paragraph 20(1)(*m*) reserve was available even though the amount might be included in income under section 9 so long as it was described in paragraph 12(1)(*a*). It is my opinion that *Ellis Vision* has settled the law with respect to this issue."

The 2013 federal Budget introduced an amendment to the reserve, clarifying that a reserve for future services cannot be used by taxpayers with respect to amounts received for the purpose of funding future reclamation obligations. Although reclamation obligations are typically incurred by corporations, the new restriction on the reserve applies to all taxpayers including individuals. The new restriction applies to amounts received after March 20, 2013, other than an amount received that is directly attributable to a reclamation obligation that was authorized by a government or regulatory authority before March 21, 2013, and that is received under a written agreement that was entered into before March 21, 2013 and not extended or renewed on or after that day, or before 2018.

(ITA: 12(1)(*a*), (*e*); 20(1)(*m*), (*m.2*), (6); IT-154R [Archived])

[¶732.10] *Payments for Undertaking Future Obligations*

Where a taxpayer who is entitled to a reserve described above pays someone else to carry out the future undertaking to which the reserve relates, the two parties may jointly elect to transfer the reserve entitlement to the party who has received the payment. This most commonly occurs on the sale of a business. There appears to be no form for making the election; a letter signed by both parties filed with the return of each (but especially with the return of the party who will take over the reserve) should suffice.

(ITA: 20(24); CRA Document No.: Subsection 20(24) of the Act, *March 7, 2005*, CRA Document No. 2005-0114981E5)

[¶732.15] *Manufacturer's Warranties*

The general reserve rule above does not permit deduction reserves in respect of guarantees, warranties or indemnities, except for extended warranties where the taxpayer seeking the reserve meets the following conditions:

(1) an amount received has been included in income from a business for the year or a previous year;

(2) the reserve is in respect of goods or services that it is reasonably anticipated will have to be delivered or rendered after the end of the year;

(3) the warranty agreement was entered into at arm's length and the only obligation of the taxpayer is to provide such goods or services with respect to property manufactured by the taxpayer, or a corporation related to the taxpayer; and

(4) the reserve does not exceed the amount paid after the end of the year to an insurer to insure the liability under the agreement.

(ITA: 12(1)(*a*), (*e*); 20(1)(*m.1*), (*m.2*), (7); IT-154R [Archived])

[¶732.17] *Repayment of Amount Previously Included in Income*

A deduction is provided, as opposed to a reserve which is brought back into income later, when a taxpayer repays an amount which was brought into income in respect of future goods or services. This deduction would apply, for example, where a taxpayer received a payment for services or goods to be delivered in the future, but was required to repay all or a portion of this amount because the services or goods were not in fact delivered.

(ITA: 20(1)(m.2) Repayment of amount previously included in income)

[¶732.18] *Reserves for Unamortized Bond Premiums*

Commentary on Legislative Proposals (Sept. 16, 2016)

Note: When Legislative Proposals, September 16, 2016, achieves Royal Assent, the commentary will be modified to read:

A taxpayer can claim a reserve in a taxation year for the unamortized amount at the end of the year for any premium received on the issuance of a new bond that arose on the re-opening of a previous issuance of bonds by the taxpayer where:

- the terms of the new bond are identical to the terms of the previously issued bonds;
- the old bonds were issued as a part of the original issuance;
- at issuance the interest rate on the old bonds was reasonable;
- the new bond is issued on the re-opening of the original issuance;
- at the time of the new bond's issuance the premium received is reasonable; and
- the premium amount has been included in income in the current or previous taxation year.

(ITA: 12(1)(d.2); 20(1)(m.3))

[¶732.20] *Food or Drink; Transportation Services*

Reserves in respect of articles of food or drink that were not delivered before the end of the year and transportation not provided before the end of the year are limited to amounts included in income at the end of the year on a received (¶713) or receivable (¶714) basis, whichever you normally use. For example, ticket reserves may not exceed the dollar amount included in income for tickets issued during the year and unredeemed at the end of it.

(ITA: 12(1)(*a*), (*e*); 20(1)(*m*), (*m*.2), (6); IT-154R [Archived])

[¶732.25] *Container Deposits*

Where your customers are entitled to a refund on the return or resale to you of containers or other articles in or by means of which goods are delivered to customers, a reasonable reserve may be deducted. Bottles are specifically excluded but such items as cable reels and paper cores which are returnable are eligible. In some cases, a reasonable reserve may be the whole of deposits made or the amount which would have to be repaid if all containers, etc., were returned. In other cases, past experience of your business may indicate that all returnable items will not be returned and a reasonable reserve should take this into account. With respect to bottles, a deduction will be allowed only when bottles are returned and the customer is paid or credited.

Support for the positions above was at one time found in Interpretation Bulletin IT-165R, "Returnable Containers". That Bulletin is now cancelled, meaning it can no longer be relied on as policy. Nevertheless, used with caution, it still presents a reasonable overview of the issues. It is not apparent which particular policy statement was considered dubious or outdated.

(ITA: 12(1)(*e*); 20(1)(*m*))

[¶732.30] *Unearned Rental Income*

You may deduct a reasonable amount as a reserve for rent received or receivable in advance at the end of your fiscal year.

(ITA: 20(1)(*m*); IT-261R [Archived])

[¶732.35] *Transfers to Reserves, Contingent Accounts or Sinking Funds*

You will not be allowed a deduction from income for any amounts set up as or on account of a reserve, contingent liability, or a sinking fund, unless the deduction is specifically authorized by one of the rules in this paragraph or ¶733.

(ITA: 18(1)(*e*))

[¶732.45] *Sale Price of Land*

Where land (including buildings and other structures on it, if any) is sold in the course of business (and so gives rise to business income and not capital gain) and all or part of the sales price is payable after the end of your fiscal year, a reasonable reserve determined in relation to the profit from the sale may be deducted. The amount of the reserve that is usually deductible is that portion of the gross profit from the sale which is reasonably attributable to the instalment payments payable after the end of the fiscal year. For example, if the selling price of certain real estate is $100,000, the gross profit is $20,000, and the purchaser pays cash of $30,000 and gives the vendor a mortgage for $70,000, the vendor's reserve would be $14,000, which is computed as follows:

$$\$ 20,000 / \$100,000 \times \$70,000 = \$14,000$$

If the real estate in the above example had an existing mortgage on it of $60,000 and the purchaser gave a second mortgage of $10,000, the reserve will normally be computed with reference to your equity in the property, as follows:

$$\$ 20,000 / \$40,000 \times \$10,000 = \$5,000$$

However, if you had clear title to the property but in contemplation of selling it you placed the $60,000 mortgage on it, your reserve will be computed with reference to the full sales price as follows:

$$\$ 20,000 / \$100,000 \times \$10,000 = \$2,000$$

If you sell land to a person or company with whom you do not deal at arm's length and claim a reserve for the unpaid sales price, the CRA may make inquiries to ensure that the terms of sale are reasonable. For example, if you sell land to a company which you own, and the company then sells the land for cash, the CRA may not consider that any reserve should be allowed with respect to the unpaid sales price owing to you by your company. Also, in non-arm's length transactions, the purchaser should be aware of the tax consequences of unpaid amounts (see ¶746).

This reserve may not be deducted if you were exempt from tax, or if you were both a non-resident and not carrying on business in Canada, at the end of the year of sale or at any time in the immediately following year.

The reserve may not be deducted if, immediately after the sale, the purchaser was:

(1) a corporation controlled by the taxpayer who would claim the reserve (or a corporation controlled by group that controlled the taxpayer, or a corporation that controlled the taxpayer, but these are typically corporate issues); or

(2) a partnership in which the taxpayer who would claim the reserve is a majority-interest partner (as defined under the subheading "Partnerships" in ¶852.25).

In both the case of a sale of land and a sale of property other than land, a reserve will be denied in any year where the sale of the property occurred more than 36 months before the end of the year. However, there is no minimum income recognition at the end of the first or second year, as there is with capital gain reserves (see ¶581). Since this income and reserve is calculated on business rather than capital account, it is reported on a fiscal period basis rather than a calendar year basis. See ¶705.

Minor changes in the wording of this provision allow a reserve for amounts "payable" after the appropriate year end even though "due" in the year. The change, effective for taxation years ending after February 21, 1994, are said to be intended to avoid penalizing creditors who exercise acceleration clauses pursuant to an agreement under which the creditor sold property and received, as part of the consideration, a note payable by the purchaser. The acceleration clause is typically exercised only if the purchaser is in default.

Note that this discussion applies to sales of land resulting in business income; where capital gains arise, provisions described in Chapter 5 apply instead.

(ITA: 20(1)(*n*), (8); IT-152R3 [Archived])

[¶732.50] *Sale Price of Property other than Land*

You may deduct a reserve if you have sold property (other than land) in the course of the business (i.e., the property was inventory and so gives rise to business income and not capital gain) and all or a portion of the sale price is payable after the end of the taxation year *and* is not due [*sic*] until a day that is more than two years after the day on which the property is sold. The reserve is calculated as a proportion of the gross profit from the sale which is reasonably attributable to the instalment payments payable after the end of the relevant fiscal year. This reserve may not be deducted if you are exempt from tax, or if you are both not resident in Canada and not carrying on a business in Canada, at the end of the year of sale or at any time in the immediately following year.

The reserve may not be deducted if, immediately after the sale, the purchaser was:

(1) a corporation controlled by the taxpayer who would claim the reserve (or a corporation controlled by group that controlled the taxpayer, or a corporation that controlled the taxpayer, but these are typically corporate issues); or

(2) a partnership in which the taxpayer who would claim the reserve is a majority-interest partner (as defined under the subheading "Partnerships" in ¶852.25).

In both the case of a sale of land and the case of a sale of property other than land, a reserve will be denied in any year where the sale of the property occurred more than 36 months before the end of the year. Accordingly, the reserve is limited to a maximum of three taxation years for individuals. Thus a property sold in 2013 would be denied a reserve in and after 2016. However, there is no minimum income recognition at the end of the first or second year, as there is with capital gain reserves (see ¶581). Since this income and reserve is calculated on business rather than capital account, it is reported on a fiscal period basis rather than a calendar year basis. See ¶705.

Minor changes in the wording of this provision made back in 1994 allow a reserve for amounts "payable" after the appropriate year end even though "due" in the year. The changes, effective for taxation years ending after February 21, 1994, are said to be intended to avoid penalizing creditors who exercise acceleration clauses pursuant to an agreement under which the creditor sold property and received, as part of the consideration, a note payable by the purchaser. The acceleration clause is typically exercised only if the purchaser is in default.

Where proceeds are capital gain rather than business income, the rules in Chapter 5 apply instead of those discussed here.

(ITA: 20(1)(*n*), (8); IT-154R [Archived])

[¶732.55] *Insurance Agents or Brokers*

Reserve

In computing income, an insurance agent or broker may deduct the lesser of 1) a reserve in respect of unearned commissions an amount computed in respect of each insurance contract (other than a life insurance contract) based on the number of days that the contract had to run after the end of the fiscal year expressed as a proportion of the whole period of the contract, and 2) a reasonable reserve in respect of amounts actually received and included in income on account of services not rendered or goods not received before the end of the year (the "regular" reserve amount under paragraph 20(1)(*m*) relating to certain types of unearned income). Accordingly, reserves may be claimed only in respect of commission income received but unearned. The reserve is added back into income in the following year, with the possibility of a further reserve.

In 1994, the CRA released revised Interpretation Bulletin IT-321R (now cancelled), setting out its interpretation of the reserve. This states that no reserve is available for commissions on life insurance contracts. The reserve for unearned commissions on other insurance contracts may not exceed the lesser of:

(1) that proportion of the amount included in income for the year or a preceding year in respect of the contract that the number of days in the contract period after the end of taxation year is of the number of days in the contract; and

(2) where amounts have been included in income for the year under the contract for services to be performed after the year end or have otherwise been considered unearned, a reasonable reserve for services to be performed after the year end. The CRA does not consider that continuing coverage under the contract is a service provided after the end of the year which justifies a reserve. Amounts that would justify a reserve must relate to a binding obligation to provide specific types of client support services after the end of the year. In the CRA's view, possible claims adjustments are not obligations justifying a reserve, since they are subject to a contingency. The CRA's logic here seems a bit tortured, since it would seem arguable that the rule permitting a reserve for services which may reasonably be expected to be performed after year end overrides the contingency rule. In any event, the CRA's view is that the amount under (2) here will in most cases "be nil, or at least significantly less than" amount (1).

Interpretation Bulletin IT-321R was archived by the CRA in 2003 and is now cancelled. The CRA's *Income Tax Technical News* No. 27 comments that "archived ITs will include those that are no longer relevant due to changes in the law or changes in our interpretation of the law, as well as those that are seldom used, either because the subject matter is covered in other CRA publications or because the information presented is no longer of interest". Accordingly, it is no longer possible to know if an IT has been cancelled because it no longer reflects policy or because it is seldom used. It may be that the latter rule is operating in this case. Or it may be that the CRA is now taking the position that a reserve is never justified on the theory that section 9 rather than section 12 applies, as discussed under the heading "Reserve for Goods or Services to be Provided after Year End" at ¶732.05 above.

(ITA: 32; IT-321R [Archived]; CRA Document No.: Insurance Broker's Reserve, *October 10, 2000*, CRA Document No. 2000-0013545)

[¶732.60] *Reserves must be Added to Income the Following Year*

If you deduct a reserve as of the end of a fiscal year, the amount of such reserve must be added to your income of the next fiscal year. A new reserve will then be claimed in that year based on the facts at the end of that year.

(ITA: 12(1)(*e*))

[¶733] DOUBTFUL ACCOUNTS AND BAD DEBTS

If you follow the accrual method of accounting (see ¶714) and, as a result, uncollected accounts receivable are included in income, you are entitled to deduct a reasonable amount as a reserve with respect to those accounts receivable which are doubtful of collection as of the end of your fiscal year. A reserve for doubtful debts claimed in a year must be included in your income for the next succeeding year.

A reserve for doubtful accounts must be distinguished from a deduction for bad debts. The reserve recognizes that collection of certain debts is in doubt and some portion of those debts will not be collected (and some portion will). The objective of the doubtful accounts reserve, therefore, is to produce a defensible estimate of accounts that are likely to become truly and finally uncollectible. Accounts receivable that have become uncollectible must be deducted as bad debts in the year the debts became uncollectible. The CRA's standards as to when a debt becomes a bad debt are fairly stringent. It would not, for example, allow as a bad debt one that has merely been outstanding for a long time. On the other hand, a debt that is doubtful of collection may be deducted as a reserve; it will thus be brought back into income annually, and must be judged either doubtful (or not) and reserved again or uncollectible and written off. It is important to note the CRA's view that only specifically identifiable debts may be subject to a doubtful account reserve or bad debt deduction; some doubt has been cast on that rule with respect to reserves by the *Coppley Noyes* case discussed below.

If a debt that has been deducted as a bad debt in a previous year is recovered during the year, the amount recovered must be included in income in the year recovered.

The right to deduct a reserve for doubtful accounts or to deduct bad debts is restricted to debts which have been included in computing your income in the year or in a previous year, except in cases where your primary business is the lending of money or where your business, by its nature or through custom, requires loans or advances to be made in the ordinary course of business.

The discussion above refers to bad or doubtful debts on income account, such as customer accounts which cannot be collected. Where proceeds of disposition from the sale of capital property become uncollectible, special rules apply depending on whether the property is capital property (¶563), depreciable property (¶847), or eligible capital property (¶768).

[¶733.05] *Receivables Assigned*

Where you have assigned a debt, but not absolutely, the debt is considered to be owing to you at the end of the taxation year even though you may be liable to furnish the assignee with other security if the assigned debt should prove to be uncollectible. In this case the assignment would be a transfer of a debt to a third party for the purpose of securing a debt owing or a loan payable to the third party, giving the third party the right to have funds collected on the assigned debt applied to payment of the debt or loan owing by you to the assignee. Therefore you may claim a reasonable reserve or deduction in the year in which the assigned debt becomes doubtful or uncollectible.

[¶733.10] *Receivables Discounted or Sold*

Where you have sold or discounted notes receivable which had arisen in the ordinary course of your business, you will not be allowed to establish a reserve against such accounts, even though the purchaser of them has recourse to you should the discounted notes prove to be uncollectible in whole or in part. If you have discounted notes receivable, you will be considered contingently liable under the debt and will be entitled to a deduction for tax purposes only when the debt actually proves to be uncollectible and the purchaser requires you to make it good.

[¶733.15] *Reserve must be "Reasonable"*

Only a "reasonable amount" may be deducted as a reserve for doubtful accounts. The reasonableness of a reserve will be decided on the basis of the facts.

When considering whether an account is doubtful it is necessary to consider such things as the period of arrears or default, the financial status of the debtor, the debtor's past credit record, the value of any security taken and any other relevant factor in determining the debtor's ability to pay. Once the doubtful debts have been identified the maximum reserve should be calculated based on an estimate of the percentage of doubtful accounts which will probably not be collected. The calculation should be based on your past history of bad debts, industry experience, and general economic conditions. You may base your reserve percentages on an age-analysis of doubtful accounts.

It is the CRA's view that a reserve which is based on a percentage of all debts, whether doubtful or not, a percentage of gross sales, or some similar calculation is not considered to be a reserve determined on a reasonable basis. In *Coppley Noyes & Randall Limited v. The Queen*, 91 DTC 5291 (F.C.T.D.), the Federal Court explicitly permitted the taxpayer to utilize a reserve for doubtful debts calculated in accordance with Generally Accepted Accounting Principles (GAAP) rather than those advocated by the CRA. The Court cited with approval an earlier Tax Appeal Board statement that a doubtful debt reserve leaves the taxpayer with a "degree of flexibility in using business judgment with regard to the inclusion of amounts in such a reserve". An appeal of this decision was taken by the CRA, and a settlement was reached which was approved by the Federal Court of Appeal (93 DTC 5508). Under the terms of that settlement, certain aspects of the Trial Division judgment supposedly based on GAAP were overturned. Specifically, GAAP principles could not justify a reserve in the taxation year for debts arising after the year on amounts which became payable after the year and therefore were not included in income in the year. It is clear that if GAAP would indeed permit this, it would contravene the law, which specifically forbids reserves against amounts not included in income, and would to that extent be invalid. On the other hand, the taxpayer's business judgment on the remaining accounts was preferred to that of the Minister, so that the Trial Division comments that management is in the best position to judge the doubtful nature of specific accounts and is entitled to a degree of flexibility in using that judgment even if not borne out by subsequent events would appear to stand.

Having determined a "reasonable" reserve for doubtful debts, it is not necessary to deduct the full amount; you may wish to deduct less, for example to reduce a loss carryover (see ¶1085–¶1087). However, bad debts as opposed to doubtful debts must be deducted in the year they are established to be uncollectible.

If you buy and sell items to which the above rules would normally apply your dealings may be considered to be business transactions and the above rules would not apply.

[¶733.20] *Special Reserve for Money Lenders*

If your ordinary business includes the lending of money, you are entitled to calculate a reserve in respect of doubtful loans or lending assets. A lending asset is, essentially, a bond, mortgage, debenture, note, or any other form of debt. Most of the features of this reserve are of special interest to banks and insurers, and therefore beyond the scope of a book aimed at individuals. In principle, however, there are features of this reserve open to anyone whose ordinary business includes lending money. Such a person can claim a reserve for doubtful loans or lending assets equal to the lesser of:

(1) a reasonable amount in respect of the "amortized cost" of the loans/assets. Amortized cost is a defined term, and includes the amount advanced by the lender, with a series of adjustments to cover the loan changing hands and to cover prior adjustments for reserves; and

(2) 90% of the reserve in respect of amortized cost reported in the financial statements.

A further reserve is allowed to persons whose business includes lending money to cover credit risks under guarantees, indemnities, letters of credit, and a broad variety of other credit facilities.

Reserves apart, money lenders are subject to superficial loss rules which restrict losses on dispositions of shares or debt held in the course of business where the disposition is temporary or to an affiliated party; these rules are very similar to the superficial loss rules for capital property discussed at ¶579.

[¶733.25] *Sale of Accounts Receivable*

If you are in business and you report your income on an accrual basis, special rules apply if you sell either the majority or all of your business assets, including accounts receivable. See ¶755.

(ITA: 12; 20; 22; IT-442R [Archived])

[¶734] MEALS, ENTERTAINMENT, CONVENTIONS, AND TRAINING COURSE EXPENSES

[¶734.05] *(A) Business Meals and Entertainment Expenses*

In principle, reasonable amounts for food, beverages and entertainment incurred in earning income from a business or property (and in some cases, from employment — ¶368; ¶369) are deductible. (In a few cases, it is conceivable that the expenses might be capitalized or treated as inventory; this is a matter of accounting policy.) However, only 50% of expenditures for meals, drinks, and entertainment may actually be deducted in computing the income of a business (or, for that matter, of an employee who is otherwise permitted to deduct the cost of meals under the rules in Chapter 3). That is to say, such expenditures are to be segregated in accounts, 50% of which must be added back to income. Exceptions complicate the basic rule.

Where the deduction in computing business income for meals and entertainment expenses is limited to 50% under subsection 67.1(1) of the *Income Tax Act*, the *Excise Tax Act* ("ETA") similarly limits the ITCs available to 50% of the GST/HST paid on such expenses.

Technically speaking, an amount paid or payable in respect of the human consumption of food or beverages or the enjoyment of entertainment is deemed to be 50% of the lesser of (i) the amount actually paid or payable, and (ii) an amount that it would be reasonable to have paid.

Exceptions

The 50% disallowance does not apply to:

(1) Amounts paid or payable for food, entertainment, etc., provided for or in expectation of compensation in the ordinary course of a business of providing food, etc., for compensation. This is intended to exempt restaurants, hotels and airlines from disallowance of their basic business costs, and to exempt the cost of providing samples of products of the taxpayer's business.

(2) Amounts related to a fund-raising event the primary purpose of which is to benefit a registered charity.

(3) Amounts for which the payer is compensated by a reasonable amount specifically identified in writing to the person who will pay the compensation. This is intended to be a flow-through provision. For example, if a lawyer takes his client to lunch and picks up the tab, the lawyer may deduct only 50% of the expense. However, if the lawyer later includes the tab in a bill to the client and identifies it as a meal expense, the lawyer will have a full deduction (offset of course by the income item on the billing) but the client will be expected to deduct only 50% of that item.

(4) Amounts required to be included in the income of an employee of the payer. That is, an employer may deduct in full the cost of a meal which is a taxable benefit to the employee. The rule permits full deduction to food and entertainment amounts included in the employment income of any person whether enjoyed by the employee or someone related to the employee, and whether paid by the employer or someone with whom the employer does not deal at arm's length. Note that where an amount is included in the employee's income, but a deduction is given to the employee (such as that for commission salesmen, transport employees, and the like), the employee's deduction will be subject to the 50% limitation.

(5) Amounts incurred by the payer for food, beverages or entertainment generally available to all employees of the payer employed at a particular location. This is intended to allow a full deduction for the costs of a Christmas party or similar event open to all employees at a particular location. The further limitation is imposed that the exception will only apply in respect of six or fewer special events held in the calendar year.

(6) Amounts for travel on an airplane, train or bus in respect of items consumed or entertainment enjoyed while travelling thereon.

(7) The cost of providing meals, etc., to an employee at a remote work location where such meals would normally be taxable benefits but for the special provisions applicable to employees at remote work locations where they cannot be expected to maintain a self-contained domestic establishment (¶360-¶361). Typically where this situation exists the exemption is identified in payroll records for T4 purposes. A further exception is provided to employers who pay meal and entertainment expenses which are not taxable benefits by virtue of the rules for "special work sites" (as opposed to "remote work locations"; both are defined at ¶360). Under this exception, a benefit which would be taxable as employment income to an employee or relative of an employee but for the special work site rules may be deducted in full by the payer provided the expenses:

- are not in respect of a conference, convention, seminar or similar event; and
- are in respect of duties performed at a work site in Canada that is both (i) outside any urban area (per the Statistics Canada definition in its Census Dictionary) that has a population of 40,000 per the last StatsCan census published before the year, and (ii) at least 30 kilometres from the nearest boundary of the nearest such urban area.

The difference between special work sites and remote work locations is discussed in ¶360. The CRA also discusses it in (the Rev. 08, i.e., 2008, version of) its *Employer's Guide — Taxable Benefits* (T4130), on pages 11 and 12.

(8) Amounts incurred after 2001 for meals provided to a taxpayer's employee at a work camp if:

(a) the site is a special work site (as opposed to a remote work location; the difference is described at ¶360) to the employee (that is, it must be far enough from the employee's principal place of residence that the employee could not be expected to return to that place of residence on a daily basis);

(b) the duties of the employee are performed at a site in Canada at which the taxpayer carries on construction activities or at a construction work camp for such a site;

(c) the employee is lodged at the work camp for the purpose of performing duties at the site;

(d) the food or beverages are provided at the work camp, which was constructed or installed for the purpose of providing meals and lodging to employees engaged in construction services at the site; and

(e) the amounts are not paid for entertainment or for a conference, convention, seminar, etc.

Exception (7), above, does not address situations where, given the large size and short duration of a construction project, the local infrastructure of an urban area is insufficient to support a large temporary workforce, and the project employer consequently establishes a temporary work camp to provide meals and accommodation at or near the construction site. Exception (8) addresses this situation, allowing full deductibility for the cost of meals provided to an employee housed at a temporary work camp constructed or installed specifically for the purpose of providing meals and accommodation to employees working at a construction site. It is intrinsic to the special work site definition that the employee cannot be expected to return home daily. The Goods and Services Tax/Harmonized Sales Tax (GST/HST) follows the income tax rules in its treatment of meal expenses. Accordingly, 100% of the GST/HST paid or payable by an employer on the cost of fully deductible meals provided at a qualifying construction work camp will be recoverable by the employer as input tax credits.

The GST Quirk

Many taxpayers account for GST paid by deducting the GST input tax credit from the total cost incurred. Where section 67.1 applies, limiting the deduction for business meals and entertainment expenses to half of the amount incurred, an input tax credit for half the GST would be claimed. For example, if the expenditure were $107 with $7 of GST, an ITC of $3.50 would be claimed. The net expenditure would be $103.50 and half of this, $51.75, would be the deduction claimed in determining income for tax purposes.

The cost of the business meal or entertainment expense in the above example, however, is $107, not $103.50. The difference, the $3.50 input tax credit, is government assistance under section 248(16) and is included in income under paragraph 12(1)(*x*). The effect of this treatment is that the net deduction with respect to the expenditure is effectively $50 (1/2 of $107, less the amount included in income under paragraph 12(1)(*x*), $3.50) not $51.75. Alternatively, the inducement is $7.00 and the $3.50 of recaptured ITC is deductible under paragraph 20(1)(*hh*), which produces the same result.

It is also the CRA's view that the result would be the same if the taxpayer elected under subsection 12(2.2), to reduce the "outlay or expense" by the government assistance. Subsection 67.1(1) uses the phrase "an amount paid or payable . . . ", which in the CRA's view would not be reduced as a result of an election under subsection 12(2.2).

Section 236 of the ETA, the provision that recaptures the input tax credit on the non-deductible portion of business meals and entertainment, is affected by an amendment contained in a Notice of Ways and Means Motion dated October 8, 1998. The amendment changes the mechanics of the formula in section 236 of the ETA and is effective in the determination of "net tax" for reporting periods after October 8, 1998.

Although the CRA fails to address the issue, it is to be assumed that HST receives the same treatment as GST; however, additional care must be taken in situations where the recapture of input tax credits rule applies for large businesses (Ontario and Prince Edwards Island) with respect to the provincial component of the HST. In accordance with section 248(18), such recapture is deemed to be assistance repaid and should be accounted for accordingly.

With respect to Quebec Sales Tax input tax refunds (ITR), in accordance with section 248(16.1) they are also treated as government assistance and therefore generally follow the federal rule. On the other hand, ITR restrictions, which may be similar to the GST/HST recapture rules, do not affect the net tax payable for QST purposes and are therefore not affected by section 248(18.1). Rather, where ITR restrictions apply, the QST which cannot be claimed as ITR is simply part of the meal or entertainment cost. Similarly, sales taxes of other provinces are also part of the cost of the meal or entertainment.

Where there is no input tax credit claimable, typically because the taxpayer's supplies are exempt for GST/HST purposes, the deduction is simply 50% of $105.

Conference Meals, etc.

Where a fee for a conference, convention, seminar, etc., entitles the participant to food, beverages or entertainment other than incidental refreshments (presumably coffee breaks), it is expected that a reasonable part of the fee will be broken out and identified as a meal etc., expense, so that the payer may add back 50% of that element when claiming the general seminar expense. Where no such identification is made to the participant, $50 per day is deemed to relate to meal costs, and the seminar fee is deemed reduced by $50. Presumably, the intended result is a $25 deduction disallowance (50% of $50). However, this rule is exceedingly general. It appears to apply even if the cost of the seminar is less than $50 (creating, among other oddities, a negative seminar fee which arguably could offset the deemed $50 meal cost). On the other hand, it appears to apply even if three substantial banquets are served in a day and their cost exceeds $50.

Long-Haul Truck Drivers

For 2006 and earlier years, and indeed for 2007 expenditures which were paid or became payable before March 19, 2007, all self-employed truck drivers were bound by the 50% limitation discussed above. That is, only 50% of the cost of meals incurred while away from home is deductible. For expenses which are paid or become payable on or after March 19, 2007, and during an "eligible travel period", the percentage deductible increased as follows:

- 60%, if the amount is paid or becomes payable on or after March 19, 2007 and before 2008;
- 65%, if the amount is paid or becomes payable in 2008;
- 70%, if the amount is paid or becomes payable in 2009;
- 75%, if the amount is paid or becomes payable in 2010; and
- 80%, if the amount is paid or becomes payable in or after 2011.

The phrase "paid or becomes payable", used in the statute, is used interchangeably with "incurred" in the Finance Technical Notes, and presumably this will be the meaning assigned by the CRA.

This rule applies to individuals (only) whose principal business is driving a long-haul truck that transports goods. A long-haul truck is a truck or a tractor that is designed for hauling freight and that has a gross vehicle weight rating (as that term is defined in subsection 2(1) of the Motor Vehicle Safety Regulations) of more than 11,788 kilograms. An eligible period is a period of at least 24 continuous hours during which (for a self-employed long-haul driver) the driver is away from the municipality or metropolitan area where he or she resides. In addition, the driver's absence from the place of residence must be for the purpose of driving a long-haul truck that transports goods to, or from, a location that is beyond a radius of 160 kilometres from the driver's place of residence.

A comparable exception for employees who are long-haul truckers is found at ¶374.30.

Tour Guides

A tour company paid the cost of meals its tour guides ate in the company of the tourists they were leading. The guides were independent contractors, not employees. Accordingly, none of the exceptions applied to them, and the company could deduct only 50% of the cost of the meals.

(ITA: 67.1; 67.1(1), (1.1), (5); Window on Canadian Tax: 1874; 5566; IT-518R [Archived]; CRA Document No.: Restricted Expenses Under 67.1 and GST, *December 8, 1998,* CRA Document No. 9830806; Goods and Services Tax, *April 9, 1992,* CRA Document No. 9209285; Food Beverages & Entertainment, *March 11, 2003,* CRA Document No. 2003-0003747)

[¶734.10] *(B) Convention Expenses*

If you are carrying on business or practising a profession, you may deduct, in computing your income, expenses of attending not more than two conventions held during the year by a business or professional organization. To be deductible, you must have attended the conventions in connection with your business or profession, i.e., you must have attended for business or professional reasons.

Expenses incurred in attending business or professional conventions held outside the geographical limits of the sponsoring organization's ordinary area of activity are not deductible for income tax purposes. This restriction is not intended to deny you a deduction for expenses that you have incurred in genuine attendance at, and participation in, a convention in another country that is organized and sponsored by a business or professional organization of that country and is related to your business or practice.

The expenses incurred must be reasonable and you should be in a position to prove your attendance and to support your expenses with vouchers.

Expenses incurred by or for your spouse and children while accompanying you to or at a convention or on a combined convention and vacation trip are normally considered to be personal. As such they are not deductible.

The deductibility of conference expenses is limited by the meal and entertainment expense rules above.

(ITA: 20(10); 67.1; IT-131R2 [Archived]; IT-357R2 [Archived])

[¶734.15] *(C) Expenses of Attending Courses*

In addition to the above rules relating to attendance at conventions, business persons and professionals may attend courses intended to develop or maintain skills. The CRA takes the view that training to acquire a new skill is a capital investment for which no deduction is allowed, although where the expense is incurred in connection with a business it may be an eligible capital expenditure depreciable under the rules at ¶766, whereas training to maintain, update or upgrade an existing skill may be a reasonable business outlay. Thus, the expenses in connection with any course taken to obtain a degree, diploma, professional qualification or similar certificate would be on capital account. On the other hand, reasonable expenses in connection with a course which enables a taxpayer to maintain, update or upgrade an existing skill or qualification with respect to his or her business or profession should be deductible. Thus, for example, costs incurred in connection with a course to allow a professional to learn the latest methods of carrying on his or her profession are allowable, even if it is an area in which the professional was not actively involved previously although qualified to be so. For example, a medical general practitioner cannot deduct the expenses of specialist training, but could deduct expenses associated with a course on the latest techniques of interest to general practitioners. A lawyer could not deduct the costs of an engineering course, but could claim costs of a course on recent tax changes.

Note that expenses of attending courses often involve two sets of expenses: first, the actual tuition costs or fees for the course, and second, the incidental costs such as travel, lodging, food and so on. The CRA takes the view (in Interpretation Bulletin IT-357R2, para. 1) that if tuition costs qualify for the personal amount credit (¶1319 *et seq.*), the tax credit rules override the deduction rules, leaving the incidental costs to be governed by the rules on income or capital expenditure as discussed above. This is good news where the tuition would otherwise be a non-deductible capital or eligible capital expense; less so if the credit must be taken in preference to a deduction from a high marginal rate. The proposition that credit-qualifying fees or tuition costs cannot be deducted but rather be claimed as a personal amount credit must be based on the principle that a specific rule overrides a general rule. There is no provision which specifically denies a deduction for fees where the credit could be claimed, although general principles would deny a claim for both deduction and credit for the same expense.

(ITA: 67.1; IT-357R2 [Archived])

[¶734.20] *(D) Club Dues and Fees*

See ¶731.

[¶734.25] *(E) Training of Employees*

Expenses you incur to train employees will generally be deductible. To the extent they are incurred to provide training which is merely for the personal interest of the employee rather than to benefit the business, they may constitute a taxable benefit to the employee, as discussed at ¶310.

[¶735] EMPLOYER'S CONTRIBUTION TO A PENSION FUND

[¶735.05] Registered Pension Plans

If you are in business or a partnership, you may establish a registered pension plan for the benefit of your employees. As a proprietor or partner, however, you are not eligible to be covered under such a plan (although if you have an incorporated business you might be eligible as an employee of the corporation). The term "registered pension plan" means an employees' pension plan which has been accepted by the Minister of National Revenue for registration in respect of its constitution and activities.

Registered Pension Plans (RPPs) are monitored by the Registered Plans Directorate of the CRA. The Directorate has its own subsection of the CRA website (www.cra-arc.gc.ca/tx/rgstrd), which features its own series of publications dedicated to the set-up and administration of RPPs. The Directorate also offers its own telephone inquiries service (1-800-267-3100, bilingual service 1-800-267-5565) to help employers, plan sponsors, administrators, and others interpret legislation and regulations related to the administering of registered plans and to help in the calculating of pension adjustments, past service pension adjustments, and pension adjustment reversals.

As you might gather from this description, the details of RPP requirements are a field of study unto themselves, and you will require professional advice and probably a professional administrator to establish and maintain a plan. For this reason, as discussed further below, small proprietors often prefer RRSPs as a vehicle for tax assisted retirement savings, and sometimes offer their employees RRSP contributions as an incentive rather than pension contributions. RRSPs are discussed in detail in Chapter 26.

[¶735.10] *Contributions by Employer*

Both past and current service contributions required under the terms of a registered pension plan to be made by the employer are deductible if made within 120 days after the end of the taxation year to which they relate. Pension contributions for "defined benefit plans" (where a formula determines the eventual benefit) are now achieved through pension plan limits based on registration restrictions on the plans themselves required by law and regulations.

Employer contributions are in theory now integrated into an overall system of tax-deferred savings which includes registered pension plans (RPPs), registered retirement savings plans (RRSPs), and deferred profit sharing plans (DPSPs). The maximum contribution (employer and employee) or benefit accrual to all three types of plans for an individual for a particular year should be 18% of earned income subject to a maximum for the year. In order to integrate RRSPs into this system, their contribution limits are based on prior year income, and the annual maximum contribution limit trails one year behind other plans. This permits reporting of prior year RPP/DPSP contributions in assessing eligible RRSP contributions. It also imposes complex new reporting requirements on employers as part of the T4 process.

Employers who have "defined benefit" (as opposed to "money purchase") pension plans may deduct all contributions necessary to fund the defined benefit plan in accordance with its terms for all periods before the end of the taxation year. The employer has 120 days following the end of a taxation year to make any current or past service contributions required for the year by the plan.

"Money purchase plans" are simpler in concept than defined benefit plans. For the employer, the rule for deductions is the same; namely, the employer may deduct amounts in accordance with the terms of the plan in respect of periods before the end of the taxation year. However, the funds which may be contributed to the plan are in effect limited by dollar amounts for each year much like RRSP contributions, rather than by actuarial calculation of the amount needed to support the defined benefits the plan must eventually provide.

Per employee contribution limits on money purchase RPP plans are 18% of pensionable earnings to a maximum of $26,010 for 2016 (for previous years, see the chart at ¶82 at the beginning of this book). Limits are to be reduced by DPSP contributions. Contributions to defined benefit RPPs are in theory equalized to these levels by complex formulae determining the current value of future benefits.

Since the rules attempt to integrate pension plan benefits with employees' RRSP contribution limits, employers face elaborate reporting requirements on their plans. The key limitation under the new rules will be the so-called Pension Adjustment. This is calculated by employers based on the tax-deferred benefits accruing to each employee annually under all of the employer's registered plans — typically pension and deferred profit sharing plans. The employee's contributions to other tax-assisted savings plans (RRSPs) are limited to the lesser of 18% of income and an annual dollar amount, minus the pension adjustment.

Where a plan permits an employee to contribute in respect of past service to acquire money-purchase benefits, such contributions are not deductible. Employee contributions in respect of past services under defined benefit plans may be deducted as discussed at ¶365.

If an employer maintains a funded but unregistered pension plan to supplement registered plan pensions, any contributions (typically made by an employer) made to the plan and any income of the plan will be subject to a special 50% tax to be refundable as pension payments are made. This second rule has been incorporated under the Retirement Compensation Arrangement rules discussed at ¶739.

To the extent that it may be possible for a tax-exempt employer (e.g., a charity, government, or non-resident) to maintain an unregistered retirement plan that is not captured by the RCA rules at ¶739, the Pension Adjustment rules should nevertheless apply to reduce allowable RRSP contributions of employees (Chapter 26).

[¶735.15] *Funding*

Pension plans are usually funded by depositing contributions with a trustee or by entering into a contract with an insurance company which undertakes to pay pensions in return for premiums paid to it annually. Where the pension plan is trusteed, the trust fund income will not be taxable year by year as it accumulates.

[¶735.20] *RRSPs Instead of RPP*

The pension rules, never simple, have become so complex that small employers increasingly prefer to contribute directly to an employee's RRSP. Since RRSP contribution limits increased to more or less match pension limits as the new rules were brought in, this is often a viable option. Where this is done the contribution is deductible to the employer as it accrues. It is salary to the employee and must be reported as such, and will be offset by the employee's RRSP deduction. Even in this simple mechanism, timing problems can arise where there is not a clear formula (e.g., 4% of salary) and contributions are not made on a pay period basis. A lump-sum annual payment will face technical withholding difficulties (solvable). There may also be timing problems in matching the RRSP deduction to the contribution, given the one-year time lag in the RRSP system (see ¶2627.25).

Since 2004, the government has tried to equalize the choice between money-purchase RPPs and RRSPs, at least for the plan member, by providing that instead of transferring funds from the money purchase plan to a RRIF or annuity on retirement, payments can be made out of the plan schedule under the rules which govern minimum RRIF withdrawals.

[¶735.25] *Pooled Registered Pension Plans (PRPPs)*

The federal government recently introduced legislation regarding PRPPs. The *Pooled Registered Pension Plans Act* received Royal Assent on June 28, 2012, and accompanying amendments to the *Income Tax Act* were passed into law on December 14, 2012. These plans will allow employers and their employees, or self-employed individuals, to make tax-deductible contributions to the plans similar to those made to money purchase RPPs described above. An employer's contribution to a PRPP in a taxation year or within 120 days after year end will be deductible (subsection 147.5(10)). The employer's contribution will reduce the employee's RRSP deduction room for the year. The employee's contribution in a year will also reduce the employee's RRSP deduction room for the year. Distributions from the PRPP and paid to the employee will be included in income and can qualify for the pension credit. See also ¶2555.

Commentary on Legislative Proposals (Sept. 16, 2016)

Note: When Legislative Proposals, September 16, 2016, achieves Royal Assent, the commentary will be modified to read:

Effective December 14, 2012, an amount of PRPP contributions refunded to a member is not included in his/her income if they were made in error or to avoid the revocation of the plan, and if the amount was not deducted as a PRPP contribution in the year of the refund or any preceding year.

In addition, a PRPP contribution is deemed not to have been made where there is a refund of a contribution made to a PRPP by a taxpayer as a result of a reasonable error or a refund to avoid the revocation of the PRPP. This contribution is not deducted as a PRPP contribution for the taxation year in which the refund is made or for any preceding taxation year.

On October 7, 2014, the Department of Finance and the Minister of State announced that five insurance companies that have federal Pooled Registered Pension Plan (PRPP) licences (Sun Life, Great West Life, Manulife, Standard Life and Industrial-Alliance) have been registered with the Office of the Superintendent of Financial Institutions (OFSI) and the Canada Revenue Agency. This was the final step necessary for the plan administrators to make federal PRPPs available to Canadians. The current list of registered PRPPs can be found on the OFSI website, under Pension Plan Administrators / Pooled Registered Pension Plans / List of Pooled Registered Pension Plans. At the time of writing, the same five companies were listed as having PRPP licences.

(ITA: 20(1)(q), (r); 147.1; 147.2; 147.5(10) Employer contributions deductible; 147.5(32.1); 149; 248(1) "registered pension plan"; ITR: 8500–8520)

[¶736] DEFERRED PROFIT SHARING PLANS

A "deferred profit sharing plan" (DPSP) is a plan registered with the CRA under which an employer sets aside an amount calculated with reference to profit for later distribution to employees. The employees are taxed only when they actually receive the funds. Employer contributions to DPSPs are restricted by a number of factors. Among these, per employee contributions are limited to 18% of pensionable earnings (as calculated for registered pension plan purposes) to a maximum of $13,005 for 2016 (for other years, see the table at ¶82). DPSP contributions reduce the contributions that can be made to other plans. Thus, for a DPSP member who also belongs to a money purchase RPP and who saves through an RRSP, the total contribution to the three plans cannot exceed 18% of earnings to a maximum of $26,010 for 2016.

Employers in particular should also note that many of the detailed rules governing DPSPs, especially as regards contributions in the year an employee is terminated, were revised under draft legislation and regulations published on July 16, 2010 and now passed into law. The degree of detail involved is typically a matter for plan administrators, not tax return preparers. Perhaps because of these changes, Interpretation Bulletin IT-363R2, dealing with DPSPs, has been cancelled, meaning it can no longer be relied on as policy. Nevertheless, used with caution, it still presents a reasonable overview of the nature of these plans. In 2007, the CRA released Information Circular IC 77-1R5, which provides extensive discussion of the CRA's policies with regard to DPSPs, and has been updated to incorporate the changes still pending as of its release date.

Since 1989, transfers by employees to other types of plans have been permitted. However, commencing with 1991, employee contributions to DPSPs (which were never deductible in any event) are prohibited. Irrevocable vesting of allocations must occur after two years.

DPSP contributions by employers must be reported as part of the Pension Adjustment on T4 slips.

[¶736.05] *Payments to Beneficiaries*

Payments out of a deferred profit sharing plan are taxable in the recipient's hands when he or she receives them. See ¶917.

(ITA: 20(1)(y); 56; 147; 147.1(1); IC 77-1R5 Deferred Profit Sharing Plans)

[¶736a] *Employees Profit Sharing Plan*

An employees profit sharing plan (EPSP) is an arrangement under which an employer pays a portion of the profits from its business to a trustee to be held and invested for the benefit of its employees who are members of the plan. The principal distinction between an EPSP and a deferred profit sharing plan (section 147) is that under the former the members pay tax each year on the contributions and trust income allocated to them, whereas in a deferred profit sharing plan they pay tax only as these amounts are actually received from the trust. In either case, the employer's contributions are deductible in the year they are made (subject to upper limits in the case of a DPSP). See ¶332 for a further discussion on EPSPs.

In its 2012 federal Budget, the government announced measures to address its concern that EPSPs have been used by business owners to direct profits to members of their families to reduce or defer payment of income tax on these profits. In particular, the new measures include a penalty tax under new Part XI.4 on a specified employee's "excess EPSP amount". See ¶332.20 for a discussion of this penalty tax.

[¶737] SUPPLEMENTARY UNEMPLOYMENT BENEFIT PLANS

A Supplementary Unemployment Benefit Plan is a plan established by an employer or group of employers to top up employees' employment insurance (EI) benefits during a period of unemployment because of training, sickness, accident or disability, maternal or parental leave, or a temporary stoppage of work (i.e., temporary lay-off).

Where you, as an employer, make payments to a trustee in trust, exclusively for the payment of periodic amounts to employees or former employees who are or may be laid off for any temporary or indefinite period, such payments are deductible in computing your business income if they were made in the year or within 30 days after the end of the year providing the plan has been registered with the Minister of National Revenue.

Any amount you receive as an employer from a trustee under a registered supplementary unemployment benefit plan to which you have made payments, resulting from an amendment, modification or termination of the plan, is to be included in your income.

The trust itself is not taxable on its income and the employee or former employee who receives the periodic payments is taxable on such amounts when received by him.

If you wish to establish such a plan, you should obtain a copy of Information Circular IC 72-5R2 from your Tax Services Office. As is recommended for new pension and deferred profit sharing plans, professional advice should be obtained before attempting to establish this type of plan.

(ITA: 145; IC 72-5R2 Registered Supplementary Unemployment Benefit Plans)

[¶738] AUTOMOBILE EXPENSES

Where you use an automobile partly to earn business income and partly for personal purposes, the deductible amount is normally that portion of the total operating expenses of the automobile incurred in the year (plus capital cost allowance and interest where applicable) that the kilometres driven to earn business income is of the total kilometres for the year. For example, assume that your total automobile expenses for a year are $1,500 and your total kilometres driven for the year are 20,000 kilometres of which 12,000 kilometres represent business kilometres. The computation of the deductible amount is as follows:

12,000 kilometres / 20,000 kilometres × $1,500 = $900

Alternatively, where there is frequent business use of the automobile during normal work hours, but the kilometres for that purpose is comparatively low, the capital cost allowance or rent only may be apportioned on the basis of a reasonable combination of kilometres and the time the automobile was used for business purposes; see ¶822. (The employee rules, which are rather more complex as to when expenses may be deducted, are discussed in Chapter 3.)

As to record-keeping requirements to prove your business-use of a vehicle, see ¶738.70 regarding the CRA's new logbook policy.

The lease costs of a leased automobile or capital cost and interest of a purchased automobile are subject to arbitrary limitations which must be calculated before applying the allocation formula. Restrictions on leasing costs and interest are considered here, and restrictions on capital cost allowance are discussed at ¶810a. The CRA provides Interpretation Bulletin IT-521R to discuss these rules, although the quantum of leasing cost, CCA, and interest expense restrictions discussed therein are out of date and reflect prior years' rates.

[¶738.05] *General Summary of Restrictions*

The *Income Tax Act* limits the capital cost allowance in respect of an automobile to an amount calculated on a prescribed maximum acquisition cost, and limits the deduction for the lease cost of a passenger vehicle to a prescribed monthly amount. Input tax credits for GST/HST paid on the acquisition or lease cost of a passenger vehicle are subject to the same limits (see paragraph 13(7)(*g*) and section 67.3 of the *Income Tax Act*).

Generally speaking, these rules are intended to disallow deduction of that portion of the lease cost of an automobile that represents the capital cost of the car in excess of the "threshold amount" determined at the time the lease is entered into, and that portion of the financing cost of a purchased car that represents interest in excess of an arbitrary daily amount fixed at the time the automobile was purchased. These threshold and daily amounts change periodically, but once a vehicle is leased or acquired under a particular set of rates, those rates continue to apply until the lease expires or is substantially altered or the car is disposed of. A table of rates applicable at different periods is set out below.

There are also provisions to disallow certain tax-free automobile allowances paid to employees to the extent those allowances exceed a set amount per kilometre; these are discussed below.

There are also elaborate rules governing the amounts taxable to employees in respect of automobiles provided for their use or allowances provided in respect of their use of their own automobiles. These employee rules are typically part of the remuneration and payroll function rather than tax return preparation; they are discussed in Chapter 3 from the employee's point of view. Insofar as they affect the employer, they are discussed below.

[¶738.10] *Which Automobiles Subject to Restrictions*

The automobile expense restrictions apply to motor vehicles that are:

(1) motor vehicles designed or adapted primarily to carry individuals and their personal luggage and which have a seating capacity of not more than the driver and eight passengers;

(2) motor vehicles which are vans, pick-up trucks, or similar vehicles, subject to the exclusions which follow. The CRA has said that a "Hummer" all-terrain vehicle is a "similar" vehicle (Wolters Kluwer *Window on Canadian Tax* at ¶3778).

A van, pick-up or similar vehicle will not be subject to the rules restricting deductions provided any one of the following three sets of conditions are met:

(1) it has in fact a seating capacity for no more than the driver and two passengers, and in the year in which it is acquired or leased it is used primarily (i.e., more than 50%) for the transportation of goods or equipment in the course of a business or for the purpose of earning income; or

(2) in the year it is acquired or leased, it is used all or substantially all for the transportation of goods, equipment or passengers in the course of gaining or producing income; the CRA uses 90% as a benchmark for "all or substantially all", although the Tax Court has interpreted the same phrase in a GST setting to be satisfied by an 80% test; see *McKay v. The Queen*, 2001 GTC 208 (T.C.C.), and *Ruhl v. The Queen*, 1998 GTC 2055 (T.C.C.). See also *Pronovost v. The Queen*, 2003 DTC 720 (T.C.C.), in which the Court dismissed the usefulness of the 90% test in finding on the facts that an employee's extended cab pick-up truck was used "all or substantially all" in the course of his work and so escaped the Class 10.1 limitation; or

(3) for 2003 and later taxation years, it is a pick-up truck regardless of capacity (i.e., an extended cab pick-up) that is used in the taxation year in which it is acquired or leased primarily for the transportation of goods, equipment or passengers in the course of earning or producing income at one or more locations in Canada that are both (i) a special or remote work site (as described in ¶360) in respect of at least one occupant of the vehicle, and (ii) at least 30 kilometres from the nearest boundary of the nearest urban area with a population of at least 40,000 (as determined in the last Statistics Canada census published before the taxation year in which the vehicle is acquired or leased). It would appear that the exclusion for extended cab pick-ups in special or remote work sites for 2003 and later years should apply to vehicles acquired in earlier years provided they met all the conditions for this exception in the year acquired or leased.

In the course of adding item (3), above, Finance also changed, for 2003 and later years, the use tests in exclusions (1) and (2). These exclusions used to depend on the extent of a motor vehicle's business use "in the taxation year in which it is acquired"; it now depends on the extent of business use "in the taxation year in which it is acquired or leased". The year of acquisition test by itself is sensible in a capital cost allowance context where a vehicle stays in the class from year to year, and changes in the degree of business use are accounted for by proration (¶822). Informal discussions with Finance officials indicate that there was no intention to change the test from one which applied once and for all in the year the vehicle is originally acquired or leased to one which, for leased vehicles, must be met again for each year in which the vehicle is leased, which is a possible construction of the new rule. The CRA had not officially opined at the time of writing, but was not expected to change its interpretation in the short run.

Motor vehicles are defined to include all automotive vehicles designed or adapted to be used on highways but to exclude trolley buses and vehicles used primarily on rails. More pertinent, the following vehicles which would otherwise be subject to restriction are explicitly excluded from the restrictions on deducting automobile expenses:

(1) an ambulance;

(2) a clearly marked emergency response vehicle used in connection with or in the course of an individual's office or employment with, for 2003 and later taxation years, a fire department or the police, and in addition, for 2005 and later taxation years, an emergency medical response or ambulance service;

(3) a motor vehicle acquired primarily for use as a taxi;

(4) a bus acquired primarily for use in a business of transporting passengers;

(5) a hearse acquired primarily for use in, or a motor vehicle used for the purpose of transporting passengers in, the course of a business of arranging or managing funerals; and

(6) a motor vehicle acquired to be sold, rented or leased in the course of carrying on a business of selling, renting or leasing motor vehicles.

The CRA has a nice chart in its *Business and Professional Income* guide distinguishing passenger vehicles perforce subject to the restrictions from motor vehicles which are not.

In the discussion below references to automobiles, cars, etc., are to all vehicles defined to be subject to the deduction restrictions.

[¶738.20] *Restriction Amounts Subject to Change*

When the deduction limitations discussed here and the capital cost allowance limitations at ¶810a were introduced in 1987, the Minister of Finance gave an undertaking that the appropriateness of the dollar limitations would be reviewed every two years, and provision would be made to adjust the amounts by regulation. Since then, changes have been made to all limitation amounts periodically; revised rates are typically now announced by press release in December, implemented by revised regulations years later. A table of effective limitations is set out below.

[¶738.25] *Table of Capital Cost/Lease Cost Threshold Amounts*

The following limitation amounts have been prescribed for automobiles leased or acquired and for kilometres incurred in the periods indicated:

Effective date	*Cost limit*	*MSLP limit (cost/.85)*	*Monthly lease limit*	*Daily interest limit*
Jan. 1, 2000	$27,000 + taxes [1]	($27,000 + taxes [1]) ÷ .85	$700 + taxes [1]	$ 8.33
Jan. 1, 2001 through 2016	$30,000 + taxes [1]	($30,000 + taxes [1]) ÷ .85	$800 + taxes [1]	$10.00

[1] taxes = GST/HST/PST/QST

(ITR: 7306 [Prescribed amount – automobile allowance]; 7307 [Prescribed amount – automobile deduction limits]; Other Publications: *Business and Professional Income* guide (T4002))

[¶738.30] *Restrictions on Automobile Leasing Expenses*

Where you incur all or part of the "actual lease charges" for an automobile directly or indirectly and you are, under general rules, entitled to deduct some amount in respect of these payments as business (or employment) expense, the "actual lease charges" on which the amount deductible would normally be calculated (where, for example, there is a proration for non-business use) cannot exceed the lesser of:

(1) for leases first entered into in or after 2001, $800 plus applicable provincial sales tax (PST or HST) and goods and services tax (GST) on $800 times the number of months during which the auto was leased in the year and preceding years, less amounts deducted in prior years in respect of the lease; (for leases entered into before 2001, substitute the *Monthly lease limit* amount from the table above for $800 plus GST/PST);

minus

(a) where the lease requires a refundable deposit, the notional interest in excess of $1,000 calculated by multiplying that deposit by the (varying) interest rates prescribed in the chart at ¶80 preceding Chapter 1 for the entire period of the lease up to the end of the taxation year during which the deposit is outstanding; and

(b) any reimbursements that became receivable by the taxpayer in respect of the lease over the entire period of the lease up to the end of the taxation year;

and

(2) for leases entered into in or after 2001, the actual lease charges for the year times $30,000 plus the applicable PST (or HST) and GST on $30,000 divided by 85% of the greater of (i) MSLP and (ii) 100/85 of $30,000 plus GST/HST/PST (as applicable in lessee's province) on $30,000; for leases entered into before 2001, substitute the *MSLP limit* amount from the table above for (ii);

minus

(a) where the lease requires a refundable deposit, the notional interest in excess of $1,000 calculated by multiplying that deposit by the prescribed interest rate in the chart at ¶80 preceding Chapter 1 for the period of the taxpayer's taxation year during which the deposit is outstanding; and

(b) any reimbursements that became receivable during the year by the taxpayer in respect of the lease.

Clearly several explanations of this formula are required.

First, the CRA is understood to take the position that it is only "actual lease charges" which are subject to the limitation; and actual lease charges do not include provincial sales tax (PST) or GST (or indeed insurance costs), where these items are shown separately from leasing charges in the lease contract. This somewhat dubious interpretation does benefit the taxpayer, who will be able to treat these costs as operating costs under the general proration rule at the beginning of ¶738, above, and not subject to the limitations here. For a more detailed discussion of the ins and outs of this policy, see ¶370g. The CRA has further said (in a memo reported in Wolters Kluwer *Windows on Canadian Tax*, 2739) that a penalty for cancellation of a lease is not included in "actual lease charges".

Second, the "actual lease charges" referred to in (2) are costs on a cash or accrual basis, depending on the method regularly followed by the taxpayer. Employees and farmers are likely to be cash basis taxpayers.

Third, the number of months in (1), above, is technically the number of days in the entire period from the commencement of the lease (in whatever taxation year) to the earlier of the end of the current year or the end of the lease period, divided by 30. A retroactive change here ensures that a cash basis taxpayer who makes a current year payment for a preceding year is not put offside, as could happen under the rule as originally formulated.

Fourth, MSLP is the manufacturer's suggested list price for the vehicle. In determining (2), above, the greater of the manufacturers list price and the $30,000 (or other prescribed) plus GST/HST/PST amount, no GST/HST/PST is added to the manufacturer's list price side of the comparison (for leases entered into after 1990). This apples-and-oranges comparison works to the taxpayer's advantage, since it permits a higher list price before the limitation amount bites.

Fifth, if the MSLP is less than 100/85 of the capital cost limitation (for 2001 through 2016 leases, less than 100/85 times $30,000 plus applicable GST/HST/PST), the formula in (2) will give a result of actual lease charges times 1 ($30,000 plus tax divided by 85/100 × 100/85 × $30,000 plus tax). If MSLP is greater than 100/85 of the capital cost limitation, the limitation will permit a deduction less than actual lease charges for the year.

Sixth, the prescribed rate of interest in (2)(a), above, is the same as other prescribed rates, that is, the quarterly rate shown in the table immediately preceding Chapter 1, not adjusted to add the 2% applicable to payments due to or from the government. Prescribed interest is multiplied by the total (if any) of all refundable deposits in excess of $1,000 to arrive at the amount subtracted in this respect from the lesser of (1) and (2).

Seventh, reimbursements are typically amounts paid by an employee to an employer in respect of personal use of a company car. However, any reimbursements from any source reduce the permissible deduction calculated as the lesser of (1) and (2). Technical amendments to the provisions attempt to ensure that reimbursement payments made are subject to the same deduction limitations to the person paying the reimbursement as to the direct lessee. The practical result seems to be that the person paying the reimbursement is considered an indirect lessee and must go through the entire limitation calculation independently.

Eighth, the alternative limitations in (1) and (2) are each reduced for notional interest on outstanding deposits from the taxpayer and for reimbursements receivable by the taxpayer. However, the calculation in (1) ($800 or whatever per month) is made each year on a cumulative basis over the lifetime of the lease, which is the period considered in prorating the number of months for which the limit applies as well as the reductions. The calculation in (2) is strictly an annual calculation insofar as these reductions are concerned.

[¶738.35] *Down Payments and Terminal Payments*

Limitation (2) of the leasing cost restriction formula above, generally speaking, disallows annual lease costs proportionally to the extent the car being leased costs more than (for 2001 through 2016 leases) $30,000 or the applicable threshold amount at the time the lease is made, assuming the lessor obtains a discount of 15% from manufacturer's suggested list price. Limitation (1) is cumulative over the period of the lease, and effectively limits lease costs to, for 2001 through 2016 leases, $9,600 per year (plus applicable GST/PST on $9,600) which is prorated on a monthly basis where the car is not leased throughout the year. Where an initial lump-sum payment is made to reduce subsequent lease costs, it appears that limitation (1) will include that payment in the initial year and may result in a disallowance even though the car costs considerably less than the applicable threshold amount and the normal monthly lease costs are less than $800 (or the applicable threshold). Where only limitation (1) is in play over the life of the lease, this will be reversed in future years since limitation (1) is calculated on a life-of-the-lease and not an annual basis.

However, as an alert reader has pointed out, this is not necessarily true where limitation (1) comes into play only at the beginning of the lease. Assume, for example, that a lease is signed in the last month (December) of the taxpayer's (calendar) taxation year, and the taxpayer makes an initial lump-sum payment, or down payment, of $3,000, and will in December and through the remainder of the lease pay a monthly charge of $300 per month. The car is not an expensive one and, ordinarily, the only limitation in play will be (2), and the limit will be the actual lease costs for the year times one. In the year of acquisition, however, the initial payment (plus the initial monthly charge of, say, $300) will create an overall limitation of $800 (ignoring GST/PST on both sides). In effect, the taxpayer may deduct the $300 monthly cost plus $500 of the initial payment. The balance of the initial payment is in effect non-deductible, and will never be recovered because only limitation (2) will apply in subsequent years, and it will limit deductions to annual lease costs of $3,600. If the lease had been entered into early enough in the year, the multiplication of the $800 limit for months in the year would have been sufficient to cover the down payment. On the other hand, if the initial payment were large enough, it could be made in January with the same result.

The same problem can in theory occur with a terminal payment at the conclusion of a lease, but this is perhaps less likely given the cumulative nature of limitation (1), which recognizes months in earlier years less payments made in earlier years.

The CRA appears to recognize this problem in a kind of backhanded way, since it gives specific alleviation for cash basis taxpayers (farmers and employees). These policies, in paragraph 11 of Interpretation Bulletin IT-521R (farmers) and in paragraph 9 (following the formula description, in a paragraph beginning "Where the total paid in a particular year...") of IT-522R (employees), appear to allow the cash basis taxpayer to amortize an advance payment over the term of the lease. By negative implication, this permission does not extend to accrual basis taxpayers (businesses). Perhaps the CRA simply accepts accrual reporting which amortizes the initial payment over the life of the lease, and is bending over backwards to give the same reasonable result to cash basis taxpayers. It is not clear that this problem occurs much in practice, since there appears to be little significant comment from the CRA or the tax practice community. One honourable exception is an article in 1998 *Canadian Tax Journal* (No. 1) 125; see pages 130-131.

[¶738.40] *Leasing Expense Deduction Calculation*

The following chart for determining leasing expenses is adapted from the form T2125, "Statement of Business or Professional Activities".

Note: Most leases do not include items such as insurance, maintenance, and taxes. You have to pay these amounts separately. Therefore, list these expenses separately when you calculate your allowable motor vehicle expenses. Do not include them on line 1 when you fill in the Chart.

The lease agreement for your passenger vehicle may include items such as insurance, maintenance, and taxes. In this case, include them as part of the lease charges on line 1 when you fill in the Chart.

Total lease charges incurred in your 2013 fiscal period for the vehicle ______	(1)
Total lease payments deducted before your 2013 fiscal period for the vehicle ______	(2)
Enter the total number of days the vehicle was leased in your 2013 and previous fiscal periods ______	(3)
The manufacturer's list price ______	(4)
Greater of line 4 and applicable MSLP limit[1] × 85% =	(5)
Applicable monthly lease limit[1] × line 3 / 30 - line 2 ______	(6)
Applicable cost limit[1] × line 1 / line 5	(7)
Your eligible leasing cost is the lesser of line 6 and line 7 ____	

[1] From "Table of Capital Cost/Lease Cost Threshold Amounts", above.

(If you are an employee, enter this amount as the leasing cost in the calculation of automobile expenses on form T777, *Statement of Employment Expenses.*) For businesses, leasing cost deductions for new system vehicles may not exceed this amount.

Note:

The calculation above may be insufficient in the following situations:

(1) You have a repayment or reimbursement owing to you for the leasing costs;

(2) You have imputed interest; that is, interest that would be owing to you if interest were paid on deposits made on the lease. Imputed interest can only occur if:

- you make one or more deposits for the leased automobile,
- the deposit is or deposits are refundable to you at the end of the lease, and
- the total deposits exceed $1,000.

If you are entitled to a reimbursement of leasing expenses, make the following calculations:

- Enter the total of all reimbursements receivable by you *for this year and previous years* in respect of the leased vehicle.
- Deduct this amount from line 6.
- Enter the total of all reimbursements receivable by you *for this year* in respect of the leased vehicle.
- Deduct this amount from line 7.

If you are subject to the imputed interest rules, make the following calculations:

- Calculate and enter the imputed interest that would have been earned *for the year and all previous years* on that part of the total of all refundable deposits for a vehicle that exceeds $1,000. It is calculated using the prescribed rate of interest for each year the refundable amounts are outstanding (see table of interest rates preceding Chapter 1).
- Deduct this amount from line 6.
- Calculate and enter the imputed interest that would have been earned *during the period for which the lease charges were paid* on that part of the total of all refundable deposits for a vehicle that exceeds $1,000. It is calculated using the prescribed rate of interest for the period during which the refundable amounts were outstanding (see table of interest rates preceding Chapter 1).
- Deduct this amount from line 7.

[¶738.45] *Restrictions on Interest on Purchased Cars*

Where money has been borrowed to purchase an automobile, the interest cost for tax purposes (and before prorations) is limited to the lesser of interest actually paid or payable in respect of the taxation year and $300 per 30-day period or $10 per day for money borrowed in respect of an automobile acquired on or after January 1, 2001 times the number of days in the taxation year in respect of which the interest was paid or payable. These amounts are noted in the table of threshold amounts above. For 2016, the $300 limitation remains in effect. (The technical rule is that the deduction may not exceed the lesser of the actual amount paid or payable for a period and $300 times the number of days in the period in respect of which the interest is paid or payable divided by 30.)

[¶738.50] *Joint Ownership of Vehicles*

In order to prevent circumvention of the above rules through shared ownership of vehicles, the rules provide that where a vehicle is jointly owned or leased, the maximum deduction available to each participant in respect of capital cost allowance, interest, or leasing costs is the proportion of the amount otherwise deductible that the fair market value of the participant's interest is of the collective fair market value of the interests of all participants.

[¶738.55] *Disallowance to Employer of Employee Allowances*

In addition to the limitations on businesses which purchase or lease automobiles, there are rules restricting the deductibility of amounts paid or payable as an allowance for the use by an individual of an automobile except where the amount is required to be included in computing the individual's income. For 2016, allowances in excess of 54¢ per kilometre for the first 5,000 kilometres of use during an employer's taxation year by the individual in the course of earning income and 48¢ per kilometre for any additional such use in the year are not deductible to the payer. An additional 4¢ per kilometre will be allowed for each kilometre travelled in the Yukon, the Northwest Territories and Nunavut. (The Department of Finance reviews these rates annually, and from time to time announces revisions. The announcement is usually made in December for the following year.)

In a technical opinion (in French, reported in English in Wolters Kluwer *Window on Canadian Tax* 8235), the CRA has confirmed that the mileage rates are prescribed for a calendar year. However, it appears that the employer would calculate its disallowance according to excess mileage incurred in the employer's fiscal period.

Although phrased in very general terms, the rules disallowing deduction of payments to individuals in respect of automobile expenses are essentially aimed at automobile allowances paid by employers. In general, the rules contemplate two situations in respect of automobile allowances:

(1) The employer may pay an allowance to the employee which is not a taxable benefit to the employee. Employees engaged in the negotiating of contracts or the selling of property for the employer may receive reasonable allowances for travelling expenses free of tax, and other employees may receive reasonable allowances from the employer for the use of a motor vehicle in the performance of their employment. In either case, the whole amount of an allowance cannot be tax-free (a) where the measurement of the *use* of the vehicle for allowance purposes is not based solely on business kilometres or (b) where the employee both receives an allowance and is reimbursed in whole or in part for expenses in respect of the same use. An employee may receive automobile cost reimbursements in respect of supplementary business insurance, parking, and toll or ferry charges without rendering the allow-

ance taxable, so long as the allowance has been determined without reference to these reimbursements. This appears to mean that the employee's allowance is not rendered taxable so long as it is not intended to cover these special reimbursements, in which case the employee would in effect be reimbursed twice. Where all employees receive the same mileage allowance, and these special items are reimbursed as incurred, it would seem clear that they should not render the allowance taxable. An employee is allowed to add an inadequate allowance to income and deduct the expenses permitted (¶369).

Note that the amount of the allowance does not enter into the issue of taxability to the employee; to be a tax-free allowance to the employee, the amount must be (i) reasonable, (ii) measured by kilometres, and (iii) not supported by additional reimbursements other than those specified above. Once an allowance becomes taxable by failing to meet even one of these criteria, the whole allowance (and not merely the unreasonable portion) becomes taxable and is dealt with under (2), below. It should thus be possible to easily disqualify an allowance if this is desirable, although since the employee has the option of treating the allowance as income when it is in his or her interest, it is rarely desirable in future to resort to this strategy.

Where the employer pays an allowance for the use of an automobile by the employee which need not be reported as a taxable benefit to the employee under the above rules, the employer may not deduct the allowance paid for automobile use in excess of the per kilometre limitations. It is irrelevant how the employer computes the automobile allowance; the deduction must be supported by reference to the employee's business use of an automobile. If the employer chooses to pay a higher allowance which otherwise complies with the tax-free rules, the excess is still not taxable to the employee (if it is "reasonable") but is not deductible to the employer.

The law distinguishes between allowances for the use of an automobile and allowances for the operation of an automobile. The latter are taxable benefits regardless of the rules above (except for the reimbursements for parking, etc., discussed above) and accordingly are not caught by the per kilometre limitation. As a practical matter, where the employer pays only a per kilometre amount for use which on its face meets the tests above, the CRA has not yet tried to separate out an operating element. Operating expenses paid by the employer for personal use of an automobile *of the employer* create a specifically defined taxable benefit to the employee (¶324), but it is the actual expenses which are deductible to the employer.

Since the tax-free allowance must be based on kilometres of business use, it presupposes a systematic employee log maintained on a current basis. Without this support, the claim may be challenged and become subject to the rules just below.

(2) The employer may pay an automobile allowance to the employee and, *provided it does not automatically qualify as a non-taxable allowance under (1), above,* report it as taxable income of the employee. In this case the employer may deduct the allowance in full. The employee should be able to deduct certain amounts in respect of operation and depreciation of the car prorated for business use of the car, provided the employer certifies that the employee meets the statutory requirements for such a deduction. Essentially, the employee's deductions will be based on his actual costs subject to the leasing cost, interest and depreciation limitations, prorated for business use. See ¶368–¶370.

In addition to the policies contemplated in the *Income Tax Act*, described above, the CRA had a policy prior to 2001, set out in its *Employer's Guide: Taxable Benefits* (T4130), which permitted a mixed allowance consisting of a flat rate portion and a reasonable per-kilometre allowance; only the flat rate portion was considered taxable to the employee. Under that policy (last in force for 2000), although the employee would by rights be disallowed any personal automobile deductions under ¶369 (because in receipt of a tax-free allowance), the CRA nevertheless permitted the employee to include both allowances in income and claim ¶369 deductions where this was advantageous. The advantage to the employer was, presumably, that it could deduct both the entire flat rate portion and the mileage portion up to the (then) 37/31 cent limit, thus exceeding in total the (then) 37/31 cent limit overall without compromising the employee's position. This policy was reversed effective January 1, 2001, and both portions of a mixed allowance which covers the same use of the same vehicle will be taxable in full to the employee. That is, the employer can (presumably) still pay a mixed allowance and achieve its deduction, but the employee will not be able to receive the mileage portion tax-free. The employee, not being in receipt of a tax-free allowance, will presumably be permitted the deductions at ¶369. In a subsequent technical opinion (CRA Document No. 2002-0176735), the CRA pointed out that its 2001 and later policy is intended to cover situation in which an employee receives both a per-kilometre and a flat-rate allowance that covers any of the same use. Where an employer had a policy of paying a flat rate on in-town use and a per-kilometre rate on out of town use, each allowance would be considered separately in determining whether it was reasonable and therefore not taxable to the employee.

There is yet another possibility not contemplated in the Act, namely, that the employee is reimbursed for specific expenditures incurred on behalf of the employer. The calculation of this reimbursement may be contested by the CRA, but it is certainly arguable that a reimbursement is not an allowance and therefore not subject to these rules. This position is supported in case law by the Federal Court of Appeal in *The Queen v. Pascoe*, 75 DTC 5427 at 5428, the Supreme Court of Canada in *Gagnon v. The Queen*, 86 DTC 6179, and the Tax Court of Canada in *Alicia and Craig Yorke v. M.N.R.*, 89 DTC 12. The issue will then shift to the measurement and reasonableness of the actual expense incurred. Presumably this would require a very explicit calculation of expense incurred on the employer's behalf by each employee, based on the employee's personal experience of costs incurred. To the extent that a payment to an employee may be characterized as a reimbursement of specific expenses incurred by the employee on behalf of the employer rather than an allowance, it should be fully deductible to the employer and not taxable to the employee.

[¶738.60] *Standby Charges and Operating Cost Benefits*

Standby charges are taxable benefits which must be reported on behalf of employees who use employer-provided automobiles for personal use. It is a payroll function of the employer to identify and report these benefits (see ¶322). These are independent of the employer's limitations on deducting the lease or depreciating the cost of automobiles.

Employers must also account for operating costs borne by the employer on account of the employee's personal use of either the employer's or employee's automobile (¶324). Again, this is a payroll function. The employer deducts actual cost (less GST if rebated to the employer).

[¶738.65] *Table of Per Kilometre Limitations*

See the table at ¶86, "Table of Per Kilometre Limitations", for current and historical rates.

The maximum deductible cents per kilometre amounts relate to the disallowance of mileage allowances paid to employees. Operating expense amounts relate to amounts which must be included in income in addition to standby charges where an employee has use of an employer's vehicle (¶324).

Self-employed individuals are expected to maintain cost records to support actual operating expense costs, and then apportion actual costs between personal and business use on a mileage basis, as discussed at the beginning of ¶738.

[¶738.70] *CRA Logbook Policy*

The CRA has historically taken the position that the best evidence to demonstrate the business use of a vehicle is a logbook maintained for the entire taxation year, recording each business trip and the distance travelled. In the 2008 federal Budget, an announcement was made that the CRA would consider allowing a sample logbook to determine business use for a taxation year. On June 28, 2010, after some consultations with business organizations, the CRA announced its new policy. It stated that it will allow businesses to use a sample logbook, covering three months of a year, to determine the business use for the entire year. The sample logbook can be used once the business has established a "base year" during which a logbook was maintained showing business travel for the entire year.

Under the policy, business owners will be expected to maintain a full logbook for one complete 12-month period (starting in 2009 or thereafter) to establish the business use of a vehicle in the base year. After completing the logbook for this period, which need not be a calendar year, a three-month sample logbook period can be used in a taxation year to determine the business use for that taxation year. However, the distances travelled and the business use of the vehicle during the three-month sample period must be within 10 percentage points of the corresponding figures for the same three-month period in the base year (which the CRA calls the "base year period"); and the calculated annual business use of the vehicle in a subsequent year cannot go up or down by more than 10 percentage points in comparison to the base year.

Where these conditions are met, the business use of the vehicle in a taxation year will be calculated by multiplying the business use as determined in the base year by the ratio of the sample period and base year period. The CRA provides the following formula for this calculation:

(Sample year period % / Base year period %) × Base year annual % = Calculated annual business use

In its June 28, 2010 release, the CRA provided the following example of the new policy.

Example

An individual has completed a logbook for a full 12-month period, which showed a business use percentage in each quarter of 52/46/39/67 and an annual business use of the vehicle as 49%. In a subsequent year, a logbook was maintained for a three-month sample period during April, May and June, which showed the business use as 51%. In the base year, the percentage of business use of the vehicle for the months April, May and June was 46%. The business use of the vehicle would be calculated as follows:

(51% / 46%) × 49% = 54%

In this case, the CRA would accept, in the absence of contradictory evidence, the calculated annual business use of the vehicle for the subsequent year as 54%. (i.e., the calculated annual business use is within 10% of the annual business use in the base year — it is not lower than 39% or higher than 59%.)

If the calculated annual business use in a subsequent taxation year increases or decreases by more than 10% relative to the base year, the CRA no longer considers the base year an appropriate indicator of annual usage in that subsequent year. In such case, the business use of the vehicle in the subsequent year would need to be determined based on an actual record of travel or alternative records. In these circumstances, the CRA recommends that the taxpayer consider establishing a new base year by maintaining a logbook for a new 12-month base period.

(ITA: 6(1)(*b*); 8(1)(*f*), (*g*), (10); 18(1)(*r*); 67.2; 67.3; 67.4; 248(1) "automobile", "motor vehicle", "personal or living expenses"; ITR: 7306 [Prescribed amount – automobile allowance]; 7307 [Prescribed amount – automobile deduction limits]; IT-521R [Archived]; IT-522R [Archived]; Other Publications: Department of Finance Releases 95-105, December 12, 1995; 96-103, December 23, 1996; 97-112, December 4, 1997; 98-127, December 16, 1998; 99-108, December 13, 1999; 2000-096, December 20, 2000; 2001-121, December 18, 2001; CRA Notice to Employers: Employers' Guides, issued December 2000, S00-007)

[¶739] EMPLOYEE BENEFIT PLANS AND SALARY DEFERRAL PLANS

[¶739.05] *Employee Benefit Plans*

Amounts paid by an employer to a "custodian" pursuant to an arrangement for the benefit of employees which is not a registered plan (¶735–¶737), an employee profit sharing plan (¶332), a salary deferral arrangement (¶307), or a retirement compensation arrangement (¶359), as these terms are defined in the *Income Tax Act*, will give rise to an "employee benefit plan". Such amounts are not currently deductible to the employer.

Amounts paid out of the plan to an employee are taxable to him when received, and a deduction may then be claimed by the employer in respect of these payments to employees (including heirs and legal representatives of employees or former employees), less income (if any) earned by the plan in the year of payment.

It appears that the salary deferral arrangement and retirement compensation arrangement rules discussed below between them leave very few employee benefit arrangements subject to the employee benefit plan rules, but there may be some. See ¶359.

[¶739.10] *Salary Deferral Arrangements*

Essentially, a salary deferral arrangement is any funded or unfunded arrangement the principal purpose of which is to defer salary or wages. This is discussed in considerable detail at ¶307. If a plan falls within the definition of a salary deferral arrangement as set out at ¶307, the employer is entitled to a deduction for amounts in respect of services rendered to him in the taxation year the amounts are taxed to the employee, whether or not the amounts have been segregated by a trustee or custodian. An employee may be taxed on amounts subject to a contingency and later forfeited. Where this happens, the employee may take a compensating deduction in the year of forfeiture and the employer must include in income for the year any amount which becomes deductible by the employee in the taxation year. All these rules are effective for 1986 and later taxation years.

[¶739.15] *Retirement Compensation Arrangements*

Essentially, these are funded unregistered pension plans. More precisely, they are plans under which an employer makes payments to another person in order that benefits may be paid to an employee or any other person on retirement, termination of employment, or a substantial change of employment services. Registered plans and other plans specifically authorized by the *Income Tax Act* are excluded, as are certain non-resident plans (see ¶359) and plans for some athletes and athletic event officials.

Employer contributions to the plans are deductible on a current basis, but the plan itself is subject to a special 50% tax which is refunded as the pensions are eventually paid out. The intent is to prevent the accumulation of income on pre-tax contributions to the plan.

Contributions to foreign pension plans may or may not fall under the Retirement Compensation Arrangement (RCA) rules. The statutory definition of an RCA excludes foreign pension plans, but there are anti-avoidance rules which can deem foreign pension plan contributions for the account of a Canadian resident to fall under the RCA rules. There is then an alleviating regulation which allows the employer to opt out of these rules by reporting Pension Adjustments and Past Service Pension Adjustments for Canadian employees under the rules for RRSPs discussed in Chapter 26. In effect, this gives the foreign employer a choice between paying 50% refundable tax or reporting a Pension Adjustment or PSPA that will reduce the Canadian employee's contributions to a Canadian RRSP. See also ¶2614a.

In *Income Tax Technical News* No. 34, dated April 27, 2006, the CRA offers the following comments:

> The CRA has recently considered arrangements to fund benefits that are to be provided to employees under the provisions of plans that are identified as unregistered pension or supplementary pension plans. CRA has taken the position that these plans will generally be RCAs if the arrangements are pension plans and the benefits being provided are reasonable. Where a plan provides benefits that are not reasonable, the CRA is of the view that a salary deferral arrangement will exist.
>
> The CRA is taking the view that benefits will not be reasonable if, for example, they are more generous than benefits that would be commensurate with the employee's position, salary and service or they do not take into account benefits that are provided through one or more registered plans.
>
> It has come to the CRA's attention that innovative tax plans purporting to be RCAs are being marketed and promoted to avoid taxes. Here are some examples: corporations that contribute excessive amounts for the benefit of owner/managers who would receive the amounts after moving offshore, corporations that are attempting to use such arrangements to streamline their long-term profits and corporations that are claiming deductions for contributions that are part of a series of contributions/loan-backs. Tax avoidance schemes purporting to be RCAs will be targeted for review with the aim of, for example, applying the salary deferral arrangement rules, denying deductibility, applying subsection 15(1) and/or subjecting the arrangements to GAAR.

More recently, the Department of Finance, in its 2012 Budget, indicated that the CRA has uncovered "tax-motivated arrangements" perceived to be an abuse of the RCA rules. Apparently, "some arrangements involve the deduction of large contributions that are indirectly returned to the contributors through a series of steps ending with the purported RCA having little or no assets but still being able to claim the refundable tax using the impaired asset exception (the 207.5(2) election). Other arrangements use insurance products to allocate costs to the arrangement for benefits that arise outside the arrangement."

As a result, the 2012 federal Budget introduced a new penalty tax on RCAs in respect of "prohibited investments", "advantages" and "stripping" rules, very similar to those applicable to RRSPs and RRIFs. See "Recent Changes" in Chapter 3. The new rules do not affect the deduction of employer's contributions to an RCA, but the penalty taxes will obviously be detrimental where they apply.

(ITA: 6(1)(*a*), (*g*), (*h*), (*i*), (10)–(14); 8(1)(*o*); 12(1)(*n*.2); 18(1)(*o*), (*o*.1), (*o*.2), (10); 20(1)(*r*), (*oo*), (*pp*); 32.1; 207.5–207.7; 248(1) "retirement compensation arrangement"; ITR: 6800 [Prescribed arrangement – employee benefit plan])

[¶740] SCIENTIFIC RESEARCH (R&D)

[¶740.05] *Overview*

Canada provides generous tax treatment for expenditures made by businesses for scientific research and experimental development (R&D) carried on in Canada. The R&D may be carried on directly by the taxpayer for use in its business, or may be commissioned and paid for by the taxpayer but carried out in Canada by others provided the results (if successful) will be used by the taxpayer in its business.

The tax benefits have two components:

(1) *Tax deductions:* R&D expenditures are allocated to a notional account or "pool" called the R&D pool. This pool may be deducted in any amount in any year. This has two advantages. For current expenditures, which could be deducted in any event, deduction may be deferred indefinitely for businesses in a loss position. For capital expenditures which would otherwise have to be deducted over time under the rules in Chapter 8, they could be deducted in full, but only for capital expenditures before 2014. See also ¶740.40 below.

(2) *Tax credits:* R&D expenses eligible for the R&D expenditure pool are also eligible for investment tax credits (¶1463). For individuals in business, the investment tax credit rate is 15%. For incorporated small businesses the rate is 35%, so that businesses substantially engaged in R&D may benefit from incorporation (see ¶2501). Where the 15% rate for individuals applies, to take that example, it means that in addition to the deductions which may be claimed from the pool under (1), above, 15% of additions to the pool are treated as reductions to tax paid. For taxation years beginning before 2014, the credit was 20%. See ¶1463. As well, 40% of the tax credit earned in a particular year, if it exceeds tax payable, is refundable to the taxpayer.

[¶740.10] *Definition of Scientific Research*

The term "scientific research and experimental development" (SR&ED), which is the formal name for the type of research and development (R&D) expenditures eligible for the treatment described here, is defined to mean a systematic investigation or search carried out in a field of science or technology by means of experiment or analysis. The following types of research will qualify:

(1) basic research, namely, work undertaken for the advancement of scientific knowledge without a specific practical application in view;

(2) applied research, namely, work undertaken for the advancement of scientific knowledge with a specific practical application in view;

(3) experimental development, namely, work undertaken for the purpose of achieving technological advancement for the purposes of creating new, or improving existing materials, devices, products or processes, including incremental improvements thereto; and

(4) work undertaken by or on behalf of the taxpayer with respect to engineering, design, operations research, mathematical analysis, computer programming, data collection, testing and psychological research, where that work is commensurate with the needs, and directly in support, of the work described (1), (2), and (3), above, that is undertaken in Canada by or on behalf of the taxpayer. For expenditures incurred after February 22, 2005, Canada for this purpose includes the exclusive economic zone of Canada as defined in the federal *Oceans Act*, as well as the airspace above and the seabed or subsoil below that zone.

Changes to (4), above, were enacted in 1998 effective for work performed after February 27, 1995, except work performed by a non-profit R&D corporation pursuant to a pre-February 27, 1995 written agreement. The changes emphasize that the work described there is limited to work undertaken by or on behalf of the taxpayer in support of work in (1), (2), or (3) that is undertaken *in Canada* by or on behalf of the taxpayer. However, expenditures which meet the definition of qualified expenditures on scientific research were always limited to research carried on in Canada. It has been held (in *Tigney v. The Queen*, 2000 DTC 6112 (F.C.A.), reversing 97 DTC 414 (T.C.C.), and *LGL Limited v. The Queen*, 2000 DTC 6108 (F.C.A.)) that where a scientific research project was carried on partly within and partly outside Canada, only the expenditures in Canada could qualify.

The term "scientific research" does not include:

- Market research;
- Sales promotion;
- Quality control or routine testing of materials, devices or products;
- Research in social sciences or the humanities;
- Prospecting, exploring or drilling for or producing minerals, petroleum or natural gas;
- Commercial production of a new or improved material, device or product or the commercial use of a new or improved process;
- Style changes; or
- Routine data collection.

The term "scientific research" was changed to "scientific research and experimental development" several years ago. In changing the name, the government said that the change recognized that the bulk of industrial R&D is concentrated on the experimental development of new products or processes rather than pure or applied research and that the phrase "experimental development", which is consistent with international usage, confirms that R&D does not include projects involving only routine engineering or routine development. Similar minor changes were intended to emphasize that development work must be experimental in nature and routine development (whatever that may be) does not qualify. It is fair to say (as the government has) that the terminology changes did not in and of themselves change existing policies.

Businesses claiming the special treatment accorded to scientific research *must* file form T661, which requires extensive information and therefore elaborate record keeping on a project-by-project basis. The CRA's *Guide to Form T661* (T4088) is essential to correct completion of the form.

The CRA has also published several Information Circulars, "Guidelines" and "Application Policies" explicating its views on specific elements of R&D tax credits (e.g., effect of provincial tax credits) and on the application of R&D tax credit rules in specialized areas (e.g., clinical research). These should be available from the CRA website area devoted to SR&ED (look under Tax Credits, Business). Readers with access to the Wolters Kluwer electronic database including the Canadian Tax Reports should be able to find a list by opening the Commentary database, the Table of Contents, the heading CRA Publications therein, and then the subheading Scientific Research and Experimental Development, and the various subheadings under that. Note in particular Application Policy SR&ED 2004-02R4, Filing Requirements for Claiming SR&ED Carried Out in Canada.

(ITA: 12(1)(*t*); 37; ITR: 2900 Interpretation; IC 86-4R3 Scientific Research and Experimental Development; IT-151R5 (Consolidated) [Archived])

[¶740.15] *Filing and Time Limit for Claims*

Only the use of form T661 can entitle you to claim either deductions from income (the "R&D pool" claims discussed below) or investment tax credit under the special rules for scientific research claims (¶1463). Moreover, form T661 must be filed on or before the day that is 12 months after the filing-due date (¶218) for the ordinary T1 return for the taxation year that includes the end of the fiscal period in which the R&D expense is incurred (regardless of whether any tax is due for the year). That is to say, for individuals, form T661 must normally be filed by June 15 of the second year following the incurring of an R&D expense. Where investment tax credits are also to be claimed on the same R&D expenditures, as is almost invariably the case, form T2038 is required as well by the same deadline. It would seem acceptable to file a T661 (and T2038) separately from (and either in advance of or after) a T1 return, but the T661 must be complete in every respect, and the T2038 complete with respect to scientific research credits.

> **Commentary on Legislative Proposals (Sept. 16, 2016)**
>
> Note: When Legislative Proposals, September 16, 2016, achieves Royal Assent, the commentary will be modified to read:
>
> Commencing on or after Royal Assent of the legislative proposals of September 16, 2016, the prescribed form T661 is required to contain claim preparer information as provided under subsection 162(5.3).

The deadline has also been modified to require identification on form T661 for a particular year of expenditures incurred in the year but not deductible for the year under the "Unpaid Salary, Wages, Bonuses, etc." rules at ¶746. That is, unpaid remuneration of Year 1 must be identified on a timely T661 for Year 1 even though it is not deductible in Year 1. The intention is that it will then be added to the scientific research expenditure pool (and eligible for investment tax credit) in the year it becomes deductible under the Unpaid Salary rules (i.e., when actually paid).

Expenditures for which no timely form T661 claim is filed are automatically classified in accordance with the general scheme of the *Income Tax Act*; that is, an ordinary claim for deduction or capital cost allowance cannot be denied on the ground that a particular expenditure was actually an R&D expenditure for which no valid T661 claim was filed. This replaces a rule (more favourable in some circumstances) that misclassified expenditures could be included in R&D by the CRA on audit.

Subsection 220(2.1) of the Act generally allows the CRA to waive a person's requirement to file a prescribed form, receipt, or other document, but the person must provide the document at the Minister's request. Subsection 220(2.2) provides that this discretion does not apply to a form T661 (or the investment tax credit form T2038) that is filed after the 12-month period described above. As the explanatory notes to the new provision explain, the "effect of new subsection 220(2.2) is that a person cannot deduct a scientific research and experimental development (SR&ED) expenditure under section 37 of the Act, or claim an investment tax credit in respect of an expenditure, if the person takes more than the additional 12 months allowed to make a claim with the Minister".

In a News Release dated February 4, 2010, the CRA announced that it will continue to accept claims with Part 2s of form T661 for only the 20 largest SR&ED projects, in dollar value, until further notice. Thus, if a taxpayer has more than 20 projects, one form is to be submitted for each of the 20 largest projects in dollar value. However, the CRA also reminded claimants of the importance of maintaining complete Part 2s of form T661 for all projects claimed, and not only for the 20 largest projects. "Upon request, claimants should be prepared to submit to the CRA a complete Part 2 of Form T661 for any, or all, of the projects claimed. Failure to provide this information will result in the disallowance of the expenditures claimed for the project as SR&ED expenditures." The CRA has updated the Application Policy SR&ED 2004-02R5, *Filing Requirements for Claiming SR&ED*, accordingly.

Owing to changes to the SR&ED program announced in the March 2012 federal Budget, the CRA revised form T661 to accommodate the legislative changes that come into effect starting January 1, 2013. The CRA has made further revisions, and the most current form can be found on its website (Forms and Publications / T661–Scientific Research and Experimental Development (SR&ED) Expenditures Claim).

In the 2013 federal Budget, the Department of Finance announced that more detailed information will be required on SR&ED program claim forms (Part 9 of T661) regarding tax preparers and billing arrangements: "In particular, in instances where one or more third parties have assisted with the preparation of a claim, the Business Number of each third party will be required, along with details about the billing arrangements including whether contingency fees were used and the amount of the fees payable. In instances where no third party was involved, the claimant will be required to certify that no third party assisted in any aspect of the preparation of the SR&ED program claim. This information will facilitate the identification of SR&ED program claims with a higher risk of non-compliance." There is a new penalty of $1,000 in respect of each SR&ED program claim for which the information regarding SR&ED program tax preparers and billing arrangements is missing, incomplete, or inaccurate. These measures apply to SR&ED program claims filed on or after January 1, 2014.

(ITA: 37(1), (11), (12); 127(9) "investment tax credit" (*m*); 220(2.1), [(2.2)])

[¶740.20] *Basic Rules*

If you are carrying on business in Canada and make any expenditures on scientific research in the year, you may deduct scientific research expenditures of a current nature incurred either in or outside of Canada and scientific research expenditures of a capital nature (except for the acquisition of land) incurred in Canada.

For scientific research carried on in Canada (which, for R&D expenditures incurred after February 22, 2005, includes the exclusive economic zone of Canada as defined in the federal *Oceans Act*, as well as the airspace above and the seabed or subsoil below that zone, the deduction is computed as the aggregate of:

(1) all expenditures of a non-capital nature incurred for R&D carried on in Canada from 1974 to the end of the current year;

(2) for expenditures made prior to 2014, the lesser of:

(a) all expenditures of a capital nature made for R&D carried on in Canada from 1959 to the end of the current year, and

(b) the undepreciated capital cost of the property so acquired at the end of the current year (the assumption here is that the property has been cumulated in a notional capital cost allowance class with a 100% write-off rate; in computing the balance (undepreciated capital cost) in the class at any time, undepreciated capital cost adjustments must be made as described at ¶811, especially investment tax credit adjustments as described at ¶827 and disposal proceeds as described at ¶839).

(c) As discussed at ¶740.05, for SR&ED capital expenditures made after 2013, a deduction is no longer allowed, such that the amounts in paragraph (1) and (2) above are not allowed.

(3) repayments in taxation years ending after 1973 of all government or non-government assistance of amounts described in (6), below;

(4) all amounts added to tax in preceding years as recapture of investment tax credit previously claimed on scientific research expenditures; such recaptures occur when property on which R&D investment tax credit has been claimed is sold or converted to commercial use; see ¶1463; and any previous income inclusions required by this research expenditure pool becoming negative.

LESS

(5) all amounts of government or non-government assistance in respect of inclusions in (1) or (2), above, that, at the time the return is filed, the taxpayer has received, is entitled to receive, or can reasonably be expected to receive;

(6) investment tax credit claims deducted or refunded in a preceding year in respect of then current scientific research expenditures and "proxy amounts" claimed under the elective rules discussed below; compare also ¶728 and ¶1463;

(7) for taxation years commencing after 1995, investment tax credit (ITC) claims deducted or refunded in a preceding year in respect of current scientific research expenditures attributable to investment tax credits transferred to the taxpayer from a non-arm's length corporation (the performer) which has been paid by the taxpayer to do the R&D; the payments themselves will have been deductible to the payer under the indirect payment rules above, but the associated investment tax credits would be those of the performer but for this transfer mechanism;

(8) previous years' scientific research expenditure deductions not accounted for by reduced balances in the notional 100% capital cost allowance class for depreciable capital property as described in (2)(b), above; and

(9) a reserve claimed for each preceding year to offset income arising from debt forgiveness under the rules at ¶565 to the extent that the taxpayer did not deduct allowable scientific research pool amounts for that year.

It will be observed that the above computation amounts to a pool of all scientific research expenditures, subject to cost base adjustments. The whole or any portion of the pool may be deducted in any year in which a business is carried on. In effect, there is an optional 100% deduction for all current and capital expenditures on scientific research, and any unclaimed amount may be carried forward to any subsequent taxation year.

Where a taxpayer sells experimental production, the CRA at one time took the position in former Interpretation Bulletin IT-151R3 that the proceeds should reduce the R&D pool rather than be treated as revenue. This treatment reduced both the R&D deduction pool and the available R&D investment tax credits, although at that time investment tax credits once claimed were not recaptured except for related assistance. The statutory authority for treating these amounts as other than revenue was dubious, and some tax practitioners were apparently successful in resisting the CRA's position; see the 1989 *Canadian Tax Foundation Journal*, No. 2, p. 320-21. In Interpretation Bulletin IT-151R4, this position was withdrawn, and the CRA explained at the end of the Bulletin how the position evolved and why it was cancelled.

(ITA: 37(1)–(1.3); IT-151R5 (Consolidated) [Archived])

[¶740.21] *Expenditures Outside Canada*

For scientific research carried on outside Canada, there is no pooling concept and no special deduction for capital expenditures. The taxpayer is allowed to deduct current-year expenditures for R&D directly undertaken by, or on behalf of, the taxpayer and related to its business, and for current year payments to an approved association, university, college, research institute, or similar organization for scientific research carried on outside Canada, related to the business of the taxpayer, and the results of which the taxpayer is entitled to exploit. Approved organizations are discussed under the subheading "Indirect Eligible Current Expenditures", below.

An exception to the general rule that R&D expenditures outside Canada do not go into the R&D pool (or become eligible for investment tax credit) has been carved out for limited salary or wages incurred by the taxpayer in respect of Canadian-resident employees carrying on R&D activities outside Canada. The activities outside Canada must be directly undertaken by the taxpayer, must be related to a business of the taxpayer, and must be done solely in support of R&D carried on by the taxpayer in Canada.

Where the taxpayer incurs salary or wage costs in respect of foreign activities which meet the above tests, and so can be included in the R&D pool (and become eligible for investment tax credit), there is a further limitation that the amount to be included in the pool may not exceed 10% of the total salary and wages directly attributable to R&D carried on in Canada by the taxpayer during the year.

Permissible salary or wages will not include remuneration based on profits or bonus. In addition, permissible salary or wages do not include salary or wages unless the payer taxpayer (the employer) "reasonably believes" the salary or wages are not subject to an income or profits tax imposed by a foreign country because of the employee's presence or activities in that country.

The exception applies only to salary or wages incurred by a taxpayer in respect of R&D carried on outside Canada on or after February 26, 2008. For the first taxation year ending on or after February 26, 2008, the 10% limit must be prorated based on the number of days that are in that taxation year that are after February 25, 2008, over days in the taxation year.

Example

A Canadian employer, A, sends his employee, B, to a foreign country for the month of December to test a prototype of A's new R&D project under the conditions in that country, which do not occur in Canada. A employs 10 employees at an annual salary of $96,000 ($8,000 per month) each, for a total annual expenditure on R&D salary and wages of $960,000. Of this, only the $8,000 was spent outside Canada. The amount which can be included in the R&D pool as deemed Canadian expenditure is the lesser of (a) the $8,000 actually paid for foreign activity, and (b) 10% of ($960,000 - $8,000) = $95,200.

Note that if the year is 2008, and A is a calendar year business, the $95,200 in (b) would be prorated by days in the taxation year after February 25, 2008 (310) over days in the taxation year (366, 2008 being a leap year), so $95,200 × 310/366 = $80,633. Note also that, for 2008, salary and wages paid before February 25, 2008 for R&D activities outside Canada would reduce the $960,000 but would not be eligible for treatment as R&D in Canada.

(ITA: 37(1.4)–(2), (9)(*b*))

[¶740.22] *Expenditure for Interest in Taxpayer*

In *Alcatel Canada Inc. v. The Queen*, 2005 DTC 387 (T.C.C.), the Tax Court ruled that a stock option benefit granted the employees of an R&D corporation constituted an R&D expenditure eligible for deduction and investment tax credit, even though the corporation had not actually laid out any expenditure in granting the options. On November 17, 2005, the Department of Finance responded with draft legislation to reverse that decision. That legislation, in somewhat revised form, was passed into law on June 26, 2013 (section 143.3). Although the matter is largely a corporate one, the new legislation sweeps in partnerships or any taxpayer who contrives to issue an option or interest in itself. Effective on or after November 17, 2005, the expense of such an option or interest is limited to the amount (if any) actually expended by the taxpayer. Such at least is the stated intention of the legislation.

(ITA: 143.3)

[¶740.25] *Direct Eligible Current Expenditures*

Current scientific research expenditures incurred in Canada are deductible in the year they are incurred, or in any subsequent year, provided the taxpayer carried on business in Canada in, and filed a timely form T661 for the year the expenditure was incurred.

The main category of expenditures which qualify as eligible current scientific research expenditures includes amounts expended on scientific research carried on in Canada, directly undertaken by or on behalf of the taxpayer, and related to a business of the taxpayer.

This very broad inclusion is modified by regulations restricting eligible expenses to those which are all, or substantially all (generally 90%), attributable to scientific research, or those permitted by regulation. The regulations in turn permit apportionment of salaries and wages between scientific research and other functions for employees who directly undertake, supervise or support the scientific research. Maintenance expenditures may also be apportioned. Some variation of the rules occurs when the election to use modified rules is made. This is described under a separate heading below.

Generally speaking, the current expenses described here are likely to be deductible in the year incurred in any event as ordinary business expenses. The prepaid expense rules at ¶753 seem also to apply to scientific research expenditures, so that no acceleration of the expense is possible by classifying it as scientific research. The advantages of including already deductible expenses in the eligible pool of expenditures are essentially (i) that they may then qualify for extremely favourable investment tax credits (¶1463), and (ii) that deduction may be deferred indefinitely at the option of the taxpayer, thus preserving loss carryforward positions. To the extent they are included in the R&D pool on form T661, current expenditures may not also be deducted in financial statement income (although, oddly, the CRA never says this in its guide). Items which have been expensed on the books and then included on form T661 and claimed again as a deduction from book income must be added back to book income to avoid double deduction.

Rental expenses in respect of a building, whether for the taxpayer itself or for the organizations described below, no longer qualify as scientific research expenditures. Exceptions may be made for prescribed special purpose buildings, which at present include only buildings designed and constructed to have a working area that has an exceptional ambient air cleanliness and an extraordinary degree of rigidity, meeting specifications in these respects set out in technical terms in Regulation 2903. Note that the restriction applies only to a "building" and not to a "structure". The CRA addresses this distinction, albeit superficially, in Interpretation Bulletin IT-79R3.

Remuneration of specified employees in excess of five times maximum pensionable earnings (MPE) under the Canada Pension Plan for the calendar year in which the taxation year ends will no longer be eligible R&D expenditures. Specified employees (non-arm's length (¶812) employees and employees of a company who are also 10% or more shareholders or their relatives) are already subject to restriction that any part of their remuneration based on bonus or profits is not an eligible R&D expenditure.

(ITA: 18(9)(*e*); 37(1), (8)–(9.1); IT-151R5 (Consolidated) [Archived])

[¶740.30] *Election to Use Modified Basic Rules re Overheads*

Businesses engaged in scientific research and experimental development in Canada can elect to use an optional treatment for scientific research expenditures and tax credits. These rules in effect permit a trade-off at the election of the taxpayer, requiring some capital expenditures of an administrative nature to be depreciated as ordinary expenses and denied investment tax credit, and treating all current administrative expenses as ordinary expenses, but allowing investment tax credits on most salaries allocated to R&D to be increased by a flat percentage to allow for administrative overhead. However, as noted below, the effect of the election has changed significantly, generally for capital expenditures made after 2013.

The election must be made annually in Part 1 of form T661 for the year. Once made with the first T661 filed for a year, the election appears to be irrevocable. The election may be beneficial to any scientific research enterprise in certain circumstances. However, it does seem aimed primarily at smaller companies with mixture of R&D and other endeavours, since these have the most difficulty qualifying a portion of administrative expenses for R&D under the general rules.

Previously, if the election was made, expenditures which could be allocated more than 90% to R&D would continue to receive full R&D treatment, with the exception of capital expenditures for general purpose office equipment or furniture, which must be depreciated in, typically, Class 8. It was intended that computers will not "necessarily" be considered office equipment. However, owing to changes introduced in the 2012 federal Budget, for expenditures made after 2013, this rule no longer applies, such that the expenditures described in this paragraph no longer qualify for R&D treatment.

Additionally, one-half of *current* expenditures for premises, facilities or equipment used primarily (more than 50% up to 90%) for scientific research (other than general office equipment) could previously receive full R&D treatment (thus 50% of normal R&D tax credit). As above, for expenditures made after 2013, this rule no longer applies, such that the expenditures described in this paragraph will not qualify for R&D treatment.

If the election is made, ordinary current expenditures which are not 90% attributable to R&D (such as office supplies, heat, electricity, telephones, management not directly involved in R&D, support staff, maintenance, etc.) are not included in the R&D pool, although they may be deducted as ordinary current expenditures. Accordingly, they are not entitled to deferred deduction or investment tax credit. The offset is that 155% of salaries directly attributable to R&D will be eligible for investment tax credits. It would seem that 100% of salaries goes into the R&D expenditure pool; the additional 55% is known as the "proxy amount" and is added directly to the amount eligible for investment tax credit. The 55% proxy amount does not, however, go into the expenditure pool eligible for deduction; it is purely an investment tax credit amount. Note that the 2012 federal Budget reduced the proxy amount to 55% from the previous 60% for 2013 and 65% before that time.

Tax credits generated on the 55% proxy amount, however, do reduce the R&D expenditure pool along with credits based on the pool. Eligible salaries or wages include those of persons engaged directly in R&D and portions of salaries which can reasonably be assigned to R&D based on time spent (including management time). However, fringe benefits and bonuses are not eligible for the 55% gross-up. Where the employee is a specified employee (that is, an employee who does not deal at arm's length (¶812) with the employer, or in the case of a corporate employer is or is related to someone who has a 10% or more interest in the business), only 75% of each such employee's salary can be included in eligible salary to a maximum for each such employee of 250% of maximum pensionable earnings for Canada Pension Plan purposes.

The proxy amount cannot exceed the total of deductions from gross revenue to arrive at net income claimed under general principles of income computation. The deductions against which the proxy amount is measured include only those made on general principles, and not specially sanctioned deductions such as capital cost allowance, interest, eligible capital expenditures, deductions based on the R&D pool, and a number of less common deductions. The intent of this limitation is that the proxy amount should not be greater than actual current overhead expenditures. Deductions from gross income to arrive at net income reduced by the special amounts specified is taken as a very rough justice measure of overhead administrative expenses.

(ITA: 37(8)(*a*)(ii)(B), (9), (10); ITR: 2900(4) [Calculation of prescribed proxy amount])

[¶740.35] *Indirect Eligible Current Expenditures*

The following expenditures also qualify as current expenditures eligible for the R&D pool:

(1) payments made to a corporation resident in Canada to be used for scientific research carried on in Canada that is related to a business of the taxpayer, but only where the taxpayer is entitled to exploit the results of that scientific research; the substitution of this rule for the virtually identical pre-1996 rule for corporations in (2), below, seems to be a function of extending exemption from the prepaid expense rules to payments described in (2), (3), and (4) while ensuring the exemption is not extended to payments to ordinary corporations described here;

(2) payments to an approved association, university, college, research institute, or similar organization or to a corporation resident in Canada, for scientific research carried on in Canada, related to the business of the taxpayer, and the results of which the taxpayer is entitled to exploit; the CRA considers all Canadian universities and affiliated colleges to be approved;

(3) payments to a corporation resident in Canada and exempt from tax as a not-for-profit organization for scientific research carried on in Canada, related to the business of the taxpayer, and the results of which the taxpayer is entitled to exploit; and

(4) payments made to an approved organization that makes payments to an association, institution or corporation described in (2) or (3), above (other than a resident profit-making corporation) to be used for scientific research carried on in Canada, related to the business of the taxpayer, and the results of which the taxpayer is entitled to exploit.

There is a specific exception to the prepaid expense rules in ¶753 for payments for all the indirect expenditures described in (2) to (4).

An "approved" association, organization, etc., is one approved by the Minister of National Revenue. Somewhat oddly, the approved status of an organization is regarded as confidential as between the CRA and the organization, so the taxpayer who makes payments to such an organization must in principle rely on its authoritative representations as to CRA approvals. The CRA provides a current list of approved entities in Appendix A to its website publication "Third-Party Payments Policy", found on the CRA website under "SR&ED / SR&ED Program policies / Third-Party Payments Policy".

The "approved organization" rules in (4), above, were added to foster joint private sector/academic research administered through organizations such as the Natural Sciences and

Research Council, the Medical Research Council, and the Social Sciences and Humanities Research Council. Corporations, but not individuals, may also be able to deduct contributions to "pre-competitive R&D consortia".

(ITA: 18(9); 37(1))

[¶740.40] *Historical Information: Capital Expenditures Previously Eligible for R&D Pool (Before 2014)*

In its 2012 federal Budget, the Department of Finance introduced changes to the SR&ED rules, one of which provides that capital expenditures made after 2013 no longer qualify for the SR&ED deduction or investment tax credit. Furthermore, the SR&ED treatment will no longer apply to expenditures (e.g., contract payments) made to another party to the extent that the other party's related expenditures are capital. Therefore, the commentary in this section is relevant only for expenditures made before 2014. After 2013, capital expenditures will only be deductible under other provisions of the Act, for example, under the capital cost allowance provisions.

Qualifying capital expenditures incurred to acquire property to be used in scientific research (except for land), may be deducted in full in the year incurred. Any amount not deducted in the current year may be carried forward to any subsequent year. Only expenditures for capital property which would otherwise be given depreciable property treatment qualify for this special scientific research treatment; land and leasehold interests in land cannot qualify.

The available-for-use rules described in detail at ¶804b may delay both the deduction of these expenditures and the related investment tax credit claims.

The capital expenditures which qualify are further limited to those incurred for the provision of premises, facilities or equipment where at the time of expenditure it was intended that the item would be used during all or substantially all (generally meaning 90%) of its operating time in its useful line in the prosecution of scientific research in Canada, or that all or substantially all of its value would be consumed in such prosecution. The 90% rule created many problems, and has been substantially revised to accommodate "mixed-use property".

Capital property acquired after December 2, 1992, for mixed use (i.e., for R&D use in the 50% to 90% range and for other uses, such as manufacturing, for the balance) will receive 25% of full investment tax credit in each of the two taxation years ending after the property has been in use for 12 and 24 months, provided the property is used at least 51% for R&D purposes in each of two periods. The first period commences with the time the property is put into use and ends with the end of the first taxation year ending at least 12 months after that time. The second period commences at the same time as the first (when the property is put in use) and ends with the end of the second taxation year ending at least 12 months after that time. Property which qualifies for the first period will receive the 25% of normal credit for that period regardless of whether it qualifies for the second period. However, property will not qualify for the second period unless it qualifies for the first. The logic of all this is to provide as broad a test period as possible. Property acquired for an ultimate commercial use will not qualify. It would seem that property which qualified for investment tax credit under this rule is not included in the R&D expenditure pool for expense purposes, and therefore is depreciated in ordinary CCA classes. It would seem to follow that investment tax credits generated under these rules would track to the class of the related assets rather than the R&D pool when computing reductions to capital cost based on investment tax credit.

Expenditures for the acquisition of a building ceased to qualify as scientific research expenditures where made after December 15, 1987, except by commitments in place at that time under the transitional rules described below. As discussed above, a structure which is not a building is not affected by this rule. Prescribed special purpose buildings described above can also qualify for scientific research treatment. Since the disallowance refers explicitly to "the acquisition of a building", one might think that expenses for additions to an existing building would not be disallowed. However, the CRA takes the contrary view, and apparently intends to assess on the basis that anything which might ordinarily be capitalized in building accounts will be denied scientific research treatment. Although there is some case law basis for their view, the matter is not beyond dispute, given the definitions elsewhere in the statute and regulations that specifically include renovations, alterations, and fixtures where these inclusions are intended. Buildings disallowed would receive ordinary depreciable property and investment tax credit treatment. The transitional rules for buildings deny expenditures effective for expenditures made after December 15, 1987 other than expenditures made after that date and before 1989 pursuant to (i) a prior written agreement, (ii) a prospectus or other offering document filed with a public authority by that date, or (iii) the terms of a detailed offering memorandum distributed by that date as part of an offering of securities, provided solicitations for sales occurred by the date and the securities sales were made as projected.

Each property included in the scientific research expenditure pool will be deemed to be a property of a separate prescribed class under the capital cost allowance regulations for purposes of the recapture rules. The result is that disposition of any particular property can give rise to recapture of the amount deducted in respect of that property (typically 100%, although the full expenditure pool may not have been deducted). See ¶843 and ¶869. Any adjustments required to capital cost under the rules at ¶811 *et seq.* must be made in computing potential recapture. Typically, federal investment tax credit related to the capital asset will be deducted from tax but added to income in the year following the year an R&D claim is made for the asset, and the credit deducted from tax will reduce cost for recapture purposes at that time. Note that the recapture arises under the general rules outlined at ¶843, and not by virtue of a reduction to the scientific research expenditure pool.

[¶740.45] *Impact of Investment Tax Credits*

Expenditures on scientific research, both capital and current expenditures, qualify for the investment tax credit as more fully discussed in ¶1463. Investment tax credits reduce the cost base of the acquisitions or expenditures to which they apply, although the reduction occurs only in the taxation year following the year in which the credits are claimed (¶827), and to the extent no cost base is available the credit must be included in income. Depreciable property covered by these rules is effectively treated (and usually reported) as a special capital cost allowance class with a 100% rate, subject to recapture on disposition (see Chapter 8). Although depreciable property used to be reported on the CCA schedule T2132, it is now accounted for on form T661 with scientific research expenditures generally. See also ¶729 regarding inducements.

(ITA: 12(1)(*t*); 37; ITR: 2900 Interpretation; IC 86-4R3 Scientific Research and Experimental Development; IT-151R5 (Consolidated) [Archived])

[¶741] SALARY, WAGES, AND BENEFITS

All amounts you pay to or on behalf of employees as salary, wages or benefits are deductible. There is an overriding rule that amounts must be reasonable, but where you are dealing with the employee at arm's length (¶812) the amount is usually presumed to be reasonable.

You may also deduct any premiums you pay on behalf of an employee for a sickness, accident, disability, or income insurance plan. Note however that contributing to a disability plan for the employee is not always to the employee's advantage; in many cases it will be preferable to have an employee-pay-all plan (see ¶328).

While you can deduct premiums paid for employees under the Ontario Employer Health Tax, it appears that you cannot deduct the premiums you must pay on account of your own personal business earnings (or could not when the EHT applied to self-employment income).

See also ¶797 and ¶798.

(ITA: 18(1)(*a*); *Business and Professional Income guide* (T4002))

[¶741.05] *Salary or Wages Paid to Spouse or Child*

If you are a proprietor of a business and you employ your spouse or child in the business, you are entitled to deduct the amounts paid as a business expense provided the services of your spouse or child are necessary to the business and are commensurate with the salary. Your spouse or child will be required to report the salary as income, which may affect the personal amount credits you can claim (see Chapter 11). If you make salary payments to your spouse, you must withhold tax, Canada Pension Plan contributions and Employment Insurance premiums as for other employees. This is also true for your children, provided they fall within the age and work limits which make such withholdings mandatory. You will also be required to prepare a T4 for your spouse or child by February 28 of the following year. Forms and employer registration numbers should be obtained from your Tax Services Office (¶287).

Note that CPP is withheld on payments deductible for income tax purposes, i.e., those considered reasonable for the work done. EI is not withheld on non-arm's length payments unless the payment arrangements are similar to what they would be in an arm's length contract. It is not clear how the EI standard differs in practice from the CPP standard. Perhaps the EI rule anticipates periodic payments of set amounts based on time or work done, while the income tax/CPP standard is only concerned with the reasonableness of the amount paid in relation to the work, and not the systematic payment (although unpaid amounts are subject to the rules in ¶746). Where payments are made to your child, the income tax rule would be the same (withhold on amounts you can deduct as reasonable), the CPP rule appears to be that you must withhold from cash remuneration regardless, and the EI rule is the same non-arm's length rule as for a spouse. As a practical matter, only the CRA can rule on the proper withholding on a particular set of facts. The withholding rules are summarized in CRA's *Employers' Guide — Payroll Deductions and Remittances* (T4001).

See also ¶746.

(ITA: 5; 18; *Employers' Guide — Payroll Deductions and Remittances* (T4001); *Employers' Guide — Filing the T4 Slip and Summary* (RC4210))

[¶741.10] *Unpaid Remuneration*

Remuneration which remains unpaid 180 days after year end is not deductible until paid, as discussed in detail at ¶746.

[¶741.15] *Group Term Life Insurance*

The general prepaid expenses rules at ¶753 (limiting deduction of prepaid expenses to the period to which they relate) will not apply to insurance premiums on group term life insurance where all or part of the premium is for insurance that is (or would be if the insured survived) in respect of a period that ends more than 13 months after the consideration is paid. Accordingly, the deduction for pre-paid premiums on a group life insurance policy do not have to be spread out over the term of the insurance, but can be deducted in the year paid. Where this exclusion does not apply, the normal limitation rules at ¶753 for prepaid expenses will apply to life insurance premiums.

Rules were also introduced to more or less match employer deductibility to employee taxability. Where premiums are paid on an annual basis in any event, employer deductibility is not a problem. However, it is apparently not uncommon for group term life insurance to be paid as an initial lump-sum amount. Explicit rules now deal with payments made under a group term life insurance policy for insurance on the life of an individual where the insurance is for the remainder of the lifetime of the individual and no further premiums are payable for the insurance. Such premiums paid by the employer are in most cases wholly deductible in the year incurred under the general rule above. This essentially matches the treatment to be given to the employee, for whom the premiums are fully taxable as paid.

Premiums are typically not deductible by the beneficiary of a life insurance policy, with limited exceptions; see ¶764.

(ITA: 18(9)(*a*)(iii), (9.01))

[¶741.20] *Demutualization Benefits*

As discussed at ¶420 and ¶537d, the Act permits mutual life insurance companies to convert to stock companies. In general, these conversion occurred in 1999. Essentially, policyholders give up rights in exchange for shares of the insurer (or a holding company) and/or other benefits. The shares received are capital assets received on a tax-free rollover basis with a cost to the policyholder of nil. Other benefits are treated as taxable dividends from a Canadian corporation.

Where an employer holds a policy for the benefit of employees, the rules contemplate that the employer can flow out the benefits received to the individuals, who in turn receives them under these rules as exchanged shares or dividends as the case may be (and not as employment income). Although this rule contemplates employer/employee situations, it is broad enough to cover any situation in which a policyholder transfers demutualization receipts to an individual who has rights or benefits under the policy and had borne part of the cost of the policy. Where a taxable conversion benefit is flowed on to the employee, it is in effect considered received by the employee and not the employer. If the benefit flowed out is a share rather than a taxable conversion benefit, the value of the amount flowed out is added to the otherwise nil ACB of the employer; the result should be no gain or loss on the transfer, with the employee receiving a share with a nil cost base.

Where the policyholder is an employer holding a group employee-paid policy on behalf of employees, which typically provides disability or other benefits which are tax free to the employee so long as the employer has not contributed to premiums, the demutualization rules contemplate that the employer can apply demutualization benefits it receives toward benefit enhancements under such policies without tainting the policy, so that benefits remain tax free. See ¶328.15.

(ITA: 139.1(4), (15)–(17); Other Publications: Department of Finance Technical Notes of December 7, 1999)

[¶741.25] *Private Health Insurance Premiums*

If as an individual you operate a business, you cannot be an employee of that business. Prior to 1998, it followed that you could not deduct from business income private health insurance premiums for yourself or your family, even if you provided such benefits to other employees. (If your spouse or other family members were *bona fide* employees, you could pay benefits on their behalf as with other employees.) The government has decided that this is inequitable, as compared to incorporated businesses, and is now prepared to permit such deductions in limited circumstances. Note that private health insurance premiums you do not deduct are eligible for medical expense tax credit (¶1245), but this may be much less beneficial than a deduction from income (as discussed at ¶2539).

Amounts which become payable as premiums (or otherwise) under a private health insurance plan (called by the government a "private health services plan", PHSP) for yourself, your spouse, or any member of your household may be deducted from the income of your business provided you are actively engaged in the business on a regular and continuous basis either directly or as a member of a partnership. There are, however, numerous conditions and qualifications.

First, the deduction is only available if, for the current taxation year or the preceding year, either (i) your income from the business exceeds 50% of your total income for the year, or (ii) your other income does not exceed $10,000. Your income from the business for this determination is determined before this deduction and before any deductions discussed in Chapter 10.

Second, the amount to be deducted must be payable under a contract between you and:

- a person licensed or authorized by the federal or a provincial government to carry on an insurance or trustee business;
- a person or partnership in the business of offering services to the public as an private health services plan (PHSP) administrator;
- a tax exempt business or professional organization of which you are a member; or
- a tax exempt trade union of which you or the majority of your employees are members.

Third, you may not claim a deduction for any amount which is deducted by another individual or which is claimed as a medical expense credit by any individual (see ¶2539).

Fourth, if an amount payable as premiums, etc., under a plan relates to a period in the year throughout which:

(1) you have one or more full-time employees (excluding seasonal and temporary employees) that have accumulated at least 3 months of service in *any* business you carry on as an individual, any partnership in which you are a majority-interest partner, or any corporation with which you are affiliated under the rules at ¶852, and

(2) the total number of *arm's length* (¶812) employees in (1) who are covered under the plan is not less than 50% of the total number of persons employed in or carrying on the business described in (1) to whom coverage is granted under the plan,

the deduction for that period is restricted to the lowest cost of equivalent coverage of an arm's length employee described in (1), above. What this seems to say is that if you have arm's length employees at all, and for some period at least 50% of your workforce (including yourself, your partners, and all arm's length and other employees) are covered by a PHSP, the amount you can deduct for your own premiums cannot exceed the lowest cost of equivalent coverage (discussed further below) for such an employee.

The next limitation is a refinement of the rule above, and applies for a period in which you do not meet all the criteria in that rule. In this case, your deduction for a such a period is limited to a dollar maximum of (on an annual basis) $1,500 for each of yourself, your spouse, and each household member over 18 at the beginning of the period, and $750 for younger household members. Where the period is less than a year, the total applicable dollar limitations are prorated by days in the period divided by 365. It would seem that if the age of a household member changes in the period, you are not permitted to end the period until the end of the taxation year. As well, if you have in this period full-time employees described in (1), above, but not arm's length employees 50% of whom are covered by a PHSP, the amount you may deduct is limited to the lowest cost of equivalent coverage for such an employee.

It would seem that if you (your partnership, etc.) have no full-time arm's length employees, this comparative aspect of the rule does not function, and you are simply limited by the dollar amounts and the first, second and third limitations above.

The cost of "equivalent coverage" of a test employee for a period is the amount that would be that employee's cost if his or her circumstances were identical to yours (i.e., spouse and dependents covered were the same), prorated by the cost payable by you or your partnership as employer. Thus, if you pay 30% of the cost of employee premiums and the employee bears the rest, you may only deduct 30% of the cost of your own premiums, subject to the limitation of cost to the cost of the employee's plan as if its circumstances were yours.

Amounts not deducted due to any of these limitations are eligible for medical expense credit calculated at ¶1235.

The CRA has a reasonably clear description of these rules in the *Business and Professional Income* guide. Perhaps there are two important rules of thumb to remember:

- First, if you are self-employed without regular employees, and your self-employment income is more than half your overall income, you may deduct private health insurance plan premiums up to $1,500 per year for each of yourself, your spouse, and members of your household 18 or older before the beginning of the year, and $750 per household member for those not yet 18 before the beginning of the year.
- Second, if you have employees in any business, or in a partnership where you are a majority partner, you probably need a good accountant anyway. In general, however, you will not be able to deduct for yourself more than you deduct for your least favoured regular full-time employee in similar circumstances.

(ITA: 20.01)

[¶741a] EMPLOYER CONTRIBUTIONS TO EMPLOYEE LIFE AND HEALTH TRUST

Premiums paid by an employer to a group sickness or accident insurance plan are generally deductible for the employer. Similarly, employer contributions to a private health insurance plan are normally deductible and, subject to the conditions discussed at ¶741.15, employer-paid premiums for group life insurance for employees are generally deductible.

On February 26, 2010, the Department of Finance announced proposals relating to the employer life and health trusts ("ELHT"), which are essentially trusts that will provide benefits from any or all of the above-noted plans for employees. The proposals to a certain extent parallel the CRA's previous administrative position regarding health and welfare trusts, as laid out in Interpretation Bulletin IT-85R2 (now archived). Draft legislation containing the proposals were released on August 27, 2010 and subsequently on September 30, 2010 as part of Bill C-47 (mainly section 144.1). Bill C-47 received Royal Assent in late 2010.

In general terms, an ELHT is a trust under which employer contributions to the trust are used to fund "designated employee benefits" for the employer's employees, their spouse or common-law partners, and related members of their households. The "designated employee benefits" are defined to mean benefits from a group sickness or accident insurance plan, a group term life insurance policy, or a private health services plan.

The new rules, which apply to trusts established after 2009, generally allow employer's contributions to the ELHT to be deductible in the year of contribution to the extent of benefits provided in those years. Basically, an employer's deduction in the year is limited to the amount of the contribution that enable the ELHT to pay premiums to a private insurance company for insurance coverage for the year or a prior year in respect of the beneficiaries, or otherwise provide group life term insurance, or designated employee benefits that are payable in the year or a prior year to the beneficiaries. Excess contributions in the year that enable the trust to provide or pay these types of benefits in a subsequent year are generally deductible in that subsequent year. Special rules apply to multi-employer ELHTs who, among other things, are required to contribute pursuant to a collective agreement and whose contributions are based on the number of hours worked by an employee or some other measure that is specific to the employee (subsection 144.1(6)).

There are various conditions required of an ELHT in order for these measures to apply. For example, the ELHT must have at least one class of beneficiaries that contains at least 25% of all of the beneficiaries of the trust who are employees of the employer, and at least 75% of the members of the class must be employees who are not "key employees". The rights under the ELHT of each key employee cannot be more advantageous than the rights of this one class of beneficiaries. In general terms, a "key employee" in a taxation year means (1) an employee who was at any time in the taxation year or in a preceding taxation year a "specified employee" of the employer (generally, an employee owning 10% or more of any class of shares in the employer, or who does not deal at arm's length with the employer), or (2) an employee whose employment income in any two of the five taxation years preceding the year exceeded five times the Year's Maximum Pensionable Earnings used for CPP purposes.

The CRA's current views on an ELTH are set out in S2-F1-C1: "Health and Welfare Trusts".

[¶742] HOME OFFICE EXPENSES

Specific restrictions are placed on deductions for the expenses of using part of your home as a place of business.

First, you may not make any claim whatever in respect of any "work space" in a "self-contained domestic establishment" in which you live unless you meet at least one of two tests:

(1) the work space is your principal place of business; or

(2) the work space is used *exclusively* for the purpose of earning income from business *and* is used on a regular and continuous basis for meeting the clients, customers or patients of your business.

A self-contained domestic establishment is merely a dwelling house, apartment or other similar place in residence in which as a general rule you eat and sleep.

Second, provided you qualify for a deduction at all under the tests above, the amount you may otherwise deduct is limited to your income from the business before claiming any deductions for work space in your home. This limitation would apply, for example, to an employee who also earns income in his spare time as, say, a freelance writer, doing this work at home. The freelancer might claim part of the home as a work space which is a principal place of business, but deductions would be limited to the amount of freelance income otherwise determined. It would not be possible to use the home expenses to reduce employment income.

Any expenses for a year which are allowable under the first rule but in excess of amounts deductible under the second may be carried forward from year to year and applied against income of the same business to the extent permitted under the two rules for a succeeding year. The expenses must be deducted at the first opportunity to the extent permitted after applying the two rules for the year.

Note that under rule (1), above, you do not have to set aside part of the house exclusively for business. Thus the freelance writer in the illustration above might use a second bedroom as both a guest room and an office. It would be a principal place of business for the writing business and therefore a claim is not prohibited by statute. The claim itself, however, would presumably have to be prorated both for square footage and time allocated to the business. For example, if the second bedroom comprised 20% of available floor space and was used as an office 60% of the time, 60% of 20% of related expenses would be deductible (or available for carryover). In this regard, Interpretation Bulletin IT-514 (now archived) specifically states that work space which qualifies under the rules in (1) can also be used for personal purposes since it need not be used exclusively in the business.

The limitations in (1) and (2), above, extend to all expenses related to the work space: rent, insurance, property taxes, mortgage interest, heat and light. Expenses such as telephone, office supplies and similar items, to the extent they are related to the business, are not considered to relate to the work space and are not subject to the restrictions in (1) and (2). That is, deductions may create a loss against other income.

Furniture and equipment used in the business is not, strictly speaking, subject to the tests in (1) and (2), above. Capital cost allowance should be available to the extent of business use.

In theory, if you own your home and set aside a separate space in it exclusively for use as an office, you can claim capital cost allowance on that proportion of the fair market value of your home at the time you so commence to use it. This is rarely desirable, however, since it is likely to impair your claim for principal residence exemption when you come to sell your house (¶553). The CRA deals with this in Income Tax Folio S1-F3-C2, sections 2.57–2.60. Essentially, if you claim capital cost allowance on the business portion of the house, or if you make structural alterations to accommodate your income-earning activities, the CRA will consider that you have a change of use (¶513) with respect to the business portion of the house, and that portion will be disqualified from principal residence treatment from the time of the change.

Quebec taxpayers should note Quebec's additional restrictions for its business taxpayers, discussed at ¶1631.

(ITA: 18(12); IT-514 [Archived]; Income Tax Folio: S1-F3-C2 Principal Residence; *Vanka v. The Queen*, 2002 DTC 3815 (T.C.C.); *Locke v. M.N.R.*, 65 DTC 223 (T.A.B.); *Heakes v. M.N.R.*, 63 DTC 667 (T.A.B.); *Merchant v. M.N.R.*, 82 DTC 1764 (T.R.B.))

[¶742.05] *Operating a Day Care Centre in Your Home*

If you operate a day care centre out of your home, it is likely to be considered a business. This will be the case where you look after a group of children and the members of the group may change over time. If you look after the children of only one family, the CRA may view this as babysitting, which they regard as "occasional employment income", although this view is arguable.

At any rate, if you do operate a day care facility as a business, you are entitled to deduct all the related expenses. For example, your expenditures for food, play supplies, field trips, etc., would be deductions. Any reimbursements for these expenses received from parents (or other sources) would be income or reduce the expense deducted (the result is the same).

Usually the most difficult calculation to make concerns expenses related to your household. Some percentage of the cost of light, heat, water, and so on should be deductible. If you own the home in which you provide day care, you should also be able to deduct something on account of taxes and insurance. If you rent, you should be able to deduct a portion of the rent (which usually includes taxes and insurance on the property). Calculating the deductible portion of these expenses is something of a challenge. If you have rooms set aside which you use only for day care, you can allocate on a square foot (or square metre) basis. That is, if your house consists of 3,000 square feet of floor space, and you regularly use 500 square feet for day care space and no other purpose, the CRA will accept an allocation of 500/3,000 × total household expenses. Many people use a room allocation regardless of size. Thus if you have a seven-room house and use two rooms for day care and no other purpose, you can deduct 2/7 × total household expenses. Although the CRA prefers the floor space allocation method, it normally accepts either result. If you provide day care in rooms you also ordinarily use for something else, e.g., the living room and dining room, or the kitchen and family room, the CRA suggests that you further prorate the expenses calculated after the space allocation by the number of hours of day care divided by 24. Thus if you offered 8 hours of day care on a normal day, you would prorate expenses calculated after the floor space allocation by 8/24.

The only legal requirement is that your allocation should be "reasonable". The CRA has indicated it will accept the above allocations as being reasonable. You may use some other method which seems reasonable to you, but you should be confident it can be explained to the CRA and makes some sense.

Note that all the technical limitations relating to deductions for a "work space" in a "self-contained domestic establishment" apply as discussed above. In general this will only be a problem if you use your home as an adjunct to another facility or if your expenses result in a loss from the day care business for the year.

If you own your home/day care facility, you might be able to claim capital cost allowance on some portion of your home. However, to do this would jeopardize the tax-free status of the capital gain you will realize when you sell your home, and it is generally not recommended. See the general comments on this situation above.

Capital cost allowance on furniture and appliances you own may be claimed, subject to proration for business use.

(Other Publications: *Using Your Home for Day Care* (CRA pamphlet P134))

[¶742.10] *Bed and Breakfast Operation*

Where you live in a bed and breakfast (B&B) home that you operate for profit, there is necessarily an allocation of deductible expenses between the commercial and personal elements of the property. By themselves, these allocations are perhaps not difficult. But the workspace-in-home provision denies the deduction of expenses against other income (although amounts so denied can be carried forward against eligible income). Thus, B&B losses (often caused by interest deductions for mortgage expenses) cannot be deducted against other income if the entire operation is viewed as a workspace in the home.

In *Sudbrack v. The Queen*, 2000 DTC 2521 (T.C.C.), the Tax Court ruled that where the taxpayer had, in effect, a separate apartment or discrete living quarters in the B&B, it was only that area that was subject to the workspace rule. In any event, the loss limitation rule did not apply to the area in which the taxpayer did not regularly live. In a technical opinion (CRA Document No. 2006-0211371E5), the CRA has said that it accepts the validity of the *Sudbrack* decision "in situations that fall within the same fact pattern". However, it repudiates the suggestion that the workspace rules simply do not apply to B&B operations.

[¶743] EXPENDITURES ON RESEARCH AND FOR BUSINESS EXPANSION

Expenditures on research and expenditures made for business expansion which are not scientific research expenditures are deductible if they are laid out to earn income from a business or property, they are not on account of capital and they are reasonable in the circumstances. Such expenditures include the cost of market research, applied research, feasibility studies and expenditures made to enhance the making of a business decision.

Expenditures made as part of your ordinary business operations to determine whether a capital asset should be created or acquired, but which by themselves are not directly linked to the creation or acquisition of a capital asset, are current operating expenses, which are deductible in the year incurred.

Where you are not presently carrying on any business and incur expenditures on research to determine whether a business should be started, such expenditures are not deductible. Where you presently carry on a business and incur expenditures on research to determine whether a new and separate business should be undertaken, these expenditures are also not deductible. In either case, if the new business is in fact commenced, the expenditures will qualify as eligible capital expenditures of that business. For treatment of eligible capital expenditures see ¶766.

(ITA: 18; IT-475 [Archived])

[¶744] EXPENSES OF LOOKING FOR A NEW BUSINESS OR BUSINESS LOCATION

Expenses incurred in investigating the suitability of a site for a building or other structure which you plan to erect and use in your business are deductible in the year the payment is made, regardless of whether the site is actually acquired. (See ¶765 for details.) In certain circumstances, the deduction of so-called soft costs is limited. For more details, see ¶771.

The expense of looking for and acquiring other types of assets will generally form part of the cost of the assets acquired. Their deductibility will be the same as for the remaining cost of acquisition of the particular assets. However, the cost of investigating the purchase of these other types of assets, which are *not* subsequently acquired, is not allowed as a deduction, but may be an "eligible capital expenditure" (see ¶766).

(ITA: 18; 20; IT-475 [Archived])

[¶745] DONATIONS

Donations made through a business normally are not deductible in computing the business income. Donations made to registered charitable organizations and registered amateur athletic organizations, certain housing corporations, Canadian municipalities, the United Nations or agencies thereof, certain universities, or charitable organizations outside Canada which the Canadian government has explicitly qualified by making its own gifts are eligible for a tax credit to the extent the amount of the gifts does not exceed 75% of your total net income. The credit is calculated on Schedule 9 of the T1 return. See Chapter 12.

Some businesses make charitable donations as a form of advertising or to attract business from the charities in the community. In these instances, you may be able to deduct the full amount of the donations as a business expense. The 75% restriction would not apply. The donations would be regarded as expenditures incurred to earn income, rather than as gifts to charities.

In a technical interpretation (CRA Document No. 2010-0388751E5, May 10, 2011), the CRA stated that the donation of property by an individual to a U.S. charity did not constitute a gift for tax purposes, because the donation was required under a distributor arrangement with a U.S. company. However, to the extent that the amount paid by the individual for the donation, as required under the terms of the distributor arrangement, was both reasonable and incurred for the purpose of gaining or producing income from a business, such amount could be deductible by the individual as a general business expense.

Certain donations made to federal or provincial political parties or candidates may be used to reduce tax payable. For discussion of the amount of political contribution tax credit available, see ¶1462 and those sections of Chapter 14 which relate to the province(s) for which you file tax returns.

Representations made directly by a business to the government on its own behalf will be covered by the rule at ¶765.20.

(ITA: 18(1)(n), 118.1; *Olympia Floor & Wall Tile (Quebec) Ltd. v. M.N.R.*, 70 DTC 6085 (Ex. Ct.); *Impenco Ltd. v. M.N.R.*, 88 DTC 1242 (T.C.C.))

[¶746] UNPAID AMOUNTS

[¶746.05] *Non-Arm's Length Debts (other than for Remuneration)*

It is fairly common for a taxpayer in business to incur debts to relatives or other persons with whom he or she is not dealing at "arm's length" (see ¶812), in return for goods or services provided by the other person. If the amounts involved are deductible business expenses for the taxpayer, and if the debt is permitted to remain unpaid for a lengthy period, the amount of the unpaid debt must be added back to the taxpayer's income (i.e., effectively, the deduction is lost). Specifically, if the debt is not paid by the end of the second taxation year after the year in which it was incurred, the unpaid portion will be added to the taxpayer's income for the third year following the year in which the debt was incurred.

Whenever an amount is added to income of the taxpayer under these provisions, there will be no further deduction allowed for the amount even when it is subsequently paid to the non-arm's length party.

The CRA has set out the administrative position that the unpaid amounts rule above will not apply to an outlay or expense:

(1) for salary, wages or other remuneration (this is clear in the statute; such payments are subject to the more rigorous rules below);

(2) for a superannuation or pension benefit, or retiring allowance (now also included in the unpaid salary rules below);

(3) for inventory, eligible capital property, or capital property (including depreciable property); or

(4) qualifying as a Canadian or foreign exploration and development expense, Canadian exploration expense, Canadian development expense, or Canadian oil and gas property expense, as those terms are explicitly defined for tax purposes (see Chapter 22).

Notwithstanding the general rule, if the taxpayer and the non-arm's length person to whom he or she owes the money file an agreement with the CRA by a stipulated date, the amount will not be added to the taxpayer's income. Instead, the debt will be deemed to have been paid on the first day of the third taxation year following the year in which the debt was incurred. The other person is deemed to have received payment on that same day, making it taxable to him or her if he or she was on the cash basis, and he or she is deemed to have loaned the amount back to the taxpayer. The stipulated date for filing this agreement is the due date of the taxpayer's income tax return for the third taxation year following the year in which the debt was incurred.

If the taxpayer and the other person sign and file an agreement in the prescribed form but it is not filed by the stipulated date, the unpaid amount will be deemed to have been paid by the taxpayer and received by the other person on the date mentioned above but the taxpayer will be required to add 25% of the unpaid amount to his or her income for the third following taxation year (unpaid amount to non-arm's length party) or to his or her income for the second following taxation year (unpaid remuneration). This can be a very costly penalty for not filing the agreement by the stipulated date, and all taxpayers in this position should take great care to ensure that they file the agreement on a timely basis. However, the late-filing procedure is open for years which are not statute-barred. Once made, a filed agreement may not be rescinded.

The prescribed form of agreement to deem these amounts as having been paid for unpaid amounts to non-arm's length parties is form T2047.

[¶746.10] *All Unpaid Salary, Wages and Other Remuneration*

A much more stringent rule applies to any salary, bonus, or other remuneration deducted in a taxation year but remaining unpaid on the day that is exactly 180 days after the last day of that taxation year (June 29 for an individual payer, or June 28 in leap years).

Unfunded obligations in respect of pension benefits and retiring allowances are also subject to this rule. That is, where an employer (rather than a registered pension plan) makes direct payments as a pension or retiring allowance (as defined in ¶923), the amounts must be actually paid within 180 days following the end of the year in which they are deducted. It is not intended to have this rule apply to contributions to registered pension plans (¶735) or retirement compensation arrangements (¶739), which in any event have their own statutory criteria.

These amounts which remain unpaid after 180 days after year end are denied a deduction in the taxation year in which they are accrued and may only be deducted in the taxation year in which they are paid. There is no requirement in this rule that the remuneration be paid to an arm's length person; all unpaid remuneration is subject to the rule. No election is available to defer or alleviate its operation, as there is for the rule for non-arm's length payments. On the other hand, an eventual deduction on payment is guaranteed under this rule, whereas it will be denied under the non-arm's length rule except on the terms permitted by the election. The remuneration rule clearly supersedes the non-arm's length rule, and applies to all remuneration whether arm's length or otherwise. The only exception is that reasonable accruals for vacation pay and amounts which are covered by the salary deferral rules (¶307 and ¶739) are excluded from the definition of remuneration for purposes of the unpaid remuneration rule.

It would appear that where an individual has a non-calendar fiscal period for a business, it is the individual's taxation year that serves as a measure rather than the fiscal period of the business, since the statute specifically refers to taxation year, and subsection 11(2), which substitutes the expression fiscal period in some cases, does not extend to section 78 which imposes these rules.

The CRA has issued an Interpretation Bulletin indicating its interpretation of these provisions in a number of special instances. Most of these interpretations apply only to the "unpaid amount" rules and not to the "unpaid salary" rules. A couple, however, such as the rules regarding promissory notes and order of payment, are generally applicable.

- Where unpaid amounts exist between a debtor and creditor who do not deal at arm's length but where both taxpayers account for income on the accrual basis and therefore the creditor has reported the amount as income, the rules regarding unpaid amounts will not be applied unless the Department considers the unpaid amount to be part of a tax avoidance scheme — e.g., if the creditor claims a bad debt reserve (¶733) or a special reserve (¶732), or if the amount is owing to a non-resident person and would be subject to withholding tax (¶2080) if paid to him.

- The unpaid amount rules will not be applied to the debtor taxpayer if an unpaid amount is reported as income in the year by a creditor taxpayer who is on the cash basis of reporting income.

- Where an amount is included in income under these rules, it is not also subject to the rules at ¶565 concerning settlement of debts for less than full value.

- An ordinary promissory note will be regarded as a promise to pay the unpaid amount at a later date and not as payment of the amount on the date the note was issued unless the agreement between the parties clearly indicates that the note has been accepted as absolute payment.

- Where an agreement is filed within the time limit in respect of unpaid remuneration and as a result the employer is required to remit non-resident withholding tax, in ordinary circumstances the Department will not levy a penalty for late payment of the withholding tax provided the tax is remitted by the 15th day of the month following the month in which the agreement is filed, even though the remuneration is considered to be paid at a much earlier date.

- In the absence of evidence to the contrary, payments will be considered to apply against the oldest amount outstanding.

- Where an amount has been included in income as an improper reserve because it does not represent a genuine current liability (¶732), it will not be subject also to the rules here.

- Where a taxpayer sells a property at a time when a deductible outlay or expense remains unpaid, and the purchaser assumes the obligation to pay the unpaid amount as full or partial consideration for the purchase, the unpaid amount rules will not apply to the vendor if the purchaser pays the unpaid amount within the time limit which would normally apply to the vendor.

The deduction claimed for the unpaid amount must be reasonable in order for the deduction to be allowed. Courts have ruled that in situations where the expense is being claimed as a deduction and there is no intention to pay the expense, the initial claim for the deduction is not allowed.

(ITA: 11; 78; IT-109R2 [Archived]; *The Queen v. Ken and Ray's Collins Bay Supermarket Ltd.*, 75 DTC 5346 (F.C.T.D.))

[¶747] ADVERTISING IN NON-CANADIAN PUBLICATIONS

[¶747.05] *Advertising in Foreign Newspapers*

Amounts paid for advertising in foreign newspapers are not deductible in computing income if the advertisement is directed primarily to a market in Canada. (This rule also applied to advertisements placed in issues of foreign periodicals dated before June 2000, but thereafter a new set of rules applies, as discussed under the next subheading below.)

Where this rule applies, advertising expense will not be deductible if paid to any newspaper:

(1) that is not owned by Canadians;

(2) that is not printed either in Canada or, after 1988 (under amendments in the Free Trade legislation), in Canada and/or the United States;

(3) that is not edited by individuals resident in Canada;

(4) for which the type is not set either in Canada or, after 1988 (under amendments in the Free Trade legislation), in Canada and/or the United States; or

(5) that is a periodical which is:

(a) produced under licence from a foreign publishing company, or

(b) substantially the same as a foreign periodical.

A periodical is considered substantially the same as a foreign periodical if over 20% of its content is the same as that of a foreign periodical.

However, you may deduct advertising payments to the following publications:

(1) an advertisement in a special issue devoted to features or news related primarily to Canada, if such special issues are not published more often than twice per year; and

(2) a publication which otherwise qualifies if the enterprise was sold to foreigners within the year preceding the placing of the advertisement.

In 1998 the World Trade Organization (WTO) ruled against various Canadian tariff and excise tax provisions by which Canada attempted to bar "split run" editions of U.S. periodicals aimed at the Canadian market. The income tax rules discussed here were not involved in those proceedings and are not affected by the WTO rulings.

(ITA: 19)

[¶747.10] *Advertising in Foreign Periodicals*

For issues of periodicals dated after June 2000, a different set of rules applies. Essentially, these deny 50% of deductions for advertising in all periodicals, Canadian or foreign owned, which do not have 80% Canadian content.

In detail, the new rules deny all ordinarily deductible expenses for advertising space in any periodical (foreign or Canadian) for advertisements directed at the Canadian market except that:

- 100% of otherwise deductible expenses may be claimed for such advertising space if the "original editorial content" in the issue is 80% or more of the of the total non-advertising content; and

- 50% of otherwise deductible expenses may be claimed in all other cases.

Original editorial content is non-advertising content (a) the author of which is a Canadian citizen or a permanent resident under the *Immigration Act* who is a writer, journalist, illustrator or photographer, or (b) that is created for the Canadian market and has not been published in any other "edition" of that issue of the periodical published outside of Canada. Where an issue of a periodical is published in several versions, each version is an "edition".

Several terms in these rules are defined by reference to the *Foreign Publishers Advertising Services Act* (FPASA). That bizarre statute prohibits foreign publishers from selling advertising services directed at the Canadian market to Canadian advertisers. Advertising services include space in a periodical or "access to a target market of consumers".

Most of the definitions are about what you'd expect. A periodical means a printed publication that appears in consecutively numbered or dated issues, published under a common title, usually at regular intervals, not more than once every week, excluding special issues, and at least twice every year. It does not include a catalogue, a directory, a newsletter or a newspaper. Advertisements "directed at the Canadian market" are those the target market for which consists primarily of consumers in Canada.

(ITA: 18(1)(a); 19.01)

[¶748] ADVERTISING ON A NON-CANADIAN TELEVISION OR RADIO STATION

Expenses incurred in respect of an advertisement expense that would otherwise be deductible will be disallowed if the advertisement is placed with a foreign broadcasting undertaking and is directed primarily to a Canadian market.

A foreign broadcasting undertaking is defined as a network operation or a broadcasting transmitting undertaking, located outside of Canada or on a ship or aircraft not registered in Canada.

(ITA: 19.1)

[¶749] PURCHASE OF CUSTOMER LISTS

Where a business is purchased as a going concern, whether or not all of the assets of that business are acquired, and the assets which are acquired include a customer list, or similar information, the cost of this list will be considered as a non-deductible, non-depreciable capital outlay, subject to the special rules discussed at ¶766. An exception is made for the dockets of a credit bureau, the cost of which will qualify for capital cost allowance as a Class 8 asset, because this information is considered to be akin to a reference library rather than a list of customers of the business.

Where it can clearly be established that a customer list has been purchased as a separate item and not as part of the purchase of a business, a full deduction will be allowed for its cost. It will be necessary to establish that the "goodwill" of the vendor has not been acquired. For example, a deduction will normally be allowed where the list is of only passing value to the purchaser because it was acquired for a specific purpose (e.g., for a promotional campaign) and its subsequent use again for that purpose would entail the expenditure of time and money to keep it up-to-date; or where the list is useful only in providing leads to prospective customers which will be valueless unless followed up by the normal selling techniques of the purchaser.

Where the payment may be considered all or partially for goodwill, the goodwill element may be amortized under the rules at ¶766.

For employees purchasing client lists, see ¶368.

(ITA: 14; 20; IT-187 [Archived])

[¶750] ADVANCES TO SUPPLIERS

Advances in the way of cash, materials, equipment or other assets are sometimes made to suppliers in order to ensure a supply of raw materials. Repayment is frequently made by means of contra (set-off) against amounts due to the suppliers for purchases from them.

Losses suffered through non-recovery of such advances will ordinarily be deductible in the year in which the loss becomes known (see ¶733).

This deduction will only be allowed if the advances are circulating amounts (i.e., are on income account). If the advances represent a form of permanent investment in the supplier, any loss will be a capital loss.

(*Ontario Culvert and Metal Products Ltd. v. M.N.R.*, 67 DTC 9 (T.A.B.))

[¶751] DISCOUNTS ON MORTGAGES, NOTES, OR SIMILAR OBLIGATIONS

If you borrowed money for use in obtaining income from a business or property, by issuing a mortgage or similar obligation which carried both stipulated interest and was issued at a discount, all or a fraction of the discount may be deducted when principal payments are made.

Discounts are deductible in full if:

(1) the debt was issued for at least 97% of the face value; and

(2) the actual yield of the debt does not exceed four-thirds of the stated interest rate.

In all other cases only one-half of the discount is deductible.

Where the debt is repayable by instalments rather than by a lump sum at maturity, you may deduct an amount in respect of a discount when the aggregate of the payments made on account of the principal exceeds the amount for which the obligation was issued.

Example of Deductible Amount:

	1	*2*
Face value of note due in one year	$10,000	$10,000
Amount received on issue	9,900	9,700
Discount	$ 100	$ 300
Stated interest rate	10%	8%
Actual yield	11.11	11.34
4/3 of stated interest rate	13.33	10.67
Deductible amount of discount	$ 100	$ 150

(ITA: 20(1)(*f*))

[¶752] FOREIGN INCOME TAXES LEVIED ON BUSINESS INCOME

If you are carrying on business in a foreign country, income taxes paid to that country with respect to the business income earned therein are not deductible in computing income but may be claimed as a direct credit against Canadian taxes payable as outlined in ¶1450.

Income taxes paid to a political subdivision (e.g., a state or a province) of a foreign country with respect to the business income earned therein are also creditable against Canadian taxes.

In certain instances, it may be difficult to distinguish between an income tax and a franchise or business tax. The distinction is important since a franchise or a business tax would be a deductible expense in computing income rather than a creditable income tax.

Non-business income taxes are in the first instance also subject to tax credit, but excess taxes may be deducted from business or property income, as discussed at ¶1455, items (C) and (D).

For issues involving penalties on foreign tax, see ¶763.

(ITA: 126; Income Tax Folio: S5-F2-C1 Foreign Tax Credit)

[¶753] PREPAID EXPENSES

Normally if you adopt the accrual method of accounting (¶714) you must deduct expenses for income tax purposes in the year in which they are incurred, subject to the timing considerations discussed at ¶730. However, if the expense is in respect of services to be rendered after the end of the year or a prepayment of rent, interest, taxes or insurance you will only be permitted to deduct the portion of the expense which relates to the taxation year. The excess must be deferred and may be deducted in the future taxation year to which the expense relates.

Prepayments of group term life insurance premiums covering a period of more than 13 months for employees are excluded from the general rule above and subject instead to the new rules at ¶741.

Pre-production or start-up costs of a new business of a non-capital nature must be claimed in the year in which they are incurred (see ¶743 and ¶744).

Payments made to reduce an interest rate or cancel a debt must be deducted over the period the obligation would have remained outstanding but for the payment. Receipts of such payments will be treated as interest income. See ¶1074.

(ITA: 18(9), (9.1); IT-417R2 [Archived])

[¶754] LOSSES FROM THEFT

A loss of trading assets such as stock in trade or cash through theft, defalcation or embezzlement normally is allowed as a deduction in computing income where a taxpayer's business involves this risk. Loss through theft, holdup or robbery by a stranger, or theft, defalcation or embezzlement by an employee (unless he is a senior official or a major shareholder) is allowed as a deduction. If the cost of assets lost is expensed in some other manner, no double deduction is permitted. Only out-of-pocket losses may be deducted; profits lost or foregone through theft, etc., are not deductible.

Losses through theft, defalcation, or embezzlement by proprietors, partners, or significant shareholders is regarded by the CRA as a withdrawal of capital and is not normally allowed as a deduction. However, the CRA has recognized the validity of a case in which deduction was allowed for amounts embezzled from operating credit by two signing officers who were minority shareholders. The court had found that the funds were not taken by the individuals in their capacity as shareholders or by exercising any overriding control.

Losses through theft, defalcation, or embezzlement by senior employees and managers may or may not be deductible. If the theft can be likened to a withdrawal of capital by someone with authority to act in lieu of the owner, a right to deduction will be resisted by the CRA. To the extent that it can be likened to an incident which might ordinarily be suffered in the course of earning income, it should be deductible.

The amount of loss allowable as a deduction is the net amount after taking into account any insurance recovery or restitution in the year in which the deduction is claimed. The loss also includes the cost to the taxpayer of discharging a liability to a third party (e.g., a customer) created by a theft or defalcation. In cases where the allowable loss is already reflected in the reported income or loss of a business (for instance, where the losses are reflected in overstated expense accounts), the amount of reported income or loss will not have to be adjusted. In any other case, an allowable loss usually is deductible in computing income of the year in which the loss is discovered. Where the application of this rule would create a hardship, the allowance may be made in the year (or years) in which the event took place if the taxpayer so requests, provided that year is not statute-barred.

Loss of a capital asset because of theft, defalcation or embezzlement is a disposition at the time of discovery. Any insurance proceeds that you receive for such losses may give rise to a recapture of capital cost allowances (¶843) and/or a capital gain or loss. See ¶525 and ¶845.

In *Hammill v. the Queen*, 2004 DTC 3271 (T.C.C.), aff'd 2005 DTC 5397 (F.C.A.), the Court ruled that where an individual engaged in lengthy activities which he thought constituted a business, or at least an adventure in the nature of trade (which the CRA had conceded), but which were from the beginning part of a scheme to defraud him, there was never a business and consequently no business loss to deduct from other income. The Tax Court decision was subject to much criticism in the tax practice community, which cited a long line of cases to the effect that it was not the business of the CRA to second guess the business judgement of the taxpayer. The Federal Court of Appeal in effect ruled that it may not be the right of the CRA, but it is the right of the courts. See also ¶705.

(ITA: 54; Income Tax Folio: S3-F9-C1 Lottery Winnings, Miscellaneous Receipts, and Income (and Losses) from Crime)

[¶755] SALE OF BUSINESS

The sale of the property used in a business will usually result in a profit or loss being realized, particularly with respect to accounts receivable, inventories, goodwill, and fixed assets.

The special treatment provided for sales of fixed assets (terminal losses or recapture) is discussed at ¶851 and ¶843 and goodwill at ¶768.

Where you are in business and report your income on the accrual basis and you sell all, or substantially all, of your business assets to a purchaser who will then carry on the business, you may, with the purchaser, elect to file form T2022 which is an agreement as to the price that was paid by the purchaser for the accounts receivable of your business. This election is available only if all the outstanding debts, which are, or will be, included in your income, are sold. If this election is made, and the sale price of the accounts receivable is less than their face value, you are permitted to deduct this difference in determining your income for the year of sale. The purchaser, on the other hand, is permitted to treat the purchased debts as if they had arisen in the ordinary course of his business. He or she is required to add to income, in the year of purchase, the difference between the price he or she paid for the accounts and their face value but may establish a reserve for doubtful accounts with respect to purchased accounts that are still outstanding at the end of his or her fiscal period and may deduct any of such accounts which became uncollectible in the year of acquisition, or thereafter. It is important to note that the amount agreed to be the sale price must be the fair market value if you are not dealing at arm's length with the purchaser.

If you and the purchaser fail to make the election and file form T2022, the purchase and sale of the debts is regarded as a capital transaction and you will be considered to have suffered a capital loss on the sale of the debts at less than their face value. The purchaser will be considered to have acquired a capital asset in the form of the purchased debts so that if he were to collect more from the debts than the price he paid for them, the excess would be treated as a capital gain. Alternatively, if he collected less, the deficiency would be a capital loss. The rules in Chapter 5 would apply to any capital gain or loss.

If inventories are sold, along with other property, to another person who uses the items as inventory in his own business, the price to be allocated to inventories should be allocated on a reasonable basis and documented by a written agreement. If you are not dealing at arm's length with the purchaser the amount allocated to inventory must be the fair market value.

If you cease to carry on the business and at a later time sell your inventory, the inventory will be deemed to have been sold in the course of carrying on the business. If you report income on the accrual basis, all of the profit from sale of the inventory must be included in computing your income in the year the inventory is sold. If you report income on the cash basis, the consideration received from sale of the inventory will be included in computing income for the year or years in which it is received.

If you are a professional and if inventory includes work in progress which you have elected to exclude from your income, see ¶780.

If you dispose of your business, you will also be entitled to elect that the last fiscal year of the business be considered to end on the date when it ordinarily would have ended (¶707). Where a taxpayer elects to extend the fiscal period of a business, any recapture of capital cost allowance, any terminal loss, and any income arising from the disposal of eligible capital property after the individual ceases to carry on the business will be included as income of the business for the extended fiscal period.

(ITA: 22; 23; 25; IT-188R [Archived]; IT-287R2 [Archived])

[¶757] INVENTORY VALUATION

The valuation of inventories is important since it has a major impact on the determination of profit. Inventory measurement is the major component of cost of goods sold, which in turn is deducted from gross revenue to give basic profit (before other costs). Generally speaking, cost of goods sold is opening inventory for the year plus cost of additions to inventory minus the value of closing inventory for the year. Since opening inventory must have the same value as closing inventory of the preceding year, it is only the value of closing inventory that can be in issue. The higher the value of closing inventory, the lower the value of cost of goods sold, giving a higher value of profit. Conversely, the lower the closing inventories, the lower your income.

Alternative methods of valuing inventories are permissible, but whatever method is used you are required to maintain records of the quantities and nature of the items included to support the valuation arrived at.

(ITA: 20; ITR: 1801–1802)

[¶758] METHOD OF VALUATION

Either of the following methods of valuation are permitted.

(1) All items may be valued at fair market value.

(2) Each item may be valued at the lower of its cost and its fair market value.

The rule specifies that in using the lower of cost or fair market value, cost must be the cost at which the taxpayer acquired the property and fair market value must be the fair market value of the inventory at the end of the year for which profit is being determined. Accordingly, businesses which have valued their property at the lower of cost and fair market value at the end of Year 1, when fair market value is less than cost, must, if fair market value has increased at the end of Year 2, write up the Year 2 value to the lower of cost and fair market value at the end of Year 2.

Taxpayers engaged in the business of breeding and raising animals may elect to use a third method, which is discussed at ¶1722.

Taxpayers who operate a retail business selling many different commodities may choose a fourth method, known as the retail inventory method. Although not sanctioned by statute, the CRA has indicated that it will accept this method provided that values are established in accordance with generally accepted accounting principles and used for financial statement as well as tax purposes. Use of this method typically presupposes professionally prepared accounting statements.

The method most commonly used is the second, which requires a valuation of each item at the lower of its cost or market value. In most cases, this method will result in the lowest valuation, and therefore the lowest income and the least tax liability.

Artists are given a special option to value inventory at nil, essentially putting them on a cash basis. See ¶789.

[¶758.05] *Inventory of Adventure in the Nature of Trade*

An "adventure in the nature of trade" is an activity devoted to making a profit but which does not have the usual *indicia* of systematic business activity. The most common example is the holding of land on the speculation that it can be sold at a profit without further development. Although one might expect in the abstract that the gain would be a capital gain, a long line of court decisions has made it clear that where the intention on acquisition was to resell at a profit rather than to hold the land for personal use or income from rental or development, holding the land is an adventure in the nature of trade and therefore a business.

(Although the holding of "raw land" is the most common adventure in the nature of trade, almost any highly speculative endeavour in which you are not systematically engaged may lend itself to being characterized as an adventure in the nature of trade, either by the Department seeking to tax gains at full rather than capital gain rates or the taxpayer seeking to deduct full losses. Examples of situations which have been categorized as adventures include acquisition of a business in distress with the intention of turning it around, and commodity market investment. In one case, the search for a particular buried treasure was held to be an adventure in the nature of trade (and the costs deductible). See also the discussion at ¶500 concerning criteria of income vs. capital transactions.)

It has long been the CRA's policy that profit or loss involved in holding real estate as an adventure in the nature of trade cannot be realized until disposition of the property. In particular, the property, which might be thought to be inventory, would not be subject to write-down if its value fell during the year. That is, the taxpayer could not claim a loss against other income from a fall in property value until there was an actual disposition. In *Friesen v. The Queen*, 95 DTC 5551, the Supreme Court of Canada ruled that such property was inventory and was subject to write-downs in years prior to disposition. The Court did not deal with the question of inventory written down which later increased in value, but there was a widespread accounting opinion that a reversal of the write-down would not occur until disposition, leaving the taxpayer in a win-win situation.

Not surprisingly, the government announced (on December 20, 1995) that it would "clarify that the rules which apply to the valuation of business inventory on an annual basis do not apply to property held as an adventure in the nature of trade". Income or loss from such property is now recognized only on disposition, for taxation years ending after December 20, 1995. Where you have claimed an inventory write-down for property held as an adventure in the nature of trade for a taxation year ending before December 21, 1995, the amount reported as fair market value (or reassessed as such) will be considered the cost for determining gain or loss on disposition.

In the same release, the Minister of Finance noted that some commentators had suggested the *Friesen* decision also stood for the proposition that in valuing inventory at the lower of cost and market, one should ignore any increase in market value. The release announced that amendments would also "clarify that business inventory valued at the lower of cost and fair market value should be reported as such, and not at the lower of cost and last lowest value of inventory". This has been done, as discussed above at the beginning of this section.

[¶758.10] *Adventure in the Nature of Trade Rule Defined*

Details of the revised inventory rules were published on June 20, 1996. In general, they carry out the government's intentions as stated. As revised, there is one rule for businesses generally, other than adventures in the nature of trade, and a separate specific rule for a business that is an adventure in the nature of trade. The general rule is discussed at the beginning of ¶758.

The specific inventory rules for an adventure in the nature of trade provide that inventory of an adventure in the nature of trade must be valued at the cost at which the taxpayer acquired it. Additions are permitted for interest and property taxes which could not be deducted under the rules at ¶665. (Since cost of goods sold is opening inventory plus additions minus closing inventory, the additions should be a wash for profit computation purposes, but will have the intended result of reducing eventual profit on disposition.)

The rules for valuing inventory of an adventure in the nature of trade contain an exception where the inventory is held by a corporation which undergoes a change of control. The rules provide that at the end of the last taxation year before the change, the inventory must be written down to the lower of cost or market, which then becomes its deemed acquisition cost. This is intended to limit loss trading in corporations.

Where property was written down at the end of a year under the pre-December 21, 1995 rules (as in the *Friesen* case), the new rule freezes the value at the end of the last taxation year in which the old rules applied as the deemed cost of the inventory for all future purposes (subject to additions for interest and property taxes denied).

Additional rules provide stop-loss rules to defer recognition of losses on transfers of adventure in the nature of trade inventory in affiliated party transactions (¶852). Essentially, recognition of the loss in the hands of the transferor is deferred until there is a final non-affiliated disposition or deemed disposition. The rules are analogous to the affiliated transaction rules at ¶851 and the superficial loss rules at ¶579.

[¶758.15] *Valuation of Work in Progress*

Specified professions are governed by a specific rule which permits work in progress (WIP), usually considered inventory, to be valued at nil, essentially permitting it to be deducted in calculating income. See ¶780. This leaves open the question of how work in progress is to be valued for taxpayers who are not members of the enumerated professions. In particular, can WIP be valued at the lesser of cost and fair market value, under the general rule above?

In *CDSL Canada Limited v. The Queen*, 2008 DTC 2812 (T.C.C.), the Court ruled that WIP had to be valued at fair market value. The general rule did not apply, as it did not give the best picture of profits in the circumstances. The taxpayers appealed to the Federal Court of Appeal, and their appeal was allowed, reversing the decision of the lower court; see 2009 DTC 5030 (F.C.A.). The taxpayers, who were consultants, were entitled to readjust their incomes, applying the lower of cost or market method of inventory valuation in accordance with subsection 10(1) of the Act, which took precedence over the general application of subsection 9(1). The application of subsection 10(1) was not confined to the professional practices enumerated under section 34. Presumably this is now the general rule for all.

(ITA: 10; 11; ITR: 1801–1802)

[¶758.20] *Derivatives Deemed not to be Inventory*

Commentary on Bill C-29 Measures (Oct. 25, 2016)

Note: When Bill C-29, October 25, 2016, achieves Royal Assent, the commentary will be modified to read:

Apparently, some taxpayers have treated derivatives held on income account as inventory and therefore reported accrued annual losses before they were realized under the inventory valuation rules. A Tax Court of Canada decision allowed this treatment in respect of certain foreign exchange option contracts (*Kruger v. The Queen*, 2015 DTC 1127), although on appeal to the Federal Court of Appeal, that Court held that the derivative contracts did not constitute inventory.

In any event, effective for agreements entered into after March 21, 2016, derivative contracts are deemed not to be inventory. In particular, new subsection 10(15) provides that "a swap agreement, a forward purchase or sale agreement, a forward rate agreement, a futures agreement, an option agreement, or any similar agreement" is deemed not to be inventory for the purposes of the inventory valuation tax rules. In addition, paragraph 18(1)(*x*) disallows the write-down or deduction for accrued losses for the foregoing types of property. As a result, the losses, if any, will be reported upon realization.

(ITA: draft 10(15); draft 18(1)(x))

[¶758.25] *Emissions Allowances*

Commentary on Bill C-29 Measures (Oct. 25, 2016)

Note: When Bill C-29, October 25, 2016, achieves Royal Assent, the commentary will be modified to read:

There previously were no specific income tax provisions dealing with emission trading transactions, and therefore the tax consequences of these transactions were determined using general income tax principles. Concern had been expressed that there was uncertainty regarding these transactions, in addition to potential double-taxation relating to emissions allowances provided by government entities for no consideration.

Regulated emitters previously treated emissions allowances as eligible capital property ("ECP") for tax purposes. With the repeal of the ECP rules in favour of a capital cost allowance system, tax policy concerns arose regarding the appropriateness of treating emissions allowances as capital property. First, capital property is generally property of an enduring nature, but most emissions allowances are commonly viewed as one-time use property. Second, the treatment of emissions allowances as capital property could have resulted in a mismatch of expenses where the obligation to remit allowances was deductible as a current expense.

Emissions allowances provided at no consideration by a government entity ("free allowances") were generally required to be included in income as government assistance. However, there was no provision that allowed the cost of the emissions allowance to be increased for this income inclusion, raising the possibility of double taxation on its disposition.

To deal with these concerns, specific rules were created in new section 27.1 to treat emissions allowances as inventory. However, the lower of cost and market valuation method cannot be used for emissions allowances, due to the potential volatility in the value of the allowances. Instead, an emissions allowance must be valued at its cost to the taxpayer for the purposes of computing the taxpayer's income from a business. The cost of identical emissions allowances will be determined based on the average cost of all identical emissions allowances held by the taxpayer. Emissions allowances will be considered identical when they can be used to settle the same emissions obligation.

Free allowances are now not required to be included in income.

The total amount deductible by a taxpayer in respect of a particular emissions obligation for a taxation year is limited to the cost of the emissions allowances that are, or could be, used to satisfy it. In particular, the amount deductible cannot exceed the taxpayer's total cost of emissions allowances either used by the taxpayer to settle the obligation in the year or held by the taxpayer at the end of the taxation year that can be used to satisfy the obligation, and the fair market value of emissions allowances, determined at the end of the taxation year, that would be needed to be acquired to settle the obligation where the taxpayer has insufficient emissions allowances on hand.

Deductions are treated in a similar manner to the current system for reserves. Each year a taxpayer claims a deduction in respect of an omissions obligation that is to be settled in a future year, the taxpayer will be required to include the deducted amount in income in the immediately following taxation year. For instance, deductions claimed in 2017 in respect of obligations that will be satisfied in the future will be required to be brought back into income in 2018, and the taxpayer will be required to evaluate the obligation each year until it is fully satisfied.

Provisions are included to ensure a taxpayer cannot realize either a gain or loss on an emissions allowance that is used to settle an emissions obligation. Specifically, where an emissions allowance is surrendered to settle an emissions obligation, the taxpayer's proceeds of disposition of the allowance are deemed to be equal to its cost.

Emissions allowances that have been disposed of, other than in satisfaction of an emissions obligation, will be included in income to the extent the proceeds of disposition exceed the cost of the emissions allowance disposed of.

Loss restriction rules on a change of control have also been included.

These new rules apply to emissions allowances acquired in taxation years beginning after 2016. However, where a taxpayer elects in their income tax return for the 2016 or 2017 taxation year, these rules will apply to taxation years ending after 2012.

(ITA: draft 27.1; draft 248(1) "emissions allowance"; draft 248(1) "emissions obligation"; ITR: draft 7300(d); IT-473R [Archived])

[¶759] CHANGE OF METHOD

Once you have adopted, or have been required to adopt, one of the foregoing methods of valuing your inventory, you must continue to use that method on a consistent basis in subsequent years. Changes in the method of valuing inventory may only be undertaken with the formal (written) consent of the CRA. The CRA's policy is that it may accept a change in the method used where it is shown that, in your particular circumstances, the new method:

(1) is a more appropriate method of computing income;

(2) will be used for financial statement purposes; and

(3) will be used consistently in subsequent years.

The valuation of your inventory at the commencement of the year must be the same as the valuation of the previous year's closing inventory.

If the Department determines that your closing inventory was not valued by one of the authorized methods, it may insist that one of such methods be used.

In 1998, the CRA appeared to modify its views as to the extent of its jurisdiction regarding permission for an inventory change. At one time it seemed to view this as extending to any change, such as changing the method of cost determination from average cost to first-in first-out (see CRA Document No. 9301695). This position is explicitly reversed ("clarified") in IT-473R, para. 7, although, rather confusingly, paragraph 16 seems to restate the old rule.

(ITA: 10; IT-473R [Archived])

[¶760] THE MEANING OF "COST"

In valuing inventories "cost" will usually be:

(1) For purchased items, the invoice price plus any foreign exchange, customs and excise duties, freight and cartage charges and other costs of bringing goods into inventory. In some cases, storage costs may be included, as where warehouse charges are incurred for storing the inventory prior to sale.

(2) For items manufactured by your business, the cost of inventory is determined by adding to the cost of purchased items, direct labour charges and overhead expenses applicable to inventoried goods.

An individual in business may not charge as an expense, or include in inventory, an amount representing the estimated value of his own services.

If the cost of each individual item in inventory can be readily ascertained, the above type of calculation should be made for each such item. However, this cannot always be done. In many cases, fairly large quantities of particular items are purchased at different times and at varying costs, and no attempt is made to record which particular item is sold or is in inventory at a given time. Consequently, some assumption must be made as to the identity of the items in inventory and their cost. The assumption adopted should be the one that produces the fairest matching of costs with the revenues, and for income tax purposes the use of either one of two assumptions is acceptable. These two methods are:

(1) *The First-In, First-Out Method (FIFO).* — Under this method, the items first acquired are considered to have been disposed of first and items in inventory are considered to be the most recently acquired.

The type of calculation required is illustrated in the following example for a business which has purchased at various times Item X for resale, and is valuing its inventory as of December 31.

Example 1

Purchases	*Number of items*
January 1	500 @ $5.00
February 9	500 @ $5.00
March 10	400 @ $5.10
June 26	500 @ $4.95
July 16	500 @ $5.05
Number in inventory as of December 31	800
Value of inventory as of December 31:	
500 @ $5.05 (most recent purchase)	$2,525

Purchases	*Number of items*
300 @ $4.95 (portion of next most recent purchase)	1,485
Inventory value at cost	$4,010

(2) *The Average Cost Method.* — Under this method the cost of each item in inventory is considered to be the weighted average cost per unit of items (a) on hand at the beginning of the year, and (b) purchased during the year.

Using the facts in the above example, the type of calculation required is illustrated as follows:

Example 2

	Number of items	*Value*
On hand January 1	500	$ 2,500
Purchased February 9	500	2,500
Purchased March 10	400	2,040
Purchased June 26	500	2,475
Purchased July 16	500	2,525
Totals	2,400	$12,040

Average cost per unit
$12,040 ÷ 2,400 = $5.02

Inventory as of December 31
800 @ $5.02 = $4,016

Other methods of costing inventory, such as the last in, first-out method (LIFO), in which the items acquired last are considered to have been disposed of first, or the base stock method, are said by the CRA to be unacceptable for income tax purposes. The CRA then goes on to say (in IT-473R, para. 16, now archived) that the method used in determining cost will "normally" be the method used for financial statement purposes. "However, if there is more than one method of determining cost according to generally accepted accounting principles, the method used for income tax purposes should be the one that gives the truer picture of the taxpayer's income." As far as it goes, this correctly acknowledges court decisions. The case cited by the CRA, however, is *West Kootenay Power and Light Company Limited v. The Queen*, 92 DTC 6023 (F.C.A), rather than the Supreme Court decision in *The Queen v. Canderel*, (98 DTC 6100), which went on to suggest that once the taxpayer chose a reasonable method for determining profit, the CRA has the onus of proving another method superior.

Some tax advisers have suggested that the GST on inventory might be included in cost, provided that GST input tax credit on the inventory has not been claimed on a timely basis and has not been claimed for a period ending in the income taxation year. This follows from the rules governing GST recognition for tax purposes (¶729), although it would seem to be contradicted by normal accounting principles. Accordingly, the matter may be regarded as uncertain at best and come into the realm of "aggressive" tax planning. That is, the CRA would probably fight such an interpretation. As well, only in limited situations of rapid inventory turnover is it likely to be beneficial.

(IT-473R [Archived])

[¶761] THE MEANING OF "FAIR MARKET VALUE"

The meaning of "fair market value" as applied to inventories is subject to some disagreement, and where an exact definition is of significance it is probably advisable to obtain professional accounting advice. However, in general it can be taken to mean either:

(1) net realizable value of the inventory; or

(2) replacement price of the inventory.

"Net realizable value" is the estimated selling price less estimated costs of completing and selling the item. It may be possible to reduce this value further to the extent of a normal profit margin for such an item. The reduction of inventory values to "net realizable value" will automatically take into account obsolescence, physical deterioration, market price reductions, etc., since these factors will be reflected in selling prices.

"Replacement" price is the amount which would be required to purchase or produce identical goods as of the year end date. A reduction to replacement value is, however, not appropriate when it is expected the items on hand can be sold at a normal profit margin. This may occur when you have a fixed price contract for sale of the items or when for other reasons the sale price of the items is not expected to reduce below what would produce a normal profit margin.

It should be noted that a reduction of inventory values to estimated market value by the deduction of a general lump-sum provision from costs is not allowed. You must be able to relate the reduction to specific inventory items, and have sound reasons for claiming that market value, as determined above, is a more appropriate basis than cost for such items.

The fair market value of property that is advertising or packaging material, parts, supplies, stationery, or similar inventory items not actually themselves held for or to be incorporated into goods for sale or lease, is deemed to be replacement cost. The purpose of this provision is to require such items to be written off over time rather than, in effect, being immediately expensed by write-down to nil fair market value.

(ITA: 10; 18; IT-473R [Archived])

[¶763] FINES, PENALTIES, AND ILLEGAL PAYMENTS

[¶763.05] *Specific Statutory Prohibitions*

Several years ago, the federal government passed legislation (section 67.6) to reverse the effects of the Supreme Court decision in *65302 British Columbia Limited v. The Queen*, 99 DTC 5799 (S.C.C.), discussed in ¶763.10, below. Section 67.6 of the Act provides that no deduction may be made for any amount that is a fine or penalty (other than a prescribed fine or penalty) imposed after March 22, 2004 under the law of a country or political subdivision (including a state, province or territory) by any person or public body that has the authority to impose the fine or penalty.

In its Income Tax Folio S4-F2-C1, "Deductibility of Fines and Penalties", the CRA says that, generally, an amount must be characterized as a fine or penalty under the relevant law in order for the section 67.6 prohibition to apply. "The legislation imposing the fine or penalty will therefore determine whether an amount is a fine or penalty that may be precluded from deduction by section 67.6."

Section 67.6 does not prohibit deduction of prescribed fines or penalties. Currently, only the penalties imposed under paragraph 110.1(1)(*a*) of the *Excise Act* are prescribed for these purposes (penalties on default in payment of any duty or penalty payable under that Act).

Paragraph 18(1)(*t*) of the Act specifically prohibits the deduction of any amount paid or payable under the Act (such as income tax, fines, penalties and interest), with the exception of tax paid or payable under Part XII.2 or Part XII.6. Paragraph 18(1)(*t*) of the Act prohibits a deduction for any amount paid or payable as interest under Part IX of the *Excise Tax Act* (relating to the goods and services tax), or as interest under the *Air Travellers Security Charge Act* (see paragraph 1.23 of the Income Tax Folio).

Otherwise, the deduction of interest charges, including interest arising on fines or penalties, is not prohibited under section 67.6 or paragraph 18(1)(*t*).

In paragraph 1.7 of the Income Tax Folio, the CRA provides that section 67.6 also does not prohibit the deduction of:

- penalties or damages paid under a private contract (for example, a penalty charged for late performance);
- interest charges, including interest arising on fines or penalties. However, certain interest charges may be precluded from deduction under another provision of the Act, such as paragraph 18(1)(*t*) [see above];
- amounts not characterized as a fine or penalty under the legislation imposing the particular amount; or
- fines or penalties imposed before March 23, 2004.

The same paragraph 1.7 in the Folio provides four examples where section 67.6 may or may not apply.

Section 67.5 of the Act explicitly prohibits the deduction of specified illegal payments. The prohibition applies to payments made or expenses incurred for the purpose of doing anything that is an offence under specified sections of the *Criminal Code*. Generally speaking, this is intended to deny any deduction in respect of illegal payments to government officials in Canada, officials engaged in the administration of justice in Canada, persons under a duty as agents or employees and persons responsible for collecting fares or admission fees. Illegal payments appear to be payments made to induce, or attempt to induce, the recipient to breach his or her duty. Deductions are also prohibited where the payment is in furtherance of a conspiracy to commit such an offence or a conspiracy in Canada to commit a similar offence under the law of another country. Special permission is given to the CRA to reassess under this provision without regard to normal time limits on reassessments.

Where section 67.5 or 67.6 does not apply, the determination of whether a fine, penalty or illegal payment will be deductible depends largely on general principles enunciated by the courts, and in particular by the Supreme Court of Canada in the *65302 British Columbia Limited* case, as discussed below.

Penalties payable on prepayment of debt may be subject to specific amortization rules of subsection 18(9.1), discussed at ¶1074. The CRA also discusses these penalties in its Income Tax Folio S4-F2-C1.

(ITA: 18(1)(*t*); 67.6; ITR: 7309 [Prescribed penalties])

[¶763.10] *Relevance of 65302 British Columbia Limited Case*

In *65302 British Columbia Limited v. The Queen*, 99 DTC 5799 (S.C.C.), the Supreme Court of Canada ruled that fines and penalties incurred in the course of earning income are deductible unless there is a specific rule in the *Income Tax Act* prohibiting the deduction. Before this ruling the courts, in Canada as elsewhere, were inclined to weigh the nature of the penalty and the public policy issues that might be involved in permitting its deduction on a case by case basis. The Supreme Court did away with this learned tradition in the interests of simplicity and straightforward interpretation of the rule that expenses to earn income are generally deductible, notwithstanding that they may be payments on account of illegal actions. Although the decision enunciated a simple principle, it had sweeping consequences for established policies, and it was always likely that the Department of Finance would step in to rescue its cherished prohibitions, as it did for fines and penalties imposed after March 22, 2004 (as discussed above at ¶763.05).

However, for fines, penalties and illegal payments not so prohibited by specific provisions of the Act, the general principles as summarized in the *65302 British Columbia* case will continue to be relevant. The CRA of course accepts this, and summarizes some of the general principles in its Income Tax Folio S4-F2-C1, "Deductibility of Fines and Penalties". The illegal nature of a payment will not preclude its deductibility. The CRA also cites the Federal Court of Appeal decision in *Canadian Imperial Bank of Commerce v The Queen*, 2013 DTC 5098 as authority for the general principle that questions relating to the morality of a taxpayer's conduct will not be relevant.

The CRA goes on to state (paragraph 1.16): "Based largely on case law [seemingly, mainly the *65302 British Columbia* case], the CRA will not consider the following factors to be relevant in determining whether a fine or penalty was incurred by a taxpayer for the purpose of gaining or producing income from the business or property:

(1) whether the taxpayer attempted to prevent the act or omission that gave rise to the fine or penalty;

(2) whether the taxpayer's income-earning purpose was achieved through the act or omission that gave rise to the fine or penalty;

(3) whether the fine or penalty was avoidable;

(4) whether it would be contrary to public policy to allow the taxpayer to deduct the fine or penalty in the circumstances; or

(5) whether the taxpayer's conduct that gave rise to the fine or penalty could be considered egregious or repulsive."

In the *65302 British Columbia* case, the Supreme Court did hold: "It is conceivable that a breach [of the law] could be so egregious or repulsive that the fine subsequently imposed could not be justified as being incurred for the purpose of producing income." The Court did not provide specific guidelines in this regard. In the subsequent decision in *Canadian Imperial Bank of Commerce v The Queen* noted above, the Federal Court of Appeal held that the taxpayer's conduct was not so egregious or repulsive so as to disallow the deduction of certain settlement payments arising out of the Enron financial scandals in the early 2000's. In the earlier case of *Ferguson-Neudorf Glass Inc. v. The Queen* (2009 DTC 1034), the taxpayer incurred a fine for improper training and guidance after one of its workers died as a result of workplace accident. The Tax Court found that the taxpayer's conduct was not egregious or repulsive so as to warrant the non-deduction of the fine.

(ITA: 18(1)(*l*.1), (*m*), (*t*); 67.5; Income Tax Folio: S4-F2-C1 Deductibility of Fines and Penalties)

[¶764] EXPENSES INCURRED IN THE BORROWING OF MONEY

To the extent that they are not deductible under any other provision of the *Income Tax Act*, certain expenses arising on the acquisition of borrowed funds to be used in the course of earning income from a business (or property), or on incurring debt on the acquisition of income producing property or otherwise to earn business income, may be deducted for tax purposes on a straight-line basis over five years at 20% per year. The 20% must be prorated for short fiscal periods by the days in the year divided by 365. Since this formula is of general application, there can apparently be a 366/365 proration for full-term leap years. Note that this rule will not normally apply to interest itself, nor to interest-rate reduction payments, since provision is made for these items elsewhere in the *Income Tax Act* (¶1063–¶1074). Interest is not deductible under this rule even if deductibility is restricted by other rules. Nor do the rules here apply to capital expenditures which may be amortized under the capital cost allowance rules (Chapter 8) or the eligible capital property rules (¶766).

If the borrowings for which the expenses were incurred are repaid in a year otherwise than as part of a refinancing, the undeducted balance of the expenses will be deductible in that year. In cases where a partnership is dissolved, the undeducted expenses will be deductible over the remainder of the five-year period in the hand of the partners, with a corresponding reduction in the adjusted cost base of the closing partnership.

To be eligible for deduction under these rules, the expense must be incurred by the taxpayer:

(1) in the course of borrowing money to earn income (other than exempt income) from a business or property;

(2) in the course of incurring indebtedness for property acquired for the purpose of gaining or producing income therefrom or for the purpose of gaining or producing income from a business (other than property from which the income would be exempt or which is an interest in a life-insurance policy, as discussed below);

(3) in the course of rescheduling or restructuring debt incurred in (1) or (2), above, where the change results in a change of conditions of the debt or a substitution of other debt or shares;

(4) in the course of assuming a debt in respect of (1) or (2); or

(5) in the course of issuing units of a unit trust, shares of a company or interests in a partnership; however, deductions under this rule must be claimed by the trust, company or partnership, as the case may be.

The following items are explicitly excluded from deduction under this rule (although they may be deducted under other rules, e.g., the interest deductibility rules):

(1) an amount paid or payable on account of principal or interest on a debt obligation;

(2) an amount that is contingent or dependent on the use of, or production from, property; and

(3) an amount that is computed by reference to revenue, profit, cash flow, commodity price or any other similar criterion or by reference to dividends paid or payable to shareholders.

Item (1), above, has always been a specified exception to the rule. Items (2) and (3) were introduced in response to a court decision (discussed under "Participating Debt", at ¶764.10 below), effective for expenses incurred after November 30, 1999, other than expenses incurred after that date pursuant to a written agreement made before December 1, 1999.

Many of the expenses that may be deducted under this provision are specifically applicable to corporations raising money by issuing shares. However, those applicable to individuals include:

(1) a commitment fee paid to a lender under an agreement committing the lender to make a specified amount available when requested;

(2) an amount paid to the guarantor of a loan either periodically or at the commencement of the loan;

(3) certain "soft costs" (see ¶771.05) incurred in financing construction of an income-earning building not otherwise added to depreciable cost, such as mortgage application, appraisal, processing, insurance, guarantee, brokerage and finder's fees, legal fees related to mortgage financing; and

(4) certification fees and certain other expenses (such as commissions) incurred in connection with the sale of bankers' acceptances.

The items above have been explicitly approved by the CRA. The list would appear to illustrate examples of the most common cases the CRA has met, rather than attempting to limit the generality of the statutory rules. It is not clear, for example, why the mortgage-related costs in (3) would apply only to soft-cost borrowing, and not to any mortgage borrowing for a (non-exempt) income-earning purpose.

Such items as prospectus costs and filing fees for regulatory bodies, also covered, would typically apply only to corporations.

In cases where a financing is aborted, the costs incurred may not be deductible although they may be considered as eligible capital expenditures.

A relieving rule overrides the five-year amortization requirement and permits a full current deduction for a standby charge, guarantee fee, registrar fee, transfer agent fee, filing fee, service fee, or any similar fee that may reasonably be considered to relate solely to the year and that relates to money borrowed by the taxpayer and used for earning income other than exempt income. The provision does not apply to contingent payments, payments dependent on use or production from property, or payments computed by reference to revenue, profit, cash flow, commodity price, dividends paid, etc.

In *Macmillan Bloedel Limited v. The Queen*, 90 DTC 6219 (F.C.T.D.), the Court ruled that foreign exchange losses on a hedging transaction were deductible under the old 100% write-off version of this provision. Presumably the loss would now be amortized over five years, although the aggressive taxpayer might argue that it was akin to the fees given 100% write-off.

(ITA: 20(1)(e), (e.1), (e.2); IT-341R4 [Archived])

[¶764.05] *Life Insurance Premiums*

The cost of premiums paid under life insurance policies is not generally deductible (except where the insurance is an employee benefit; see ¶741). However, a deduction is permitted under paragraph 20(1)(*e.2*) of the Act in respect of life insurance premiums under a policy that is assigned as collateral for a loan, provided (1) the assignment is required by the lender; (2) the lender is a Canadian (or Quebec) licensed bank, trust company, credit union, insurance company, or any other corporation whose principal business is lending money to or purchasing debt obligations from arm's length persons; and (3) the interest payable on the loan is either deductible or would be deductible but for the limitations on interest and property on vacant land (¶665), the soft cost limitations (¶771), or the capitalized interest election (¶1073).

Pursuant to amendments first announced in the 2013 federal Budget, the deduction is not allowed for premiums paid in respect of an "LIA policy" or a "10/8 policy". See ¶764.07, below.

Under the rules permitting deduction of premiums, a whole life policy could be assigned as collateral, but only the "net cost of pure insurance" for the period would be deductible. However, an alternative limitation provides that the full premiums paid will only be deductible to the extent they may reasonably be considered to relate to the amount owing under the loan for which the policy is collateral. Thus if the policy is for $500,000, but the average loan balance during the taxation year is $200,000, the deduction for premiums will be limited to the lesser of (a) $^2/_5$ (40%) of the premiums payable and (b) the net cost of pure insurance for the policy in respect of the year. The net cost of pure insurance is determined by the insurer in accordance with regulations. Typically the insurer will provide this information on request.

Although a self-employed person cannot usually deduct the cost of life insurance on his or her own life (subject to the rules above), it is possible to deduct premiums paid for an employee's life insurance policy under ordinary rules concerning the payment of remuneration. Typically, this occurs where the employee or employee's family is a beneficiary, and the premiums paid by the employer are a taxable fringe benefit to the employee. By far the most common example of this is group term life insurance provided by employers for employees. In all cases where an employer may deduct insurance payments, whether for employees' life insurance or otherwise, there may be restrictions to the company on the timing of the deductions; see ¶741 and ¶753.

(ITA: 20(1)(e), (e.1), (e.2); Window on Canadian Tax: 8228; IT-309R2 [Archived])

[¶764.07] *Restrictions in Respect of LIA Policies and 10/8 Policies*

Amendments first announced in the 2013 federal Budget will deny the deduction under paragraph 20(1)(*e*.2) of life insurance premiums payable in respect of "LIA policies" (leveraged insured annuity policies) and "10/8 policies". For LIA policy premiums, the deduction is denied for taxation years ending after March 20, 2013, other than in respect of LIAs for which all borrowings were entered into before March 21, 2013. The denial in respect of 10/8 policies applies to periods after 2013. In addition, the deduction of any interest payable in respect of a borrowing in a 10/8 policy arrangement is denied for periods after 2013 (see subsection 20(2.01)). For further details regarding these policies and the amendments, see ¶432a.05 (LIA policies) and ¶1063.15 (10/8 policies).

[¶764.10] *Participating Debt as a Borrowing Expense*

Participating debt (normally issued by corporations) is, generally speaking, a hybrid debt obligation in which normal interest expressed as a percentage of principal is supplemented or replaced by payments based on other criteria, such as cash flow or gross or net profits above a certain level. Generally speaking, the CRA's view has been that payments based on criteria other than principal are not deductible by the payer as interest, but rather are returns of profit on an equity investment.

Where participation payments are not deductible as interest, it is the CRA's view that they are also not deductible over a five-year period as expenses incurred to borrow money. The CRA views these rules as applicable to incidental expenses incurred at the time of the borrowing and not to compensation for money borrowed. However, in *Sherway Centre Limited v. The Queen*, 96 DTC 1640, the Tax Court ruled that participation payments designed to augment the stated rate of interest where operating surplus exceeded a specified amount were deductible under an earlier but similar version of the five-year rule under paragraph 20(1)(*e*) of the Act. The *Sherway* case was appealed to the Federal Court of Appeal 98 DTC 6121, which ruled that the payments were deductible as interest, but had they not been, the Tax Court would have been correct that they qualified as expenses incurred to borrow money. In response to the *Sherway* decision, statutory changes to paragraph 20(1)(*e*) effective after November 1999 expressly disallow the deduction of participation payments under that provision (see ¶764 above).

However, the CRA has historically taken the position that participation payments can be considered interest, and therefore potentially deductible under paragraph 20(1)(*c*), if they are limited to a stated percentage of principal amount of the debt, the limiting percentage reflects commercial interest rates prevailing at the time the loan is entered into, and no other facts can indicate the presence of an equity investment (for example, see Income Tax Technical News No. 16). Furthermore, in light of the *Sherway* decision, the CRA provides that where the participation payments do not satisfy all the criteria mentioned above "but there is clear evidence that the payments are paid in lieu of interest, as for example where they are intended to increase the interest rate of a loan to the prevailing market rate, we will allow the deductibility thereof as interest under paragraph 20(1)(*c*) of the Act. If, however, the payments are such that they result in the yield on the loan exceeding the prevailing market rate and the evidence establishes that the parties did not genuinely attempt to estimate whether the payments would approximate this rate, we might deny the deduction of the participating loan payments under paragraph 20(1)(*c*) of the Act on the grounds that they are distributions of profit and not interest" (CRA Document No. 9823880).

[¶764.20] *Interest Expense*

Interest expense is discussed in detail at ¶1063–¶1075.

[¶765] MISCELLANEOUS DISBURSEMENTS

[¶765.05] *Conversion of Retailers' Equipment to Account for GST*

Certain expenditures for point-of-sale equipment to calculate the Goods and Services Tax will be given a full 100% write-off under applicable capital cost allowance rules.

[¶765.10] *Interest Expense*

For a discussion on interest expense, see ¶1063–¶1075.

[¶765.20] *Capital Expenditures Which May be Deducted*

There are expenditures which even though of a capital nature, may be deducted for income tax purposes. These include:

Site Investigation

Costs of investigating a site for a new plant are deductible currently. These include costs of surveying, soil testing, engineer's reports, etc.

Landscaping

Amounts paid for landscaping of grounds around a building or other structure used in your business are deductible. Landscaping costs for this purpose include fees to a professional landscape architect. The landscaping deduction was at one time discussed in former Interpretation Bulletin IT-296. That Bulletin was cancelled, meaning it can no longer be relied on as policy. Nevertheless, used with caution, it still presents a reasonable overview of the issues. It is not apparent which particular policy statement was considered dubious or outdated.

Representation Expenses

Expenses incurred in making representations in respect of your business to a government (municipal, provincial or federal) or to an agency of such a body are deductible even if for the purpose of obtaining a franchise or trademark. Alternatively you may deduct the expenses in 10 equal instalments over a period of 10 consecutive years. This may be advantageous if claiming the expense in its entirety in the year would result in a loss carry forward which cannot be used. A deduction for representation expenses incurred on acquisition of depreciable property will be deemed to be allowed as a deduction to you as capital cost allowance (Chapter 8). When the property is disposed of, the sale may give rise to a recapture of this deduction (see ¶843).

Utilities Connection

Amounts paid for making a service connection to your place of business for the supply of electricity, water, sewer, gas or telephone service are deductible if they were paid to the supplier of that service and if, as a result of the payment, you did not acquire any property nor become entitled to any of the goods or services to be supplied by the utility.

Improvements to Benefit the Disabled

Businesses may deduct several expenditures on behalf of disabled employees, clients or customers which are capital outlays and would otherwise be depreciated through the capital cost allowance system (Chapter 8). First, you may deduct amounts paid in the year for "prescribed" renovations or alterations to an income (as opposed to personal use) building made to enable individuals who have a mobility impairment to gain access to the building or to be mobile within it. This rule allows such expenses to be deducted by any person who has paid them and who uses the building primarily to gain or produce income from the building or from a business. Prescribed modifications include the installation of interior and exterior ramps and hand-activated electric door openers, the widening of doorways and modifications to bathrooms, elevators or doorways to accommodate use by a person in a wheelchair.

A further rule allows a current deduction from business or property income for any expenses paid in the year for any "prescribed disability-specific device or equipment". Prescribed devices in this category include elevator car position indicators (such as Braille or audio signal) for individuals having a sight impairment, and visual fire alarm indicators, listening devices for group meetings or telephone devices, for individuals having a hearing impairment. The Department of Finance notes on this provision stated that disability-specific computer software and hardware attachments would be prescribed. In fact, this item was not included in the original regulations, but it was added for computer attachments for which amounts are paid after February 25, 1992 by the taxpayer claiming the deduction. Some of the items in this list might normally be paid for by businesses for their employees or customers; some (elevator car position indicators and visual fire alarm indicators) might more commonly be paid for by landlords; regardless of whether the landlord or business pays, however, the amounts paid should be deductible from business or property income of the payer.

It would appear that any expenses which are deductible from income under these rules *must* be deducted from current income rather than depreciated under the capital cost allowance system. This is because the CCA regulations specifically exclude from CCA classes any property the cost of which is "deductible" in computing the taxpayer's income, whether or not the deduction from income is claimed.

Employers of the Disabled

Employers of the disabled should note that certain types of benefits may be paid to or for the disabled which will not create a taxable fringe benefit for them; see ¶361d.

Real Estate Development

See ¶771 for a discussion of restrictions on the deductibility of costs relating to real estate development.

(ITA: 6(16); 20(1)(*aa*), (*cc*), (*dd*), (*ee*), (*qq*), (*rr*); 20(9); ITR: 1102(1)(*a*); 4100 [Election]; 8800 [Prescribed renovations and alterations]; 8801 [Prescribed devices and equipment]; IT-350R [Archived]; IT-485 [Archived]; IT-99R5 (Consolidated) [Archived])

GOODWILL AND OTHER "NOTHINGS"

[¶766] GENERAL

There are some types of expenditures incurred in connection with a business which are neither deductible in full (because they are capital in nature) nor subject to the capital cost allowance provisions (since they are not defined in any of the prescribed classes).

Many of these expenditures will qualify for a partial deduction as "eligible capital expenditures" and the discussion below, through ¶770, discusses the treatment of these expenditures prior to 2017.

Effective January 1, 2017, these expenditures will be subject to the capital cost allowance provisions under new Class 14.1. See ¶770a.

To qualify as an eligible capital expenditure an expenditure must meet a number of conditions, the most important of which are:

(1) It must result from a transaction occurring after 1971.

(2) It must relate to a business of the taxpayer.

(3) It must be capital in nature (accordingly if you deal in properties of this type the transactions may give rise to ordinary business income or loss rather than eligible capital expenditures).

(4) It must be incurred for the purpose of gaining or producing income from a business.

(5) The income gained or produced must not be exempt income.

(6) It must not be deductible or depreciable under any of the other income tax rules.

(7) It must be for the purchase of intangible property or tangible property not owned by the taxpayer.

(8) It must not be an expense otherwise specifically disallowed by the *Income Tax Act*.

Expenditures that would be included in this category are:

[¶766.05] *Goodwill*

Where goodwill is purchased as one of the assets of a business it qualifies as an eligible capital expenditure. Where shares of an incorporated company are purchased and some of the cost of the shares reflects the value of the goodwill of the company, this part of the cost is not considered to be "goodwill" but is just a part of the cost of the shares.

[¶766.10] *Customer Lists*

Generally the cost of a list bringing an enduring benefit to the business of the purchaser is a capital outlay and is an eligible capital expenditure (see ¶749).

[¶766.15] *Trademarks*

The cost of registering a trademark to protect a trade name, design or product is available as a deduction in computing income. Where, however, the taxpayer buys a trademark from another person who has developed a trademark of enduring value, the amount paid for it is an eligible capital expenditure.

[¶766.20] *Franchises, Concessions, or Licences*

A payment for a franchise, concession, or licence for an unlimited period that is not a depreciable property under Class 14 (see ¶880) qualifies as an eligible capital expenditure.

[¶766.25] *Initiation or Admission Fees*

Initiation or admission fees paid to an organization (e.g. for call to the Bar or for membership in a professional accounting institution) are eligible capital expenditures where it can be shown that the annual membership fees of the organization are allowable deductions in computing income of a business.

The entrance or initiation fees paid to a stock exchange are eligible capital expenditures.

Some expenditures which would not be included are:

(1) fines and penalties;

(2) political contributions, even if they do not qualify for a tax credit (¶1462);

(3) employer's contributions to pension and other retirement funds to the extent they exceed the allowable limits;

(4) carrying costs of excess land held for future expansion; and

(5) expenses specifically not allowed as deductions such as club dues or advertising in non-Canadian periodicals.

[¶766.30] *Quotas or Other Government Rights*

Milk quotas issued by provincial milk marketing boards are generally issued originally at no cost to the producer. However, transfers of quotas for value may generally be made, subject to the terms and approval of the board. The cost of a milk quota purchased after 1971 is an eligible capital expenditure. The cost of other similar rights or licences issued under governmental authority are also eligible capital expenditures.

[¶766.35] *Others*

Other eligible capital expenditures include payments:

- for an easement or right of access (but see ¶810d);
- to increase operational efficiency of a business by improving property owned by some other person with which the corporation deals at arm's length (but see ¶810d for circumstances where capital cost allowance may be permitted); and
- to obtain non-competition covenant. Note that the recipient of payments for a non-competition covenant is subject to special rules in ¶929, and that the person who pays to obtain the agreement may enter into an agreement and tax election which will govern the tax consequences, overriding the general rule, although in many cases the payment would remain an eligible capital expenditure under the election.

A number of other items may in some circumstances constitute eligible capital property. Interpretation Bulletin IT-143R3 (now archived) includes both a useful discussion and (in paragraph 33) a list of references to 10 other bulletins in which the concept is discussed. Probably the most generally useful of these is IT-386R, but specific items are dealt with in each of the bulletins listed.

(ITA: 14; IT-143R3 [Archived]; IT-386R [Archived])

[¶766.40] *Emissions Allowances*

Commentary on Bill C-29 Measures (Oct. 25, 2016)

Note: When Bill C-29, October 25, 2016, achieves Royal Assent, the commentary will be modified to read:

There were previously no specific income tax provisions dealing with emission trading transactions, and therefore tax consequences were determined using general income tax principles. Regulated emitters previously treated emissions allowances as eligible capital property ("ECP") for tax purposes, but concern had been expressed that there was uncertainty regarding these transactions in addition to potential double-taxation relating to emissions allowances provided by government entities for no consideration.

To deal with these concerns, there are specific rules now in new section 27.1 to treat emissions allowances as inventory. See ¶758.25 for an overview of these rules.

[¶767] DEDUCTION OF COSTS OF ACQUISITION

The mechanics of amortizing "eligible capital expenditures" are almost identical to those for claiming capital cost allowances (see Chapter 8). The pool system for accumulating costs and proceeds of disposal is used, as is the declining balance method of calculating deductions.

The rules for amortizing these costs changed substantially for fiscal periods commencing after December 31, 1987. This remains important where eligible capital expenditures were made before 1988 but are sold currently, as illustrated in Example 2 at ¶768.

The rules which apply currently require that:

(1) Three-fourths of all actual qualifying expenditures are grouped in one "class" subject to a 7% declining balance rate, except that separate classes are prescribed for each separate business (see ¶702). Any expenditures in this class, which is called "cumulative eligible capital", at the end of the last fiscal period commencing before 1988 were to be "grossed up" or increased by 50% at the beginning of the first fiscal period commencing after 1987. This gross-up offset the new lower rate of 7% and, more important, trued up the expenditure pool so that proceeds of dispositions are correctly accounted for under new inclusion rate of 75%.

(2) Three-fourths of proceeds of disposals are deducted from the pool; negative balances are business income to the extent of previous deductions from income (i.e., negative proceeds go first to *recapture*). Excess negative balances (i.e., in excess of previous deductions) are, to the extent the proceeds are related to qualified farm property (typically farm quotas), eligible for the capital gains exemption (¶502f), deemed to be taxable capital gain and carried directly to Schedule 3. To the extent the proceeds do not relate to eligible farm property, the excess over recapture is business income, and is adjusted to match capital gain rates if the disposition occurs after February 27, 2000. (On earlier dispositions no such adjustment is required because the income is already set at the 75% mode in which the pool operates, matching the then-current 75% capital gain inclusion rate.)

(3) When you cease a business the unamortized balance for that business is deductible in full in the year the business is terminated unless your spouse or a corporation controlled by you continues the business (see ¶770).

(4) When eligible capital expenditures are incurred on a "non-arm's length" acquisition (see ¶812) the amortization base for the purchaser is deemed to be $^4/_3$ of the proceeds credited to the vendor's expenditure pool reduced by any amount on which the vendor has claimed capital gains is exemption (see ¶768).

(5) When you sell an eligible capital property and replace it with similar property, you may deduct the cost of the replacement property from the net proceeds of the former property (see ¶769).

(6) Taxpayers with short taxation years must (for taxation years commencing after December 21, 2000) prorate the maximum permissible claim by days in the taxation year divided by 365.

Proposed Change

In the 2014 Budget, the government announced a consultation process to consider its proposal to eliminate the rules governing the deduction of cumulative eligible capital (CEC). Under the proposal, a new class of depreciable property for CCA purposes would be introduced. Expenditures that are currently added to CEC (at a 75 per cent inclusion rate) would be included in the new CCA class at a 100 per cent inclusion rate. Because of this increased expenditure recognition, the new class would have a 5 per cent annual depreciation rate (instead of 7 per cent of 75 per cent of eligible capital expenditures). The government reiterated its proposal in the 2015 Budget, adding that it "is the intention of the Government to release detailed draft legislative proposals for stakeholder comment before their inclusion in a bill." At the time of publication, draft proposals had not been released.

[¶767.10] *Government Assistance*

The treatment of government assistance received to assist in the acquisition of eligible capital property is clarified to ensure that assistance the taxpayer received or is entitled to receive will reduce the cost of such property eligible for the cumulative eligible capital pool; repayments of assistance are added to the pool when made. Special rules operate where the taxpayer ceases to carry on the business related to the eligible capital property (¶770). It is not clear that this much changes the rules previously in place. Assistance which does not reduce a related expenditure (such as an eligible capital expenditure) will be income; see ¶729.

[¶767.15] *Forgiveness of Debt*

The eligible capital expenditure pool may be reduced where any debt owed by the taxpayer is settled for less than its principal amount; see ¶565.

[¶767.20] *Non-Arm's Length Acquisitions*

This adjustment to the acquiror's cost of eligible capital property is applicable where property is acquired from a person or partnership with which the acquiror does not deal at arm's length (¶812). The adjustment is intended to ensure that the acquiror's pool does not include any portion of the non-taxable part of a gain realized by the transferor on the transfer.

Although the adjustment rule applies on its face to taxation years that end after February 27, 2000, the reduction it generally applies in respect of the disposition after December 20, 2002, of property acquired from the transferor and not disposed of by the taxpayer before that time.

A grandfathering clause provides, essentially, that the "after December 20, 2002" date noted above is read as "after 2003" in the case of an acquisition pursuant to a written agreement in place before December 21, 2002, provided there was no clause in the agreement or otherwise that allowed its obligations to be altered in consequence of an adverse tax assessment.

(Note that where property is acquired in a non-arm's length transaction from an individual who claimed the capital gains exemption, there can be a further adjustment, described under the next subheading below.)

The non-arm's length adjustment discussed here reduces the acquiror's cost (i.e., the cost $^3/_4$ of which is included in the acquiror's pool) by, generally speaking, $^1/_2$ of that portion of the transferor's gain that is taxed at capital gain rather than recapture rates. This is true whether the transferor has accounted for this portion of its proceeds under the ordinary disposition of capital property rules or withdrawn it from the pool and treated the excess over recapture as capital gain. However, where the transferor is an individual who has claimed capital gains exemption, so that the adjustment for that situation operates as described below, the reduction to the acquiror's cost does not include $^1/_2$ of the amount of that claim. That is, the acquiror's reduction amount is the transferor's excess over recapture minus the exemption claimed by the transferor, multiplied by $^1/_2$.

The reduction under this formula cannot exceed the potential addition to the pool. That is, it cannot reduce the addition to less than nil.

Where the transferor has realized such a gain in a taxation year in respect of more than one property, the amount of the gain of the transferor for the purposes of this calculation is that proportion of the gain that the proceeds of disposition of the eligible capital property acquired by the taxpayer is of the total proceeds of disposition of all such property disposed of in the transferor's taxation year.

Presumably the objective is to prevent the acquiror from depreciating an amount which is larger than the amount the transferor could have depreciated plus the amount actually taxable to the transferor (i.e., the taxable portion of the transferor's gain in excess of recapture). The technical language of the reduction provision can be confusing when the acquiror in turn sells the property. It is intended that the acquiror's reduction is reversed on the acquiror's resale. Immediately after the resale, the property is one "disposed of by the taxpayer before that time", and the reduction self-destructs. Since the pool is measured to determine gain only at the last instant of the year, the reduction has been restored and the acquiror's gain on resale is correctly measured.

Department of Finance technical notes provide the following basic examples, to which some format revisions and some comments have been added:

Example 1

Mr. X purchased a farm production quota several years ago for $300,000 and claimed no cumulative eligible capital amounts, so his cumulative eligible capital at the end of his previous taxation year was $225,000. This year he sold the production quota to his sister, Mrs. Y, for its fair market value of $1,200,000. Mr. X reported income of $450,000 under the general rules for disposition of eligible capital property, and did not make any claim under the $500,000 capital gains exemption rule. (Alternatively, Mr. X could have made an election to remove the property from his pool and report a taxable capital gain of $450,000; the result would be the same except that he could offset allowable capital losses if the election were made.)

Because Mrs. Y purchased the production quota in a non-arm's length transaction, the amount included in her cumulative eligible capital balance at the end of the year in respect of the acquisition would be $675,000 (i.e., $^3/_4$ of $1,200,000, less $^1/_2$ of the taxable gain of Mr. X of $450,000). Looked at another way, the amount on which she can claim an annual deduction is limited to Mr. X's $225,000 plus his reported income of $450,000, which presumably is the point of the exercise.

If Mrs. Y in turn claimed no deduction for cumulative eligible capital amounts and in the following year sold the same property at her actual cost of $1,200,000, her pool balance would be restored to $900,000 at the time of (or at least, immediately after) the disposition and before her income inclusion is measured at the end of the year. If this reversal did not occur, Mrs. Y would in turn be taxed on the same gain on disposition already taxed to Mr. X. Technically, the reversal occurs because at the end of the year when her income inclusions are measured, she is a taxpayer "who has disposed of the property before that time".

Example 2

Assume the same facts as Example 1, except that Mr. X claimed a capital gains exemption of $250,000 in respect of his $450,000 taxable gain under paragraph 14(1)(b) of the Act.

Mrs. Y's eligible capital expenditure under subsection 14(3) of the Act is deemed to be $700,000, calculated as $^4/_3$ of the excess of

- $^3/_4$ of the actual proceeds of disposition of $1,200,000 (i.e., $900,000) over
- $^3/_2$ of the $250,000 capital gains exemption of Mr. X (i.e., $375,000)

The amount included in A of Mrs. Y's cumulative eligible capital balance is calculated as follows:

• $^3/_4$ of her deemed eligible capital expenditure of $700,000		$525,000
less $^1/_2$ of the amount by which		
• the taxable gain of Mr. X	$450,000	
exceeds		
• the capital gains exemption claimed by Mr. X	250,000	
	200,000	
	× $^1/_2$	
		$100,000
Amount included in cumulative eligible capital		$425,000

[¶767.25] *Non-Arm's Length Acquisitions from Individuals*

Consistent with the rules which permitted individuals to treat certain negative pool balances as taxable capital gains and therefore eligible for an individual's lifetime capital gains exemption (¶768), and still permit eligible farm or fishing property to qualify for the capital gains exemption (¶502f), a cost adjustment is required by the acquiror of eligible capital property from a non-arm's length individual who has utilized this exemption. The acquiror must reduce his cost of the property to the extent the vendor has claimed capital gains exemption. This remains true for non-arm's length acquisitions after the general capital gains exemption was shut down on February 22, 1994, where the non-arm's length vendor made a final election with respect to property on hand on that date. Accordingly, there can now be a lengthy time between the capital gains election by the vendor and the acquisition and required adjustment by the acquiror. The non-arm's length adjustment can also continue to occur on dispositions of qualified farm property, which includes some eligible capital expenditures.

This adjustment to reduce additions to the pool for non-arm's length acquisitions will not occur where the property is acquired as a consequence of the death of the transferor. Rather, specific rules discussed in Interpretation Bulletin IT-313R2 (now archived) apply to the acquiror in this situation. (See ¶770.)

Where the taxpayer acquires property in a non-arm's length transaction in a taxation year ending after February 27, 2000, the cost of the property to the acquiror will be deemed to be $^4/_3$ of:

(1) the vendor's pool reduction on the disposition [or, if the vendor has elected to withdraw the asset from the pool in order to recognize capital gain as described in ¶768.20, $^3/_4$ of the actual proceeds of disposition under the election]

REDUCED BY THE TOTAL OF

(2) any capital gains exemption claimed by the non-arm's length vendor on the disposition, or by any other non-arm's length person on an earlier non-arm's length transaction, for a taxation year ending before February 28, 2000, plus

(3) $^9/_8$ of any capital gains exemption claimed by the non-arm's length vendor on the disposition, or by any other non-arm's length person on an earlier non-arm's length transaction, for a taxation year ending after February 28, 2000 and before October 18, 2000, plus

(4) $^3/_2$ of any capital gains exemption claimed by the non-arm's length vendor on the disposition, or by any other non-arm's length person on an earlier non-arm's length transaction, for a taxation year ending after October 17, 2000.

Example

Mr. A acquires an eligible capital property (ECP) for his business. The purchase price for the property is $100 and thus he adds $75 to the EC property pool for the business. The balance in the pool at the end of the year is $75 and Mr. A claims a paragraph 20(1)(*b*) deduction of $5, reducing the pool balance to $70. Assume for the sake of simplicity there are no further depreciation claims. In a later year, after 2000, Mr. A sells the ECP to A Jr., his son, for $200 (the fair market value at that time). Mr. A's proceeds credited to the pool from the disposition is $150 (assume that there are no costs for the disposition), which causes a negative balance of $80 in his

EC pool at the end of that year. Five dollars of that negative balance is included in Mr. A's income as a recapture of the prior year's deduction. The remaining $75 is either (i) subject to an offset of $75 from his exempt gains balance if he made a 1994 election to have a deemed disposition then, or (ii) stepped down to $50 and included in Mr. A's income, offset by a $50 capital gains deduction if the property is qualified farm property. A Jr.'s EC expenditure for the EC property acquired for his business is determined to be $^4/_3$ of (his father's $150 EC amount minus, if the property was subject to a 1994 election, the $75 on which a 1994 capital gains exemption was claimed, or, if the property is qualified farm property, $^3/_2$ of his father's $50 capital gains deduction). In either case, A Jr.'s EC actual EC expenditure of $200 is reduced by ($^4/_3$ of $75 =) $100, and is therefore deemed to be $100, and $75 rather than $150 is added to the pool for his business.

As if this were not enough, there is a further element to this rule which reverses the transferee's cost reduction on the transferee's subsequent disposition for proceeds in excess of the reduced cost. That is, the reduction in (2), above (and (3) and (4) where they applied) is deemed to be the lesser of (i) the original reduction determined at the time of the transfer and (ii) the original transferor's proceeds in (1), above, in excess of the transferee's pool proceeds on the transferee's disposition. Thus, in the example above, if A Jr. sold the property for $120, with consequent proceeds to the pool of $90, he would find the original cost reduction of $75 in the original formula had become the lesser of $75 and (Mr. A's original pool proceeds of $150 minus A Jr.'s pool proceeds of $90 =) $60. A Jr.'s cost is now $^4/_3$ of (his father's $150 EC amount minus the new reduction of $60 =) $90, or $120. His new pool cost is $90 immediately after the disposition, and his pool proceeds are $90, so he has no income inclusion. In short, he is not obliged to pay tax on the gain his father already recognized, even though his father was able to shelter the gain. He is simply not allowed to take depreciation on the non-arm's length price bump. All this is much easier to visualize if you work in terms of whole gains.

The formula above replaced a less complex formula, which was adequate to adjust for non-arm's length transactions before February 28, 2000, when the capital gains inclusion rate on the earlier transactions was 75%, but did not properly adjust for capital gains claims by the vendor (or the vendor's non-arm's length antecedents) where that rate was less (and there is a greater exempt gain which should reduce the transferee's cost). The mechanics of the pre-February 28, 2000 adjustment were that the cost of the property to the acquiror was deemed to be $^4/_3$ of:

(1) the vendor's pool reduction (i.e., the $^3/_4$ of proceeds debited to the pool) on the disposition [or, if the property is the subject of an election by the vendor to remove it from the pool in the year of disposition, as described under the subheading "Withdrawing Property from the Pool to Utilize Capital Losses or Obtain a Reserve" in ¶768, below, $^3/_4$ of the actual proceeds under that election]

REDUCED BY

(2) any capital gains exemption claimed by the non-arm's length vendor on the disposition, or by any other non-arm's length person on an earlier non-arm's length transaction.

The $^4/_3$ grosses up the vendor's pool adjustments to a notional cost.

(ITA: 14(1), (3), (5), (9), (10); 20(1)(*b*), (*hh*); 24(1)(*a*); ITAR: 21(2); IT-123R6 [Archived])

[¶768] TAXATION OF DISPOSITIONS

[¶768.05] *Which Dispositions Give Rise to "Eligible Capital Amounts"*

When you dispose of "eligible capital property", the proceeds of disposition are classified as an eligible capital amount (ECA) and reduce your eligible capital expenditure pool. This is true even if your pool is zero to begin with; that is, if you had never purchased the eligible capital property.

For example, suppose you have built up a business from scratch and never purchased goodwill, customer lists, or similar assets. When you sell the business, however, you are paid more than the value of the "hard" assets, such as inventory and business machinery. You are also paid for the reputation of the business, favourable business contracts, and perhaps a non-competition provision. These items are included (along with some others) in the concept of goodwill. They are not items you have bought, but they are part of the business value you can sell when you sell the business as a whole. The price the purchaser pays you in excess of the "net asset value" for this goodwill is an eligible capital amount. It creates a negative eligible capital expenditure pool, which in turn creates an income inclusion geared to the capital gains inclusion rate, as discussed below. For actual dispositions after February 22, 1994, and subject to an exception for eligible farm or fishing property (typically quotas; see ¶502f.15), this income inclusion is business income, but may be offset by amounts on which you made an election in respect of eligible property on hand at February 22, 1994.

An "eligible capital property" is, strictly speaking, property the disposition of which gives rise to an "eligible capital amount". The definition of this property changed somewhat in 2006. Originally, such property was defined as property the cost of which would be an eligible capital expenditure of your business if you bought it rather than sold it. This led to some court cases in which the taxpayer who disposed of the property was put in the shoes of the taxpayer who acquired it. In particular, where property was expropriated by a municipality for civic purposes, the corporation that disposed of the property did not have to treat it as an eligible capital amount on disposition, essentially because the municipality's purpose was attributed to the corporation. The Department of Finance took exception to the implications of this, and replaced the "mirror image test", effective for amounts receivable after May 2, 2006, except that the taxpayer could elect to be covered by the old definition for amounts received before August 31, 2006 if it elected in writing before the filing due date for its return for the year which included August 31, 2006.

Under the current definition, amounts are eligible capital amounts you have received or become entitled to receive on account of capital in respect of the business you carry on, or formerly carried on, unless the amount:

(1) is otherwise included in your income or otherwise deducted from any balance of undeducted outlays, expenses or other amounts for the year or a preceding year,

(2) reduces your cost or capital cost of a property or the amount of an outlay or expense, or

(3) is included in computing any gain or loss on the disposition of capital property.

An amount which meets these tests is net of any expenses made or incurred for obtaining it, provided the amount is not otherwise deductible.

In basic terms, an eligible capital amount is an amount received on account of capital of a business which is not otherwise accounted for as income, deduction, or reduction of expense (i.e., a "nothing"). Essentially, the receipts which give rise to these amounts should still be for dispositions of the same kind of things which would give rise to eligible capital expenditures if purchased, except that the vendor is not put in the purchaser's shoes. Or at least, this is the intention. Whatever problems may lurk in the new definition have yet to surface. In any event, eligible capital property is essentially the kind of property described in ¶766.

Strictly speaking, an eligible capital amount is 75% of the net amount described above, which simply matches the inclusion and deduction rates for additions to and deductions from the eligible capital expenditure pool.

(ITA: 14(5), amount E)

[¶768.15] *Amount of Income Inclusion*

Returning from the election to the general rules, if you already have an eligible capital expenditure pool, you may sell an item which reduces that pool. (The item need not be one which you are actually depreciating in the pool, although it often will be. For example, in a farming business you might have a milk quota. If it was granted to you at no cost, it would have no impact on your eligible capital expenditure pool, which might contain other items. On the other hand, if you purchased it, it would be included in the pool. In either case, if you sell the quota the proceeds of disposition would be an eligible capital amount and reduce the pool.) A pool reduction operates very much like a capital cost allowance class. The negative balance represents income to the extent of the original cost of assets in the pool at the time immediately preceding the disposition. That is, all amounts of depreciation taken on the pool are "recaptured" to the extent of proceeds of disposition which reduce it below zero.

However, once all depreciation has been recaptured (which is to say once proceeds of disposition exceed the actual costs of pool assets) any further proceeds of disposition are treated similarly to taxable capital gains in that only one-half of the excess over the original cost of the assets are included in income.

The current rules work generally as follows. Where a negative pool arises by virtue of the sale of items in the pool which do not represent the sale of the entire business, any negative pool balance after recapture (and assuming the qualified farm or fishing property rules do not apply) is stepped down by a factor of $^2/_3$ to parallel the $^1/_2$ capital gains inclusion rate for that period. That is, $^2/_3$ of the 75% of proceeds credited to the pool and surplus to recapture yields an effective $^1/_2$ (50%) inclusion rate ($^2/_3 \times ^3/_4 = ^1/_2$). The system permits you to notionally withdraw a property from the pool at cost immediately prior to disposition, and treat it as a capital property. The logic and consequences are discussed under ¶768.20. As well, the qualified farm property rules still operate to deem an appropriate amount of proceeds in excess of recapture to be taxable capital gain (to the extent of the available capital gains exemption).

Historical Information Regarding Treatment After Recapture

The historical rules are as follows:

(1) For taxation years ending prior February 23, 1994, these amounts simply went directly into the taxable capital gain category for the year (again, provided you are an individual carrying on the business directly or through a Canadian partnership).

(2) For taxation years ending after February 22, 1994, and before February 28, 2000, where a negative pool arises in by virtue of the sale of items in the pool which do not represent the sale of the entire business, the negative balance is included in business income, although it may be sheltered by an exempt gains balance as discussed above. There is an exception for qualified farm or fishing property (typically quotas or licences), which continues to be eligible for the capital gain exemption described at ¶502f. Proceeds of disposition of qualified farm property in excess of recapture are deemed to be taxable capital gain to the extent of the exemption. By its own terms, the capital gains exemption is typically not available to non-residents. Note that where the 75% of proceeds credited to the pool (in excess of recapture) were treated as business income, this was equivalent to a capital gain included in income at a 75% inclusion rate.

(3) For taxation years ending after February 27, 2000, and before October 18, 2000, where a negative pool arises by virtue of the sale of items in the pool which do not represent the sale of the entire business, any negative pool balance after recapture (and assuming the qualified farm property rules do not apply) is stepped down by a factor of $^9/_8$ to parallel the $^2/_3$ capital gains inclusion rate for that period. That is, $^8/_9$ of the 75% of proceeds credited to the pool and surplus to recapture yields an effective $^2/_3$ inclusion rate ($^8/_9 \times ^3/_4 = ^2/_3$). Now, however, there is a new wrinkle. The system now permits you to notionally withdraw a property from the pool at cost immediately prior to disposition, and treat it as a capital property. The logic and consequences are discussed under the next subheading below. As well, the qualified farm property rules still operate to deem an appropriate amount of proceeds in excess of recapture to be taxable capital gain (to the extent of available $500,000 exemption).

(4) For taxation years ending after October 17, 2000, the current rules apply.

The result of these considerations should be that where you are in business and you sell some asset of the business which has the nature of eligible capital property as described in ¶766, the proceeds of disposition must be accounted for under the machinery described here. The result will typically be the same as if the property had been a capital property. Where the entire business is sold or otherwise ceases, see ¶770.

[¶768.20] *Withdrawing Property from the Pool to Utilize Capital Losses or Obtain a Reserve*

The rules above only apply where a taxpayer has a negative CEC pool balance. Moreover, the pool still operates in 75% mode even where proceeds actually included in income are adjusted to match capital gain inclusion rates. That is, additions to the CEC pool are still made at the $^3/_4$ rate and dispositions of eligible capital property still reduce pool balances on a $^3/_4$ basis.

The current system recognizes that there may be circumstances in which a taxpayer would prefer to recognize the inherent capital gain on an eligible capital property disposition regardless of whether or the extent to which it creates a negative CEC pool; for example, if a taxpayer has outstanding capital losses to be used but wants to conserve the CEC pool balance. Accordingly, the system now permits a taxpayer to elect to, in effect, remove a particular asset from the CEC pool and recognize a capital gain on the particular asset in the year as if it were ordinary non-depreciable capital property. A perhaps unintended effect is that the capital gain element resulting from the election is a true capital gain, and so eligible for the capital gain reserve described in ¶581 (see CRA Document No. 2002-0133797).

This election is only available to recognize gains, not losses, and is not available for goodwill or for other types of property for which the original cost cannot be determined.

The mechanics of this rule are that where you dispose of an eligible capital property (other than goodwill or property the cost to you of which cannot be determined), and your exempt capital gains balance at the time is nil, and the proceeds of disposition exceed the original cost, you can elect ("under subsection 14(1.01)") to have the following consequences:

(1) there is deemed to be a disposition of the property from the pool at original cost (so there is recapture but no gain in the pool);

(2) you are deemed to have disposed of a capital property (not an eligible capital property) with an adjusted cost base equal to the original cost, for proceeds of disposition equal to the actual proceeds, at the time of the actual disposition; and

(3) if the property was qualified farm or fishing property, the notional capital property (in (2)) is also qualified farm or fishing property, as the case may be.

According to the CRA's *Business and Professional Income* guide (T4002), the election is made by attaching a note to your return. No provision is suggested for electronically filed returns; perhaps qualifying software provides for such notes.

Another provision permits you to make a similar election (to remove a particular asset from the CEC pool and recognize a capital gain on it) in respect of property acquired before 1971 which would have been eligible capital property if acquired after 1971. The problem arose in the first place because pre-1972 acquisitions are not automatically included in the definition of eligible capital property. The conditions and consequences of the election are essentially the same as for post-1971 property.

A further amendment prevents a corporation from making the above-noted election on property acquired in a section 85 rollover if (i) the elected amount was less than fair market value at the time of the election, and (ii) the property was acquired by the corporation from a non-arm's length person for whom the eligible capital expenditure cannot be determined. The point is to prevent a taxpayer from rendering a property with an indeterminable cost into a property with a determinable cost by passing it through a corporation.

[¶768.25] *Mechanics of Accounting for Eligible Capital Property Dispositions*

For dispositions in fiscal periods commencing in 1988 or later years, it is essential to be sure that any eligible capital expenditure pool existing at the end of the last fiscal period commencing before 1988 was increased, at the beginning of the first fiscal period commencing after 1987, by 50% of the closing balance at the end of the last fiscal period commencing before 1988. This step was essential to ensure that 1988 and later proceeds of disposition are correctly matched to original costs. Note that the pool deals only with depreciable percentages (one-half before 1988 and three-fourths after 1987), and amounts which fall outside the pool simply have no tax status whatsoever on acquisition or disposition.

For dispositions of eligible capital property occurring in taxation years which commenced after 1987, three-fourths of the proceeds of dispositions of any eligible capital properties reduce the new pool balance. If the pool reductions result in a negative pool, the negative amount is business income to the extent it does not exceed all prior income deductions claimed after 1971. Any negative pool excess over prior income deductions is deemed to be:

(1) if arising from dispositions occurring in taxation years ending prior to February 23, 1994, pure taxable capital gain, and therefore income but eligible for the capital gains exemption;

(2) if arising from actual dispositions of a business before February 23, 1994, pure taxable capital gain, and therefore income but eligible for the capital gains exemption;

(3) if arising from the disposition at any time of eligible capital property which is qualified farm or fishing property (¶502f), pure taxable capital gain to the extent of available lifetime farming or fishing capital gain exemption, and therefore income eligible for the relevant capital gains exemption;

(4) in all other cases, for taxation years ending after February 27, 2000, the amount of business income is stepped down, to $^8/_9$ of the amount otherwise so included for taxation years ending after February 27, 2000 and before October 18, 2000 (irrelevant for most individuals unless there is a non-calendar taxation year), and to $^2/_3$ of the amount otherwise so included for taxation years ending after October 17, 2000. This matches the income to capital gain inclusion rates (¶500a).

In brief, proceeds in excess of pool balances (all calculated on the 75% basis) are recaptured to the extent of prior income deductions, and are income eligible for capital gains exemption or exempt gains balance offset thereafter (see Example 2 below). This carve-out of a capital gain element was, before February 28, 2000, limited to individuals; there was simply no such rule for corporations.

The cumulative eligible capital pool under the current rules is measured as follows:

ADD:

(1) $^3/_4$ of eligible expenditures made under the new rules (i.e., for fiscal periods commencing after 1987); technical amendments described at ¶767.20 ensure that the amount included here includes only taxable portion of the gain realized by the non-arm's length transferor on the disposition after December 20, 2002 of eligible capital property.

(2) all negative pool balances previously accounted for under the rules beginning with fiscal periods commencing after 1987; this includes amounts accounted for as:

(a) gain in excess of recapture; since gains are identified by income inclusion, it follows that for taxation years ending after February 27, 2000, the gain element of income inclusions must be grossed up to reverse the stepped-down income inclusions after that date and ensure that all negative pool balances are accounted for,

(b) offsets claimed from the unused balance of an exempt gains balance arising from a capital gains exemption election in 1994, and

(c) taxable capital gain for taxation years that began prior to February 23, 1994;

(3) 150% of the closing balance under the old rules (i.e., for fiscal periods commencing before 1988);

(4) all deductions claimed under the old rules minus all business income inclusions under the old rules, but any negative balance from the old rules must be entered at nil; and

(5) where (2), above, is a positive number, 50% of (7)(b), below;

SUBTRACT:

(6) $^3/_4$ of all proceeds (net of related undeductible expenses) which you receive or may be entitled to receive under the new rules (i.e., for individuals, for fiscal periods commencing after 1987) on the disposition of eligible capital property from a business or former business, whether or not acquired before 1972 (note that the definition of eligible capital property has been modified for dispositions after May 1, 2006, as discussed at ¶768.05); and

(7) the total of:

(a) all new system deductions from income (i.e., for fiscal years commencing after 1987), and

(b) all old system deductions minus all old system income inclusions, and

(c) all reductions required under the settlement of debt rules at ¶565,

minus

(d) the recapture portion of all new system income inclusions.

In principle, the system is fairly clear: when eligible capital property is sold, 3/4 of proceeds are included in income to the extent of all prior income deductions in respect of eligible capital property (not just those on the property sold), and any balance in excess of prior deductions is deemed capital gain prior to the fiscal year including February 22, 1994 (or where the business is actually sold before that date), and income (adjusted for capital gains inclusion rates) eligible for exempt gains balance offset thereafter. Qualified farm or fishing property in excess of recapture remains eligible for taxable capital gains exemption, and also for exempt gains balance offset (which will reduce the amount eligible for capital gains exemption). However, the pool mechanics must be strictly complied with to obtain this result.

Eligible capital property acquired by a spouse under the rules at ¶770 upon ceasing to carry on business will, when disposed of by the acquiring spouse, take account of the claims made by the disposing spouse, so that capital gain and income inclusions will not be overstated on final disposition by the spouse who continued to carry on the business.

The following examples illustrate the rules using four different times periods. Examples 3 and 4 cover the current treatment of sales of eligible capital property.

Example 1: Eligible Capital Property Acquired before 1972

Mr. Johnson acquired a plumbing business in December 1970. Included in the purchase price was $10,000 for goodwill. Since the original goodwill was acquired before 1972, it was never eligible for depreciation, although proceeds of disposition are subject to taxation. No other eligible capital expenditures were made after 1970. On November 30, 2000, Mr. Johnson sold his plumbing business and received $10,000 for goodwill. Mr. Johnson should debit $7,500 to cumulative eligible capital, creating a negative balance of $7,500, of which, since the taxation year ends after October 17, 2000, 2/3 ($5,000) is included in business income.

Example 2: Dispositions of Eligible Capital Property Acquired in Fiscal Periods Commencing Before 1988

Mr. Williams acquired a florist shop in 1986 and paid $20,000 for goodwill. He sold the shop in 1991 and received $24,000 for the goodwill. (The example ends in 1991 to avoid an unnecessary accumulation of annual deductions.) The business had a fiscal period of January 1 to December 31. Mr. Williams' income for the relevant years is calculated as follows:

1986		
Expenditure		$20,000
Less — One-half not deductible		10,000
		$10,000
1986 allowable deduction of 10%		1,000
Cumulative eligible capital		$ 9,000
1987		
1987 allowable deduction of 10%		900
Cumulative eligible capital		$ 8,100
1988		
Old pool balance		$ 8,100
1988 gross-up (50%)		4,050
Restated cumulative eligible capital.		$12,150
1988 allowable deduction of 7%		850
Cumulative eligible capital		$11,300
1989		
1989 allowable deduction of 7%		
Cumulative eligible capital		$10,509
1990		
1990 allowable deduction of 7%		736
Cumulative eligible capital		$ 9,773
1991		
Proceeds of sale	$24,000	
Deduction from cumulative eligible capital account 75%		18,000
Cumulative eligible capital		$(8,227)
Allocation to income: lesser of		
Negative CEC	$8,227	
Net prior claims	$4,277	
Recapture (1991 business income)		$ 4,277
Allocation to capital gain:		
Negative CEC		$ 8,227
Minus: recapture		4,277
50% of net pre-1988 claims		950
1991 taxable capital gain		$ 3,000

All previous deductions of $4,277 are recaptured as income. The remaining negative pool amount of $3,950 must be further reduced by 50% of the old system claims of $1,000 in 1986 and $900 in 1987, which in effect grosses up old system claims to new system rates. The result is $3,000, or 75% of the $4,000 actual gain on the sale for $24,000 of an asset which cost $20,000. It is this amount (which has already been reduced to 75% of the actual gain) that was, for 1991, treated as taxable capital gain. After February 22, 1994, there would have been $4,277 of recapture and $3,000 of other business income. For a fiscal period ending after February 27, 2000 and before October 18, 2000, the $3,000 gain portion would be stepped down by 8/9 to $2,667 (2/3 of the actual $4,000 gain). For a fiscal period ending after October 17, 2000, the $3,000 gain portion would be stepped down by 2/3 to $2,000 (1/2 of the actual $4,000 gain).

Example 3: Current Sale Where Property Acquired in Fiscal Period Commencing After 1987

This illustration assumes that no eligible capital expenditures were made before the 1988 rules came into force, or that all balances carried forward from taxation years commencing under the old rules have been absorbed on subsequent dispositions. If this is not the case, tax will be overpaid unless old balances are taken into account as shown in Example 2.

Actual cost (purchased in 1996 taxation year)	$50,000	
Proceeds of disposition (sold in 1999 taxation year)	80,000	
Calculation:		
Deemed proceeds of disposition (75% of the actual proceeds)		$60,000
Cumulative eligible capital (75% of the original cost less each year's cumulative eligible capital amount)		
75% of original cost	$37,500	
CEC amount — 1996	2,625	
	$34,875	
CEC amount — 1997	2,441	
	$32,434	
CEC amount — 1998	2,270	30,164
Inclusion in income — 1999		$29,836

The income inclusion is made up of recapture of the $7,336 previously deducted (2,625 + 2,441 + 2,270 = 7,336) plus $22,500, or 75% of the $30,000 proceeds of disposition in excess of actual cost ($80,000 proceeds - $50,000 cost = $30,000, × 75% = $22,500). Cumulative gains balance, if any, could be used to reduce the $22,500 only.

If the property were acquired in 1998 and sold in 2000, the results would be the same for a 2000 fiscal period ending before February 28, 2000. For a fiscal period ending after February 27, 2000 and before October 18, 2000, the $22,500 gain portion ($29,836 proceeds in excess of pool minus accumulated depreciation recaptured of $7,336) would be stepped down by $^8/_9$ to $20,000 ($^2/_3$ of the actual $30,000 gain). For a fiscal period ending after October 17, 2000, the $22,500 gain portion would be stepped down by $^2/_3$ to $15,000 ($^1/_2$ of the actual $30,000 gain).

Example 4: Property Acquired in Fiscal Period Commencing after 1987, Sold after February 27, 2000

This illustration assumes that no eligible capital expenditures were made before the 1988 rules came into force, or that all balances carried forward from taxation years commencing under the old rules have been absorbed on subsequent dispositions. If this is not the case, tax will be overpaid unless old balances are taken into account as shown in Example 2.

Margo has a calendar taxation year. She acquired her only eligible capital property in her 1999 taxation year for $50,000. Of this, $37,500 was posted to cumulative eligible capital, and 7% thereof deducted ($2,625), leaving a balance of $34,875. No further depreciation has been claimed for tax purposes. In the current taxation year, the property was sold for $80,000, of which 75% ($60,000) is credited to the CEC pool. Since it exceeds the pool balance, there is recapture up to the lesser of the $60,000 and the full amount of $2,625 claimed, so income from the recapture element of $2,625. To the extent the $60,000 exceeds both the closing pool and the recapture element ($60,000 - ($34,875 + $2,625) = $22,500), that excess is stepped down by $^2/_3$ to arrive at an income inclusion of ($^2/_3$ × $22,500 =) $15,000 for the gain element. The total income inclusion is $15,000 + $2,625 = $17,625, representing half the actual gain of $30,000 ($80,000 actual proceeds - $50,000 actual cost) plus all depreciation previously taken. If 75% of the proceeds had exceeded $34,875 but not $37,500, there would be recapture only.

If Margo had a June 30, 2000 year end, the calculations would be identical but the income inclusion element on the gain would be only $^8/_9$ × $22,500 = $20,000, which is of course $^2/_3$ of the $30,000 actual gain. To this would be added the recapture element of $2,625.

See also the Sophie example below under the heading "Uncollectible Proceeds on Cumulative Eligible Capital".

[¶768.30] Reserves where Some Proceeds not Due until Future Year

Proceeds of disposition of eligible capital property (unless pursuant to a pre-June 18, 1987 written agreement) are treated as having become payable at the time of the disposition; that is, the applicable portion of proceeds must be credited to the pool and any income resulting from a negative pool must be recognized in the year of disposition regardless of whether the proceeds have been fully received. In short, no reserve is permitted.

However, where an election is made to recognize capital gain on a disposition pursuant to the rules under the subheading "Withdrawing Property from the Pool to Utilize Capital Losses or Obtain Reserve" at ¶768.20, the capital gain element calculated under that provision is a true capital gain eligible for the capital gain reserve described in ¶581. This result of the election, perhaps unintended, is confirmed in CRA Document No. 2002-0133797.

(ITA: 14; 20(1)(*l*), (p), (4.2); ITAR: 21; IT-123R6 [Archived]; IT-386R [Archived]; *The Queen v. Timagami Financial Services Ltd.*, 82 DTC 6268 (F.C.A.); Other Publications: Canadian Tax Foundation, *1983 Conference Report*, p. 789)

[¶768.40] Uncollectible Proceeds on Cumulative Eligible Capital

The procedure above for dealing with bad debts on dispositions of eligible capital property is complex due to the changes of income inclusion rates on the dispositions. The already complex formula above is restated so that deductions for these bad debts accumulate at a rate that reflects changing inclusion rates. Unfortunately this requires a formula so complex that it seems beyond simple explanation. Accordingly, we have borrowed liberally from the Department of Finance's own explanation and example, from its Technical Notes.

Because the eligible capital property system after February 27, 2000, incorporates three fractions on dispositions for proceeds in excess of pool balances, one for calculating cumulative eligible capital pool balance ($^3/_4$) and two others ($^2/_3$ and $^1/_2$) for calculating income inclusions for a negative pool in excess of recaptured depreciation, the reserve for bad debts arising from these dispositions recognizes three different proportions of bad debts as deductible, depending on how the recognition of the proceeds of disposition originally affected the taxpayer. The amount deductible in respect of bad debts is (after February 27, 2000) determined by the formula (A + B) - (C + D + E + F + G + H). The formula operates as a pool that takes into account bad debts in the year and in preceding years.

Variable A applies for taxation years that end after February 27, 2000. It is equal to the lesser of $^1/_2$ of total bad debts ($^2/_3$ for taxation years ending after February 27 and before October 18, 2000) and, generally, that portion of the taxpayer's income inclusion, which reflects the taxable portion of the taxpayer's gain in respect of eligible capital property (before shelter from exempt capital gains balance, if any). This portion of the taxpayer's income inclusion reflects the $^2/_3$ or the $^1/_2$ inclusion rate for capital gains.

Variable B is the amount by which $^3/_4$ of the bad debt exceeds $^9/_8$ or $^3/_2$ of variable A. The $^9/_8$ fraction of course applies to that portion of A arising in taxation years ending after February 27 and before October 18, 2000 (the interim period); the $^3/_2$ fraction to that portion of A arising in later taxation years (the new period). For earlier taxation years, B is nil. This ensures that only the appropriate fraction of the bad debt is recognized. Multiplying A by $^9/_8$ or $^3/_2$ converts it from a $^2/_3$- or $^1/_2$-based amount to a $^3/_4$-based amount.

Variables C through H reduce the amount of the taxpayer's deduction to reflect otherwise taxable amounts that have been sheltered by deductions in respect of capital gains. Variables F and G relate to the taxpayer's claim in respect of his or her exempt gains balance, related to the lifetime capital gains exemption (and so are only relevant for individuals). The claim will be the whole amount of old system gain so sheltered, $^8/_9$ of interim period gain, and $^2/_3$ of new period gain. Variables C, D and E describe amounts that have been sheltered by the deduction in respect of capital gains on qualified farm property in each of the old, interim, and new periods. Variable H reduces the deduction by amounts deducted under the provision for prior years, to appropriately adjust the pool, which reflects all bad debts owing to the taxpayer in respect of eligible capital property.

Variables C to G are used to calculate the taxpayer's allowable capital loss, as described below.

Example 5

Sophie has a cumulative eligible capital pool balance of $750,000 in 1999. This pool balance reflects $100,000 of depreciation claimed since Sophie began carrying on business in 1989. In January 2000, Sophie disposes of eligible capital property to Acme Corporation for proceeds of disposition of $2 million. Sophie claims no depreciation in 2000. Sophie has an exempt gains balance of $50,000, which she claims to reduce the gain element of her income inclusion for 2000.

The 2000 taxation year results are as follows:

- opening balance: $750,000
- less $^3/_4 \times$ $2 million proceeds of disposition
- credit balance: ($750,000)
- recapture of depreciation claimed:
- $100,000 income inclusion
- residual income inclusion (gain element):

$^2/_3 \times$ (A - B - C - D)

A is $750,000

B is $100,000 of depreciation

C ($^1/_2$ of depreciation claimed before adjustment time) is nil, and

D is $50,000 (exempt gains balance that Sophie is claiming).

$^2/_3 \times$ ($750,000 - $100,000 - $50,000) = $400,000 income inclusion.

In 2001, the $2 million owed to Sophie becomes a bad debt when Acme Corporation goes bankrupt.

Sophie applies the magic formula to calculate her deduction and allowable capital loss in respect of the bad debt.

Deduction ((A + B) - (C + D + E + F + G + H)).

A is the lesser of

(a) $^1/_2$ of the bad debt ($^1/_2$ of $2 million), plus $^1/_2$ of bad debts from prior years (none), so: $1,000,000, and

(b) the gain (not recapture) inclusion on the disposition, read without reference to variable D (exempt gain balance) in the gain formula: $^2/_3 \times$ ($750,000 - $100,000) = $433,333

the lesser of (a) and (b) is $433,333

B is the amount by which $^3/_4$ of the bad debt, plus $^3/_4$ of the bad debts from prior years — $1.5 million — exceeds $^3/_2$ of the amount determined for A: $^3/_2 \times$ $433,333 = $650,000, therefore B is $1.5 million - $650,000 = $850,000

(A + B) is $433,333 + $850,000 = $1,283,333

C is nil, because Sophie has not claimed a capital gains exemption in respect of capital gains related to an income inclusion on disposition of eligible capital property.

F(a) is $^2/_3$ of the exempt gains balance that Sophie claimed. $^2/_3$ of $50,000 is $33,333.

D, E, F(b), and G are generally the same as C and F(a), except that they apply in respect of taxation years that ended before February 28, 2000 or taxation years that ended after February 27, 2000 and before October 18, 2000. Sophie has not claimed a deduction in respect of capital gains, or claimed anything in respect of her exempt gains balance, for taxation years that ended before February 28, 2000 nor for taxation years that ended after February 27, 2000 and before October 18, 2000.

H is nil because Sophie has not claimed an amount under these rules for bad debts in prior years.

The formula therefore allows Sophie a deduction of $1,283,333 - $33,333 = $1,250,000. This deduction corresponds to Sophie's $400,000 income inclusion of the gain element of the disposition, plus her recaptured depreciation of $100,000, plus the elimination of her $750,000 pool balance; these three amounts total $1,250,000.

Sophie used her exempt gains balance of $50,000 in the 2000 taxation year sale of eligible capital property to shelter a portion of the gain. The $33,333 determined by variable F(a) reduces Sophie's deduction as described above in recognition of this sheltering. The amount of the reduction is $33,333, rather than $50,000, because the new formula for the calculation of Sophie's 2000 taxation year (December 31 year-end) income inclusion introduces the factor $^2/_3$ to the calculation. (In other words, $33,333 will shelter the same amount of gain under a $^1/_2$ inclusion rate system as $50,000 did under a $^3/_4$ inclusion rate system. In both cases $66,667 can be sheltered.) The amount of the reduction in variable F(a) is deemed to be an allowable capital loss, as discussed below.

As before, where a taxpayer's deduction for bad debts on eligible capital property dispositions is reduced to recognize the taxpayer's use of a capital gains deduction to offset an income inclusion or the original disposition, the taxpayer is deemed to have an allowable capital loss. The allowable capital loss, in effect, restores the capital gains deduction that was used up in sheltering a gain on what turned out to be a bad debt. The allowable capital loss is equal to the lesser of two amounts. The first amount is the value of A in the bad debt formula plus $^2/_3$ of the value of B in the bad debt formula (in general this will be $^1/_2$ of the total bad debts). The second amount is the capital gains exemption amounts or exempt gains balance used up in respect of dispositions of eligible capital property under the $^1/_2$ inclusion rate system, plus $^3/_4$ of capital gains exemption or exempt gains balance used up in respect of dispositions of eligible capital property under the $^2/_3$ inclusion rate system plus $^2/_3$ of capital gains exemption or exempt gains balance used up in respect of dispositions of eligible capital property under the $^3/_4$ inclusion rate system. The use of the fraction $^3/_4$ converts the $^2/_3$-based exemption claims to a $^1/_2$ basis for the purpose of calculating an allowable capital loss that will be used to offset capital gains that are included at $^1/_2$. The fraction $^2/_3$ converts the $^3/_4$-based exemption claims to the same rate basis.

The fractions immediately above apply in respect of taxation years that end after February 27, 2000 except that, for taxation years that end after February 27, 2000 and before October 18, 2000, the fractions used will be adjusted to reflect the $^2/_3$ inclusion rate. In particular, the references to $^1/_2$, $^3/_2$ and $^2/_3$ are to be read as references to $^2/_3$, $^9/_8$ and $^8/_9$, respectively, the $^3/_4$ fraction is read as nil.

Where an amount is received in a taxation year ending after October 17, 2000, on account of a bad debt deducted in an earlier year, there is an income inclusion of half the amount received prorated by the earlier deduction in respect of that particular debt over the sum of the earlier deduction and the allowable capital loss in respect of the particular debt. The portion of the recovered amount that relates to the allowable capital loss is deemed to be taxable capital gain.

(ITA: 12(1)(*i.*1); 14; 20(4.2), (4.3); 39(11); Other Publications: Department of Finance Technical Notes of March 16, 2000)

[¶769] REPLACEMENT PROPERTY

If you voluntarily dispose of eligible capital property in a particular taxation year (fiscal period of a business), you may be able to defer the amount required to be deducted by you in calculating your cumulative eligible capital for the year by purchasing a replacement property before the later of: (1) the end of the following taxation year, or (2) 12 months after the end of the taxation year (fiscal period) in which the disposition occurred. The second rule has been added to provide for short taxation years.

If the proceeds of disposition are equal to or less than the cost of the replacement property, the entire proceeds may be deferred to the following year. If the proceeds of disposition are greater than the cost of the replacement property, the excess must be recognized as proceeds of disposition in the year of disposition.

An eligible capital property will be considered a replacement property if all the following conditions are met:

(1) it is reasonable to conclude that the property was acquired to replace the former property;

(2) it was acquired by the taxpayer for a use that is the same as or similar to the use to which the former property was put;

(3) it was acquired for the purpose of gaining or producing income from the same or similar business in which the former property was used; and

(4) if you used the former property in a business carried on in Canada, the replacement property must be acquired for use, at least in the first instance, in a business you are carrying on in Canada. Under this rule, Canadian residents are also covered, but taxpayers taxable in Canada but also doing business elsewhere may replace foreign-use property with other foreign-use property.

The election to utilize these rules must be made in your income tax return in the year you acquire the replacement property. You will file your income tax return in the year you sell your eligible capital property as though you were not going to purchase a replacement property. In the subsequent year, when you purchase a replacement property, you will file an amended income tax return for the prior year (see ¶221).

Example

Janet Hunter sold a list of customers of her mail order business in 2007 for $20,000. On January 2, 2008, she purchased another customer list for $25,000. She had purchased other customer lists after 1971, and the balance in her cumulative eligible capital account at the beginning of 2007 was $10,000. Her business has a calendar-year fiscal period.

2007

Cumulative eligible capital account, beginning of year		$ 10,000
Proceeds of disposition of customer lists	$20,000	
Eligible capital amount		(15,000)
Cumulative eligible capital account, end of year		Nil

Janet will not be allowed a deduction in respect of her eligible capital property on her original tax return for 2007, and the 75% of proceeds ($15,000) credited to the account creates a negative balance which will result in income (recapture), as illustrated at Example 5 in¶768.40. You may assume she had to report the $5,000 negative balance as income. However, in 2008, she may file an election to utilize the replacement property rules.

2007 AMENDED

Cumulative eligible capital account, beginning of year		$10,000
Allowable deduction — 7%		700
		$ 9,300

2008

Revised cumulative eligible capital account, beginning of year		$ 9,300
Eligible capital expenditure	$25,000	
Less: Proceeds of disposition of former property in 2006	20,000	
	$ 5,000	
75% thereof		3,750
		$13,050
Allowable deduction — 7%		914
Cumulative eligible capital account, end of year		$12,136

Janet will report, in her amended income tax return for 2007, an allowable deduction of $700 as eligible capital expenditure, and no income (recapture) or capital gain on account of the original disposition. She will receive an allowable deduction of $914 in 2008 unless she acquires or disposes of additional eligible capital property. Using the above example as an illustration, you should note that as long as the cost of the replacement property ($25,000) equals or exceeds the proceeds of disposition of the former property ($20,000), you are able to defer recognition of the entire proceeds of disposition to the next year.

The CRA states in Interpretation Bulletin IT-259R4 (paragraph 3) that this amended return procedure must be followed even where the replacement property has been acquired prior to the filing of the 2007 return. It does go on to say that it is prepared to alleviate the prior year problem by accepting security in lieu of tax "until the time for the final determination of taxes is made or the time period for acquiring the replacement property has expired. Where this practice is followed, the full cost of providing such security is borne by the taxpayer and the interest on the unpaid taxes will continue to accrue at the appropriate prescribed rates subject to being reduced by interest credited on any subsequent reassessment giving effect to the deferral". Providing security is all very well for the sophisticated taxpayer doing business on a large scale. Some taxpayers have apparently found that, at least where the replacement property is acquired before the prior year return is filed, the CRA does not insist on its stated position. Some technical support for the proposition that it is not necessary to file a return ignoring a replacement property acquired after year end will be found in the 1985 *Canadian Tax Journal* (January/February) at page 15. However, failure to follow the CRA procedures runs some risk of assessment and interest charges, or at least prolonged argument.

(ITA: 14; IT-123R6 [Archived]; IT-259R4 [Archived])

[¶769.05] *Business Expansion*

The CRA announced in 2002 a modification of its policies concerning the operation of the replacement property rules in the context of a business expansion. The change is discussed in detail in the context of capital cost allowance under the subhead "Business Expansion" at ¶846.25, but those comments apply equally to the replacement property rules for eligible capital property.

[¶770] CEASING TO CARRY ON BUSINESS

In a year in which you (a) cease to carry on business activities and (b) no longer have eligible capital property that has any value, you must deduct in computing your income for the taxation year during which the business ceased, the amount of any unclaimed cumulative eligible capital you may have. This deduction is sometimes called the "terminal allowance" and is similar in principle to the terminal loss rules for capital cost allowance except that under these rules the business must cease. In the year a terminal allowance is required, no deduction may be made for ordinary depreciation of eligible capital property. Thereafter, the pool balance is deemed to be nil. Nevertheless, the pool continues to exist so that any subsequent sale of pool items which have acquired value in the interim will give rise to income.

You will not be allowed this deduction if, after you cease to carry on the business, your spouse or common-law partner (¶1113), or a corporation controlled by you, does carry on the business. However, your spouse or common-law partner, or the corporation, will take over the positive pool balance and history, and so be able to claim continuing deductions or be subject to recapture/capital gain inclusions on disposition. This is true whether you cease to carry on the business by virtue of death or for any other reason.

Similar but not identical rules apply on the death of an individual, if as a consequence of the taxpayer's death, a person other than the spouse or common-law partner or controlled corporation acquires a property that was an eligible capital property of the taxpayer for the business that was carried on by the taxpayer until his or her death. These rules operate on each property and not on the pool as a whole, and allocate pool amounts to each property based on its *pro rata* share of fair market value of the pool. Essentially, there is no terminal loss on death, but a beneficiary who continues to carry on the business will take over the decedent's tax position with respect to the property. If the beneficiary does not carry on the business, he or she acquires the property as a capital property with a cost base of $^4/_3$ its share of pool value.

(ITA: 24; 25; IT-313R2 [Archived])

[¶770.05] *Stop-Loss Rules and Affiliated Party Transactions*

The stop-loss rules operate where a corporation, trust or partnership disposes of eligible capital property. They do not apply where an individual disposes of eligible capital property (as did the old rules), but do apply to transfers to individuals, corporations and partnerships. Unlike the old rules, which denied the deduction to the transferor and shifted the potential loss to the recipient through cost base adjustments, the current rules leave the deduction with the transferor but defer it.

The rules apply where:

(1) a corporation, trust or partnership (the transferor) disposes of eligible capital property and in consequence a deduction could be claimed under the cessation of business rules for eligible capital property; and

(2) the transferor or an affiliated person (¶852) acquires or has the right to acquire the property (or an identical property) within the period that begins 30 days before the disposition and ends 30 days after the disposition. An identical property for these purposes is defined to include a right to acquire property, other than a security right derived from a mortgage, sale agreement or the like. The meaning of identical properties generally is discussed in ¶512.

Once these conditions are met, the transferor is deemed to continue to own the property and to carry on the business until immediately before the earliest of the following times:

(1) the beginning of a 30-day period throughout which neither the transferor nor a person affiliated with the transferor owns (a) the property or (b) an identical property acquired after the day that is 31 days before the period begins;

(2) when the transferred property or identical property ceases to be used by the transferor or a person affiliated with the transferor in respect of a business (for example on a change in use);

(3) when there is (or would have been if the transferor still owned the property) a deemed disposition of the property or identical property by the transferor under the emigration rules or, in the case of a Crown corporation, the change of status rules;

(4) when there is change of control of the transferor corporation; or

(5) if the transferor is a corporation, generally the beginning of a wind-up or dissolution of the corporation (other than a subsection 88(1) wind-up or certain dissolutions of foreign affiliates).

The result is that the transferor continues to depreciate the eligible capital property (assuming there is income against which to do so) and is entitled to the eventual deduction until there is an ultimate disposition to an unaffiliated party or an event which triggers a recognition of all gains and losses in the transferor.

(ITA: 14(12) Loss on certain transfers; 14(13) Deemed identical property; 24 Ceasing to carry on business; 25 Fiscal period of business disposed of by individual; 85(4) Loss from disposition to controlled corporation; S.C. 1998, c. 19, s. 247; IT-291R3, para. 23, 24 [Archived])

SPECIAL BUSINESSES

[¶770a] CCA RULES APPLICABLE BEGINNING JANUARY 1, 2017

Commentary on Bill C-29 Measures (Oct. 25, 2016)

Note: When Bill C-29, October 25, 2016, achieves Royal Assent, the commentary will be modified to read:

A new class of depreciable property for CCA purposes is to be introduced. Eligible capital property (ECP) that is currently added to the CEC pool (at a 75 per cent inclusion rate) will be included in the new CCA class at a 100 per cent inclusion rate. Because of this increased expenditure recognition, the new class will have a 5 per cent annual depreciation rate (instead of 7 per cent of 75 per cent of eligible capital expenditures).

A summary of the new rules, generally applicable on January 1, 2017, is provided below. There are various transitional rules that apply to expenditures incurred before 2017 and that generally convert the former CEC pools to the new Class 14.1 pool.

Basically, amounts formerly treated as ECP will now be added to new Class 14.1 of Schedule II of the *Income Tax Regulations* effective January 1, 2017. Property that was ECP will be classified as depreciable capital property and expenditures and receipts will also receive depreciable capital property treatment.

Class 14.1 will include goodwill, property that was ECP before January 1, 2017, and any property acquired January 1, 2017 or later that would have otherwise been treated as ECP. The full cost of property acquired is added to Class 14.1 versus the 75% addition for ECP.

Subparagraph 1100(1)(a)(xii.1) of the *Income Tax Regulations* provides for CCA on Class 14.1 property at the rate of 5% on a declining balance basis deductible under paragraph 20(1)(*a*). A separate Class 14.1 must be maintained in respect of each business of the taxpayer, which is consistent with depreciable property and ECP rules.

The recapture rules, terminal loss rules and similar provision applicable to depreciable property will apply. If a Class 14.1 property is sold for more than its original cost, half of the excess will be treated as a taxable capital gain. This treatment contrasts with the pre-2017 treatment under the CEC rules, under which half of the excess is sometimes treated as income from a business (see ¶768.15 through ¶768.30).

Transitional Rules

There are a number of transitional rules that will apply in respect of expenditures incurred before 2017. Basically, the end result of the transitional provisions appears to be to place taxpayers in a position similar to what they would have been in if the ECP rules never existed and Class 14.1 existed all along. The transitional provisions include the following:

(1) Additional depreciation — Prior to the 2027 taxation year, expenditures incurred prior to January 1, 2017 are depreciable at a 7% rate vs. the 5% rate.

(2) Capital cost — On January 1, 2017, the capital cost of property will be determined to be $^4/_3$ of the CEC balance at that time plus $^4/_3$of previously claimed deductions that have not been recaptured, less $^4/_3$ of any negative CEC balance at that time.

(3) Undepreciated capital cost — In most cases the balance in CEC will become the UCC with the difference between capital cost and UCC being deemed to have been claimed as a deduction under paragraph 20(1)(*a*). The amount deemed to have been deducted under paragraph 20(1)(*a*) is calculated as the amount by which total capital cost and any negative CEC balance exceeds any positive CEC balance.

(4) Allocation of capital cost — Paragraph 13(37)(*b*) provides rules for allocating the total capital cost of properties as between a goodwill property and each identifiable property in the class.

(5) Deemed gain immediately before January 1, 2017 — Where a taxation year straddles January 1, 2017 and the taxpayer entered into a transaction prior to January 1, 2017 that resulted in an income inclusion under the ECP rules, the taxpayer can elect to report the transaction as business income (old rules) or as a taxable capital gain (new rules).

(6) Deferral of gains realized before January 1, 2017 — A taxpayer can elect to reduce the income inclusion under the ECP rules where a property described in Class 14.1 has been acquired in the same taxation year the income inclusion arose. These rules operate much the same as the ECP rules would have if a replacement property were acquired before the end of the taxation year in which an income inclusion arose.

(7) Dispositions of former ECP — To avoid excess recapture when disposing of former ECP, subsection 13(38) increases the UCC of Class 14.1 by 25% of the lesser of the proceeds of disposition and the cost of the property disposed of.

(8) Non-arm's length dispositions of former ECP — subsection 13(39) is intended to prevent the use of non-arm's length transfers to increase the amount that can be depreciated in Class 14.1. In effect, only $^3/_4$ of the cost of the former ECP is included in the UCC of Class 14.1 where the property was formerly an ECP of the taxpayer (or certain non-arm's length persons) and subsection 13(38) applied

to increase the UCC in respect of an earlier disposition of the property.

In its explanatory notes to Bill C-29, the Department of Finance provides the following examples illustrating how the capital cost and CEC pool for expenditures incurred before 2017 will be effectively converted to depreciable property in the new Class 14.1 class.

Example 1 — Deemed Capital Cost

Before January 1, 2017

In a taxation year ending before January 1, 2017, a taxpayer incurred an eligible capital expenditure of $100, resulting in a cumulative eligible capital balance of $75 (i.e., $^3/_4$ × $100), to acquire a government licence of unlimited duration. In taxation years ending before January 1, 2017, the taxpayer deducted a total of $35 from cumulative eligible capital under paragraph 20(1)(*b*), resulting in a cumulative eligible capital balance of $40.

On January 1, 2017

The government licence and goodwill are property included in new Class 14.1 of Schedule II to the Regulations.

Paragraph 13(37)(*a*) provides that the total capital cost of property of the new class at the beginning of January 1, 2017 that is goodwill or that was eligible capital property before January 1, 2017 is $^4/_3$ of the amount that would be the cumulative eligible capital at the beginning of January 1, 2017; plus 4/3 of the amount of deductions taken that have not been recaptured; less $^4/_3$ of any negative cumulative eligible capital balance at the beginning of January 1, 2017. The total capital cost of the class is equal to $100 (i.e., $^4/_3$($40+$35-$0)). Subparagraph 13(37)(*b*)(ii) deems the capital cost of the government licence to be $100 and subparagraph 13(37)(*b*)(iii) deems the capital cost of the goodwill of the business to be nil.

Example 2 — Deemed Capital Cost

Before January 1, 2017

In a taxation year ending before January 1, 2017, a taxpayer incurred an eligible capital expenditure of $100 to acquire a government licence of unlimited duration, an eligible capital expenditure of $150 to acquire a customer list and an eligible capital expenditure of $50 for incorporation expenses, resulting in a cumulative eligible capital balance of $225 (i.e., $^3/_4$ × ($100+$150+$50)). In taxation years ending before January 1, 2017, the taxpayer deducted a total of $45 from cumulative eligible capital under paragraph 20(1)(*b*), resulting in a cumulative eligible capital balance of $180 (i.e., $225 – $45). Also in a taxation year ending before January 1, 2017, the taxpayer disposed of the customer list for $112, resulting in a cumulative eligible capital balance of $96 (i.e., $180 – $^3/_4$ ($112)).

On January 1, 2017

The government licence and goodwill would be property included in new Class 14.1 of Schedule II to the Regulations. The customer list and the incorporation expenses would not be property of the new class: the customer list was disposed of before January 1, 2017 and the incorporation expenses were not the cost of an acquisition of property.

Paragraph 13(37)(*a*) provides that the total capital cost of property of the new class at the beginning of January 1, 2017 that is goodwill property or that was eligible capital property before January 1, 2017 is $^4/_3$ of the amount that would be the cumulative eligible capital at the beginning of January 1, 2017; plus $^4/_3$ of the amount of deductions taken that have not been recaptured; less $^4/_3$ of any negative cumulative eligible capital balance at the beginning of January 1, 2017. The total capital cost equals $188 (i.e., $^4/_3$ × ($96+$45-$0)). Subparagraph 13(37)(*b*)(ii) deems the capital cost of the government licence to be $100 (i.e., the lesser of the total capital cost and the eligible capital expenditure to acquire the licence) and subparagraph 13(37)(*b*)(iii) deems the capital cost of the goodwill of the business to be $88 (i.e., $188-$100).

Example 3 — Undepreciated Capital Cost Balance

Before January 1, 2017

In a taxation year ending before January 1, 2017, a taxpayer incurred an eligible capital expenditure of $100, resulting in a cumulative eligible capital balance of $75 (i.e., $^3/_4$ × $100) to acquire a government licence of unlimited duration. In taxation years ending before January 1, 2017, the taxpayer deducted a total of $35 from cumulative eligible capital under paragraph 20(1)(*b*), resulting in a cumulative eligible capital balance of $40.

On January 1, 2017

The government licence and goodwill are property included in new Class 14.1 of Schedule II to the Regulations.

Paragraph 13(37)(*a*) provides that the total capital cost of property of the new class at the beginning of January 1, 2017 that is goodwill or that was eligible capital property before January 1, 2017 is $^4/_3$ of the amount that would be the cumulative eligible capital at the beginning of January 1, 2017; plus $^4/_3$ of the amount of deductions taken that have not been recaptured; less $^4/_3$ of any negative cumulative eligible capital balance at the beginning of January 1, 2017. The total capital cost would equal $100 (i.e., $^4/_3$ × ($40+$35-$0)). As a result, the amount described by A in the definition "undepreciated capital cost" in subsection 13(21) would be $100.

Paragraph 13(37)(*c*) would deem an amount to have been allowed to the taxpayer under paragraph 20(1)(*a*) for taxation years ending before January 1, 2017, equal to the amount by which total capital cost and any negative cumulative eligible capital balance exceed any positive cumulative eligible capital balance. In this example, this excess equals $60 (i.e., $100+$0-$40). This is, therefore, the amount determined by E in the definition "undepreciated capital cost" in subsection 13(21).

As a consequence, the undepreciated capital cost of the new class at the beginning of January 1,

2017 is $40, which is equal to the amount that would be the CEC balance at the beginning of January 1, 2017.

[¶771] LAND DEVELOPERS

(1) Interest and Property Taxes — These expenses are not deductible to the extent they exceed income from the related land. This is true for all taxpayers, except that there is a partial exception for corporations whose principal business is the leasing, sale, or development of real property.

(2) Utility Service Connections — Interpretation Bulletin IT-452 (now cancelled) commented that the general rule that service connections are deductible applies only to those on capital account, and subdivision connections would be on inventory account. IT-452 has been archived and cancelled; it is probable that it is still the CRA's view that these costs are inventory, and are governed by paragraph 13 of IT-153R3.

(3) Installations within Subdivision Area — Costs of installations, such as roads, sewers, water mains, are considered part of inventory cost.

[¶771.05] *Soft Costs*

In general, no deductions may be taken for expenditures that relate to the period in which a building is undergoing construction, renovation or alteration, and that relate to that construction, alteration or renovation, except to the extent of related income. There are exceptions to the disallowance for capital cost allowance, landscaping, and costs related modifications to accommodate the disabled. The most common expenditures captured under this rule are "soft costs", which include interest, legal and accounting fees, and property taxes. For such costs related to vacant land, see ¶1073.

Expenditures that relate to the period in which a building is undergoing construction, renovation or alteration are deductible only to the extent of income in the year from the building on which they are incurred; see ¶804b. Costs over and above rental income from the project are a non-deductible item which must be added to the capital cost of the property for depreciation (see Chapter 8, and capitalization of interest rules at ¶665) or, if related to land, to the cost. Soft costs include interest not only on funds directly traceable to building costs, but also on funds which may "reasonably be considered" borrowed for such use, whether borrowed directly or through a chain of related parties.

Furthermore, a rule provides that only soft costs which would have been deductible but for the soft cost rule itself can be capitalized under the soft cost rule. This rule is said to be an extension of the weak currency borrowing rules discussed at ¶1064.30; the point is that a cost made non-deductible by other rules (such as but not limited to weak currency borrowings) cannot be capitalized because it is also a soft cost.

For the period after November 12, 1981 and before 1990, all costs (other than capital cost allowance and landscaping costs) incurred during the construction, renovation or alteration of buildings were not deductible, and had to be capitalized as above.

The rules do ensure that a taxpayer who owns land may continue to deduct expenses such as taxes and interest during a period in which an arm's length person constructs, renovates or alters a building on that land on that arm's length person's own behalf. Were it not for these corrections, the arm's length owner would be denied ordinary expenses which might fall under the heading of soft costs.

These rules are applicable to all taxpayers, whether they are developers or are building facilities for their own business premises or for investment purposes. Capitalization is required for expenses that are attributable to the period even though incurred outside the period. That period is considered to end at the earlier of the day the construction, renovation or alteration is actually completed and the day on which substantially all of the building is used for the purpose for which it was constructed, renovated or altered. It is the CRA's view that "substantially all" means 90% or more. (The Tax Court of Canada, in interpreting the same phrase for GST purposes, has been satisfied with an 80% test (see *McKay v. The Queen*, 2001 GTC 208, and *Ruhl v. The Queen*, 1998 GTC 2055. Thus, while it is always desirable to arrange matters to meet the 90% test, it is possible to argue for some other benchmark.)

For developers, if the land is inventory, undeductible soft costs may be added to the cost of inventory.

Certain interest payments, which otherwise might not be specifically identified with the construction, renovation or alteration of a particular building or the ownership of a particular parcel of land, are nonetheless subject to the rules relating to soft costs. The rules require the capitalization of interest paid or payable by a taxpayer on borrowed money in circumstances where the borrowed money can reasonably be considered to have been used by the taxpayer in the construction, renovation or alteration. For example, where a taxpayer uses available cash to fund the construction of a building and borrows money to finance its trade receivables, a portion of the interest paid in respect of the money borrowed would fall within this rule.

The rules also deal with indirect borrowings. If, for example, a taxpayer pays interest on borrowed money which is invested in a non-arm's length corporation or otherwise used to assist a non-arm's length person or partnership that uses the funds to construct a building, the interest will not be deductible by the taxpayer. The same rule applies if the borrowed funds are invested in the shares of a corporation for the construction of a building. In both cases there are exceptions. In the case of shares, the deduction is only denied if the investor is a specified shareholder of the corporation. A "specified shareholder" generally means a person who has, or is related to a person who has, an interest of 10% or more in the corporation. Similarly, for taxation years commencing after April 1988, the deduction is denied to an investor in a non-arm's length partnership only if the investor has a 10% or greater interest in the partnership. The rules do not apply to interest on money borrowed by a corporation where it reloans the money to the person, partnership or corporation doing the construction at a reasonable rate of interest. However see ¶1063 on a reasonable rate.

(ITA: 10; 18(3.1)–(3.7); 20; IT-153R3 [Archived])

[¶773] CONTRACTORS

[¶773.05] *Reporting Payments Made*

Businesses whose income derives primarily from construction activities must ensure they keep a record of the name, address, amount paid, and GST Registration Number, Business Number or Social Insurance Number of their subcontractors. The reporting business may report on either a calendar year basis or a financial year basis, although for unincorporated businesses this will usually be a distinction without a difference.

In general, returns (consisting of a T5018 summary and slip(s)) are required on or before the date that is six months after the end of the reporting period. Therefore, if a business is reporting on a calendar year basis, reporting is always required at the end of the following June. Once a reporting period is chosen, it cannot be altered without the express authorization of the CRA.

Construction is defined for purposes of this reporting requirement as including the erection, excavation, installation, alteration, modification, repair, improvement, demolition, destruction, dismantling, or removal of all or any part of a building, structure, surface or subsurface construction, or any similar property. A subcontractor is an individual, partnership or corporation which provides goods or services in the course of construction activities in the reporting period.

The construction business must report total amounts paid or credited to each subcontractor for a calendar year, except that the governing regulation specifically exempts from reporting amounts paid or credited in the period for goods for sale or lease by the reporting entity, amounts subject to withholding (either on account of wages or under non-residents rules), and amount paid to a non-resident of Canada during a period when the reporting entity was a non-resident.

The CRA policy, set out as part of the T5018 Summary, seems to create somewhat broader exemptions. The T5018 Summary says flatly that payments for goods only do not have to be reported. Payments for mixed goods and services need not be reported if the total annual service component is less than $500. Payments to individual contractors need not be reported if the total payment for the reporting period for that particular subcontractor is less than $500.

Where cheques are made out in the name of more than one subcontractor, typically to a subcontractor and its subcontractor, the writer of the cheque reports the payment to the subcontractor it deals with directly, and that subcontractor reports the payment to its sub-subcontractor.

Where a subcontractor refuses to provide a business or Social Insurance Number, the CRA suggests that the contractor should protect itself by making the request in writing. The onus then shifts to the subcontractor, who is subject to a separate penalty for failing to provide the information.

The CRA provides form T5018 (T1204 for federal departments, agencies and Crown corporations), which is similar to the T4 or T4A in providing an information slip and a summary of slips issued. However, use of the T5018 is not mandatory, at least for the time being, nor is it mandatory to provide copies of the data to the subcontractors themselves. You can provide the data to the CRA in any format so long as is in a column format with one line providing the requisite information for each contractor, and is backed up by a summary that states the number of contractors and the total paid.

If you file more than 50 T5018 slips for a calendar year, you must file the T5018 return over the Internet. You can use either the Internet File Transfer (XML) format, or the Web Forms format. Information about filing slips and returns electronically can be found on the CRA website, at www.cra.gc.ca/iref.

(ITR: 238 Reporting of Payments in respect of Construction Activities; Other Publications: CRA website, www.cra-arc.gc.ca/contract)

[¶773.10] *Computation of Income*

On the completed contract basis, the profit or loss on a contract would be accounted for only in the year the contract was completed. On the percentage of completion basis, profit or loss is taken into account over the term of the contract, on the basis of progress estimates.

The CRA's general position with respect to the treatment of contract income where the completed contract method cannot be used is as follows:

(1) All amounts which have been billed, or which could have been billed, under the contract terms, during the taxation year, must be included in income. Generally, this will mean the inclusion of: (a) progress billings with respect to work performed during the year, (b) unbilled amounts with respect to work performed during the year which could have been billed and (c) advance payments received with respect to work yet to be performed. Refer to paragraph (4), below, for reserve allowed on advance payments.

(2) Amounts not received in the year which are not legally receivable at the end of the year may be excluded from income. Whether or not an amount is legally receivable will depend upon the contract terms. However, holdbacks are usually not legally receivable until an engineer's or architect's certificate has been issued. Therefore, the portion of billings represented by holdbacks for which such a certificate has not been issued prior to the year end may be excluded from income in most cases.

(3) All outlays or expenses made or incurred during the year with respect to the contracts (except for depreciable assets) are deductible in the year, including the cost of work in process which is unbilled at the year-end. No deduction is permitted for holdbacks payable to subcontractors as at the end of the year because you are permitted to exclude holdbacks receivable from your income.

(4) A contractor may claim a reserve in respect of work not done but for which the customer has been billed. Such a reserve is only allowable where the contractor can identify specific costs that will have to be incurred after the year end for which the billings were made.

Where you choose to adopt the completed contract method of accounting, you must consistently use this method from year to year for all contracts. You should consider whether or not changing to the basis described above would be advantageous. If you change your basis of accounting from a completed contract or percentage completion basis to the basis described above, the Department will not permit you to change back again.

(IT-92R2 Income of Contractors; CRA Document No.: Income of a Contractor, *October 10, 2002*, CRA Document No. 2002-0158335)

[¶774] CALCULATION OF CONTRACT INCOME

A Plumbing Contractor's Business (December 31 Year End)

A plumbing contractor's business included the following contracts in 2009:

Contract 1

A $10,000 contract on which he commenced work July 18, 2009, and completed November 29, 2009. The full contract price was received by him before the end of the year.

Contract 2

A cost plus contract on which he had commenced work in November 2008, half-completed by December 31, 2008, and completed on May 15, 2009. Costs totalled $45,000 of which $22,500 were incurred in 2008. The contract provided that he would render bills monthly equal to the cost of the work performed that month plus 20%. Each bill was subject to a holdback by his customer of 15%, payable after the work was approved by the customer's architect. The architect's approval was issued in October 2009, and the amount of the holdback was paid to the contractor in January 2010.

Contract 3

A cost plus $4,000 fixed fee contract on which he commenced work on December 5, 2009, and which was not completed by the year end. In December 2009 he incurred costs of $11,000. Total costs were estimated at $36,000. He was entitled to bill his customers $10,000 per month, for four months, beginning in December 2009, with the balance of the price (if any) being payable after completion of the contract, subject to approval by the customer's engineer.

Contract 4

A $15,000 contract upon which work had not started as of December 31, 2009. The estimated cost was $12,000 and an advance of $5,000 on the contract price was received in 2008.

As of December 31, 2009, the contractor owed various sub-contractors a total of $7,000 which was not to be paid them unless and until certain contracts undertaken by the contractor were approved by architects and engineers of customers.

The current income tax treatment of the above contracts (and a comparison with the "completed contract" basis and the "percentage of completion" basis) is as follows:

Contract 1

Any income or loss on this contract would be reported in full on the contractor's 2009 income tax return.

All three methods of computing contract income would have the same result in this case.

Contract 2

The income from this contract would be partially taxable in each of the 2008 and 2009 taxation years, under the current method of computing income.

In 2008, the contractor would report net income of $450, comprising:

Amounts billable in 2008 for costs incurred		$22,500
20% Profit billable		4,500
Total billable		$27,000
Less — 15% holdback on billings	$ 4,050	
Costs incurred	22,500	26,550
Net income		$450

In 2009, the contractor would report net income of $8,550, comprising:

Amount billable in 2009 for costs incurred in 2009	$22,500
20% Profit billable	4,500
2008 holdback approved for payment in 2009	4,050
	$31,050
Less — Costs incurred in 2009	22,500
Net income	$ 8,550

Note that no income on this contract is reportable in 2010, although the holdbacks were not collected until that year. Holdbacks are due on the later of the architect's certification or completion or the expiration of the Mechanics Lien period. The holdbacks became *legally receivable* when the architect issued his approval in 2009. The actual date of *collection* is not important.

The effect of the tax treatment described above is that the largest portion of the net income is taxable in 2009 although the contract was half-completed in 2008.

The pure "percentage-of-completion" method would have required the contractor to report one-half the net income in each of the 2008 and 2009 tax returns since the contract was half-completed in 2009.

Contract 3

For 2009 the contractor will report on his income tax return a net loss of $1,000. He must include in income the $10,000 billable in December 2009, but may deduct the $11,000 in costs incurred.

The three remaining monthly billings of $10,000 each will be reported as income for 2010, and any 2010 costs can be deducted in that year.

The balance of the contract price will be reported as income in the year approval for payment is issued.

Note that a loss is reported for 2009, although the contract is a profitable one.

The taxpayer here is relying on the general rules for deduction of expenses actually incurred, and on the CRA's position that if billings for a fixed fee contract are made as amounts are approved, and a reasonable proportion of profit is included, the reporting of income on the basis of billings is acceptable.

Contract 4

The advance of $5,000 had to be included in income for 2008. However, a reasonable reserve equal to the advance, for costs to be incurred in the future, could be deducted.

If the advance had exceeded estimated future costs, the excess would not be allowed as a reserve.

Under the "completed contract" method or the "percentage-of-completion" method no income or loss would be reported for 2009 on this contract.

The amount of $7,000 held back from the contractor's sub-contractors would not be allowed as a deductible expense for 2009 under the current method of computing contract income. It would be deductible in later years as approvals were obtained for work done.

[¶776] PROSPECTORS

If you are a prospector (or a grubstaker) and receive proceeds from the sale of mining properties you discover, any income you receive is subject to tax, either as ordinary income or as a capital gain, depending on the nature of the property received in exchange for the mining property and when the property was received.

If the mining property was sold to a corporation in exchange for shares and the shares were received before May 23, 1985, the shares are treated as having no cost for tax purposes. The proceeds from a subsequent sale of the shares would be taxed either as income or as a capital gain depending on the circumstances. (See Chapter 5 for a discussion of capital gains.) If you are a promoter or dealer in shares, all of your proceeds on the disposition of such shares less the applicable disposal expenses would be taxed as income. Note that income subject to tax arises when the shares are sold, not when the mining property is sold.

Where shares are received for an interest in mining property, the lesser of the fair market value of the shares at the time of acquisition and the proceeds received on the eventual sale of the shares will be included in income at the time of the sale. A special offsetting deduction of $^1/_2$ of the amount included in income is allowed in computing taxable income. The shares received will have an adjusted cost base equal to the amount included in income.

The special deduction is claimed on line 249 of page 3 of the T1 General, and the capital gain or loss is reported on Schedule 3.

If property other than shares (e.g., cash) is received in exchange for a mining property, the entire amount of the property received must be included in income unless the mining property was owned on December 31, 1971, in which case only a portion of the proceeds need be taken into account for a discussion of the application of this rule to the sale of oil and gas properties).

Expenses incurred by the prospector (net of funds supplied by grubstakers) in the course of his work and amounts paid to prospectors by grubstakers may not be fully deductible in the year incurred. See Chapter 22 for more details.

(ITA: 35; 110(1)(*d.2*))

[¶777] AMATEUR ATHLETES

Commencing January 1, 1992, a regime was added to deal specifically with tax payable on amounts received by or on behalf of individuals who are amateur athletes. An amateur athlete is defined as an individual (other than a trust) who is a member of a registered Canadian amateur athletic association, who is eligible to compete as a Canadian national team member in an international sporting event sanctioned by an international sports federation, and who is not a professional athlete who receives compensation for, or income attributable to, activities as a player or athlete in a professional sport.

Where an individual who is an amateur athlete enters into an arrangement to deposit specific types of income into a qualifying account administered by either an eligible national sports organization or another third-party issuer, a trust ("amateur athlete trust") is deemed to be created for the benefit of that individual. Property held under the arrangement is considered to be property of the trust, with the Canadian sports organization or other third-party issuer as trustee and the athlete as beneficiary. The trust would be exempt from income tax. However, any amounts distributed by the organization under the arrangement, or for the benefit of the athlete, are deemed to be payments from the trust received by the athlete and subject to tax as income from business or property. Accordingly, associated expenses incurred by the athlete can be deducted in computing income.

Under the eligibility standards of certain international sport federations, in order to preserve the eligibility status of an athlete for international competition, certain types of income earned by the athlete must be deposited with, controlled and administered by the applicable national sport organization. In Canada, such national sport organizations are typically registered charities for income tax purposes (see Chapter 12). Under these rules, to preserve international competition eligibility, any arrangement under which amounts earned by an athlete are required by international sport rules to be held by a tax-registered Canadian national sport organization will result in the creation of a trust for tax purposes with the national sport organization as trustee. The trust is deemed to be created on the later of the day the first payment is received and January 1, 1992.

For 2008 and subsequent taxation years, a trust can also be created where an athlete enters into a "qualifying arrangement" with a third-party issuer to deposit qualifying performance income, interest, or other income attributable to property of the trust into an eligible account controlled and administered by the issuer for the benefit of the individual. The third-party issuer is deemed to be the trustee of the trust and must be a mandatory signatory on any payment from the account. A "qualifying arrangement" generally includes an account offered by a financial institution, credit union, or insurance company that is maintained for the exclusive benefit of an individual, but does not include an RRSP or TFSA. "Qualifying performance income" is defined as endorsement income, prize money, or income from public appearances or speeches received by an individual who was, at any time in the year, an amateur athlete and was not at any time a professional athlete, and which may reasonably be considered to be in connection with the individual's participation as an amateur athlete in one or more international sporting events.

Previously, since the contributed qualifying performance income was not included in the individual's income, it did not form part of the individual's earned income for RRSP purposes. The 2014 federal Budget amended this situation such that the contributions to the trust will now form part of earned income for RRSP purposes (even though they still are not included in the individual's income). The amendment applies to the 2014 taxation year, but individuals can elect that it apply to contributions made in the 2011, 2012, or 2013 years if they file the election by March 3, 2015.

Where an individual has not competed in an international sporting event as a Canadian national team member for eight years, the trust will be deemed to be wound up and the amounts held by the trust at the end of the year are deemed to be distributed to the athlete at that time, and are therefore subject to tax. The eight-year period commences with the later of the last year in which the athlete so competed and the year in which the trust was created. For an arrangement entered into prior to 1992, the trust is nevertheless deemed to be created on January 1, 1992.

Where the athlete is a non-resident at the time of deemed wind-up of the trust, the amount of the deemed distribution is reduced to 60% of the value of the trust. This is intended to provide the trustee with the tax payable at a 40% rate, and this tax will be required of the trustee organization at that time. For years prior to 2016, the deemed distribution was 64% of the value of the trust.

Where the athlete dies, the trust is effectively considered wound up immediately before death, with its value included in income for the year of death or, if the athlete is non-resident at the time of death, deemed distribution of 60% with the balance assessed as a special tax payable by the trustee. For years prior to 2016, this deemed distribution rate was 64%.

For professional athletes who are employees, see ¶390.

(ITA: 12(1)(z) Amateur athlete trust payments; 143.1 [Amateur athletes' reserve funds]; 146.2(1) Definitions; 149(1)(l) Non-profit organizations; 149(1)(v) Amateur athlete trust; 210.1 Application of Part; 210.2(2) Amateur athlete trusts; 212(1)(u) Amateur athlete trust payments; 214(3) Deemed payments)

[¶777c] MESSENGERS AND RICKSHAW DRIVERS

The CRA published in late 2004 an opinion to the effect that *self-employed* foot and bicycle messengers and rickshaw drivers are allowed to deduct food and beverage expenses subject to the dollar limits applied to transport employees (¶374).

Citing the Federal Court of Appeal decision in *Alan Wayne Scott v. The Queen*, 98 DTC 6530, the CRA affirmed that foot and bicycle messengers and rickshaw drivers can deduct the cost of extra food and beverages that are consumed to enable them to carry on their business.

The messenger or driver may deduct the actual expenses above and beyond normal costs of food and beverages, if such costs are supported by receipts. Alternatively, he or she may claim a flat rate amount without providing receipts. For 2006 and subsequent taxation years, the flat rate is $17.50. The CRA notes (on its website at "Businesses/Sole proprietorships and partnerships/Reporting/T2125/Expenses/Line 8523 — Meals and entertainment (allowable part only)") that by "using this flat rate deduction, you will not be required to maintain or submit receipts for the extra meal and beverage consumed". Furthermore, the CRA notes:

> If you want to claim more than the flat-rate amount, the CRA will also need:
>
> - supporting receipts for all food and beverage claimed; and
> - a clear demonstration of the extra amount of food and beverage requested because of the nature of your work, and how this amount exceeds what the average person would consume both in terms of cost and quantity.

The $17.50 flat rate is expected to change from time to time, and if such change is made prior to publication, it will be provided in ¶87 at the front of this book.

(CRA Document No.: Extra Food & Bev. Self-Emp. Foot & Bicycle Mess., *December 7, 2004*, CRA Document No. 2004-0103271E5)

PROFESSIONALS — CALCULATION OF INCOME

[¶778] GENERAL RULES

Income for tax purposes from a professional business must be calculated according to a modification of the "accrual" method, and use of the cash method is discontinued.

In computing income under the accrual method, every amount which becomes receivable during the business' fiscal period for services rendered is included in the income of that tax year whether payment has been received or not. Similarly, all expenses incurred during the fiscal period, whether actually paid or not, are deductible in that year. In determining what is receivable, an amount for services rendered will be deemed to have become receivable on either the date when the bill for services is presented, the date when the bill would have been presented if there were no delay in presenting it, or the date when payment is received, whichever is earliest.

The modification to the accrual method, for certain professionals, applies to work in progress — an election can be made not to include any value in income (see ¶780).

It is clear that (subject to the election at ¶780) professionals may compute their income in the same manner as other businesses (see ¶714, ¶716 and ¶732). That is, amounts received are income subject to a reserve for work not yet performed; amounts receivable for work performed are income although not yet received.

(ITA: 10; 34; 96; ITAR: 23)

[¶780] INVENTORY OF WORK IN PROGRESS

Ordinarily, work in progress at the end of a fiscal period is treated like inventory and the related costs are not allowed as a deduction in computing income. Put another way, an inventory of unbilled service costs plus a profit mark-up would normally be included in the income of a professional, offset (except for the profit element) by the inventory costs themselves.

However, as a professional you may elect not to be subject to this general rule and deduct the cost of work in progress at the end of a fiscal period.

This election may be made by certain professional taxpayers, including those who previously used the accrual basis and treated work in progress as inventory. The professional taxpayers who are eligible to make this election are as follows:

(a) an accountant;

(b) a dentist;

(c) a lawyer (including a Quebec notary);

(d) a medical doctor;

(e) a veterinarian; or

(f) a chiropractor.

If you did not make this election in the previous year the value of work in progress at the beginning of the current year is deemed to be the same value used by you in computing your previous year's income.

Where you are a member of a professional partnership all of the partners must make the same election (see ¶1876).

Once the election is made it may not be revoked without the permission of the Minister of National Revenue through your local Tax Services Office.

The CRA takes the view that the cost of work in progress is included in inventory regardless of whether an election is made to exclude the related profit from income.

The CRA does not provide a form to be used for making this election. A written statement worded as follows, and either attached to your income tax return or shown in the financial statements or income reconciliation submitted with your return should suffice:

> (Date)
>
> "I elect under the provisions of paragraph 34(1)(*d*) of the *Income Tax Act* to exclude work in progress from the computation of income for the year."
>
> (Signed)

For work in progress of taxpayers who are not members of the enumerated professions, see ¶758.15.

(ITA: 10; 34; 96; IT-457R [Archived])

[¶781] ACCOUNTS PAYABLE

Expenses incurred in, but unpaid at the end of, a taxpayer's fiscal period may be deducted in the fiscal period. They may not be deducted when subsequently paid.

(ITA: 9)

[¶782] LAWYERS' TRUST ACCOUNTS

Special rules apply to lawyers who receive trust funds on behalf of, or from, clients. Advances received from a client in anticipation of services to be rendered or disbursements to be made, if placed in a trust bank account, will not be included in income. Any amounts which the lawyer is entitled to treat as his or her own funds, including funds received by way of retainer, must be included in his or her income whether or not he or she has deposited them in a trust account. Amounts which can legally be transferred out of a trust account for the use and benefit of the lawyer must be included in his or her income, even if the amounts have not actually been transferred. Any amount actually withdrawn from a trust account for the use and benefit of the lawyer must be included in his or her income unless a corresponding amount has already been reported as income at a previous time.

Disbursements customarily made by a lawyer in the ordinary course of his practice will generally form part of his work in progress if they are not billable at the end of his fiscal year. If the amounts are billable they should be included in receivables. If they are recoverable from a client who has a trust account, it is considered that an amount equal to the disbursement can legally be withdrawn from the trust account and consequently the amount will be considered to have been billed and received as income of the year.

Interest on trust accounts which, by provincial law, is required to be paid to a Law Society or Bar Association or some foundation or fund related thereto is not taxable. Where no such law is applicable and no arrangement to the contrary exists between the lawyer and his or her client, interest credited on a trust account to which the client's advances have been deposited belongs beneficially to the client and the interest is therefore not considered to be income of the lawyer. If there is a specific agreement between the lawyer and his client that the interest credited to a particular trust account will accrue to the lawyer for his or her own use and benefit, then the interest will be income of the lawyer at the time when it is credited to the account.

(IT-129R [Archived])

[¶782c] LAWYERS APPOINTED TO THE BENCH

The CRA has a document called "Report on the tax treatment of lawyers' income on their appointment to the bench", issued by the Business and Partnerships Division of the Income Tax Rulings Directorate (2005-0113961E5). The document reviews such things as the sale of a proprietorship, the disposition of a partnership interest, and so on. There is nothing very surprising in the document, but it may be a useful checklist for the lawyer in this situation.

(CRA Document No.: 2005-0113961E5 (2005 version))

[¶783] PROFESSIONAL'S DEDUCTIONS

Doctors, dentists, lawyers, architects, engineers, accountants and other professionals deriving income from a business are allowed to deduct expenses incurred in earning such income.

In order that an expense may be deducted in computing the income of a professional from a business, it must have been incurred for the purpose of earning income from the business; it must not be a capital expenditure; and it must have been reasonable in the circumstances. Subject to these limitations, the following rules are, generally speaking, applicable in determining what amounts may be deducted in computing income from a professional business. In all cases adequate books and records should be kept to substantiate the amounts claimed.

(1) *Annual fees* paid to professional and scientific associations or societies are deductible. However, an entrance fee payable on admission to a professional society, e.g., a fee for a call to the bar, may not be deducted currently, but may qualify for the special treatment outlined in ¶766 and ¶767.

(2) *Rent* for business premises is deductible. Where rent is prepaid and relates to a future year, part or all of the expense should be deferred and written off in the years to which it is applicable (see ¶753).

(3) *Office maintenance expenses* and carrying charges on business premises are deductible. These include business and property taxes, light, heat, insurance, repairs, capital cost allowance and mortgage interest. If a professional has his or her office in a house which he owns and in which he or she resides, he or she may deduct carrying charges and other expenses properly applicable to the part of the house which he or she can prove he or she used for professional purposes, subject to the limitations discussed at ¶742.

If you are maintaining an office in your home you should refer to ¶554 since this may affect your capital gain exemption on the sale of your principal residence.

(4) *Salaries to employees* such as professional assistants or associates, secretaries, bookkeepers, and medical and dental assistants are deductible. The names and addresses of such employees are to be furnished annually to the CRA on form T4, Statement of Remuneration Paid.

(5) *Contributions to superannuation or pension funds*, profit sharing plans, supplementary unemployment benefit plans, registered retirement savings plans and deferred profit sharing plans, for employees are deductible (¶735–¶737; ¶739).

(6) *Fees of consultants* may be deducted.

(7) *Legal and accounting expenses*, if related to the earning of income, are deductible; if related to capital, they are not deductible currently, but may qualify for the special treatment outlined in ¶766 and ¶767 or may be capitalized as part of the cost of a capital asset acquired.

(8) *Telephone and postage expenditures* are deductible, but *stationery* is supposed to be inventoried and valued at its replacement cost. That is, it is to be expensed as it is consumed rather than as it is ordered.

(9) *Insurance premiums* are deductible in two cases. One is where the insurance is against a loss of a revenue nature, e.g., malpractice insurance. The other is where it is regular commercial practice to carry the insurance — e.g., fire insurance on business property. Premiums on partnership insurance, i.e., where the partnership insures the life of each partner, the surviving partner becoming beneficiary in event of the death of the other partner, are *not* deductible, nor is the benefit taxable. But see ¶764.

(10) *The cost of a professional library* is not deductible but depreciation is allowed on the capital cost of a library; see point 16 below. The Department ordinarily permits the deduction of the cost of professional periodicals and library books purchased individually. Professional library fees may be deducted.

(11) *Tuition fees.* See Chapter 13.

(12) *Automobile expenses* may be claimed by a professional who uses his or her car in the course of carrying on his or her business. Automobile expenses incurred in driving to and from work are not deductible. If a professional uses his or her car partly in the course of his or her business and partly for personal transportation, the proportions of each would have to be proved and the expenditures apportioned. See ¶738. Depreciation may also be deducted; see point 16 below. All automobile expenses may be subject to limitations discussed at ¶738.

(13) *Expenses of attending conventions* of professional bodies. Expenses of attending up to two conventions a year, in connection with the taxpayer's profession, are deductible. The deduction must be claimed in the year in which the expense is paid. It would appear, however, that where expenses incurred through attendance at conventions can be shown to have been made for the purpose of earning income (as advertising or similar expenses), the taxpayer might succeed in claiming their deduction as ordinary business expenses, thus avoiding the necessity of claiming them under the specific section which limits their deduction to two conventions a year (see ¶734).

(14) *Christmas gifts*, entertainment expenditures and the like are deductible if it can be proved that they were incurred for the purpose of earning income.

(15) *The cost of medical, surgical and like supplies* other than capital expenditures is deductible in computing the income of a doctor or dentist.

(16) *Capital cost allowance* is allowed on the undepreciated cost of capital assets of professionals as follows:

(a) office furniture and fixtures, 20% *per annum* (Class 8);

(b) computers, 100% *per annum* (half-year rule does not apply) if acquired after January 27, 2009, and before February 2011 (Class 52); 55% if acquired after January 2011 (see ¶886t for computers acquired at other times);

(c) library, 20% *per annum* (Class 8);

(d) medical and dental instruments costing less than $500, 100% (Class 12);

(e) medical or dental instruments costing $500 or more, 20% *per annum* (Class 8);

(f) the proportion of the capital cost of an automobile which the use regularly made of the automobile in earning income is of the whole use regularly made of it (¶822), 30% *per annum* (Class 10 or 10.1); note that capital cost may not exceed the applicable threshold amount discussed at ¶810a;

(g) office building or office portion of house, 4% *per annum* (6% for non-M&P non-residential buildings acquired after March 18, 2007, see ¶875.03) (Class 1), 5% *per annum* (Class 3), or 10% *per annum* (Class 6); and

(h) a leasehold interest, evenly over the period of the lease with a maximum of 20% *per annum* (Class 13); see ¶879.

Except in the case of (h) the percentages are to be applied to the undepreciated portion of the cost of all the capital assets in each class. There are limitations which restrict the capital cost allowance which could otherwise be claimed in the year in which assets are purchased. See Chapter 8 for further details.

(17) *A reserve for doubtful debts* and *bad debts* may be deducted (see ¶733).

(18) *Sundry expenses* not otherwise classified may be deducted if incurred for the purpose of earning income.

The above paragraphs relate to deductions which might be claimed in computing the income of a professional whose income is derived from a business. In addition he or she will be entitled to claim certain deductions available to taxpayers generally; see Chapter 10.

(ITA: 18; 20; 96; 230; ITR: 1100 [Capital cost allowance – deductions allowed]; Schedule II Capital Cost Allowances)

[¶784] SERVICE CORPORATIONS

For most professions (e.g., medicine, law, etc.), provincial law or the profession's code of ethics requires that they be practised only by individuals properly registered or qualified, either alone or in partnership. Where this restriction exists, an individual cannot incorporate a company to carry on his profession.

However, a corporation could normally be formed to:

(1) collect or receive the amounts billed in the name of the individual practitioner or partnership for services rendered; and

(2) provide the practitioner with premises and/or services.

Under such arrangements, clients would be billed for services in the name of the individual practitioner, or the partnership, and amounts received may come directly to the corporation from the clients. Since the corporation is entitled to a reasonable profit for the services it provides for the practitioners, profits from this source are taxable in the hands of the corporation. The individual's income from his practice is determined allowing a reasonable charge for the services and premises provided by the corporation. Generally the CRA accepts any reasonable method for determining this charge provided it does not:

(1) permit a practitioner to defer or avoid tax on significant amounts of income; or

(2) allocate unreasonably high charges to the practitioner for premises and/or services.

The corporation should remunerate appropriately its employees, who could include the particular professionals or their relatives, and charge its clients (the practice of the particular professionals and perhaps other persons) an appropriate total amount for the premises and services provided, which would include a reasonable profit to the corporation. The deduction of the amount paid to the corporation by the practice of the particular professionals is acceptable provided that the charges for the premises and services are reasonable. The corporation is taxable on its income arising from the performance of its assigned functions. You should note that where the employees of the corporation include a spouse or relatives of the professionals, the corporation may be tainted as a personal services business (see ¶785) and there would be a tax disadvantage.

A service corporation (other than a personal service business; see ¶785) which is a Canadian-controlled private corporation is entitled to the full small business deduction on the first $500,000 of active business income earned in the year. Typically, this result is in an effective tax rate of 14% to 20%, depending on the province.

The introduction of the Goods and Services Tax (GST) rules sometimes had adverse effects on pre-existing service corporations. Service corporations which charge salary costs through to professional practices which cannot register for GST, such as medical practices, may have been disadvantaged by GST. Professional advice, usually instrumental in setting up these systems in the first place, was necessary to palliate the GST effects insofar as possible.

(ITA: 125; 248)

[¶785] PERSONAL SERVICES BUSINESSES

A personal services business is an "incorporated employee". That is, it means an incorporated business of providing services where an individual who performs such services on behalf of the corporation, or a person related to that individual, owns 10% of any shares of the corporation and, but for the existence of the corporation, the relationship between the individual and the person to whom the corporation provides such services could reasonably be considered to be that of an officer or employee and his employer. A corporation will not be a personal services business where it employs *more than five* full-time employees throughout the year. In *489599 B.C. Ltd. v. The Queen*, 2008 DTC 4107 (T.C.C.), it was held that a company meets the five or more employee test if it employs five full-time employees and at least one part-time employee. The CRA now accepts this decision; see CRA Document No. 2008-0300581C6 (March 5, 2009). Full-time employees (or persons related thereto) who own shares of the corporation are included in the count of employees in spite of their shareholdings. (There is also an exception where the corporation's income is received from an associated corporation; that is, a controlling shareholder of a corporation may use a second corporation to provide employment services to the first corporation. This is sensible, since the controlling shareholder could take corporate treatment directly from the first corporation.)

The purpose of these rules is to prevent an employee from obtaining beneficial tax treatment provided to small business corporations by interposing a corporation to provide the employment services. Accordingly, no deduction is allowed to the incorporated personal services business except in respect of the salary, wages and other benefits provided to the individual who performed such services, certain amounts expended by the corporation in connection with the selling of property or negotiation of contracts and certain amounts paid by the corporation on account of legal fees in connection with the collection of amounts owing on account of services rendered. The rules also deny the corporate small business deduction to personal services businesses.

The incorporated employee rules may affect employees who have been terminated by their companies but allowed to continue what are essentially their old functions through a corporation. This sometimes happens with executives. It permits the company to escape payment of fringe benefits, payroll taxes, and the like, and often to (in effect) hire the executive back through service payments to the executive's company for less than original salary. Where the executive's services are provided exclusively to one "employer" (including related companies of the employer) in much the same circumstances as if the executive were still personally an employee, the executive's corporation is likely to be a personal services business. If the employee does not take all his or her remuneration out of the corporation in salary, there is a considerable risk of double taxation if funds are removed as benefits or dividends.

Changes spread over the period of 2006 through 2011, including the 2006 enhancement of the dividend tax credit on "eligible" dividends (¶404) and scheduled reductions in the general corporate tax rate through 2011, significantly reduced the penalty on dividend as opposed to salary income, which has been one of the main elements deterring the use of personal services business corporations. That is, in the past, it has never been worth leaving funds in such a corporation to be paid as dividends because there would have been significant double taxation as the dividends were paid out. In some cases, depending on the provincial tax component, the dividend tax credit and corporate tax rate changes made such a corporation worth considering as a tax planning device. This is discussed at ¶2550. Unfortunately, technical amendments released on October 31, 2011 have effectively negated this type of tax planning as they provide that income from a personal services business is not eligible for the general corporate rate reduction, meaning that such income will be taxed at significantly higher levels than regular corporate income. See ¶2550.

(ITA: 18; 125)

[¶785.50] *Specified Investment Business*

Although strictly speaking a corporate rather than a personal tax matter, it is worth noting that the *489599 B.C. Ltd.* decision discussed above should also be persuasive in the identical five-employee test which appears in the definition of "specified investment business". As a personal investment business is intended to transmute employment income into small business income, a specified investment business is a corporation intended to transmute corporate investment income into corporate small business income for corporate tax purposes, and it is similarly denied small business treatment unless, among other exceptions, it has five or more full-time employees. See the companion Wolters Kluwer volume *Preparing Your Corporate Tax Returns*, ¶4376.

INTELLECTUAL AND ARTISTIC BUSINESSES

[¶787] ROYALTIES

Royalties are generally considered to be investment income and should be reported as outlined in ¶490. There are a number of cases, however, where royalty income constitutes business income because royalties are the form in which an individual collects the revenue from his or her business. Examples of such cases are authors, musicians, inventors and actors. Creators of computer programs may also be in a business which gives rise to royalty income. This is discussed in ¶789.

In these circumstances royalties collected should be reported as business income and all allowable deductions should be taken in computing the net income from the business, as indicated on form T2125. For a discussion on what constitutes a business and the timing of expenses and deductions, refer to ¶700 through ¶714.

Artists in Quebec will find that Quebec provides tax incentive relief for the first $15,000 of first-holder royalty income. Relief decreases as royalty income exceeds $30,000. See ¶1641.25.

You should note that any amount you receive based on the use of or production from property, even if such amount is an instalment of the sale price of the property, will be included in your income (¶490). This rule does not apply to the sale of agricultural land. In certain circumstances (outlined in Interpretation Bulletin IT-426R), the CRA will permit capital treatment of a sale of shares where price is based on an "earn out" formula notwithstanding the general rule.

Where the royalty is reported to you on a T5 slip, the CRA states that it should be reported at line 104 as miscellaneous employment income, which is dubious if there are offsetting expenses.

(ITA: 12(1)(*g*); IT-426R [Archived])

[¶789] AUTHORS, ARTISTS, AND COMPOSERS

[¶789.05] *Is the Artist in Business?*

Often the income of an artist, writer, entertainer, etc., will be sporadic at best, so that for a particular year or several years expenses will exceed income. The artist may meet these expenses and support himself/herself through employment or other business activities which may or may not be related to the artistic endeavour. In these cases, the losses from artistic endeavour (as calculated on form T2125 or in any appropriate format) will usually be deducted (on line 135 of the T1) from employment and other income. Where there is income from one business and loss from another, a separate income statement should be prepared for each; the gross revenue of all businesses will be entered at box 162 on the T1 and the net loss at line 135.

The CRA has often challenged the loss claim from an artistic endeavour on the grounds that the activity constituted a hobby rather than a business, as discussed at ¶700 and ¶704. In order to be considered a business, an activity has to be carried on "with a reasonable expectation of profit". (Or at least, after the 2002 Supreme Court decisions in the *Stewart* case at ¶690 and the *Walls* case at ¶704, an activity which has a substantial personal element, meaning one that might normally be undertaken for pleasure as opposed to profit, must be carried on in a "sufficiently commercial manner to constitute a source of income", for which reasonable expectation of profit remains one test.)

The CRA appeared to embark on a systematic campaign of challenging loss claims of artists in the early 1980s, and a protracted public dispute with the artistic community resulted. Eventually the issues were resolved, or at least muted, by the technical amendments discussed below but more significantly by the issuance of Interpretation Bulletin IT-504R, in which the CRA sets out an assessing policy for the guidance of its own auditors as well as the general public. The replacement of IT-504R with IT-504R2 (Consolidated) in 1995 did not appreciably alter current policy.

In Interpretation Bulletin IT-504R2, the CRA specifically acknowledges that "the nature of art and literature is such that a considerable period of time may pass before an artist or writer becomes established and profitable. Although the existence of reasonable expectation of profit is relevant in determining the deductibility of losses, in the case of artists and writers it is recognized that a longer period of time may be required in establishing that such reasonable expectation does exist".

Interpretation Bulletin IT-504R2 goes on, in paragraph 5, to list indices of a reasonable expectation of profit, which include time devoted to the activity, showings or publication, recognition in the way of awards or grants, and so on.

If the CRA challenges your loss claim from an artistic endeavour, you should obtain a copy of Interpretation Bulletin IT-504R2 (by mail or in person from any Tax Services Office listed at ¶287) and try to match your situation to the standards set out by the CRA.

If you are challenged by the CRA, you may initially want to write out your response. If you do this, you should both clarify your position as being a business with a reasonable expectation of profit within the terms in Interpretation Bulletin IT-504R2, and ask the CRA to be explicit about any deductions it proposes to deny, and the grounds for denial in each case. You should also make clear in your initial response that you will want an opportunity to meet personally with the CRA assessor to discuss the issues the CRA decides to contest. If you do not do this, the CRA has a tendency to accept your written submission as your last word and move ahead to the assessment stage.

If you are challenged by the CRA and are not confident about your ability to understand their case clearly or to put your own case effectively, you should consider obtaining professional advice at the earliest possible stage. Remember that if the CRA does issue a formal Notice of Assessment or Reassessment (usually on form T451) increasing your tax, you have only 90 days from the date on the Notice to file a Notice of Objection in order to continue the presentation of your case.

Remember that your claim to be in business with a reasonable expectation of profit will probably appear more plausible if you keep businesslike books and records in the first place. The burden of proof is always on the taxpayer to show that particular expenditures were in fact made and were made in aid of a business endeavour. A visit to a bookkeeper or accountant, or even the purchase of a book on the subject of basic bookkeeping, is advisable at an early stage in your artistic pursuit.

See also the comments at ¶793 regarding statements of the CRA's position.

Note that if you receive grants to produce a work of art, you may be able to deduct related expenses from the grants, regardless of whether you are otherwise considered in business; see ¶953 and ¶966.

[¶789.10] *Valuation of Artists' Inventories*

Artists may exclude the value of inventory in computing income instead of having to include the cost or fair market value of such inventory. This change allows artists to write off the costs involved in a work of art in the year they are incurred, rather than waiting until the work is sold. This recognizes artists' problems in valuing their works of art on hand, attributing costs to particular works, and carrying inventories over long periods of time. Technically, the rules allow an individual to value his or her inventory at nil in computing income from "an artistic endeavour". The individual must elect to make this valuation, presumably by filing a letter so stating with his or her return, although in an opinion reported in Wolters Kluwer *Window On Canadian Tax* 8230, the CRA accepted the consistent reporting of a closing inventory of zero on form T2125 as the making of an election. Once made, the election cannot be revoked in subsequent years without the concurrence of the CRA.

An "artistic endeavour" is defined as the business of an individual in creating paintings, prints, etchings, drawings, sculptures or similar works of art, other than the business of reproducing such works. In the case of prints, it is apparently intended that a series of original prints would qualify for the new inventory treatment whereas reproductions of those prints or of other original works would not.

[¶789.15] *Charitable Donations from Artists' Inventories*

Subsection 118.1(7) of the Act allows an artist to value a gift of art from inventory at any amount that is not less than its inventory value but not more than its fair market value. This amount will be used in determining the proceeds of disposition of the art and the amount that qualifies as a charitable donation. Typically the resulting transaction is a wash; that is, the income will be exactly offset by the charitable donation credit, subject to minor variations because the credit does not exactly offset the income at various levels of income and donation (see ¶1263). Another rule for gifts of artist's inventory that qualify as gifts of Canadian cultural property permits a charitable donation credit without an income inclusion; see ¶1291.

Prior to 2016, where the charitable donation is donated as a result of death, the donation is deemed to be made immediately before death, so that these rules will clearly apply to the year of death return rather than to the estate. As well, where the art in question is transferred to a beneficiary under the "rights or things" rules in ¶1908, so that proceeds would be taxable to the beneficiary and not the deceased, the beneficiary can make the same donation with the same results for the beneficiary as if the artist had made the donation. These changes are generally effective for 2000 and later years, but the legal representative of the deceased taxpayer, or the beneficiary under the rights or things rule, can elect to have them apply in respect of any year after 1996 and before 2000. The election must have been made in writing before 2002.

Starting in 2016, new rules apply to a gift of artwork made by an artist's graduated rate estate where immediately before the artist's death the fair market value of the artwork exceeds its cost amount to the artist. If the artwork is a cultural gift, the artist is deemed to receive immediately before death proceeds of disposition in respect of the artwork equal to its cost amount to the artist at that time and the graduated rate estate is deemed to have acquired the work of art at a cost equal to those proceeds. As a result, no income in respect of the artwork's value is recognized under section 70 by the artist for the year of death. If the gift of artwork is a charitable gift, the artist's legal representative may designate a value between the cost amount and the fair market value of the artwork to be treated as the proceeds of disposition for the purpose of calculating the artist's income in respect of the artwork's value for the year of death. The artist's graduated rate estate is deemed to have acquired the work of art at a cost equal to those proceeds.

(ITA: 10(6), (7), (8); 118.1(7), (7.1); IT-504R2 (Consolidated) [Archived])

[¶791] INVENTORS

Royalties received by an inventor must be included in computing income. If a lump-sum payment or a series of fixed payments not dependent on production or use of the invention are received on sale of a patent or invention, these amounts must also be included in computing income if the recipient is a professional inventor carrying on a business of inventing, but will be taxed as a capital gain if of a windfall or non-business nature. A professional inventor is allowed a deduction for expenses incurred in carrying on his business, and is permitted to claim capital cost allowance on costs incurred in patenting his inventions (¶898 — Class 14).

(ITA: 9; 12)

[¶793] PERFORMING ARTISTS

[¶793.05] *Employed or Self-Employed*

Performing artists, such as musicians and actors, may be considered employed or self-employed with respect to their earnings from their performances.

The question as to whether the artist is an employee or self-employed will depend upon the terms of the contract. All the comments at ¶304 apply in full to entertainers and performing artists, and indeed to related positions in the arts, such as stage managers, film editors, and so on. Artists who are unmistakably employees are entitled to special deductions noted at ¶379.

The CRA recognizes that special considerations arise in the case of performing artists, and addresses these in Interpretation Bulletin IT-525R (consolidated). That bulletin sets out a number of employee/self-employment criteria addressed specifically to performing artists. It should be read, however, with a certain caution. In the first place, it stresses the relationship between Employment Insurance/CPP contributions and income tax deductions. It is true that consistency is desirable, and a person who claims that certain income is not employment income will not be able to deduct EI withholdings (but these should be refunded). On the CPP side, a self-employed person may have to make a larger share of CPP contributions than an employee, so some tax cost may be associated with the claim. However, it is open to an individual to object on the income tax side (¶266) to being treated as an employee even if that person has been treated as such for EI/CPP purposes. It is important to remember, however, that this may result in CPP assessments and denial of EI benefits.

The CRA also does not choose to address the situation in which an artist may be an employee with respect to one position but self-employed with respect to others. A director, for example, who had a full-time position every summer for four months with a particular company might (or might not) be an employee of that company, but self-employed with respect to other work in the year. If the expenses of that other work exceeded its income, the net loss (subject to limitations for home-in-office expenses) should be a business loss offsetting employment income (¶795).

In the prior version of Interpretation Bulletin IT-525R (item 9), the CRA says that it relies on the quasi-judicial decision in the *Mermaid Theatre Society* case. This was the decision of an Umpire in an Employment Insurance proceeding. Accordingly, it is not published in the usual tax sources. This is unfortunate, since the Umpire was a respected federal judge and his decision, although limited in scope, was a sensible one. As well, it has sometimes been misunderstood or misrepresented by the CRA. Usually the CRA itself can be persuaded to provide a copy; their CPP/EI assessment officers are the persons most likely to be able to do this. Briefly, the *Mermaid* decision held that the director of a Nova Scotia theatre company was an employee of the theatre by virtue of a three-year non-exclusive contract, which meant that he had a continuing relationship with the theatre over several series of productions. By contrast, the actors and actresses who typically signed on for a particular production were held not to be employees, even if they happened to be engaged by the same company several times during the course of a year.

Note that the *Mermaid* decision cannot be stretched too far. It specifically related to the theatre. It addressed only the situation of the director and cast. One supposes that backstage personnel, e.g., a stage manager, might have fallen in either category, depending on whether taken on for a particular production or for a season. It remains a leading case, however, because there are virtually no others.

Interpretation Bulletin IT-525R (consolidated) reiterates that the artist will generally be considered self-employed when he or she is engaged to achieve a prescribed objective and is given all the freedom he requires to attain the desired results.

In the decision of *Royal Winnipeg Ballet v. MNR* (2006 DTC 6323), the Federal Court of Appeal overturned the previous Tax Court of Canada decision, which had held that the dancers of the ballet company were employees. In finding that the dancers were independent contractors, the Federal Court of Appeal conceded that the ballet company exerted extensive control over the dancers. However, similar control would be exerted over a guest dancer who was clearly not an employee. The Federal Court of Appeal concluded that the common understanding between the dancers and the ballet company that the legal relationship was one of independent contractor was "borne out by the contractual terms and the other relevant facts". The Federal Court held that the Tax Court judge was incorrect in disregarding "the uncontradicted evidence that the parties shared a common understanding that the dancers were self-employed and were not employees of the RWB".

[¶793.10] *Deductible Expenses*

If the artist is employed, see Chapter 3 for allowable deductions in determining net income. Note that musicians who are employees are allowed specific deductions for their instruments; see ¶379.

If the artist is self-employed he or she would be allowed to deduct all expenses which are laid out to earn income as previously described above.

Such expenses would include:

(1) insurance premiums on musical instruments and equipment;

(2) the cost of repairs to instruments and equipment, including the cost of new reeds, ligatures, pads and accessories;

(3) legal and accounting fees;

(4) travelling expenses;

(5) union dues and professional membership dues;

(6) commissions to agents;

(7) remuneration paid to a substitute or assistant;

(8) the cost of make-up and hair-styling required for public appearances;

(9) publicity — including photographs and other materials sent to news media and producers, and the cost of advertisements in talent magazines;

(10) transportation expenses related to an engagement (including an audition) under one of the following conditions:

(a) where an engagement is out of town, in which case board and lodging would also be deductible subject to the limitation in ¶734,

(b) where a large instrument or equipment must be carried to the engagement,

(c) where dress clothes must be worn from a residence to the place of engagement, or

(d) where one engagement follows another so closely that a car or taxi is the only means by which the engagement can be fulfilled;

(11) the cost of videotaping or recording performances where required for their preparation or presentation;

(12) telephone expenses, including an applicable portion of the cost of a telephone in a residence where the number is listed as a business phone (per CRA, although the restriction may be doubtful);

(13) capital cost allowance (Class 8, 20% — see ¶801) on wardrobe that is acquired by the artist specifically to earn self-employment income and that is used solely for performances, when the cost of such wardrobe gives rise to an enduring benefit to the artist (where there are recurring expenditures for replacement or renewal indicating an article has a short useful life, it is generally not considered an item of enduring benefit);

(14) the cost of wardrobe used solely for performances when such cost does not give rise to an enduring benefit to the artist;

(15) capital cost allowance (Class 8, 20%) on instruments, sheet music, scores, scripts, transcriptions, arrangements and equipment;

(16) the cost of repairs, alterations and cleaning of clothes for the purpose of their use in self-employment, or required as a result of such use;

(17) costs to maintain that part of the artist's residence used for professional purposes, subject to the restrictions at ¶742;

(18) the cost of music, acting or other lessons incurred for a particular role or part or for the purpose of general self-improvement in the individual's artistic field;

(19) the cost of industry-related periodicals.

In the transportation item above, the CRA is attempting to strike a balance between its usual position that transportation from home to place of business is not a business expense and the special needs of performers. Motor vehicles used in the situations described may be eligible for leasing or interest cost deductions within the limits at ¶738 or capital cost allowance as discussed at ¶810a.

Where the CRA takes the position that capital cost allowance (¶801) may be claimed on instruments, sheet music, scores, arrangements, transcriptions, recordings and certain wardrobe, it means these costs may be deducted to the extent of 20% per year (Class 8) on a declining balance basis, subject to the numerous restrictions in Chapter 8. It follows that these items may not be expensed in full, but must be claimed over time. In the case of such things as scripts and sheet music for a particular performance, it is not clear that there is merit in the requirement that such things cannot be expensed, on analogy to its position on wardrobe which does not create an enduring benefit.

In April 2001, the CRA revised its comments on the wardrobe of performing artists. Previously it had said that wardrobe acquired "specifically to earn self-employment income" would qualify for Class 8 (20%) capital cost allowance. The revised rule is that wardrobe that is "used solely for performances" will be 100% deductible where it does not give rise to enduring benefit for the artist (presumably where it is used for one performance, or perhaps a series of performances in one year, but will not be used again), and will be Class 8 property where there is an enduring benefit for the artist. The "solely for performances" criterion appears more restrictive than the old rule, but of course the 100% rule is more generous.

The CRA takes the position that videotaping and recording costs related to study and general self-improvement (as opposed to those in (10), above) are not deductible.

The positions discussed above are set out in Interpretation Bulletin IT-525R. Essentially the same policies were set out in the original version of IT-525, issued in 1990, which in general confirmed (at long last) a 1984 announcement by the Minister of National Revenue of acceptance of certain recommendations made by a Parliamentary committee regarding the taxation of artists and writers.

The Minister of National Revenue also reflected the Department's current view that continuous losses for many years are not alone sufficient to establish that there is no "reasonable expectation of profit". All the facts and circumstances surrounding the reasonable expectation of profit will be evaluated. Previously, the CRA had endeavoured to disallow certain expenses of artists and writers on the premise that they had no reasonable expectation of profit if such profits were not earned within a reasonable time frame. The CRA's latest position on artists and writers is set out in Interpretation Bulletin IT-504R2, available from Tax Services Offices (see ¶287 and ¶789).

(IT-504R2 (Consolidated) [Archived]; IT-525R (Consolidated) [Archived]; Other Publications: CRA Press Release, June 27, 1984)

BUSINESS LOSSES

[¶795] BUSINESS LOSSES

If expenses exceed revenues, the resulting business loss may be deducted from any other income for the year the loss occurred. The amount of the loss should be entered, as a negative figure, on page 2 of the T1 return in the same manner as business income is entered.

To the extent losses on the T1 exceed income, resulting in a negative income at line 150, you will probably have a "non-capital loss carryover". Such a carryover may be carried back three years to recover prior years' taxes paid or carried forward

- 20 years for losses arising in and after the 2006 taxation year,
- 10 years for losses arising in taxation years ending after March 22, 2004, and before 2006,
- seven years for losses arising in taxation years ending before March 23, 2004,

to offset future taxes. Calculation of the loss carryover is discussed and utilization of the loss carryover is considered in Chapter 10; see ¶1083–¶1091.

For a further discussion of business and other losses refer to Chapter 10.

(ITA: 3)

BOOKS AND RECORDS

[¶796] BOOKS AND RECORDS

If you carry on a business, you are required to keep records and books of accounts. The books and records, including supporting documents such as sales and purchase invoices, contracts, bank statements, annual inventory and cancelled cheques, must be kept in an orderly manner at your place of business, your residence in Canada or, under certain circumstances, such other place as may be requested by the Minister of National Revenue.

These books and records should contain sufficient information to enable you to determine the amount of income taxes payable and the income taxes, CPP, EI and so on you were required to have withheld and remitted to the Receiver General of Canada on behalf of others. Records must be supported by source documents that verify the information in records and accounts. Source documents include such things as sales invoices, purchase invoices, cash register receipts, contracts, work orders, cheques, bank statements, tax returns, etc.

In general, most books and records must be kept for a minimum of six years from the end of the last taxation year to which they relate. The taxation year for an individual is the calendar year, even if the fiscal period of a business ended early in the taxation year. The *Income Tax Regulations* extend the six-year limit for certain "permanent" books and records of businesses (and also of corporations, registered charities and registered Canadian amateur athletic associations). Permanent records of an unincorporated business include the general ledger (or other book of final entry containing summaries of year-to-year transactions) and any special contracts or agreements necessary to an understanding of the entries in the ledger or summary. These must be kept to the end of the period ending of the day that is six years after the last day of the taxation year of in which the business ceased.

If you wish to destroy books and records other than as permitted under the rules above, you must apply in writing to the Director of the Tax Services Office in your area for permission. Form T137 is available for this purpose. The request should be signed by you and provide at least the following

- a clear identification of the books, records and other documents to be destroyed;
- the tax years for which the request applies;
- details of any special circumstances which justify destroying records earlier than normally permitted; and
- any other pertinent information.

Before permission to destroy records is granted, all returns for the taxation years concerned must have been filed, if required, and assessed. The periods allowed for filing notices of objection or appeal must have expired, and there must be no notice of objection or appeal outstanding for the taxation years involved under either the *Income Tax Act*, *Employment Insurance Act* or the *Canada Pension Plan*.

You should note that the CRA can only grant permission to destroy records for income tax purposes. Permission may also be required from other federal departments and provincial or municipal governments.

If you are considering microfilming your records, you should contact your Tax Services Office for requirements and procedures.

Information Circular IC 78-10R5, dated June 2010, provides guidelines regarding records retention and accessibility. The Circular is available in electronic format on the CRA website.

The CRA recognizes that books and records may be kept in electronic form and offers separate Information Circulars to guide taxpayers maintaining traditional paper records (IC 78-10R5) and those maintaining primarily electronic records (IC 05-1R1). The rules in both circulars are essentially the same, but the electronic records version includes additional data on the storage and readability/accessibility of electronic records. Prior to 2010, both sets of information were provided in paper copies as well. Copies of these circulars could be obtained from any Tax Services Office (see ¶287).

(ITA: 230; ITR: 5800 [Required retention period]; IC 78-10R5 Books and Records Retention/Destruction; IC 05-1R1 Electronic Record Keeping)

[¶796.05] *Special Documentation Requirements: Transactions with Non-Arm's Length Non-Residents (Transfer Pricing)*

(1) Overview

Transactions in property, goods and services with non-arm's length non-residents must be documented as to the arm's length nature of the price at the time of the transaction, with potentially severe penalties if the CRA later adjusts the price to increase your taxes and the contemporaneous documentation is not on hand. In addition to this general rule, there are new reporting requirements for individuals and partnerships conducting over C$1 million worth of business in the year with non-arm's length non-residents.

(2) Background

There are various rules throughout this book that ensure gain or defer loss recognition on transactions between non-arm's length parties; see ¶812.

One such area, which is usually more the concern of corporations than individuals, involves commercial transactions with non-arm's length non-residents. Typically, these "transfer pricing" issues arise on prices charged between related parties in international commercial transactions; for example, where goods or services are bought from or sold to a related non-resident by a Canadian resident for commercial purposes. The government's main concern with these transactions is that, especially where they occur on a large scale, the prices charged should reflect arm's length principles so that taxable profit cannot simply be shifted to another jurisdiction by minimizing the Canadian profit component. All high tax jurisdictions share this concern, even where transactions are exclusively with other high tax jurisdictions. In 1995, the Organisation for Economic Co-operation and Development (OECD) issued revised guidelines which are generally accepted by major taxing jurisdictions.

In its Budget of February 18, 1997, the federal government announced that it would take steps:

(a) to harmonize Canadian tax legislation with the "arm's length" principle as defined by the OECD as the standard for determining transfer pricing, and

(b) to introduce new reporting requirements to ensure *contemporaneous documentation* by the taxpayer of cross-border related party transactions

effective for taxation years commencing in or after 1998.

On September 27, 1999, the CRA released Information Circular IC 87-2R, discussing at length its views on the application of the transfer pricing rules under Canadian law and their views on the application of OECD guidelines on transfer pricing.

Commentary on Bill C-29 Measures (Oct. 25, 2016)

Note: When Bill C-29, October 25, 2016, achieves Royal Assent, the commentary will be modified to read:

Canada has been actively engaged with other G20 members and with the OECD in recent years in exploring ways to combat what is termed "base erosion and profit shifting" (BEPS). BEPS refers to international tax planning undertaken by multi-national entities (MNEs) to shift taxable profits away from the typically high tax jurisdiction where the underlying economic activity is taking place to low or no tax jurisdictions.

As part of the BEPS project, the OECD made changes to its Transfer Pricing Guidelines, which include an improved interpretation of the arm's length principle. The CRA has stated that it will be applying these changes as they generally support its current interpretation and audit and assessing practices. In two areas, though, the CRA will not be adjusting its administrative practices as yet. The BEPS project is still engaged in follow-up work on developing a threshold for a proposed simplified approach to low value-adding services, as well as in clarifying the definition of risk-free and risk-adjusted returns for minimally functional entities (cash boxes). Canada will decide on a course of action relating to these two measures once the work is completed.

The BEPS project also recommended the adoption of county-by-country reporting to enhance transparency for tax administrations through having large MNEs provide adequate information for them to assess high-level transfer pricing and other BEPS risks. Canada adopted these recommendations in Budget 2016 for reporting fiscal years of MNE groups having total consolidated group revenue of 750 million Euros or more in the immediately preceding fiscal period that begin on or after January 1, 2016. The country-by-country report generally must be filed by the parent entity of the group and must include the global allocation, by country, of key economic variables, such as revenue, profit, tax paid, stated capital, accumulated earnings, number of employees and tangible assets, as well as the main activities of each subsidiary.

Information Circular IC 87-2R also discusses at length the penalties for failing to use arm's length pricing, whether or not T106 filing (see below) is required, and the requirements for contemporaneous documentation which will alleviate those penalties.

(3) Filing Requirements

Under these rules, reporting requirements for corporations have been replaced by a filing requirement which also applies to businesses carried on by individuals and partnerships. Any Canadian resident carrying on business (here called a "filer") is required to file a return (form T106) for any year in which it has international non-arm's length transactions of sufficient value. A non-resident may also be required to file in respect of a series of transactions of the year if it carried on business in Canada in the year or a preceding year.

This extension of the filing requirement is offset by a $1 million *de minimis* exception, which excuses a filer from filing if the total fair market value of the property and services involved in reportable transactions with all non-arm's length non-residents (and partnerships of which non-arm's length non-residents are members) does not exceed $1 million. That is, no filing is required so long as the aggregate of all reportable transactions with all related non-residents is $1 million or less.

Once the $1 million threshold is met, the rules contemplate a separate T106 filing for each non-resident with which there are reportable transactions.

(4) Documentation Required Even If Filing is Not Required (Transfer Pricing)

Although the $1 million filing exemption should eliminate the filing requirement for most individuals, being excused from filing does not excuse the individual from contemporaneous documentation requirements. The new rules require that all (not merely reportable) cross-border transactions with non-arm's length parties be priced on an arm's length basis, and give the CRA the authority to tax transactions on a reconstructed arm's length basis where arm's length criteria are not met. As well, if the transaction would not be entered into at all by arm's length parties, and it appears that the taxpayer cannot show a primary *bona fide* purpose beyond a tax advantage, the CRA can for tax purposes restructure the transaction as it sees fit. It has been suggested that in these circumstances it could for example treat an investment in shares as a loan subject to imputed interest, although the *bona fide* test might offer some protection. The authority to restructure transactions for tax purposes appears to be restricted (at least in practice) to transfer pricing with non-residents, and cannot be extended to other types of transactions. There is a useful discussion of this issue in the Wolters Kluwer Newsletter *Tax Topics* No. 1783, dated May 11, 2006.

To ensure contemporaneous documentation of transfer pricing arrangements, a penalty of 10% of any adjustments made in the CRA's favour (to a maximum penalty of $5 million) is provided in the absence of contemporaneous documentation spelling out details of the transactions and transfer pricing methods adopted. Such documentation must be provided to the CRA within 60 days of a request for it. However, the penalty provision is only applicable if the net transfer pricing adjustments for a particular year exceed the lesser of $5 million or 10% of a taxpayer's gross revenue. If applicable, the penalty is equal to 10% of the amount of the net transfer pricing adjustments (not merely the excess over $5 million).

Although the rules are aimed at large scale international commercial transactions, there is no such limitation in the statute. Consider, for example, the case of a Canadian individual who buys, say, a condominium in Florida for rental purposes from a brother resident in the U.S. It was always true that, in claiming depreciation for Canadian purposes, or realizing capital gain or loss on eventual resale, the original purchase had to be valued at fair market value. Now, however, it seems that the new documentation and penalty rules would also apply after 1997. (They will not, of course, apply where there are no consequences subject to Canadian tax.) Note that, assuming the condo is used for rental but not business purposes (e.g., assuming it was not purchased for real estate speculation), there is no filing requirement even if the $1 million filing threshold is met. Nevertheless, the CRA will have the power to reprice the transaction, and possibly to impose the 10% penalty, where contemporaneous documentation justifying the purchase price as arm's length was not provided. It is even arguable, although not clear, that documentation would have to include an operating plan justifying the price in commercial terms.

The ramifications these rules will have for non-commercial individual situations, say for example the purchase of a non-resident brother's interest in the Canadian family cottage, simply have not been addressed at this time by either tax authorities or practitioners.

(ITA: 69; 233.1; 247; IC 87-2R International Transfer Pricing; IC 06-1 Income Tax Transfer Pricing and Customs Valuation)

PROVINCIAL TAX PAYABLE AND CANADA PENSION PLAN AND EMPLOYMENT INSURANCE PAYMENTS

[¶797] PROVINCIAL TAX PAYABLE

All of the provincial governments levy income taxes similar to the federal income tax.

Where a person has a business with establishments in more than one province, he or she must allocate the business income to the provinces by use of a formula. See ¶1440.

Provincial taxes other than income tax, such as sales taxes and payroll taxes, are expenses of doing business and deductible as such.

Normally this means you may deduct any amounts you must pay to any province on account of provincial heath care premiums charged to you for your employees. If a province also requires you to withhold and contribute an amount on behalf of an employee, that amount is not a deduction to you except insofar as it forms part of gross wages paid to the employee.

There appears to be an exception for the Ontario Employee Health Tax you must pay on your own personal earnings from a business. By agreement between Ontario and the federal government, this amount appears not to be deductible, although it is not entirely clear why not. You may deduct amounts you must pay on behalf of employees.

(ITA: 18(1)(*a*), (*t*))

[¶798] CANADA PENSION PLAN AND EMPLOYMENT INSURANCE PAYMENTS

As a self-employed individual you must distinguish between Canada Pension Plan payments on your own behalf and those on behalf of your employees. You are required to make two sets of CPP payments on behalf of your employees: their own contributions paid through withholding, and your contributions on their behalf. Both are deductible by you as an employer. The employees' withholding is essentially an amount paid as salary or wages to the employee and therefore deductible, and your own contribution is in the nature of a business tax and therefore deductible. Similarly, Employment Insurance payments made by you for your employees, both the withholding portion and your own contributions on their behalf, are deductible.

See ¶741 if you pay salary to your spouse.

You may deduct one-half of the lesser of (i) your personal CPP/QPP payments *on your self-employment earnings* only, and (ii) the maximum amount you can contribute for the year on your self-employment. The amount deductible under this rule is subtracted from the personal amount eligible for credit under the rules at ¶1305. Since the personal amount credit is equivalent to a deduction only if income does not exceed the lowest marginal tax rate bracket, you will benefit from this rule if your income exceeds that level. The rule appears to be mandatory, in that the amount "deductible" under this rule reduces the personal amount credit whether or not you deduct it. Although the deduction only applies to CPP/QPP payments on self-employment (business) income, it does not actually reduce that income, but is deducted separately, and thus does not add to losses for the year.

Commentary on Bill C-26 Measures (Oct. 6, 2016)

Note: When Bill C-26, October 6, 2016, achieves Royal Assent, the commentary will be modified to read:

Effective January 1, 2019, a deduction is allowed for 100% of the enhanced contributions to the CPP payable on the taxpayer's self-employed earnings for the year. A deduction is also allowed on such additional contributions made in respect of a taxpayer's employment income other than self-employed earnings. They will be subject to applicable constraints based on the maximum of such contributions payable by the taxpayer for the year under the plan.

Effective as of 2006, Quebec self-employed individuals and residents who work outside of Quebec who pay Quebec Parental Insurance Premiums may deduct the amount by which

(1) the amounts payable by a taxpayer in respect of self-employed earnings for the taxation year as a premium under the Quebec Parental Insurance Plan exceeds

(2) the amounts that would be payable by the taxpayer as an employee's premium under that Plan if those earnings were employment income of the taxpayer for the taxation year.

See Schedule 10 of the T1 return for the calculation.

(ITA: 18(1)(*a*), (*t*); 60(*e*); 60(*g*))

HOW TO REPORT INCOME FROM A BUSINESS

[¶798a] BUSINESS INCOME

If you are in business (this term includes professions) you report the business income for the year on page 2 of the T1 return.

Both gross and net income must be reported. Gross income is the total revenue of the business. Net income is the gross income less all deductions allowable for tax purposes. If you are a member of a partnership, enter the total gross income of the partnership but only your share of the net income.

[¶798b] OTHER INFORMATION WHICH MUST BE REPORTED

- You must fill out the Calculation of Canada Pension Plan Contributions on Self-Employment and Other Earnings on Schedule 8 of the T1 General.
- Details of the revenue, expenses, and other adjustments making up the "net income" figure must be supplied. (Farmers and fishers should refer to Chapter 17.)
- You should prepare a Statement of Income and Expenses for your business and, where income and expenses on that Statement must be further adjusted for tax purposes, a schedule of Adjustments to Income. The most common difference is capital cost allowance, which often differs from book depreciation. Even if these are the same, you should support your capital cost allowance claim with a schedule similar to page 4 of form T2125.
- The CRA has prepared a *Business and Professional Income* guide (T4002) which (at least in the version available at press time) includes form T2125 (Statement of Business or Professional Activities). Use of these forms is optional — you may continue to use an acceptable format of your own if you prefer. However, the CRA Guide is helpful, and can be obtained from any Tax Services Office (¶287). The guide does not include form T2038 (Ind.), which is mandatory if you claim investment tax credit (¶1463), or T1A, which you should use if you claim loss carrybacks.
- You should be prepared to support the details reported with invoices and any other relevant documentary evidence, although it is not necessary to file this evidence with the return.
- Partners must file either partnership financial statements or form T5013; see ¶1880.

SPECIFIC QUESTIONS AND ANSWERS

[¶798c] SPECIFIC QUESTIONS AND ANSWERS

Salary to Spouse and Self

Mr. Carrie is the proprietor of a daycare centre showing a net profit of $10,000 for the year. During the year he paid his wife, who works for him, a salary of $5,000. In addition, he withdrew $5,000 from the business as remuneration for his own services and charged this as an expense; it (along with the other salaries and expenses) has been deducted to arrive at the $10,000 net profit. How should Mr. Carrie calculate his income for tax purposes?

He should calculate his income for the year for tax purposes as follows:

Net profit for year	$10,000
Salary for Mr. Carrie	5,000
Net income for tax purposes	$15,000

The "salary" Mr. Carrie paid to himself is a distribution of profit; it is part of his business income and it is not employment income. A reasonable salary paid to a spouse is deductible in arriving at income. A reasonable salary paid to a son or daughter is also deductible. Where, however, salary is provided to a person you normally claim as a dependant for purposes of personal exemption tax credits, the income may reduce the credit you may claim. See Chapter 11.

Automobile Expenses

Mike Blane purchased an automobile to be used 60% for business and 40% for pleasure. In the first year, he has an accident while in the course of business, with damages amounting to $800, for which he is not insured. Can he claim the uninsured loss?

He may claim the full $800 damages, as the car accident took place in the normal conduct of business. If he had been insured he could only claim the damages not covered by insurance. If the accident did not occur while driving in the course of business, no portion of the damages would be deductible.

Expense of Trip to Europe

Jones is the proprietor of an iron and steel company. He takes a three month trip on business to Europe, accompanied by his wife. The cost of the trip is $20,000 and he spends 40% of his time doing business. Is Jones able to claim the full $20,000 as a deduction?

He may claim only that portion of his expenses actually incurred to earn revenue and promote his business income. He may not claim expenses for his wife, and of the remaining $10,000, he may claim only 40%, i.e., $4,000, representing that portion of his trip devoted to earning income. He could claim a larger deduction if he could substantiate the fact that less than half the expenses applied to his wife, or that his wife was present in a capacity related to the business.

Professionals — Work in Progress

Ed Kraft conducts his own law practice and employs a lawyer who is paid $20 per hour, including fringe benefits. As of the end of Mr. Kraft's current fiscal period the following work is incomplete:

Client A — four hours of Mr. Kraft's time billable at $100 per hour; — twenty hours of the employee's time billable at $60 per hour.

If Mr. Kraft does not elect to exclude his work in progress for tax purposes, how should he value it?

Mr. Kraft's work in progress may be valued at cost of $400 ($20 × 20 hours). Mr. Kraft's time is not included in the cost of inventory since no actual cost of inventory is incurred by Mr. Kraft with respect to his time.

Entertainment Expenses

Bub Lewis, for promotional reasons, entertains one of his customers by taking him to his club to play a round of golf. Bub pays $15 for his customer's golf club rental and $50 for a meal after the game. What amount, if any, may Bub deduct in computing income?

It would seem that Bub may deduct $25 (50% of the $50 meal cost). It has long been clear that Bub's club dues, greens fees and initiation fees would not be deductible. In 1997 the CRA went further and said that meal expenses (and presumably rental fees also) at a golf facility "in conjunction with a game of golf" are not deductible. (Interpretation Bulletin IT-148R3 still contained this statement at the time of writing.) However, in early 1998 the CRA recanted and said (in *Income Tax Technical News* No. 12) that the deduction is denied only in respect of recreational amenities and not dining or conference facilities of the club. It would seem to follow that the club rental is not deductible but lunch is, subject to the usual 50% disallowance for meals and entertainment expenses. See ¶731 and ¶734.

Chapter 8

Capital Cost Allowance

THESE POINTS ARE COVERED IN THIS CHAPTER

CRA REFERENCES RELATING TO THIS CHAPTER

T1 Lines

- Line 135 — Business income (Net)
- Line 137 — Professional income (Net)
- Line 139 — Commission income (Net)
- Line 229 — Other employment expenses

CRA Guides

T4002, "Business and Professional Income"; **T4036**, "Rental Income — Includes Form T776"; **T4044**, "Employment Expenses — Includes Forms T777, TL2, T2200, and GST370."

CRA Forms

T776, "Statement of Real Estate Rentals"; **T777**, "Statement of Employment Expenses"; **T1030**, "Election to Claim A Capital Gains Reserve For Individuals (Other Than Trusts) When Calculating The Amount Of A Capital Gain Using The Replacement Property Rules"; **T1031**, "Subsection 13(29) Election in Respect of Certain Depreciable Properties, Acquired for Use in a Long Term Project"; **T2125**, "Statement of Business or Professional Activities"; **T2145**, "Election in Respect of the Leasing of Property"; **T2146**, "Election in Respect of Assigned Leases or Subleased Property"

Income Tax Folios

S1-F3-C2, "Principal Residence"; **S1-F5-C1**, "Related Persons and Dealing at Arm's Length"

Interpretation Bulletins

IT-79R3, "Capital Cost Allowance — Buildings or Other Structures" [Archived]; **IT-99R5 (Consolidated)**, "Legal and Accounting Fees" [Archived]; **IT-102R2**, "Conversion of Property, Other than Real Property, from or to Inventory" [Archived]; **IT-128R**, "Capital Cost Allowance — Depreciable Property" [Archived]; **IT-147R3**, "Capital Cost Allowance — Accelerated Write-off of Manufacturing and Processing Machinery and Equipment" [Archived]; **IT-159R3**, "Capital Debts Established to be Bad Debts" [Archived]; **IT-190R2**, "Capital Cost Allowance —

Transferred and Misclassified Property" [Archived]; **IT-209R**, "Inter-Vivos Gifts of Capital Property to Individuals Directly or Through Trusts" [Archived]; **IT-220R2**, "Capital Cost Allowance — Proceeds of Disposition of Depreciable Property" [Archived]; **IT-259R4**, "Exchange of Property" [Archived]; **IT-267R2**, "Capital Cost Allowance — Vessels" [Archived]; **IT-273R2**, "Government Assistance — General Comments" [Archived]; **IT-274R**, "Rental Properties — Capital Cost of $50,000 or More" [Archived]; **IT-285R2**, "Capital Cost Allowance — General Comments" [Archived]; **IT-304R2**, "Condominiums" [Archived]; **IT-306R2**, "Capital Cost Allowance — Contractor's Movable Equipment" [Archived]; **IT-359R2**, "Premiums and Other Amounts With Respect to Leases" [Archived]; **IT-418**, "Capital Cost Allowance — Partial Dispositions of Property" [Archived]; **IT-443**, "Leasing Property — Capital Cost Allowance Restrictions" [Archived]; **IT-464R**, "Capital Cost Allowance — Leasehold Interests" [Archived]; **IT-469R**, "Capital Cost Allowance — Earth-Moving Equipment" [Archived]; **IT-472**, "Capital Cost Allowance — Class 8 Property" [Archived]; **IT-476R**, "Capital Cost Allowance — Equipment Used in Petroleum and Natural Gas Activities" [Archived]; **IT-477 (Consolidated)**, "Capital Cost Allowance — Patents, Franchises, Concessions and Licenses" [Archived]; **IT-478R2**, "Capital Cost Allowance — Recapture and Terminal Loss" [Archived]; **IT-481 (Consolidated)**, "Timber Resource Property and Timber Limits" [Archived]; **IT-485**, "Cost of Clearing or Levelling Land" [Archived]; **IT-491**, "Former Business Property" [Archived]; **IT-492**, "Capital Cost Allowance — Industrial Mineral Mines" [Archived]; **IT-501**, "Capital Cost Allowance — Logging Assets" [Archived]; **IT-521R**, "Motor Vehicle Expenses Claimed by Self-Employed Individuals" [Archived]; **IT-522R**, "Vehicle, Travel and Sales Expenses of Employees" [Archived]; **IT-532**, "Part I.3 — Tax on Large Corporations" [Archived]

Information Circulars

84-1, "Revision of Capital Cost Allowance Claims and Other Permissive Deductions"

Income Tax Technical News

No. 25, October 30, 2002, "Replacement Property Rules and Business Expansions"

WHAT YOU SHOULD KNOW ABOUT CAPITAL COST ALLOWANCE

RECENT CHANGES

Capital cost allowance ("CCA") is an area that is particularly susceptible to change. Because it permits depreciation of capital assets for tax purposes, it has a major impact on the cash flow position of companies making new investments. On the one hand, where the government wants to stimulate capital investment, it frequently resorts to accelerated tax depreciation. On the other hand, where the government wants more money itself, one of its quickest revenue raisers is a reduction in tax depreciation. Moreover, the rates of depreciation for particular properties are prescribed by regulation rather than legislation, so that in theory at least the government has the capability to make rapid adjustments to these items.

An overview of the CCA system commences at ¶801. Because of its flexibility and generally accelerated rates of CCA, the system is extremely important to the tax position of most business enterprises.

The following summary is a review of recent changes, and assumes a familiarity with the system. Detailed discussions follow ¶802. Statements based on law and regulations not formally enacted at the time of writing (except those in the summaries immediately below) are indicated in square brackets, thus: [].

Summary of Changes

2016 Federal Budget

Enhancing Tax Support for Clean Energy

Budget 2016 again expanded CCA Classes 43.1 and 43.2 to allow for accelerated CCA rates for electric vehicle charging stations and electrical energy storage property acquired after March 21, 2016 that were not used or available for use before March 22, 2016. See ¶889.05.

Bill C-29 (Introduced October 25, 2016)

Eligible Capital Property Rules

The eligible capital property rules will be replaced effective 2017. For 2017 and later years, eligible capital property will be treated as depreciable capital property and included in CCA Class 14.1 (5%). Many accompanying transitional rules are proposed to allow for the shift to the new regime. For example, as a transitional measure, any expenditure incurred before January 1, 2017 will be depreciable at a rate of 7% instead of 5% before the 2027 taxation year. See ¶880a.

2016 Automobile Capital Cost Limit

For automobiles acquired in 2016, the maximum amount which you can add to the capital cost of that automobile remains at $30,000. See ¶810a.

Filing Based on Pending Changes

In general, the CRA will accept CCA claims based on pending changes. See ¶222.

[¶801] WHAT IS CAPITAL COST ALLOWANCE?

CCA Explained

With a few exceptions, expenditures of a capital nature may not be deducted in full in computing income for tax purposes in the year the expenditures are made. Instead, most capital expenditures must be deducted from income over a period of several years. The annual deductions which may be claimed will eventually result in the cost of capital assets being allowed as a deduction to the taxpayer. These deductions are known as "capital cost allowances" (often referred to as CCA).

The amount which may be depreciated for tax purposes is the "capital cost" of depreciable property. This amount is subject to a number of adjustments, described at ¶811 et seq. CCA claimed reduces the "undepreciated capital cost" ("UCC") of depreciable property. The UCC is therefore the balance left for further depreciation in future years. CCA deductions are not calculated using a single property's capital cost, but rather using the UCC of a pool ("class") of similar property, as described at ¶866 et seq.

Depreciable Property

Most classes of depreciable property have a CCA rate prescribed by regulation. The prescribed rate multiplied by the UCC of the depreciable property in the class after additions, deductions, and adjustments for the year gives the tax deduction available ("CCA claim") for that class for the year.

Depreciable property in itself is simply property which is entitled to depreciation for tax purposes under any of the regulations described in this section. Depreciable property can only be depreciated in computing the income from a business or from property, with the exception of automobiles and aircraft required in the course of employment, which can be depreciated against employment income. Property which is eligible for depreciation is described further at ¶807 et seq.

Disposing of Depreciable Property

When you dispose of depreciable property, the proceeds of disposition up to the capital cost of the property sold are subtracted from the UCC of the class. Where the pool balance is negative at the end of the taxation year, the negative balance is included in income as "recapture" of CCA. Proceeds received for property sold in excess of its capital cost are considered capital gains and are accounted for separately on Schedule 3 (see ¶841).

Where all the property in a class is disposed of in a taxation year and a positive balance remains after accounting for proceeds of disposition, that balance is a "terminal loss" and is deductible from income (¶851).

Certain exceptions, notably for Class 10.1 automobiles (¶810a), exist to the recapture/terminal loss rules. As well, special rules vary the general result in a number of specific cases discussed in the paragraphs following ¶839.

(ITA: 13; 18; 20; ITR: 1100)

[¶801a] CAPITAL COST ALLOWANCE VERSUS ACCOUNTING DEPRECIATION

Do not record depreciation in your accounting records in the same amounts as you claim with respect to CCA for tax purposes. Conversely, accounting depreciation or amortization is not relevant for income tax purposes.

CCA rates are prescribed by tax law which is often influenced by government and politics, so these rates are not always designed to reflect an accurate measure of the decrease of an asset's value as is calculated for accounting purposes. In some cases, prescribed rates may be higher than would be appropriate for proper accounting, particularly where accelerated rates are granted to stimulate purchases of capital assets.

The generally accepted method of calculating accounting depreciation requires the amortization of the cost of the assets, less their estimated eventual salvage value, divided by the estimated useful life of the assets. When the variation in useful lives and salvage values of assets is considered, this calculation will rarely produce a result identical to a CCA calculation where many different assets are grouped in one class at one rate.

(ITA: 20)

[¶802] GENERAL METHOD OF CALCULATION

The calculation begins with the UCC of a particular class of assets as determined at the beginning of the tax year. To this value, the capital cost of assets acquired during the year is added and the proceeds received from disposing of any assets in the Class (up to the original cost of the asset) are subtracted. Last, the prescribed CCA rate is applied to the resulting value, which will yield the CCA amount which is deducted from income. One must be cognizant of the "half-year rule" (discussed at ¶802.10) while making this calculation. Further, property acquired but not yet put into use also adds complexity (¶804b).

Before these calculations can be made, however, it is necessary to determine which amounts and rates are applicable. This chapter includes a discussion of the meaning of "capital expenditures", "capital cost", "undepreciated capital cost", and "proceeds of disposal", and the means of arriving at the appropriate rate of allowance. It is, of course, necessary to determine whether your property qualifies for CCA.

[¶802.05] *Capital Cost Allowance Claims Optional*

The rates of CCA prescribed are the maximum rates which may be claimed in the year. You are not obliged to claim the maximum CCA in any year, but you may claim any amount you wish, from Nil up to the maximum amount. Given the mechanics of the CCA system, unclaimed amounts remain on hand for claims in any future year subject to the maximum allowance calculation in that future year.

Planning Opportunity

You may not wish to claim the maximum amount of CCA available for the year if, by doing so, a loss would be created which could not be offset against other income. If you are claiming some but not all of the CCA available to you, it may be to your advantage to claim the maximum amount in the lower rate classes (e.g., Class 1, 3, etc.) rather than in the higher rate classes (e.g., Class 8, 10, 29, etc.) as this will maximize the deductions available to you in the immediately succeeding years. The CCA claimed can in some circumstances be revised in the future (see ¶802b).

[¶802.10] *The "Half-Year Rule"*

How the Rule Works

For most classes of depreciable property, you may not claim a full year's CCA in the year a depreciable asset is acquired. The maximum CCA you may claim in the year of acquisition is limited to one-half of the normal CCA. The half-year rule is an average measure, reflecting the fact that assets can be acquired at any time during a taxation year and therefore do not always warrant a full depreciation deduction in the year of acquisition.

An asset is considered to be acquired at the earlier of: (i) the date title is obtained under provincial law, or (ii) the date the incidents of title such as possession, use, and risk are obtained.

Where the Half-Year Rule Does Not Apply

- Canadian Vessels placed in class 7.
- Certified productions acquired after 1987 and before March 1996 placed in Class 10.

- Most Class 12 property, which often may be depreciated at 100%, except where otherwise noted (see ¶898).
- Classes 13, 14, and 15 — where the claims are calculated in accordance with other rules. See ¶879, ¶880, and ¶882, respectively.
- Classes 24, 27, and 34 — certain pollution control and energy conservation equipment placed in these classes. See ¶899a.
- Class 29 — designated manufacturing equipment acquired after March 18, 2007 and before 2016. See ¶899a.
- Class 52 — certain general purpose data processing equipment and systems software for that equipment, acquired after January 27, 2009, and before February 2011 (see ¶886t.05).
- Specified leasing property of taxpayers who have elected to capitalize the lease (¶873a.10) if the property is deemed acquired in a preceding taxation year.

Additionally, the half-year rule will not apply where property has been transferred in either:

(1) a non-arm's length transaction (as defined in ¶812) except where the non-arm's length status between the transferee and transferor arises from contingent rights (i.e., options or cancellation rights), or

(2) a "butterfly transaction" (which is a complex divisive reorganization of corporations, usually dividing the assets of one corporation among two or more shareholder corporations),

provided that in either case, the transferor held the property continuously from the day that was at least 364 days before the end of the taxation year of the transferee in which the transferee acquired the property to the day it was acquired by the transferee.

Non-arm's length or butterfly transfers which escape the half-year rule in the hands of the transferee will be deemed to have been acquired by the transferee at the beginning of the transferee's first taxation year commencing after the time the property was acquired by the transferor. This is intended to allow the transferee to claim accumulated but unclaimed CCA of the transferor in straight-line classes such as Class 29 (and previously for Classes 24, 27, and 34) where it is possible to "catch up" previously unclaimed amounts. That is, if the transferor had held a Class 29 asset for three years but claimed no CCA on it and then transferred it to the transferee, the transferee could claim 100% CCA in the year of acquisition (as could the transferor if it had held the property). See ¶878.

The Half-Year Rule and CCA Calculation

For most classes, disposals made are first netted against acquisitions made before computing CCA for the year. Consequently, the effect of the "half-year rule" will be mitigated when there are major disposals of fixed assets which can be netted against additions.

For most classes, additions, adjustments, and disposals are applied to the opening UCC before CCA is claimed for the year. Then, for each class, the following reduction is applied:

50% of:

(1) cost of acquisitions net of adjustments (e.g., for investment tax credit) of property acquired in the year

minus

(2) proceeds of property disposed of in the year.

Miscellaneous Rules

Government assistance in respect of property disposed of in a preceding year may give rise to additions (if the assistance is repaid) or deductions (if the assistance is received in the current year) to UCC (see ¶825). These adjustments are included in (a) and (b) when calculating the reduction to CCA for the year.

Special rules apply to proceeds for Classes 14, 15, and 29. These are discussed at ¶880, ¶882, and ¶899a. With respect to assets in Class 29, the maximum CCA is 25% in the year of acquisition, 50% in the subsequent year, and the remaining balance in the third year. Any claim foregone in one year may be claimed in full in the following year. For example, if no claim is made in the year of acquisition, the rate will be 75% in the subsequent year and the balance in the third year. Similarly, the entire amount may be deducted in the third year if no claim is made in the year of acquisition and the subsequent year.

See also the application of the half-year rule where the available-for-use rule applies, described at ¶804b.10.

(ITA: 13, 251(5)(*b*)(i); ITR: 1100(1), (2), (2.1), (2.2), (2.3); IT-285R2 Capital cost allowance — General comments)

[¶802a] SHORT TAXATION YEARS

If the fiscal period of your business is less than 12 months, the amount of CCA that may be claimed for depreciable property used in a business is prorated. CCA in short taxation years is limited to that portion of the maximum amount otherwise allowable that is proportionate to the number of days in your fiscal period out of 365.

Proration for short taxation years is not required for CCA taken on the following depreciable properties:

(a) allowances for Class 14 assets (patents, franchises, etc.);

(b) allowances for timber limits and cutting rights (Schedule VI);

(c) allowances for Class 15 assets (woods assets);

(d) allowances for industrial mineral mines (Schedule V);

(e) additional allowances for certified productions assets;

(f) additional allowances for Canadian film or video production assets;

(g) additional allowances for mining assets placed in Classes 28 and 41; and

(h) allowances for year 2000 computer software.

Allowances respecting timber limits, woods assets, and industrial mineral mines will vary according to the number of units of timber cut or mineral mined in the taxation year. The additional allowances for certified productions, Canadian film or video productions, and mining assets are limited by income which presumably will be reduced in a short taxation year in any event.

(ITR: 1100(3))

¶802b REVISION OF CAPITAL COST ALLOWANCE CLAIMS

As mentioned at ¶802, you may claim any amount of CCA for a year provided that you do not exceed the maximum annual rate of allowance prescribed for the particular class of asset involved. In some cases, the amount of CCA claimed for a year may subsequently prove to be higher or lower than the desired amount. For example, you might have claimed maximum CCA for a particular year, with the result of increasing a business loss for that year and subsequently find that you cannot generate sufficient income within the allowable carry-forward period to fully utilize the loss (see ¶1087). In this case, you will want to revise your CCA claim for the earlier year, and this may be done in some circumstances.

Many of the administrative policies discussed in this section and ¶802b.05 are derived from CRA information circular IC 84-1. In 2014, the CRA expressed that the policies contained in IC 84-1 were under review. Until the time when new policies are released, each request will be reviewed on a case-by-case basis.

Revision Options and Timing

Where the Minister has not issued a Notice of Assessment (¶257) for a taxation year, you can simply file a revised CCA claim for that year. The revision should be requested in a letter sent to your local Tax Services Office, accompanied by revised schedules of CCA and any other schedules which are affected by the revision of the CCA claim. The CRA will normally agree to such a request, and if, for some reason, it does not, you have the right to file a Notice of Objection (¶266) with respect to any assessment issued which does not reflect the revised CCA claim.

If the revision is desired for a taxation year which has been assessed by the Minister, and the 90-day period allowed for filing a Notice of Objection to the assessment has not yet expired, you should follow the same procedure described above, and write a letter to the local Tax Services Office requesting the desired revision of your CCA claim. However, keep in mind that you will have no legal right to obtain such a revision once the 90-day period has expired, and therefore in these situations you may wish to file a protective Notice of Objection if it appears the CRA may not agree to the revision before the 90-day period expires.

If the revision is desired for a year which has been assessed by the Minister, and the 90-day period for filing a Notice of Objection has already expired, the revision will normally only be permitted if it does not result in a change in the tax assessed for the year of revision, or any other year affected by the revision for which the time has expired for filing a Notice of Objection.

If you receive a Notice of Determination of a Loss from the Minister regarding the amount of your non-capital loss, capital loss or restricted farm loss for any particular taxation year, you have 90 days from the day of sending of this Notice to advise the Minister that you wish to revise the amount of CCA claimed for that year. Once the period expires, your request to revise the CCA will normally not be accepted as a matter of CRA policy.

(ITA: 165; CRA Document No.: 2014 TEI Liaison Meeting, Q.E2, *November 18, 2014*, CRA Document No. 2014-0550381C6)

[¶802b.05] *Revisions to Statute-Barred Years*

See ¶267 and ¶268 for rules relating to the normal reassessment period and when revisions can be made.

Where a request is made to revise the capital cost of a depreciable property acquired during a taxation year which is statute-barred, the amount of CCA deducted with respect to that property in any statute-barred year will not be adjusted. Instead, the CRA will recalculate the UCC as of the beginning of the oldest non-statute-barred year using the revised capital cost. Therefore, the recalculated UCC at the beginning of that year will reflect the upward or downward revision. Moreover, the CRA will make the necessary upward adjustments to the CCA claimed in the current and subsequent non-statute-barred years if provided with a written request. If the revision results in a reduction of UCC, the CRA will automatically make the downward adjustments to CCA claimed in those years.

As previously mentioned, this administrative policy is stipulated by the CRA in IC 84-1, which is currently under review. However, until updated policies are released, the policy described above will continue to apply.

Reassessments Outside the Normal Period

Subsection 152(4.2) gives the Minister the discretion to reassess or redetermine beyond the normal reassessment period in order to give a refund or to reduce taxes payable for the taxation year in question. The reassessment or redetermination will generally be made upon receipt of your written request after the normal reassessment period has expired and where the Minister is satisfied that the request would have been honoured had it been made within the normal reassessment period.

Either you or the CRA can request a reassessment of statute-barred year under subsection 152(4.3) if an assessment (where issues have been in dispute with the CRA and an agreement is reached) or a court decision is to change your balances. A "balance" means income, taxable income, taxable income earned in Canada, loss, or any tax or other amount payable or refundable or deemed paid. The request must be made within one year after all rights of objection and appeal have expired. Revisions to the statute-barred year can only be made to the extent the changes can reasonably be considered to relate to the changed balances for the settlement year. This provision also allows the modification of a refund or other amount payable for another year, applicable to reassessments, redeterminations, and modifications in respect of taxation years that relate to changes in balances for that other taxation year as a result of assessments made, or decisions on appeal rendered, after November 5, 2010.

(ITA: 152(4.2), (4.3); IT-478R2, para. 14)

¶803 TAXPAYERS ELIGIBLE FOR CAPITAL COST ALLOWANCE

CCA may be claimed if you have income from a business or from property. If you are an employee and are required to travel extensively in the course of employment, you can claim CCA with respect to the cost of automobiles and aircraft used in the performance of your duties. The requirements which an employee must meet in order to claim CCA are discussed at ¶368, ¶369, and ¶370.

Unique Situations

If you are in business as a proprietor, and the business has a fiscal period which does not coincide with the calendar year, the CCA rules will apply, in respect to your business assets, to capital assets owned, acquired or disposed of during the business fiscal year and not during your personal taxation year (which is the calendar year).

CCA must be claimed by the person who owns the property being depreciated. Expenditures to improve a leasehold interest may also give rise to CCA to the lessee, as discussed in ¶879. There may be circumstances in which a lease is treated as a sale and the lessee is allowed to depreciate the property; see ¶833 and ¶873a.

Where your spouse obtains a loan and purchases an automobile for use in your business, and the funds used to make the loan payments and maintain the vehicle would be exclusively yours, you could claim CCA on the vehicle. This results because you are considered to have acquired beneficial ownership of the automobile (that is, all the incidents of possession, use, and risk).

(ITA: 20; ITR: 1100; IT-128R Capital Cost Allowance — Depreciable Property; IT-521R Motor Vehicle Expenses Claimed by Self-Employed Individuals; IT-522R Vehicle, Travel and Sales Expenses of Employees; CRA Document No.: Cca on a Vehicle in the Spouse's Name, *June 28, 2005*, CRA Document No. 2005-0122211E5)

¶804 EXPENDITURES QUALIFYING FOR CAPITAL COST ALLOWANCE

Only expenditures incurred to acquire property of a capital nature for the purpose of producing income may be added to a capital asset class. However, not all such expenditures qualify for CCA claims. Consequently, we will first discuss the meaning of "capital" expenditures, and the requirement that they be made to produce income, and then describe the conditions under which CCA may, or may not, be deducted as a result of such expenditures.

(IT-128R Capital Cost Allowance — Depreciable Property)

¶804a WHEN A DEPRECIABLE ASSET IS ACQUIRED

Where a year-end intervenes between the order and the physical acquisition of property, you are considered to acquire property at the earlier of:

(1) the date you obtain legal title; and

(2) the date you acquired all the incidents of ownership, such as possession, use, and risk.

Purchase Contracts

A contract for purchase may or may not indicate when title will pass. If the contract is an unconditional contract for the sale of specific assets which are in a deliverable state, property passes to the purchaser when the contract is made. If the contract is for the sale of specific assets which must be processed to be deliverable, or measured to determine price, property passes when that is done and the purchaser has notice thereof. The property must exist and be specifically identifiable (for example, by serial number) as the object of the contract.

The date of acquisition remains important for crediting assets to a class. CCA claims with respect to certain assets may be deferred until the assets are available for use, or until the taxation year following a full-length taxation year following acquisition (see ¶804b).

[¶804a.05] *Assets under Construction*

The acquisition of a capital asset may have commenced but not be completed by the end of the taxation year (e.g., a large construction project which spans several years). It may, however, also occur in the case of other types of assets, such as machinery, where a purchase has been decided upon, but one or more of the order, delivery, approval, or payment steps have not been completed at year end. For such purchases, there may be a question when CCA may first be claimed. This issue turns in the first instance on the passage of title, as discussed above. Even where title appears to have passed, the CRA is of the view that property can pass and acquisition take place only if the asset is in existence and it is a specific asset which can be identified as the object of the contract.

In the case of construction projects, rights are usually acquired gradually over the construction term as construction progresses, and the cost of such rights is usually reflected in progress billings made by the contractor. Consequently, CCA may be claimed on the amount of progress billings rendered by the end of the year for completed construction. In *Newfoundland Light and Power Co. Ltd. v. The Queen*, 90 DTC 6166 (FCA), the Court found that a holdback of price pending was not a capital cost until actually paid.

For other assets, the time at which a right to the asset exists will depend upon the terms of the agreement between the seller and buyer. Usually the delivery date will be the time the buyer acquires a right to an asset. However, a purchase order for a specific item, which can be specifically identified (e.g., by serial number) and has been accepted by the seller, may give the buyer an enforceable right to the asset before delivery. On the other hand, in some industries, notably automotive and other heavy equipment manufacturing, it is customary to issue contracts that describe property being purchased by make, model, and serial number at a time when the property does not exist but is scheduled for production. Under this type of contract, the purchaser acquires the property when it has been produced and the purchaser has knowledge that it is in a deliverable state.

(IT-285R2, paras. 15-22)

¶804b WHEN TAX DEPRECIATION MAY COMMENCE: THE "AVAILABLE-FOR-USE" RULES

[¶804b.05] *Overview*

The basic principle of the "available-for-use" rules is that property may not be depreciated for income tax purposes until the earlier of the time it is put in use or in the second taxation year following the year of acquisition. You may depreciate buildings when they are either complete or "substantially" (usually 90%) in use.

The available-for-use rules also defer the right to claim the investment tax credit or scientific research deductions on acquisitions of depreciable property until the property becomes available for use, as described below.

Although the property may not be credited to capital cost allowance classes at the time of acquisition for purposes of claiming CCA, the property has still been acquired for tax purposes (e.g., an asset which is not yet available for use is subsequently sold and you report a capital gain). Accordingly, such cost might provide shelter from recapture of CCA or prevent a terminal loss, even though CCA claims on the new property have not yet commenced.

Lengthy and complex rules will define when a property becomes available for use. The rules are being divided into the following groups:

- the general rules (for property other than buildings);
- the general building rules, which applies to all buildings;
- the long-term project rule (which involves electing on form T1031), which accelerates the amount considered available for use on long-term construction projects involving buildings or other assets but not rental buildings;
- the rental income rule for buildings, which allows an acceleration of deductions over the general building rule to the extent of rental income from the building; and
- the non-arm's length (and butterfly) transfer rules, which provide overriding exceptions, positive and negative, to the preceding rules.

(ITA: 13(26)–(30); 20(28), (29); 37(1.2); 127(11.1); 248(19))

[¶804b.10] *Application of the Half-Year Rule Where Available-For-Use Rule Applies*

The half-year rule (¶802) applies when property is recognized for UCC purposes under the available-for-use rules. There is an exception, however, for property recognized only under the two-year deferral rule ("rolling start" rule) described in ¶804b.15 of the general rule and ¶804b.20 of the general building rule below. Property recognized by virtue of these rules will not be subject to the half-year rule in the year it becomes eligible for CCA. The following example illustrates the half-year rule in relation to the available-for-use rule.

Example

Mac Chivers constructed a piece of machinery for his business (which operates on a calendar year fiscal period). He spent $25,000 on the machinery in Year 1, $50,000 in Year 2, and $25,000 in June of Year 3. The machinery was put into use in September of Year 3. You may assume that the property was "acquired" in these years in these amounts under the rules at ¶804a.

In Year 1 and Year 2, CCA cannot be claimed due to available-for-use rules. In Year 3, Mac Chivers may claim CCA on the $100,000 of capital asset additions as follows:

The $25,000 expended in Year 1 is added to Class 8 (since it was "acquired" in Year 1) and is deemed available for use at one instant past midnight on January 1, Year 3 under the "rolling start" rule. Accordingly, it is not subject to the half-year rule, even though it would also qualify in Year 3 since it was put in use in that year.

The $50,000 spent in Year 2 is included in Class 8 and eligible for CCA in Year 3 since it was put in use in that year. The half-year rule will apply to Year 3 CCA claims on this amount.

The $25,000 expended in Year 3 will be added to Class 8. Since the machinery has been put in use in Year 3, this amount is eligible for CCA in Year 3, subject to the half-year rule.

(ITR: 1100(2))

[¶804b.15] *The General Rules*

For assets other than a building or part of a building, an asset is considered to become available for use and therefore eligible for CCA and investment tax credit at the earliest of the times described below. This list is intended for individual taxpayers; its contents are not exhaustive.

Although there are numerous rules described below, the general principle is that you may depreciate property for tax purposes at the earlier of the time it is put in use or in the second taxation year following the year of acquisition.

1. Property Put Into Use

The time when you first used the property for the purpose of earning income.

2. Rolling Start

Your property is considered available for use at the beginning of the taxation year that is more than 357 days after the end of the taxation year which you acquired it. That is, property acquired in taxation Year 1 may be depreciated for tax purposes in taxation Year 3 provided there is no intervening short taxation year.

3. Time of Disposition

The time that is immediately before the disposition of the property.

4. Delivered and Ready to Produce Income

The time at which:

(a) you accept delivery of the property, or where the property is not the deliverable type, it is available for you to use, and

(b) you are capable, either alone or in combination with other property in your possession, of producing a commercially saleable product or performing a commercially saleable service, including an intermediate product or service that is that can be used or consumed.

This rule allows CCA on property delivered or available for delivery if the property (together with other property on hand) has the capability of making a saleable intermediate product even if that product is not sold. For example, suppose a production plant takes raw wood and makes paper. An intermediate stage is the production of wood chips, which could be sold commercially, although the plant does not sell them. If the plant acquires a machine which is necessary to the manufacture of saleable chips and in fact has the capacity to make them, it can depreciate the machine even though it has not acquired the additional machinery necessary to make paper from the chips, and does not in fact sell the chips.

5. Pollution-Control Equipment

With respect to property acquired for the prevention, reduction, or elimination of air or water pollution carried on by your business operations, the time that the property is installed and functional.

6. Farming or Fishing Property

If you acquire property to be used in carrying on a business of farming or fishing, the time at which the property has been delivered and is capable of performing the function for which it was acquired even though the seasonal timing may prevent its immediate use.

7. Vehicles which Require Licensing

Where you acquire a motor vehicle, trailer, trolley bus, aircraft, or vessel, and you are required to obtain a permit, certificate, or license to operate that machine, it is available for use at the time which these necessary credentials are obtained.

8. Spare Parts

If you acquire a spare part which is intended to replace an existing part of your property due to a breakdown, the spare part is available for use at the time which the property is available for use.

9. Replacement for Involuntarily Disposed Property

This rule applies where you have involuntarily disposed of your property (i.e., by fire, theft, or expropriation), and you acquired replacement property. Provided that the original property was acquired before 1990 or was available for use at or before the time which the replacement property is acquired, your replacement property is considered available for use at the time it is acquired. The replacement property must meet the tests set out for purposes of the rollover rules at ¶846. While a replacement property must meet the criteria at ¶846, it is not necessary to actually make a replacement property election under those rules for this available-for-use rule to apply. The election is unnecessary where depreciable property with no inherent capital gain is replaced with property of the same class, since the same result generally occurs whether or not an election is made.

(ITA: 13(26), (27); IT-259R4 Exchanges of Property)

[¶804b.20] *The General Rules for Buildings*

A building or part of a building is considered to become available for use and therefore eligible for CCA and the investment tax credit at the earliest of the following five times:

(1) *The time at which all or substantially all of the building is used for the purpose for which you acquired it*; "all or substantially all" generally refers to at least 90%.

(2) *In the case of the construction, renovation or alteration of a building, the time of completion.*

(3) *The time that is immediately after the commencement of the first taxation year of the taxpayer commencing more than 357 days after the end of the taxation year in which you acquired the property.* This is identical to the rolling start rule discussed at ¶804b.15.

(4) *The time that is immediately before you dispose of the building.*

(5) *Where the building is a replacement for a building which you involuntarily disposed of (i.e., theft, fire, or expropriation), the replacement building is available for use at the time which you acquired it, provided that the original property had been acquired before 1990 or was available for use at or before the time you acquired the replacement property.* This rule is identical to the involuntary disposition rule discussed at ¶804b.15.

For purposes of the general rules for buildings, a renovation, alteration, or addition to a building is considered a separate building.

(ITA: 13(26), (28))

[¶804b.25] *The Long-Term Project Election*

This is the most complex of these rules. It is an election which applies to both property in general and to buildings, but not to rental buildings. The buildings excluded as rental buildings are buildings used or to be used by the taxpayer who would make the election principally for the purpose of gaining or producing gross revenue that is rent. "Principally" is usually interpreted to mean more than 50%.

Essentially this election appears to allow a double-up of amounts claimed under the rolling start (two-year deferral) rule commencing with Year 3 of a long-term construction project, but only to the extent property acquired (under the old rules) in Year 3 onward has not become available for use under other rules (or earlier uses of this rule). Probably the rule can only be understood by examples, and the government's illustrations are provided below. In principle, however, the election rule operates as follows:

STEP 1

Is there property acquired in taxation Year 3 that is part of the project for which property was first acquired in Year 1 and has not yet become available for use? If so, the terms necessary for the election are met. It appears that property first acquired in Year 1 must in fact mean property first acquired after 1989, so that 1990 taxation years will usually be Year 1 for projects already under way. Accordingly, it appears that elections cannot be made before 1992. This would be because the rules apply to "property acquired after 1989" and it is only that project property which starts the whole machinery of the rules running. Technically speaking, all references to property in subsection 13(29) must be references to property acquired after 1989.

STEP 2

Elect in Year 3. Where a project commences in Year 1 (say, 1990) and is continuing in Year 3 (1992) and Year 3 commenced more than 357 days after the end of Year 1, the taxpayer can elect in Year 3 to claim that extra amounts have become available for use. This assumes that there remain amounts incurred in both Year 3 and prior years that are not otherwise available for use under any rule. It appears that this election can only be made in Year 3 of a project, and then applies for all subsequent years. Since the election can normally only accelerate access to capital cost allowance (and investment tax credit if available), there appears to be no downside to making the claim in most circumstances. Where the taxpayer is a loss company likely to be subject to takeover, consideration should be given to the interplay of these deferral rules and the loss carryover rules on a change of control (¶2526). Where Year 3 commences 357 days or less after the end of Year 1, the first year that does commence more than 357 days later is the election year.

STEP 3

Determine the additional amount available for use under the election. This calculation consists of two limitations.

The first limitation is the property acquired (under the old rules) in Year 3 that is part of the project minus amounts of Year 3 property only that have otherwise become available for use under any rule.

The second limitation is:

(1) the amount of project property acquired in Year 1 that has not become available under other rules except this election or the rolling start rule; that is, if Year 1 property has become available in Year 3 only because of the rolling start rule for either buildings or other projects, it is nevertheless counted here as property that has not yet become available for use and so may be included in this calculation

minus

(2) prior claims under this election (nil in Year 3 itself).

The technical rule is that the first limitation amount may be considered available for use to the extent it does not exceed the second limitation amount. This appears to be the same as saying that the lesser of the two limitations may be claimed as capital cost allowance in Year 3 in addition to amounts which have become available for use under the rolling start rule. The amounts available under the rolling start rule are amounts calculated under rule (2) of the general rules and rule (3) of the general rule for buildings.

STEP 4

Repeat Step 3 for Year 4 and later years. For Year 4, the Year 3 election continues to be valid. The amount calculated under the election rule is again the lesser of two limitations.

The first limitation is the aggregate of property acquired (under the old rules) as part of the project in Years 3 and 4 together which has not otherwise become available for use under any rule. That is, it is the property of Year 3 and Year 4 minus amounts claimed for Year 3 and 4 property only under other rules for those years. The subtracted amount will therefore not include amounts under the rolling start rule for Years 1 and 2 property but will include amounts claimed in Year 3 under the election.

The second limitation is:

(1) the amount of project property acquired in Years 1 and 2 that has not become available under other rules except this rule and the rolling start rule; that is, if Years 1 and 2 property has become available in Year 4 only because of the rolling start rule for either buildings or other projects, it is nevertheless counted here as property that has not yet become available for use and so may be included in this calculation

minus

(2) prior claims under this election (in Year 4 the Year 3 election claim).

STEP 5

Repeat. In calculating part (1) of the second limitation in Year 5, property acquired in Years 1, 2, and 3, will be counted if it has become available for use under either the rolling start rule or the election rule, but not if it has become available under any other rule.

To repeat, this election would seem only to work in the taxpayer's favour; aside from its deliberate complexity, it is difficult to imagine circumstances in which it is not beneficial. Remember that it is not available for rental buildings.

Examples of Long-Term Project Election

Example A:

A $160 million industrial project is completed and put in use to earn income in its sixth year. It is assumed that none of the property included in the project will be otherwise available for use until the project is completed (other than property which becomes available for use during the construction period under this rule or the two-year rolling start rule). The taxpayer elects in Year 3 of the project to have the long-term project rule apply. The application of subsection 13(29) in these circumstances is shown below.

Year	Expend itures	Additions to UCC: Long-term project	Rolling start	Other	Current year expenditures deferred
1	10	0	n/a		10
2	20	0	n/a		20
3	70	10[1]	10[2]		60
4	50	20[3]	20[4]		30
5	5	35[5]	60[6]		0
6	5	0	0	5[7]	0
Total	160	65	90	5	

[1] Lesser of 70 (Year 3 expenditures not available for use before the end of the year)

and 10 - 0 = 10 (Year 1 expenditures less amounts previously determined to be available for use under this rule)

= 10

[2] Year 1 expenditures available for use under the rolling start rule

[3] Lesser of 120 - 10 = 110 (Year 3 and 4 expenditures not available for use before the end of the year)

and 30 - 10 = 20 (aggregate of Year 1 and 2 expenditures less amount calculated under 1, above)

= 20

[4] Year 2 expenditures available for use under the rolling start rule

[5] Lesser of 125 (aggregate of Year 3, 4 and 5 expenditures) less (10 + 20 + 60) (portion of Year 3, 4, and 5 expenditures already available for use at the end of the year) = 35 (Year 3, 4, and 5 expenditures not available for use before the end of the year)

and 100 (aggregate of Year 1, 2, and 3 expenditures) less 30 (aggregate of amounts calculated under 1 and 3, above) = 70 = 35

[6] Remainder of Year 3 expenditures available for use under the rolling start rule

[7] Year 6 expenditures available for use when the project is put in use (paragraph 13(27)(a) of the Act) during the sixth year.

Property available for use by reason of the two-year rolling start rule is not subject to the half-year convention.

Example B:

Another long-term project has a different expenditure pattern. It is assumed that one-half of the property acquired in Year 2 of the project becomes available for use during Year 3 pursuant to paragraph 13(27)(*d*) (the intermediate product rule). None of the other property included in the project will be otherwise available for use until the project is put in use in the fifth year (other than property which becomes available for use under this rule or the two-year rolling start rule). This taxpayer also elects in Year 3 to have the long-term project rule apply. The application of the rules in subsection 13(29) in these circumstances is shown below.

Year	Expend itures	Additions to UCC: Long-term project	Rolling start	Other	Current year expenditures deferred
1	25	0	n/a	0	25
2	30	0	n/a	0	30
3	20	20[8]	25[9]	15[10]	0
4	40	20[11]	15[12]	0	20
5	10	0	0	30[13]	0
Total	125	40	40	45	

[8] Lesser of 20 (Year 3 expenditures not available for use before the end of the year)

and 25 - 0 = 25 (Year 1 expenditures less amounts previously determined to be available for use under this rule)

= 20 (subject to the half-year convention)

[9] Year 1 expenditures available for use under the rolling start rule, not subject to the half-year convention

[10] Portion of Year 2 expenditures available for use during Year 3 under the intermediate product rule (subject to the half-year convention)

[11] Lesser of 60 - 20 = 40 (Year 3 and 4 expenditures not available for use before the end of the year)

and (55 - 15) - 20 = 20 (aggregate of Year 1 and 2 expenditures less Year 1 or 2 expenditures already available for use without regard to the rolling start rule (see 7) less amount calculated under 1, above)

= 20 (subject to the half-year convention)

[12] Portion of Year 2 expenditures not already available for use (see 7) available for use under the rolling start rule, not subject to the half-year convention

[13] Year 5 expenditures and remainder of Year 4 expenditures available for use when the project is put in use (paragraph 13(27)(a) of the Act) during the fifth year, subject to the half-year convention

(ITA: 13(26), (29))

[¶804b.30] *The Rental Income Rules for Buildings*

Soft Cost Deduction

Certain provisions in the Act provide the potential for additional deductions from rental income with respect to soft costs (i.e., cost that to relate to the period of construction, renovation, or alteration of a building) and CCA that is otherwise disallowed under the general available-for-use rules which pertain to all buildings. These provisions require that soft costs are deducted before otherwise unavailable CCA claims.

Although soft costs incurred in constructing a building must generally be capitalized, subsection 20(29) permits the deduction of these soft costs to the extent of net rental income for the year (after CCA has been deducted, but before the additional CCA claim under subsection 20(28), which is discussed below). If any current year soft costs remain after this deduction, they will be capitalized in accordance with the rules described at ¶771, and will then be subject to the previously-discussed available-for-use rules.

Additional CCA Claim

If all current soft costs have been deducted from net rental income and there remains both rental income and CCA which has been restricted as at the end of the taxation year by the available-for-use rules, subsection 20(28) allows a further deduction from income.

Subsection 20(28) allows you to deduct the amount by which A exceeds B, where:

A = the lesser of:

(1) The amount of CCA that would otherwise be deductible for the year if it was not denied by the available-for-use rules; or

(2) Your net rental income for the year after deducting soft costs under subsection 20(29)

B = the amount of CCA that you can deduct in the current year (not including what is deductible because of this subsection).

This CCA claim is in addition to any CCA on the building which was permitted under the available-for-use rules.

Example 1: Deduction of Soft Costs and Additional CCA

An office tower is under construction. Only a portion of the building (less than 90%) is occupied and producing rental income. The owner of the building has received rental income of $200,000, before any deduction of CCA, and has incurred soft costs of $150,000 in the year. The owner may claim $40,000 of CCA in respect of costs and could have claimed additional CCA of $80,000 in respect of costs incurred had the available-for-use rule not applied. Pursuant to subsections 20(28) and (29), the taxpayer may deduct from his or her rental income the following amounts:

Soft costs

- lesser of
  - (a) soft costs ($150,000), and
  - (b) rental income ($200,000 - $40,000 = $160,000)

= $150,000

Plus CCA

- amount by which lesser of:
  - (a) rental income net of deductible soft costs ($200,000 - $150,000 = $50,000), and
  - (b) total CCA had the available-for-use rules not applied ($120,000) = $50,000

exceeds

- (c) CCA deductible had s. 20(28) not applied ($40,000)

= $10,000

Therefore, the taxpayer is allowed to deduct $150,000 with respect to soft costs and $10,000 with respect to CCA that otherwise would not have been deductible due to the available-for-use rules.

Example 2: Deductible Soft Costs Exceed Net Rental Income

If the soft costs associated with the building were $225,000, the taxpayer could deduct from his rental income the following amounts:

Soft costs

- lesser of
  - (a) soft costs ($225,000), and
  - (b) rental income ($160,000)

= $160,000

Plus CCA

- amount by which lesser of:
  - (a) rental income net of deductible soft costs ($200,000 - $160,000 = $40,000), and
  - (b) total CCA had the available-for-use rules not applied ($120,000) = $40,000

exceeds

- (c) CCA deductible had s. 20(28) not applied ($40,000)

= $0

The undeducted balance of the taxpayer's soft costs ($65,000) would be added to the capital cost of the building pursuant to subsection 18(3.1) of the Act.

To be eligible for these deductions, the building need not be solely used for earning rental income. Rather, if a portion of the building is used to earn rental income, you are eligible for the deductions for soft costs and additional CCA otherwise restricted under the available-for-use rules.

(ITA: 13(29); 18(3.1); 20(28), (29))

[¶804b.35] *The Non-Arm's Length Transfer Rules*

Non-Arm's Length Transfers

If you acquire property from a person who you did not deal with at arm's length (other than because of contingent rights), that property is deemed to be available for use at the time you acquired it, provided that it was available for use before the transfer occurred (except by reason of disposition). Also, with respect to the rolling start and long-term project election rules, you are deemed to have acquired the property at the time the original owner had acquired it. See ¶812 for a description of non-arm's length.

Butterfly Transactions

A butterfly transaction is a complex divisive reorganization, in which typically the assets of one company are divided into separate companies. An individual is unlikely to acquire depreciable property in a butterfly transaction. That said, where there has been a butterfly transaction and the property had met the available-for-use tests of the transferor, it will be considered available for use by the transferee at the time the asset was acquired (again, except by reason of disposition). Similarly, in butterfly transactions involving rolling start and long-term project election rules, the transferee is deemed to have acquired the property at the time that the transferor originally acquired it.

If the half-year rule has already applied with respect to the transferred property in the hands of the transferor, it will not apply again to the transferee; see ¶802.

Leasing at Non-Arm's Length

If you lease depreciable property from any non-arm's length person and the property would have been subject to available-for-use restrictions if you had acquired rather than leased it, any lease payments made prior to the time it would have been available for use, if acquired, will be classified as Class 13 (leasehold improvements) rather than treated as an expense. This will force depreciation of the payments subject to the available-for-use restrictions and the Class 13 rules (¶879).

(ITA: 13(30), (31), (32))

¶805 MEANING OF "CAPITAL EXPENDITURES"

Where you incur a cost to acquire property which will produce an enduring benefit, this cost is a capital expenditure. Property with a useful life of more than one year is considered to produce an enduring benefit. In contrast, expenditures of a current nature produce an immediate benefit, but have little or no long-term usefulness. Further, a "capital expenditure" does not include the cost of acquiring a property which is of capital nature where you will not use this property. An example of this type of expenditure would be the purchase of machinery for the purpose of resale. The cost of the machinery is deductible from the proceeds of resale when resale occurs, but is not a capital expenditure to the original purchaser.

[¶805.05] *Deductible Repair Versus Capital Improvement*

The cost of repairs to existing property may be classified as a current deductible expense or a capital expenditure. Minor repair and routine maintenance expenses would normally be treated as expenditures which can be deducted in the current year. However, major repairs may result in a substantial alteration of the character of the asset, or an extension to its useful life, and they will be treated as capital expenditures.

Whether a repair expenditure is capital in nature or deductible in the current year depends on the following factors (which the CRA has summarized in IT-128R):

(1) **Enduring Benefit** — whether the expenditure results in a long term benefit

(2) **Maintenance or Betterment** — whether the expenditure restores the property's original condition or improves it beyond its initial state

(3) **Integral Part or Separate Asset** — an integral part would be a deductible expense but a separate asset is capital in nature

(4) **Relative Value** — does the repair represent a significant proportion of the asset's value?

(5) **Used Property** — necessary repairs to put newly-acquired used property in working order are capital expenditures

(6) **Anticipation of Sale** — repairs made in anticipation of sale of the property are capital expenditures

(IT-128R Capital Cost Allowance — Depreciable Property; *Rainbow Pipeline Co. v. The Queen*, 99 DTC 1081 (TCC), aff'd 2002 DTC 7124 (FCA); *Atco Electric Ltd. v. The Queen*, 2007 DTC 974 (TCC), aff'd 2008 DTC 6438 (FCA))

[¶805.10] *Impact of Accounting Treatment*

Ambiguity surrounds the importance of book treatment and accounting principles when determining whether an expense is a capital expenditure or currently deductible. The courts must decide on the basis of "ordinary commercial principles", as was decided by the Supreme Court in *Dominion Taxicab Association v. M.N.R.* and numerous subsequent decisions. Implicit in these cases is that the courts, and not the accounting profession, determine ordinary commercial principles. Realistic limitations on the importance of accounting principles were imposed when the Supreme Court affirmed the lower courts' decisions in *Ikea Limited v. The Queen*. The Supreme Court encouraged the idea that the courts will continue to look to accounting treatment for insights into the computation of profit. Accounting treatment, however, is an influencing rather than deciding principle.

See also the discussion of timing of expense claims at ¶730.

(*Dominion Taxicab Association v. M.N.R.*, 54 DTC 1020 (SCC); *Ikea Limited v. The Queen*, 94 DTC 1112 (TCC), aff'd 96 DTC 6526 (FCA), aff'd 98 DTC 6092 (SCC))

¶806 DEPRECIABLE ASSETS VERSUS INVENTORY

The tax treatment of the disposition of capital property differs from that of inventory. This section examines the determination of whether the property is capital property or inventory, and the tax rules which apply to the disposition of that property. In some situations, the property may be converted from capital property to inventory, or vice versa. The CRA expressed its various policies pertaining to this topic in interpretation bulletin IT-102-R2, pertinent sections of which are summarized below.

With respect to selling capital property, the proceeds are generally recognized on the account of capital, so the sale would be computed as a capital gain (or loss) for tax purposes. Conversely, the sale of inventory is recognized on the account of income. Various rules will affect, upon the disposition of property, whether the property sold will be considered capital property or inventory; this classification determines the tax consequences.

Selling and Renting/Leasing the Same Property (Other than Real Property)

If you both (i) sell and (ii) either rent or lease the same kind of property, proceeds from the sale are taxable as income. For example, car dealerships often sell automobiles, as well as lease them to consumers. However, the CRA stated that it will make an exception to this treatment where all of the following criteria are met:

(1) You operate a separate and clearly distinguishable leasing division which includes separate record-keeping;

(2) You set aside specific property for the sole purpose of renting or leasing; and

(3) After being rented or leased, properties are normally sold for proceeds that are less than your original acquisition cost

Notwithstanding the other rules discussed, if all three conditions are met, the exception would allow the sale of the property to be treated as a disposal of capital property.

Solely in the Business of Renting or Leasing Property (other than Real Property)

The CRA acknowledges that businesses that solely rent or lease property will often purchase new property to replace property that has been rented or leased for a significant length of time. If the proceeds from disposing of the old property normally exceed its cost of acquisition, the proceeds are received on the account of income.

For example, if a canoe rental business generally buys the canoes for $500 each, rents them for several years, and often sells them afterwards for proceeds in excess of $500, these proceeds are included in its income for tax purposes.

However, if property is leased:

(1) without any option to purchase;

(2) for a long period of time sufficient to reasonably anticipate that the selling price at the lease's expiration will not normally be greater than the lessor's cost; and

(3) the property is not normally replaced by other property during the lease's duration,

that property will be treated as capital property. As is implied in these various rules, the facts pertaining to how your business operates will determine the income or capital treatment upon the sale of rented or leased property.

Conversion of Capital Property to Inventory

When the treatment of property is converted from capital property to inventory, no disposition is deemed to occur for tax purposes at the time of conversion. However, upon the eventual disposition of the property, a capital gain (or loss) will be recognized in the year of disposition with the proceeds of disposition being equal to the property's FMV on the conversion day. A gain or loss on the account of income is also recognized upon the sale of the property with the initial cost of the inventory being the FMV on the date of conversion.

Conversion of Inventory to Capital Property

If by application of the rules discussed above, inventory is converted to capital property, the capital cost of the property will be the inventory's FMV on the date of conversion. Again, this conversion is not a disposition or acquisition for tax purposes, so for the purpose of the half-year rule, acquisition year is the actual year which the property was acquired and not the conversion date. Moreover, a conversion from inventory to capital property does not occur when property that was purchased for resale is temporarily withdrawn from inventory to be used in the business.

Relevant Case Law

According to the decision in *Wang v. M.N.R.*, 91 DTC 1279 (TCC), where a lessor/vendor disposes of property that was previously converted to inventory, the amount to be credited to the CCA class as proceeds of disposition on the final sale is the net book value of the assets sold rather than the usual lesser of cost or proceeds.

(IT-102R2 Conversion of Property, Other than Real Property, from or to Inventory; *Wang v. M.N.R.*, 91 DTC 1279 (TCC); *C.A.E. Inc. v. The Queen*, 2013 DTC 5084 (FCA))

CAPITAL EXPENDITURES ELIGIBLE FOR CAPITAL COST ALLOWANCE

¶807 CAPITAL EXPENDITURES CLASSIFIED

Capital expenditures are generally classified as one of the following:

(1) expenditures for which CCA may be claimed;

(2) expenditures which are ineligible for CCA claims, but special rules are provided which permit a deduction in computing income; or

(3) expenditures for which no deduction in computing income is allowed.

(ITA: 18; 20; IT-128R Capital Cost Allowance — Depreciable Property)

¶808 ASSETS FOR WHICH CAPITAL COST ALLOWANCE MAY BE CLAIMED

An asset must fall within one of the classes prescribed by the *Income Tax Regulations* in order to be eligible for CCA claims. These classes include descriptions of a lengthy list of assets, comprising a mixture of specific types of items and general categories which cover most, but not all, of the assets which you might acquire. A list of these asset descriptions is provided at ¶898.

Special Treatment

You can claim CCA only with respect to property you have acquired and continue to own, but there are exceptions. Leasehold costs may continue to be depreciated after termination of the lease, unless there are no other leasehold costs left (¶879). In some cases, taxpayers (especially in the mining and oil and gas sectors) pay for township sites, roads, bridges, and the like, either by paying the local government to do the construction or by doing it themselves, but then turning the property over to local government. Special rules for these expenditures are discussed at ¶810d.

Of particular interest is Class 8. This class includes all tangible capital assets not specifically included in another class, with a relatively short list of exclusions (see ¶898 for Class 8).

(IT-128R Capital Cost Allowance — Depreciable Property; IT-285R2 Capital cost allowance — General comments; IT-472 Capital cost allowance — Class 8 property)

¶809 ASSETS FOR WHICH SPECIAL RULES ARE PROVIDED

Expenditures Addressed in Non-CCA Provisions

Certain expenditures on capital assets do not qualify for CCA because the deduction from income is permitted by another provision. Such expenditures include:

- Capital expenditures in Canada on scientific research (see ¶740).
- Expenditures relating to an interest in respect of minerals, petroleum, natural gas, other related hydrocarbons or timber and property relating thereto, or in respect of a right to explore for, drill for, take, or remove such products (see Chapter 22).
- Expenditures on goodwill and most other intangible assets not included in a capital cost class (see ¶766).

Current Deductible Expenditures

The following expenditures, although not eligible for CCA, are fully deductible when incurred (¶765):

- Prescribed equipment or building modifications to assist disabled individuals;
- Landscaping grounds around a building or structure that you use for gaining or producing business income;
- Payments, which relate to your business, to a Canadian government body or an agency thereof (you can alternatively elect to deduct 1/10th of the amount each year for the next 10 years);
- Costs incurred to investigate the suitability of a site for a building or other structure to be used in connection with your business; and
- Costs of making a service connection (i.e., wires, pipes, or conduits) to your place of business for the supply of electricity, gas, telephone service, water, or sewers. This deduction is subject to restrictions (see ¶765.20).

(ITA: 20; ITR: 1102(1); IT-99R5 Legal and Accounting Fees)

¶810 ASSETS FOR WHICH NO CCA CLAIM IS ALLOWED

Certain capital expenditures are not deductible from income to any extent except in determining a gain or loss when the asset is sold. For some assets, there is a specific disallowance of the deduction. For others, no deduction is allowed because they cannot be fit into a capital cost class, and no special provision has been made for the deduction of their cost. Assets which will be deducted in computing income, such as inventory acquisitions, are not capitalized and depreciated.

Capital Expenditures that are Ineligible for CCA:

- Expenditures for land (except where the land has been purchased for resale, in which case its cost may be deducted in full when the land is sold).
- Expenditures by a non-resident on capital property situated outside of Canada.
- Expenditures for real estate, including a building, if the building is torn down within a relatively short time after purchase. See IT-220R2.
- Expenditures for shares of a corporation.
- Expenditures for a yacht, a camp, a lodge or a golf course or facility, unless you are in the ordinary business of providing these properties.
- Expenditures for property not acquired for the purpose of gaining or producing income.
- Expenditures to purchase inventory.
- Expenditures which are already deductible for tax purposes under different provisions of the Act.
- Expenditures for specified art and antiques (see ¶891).

(ITR: 1102; IT-128R Capital Cost Allowance — Depreciable Property; IT-220R2 Capital Cost Allowance — Proceeds of Disposition of Depreciable Property)

¶810a ASSETS FOR WHICH CCA CLAIM IS LIMITED: AUTOMOBILES

For automobiles acquired to produce income at a cost exceeding a threshold that is prescribed annually by the Department of Finance, each automobile is included in a separate Class 10.1. This threshold has remained at $30,000 for years. Motor vehicles with a cost not exceeding $30,000 are rather included in Class 10 and, along with other property included in Class 10, are depreciated as per the usual rules.

Motor vehicles acquired for lease or renting are included in Class 16.

Where you acquire a motor vehicle which is not used 100% for the purpose of earning income, the capital cost is subject to proration. See ¶822.

Determining Capital Cost for Class 10.1

Although not specifically prescribed by legislation, the generally accepted commercial and accounting practice is to include federal and provincial sales taxes in the capital cost of an asset. The cost must be compared to the threshold amount (which also includes sales taxes) to determine whether the automobile belongs in Class 10.1. If the cost is below the threshold, the automobile is added to Class 10. Conversely, if the cost exceeds the threshold, the automobile is added to Class 10.1 and the amount to be capitalized is subject to a limitation that is illustrated in Example 2.

Example 1

You acquire an automobile which costs $29,000 plus PST of $2,320 (8%) and GST of $1,450 (5%). The total cost is therefore $32,770. This total cost is compared to the threshold plus the sales taxes that would hypothetically apply to that amount: $30,000 + $2,400 in PST + $1,500 in GST = threshold of $33,900. Since the cost of the automobile ($32,770) is less than the threshold ($33,900), the automobile is added to Class 10 which may include other existing assets.

Example 2

If you acquire an automobile for $31,000 plus PST of $2,480 (8%) and GST of $1,550 (5%), for a total of $35,030, the automobile exceeds the previously-described threshold, so it will be included in Class 10.1. The maximum amount that may be capitalized in Class 10.1 is $30,000 plus sales tax thereon, so $30,000 plus $2,400 PST (assuming 8%) and $1,500 GST (assuming 5%) = $33,900.

Effect of Input Tax Credits

Once the determination is made as to whether Class 10 or Class 10.1 is appropriate, the amount to be included in the class must be determined, taking into account any applicable GST/HST input tax credits. For Class 10 the cost paid for the vehicle less the actual input tax credit received or receivable can actually be included in Class 10. For Class 10.1, the most that can be included in the class is the threshold amount plus GST/HST/PST on the threshold amount less actual input tax credit received or receivable. The HST applies in the same fashion as the GST in a participating province for Class 10.1 purposes.

Employed Individuals and Partners

For employees or partners in partnerships, even if use of the vehicle is more than 90% for commercial purposes, GST/HST input tax credits should arise only in succeeding years in accordance with the rules at ¶363, so that the entire cost, including tax, is entered in Class 10, or the threshold cost plus tax thereon in Class 10.1, in the year of acquisition.

Self-Employed Individuals

For the self-employed, if the vehicle is used less than 90% for business purposes, the results are essentially the same; GST/HST (up to the threshold limits) is included in cost and input tax credits are deferred and received piecemeal as illustrated at ¶828. However, if the vehicle is used 90% or more for business purposes, it is in effect immediately eligible for GST/

HST input tax credits, and any GST/HST entitlement (whether or not received in the year) must not be included in Class 10 or 10.1 capital cost since it will be otherwise recovered.

Example: Self-Employed

Albert is self-employed and uses his car 90% or more for business purposes. The car was acquired in a non-participating province in 2013 at a cost of $29,000, plus 5% GST of $1,450 and PST of $2,320, for a total cost of $32,770. Assume, because business use is 95%, the full $1,450 is recovered almost immediately as a GST input tax credit. The amount to be included in Class 10 is $32,770 - $1,450 = $31,320.

If the cost of acquiring the car consisted of $31,000 plus $1,550 (5%) GST and $2,480 (8%) PST (so $35,030 in total), the most that can be included in Class 10.1 is $30,000 plus GST/PST thereon, so $30,000 plus $1,500 GST and $2,400 PST, or $33,900. However, if $1,500 GST is to be recovered as an input tax credit (and that is the maximum permitted recovery, since GST/HST restricts input tax credits to the threshold maximum), then the capital cost addition is the $30,000 permitted in Class 10.1 plus only the $2,400 PST for a total of $32,400.

Less Than 90% Business Use

In both cases above, the same results would not apply for a car owned by an employee or a partner, or a self-employed individual with less than 90% business use. For employees, partners, and mixed use proprietors, the full cost would be capitalized and input tax credits would be claimed piecemeal based on CCA, with the credits in one year included in income of the next. See ¶828.

For restrictions on leased vehicles and on interest on acquired vehicles, see ¶738.

(ETA: 201; ITA: 13(7)(g), (7.1); 248(16); ITR: 7307; Sch. II Class 10.1; CRA Document No.: Class 10.1, *January 24, 1992*, CRA Document No. 9133015; Minivan Fitted with Mobile "Office" — Capital Cost and CCA, *April 6, 1994*, CRA Document No. 9401872; GST on Class 10.1 Asset, *March 22, 2002*, CRA Document No. 2002-0126455)

[¶810a.05] *Table of Threshold Amounts*

As the information above makes clear, the restrictions concerning cars costing more than $30,000 are subject to periodic revision as to this threshold amount. The amount is set out in subsection 7307(1) of the *Income Tax Regulations* and is also published in year-end press releases from the Department of Finance. As set out in the following list, the amount has remained the same since 2001.

Automobile acquired on or after	*Threshold amount*
June 17, 1987	$20,000
September 1, 1989	$24,000
January 1, 1991	$24,000 + taxes* payable on $24,000
January 1, 1997	$25,000 + taxes* payable on $25,000
January 1, 1998	$26,000 + taxes* payable on $26,000
January 1, 2000	$27,000 + taxes* payable on $27,000
January 1, 2001	$30,000 + taxes* payable on $30,000

taxes* = GST/HST/QST/PST

Cars costing in excess of the threshold are placed in Class 10.1 at the threshold value.

Under the rules enacted to prevent recapture/terminal loss claims on Class 10.1 cars, some very odd things happen. See discussion of "Special Rules on Disposition" and "Trade-ins" below.

For restrictions on leased vehicles and on interest on acquired vehicles, see ¶738.

(ITA: 13(7)(g); ITR: 7307; Sch. II Class 10.1)

[¶810a.10] *Which Automobiles Subject to Restrictions*

The term "automobile", to which Classes 10 and 10.1 apply, is defined specifically in the Act. This definition excludes certain types of motor vehicles. If a motor vehicle is not considered an automobile, it is not subject to inclusion in Classes 10 and 10.1 and will rather be included in a less-restrictive class. In determining whether property acquired belongs in these classes, you must apply the following tests.

1. Is the property a "motor vehicle?"

As defined in the Act, a motor vehicle is an automotive vehicle designed or adapted to be used on highways and streets. Trolley buses and vehicles that use rails are excluded.

2. Is the motor vehicle an "automobile?"

Once you are confident that the property is a motor vehicle, the property must meet the definition of an automobile to be included in Class 10 or 10.1. An automobile is a motor vehicle that is designed or adapted primarily to carry individuals and their personal belongings which has a seating capacity of not more than the driver plus 8 passengers. Although this definition is simple, it is subject to various exclusions.

Exclusions from the Definition of "Automobile"

The following types of motor vehicles are specifically excluded:

- emergency response vehicles;
- a motor vehicle used acquired primarily for use as a taxi
- a bus used in a business of transporting passengers;
- a hearse used in the course of a funeral business; and
- any motor vehicle acquired to be sold, leased, or rented in the course of carrying on the business of selling, leasing, or renting motor vehicles.

Further, a van, pick-up truck, all-terrain vehicle, cross-over vehicle, or similar vehicle is excluded from the definition of an automobile, provided that one of the following three conditions are met:

(1) the motor vehicle has a seating capacity for no more than the driver and two passengers and in the year of acquisition or lease initiation, is used primarily (i.e., more than 50%) for the transportation of goods or equipment to produce income;

(2) the motor vehicle is used all or substantially all (i.e. at least 90%) of the time for the transportation of goods, equipment, or passengers to produce income in the tax year in which it was acquired or leased; or

(3) the motor vehicle is a pick-up truck used in the tax year in which was acquired or leased primarily for the transportation of goods, equipment, or passengers in

the course of earning income at one or more locations in Canada that are both (i) a special work site and (ii) subject to a requirement of being a certain distance from the nearest city.

(ITA: 13(7)(*g*); 248(1) "automobile", "motor vehicle", "passenger vehicle"; ITR: 1101(1af); Sch. II Class 10.1; IT-521R Motor Vehicle Expenses Claimed by Self-Employed Individuals; IT-522R Vehicle, Travel and Sales Expenses of Employees; CRA Document No.: Definition of Automobile, *July 14, 1995,* CRA Document No. 9507975; Crossover Utility Vehicles, *June 29, 2011,* CRA Document No. 2011-0408171I7)

[¶810a.15] *Special Rules on Disposition of Class 10.1 Automobiles*

No Recapture or Terminal Loss

Automobiles costing more than the applicable threshold amount (mentioned at ¶810a) are placed in a separate Class 10.1, and special rules ensure that on the disposition of any Class 10.1 vehicle, there can be neither recapture nor terminal loss. Upon the disposition, the balance of the class is reduced to nil.

Exception Allowing CCA Claim

Normally, no CCA is allowed in the year of disposition, but a rule allows one-half of the CCA that would have been permitted on each Class 10.1 automobile disposed of in the year. That is, where any Class 10.1 automobile owned at the end of the preceding year is disposed of in the current year, you may make a special claim of one-half the CCA claim for the automobile which could normally be made if it were still on hand.

Employed Individuals

If you are an employee, you are subject to recapture rules, but you cannot deduct a terminal loss from your employment income; the deduction for a terminal loss is only permitted in computing income from business or property, as the section of the Act that pertains to employment deductions does not include a provision for terminal losses.

(ITA: 13(2), (11); 20(16.1); ITR: 1100(2.5); IT-478R2 Capital Cost Allowance — Recapture and Terminal Loss; IT-521R Motor Vehicle Expenses Claimed by Self-Employed Individuals; IT-522R Vehicle, Travel and Sales Expenses of Employees)

[¶810a.20] *Trade-ins*

A trade-in arrangement adds complexity to determining the cost of an automobile for the purpose of the threshold amount (referred to in ¶810a). Generally, the agreed purchase price that is stipulated in the contract is the purchaser's capital cost.

Pitfalls of Trade-Ins

Potential problems arise where a Class 10 automobile is traded in for a Class 10.1 automobile. Since the new automobile is included in a different class, the recapture (or perhaps even a terminal loss) will be triggered with respect to the automobile that is traded, which is often the only asset in the class. Thus, where a CCA recapture occurs as a result of the trade-in, the higher the trade-in value assigned to the automobile, the higher the recapture amount.

Therefore, it is prudent to consider the potential recapture from disposing of a Class 10 automobile when negotiating the purchase contract to acquire a Class 10.1 automobile. That said, attempting to negotiate tax-favorable trade-in value with the vendor or arguing that the trade-in price was inflated with the CRA may prove to be difficult.

Where a trade-in reduces the net sales tax paid on a vehicle, it is the CRA's view that it is the reduced sales tax which is to be included in the capital cost of the acquired vehicle.

See also ¶816.

(Window on Canadian Tax: ¶3210; *Myrdan Investments Inc. v. The Queen,* 2013 DTC 1058 (TCC))

[¶810a.25] *Anti-Avoidance Rules*

Anti-avoidance rules limit the depreciable capital cost of an automobile acquired in a non-arm's length transaction (¶812) to the least of:

(1) its fair market value ("FMV") at the time of transfer;

(2) the UCC of the vehicle to the transferor at the time of transfer; and

(3) the applicable threshold amount (see ¶810a).

As well, where an automobile is jointly owned, the applicable deemed capital cost must be apportioned according to the value of each interest.

(ITA: 13(7)(*h*); 67.4)

¶810d ROADS, TOWNSITE COSTS, AND RELATED INTANGIBLES

With respect to costs incurred for public roads, townsites, or related intangibles such as access rights, you have no legal ownership of the assets and therefore have no property to depreciate for tax purposes. Some taxpayers have been allowed by the courts to expense these costs. Resource development costs may qualify for special deductions (see ¶2210 and ¶2215). In other cases, intangibles are capitalized as eligible capital expenditures (see ¶766).

These types of property acquired after March 6, 1996 may be capitalized and added to Class 8(i), 10(*n*) or (*p*), 15, 17 or 41 (¶898), depending on the use to which they are related.

Example

In order to establish a factory at a particular site, a taxpayer builds a road to the factory at a cost of $10 million. The road is owned by the municipality, which provides the taxpayer with exclusive access to two parts of the road indefinitely. These access rights are valued at $200,000 and $300,000.

The taxpayer is deemed to acquire a Class 17 road for $10 million. The access rights are considered part of the road, but are each given identifiable capital costs based on the overall $10 million payment prorated by the fair market value of each right divided by the fair market value of all the intangibles acquired (which in this case works out to be $200,000 and $300,000).

(ITA: 13(7.5); ITR: 1102(14.2), (14.3); Sch. II Class 8(*i*)(*vi*))

DETERMINATION OF CAPITAL COST

[¶811] GENERAL

General Expenses Included in Capital Cost

The following expenses are added to the property's capital cost:

(1) the purchase price of the property;

(2) actual costs of preparing the property for use in the desired location;

(3) freight and other delivery expenses;

(4) installation;

(5) customs duties on imported items;

(6) purchase taxes;

(7) legal, accounting, and other fees; and

(8) any additional costs incurred in preparing the property for use.

If you manufacture, install, or modify the property for use, the cost of materials, labour, and overhead are also capitalized.

For GST/HST considerations where tax is paid but is generally recovered, see ¶828.

Soft Costs for a Building

Where your building is currently under construction, renovation, or alteration, no current deduction is allowed for financing costs incurred. Such costs, commonly referred to as "soft costs", include, among other items, interest, legal, and accounting fees and property taxes which must be capitalized.

The current deduction, however, is allowed for:

- landscaping costs;
- modifications to the building to improve accessibility for disabled individuals; and
- deduction allowed to the extent of rental income earned during the aforementioned period (see ¶804b.30).

The construction, renovation, or alteration of a building is deemed to be completed at the earlier of the day on which the construction, renovation, or alteration is actually completed and the day on which all or substantially all (at least 90%) of the building is used for the purpose for which it was constructed, renovated, or altered. For further details see ¶771 and ¶1073.

Foreign Currency Paid for Property

Where the purchase price of a capital asset is payable in a foreign currency, the capital cost of the asset will be determined in Canadian dollars by reference to the rate of foreign exchange at the time the asset is acquired.

Any foreign exchange gain or loss made or incurred by payments on the purchase price at a subsequent date are regarded as capital gains or losses, and not as adjustments of the capital cost of the asset. See ¶556.

Immigration

If you immigrate and bring capital assets into Canada on immigration on or after 1993, the capital cost of the assets is deemed to be the fair market value at the time of immigration. This does not apply to assets already being used in a business in Canada and already subject to Canadian CCA rules. See Chapter 21.

Demolishing a Building to Build Another

Costs of demolishing an old building which has been used for a considerable period of time for the purpose of earning income may be treated in either of two ways provided that the demolition occurs in order to erect a new building. The demolition costs may be treated as part of the capital cost of the new building, or alternatively these costs may be claimed as an expense.

If you buy real estate and intend to demolish the building without having used it to earn income, the demolition costs less the amount of any salvaging proceeds will be added to the cost of the land.

Special Rules

Certain rules are provided for the determination of "capital cost" in the following circumstances:

- property is acquired at non-arm's length (see ¶812 and ¶813);
- property is acquired by gift, bequest, or inheritance (see ¶817);
- property is acquired for some combination of producing income and for some other purpose (see ¶819, ¶821, and ¶823);
- property is acquired of which the cost is partly or entirely offset by a government grant, subsidy, or tax credit (see ¶825);
- an amount paid is partly for depreciable property and partly for another type of property (see ¶829); or
- an automobile is acquired which exceeds the threshold amount (see ¶810a).

(ITA: 13; 69; ITAR: 18; 20; IT-102R2 Conversion of Property, Other than Real Property, from or to Inventory; IT-273R2 Government Assistance — General Comments; IT-285R2 Capital cost allowance — General comments; IT-485 Cost of clearing or levelling land)

¶812 NON-ARM'S LENGTH TRANSACTIONS

At various places in this chapter and in other chapters of this book, special rules are mentioned which apply when persons are not dealing with each other at "arm's length". There are some complicated rules provided in the *Income Tax Act* for determining whether or not persons are dealing with each other at "arm's length" in specific situations. Where these rules do not apply, it is a question of fact whether a transaction was at "arm's length", and all the circumstances related to the parties concerned must be considered.

[¶812.05] Related Individuals

Two or more individuals are deemed to be related persons, and therefore not dealing at arm's length, if:

(1) one is the child or other descendant of the other;

(2) they are brothers or sisters;

(3) they are married to each other or are common-law partners (as discussed at ¶1113);

(4) one is married to or in a common-law partnership with a person who is connected to the other as described in (1) or (2), above; or

(5) one has been adopted by the other, or by some person connected to the other as described in (1), above.

Meaning of "Child"

"Child", for purposes of (1), above, is broadly defined to include:

(1) a person of whom the taxpayer is the legal parent;

(2) a person who is dependent on the taxpayer for support up until the person turned 19 and of whom the taxpayer had custody;

(3) a child of the taxpayer's spouse or common-law partner; and

(4) the spouse or common-law partner of the taxpayer's child.

See also ¶1122.

(ITA: 251(6); 252(1))

[¶812.10] *Individuals Related to Corporations*

You do not deal at arm's length with a corporation if you or persons related to you control the corporation. Although a complex topic, "control" generally means control of a majority of voting shares. The technical rules go further in terms of providing for (i) control by a subgroup of a related group, (ii) control by virtue of option rights or share cancellation or redemption rights, and (iii) a shareholder of more than one corporation to be related to itself.

(ITA: 251(2), (4))

[¶812.15] *Corporations Related to Each Other*

In the case of two or more corporations, they are deemed to be related persons, and, therefore, not dealing at arm's length:

(1) if they are controlled by the same person or group of persons;

(2) if each of the corporations is controlled by one person, and the person who controls one of the corporations is related to the person who controls the other corporation;

(3) if one of the corporations is controlled by one person and that person is related to any member of a related group that controls the other corporation;

(4) if one of the corporations is controlled by one person and that person is related to each member of an unrelated group that controls the other corporation;

(5) if any member of a related group that controls one of the corporations is related to each member of an unrelated group that controls the other corporation; or

(6) if each member of an unrelated group that controls one of the corporations is related to at least one member of an unrelated group that controls the other corporation.

Related Group

A related group is a group of persons, each member of which is related to every other member of the group. For example, a group consisting of two common-law partners and their children would be a related group. Conversely, an unrelated group (in 4, 5, and 6, above) refers to a group of persons that is not a related group.

For a group of unrelated persons to constitute "a group of persons which controls a corporation", there must be:

(1) a common link or interest between the persons (which must involve more than their mere status as shareholders); or

(2) there must be evidence that those shareholders act together to exert control over the corporation.

With respect to a closely-held corporation (i.e., where there are only a few unrelated shareholders, none of whom individually controls the corporation), the CRA presumes that the shareholders act together to control the corporation. You would be required to prove that no one controls the corporation and that the decision-making process is deadlocked in order to rebut this presumption.

(ITA: 251(2); Income Tax Folio: S1-F5-C1 Related Persons and Dealing at Arm's Length)

[¶812.20] *Consequences of Non-Arm's Length Transactions*

When transactions occur among non-arm's length parties, agreed prices may be adjusted to provide the tax results that would have occurred if the transaction had occurred at fair market value between unrelated parties. As well, there are numerous specific tax rules that prescribe tax adjustments to non-arm's length transactions. Transactions with non-arm's length non-residents can give rise to special reporting requirements as well as pricing adjustments; see ¶796 et seq.

[¶812.25] *Other Related Party Rules*

In addition to the non-arm's length rules, several other sets of rules may affect transactions or tax results among parties with some degree of inter-relationship. These include:

- affiliated person rules, which in general defer losses on transactions among parties with a specified degree of relationship (¶852);
- control rules, which to some extent have been replaced by affiliated person rules but still may govern losses where there is a change of control of a corporation; control rules also govern the definitions of other relationships, as previously-discussed;
- associated corporation rules, which force the sharing of certain tax benefits among corporations with a specified degree of relationship.

(ITA: 69; 251; Income Tax Folio: S1-F5-C1 Related Persons and Dealing at Arm's Length)

¶813 NON-ARM'S LENGTH TRANSFERS OF DEPRECIABLE PROPERTY

This section discusses the various rules that affect the capital cost of property you acquire in a non-arm's length transaction. In the unlikely scenario that you acquired your depreciable property several decades ago, note that the provisions discussed here only applied to non-arm's length transfers that occurred after May 22, 1985. If these provisions apply, your capital cost will be equal to the result of the calculations discussed below. These rules are intended to prevent you from obtaining the benefit of capital cost in excess of fair market value and will alter your CCA calculation.

These rules do not apply to transfers occurring as a consequence of the death of the transferor. Also, the rules do not apply to transfers of timber resource properties (¶881). Special rules apply to depreciable property acquired by way of gift or bequest, or from a spouse, and are described at ¶532 and ¶510.

Cost to Purchaser Exceeds Transferor's Capital Cost

If you purchase depreciable property at non-arm's length for a price that exceeds the transferor's capital cost, then the following rules apply:

a) Transfer of Depreciable Property from Resident of Canada

This transfer rule applies where you acquire property as a result of a non-arm's length transaction from:

(1) an individual resident in Canada;

(2) a partnership of which any member was a resident of Canada; or

(3) a partnership of which any members was another partnership.

If any of those three situations is true, your capital cost is equal to:

A + B

where

A = the transferor's capital cost

B = ½ the amount, if any, by which

i) the transferor's proceeds of disposition exceeds

ii) the sum of

- the transferor's capital cost and
- twice the amount of any capital gains exemptions claimed by the transferor in respect to the property.

b) Transfer of Depreciable Property from a Non-Resident or a Corporation

Where the rule described in (a) above does not apply and the purchase price of depreciable property exceeds the transferor's capital cost as determined immediately before the transfer, a simplified version of the formula described above applies and your capital cost is deemed to be the sum of:

(1) the capital cost of the property to the transferor immediately before the transaction; plus

(2) ½ the amount, if any, by which the transferor's proceeds of disposition exceed its capital cost.

Conceptually speaking, these two mechanisms ensure that the transferor's non-taxable portion of any capital gains is not added to your capital cost.

Example of Rule 1

In 2012, Mr. A bought a depreciable asset for $1,000 for use in his business. In 2012 and 2013, he claimed a total of $300 in CCA claims, so that the opening value for UCC in 2014 is $700. However, the FMV of the property has actually increased; he could buy an identical second-hand one in 2014 for $1,500.

In January 2014, he decided to replace the asset with an upgraded one, and sold the old one to his son, who is in a similar but separate business, for $1,500. Mr. A will reduce his UCC pool by $1,000. If there were no other assets in the pool, he would have a recapture of $300 (¶843). This represents the original cost to him of the asset. He will also have a capital gain of $500 (taxable capital gain of $250). The son's capital cost for the acquired asset is $1,250 for UCC and CCA purposes.

Mr. A's Position

Actual cost		$1,000	
CCA claimed		$ 300	
UCC		$700	
Proceeds of disposition		$1,500	
Capital gain			
Proceeds	$1,500		
less cost	1,000		
	$ 500		($250 taxable capital gain)

Son's Position

Actual cost	$1,500	(equal to Mr. A's proceeds)	
Deemed cost:			
Vendor's (Mr. A's) original capital cost			$1,000
Plus 1/2 of:			
Mr. A's proceeds	$ 1,500		
Less Mr. A's cost	1,000		
	$ 500		250
			$1,250

However, for the purposes of determining a subsequent capital gain (or loss), the son's adjusted cost base will equal $1,500. Thus, if the son later sells the asset for $1,400, he will reduce his UCC by $1,250 and will have no capital gain, since proceeds of disposition ($1,400) are less than the adjusted cost base ($1,500). The son will have no capital loss, since such a loss cannot be claimed with respect to depreciable property (¶558).

Transferor's Capital Cost Exceeds Purchase Price

If the transferor's capital cost immediately before the transfer exceeds the purchaser's acquisition cost, the purchaser is deemed to have acquired the property at a capital cost equal to that of the vendor's and is also deemed to have claimed the difference as a previous CCA claim. Typically this situation arises where property is transferred to a company at an elected value less than cost.

As a result, the transferee is in the same position as the transferor with respect to a potential CCA recapture upon a subsequent disposition of the property. The purpose of this mechanism is to ensure that the potential for a CCA recapture in the future is not diminished by transferring the asset.

Example

Suppose Mr. A sells an asset with an FMV of $300, a cost of $240, and a UCC of $220 to his company at an elected value (under section 85) of $220. The company would have otherwise had a deemed cost of $220, which is less than Mr. A's cost.

However, due to this rule, the company is considered to have acquired the asset for a cost of $240 and to have previously claimed $20 in CCA, so that it will have $220 available for capital cost allowance, but on its eventual disposition of the asset up to $240 will be subtracted from the UCC pool.

(ITA: 13(7); 20; 69)

¶814 RELATIONSHIP OF CAPITAL COST AND ADJUSTED COST BASE

The capital cost for depreciation purposes is often equal to the adjusted cost base (¶506–¶508) for capital gains purposes. For example, when the capital cost for depreciation purposes is reduced for investment tax credit (¶827), adjusted cost base is similarly reduced. Thus, if you bought a depreciable asset for $100 and claimed $7 investment tax credit, both capital cost and adjusted cost base would be $93.

If you depreciated the asset to zero and sold it for $95, you would have potential recapture (¶843) of $93 and capital gain of $2. However, some adjustments to capital cost for depreciation and recapture purposes do not apply to alter adjusted cost base for capital gains purposes. The previously-discussed rules (in ¶813) for non-arm's length transfers are an example of this.

(ITA: 13; 53)

¶815 FAIR MARKET VALUE

The FMV of an asset is a question of fact. The CRA generally refers to the FMV of an asset as "the highest price expressed in terms of money or money's worth, obtainable in an open and unrestricted market between knowledgeable, informed and prudent parties acting at arm's length, neither party being under any compulsion to transact."

When the FMV of property has not been established by an arm's length sale, it may be necessary to make a determination. Some of the factors considered include the respective locations of the parties, the course of dealing between them, the volume of business done between them, whether the property is sold on a long term contract basis, and special terms in the contract, if any, between them. Market quotations would not necessarily be conclusive.

(ITA: 69; CRA Document No.: Post-Mortem Planning, *2014-XX-XX*, CRA Document No. 2013-0503611R3)

¶816 TRADE-INS

The value assigned to a trade-in is generally immaterial for CCA purposes when both the proceeds of disposition of the disposed property and the cost of the acquired property are accounted for in the same CCA pool. As previously discussed at ¶810a.20, the value assigned to a trade-in may carry the implications with respect to CCA recapture when trading-in a Class 10 automobile to acquire a Class 10.1 automobile.

Limitation of Trade-In Value

Where property is transferred to the vendor as a part of consideration to acquire depreciable property, the capital cost of the depreciable property purchased may not exceed the FMV of the transferred property. This upper-limit to the value assigned to a trade-in prevents the cost of the depreciable property acquired from being inflated by overstating the trade-in value and hence preventing excessive investment tax credit claims and CCA claims based on otherwise inflated value.

(ITA: 13(33); 20(16), (16.1); 127(9) "investment tax credit"; IT-285R2 Capital cost allowance — General comments; *Zeiben v. M.N.R.*, 91 DTC 886 (TCC))

¶817 ASSETS ACQUIRED BY GIFT OR BEQUEST

The capital cost of assets acquired by gift or bequest is determined under special rules as outlined in ¶532.

¶819 CONVERSION OF ASSET TO OR FROM USE IN PRODUCING OR GAINING INCOME

[¶819.05] *Asset Later Converted to Use in Producing or Gaining Income*

Where an asset is converted to use in producing or gaining income from some other use, paragraph 13(7)(*b*) of the Act provides for the determination of the asset's capital cost. As previously discussed, when the asset is used to gain or produce income, it becomes eligible for CCA. The following rules apply where an asset acquired entirely for non-income-earning use is converted to income-earning use.

For assets acquired partially for income and partially for non-income purposes, see ¶821.

Where income-producing to non-income-producing proportion changes, see ¶823.

Deemed Disposition from Complete Change-In-Use

First, paragraph 45(1)(*a*) of the Act deems property to have been disposed of in the event of a change-in-use to or from an income-earning purpose. You are deemed to have disposed of the property at FMV which triggers a capital gain (or loss) and to have reacquired the property at a cost equal to its FMV at that time.

CCA Treatment from Complete Change-In-Use

Accordingly, when an asset's use has changed from income-producing to non-income-producing, the lesser of the proceeds of disposition and the asset's capital cost is subtracted from the CCA pool to which that asset belongs. When the asset's use has changed from completely non-income-producing to income-producing, the following section reviews the determination of the asset's capital cost.

Calculation of Capital Cost

Where your property converts to an income-earning use from an entirely non-income-earning use, your capital cost of that property is the lesser of A and B,

where

A = the property's FMV at that time; and

B = the total of:

(i) the property's cost

plus

(ii) 1/2 of the amount, if, any, by which the FMV at that time

exceeds

- the property's cost

plus

- twice any amounts claimed using the capital gains deduction with respect to capital gains triggered from this change-in-use

The purpose of this formula is to limit the capital cost to the initial cost plus the taxable portion of any capital gains recognized from the deemed disposition triggered by the change-in-use. Moreover, as a result of this formula, capital gains that were exempt from tax under the capital gains exemption are not added to the capital cost.

Electing Out Of Change-In-Use Disposition

Where a conversion is made from an asset wholly devoted to a non-income purpose into an income-earning purpose, you can elect not to have the change-of-use rules apply. You would not be allowed to deduct CCA amounts but the capital gains would be deferred. See ¶555.

(ITA: 13(7)(*a*), (*b*); 45(1)(*a*), (2))

[¶819.20] *Conversion of Whole Asset to Non-Income Use*

Where there is a change of use in an asset wholly acquired for income-earning use to an "other" purpose, the whole property is deemed to be disposed of at FMV at the time of the conversion. Accordingly the proceeds of disposition are equal to the lesser of FMV and original cost credited to the CCA class (if any) to which the asset belonged. Similarly, there is recognition of a capital gain or loss.

(ITA: 13(7)(*a*); 45(1)(*a*))

[¶819.25] *Change-In-Use and Principal Residence*

Principal Residence to Income-Producing

Where a property which has been used as a principal residence is converted to an income-producing asset (i.e., earning rental income) you are deemed to have disposed of the property at FMV and reacquired it immediately thereafter at the same amount. Any gain realized on this deemed disposition may be eliminated or reduced by the principal residence exemption. You can elect to defer under 45(2) to be deemed not to have made the change in use for up to four years provided that CCA is not claimed; see ¶555. If this election is not made, or it is rescinded, the capital cost must be determined subject to the rules above.

Income-Producing to Principal Residence

Where an income-producing asset is converted in whole or in part to use as a personal residence, an election for this situation allows the deferral of the capital gain, provided that no CCA has been claimed on the asset. See ¶555.

(ITA: 45(3); 45(1); 45(2); Income Tax Folio: S1-F3-C2 Principal Residence)

¶821 ASSETS ACQUIRED BOTH FOR THE PURPOSE OF GAINING OR PRODUCING INCOME AND FOR SOME OTHER PURPOSE

An automobile may be acquired both for personal use by the taxpayer and for use in his business. This is an example of an asset acquired for gaining or producing income and for some other purpose.

In such cases, the capital cost upon which CCA may be claimed is that proportion of the asset's cost equal to the ratio of its income producing use to its total use. When calculating this ratio the most appropriate basis should be used. For an automobile, this will probably be kilometres driven for a specific purpose. For other assets, use may be calculated on a time, space, or other reasonable basis.

(IT-521R Motor Vehicle Expenses Claimed by Self-Employed Individuals)

¶822 AUTOMOBILES USED BOTH FOR PERSONAL AND BUSINESS PURPOSES

When an automobile is used by an individual partly to earn business income (or employment income by an employee eligible for travel deductions — see ¶369 and ¶370) and partly for personal purposes, you can deduct the portion of CCA for the kilometres driven to earn business income over the total kilometres driven in the year. When you acquire an automobile, you will calculate the annual CCA amount on the full UCC, but only the business portion of the full annual CCA amount is deductible for tax purposes.

Example: Calculating Business Portion

At the end of last year, your automobile had a UCC of $10,000. Since the automobile is included in Class 10 (30%), you are eligible for a $3,000 CCA claim this year. This year you drove the automobile 50,000 kilometres of which 20,000 was for business purposes, so you may only deduct $1,200 ((20,000 ÷ 50,000) × $3,000) for tax purposes; the proportion of the CCA attributable to non-business travel is not deductible.

Alternative Proportion Method

If you frequently use an automobile while earning business income but this use represents a small amount of the total distance travelled, you may instead calculate the business portion as a reasonable combination of the automobile's kilometres driven and time used for business purposes. IT-521R provides an example of this: where an automobile was used 65% of the year for business purposes and 25% of the total distance was during these hours. Thus, the average of these two figures is 45%, which was the proportion of CCA that could be deducted.

Tax Filing

When completing a tax return, it is often necessary to include the business proportion in various CRA forms. Employees looking to claim employment expenses can do so on T777 and are required to compute the total CCA claim with respect to an automobile and then apply the business proportion in order to compute the amount which may actually be deducted.

For self-employed individuals earning business income, several boxes on form T2125 require you to separate the personal and business proportions of the capital cost upon acquisition and disposition. When depreciable property is acquired, columns 4 and 5 of the T2125 capital asset addition section require inputting the personal and business portions of the property. Therefore, if an automobile is acquired in the year, only the business portion of its capital cost is added to the UCC of the class under Area A (calculation of CCA).

This method of reporting also applies if you are earning rental income and are deducting CCA with respect to an automobile, but you would rather report these amounts in Area A of form T776.

However, where this portion of the capital cost is unlikely to remain constant (i.e., because of changes in use), it may be prudent to include the automobile's total capital cost in Area A and compute the business portion of the CCA claim annually. Otherwise, recalculating an automobile's UCC following a change-in-use may become an onerous task.

Example: Changing Proportion of Business Use

Bart Jones purchased a new car, which had a capital cost of $35,000, plus HST of 13% ($4,550). By virtue of ¶810a, capital cost is limited to $30,000 plus HST on $30,000, so $30,000 + $3,900 = $33,900. The applicable Class 10.1 CCA rate is 30%. Bart used the car 65% for business purposes. Note that because business use is less than 90%, Bart cannot claim immediate HST input tax credit (which would reduce capital cost), but rather must claim input tax credits (if he chooses to do so) piecemeal over succeeding years. The input tax credit calculations are illustrated at ¶363 for employees and ¶828 for the self-employed.

(1) If the 65% rate will be constant, Bart can add 65% × $33,900 (= $22,035) to the class and claim 30% CCA on $22,035 ($6,610) subject to the half-year rule. His claim therefore will be $3,305 (half of $6,610) and his closing UCC will be $22,035 - $3,305 = $18,730. Next year, the 30% rate will be applied to $18,730 and so on. Remember that the 65% rate is, by hypothesis, constant.

(2) Where the 65% rate may be different from year to year, Bart may add the full $33,900 to the appropriate class (Class 10.1). His CCA will be $10,170 ($33,900 × 30%) subject to the half-year rule, or $5,085. This $5,085 is the amount which must be deducted from the class UCC to arrive at the closing UCC, which will thus leave $28,815 for depreciation next year. However, his actual deduction for the $5,085 CCA is limited to 65% thereof, or $3,305 (rounded). Next year his CCA claim will be 30% × $28,815 = $8,645, but his actual deduction will be limited to his business percentage for that year times $8,645.

For comment on the effect of GST/HST on the capital cost of cars acquired for mixed use, see ¶828; for employees, see ¶363.

(IT-521R Motor Vehicle Expenses Claimed by Self-Employed Individuals; IT-522R Vehicle, Travel and Sales Expenses of Employees)

¶823 CHANGES IN THE PROPORTION OF ASSETS USED FOR GAINING OR PRODUCING INCOME

An asset may be acquired at a time when its proportion of use for gaining or producing income is, for example, 50%. Subsequently the use may increase to, say, 75%, or decrease to 25%. Specific rules provide for both capital gain consequences on the non-business portion and capital cost consequences on the business portion. Although the rules themselves are complex, the concepts are simple.

Upon acquisition, the asset is notionally separated in two according to the proportion of its business and non-business use as a portion of total use (¶821). The CRA provides little guidance on this, although in the case of automobiles, distance is a common measure. As the proportions change, there are deemed dispositions or acquisitions of non-business property (where the capital loss generally is limited to nil by personal-use property rules but capital gain is recognized), and corresponding deemed acquisitions or dispositions of depreciable property (assuming the property is by its nature depreciable).

When the mixed-use asset is eventually sold or otherwise disposed of in fact, for capital gain purposes the entire proceeds of disposition are accounted against its cost which was adjusted by the changes in use. Similarly, for CCA purposes, the proportion of proceeds of disposition applicable under the most recent allocation is credited to the CCA class, to the extent of the cumulative cost credited to the class.

[¶823.05] *Increase in Business Use*

Where the percentage of business use increases, for capital gain purposes you are deemed to have disposed of the non-business portion for proceeds of disposition equal to the percentage change multiplied by the property's FMV at that time. These deemed proceeds of disposition and the same proportion of the non-business portion's adjusted cost base ("ACB") will be used to calculate any capital gain.

Example

A Class 10 asset costs $100 and was originally devoted 60% to business use. $60 is assigned to Class 10, and $40 to non-business use. The FMV of the asset subsequently falls to $90 and there is now a change of use so the asset is devoted 75% to business use and 25% to non-business.

Capital Gains/Losses Treatment

For capital gain/loss purposes, there is a disposition with proceeds of disposition equal to:

FMV ($90) × [amount of non-business decrease (40 - 25 = 15) ÷ total use (100)]

Thus the proceeds are 15% of the new $90 FMV, or $13.50. Although unclear in the *Income Tax Act*, the capital gain or loss would logically be determined by comparing the deemed proceeds to the 15% change in use multiplied by the original ACB of $100, or $15. Accordingly, there is a recognized capital loss of $1.50 (15.00-13.50), of which is subject to the stop-loss rules for personal-use property.

The ACB of the business use portion is increased by the $13.50 notional addition, to $73.50, and the ACB of the non-business use portion is reduced by the notional disposition of $15.00 to $25.00. These reconcile to the new aggregate ACB of $98.50 for both portions combined.

CCA Treatment

As a result of the change in proportion of business use, there is a deemed acquisition of the depreciable property of the class. Your capital cost of this newly acquired property is equal to the sum of:

- the percentage change in business use multiplied by the lesser of the property's FMV and its cost; and
- 1/2 the amount, if any, that is a capital gain resulting from this disposition (this amount is reduced where part of the capital gain is reduced under the capital gains exemption)

Therefore, in this example, the taxpayer is deemed to have acquired Class 10 property at a cost of $13.50 (15% × $90) which is added to Class 10. Assuming no depreciation has been claimed yet, the new UCC equals $73.50 ($60 + $13.50).

(ITA: 13(7)(*d*)(i); 45(1)(*c*)(ii))

[¶823.10] *Decrease in Business Use*

Compared to the previously discussed rules, the provisions that apply to a decrease in business use are generally simpler.

Capital Gains/Losses Treatment

The proportion of the property that is changing use is deemed to have been disposed of for proceeds equal to the appropriate proportion of the property's FMV. This same percentage is applied to the most recently determined ACB. The deemed proceeds are compared to the proportion of the property's ACB to determine the amount of your capital gain or loss.

CCA Treatment

You are deemed to have disposed of the appropriate proportion of the property's FMV. As with any disposition of property of a depreciable class, you reduce that CCA class by the lesser of the cost and the proceeds of disposition.

Example

Assume that in the case above, the property is acquired for $100 and used 75% for business. $75 is credited to Class 10 and $25 is "other" property. The use proportions subsequently change to 60% business and 40% other and the FMV of the asset falls to $90.

For capital gain/loss purposes, there is a 15% change in use and notional proceeds of disposition of 15% of $90, or $13.50. This is compared to 15% of original cost, or $15, so this disposition results in a $1.50 capital loss, of which is subject to stop-loss rules. For UCC purposes, $13.50 is treated as proceeds of disposition in the year, leaving a balance of $61.50 less any depreciation already taken.

(ITA: 13(7)(*d*)(ii); 45(1)(*c*)(i))

¶825 GOVERNMENT GRANTS, SUBSIDIES, AND OTHER ASSISTANCE

Government assistance received (or that you are entitled to receive) for acquiring depreciable property reduces the capital cost of that depreciable property. This includes assistance from federal, provincial, and municipal governments or other public authorities, whether received as a grant, subsidy, forgivable loan, deduction from tax, or investment allowance; amounts received under a Government of Canada program relating to home insulation or energy conversion are specifically excluded.

Government assistance is often paid in a year subsequent to that of acquisition of the depreciable property. If you have not received and are not entitled to receive any assistance in the year in which depreciable property was acquired, you can deduct CCA based on the capital cost of the property without the adjustment for assistance. The capital cost of the property is reduced by the amount of assistance that you receive or are entitled to receive in a subsequent year, but not for any year prior to that in which the assistance was made. If the property is disposed of before you receive or are entitled to receive the assistance, the amount of the assistance is deducted from the UCC of the former property.

If, in a subsequent year, you are required to repay a government assistance which previously reduced the capital cost of your property, the capital cost of the property is increased by the amount of the repayments in the year they are made. If the property has been disposed when the assistance is repaid, the repayments are added to the UCC of the former property.

See ¶827 regarding treatment of the investment tax credit. Government or other assistance which does not reduce the capital cost or adjusted cost base of related property is likely to be income and subject to the rules at ¶729.

(ITA: 13(7.1); IT-273R2 Government Assistance — General Comments)

¶826 OTHER PRIVATE AND PUBLIC SUBSIDIES, INDUCEMENTS, REIMBURSEMENTS, AND DAMAGES

[¶826.20] *Election to Treat Income Items as Reduction of Cost*

You are required to include an amount in your income if it was received as an inducement, grant, subsidy, forgivable loan, deduction from tax, allowance, or other form of inducement in the course of earning business or property income if it was received from:

(1) a person or partnership who paid the amount in the course of earning business or property income in order to obtain a benefit; or

(2) a government, municipality, or other public authority.

Electing Out of Income Inclusion

Rather than including the inducement amount in your income, you can elect to reduce the ACB of the capital property or capital cost of the depreciable property by the amount provided that it was paid with respect to the cost of acquiring that property.

The elected amount cannot exceed the least of:

(1) capital cost (or adjusted cost base, as the case may be);

(2) the amount received; and

(3) where the property has been disposed of before the year, nil.

The formalities of the election are set out in Interpretation Bulletin IT-273R2 at paragraph 10, and are discussed at ¶729.

If you reduced your capital cost or ACB by using this election and subsequently repay the grant, subsidy, etc., because of a legal obligation, the reduction to the property's capital cost or ACB is reversed if you still own the property at that time. If you disposed of the property before the amount was repaid, the repayment is credited to its CCA class. Repayments of amounts that were included in income and not subject to an election are deductible from income.

(ITA: 12(1)(*x*); 13(7.4); 20(1)(*hh*); IT-273R2 Government Assistance — General Comments; IT-359R2 Premiums and other amounts with respect to leases)

[¶826.30] *Damages*

The courts have held that amounts received as damages are not only tax-free, but they are not considered a form of assistance that would reduce your ACB or capital cost. That is, they are not included in income and necessitate an election for capital treatment even if they clearly offset capital expenditures in fact. See the discussion at ¶729.

(*Ipsco Inc. v. The Queen*, 2002 DTC 1421 (TCC))

[¶826.50] *Lease Cancellation Payments*

See ¶603.

¶827 INVESTMENT TAX CREDIT

The investment tax credit which is deducted in computing your tax payable for the year reduces the capital cost of your depreciable property in the year following the year the credit is claimed.

Where investment tax credit is claimed in a year later than that in which the property is acquired, the capital cost may be recorded without adjustment in the year of acquisition. Deduction from the pool will be required only in the year following the year in which the credit is subsequently claimed.

(ITA: 13(7.1); 127(5); IT-273R2 Government Assistance — General Comments)

¶828 CAPITAL COST AND GST/HST

The federal GST is a broad-based consumption tax that applies to most goods and services supplied in Canada at a rate of 5%. The HST is an extension of the GST, administered under the same legislation, but levied at a higher rate in harmonized ("participating") provinces.

Under value-added tax ("VAT") sales tax systems such as the QST and GST/HST, a manufacturer pays the tax on machinery, but that tax is deducted from the tax remittable by the manufacturer on the sale of its product. Similarly, a barber pays tax on scissors, but deducts that tax from tax charged to customers and remitted to the government. Certain industry sectors, most notably the financial sector, are not entitled to full input tax credits ("ITCs") because they receive ITCs only to the extent of use of inputs in taxable (not exempt) activities.

How GST/HST Affects Capital Cost

For income tax purposes, the cost of depreciable assets initially includes the GST/HST paid or payable on the asset. However, the income tax rules dealing with GST/HST paid or payable treat the GST/HST recoveries as government assistance. It follows that the capital cost of depreciable property which includes GST/HST must be reduced to the extent that GST/HST is recovered. These complex rules which govern the timing of the receipt of these items are discussed in ¶729.45 under the subheading "GST/HST Credits and Rebates as Government Assistance".

Suffice it to say here that when a GST/HST input credit or rebate is determined to occur in the same taxation year an asset is acquired, it offsets the cost of the asset for CCA purposes in that year. That is, for income tax purposes, the credited or rebated GST/HST vanishes as if it had never been part of the cost of the asset. However, if the GST/HST input tax credit for a particular asset (or service) is considered received in a later taxation year, the original GST/HST paid is included in capital cost in the year of acquisition and the credit reduces it in the subsequent year. The following example is set in a non-participating province, but applies equally in all provinces at the applicable GST/HST rate.

Example: GST/HST Recovery

Mac Chivers has a fiscal period ending February 28. On February 1, he purchased a new computer in a non-participating province for $3,000, and paid an additional $240 provincial sales tax and $150 GST. Mac Chivers is in a fully "commercial" business, on a quarterly reporting system for GST/HST, and has a GST/HST threshold amount of less than $500,000; he accounts for GST/HST on sales and purchases for each three-month period beginning with January 1. Accordingly he will account for GST/HST for the period January 1 to March 31 in a GST/HST return to be filed by April 30.

If Mac claims his GST/HST input tax credit in the GST/HST return for the January-March period, his income tax cost eligible for capital cost allowance for the computer in the year of acquisition will be $3,240. The GST will be treated as if it had never been part of the cost. However, if Mac Chivers defers the input tax credit claim until his April 1 to June 30 GST reporting period, his income tax cost for the year of acquisition will be $3,390 ($3,000 + $240 + $150). The $150 will be considered to be received and to reduce the income tax cost of the computer on June 30. Whether the one-year tax deferral of $22.50 ($^1/_2$ × 30% × $150) is worth the delay in receiving a $150 credit (plus the aggravation of the calculations) is a question Mac must decide for himself.

Miscellaneous Rules

Where the GST/HST paid is rebated to the company which paid it (i.e., recovered other than through the input tax credit mechanism), it is considered received when the amount is actually received or credited. In general, then, the GST/HST will have a net effect of zero on CCA classes, although timing differences may mean that it will be included in a CCA pool in one year and reduce the pool in a later year.

Where GST/HST is paid on capital property which is not depreciable, the same rules will apply in principle to the adjusted cost base.

Where a GST/HST input tax credit is later reduced, possibly due to a denial through a CRA audit assessment, the adjustments will be treated as government assistance repaid, that is, will increase the cost base of related property (or reduce income if there is no related property). Where GST/HST becomes payable or refundable by virtue of a change of use of property, cost or capital cost is adjusted upward or downward accordingly immediately following the change of use.

Historical Notes — Harmonization

The first provinces to harmonize were New Brunswick, Nova Scotia, and Newfoundland and Labrador in 1997, bringing in one HST rate in these provinces. Ontario and British Columbia followed in 2010, but at different rates, and Nova Scotia also increased their rate at that time. The combined tax is referred to as GST/HST. Following the 2011 British Columbia provincial referendum on the subject, the government "deharmonized" its sales tax and returned to a separate PST regime on April 1, 2013. Following its 2012 Budget proposal, Prince Edward Island also harmonized its PST and merged its PST as a participating province for HST purposes effective April 1, 2013. Quebec, which already had a sales tax regime similar to the GST, further harmonized its QST with the GST on January 1, 2013; however, the QST has not been merged into the GST/HST as a participating province and remains a separate tax equivalent to the GST.

[¶828.02] Mixed Use Property

Where you are registered for GST/HST purposes and you acquire capital personal property (i.e., capital property for income tax purposes other than real property) other than an automobile or aircraft (as to which the special rules at ¶828.05 apply) which will be used partly for commercial and partly for non-commercial use, section 199 of the *Excise Tax Act* ("ETA") provides that the use for which the property is primarily acquired will determine whether you are entitled to GST/HST input tax credits. (This overrides the general apportionment rules of subsection 169(1) of the ETA.) Primarily means more than 50%. If the property is acquired primarily for commercial use, you are entitled to a full ITC. If 50% or less, no ITC is available. As the capital personal property crosses the 50% threshold from year to year, there may be deemed acquisitions and dispositions. These rules are discussed in GST/HST Memoranda Series Chapter 8.1. They are also discussed in original memorandum GST 400-3-9, which is scheduled to eventually be replaced by Chapter 11 in the Memoranda Series.

Rules respecting eligibility of ITCs with respect to capital real property are outlined in section 206 of the ETA; basically, ITCs are available (in accordance with general eligibility rules) to the extent the capital real property is used in commercial activities. (Different rules apply to public sector bodies.)

[¶828.05] Special Rules for Automobiles and Aircraft

Special rules apply to automobiles or aircraft owned by yourself (or a partnership) where the automobile (or aircraft) is partly for commercial and partly for non-commercial use. In the first place, if you (or the partnership of which you are a member) are registered under the GST/HST, you may be entitled to an ITC. The ITC will itself be prorated where commercial use is less than 90% of total use, but may be claimed in full (100%) where commercial use is 90% or more.

Where commercial use is less than 90%, you will be deemed to have paid an amount of GST/HST (for purposes of calculating the ITC only, and not for purposes of determining the amount originally included in Class 10 or Class 10.1) determined by applying the specified GST/HST rate to the CCA claim for income tax purposes.

The specified rate is calculated as follows:

Applicable tax rate on acquisition (e.g., 13%) / Applicable tax rate on acquisition plus 100% (e.g., 113%)

Any CCA claim will of course be subject to the half-year rule and, if applicable, the $30,000 depreciation limitation (¶810a), so this is a very parsimonious (or at least slow) recovery. On the other hand, it appears that the ITC so claimed will not be subject to recovery when the percentage of commercial use changes, as would be the case where a car is used 90% or more for commercial purposes when acquired but later ceases to meet the 90% test. As well, it is intended that this rule will allow you (or the partnership) to claim an ITC even where a vehicle or aircraft is not primarily (more than 50%) used in commercial activities, contrary to the usual rule.

On the income tax side, the basic rules including GST/HST in cost and reducing cost for GST/HST input tax credits will apply. In participating provinces where recapture of input tax credits rules apply (i.e, Ontario and Prince Edward Island), it should be noted that in accordance with subsection 248(18), the recaptured amount is considered as repaid government assistance.

Timing of Credit Adjustment

Where commercial use is less than 90%, and where you are GST/HST registered and eligible for ITCs, special rules govern the timing of the credit adjustment. Briefly, where business use is less than 90%, it is necessary to defer the capital cost reduction for the GST/HST credit to the year following the year the credit is claimed. Thus, where GST/HST is paid on such a vehicle (or aircraft), it is included in the initial capital cost. However, an ITC (which would reduce capital cost when applied) is considered received only in the year following the year that credit is applied to reduce GST/HST remittable by the taxpayer. That is, the ITC on a less than 90% commercial use car is typically to be claimed in the return for the reporting period which includes the last day of the taxation year for the year of acquisition of the car, and would apply for income tax purposes to reduce capital cost in the following year.

It appears that the logic of this rule is to put partially commercial businesses under parallel rules to those for employees at ¶363. If for some reason no GST/HST is payable or deemed payable on the car in the GST/HST reporting period for which the ITC is claimed, the credit is considered received in that reporting period. The following example is set in a non-participating province, but applies equally in all provinces at the applicable GST/HST rate.

Example

Joe Brown, a self-employed accountant, bought a new car in a non-participating province in 2015 for $30,000 plus GST of $1,500 and PST of $2,400. In 2015, he reported 40% commercial use for the car. His GST input tax credit for 2014 will be limited to 5/105 × 40% commercial use × 30% CCA rate × 1/2 (half-year rule) × $33,900 allowed in Class 10, or $97, which will reduce his GST remitted for his last reporting period for 2015. However, this $97 will only appear as a reduction of (opening) capital cost at the beginning of 2014. Perhaps a simpler way to look at this is to say that Joe's GST credit will be 5/105 × $2,034 (his capital cost allowance for 2015).

In 2015, Joe's capital cost allowance was $2,034 ($33,900 × 30% × 1/2 × 40%). In 2016, his capital cost should be reduced by $97, and his opening UCC will be $33,900 - $97 (GST credit) - $5,085 (CCA before 40% proration) = $28,718. For 2016 the credit cycle is repeated. Suppose this year Joe's commercial use is 60%. His CCA will be $28,718 × 30% × 60% = $5,169. His input tax credit will be 5/105 × $5,169 = $246, and so on.

(ETA: 202(4), (5); ITA: 12(1)(x), (2.2); 13(7.1), (7.4); 248(15)–(18); IT-273R2, para. 22)

¶828a CAPITAL COST AND QUEBEC SALES TAX ("QST")

Although the QST regime was further harmonized with the GST/HST on January 1, 2013, the two separate taxes remain, with the GST rate at 5% and the QST rate at 9. 975%. Hence, the QST issue discussed herein remains.

Technical amendments that were enacted in June 2013 deem QST input tax refunds to be government assistance and impose timing rules for the recognition of those credits which exactly parallel the federal rules for GST/HST. Those rules are discussed in detail in ¶729 (under the subheading "GST/HST Credits and Rebates as Government Assistance"), and the result for capital cost allowance purposes should be identical to that in ¶828. The amendments are effective for taxation years commencing after February 27, 2004.

QST "input tax refunds" (the term for QST, as opposed to "input tax credits", the term for GST/HST) or QST rebates present a similar issue for income inclusion. Where there are no input tax refunds, sales tax paid on expenditures is simply part of the cost for income tax purposes, as with any other provincial sales tax. This is also true where ITR restrictions apply. Where there are Quebec input tax refunds claimed, these refunds fall into the definition of "government assistance" to be included in income, thus offsetting the deduction claimed for the tax-included expenditure. Hence, the treatment is similar to that for GST/HST credits and rebates.

(ITA: 12(1)(x); 13(7.1), (7.4); 248(15)–(18))

¶829 PAYMENTS PARTLY FOR DEPRECIABLE PROPERTY AND PARTLY FOR SOME OTHER TYPE OF PROPERTY

It is quite common for a purchase transaction to cover the purchase of depreciable property along with some other type of property. This often occurs if you purchase the entire business of another person. Another example is the purchase of land and buildings, where the building is depreciable but the land is not. The purchase price may, or may not, be allocated by the purchaser and seller between depreciable property and other property.

If there is evidence of bargaining between the arm's length buyer and seller, a purchase agreement which specifies values to each asset may be a basis upon which you can allocate the costs. However, the CRA may reassess the values assigned to each asset because they are otherwise unreasonable.

Relevant Case Law

In *Golden v. The Queen*, 86 DTC 6138, the Supreme Court of Canada ruled that an allocation agreement by arm's length parties is entitled to considerable weight as evidence of value, and cannot be arbitrarily upset by the CRA in the absence of sham or subterfuge. See also ¶859.

(ITA: 68; IT-220R2 Capital Cost Allowance — Proceeds of Disposition of Depreciable Property)

[¶829.05] *Condominium Units*

Condominium units typically rest on or above common land. The rights of a unit owner will typically include an undivided interest in the common elements or property pertaining to the unit or lot. The CRA is also of the view that a unit held for rental may include both depreciable and non-depreciable elements. This may occur, for example, where a ground floor apartment includes an outdoor patio or yard which is not part of the common property. The value of this element would be land and not eligible for CCA.

More often, to the extent that the unit owner's rights include an interest in common elements or property that includes both land and building (a parking lot, perhaps), an allocation of these elements must be made to find the element available for CCA and, presumably, subject to recapture or terminal loss on disposition (¶859).

See also ¶876.

(IT-304R2 Condominiums)

¶833 CAPITALIZED LEASES AND LEASE OPTIONS

Lease transactions are generally given the same treatment for tax and accounting purposes, but, in some circumstances, leases may be required to be capitalized for accounting purposes and not capitalized for tax purposes. According to the CRA, the Supreme Court's decision in *Shell Canada Limited v. The Queen*, 99 DTC 5669, and various lower court decisions to follow, whether or not a lease should be capitalized for tax purposes depends on the terms of the legal agreement. Therefore, the arrangement is either a lease or a sale of an asset based on the legality of the arrangement rather than the economic reality.

If the legality of the arrangement is a sale of the asset, you (the acquirer) can add the asset to its appropriate class and deduct CCA. A portion of your payments is considered interest which you deduct separately from income and the remainder is considered a repayment of the principal. If the arrangement constitutes a lease, the lease payments are deductible from income and you cannot deduct any CCA amounts.

Lease Options

Exercising an Option

Subsection 13(5.2) of the Act provides that where you acquire depreciable property which you have previously made deductible rental or lease payments for the use of, your capital cost is deemed to be different from what you paid for the property. The capital cost is deemed to be the lesser of:

(1) the property's FMV; and

(2) the cost of the property plus the total of all amounts previously paid for the use of the property.

The amount by which the deemed capital cost exceeds the actual cost is deemed to have been previously deducted as CCA, so upon the eventual disposition of the property, the excess may be treated as a recapture subject to tax at full rates rather than as a capital gain. Land acquired under a lease-option agreement will be considered to be depreciable property of a separate class (Class 36) for purposes of taxation upon disposition.

Disposing of an Option

If you dispose of (rather than exercise) an option to acquire depreciable property or real property which you previously rented or leased and you deducted the rent or lease payments from income, subsection 13(5.3) of the Act triggers a deemed CCA recapture. The excess of the proceeds of disposition over the option's cost is included in your income as a CCA recapture.

(ITA: 13(5.2), (5.3); ITR: Sch. II Class 36)

[¶833.05] *Leases on Specified Property*

Specific rules treat leases on certain property as sales by the lessor; the lessee may elect to treat the transaction as a purchase; see ¶873a.

¶835 LIMITED RECOURSE FINANCING

The amount of CCA which you can deduct may be limited if the deduction is with respect to your investment in a tax shelter. If you have indeed invested in a tax shelter, the cost of your investment is reduced where the investment is financed on a "limited recourse" basis. These rules are particularly complex. See ¶2521 for further information.

Investors in projects involving projected short term losses, especially where recourse on the financing is limited to investment assets, must be cautious and seek professional tax advice on the deductibility of depreciation and financing costs.

Financing and capital cost allowance deductions in excess of profit, whether or not they reduce the tax cost of investments, may trigger alternative minimum tax (see ¶2420–¶2427). Where the investments are made through limited or passive partnership arrangements, the rules at ¶1818 and ¶1842 may also apply.

(ITA: 143.2; 237.1)

DISPOSAL OF CAPITAL ASSETS

¶839 GENERAL RULE

Upon the disposition of depreciable property that belongs to a CCA class, you must deduct from that class the lesser of the proceeds of disposition or the property's original capital cost. This reduction is made before computing the CCA for the year.

In most cases, proceeds of disposition will be the sale price, less expenses of sale. Expenses might include such things as commissions and legal fees.

Where the proceeds from disposition of depreciable property cannot be determined at the time of disposition, a reasonable estimate of the proceeds of disposition should be used for the purpose of filing your income tax return for the year of disposition (see also ¶845 for involuntary dispositions). If the final amount of proceeds differs from the estimate, the CRA will reassess that year to give effect to an increase or decrease in the amount of the proceeds, if the final determination is made within the period before the return becomes statute-barred (normally three years from assessment date, but longer if you have filed a waiver; see ¶268 and ¶277).

(ITA: 13; 152(4))

[¶839.05] *Timing of Disposition*

Generally speaking, where there is a disposition to another party, its timing is determined under local law; typically, disposition occurs when the parties intend it should occur, or when the incidents of ownership (use and risk) pass.

Relevant Case Law

There is a slight variation in the case of recapture of CCA. As established in *Victory Hotels Ltd. v. M.N.R.*, 62 DTC 1378 (Ex. Ct), cited with approval in *Hewlett Packard (Canada) Ltd. v. The Queen*, 2004 DTC 6498 (F.C.A.): "it would indeed appear that the meaning of 'disposition of property' had been somewhat restricted by the Act when a disposal of property takes place by means of a sale; in such a case there is a disposal of property as soon as a taxpayer is entitled to the sale price of property sold."

¶841 CAPITAL GAIN

When an asset is disposed of, the amount to be deducted from the UCC of the class is limited to the original capital cost of the asset. Any excess over this amount represents a capital gain and does not affect future CCA claims. Capital losses cannot arise from depreciable property — rather when the last item in a particular class is disposed of, a terminal loss may become available as described at ¶851.

(ITA: 13; 40)

¶843 RECAPTURE

As mentioned in ¶839, a disposition of asset of a class will reduce the UCC of the class. If the amount to otherwise reduce the UCC of a class would result in a negative UCC, your total CCA claims for that class have exceeded the net cost of the assets (i.e., original cost less proceeds of disposition).

The UCC can only be reduced to nil, and the remaining excess amount of the reduction is included in your income as a recapture of CCA. The inclusion of the recapture in your income may result in a higher-than-expected tax bill for that year. Where special classes are provided for each asset in a class, recapture may occur on the disposition of each asset, rather than the last asset in the rate pool; see ¶869.

[¶843.05] *Where Recapture Not Applicable*

There are several situations in which the recapture rules will not automatically apply where there is an excess reduction after reducing the UCC to nil. The most common relates to automobiles with an original cost greater than currently prescribed limits, as discussed at ¶810a.

Where the last property of one class is replaced with similar property which is in a different class only by virtue of a change in class rules, any of several special rules may permit a deferral of recapture; see ¶870.

Where you dispose of a capital property that is real property (other than a rental property) or a limited period franchise, concession, or licence used by you primarily for the purpose of gaining or producing income from a business, recapture can be deferred provided that, by the end of the taxation year following the year in which the property was disposed of, you acquired a replacement property.

Recapture can be eliminated where the cost of the replacement property exceeds the recapture otherwise determined. The effect of the purchase of the replacement property is to prevent (or reduce) the inclusion of recapture in income. This benefit is somewhat offset by reduced CCA in the future. See ¶846. A deferral of tax arising on the disposal of eligible capital property before 2017 is also available if a replacement property is acquired. See ¶769.

(ITA: 13; ITR: 1101; 1103; IT-478R2 Capital Cost Allowance — Recapture and Terminal Loss)

¶844 CALCULATION OF PROCEEDS OF DISPOSITION FOR DEPRECIABLE PROPERTY OWNED ON DECEMBER 31, 1971

Prior to 1972, the disposition of depreciable property could produce income by way of "recapture" as described in ¶843, when the proceeds of disposal exceeded the undepreciated capital cost of the particular capital cost class of property involved. However, if the proceeds of disposition exceeded the capital cost of the asset involved, the excess constituted a non-taxable capital gain. With the introduction of a tax on capital gains, as described in Chapter 5, special rules apply with respect to the determination of the amount of capital gain involved in any disposition of depreciable property. Since capital gains accruing to December 31, 1971, remain non-taxable, it may also become necessary to distinguish between the taxable and non-taxable portion of any such gain, in addition to determining the amount of recapture arising from a disposition.

Generally speaking, only capital gains in excess of an asset's value on Valuation Day (December 31, 1971) are taxable. This is achieved by a tax provision that deems your proceeds of disposition to be equal to the result of a specific formula. Moreover, unique rules will apply to you if you receive a non-arm's length transfer of depreciable property which was initially acquired by the transferor before Valuation Day.

(ITA: 20(1))

[¶844.15] *Where Election Made to Have Deemed Disposition on February 22, 1994*

Where you elected to dispose of a property on February 22, 1994 in order to utilize the $100,000 capital gains exemption which expired thereafter, and the property has been owned continuously since the end of 1971 (or has been acquired since in non-arm's length transactions), special rules apply.

(ITA: 20; IT-209R Inter-vivos gifts of capital property to individuals directly or through trusts)

¶845 INVOLUNTARY DISPOSITIONS

Special rules apply to proceeds received for depreciable property that has been disposed of involuntarily. These rules apply to:

- insurance proceeds for depreciable property which was lost or destroyed;
- other compensation for depreciable property which was destroyed;
- compensation for property unlawfully taken (typically, stolen);
- compensation for depreciable property taken under statutory authority (typically by expropriation, but bankruptcy, or corporate squeeze-out under the authority of a *Corporations Act*, are also possibilities); and
- sale proceeds, where a notice of intention to take under statutory authority was received and the property was then sold to the entity which gave the notice.

Timing of Proceeds

The date of disposition of the property and for which the proceeds are considered to be receivable is the earliest of:

(1) the date on which you agree with the settlement;

(2) the date on which your compensation is determined by a court or tribunal; or

(3) two years after the expropriation, loss or destruction if no claim, suit or appeal is launched by that date.

Emigration or Death

If you emigrate from Canada or die between the time when the property is actually lost, taken, or destroyed and the time when it would be considered to have been disposed of under this special rule, it will be deemed to have been disposed of at the time of emigration or death, for proceeds based on the amount of any compensation received to that date plus the fair market value of the taxpayer's uncollected rights to or claim for compensation at that time.

Deferral of Recapture

If the deemed proceeds result in a recapture of CCA, the amount of this recapture may be excluded from income. This "rollover" rule is discussed at ¶846, below. Where capital gain as well as recapture may result from an involuntary disposition, and the property is to be replaced, see also ¶523-¶525.

(ITA: 13(4); 44(2))

¶846 REPLACEMENT PROPERTIES

When any depreciable property is disposed of involuntarily as described at ¶845, or when a "former business property" is disposed of, it can be replaced by a similar property on a tax-deferred basis within specified time limits. Further, this rule allows recapture (¶843) to be deferred to the extent proceeds of disposition giving rise to the recapture are reinvested in replacement property. A former business property includes real property or an interest in real property, such as land and building that is used primarily in a business.

Former business property also includes a limited period franchise, concession, or licence that is wholly attributable to carrying on a business at a fixed place if a joint election (described in subsection 13(4.2)) is made between the transferor and transferee of the property. A limited period franchise, concession, or licence is generally included in Class 14. See ¶880 for details.

[¶846.05] *Definition of Replacement Property*

To qualify for the deferral of CCA recapture from the property's disposal, voluntarily (with respect to former business property) or involuntarily, there must (eventually) be a replacement property. Several conditions must be met with respect to the replacement property:

(1) You acquired the replacement property to replace a former property;

(2) You acquired the replacement property for use, by yourself or by a person related to you, that is the same or similar to the use of the former property;

(3) Where the property disposed of was used to earn business income (rather than merely as an income producing — i.e., rental property) by the taxpayer or a related person, the replacement property must be acquired for use in the same or a similar business;

(4) Where the former property was taxable Canadian property as described in ¶2040, the replacement property must also be taxable Canadian property; and

(5) If the former property was taxable Canadian property that was not treated-protected (i.e., exempt from Part I tax under a treaty), the replacement property must similarly be taxable Canadian property which is not treaty-protected property.

The tests in (3) through (5) are conditional; that is, if the conditions do not apply, the tests need not be met.

Where the cost of the replacement property is less than the amount of the recapture, then only an amount equal to the cost of the replacement property is subject to the special treatment and the balance of the recapture is included in income in the year the original property is considered to have been disposed of.

(IT-259R4 Exchanges of Property)

[¶846.10] *Specified Time Limits for Acquiring Replacement Property*

In the case of an involuntary disposition, the replacement property must be acquired before the later of:

(1) the end of the second taxation year following the year when the original property is disposed of; and

(2) 24 months after the end of the taxation year in which the involuntary disposition occurred (to accommodate short tax years).

In a situation other than an involuntary disposition, (e.g., the case of the voluntary disposition of a building), the replacement property must be acquired before the later of:

(1) the end of the first taxation year following disposition; and

(2) 12 months after the end of the taxation year in which the disposition occurred (to accommodate short tax years).

Additional Timing Rules

The replacement property might be acquired either before or after the original property is considered to have been disposed of, and need not be of the same CCA class as the original property provided it can reasonably be considered as a replacement for the original property. If the replacement property is acquired before the original property is considered to have been disposed of, it must still be owned at the date of that deemed disposition in order for the special rule to apply.

(ITA: 13(4), (4.1), (4.2), (4.3); 44; 248(1) "former business property"; IT-259R4 Exchanges of Property; IT-491 Former business property)

[¶846.15] *Mechanics of Rollover*

Where you dispose of former property and acquire a replacement property within the time limits defined above and elect under subsection 13(4) of the Act, your proceeds of disposition from the former property are reduced by the lesser of:

(1) any recapture which would otherwise have arisen in the class to which the former property belonged; and

(2) the amount reinvested in the replacement property.

Thus, the election will eliminate any recapture to the extent of the cost you incurred to acquire the replacement property. Moreover, the election will reduce the capital cost of the replacement property by a specified amount. The calculations involved in these replacement property rules are complex, but you can find a comprehensive example of how the rules are applied in IT-259R4.

Alternative Election

An alternative election is available under Regulation 1103(2d) to alleviate recapture where property of one class is replaced with property of another class, and that election may yield a preferable result if disposition of old and acquisition of new property occur in the same year and capital gain deferral is not an issue. This alternative rule is discussed at ¶870.

Capital Gains

If you also have a capital gain on a depreciable property disposed of involuntarily, or a former business property, similar rules relating to capital gains also apply. The capital gain deferral rules are discussed at ¶523–¶525. Where there is a disposition of land and a building, the capital gain deferral rules are available not only to defer gain on the land, but to reallocate proceeds of disposition between the land and building if necessary to achieve a deferral of capital gain; see ¶524. An election to apply the rollover to defer recapture necessarily requires an election to apply the rollover to defer capital gain, if any, as described at ¶523–¶525.

Example

An example of the capital gain rollover provision is found at ¶523. In that example, a Class 3 building with a cost of $100,000 was sold for $125,000 and replaced with a Class 1 building costing $150,000. The $25,000 capital gain on the former property was deferred, and the deferral reduced the capital cost of the replacement building for capital cost allowance purposes to $125,000.

To complete this example, assume that the undepreciated capital cost of Class 3 immediately before the disposition of the former property was $50,900. Accordingly, the disposition of the former building would normally result in a subtraction from the class of $100,000 (proceeds of disposition up to original cost), and a negative balance (recapture) of $49,100. However, since an election under section 44 (¶523) was made, the rollover rules for depreciable property (subsection 13(4)) must also operate. These will provide that the $100,000 proceeds of disposition up to capital cost must be reduced by the lesser of (i) recapture ($49,100) and (ii) cost of replacement property ($150,000). Accordingly, the proceeds are reduced to $50,900 ($100,000 - $49,100). This equals the undepreciated capital cost of Class 3, which is therefore reduced to nil. The reduction of $49,100 becomes the notional proceeds of disposition of a property in Class 1. The Class 1 undepreciated capital cost at the end of the year is therefore:

Add: opening Class 1 balance	$Nil
cost of replacement property (deemed by capital gain election) opening Class 1 balance	125,000
Subtract: notional proceeds of disposition	(49,100)
UCC before current CCA	$ 75,900

[¶846.20] *Election Required*

These replacement property rules are not automatic but will only apply if you make an election. In the absence of an election, ordinary recapture and capital gain rules will apply.

Where the disposition and replacement occur in the same year, a correct accounting of the results of the rollover in your return will be considered a proper election.

Replacement Property Acquired Before or After Year of Disposition

If no replacement property has been acquired in the year of disposition, you should file a letter with your T1 return for the year of replacement describing the former and replacement properties and asking for an adjustment for the year of disposition.

If the replacement property is acquired in an earlier year than the disposition, you should file a letter with your T1 return for the year in which the replacement property is acquired describing both properties. The CRA will accept a late-filed election where the replacement acquisition precedes the disposition. This being said, the CRA has outlined a specific administrative process for filing a prior year election, which can be found in paragraph 3 of IT-259R4.

(IT-259R4, paras. 3, 7)

[¶846.22] *Limited Period Franchise, Concession, or Licence*

See ¶880.20.

[¶846.25] *Business Expansion*

One of the basic requirements of the replacement property rules is that it must be reasonable to conclude that the property was acquired to replace a former property. The CRA has taken the position that a business expansion is not necessarily indicative that the replacement property rules do not apply, but rather a substitution must take place for the purposes of the rules. There must be a direct substitution or causal relationship between the properties for one to be considered a replacement of the other.

(IT-259R4, para. 15)

¶847 UNCOLLECTIBLE PROCEEDS OF DISPOSITION

Proceeds of disposition of depreciable property are typically credited to a CCA class rather than being included in income (see ¶839); accordingly, no deduction for uncollectible proceeds could be made under this general rule. However, another rule provides a deduction from income specifically for uncollectible proceeds of disposition. This rule may apply if you disposed of your depreciable property for consideration in some form of debt which subsequently went bad.

Deduction from Income

Uncollectible proceeds of disposition from a depreciable property may be deducted from income only to the extent of capital cost less amounts actually realized. That is, a deduction may be taken for the lesser of

(1) the uncollectible proceeds; and

(2) the amount, if any, by which the capital cost exceeds the total amount of the proceeds of disposition that you actually received.

However, no deduction under this provision is allowed with respect to proceeds of disposition of Class 10.1 automobiles that were in the form of a debt that since went bad.

Special rules apply where the bad debt is non-arm's length; see Interpretation Bulletin IT-159R3.

Deemed Disposition of Bad Debt

In addition to the income deduction, a debt going bad results in a deemed disposition of the debt for nil proceeds (followed by a deemed reacquisition at nil). This in turn creates a capital loss on the debt to the extent amounts have not already been deducted from income under the rule above. Since the loss is on the debt and not on the depreciable property, it will be a capital loss for the year.

Recovery of Bad Debt

Recovery of debt deducted under these provisions will be income to the extent of prior income deductions, and capital gain to the extent of any excess.

(ITA: 12(1)(*i*); 20(4), (5); 40(1); 50(1); ITR: 7307(1); IT-220R2 Capital Cost Allowance — Proceeds of Disposition of Depreciable Property; IT-159R3 Capital debts established to be bad debts)

[¶847.10] *Other Uncollectible Proceeds*

For uncollectible proceeds on non-depreciable capital property, see ¶518 and ¶563. For eligible capital property, see ¶768. For bad debts generally, see ¶733.

¶851 TERMINAL LOSSES

It may be that all assets of a particular class have been disposed of, but a UCC balance remains in the class at the end of the taxation year. This indicates that your actual cost of using assets of this class (i.e., original cost less proceeds of disposal) has exceeded the total of capital cost allowances claimed to date. The balance of the UCC of the class is reduced to nil as a result.

Deduction from Income

In these circumstances, the remaining balance of the UCC for the class is deductible from income in the year when the last asset of the class is disposed of. This final allowance with respect to a class is commonly known as a "terminal loss". A terminal loss reduces income from all sources, and if it creates or increases a net loss for the year, it is included in the non-capital loss carryover pool for the year, as discussed at ¶1087.

Where a Terminal Loss is Not Permitted

If some assets of the class have not been disposed of, a terminal loss may not be claimed and the deduction for the year will be limited to the normal CCA, computed on the remaining UCC of the class. A disposal is considered to occur in situations where depreciable property has been abandoned, scrapped, stolen or destroyed, even though no proceeds may be received.

If you discontinue your business, you may not claim a terminal loss unless you dispose of the property or the property is converted to personal use. That is, if you retain the property but do not use it for any other purpose, you are not deemed to have disposed of it and may not continue to deduct CCA either.

A terminal loss is not permitted with respect to the disposition of Class 10.1 automobiles. See ¶810a.

Finally, a terminal loss is not available for a limited period franchise, concession, or licence that is a former business property pursuant to the election available in subsection 13(4.2).

Planning Opportunity

If a loss carryforward seems unlikely to be used in the carryforward period, it might be advantageous to retain a few assets of the same class in order to avoid a "terminal loss" claim. Thus, the deduction can be deferred to a subsequent year in which it may produce a usable tax reduction. If all assets of a class have been disposed of, the "terminal loss" must be claimed in the year of disposal.

(ITA: 13(1), (21), (21.1); 20(16), (16.1); IT-220R2 Capital Cost Allowance — Proceeds of Disposition of Depreciable Property; IT-478R2 Capital Cost Allowance — Recapture and Terminal Loss; IT-521R Motor Vehicle Expenses Claimed by Self-Employed Individuals; IT-522R Vehicle, Travel and Sales Expenses of Employees; *Benedict v. The Queen*, 2012 DTC 1170 (TCC))

[¶851.05] *Employees*

If you deduct CCA for the use of an automobile because you are required to travel extensively in the course of employment, you are not permitted to deduct a terminal loss with respect to that automobile. However, as an employee, you are subject to CCA recapture if it arises in a class other than Class 10.1.

(ITA: 20(16); IT-522R, para. 26)

[¶851.15] *Dispositions to Affiliated Persons*

The rules described in this section pertain to the denial of a terminal loss incurred where you or someone affiliated with you own the property 30 days after you initially disposed of it. More often than not, the denial of a terminal loss will occur where you transfer your depreciable property to an affiliated person. In order to eventually realize the loss, one of several conditions must be met. A detailed discussion and an example of these rules are found below.

The definition of an affiliated person is discussed in detail at ¶852.

Where the Loss Denial Rule Applies

Your terminal loss will be denied if all three of the following conditions are met:

(1) you disposed of depreciable property;

(2) the "tax cost" of that property exceeds the proceeds of disposition; and

(3) on the 30th day after the disposition, you or a person or partnership that is affiliated with you owns the property or a right to acquire it.

The property's "tax cost" is the lesser of the two amounts:

(1) the property's capital cost; and

(2) (the property's FMV at the time of the transfer ÷ the FMV of all property of the CCA class) multiplied by the UCC of the class at the time of the transfer.

Tax Consequences to the Transferor

If the above conditions are met, you are deemed to have disposed of the property for proceeds equal to its tax cost (defined above), and thus the terminal loss is denied. The UCC is reduced by an amount equal to the tax cost.

These rules override the rollover provisions on transfers of property to corporations (section 85) and to partnerships (section 97).

You (the transferor) are also deemed to own a new property of the same class with a capital cost equal to the loss that was denied (that is, to the excess of tax cost over proceeds of disposition). Since the "property" is added to the UCC, it will be included in the future calculations of CCA claims with respect to that class. The "property" will be deemed disposed of at the times described in the section below.

Tax Consequences to the Transferee

If you are the transferee where these rules apply, the property's capital cost for CCA purposes is its original cost to the transferor. You are also deemed to have previously deducted CCA equal to that capital cost in excess of FMV, which increases the potential for a recapture upon the subsequent disposition.

Subsequent Disposition of the Property

You (the transferor) are deemed to have disposed of the notional property immediately before the earliest of the following times:

(1) the beginning of a 30-day period throughout which neither yourself nor a person affiliated with you own or has a right to acquire the property;

(2) when the transferred property is no longer used for the purpose of earning income and is used for another purpose; or

(3) when you are deemed to have disposed of the property under the emigration rules (¶2153).

These rules leave the loss with the transferor but defer it until there is an ultimate disposition to an unaffiliated party or an event which triggers recognition of all gains and losses to the transferor.

Again, you can find the definition of an "affiliated person" at ¶852.

Capital property and depreciable property not of a prescribed class is governed by similar rules (¶585).

Example

Person A sells a depreciable property to affiliated Person B. The property had a cost of $100, a UCC immediately before disposition of $70, and a FMV of $50.

A is deemed to have received proceeds of disposition of $70 (assuming no other property in the class). The balance of the class is therefore reduced by $70. However, A also is deemed to have acquired a property of the same class at a cost equal to the $20 loss that is denied (UCC of $70 minus proceeds of $50). A can compute CCA claims with respect to this property.

B is deemed to have originally acquired the property at $100 and to have already claimed $50 (original cost of $100 minus fair market value of $50) as CCA, which increases the probability of a recapture of CCA. B can claim CCA on the $50 addition to UCC.

When there is finally a non-affiliated disposition, actual or deemed, A is deemed to no longer own the notional property with its remaining UCC of $20 less any further depreciation claimed. Provided that no other property belongs to the CCA class, the remaining UCC balance will be the amount of A's realized terminal loss.

(ITA: 13(21.2))

[¶851.20] *Land and Building Dispositions*

Dispositions of land and building where there is a loss on the building but a gain on the land are governed by rules at ¶859 which operate before the affiliated person rules but not in place of them. That is, if a terminal loss remains on a building after the operation of the rules at ¶859, the rules above would apply if the respective conditions are met.

(ITA: 13(21.1))

¶852 AFFILIATED PERSONS

The affiliated person rules supplement the concepts of non-arm's length transactions (¶812). They deal with the losses inherent in affiliated party transfers of depreciable property (¶851), capital property (¶579 and ¶585), and eligible capital property (¶770). Where the conditions of each rule are met, persons are affiliated for tax purposes, which will affect the application of the rules listed above. Expect that many of these rules will not apply to you as they cover a significant breadth of scenarios.

[¶852.05] *General Affiliated Person Rules*

A "person" includes not only an individual, a trust, and a corporation, as is commonly the case, but a partnership as well. Persons are automatically affiliated with themselves.

Control means de facto control; that is, you control a corporation not only if you have a majority of shares, but if you have any direct or indirect influence that, if exercised, would result in control in fact of the corporation.

An "affiliated group" means a group of persons, each member of which is affiliated with every other member.

(ITA: 248(1) "person"; 251.1(1); 251.1(3) "affiliated group of persons"; 256(5.1))

[¶852.10] *Individuals*

An individual is affiliated with him or herself and with a spouse or common-law partner. Presumably, this includes any current spouse or common-law partner, and there may be more than one under the rules at ¶1113.

(ITA: 251.1(1))

[¶852.15] *Corporations and Persons*

Remember that a person includes an individual, trust, corporation, or partnership.

A corporation is affiliated with:

(1) a person by whom the corporation is controlled;

(2) each member of an affiliated group that controls the corporation; and

(3) a spouse or common-law partner of a person described in (1) or (2).

(ITA: 248(1) "person"; 251.1(1))

[¶852.20] *Two Corporations*

In addition to being affiliated under the rules above (i.e., where one corporation controls the other), two corporations are affiliated if:

(1) each corporation is controlled by a person, and the person by whom one is controlled is affiliated with the person by whom the other is controlled;

(2) one corporation is controlled by a person, the other is controlled by a group of persons, and each member of that group is affiliated with that person; and

(3) each corporation is controlled by a group of persons, and each member of each group is affiliated with at least one member of the other group.

(ITA: 251.1(1))

[¶852.25] *Partnerships*

Majority-Interest Partner

Essential to the affiliated person rules for partnerships is the concept of a majority-interest partner. A person or partnership is a majority-interest partner if:

(1) its share of the partnership's income for the last fiscal period exceeded 1/2 of the entire partnership's income (for the purpose of this determination, the person's share of partnership income is computed assuming that they also hold the interests in the partnership that belong to persons that they are affiliated with); or

(2) the share (including the share of affiliated persons) of the total payment that would be made from the partnership in the event of a wind-up exceeds 1/2 of the total hypothetical payment to all partners.

Majority-Interest Group of Partners

A majority-interest group of partners of a partnership means a group of persons each of whom has an interest in the partnership, where:

(1) if one person held the interests of all members of the group, that person would be a majority-interest partner; and

(2) if any member of the group were not a member, the test described in (1) would not be met.

The affiliated person rules extend their reach to partnership-related situations, so it is important to understand these definitions.

(ITA: 248(1) "majority-interest partner"; 251.1(1); 251.1(3) "majority-interest group of partners")

[¶852.30] *A Corporation and a Partnership*

A corporation and a partnership are affiliated if:

(1) the corporation is controlled by a particular group of persons;

(2) each member of the group is affiliated with at least one member of a majority-interest group of partners of the partnership; and

(3) each member of that majority-interest group is affiliated with at least one member of the particular group.

(ITA: 251.1(1))

[¶852.35] *A Partnership and a Majority Interest Partner*

A partnership and its majority interest partner are affiliated persons.

(ITA: 251.1(1))

[¶852.40] *Two Partnerships*

Two partnerships are affiliated if:

(1) the same person is a majority-interest partner of both partnerships;

(2) a majority-interest partner of one partnership is affiliated with each member of a majority-interest group of partners of the other partnership; or

(3) each member of a majority-interest group of partners of each partnership is affiliated with at least one member of a majority-interest group of partners of the other partnership.

(ITA: 251.1(1))

[¶852.45] *A Person and a Trust*

A person and a trust will be affiliated if the person:

(1) is a majority-interest beneficiary of the trust; or

(2) is affiliated with a majority-interest beneficiary of the trust.

A trust is a person, so it may be affiliated with a corporation or partnership under the rules above.

Majority-Interest Beneficiary

A person is a "majority interest beneficiary" of a trust at any time if that person's income or capital interest as a beneficiary together with the income or capital interests of all persons with whom the person is affiliated, is greater than 50% of the FMV of all the interests as a beneficiary in the income or capital of the trust.

(ITA: 251.1(1); 251.1(3) "majority-interest beneficiary")

[¶852.50] *Two Trusts*

Two trusts are affiliated if a contributor to one of the trusts is affiliated with a contributor to the other trust and:

(1) a majority-interest beneficiary of one of the trusts is affiliated with a majority-interest beneficiary of the other trust;

(2) a majority-interest beneficiary of one of the trusts is affiliated with each member of a majority-interest group of beneficiaries of the other trust; or

(3) each member of a majority-interest group of beneficiaries of each of the trusts is affiliated with at least one member of a majority-interest group of beneficiaries of the other trust.

Majority-Interest Group of Beneficiaries

A group of persons is a "majority interest group of beneficiaries" of a trust at any time where all the conditions are met:

(1) each member of the group is a beneficiary under the trust;

(2) if one member held all the interests of the members of the group, that person would be a majority interest beneficiary of the trust; and

(3) if any member were not a member of the group, the test described in item (2) would not be met.

For the purposes of this definition, only persons acting in concert are considered to be a group. Again, in determining whether a group is a majority interest group, the specific rules of interpretation below must be taken into consideration.

Contributor

A contributor is defined as a person who has at any time made a loan or transfer of property, either directly or indirectly, in any manner whatever, to or for the benefit of the trust. This excludes a loan made at a reasonable rate of interest or a transfer made for fair market value consideration if the person deals at arm's length with the trust at that time and is not immediately after that time a majority-interest beneficiary of the trust.

(ITA: 251.1(1); 251.1(3) "majority-interest group of beneficiaries", "contributor")

[¶852.55] *Rules of Interpretation for Trusts*

In addition to the general rules set out under the subheading "General Affiliated Person Rules" above, in determining whether a person is affiliated with a trust, the following rules also apply:

(1) if a beneficiary's entitlement to income or capital depends on the exercise of discretion by any person, that person is deemed to have fully exercised that discretion (i.e., the trustee is assumed to have fully paid out capital or income to the beneficiary within his or her discretion);

(2) the interest of a person in a trust as a beneficiary is disregarded in determining whether the person deals at arm's length with the trust if the person would otherwise be considered to deal at arm's length with the trust;

(3) a trust is not a majority interest beneficiary of another trust unless the trust has an interest as a beneficiary in the income or capital, of the other trust; and

(4) in determining whether a contributor to one trust is affiliated with a contributor to another trust, individuals connected by blood, marriage, common-law partnership, or adoption are deemed to be affiliated with one another.

Additional Guidance on Trust Affiliation

Department of Finance technical notes published September 16, 2004, assert that several generalizations can be drawn from the trust and interpretation rules above. These include:

- Two trusts are affiliated where a corporation that is a majority interest beneficiary of one trust is controlled by the other trust.
- Two trusts are not affiliated, at least under the rule affiliating a person with a trust, simply because they share a majority interest beneficiary.
- Two trusts are not affiliated simply because they share the same trustee.
- A person is not affiliated with a trust simply because that person is affiliated with the trustee of the trust.
- The spouse of the sole beneficiary of a trust is affiliated with the trust even if the spouse is not affiliated with the trustee of the trust.
- A trust that shares a majority interest beneficiary with another trust is not a majority interest beneficiary of the other trust unless the person has an interest as a beneficiary in either the income or capital of the other trust.

(ITA: 248(1) "majority interest partner"; 251.1; 251.1(4)(*d*))

¶853 GIFTS AND BEQUESTS

Where you give away or bequeath depreciable property, you are deemed to have disposed of the property for an amount as determined by special rules discussed at ¶530 and ¶532. This may result in "recapture", terminal loss, or a capital gain.

(ITA: 69; 70; 73)

¶855 CONVERSION OF DEPRECIABLE PROPERTY TO PERSONAL-USE PROPERTY

You might have purchased depreciable property for use in your business and subsequently converted the property to personal use. If this happens, you are deemed to have disposed of the property at that time for an amount equal to its FMV.

The same rule applies where you use property for both personal and business purposes, and the proportion of business use decreases. A portion of the property's FMV will be deemed to be proceeds of disposition (see ¶823, ¶843, and ¶844).

Where you cease to use property to earn income and retain the property for a period of time without making any use of it, you are not deemed to have disposed of the property until such a time where you begin to use it for some other purpose.

See further details at ¶819.

(ITA: 13(7))

¶857 SALE OF PROPERTY USED PARTLY FOR BUSINESS PURPOSES AND PARTLY FOR PERSONAL PURPOSES

When property has been used partly for business, and partly for personal purposes, and it is subsequently sold, only a part of the sale price is considered proceeds of disposition to be deducted from the UCC of the class. This portion is calculated by applying the ratio of its business use to total use to the sale price. See details at ¶823.

(ITA: 13(7)(*c*))

¶859 DISPOSITION OF A COMBINATION OF DEPRECIABLE AND NON-DEPRECIABLE PROPERTY

You may dispose of both depreciable and non-depreciable property in a single transaction. The most common example of this is where buildings (depreciable) and land (non-depreciable) are sold together. You and the buyer may, or may not, stipulate an allocation of the sale price between the land and building in the sale agreement.

With respect to replacing business property, you are permitted to allocate proceeds between land and building on the disposition of qualifying business property consisting of land and building where you have purchased a qualifying replacement property (see ¶523, ¶524, and ¶846).

Allocation of Proceeds of Disposition

The part of the consideration which can be reasonably regarded as the consideration for the depreciable property is its proceeds of disposition regardless of the allocation in the sale agreement. A "reasonable" allocation depends on the facts relating to the transaction.

This being said, where you and the buyer are dealing at arm's length, the sale agreement is *prima facie* ("at first glance") evidence of the reasonableness of the allocation. Therefore, an allocation of the proceeds to the depreciable property in the sale agreement and proof of hard bargaining between yourself and the buyer are both evidence which support the reasonableness of your allocation of the proceeds.

If the CRA deems that the allocation of the proceeds to be unreasonable, it may reallocate the proceeds between the assets sold to achieve a more reasonable allocation.

See also the discussion at ¶829.

Selling Land and Building — Buyer Demolishes the Building

If land and a building are sold and the buyer demolishes the building shortly after the sale, the CRA will consider this fact in determining what allocation of proceeds between the land and building is reasonable.

Where the total sale price does not exceed the FMV of comparable land, the CRA will not normally consider any portion of the proceeds to be allocated to the building.

However, where the total selling price exceeds the FMV of comparable land, the CRA will normally consider the amount of the excess to be the seller's proceeds of disposition from the building. Since the purchaser will demolish the building, they will likely be ineligible for a CCA claim or terminal loss.

(ITA: 44; 68; IT-220R2 Capital Cost Allowance — Proceeds of Disposition of Depreciable Property)

[¶859.05] Land and Building Dispositions: Where Building Proceeds are Less than UCC

Where the proceeds of disposition of a building are less than both its capital cost and its cost amount (the building's proportionate share of the UCC) and if the land on which the building is situated is also disposed of in the same year, the terminal loss on the sale of the building is reduced to the extent of any gain on the sale of land.

Although this provision is highly technical, in effect it prevents you from recognizing a terminal loss from the building to the extent that you recognize a capital gain from the disposition of the land. Complexities aside, in effect, the terminal loss on the building is reduced by any capital gain on the land.

This adjustment applies to proceeds of disposition but not to related outlays and expenses of disposition. These may be allocated in a reasonable manner and may create some terminal loss on land and building.

The following example best illustrates not only how this mechanism works, but its ultimate effect for tax purposes.

Example

Ms. Y owns a rental property. As a result of a booming real estate market, this year she decided to dispose of the building and the property on which it is situated for a sum of $900,000. The relevant tax information is as follows:

ACB of Land	$350,000
Building's Capital Cost	$400,000
UCC	$350,000

Proceeds of Disposition — Allocation

Building	$300,000
Land	$600,000
Total	$900,000

In absence of the rule currently being discussed, Ms. Y would recognize a terminal loss of $50,000 (350,000 UCC - 300,000 proceeds) from the building and a taxable capital gain of $125,000 ($^1/_2$ × (600,000 proceeds – 350,000 ACB)) from the land. Thus, when negotiating the sale agreement, Ms. Y has incentive to allocate the proceeds to the land as only one-half of the gain is taxable and the terminal loss is fully deductible from income.

This being said, the rule discussed above will reduce the terminal loss on the building to the extent of the capital gain. This rule is found under subsection 13(21.1) of the Act.

Deemed Proceeds of Disposition — Building

Under paragraph 13(21.1)(*a*), the proceeds of disposition of the building are deemed to be the lesser of:

A)	The combined FMV of the building and land			900,000
	minus the lesser of:			
	i) the land's ACB	350,000		
	ii) the land's FMV	600,000	(350,000)	
				550,000
AND				
B)	The greater of			
	i) the building's FMV		300,000	
	ii) the lesser of			
	a) the building's capital cost; and	400,000		
	b) the building's UCC	350,000	350,000	
				350,000

Therefore, the proceeds of disposition of the building are deemed to be $350,000 (they otherwise would have been $300,000). Moreover, this provision deems the proceeds of disposition of the land to be the total proceeds minus the deemed proceeds for the building (i.e., total proceeds of $900,000 minus the $350,000 proceeds for the building = $550,000 deemed proceeds for the land).

Ms. Y will recognize no terminal loss or recapture since the deemed proceeds of disposition and the building's UCC are both $350,000. Her taxable capital gain on the sale of land is $100,000 (1/2 × (550,000 − 350,000)). The following chart illustrates the net tax effect that this rule has on the disposition of a building and its land:

	In Absence of 13(21.1)(a)	*Deemed Proceeds under 13(21.1)(a)*
Terminal Loss	$50,000	$0
Taxable Capital Gain	$125,000	$100,000
Total Income Inclusion	$75,000	$100,000

Therefore, this rule has effectively denied the terminal loss from the building by reducing the taxable capital gain for the land.

(ITA: 13(21.1); Window on Canadian Tax: ¶9202; IT-220R2 Capital Cost Allowance — Proceeds of Disposition of Depreciable Property)

¶860 PARTIAL DISPOSITION

If you dispose of a part of a depreciable property, the capital cost of that part of the property must be calculated so that you may determine the remaining UCC of the class as well as the amount of any CCA recapture and capital gains resulting from the disposition.

The cost of the part of the property is determined by apportioning the cost of the entire property on a reasonable basis. The following example illustrates how the allocation is done.

Note that this administrative policy was communicated by the CRA in IT-418. The position in this archived bulletin, which relies on repealed legislation, is assumed to still apply since it has yet to be formally revoked by the CRA.

Example

Mr. Q has a depreciable property which is the only property in its class.

Capital cost	$100,000
less:	
Total depreciation to date	(75,000)
UCC of the class	$ 25,000

This year Mr. Q sells exactly 1/2 of the property for $55,000 without incurring any selling costs. Clearly the capital cost with respect to the part of the property that was sold is 50% of its total capital cost. Assuming the ACB of the property is equal to its capital cost and no subsequent adjustments were made, the ACB of the disposed part of the property is $50,000 ($100,000 × 1/2).

Determining the Capital Gain

Proceeds of disposition		$ 55,000
less:		
ACB	$50,000	
Selling expenses	Nil	50,000
Capital gains		$ 5,000

Determining the Recaptured CCA

Capital cost of all property in class			$100,000
Recaptured CCA in previous taxation years			Nil
			$100,000
less:			
Total CCA claims to date		$75,000	
The lesser of:			
Proceeds of disposition	$55,000		
Capital cost of part of the disposed property	$50,000	50,000	125,000
Recaptured CCA			$25,000
Remaining UCC Balance			Nil

Since the UCC of the class has been reduced to zero, any proceeds resulting from a future disposition of the other half of the property will trigger a CCA recapture of up to $50,000 ($75,000 in CCA claims minus the $25,000 already subject to recapture).

Where Capital Cost for Disposed Part is Uncertain

If you dispose of a part of depreciable property and its capital cost cannot be accurately determined, a reasonable estimate of the amount can be used. You may wish to estimate the capital cost on a *pro rata* basis. This estimate of capital cost is made by apportioning the property's total capital cost on a FMV basis.

For example, you disposed of a part of your depreciable property for $20,000. The entire property's total capital cost is $50,000. The FMV of the remaining portion of the property is $80,000. Accordingly, the capital cost of the part disposed of was $10,000 and is calculated as follows:

$$[\$20,000 / (\$20,000 + \$80,000)] \times \$50,000 = \$10,000$$

(ITA: 13; 43; IT-418 Capital Cost Allowance — Partial Dispositions of Property)

¶861 PARTNERSHIPS

For a discussion of the rules applicable to depreciable property owned by a partnership, see Chapter 18.

CAPITAL COST CLASSES AND RATES

¶866 CLASSES

When computing CCA, all depreciable assets owned must be included into their respective CCA classes. The CCA is then calculated by applying the rate for the classes involved to the UCC of each class. Since the CCA claim reduces UCC for subsequent calculations, the system is in general a declining balance depreciation system.

Although these calculations are relatively simple, there are some special rules which are discussed below.

(ITR: Sch. II)

¶868 SPECIAL RULES

There are three general types of exceptions to the general rule that depreciation is taken on a class basis by applying a declining balance method.

The first set of exceptions is intended to accelerate (or in a few cases decelerate) the application of recapture and terminal loss rules. These rules have to do with requiring or permitting separate classes for each property within a general class, and with permitting transfers between classes. These special rules are discussed at ¶869 to ¶873 below, and include the following situations:

- when similar properties are acquired for different income-producing purposes (¶869.05);
- where you adopt one general classification for a group of your assets (¶870);
- where property has originally been assigned to an incorrect class and is transferred to the correct class (¶871);
- where you dispose of property of one class and acquire similar property of another class (¶871);
- where you own rental buildings costing over $50,000 (¶872);
- where you own leasing property and other property of the same class (¶873); and
- where you own other assets for which a separate class is required for each asset (¶869.10).

The second category of exceptions limits CCA on property to income from that property, or in the case of specified leasing property, to a formula amount. This category includes:

- rental buildings (¶630);
- leasing property (¶873); and
- specified leasing property (¶873a).

The third set of exceptions is in most cases beneficial, and creates exceptions to statutory, accounting, or case law rules which would otherwise be more restrictive. In many cases, these special rules are intended to provide tax incentives, and this may be done merely through the creation of special classes with high depreciation rates. In some cases, the benefit may be created or enhanced through an exception to the declining balance rules, thus permitting an asset to be written off completely in a specified period. Assets subject to these special rules include:

- manufacturing and processing machinery and equipment (¶878);
- leasehold interests (¶879);
- patents, franchises, concessions and licences (¶880);
- timber limits (¶881);
- woods assets (¶882);
- industrial mineral mines (¶883);
- ships or other vessels (¶884);
- water and air pollution control (¶886);
- computers and office equipment (¶886t);
- computer software (¶887);
- telephone equipment (¶887a);
- contractor's movable and earth-moving equipment (¶888);
- energy-efficient equipment (¶889);
- railway cars (¶890);
- art and antiques (¶891); and
- accelerated allowance for qualifying mines (¶892).

¶869 SEPARATE CLASSES FOR EACH BUSINESS; SEPARATE CLASS FOR EACH PROPERTY

[¶869.05] *Separate Businesses*

You can operate more than one business, or can operate a business and also own some income-producing property. In such cases, depreciable assets acquired must be allocated to the appropriate business or other use, and included in separate classes, even though they would otherwise have been included in only one class. For example, you might acquire two brick buildings, one for use in your manufacturing business and one to be rented to other persons. Both buildings are Class 1 assets, but separate classes must be established.

In such a case, the assets would be reported on separate CRA forms (e.g., Class 1 building used for business purposes on T2125 and Class 1 building used to earn rental income on T776). Therefore, when calculating whether you have realized a terminal loss (¶851) or recapture of CCA (¶843), the calculations must also occur separately.

(ITR: 1101(1); IT-206R Separate businesses)

[¶869.10] *Other Situations Where Separate Classes are Permitted or Required*

In addition to separate businesses, there are a number of types of property for which a separate class is required for each asset in the class. Some of these include (but are not limited to):

- automobiles which exceed the $30,000 threshold amount (¶810a);
- rental buildings (¶872);
- non-residential buildings (¶875.03);
- fishing vessels;
- electronic office equipment (¶886t.15);
- outdoor signs; and
- specified leasing property (¶873a).

(ITR: 1101)

¶870 INCLUDING ASSETS OF DIFFERENT CLASSES IN ONE CLASSIFICATION; DEFERRING RECAPTURE IN CLOSED CLASSES

There are several potential scenarios which you may include otherwise differently classified depreciable properties under one class, or shift proceeds of disposition from one class to another:

(1) Where a change in regulations requires a type of property to be in one class before the date of change and different class after that date. Where a recapture of CCA would occur from disposing of the property in the former class and you acquired another property of the new class that would have been included in the former class before the change, you may elect to transfer the disposed property (before having been considered to dispose of it) to the new class in the year of disposition.

This election to transfer is not available where a particular class of property is required to be included in separate classes.

(2) You may elect to include in Class 1 all assets which would otherwise be included in Classes 2 to 12 that were acquired for use in the same business.

(3) You may elect to transfer to Class 8 in a taxation year all property in Class 19 or Class 21 at the commencement of the year.

(4) You may elect to transfer Class 20 assets owned at the commencement of the year to Class 1, 3, or 6.

In general, these rules permit a deferral of recapture (¶843) by permitting proceeds in excess of the UCC of one class to be credited to another class.

How to Make the Election

The above elections must be made by the due date for filing your tax return for the taxation year for which the change is sought. The rules specify that you can only make the elections by attaching a letter to your tax return stating your intention to make the election to reclassify certain assets or proceeds.

Benefits of the Election

Utilizing these provisions may yield the following advantages:

(1) Simplification of CCA calculations.

(2) The avoidance, or postponement, of recapture (see ¶843).

Example

Josephine Apricot operates a business, in the course of which she uses a Class 1 building (which she owns) with a substantial amount of remaining UCC, and Class 8 and 10 equipment which is substantially depreciated. She plans on selling the equipment, which would normally result in recapture, since the proceeds will exceed the UCC of each class.

Josephine elects to include the Class 8 and 10 equipment in Class 1. Therefore, by electing to include all assets in Class 1 in the year of sale (or in a prior year), no recapture occurs immediately since Class 1 continues to carry a positive UCC balance after the disposition.

See ¶871 below for a discussion of how transferring property between classes is treated for tax purposes.

(ITR: 1103)

¶871 TRANSFERS BETWEEN CLASSES

As a result of transferring a depreciable property (or group of properties) from one class to another, you must be mindful of accounting for the tax effects of the transfer. Notably, the transfer will affect the UCC of each class and the amount of CCA previously allowed with respect to that class. A depreciable asset may be transferred from one class to another in any of the following situations:

(1) you have placed depreciable property in the wrong class, the CRA has reassessed you within the required time limitation, and has placed the property in the correct class;

(2) you make an election under the rules discussed previously at ¶870;

(3) where property properly included in one class is transferred because of a change of its use in the income earning process; or

(4) where an amendment to the Act or Regulations requires that a transfer should occur.

Accounting for the Transfer

The transfer rules require a few adjustments. First, the capital cost of the property is transferred to the new class as it is assumed that the property originally belonged to the new class and had never been included in its old class. Second, any previously-deducted CCA with respect to that property is deemed to have been allowed for property of the new class and not of the old class. This essentially results in an adjustment to the UCC of each class.

The basic steps, which are thoroughly explained in the subsequent example, are involved in accounting for the transfer from one class to the other:

(1) Determine the property's capital cost (often simple) and CCA deducted with respect to the transferred property up to that time.

(2) Use these amounts to adjust the UCC of the old class.

(3) Use these amounts to adjust the UCC of the new class.

Determining Previously-Deducted CCA

The determination of the accumulated CCA associated with a particular asset which has been grouped together in a class of several assets is problematic. The rules specify that the accumulated CCA of a particular asset is the greater of:

(1) the total amount of CCA deducted if the property had been of a separate class depreciated at the "effective rate" used to depreciate the old class; and

(2) the property's capital cost minus UCC of the entire class immediately before the calculation.

The effective rate (referred to in (a)) is the amount of CCA taken divided by the available UCC for a given year. For example, if in a taxation year you claimed (with respect to a class with a 20% maximum rate), only $125 CCA on a UCC balance of $1,000, the effective rate for the year for the class was 12.5%. That 12.5% would be used as the depreciation rate on the notional separate class for that year. The calculation in (b) prevents recapture in the old class by limiting the UCC addition where the excess of original cost of the transferred asset over UCC is greater than in (a).

Example: Transfer Between Classes: Class 3 to Class 1

A Class 3 building with a capital cost of $100,000 has been sold for proceeds of $100,000. The building has been used in a business and not primarily to produce rental income (otherwise the separate class rules at ¶872 would prevent this election).

The opening UCC of Class 3 for the year is $50,900. The UCC of this particular building, had it been the only asset in the class and fully depreciated at all times, would be $63,000 (i.e., CCA of $37,000 would have been claimed had the building been in a separate class). In the same year, a Class 1 building has been acquired for $150,000. In the absence of a class transfer, $49,100 of recapture would arise on Class 3 and $3,000 of CCA would be available on Class 1.

If the taxpayer makes the election from (2) of ¶870, the taxpayer can elect to transfer the whole Class 3 asset disposed of to Class 1 immediately before disposition.

(1) Computing the Adjustment Amounts

We begin by computing the greater of the notional CCA taken on the Class 3 building alone (i.e., (a) as described previously) and the capital cost of the building minus the UCC of Class 3 before the transfer (i.e. (b) as described previously). Thus, we compute the greater of:

(a)	Capital cost	$100,000
	Minus: UCC of Class 3 immediately before transfer	$ 50,900
	Equals (cannot be less than nil)	$ 49,100
(b)	Notional CCA that would have been deducted in all prior years for A and B had each been the only asset in the class	$ 37,000

(2) Removing Building from Class 3

We reverse the balances in Class 3 so that the original cost of the building ($100,000) is deducted from prior additions to the UCC and notional depreciation computed above is deducted from depreciation taken in the UCC calculation. That is, adjust the opening UCC of the former class (Class 3) as follows:

UCC immediately before disposition		$ 50,900
Less: Capital cost to be transferred out	$100,000	
Plus: greater of (a) and (b) from Step One	49,100	
Net Adjustment	$ 50,900	50,900
Adjusted Class 3 UCC immediately after disposition		Nil

(3) Adding Building to Class 1

We revise the balances in Class 1 by adding the capital cost of the building to UCC and subtracting the notional CCA from the first step (which is now considered CCA already taken with respect to Class 1). That will adjust the opening balance of the new class as follows:

Add: Cost of old building	$100,000
Less: Notional CCA previously claimed	$ 49,100
Class 1 addition	$ 50,900

The result is that Class 1 UCC for the year before depreciation is $50,900 + $150,000 = $200,900, and $49,100 recapture will have been avoided.

Note that an alternative calculation is available for sheltering recapture in some situations under the replacement property rules, provided the that conditions for using those rules are met (¶846).

(ITA: 13(5), (6); 52; IT-190R2 Capital Cost Allowance — Transferred and Misclassified Property)

¶872 SEPARATE CLASSES FOR RENTAL BUILDINGS

If you acquire a rental property at a cost of $50,000 or more, it must be included in a separate CCA class. A rental property is a building that is used principally (more than 50%) for the purpose of gaining or producing gross revenue that is rent. Floor space allocation is often used to measure the percentage use with respect to rental buildings. Further, the $50,000 test refers to the cost of the building alone, and does not include land or furnishings.

By the application of this rule, an immediate recapture or terminal loss will occur when you sell a rental property of a separate class.

Example

Jack Jones acquired, for rental purposes, two apartment buildings in Year 1, each building costing $102,000. In Year 2, he deducted $2,000 in CCA for each building (without exceeding the deduction limit discussed at ¶630). In Year 3, he deducted another $4,000 in CCA for each building. In Year 4, Jack sold one of the buildings for $100,000. Jack's recapture is calculated as follows:

	Apartment 1	*Apartment 2*
Capital cost — Year 1	$102,000	$102,000
CCA — Year 2	(2,000)	(2,000)
CCA — Year 3	(4,000)	(4,000)
UCC — end of Year 3	$ 96,000	$ 96,000
Less: Lesser of 1) Year 4 proceeds of disposal or 2) Capital cost	(100,000)	—
Recapture — Year 4	$ 4,000	—
CCA — Year 4	—	(3,840)
UCC — end of Year 4	—	$ 92,160

In Year 4 Mr. Jones will have income (recapture) of $4,000 and deduction (CCA) of $3,840, for a net income position of $160 in Year 4. This is of course a less favorable result than if both buildings had been included in a single class. In this case, there would have been no immediate recapture and a UCC balance of $92,000 available for CCA, so there would be a net deduction position of approximately $3,680 in Year 4.

The rollover rules discussed at ¶846 and ¶870 cannot be used to circumvent the recapture since these rules do not apply to rental property. The one exception is in cases of involuntary dispositions (¶846). You should also be mindful of the restriction at ¶630, which limits the annual CCA claim to net real estate rental income.

(ITR: 1101(1ac); IT-274R Rental properties — Capital cost of $50,000 or more; *Mother's Pizza Parlour Ltd. v. The Queen*, 88 DTC 6397 (FCA))

¶873 LEASING PROPERTIES

The aggregate CCA claim in respect of a prescribed class of "leasing property" is limited to the net income for the year from renting, leasing, or earning royalties from leasing properties. This rule is designed to prevent you from deducting CCA to increase or create a loss from leasing properties which could be used to shelter other unrelated income.

What is Leasing Property?

"Leasing property" is defined as depreciable property which is used principally to obtain gross revenue from rent, royalties, or leasing. It does not include property leased in your ordinary course of business to a lessee who uses the property in furtherance of your business.

Leasing property also excludes buildings and leasehold interests in Class 1, 3, 6, or 13, which are covered by their own set of restrictions discussed at ¶630. Similarly, leasing property does not include computer tax shelter property discussed in ¶886t.08 and ¶887.05.

A CCA claim may be restricted under these rules where you use as well as rent out an office building. In this situation the entire building may be classified as a leasing property, thereby restricting the CCA claim on the entire building and not only the portion which is rented.

Example

A taxpayer leases industrial equipment which would otherwise be eligible for a $150,000 CCA claim this year. However, the total income from the leasing property was a mere $90,000. Assuming that the taxpayer earned no other income from any other leasing properties in that year, his or her CCA claim will be limited to $90,000.

(ITR: 1100(14)–(20); 1102; IT-443 Leasing property — Capital cost allowance restrictions; *Canada Trust Company v. M.N.R.*, 85 DTC 322 (TCC))

¶873a SPECIFIED LEASING PROPERTY: ELECTION TO CAPITALIZE CERTAIN LEASES

Generally speaking, leases may not be capitalized for tax purposes, as discussed in ¶833. Certain leases, however, are treated as a fully financed sale by the lessor for the purposes of calculating the lessor's CCA. The lessee is not affected by these provisions, except that a statutory provision allows the lessee to elect to capitalize the lease at his or her option.

[¶873a.05] *Capital Cost Allowance Restrictions on Lessors*

If you are the lessor of "specified leasing property", your CCA claim with respect to that property is subject to a limitation. Specified leasing property is depreciable property (other than exempt property) that is:

(1) used by yourself or a person with whom you do not deal at arm's length principally for the purpose of gaining or producing gross revenue that is rent or leasing revenue;

(2) the subject of an arm's length lease with a term of more than one year; and

(3) tangible property with, at the time the lease was made, an aggregate FMV in excess of $25,000.

Intangible property is specifically excluded from this restrictive rule. For example, computer software that is systems software (see ¶887) or Class 12 software applications are intangible property.

Exempt Property

"Exempt property" is specifically excluded from the specified leasing property rules. Its definition encompasses a wide breadth of properties and can be found under Regulation 1100(1.13). That said, some of the following assets fall under the definition of exempt property:

(1) Class 8 office furniture or equipment and Class 10(*f*), 45, 50, or 52 electronic equipment other than any individual item with a capital cost in excess of $1 million;

(2) furniture, appliances, television or radio receivers, telephones, furnaces, hot-water heaters and other similar properties designed for residential use;

(3) automobiles of all kinds, including vans, pick-up trucks, ambulances, funeral vehicles, taxis, and vehicles for rental use;

(4) trucks or tractors for highway use;

(5) trailers designed to be hauled under normal operating conditions by a truck or tractor;

(6) a building or part of a building included in Class 1, 3, 6, 20, 31, 32 (including components such as electric wiring, plumbing, sprinkler systems, air-conditioning and heating equipment, lighting fixtures, elevators and escalators) with the exception of buildings leased to certain tax-exempt entities;

(7) vessel mooring space; and

(8) a railway car included in Class 35 (see ¶890).

Notwithstanding the above, certain property that would otherwise be "exempt property" is excluded from the definition. The specified leasing property rules are extended to property with an aggregate FMV in excess of $1 million that is leased to a person who:

(1) is exempt from tax by reason of section 149 of the Act;

(2) uses the property in the course of carrying on a business where the income is exempt from Part I tax;

(3) is a Canadian government; or

(4) is a non-resident of Canada.

Limitation of CCA Claim

Where you have leased specified leasing property, your CCA claim with respect to that property in any year is limited to the lesser of:

(1) the amount of the repayment of principal as determined under the "notional sale rule" minus the aggregate of all CCA claims made with respect to the property in prior years; and

(2) the maximum amount of CCA you could have otherwise deducted for this year and all prior years minus the total of all prior years' actual CCA claims with respect to the property.

This rule does not affect the income character of the lease payments that you receive. Rather, it merely limits the CCA which you can deduct with respect to the specified leasing property.

Notional Sale Rule

Complex calculations aside, this rule assumes that you have loaned the property to the lessee and are charging interest on the loan. A prescribed rate of interest is applied to the loan's FMV to determine the interest portion of all "loan payments" for the year. Second, this notional interest is subtracted from the total of all payments made with respect to the lease for the year. The net amount is considered repayments of principal, and for the purpose of the CCA claim limits above, this amount is (A).

Example

Year One

Ms. Jackson, a lessor, leases a specified leasing property to a customer. The CCA rate for the property is 20% and the FMV of the property is $100,000. The annual lease payments are $13,140. Under the rules, the $13,140 payment is considered a blended payment of interest and principal.

The interest is determined by the formula: FMV × prescribed interest rate. Assuming the prescribed interest rate is 10%, and ignoring the compounding, the interest portion is $100,000 × 10% = $10,000. What remains of the $13,140 payment, $3,140, is deemed amortization. This is compared to CCA available under normal rules ($100,000 × 20% × half-year rule = $10,000), and the lesser ($3,140) is the maximum CCA for the year.

Year Two

In the following year, the interest formula is applied to an unamortized balance of $96,860, yielding notional interest of $9,686. Subtracting this from the $13,140 payment leaves a notional amortization of $3,454. However, return of principal is considered to be cumulative with actual claims deducted, so the actual calculation is last year's return of principal ($3,140) plus this year's ($3,454) minus last year's actual claim ($3,140). Accordingly, the limitation under this part of the formula will be $3,454. The "ordinary" cumulative CCA will be ($90,000 × 20% = $18,000), plus $10,000 from last year, less $3,140 actually claimed from last year, or

$24,860. The current year maximum CCA claim is the lesser of these, $3,454.

Prescribed Rate of Interest

The prescribed interest rate is determined at the time the lease is entered into or, if an agreement to lease is made before the commencement of the lease, at the time of the agreement. If the lease contains a floating interest rate, the lessor may elect to use the rate prescribed at the beginning of the period for which each calculation is made. This election can be made on a lease-by-lease basis, but must be made in the first year of the lease. The prescribed interest rate will not be the usual quarterly rate, but will be adjusted monthly to be one point above the government rate on certain bonds for the preceding month.

The prescribed rate for each month is published by the CRA on its website at http://www.cra-arc.gc.ca/tx/ndvdls/fq/ls-eng.html.

Separate Class Requirement

Each specified leasing property must be placed in a separate class (see ¶869), so that recapture and terminal loss will be calculated separately for each property. However, you might be able to utilize the transfer rule to avoid recapture under ¶870(1) provided that the necessary conditions are met.

Additional Miscellaneous Rules

There are a number of miscellaneous anti-avoidance and administrative provisions which affect the specified leasing property rule:

- Reg. 1100(1.17) applies where the property has been replaced;
- Reg. 1100(1.19) applies where an addition or alteration has been made to the property;
- Reg. 1100(1.13)(*b*) is an anti-avoidance rule that prevents you from intentionally entering into short-term leases (i.e., less than one year) to avoid the application of the rule; and
- Reg. 1100(1.13)(*a.2*) an anti-avoidance rule if it is reasonable to conclude that two or more leases were entered into in order to avoid the application of the $1 million threshold.

(ITR: 1100(1.1)-(1.3); 1100(1.13); 1100(1.17); 1100(1.19); 1101(5n), (5o); 4302)

[¶873a.10] *Lessee May Elect to Capitalize Specified Leasing Property Leases*

If you are the lessee of specified leasing property (as defined at ¶873a.05), you may elect to capitalize the lease so that you may claim CCA and interest deductions rather than deducting the lease payments for tax purposes. As discussed at ¶833, a lease may be capitalized without making this election provided that the legal form of the transaction is indicative of a sale rather than a lease.

Although the term "specified leasing property" is not used with respect to these rules, the property which may be subject to this election is nearly identical. Regardless, we will outline all of the criteria necessary to make the election.

Conditions to Make The Election

You (the lessee) may capitalize the lease if:

- the leased property is tangible property that is not prescribed property;
- the leased property would be depreciable property had you acquired it;
- the lessor is a resident of Canada (and not tax-exempt) or a non-resident carrying on a business through a permanent establishment in Canada;
- the lease term exceeds one year; and
- you and the lessor jointly elect and file form T2145 for your respective tax years in which the lease began.

Prescribed property may not be capitalized under this election and includes the following:

- exempt property (as defined at ¶873a.05);
- property with an FMV that is $25,000 or less; and
- intangible property.

Tax Consequences of The Election

Provided that the previous conditions are met and you (the lessee) made the joint election, the resulting tax consequences are as follows:

- you are considered to have acquired the property at its FMV and borrowed the same amount from the lessor;
- you can depreciate the property under the usual rules (including the half-year rule); and
- your lease payments are considered a blend of interest and principal portions, with the interest factor deemed to accrue on principal outstanding, compounded semi-annually not in advance, at a prescribed interest rate.

The interest rate is determined using the prescribed rate at the time the lease is made, or, if an agreement to the lease is made before the commencement of the lease, the prescribed rate at the time of that agreement will be used. If the lease is a floating rate lease, interest is the rate prescribed at the beginning of the period for which the calculation is made. Interest will not be the usual prescribed rate, but will be prescribed quarterly.

Thus, you can deduct the CCA and interest amounts rather than the entire lease payment. Unlike in the case of a lessor of specified leasing property, you do not have to put the property into a separate class. Rather, the property's FMV is added to the respective CCA class as if you had acquired it.

Example 1: Acquisition and Depreciation

Mr. West is the lessee of an asset with a FMV of $100,000 for a period of five years. The prescribed rate in effect at the time of the commencement of the lease is 10%. The annual payment is $13,140 and the applicable CCA rate is 25%, on a diminishing balance basis, subject to the half-year rule. He jointly elects with the lessor to treat the lease as a loan and purchase for the lease term and deducts interest expense and CCA as follows:

Year	*Lease payment*	*Principal*	*Interest*	*CCA*	*UCC*
	$	$	$	$	$
					100,000
1	13,140	3,140	10,000	12,500	87,500
2	13,140	3,450	9,690	21,880	65,620
3	13,140	3,800	9,340	16,410	49,210
4	13,140	4,180	8,960	12,300	36,910
5	13,140	4,600	8,540	9,230	27,680
Total	65,700	19,170	46,530	72,320	

Post-Election Disposition of Property — Tax Consequences

At the time of the expiration, cancellation, assignment, or sublease of a lease in respect of which an election has been made under this subsection, you are deemed to have disposed of the leased property for proceeds equal to the outstanding principal of the loan plus or minus any amounts actually received or paid by the lessee in respect of the cancellation, assignment, or sublease. The normal rules relating to recapture and terminal losses will apply at that time.

> *Example 2: Subsequent Disposal*
>
> At the end of the five-year lease described in the above example, Mr. West is deemed to have disposed of the property for the remaining principal amount of the demand loan — $80,830 ($100,000 original loan less $19,170 principal repayments). If the property is the only property in that class, he will include $53,150 ($80,830 deemed proceeds of disposition less $27,680 UCC) of CCA recapture in his income.
>
> His total deductions allowed with respect to the property over the term of the lease are $65,700 (interest of $46,530 and CCA of $72,320 less recapture of $53,150). You might notice that this total deduction is equal to the amount of total lease payments that he would have deducted had he not made the election ($13,140 × 5 years = $65,700). The difference between each outcome is the timing of the deductions.

Assigning or Subleasing

Where a lessee has elected under these rules (made a section 16.1 election) and assigns or subleases the subject property, the assignment or sublease is treated as a disposition to the sublessor. An arm's length sublessee in turn has the option to make a joint election with the sublessor to capitalize the sublease at the fair market value of the sublease at the time the sublease is made. However, if the sublessee is not dealing at arm's length with the sublessor, the sublessee always steps into the sublessor's position with respect to the loan interest rate, and deemed proceeds to the sublessor become deemed cost to the sublessee.

Miscellaneous Rules

On a non-arm's length rollover under section 87 or 88, the survivor steps into the old position with respect to the interest rate, original cost, and CCA rate.

Where similar property is substituted and the lease terms do not change, the new property is considered the same as the old. Where the lessor provides an addition or alteration at an increased rent, the new property takes on the characteristics of the original and the FMV of additions or alterations is added to the depreciable capital cost of the lessee.

(ITA: 16.1; ITR: 8200; 8201)

[¶873a.15] *Capitalization for ITC/M&P Credits*

Section 16.1 specifically permits the capitalization of leases (as described above) for purposes of computing income. Thus, property subject to the election is therefore eligible for CCA. As well, the CRA appears to allow a valid section 16.1 election to treat capitalized property as eligible for investment tax credit (if previously unused) and to be included in the cost of capital for manufacturing and processing tax credit.

(CRA Document No.: Leasing Properties and R&D, *June 8, 1993*, CRA Document No. 9315705; Cost of Capital, *December 24, 1999*, CRA Document No. 9932567)

¶874 MOTION PICTURE FILMS AND VIDEOTAPES OR DISKS

[¶874.05] *Videotapes and Laser-Disks for Rental*

A videocassette, a video-laser disk or a digital video that is acquired for the purposes of short-term rental is a Class 12 item. They are exempt from the half-year rule, so they can be written off 100% in the year of acquisition. Short-term rentals are rentals that are not expected to be made to any one person for more than 7 days in any 30-day period.

(ITR: Sch. II Class 12(*r*))

[¶874.10] *TV Commercial Message*

A "television commercial message" is a commercial message as defined in the *Television Broadcasting Regulations* under the *Broadcasting Act*. The *Television Broadcasting Regulations* define a "commercial message" to mean any commercial announcement. A television commercial message is a Class 12 asset subject to the half-year rule, which means that it can be fully deducted within two years.

(ITR: 1100(2); Sch. II Class 12(*m*))

[¶874.15] *Other Uncertified Film or Videotape*

Any motion picture film or videotape which is neither eligible for Class 12 or a Canadian film or video production (see ¶874.20) is depreciable at 30% under Class 10 and subject to the half-year rule.

(ITR: Sch. II Class 10(*s*))

[¶874.20] *Canadian Film or Video Productions*

These are films eligible for the refundable tax credits claimed by prescribed corporations carrying on a Canadian film or video production business in Canada (see ¶9747 in the Wolters Kluwer companion volume Preparing Your Corporate Tax Returns). Qualifying films acquired (i.e., produced) by qualifying companies are Class 10 assets, subject to the half-year rule. Capital cost eligible for capital cost allowance is explicitly reduced by tax credit incentives in the year for which the incentives are claimed. The CCA for these films cannot be syndicated to passive investors. A separate class is prescribed for Canadian film or video production property owned by a corporation and an additional allowance can be claimed on such property in the separate class.

(ITA: 125.4(5); ITR: 1100(1)(*m*); 1101(5k.1); Sch. II Class 10(*x*))

¶875 BUILDINGS AND STRUCTURES

Generally, buildings and structures are included in Class 1 (4%). However, older buildings that exhibit specific characteristics may instead be included in Class 3, 6, or 20. See ¶875.05, ¶875.10, ¶875.15 for guidance on these classifications and ¶898 for complete details on what buildings are included in these classes.

What Constitutes a Building or Structure?

There can be a number of occasions when doubt may arise as to whether an asset is a "building or other structure" and should therefore be included in any of the building CCA classes. A building is a structure with walls and a roof which provides shelter and protection. "Structure" includes anything of substantial size which is built up from component parts and intended to remain on a permanent foundation.

Structures on Leased Land

If you build a structure on leased land, it is included in its usual class and not in Class 13 as a leasehold interest. For example, a bridge built on leased land would be included in Class 2.

Portable Shelter

Portable shelters such as housing, office, and other service units are regarded as buildings if they are installed and intended to remain at a particular location. Such things as tents, canvas marquees, and air supported fabric domes that are not part of a rigid structure are not considered to be buildings.

Component Parts

Also included in a building's class are its component parts, some of which are specifically outlined in the class description. These generally include:

- electric wiring;
- plumbing;
- sprinkler systems;
- air-conditioning equipment;
- heating equipment;
- lighting fixtures; and
- elevators and escalators.

In addition to this list, other component parts that ordinarily go with the building when it is bought or sold, or which relate to the functioning of the building, are included in the building class. These may include:

- storm doors and windows;
- automatic stokers;
- sump pumps;
- combination heating and cooling units; and
- fire alarm systems.

Lease of Component Parts

If you own what would normally be regarded as component parts of a building and lease these to customers under leases which provide that the components remain your property, you generally add this property to Class 8. However, where the purported lease of component parts is considered to be a sale, these component parts are considered to be owned by the lessee. Thus, the lessee would include these components in the same class as the building or other structure.

(IT-79R3 Capital Cost Allowance — Buildings or Other Structures)

[¶875.03] *Additional Allowances for Manufacturing and Processing Buildings and Other Non-Residential Buildings*

You can claim an additional CCA deduction with respect to non-residential buildings acquired after March 18, 2007. If the building is used for manufacturing and processing ("M&P") you may elect to claim an additional 6% of CCA, and you may claim an additional 2% in the case of all other non-residential buildings.

Other Non-Residential Building Eligibility Criteria (all must apply):

In order for a building to constitute a "non-residential building", it must meet all of the following criteria:

- it must be located in Canada;
- it must be included in a separate CCA Class 1;
- at least 90% of the building is used for non-residential purposes (measured by floor space)
- you must have acquired it after March 18, 2007; and
- its use must be for non-residential purposes.

M&P Building Eligibility Criteria

A building is eligible for the additional 6% CCA claim if, at the end of the tax year, at least 90% of the building (measured by floor space) is used for manufacturing or processing in Canada (see its definition at ¶878.01) of goods for sale or lease.

Election

By attaching a letter to your tax return for the year in which you acquire the building, you can elect to include the building in a separate Class 1. Since Class 1 normally allows for a 4% CCA claim, you may claim CCA at a total rate of 10% (4% + 6%) with respect to non-residential M&P buildings and 6% (4% + 2%) with respect to all other non-residential buildings.

Additions, Alterations, and Buildings Under Construction

If a qualifying building was under construction on March 19, 2007, its capital cost incurred prior to that date will also be eligible for the additional CCA claim. Further, additions or alterations made to a building after this date will be eligible for the additional deduction too. These costs are deemed to be a separate building and will be placed into a separate Class 1 provided that the use of the building meets the aforementioned 90% test.

(ITR: 1100(1)(a.1), (a.2); 1101(5b.1); 1102(23)–(25); 1104(2) "eligible non-residential buildings"; 1104(9))

[¶875.05] *Additions or Alterations to Class 6 Buildings*

Buildings acquired before 1979 of frame, log, stucco on frame, or galvanized or corrugated iron were generally included in Class 6. See ¶898 for further information on the criteria for this class. Where you acquired a Class 6 building before 1979, you can reasonably assume that the building would have been fully depreciated as of years ago.

Provided that you acquired and still own a Class 6 building, any alterations or additions made to that building after 1978 (subject to a $100,000 lifetime limit) are included in Class 6 and can be depreciated at a 10% rate. Addition or alterations costs in excess of that limit will be included in Class 3 (subject to its limit discussed at ¶875.10) and the excess over that limit is included in Class 1.

[¶875.10] *Additions or Alterations to Class 3 Buildings*

Buildings acquired after 1978 and before 1988 were included in CCA Class 3. Buildings acquired after 1987 are included in Class 1. There are also various grandfathering provisions which may apply. In determining whether a building belongs in Class 3, ¶898 provides a comprehensive summary of the necessary criteria.

Additions and alterations to a Class 3 building made after 1987 may continue to be capitalized and depreciated at a rate of 5%. However, the amount which can be capitalized may not exceed the lesser of:

(1) $500,000 for each building; and

(2) 25% of the capital cost of the building.

If your additions and alterations exceed this limit, they will be included in Class 1 and depreciated at a rate of 4%. The $500,000 limitation is cumulative over the entire life of the asset after 1987.

[¶875.15] *Class 20 Buildings*

Certain buildings acquired between December 5, 1963 and April 1, 1967 in designated areas were given accelerated (20%) depreciation in Class 20. To the extent such buildings are still on hand in Class 20, additions track through Class 20 and then through Class 3 under rules similar to those for Class 6 above.

[¶875.20] *Recapture on Reclassified Buildings*

Recapture on dispositions of buildings in Classes 3, 6, or 20 may be sheltered as described at ¶870, where there are buildings of succeeding classes on hand. See also the general discussion of recapture on sale of land and building at ¶859.

(ITR: Sch. II Classes 1, 3, 6, 20; IT-79R3 Capital Cost Allowance — Buildings or Other Structures)

¶876 CONDOMINIUMS

Your holdings of a condominium (excluding your proportion of the land) are included in Class 1 as a building for CCA purposes. For example, a single unit within a building, which would be a Class 1 building if it were not a condominium, is itself considered to be a Class 1 building.

If you happen to own two or more condo units within the same building, they are together considered to be a single building for CCA purposes. Provided that their combined capital cost exceeds $50,000, they will be included on their own separate Class 1. If you dispose of a portion of the holdings of that condominium building, the partial disposition rules discussed at ¶860 will apply.

(IT-304R2 Condominiums)

¶877 CERTAIN TYPES OF ASSETS

For most assets, the CCA rate will simply be the percentage prescribed in the *Income Tax Regulations*. However, certain types of assets are given special CCA treatment or do not use the general percentage rate system. These types of assets are discussed as follows:

- Manufacturing and processing machinery and equipment, ¶878
- Leasehold interests, ¶879
- Patents, franchises, concessions and licences, ¶880
- Timber limits, ¶881
- Woods assets, ¶882
- Industrial mineral mines, ¶883
- Ships or other vessels, ¶884
- Water and air pollution control, ¶886
- Computers and office equipment, ¶886t
- Data network infrastructure equipment, ¶886v
- Computer software, ¶887
- Contractor's movable and earth moving equipment, ¶888
- Energy-efficient equipment, ¶889
- Railway cars, ¶890
- Art and antiques, ¶891
- Accelerated allowances for qualifying mines, ¶892

(ITR: 1100)

¶878 MANUFACTURING AND PROCESSING MACHINERY AND EQUIPMENT

[¶878.01] *Meaning of Manufacturing and Processing*

The term "manufacturing and processing" is not specifically defined in the Act. Consequently, the ordinary everyday meanings of "manufacture" and "process" are applicable. Generally, "manufacture" involves the creation of something (e.g., making or assembling) or the shaping, stamping, or forming of an object out of something. "Processing" refers to the technique of preparation, handling, or other activity designed to effect physical or chemical change in an article or substance, other than by natural growth.

The activities of breaking bulk and repackaging for subsequent resale where there is a systematic procedure to make a product more marketable are generally considered to be processing. However, the filling of orders from bulk inventories is not viewed as processing where the activities involved are nothing more than counting or measuring and packaging.

List of Statutory Exclusions

For CCA purposes, Regulation 1104(9) specifically excludes the following activities from the definition of manufacturing and processing:

(1) farming or fishing;

(2) logging;

(3) construction;

(4) operating an oil or gas well or extracting petroleum or natural gas from a natural accumulation of petroleum or natural gas;

(5) extracting minerals from a mineral resource;

(6) processing

(a) ore (other than iron ore or tar sands ore) from a mineral resource located in Canada to any stage that is not beyond the prime metal stage or its equivalent;

(b) iron ore from a mineral resource located in Canada to any stage that is not beyond the pellet stage or its equivalent; or

(c) tar sands ore from a mineral resource located in Canada to any stage that is not beyond the crude oil stage or its equivalent;

(7) producing industrial minerals;

(8) producing or processing electrical energy or steam for sale;

(9) processing natural gas as part of the business of selling or distributing gas in the course of operating a public utility;

(10) processing heavy crude oil recovered from a natural reservoir in Canada to a stage that is not beyond the crude oil stage or its equivalent; or

(11) Canadian field processing.

(ITR: 1104(9); CRA Document No.: Manufacturing and processing, *March 25, 2013*, CRA Document No. 2012-0470501E5)

[¶878.02] *Revised Class 29: Manufacturing and Processing Machinery and Equipment Acquired after March 18, 2007*

M&P equipment acquired after March 18, 2007 and before 2016 is eligible for a straight-line write-off over three years on a 25%/50%/25% basis. Generally, property which qualifies for revived Class 29 treatment is property that would initially be described in Class 8 (but excluding railway rolling stock and radio-communication equipment), or is an oil or water storage tank or powered industrial lift truck.

Class 8 generally excludes buildings (generally Class 1(*q*)), but does permit the inclusion of a "structure that is manufacturing or processing equipment".

The various classes and their respective assets are described in full at ¶898. In determining which class an asset belongs to, it is imperative that you consult that section.

Other Depreciable Property Included in Class 29

Since property included in Class 8 may be "overridden" by other classes and still be described in Class 8, technical rules specifically ensure that Canadian field processing equipment and liquefied natural gas ("LNG") facilities (¶889f.40) are excluded.

Energy Efficient Equipment

Property included in Classes 43.1 or 43.2 (¶889), which offer high CCA rates for energy efficient equipment, may also be included in Class 29 if the property is used in manufacturing and processing. However, by default, such property is included in Classes 43.1 or 43.2. Therefore, an election is available so that property can be more quickly depreciated in Class 29.

The Regulation 1102(16.1) election allows you to elect to include M&P machinery and equipment in Class 29 provided that it would otherwise qualify for Class 29 if it did not first fall into Class 43.1 or 43.2. The election must be made by letter attached to the return of income for the taxation year in which the property is acquired.

Class 29 — Inclusion Criteria

Any property described above as eligible for Class 29 must satisfy the general Class 29 conditions. These conditions are that you must manufacture or acquire the property:

(1) to use it directly or indirectly in Canada primarily in the manufacturing or processing of goods for sale or lease; or

(2) **(only applies to corporations)** to lease it in the ordinary course of carrying on a business in Canada to a lessee who can reasonably be expected to use the property in Canada primarily in the manufacturing or processing of goods for sale or lease, if the principal business of your corporation is:

(a) leasing property;

(b) manufacturing of property that it sells or leases;

(c) lending money;

(d) financing the purchase by others of merchandise or services by purchasing conditional sales contracts, chattel mortgages, receivables, and so on;

(e) selling or servicing a type of property that it also leases; or

(f) any combination of the above activities.

Depreciation Rate

CCA claims with respect to property included in Class 29 are determined using a 50% straight-line (as opposed to the common diminishing balance) basis, subject to the half-year rule. In the year the property is acquired, you can depreciate 25% of the capital cost (i.e.: $^1/_2$ of 50%). In the second year you can depreciate 50%, and the remaining 25% is depreciated in the third year.

If the half-year rule does not apply (perhaps because the property has become available for use only in the third year following acquisition), it may be written off 50% in the year it becomes available for use and 50% in the following year. Property which becomes available because it has been unavailable for use in the two preceding years (among other circumstances) is known as "designated property". The technical calculation of Class 29 property where there are additions of designated property, and especially dispositions credited to the class in the year, is described in ¶899a.

CCA is always an optional claim, so you are not obliged to claim the full amount available in the year. Unlike most other classes, which operate on a diminishing balance basis, you can catch up in the current year claims forgone in earlier years.

Example

An enterprise acquired in June of Year 1 has property with a cost of $200,000, which is eligible for the Class 29 CCA provisions for manufacturing and processing property. The property is available for use when acquired.

Case A — The enterprise claims maximum capital cost allowance in the year of acquisition.
Schedule of CCA

	Class	UCC opening	Additions	Proceeds	UCC before allowance	Rate[1]	CCA	UCC
Year 1	29	$—	$200,000	—	$200,000	25%	$ 50,000	$150,000
Year 2	29	150,000	—	—	150,000	50%	100,000	50,000
Year 3	29	50,000	—	—	50,000	25%	50,000	—

[1] Based on the original cost.

Case B — The enterprise does not claim any capital cost allowance in the year of acquisition, but claims maximum capital cost allowance in the following years.
Schedule of CCA

	Class	UCC opening	Additions	Proceeds	UCC before allowance	Rate[2]	CCA	UCC
Year 1	29	$—	$200,000	—	$200,000	25%	$—	$200,000
Year 2	29	200,000	—	—	200,000	50%	150,000	50,000
Year 3	29	50,000	—	—	50,000	25%	50,000	—

[2] Based on the original cost.

Case C — The enterprise does not claim any capital cost allowance in the year of acquisition and in the following year, but claims maximum capital cost allowance in the third year.
Schedule of CCA

	Class	UCC opening	Additions	Proceeds	UCC before allowance	Rate[3]	CCA	UCC
Year 1	29	$—	$200,000	—	$200,000	25%	$—	$200,000
Year 2	29	200,000	—	—	200,000	50%	—	200,000
Year 3	29	200,000	—	—	200,000	25%	200,000	—

[3] Based on the original cost.

For an illustration of the calculation required where there is designated property, see ¶899a.

[¶878.03] *Class 53: Manufacturing and Processing Machinery and Equipment Acquired After 2015*

Class 29 is closed for new additions of any property acquired after 2015. The 2015 federal Budget introduced the new corresponding Class 53. Manufacturing and processing equipment and machinery acquired after 2015 and before 2026 that would have otherwise been included in Class 29 is included in Class 53. Like Class 29, Class 53 will retain its 50% CCA rate, but it will instead depreciate on a declining balance basis and will be subject to the half-year rule. Beginning in 2026, these properties will be subject to the former 30% rate under Class 43.

Planning Opportunity

You can elect to transfer property from one class (the old class) to another (the new class) where new property has been acquired in the new class and the old property would be in the new class if acquired when the new property was acquired (see the discussion in ¶870).

The election may be useful when, in a taxation year, you dispose of Class 29 property, and before the end of that taxation year (even in previous years) you acquire a new Class 53 property. The effect of the election is that the old property is transferred to the new class before its disposition. This election may allow you to defer a recapture of CCA (because Class 53's UCC may shelter the proceeds of disposition of the Class 29 property). See ¶870.

The election is made by letter in the tax return for the taxation year of disposition. It must be made by the deadline for filing the tax return for the year, but pursuant to Regulation 600(*d*), this election is eligible for late filing under subsection 220(3.2) of the Act

(ITR: 600(*d*); 1100(1)(*ta*); 1102(16.1); 1103(2d); Sch. II Classes 8, 29, 43, 53)

[¶878.04] *Class 43(a)*: Other Manufacturing and Processing Property

Manufacturing and processing property which fails to fall into Class 29, either because it is Canadian field processing property and so specifically excluded from the 2007 through 2015 version of Class 29, or because it was acquired before March 19, 2007 is generally included in Class 43. Class 43 assets are eligible for a 30% CCA rate on the usual declining balance basis.

Class 43 is divided into two sections. Class 43(*a*) deals with manufacturing and processing property (discussed here). Class 43(*b*) deals with machinery and equipment to process ore from foreign mines, and is discussed at ¶878.10.

Property Which Belongs in Class 43(a)

Class 43(*a*) manufacturing and processing property is essentially (but not entirely) similar to Class 29 property. As with Class 29 (except for the addition in Class 43 of a reference to field processing in the preamble to (b), below), you must acquire or manufacture the property:

(1) for direct or indirect use in Canada primarily in the manufacturing or processing of goods for sale or lease; or

(2) **(applicable only to your corporation)** to lease it in the ordinary course of carrying on a business in Canada to a lessee who can reasonably be expected to use the property in Canada, primarily in Canadian field processing or in the manufacturing or processing of goods for sale or lease, if the principal business of your corporation is:

(a) leasing property,

(b) manufacturing of property that it sells or leases,

(c) lending money,

(d) financing the purchase by others of merchandise or services by purchasing conditional sales contracts, chattel mortgages, receivables and so on,

(e) selling or servicing a type of property that it also leases, or

(f) any combination of the above activities.

Further, to be included in Class 43(*a*), the property itself must be: machinery or equipment that otherwise would fall into Class 8 (¶898), but excluding railway rolling stock and radio-communication equipment; or an oil or water storage tank. Class 8 is, among other things, an all-purpose default class for items not otherwise specifically assigned a CCA class.

(ITR: Sch. II Classes 8, 29, 43; IT-147R3 Capital cost allowance — Accelerated write-off of manufacturing and processing machinery and equipment)

[¶878.05] *Separate Class Election for Class 43(a) Property*

You may elect to set up a separate Class 43 for each item of manufacturing and processing property in Class 43(*a*) costing over $1,000. Thus, where the specific equipment is sold at a loss (or merely given away or junked), the loss will be fully recognized for tax purposes when incurred, rather than having the proceeds credited to the general Class 43 which will be depreciated at the 30% declining balance rate indefinitely.

The election to include Class 43(*a*) property in a separate class must be made in the year of acquisition (regardless of whether it is available for use) by including a letter with your tax return for that year.

Property in any of the separate classes created under this rule which is still on hand at the beginning of the fifth taxation year after the property first became available for use is forcibly relocated to the general Class 43 immediately after the beginning of that fifth year.

(ITR: 1101(5q), (5s); 1103(2g))

[¶878.10] *Class 43(b): Assets Acquired to Process Foreign Ore in Canada*

To be included in Class 43(*b*), your property must meet the following criteria:

- it is machinery, equipment, or a Class 8 structure;
- it is reasonably expected to be used entirely in Canada; and
- its use is primarily for the purpose of processing ore extracted from a mineral resource outside Canada.

Class 43(*b*) assets are also amortized at a 30% CCA rate on a declining balance basis.

[¶878.15] *History of Manufacturing and Processing CCA Rates*

M&P machinery and equipment has been through a long cycle of shifting rates. That being said, the history discussed here is not a complete timeline.

M&P machinery and equipment (with some exceptions) acquired after 1987 and before February 26, 1992 were mostly assigned to Class 39. Class 39 was shut to new additions after February 25, 1992, and the same items were instead included in Class 43, which is depreciated at a 30% rate. M&P assets acquired after March 18, 2007, and before 2016 are included in the reopened Class 29 (see ¶878.02). Class 43 remains for some types of assets (see ¶878.04 and ¶878.10) that are not included in the reopened Class 29. Property acquired after 2015 and before 2026 that would otherwise belong in Class 29 is included in Class 53 (see ¶878.03).

¶879 LEASEHOLD INTERESTS

[¶879.05] *What is a Leasehold Interest?*

A leasehold interest, which is included in Class 13, is the interest of a tenant in any leased tangible property. Such property includes:

- improvements to leased property;
- the assignment of a lease from a tenant; and
- a lease itself.

Improvements that are considered part of a building or structure are specifically excluded from the definition of leasehold interests. Further, leasehold interest does not include an interest in:

- minerals;
- petroleum;
- natural gas;
- other related hydrocarbons;
- timber; and
- property related to any of the above.

If you are the lessee of any property, you have acquired a leasehold interest in that property regardless of whether or not you paid anything to acquire the interest. However, you are considered to have acquired a depreciable leasehold interest only when you have incurred a capital cost to acquire the property.

The Capital Cost of a Leasehold Interest

The capital cost of a Class 13 leasehold interest includes:

(1) any capital amounts that you (the tenant) incur to improve or alter the leased property (excluding amounts that are capitalized as a part of a building or structure); and

(2) amounts that you (the tenant) incur to obtain or extend the lease/sublease or pay the lessor for permission to sublease the property.

Class 13 also includes property that you acquire (after December 23, 1991) from a person that you do not deal at arm's length with, provided that the property would have been considered a leasehold interest if it were owned by that person. Thus, you can depreciate leasehold improvements that you made to property where a non-arm's length person is the lessee.

Example

Suppose you lease space personally and you and your son both operate separate businesses using that space. Your son pays you for use of the space, but is not a party to the lease and has in effect only a monthly tenancy held from you. If your son makes leasehold improvements to the space and pays for them, he can claim CCA with respect to the improvements even though he has no leasehold interest to which the expenditures can attach.

Improvements to Buildings and Structures

Where you have incurred a capital cost that would otherwise be a leasehold interest, it is not included in Class 13 and is instead included in the appropriate CCA class for a building (¶875) if the leasehold interest is acquired because:

(1) you erected a building or structure on leased land;

(2) you made an addition to a leased building or structure; or

(3) made alterations to a leased building or structure that substantially changed its nature.

Moreover, as discussed above, you can depreciate leasehold improvements that you acquire and include in a building CCA class even if you are not the lessee. This is permitted when the lessee deals with you at non-arm's length.

For example, you lease a building personally and your wholly owned corporation builds an addition for its use. The company may depreciate the cost of the addition even though it has no leasehold interest to which the expenditures can attach.

[¶879.10] *Leasehold Depreciation and the Half-Year Rule*

The application of the half-year rule only permits you to deduct one-half of normally calculated CCA (as computed in ¶879.15) in the year which you acquire a leasehold interest. The same exceptions which apply generally for specified leasing property (¶873a), property capitalized by the lessee under the specified leasing rules (¶873a), and property where CCA has been deferred under the available for use rules but may now be claimed (¶804b).

[¶879.15] *How is Leasehold Depreciation Calculated?*

The maximum annual CCA claim amount for Class 13 leasehold interests is the aggregate of the "prorated portions" of the capital costs of the individual leasehold interests and may not exceed the UCC of Class 13 immediately before any deductions. The CCA amount for each capital cost incurred to acquire a leasehold interest must be calculated individually and the sum of the prorated portions is the amount which can be deducted for tax purposes.

To comprehend the methodology of these calculations, it is crucial to understand that CCA, with respect to capital costs incurred to acquire a leasehold interest, must be calculated separately on the basis of not only the year the cost was incurred in, but also which lease the cost relates to. The sum of these individually calculated prorated portions will result in the total Class 13 CCA claim for the year.

Prorated Portion Calculation

For each taxation year in which you incur a capital cost to acquire leasehold interest, a separate CCA calculation is required. Moreover, if in the same year you incur leasehold costs with respect to multiple leases, then a separate calculation is necessary for each lease. Understanding the calculation described below will provide more clarity on this concept.

The prorated portion of a capital cost incurred in a particular tax year for a particular leasehold interest is the lesser of:

(1) $^1/_5$ of the capital cost; and

(2) the capital cost divided by the number of 12-month periods, to a maximum of 40, which the lease has to run.

Example: Prorated Portion

To illustrate the calculation of the "prorated portion", assume that you have a December 31 year end and have entered into a 20-year building lease on June 1 of Year 1, and on June 30 of Year 1 spent $5,000 on leasehold improvements. The "prorated portion" of this expenditure is calculated as follows:

Expenditure	$ 5,000
Number of months in period from January 1 of Year 1 to June 1 of Year 20	245
Number of 12-month periods in above period = 245 ÷ 12	20
Prorated portion = $5,000 ÷ 20	$ 250

If this is your only leasehold interest, your Year 1 CCA claim with respect to Class 13 is $125 ($250 × 50%, due to the half-year rule). In each subsequent year until Year 20, you can deduct CCA of $250. Upon deducting the remaining $125 in Year 21, the entire $5,000 will have been deducted from income. Since the leasehold interest is depreciated on a straight-line basis, the half-year rule results in an extra year to depreciate the lease fully (i.e., a 20-year lease is actually written-off over 21 years).

Example: Subsequent Improvements

If you spend another $1,000 in Year 2 on improvements, you will make a similar calculation. In this case, the expenditure of $1,000 is divided by 19 (the number of 12-month periods remaining in the lease after January 1 of Year 1) and the prorated portion of the Year 2 expenditure is $1,000 ÷ 19 = $52.63.

The Year 2 CCA claim for Class 13 is the aggregate of the "prorated portions" adjusted for the half-year rule on Year 2 expenditures. Thus, the Year 2 CCA deduction is ($250 + $^1/_2$ × $52.63) or $276.32. In subsequent years, assuming no additional expenditures, the deduction will be $302.63. In Year 21, the CCA claim will be $151.31 ($125 + $26.31), picking up the leftover balances from the half-year rule.

Disposition of a Leasehold Interest

If you have an interest in more than one lease, each lease is not considered to be a separate class. As a result, the disposal of one or more of the interests does not permit a "terminal loss" to be claimed in that year unless all leasehold interests have been disposed of. The expiry of a leasehold interest is treated as a disposal, and when the last lease owned by you expires, you deduct the remaining UCC as a terminal loss.

Miscellaneous Rules

If you have the right to renew a lease for one or more periods, the length of the first renewal term must be added to the remaining term of the lease for the purpose of calculating the prorated portion. The number of 12-month periods to be used in the above calculations is limited to a maximum of 40. On the other hand, the maximum claim in any year is limited to one-fifth of the particular cost, so that, for instance, an expenditure with respect to a lease with only two years to run must be deducted over a five-year period, rather than a two-year period.

If you incur the cost before the leasehold interest itself is acquired, the cost is deemed to have been incurred in the year the leasehold interest was acquired (i.e., improving property before you lease it).

Special tenant inducements may reduce the capital cost of leasehold additions (see ¶826).

(ITA: 13; 20; ITR: Sch. II Class 13; Sch. III; 1100(1)(*b*); 1102(5), (5.1); IT-464R Capital Cost Allowance — Leasehold Interests)

¶880 LIMITED LIFE PATENTS, FRANCHISES, CONCESSIONS, AND LICENCES

[¶880.05] *General Rules: Class 14*

Assets Belonging in Class 14

Patents, franchises, concessions, and licences, provided that they are granted for limited periods, are included in Class 14. However, patents generally fall into Class 44 by default, but may be included in Class 14 by making the election described at ¶880.10. Specifically excluded from Class 14 are the following:

(1) a franchise, concession, licence, or right in respect of minerals, petroleum, natural gas, other related hydrocarbons, or timber;

(2) a leasehold interest;

(3) a property belonging in Class 23; or

(4) a licence to use computer software.

Notably, expenses paid in the year to a government or government body for the purpose of obtaining a licence, permit, franchise or patent are currently deductible if they are incurred to make representations relating to your business.

Unlimited life franchises, concessions, or licences are eligible capital expenditures (see ¶766.20), amortized under the rules at ¶767.

Commentary on Bill C-29 Measures (Oct. 25, 2016)

Note: When Bill C-29, October 25, 2016, achieves Royal Assent, the commentary will be modified to read:

Prior to 2017, unlimited life franchises, concessions, or licences are eligible capital expenditures (see ¶766.20), amortized under the rules at ¶767. Effective January 1, 2017, all eligible capital property will be reclassified as depreciable property and included in CCA Class 14.1. See ¶880a.

See ¶887 regarding licences to use computer software.

Determining the Capital Cost

The following amounts are added to the capital cost of Class 14 property:

- its purchase price;
- any legal fees and disbursements incurred to acquire the asset;
- any registration fees and representation costs incurred to acquire the asset; and
- research and development expenses incurred in developing and designing a patent or industrial design (to the extent that these expenses have not been deducted under another provision and were incurred before the patent or industrial design is registered).

Where these costs are incurred prior to the year in which the property is acquired, they are added to the capital cost of the property in the year of its acquisition. No CCA claim may be made in a year prior to the year of the actual acquisition of the relevant property.

Determining the CCA Amount

The annual CCA claim is calculated for each asset by apportioning the cost of the asset over its life remaining at the time the cost was incurred. That is, unlike many other CCA classes, a specified percentage is not applied to the UCC of Class 14. The half-year rule also does not apply to Class 14 property.

Since the assets are depreciated by apportioning them over their useful lives, Class 14 treatment applies only to a patent, franchise, concession, or licence with a limited life.

Apportioned amount for a single asset = asset's capital cost / asset's life at time the cost was incurred

Therefore, the maximum CCA amount which you can deduct with respect to Class 14 property is the lesser of:

(1) the total of all the apportioned amounts; and

(2) the UCC of Class 14 for the year before making any CCA claims.

Deducting Less Than the Maximum CCA Amount

If you choose to depreciate less than the maximum amount in a given tax year, the remainder can only be deducted as a terminal loss when all Class 14 property has been disposed of. You may not "catch-up" on CCA claims with respect to Class 14 assets in subsequent years. Therefore, if you anticipate having at least one Class 14 asset on hand for the foreseeable future, it may be prudent to claim the maximum annual deduction if you wish to realize this tax deduction in the short-term.

Ability to Renew a Franchise, Concession, or Licence

If the franchise, concession, or license automatically renews or can be renewed with your complete autonomous consent (i.e., no negotiation is required to renew), the life of the period includes the renewal period for the purpose of the CCA calculation. However, if the renewal is dependent on certain conditions being met, the facts of each case will determine whether the additional period is included in the life of the asset.

Where renewal of extension periods are considered part of the life of the property and where the number of such renewals or extensions are indefinite, the property right is not for a limited period and is therefore not Class 14 property.

Alternate Depreciation Methods

The capital cost of a Class 14 property may be apportioned on another basis where, based on the legal agreements and other relevant factors, you can clearly demonstrate that the alternative method is reasonable. For example, where a three-year licence provides that a television program may be broadcasted three times in Year 1, and once in each of Years 2 and 3, it would be appropriate to allocate 3/5 of the capital cost to Year 1 and 1/5 to each of Years 2 and 3.

> *Example*
>
> Jack acquires a patent for the purpose of earning business income. He paid $5,000 in legal fees, $10,000 in development costs, and $2,000 in registration fees to the patent office. All of these amounts are added the capital cost of the patent. Therefore, Jack includes the total of $17,000 to Class 14. The patent's life is 17 years.
>
> Apportioned amount = capital cost / remaining useful life at time of acquisition = $17,000 / 17 years = $1,000.
>
> Therefore, assuming no other property is included in Class 14, Jack may deduct a CCA amount of $1,000/year with respect to Class 14 for the next 17 years. As previously mentioned, the half-year rule does not apply to Class 14 property.

Where Patent's Cost is Dependent Upon its Use

An additional provision allows for an alternate CCA calculation with respect to patents where the patent's cost is dependent upon its use. The CCA claim (limited to the UCC of Class 14) is the sum of the two following amounts:

(1) the capital cost incurred in that tax year by having used the patent; and

(2) the amount computed under the normal CCA calculation method described previously assuming that the capital cost of the property used in this computation does not include any costs incurred with respect to the use of the patent.

(ITR: Sch. II Class 14, Class 44; 1100(1)(c), (9); IT-477 (Consolidated) Capital cost allowance — Patents, franchises, concessions and licences — Consolidated)

[¶880.10] *Patents — Inclusion in Class 44*

A patent, or a right to use patented information for a limited or unlimited period, may be included in Class 44 rather than Class 14. The rate of depreciation is 25%, subject to the half-year rule (¶802), on the standard declining balance basis.

You may elect to have a patent or right excluded from Class 44 and instead included in Class 14 (where it has a finite life) or as eligible capital property in years before 2017 (provided that its life is unlimited). The election to exclude a property from Class 44 must be made in the year the property is acquired, by letter attached to the return of income for that year.

Where Patent's Cost is Dependent Upon its Use

Mirroring the rule for Class 14 patents, a similar provision modifies the CCA calculation with respect to a patent where its cost is dependent upon its use. Therefore, the CCA claim (limited to the UCC of Class 44), with respect to such a patent, is the sum of the two following amounts:

(1) the capital cost incurred in that tax year by having used the patent; and

(2) the amount computed under the normal CCA calculation method described previously (25% declining-balance) assuming that the capital cost of the property used in this computation does not include any costs incurred with respect to the use of the patent.

(ITR: Sch. II Class 14, Class 44; 1100(9.1); 1103(2h); CRA Document No.: Sale — Intellectual property — Patent pending, *April 17, 1998*, CRA Document No. 9720785)

[¶880.20] *Election to Defer Recapture on Disposition or Termination*

Where a limited period franchise, concession, or licence is disposed of or terminated after December 20, 2002, it is considered a "former business property" for purposes of the deferral of recapture of CCA under the rules at ¶846. If you are the transferor of such property, by making an election, you can potentially defer the recapture of CCA by acquiring replacement property as described under these rollover rules. An overview of how the election works and detailed examples of the consequences of the election and rollover are provided below.

Since the election makes the franchise, concession, or licence a former business property by definition, the rules for the deferral of a capital gain also apply. See the corresponding "Replacement Properties" rules at ¶523.

Such property that has an indefinite life is generally an eligible capital property, and as such is eligible for the rollover for former business properties (¶769). It may also be eligible for capital gain treatment, as discussed under the subheading "Withdrawing Property from the Pool to Utilize Capital Losses or Obtain a Reserve" at ¶768.20.)

Where the Election Can Be Made

The election applies only to a franchise, concession or licence for a limited period that is wholly attributable to the carrying on of business at a fixed place. The election in respect of a limited period franchise, concession or licence is available only in circumstances where such a franchise, licence or concession is:

(1) disposed of directly by the owner (the "transferor") to another person (the new owner or "transferee"); or

(2) terminated by the owner (transferor), and the other person (transferee) acquires a similar property in respect of the same fixed place of business.

If the conditions above are met, the transferor and transferee can jointly elect in respect of the acquisition and disposition (or termination). If the election is made, the transferor has disposed of a former business property, which can be replaced under the rollover rules at ¶523 and ¶846.

Consequences to the Transferee

If the actual property was transferred, the transferee is deemed to own that property until the time that he or she owns neither the former property nor a similar property in respect of the same fixed place to which the former property related.

If the transferee, instead, acquires a similar property in respect of the same fixed place (i.e., the life of the former property was terminated), the transferee is deemed to have also acquired the former property and to continue to own it until the transferee no longer owns the similar property.

For the purpose of claiming CCA in either situation, the life of the former property in the hands of the transferee is deemed to be the term remaining at the time the transferor originally acquired the property. For example, a licence, with a 20-year life when it was originally acquired by the transferor with five years remaining at the time of the transfer, is considered to have a 20-year life in the hands of the transferee for purposes of the transferee's CCA calculation.

A separate class is prescribed for each property which the transferee has acquired under this election.

Eligible Capital Property Treatment — Prior to 2017

There may be circumstances where, but for this election, a portion of the consideration given by a transferee might reasonably be considered to be an eligible capital amount (¶768) to the transferor and an eligible capital expenditure (¶767) to the transferee prior to 2017. For example, a portion of the consideration may relate to the preferred status that the transferee receives in obtaining a new property at the end of the term.

Where the joint election is made, such an amount will be neither an eligible capital amount to the transferor, nor an eligible capital expenditure to the transferee, but will instead be included in the cost to the transferee and the proceeds of disposition of the transferor.

Post-Election Denial of Terminal Loss to Transferee

After the transfer occurs, the life of the property expires and a similar property in respect of the same fixed place is not acquired by the transferee, the transferee would normally be entitled to a terminal loss, and generally that will be true under the election. However, no terminal loss may be claimed by the transferee on property acquired on which a joint election has been made, if:

- within 24 months after the transferee last owned the former property, the transferee or a person not dealing at arm's length with the transferee acquires a similar property in respect of the same fixed place to which the former property applied; and
- at the end of the taxation year, the transferee or the person owns the similar property or another similar property in respect of the same fixed place to which the property subject to the election applied.

The following examples were prepared by the Department of Finance and published in the technical notes to this legislation. They have been edited to provide internal cross-references.

Example 1

Ms. Patel owns a franchise with 5 years remaining of a 20-year agreement. The original cost was $60,000, and the UCC is $15,000. The agreement is transferable, so she agrees to sell the franchise to Mr. Grando at its FMV of $85,000. Ms. Patel will, in the same taxation year, purchase from Ms. Vincent a replacement franchise that has 15 years remaining of a 20-year term, for $100,000.

No 13(4.2) Election

Ms. Patel would have a capital gain of $25,000 (i.e., $85,000 - $60,000) and a UCC balance of $55,000 ($15,000 + $100,000 - $60,000) before deducting any CCA for the year. The ACB of her replacement franchise is $100,000. Mr. Grando acquires a Class 14 property with an ACB and capital cost of $85,000, depreciable over five years.

Joint 13(4.2) Election

If Ms. Patel and Mr. Grando jointly elect under subsection 13(4.2), Ms. Patel may elect under the rules at ¶523 and ¶846 to defer the capital gain, such that the ACB and capital cost of the replacement franchise will be deemed to be $75,000 ($100,000 less the $25,000 deferred capital gain). Further, Ms. Patel's UCC balance for Class 14 is $30,000 ($15,000 UCC plus $100,000 cost of the replacement franchise less $85,000 proceeds from the former property), to be amortized over the remaining 15-year term.

You might have noticed that the term for amortizing Ms. Patel's replacement franchise is unaffected by her and Mr. Grando's joint election in respect of the former property. Mr. Grando, on the other hand, will be required to amortize his $85,000 cost of the former property over 20 years, which was the term of the former property when it was first acquired by Ms. Patel.

If Mr. Grando does not enter into a new agreement with the franchisor after the five-year period, he will be eligible for a terminal loss with respect to the remaining UCC of the separate Class 14. However, a terminal loss will not be available if a person dealing at non-arm's length with Mr. Grando, at any time before the time that is 24 months after the expiry of the old agreement, enters into a new franchise agreement in respect of the same fixed place.

Example 2

Consider the above example, except that the original franchise agreement of Ms. Patel (the former property) is not transferable, but instead terminated and renewed with the franchisor. Suppose that it is renewed by Mr. Grando for a period of 12 years, with an additional amount of $120,000 paid by Mr. Grando to the franchisor for the new agreement.

Potential Eligible Capital Property Treatment — prior to 2017

In this case it is arguable that, for Mr. Grando, the $85,000 payment to Ms. Patel is, absent an election under subsection 13(4.2) and prior to 2017, an eligible capital expenditure by Mr. Grando. That is, Mr. Grando will pay a separate amount of $120,000 to the franchisor for a Class 14 asset, but the $85,000 payment to Ms. Patel is, in effect, incurred to acquire the right to renew the franchise, not to acquire a Class 14 property.

Prior to 2017, Ms. Patel has likewise received proceeds of disposition of an eligible capital property (i.e., an eligible capital amount, $^{3}/_{4}$ of which would reduce her CEC balance), not proceeds of disposition of a Class 14 property. Absent an election under subsection 13(4.2), Ms. Patel would not be entitled to acquire a replacement eligible capital property, but could be entitled to claim a terminal loss on the termination of the original franchise agreement (if she had no other Class 14 assets on hand at the end of the taxation year of disposition). The recapture rules for dispositions of eligible capital property would apply to the eligible capital amount received by Ms. Patel.

Joint 13(4.2) Election

The $120,000 cost of the new agreement to Mr. Grando, paid to the franchisor, is depreciable by Mr. Grando over its 12-year term.

If Ms. Patel and Mr. Grando jointly elect under subsection 13(4.2), no part of the proceeds of disposition for the former property will be an eligible capital amount or an eligible capital expenditure. The results are the same as in Example 1, except that Mr. Grando will now have two Class 14 properties:

- the new franchise agreement, the $120,000 cost of which may be written off by him over its 12-year term; and
- the former property, deemed to have been acquired by him and included in a separate class, the $85,000 cost of which may be written off by him over its deemed 20-year term.

Commentary on Bill C-29 Measures (Oct. 25, 2016)

Commentary on Bill C-29 Measures (Oct. 25, 2016)

Note: When Bill C-29, October 25, 2016, achieves Royal Assent, the commentary will be modified to read:

Effective January 1, 2017, eligible capital property will be treated as depreciable property under the CCA rules. See ¶880a.

Example 3

Consider again Example 1, but suppose that the replacement franchise, purchased by Ms. Patel from Ms. Vincent, is itself the subject of a joint election by them under subsection 13(4.2). Ms. Patel is required to amortize her $30,000 UCC (see Example 1) over the original 20-year term of Ms. Vincent, not over its remaining 15 years.

(ITA: 13(4.2), (4.3); 20(16.1)(*b*); ITR: 1101(1ag))

¶880a ELIGIBLE CAPITAL PROPERTY

Commentary on Bill C-29 Measures (Oct. 25, 2016)

Note: When Bill C-29, October 25, 2016, achieves Royal Assent, the commentary will be modified to read:

New Regime

Following an initial public consultation announced in Budget 2014, Budget 2016 announced that the eligible capital property ("ECP") rules would be replaced by a new CCA class, effective January 1, 2017. Amounts formerly treated as ECP are added to new Class 14.1 of Schedule II of the Income Tax Regulations .This overhaul of the treatment of ECP (generally, goodwill and other intangibles) requires complex legislative provisions to enact in a manner that is fair and equitable to taxpayers. See ¶766 for full explanation of the pre-2017 rules.

Overview of New Rules

Property that was ECP is classified as depreciable capital property and expenditures and receipts also receive depreciable capital property treatment. Class 14.1includes goodwill, property that was ECP before January 1, 2017 and any property acquired January 1, 2017 or later that would have otherwise been treated as ECP. See ¶766 for a list of what types of expenditures are capitalized as ECP. The full cost of property acquired is added to Class 14.1 versus the 75% addition for ECP. Class 14.1 property will be subject to a CCA rate of 5% on a declining balance basis. A separate Class 14.1 must be maintained in respect of each business of the taxpayer, which is consistent with depreciable property and ECP rules.

CCA claimed on Class 14.1 property is subject to recapture on disposition. The lesser of the proceeds and capital cost of the property disposed is credited to the Class 14.1 pool and negative amounts are treated as ordinary income. To the extent that proceeds of disposition are greater than the capital cost of the property disposed of, the difference is treated as a capital gain. Importantly, because existing dispositions of ECP are considered to give rise to income from an active business, the change will result in an additional tax of approximately 10% to a Canadian-controlled private corporation that disposes of goodwill after 2016, as capital gains are treated as "aggregate investment income" for these purposes.

Special rules have been created to account for receipts and expenditures of a business that do not relate to property (such as incorporation costs) that would have adjusted the cumulative eligible capital balance under the ECP rules. Every business will have a goodwill property associated with it even if the business has not previously acquired goodwill. Expenditures increase the capital cost and undepreciated capital cost of Class 14.1 property pools.

Transitional Rules

There are a number of transitional rules of varying degrees of complexity that will require careful consideration by taxpayers in subsequent taxation years. That being said, the end result of the transitional provisions appears to be to place taxpayers in a position similar to what they would have been in if the ECP rules never existed and Class 14.1 existed all along.

(1) Additional depreciation — Prior to the 2027 taxation year, expenditures incurred prior to January 1, 2017 are depreciable at a 7% rate vs. the 5% rate.

(2) Capital cost — On January 1, 2017, the capital cost of property will be determined to be $^4/_3$ of the CEC balance at that time plus $^4/_3$ of previously claimed deductions that have not been recaptured less $^4/_3$ of any negative CEC balance at that time.

(3) Undepreciated capital cost — In most cases the balance in CEC will become the UCC, with the difference between capital cost and UCC being deemed to have been claimed as a deduction under paragraph 20(1)(*a*). The amount deemed to have been deducted is calculated as the amount by which total capital cost and any negative CEC balance exceeds any positive CEC balance.

(4) Allocation of capital cost — A new rule allocates the total capital cost of properties between a goodwill property and each identifiable property in the class.

(5) Deemed gain immediately before January 1, 2017 — Where a taxation year straddles January 1, 2017 and the taxpayer entered into a transaction prior to January 1, 2017 that resulted in an income inclusion under the ECP rules, the taxpayer can elect to report the transaction as business income (old rules) or as a taxable capital gain.

(6) Deferral of gains realized before January 1, 2017 — A taxpayer can elect to reduce the income inclusion under the ECP rules where a property described in Class 14.1 has been acquired in the same taxation year the income inclusion arose. These rules operate much the same as the ECP rules would have if a replacement property were acquired before the end of the taxation year in which an income inclusion arose.

(7) Dispositions of former ECP — To avoid excess recapture when disposing of former ECP, the UCC of Class 14.1 increases by 25% of the lesser of the proceeds of disposition and the cost of the property disposed of.

(8) Non-arm's length dispositions of former ECP — a new rule is intended to prevent the use of non-arm's length transfers to increase the amount that can be depreciated in Class 14.1. In effect, only $^3/_4$ of the cost of the former ECP is included in the UCC of Class 14.1 where the property was formerly an ECP of the taxpayer (or certain non-arm's length persons) and subsection 13(38) applied to increase the UCC in respect of an earlier disposition of the property.

¶881 TIMBER LIMITS AND TIMBER RESOURCE PROPERTY

[¶881.05] *Timber Limits*

A timber limit is a parcel of land with timber on it, a right or licence to cut or remove timber from an area in Canada which was acquired prior to May 7, 1974, or such a right or licence acquired after May 6, 1974 which is not a "timber resource property" (defined at ¶881.10).

A timber limit or cutting right may be acquired with or without title to the land on which the timber stands. Contrary to the general rule for land (that it may not be depreciated), land acquired with standing timber is a timber limit or part of a timber limit and is depreciable.

A timber limit or a right to cut timber from a limit is deemed to be a separate class of property, so if you have more than one timber limit or rights to cut timber from more than one limit, each limit or right is deemed to be a separate class of property. Accordingly, recapture, capital gain, or terminal loss may result from each individual disposition.

Determining Your CCA Claim

The annual CCA claim with respect of a timber limit is the lesser of:

(1) the UCC of the timber limit (as of the end of the year and before making any deductions under this provision); and

(2) the aggregate of (i) an amount computed on the basis of a rate per cord, board foot or cubic metre cut in the year and (ii) certain allowances in respect of survey and cruise expenses.

The computation of the rate per cord, board foot or cubic metre will depend on whether or not you have been granted an allowance in respect of the timber limit for a previous taxation year.

Rate with No Allowance

Where such an allowance has not been granted, the CCA rate is equal the following amount:

(capital cost – the residual value of the timber limit – survey expenses included in the capital cost) ÷ the quantity of timber in the limit or by the quantity of timber that you have the right to cut

Residual value is the estimated value of the property if the merchantable timber were removed.

Rate with Allowance

Where an allowance has been granted in respect of the limit in a previous taxation year, the rate is ascertained in two ways, depending on the circumstances.

If it has been established that the quantity of timber in the limit or its capital cost was in fact substantially different from that used for the computation of the rate in the previous year, the rate will be determined by deducting the residual value of the timber limit from its UCC as of the commencement of the year and dividing the result by the estimated quantity of timber that is in the limit or that the you have the right to cut at the commencement of the year. Where there is no difference as described above, the rate will be that employed to determine the allowance for the most recent year for which an allowance was granted.

The allowance in respect of the survey and cruise expenses ((ii) above) is the lesser of:

(1) 1/10 of the amount expended for surveys, cruises or preparation of prints, maps and plans for the purpose of obtaining a licence or a right to cut timber (provided that the expense was included in the capital cost of the limit); and

(2) the amount as described above under (1) minus any amounts deducted in previous years.

Alternate CCA Amount

Instead of the allowances described above, you may elect to deduct an amount that is the lesser of (a) $100, or (b) the amount received in the current tax year from the sale of timber.

(ITA: (1), (21) "timber resource property"; 20(1)(*a*); ITR: 1100(1)(*e*); 1101(3); 1102(14); Sch. VI; IT-481)

[¶881.10] *Timber Resource Property*

A timber resource property is:

(1) a right or licence to cut or remove timber from a limit or area in Canada (acquired after May 6, 1974) if, at the time you acquired it, you also directly or indirectly acquired a right to extend or renew it or to acquire another right or licence as a substitute for it; or

(2) any right or licence which may reasonably be regarded as an extension of, renewal of, or substitution for any previous timber right or licence which you owned.

Timber resource properties are included in Class 33, are subject to the half-year rule, and depreciated at a rate of 15%.

Disposing of Timber Resource Property

When you dispose of a timber resource property, you must include in proceeds of disposition the entire proceeds, not merely the portion up to original capital cost as is generally the case (¶841). Thus, if proceeds exceed the UCC of timber resource property in Class 33 at the end of the taxation year, the entire difference will be recapture of CCA (¶843).

(ITA: 13(1), (21) "undepreciated capital cost" (G), "timber resource property"; ITR: Sch. II Class 33; 1100(1)(*a*)(xxiv); IT-481; *Daishowa-Marubeni International Ltd. v. The Queen*, 2013 DTC 5085 (SCC))

¶882 WOODS ASSETS

The classes discussed here relate to assets related to timber removal that will be obsolete and of no use once all of the timber is removed. A more definitive description is provided below. You have the choice to include such assets in either Class 10 or Class 15.

Wood Assets — Included in Class 15

Class 15 includes property which was acquired for the purposes of cutting and removing merchantable timber from a timber limit and will be of no further use to you after all of the merchantable timber which you are entitled to cut and remove has been cut and removed from the limit. However, it specifically excludes such property that you elected to include in Class 10 or any timber resource properties (¶881).

Rather than applying a prescribed percentage to depreciate the property, a formula (prescribed in Schedule IV of the *Income Tax Regulations*) determines the CCA claim which is described below. Class 15 assets are not subject to the half-year rule for CCA purposes.

Calculating the CCA Claim

The amount that may be deducted as CCA in respect of wood assets included in Class 15 is an amount computed on the basis of a rate per cord, board foot, or cubic metre cut in the taxation year with the maximum CCA being limited to the UCC of the class at the end of the taxation year before subtracting depreciation.

If all the property of the class is used in connection with one timber limit (or a section of it), the rate per cord, board foot, or cubic metre is determined by dividing the UCC of the property by the number of cords, board feet or cubic metres of timber in the limit at the beginning of the year.

Where different parts of the property of the class are used in connection with different timber limits or sections thereof, separate rates are computed for each part of the property as though each part of the property was your only property of that class.

Wood Assets — Included in Class 10

Class 10 includes property which was acquired for the purposes of cutting and removing merchantable timber from a timber limit and will be of no further use to you after all merchantable timber which you are entitled to cut and remove has been cut and removed from the limit. However, it specifically excludes such property that you instead included in Class 15 (i.e., you did not make an election to exclude it from Class 15) or any timber resource properties (¶881).

Class 10 property is subject to the half-year rule, and is depreciated at 30% on a declining balance basis.

Alternate Depreciation Method

Also, according to IT-501, the CRA will allow immovable wood assets to be deducted as current expenses when incurred, provided that the assets will have a useful life of three years or less by virtue of the fact that all merchantable timber will have been removed in that time from the area serviced by the assets.

(ITR: Sch. II Class 10, Class 15; Sch. IV; 1100(1)(*f*); IT-501 Capital cost allowance — Logging assets)

¶883 INDUSTRIAL MINERAL MINES

Industrial minerals are essentially non-metallic minerals such as asbestos, gravel, clay, stone, talc, or feldspar. You can find a comprehensive definition of industrial minerals in IT-492. Equipment used in industrial mineral mines is classified according to its nature; Class 41(*b*) (through Class 10(*k*)) is the most common class. Class 41 is depreciated at a rate of 25% and is subject to the half-year rule.

In addition to depreciating equipment, you can claim CCA claims with respect to your cost of acquiring an industrial mineral mine (including the right to remove industrial minerals from an industrial mineral mine). An industrial mineral mine does not include:

- coal mines;
- bituminous sands deposits;
- base or precious metal mines;
- mineral deposits which the Minister of Natural Resources has certified that the principal mineral extracted is an industrial mineral contained in a non-bedded deposit;

- where the principal mineral extracted is sylvite, halite or gypsum; or
- where the principal mineral extracted is silica and it is extracted from sandstone or quartzite.

Where you have one or more industrial mineral mines as described here, each mine is deemed to be a separate class of property.

Computing the CCA Claim

You may deduct the lesser of the two following amounts:

(1) the UCC of the class at the end of the taxation year before subtracting depreciation; and

(2) an amount computed by applying a rate per unit of mineral mined in the tax year (see below for rate calculations).

The applicable rate is calculated differently depending on whether you received an allowance in respect of the mine for any previous year.

Rate per unit — No Allowance

If there has been no previous allowance, the rate is the amount determined by dividing the capital cost of the mine minus its residual value, by the total number of units of commercially minable material estimated as being in the property. In the case of an industrial mineral mine, the residual value means its estimated value of the property if all the commercially minable material is removed.

Rate per unit — Allowance

If you have had a previous allowance in respect of the mine, the rate applied in computing the CCA claim is that which was used for the most recent year for which an allowance was granted. However, if it is shown to the satisfaction of the Minister that the quantity of commercially minable material in the mine is in fact a different quantity from that employed in determining the earlier rate or that the capital cost of the mine or right is different, the rate is reestablished using the formula described above.

Alternate Depreciation Method

In lieu of the aggregate deductions otherwise determined, you may elect that the CCA deduction for a taxation year shall be the lesser of $100 or the amount you have received in the taxation year from the sale of the mineral.

(ITR: 1100(1)(*g*); 1101(4); Sch. V; IT-492 Capital cost allowance — Industrial mineral mines)

¶884 SHIPS OR OTHER VESSELS

The term "vessel" is defined under the *Canada Shipping Act, 2001*, as a boat, ship, or craft designed, used or capable of being used for navigation in, on, through or immediately above water. A vessel is included in Class 7 and is subject to a maximum CCA rate of 15% (subject to the half-year rule in the year of acquisition; see ¶802.10). This same rate applies to the furniture, fittings, and equipment (other than radio communication equipment) attached to such a vessel.

Accelerated CCA for Certain Vessels

An exception to this general rule is a vessel all or part of the cost of which qualifies as a separate prescribed class at a rate designed to create an incentive for the acquisition, construction, or conversion of the vessel.

Accelerated CCA on a straight-line basis at a maximum rate of 33 1/3% of the capital cost of the property (subject to the half-year rule in the year of acquisition) is available in respect of each vessel, including furniture, fittings, radio communication equipment, and other equipment attached to it, that:

(1) was constructed in Canada;

(2) is registered in Canada; and

(3) has not been used for any purpose whatever before acquisition by the owner.

Costs of a conversion or major alteration to a vessel in Canada also qualify for this accelerated CCA provision. Qualifying conversion costs form a separate CCA class for each vessel converted or altered.

Structured Financing Facilities

Only the basic Class 7 CCA rate of 15% will apply to a vessel or its equipment where a structured financing facility (under Industry Canada's Structured Financing Facility Program) relating to the property has been agreed to by Industry Canada.

Offshore Drilling Vessels

An offshore drilling vessel is included in Class 41(*b*), rather than Class 7, which has a CCA rate of 25% and is subject to the half-year rule.

(ITR: 1100(1)(v), (va), (2); 1101(2a), (2b), (2c); IT-267R2 Capital cost allowance — Vessels)

¶886t COMPUTERS AND OFFICE EQUIPMENT

[¶886t.05] Computers

CCA Classification of Computers

Computers, systems software (¶887), and ancillary data processing equipment are included in Class 50 at a 55% rate (subject to the half-year rule in the year of acquisition; see ¶802.10) if they are acquired after March 18, 2007 (other classes apply with respect to prior years).

What Is Considered a Computer?

"General-purpose electronic data processing equipment", "systems software", and "ancillary processing equipment" are all defined in 1104(2) of the *Income Tax Regulations*. Computers are generally considered to be "general-purpose electronic data processing equipment", which is defined as electronic equipment that, in its operation, requires an internally stored computer program that:

(1) is executed by the equipment;

(2) can be altered by the user of the equipment;

(3) instructs the equipment to read and select, alter, or store data from an external medium such as a card, disk or tape; and

(4) depends upon the characteristics of the data being processed to determine the sequence of its execution.

(ITR: 1101(5q); 1104(2) "general-purpose electronic data processing equipment", "systems software"; Sch. II Classes 10(*f*), 45, 50, 52; CRA Document No.: Expensed Vs. Capitalized, *July 16, 2004*, CRA Document No. 2004-0070211E5; Cca - Printer, *February 22, 2005*, CRA Document No. 2005-0112331E5)

Relevant CRA Documents

Evidently, this definition results in a broad interpretation of what may constitute a computer for tax purposes. In Document No. 2005-0163331I7, the CRA set out its views on the context and purpose of the definition of general-purpose electronic data processing equipment. The two notable conclusions made in this document are:

(1) "Equipment that contains a computer or computer chip, but the bulk of the value is in the physical machinery rather than the electronics," is not general-purpose electronic data processing equipment. Rather, it should be included in another CCA class based on its use.

(2) The term "general-purpose" is relevant to what property may be included. Therefore, equipment that is to be put to a special use will naturally be excluded from this classification.

Ancillary data processing equipment is not a defined term, but the CRA noted (in Document No. 2007-0243381C6) that it includes equipment that is subordinate to general-purpose electronic data processing equipment.

Exclusions from Class 50

Class 50 specifically excludes property that is principally or used principally as:

(1) electronic process control or monitor equipment;

(2) electronic communications control equipment;

(3) systems software for equipment referred to in (1) and (2); or

(4) data handling equipment

These exclusions intend to distinguish equipment which are used for routine monitoring, switching, and similar activities.

Historical Notes Information

Acquisitions After January 27, 2009 and Before February 2011

A computer would have been included in Class 52 at a 100% rate (not subject to the half-year rule) if it:

- was acquired after January 27, 2009, and before February 2011;
- was situated in Canada;
- had not been previously used or acquired for use; and
- was acquired to carry on a business or to earn property income in Canada
  - by yourself; or
  - by a lessee to which you leased the property.

Acquisitions Before March 19, 2007

Prior to the introduction of Class 50, computer equipment, as described above, was placed in the following classes:

- Class 45 (45%) — acquired after March 22, 2004, and before March 19, 2007, subject to the half-year rule
- Class 10(*f*) (30%) — acquired before March 23, 2004, subject to the half-year rule

[¶886t.08] *Computer Tax Shelter Rules*

Generally, if an investment's tax benefits over the first four years equal or exceed the amount paid for it, the investment is considered a tax shelter. The computer tax shelter rules apply to computer equipment and software that are included in Class 50 (and until recently, Class 52). For details on what constitutes a tax shelter, see ¶2521.10 and ¶2521.15.

Tax Treatment of Computer Tax Shelters

First, equipment and software that are computer tax shelters are lumped into a separate class, so that the tax shelter property will have its own recapture/terminal loss characteristics.

Second, CCA on computer equipment tax shelter property cannot be used except to reduce the income from the business in which that property is used to zero. Therefore, no loss may be created from CCA claims on tax sheltered computer equipment that would otherwise be used to reduce income from other sources.

(ITR: 1100(20.1), (20.2); 1101(5r); Other Publications: Department of Finance News Releases 97-069, 97-094)

[¶886t.10] *Office Equipment*

Office equipment which fails to qualify as being used for a special purpose, such as manufacturing and processing (¶878) or scientific research (¶740), is relegated to Class 8(*i*) as tangible property not otherwise classified. Telephone equipment of a sophisticated enough type may conceivably be included with computer equipment, as discussed at ¶887a.

[¶886t.12] *Printers*

In Document No. 2005-0163331I7, the CRA expressed its opinion regarding the classification of printers for CCA purposes. The taxpayer had three general types of printers, and the CRA's position with respect to each type is summarized below:

(1) The smaller multi-functional printers (with a cost of approximately $3,000 to $10,000), that were connected through a LAN system. Their capabilities included faxing, photocopying, scanning and printing. These smaller printers would be included in Class 50.

(2) The medium multi-functional printers with a cost in excess of $10,000, which were used in printing low volume presentation documents and also used for photocopying and faxing. These medium sized printers would be included in Class 50, as ancillary data processing equipment "to the extent that they are used in a similar fashion as the small printers." To the extent that the medium sized printers were not ancillary data processing equipment, they would not qualify as general-purposes electronic data processing equipment.

(3) Large printers with a cost exceeding $100,000, with their own CPU that are typically used in print shops and larger businesses. The CRA took the view that these large printers should be included in Class 8. The position is based on the fact that the printers were for a special use and the majority of their value was derived from the mechanical parts rather than the electronic components.

[¶886t.15] *Separate Classes for Computers, Faxes, Copiers*

You can elect to include in a separate class for one or more properties, each of which has a capital cost of at least $1,000 that is computer software (see ¶887), a photocopier, or electronic communications equipment (such as facsimile transmission devices or telephone equipment) that is normally included in Class 8. These assets would, in the event of your election, be included in separate Class 8 classes.

Making the Election

The election to include an item in a separate class must be made in the year of actual acquisition by letter filed with your tax return for that year. A separate class may be chosen for each or any group of qualifying Class 8 assets.

The advantage of a separate class election is that where the specific equipment is sold at a loss (or merely given away or junked), the terminal loss will be immediately recognized when incurred, rather than waiting until the UCC of Class 8 is completely depleted. This election recognizes that qualifying assets often depreciate at a rate exceeding that for tax purposes.

Property That Does Not Require Rapid Replacement

Where the equipment does not in fact require rapid replacement, each separate class is merged into the general class after five years. The counting of the five years does not begin until the class becomes available for use (¶804b). Transfers to the appropriate general class will occur under the general rules for transfers between classes; see ¶871.

For a discussion of separate classes generally, see ¶869–¶871.

(ITR: 1101(5p), (5q); 1103(2g))

¶886v DATA NETWORK INFRASTRUCTURE EQUIPMENT

"Data network infrastructure equipment" is included in Class 46 and depreciated at a rate of 30%. Data network infrastructure equipment is network infrastructure equipment that controls, transfers, modulates, or directs data, and that operates in support of telecommunications applications such as e-mail, instant messaging, audio- and video-over-internet protocol or web browsing, web searching and web hosting, including data switches, multiplexers, routers, remote access servers, hubs, domain name servers, and modems.

Excluded Property

The following assets are excluded from the definition of data network infrastructure equipment and hence not included in Class 46:

(1) network equipment (other than radio network equipment) that operates in support of telecommunications applications (subject to a speed limitation);

(2) radio network equipment that operates in support of wireless telecommunications applications unless the equipment supports digital transmission on a radio channel;

(3) network equipment that operates in support of broadcast telecommunications applications and that is unidirectional;

(4) network equipment that is end-user equipment, including telephone sets, personal digital assistants and facsimile transmission devices;

(5) telecommunications satellites or cablevision connection boxes (Class 10 assets) or computers and ancillary equipment and systems software (Class 50);

(6) wires or cables; and

(7) structures.

Relevant CRA Documents

According to Document No. 2007-0243381C6, the CRA would exclude an internet fax (FOIP) and IP(VoIP) telephone from Class 46 because of paragraph (d), above, which excludes "network equipment that is end-user equipment, including telephone sets, personal digital assistants and facsimile transmission devices".

(ITR: Sch. II Class 46; 1104(2) "data network infrastructure equipment"; CRA Document No.: Classification des Équipements de Bureautique, *October 5, 2007*, CRA Document No. 2007-0243381C6)

¶887 COMPUTER SOFTWARE

If you acquire computer software primarily for the purpose of use in your business, its nature, purpose, and anticipated life should be examined to determine whether it should be deducted in the year as a current expense or, because it is of an enduring nature (i.e., its useful life is anticipated to last beyond one year), capitalized as depreciable property.

Software Included in Class 12

Computer software includes system software and a right or licence to use software. Where software is considered to be a capital expenditure, the CCA class in which it is to be classified depends on whether or not it is system software. Computer software other than system software is included in Class 12, and is depreciated at a rate of 100% but subject to the half-year rule.

CCA Classification of Systems Software

Systems software includes computer programs and associated procedures, related documentation, and data that facilitate the functioning of a computer system by other programs. That is, systems software generally refers to the operating system that enables the computer to run, and directs and coordinates its different operations, including input and output between keyboard, screen, printer, external drives, and other peripherals.

Systems software is classified as follows:

(1) Class 50 (55%) if not used primarily in manufacturing and processing in Canada;

(2) Class 52 (100% with no half-year rule) if acquired after January 27, 2009 and before February 2011 and used in a business by you (or by a lessee) in Canada or for earning income from property situated in Canada; or

(3) Class 8 (20%) if it is used principally as electronic process control equipment, electronic communications control equipment, or data handling equipment not ancillary to general purpose computer equipment (included under Class 8(*i*) as tangible capital property not included in another class).

See ¶878 for details of qualification for manufacturing and processing classes. If you incur costs that are capital in nature in the development of software program for your own use, your capital cost with respect to that property includes labour, material, and overhead costs that are reasonably attributable to its development.

(ITR: Sch. II Classes 8, 10, 12, 29, 39, 40, 43, 45, 50, 52; 1104(2) "systems software")

¶887a TELEPHONE EQUIPMENT

Telephone equipment is generally included in Class 8 (20%). However, depending on the elements of the system, the equipment may be classified as "general purpose electronic data processing equipment" and therefore included in Class 50 (see ¶886t.05). For example, according to CRA Document No. 2009-0344551I7, an iPhone is included in Class 50 regardless of the fact that it is indeed a phone.

Telephone and fibre-optic wire or cable that was acquired after February 22, 2005 is specifically included in Class 42 (12%).

Separate Class Election

Telephone equipment may be eligible to be included in a separate Class 8 if it costs more than $1,000, which would allow for earlier terminal loss recognition if it proves to have a useful life of no more than five years. See ¶886t.

(ITR: Sch. II Classes 3, 8, 10, 17, 42, 45, 50, 52)

¶887c AUTOMOBILES

Automobiles are generally included in Class 10. However, automobiles with a capital cost exceeding $30,000 must be placed in a separate Class 10.1 and will have a deemed capital cost of $30,000. See ¶810a.

¶887d TRUCKS

Trucks are generally in Class 10 (30%) along with other automotive equipment. CCA claims with respect to small trucks, vans, and other vehicles may also be subject to the limitation discussed at ¶810a. Large trucks may rather be included in Class 16 (40%).

Large Trucks — Class 16

Tractors and trucks with a gross vehicle weight rating in excess of 11,788 kg. (or 26,000 lb.) may be included in Class 16 and depreciated at a higher rate of 40%. To qualify for Class 16, the truck or tractor must be designed to haul freight and be primarily used by yourself or a person with whom you do not deal with at arm's length in a business that includes hauling freight.

(ITR: Sch. II Classes 10, 16)

¶888 CONTRACTOR'S MOVABLE EQUIPMENT AND EARTH-MOVING EQUIPMENT

Contractor's Movable Equipment

Contractor's movable equipment is generally included in Class 10 (30%). The equipment generally includes any equipment that is normally moved from place to place in the course of construction and has been acquired for use in a construction business or for lease to another person for use in a construction business. Whether or not a large piece of equipment is movable is a question of the function of its particular use.

If the above conditions are not met, the property is included in the relevant manufacturing and processing class if used for such a purpose (see ¶878), or failing that will otherwise be included in Class 8.

Earth-Moving Equipment

Earth-moving equipment is power-operated movable equipment that is designed for the purpose of excavating, moving, placing or compacting earth, rock, concrete or asphalt. Earth-moving equipment is included in Class 38 (30%) provided that it does not belong in Class 7 (presumably only a dredging vessel would meet this exception; see ¶898).

The actual use of property is not a factor in determining whether or not it qualifies for inclusion in Class 38. Rather, it must simply be designed for the aforementioned use. Equipment is "powered-operated" where it is driven or handled by its own motor or a closely associated separate power source. Further, such equipment is considered "movable" if it is designed to move on its own wheels, treads or skids, or to be carried.

Relevant Case Law

A notable Tax Court case pertaining to earth-moving equipment, *L & R Asphalt Ltd. v. M.N.R.*, 89 DTC 266 (TCC) established some clarity with respect to the CCA classification of such equipment. The movability of equipment is sufficient — it need not be self-propelled; and equipment need not be designed exclusively or even primarily for the purposes set out in Class 38 in order to come within that class.

Separate Class for Earth-Moving Equipment

You may elect to put any particular Class 38 property in a separate class. The election must be made by a letter filed with a timely return for the year of acquisition. The advantage would be the ability to claim terminal loss on the particular piece of equipment if, for example, it were to be used for a season or two and abandoned. However, this may also accelerate the recapture of previously-deducted CCA.

(ITR: Sch. II Classes 22, 38; 1101(5l); 1100(1)(*zd*); IT-306R2 Capital cost allowance — Contractor's movable equipment; IT-469R Capital cost allowance — Earth-moving equipment)

¶889 FAST WRITE-OFF FOR ENERGY-EFFICIENT EQUIPMENT

[¶889.05] *Class 43.1*

There are two fast write-off classes in which energy-efficient equipment may be included. The first, Class 43.1 (30%), is regarded as the primary class for such equipment. The half-year rule applies. Historically, Class 43.1 has been subject to frequent amending over the years. There are various complex conditions that property must meet to be included in this class, but a general summary of this criteria is provided below.

For a more definitive description of what property may be included in Class 43.1, see ¶898. Although an effort has been made to keep track of changing acquisition dates in ¶898, there is no substitute for reading the actual regulations and their histories in a commercial version of the Act, such as Wolters Kluwer's Canadian Income Tax Act with Regulations.

Class 43.1 Property — Conditions

Property included in Class 43.1 (and by extension Class 43.2, see ¶889.10) must be:

- situated in Canada;
- acquired for the purpose of earning income from a business carried out in Canada or from property situated in Canada; and
- not have been previously used for any other purpose before being acquired.

There is an exception to the third condition of not being previously used. You may include the property in Class 43.1 if:

- the vendor had included it in Class 34, 43.1, or 43.2;
- the property remains in the same location where it was used by the vendor; and
- you acquired it within five years of the time that it became available for use by the vendor.

The CRA has stated in various technical interpretations that equipment that is demonstrated or tested for a taxpayer prior to it being acquired by the taxpayer will be considered to have not been previously used. However, equipment that is used by a vendor regularly for demonstration purposes will be considered to have been used by the vendor and so will not meet the "not previously used" condition.

Types of Property Included in Class 43.1

The types of assets that are included in Class 43.1 are described in paragraphs (a) to (d) of that Class under Schedule II of the *Income Tax Regulations* (see ¶898). The information contained here is not exhaustive. Depending on the use to which the equipment is put and various other conditions set out in paragraph (d), the equipment could qualify for Class 43.1, and by extension, Class 43.2.

Paragraphs (a) and (c) describe criteria relating to high efficiency cogeneration systems used to generate electricity or both electricity and heat using various fuels, including fossil fuel and eligible waste fuel and waste heat. The heat rate of an eligible co-generation system attributable to fossil fuel cannot exceed 6,000 BTUs.

Paragraph (d) sets out criteria for various types of renewable energy property, including:

- active solar heating equipment;
- fixed location wind energy conversion equipment;
- fixed location photovoltaic equipment;
- small-scale hydro-electric installations;
- equipment that converts wood waste or plant residue into bio-oil;
- equipment used to generate electrical energy from geothermal energy;
- equipment used to generate heat energy from eligible waste fuel;

Commentary on Legislative Proposals (July 29, 2016)

Note: When Legislative Proposals, July 29, 2016, achieves Royal Assent, the commentary will be modified to read:

- electrical energy storage property; and
- electric vehicle charging stations.

Anti-avoidance Rules

Note that Class 43.1 and 43.2 assets are subject to anti-avoidance rules to prevent passive investors from reducing other sources of income with CCA on Class 43.1 assets. These "specified energy property" rules are described at ¶889.25.

Determining Eligibility

For purposes of determining eligibility of energy conservation equipment for Class 43.1, the CRA may consult with Natural Resources Canada to determine if property is qualified. The Natural Resources Canada publication Technical Guide to Class 43.1 is deemed (by subsection 13(18.1) of the *Income Tax Act*) to be conclusive on engineering and scientific matters. Although not completely up-to-date, the Class 43.1 Technical Guide and Technical Guide to Canadian Renewable and Conservation Expenses (CRCE) can be found at the following URL:

https://www.nrcan.gc.ca/energy/efficiency/industry/financial-assistance/5147

In addition to what is discussed in the Technical Guide, many of the terms used in the description of Class 43.1 have explicit definitions set out in subsection 1104(13) of the *Income Tax Regulations.*

Historical Notes

For many years this class has been subject to various legislative amendments, which often expand the kinds of property that may be included in Class 43.1. Significant recent changes are summarized here.

2016 Changes

Commentary on Legislative Proposals (July 29, 2016)

Note: When Legislative Proposals, July 29, 2016, achieves Royal Assent, the commentary will be modified to read:

Classes Class 43.1 and Class 43.2 were expanded to include fixed location electric vehicle charging stations (and related equipment) and electrical energy storage property (i.e., batteries, compressed air storage, flywheels, ancillary equipment, and related structures) that are acquired after March 21, 2016 that had not been used or available for use before March 22, 2016. Existing references to similar electrical energy storage equipment located elsewhere in Class 43.1 were removed for clarity, so there is a single all-encompassing definition of such property now. The inclusion of fixed location fuel cell equipment was also expanded to include additional equipment that can be used to generate energy for ancillary electrolysis equipment.

Commentary on Legislative Proposals (Sept. 16, 2016)

Note: When Legislative Proposals, September 16, 2016, achieves Royal Assent, the commentary will be modified to read:

A retroactive change applies to heat recovery equipment included in Class 43.1(*d*)(iv). Previously, such equipment had to be used primarily for the purpose of conserving energy or reducing the requirement to acquire energy by extracting for reuse thermal waste that is generated by an industrial process. Applying retroactively to such equipment acquired after March 3, 2010, Class Class 43.1(*d*)(iv) was expanded to include heat recovery equipment used primarily for the purpose of extracting heat for sale.

2014 Changes

Effective for new equipment acquired after February 10, 2014, the 2014 federal Budget expanded Class 43.1 to include equipment used to gasify eligible waste fuel and equipment that generates energy from water currents.

2013 Changes

The 2013 federal Budget expanded what types of property may be included in Class 43.1. Acquired after March 20, 2013, the following assets may also be included in the class:

(1) biogas production equipment that uses pulp and paper waste, wastewater, beverage industry waste and wastewater, and separated organics from municipal waste; and

(2) cleaning and upgrading equipment that transforms biogas, landfill gas, or digester gas into biomethane.

Further, to be included in Class 43.1, both of these types of equipment must comply with environmental laws and regulations at the time the equipment becomes available for use.

2012 Changes

The section of Class 43.1 that pertains to waste-fueled thermal energy equipment was amended. After March 28, 2012, it includes such equipment that uses plant residue to generate electricity and heat.

[¶889.10] *Class 43.2*

Certain equipment acquired after February 22, 2005 and before 2020 that would otherwise be included under specific provisions of Class 43.1 is eligible for inclusion in Class 43.2, which is depreciated at a 50% declining balance rate and subject to the half-year rule. Property in this class is also subject to the anti-avoidance rules discussed at ¶889.25.

Property Included in Class 43.2

Class 43.2 operates by reference to Class 43.1. Assets in Class 43.2 are those assets that are described in paragraphs (a) to (c) of Class 43.1 (i.e., energy conservation equipment) if the heat rate of a cogeneration system attributable to fossil fuel (defined in Regulation 1104(13)) does not exceed 4,750 BTUs and assets that are described in paragraph (d) of Class 43.1 (i.e., alternative fuel energy equipment or other renewable energy equipment).

Commentary on Legislative Proposals (July 29, 2016)

Note: When Legislative Proposals, July 29, 2016, achieves Royal Assent, the commentary will be modified to read:

Class 43.2 operates by reference to Class 43.1. Assets in Class 43.2 are those assets that are described in paragraphs (*a*) to (*c*) of Class 43.1. With respect to equipment included under 43.1(*c*)(i), the heat rate attributable to fossil fuel cannot not exceed 4,750 BTUs in order to be included in Class 43.2. Assets described in paragraph (*d*) of Class 43.1 (i.e., alternative fuel energy equipment or other renewable energy equipment) are also eligible for inclusion in Class 43.2. With respect to electric vehicle charging stations and fixed location energy storage property acquired after March 21, 2016 that would otherwise be included in Class 43.1, these types of equipment must meet additional criteria in order to be included in Class 43.2. Electric vehicle charging stations must meet certain requirements with respect to supplying power (see 43.2(*b*)(ii)) and fixed location energy storage property must store energy in connection with Class 43.2 property.

Since Class 43.2 operates by reference to Class 43.1, the Technical Guide and the definitions in subsection 1104(13) and 1104(17) of the *Income Tax Regulations* referred to in ¶889.05 also govern Class 43.2 inclusions.

If the majority of tangible property in a project is eligible for inclusion in Class 43.1 or 43.2, then certain intangible expenses related to the project such as engineering and design work and feasibility studies qualify as Canadian Renewable and Conservation Expenses (see ¶889.30).

(ITA: 13(18.1); ITR: Sch. II Classes 43.1, 43.2; 1100(24), (25); 1102(8), (9); 1103(4); 1104(13), (14), (17); 8200.1; CRA Document No.: Renewable Energy Property, *March 9, 2007*, CRA Document No. 2007-0225661E5; Geothermal Heating and Cooling Systems, *June 11, 2012*, CRA Document No. 2012-0433611E5; Installation of Solar Panels, *February 29, 2012*, CRA Document No. 2012-0435151E5; Ontario FIT / microFIT Programs, *October 15, 2012*, CRA Document No. 2012-0458201E5; Clarification of Class 43.2 Project Eligibility, *December 18, 2012*, CRA Document No. 2012-0468301E5)

[¶889.15] *Classes 43.1 and 43.2 Versus Class 29*

It is possible that property may be included in Class 43.1 and/or 43.2 and also in Class 29 (for property acquired before 2016) for manufacturing and processing property (¶878). Class 43.1 and 43.2 prevail in these circumstances, but an election is available so that such dual qualifying property can be more quickly depreciated in Class 29. The Regulation 1102(16.1) election permits a taxpayer to elect to include in Class 29 particular items of M&P machinery and equipment which would qualify for Class 29 if they did not first fall into Class 43.1 or 43.2. The election must be made by letter attached to the return of income for the taxation year in which the property is acquired. This being said, the election is unavailable for property acquired after 2015 as Class 29 will be closed for new additions at that time.

Manufacturing and processing equipment acquired after 2015 and before 2026 will instead be included in Class 53, which does not have an equivalent election.

(ITR: 1102(16.1))

[¶889.20] *Combustion Turbines*

The kinds of combustion turbine generators discussed here are, generally speaking, large generators used in the business of producing electrical energy for sale to others. Combustion turbines (including associated burners and compressors) which generate electrical energy are included in Class 48 (15%) provided that they are acquired after February 22, 2005. The half-year rule applies to Class 48.

Exclusions from Class 48

Some energy-efficient electrical generating equipment will qualify for Class 43.1 or Class 43.2; any turbines which might fall into these classes will not be subject to the rules here. Class descriptions are found at ¶898. Small generators (less than 15kw), portable generators, auxiliary generators, and generators not used as a main source of supply are included in Class 8 (20%).

Historical Notes — Transition from Class 17

Combustion turbines were, if acquired after February 27, 2000 and before February 23, 2005, included in Class 17(*a*.1)(i) (8%) with other electrical generating equipment. Turbines acquired after this date are included in Class 48. Class 17 combustion turbines that generate electricity were, prior to February 23, 2005, eligible for a separate class election. To accommodate taxpayers who had already planned purchases based on the availability of the separate class election, the election was left in force until 2005 ended. Thus, if you purchased a combustion turbine in 2005 in contemplation of including it in the separate Class 17, but the new rule would have included it in Class 48, you may have elected to include the property in Class 17 as long as you acquired it before 2006.

(ITR: 1103(2g))

[¶889.25] *"Specified Energy Property" Restrictions*

Under these rules, the total of all CCA claims in a year with respect to "specified energy property" cannot exceed income for the year from that property. Specified energy property includes Class 43.1, Class 43.2, Class 47 (electricity transmission assets which carry an 8% CCA rate), and Class 48 (combustion turbines which carry a 15% CCA rate). It is the total amount of all expenditures for such property in a year and income from all such property that is subject to the limitation.

Specified energy property excludes property that you acquired to be used primarily to earn income from a business carried on in Canada (other than the business of selling the product of that property) or property that you acquired to lease to a lessee who will use it for the same aforementioned purpose. For example, a farmer buying Class 43.2 wind energy conversion equipment for supplementary farm energy to be used in his or her farming operation can deduct the full CCA amount from all sources of income.

(ITR: 1100(24)–(27); 1101(5m))

[¶889.30] *Canadian Renewable and Conservation Expenses ("CRCEs")*

CRCEs are expenses incurred within the preparatory phase of renewable energy and energy conservation projects for which the equipment will likely to be included in Class 43.1 and 43.2. CRCE expenditures are deemed to be Canadian Exploration Expenses (CEE — ¶2210) and indeed are similar in kind to those expenses except that the nature of the projects is different. Eligible expenses are defined from time to time by the Department of Natural Resources in a Technical Guide to Canadian Renewable and Conservation expenses, which is deemed (by the definition of "Canadian renewable and conservation expense" in subsection 66.1(6) of the *Income Tax Act*) to be conclusive with regard to engineering and scientific matters.

Tax Treatment of CRCEs

Since they are deemed to be CEE, CRCEs form a pool of expenses which can be deducted to the extent chosen up to 100% in a year and can be syndicated to investors through flow-through share mechanisms (¶2521.50). CRCEs qualify for the "look-back" rule under which companies can renounce expenses to be incurred in the coming year, subject to a transaction tax. The look-back rule is discussed in ¶227.35 under the subheading "Instalments and Flow-Through Shares".

Natural Resources Canada's Technical Guide to Class 43.1 and 43.2, and Technical Guide to Canadian Renewable and Conservation Expenses (CRCE) are available at the following URL:

https://www.nrcan.gc.ca/energy/efficiency/industry/financial-assistance/5147

(ITA: 66.1(6) "Canadian renewable and conservation expense"; ITR: 1219)

¶889f PIPELINES AND RELATED EQUIPMENT; LIQUEFIED NATURAL GAS FACILITIES

Transmission Pipelines

A pipeline that is used for the transmission (but not distribution) of petroleum, natural gas, or related hydrocarbons is eligible for inclusion in Class 49 (8%) provided that it was acquired after February 22, 2005 and that it had not been used or acquired for use before that date. An amendment was made to include transmission pipelines for carbon dioxide acquired after February 25, 2008.

Control and monitoring devices, valves, and other equipment ancillary to the pipeline is also included in Class 49.

Class 49 specifically excludes:

- distribution pipelines (see ¶889f.15);
- property acquired before February 23, 2005 for petroleum related pipelines;
- property acquired before February 26, 2008 for carbon dioxide related pipelines;
- related pumping and compression equipment, or equipment ancillary to pumping and compression equipment (Class 7 property); and
- a building or other structure.

Pumping and Compression Equipment

Pumping and compression equipment, and equipment ancillary to pumping and compression, are included in Class 7 (15%) provided that they were acquired after February 22, 2005 for petroleum-related pipelines and after February 25, 2008 for carbon dioxide pipelines. The equipment must pump or compress petroleum, natural gas, carbon dioxide, or related hydrocarbons to move it:

(1) through a transmission pipeline;

(2) from a transmission pipeline to a storage facility; or

(3) to a transmission pipeline from a storage facility.

The half-year rule applies to Class 49 and Class 7.

Historical Notes

Prior to February 24, 2005, transmission pipelines were included in Class 1 (4%). However, a pipeline for oil or natural gas would be included in Class 8 (20%), "if the Minister, in consultation with the Minister of Natural Resources, is or has been satisfied that the main source of supply for the pipeline is or was likely to be exhausted within 15 years after the date on which operation of the pipeline commenced". Ministerial exclusions apart, petroleum pumping and compression equipment on such pipelines was generally not included in Class 1, on the argument that it is not specifically referred to anywhere in the CCA regulations. According to the 2005 federal Budget papers, the owners of such equipment had generally been successful in including it in Class 8, the default class for unlisted tangible property

[¶889f.10] *Separate Classes*

You may elect to include each of one or more Class 49 transmission pipelines and Class 7(*j*) and (*k*) items of pumping and compression equipment in a separate CCA class. The election must be made by attaching a letter to your tax return for the year in which the property is acquired. The separate class election allows any remaining undepreciated balance in the class to be fully deducted as a terminal loss following the disposition of the property.

(ITR: 1101(5u), (5v))

[¶889f.15] *Natural Gas Distribution Pipelines Acquired after March 18, 2007*

Natural gas distribution (as opposed to transmission) pipelines were left in Class 1 (4%) by the 2005 changes. However, natural gas distribution pipelines acquired after March 18, 2007 (including control and monitoring devices, valves, metering, and regulating equipment and other equipment ancillary to a distribution pipeline, but not buildings or other structures) which have not been used, or acquired for use, before that date, are included in Class 51 (6%).

(ITR: 1101(5u), (5v))

[¶889f.30] *Pipelines Generally*

Subject to the exceptions above, the general rule remains that pipelines are a Class 1 property, subject to the ministerial determination which can include them in Class 8.

[¶889f.40] *Liquefied Natural Gas ("LNG") Equipment*

LNG equipment acquired after March 18, 2007 that is part of an LNG facility that liquefies the gas prior to shipment or regasifies it after transportation is included in Class 47 (8%). LNG equipment includes:

- controls;
- cooking equipment;
- compressors;
- pumps;
- storage tanks;
- vaporizers and ancillary equipment;
- loading and unloading pipelines; and
- related structures.

However, LNG equipment does not include:

- property acquired to produce oxygen or nitrogen;
- a breakwater, dock, jetty, wharf, or similar structure; or
- a building.

LNG equipment acquired prior to March 19, 2007 was included in Class 1 (4%).

The half-year rule applies to Class 47.

[¶889f.41] *Accelerated Depreciation of LNG Equipment*

On February 19, 2015, the government announced new regulations that accelerate the CCA claims of LNG equipment and facilities. The additional allowance for Class 47 LNG equipment is 22%, which raises the total CCA rate for such equipment to 30%. Further, an additional 6% CCA rate applies to buildings that are part of an LNG facility, bringing the total CCA rate to 10%.

If you acquire any LNG equipment that belongs in Class 47, you may be eligible to accelerate the CCA rate for that equipment. You are allowed to claim an additional 22% of annual CCA with respect to LNG equipment if:

- you acquired that property after February 19, 2015, and before 2025;
- the property is included in Class 47;
- the property has not been used or acquired for use for any purpose before you acquired it;
- the property is not excluded equipment (see below); and
- the property is used as a part of an eligible liquefaction facility (see below also)

Excluded equipment is comprised of pipelines (other than those used within the facility or used to move the LNG), regasification equipment, and electrical generation equipment. An eligible liquefaction facility is a self-contained system located in Canada (including buildings, structures, and equipment) that is used or intended to be used for the purpose of liquefying natural gas.

Accelerated CCA for LNG Equipment

The 8% normal Class 47 CCA rate in tandem with the 22% accelerated amount allows you to claim CCA on your LNG equipment at a rate of 30%. The half-year rule also applies to the calculation of the accelerated amount. Class 47 property that is eligible liquefaction equipment used as a part of an eligible liquefaction facility must be included in a separate class. Thus, recapture is not deferred upon the disposition of that equipment.

The accelerated amount can only be deducted to the extent of your income from liquefaction activities. This includes income from selling the LNG that you liquefied if you owned the gas when it entered the facility, from selling related byproducts, and from providing liquefaction services to natural gas owned by a third-party.

Accelerated CCA for Liquefaction Buildings

In addition to the accelerated CCA rates for LNG equipment discussed above, you may claim an additional 6% CCA claim with respect to Class 1 (4%) buildings that are eligible liquefaction buildings. Therefore, the combined CCA rate with respect to these buildings is 10%. The half-year rule also applies. An eligible liquefaction building is a building that meets the following criteria:

- it has not been used or acquired for use for any purpose before you acquired it;
- it is not a residential building;
- you acquired it after February 19, 2015, and before 2025;
- it is included in Class 1 because of paragraph (q) of that class; and
- it is used as a part of the eligible liquefaction facility.

Again, the CCA claim from the accelerated amount is limited to your income from liquefaction activities, which is explained above. Eligible liquefaction buildings must each be included in a separate class and the election out of this treatment is unavailable for such buildings.

(ITR: 1100(1)(*a*.3), (*yb*), (4i); 1104(2), (18))

¶890 RAILWAY CARS, TRACKS, AND TRACK-RELATED ASSETS

Railway Locomotives

Railway locomotives that have not been used or acquired for use before February 26, 2008, are included in Class 10(*y*) (30%). Regulations 1102(19.1) and (19.2) provide, in effect, that property to be incorporated into an older (pre-Class 10) class in the course of its refurbishment or reconditioning is also included in Class 10(*y*). Railway locomotives that had been used or acquired before February 26, 2008 were previously included in Class 7 (15%). In all cases, the rules specify that, for greater certainty, locomotives do not include automotive railway cars.

Railway Cars

Railway cars and railway suspension devices are included in Class 7 (15%). Certain "suspension devices" (which carry trailers suitable for both highway and rail track) are also included in Class 7. Previously, such property was included in Class 35 (7%).

Railway trestles are included in Class 3(*d*) (5%), and much other railway equipment, such as track, signals, and so on, is included in Class 1(*h*) and Class 1(*h*)(i) (4%).

For particulars of these classes, see ¶898. The half-year rule applies in all cases; see ¶802.

Planning Opportunity

You might be eligible for an election to include railway cars in Class 35 rather than Class 7 and depreciate them at a slightly lower rate of 13% (i.e., 6% + usual 7% for Class 35). The property must otherwise be eligible for the additional 6% allowance for railway cars (in the case of lessors) or for railway cars and suspension devices (in the case of common carriers) to make the election. See ¶890.05 and ¶890.10 for further details on these additional allowances.

Including railway cars in Class 35 would exempt them from the specified leasing property treatment discussed at ¶873a. Failure to elect leaves the property in Class 7 (15%), but the specified leasing property rules will apply. The election must be made by a letter filed with your return for the year of acquisition.

The half-year rule applies to Class 35.

(ITR: 1100(1.13); 1102(19.1), (19.2); 1103(2i); Sch. II Classes 1, 3, 6, 7, 10, 35)

[¶890.05] *Additional Allowance: Other than Common Carriers*

In addition to ordinary Class 35 depreciation (7%), railway cars included in Class 35 that you rent out, lease, or own, and are used in Canada (other than railway cars owned by a corporation that is a common carrier that owns or operates a railway, or a corporation associated with such a corporation) are included in a separate class and are eligible for an additional 6% of CCA.

Although the term "common carrier" is not defined in the Act, Black's Law Dictionary (8th ed.) defines it as "[*a*] *commercial enterprise that holds itself out to the public as offering to transport freight or passengers for a fee.*" All of the railway cars for rent or lease are included in their own separate Class 35 and all the cars not for rent or lease are given their own separate Class 35. The half-year rule also applies to the additional allowance.

(ITR: Sch. II Class 35; 1100(1)(*z*.1*a*); 1101(5*d*); 1103(2*d*))

[¶890.10] *Additional Allowance: Common Carriers*

Additional allowances are available for railway property acquired by common carriers that own and operate a railway. The definition of a "common carrier" is described in ¶890.05. The additional allowances are achieved by providing separate classes for various types of railway property and attaching an additional allowance to each. If your business is that of a common carrier, the separate classes are as follows:

(1) a separate class which carries a 6% allowance (in addition to the 7% Class 35 rate) is prescribed for all Class 35 property;

(2) a separate class which carries a 6% allowance (in addition to the 4% Class 1 rate) is prescribed for all Class 1 property, which is described in paragraph (h) or (i) of Class 1 or is a Class 1 bridge, culvert, subway or tunnel that is ancillary to railway track and grading; and

(3) a separate class which carries a 5% allowance (in addition to the 5% Class 3 rate) is prescribed for Class 3 trestles ancillary to railway track and grading.

For particulars of these classes, see ¶898. The half-year rule applies in all cases; see ¶802.

The normal restrictions on separate classes described at ¶869 apply, as does the restriction against use of the deferral of recapture provision described in ¶870, item (1).

(ITR: Sch. II Classes 1, 3, 35; 1100(1)(*z*.1*c*), (*za*.1), (*za*.2); 1101(5*d*.2), (5*e*.1), (5*e*.2); 1103(2*d*))

¶891 ART AND ANTIQUES

You will not be able to claim CCA on certain antiques and art purchased for your business. Such property where CCA cannot be claimed is:

(1) a print, etching, drawing, painting, sculpture, or other similar work of art, the cost of which was $200 or more;

(2) a hand-woven tapestry or carpet or a handmade appliqué, the cost of which was $215 per square metre or more;

(3) an engraving, etching, lithograph, woodcut, map or chart, made before 1900; or

(4) antique furniture, or any other antique object, produced more than 100 years before the date it was acquired, the cost of which was $1,000 or more.

There are, however, no restrictions on CCA on property described in (1) and (2), above, where the person who created the property was a Canadian at the time the property was created. A Canadian for this purpose is a Canadian citizen as defined in the *Citizenship Act* or a permanent resident within the meaning of the *Immigration Act*.

Generally speaking, works of art which do qualify for CCA (specified Canadian art) are Class 8 assets, are depreciated at a rate of 20%. For the Quebec rules with respect to the depreciation of art, see ¶1633.55.

(ITR: 1102(1)(*e*); 1104(10)(*a*))

¶892 ACCELERATED ALLOWANCES FOR QUALIFYING MINES (INCLUDING OIL SANDS)

CCA Classification of Mining Property

Most machinery, equipment, and structures used to produce income from resource extraction including buildings and community infrastructure related to worker accommodations are included in Class 41 (25%). Oil sands property that would otherwise be included in Class 41 is included in Class 41.1 (25%) if acquired after March 18, 2007 (see ¶892.10). Mining assets, other than "eligible mine development property", that would otherwise be included in Class 41 are included in Class 41.2 (25%) if acquired after March 20, 2013.

"Eligible mine development property" is defined in Regulation 1104(2) as mining assets acquired after March 20, 2013 and before 2018 for a new mine or mine expansion under a written agreement entered into before March 21, 2013 or where the construction or engineering work was started before March 21, 2013. Eligible mine development property can be included in Class 41 and will not be subject to the phase out of the additional allowance (see below).

If mining equipment does not fall into Class 41, 41.1, or 41.2, it qualifies for a 30% rate under Class 10(*k*) with no additional allowance. Equipment for processing foreign ore in Canada is eligible for Class 43 (30%) treatment (see ¶878.10).

A "mine" and "income from a mine" are variously defined in Regulations 1104(3)–(8.1), and these definitions determine what type of mining and what stage of production is involved in assigning equipment to Class 10, 41, 41.1, 41.2 or 43. These regulations are so detailed that there is no substitute for reading them.

Additional Accelerated Allowance

In addition to the 25% allowance provided in Class 41, Class 41.1 and Class 41.2, you may claim an additional allowance in respect of a mine which came into production in reasonable commercial quantities after November 7, 1969, or was the subject of a major expansion thereafter. A major expansion is one in which output of the mine is increased by at least 25%,

The additional CCA accelerates the write-off of the mining property and is equal to the lesser of:

(1) the remaining UCC of property of the class; and

(2) your income for the year from the mine.

For this provision, income for the year from the mine is determined before making any deductions for depletion or exploration and development expenses, or the additional CCA mentioned in this paragraph.

Separate Class Rules

If you own property which qualifies for inclusion in Class 41 or Class 41.2, and the properties you own were acquired for use in more than one qualifying mine, you must establish separate classes of property for the fixed assets applicable to each of such mines. The limitation on the additional allowance each year is then calculated separately on the basis of the UCC of each such separate class, and the income and exempt income of each mine. In addition, separate classes are required to be maintained for each mine where the additional allowance provisions are applicable.

Property Ineligible for Accelerated CCA

For purposes of accelerated CCA amounts, qualifying mines exclude:

- sand pit;
- gravel pit;
- clay pit;
- shale pit;
- peat bog;
- deposit of peat; or
- stone quarry.

Equipment for these uses would most commonly fall into Class 41 (but without the accelerated write-off), being included by virtue of Class 41(*b*) from its initial description in Class 10(*k*), (*l*), or (*m*). See the discussion of industrial mineral mines at ¶883. On the other hand, extraction of oil from bituminous sands (oil sands) by surface mining techniques, as well as by in situ extraction, is considered mining (but not industrial mineral mining) rather than operating an oil well (see ¶892.10).

Phase-Out of Additional Allowances in Class 41.2

Mining assets acquired after March 20, 2013 and before 2021 are included in Class 41.2(*a*) and are eligible for the full additional accelerated CCA in addition to the 25% until 2016, after which it is phased out from 2017 to 2021. The additional allowance will be phased out on a calendar year basis as follows:

- 2013-2016, 100%
- 2017, 90%
- 2018, 80%
- 2019, 60%
- 2020, 30%
- 2021, nil

Mining assets acquired after 2020 are included in Class 41.2, however they are not eligible for additional accelerated CCA in addition to the 25%.

[¶892.05] *Alternative Classification*

Some expenditures related to depreciable property for mining may be available as development expenses rather than through CCA. Where this is true, it will permit not only accelerated write-offs, but syndicated or tax-sheltered financing through flow-through shares (¶2521).

[¶892.10] *Oil Sand Assets*

Assets acquired before March 19, 2007 for use in the extraction of oil from bituminous sands (oil sands), including surface mining and in situ extraction, were previously included in Class 41 (25%). Oil sand assets acquired after March 18, 2007 and before 2016 are included in Class 41.1 and are eligible for the full additional accelerated CCA in addition to the 25% until 2010, after which it is phased out from 2011 to 2015. The additional allowance will be phased out on a calendar year basis as follows:

- 2007-2010, 100%
- 2011, 90%
- 2012, 80%
- 2013, 60%
- 2014, 30%

- 2015, nil

Oil sand assets acquired after 2015 are included in Class 41.1, however they are not eligible for additional accelerated CCA in addition to the 25%. The calculation of the accelerated CCA amount is the same as Class 41 mining assets described at ¶892.

(ITR: 1100(1)(y), (y.1), (ya), (ya.1); 1101(4c), (4d), (4e), (4f); 1102(14), (14.1), (14.11), (14.12); 1104(2)–(8.1); Sch. II Classes 41, 41.1, 41.2; IT-469R Capital cost allowance — Earth-moving equipment)

¶897c CLASSIFICATION OF ASSETS RECEIVED IN NON-ARM'S LENGTH TRANSACTION

The *Income Tax Regulations* require property received in non-arm's length transactions to be assigned to the same class in the hands of the transferee that it occupied in the hands of the transferor. For example, a Class 29 property to the transferor will become Class 29 to the transferee, although it might otherwise have been Class 8 or 39 to the transferee.

Non-Arm's Length Transfer of Mining or Oil Sands Property

An exception to the same class rules applies for Class 41 property with respect to oil sands property acquired after March 18, 2007 and mining property acquired after March 20, 2013. The transferee can include in Class 41 the lesser of the transferor's UCC of the property prior to disposition and the amount, if any, that the UCC is reduced as a result of the transfer. Any remaining portion is included in Class 41.1 or 41.2 as the case may be.

These rules apply to non-arm's length transactions described at ¶812, except those transactions which are non-arm's length only by reason of "control" existing through the existence of share options or redemption/cancellation rights. They also apply to butterfly transactions.

(ITR: 1102(14), (14.1); 1102(14.11); 1102(14.12))

[¶898] CAPITAL COST ALLOWANCE CLASSES AND RATES

The following are the capital cost classes and rates prescribed for 2016. Notes have been added throughout to clarify some of the descriptions or to indicate other classes where certain assets may also be described.

Class 1 (4 per cent)

Property not included in any other class that is

(*a*) a bridge;

(*b*) a canal;

(*c*) a culvert;

(*d*) a dam;

(*e*) a jetty acquired before May 26, 1976;

(*f*) a mole acquired before May 26, 1976;

(*g*) a road, sidewalk, airplane runway, parking area, storage area or similar surface construction, acquired before May 26, 1976;

(*h*) railway track and grading, including components such as rails, ballast, ties and other track material,

(i) that is not part of a railway system, or

(ii) that was acquired after May 25, 1976;

(*i*) railway traffic control or signalling equipment, acquired after May 25, 1976, including switching, block signalling, interlocking, crossing protection, detection, speed control or retarding equipment, but not including property that is principally electronic equipment or systems software therefor;

(*j*) a subway or tunnel, acquired after May 25, 1976;

(*k*) electrical generating equipment; (except as specified elsewhere in this Schedule); (Note: e.g., Classes 8(f) to (h), 17, 43.1, 43.2, or 48);

(*l*) a pipeline, other than:

(i) a pipeline that is gas or oil well equipment, and

(ii) a pipeline that is for oil or natural gas if the Minister, in consultation with the Minister of Natural Resources, is or has been satisfied that the main source of supply for the pipeline is or was likely to be exhausted within 15 years after the date on which the operation of the pipeline commenced;

(Note: Transmission pipelines (as contrasted with distribution lines) for petroleum, natural gas or related hydrocarbons acquired on or after February 23, 2005 that are not used or acquired for use before that date are eligible for an 8% rate in Class 49. Property eligible for the 8% rate will include control and monitoring devices, valves and other ancillary equipment (other than pumping and compression equipment, which will be given a 15% rate (in Class 7(j)). Transmission pipelines are eligible for a separate class election in the year of acquisition (see ¶869), allowing a terminal loss on disposition. Distribution pipelines to the ultimate consumers continue to be included in Class 1, eligible for a 4% CCA rate, except that natural gas distribution pipelines acquired after March 18, 2007 are included in Class 51 instead. See ¶889f.)

(*m*) the generating or distributing equipment and plant (including structures) of a producer or distributor of electrical energy; *(Note: For new generating equipment (other than buildings and structures) acquired after February 27, 2000, see Class 17; for transmission and distribution assets acquired on or after February 23, 2005, and not used or acquired for use before that date, see Class 47; for combustion turbines, see Class 48)*

(*n*) manufacturing and distributing equipment and plant (including structures) acquired primarily for the production or distribution of gas, except:

(i) a property acquired for the purpose of producing or distributing gas that is normally distributed in portable containers,

(ii) a property acquired for the purpose of processing natural gas, before the delivery of such gas to a distribution system, or

(iii) a property acquired for the purpose of producing oxygen or nitrogen;

(Note, however, that liquefied natural gas facilities acquired after March 18, 2007 are allowed an 8% rate in Class 47.)

(*o*) the distributing equipment and plant (including structures) of a distributor of water (Note: For new equipment (other than buildings and other structures) acquired after February 27, 2000 other than by a distributor of water for consumption, disposal or treatment, see Class 17);

(*p*) the production and distributing equipment and plant (including structures) of a distributor of heat; or (*Note: For new equipment (other than buildings and other structures) acquired after February 27, 2000, see Class 17)*

(*q*) a building or other structure, or a part of it, including any component parts such as electric wiring, plumbing, sprinkler systems, air-conditioning equipment, heating equipment, lighting fixtures, elevators and escalators (except property described in any of paragraphs (k) and (m) to (p) of this Class or in any of paragraphs (a) to (e) of Class 8). (Note: For additional allowances on non-residential buildings, see ¶875.03.)

Class 2 (6 per cent)

(Note: Class 2 does not include property acquired after 1987, subject to certain grandfathering provisions for property acquired before 1990.)

Property that is:

(*a*) electrical generating equipment (except as specified elsewhere in this Schedule);

(*b*) a pipeline, other than gas or oil well equipment, unless, in the case of a pipeline for oil or natural gas, the Minister in consultation with the Minister of Energy, Mines and Resources, is or has been satisfied that the main source of supply for the pipeline is or was likely to be exhausted within 15 years from the date on which operation of the pipeline commenced;

(*c*) the generating or distributing equipment and plant (including structures) of a producer or distributor of electrical energy, except a property included in Class 10, 13, 14, 26, or 28;

(*d*) manufacturing and distributing equipment and plant (including structures) acquired primarily for the production or distribution of gas, except

(i) a property included in Class 10, 13, or 14,

(ii) a property acquired for the purpose of producing or distributing gas that is normally distributed in portable containers,

(iii) a property acquired for the purpose of processing natural gas, before delivery of such a gas to a distribution system, or

(iv) a property acquired for the purpose of producing oxygen or nitrogen;

(*e*) the distributing equipment and plant (including structures) of a distributor of water, except a property included in Class 10, 13, or 14; or

(*f*) the production and distributing equipment and plant (including structures) of a distributor of heat, except a property included in Class 10, 13, or 14;

acquired by the taxpayer

(*g*) before 1988, or

(*h*) before 1990

(i) pursuant to an obligation in writing entered into by the taxpayer before June 18, 1987,

(ii) that was under construction by or on behalf of the taxpayer on June 18, 1987, or

(iii) that is machinery or equipment that is a fixed and integral part of a building, structure, plant facility or other property that was under construction by or on behalf of the taxpayer on June 18, 1987.

Class 3 (5 per cent)

Property not included in any other class that is

(*a*) a building or other structure, or part thereof, including component parts such as electric wiring, plumbing, sprinkler systems, air-conditioning equipment, heating equipment, lighting fixtures, elevators and escalators, acquired by the taxpayer

(i) before 1988, or

(ii) before 1990

(A) pursuant to an obligation in writing entered into by the taxpayer before June 18, 1987,

(B) that was under construction by or on behalf of the taxpayer on June 18, 1987, or

(C) that is a component part of a building that was under construction by or on behalf of the taxpayer on June 18, 1987;

(*b*) a breakwater;

(*c*) a dock;

(*d*) a trestle;

(*e*) a windmill;

(*f*) a wharf;

(*g*) an addition or alteration, made during the period that is after March 31, 1967 and before 1988, to a building that would have been included in this class during that period but for the fact that it was included in Class 20;

(*h*) a jetty acquired after May 25, 1976;

(*i*) a mole acquired after May 25, 1976;

(*j*) telephone, telegraph or data communication equipment, acquired after May 25, 1976, that is a wire or cable; (Note: New wire or cable acquired after February 22, 2005, is allowed a 12% rate in Class 42; there is no suggestion that ancillary equipment in (l), below, qualifies for the higher rate)

(*k*) an addition or alteration, other than an addition or alteration described in paragraph (k) of Class 6, made after 1987, to a building included, in whole or in part,

(i) in this class,

(ii) in Class 6 by virtue of subparagraph (a)(viii) thereof, or

(iii) in Class 20,

to the extent that the aggregate cost of all such additions or alterations to the building does not exceed that lesser of

(iv) $500,000, and

(v) 25% of the aggregate of the amounts that would, but for this paragraph, be the capital cost of the building and any additions or alterations thereto included in this class or Class 6 or 20; or

(*l*) ancillary to a wire or cable referred to in paragraph (j) or Class 42 and that is supporting equipment such as a pole, mast, tower, conduit, brace, crossarm, guy or insulator.

Class 4 (6 per cent)

Property that would otherwise be included in another class in this Schedule that is (*a*) a railway system or a part thereof, except automotive equipment not designed to run on rails or tracks, that was acquired after the end of the taxpayer's 1958 taxation year and before May 26, 1976; or

(*b*) a tramway or trolley bus system or a part thereof, except property included in Class 10, 13 or 14.

Class 5 (10 per cent)

(Note: Class 5 does not include property acquired after taxpayer's 1962 taxation year.)

Property that is

(*a*) a chemical pulp mill or ground wood pulp mill, including buildings, machinery and equipment, but not including hydro-electric power plants and their equipment, or

(*b*) an integrated mill producing chemical pulp or ground wood pulp and manufacturing therefrom paper, paper board or pulp board, including buildings, machinery and equipment, but not including hydro-electric power plants and their equipment,

but not including any property that was acquired after the end of the taxpayer's 1962 taxation year.

Class 6 (10 per cent)

Property not included in any other class that is

(*a*) a building of

(i) frame,

(ii) log,

(iii) stucco on frame,

(iv) galvanized iron, or

(v) corrugated metal

construction, including component parts such as electric wiring, plumbing, sprinkler systems, air-conditioning equipment, heating equipment, lighting fixtures, elevators and escalators, if the building

(vi) is used by the taxpayer for the purpose of gaining or producing income from farming or fishing,

(vii) has no footings or any other base support below ground level,

(viii) was acquired by the taxpayer before 1979 and is not a building described in subparagraph (vi) or (vii),

(ix) was acquired by the taxpayer after 1978 under circumstances such that

(A) he was obligated to acquire the building under the terms of an agreement in writing entered into before 1979, and

(B) the installation of footings or any other base support of the building was commenced before 1979, or

(x) was acquired by the taxpayer after 1978 under circumstances such that

(A) he commenced construction of the building before 1979, or

(B) the construction of the building was commenced under the terms of an agreement in writing entered into by him before 1979, and

the installation of footings or any other base support of the building was commenced before 1979;

(*b*) a wooden breakwater;

(*c*) a fence;

(*d*) a greenhouse;

(*e*) an oil or water storage tank;

(*f*) a railway tank car acquired before May 26, 1976;

(*g*) a wooden wharf;

(*h*) an aeroplane hangar acquired after the end of the taxpayer's 1958 taxation year;

(i) an addition or alteration, made

(A) during the period that is after March 31, 1967 and before 1979, or

(B) after 1978 if the taxpayer was obligated to have it made under the terms of an agreement in writing entered into before 1979,

to a building that would have been included in this class during that period but for the fact that it was included in Class 20;

(*j*) a railway locomotive that is acquired after May 25, 1976, and before February 26, 2008, and that is not an automotive railway car *(Note: See Class 7(i) for locomotives acquired after February 27, 2000, and Class 10(y) for new locomotives acquired after February 25, 2008; also ¶890)*;

(*k*) an addition or alteration, made after 1978 to a building included in this class by virtue of subparagraph (a)(viii), to the extent that the aggregate cost of all such additions and alterations to the building does not exceed $100,000.

Class 7 (15 per cent)

(Note: *You* may elect separate class treatment for property in class 7(j) or (k), see ¶869.)

Property that is

(*a*) a canoe or rowboat;

(*b*) a scow;

(*c*) a vessel, but not including a vessel

(i) of a separate class prescribed by subsection 1101(2a), or

(ii) included in Class 41;

(*d*) furniture, fittings or equipment attached to a property included in this class, but not including radiocommunication equipment;

(*e*) a spare engine for a property included in this class;

(*f*) a marine railway;

(*g*) a vessel under construction, other than a vessel included in Class 41;

(*h*) subject to an election made under subsection 1103(2i), property acquired after February 27, 2000 that is

(i) a rail suspension device designed to carry trailers that are designed to be hauled on both highways and railway tracks, or

(ii) a railway car;

(*i*) property that is acquired after February 27, 2000 (other than property included in paragraph (y) of Class 10), that is a railway locomotive, and that is not an automotive railway car (Note: Class 10(y) (30%) includes new railway locomotives acquired after February 25, 2008; see ¶890);

(*j*) pumping or compression equipment, including equipment ancillary to pumping and compression equipment, acquired after February 22, 2005 if the equipment pumps or compresses petroleum, natural gas or a related hydrocarbon for the purpose of moving it

(i) through a transmission pipeline,

(ii) from a transmission pipeline to a storage facility, or

(iii) to a transmission pipeline from a storage facility, or

(*k*) pumping or compression equipment that is acquired after February 25, 2008, including equipment ancillary to pumping and compression equipment, that is on a pipeline and that pumps or compresses carbon dioxide for the purpose of moving it through the pipeline.

Class 8 (20 per cent)

Property not included in Class 1, 2, 7, 9, 11, 17, or 30 that is

(*a*) a structure that is manufacturing or processing machinery or equipment;

(*b*) tangible property attached to a building and acquired solely for the purpose of

(i) servicing, supporting or providing access to or egress from, machinery or equipment,

(ii) manufacturing or processing, or

(iii) any combination of the functions described in subparagraphs (i) and (ii);

(*c*) a building that is a kiln, tank or vat, acquired for the purpose of manufacturing or processing;

(*d*) a building or other structure, acquired after February 19, 1973, that is designed for the purpose of preserving ensilage on a farm;

(*e*) a building or other structure, acquired after February 19, 1973, that is

(i) designed to store fresh fruits or fresh vegetables at a controlled level of temperature and humidity, and

(ii) to be used principally for the purpose of storing fresh fruits or fresh vegetables by or for the person or persons by whom they were grown;

(*f*) electrical generating equipment acquired after May 25, 1976, if

(i) the taxpayer is not a person whose business is the production for the use of or distribution to others of electrical energy,

(ii) the equipment is auxiliary to the taxpayer's main power supply, and

(iii) the equipment is not used regularly as a source of supply;

(*g*) electrical generating equipment, acquired after May 25, 1976, that has a maximum load capacity of not more than 15 kilowatts;

(*h*) portable electrical generating equipment acquired after May 25, 1976;

(*i*) a tangible capital property that is not included in another class in this Schedule except

(i) land or any part thereof or any interest therein,

(ii) an animal,

(iii) a tree, shrub, herb or similar growing thing,

(iv) an oil or gas well,

(v) a mine,

(vi) a specified temporary access road of the taxpayer, (Note: As defined in Regulation 1104(2) in relation to an oil or gas well or exploration therefor)

(vii) radium,

(viii) a right of way,

(ix) a timber limit,

(x) a tramway track, or

(xi) property of a separate class prescribed by subsection 1101(2a);

(*j*) property not included in any other class that is radio-communication equipment acquired after May 25, 1976;

(*k*) a rapid transit car that is used for the purpose of public transportation within a metropolitan area and is not part of a railway system;

(*l*) an outdoor advertising poster panel or bulletin board; or

(*m*) a greenhouse constructed of a rigid frame and a replaceable, flexible plastic cover.

Class 9 (25 per cent)

Property acquired before May 26, 1976, other than property included in Class 30, that is

(*a*) electrical generating equipment, if

(i) the taxpayer is not a person whose business is the production for the use of or distribution to others of electrical energy,

(ii) the equipment is auxiliary to the taxpayer's main power supply, and

(iii) the equipment is not used regularly as a source of supply,

(*b*) radar equipment,

(*c*) radio transmission equipment,

(*d*) radio receiving equipment,

(*e*) electrical generating equipment that has a maximum load capacity of not more than 15 kilowatts, or

(*f*) portable electrical generating equipment,

and property acquired after May 25, 1976 that is

(*g*) an aircraft;

(*h*) furniture, fittings or equipment attached to an aircraft; or (*i*) a spare part for an aircraft, or for furniture, fittings or equipment attached to an aircraft.

Class 10 (30 per cent)

Property not included in any other class that is

(*a*) automotive equipment, including a trolley bus, but not including

(i) an automotive railway car acquired after May 25, 1976,

(ii) a railway locomotive, or

(iii) a tramcar,

(*b*) a portable tool acquired after May 25, 1976 for the purpose of earning rental income for short terms, such as hourly, daily, weekly or monthly, except a property described in Class 12,

(*c*) harness or stable equipment,

(*d*) a sleigh or wagon,

(*e*) a trailer, including a trailer designed to be hauled on both highways and railway tracks,

(*f*) general-purpose electronic data processing equipment and systems software for that equipment, including ancillary data processing equipment, acquired after May 25, 1976 and before March 23, 2004 (or after March 22, 2004 and before 2005 if an election in respect of the property is made under subsection 1101(5q))(Note: See ¶886t.05), but not including property that is principally or is used principally as

(i) electronic process control or monitor equipment,

(ii) electronic communications control equipment,

(iii) systems software for a property referred to in subparagraph (i) or (ii) (Note: See ¶887), or

(iv) data handling equipment unless it is ancillary to general-purpose electronic data processing equipment,

(*f.1*) a designated underground storage cost, or

(*f.2*) an unmanned telecommunication spacecraft designed to orbit above the earth,

and property (other than property included in Class 41, 41.1 or 41.2 or property included in Class 43 that is described in paragraph (b) of that Class) that would otherwise be included in another Class in this Schedule, that is

(*g*) a building or other structure (other than property described in paragraph (l) or (m)) that would otherwise be included in Class 1, 3 or 6 and that was acquired for the purpose of gaining or producing income from a mine, except

(i) a property included in Class 28,

(ii) a property acquired principally for the purpose of gaining or producing income from the processing of ore from a mineral resource that is not owned by the taxpayer,

(iii) an office building not situated on the mine property, or

(iv) a refinery that was acquired by the taxpayer:

(A) before November 8, 1969, or

(B) after November 7, 1969 and that had been used before November 8, 1969 by any person with whom the taxpayer was not dealing at arm's length;

(v) (Revoked.)

(*h*) contractor's movable equipment, including portable camp buildings, acquired for use in a construction business or for lease to another taxpayer for use in that other taxpayer's construction business, except a property included in

(i) this Class by virtue of paragraph (t),

(ii) a separate class prescribed by subsection 1101(2b), or

(iii) Class 22 or 38;

(*i*) a floor of a roller skating rink;

(*j*) gas or oil well equipment;

(*k*) property (other than property included in Class 28 or property described in paragraph (l) or (m)) that was acquired for the purpose of gaining or producing income from a mine and that is

(i) a structure that would otherwise be included in Class 8, or

(ii) machinery or equipment,

except a property acquired before May 9, 1972 for the purpose of gaining or producing income from the processing of ore after extraction from a mineral resource that is not owned by the taxpayer;

(*l*) property acquired after the 1971 taxation year for the purpose of gaining or producing income from a mine and providing services to the mine or to a community where a substantial proportion of the persons who ordinarily work at the mine reside, if such property is

(i) an airport, dam, dock, fire hall, hospital, house, natural gas pipeline, power line, recreational facility, school, sewage disposal plant, sewer, street lighting system, town hall, water pipeline, water pumping station, water system, wharf or similar property,

(ii) a road, sidewalk, airplane runway, parking area, storage area or similar surface construction, or

(iii) machinery or equipment ancillary to any of the property described in subparagraph (i) or (ii),

but is not

(iv) a property included in Class 28, or

(v) a railway not situated on the mine property;

(*m*) property acquired after March 31, 1977, principally for the purpose of gaining or producing income from a mine, if such property is

(i) railway track and grading including components such as rails, ballast, ties and other track material,

(ii) property ancillary to the track referred to in subparagraph (i) that is

(A) railway traffic control or signalling equipment, including switching, block signalling, interlocking, crossing protection, detection, speed control or retarding equipment, or

(B) a bridge, culvert, subway, trestle or tunnel,

(iii) machinery or equipment ancillary to any of the property referred to in subparagraph (i) or (ii), or

(iv) conveying, loading, unloading or storing machinery or equipment, including a structure, acquired for the purpose of shipping output from the mine by means of the track referred to in subparagraph (i),

but is not

(v) property included in Class 28, or

(vi) for greater certainty, rolling stock,

(*n*) property that was acquired for the purpose of cutting and removing merchantable timber from a timber limit and that will be of no further use to the taxpayer after all merchantable timber that the taxpayer is entitled to cut and remove from the limit has been cut and removed, unless the taxpayer has elected to include another property of this kind in another class in this Schedule;

(*o*) mechanical equipment acquired for logging operations, except a property included in Class 7;

(*p*) an access road or trails for the protection of standing timber against fire, insects or disease;

(*q*) property acquired for a motion picture drive-in theatre;

(*r*) property included in this class by virtue of subsection 1102(8) or (9), except a property included in Class 28;

(*s*) a motion picture film or video tape acquired after May 25, 1976, except a property included in paragraph (w) or (x) or in Class 12;

(*t*) a property acquired after May 22, 1979 that is designed principally for the purpose of

(i) determining the existence, location, extent or quality of accumulations of petroleum or natural gas,

(ii) drilling oil or gas wells, or

(iii) determining the existence, location, extent or quality of mineral resources,

except a property included in a separate class prescribed by subsection 1101(2b);

(*u*) property acquired after 1980 to be used primarily in the processing in Canada of heavy crude oil recovered from a natural reservoir in Canada to a stage that is not beyond the crude oil stage or its equivalent that is

(i) property that would otherwise be included in Class 8 except railway rolling stock or a property described in paragraph (j) of Class 8,

(ii) an oil or water storage tank,

(iii) a powered industrial lift truck that would otherwise be included in paragraph (a), or

(iv) property that would otherwise be included in paragraph (f);

(*v*) property acquired after August 31, 1984 (other than property that is included in Class 30) that is equipment used for the purpose of effecting an interface between a cable distribution system and electronic products used by consumers of that system and that is designed primarily

(i) to augment the channel capacity of a television receiver or radio,

(ii) to decode pay television or other signals provided on a discretionary basis, or

(iii) to achieve any combination of functions described in subparagraphs (i) and (ii);

(*w*) a certified production acquired after 1987 and before March 1996 (see ¶874);

(*x*) a Canadian film or video production; or

(*y*) a railway locomotive that is not an automotive railway car and that was not used or acquired for use for any purpose by any taxpayer before February 26, 2008. (Note: Regulations 1102(19.1) and (19.2) provide, in effect, that property that is incorporated into an older (pre-Class 10(y)) locomotive in the course of its refurbishment or reconditioning may also be included in Class 10(y). See ¶890.)

Class 10.1 (30 per cent) (see ¶810a)

Property that would otherwise be included in Class 10 that is a passenger vehicle, the cost of which to the taxpayer exceeds $20,000 or such other amount as may be prescribed for the purposes of subsection 13(2) of the Act. (Note: Each of these vehicles is required to be in a separate class, see ¶869.)

Class 11 (35 per cent)

(Note: Class 11 does not include property acquired after 1987, subject to grandfathering provisions for certain property acquired before 1990.)

Property not included in any other class that is used to earn rental income and that is

(*a*) an electrical advertising sign owned by the manufacturer thereof, acquired before May 26, 1976; or

(*b*) an outdoor advertising poster panel or bulletin board acquired by the taxpayer

(i) before 1988, or

(ii) before 1990

(A) pursuant to an obligation in writing entered into by the taxpayer before June 18, 1987, or

(B) that was under construction by or on behalf of the taxpayer on June 18, 1987.

Class 12 (100 per cent)

Property not included in any other class that is

(*a*) [1]a book that is part of a lending library;

(*b*) [1]chinaware, cutlery, or other tableware;

(*c*) [1]a kitchen utensil costing less than

(i) $100, if acquired before May 26, 1976,

(ii) $200, if acquired after May 25, 1976 and before May 2, 2006; or

(iii) $500, if acquired after May 1, 2006;

(*d*) a die, jig, pattern, mould, or last;

(*e*) [1]a medical or dental instrument costing less than

[1] Not subject to the half-year rule, so that property described in them may be written off in full in the year of acquisition (see ¶802.10). Property described in other paragraphs of Class 12 is subject to the half-year rule; in effect it may be written off over two years at 50/50 straight-line.

(i) $100, if acquired before May 26, 1976,

(ii) $200, if acquired after May 25, 1976 and before May 2, 2006, or

(iii) $500, if acquired after May 1, 2006;

(*f*)[1]a mine shaft, main haulage way or similar underground work designed for continuing use, or any extension thereof, sunk or constructed after the mine came into production, to the extent that the property was acquired before 1988;

(*g*)[1]linen;

(*h*)[1]a tool (other than an electronic communication device or electronic data processing equipment (Note: See ¶886t.05) that is acquired after May 1, 2006, and that can be used for a purpose other than any of measuring, locating and calculating) costing less than

(i)[1]$100, if acquired before May 26, 1976,

(ii) $200, if acquired after May 25, 1976 and before May 2, 2006, or

(iii) $500, if acquired after May 1, 2006;

(*i*)[1]a uniform;

(*j*) the cutting or shaping part in a machine;

(*k*)[1]apparel or costume, including accessories used therewith, used for the purpose of earning rental income;

(*l*)[1]a video tape acquired before May 26, 1976;

(*m*) a motion picture film or video tape that is a television commercial message;

(*n*) a certified feature film or certified production (Note: Acquired before 1988 — see ¶874);

(*o*) computer software acquired after May 25, 1976, but not including systems software and property that is described in paragraph (s) (Note: See ¶887);

(*p*)[1]a metric scale or a scale designed for ready conversion to metric weighing, acquired after March 31, 1977 and before 1984 for use in a retail business and having a maximum weighing capacity of 100 kilograms;

(*q*)[1]a designated overburden removal cost; or

(*r*)[1]a video-cassette, a video-laser disk or a digital video disk, that is acquired for the purpose of renting and that is not expected to be rented to any one person for more than 7 days in any 30-day period;

and property that would otherwise be included in another class in this Schedule that is

(*s*)[1]acquired by the taxpayer after August 8, 1989 and before 1993, for use in a business of selling goods or providing services to consumers that is carried on in Canada, or for lease to another taxpayer for use by that other taxpayer in such a business, and that is

(i) electronic bar code scanning equipment designed to read bar codes applied to goods held for sale in the ordinary course of the business,

(ii) a cash register or similar sales recording device designed with the capability of calculating and recording sales tax imposed by more than one jurisdiction in respect of the same sale,

(iii) equipment or computer software that is designed to convert a cash register or similar sales recording device to one having the capability of calculating and recording sales tax imposed by more than one jurisdiction in respect of the same sale, or

(iv) electronic equipment or computer software that is ancillary to property described in subparagraph (i), (ii) or (iii) and all or substantially all the use of which is in conjunction with that property.

Class 13 (see ¶879)

Property that is a leasehold interest and property acquired by a taxpayer that would, if that property had been acquired by a person with whom the taxpayer was not dealing at arm's length at the time the property was acquired by the taxpayer, be a leasehold interest of that person, except

(*a*) an interest in minerals, petroleum, natural gas, other related hydrocarbons or timber and property relating thereto or in respect of a right to explore for, drill for, take or remove minerals, petroleum, natural gas, other related hydrocarbons or timber;

(*b*) that part of the leasehold interest that is included in another class in this Schedule by reason of subsection 1102(5) or (5.1); or

(*c*) a property included in Class 23.

Class 14 (see ¶880)

Property that is a patent, franchise, concession or licence for a limited period in respect of property, except

(*a*) a franchise, concession or licence in respect of minerals, petroleum, natural gas, other related hydrocarbons or timber and property relating thereto (except a franchise for distributing gas to consumers or a licence to export gas from Canada or from a province) or in respect of a right to explore for, drill for, take or remove minerals, petroleum, natural gas, other related hydrocarbons or timber;

(*b*) a leasehold interest;

(*c*) a property included in Class 23;

(*d*) a licence to use computer software; or

(*e*) a property that is included in Class 44.

Bill C-29 Measures (Oct. 25, 2016)

Note: When Bill C-29, October 25, 2016, achieves Royal Assent, the legislation will be modified to read:

Class 14.1 (5 per cent)

(see ¶880a)

Property of a taxpayer that, in respect of a business of the taxpayer,

(*a*) is goodwill;

(*b*) was eligible capital property of the taxpayer immediately before January 1, 2017 and is owned by the taxpayer at the beginning of that day; or

(*c*) is acquired after 2016, other than

(i) property that is tangible or, for civil law, corporeal property,

(ii) property that is not acquired for the purpose of gaining or producing income from business,

(iii) property in respect of which any amount is deductible (otherwise than as a result of being included in this class) in computing the taxpayer's income from the business,

(iv) property in respect of which any amount is not deductible in computing the taxpayer's income from the business because of any provision of the Act (other than paragraph 18(1)(*b*)) or these Regulations,

(v) an interest in a trust,

(vi) an interest in a partnership,

(vii) a share, bond, debenture, mortgage, hypothecary claim, note, bill or other similar property, or

(viii) property that is an interest in, or for civil law a right in, or a right to acquire, a property described in any of subparagraphs (i) to (vii).

Class 15 (see ¶882)

Property that would otherwise be included in another class in this Schedule and that

(*a*) was acquired for the purpose of cutting and removing merchantable timber from a timber limit, and

(*b*) will be of no further use to the taxpayer after all merchantable timber that the taxpayer is entitled to cut and remove from the limit has been cut and removed,

except

(*c*) property that the taxpayer has, in the taxation year or a preceding taxation year, elected not to include in this class, or

(*d*) a timber resource property.

Class 16 (40 per cent)

Property acquired before May 26, 1976 that is

(*a*) an aircraft,

(*b*) furniture, fittings or equipment attached to an aircraft, or

(*c*) a spare part for a property included in this class,

property acquired after May 25, 1976 that is

(*d*) a taxicab,

property acquired after November 12, 1981 that is

(*e*) a motor vehicle that

(i) would be an automobile as that term is defined in subsection 248(1) of the Act, if that definition were read without reference to paragraph (*d*) thereof,

(ii) was acquired for the purpose of renting or leasing, and

(iii) is not expected to be rented or leased to any person for more than 30 days in any 12 month period,

property acquired after February 15, 1984 that is

(*f*) a coin-operated video game or pinball machine,

and property acquired after December 6, 1991 that is

(*g*) a truck or tractor designed for hauling freight, and that is primarily so used by the taxpayer or a person with whom the taxpayer does not deal at arm's length in a business that includes hauling freight, and that has a "gross vehicle weight rating" (as that term is defined in subsection 2(1) of the Motor Vehicle Safety Regulations) in excess of 11,788 kg.

Class 17 (8 per cent)

Property that would otherwise be included in another class in this Schedule that is

(*a*) a telephone system, telegraph system, or a part thereof, acquired before May 26, 1976, except

(i) radiocommunication equipment, or

(ii) a property included in Class 10, 13, 14 or 28, or

(*a.1*) property (other than a building or other structure) acquired after February 27, 2000 that has not been used for any purpose before February 28, 2000 and is

(i) electrical generating equipment (other than electrical generating equipment described in Class 43.1, 43.2 or 48 or in Class 8 because of paragraph (f), (g) or (h) of that Class or

(ii) production and distribution equipment of a distributor of water or steam (other than such property described in Class 43.1 or 43.2) used for heating or cooling (including, for this purpose, pipe used to collect or distribute an energy transfer medium but not including equipment or pipe used to distribute water that is for consumption, disposal or treatment),

and property not included in any other class, acquired after May 25, 1976, that is

(*b*) telephone, telegraph or data communication switching equipment, except

(i) equipment installed on customers' premises, or

(ii) property that is principally electronic equipment or systems software therefor; or

(*c*) a road (other than a specified temporary access road of the taxpayer), sidewalk, airplane runway, parking area, storage area or similar surface construction.

Class 18 (60 per cent)

(Note: Class 18 does not include property acquired after May 25, 1976.)

Property that is a motion picture film acquired before May 26, 1976, except

(*a*) a television commercial message; or

(*b*) a certified feature film.

Class 19 (50 or 20 per cent)

(Note: Class 19 does not include property acquired after 1966.)

Property acquired by the taxpayer after June 13, 1963 and before January 1, 1967 that would otherwise be included in Class 8 if, (*a*) in the taxation year in which the property was acquired,

(i) the taxpayer was an individual who was resident in Canada for not less than 183 days, or

(ii) the taxpayer was a corporation that had a degree of Canadian ownership;

(*b*) the property was acquired for use in Canada in a business carried on by the taxpayer that,

(i) for the fiscal period in which the property was acquired, or

(ii) for the fiscal period in which the business first commenced selling goods in reasonable commercial quantities,

whichever was later, was a business in which the aggregate of

(iii) its net sales, as they would be determined under paragraphs 71A(2)(*d*) and (*f*) of the former Act (within the meaning assigned by paragraph 8(*b*) of the *Income Tax Application Rules, 1971*), from the sale of goods processed or manufactured in Canada by the business,

(iv) an amount equal to that part of its gross revenue that is rent from goods processed or manufactured in Canada in the course of the business, and

(v) its gross revenue from advertisements in a newspaper or magazine produced by the business,

was not less than 2/3 of the amount by which the gross revenue from the business for the period exceeded the aggregate of each amount paid or credited in the period to a customer of the business as a bonus, rebate or discount or for returned or damaged goods, and was not a business that was principally

(vi) operating a gas or oil well,

(vii) logging,

(viii) mining,

(ix) construction, or

(x) a combination of two or more of the activities referred to in subparagraphs (vi) to (ix); and

(*c*) the property had not been used for any purpose whatever before it was acquired by the taxpayer.

Class 20 (20 per cent)

(Note: Class 20 does not include property acquired after March 31, 1967.)

Property that would otherwise be included in Class 3 or 6

(*a*) that was acquired after December 5, 1963 and before April 1, 1967 that is

(i) a building,

(ii) an extension to a building, outside the previously existing walls or roof of the building, if the aggregate cost of the extensions added in the aforementioned period exceeded the lesser of

(A) $100,000, and

(B) 25% of the capital cost to the taxpayer of the building on December 5, 1963, or

(iii) an addition or alteration to a property described in subparagraph (i) or (ii),

and that has been certified by the Minister of Industry, upon application by the taxpayer in such form as may be prescribed by the Minister of Industry,

(iv) to be situated in an area that was a designated area, as determined for the purposes of section 71A of the former Act (within the meaning assigned by paragraph 8(*b*) of the *Income Tax Application Rules, 1971*),

(A) at the time the property was acquired,

(B) in a case where the property was built by the taxpayer, at the time construction was commenced, or

(C) in a case where the property was built for the taxpayer pursuant to a contract entered into by the taxpayer, at the time the contract was entered into, and

(v) to have not been used for any purpose whatever before it was acquired by the taxpayer; or

(*b*) the capital cost of which was included in the approved capital costs as defined in the *Area Development Incentives Act* upon which approved capital cost the Minister of Industry has based the amount of a development grant authorized under that Act.

Class 21 (50 per cent)

(Note: Class 21 does not include property acquired after March 31, 1967.)

Property that would otherwise be included in Class 8 or Class 19

(*a*) that was acquired after December 5, 1963 and before April 1, 1967 and that

(i) was acquired for use in a business carried on by the taxpayer that has been certified by the Minister of Industry, for the purposes of section 71A of the former Act (within the meaning assigned by paragraph 8(*b*) of the *Income Tax Application Rules, 1971*), to be a new manufacturing or processing business in a designated area for the fiscal period in which the property was acquired or for a subsequent fiscal period, and

(ii) had not been used for any purpose whatever before it was acquired by the taxpayer; or

(*b*) the capital cost of which was included in the approved capital costs as defined in the *Area Development Incentives Act* upon which approved capital cost the Minister of Industry has based the amount of a development grant authorized under that Act.

Class 22 (50 per cent)

(Note: Class 22 does not include property acquired after 1987, subject to grandfathering provisions for certain property acquired before 1990. See Class 38 and ¶888.)

Property acquired by the taxpayer after March 16, 1964 and

(*a*) before 1988, or

(*b*) before 1990

(i) pursuant to an obligation in writing entered into by the taxpayer before June 18, 1987, or

(ii) that was under construction by or on behalf of the taxpayer on June 18, 1987 that is power-operated movable equipment designed for the purpose of excavating, moving, placing or compacting earth, rock, concrete or asphalt, except a property included in Class 7.

Class 23 (100 per cent)

(Note: Class 23 includes property relating to leaseholds only with respect to Expo 86 and the 1967 World Exhibition.)

Property that is

(*a*) a leasehold interest or a concession in respect of land granted under or pursuant to an agreement in writing with the Canadian Corporation for the 1967 World Exhibition where such leasehold interest or concession is to expire not later than June 15, 1968;

(*b*) a building or other structure, including component parts, erected on land that is the subject matter of a leasehold interest or concession described in paragraph (a) where such building or other structure, including component parts, is of a temporary nature and is required by the agreement to be removed not later than June 15, 1968;

(*c*) a leasehold interest or licence in respect of land granted under or pursuant to an agreement in writing with the Expo 86 Corporation where such leasehold interest or licence is to expire not later than January 31, 1987; or

(*d*) a building or other structure, including component parts, erected on land that is the subject matter of a leasehold interest or licence described in paragraph (c) where such building or other structure, including component parts, is of a temporary nature and is required by the agreement to be removed not later than January 31, 1987.

Class 24

(Note: Class 24 does not include property acquired after 1998)

Property acquired after April 26, 1965 and before 1971

(*a*) that would otherwise be included in Class 2, 3, 6 or 8 and that

(i) was acquired primarily for the purpose of preventing, reducing or eliminating pollution of

(A) any of the inland, coastal or boundary waters of Canada, or

(B) any lake, river, stream, watercourse, pond, swamp or well in Canada,

by industrial waste, refuse or sewage created by operations in the course of carrying on a business by the taxpayer or that would be created by such operations if the property had not been acquired and used, and

(ii) had not been used for any purpose whatever before it was acquired by the taxpayer,

but not including property acquired for use in the production of by-products or the recovery of materials unless the by-products are produced from, or the materials are recovered from, materials that after April 26, 1965,

(iii) were being discarded as waste by the taxpayer, or

(iv) were commonly being discarded as waste by other taxpayers who carried on operations of a type similar to the operations carried on by the taxpayer,

and property acquired before 1999

(*b*) that would otherwise be included in another class in this Schedule

(i) that has not been included by the taxpayer in any other class,

(ii) that had not been used for any purpose whatever before it was acquired by the taxpayer,

(iii) that was acquired by the taxpayer after 1970 primarily for the purpose of preventing, reducing or eliminating pollution of

(A) any of the inland, coastal or boundary waters of Canada, or

(B) any lake, river, stream, watercourse, pond, swamp or well in Canada,

that is caused, or that, if the property had not been acquired and used, would be caused by

(C) operations carried on by the taxpayer at a site in Canada at which operations have been carried on by him from a time that is before 1974,

(D) the operation in Canada of a building or plant by the taxpayer, the construction of which was either commenced before 1974 or commenced under an agreement in writing entered into by him before 1974, or

(E) the operation of transportation or other movable equipment that has been operated by the taxpayer in Canada (including any of the inland, coastal or boundary waters of Canada) from a time that is before 1974,

or that was acquired by him after May 8, 1972, that would otherwise have been property referred to in this subparagraph except that

(F) it was acquired

(I) for the purpose of gaining or producing income from a business by a taxpayer whose business includes the preventing, reducing or eliminating of pollution of a kind referred to in this subparagraph that is caused or that otherwise would be caused primarily by operations referred to in clause (C), (D) or (E) carried on by other taxpayers (not including persons referred to in section 149 of the Act), and

(II) to be used in a business referred to in subclause (I) in the preventing, reducing or eliminating of pollution of a kind referred to in this subparagraph, or

(G) it was acquired

(I) for the purpose of gaining or producing income from a property by a corporation whose principal business is the purchasing of conditional sales contracts, accounts receivable, bills of sale, chattel mortgages, bills of exchange or other obligations representing part or all of the sale price of merchandise or services, the lending of money, or the leasing of property, or any combination thereof, and

(II) to be leased to a taxpayer (other than a person referred to in section 149 of the Act) to be used by him, in an operation referred to in clause (C), (D), (E) or (F), in the preventing, reducing or eliminating of pollution of a kind referred to in this subparagraph, and

(iv) that has, upon application by the taxpayer to the Minister of the Environment, been accepted by that Minister as property the primary use of which is to be the preventing, reducing or eliminating of pollution of a kind referred to in subparagraph (iii)

and for the purposes of paragraphs (a) and (b)

(*c*) where a corporation (in this paragraph referred to as the "predecessor corporation") has, as a result of an amalgamation within the meaning assigned by subsection 87(1) of the Act, merged at any time after 1973 with one or more other corporations to form one corporate entity (in this paragraph referred to as the "new corporation"), the new corporation shall be deemed to be the same corporation as, and a continuation of, the predecessor corporation;

(*d*) where a corporation (in this paragraph referred to as the "subsidiary") has been wound up at any time after 1973 in circumstances to which subsection 88(1) of the Act applies, the parent (within the meaning assigned by that subsection) shall be deemed to be the same corporation as, and a continuation of, the subsidiary; and

(*e*) this class shall be read without reference to subparagraph (b)(i) where paragraph (c) or (d) applies to the taxpayer and the property was acquired before 1992.

Class 25 (100 per cent)

(Note: Class 25 does not include property acquired after 1973.)

Property that would otherwise be included in another class in this Schedule that is property acquired by the taxpayer

(*a*) before October 23, 1968, or

(*b*) after October 22, 1968 and before 1974, where the acquisition of the property may reasonably be regarded as having been in fulfilment of an obligation undertaken in an agreement made in writing before October 23, 1968 and ratified, confirmed or adopted by the legislature of a province by a statute that came into force before that date,

if the taxpayer was, on October 22, 1968, a corporation, commission or association to which, on the assumption that October 22, 1968 was in its 1969 taxation year, paragraph 62(1)(*c*) of the former Act (within the meaning assigned by paragraph 8(*b*) of the *Income Tax Application Rules, 1971*),

(*c*) would not apply; and

(*d*) would have applied but for subparagraph (i) or (ii) of that paragraph.

Class 26 (5 per cent)

Property that is

(*a*) a catalyst; or

(*b*) deuterium enriched water (commonly known as "heavy water") acquired after May 22, 1979.

Class 27

(Note: Class 27 does not include property acquired after 1998)

Property acquired before 1999 that would otherwise be included in another Class in this Schedule

(*a*) that has not been included by the taxpayer in any other class;

(*b*) that had not been used for any purpose whatever before it was acquired by the taxpayer;

(*c*) that was acquired by the taxpayer after March 12, 1970 primarily for the purpose of preventing, reducing or eliminating air pollution by

(i) removing particulate, toxic or injurious materials from smoke or gas, or

(ii) preventing the discharge of part or all of the smoke, gas or other air pollutant,

that is discharged or that, if the property had not been acquired and used, would be discharged into the atmosphere as a result of

(iii) operations carried on by the taxpayer at a site in Canada at which operations have been carried on by him from a time that is before 1974,

(iv) the operation in Canada of a building or plant by the taxpayer, the construction of which was either commenced before 1974 or commenced under an agreement in writing entered into by him before 1974, or

(v) the operation of transportation or other movable equipment that has been operated by the taxpayer in Canada (including any of the inland, coastal or boundary waters of Canada) from a time that is before 1974,

or that was acquired by him after May 8, 1972, that would otherwise have been property referred to in this paragraph except that

(vi) it was acquired

(A) for the purpose of gaining or producing income from a business by a taxpayer whose business includes the preventing, reducing or eliminating of air pollution that is caused or that otherwise would be caused primarily by operations referred to in subparagraph (iii), (iv) or (v) carried on by other taxpayers (not including persons referred to in section 149 of the Act), and

(B) to be used in a business referred to in clause (A) in the preventing, reducing or eliminating of air pollution in a manner referred to in this paragraph, or

(vii) it was acquired

(A) for the purpose of gaining or producing income from a property by a corporation whose principal business is the purchasing of conditional sales contracts, accounts receivable, bills of sale, chattel mortgages, bills of exchange or other obligations representing part or all of the sale price of merchandise or services, the lending of money, or the leasing of property, or any combination thereof, and

(B) to be leased to a taxpayer (other than a person referred to in section 149 of the Act) to be used by him, in an operation referred to in subparagraph (iii), (iv), (v) or (vi), in the preventing, reducing or eliminating of air pollution in a manner referred to in this paragraph; and

(*d*) that has, upon application by the taxpayer to the Minister of the Environment, been accepted by that Minister as property the primary use of which is to be the preventing, reducing or eliminating of air pollution in a manner referred to in paragraph (c);

and for the purposes of paragraphs (a) to (d),

(*e*) where a corporation (in this paragraph referred to as the "predecessor corporation") has, as a result of an amalgamation within the meaning assigned by subsection 87(1) of the Act, merged at any time after 1973 with one or more other corporations to form one corporate entity (in this paragraph referred to as the "new corporation"), the new corporation shall be deemed to be the same corporation as, and a continuation of, the predecessor corporation;

(*f*) where a corporation (in this paragraph referred to as the "subsidiary") has been wound up at any time after 1973 in circumstances to which subsection 88(1) of the Act applies, the parent (within the meaning assigned by that subsection) shall be deemed to be the same corporation as, and a continuation of, the subsidiary; and

(*g*) this class shall be read without reference to paragraph (a) where paragraph (e) or (f) applies to the taxpayer and the property was acquired before 1992.

Class 28 (30 per cent)

(Note: Class 28 does not include property acquired after 1987, subject to grandfathering provisions for certain property acquired before 1990.)

Property situated in Canada that would otherwise be included in another class in this Schedule that

(*a*) was acquired by the taxpayer:

(i) before 1988, or

(ii) before 1990

(A) pursuant to an obligation in writing entered into by the taxpayer before June 18, 1987,

(B) that was under construction by or on behalf of the taxpayer on June 18, 1987, or

(C) that is machinery or equipment that is a fixed and integral part of a building, structure, plant facility or other property that was under construction by or on behalf of the taxpayer on June 18, 1987,

and that

(*b*) was acquired by the taxpayer principally for the purpose of gaining or producing income from one or more mines operated by the taxpayer and situated in Canada and each of which

(i) came into production in reasonable commercial quantities after November 7, 1969, or

(ii) was the subject of a major expansion after November 7, 1969

(A) whereby the greatest designed capacity, measured in weight of input of ore, of the mill that processed the ore from the mine was not less than 25% greater in the year following the expansion than it was in the year preceding the expansion, or

(B) where in the one year period preceding, the expansion

(I) the Minister, in consultation with the Minister of Natural Resources, determines that the greatest designed capacity of the mine, measured in weight of output of ore, immediately after the expansion was not less than 25% greater than the greatest designed capacity of the mine immediately before the expansion, and

(II) either

1. no mill processed the ore from the mine at any time, or

2. the mill that processed the ore from the mine processed other ore,

(*c*) was acquired by the taxpayer

(i) after November 7, 1969,

(ii) before the coming into production of the mine or the completion of the expansion of the mine referred to in subparagraph (b)(i) or (ii), as the case may be, and

(iii) in the case of a mine that was the subject of a major expansion described in subparagraph (b)(ii), in the course of and principally for the purposes of the expansion,

(*d*) had not, before it was acquired by the taxpayer, been used for any purpose whatever by any person with whom the taxpayer was not dealing at arm's length, and

(*e*) is any of the following, namely,

(i) property that was acquired before the mine came into production and that would, but for this class, be included in Class 10 by virtue of paragraph (g), (k), (l) or (r) of that class or would have been so included in that class if it had been acquired after the 1971 taxation year,

(ii) property that was acquired before the mine came into production and that would, but for this class, be included in Class 10 by virtue of paragraph (m) of that class, or

(iii) property that was acquired after the mine came into production and that would, but for this class, be included in Class 10 by virtue of paragraph (g), (k), (l) or (r) of that class,

or that would be described in paragraphs (b) to (e) if in those paragraphs each reference to a "mine" were read as a reference to a "mine that is a location in a bituminous sands deposit, oil sands deposit or oil shale deposit from which material is extracted", and each reference to "after November 7, 1969" were read as "before November 8, 1969".

Class 29 (see ¶878)

Property (other than property included in Class 41 solely because of paragraph (c) or (d) of that Class or property included in Class 47 because of paragraph (b) of that Class) that would otherwise be included in another Class in this Schedule

(*a*) that is property manufactured by the taxpayer, the manufacture of which was completed by him after May 8, 1972, or other property acquired by the taxpayer after May 8, 1972,

(i) to be used directly or indirectly by him in Canada primarily in the manufacturing or processing of goods for sale or lease, or

(ii) to be leased, in the ordinary course of carrying on a business in Canada of the taxpayer, to a lessee who can reasonably be expected to use, directly or indirectly, the property in Canada primarily in Canadian field processing carried on by the lessee or in the manufacturing or processing by the lessee of goods for sale or lease, if the taxpayer is a corporation whose principal business is

(A) leasing property,

(B) manufacturing property that it sells or leases,

(C) the lending of money,

(D) the purchasing of conditional sales contracts, accounts receivable, bills of sale, chattel mortgages, bills of exchange or other obligations representing part or all of the sale price of merchandise or services, or

(E) selling or servicing a type of property that it also leases,

or any combination thereof, unless use of the property by the lessee commenced before May 9, 1972;

(*b*) that is

(i) property that, but for this class, would be included in Class 8, except railway rolling stock or a property described in paragraph (j) of Class 8,

(ii) an oil or water storage tank,

(iii) a powered industrial lift truck,

(iv) electrical generating equipment described in Class 9,

(v) property that is described in paragraph (b) or (f) of Class 10, or

(vi) property that would be described in paragraph (f) of Class 10 if the portion of that paragraph before subparagraph (i) read as follows: "(f) general-purpose electronic data processing equipment and systems software for that equipment, including ancillary data processing equipment, acquired after March 18, 2007 and before January 28, 2009, but not including property that is principally or is used principally as"; and

(*c*) that is property acquired by the taxpayer

(i) before 1988,

(ii) before 1990

(A) pursuant to an obligation in writing entered into by the taxpayer before June 18, 1987,

(B) that was under construction by or on behalf of the taxpayer on June 18, 1987, or

(C) that is machinery or equipment that is a fixed and integral part of a building, structure, plant facility or other property that was under construction by or on behalf of the taxpayer on June 18, 1987, or

(iii) after March 18, 2007 and before 2016 if the property is machinery, or equipment,

(A) that would be described in paragraph (a) if subparagraph (a)(ii) were read without reference to "in Canadian field processing carried on by the lessee or", or

(B) that is described in any of subparagraphs (b)(i) to (iii) and (vi).

Class 30 (40 per cent)

Property of a taxpayer that is

(*a*) an unmanned telecommunication spacecraft that was designed to orbit above the earth and that was acquired by the taxpayer

(i) before 1988, or

(ii) before 1990

(A) pursuant to an obligation in writing entered into by the taxpayer before June 18, 1987, or

(B) that was under construction by or on behalf of the taxpayer on June 18, 1987; or

(*b*) equipment used for the purpose of effecting an interface between a cable or satellite distribution system (other than a satellite radio distribution system) and electronic products used by consumers of that system if the equipment

(i) is designed primarily

(A) to augment the channel capacity of a television receiver, or

(B) to decode pay television or other signals provided on a discretionary basis,

(ii) is acquired by the taxpayer after March 4, 2010, and

(iii) has not been used or acquired for use for any purpose by any taxpayer before March 5, 2010.

Class 31 (5 per cent)

(Note: Class 31 does not include property acquired after June 17, 1987, subject to grandfathering provisions for certain property acquired after June 17, 1987.)

Property that is a multiple-unit residential building in Canada that would otherwise be included in Class 3 or Class 6 and in respect of which

(*a*) a certificate has been issued by Canada Mortgage and Housing Corporation certifying

(i) in respect of a building that would otherwise be included in Class 3, that the installation of footings or any other base support of the building was commenced

(A) after November 18, 1974 and before 1980, or

(B) after October 28, 1980 and before 1982,

as the case may be, and

(ii) in respect of a building that would otherwise be included in Class 6, that the installation of footings or any other base support of the building was commenced after December 31, 1977 and before 1979,

and that, according to plans and specifications for the building, not less than 80% of the floor space will be used in providing self-contained domestic establishments and related parking, recreation, service and storage areas;

(*b*) not more than 20% of the floor space is used for any purpose other than the purposes referred to in paragraph (a);

(*c*) the certificate referred to in paragraph (a) was issued on or before the later of

(i) December 31, 1981, and

(ii) the day that is 18 months after the day on which the installation of footings or other base support of the building was commenced; and (*d*) the construction of the building proceeds, after 1982, without undue delay, taking into consideration acts of God, labour disputes, fire, accidents or unusual delay by common carriers or suppliers of materials or equipment;

and that was acquired by the taxpayer

(*e*) before June 18, 1987, or

(*f*) after June 17, 1987 pursuant to

(i) an obligation in writing entered into by the taxpayer before June 18, 1987, or

(ii) the terms of a prospectus, preliminary prospectus, registration statement, offering memorandum or notice required to be filed with a public authority in Canada and filed before June 18, 1987 with that public authority.

Class 32 (10 per cent)

(Note: Class 32 does not include property acquired after 1979.)

Property that is a multiple-unit residential building in Canada that would otherwise be included in Class 6 if the reference to "1979" in subparagraph (a)(viii) of that Class were read as a reference to "1980", and in respect of which

(*a*) a certificate has been issued by Canada Mortgage and Housing Corporation certifying

(i) that the installation of footings or any other base support of the building was commenced after November 18, 1974 and before 1978, and

(ii) that, according to plans and specifications for the building, not less than 80% of the floor space will be used in providing self-contained domestic establishments and related parking, recreation, service and storage areas; and

(*b*) not more than 20% of the floor space is used for any purpose other than the purposes referred to in subparagraph (a)(ii).

Class 33 (15 per cent)

Property that is a timber resource property.

Class 34 (see ¶889)

(Note 1: Class 34 does not include property acquired after February 21, 1994, subject to grandfathering provisions for certain property acquired before 1996. See Classes 43.1 and 43.2.)

(Note 2: Property described in this class and acquired after February 27, 2000, carries a 15% capital cost allowance rate in Class 7(h) unless an election is made to maintain the property in Class 35 for the reasons discussed in ¶890.)

Property that would otherwise be included in Class 1, 2 or 8

(*a*) that is

(i) electrical generating equipment,

(ii) production equipment and pipelines of a distributor of heat,

(iii) steam generating equipment that was acquired by the taxpayer primarily for the purpose of producing steam to operate property described in subparagraph (i), or

(iv) an addition to a property described in subparagraph (i), (ii) or (iii),

but not including buildings or other structures,

(*b*) that was acquired by the taxpayer after May 25, 1976,

(*c*) that

(i) was acquired by the taxpayer for use by him in a business carried on in Canada, or

(ii) is to be leased by the taxpayer to a lessee for use by the lessee in Canada, and

(*d*) that is property in respect of which a certificate has been issued

(i) before December 11, 1979 by the Minister of Industry, Trade and Commerce certifying that the property is part of a plan designed to

(A) produce heat derived primarily from the consumption of wood wastes or municipal wastes,

(B) produce electrical energy by the utilization of fuel that is petroleum, natural gas or related hydrocarbons, coal, coal gas, coke, lignite or peat (in this clause referred to as "fossil fuel"), wood wastes or municipal wastes, or any combination thereof, if the consumption of fossil fuel (expressed as the high heat value of the fossil fuel), if any, chargeable to electrical energy on an annual basis in respect of the property is no greater than 7,000 British Thermal Units per kilowatt-hour of electrical energy produced, or

(C) recover heat that is a by-product of an industrial process, or

(ii) after December 10, 1979, by the Minister of Energy, Mines and Resources certifying that the property is part of a plan designed to

(A) produce heat derived primarily from the consumption of natural gas, coal, coal gas, lignite, peat, wood wastes or municipal wastes, or any combination thereof,

(B) produce electrical energy by the utilization of fuel that is petroleum, natural gas or related hydrocarbons, coal, coal gas, coke, lignite or peat (in this clause referred to as "fossil fuel"), wood wastes or municipal wastes, or any combination thereof, if the consumption of fossil fuel (expressed as the high heat value of the fossil fuel), if any, chargeable to electrical energy on an annual basis in respect of the property is no greater than 7,000 British Thermal Units per kilowatt-hour of electrical energy produced, or

(C) recover heat that is a by-product of an industrial process,

and property that was acquired by the taxpayer after December 10, 1979 (other than property described in paragraph (a)) and would otherwise be included in another Class in this Schedule

(*e*) that is

(i) active solar heating equipment including solar collectors, solar energy conversion equipment, storage equipment, control equipment, equipment designed to interface solar heating equipment with other heating equipment, and solar water heaters, used to

(A) heat a liquid or air to be used directly in the course of manufacturing or processing,

(B) provide space heating when installed in a new building or other new structure at the time of its original construction where that construction commenced after December 10, 1979, or

(C) heat water for a use other than a use described in clause (A) or (B),

(ii) a hydro electric installation of a producer of hydro electric energy with a planned maximum generating capacity not exceeding 15 megawatts upon completion of site development that is the generating equipment and plant (including structures) of that producer including a canal, a dam, a dyke, an overflow spillway, a penstock, a powerhouse complete with generating equipment and other equipment ancillary thereto, control equipment, fishways or fish bypasses and transmission equipment, except distribution equipment and a property included in Class 10 or 17,

(iii) heat recovery equipment that is designed to conserve energy or reduce the requirement to acquire energy by extracting and reusing heat from thermal waste including condensers, heat exchange equipment, steam compressors used to upgrade low pressure steam, waste heat boilers and ancillary equipment such as control panels, fans, instruments or pumps,

(iv) an addition or alteration to a hydro electric installation described in subparagraph (ii) that results in a change in generating capacity if the new maximum generating capacity at the hydro electric installation does not exceed 15 megawatts, or

(v) a fixed-location device acquired after February 25, 1986, that is a wind energy conversion system designed to produce electrical energy, consisting of a wind-driven turbine, generating equipment and related equipment, including control and conditioning equipment, support structures, a powerhouse complete with equipment ancillary thereto, and transmission equipment, but not including distribution equipment, equipment designed to store electrical energy or property included in Class 10 or 17,

(*f*) that

(i) was acquired by the taxpayer for use by him for the purpose of gaining or producing income from a business carried on in Canada or from property situated in Canada, or

(ii) is to be leased by the taxpayer to a lessee for use by the lessee in Canada, and

(*g*) that is property in respect of which a certificate has been issued by the Minister of Energy, Mines and Resources,

but not including

(*h*) property in respect of which a certificate issued under paragraph (d) or (g) has been revoked pursuant to subsection 1104(11),

(*i*) property that had been used before it was acquired by the taxpayer unless the property had previously been included in Class 34 for the purpose of computing the income of the person from whom it was acquired.

(*j*) property acquired by the taxpayer after February 21, 1994 other than

(i) property acquired by the taxpayer

(A) pursuant to an agreement of purchase and sale in writing entered into by the taxpayer before February 22, 1994,

(B) in order to satisfy a legally binding obligation entered into by the taxpayer in writing before February 22, 1994 to sell electricity to a public power utility in Canada,

(C) that was under construction by or on behalf of the taxpayer on February 22, 1994, or

(D) that is machinery or equipment that is a fixed and integral part of a building, structure or other property that was under construction by or on behalf of the taxpayer on February 22, 1994, and

(ii) property acquired by the taxpayer before 1996

(A) pursuant to an agreement of purchase and sale in writing entered into before 1995 to acquire the property from a person or partnership in circumstances where

(I) the property was part of a project that was under construction by the person or partnership on February 22, 1994, and

(II) it is reasonable to conclude, having regard to all of the circumstances, that the person or partnership constructed the project with the intention of transferring all or part of the project to another taxpayer after completion, or

(B) pursuant to an agreement in writing entered into before 1995 by the taxpayer with a person or partnership where the taxpayer agrees to assume a legally binding obligation entered into by the person or partnership before February 22, 1994 to sell electricity to a public power utility in Canada, or

(*k*) property in respect of which a certificate has not been issued under paragraph (d) or (g) before the time that is the later of

(i) the end of 1995, and

(ii) 2 years after the property is acquired by the taxpayer or, where the property is property acquired in circumstances to which paragraph (j) applies, 2 years after substantial completion of the property.

Class 35 (7 per cent)

(see ¶890)

Property not included in any other class that is

(*a*) a railway car acquired after May 25, 1976; or

(*b*) a rail suspension device designed to carry trailers that are designed to be hauled on both highways and railway tracks.

Class 36 (see ¶833)

Property acquired after December 11, 1979 that is deemed to be depreciable property by virtue of paragraph 13(5.2)(*c*) of the Act.

Class 37 (15 per cent)

Property that would otherwise be included in another class in this Schedule that is property used in connection with an amusement park, including (*a*) land improvements (other than landscaping) for or in support of park activities, including

(i) roads, sidewalks, parking areas, storage areas, or similar surface constructions, and

(ii) canals,

(*b*) buildings (other than warehouses, administration buildings, hotels or motels), structures and equipment (other than automotive equipment), including

(i) rides, attractions and appurtenances associated with a ride or attraction, ticket booths and facades,

(ii) equipment, furniture and fixtures, in or attached to a building included in this class,

(iii) bridges, and

(iv) fences or similar perimeter structures, and

(*c*) automotive equipment (other than automotive equipment designed for use on highways or streets),

and property not included in another class in this Schedule that is a waterway or a land improvement (other than landscaping, clearing or levelling land) used in connection with an amusement park.

Class 38 (see ¶888)

Property not included in Class 22 but that would otherwise be included in that Class if that Class were read without reference to paragraphs (a) and (b) thereof.

Class 39 (see ¶878)

(Note: Class 39 does not include property acquired after February 25, 1992.)

Property acquired after 1987 and before February 26, 1992 that is not included in Class 29, but that would otherwise be included in that Class if that Class were read without reference to subparagraphs (b)(iii) and (v) and paragraph (c) thereof.

Class 40 (see ¶878)

(Note: Class 40 does not include property acquired after 1989.)

Property acquired after 1987 and before 1990 that is a powered industrial lift truck or property described in paragraph (b) or (f) of Class 10 and that is property not included in Class 29 but that would otherwise be included in that class if that class were read without reference to paragraph (c) thereof.

Class 41 (25 per cent)

(Additional allowances: see ¶892)

Property (other than property included in Class 41.1 or 41.2)

(*a*) not included in Class 28 that would otherwise be included in that Class if that Class were read without reference to paragraph (a) of the Class and if subparagraphs (e)(i) to (iii) of that Class were read as follows:

"(i) property that was acquired before the mine came into production and that would, but for this Class, be included in Class 10 because of paragraph (g), (k), (l) or (r) of that Class or would have been so included in that Class if it had been acquired after the 1971 taxation year, and property that would, but for this Class, be included in Class 41 because of subsection 1102(8) or (9),

(ii) property that was acquired before the mine came into production and that would, but for this Class, be included in Class 10 because of paragraph (m) of that Class, or

(iii) property that was acquired after the mine came into production and that would, but for this Class, be included in Class 10 because of paragraph (g), (k), (l) or (r) of that Class, and property that would, but for this Class, be included in Class 41 because of subsection 1102(8) or (9));"

(*a.1*) that is the portion, expressed as a percentage determined by reference to capital cost, of property that

(i) would, but for this Class, be included in Class 10 because of paragraph (g), (k) or (l) of that Class, or that is included in this Class because of subsection 1102(8) or (9),

(ii) is not described in paragraph (a) or (a.2),

(iii) was acquired by the taxpayer principally for the purpose of gaining or producing income from one or more mines that are operated by the taxpayer and situated in Canada, and that became available for use for the purpose of subsection 13(26) of the Act in a taxation year, and

(iv) had not, before it was acquired by the taxpayer, been used for any purpose by any person or partnership with whom the taxpayer was not dealing at arm's length,

where that percentage is determined by the formula

$$100 \times (([A - (B \times 365 / C)]) / A)$$

where

A is the total of all amounts each of which is the capital cost of a property of the taxpayer that became available for use for the purpose of subsection 13(26) of the Act in the year and that is described in subparagraphs (i) to (iv) in respect of the mine or mines, as the case may be,

B is 5% of the taxpayer's gross revenue from the mine or mines, as the case may be, for the year, and

C is the number of days in the year;

(*a.2*) that

(i) is property that would, but for this Class, be included in Class 10 because of paragraph (g), (k) or (l) of that Class or that is included in this Class because of subsection 1102(8) or (9),

(ii) was acquired by the taxpayer in a taxation year principally for the purpose of gaining or producing income from one or more mines each of which

(A) is one or more wells operated by the taxpayer for the extraction of material from a deposit of bituminous sands or oil shales, operated by the taxpayer and situated in Canada.

(B) was the subject of a major expansion after March 6, 1996, and

(C) is a mine in respect of which the Minister, in consultation with the Minister of Natural Resources, determines that the greatest designed capacity of the mine, measured in volume of oil that is not beyond the crude oil stage or its equivalent, immediately after the expansion was not less than 25% greater than the greatest designed capacity of the mine immediately before the expansion,

(iii) was acquired by the taxpayer

(A) after March 6, 1996,

(B) before the completion of the expansion, and

(C) in the course of and principally for the purposes of the expansion, and

(iv) had not, before it was acquired by the taxpayer, been used for any purpose by any person or partnership with whom the taxpayer was not dealing at arm's length;

(*a.3*) that is property included in this Class because of subsection 1102(8) or (9), other than property described in paragraph (a) or (a.2) or the portion of property described in paragraph (a.1);

(*b*) that is property, other than property described in subsection 1101(2c),

(i) described in paragraph (f.1), (g), (j), (k), (l), (m), (r), (t) or (u) of Class 10 that would be included in that Class if this Schedule were read without reference to this paragraph; or

(ii) that is a vessel, including the furniture, fittings, radio communication equipment and other equipment attached thereto, that is designed principally for the purpose of

(A) determining the existence, location, extent or quality of accumulations of petroleum, natural gas or mineral resources, or

(B) drilling oil or gas wells,

and that was acquired by the taxpayer after 1987 other than property that was acquired before 1990

(iii) pursuant to an obligation in writing entered into by the taxpayer before June 18, 1987,

(iv) that was under construction by or on behalf of the taxpayer on June 18, 1987, or

(v) that is machinery and equipment that is a fixed and integral part of property that was under construction by or on behalf of the taxpayer on June 18, 1987.

(*c*) acquired by the taxpayer after May 8, 1972, to be used directly or indirectly by the taxpayer in Canada primarily in Canadian field processing, where the property would be included in Class 29 if

(i) Class 29 were read without reference to

(A) the words "property included in Class 41 solely because of paragraph (c) or (d) of that Class or",

(B) its subparagraphs (b)(iii) and (v), and

(C) its paragraph (c),

(ii) subsection 1104(9) were read without reference to paragraph (k) of that subsection, and

(iii) this Schedule were read without reference to this Class, Class 39 and Class 43; or

(*d*) acquired by the taxpayer after December 5, 1996 (otherwise than pursuant to an agreement in writing made before December 6, 1996) to be leased, in the ordinary course of carrying on a business in Canada of the taxpayer, to a lessee who can reasonably be expected to use, directly or indirectly, the property in Canada primarily in Canadian field processing carried on by the lessee, where the property would be included in Class 29 if

(i) Class 29 were read without reference to

(A) the words "property included in Class 41 solely because of paragraph (c) or (d) of that Class or",

(B) its subparagraphs (b)(iii) and (v), and

(C) its paragraph (c), and

(ii) this Schedule were read without reference to this Class, Class 39 and Class 43.

Class 41.1 (25 per cent)

(Additional allowances: see ¶892)

Oil sands property (other than specified oil sands property) that,

(*a*) is acquired by a taxpayer after March 18, 2007 and before 2016 and that if acquired before March 19, 2007, would be included in paragraphs (*a*), (*a.1*) or (*a.2*) of Class 41, or

(*b*) is acquired by a taxpayer after 2015 and that if acquired before March 19, 2007 would be included in Class 41.

Class 41.2 (25 per cent)

(Additional allowances: see ¶892)

Property, other than an oil sands property or eligible mine development property,

(*a*) that is acquired by a taxpayer after March 20, 2013 and before 2021 and that, if acquired on March 20, 2013, would be included in paragraph (a) or (a.1) of Class 41, or

(*b*) that is acquired by a taxpayer after 2020 and that, if acquired on March 20, 2013, would be included in paragraph (a) or (a.1) of Class 41.

Class 42 (12 per cent)

(see ¶887a)

Property that is

(*a*) fibre-optic cable; or,

(*b*) telephone, telegraph or data communication equipment that is a wire or cable (other than a cable included in this class because of paragraph (a), acquired after February 22, 2005, and that has not been used, or acquired for use, for any purpose before February 23, 2005.

Class 43 (30 per cent)

(see ¶878, ¶892)

Property acquired after February 25, 1992 that

(*a*) is not included in Class 29 or 53, but that would otherwise be included in Class 29 if that Class were read without reference to its subparagraphs (b)(iii) and (v) and paragraph (c)); or

(*b*) is property

(i) that is described in paragraph (k) of Class 10 and that would be included in that Class if this Schedule were read without reference to this paragraph and paragraph (b) of Class 41, and

(ii) that, at the time of its acquisition, can reasonably be expected to be used entirely in Canada and primarily for the purpose of processing ore extracted from a mineral resource located in a country other than Canada.

Class 43.1 (30 per cent)

(see ¶889)

(Note: Many of the terms used in this class have definitions set out in regulation 1104(13). Note also that this class is subject to frequent change, and so it is essential to use an official text and refer the history notes to the amendments when making determinations regarding assets in this class. This is especially true as changes may be made to definitions as well as to Class 43.1 itself.)

Property, other than reconditioned or remanufactured equipment, that would otherwise be included in Class 1, 2, 8, or 48 or in Class 17 because of paragraph (a.1) of that Class

(*a*) that is

(i) electrical generating equipment, including any heat generating equipment used primarily for the purpose of producing heat energy to operate the electrical generating equipment,

(ii) equipment that generates both electrical and heat energy other than, for greater certainty, fuel cell equipment,

(ii.1) fixed location fuel cell equipment that uses hydrogen generated only from internal, or ancillary, fuel reformation equipment (Note: Equipment acquired before March 19, 2007, also had to have a peak capacity of not less than 3 kilowatts of electrical output),

(iii) heat recovery equipment used primarily for the purpose of conserving energy, or reducing the requirement to acquire energy, by extracting for reuse thermal waste that is generated by equipment referred to in subparagraph (i) or (ii),

(iii.1) district energy equipment that is part of a district energy system that uses thermal energy that is primarily supplied by electrical cogeneration equipment that would be property described in paragraphs (*a*) to (*c*) if read without reference to this subparagraph,

(iv) control, feedwater and condensate systems and other equipment, if that property is ancillary to equipment described in any of subparagraphs (i) to (iii), or

(v) an addition to a property described in any of subparagraphs (i) to (iv),

other than buildings or other structures, heat rejection equipment (such as condensers and cooling water systems), transmission equipment, distribution equipment, fuel handling equipment that is not used to upgrade the combustible portion of the fuel and fuel storage facilities,

(*b*) that

(i) is situated in Canada,

(ii) is

(A) acquired by the taxpayer for use by the taxpayer for the purpose of gaining or producing income from a business carried on in Canada or from property situated in Canada, or

(B) leased by the taxpayer to a lessee for the use by the lessee for the purpose of gaining or producing income from a business carried on in Canada or from property situated in Canada, and

(iii) has not been used for any purpose before it was acquired by the taxpayer unless

(A) the property was depreciable property that

(I) was included in Class 34, 43.1 or 43.2 of the person from whom it was acquired, or

(II) would have been included in Class 34, 43.1 or 43.2 of the person from whom it was acquired had the person made a valid election to include the property in Class 43.1 or 43.2, as the case may be, under paragraph 1102(8)(d) or 1102(9)(d), and

(B) the property was acquired by the taxpayer not more than five years after the time it is considered to have become available for use, for the purpose of subsection 13(26) of the Act, by the person from whom it was acquired and remains at the same site in Canada as that at which that person used the property, and

(*c*) that is

(i) part of a system (other than an enhanced combined cycle system) that

(A) is used by the taxpayer, or by a lessee of the taxpayer, to generate electrical energy, or both electrical and heat energy, using only fuel that is eligible waste fuel, fossil fuel, producer gas, spent pulping liquor or any combination of those fuels (Note: Most of the terms here are defined in regulation 1104(13) and the definitions change frequently over time. Producer gas may only be used for new property acquired after February 10, 2014.), and

(B) has a heat rate attributable to fossil fuel (other than solution gas) not exceeding 6,000 BTU per kilowatt-hour of electrical energy generated by the system, which heat rate is calculated as the fossil fuel (expressed as the high heat value of the fossil fuel) used by the system that is chargeable to gross electrical energy output on an annual basis (Note: Fossil fuel is defined in regulation 1104(13) and the definition has changed over time),

(ii) part of an enhanced combined cycle system that

(A) is used by the taxpayer, or by a lessee of the taxpayer, to generate electrical energy using only a combination of natural gas and thermal waste from one or more natural gas compressor systems located on a natural gas pipeline,

(B) has an incremental heat rate not exceeding 6,700 BTU per kilowatt-hour of electricity generated by the system, which heat rate is calculated as the natural gas (expressed as its high heat value) used by the system that is chargeable to gross electrical energy output on an annual basis, and

(C) does not have economically viable access to a steam host

(Note: Applicable to property acquired after March 21, 2011.), or

(iii) equipment that is used by the taxpayer, or by a lessee of the taxpayer, to generate electrical energy in a process all or substantially all of the energy input of which is thermal waste, other than

(A) equipment that uses heat produced by a gas turbine that is part of the first stage of a combined cycle system, and

(B) equipment that, on the date of its acquisition, uses chlorofluorocarbons (CFCs) or hydrochlorofluorocarbons ("HCFCs"), within the meaning assigned by the *Ozone-Depleting Substances Regulations, 1998*,

and property, other than reconditioned or remanufactured equipment, that would otherwise be included in another Class in this Schedule

(*d*) that is (Note: The changes in (d) have been frequent; be sure to check the actual regulation and its history.)

(i) property that meets the following conditions:

(A) it is used by the taxpayer, or by a lessee of the taxpayer, primarily for the purpose of heating an actively circulated liquid or gas and is

(I) active solar heating equipment, including such equipment that consists of above ground solar collectors, solar energy conversion equipment, solar water heaters, energy storage equipment, control equipment and equipment designed to interface solar heating equipment with other heating equipment, or

(II) equipment that is part of a ground source heat pump system that transfers heat to or from the ground or groundwater (but not to or from surface water such as a river, a lake or an ocean) and that, at the time of installation, meets the standards set by the Canadian Standards Association for the design and installation of earth energy systems, including such equipment that consists of piping (including above or below ground piping and the cost of drilling a well, or trenching, for the purpose of installing that piping), energy conversion equipment, energy storage equipment, control equipment and equipment designed to enable the system to interface with other heating or cooling equipment, and

Legislative Proposals (July 29, 2016)

Note: When Legislative Proposals, July 29, 2016, achieves Royal Assent, the legislation will be modified to read:

(I) active solar heating equipment, including such equipment that consists of above ground solar collectors, solar energy conversion equipment, solar water heaters, thermal energy storage equipment, control equipment and equipment designed to interface solar heating equipment with other heating equipment, or

(II) equipment that is part of a ground source heat pump system that transfers heat to or from the ground or groundwater (but not to or from surface water such as a river, a lake or an ocean) and that, at the time of installation, meets the standards set by the Canadian Standards Association for the design and installation of earth energy systems, including such equipment that consists of piping (including above or below ground piping and the cost of drilling a well, or trenching, for the purpose of installing that piping), energy conversion equipment, thermal energy storage equipment, control equipment and equipment designed to enable the system to interface with other heating or cooling equipment, and

(B) it is not a building, part of a building (other than a solar collector that is not a window and that is integrated into a building), equipment used to heat water for use in a swimming pool, energy equipment that backs up equipment described in subclause (A)(I) or (II) nor equipment that distributes heated or cooled air or water in a building,

(ii) a hydro-electric installation of a producer of hydro-electric energy, where that installation

(A) has, if acquired after February 21, 1994 and before December 11, 2001, an annual average generating capacity not exceeding 15 megawatts upon completion of the site development, or, if acquired after December 10, 2001, a rated capacity at the hydro-electric installation site that does not exceed 50 megawatts, and

(B) is the electrical generating equipment and plant (including structures) of that producer including a canal, a dam, a dyke, an overflow spillway, a penstock, a powerhouse (complete with electrical generating equipment and other ancillary equipment), control equipment, fishways or fish bypasses, and transmission equipment,

other than distribution equipment, property otherwise included in Class 10 and property that would be included in Class 17 if that class were read without reference to its subparagraph (a.1)(i),

(iii) an addition or alteration, which is acquired after February 21, 1994 and before December 11, 2001, to a hydro-electric installation that is described in subparagraph (ii) or that would be so described if that installation were acquired by the taxpayer after February 21, 1994, and which results in an increase in generating capacity, if the resulting annual average generating capacity of the hydro-electric installation does not exceed 15 megawatts,

(iii.1) an addition or alteration, which is acquired after December 10, 2001, to a hydro-electric installation that is described in subparagraph (ii) or that would be so described if that installation were acquired by the taxpayer after February 21, 1994, and which results in an increase in generating capacity, if the resulting rated capacity at the hydro-electric installation site does not exceed 50 megawatts,

(iv) heat recovery equipment used by the taxpayer, or by a lessee of the taxpayer, primarily for the purpose of conserving energy, or reducing the requirement to acquire energy, by extracting for reuse thermal waste that is generated directly in an industrial process (other than an industrial process that generates or processes electrical energy), including such equipment that consists of heat exchange equipment, compressors used to upgrade low pressure steam, vapour or gas, waste heat boilers and other ancillary equipment such as control panels, fans, instruments or pumps, but not including property that is employed in re-using the recovered heat (such as property that is part of the internal heating or cooling system of a building or electrical generating equipment), is a building or is equipment that recovers heat primarily for use for heating water in a swimming pool.

Legislative Proposals (Sept. 16, 2016)

Note: When Legislative Proposals, September 16, 2016, achieves Royal Assent, the legislation will be modified to read:

(iv) heat recovery equipment used by the taxpayer, or by a lessee of the taxpayer, primarily for the purpose of conserving energy, reducing the requirement to acquire energy or extracting heat for sale, by extracting for reuse thermal waste that is generated directly in an industrial process (other than an industrial process that generates or processes electrical energy), including such equipment that consists of heat exchange equipment, compressors used to upgrade low pressure steam, vapour or gas, waste heat boilers and other ancillary equipment such as control panels, fans, instruments or pumps, but not including property that is employed in re-using the recovered heat (such as property that is part of the internal heating or cooling system of a building or electrical generating equipment), is a building or is equipment that recovers heat primarily for use for heating water in a swimming pool,

(v) a fixed location device that is a wind energy conversion system that

(A) is used by the taxpayer, or by a lessee of the taxpayer, primarily for the purpose of generating electrical energy, and

(B) consists of wind-driven turbine, electrical generating equipment and related equipment, including

(I) control, conditioning and battery storage equipment,

Legislative Proposals (July 29, 2016)

Note: When Legislative Proposals, July 29, 2016, achieves Royal Assent, the legislation will be modified to read:

(I) control and conditioning equipment,

(II) support structures,

(III) powerhouse complete with other ancillary equipment, and

(IV) transmission equipment,

other than distribution equipment, auxiliary electrical generating equipment, property otherwise included in Class 10 and property that would be included in Class 17 if that Class were read without reference to its subparagraph (a.1)(i),

(vi) fixed location photovoltaic equipment that is used by the taxpayer, or a lessee of the taxpayer, primarily for the purpose of generating electrical energy from solar energy if the equipment consists of solar cells or modules and related equipment including inverters, control, conditioning and battery storage equipment, support structures and transmission equipment, but not including

Legislative Proposals (July 29, 2016)

Note: When Legislative Proposals, July 29, 2016, achieves Royal Assent, the legislation will be modified to read:

(vi) fixed location photovoltaic equipment that is used by the taxpayer, or a lessee of the taxpayer, primarily for the purpose of generating electrical energy from solar energy if the equipment consists of solar cells or modules and related equipment including inverters, control and conditioning equipment, support structures and transmission equipment, but not including

(A) a building or a part of a building (other than a solar cell or module that is integrated into a building),

(B) auxiliary electrical generating equipment, property otherwise included in Class 10 and property that would be included in Class 17 if that Class were read without reference to its subparagraph (a.1)(i), and

(C) distribution equipment,

(vii) equipment used by the taxpayer, or by a lessee of the taxpayer, primarily for the purpose of generating electrical energy solely from geothermal energy, including such equipment that consists of piping (including above or below ground piping and the cost of drilling a well, or trenching, for the purpose of installing that piping), pumps, heat exchangers, steam separators, electrical generating equipment and ancillary equipment used to collect the geothermal heat, but not including buildings, transmission equipment, distribution equipment, equipment designed to store electrical energy, property otherwise included in Class 10 and property that would be included in Class 17 if that Class were read without reference to its subparagraph (*a*.1)(i),

Legislative Proposals (July 29, 2016)

Note: When Legislative Proposals, July 29, 2016, achieves Royal Assent, the legislation will be modified to read:

(vii) equipment used by the taxpayer, or by a lessee of the taxpayer, primarily for the purpose of generating electrical energy solely from geothermal energy, including such equipment that consists of piping (including above or below ground piping and the cost of drilling a well, or trenching, for the purpose of installing that piping), pumps, heat exchangers, steam separators, electrical generating equipment and ancillary equipment used to collect the geothermal heat, but not including buildings, transmission equipment, distribution equipment, property otherwise included in Class 10 and property that would be included in Class 17 if that Class were read without reference to its subparagraph (*a*.1)(i),

(viii) equipment used by the taxpayer, or by a lessee of the taxpayer, primarily for the purpose of collecting landfill gas or digester gas (Note: These terms are defined in Regulation 1104(13)), including such equipment that consists of piping (including above or below ground piping and the cost of drilling a well, or trenching, for the purpose of installing that piping), fans, compressors, storage tanks, heat exchangers and related equipment used to collect gas, to remove non-combustibles and contaminants from the gas or to store the gas, but not including property otherwise included in Class 10 or 17,

(ix) equipment used by the taxpayer, or by a lessee of the taxpayer, for the sole purpose of generating heat energy, primarily from the consumption of eligible waste fuel, producer gas or a combination of those fuels (Note: Eligible waste fuel is defined in Regulation 1104(13) and the definition has changed over time) and not using any fuel other than eligible waste fuel, fossil fuel, or producer gas, including such equipment that consists of fuel handling equipment used to upgrade the combustible portion of the fuel and control, feedwater and condensate systems, and other ancillary equipment, but not including equipment used for the purpose of producing heat energy to operate electrical generating equipment, buildings or other structures, heat rejection equipment (such as condensers and cooling water systems), fuel storage facilities, other fuel handling equipment, and property otherwise included in Class 10 or 17 (Note: Producer gas may only be used for new equipment acquired after February 10, 2014.),

(x) an expansion engine with one or more turbines, or cylinders, that convert the compression energy in pressurized natural gas into shaft power that generates electricity, including the related electrical generating equipment and ancillary controls, where the expansion engine

(A) is part of a system that is installed

(I) on a distribution line of a distributor of natural gas, or

(II) on a branch distribution line of a taxpayer primarily engaged in the manufacturing or processing of goods for sale or lease if the branch line is used to deliver natural gas directly to the taxpayer's manufacturing or processing facility, and

(B) is used instead of a pressure reducing valve,

(xi) equipment used by the taxpayer, or by a lessee of the taxpayer, in a system that converts wood waste or plant residue into bio-oil (Note: These terms are defined in Regulation 1104(13)), if that bio-oil is used primarily for the purpose of generating heat that is used directly in an industrial process or a greenhouse, generating electricity or generating electricity and heat, other than equipment used for the collection, storage or transportation of wood waste or plant residue, buildings or other structures and property otherwise included in Class 10 or 17,

(xii) fixed location fuel cell equipment used by the taxpayer, or by a lessee of the taxpayer, that uses hydrogen generated only from ancillary electrolysis equipment (or, if the fuel cell is reversible, the fuel cell itself) using electricity all or substantially all of which is generated by photovoltaic, wind energy conversion or hydro-electric equipment, of the taxpayer or the lessee, and equipment ancillary to the fuel cell equipment other than buildings or other structures, transmission equipment, distribution equipment, auxiliary electrical generating equipment and property otherwise included in Class 10 or 17,

Legislative Proposals (July 29, 2016)

Note: When Legislative Proposals, July 29, 2016, achieves Royal Assent, the legislation will be modified to read:

(xii) fixed location fuel cell equipment used by the taxpayer, or by a lessee of the taxpayer, that uses hydrogen generated only from ancillary electrolysis equipment (or, if the fuel cell is reversible, the fuel cell itself) using electricity all or substantially all of which is generated by using kinetic energy of flowing water or wave or tidal energy (otherwise than by diverting or impeding the natural flow of the water or by using physical barriers or dam-like structures) or by geothermal, photovoltaic, wind energy conversion, or hydro-electric equipment, of the taxpayer or the lessee, and equipment ancillary to the fuel cell equipment other than buildings or other structures, transmission equipment, distribution equipment, auxiliary electrical generating equipment and property otherwise included in Class 10 or 17,

(xiii) property that is part of a system that is used by the taxpayer, or by a lessee of the taxpayer, primarily to produce and store biogas (Note: Biogas is defined in Regulation 1104(13) and the definition has changed over time), including equipment that is an anaerobic digester reactor, a buffer tank, a pre-treatment tank, biogas piping, a fan, a compressor, a heat exchanger, a biogas storage tank and equipment used to remove non-combustibles and contaminants from the gas, but not including

(A) property (other than a buffer tank) that is used to collect, move or store organic waste,

(B) equipment used to process the residue after digestion or to treat recovered liquids,

(C) buildings or other structures, and

(D) property otherwise included in Class 10 or 17,

(xiv) property that is used by the taxpayer, or by a lessee of the taxpayer, primarily for the purpose of generating electricity using kinetic energy of flowing water or wave or tidal energy (otherwise than by diverting or impeding the natural flow of the water or by using physical barriers or dam-like structures), including support structures, control, conditioning and battery storage equipment, submerged cables and transmission equipment, but not including buildings, distribution equipment, auxiliary electricity generating equipment, property otherwise included in Class 10 and property that would be included in Class 17 if that class were read without reference to its subparagraph (*a*.1)(i),

Legislative Proposals (July 29, 2016)

Note: When Legislative Proposals, July 29, 2016, achieves Royal Assent, the legislation will be modified to read:

(xiv) property that is used by the taxpayer, or by a lessee of the taxpayer, primarily for the purpose of generating electricity using kinetic energy of flowing water or wave or tidal energy (otherwise than by diverting or impeding the natural flow of the water or by using physical barriers or dam-like structures), including support structures, control and conditioning equipment, submerged cables and transmission equipment, but not including buildings, distribution equipment, auxiliary electricity generating equipment, property otherwise included in Class 10 and property that would be included in Class 17 if that class were read without reference to its subparagraph (*a*.1)(i),

(xv) district energy equipment that

(A) is used by the taxpayer or by a lessee of the taxpayer,

(B) is part of a district energy system that uses thermal energy that is primarily supplied by equipment that is described in subparagraphs (i), (iv) or (ix) or would be described in those subparagraphs if owned by the taxpayer, and

(C) is not a building, or

(xvi) equipment used by the taxpayer, or by a lessee of the taxpayer, primarily for the purpose of generating producer gas (other than producer gas that is to be converted into liquid biofuels or chemicals), including related piping (including fans and compressors), air separation equipment, storage equipment, equipment used for drying or shredding eligible waste fuel, ash-handling equipment, equipment used to upgrade the producer gas into biomethane and equipment used to remove non-combustibles and contaminants from the producer gas, but not including buildings or other structures, heat rejection equipment (such as condensers and cooling water systems), equipment used to convert producer gas into liquid biofuels or chemicals, and property otherwise included in Class 10 or 17,

(Note: Equipment may only be included if new and acquired after February 10, 2014.)

Legislative Proposals (July 29, 2016)

Note: When Legislative Proposals, July 29, 2016, achieves Royal Assent, the legislation will be modified by striking out "or" at the end of subparagraph (xv) and "and" at the end of subparagraph (xvi) and by adding the following:

(xvii) equipment used by the taxpayer, or by a lessee of the taxpayer, for the purpose of charging electric vehicles, including charging stations, transformers, distribution and control panels, circuit breakers, conduits and related wiring, if

(A) the equipment is situated

(I) on the load side of an electricity meter used for billing purposes by a power utility, or

(II) on the generator side of an electricity meter used to measure electricity generated by the taxpayer or the lessee, as the case may be,

(B) more than 75 per cent of the electrical equipment capacity is dedicated to charging electric vehicles, and

(C) the equipment is

(I) an electric vehicle charging station that supplies more than 10 kilowatts of continuous power, or

(II) used primarily in connection with one or more electric vehicle charging stations each of which supplies more than 10 kilowatts of continuous power, or

(xviii) fixed location energy storage property that

(A) is used by the taxpayer, or by a lessee of the taxpayer, primarily for the purpose of storing electrical energy

(I) including batteries, compressed air energy storage, flywheels, ancillary equipment (including control and conditioning equipment) and related structures, and

(II) not including buildings, pumped hydroelectric storage, hydro electric dams and reservoirs, property used solely for backup electrical energy, batteries used in motor vehicles, fuel cell systems where the hydrogen is produced via steam reformation of methane and property otherwise included in Class 10 or 17, and

(B) either

(I) if the electrical energy to be stored is used in connection with property of the taxpayer or a lessee of the taxpayer, as the case may be, is described in paragraph (c) or would be described in this paragraph if it were read without reference to this subparagraph, or

(II) meets the condition that the efficiency of the electrical energy storage system that includes the property – computed by reference to the quantity of electrical energy supplied to and discharged from the electrical energy storage system – is greater than 50%, and

(Note: when enacted, (xvii) and (xviii) will apply to property acquired after March 21, 2016 that has not been used or acquired for use before March 22, 2016.)

(*e*) that

(i) is situated in Canada,

(ii) is

(A) acquired by the taxpayer for use by the taxpayer for the purpose of gaining or producing income from a business carried on in Canada or from property situated in Canada, or

(B) leased by the taxpayer to a lessee for the use by the lessee for the purpose of gaining or producing income from a business carried on in Canada or from property situated in Canada, and

(iii) has not been used for any purpose before it was acquired by the taxpayer unless

(A) the property was depreciable property that

(I) was included in Class 34, 43.1 or 43.2 of the person from whom it was acquired, or

(II) would have been included in Class 34, 43.1 or 43.2 of the person from whom it was acquired had the person made a valid election to include the property in Class 43.1 or 43.2, as the case may be, under paragraph 1102(8)(*d*) or 1102(9)(*d*), and

(B) the property was acquired by the taxpayer not more than five years after the time it is considered to have become available for use, for the purpose of subsection 13(26) of the Act, by the person from whom it was acquired and remains at the same site in Canada as that at which that person used the property, or

Class 43.2 (50 per cent)

(see ¶889)

Property that is acquired after February 22, 2005 and before 2020 (other than property that was included, before it was acquired, in another class in this Schedule by any taxpayer) and that is property that would otherwise be included in Class 43.1

(*a*) if the expression "6,000 BTU" in clause (*c*)(i)(B) of that Class were read as the expression "4,750 BTU"; or

(*b*) because of paragraph (*d*) of that Class.

Legislative Proposals (July 29, 2016)

Note: When Legislative Proposals, July 29, 2016, achieves Royal Assent, the legislation will be modified to read:

(*a*) otherwise than because of paragraph (*d*) of that Class, if the expression "6,000 BTU" in clause (*c*)(i)(B) of that Class were read as "4,750 BTU"; or

(*b*) because of paragraph (*d*) of that Class, if

(i) the expression "6,000 BTU" in clause (*c*)(i)(B) of that Class were read as "4,750 BTU",

(ii) subclauses (*d*)(xvii)(C)(I) and (II) of that Class were read as follows:

(I) an electric vehicle charging station that supplies at least 90 kilowatts ofcontinuous power, or

(II) used

1. primarily in connection with one or more electric vehicle charging stations each of which supplies more than 10 kilowatts of continuous power, and

2. in connection with one or more electric vehicle charging stations each of which supplies at least 90 kilowatts of continuous power, or

and

(iii) clause (*d*)(xviii)(B) of that Class were read without reference to its subclause (II).

(Note: when enacted, the proposed replacements to (a) and (b) will apply to property acquired after March 21, 2016 that has not been used or acquired for use before March 22, 2016.)

Class 44 (25 per cent)

(see ¶880)

Property that is a patent, or a right to use patented information for a limited or unlimited period.

Class 45 (45 per cent)

(see ¶886t)

Property acquired after March 22, 2004 and before March 19, 2007 (other than property acquired before 2005 in respect of which an election is made under subsection 1101(5q)) that is general-purpose electronic data processing equipment and systems software for that equipment, including ancillary data processing equipment, but not including property that is principally or is used principally as (*a*) electronic process control or monitor equipment,

(*b*) electronic communications control equipment,

(*c*) systems software for equipment referred to in paragraph (a) or (b), or

(*d*) data handling equipment (other than data handling equipment that is ancillary to general-purpose electronic data processing equipment).

Class 46 (30 per cent)

(see ¶886v)

Property acquired after March 22, 2004 that is data network infrastructure equipment, and systems software for that equipment, that would, but for this Class, be included in Class 8 because of paragraph (i) of that Class.

Class 47 (8 per cent)

(see ¶886t)

Property that is

(*a*) transmission or distribution equipment (which may include for this purpose a structure) acquired after February 22, 2005 that is used for the transmission or distribution of electrical energy, other than

(i) property that is a building; and

(ii) property that has been used or acquired for use for any purpose by any taxpayer before February 23, 2005, or

(*b*) equipment acquired after March 18, 2007 that is part of a liquefied natural gas facility that liquefies or regasifies natural gas, including controls, cooling equipment, compressors, pumps, storage tanks, vaporizers and ancillary equipment, loading and unloading pipelines on the facility site used to transport liquefied natural gas between a ship and the facility, and related structures, other than property that is *is (Note: certain LNG equipment and buildings may be eligible for accelerated CCA, see ¶889f.41)*:

(i) acquired for the purpose of producing oxygen or nitrogen,

(ii) a breakwater, a dock, a jetty, a wharf, or a similar structure, or

(iii) a building.

Class 48 (15 per cent)

(see ¶889.20)

Property acquired after February 22, 2005 that is a combustion turbine (including associated burners and compressors) that generates electrical energy, other than

(*a*) electrical generating equipment described in any of paragraphs (f) to (h) of Class 8;

(*b*) property acquired before 2006 in respect of which an election is made under subsection 1101(5t); and

(*c*) property that has been used or acquired for use for any purpose by any taxpayer before February 23, 2005.

Class 49 (8 per cent)

(see ¶889f)

Property that is a pipeline, including control and monitoring devices, valves and other equipment ancillary to the pipeline, that

(*a*) is acquired after February 22, 2005, is used for the transmission (but not the distribution) of petroleum, natural gas or related hydrocarbons, and is not

(i) a pipeline described in subparagraph (l)(ii) of Class 1,

(ii) property that has been used or acquired for use for any purpose by any taxpayer before February 23, 2005,

(iii) equipment included in Class 7 because of paragraph (*j*) of that Class, or

(iv) a building or other structure; or

(*b*) is acquired after February 25, 2008, is used for the transmission of carbon dioxide, and is not

(i) equipment included in Class 7 because of paragraph (k) of that Class, or

(ii) a building or other structure.

Class 50 (55 per cent)

(see ¶886t.05)

Property acquired after March 18, 2007 that is general-purpose electronic data processing equipment and systems software for that equipment, including ancillary data processing equipment, but not including property that is included in Class 52 or that is principally or is used principally as

(*a*) electronic process control or monitor equipment;

(*b*) electronic communications control equipment;

(*c*) systems software for equipment referred to in paragraph (a) or (b); or

(*d*) data handling equipment (other than data handling equipment that is ancillary to general-purpose electronic data processing equipment).

Class 51 (6 per cent)

(see ¶889f.15)

Property acquired after March 18, 2007 that is a pipeline, including control and monitoring devices, valves and other equipment ancillary to the pipeline, used for the distribution (but not the transmission) of natural gas, other than

(*a*) a pipeline described in subparagraph (l)(ii) of Class 1 or in Class 49;

(*b*) property that has been used or acquired for use for any purpose by a taxpayer before March 19, 2007; and

(*c*) a building or other structure.

Class 52 (100 per cent)

(and no half-year rule (¶802.10)

(see ¶886t.05))

Property acquired by a taxpayer after January 27, 2009 and before February 2011 that

(*a*) is general-purpose electronic data processing equipment and systems software for that equipment, including ancillary data processing equipment, but not including property that is principally or is used principally as

(i) electronic process control or monitor equipment,

(ii) electronic communications control equipment,

(iii) systems software for equipment referred to in paragraph (i) or (ii), or

(iv) data handling equipment (other than data handling equipment that is ancillary to general-purpose electronic data processing equipment);

(*b*) is situated in Canada;

(*c*) has not been used, or acquired for use, for any purpose whatever before it is acquired by the taxpayer; and

(*d*) is acquired by the taxpayer

(i) for use in a business carried on by the taxpayer in Canada or for the purpose of earning income from property situated in Canada, or

(ii) for lease by the taxpayer to a lessee for use by the lessee in a business carried on by the lessee in Canada or for the purpose of earning income from property situated in Canada.

Class 53 (50 per cent)

Property acquired after 2015 and before 2026 that is not included in Class 29, but that would otherwise be included in that Class if

(*a*) subparagraph (*a*)(ii) of that Class were read without reference to "in Canadian field processing carried on by the lessee or"; and

(*b*) that Class were read without reference to its subparagraphs (*b*)(iv) to (vi) and paragraph (*c*).

(Note: see ¶878.03)

(ITR: Sch. II)

[¶899] ALPHABETICAL LIST OF ASSETS BY CAPITAL COST ALLOWANCE CLASS AND RATE

The following table sets out the capital cost allowance rates and classes for certain types of assets — listed alphabetically. This table is for use only as a quick reference guide. See Part XI and Schedules II, III, IV, V, and VI of the *Income Tax Regulations* for detailed rules relating to capital cost allowance.

Item	Rate	Class
Access roads and trails for the protection of standing timber	30%	10
Air conditioning equipment — same rate as building[1]		
Aircraft	25%	9
furniture and fittings	25%	9
hangars[1]	10%	6
Airplane runways	8%	17
Amusement park components (including fences, bridges, canals, stalls, tractors, etc.)	15%	37
land improvements[35]	15%	37
Apparel, used for earning rental income[1,26]	100%	12
Asphalt surface, storage yard	8%	17
Assets, tangible capital[1,2]	20%	8
used primarily in manufacturing or processing[10,15]		29, 39, 40, 43, 53
Automobiles[1]	30%	10
in excess of prescribed amount (Reg. 7307(1))[1,7]	30%	10.1
for lease or rental[22]	40%	16
Automotive equipment[1]	30%	10
designed for and used in amusement parks	15%	37
Bar code scanners — see Cash registers		
Billboards	20%	8
Boats — see Vessels		
Boilers		
heating use — same rate as building		
used primarily in manufacturing or processing[10,15]		29, 39, 43, 53
Books of lending libraries[26]	100%	12
Breakwaters		
wooden	10%	6
other	5%	3
Bridges[1]	4%	1
Buildings[1]		
addition or alteration — same class as buildings[13]		
amusement park stalls	15%	37
brick, stone, cement, etc., acquired before 1988	5%	3
brick, stone, cement, etc., acquired after 1987	4%	1
component parts — generally same class as building (see individual items)		
farm ensilage storage	20%	8
foundation excavation — same rate as building		
frame, log, stucco on frame, galvanized iron or corrugated metal[25]	10%	6
kiln, tank, vat used in manufacturing or processing	20%	8
liquefaction buildings acquired after Feb. 19, 2015, and before 2025.[5]	4%	1
manufacturing or processing[39]	4%	1

Item	Rate	Class
mining (except refineries and office buildings not at mine)	30%	10
multiple-unit residential[7,18]	4%	1
non-residential[39]	4%	1
portable camp	30%	10
rental property[7]		
storage of fresh fruits and vegetables	20%	8
Buses	30%	10
Cable TV converters and descramblers	40%	30
Cables — telephone, telegraph or data communication		
acquired after Feb. 22, 2005	12%	42
fibre optic	12%	42
Calculator	20%	8
Canals[1]	4%	1
Canoes	15%	7
Capital tangible assets[1,2]	20%	8
used primarily in manufacturing or processing[10,15]		29, 39, 40, 43, 53
Cash registers	20%	8
electronic, to record multiple sales taxes acquired after Aug. 8, 1989 and before 1993	100%	12
Catalyst	5%	26
Cattle	nil	—
Chinaware[26]	100%	12
Cold storage structures	20%	8
Computer hardware and systems software	55%	50
acquired after Jan. 27, 2009 and before Feb. 2011[40]	100%	52
Computer software[10,24]	100%	12
Concessions, for a limited period		14
Contractors' movable equipment, heavy	30%	10
Power-operated and designed for the purpose of excavating, moving, placing or compacting earth, rock, concrete or asphalt.	30%	38
Conversion cost — see Vessels		
Copyrights, for a limited period		14
Costume and accessories for earning rental income[1,26]	100%	12
Culverts[1,10]	4%	1
Customer lists [Proposed][21]	5%, 7%	14.1
Cutlery[26]	100%	12
Cutting part of a machine[1]	100%	12
Dams[1]	4%	1
Data communication equipment — wire and cable		
acquired after Feb. 22, 2005	12%	42
Data communication switching equipment[16]	8%	17
Dental instruments costing less than $500[1,26,28]	100%	12

Item	Rate	Class
Dies[1]	100%	12
Digital video disk — See DVD		
Display fixtures (window)	20%	8
Distribution equipment for heat, electrical energy, or water[4]	4%	1
for water or steam, acquired after Feb. 27, 2000	8%	17
for electrical energy, acquired after Feb. 22, 2005[32]	8%	47
Docks[1]	5%	3
Drive-in theatre property	30%	10
DVD, for rental[23,26]	100%	12
Electric vehicle charging stations	20%	8
greater than 10kw but less than 90kw [Proposed]	30%	43.1
at least 90kw [Proposed]	50%	43.2
Electrical advertising signs[10,16]	20%	8
Electrical energy storage equipment [Proposed]	30%	43.1
[Proposed]	50%	43.2
Electrical generating and distributing equipment[6,10]		
acquired after 1987	4%	1
acquired after Feb. 27, 2000 for generation[10]	8%	17
acquired after Feb. 22, 2005 for transmission or distribution[32]	8%	47
combustion turbines acquired after Feb. 22, 2005[32]	15%	48
energy efficient generating equipment[19,32,33]	30%, 50%	43.1, 43.2
portable or maximum load 15 kw	20%	8
Electric wiring — same rate as building		
Electronic communications equipment including fax machines and telephone equipment[10]	20%	8
Electronic data processing equipment[1,15,16,40]		
used primarily in manufacturing or processing[15]		10, 29, 40
Electronic data processing equipment — data network infrastructure and systems software	30%	46
Electronic data processing equipment — general purpose and systems software	55%	50
acquired after Jan. 27, 2009 and before Feb. 2011[40]	100%	52
Elevators — same rate as building		
Equipment (see specific types)		
if not specifically mentioned[2]	20%	8
manufacturing or processing[10,15]		29, 39, 40, 43, 53
Escalators — same rate as building		
Fences[1]	10%	6

Item	Rate	Class
Fibre-optic cable	12%	42
Films, motion pictures	30%	10
Canadian production[7]	30%	10
certified production	100%	12
television commercials	100%	12
Franchises		
for a limited period		14
for an unlimited period [Proposed]	5%, 7%	14.1
Furniture (not otherwise listed)	20%	8
Gas manufacturing and distributing equipment, plants and pipelines acquired after 1987[8]	4%	1
distribution pipelines acquired after Mar. 18, 2007[31]	6%	51
liquefied natural gas equipment acquired after Mar. 18, 2007[32]	8%	47
liquefied natural gas equipment acquired after Feb. 19, 2015, and before 2025.[11]	8%	47
liquefaction buildings equipment acquired after Feb. 19, 2015, and before 2025.[16]	4%	1
transmission pipelines acquired after Feb. 22, 2005[10,31]	8%	49
Gas well equipment acquired after 1987	25%	41
Generating equipment and plant of producer or distributor of electrical energy[4,6]		
acquired after 1987	4%	1
acquired after Feb. 27, 2000	8%	17
energy efficient[32,33]	30%, 50%	43.1, 43.2
wave and tidal energy equipment[32,33]	30%, 50%	43.1, 43.2
Glass tableware[1,26]	100%	12
Goodwill [Proposed]	5%, 7%	14.1
Grain storage facilities — see buildings		
Greenhouses[1]	10%	6
rigid frame with plastic cover	20%	8
Hangars[1]	10%	6
Harness equipment[1]	30%	10
Heat production and recovery equipment[19,32,33]	50%, 30%, 50%	34, 43.1, 43.2
Heating equipment		
distribution plant, acquired after 1987	4%	1
general — same rate as building		
solar or energy efficient[19,32,33]	30%, 50%	43.1, 43.2
Herbs	nil	—
Horses	nil	—
Instruments, dental or medical costing less than $500[1,26,28]	100%	12
Jetties	5%	3
wood	10%	6
Jigs[1]	100%	12

Item	Rate	Class
Kitchen utensils costing less than $500[1,26,28]	100%	12
Land	nil	—
deemed depreciable[7]	nil	36
Lasts[1]	100%	12
Leasehold interest		13
Lending library books[1,26]	100%	12
Licences		
for a limited period		14
for an unlimited period [Proposed]	5%, 7%	14.1
Lighting fixture — same rate as building		
Linen[1,26]	100%	12
Logging mechanical equipment[3]	30%	10
Machinery and equipment		
additional capital cost allowance on grain elevators	14%	8
not specifically listed	20%	8
used primarily in manufacturing or processing[10,15]		29, 39, 40, 43, 53
Marine railways	15%	7
Medical instruments costing less than $500[1,26,28]	100%	12
Mining equipment	30%	10
Mining equipment, acquired for processing foreign ore in Canada	30%	43
Mining equipment, new or expanded mines[7,14]		
mining property acquired after 1987	25%	41
oil sands property acquired after March 18, 2007	25%	41.1
mining property acquired after March 20, 2013, other than "eligible mine development property"	25%	41.2
Moles[1]	5%	3
Motion picture drive-in theatres	30%	10
Motion picture films — see Films		
Moulds[1]	100%	12
Multiple-unit residential buildings[7,18]	5%, 10%	31, 32
Office equipment	20%	8
Offshore drilling platforms		
acquired after 1987	25%	41
Offshore drilling vessels[7,17]		
acquired after 1987	25%	41
Oil pipelines		
acquired after 1987	4%	1
acquired after Feb. 22, 2005 — transmission[31]	8%	49
Oil sands — see Mining equipment, new or expanded mines		
Oil storage tanks[1,15]	10%	6

Item	Rate	Class
used primarily in manufacturing or processing[15]		29, 39, 43, 53
Oil well equipment[1]		
acquired after 1987[14]	25%	41
Overburden removal cost, designated[1,26]	100%	12
Parking area	8%	17
Passenger vehicles — see Automobiles		
Patents[20]		14
	25%	44
	5%, 7%	14.1
Patterns[1]	100%	12
Photocopy machines[10]	20%	8
Pinball machines — see Video games		
Pipelines		
acquired after 1987	4%	1
acquired after February 22, 2005 and used for transmission of oil and natural gas[31]	8%	49
acquired after March 18, 2007 for distribution of natural gas[31]	6%	51
acquired after Feb. 25, 2008 for transmission of carbon dioxide	8%	49
Plumbing — same rate as building		
Pollution control equipment[12]		
Portable construction camp buildings	30%	10
Portable electrical generating equipment	20%	8
Portable tool used for temporary rentals	30%	10
Power operated movable equipment[15]		
acquired after 1987	30%	38
Power plants — see Electrical power plants		
Producer gas generating equipment	30%	43.1
acquired after February 10, 2014	50%	43.2
Production equipment of distributor of heat (including structures)		
acquired after 1987	4%	1
acquired after Feb. 27, 2000	8%	17
Pumping and compression equipment		
Gas and oil acquired before Feb. 23, 2005	20%	8
Gas and oil acquired after Feb. 22, 2005[10,31]	15%	7
Carbon dioxide acquired after Feb. 25, 2008[31]	15%	7
Radar equipment	20%	8
Radio communication equipment (excluding satellites)	20%	8
Radium	nil	—
Railway car and rail suspension devices[1,7,29]		
acquired before Feb. 28, 2000[29]	7%	35
acquired after Feb. 27, 2000[29]	15%	7
Railway locomotive (excluding automotive railway car)		

Item	Rate	Class
acquired after Feb. 27, 2000[29]	15%	7
acquired after Feb. 25, 2008[29]	30%	10
Railway, marine	15%	7
Railway track or grading[1,7,29]	4%	1
Railway traffic control or signaling equipment[1,7,29]	4%	1
Rapid transit car[36]	20%	8
Refrigeration equipment	20%	8
Renewable energy generation equipment[6,19,32,33]		
acquired after Feb. 22, 2005 and before 2020[33]	50%	43.2
Rental property[7]		
Roads[1]	8%	17
acquired in relation to a mine	25%	41
forestry (may be depreciated with timber limit)[3]		
oil and gas mining temporary access[37]		
Roller rink floors	30%	10
Rowboats	15%	7
Satellites	30%	10
Scows	15%	7
Shaping part of a machine[1]	100%	12
Ships, including ships under construction[17]	15%	7
Shrubs	nil	—
Sidewalks	8%	17
Sleighs[1]	30%	10
Smart phone	55%	50
Solar heating equipment acquired after Feb. 22, 2005 and before 2020[32,33]	50%	43.2
Spare parts for an aircraft	25%	9
Sprinkler systems — same rate as building		
Stable equipment[1]	30%	10
Storage area	8%	17
Storage tanks, oil or water[1]	10%	6
direct manufacturing use[15]		29, 39, 43, 53
Subway or tunnel[1]	4%	1
Systems software — general purpose electronic data processing equipment[1,40]		
acquired after Mar. 22, 2004 and before Mar. 19 2007[40]	45%	45
acquired after Mar. 18, 2007[40]	55%	50
acquired after Jan. 27, 2009 and before Feb. 2011[40]	100%	52
primary manufacturing purpose, acquired after March 18, 2007 and before January 28, 2009[15,40]		10, 29, 40
Tableware, glass[1,26]	100%	12
Tangible capital assets[1,2]	20%	8
Tank cars, railway[1,7]	7%	35
Tanks, oil and water storage[1]	10%	6

Item	Rate	Class
used primarily in manufacturing or processing[15]		29, 39, 43, 53
Taxicabs	40%	16
Telecommunication spacecraft	30%	10
Telegraph and telephone equipment, wires and cables		
acquired before Feb. 23, 2005[1]	5%	3
new and acquired after Feb. 22, 2005	12%	42
poles and masts[1]	5%	3
fibre-optic cable	12%	42
Telephone or telegraph communication non-electronic switching equipment	8%	17
Telephone system (purchased)	20%	8
Television aerial	20%	8
Television commercials	100%	12
Television set-top boxes	40%	30
Timber cutting and removing equipment[3]		10, 15
Timber limits — see Sched. VI of the *Income Tax Regulations*[3,7]		
Timber resource property[3]	15%	33
Tools costing less than $500[1,26,28]	100%	12
Tractors[1]	30%	10
for hauling freight[27]	40%	16
Trailers[1,34]	30%	10
Tramways[4,9]	6%	4
Trees	nil	—
Trestles[1]	5%	3
Trolley bus	30%	10
Trolley bus system[4]	6%	4
Trucks, automotive[1]	30%	10
for hauling freight[27]	40%	16
Tunnel[1]	4%	1
Uniforms[1,26]	100%	12
Vessels[7,17]	15%	7
furniture, fittings and spare engines[17]	15%	7
offshore drilling after 1987[30]	25%	41
Video cassettes, video laser disks and DVDs[23,26]	100%	12
Video games (coin operated)	40%	16
Video tapes[1]	30%	10
television commercial	100%	12
Wagons[1]	30%	10
Water current energy equipment	30%	43.1
acquired after Feb. 10, 2014	50%	43.2
Water pipelines	4%	1
Water pollution control equipment — see Pollution control equipment		
Water storage tanks[1]	10%	6
primary manufacturing purpose[15]		
Water distribution plant and equipment	4%	1

Item	Rate	Class
Well equipment, oil or gas (for use above ground)		
acquired after 1987	25%	41
oil sands property acquired after Mar. 18, 2007	25%	41.1
certain mining property acquired after March 20, 2013[14]	25%	41.2
Wharves[1]	5%	3
wooden[1]	10%	6
Wind energy conversion system acquired after Feb. 22, 2005 and before 2020[32,33]	50%	43.2
Windmills[1,38]	5%	3
Wiring, electric — same rate as building		

[1] Unless included in another class of assets subject to a different rate.

[2] Not applicable to land, animals, herbs, trees, shrubs or similar growing things, gas wells, mines, oil wells, radium, rights of way, timber limits, tramway track or certain vessels.

[3] See IT-481 and IT-501 regarding timber limits, timber resource property, and logging assets.

[4] Except property included in Class 10, 13, 14, 26 or 28. For distributors of gas, not including a property acquired to produce or distribute gas normally distributed in portable containers, to process natural gas before its delivery to a gas distribution system and to produce oxygen or nitrogen. See also under Gas manufacturing and distribution equipment, plants and pipelines; and Pipelines.

[5] Additional allowances are available for buildings in Class 1 acquired after February 19, 2015, and before 2025 that are considered eligible liquefaction buildings. The additional allowances are 6% for such buildings, and additions are required to be placed in a separate class in order to claim the additional allowance.

[6] Electrical generating equipment may be allocated to one of the following different classes: Class 1, if large and acquired by a producer; Class 8, if small; or Class 17, if new and acquired after February 27, 2000 (with certain exclusions). Energy-efficient equipment may be in Class 43.1; or Class 43.2, if acquired after February 22, 2005 and before 2020, and certain requirements are met (see note 35). Only a detailed reading of the classes can determine the appropriate one; see Schedule II of the *Income Tax Regulations*. If used in manufacturing or processing, see note 15.

[7] Separate classes may be required for each asset, including: certain rental properties costing $50,000 or more; automobiles in Class 10.1; certain vessels, including Canadian vessels and offshore drilling vessels; and Class 28, 41, 41.1, or 41.2 property relating to a particular mine or group of mines. See Regulation 1101 for the provisions regarding separate classes.

[8] Unless, in the case of a pipeline for oil or natural gas, the Minister is satisfied that the main source of supply for the business is likely to be exhausted within 15 years; such pipelines, not being specifically listed, fall under the general rate of 20% (Class 8).

[9] Tramway tracks: 100% on cessation of tramcar operation.

[10] Separate class elections may be available for certain assets or groups of assets, including: non-residential buildings in Class 1; certain electronic equipment in Class 8; transmission pipelines in Class 49; and equipment relating to transmission pipelines in Class 7. See Regulation 1101 for the provisions regarding separate classes.

[11] Additional allowances are available for equipment in Class 47 acquired after February 19, 2015, and before 2025 that are considered eligible liquefaction equipment. The additional allowance is 22% for such equipment, and additions are required to be placed in a separate class in order to claim the additional allowance.

[12] The equipment may be Class 8, 39 or 43 if used primarily in manufacturing, or Class 1, 3 or 6, depending on its nature.

[13] An addition or alteration to a building originally placed in Class 3, 6 or 20, but which would no longer be in that class under current rules, may be added to the old class within certain dollar and transitional rule limitations. See IT-79R3 and Regulation 1102(19).

[14] Qualifying assets are included in a special class for each mine. The full amount of UCC up to the amount of income from a mine may be claimed on property for new or expanded mines. This additional allowance is being phased out for oil sands property acquired after March 18, 2007 and for

certain mining property acquired after March 20, 2013. See paragraphs 1100(1)(*w*) to (*ya.2*) of the *Income Tax Regulations*.

[15] Specified property used primarily in manufacturing or processing may be allocated to one of the following classes: Class 53, if acquired after 2015 and before 2026, Class 29 (25%/50%/25% straight line), if acquired after March 18, 2007 and before 2016. See note 44 for general-purpose electronic data processing equipment and system software used primarily in manufacturing or processing (Class 29 if acquired after March 18, 2007 and before January 28, 2009). The description of the specified property varies depending on the date it is acquired and the class. See the descriptions of the classes in Schedule II of the *Income Tax Regulations*.

[16] Additional allowances are available for buildings in Class 1 acquired after February 19, 2015, and before 2025 that are considered eligible liquefaction buildings. The additional allowances are 6% for such buildings, and additions are required to be placed in a separate class in order to claim the additional allowance.

[17] Accelerated capital cost allowances of 33$^1/_3$% are provided on certain prescribed vessels and conversion costs (generally, Canadian vessels and furniture and fittings attached thereto). See Regulations 1100(1)(*va*) and 1101(2a).

[18] Multiple-unit residential buildings acquired after June 17, 1987 are Class 1 (4%).

[19] Such assets acquired after February 21, 1994 are eligible for CCA at 30% in Class 43.1. Certain Class 43.1 assets acquired after February 22, 2005 and before 2020 may be eligible for a CCA rate of 50% in Class 43.2. See Regulation 1102(16.1) that would allow a taxpayer to elect Class 29 treatment for property acquired after March 18, 2007 and before 2016 that would otherwise be in Class 43.1 or Class 43.2 and is used in manufacturing or processing.

[20] Patents for a limited or unlimited period acquired after April 26, 1993 are in Class 44 (25%). Patents for a limited period acquired before April 27, 1993 are in Class 14, written off on a straight-line basis over the life of the patent, but a taxpayer can elect out of Class 44 into Class 14 for limited period patents acquired after April 26, 1993. A taxpayer can make the same election out of Class 44 with respect to unlimited life patents acquired before 2017 to treat them as eligible capital property.

[21] The 2016 federal Budget proposes to replace the eligible capital property ("ECP") regime. Effective January 1, 2017, property that was ECP will be added to Class 14.1 and subject to a 7% CCA rate in years prior to 2027. Property acquired in 2017 and going forward that would have been considered ECP is also added to Class 14.1 and is subject to a 5% CCA rate.

[22] Automobiles acquired for lease or rental other than to any one person for more than 30 days in a 12-month period.

[23] Items must be acquired for the purpose of renting to any one person for no more than 7 days in any 30-day period.

[24] Computer software in Class 12 is subject to the half-year rule. Systems software is in Class 10, 29, 45, 50, or 52, depending on the date acquired. See note 44.

[25] Building must be used in farming or fishing business, or be unsupported below the ground, or have been acquired before 1979.

[26] The half-year rule does not apply to this item. It may be written off in full in the first year claimed.

[27] Trucks or tractors acquired after December 6, 1991 that have a gross vehicle weight rating in excess of 11,788 kg.

[28] Tools, kitchen utensils, and medical and dental instruments costing more than the $500 limit are Class 8. Portable tools acquired to earn short-term rental income are Class 10 (30%).

[29] Railway equipment may be subject to additional allowances over and above the class rate. Railway locomotives, railway cars and railway suspension devices acquired after February 27, 2000, (other than property included in paragraph (*y*) of Class 10) are eligible for Class 7 (15%) rather than a combined rate of 10% or 13% (7% + additional allowance of 3% or 6%) previously available for Class 35 assets. Leased assets are included in Class 7 (15%) only if the lessor elects specified leasing property treatment. Railway locomotives acquired after February 25, 2008 and not used previously by any taxpayer for any purpose are Class 10(*y*) (30%).

[30] After November 7, 2001, Class 41 for offshore drilling vessels is not available if the Minister of Industry has agreed to a structured financing facility. In such a case, the maximum CCA rate applicable to the vessel and its attachments will be 15% under Class 7 (see Regulation 1101(2c)).

[31] Class 49 applies to new transmission pipelines. Taxpayers may elect in the year the pipelines are acquired, to place them in a separate CCA class. The rate for new natural gas distribution pipelines acquired after March 18, 2007 changed from Class 1 (4%) to Class 51 (6%). Eligible assets will include control and monitoring devices, valves, metering and regulating equipment and other equipment ancillary to a distribution pipeline, but not buildings or other structures. See Class 7 for pumping and compression equipment used to move product along a transmission pipeline.

[32] Specified energy property rules may apply. See Regulations 1100(24) to (29).

[33] Class 43.2 (50%) applies to certain assets in Class 43.1 (30%) if they are acquired after February 22, 2005 and before 2020. Co-generation equipment described in paragraphs (*a*) to (*c*) of Class 43.1 will be eligible for Class 43.2 if the equipment has a heat rate attributable to fossil fuel not exceeding 4,750 BTU (Class 43.1 allows up to 6,000 BTU). Paragraph (*d*) of Class 43.1 sets out various other types of renewable energy assets that are eligible for Class 43.2, including active solar equipment, geothermal equipment, photovoltaic equipment, ground source heat pump systems, wind energy conversion systems, equipment used to collect, store, clean, or upgrade landfill gas and digester gas, equipment used to generate heat energy from eligible waste fuel, equipment used to generate electricity using waste heat, equipment used to produce and store biogas, and cleaning and upgrading equipment used to produce biomethane.

[34] Includes trailers designed for use on both highways and railway tracks.

[35] This item excludes landscaping costs deductible under paragraph 20(1)(*aa*) of the Act.

[36] Used for public transportation within a metropolitan area and not part of a railway system.

[37] Temporary access roads in the oil and gas mining sectors may qualify as Canadian exploration or development expenses.

[38] Not to be confused with wind energy conversion systems included in Class 43.1 or 43.2.

[39] Additional allowances are available for buildings in Class 1 acquired after May 18, 2007 (including new buildings which are under construction on March 19, 2007) that are used at least 90% (measured by square footage) for manufacturing or processing in Canada or for other non-residential purposes at the end of the year. The additional allowances are 6% for such a building used for manufacturing or processing and 2% for other non-residential buildings. In each case, the building is required to be placed in a separate class in order to claim the additional allowance.

[40] Class 52 (100%) applies to certain general-purpose electronic data processing equipment and systems software for that equipment, acquired after January 27, 2009 and before February 2011 (i.e., situated in Canada and not previously used). Property that is general-purpose electronic data processing equipment and systems software for that equipment is included in Class 29 if acquired after March 18, 2007 and before January 28, 2009 and used primarily in manufacturing or processing. Property that is general-purpose electronic data processing equipment and systems software for that equipment acquired after March 18, 2007, that is not in Class 29 or Class 52, is Class 50 (55%).

[¶899a] DESIGNATED PROPERTY AND CALCULATION OF CLAIM FOR CLASS 29

Classes 24, 27, and 34, which dealt with pollution control equipment and energy efficient equipment, have long been closed to new additions. Class 29, manufacturing and processing property, was long dormant as well but has been resuscitated for acquisitions after March 18, 2007 and before 2016. Classes 24, 27 and 34 (and indeed 29) continue to exist, although all old acquisitions should long since have been fully depreciated. The classes could give rise to recapture on dispositions of property.

Designated property is not subject to the half-year rule and includes:

(1) property which has become available under the "rolling start" available-for-use rule (¶804b);

(2) specified leasing property of corporations which are principal business (leasing) corporations;

(3) specified leasing property where you elected to capitalize the lease (¶873a.10), if the property is deemed acquired in a preceding taxation year;

(4) property acquired in a non-arm's length transaction from a transferor who had held it for at least 364 days before the end of the taxation year of the transferee in which the transfer occurred (be warned this description simplifies a complex rule); the property is deemed acquired by the transferee at the beginning of the first taxation year following the transfer; and

(5) property acquired in the course of a sanctioned divisive reorganization (butterfly transaction) from a transferor who had held it for at least 364 days before the end of the taxation year of the transferee in which the transfer occurred; the property is deemed acquired by

the transferee at the beginning of the first taxation year following the transfer.

Note that property acquired under standard rollover provisions is not designated property and does not escape the half-year rule.

For Class 29, the rules incorporating the effects of designated property are complex, although the principles are simple enough: designated property is not subject to the half-year rule, and so when brought into a Class should be eligible for 50/50 straight-line depreciation rather than the 25/50/25 depreciation which the half-year rule requires. The form below has been designed to follow the wording of the regulations.

COMPUTATION OF CLAIM — CLASS 29

Designated property Additions	(1)	(A)	Capital cost[1] of current year additions of designated property	$	x 50% =	$	(A)
		(B)	UCC of class before CCA claim[2]			$	(B)
			Lesser of (A) & (B)			$	(X)
Other Current Year Additions	(2)	(C)	UCC of class before CCA claim, excluding any amount related to designated property acquired during the year[3]			$	(C)
		(D)	Capital cost of current additions not including designated property additions			$	(D)
			Lesser of (C) & (D)	$	x 25% =	$	(Y)
Deduction of Carry-forward	(3)	(E)	UCC of class before CCA claims[4]			$	(K)
			Capital cost of all current year additions			$	(L)
			Adjusted UCC: (K) - (L)			$	(E)
		(F)	(I) Capital cost of all immediately prior year additions	$	x 50% =	$	(F)(I)
			(II) Adjusted UCC above (E)				
			Minus				
			— Capital cost of all non-designated property additions in immediately prior year	$	x 75% =	$	(M)
			— Capital cost of all designated property additions in immediately prior year	$	x 50% =	$	(N)
			Subtotal: (E) - (M & N)			$	(F)(II)[5]
			(F)(I) plus (F)(II)			$	(G)
			Lesser of (E) & (G)			$	(Z)
			Total CCA claim for the year (X + Y + Z)			$	[6]

[1] Capital cost is cost net of adjustments, e.g., for investment tax credit. See ¶811 and ¶827.

[2] Opening balance, plus all additions, less all proceeds and adjustments, except that if any designated property is included which has been acquired on a rollover, then only designated property acquired in the year is considered (but all such property whether or not acquired on the rollover).

[3] Opening balance, plus additions, less all proceeds of disposition and adjustments (e.g., investment tax credit) except proceeds and adjustments related to designated property acquired in the year. The regulations are perhaps ambiguous enough to argue that proceeds of dispositions of designated property acquired in the year are not deducted here, but such a result is not intended.

[4] Opening balance, plus all additions, designated and non-designated, less all proceeds and adjustments in the year.

[5] If negative, enter nil.

[6] If the taxation year is less than 365 days, then the CCA claim must be prorated accordingly (see ¶802a).

(ITR: 1100(1), (1)(*ta*), (2)–(2.4))

HOW TO CLAIM CAPITAL COST ALLOWANCE

[¶899a.01] HOW TO CLAIM CAPITAL COST ALLOWANCE ("CCA")

The general method for computing CCA is as follows:

- For all capital assets eligible for CCA which were acquired during the year, determine the appropriate capital cost class by consulting the list at ¶899 and the details at ¶898.
- Segregate the assets acquired by class, and add their capital cost to the undepreciated cost in the respective classes at the beginning of the year (typically these are

the closing balances taken from last year's capital cost allowance form).

- Deduct the *proceeds* of any disposals of capital assets, up to original cost, from the undepreciated cost of the applicable class before the disposal.
- Calculate the undepreciated cost of each class, after adding the cost of assets acquired and deducting proceeds of disposals (but for Class 29, see ¶899a).
- Adjust the balance reached in the preceding step as follows: (1) Subtract the full cost of any assets acquired but not available for use in the year (¶804b); (2) Add the cost of assets which have been previously acquired but have only become available for use in the year (provided this amount is not already included in opening UCC of the class); (3) Subtract one-half of the cost of assets acquired in the year (provided the cost has not already been subtracted in adjustment (1)), subject to the exceptions discussed in ¶802; this final adjustment gives effect to the "half-year" rule.
- Determine the CCA by applying the rates prescribed for each class (see ¶898) to the UCC of each class, as adjusted in the preceding steps.

The CCA claimed should then be deducted from the undepreciated cost of each class, and the net balance carried forward to the next year. Note that government reassessments may require adjustment of opening balances. If no further purchases of capital assets were made in subsequent years, the UCC of each class would steadily decline and the CCA would correspondingly decline. The method is therefore known as a "declining balance" system, as opposed to a "straight-line" basis of allowance in which equal portions of the initial cost of assets would be amortized each year.

The declining balance method is used for all CCA classes except Classes 13, 14, 15, 19, 20, 21, 24, 27, 29, and 34 which use the straight-line method.

Most assets purchased in the year will only be allowed one-half of the normal CCA for the first year (see ¶802). To accelerate the recognition of CCA claims, you can purchase assets near the end of the taxation year rather than at the beginning of the following taxation year.

Individuals claiming CCA should complete one of the capital cost allowance forms applicable to the type of income against which the claim is made. Thus, if you are claiming CCA in connection with a business, you may use page 4 of form T2125, provided by the CRA as part of their *Business and Professional Income* guide (see Chapter 7). Employees may use form T777 supplied with the *Employment Expenses* guide, and real estate owners may use form T776 supplied with the *Rental Income Tax* guide (see Chapter 6). However, no particular form need be chosen, provided the essential information to determine the claim is presented in a clear format. CCA calculations are the amounts deductible in computing income for tax purposes.

Chapter 9

Other Income

THESE POINTS ARE COVERED IN THIS CHAPTER

CRA REFERENCES RELATING TO THIS CHAPTER

T1 Lines

- Line 104 — Other employment income
- Line 113 — Old Age Security pension (box 18 on T4A(OAS) slips)
- Line 114 — CPP or QPP benefits (box 20 on T4A(P) slips)
- Line 115 — Other pensions or superannuation
- Line 116 — Elected split-pension amount
- Line 117 — Universal Child Care Benefit
- Line 119 — Employment Insurance and other benefits (box 14 on T4E slips)
- Line 129 — RRSP income (from all T4RSP slips)
- Line 130 — Other income
- Line 139 — Commission income (Net)
- Line 144 — Workers' compensation benefits (box 10 on T5007 slips)
- Line 145 — Social assistance payments
- Line 146 — Net federal supplements (box 21 on T4A (OAS) slips)
- Line 152 — Disability benefits included on line 114
- Line 166 — Commission income (Gross)
- Line 206 — Pension adjustment (box 52 on all T4 slips and box 34 on all T4A slips)
- Line 207 — Registered pension plan deduction (box 20 on all T4 slips and box 32 on all T4A slips)
- Line 235 — Social benefits repayment
- Line 236 — Net income
- Federal Worksheet, Line 314 — Pension income amount

CRA Guides

5000-G, "General Income Tax and Benefit Guide"; **P105**, "Students and Income Tax"; **P119**, "When You Retire"; **RC4092**, "Registered Education Savings Plans (RESPs)"; **RC4112**, "Lifelong Learning Plan (LLP)"; **RC4157**, "Deducting Income Tax on Pension and Other Income, and Filing the T4A Slip and Summary"; **T4013**, "T3 — Trust Guide"; **T4015**, "T5 Guide — Return of Investment Income"; **T4040**, "RRSPs and Other Registered Plans for Retirement"; **T4041**, "Retirement Compensation Arrangements Guide"; **T4079**, "T4RSP and T4RIF Guide"; **T4084**, "Pension Adjustment Guide"

CRA Forms

T3, "Statement of Trust Income Allocations and Designations"; **T4**, "Statement of Remuneration Paid"; **T4A**, "Statement of Pension, Retirement, Annuity and Other Income"; **T4A (OAS)**, "Statement of Old Age Security"; **T4A (P)**, "Statement of Canada Pension Plan Benefits"; **T4E**, "Statement of Employment Insurance and Other Benefits"; **T4PS**, "Statement of Employee Profit Sharing Plan Allocations and Payments"; **T4RIF**, "Statement of Income from a Registered Retirement Income Fund"; **T4RSP**, "Statement of Registered Retirement Savings Plan Income"; **T5**, "Statement of Investment Income"; **T1032**, "Joint Election to Split Pension Income"; **T1198**, "Statement of Qualifying Retroactive Lump-Sum Payment"; **T2078**, "Election Under Subsection 147(10.1) in Respect of a Single Payment Received from a Deferred Profit Sharing Plan"; **T2205**, "Amounts from a Spousal or Common-Law Partner RRSP or RRIF to Include in Income"

Income Tax Folios

S1-F2-C3, "Scholarships, Research Grants and Other Education Assistance"; **S1-F5-C1**, "Related Persons and Dealing at Arm's Length"; **S3-F9-C1**, "Lottery Winnings, Miscellaneous Receipts, and Income (and Losses) from Crime"; **S1-F3-C3**, "Support Payments"; **S3-F10-C1**, "Qualified Investments — RRSPs, RESPs, RRIFs, RDSPs and TFSAs"

Interpretation Bulletins

IT-99R5 (Consolidated), "Legal and Accounting Fees"; **IT-167R6**, "Registered Pension Funds or Plans — Employee's Contributions"; **IT-202R2**, "Employees' or Workers' Compensation"; **IT-220R2**, "Capital Cost Allowance — Proceeds of Disposition of Depreciable Property"; **IT-257R**, "Canada Council Grants"; **IT-273R2**, "Government Assistance — General Comments"; **IT-307R4**, "Spousal or Common-Law Partner Registered Retirement Savings Plans"; **IT-335R2**, "Indirect Payments"; **IT-337R4 (Consolidated)**, "Retiring Allowances"; **IT-365R2**, "Damages, Settlements, and Similar Receipts"; **IT-379R**, "Employees Profit Sharing Plans — Allocations to Beneficiaries"; **IT-397R**, "Amounts Excluded from Income — Statutory Exemptions and Certain Service or RCMP Pensions, Allowances and Compensation"; **IT-440R2**, "Transfer of Rights to Income"; **IT-499R**, Superannuation or Pension Benefits; **IT-500R**, "Registered Retirement Savings

Plans — Death of an Annuitant"; **IT-508R**, "Death Benefits"; **IT-510**, "Transfers and Loans of Property Made After May 22, 1985 to a Related Minor"; **IT-511R**, "Interspousal and Certain Other Transfers and Loans of Property"; **IT-528**, "Transfers of Funds Between Registered Plans"

Information Circulars

72-22R9, "Registered Retirement Savings Plans"; **93-3R1**, "Registered Education Savings Plans"

WHAT YOU SHOULD KNOW ABOUT OTHER INCOME ITEMS

RECENT CHANGES

2016 Federal Budget

Pursuant to the 2016 Federal Budget, Bill C-29 introduced a new rule applicable to dispositions of interests in life insurance policies after March 21, 2016, to non-arm's length persons. See ¶981.

2015 Federal Budget

The Budget changed the withdrawal rules for Registered Retirement Income Funds ("RRIFs"). The minimum amounts that need to be withdrawn are decreased in percentage terms between the ages of 71 and 94, beginning in 2015. See Chapter 26 at ¶2630–¶2634.10 for details.

The Budget also implemented previously announced increases to the Universal Child Care Benefit ("UCCB") for children under the age of 6 to $160 per month beginning in 2015, up from the previous $100 amount. Additionally, a monthly UCCB of $60 per child will be paid for children aged 6 through 17. See ¶935.

PENSION AND RETIREMENT BENEFITS

[¶903] BENEFITS RECEIVED FROM A REGISTERED RETIREMENT SAVINGS PLAN ("RRSP")

[¶903.05] *Basic Rules*

All amounts received as a benefit from an RRSP must be included in income and reported on line 129 of the T1 return. A benefit is any money you withdraw from the plan, either as a lump-sum or periodic payment. It does not include amounts transferred directly from one plan to another held by the same person, or qualifying amounts withdrawn under the Home Buyers' Plan or the Lifelong Learning Plan. Annuity payments received from a registered retirement savings plan may be eligible for the tax credit on the first $2,000 of pension income (see ¶1311).

If you take property, as opposed to money, out of an RRSP, the fair market value of the property will be included in your income (see also ¶905).

A provision exists in subsection 146(15) of the *Income Tax Act* for not taxing a portion of the benefits received from an RRSP if contributions were made to the plan before it was registered and were therefore not deductible. Although regulations have not been issued to make this provision effective, it is understood that the CRA will allow an appropriate reduction of the amount taxable in these circumstances.

This section of the commentary provides an overview of the inclusion of benefits received from an RRSP and related issues. RRSPs are discussed in detail in Chapter 26.

(ITA: 56(1)(*h*); 146(1) "benefit", (8), (9); 248(1) "amount")

[¶903.10] *Special Rules on Death of Plan Holder*

If a plan holder dies, special rules come into play to govern the taxation of assets in the plan. These are discussed in detail in ¶1914. Essentially, if the plan has not matured (as is generally the case, until the end of the year in which the plan holder reaches age 71), the assets may be left to a surviving spouse (which in this discussion includes a common-law spouse and a common-law partner as discussed at ¶1113) and taxed to the surviving spouse rather than the deceased plan holder or his (her) estate. These assets so paid to the spouse are referred to by definition as a "refund of premiums", and the surviving spouse may put all or any part of the refund of premiums into his or her own RRSP, or indeed any of the other qualifying tax deferred plans described below (¶903.15), without current tax. These "refunds" are not to be confused with annuity or RRIF payments out of a plan which has "matured" as described at ¶1005. Typically, an annuity out of a mature plan will continue to be payable to a surviving spouse and the annuity payments will be taxable to that surviving spouse. See ¶1914. Note that where the surviving spouse receives refunds from an unmatured plan after the year in which the surviving spouse has turned 71 years of age, the age limits on RRSPs will prevent the surviving spouse from rolling over the refunds to his or her own RRSP, but the alternative investments described below will be available.

Any payment received out of an RRSP or RRIF by a child or grandchild financially dependent on the deceased at the time of death by virtue of physical or mental infirmity can be transferred to any of the investments described below at ¶903.15. The infirm dependent child or grandchild can also apply this treatment to lump-sum payments received out of a registered pension plan on the death of the supporting parent/grandparent. This allows money purchase RPPs to pay retirement income in the same manner as a RRIF. Presumably spouses do not have this option because, as with a RRIF, they would normally receive continuing periodic payments.

Any amounts paid from the RRSP, etc., of the deceased to any child or grandchild who was financially dependent on the RRSP annuitant for support at the time of the annuitant's death will be taxable to the child rather than the deceased, and will be eligible for rollover by the child only to purchase a special annuity consisting of equal annual payments until the child reaches age 18. The annuity must name as annuitant either the child or a trust of which the child is the sole beneficiary. This provision allows a minor child to spread a lump-sum payment received on the death of a parent or grandparent who provided support over the years remaining to age 18. Note that in the case of such a child, it is irrelevant whether or not the plan has "matured", although it is doubtful whether a matured plan would ever provide for payments after death to persons other than a spouse. This option does not eliminate the right of an infirm child of any age to make the wider range of deferral investments permitted below. However, the child or grandchild who is not infirm has only this option available, and consequently there is no rollover option for children 18 and over. "Child" has a fairly broad meaning, as discussed at ¶1122. For more detail on this rollover, see ¶1914.

For the above purposes, it is assumed, unless the contrary is established, that the child or grandchild was not financially dependent on the deceased individual for support immediately before the death if the income of the child or grandchild for the taxation year preceding the taxation year of death exceeded the basic personal credit amount plus, where the dependency was because of mental or physical infirmity, the disability credit amount. See ¶65 for the current year tax credit amounts.

A RRIF, generally speaking, will provide for continuing payments to a surviving spouse, as described at ¶1916. Payments to the estate of the RRIF holder may be taxed to the surviving spouse where there is an election to do so; the surviving spouse may roll them over to one of the investments below. In general they maintain treatment parallel to the RRSP refund of premium rules, although RRIF payments are "designated benefits" rather than "refund of premiums". Where there is no surviving spouse, a dependent child receiving amounts from the RRIF must, in effect, treat them as if they were a refund of RRSP premiums, subject to identical restrictions and options as described above (and the investments below). For more detail, see ¶1916.

The government recently introduced a similar transfer (and deduction) for refunds of premiums from an RRSP or eligible amounts from a RRIF received on the death of the annuitant by financially dependent children or grandchildren who were dependent by reason of mental or physical infirmity and who contribute such amounts to their registered disability savings plans (RDSPs). Other taxpayers, such as the deceased's spouse or common-law partner, who received such amounts upon the death and contributed the proceeds to an RDSP of a financially dependent infirm child or grandchild, may also receive a deduction. This new transfer/deduction is discussed below at ¶903.15.

[¶903.15] *Permitted Tax Deferred Investments*

Recipients of a "refund of premiums" as described above (other than financially dependent children/grandchildren who were not dependent by reason of infirmity, who are limited to option (5)) may make a broad range of tax-deferred investments by "rolling over" all or a portion of the amounts received. A refund of premiums is in the first instance included in the recipient beneficiary's income, but may be deducted if paid within 60 days of year end:

(1) into an RRSP of the recipient (except where the receipt occurs after the year in which the recipient's RRSPs must mature or be converted to retirement income because of the recipient's age (¶2616.05));

(2) for an annuity for the life of the recipient (or the last survivor of the recipient and his or her spouse or common-law partner) sold by a person licensed in Canada or a province to sell annuities;

(3) for a term annuity for the recipient to age 90 (or to age 90 of the recipient's spouse or common-law partner, if later) sold by a licensed annuity seller;

(4) into a registered retirement income fund (RRIF) of the recipient (see ¶2630); or

(5) for an annuity for a fixed number of years not exceeding 18 minus the contributor's age at the time the annuity is acquired. Note that this is the only investment permitted to a minor child or grandchild who was financially dependent on the deceased but was not dependent by reason of physical or mental infirmity.

The annuities listed in (2), (3), and (5), above, must (subject to the rules below regarding trusts) name as the annuitant the recipient of the refund of premiums.

Recently, the government introduced section 60.02, allowing the rollover for permitted deferred investments to be extended to include amounts contributed to an RDSP of a financially dependent child or grandchild who was dependent upon the deceased annuitant by reason of mental or physical infirmity. The new general rule applies to amounts received as a refund of premiums out of an RRSP or as designated benefits out of a RRIF or a lump sum from a pension plan as consequence of the death of the annuitant or plan holder after March 3, 2010, where the contribution is made to the RDSP after June 2011. The contribution can be made by the child or grandchild receiving the refund of premiums (or RRIF designated benefit or pension amount). See the discussions at ¶1914.15 and ¶2612.60 for more details of this rollover into an RDSP.

For annuities obtained for minors as described in item (5) above, the rollover can apply if the annuitant is a trust under which the taxpayer (the minor) is the sole beneficiary (determined without regard to any right of a person to receive amounts from the trust only on or after the death of the taxpayer). The annuity must require that, in the event of the death of the taxpayer during the term of the annuity, amounts otherwise payable after the death be commuted into a single payment.

For annuities acquired in respect of taxpayers described in items (2) and (3) above, the rollover can apply if the annuitant is a personal trust under which the taxpayer (the surviving spouse or common-law partner, or financially dependent infirm child or grandchild) is the sole beneficiary during the taxpayer's lifetime, i.e., no one else may receive any of the trust capital or income during the taxpayer's lifetime. The annuity in this case must be either for the life of the taxpayer or for a fixed term to the age of 90 of the taxpayer. If the annuity is guaranteed or for a fixed term, it must require that in the event of the death of the taxpayer during the term of the annuity, amounts otherwise payable after the death be commuted into a single payment. The taxpayer must be mentally infirm.

For annuities acquired after 2000 and before 2006 in respect of taxpayers described in items (2) and (3) above, the rollover can apply if the annuitant is a trust under which the taxpayer is the sole beneficiary (determined without regard to any right of a person to receive amounts from the trust only on or after the death of the taxpayer). The annuity must be for the life of the beneficiary or to the age of 90 of the beneficiary. For annuities acquired in 2001 through 2004, the taxpayer must be mentally or physically infirm; for annuities acquired in 2005, the taxpayer must be mentally infirm.

The refund of premiums will normally be reported to you on form T4RSP and must be reported on line 129. Remember that you have only 60 days from the end of the year in which a refund of premiums is paid to you to make your special contribution to an RRSP, RRIF, or annuity even if you haven't received your T4RSP on a timely basis.

If you make a timely contribution of this refund to an RRSP, you must "designate" this special contribution. Apparently a contribution is designated if it is entered on line 14 (box 240) of Schedule 7 of your T1 return. At any rate, the CRA describes no other options, although it also does not refer to the entry as a "designation". On Schedule 7, the special contribution is added to other allowable contributions, and the total carried to line 208 for deduction. The RRSP receipt for the special contribution is kept on file, together with any other RRSP contribution slips, for verification by the CRA. The CRA specifies in the T1 Guide that RRSP slips should not be filed with your T1 return. Although the CRA does not specify this, you might want to write "refund of premium contribution" on slips representing these special contributions, or even keep with your receipts a designation letter, as much for your own information as for the CRA.

If you contribute a refund of premiums to any of the permitted rollover investments other than an RRSP, i.e., to a RRIF or an annuity, the issuer should provide you with an appropriate tax receipt. Claim this deduction on line 232 of your T1 and support it by filing the tax receipt with your returns.

An annuity may provide for full or partial commutation; the annuity income will, of course, be recognized as received, whether in regular payments or on commutation.

(ITA: 60.02)

[¶903.20] *Other Permitted Transfers*

The RRSP rules also allow individuals to transfer amounts from one plan to another. This also includes transfers made to an RRSP belonging to your spouse or common-law partner, or former spouse or common-law partner, provided the transfer takes place on or after the breakdown of the marriage, pursuant to a decree, order, or judgment of a competent tribunal, or a written separation agreement. Unlike the rule for refunds or benefits paid to a surviving spouse or common-law partner, transfers of this kind *must* be made directly from one plan to another; they cannot be paid to the annuitant and then recontributed by him to another plan. A form T2033(E) should accompany a transfer of this kind. No transfers on marriage breakdown can be made from a matured RRSP, but the same result can be accomplished indirectly if necessary. See ¶1021.

[¶903.25] *Other Rules*

If refunds or benefits are paid to the estate of a deceased taxpayer or to anyone other than a spouse, common-law partner, or dependent child, they are probably taxable to the deceased. This is discussed in ¶1914.

If your plan is revised, amended or a new plan is substituted for it and the revised, amended, or new plan does not comply with the requirements for registration, the plan is considered to be deregistered.

Where a plan is deregistered you must include in your income the fair market value of the property of the plan at the time of deregistration. A portion of the amount to be taken into your income is reduced if that portion is required to be included in your spouse's or common-law partner's income.

The plan trust may, depending upon its terms, continue after the plan is deregistered. It will then be taxed as any other trust, and income earned by the plan will be taxed at the highest marginal tax rate.

Any amounts received by your spouse or common-law partner from that person's registered retirement savings plan (other than to purchase a "retirement income", a withdrawal in the year of your death, or when either you or your spouse or common-law partner is not resident in Canada) must be included in your income rather than your spouse's/partner's, to the extent that spousal contributions were deductible by you in the year of withdrawal or any of the two immediately preceding years.

(ITA: 56(1)(*h*); 60(*l*); 110.2(1), (2); 118(7), (8); 122(1); 146(1), (1.1), (8.3), (8.8), (12), (15), (16); 146.3(6), (6.1), (6.11), (6.2); IT-307R4 Spousal or Common-Law Partner Registered Retirement Savings Plans; IT-500R Registered Retirement Savings Plans — Death of an Annuitant)

[¶905] DEEMED BENEFITS FROM A REGISTERED RETIREMENT SAVINGS PLAN

If your registered retirement savings plan acquired a non-qualified investment before March 23, 2011 (¶2618), the fair market value at the time of purchase of such investment will be included in your income in the year of acquisition.

For non-qualified investments acquired after March 22, 2011, there is no income inclusion, but the 50% Part XI.01 penalty tax applies.

If your registered retirement savings plan pledges property held in the trust as security for a loan, the fair market value of the property pledged will be included in your income.

If your RRSP disposes of property for an amount less than fair market value or acquires property at an amount greater than fair market value, the difference between the fair market value and the amount of consideration will be included in your income.

The trust company or insurance company which holds your investments is required to notify you of any amount that must be included in your income under these rules.

For more details, see ¶2618 to ¶2622.10, inclusive.

(ITA: 146(9), (10), (10.1); ITR: 214(2))

[¶907] BENEFITS RECEIVED FROM A REGISTERED RETIREMENT INCOME FUND

Amounts received by you as an annuitant under a registered retirement income fund are taxable in the year received. However, payments received out of or under a registered retirement income fund may be eligible for the tax credit of up to $2,000 of pension income. (See ¶1311). These plans are an alternative to an annuity or lump-sum payment on maturity of an RRSP. Details of their required payment schedule are provided at ¶2632.05. Income earned by the fund is generally not taxable, but these funds are subject to the same provisions as RRSPs with respect to the acquisition of non-qualified investments and the pledging of property held in the trust as security (see ¶905).

If your RRIF disposes of property for an amount less than the fair market value or acquires property at an amount greater than fair market value, two times the difference between the fair market value and the amount of consideration shall be included in your income.

If a RRIF holder dies, the remaining benefits under the arrangement may pass to others under the terms of the arrangement or by his or her will. If these benefits pass to the plan holder's spouse or common-law partner, the yearly payments may continue and the spouse/partner will pay tax on the payments as they are received. The definition of common-law spouse or partner for this purpose has changed from time to time, as discussed in detail at ¶1113. Note that "parent" and "child" have fairly broad meanings for tax purposes. See ¶1122.

If the property in the plan passes on the death of the plan holder to a person other than the plan holder's spouse or common-law partner, the fair market value of the property in the plan immediately before his death must be included in the plan holder's income. The person receiving the property will only be taxed on any increase in value after the date of death of the plan holder. Certain exceptions to this are made if the beneficiary is a minor or dependent child or grandchild (see ¶903.10 and ¶903.15). Further details on taxation of RRIF property at death are found at ¶1916.

For a more detailed discussion of registered retirement income funds, see ¶2630–¶2634.10.

(ITA: 56(1)(*h*); 118(3), (7); 146.3)

[¶908] ANNUITIES

Annuities are defined to include all amounts payable on a periodic basis, whether payable at intervals longer or shorter than a year, and whether payable under a contract, will, trust or otherwise. The method of taxing annuity income changed with the introduction of income accrual rules for life insurance policies and annuities (see ¶432).

Under the general rules, amounts received as annuity payments are included in income, but a deduction may be claimed for the capital portion of that payment (see ¶481). These rules apply to those contracts which are excluded from the income accrual rules. These contracts include exempt policies, prescribed annuity contracts, contracts arising under the settlement option of a life insurance policy acquired before December 2, 1982 and annuities where payments have been commenced before December 2, 1982.

Annuities not exempt under the above conditions are subject to income accrual rules which require income accrued but not received to be reported every three years. For annuities acquired after 1988, annual accrual reporting of income will generally be required. These rules are described in detail at ¶432.

Amounts received from, or as proceeds of disposition of an annuity contract that was acquired with a refund of premiums from an RRSP, the payment for which was deductible in computing income, must be included in income (see ¶903). This rule also applies to annuities under the old rule allowing the purchase of an annuity to shelter proceeds of disposition of qualified farm property. For 1996 and later years it also applies to DPSP annuities (¶917), ensuring that proceeds of disposition will be taxed as well as regular annuity payments (which were always taxed).

Some annuity income may qualify for the tax credit on the first $2,000 of pension income (¶1311). The interplay of claims for these deductions actually determines on which line of the T1 the annuity income should be reported. This is described at ¶480.

Note that amounts received out of an annuity contract that is a tax-free savings account (TFSA) are not taxable as income. This is effective for 2009 and subsequent taxation years under subparagraph 56(1)(*d*)(iii). TFSAs are discussed in ¶478, ¶2532c, and ¶2635 to ¶2640.

(ITA: 12.2(1); 56(1)(*d*), (*d.2*); 60(*a*); 118(3), (7); 248(1) "annuity")

[¶911] SUPERANNUATION AND PENSION BENEFITS

Superannuation or pension benefits received must be included in computing income. This is true for income out of all registered pension plans and most other plans, and includes not only regular pension payments, but also special lump-sum payments, refunds of contributions, etc. For OAS, CPP, DPSP, and foreign pension income, see the separate headings below.

Pension benefits will generally qualify for the pension tax credit providing you meet the other requirements for that credit. See ¶1311.

You may deduct contributions to an RRSP or RPP from certain pension benefits received (see ¶1021). These contributions may be paid in the year that you received the benefits or within 60 days after the end of the year. These special contributions are not affected by the normal deductibility restrictions applicable to RPPs and RRSPs. Also refer to ¶903 which discusses the waiving of withholding taxes on such a transfer.

You may not transfer ordinary periodic pension payments to an RRSP or RPP, although some special lump-sum payments are transferable provided the transfer is made directly between plans. See ¶1021 and ¶2616.05. In the 2014 federal Budget, the lump-sum transfer rule from RPPs to other plans was relaxed somewhat for underfunded defined benefit RPPs; see ¶1021.20 and ¶2612.05.

A number of military pensions, primarily relating to service in the World Wars, are exempt from tax. See ¶991.

If you belong to a funded but unregistered pension plan in Canada, the plan will probably fall within the definition of a Retirement Compensation Arrangement (¶359). You will be taxed on the benefits you receive out of the plan, but if the plan calls for payments to someone else (such as your spouse) in respect of your employment, those payments will be taxed to you rather than to the recipient. If you are a non-resident at the time of the payment, it may instead be taxed to the recipient. It is not clear if double taxation can arise in this situation. If you sell an interest in a retirement compensation arrangement, the proceeds are income to you, except to the extent that money is returned and taxed to your employer in the transaction. If you have made non-deductible contributions to an RCA, payments out of the plan to you are taxable but may be offset by deductions to the extent they constitute a refund of your own non-deductible contribution; see ¶365a.

If you receive an amount that represents several periodic payments lumped together, some of which would ordinarily have been received in *preceding* taxation years, you may be eligible for a form of income averaging to spread the applicable tax calculation over those years. Note that lump-sum payments received as commutations of future payments are not eligible for this treatment. Eligible amounts should be reported to you on form T1198, and the CRA should do the averaging automatically if you deal with form T1198.

The federal government recently introduced legislation regarding pooled registered pension plans ("PRPPs"). These plans allow employers and their employees, or self-employed individuals, to make tax-deductible contributions to the plans similar to those made to money purchase RPPs. An employer's contribution to a PRPP in a taxation year will not be a taxable benefit to the employee, although it will reduce the employee's RRSP deduction room for the year. The employee's contribution in a year will also reduce his or her RRSP deduction room for the year. Distributions from the PRPP and paid to the employee will be included in income and can qualify for the pension credit. See also the discussion on PRPPs in Chapter 25 at ¶2555, and in Chapter 26 at ¶2655 to ¶2655c.

Commentary on Legislative Proposals (Sept. 16, 2016)

Note: When Legislative Proposals, September 16, 2016, achieves Royal Assent, the commentary will be modified to read:

Effective December 14, 2012, an amount of PRPP contributions refunded to a member is not included in his/her income if the contributions were made in error or to avoid the revocation of the plan, and if the amount was not deducted as a PRPP contribution in the year of the refund or any preceding year.

(ITA: 56(1)(*a*), (*x*), (*y*), (*z*); 57(1), (2), (3); 60(*j*), (*j*.2); 146(5); IT-397R Amounts Excluded from Income — Statutory Exemptions and Certain Service or RCMP Pensions, Allowances and Compensation; IT-499R Superannuation or pension benefits)

[¶911a] REGISTERED DISABILITY SAVINGS PLAN ("RDSP") RECEIPTS

Under these plans, non-deductible contributions to a trust, similar to an RESP or RRSP trust, are made for the benefit of a disabled person (usually but not necessarily a relative). The government will, up to a point, make matching and supplementary contributions. Although contributions are not deductible, income earned in the trust accumulates free of tax, and payments of accumulated income are included in the tax of the disabled beneficiary. (Payments are considered blended payments of income and capital, and only the income portion is taxed.) Line 125 of the T1 Return is provided to report such income. Contributions to the plan may also arise from government grants. These grants may be subject to recapture by the government in certain circumstances. Where amounts subject to recapture have already been paid out and included in the beneficiary's income, the beneficiary will have to make the repayment. Such repayments are deductible (on line 232) in the year of repayment. RDSPs are discussed in greater detail in ¶1255.50 and ¶2529h.

As discussed therein, changes first announced in the 2012 federal Budget and now passed into law include the following:

- The introduction of a "proportionate repayment rule", replacing the current 10-year repayment rule, which applies when RDSP withdrawals are made within 10 years of government grants or bonds being contributed to the plan;
- Changes to rules regarding minimum and maximum withdrawals from an RDSP;
- Allowing a rollover from an RESP to an RDSP in certain circumstances; and
- The extension, in certain circumstances, in the period for which an RDSP may remain in place without being terminated, when a beneficiary becomes ineligible for the disability tax credit.

See also the discussion on RDSPs in Chapter 26 at ¶2670 to ¶2677.

(ITA: 56(1)(*q*.1); 60(*z*); 146.4(1), (6), (7); Department of Finance News Release 2008-110, dated December 23, 2008)

[¶912] WITHDRAWALS FROM A SPECIFIED DISABILITY SAVINGS PLAN ("SDSP")

The purpose of an SDSP is to provide beneficiaries with shortened life expectancies greater flexibility in accessing their funds in Registered Disability Savings Plans (RDSPs) by allowing them to make withdrawals without being required to repay the assistance holdback amount. The assistance holdback amount is the amount that an RDSP would be required, under the *Canada Disability Savings Act*, to repay to the government if a withdrawal were made from the RDSP. The assistance holdback amount is generally equal to the total amount of Canada Disability Savings Grants and Canada Disability Savings Bonds paid into an RDSP in the 10 years that precede the withdrawal of funds from the RDSP, less any amount that has already been repaid to the government (CDSA regulations).

An SDSP is formed from an RDSP if the following conditions are met:

(1) a medical doctor (licensed to practise under the laws of a province or where the beneficiary resides) certifies that the beneficiary of an RDSP is unlikely to survive more than five years;

(2) the holder of the RDSP elects in prescribed form and provides the election and medical certification to the issuer of the RDSP; and

(3) the issuer of the RDSP notifies the specified Minister (the Minister of Human Resources and Skills Development) in a manner and format acceptable to that Minister.

If the above conditions are met, then the RDSP becomes an SDSP at the time the notification is received by the specified Minister, and the SDSP is not required to repay an assistance holdback amount.

A plan will cease to be an SDSP on the occurrence of the earliest of the following events:

(1) when the specified Minister (the Minister of Human Resources and Skills Development) receives notification in a manner and format acceptable to that Minister that the holder of the SDSP elects that the plan cease to be an SDSP;

(2) when the total of the taxable portions of disability assistance payments made from the SDSP in the year while it was an SDSP exceeds $10,000 (there is a transitional provision that raises this threshold from $10,000 to $20,000 if the required medical certification mentioned in subsection 146.4(1.1) is obtained before 2012);

(3) when a contribution is made as defined in paragraph (*a*) or (*b*) of the definition of "contribution" found in subsection 146.4(1), which is an amount (i) paid into the plan under or because of the *Canada Disability Savings Act* or a designated provincial program, or (ii) any other program that has a similar purpose to a designated provincial program and that is funded directly or indirectly by a province;

(4) when the SDSP is terminated or when the SDSP ceases to be an RDSP as a result of the application of paragraph 146.4(10)(*a*), which is the plan ceases to be an RDSP;

(5) when lifetime disability assistance payments have not begun to be paid before the end of the particular calendar year following the year in which the plan last became an SDSP (i.e., if a plan becomes an SDSP in 2012, the plan will cease to be an SDSP if lifetime disability assistance payments have not begun to be paid before the end of 2013); or

(6) when the plan is a "primarily government assisted plan" as set out in paragraph 146.4(4)(*n*) and the total amount of disability assistance payments made from the SDSP to the beneficiary in the calendar year is less than the amount determined by the formula in paragraph 146.4(4)(*l*) in respect of the SDSP for the calendar year.

If a plan ceases to be an SDSP, then, under the criteria listed above, there is a waiting period for a holder of a plan to make a new election for the plan to be an SDSP again. The holder of the plan may not make an election that the plan be qualified as an SDSP until 24 months after the plan has ceased to be an SDSP. However, the Minister of National Revenue may waive the application of the above criteria nullifying the plan's SDSP status or the waiting period where it is just and equitable to do so.

(ITA: 146.4(1.1), (1.2), (1.3), (1.4))

[¶913] OLD AGE SECURITY PENSIONS ("OAS")

Old Age Security (OAS) pensions are payable to Canadians who have attained age 65. In addition, some persons receive additional payments as Guaranteed Income Supplements or Spouse's Allowance, either from the federal government or from a provincial government. If your net income exceeds a threshold amount, you will be required to repay part or all of the OAS through a special clawback tax; see ¶913.10.

If you have received the OAS pension, you must include it in your income. This is the basic amount which is paid to Canadians 65 or over.

If your return indicates that you are 65 or older, but shows no social security income, the CRA's computers will likely flag the return for a manual check. You will speed up the processing of your return if you attach a letter stating that you are not receiving the OAS pension for whatever reason.

The income tax law also requires that if you receive the Guaranteed Income Supplement or Spouse's Allowance you must include it in income, but that an equal amount may be claimed as a deduction from "net income" of Division B in the Act to arrive at "taxable income" after the deduction found in Division C. The effect of this rule is that the Guaranteed Income Supplement or Spouse's Allowance is not taxed in your hands, but it must be included in your income for purposes of determining whether, and for how much, you may be claimed as an exemption by other taxpayers on whom you are dependent.

Guaranteed Income Supplement and Spouse's Allowance are collectively referred to as "net federal supplements" on the T1 return; they are reported separately (on line 146) from basic Old Age Security payments (which are reported on line 113).

On its website, the CRA notes that you do not automatically get the OAS or Guaranteed Income Supplement (GIS). You must apply to receive them using the Application Form ISP-3000. You do not have to renew your application for the GIS each year. If you are eligible for the GIS, you will get it as long as you file your income tax and benefit return each year.

The inclusion of your own GIS or Spouse's Allowance ("SA") in your income can affect your claim for the age credit amount (reduced by net income over a threshold amount; see ¶65), medical expenses (amount of expenses less 3% of net income) or, although less likely, your credit for donations (maximum 75% of net income), and might have some effect on other tax calculations, especially provincial tax credits which refer to your net income. It also enters into the calculation of family income for determining GST credit (¶1496) and Canada Child Benefit (¶1498).

It may happen that you have received OAS payments in error in the year or earlier years. Where you have repaid Old Age Security amounts in the year for which your T1 is filed, you may claim a deduction on line 232 for the amounts repaid to the extent they were included in your income on that return or returns for earlier years.

The maximum OAS payable per month can be found at http://www.servicecanada.gc.ca/eng/services/pensions/oas/payments/index.shtml.

[¶913.05] *Non-Residents*

OAS benefits paid to non-residents are subject to non-resident withholding tax, but subject to treaty protection. See ¶2076, ¶2080.04, and ¶2086.

[¶913.10] *Old Age Security Pension Clawback*

There is a special tax on OAS pension amounts received by a taxpayer with net income for the year in excess of a threshold amount as indexed annually, and for 2016 the threshold is $73,756. (See ¶65 preceding Chapter 1 for a table of earlier and following year rates.) The special tax is 15% of your net income in excess of the threshold for the year up to the amount of your OAS pension on line 113. This special tax is added to the other clawback taxes on line 422 of your return. The tax does, however, reduce your net income otherwise calculated. This deduction is taken at line 235, so that full OAS pension taxable to you under the rules above is reported on line 113, and the amount of the clawback tax, if any, deducted at line 235. "Net income in excess of" the threshold for this purpose is, in effect, the amount by which line 234 income, including grossed-up dividends, and before the deduction allowed for the OAS tax, and not including payments included in income from an RDSP and any inclusion of the Universal Child Care Benefit ("UCCB"), and adding back any deductions for repayments of amounts to an RDSP or UCCB, exceeds the threshold. The CRA provides a "Line 235" chart for clawback calculations in the worksheets which accompany the T1 package; see also ¶1419. Where net federal supplements (GIS or SA) are included in OAS income subject to clawback, see ¶1026.

Old Age Security payments are subject to withholding on the potential clawback where net income has in prior years exceeded the threshold as indexed for the current year (¶1419). Withholding for the January–June period of any year will be based on income calculated on second prior year returns; withholding for July–December will be based on prior year returns. The clawback system applies to non-residents, and may result in 100% withholding where the non-resident files no base year tax return, subject to any treaty protection which may be available. See ¶225.

(ITA: 56(1)(*a*); 60(*j*), (*n*); 110(1)(*f*); 180.2; 5000-G, "General Income Tax and Benefit Guide" (T1 Guide))

[¶915] CANADA AND QUEBEC PENSION PLANS (CPP, QPP)

If you have received a pension payment (or any benefit) under the *Canada Pension Plan Act* or the *Quebec Pension Plan Act*, the amount must be included in your income. A T4A(P) information slip will be sent to you showing the amounts you have received in the taxation year.

It may happen that you have received Canada or Quebec Pension Plan payments (especially disability payments) in error in the year or earlier years. Where you have repaid those amounts in the year for which your T1 is filed, you may claim a deduction on line 232 for the amounts repaid to the extent they were included in your income on that return or returns for earlier years. See ¶1029.

On the other hand, you may receive CPP/QPP payments (especially disability payments) in a lump-sum which represent payments for more than one calendar year. Where this is the case, you are in theory entitled to deduct the payments from taxable income (thus lowering current tax) and be subjected to an offsetting tax adjustment (increase) which represents the tax you would have paid at lower marginal rates in the preceding years. In practice, the CRA asks to report the benefits in full, and itself makes the adjustment, if beneficial, in calculating your refund (or reducing your tax owing). The adjustment is described as a line 423 adjustment.

CPP/QPP benefits paid to non-residents are taxable, subject to treaty protection. See ¶2080.04 and ¶2086.

(ITA: 56(1)(*a*); 60(*j*))

[¶917] BENEFITS RECEIVED FROM A DEFERRED PROFIT SHARING PLAN ("DPSP")

Amounts received by you as a beneficiary under a deferred profit sharing plan (¶736) must be included in your income. If funds of a plan are used to purchase an annuity for you, you will not be taxable on the amount paid for the annuity but you will be taxable on the full amount of each annuity payment you receive. However, annuity payments received from a deferred profit sharing plan may be eligible for the tax credit on the first $2,000 of pension income. See ¶1311.

Under certain circumstances, deductions may be allowed from this income. These are:

(1) If you have made payments into the plan for which you have received no tax deduction, you may deduct the lesser of:

(a) the amount received from the plan during the year minus any amount deductible by virtue of subparagraph (2) below; or

(b) the amount of the above-mentioned payments to the plan to the extent that they have not been deducted in a previous year.

(2) If you were a beneficiary of the plan at a time when it was an employees' profit sharing plan rather than a deferred profit sharing plan, you may deduct the total of:

(a) amounts previously included in your income under the employees' profit sharing plan;

(b) amounts paid into the employees' profit sharing plan by you; and

(c) pre-1972 capital gains allocated to you under the employee's profit sharing plan;

minus the total of:

(d) pre-1972 capital losses allocated to you under the employee's profit sharing plan; and

(e) amounts previously received by you from the plan while it was either an employee's profit sharing plan or a deferred profit sharing plan.

If you receive a lump-sum settlement from a deferred profit sharing plan upon withdrawal from the plan, retirement from employment, or death, and the settlement includes shares or other securities, the income which you will be deemed to have received would normally be equal to the value of the property you received as settlement. Your deemed cost of the securities would also be their value when received. If you are a resident of Canada, you may elect to defer the unrealized gains on the securities and reduce the deemed cost of the securities accordingly. The form you must file is T2078, available from your Tax Services Office. When you eventually dispose of the shares on which you have elected, the difference between their tax cost to the plan and their fair market value at the time you received them will be ordinary income to you, but you will be allowed an offsetting deduction in computing taxable income of one-half of that amount on line 249 of the T1 return. This deduction is intended to match capital gain inclusion rates (¶500) but deny the capital gains exemption on the income element. Although the income element is fixed when you receive the shares, the offsetting deduction is fixed according to the year of disposition. As well, any gains or losses on the shares subsequent to your receipt of them will be ordinary capital gains or losses.

If you are related to your employer, and your employer contributes to a DPSP on your behalf or where an amount forfeited under a plan is allocated to you, the amounts contributed or allocated will be included in your income for the year (see ¶736).

DPSP benefits must commence at the same age at which RRSPs must mature and be converted to retirement income (¶2616.05).

[¶917.05] *Transfer of Lump-Sum Payments Received*

You may direct that lump-sum amounts you are entitled to receive from a deferred profit sharing plan be transferred directly into your RRSP, RRIF, RPP, PRPP, SPP, or another DPSP (see ¶1021). Only lump-sum transfers directly between DPSPs or from DPSPs to RRSPs or RPPs are permitted. The ability to receive periodic payments and transfer them in part or full under the rollover rules at ¶1021 has been removed. See ¶1021.

If you are the spouse or common-law partner at the time of death of an employee or former employee covered by a DPSP, and accordingly receive a lump-sum payment from a DPSP on the death of the employee or former employee, you can have the plan make a direct transfer of the amount to your own DPSP, RRSP, RRIF, RPP, PRPP, or SPP, thus avoiding immediate tax on the payment to the estate, and deferring tax until such time as you make arrangements for retirement income or other withdrawals from your plan. Such transfers may also be made where you receive such an amount on the death of a former spouse or common-law partner. Moreover, provisions are added to accommodate the division of DPSP assets on the breakdown of a marriage or common-law partnership. As well, the rules permit direct transfers from DPSPs to RRIFs. This is primarily of relevance where the surviving spouse or common-law partner of a deceased employee is over 71 years of age and, therefore, cannot transfer the DPSP assets to an RRSP.

(ITA: 56(1); 60(*j*); 110(1)(*d.3*); 118(3), (7), (8); 147(10), (10.1), (10.2), (10.3), (11), (12); CRA Guide to *RRSPs and Other Registered Plans for Retirement* (T4040), Chapter 5)

[¶919] PENSIONS FROM FOREIGN SOURCES

Pensions received by Canadian residents from a foreign source are subject to tax in Canada in the same way as private pensions received from a Canadian source, subject to the "foreign retirement arrangement" rules below.

If there is an income tax treaty between Canada and the foreign country, it may alter the taxation of pensions received from that country. See the list of tax treaties at ¶2005 and the discussion of pensions at ¶2080.04. Although the latter is directed at non-residents, the rules are generally reciprocal; that is, similar rules will apply to Canadians receiving foreign pensions.

In general, foreign pension income would seem to qualify for the $2,000 pension income credit (¶1311) to the extent the income is not protected by treaty. Foreign pension income is reported on line 115; the entire amount should be reported there; to the extent foreign pension income is treaty-protected, an offsetting deduction is claimed at line 256. That deduction is also backed out of foreign pension income when claiming pension income credit; the CRA provides a "Line 314 — Pension income amount" chart for this calculation in the worksheets which accompany the T1 package.

Foreign source government pensions similar to OAS may receive special treatment under social security treaties; see ¶2111.

Where you receive a lump-sum payment from a non-registered (typically a foreign) pension plan and the payments are attributable to services rendered outside Canada, the lump-sum payments will be income but you can defer taxation on the receipts to the extent you make offsetting contributions to a registered retirement savings plan ("RRSP"), pooled registered pension plan ("PRPP"), or registered pension plan ("RPP") within 60 days following the end of the year in which you receive the lump-sum payments; see ¶2612.05. However, you cannot deduct RRSP/PRPP/RPP contributions based on foreign pension income to the extent you have claimed treaty-protection on that income.

If you receive an amount that represents several periodic payments lumped together, some of which would ordinarily have been received in *preceding* taxation years, you may be eligible for a form of income averaging to spread the applicable tax calculation over those years. Note that lump-sum payments received as commutations of future payments are not eligible for this treatment. Income is not eligible for this treatment to the extent it is exempt under a tax treaty. Normally, the CRA expects eligible amounts to be reported to you on form T1198, but this may not be practical with foreign plans. The CRA does allow a letter or other explanation from the payer to serve in lieu of form T1198.

For deductibility of contributions to foreign plans, see ¶365a. For foreign social security payments received, see ¶921 (U.S.) and ¶922 (other).

[¶919.05] *Foreign Retirement Arrangements ("IRAs")*

A foreign retirement arrangement is any plan prescribed by regulation to be such. Currently, only Individual Retirement Accounts (IRAs) referred to in subsections 408(a) and (b) of the U.S. *Internal Revenue Code* are prescribed. An IRA is similar in concept to an RRSP.

Payments out of a foreign retirement arrangement established under the laws of a country are not taxable in Canada to the extent they would not be taxable in that country to a resident of that country. That is, payments out of an IRA to a Canadian resident will not be taxed in Canada to the extent they would not be taxed under U.S. law if the Canadian were a U.S. resident. This is intended to allow payments to be transferred from one such foreign plan to another. It may also apply where an individual receives a return of contributions from an IRA in respect of which the individual was not initially entitled to a deduction under U.S. law.

Technical amendments passed into law on June 26, 2013 ensure that for 2002 and later taxation years amounts treated as income distributions from IRAs at any particular time under U.S. rules are similarly treated as income under Canadian rules. This is mainly relevant to conversions of ordinary IRAs to "Roth IRAs", as such is discussed further under the next subheading below. However, the U.S. rules also deem a taxable distribution to occur when money is borrowed from an IRA, or an IRA is used as security for a loan, and such income inclusions would be matched in Canada when they occur under U.S. rules.

This matching rule for deemed distributions is of general application (which is to say it would apply to foreign retirement arrangements other than IRAs if there were any), and treats any amount in respect of a foreign retirement arrangement ("FRA") which is, as a result of a transaction, event or circumstance, deemed under the laws of the country in which it is established to be a distribution to an individual, as income in Canada under the FRA rules for the taxation year that includes the transaction, event or circumstance.

A lump-sum payment out of an IRA which is taxable in Canada (because it would be taxable to a U.S. resident) will be eligible for recontribution to a Canadian registered pension plan ("RPP"), registered retirement savings plan ("RRSP"), pooled registered pension plan ("PRPP"), or specified pension plan ("SPP") if it derives from contributions made to the IRA by the Canadian taxpayer or the taxpayer's spouse or former spouse; see ¶2612.20. The taxpayer's spouse includes a common-law spouse or partner, as defined at various times under the rules at ¶1113.

Transfer to an RPP, RRSP, PRPP, or SPP can be made by contribution within 60 days following the end of the year in which the payment from a foreign retirement arrangement is received (see subheading "Receipts from a United States IRA" in ¶2612.20).

The foreign retirement arrangement rules should apply to payments received after July 13, 1990. Payments received before that time were, under CRA policy, income except to the extent they were returns of capital made by the sole contributor to an IRA. However, from July 13, 1990 on, all such payments are regarded as taxable. It is understood that payments from an IRA received prior to July 14, 1990 would be treated as income from a foreign pension plan, so that lump sums for services attributable to periods of non-residence in Canada would qualify for rollover treatment under the general rule above, although no formal confirmation of this position was available at the time of writing. Note that a more favourable result on an IRA withdrawal prior to July 13, 1990, was obtained in the case of *Abrahamson v. M.N.R.*, 91 DTC 213, in which the Tax Court of Canada ruled that the IRA was essentially a trust rather than a pension and withdrawals were considered to come out of capital first except to the extent of trust income in the year. Since the IRA had been financed while the taxpayer was non-resident by a rollover from a U.S. pension plan, the capital element was considerable. However, the result in the *Abrahamson* case would seem to be overridden by the new rules making such payment taxable except to the extent of U.S. exemption. This is the conclusion in *Kaiser v. the Queen*, 95 DTC 13 (T.C.C.).

The foreign retirement arrangement rules also ensure that obligations held by a Canadian taxpayer through an IRA are not subject to income accrual rules, foreign passive income rules, or Canadian taxable trust rules. Where income was taxed under these rules prior to July 13, 1990, it is not taxed again upon withdrawal under the general rule prohibiting double taxation.

The CRA is of the view that the value of an IRA on death is a "right or thing"; see ¶1908.

For deductibility of contributions to foreign plans, see ¶365a; for rollover of lump sums to RRSP, see ¶2612.05. The CRA takes the view (in the T1 Guide) that IRA payments taxable in Canada are not eligible for the $2,000 pension income credit.

Where amounts are transferred from a U.S. employer's pension plan to an IRA on behalf of a Canadian resident employee, the amount on its face is taxable in Canada. However, where the transfer is exempt under U.S. rules, it would appear that the Canadian resident is entitled to an offsetting deduction for treaty-protected income, pursuant to Article XVIII(1) of the Canada–U.S. Tax Treaty. It may be, however, that the amount is included in net income for the purpose of limiting tax benefits and, perhaps, calculating clawback taxes (see ¶1419).

[¶919.10] *Roth IRAs*

The United States has an alternative IRA, called a "Roth IRA". Contributions to a Roth IRA are not deductible for U.S. taxpayers under U.S. rules, but investment income accrues tax-free and distributions generally are not taxable. Under certain circumstances, an individual may convert an ordinary IRA into a Roth IRA, but is required to include in income the value of the IRA at the time of conversion. If the conversion was made in 1998, the income inclusion could be spread over a four-year period. On December 18, 1998, Canada announced (by press release) changes that would ensure the conversion amount is taxed in Canada, and that the amount and timing of Canadian income inclusions match that of U.S. inclusions on the conversion, thus permitting Canadian foreign tax credits to arise in synchronization with U.S. taxes.

In technical amendments passed into law on June 26, 2013, new rules provide that:

(1) On conversions under U.S. rules in 1998 (when the resulting income could be spread over four years), the amount and timing of income for Canadian purposes will match the amount and timing of income for U.S. purposes. However, if an individual became resident in Canada after having converted an IRA into a Roth IRA in 1998, the individual will not be subject to taxation in Canada on any amounts relating to the conversion that remain taxable for U.S. purposes before 2002.

(2) For conversions in 1999 through 2001 inclusive, on conversions from an IRA to a Roth IRA only, amounts considered distributed for U.S. purposes as a result of a conversion are considered payments received in the taxation year of the conversion.

For 2002 and later taxation years, these rules are overtaken by the general rule, discussed under the heading "Foreign Retirement Arrangements" above, that any deemed distributions from an IRA considered income in the United States are considered income at the same time in Canada.

A Roth IRA is not a foreign retirement arrangement and therefore distributions from it are not taxable under the rule discussed at ¶919.05. However, income accruing in the Roth IRA may technically be included in the Canadian holder's income, although treaty relief is available, as discussed below. If the Roth IRA is a custodial account, the CRA takes the position that interest credited or accrued under the account will, subject to the Canada–U.S. income tax treaty, be taxable on an annual basis to the individual holder under paragraph 12(1)(*c*) or subsection 12(4) of the Act. A subsequent distribution is not taxable in Canada in the year it is received.

Notwithstanding the above, a Roth IRA is now considered a "pension" for purposes of the Canada–U.S. tax treaty (as long as no contribution is made to the Roth IRA after December 31, 2008, by or on behalf of the holder while the holder is resident in Canada). As such, it is eligible for relief under the treaty. Under paragraph 1 of Article XVIII of the treaty, distributions from a Roth IRA are exempt from taxation in Canada to the extent that they would be excluded from taxable income in the U.S., meaning that they are generally tax free in Canada. Furthermore, an election under paragraph 7 of that Article is available which defers Canadian taxation with respect to the income accrued in the Roth IRA. Effectively, this means that Canadian resident holders of a Roth IRA are exempt from taxation on accrued income and distributions from a Roth IRA, provided that a valid election is filed and distributions would not be taxable in the U.S. if the individual were resident in the U.S.

In its Income Tax Technical News No. 43, dated September 24, 2010, the CRA provides the filing requirements for the election. If you were resident in Canada before January 1, 2010 and had a Roth IRA before that time, you have until April 30, 2011 to make the election. The election will be valid for all taxation years. If you became resident in Canada in a taxation year ending after December 31, 2009, you have until the filing due-date for the first year of residence to make the election in respect of the Roth IRA. The election will be valid for the first year of residence and all subsequent taxation years. There is no prescribed form to make the election. A letter is sufficient, with information regarding the Roth IRA as set out in the Income Tax Technical News No. 43 (available on the CRA website).

The election in respect of the Roth IRA will be valid only if no contributions are made to the Roth IRA while the holder is resident in Canada. If contributions are made while you are resident in Canada, the election is no longer valid and subsequent income in the Roth IRA will be subject to taxation in Canada in accordance with the rules discussed above.

(ITA: 12(11); 56(1)(*a*), (12); 60(*j*); 60.01; 248(1) "foreign retirement arrangement", (28); ITR: 6803 [Prescribed plan or arrangement – foreign retirement arrangement]; Window on Canadian Tax: 2247; 2851; 5657; IT-528 Transfers of Funds Between Registered Plans; CRA Document No.: U.S. Roth Individual Retirement Arrangement, Education Individual Retirement Arrangement (4125-U5-100-21), *February 3, 1999*, CRA Document No. 9810656)

[¶919.20] *U.S. War Hazards Compensation Act (Foreign Workers' Compensation)*

It is the CRA's view that the *U.S. War Hazards Compensation Act*"provides workers' compensation payments in the form of annuities to surviving spouses and dependants of certain employees who are killed on the job". Such payments are included in income as ordinary annuity income (and not as workers' compensation, which includes in income only payments received under an employees' or workers' compensation law of Canada or a province). The payments are not treaty-protected. As an annuity, the income would seem to be eligible for the pension income deduction for eligible taxpayers; see ¶1311. On the other hand, it will not be deductible in full from taxable income as workers' compensation (¶990).

(CRA Document No.: workers' compensation and annuities, *July 24, 2007*, CRA Document No. 2006-0217681E5)

[¶921] U.S. SOCIAL SECURITY

U.S. Social Security payments (including tier 1 railroad retirement benefits) received by Canadian residents are taxed under the provisions of the Fourth Protocol to the Canada–U.S. Tax Treaty, which provides that the United States will impose no tax on the benefits and Canada will follow U.S. rules under which only 85% of the benefits are taxable.

For Canadian purposes, income exempt under a tax treaty is claimed as a deduction from taxable income. Accordingly, U.S. Social Security benefits are taxed in full on line 115 of your T1 return, but 15% of the benefits so reported may be deducted at line 256. If you have other pension income reported on line 115, you may only deduct 15% of the U.S. Social Security component of that income.

Additionally, starting in 2010, Canadian resident persons who have been receiving U.S. Social Security payments since before 1996 and continually up to the relevant taxation year are entitled to deduct an additional 35% of such benefits in computing their taxable income for the taxation year. The deduction is also allowed for resident surviving spouses or common-law partners of such persons. Since, as noted, 15% of such amounts is already deductible by virtue of the treaty, the new deduction restores the pre-1997 tax treatment for such residents who received U.S. Social Security benefits and were subject to a 50% inclusion rate. This additional deduction is also claimed on line 256 if applicable.

Canadian courts have repeatedly affirmed that it is only the U.S. Social Security benefits mentioned above that qualify for the 15% treaty deduction. Income from U.S.-source private pension plans does not qualify. See *Donnelly v. The Queen,* 2007 DTC 1281 (T.C.C.), and cases cited therein.

By asking you to report U.S. Social Security on line 115, the CRA is declaring it eligible for the pension income credit claimed at line 314 (discussed at ¶1311). This is technically dubious, since the Fourth Protocol specifies that these benefits are taxed as if they were benefits under the Canada Pension Plan (CPP), and CPP benefits are not eligible for the pension income credit. However, the CRA has chosen not to impose this interpretation and so, at least for the time being, the U.S. Social Security benefits may be treated as eligible for the credit.

As you might expect, it is only the taxable 85% (or 50%, as the case may be) of these benefits that is eligible for the pension credit. The CRA provides a "Line 314 — Pension income amount" chart (on the federal worksheet which accompanies the T1 Return package), on which, at line 4, you back out the 15% of benefits deducted at line 256.

Since U.S. Social Security is treated as CPP income and not Old Age Security income, it is not subject to the clawback taxes on Old Age Security benefits (¶1419).

In general, the payment of U.S. Social Security tax by a Canadian employer on your behalf without deducting it from your salary or wages constitutes a taxable benefit to you. However, if you are making CPP contributions, you should be able to apply for exemption from U.S. Social Security tax (or *vice versa*). See also ¶2111 and ¶2183.

U.S. citizens resident in Canada (and perhaps U.S. green card holders) may have to report U.S. Social Security to the United States as well, but should receive offsetting credits, and Canada will not normally give foreign tax credit (¶1455) for U.S. tax on these amounts, expecting it to be eliminated by credits. The situation may be different for U.S. Alternative Minimum Tax on the Canadian resident U.S. citizen. CRA Document No. 9827211 suggests that Canada will provide foreign tax credit for the portion of U.S. AMT related to Social Security benefits. Non-U.S. citizens resident in Canada should have no U.S. withholding tax and no U.S. liability.

(Notice of Ways and Means Motion of December 10, 1998, Clause 83; Canada–U.S. Tax Treaty, Art. XVIII 5, as amended effective December 16, 1997; Canada–U.S. Totalization Agreement; ITA: 6(1)(*a*); 56(1)(*a*); 110(1)(*f*); IT-122R2 (Archived pursuant to *Income Tax Technical News* No. 31, as discussed at ¶1455(3)); Dept. of Finance News Releases Nos. 97-062,97-122, 97-125)

[¶922] OTHER FOREIGN SOCIAL SECURITY INCOME

United States Social Security payments are far and away the most common foreign social security payments received by Canadian residents, and for that reason they are discussed at ¶921 in some detail. Canadian taxation of social security payments received from other countries may be dealt with in a tax treaty between Canada and the country from which the payment originates. Canada has a web of more than 90 such treaties, and at any given time several of those treaties will be under renegotiation and several new treaties are in the process of negotiation or ratification. A complete list of existing and pending treaties, and those in the process of revision or recently revised, is found on the Department of Finance website under "Home/Topics/Status of International Tax Treaty".

Treaty revisions in particular can affect longstanding treatment of foreign social security pensions, and the details as well as the principles must be examined with care.

As an example, the Canada–Germany Tax Treaty was revised effective March 28, 2002, to render German Social Security payments taxable in Canada to the extent they would have been taxable by Germany. (However, coming-into-force provisions of the treaty itself generally deferred the change to the 2003 Canadian taxation year.) For 2003 and 2004, Germany in effect taxed the income earned in the pension but not the capital contributed. In practice, the CRA published a list of the taxable element of the pension determined according to the age of the pensioner at the time the pension commenced. The list was published in a CRA technical opinion; see CRA Document No. 2002-1125885, or the CRA website. At the time of writing, the website memo could be found (with some difficulty) by typing into the CRA search engine "non-residents", following the link to International and Non-Resident Taxes, then to Tax Treaties, then to Important Notices. The URL at the time of writing was: www.cra-arc.gc.ca/tx/nnrsdnts/ntcs/grmny-eng.html.

For 2005 and later years, Germany revised its taxation of pension income, and consequently Canadian treatment of social security pensions received from Germany changed as well. Under these rules, 50% of the German social security benefits covered by the German treaty were taxable in 2005. For those who start receiving a pension after 2005, the rate to be used in calculating the taxable portion of the pension, based on the first year of receipt, will increase by two per cent a year from 2006 to 2020. From 2021 to 2040, that rate will increase by one per cent a year. The document can be found on the CRA website, under "Individuals and families/Individuals — Leaving or entering Canada and non-residents/Important notices/Change to the taxation of social security pensions received from Germany by a resident of Canada". The most recent CRA document on the revisions, "Additional information regarding the change to the taxation of German social security pensions", published on September 15, 2014, can be found under the same "Important Notices" referred to above.

Treaties provide special tax treatment for a myriad of income items in addition to pension income. Because the items dealt with are so extensive, and there are so many treaties, it is beyond the scope of this book to deal with each treaty or even to flag in detail each set of changes. The fact that a treaty is being revised will be flagged in ¶2005, but the recipient of income from such a treaty country must consult the treaty itself for consequential changes. The treaties are public documents, available on the Department of Finance website.

In the absence of treaty provisions, one would normally assume that the general foreign pension rules at ¶919 should apply, unless the payment for some reason cannot be characterized a pension income.

In addition to the tax treatment of such income, governed by treaty, another set of international agreements attempts to integrate the treatment of contributions and pension credits where residents of one country are working in another. A list of such agreements is found at ¶2111.

Tax credits are generally not allowed for foreign social security taxes paid; there is a major exception for U.S. social security taxes related to U.S. employment income. See ¶1455(3).

[¶923] RETIRING ALLOWANCES; TERMINATION PAYMENTS

You must include in your income any amounts received as a retiring allowance. A retiring allowance is an amount received upon or after retirement from an office or employment in recognition of long service or in respect of loss of office or employment. Amounts received on a termination of an office or employment, whether or not received as damages, are included within the definition of a retiring allowance (these payments were formally known as termination payments). You may, if your employment with the employer began in a taxation year before 1996, transfer part of the allowance into a registered retirement savings plan or registered pension plan. The calculation of the amount which may be so transferred is discussed in ¶2612.10. A retiring allowance eligible for transfer to an RRSP, RPP, PRPP, or SPP must be made either by your employer or a retirement compensation arrangement (¶359) to which your employer contributed.

As noted above, a "retiring allowance" must be paid either on retirement or for loss of office. Cases on the first part of the definition have suggested that amounts received by an individual as a retirement allowance may not be eligible for tax deferral through the use of a registered retirement savings plan or registered pension plan if the individual left his employment before a mandatory retirement age and then carried on an active business life. On the other hand, the cases are not uniform on this point; *Berlinski v. M.N.R.*, 89 DTC 433 (T.C.C.), limits "retirement" to "withdrawal from occupation" and suggests that it does not follow the taxpayer must vegetate thereafter. The CRA's Interpretation Bulletin IT-337R4 (consolidated) expands on this issue.

It is the CRA's view that retirement or loss of an office or employment does not include a transfer from one office or position to another with the same employer (or an affiliate), in a different capacity (including one with diminished responsibilities). However, a termination of employment which otherwise qualifies as a retirement or loss of office will not be excluded solely because a taxpayer continues as a corporate director (other than a director of a public company) at nominal compensation. Similarly, where after the sale of the employer's active business an individual carries on certain administrative duties for the former employer for which no remuneration or director's fees are received, the individual may still be considered to have retired or have lost an office or employment. Such administrative duties include collecting rents, hiring trades for general maintenance of a building, day-to-day banking and general bookkeeping.

Similarly, the CRA sets out a general rule that a retiring allowance does not include a payment of termination of employment with an employer followed by (1) re-employment with the employer (on a full- or part-time basis), or (2) employment with an affiliate of the employer pursuant to an arrangement made prior to the termination of employment. However, the CRA will recognize exceptions where, for example, the termination of employment is followed by part-time re-employment which is not pensionable.

The second part of the definition, "in respect of loss of office or employment", covers awards made by an employer who terminates your employment. The CRA adopts a general rule that the words "in respect of" imply a connection between the loss of employment and the subsequent receipt, where the primary purpose of the receipt was compensation for the loss of employment. Two questions determine whether such a connection exists:

(1) But for the loss of employment would the amount have been received?

and

(2) Was the purpose of the payment to compensate a loss of employment?

Only if the answer to the first question is no and the answer to the second question is yes will the amount received be considered a retiring allowance.

The CRA goes on to say that "A payment in respect of loss of office or employment usually refers to the elimination or expiration of a particular office or employment; e.g., the abolition of a job or position for economic reasons or as the consequence of an employer's withdrawal from a particular business." However, the term may also refer to the loss of an income source of an employee who is released from an office or employment whether unilaterally or not. Since "early retirement incentive plans" are essentially designed to eliminate a number of office or employment positions (albeit on an elective basis), the CRA accepts payments made upon such "retirements" as being in respect of a loss of office or employment.

Legal expenses incurred to obtain a termination payment (e.g., damages for loss of office) or other retiring allowance are deductible to the extent of payments obtained and not transferred on a rollover basis to an RRSP or RPP; see ¶924.

If a taxpayer dies prior to receiving all of the retiring allowance payments to which he or she is entitled, the subsequent payment of this allowance made to a dependant, relation or legal representative of the taxpayer will normally be included in the recipient's income as a retiring allowance. However, as an alternative, the CRA will allow the value of any retiring allowance not received at the time of the taxpayer's death to be included in his or her income for the taxation year in which he died as a "right or thing" (see ¶1908).

If an officer or employee dies prior to his or her retirement, then any payments made by the company, similar to these retiring allowances, are considered "death benefits" rather than a retiring allowance (see ¶925).

If an employee, after retirement, receives a payment from his or her employer which represents a settlement of the accumulated sick leave credits to which he or she is entitled, the CRA considers the payment to qualify as a retiring allowance; however, accumulated vacation leave credit payments are considered to be ordinary employment income.

If you receive (or another person receives by virtue of your employment) a payment on retirement or termination out of a funded pension plan called a Retirement Compensation Arrangement (¶359), this will not be considered a retiring allowance but will typically be ordinary income to you (¶911), and not eligible for transfer to an RRSP under ¶2612.05.

If you repay all or part of a retiring allowance included in your income in the year or an earlier year, the repayment may be deducted in the year made. It is not clear what would happen if you had contributed the entire amount to an RRSP. It seems that you are not required to withdraw from the RRSP; you can (if you have the necessary funds) leave the RRSP funds in the RRSP and make the repayment out of cash on hand, and take the deduction. Presumably, the general rules against tax evasion and tax avoidance will prevent collusive transactions.

If you receive income under order of a court or other competent tribunal, under an arbitration award, or under a contract terminating a legal proceeding (i.e., an out of court settlement), and the income is characterized as employment income *or* is received on account of damages for loss of office, and part or all of the amount relates to other years, the amount (less any associated deductions for legal expenses) to which you had a right in earlier years may be eligible for averaging. Income related to other years must exceed $3,000 for the rule to apply. In theory, at least, eligible amounts should be reported to you on form T1198, and the CRA should do the averaging automatically if you deal with form T1198.

(ITA: 56(1)(*a*), (*l*.1); 60(*j*.1), (*n*), (*o*.1); 110.2(2); 248(1) "retiring allowance"; IT-337R4 Retiring Allowances (Consolidated); CRA Document No.: Reorganization FMV of Phantom Stock Units, *March 6, 2002*, CRA Document No. 2001-0085613)

[¶923.05] *Damages as Termination Payments*

Generally speaking, compensation received by an individual from the individual's employer or former employer on account of damages may be employment income, a retiring allowance, non-taxable damages, or a combination thereof. Such a determination is a question of fact, which requires a review of all relevant facts and documentation of each particular case.

Special damages, such as those received for lost (unearned) wages or employee benefits, are taxable as employment income if the employee retains his or her employment or is reinstated.

The definition of a retiring allowance includes an amount received in respect of a loss of office or employment of a taxpayer, whether or not received as, on account or in lieu of payment of damages or pursuant to an order or judgment of a competent tribunal. As discussed above, the CRA perceives that the words "in respect of" denote a connection between the loss of employment and the subsequent receipt. Accordingly, where an individual receives compensation on account of damages as a result of a loss of employment, the amount received will be taxed as a retiring allowance. This applies to both special damages, as well as general damages received for loss of self-respect, humiliation, mental anguish, hurt feelings, etc.

Where personal injuries have been sustained before or after the loss of employment (for example, in situations of harassment during employment, or defamation after dismissal), the general damages received in respect of these injuries may be viewed as unrelated to the loss of employment and therefore non-taxable (see ¶991, under the subheading "Damages for Personal Injury or Death"). In order to claim that damages received upon loss of employment are for personal injuries unrelated to the loss of employment, it must be clearly demonstrated that the damages relate to events or actions separate from the loss of employment. In making such a determination, the amount of severance that the employee would reasonably be entitled to, will be taken into consideration.

Similarly, general damages relating to human rights violations can be considered unrelated to a loss of employment, despite the fact that the loss of employment is often a direct result of a human rights violations complaint. If a human rights tribunal awards a taxpayer an amount for general damages, the amount is normally not required to be included in income. When a loss of employment involves a human rights violation and is settled out of court, a reasonable amount in respect of general damages can be excluded from income. The determination of what is reasonable is influenced by the maximum amount that can be awarded under the applicable human rights legislation and the evidence presented in the case. Any excess will be taxed as a retiring allowance.

In *Forest v. The Queen*, 2008 DTC 6506 (F.C.A.), reversing 2007 DTC 632 (T.C.C.), the taxpayer had received a payment in settlement of a dispute about workplace harassment. As part of the settlement, the taxpayer agreed to a termination of employment. The CRA assessed the entire amount as a retiring allowance, refusing to allocate any amount to damages. The Court ruled that the situation required an apportionment of the settlement between damages and a retirement allowance. The taxpayer had met the burden of proof as to the determination of the allocation by introducing evidence from which the apportionment could be deduced by the Court. It was incumbent upon the Court to make such an allocation as long as there was some evidence, in whatever form, from which the trial judge could infer, on a balance of probabilities, which part of that general award was intended to compensate for specific types of damages.

(IT-337R4 Retiring Allowances (Consolidated))

[¶923.10] *Prejudgment Interest on Wrongful Dismissal*

Prejudgment interest generally refers to the element in a court order or settlement characterized as interest up to the time of the order or settlement. It was traditionally CRA policy to exclude prejudgment interest in wrongful dismissal orders or settlements from income. (Post-judgment interest, by contrast, the CRA has always viewed as taxable.) At the Canadian Tax Foundation Annual Conference in September 2003, the CRA announced that, commencing in 2004, prejudgment interest in wrongful dismissal suits will no longer be excluded from income. It is understood to be the CRA's view that the interest is taxable by virtue of paragraph 12(1)(*c*) of the *Income Tax Act* and is not necessarily swept into the definition of retiring allowance and is therefore not eligible for contribution to an RPP or RRSP. This view has the advantage for the employer that prejudgment interest is not subject to withholding, but of course deprives the employee of the ability to transfer the amount to an RRSP. Given that the RRSP/RPP transfer is only available *pro rata* to the extent the employment began before 1996, this is perhaps not a major consideration. The CRA has suggested, informally, that it probably would not resist the employee's effort to characterize prejudgment interest as retiring allowance eligible for the now somewhat truncated transfer. In view of the broad sweep of the retiring allowance definition, one would think the employee could properly insist on this, although of course nothing can be taken for granted without at least a written opinion from the CRA.

The CRA's comments on this subject have been published in *Income Tax Technical News* No. 30, dated May 24, 2004.

Note that prejudgment interest in cases involving damages for personal injury or death continues to be treated as non-taxable, as discussed under the subheading "Damages for Personal Injury or Death" in ¶991.

[¶924] LEGAL EXPENSES OF OBTAINING TERMINATION PAYMENTS, RETIRING ALLOWANCES, OR PENSION BENEFITS

When termination payments were incorporated in the concept of retiring allowances in 1981, the government failed to take account of the fact that these payments, on account of loss of office or employment, could result from genuine and costly legal proceedings, whether or not they involved actual litigation. Accordingly, although the government was greatly concerned that the payments should be treated as income, no provision was made for deduction of the related legal costs. The result was that the whole payment was considered income (but not employment income), and the legal costs received no recognition. It followed that where legal costs were sufficiently high, the tax on termination payments could exceed the amount actually received by the taxpayer.

Although aware of this situation, the government did not act to give redress until the courts confirmed it, as they did in *Lyonde v. M.N.R.*, 88 DTC 1397 (T.C.C.).

Eventually, the government enacted legislation under which legal expenses incurred to collect or establish (i) a right to a retiring allowance (including a termination payment), or (ii) a right to pension benefits (other than CPP or provincial pension plan benefits) arising from employment will reduce any income from those sources. Note that these legal expenses are not deductible against other income, but only against the pension income or retiring allowances to which the legal expenses relate. However, to the extent income is not available to permit the deduction of legal expenses *paid*, the expense may be carried forward seven years and matched to appropriate income. Conversely, where the income has been received in one year and the legal expense paid in a later year, the expense may be deducted in the year paid.

Where the taxpayer is rolling over the retiring allowance or pension income under the rules at ¶1021 (as they apply in the particular year the income is received), the amount designated as a contribution out of those amounts reduces the amount eligible for deduction of legal expenses.

Where the taxpayer receives an award or reimbursement in respect to the legal costs paid to establish or collect a termination payment or pension benefit, the award or reimbursement is clearly income and is part of the pool of income against which the legal expense may be deducted.

If you have been denied a deduction for legal expenses of this type in prior years, you should put in a refund claim promptly; see ¶221. You will not be entitled to the refund if you do not request it before the year in question becomes statute-barred. You may want to file a waiver (¶277) to ensure the year remains open if the three-year time limit on your original notice of assessment for the year is approaching.

Technically, retiring allowances and pension benefits are not "employment income". Parallel rules permit the deduction of legal expenses to establish or collect salary or wages retroactive to 1986; previously a deduction was permitted only for expenses of collecting unpaid remuneration. See ¶371.

These rules explicitly do *not* apply to allow deduction of legal expenses related to establishing pension rights on divorce or separation; accordingly, these remain non-deductible under the explicit rules discussed here. The CRA has opined (in CRA Document No. 2002-0177827) that the legal expenses of obtaining a pension division order would accordingly not be deductible notwithstanding its change in position with respect to other legal expenses of separation in *Income Tax Technical News* No. 24, discussed at ¶2355.

(ITA: 56(1)(*l*.1); 60(*o*.1); 248(1) "retiring allowance"; IT-99R5, paras. 25–28; IT-337R4 (consolidated), para. 23)

[¶925] DEATH BENEFITS

Where an employee dies and subsequently a payment is made to his or her spouse, common-law partner, or other beneficiary in recognition of his or her service in an office or employment, the amount or amounts received (called the "gross death benefit") are subject to special tax treatment. If there is only one recipient of all such payments in respect of the deceased, the amount to be included in that recipient's income is only that portion of the gross death benefit received in the year which exceeds $10,000 minus any amounts excluded by the recipient under this rule in prior years in respect of the death of that employee. That is, if the death benefit is payable in more than one year and the amount received in the first year is less than the amount of the $10,000 exemption, the unused exemption may be carried over and deducted from amounts received in subsequent years until it is completely used.

If gross death benefits are received in respect of service in more than one office or employment, the $10,000 exemption applies to the aggregate of all such amounts.

Although the payment of the death benefit must be in recognition of service in office or employment, it need not be made directly by the employer; it follows that an otherwise qualifying payment made after death to a testamentary trust of the employee and thence to a beneficiary may qualify provided the trust rules are met and the gross amount is paid or payable to the beneficiary.

Payments made out of a pension or superannuation fund, a salary deferral arrangement (¶307) or a retirement compensation arrangement (¶365a) upon or after the death of an officer or employee are not taxed as a death benefit but as pension or superannuation benefits. Similarly, a death benefit for purposes of the $10,000 exclusion does not include death benefits under the Canada or Quebec Pension Plan.

Accumulated sick leave credits owing to an employee who dies prior to retirement and are paid after his or her death are subject to the special treatment accorded to death benefits. (Sick leave credits are also apparently qualified as retiring allowances (¶923), although the same amount cannot qualify for both treatments.) Amounts paid after the death of the employee on account of accumulated vacation leave credits, overtime pay, and items taxable as employment income under the rules at ¶307, do not qualify as death benefits and must be considered employment income.

(ITA: 56(1)(*a*)(iii); 248(1) "death benefit"; IT-508R Death Benefits)

[¶925.05] *Multiple Beneficiaries*

The rules above are clear and simple as long as only one person ever receives a "death benefit" on account of the death of a particular employee. Where death benefits are paid to more than one survivor, however, the rules are necessarily more complex.

Where the death benefit is divided between one surviving spouse or common-law partner and other beneficiaries (usually children), the spouse or common-law partner in effect gets first crack at the $10,000 exemption and the children take any remainder, which (if there is more than one beneficiary in addition to the spouse) must be divided among them *pro rata* to the benefits paid to the non-spouse or common-law-partner beneficiaries.

Where a gross death benefit is paid out over more than one year, any unused portion may be carried forward. The rule that a spouse or common-law partner has priority on the whole $10,000 amount may require other taxpayers to be reassessed in later years.

Example

Employee A died and the employer paid a $15,000 death benefit, as A had directed: $8,000 to A's spouse, $5,000 to A's son, and $2,000 to A's niece. The spouse is allowed $8,000 of the $10,000 death benefit exemption. The son and the niece must split the remaining $2,000 death benefit exemption in proportion to their shares of the $7,000 paid to them. Accordingly, the son may claim an exemption of $5,000/$7,000 × $2,000 = $1,429, and the niece may claim $2,000/$7,000 × $2,000 = $571.

If the death benefit had been paid out in equal instalments over two years, $4,000 to the spouse, $2,500 to the son, and $1,000 to the niece in each year, each beneficiary would, in Year 1, have been able to claim an exemption for the full amount received, since the total of all such amounts was less than $10,000. However, when the balance was paid out in Year 2, the son and the niece would be reassessed to reduce their Year 1 claims to $1,429 and $571 respectively.

Where there is no spouse or common-law partner, there is no priority claimant and, as you might expect, the $10,000 death benefit exemption is divided *pro rata* among the recipients according to the amounts received by each.

Under the common-law spouse/common-law partner rules at ¶1113, there can be more than one spouse at a time. Typically this will be the case where there is both a common-law and a legal spouse not yet divorced, although no doubt other variations are possible. Where more than one spouse or common-law partner receives a death benefit, the spousal priority rule simply does not apply, and the death benefit exemption is divided under the general rule, i.e., *pro rata* among all recipients according to the amounts received by each. It follows that where there are two surviving spouses, and one receives $10,000 in Year 1 and the other $10,000 in

Year 2, the second can claim a Year 2 exemption of $5,000 and force the first to be reassessed for Year 1 to limit the claim of the first to $5,000.

(ITA: 56(1)(*a*)(iii); 248(1) "death benefit"; IT-508R Death Benefits)

[¶925.10] *Mechanics of Claiming Death Benefit Exemption*

Normally, a death benefit will be reported to you on either a T3 slip (in box 26, identified in box 35) or a T4A slip (in box 28, identified by footnote 06). It is up to you to identify the amount of the death benefit which you can exclude from income and exclude it by not including it in the amount you carry from the slip to line 130 of your T1 return. You must attach to your T1 return a note indicating the amount you have excluded as a death benefit. The CRA says you merely have to identify the amount and not provide the calculation, but providing the calculation may save time in the long run, and will at least remind you of what you did and why.

(5000-G, "General Income Tax and Benefit Guide" (T1 Guide) for line 130)

RESTRICTIVE COVENANTS

[¶929] COVENANTS NOT TO COMPETE

[¶929.05] *Restrictive Covenant Defined*

The general rule is that amounts received or receivable in a particular year under a "restrictive covenant", as defined, are included in income in full in that year unless some other specified treatment is explicitly provided for by the legislation. The general rule applies only to amounts received or receivable by the taxpayer or a person or partnership not dealing at arm's length with the taxpayer. There is no comparable rule for the person paying these amounts except where a joint election is provided for or the amount is considered employment income as discussed in the exceptions below. In the absence of a rule, one would assume the payer is obtaining an eligible capital property which can be amortized if the payer is engaged in business.

Commentary on Bill C-29 Measures (Oct. 25, 2016)

Note: When Bill C-29, October 25, 2016, achieves Royal Assent, the commentary will be modified to read:

Effective January 1, 2017, the eligible capital property rules have been repealed and replaced by a new Class 14.1 of depreciable property. Property that previously was eligible capital property is now depreciable capital property, and expenditures and receipts that previously were accounted for under the eligible capital property rules are now accounted for under the rules for depreciable property and capital property.

A restrictive covenant is defined in relation to a particular taxpayer (which, for these purposes, includes a partnership), and means an agreement entered into, an undertaking made, or a waiver of an advantage or right by that taxpayer, whether enforceable or not, that affects or is intended to affect, in any way whatever, the acquisition or provision of property or services by a taxpayer or by another taxpayer that does not deal at arm's length with the taxpayer. There are exceptions. A restrictive covenant does not include (i) an agreement or undertaking for the disposition of the taxpayer's property, or (ii) a limited class of deemed non-dispositions where a right acquired for not less than fair market value is exchanged for property under an arrangement to establish the right. The fair market value requirement in (ii) only applies to restrictive covenants granted after November 8, 2006.

The definition is broad enough to capture covenants attached to land and to employment as well as covenants attached to the purchase and sale of shares or business assets. The phrase "restrictive covenant … whether enforceable or not" brings to mind discriminatory covenants that at one time attached to land to restrict its sale, typically, to white protestants, and which are presumably no longer enforceable, although this may not have been in the minds of drafters fortunately too young to remember such things.

An essential part of the legislation specifically applies the allocation rules (section 68 of the *Income Tax Act*) to restrictive covenants. These rules say that where part of an amount received or receivable by a taxpayer may be considered consideration for a disposition or for services rendered by the taxpayer, and part may be considered for a restrictive covenant, the proceeds must be allocated on a reasonable basis regardless of the form or effect of a contract or agreement governing the disposition and proceeds.

The allocation rule, together with the exclusions from the restrictive covenant definition, are apparently designed to carve up an agreement for a disposition of assets which includes a covenant not to compete into (i) the agreement in respect of the disposition, which is presumably on capital account, giving rise in most cases to capital gain or loss or a disposition of eligible capital property, and (ii) the agreement not to provide the specified arm's length services to anyone, which latter agreement the courts have held not to be a disposition of property.

There are now several exceptions to the compulsory allocation of proceeds to a non-competition agreement rather than to proceeds of disposition. These are discussed under subheadings ¶929.30 through ¶929.40, below. The most recent exception is at ¶929.42.

Since the general rule can tax amounts receivable but not yet received, it is of course possible that there will be intervening events and the amounts will never be received. In this case there is an offsetting deduction from income from all sources in the year the amount owing is established to be a bad debt. If an amount deducted as a bad debt under this provision is later recovered, the recovery is included in income when received.

(ITA: 56(1)(*m*); 56.4(1)(*a*)(iii); 60(*f*); 68(1)(*c*))

[¶929.10] *Historical Information: Background Litigation Giving Rise to the Restrictive Covenant Rules*

In *The Queen v. Fortino et al.*, 2000 DTC 6060 (F.C.A), affirming 97 DTC 55 (T.C.C.), the shareholders of a grocery business sold the shares of the business under an agreement which included a non-competition clause binding on the individual shareholders. The CRA treated amounts received for the non-competition clause as business income, but the Court found that whatever the expenditure might be, the amount received was not income (as opposed to capital gain) of the recipient. Nor was it an eligible capital expenditure, since the agreement was for the sale of shares and not for the sale of a business carried on by individual shareholders as such. The eligible capital property rules could not pierce the corporate veil and attribute the business activity to the shareholders. Since the CRA neglected to plead the alternative that the amount might be capital gain to the recipient, it went untaxed.

In its discussion of the *Fortino* case in CRA Document No. 2000-EM20425, which also appears in 2000 Canadian Tax Foundation Annual Conference Report 36 at 36:3, the CRA in effect accepted that receipts for a non-competition clause are not eligible capital property, and staked out the position that they are proceeds of disposition of capital property instead: "It is the CRA's view that non-competition payments will generally constitute proceeds of disposition of capital property, that being the right to compete with the purchaser".

Inevitably, adventurous vendors argued in later cases that the vendor's receipts were not capital gain either, but essentially a non-taxable amount.

In *Manrell v. The Queen*, 2002 DTC 1222 (T.C.C.), the Tax Court dismissed this line of reasoning and upheld the CRA position that amounts allocated to a non-competition clause on the sale of shares are proceeds from the disposition of a capital property (the right to compete) and therefore give rise to capital gain. The Federal Court of Appeal reversed in 2003 DTC 5225 (F.C.A.), holding, with logic only a lawyer could love, that the right to compete was not "a right of any kind whatever" included in the definition of property. Accordingly, "non-competition payments are non-taxable capital receipts". See also the article in Wolters Kluwer's *Tax Topics* No. 1621, April 3, 2003, for a discussion of the foregoing cases.

[¶929.15] *Historical Information: Legislation to Reverse Litigation Results; Timing of Implementation*

The notion of proceeds of disposition falling through the tax net altogether proved too much for the Department of Finance to bear, and on October 7, 2003, it announced that it would reverse the *Manrell* decision by statute. Although no draft legislation was published, the announcement did indicate that the basic rule will be that, in the first instance, any amount receivable in respect of a restrictive covenant will be treated as ordinary income for income tax purposes. However, exceptions will be provided in certain situations — for example, where proceeds are receivable by a taxpayer in respect of an arm's length disposition of shares in a corporation, and other proceeds are receivable by the taxpayer for a restrictive covenant relating to the business carried on by the corporation. In these cases, the amount receivable for the covenant may be treated as part of the proceeds for the disposition of the shares, to the extent that the covenant increases the fair market value of the shares. Only the portion of the amount receivable for the covenant that is in excess of that treated as share proceeds will be taxable as ordinary income. This mechanism will also apply to dispositions of partnership interests.

Most of these proposals, now passed as law, apply to amounts received or receivable after October 7, 2003, other than to amounts received before 2005 pursuant to a written agreement made on or before that date between parties dealing at arm's length. However, the proposals relating to employment income apply to amounts receivable after October 7, 2003, without further qualification.

(Department of Finance Release No. 2003-049, dated October 7, 2003)

[¶929.20] *Details of Legislation: Covenants Related to Dispositions of Shares or Partnership Interest*

Generally speaking, where a taxpayer (the vendor) gives a covenant to an arm's length purchaser of the vendor's shares in a corporation which carries on business, or the vendor's partnership interest in a partnership that carries on business, and the covenant relates to the business, the purchaser and the vendor may jointly elect that amounts paid under the covenant will be treated as part of the vendor's proceeds of disposition of the shares or partnership interest, and will be treated as part of the purchaser's cost of the shares or partnership interest. It follows that the vendor will receive capital gains treatment, conceivably eligible for capital gains exemption or rollover, and the purchaser will have a reduction in gain on a later sale, but the purchaser will not have an eligible capital property which can be amortized.

Commentary on Bill C-29 Measures (Oct. 25, 2016)

Note: When Bill C-29, October 25, 2016, achieves Royal Assent, the commentary will be modified to read:

Effective January 1, 2017, the eligible capital property rules have been repealed and replaced by a new Class 14.1 of depreciable property. Property that previously was eligible capital property is now depreciable capital property, and expenditures and receipts that previously were accounted for under the eligible capital property rules are now accounted for under the rules for depreciable property and capital property.

This exception to the general rule that amounts received under a restrictive covenant (as defined above) are fully taxable as income only applies if certain conditions are met. These are:

- the covenant must be related to a disposition to the arm's length purchaser or to a person related to the purchaser;
- the covenant must be an undertaking not to provide, directly or indirectly, property or services in competition with the purchaser or a person related to the purchaser;
- the covenant may reasonably be considered to have been granted to maintain or preserve the value of the interest disposed of to the purchaser;
- for covenants granted after July 18, 2005, the deemed dividend rules of subsection 84(3) do not apply;
- the amount is added to the vendor's proceeds of disposition;
- the joint election is filed "in prescribed form" as discussed under that subheading below (see ¶929.45).

Absent the joint election, the legislative rule for restrictive covenants would deem payments under the covenant to be ordinary income to the vendor. Presumably general rules would in most cases determine the expenditure to be an eligible capital expenditure of the purchaser. The insistence on determining a fair market value for the covenant presumably prevents the purchaser from inflating the eligible capital expenditure aspect of the purchase, and forces the vendor to participate in this effort or risk ordinary income treatment.

(ITA: 56.4(1); (2); (3)(c); (4)(c))

[¶929.25] *Details of Legislation: Covenants Related to Dispositions of Eligible Capital Property*

Where a taxpayer (the vendor) gives a covenant to a purchaser of the vendor's eligible capital property on a sale of the assets of a business (literally, where amounts paid under the covenant must normally be accounted for as a reduction of the cumulative eligible capital of the vendor, which is to say where the amount paid results from a disposition by the vendor of eligible capital property under the rules at ¶768), the purchaser and the vendor may jointly elect to treat amounts paid under the covenant as proceeds of disposition of eligible capital property by the vendor. (Where the amount is not paid by a purchaser in respect of a business carried on in Canada by the purchaser, the vendor may elect on its own, without consent of the purchaser.) It follows that the vendor will have recapture of any previous tax amortization of the property and the equivalent of capital gains treatment on any excess over cost, as discussed at ¶768. The purchaser is said only to have made an outlay on account of capital. Generally speaking, the purchaser will have an eligible capital property which can be amortized under the rules at ¶767, assuming that from the purchaser's point of view the property meets the criteria at ¶766. Again from the purchaser's point of view, this is essentially the same treatment that would have obtained in the absence of legislation, but now the vendor and purchaser must jointly elect "in prescribed form" as described under subheading ¶929.45, below.

In the absence of the election, payments under the covenant seem to be ordinary income to the vendor and, presumably, eligible capital expenditures of the purchaser.

> **Commentary on Bill C-29 Measures (Oct. 25, 2016)**
>
> Note: When Bill C-29, October 25, 2016, achieves Royal Assent, the commentary will be modified to read:
>
> Effective January 1, 2017, the eligible capital property rules have been repealed and replaced by a new Class 14.1 of depreciable property. Property that previously was eligible capital property is now depreciable capital property, and expenditures and receipts that previously were accounted for under the eligible capital property rules are now accounted for under the rules for depreciable property and capital property.

(ITA: 56.4(1); (2); (3)(*b*); (4)(*b*))

[¶929.30] *Details of Legislation: Covenants Given on Arm's Length Sale of Goodwill by Taxpayer or Taxpayer's Corporation*

The new legislation includes an exception to the covenant rules for certain arm's length sale of goodwill. It deals with the situation where a business is sold at arm's length and any proceeds which might be attributable to the covenant are included in the good will of the vendor or of, in effect, the vendor's corporation, and will be included in potential eligible capital property recapture on the disposition. The exception is retroactive to the start-up of the restrictive covenant system.

As discussed under the subheading "Restrictive Covenant Defined" above, the basic machinery of the restrictive covenant rules specifically applies the allocation rules (section 68 of the *Income Tax Act*) to restrictive covenants. These rules say that where part of an amount received or receivable by a taxpayer may be considered in part consideration for a disposition or for services rendered by the taxpayer, and in part may be considered payment for a restrictive covenant, the part which can reasonably be regarded as consideration for the covenant is deemed to be received or receivable in respect of the covenant regardless of the form or effect of a governing contract or agreement.

The legislation now says that in very limited circumstances, this rule does not apply to, and therefore effectively exempts from the application of section 68, a covenant granted by a vendor to an arm's length purchaser not to provide property or services in competition with the purchaser or a person related to the purchaser. Provided the consideration for the restrictive covenant is included in the vendor's goodwill amount (or that of the vendor's corporation), and the vendor (or the corporation) and the purchaser jointly elect to have this exception (subsection 56.4(5)) apply, any consideration which might be considered to arise is included in the vendor's (or its corporation's) calculation of recaptured eligible capital, if any. However, this joint election is not required in respect of a restrictive covenant granted on or before October 24, 2012.

Provided all the conditions are met (see subsection 56.4(7)), the allocation rules do not apply to consider part of the consideration for the sale to be on account of the covenant. Presumably, the sale agreement must allocate no proceeds to the covenant to meet the conditions, and must allocate any consideration which might be considered for the covenant to be on account of goodwill. This should bind both vendor and purchaser to goodwill treatment.

An anti-avoidance rule effective for covenants granted after November 8, 2006, is meant to preclude this exception from applying to consideration in respect of a restrictive covenant that is taxable as ordinary income.

(ITA: 56.4(1); (5); (7); 68(1)(*c*))

[¶929.32] *Details of Legislation: Covenants Related to the Arm's Length Disposition of Property Generally*

This rule is generally retroactive to the start of the system after October 7, 2003. It deals with covenants related to dispositions of property generally, and so seems to overlap the rules relating to goodwill described above. Property is not specifically defined for this purpose, so the general *Income Tax Act* definition should apply. That definition is very broad: property is "property of any kind whatever whether real or personal, [movable or immovable, tangible or intangible,] corporeal or incorporeal ...". Without limiting the breadth of that definition, it explicitly includes a "right of any kind whatever" and a share.

In order for this exception to apply, such that section 68 does not apply, the conditions include the following:

- the covenant must be granted by a taxpayer (the vendor) to an arm's length taxpayer (the purchaser);
- the covenant must be an undertaking not to provide, directly or indirectly, property or services in competition with the property or services provided by the purchaser or a person related to the purchaser in the course of carrying on the business to which the covenant relates;
- if the covenant relates to a disposition of shares to the purchaser, it must be reasonable to conclude that the restrictive covenant is integral to an agreement in writing under which the shares of the corporation are disposed of to the purchaser. If this is the case, the amount received in respect of the shares is included in the vendor's proceeds of disposition from the shares;
- if the covenant relates to a disposition of property other than shares to which the condition above applies, it must be reasonable to conclude that the restrictive covenant is integral to an agreement in writing under which the vendor disposes of property to the purchaser for consideration received or receivable by the vendor. If this is the case, the consideration that can reasonably be regarded as being for the restrictive covenant must be received or receivable by the vendor as consideration for the disposition of the property, and if it includes a goodwill amount, that amount must be included as proceeds of eligible capital property (or included as ordinary income);
- in order to be able to add the restrictive covenant amount to the proceeds of disposition of property, the disposition cannot be a redemption, acquisition or cancellation of the share to which subsection 84(3) applies to deem a dividend on a redemption, acquisition or cancellation by a corporation of its own shares;
- for covenants granted after July 16, 2010, no proceeds are received or receivable by the vendor for granting the restrictive covenant; and

- the restrictive covenant must be granted to maintain or preserve the fair market value of the vendor's property disposed of to the purchaser, or of the shares of the corporation disposed of to the purchaser.

An anti-avoidance rule effective for covenants granted after November 8, 2006, is meant to preclude this exception from applying to consideration in respect of a restrictive covenant that is taxable as ordinary income. For example, if a taxpayer were to grant a restrictive covenant to a purchaser in circumstances where another taxpayer disposes of shares to the purchaser, section 68 would apply to the consideration that can reasonably be regarded as being for the restrictive covenant if that consideration would be ordinary income to the other taxpayer — which would be the case, for example, if those shares were held by the other taxpayer on income account.

(ITA: 56.4(8); (11); 68(1)(c))

[¶929.35] *Details of Legislation: Covenants Related to Employment*

The general employment income exception applies if an amount is receivable at the end of a year in respect of a restrictive covenant, and the amount is included or would be included in the recipient's income from employment under section 5 or 6 if it were received in the year. In such case, the amount is included under one of those provisions in the year of receipt. Furthermore, if the amount has not otherwise been received but is receivable at the end of the year, and the restrictive covenant was granted more than 36 months prior, the amount is deemed to be received and therefore included in income.

Note that the rule forcing payments receivable in the year under a covenant to be treated employment income (and therefore not covered by the general restrictive covenant rule) only operates on income that would be employment income if received in the year. This would be the case, for example, where a covenant not to compete is part of the termination provisions of an employment contract. The CRA always took the position that this was so (see CRA Document No. 2002-0147967), but was perhaps sufficiently shaken by the implications of the *Fortino* and *Manrell* decisions that it welcomes the support of the legislation.

Where an amount paid or payable under a covenant is specifically considered to be employment income, it is considered wages paid or payable by the purchaser, and is presumably deductible subject to the unpaid remuneration rule at ¶746.

Since the provision can include employment income not yet received, it is of course possible that there will be intervening events and the amounts will never be received. In this case there is an offsetting deduction from income from all sources in the year the amount owing is established to be a bad debt. If the bad debt is later recovered in part or in full, the recovery is included in income when received.

See also discussion under the subheading "Amounts Receivable under Covenant" in ¶308.

(ITA: 6(3.1); 56(1)(*m*); 56.4(1); (2); (3)(*a*); (4)(*a*); 60(*f*))

[¶929.40] *Details of Legislation: Covenants Given by Third Party Employee*

The legislation includes an exception to the employee covenant rules where a business which operates at arm's length from its employee is sold, and the employee gives a covenant to the purchaser. The exception is retroactive to the start-up of the restrictive covenant system.

As discussed under the subheading "Restrictive Covenant Defined" above, the basic machinery of the restrictive covenant rules specifically applies the allocation rules (section 68 of the *Income Tax Act*) to restrictive covenants. These rules say that where part of an amount received or receivable by a taxpayer may be considered in part consideration for a disposition or for services rendered by the taxpayer, and in part may be considered payment for a restrictive covenant, the part which can reasonably be regarded as consideration for the covenant is deemed to be received or receivable in respect of the covenant regardless of the form or effect of a governing contract or agreement.

The legislation now says that in very limited circumstances, this section 68 allocation rule does not apply to, and therefore effectively exempts, certain employee covenants from the new allocation rules. The exemption applies only to a covenant granted by an individual employee who deals at arm's length with both the employer and with the purchaser of an interest in the employer or in a related party. Where the employee provides a covenant to the purchaser not to provide property or services in competition with the purchaser (or a party related to the purchaser), and does not personally receive any proceeds for granting the covenant, any consideration for the covenant received by the vendor (typically the employer) is added to the vendor's proceeds of disposition rather than being income. Why the employee grants a covenant for no proceeds is not clear, but perhaps in consideration of an employment contract with the purchaser or a termination payment from the employer. It seems to be intended that by overriding the language that sets aside the form or legal effect of an agreement, it cannot be argued that such a contract or payment is in fact wholly or in part consideration for a covenant, but rather the character determined by the employee's agreement will be honoured.

It would seem that if the employee's agreement does not characterize any part of a payment as receivable on account of a covenant, then the employee rules concerning receivables would not come into play, and payments could be spread out over more than three years.

(ITA: 6(3.1); 56.4(1); (5); (6); 68(1)(*c*))

[¶929.42] *Details of Legislation: Covenants Given to Eligible Individual*

An exception to the section 68 allocation rules exists, which is generally retroactive to the start-up of the restrictive covenant system. In general terms, this exception deals with the situation where the covenant is granted in connection with an individual vendor's sale of property or shares in a corporation to an "eligible individual" in respect of the vendor — a person who is related to the vendor and at least 18 years of age. More particularly, this exception applies, such that section 68 does not apply to deem consideration to be received or receivable for granting the restrictive covenant, if the restrictive covenant is granted by an individual (the "vendor") who is resident in Canada at the time of the grant to the eligible individual, and the following conditions are met:

- the restrictive covenant is an undertaking of the vendor not to provide, directly or indirectly, property or services in competition with the property or services provided or to be provided by the eligible person (or by an eligible corporation of the eligible person) in the course of carrying on the business to which the restrictive covenant relates;
- the amount that can reasonably be regarded as being consideration for the restrictive covenant is included by the vendor or the vendor's eligible corporation in computing its goodwill amount and therefore treated as proceeds of disposition of eligible capital property, and a joint election is made with the eligible individual or that individual's eligible corporation (the most recent Department of Finance explanatory notes indicate that the joint election is not required in respect of a restrictive covenant granted on or before October 24, 2012). Alternatively, it is reasonable to conclude that the restrictive covenant is integral to an agreement in writing under which shares of the vendor's eligible corporation ("family corporation") are disposed of to the eligible individual or the eligible

individual's eligible corporation, or under which property other than such shares are disposed of to the eligible individual or eligible individual's eligible corporation; in the latter case, the proceeds will be consideration for the disposition of the property and to the extent the consideration includes a goodwill amount, that amount must be included as proceeds of eligible capital property (or included as ordinary income);

- the vendor does not retain a direct or indirect interest in the family corporation or in the eligible corporation;
- no proceeds are received or receivable by the vendor for granting the restrictive covenant;
- the disposition cannot be a redemption, acquisition, or cancellation of target shares to which subsection 84(3) applies;
- the restrictive covenant can reasonably be regarded to have been granted to maintain or preserve the fair market value of the property or shares of the family corporation disposed of to the eligible person; and
- for the purposes of applying section 69 to the disposition, the fair market value of the property is to be determined on the basis that the restrictive covenant is part of the share.

Commentary on Legislative Proposals (Sept. 16, 2016)

Note: When Legislative Proposals, September 16, 2016, achieves Royal Assent, the commentary will be modified to read:

Minor technical amendments were released on September 16, 2016, to clarify the "goodwill amount" that is relevant for the above purposes.

Commentary on Bill C-29 Measures (Oct. 25, 2016)

Note: When Bill C-29, October 25, 2016, achieves Royal Assent, the commentary will be modified to read:

Effective January 1, 2017, the eligible capital property rules have been repealed and replaced by a new Class 14.1 of depreciable property. Property that previously was eligible capital property is now depreciable capital property, and expenditures and receipts that previously were accounted for under the eligible capital property rules are now accounted for under the rules for depreciable property and capital property.

(ITA: 56.4(7); (8))

[¶929.45] *Election in Prescribed Form*

The joint elections referred to in ¶929.20, ¶929.25, ¶929.30, and ¶929.42 are to be made in prescribed form along with a copy of the restrictive covenant. If the person granting the covenant was resident in Canada, the filing deadline is the filing-due date of that person for the year in which the covenant was granted. In any other case, the joint election must be filed within six months of the day on which the covenant was granted. However, in either case the elections are deemed to be made on a timely basis if they are made within 180 days after June 26, 2013. Furthermore, the Department of Finance explanatory notes to the most recent version of the legislation indicate that these joint elections in ¶929.30 and ¶929.42 (in subsection 56.4(7)) are not required in respect of a restrictive covenant granted on or before October 24, 2012.

[¶929.50] *Withholding Tax*

All payments to non-residents to which the restrictive covenant rules apply are subject to withholding tax (¶2080.04). It is perhaps doubtful if treaty relief would apply to reduce the 25% withholding rate, but where payments are made to a treaty country, the applicable treaty should always be studied to see if a payment can be fitted within its parameters.

The withholding rules which impose tax where one non-resident makes payments to another (¶2080.10) will also apply where payments for a restrictive covenant affect:

- the acquisition or provision of property or services in Canada;
- the acquisition or provision of property or services outside Canada by a person resident in Canada; or
- the acquisition or provision outside Canada of a taxable Canadian property.

(ITA: 212(13)(*g*); 212(1)(*i*))

[¶929.55] *Allocation of Proceeds of Disposition in Agreement*

The allocation of proceeds issue deserves some comment.

In *Manrell*, virtually the whole proceeds of disposition were assigned to the non-competition agreement, and the issue of the correct allocation of proceeds of disposition to the non-taxable agreement as opposed to other assets giving rise to capital taxable gain was not in dispute. One assumes that it will be very much in dispute in future. The allocation of proceeds in an agreement between an arm's length purchaser and seller will no doubt carry some weight in the courts, but it remains to be seen how much. For agreements made before October 8, 2003, the vendor's interest in assigning proceeds to a non-taxable capital receipt will be great; the purchaser's interest in assigning proceeds to a cost base which in many cases will be non-depreciable, rather than to depreciable (albeit slowly) eligible capital property, will be less certain. The CRA has said, in Ruling 9800145:

> Finally, we wish to stress to you that under section 68 of the Act the parties must make a reasonable allocation of the consideration among the assets sold. If the allocation is unreasonable, the Department can apply the provisions of section 68 to deem what may reasonably be regarded as the proceeds for the various assets, including the goodwill.

Of course, for agreements after October 7, 2003, the shoe will be on the other foot, and the vendor will want to assign as much as possible to the proceeds of disposition.

A general discussion of the principles to be followed in valuing a non-competition agreement will be found in Wolters Kluwer *Tax Topics* No. 1638, dated July 31, 2003.

UNIVERSAL CHILD CARE BENEFIT

[¶935] HISTORICAL INFORMATION — UNIVERSAL CHILD CARE BENEFIT ("UCCB")

Effective for the final payment of the UCCB on June 20, 2016, the UCCB was repealed and replaced by the non-taxable Canada Child Benefit ("CCB") (see ¶1498). For historical reference, information on the UCCB amount is provided below.

Prior to 2015, the federal government paid a benefit of $100 per month for each child in your family under the age of six years at the beginning of any particular month. Unlike a tax credit, the UCCB is a direct payment from the government. Accordingly, the UCCB is taxable and is not means tested (i.e., is not reduced as family income increases).

As announced on October 30, 2014, for the 2015-2016 payment period, the UCCB for children under the age of 6 was increased to $160 per month, up from the previous $100 amount. Also, a monthly UCCB of $60 per child was introduced for children aged 6 through 17.

Concurrent with the 2015 UCCB enhancement, the child tax credit was repealed starting in 2015. However, individuals continued to be eligible for the family caregiver amount credit for a disabled child under 18. In general terms, this provides credit for an eligible child who, by reason of mental or physical infirmity, is likely to be, for a long and continuous period of indefinite duration, dependent on others in attending for the child's care. See ¶1124.

On the other hand, the UCCB was integrated with the child tax benefit system administered by the CRA, so that if you were receiving child tax benefits for a child under six, you should have automatically received the UCCB as well. If you did not receive the benefit automatically, you had to apply on CRA Form RC66, *Canada Child Tax Benefit Application*. Depending on your residency and immigration status, you may also have had to complete CRA Schedule RC66, *Status in Canada/Statement of Income*. The benefit was available to Canadian citizens, to permanent residents, and to "protected persons" as defined in the *Immigration and Refugee Protection Act*. For more information on applying and eligibility, see also the CRA website under "Home/Benefits/Universal child care benefit (UCCB)".

The basic requirements to obtain the UCCB were (except for the income test) essentially the same as for the CCB. The payment is made to the "custodial parent", who must be a parent who resides with the child and who primarily fulfills the responsibility for care and upbringing. The definition of parent is broad, and can include parents, grandparents, or anyone on whom the child is wholly dependent for support. The definition of parent is discussed in more detail at ¶1122.

Where the recipient parent had a spouse or common-law partner on the last day of the taxation year, the UCCB received by that parent was taxed in the hands of the spouse or common-law partner with the lower income. This appeared to be true regardless of any relationship between the spouse/partner and the child. It also seemed to be quite clear that status on the last day of the taxation year was definitive. Effective for 2010 and subsequent years, the spouse or common-law partner had to be a "cohabiting spouse or common-law partner" at the end of the year, which means that the two spouses or common-law partners were not living separate and apart at that time. For these purposes, they would not be considered to be living separate and apart at that time unless they had been living separate and apart for at least 90 days because of a breakdown in the marriage or common-law partnership.

Where the recipient parent had no cohabiting spouse or common-law partner on the last day of the taxation year, amounts received by that parent were taxable to that parent. However, the parent could designate, in his or her return for the year, that all of the benefits be included in the income of the parent's dependant for whom the wholly dependent person credit (eligible dependant credit) is claimed. If that credit was not claimed, the parent could designate that all of the benefits be included in the income of any one of the children for whom the benefit was paid. Assuming the child has little or no other income, it would not be subject to tax because the child would be entitled to the personal basic credit.

It would seem that it was incumbent on the recipient(s) to inform the CRA of changes in status; for example, where custody of a child shifted from one separated parent to the other during the year. It is status on the first day of the month that should have determined who received the payment for that month.

The CRA advises that the requirement to report UCCB income will not by itself require you to file an income tax return, since the UCCB is not means tested. If you must file a return for any other reason (for example, if the additional income itself makes you subject to tax) and you are the person in whose hands the UCCB is taxed, you must report it (on line 117). Of course, if you are receiving child tax benefits as well, you must file a return to ensure you receive those payments, so it is generally higher income families with only one working spouse who will benefit from the freedom from filing rule.

Although UCCB is included in taxable income, special provisions have been added to ensure that it will be reversed out again for the purposes of calculating your GST/HST credit (¶1496), your child tax benefit payments (¶1498) including provincial components of those payments (Chapter 15), social benefits repayment (¶1026), and the refundable medical expense supplement (¶1237).

Separated parents are each allowed a one-half entitlement to the UCCB payments if the child lives more or less equally with the two separated parents.

(*Universal Child Care Benefit Act*, S.C. 2006, c. 4; ITA: 56(6); 56(6.1); 122.62; ITR: 6301 Non-Application of Presumption; 6302 Factors)

[¶935.10] *UCCB Repayments*

If for any reason the universal child care benefits paid to you have been in excess of the amount to which you were entitled, the CRA can demand repayment of the excess. Amounts repaid in a particular year are deductible in computing income of that year (at line 213 of your T1). Repayments should be shown on Box 12 of the RC62 slip furnished to you by the CRA.

(ITA: 60(y))

EMPLOYMENT INSURANCE BENEFITS

[¶941] EMPLOYMENT INSURANCE BENEFITS

Any benefits received from the government's Employment Insurance ("EI") plan must be included when calculating your income (line 119 of the T1). It is intended that EI payments made to or on behalf of an individual for tuition costs to educational institutions for programs to facilitate re-entry into the labour force should be subject to an offsetting deduction, as described in ¶971.

EI benefits may be reduced where you have been overpaid by EI and have returned the overpayments. If the EI authorities have offset later payments to account for earlier overpayments, the offset should simply reduce EI benefits shown on your T4E slip. If you actually repaid amounts, your T4E slip should specify the repayments, and you can deduct the amount shown at line 232 of your T1 return.

You may deduct (on line 232) fees and expenses incurred in connection with an objection or an appeal from a decision under the *Employment Insurance Act*. If a reimbursement of costs is awarded to you by an EI board or umpire, or legal costs are awarded to you by a court, to reimburse you for costs which you had deducted or may deduct, the amounts so awarded will be included in your income.

If your net income for the year (line 236 on page 3 of your return) exceeds 125% of the "maximum insurable earnings" for the year (125% × $50,800 = $63,500 for 2016; see ¶84 for information on maximum insurable earnings for prior years), a portion of any government Employment Insurance benefit you received *in the year* (as reported in box 15 of the T4E) is repayable to the government, but the amount you have to repay to the government is deducted from your income. The calculation of this repayment is found on charts on the back of your T4E slip. These repayments apply to the net benefit received in the year, that is, the total of all benefits received (T4E slip) less any refund the government may have required if it paid you benefits to which you were not entitled (¶1029). See also ¶1419.

Contributions payable for EI are eligible for the EI tax credit (equivalent to a deduction from income for taxpayers in the lowest tax bracket). Overpayments of EI contributions which may arise if you had more than one job in the year are not included in amounts eligible for credit at line 312 but rather are refunded by claiming the excess on line 450. This is fully discussed at ¶1307.

(ITA: 56(1)(*a*), (*l*); 60(*o*); 5000-G, "General Income Tax and Benefit Guide" (T1 Guide))

[¶941.05] *Lump-Sum EI Receipts*

If you receive an amount that represents several periodic EI payments lumped together, some of which you were actually entitled to receive in other taxation years, you may be eligible for a form of income averaging to spread the applicable tax calculation over those years. The eligible amount is reduced by any repayment deductions taken in respect of the amounts received. Income related to other years must exceed $3,000 for the rule to apply. Eligible amounts should be reported to you on form T1198, and the CRA should do the averaging automatically if you deal with form T1198.

(ITA: 110.2; 120.31)

[¶943] SUPPLEMENTARY UNEMPLOYMENT PLAN BENEFITS

Any amount received from a supplementary unemployment benefit plan (sometimes referred to as a guaranteed annual wage plan) must be included in your income.

(ITA: 56(1)(*g*))

SCHOLARSHIPS, PRIZES, AND RESEARCH GRANTS

[¶951] REGISTERED EDUCATION SAVINGS PLAN ("RESP")

Contributions to a registered education savings plan ("RESP") are not tax-deductible. Income earned while in the RESP is not subject to tax. The beneficiary of the plan will be taxable on payments received from the plan only to the extent that the payments represent income or government grants paid into the plan, but not capital contributed to the plan.

Contributions to these plans (even though non-deductible) may not exceed $50,000 per beneficiary, and plans must provide for benefits only for full-time qualifying students, and must terminate after 35 years. Contributions can be made until the plan beneficiary is 31 years of age (35 years in the case of a single beneficiary plan for a disabled beneficiary).

The government encourages the use of these plans to provide savings for the education of children by offering various inducements in the form of matching grants and in some cases direct unmatched grants to the plan.

Details of these RESP plans and related government inducements are discussed at ¶2529d and ¶2660 to ¶2667.

(ITA: 56(1)(*q*); 146.1(7); RC4092 Registered Education Savings Plans; IC 93-3R1)

[¶953] SCHOLARSHIPS, FELLOWSHIPS, BURSARIES, PRIZES, AND RESEARCH GRANTS

[¶953.05] *General Rules and Employer-Provided Amounts*

Amounts received in a year as, or on account of, a scholarship, fellowship, bursary, or prize for achievement in a field of endeavour are tax-free to the extent they equal the recipient's "scholarship exemption" for the year (see ¶953.10). For scholarships, fellowships, and bursaries received in connection with a qualifying student's enrolment (see ¶1337.25) in a full-time educational program (for the taxation years from 2007 to 2016, prior to the repeal of the education tax credit, enrolment had to be in a program which entitled the student to the education tax credit), or in connection with enrolment in secondary or elementary school, the entire amounts are exempt. The entire exemption also applies to part-time students who are eligible for the disability tax credit or who cannot be enrolled in an educational program on a full–time basis because of a mental or physical impairment. For other part-time qualifying students (or, prior to 2017, part-time students entitled to the education tax credit), the exemption covers only the amounts paid for tuition and program-related materials. For other situations, see ¶953.10. Prescribed prizes discussed at ¶960 are tax-exempt.

In *The Queen v. DiMaria*, 2009 DTC 5019 (F.C.A.), affirming 2008 DTC 3027 (T.C.C.), it was ultimately held that the $3,000 scholarship award paid by the employer to the employee's child was not an employment benefit taxable in the hands of the employee. The purpose of the award was to recognize scholastic achievement and, accordingly, the award was scholarship income in the hands of the employee's child.

As a result of this and similar decisions, in 2007 the CRA changed its position regarding the reporting of taxable benefits by a post-secondary educational institution that offers free tuition to an employee's dependant and by other employers that offer scholarship programs for employees' dependants. Under these changes, instead of being taxable benefits to the employees, the amounts will be reported as scholarships for the children, which are normally tax-exempt. See ¶953.75.

Furthermore, effective October 31, 2011, this tax-free treatment is also extended to an employer's payment of tuition for a family member's attendance at an elementary, secondary, or post-secondary school (private or otherwise). It will also apply to tuition discounts provided by such educational institutions to the family members of its employees. See ¶10.05.

The CRA position regarding employer-provided scholarships and the legislative treatment described above do not apply to amounts paid by a corporation to a relative of a shareholder who is not an employee of the corporation. In a recent technical interpretation, the CRA held that a corporation's payment of tuition and living expenses to an 18-year-old individual who is a relative of a shareholder of the corporation was a shareholder benefit included in the shareholder's income; see CRA Document No. 2013-0502151E5, "Deductible Business Expenses", August 26, 2013. Furthermore, as a shareholder benefit, it would not be deductible for the corporation.

[¶953.10] *Exemption for Scholarships, Fellowships, and Bursaries*

The general tax exemption applies to scholarships, fellowships, and bursaries for elementary and secondary school education, as well as for post-secondary education. The exemption for post-secondary enrolment is broadened to apply where you are a qualifying student (see ¶1337.25) (prior to its repeal, effective January 1, 2017, you must be entitled to the education credit) in the year preceding or following the year of receipt of the scholarship, fellowship, or bursary.

The amount which reduces the basic inclusion of all scholarships, fellowships, bursaries, and prizes for achievement (that is, the general exemption) is the total of the following items:

(1) the total of all scholarships, fellowships, and bursaries received in the taxation year (and included in your income by virtue of the basic inclusion at ¶953.05) in connection with your enrolment at

(a) a designated educational institution in an educational program in which you are a "qualifying student" (for the taxation years from 2007 to 2016, prior to the repeal of the education tax credit, enrolment must be in an educational program for which you can claim an education amount under the rules at ¶1337) in (1) the year the scholarships, fellowships, and bursaries are received (i.e., the year they are necessarily included in income), or (2) the year preceding or the year following such receipt (note that prizes for achievement in your ordinary field of endeavour are not included here; generally, however, students at recognized post-secondary educational institutions will be able to claim exemption on all scholarships, etc., by virtue of this provision); or

(b) an elementary or secondary school educational program;

PLUS

(2) the lesser of (i) your scholarships, fellowships, bursaries, and prizes to be used by you in the production of a literary, dramatic, musical, or artistic work, and (ii) expenses in connection with an artist's grant, with certain exceptions for personal expenses, as discussed at ¶966; essentially, this rule taxes amounts granted for the production of artistic work in excess of the amounts expended to produce the work;

PLUS

(3) the lesser of $500 and the amount included in income before exemptions in excess of the exemptions in (1) and (2), above; essentially, this preserves a $500 exemption for prizes for achievement in your field (¶959), other than amounts received in the course of business or employment, as discussed in ¶953.20, below, and other than wholly exempt prizes discussed in ¶960.

You cannot reduce this income below zero for the year; that is, if your scholarship, etc., income is less than the total of exemptions listed above, you cannot create a loss against other income.

In effect, the CRA asks you to compute the income eligible for this exemption yourself, deduct the correct exemption, and report the balance (if any) on line 130 of the T1 return. In the common case where you are a student and the income is wholly exempt, there is no entry to make on line 130 and that is effectively the end of the matter. If, however, you are in receipt of a research grant or prize, where there is a calculation to make regardless of whether it yields a nil result, you should keep a record of this calculation with your copy of the return.

Historical Information: Recent Amendments

Recent legislative amendments "clarified" (see below) that a post-secondary program that consists principally of research will be eligible for the education tax credit (which is repealed effective January 1, 2017) and the scholarship/fellowship/bursary exemption, only if it leads to a college or CEGEP diploma, or a bachelor, masters, or doctoral degree (or an equivalent degree). As a result, post-doctoral fellowships are fully taxable and not eligible for the exemption. The amendments also provide that an amount will be eligible for the exemption only to the extent it can reasonably be considered to be received in connection with enrolment in the relevant educational program for the duration of the period of study related to the scholarship or other amount.

Lastly, the recent amendments provide that if a scholarship, fellowship, or bursary is provided in connection with a part-time program, the exemption will be limited to the amount of tuition paid for the program plus the costs of program-related materials, except if the part-time program is undertaken by a student entitled to the disability tax credit or a student who cannot be enrolled on a full-time basis because of a mental or physical impairment.

These measures are effective for 2010 and subsequent taxation years. However, the CRA's administrative position is that post-doctoral fellowships have always been taxable, and that the recent amendments relating to these fellowships merely confirms that administrative position (CRA Document No. 2008-0301601M4, June 1, 2010).

(ITA: 56(1)(n), (3))

[¶953.20] *Other General Rules*

The exemption does not apply to:

(1) amounts received out of a registered education savings plan (¶951);

(2) research grants, which are included in income under a separate provision discussed at ¶961;

(3) financial assistance under government programs described in ¶971; and

(4) amounts received in the course of a business or in the course of or by virtue of employment (¶959).

Note that for scholarships, fellowships and bursaries and prizes awarded to artists to be used in the production of a work of art an alternative treatment is available; see ¶966.

Where a grant is received by you to enable you to carry on research or any similar work, the amount so received, to the extent that it exceeds the aggregate of allowable expenses incurred by you in the year for the purposes of carrying on the work, must be included in your income. The CRA wants net income from research grants reported on line 104 rather than 130, although strictly speaking this may not be employment income. See ¶961–¶965.

Where you receive as a scholarship, fellowship, bursary, prize for achievement or a research grant, a fixed sum plus additional amounts as allowances for expenses such as equipment, travel, accommodation, conferences or other expenses, these additional amounts are considered to be part of the scholarship, fellowship, bursary, prize for achievement or research grant, as the case may be. Where such expenses are incurred for the purpose of carrying on research or other similar work they may be deducted from the research grants received in that year, to the extent that they are deductible as described in ¶961.

If you leave Canada on a temporary basis to study or teach you will continue to be taxed by Canada. Generally, you will be regarded as continuing to have Canadian residence and therefore will be taxable by Canada on your world income (¶115). Even if you cease to be resident in Canada for tax purposes, you may be taxable on certain scholarships, etc. received from Canadian sources (¶2024).

Individuals from other countries who come to Canada for education or training and become residents (¶115) or are deemed to be residents (¶117) are taxed on their world income, which would include both Canadian and foreign source awards as described in these paragraphs. However, foreign source awards are often exempt from Canadian tax by virtue of a tax treaty (¶2005) between Canada and the individual's home country. Such provisions are common in tax treaties (typically in Article XX), but should not be taken for granted; the appropriate treaty must be consulted in each case. The Canada–U.S. Tax Treaty provides an exemption from tax in Canada in respect of amounts received from within the United States by American students for the purpose of their maintenance or studies in Canada.

(ITA: 56(1)(n), (o), (3); 115(2)(e); 5000-G, "General Income Tax and Benefit Guide" (T1 Guide) for line 130; Income Tax Folio: S1-F2-C3 Scholarships, Research Grants and Other Education Assistance)

[¶953.75] *T4A Reporting*

Scholarships, fellowships, bursaries, research grants, and prizes are generally not subject to withholding by the payer, but are to be reported on T4A slips issued to you (and to the CRA). The amounts are included in box 28.

As discussed in ¶953.05, if a post-secondary educational institution provides free tuition to an employee's family members, the fair market value of such a benefit is not included in the employee's income. Instead, the amount is reported as a scholarship on a T4A slip for the family member. Similarly, if an employer operates a scholarship program for the family members of employees, any awards paid would not be included in the income of the employee. Instead, the amount would be reported on a T4A slip for the family member.

(RC4157, "Deducting Income Tax on Pension and Other Income, and Filing the T4A slip and Summary"; Pamphlet P105E, "Students and Income Tax"; Income Tax Folio: S1-F2-C3 Scholarships, Research Grants and Other Education Assistance)

[¶955] WHAT ARE SCHOLARSHIPS AND BURSARIES?

Scholarships and bursaries for purposes of the *Income Tax Act* may be defined as amounts paid or benefits given to students to enable them to continue their education, usually at a university, college, technical institute or other educational institution. However, scholarships and bursaries may sometimes be awarded below the post-secondary level. Scholarships and bursaries normally assist the student to proceed towards obtaining a degree, diploma, or other certificate of graduation. Scholarships and bursaries may apply to any field of study, including an academic discipline, a professional program, or a trade or skill. Normally, a student is not expected to do specific work for the payer in exchange for such amounts. If a scholarship and bursary program provides allowances or reimbursements to pay for specific educational costs, such as lodging, travel, tools, books or equipment, those amounts are generally included in income and subject to the amounts eligible for the exemption/income offset.

Where a student is or was employed, and he or she received a scholarship or bursary from an employer on the condition that he or she returns to that employment, the amount he or she receives is considered to be employment income and not scholarship or bursary income.

On the other hand, if an employer–employee relationship has not been established and a student receives a scholarship or bursary in return for undertaking to enter the employment of the person granting the award upon completion of the studies or training, the payments are considered to be a scholarship.

Where an employer provides scholarships for the children of employees, or for other issues involving the taxability of employer-paid education, see ¶310.

(Income Tax Folio: S1-F2-C3 Scholarships, Research Grants and Other Education Assistance)

[¶957] WHAT IS A FELLOWSHIP?

Fellowships are similar to scholarships and bursaries in that they are amounts paid or benefits given to persons to enable them to pursue their education. However, the recipient is generally a graduate student and the payer is generally a university, charitable organization, or similar body. However, when the primary purpose of the fellowship is not education and training but carrying out research, the award is considered to be a research grant. In this situation, only the portion that exceeds allowable expenses is taken into income (see ¶961).

In some cases the recipient of a fellowship may receive remuneration from the payer in addition to the fellowship. For example, in addition to pursuing your studies as a graduate student you may agree, as a condition of receiving a fellowship, to do some teaching, marking of examination papers, demonstration of work, or research as a member of the staff of the university. In these circumstances, the amount received as a fellowship will be included in the computation of your income under the fellowship rules and be included in amounts eligible for the exemption, and the portion received for services rendered as an employee will be fully included in the computation of income as employment income.

If the university has not provided for separate payments of the fellowship and employment components of the financial assistance, the whole amount so paid to the student would technically be employment income, since the terms of the agreement require the student to render service in return for it. However, if this results in a rate of pay that is considerably in excess of the going rate for similar services, the CRA will permit the student to include in his or her income from employment only the amount that is equal to what the university would have paid for similar services rendered by a person not receiving a fellowship or similar assistance. The remainder of the financial assistance is regarded as a fellowship and is included in amounts eligible for the exemption.

(Income Tax Folio: S1-F2-C3 Scholarships, Research Grants and Other Education Assistance)

[¶959] WHAT IS A "PRIZE FOR ACHIEVEMENT IN A FIELD OF ENDEAVOUR ORDINARILY CARRIED ON BY A TAXPAYER"?

The issue of what is a prize has been litigated to the Supreme Court of Canada in a case in which an employee of an insurance company received an award of $100 for successful completion of a course on insurance matters. The award was open to all employees who succeeded; typically only 61% or so who wrote the course examination would pass. The CRA contended that:

(1) a prize implies a reward for superiority in a contest or competition, and mere successful completion of the course did not qualify; and

(2) in any event, the prize was employment income and income from employment or business was not subject to the $500 exemption.

The Supreme Court held for the taxpayer on both issues (*The Queen v. Savage*, 83 DTC 5409). The Court said:

> In my view, a "prize for achievement" does not necessarily connote an award for victory in a competition or contest with others. That places too narrow and inflexible a meaning on the words. In the case at bar the award was in recognition of *bona fide* accomplishment, successful completion of course studies, and examinations in a challenging field of endeavour, in which about 61 per cent of those writing were successful and about 39 per cent failed. Only the successful candidates were eligible to receive a prize.
>
> It is important also to say that it is not suggested here that the system of awards was introduced as a colourable device intended to provide the employer with an opportunity of increasing the statutory exemption of employees by $500 per year. If and when such a case arises it can be considered on its facts.

The CRA now accepts that the $500 exemption applies to a prize awarded for success in an area in which the recipient regularly applies effort. Generally, the $500 exemption will apply to prizes paid in recognition of *bona fide* accomplishment in a challenging area, whether it is of an academic, vocational, or technical nature, as long as it is not excluded as described at ¶953. (Note that some prizes may be exempt from tax altogether; see ¶960.)

The Court also held that although the prize was employment income, it nevertheless qualified for the exemption. On this latter point, subsequent legislation has reversed the Court decision and ensures that work- and business-related awards *received* after May 23, 1985, will not qualify for the exemption. Awards received before that date were governed by the *Savage* case.

Note that the legislation does not affect the issue of what constitutes a prize, as to which the Court's comments remain valid.

Where you are self-employed, the facts will determine whether the amount is received in the course of business or whether it is received as a prize. If it can be established that the amount is a business receipt, then the amount must be included in the computation of your business income. Where the amount received is a prize for achievement in a field of endeavour ordinarily carried on by you and cannot be regarded as a business receipt, then the amount will be included in income to the extent that it exceeds $500.

See also the deduction alternative for artist's grants at ¶966.

(ITA: 56(1)(n), (3); IT-257R Canada Council Grants; IT-273R2 Government Assistance — General Comments; Income Tax Folio: S1-F2-C3 Scholarships, Research Grants and Other Education Assistance)

[¶960] EXEMPT PRIZES

Prizes recognized by the general public and awarded for meritorious achievement in the arts, sciences or service to the public are exempt from tax altogether. However, this rule does not apply to any amount that can reasonably be regarded as having been received as compensation for services rendered or to be rendered.

It would appear that this exemption is aimed at high-profile awards such as a Nobel Prize or the Governor General's Literary Award. However, the rule is general and presumably will apply to such things as community service awards provided they cannot be considered compensation for services. Specifically exempt prizes are not listed; only the general rule is set out.

Remember that a prize must first be a prize under ¶959 before it can be an exempt prize. Accordingly, prizes received in the course of or by virtue of employment or business activity will not qualify.

It appears that the CRA has been very restrictive in applying this exemption. However, in the case of *Labelle v. The Queen* (a case under the informal Tax Court procedure decided on September 27, 1994, 96 DTC 1115), the Tax Court allowed the taxpayer to claim exemption on a prize for winning the Second International Accounting Case Writing competition organized by the University of Lethbridge. The taxpayer argued that the CRA had allowed the exemption for the same prize in other cases. The CRA apparently did not deny the allegation, but merely argued that its position in other cases was irrelevant. The Tax Court agreed that this would usually be true, but here determining whether a prize was generally recognized required an element of evaluation which must be applied on a consistent basis. In seemingly general terms, the Tax

Court ruled that the CRA could not arbitrarily dismiss an exemption claim by simply saying it did not think a prize was sufficiently widely recognized; it had to provide some reason and rationale which could be applied on a consistent basis. "In other words, the Minister must adopt only one position with respect to a prize, which he must be capable of explaining." Although Informal Procedure cases do not have precedent value, one would expect the CRA to feel obliged to take up the Court's challenge of producing suitable guidelines, but so far no public response has been discernible.

The CRA has said that the Prime Minister's awards for teaching excellence qualify as exempt prizes. It has also given an opinion that prescribed prizes would not include awards by an employer which are only available to its employees.

In a technical opinion (not a ruling), CRA Document No. 2000-0002565, the CRA considered 23 specific Canada Council awards and tentatively determined that 16 of them would be prescribed prizes exempt under these rules provided they cannot be considered business or employment income to a particular recipient, which will be a question of fact in each case.

(ITA: 56(1)(*n*)(i); ITR: 7700 [Prescribed prize]; Window on Canadian Tax: 3809; CRA Document No.: XXXXXXXXXX, *December 23, 1997*, CRA Document No. 9725873; Income Tax Folio: S1-F2-C3 Scholarships, Research Grants and Other Education Assistance)

[¶961] WHAT IS A RESEARCH GRANT?

A research grant is generally a sum of money given to enable a grantee to pay expenses (which may include personal or living expenses) that are necessary to carry out a research project. The grant may also include an element of remuneration to the recipient. In order for a grant to be considered a research grant, its terms must establish that the primary purpose of the grant is the carrying out of research. Research must involve a critical or scientific inquiry having for its aim the discovery of new facts and their correct interpretation or practical application. It does not include research carried out for the sake of acquiring the experience or skill of conducting research, as may be the case with research carried out by undergraduate students.

To the extent that the research grant exceeds allowable expenses (outlined below), it must be included in income. The total amount of allowable research expenses reported on your tax return may not exceed the total taxable amount of the research grant.

Where a corporation or other entity, such as a university or college, makes a grant to a person outside its own organization to do specific research, the grant is considered to be a research grant whether or not the results of the research belong to the grantor or the grantee. Where you are an employee of the grantor and are also retained on salary, the salary will be included in your income as employment income and the research grant will be included in your income to the extent it exceeds allowable expenses.

The allowable expenses include cost of equipment, fees, laboratory charges, etc. For this purpose the term expenses is interpreted to include not only current expenses but also expenditures of a capital nature. However, the allowable expenses do not include:

(1) personal living expenses (other than the travelling expenses mentioned below);

(2) expenses in respect of which you have been reimbursed, except to the extent that the reimbursement is considered to be part of a grant received;

(3) expenses that are otherwise deductible in computing your income for the year;

(4) expenses that are unreasonable under the circumstances; and

(5) expenses paid by the university, hospital or similar institution on your behalf.

Travelling expenses (including all amounts spent for transportation and lodging while travelling) you incur while away from home in the course of carrying on the work are allowable research expenses. If, while engaged in the research work, you establish a temporary base in a place other than your home, you may be considered to be temporarily residing in that place (sojourning) rather than travelling. This is a question of fact in each case that depends on factors such as the type of accommodation, the length of stay, the existence of a permanent home elsewhere and the location of your family. If you are temporarily residing in a place, amounts paid for meals and lodging in that place are considered to be personal and living expenses rather than travelling expenses, and so are not allowable research expenses. You may claim your own expenses for: travel between your home and the place where you temporarily reside while engaged in the research work; travel from one temporary location to another; and travel on field trips connected with the work. You may not claim the travelling expenses of your spouse, common-law partner or children or other third parties (see *Subbarao v. M.N.R.*, 86 DTC 1554 (T.C.C.)).

If you are temporarily residing in a place other than your home while engaged in research, you are considered to be sojourning rather than travelling. Therefore, amounts paid for meals and lodging are personal living expenses and are not allowable.

Technically, the *Income Tax Act* provides that research expenses must be incurred in the same year in which the research grant is received in order to be deductible from the grant. In some cases, research expenses may be incurred in the year immediately preceding or immediately following the year in which the grant is received. While those expenses are not deductible in the year in which they are incurred, the CRA will consider that they are deductible in the year in which the grant is received except for those expenses incurred prior to receipt of notification that the grant would be paid. Research expenses incurred more than one year before or after the year in which the grant is received are not deductible from the grant.

Note that the CRA asks you to report the net income from these grants on line 104 of the T1 return, although it is technically not employment income. If you are claiming the related expenses, make an itemized list of those expenses and deduct them from the grant income received (¶965), reporting only the balance at line 104. You should attach the list of itemized expenses to your return. It will probably be best if you start your list with "Grant Income", then show each expense deducted, and show the balance as "Income reported at line 104".

(ITA: 56(1)(*o*); T1 Guide; Income Tax Folio: S1-F2-C3 Scholarships, Research Grants and Other Education Assistance)

[¶963] RESEARCH ASSISTANTS

In some cases, a researcher may engage one or more assistants whose relationship to the researcher may be that of a co-researcher, employee, or student.

Where the relationship is that of a co-researcher to a researcher, payments made out of a research grant to the co-researcher will be regarded as a research grant received by the research assistant.

Where the relationship is that of an employee to an employer, payments made to the assistant will be regarded as employment income of the research assistant.

Where the relationship is that of a student to a professor, the student receiving payment for his share in the project may have undertaken the work not primarily for financial gain but because his participation in it will assist him in qualifying for a degree or other scholastic recognition in the field in which the research is being carried on. Generally speaking, in this situation the direction given by the researcher will be of a general or consultative nature, and the student-assistant will have more freedom in carrying on his part of the project than would an assistant under an employee–employer relationship. Where this is the case, payments made out of a research grant to the assistant (student) will be considered research grant income in the hands of the recipient.

On the other hand, assistance may be required that need not necessarily be performed by a student participating in the research to further his or her own education. Certain types of clerical or laboratory work, for example, may require skills of some degree, but if that work is performed by a student-assistant under the specific direction of a researcher or co-researcher and primarily for financial gain, the amount received by the student-assistant out of the grant is considered to be employment income of the recipient.

(Income Tax Folio: S1-F2-C3 Scholarships, Research Grants and Other Education Assistance)

[¶965] WHEN IS A RESEARCH GRANT RECEIVED?

The taxation authorities will not consider a research grant to be "received" at any time if *all* of the following circumstances apply:

(1) Funds are made available to an individual who holds an academic appointment at a university, hospital or similar institution to enable the individual to carry on research or similar work.

(2) The funds are paid directly to the university, hospital, or similar institution.

(3) The funds are provided only for the purpose of defraying the costs of the research project.

(4) The funds were not used by or otherwise available for the personal benefit of the individual.

In circumstances where part of the research grant is paid to a researcher, or otherwise made available for his personal benefit, and the remainder of the funds meet the above circumstances, only that part of the grant paid to, or otherwise available for, the researcher will be considered to be "received" by him as a research grant.

(Income Tax Folio: S1-F2-C3 Scholarships, Research Grants and Other Education Assistance)

[¶966] SPECIAL RULES FOR ARTISTS' GRANTS, ETC.

[¶966.05] *Basic Rules*

If you receive payment in the year of a scholarship, fellowship, bursary, or prize which is to be used by you in the production of a literary, dramatic, musical, or artistic work, you may claim an exemption for the lesser of the prize (etc.) itself and specified allowable expenses.

Note that neither the income inclusion nor exemption rules apply to amounts received in the course of a business or by virtue of employment. In such cases, the business or employment deduction rules would apply; see, respectively, ¶789 and ¶379.

In calculating the artistic production exemption, you include the prize (or scholarship, etc., but typically a prize, since a scholarship received in connection with an educational program for which you could claim the education amount would generally be 100% exempt in any event) in income and claim an exemption for the lesser of the prize itself and allowable expenses. The effect is that the income is reduced by allowable expenses to the extent they do not exceed the prize, but cannot be reduced below nil. The allowable expenses which may be claimed to reduce your income inclusion in respect of the prize, etc., are all amounts incurred in the year for the purpose of creating or producing the artistic work for which the prize was offered, *except*

(1) personal or living expenses, but you may deduct expenses for travel, meals, and lodging incurred in the course of fulfilling the conditions of the prize, etc., while absent from your usual place of residence for the period to which the prize (grant, etc.) relates; however, travelling expenses of your spouse, common-law partner, children, or other third parties would not normally qualify; other considerations are probably much the same as for travel in relation to research grants, discussed in ¶961, above;

(2) expenses for which you have been otherwise reimbursed; and

(3) expenses that are otherwise deductible.

If you are claiming a prize net of related expenses, accepted practice is to make an itemized list of those expenses and deduct them from the grant income, reporting only the balance at line 130. Although it is not required, you may want to attach the list of itemized expenses to your return. In any event, you must be able to produce such a list, and, of course, the receipts which support it. It will probably be best if you start your list with "Grant Income", then show each expense deducted, and show the balance as "Income reported at line 130".

Technically, only income received in the year is included in income, and the exemption from that income is only available to the extent of expenses "incurred in the taxation year" for the purpose of fulfilling the grant conditions. The CRA has an administrative policy (in Income Tax Folio S1-F2-C3, paragraph 3.77) which allows grant-related expenses incurred in the preceding or following year to be considered an allowable expense related to a grant in a particular year where they cannot otherwise be claimed because no grant was given in the year they were actually incurred. Expenses incurred before notification of the grant do not qualify.

(ITA: 56(1)(n), (3); Income Tax Folio: S1-F2-C3 Scholarships, Research Grants and Other Education Assistance)

[¶967] REPAYABLE AWARDS

You may be in receipt of a prize, award or grant which is repayable by you if its conditions are not fulfilled. Where the award has been included in your income under the various rules above, you may deduct repayments in the year you make them under certain conditions. These are:

(1) You must deal at arm's length (¶812) with the person you are repaying.

(2) Repayment must arise from failure to meet conditions specified at the time of the award.

(3) You must not have provided services (other than occasional services) as an officer or employee of the payer while you held the award.

(4) The award was originally received to help further your education.

In distinguishing between repayable awards and forgivable loans, the CRA provides the following in Income Tax Folio S1-F2-C3:

> **3.40** Forgivable loans and repayable awards have similar characteristics, however, they may be distinguished as follows: A forgivable loan refers to a loan made to enable a borrower to pursue an education or to carry out a research project and which the lender is committed to forgive if certain conditions are met by the borrower; on the other hand, a repayable award is a scholarship, fellowship, bursary or research grant which the recipient is committed to return if certain conditions are not met.
>
> **3.41** In order to determine whether an amount is a forgivable loan or a repayable award, the rights and obligations flowing from the agreement between the grantor and the recipient must be examined. If the agreement under which an amount is paid gives rise at the time of payment to an enforceable debt, the amount is generally considered to be a loan for tax purposes. If the agreement specifies that the amount paid does not become a debt of the recipient unless the recipient fails to fulfill certain conditions, the amount is generally considered to be a repayable award. In determining whether a bona fide loan or enforcable debt exists, the intent of the parties should be considered (i.e., was the intention to provide a grant that would be repayable in certain circumstances or to provide a loan that would cease to be repayable in certain circumstances). Establishing the intent of a particular agreement can be difficult as both repayable awards and forgivable loans rely on future conditions to determine whether or not the amount will be repaid.

The amount you may deduct under this provision cannot exceed amounts previously taxed to you — that is, they will be net of any exemption you originally claimed under the rules at ¶953, and of deductions claimed against research grants.

(ITA: 56(1)(*n*), (*o*), (*p*); 60(*q*); Income Tax Folio: S1-F2-C3 Scholarships, Research Grants and Other Education Assistance)

[¶969] STUDENT LOANS

Where a student is in receipt of a *bona fide* loan which is repayable under any condition, for the purpose of assisting him or her in financing his or her studies, the loan is not considered to be an amount received as or on account of a scholarship, fellowship or bursary, and is not included in income.

Where an employee receives a loan from his or her employer to further his or her education, and the loan is forgivable on condition that he or she return to employment with the employer upon completion of the education period, the amount received as a loan generally is not income when received. If the loan is subsequently forgiven because the employment conditions are met, the amount forgiven constitutes employment income of the employee in the year of forgiveness (see ¶1034).

Where the recipient of a scholarship, fellowship, bursary or research grant is required to repay the amounts only if certain conditions are not met, the receipt is considered to be a "repayable award" as discussed in ¶967 above. A repayable award is included in computing the recipient's income in the year it is received. Where a recipient repays part or all of the award, the amount repaid is deductible in computing his income for the year of repayment.

(Income Tax Folio: S1-F2-C3 Scholarships, Research Grants and Other Education Assistance)

MISCELLANEOUS ITEMS INCLUDED IN INCOME

[¶971] TRAINING ALLOWANCES

Payments may be made under a number of federal and provincial programs for training assistance. Essentially, four types of tax treatment are available for these payments:

(1) They may be classified as social assistance to the beneficiary, in which case they are included in income but deducted to arrive at taxable income as discussed at ¶990. It would appear that payments under the Alberta Skills Development Program (CRA Document No. 9832995) and the Saskatchewan Provincial Training Program (CRA Document No. 9803958) receive this treatment, although the Saskatchewan program has received inconsistent rulings.

(2) If paid under Part I of the federal *Employment Insurance Act* or under any government or government agency program in Canada to encourage individuals to obtain or keep employment (presumably other than those described in (3), below), payments are taxable and no offset is available; Part I benefits are those normally thought of as ordinary EI benefits, i.e., those paid periodically to all similarly situated workers who are currently unemployed.

(3) If paid under Part II of the federal *Employment Insurance Act* or under provincial programs which operate under the terms of an agreement with the Canada Employment Insurance Commission, the amounts are taxable under paragraph 56(1)(*r*) of the Act, but to the extent the benefits are financial assistance for the payment of tuition fees not otherwise deductible, an offsetting deduction is available as described under the next subheading below; Part II benefits are those paid under specialized programs under the EI mandate to experiment with programs such as programs to encourage the unemployed to improve their job application abilities, to become self-employed, and, most significantly for these purposes, help them obtain skills for employment, ranging from basic to advanced skills.

(4) Payments which are not caught under any of the provisions above might qualify as bursaries and be subject to the exemption discussed in ¶953. It is the CRA's view that payment of training/tuition costs under the Employment Supports Program of the Ontario Disability Support Program (CRA Document No. 9901955) and the Prince Edward Island EAPD and FS programs (CRA Document No. 9904707) fall into

this category (see also ¶975). This treatment predated the offsetting deduction for adult training referred to in (3), and may in some cases be overtaken by it. See also paragraphs 3.79 to 3.83 of Income Tax Folio S1-F2-C3, "Scholarships, Research Grants and Other Education Assistance".

In general, it is up to the government agency to determine the tax treatment in specific cases and issue the appropriate reporting slip. If you feel the payment has not been classified correctly in your case, you should both take it up with the paying agency and object to the assessment by the CRA.

Payments under some programs may fall under different rules depending on the circumstances of the payment. Thus, participants in the federal Youth Internship Program may come in as continuing Employment Insurance recipients, in which case the payments continue to be taxable under the EI rules, as continuing social assistance recipients, in which case the payments maintain that character, or as bursaries during off the job training periods. On-the-job training payments are employment income (CRA Document No. 9433116).

(ITA: 56(1)*(a)*, *(m)*, *(n)*, *(r)*, *(u)*; Income Tax Folio: S1-F2-C3 Scholarships, Research Grants and Other Education Assistance)

[¶971.05] *Offsetting Deduction for Adult Education Training Tuition*

Where adults take basic education courses to upgrade their skills, they may receive direct financial assistance from governments to pay their tuition fees. This tuition assistance must be included in income under the rules above. Because the fees are for basic education and not post-secondary or vocational education, they do not qualify for the tuition tax credits discussed at ¶1321.

Individuals may deduct (at line 256 in computing taxable income) certain tuition assistance received for adult basic education that has been included in their income. In order to be eligible, the tuition assistance must be provided under:

(1) Part II of the *Employment Insurance Act* (or a similar program provided by a province or territory under a Labour Market Development Agreement); or

(2) another prescribed training program established under the authority of the Minister of Human Resources Development.

It is understood that, in addition to the programs described in (a) above, the following programs have in fact been determined by the Department of Employment and Social Development as qualified under these rules:

- Employability Assistance for People with Disabilities (EAPD);
- Opportunities Fund for Persons with Disabilities (OF); and
- Fisheries Restructuring and Adjustment Measures.

See also paragraphs 3.81 to 3.83 of Income Tax Folio S1-F2-C3, "Scholarships, Research Grants and Other Education Assistance".

To be eligible for the offsetting deduction, the assistance must be for tuition fees not eligible for tuition fee credit or any other deduction.

Both the income and the amount eligible for offsetting deduction should be reported to you on a T4E slip.

The offsetting deduction is retroactive, permitting deduction of eligible tuition assistance received after 1996. The normal period limits on reassessment (see ¶268) are waived to give effect to this provision.

Note that where government tuition assistance for post-secondary education has been received in the past, it was always eligible (and will continue to be eligible) for tuition tax credit. However, that assistance barred the recipient from claiming the flat rate education amount credit at ¶1337. This rule has changed for 2002 and later years (see "Other Conditions" at ¶1337), so that recipients of government tuition assistance for post-secondary/vocational education may now claim both tuition and education credits (the education and textbook tax credits are repealed effective January 1, 2017). Recipients taking basic education courses, however, do not qualify for either of those credits, and must instead claim the offsetting deduction for tuition assistance under this provision.

(ITA: 60*(n)*; 110(1)*(g)*; Income Tax Folio: S1-F2-C3 Scholarships, Research Grants and Other Education Assistance)

[¶972] ARTS SEMINARS

The value of benefits you "received or enjoyed" in the year in respect or workshops, seminars, training programs, and similar development programs by reason of your membership in a registered national arts service organization (a kind of arts charity) is to be included in your income. However, where the organization paid you a scholarship, fellowship, bursary, or a prize related to the sector it represents, one of the exemptions at ¶953 should apply.

(ITA: 56(1)*(z.1)*; 149.1(6.4); 248(1) "registered national arts service organization"; Income Tax Folio: S1-F2-C3, para. 3.105)

[¶973] AUTO PACT ASSISTANCE BENEFITS

Any assistance benefits received as a result of the 1965 Canada–United States Agreement on automotive products must be included in the computation of your income.

(ITA: 56(1)*(a)*(v))

[¶974] APPRENTICESHIP GRANTS

Any amounts received under the federal government's apprenticeship grant program must be included in the computation of your income. Repayments you made in the taxation year of amounts included in the year or a previous year may be deducted.

(ITA: 56(1)*(n.1)*; 60*(p)*)

[¶975] BENEFITS UNDER GOVERNMENT PROGRAMS

Any benefits received under prescribed legislation must be included in income. Prescribed legislation includes the *Labour Adjustment Benefits Act* and the *Department of Labour Act*, and section 5 of the *Department of Fisheries Act* and the Northern Cod Compensation and Adjustment Program. Any payments received which have been included in income but must be refunded are deductible in the year the refund is made.

Under this rule, benefits you received under the following government assistance programs must be included in your income:

- Program for Older Worker Adjustment;
- Plant Workers Adjustment Program;
- Northern Cod Adjustment and Recovery Program;

- Atlantic Groundfish Adjustment Program; and
- Atlantic Groundfish Strategy.

In addition, social assistance under a project sponsored by the government of Canada under which the only benefits paid are intended to supplement individual's income from employment must be included in income.

Note that to the extent any of the above amounts might be considered social assistance, they are specifically included in income of the recipient and thus override the social assistance rule that payments are taxed to the higher income spouse (¶990).

(ITA: 56(1)(*a*)(vi), (*r*); 153(1)(*m*); ITR: 5502 Benefits under Government Assistance Programs; Tax Topics: 1219; CRA Document No.: Govt Assistance - Fishers, *September 22, 2000*, CRA Document No. 2000-0045465)

[¶975.03] *Wage Earner Protection Program Act (WEPP)*

The WEPP provides a level of compensation for lost employee wages due to employer bankruptcy or insolvency. Amounts received under the WEPP place employees in a similar position to the one they would have been in had they been fully compensated by their employer.

Paragraph 56(1)(*r*) of the Act requires that certain amounts received as earnings supplements under government-sponsored projects, as financial assistance under programs established by the Canada Employment Insurance Commission, or under certain similar programs are to be included in computing the recipient's income. Effective for 2008, a new subparagraph, 56(1)(*r*)(v), clarifies that payments received under the *Wage Earner Protection Program Act* are to be included in a recipient's income.

[¶975.05] *Provincial Disability Programs*

The CRA has issued similar opinions with respect to the Ontario (CRA Document No. 9901955) and the Prince Edward Island Employability Assistance for People with Disabilities (EADP) Program and Family Support (FS) Program (CRA Document No. 9904707) that:

- payment for tuition and training costs is taxable as a bursary (per ¶971);
- payment for wages subsidies is taxable as employment income;
- assistance to self-employed individuals is taxable under the government assistance rules at ¶729; and
- other payments are not taxable.

The opinions above were issued prior to the announcement of the adult education tuition deduction described under the subheading "Offsetting Deduction for Adult Education Training Tuition" at ¶971. It is possible that they will be overtaken by those rules. In general, it may be a distinction without a difference, unless the amount treated as a bursary under these opinions exceeds the bursary exemption described at ¶953 but would be deductible in full under the adult education rules at ¶971.

[¶977] TRANSFER OF PROPERTY AND RIGHTS TO INCOME

If, at any time, you have transferred or assigned to a person with whom you were not dealing at arm's length the right to an amount which would otherwise have been included in your income, the amount transferred must be included in your income for the year (see ¶741 for a discussion of salaries or wages paid to your spouse or common-law partner). Income that relates to a period of the year during which you were a non-resident is taxed to the transferee and not to you.

The main exception to this rule arises where the income is from property and the property has also been transferred. Even in this case, the income or loss from the property transferred is taxable in your hands if the property is transferred directly or indirectly:

(1) to your spouse or common-law partner or to a person who has since become your spouse or common-law partner, or to a trust for your spouse or common-law partner;

(2) to a person under 18 years of age with whom you do not deal with at arm's length (this includes your minor children, grandchildren, nieces and nephews); the concept of arm's length is considered at ¶812; or

(3) to a trust under the terms of which the property may revert to you, or it may pass to persons to be determined by you at a time subsequent to the creation of the trust, or it can only be disposed of by the trust during your lifetime with your consent or in accordance with your direction.

The income or loss will continue to be taxed in your hands:

(1) in the case of property transferred to your spouse or common-law partner, or to a trust for your spouse or common-law partner, until the earlier of the death of either you or your spouse/partner, your emigration from Canada, your divorce, or your separation by reason of the breakdown of your marriage/relationship;

(2) in the case of property transferred to a non-arm's length minor, or a trust for a minor, until the commencement of the year when the minor reaches 18 years of age (or upon your death or your emigration if sooner); and

(3) in the case of property transferred to any other trust, until distribution of the property by the trust (or upon your death or emigration, if sooner).

However, benefits received by your spouse or common-law partner out of a registered retirement savings plan as a result of your contribution to your spouse's or common-law partner's plan will normally be income to your spouse or common-law partner and not to you. See ¶903.

In all of these rules, the tax law provides that if the transferred property is disposed of and new property is substituted for it, the rules also apply to the income from the substituted property. It does appear, however, that the CRA's assessing provision would deny proration. Note that in any event, capital gain is also attributed to the transferor on transfers to a spouse, although not to a child. See ¶531 and ¶532.

Income earned on accumulated earnings of the transferred property or substituted property is not attributed back to you.

For loans made to a spouse, common-law partner, or non-arm's length minor (including a child, grandchild, niece or nephew), income earned on the loan or property substituted for it will be taxed to the transferor. The income attributed will be net of any interest paid by the spouse, common-law partner, or minor to the transferor. However, where the loan is made at commercial or prescribed rates of interest, there will be no attribution of income. Where such existing loans were not repaid within these time limits, there will be attribution of income derived from the loaned property.

Additional rules apply to non-arm's length loans not already subject to attribution under the rules above. Under these rules, if any loan is made by you to a non-arm's length person (or any debt to you is otherwise incurred by a non-arm's length person) and one of the main reasons for the loan or debt is to reduce or avoid tax on income from (i) the loan, or (ii) property the loan or debt enabled the non-arm's length person or a trust in which the person is beneficially interested to acquire, or (iii) property substituted for (i) or (ii), the income will be taxable in the hands of the lender/creditor and not the borrower/debtor. Again, there is an exception for loans made or debt incurred which is subject to the lesser of the prescribed rate of interest at the time the loan is made or debt incurred or ordinary commercial interest rates, provided the interest is always actually paid within 30 days of year end. There are provisions to prevent using a new interest-bearing loan to replace an old non-interest-bearing loan. One of the main concerns about these rules is that they will apply to loans to adult children, although only if the "main reason" test is met. The extension of these rules to indebtedness arising otherwise than by loan is created by technical amendments dated July 13, 1990, but revised February 18, 1991, and applies to income relating to periods after December 31, 1990. The extension is seen as an anti-avoidance measure dealing with an unpaid balance of purchase price, and is essentially retroactive to arrangements in place before the changes were announced. The February 18, 1991, amendments also extend the scope of the rules to include loans to or indebtedness incurred by a trust with any non-arm's length (to the lender/creditor) resident beneficiary for income related to periods after 1990.

It is also important to note that "transfer" includes a sale, even if it was a genuine sale, and the rules outlined above would apply. Transfers made at fair market value, as well as income derived from loans outstanding then or thereafter which bear a commercial rate of interest, will not be subject to the attribution rules.

For rules regarding attribution of capital gains and losses, see ¶531.

For a further discussion of income splitting and attribution rules, see ¶2529.

(ITA: 56(4)–(4.3); 74.1–74.4; 75(2); 146(8.3); IT-440R2 Transfer of Rights to Income; IT-510 Transfers and loans of property made after May 22, 1985 to related minor; IT-511R Interspousal and certain other transfers and loans of property; Income Tax Folio: S1-F5-C1 Related Persons and Dealing at Arm's Length)

[¶978] PENSION INCOME TRANSFERRED FROM SPOUSE OR COMMON-LAW PARTNER (LINE 116)

For 2007 and later taxation years, you and your spouse (or common-law partner) can agree to split up to 50% of your spouse/partner's *eligible* pension income. If your spouse/partner is 65 years of age at the end of the taxation year, all his/her pension income is eligible, and up to 50% of it can be transferred to you. If your spouse/partner is not 65 at the end of the year, only his/her income eligible for the $2,000 pension income credit ("qualified pension income", ¶1311) is eligible income for purposes of the income splitting election.

There are two possible benefits to splitting income. First, if you are in a lower tax bracket than your spouse/partner, as a couple your tax will be lower overall. That is, your spouse/partner's income taxed at the higher rate will be reduced, and your income taxed at the lower rate will be increased. For 2016 tax rates, see the tables preceding Chapter 1, particularly ¶62. Provincial tax will also have a bearing on the tax savings involved, but generally speaking the federal rate brackets will determine whether the election is beneficial in terms of tax rates.

Second, if you are 65 or over at the end of the taxation year for which you are splitting pension income, you may include the transferred income along with your own pension income in claiming the $2,000 pension income credit. Thus, to the extent you do not already have $2,000 of pension income of your own before the transfer, you can increase this credit. To the extent your spouse/partner has more than $2,000 of eligible pension income, this will increase the credit available to you as a couple. If you are not yet 65 at the end of the relevant taxation year, you may still claim the credit in respect of "qualified pension income" transferred from your spouse. This is defined in ¶1311. Essentially, it is your spouse's private pension or annuity income, not including RRSP, RRIF, or DPSP (deferred profit sharing plan) income, plus certain amounts received as a consequence of the death of your spouse/partner's (former) spouse/partner.

The two elements of benefit should each be considered in deciding how much (if any) pension income should be transferred. If you are both in the same income bracket and both fully using the $2,000 pension credit with your own pension income, there is typically not much point to the transfer. If your spouse/partner is in a higher income bracket, you will, as a couple, benefit from a transfer at least to the point where you are both in the same bracket. Even if you are both in the same bracket, there may be an advantage to receiving at least enough pension income to fully utilize the $2,000 credit, assuming you do not have $2,000 of pension income of your own.

Commentary on Legislative Proposals (Sept. 16, 2016)

Note: When Legislative Proposals, September 16, 2016, achieves Royal Assent, the commentary will be modified to read:

Effective for 2015, retirement income security benefits ("RISBs") received by veterans and members of the *Canadian Forces under the Canadian Forces Members and Veterans Re-establishment and Compensation Act* may be included in their eligible pension income and split with their spouse or common-law partner, but only if they do not exceed the difference between (1) 35 times the defined benefit limit (i.e., $2,290 for 2016) and (2) the total of their other eligible pension income and income received under a retirement compensation arrangement ("RCA").

The election is made on form T1032. You must report on line 116 of your return your share of the income transferred, and form T1032 will show you the pension amount you can claim (both on your own account and on account of the transfer) on line 314.

The transfer from the transferor's point of view is discussed at ¶1076.

(ITA: 56(1)(*a.2*); 60(*c*); 60.03)

[¶979] INDIRECT PAYMENTS

The payment or transfer of property to others which ordinarily would be regarded as your income had it been paid to you will be deemed to be your income in certain circumstances. This provision applies to a payment or transfer made to another person at your direction or with your concurrence, for your benefit, or as a benefit which you wished to confer on the other person.

For example, consider an employee who does not actually receive all or part of the income earned by him or her, but instead asks his or her employer that it be paid to someone else. In this case, the employee would be considered to have received that part of his or her income which he or she has transferred to another person.

The indirect payments rule is so obvious that it generally causes little difficulty. Where it does get an airing, however, it is often in the context of family income splitting plans involving private corporations; see ¶2501.05.

(ITA: 56(2); IT-335R2 Indirect payments)

[¶981] PROCEEDS OF LIFE INSURANCE POLICIES

If you have an interest in a life insurance policy and become entitled to receive proceeds in respect of a disposition of your interest in the policy during the lifetime of the insured, a portion of the amounts received may be subject to tax. The taxable portion will be the excess of the "proceeds of disposition" over the "adjusted cost basis" of your interest in the insurance policy. (For a disposition to a non-arm's length person, see "Commentary on Bill C-29 Measures (October 25, 2016)" below.) Your insurance company will advise you annually of the amount of any "proceeds" you have become entitled to receive under the income tax rules. Technically, you are required to make your own calculation of "adjusted cost basis" to determine the portion of the proceeds, if any, which must be included in income, but most insurance companies will assist their policyholders in making this calculation.

There is no income inclusion in respect of a disposition of the following life insurance policies:

(1) a policy that is issued pursuant to a registered pension fund or plan, a registered retirement savings plan, a registered retirement income fund, an income averaging annuity contract, a deferred profit sharing plan, or a tax-free savings account; and

(2) an annuity contract that is purchased with the proceeds of a registered retirement savings plan received as a refund of premiums by a surviving spouse or common-law partner over 71 years of age, or by a child that was dependent by virtue of physical or mental infirmity.

A disposition of a term certain annuity contract after November 12, 1981 will be subject to tax as set out above.

"Proceeds of disposition" of an interest in an insurance policy include all amounts which you become entitled to receive as a result of surrender, disposition by operation of law, the maturity of the policy, policy dividends except policy dividends after December 20, 1991 automatically applied to pay a premium or pay down a policy loan, or certain amounts received in respect of policy loans after March 31, 1978. "Proceeds of disposition" with respect to a policy loan after March 31, 1978 will be equal to the lesser of the amount of the loan and the excess of the cash surrender value of the policy immediately before the loan was made over the policy loans outstanding at that time. However, an assignment of the policy for the purpose of securing a loan will not, in itself, be considered as the disposition of an interest in the policy, nor will a lapse of the policy as a result of unpaid premiums if the policy is reinstated within 60 days after the end of the calendar year in which the lapse occurred. Nor will payments under a policy received as a disability benefit or an accidental death benefit, annuity payments and payments on death for policies, other than annuity contracts, acquired prior to December 2, 1982 or for exempt policies or prescribed annuities that are issued after December 1, 1982. (Exempt policy is a complex technical term prescribed by regulations. Your insurance company will inform you as to whether or not your policy is exempt.)

There are certain additional circumstances in which a life insurance policy or annuity contract is deemed to have been disposed of. These include:

(1) On the death of a holder of a life insurance policy, or of the insured or the annuitant under a life insurance policy (other than an exempt policy) issued after December 1, 1982 or an annuity contract (other than a life annuity contract issued prior to November 13, 1981 or a prescribed annuity contract) the policyholder is deemed to have disposed of the interest in the policy or the annuity immediately before his or her death for proceeds equal to the accumulating fund. The policyholder acquires the policy at a cost equal to the accumulating fund after death.

(2) When a life insurance policy acquired after December 1, 1982 or a life insurance policy acquired before December 2, 1982 which becomes subject to the income accrual rules, as a result of a premium payment and increase in the death benefit on death after that date, ceases to be an exempt policy, the policyholder is deemed to dispose of it for proceeds equal to the accumulating fund and to reacquire it at a cost equal to the proceeds at that time. Exceptions to this deemed disposition rule apply where the policy ceases to be an exempt policy as a consequence of the death of the insured or at a time when the insured is totally and permanently disabled.

(3) A recent amendment, to be applicable to exempt policies issued after 2016, provides for a deemed disposition, generally, if after issuance of the policy (i) a benefit on death under a coverage under the policy is paid at a particular time, (ii) the payment results in the termination of the coverage but not the policy, and (iii) the amount of the fund value benefit (as defined in the *Income Tax Regulations*) paid in respect of the coverage exceeds the "maximum fund value benefit" (determined on the policy anniversary that is on or that first follows the date of death of an individual whose life is insured under the coverage that would be payable under the policy if no other coverage were offered).

Commentary on Legislative Proposals (Sept. 16, 2016)

Note: When Legislative Proposals, September 16, 2016, achieves Royal Assent, the commentary will be modified to read:

(3) A recent amendment, to be applicable to exempt policies issued after 2016, provides for a deemed disposition, generally, if after issuance of the policy

(i) a benefit on death under a coverage under the policy is paid at a particular time,

(ii) the payment results in the termination of the coverage but not the policy, and

(iii) the amount of the fund value benefit (as defined in the Income Tax Regulations) paid in respect of the coverage exceeds the "maximum fund value benefit" as calculated on the policy anniversary date. The determination of that maximum will be:

- in the case where there is no policy anniversary before the date of death of the individual whose life is insured under the coverage, on the policy anniversary that is on or that first follows that date; and
- in any other case, on the last policy anniversary before the date of death.

The policyholder entitled to receive this excess is deemed to have disposed of a part of his or her interest and included the excess in income. These amendments are effective on the Royal Assent Date of the Proposed Legislation.

If you dispose of a part of a policy or annuity contract acquired after December 1, 1982, only the proportion of the adjusted cost basis attributable to the part disposed of will be deductible in determining the income resulting from the disposition. This rule does not apply to a deemed disposition arising as a result of an entitlement to a policy dividend or to a policy loan. The proportion of the adjusted cost basis of a policy that may be deducted on a partial disposition is the ratio of the proceeds to its accumulating fund. For a policy issued after 2016, recent amendments provide that the ratio will be the ratio of the proceeds to cash surrender value of the interest less any amount payable, immediately before the disposition, by the taxpayer in respect of policy loans in respect of the policy.

A payment out of a life annuity contract entered into after November 16, 1978 and before November 13, 1981 that is not an annuity payment, loan or a dividend will be treated as a disposition of an interest in a life insurance policy. If you are in receipt of such payment from a life annuity contract, you will be taxed to the extent the payment exceeds the adjusted cost basis of the policy.

"Adjusted cost basis" of your interest in an insurance policy includes:

(1) Cost of acquiring your interest in the policy (including amounts paid to another person from whom the policy was purchased); plus

(2) All amounts paid by you or on your behalf as premiums under the policy and any non-refundable prepaid premium paid after November 12, 1981. Excluded are costs incurred after May 31, 1985 that relate to accidental death and disability benefits and to certain additional risks for policies acquired after December 1, 1982; plus

(3) Interest paid after 1977 on a policy loan, if the interest was not deductible in computing income (see ¶1063); plus

(4) All portions of annuity payments made to a non-resident that were subject to withholding tax; plus

(5) Amounts previously taxed on a partial disposition of the policy; plus

(6) Amounts included in income from a policy subject to the income accrual rules; plus

(7) Repayments of policy loans outstanding at that time or received after that time to the extent they constituted proceeds of disposition, except for the portion of such repayments which is deductible; for policies issued after 2016, recent amendments add the repayment of the portion of a policy loan used immediately after the loan to pay a premium under the policy (except to the extent that the portion has reduced the proceeds of disposition of a partial surrender of the interest); plus

(8) The mortality gain with respect to life annuity contracts that are subject to the income accrual; plus

MINUS the aggregate of:

(10) Prior proceeds of disposition;

(11) Policy loans owing on March 31, 1978 including interest owing;

(12) The capital element of an annuity payment previously deducted;

(13) The net cost of pure insurance, as determined by prescribed regulations at the end of each calendar year for taxation years that commence after May 31, 1985 of a life insurance policy acquired after December 1, 1982 that is not an annuity contract (this will be supplied by your insurance company);

(14) Annuity payments made after 1982 in respect of annuity contracts which are subject to the income accrual rules;

Commentary on Legislative Proposals (Sept. 16, 2016)

Note: When Legislative Proposals, September 16, 2016, achieves Royal Assent, the commentary will be modified to read:

(14) Annuity payments made after 1982 in respect of annuity contracts which are subject to the income accrual rules (effective on Royal Assent Date of the Proposed Legislation this variable does not apply to the payment of an endowment benefit);

(15) The mortality loss in respect of a life annuity contract; and

(16) For policies issued after 2016 that are not annuity contracts, certain other reductions will apply (see the Department of Finance notes to subsection 148(9) at http://www.fin.gc.ca/drleg-apl/2014/bia-leb-oct20-1014-l-eng.asp.

Where under the terms of a life insurance policy last acquired before December 2, 1982, you become entitled before the death of the insured to receive an annuity in respect of all of your interest in the policy (except policy dividends), then you will determine the amount to be included in income under the rules for annuities (see ¶480) and the cost of the annuity contract will be deemed to be your "adjusted cost basis" in the insurance policy immediately before the first annuity payment. Where an insurance policy is acquired after December 1, 1982, its conversion into an annuity triggers a disposition with proceeds equivalent to cash surrender value.

There are provisions to transfer a policy to an insured spouse, common-law partner, or child on a rollover basis. Where a spouse or common-law partner is not also insured under a life insurance policy or annuity, provision is made for transfers to a spouse or common-law partner or former spouse or common-law partner on the same tax basis as the transfer of other capital property (¶531), except that the provisions for transfer at cost are mandatory rather than elective. Special cost base adjustments to the policy may apply on the spousal rollover.

Commentary on Bill C-29 Measures (Oct. 25, 2016)

Note: When Bill C-29, October 25, 2016, achieves Royal Assent, the commentary will be modified to read:

Dispositions to non-arm's length persons

For dispositions of an interest in a life insurance policy before March 22, 2016, to a non-arm's length person, you will be deemed to have received proceeds of disposition equal to the cash surrender value of your interest in the policy at the time of transfer, and the transferee will be deemed to have acquired the policy at its cash surrender value. The same rule will apply if you dispose of the policy by gift, bequest, distribution from a corporation, or by operation of law to any person, including persons with whom you deal at arm's length. These rules do not apply to a deemed disposition that arises on death in respect of life insurance policies acquired after December 1, 1982, other than exempt policies and in respect of annuities (other than life annuity contracts acquired prior to November 13, 1981).

For dispositions of an interest in a life insurance policy after March 21, 2016, to a non-arm's length person, the legislation was updated to ensure that amounts are not inappropriately received tax-free by a policyholder as a result of a disposition of an interest in a life insurance policy. These rules provide that the proceeds of disposition will equal the greatest of the adjusted cost base of the interest, the cash surrender value, and the fair market value of the interest.

(ITA: 148(1), (2), (4), (6), (7), (9); ITR: 300 Capital Element of Annuity Payments)

[¶981.01] *Leveraged Insurance Annuities (LIAs)*

Proposals first announced in the 2013 federal Budget target the "unintended tax benefits" in respect of arrangements known as life insurance annuities or "LIA policies". Prior to the proposals, income earned on the invested capital in such policies was generally not taxed under the accrual rules described earlier because most life insurance policies were exempt policies. Under the proposals, LIA policies will no longer be exempt policies, such that the accrued income will be subject to the annual accrual rules, effective for taxation years that end after March 20, 2013. See also ¶432a.05.

[¶981.05] *Insurance Advances to the Terminally Ill*

In a Technical Opinion (found in CRA Document No. 2002-0138895), the CRA said:

> We understand that the Financial Services Commission of Ontario has adopted a recommendation that life insurance companies should provide funds to terminally ill policyholders who have a life expectancy of less than 24 months. While not legally obligated to provide funding to these policyholders, many life insurers are considering implementing the recommendation by providing loans to the policyholders out of the insurer's general funds. As security for the loan payment received from the life insurer, the policyholder assigns the life insurance policy to the life insurer. Provided there is no amendment made to the life insurance policy, it is our general view that the payment of the loan proceeds by the life insurer would not cause the CRA to view the life insurance policy to have been disposed of by the individual for purposes of section 148 of the Act and a new life insurance policy to have been issued. However, where such a loan is provided for under the terms and conditions of the life insurance policy, the loan would be a "policy loan" as defined in subsection 148(9) of the Act, and would result in a disposition of an interest in the policy pursuant to paragraph (*b*) of the definition of "disposition" in subsection 148(9) of the Act.

[¶983] SEGREGATED FUND LIFE INSURANCE POLICIES

A segregated fund life insurance policy is a policy which fluctuates in value depending upon the fair market value of investments held by the insurance company in a "segregated fund" for the benefit of the policyholders. It is similar in concept to a combination of an insurance policy plus an interest in a mutual fund. For tax purposes the fund is treated as a trust.

If you have an interest in a segregated fund life insurance policy, you will be taxable each year on amounts allocated to you by the insurance company in respect of the income from the investments in the segregated fund. This allocation may include an allocation of capital gains, capital losses, dividends from taxable Canadian corporations, or income from foreign sources and foreign income tax thereon, in which case you will be entitled to claim a dividend tax credit (¶1425) or foreign tax credit (¶1450) respectively. The amounts allocated to you which must be included in your income will not necessarily be paid to you by the insurance company.

Your insurance company will advise you by form T3 of all amounts allocated to you from income of the segregated fund, and the amount of dividends from taxable Canadian corporations, foreign source income, and foreign tax paid included thereon. Taxation and reporting of these items are discussed in Chapter 4.

When you dispose of your segregated fund policy, you may have a capital gain or a capital loss. This will be determined by subtracting your adjusted cost base from your proceeds of disposition. The rules in Chapter 5 will be applicable.

[¶984] REFUNDS FROM ELIGIBLE FUNERAL ARRANGEMENTS

Statutory rules provide for the tax-free accrual of income on prepaid funeral expenses under an "Eligible Funeral Arrangement" ("EFA"). The rules contemplate that an eligible funeral arrangement may be established with any person (or company) licensed or authorized under provincial law to provide funeral or cemetery services for individuals. For simplicity, the authorized provider of such services will be referred to here as the provider.

For details of the contribution limits and the benefits of using these plans, see ¶2532f.

The provider may offer a plan for the purpose of funding funeral or cemetery services (as defined at ¶2532f) for one or more individuals (called here the beneficiary). The provider may establish a formal trust to hold prepayments of funeral or cemetery expenses, or may simply hold them as custodian. The provider need not be the trustee or custodian. In either case, contributions to the plan by or for the beneficiary (which are limited to $35,000 overall as discussed at ¶2532f) are not deductible, since funeral expenses are personal and not deductible. However, funds in the plan may earn income (typically interest). The income will not be taxed while the plan is in force.

Normally, on death the plan will pay the funeral and/or cemetery expenses of the beneficiary, and the service provider will recognize the income as business income at that time. If there is any payment out of the plan for anything other than the provision of funeral or cemetery services as defined, there will be an income inclusion to the recipient. This rule contemplates (but does not specify) either (i) cancellation of the plan by the contributor, or (ii) a refund owing the estate, presumably because the funeral cost less than the funds in the plan. Essentially, the rule assumes that any such non-funeral payments out of the plan represent taxable income to the extent of earnings in the plan, and then a refund of contributions. That is, where there is a payment otherwise than for funeral services, the recipient must include in income *the lesser of* the amount received and:

(1) the remaining balance in the plan immediately before payment

PLUS

(2) all payments made from the EFA for the provision of funeral or cemetery services for the individual (beneficiary) covered by the plan before the payment

MINUS

(3) contributions made to the plan for the purpose of funding funeral arrangements for the beneficiary, or the contribution portion of transfers from other eligible plans for the beneficiary, [reduced, for transfers, credits or additions occurring after December 20, 2002, by the portion of the transferred amount that was not previously included in income, i.e., the portion that represents a return of contributions.]

Example 1

Mr. Gilbert contributed $8,000 to a prepaid funeral arrangement. The balance grew to $10,000 before his death. The plan paid $9,500 for funeral services. The $500 balance was refunded to the estate. The EFA should report $500 on a T5 issued the estate. This is the lesser of (i) $500 (the amount of the refund), and (ii) $2,000 ($500 + $9,500 - $8,000).

Property in a cemetery care trust in not included in the computation.

Income received under these rules is considered to be income from property (see Chapter 4).

For taxable cancellation/refund, etc., payments made under these rules after 1995, the payer must file a T5 information return (illustrated in Chapter 4). These amounts are included in box 14 of the T5 and are considered investment income.

On the other hand, a trust or other fiduciary governed by an eligible funeral arrangement is not required to file a T3 return.

A trust established under these rules is not subject to the 21-year deemed disposition rule.

[¶984.05] *Transfers Between Plans*

The eligible funeral arrangement (EFA) rules are amended to provide specific rules relating to transfers from one EFA account to another. In general terms, the changes are as follows:

- A new provision (paragraph 148.1(4)(*a*)) deems the transferred amount to be distributed to the individual from whose EFA account the amount is transferred. However, if that individual is deceased, the amount is deemed to be distributed to the individual to whose EFA account the amount is transferred. This ensures that the transfer is included in income (to the extent that it does not exceed the income accumulated in the transferor account).
- A new provision (paragraph 148.1(4)(*b*)) deems the transferred amount to be a contribution made to the recipient EFA account other than by way of transfer. This ensures that the earnings portion of the transferred amount is not taxed again when it is distributed from the recipient EFA account.
- The provision that requires EFA distributions to be included in income (described above) is amended to ensure that the determination of the amount that can subsequently be distributed from the transferor EFA account on a tax-free basis is reduced by the portion of the transferred amount that was not included in income (i.e., that portion of the transferred amount that represents a return of contributions).
- A new provision provides that these new rules do not apply if the transferor and the recipient EFA accounts are in respect of the same person, the entire balance in the transferor account is transferred to the recipient account and the transferor EFA account is terminated immediately after the transfer.

Department of Finance Technical Notes published December 20, 2002 (and republished in identical form July 18, 2005) provide the following examples to illustrate the application of the workings of these amendments.

Example 1

Paul sets up an EFA account for the pre-funding of his funeral expenses. He contributes $10,000 to his account, and earns $7,000 of interest in the account. Paul transfers $3,000 to an EFA account which he establishes for his daughter, Gaby.

The transferred amount is deemed to be a distribution to Paul under the new deemed distribution rule. Consequently, Paul includes in his income, under the general inclusion rule formula above, an amount of $3,000, which is the lesser of

- $3,000, which is the amount distributed; and
- $7,000, which is the amount determined by the formula (1) + (2) - (3) set out above, which is the plan balance immediately before the transfer ($17,000) + allowable payments ($0) - [contributions made to the plan ($10,000) - distributions in excess of previous additions to income ($0)].

The transfer is treated, in effect, as a distribution of a portion of the income accumulated in the plan.

The transferred amount is also deemed to be a contribution made, other than by way of transfer, to Gaby's EFA account. Thus, the $3,000 is considered to be a "relevant contribution" in respect of Gaby's EFA account, and can subsequently be withdrawn tax free.

Example 2

The facts are the same as in Example 1, except that Paul transfers $13,000 to Gaby's EFA.

The transferred amount is deemed to be a distribution to Paul. Consequently, Paul includes in his income, under subsection 148.1(3), an amount of $7,000, which is the lesser of

- $13,000, which is the amount distributed; and
- $7,000, which is the amount determined by the formula (1) + (2) - (3) set out above, which is the amount of the plan balance immediately before the transfer ($17,000) + allowable payments ($0) - [contributions made to the plan ($10,000) - distributions in excess of previous additions to income ($0)].

The transfer is treated, in effect, as a distribution of all of the income accumulated in the plan ($7,000), which is taxable, plus a return of a portion of the relevant contributions in respect of the EFA ($6,000), which is not taxable.

Under the post-December 20, 2002 rules, the transferred amount is also deemed to be a contribution made, other than by way of transfer, to Gaby's EFA account. This has no particular significance with respect to the portion of the transfer that represents relevant contributions in respect of Paul's EFA account, since this amount would be considered to be a relevant contribution to Gaby's EFA account under the existing rules. However, it does have significance with respect to the portion of the transfer that represents income in Paul's EFA account, in that it allows that portion to become a relevant contribution in respect of Gaby's EFA account which can then be withdrawn from Gaby's account tax-free.

Example 3

The facts are the same as in Example 2. After the transfer of $13,000, the balance in Paul's EFA account is $4,000, all of which represents relevant contributions in respect of the account. Over the next few years, the account earns an additional $2,500 of interest. Paul then withdraws the entire balance from the account.

The withdrawal is a distribution under subsection 148.1(3). Consequently, Paul includes $2,500 in his income, which is the lesser of:

- $6,500, which is the amount of the withdrawal; and
- $2,500, which is the amount determined by the formula (1) + (2) - (3) set out above, which is the plan balance immediately before the withdrawal ($6,500) + allowable funeral payments ($0) - [contributions made to the plan ($10,000) - distributions in excess of previous additions to income ($6,000)].

The $6,000 reduction in (3) is the excess of the amount that was previously transferred and to which the transfer rules applied ($13,000) over the portion of that amount that was previously included in income ($7,000).

(ITA: 108(1) "trust" (e.1); 148.1; ITR: 201(1)(f); 204(3)(d); T4015, "T5 Guide — Return of Investment Income")

[¶985] SUPPORT PAYMENTS RECEIVED ON SEPARATION OR DIVORCE

These rules are discussed in detail in Chapter 23.

[¶987] PARTICIPATION IN CLINICAL TESTS

The CRA commented in a technical opinion on payments received by individuals recruited by pharmaceutical companies for testing certain drugs and receiving certain amounts of money for participating in clinical studies. After their first test, the individuals could have their names included on a recall list and participate in the studies several times during the same year. All the studies were conducted on the premises of the companies and the time spent by the individuals at those premises varied with each test. The CRA was asked if the individuals had to include those amounts in their income for tax purposes. The CRA considers that the amounts were received for services rendered by the individuals to the companies and should be included in their income. Those testing services were of a commercial, not personal or voluntary, nature and were motivated by the receipt of money from the companies. The money was also not received as a compensation for personal expenses to participate in the studies. In the circumstances, the testing activities performed by the individuals constituted a source of income from a business. The amounts could also be considered employment income if there was an employer–employee working relationship between the companies and the individuals, but the CRA did not have enough information to make that determination. If the amounts qualified as employment income, the employer companies would have to report the amounts on a form T4 and make the necessary source deductions. If the amounts qualified as service fees, the client companies would have to report the fees on a form T4A (without source deductions) but only for amounts in excess of $500.

Although the opinion does not appear to discuss the issue, it is presumably the recall feature that makes the difference. One might doubt that a volunteer who received compensation for test participation but was not subject to systematic recall would rise to the level of engaging in a business, much less being an employee.

(Window on Canadian Tax: 8240, reporting technical opinion 2004-0107991E5, in French only)

[¶987.05] *Focus Groups or Product Review Groups?*

One might speculate that the rules above would apply to participants in focus groups who are typically paid small sums to participate in a review of a product, ad campaign, etc. Once you have made your way onto a list for such a group there is probably a reasonable chance of recall. Although, the sums paid are rather smaller than for clinical trials, it seems likely that the CRA would say, if asked, that the same principles would apply.

[¶988] HOME INSULATION AND ENERGY CONVERSION GRANTS

Grants received under the Canadian Home Insulation Program and the Canada Oil Substitution Program must be included in your income (or the income of your spouse or common-law partner, if higher, if you resided together at the time the grant was received).

(ITA: 12(1)(*u*); 56(1)(*s*); ITR: 5500 Canadian Home Insulation Program; 5501 Canada Oil Substitution Program)

[¶989] GAINS FROM THEFT OR EMBEZZLEMENT

Amounts received from criminal or illegal activity are taxable. If property (other than cash) is received, the fair market value thereof should be included in income.

If you repay amounts which were previously included in your income, it is normally the policy of the CRA to allow a deduction for the amount repaid, in the year of repayment.

(Income Tax Folio: S3-F9-C1 Lottery Winnings, Miscellaneous Receipts, and Income (and Losses) from Crime)

[¶990] WORKERS' COMPENSATION, SOCIAL ASSISTANCE PAYMENTS, AND TREATY-EXEMPT INCOME

The following items are technically included in your income subject to tax, but may then be deducted again in arriving at "taxable income" (¶1000). The purpose of this circuitous procedure is to ensure that the amounts are counted when you claim means-tested tax credits or benefits such as the CCB or GST credit (Chapter 14), and to determine whether someone else can claim you as a dependant (Chapters 11 and 12).

The receipts which should be treated in this way include:

- Social assistance payments made in the year on the basis of a means, needs or income test (whether made by an organized charity or under a government program) where the payment is received by the individual or the individual's spouse or common-law partner (as defined at ¶1113), provided they reside together at the time the payment was received. Note that these payments must be included in your income or your spouse's or common-law partner's income, whichever is higher unless the amount is already included in one income or the other under another provision (such as that at ¶975). Note that some but not all provincial training assistance programs may qualify as social assistance; see ¶971. The CRA has said that payments under the "Financial Assistance to Pregnant Minors Measure" provided under Quebec's *Individual and Family Assistance Act* are social assistance payments; see Wolters Kluwer *Window on Canadian Tax* 9204.
- Federal supplements received, such as spouse/common-law partner allowance and guaranteed income supplement (see ¶913).
- Compensation received as (Canadian) federal or provincial workers' compensation in respect of an injury, disability or death must be included in your income. Complexities arise where an employer continues the injured employee's wages and is recompensed out of worker's compensation awards; these are discussed at ¶358.
- Amounts received or receivable by you that are exempt by virtue of a provision contained in a tax convention or agreement with another country. Note that they may increase the limitation on your charitable donation claims, but decrease medical expense claims and the claims of others who might claim you as a dependant.
- Amounts received as an employee of the United Nations or its affiliates or as a visiting employee of the International Air Transport Association or the Société internationale de telecommunications aéronautiques; see ¶1456.

Workers' compensation, social assistance, and federal supplements, as reported to you on a T5007 information slip, should be entered on line 144, 145, or 146, respectively, of the T1 Return and deducted again at line 250. The result for persons claiming you as a dependant is the same; the difference is that the true net income can now be determined from line 236 of the return of the recipient of the income. Amounts cannot be deducted on line 250 unless they are matched to income inclusions on lines 144 to 146.

The CRA does not comment specifically on treaty-exempt or international employee income, but it is understood that the preferred procedure is to include the amounts in income on the appropriate line of the T1 return, and claim the offsetting deduction on line 256 (with an explanation).

It is possible that net federal supplements paid in addition to basic OAS may be reduced at line 235 where your line 234 income for the year exceeds the OAS clawback threshold ($73,756 for 2016). It is rare for supplements to be paid at all in such a case, but it can occur where you suddenly get a high-paying job, or more probably when you sell a capital property, such as a cottage, and have a capital gain added to your income. The CRA takes the position that where net federal supplements are reduced by clawback taxes at line 235, the offsetting deduction at line 250 is similarly reduced. This is reasonable as far as it goes, but the CRA's rule seems to be that any deduction for OAS payments at line 235 reduces line 250 deductions dollar for dollar to the extent of line 146 inclusions. That is, rather than apportioning the line 235 OAS deductions between ordinary OAS benefits and net federal supplements, the reduction is applied to supplements first. It is not clear that this position is justified.

Note that the inclusion of these items as income will not only increase your 20% limitation in computing charitable donations (¶1270), but will also increase your income for purposes of computing the 3% floor on medical expense claims (¶1225). Regardless of whether the T1 return itself does or does not provide for these items for a particular year, you are entitled to insist on income inclusion if it is actually to your benefit. Similarly, the CRA can insist on it to their benefit.

Note that social assistance payments (if they are income at all because means tested) are taxed to the higher-income spouse or common-law partner for any payments received while the spouses/partners are living together. It follows that in the year of marriage, etc. (see ¶1113), payments received prior to the marriage are income of the recipient and not the new spouse or partner. Technically, the payments received before marriage should be included in the recipient's income for purposes of calculating personal amount credits for the recipient, but the T1 Guide does not require this; see ¶1103.

[¶990.05] *Training Allowances*

See ¶971.

(S.C. 1993, c. 24, s. 159; ITA: 56(1)(*u*), (*v*); 81(1)(*h*); 110(1)(*f*))

[¶991] YOU SHOULD NOT INCLUDE THESE AMOUNTS IN YOUR INCOME

- Civil and military service pensions, allowances or compensation under the following Acts or Orders:

  (1) *Pension Act* — which provides for pensions payable on the death or disability of members of the armed forces owing to service therein.

(2) *Civilian War Pensions and Allowances Act* — which provides for pensions for certain civilians who suffered injury during the Second World War.

(3) *War Veterans Allowance Act* — which provides for pensions for certain veterans and their widows, widowers, and orphans.

(4) Gallantry Gratuities and Annuities Order — which provides awards to members of Canadian Forces for conspicuous and distinguished service during war.

(5) *Aeronautics Act* — which provides for pensions on the death or disability of a person resulting from an unscheduled flight undertaken in the course of public duty.

- War service (or, for 1988 and later years, other) pensions on account of disability or death arising out of a war received from another country if allied with Canada at the time of the war and similar relief is accorded by that country with respect to any pensions and allowances mentioned in (1) to (5) above. A list of allied countries is provided in Interpretation Bulletin IT-397R.

- *Per diem ex gratia* payments made (apparently in or after 1998) by Veterans Affairs Canada to veterans who were prisoners of the Japanese during the Second World War, or their surviving spouses, or to Canadian airmen who were incarcerated in Buchenwald or their surviving spouses; see CRA Document No. 9833395.

- Certain employees' fringe benefits. See Chapter 3 for details.

- Gifts and inheritances.

- Lottery winnings (see the discussion of *Leblanc v. The Queen*, 2007 DTC 307 (T.C.C.), at ¶704).

- Proceeds from accident, disability, sickness or income maintenance insurance policies if your employer pays no part of the premiums. If you are a member of a group plan and your employer has contributed premiums on your behalf, then benefits must be included in your income (see ¶328). Note that premiums are considered personal living expenses and are therefore not deductible.

- Credits received under the Ontario Electricity Support Program after December 31, 2015 (s. 81(1)(g. 6))

- Payments from Régie de l'assurance du Québec — automobile.

- Capital element of annuities. See ¶481 for details.

- Non-taxable dividends paid by a Canadian corporation. See ¶415 for details.

- Profits from betting or gambling for mere pleasure or enjoyment. By the same token losses are not deductible. This would apply even though the bets were substantial and the gains or losses sizable. However, where the betting is organized and conducted as an enterprise of a commercial character any winnings will be taxable.

- Receipts from an Employees Profit Sharing Plan — if tax has previously been paid when such amounts were credited to your account (see ¶332).

- Expense allowances of:

(1) elected members of a provincial legislative assembly;

(2) elected officers of incorporated municipalities, municipal utilities boards, corporations, commissions, or similar bodies; and

(3) members of public or separate school boards or similar bodies governing a school district to the extent the allowances do not exceed one-half of your salary received from this office.

to the extent the allowances do not exceed one-half of your salary received from this office.

- Expense allowances of Members of Parliament, Ministers of the Crown, etc. (see ¶339).

- RCMP pensions or compensation if paid under specified sections of the *Royal Canadian Mounted Police Pension Continuation Act* or the *Royal Canadian Mounted Police Superannuation Act* in respect of injury, disability, or death. An opinion by the CRA suggests that the taxpayer must determine the qualification of the pension with the help of the payer (Wolters Kluwer *Window on Canadian Tax* 9634, providing an English summary of the French opinion in CRA Document No. 2008-0286341E5).

- Halifax Disaster pensions.

- Compensation by Federal Republic of Germany to a victim of National Socialist persecution if no income tax is payable on the payment in Germany.

- Allowances to service veterans during vocational or technical training or while attending university.

- Income of an Indian living on a reserve, if earned on the reserve; also income of a status Indian if the income has *situs* on the reserve, and income of status Indians on income derived from the performance of services on a reserve. This exemption was expanded somewhat by the decision in *Williams v. The Queen*, 92 DTC 6320 (S.C.C). The CRA has now issued guidelines in light of that decision, available from Tax Services Offices. The issue is: when is off-reserve income nevertheless sufficiently connected with a reserve to be protected. See Wolters Kluwer *Window on Canadian Tax*, 2785.

- A member of a visiting force — under the *Visiting Forces Act* Treaty — is exempt from Canadian tax on salary and emoluments paid to him by an associated state, unless he was a Canadian citizen who is resident or ordinarily resident in Canada.

- Remuneration received by officials of international organizations such as the United Nations is exempt from tax if received by persons who are resident in Canada but who are not Canadian citizens. Remuneration received by officials of NATO will also be exempt from tax unless employed by Canada, and resident or deemed to be resident in Canada; see ¶1456.

- Amounts received from Canadian War Savings Certificates, or from similar certificates issued by Newfoundland before April 1, 1949.

- Income earned in Canada by a non-resident from the operation of a ship or aircraft in international traffic if he resided in certain specified countries.

- Income earned or taxable capital gains from property received as a personal injury award, or substituted property, provided the taxpayer is not yet 22 years of age at any time in the year.

- The first $1,000 of the indemnity paid in any year to an elected or appointed member of the Council of the Northwest Territories, the Council of Nunavut, or Council of the Yukon Territory.

- Amounts received in respect of a dwelling insulated with urea formaldehyde foam insulation under the *Urea Formaldehyde Insulation Act*.

- Amounts claimed as child tax credits or federal sales tax credits.

- Quebec work income supplement.

- Under a 1993 multi-provincial assistance package for persons affected with HIV through the blood supply program, qualified individuals will receive a payment of $20,000 upon signing a release of further liability. Additional payments of $30,000 *per annum* will also be received. On death, the spouse of the deceased will receive an annual payment of $20,000 and other dependants will receive $4,000. The CRA has confirmed that the payments will not be taxable. See Wolters Kluwer *Window on Canadian Tax*, 2796.

- Payments under the Ontario Hepatitis C Assistance Plan (per CRA Document No. 9833955).

- Amounts received under Part 1 of the *Energy Costs Assistance Measures Act*, introduced in October 2005; Part 1 provides for income supplements of $250 to be paid to low-income families and $125 to low-income seniors ($250 to low-income senior couples) in January 2006.

(ITA: 6(1)(*b*), (*f*); 81(1); 144(6); IT-397R Amounts Excluded from Income — Statutory Exemptions and Certain Service or RCMP Pensions, Allowances and Compensation; Income Tax Folio: S3-F9-C1 Lottery Winnings, Miscellaneous Receipts, and Income (and Losses) from Crime)

[¶991.05] *Payments to Foster Parents*

In its Budget of February 10, 1988, the government announced that it would change the fact that payments to foster parents were taxable, but foster parents could not claim foster children as dependants. The change, which was retroactive to 1982, specified that social assistance payments ordinarily made on the basis of a means, needs or income test under a program provided for *under the laws of Canada or a province* are specifically exempt income provided they meet the following tests:

(1) payments are exempt to the extent the payments were received directly or indirectly for the benefit of an individual (the beneficiary) who is neither the recipient, the spouse or common-law partner of the recipient, nor related to the recipient, spouse or common-law partner; note that the definition of common-law partner has changed from time to time, as discussed at ¶1113;

(2) no family allowance payments (or similar provincial payments by Quebec or Alberta) are paid to anyone in respect of the beneficiary for the period for which the payment is made; and

(3) the beneficiary resides in the recipient's principal place of residence, or that residence is maintained for use as a residence of the beneficiary, throughout the period for which the social assistance is paid.

Presumably, the rule in (2) was based on the theory that a foster child is not related to its foster parents and no one should have received the (now defunct) family allowance for it, although both these premises may have been doubtful in some cases. The rules have not been revised to refer to the Canada Child Benefit (¶1498), although again in most cases the criteria for that program will ensure that foster parents do not receive the benefit. Nevertheless, it is not a specific statutory rule that the Canada Child Benefit and the exempt foster parent payments are mutually exclusive, even if the possibility is remote.

In any event, if these criteria are met, the foster child payments will not be taxable in the first place and thus will not add to anyone's net income in any circumstances. The same would be true of a person providing care to, for example, a disabled adult under a program which provides payments to you for so doing.

Note that the tests above reflect 1991 technical amendments to the revisions enacted in 1988. Although the intent of the provisions appears to be the same, the new rules specify that only social assistance provided under the laws of Canada or a province are subject to this exemption, which requirement was not made in the 1988 version. The new version is nevertheless retroactive to 1982.

In the 1989 T1 Guide, the CRA indicated that social assistance payments had to be minimal enough to be considered an offset of expenses and not a source of business or employment income in order to escape taxation. While this position had merit under the 1989 version of the income exclusion, it would not seem to be valid in the face of a statutory provision which makes such income absolutely exempt from tax (when received by an individual) as long as it meets the specified tests. In the CRA's *Income Tax Technical News* No. 17, dated April 26, 1999, it said that it had originally taken the position that exempt payments could be made by non-profit organizations responsible for recipients and foster homes, but in these situations only *per diem* amounts paid to the individual responsible for a foster home were exempt income; base payments were employment income if an employer–employee relationship existed between the individual and the payer. However, the CRA has reversed its position and now accepts that the exemption "can apply to base amount payments made by a non-profit organization to an individual responsible for a foster home, even when the amount has the features of employment income".

(S.C. 1993, c. 24, s. 159; ITA: 81(1)(*h*))

[¶991.10] *Windfall Gains*

It is possible that amounts received will fall outside the scope of the tax system altogether, being neither ordinary income nor capital gain. Occasional profits from a hobby, for example, will fall into this category (see ¶704).

Another example of non-taxable income is the windfall gain. The CRA has said that the following factors may be indicative that a particular receipt is a non-taxable "windfall":

(1) the taxpayer had no enforceable claim to the payment;

(2) the taxpayer made no organized effort to receive the payment;

(3) the taxpayer neither sought after nor solicited the payment;

(4) the taxpayer had no customary or specific expectation to receive the payment;

(5) the taxpayer had no reason to expect the payment would recur;

(6) the payment was from a source that is not a customary source of income for the taxpayer;

(7) the payment was not in consideration for or in recognition of property, services or anything else provided or to be provided by the taxpayer; and

(8) the payment was not earned by the taxpayer as a result of any activity or pursuit of gain carried on by the taxpayer and was not earned in any other manner.

The factors above are based on those set out in the decision of *The Queen v. Cranswick*, 82 DTC 6073 (F.C.A.). *Fortino et al. v. The Queen*, 97 DTC 55 (T.C.C.), aff'd 2000 DTC 6060 (F.C.A.), includes a more recent discussion of case law on the windfall issue. The aspect of the *Fortino* case relating specifically to non-competition clauses has been reversed by legislation (see ¶929). However, where a non-competition clause or restrictive covenant is not in issue, the *Cranswick* doctrine, and the discussion of windfall in *Fortino*, would appear to remain sound.

The CRA has at times attempted to tax systematic gambling winnings as business income (which of course implies the deduction of losses). Where games of sheer chance are involved, the case of *Leblanc v. The Queen*, 2007 DTC 307 (T.C.C.), discussed at ¶704, suggests that the case is a difficult one for the CRA to make.

Note the separate comments on prizes for achievement at ¶953.

(Income Tax Folio: S3-F9-C1 Lottery Winnings, Miscellaneous Receipts, and Income (and Losses) from Crime)

[¶991.15] *Damages for Personal Injury or Death*

Amounts in respect of damages for personal injury or death may be received by an injured taxpayer or by a dependant of a deceased taxpayer on account of special damages (e.g., compensation for out-of-pocket expenses such as medical and hospital expenses, and accrued or future loss of earnings) and general damages. Examples of general damages are compensation for pain and suffering, the loss of amenities of life, the loss of earning capacity, the shortened expectation of life, and the loss of financial support caused by the death of the supporting individual.

All amounts received by a taxpayer or the taxpayer's dependant, as the case may be, that qualify as special or general damages for personal injury or death will be excluded from income regardless of the fact that the amount of such damages may have been determined with reference to the loss of earnings of the taxpayer in respect of whom the damages were awarded. However, an amount which can reasonably be considered to be income from employment rather than an award of damages will not be excluded from income; see ¶328. The tax treatment of an award of compensation, as adjudicated by a compensation board or commission in Canada which is received as a result of a worker having suffered injury, disability or death while performing the duties of employment, is taxable in the first instance but subject to an offsetting deduction. See ¶358.

An award of damages for personal injury or death that decrees that it be paid in periodic payments is not, despite such periodic payments, considered to be an annuity contract and the periodic payments themselves are not considered to be taxable annuity payments. However, an annuity contract purchased by a taxpayer or a taxpayer's representative with proceeds of a lump-sum award received for damages for personal injury or death will be an annuity contract for all purposes of the Act and will, except where the award is received by a person under 21 as described in ¶570, give rise to income in the taxpayer's hands.

Where an amount in respect of damages for personal injury or death has been awarded by a court or resolved in an out-of-court settlement, no part of such amount will be income to the recipient even though the amount includes or is augmented by an amount which, pursuant to the terms of the court order or the settlement agreement, is referred to as interest. However, where an amount that has been awarded for damages is held on deposit, the amount of interest earned will be included in the income of the injured taxpayer (again subject to the exception at ¶570 for recipients under 21). Where an amount that has been awarded for damages is held in trust, any interest earned on the amount is income of the trust or of the beneficiary, depending on the circumstances.

A number of provinces make crime-compensation awards pursuant to the authority of criminal-injury compensation laws. The CRA considers that such crime-compensation awards are non-taxable.

For damages received in a business context, see ¶719 and ¶728.

For damages received on the termination of employment, especially wrongful dismissal damages, see ¶309, ¶923 and ¶924.

(IT-202R2 Employees' or workers' compensation; IT-365R2 Damages, settlement, and similar receipts)

Chapter 10

Other Deductions

THESE POINTS ARE COVERED IN THIS CHAPTER

CRA REFERENCES RELATING TO THIS CHAPTER

T1 Lines and Schedules

- Line 207 — Registered pension plan deduction (box 20 on T4 slips and box 32 on T4A slips)
- Line 208 — RRSP/ pooled registered pension plan (PRPP) deduction (see also chapter 26 of this book)
- Line 210 — Deduction for elected split-pension amount
- Line 213 — Universal Child Care Benefit repayment
- Line 214 — Child care expenses
- Line 215 — Disability supports deduction
- Line 219 — Moving expenses
- Line 220 — Support payments made
- Line 221 — Carrying charges and interest expenses
- Line 222 — Deduction for CPP or QPP contributions on self-employment and other earnings
- Line 224 — Exploration and development expenses
- Line 229 — Other employment expenses
- Line 231 — Clergy residence deduction
- Line 232 — Other deductions
- Line 235 — Social benefits repayment
- Line 244 — Canadian Forces personnel and police deduction
- Line 250 — Other payments deduction
- Line 251 — Limited partnership losses of other years
- Line 252 — Non-capital losses of other years
- Line 253 — Net capital losses of other years
- Line 256 — Additional deductions
- Schedule 4 — Statement of Investment Income
- Schedule 7 — RRSP and PRPP Unused Contributions, Transfers, and HBP or LLP Activities
- Schedule 8 — CPP Contributions on Self-Employment and Other Earnings

CRA Guides

5000-G, "General Income Tax and Benefit Guide"; **P105**, "Students and Income Tax"; **P119**, "When You Retire"; **RC4064**, "Medical and Disability-Related Information — Includes Form T2201"; **T4037**, "Capital Gains"; **T4040**, "RRSPs and Other Registered Plans for Retirement"; **T4044**, "Employment Expenses — Includes Forms GST 370, T777, TL2, and T2200"; **T4130**, "Employers' Guide — Taxable Benefits and Allowances"

CRA Forms

T1A, "Request for Loss Carryback"; **T1-ADJ**, "T1 Adjustment Request"; **T1-M**, "Moving Expenses Deduction"; **T3**, "Statement of Trust Income Allocations and Designations"; **T4**, "Statement of Remuneration Paid"; **T4A**, "Statement of Pension, Retirement, Annuity and Other Income"; **T4E**, "Statement of Employment Insurance and Other Benefits"; **T4A (OAS)**, "Statement of Old Age Security"; **T777**, "Statement of Employment Expenses"; **T778**, "Child Care Expenses Deduction"; **T929**, "Disability Supports Deduction"; **T1032**, "Joint Election to Split Pension Income"; **T1136**, "Old Age Security Return of Income"; **T1223**, "Clergy Residence Deduction"; **T1229**; "Statement of Resource Expenses and Depletion Allowance"; **T2030**, "Direct Transfer under Subparagraph 60(l)(v)"; **T2200**, "Declaration of Conditions of Employment"; **T2201**, "Disability Tax Credit Certificate"; **T2210**, "Verification of Policy Loan Interest by the Insurer"

Income Tax Folios

S1-F2-C3, "Scholarships, Research Grants and Other Education Assistance"; **S3-F6-C1**, "Interest Deductibility"; **S3-F9-C1**, "Lottery Winnings, Miscellaneous Receipts, and Income (and Losses) from Crime"; **S6-F1-C1**, "Residence of a Trust or Estate"; **S1-F3-C1**, "Child Care Expense Deduction"; **S1-F1-C3**, "Disability Supports Deduction"; **S1-F3-C3**, "Support Payments"; **S1-F3-C4**, "Moving Expenses"

Interpretation Bulletins

IT-86R, "Vow of Perpetual Poverty"; **IT-99R5 (Consolidated)**, "Legal and Accounting Fees"; **IT-141R (Consolidated)**, "Clergy Residence Deduction"; **IT-167R6**, "Registered Pension Plans — Employee's Contributions"; **IT-202R2**, "Employees' or Workers' Compensation"; **IT-232R3**, "Losses — Their Deductibility in the Loss Year or in Other Years"; **IT-238R2**, "Fees Paid to Investment Counsel"; **IT-322R**, "Farm Losses"; **IT-346R**, "Commodity Futures and Certain Commodities"; **IT-396R**, "Interest Income"; **IT-528**, "Transfers of Funds Between Registered Plans"

Information Circulars

78-5R3, "Communal Organizations"; **84-1**, "Revision of Capital Cost Allowance Claims and Other Permissive Deductions"

WHAT YOU SHOULD KNOW ABOUT OTHER DEDUCTIONS FROM INCOME

RECENT CHANGES

Draft legislation released on September 16, 2016, proposes to amend the definition of "eligible pension income " (¶1076) to include amounts received by the taxpayer on account of a retirement income security benefit under Part 2 of the Canadian Forces Members and Veterans Re-establishment and Compensation Act.

2016 New Income Tax Folios

In 2016, the CRA released or updated the following income tax folios:

- S1-F1-C3, Disability Supports Deduction issued January 20, 2016 (Update)
- S1-F3-C4, Moving Expenses issued April 5, 2016 (New)
- S1-F3-C1, Child Care Expense Deduction issued June 21, 2016 (Update)

[¶1000] NET INCOME AND TAXABLE INCOME

The *Income Tax Act* contemplates a two-stage income calculation. Certain deductions and losses are applied in arriving at "Net Income" (line 236 of the T1 return), which may generally be regarded as all actual earnings net of related expenses and current year deductible losses. Net income is sometimes referred to as "Division B income", because it is the income computed under that Division of the Act, as mandated by section 3 of the Act.

Following this is a series of further deductions under Division C to arrive at "Taxable Income". These adjustments are considered to be related not so much to earnings generally as to the special quality of certain deductions, for example by treating employee stock option benefits on an equivalent to capital gain basis. A complete list of taxable income deductions is found at ¶1077. In general, it is felt that these special status deductions should not reduce net income for purposes of measuring eligibility for a number of tax credits and benefits. Thus, net income is used in many calculations (e.g., certain tax credits, dependant exemptions, see ¶1103, and amount of Canada Child Benefit (¶1498)) required in the Act, and in many provincial tax credit calculations. Net income is a closer measure of actual economic income than taxable income. Taxable income is the actual tax base on which tax is calculated.

Another level of calculation applies to the clawback taxes and deductions for Old Age Security and Family Allowance payments. This is preliminary net income (line 234) before these deductions are taken, and is relevant primarily in the calculation of the clawback taxes and deductions themselves. The Employment Insurance clawback is also part of this group of special deductions from preliminary net income. See ¶1419.

The deductions below are made in the first stage of the income computation process, to arrive at net income. Note, however, that most of the deductions discussed below do not relate directly to a source of income, such as employment income, or income from a property or business. Most of the deductions relating directly to these sources are discussed in the chapters dedicated to those sources (Chapters 3, 4, and 6 through 8). The deductions discussed in this chapter are mainly found in subdivision "e" of Division B of Part 1 of the Act (many of the lines between lines 206 and 236 of the T1 return), although there is also a discussion on the deductibility of interest (¶1063 through ¶1075) which generally does relate to a source of income that is either investment or business (line 221 of the return if related to investment income). Exploration and development expenses, which are also subdivision "e" expenses, are discussed in Chapter 22.

Taxable income deductions in Division C are discussed at ¶1077 *et seq.*

TAX-DEFERRED SAVINGS PLANS

[¶1001] WHAT IS A TAX-DEFERRED SAVINGS PLAN?

A tax-deferred savings plan in general is any plan that allows you to set aside money you earn currently without paying tax until you use the funds in some future year. There are essentially two types of plans. Registered plans are explicitly sanctioned by the government to provide savings to supplement retirement income. The amounts that can be contributed without current tax (or as deductions from current tax) are strictly regulated, as are the investments the plan may make. There are also unregistered plans of various types. These are usually devised by employers as employee incentives.

Registered tax-deferred savings plans are discussed in detail in chapter 26. The following is a summary of the plans and the deductions allowed for contributions to the plans.

[¶1001.05] *Registered Tax-Deferred Savings Plans*

There are essentially seven types of government-sanctioned registered tax-deferred savings plans. Each is discussed briefly below.

(1) Registered Pension Plans (RPPs)

RPPs are plans established by an employer to provide retirement income. They (and their investments) are usually administered by the employer or by an administrator appointed by the employer.

Defined benefit RPPs typically provide a retirement income by reference to salary in the last years of employment. The employer generally makes the bulk of the contributions necessary to fund these plans, and these contributions are not taxed to the employees; rather, the pension income provided is taxable as received. In some defined benefit RPPs it is possible (or mandatory) for employees to make supplementary contributions, which they may deduct from income. It may also be possible to "buy back" past service where an employee leaves an employer and returns, or transfers between certain plans, or where plan benefits are retroactively upgraded. Where employees make qualifying contributions, they may deduct these amounts from employment income; see ¶365.

Money purchase RPPs provide a retirement income based on the total contributions to the plan in the same manner as Registered Retirement Savings Plans. The employer may contribute according to the terms of the plan as long as the annual contributions do not exceed specified limits. If the plan permits, employees may also make contributions (which will be deductible from employment income) to bring the total contributions up to the legally specified annual limits; see ¶365. The deductible employee contributions are claimed on line 207 of the T1 return. Retirement income is taxable as received.

(2) Deferred Profit Sharing Plans (DPSPs)

DPSPs are similar to RPPs but the employer contributions must be calculated by reference to the profits of the employer, subject to overall statutory limits. They are therefore oriented somewhat more towards providing the employees with an incentive to maximize employer profitability. Employees can no longer contribute directly to these plans. Earnings of the plan must be allocated to employees annually and the eventual benefits will depend on these allocations. To a greater extent than other plans, DPSPs may invest in shares of the employer company, presumably increasing the incentive feature. Benefits received by employees are taxable as described at ¶917.

(3) Registered Retirement Savings Plans (RRSPs)

RRSPs are plans under which individuals contribute deductible amounts directly to a trust that will provide income for retirement. The plan may hold cash or invest in specified investments, but investment in unqualified investments results in harsh penalty taxes. The general RRSP deduction limit for 2016 is the lesser of $25,370 and 18% of the individual's earned income for 2015, minus the pension adjustment for 2015, if any. Unused deduction room is carried forward indefinitely. The general deduction limit is discussed in Chapter 26 at ¶2604, and other allowable deductions are discussed at ¶2612.05. The deduction is claimed on line 208 of the T1 return.

Chapter 26 of this book deals with the RRSP rules in detail.

(4) Pooled Registered Pension Plans (PRPPs)

The federal government recently introduced legislation regarding PRPPs. The *Pooled Registered Pension Plans Act* received Royal Assent on June 28, 2012, and accompanying amendments to the *Income Tax Act* have been passed into law and are generally effective as of the same date. These plans will allow employers and their employees, or self-employed individuals, to make tax-deductible contributions to the plans similar to those made to money purchase RPPs described above. An employer's contribution to a PRPP in a taxation year will reduce the employee's RRSP deduction room for the year. The employee's contribution in a year will also reduce the employee's RRSP deduction room for the year. Distributions from the PRPP and paid to the employee will be included in income and can qualify for the pension credit. See also the discussion on PRPPs in Chapter 26.

(5) Registered Retirement Income Funds (RRIFs)

RRIFs provide an alternative form of retirement income for funds accumulated in an RRSP or other registered tax deferred plan. These plans are discussed in detail at ¶2630.10 to ¶2634.10, inclusive. The investment limitations are identical to those for RRSPs. See ¶2618.

(6) Registered Education Savings Plans (RESPs)

RESPs are savings vehicles for higher education. The RESP itself is a trust to which contributions are made (usually but not necessarily by a relative) for the benefit of the potential student. The government will, up to a point, make matching and supplementary contributions. Contributions are not deductible, but income earned in the trust accumulates free of tax, and payments of accumulated income are included in the tax of the student once the student reaches the post-secondary level of education. Income inclusions are reported as miscellaneous income on line 130 of the T1 Return. Where payments from a plan have been included in income in a year, and the amounts are repaid to the plan in the year or a subsequent year, the repayments are deductible (on line 232). This is only likely to occur when government contributions which have proved excessive have been flowed out to beneficiaries. RESPs are discussed in greater detail in ¶2529d.

(7) Registered Disability Savings Plans (RDSPs)

RDSPs are trusts to which contributions are made (usually but not necessarily by a relative) for the benefit of a disabled person. The government will, up to a point, make matching and supplementary contributions. Contributions are not deductible, but income earned in the trust accumulates free of tax, and payments of accumulated income are included in the tax of the disabled beneficiary. (Payments are considered blended payments of income and capital, and only the income portion is taxed.) Line 125 of the T1 Return is provided to report such income. Contributions to the plan may also arise from government grants. These grants may be subject to recapture by the government in certain circumstances. Where amounts subject to recapture have already been paid out and included in the beneficiary's income, the beneficiary will have to make the repayment. Such repayments are deductible (on line 232) in the year of repayment. RDSPs are discussed in greater detail in ¶2529h.

(8) Tax-Free Savings Accounts (TFSAs)

TFSAs permit individuals to contribute limited amounts to trusts for their own benefit. Contributions are not deductible but income earned in the trust is not taxable. Payments to the beneficiary of amounts in the trust, including both contributions and earnings, are not taxable. Trust investments are limited to a subset of investments which are eligible for RRSP investments. Tax reporting is generally the responsibility of the trustee, although there can be penalties for the beneficiary for inappropriate investments. TFSAs are discussed in ¶2532c and ¶478.

[¶1001.10] *Other Tax-Deferred Savings Plans*

There are a number of situations in which it may be possible to earn income, or an entitlement to potential income or benefits, and not be taxed currently. Typically these plans do not depend on current deductions from income but rather on the fact that tax is not currently required in the first place. Often these situations survive as exceptions to rules seeking to limit such tax deferral. The following tax deferral situations are discussed in this book:

- Foreign pension plans, ¶365a
- Unregistered pension plans, ¶359
- Retirement compensation arrangements, ¶359
- Phantom pension plans, ¶359
- Employee benefit plans, ¶359
- Salary deferral arrangements, ¶307
- Stock option plans, ¶2559
- Life insurance, ¶2557
- Employee profit sharing plans, ¶332
- Death benefits, ¶925
- Retiring allowances, ¶923; ¶2612.05.

Tax planning opportunities generally are discussed in Chapter 25.

[¶1019] TAX-ASSISTED HOME OWNERSHIP SAVINGS

The provinces of Ontario and Nova Scotia have tax credit provisions or rebates to assist first-time home buyers.

Furthermore, some provinces operate programs to abate land transfer taxes for first time home purchasers, or to abate sales taxes on new houses. Such programs are beyond the scope of this book. They are usually well known to real estate lawyers and realtors where they are in effect, and details of any programs currently in effect should be available from the provincial housing ministry.

The federal government has provided for individuals to borrow limited amounts from their RRSPs for use toward the purchase of a Canadian residence which will be the individual's primary place of residence. See ¶2625.05 *et seq.* regarding the Home Buyers' Plan.

See also ¶2543 on tax planning for home ownership.

TRANSFERS BETWEEN REGISTERED PLANS

[¶1021] TRANSFER OF PENSION FUND CONTRIBUTIONS, RETIREMENT ALLOWANCES, TERMINATION PAYMENTS, OR DEFERRED PROFIT SHARING PLAN CONTRIBUTIONS

[¶1021.10] *Overview of Current Transfers*

The transfers permitted from other tax-deferred plans to RRSPs are discussed in detail in Chapter 26; see ¶2612.05 *et seq.* Transfers of certain RRSP payments received are also discussed at ¶903.

The discussion below is given over primarily to inter-plan transfers not covered elsewhere in this book, and to cross-references to transfers which are covered elsewhere.

Transfers between plans or of special types of income to plans are often referred to as "rollovers" because they result in no tax payable.

[¶1021.15] *General Information*

Excellent charts of the various transfer rules are found in the CRA's *RRSPs and Other Registered Plans for Retirement Tax Guide* (T4040). An even more comprehensive discussion of transfer rules is found in Interpretation Bulletin IT-528. The current guide always has the advantage of being updated annually, but IT-528 is more detailed.

[¶1021.20] *Rollovers of Lump Sums Owing from Registered Pension Plans*

Except where spouses, common-law partners, or certain children or grandchildren (see below) are recipients, transfers of lump-sum amounts must normally be made directly between plans. The most common situation in which this will arise is on a change of employment. Since there are two types of RPPs, defined benefit and money purchase, the rules must contemplate payments out of each type of plan to the other or to an RRSP. A defined benefit plan is the most common, and provides for specific benefits on retirement, usually measured by the average salary for a period preceding retirement. Where an employee moves from this type of a plan to another employer that also provides a defined benefit plan, funds (including actuarial surplus) may be transferred between plans for the benefit of the employee, and to the extent that the plans do not mesh in terms of benefits, the difference is supposed to be reflected in RRSP pension room, that is, in allowable contributions to an RRSP. It is also possible for an employee to direct (subject to the terms of his pension plans) the payment of lump sums from a defined benefit RPP to an RRSP or a RRIF in full or partial satisfaction of the employee's rights under the defined benefit plan. The amount transferable will be prescribed by regulation and will be lifetime retirement benefits commuted multiplied by an arbitrary present value factor to be set out in regulations. The amount will not include actuarial surplus in the defined benefit plan, and will reduce RRSP contribution room. Where the new employer offers a money purchase RPP, transfer may be made to this on the same terms as to an RRSP.

For excess direct transfers, that is, transfers exceeding the permissible limits, see ¶2612.45.

Previously, if an individual was a member of a defined benefit RPP and there was a shortfall in the member's commutation payments such that only a lower amount was available (say, owing to underfunding of the pension), the amount that could be transferred tax-free to the member's RRSP, RRIF or money purchase RPP was based on that lower amount. However, since 2011, a new rule allows the maximum transferable amount for a plan member who is leaving an underfunded RPP to be the same as if the RPP were fully funded. In general terms, this rule applies where the underfunded RPP has broad membership, is sponsored by an insolvent employer that is being wound up, and the Minister of National Revenue has given approval. Furthermore, the 2014 federal Budget extended the circumstances in which the new rule will apply, effective after 2012. The rule will also apply, if approved by the Minister, to a plan member who is leaving an RPP if the payment has been reduced due to plan underfunding and either (i) where the plan is an RPP other than an individual pension plan, the reduction in the estimated pension benefit that results in the reduced commutation payment is approved pursuant to the applicable pension benefits standards legislation, or (ii) where the plan is an individual pension plan, the commutation payment to the plan member is the last payment made from the plan and all the property is distributed from the plan within 90 days.

Where an employee is leaving employment which provided a money purchase RPP (one in which the eventual benefits are a direct function of employer/employee contributions rather than final period salary), lump sum amounts may be transferred directly to the employee's RRSP, PRPP, SPP, or RRIF or, if there is an RPP with the new employer, to the new RPP. There is no limit to these transfers, but, as with almost all transfers out of RPPs, they must be directly to the new plan. See ¶1028 for information on the Saskatchewan Pension Plan (SPP).

There is no actual requirement that an employee leave his or her employment to make transfers from an RPP to another RPP, PRPP, SPP, RRIF, or RRSP under the rules above; this is merely the most likely time for such a transfer. Generally, the terms of the plans will discourage such transfers in other situations; but that is not a function of tax law, which simply provides that the transfers can be made on a tax-free basis provided the transfer rules are complied with as to amount and RRSP room calculations.

In addition to changes of employment, the rules contemplate three situations in which direct transfers of lump sum amounts from RPPs may be made directly to another RPP, a PRPP, an SPP, an RRSP or an RRIF. First, a lump-sum transfer may be made to the plan of a spouse or common-law partner or former spouse or former common-law partner pursuant to either a court order or a written separation agreement relating to a division of property on marriage breakdown. Second, a direct transfer may be made to the RPP, PRPP, SPP, RRSP, or RRIF of a spouse or common-law partner in consequence of the death of the plan holder. The above transfers may not include actuarial surplus. Finally, a direct transfer may be made as a return of pre-1991 employee contributions (and interest thereon) to an RPP, an RRSP, or a RRIF of the plan holder. The intention of this last rule is apparently to allow transfer of such contributions when a defined benefit RPP is amended to retroactively reduce or eliminate the requirement for members to make contributions.

There is another general transfer rule for RPP amounts, and this involves the situation where a lump sum becomes payable to minor children or grandchildren, or children or grandchildren who were financially dependent on the plan holder for support because of mental or physical infirmity, on the death of a plan holder. Typically this arises where there is no surviving spouse, although that may not always be the case. Where non-infirm children or grandchildren under the age of 18 become entitled to a lump sum out of an RPP on the death of the plan holder, each child (or a trust for the child) may use the payment to purchase a special annuity making at least annual payments to the child (or a trust for the child) to age 18. Although the RPP amount will be included in the child's income in the year, an offsetting deduction equal to the amount paid to acquire the annuity is allowed if it is paid in the year or within 60 days after the end of the year. For a financially dependent infirm child or grandchild, a similar deduction is allowed if the amount is contributed to the child's own RRSP or used to acquire an annuity payable for life or to age 90.

Lastly, there is a similar rollover for lump-sum RPP amounts (and similar amounts from an RRSP or RRIF) received on the death of the plan holder by financially dependent children or grandchildren who were dependent upon the holder by reason of mental or physical infirmity and who contribute such amounts to their RDSPs. The rules for this rollover are found in section 60.02. The rollover — an inclusion for the dependant with an offsetting deduction for the contribution to the RDSP — applies to amounts received as a consequence of the death of the parent or grandparent after March 3, 2010 where the contribution is made to the RDSP after June 2011. However, the rollover is allowed only to the extent that there is existing contribution room for the RDSP (a lifetime $200,000 limit applies). A transitional rollover rule applies for amounts received after 2007 and before 2011. The transitional rule allows the child or grandchild who received such amounts out of an RPP (or RRSP or RRIF) on the death of the parent or grandparent (in respect of deaths before March 4, 2010) to deduct the amounts in the year of receipt if the amounts are contributed to the child's RDSP after June 2011 and before 2012. The transitional rule also allows the child or grandchild to withdraw amounts from their RRSP that were previously deducted under the rule described in the paragraph above (i.e., rollover into their RRSPs upon the death of the plan holder) and contribute them to their RDSPs after June 2011 and before 2012. The transitional rule similarly allows the spouse or common-law partner of the deceased or a beneficiary of the deceased to contribute amounts received out of an RPP, RRSP, or RRIF after 2007 and before 2011 as a consequence of the death of the deceased plan holder to the child's or grandchild's RDSP after June 2011 and before 2012 and to receive an offsetting deduction. The details of this RDSP rollover are also discussed in Chapter 19 at ¶1913 and ¶1914.15.

Single amounts payable to beneficiaries of deceased RPP members (other than spouses, common-law partners, or children or grandchildren as described above) are not eligible for transfer to RPPs or RRSPs.

(ITA: 60(*j*), (*l*); 147.3)

[¶1021.30] *Rollovers of DPSP Payments*

Lump-sum entitlements from a DPSP may be transferred directly to another DPSP or to an RPP, PRPP, SPP, RRSP or RRIF on behalf of an employee or on behalf of a person who was the current spouse or common-law partner of an employee in the event of the employee's death. (For transfers after March 20, 2003, the transfer may also be made for direct transfers to any of these plans on behalf of a former spouse or common-law partner.) Amounts may be transferred only to the extent that they would be included in income if paid directly to the individual. Thus, employee contributions made to a DPSP are not transferable. On the other hand, the *cost* of DPSP shares included in income is transferable (see also ¶917). Direct transfer is not required where the payments pass through a testamentary trust; in this case, a contribution to the surviving spouse's/partner's RPP, PRPP, SPP, RRSP, or DPSP must be made within 60 days of year end and a designation made on Schedule 7 of the T1 return. See ¶1028 for information on the Saskatchewan Pension Plan (SPP).

Periodic payments from a DPSP are permitted no special transfers to any tax-deferred plan.

(ITA: 60(*j*); 147(19)–(22))

[¶1021.35] *Receipts from Trusts Representing Pension or DPSP Income*

Where a taxpayer has died and a testamentary trust receives certain pension or DPSP amounts which the trust has allocated as income to a spouse or common-law partner of the deceased, these amounts are eligible for special contribution by the surviving spouse or common-law partner, etc. to the surviving spouse's or common-law partner's RPP, PRPP, SPP, RRSP, or RRIF. The trust should identify these amounts on the T3 to the surviving spouse in box 22 of the T3 Supplementary. The surviving spouse or common-law partner, if not disqualified by age from having an RRSP, may deduct as a special contribution any amount up to the amount in box 22 contributed to an RRSP within 60 days of the end of the year to which the T3 relates. The special contribution must be designated on Schedule 7 of the T1 return. See ¶2612.05. See ¶1028 for information on the Saskatchewan Pension Plan (SPP).

Beginning in 2016, the foregoing rules apply only to a graduated rate estate and not to other testamentary trusts. In general terms, a graduated rate estate is a deceased individual's estate for up to 36 months after death.

(ITA: 60(*j*); 104(27), (27.1); 147(10.2))

[¶1021.40] *Rollovers from RRSPs to Plans of the Same Annuitant*

The "annuitant" (plan holder) of an RRSP may transfer lump sum funds freely from one plan to another or to a RRIF, RPP, PRPP, or SPP provided the annuitant is the same. Note that this requires a direct transfer. The transfer is certified on form T2033, and has no tax consequences (although transfer to a RRIF will ensure commencement of taxable payments in the following year). This policy continues. A similar direct transfer may be made to any of the old-age annuities discussed at ¶903, including a joint annuity providing for continuing payments to a surviving spouse or common-law partner. These rules continue. Form T2030 reports the transfer. Where a plan has been annuitized or "matured" to provide retirement income, a direct transfer of plan funds may be accomplished by commuting the annuity and transferring the commutation payment to any of the investments described at ¶903, including an unmatured RRSP provided the taxpayer is not precluded by age from having such a plan. See ¶1028 for information on the Saskatchewan Pension Plan (SPP).

If an RRSP had been "annuitized" to provide periodic retirement income payments, these payments could, prior to 1990, be transferred directly to another RRSP or to a RRIF of the same plan holder under the age of 72. This right has been terminated so that periodic payments from a "mature" RRSP cannot be transferred to another plan after December 31, 1989. Commutation of part or all of the annuity and direct transfer of the commutation payment to any of the permitted investments described at ¶903 continues to be permitted.

Since an RRSP or an RRIF is not normally taxable, the annuitant is generally indifferent to the cost base of assets in the plan when transfers are made from one plan to another on a tax-free basis. New trust rules effective December 23, 1999, subject to certain transitional rules, permit the transfer of assets between plans of the same annuitant with a complete rollover of the cost base of all assets in the old plan, provided certain conditions are met. (This occurs because such a transfer is defined not to be a disposition at all under the definition of "disposition" under subsection 248(1), and therefore there is no effect on asset costs.) Two of the conditions of this rule are that the transferor plan ceases to exist, and that the transferee plan held no substantial assets before the transfer; that is, all assets are transferred from one plan to a new plan or plans. This makes a certain amount of sense in terms of preserving the relative cost of foreign assets. It follows, however, that where there is only a partial transfer, there is a disposition, which occurs under the applicable rollover rule at cost unless the transferor elects to use another value, which may be anywhere between cost and fair market value. The election, however, cannot be used to circumvent the foreign property rules. Care must be taken in any partial transfer that the cost base of transferred property in both new and old plans is not excessive. The election presumably allows some scope for transferring a selection of property and electing to have transfer values so that the relative value of foreign assets in each plan does not trigger foreign property tax in the trust.

(ITA: 60(*l*); 107.4; 146(16); 206(4); 248(1) "disposition" (*f*))

[¶1021.45] *Rollovers from RRSPs to Plans of the Spouse or Common-Law Partner on Marriage Breakdown*

See ¶2330.

[¶1021.50] *Rollovers of RRIF Amounts*

Direct transfer of capital amounts in an RRIF can be made to any other RRIF. In addition, withdrawals from a RRIF in excess of required minimum RRIF payments can be made *by direct transfer only* to any of the permitted investments described at ¶903, that is, to an RRSP, PRPP, SPP, or another RRIF of the same plan holder, or an old age annuity including one that provides for continuing payments to a spouse or common-law partner. See ¶1028 for information on the Saskatchewan Pension Plan (SPP).

Direct transfer of amounts in an RRIF may be made on marriage breakdown to the RRSP, PRPP, SPP, or RRIF of a spouse or common-law partner as defined at ¶1113. Further detail is provided at ¶2330.

For transfers on the death of a spouse or common-law partner, parent or grandparent, see ¶1916 and ¶2612.05.

(ITA: 60(*l*); 146.3(14))

[¶1021.53] *Rollover from RESP to RDSP*

The rules first announced in the 2012 federal Budget provide that accumulated income earned in an RESP (see ¶1001.05) can be rolled over on a tax-free basis to an RDSP (¶1001.05). The new rules provide that a subscriber of an RESP and a holder of an RDSP may make a joint election in prescribed form to transfer the income of the RESP to the RDSP if, at the time of the election, the RESP beneficiary is the beneficiary under the RDSP and

- the beneficiary has a severe and prolonged mental impairment that prevents him or her or can reasonably be expected to prevent him or her from enrolling in post-secondary education; or
- the payment is made in the 35th year after the year in which the RESP began, or it is made in the 10th or subsequent year after the RESP began and each beneficiary under the RESP is at least 21 years old of age and is not eligible to receive educational assistance payments.

The legislation provides that the promoter of the RESP must file the election with the Minister "without delay". If the election is properly made, the income transferred from the RESP to the RDSP will not be included in the beneficiary's (or any other person's) income. The amount so transferred on a rollover basis is subject to the lifetime $200,000 contribution limit for RDSPs.

The rollover applies beginning in 2014.

[¶1021.55] *Rollovers of RRSP Refund of Premiums or RRIF Designated Benefits*

See ¶1914 on RRSPs and ¶1916 on RRIFs; also ¶2612.05 on both. Generally, these rollovers are amounts received out of an RRSP or RRIF on the death of the annuitant by the surviving spouse or common-law partner, a financially dependent child or grandchild under the age of 18, or a child or grandchild who was financially dependent for support because of a mental or physical infirmity. The recipient includes the amount received in income, but gets an offsetting deduction to the extent the amount is contributed to an RRSP, PRPP, SPP, or RRIF, or used to acquire an annuity payable for life or to age 90 (spouses and infirm children and grandchildren) or to acquire an annuity to age 18 (non-infirm children and grandchildren). In the 2010 federal Budget, the rollover was extended for amounts contributed to an RDSP of a financially dependent infirm child or grandchild, effective for contributions made after June 2011; see ¶1914.15. See ¶1028 for information on the Saskatchewan Pension Plan (SPP).

[¶1021.60] *Retiring and Termination Payment Rollovers*

You may transfer or contribute to an RRSP, PRPP, SPP, or RPP, in addition to the amounts based on earned income and rollovers of pension plan or DPSP amounts, specific amounts received as a retiring allowance (which includes damages on termination), as defined at ¶923. The amount of the additional contribution is based on the number of pre-1996 years that you were employed by the employer. The transfer is usually indirect; that is, the amounts are paid to you and must be contributed to the plan within 60 days following the end of the year of receipt, and designated by you on Schedule 7 filed with your tax return. In certain circumstances the amount may be transferred directly between plans, but you must still report the receipt as income and make the designation on Schedule 7. See ¶1028 for information on Saskatchewan Pension Plan (SPP).

Details of these rules as well as a detailed example of this rollover are provided at ¶2612.05.

[¶1021.65] *Rollovers of Foreign Pension Plan Amounts*

Where you receive a lump sum payment out of a foreign pension plan for services attributable to a period of non-residence in Canada, the amount can be rolled over to a Canadian RPP, PRPP, SPP, or RRSP by making a contribution within 60 days from the end of the year of receipt. See ¶1028 for information on the Saskatchewan Pension Plan (SPP).

Payments out of certain quasi-pension plans such as U.S. Individual Retirement Accounts may also be eligible for rollover treatment; see ¶919.

(ITA: 60(*j*))

[¶1021.70] *Recontributions of Past Service Event Excess Withdrawals*

Under the complex new registered pension plan (RPP) rules, a "past service event" may be permitted to increase the benefits to employees under a *defined benefit RPP.* A retroactive increase in benefits is the most obvious example. For these benefits to be permitted under the plan, the employees affected must have sufficient unused RRSP room (¶2610.15). Where the employee has insufficient room, a special (taxable) RRSP withdrawal may be made. Where the withdrawal proves excessive, for example because the past service event does not in fact qualify, a recontribution of the withdrawal can be made and deducted. See ¶2614c.10.

(ITA: 146(6.1); 147.1(10); ITR: 8307(1) Application for Certification)

[¶1021.75] *Cross-References*

Other sections of this book relating to RRSP rollovers include:

¶903 — Income items from RRSPs and RRIFs

¶907 — RRIF income

¶913, ¶915 — OAS/CPP pensions

¶917 — DPSP receipts

¶923 — Retiring allowances (and termination payments)

¶1914 — RRSP balances on death of annuitant

¶1916 — RRIF balances on death of annuitant

¶2330 — Transfer of RRSP or RRIF on marriage breakdown

¶2611.15 — Penalties on excess contributions

Chapter 26 — Calculating your RRSP deduction on your current return and contributions for future years.

(ITA: 60(*j*), (*j*.1); (*l*); 146(5); IT-528 Transfers of Funds Between Registered Plans)

MISCELLANEOUS DEDUCTIONS

[¶1026] SOCIAL BENEFIT (OAS AND EI) CLAWBACK DEDUCTIONS

Special deductions from income are allowed for clawback taxes applied to Old Age Security (OAS) and Employment Insurance (EI) payments. These are claimed at line 235 and are discussed in detail at ¶1419.

[¶1026.05] *Net Federal Supplements Deduction*

Net federal supplements are means-tested supplementary payments made under the OAS program in addition to basic pension entitlements. These must be reported as income (on line 146 of the T1 return) separately from basic non-means-tested OAS benefits (reported at line 113). The net federal supplements may then be deducted again (at line 250) in calculating taxable income. The purpose of this inclusion and deduction is to include the supplements in measuring net income to determine various tax and other benefits such as the age amount (line 301), Canada Child Benefit (¶1498) and GST credit (¶1496).

An odd technical problem arises where a taxpayer has net federal supplements (NFS) in the same year that income exceeds the threshold for OAS recapture. This would normally be very rare, but where it does occur, the offsetting deduction for net federal supplements (at line 250) must be reduced since it is only allowed "to the extent that it [the NFS] is included in the taxpayer's income". The CRA interprets this to mean that the offsetting reduction (at line 250) must itself be reduced to the extent that net federal supplements are deducted (at line 235) under the OAS clawback rules.

There are two problems with this. The first is that it is not quite what the statute says. The NFS have been included in income as required, and it is not clear that the offsetting clawback deduction changes that. Even allowing, however, that general principles would argue against permitting a double deduction for supplements under both the clawback (line 235) and offset (line 250) rules, it is not clear how an allocation should be made between ordinary and NFS payments where only part of total OAS payments are being clawed back. The CRA takes the position that net federal supplements are clawed back first, and accordingly the line 250 offset deduction must be reduced dollar for dollar to the extent of OAS clawback. It is by no means clear why net federal supplements should be considered clawed back before ordinary OAS benefits, as opposed to the other way around. A more reasonable position might apportion the OAS clawback in proportion to the mix of ordinary and NFS payments received as OAS in the year. If this issue has ever arisen in practice, it is not apparent in any reported cases.

[¶1027] SUPPORT PAYMENTS ON SEPARATION OR DIVORCE

The tax consequences of divorce and separation are discussed in detail in Chapter 23. Treatment of payments to third parties in particular is covered at ¶2315.

[¶1028] SASKATCHEWAN PENSION PLAN CONTRIBUTIONS

The Saskatchewan Pension Plan (SPP) is a voluntary money purchase pension plan that is intended to extend pension coverage over and above OAS/CPP to those who might not otherwise belong to private pension plans, such as homemakers, part-time employees, farmers, and the self-employed. SPP membership is available to all Canadians (not just Saskatchewan residents) aged 18 to 71 with available RRSP contribution room. Your contributions to the plan on behalf of yourself and/or your spouse or common-law partner are generally deductible within RRSP limits (see the SPP guide at http://www.saskpension.com/pdfs/documents/member_guide.pdf).

T1 returns for 2010 and prior years had a separate line for recording SPP contributions (line 209). However, for 2011 and subsequent years, SPP contributions are subject to the same rules as RRSP contributions. SPP contributions are reported on Schedule 7 and may be used to claim the RRSP tax deduction on line 208 of the T1 return.

SPP members can also transfer up to $10,000 per year from an existing RRSP, RRIF, or unlocked RPP, but there are no tax deductions for these direct transfers between plans.

Where there has been a marriage breakdown, *The Saskatchewan Pension Plan Act* (section 19.1) stipulates that, in the case of an unretired member, the receiving spouse must become a member of the Plan. The funds in both accounts remain locked-in until retirement. In the case of a retired member, pension payments are split and then issued to the respective parties.

Death benefits transferred to a tax-deferred plan must use the direct transfer to RRSP, etc. (¶2612.35).

Member contributions are pooled in a managed investment fund and members continue to be credited with plan earnings. At any time between ages 55 and 71, plan members who retire can commence to take retirement benefits based on contributions and earnings. Members can choose a SPP annuity or transfer to a locked-in option (LIRA, PRRIF (Prescribed RRIF), LAC (life annuity contract)). Where the member's annuity payment is less than the amount prescribed in SPP Regulations, the member may elect to received their pension in a one-time lump-sum payment. This one-time payment may be transferred to a tax-deferred plan using the direct transfer to RRSP, etc. or received in cash, less withholding tax.

(ITA: 118.7; ITR: 7800 [Prescribed arrangement])

[¶1029] OVERPAYMENTS OF EMPLOYMENT INSURANCE, OLD AGE SECURITY, CANADA OR QUEBEC PENSION, AND AMOUNTS RECEIVED UNDER THE LABOUR ADJUSTMENT BENEFITS ACT

You may deduct in computing your income any amount repaid by you on account of an overpayment which you previously received under the *Old Age Security Act*, the *Canada Pension Plan*, the *Quebec Pension Plan*, the *Labour Adjustment Benefits Act* and the *Employment Insurance Act*. With regard to workers' compensation, however, see ¶358. These claims for your repayment of excess benefits received should not be confused with repayments of overcontributions withheld from your pay on account of *Canada Pension Plan* or Employment Insurance, as to which see ¶1491 and ¶1492, nor with the recapture of Employment Insurance described at ¶1419. Quebec taxpayers should note the special rules at ¶1676d.

(ITA: 60(*n*))

[¶1030] REFUND OF RETIREMENT COMPENSATION AMOUNTS

A retirement compensation arrangement (RCA) is essentially an unregistered pension plan, as discussed at ¶359. If you make non-deductible contributions to the plan while resident in Canada, your payments out of the plan (all of which are taxable) will be offset by deductions to the extent they represent a return of non-deductible contributions. These returns are considered to be the first payments out of the plan.

For 1996 and later years, the transfer of amounts from one RCA to another on a tax-free basis has been facilitated, and the deduction for the return of non-deductible contributions will track the funds from plan to plan.

(ITA: 60(*t*), (*u*); 207.6(7))

[¶1031] EXPENSES OF TAX RETURN PREPARATION, OBJECTION, OR APPEAL

Where you incur fees or expenses in preparing, instituting or prosecuting an objection to or an appeal in relation to:

(1) an assessment of tax, interest or penalties under the federal *Income Tax Act* and/or any provincial *Income Tax Act*;

(2) a decision of the Canada Employment and Immigration Commission, the Employment and Insurance Commission, a board of referees or an umpire under the *Employment Insurance Act* or the *Unemployment Insurance Act*;

(3) any foreign income tax assessment where the foreign tax is deductible; or

(4) an assessment or decision under the *Canada Pension Plan* or a provincial pension plan,

you are entitled to deduct such expenses in computing your income in the year in which they are paid.

In general, this rule does not permit a deduction for personal tax return preparation fees or personal tax planning advice. There are exceptions. If you are self-employed, reasonable fees and expenses incurred for advice and assistance in preparing and filing income tax returns are normally deductible under the general rules for expenses laid out in the course of earning income. Also, commission salespersons who qualify for deductions under the rules at ¶368 may similarly claim reasonable fees and expenses for tax return advice and assistance.

The rule here does permit any taxpayer to deduct legal and accounting fees incurred for advice and assistance in making representations after he or she is informed that income or tax for a particular year is to be reviewed, whether or not a formal notice of objection or appeal is subsequently filed.

You must include in your income any amounts received by you as legal costs awarded to you by a court because of an appeal in relation to an assessment of tax, interest or penalties under the federal or provincial income tax acts, a decision of either Commission in (2), above, or an assessment or decision under the *Canada Pension Plan* or provincial plan, provided the expenses were deductible as described in ¶1081.

Where your objection or appeal is in respect of issues connected with your business, the same results would seem to obtain on an accrual rather than cash basis (¶714) under general business expense rules. For expenses of representations to government in respect of a business, see ¶765.

Individuals with legal expenses incurred to collect or establish a right to a retiring allowance (termination payment) or to a private pension plan are subject to similar rules discussed in ¶371.

(ITA: 56(1)(*l*); 60(*o*); IT-99R5 (Consolidated) Legal and Accounting Fees (Consolidated))

[¶1032] SUCCESSION DUTIES APPLICABLE TO CERTAIN PROPERTY

If you, as a beneficiary, receive a superannuation, pension or death benefit, or a benefit under a Registered Retirement Savings Plan, a deferred profit sharing plan or an income-averaging annuity contract, you may deduct in computing income the portion of succession duties payable which applies to these benefits. Although succession duties have been withdrawn long since, it is conceivable that this provision will continue to apply to continuing period payments arising from a death occurring while duties were still in effect.

The amount of the succession duties which may be deducted is computed as follows:

$$\text{Benefits (as enumerated above) received by you during the year} \times \frac{\text{Succession duties reasonably applicable to the rights of the deceased from which these benefits were paid}}{\text{Value of the right passing from the deceased as computed for succession duty purposes}}$$

(ITA: 60(*m.1*))

[¶1034] DEDUCTION FOR REFUND OF INCOME PAYMENTS

Payments made by you to an arm's length person will be deductible if they were included in your income in a previous year as salary, scholarship or research grant and were repayable because certain conditions were not fulfilled. In addition, the original sum paid to you must have been paid for the purpose of furthering your education and, in the year you received the sum, you must not have performed other than occasional services for the payer. The repayments are taxable in the hands of the arm's length recipient. See ¶967.

(ITA: 56(1)(*p*); 60(*q*))

[¶1036] DISABILITY SUPPORT AND ATTENDANT CARE COSTS — LINE 215; FORM T929

[¶1036.05] *Circumstances which Entitle You to "Disability Supports Deduction"*

You may claim this deduction for amounts you personally have paid during the taxation year to enable you to:

(1) perform the duties of an office or employment,

(2) carry on a business either alone or as a partner actively engaged in the business,

(3) attend a designated educational institution or a secondary school at which you are enrolled in an educational program, or

(4) carry on research or any similar work in respect of which you received a grant.

A designated educational institution, for the purposes of (3) above, has the same meaning here as it does in ¶1337 for purposes of the education amount credit (although the education credit is repealed as of January 1, 2017, a revised definition of designated educational institution remains in effect). On the other hand, the term "educational program" here seems to have only its dictionary meaning, since none of the defined terms used in ¶1337 is used here.

[¶1036.10] *Amounts Eligible for Deduction since 2004*

You may deduct all the amounts you have personally paid to allow you to engage in any of the activities above to the extent those amounts fall into any of the following categories:

- if you have a speech or hearing impairment, the cost of sign-language interpretation services or real time captioning services paid to a person engaged in the business of providing such services,
- if you are deaf or mute, the cost of a teletypewriter or similar device, including a telephone ringing indicator,

prescribed by a medical practitioner, to enable you to make and receive phone calls,

- if you are blind, the cost of a device or equipment, including synthetic speech systems, Braille printers, and large print on-screen devices, prescribed by a medical practitioner, and designed to be used by blind individuals in the operation of a computer,

- if you are blind, the cost of an optical scanner or similar device, prescribed by a medical practitioner, and designed to be used by blind individuals to enable them to read print,

- if you are mute, the cost of an electronic speech synthesiser, prescribed by a medical practitioner, and designed to be used by mute individuals to enable them to communicate by use of a portable keyboard,

- if you have an impairment in physical or mental functions, the cost of note-taking services and to a person engaged in the business of providing such services, if you have been certified in writing by a medical practitioner to be a person who, because of that impairment, requires such services,

- if you have an impairment in physical functions, the cost of voice recognition software, if you have been certified in writing by a medical practitioner to be a person who, because of that impairment, requires that software,

- if you have a learning disability or an impairment in mental functions, the cost of tutoring services that are rendered to, and supplementary to the primary education of, the taxpayer and to a person ordinarily engaged in the business of providing such services to individuals who are not related to the person, if the taxpayer has been certified in writing by a medical practitioner to be a person who, because of that disability or impairment, requires those services,

- if you have a perceptual disability, the cost of talking textbooks used by the taxpayer in connection with the taxpayer's enrolment at a secondary school in Canada or at a designated educational institution, if the taxpayer has been certified in writing by a medical practitioner to be a person who, because of that disability, requires those textbooks, and

- if you have an impairment in physical or mental functions, the cost of attendant care services provided in Canada if paid to a person who is neither your spouse or common-law partner nor under 18 years of age, provided you either have a medical certificate making you eligible for the disability deduction discussed in ¶1255, or you have been certified in writing by a medical practitioner to be a person who, because of that infirmity is, and is likely to be indefinitely, dependent on others for their personal needs and care and who as a result requires a full-time attendant. Both the disability certificate requirements and the infirmity test are discussed in ¶1209, and the requirements for either are the same for these purposes as for the tax credit purposes discussed in Chapter 12.

Note that, except for the cost of sign-language interpretation or real time captioning services in the first item above, each of the items above involves a prescription or certification by a medical practitioner. Which medical practitioners can prescribe or certify the conditions is discussed in ¶1209. Similarly, what constitutes a severe and prolonged impairment is discussed at ¶1209.

[¶1036.15] *Amounts Eligible for Deduction since 2005*

The categories of expense eligible for deduction have been expanded for 2005 and later years. In addition to deductions listed above, you may deduct all the amounts you have personally paid in the year to allow you to engage in any qualifying activities, such as employment, listed above, to the extent those amounts fall into any of the following categories:

- if you have a severe and prolonged impairment in physical or mental functions, the cost of job coaching services (not including job placement or career counselling services) paid to a person engaged in the business of providing such services, if you have been certified in writing by a medical practitioner to be a person who, because of that impairment, requires such services,

- if you are blind or have a severe learning disability, for cost of reading services paid to a person engaged in the business of providing such services, if you have been certified in writing by a medical practitioner to be a person who, because of that impairment or disability, requires those services,

- if you are blind *and* profoundly deaf, the cost of deaf-blind intervening services paid to a person engaged in the business of providing such services,

- if you have a speech impairment, the cost of a device that is a Bliss symbol board that is prescribed by a medical practitioner to help you communicate by motioning at the symbols or spelling out words,

- if you are blind, the cost of a device that is a Braille note-taker, prescribed by a medical practitioner to allow you to take notes (that can be read back to you or printed or displayed in Braille) with the help of a keyboard,

- if you have a severe and prolonged impairment in physical functions that markedly restricts your ability to use your arms or hands, the cost of a device that is a page-turner prescribed by a medical practitioner to help you turn the pages of a book or other bound document, and

- if you are blind, or have a severe learning disability, the cost of a device or software that is prescribed by a medical practitioner and designed to enable you to read print.

Note that, except for the cost of deaf-blind intervening services, each of the items above involves a prescription or certification by a medical practitioner. Which medical practitioners can prescribe or certify the conditions is discussed in ¶1209. Similarly, what constitutes a severe and prolonged impairment is discussed at ¶1209.

[¶1036.20] *Reduction for Reimbursements*

Eligible expenses must be reduced by any reimbursement or other form of assistance that you (or indeed anyone else) are or were entitled to receive in respect of the expenses included in your claim. Typically these would be insurance payments, and they reduce your claim whether or not you have actually received them. On the other hand, if they are in dispute, you are presumably not yet entitled to receive them and they do not reduce your claim. When if ever they would do so, especially in regard to statute barred claims, is not clear.

Training allowances and scholarships might also be subject to this rule to the extent they are not taxable; see ¶953 and ¶971.

You need not reduce your claim for reimbursements or assistance which are otherwise taxable, i.e., which are included in your (or someone else's) income and not deducted from taxable income. The statute also provides that prescribed assistance will not reduce your claim, but as it appears that no regulations have ever appeared to have been issued give content to this exception, and for the time being it is a dead letter.

[¶1036.25] *Medical Expense Credit as an Alternative*

You will note that for most of the expenses above, you must have a prescription by a medical practitioner. The rules as to who can prescribe what are the same as those for medical expense credit, which are described in ¶1209.

Virtually all the above expenses can be claimed as medical expenses eligible for credit rather than as a deduction from income (see ¶1205 and ¶1215). However, the deduction from income is usually preferable, first because the medical expenses available for credit are reduced by 3% of your net income (to a maximum indexed value described in ¶1235), a reduction which does not apply to this income deduction, and second because if your taxable income exceeds the minimum tax bracket value, the value of the deduction will be higher than the value of the medical expense credit, even leaving apart the 3% of income disallowance, because the medical expense credit only offsets income taxed at the lowest federal rate.

On the other hand, you can only claim under these rules expenses you have paid yourself on account of your own disability. The medical expense credit can be claimed by other relatives who are entitled to claim you as a dependant, as discussed in ¶1225.

As you might expect, any particular expense claimed under these rules cannot be claimed again in any year, by you or anyone else, under the medical expense credit rules in Chapter 12. However, particular expenses which you could claim under this rule but chose not to remain available for claim by yourself or others under the medical expense rules. This could be relevant if you are subject to the income limits discussed below. You could claim deductions up to those limits under these rules, and if additional expenses have been incurred but are not eligible for claim, they could be claimed by you or others under the medical expense rules.

[¶1036.30] *Attendant Care and Disability Credit*

Attendant care expenses not claimed as a deduction under these rules may be available as medical expenses under any one of several different rules in ¶1207. Note, however, that certain of those claims are incompatible with the disability credit in ¶1255. A claim for attendant care deduction under the rules here is not incompatible with the ¶1255 disability claim. However, where there are excess attendant care expenses to be claimed as well, you must exercise caution if you want to claim (or allow someone else to claim) those expenses as well as the disability credit. The rules are explained in ¶1255.

[¶1036.35] *Non-Residents (Care outside Canada)*

In general, the deduction for attendant care under these rules is available only for attendant care provided in Canada. However, if you are a deemed resident of Canada (¶117) or otherwise absent from Canada for a period during which you are considered a resident for tax purposes, this restriction does not apply. It would appear that if you are a non-resident paying tax in Canada (for example an employee living in the U.S. and commuting to work in Canada), you can make the claim only for attendant care in Canada.

[¶1036.40] *Income Limitations*

The amount you may deduct in a particular year under these rules cannot exceed the total of:

(1) your earned income for the year, consisting of:

(a) net income from a business carried on alone or as a partner actively engaged in the business;

(b) gross employment income (i.e., all amounts included as income described in Chapter 3; usually this is box 14 from your T4 slip, but could include other (line 104) items as well; employment income is not reduced by related deductions but does not include employer-paid transportation or attendant care allowances for the disabled which are not included in employment income per ¶361d);

(c) net research grants (¶961);

(d) the taxable amount of scholarships, fellowships, bursaries and similar awards (apparently this is also gross income, reduced by the exemption but not by award repayments; see ¶953–¶959); and

(e) earnings supplements under a government program to encourage individuals to find or keep employment, and financial assistance (usually related to training programs and not including ordinary EI payments) under the *Employment Insurance Act* and similar provincial programs, and amounts received under the *Wage Earner Protection Program Act.*

Plus

(2) if you were in attendance at either a designated educational institution (as defined in ¶1337 for purposes of the education amount; although the education credit is repealed as of January 1, 2017, a revised definition remains in effect) or a secondary (high) school, at which you were enrolled in an education program, the least of (A) $15,000, (B) $375 times the number of weeks you were in attendance at the institution or school, and (C) your earned income under (a), above (see computation given in form T929).

[¶1036.45] *Receipts*

You are required to have evidence of the payments claimed in the form of receipts issued by the payee. If the payments were made to an individual providing attendant care, under the last item above, the receipt must include that individual's social insurance number. There is an exception if you are technically resident in Canada for tax purposes but temporarily absent; as described under the subheading "Non-Residents (Care outside Canada)". In these circumstances amounts paid to a non-resident attendant are excused from the requirement to provide a social insurance number. Restrictions as to the age and non-family status of the attendant continue to apply.

The law says that the receipts must be filed with your return, but the CRA has the authority to dispense with this requirement, and for other medical expenses usually does so. Only the T1 Guide and the claim form (T929) can tell you whether to file receipts; neither was available as this was written. Regardless of whether you are required to file the receipts, you must keep them on hand for several years in case the CRA decides to review your claim. Unreceipted expenses can be denied out of hand.

(ITA: 64; 64.1)

MOVING EXPENSES

[¶1039] WHO MAY DEDUCT MOVING EXPENSES?

If you move to a new location, you may be eligible to deduct your moving expenses from income earned at the new location. The deduction is claimed on line 219 of the T1 return.

The general rule is that you may deduct moving expenses from your income if:

(1) You move your residence in order to earn salary, wages, or self-employment income in a new location in Canada, even if you will be working for the same employer (see also ¶1039.05 below where the "in Canada" requirement is waived);

(2) Your move results in your new residence being at least 40 kilometres closer than your former residence to your new place of work or business (via the shortest normal route open to the travelling public);

(3) You ordinarily resided in the former home before the move and you ordinarily resided in the new home after the move; and

(4) You cease your business or employment at the former location.

Moving expense deductions may also be claimed by individuals who were unemployed immediately before moving to a new employment or business for relocations within Canada.

Students, under certain circumstances, may also claim moving expenses. See ¶1047.

The CRA's policies on moving expenses are set out in Income Tax Folio S1-F3-C4, "Moving Expenses" (they were formerly set out in Interpretation Bulletin IT-178R3 (consolidated), "Moving Expenses". The Folio is effective as of April 5, 2016, while the former Interpretation Bulletin was effective prior to that date. The CRA also summarizes its policies on several pages of notes included as part of the T1-M form for claiming moving expenses. Both should be available from the CRA website. Since the T1-M form is updated regularly, its notes are more current than the more extensive comments in the Interpretation Bulletin.

In *Giannakopoulos v. The Queen*, 95 DTC 5477 (F.C.A.), the Federal Court of Appeal set aside the CRA's administrative policy that in determining whether the taxpayer had moved 40 kilometres closer to its place of work, the distance from each place to the worksite had to be measured in a straight line. The Court ruled that the distance should be measured by the shortest normal route open to the travelling public. The CRA has accepted the new requirement, as indicated by their comments on form T1-M and in Interpretation Bulletin IT-178R3, paragraph 1.

Where you include the costs of using your personal automobile for travel related to moving, the CRA now gives you two options. The traditional method of costing the use of a car is to keep full records of automobile expenditures and then prorate the costs of deductible mileage over total mileage for the year. This is always acceptable, and is required if you deduct mileage for business or employment use. However, if you do not keep such records, the CRA is prepared to accept a record of mileage associated with the move and allow you a per kilometre deduction. The table of applicable per kilometre rates under this option is shown at ¶87 preceding Chapter 1. Similarly, the CRA is prepared to accept meal deductions at a flat rate (it has been $17 per meal to a maximum of $51 per day; the 2016 rate will be posted on the CRA website in early 2017) without supporting receipts; actual "reasonable" costs may be claimed if supported by receipts. See ¶87.

[¶1039.05] *"In Canada" Requirement*

A taxpayer who is, throughout all or part of a year, absent from Canada but resident in Canada for tax purposes is not subject to any of the "in Canada" requirements above. A move to and/or from a foreign location will qualify, and the new income location need not be in Canada. Taxpayers absent from but resident in Canada include both factual residents who may live abroad but are not considered to have severed ties with Canada as discussed in ¶115, and deemed residents as defined in ¶117.

(ITA: 62(1); 64.1(*a*); 248(1) "eligible relocation"; Income Tax Folio: S1-F3-C4 Moving Expenses)

[¶1041] WHAT EXPENSES ARE DEDUCTIBLE?

Moving expenses are limited to reasonable amounts paid for moving yourself, members of your household and your household effects from your old to your new residence.

Travelling costs from your former to your new residence are eligible. These include meals and lodging for yourself and your family while en route. Transportation and storage costs for moving your household effects from your former house to your new residence are also eligible. These would include packing, hauling, in-transit storage and insurance. If you stayed in temporary quarters, the cost of up to 15 days temporary board and lodging near your former or your new residence is eligible. When claiming your meal and travel expenses, you can either claim your actual expenses or use the "simplified method" described above at ¶1039.

Any costs that you have incurred for cancelling an unexpired lease on your former residence, not including any rental payments for a period during which you occupied the residence, are eligible as a moving expense.

The costs of selling a former residence, including advertising, notarial or legal fees, real estate commissions and a mortgage penalty incurred because the mortgage was paid off before maturity are eligible. The cost of selling your former residence will not include expenses for any work done to make the property more saleable, or a loss incurred on the sale of your former residence. As stated in Income Tax Folio S1-F3-C4, "Moving Expenses" (paragraph 4.26), the CRA allows individuals to deduct of the costs of selling the former residence

> . . .even if they did not take immediate action to sell the residence, due to specific circumstances. However, individuals must be able to explain the reasons for the delay and demonstrate that the costs were actually incurred because of the move. On the other hand, the selling costs of the old residence are not eligible if it is determined that the individual intended to keep the old residence as an investment or until its market value increased. In general, the more time that passes between the move and the sale of the old residence, the less likely it is that the selling costs were incurred because of the move.

In a recent technical interpretation (CRA Document No. 2014-0527271E5, August 14, 2014), the CRA expressed the view that rental payments required to be made under a lease at the taxpayer's former residence until the end of the lease term (but after the taxpayer's move) were not lease cancellation payments because they did not have the effect of terminating the lease. As such, they did not qualify as eligible moving expenses.

Interestingly, in a recent Tax Court decision under its informal procedure (which unfortunately has no precedential value), the Court interpreted the 15-day restriction noted above regarding food and lodging as not applying to lodging when considered by itself. As such, the taxpayer in that case was allowed to deduct rental costs covering more than 15 days in the city in which his new work began; see *Sirivar v. The Queen*, 2014 DTC 1052 (T.C.C.). However, the CRA has not explicitly approved of this decision.

If you or your spouse or common-law partner have sold your old residence, you may also deduct the cost of any taxes other than a goods and services tax or any other value added tax (VAT) on transfer or registration of title to a new residence, together with legal fees associated with the purchase of the new residence. Apparently, the reference to any value-added tax is intended to ensure that you also cannot deduct Quebec sales tax (TVQ), in place as a value-added tax since 1992, nor any HST (harmonized sales tax) imposed by certain provinces. The exclusion would also seem, quite by accident, to pick up any of the European or other value-added taxes imposed by many other countries.

The following expenses also qualify for deduction:

- if you and your family have moved out of your old residence (so that it is no longer "ordinarily occupied" by you or anyone else who ordinarily resided with you at the old residence immediately before the move) and you have not rented it out, and are making reasonable efforts to sell it, you may deduct expenses incurred on the old residence for the period for which those conditions are met for interest, property taxes, insurance premiums, heating and utilities to a maximum of $5,000; and
- the cost of revising legal documents to reflect your new address, of replacing driver's licences and non-commercial vehicle permits (but no deduction is allowed for vehicle insurance costs), and of connecting or disconnecting utilities.

In circumstances where title registration on sale of the former home was delayed, the taxpayer was obliged to obtain bridge financing for the new home and received interest income for the interim, in which funds from sale of the old home were delayed. In a technical opinion, the CRA ruled (in CRA Document No. 9907486) that the interest received was indeed taxable, but the bridge financing interest paid was not deductible, since it was a financing expense of the new home and not the old one. Moreover, there was no basis on which to reduce the taxable interest received by the non-taxable interest paid, since the bridge financing on its face was not laid out to earn income.

No deduction is allowed as a moving expense for losses incurred as the result of damage to household possessions during a move, according to a case decided by the Federal Court of Appeal.

(ITA: 62(3); CRA Document No.: Moving Expenses — GST on New Home Purchase, *December 2, 1993*, CRA Document No. 9313197; *Rath v. The Queen*, 82 DTC 6175 (F.C.A.))

[¶1043] WHEN ARE MOVING EXPENSES DEDUCTIBLE?

The CRA says, in former Interpretation Bulletin IT-178R3, that moving expenses paid must first be deducted in the year of the move from income at the new location, and may be deducted only to the extent of income earned at the new location (this now includes any amounts received under the *Wage Earner Protection Program Act* (WEPP) at the new location). However, if your moving expenses were greater than income earned at the new location in that year, the difference may be carried forward and deducted from such income in the following years. Income earned at the new work location includes both income from employment and from carrying on business, and may include income from more than one employment or business at the new location.

In Income Tax Folio S1-F3-C4, "Moving Expenses", the CRA further provides that an individual may not deduct moving expenses until they are paid. For example, where an individual moves and incurs a moving truck expense in year 1, but does not pay the invoice for the moving truck expense until year 2, the earliest that the moving expense could be deducted is in year 2. Similarly, an individual may not deduct moving expenses paid in a year until the eligible relocation has occurred. For example, where an individual pre-pays a one-way airfare in year 1 in respect of an eligible relocation that does not occur until year 2, the earliest that the airfare expense may be deducted is in year 2.

Some expenses may be paid in a year after your move. In this regard, the information sheet that forms part of form T1-M, on which moving expenses are claimed, says:

> If. . .your moving expenses were paid in a year after the year of your move, you now may be able to claim them on your return for the year you paid them against income earned in the new location. Any unused amounts may be carried forward and deducted only against income earned at the new location in the following years. . .This may apply if your old residence did not sell until after the year of your move. If this is the case, we may ask you to submit this form with the receipts and explain the delay in selling your home.

You are not required to move in the year you commence work at a new location. The CRA takes the view that moving expenses may be claimed provided you commence your new employment (or education) within a reasonable period of time either before or after the move. In *Beyette v. M.N.R.*, 89 DTC 701 (T.C.C.), the taxpayer was permitted to deduct expenses for a move 40 kilometres closer to a place of work even though the work had commenced five years before the move. The taxpayer introduced evidence to show that he had always intended to make the move, but had put it off due to a poor housing market, lack of equity, high interest rates and health problems. The Court noted that there was no time limit imposed in the law, and ruled that as long as the basic conditions of the law were met, the CRA could not impose a "reasonable" time limit on the move. The CRA more or less accepted the *Beyette* decision in a technical opinion (CRA Document No. 9905726), although it did stress that there must be some nexus between the new work location and the decision to move, so that it would still require an explanation in cases of inordinate delay. The statute would seem to support this position. See also *Beaudion v. The Queen*, 2005 DTC 282 (TCC), which followed the reasoning in the *Beyette* case and allowed a taxpayer to deduct moving expenses incurred in a move that occurred seven years after his employer relocated to a new location (the taxpayer had commuted to the new work location up until the time of his move).

The CRA asks you to compute your claim for moving expenses on form T1-M, which should ensure that you pick up the relevant items and calculate the claim correctly. You are asked not to file form T1-M with your tax return, but rather to keep it on hand together with supporting receipts or other documentation of all eligible expenses should the CRA ask you to verify your claim. For example, you should keep a record of and receipts for gasoline expenses if you use your own automobile when moving. The CRA does not specify a period through which the form and receipts should be kept. Three years from the date of notice of assessment of the return on which the claim is made is a reasonable minimum; longer if the statutory reassessment period (¶268) is kept open for some reason. Form T1-M can be obtained from the CRA website.

(ITA: 62(1), (3); 248(1) "eligible relocation")

[¶1045] ADDITIONAL RULES INCLUDING PAYMENTS BY EMPLOYER

No moving expense that is paid by your employer may be claimed as a deduction.

Where an employer gives the employee a non-accountable allowance for moving or pays or reimburses an employee for only part of the moving expenses, the employee may deduct all eligible moving expenses but must include the employer's payments in income, whether or not they are paid to the employee directly.

Example

Robert Simpson moved from Halifax to Toronto in Year 1, in order to secure a new job. He incurred moving expenses of $1,000. His earnings from employment for Year 1 were $5,400 from his old job and $600 from the new one.

Robert is entitled to deduct $600 of his moving expenses from his earned income in Year 1 and can carry the remaining $400 forward and deduct it from his earned income in Year 2.

If Robert had moved to Toronto to work for the same employer, and his employer had paid him an allowance of $800 of his moving expenses, he would then be entitled to deduct the $1,000 of moving expenses from his Year 1 income as the income from his new employment is greater ($1,400 consisting of $600 in earnings and $800 of allowance). Where the employer reimbursed all moving expenses, there is of course no claim under this provision, and no income inclusion except to the extent required by ¶356.

Alternatively, if an individual does not include the amount of a partial reimbursement or allowance, it is the CRA's practice to allow the individual to deduct the amount of the expenses in excess of the allowances or reimbursements (paragraph 4.13, Income Tax Folio S1-F3-C4.

No moving expense deductions will be allowed for moves into or out of Canada, except for certain students (¶1047) and for taxpayers who are absent from Canada but are nevertheless considered factual or deemed residents of Canada under the rules in ¶115 to ¶117.

[¶1045.05] *Reimbursements by Employer*

Where an employer pays or reimburses an employee for reasonable moving expenses which are not eligible for the moving expense deduction, the CRA has always taken the view that the reimbursement is normally not a taxable benefit.

However, if the employer reimburses an employee for the loss on the sale of the employee's house incurred in the course of the move, specific rules under the Act apply. Basically, for moves that bring the employee at least 40 kilometres closer to the new work location, the first $15,000 of the reimbursement is tax-free while $1/2$ of any excess is taxable. For other moves, the entire reimbursement is taxable. These rules are discussed in detail at ¶356.

(ITA: 6(20); 62(1); T4130 Employer's Guide — Taxable Benefits and Allowances; Income Tax Folio: S1-F3-C4 Moving Expenses)

[¶1046] LOW-INTEREST LOANS

Employees who received a low-interest loan from an employer when relocating to a new work location can exclude deemed interest on up to $25,000 of the loan from the deemed interest rules. See ¶353.05.

(ITA: 110(1)(*j*); 248(1) "home relocation loan ")

[¶1047] SPECIAL RULES FOR STUDENTS

If you have been in full-time attendance at a university or other post-secondary educational institution in Canada, and you move within Canada to take a job, including summer employment or to start a business, you may claim a moving expense deduction under the same general rules as those for persons who have been earning income. In other words, the moving expenses can be deducted against such employment or business income.

However, if you move to attend full-time courses at a university or other post-secondary educational institution in Canada and not to work or carry on business, you may deduct moving expenses only against scholarships, fellowships, research grants, and similar awards that are included in your income. Most scholarships and fellowships are now tax-exempt (see ¶953), meaning that the moving expense deduction for many students is limited.

Students leaving Canada to study full-time at a post-secondary educational institution abroad are also entitled to deduct moving expenses from scholarships, fellowships, research grants, and similar awards, but only to the extent that these amounts are included in income. Similar rules apply to foreign students coming into Canada to study at a post-secondary educational institution.

In all cases, moving expenses of a student may only be deducted if the move results in the student residing at least 40 kilometres closer to the educational institution.

The CRA considers a student registered in a particular session in courses of a program at an educational institution to be in full-time attendance if the number of those courses is at least 60% of the number of courses which is the normal course load for the program in that session.

(ITA: 62(2); 248(1) "eligible relocation"; Income Tax Folio: S1-F3-C4 Moving Expenses)

CHILD CARE EXPENSES

[¶1048] CASE LAW AND CHILD CARE EXPENSES

In general, the expenses of child care are considered a personal or living expense, and may not be deducted from income except in strict compliance with the rules at ¶1049 *et seq.*, below. Two court cases for a time cast doubt on important aspects of the basic rules, but in both cases the CRA prevailed, in one case by amending the law, and in the other through appeals through higher courts. In a third line of cases, however, the taxpayer has so far prevailed; see "Expenses Incurred during Maternity Leave" immediately below.

[¶1048.05] *Expenses Incurred during Maternity Leave*

In one line of cases, the Tax Court has ruled that particular circumstances may justify a claim for child care expenses incurred to enable the taxpayer to execute or perform a particular job but not necessarily only during a period of actual performance of the job. For example, in *McLelan v. The Queen*, 95 DTC 856 (T.C.C.), the taxpayer had taken maternity leave combined with annual leave, and returned to work on October 11. However, she hired a nanny on August 1. She was permitted to deduct child care expenses for the period August 1 to October 10 as well as later expenses. The Court noted several unusual circumstances. The taxpayer had signed an agreement that she would return to work for at least six months as a condition for receiving maternity allowance. For health reasons, she had deferred the original return date by taking additional leave entitlement. The taxpayer lived in a remote suburb and when the opportunity to hire a suitable nanny arose, she took it rather than risk not finding one at a later date. In *McCluskie v. The Queen*, 94 DTC 1735 (T.C.C.), a taxpayer similarly hired a baby sitter a month or more before returning to work. There the Court held that a week of orientation before returning to work would have been sufficient, and allowed expenses for that period in addition to the actual period of job performance. In *D'Amours v. M.N.R.*, 90 DTC 1827 (T.C.C.), the taxpayer was allowed a deduction for a four-month period during which a more-or-less permanent sitter was kept on while the taxpayer was on maternity leave. The reason was to keep the services of the sitter, who was accustomed to attending to three previous children. The Court noted in this case that the taxpayer continued to receive employment income (the employer making up the difference between UI benefits and normal salary). The trend of these cases is clear in maternity leave cases where the taxpayer can show cause why payments were made during a period of leave. The CRA originally appealed the *D'Amours* case to the Federal Court–Trial Division, indicating at a minimum that it was dissatisfied with some aspects of this line of cases, but the appeal appears to have been dropped without a hearing.

[¶1049] CHILD CARE EXPENSES

The cost of caring for children will be allowed as a deduction for tax purposes from the income of a working parent. Generally speaking, the effect of the child care provision is to allow a deduction for child care expenses to the supporting individual with the lower income, within certain limitations.

A claim for child care expenses should be made on form T778 and carried to line 214 of your T1 tax return. Form T778 is available from Tax Services Offices; you can also obtain with it the Child Care Expenses Information Sheet (also designated T778) published by the CRA. The T778 form is also sent to taxpayers with their personalized tax return packages where government computers identify them as likely to file this claim based on prior year's returns.

The CRA discusses the child care expense deductions in Income Tax Folio S1-F3-C1. The CRA's Child Care Expenses Information Sheet is published annually and may be a more reliable summary of the CRA's views on the current rules.

(ITA: 63(1); S1-F3-C1 Child Care Expense Deduction)

[¶1050] WHO IS AN ELIGIBLE CHILD?

An eligible child of a taxpayer includes:

(1) a child (as defined at ¶1122.15) of the taxpayer or the taxpayer's spouse (including common-law spouse or partner as discussed at ¶1113), and

(2) any child who was, in fact, dependent (¶1122) on the taxpayer or the taxpayer's spouse (including common-law spouse or partner as discussed at ¶1113) at some time during the year, and whose income for the year did not exceed the amount of the basic personal credit amount on line 300 of the T1 return. See the basic personal amount in the table at ¶65 preceding Chapter 1),

if at any time in the year the child was under 16 years old or, if over 16, was dependent on the taxpayer or the taxpayer's spouse or common-law partner and had a physical or mental infirmity (¶1122.40). A child will be under 16 at some time in the year even if its birthday is January 1st.

It is not required that an eligible child be in the custody of the person claiming the child care deduction. Child care expenses qualify for a deduction by a taxpayer in any case where the expenses relate to an eligible child.

(ITA: 63(3) "eligible child")

[¶1051] WHAT EXPENSES ARE DEDUCTIBLE?

The CRA's policy is that child care expenses include payments to:

- an eligible person (see below) providing child care services;
- a day nursery school or day-care centre;
- a day camp or sports school;
- a boarding school or camp (including a sports school where lodging is involved); and
- an educational institution *for the purpose of providing child care services*. Where the institution offers child care as well as an educational program, only that portion of the fees relating to child care qualify. This would include such things as supervision before and after class or during lunch. However, when the payment is made for a child under compulsory school age, it is generally considered to be for child care rather than education "unless the facts indicate otherwise".

As might be expected, the last item in the list causes the most difficulty. Clearly what the CRA has in mind is that the costs of private school education, as such, cannot be deducted under this provision, but the programs of private or public schools to care for children outside of normal school hours should qualify. The resulting contortions are well illustrated in a technical opinion (CRA Document No. 9830065) which says that a school's sports training program for gifted athletes outside school hours is probably training and not child care, depending on the facts.

This difficulty is extended to camp situations in CRA Document No. 2004-0086251E5. Camps are ordinarily qualified, but there would come a point of specialized expert training where the expense would be considered educational rather than child care.

In *Bailey v. The Queen*, 2005 DTC 673 (T.C.C.), a parent was allowed to claim the child care expense deduction for the full fees for her daughter in grade primary. The child was by a few days too young to be enrolled in the provincial school system, and the parent had a choice of returning her to a day care facility or enrolling her in grade primary in a private school, where, as it happened, the fees were actually less and care was provided from 7:30 a.m. to 5:00 p.m., although grade primary education was provided within that period. The governing consideration was whether the parent's intent was to pay the fees "for" child care, and that was clearly the case here. The case was heard under informal procedure, and so in theory has no precedent value. In the circumstances, the CRA may accept it as confined to the particular grade primary fact situation. It is doubtful that the CRA, or Finance if the CRA cannot hold the line, will permit a major expansion of the child care deduction for private education. In *Chan v. The Queen*, 2005 DTC 624 (T.C.C.), the Court had no hesitation in dismissing a child care expense deduction claimed by a parent who sent a child to a expensive private school in lieu of a local day care facility.

Board and lodging expenses are only included as child care expenses to the extent they are included in total charges for attendance at an overnight sports school or a boarding school or camp, and then only to a maximum of one-fortieth per week of the basic amounts at ¶1053. For 2015 and subsequent years, this works out to:

(1) $200 per week per eligible child under seven at the end of the year, other than a child claimed in (3); plus

(2) $125 per week per eligible child for children over six but not yet 17 at the end of the year, other than a child claimed in (3); plus

(3) $275 per week per eligible child not yet 17 at the end of the year for whom anyone is entitled to claim disability credit described at ¶1255. That credit requires certification of disability on form T2201; see ¶1209.

However, the cost of meals included in the cost of babysitting, day nursery or day camp is permitted.

Subject to the limitations below, expenses for advertising and placement agency fees incurred to locate a child care provider should qualify as child care expenses.

[¶1051.05] *Purposes for Which Child Care Expenses Must be Incurred*

To be deductible, the expenses must have been incurred to either the taxpayer, or the "supporting person" with respect to the child for the year, who resided with the child at the time the expense was incurred, to be employed, to carry on a business, to carry on research or similar work for which a grant was received, or to attend a secondary school or designated educational institution. A designated educational institution is one which would entitle its students to a tuition fee credit; these are described in ¶1323. The educational attendance criterion will be met where you are in attendance at a secondary or designated school and enrolled in a program not less than three consecutive weeks long which requires of all students not less than (i) 10 hours per week of course or program work, or (ii) 12 hours per month on courses in the program.

As to what constitutes secondary education, see ¶1053(3).

A supporting person in respect of an eligible child is a person other than the taxpayer who is a parent of the parent of the child, the spouse or common-law partner of the taxpayer, or a person who claimed a non-refundable credit for the child under the rules in Chapter 11, provided that parent, spouse, etc. resided with the taxpayer at any time during the year *and* at any time within 60 days after the end of the year. The upshot here is that child care expenses must be incurred to allow either you or the supporting person (if any) to engage in an eligible activity. The definition is also used in rules described in ¶1053, and is discussed in greater detail there under the subheading "(2) Separation or Divorce".

[¶1051.10] *Services Must be Provided in Canada (with some exceptions)*

Generally, expenses must be for care in Canada, and are deductible only for the year in which they are paid.

However, if you are absent from Canada for all or part of a year but are nevertheless considered to be a resident of Canada under the rules discussed at ¶115 to ¶117, you may deduct the qualifying amount of child care expenses incurred outside of Canada whether or not paid to a resident of Canada. This rule was expanded in 1989; for 1988 and earlier years only a deemed resident could pay child care expenses to a non-resident.

As well, if you live in Canada near the U.S. border, you can claim expenses of child care provided in the U.S. on the same terms and conditions as if it were provided in Canada, provided the U.S. child care facility is closer to your principal place of residence by a reasonably accessible route than any place in Canada where "such services" are available. The rule cannot be used to claim expenses at a boarding school or camp outside Canada. You do not have to provide Social Insurance Numbers of individuals to whom you pay child care expenses where those expenses are for care outside Canada, although you do have to be able to provide other proof of payments described at ¶1061.

[¶1051.15] *Expenses Not Allowed*

Payments for board and lodging (except as mentioned above), clothing, transportation, education, medical or hospital care are *not* eligible child care deductions. Note, however, that certain medical and disability credits may be available to parents of children under another set of rules (¶1205, ¶1207, ¶1225, and ¶1255) in addition to expenses that may be deducted here.

Child care payments may be made to any person resident in Canada except:

(1) the father or mother of the child;

(2) a person who was under 18 and related (see ¶1122) to you or your spouse or common-law partner; and

(3) a person in respect of whom any dependant deduction (Chapter 11) was claimed by the person deducting the child care expenses or a "supporting person" as defined at ¶1053.

(ITA: 63(3) "child care expense", (4); 64.1; S1-F3-C1 Child Care Expense Deduction)

[¶1051.20] *Quebec Expenses for Federal Purposes*

In a technical opinion, the CRA explains to a Quebec day-care employee issuing receipts for federal tax purposes what child care expenses are deductible. The opinion (in French, CRA Document No. 2005-0114421E5) is summarized in English in Wolters Kluwer *Window on Canadian Tax* 8429 as follows:

> The CRA was asked if certain expenses paid by the parents to the centre would qualify as child care expenses under section 63 of the Act. The CRA provided the following comments:
>
> - The $7 per diem amount charged to Quebec resident taxpayers is not deductible for Quebec purposes but is deductible for federal purposes as long as it meets the conditions of section 63 of the Act.
> - Any extra charge paid by a parent picking up his child after the day-care centre regular

hours is deductible provided it also meets the other conditions of section 63 of the Act.

- Expenses associated with the breach of a child care contract as well as expenses for sunscreen, insect repellent, bibs and mattress covers are deductible under section 63 of the Act.
- Expenses incurred by the parents for various day trips, outings or other recreational activities of their children (either within or outside the day-care centre) are not deductible under section 63 of the Act because the main purpose of the activities is to develop their physical, social and artistic skills not to take care of them to enable the parents to earn some employment income.
- The annual dues paid by the parents participating to the management of the day-care centre and the interest charges imposed for late payments are not eligible child care expenses because they are not paid as such for taking care of the children.

[¶1053] HOW MUCH MAY BE DEDUCTED?

Bill C-59 amended the annual child care expense deduction limits ($1,000 annual increase for each limit). This amendment applies to the 2015 and later taxation years. The information below is updated to reflect the new deduction limits.

(1) Parents Living Together

In typical circumstances, where the child lives with both parents, the child care expense deduction will be available to the parent with the lower income. There is an exception (in addition to those shown just below) where the higher-income parent is enrolled in certain courses; see subheading (3), below.

The lower income spouse may deduct the amount the couple actually spent on child care, provided that it does not exceed the lesser of (a) and (b) below:

(a) the sum of:

(i) $8,000 per eligible child for children who were not seven years old at the end of the year, other than a child claimed in (iii), plus

(ii) $5,000 per eligible child for unimpaired children who were seven years old but not yet 17 years old at the end of the year, other than a child claimed in (iii), plus

(iii) $11,000 per eligible child not yet 17 at the end of the year for whom anyone is entitled to claim disability credit described at ¶1255. That credit requires certification of disability on form T2201; see ¶1209, or

(b) two-thirds of your earned income for the year.

However, the supporting individual with the higher income may claim a deduction based on the number of weeks in the year throughout which the lower-income individual is separated, infirm, confined to a bed or a wheelchair, in prison or in attendance at a secondary school or designated educational institution. The number of weeks is multiplied by the $125, $200 or $275 figures, as the case may be, as noted in ¶1051. Where the lower-income spouse is in part-time attendance at school, the deduction is based on the number of months rather than weeks.

Where the claim of the higher income supporting individual is based on the medical condition of the lower income individual, a medical doctor must certify in writing that the lower income individual was either (i) incapable of caring for children because of mental or physical infirmity and confinement throughout a period of not less than two weeks in the year to bed, to a wheelchair, or as a patient in a hospital, asylum, or similar institution, or (ii) was in the year (and is likely to be for a long, continuous and indefinite period), incapable of caring for children because of that person's mental or physical infirmity. The infirmity test is a different and perhaps less difficult test than the impairment test used for disability claims, as discussed at ¶1209. In an opinion summarized in Wolters Kluwer *Window on Canadian Tax* (8234), the CRA says that a period of two weeks means two consecutive weeks; a period is a continuous and uninterrupted space of time.

A designated educational institution is one which entitles its students to a tuition fee credit; these are described in ¶1323. The educational attendance requirement will be met where the lower-income spouse is in attendance at a secondary or designated school and enrolled in a course not less than three consecutive weeks long which requires of all students not less than 10 hours per week of course or program work.

The deduction limits under the higher income rule are restricted to one-fortieth per week of the basic amounts at ¶1053. This works out to:

(i) $200 per week per eligible child under seven at the end of the year, other than a child claimed in (e), plus

(ii) $125 per week per eligible child for children over 6 but not yet 17 at the end of the year, other than a child claimed in (e), plus

(iii) $275 per week per eligible child not yet 17 at the end of the year for whom anyone is entitled to claim disability credit described at ¶1255. That credit requires certification of disability on form T2201. See ¶1209.

for each week throughout which the higher-income individual was eligible to claim. The lower-income individual's claim is then reduced by the amount of this claim.

Example

Debbie and Randy Sinclair are the parents of three children (none disabled), who are four, six and nine years old. During the year, they paid a day nursery $4,000 to care for one child, and paid babysitting fees of $3,500 for the other two children. Debbie and Randy earned salaries of $55,000 and $21,000 respectively in the year. Randy was confined to a wheelchair for 16 weeks during the year.

Randy can claim child care expenses equal to the least of three factors calculated as follows:

(a) Total spent for child care		$ 7,500
(b) $8,000 per child under 7	$16,000	
(c) plus $5,000 per child 7 and over	5,000	$21,000
Two-thirds of his earned income (two-thirds × $21,000)		$14,000

According to these calculations, Randy's deduction for child care expenses is limited to the least of these factors which is $7,500.

Because Randy was confined to a wheelchair for 16 weeks, the $7,500 deduction may be shared between himself and Debbie. Debbie can claim child care expenses equal to the lesser of two factors calculated as follows:

(a) same calculations as Randy which a deduction of yields		$ 7,500
(b) number of weeks × number of children under 7 × $200 (16 × 2 × $200)	$6,400	
plus number of weeks × number of children 7 and over × $125 (16 × 1 × $125)	2,000	$ 8,400

According to these calculations, Debbie's deduction for child care expenses is limited to the lesser of two factors which is $7,500. If Debbie deducts $7,500, Randy's deduction will be reduced to $0 ($7,500 - $7,500).

Since Debbie's 2016 income in excess of $45,282 will be taxed at a higher rate, it will be beneficial for her to take the maximum possible deduction.

It is not required that an eligible child be in custody of the person claiming the child care deduction. Child care expenses qualify for a deduction by a taxpayer in any case where the expenses relate to an eligible child. An eligible child of a taxpayer includes a child of the taxpayer or his spouse or any child whom the taxpayer claimed as a dependant.

Where the incomes of the parents of an eligible child are equal (as determined at line 234 of the T1, i.e., before social benefit clawback deductions), the Act provides that no child care expense deduction will be allowed to either person in respect of the child unless they jointly elect to treat the income of one of them as exceeding the income of the other for the year. The election can be made by having either one, but not both, claim the deduction.

[¶1053.05] *Part-Time Student With Lower Income*

The higher income spouse or common-law partner may claim, in addition to any weekly amounts the higher income spouse/partner may claim under the rules above, child care expenses for eligible children of $200 per child under seven at the end of the year (and not disabled) plus $125 per child over six but under 17 (not disabled) plus $275 for disabled children not yet 17 for each *month* the other spouse/partner is a student in attendance at a designated educational institution (as described above) or secondary school and enrolled in a program of not less than three consecutive weeks duration and that requires not less than 12 hours in the month on courses in the program. This monthly amount is not available for any month that includes any days included in a weekly calculation by the higher income spouse as described above.

(2) Separation or Divorce

Complexities arise where the parents of an eligible child have separated or divorced. A taxpayer may claim any child care deduction only for an "eligible child" (¶1049) — essentially a child not yet 17 at the end of the year, of his own or his spouse or for whom he can claim a personal exemption (e.g., a grandchild, nephew or niece). In complex situations, one must also look to the definition of "supporting person" to see who is entitled to what deduction.

A "supporting person" of an eligible child of a taxpayer for a taxation year means a person (other than the taxpayer) who is:

(1) a parent of the child;

(2) the taxpayer's spouse or common-law partner (as defined at ¶1113); or

(3) any other individual who claimed the child as a dependant under section 118 (Chapter 11, ¶1120, ¶1124, and ¶1126) for the year

if the parent, spouse or other individual, as the case may be, resided with the taxpayer at any time during the year and at any time within 60 days after the end of the year.

The definition of spouse for purposes of the child care expense deduction includes common-law relationships, as defined at ¶1113.

The taxpayer with the higher income is permitted to claim child care expenses during the period that the supporting person with the lower income is living separate and apart from the taxpayer with the higher income by reason of breakdown of the marriage (or similar domestic relationship) provided that:

(1) the breakdown is for a period of at least 90 days commencing in the year;

(2) the parties were living separate and apart at the end of the year; and

(3) the taxpayer with the higher income for the year has paid those child care expenses.

Where there is separation (and no other marital or common-law relationship) throughout the year, there is no "supporting person" by definition and the payer of child care expenses may claim them for an "eligible child" provided all the general requirements are met. The limitations will be the $8,000/$5,000/$11,000/$^2/_3$ of income limitations. Where there is no supporting person, the definition of "child care expense", which provides that it must be an expense incurred "to enable the taxpayer, or the supporting person of the child for the year, who resided with the child at the time the expense was incurred . . ." to carry out the activities detailed under the subheading "Purposes for Which Child Care Expenses Must be Incurred" in ¶1051 (e.g., to be employed, carry on business, etc.). It follows that where there is no supporting person, the taxpayer may deduct only those expenses that relate to a period where the taxpayer and the child reside together.

The CRA takes the position, in CRA Document Nos. 9928395 and 2000-0048145, as well as in Interpretation Bulletin IT-495R3, para. 18, that in cases of separation or divorce throughout the year, only the custodial parent can claim child care expenses. Where there is joint custody, i.e., the child lives with each parent for a period of the year, the parent paying the expenses for the relevant period can claim them for that period (CRA Document No. 2003-0018815), providing of course all other criteria are met.

Where there is a reconciliation in effect at the end of the year, the general rules for couples living together apply, and no claim can be made by the higher-income partner based on the period of separation. Claims must be made by the parents living together rules above.

Where separation occurs in the year, the higher-income partner may claim the deductions based on $200/$125/$275 general limits for the period of separation to the extent actually paid by the higher-income partner. The lower-income partner may deduct amounts paid by the lower-income partner.

(3) Parent Enrolled in Education

You can deduct child care expenses in respect of periods during which you are a qualifying student and are either:

- the sole supporting person of an eligible child; or
- if there is another supporting person, you are the supporting person with the higher income for the year.

If you are a student eligible to make a claim under this rule for part of the year and employed or earning business income for part of the year, you can add this claim to your general claim under (1) or (2), above, subject to the limitations below. In general, the limitations below ensure that your total child care expense claims will not exceed the overall $8,000/$5,000/$11,000/²/₃ of income limitations described in (1), above.

To be a qualifying student you must be a student in attendance at a secondary school or designated educational institution. A designated educational institution is one which would entitle its students to a tuition fee credit; these are described in ¶1323. The educational attendance requirement will be met where you were in attendance at a secondary or designated school and enrolled in a course no less than three consecutive weeks long which requires of all students no less than:

(1) 10 hours per week of course or program work; or

(2) for 1998 and later years, 12 hours per month on courses in the program.

One might have thought, since the government has gone to great lengths to define designated post-secondary education in ¶1323, it would have addressed what constitutes secondary education. This has not been done. Clearly, a high school is a secondary school. In some parts of the country, high school includes grades 9–12; elsewhere there are "junior high" or "intermediate" schools covering grades 7–9 and high school includes grades 10–12. Neither the CRA nor the Department of Finance have addressed the inconsistencies or the status of junior high schools.

The overall limits are essentially the same as the $200/$125/$275 per week limits in (1), above, and are constructed so that the overall $8,000/$5,000/$11,000/²/₃ of income limits cannot be exceeded. Thus, the maximum deduction under this rule is the least of:

(a) actual qualifying child care expenses (¶1051) minus deductions claimed under (1) or (2), above;

(b) two-thirds of your actual net income (not earned income) for the year before deductions for clawback tax and child care expense itself; that is, net income from line 239 of your T1 return plus amounts already deducted on page 2 of the return at lines 214 and 235;

(c) one-fortieth of the basic $8,000/$5,000/$11,000 per year amounts, which is to say:

(i) $200 per week per eligible child under seven at the end of the year, other than a child claimed in (c)(iii), plus

(ii) $125 per week per eligible child for children over six but not yet 17 at the end of the year, other than a child claimed in (c)(iii), plus

(iii) $275 per week per eligible child of any age for whom anyone is entitled to claim disability credit described at ¶1255. That credit requires certification of disability on form T2201. See ¶1209.

with (c)(i), (ii), and (iii) multiplied by (A) where there is a another supporting person, the number of weeks in the year in which both you (as the claimant) and the other supporting person were students meeting the 12 hour per month but not 10 hour per week criterion above, or (B) where there is no other supporting person, the number of weeks in the year in which you were a student meeting the 12 hour per month but not 10 hour per week criterion above;

(d) any amount remaining after the amounts claimed by you under subheadings (1) or (2), above, are deducted from the maximum claim permitted under the $8,000/$5,000/$11,000/²/₃ of earned income tests in (1)(a) and (b), above; and

(e) where there is another (lower-income) supporting person of an eligible child, the amount by which the claims made by you for that supporting person under subheadings (1) or (2), above, in respect of periods during which the supporting person was ill, in school, etc., exceed two thirds of your earned income.

Since net income in (b), above, will include a number of deductions, two-thirds of it may well be less than two-thirds of earned income which is one of the limits in (e). Why this additional limitation is important for students but not employees or business income earners is less than transparent.

These rules seem to yield some odd results. Where the other supporting person is working regularly but the student nevertheless has the higher income for the year, the deduction will seemingly stay with the lower-income spouse by virtue of the multiplier in (c) or (d), above.

(4) *Claiming Less Than the Full Amount*

You may claim less than the full amount you are entitled to if this should be beneficial. Usually you would want to make the entire claim, but there might be cases, perhaps involving alternative minimum tax (Chapter 24), where a partial claim would be preferable. There is no carryover of amounts not claimed for a year.

(ITA: 63(1)–(3); 118.6(1); S1-F3-C1 Child Care Expense Deduction)

[¶1055] WHAT IS EARNED INCOME?

For purposes of calculating the child care expense deduction, your earned income includes:

- salary, wages, tips (reported as income) and taxable benefits from an office or employment;
- income from all businesses carried on either alone or as a partner actively engaged in the business;
- exempt income of volunteer firefighters, ambulance technicians and other emergency personnel, as discussed at ¶338;
- amounts allocated under an employees' profit sharing-plan;
- benefits received under a stock option plan;
- disability pension amounts received under the *Canada Pension Plan* or *Quebec Pension Plan*;
- research grants (net of deductions) and the taxable portions of awards such as scholarships, fellowships, bursaries or prizes (¶953 *et seq.*; also ¶971);
- disability pension amounts received under the Canada or Quebec Pension Plan; other disability payments may be or may not be included in income, depending on whether they are taxable as employment income; see ¶328;
- amounts received as social assistance under a project sponsored by the government of Canada under which the only benefits paid are intended to supplement individual's income from employment (¶975);

- taxable earnings supplements received under programs sponsored under Part II of the *Employment Insurance Act* or similar programs;
- training allowances paid under the *National Training Act* (which expired after 1997; see ¶971);
- apprenticeship grants received in the year under the federal Apprenticeship Incentive Grant program, instituted in 2006; and
- amounts received in the year under the *Wage Earner Protection Program Act* (WEPP) (subparagraph 56(1)(*r*)(v)) for 2008 and subsequent years.

Although the above list is quite inclusive, there are items not included, such as the universal child care benefit (UCCB) introduced in 2006.

(ITA: 6(1)(*g*); 7(1.1); 56(1)(*r*); 63(3) "earned income")

[¶1061] RECEIPTS REQUIRED

To be allowed deductions for child care expenses, you must support these expenses with receipts. Each receipt must include the following information:

(1) The name, address and Social Insurance Number of the person to whom the taxpayer made payments for child care. (The Social Insurance Number is not necessary for organizations such as a day nursery, or where payments are properly paid to non-residents under the exceptions at ¶1051.)

(2) The name of the parent.

(3) The amount paid for child care.

(4) The date of the payment.

(5) The signature of the person who provided the child care services.

The receipts do not have to be filed with your return but should be retained in case, at a later date, the CRA wishes to examine them.

(ITA: 63(1); 220(2.1))

INTEREST DEDUCTIONS

[¶1063] WHEN IS INTEREST DEDUCTIBLE?

Generally, interest is deductible under the following conditions:

(1) it must have been paid or payable in respect of the year pursuant to a legal obligation to pay interest; and

(2) the borrowed money must have been used for the purpose of earning income from a business or property or the interest must have been on an amount payable for property acquired for the purpose of gaining or producing income from the property or from a business.

In certain circumstances, the interest deduction is limited with respect to annuities taxable at three-year intervals on an accrual basis (see ¶432 and ¶908). Subsequent to the year in which the annuity payments commence, a deduction for interest will be limited to the amount included in income. For years prior to the commencement of the annuity payments, and for the year in which the annuity payments commence, the deductibility of interest is not limited.

Interest may be deducted either when it is paid or when it is payable depending on the method regularly followed in computing your income. If you are following the accrual method of keeping your accounts (¶714), you would deduct interest in the year that it was accrued whether or not it had actually been paid during that year.

Taxpayers claiming interest deductions on investment income should list the interest as "carrying charges" on Part III of Schedule 4. Where these amounts are significant, the CRA may require further detail. As noted at ¶445, carrying charges include certain items in addition to interest, although interest is often the main component.

There is a provision in the interest deductibility rules to the effect that if the interest payable is unreasonable in relation to the borrowing, only a reasonable amount in respect of the borrowing is deductible. This is discussed further under the subheading "Tax Planning and Interest Deductibility" (¶1063.10), below.

It may happen that your total carrying charges will exceed your investment income producing a net loss from investments. So long as the carrying charges meet the conditions for deductibility, such a loss is fully deductible from your income from other sources such as salary, wages, or income from a business. You should include in your claim all types of interest. For example, in addition to the normal bank loan interest, you may be paying interest to your broker and this should be claimed as deduction.

Note that where interest exceeds related investment income, the net loss will be deductible against other income but will go into the "cumulative net investment loss (CNIL)" account and reduce the cumulative gains limit for capital gains deduction purposes (¶502). Net investment income, on the other hand, reduces the CNIL limitation. Accordingly, it is necessary to keep a lifetime running record of net investment income and loss, beginning in 1988, in order to ever claim the capital gains deduction. See ¶1071.

No difficulty should be encountered in gaining a deduction for interest on money borrowed in connection with financing an unincorporated business of any kind.

Historical Note:

On October 31, 2003, the Department of Finance announced draft legislation to reverse a series of Supreme Court decisions. The legislation would impose a statutory requirement that, for taxation years commencing in or after 2005, losses from business or property would only be deductible in a year if it is reasonable to expect that the taxpayer will realize a cumulative profit over the period during which he or she may reasonably be expected to carry on the business or hold the property in that year. Profit would not include capital gain or loss. In short, the "reasonable expectation of profit" test would be legislated back into existence. The most common use of this test would deny interest deductions which exceeded the income from the particular source related to the interest. The legislation was said to be deferred to 2005 so that the Department could listen to arguments on the merits of its approach; however, the consultation period went on for several years after which no new legislation passed. Ultimately, the Department withdrew the draft legislation by way of a release date of November 17, 2014 (since it was excluded from the "List of outstanding specific legislative proposals for listed tax laws announced prior to April 1, 2013").

[¶1063.05] *Interest on Non-Capital Borrowings*

In general, the interest deduction provision is viewed as a relieving provision, permitting the taxpayer to deduct interest on money borrowed to make capital investments. In the absence of a specific provision, case law suggests that such borrowings would be on capital account and the related interest would not be deductible.

In this regard, it is a contentious point whether interest on funds borrowed to make a current rather than a capital expenditure are subject to the restrictions above, or can be deducted on the general principle that an expenditure laid out to earn income from business or property is deductible. In *Gifford v. The Queen*, 2001 DTC 168 (T.C.C.), the Tax Court came down fairly clearly on the side of the principle that interest follows the nature of the expenditure for which funds are borrowed and need not always be on capital account. The Federal Court of Appeal reversed the ruling, 2002 DTC 7197 (F.C.A.), holding that it was bound by Supreme Court precedents to take the view that interest is virtually always on capital account and consequently may only be deducted in strict accordance with specific provisions of the *Income Tax Act* permitting an interest deduction. What is interesting is that the Federal Court of Appeal (F.C.A.) virtually invited the Supreme Court to review this issue specifically. The F.C.A. set out its own views that in the absence of binding Canadian precedent it would incline to the view that interest is almost always on income account. For a detailed commentary, see Wolters Kluwer *Tax Topics* 1591 of September 5, 2002. The Supreme Court handed down its judgement in *Gifford* in 2004 (2004 DTC 6120). The Court ruled that: (1) it had not previously determined that an interest payment is always on account of capital; (2) the various interest deductibility provisions of the *Income Tax Act* do not provide a complete code on the deductibility of interest; and (3) under the *Income Tax Act*, if money borrowed adds to financial capital (usually the case) it is on capital account, and can only be deducted in accordance with the strict rules of the Act; however, if loan proceeds constitute inventory of the borrower, as is the case with moneylenders, the interest is on current account and deductible under general principles. Moneylenders apart, this result seems offhand not particularly favourable to taxpayers.

In Interpretation Bulletin IT-533, discussed above and below, the CRA comments (in para. 4) that, notwithstanding the general rule that interest is always on capital account, it recognizes an exception for financing businesses (e.g., money-lending) interest expense for borrowed money that constitutes stock in trade is on income account. It also says (in para. 36) that the deduction of interest expense on amounts payable for service costs will be permitted on income account. This bulletin was replaced on June 3, 2015 by Income Tax Folio S3-F6-C1.

[¶1063.10] *Tax Planning and Interest Deduction*

It is evident that given a choice between borrowing for business or investment use and borrowing for personal expenses, the former is always preferable because the interest is deductible. The question arises as to how far you can go in rearranging existing borrowings to improve your interest deductions. A series of Supreme Court cases in 1999 and 2001 suggested that the Court takes quite a literal view of the statutory requirements, and will reject any argument advanced by the CRA that it should look past the use to which borrowed money is put (or to which it is "directly linked") and view the economic realities of a transaction. This gives great scope to the taxpayer to rearrange borrowings to fit the statutory requirements. The Court has been so definitive in its reading as to suggest to some observers that the government will be moved to undertake a wholesale revision of the interest deduction provisions, laying down much more detailed provisions as to when interest can be deducted. It has failed in a previous attempt, as discussed below in the context of the *Bronfman Trust* case, but may be tempted to revisit the issue. In the meantime, however, the Supreme Court's view gives new scope for tax planning in rearranging borrowings.

The cases referred to are:

In *The Queen v. Shell Canada Limited*, 99 DTC 5669 (S.C.C.), the Court identified the basic requirements for interest deductibility as follows:

(1) the amount must be paid in the year or be payable in the year in which it is sought to be deducted;

(2) the amount must be paid pursuant to a legal obligation to pay interest on borrowed money;

(3) the borrowed money must be used for the purpose of earning non-exempt income from a business or property; and

(4) the amount must be reasonable, as assessed by reference to the first three requirements.

In *Shell*, reasonableness was under attack. The company had, in effect, borrowed New Zealand dollars at 15.4% interest rather than the U.S. dollars it needed at 9%, hedging the transaction so that the difference, more or less, came back to it as capital gain. The Court found that the interest was reasonable, since it was an arm's length borrowing at the going rate for New Zealand dollars. It declined to look beyond the borrowing transaction itself. Note that the general anti-avoidance rule (GAAR) was not at issue in *Shell*. The GAAR issue was raised, however, on facts identical to the *Shell* case, above, in *The Queen v. Canadian Pacific Ltd.*, 2002 DTC 6742 (F.C.A.), aff'g 2000 DTC 2428 (T.C.C.), which was decided in favour of the taxpayer. For GAAR decisions generally, see ¶285. (The government has since responded by legislating against weak currency borrowings; see ¶1064.)

In *Ludco v. The Queen*, 2001 DTC 5518 (S.C.C.), the taxpayer borrowed money to invest in offshore investment companies with the purpose of earning investment income which would not be taxed currently in Canada (unless remitted to Canada) and realizing the eventual profit as capital gain on the disposition of the offshore shares. The offshore companies did in fact pay nominal interest, but the borrowing cost to Ludco far exceeded the dividend income (but not the eventual capital gains, which were substantial). The CRA attacked the interest on the ground that the purpose of the transaction was not to earn income, since it was always intended that the transaction should be underwater as an income flow matter. The Court found, in effect, that income is income. If Parliament had wanted to allow an interest deduction only on profitable transactions, it could have said so. The fact that there was a reasonable expectation of dividend income made the CRA's position untenable.

In *Singleton v. The Queen*, 2001 DTC 5533 (S.C.C.), the taxpayer had $300,000 in a partnership capital account. He withdrew the funds to pay for a house and borrowed money to replace them. The CRA argued that looking at the transaction as a whole, the taxpayer had borrowed to purchase the house, so the funds were not used to earn income. The Supreme Court held that looking at the use to which the borrowed funds were in fact put (i.e., into the partnership) was sufficient to decide the case in favour of the taxpayer. (One interesting commentary on this case suggests that it is not the tracing of funds that is at issue. Rather, it affirms the longstanding decision in *Trans-Prairie Pipelines Ltd. v. M.N.R.*, 70 DTC 6351 (Ex. Ct.), that a taxpayer can replace tax-paid money used in a business with borrowed money used in the business; as such, the decision is unexceptional. It merely places the taxpayer who invests borrowed money on a level with a taxpayer who invests tax-paid money.

These cases taken together suggest that, broadly speaking, where the taxpayer meets the basic words of the statute, interest will be deductible regardless of the circumstances surrounding the transaction as whole. The Supreme Court seems to find the statute clear and unambiguous. The CRA has one more string to its bow: the general anti-avoidance rule (see ¶285), which was not at issue in the transactions above (except for *Canadian Pacific*, as noted). The GAAR issue continues to be litigated, with mixed results; see ¶285.

In the wake of several cases in which the Supreme Court expressed its opinion on the uses of GAAR (see ¶285), the Tax Court ruled in 2006, in *Lipson et al. v. The Queen*, 2006 DTC 2687 (T.C.C.), that a tax plan to render personal mortgage interest deductible violated the clear statutory policy "to permit interest on money borrowed for commercial purposes to be deducted. The corollary is that interest on money borrowed for personal use (such as buying a residence) is not deductible." The Tax Court decision was affirmed by the Federal Court of Appeal (2007 DTC 5172). The Supreme Court heard an appeal from the Federal Court decision on April 23, 2008. In January 2009, the Supreme Court affirmed prior decisions, and the taxpayers' appeal was dismissed (2009 DTC 5015).

As noted at ¶1063 above, on October 31, 2003, the Department of Finance announced draft legislation to reverse the Supreme Court and impose a statutory requirement that *losses* from business or property would only be deductible in a year if it is reasonable to expect in that year that the taxpayer will realize a cumulative profit over the period during which the taxpayer may reasonably be expected to carry on the business or hold the property. Profit would not include capital gain or loss. In short, the reasonable expectation of profit test would be legislated back into existence. Interest would remain deductible to the extent of related profit, but could not be used to create losses in the absence of a reasonable expectation of cumulative profit. The good news was that the legislation was not scheduled to come into effect in 2004, but only for taxation years commencing in or after 2005. In the meantime, the Department was prepared to listen to arguments, most of which were submitted by the Joint Taxation Committee (of the Canadian Bar Association and Canadian Institute of Chartered Accountants) and the Tax Executives Institute. Several years went by without an enactment of the legislation. Finally, the Department withdrew the draft legislation by way of a release date of November 17, 2014 (since it was excluded from the "List of outstanding specific legislative proposals for listed tax laws announced prior to April 1, 2013").

Interpretation Bulletin IT-533, also released October 31, 2003, guided taxpayers trying to live with the current rules; this bulletin was recently replaced by Income Tax Folio S3-F6-C1. In many cases, even if the reasonable expectation of profit test is in fact legislated back into existence, the folio will presumably remain the main guide to administrative policy in regard to the deductibility of interest.

Given that the pending legislation was withdrawn, one must assume that in general terms Finance and the CRA are prepared to live with the other implications of the cases discussed above. Some of the salient points of IT-533 are summarized below. These concepts have generally been carried over to the new Income Tax Folio S3-F6-C1.

Reasonable Interest

In terms of establishing whether or not an amount of interest is reasonable, as required in the post-amble to paragraph 20(1)(*c*), the bulletin states that "consideration will be given to prevailing market rates for debts with similar terms and credit risks, and the existence of any issue premiums". As well, the bulletin quotes from the *Shell* decision (99 DTC 5669 at 5675) to the effect that a rate established between arm's length parties is generally considered to be a reasonable rate.

Use of Borrowed Funds

One of the major stumbling blocks in the deductibility of interest under subparagraph 20(1)(*c*)(i) is the use to which the borrowed money has been put. Paragraphs 1.35 through 1.40 of the Income Tax Folio refer to the *Bronfman Trust* case (87 DTC 5059), the *Singleton* case (2001 DTC 5533), and the *Shell* case (99 DTC 5669), and conclude that with certain exceptions enumerated in paragraphs 22 to 26, the borrowed funds must be used directly for the purpose of earning income from a business or property. In addition, the use of the funds refers to the current use, rather than the original use. It is up to the taxpayer to link the borrowed money to the eligible use.

Restructuring Borrowings

Paragraph 1.33 of the folio says flatly that a taxpayer may restructure borrowings and the ownership of assets to meet the use test.

In paragraph 1.34 of the folio, the CRA describes the practice of "cash damming" as an acceptable method of tracing borrowed funds to eligible uses. This technique requires keeping separate bank accounts to pay amounts for eligible and ineligible uses. Expenditures incurred for the purpose of earning income from a business or property will be paid from an account using borrowed funds while ineligible expenditures will be paid from an account funded by other receipts. This requires accurate and vigilant banking procedures to ensure that only expenditures for eligible uses are paid from the account that contains the funds from borrowed money. There is a technical interpretation (CRA Document No. 2002-0180523, dated May 7, 2003) where the CRA accepted an ongoing cash damming arrangement carried out by a real estate agent.

Paragraphs 1.42 to 1.44 of the folio outline the CRA's acceptance of linking borrowed money in order to establish the use to which it is currently being put. Where both borrowed funds and non-borrowed funds are in one account, the CRA will allow a taxpayer to assign expenditures which were made for eligible uses to the borrowed funds. This becomes difficult in complicated situations where large numbers of transactions with mixed uses of funds are going through one account. The folio sets out a number of examples of linking and tracing of borrowed money, including situations of investments in shares, trust units, and a partnership interest where there is a return of capital.

Under the heading of "Exceptions to the direct use test", paragraphs 1.45 to 1.58 of the folio set out the CRA's acceptance of deducting interest on money that has been borrowed to reduce capital or pay dividends where the borrowed funds replace the capital or retained earnings that were being used for an eligible purpose — the so-called "filling the hole" concept. This type of indirect use, as well as using borrowed money to make interest free loans (described in paragraphs 1.54 to 1.57 of the folio), may result in the interest on the borrowed funds being deductible. In the case of reducing capital, the interest will be deductible where the borrowed money just replaces the contributed capital that would have been used in the carrying out of the business. This also applies to a partner's capital account. With respect to funds borrowed to make an interest-free loan, such as in the case of *Canadian Helicopters* (2002 DTC 6805), interest will be deductible if it can be shown that the interest-free loan will affect the taxpayer's ability to earn income. It is pointed out in paragraph 1.65 of the folio, however, that interest on notes issued to pay dividends or to return capital would not be deductible since no property is acquired in these types of transactions as is required under subparagraph 20(1)(*c*)(ii).

Other Issues

The folio notes other issues surrounding interest deductibility such as: borrowing for investments; loss utilizations within a corporate group; honouring guarantees; discounts or premiums arising on the issuance of debt obligations; and interest on death duties. For interest bearing investments or preferred shares, the CRA will allow interest to be deducted even if the income from the investments does not exceed the interest expense — subject to the proviso expressed in *Ludco* (2001 DTC 5505) that the transaction is "absent a sham or window dressing or similar vitiating circumstances".

Redemption of Shares Acquired with Borrowed Money

In 2007, the CRA issued a number of opinions on this subject.

(1) Where a property acquired with borrowed money is disposed of and a replacement property is acquired, it is the CRA's view that there is a link between the borrowed money and the replacement property. In a situation the CRA was asked to comment on, the taxpayer had borrowed to acquire preferred shares that were redeemed. On the redemption, the taxpayer received an interest-bearing note that was repayable over two years. The taxpayer used the principal repayments on the note for personal use.

It is the CRA's view that:

> [T]he amount of interest deductible on the loan for the year should be calculated as if the monthly principal repayments on the note for the year have reduced the loan balance. This should accurately reflect our view that the interest on the portion of the loan that represents a repayment of principal on the note would not be deductible since the current use is personal and not for an income earning purpose.

(2) In another interpretation concerning a return of capital by a mutual fund, the CRA indicated "if we assume that the ROC by the mutual fund to the investor is not used for an income-earning purpose but is used for personal use, in our view, the interest on that portion of the borrowed money that relates to the return of capital from the mutual fund would not be deductible since its current use is personal and not for an income-earning purpose".

(3) The CRA took a similar view in another interpretation where a taxpayer reinvested income distributions from a mutual fund trust in additional units and then sold an equivalent number of units. Given the fungible nature of mutual funds, it was the CRA's view that the proportional method should be used to determine the number of original mutual fund trust units disposed of.

The following example was provided in the interpretation:

Original cost of borrowing $100,000

Original units purchased (say) 80,000

Income reinvested $3,000

Units acquired on reinvestment (say) 2,400

Units subsequently disposed of 2,400

Under the proportional method, the 2,400 units subsequently disposed of would be allocated between those units purchased originally and those purchased with reinvested income as follows:

80,000 × 2,400 ÷ 82,400 = 2,330 units purchased originally

2,400 × 2,400 ÷ 82,400 = 70 units purchased with reinvested income

Given the above, only 97.09% ((80,000 - 2,330) ÷ 80,000) of the source of income acquired with the original debt remains, whereas 2.91% has been disposed of. Whether or not interest on the entire $100,000 original cost of borrowing remains deductible, depends on the current use of the proceeds from the 2,330 original units disposed of. Where, however, the investor chose to receive the mutual fund distributions in cash, "the fact that the income earned by the mutual fund trust is paid out to the unit holder is not relevant to determining the current use of the borrowed money".

(Window on Canadian Tax: 9185)

[¶1063.15] *New Restriction on Interest Deduction Relating to "10/8 Arrangements"*

In the 2013 federal Budget, the Department of Finance identified this type of arrangement as being unacceptable from a tax policy perspective. As the Department described, the arrangement is generally one as follows:

> In a typical 10/8 arrangement now defined as a "10/8 policy" in subsection 248(1), a taxpayer (usually an individual or a closely-held private corporation) creates an annual tax deduction for interest expense by entering into transactions that result in a circular flow of funds. Specifically:
>
> - the taxpayer invests an amount of money in a life insurance policy;
> - the taxpayer then borrows an equal amount and the borrowing is secured by the policy or an investment account in respect of the policy; and
> - the taxpayer then invests the borrowed amount in income-producing assets (to ensure that interest paid or payable on the borrowed amount is tax-deductible).
>
> Under a 10/8 arrangement, the taxpayer pays interest expense on the borrowed amount and earns interest income on the amount invested in the policy. The interest rate earned by the taxpayer (typically eight per cent) on the amount invested in the policy is equal to the interest rate on the borrowed amount (typically ten per cent) less a fixed spread (typically two percentage points). The taxpayer takes the position that the interest expense on the amount borrowed is deductible while the interest income earned on the amount invested in the policy is not included in income (because the policy is an exempt policy for income tax purposes).

As a result, new rules will provide that the deductibility of interest paid or payable after March 20, 2013 on the borrowing in these arrangements will be denied, to the extent that it relates to a period after 2013. The restriction is found in subsection 20(2.01). Furthermore, the deductibility of a premium that is paid or payable under the policy that relates to a period after 2013 will be denied, as will the increase in the capital dividend account by the amount of the death benefit that becomes payable after 2013 under the policy and that is associated with the borrowing.

[¶1064] INTEREST WHICH IS NOT DEDUCTIBLE

[¶1064.05] *Tax-Deferred Plans*

Interest is not deductible on money borrowed to:

(1) make a payment for an income-averaging annuity contract, unless the contract was acquired pursuant to an agreement in writing entered into before November 13, 1981;

(2) pay a premium under a registered retirement savings plan, or to finance a repayment to an RRSP of an amount withdrawn under the RRSP Home Buyers' Plan (¶2625.05);

(3) make an employee contribution to a registered pension fund, pooled registered pension plan, or deferred profit sharing plan;

(4) make a payment for an annuity whose cost is deductible under the provision allowing a refund of RRSP premiums to be rolled over to an annuity (see ¶903);

(5) make a contribution under a "retirement compensation arrangement" (RCA); see ¶359;

(6) make a contribution to a "net income stabilization account";

(7) make a contribution to the Saskatchewan Pension Plan (see ¶1029);

(8) make a contribution to a registered education savings plan (see ¶2529.05); this rule applies to interest paid in or after 1998, but it would seem to apply in 1998 or later even if the borrowing and contribution were made earlier; this is yet another example of the government's constant chipping away of the principle that legislation should not be retroactive; or

(9) make a contribution to an RDSP or tax-free savings plan.

A 1994 "technical correction" to this rule, effective for 1990 and later years, makes it clear that where money is borrowed to purchase income-earning assets, such as shares, which are then contributed to a tax deferred plan listed above, no interest can be deducted for any period after the property is transferred to the plan. A further correction, effective for 1991 and later years, provides that interest deductibility is denied only to the extent that property is used for a prohibited purpose. Thus, for example, if you borrow to buy 100 shares and contribute 50 of them to an RRSP, only half the interest would become non-deductible.

The CRA has indicated that the refinancing of a loan where interest was deductible because the loan predated the implementation of the above rules would not by itself prohibit continuing deductibility.

(ITA: 18(11); 20(3); Window on Canadian Tax: 2725)

[¶1064.10] *Soft Costs*

Interest may not, in general, be deducted where it is related to money borrowed to construct, alter or renovate buildings or to own the related land during the period prior to the completion of the construction, alteration or renovation (see ¶771).

[¶1064.15] *Life Insurance Policy Loans*

Even though certain proceeds on the disposition of life insurance policies are taxable, the *Income Tax Act* specifically provides that interest on funds borrowed to acquire an interest in a life insurance policy (e.g., to purchase a policy or to pay premiums thereunder) is not deductible in computing income. There are exceptions for certain policies issued before 1978, and for policies issued before November 13, 1981 under certain tax-deferred plans, and for segregated fund annuity contracts (¶983). In addition, interest on annuity contracts may be deductible if the contract is one under which the taxpayer must recognize income on an accrual basis (¶432).

Interest paid (not payable) on a policy loan from an insurance company is deductible if the funds were used to acquire income-earning assets, or to carry on a business, and is not prohibited by other rules such as those limiting interest on automobiles (¶738), raw land (¶665), or soft costs (¶771). However, you must have the insurance company verify that this interest was not added to the adjusted cost base of the insurance policy (see ¶981). Form T2210, available from the CRA website, is used by the insurer to provide the verification. See also the new restriction on interest deductions relating to "10/8 polices", above at ¶1063.15.

(ITA: 20(1)(c), (d), (2.1), (2.2); 138(12); 138.1)

[¶1064.20] *Limited Partnership and Limited Recourse Financing*

The government has numerous rules in place to combat "tax shelters" by limiting the loss deductions for interest (and other things) flowed out by partnerships to limited or passive partners (¶1818 and ¶1842), and by reducing the amount of any expenditure or cost of property by the amount borrowed on a "limited recourse" basis to invest in projects which do not have short-term profitability (¶835). The limited partnership rules can, in effect, undermine the deductibility of interest where it contributes to a loss, and the limited recourse rules can, by virtue of the financing arrangements associated with a project, undermine its financial viability by reducing the deductions (including interest deductions) associated with its cost.

Even if the interest on money borrowed to make limited recourse investments should in the first instance be deductible, whether because the investment is grandfathered or otherwise, the interest deductions may trigger alternative minimum tax where the interest (or other financing charges) and capital cost allowance (if any) exceed income from the investment (see ¶2420–¶2427).

See also the discussion of tax shelter restrictions at ¶2521.

[¶1064.25] *Bonds Bought or Sold with Accrued Interest*

See ¶440.

[¶1064.30] *Weak Currency Borrowings*

Note that the transactions discussed here are in practice done by large corporations and rarely if at all by individuals. Nevertheless, the rules are general and, for the sake of thoroughness, included here.

In general, borrowing in a foreign currency carries the same interest deductibility as borrowing in Canadian currency; so long as the money is borrowed to earn income, even if through capital investment, the interest should be deductible. In *The Queen v. Shell Canada Limited*, 99 DTC 5669 (S.C.C.), the Supreme Court of Canada ruled that interest was deductible in a transaction in which the taxpayer borrowed in a weak currency (one which carried a high rate of interest because its value was expected to fall) and immediately exchanged the dollars for U.S. dollars (the currency it actually needed for its investment), and hedged the transaction so that a capital gain would be realized when currency was reconverted to pay off the weak currency debt. The company was able to deduct the high interest rate paid on the weak currency borrowing, and realize a capital rather than income gain on the hedge.

The *Shell* case was decided on facts that arose before the introduction of the general anti-avoidance rule (GAAR), and the government promised to continue litigation on these types of transactions on the issue that they are avoidance transactions subject to GAAR. Precisely the same facts were litigated under GAAR in the case of *The Queen v. Canadian Pacific Ltd.*, 2002 DTC 6742 (F.C.A.), aff'g 2000 DTC 2428 (T.C.C.), which held in favour of the taxpayer. In light of the rules discussed below, the outcome of these cases affects only transactions prior to February 28, 2000.

In its February 28, 2000 Budget, the government announced that it would reverse the results of these court decisions effective July 1, 2000 in respect of indebtedness incurred after February 27, 2000. The new weak currency borrowing rules apply where a taxpayer incurs foreign currency indebtedness that meets the following conditions:

- the proceeds from the indebtedness are not used directly in the currency of the debt, but rather are converted into another currency and used in that form by the taxpayer;
- the interest rate on the debt is more than two percentage points above the rate on an equivalent borrowing in the currency used to earn income; and
- the principal amount of the debt exceeds $500,000.

Where these conditions are met, the following rules will apply:

(1) deductible interest on the indebtedness will be limited to the interest that would have been payable if the taxpayer had incurred an equivalent debt directly in the currency of use;

(2) the total of interest expenses disallowed over the term of the indebtedness will be subtracted from the foreign exchange gain or loss realized when the debt is repaid; and

(3) any foreign exchange gain or loss realized on repayment of the debt, and the gain or loss on any associated hedge, will be on income account.

The measure does not apply to a bank, credit union, trust company, or a corporation whose principal business is the lending of money and/or purchasing of debt at arm's length.

(ITA: 20.3)

[¶1064a] CONTINGENT AMOUNTS

As a general rule, paragraph 18(1)(*e*) of the Act prohibits the deduction of a contingent amount. In this regard, the courts have generally held that a condition subsequent to an otherwise non-contingent expenditure — that is, where a condition in the future may allow the expenditure to be returned, or the liability to pay absolved or reduced — does not, in itself, make the expenditure currently contingent. This distinction was the crux of the Collins case, discussed below, which provided an unsatisfactory result in the eyes of the Department of Finance, which then responded with an amendment to the Act.

The changes to the legislation were first released on March 16, 2011 and passed into law on June 26, 2013 (section 143.4). Basically, the new rule provides that a taxpayer's interest expense will be a "contingent amount" and therefore reduced to the extent that the taxpayer has a right to reduce or eliminate the amount that is required to be paid in respect of the expense. The new rules were introduced by the Department of Finance in response to the decision in *Collins v. The Queen* (2010 DTC 5028). In *Collins*, the Federal Court of Appeal allowed the taxpayers to deduct the full face amount of interest expenses in the years in which it accrued, even though the taxpayers had the right to subsequently reduce the amounts of that interest. In particular, *Collins* involved two taxpayers with a 20-year $1.5 million loan with 10% annual interest payable on the loan. The terms of the loan allowed the taxpayers to make much smaller annual interest payments for the first 15 years ($20,000 per year), which the taxpayers made, with the remaining unpaid interest being added to the total indebtedness. Moreover, the terms of the loan provided the taxpayers with the right, at any time before the end of the first 15 years, to make a lump-sum payment that would terminate their liability to pay any remaining interest and principal (the "settlement option"). The lump-sum payment was significantly less than the total of accrued interest and principal owing; the settlement option allowed the taxpayers to reduce the amount of accrued and unpaid interest owing on the loan. The taxpayers subsequently exercised the settlement option and reduced the amount of interest to be paid on the loan to an amount significantly less than the 10% annual amount. Nonetheless, the Federal Court of Appeal allowed the taxpayers to deduct the 10% annual interest expense in each year it accrued. The Court felt that the liability to pay the interest was not contingent in each such year.

The new rules apply to an otherwise unconditional expenditure in respect of which there is a contingent amount. Subsection 143.4(1) defines the "contingent amount" of a taxpayer at any time (other than a time at which the taxpayer is a bankrupt) to include an amount to the extent that the taxpayer, or another taxpayer who does not deal at arm's length with the taxpayer, has a right to reduce the amount at that time. An "expenditure" of a taxpayer means an expense, expenditure, or outlay made or incurred by the taxpayer, or a cost or capital cost of property acquired by the taxpayer. Obviously, then, the legislation can apply to a broader category of expenditures, rather than just to interest. The "right to reduce" an amount of expenditure means a right to reduce or eliminate the amount, including a right that is contingent upon the occurrence of an event, or in any other way, but only if it is reasonable to conclude, having regard to all the circumstances, that the right will become exercisable.

Subsection 143.4(2) will reduce the amount of a taxpayer's expenditure incurred in a taxation year by the amount of the contingent amount in respect of the expenditure net of any amount paid by the taxpayer to obtain the right to reduce the amount of the expenditure. Under subsection 143.4(3), if the taxpayer pays the contingent amount in a subsequent year, the amount is deemed to have been incurred in and become payable in respect of that subsequent year. The amount paid is deemed to have been incurred for the same purpose and to have the same character as the expenditure that was reduced.

Subsection 143.4(4) applies where the taxpayer, or a person not dealing at arm's length with the taxpayer, has at any time in a taxation year after the year in which the expenditure was incurred, a right to reduce the amount of the expenditure (where the right would have reduced the expenditure under subsection 143.4(2), had it been in existence in the year of expenditure). The taxpayer is deemed to receive a "subsequent contingent amount" in respect of the "prior expenditure" in the course of earning income from a business or property under paragraph 12(1)(*x*), and the amount is deemed to be a refund, reimbursement, or similar amount in respect of the expenditure as described in subparagraph 12(1)(*x*)(iv). The subsequent contingent amount is therefore included in the taxpayer's income. The amount of the subsequent contingent amount is the maximum amount of the prior expenditure that may be reduced under the right to reduce net of any amount paid to obtain the right to reduce.

However, subsection 143.4(4) does not apply if it is reasonable to conclude, having regard to all the circumstances, that one of the purposes for having a right to reduce an amount in respect of an expenditure after the end of the taxation year in which an expenditure occurred was to avoid a reduction under subsection 143.4(2) in respect of the expenditure. In such case, subsection 143.4(6) provides that the taxpayer is deemed to have the right to reduce in the year in which the expenditure occurred, effectively subjecting the expenditure to the reduction under subsection 143.4(2) in the year in which the expenditure occurred.

The new legislation applies in respect of taxation years that end on or after March 16, 2011. See also the lead article in *Tax Topics* No. 2037, March 24, 2011, which discusses the new rules.

[¶1065] NO DEDUCTION FOR INTEREST ON HOME MORTGAGES FOR PERSONAL USE

Interest on a mortgage or other loan to finance the purchase of your home is not deductible.

However, interest on a mortgage to finance the purchase of rental property is fully deductible. Therefore, if you rent part of your residence, a portion of your mortgage interest will be deductible from that rental income. The apportionment is usually made on the basis of the number of rooms or total floor space rented to the total number of rooms or floor space in your home.

If you mortgage your home to obtain a loan that is used to purchase investments (e.g., stocks or bonds) or to finance a business, the interest is deductible.

If you use part of your home as a business office, you may be able to deduct a portion of the mortgage interest, provided you meet the tests in ¶742.

If as an employee you are required to use part of your home as an office, you may deduct some related expenses, but not any portion of mortgage interest, if you meet the tests in ¶373.

For a discussion of rearranging borrowings to achieve deductibility, see ¶2517. For a discussion of the tax implications of financing home ownership, see ¶2543.

(ITA: 20(1)(c))

[¶1067] INTEREST DEDUCTION WHERE SOURCE OF INCOME IS LOST

As discussed at ¶1063, interest on borrowed money is only deductible, in effect, on money borrowed for the purpose of earning income from business or property. A specific tracing rule provides "for greater certainty" that money borrowed to repay previously borrowed amounts or pay for previously acquired property will be considered to take on the character of the original borrowing, thus continuing its deductible character (if any).

In the mid-1980s, the courts established with finality that where a source of income disappeared, the deductibility of interest on the money borrowed to acquire the source ceased. (See *Lyons v. M.N.R.*, 84 DTC 1633; *Emerson v. The Queen*, 86 DTC 6184). Thus where, for example, shares were acquired wholly with borrowed money and later sold at a loss and the proceeds reinvested, only the proportion of interest on the surviving funds remained deductible. In the case of bankruptcy, borrowed money invested in a business was not only lost, but interest ceased to be deductible. From the taxpayer's point of view, of course, this merely added insult to injury. Moreover, an aura of uncertainty as well as inequity arose on further transactions. Suppose the surviving borrowed funds were reinvested in property which regained the original value. It seemed particularly unfair that lost deductibility could not be regained, if indeed it could not.

Detailed rules now permit the lost portion of money borrowed for an income earning purpose to be deemed to be used for the purpose of earning income, and therefore the interest thereon to continue to be deductible (unless the original interest was not deductible for some other reason). The rules deal with two distinct situations. The first is where the borrowed funds were used to acquire a capital asset other than real or depreciable property. The second is where borrowed funds were invested in a business. Depreciable property (or real property for that matter) if used in a business is essentially protected under the second rule. But real and depreciable property — essentially land and building — acquired as a passive investment (i.e., for rent only) seem to be excluded from the protection of these rules.

(1) Where Source of Income was Capital Asset (other than Real or Depreciable Property)

The first main heading concerns money originally borrowed for the purpose of earning income from a capital property other than real property or depreciable property. Where the borrowed money ceases to be used for the purpose of earning income (typically because the property is sold), the basic rule seems to be that the amount of borrowed money contributed to the original cost of the asset, in excess of the surviving amount of borrowed funds that may be attributed to the consideration received on disposition of the asset, is deemed to continue borrowed for an eligible purpose thereafter to the extent it remains outstanding. What the statute does not actually tell you but requires you to infer is that the surviving amount of borrowed funds attributed to the consideration is the proportion obtained by dividing final proceeds by original cost. Essentially, this seems to say that, where the income earning capital asset is sold at a loss, the original borrowing is divided into a lost share and a surviving share. The surviving share is calculated as consideration for the disposition over original cost times original borrowing. The remaining portion of the original borrowing is the lost share. The surviving portion of the borrowed funds continues to have deductibility of related interest traced to the use to which the surviving funds are put (under general rules). The lost share is deemed to continue deductible while outstanding.

Thus, for example, assume a taxpayer borrowed $1,000 toward the purchase of shares costing $1,600. The shares are sold for $900. Department of Finance technical notes say that $^{9}/_{16}$ of the original borrowing of $1,000 ($563) represents the surviving borrowed money, and deductibility of the interest on that portion of the funds depends on the new use to which they are put. If reinvested, interest on that $563 remains deductible; if the $563 is not used for a qualifying purpose, the interest is no longer deductible. The lost portion of the original $1,000 ($437) is deemed to continue to be used for an income producing purpose, so long as it is outstanding, regardless of whether the entire proceeds are put to an ineligible use. This is explicitly stated in the Department of Finance notes.

The legislation itself operates by identifying the portion deemed to continue deductible, being the original (or a substituted) qualified borrowing minus the proportion of the original borrowing represented in the consideration. This subtraction gives the amount of borrowing attributable to lost funds ($437 in the example above) and the law operates to deem this amount used for the purpose of earning income. It does not categorize the amount relating to surviving funds at all, presuming that the ordinary tracing rules will characterize the use of those funds as deductible or not. Unfortunately, the legislation itself is less clear than it might be. Perhaps the best that can be said is that it appears susceptible of this interpretation.

Several issues are not clarified by either the legislation or official commentary. Where the surviving funds are not used for an eligible purpose and the borrowed money is partially repaid, how is repayment allocated between surviving and lost funds? No doubt the taxpayer will want to allocate all repayments to surviving funds first, and the CRA will want *pro rata* allocations. Suppose, for instance, in the example above, the taxpayer sells the shares for $900 and immediately repays that amount to the lender. There is now $100 of borrowed money outstanding. The law seems to say that so long as any part of the $437 is outstanding, interest thereon is deemed deductible. It is implied that the whole interest on the remaining $100 is deductible, which might seem a sensible answer here. Suppose, however, that the taxpayer repays $463 of its $900 consideration and uses the remainder ($437) for ineligible purposes. Do the rules require that so long as $437 remains outstanding, interest on that amount is deductible? Or can the CRA argue that repayments must be allocated between lost and surviving funds?

Informal discussions with Department of Finance officials suggest that they, or some of them, intend that all subsequent repayments of the indebtedness outstanding at the time of sale must be allocated between surviving and lost funds. Thus, in the example above where $900 is returned to the bank after the sale and $100 remains outstanding, interest on 7/16 of the remaining debt ($43.75) would be attributed to lost funds and fully deductible and interest on the $56.25 attributable to surviving funds would be ... what? Would be determined under the old rules, presumably, which said that a loss of source renders the funds non-deductible. It should be said that neither the law nor the Department of Finance notes clearly require this position. The law says that "the amount of the borrowed money equal to the excess [i.e., the $437] shall, to the extent that the amount is outstanding after that time, be deemed to be used" for the purpose of earning income. This could perhaps be taken to imply that interest on that amount to the extent outstanding is deductible regardless of other circumstances. This view is perhaps not without merit. At this stage, one can only say that the question of allocating repayments to determine the amount of the deemed eligible borrowing which has been repaid is not beyond question.

The exclusion of real and depreciable property will also create problems, especially for individuals. In the case of real or depreciable property acquired for use in a business, Department of Finance officials take the view that a problem does not arise because so long as the business survives, that may be said to be the source of the income for which the money was borrowed, rather than any particular item of property, and so deductibility continues under general rules. Where the business does not survive, there are special rules below. Where the property is rental property, however, and clearly does not constitute a business, the purpose of the exclusions is not entirely clear. They seem to be aimed at the individual real estate investor, who is felt not to deserve protection. Corporations, at least, have some presumption that they are engaged in business, even if it is not an active business.

Although they leave many uncertainties and are likely to be subject to continuing revision, the rules do address some additional specific issues. For example, they specify that where the capital property was disposed of for "not less than fair market value", it is the actual consideration (even if greater than fair market value) that is used to prorate the surviving and lost portions of the borrowed money. If the disposition is for less than fair market value, however, it is fair market value that is used in the proration. If the proceeds or consideration on the disposition include a reduction in the amount of the borrowed money (presumably on disposition to a creditor), the reduction is first subtracted from the total borrowed money before applying the proration rules. Finally, if the consideration on disposition is less than fair market value *and* there is a reduction of the debt as part of the consideration, the reduction is also subtracted from fair market value in determining consideration to be prorated.

Where the taxpayer does not actually dispose of the property, but the borrowed money ceases to be used for an eligible purpose, presumably because of a change of use in the property or its inability to continue to generate income (e.g., where the taxpayer borrowed to acquire shares of a company which has become bankrupt), there is in effect a deemed disposition at fair market value at that time. The rules above separate the original borrowed funds into surviving and lost portions as if the fair market consideration had been received. The lost portion continues deductible, although it would seem that the surviving portion does not.

(2) Loss of Source of Income Where Money Borrowed to Earn Income from Business

The second main element in the new rules deals with the situation where money had been borrowed to earn income from a business and the taxpayer ceases to carry on the business and in consequence the money ceases to be used for the purpose of earning income from the business. Where this condition is met, the basic rule is that money which had been borrowed to earn income from the business and remains outstanding at the time of cessation is deemed to continue to be used by the taxpayer for the purpose of earning income from the business. However, as property of the business is disposed of at or after the cessation, either in fact or through change of use (for example, where property commences to be used in another business of the taxpayer), the fair market value of each property at the time of disposition is subtracted from the amount protected by the basic deeming rule. It is intended that ordinary tracing rules will then determine the deductibility of interest on the borrowed funds deemed to be associated with a particular disposition.

It is evident that this scheme will put a premium on the careful ordering of dispositions following the cessation of a particular business. The rule operates on a completely mechanical basis; that is, allocations must be made in order of disposition regardless of whether particular funds are traceable to particular properties.

Note that real or notional disposition of *any* "property" will incur the allocation of its value from the pool of borrowed money deemed used in the former business. "Property" is broadly defined in the *Income Tax Act* to include any kind of property, tangible or intangible, including rights, timber resource properties, and work in progress of a profession. Money itself is property "unless a contrary intention is evident".

The rules governing deductibility of interest on cessation of business contain a number of detailed provisions to support the basic concept. They have their own deemed disposition rules to ensure that any property which has not been actually disposed of is deemed to be disposed of when the taxpayer begins to use the property in another business or for any other purpose. Where a taxpayer disposes of two or more properties at the same time and the pool of borrowed money to be matched with those properties is less than their aggregate fair market value, the taxpayer may choose the properties to which the remaining borrowed money is matched. This permits allocation to properties which will continue to serve a business purpose in this situation. Similarly, where borrowed money is owed under two or more debt obligations, the taxpayer may determine the amount of borrowed money under each obligation that is to be matched with property.

The rules do permit refinancing of borrowed money without impairing the status of deductibility.

A rather odd rule requires that the fiscal period of the discontinued business must after the discontinuance coincide with the fiscal period of the taxpayer. Apparently the rule exists so that there will be a "year" in which there is an obligation to pay interest, so that the deeming rule will operate. Unfortunately, the deemed year end chosen seems to produce bizarre results. First, the first coinciding year end seems intended to commence with the day after the business was discontinued but to end with fiscal year end of the taxpayer. This assumes, however, that there is an automatic termination of fiscal period where a business ceases; something which is not at all clear. Certainly the Act makes no such specific provision. If the fiscal period did not cease at the termination of the business and the discontinuance occurred after the taxpayer's year end, the rule would lead to a fiscal period of more than 53 weeks, placing the rule in conflict with the general restriction. Moreover, the rule appears to operate generally for all purposes of the Act provided there is borrowed money for the rule to act on in the first place. It is not clear that this has much practical significance; in general a discontinued business has no further need for a fiscal period. On the other hand, if there is a need, it is not clear why the old fiscal period is not notionally continued.

(ITA: 20(1)(c), (3); 20.1; 249)

[¶1069] INTEREST ON LATE INCOME TAX PAYMENTS

Unpaid income taxes and late or deficient instalments of income taxes bear interest at a prescribed rate per annum from the day on which payment should have been made until the date of payment. Such interest is a non-deductible item.

The Minister of Finance establishes the prescribed rate on a quarterly basis. The rate is four percentage points above the average rate earned on 90-day treasury bills during the first month of the preceding quarter. A table of prescribed interest rates is reproduced immediately preceding Chapter 1.

(ITA: 161(1); ITR: 4300 [Interpretation]; 4301 Prescribed Rate of Interest)

[¶1071] INTEREST WHICH CREATES A LOSS

Generally speaking, interest on money borrowed for an income-producing purpose will be deductible even though there is a net loss position for the current year from that source. That is, where interest (and other expenses, if any) exceeds revenue from the property or business in which the funds were invested, the loss from that source reduces other income, for example, employment income. If such losses exceed other income altogether they may be carried over to other years as discussed in the section on losses below. This general rule is subject to the limitations discussed at ¶1063 where the income source disappears or where there is no reasonable expectation of profit because the property has an element of personal use. It is also subject to the limitations discussed in ¶1064 under the subheading "Limited Partnership and Limited Recourse Financing" where funds are borrowed for investment in tax shelters or, perhaps, other projects where short term tax losses will exceed medium term profitability.

Where interest exceeds related investment income, the net loss will be deductible against other income but will go into the "cumulative net investment loss (CNIL)" account and reduce the cumulative gains limit for capital gains deduction purposes (¶502). Net investment income, on the other hand, reduces the CNIL limitation. The implications of maintaining a lifetime record of net investment gains and losses are discussed at ¶400.

Quebec taxpayers should note that Quebec has imposed additional restrictions on the deduction of aggregate investment expenses (typically interest) in excess of aggregate investment income; see ¶1635.

(ITA: 3; 20(1)(c); 110.6(1))

[¶1073] INTEREST RELATED TO DEPRECIABLE ASSETS (CAPITALIZED INTEREST)

Interest and other deductible borrowing costs on funds borrowed to acquire depreciable assets may, if you elect in your income tax return, be treated as additional capital cost of the assets acquired (and thereby eligible for capital cost allowance) rather than as a deduction in computing income.

It should be noted that interest related to the costs of construction, renovation or alteration of a building or ownership of related land during the period prior to the completion of the construction, renovation, or alteration is not deductible and must be included in the cost of the land and building, i.e., capitalized (see ¶771).

You may elect to capitalize interest incurred in the year the asset was acquired and in any of the three preceding years if interest was incurred in those preceding years in respect of the asset acquired during the year of election. For example, if you obtained a loan in Year 1 which you have used to acquire depreciable assets in Year 2, you may elect to capitalize the interest paid both in Year 1 and Year 2. If you have already claimed the Year 1 interest as an expense and then with your Year 2 return you elect to capitalize it, you will receive a reassessment for Year 1 disallowing the interest and charging any applicable additional taxes and interest thereon. If you wish, you may elect to capitalize part of the interest only, and claim the balance as a deduction.

If in a previous taxation year you have made an election to capitalize interest relating to a depreciable asset acquired during that year, or have been required by law to capitalize interest (¶771), you may elect for the current year to also capitalize the interest or a portion of the interest relating to that asset acquisition. You may make a similar election for each succeeding year providing you have elected to capitalize the total interest in each year since the asset was acquired.

The election is made by filing with your income tax return for the Year 2 copies of a letter stating that you are electing to capitalize interest under subsection 21(3) of the *Income Tax Act* and specifying each amount of interest which you elect to capitalize.

For example, if funds are borrowed in Year 1 to acquire an asset in Year 2, elections to capitalize interest could be made as follows:

Year 1 — No election possible because the depreciable asset has not been acquired.

Year 2 — May elect to capitalize all or any part of the interest paid in Year 1 and/or Year 2.

Year 3 — May elect to capitalize all or any part of the interest paid in Year 3 providing an election has been made in Year 2 (Year 2 election need not necessarily have been for the total amount of the interest paid).

Year 4 — May elect to capitalize all or any part of the interest paid in Year 4 providing a valid election has been made for Year 3 in respect of *all* interest paid in that year.

Year 5 — May elect to capitalize all or any part of the interest paid in Year 5 providing a valid election has been made for Year 4 in respect of *all* interest paid in that year.

Interpretation Bulletin IT-121R3, dealing with this subject, was "archived" in late 2003 or 2004, for reasons unknown. Accordingly, while it may still provide valid guidance on some details, it must be used with extreme caution, as an aid to informed understanding only. It has no further authority in the eyes of the CRA.

(ITA: 18(3.1); 21(1), (3))

[¶1073c] INTEREST RELATED TO RESOURCE EXPENDITURES

You may elect on the amount of expense incurred in respect of borrowed money used for the purpose of exploration, development, or the acquisition of property, provided the expense is a:

(1) Canadian exploration and development expense;

(2) foreign exploration and development expense;

(3) Canadian exploration expense;

(4) Canadian development expense; or

(5) Canadian oil and gas property expense.

These expenses are defined in Chapter 22.

Where you make this election, costs in respect of the borrowed money are not deductible under any of the normal interest or financing cost provisions. Instead, those costs are added to the category of resource expenses that the borrowed money was used to incur. The rule does not apply where the deduction normally applicable relates to exempt income. For taxation years beginning after 2000, these rules are amended so that the exception referred to above for exempt income extends to all income that is exempt from ordinary income tax. This ensures that the election cannot be made where the borrower rather than the income is exempt from tax (under subsection 149(1)).

The rules are also amended so that the specified resource expenses include foreign resource expenses determined on a country-by-country basis. This amendment is consequential on the introduction of new rules for the deduction of foreign resource expenses, discussed in Chapter 22.

The election must initially be made in connection with financing costs incurred in the taxation year during which the related resource expenses were incurred (but may be made within three years of the time the actual costs are incurred). For example, if you obtained a loan in Year 1 which you have used to finance resource expenses in Year 2, you may elect in respect of the interest paid both in Year 1 and Year 2. If you have already claimed the Year 1 interest as an expense and then with your Year 2 return you elect to capitalize it, you will receive a reassessment for Year 1 disallowing the interest and charging any applicable additional taxes and interest thereon. If you wish, you may elect on part of the interest only, and claim the balance under normal rules.

If in a previous taxation year you have made this election, you may elect for the current year as well with respect to the same resource endeavour. You may make a similar election for each succeeding year providing you have elected to capitalize the total interest in each year since the asset was acquired.

Interpretation Bulletin IT-121R3, dealing with this subject, was "archived" in late 2003 or 2004. Accordingly, while it may still provide valid guidance on some details, it must be used with extreme caution, as an aid to informed understanding only.

(ITA: 21(2), (4))

[¶1074] PREPAID INTEREST, PAYMENTS TO REDUCE FUTURE INTEREST, AND PENALTIES ON DEBT CANCELLATION

Under the rules at ¶608 and ¶753, prepaid expenses (including interest) can only be deducted in the year to which the expense relates.

In general (and for individuals, but not necessarily partnerships, corporations, or trusts), the prepaid interest rules require that prepayments of interest made are matched to (and only deductible in) the period to which the expenditure relates, under the rules in ¶753. Generally this will mean that book and tax expenditures should be the same, provided generally accepted accounting principles are followed. In any event, a prepayment of interest is denied deduction in the year it is incurred and deduction is permitted in the year to which the expenditure relates.

The line between a prepayment of interest and a payment to reduce future interest or cancel a debt may be difficult to draw. A payment that falls into the latter camp rather than the former is now governed by rules discussed below at ¶1074.05.

Interest prepayments made by a partnership, corporation, or trust are governed by complex rules intended to require immediate recognition and reduction of interest deductions in the year the prepayment is made, even if it purports to relate to years far in the future.

Prepayments of interest received by a lender would seem to be taxable income when received if they have not been included in income earlier under the accrual rules at ¶432, or the general rule that interest must be included in income when received or receivable, depending on the method usually followed by the taxpayer.

(ITA: 12(1)(c), (3); 18(9), (9.2)–(9.8); IT-396R Interest Income; *Freeway Properties Inc. v. The Queen*, 85 DTC 5183 (F.C.T.D.))

[¶1074.05] *Payments Made To Reduce Interest or for Early Repayment of Debt*

It seems that the government felt that payments made either to reduce interest or as interest penalty on payment to cancel the underlying debt might not be deductible, either because they would not have the character of interest but rather would be capital payments, or because upon cancellation there would be no underlying debt and so no character of interest in future years. Accordingly, subsection 18(9.1) was introduced several years ago to allow a deduction on the basis that prepayments of future interest may be distinct from payments made to buy down or reduce a future interest rate or payments made as a penalty or bonus on the early repayment of a debt.

Subsection 18(9.1) applies to amounts paid in the course of carrying on business or earning income from property, either:

(1) as consideration for a reduction in the rate of interest payable on a debt obligation incurred, either through borrowing money or on the acquisition of property; or

(2) as a penalty or bonus payable by reason of the repayment before maturity of all or part of the principal amount of a debt incurred, either through borrowing money or on the acquisition of property.

The rules will not apply to any fee, penalty, or bonus that may reasonably be considered to have been paid for the extension of a debt or as consideration for the substitution or the conversion of one debt obligation into another debt or a share. Also excluded is any fee, penalty, or bonus that is contingent upon use or production from property or is computed by reference to revenue, profit, etc. This is intended to leave in place the rules governing certain "earn-out" agreements.

The net effect of the rule is that where a payment is made that is covered by these rules, the amount paid will be treated as deductible interest in the future years to which the interest would have related but for the payment, but only to the extent of the present value at the time of the payment of the interest that would otherwise have been payable in future years. That is, the present value of the future interest payments must be deducted over the life of the debt as it existed before the interest prepayment or principal repayment. The present value of the payment as it relates to each future year of the debt should be deductible in that future year.

It is not entirely clear what becomes of penalty payments in excess of the present value of interest cancelled. Presumably, these would be governed by ordinary case law. They might be deductible if related to money borrowed on current account, and non-deductible if related to capital borrowings. Some argument might be made that they would qualify for five-year tax amortization under paragraph 20(1)(*e*) (see ¶908).

[¶1074.10] *Payments Made To Reduce Interest or Cancel Debt: Taxability to Recipient*

Where subsection 18(9.1) applies to a payment to reduce future interest or as a penalty on the early repayment of a debt, the recipient is treated, for the purposes of the Act, to have received the payment at that time as interest. As such, the amount will be included in the recipient's income, with no apparent reserve mechanism to spread out the inclusion over the remaining term of the debt.

(ITA: 18(9), (9.1))

[¶1075] INTEREST ON DEATH DUTIES

Interest accruing on succession duties, inheritance taxes, and estate taxes is deductible in computing the income of the person who is primarily liable or upon whom the incidence of death duties and accrued interest falls. The deduction must be taken each year for the interest accruing during the taxation year.

Interest on borrowed money to pay succession duties or estate taxes is, however, not deductible.

(ITA: 60(*d*); S3-F6-C1 Interest Deductibility)

PENSION INCOME SPLITTING

[¶1076] PENSION INCOME TRANSFERRED TO SPOUSE OR COMMON-LAW PARTNER — LINE 210

You can transfer to your spouse (or common-law partner), provided you sign a joint agreement on form T1032, up to 50% of your *eligible* pension income. If you are 65 years of age at the end of the taxation year, all of your pension income is eligible ("eligible pension income"), and up to 50% of it can be transferred. If you are not 65 at the end of the year, only your income eligible for the $2,000 pension income credit ("qualified pension income", ¶1311) is eligible income for purposes of the income splitting election.

To be effective, you and your spouse or common-law partner must have been resident in Canada at the end of the calendar year (or the time of death if this occurred during the year). As well, you must be living together at the end of the year. If at the end of the year you are living separate and apart by reason of a breakdown of the relationship which proves to have lasted for at least 90 days, no transfer is permitted. If you have more than one partner at the end of the year, only one transfer is permitted.

If you were married or commenced living common-law (for tax purposes, as discussed at ¶1113) during the year, or your spouse or common-law partner died during the year, you must prorate the amount eligible for transfer by the number of months during which the relationship existed. The month in which in relationship began or your spouse/partner died (or both) counts as a full month, and the number of months in which the relationship existed is divided by 12 to determine the amount you can transfer.

There are two possible benefits to splitting income. First, if your spouse/partner is in a lower tax bracket than you are, as a couple your tax will be lower overall. That is, your income taxed at the higher rate will be reduced, although your spouse/partner's income taxed at the lower rate will be increased. For current year tax rates, see the tables preceding Chapter 1, particularly ¶62. Provincial tax will also have a bearing on the tax savings involved, but generally speaking the federal rate brackets will determine whether the election is beneficial in terms of tax rates.

Second, if your spouse/partner is 65 or over at the end of the taxation year for which you are splitting pension income, the spouse/partner may include the transferred income along with his or her own pension income in claiming the $2,000 pension income credit. Thus, to the extent your spouse/partner does not already have $2,000 of pension income of his or her own before the transfer, he or she can increase this credit. To the extent you have more than $2,000 of eligible pension income, this will increase the credit available to you as a couple.

If your spouse/partner is not yet 65 at the end of the relevant taxation year, he or she may still claim the amount of "qualified pension income" you transfer. This is defined in ¶1311. Essentially, it is your private registered pension plan or annuity income, not including RRSP, RRIF, or DPSP (deferred profit sharing plan) income, plus certain amounts received as a consequence of the death of a former spouse/partner.

The two benefits should each be considered in deciding how much (if any) pension income should be transferred. If you are both in the same income bracket and both fully using the $2,000 pension credit with your own pension income, there is typically not much point to the transfer. If you, as the transferor, are in a higher income bracket, you will, as a couple, benefit from a transfer at least to the point where you are both in the same bracket. Even if you are both in the same bracket, there may be an advantage to transferring at least enough pension for your spouse/partner to fully utilize the $2,000 credit, assuming he or she does not have $2,000 of pension income of his or her own and assuming the pension income transferred is eligible in the hands of your spouse/partner if he or she is under 65.

Commentary on Legislative Proposals (Sept. 16, 2016)

Note: When Legislative Proposals, September 16, 2016, achieves Royal Assent, the commentary will be modified to read:

Effective for 2015, retirement income security benefits ("RISBs") received by veterans and members of the Canadian Forces under the Canadian Forces Members and Veterans Re-establishment and Compensation Act may be included in their eligible pension income and split with their spouse or common-law partner, but only if they do not exceed the difference between (1) 35 times the defined benefit limit (i.e., $2,290 for 2016) and (2) the total of their other eligible pension income and income received under a retirement compensation arrangement ("RCA").

Remember that a low-income spouse or common-law partner can transfer pension, age, child, and tuition/education/textbook amounts (the education and textbook credits are repealed effective January 1, 2017) in excess of income to the higher-income spouse/partner (¶1361), and to the extent that income transfers simply grind amounts that would otherwise be transferred, the result is neutral; that is, there is neither benefit nor cost to the couple as a whole. On the other hand, to the extent the lower-income spouse has other unused non-refundable and non-transferable amounts eligible for credit to soak up transferred pension income, there is a net benefit. As well, the transferor may be able to increase some non-refundable credits, such as the age amount, which would otherwise be reduced by the income which has been transferred. The transfer of unused spousal/partner credits is discussed at ¶1361, and the examples there discuss the interplay of the income and credits transfer mechanisms.

To make the election, you must each complete the line 314 federal worksheet calculation (the worksheet comes with the T1 package). The actual election is then made on form T1032. You deduct on line 210 of your T1 return your share of the income transferred (and your spouse/partner adds the same amount to income on line 116 of his or her T1 return). Form T1032 will show you how much pension credit each of you can claim on line 314.

The transfer from the transferee's point of view is discussed at ¶978, although the considerations are the same.

(ITA: 56(1)(*a.2*); 60(*c*); 60.03)

DEDUCTIONS FROM NET INCOME TO ARRIVE AT TAXABLE INCOME

[¶1077] MISCELLANEOUS ADJUSTMENTS FOR TAXABLE INCOME

The T1 General shows numerous deductions allowed to reduce net income to taxable income. These are discussed in this book as follows:

Employee relocation loan	¶409
Stock options	¶330
Prospector's claims	¶776
DPSP shares disposed of	¶917
Employment Insurance repayments	¶941
Non-capital losses of other years	¶1085, ¶1087
Net capital losses of other years	¶1093
Limited partnership losses of other years	¶1091
Capital gains deduction	¶502
Northern residents deduction	¶361a
Vow of perpetual poverty claims	¶1080
Social assistance payments	¶990
Workers' Compensation payments	¶358, ¶990
Net federal supplements	¶990, ¶1026
U.S. Social Security benefits	¶921

In the 2010 federal Budget, the deduction in computing taxable income in respect of U.S. Social Security benefits was increased by another 35% (to a total of 50%) for resident taxpayers receiving such benefits since before 1996 and up to the relevant taxation year; the increased deduction applies to 2010 and subsequent years. See the discussion at ¶921.

As well, certain items not listed on the T1 return are actually included in net income and deducted to reach taxable income. These include:

Treaty exempt income	¶990
UN employment income	¶1456
Tuition assistance received under government programs (such as EI)	¶971
IATA or ISAT income	¶1456

See ¶990 and ¶1103.

[¶1078] ORDER OF ADJUSTMENTS TO TAXABLE INCOME

The order in which you must make adjustments in calculating your taxable income is as follows:

(1) Deductions for employee stock options, home relocation loans, Canadian Forces personnel and police deduction (a deduction may be claimed for certain members of the Canadian Forces and Canadian police services deployed outside Canada on a high-risk or current moderate-risk operational mission; the amount is shown in box 43 of the T4 slip and claimed in line 244), prospectors' claims, DPSP shares disposed of, Employment Insurance repayments, vow of perpetual poverty claims, social assistance payments, workers' compensation, and treaty exemptions (if included in income). Within this group, claims may be made in any order. References are given at ¶1077, above.

(2) Deduction of payments related to prior years entitled to income averaging. You do not normally make this adjustment yourself; rather, the CRA makes the adjustment on the basis of information supplied by the payer.

(3) Non-capital losses (see ¶1085), restricted farm losses (see ¶1089), farm losses (see ¶1085 and ¶1720), limited partnership losses (¶1091), and net capital losses (see ¶1093) of other years.

(4) Lifetime capital gains deduction claim for the year (¶502).

(5) Northern residents' allowances (¶361a).

The main function of this ordering provision is in the determination of loss carryover amounts, as discussed at ¶1085.

(ITA: 111.1)

[¶1079] SPECIAL DEDUCTION FOR RESIDENCE IN REMOTE LOCATIONS

If you live in certain remote areas of Canada, primarily in the far north, you are eligible for special deductions, provided you lived in such an area for a continuous period of at least six months. This basic deduction is available to all taxpayers who meet the residence conditions. Certain additional deductions for taxable travel costs provided by an employer may be claimed by employees only. Both these deductions are described in detail at ¶361a.

[¶1080] CHARITABLE GIFTS BY MEMBERS OF RELIGIOUS ORDERS (VOWS OF PERPETUAL POVERTY)

An individual who is a member of a religious order at any time during the year and who has taken a vow of perpetual poverty may deduct the entire amount of his or her earned income paid in the year to the order. "Earned income" has the same meaning here as at ¶1055 for purposes of computing deductible child care expenses. It would appear that where the individual joins or leaves the order in a year, there is no limitation on this deduction on amounts paid to the order in the year while not a member. On the other hand, where any deduction is claimed under these rules for a year, no charitable donation tax credit can be claimed for *any* gift made in the year, either currently or on a carryover basis.

It should be noted that this special deduction applies only to earned income and it would not include investment income such as dividends and interest, even though this income may also be paid over to the religious order. A claim for this special deduction must generally be substantiated by a letter from the religious order, stating that the taxpayer is a member of the order and, as such, has taken a vow of perpetual poverty and has given his or her entire earned income for the year to the order. A person who has not taken a vow of perpetual poverty will not be allowed this special deduction even though he or she may turn over all of his or her earned income to a religious order. If a person who has taken a vow of perpetual poverty receives earned income from which he or she deducts the cost of his or her board, lodging and a small living allowance and remits the balance to his or her religious order, the special deduction will not apply because he or she has not turned over his or her *entire* earned income for the year to the religious order, but he or she is allowed a donation credit under the general rules in Chapter 12.

The CRA states, in Interpretation Bulletin IT-86R, that a member of a religious order who was under a vow of perpetual poverty for only part of the year may deduct the amount of his earned income and superannuation or pension benefits for that part of the year, if the whole of that amount was paid over to his order. To the extent this implies that the member cannot deduct all amounts paid to the order in the year, it would appear to contradict the statute, and it is worth noting that the Interpretation Bulletin does not explicitly state such a proposition. The bulletin does note that the taxpayer may choose to forgo a deduction under this provision and claim ordinary charitable donation credits for the year under the general rules.

Residents of Quebec should note that its rules for the members of religious orders in these circumstances are quite different, as discussed under the subheading "Vow of Perpetual Poverty" in ¶1657.

(ITA: 110(2); IT-86R Vow of Perpetual Poverty)

[¶1081] COMMUNAL ORGANIZATIONS

The rules at ¶1080 are intended to apply primarily to certain Catholic orders, although of course they apply to members of any religious order which falls within the definition. Rather different rules apply to religious communities, such as the Hutterites, which operate taxable businesses but do not recognize ownership by individual members of the community. Such organizations are taxed as trusts, and income and charitable donations may be allocated to members on a specified basis.

(ITA: 143; IC 78-5R3 Communal organizations)

WHAT YOU SHOULD KNOW ABOUT LOSSES

[¶1083] DEDUCTIBLE LOSSES

You are allowed to deduct certain types of losses in computing your taxable income for the year, namely:

- non-capital losses (¶1085);
- restricted farm losses (¶1089);
- farm losses (¶1720);
- limited partnership losses (¶1091); and
- net capital losses (¶1093).

There are specific rules that allow you to carry these losses back to the preceding taxation years or forward to succeeding taxation years if you cannot use them in the current year.

Except for limited partnership losses, the losses discussed here are assumed to arise from a source where the expenses exceed the revenue and no anti-avoidance restrictions have been placed on the loss. You should know that there are many loss restrictions intended primarily to limit syndication of losses through tax shelter investments (¶835, ¶2521) or losses on dispositions to affiliated parties (¶852). The alternative minimum tax rules in Chapter 24 can also restrict losses otherwise claimed.

(ITA: 111)

[¶1085] NON-CAPITAL LOSSES

You may have a non-capital loss if you have incurred a loss from employment, property or a business. A non-capital loss also includes the amount of an allowable business investment loss. See ¶580 for details.

Net incomes and losses from each source are calculated using the rules outlined in the appropriate chapters of this book. The rules governing the determination of a non-capital loss are detailed and complex, and the CRA discusses them in Interpretation Bulletin IT-232R3. Form T1A, available from the CRA website, is designed to assist you to calculate your non-capital loss for the year, as well as to actually carry back the losses and claim refunds for prior years. It is not necessary to file a complete amended return for previous years to carry back a loss, and in general, the CRA would prefer that you simply file T1A with your current year return. However, you may want blank returns from the prior year to which your current losses will be applied to do your own calculations; T1 returns for several preceding years are posted on the CRA website.

There are several things you should note about T1A. First, you must report total income or loss from each listed source. Thus, if you have $5,000 as the taxable amount of dividends at line 120 of the T1, $2,000 of interest at line 121, and $8,000 of carrying charges at line 221, you would report no investment income on T1A but rather a net investment loss of $1,000.

Generally speaking, investment income from lines 120 and 121, minus carrying charges at line 221 will be investment income or loss on T1A.

Similarly, employment income from lines 101 plus 104 minus pension plan contributions (line 207), minus employment expenses at lines 212, 229, and 231 will be employment income or loss on T1A.

You should note that most of the other deductions from income (lines 208, 210, 213, 214, 215, 219, 220, 224, 232, and 235) will reduce positive amounts of income but will not augment a loss to the extent positive income amounts are not enough to absorb them. Allowable business investment losses (line 217) are an exception. On the other hand, several deductions from net and taxable income will augment a loss.

[¶1085.05] *Farming and Fishing Losses Determined Separately*

If you are ordinarily in the business of farming or fishing, your farming or fishing loss for the year is your net loss from all such businesses (see Chapter 17).

The reason for this separate loss pool was originally to allow such losses a longer carryover period than was available for other non-capital losses. The carryforward period for farm losses arising in taxation years ending years prior to March 23, 2004, is 10 years, whereas the carryforward for losses from other businesses for such taxation years is seven years (see ¶1087). Farm losses arising in taxation years ending before March 23, 2004, remain subject to special carryover rules of 10 years forward and three years back. Accordingly, these losses form a separate pool; to the extent all non-capital losses for the year as determined in ¶1085, above, exceed these farm losses, the excess remains in the non-capital loss pool for the year.

The farm loss pool remains in use, but the carryover period now matches the carryover periods for other non-capital losses, i.e., three-year carryback in all cases, 10-year carryforward for losses arising in taxation years ending after March 22, 2004, and 20-year carryforward for losses arising in 2006 and later taxation years. Since both farm losses and non-capital losses can be deducted from income generally, this is for currently generated losses a distinction without a difference.

Yet another category of losses relating to farm income is called restricted farm losses. These are described at ¶1750. These losses are applied in the calculation of farm income at line 141 of your return and form yet a separate pool which is not to be included in either the non-capital loss or farm loss pool.

[¶1085.10] *Technical Calculation of Non-Capital Loss*

As stated above, the technical rules for determining your non-capital loss for a year are somewhat more complex, in that you must aggregate separate positive and negative incomes from various sources, and apply deductions at various stages. Here you are in effect working with losses and deductions as positive entries and income as a negative entry to come up with an effective loss balance. The result should be the same as that above. For those interested, the technical rules are:

(1) Determine the total of your incomes from the miscellaneous sources outlined in Chapter 9 (before any offsetting deduction, which are claimed below) plus your incomes from each separate employment, business or property, calculated in accordance with the rules outlined in the chapters covering these items. For purposes of this calculation, incomes and losses from each different employment, business or property should be separately determined.

Example 1

Income from business A	$10,000
Loss from business B	(5,000)
Net income from all businesses	$ 5,000

In this case the $10,000 of income from business A will be accumulated with income from other sources. The $5,000 loss from business B is to be included in item (4) below.

(2) Add to the amount determined in Step (1) your net taxable capital gains for the year (see Chapter 5).

(3) From the total of Step (1) and Step (2) above deduct the amounts identified at lines 207 to 235 of your return not already deducted in Step (1). The amounts at lines 207, 212, 221, 229, and 231 should generally be accounted for in Step (1) above; if not, deduct here. The result of this calculation cannot be a negative number; if the deductions exceed the income the result is considered to be zero.

(4) Determine the total of each loss from employment, business or property and your allowable business investment loss. At this point, the $5,000 loss calculated in Step (1) is taken into account. Also included here are the following amounts to the extent they are eligible for deduction from net income in arriving at taxable income, regardless of whether there is sufficient net income to absorb them:

- offsetting deduction for employee stock option benefits (¶330);
- offsetting deduction for prospector's and grubstaker's gains on dispositions for shares (¶776);
- offsetting deduction on sale of shares rolled out of DPSP on termination of a plan (¶917);
- offsetting deduction for interest imputed on home relocation loans (¶409);
- amount protected by tax treaties (to the extent not deducted in Step (1); ¶990);
- offsetting deduction for workers' compensation awards (¶990); and
- offsetting deduction for social assistance (welfare) payments (¶990).

You may also include here any amount actually deducted under (rather than eligible for) the lifetime capital gains deduction (¶502) rule for the year.

The reason for increasing losses with these items is that they represent income items which in a sense should not be included in income in the first place, since they are later allowed as deductions in arriving at taxable income. They exist as income items only to measure other taxpayers' claims for the loss taxpayer as a dependant. Since income is deducted from losses below (Step (5)), these addbacks permit a netting out so that losses are not impaired by the income inclusions. Contrast this with the treatment of Northern residents' allowances, RRSP contribution deductions, and a number of other special deductions (and, before 1988, personal exemptions), which, although they can reduce positive income amounts, are not preserved in the loss carryover pool if they cannot be utilized in the current year.

(5) Subtract the amount, if any, determined in Step (3) from the total losses calculated in Step (4).

(6) Subtract from the amount determined after Step (5) any amounts of previously elected forward averaging and drawn down in the current year, and any amounts carved out as farming or fishing losses for the year. The remaining balance is your non-capital loss for the year available for carryover.

Example of Technical Non-Capital Loss Calculation:

Business loss	$(10,000)
Rental income, net	4,000
Employment income	2,000
	$ (4,000)
Deductible alimony payments	(8,000)
Net income (loss), per return	$(12,000)
Rental income is analyzed further as:	
Property A income	$ 5,000
Property B loss	(1,000)
Net rental income	$ 4,000
Calculation of non-capital loss:	
Rental income, property A	$ 5,000
Employment income	2,000
	$ 7,000
Net taxable capital gains	—
Total of income	$ 7,000
Less — deductible alimony	(8,000)
Total of income less miscellaneous deductions, see (3) above	Nil
Losses:	
Business	$ 10,000
Rental, property B	1,000
	$ 11,000
Deduct total of incomes less miscellaneous deductions	Nil
Non-capital loss	$ 11,000

[¶1085.15] *Regenerating Non-Capital Losses Used against Capital Gains*

If a non-capital loss arises in a year in excess of ordinary income, the mechanics of income computation will automatically use the excess against the taxable portion of any net taxable capital gain for the year (i.e., against the income inclusion portion of capital gains in excess of capital losses of the year). Prior to 1991, capital losses of other years applied to the year in question could not alter this result, because such losses affect only taxable income after income computations. Under amendments effective for 1991 and later taxation years, this result is altered by adding directly to the non-capital loss pool any net capital losses of other years applied to reduce net capital gains in a particular year. The result is that capital losses available for carryover to a year can be substituted for non-capital losses which might otherwise have to be used against net capital gains. This is true retrospectively in that a capital loss arising after the year of computation can be carried back to displace a non-capital loss used against net capital gains, thus effectively regenerating non-capital losses.

(ITA: 3; 4; 56; 60–66.4; 110; 111; IT-232R3 Losses — Their Deductibility in the Loss Year or in Other Years)

[¶1087] CARRYFORWARD AND CARRYBACK OF NON-CAPITAL LOSSES

The amount of non-capital losses determined in ¶1085 for a taxation year may be deducted against income from all sources for the three preceding years and, depending on the taxation year in which the loss originated, may be carried forward for 7, 10, or 20 years, as discussed below.

[¶1087.05] *Losses Arising in Taxation Years Ending Before March 23, 2004 (Seven-Year Carryforward)*

The amount of non-capital losses determined in ¶1085 for a taxation year may be deducted against income from all sources for the three preceding years and, where the loss arose in a taxation year ending before March 23, 2004 (so, for individuals, a loss which arose in 2003 or earlier), the loss or any portion of the loss not carried back may be carried forward and deducted against income of the seven following years. You are not obliged to carry back a loss or any part of it rather than carrying it forward. Carrying a loss back has the advantage of gaining you an immediate refund of prior year taxes, but this must be weighed against the possibility of using some or all of the loss against higher tax brackets in future, as illustrated in the example below and in ¶1095.

If the non-capital loss is attributable to farming or fishing, the loss is deductible (from all sources of income) for the three preceding years and the 10 following years. See also ¶1720. The special category of restricted farm losses may only be carried over against farming income; see ¶1750.

[¶1087.10] *Losses Arising in Taxation Years Ending After March 22, 2004, and Before 2006 (10-Year Carryforward)*

As with earlier losses, the amount of non-capital losses determined in ¶1085 for a taxation year may be deducted against income from all sources for the three preceding years. Where the loss arose in a taxation year ending after March 22, 2004 and before 2006 (so, for individuals, a loss arising in 2004 or 2005), any portion of the loss not carried back may be carried forward and deducted against income of the *ten* following years. As before, you are not obliged to carry back any portion of a loss rather than carrying it forward. As before, carrying a loss back has the advantage of gaining you an immediate refund of prior year taxes, but this must be weighed against the possibility of using some or all of the loss against higher tax brackets in future, as illustrated in the example below and in ¶1095.

There is no change in the status of farming or fishing losses, which remain eligible for three-year carryback and ten-year carryforward. As before see also ¶1720 and ¶1750 regarding losses from farming or fishing.

[¶1087.12] *Losses Arising in 2006 and Later Taxation Years (20-Year Carryforward)*

As with earlier losses, the amount of non-capital losses determined in ¶1085 for a taxation year may be deducted against income from all sources for the three preceding years. Where the loss arose in a taxation year in or after 2006 (so, for individuals, a loss arising in 2006 or later), any portion of the loss not carried back may be carried forward and deducted against income of the *20* following years. As before, you are not obliged to carry back any portion of a loss rather than carrying it forward. Carrying a loss back has the advantage of gaining you an immediate refund of prior year taxes, but this must be weighed against the possibility of using some or all of the loss against higher tax brackets in future, as illustrated in the example below and in ¶1095.

Farming or fishing losses, which remain as a distinct category, are (for losses arising in and after 2006) eligible for three-year carryback and 20-year carryforward against all sources of income. See also ¶1720 regarding losses from farming or fishing. As before, restricted farm losses may only be carried over (back three or forward 20 years) against farming income; see ¶1750.

[¶1087.14] *Effect of Rate Changes*

The lowest marginal tax rate was 16% before 2005, 15% in 2005, 15.25% in 2006, and 15% in and after 2007. This has some effect on the choices made in deciding to carry losses forward or back. Loss carryovers arising in 2007, to the extent they reduce low-bracket income, can be carried back against 16%, 15%, or 15.25%, depending on the year to which they are applied. Similarly, losses arising in 2008 can (to the extent applied against low-rate income) be carried back against a rate of 15%, 15.25%, or 15%, depending on the year to which they are applied. If carried forward, they will (if applicable to low-bracket income) apply only against a 15% rate. Although the effects are not large, and apply only to the extent losses reach into income far enough to reduce low bracket income, the rate changes do in some slight degree affect the decision as to which year losses should be carried.

Changing provincial tax rates should also be considered.

[¶1087.15] *General Rules*

The following rules apply regardless of when the loss was incurred.

If you owed a debt, but settled your liability for an amount which was less than the principal amount of the debt, the amount of losses you can carry forward may be reduced. For details, see ¶565.

If you are carrying a loss back to the 1st, 2nd, or 3rd preceding taxation year, a Request for Loss Carryback can be filed by the due date for the return for the year in which the loss arose (but see ¶1097). Form T1A is available from the CRA website.

The CRA will calculate your income tax refund, if any, for you. For interest arising on a loss carryback, see ¶1098. Although the CRA requests that form T1A be used, you may file an amended return. An amended return must be prepared using the appropriate year's form (e.g., a 2008 loss deducted from 2005 income would be reported by preparing an amended return on a 2005 form) but there is no need to include all of the schedules filed with the original return since the CRA will already have this information on file. The amended return is essentially for your own information in calculating your refund; the CRA prefers you to file only the T1A.

Note that, although the allowable business investment loss carryforward period was extended (along with other non-capital losses) to 10 years in 2004, it has not been extended to 20 years in 2006. The carryforward period for these losses incurred in and after 2006 remains 10 years, after which unutilized amounts revert to net capital losses.

That is, any unutilized allowable business investment loss in respect of which the carryover period expires in a taxation year will be included in the taxpayer's net capital loss for that year. Thus, allowable business investment losses which cannot be deducted in the carryforward period for non-capital losses can be carried forward indefinitely as net capital losses.

In the example of loss carrybacks below, Robert Stellar carried the non-capital loss incurred in 2009 back and apportioned it over the past three years. However, he could have chosen instead to carry all or a portion of the loss forward for up to 20 years, if it was beneficial to him. This might occur if he anticipated much higher levels of income taxed at much higher rates within the carryforward period.

You need not lose the availability of your personal amount credits where losses are carried back to earlier years, as you have the option of only utilizing a portion of your non-capital loss. In general, you would not want to eliminate a personal amount credit (most of which have no carryover) by applying a loss which could be carried to a different year.

You have the choice of whether to deduct all, or a portion of, a loss in a particular year or to carry it back to a previous year or forward to a subsequent year, up to the time limitation.

The one restriction which does remain is that losses arising in Year 1 must be applied before losses arising in Year 2. It appears to follow that if Robert Stellar had carried back 2008 losses to 2007, he could not later carry back 2009 losses to 2006, because he would not be applying 2008 losses first in 2006. It appears, however, that the CRA does not normally apply this restriction, which, arguably, could in any event be overcome by the rejigging of carrybacks to apply 2008 to 2006 and then 2009 to 2007.

Carryback of Losses using Form T1A

In 2006, Robert Stellar had taxable income of $26,000 (before personal amount computations), including a taxable capital gain of $3,000 (at an inclusion rate of 50%). That is, he had ordinary income of $23,000, plus taxable capital gain of $3,000. In 2007, he had taxable income of $27,400 with no capital gain or loss. In 2008, he had taxable income of $39,000, with no taxable capital gain or loss.

In 2009, he had net employment income of $10,000. He sold his remaining investments at the end of the year for a net loss for the year of $11,400, giving rise to a net allowable capital loss ($^1/_2$ of actual loss) of $5,700, and started his own business, which has a calendar year end and a loss of $34,100.

Robert Stellar would be entitled to claim a non-capital loss carryback of $24,100 (business loss minus employment income) to his 2008, 2007, or 2006 taxation year to the extent of taxable income in any of those years. Usually he would spread the loss back over preceding years to the extent of the highest marginal rate to which he had been subjected, as illustrated after the capital loss carryback discussion below.

Capital Loss Carryback

In addition to his non-capital loss carryback, discussed below, Mr. Stellar would have a net capital loss available for carryback to 2006, 2007, or 2008 of $5,700. Since the 2009 loss had a 50% inclusion rate and the 2006 gain also had a 50%

inclusion rate, he need not adjust the carryback for a differential inclusion rate, as had to be done when carrying 2000 or later capital losses back to offset 2000 or earlier capital gains. (Where losses arose in 2000, 2001, 2002, and/or 2003, an adjustment could be required where a loss was carried back to an earlier year with a different inclusion rate. In theory, that adjustment operation is still conducted for all losses applied to an earlier year. However, for 2004 and later losses, the inclusion rate in the loss year must necessarily be the same as that in the year to which the loss is carried back. It must follow that the outcome, which is that there is no adjustment, is known in advance, and as a practical matter the operation is ignored.) Accordingly, $3,000 of the $5,700 loss incurred in 2009 at a 50% inclusion rate is needed to wipe out the $3,000 gain realized in 2006 at a 50% inclusion rate, and the remaining $2,700 of net capital loss ($5,400 of actual capital loss) will remain on hand to be used against net capital gains in future years.

Non-Capital Loss Carryback

Mr. Stellar has elected to carry back to 2006 enough of his 2009 net (allowable) capital loss to offset the taxable capital gain of that year, leaving at that stage an effective 2006 taxable income of $23,000. He might determine the application of the business loss as follows: $1,115 applied to 2008 will lower his 2008 taxable income to $37,885 eliminating all tax at rates above the lowest bracket ($37,885 for 2008; tables of rate brackets for earlier years are found at ¶1415). There remains for loss carryback $22,985 ($24,100 loss minus $1,115 applied to 2008). Mr. Stellar next calculates the amount he can carry furthest back without losing tax credits. For 2006, his federal tax on $23,000 before personal non-refundable credits would be $3,507. Assuming personal amounts of, say, $8,900, converted at 15.25% to tax credits of $1,357, he wants to eliminate tax of $3,507 - $1,357 = $2,150. He can find the income number to offset this tax by dividing the tax by the effective 15.25% rate, thus: $2,150/.1525 = $14,100 (rounded). Accordingly, he will apply $14,100 of his 2009 loss to 2006, reducing his 2006 income to $8,900, at which level, tax of $1,357 will be fully offset by his personal amount credits. (Rounding can lead to marginal differences; he could as well carry back $23,000 - $8,900 = $14,100, leaving $8,900 of income, to be exactly offset by the total of his personal amounts. As long as no higher rate bracket is involved, this yields the correct answer more simply.) Having used $1,115 of his loss against 2008 and $14,100 against 2006, the remaining loss is $8,885 ($24,100 - $1,115 - $14,100). His 2007 income of $27,400 is compared with his 2007 basic personal amounts of, say, $9,600, and it is evident that he can apply the whole remaining loss to 2007 and not worry about wasting carryback against tax credits. The $8,885 could be applied equally to 2008. Normally, it is preferable to use losses against the oldest year and so preserve later years to absorb later losses. There is, for these particular years, the additional consideration that losses applied to the lowest tax bracket in 2006 will reduce income taxed at 15.25%, whereas losses applied to the lowest bracket in 2007 or 2008 will reduce income taxed at 15%. The overall effect may not be substantial enough to override other considerations.

(ITA: 80; 111; 164)

[¶1089] RESTRICTED FARM LOSSES

The meaning, and calculation, of restricted farm losses is discussed at ¶1750.

A restricted farm loss may be deductible against income from all farming businesses in either the three taxation years preceding the year of the loss or the 20 taxation years following the year of the loss. Use form T1A to calculate carryovers and claim carrybacks.

(ITA: 111)

[¶1090] REASONABLE EXPECTATION OF PROFIT

Overview and Development of Reasonable Expectation of Profit ("REOP") Doctrine

As discussed at ¶704, activities (such as hobbies) which generate occasional income or loss but do not have a "reasonable expectation of profit" overall are not considered businesses, and accordingly the occasional income is not taxed. It follows that the expenses, or losses, are similarly not deductible. The logic is that since there is no business, there is no "source" for the income or loss.

Over time, a similar doctrine had developed for investment losses. Where a capital property (often but not necessarily real property, such as a condominium unit) earns a return (e.g., rental income) on a regular basis, the income is considered income from property and is taxable. Where a similar property incurred regular losses, however, the CRA looked at the investment to determine whether there was a "reasonable expectation of profit" from the investment and, if there was not, the losses were denied. So common was this argument that "reasonable expectation of profit" acquired the acronym REOP.

It had become established that the reasonable expectation of profit (REOP) test is not annual but must be based on a fair length of time. It was also established that profit means a return of positive income over the lifetime of the investment. However, the actual return of income over the period of holding the investment is not in fact the measurement of REOP. Rather, REOP is a subjective test of whether the investor could plausibly ("reasonably") have had an expectation of profit over the life of the investment. Note that a reasonable expectation of capital gain will not suffice, although where a property is purchased with the expectation of resale at a profit (as opposed to earning a profit over time), the acquisition may be an "adventure in the nature of trade" (i.e., a speculation; see ¶758), which is considered a business. Profit from an adventure in the nature of trade is income (not capital gain), and losses are deductible as business losses.

Real estate investments have been the most common target of assessments denying an investment loss under the REOP test. Real estate is expensive, and financing (mortgage costs) may exceed income for many years.

The waters here are muddied where there is an element of personal use. For example, if you buy a condominium in Florida and you and/or your family live in it for six months in the winter, and you try to rent it out for the summer when there is no market for such rentals, the CRA is likely to take the view that the condo has no reasonable expectation of profit to you and that an effort to deduct, say, mortgage interest for the six months of non-personal use is merely an effort to deduct personal or living expenses.

Even where there was no element of personal use, the CRA frequently disallowed rental losses on REOP grounds. Case law challenging these assessments could be said, at least prior to 2002, to have come down firmly on both sides of the issue, depending on the courts' view of the salient facts in a particular case.

In *Shaughnessy v. The Queen*, 2002 DTC 1272 (T.C.C.), the Tax Court made a singularly valiant effort to reconcile the cases into a coherent doctrine which, in the absence of personal use issues, is extremely favourable to the taxpayer. The Court also pointed out that losses are usually created largely by interest expense, and after the 2001 Supreme Court decision in *Ludco Enterprises Ltd. v. the Queen*, 2001 DTC 5505 (S.C.C.), holding that if an investment creates an income flow that is sufficient to justify an interest deduction even if the income will always be less than the interest (see *Tax Planning and*

Interest Deduction at ¶1063.10), it is difficult to deny interest expense on REOP grounds.

Demise of REOP Doctrine as a Definitive Test

In two 2002 cases, *Stewart v. The Queen*, 2002 DTC 6969 (S.C.C.), and *The Queen v. Jack Walls and Rupert Buvyer*, 2002 DTC 6960 (S.C.C.), the Supreme Court demolished the REOP doctrine in any case where an investment or business venture is purely commercial in nature. It held that in the absence of a "personal element" in the enterprise (such as a hobby in which profit or loss is incidental, or personal use of a rental property), the CRA may not second-guess the taxpayer's wisdom in pursuing an unprofitable venture. It is sufficient that the taxpayer made a commercial decision, however ill-advised, to create a source of income and therefore a source of deductible loss. Specific expenditures may be challenged on specific grounds (such as being intrinsically unreasonable), but so long as the venture has no personal element and does generate an income flow (even if it is and always must finally be negative due to associated expenses), the losses cannot be denied on REOP grounds. Where there is a personal element, the REOP test is one element in determining whether the enterprise was sufficiently commercial in nature to create a source of income or loss, or whether it was indeed merely a hobby or personal expense. For more detail, see the discussions of *Walls* (a business partnership case) at ¶704 and *Stewart* (a real estate investment) at ¶690.

In *Hammill v. the Queen*, 2004 DTC 3271 (T.C.C.), aff'd 2005 DTC 5397 (F.C.A.), the Court ruled that where an individual engaged in lengthy activities which he thought constituted a business, or at least an adventure in the nature of trade (which the CRA had conceded), but which were from the beginning part of a scheme to defraud him, there was never a business and consequently no business loss to deduct from other income. The Tax Court decision was subject to much criticism in the tax practice community, which cited a long line of cases to the effect that it was not the business of the CRA to second guess the business judgement of the taxpayer. The Federal Court of Appeal in effect ruled that it may not be the right of the CRA, but it is the right of the courts. There is some sentiment in the tax practice community that this will ultimately reintroduce a reasonable expectation of profit test in another guise, although the facts of the case would seem to limit it to cases of fairly spectacular gullibility, supported by an absence reasonable business practice.

Farming losses stand on separate ground, to which the REOP test does apply for certain purposes; see ¶1750.

(ITA: 3 Income for taxation year; 4 Income or loss from a source or from sources in a place; 9(3) Gains and losses not included)

[¶1091] LIMITED PARTNERSHIP LOSSES

Losses incurred by a limited partner are restricted to the amount the limited partner has "at risk". To the extent that these losses are restricted in the current year, they may be carried forward indefinitely for use against future income from the partnership or for deduction as the "at-risk" amount increases. The purpose of these rules is to restrict the deductibility of tax shelter investments (¶2521). The rules are discussed in detail at ¶1818.

Losses from partnerships other than limited partnerships will typically be non-capital, net capital, farm or restricted farm losses of the partners to the extent of their partnership interests, and will be treated by them as described in other sections of this chapter. Note, however, that the limited partnership restrictions extend the definition of limited partnership beyond the strict legal form. See ¶1818.

[¶1093] NET CAPITAL LOSSES

[¶1093.05] *Current Year Losses*

Your capital gains and losses are to be reported on Schedule 3 of the return. Most of Chapter 5 is devoted to calculating your capital gains and capital losses. Briefly, capital gains are proceeds of disposition of capital property in excess of the adjusted cost base of the property. However, gains on eligible capital property (¶768), cultural property disposed of to specified organizations (¶547), Canadian resource properties (¶2202), foreign resource property (¶2225), certain insurance policies (¶981), and timber resource property (¶881) are not capital gains but are dealt with under other provisions discussed in the paragraphs cited. Similarly, capital losses arise where the adjusted cost base of capital property disposed of exceeds proceeds of disposition. However, capital losses do not include losses from depreciable property (¶557) or eligible capital property, Canadian resource property, or insurance policies.

If your capital losses exceed your capital gains, a fraction or percentage (called the inclusion rate) of this excess will be your "net capital loss". That fraction was $^2/_3$ (75%) for 1990 through 1999 inclusive, and is $^1/_2$ (50%) for 2001 and later years. For 2000, however, the fraction may be $^2/_3$, $^1/_2$, or any fraction in between. This determination is discussed at ¶500a. It is important that you keep a record of the year of origin of your loss and, in the case of capital losses arising in 2000 in particular, the applicable inclusion rate, prominently on file in your tax records, since capital losses arising at one rate must be adjusted when applied to capital gains arising at a different rate. Capital losses carry forward indefinitely (i.e., as long as you live), so that even where all your losses arise after 2000, it is possible that future inclusion rate adjustments will affect current loss applications in future years.

You may not deduct net allowable capital losses (the inclusion portion of current year capital losses net of the taxable portion of current year capital gains) from other income for the current year. The losses, termed "net capital losses", are only available to carry back or forward against the taxable portion of capital gains of other years as discussed below.

Net capital losses may be carried back to any of the three preceding years for which there are taxable capital gains remaining after capital gains deduction applied for that preceding year. Thus, for example, 2016 net capital losses may be applied to 2013, 2014, or 2015, using form T1A. At present, these limits mean that current year losses can only be applied to earlier years in which the inclusion rate was the same.

It is common to carry losses back where possible to obtain refunds, although you would be influenced by your marginal tax rate on the gains in the year to which you consider applying losses, as in the Robert Stellar example at ¶1087. However, the fact that capital losses can only be used against capital gains will cut the other way where capital transactions and therefore capital gains are rare.

Net capital losses of a year which are not used by carrying them back to earlier years remain available for carryforward to any future year. There is no time limit on such carryforwards.

Carrybacks of allowable net capital losses to prior years are accomplished by filing form T1A (Area III) with your T1. There is no form for carryforwards, although T1A will help you to calculate the correct amount available; however, you must keep track of the amounts available to you and deduct them in future years on line 253, to the extent you have capital gains in that year on line 127 on which you are not claiming the capital gains deduction (see ¶502). The CRA does maintain a computerized record of your unused capital losses, and you may obtain this information from your Tax Services Office (¶287). You may carry capital losses back three years and forward indefinitely, and you may apply any amount of loss in any open year to the extent of gains on which exemption is not claimed, so long as losses are applied in order. For example, your 2015 (and earlier) net capital losses must be applied to other years before 2016 net capital losses are applied.

[¶1093.10] *Applying Loss Carryforwards in the Current Year*

As explained above, net capital losses of prior years carry forward indefinitely. To the extent previously unused, they may be claimed on line 253, to the extent of taxable capital gains on line 127 for which no deduction is claimed on line 254.

Because the inclusion portion of actual capital losses for 2000 and later years will generally differ from the inclusion portion for 1999 and earlier years (see ¶500a), an adjustment is required when applying in the current year a loss from a year which had a different inclusion rate. The underlying principle of this adjustment is simple: a dollar of actual loss (before applying the inclusion rate) from one year should offset a dollar of actual gain (before applying the inclusion rate) of another year. Keeping this principle in mind is a useful check on the actual calculation results.

Technically, where you have a target taxable capital gain (say, in 2016) which you want to offset with a prior year (say, in 1999) net capital loss, you determine the loss required to offset that gain with the formula

target gain × loss year inclusion rate / gain year inclusion rate

Assume, for example, that you had a 2016 capital gain of $4,000 at the inclusion rate of 50%, and so a taxable capital gain of $2,000. You want to apply a 1999 capital loss of $10,000, which had an inclusion rate of 75%. Using the formula you would calculate the amount of 1999 loss needed to eliminate the 2016 gain as:

$2,000 × 75%/50% = $3,000

From this you learn that using $3,000 of 1999 net capital loss (at a 75% inclusion rate) will offset $2,000 of 2016 gain (at a 50% rate). Your 1999 net capital loss of $7,500 will accordingly be reduced by $3,000 to eliminate the $2,000 taxable capital gain in 2016, leaving a carryforward of $4,500. The proof is that to absorb $4,000 of actual 2016 gain, you used $4,000 of actual 1999 loss, leaving an actual 1999 loss of $10,000 - $4,000 = $6,000, which at a 1999 inclusion rate of 75% is 75% × $6,000 = $4,500.

The rules of course prevent you from carrying forward to the current year more net capital loss than will eliminate capital gains of the current year.

If your loss is inadequate to eliminate the current year taxable capital gain, you simply apply the whole loss to the target year. To determine how much target year gain has been eliminated by your loss, you stand the formula on its head:

current year loss applied × gain year inclusion rate / loss year inclusion rate

Thus, if you had a $2,500 loss ($1,875 net capital loss) in 1999 carried forward against a $4,000 gain in 2016 ($2,000 taxable capital gain), applying the whole loss would eliminate

$1,875 × 50%/75% = $1,250

From this you learn that using your $1,875 allowable capital loss from 1999 will eliminate $1,250 of your $2,000 taxable capital gain in 2016, leaving a taxable capital gain of $750. Again, the proof is that an actual loss of $2,500 from 1999 has reduced an actual gain of $4,000 from 2016, leaving $1,500 of actual gain at an inclusion rate of 50% (50% × $1,500 = $750).

Note that losses from taxation years before 1990 have lower inclusion rates than losses from 1990 through February 27, 2000 inclusive. You cannot always assume the inclusion rate of a carryforward is 75%; rather, you must identify the year of origin and apply the correct rate in the formula.

The CRA does things somewhat differently. In Charts 4 and 5 in Chapter 5 of its *Capital Gains Guide* (T4037), it has you step down all your net capital loss carryforwards from earlier years with higher inclusion rates and restate them as if the current year inclusion rate applied. Thus, for losses of 1990 through 1999 applied after 2000, the earlier loss is divided by its 75% inclusion rate to restore it to a whole gain amount, and then multiplied by the current year inclusion rate (50% when applied to 2001 and later). This two-step process is combined into one step by using an adjustment factor of, for 1990 through 1999 losses carried to 2001 and later, 50%/75% (old loss ÷ 75% × 50%), or $^2/_3$.

The adjustment factor in Chart 5 of the CRA Guide to step down pre-2001 losses applied to 2001 and later years is:

- for 1987 and earlier net capital losses, 50%/50%, or 1;
- for 1988 and 1989 net capital losses, $^1/_2 \div {}^2/_3 = {}^3/_4$;
- for 1990 through 1999 net capital losses, $^1/_2 \div {}^3/_4 = {}^2/_3$;
- for 2000, 50% divided by your 2000 inclusion rate, which, by the simple expedient of multiplying the fraction by $^2/_2$, the CRA shows as 1 ÷ (2 × your 2000 inclusion rate); and
- for 2001 and later net capital losses carried forward to later years, 50%/50%, or 1.

In the CRA chart, you then total the prior year losses, apply as much as you wish to the current year, subtract the oldest losses first, from your remaining loss balance (if any), and restore the losses to their year-of-origin value by multiplying the remaining balance by the reciprocal of the step-down, so that you can repeat the process again in later years in which you have taxable capital gains.

You will note that the CRA chart distinguishes between capital losses before May 23 and after May 22, 1995. This is because the older losses form a pool of "pre-1986 capital losses" which to some extent are deductible from other income, as discussed below. It follows that the pool must be separately measured as it is consumed against capital gains.

[¶1093.15] *Applying Allowable Business Investment Losses*

Note that "allowable business investment losses" (ABILs) as described at ¶580 are normally not reported on Schedule 3 (except, for 1994 and earlier T1 returns, as addbacks at line 535 where their nature was changed by use of the capital gains deduction), but rather are deducted currently at line 217 with carryover amounts forming part of non-capital losses described at ¶1085. Once the allowable business investment loss is fixed by its year of origin, no further adjustment is required as it is carried forward or back against income of other years, nor when it rejoins the net capital loss pool after a specified period in the non-capital loss pool.

Example

Lynne Allen had a business investment loss (¶580) on shares of her private company of $100,000, sold in July 2000. Two-thirds of this, or $66,667 is an allowable business investment loss. $50,000 was used to eliminate all other income for 2000. The remaining

$16,667 becomes a non-capital loss, which can be applied against ordinary income for any of the past three or next seven years. The full $16,667 will be available, neither more nor less, to offset $16,667 of ordinary income earned before or after 2000. No adjustment is made to match changes in the ⅔ inclusion rate. If the loss is not used before 2008, it (or what remains of it) will cease to be a non-capital loss and become a net capital loss carryover in 2008, with no further inclusion rate adjustment. The inclusion rate was fixed by the year the loss arose.

Similarly, a 1999 business investment loss of $100,000, giving rise to an allowable business investment loss of $75,000 and eliminating $50,000 of 1990 income, would leave $25,000 for carryover against ordinary income with no further adjustment.

The specified period for which an ABIL remains in the non-capital loss pool before any unused portion reverts to the capital loss pool is:

- for ABILs arising in taxation years ending before March 23, 2004, seven years; and
- for ABILs arising in taxation years ending after March 22, 2004 (including ABILs arising in 2009, notwithstanding the 20-year carryforward period for other non-capital losses), 10 years.

This has no effect on the example above, which relates to such losses arising before 2001.

[¶1093.25] *Applying Loss Carryovers of Listed Personal Property*

Losses arising on the disposition of "listed personal property" (¶546) are governed by special rules discussed at ¶548.

Listed personal property losses are carried over in full against full listed personal property gains of the three preceding or seven following taxation years, and then the taxable capital gain rate is applied to the resulting whole listed personal property gain. Accordingly, there is no adjustment required for changing taxable capital gain inclusion rates.

Since listed personal property loss carryovers are applied directly to reduce listed personal property gains, they effectively reduce net income (at line 127 and Schedule 3) rather than taxable income (at line 253), and so beneficially reduce income for purposes of calculating Old Age Security clawback (¶1419), personal amount credit for age (¶1108), Canada Child Benefit (¶1498), GST credit, and similar means-tested provincial credits (Chapter 15).

Listed personal property is a subset of personal-use property, losses from which cannot otherwise be used at all (¶548).

[¶1095] DEDUCTION OF LOSSES

There is no provision ordering deductions for losses; accordingly, you may choose which type or types of loss to deduct in computing your taxable income, subject to the restrictions applicable to the deduction of net capital losses and restricted farm losses (see ¶1089 and ¶1093). In addition, you may choose not to claim all or part of a loss carryover in computing your taxable income for a taxation year but rather to carry losses forward to be deducted in later years in the carryover period.

Example

John Purdy has incurred the following income (non-capital loss):

2004	($20,000)
2005	($10,000)
2006	($30,000)
2007	$10,000
2008	$40,000
2009	$70,000

For purposes of this example, it is assumed that John's 2004 to 2006 non-capital losses were not deducted in earlier years for lack of income.

John can choose to utilize his above losses as follows:

	2007	*2008*	*2009*
Income	$10,000	$ 40,000	$ 70,000
2004 loss utilization	—	(2,115)	(17,885)
Portion of 2005 loss utilized	—	—	(10,000)
Portion of 2006 loss utilized	—	—	(1,389)
Taxable income before personal amounts	$ 10,000	$ 37,885	$ 40,726

(1) In 2007, John chose not to deduct any of the 2004 loss since he had sufficient personal amount and other tax credits to reduce the tax on his $10,000 taxable income to nil.

(2) In 2008, John used $2,115 of the 2004 loss to reduce his income to $37,885 (the top of the low-rate bracket for that year). He did not use the full loss because he was confident that his losses would not expire before he could use them, and that his income would continue to rise. He chose to preserve the loss for use against a higher income bracket.

(3) In 2009, the balance of the 2004 loss is claimed ($17,885) plus all of the 2005 loss ($10,000) and $1,389 of the 2006 loss, to reduce income to $40,726, where a higher tax rate commences. Note that all of the 2004 loss must be deducted before any portion of any subsequent year's loss can be utilized, and similarly the 2005 loss must be used before 2006 is applied. John anticipates that his 2010 income will continue at a high marginal tax rate and therefore chooses to save some of his 2006 loss to carry forward to 2010.

(4) The non-capital loss carryforward at the end of 2009 is $28,611, all of it from 2006. John can utilize this non-capital loss carryforward in subsequent taxation years, up to and including the 2026 taxation year. Because the loss arose in 2006, the carryforward period is 20 years.

Note that while John can optimize losses against high marginal rates for federal purposes, his resulting federal taxable income is binding for provincial tax as well (except of course if he is a Quebec taxpayer). Quebec apart, an individual cannot optimize losses against both federal and provincial marginal rates and personal tax credits (unless the province happens to have a rate credit structure identical to the federal one for the year). Since federal rates are generally a good deal higher, you will generally optimize your loss claims for federal purposes and let the provincial chips fall where they may.

It is not entirely clear what happens if John cannot utilize his losses after 2009 in the carryforward period because his income expectations do not materialize. In Information Circular 84-1, the CRA takes a stand of sorts against the revision of "permissive deductions" such as capital cost allowance or capital gain reserves, at least once the time for filing notice of objection for the year in which they were originally claimed has expired, although there are notable exceptions in the case of reassessment for other reasons. The Circular notably fails to comment on loss carryovers. In general, the CRA is ill-disposed to what it regards as retroactive tax planning, but it simply does not appear to be on record about revisions of earlier carryforward claims to prevent losses from expiring in later years. It is particularly doubtful this would be allowed where the earlier years are statute-barred.

(ITA: 111)

[¶1097] TIMELY APPLICATION FOR LOSS CARRYBACK

It is arguable on the words of the *Income Tax Act* that the right to carry back losses of all descriptions (non-capital, net capital, etc.) technically depends on timely application for the carryback. The loss carryback request must be made by the filing deadline for the year in which the loss arises. Typically, the request is made by filing a T1A form with the return for the year in which the loss arises. However, if this is overlooked, or for some reason the return cannot be filed on a timely basis, it is essential to communicate to the CRA in writing by the filing deadline the intention to carry back a loss.

This rather harsh rule has in the past been administered by the CRA in a reasonable fashion, so that as long as a prior year is open to reassessment, the CRA would normally use its statutory discretion (¶221) to honour carryback requests. This was restated in 1985. Nevertheless, it is preferable to comply with the strict rule wherever possible.

In *Burleigh v. The Queen*, 2004 DTC 2399 (T.C.C.), the Tax Court dismissed out of hand a contention by the CRA that an individual taxpayer could not obtain recognition of a loss unless a timely return for the loss year had been filed. The Court appeared to rule that since an individual is not required to file a return for a loss year, it is open to him or her to appeal the year to which a loss has been carried, regardless of whether a timely return, or perhaps any return, has been filed for the loss year. With respect, the Court saw this as so obvious that it simply ignored any analysis of statutory language. No appeal was filed by the CRA. On the other hand, neither has the CRA commented on the case. The case is welcome for taxpayers who do not, for whatever reason, file a timely return for a loss year. Nevertheless, the issue has never been carried past the Tax Court level, and the cautious taxpayer will want to file a timely loss year return in any event.

This rule also applies (if indeed it applies at all) to carrybacks of year-of-death charitable donations (¶1931) and to tax credits eligible for carryback (¶1455 and ¶1463).

(ITA: 152(6); IC 84-1 Revision of capital cost allowance claims and other permissive deductions; Other Publications: CTF Round Table 49:2, Question 3)

[¶1098] INTEREST ON REFUNDS ARISING FROM LOSS CARRYBACKS

Where a loss is carried back, it typically gives rise to a retroactive overpayment in the year to which the loss has been applied. Interest on that overpayment arises commencing at the latest of:

- the first day following the actual loss year;
- the day on which the return for the actual loss year was filed;
- where an amended return or T1A is filed, the day it is filed; and
- where a written request to the CRA resulted in reassessment to take account of the carryback, the day on which the request was made.

The list above restates the statute; as a practical matter it appears that interest commences to run on a carryback at the time the CRA is notified in writing of the request for the carryback. Typically this will be by T1A filed with the return for the loss year, although it could be later if the actual carryback request is not made at that time.

(ITA: 164(5))

SPECIFIC QUESTIONS AND ANSWERS

[¶1098a] SPECIFIC QUESTIONS AND ANSWERS

I incurred losses in a business in Year 1, so I have now sold the business and found a job. Can I claim my Year 1 business loss against my employment income in Year 5?

Yes — the tax rules permit a non-capital loss to be claimed against income from any source.

In February of Year 2, I incurred a $5,000 capital loss on the sale of some shares. I had a capital gain in Year 1. Can I file my Year 1 return now to claim a carryback of the Year 2 net capital loss deduction?

No — you must wait until after the end of Year 2. This capital loss must first be deducted from any capital gains you may have in Year 2. Only after the end of Year 2 will you be able to demonstrate that some portion of this loss is a net capital loss which is deductible in Year 1. See ¶1095.

I incurred a capital loss on the sale of a painting in Year 2. I realized capital gains on shares disposed of in Year 1 and in Year 2. Will I be able to deduct the loss from the Year 2 gain and carry back any excess to deduct from my Year 1 gain?

No — capital losses on paintings, which are listed personal property, can only be deducted from capital gains on listed personal property. See ¶576 and ¶577.

Chapter 11

Personal Tax Credit Amounts

THESE POINTS ARE COVERED IN THIS CHAPTER

CRA REFERENCES RELATING TO THIS CHAPTER

T1 Lines and Schedules

- Line 113 — Old age security pension [¶1110] [¶1195]
- Line 144 — Workers' compensation benefits [¶1110] [¶1108]
- Line 145 — Social assistance payments [¶1103]
- Line 146 — Net federal supplements [¶1110]
- Line 236 — Net income [¶1103]
- Line 250 — Other payments deduction [¶1110]
- Federal Worksheet, Line 301, Age amount [¶1108]
- Federal Worksheet, Line 316, Disability amount (for self if under 18 at year-end) [¶1255]
- Federal Worksheet, Line 318, Disability amount transferred from a dependant [¶1255]
- Schedule 1, Line 300 — Basic personal amount [¶1100] [¶1106]
- Schedule 1, Line 301 — Age amount (if you were born in 1950 or earlier) [¶1108]
- Schedule 1, Line 303 — Spouse or common-law partner amount [¶1113] [¶1114]
- Schedule 1, Line 305 — Amount for an eligible dependant [¶1120]
- Schedule 1, Line 306 — Amount for infirm dependants age 18 or older [¶1126]
- Schedule 1, Line 315 — Caregiver amount [¶1140]
- Schedule 1, Line 316 — Disability amount (for self) [¶1255]
- Schedule 1, Line 318 — Disability amount transferred from a dependant [¶1255]
- Schedule 1, Line 367 — Family caregiver amount for children under 18 years of age [¶1124.05]
- Schedule 5, Line 303 — Amounts for spouse or common-law partner and dependants

CRA Guides

5000-G, "General Income Tax and Benefit Guide"; **RC4064**, "Disability-Related Information"; **RC4065**, "Medical Expenses"

CRA Forms

T2201, "Disability Tax Credit Certificate"

Income Tax Folios

S1-F5-C1, "Related Persons and Dealing at Arm's Length"; **S1-F3-C3**, "Support Payments"

Interpretation Bulletins

IT-513R, "Personal Tax Credits" [Archived]

WHAT YOU SHOULD KNOW ABOUT PERSONAL TAX CREDIT AMOUNTS

RECENT CHANGES

Indexation Adjustments

2016 factor for indexing personal credit amounts and net income thresholds: 1.3%

On December 8, 2015, the CRA announced in a fact sheet the factor to be used to index certain personal credit amounts and net income thresholds for 2016. You will find in ¶65 a list of the 2016 revised amounts discussed in Chapter 11.

Caregivers of dependants with a mental or physical disability claiming the spouse or common-law partner amount, the amount for an eligible dependant, or the caregiver amount may claim the additional family caregiver amount listed in ¶1150. Those having a disabled child under 18 may not claim the amount for children under age 18 (for 2015 and subsequent years) but may continue to claim the family caregiver amount. Taxpayers claiming the infirm dependant amount (see ¶1126) cannot claim an additional family caregiver amount since it is deemed to be already included in the infirm dependant amount.

Personal amounts and net income thresholds are adjusted annually to reflect increases in the cost of living. For more details on how to calculate those adjustments, refer to ¶1101. For a list of indexed amounts and thresholds for the current year, the preceding year, and the three preceding years, see ¶65, preceding Chapter 1.

[¶1100] WHAT IS A PERSONAL TAX CREDIT OR PERSONAL AMOUNT? — LINE 300

Individuals meeting certain conditions may claim personal amounts and personal tax credits on Schedule 1 of their return to calculate their income tax liability. Those tax credits are non-refundable, which means that they are generally lost if the taxpayer's tax payable is insufficient to claim them in the current year. There are exceptions for charitable donations qualifying for a carryover to another taxation year, and tuition, education, or textbook amounts (the education and textbook credits were repealed effective January 1, 2017) qualifying for a transfer to another person.

Reporting

Personal amounts are:

(1) reported on lines 300 to 332 of Schedule 1 of your return;

(2) added and reported on line 335; and

(3) converted into personal tax credits by multiplying line 335 by the rate of 15% (i.e., lowest personal marginal tax rate) and reporting the result on line 338.

Conditions

The following factors are considered to determine if an individual may claim a particular personal amount:

- Age.
- Support of dependants.
- Physical or mental infirmity.
- Marital or common-law partnership status.

Most Common Personal Amounts

The most common personal amounts are the following:

- Basic personal amount (for all individuals) claimed under paragraph 118(1)(*c*) of the Act and reported on line 300 of your return.
- Age amount (for individuals over 64) claimed under subsection 118(2) of the Act and reported on line 301 of your return.
- Spouse or common-law partner amount (for individuals married or in a common-law partnership) claimed under paragraph 118(1)(*a*) of the Act and reported on line 303 of your return.
- Eligible dependant amount (for a single parent with a dependent child or other relative) claimed under paragraph 118(1)(*b*) of the Act and reported on line 305 of your return.
- Amount for infirm dependant over 17 (for individuals taking care of disabled children, parents, brothers, sisters, aunts, and uncles over 17) claimed under paragraph 118(1)(*d*) of the Act and reported on line 306 of your return.
- Caregiver amount (for individuals taking care of parents over 64 or disabled relatives) claimed under paragraph 118(1)(*c*.1) of the Act and reported on line 315 of your return.

(ITA: 118(1), (2))

[¶1101] CONSUMER PRICE INDEX ADJUSTMENTS

Federal adjustments

All federal personal amounts and limits (i.e., income limits above which you must reduce the personal amounts you may claim for a dependant) discussed in this chapter are indexed annually to the nearest dollar under subsection 117.1(1) of the Act to reflect any increase in the

Consumer Price Index. The average Consumer Price Index for a 12-month period ending on September 30 of the preceding year determines the adjustments.

The government may decide for various reasons to ignore the indexation normally applicable to a personal amount for a particular year and increase it by an amount greater than inflation.

For a list of federal personal amounts and limits for the current and four preceding years, see ¶65.

Provincial adjustments

Provinces do not have to use and index the federal personal amounts to calculate the provincial income tax liability of their residents and, if they do, they may use their own amounts and indexing criteria. The only way to know the value of a provincial personal amount for a particular taxation year is to look at the tax credits form included in the provincial tax package released by the CRA for that year. This package is normally released in the fall of that year.

(ITA: 117.1)

[¶1102] WHO CAN QUALIFY AS A DEPENDANT?

Eligible dependants

You may claim personal amounts for the following dependants:

- Your spouse or common-law partner under paragraph 118(1)(*a*) of the Act (see ¶1113–¶1118).
- Your eligible dependent child or relative under paragraph 118(1)(*b*) of the Act if you are single or separated (see ¶1120).
- Your relatives by blood, marriage, or adoption under paragraph 118(1)(*d*) of the Act, provided they are at least 18 and dependent on you for support by reason of physical or mental infirmity (see ¶1126–¶1140).

Relationship and support during the year

You can only claim personal amounts for dependants if you had a relationship with them and supported them at any time during the year, which is not necessarily throughout the year. Even if you had no relationship with the dependants for the whole year or did not support them for the whole year, you could still make your claim.

(ITA: 118; IT-513R [Archived])

[¶1103] WHAT IS MEANT BY "INCOME"? — LINES 145 AND 236

Income Inclusions

Income earned by your spouse, common-law partner, or other dependants may reduce the amount you claim as a personal amount eligible for a credit.

The income used to calculate the reduction is the net income shown on line 236 of their return, if they file one. The following items are included in the income of your dependant, whether or not they file a T1:

- salary, wages, commissions, tips, and other employment income;
- taxable dividends;
- interest to be reported in the year, and other investment income;
- pensions, including Old Age Security pension and CPP/QPP benefits;
- elected split-pension amount received from spouse;
- Employment Insurance and QPIP benefits;
- Universal Child Care Benefit (for the first 6 months of 2016);
- taxable portion of capital gains (even if lifetime exemption was claimed);
- self-employment net income from a business, profession, farming, or fishing;
- net rental or partnership income;
- support payments, following a relationship breakdown, deductible to the payer;
- taxable scholarships, grants, and prizes; and
- any income item covered in Chapter 9 or normally reported as income on page 2 of their returns; and
- amounts received but exempted under a tax treaty even if they are deductible on line 256 of their returns.

Income Exclusions

The following income items are excluded from the net income of your dependants:

- payments for being a foster parent (see ¶991.05);
- items listed at ¶991 (see discussion of *Sinclair v. M.N.R.* at ¶1114.10);
- lottery winnings; and
- Quebec work income supplement.

Allowed Deductions

The following items shown above line 236 of your dependants' returns may be deducted to calculate their net income which is then used to calculate your personal amounts:

- deductible business expenses;
- annual union or professional dues;
- allowable business investment losses ("ABIL") (see ¶580);
- deductions associated with resource investments in flow-through shares;
- RRSP, PRPP, and RPP deductions;
- support payments made (see Chapter 23);
- elected split-pension amount deduction; and
- generally, deductions discussed at ¶1001 to ¶1076.

Disallowed Deductions

The following items listed below line 236 of your dependants' returns may not be deducted to calculate their net income:

- capital gains exemptions;
- loss carryovers; and
- deductions for social assistance payments like workers' compensation and guaranteed income supplement.

Social Assistance Payments

Social assistance payments received by your spouse or common-law partner in the year but prior to marriage or beginning of common-law partnership can cause confusion.

The general rule is that social assistance payments received by spouses/partners while married or in common-law partnership and living together must be included in the income of the higher-income taxpayer (see ¶990) and are not included in the income of the lower-income spouse or common-law partner.

If you married or entered into a common-law partnership during the year, your spouse's or common-law partner's social assistance payments received prior to marriage or common-law partnership are subject to the general rule that all your spouse's or common-law partner's income for the year is counted in determining your personal amount for your spouse or common-law partner, regardless of when in the year you married or began the common-law partnership. Your spouse's or common-law partner's social assistance payments prior to marriage or common-law partnership should be included in your spouse's or common-law partner's income in computing the personal credit, whereas those received after marriage or partnership will not be included in your spouse's or common-law partner's income but in yours (assuming that your income is higher).

To determine if a person is a spouse or common-law partner, see ¶1113.

(ITA: 3; 56; 60; 81; 118; 5000-G, "General Income Tax and Benefit Guide" (T1 Guide); IT-513R [Archived])

[¶1106] BASIC PERSONAL TAX CREDIT — LINE 300 (SCHEDULE 1)

All individuals may claim the basic personal amount on their tax return. Unlike other personal amounts discussed in this chapter, you do not need to meet any conditions to claim the basic personal amount.

The basic personal amount is:

- claimed under paragraph 118(1)(*c*) of the Act; and
- reported on line 300 of Schedule 1 of your return.

Value for Current Year

For 2016, the basic personal amount is $11,474 and does not have to be reduced by your net income or the net income of any other person.

Value for Preceding Years

Year	*Basic personal amount*
2015	$11,327
2014	$11,138
2013	$11,038
2012	$10,822

Calculation

The basic personal tax credit is calculated at the rate of 15% of the basic personal amount.

Indexation

The basic personal amount is indexed annually (see ¶65 and ¶1101).

Non-Refundability

The credit is non-refundable which means that it cannot be claimed if the taxpayer has no income tax payable before claiming the credit.

(ITA: 118(1)(c))

[¶1107] PERSONAL AMOUNTS OF NON-RESIDENTS

Non-Residents

Non-resident individuals may only claim tax credits for personal amounts if all or substantially all of their employment and business income is from Canada and is not treaty-protected. The CRA generally considers that the "all or substantially all" test is met if 90% of that income is from Canada and not treaty-protected.

For more information on this topic, see ¶2062a to 2069.

Part-Year Residents

Part-year residents are similarly restricted on personal amounts claimed for the period of non-residence and must prorate those amounts for the period of residence.

For more information on this topic, see ¶2107.

(ITA: 118.91; 118.94)

[¶1107c] PERSONAL AMOUNTS OF BANKRUPTS

Taxpayers becoming bankrupt in the year must file two returns for that year:

- one for the period of January 1 to the date before the bankruptcy; and
- one for the remainder of the calendar year.

All personal amounts must be prorated between the two returns according to the days in each period.

For more information on this topic, see ¶286.

(ITA: 118.95)

[¶1108] AGE TAX CREDIT — LINE 301 (FEDERAL WORKSHEET)

If you were 65 or older at the end of the year you may claim the age amount.

The age amount is:

- claimed under subsection 118(2) of the Act;
- calculated on the federal worksheet of your return; and
- reported on line 301 of Schedule 1 of your return.

Value for Current Year

For 2016, your age amount is $7,125 but is reduced by 15% of your net income over $35,927. This means that your age amount is eliminated completely when your net income reaches $83,427.

To calculate the net income level at which the age amount disappears, you divide the age amount by 15% and add the net income threshold amount (e.g., $7,125/.15 +35,927 = $47,500 + $35,927 = $83,427).

See ¶1103 and line 236 of your return to determine your net income.

Value for Preceding Years

Year	*Age Amount*	*Net Income Threshold*	*Net Income Level at Which Age Amount is Eliminated*
2015	$7,033	$35,466	$82,352
2014	$6,916	$34,873	$80,979
2013	$6,854	$34,562	$80,255
2012	$6,720	$33,884	$78,684

Calculation

The age tax credit is calculated at the rate of 15% of the age amount.

Indexation

The age amount and net income threshold are indexed annually (see ¶65 and ¶1101).

Non-Refundability

The credit is non-refundable which means that it cannot be claimed if the taxpayer has no income tax payable before claiming the credit.

Capital Gain on Acquisition of Mortgaged Property

If you realize a capital gain on the acquisition or reacquisition by the creditor of a mortgage property on which you defaulted (see ¶518), you may exclude the gain from your net income to calculate the15% net income reduction.

Transfer to Spouse or Common-Law Partner

If your spouse or common-law partner reached the age of 65 by year-end and does not completely use the age amount, the unused portion of the age amount may be transferred to you as an additional personal amount (see ¶1361). This additional personal amount is calculated on Schedule 2 of your return. The age amount of your spouse or common-law partner is reduced by his or her net income over $35,927, leaving a reduced amount available for transfer. The transferred amount cannot be reduced again in your hands, regardless of your income.

For more information on this topic, see ¶1361.

Relevant Case Law

Workers' Compensation Payment

In *Sveinson v. The Queen*, 2011 DTC 1061 (TCC), the Court concluded that an individual had to include a lump-sum workers' compensation payment in his net income to reduce his age amount in calculating his age amount credit, and disagreed that the payment was simply compensation for injuries that did not reduce the age amount.

(ITA: 118(2); 118.8)

[¶1110] OLD AGE SECURITY AND GUARANTEED INCOME SUPPLEMENTS — LINES 113 AND 146

Under the federal *Old Age Security Act*, general Old Age Security ("OAS") pensions are paid commencing at age 65 to most Canadians, and in addition, guaranteed income supplements are paid to certain persons who qualify because of low income. Some provinces also pay old age pension supplements.

Taxation of Old Age Security Payments

The general pension amounts are income reported on line 113 of your return and are subject to tax. The only offset comes from the age amount reported on line 301 (see ¶1108).

Taxation of Guaranteed Income Supplements

The means-tested guaranteed income supplements received during the year are included in your income on line 146 but deducted on line 250 for no effect on your taxable income. The treatment is the same as for workers' compensation benefits reported on line 144 and social assistance payments reported on line 145. The logic is to force anyone claiming you as a dependant to take the supplements into account in calculating his/her personal amount without forcing you to pay tax on the supplements. However, the supplements are not subject to the rule requiring social assistance receipts to be included in the income of the higher income spouse or common-law partner, and remain taxable only for the taxpayer who received them.

For more information on this topic, see ¶913, ¶990, and ¶1103.

(ITA: 56(1)(*a*); 110(1)(*f*))

[¶1113] MEANING OF SPOUSE OR COMMON-LAW PARTNER — LINE 303

Only an individual supporting and having a relationship with a spouse or common-law partner may report the spouse or common-law partner amount on line 303 of Schedule 1 and claim the related tax credit. Even if the two terms are discussed separately in the paragraphs below, they are treated the same for tax purposes.

[¶1113.05] *Meaning of "Spouse"*

The term "spouse", which is not defined in the Act, refers to an individual to whom a taxpayer is legally married under a civil or religious celebration. Unless they divorce, two spouses remain legally married even if they do not live together or live with someone else.

[¶1113.15] *Meaning of "Common-Law Partner"*

The concept of "common-law partner" is more complicated, but the term is defined in subsection 248(1) of the Act. To qualify as a taxpayer's common-law partner at a particular time, an individual must meet all the following conditions:

(1) be a person of the same or opposite sex;

(2) cohabit in a conjugal relationship with the taxpayer at the particular time; and

(3) meet one of the following two conditions:

(a) have cohabited with the taxpayer throughout the 12-month period ending at that time; or

(b) be the parent of a child of whom the taxpayer is a parent, otherwise than by virtue of the rule that:

(i) a parent includes a person who is a parent of the taxpayer's spouse or common-law partner,

(ii) a child includes the spouse or common-law partner of a child of the taxpayer, or

(iii) a child includes the child of a taxpayer's spouse or common-law partner.

Conjugal Relationship

Conjugal relationships between two individuals include some, but not necessarily all, of the following characteristics:

- shared shelter;
- sexual and personal relations;
- social activities;
- economic support;
- having children; and
- social perception as a couple.

Those relationships are normally considered spousal relationships, regardless of whether the two parties involved wish it or not, and are not easy to sever unless the two parties divorce or stop living together.

The courts have concluded that one could have a conjugal relationship without sex, or sex without a conjugal relationship. Sexual relations are one element but not the only element of a conjugal relationship.

The question of whether two individuals are common-law partners or not is one of fact and not one to be decided by the taxpayers to gain certain tax benefits. Depending on the benefits involved, it may be advantageous or disadvantageous to two individuals to be considered common-law partners. However, they cannot decide on their own to be treated as common-law partners to obtain certain tax advantages.

Elements of Conjugal Relationship

In *Moldowich v. Penttinen* (1980), 17 RFL (2d) 376 (Ont. Dist. Ct.), the Court held that all the elements of a conjugal relationship (i.e., shared shelter; sexual and personal behaviour; social activities, economic support; children; and societal perception of the couple) did not have to be present and could be present in varying degrees for the relationship to be considered a conjugal one. Neither opposite-sex couples nor same-sex couples need to fit the traditional marital model to be considered in a conjugal relationship. For example, two individuals having lived together for many years are still considered to be in a conjugal relationship even if they have no children and no sexual relations. Courts are flexible in applying the factors to determine the existence of a conjugal relationship.

CRA Position on Common-Law Partnerships

The CRA addressed the following common-law partnership issues in a February 2000 press release.

> We have a self-assessment system in which taxpayers are expected to tell the truth and in which persons who make false declarations can be penalized. Whether or not two individuals (opposite-sex or same-sex) are living in a conjugal relationship is a question of fact, and this can include whether or not the couple presents itself publicly as a conjugal couple, has claimed the status of a couple for purposes of a pension or health plan. Taxpayers failing to identify themselves as common-law partners in order to avoid losing some benefits may deprive themselves of important fiscal advantages and pension rights as well.

There is no mention in the press release of sexual relations, a subject the CRA does not want to mention, let alone investigate. The notion that taxpayers hold themselves out as a couple is as far as the CRA wants to go in this direction. One can easily appreciate a reluctance to elucidate further. The courts will look at sexual relations as an element of a conjugal relationship but not the only element.

The CRA is more concerned that couples would fail to report their common-law relationship to be able to claim a greater Canada Child Benefit, eligible dependant personal amounts, and multiple permanent residence exemptions, than it is with couples claiming the common-law relationship to be able to claim a spousal RRSP contribution or tax-free rollover upon death of the other partner. Its enforcement efforts will be directed to the former situation rather than the latter.

Women Sharing an Apartment

Two women acting independently, sharing an apartment, and contributing to upkeep and household chores, but without having sexual relations with each other, are not common-law partners and do not have any interest in being treated as such. After a while they come to rely on each other, decide to remain together more or less indefinitely, decide to buy a house together, and make each other beneficiaries of their pension plans, RRSPs, and the like. They do not have sexual relations together but sometimes act as a couple, taking vacations together, etc. The existence of a common-law partnership does not turn on the presence of sexual relations. A joint declaration of common-law partnership by two partners on their returns is generally accepted by the CRA as a proof of common-law partnership status.

Beneficiary Designation

Accepting self-declarations of common-law status for pension or health plan benefits as indicative on its face of a common-law partnership seems realistic enough, in that the desire to name a partner as a pension, RRSP, or asset beneficiary seems to imply a relationship of some substance, regardless of its sexual content. One thing that is certainly being made clear, however, is that you cannot pick and choose among tax benefits; once you claim common-law status in matters such as pension or health plan rights, the declaration will be considered evidence of the relationship for all tax purposes.

Relationships Between Relatives

The common-law partnership status may apply to cousins or siblings depending on the facts of the situation but will not apply to a situation involving a parent and a child, or other lineal descendants because there is a policy in tax law preventing spousal or common-law partner rollovers on death that would allow properties to pass tax-free to the next generation. The courts should consider the concepts of conjugal relationship and parent -child relationship mutually exclusive.

Deemed Cohabitation

Where two individuals cohabit in a conjugal relationship, that relationship status continues until they have not been cohabiting together for at least 90 days because of a breakdown of their relationship.

Parent of Child

A taxpayer's child is specifically defined and includes not only his/her natural or adopted child but also an individual wholly dependent on him/her for support and of whom he/she has in law or in fact custody and control (see ¶1122). If a taxpayer begins cohabiting with an individual having a child and providing full support to the child, he/she could treat the cohabiting parent as his/her common-law partner immediately, ignoring the requirement to be cohabiting for a the 12-month period.

(ITA: 248(1) "common-law partner", "common-law partnership"; Income Tax Folio: S1-F5-C1 Related Persons and Dealing at Arm's Length)

[¶1113.30] More Than One Spouse or Common-Law Partner

Legal Spouse and Common-Law Partner

You may have a spouse and several common-law partners at once. For example, a taxpayer who leaves a legal spouse to cohabit with the parent of the taxpayer's child could treat the first one as a spouse and the second one as a common-law partner. This situation could continue until the taxpayer obtains a divorce from the legal spouse or there is a breakdown of the common-law relationship.

Religion Allowing Many Spouses

Your religion may allow or encourage you to have several spouses. If this is the case, all of them will be considered to be your spouses for income tax purposes. Even if the marriages are declared bigamous and void by provincial law, they will still be considered valid for income tax purposes until their dissolution.

Limitation of Tax Benefits from Multiple Spouses or Common-Law Partners

You cannot extend the multiple spouse principle too far, since it is limited by the technical wording of the Act. For example, you can claim only one spouse or common-law partner amount even if you have more than one spouse or common-law partner. Furthermore, it is not always clear which spouse's income must be used to reduce the spouse or common-law partner amount. If you have many former spouses or common-law partners dependent on you for support and not covered under the support payment rules (see ¶1118), you could choose the spouse with the lowest income to calculate your spouse or common-law partner amount.

Disability Credit

In disability credit situations, you could pick up excess disability credits from all of your disabled spouses. In cases involving a claim of medical expenses, those expenses could be transferred among all the individuals linked by a marriage relationship (e.g., you or any of your spouses could claim medical expenses for all of you).

[¶1113.35] Social Insurance Numbers of Spouses and Common-law Partners

To make the common-law partner system work for purposes of the Canada Child Benefit (¶1498) and refundable GST credit (see ¶1496), you must disclose the Social Insurance Number of your common-law partner on your return if you had a common-law partner at the end of the year for which the return is filed. Report that number in Step 1 of your return. The return provides space for only one number. If you have more than one common-law partner at the end of the year for which the return is filed, provide the number of the one cohabiting with you at that time. If other common-law partners are relevant for you, attach an explanation of their relevance and identify them by their Social Insurance Number. The same rules apply if you have more than one spouse.

(ITA: 252(3))

[¶1114] SPOUSE OR COMMON-LAW PARTNER TAX CREDIT — LINE 303 (SCHEDULE 1)

Individuals meeting the following conditions at any time during the year may claim a spouse or common-law partner amount on their return:

- being married or in a common-law partnership;
- supporting his/her spouse or common-law partner; and
- not living separate from him/her because of a breakdown in their relationship.

The spouse or common-law partner amount is:

- claimed under paragraph 118(1)(*a*) of the Act;
- calculated on Schedule 5 of your return; and
- reported on line 303 of Schedule 1 of your return.

For a definition of "spouse" or "common-law partner", see ¶1113.

Value for Current Year

For 2016, your spouse or common-law partner amount is $11,474 but is reduced by any net income earned by your spouse or common-law partner. This means that it is eliminated completely when his/her net income reaches $11,474.

See ¶1103 and line 236 of your return to determine the net income of your spouse or common-law partner and ¶65 for the indexed values of the spouse or common-law partner amount.

To determine the net income earned by your spouse or common-law partner during the year, see ¶1103.

If your spouse/common-law partner's net income is:	*The spouse or common-law partner amount will be:*
$0	$11,474
$5,000	$6,474
$11,474	$0

Value for Preceding Years

Year	*Spouse or common-law partner amount*
2015	$11,327
2014	$11,138
2013	$11,038
2012	$10,822

Family Caregiver Amount

Each spouse or common-law partner amount is increased by a family caregiver amount if your spouse or common-law partner is dependent on you by reason of a mental or physical infirmity. Only one family caregiver amount may be claimed for each spouse or common-law partner. If eligible, the family caregiver amount is added to the spouse or common-law partner amount and reported on line 303.

The family caregiver amount is claimed under paragraph 118(1)(*a*) of the Act. For more information see ¶1150.

Calculation

The spouse or common-law partner tax credit is calculated at the rate of 15% of the spouse or common-law partner amount.

Indexation

The spouse or common-law partner amount is indexed annually (see ¶65 and ¶1101).

Non-Refundability

The credit is non-refundable, which means that it cannot be claimed if the taxpayer has no income tax payable before claiming the credit.

Income Inclusions

The net income of your spouse or common-law partner for the year includes the following items:

- salary;
- wages;
- commissions;
- tips;
- other remuneration;
- dividends;
- interest;
- old age security pension or supplement;
- rents;
- business income;
- workers' compensation payments (see ¶358);
- social security payments including spouse's allowances (see ¶990);
- guaranteed income supplements (see ¶1110); and
- taxable portion of capital gains received by spouse or common-law partner and not attributed to you (see ¶531) even if he/she claims a lifetime capital gains exemption (see ¶502).

Income Exclusions

The net income of your spouse or common-law partner for the year excludes the following items:

- items listed at ¶991;
- income attributed to you on loans made or property transferred to him/her (see ¶977); and
- dividends received by him/her which you have elected to include in income (see ¶408).

Deduction Exclusions

The net income of your spouse or common-law partner excludes prior years' business losses.

Special Situations

Pension Refund Received After Marriage or Common-Law Partnership

If your spouse or common-law partner received a pension or superannuation refund after getting married or entering into a common-law partnership and the pension plan membership dated back before 1972, he/she may elect to take advantage of the special tax-averaging provisions applicable to such lump-sum payments (see ¶1472). If this election is made, the payment received is not included in his/her income while married for purposes of calculating the availability of the credit.

Special Events During the Year

If you married or entered into a common-law partnership during the year, or if your spouse or common-law partner died during the year, you may claim the spouse or common-law partner regular amount for the year without any reduction for the period during which you were not married or did not have a common-law partner. The amount must be reduced by any income earned by your spouse or common-law partner for the whole year.

If you separate from your spouse or common-law partner in the year because of a marriage or relationship breakdown and are not reconciled in the year, you do not need to take into account the entire income of your spouse or common-law partner for the year to calculate your spouse or common-law partner amount. If you were separated at year-end, you need only to include your spouse's or common-law partner's income earned before the separation. You cannot claim a spouse or common-law partner amount if you also claim support payments (see ¶1118).

After the year of separation, you cannot claim a spouse or common-law partner tax credit for a spouse or common-law partner from whom you are living separate throughout the year because of a marriage or relationship breakdown, even if you continue to provide him/her with support. This is true regardless of whether the support paid to him/her is deductible from your income (see Chapter 23).

Example 1: One Spouse Earned $2,000 Net Income

Jane and Bill Wiggens have been married for 10 years. For the year, Bill had income of $25,000 and Jane worked part-time, earning $2,000. Jane's employer deducted $200 tax from her earnings.

Bill may claim credits for the following personal amounts in the year:

Basic amount		$11,474
Spousal amount — maximum	$11,474	
Jane's income	2,000	
Reduced spousal amount	9,474	9,474
Total claim		$20,948

Jane Wiggens should file a tax return of her own showing $2,000 taxable income (which was the same as her net income). Her federal tax of $300 (15% × $2,000) will be more than offset by the tax credit on her $11,474 basic personal amount, so she will have nil tax payable. She should then insert (at line 437 of her return) the tax deducted at source of $200, thus claiming a full refund of that amount.

If both spouses or common-law partners had incomes over $11,474, they could each claim their basic personal amount of $11,474 (see ¶1106) but would be denied the $11,474 spousal or common-law partner amount.

Example 2: Couple Separated During the Year

John and Mary Jenkins separated on April 1. John earned $25,000 during the year and Mary earned $3,000 in the first 3 months and $9,000 in the last 9 months. John made no support payments to Mary.

John may claim personal amounts as follows:

Basic amount		$11,474
Spousal amount — maximum	$11,474	
Mary's earnings while married	3,000	
Reduced spousal amount		8,474
Total claim		$19,948

Mary must file her own return, reporting income of $12,000 and claiming a full basic amount of $11,474. If John was unemployed before April 1 or earned less than $11,474, Mary was supporting John while they were living together and could claim the spousal amount. The CRA considers that only one spouse or common-law partner may make the claim for the other. For more information on the meaning of "support", see ¶1116.

Example 3: Common-Law Relationship Commenced During the Year

Dick and Jane commenced to live together in a conjugal relationship on February 1st of Year 1. They had no children. They are not considered common-law partners for purposes of their Year 1 tax returns because they have not lived together for 12 months. If their relationship continued until, say, March of Year 2, and then ceased, they would be considered common-law partners having entered into a common-law partnership on February 2nd of Year 2, and separated in March of Year 2. Their Year 2 claims would be determined as if they had married on February 2 of Year 2 (and so could claim the common-law partner amount). Their Year 2 common-law partner claims would be governed by the rule in the preceding separation example. For more information on the meaning of "common-law partner", see ¶1113.

Example 4: Spouse Died During Year

Martha Jones died on April 1, and had income of $2,000 prior to her death. Her husband, Howard, was employed throughout the year and earned $25,000.

Howard may claim his own basic personal amount of $11,474, plus a married amount of $11,474 less his wife's income ($11,474 – $2,000 = $9,474).

(ITA: 118(1)(*a*); IT-513R [Archived])

[¶1114.05] *Common-Law Partners Separated at Year-End for Less than 90 Days*

In CRA Document No. 2001-0114117, the CRA confirmed that a common-law partner who was separated on December 31 but was reunited with his/her partner within 90 days need only to consider the income of his/her partner up to the date of separation in calculating his/her common-law partner amount. This seems a fair result since it puts spouses and common-law partners on the same footing. This opinion applies to non-refundable credits if the issue turns on your marital status at year-end but does not apply to the Canada Child Benefit (see ¶1498), GST credits (¶1496), or similar refundable credits which depend on whether you have a cohabiting spouse or common-law partner at a given time. Form RC65, which deals with changes in marital status for Canada Child Benefit and GST credit purposes, states clearly that separation begins on the first day of a period having lasted at least 90 days. You would still have to wait 90 days to file the form. This would be correct not only in determining refundable credit payments at a particular time but also in determining the year-end adjusted income for those credits and year-end net family income for provincial credits. See ¶213 for a discussion on the identification of spouses and common-law partners.

[¶1114.10] *Exempt Income of Status Indian*

Relevant Case Law

Exempt Income (1)

In *Sinclair v. M.N.R.*, 91 DTC 960 (TCC), the Court concluded that the male spouse of a treaty Indian had to include in his spouse's income, when calculating his spousal credit, payments not taxable to her by reason of a status Indian exemption. This opinion neither discusses the issues nor cites authority, and appears to contradict the CRA's directions contained in the T1 Guide and IT-513R (archived content), which states that the income of a spouse, common-law partner, or dependant is the amount shown on line 236 of their return, or the amount that would be there if they filed a return.

In *Robinson et al. v. The Queen*, 2011 DTC 1046 (TCC), the Court stated that status Indian taxpayers should be denied a spousal amount if they claimed the credit without reducing it by income earned by their spouse from work not done on the reserve for an employer having a head office on the reserve. This income was not exempt because it was not income from property situated on a reserve and exceeded the spouse amount. The credit was correctly denied.

Relevant CRA Documents

Exempt Income (2)

In CRA Document No. 9833137, the CRA confirmed that a spouse's income which is exempt under the status Indian rules was ignored in calculating the spouse's income for purposes of calculating a spousal amount. The CRA noted the above Sinclair decision actually involved a pension refund in circumstances not likely to happen today. Even if the case itself may have been correctly decided, exempt income must normally be included in calculating the spouse's personal amount.

[¶1116] SUPPORT OF A SPOUSE OR COMMON-LAW PARTNER

To qualify for the spouse or common-law partner tax credit, you must not only have a spouse or common-law partner but also support him/her. The meaning of the term "support" is discussed below.

Support Rule

You support your spouse or common-law partner if you contribute to his/her support even though he/she may supply some money towards the cost of maintenance of the household. For example, you are still considered to support your spouse or common-law partner if you pay utilities, taxes, insurance, and repairs on the family residence and he/she uses his/her income to pay for the family's food, clothing, and household necessities. The support must be more than a trifling amount and bear a reasonable relationship to the total cost of support. Therefore, you do not need to support your spouse or common-law partner wholly to claim the spouse or common-law partner amount.

Income Rule

Even if the support rule remains in place, the income earned by your spouse or common-law partner is the factor that will determine if you may claim the spouse or common-law partner amount. For 2016, you cannot claim the amount if your spouse or common-law partner earned $11,474 or more. The CRA does not normally deny the spouse or common-law partner amount on the basis that the taxpayer did not actually provide support to his/her spouse or common-law partner, but the rule remains and could be invoked in certain circumstances.

Relevant Case Law

Administrative Position

The CRA confirmed in paragraph 8 of Interpretation Bulletin IT-513R (now archived) that either spouse or common-law partner, but not both, could claim the spouse or common-law partner amount for the other, provided the spouse or common-law partner making the claim was the one supporting the other. This is based on the assumption that only one spouse or common-law partner may be considered to support the other (see *The Queen v. Robichaud*, 83 DTC 5265 (FCTD)). Based on this administrative position, it is difficult to see how a lower income spouse or common-law partner could be considered to be supporting a higher income spouse or common-law partner.

(IT-513R [Archived])

[¶1118] IF YOU WERE DIVORCED OR SEPARATED DURING THE YEAR

Where you were divorced or separated throughout the year, the rules governing your ability to claim personal amounts with respect to your former spouse or common-law partner and/or children are fairly clear. The general rules are:

(1) you cannot make a claim for a personal amount relating to an individual for whom you pay either child or spousal support if you have been living separate and apart from your spouse or common-law partner throughout the year as a result of the breakdown of the marriage; and

(2) you cannot claim a personal amount for a former spouse or common-law partner if you deduct support payments made in the year.

In the year of separation or divorce, the first condition will not be met, and therefore it may be possible to make a claim for a former spouse or common-law partner or child in that year so long as you otherwise qualify. Similarly, you may be able to make a claim for a former spouse or common-law partner in the year of separation or divorce, provided you supported that person at some time in the year and you do not deduct any spousal support payments made in the year.

Additional issues arise in shared custody relationships. These are discussed at ¶1120.

[¶1118.05] *If You Became Divorced or Separated During the Year*

Impact on Spouse or Common-Law Partner Amount

If you divorced or separated in the year and made deductible support payments to a spouse or common-law partner, you can deduct the payments from your income but, if you do, you cannot also claim a spouse or common-law partner amount. However, if you choose not to deduct the payments, you will be able to claim your former spouse or common-law partner's amount under the rules described at ¶1114, provided you otherwise qualify including, in particular, if you supported your former spouse or common-law partner. Thus, in the year of separation or divorce, you will have a choice and you can claim either the deduction for support or the spousal or common-law partner credit, whichever is more beneficial, but not both.

Example

Nelson and Louisa separated on August 1. Prior to that time, Nelson had no income and was wholly dependent on Louisa for support. From August 1 Louisa paid spousal support of $1,500 a month to Nelson pursuant to a written separation agreement. In the year of separation, Louisa may claim the spousal amount for Nelson as she supported him at some point in the year, or she can deduct the spousal support she paid, but not both. In subsequent years, she will not be able to claim the spousal amount for Nelson, as they will be living separately as a result of the breakdown of the marriage.

Impact in Eligible Dependant Amount

If you make support payments for a child, you cannot claim a personal amount with respect to that child. This is true whether or not the child support payments are deductible, although deductible payments should now be very rare (see Chapter 23). If you make such a child support payment in the year of separation or divorce, you will not be able to claim any personal amount with respect to that child.

Types of Separation

Separation may occur by mutual consent (i.e., without a written agreement), by desertion, or in more formal ways. However it occurs, separation will be taken into account in calculating the portion of the income of your spouse or common-law partner that is deducted from your spouse or common-law partner amount. However, if you separated in the year but were reconciled before year-end, you are considered to have been married or common-law partners for the whole year, and all the income earned by your spouse or common-law partner in the year will be taken into account in calculating your spouse or common-law partner amount. If you made deductible spousal support payments for the separation period, the either-deduction-or-personal-amount rule seems to function.

[¶1118.10] *If You Received Support Payments During the Year*

If you received taxable spousal support payments from your former spouse or common-law partner during the year you must include these payments in your income (see ¶2307).

After the year in which you divorce or separate, you may claim dependant amounts (including the eligible dependant amount) for your child (see ¶1120) so long as you do not make a support payment for the child and you otherwise qualify.

In the year of separation, even if your former spouse or common-law partner chooses not to deduct spousal support payments made to you, you may not be entitled to claim an eligible dependant amount for a child (even though you do not make support payments with respect to the child) since it may be difficult to identify a period in the year when you are not supported.

[¶1118.15] *If You Reconciled During the Year*

If you separated during the year but reconciled before year-end, each spouse or common-law partner will be able to claim a spouse or common-law partner amount based on the income of the other spouse or common-law partner for the whole year. They may also claim an eligible dependant amount if all the other conditions to claim the amount are met at some point during the year and they do not claim a spouse or common-law partner amount.

[¶1118.20] *If You Were Divorced or Separated Throughout the Year*

If you were divorced or separated throughout the year, the deduction of support payments made to your former spouse or common-law partner will prevent you from claiming a spouse or common-law partner amount.

(ITA: 56(1)(*b*), (c.2); 56.1(4); 60(*b*), (c.2); 60.1; 118(5); 5000-G, "General Income Tax and Benefit Guide" (T1 Guide), line 303; IT-513R [Archived])

[¶1120] ELIGIBLE DEPENDANT TAX CREDIT — LINE 305

You may claim the eligible dependant amount if you met the following conditions at any time in the year:

- you did not claim the spouse or common-law partner amount;
- you were not married or were separated from your spouse or common-law partner, were not supporting him/her, and were not being supported by him/her; and
- you maintained a "self-contained domestic establishment" in which you lived with one of the following related persons who was "wholly dependent" on you for support:
  - Canadian resident parent or grandparent;
  - child under 18 even if not Canadian resident;
  - disabled child even if not Canadian resident; or
  - other Canadian resident relative under 18 or disabled.

The credit is usually claimed by a single parent for a child, a child for a parent, or a sibling for a sibling etc.

For a definition of certain terms, see:

Definition	*Paragraph*
"spouse" or "common-law partner"	¶1113
"self-contained domestic establishment"	¶1122.10
"wholly dependent"	¶1122.25

The eligible dependant amount is:

- claimed under paragraph 118(1)(*b*) of the Act;
- calculated on Schedule 5 of your return, and
- reported on line 305 of Schedule 1 of your return.

Value for Current Year

For 2016, your eligible dependant amount is $11,474 but is reduced by any net income earned by your eligible dependant. This means that it is eliminated when his/her net income reaches $11,474.

See ¶1103 and line 236 of your eligible dependant's return to determine his/her net income.

If your eligible dependant's net income is:	*Your eligible dependant amount will be:*
$0	$11,474
$5,000	$6,474
$11,474	$0

Value for Preceding Years

Year	*Eligible dependant amount*
2015	$11,327
2014	$11,138
2013	$11,038
2012	$10,822

Family Caregiver Amount

Each eligible dependant amount is increased by a family caregiver amount if your eligible dependant is dependent on you by reason of a mental or physical infirmity. Only one family caregiver amount may be used for each eligible dependant. If eligible, the family caregiver amount is added to the eligible dependant amount and reported on line 305.

The family caregiver amount is claimed under paragraph 118(1)(*b*) of the Act. See ¶1150 for detailed information on this amount.

Calculation

The eligible dependant tax credit is calculated at the rate of 15% of the eligible dependant amount.

Indexation

The eligible dependant amount is indexed annually (see ¶65 and ¶1101).

Non-Refundability

The credit is non-refundable, which means that it cannot be claimed if the taxpayer has no income tax payable before claiming the credit.

Special Situations

Single Claim

Taxpayers that were married during the year may claim a spouse or common-law partner amount or an eligible dependant amount, but they cannot claim both.

Eligible Dependant Amount Claimed by Common-Law Partner

If you had a common-law partner in a given year, you will only qualify for an eligible dependant amount if you met the following conditions at some time during the year:

- you were unmarried and were not living in common-law partnership, or were married or in common-law partnership, but neither of you supported or lived with the other or was supported by the other; and
- you supported a qualified dependant in your home.

A taxpayer married or in common-law partnership in the year may only claim the eligible dependant amount once.

The eligible dependant is normally a child under 18 or another eligible relative living with you.

Deemed Separation

If you are separated from your common-law partner for 90 days, you are treated as if you were divorced at the beginning of the separation once the 90 days are up.

If you had a valid separation lasting for less than 90 days (i.e., in a common-law partnership or legal marriage), you could still qualify for the eligible dependant amount, although, unless there were significant evidence of the validity of the separation, this could be challenged by the CRA.

(ITA: 118(1)(*b*); IT-513R [Archived])

[¶1120.05] *Where Support Payments Made*

As discussed at ¶1118, if you must make periodic support payments for the maintenance of your spouse or common-law partner, or your children, you cannot claim personal amounts for any person covered by the payments if:

- you are separated from the recipient throughout the year by reason of relationship breakdown; or
- you claim a tax deduction for the support payments.

You may claim an eligible dependant amount for a dependant not covered by the support payments.

Separation or Divorce

A separated or divorced spouse or common-law partner receiving support payments is in a similar position. If you were separated throughout the year or if the payments were deducted by you as the payer, you cannot claim a personal amount for anyone covered by those payments. The recipient can claim the eligible dependant amount for a dependant not claimed by anyone else as a dependant of any kind.

Support Payments for Wife and Children

Probably the most common case is still that the husband makes support payments to his wife for her and the children. After the year in which they separate, he may claim no personal amounts for his wife and his children. His wife can claim the basic personal amount for herself, the eligible dependant amount for one of her children, and ordinary personal amounts for any other children. The rules are different where separation begins or ends in a year (see ¶1118).

Same Child Supported by Both Parents

If both parents make support payments with respect to the same child in the same year, the general rule is to deny the eligible dependant amount to both parents. In this event, an override rule allows one of the parents to make the claim, provided they can agree on who should make the claim. Otherwise, the claim will be denied.

Relevant Case Law

Both Parents Paying Child Support

In *Verones v. The Queen*, 2013 DTC 5061 (FCA), the Court disagreed that both parents paid child support and that the override in subsection 118(5.1) allowed a taxpayer to claim an eligible dependant tax credit. Even though his spouse was required by the *Federal Child Support Guidelines* to contribute $439 for the child's support and his own support payment ordered by the Court was reduced by the same amount, he was still considered the only one ordered to pay child support and could not therefore claim the eligible dependant tax credit for his child.

Shared Custody of Two Children

In *Ladell v. The Queen*, 2011 DTC 1240 (TCC), the Court held that the eligible dependant and child tax credits were properly denied where a taxpayer and his spouse had been divorced for many years, with shared custody of their two children. The taxpayer was required by a divorce agreement to pay child support to his former spouse but continued to claim the above credits. The Court dismissed his arguments that both spouses paid child support, that his payment was a net payment, and that subsection 118(5) of the Act allowed him to claim the credits.

Relevant CRA Documents

Side Agreement with Spouse vs. Court Order

In CRA Document No. 2014-0516711E5, a taxpayer, required by a court order to pay child support to his former wife for their two children, signed a separate agreement with her exempting him from paying support and allowing him to claim an eligible dependant tax credit for his child. The CRA confirmed that, since the court order was still in force, the taxpayer was prevented by subsection 118(5) of the Act from claiming the credit.

Credits Claimed Every Other Year by Separated Payments

In CRA Document No. 2012-0443301E5, the CRA confirmed that separated parents living apart, having shared custody of a minor child, living 50% of the time with the child, and with both required to pay child support, could claim the eligible dependant and child credit every other year. One parent claimed both credits in even years and the other parent claimed both credits in odd years.

Separated Parents Living in Same Domestic Establishment

In CRA Document No. 2010-0364841E5, the CRA confirmed that two separated spouses living in the same residence could not claim the eligible dependant and child tax credits twice even if they had two children living with them in that residence, did not claim the spouse amount tax deduction, and did not pay child support. Since they were living in the same domestic establishment, only one spouse could claim the credits and they would have to agree on who would claim them or lose them completely. This was the case even if the spouses had little, if any, communication, lived in separate bedrooms, and had no sexual relationship.

(IT-513R [Archived]; ITA: 118(1)(*b*), (4), (5), (5.1))

[¶1120.10] *General Conditions for Claim*

To claim the eligible dependant amount you must meet the following conditions:

- be unmarried or separated, and not in a common-law partnership; and
- contribute to the support of an individual:
  - who is related to you (see ¶1122);
  - who lives with you in a self-contained domestic establishment maintained either solely or partially by you (see ¶1122);
  - who is wholly dependent for support upon you or upon you and one or more other persons with whom you jointly maintain the establishment (see ¶1122); and
  - who at the time the above conditions are met is either (i) under 18 years of age at any time in the year or dependent by reason of physical or mental infirmity (see ¶1122), or (ii) a parent or grandparent (see ¶1122).

Claim for Parents or Grandparents

The eligible dependant amount may be claimed by you for a parent or grandparent regardless of the age of the individual being supported, but is only available for any other relative if the supported individual (i) was under 18 years of age at any time in the year during which the other conditions are met or (ii) was dependent by reason of mental or physical infirmity.

Self-Contained Domestic Establishment

In CRA Document No. 2012-0443301E5, the CRA confirmed that for the purpose of claiming the related credit tax credit, a taxpayer was only considered to maintain a self-contained domestic establishment for an eligible dependant if the taxpayer was responsible for the upkeep of the establishment. This did not cover a situation where a taxpayer only reimbursed upkeep expenses to the actual owner or renter of the establishment.

Wholly Dependent

The term "wholly dependent" is not clearly defined, but where a dependant does not have sufficient income to eliminate the eligible dependant amount and some degree of support is provided to him/her during the year, the amount may be claimed if all other conditions are met. The term "wholly dependent" means that the dependant is dependent on you, as opposed to someone else, for support. If no one else can claim the dependant for a personal amount and you support him/her, he/she should be wholly dependent on you for support.

Canadian Residence

To qualify for the eligible dependant amount, the dependant does not need to live with you throughout the year but must be resident in Canada at some time during the year unless the dependant is your child, in which case Canadian residence is not required (see ¶1122). See Chapter 1 for a discussion on residence.

Example 1

A dependant residing at school for part of the year and living with you for the non-school part of the year would be considered to have lived with you in the year and would qualify for the credit if all the other conditions were met.

Multiple Claims

If more than one person is eligible to claim the eligible dependant amount for the same dependant, they must agree on who will make the claim or lose it entirely. The claim cannot be split between them, but nothing prevents them from splitting the tax value of the credit after one of them had made the claim on his/her tax return.

Single Claim per Household

Only one eligible dependant amount can be claimed per household or self-contained domestic establishment. Thus, if two individuals are supported in one establishment by two or more persons, only one eligible dependant claim can be made since the law allows only one claim for the same person or the same establishment.

Example 2

John Wiley and his sister, both unmarried, live in a house with their mother and father. The mother and father are wholly dependent for support upon John and his sister. Although it would appear that John could claim eligible dependant status for one parent and his sister could do likewise for the other parent, such is not the case since only one claim may be made with respect to the same household. In this situation, either John or his sister would claim the eligible dependant amount for one parent and the other sibling could claim the caregiver amount for the other parent, if the conditions in ¶1140 or ¶1126 are met.

Example 3

Alex and Evelyn are a same-sex couple, living together in a conjugal relationship in the same household. Each has a child from a former relationship living in the household. Each has an independent income. Alex and Evelyn are deemed to be common-law partners for tax purposes under the rules at ¶1113 and neither of them may claim the eligible dependant amount.

Any Time in the Year vs. Throughout the Year

The eligible dependant amount may be claimed if the required conditions are satisfied at any time during the year as opposed to throughout the year. If a widowed father lived with and provided the sole support to a daughter (who turned 18 in the year), he could claim the eligible dependant amount for her even if she married and moved away during the year. In this case, her husband would also be able to claim the spouse amount for her. Here, one person (the husband) is claiming the spouse amount and another person (the father) the eligible dependant amount. The spousal claim would be reduced by the wife's net income earned during the whole year (unless they were separated by year-end) and the eligible dependant claim would also be reduced by the daughter's net income earned for the entire year.

Spouse or Common-Law Partner and Eligible Dependant Amounts Cannot Both Be Claimed

Where (i) an amount is claimed for a person as a spouse or common-law partner who was married or living in a common-law partnership, and (ii) throughout the year they were not living separate and apart by reason of marriage or common-law partnership breakdown, no one can claim an eligible dependant amount for the person.

(IT-513R [Archived]; ITA: 118(1)(*b*), (4), (5), (5.1))

[¶1120.15] *Joint or Alternate Custody*

Where you must make periodic support payments for the maintenance of your spouse, common-law partner, or children, you may not claim a personal amount for any person covered by those payments if:

- you are separated from the recipient throughout the year because of a relationship breakdown; or
- you claim a tax deduction for the year for those payments.

You may claim an eligible dependant amount for a dependant not covered by support payments provided certain conditions are met (e.g., dependant lives with and is dependent on you for some period during the year).

Multiple Claims

If more than one person is eligible to claim the eligible dependant amount for the same dependant, they must agree on who will make the claim or lose it completely, since the claim cannot be made twice and cannot be split between taxpayers. However, nothing prevents them from splitting the tax value of the claim after one of them has made it. In cases of joint custody, the claimant will be determined by the existence of maintenance payments.

Where parents are separated, do not live with anyone else, have shared custody of a child spending part of the year with each of them, and no child support payments are made, they must agree on who will claim the eligible dependant amount. Otherwise, neither of them will be able to make the claim it. However, nothing prevents one parent from making the claim and paying half of its value to the other parent.

Where two children spend part of the year with each parent, or each of them spends the whole year with one of them, and no child support is paid, each parent may claim the eligible dependant amount for one of children.

For payments made during the year of separation, see ¶1118.

Relevant Case Law

Payment of Child Support

In *Abiola v. The Queen*, 2013 DTC 1141 (TCC), the Court concluded that a taxpayer was allowed to claim the child and eligible dependant amount in the following situation. Following her divorce in January 2009, she had to pay child support for the child staying with her former husband. Shortly after the court order was issued, the child moved back with her, she stopped having to pay child support, and was thus allowed to claim the amount.

(IT-513R [Archived]; ITA: 118(1)(*b*), (4), (5), (5.1))

[¶1122] DEFINITION OF CERTAIN TERMS

The meaning of certain terms used to determine your ability to claim various amounts including the eligible dependant amount is discussed below.

[¶1122.05] *Definition of "Person Related"*

Only a person connected by blood, marriage, or adoption may qualify as an eligible dependant.

Blood Relationship

Persons connected by blood are limited to:

- children and similar direct descendants like grandchildren (see ¶1122), and
- brothers and sisters.

You are connected by marriage to the blood relatives of your legal spouse or common-law partner.

A blood relationship describes a relationship between persons in lawful descent from a common ancestor and may be broader than indicated above. The CRA accepts claims for more distant relatives if all other conditions are met and if there is evidence to substantiate the relationship.

Marriage

A connection by marriage continues after the marriage is dissolved by death. For example, a man or woman remains connected by marriage with the mother or father of his or her deceased spouse.

Adoption

Adoption includes a factual and legal adoption. A child may be related to a person by adoption even though the legal requirements to effect the adoption under the relevant provincial laws have not been completed.

In the case of a child, a broad scope is given to include a variety of factual situations (see ¶1122) and the child definition applies for all purposes of the Act including the claim of an eligible dependant amount.

Two persons are connected by adoption if one is the adopted child of:

- the other person, or
- a direct line ancestor or descendant of the other person.

The following relationships should qualify for claiming an eligible dependant amount:

(1) Blood Relationship

— father	— grandmother
— mother	— grandson
— son	— granddaughter
— daughter	— great-grandson
— brother	— great-granddaughter
— sister	— illegitimate son
— grandfather	— illegitimate daughter

(2) Marriage

— parent of spouse	— sister of spouse
— brother of spouse	— spouse of sister
— spouse of brother	— spouse of grandparent
— grandparent of spouse	— child or grandchild of spouse
— spouse of parent	— spouse of child or grandchild (of self or spouse)

Remember that "spouse" above includes a common-law partner, as defined at ¶1113.

(3) Adoption

— adopted father	— adopted daughter
— adopted mother	— adopted brother
— adopted son	— adopted sister

(ITA: 251(2))

[¶1122.10] *Definition of "Self-Contained Domestic Establishment"*

A self-contained domestic establishment is a:

- dwelling house,
- apartment,
- or other similar place of residence

in which a person sleeps and eats.

An establishment like a hotel room or boarding house that is not self-contained and where a person sleeps but does not eat does not qualify as a self-contained domestic establishment.

To show that you maintain a self-contained domestic establishment is easy if you own or rent the dwelling. If you do not own or rent it, you will need to demonstrate that you paid the property taxes or rent, utility bills, and insurance and that all receipts were issued in your name.

(ITA: 248(1) "self-contained domestic establishment"; 251; 252; IT-513R [Archived]; Income Tax Folio: S1-F5-C1 Related Persons and Dealing at Arm's Length)

[¶1122.15] *Definition of "Child"*

The meaning of the term "child" is extended to include:

- a person of whom the individual is the legal parent (including a natural or adoptive parent);
- a person wholly dependent on the individual for support and of whom the individual has the legal or factual custody and control immediately before the person attained the age of 19;
- a child of the individual's spouse or common-law partner; and
- a spouse or common-law partner of the individual's child.

The CRA considers that a child excludes a foster child, since a foster child is not wholly dependent on the foster parents because of they receive support payments from an agency responsible for the child's care.

(ITA: 252(1))

[¶1122.20] *Definition of "Parent or Grandparent"*

A parent is an individual who has a child within the definition in ¶1122.15.

A grandparent includes:

- a grandmother or grandfather of your spouse or common-law partner, and
- the spouse or common-law partner of your grandmother or grandfather.

This latter relationship will continue even if the connecting marriage or common-law partnership is dissolved by death.

(ITA: 252(2)(*a*), (*d*))

[¶1122.25] *Definition of "Wholly Dependent"*

The term "wholly dependent" is relevant in two situations:

- to make an eligible dependant claim; and
- to define the term "child".

To Make an Eligible Dependant Claim

To be able to claim the eligible dependant amount for an individual, he/she must be wholly dependent on you or on you and another person in your household. This means that he/she must be dependent on your household rather than on other persons during the year. This does not mean that he/she has no other sources of income but that the support must be more than just a trifling amount.

To Define the Term "Child"

An individual who is neither a natural child nor an adopted child may still be considered your child if the following conditions are met:

- he/she is under your custody and control before reaching the age of 19, and
- he/she is wholly dependent on you for support.

In this context, the meaning of "wholly dependent" is the same as in the "Eligible Dependant Claim" section.

Division of Claim Between Two individuals

The "wholly dependent" concept does not allow for the division of the eligible dependant amount between two persons, since a dependant cannot be wholly dependent on two people at the same time. Because it is sufficient for the condition to be met at any time in the year, a dependant could be wholly dependent on two individuals in sequence during the same year. However, only one eligible dependant amount may be claimed for one individual in a particular year. If this claim is made, no other personal amount may be claimed for that same individual.

Relevant CRA Documents

Claim for Grandchild

In CRA Document No. 2012-0433851M4, the CRA confirmed that a grandmother taking care of a grandchild under a kinship care arrangement and receiving social services payments for him/her could not claim the eligible dependent amount for him/her because he/she was not wholly dependent on her for support.

[¶1122.30] *Definition of "Dependant"*

The term "dependant" means one of the following persons dependent on you for support at any time in the year (but not necessarily throughout the year):

- a child or grandchild of you or your spouse or common-law partner, or
- a parent, grandparent, brother, sister, uncle, aunt, niece or nephew of you or your spouse or common-law partner who is resident in Canada at any time in the year.

This definition is relevant for ¶1124 and ¶1126, and is also used to establish the dependants, other than your spouse, common-law partner, or children under 18, for whom you may claim medical expenses (see ¶1225).

(ITA: 118(6))

[¶1122.35] *Definition of "Dependent"*

A dependant is someone related to you who is dependent on you for support at some time in the year but not necessarily throughout the year. There is no precise definition of the expression "dependent for support" which has usually been interpreted broadly, since the personal amounts are reduced by the dependant's net income.

Dual Test to Determine Dependency

The legislation uses a dual test to determine an individual's dependency on you. The individual must:

- be dependent on you for support; and
- have a personal net income not greater than the basic personal amount (see ¶1106).

The first leg of the test is met if you contribute to the maintenance of the dependant. In other words, the main condition is that you must have made some contribution to support him/her (see ¶1116).

The second leg of the test eliminates most claims in cases of non-dependency, but is not necessarily used in all cases. If it is not mentioned in the context of a personal tax credit, the second test does not apply.

Support for Relative in Hospital

Where a person is confined to a hospital for the whole year because of an infirmity, and the cost is borne by the government or an insurance plan, but a relative incurs expenses for the person's medical premiums, clothing, and comforts, there may be a case to argue that the hospitalized person is dependent on the relative for support.

CRA Position

The CRA considers that an individual contributing to a household only for his/ her own accommodation and meals does not support other members of the household. For example, an adult daughter living in her mother's home with a disabled brother would not be considered to support him if she only contributed amounts covering her own accommodation and meals.

[¶1122.40] *Definition of "Infirmity"*

Special claims may be made for dependants over 17 at year-end, provided they are dependent by reason of physical or mental infirmity. To qualify for these claims, the dependency must be brought about solely by reason of such infirmity. The expression "physical or mental infirmity" is not defined in the Act.

Documentation of Infirmity Claims

You do not need a medical certificate to support your infirm dependant amount claim, but should keep on file (not enclose with your return) a doctor's statement confirming the nature, commencement, and duration of your dependant's infirmity. This may cause some confusion, since a form T2201 must be prepared by a doctor to support the credit for mental or physical impairment (see ¶1225).

CRA Position

The CRA has offered the following comments in its interpretation bulletins and technical interpretations:

- a temporary illness is not considered an infirmity; and
- an infirmity is not the same and is less severe than a severe impairment (see ¶1209).

[¶1122.45] *Definition of "Under the Age of 18 in the Year"*

Eligible Dependant Amount

The expression "under the age of 18 in the year", used to qualify a category of dependant for whom you can claim the eligible dependant amount, seems to cause confusion for dependants turning 18 or 19 in the year. The CRA solves the problem in the T1 return by referring to the year of birth, but that is only valid for a particular year and not useful for a general discussion.

The following expressions have the same meaning:

- a dependant who is under 18 at any time in the year;
- a dependant who is under 19 on the last day of the year; and
- a dependant born in 1998 or later (for the year 2016).

A child turning 18 during the year qualifies for the eligible dependant amount. Technically, to qualify for the amount, the child must meet the following conditions:

- be under 18 while living with you, and
- be wholly dependent on you.

As long as those conditions are met at any time in the year, you may claim the eligible dependant amount.

Infirm Dependant Amount

An older child will be one turning 19 or more in the year. A different standard applies for infirm dependant amounts (i.e., where a claim is not for an eligible dependant amount on line 305, but for an infirm dependant amount on line 306). Here, a child turning 18 or older in the year qualifies for the claim (see ¶1126).

For 2016, a person born in 1998 or earlier qualifies for the claim. The line 306 claim meshes with the line 367 claim for younger children (i.e., children under 18 at year-end who are, for 2016, born in 1999 or later).

Mutually Exclusive Claims

The eligible dependant and infirm dependant claims are mutually exclusive (i.e., if you make an eligible dependant claim for a dependant on line 305, you cannot make an infirm dependant claim for the same dependant on line 306). Where there is more than one child and the older is infirm, choosing the younger child for the eligible dependant claim will maximize the value of the claims in the year the older turns 18, since the claim for the infirm dependant can be made for the older child.

(ITA: 118(4), (6); 251; 252; IT-513R [Archived]; Income Tax Folio: S1-F5-C1 Related Persons and Dealing at Arm's Length)

[¶1124] AMOUNTS FOR CHILDREN UNDER 18

[¶1124.05] *Amounts for Infirm Children Under 18 at the End of the Year — Line 367 (Schedule 1)*

You may claim the family caregiver amount for a child who:

- is under 18 at year-end; and
- is dependent on you by reason of mental or physical infirmity for a long and continuous period of indefinite duration.

For a definition of the term "child", see ¶1122.15.

Please see ¶1150 for an in-depth discussion of the family caregiver amount.

(ITA: 118(1)(*b*.1), (4)(*a*), (4)(*b*), (5), (5.1), (9.1))

[¶1124.10] *Child Amount (for years before 2015)*

Before 2015, taxpayers with a child under 18 at year-end could claim the child tax credit for that child, and also the family caregiver tax credit (see ¶1150) if that child was dependent on them by reason of mental or physical infirmity.

Effective for 2015, taxpayers may only claim the family caregiver tax credit if the child is under 18 at year-end and dependent on them by reason of mental or physical infirmity (see discussion above).

The following information on the calculation of the regular child tax credit is only applicable for the years before 2015.

Child Amount

Before 2015, a child amount could be claimed for each child under 18 at year end, was not reduced by the child's net income, and was subject to annual indexation (see ¶65 and ¶1101).

Multiple Claimants

If parents lived together with the child throughout the year, either parent could make the claim. However, they could not split the claim. If they both tried to make the same claim, it would be denied to both of them. Any excess credit not utilized by a parent could be transferred to the other one on Schedule 2 of the tax return (see ¶1361). The expression "throughout the year" was modified by the CRA to count only the period of the year following a birth or adoption, or preceding death. The credit would not be denied for the sole reason that a person was not yet born or adopted, or had died.

In CRA Document No. 2013-047830117, the CRA confirmed that if a child lives with both parents and one of them dies during the year, either parent can claim the child tax credit. If the child resided with both parents before the death of one of them, the surviving parent could claim the eligible dependant credit provided it was not claimed on the deceased's final tax return.

Separation

Where parents do not live together, the claim can be made by the parent allowed to claim the child as an eligible dependant or allowed to make that claim if the child were his/her only child with no net income.

Single Parents

The rule for single parents was that the child amount could be claimed for each child by the parent who, at any time in the year, was:

- unmarried and not living in a common-law partnership, or
- married or in a common-law partnership, but neither supporting nor living with the spouse or common-law partner nor being supported by the spouse or common-law partner,

and who, at some time in the year, maintained and lived with the child in a self-contained domestic establishment.

The child had also to be, at some time during the year, wholly dependent on the parent.

The rule also applied when the parent maintained the self-contained domestic establishment with other persons like friends, grandparents of the child, or other relatives living and sharing a home together.

If a single parent supports, at any time in the year, wholly dependent children who were under 18 at year-end, the parent may claim a child amount for each child, including one for whom the eligible dependant amount is claimed. This could be done regardless of the children's net income provided only one person makes the claim for any particular child.

Shared Custody

Each parent could claim the child amount under the separation rules, where custody was shared and the child lived with each parent for part of the year. In this situation, the parents would have to decide who would make the claim since the legislation prevented both parents from making the claim. If they did, the credit would be lost to both of them. However, one parent could make the claim and share its value with the other parent.

In CRA Document No. 2012-0443301E5, the CRA confirmed that parents who were separated, had shared custody of a minor child, lived 50% of the time with the child, and were both required to pay child support, could claim both the eligible dependant credit and child credit every other year (e.g., one could claim the two credits in odd years and the other one in even years). Only the parent claiming the eligible dependant credit for a year could also claim the child credit for that year.

Support Amount

You could not claim the child amount for a child in respect of whom you paid child support to your current or former spouse or common-law partner (see ¶1120.05). Both parents could pay child support at some time for the same child. If this was the case, the credit was not denied and one of the parents (not both) could make the claim.

Shared Self-Contained Domestic Establishment

If more than one family/single parent shared the same self-contained domestic establishment, each family or single parent could claim a separate child amount. Sharing a home did not disqualify an eligible family or parent from claiming the amount. The rule was different for claiming an eligible dependant amount. In this particular case, only one family or single parent could claim the amount.

For example, two single parent sisters sharing the same residence could claim separate child amounts for their respective children, but would have to decide who would claim the eligible dependant amount because only one such amount could be claimed for the self-contained domestic establishment. Otherwise, the eligible dependant amount would be denied to both of them. Nothing would prevent them from having one of them claim the related tax credit and then divide the tax value of the credit between themselves.

In CRA Document No. 2012-0452131E5, the CRA noted that two spouses or common-law partners living together in the same self-contained domestic establishment with more than one child could claim the child tax credit (not the eligible dependant tax credit) for a different child if all other conditions were met. For example, parents X and Y living in the same establishment with children A and B could each claim a child tax credit (not an eligible dependant tax credit) for A and B (e.g., X could claim it for A and Y could claim it for B).

Relevant CRA Documents

Death of Child

In CRA Document No. 2012-0440261E5, the CRA confirmed that a taxpayer could not claim a child tax credit for a child having passed away before reaching the age of 18 in the year. Since the child, had he/she lived, would not have been under18 at year-end, the taxpayer did not qualify for the credit.

Foster Parents

In CRA Document No. 2010-0382341E5, the CRA confirmed that foster children were not wholly dependent on their foster parents for support and thus were not considered to be their children for the purpose of claiming a child tax credit for them in 2009. The parents received monthly payments from the government for them in 2009 and 2010, before they adopted them in 2010. Because of the payments made by the government to the foster parents in 2009, the children were not wholly dependent on them for support and were thus not considered to be their children.

[¶1126] INFIRM DEPENDANT TAX CREDIT — LINE 306 (SCHEDULE 1)

Individuals may claim the infirm dependant amount on their return for a dependant who is:

- over 17 at year-end;
- dependent on them by reason of mental or physical infirmity; and
- their child or grandchild, or the same of their spouse or common-law partner, or
- their Canadian resident parent, grandparent, brother, sister, uncle, aunt, nephew, or niece, or the same of their spouse or common-law partner.

The infirm dependant amount is:

- claimed under paragraph 118(1)(*d*) of the Act:

- calculated under Schedule 5 of your return; and
- reported on line 306 of Schedule 1 of your return.

For a definition of certain terms, see:

Definition	*Paragraph*
"spouse" or "common-law partner"	¶1113
"child"	¶1122.15
"parent" or "grandparent	¶1122.20
"dependent"	¶1122.35
"infirmity"	¶1122.40

Value for Current Year

For 2016, your infirm dependant amount is $6,788 but is reduced by any net income of your dependant over $6,807. This means that your infirm dependant amount is eliminated completely when your dependant's net income reaches $13,595.

See ¶1103 and line 236 of your dependant's return to determine his/her net income.

To calculate the net income level at which the infirm dependant amount is eliminated completely, you add the net income threshold above which the amount is reduced to the amount itself (i.e., $6,788 + 6,807 = $13,595).

Value for Preceding Years

Year	*Infirm dependant amount*	*Net Income Threshold*	*Net Income Level Where Infirm Dependant Amount Eliminated*
2015	$6,700	$6,720	$13,420
2014	$6,589	$6,607	$13,196
2013	$6,530	$6,548	$13,078
2012	$6,402	$6,420	$12,822

Family Caregiver Amount

Unlike the spouse or common-law partner amount, eligible dependant amount, and caregiver amount, the infirm dependant amount is not increased by the family caregiver amount because it is already included in both the infirm dependant amount and the net income threshold, above which the amount is reduced.

Calculation

The infirm dependant tax credit is calculated at the rate of 15% of the infirm dependant amount.

Indexation

The infirm dependant amount is indexed annually (see ¶65 and ¶1101).

Non-Refundability

The credit is non-refundable which means that it cannot be claimed if the taxpayer has no income tax payable before claiming the credit.

[¶1126.05] Children and Grandchildren

Advantage of Caregiver Amount Over Infirm Dependant Amount

If you have disabled children or other relatives qualifying for the infirm dependant amount but living with you in your household at any time during the year, you should instead claim the caregiver amount (see ¶1140), since it will provide you with a tax credit worth the same or more that the infirm dependant tax credit. The major difference is the net income threshold which is much higher for the caregiver amount than the infirm dependant amount. If you claim the caregiver amount, your dependant may earn much more income before your caregiver amount is reduced.

Documentation for Non-Resident Child

If the child or grandchild in respect of whom you claim the infirm dependant amount does not reside in Canada, you must file proof of support paid (see ¶1127).

(ITA: 118(1)(*d*), (4))

[¶1126.15] Rules Applicable to Children, Grandchildren, and Other Dependants

Meaning of Infirmity

To qualify for the infirm dependant amount, your child, grandchild, or other dependant must be dependent on you by reason of physical or mental infirmity. The expression "mental or physical infirmity" is not defined in the Act and should normally take its ordinary meaning. The degree of infirmity does not have to prevent the dependant from being employed for a considerable period of time. However, the dependency must be brought about solely by reason of the infirmity, and a temporary illness would not qualify as an infirmity. An infirmity for the purpose of claiming the infirm dependant amount is not the same as a severe impairment or disability, which is the standard for the purpose of claiming the disability amount (see ¶1209).

Certification

No medical certificate is required to claim the infirm dependant amount but you must still have a doctor's statement confirming the nature, commencement, and duration of the infirmity.

This could cause some confusion, since taxpayers claiming the disability amount for dependants affected by a more severe disability would have to file form T2201 filled in by a doctor (see ¶1255).

You may want to get a copy of Interpretation Bulletin IT-513R (archived content) and mark the discussion of "Mental or physical infirmity" in Appendix A to show the doctor what the criteria are for this claim as opposed to the disability claim.

Do not attach the doctor's statement to your return but keep it on hand in case you are audited by the CRA.

Example

Ellen Reed is 24 years old and dependent upon her Aunt Julia by reason of having multiple sclerosis. The disease was in remission for part of the year, during which Ellen lived with friends and earned $7,500. Aunt Julia may claim a personal amount for Ellen as follows:

Maximum personal amount		$6,788
Ellen's Income	$7,500	
Minus	6,807	693
Reduced personal amount		$ 6,095

Line 306 of Schedule 5 arrives at the same amount through a different calculation. If Ellen also files a tax return, for example to recover tax withholdings, she may claim the $11,474 basic personal amount. Ellen may also qualify for the disability amount. If she does, certain relatives could claim that amount if she is claimed as a dependant.

For more information on the disability amount, see ¶1255.

(ITA: 118(1)(*d*); IT-513R Appendix A [Archived])

[¶1126.20] *Special situations*

Eligible Dependant Amount and Support Payments

You cannot claim the infirm dependant amount for a child in respect of whom you already claimed the eligible dependant amount or made support payments.

Choice Between Eligible Dependant Credit and Caregiver Credit

If you supported a disabled relative in a self-contained domestic establishment at any time in the year, you should explore the possibility of claiming the $11,474 eligible dependant amount (see ¶1120), or the $4,667 caregiver amount (see ¶1140) instead of the infirm dependant amount in respect of that relative. You may have to choose one of those claims or you may benefit from one of those claims depending on your personal situation.

If someone else is entitled to make the eligible dependant or caregiver claim for the infirm dependant, that will bar you or anyone else from making this claim for the same dependant. However, two individuals qualifying for the caregiver amount may divide it between them. Such allocation is not possible for the eligible dependant amount.

Multiple Claimants

If more than one person supports the dependant, they must allocate the infirm dependant amount between themselves. Otherwise, the CRA may allocate the amount arbitrarily. Under no circumstances can the sum of the allocations exceed the amount which could be claimed by a single person for that dependant.

For example, where both parents contribute to the support of a 20-year-old child dependent by reason of infirmity, whose income does not exceed $13,595, they may divide the infirm dependant amount between themselves so long as the total of their claims does not exceed that amount. It does not matter which parent claims what proportion of the personal amount, as long as the parent has enough tax payable to absorb the full credit.

Meaning of Dependant

Persons may be dependent on you for support even if they provide some contribution toward their own support. However, you must provide more than merely a trifling amount. Your support must bear some reasonable relationship to the total cost of support. For example, children may have income of their own and still be claimed as dependent children.

(ITA: 118(1)(*d*), (4), (6)(*a*))

[¶1126.25] *Dependants for Whom You May Claim an Infirm Dependant Amount*

You may claim the infirm dependant amount for the following persons:

- Father of you or your spouse or common-law partner
- Stepfather of you or your spouse or common-law partner
- Mother of you or your spouse or common-law partner
- Stepmother of you or your spouse or common-law partner
- Grandfather of you or your spouse or common-law partner
- Grandmother of you or your spouse or common-law partner
- Brother of you or your spouse or common-law partner
- Sister of you or your spouse or common-law partner
- Uncle of you or your spouse or common-law partner
- Aunt of you or your spouse or common-law partner
- Niece of you or your spouse or common-law partner
- Nephew of you or your spouse or common-law partner

To entitle you to an infirm dependant amount for any of the above relatives, the relative must be:

- over 17 at the end of the year for which your tax return is filed;
- resident in Canada at some time during the year;
- dependent on you by reason of physical or mental infirmity; and
- dependent on you for support at some time in the year.

Stepbrothers and Stepsisters

The interpretation authorizing claims for stepbrothers or stepsisters has been withdrawn, and, indeed, it is not clear from the statute that these relations qualify. On the other hand, it is not clear either that there has been any intention to eliminate them.

Extended Definition of Child

Given the extended definition of child (see ¶1122), where you have a parent in common by virtue of that definition, you have a brother or sister for tax purposes. However, this is merely an argument and the contrary view is possible since the CRA has chosen to be silent on the issue. A half-brother or half-sister or a brother or sister by virtue of legal adoption of a child should qualify.

Other Relatives

You cannot claim an amount for the support of any relative more distant than nieces or nephews (e.g., cousins will not qualify) unless, before his or her 19th birthday, he or she was wholly dependent on you for support, and he or she was under your custody and control (see definition of child at ¶1122).

[¶1127] NON-RESIDENT DEPENDANTS

You may claim personal amounts for non-resident dependants if certain conditions are met.

Spouse or Common-Law Partner Amount

You may claim the spouse or common-law partner amount for your spouse or common-law partner regardless of whether he/she is resident in Canada or not. For a definition of "spouse" or "common-law partner", see ¶1113.

Eligible Dependant, Infirm Dependant, or Caregiver Amount

You may claim the following personal amounts for an infirm child or grandchild of yourself or your spouse or common-law partner, regardless of whether he/she is resident in Canada:

- eligible dependant amount (see ¶1120);
- infirm dependant amount (see ¶1126); or
- caregiver amount (see ¶1140).

Canadian Residence Condition

Dependants other than your spouse or common-law partner, or your spouse's or common-law partner's infirm children or grandchildren, must have resided in Canada at one point during the year to allow you to claim a personal amount for them. The term "resided" means that they must have been resident of Canada for tax purposes (as discussed in Chapter 1) and not only made a visit to Canada. However, the term "resided" is not the same thing as for immigration purposes. A dependant could be resident for tax but not immigration purposes (see ¶117).

Evidence of Support

If you claim a personal amount for a non-resident spouse or non-resident infirm child, you must be able to provide some evidence of the amount you spent for their support. Such evidence will usually consist of:

- receipts for post office orders or
- bank money orders;
- cancelled cheques payable to and negotiated by the dependant; or
- receipts from private agencies established to transfer money or goods to residents of other countries.

Receipts provided by the non-resident dependant are not sufficient. Proof of payment must show your name, the amount, the date of the payment, and the dependant's name and address. If you sent the funds to a guardian, the guardian's name and address also have to appear on the proof of payment.

You should make copies of documents submitted. If you file electronically, you do not need to attach a copy of those documents to your return, but should keep them on file to be able to produce them upon request.

Dependence

A spouse, common-law partner, or infirm child claimed as a non-resident dependant must be dependent on you for support (see ¶1122). Those with enough income from other sources to have a reasonable standard of living in their own country are not considered dependants. Gifts to non-resident dependants do not constitute support.

(ITA: 118(1)(*d*), (4), (6)(*b*); IT-513R [Archived]; 5000-G, "General Income Tax and Benefit Guide" (T1 Guide), Federal non-refundable tax credits)

[¶1140] CAREGIVER AMOUNT — LINE 315 (SCHEDULE 1)

You may claim the caregiver amount if you met the following conditions at any time in the year:

- you did not claim the eligible dependant amount;
- you provided in-home care to an adult relative;
- you maintained a "self-contained domestic establishment" in which you live with the adult relative; and
- the adult relative was one of the following persons for you or your spouse or common-law partner:
  - child or grandchild over 17 dependent on you or your spouse or common-law partner because of an infirmity,
  - parent or grandparent who is at least 65 and resides in Canada; or
  - brother, sister, uncle, aunt, nephew, niece, and parent or grandparent (regardless of their age) who is dependent on you or your spouse or common-law partner because of an infirmity.

For a definition of certain terms, see:

Definition	*Paragraph*
"spouse" or "common-law partner"	¶1113
"self-contained domestic establishment"	¶1122.10
"child"	¶1122.15
"parent" or "grandparent	¶1122.20
"dependent"	¶1122.35
"infirmity"	¶1122.40

The caregiver amount is:

- claimed under paragraph 118(1)(*c*.1) of the Act;
- calculated on Schedule 5 of your return, and
- reported on line 315 of Schedule 1 of your return.

Value for Current Year

For 2016, your caregiver amount is $4,667 but is reduced by any net income earned by your dependant over $15,940. This means that it disappears completely when his/her net income reaches $20,607.

See ¶1103 and line 236 of your return to determine the net income of your dependant.

To calculate the net income level at which the caregiver amount is eliminated completely, you add the net income threshold above which the amount is reduced to the amount itself (i.e., $15,940 + 4,667 = $20,607).

Value for Preceding Years

Year	*Caregiver amount*	*Net Income Threshold*	*Net Income Level Which Eliminates the Caregiver Amount*
2015	$4,608	$15,735	$20,343
2014	$4,530	$15,472	$20,002
2013	$4,490	$15,334	$19,824
2012	$4,402	$15,033	$19,435

Family Caregiver Amount

Each caregiver amount is increased by a family caregiver amount if your dependant is dependent on you by reason of a mental or physical infirmity. Only one family caregiver amount may be used for each dependant. If eligible, the family caregiver amount is added to the caregiver amount and reported on line 315.

The amount is claimed under paragraph 118(1)(*c*.1) of the Act. See ¶1150 for rates and more information.

Calculation

The caregiver tax credit is calculated at the rate of 15% of the caregiver amount.

Indexation

The caregiver amount is indexed annually (see ¶65 and ¶1101).

Non-Refundability

The credit is non-refundable which means that it cannot be claimed if the taxpayer has no income tax payable before claiming the credit.

Special Situations

Parents Living in Retirement Home

In *Tcheng v. The Queen*, 2013 DTC 1165 (TCC), the Court held that the taxpayer did not qualify for a caregiver amount in respect of her parents living in a retirement home because she was unable to prove that she lived with them.

Ex-Spouse not Qualifying for Caregiver Credit

In CRA Document No. 2013-0479671E5, the CRA confirmed that the taxpayer could not claim the caregiver amount for an ex-spouse (whom she helped at his home and accompanied on his hospital visits) who was dying from cancer. The following conditions were not met: (1) her ex-spouse did not live with her; and (2) an ex-spouse is not included in the list of dependants qualifying a taxpayer for the caregiver amount.

Self-Contained Domestic Establishment

The definition of "self-contained domestic establishment" is the same for the eligible dependant amount and the caregiver amount. However, unlike the eligible dependant amount, you do not have to be unmarried or separated from your spouse or common-law partner to claim the caregiver amount.

Separate Claim for Each Dependant

You may claim the credit for each qualified dependant meeting the conditions at any time during the year. You should calculate a separate claim in Schedule 5 of your return for each such dependant and provide details for each such dependant. Use a separate sheet if you have more than one dependant.

Multiple Claimants

If you and someone else claim a caregiver amount for the same person, you may divide the claim between you as long as the total claimed does not exceed the maximum amount that could be claimed by one person. If you cannot agree on how to split the claim, the CRA has the authority to make an arbitrary division.

Choice Between Caregiver Amount and Infirm Dependant Amount

If you are allowed to claim the caregiver amount for a particular individual, neither you nor anyone else can claim the infirm dependant amount (see ¶1126) for the same individual. This solves the problem of trying to divide two potentially unequal credits at the cost of guaranteeing the credit to the live-in relative, even if someone else is contributing substantial support.

The conditions for determining the qualifying relatives and minimum infirmity required for both the caregiver and infirm dependant amount are basically the same, except for the following differences:

- a parent over 64does not need to be infirm to qualify for the caregiver amount; and
- for an infirm dependant, the two special conditions for the caregiver amount (vs. infirm dependant amount) are: (i) the dependant must live with you in a self-contained domestic establishment, but (ii) the dependant may have substantially more net income before the amount begins to be eroded.

Where a relative qualifies for both the caregiver amount and another personal amount, the relative's income will be the determining factor in choosing between the two amounts, since the $20,607 (the caregiver amount of $4,667 plus the net income threshold of $15,940) net income limit over which the caregiver amount is completely eliminated is appreciably higher than the one for which other personal amounts (e.g. eligible dependant amount or infirm dependant amount) are eliminated. If you can claim the infirm dependant amount or the caregiver amount for an individual, you must choose the caregiver amount. The eligible dependant rules are more complex, since the initial amount is higher. For a relative with net income below $6,807 (i.e., eligible dependant amount of $11,474 minus the $4,667 caregiver amount) the eligible dependant amount is preferable to the caregiver credit. In fact, you may choose the amount that is more beneficial for your particular situation.

If your live-in relative qualifies you for the eligible dependant and caregiver amounts, you will get the best result by claiming the eligible dependant amount for a relative with income below $6,807 and the caregiver amount for a relative with income above $6,807. For a relative earning $6,807 in income, the tax implications are identical.

Example

> Mary has a parent, dependent by reason of infirmity, living with her in her home during the year and whose income is $7,227. No one else makes a claim for the parent, and Mary does not make a claim for a spouse, common-law partner, or other eligible dependant. The parent qualifies Mary for an eligible dependant amount and the family caregiver amount, which totals $6,368 ($11,474 + $2,121 - $7,227). In the alternative, she could claim an infirm dependant

amount of $6,368 ($13,595 - $7,227). In these circumstances, she will prefer to claim the caregiver amount plus the family caregiver amount of $6,788 ($4,667 + $2,121). As between the infirm and caregiver amounts, she has no choice because the rules demand that if she could take either the infirm dependant amount or the caregiver amount for the same person, she must choose the caregiver amount. If she has a spouse or common-law partner and is living with him/her, either of them could claim the credit or they could divide it between themselves.

The eligible dependant amount rules state that where such an amount may be claimed for a person, no other personal amount can be claimed for that person even if it would be more beneficial for the taxpayer not to claim the eligible dependant amount and claim another personal amount. In this example, it makes no sense to deny Mary the $6,788 higher amount since all the conditions to claim a caregiver amount are met. To prevent this unfair situation, the Department of Finance decided many years ago not to amend the eligible dependant amount rules but to provide taxpayers in that situation with an additional amount (called "top-up") that would place them in the same position as if they had claimed a caregiver amount. Technically, Mary claims the eligible dependant amount of $6,368 for the parent plus the "top-up" additional amount. The top-up amount is calculated as caregiver amount less the eligible dependant amount:

(i) Caregiver amount as calculated: $6,788 minus net income in excess of the threshold = $6,788 - [$7,227 income in excess of $15,940 = nil] = $6,788 (subject to a maximum of $6,788) = 6,788.

(ii) Less: Eligible dependant amount as calculated: $6,368

(iii) Equals: Additional "top-up" amount: $420.

The total of the eligible dependant amount of $6,368 and the additional "top-up" amount is $6,368 + $420 = $6,788, which is the higher amount to which Mary was entitled in the first place.

The eligible dependant claim could also be denied if Mary claimed another dependant under the same rule. If she was a single parent with a young child living with her, she could claim the eligible dependant amount for the child.

There is no limit on the number of live-in relatives for whom Mary can claim the caregiver credit so long as each relative meets the conditions.

(ITA: 118(1)(c.1), (1)(e), (4))

[¶1150] FAMILY CAREGIVER AMOUNT

You may claim the family caregiver amount (in addition to the regular personal amount) if you have a dependant with a mental or physical infirmity and already claim one of the following personal amounts:

- spouse or common-law partner amount;
- eligible dependant amount;
- child amount*; and
- caregiver amount.

The family caregiver amount is:

- claimed under paragraph 118(1)(*a*), 118(1)(*b*), 118(1)(*b*.1), and 118(1)(*c*.1) of the Act;
- calculated on Schedule 5 of your return, and
- reported on lines 303 (with the spouse or common-law partner amount), 305 (with the eligible dependant amount), 367 (for children born in 1999 or after), and 315 (with the caregiver amount) of Schedule 1 of your return.

Only one family caregiver amount may be used for each dependant.

*Effective for 2015 and subsequent taxation years, you may not claim the regular child amount but may still claim the family caregiver amount for a disabled child under 18 at year-end.

Value for Current year

The family caregiver amount is $2,121 for 2016.

Value for preceding years

Year	*Family caregiver amount*
2015	$2,093
2014	$2,058
2013	$2,040
2012	$2,000

The family caregiver amount was not available before 2012.

Calculation

The family caregiver tax credit is calculated at the rate of 15% of the family caregiver amount.

Indexation

The family caregiver amount is indexed annually (see ¶65 and ¶1101).

Non-Refundability

The credit is non-refundable, which means that it cannot be claimed if the taxpayer has no income tax payable before claiming the credit.

Net Income Thresholds

For the caregiver amount and infirm dependant amount, the net income thresholds at which the credits are phased out are increased to take into account those amounts.

Infirm Dependants

Meaning of Infirmity

For the family caregiver amount claimed for a disabled child under 18, the child for which the amount is claimed is only considered infirm if he/ she is dependent on others for significantly more assistance than other non-disabled dependants of the same age, and if the dependence is for a long, continuous, and indefinite period.

Infirm Dependant Amount

The infirm dependant amount already includes the family caregiver amount because the dependant must necessarily be disabled to qualify for the infirm dependant credit.

Personal Amounts Including and Excluding Family Caregiver Amount

Personal tax credit amount	*Not-Infirm*	*Infirm*
Spouse or common-law partner amount	$11,474	$13,595
Eligible dependant amount	$11,474	$13,595
Child amount*	Nil	$2,121
Caregiver amount	$4,667	$6,788

*Following the repeal of the child tax credit, parents may only claim the family caregiver amount for a disabled child under 18 at year-end.

SPECIFIC QUESTIONS AND ANSWERS

[¶1195] SPECIFIC QUESTIONS AND ANSWERS

Support of Brother's Child

I was single during the taxation year but had the care and control of my brother's child, whose parents were divorced three years ago. He lives with me in a residence maintained by me. The child was wholly dependent on me for support. Am I allowed any personal amount for the child?

Yes. You may claim the eligible dependant amount of $11,474, even though you did not formally adopt the child. See ¶1122. If the child is dependent on you by reason of mental or physical infirmity, the amount you may claim is increased to $13,595.

Brothers Jointly Supporting Mother

My brother and I were both single throughout the year and we jointly supported our mother who lived with us in our apartment. We cannot agree on who will claim the $11,474 eligible dependant amount. May we each claim one-half of the $11,474?

No. You must agree as to who will claim the full $11,474; otherwise, no deduction will be allowed to either of you. Under such circumstances, one of you could make his claim and pay the other one half of the tax saving achieved. There would be no tax consequence to this payment; it would not be a deduction to the payer or income to the recipient. However, if your mother reached the age of at least 65 during the year, or was dependent on you by reason of infirmity, and her income is above $6,807, you would do better in any event to claim the caregiver credit, which can be divided. If the mother is dependent on you by reason of mental or physical infirmity, the eligible dependant amount you may claim is increased from $11,474 to $13,595.

Single Parent with Infirm Child

I am a single parent with two children living at home. The children turned 7 and 18 years old, respectively, during the year. They had no income. The older child is dependent on me by reason of infirmity. Last year I claimed an eligible dependant amount for the older child. May I continue to do so?

Yes, you may continue to claim the eligible dependant amount for a child who is under 18 at any time in the year, and for an infirm child you can continue to make the claim indefinitely. However, once your child has turned 19 you can claim the $6,788 amount for that child on line 306 or, in your case, line 315, and the eligible dependant amount for the younger child. You are not bound to continue using the eligible dependant claim for the same child from year to year.

Non-Resident Carrying on Business in Canada

I was a non-resident of Canada for the year but taxable since I carried on business here. Am I allowed any personal amounts for the support of my wife and children?

A non-resident of Canada will only be permitted personal amounts where all or substantially all of his or her income for the year is from Canada. Therefore, the answer is yes, if the business income from Canada during the year represents all or substantially all your income. The CRA generally considers that the "all or substantially all" test is met if 90% of that income is from Canada and not treaty-protected. See ¶2060 et seq.

Support "During the Year"

To claim an amount for a dependant, must I support that person for the whole of the taxation year?

No. Such support must have been supplied "during the year" which means at any time in the course of the year and not throughout the year.

Joint Support of Mother

My brother and I were both married throughout the year but jointly supported our mother, who was infirm. She has no income of her own. Is my mother considered a dependant, and, if so, may we split the "personal amount"?

Yes. You may split the $6,788 infirmity amount (¶1126) between you in any proportion you wish. On the other hand, if your mother is living with one of you only, that person must claim the caregiver amount (¶1140) and the infirmity amount is denied to the other. If your mother lives with one of you for part of the year and the other for another part of the year, you may divide the caregiver amount between you. If you cannot agree on the division, the CRA has the authority to apportion the amount as it sees fit.

Old Age Security and Supplement

My wife and I each received $12,000 of Old Age Security pension and guaranteed income supplement in 2016. My wife had no other income. What amount can I claim for my wife?

You are not allowed to claim any amount for your wife. The total old age security pension and guaranteed income supplement paid in 2016 to your wife was more than $11,474, which disqualified her from being dependent on you for support. You should report the Old Age Security pension as pension income on line 113 of your T1. The guaranteed income supplement should be reported on line 146 and subtracted on line 250. Your taxable income may be below the taxable limit. You may be eligible to claim the unused portion of your wife's age amount (see ¶1108 and ¶1361). You should qualify for future payments of the Goods and Services Tax ("GST") credit, provided you filed an income tax return for the year. Either you or your spouse (but not both) may receive the GST credit based on your 2015 T1. The CRA will send a Notice of Determination to those individuals who are eligible for the credit. The CRA will, in the case of eligible couples, pay the GST credit to the spouse or partner whose return is assessed first.

Chapter 12

Medical Expenses and Charitable Donations

THESE POINTS ARE COVERED IN THIS CHAPTER

CRA REFERENCES RELATING TO THIS CHAPTER

T1 Lines and Schedules

- Line 452 — Refundable medical expense supplement
- Federal Worksheet, Line 316 — Disability amount (for self if under 18 at year end)
- Federal Worksheet, Line 318 — Disability amount transferred from a dependant
- Federal Worksheet, Line 452 — Refundable medical expense supplement
- Schedule 1, Line 316 — Disability amount (for self)
- Schedule 1, Line 318 — Disability amount transferred from a dependant
- Schedule 1, Line 330 — Medical expenses for self, spouse or common-law partner, and your dependant children born in 1997 or later
- Schedule 1, Line 331 — Allowable amount of medical expenses for other dependants
- Schedule 1, Line 332 — Total allowable portion of medical expenses
- Schedule 1, Line 349 — Donations and gifts
- Schedule 5 — Amounts for spouse or common-law partner and dependants
- Schedule 9 — Donations and gifts

CRA Guides

5000-G, "General Income Tax and Benefit Guide"; **P113**, "Gifts and Income Tax"; **RC4064**, "Disability-Related Information"

CRA Forms

T3, "Statement of Trust Income Allocations and Designations"; **T4**, "Statement of Remuneration Paid"; **T4A**, "Statement of Pension, Retirement, Annuity and Other Income"; **T1170**, "Capital Gains on Gifts of Certain Capital Property"; **T2201**, "Disability Tax Credit Certificate"; **T5013**, "Statement of Partnership Income"

Income Tax Folios

S1-F1-C1 "Medical Expense Tax Credit"; **S1-F1-C2** "Disability Tax Credit"; **S1-F1-C3** "Disability Supports Deduction"

Interpretation Bulletins

IT-110R3, "Gifts and Official Donation Receipts"; **IT-226R**, "Gift to a Charity of a Residual Interest in Real Property or an Equitable Interest in a Trust"; **IT-244R3**, "Gifts by Individuals of Life Insurance Policies as Charitable Donations"; **IT-288R2**, "Gifts of Capital Properties to a Charity and Others"; **IT-297R2**, "Gifts in Kind to Charity and Others"; **IT-339R2**, "Meaning of Private Health Services Plan"; **IT-407R4 (Consolidated)**, "Dispositions of Cultural Property to Designated Canadian Institutions"; **IT-504R2 (Consolidated)**, "Visual Artists and Writers"; **IT-513R** "Personal Tax Credits"

Information Circulars

75-23, "Tuition Fees and Charitable Donations Paid to Privately Supported Secular and Religious Schools"; **84-1**, "Revision of Capital Cost Allowance Claims and Other Permissive Deductions"

Income Tax Technical News

No. 26, December 24, 2002, "Proposed Guidelines on Split Receipting"

WHAT YOU SHOULD KNOW ABOUT MEDICAL EXPENSES

[¶1205] REQUIREMENTS FOR CLAIMING MEDICAL EXPENSES

In order to claim a medical expense tax credit for medical expenses paid in respect of a patient for the year, you must meet the following conditions:

(1) the medical expenses must be eligible medical expenses (see ¶1205.05, ¶1207, and ¶1215);

(2) the medical expenses must have been paid or deemed to have been paid by you or your legal representative (see ¶1225);

(3) the medical expenses must have been paid within a 12-month period ending in the calendar year, or a 24-month period if the patient died in the year (see ¶1250);

(4) the medical expenses must not have been used to calculate your medical expense tax credit under section 118.2, disability supports deduction under section 64, or refundable medical expense supplement under section 122.51 for a previous year;

(5) the medical expenses must not have been used to calculate anyone else's medical expense tax credit under section 118.2, disability supports deduction under section 64, or refundable medical expense supplement for the year or a previous year;

(6) the medical expenses must generally be supported by receipts filed with your return, unless you EFILE, in which case you should retain your receipts as they may be requested (see ¶1260); and

(7) generally, you must not have been reimbursed for the medical expenses, or be entitled to reimbursement (see ¶1225).

Meaning of the Term "Medical Practitioner"

The term "medical practitioner", used throughout the relevant provisions of the Act, refers to a person authorized to practice under provincial or, if relevant, applicable foreign law. The legislation must enable, authorize, or empower the individual to perform medical services. Generally, such legislation will also provide for licensing or certification and establish a governing body empowered to determine competency, enforce discipline, and set basic standards of conduct.

Certain specialists (for example, an audiologist) are specifically permitted by income tax rules to certify and prescribe treatment for certain medical conditions, as described in ¶1209.

The importance of provincial determinations of who is a medical practitioner is illustrated in *Noddin v. The Queen*, 2004 DTC 3577 (T.C.C.), and *Davar v. The Queen*, 2005 DTC 1671 (T.C.C.). In those cases, New Brunswick taxpayers paid for, variously, the services of naturopaths, a massage therapist, and an acupuncturist. While conceding that at least some of these services would have been eligible for credit in Ontario (and indeed some of the practitioners were qualified in Ontario), the services were performed in New Brunswick, which had no statute recognizing these specialists as medical practitioners. Accordingly, amounts paid to them were not eligible for credit. The result might be unfair, but it was not unconstitutional, and any remedy lay with the federal and provincial governments.

The following is a non-exhaustive list of practitioners authorized to practice as medical practitioners in a province or territory:

- Acupuncturist: Alberta, British Columbia, Newfoundland and Labrador, and Quebec.
- Audiologist: Alberta, British Columbia, Manitoba, New Brunswick, Ontario, Quebec, and Saskatchewan.
- Chiropodist: Manitoba, New Brunswick, and Ontario.
- Chiropractor: Alberta, British Columbia, Manitoba, New Brunswick, Newfoundland and Labrador, Nova Scotia, Ontario, Prince Edward Island, Quebec, Saskatchewan, and Yukon.
- Combined lab and X-ray technologist: Alberta.
- Counselling therapist: Nova Scotia
- Dental assistant: Alberta, Manitoba, New Brunswick, Newfoundland and Labrador, Nova Scotia, Prince Edward Island, and Saskatchewan.
- Dental hygienist: all provinces and territories.
- Dental nurse: Manitoba.
- Dental technician or technologist: Alberta, British Columbia, Manitoba, New Brunswick, Newfoundland and Labrador, Nova Scotia, Ontario, Quebec, and Saskatchewan.
- Dental therapist: Newfoundland and Labrador, Northwest Territories, Nunavut, Saskatchewan, and Yukon.
- Dentist: all provinces and territories.
- Denturist, dental mechanic, denturologist: all provinces and territories.
- Dietician: Alberta, British Columbia, Manitoba, New Brunswick, Newfoundland and Labrador, Nova Scotia, Ontario, Prince Edward Island, Quebec, and Saskatchewan.
- Emergency medical technician: Alberta, British Columbia, Prince Edward Island, and Saskatchewan.
- Hearing aid practitioner: Alberta, British Columbia, Manitoba, Newfoundland and Labrador, and Quebec.
- Licensed or registered practical nurse: all provinces and territories.
- Massage therapist: British Columbia, Newfoundland and Labrador, and Ontario.
- Medical laboratory technologist: Alberta, Manitoba, New Brunswick, Newfoundland and Labrador, Nova Scotia, Ontario, Quebec, and Saskatchewan.
- Medical radiation technologist: Alberta, New Brunswick, Nova Scotia, Ontario, Quebec, and Saskatchewan.
- Midwife: Alberta, British Columbia, Manitoba, New Brunswick, Nova Scotia, Northwest Territories, Nunavut, Ontario, Quebec, and Saskatchewan.
- Naturopath: Alberta, British Columbia, Manitoba, Nova Scotia, Ontario, and Saskatchewan.
- Occupational therapist: Alberta, British Columbia, Manitoba, New Brunswick, Newfoundland and Labrador, Nova Scotia, Ontario, Prince Edward Island, Quebec, and Saskatchewan.
- Ophthalmic medical assistant: Northwest Territories and Nunavut.
- Optician: Alberta, British Columbia, Manitoba, New Brunswick, Newfoundland and Labrador, Nova Scotia, Ontario, Prince Edward Island, Quebec, and Saskatchewan.
- Optometrist: all provinces and territories.
- Pharmacist: all provinces and territories.
- Physician: all provinces and territories.
- Physiotherapist or physical therapist: Alberta, British Columbia, Manitoba, New Brunswick, Newfoundland and Labrador, Nova Scotia, Ontario, Prince Edward Island, Quebec, Saskatchewan, and Yukon.
- Podiatrist: Alberta, British Columbia, Manitoba, New Brunswick, Ontario, Quebec, and Saskatchewan.
- Psychological associate: British Columbia, Manitoba, and Ontario.
- Psychologist: Alberta, British Columbia, Manitoba, New Brunswick, Newfoundland and Labrador, Nova Scotia, Northwest Territories, Nunavut, Ontario, Prince Edward Island, Quebec, and Saskatchewan.
- Registered nurse: all provinces and territories.
- Registered nursing assistant: Manitoba, Northwest Territories, and Quebec.
- Registered nutritionist: Alberta, New Brunswick, Nova Scotia, and Quebec.
- Registered psychiatric nurse: Alberta, British Columbia, Manitoba, Saskatchewan, and Yukon.
- Respiratory therapist: Alberta, Manitoba, New Brunswick, Newfoundland and Labrador, Nova Scotia, Ontario, Quebec, and Saskatchewan.
- Social worker: Alberta, British Columbia, Manitoba, New Brunswick, Newfoundland and Labrador, Nova

Scotia, Ontario, Prince Edward Island, Quebec, and Saskatchewan.

- Speech language pathologist: Alberta, British Columbia, Manitoba, New Brunswick, Ontario, Quebec, and Saskatchewan.

- Surgeon: all provinces and territories.

- Traditional Chinese medicine practitioner: British Columbia.

(ITA: 118.2(2); 118.4(2); ITR: 5700 [Prescribed devices and equipment]; Window on Canadian Tax: 2010; 4319; CRA Document No.: Medical practioner — Massage therapists, *October 30, 1995*, CRA Document No. 9524708; Frais médicaux- déplacements- pénurie de médecins, *April 5, 2013*, CRA Document No. 2013-0478271E5; Income Tax Folio: S1-F1-C1, Medical Expense Tax Credit; *Noddin v. The Queen*, 2004 DTC 3577 (T.C.C.); *Davar v. The Queen*, 2005 DTC 1671 (T.C.C.))

[¶1205.05] *Transportation to Obtain Medical Services*

In addition to claiming ambulance charges to and from a hospital, you may also claim amounts paid to commercial transport services such as taxicabs and trains for transportation of a patient (you, your spouse or common-law partner, or a dependant) and an attendant (if the necessity of the attendant is certified in writing by a qualified medical practitioner) to and from a hospital, clinic or doctor's office, provided the patient has travelled a distance in excess of 40 kilometres to obtain medical services not otherwise available nearer to home. Such medical services may include the services of a general practitioner where one is not available in the patient's locality.

If public transportation is not readily available, you may claim reasonable expenses incurred for the use of a private vehicle (your own or someone else's) to provide transportation for you, your spouse or common-law partner, or dependant, and an attendant if certified as necessary in the circumstances described above. A vehicle may include any type of conveyance used to transport a person by land, water or air.

In addition to transportation expenses, if medical services are not available locally and you (or your spouse or common-law partner, or a dependant for whom you are claiming medical expenses — see ¶1255) must travel at least 80 kilometres to obtain them, reasonable travelling expenses such as meal and accommodation costs for the patient and, if certified in writing by a physician, an accompanying individual, may also be deducted. Travelling expenses should be substantiated by receipts, and must be necessitated by the distance travelled.

In measuring 40 or 80 kilometres, as the case may be, there would seem to be a case for measuring the distance by the shortest normal route open to the travelling public rather than as the crow flies. The CRA does comment (in Income Tax Folio S1-F1-C1, paras. 1.65 and 1.68) that in applying the distance tests the patient must take "a reasonably direct route", which would seem to support this interpretation.

In the case of *Mullin v. the Queen*, 99 DTC 748 (T.C.C.), the Court found that the "reasonable" cost of using a vehicle for medical travel (under the 40 kilometre rule where no public transportation was available) was the amount employers, notably the Treasury Board, normally pay as allowances (30 cents a kilometre or more) rather than the 16 cents the CRA had argued for. The CRA has accepted the logic of this case, and announced that it will permit taxpayers to calculate mileage for automobile use, where general conditions are met under either the 40 or 80 kilometre rule, on a fixed per kilometre amount. It has fixed amounts for each province and territory, apparently based on Treasury Board mileage allowance rates for civil servants. These are updated periodically. The most recent rates available at the time of publication are shown in the table at ¶87 preceding Chapter 1.

It is always open to the taxpayer to keep records of actual ownership costs (fuel, maintenance, insurance, licensing, depreciation) and prorate these actual expenses based on mileage for medical purposes over total mileage for the year, or for the 12-month period for which medical expenses are claimed. It is doubtful that this would often give a better result, but you may do it if you wish.

In addition, the CRA apparently will allow meal expenses (under the 80 kilometre rule) of $17 per meal to a maximum of $51 per day (per person), as an alternative to providing receipts for the actual "reasonable" cost of meals. See the table at ¶87 preceding Chapter 1.

In *Tallon v. The Queen*, 2014 DTC 1148 (T.C.C.), the Court held that the travel expenses incurred by a taxpayer who suffered from severe chronic pain and her husband were eligible medical expenses for the purpose of claiming the medical expense tax credit (METC). The expenses amounted to $17,494 and were incurred for flights, accommodation, and meals for a trip to Thailand and Indonesia. The taxpayer had received medical advice to spend winters in warmer climates. In this case, the travel expenses were eligible because the medical services (use of warmer climates) were not available locally, it was reasonable for her to travel to obtain the services, and the route taken to obtain those services was direct. Because the taxpayer provided a physician's letter stating that she could not travel on her own, the travel expenses incurred for her husband were also eligible to calculate the METC.

In *Jordan v. The Queen*, 2013 DTC 1015 (T.C.C.), the Court held that the taxpayer's motor vehicle and meal expenses incurred during 102 round trips to visit his spouse, who suffered from brain damage, at the long-term care facility in which she resided were eligible for the METC. The Court held that travel expenses were not limited to the initial cost of attending at a place for medical treatment, but that they covered travel expenses incurred during the period of treatment. The taxpayer's spouse required treatment over a prolonged period of time and the taxpayer's presence contributed significantly to his spouse's recovery.

In CRA Document No. 2013-0510121E5, the CRA confirmed that travel expenses incurred by a taxpayer to purchase a specific type of contact lens not available in his locality were not eligible medical expenses for the purpose of claiming an METC. The CRA was not convinced that substantially equivalent medical services (availability of contact lenses) were not available in the taxpayer's locality and that it was reasonable for the taxpayer to travel to another location to purchase contact lenses.

In CRA Document No. 2013-0478271E5, an individual with a medical condition requiring him to see a physician on a regular basis was able to in City A but was not able to see a physician after moving to City B, which is located 330 kilometres from City A and has a shortage of physicians. The CRA confirmed that the individual would be allowed to claim an METC for the meal, travel, and accommodation expenses incurred to travel back to City A to see his family physician if he could not get substantially equivalent medical services in City B, if the route travelled to City A was direct, and if it was reasonable for him to travel to City A to get those services.

(ITA: 118.2(2)(*g*), (*h*), (4); Income Tax Folio: S1-F1-C1, Medical Expense Tax Credit; *Mullin v. the Queen*, 99 DTC 748 (T.C.C.); *Jordan v. The Queen*, 2013 DTC 1015 (T.C.C.); Other Publications: "Meal and vehicle rates used to calculate travel expenses" and "Authorized medical practitioners by province or territory for the purposes of claiming medical expenses" on CRA website)

[¶1207] PAYMENTS FOR ATTENDANT, NURSING HOME, OR INSTITUTIONAL CARE

Three separate but overlapping rules permit the inclusion as medical expenses of remuneration paid to a full-time attendant. A fourth rule permits credit for attendant care for the disabled which need not be full-time. A fifth rule permits credit for payments to a school, institution or other place which provides special care and training certified as required for the patient by a qualified practitioner to require. A sixth rule allows medical expense credit for remuneration paid for care or supervision provided in a group home in Canada maintained exclusively for the benefit of individuals who have a severe and prolonged impairment qualifying for the disability credit.

Under the *first rule*, you (or a supporting person, see ¶1225) may claim as a medical expense the remuneration of a full-time attendant or the expenses for *full-time care in a nursing home* if you have obtained a certificate, generally from a medical doctor (¶1209). The certificate must be on form T2201 and must certify that you have a severe and prolonged mental or physical impairment as defined at ¶1209. The certificate must generally be provided by a medical doctor, but certain impairments may be provided by other medical practitioners. For example, if the impairment is one of sight, the certificate may be signed by either a medical doctor or optometrist. The attendant cannot be the spouse or common-law partner of the payer and cannot be under 18 at the time the remuneration is paid. However, the attendant can be the spouse or common-law partner of the patient, or another relative of the patient. The relative must be over 18.

The tax courts have defined remuneration paid to "one full-time attendant" as the total remuneration paid to any number of attendants in the relevant period, provided the total remuneration so claimed only covered the services of one attendant at any given time (*Wakelyn v. M.N.R.*, 71 DTC 35 (T.A.B.)). The CRA has commented that an attendant may perform tasks including cleaning and transportation services, but that if a person is employed as a single service provider, such as a housekeeper or driver, such person will not be considered an attendant (see Income Tax Folio S1-F1-C1). You can claim attendant care expenses necessary for you to earn business or employment income as a deduction from income rather than an expense eligible for medical expense credit, although you cannot claim any attendant care under the medical expense credit rules if you do so. The impairment criteria and form T2201 certification requirements are the same. The limitations on that claim and the circumstances in which it might be beneficial are discussed at ¶1036.

The CRA has commented in a tax opinion (CRA Document No. 2003-0030965) that "all regular fees paid to a nursing home, including food, accommodation, nursing care, administration, maintenance and social programming, qualify as medical expenses which are eligible for the medical expense tax credit. Additional personal expenses, *which are separately identifiable*, such as hairdresser fees, are not allowable expenses".

The *second rule* permitting a deduction for a full-time attendant for you, your spouse or common-law partner, or your dependant requires that the attendant be for a patient in a "self-contained domestic establishment in which the patient lives". Self-contained domestic establishment is defined in ¶1122. This rule does not require a disability certificate on form T2201, but does require a qualified medical practitioner (¶1209) to certify in writing that by reason of physical or mental infirmity the patient is or is likely to be "for a long-continued period of indefinite duration" dependent on others for personal care and, consequently, in need of a full-time attendant. The attendant cannot be the spouse or common-law partner of the payer and cannot be under 18 at the time the remuneration is paid. However, the attendant can be the spouse or common-law partner of the patient, or another relative of the patient. The relative must be over 18. You must have receipts on hand showing, if the payee is an individual, a Social Insurance Number.

It would seem that the first rule is aimed at institutional care and the second is aimed at home care, but the first rule would seem applicable to attendant care in any setting. The main distinction between these two rules seems to be that the first rule requires "impairment" whereas the second requires "infirmity". Impairment is a defined term, and requires the sufferer to be "markedly restricted in his activities of daily living" and that the condition is reasonably expected to last at least 12 months. See ¶1209. The CRA has the right to obtain its own professional advice on whether "impairment" exists. The expression "mental or physical infirmity" is not defined in the Act and must take its ordinary meaning (see Appendix A of Interpretation Bulletin IT-513R). The CRA noted in IT-513R that a temporary illness was not considered an infirmity and that the degree of infirmity had to be such that it required a person to be dependent on another person for a considerable period of time. As the test under the second rule would seem to be at least as onerous as the test for the first rule, and the restrictions are more onerous, it is difficult to see when it will be invoked. The CRA has redesigned form T2201 with only the first rule in mind. Previously issued certificates under the second rule apparently continue to be valid assuming, of course, the disability continues.

The *third rule* provides for the deduction of the cost of full-time nursing home care for a person certified in writing by a medical practitioner to lack "normal mental capacity " and consequently be dependent now and in the foreseeable future on others for personal needs and care.

The Tax Courts have defined remuneration paid to "one full-time attendant" as the total remuneration paid to any number of attendants in the relevant period provided the total remuneration so claimed only covered the services of one attendant at any given time (*Wakelyn v. M.N.R.*, 71 DTC 35 (T.A.B.)).

The *fourth rule* allows a medical expense credit for remuneration for attendant care (which need not be full-time attendant care) provided in Canada for a person with a severe and prolonged impairment of physical or mental functions to the extent the cost for the year does not exceed $10,000 (or $20,000 in the year of death *of the payer*). Ontario, uniquely, indexes the $10,000/$20,000 values, and the CRA usually publishes the current Ontario values in its notes to line 5868 in the Ontario T1 package; for 2016 they are $13,844 and $27,687.

The claim under this rule is only permitted if the patient is someone for whom a disability credit described in ¶1255 can be claimed for the year in question. This in turn requires a disability certificate described in ¶1209. The remuneration paid for attendant care cannot also be included in any of the other claims described here, nor in claims for child care expense or disability supports. The attendant cannot be the spouse or common-law partner of the payer and cannot be under 18 at the time the remuneration is paid. However, the attendant can be the spouse or common-law partner of the patient, or another relative of the patient. The relative must be over 18. Finally, you must have receipts on hand showing, if the payee is an individual, a Social Insurance Number. Also see ¶1255.05.

If a credit for full-time attendant or nursing home care is claimed under any of the first three rules above, the disability deduction under ¶1255 may not be claimed by anyone for the same disabled person. The higher of the actual cost (in excess of the threshold) or the disability amount can be claimed, but not both. This is not true for credit claimed under the fourth rule, which can be doubled up with the disability amount.

Although a claim will generally be made under the fourth rule where the remuneration paid is for part-time care, a claim may be made under the fourth rule in respect of remuneration paid for full-time attendant care so that the disability tax credit may also be claimed.

In CRA Document No. 2003-0030965, the CRA comments that a resident of a retirement home may make a claim under this rule in respect of attendant care, provided the resident meets the requirements of the disability credit provision and provided the resident can establish that an amount, in addition to the amount paid as rent, is paid as remuneration for attendant care. To qualify under this rule, a claim must be accompanied by proof of payment, generally by means of a receipt, and must pertain to actual remuneration paid for attendant care. The CRA opinion goes on to say:

> The home, as the service provider, must determine the total amount paid for attendant care and allocate such amounts to the residents on a reasonable basis. In our view, the amounts that may be so allocated would generally be limited to salaries and wages paid to employees engaged in providing attendant care services. Attendant care is care provided by a person who performs those personal tasks that the individual with a disability is unable to do. Depending on the situation, such tasks could include meal preparation, housekeeping for the resident's personal living space, laundry services for the resident's personal items, transportation and personal services such as banking and shopping. However, fees paid for identifiable personal expenses, such as hairdresser fees, would not qualify as a medical expense.

In CRA Document No. 2004-0101081E5, the CRA provides somewhat more detail, saying that under the fourth rule a retirement home can aggregate the salaries and wages paid to its employees who provide the following services: health care, meal preparation, housekeeping for the resident's personal living space, laundry services for the resident's personal items, transportation driver, and security (in secured units). The home must then allocate the claim among its residents: "The claim for attendant care is the portion of the salary and wages of all such attendants that can reasonably apply to the senior."

The *fifth rule* provides that payments to a school, institution, or other place for the care, or care and training of an individual will qualify as medical expenses if an "appropriately qualified person" has certified in writing that the patient requires the equipment, facilities, or personnel provided by that institution because of a physical or mental handicap and if the equipment, facilities, or personnel are specially provided by that institution for the care or care and training of individuals suffering from the same handicap as the patient. Note that the conditions here are not those at ¶1209, in terms of either the degree of infirmity or the person who must certify the condition. In *Lister v. The Queen*, 2006 DTC 6721, the Federal Court of Appeal disallowed the taxpayer's claim under this rule for expenses paid to a retirement home. The Court found that the principal function of the institution was to provide residential accommodation and that the medical services provided by the institution were incidental to this purpose, and further that the medical services were available to all residents and were not specially provided for residents requiring such services.

Finally, a *sixth rule* allows medical expense credits for remuneration paid for care or supervision provided for a patient qualifying for the disability credit in ¶1255 in a group home in Canada maintained exclusively for the benefit of individuals who have a severe and prolonged impairment. You must have receipts on hand showing, if the payee is an individual, a Social Insurance Number. Remuneration eligible under this rule cannot include any amount claimed under any of the other five rules discussed here, or under the attendant care provision at ¶1036. Amounts deducted as a child care expense or disability supports deduction are also excluded. It was originally thought to be the government's intention that, since there is no dollar limit on this amount, it would be incompatible with the disability credit at ¶1255. That is, you could claim remuneration paid under this rule as a medical expense, or you could claim the disability credit, but not both. However, the actual legislation does not seem to impose this limitation and, as it stands, appears to permit both claims. The CRA has commented that a claim may be made both for the medical expense tax credit under this rule and for the disability tax credit (see Income Tax Folio S1-F1-C1).

In all the above rules, the expense transfer provisions described at ¶1225 apply to permit deductions to be transferred to a spouse or common-law partner or person claiming the disabled person as a dependant.

(ITA: 118.2(2)(*b*)–(*e*); 118.4(1); 5000-G General Income Tax and Benefit Guide — 2015; RC4064 Disability-Related Information 2015; CRA Document No.: Attendant Care, *September 25, 2003*, CRA Document No. 2003-0030965; Income Tax Folio: S1-F1-C1 Medical Expense Tax Credit; S1-F1-C2 Disability Tax Credit; *Wakelyn v. M.N.R.*, 71 DTC 35 (T.A.B.); *Lister v. The Queen*, 2006 DTC 6721 (F.C.A.))

[¶1207.05] *Threading through the Care Requirements*

Threading through the various care requirements above can require painstaking attention but can occasionally be rewarding. In CRA Document No. 2006-0172181I7, the CRA addressed a case where the patient (who qualified for the disability credit) paid nursing home fees, and, in addition, her son shared in the cost of a paid companion for the patient. The CRA's opinion was that the patient could claim the medical expense credit for the nursing home fees under the first rule above (but not, of course, the disability credit as well). In addition, the son could deduct up to $10,000 under the fourth rule for remuneration paid to a companion for the patient, provided the companion's remuneration was not included in the nursing home fees and the companion was providing some form of additional attendant care, i.e., "some form of direct care or personal service provided to the patient". In the alternative, if the nursing home broke out the cost of attendant care, the patient could claim up to $10,000 of that cost, the son could claim up to $10,000 of companion cost, and the patient could claim the disability credit. "The wording of the Act supports the position that the $10,000 limit found in paragraph 118.2(2)(*b.1*) is intended to apply per paying individual in respect of a particular patient. We note in particular that the limit is raised to $20,000 in the year of the individual's death, rather than in the year of the patient's death."

The opinion seems fixated on the fact pattern given, with the patient paying the nursing home and the son paying a separate attendant. It seems to be assumed that the patient could not make a claim for nursing home care under the first rule and a separate claim for up to $10,000 paid for attendant care to someone not remunerated by the nursing home. So long as the remuneration is not paid to the same attendant under both provisions, it is not clear that this assumption is correct.

[¶1209] WHO MAY ISSUE A DISABILITY CERTIFICATE? FOR WHAT CONDITIONS?

Where a certificate of impairment or infirmity by a "medical practitioner" is required to claim a disability allowance (¶1255), exemption of disability-related employment benefits (¶361d), the high rate of child care expense for an eligible child (¶1053), a particular medical expense credit (¶1207), or a particular listed deduction which enables a person with a specified disability to work or study (¶1036), the certificate must generally be provided by a medical doctor.

In addition, the following practitioners can certify or prescribe in their fields:

- an optometrist can certify an impairment of sight;
- an audiologist can certify an impairment of hearing;
- an occupational therapist can certify an impairment with respect to an individual's ability in walking or in feeding or dressing one's self;
- a psychologist can certify an impairment with respect to an individual's ability in mental functions necessary for everyday life;
- a speech-language pathologist can certify a speech impairment; and
- a physiotherapist can certify an impairment in walking.

In CRA Document No. 2005-0126931E5, the CRA says that "We are not aware of any province in Canada that specifically authorizes Christian Science practitioners or nurses to act as medical practitioners" and consequently such persons would not be medical practitioners or nurses for income tax purposes (unless, of course, they had other credentials). Several provinces provide in their legislation authorizing certain persons to practice medicine that the authority so provided does not take away from a person's freedom practise the religious tenets of his or her church. This does not, in the CRA's view, mean that the jurisdiction has authorized religious groups to perform medical services.

As discussed in more detail in ¶1205, the determination of who is a medical practitioner is a matter to be defined by provincial law. In the case of certificates issued by a medical practitioner, it is the province in which the taxpayer resides that determines eligibility.

Note that payments to a school, institution, or other place for the care and training of a person with a mental or physical handicap require only the certificate of an "appropriately qualified person" and not a medical practitioner.

(ITA: 118.3(1)(*a*.2); 118.4(2); CRA Document No.: Christian Science Practitioners, *June 21, 2005*, CRA Document No. 2005-0126931E5; Income Tax Folio: S1-F1-C1 Medical Expense Tax Credit; S1-F1-C2 Disability Tax Credit)

[¶1209.05] *What is "a Severe and Prolonged Mental or Physical Impairment"?*

Where a doctor (or optometrist, etc.) is required to certify "one or more severe and prolonged impairments in physical or mental functions", the criteria for certification are spelled out with some clarity in the law. By contrast, there is no statutory definition of "infirmity" or "lack of normal mental capacity" where a medical practitioner is required to certify these conditions.

The CRA requires you to use form T2201 to obtain certification of a severe or prolonged mental or physical impairment (but not of mere infirmity).

The legislative definition of "severe and prolonged mental or physical impairment" asserts that an impairment is prolonged if it has lasted or may reasonably be expected to last for a continuous period of at least 12 months.

A severe impairment is not itself defined, but for several purposes, notably the disability credit (¶1255), one of the several full-time attendant care provisions, and the exemption of disability-related employment benefits (¶361d) an impairment must not only be severe but have effects such that the individual's ability to perform a basic activity of daily living is markedly restricted.

A marked restriction is defined to be blindness or the inability to perform any particular one of the basic activities of daily living on the list below. That is, if there is only one activity that cannot be performed, that constitutes a marked impairment.

It is also recognized that individuals may have several limitations none of which produces a "marked" restriction by itself but which have a cumulative effect equivalent to the individual having a marked restriction in a basic activity of daily living.

A marked restriction occurs only where all or substantially all of the time, even with therapy and the use of appropriate devices and medication, the individual is blind or is unable (or requires an inordinate amount of time) to perform a basic activity of daily living. The CRA generally considers that "all or substantially all of the time" means "90% of the time".

A basic activity of daily living is defined to mean:

- mental functions necessary for everyday life; these include (i) memory, (ii) problem solving, goal-setting and judgment (taken together), and (iii) adaptive functioning;
- feeding oneself or dressing oneself (subject to the limitations discussed below);
- speaking so as to be understood, in a quiet setting, by another person familiar with the individual;
- hearing, so as to understand, in a quiet setting, another person familiar with the individual;
- eliminating (bowel or bladder functions); or
- walking.

The rules also specify that:

- feeding oneself does not include: (i) any of the activities of identifying, finding, shopping for or otherwise procuring food; or (ii) the activity of preparing food to the extent that the time associated with the activity would not have been necessary in the absence of a dietary restriction or regime; and
- dressing oneself does not include any of the activities of identifying, finding, shopping for or otherwise procuring clothing.

The limitations above effectively reverse the decision in *The Queen v. Ray F. Hamilton*, 2002 DTC 6836 (F.C.A.), affirming 2001 DTC 3720 (T.C.C.), in which a person with celiac disease required a gluten-free diet, and argued successfully that he had a marked restriction in daily living because he required an inordinate amount of time to find, procure, and prepare foods that he could safely eat. Apparently the CRA found this an intolerable expansion of the definition of feeding oneself, and prevailed upon the Department of Finance to introduce the limitations above, offset in some degree by allowing a medical expense credit for the incremental cost of gluten-free food as compared to the cost of similar non-gluten-free food if a medical practitioner certifies in writing that the person requires a gluten-free diet because of celiac disease. In their final form, the limitations at least seem to ensure that individuals who are markedly restricted in their ability to prepare a meal for reasons other than a dietary restriction or regime (such as severe arthritis) will continue to be eligible for the disability credit.

General activities, such as working, housekeeping, or a social or recreational activity, do not constitute a "basic activity of daily living", and disability in regard to these activities is not by itself sufficient to qualify you for a disability credit or other tax benefits based on this definition.

An individual is also considered impaired if he or she would be markedly restricted in a basic activity of daily living but for a therapy administered at least three times a week for a total time of at least 14 hours per week. The therapy must be essential to sustain a vital function of the patient, and must be one that could not reasonably be expected to be of significant benefit to a person not so impaired. Dialysis and cystic fibrosis patients, for example, are likely beneficiaries of this policy.

The activities which make up the 14 hours per week of therapy time are themselves defined. Time spent by an individual which counts toward the administration of therapy:

(1) includes only time spent on activities that require the individual to take time away from normal everyday activities in order to receive the therapy;

(2) in the case of therapy that requires a regular dosage of medication that is required to be adjusted on a daily basis, includes (subject to (4) below) time spent on activities that are directly related to the determination of the dosage of the medication;

(3) in the case of a child who is unable to perform the activities related to the administration of the therapy as a result of the child's age, includes the time, if any, spent by the child's primary caregivers performing or supervising those activities for the child; and

(4) does not include time spent on activities related to dietary or exercise restrictions or regimes (even if these restrictions or regimes are a factor in determining the daily dosage of medication), travel time, medical appointments, shopping for medication or recuperation after therapy.

Children with very severe cases of Type 1 diabetes — who require many insulin injections (which requires knowledge of current blood sugar levels at the time of each injection), as well as several additional blood sugar tests to monitor their condition — may be eligible for the disability credit.

At one time, the CRA took the view that an impairment certificate could not be written after death, since there could not then be a reasonable expectation that the condition would last for 12 months. This position was modified in CRA Document No. 2002-0151185 to the more reasonable view that "a certificate may be completed after death if it is based on a prognosis, made by an appropriately qualified person before the individual died, that the individual's severe impairment was reasonably expected to last for a continuous period of at least one year."

Where the disability credit at ¶1255 is claimed by or for an individual, the CRA has authority to make a written request for additional information on the impairment, its effects on the individual, and where relevant, the therapy which itself qualifies the individual for the credit. The CRA has an in-house medical staff making it possible to make this type of request. It appears that the request may be made to the individual, the person making the claim for the individual, or the doctor, optometrist, etc. who initially completed form T2201. Such a request must be answered in writing, and the information so provided is considered part of the disability certificate.

In *Poehlke v. The Queen*, 2011 DTC 1001, the Tax Court of Canada concluded, based on an evaluation by two cognitive experts, that the taxpayer's son suffered from only a mild intellectual disability and could adequately perceive, think, and remember. His disability was not considered serious enough to enable his father to claim the disability tax credit.

In *Brazeau v. The Queen*, 2011 DTC 1012, the Tax Court of Canada concluded that the taxpayer could claim the disability tax credit in respect of his son, who suffered from insulin-dependent diabetes because he spent at least 15 hours per week in maintaining his proper blood sugar levels. The Court relied on the son's testimony to reach that conclusion.

In *Wood v. The Queen*, 2011 DTC 1131, the Tax Court of Canada held that a taxpayer who was experiencing migraine headaches after a laboratory accident and was unable to perform one or more basic daily activities was not disabled and did not qualify for a disability tax credit. Although those migraines were frequent, they did not prevent him from performing his basic daily activities all or substantially all of the time (i.e., 90% of the time).

In *Ostlund v. The Queen*, 2011 DTC 1147, the Court denied the disability tax credit to a father whose son was diagnosed with Asperger's syndrome. Since the father admitted during his testimony that his son was not markedly restricted from performing daily life skills or mental functions and could only claim that the overall result was unfair to him and his wife, the Court concluded that his son was not truly disabled.

(ITA: 118.3; 118.4; Income Tax Folio: S1-F1-C1, Medical Expense Tax Credit; S1-F1-C2, Disability Tax Credit)

[¶1209.10] *Infirmity Test*

The disability certificate described above is required for the disability credit described at ¶1255 and for a number of other tax benefits described in this book. Other benefits, such as the tax credit at ¶1126 or the rollover of RRSP funds from a deceased taxpayer to a child (¶1914), are available if someone is dependent by reason of infirmity. This is quite a different standard from the disability standard above, and is not a defined term.

As to infirmity, as opposed to impairment, the CRA says that to establish dependency the degree of infirmity must be such that it requires the infirm person to be dependent "for a considerable period of time. Temporary illness is not classified as infirmity." Presumably, infirmity is a less strictly defined and less onerous test than impairment.

(IT-513R, Appendix A; Income Tax Folio: S1-F1-C1, Medical Expense Tax Credit; S1-F1-C2, Disability Tax Credit)

[¶1209.15] *CRA Guide*

The CRA has published a general guide, *Disability-Related Information* (RC4064), which groups together information on the various income tax and GST benefits, and some of the tax-related services, available to individuals with disabilities. The guide can be downloaded from the Internet.

[¶1210] MEDICAL EXPENSES INCURRED OUTSIDE CANADA WILL QUALIFY

Allowable medical expenses are generally not restricted to those incurred or paid for treatment in Canada. For example, if you were sick while on a vacation in the United States, you should include any medical expenses incurred or paid in the United States along with your other medical expenses. However, if you are a non-resident, see ¶2062a and ¶2065; if you are a part-year resident, see ¶2107.

(Income Tax Folio: S1-F1-C1, Medical Expense Tax Credit, para. 1.12)

[¶1215] CHECKLIST OF ALLOWABLE MEDICAL EXPENSES

[¶1215.05] *Professional Services*

Eligible medical expenses include amounts paid to a medical practitioner, dentist, nurse, or a public or licensed private hospital for medical or dental services.

A medical service is a service relating to the diagnosis, treatment, or prevention of disease performed by a medical practitioner acting in the scope of his or her training.

As discussed in more detail in ¶1205 and ¶1209, the determination of who is a medical practitioner is a matter to be defined by provincial law (or the laws of a foreign jurisdiction, where applicable). Thus practitioners of some specialized therapies, such as naturopaths, massage therapists, and acupuncturists, may be recognized in some provinces but not others. In the case of payments for services, it is the law of the province where the services are performed that governs eligibility for medical expense credit.

In CRA Document No. 2012-0465171E5, the family physician suggested speech therapy for the taxpayer's child who had a severe and prolonged impairment which qualified him for the disability tax credit. Because of the long waiting list in the public sector and limited time availability of the speech-language pathologist hired from the private sector, he used the services of a specialized speech therapy technician. The CRA was asked if the expenses incurred for the technician qualified for the medical expense tax credit. The CRA confirmed that those expenses would not qualify for the credit since there was no indication that the treatment was prescribed by a medical practitioner or would help the speech-language pathologist reach a diagnosis.

[¶1215.10] *Laboratory Examinations and Tests*

Medical expenses include amounts paid for laboratory, radiological, or other diagnostic procedures or services, and the necessary interpretations, for maintenance, prevention, diagnosis, or treatment, if prescribed by a medical practitioner or dentist. Examples include:

- Blood tests
- Cardiographs
- Metabolism tests
- Spinal fluid tests
- Stool examination
- Urine analyses
- X-ray examinations

[¶1215.15] *Dental Services*

Medical expenses include amounts paid to a dentist for dental services including:

- Dental X-rays
- Extracting teeth
- Filling teeth
- Gum treatment
- Oral surgery
- Straightening teeth
- Dental implant

Amounts paid to a dental mechanic for the making or repairing of a denture or for the taking of impressions, bite registrations, and insertions in respect of the making of a denture are also eligible for medical expense tax credit.

[¶1215.20] *Hospital Services*

Medical expenses include amounts paid to public or private hospitals in respect of medical or dental services. For example:

- Anaesthetist
- Hospital bills
- Oxygen masks, tent — prescription required
- Use of operating room
- Vaccines — prescription required
- X-ray technician

[¶1215.25] *Medicines*

Medical expenses include the following medicines:

- Insulin or substitutes — prescription required
- Oxygen (and related equipment to administer oxygen) for medical purposes — prescription required
- Liver extract injections prescribed for pernicious anaemia
- Vitamin B12 — for pernicious anaemia
- Drugs obtained under Health Canada's Special Access Programme in accordance with sections C.08.010 and C.08.011 of the *Food and Drug Regulations*
- Any medicine or drug purchased by you, your spouse, or a dependant, as prescribed by a medical practitioner or dentist, recorded by a licensed pharmacist, and only available on medical prescription. For more detail, see ¶1220.10. As to who is a medical practitioner qualified to prescribe, see ¶1205.
- Medical marijuana, if purchased from either Health Canada or a designated grower, and marijuana seeds, if purchased from Health Canada, purchased by a patient authorized to use the drug for medical purposes under Health Canada's *Marihuana Medical Access Regulations* or who possesses an exemption under section 56 of the *Controlled Drug and Substances Act.* The designated grower must possess, on behalf of the particular patient, a designated person production licence to produce marijuana under the *Marihuana Medical Access Regulations* or an exemption for cultivation or production under section 56 of the *Controlled Drugs and Substances Act.*

Commentary on Legislative Proposals (Sept. 16, 2016)

Note: When Legislative Proposals, September 16, 2016, achieves Royal Assent, the commentary will be modified to read:

- Prior to the date of Royal Assent of the Legislative Proposals from September 16, 2016, medical marijuana, if purchased from either Health Canada or a designated grower, and marijuana seeds, if purchased from Health Canada, purchased by a patient authorized to use the drug for medical purposes under Health Canada's *Marihuana Medical Access Regulations* or who possesses an exemption under section 56 of the *Controlled Drug and Substances Act.* The designated grower must possess, on behalf of the particular patient, a designated person production licence to produce marijuana under the *Marihuana Medical Access Regulations* or an exemption for cultivation or production under section 56 of the *Controlled Drugs and Substances Act.*

- Effective June 19, 2013, the cost of marijuana will be an eligible expense if it is purchased on behalf of a patient who is authorized to possess marijuana for medical purposes under the *Marihuana for Medical Purposes Regulations* or section 56 of the *Controlled Drug and Substances Act* from a licensed producer, a health care practitioner, a hospital, or an individual who possesses an exemption for cultivation or production under section 56 of the *Controlled Drug and Substances Act.*

[¶1215.30] *Apparatus and Materials (including repairs thereto and replacement batteries)*

Note that all items prescribed by regulation must be prescribed by a medical practitioner, whereas those items prescribed by statute may or may not require medical prescription; in all cases where a medical prescription is required, this is indicated by an asterisk (*) below (see ¶1205).

- Air conditioner — 50% of the cost of an air conditioner for an individual with a severe chronic ailment, disease, or disorder, to a limit of $1,000*
- Air or water filter or purifier for use by an individual suffering from a severe chronic respiratory ailment or a severe chronic immune system disregulation*
- Altered auditory feedback device designed for use by an individual who has a speech impairment*.
- Artificial eye[1]
- Artificial kidney machine, including reasonable installation and home alteration costs
- Artificial limb
- Baby breathing monitor designed to sound an alarm if an infant stops breathing — a medical practitioner must certify in writing that the infant is prone to sudden infant death syndrome*
- Bathroom aids — devices designed to assist a person to enter or leave a bathtub or shower, or to get on or off a toilet*
- Bliss symbol board or similar device designed to help an individual with a speech impairment to communicate by selecting symbols or spelling out words*
- Blood coagulation monitors (including disposable peripherals) for use by patients requiring anti-coagulation therapy*
- Blood sugar level measuring devices for diabetics
- Brace for a limb
- Braille note-taker designed to allow a blind individual to take notes with the help of a keyboard*
- Canes, walkers, and other devices exclusively designed as walking aids, where the patient has a mobility impairment*
- Catheters, catheter trays, tubing, or other products required by persons who are incontinent by virtue of illness, injury, or affliction
- Colostomy pads
- Contact lenses*
- Crutches
- A device, including replacement parts, designed exclusively for use by an individual who is suffering from a chronic respiratory ailment or a severe chronic immune system disregulation, not including an air conditioner, humidifier, dehumidifier, heat pump, or heat or air exchanger*
- A device designed exclusively to enable an individual with a mobility impairment to operate a vehicle*
- Diapers, disposable briefs, or other products required by persons who are incontinent by virtue of illness, injury, or affliction
- Electronic or computerized environmental control systems designed exclusively for the use of an individual with severe and prolonged mobility restrictions (apparently this is to include electronic control systems for quadriplegics)*
- Electronic speech synthesizers that enable mute individuals to communicate using a portable keyboard*
- Electrotherapy device designed to be used by an individual with a medical condition or a severe mobility impairment*
- Eye glasses or other devices for the treatment or correction of a vision defect*
- External breast prosthesis that is required because of a mastectomy*
- Extremity pump or elastic support hose designed exclusively to reduce swelling caused by lymphedema*
- Furnace — electric or sealed combustion furnace to replace a furnace that is not either where replacement is necessary because of a severe chronic respiratory ailment or a severe chronic immune system disregulation*
- Hearing aid, or in fact any "aid to hearing", which can include audible signals, cochlear implants, telephone volume enhancers, bone-conduction telephone receivers, and devices to reduce sound distortions; see also the separate item below for telephone assistance devices for the deaf or mute
- Heart monitoring or pacing devices*
- Hospital bed and attachments included in the prescription, if required in home*
- Infusion pumps, including disposable peripherals, used in the treatment of diabetes or to measure a diabetic's blood sugar level*
- Iron lung
- Ileostomy pads
- Laryngeal speaking aid

[1] Eligible expense includes the purchase price or rental cost, and related expenses such as maintenance, repairs, and supplies.

- Medical devices obtained under Health Canada's Special Access Programme in accordance with Part 2 of the Medical Devices Regulations
- Needles and syringes*
- Optical scanners or similar devices to enable a person who is blind to read print and devices or software designed to enable a person who is blind or who has a severe learning disability to read print*
- Orthopedic shoes, boots, and inserts*
- Osteogenesis stimulator (inductive coupling) for treating non-union of fractures or aiding in bone fusion*
- Oxygen tent and equipment*
- Oxygen concentrator and the expenses in respect of it, such as the cost of electricity
- Page-turner device designed for use by an individual who has a severe and prolonged impairment that markedly restricts his or her ability to use his or her arms or hands to turn pages*
- Phototherapy equipment for the treatment of psoriasis or other skin disorders, and expenses to operate and maintain such equipment
- Portable chest respirator that performs the same function as an iron lung; also a machine for supplying air (possibly in combination with oxygen or medication) to the lungs under pressure, for therapeutic use
- Power-operated guided chair installation to be used solely in a stairway*
- Power-operated lifts or transportation equipment designed exclusively for use by or for a disabled individual to allow the individual access to different areas of a building or to assist the individual to gain access to a vehicle or to place his or her wheelchair in or on a vehicle (apparently this includes track electrical systems to move quadriplegics about the home, e.g., from bed to bath)*
- Pressure pulse therapy device designed to be used by an individual for the treatment of a balance disorder*
- Rocking bed for polio victim
- Spinal brace
- Standing device designed to be used by an individual for standing therapy in the treatment of severe mobility impairment*
- Synthetic speech systems, braille printers, large print-on-screen devices, and other devices designed to enable blind persons to use computers*
- Talking textbook for use by an individual with a perceptual disability in connection with the individual's enrolment at an educational institution in Canada (¶1323) or a designated educational institution (¶1323)*
- Tapes or tablets for sugar content tests by diabetics, if the procedure has been required by a physician
- Teletypewriter, telephone ringing indicator, or similar device that enables a deaf or mute person to make and receive telephone calls. Amounts paid in providing additional equipment and accessories to others in order to make telephone communication possible with those other persons are also allowed as medical expenses*
- Television closed caption decoders for the deaf*
- Truss for hernia
- The lesser of $5,000 and 20% of the cost of a van (minus any portion of the cost for which credit is claimed under the rule above) that, at the time of acquisition or within six months thereafter, has been adapted for the transportation of a patient who requires a wheelchair (Ontario, uniquely, indexes the $5,000 value, and the CRA usually publishes the current Ontario values in its notes to line 5868 in the Ontario T1 package; for 2016, the value is $6,922)
- Visual or vibratory signaling device, such as a visual fire alarm indicator, for an individual with a hearing impairment*
- Voice recognition software for a patient certified by a medical practitioner to require it because of a physical impairment
- Wheelchair, including a scooter or wheel-mounted geriatric chair
- Wigs made for individuals who have suffered abnormal hair loss owing to disease, accident or medical treatment*

[¶1215.35] *Medical Services*

Medical expenses include an amount paid to a medical practitioner or nurse for medical services such as:

- Blood transfusion
- Diathermy
- Electric shock treatments
- Healing services
- Hydrotherapy
- Injections
- Insulin treatments
- *In vitro* fertility program, including the cost of sperm and egg freezing and storage
- Laser eye surgery
- Pre-natal; post-natal treatments
- Psychotherapy
- Radium therapy
- Speech pathology or audiology
- Transplants: on behalf of a patient who requires a bone marrow or organ transplant, including the reasonable costs of locating a compatible donor and arranging for the transplant, and reasonable travelling, board and lodging expenses for the donor and a companion as well as the recipient and a companion incurred in respect of the transplant
- Ultra violet ray treatments

- Weight loss program, if provided by a medical practitioner for therapeutic or rehabilitative reasons (see CRA Document No. 2011-0429001E5)

- Whirlpool baths treatments, not including home installation of a hot tub

- X-ray treatments

In *Ismael v. The Queen*, 2014 DTC 1140 (T.C.C.), the Minister conceded that the amounts paid by a taxpayer to *in vitro* fertilization treatment clinics in the U.S. and Ukraine qualified for the medical expense tax credit (METC). However, the egg donor fees, transportation, food, and accommodation costs, and wiring and banking charges were considered ineligible to calculate the METC. The Court concluded that, because substantially similar *in vitro* fertilization treatments were already available in Canada, the travel expenses for the taxpayer and her husband did not qualify for the METC.

[¶1215.40] *Miscellaneous*

Medical expenses also include the following miscellaneous expenses:

- Ambulance charges — to or from hospital

- Deaf-blind intervening services for a patient who is blind and profoundly deaf if the payment is made to a person normally engaged in the business of providing such services

- Prescription birth control pills

- Premium paid to a private health services plan (Interpretation Bulletin IT-339R2 says the plan must be in respect of hospital care or expense or medical care or expense which normally would otherwise have qualified as a medical expense)

- Reading services for a patient who is blind or has a severe learning disability, if the need is certified by a medical practitioner and the amount is paid to a person normally engaged in the business of providing such services

- Remuneration for therapy prescribed by, and administered under the general supervision of, a medical doctor or psychologist, in the case of a mental impairment, or a medical doctor or occupational therapist, in the case of a physical impairment, where the patient is an eligible person with a disability. The payee must not be the individual's spouse or common-law partner or under the age of 18. Where the payee is an individual, the receipt must include the payee's Social Insurance Number

- Remuneration for designing an individualized therapy plan but only if the following conditions are met: (1) the therapy is prescribed by a medical doctor, occupational therapist, or psychologist; (2) the plan is required to get public funding for a specialized therapy or is prescribed by a medical doctor, occupational therapist, or psychologist, and is designed for an individual with a severe and prolonged impairment qualifying for the disability tax credit; and (3) the payments are made to persons normally engaged in the business of designing such plans for unrelated individuals.

- Remuneration for tutoring services that are supplementary to the primary education of the patient, for a patient with a learning disability or mental impairment, if the need is certified by a medical practitioner and the amount is paid to an unrelated person normally engaged in the business of providing such services (in *Hoare v. The Queen*, 2007 DTC 992 (T.C.C.), credit was allowed for expenses for a professional teacher who taught the patient at home, on a full-time basis, a curriculum developed and graded elsewhere; it was held that the teacher's activities were supplementary)

- Reasonable expenses relating to renovations or alterations to a dwelling, including the driveway, of a patient who lacks normal physical development or has a severe and prolonged mobility impairment (one that may be expected to last 12 months or more), to enable the patient to gain access to, or to be mobile or functional within, the dwelling, provided that the expenses would not typically be expected to increase the value of the dwelling, and that the expenses would not normally be incurred by persons without the lack of development or the impairment described

- Reasonable moving expenses (not to exceed $2,000) of a patient who lacks normal physical development or has a severe and prolonged mobility impairment if incurred for moving to a dwelling more accessible by the patient or in which the patient is more mobile and functional (eligible moving expenses are those discussed at ¶1041); however, the same expense cannot be claimed under both this provision and the rules of moving to a new work location at ¶1039. Ontario, uniquely, indexes the $2,000 value, and the CRA usually publishes the current Ontario values in its notes to line 5868 in the Ontario T1 package; for 2016, the value is $2,769.

- Reasonable expenses relating to rehabilitative therapy, including training in lip reading and sign language, if incurred to adjust for the patient's loss of hearing or speech

- Sign language interpretation services or real-time captioning services, where the payment is made to a person engaged in the business of providing such services on behalf of a patient who has a speech or hearing impairment

- Special access items — amounts paid for drugs or devices purchased under Health Canada's *Special Access Programme* on behalf of the patient. This programme allows access to drugs or medical devices that have not yet been approved for sale in Canada. Special access can be requested in emergency cases or when conventional therapies have failed, are unsuitable or are unavailable

- The cost of an animal specially trained to assist a person who is blind or profoundly deaf, or has severe autism, severe epilepsy, severe diabetes, or a severe and prolonged impairment that markedly restricts the use of the patient's arms or legs. In addition to the cost of the animal, its care and maintenance (including food and veterinary care) are eligible expenses, as are travel expenses to a training facility to learn how to handle the animal, and, if full-time attendance at the training facility is required, reasonable board and lodging incurred in the full-time attendance

- Training — reasonable expenses (other than amounts paid to your spouse or to a person under 18) to train you or a person related to you (as defined at ¶1122) if the training relates to the physical or mental infirmity of a person who is related to you and is either (i) a member of your household or (ii) dependent on you for support. "Infirmity" as used here is infirmity as defined in ¶1122.40 and not impairment. In order to claim these medical expenses you need not claim a personal amount in Chapter 11 for the person the training relates to; however, it will often be possible to make a claim for that person under the rules in ¶1120, ¶1126, or ¶1140.

- Transportation costs — to or from a hospital, clinic, or doctor's office to obtain services not otherwise available nearer the individual's home (see ¶1205.05)
- The cost of note-taking services on behalf of a person certified in writing by a medical practitioner to require such services because of physical or mental infirmity, if paid to a person in the business of providing such services
- The incremental cost of gluten-free food as compared to the cost of similar non-gluten-free food, if a medical practitioner has certified in writing that the person requires a gluten-free diet because of celiac disease

In *Sotski v. The Queen*, 2013 DTC 1229 (T.C.C.), the cost of replacing carpeting with laminate flooring to improve the mobility and safety for the taxpayer's husband, who suffered from Parkinson's disease, was held to be eligible for the medical expense tax credit. The Court considered the requirement that the renovations not be of the type normally incurred by people without impairment. The Court found that the purpose of this requirement was to ensure that the medical expense tax credit could not be used to subsidize personal consumption and personal choices. The renovations were restricted to those necessary to alleviate the taxpayer's husband's impairment and did not represent a personal consumption choice; the laminate flooring was modestly priced and was only installed in the area of the home used by the taxpayer's husband. As such, there was no abuse and the conditions to claiming the medical expense tax credit were met. However, see CRA Document No. 2011-0422991E5.

In *Shapiro v. The Queen*, 2014 DTC 1080 (T.C.C.), the Court concluded that the cost incurred by a taxpayer for storing the umbilical cord blood of her child at a hematology lab did not qualify as an eligible medical expense to calculate the METC. Even if the blood was stored at the lab for future use in stem cell therapy or treatment of illnesses like leukemia, the storing procedure was not prescribed by a medical practitioner and therefore the related expense could not qualify as an eligible medical expense. Even if the obstetrician extracted the blood from the cord, this would not be considered as a prescribed medical procedure.

In CRA Document No. 2013-0507021E5, the CRA confirmed that the tuition fees paid to a private school providing a safe allergen-free environment to the taxpayer's son who had multiple severe allergies would not qualify as medical expenses for the purpose of claiming the METC. The taxpayer put forth that the public school system could not provide this type of environment. To qualify for the credit, the son had to suffer from a handicap requiring equipment, facilities, and personnel provided by the private school for his care, and a medical practitioner or school principal had to confirm the requirement in writing. Since those conditions were not met, the tuition fees did not qualify as eligible medical expenses.

In CRA Document No. 2013-0499731E5, the CRA confirmed that any fee paid to a medical practitioner for a Special Authority status for a prescription medication was ancillary to the medical service, thus qualifying as an eligible medical expense. Since certain provincial prescription drugs programs and private health services plans only reimburse prescription medication, the patient may require a Special Authority status form prepared by his/her doctor for a fee to obtain such special medication.

(ITA: 118.2(2); ITR: 5700 [Prescribed devices and equipment]; IT-339R2 Meaning of "private health services plan"; CRA Document No.: weight loss program - METC, *January 25, 2012,* CRA Document No. 2011-0429001E5; In vitro fertility program, *September 30, 2011,* CRA Document No. 2011-0415601E5; Sperm Banking — Whether Medical Expense, *August 6, 2002,* CRA Document No. 2002-0148245; Income Tax Folio: S1-F1-C1 Medical Expense Tax Credit; *Sotski v. The Queen,* 2013 DTC 1229 (T.C.C.))

[¶1220] WHAT YOU CANNOT CLAIM AS MEDICAL EXPENSES

The following is a non-exhaustive list of non-eligible expenses:

- Athletic or fitness club fees
- Birth control devices, non-prescription
- Blood pressure monitors
- Diaper services
- Funeral, cremation or burials, cemetery plot, monument, mausoleum
- Health plan premiums paid by an employer and not included in your income
- Health programs, such as those offered by resort hotels, health clubs, and gyms
- Illegal operations, treatments, or drugs illegally procured
- Maternity clothes
- Medical expenses for which you, the patient, a person related to you or the patient, or a legal representative of any of the aforementioned individuals are reimbursed or are entitled to be reimbursed, unless the amount of the reimbursement is required to be included in income and is not deductible
- Organic food
- Over-the-counter medications, vitamins, and supplements, even if prescribed
- Personal response systems such as Lifeline and Health Line Services
- Premiums and contributions paid to provincial or territorial medical or hospitalization insurance plans
- Scales for weighing food
- Toothpaste
- Wigs — unless made to order for individuals who have suffered abnormal hair loss owing to disease, medical treatment, or accident

In *Anthony v. The Queen*, 2012 DTC 1275 (T.C.C.), the cost of a hot tub purchased on the advice of the taxpayer's doctor to assist with mobility impairment caused by severe chronic pain was held not to be an eligible medical expense. A medical expense tax credit may be available for home renovations to increase mobility; however, the renovations must not be of the type that would normally be incurred by people with no impairments. A medical expense tax credit may also be available for the purchase of a device designed exclusively to help a person to walk. Although the hot tub increased mobility and improved the taxpayer's ability to walk, it was of a type not exclusively designed for this purpose and commonly purchased by people with no impairments. See also *Johnston v. The Queen*, 2012 DTC 1175 (T.C.C.).

In *Mongillo v. The Queen*, 95 DTC 199 (T.C.C.), the cost of specialized food required by an allergy sufferer in accordance with a doctor's advice was held not to be an eligible medical expense. Although admittedly required by the patient's medical condition, there was simply no provision permitting such a deduction. The closest permissive provision, for substances for the treatment of disease, requires the substances to be provided by a licensed pharmacist. Note that a statutory exception now exists for the incremental cost of gluten-free food required by a person with celiac disease.

In CRA Document No. 2011-0422991E5, the CRA noted that the cost of replacing carpet with hardwood flooring to alleviate the patient's asthma was not a renovation qualifying for the medical expense tax credit since it was of the type expected to increase the value of the home and would normally be incurred by persons without impairment. However, see *Sotski v. The Queen*, 2013 DTC 1229 (T.C.C.), discussed above.

In CRA Document No. 2012-0440931E5, the CRA confirmed that the purchase cost of a motorized stationary bicycle was not an eligible medical expense even if the device was prescribed by a doctor to an individual suffering from an illness significantly restricting his ability to walk. The purpose of the device was to improve the individual's muscular tone, blood circulation, and flexibility of movement, and reduce muscular spasms and inflammation. However, since it was not exclusively designed to help an individual with mobility impairment in walking, it was not covered under Regulation 5700(*i*) and would not qualify as a medical expense under paragraph 118.2(2)(*m*) of the Act.

In CRA Document No. 2011-0416651I7, the CRA noted that the interest expense paid on a bank loan to finance the cost of a dental implant surgical procedure was not an eligible medical expense for the purpose of claiming the medical expense tax credit. To qualify as an eligible medical expense, the expense had to be paid to a medical practitioner, dentist, nurse, public hospital, or licensed private hospital. In this case, the expense was instead paid to a bank.

In CRA Document No. 2011-0392401E5, the CRA noted that expenses paid to a massage therapist were not eligible medical expenses since the therapist was not authorized under the provincial legislation (i.e., *Medical Act* in Quebec) to practice. In *Chevalier v. The Queen*, 2008 DTC 2477, the Tax Court Canada concluded for the same reason that expenses paid to naturopaths and osteopaths did not qualify to claim a medical expense tax credit.

In CRA Document No. 2010-0385911E5, the CRA confirmed that the purchase cost of equipment used to treat an individual's high cholesterol level was not an eligible medical expense, even though it was prescribed by a medical practitioner, because it was not listed in subsection 118.2(2) or prescribed under Regulation 5700.

In CRA Document No. 2010-0386621E5, the CRA confirmed that the costs related to the retrieval and storage of stem cells did not qualify as eligible medical expenses because: (1) they were not procedures related to an existing injury or medical condition, and (2) they were not procedures for maintaining health, preventing diseases, or diagnosing or treating injuries. Therefore, no medical expense tax credit could be claimed. Also, see CRA Document No. 2011-0422941E5, where the CRA noted that amounts paid for the collection and storage of umbilical cord blood did not qualify as medical expenses.

In CRA Document No. 2010-0383021E5, the CRA indicated that the cost of an Apple iPad acquired to help autistic children and other special needs children to communicate more effectively did not qualify for the medical expense tax credit. To qualify under paragraph 118.2(2)(*m*), a device or equipment must be prescribed by a medical practitioner, listed under Regulation 5700, and meet certain conditions regarding its use and reason of acquisition.

In CRA Document No. 2010-0378071E5, the CRA confirmed that the purchase cost of a four-wheel scooter for an individual unable to drive a car or walk long distances because of a partial vision reduction did not qualify as an eligible medical expense. The purchase of the scooter would only qualify for the medical expense tax credit if the individual had difficulty walking or was unable to walk and the scooter was bought in place of a wheelchair.

(ITA: 118.2(3)(*b*); RC4064 Disability-Related Information 2015; Income Tax Folio: S1-F1-C1 Medical Expense Tax Credit)

[¶1220.10] *Over-the-Counter Drugs, Even if Prescribed*

Over-the-counter drug store purchases, i.e., those which do not require a prescription, such as vitamins, mouth rinse, and the like, do not qualify for the medical expense credit even when recommended by a medical practitioner or dentist and recorded by a licensed pharmacist. Over-the-counter drug store purchases, i.e., those which do not require a prescription, such as vitamins, mouth rinse, and the like, do not qualify for credit even when recommended by a medical practitioner as essential to the patient's well-being, since they do not meet the "recorded by a licensed pharmacist" test. See *The Queen v. Rhonda Ray*, 2004 DTC 6028 (F.C.A.), rev'g 2004 DTC 2120 (T.C.C.), followed in *Rasler v. The Queen*, 2005 DTC 1096 (T.C.C.).

Prescribed medications are only eligible for credit if they meet the following criteria:

(1) they are manufactured, sold or represented for use in the diagnosis, treatment or prevention of a disease, disorder or abnormal physical state, or its symptoms, or in restoring, correcting or modifying an organic function,

(2) they can lawfully be acquired for use by the patient only if prescribed by a medical practitioner or dentist, and

(3) the purchase is recorded by a pharmacist.

As to who is a medical practitioner qualified to prescribe, see ¶1205.

Paragraph 118.2(2)(*k*) provides exceptions for insulin, oxygen, liver extract injectable for pernicious anaemia, or vitamin B12 for pernicious anaemia, which need only be prescribed by a medical practitioner to be eligible for the medical expense credit.

(ITA: 118.2(2)(*k*); 118.2(2)(*n*); ITR: 5701 [Prescribed drugs and medicaments]; *The Queen v. Rhonda Ray*, 2004 DTC 6028 (F.C.A.); *Norton v. The Queen*, 2008 DTC 2605 (T.C.C.))

[¶1220.15] *Cosmetic Procedures*

Medical, dental, or other related expenses cannot be claimed if they are provided only for cosmetic purposes (e.g., liposuction, hair replacement, etc.). Expenses for procedures required for medical or reconstructive purposes (e.g., services to ameliorate a deformity related to a congenital abnormality, a disfiguring disease, or an injury resulting from an accident or trauma) are eligible. It is a question of fact as to whether a procedure is for cosmetic purposes only, or required for medical or reconstructive purposes; however, the CRA has indicated that the expenses for the following procedures may be eligible for the medical expense tax credit: sexual reassignment surgery; treatment of severe acne; removal of hair caused by polycystic ovarian syndrome; and removal of excess skin after rapid weight loss.

In CRA Document No. 2013-0477051E5, the CRA confirmed that the cost of an endovenous laser treatment of varicose veins that was paid to a medical practitioner, public hospital, or licensed private hospital would qualify as an eligible medical expense to claim the medical expense tax credit since it was not undertaken purely for cosmetic purposes.

(ITA: 118.2(2.1); CRA Document No.: Cosmetic procedures - Hair removal, *June 15, 2011*, CRA Document No. 2011-0401221E5; METC - Cosmetic - Acne, *September 27, 2011*, CRA Document No. 2011-0412591E5; medical expenses - sex reassignment surgery, *September 25, 2012*, CRA Document No. 2012-0463201E5; Frais médicaux - chirurgie esthétique, *April 16, 2013*, CRA Document No. 2013-0480831E5)

[¶1225] YOU MAY CLAIM MEDICAL EXPENSES FOR YOURSELF, YOUR SPOUSE OR COMMON-LAW PARTNER, AND YOUR DEPENDANTS

You may claim medical expenses in your return which have been incurred by yourself, your spouse or common-law partner, your children under the age of 18 at the end of the tax year, or specified relatives who were dependent (but not necessarily wholly dependent) on you for support at some time during the year.

[¶1225.05] *Basic Test for Medical Expense Credit*

In order to claim a medical expense, the expense must have been paid by you or your legal representative, or by your spouse or common-law partner (see ¶1225.10).

To the extent you, the patient, a person related to you or the patient, or a legal representative of any of the aforementioned individuals are reimbursed or are entitled to be reimbursed for the expense, whether by insurance or another family member, you may not claim the expense. There is an exception to this rule where the amount of the reimbursement is required to be included in income and is not deductible. Medical expenses eligible for the medical expense tax credit are not reduced by the Ontario Healthy Homes Renovation Tax Credit.

As you might expect, amounts claimed in an earlier year are not available again in a later year. As well, where the medical expenses are for expenses covered by the rules in ¶1036 or under the refundable medical supplement rules in ¶1237 and were claimed by you in an earlier year under those rules, they are not available for further credit.

Where a claim for the same expenses is made by anyone else for any year as a medical expense or under the rules in ¶1036 or under the refundable medical supplement rules in ¶1237, they are not available to you as current medical expense claims. In short, issues of who is to claim a particular expense must be resolved in advance.

[¶1225.10] *Allocating Medical Expenses between Spouses or Common-Law Partners*

You may claim a medical expense credit for expenses incurred by your spouse or common-law partner and paid by you or your legal representative. Even if you are not able to claim any personal amount for your spouse or common-law partner's support, you may still claim medical expenses incurred by him or her.

If you have a spouse and a common-law partner at the same time, you may only claim the medical expenses of your spouse or common-law partner but not both (i.e., if you are still married but have a common-law partner, you may not claim medical expenses for both the spouse and the common-law partner) in calculating their medical expense tax credit for a particular taxation year.

The CRA, as an administrative policy, provides in paragraph 1.11 of Income Tax Folio S1-F1-C1 that an individual may claim the medical expenses paid by his or her spouse or common-law partner; the CRA states that: "A receipt in the name of either spouse or common-law partner is considered acceptable evidence of a medical expense of either, and the amount of that expense may be used by either, as agreed between them".

In CRA Document No. 2005-0131681I7, the CRA has confirmed that this policy extends to expenses incurred for a dependent child who has attained the age of 18. It must follow that expenses incurred for younger children can also be allocated between spouses or common-law partners.

As a result of the above rules, either spouse or common-law partner may claim the medical expenses of both.

If both spouses or common-law partners have a tax liability and are therefore filing a return, it may be advantageous to have the lower-income spouse or common-law partner claim the medical expenses of both because only eligible medical expenses exceeding the lesser of $2,237 and 3% of the claimant's net income qualify for the medical expense tax credit (see ¶1235).

Wife Claims Medical Expenses

Rammy Rochman and his wife Doris, who have no children, each had income and incurred medical expenses for the year as follows:

	Doris	Rammy
Net income	$15,000	$28,000
3% of net income	450	840
Medical expenses	$300	$425

By combining Doris's and Rammy's expenses in Doris's return, a tax credit for medical expenses of $275 ($725 – $450) can be claimed (on line 332). No credit would be available by combining expenses and claiming them in Rammy's return, since the $725 expenses do not exceed his $840 threshold. If Doris and Rammy each claimed their own medical expenses, the income threshold would apply twice.

[¶1225.15] *Medical Expenses of Dependent Children Under 18*

You may claim the expenses you paid on behalf of your children under 18 at the end of the taxation year regardless of the child's income. "Your child" for this purpose is broadly defined, as discussed in ¶1122.15.

The CRA has offered no ascertainable comment on whether receipts issued to minor children can be claimed by a parent. Where the child is in fact dependent on the parent, even if he or she has some independent income, it is difficult to see why the CRA should make an issue of this, especially if the parent appears to be the ultimate source of the particular payment. For example, if a child at a boarding school incurs medical expenses paid by the school and added to the parent's bill, the fact that a receipt is issued to the child rather than the parent would seem an inadequate reason to deny the parent's medical claim. As well, in the case of a minor child, the CRA's theory (that the parent is always an agent for a minor dependant) might have some merit.

Although the CRA has not yet commented on whether amounts paid by one spouse or common-law partner on behalf of a minor child can be attributed to the other spouse or common-law partner, in the absence of a negative comment one would assume that this would be allowed (see ¶1225.10).

[¶1225.20] *Medical Expenses of Dependants Other Than Spouse and Children under 18*

Medical expenses you pay for each of your dependent children 18 and over, and for other dependants, may be included in your own medical expense claim to the extent of the amount by which the expenses you paid on behalf of the dependant exceed that dependant's medical expense threshold of the lesser of 3% of the dependant's net income and $2,208 (see ¶1235).

The reduction for the dependant's "3%/$2,237" threshold is a substitute for, and not in addition to, your own threshold (see ¶1235). That is, medical expenses you paid for each dependant other than your spouse, common-law partner, or children under 18 at the end of the year forms a separate basket of expenses which must be reduced by the dependant's threshold amount. However, the entire remaining basket is then added to your medical expense claim, and is not further reduced by your own threshold amount.

Your dependant includes anyone who meets the definition under the subheading "Definition of Dependant" in ¶1122, except of course it does not include your spouse or your children under 18 at the end of the taxation year, since they are covered by the more generous rule above.

Where a person is dependent on more than one person, the supporting persons may divide medical expense claims among them. In CRA Document No. 2005-0131681I7, the CRA commented on a situation where a parent was dependent on more than one child. "If the parent was dependent on support from each of the children, it would be our view that each child could include the portion of permissible costs ... as a medical expense, to the extent such medical expenses were paid or deemed to be paid by each child, the child's spouse or the child's common-law partner."

The expenses that qualify are subject to the rules under ¶1225.05. Essentially, as you might expect, this means that a particular expense once claimed by you, your dependant, or anyone else as a medical expense credit, attendant care credit, or refundable medical expense supplement cannot be claimed a second time by anyone in any year.

[¶1225.30] *Timing*

Where medical expenses are incurred in one year on behalf of a spouse, common-law partner, or dependant but are not paid until the following year at a time when such person is no longer a spouse, common-law partner, or dependant, the expenses nevertheless qualify in the year of payment, since the person referred to is only required to be a spouse, common-law partner, or dependant when the expenses are incurred.

See also ¶1250 on choosing a non-calendar period to measure medical expenses.

(ITA: 118.2(1); 118.2(3)(*b*); CRA Document No.: Medical Expenses of Dependents, *May 31, 2005,* CRA Document No. 2005-0131681I7; medical expense tax credit, *August 19, 2013,* CRA Document No. 2013-0490901I7; Income Tax Folio: S1-F1-C1 Medical Expense Tax Credit)

[¶1225.35] *Deemed Medical Expenses*

If your employer has included in your income medical expenses it provided or paid on your behalf, the expenses are deemed to be expenses you paid at the time the medical expenses were paid or provided by your employer.

(ITA: 118.2(3)(*a*))

[¶1235] YOU MAY CLAIM ALL OF YOUR MEDICAL EXPENSES IN EXCESS OF $2,171 OR 3% OF YOUR NET INCOME

There is no limit on the total amount of medical expenses you may claim for the year. The only restriction is that you may claim only the excess of your expenses over the lesser of $2,237 and 3% of your net income for the year. Your "net income" is determined at line 236 of your T1, before deducting such items as the capital gain exemption, stock option benefits, and losses of other years (except capital losses on listed personal property).

Example

Barry Howson's net income for Year 2 was $30,000. He had a non-capital loss carryforward from Year 1 available for deduction this year in the amount of $1,100. Barry was married and was the sole supporter of his wife and two children aged 6 and 8. The Howson family's medical expenses were $1,000 for the year.

Calculation of Barry Howson's Medical Amount for Year 2

Net income	$30,000
Non-capital loss carried forward	1,100
Taxable income	$28,900
Medical expenses:	
Expenses incurred	$ 1,000
Less: lesser of	
(a) 3% of net income (3% × $30,000 = $900)	
(b) $2,237	900
Amount eligible for conversion to credit:	$100

Generally, the amount of net income on which you calculate the 3% deduction will be the amount shown on page 3 of your T1 return opposite the words "Net Income" at line 236. You should include in your net income for purposes of the 3% limit any treaty-exempt amounts (discussed at ¶990) for which no provision is made on your T1 return but which, strictly speaking, are added to net income and deducted again in arriving at taxable income on line 260.

The allowable "personal amount" for medical expenses, finally computed and entered at line 332 of Schedule 1 of your T1, is then converted to credit, along with other "personal amounts", at line 338. For ordering of credits, see ¶1365.

[¶1235.05] *Indexation*

Although the 3% element of the medical expense reduction is constant from year to year, the $2,237 amount is indexed from year to year. For more details on the indexation methodology and the value of this amount in preceding years, see ¶1101 and ¶65.

[¶1235.10] *Provincial Variation of Income Threshold Amount*

Most provinces do not index the income threshold amount in lockstep with the federal government. For those which do not, the current value will be given in the notes to line 5868 of the provincial form 428. These notes, like the provincial form 428, will be unique to the T1 package for each province. The few provinces which do use the federal number may not have a line 5868.

Most provinces have eliminated the $10,000 limit previously imposed on claims for medical expenses incurred by dependants other than a spouse or common-law partner, or children under 18 at the end of the tax year.

(ITA: 118.2(1); 5000-G General Income Tax and Benefit Guide — 2015; Income Tax Folio: S1-F1-C1 Medical Expense Tax Credit)

[¶1237] REFUNDABLE MEDICAL EXPENSE SUPPLEMENT

Once you have determined that there is an amount eligible for non-refundable medical expense credit at line 332 of Schedule 1 of your return and/or you have claimed a deduction from income on line 215 for expenses deducted under the rules in ¶1036, you may be entitled to an additional refundable medical expense credit (called the "refundable medical expense supplement") for that amount, but only if your business and employment income is at least $3,465. For more information, see the detailed calculation below.

The refundable medical expense supplement is calculated on the *Federal Worksheet* chart for line 452 and will apply whether or not you have tax payable from which the non-refundable credit at line 332 can be deducted. The supplement is equal to the lesser of: (1) $1,187; and (2) 25% of the allowable medical expenses claimed under the medical expense tax credit and disability support deduction. This supplement is reduced by 5% of the taxpayer's adjusted net family income exceeding $26,277, which means that no supplement may be claimed if the taxpayer's adjusted net family income exceeds $50,017 ($26,277 + $23,740 [$1,187 / 5%=$23,740]). For more information, see the detailed calculation below.

Adjusted net family income is, strictly speaking, net family income as defined for purposes of the Canada Child Benefit at ¶1498. As a practical matter, it is the aggregate income of you and your spouse from line 236 of each return (or what would be line 236 income of your spouse if he or she was required to file a return). Note that each reference in this paragraph to the term "spouse" includes a common-law partner, as defined at ¶1113.

There are four exceptions to the rule that adjusted net family income includes all line 236 income from your return and your spouse's return.

First, you back out of income the former universal child care benefit ("UCCB") received during the year and reported as income on line 117 of your return or the return of your spouse (or what would have been reported on the return of your spouse if your spouse had filed a return). This spousal information for the UCCB is captured in a box on the right side of page 1 of your return. You also back out any registered disability savings plan ("RDSP") benefits you or your spouse received in the year and reported as income on line 125 of the return of yourself and your spouse (or would have been reported if a return had been filed). The federal worksheet calculation for line 452 provides for these reductions.

Second, you need not include the income of your spouse, if you were separated by reason of a breakdown in your relationship for a period of at least 90 days that included the end of the year; for more detail see ¶1498.10.

Third, you exclude income from a gain on the disposition of property to which section 79 applies or a gain described in subsection 40(3.21) in respect of a deferred stock option benefit election.

Fourth, you do not deduct any amounts in respect of repayments of child care benefits under the former *Universal Child Care Benefits Act* deductible under paragraph 60(*y*) or repayments under the *Canada Disability Savings Act* or a designated provincial program (defined in subsection 146.4(1)) deductible under paragraph 60(*z*).

In addition to the net family income limitation, you must meet the following conditions to qualify for the supplement:

(1) you must have been resident in Canada throughout the taxation year (or resident to the date of death for an individual who died during the year); resident means a factual or deemed resident, as discussed in Chapter 1;

(2) you must have reached the age of 18 by the end of the taxation year; and

(3) your income for the taxation year from the following sources must total at least $3,465 (for earlier tax years and for the next tax year, see the table at ¶65 preceding Chapter 1):

(a) office or employment; this is net employment income except that it excludes taxable (and of course non-taxable) benefits under a wage loss replacement plan (¶328); in calculating net employment income you aggregate lines 101 and 104 and deduct lines 207 (pension plan contributions), 212 (union or professional dues), 229 (employment expenses), and 231 (clergy residence deduction) to reach net employment income, but this may still overstate employment income where line 104 has included items which technically are not employment income, as discussed at ¶308; whether the CRA's computers will pick up the discrepancies remains to be seen;

(b) net business (self-employment) income from business carried on by you alone or as a partner actively engaged in partnership business; typically this is business income from line 135 to 143 of the T1 return after deductions, but if net income is negative it is included as zero; that is, business losses (and for that matter employment losses) do not reduce aggregate income from other businesses or employment; and

(c) the program established under the *Wage Earner Protection Program Act*; this program reimburses eligible workers for unpaid wages, vacation pay, severance pay, and termination pay they are owed when their employer declares bankruptcy or becomes subject to a receivership under the *Bankruptcy and Insolvency Act*; include the amount shown in the "Other Information" area of your T4A slip with a code 132 on line 104 of your T1 return.

Once you have established that you are eligible for the refundable medical expense supplement, it remains only to calculate it. The *Federal Worksheet* chart for line 452 starts the calculation with your adjusted net family income and subtracts the base amount of $26,277. Five per cent (5%) of the excess (if any) is subtracted from the maximum amount which may be claimed, which is the lesser of $1,187 and 25% of the sum of (i) your total amount eligible for the non-refundable medical expense credit on line 332 (¶1235), and (ii) any amounts you have deducted from income on line 215 under the disability supports rules at ¶1036. This means that only $4,748 ($1,187 ÷25%) of the total of the medical expenses at line 332 (after deduction of the "3%/$2,237" reduction) and the disability supports deduction at line 215 can qualify for the refundable credit. The amount of the refundable medical expense supplement you are entitled to is based on the full amount of your allowable medical expenses and disability supports deduction, whether or not you have sufficient income to utilize the full deductions.

The 12-month rule discussed at ¶1250 thus governs both the non-refundable medical expense tax credit and refundable medical expense supplement. Once you select expenses for a period for the refundable supplement, you cannot use them again in a different 12-month period for the non-refundable credit.

You should claim both the non-refundable medical expense credit at line 332 of Schedule 1 and the refundable medical expense supplement (if any) at line 452 of the T1. You need not file the *Federal Worksheet* calculation.

Typically, a couple will aggregate medical expenses on one return, usually the lower income return, as described at ¶1225. The refundable medical expense supplement provides an additional reason to do this, since if the credit is divided between two returns the net family income reduction will occur twice. However, if a couple chooses for whatever reason to separate medical expenses between their returns, each could claim credit for their share of expenses claimed.

All the amounts used in this calculation, that is, the $1,187 limit, the $3,465 and $26,277 thresholds, and the $50,017 threshold which is merely a by-product of the $26,277 amount, are indexed annually, as discussed in ¶1101. A table of these amounts for earlier years and for next year is found at ¶65 preceding Chapter 1.

Many provinces have a unique refundable medical expense supplement calculation on the provincial worksheet which accompanies each different provincial T1 package for those provinces that have personal amount values different from federal personal amount values. Where there are such differences, they will be described in the notes to line 5872 of the provincial form 428. The few provinces which do use the federal number may not have a line 5872. The description above uses federal values. The principles will be the same in all cases, but provincial values may differ.

(ITA: 117.1; 122.51; 5000-G General Income Tax and Benefit Guide — 2015; Income Tax Folio: S1-F1-C1, Medical Expense Tax Credit)

[¶1245] HEALTH INSURANCE PLANS

Medical expenses, including hospital and surgical expenses, paid on your behalf by any medical plan, private or government sponsored, may not be included in your medical expense claim. However, you are entitled to deduct premiums paid to a private insurer for medical or hospital coverage ("private health services plan") for yourself, your spouse or common-law partner, or a member of your household to whom you are connected by blood, marriage, common-law partnership, or adoption.

In some instances medical plans pay only a portion of the total expense and you are required to pay the remainder. The difference between the amount you have paid and the amount for which you have been or are entitled to be reimbursed may be claimed as a medical expense.

Example

During Year 1, Renée Gallant paid $25 a month to a government medical plan and $12 a month to a private health services plan. Renée was hospitalized during the year and paid medical expenses of $2,000 of which $1,500 was reimbursed by the medical plans.

Renée may claim the following as medical expenses:

Medical expenses paid	$2,000
Less: Expenses reimbursed	1,500
Claim	$ 500
Plus: Premiums to the private health services plan (12 × $12)	144
Total	$644

The eligible expenses must of course be measured against the income threshold to determine the amount eligible for credit.

To qualify as a private health services plan, the plan must be one of insurance and have an element of risk. A plan that provides for the refund of unused contributions is not a private health services plan (see CRA Document No. 2011-0417671E5).

(ITA: 118.2(2)(q); 248(1) private health services plan; IT-339R2 Meaning of "private health services plan"; CRA Document No.: Balance in a health spending account, *June 7, 2012*, CRA Document No. 2011-0417671E5; Income Tax Folio: S1-F1-C1, Medical Expense Tax Credit)

[¶1245.05] *Medical Plan Administration Fees*

Apparently, it is now not uncommon for medical practitioners to charge administration fees to their clients for services that are not covered by provincial health plans. In a situation the CRA was asked to comment on, a membership fee was charged by a private medical clinic that allowed the individual access to private medical services when these were required. The fee did not relate to any existing condition of the taxpayer. Where private medical services were provided, a fee over and above the membership fee would be charged to the individual for the services (unless the service was covered by provincial medical insurance).

In this situation, the CRA was of the view that the membership fee "cannot be attributed to any particular medical service provided to an individual and would not qualify as a medical expense", because an expense for medical services must relate to an existing medical condition or illness. Nor would the expense be deductible under the definition of a private health services plan, presumably because it is not a contract of insurance or an insurance plan, since it does not actually provide coverage, but access to services.

It is conceivable that an administration fee could be drafted to meet the conditions for credit eligibility if, for example, it did constitute a prepayment of expenses later incurred (although the timing of the credit would then become an issue).

(CRA Document No.: Medical Expenses, Private Health Clinic Access Fee, *April 20, 2006*, CRA Document No. 2006-0166961E5)

[¶1250] YOU MAY CLAIM EXPENSES FOR ANY 12-MONTH PERIOD ENDING IN THE YEAR

Because only medical expenses in excess of the lesser of $2,237 and 3% of your net income are eligible for conversion to credit, it is to your advantage to lump medical expenses together as much as possible. It is recognized that abnormally large medical expenses may be spread out over several months and may overlap a calendar year end. Therefore, you may pick any 12-month period ending in the year and claim the medical expenses paid during that period.

It would seem that the 12-month (or 24-month) period is always chosen by reference to the payer claiming the medical expense credit. That is, if you are claiming medical expenses for several dependants, you cannot select a different period for each; you must select one period and aggregate all expenses not previously claimed in that period.

Where an individual, including the taxpayer, has died, the taxpayer may claim medical expenses for that individual for a 24-month period that includes the date of death. It would seem that the 24-month period selected for the deceased need not have a relationship to the 12-month period selected for the taxpayer (if not the deceased) and other dependants. Although this is not entirely clear, it is difficult to put any other construction on the statute.

Choosing a 12-Month Period

Walt Murray's wife Ethel had a serious operation in December of Year 1. Walt paid doctors' bills and hospital bills as follows for Year 1 and Year 2:

Year 1		
November	$100	
December	130	$230
Year 2		
January	$460	
February	60	
March	70	590
Total		$820

Walt's total medical expenses for Year 1 of $230 afforded him a very small claim. By choosing a 12-month period ending March 31 of Year 2, he was able to include all $820 in his medical expenses for Year 2, thus obtaining a deduction for medical expenses which might otherwise have been lost because of the income threshold.

An important point to remember — The 12-month period ending in the year may be varied from year to year and these periods may overlap. However, you may not claim the same expense twice.

12-Month Periods May Overlap

Keith Flanagan paid medical expenses in Year 1 and Year 2 as follows:

Year 1	
May	$100
June	150
July	300
December	70
Year 2	
January	$100
February	70
August	200
September	300

Keith used a 12-month period ended December 31, in his Year 1 return.

In his Year 2 return he may use a 12-month period ending September 30 of Year 2, but may not include the $70 paid in December of Year 1 in the claim for that period.

Reduction of Claim for Dependant other than Spouse or Child under 18

Jack Black paid $2,500 in September of Year 1 and another $5,000 in January of Year 2, for the medical expenses of his 20-year-old son, who was studying in the United States and had no net income in Year 1. Jack had no other medical expenses. All things being equal, he would want to aggregate the medical expenses, since otherwise he would have to deduct the income threshold in Year 1 and again in Year 2.

However, if we suppose his son will graduate and obtain a well-paying job in Year 2, the son's net income could erode the Year 2 medical expense amount under the dependant income limitation rules at ¶1225 and eliminate the benefit of not double counting the income threshold.

(ITA: 118.2(1); Income Tax Folio: S1-F1-C1, Medical Expense Tax Credit)

[¶1255] DISABILITY AMOUNT AND SUPPLEMENT FOR DISABLED CHILDREN — LINES 316, 318, AND 338

There is a special personal amount of $8,001 available for persons who have "a severe and prolonged mental or physical impairment". A second component can be added to that basic disability amount for a disabled person who was under 18 at the end of the year. That supplement is $4,667 and is reduced by the amount by which amounts paid for the care of the disabled person and claimed by any person as a child or attendant care expense exceed $2,734. The reduction applies regardless of whether the child care or attendant care expenses are claimed as a child care expense deduction, attendant care expense deduction, or medical expense tax credit. As a result, no supplement may be claimed if the total amount of child care and attendant care expense exceeds $7,401 (i.e., $4,667 + $2,734). For a table of these amounts over a five-year period, see ¶65 preceding Chapter 1.

The personal amount is claimed on line 316 of Schedule 1 of the T1 return of the person suffering the impairment, and converted to credit along with other such amounts on line 338. A person under 18 suffering an impairment calculates the additional disability supplement on the *Federal Worksheet* chart for line 316; the *Federal Worksheet* is provided as part of the T1 return package.

Many provinces will have a unique disability amount calculation on the provincial worksheet which accompanies each different provincial T1 package for those provinces which have personal amount values which differ from federal personal amount values. Where there are such differences, they will be described in the note to line 5844 of the provincial form 428. The few provinces which do use the federal number may not have these lines. The description below uses federal values. The principles will be the same in all cases, but provincial values may differ.

To the extent that the credit (and supplement) exceed the tax payable by the person suffering the impairment, the unused balance may be claimed on line 318 of the T1 return of a spouse or common-law partner, or a supporting individual, as discussed below.

To qualify for the disability credit, a doctor (or in certain cases a person with special qualifications in regard to a particular disability, as discussed at ¶1209) must certify on the prescribed form T2201 that you have a severe and prolonged impairment in physical or mental functions by reason of which you are "markedly restricted" in your "activities of daily living" and that the impairment has lasted or can reasonably be expected to last for a continuous period of 12 months. The meaning of being markedly restricted is defined in some detail at ¶1209.05. The credit may also be claimed by or on behalf of someone who would be markedly restricted but for a therapy administered at least three times a week for a total time of at least 14 hours per week. The therapy must be one which is essential to sustain the vital functions of the patient, and could not reasonably be expected to be of significant benefit to persons without the particular disability.

You (or the person claiming the credit for you — see below) must file the T2201 certificate with the return on which the claim is made. The certificate must be an original; the CRA does not accept photocopies or facsimile copies. Once obtained, a certificate continues to be valid until the cessation date on its face, or until your condition changes. You do not need to obtain a new certificate each year.

No claim may be made under this provision if *any* credit is claimed by anyone for remuneration for a full-time attendant or care in a nursing home for the disabled person under the provisions at ¶1207, except the dollar limited attendant care provision discussed below. You may claim the higher of the actual attendant or nursing home expense (minus the amount of the income threshold) or the disability amount (plus the supplement, if any), but not both. On the other hand, it appears that you may claim attendant care deductions under the rules at ¶1036 to the extent of earned income and the disability amount as well, as long as no additional attendant or nursing home claim is made by you or for you under ¶1207.

It does appear that you can claim both the disability credit and the credit for remuneration paid for care or supervision in a group home for the disabled, although that claim in turn will be incompatible with the attendant care claim described immediately below.

In *Pekofsky v. The Queen*, 2014 DTC 1151 (T.C.C.), the Court concluded that the taxpayer qualified for a disability tax credit since her daughter, who was dyslexic and suffered from Tourette's syndrome, had a severe and prolonged mental disability that restricted her ability to perform basic daily living activities. Medical reports were produced to document the daughter's problems. The Court dismissed the Minister's arguments that the daughter was not impaired and had only academic difficulties.

In *Benoit v. The Queen*, 2014 DTC 1141 (T.C.C.), the Court held that a taxpayer with bipolar disorder had suffered a severe and prolonged mental disability for at least 12 months and was therefore entitled to claim the disability tax credit. He had a cyst in his brain and suffered from tremors, serious depressions, and anxiety and panic attacks. The Court was therefore convinced that his ability to perform basic daily living activities was markedly restricted more than 90% of the time.

In *Brassard v. The Queen*, 2014 DTC 1096 (T.C.C.), the Court concluded that a taxpayer suffering from severe allergies leading to eczema that was aggravated when the weather changed was not entitled to claim the disability tax credit, since his physician did not certify in the medical certificate that his disability was sufficiently severe and prolonged to markedly restrict his ability to perform basic daily living activities.

(Income Tax Folio: S1-F1-C1, Medical Expense Tax Credit; S1-F1-C2, Disability Tax Credit)

[¶1255.05] *Additional Credit for Attendant Care*

Notwithstanding the general rule that you cannot claim both the medical expense credit for full-time attendant care (¶1207) and the disability amount, there is a provision which allows a medical expense credit for attendant care provided the total expenses for such care for the year do not exceed $10,000 (or $20,000 in the year of death). (Ontario, uniquely, indexes the $10,000/$20,000 values, and the CRA usually publishes the current Ontario values in its notes to line 5868 in the Ontario T1 package; for 2016 they are $ 13,844 and $27,687.) The care must be provided for a patient who is eligible for the disability amount (although someone else may actually claim the disability amount under the transfer rules), and this attendant care credit is not available if any expense is deducted from the disabled person's income under the rules at ¶1036 (line 215 of your T1 return), or if any deduction for child care for the disabled person is claimed under the rules at ¶1049. As well, this particular attendant care credit cannot be claimed in combination with any of the other patient care credits (full-time attendant, nursing home care, training facility care) described at ¶1207. This credit can, however, be combined with the disability credit itself, although the amount claimed will (to the extent it exceeds the threshold) reduce the supplemental component of the disability credit available for children under 18, as discussed above.

Although the statute says that remuneration paid for attendant care only qualifies to the extent that the total amounts paid do not exceed the limits above, the CRA appears to interpret this as merely limiting the amount of expenses which can be claimed under this provision, so that if you actually paid, say, $12,000, you could claim $10,000 ($12,000 if the disabled person dies in the year) under this provision as well as the disability amount.

At one time, the T1 Guide referred to this as a claim for "part-time attendant" to distinguish it from the full-time care claims discussed at ¶1207. However, this terminology was misleading and has been discarded. Although the provision was intended to accommodate part-time attendant care, the CRA says (in Income Tax Folio S1-F1-C1, para. 1.42) that claims can be made for full-time attendant care as long as the above mentioned dollar limit is observed. The implication seems to be, reading paragraph 1.42 as a whole, is that you can spend more than the limit without impairing the disability claim as long as you don't claim more than the limit.

Remuneration paid for the attendant under this rule does not qualify unless the attendant is 18 years old when paid and is not the spouse or common-law partner of the payer.

Receipts must be filed to prove payment and, if the payments are made to an individual, must include the Social Insurance Number of the attendant(s) paid. Receipts are not filed with an E-filed return (¶219) but are to be shown to the preparer and retained for inspection by the CRA.

The attendant care credit is claimed under the medical expense rules, which means that it is subject to the income threshold and should be claimed by the person who pays it (or the spouse or common-law partner of the person), which may be the disabled person or a relative whom the disabled person is dependent upon. Transfers of this and the disability credit are discussed in greater detail below.

In CRA Document No. 2011-0418081E5, the CRA confirmed that the amounts paid by a taxpayer to a nursing home but not supported by receipts detailing the portion related to attendant care would not qualify as eligible medical expenses for the purpose of claiming the medical expense tax credit (METC). Payments to nursing homes may cover not only attendant care remuneration (eligible to claim an METC) but also room and board (ineligible to claim an METC). If receipts were available, the remuneration paid for attendant care not exceeding $20,000 in the year of death and $10,000 in other circumstances could be used to claim the METC. The disability tax credit is only claimable if no METC is claimed for attendant care remuneration.

[¶1255.10] *Transfer of Credits to a Spouse or Common-Law Partner*

Any portion of the disability amount unused by the disabled person may be transferred to the spouse or common-law partner of the disabled person under the provisions described at ¶1361. The special $10,000/$20,000 claim for attendant care can be claimed by either spouse or common-law partner as of right. Accordingly, the attendant care claim is not subject to the limitation of being used against the patient's income first.

[¶1255.15] *Transfer of Credits Where Disabled Person Claimed as Eligible Dependant*

Provided that the disabled person's spouse or common-law partner is not claiming either the spouse/partner amount (on line 303 of the spouse or common-law partner's return) or any of the transfer provisions on Schedule 2 of the T1 return (¶1361), the unused portion of the disability credit under this provision may be transferred to anyone who claims the disabled person as a dependant under the "eligible dependant" provision (on line 305, ¶1120), in the manner illustrated in the example below.

[¶1255.20] *Transfer of Credits to Other Relatives*

If a disabled person's spouse or common-law partner is not claiming the spousal amount (line 303) or the disabled person's unused credits, including the disability credit, under section 118.8 (see ¶1361), you may claim all or a part of the disabled person's unused disability amount if he or she was resident in Canada at any time during the year and:

(1) you could have claimed the eligible dependant amount (on line 305, ¶1120) for that dependant if you did not have a spouse or common-law partner and/or if the dependant had no income; or

(2) the dependant was your or your spouse's or common-law partner's parent, grandparent, child, grandchild, brother, sister, uncle, aunt, nephew, or niece, and you claimed an amount for an infirm dependant (line 306, ¶1126) or the caregiver amount (line 315, ¶1140) for that dependant, or could have if the dependant had no income or had been 18 years of age or older in the year (line 318).

For example, if you have a disabled parent, child, brother, or sister living with you in a self-contained domestic establishment and wholly dependent on your household for support, you may (if there are no spousal claims) claim the unused portion of the disability credit under the first rule, as calculated below. This is true even if you yourself have a spouse, and even if the disabled person has enough income to disallow the eligible dependant claim under ¶1120, although both these conditions would normally disallow the eligible dependant claim. On the other hand, if there is some other factor at work which would disallow your eligible dependant claim for the disabled person, for example someone else is making a claim for the disabled person as a dependant, you cannot claim the transfer under this provision.

Under the second rule, you can, for instance, make this claim for each (resident Canadian) parent or child of yours or your spouse who either lives with you in a self-contained domestic establishment or is dependant on you by reason of infirmity, whether residing with you or not. Of course, if the disabled person's income is high enough to absorb the credit, there will be no credit left to transfer.

Example

Helen and Dennis are married and Helen's mother and Dennis' father live with them, and both are disabled. The parents each have $12,000 of income, as in the example below, so no eligible dependant claim can be made. As the rules now stand, one parent can be claimed under the first rule above and one under the second rule (as eligible for the caregiver credit on line 315). It would seem that either Helen or Dennis could claim the transfer from both parents, or they could claim one each, as they agree. In this case, there should also be a line 315 claim for the parents, but the transfers of disability credits would be permitted even if the parents' incomes were high enough that no line 315 claims were allowed.

The CRA has issued an opinion (reported in Wolters Kluwer's *Window on Canadian Tax* 8359) saying that where a disabled child over 18 is in a special care facility and receives government social assistance, the child is not considered dependent on a parent for support, and no credit is available to the parent. So long as it is clear that a child is not dependent on the parent for support, the same result should be obtained regardless of the age of the child.

[¶1255.30] *General Rules on Transfers to Relatives*

Where more than one supporting person is entitled to make a claim for the same disabled person, the personal amount available after reducing the income of the disabled person may be divided among the possible claimants. If they cannot agree, the CRA may allocate the available amount arbitrarily. However, if the spouse of the disabled person makes any claim for married status or transfer of personal amounts, no one else can make a claim for the transfer of the disability credit. Also, where a claim is made by virtue of the eligible dependant rules, as varied above, there can be only one such claimant. Note that each reference in this paragraph to the term "spouse" includes common-law partner as defined in ¶1113.

Where a claim is being divided among transferees, each transferee is expected to attach a note to his or her return disclosing the name and Social Insurance Number of other transferees.

The amount of a disabled person's credit which may be transferred to a supporting person is the amount in excess of that needed to reduce the disabled person's tax to zero, after credits have been taken by the disabled person under section 118 to 118.07 (including personal amounts and the pension credit), and under section 118.7 for the CPP/EI credit, but before any other credits.

Example

John Wilson's 20-year-old son is confined to a wheelchair. The son, who does not live with John, has a taxable income of $15,000, and made Canada Pension Plan contributions of $120 and Employment Insurance contributions of $224. John cannot claim the son as a dependant under ordinary rules, even for the infirm (because the son's income exceeds the threshold for the infirm credit at ¶1126). However, John can claim part of the special disabled deduction as follows:

Son's net income	$15,000
Less: Son's basic personal amount ($11,474), dependant amounts (none), CPP and EI contributions ($344)	11,818
Amounts needed to reduce son's income (and therefore tax) for the year to zero	$3,182

John may claim:

Disabled exemption	$8,001
Less: Amount absorbed by son's income	3,182
	$4,819

If John had incurred $4,000 in attendant care expenses, or indeed any amount up to $10,000, he could claim this amount as medical expense credit in addition to making the disability claim, allowing for the son's 3%/$2,237 deductible amount (under the fourth rule in ¶1207).

Technically, it is not clear whether the tests for "full-time care" under the first three rules at ¶1207 are more or less rigorous than the infirmity test at ¶1126. See the discussion at ¶1209.10. As a practical matter, an infirmity claim at ¶1126 will almost certainly be accepted where there is a disability credit certificate, and presumably in a somewhat wider range of circumstances as well.

It appears that the category of persons who can make the $10,000/$20,000 attendant care expense claim is somewhat broader than the category of persons who can claim the transfer of disability credit. Any person who pays the attendant care expenses and is entitled to claim the disabled person as a dependant may make this claim for attendant care as a medical expense credit (see ¶1225). Thus it would seem possible for a spouse, for example, to take over a transfer of disability credit and a parent to pay for and claim medical expense credit under the $10,000/$20,000 attendant care expense rule. Similarly, an uncle who could claim the disabled person as a dependant at line 306 could claim the $10,000/$20,000 attendant care expense, even though he could not claim a transfer of disability credit.

In short, the $10,000/$20,000 attendant care provision is independent of the disability credit. The $10,000/$20,000 attendant care rule operates under the general medical expense credit rules at ¶1225. Any claims made by anyone under the part-time attendant care rule do not affect any claims or transfers made under the disability credit rules. The only link is that the disabled person or someone else must be able to claim disability credit for the disabled person for the part-time attendant care expenses to be eligible expenses for medical care credit.

[¶1255.35] *Filing Disability Certificates (form T2201)*

To obtain a disability credit, you must have your disability certified "in prescribed form". The form prescribed is T2201. Form T2201 is merely an application; the CRA is to review the form and, if it is approved, give you written permission to claim the credit.

In general, the CRA administers the disability credit provision on the basis that a certificate once obtained remains valid for the period on its face as long as you continue to suffer from the impairment at any time during the year. You need not obtain a new certificate each year, but if the conditions of impairment do not apply at all in a year, you will of course not be entitled to a deduction. On the other hand, if your impairment has continued for 12 months but has been cured in the year, you may take the deduction. It follows that if your certificate ceased to be valid in the preceding year (say, Year 1) you must obtain a new certificate to claim the disability amount for the current taxation year (Year 2).

The CRA retains the right to verify a certificate at any time, and to require you to obtain a new one.

Form T2201 can be filed at any time in the year, and in theory at least, the earlier it is filed the earlier it will be approved (or disapproved).

If you are the transferee of a disability credit and you are not filing form T2201 with your own return, you should attach a note to your return disclosing the name and Social Insurance Number of the disabled person. The CRA will use this to verify the existence of a disability certificate on file for that person. Indeed, it should be evident that everyone other than the disabled person who files a claim for which that person's disability credit entitlement is a prerequisite (see ¶1209) has to adequately identify the disabled person so that the claim can be verified.

(ITA: 118.2(1), (2)(*b*), (*b*.1), (*c*); 118.3; Income Tax Folio: S1-F1-C1, Medical Expense Tax Credit; S1-F1-C2, Disability Tax Credit)

[¶1260] WHAT PROOF IS REQUIRED OF MEDICAL EXPENSES CLAIMED?

The CRA says that if you file paper returns (as opposed to EFILE or NETFILE returns), you must file formal receipts with your return in support of medical expenses claimed. Receipts are also not needed for transportation and travel expenses if the simplified method of calculating meal and vehicle expenses is chosen. However, you need not file health services plan premium receipts, although you should keep them on file. It is your responsibility to obtain such receipts. If you EFILE, keep the receipts on file as they may be requested.

If you are unable to obtain a credit for medical expenses for the year because of the income limitation, you should keep your receipts for possible use in the next year.

(5000-G General Income Tax and Benefit Guide — 2015)

IMPORTANT POINTS TO REMEMBER — MEDICAL EXPENSES

[¶1260a] IMPORTANT POINTS TO REMEMBER — MEDICAL EXPENSES

- Medical expenses for you, your spouse or common-law partner, and your dependent children under 18 may be lumped together and claimed by either spouse (or common-law partner), but only to the extent that the total of the allowable expenses exceeds the lesser of $2,237 and 3% of the amount shown on the return opposite the words "Net Income" at line 236. Of course, each spouse/partner may claim its own expenses, but this means the $2,237/3% limit applies twice, rather than once to the aggregate amount. See ¶1225.10.
- You may claim medical expenses you paid on behalf of other relatives dependent on you for support (those relatives described in the definition of "Dependant" at ¶1122.30), but for each such dependant you may claim only the expenses you paid for that dependant in excess of the lesser of $2,237 and 3% of the amount shown on the return opposite the words "Net Income" at line 236 of that dependant's return (or what would have been the dependant's return if it were obliged to file one). See ¶1225.20.
- Medical expenses need not be accumulated on a calendar year basis; any 12-month period ending in the year will do. Accordingly, you may want to forgo expense claims in a year if they are grouped with expenses that fall on both sides of December 31 in order to exceed the income threshold or avoid its applying twice. See ¶1250.
- If you have a claim at line 332 and your net family income (income from line 236 of you and your spouse

or common-law partner) is less than $50,017, complete the Federal Worksheet chart for line 452 to obtain the refundable medical expense supplement. You can receive this credit even if you have no tax payable.

- Attach your receipts in support of any medical expenses claimed (other than health services plan receipts). Receipts for attendant care should show the individual's name and Social Insurance Number. If you are filing electronically, keep the receipts with your tax records so you can show them to the CRA on request.

SPECIFIC QUESTIONS AND ANSWERS — MEDICAL EXPENSES

[¶1260b] SPECIFIC QUESTIONS AND ANSWERS

Medical Plan Paid Expenses

During the tax year, I incurred substantial medical expenses which were not actually paid by my medical plan until the following year. May I claim these amounts in my tax return?

No. You may not claim medical expenses which have been or will be reimbursed by a medical plan. In the case of a private health services plan, however, you may deduct the premiums paid.

Expenses Paid for Non-Dependant

During the year, I paid for my mother's operations. Although my father claims her as a dependant, may I claim these medical expenses in my return?

It certainly seems worth trying. The fact that you paid these expenses indicates that your mother was in some sense dependent on you during the year. Neither your claim nor your father's claim requires the dependant to be "wholly dependent". The CRA has stated that where a person is dependent on more than one person, medical expense claims may be divided between them. Accordingly, there is a case to be made that you may make this claim. See ¶1225.20.

Premiums Paid to a Provincial Plan

During the year, I paid $150 in premiums to a provincial health plan. May I deduct the premiums on my tax return?

No. Premiums to a government health plan are not deductible, although premiums to a private health services plan are.

Temporary Blindness

During the year, I was temporarily blinded for three days due to an industrial accident. May I claim the special disability deduction?

No. Temporary loss of sight is not prolonged impairment.

Payments to Non-Licensed Person

During the year, I visited a psychoanalyst twice a month. The psychoanalyst was not a doctor and did not have a licence to practice. I paid $1,200 in the year. Can I deduct this amount as medical expenses?

No. The payment must be made to a medical practitioner licensed to practice under the laws of the province where he or she operates.

WHAT YOU SHOULD KNOW ABOUT DONATIONS

RECENT CHANGES

Bill C-2 (2015)

Effective for 2016 and subsequent taxation years, individuals with a taxable income over $200,000 making charitable donations over $200 qualify for the following higher charitable donations tax credit:

- 15% of their donations up to $200;
- 33% of lesser of (1) their donations over $200, and (2) their taxable income over $200,000; and
- 29% of their donations over $200 not qualifying for the 33% tax credit rate.

Individuals with a taxable income under $200,000 will continue to calculate their credit at 15% of donations up to $200 plus 29% of their donations over $200.

The same calculation is applicable to Crown gifts, cultural gifts, and ecological gifts.

The $200,000 top taxable income threshold is subject to annual indexation.

Bill C-15 (2016)

Effective for 2016 and subsequent taxation years, trusts subject to the 33% top marginal tax rate on all their taxable income (i.e., excluding graduated rate estates and qualified disability trusts) and making charitable donations in excess of $200 qualify for the following higher charitable donations tax credit:

- 15% of their donations up to $200; and
- 33% of their donations over $200.

[¶1261] WHAT IS A GIFT?

Essential to the charitable donation rules discussed below is the concept of a "gift". Tax credits for charitable contributions only arise in respect of gifts. Where you simply donate cash to a registered charity and receive and expect to receive nothing back, the issue does not arise; you have clearly made a gift. Where you donate property and receive and expect to receive nothing back, you have made a gift. Where, however, you do get something back, matters become more complex.

It is generally the view at common law that a gift includes only a voluntary transfer, without any contractual obligation and with no advantage of a material character returned to the transferor. Generally speaking, common law does not allow for separating the rights of ownership of a single property in the course of making a gift. Hence, at common law, a contract to dispose of a property to a charity at a price below fair market value would not generally be considered to include a gift. Nevertheless, there have been certain decisions made under the common law where it has been found that a transfer of property to a charity was made partly in consideration for services and partly as a gift. By contrast, under section 1806 of the *Civil Code of Quebec* ("CCQ"), a gift in Quebec is a contract by which ownership of property is transferred by gratuitous title. However, the rights of ownership may be separated, so that it may be possible for a transferor to transfer part of the rights of ownership without any material advantage returned (i.e., by way of gift) and to transfer the other part separately for consideration. It is therefore possible, in Quebec, to sell a property to a charity at a price below fair market value, resulting in a gift of the difference.

In an effort to make the tax treatment of such gifts more uniform, specific provisions are included in the *Income Tax Act* so that it is possible to make a gift and take back consideration without wholly disqualifying the gift for charitable donation status. In particular, the legislation provides that the existence of an amount of an "advantage" (see below) in respect of a transfer of property does not in and by itself disqualify the transfer from being a gift, if the amount of the advantage does not exceed 80% of the fair market value of the transferred property, or the transferor of the property establishes to the satisfaction of the Minister that the transfer was made with the intention to make a gift.

The value of the advantage is carved out from the total value of the property donated by referring to the "eligible amount" of a gift. Thus, the eligible amount of a gift is defined (in subsection 248(31)) to be the fair market value of the gift less the "advantage" the donor receives in respect of the gift. The "advantage" in respect of a gift or contribution is, in general, the total value of all property, services, compensation or other benefits to which the donor of a property is entitled as partial consideration for, or in gratitude for, the gift or contribution. The advantage may be contingent or receivable in the future, either to the donor or to a person not dealing at arm's length with the donor. It is not necessary that the advantage be receivable from the donee. However, a tax credit or deduction resulting from a charitable donation is not considered a benefit.

Example 1 (provided by Department of Finance):

Mr. Short transfers land and a building with a fair market value of $300,000 to a registered charity. The charity assumes liability for an outstanding $100,000 mortgage on the property. The assumption of the mortgage by the charity does not necessarily disqualify the transfer from being a gift for the purposes of the Act. If the value of the mortgage is equal to the outstanding amount (e.g., the interest rate and terms and conditions are representative of current market conditions), the eligible amount of the gift, in respect of which Mr. Short may be entitled to a charitable donation credit (subject to the general rules and limitations for charitable donations, discussed below) is $200,000.

If the amount of an advantage in respect of a transfer of property exceeds 80% of the fair market value of the transferred property, the transfer will not necessarily be disqualified from being a gift if the transferor can establish to the satisfaction of the Minister of National Revenue that the transfer was made with the intention to make a gift.

Example 2

In the above example, if the amount of the mortgage outstanding had been greater than $240,000, Mr. Short (or the charity on the donor's behalf) could apply to the Minister of National Revenue for a determination as to whether the transfer was made with the intention to make a gift.

The regulations governing charitable receipts require a description of and the amount of the "advantage", if any, and the eligible amount of the gift.

It is incumbent upon the donor to inform the charity of any information that would result in an eligible amount lower than the value of the gift before a receipt is issued. The penalty for failure to do so is that the value of the gift for donation purposes will be nil, so that no credit at all will be allowed.

(ITA: 110.1(1)(*a*); 248(30)–(33); 248(40); 248(41))

[¶1262] ELIGIBLE AMOUNT OF THE GIFT

As discussed above, the amount of a gift that qualifies for the credit is the "eligible amount" of the gift, which is generally the fair market value of the gift in excess of the "advantage", if any, received in respect of the gift.

Furthermore, an anti-avoidance rule in subsection 248(35) may decrease the fair market value of donated property for these purposes. Under this provision, the fair market value of a donated property for these purposes is deemed to be the lesser of the fair market value of the property otherwise determined and the cost, or in the case of capital property, the adjusted cost base, or in the case of a life insurance policy in respect of which the taxpayer is a policyholder, the adjusted cost basis (as defined in subsection 148(9)), of the property to the taxpayer immediately before the gift of the property is made if:

(1) the taxpayer acquired the property under a gifting arrangement that is a tax shelter (see ¶2521.40); or

(2) unless the gift is made as a consequence of the taxpayer's death,

(a) the taxpayer acquired the property less than 3 years before the day that the gift is made, or

(b) the taxpayer acquired the property less than 10 years before the day that the gift is made and it is reasonable to conclude that, at the time the taxpayer acquired the property, one of the main reasons for the acquisition was to make a gift of the property to a qualified donee.

Where one of the above scenarios applies, the lesser of the cost (or adjusted cost base or adjusted cost basis, as the case may be) and the fair market value of the property is deemed to be the fair market value of the gift for the purposes of the credit, and is also deemed to be the taxpayer's proceeds of disposition for capital gains purposes. The anti-avoidance rule does not apply to gifts of inventory, real property, or an immovable situated in Canada, qualifying publicly listed securities (¶1290d), qualifying ecological gifts and certain certified cultural property gifts (1268 and ¶1268d and ¶1268d), and certain other gifts described at ¶2521.40.

In some circumstances, an election is available that can deem the fair market value of a gift to be any amount generally between its cost and fair market value; see ¶1269.10.

[¶1263] CALCULATION OF THE CHARITABLE DONATION CREDIT

Most donations are subject to a limitation that total donations are not eligible for credit in the current year to the extent they exceed 75% of net income; unused donations can generally be carried forward for up to five years (ten years for ecological gifts made after February 10, 2014). In the case of donated capital property, the donation limit is normally increased by 25% of the resulting taxable capital gain or recapture, if any; see ¶1270. Note that the 75% income limitation does not apply in the individual's year of death or in the immediately preceding year (see ¶1931). Rather, the limitation is the individual's income for the year. Furthermore, for certain donations of ecologically sensitive land and certified cultural property, there is no income limit (see ¶1268 and ¶1268d).

Basic Credit Calculation for 2015 and Preceding Taxation Years

The donation credit is unusual in that it is calculated at two rates. The first $200 of donations in a year is allowed a credit at the lowest marginal tax rate (15% for federal purposes), so that it is the equivalent of a full deduction for incomes that are subject to that lowest tax rate. However, donations in excess of $200, to the extent allowable in the year under the 75% rule, receive a credit at the highest marginal tax rate (29%), so that donors with incomes that are subject to the highest tax rate receive the full value of the credit, as if it were a deduction, and donors with lower incomes can actually receive a tax benefit on the excess over $200.

Example 1:

John has taxable income in the lowest tax bracket, say $25,000. His effective combined federal and provincial tax rate is approximately 26%. If John contributes $200 to charity, he will be giving up money which carries a tax cost to him of $52 ($200 × 26%) and receiving a tax credit of $52. For every $100 John gives over $200, he will receive about $44 of tax credit (depending on his province of residence) although his tax cost of earning the $100 was only $26. This assumes all amounts are creditable in the year; if there is a carryforward the first $200 will be subject to the lower rate in the year it is applied.

Example 2:

Marissa has taxable income in the second rate bracket, say $50,000. Her marginal tax rate (including her provincial tax) is approximately 40% on the income in that bracket. On her first $200 contribution she will have a credit of $52, but her tax paid to earn the income donated will be $80, so that she has a net tax cost of $28 on her $200 contribution. If she contributes an additional $700, for a total of $900, her total credit will be $52 + 44% × $700 = $360, which matches her tax cost of 40% of $900 = $360. Past this point, contributions will earn credit at 44% while the tax cost will be 40%, so there will be a $4 benefit on every $100 contribution.

Example 3:

Bill is in the top rate bracket of 48% in his province. On his first $200 of donations, he will have a tax credit of (with the provincial credit, say) 26% but a tax cost of 48%; that is, there is a 22% penalty on every dollar contributed up to $200. This penalty is capped at $44 on a $200 contribution, which represents a permanent tax cost, no matter what his additional contributions. However, for all additional contributions his credits will fully offset the cost of earning the income.

The lesser of your total eligible amounts of donations for the year (plus carryforward amounts) and 75% of net income (line 236 of your return, subject to the comments at ¶1270) is carried to line 340 on Schedule 9 of the T1 return. The result carried to line 340 is added to gifts not subject to the 75% rule (line 342, see ¶1268), and the total converted to credits at lines 346 and 348.

The credit claim for charitable donations is optional. It follows that donations may be accumulated within the five-year carryforward period and claimed when they aggregate more than $200, and thereby avoid the low rate of credit where gifts in a particular year are less than $200.

Basic Credit Calculation for 2016 and Subsequent Taxation Years

Effective for 2016 and subsequent taxation years, individuals with a taxable income over $200,000 and making charitable donations over $200 qualify for the following higher charitable donations tax credit:

- 15% of their donations up to $200;
- 33% of lesser of (1) their donations over $200, and (2) their taxable income over $200,000; and
- 29% of their donations over $200 not qualifying for the 33% tax credit rate.

Individuals with a taxable income under $200,000 will continue to calculate their credit at 15% of donations up to $200 plus 29% of their donations over $200.

The same calculations apply to Crown gifts, cultural gifts, and ecological gifts.

The $200,000 top taxable income threshold is subject to annual indexation.

Example 1:

John has a taxable income of $220,000 and charitable donations of $10,000. To calculate his charitable donations tax credit, the 15% tax credit rate would apply to the first $200 and the 33% rate would apply to the remaining amount of $9,800. His total tax credit would be $3,264 (i.e., [$200 × 15%= $30] + [$9,800 × 33%]= $3,234]).

Example 2:

Mary has a taxable income of $220,000 and charitable donations of $30,000. To calculate her charitable donations tax credit, the 15% tax credit rate would apply to the first $200, the 33% tax credit rate would apply to the next $20,000, and the 29% rate would apply to the remaining amount of the donation of $9,800. Her total tax credit would be $9,472 (i.e., [$200 × 15%= $30] + [$20,000 × 33%= $6,600] +[$9,800 × 29%= $2,842]).

Calculation of Super First-Time Donor Credit

The federal "super first-time donor credit" applies to gifts made after March 20, 2013, and before 2018. The credit is an additional 25% of the gift, to a maximum additional credit of $250. This credit is discussed at ¶1264.

(ITA: 118.1)

[¶1263.05] *A Calculation Format*

The CRA provides Schedule 9 to calculate the donation limit and credit entitlement. Where gifts of capital (including depreciable) property are made, Schedule 9 in turn depends on a calculation provided in the pamphlet *Gifts and Income Tax* (P113).

There is no provision in the T1 return to list donations, although the mandatory donation receipts provide all the essential information. Nevertheless, a list of donations is a useful check for you that you have included everything and added correctly, and is essential if you will have carryforward amounts (¶1270). A general format for listing donations, applying the 75% of net income limitation, and determining your carryforward if any, is suggested below:

	Registration No.	*Amount*
Charitable donations to qualifying institutions per ¶1265 and to Canadian and provincial governments (¶1266)		
______________________	______	$__
______________________	______	$__
______________________	______	$__
Total		$__ (A)
Foreign donations allowed per tax treaty (¶1287), Country 1	$__ (W)	
Add: Prior years' foreign donations carried forward	$__ (X)	
Total: (W) + (X)	$__ (Y)	
Foreign source income, Country 1 $______ × 75% (or applicable treaty limitation)	$__ (Z)	
Add: Lesser of (Y) and (Z)		$__ (B)
¶1267 donations of prior years carried forward		$__ (C)
Total: (A) + (B) + (C)		$__ (D)
Net income, line 236 of T1	$__	
Add: Other net income[1]	$__	
Revised net income	$__ (N)	
Taxable capital gains arising on gifts of property in the year, net of capital gains exemptions (as described at ¶502) deductible in the year on those gifts	$__ (O)	
Deferred taxable capital gains on gifts of non-qualified property arising on a final arm's length disposition (¶1290) .	$__ (P)	
Recapture of capital cost allowance on gifts of depreciable property made in the year to the extent included in income as recapture of that class of property	$__ (Q)	
Current year limitation: 75% of (N) + 25% of ((O) + (P) +(Q))		$__ (E)

Carry the lesser of (D) and (E) to line 340 of the T1.

If (D) is greater than (E), analyze the remaining carryforward amount by year (¶1272).

[1] Strictly speaking, all net income should be included at line 236. However, it sometimes happens that amounts which should be included in net income and deducted in taxable income are simply omitted; for example, income which is treaty exempt. Net income generally has the same meaning for an individual as for a dependant as described at ¶1103.

[¶1264] FIRST-TIME DONOR'S SUPER CREDIT

This federal "super credit" applies to cash gifts — it does not apply to gifts in kind — made after March 20, 2013, and before 2018. It applies only to a "first-time donor", defined as an individual (other than a trust) that has not claimed the regular donation credit in a preceding taxation year after 2007, and whose spouse or common-law partner has not claimed such a credit after 2007.

The credit is 25% of the eligible amount of the cash gift on up to $1,000 of donations, for a maximum additional credit of $250. When combined with the regular donations credit, the first $200 of cash gifts in a year will earn a 40% federal credit and the remaining amount, up to $1,000 of gifts, will earn a 54% or 58% federal credit depending on whether the taxpayers qualify for a 29% or 33% federal credit for their charitable donations in excess of $200.

The super credit may be claimed only once and it is claimed only in a year in which the regular donations credit is also claimed. Where a cash gift is made in one year and the additional super credit is not claimed in that year, the amount of the gift can be carried forward and earn the super credit in one of the subsequent four years (although the credit cannot be claimed after 2017).

In the case of married persons or common-law partners, the super credit can be claimed by either person, or it can be shared between the two persons.

[¶1264a] GIFTS MADE BY THE WILL

A donation made by an individual's will is deemed to be made by the individual in the year of their death. The donation can qualify for the credit in the individual's year of death or the immediately preceding year, and as discussed above is subject to a 100% income limit rather than the usual 75% income limit. See also ¶1263 and ¶1931.

Beginning in 2016, the rules regarding gifts made as a consequence of death are amended. A gift made of property by a graduated rate estate of an individual, where the property or property for which it was substituted was acquired as a consequence of the death of the individual, will be claimable for the purposes of the donation credit by either the individual in the year of death or the preceding year, or by the estate in the year of donation or a previous year.

Commentary on Bill C-29 Measures (Oct. 25, 2016)

Note: When Bill C-29, October 25, 2016, achieves Royal Assent, the commentary will be modified to read:

Effective for 2016 and subsequent years, there is more flexibility for gifts by estates. See ¶1931.10.

[¶1265] QUALIFIED DONEES OF CHARITABLE GIFTS

The charitable gift tax credit applies to gifts made to qualified donees, which include certain organizations in addition to registered charities. The list of qualified donees is provided below.

From January 1, 2012, all qualified donees are required to be on a publicly available list maintained by the CRA. In this regard, the Department of Finance stated:

> As is the case for registered charities, these measures will enable members of the public to determine which organizations may issue an official donation receipt and will enable registered charities, which may only make gifts to qualified donees, to determine whether an organization is a qualified donee for grant-making purposes

You may take into account donations to the following organizations for the purposes of the credit.

(1) Registered Charities and Canadian Amateur Athletic Organizations

In order to obtain a deduction for donations to one of these organizations, the organization must have been devoted to the specified activity and no part of its income could have been available for the personal benefit of any proprietor, member or shareholder. In addition, the organization must be resident in Canada and be registered with the CRA. As noted above, a list of registered organizations is maintained by the CRA.

The requirement that Canadian organizations be registered in order for donations to them to be creditable may represent a pitfall to some individual donors. Registration is the responsibility of the organization, but there is no relief granted to a person who has given to an organization on the assumption that it is a properly registered charity. If the organization has not complied with the registration requirements, the credit will be denied to the donor. Each donation receipt issued by a registered charitable organization should indicate the organization's registration number. Where there is any doubt as to whether a charity has registered, and the tax credit for the donation is a prime consideration, it is advisable to check the organization's registration status.

The CRA maintains a list of registered charities on its website, at www.cra-arc.gc.ca (see "Charities and Giving"). Presumably the list is updated as charities are registered or deleted, although at the time of writing the website did not specify this. You can also obtain information on whether a charity is registered (as well as other public information about it) by calling 1-800-267-2384 or, in Ottawa, (613) 954-0410. Alternatively, you can mail the Charities Directorate at:

Charities Directorate
Canada Revenue Agency
Ottawa ON
K1A 0L5.

Examples of organizations which qualify under this category include:

- The Canadian Red Cross
- The Canadian Cancer Society
- Heart and Stroke Foundation of Canada
- United Way
- Salvation Army
- Y.M.C.A.–Y.W.C.A.
- Boy Scouts
- The Royal Life Saving Society of Canada
- Hospitals operating on a non-profit basis
- Churches, temples, synagogues and affiliated or associated organizations, formed for the advancement of religious purposes
- Schools, colleges, universities, libraries, or museums not operated for private gain or profit.

Other lesser-known charities may also qualify as charitable organizations if they have registered with the CRA and if their objects are:

- The relief of poverty
- The advancement of religion
- The advancement of education
- Other purposes beneficial to the community.

(2) Low-Cost Housing Corporations

These corporations must be exempt from tax and resident in Canada. The corporations must be constituted exclusively for the purpose of providing low-cost housing accommodation for the aged.

(3) The United Nations or Agencies Thereof

The main United Nations specialized agencies are the following:

- World Bank ("WB")
- International Monetary Fund ("IMF")
- World Health Organization ("WHO")
- United Nations Educational, Scientific and Cultural Organization ("UNESCO")
- International Labor Organization ("ILO")
- Food and Agricultural Organization ("FAO")
- International Fund for Agricultural development ("IFAD")
- International Maritime Organization ("IMO")
- World Meteorological Organization ("WMO")
- World Intellectual Property Organization ("WIPO")
- International Civilian Aviation Organization ("ICAO")
- International Telecommunication Union ("ITU")
- United Nations Industrial Development Organization ("UNIDO")
- Universal Postal Union ("UPU")
- United Nations World Tourist Organization ("UNWTO")

For more information, see:
http://www.un.org/en/sections/about-un/funds-programmes-specialized-agencies-and-others/index.html

(4) Canadian Municipalities and Municipal or Public Bodies Performing Government Functions

It is the CRA's view (in CRA Document No. 9827515) that a gift of property made to a municipality for use by a community association would, provided it qualifies generally, qualify for a charitable receipt under this rule, provided the association operates under authority of the municipality (e.g., a committee established under a municipal by-law). A municipality would not be entitled to issue a receipt for the donation where it was merely acting as a conduit for the organization receiving the gift.

Indian Band Councils which are authorized under the Indian Act to make by-laws for the raising of money by the taxation of land and the licensing of businesses, callings, trades and occupations are considered to qualify as municipalities.

(5) Foreign Universities

Certain prescribed universities outside Canada whose student bodies normally include students from Canada are qualified donees, so that gifts made to such institutions will generate a credit, subject to the normal income limitations. These are known as "Schedule VIII Universities", because they are listed in Schedule VIII of the Income Tax Regulations. Note that a credit may be available for a gift made to non-resident charities under item (6), below. Also, certain contributions to U.S. charities and unlisted U.S. universities may be made under the rules at ¶1285 below, although contributions under ¶1285 are limited to 75% of U.S. income taxed in Canada.

It is a requirement for these donations that they be receipted by serialized receipts showing the name and address of both the donor and the recipient, the place of issue of the receipt, the amount of the donation and at least the year in which the donation was received, and a signature authorized by the recipient.

The CRA also maintains a list of Schedule VIII Universities on its website, at www.cra-arc.gc.ca; see "Charities and Giving/Qualified donees/Other qualified donee listings/List of prescribed universities outside Canada".

(6) Charitable Organizations Outside Canada to Which the Government of Canada Has Made a Gift

If the Government of Canada has made a gift to a foreign charity, that charity may also become a qualified donee for other donors. Accordingly, the credit can be claimed for contributions to that charity by Canadian taxpayers. As with other donations, you must obtain a receipt from the foreign charity issued in its name and signed by a person authorized by that organization to acknowledge donations. Prior to June 23, 2015, a gift only qualified if the foreign donee was a charitable organization – an entity that carried on charitable activities itself. From that date, the rule is amended to refer to a "foreign charity", so that a foreign foundation – an entity that does not itself carry on charitable activities, but which makes gifts to organizations that do – can also be a qualified donee.

The CRA publishes "Charitable Organizations Outside Canada that Have Received a Gift from Her Majesty in Right of Canada" (CG0915), which summarizes the rules governing these donations. The publication includes the list of charitable organizations outside Canada that have received a gift from the government of Canada and which therefore are eligible donees.

For a detailed current list of registered foreign charities which have received a gift from the Canadian government, see:
http://www.cra-arc.gc.ca/chrts-gvng/qlfd-dns/qd-lstngs/gftsfrmhrmjsty-lst-eng.html

From January 1, 2013, a foreign charitable entity becomes a qualified donee if it applies to the Minister for registration and it is registered. The Minister can register the charity for a 24-month period that includes the time at which the federal government has made a gift to the organization, so that a gift made in this time period will qualify for a donation credit. The list referred to above sets out the time periods for which the foreign charity is a qualified donee. Previously, individuals could claim the credit for gifts made in the calendar year the government made its gift or in the following calendar year. This timing rule was revised, but only for the 2012 calendar year, so that a charitable organization outside Canada was a qualified donee at a particular time if the Government of Canada had made a gift to it in the 36-month period that began 24 months before that time.

(7) Crown Gifts to Government of Canada or a Province

Gifts made to the Government of Canada, a province, or a territory are also eligible for the credit.

(ITA: 110(1), (2); 118.1; 248(1))

[¶1267] DONATIONS OF LIFE INSURANCE POLICIES AND ANNUITIES

[¶1267.05] *Annuities*

Where an amount is contributed to a charitable organization by a donor, and the advantage received by the donor is a stream of guaranteed payments for a period of time – that is, the donor purchases an annuity from the charity – the eligible amount of the gift will be the excess of the amount contributed over the amount that would be paid at that time to an arm's length third party to acquire an annuity to fund the guaranteed payments.

Example

Facts:

- A donor makes a $100,000 contribution to a charitable organization.
- The donor's life expectancy is 8 years (assume the donor lives 8 years).
- The donor is to be provided annuity payments of $10,000 per year ($80,000).
- The cost of an annuity that will provide $80,000 over 8 years is $55,000.

Tax treatment:

- The donor receives a tax receipt for $45,000 for the year of donation, the excess of the $100,000 contribution over the $55,000 cost of the annuity.
- The donor receives in total $80,000 in annuity payments, of which $25,000 will be included in income over 8 years.

(ITA: 248(30)–(32); ITTN: No. 26 [Archived])

[¶1267.10] *Life Insurance*

The donation of a life insurance policy (both "whole life" and "term life") to a registered charitable organization is eligible for credit provided the policy has been absolutely assigned to the charitable organization and the charity is the registered beneficiary of the policy. Any consents that are required to change a beneficiary must be signed before there is a valid charitable donation.

The amount eligible for credit as a charitable donation is the lesser of the total of the cash surrender value of the policy plus any accumulated dividends and interest thereon at the time of the transfer, and its adjusted cost basis, as discussed at ¶1262. If there is no cash surrender value, there is no charitable donation when the policy is transferred.

If premiums on the policy are paid by the charitable organization with monies donated to it by you, you can claim a credit for the donation of these amounts. If you pay the premiums on the policy directly to the insurance company at the request of, or with concurrence of, the charitable organization, the CRA considers this action to be constructive payment of a donation to the organization and therefore a charitable donation.

Where a donor has assigned a life insurance policy to a charitable or non-profit organization, the donor's proceeds of disposition will be the cash surrender value of the policy plus any accumulated dividends assigned to the charity. See ¶981.

(IT-244R3 [Archived])

[¶1268] GIFTS OF CULTURAL PROPERTY

The *Cultural Property Export and Import Act* (CPEIA) contains provisions to encourage the retention of national treasures (Canadian cultural property) within Canada. Under these provisions, taxpayers are encouraged to dispose of such property to designated institutions or public authorities in Canada. Gifts of cultural property to a designated public authority or institution in Canada and certified by the Canadian Cultural Property Export Review Board will entitle you to a tax credit as a donation. Certification should be received on form T871. Your deduction will be for the fair market value of the property at the date of the disposition.

Capital gains from gifting Canadian cultural property to such designated institutions or public authorities are not taxable. Capital losses will be treated in the ordinary manner described in ¶576. As a result of these rules, a gift of qualified cultural property that is capital property of the donor will generally result in a donation tax credit that offsets tax on other income. However, there could be an income inclusion if the cultural property donated was a trading asset such as inventory. Artists gifting property they have created should see the special rules at ¶1291.

The amount eligible for credit is not limited to a percentage of your net income for the year (see ¶1263 and 1270). Any portion not claimed in a year may be carried forward to the next five years (¶1272).

The fair market value of a donated cultural property is deemed to be the fair market value set by the Cultural Property Export Review Board. Appeals of such valuations may be taken to the Tax Court of Canada.

The rules here override the rules for ecological property in ¶1268d in the unlikely event that a gift should be certified under both rules. However, if the cultural property claim overrides the ecological claim, the individual taxpayer cannot then go on to claim the ecological credit based on the ecological valuation rules. It is at least arguable that the problem can be eliminated simply by not claiming the item as cultural property; it is therefore not "included" in cultural gifts and can be claimed under ecological rules. That is, the rule may be simply an ordering rule ensuring that the same claim cannot be made under both rules. (If this is true for individuals, it is not necessarily true for corporations.)

Where the Board makes a determination of fair market value of a property that is a charitable donation but not a gift of cultural property, that amount will be deemed to be fair market value for all provisions related to charitable donations for a period of two years from the date of determination. In general, this means that if the Board makes a determination of value unacceptable to the taxpayer, the taxpayer cannot then rescind the transaction and make a gift under the ordinary rules at a different value within the two year limitation. Exceptions permit (i) the election (described in ¶1269.10) to value property between fair market value and cost, and (ii) the artist's inventory rules (at ¶1291) to override the determination of proceeds of disposition (but not, it would seem, the fair market value of the gift) set by the Board. It would apparently still be open to the taxpayer to appeal the value. The Board also has its own procedures for revaluation where market or other circumstances change (the Grandma Moses turns out to be a Van Gogh).

The recipient of certified cultural property is required to hold it for a period of 10 years or be subject to penalty tax.

Prior to February 11, 2014, the anti-avoidance rule discussed at ¶1262 (deeming the fair market value of gifts to be their cost rather than fair market value) did not apply to cultural gifts made under a gifting arrangement that is a tax shelter. Such gifts made after February 10, 2014 are not exempt from the rule.

(ITA: 39(1)(*a*)(i.1); 110(1)(*b*.1); 118.1(1)–(3), (10)–(11); 207.3; IT-110R3 [Archived]; IT-407R4 (Consolidated) [Archived]; *Friedberg v. The Queen*, 92 DTC 6031 (F.C.A.))

[¶1268d] GIFTS OF ECOLOGICALLY SENSITIVE LAND

Gifts of ecologically sensitive land (including related servitudes, and a covenant or easement) may in certain circumstances be eligible for

(1) charitable donation tax credit for the eligible amount without regard to the normal percentage-of-net-income limitation discussed in ¶1270; and

(2) an exemption from any capital gain realized on the gift (that is, the taxable capital gain on such a gift is nil).

To qualify for the special treatment for ecological gifts, such gifts must:

(1) be made either to Canada, a province or territory of Canada, a Canadian municipality, a municipal or public body performing a function of government in Canada, or a registered charity one of the main purposes of which is, in the opinion of the Minister of the Environment, the conservation and protection of Canada's environmental heritage and which is approved by the Minister of Environment or a person designated by that Minister to receive the particular gift; and

(2) be gifts of land, including a servitude for the use and benefit of dominant land, and a covenant or easement, certified by the Minister of the Environment, or a person designated by the Minister, to be ecologically sensitive land important to the preservation of Canada's environmental heritage, the fair market value of which is certified by the Minister.

Where an advantage has been conferred on the donor, so that the eligible amount of the gift is less than its fair market value (as discussed in ¶1261), only that proportion of the gain on the gift that the eligible amount is of the fair market value (more specifically, of the deemed or elected proceeds of disposition) is eligible for the exclusion. See the example at ¶1290d.05.

If you make a gift in compliance with these rules, you may claim the charitable donation credit for the full eligible amount of the gift. To the extent you choose not to take the entire deduction in the year the gift is made, any unclaimed portion may be carried forward and credited to the extent chosen in any of the following 10 years. For gifts made before February 11, 2014, the carry-forward period was five years.

Note that the property will typically be capital property subject to the deemed disposition rules at ¶1269; if it is not capital property, see ¶1290g. In the unlikely event that a property could qualify for either the cultural property or ecological credit, the cultural property rules take precedence; a property claimed under the cultural property rules cannot also be claimed under the ecological rules.

Since the fair market value of the gift of a servitude, covenant, or easement may be difficult to establish, a specific rule provides that the fair market value of the gift of a servitude, etc., is the greater of (a) its fair market value otherwise determined, and (b) the amount by which the fair market value of the land is reduced as a consequence of the gift. This ensures that the value of a gift of servitude, covenant, or easement cannot be less than the resulting decrease in value of the land which is subject to it. Where the value of a servitude, covenant, or easement is fixed by this rule, that value will also be eligible for the election (discussed at ¶1269.10) to designate both the value of the gift and the proceeds of disposition at any amount between adjusted cost base and fair market value of the gift. Similarly, a portion of the adjusted cost base of the land to which the covenant, easement or servitude relates is to be allocated to the donated covenant, etc., so the gain on such a gift can be reasonably measured. For this purpose, the adjusted cost base allocated to the covenant, etc. is the adjusted cost base of the land immediately before the gift prorated by the value of the covenant as just discussed (the greater of (a) and (b) subject to a designated value election) over the fair market value of the land immediately before the gift. That amount reduces the adjusted cost base of the land and becomes the adjusted cost base of the covenant, etc., for capital gain purposes.

As noted above, the donor must obtain from the Minister of the Environment (MOE) not only a certification regarding the qualified nature of the property, but a valuation as well. The taxpayer can obtain a prospective valuation from the MOE, and can within 90 days ask for a redetermination. However, the MOE can also make a redetermination on its own initiative at any time, which seems to add an excessive note of uncertainty. The MOE-determined value is not subject to the normal notice of objection procedure; rather, it may be appealed directly to the Tax Court (within 90 days of the determination or redetermination by MOE), but only after an irrevocable gift has been made. Only the taxpayer will have this right of appeal; the CRA does not have authority to appeal a valuation by the Minister of the Environment.

The recipient of a gift of certified ecological property faces penalty taxes if it in turn disposes of the gift without federal government approval.

Environment Canada publishes an Information Circular entitled "The Ecological Gifts Program" as well as "The Canadian Ecological Gifts Program Handbook". Both describe, in greater or lesser detail, the full program, criteria for the ecological character of such gifts, certification authorities in each province or territory, and a list of qualified recipient charities, including land trusts and conservancies. These publications and other useful information are available on a dedicated portion of the Canadian Wildlife Service section of the Environment Canada website.

(ITA: 38(*a.2*); 43(2); 118.1; 165(1.2); 169(1.1); 207.31; Window on Canadian Tax: 9663)

[¶1268g] ORDERING OF GIFT CATEGORIES

Where a gift is described in two or more categories of "charitable", "cultural", or "ecological", the law provides for the following order of precedence: cultural, ecological, charitable. Thus, a gift of property which had received both cultural and ecological designations, would be considered a cultural gift. It would seem that a gift which has a cultural designation will receive its exemption from capital gains tax regardless of the provision under which it is claimed; however, if it is also designated under the ecological property rules (or perhaps claimed under the general rule), it is conceivable that a different valuation might apply if those rules prevailed for donation purposes. The ecological rules too have their own valuation standards. Arguably, the ordering provision merely prevents the taxpayer from claiming the same gift in two categories at once, so that if you decline to place it in a particular category it will simply bounce along to the next one. (This would not necessarily be true for corporations even if true for individuals.) The CRA has not clearly opined on whether it will accept this permissive approach.

There is also an ordering rule which requires the oldest carryforward in any category to be considered to be used first; this is the result most favourable to the taxpayer.

For the ordering of donation credits vis-à-vis other personal tax credits, see the subheading "Ordering of Credits" at ¶1270.

(ITA: 118.1(1), (2.1); IT-407R4 (Consolidated) [Archived])

[¶1269] GIFTS OF PROPERTY OTHER THAN CASH

You are allowed a donation credit for gifts of property other than cash. However, when you donate property you are also deemed to receive proceeds equal to the value of the property. Accordingly, if the property given away was capital property you may be subject to tax on a deemed capital gain (see ¶530), and furthermore, if the property given away was property for which you claimed capital cost allowance, the gift may result in a recapture of capital cost allowance (see ¶532). The potential capital gain or recapture may be mitigated by the right to designate a disposition value for the property at any point between adjusted cost base and fair market value (if higher); see ¶1269.10.

Although you will be deemed to have disposed of the gifted property for proceeds equal to its fair market value, the amount of the gift for purposes of the donation credit is the "eligible amount" of the gift, which equals the fair market value of the gift less the "advantage", if any, received in respect of the gift (see ¶1261 and ¶1262). For these purposes, in certain cases the fair market value of the property is deemed to be the lesser of the fair market value otherwise determined and the cost of the property (see ¶1262 and ¶1269.05 below). Also, as noted, there is an election available that allows you to elect that the proceeds of disposition and the fair market value of the gift be an amount between the cost of the property and its fair market value, as discussed below at ¶1269.10.

If the property disposition does give rise to capital gain, the capital gains exemption rules (¶502) will apply to qualified farm and fishing property and qualified small business shares.

For gifts of capital property which are non-arm's length shares, debt, or other rights or securities, see the subheading "Gifts of Non-Qualified Securities" at ¶1290d.

If you dispose of property which is inventory of a business, see the discussion at ¶1290g. Gifts of services are also discussed at ¶1290g.

Property that is inventory of an artist is subject to a special rule at ¶1291.

(ITA: 69(1)(*b*)(ii); 118.1; IT-297R2 [Archived])

[¶1269.03] *Gifts of Barter Dollars*

In a technical opinion (CRA Document No. 2008-0274411I7), the CRA considered whether a gift of "barter dollars" to a charity would generate charitable donation credit. The CRA first laid down its understanding that the barter dollars were acquired by the individual in return for services rendered or goods sold in the course of carrying on his business during a particular taxation year, and that the fair market value of the transaction that caused the receipt of the barter dollars by the taxpayer would have been included in computing the taxpayer's business income for the particular taxation year. Moreover, the registered charity would use the barter dollars to acquire goods necessary for its charitable activities from other barter club members. The CRA went on to say that in its opinion the barter dollars were property and therefore could be the subject of an eligible gift provided the fair market value of the gift could be established. The registered charity could issue an official receipt for an amount equal to the fair market value of the barter dollar units received (less the advantage received in respect of the gift, if any). "When proposed [at that time] subsection 248(35) applies, the fair market value of a property that is the subject of a gift is deemed, for determining the eligible amount of a gift, to be the lesser of the fair market value of the property and the cost of the property to the taxpayer." While the determination of the cost to the individual was a question of fact, "it is our view that the cost of the Units to the individual could be equal to the total value of the goods, property or services given up in order to obtain the Units, plus or minus any cash paid or received as part of the barter".

[¶1269.05] *Gifts of Appreciated Property*

As part of the government's shutdown of certain tax shelter schemes involving donations of property, the value of a gift is deemed to be the lesser of its fair market value and its cost or adjusted cost base if the gift is made:

(1) as part of a tax shelter gifting arrangement, as defined, OR

(2) unless the gift is made in consequence of death

(a) within three years of the acquisition of the property, OR

(b) if the property is held for less than 10 years, it is reasonable to conclude that at the time the taxpayer acquired the property the taxpayer expected to make a gift of it.

The last condition could be rather extreme, depending on how it is interpreted by the CRA and the courts. If either should adopt the line of reasoning that has been used in assessing whether capital gain or income is realized on the sale of unimproved real estate — a line of reasoning that takes into account any possible secondary intention at the time of acquisition to dispose of the property later at a profit — the rule could make it difficult to realize a tax benefit in respect of the gift of an appreciated property made within 10 years of its acquisition, except on death. Until the CRA establishes a pattern, either through advance rulings or litigation, this uncertainly will hang over the head of the potential donor.

The rule technically applies to all gifts of property except:

- inventory (see ¶1290g);
- real property situated in Canada;
- certified cultural property, discussed at ¶1268;
- publicly traded shares, debt, or rights which are eligible for the zero gain inclusion rate discussed at ¶1290d;
- ecological gifts which qualify for the zero gain inclusion rate, discussed at ¶1268d.

A gifting arrangement is an arrangement under which a person makes a charitable donation (or election campaign contribution) of property acquired under the arrangement, or an arrangement under which a gift is made in circumstances involving limited recourse debt.

The background of this rule, and other rules involving contributions which may be construed as tax shelters, are described under the subheading "The Great Tax Shelter Fight: Round Five", and in more specific detail in ¶2521.35.

[¶1269.10] *Election for Gifts of Capital Property*

If a taxpayer makes a gift of capital property that is a charitable gift to a qualified donee (see ¶1265) or a gift of ecologically sensitive land (¶1268d), an election is available that can lower the proceeds of disposition for capital gains purposes and the fair market value of the gift for purposes of the credit. The election is available if the fair market value of the property exceeds

- in the case of depreciable property of a prescribed class, the lesser of (i) the undepreciated capital cost ("UCC") of the class at the end of the taxation year of the gift (before accounting for the proceeds of disposition), and (ii) the adjusted cost base of the property immediately before the gift, and
- in any other case, the adjusted cost base of the property immediately before the gift.

In the election, the taxpayer may designate an amount which is not less than the greater of the applicable amount described above and the advantage, if any, received in respect of the donation, and not greater than the fair market value of the property. The designated amount is deemed to be both the fair market value of the gift (and therefore used in determining the eligible amount of the gift) and the taxpayer's proceeds of disposition of the property. The election is made in the tax return for the year of the donation.

The election also applies to gifts by non-resident individuals of Canadian real or immovable property made to a prescribed donee charity that provides an undertaking that it will hold the land for use in the public interest. Although the gift will not be eligible for the credit in Canada if the donee is non-resident, the election can nonetheless be used to avoid any Canadian tax on the resulting disposition without affecting the eligibility of a credit in the individual's country of residence. The Nature Conservancy (a U.S. charity), the Friends of Nature Conservancy of Canada, Inc., and the American Friends of Canadian Land Trusts are prescribed charities for these purposes.

[¶1269.15] *Grant of Options to Qualified Donees*

Where the option was granted after March 21, 2011, no amount is included as a charitable gift of a donor granting an option to a qualified donee until the qualified donee exercises or disposes of the option.

At the time the option is exercised, the donor is deemed to receive proceeds of disposition equal to the fair market value of the property, and there is included in the donor's total gifts the amount by which that fair market value exceeds the total of the consideration, if any, paid by the qualified donee to the donor for the property and the amount, if any, paid by the donee to the donor for the option. The normal limitations described at ¶1261 apply in determining the eligible amount of the gift.

Where the donee disposes of the option (other than by exercise) at a particular time, the donor is deemed to have disposed of a notional property at that time. The proceeds of disposition are deemed to be the lesser of the fair market value of the option at that time and the fair market value of any consideration (other than a non-qualified security — see ¶1290d.15) received by the qualified donee for the option. The adjusted cost base of the property is deemed to be the amount, if any, the qualified donee paid for the option. The donor is deemed to have made a gift at that time equal to the amount by which those proceeds of disposition exceed the amount, if any, paid by the donee for the option.

There were no specific rules governing options where an option was donated prior to March 12, 2011.

[¶1269.20] *Donations of Flow-Through Shares*

An investor who subscribes for flow-through shares ("FTS") is deemed to have acquired such shares at a cost of nil. Consequently, an investor in FTS could realize a significant capital gain on the disposition of the FTS to a qualified donee which, if the shares were listed on a designated stock exchange, would be tax-free owing to the zero inclusion rate for such gains (see ¶1290d.05). This could be the case even if the investor had claimed significant flow-through deductions or credits in respect of the FTS (see Chapter 22).

Where FTS are gifted on or after March 22, 2011, the zero inclusion rate effectively applies only to the amount by which the capital gain exceeds the actual amount paid for the FTS. More particularly, the donor accounts for a zero capital gain inclusion on the donation of the FTS but is deemed to have a separate capital gain from a disposition of another capital property equal to the lesser of (a) the donor's "exemption threshold" at that time in respect of the "flow-through share class of property"; and (b) the total of the capital gain from such actual disposition at that time by the donor. The exemption threshold generally equals the actual amount paid by the investor for all of the FTS of the class of shares in excess of capital gains previously realized on the disposition of an FTS of the same class.

Additionally, a specific anti-avoidance rule deals with circumstances under which an FTS has been acquired during a tax-free reorganization completed under any of sections 51, 73(1), 85, 85.1, 86, and 87, and the FTS is part of a gifting arrangement.

[¶1270] HOW MUCH CAN YOU CLAIM?

[¶1270.05] *Donations Made in Taxation Year*

Normally, you can only claim donation credits for gifts made in the taxation year, which for an individual will be the calendar year (although for gifts made by a partnership the partner may only claim for gifts made in the partnership taxation year ending in the individual's calendar year). Gifts not claimed in the year are eligible for a five-year carryforward (10 years for ecological gifts) as discussed below. For gifts made or deemed to have been made in the year of death, the credit in respect of the gifts is allowed in the year of death or in the immediately preceding year, and the 75% income limitation described below does not apply. Where the gift is made by will and death occurs prior to 2016, the gift is deemed to have been made immediately prior to death. Gifts made by will where death occurs after 2015 are subject to more flexible rules — see Chapter 9.

[¶1270.10] *Donation Limits*

The amount of donations for which you can claim a federal tax credit of 15%, 29%, or 33% (as explained in ¶1263) is:

(1) the least of:

(a) the actual amount of donations made to any of the organizations noted in ¶1265, plus gifts in this category made in the past five years to the extent full credit has not been claimed for them in prior years;

(b) in the year of death or the immediately preceding year, 100% of net income (see ¶1931);

(c) where the year of death and preceding year rules in (b) above do not apply, the lesser of your net income for the year and the result of the following computation:

(i) 75% of your net income for the year (as described below); plus

(ii) 25% of the aggregate of your:

(A) taxable capital gains for the year on account of creditable gifts of capital property; plus

(B) taxable capital gains for the year from the final recognition of a prior year reserve on a creditable gift of non-qualified property as discussed in ¶1290d.15; plus

(C) income for the year from recapture of capital cost allowance on creditable gifts of depreciable property; minus

(D) any claimed capital gains exemption (¶502) for the year to the extent it relates to a gift referred to in (B) or (C) above;

(2) the full amount of gifts of ecologically sensitive property, provided the appropriate certifications have been obtained (¶1268d), plus gifts in this category made in the past 10 years to the extent the credit has not already been claimed for them (for gifts made before February 11, 2014, the carry-forward period is 5 years; see ¶1268d); plus

(3) the full amount of gifts of certified cultural property donated in compliance with the rules at ¶1268, plus gifts in this category made in the past 5 years to the extent the credit has not already been claimed for them.

Your "net income" — to which the 75% limit in (1) above applies — is usually the number at line 236 of your T1 return. Accordingly, it does not include deductions for such items as capital gains exemption, prior years' losses or any of the items listed at ¶1080, which enter into the calculation of "taxable income" rather than "net income".

On the other hand, the income items discussed at ¶990 (except foster parents' payments received) should be included in net income for purposes of the limitation calculation even if for some reason they are not reported on your return.

¶1270.15] *First-Time Donor "Super Credit"*

For gifts made after March 20, 2013 and before 2018, a "first-time donor" is eligible for an additional credit of 25% for up to $1,000 of cash gifts. See ¶1264.

[¶1270.25] *Ordering of Credits*

There is an ordering provision for tax credits (¶1365); charitable contribution credits are deducted after all other credits except the student loan interest credit and the dividend tax credit. This is typically beneficial to the taxpayer in that it preserves unused donations for carryover.

Example

Barry has $16,227 of taxable income (line 260) for the year. He is unmarried with no dependants. His CPP contributions for the year were $157, and his EI contributions were $203. He also incurred $3,000 of tuition fees and is entitled to a $1,200 education amount as a student. He made $600 of charitable contributions in the year. He must claim credits for personal amounts in the following order:

- Basic personal amount, $11,327
- CPP/EI, $360
- Tuition, $3,000
- Education amount, $1,200

The creditable amounts to this point total $15,887, leaving $340 which will, in effect, be subject to tax. Because the charitable donation credit on his gift in excess of $200 will be given at the highest tax rate, his $600 gift will more than eliminate his remaining tax. What he wants to find is the amount that will reduce his tax to zero, and carry forward the excess to next year.

Before the charitable donation credit, Barry has tax of 15% of $16,227, or $2,434, and credits of $15,887 × 15% = $2,383. He now must find the necessary donation credit to eliminate the remaining tax of ($2,434 - $2,383 =) $51. If Barry now uses the first $200 (credited at the 15% rate) of charitable donation, he can generate an additional $30 of credit; he now must offset the remaining tax of $51 - $30 = $21 with credit at the 29% rate. The amount can be found by dividing $21 by.29, thus: $21 ÷.29 = $72.41. Thus, $200 of charitable donation at the 15% rate plus $72 (rounded down) at the 29% rate will eliminate tax for the year. The remaining donation of $328 ($600 - $200 - $72) can be carried forward to next year.)

Note that if the charitable contribution claim came earlier in the ordering, Barry would be compelled to take his contribution amount this year and would lose credit for $328 on some other item which permits no carryforwards.

(ITA: 118.92)

[¶1270.30] *Donations Made by Your Business*

If you operated an unincorporated business during the year or were a member of a business partnership, charitable donations may have been made by the business. If so, these donations may be claimed by you (subject to your overall 75% income limit) in addition to any donations you made personally — i.e., outside of the business.

An exception to the income limitation occurred in a few court cases where a taxpayer in business proved that his donations were made for the purpose of increasing or maintaining the business' sales and only secondarily, if at all, for charitable or benevolent reasons. However, the facts in these cases were unusual and it would seem that few taxpayers will be able to claim donations in excess of the limitation on the grounds that they are a business expense (see *Olympia Floor & Wall Tile (Quebec) Ltd. v. M.N.R.*, 70 DTC 6085 (Ex. Ct.); *Impenco Ltd. v. M.N.R.*,88 DTC 1242 (T.C.C.)).

A partner will have available for claim the same percentage share of the partnership's donations as his or her percentage share of the partnership's profits. In order for you to claim a share of donations made by a partnership you must be a member of the partnership at the end of its fiscal year. Your claim for donations should be made in your taxation year in which the partnership's fiscal year ends. If your business suffered a loss in the year you may still be able to claim the donations made by the loss business if you had sufficient income from other sources.

The important thing to remember is that you must aggregate all of your charitable donations — those made by your unincorporated business and directly by you — and all of your income from unincorporated business and other sources to determine the amount of your claim.

Example — Donations by a Partnership

Bill Davis and Jack Moore were partners in a law practice throughout the year. For their fiscal year ended December 31, the partnership earned a net profit of $20,000, after deducting charitable donations of $2,000. They shared profits on a 60-40 basis.

	Davis 60%	*Moore 40%*	*Total 100%*
Income from partnership	$13,200	$ 8,800	$22,000
Charitable donations made by partnership available for individual claim	1,200	800	2,000

(ITA: 118.1(1)–(3), (8))

[¶1271] RETURNED OR RECOVERED GIFTS

A donation credit is denied or restricted where an individual transfers property on or after March 22, 2011, to a qualified donee and the donated property or another property is subsequently returned by the donee to the donor. Specifically, this rule applies if the donee has issued a receipt to the donor in respect of a transfer of property and the property, or another property that may be reasonably considered to be transferred in substitution or compensation for the donated property, is later transferred by the donee to the donor. However, the rule does not apply if the later transfer of the property to the donor is reasonable consideration for other property or services rendered.

When the rule applies, the original gift is deemed not to have been made and the property is deemed not to have been disposed of. If the returned property is identical to the donated property, there will be no gift and the returned property will be deemed to be the donated (original) property. If the returned property is not the donated property, there will be a deemed gift at the time of the original transfer, and the gift will have a deemed fair market value equal to the fair market value of the original property at the time of its transfer to the donee in excess of the fair market value of the returned property at the time of its transfer to the donor. The donor is deemed to have disposed of the original property at the time the returned property is transferred to the donor for proceeds equal to the greater of the fair market value of the returned property at that time and the fair market value of the original property at the time of the original transfer. A revised donation receipt must be issued by the donee to the donor and a copy sent to the Minister of National Revenue if the value of the returned property is greater than $50. The Minister has the authority to reassess any person whose income would reasonably be regarded as relating to the return of property.

[¶1272] EXCESS DONATIONS CAN BE CARRIED FORWARD

Donations not claimed in a taxation year can generally be carried forward to any of the five subsequent years, although ecological gifts made after February 10, 2011 carry forward for 10 years. This is implicit in the eligible amounts pool for the year described at ¶1270. As well, the claim for these credits is optional, so that any donation not credited in the current year is eligible for carryforward, subject to the annual 75% income test and the low credit rate on the first $200. It follows that donations can be accumulated and claimed together in a year to generate credits in excess of the low rate on the first $200 of donations. Excess contributions made in the year of death of a taxpayer (whether made before death or by will) will be permitted as a donation in the preceding year.

Example 1: Carryforwards of Cash Gift

Bruce Nolan had income and donations for three years as follows:

	Net income	*Donations*
Year 1	$1,600	$1,400
Year 2	5,800	4,500
Year 3	10,000	2,300

For Year 1, his donation was limited to 75% of $1,600	$1,200
For Year 2, Bruce had available to claim:	
First: Carryforward from Year 1 ($1,400 - $1,200)	$ 200
Second: Year 2 donations	4,500
	$4,700
Year 2 limitation was 75% of $ 5,800	$4,350

In effect, Bruce has used the $200 carryforward from Year 1 first in Year 2 and then $4,150 from his Year 2 donations to make up the $4,350 claim for Year 2. The excess Year 2 donations of $350 ($4,700 - $4,350, or, if you like, the $4,500 of Year 2 donations less the $4,150 utilized) is considered to come entirely from Year 2 donations and so the whole $350 will be available for carryforward to the next five years.

For Year 3 Bruce will have available to claim:	
First: Carryforward from Year 2	$ 350
Second: Year 3 donations	2,300
	$2,650
Year 3 limitation is 75% of $10,000	$7,500

With the 75% limit effective in Year 3, Bruce can claim all donations, both carryforwards and current.

Of course, the example in these terms is not realistic from a practical perspective, because other personal tax credits would eliminate taxes in any event at the numbers given. But the principles are correct, and if you multiply all the numbers by 100, it will solve the personal tax credit issue.

Example 2: Carryforwards on Gift of Depreciable Capital Property

Mary Scot made a gift in the current year of depreciable property which had fair market value of $110,000, a cost of $100,000, and an undepreciated capital cost of $93,000. She had no net income for the year other than the $7,000 of recapture on the disposition plus the $5,000 taxable capital gain (50% taxable portion of the $10,000 gain). Her donation limit is the least of (i) her $110,000 gift, (ii) her net income of $12,000, and (iii) 75% of $12,000 net income ($9,000) plus 25% of $5,000 taxable capital gain ($1,250) plus 25% of the $7,000 recapture ($1,750), or $12,000. Accordingly, she may claim a credit on $12,000 and will carry the balance of $98,000 forward for five years against, in effect, 75% of any income arising in those years (assuming no further capital gifts).

(ITA: 110(1)(*a*), (*b*), (1.2); 118.1(1)–(3))

[¶1275] DONATIONS MADE BY SPOUSE

Donation receipts made out to your spouse will normally, as a result of administrative practice, be accepted if claimed in your return. The CRA affirms this policy in its T1 Guide (for line 349), and the policy explicitly extends to common-law spouses or partners as defined in ¶1113. Aggregating the credits for donations made by spouses and partners in the return of one spouse results in the low rate of credit which applies to the first $200 of gifts being incurred only once; if you each claim separate donations it is incurred twice. Under $200 of aggregate donations the dollar value of the credit is the same and the division of credits is immaterial, provided someone can claim them. For gifts in kind, see also ¶1269.

The administrative concession extends to allowing spouses/partners to allocate donations between them in the proportions they choose. Claiming donations on both returns means that the $200 low-rate credit applies twice. However, taxpayers may still choose to report in this manner if, for example, the intent is to eliminate the tax payable by both rather than generating a refund for one and a liability for the other.

(ITA: 110(1)(*a*); 118.1)

[¶1278] WHAT YOU CANNOT CLAIM

The following donations do not in general qualify for credit (although a few qualify to the extent described):

(1) Donations to charitable organizations outside Canada (except for foreign organizations mentioned in ¶1265, ¶1287, and ¶1285).

(2) Donations to individuals.

(3) Gifts in the form of services. Only gifts of money or property are eligible for credit. A charity may pay for services and accept a return of the payment as a gift for which a receipt is issued, provided the gift was voluntary. The payment will be income to the donor, the tax on which will be offset by the donation credit, within normal limits.

(4) The value of merchandise where its cost has been deducted in computing business income (but see ¶1290g).

(5) Donations subject to a direction by the donor that they benefit a particular person or family, or be in turn donated to a non-qualified donee such as a foreign charity. Donations can be directed to a particular program operated by the charity provided there is no benefit for the donor or persons not at arm's length with the donor.

(6) Amounts paid for card parties, bingos, and lotteries — even where such activities may be held for the benefit of charity.

(7) Donations of blood.

(8) Unreimbursed expenses of volunteer workers.

(9) Donations to patriotic, fraternal or benevolent organizations.

(10) Political donations (but see ¶1462).

(11) Payment of membership fees. Whether or not there is an eligible amount associated with the payment of membership fees or other amounts to a registered charity of which an individual is a member will be determined on the basis of whether the membership fee or other amounts exceed the amount of the advantage the member receives. If the amount of the advantage is 80% or less of the payment to the charity, a tax receipt may be issued for the eligible amount (the payment minus the value of the advantage(s)).

(12) Amounts expended in private acts of benevolence no matter how worthy the cause.

(13) Purchase of tickets to a charity fundraiser. While a particular event may be a charity fund raiser and all or a portion of the proceeds designated in favour of a charity, there will need to be clear evidence that the ticket price is in excess of the usual and current ticket price to allow a finding that there is an eligible amount. Where the amount of the advantage (including the usual and current ticket price) is 80% or less of the actual ticket price, a tax receipt may be issued for the difference.

(14) Purchase of items at a charity auction. Generally, it is the CRA's position that there will not be an eligible amount with respect to items obtained at charity auctions on the basis that the bid determines the value of the various items put up for auction. However, where the value of an item is clearly otherwise ascertainable (e.g., there is a retail price for the item) and is made known to all bidders in advance, an eligible amount exists where the amount bid is in excess of the posted value. Where a donative intent can be established, which may be the case where the posted value of the item does not exceed 80% of the accepted bid, a tax receipt may be issued for the eligible amount.

(15) In general, donations where you expect any kind of return or personal benefit of more than nominal value, and only the value in excess of the benefit expected qualifies, as discussed at ¶1261. Thus, except as noted in (13) and (14), payments for goods or services were not generally eligible for credit and may only be eligible for a reduced credit where you paid more than what the items are worth.

(16) Donations where the value to the donor cannot be ascertained. In general, it is the CRA's initial view that any advantage received by the donor must be clearly identified and its value ascertainable. If its value cannot be reasonably ascertained, no credit is allowed.

(17) A pledge or undertaking to pay a donation over a period of years does not entitle you to a credit in the year you made the pledge. However, you can make a claim in a year for monies actually paid pursuant to a pledge made in that year or prior years.

(18) The loan of property (including money) is not a gift. A charity may, however, pay rent or interest on a loan and later accept the return of all or a portion of that payment as a gift, provided it is returned voluntarily. The donor would have to account for the taxable income received, the tax on which can be offset by the charitable donation credit. This makes the treatment of loans comparable to gifts of inventory or services, discussed at ¶1290g.

(IT-110R3 [Archived]; IT-297R2 [Archived]; ITTN: No. 17, 26 [Archived])

[¶1278.05] *Charitable Donation Schemes (and Sometimes Scams)*

Over the years, a number of schemes have arisen to use the charitable donation rules to obtain inflated deductions. Some of these, such as giving a kickback of part of the tax savings to someone in a position to offer a charitable receipt, are patently illegal. The donation credit is denied, and the person offering the receipt may be subject to criminal prosecution.

More often, the process has involved acquiring an item, such as a work of art, at one price, and donating it at a vastly inflated price, justifying the difference under various valuation theories. The government has fought these schemes with varying degrees of success. Such schemes have effectively been legislated out of existence by the rules described at ¶1269.05, which limit the donation amount to the cost of the property donated.

A much more detailed discussion of various donation transactions which the government finds abusive, and its legislative rules against them, as well as some recent case law, is found in ¶2521; see particularly the discussions under the subheadings "The Great Tax Shelter Fight: Round Five" and "(5) Acquisitions for Charitable Donations".

[¶1279] PAYMENTS TO RELIGIOUS SCHOOLS AND SPORTING ORGANIZATIONS

These issues were at one time very contentious, but have been effectively settled by the courts. The CRA's position is that fees paid to a school which teaches only religion are charitable contributions (and may be paid and claimed by parents) whereas fees paid to secular schools with a religious component or bias are eligible for credit only to the extent they represent identifiable costs of the religious components of the curriculum. The courts have upheld this view. (See also the argument as to whether tuition fees may be deducted under tuition fee credit rules at ¶1339.)

Donations to a sporting organization in which the taxpayer's child was actively involved were held to involve a consideration or benefit for the taxpayer, consisting of the training of his child, and so were not true gifts and not eligible for deduction or credit.

(IC 75-23 Tuition fees and charitable donations paid to privately supported secular and religious schools; IT-110R3 [Archived]; *The Queen v. McBurney*, 85 DTC 5433 (F.C.A.); *Burns v. M.N.R.*, 88 DTC 6101 (F.C.T.D.); aff'd by 90 DTC 6335 (F.C.A.))

[¶1280] WHAT PROOF OF DONATIONS IS REQUIRED?

Your claim must be supported by formal receipts issued by the qualified donees to which the gifts were made. If your return is filed electronically, you must maintain the receipts and have them available for review by the CRA, should they request them. If your return is filed on paper, you must attach your receipts to your return.

If your employer withheld amounts from your pay for charitable donation purposes, it will report the amounts on your T4 Supplementary form and no further proof is required. In a few cases, charitable donations on your behalf may be reported to you on T5013 or T4A slips, and these too need no further proof of donation. You may have had amounts withheld from your pay for contributions to be made through your employees' association. To claim these contributions you must obtain a formal receipt from the association and file it with your return (unless a T4, T4A or T5013 slip has been issued on which the donation is reported).

If you are claiming the balance of a donation claimed in part on an earlier return, you should attach or retain a note identifying the year of the earlier donation and reconciling it with the amount being claimed currently. It helps to keep photocopies of receipts already submitted and write on them the amount claimed in each taxation year.

Receipts from Canadian charities and athletic associations must contain a statement that it is an official receipt for income tax purposes and show the name of the organization, its address, the registration number assigned to it by the Minister, the date and the amount of the donation. Your name (or that of your spouse or partner), including first name and initial, and full address should be clearly indicated. The receipt should be signed by a duly authorized officer of the organization, should be serially numbered, and should show where the receipt was issued from.

Receipts from other recipients of a gift such as foreign universities, Canadian municipalities or the United Nations, must also contain the above information with the exception of the registration number assigned by the Minister. Note that this requires these receipts to be either signed personally by an official of the recipient organization or serialized.

Where the donation is a gift of property other than cash, a brief description of the property should be included, as well as an estimate of the fair market value of the property if an appraisal has been performed. The name and address of the appraiser should also be included.

(ITR: Part XXXV Gifts)

[¶1285] DONATIONS TO U.S. ORGANIZATIONS

[¶1285.05] *General Rule Under Tax Treaty*

The denial of credits for donations to organizations outside Canada (except the United Nations (¶1265(3)) and certain foreign universities (¶1265(5)) and listed organizations (¶1265(6)) is modified somewhat for donations by Canadian residents to U.S. charitable organizations which are recognized as such by U.S. law and would have qualified in Canada if they had been Canadian organizations. Any donations to such U.S. charitable organizations are eligible for credit, subject to a specific restriction: the credit may not exceed the amount that would be allowed under the rules at ¶1270 if your only income in the year were your U.S.-source net income which is taxable in Canada. That is, you may claim gifts to U.S. charities subject to a limitation of 75% of your U.S.-source income. The Canada–U.S. Tax Treaty requires Canada to provide the equivalent of Canadian treatment to the extent of U.S.-source income, so that in the remote event that a U.S. taxable capital gain or recapture of capital cost allowance on the gift is included in U.S.-source income, it would seem that 25% of these amounts should be added to the 75% of U.S.-source income limitation.

Example

Throughout the year, Lou Jensen was single and resident in Canada. During the year, he made contributions to U.S. and Canadian charities of $750 and $290 respectively. His eligible donations for the year are calculated as follows:

Net income from Canadian sources		$ 8,750
Net income from U.S. sources		800
World net income		$ 9,550
Charitable donations eligible for tax credit:		
Canadian — lesser of:		
gifts made	$ 290	
75% of world net income	7,162	$ 290
U.S. — lesser of:		
gifts made	$ 750	
75% of U.S. net income	600	600
Charitable donations		$890

The excess donations to U.S. organizations, i.e., $150 ($750 - $600) will be available for carry forward against U.S. source income to the next five years.

The CRA has indicated that this special deduction for donations to U.S. charities is in addition to any deductible amounts contributed to a prescribed U.S. university (see ¶1265), although the overall limitation of 75% of net income may never be exceeded. In the above example, if Lou Jensen's $750 of U.S. donations included $200 to Harvard University, he could claim all of his donations in the year, since the donation to Harvard University would be included with the charitable Canadian donations.

(Other Publications: 1980 Canada–U.S. Tax Convention, Art. XXI(7))

[¶1285.10] *Special Rule for U.S. University Alumnae; Canadians with Relatives in U.S. Colleges and Universities*

The Canada–U.S. Tax Treaty further permits a Canadian resident to deduct donations to U.S. colleges and universities which are or were *attended by* donating Canadian taxpayers or their family members (siblings, spouses, parents, children) regardless of whether the universities are prescribed (see ¶1265(5)). Donations to U.S. universities (whether or not prescribed) in these circumstances are not subject to the 75% of U.S. income limitation, but only to the normal 75% of net world income (plus capital gain, etc.) limitation. Your family members for purposes of this rule include your brothers and sisters, whether by whole or half blood or by adoption, as well as your spouse, ancestors, lineal descendants, and adopted descendants.

(Other Publications: 1980 Canada–U.S. Tax Convention, Art. XXI(7))

[¶1285.15] *Special Rule for Commuters to the United States*

If, throughout the year, you were resident in Canada near the Canada–U.S. border and commuted to the U.S., where you worked or carried on business, and this business or employment was your chief source of income, a special provision governs your contributions to U.S. organizations. Your gifts to religious, charitable, scientific, literary or educational organizations in the U.S. — that would be deductible under the U.S. *Internal Revenue Code* — will be allowed as charitable donations in Canada subject to the 75% of net world (including Canadian) income limitation.

(ITA: 118.1(9))

[¶1287] DONATIONS TO OTHER FOREIGN CHARITIES

In general, gifts to foreign charities are not eligible for the credit. However, there are some exceptions. Donations may be claimed, subject to the general 75% of world income limitation, if made to:

(1) a university listed in Schedule VIII of the Income Tax Regulations (¶1265(5));

(2) an organization to which the government of Canada has made a contribution in the year or the preceding year (¶1265(6)); or

(3) the United Nations or agencies thereof (see ¶1265 (3)).

[¶1290] GIFT OF CAPITAL PROPERTY

As discussed earlier (¶1269), property other than cash that is gifted is deemed to have been disposed of for proceeds equal to its fair market value. The eligible amount of the gift is the fair market value less the advantage, if any, received in respect of the gift. As a consequence, where a capital property is donated, a capital gain or loss can arise. Where the property is depreciable, recapture of capital cost allowance or terminal loss can also arise. If the gift is a cultural gift (¶1268), there is no capital gain. If the gift is a qualifying ecological gift, any resulting taxable capital gain will be nil and therefore not taxable (¶1268d). Also, where a gift is made of publicly traded shares or debt, mutual fund interests, or government bonds, any taxable capital gain will be nil; see ¶1290d.05 below. Conversely, gifts of non-arm's length securities may create adverse tax consequences, as discussed at ¶1290d.15 below.

As discussed earlier, the general donation limit for charitable gifts is 75% of net income plus 25% of taxable capital gain and 25% of recapture of any capital cost allowance arising on the gift. The amount of recapture eligible for this 25% claim is specified to be the lesser of (i) recapture of that property class included in income, and (ii) the total of amounts for each gift equal to the lesser of its proceeds of disposition (minus related expenses of disposition) and its capital cost to the taxpayer. The donor still faces tax on any taxable capital gain and recapture under these rules; the benefit is that the charitable donation credit can be used on current basis to offset the current income, rather than having to suffer tax currently and use the deduction in the future.

Example

Jenny Jerome had a net income of nil in a taxation year apart from the capital gain and recapture on her gift of depreciable capital property. She donated a capital property with an adjusted cost base of $20, an undepreciated capital cost of $8 and a fair market value of $100. In the absence of capital gain and recapture, she would have had no tax for the year and been able to carry forward the $100 deduction over the next five years. However, Jenny is deemed to dispose of the property at fair market value. The capital gain is therefore $80, and the taxable capital gain (and net income) is 50% of $80 = $40. Recapture is $20 - $8 = $12. Total income is now $52. Jenny's donation is limited to 75% of net income $52 = $39, plus 25% of the taxable capital gain of $40 = $10, plus 25% of the recapture of $12 = $3, or $52. The overall limit of $52 permits Jenny to utilize credit to the extent of all the income arising from the gift in the year. There now remains a $48 carryforward.

[¶1290.05] *Losses on Donation*

Where a capital or terminal loss is created on a gift of capital property, there are no special loss limitation rules, although the general loss limitation rules on superficial loss and affiliated person transactions could apply. The loss could, of course, reduce net income and so create problems with the donation limitation, but there is no special solution for these problems.

(ITA: 69(1)(b)(ii); 118.1(6); IT-288R2 [Archived]; IT-297R2 [Archived])

[¶1290.15] *Gifts of Depreciable Property*

Since a gift involves a deemed disposition at fair market value, a gift of depreciable property used to earn income may involve recapture or terminal loss. As a general matter, where a gift of depreciable property has been made, the charitable donation credit will offset the tax in respect of any recapture and more than offset any tax in respect of capital gain, since the whole capital gain is not included in income. To the extent the deemed proceeds of disposition are less than the cost, the transaction should be a wash for tax purposes overall, although there may be a timing benefit for the donor. For example, suppose Businessman A donates an asset with a cost of $1,000, a UCC of $700, and a fair market value of $800. On a current basis he will have recapture of $100 and a donation of $800. This is the right result in a general sense, since A has tax effected a total of $1,000, composed of $200 of capital cost allowance and $800 of donation, and no longer has the asset. The important point is that proceeds of disposition of an asset on which capital cost allowance has been claimed must always be accounted for on your capital cost allowance schedule (Chapters 6, 7) and, where the asset has appreciated, on Schedule 3 (Chapter 5).

[¶1290.20] *Gifts of Property Previously Valued by Cultural Property Board*

As discussed at ¶1268 where property has been valued or revalued by the Canadian Cultural Property Export Review Board, the value last determined by the Board is binding on the donor for a period of two years for purposes both of determining the value of a gift of the property and the proceeds of disposition. However, the proceeds of disposition (but not the amount that is deemed to be the gift) may be set in accordance with the election discussed at ¶1269.10. Such a designation would be useful, for example, where the property is deemed to have been disposed of on death but has not been donated to a qualifying institution.

(ITA: 118.1(10.1))

[¶1290.25] *Gifts of Personal-Use Property*

Personal use property is defined in ¶545. It is essentially property held for the use or enjoyment of an individual, although a corporation may also hold such property for the use or enjoyment of a shareholder or related individual. As discussed at ¶547, generally the adjusted cost base and proceeds of disposition of each such property are deemed to be not less than $1,000, so where the actual adjusted cost base is less, there can be an element of tax-free capital gain. This will be true whether the property is donated or otherwise disposed of. At one time, certain tax shelters contrived to take advantage of this rule for multiple transactions (i.e., a series of works of art valued separately) to achieve a substantial charitable donation credit. However, the $1,000 cost base exemption and deemed proceeds rules simply do not apply as part of an arrangement in which the property is donated as a charitable, cultural, or ecological gift. For more detail, see ¶547. Note that Quebec has had rather different rules in place for some time to deal with such situations (see ¶1657).

(ITA: 46; 54)

[¶1290.30] *Gifts in Kind by Spouses*

Where gifts in kind (rather than in money) are made and the property gifted was held jointly by husband and wife, other than as partners in a partnership, they may choose whichever allocation is most advantageous to them for the purpose of a claim by each of them under the tax credit provisions. This discretionary allocation applies as well to subsequent year claims in respect of any unused portion of the donations. The CRA, which is being reasonably generous in this interpretation, asks that these claims should be adequately explained upon filing of the applicable income tax returns, particularly by the individual who uses the original receipt to support the claim. This position is set out in Interpretation Bulletin IT-297R2, paragraph 3.

(IT-297R2 [Archived])

[¶1290d] GIFTS OF SECURITIES

[¶1290d.05] *Gifts of Publicly Traded Securities*

Where a donor makes a gift to a qualified donee and the gift consists of:

- shares, rights, or debt obligations (typically bonds or debentures) listed on a designated stock exchange;
- shares of the capital stock of a Canadian public mutual fund corporation;
- a unit of a Canadian mutual fund trust;
- an interest in a segregated (insurance) fund trust; or
- a prescribed debt obligation, i.e., a bond, debenture, note, mortgage, or similar obligation issued or guaranteed by the government of Canada or an agent or province of Canada

the taxable capital gain on that property is nil.

Where you have made gifts which qualify for the nil capital gains inclusion rate, you do not report the disposition in the general section of Schedule 3, but rather you calculate the reduced gain on form T1170 and carry the result to the specially designated line on Schedule 3.

A designated stock exchange is one listed in items (2) and (3) at ¶2618; these include most of the world's recognized markets.

Note that there is no corresponding adjustment for capital losses; that is, a gift of securities resulting in a capital loss will yield an allowable capital loss of 50% of the loss regardless of the rate at which a gain on the same disposition would have been taxed.

Where an advantage has been conferred on the donor, so that the eligible amount of the gift is less than its fair market value (as discussed in ¶1261), only that proportion of the gift that the eligible amount is of the fair market value (actually, of the deemed or elected proceeds of disposition) is eligible for the special inclusion rate. For example, assume an individual donated public shares worth $300,000 and the donee provided the individual with a $100,000 advantage, so that the eligible amount for charitable donation deduction was $200,000. The deemed proceeds of disposition of the gift would remain $300,000. If the property originally cost $150,000, there would be a capital gain of $150,000. Of this $150,000 gain, $200,000/$300,000 = 2/3 = $100,000 will be eligible for the zero gift inclusion rate, and the remaining $50,000 will be subject to the normal capital gains inclusion rate of 50% (resulting in $25,000 of income). Accordingly, there will be a credit in respect of $200,000 (the eligible amount), more than offsetting the tax resulting from an income inclusion of $25,000.

(ITA: 38(*a*.1); 38.2; ITR: 6210 Prescribed Shares)

[¶1290d.07] *Gift of Publicly Traded Securities Received on Exchange of Other Shares or Partnership Interest*

The nil capital gain inclusion rate for gifts of publicly traded securities is extended to permit holders of unqualified (unlisted) securities, which have an exchange feature permitting conversion to a publicly traded security, to exercise the exchange feature free of capital gain provided the publicly traded shares received on the exchange are donated to a qualified charity within 30 days of the exchange.

In particular, this nil capital gains inclusion rate will apply to gains arising on the exchange of securities where the securities received are qualified publicly traded securities, provided

(a) the exchange occurs pursuant to an exchange feature of the shares given up, which exchange provision was included in the shares given up at the time they were issued and at the time of disposition;

(b) no consideration is received by the donor on the exchange except the exchanged shares; and

(c) the publicly traded securities received meet the conditions in ¶1290d.05, above, and are donated to a qualified donee not more than 30 days after the exchange.

A similar rule applies where partnership interests are exchanged for publicly traded shares, subject to rules intended to limit the nil capital gains inclusion to gains that reflect economic appreciation of the partnership interest and not gains arising from adjusted cost base reductions to the partnership interest. For the partnership exchange rule to apply, the partnership interest must first meet the three rules ((a) to (c)) above (on the assumption that the partnership interest were shares). Where the partnership interest meets those conditions, the taxable capital gain on the exchange is the lesser of

(d) the taxable capital gain that would be determined under the exchange rules for shares, and

(e) one-half of the amount (if any) by which

(1) the cost to the donor of the exchanged partnership interest (including any contributions to partnership capital by the donor) exceeds

(2) the adjusted cost base to the donor of that interest (determined without reference to distributions of partnership capital).

(ITA: 38(*a*.1)(iii), (*a*.3))

[¶1290d.10] *Gifts of Shares Acquired with Employee Options*

As discussed at ¶330, employee stock or mutual fund options normally involve an employment benefit either when the options are exercised or when the shares acquired with them are sold. That benefit is reduced by an offsetting deduction from taxable income so that it is in effect taxed at capital gain rates rather than employment income rates.

If you make a charitable donation to a qualified donee of publicly traded shares or units acquired under a stock or mutual fund option plan to which the employee income inclusion/deduction rules at ¶330 apply, and the shares or units are donated within 30 days of acquiring them through the exercise of the options (and within the same taxation year), the other half of the benefit is deductible in computing your taxable income, meaning that the net taxable income inclusion is nil.

This treatment is intended to be comparable to the capital gain treatment on share/unit donations discussed above.

These rules are discussed in greater detail at ¶330.

(ITA: 110(1)(*d*.01))

[¶1290d.15] *Gifts of Non-Qualified Securities*

These are not the mirror image of the securities described above; rather, non-qualifying securities are essentially securities issued by a non-arm's length party.

Specifically, a non-qualifying security in relation to an individual or an estate or trust at a particular time (such as the time of a donation) means:

(1) an obligation (except (i) an obligation of a financial institution — i.e., a member of the Canadian Payments Association or a credit union that is part of an organization that is a member — to repay an amount deposited with the institution, or (ii) an obligation listed on a designated stock exchange) of the individual or the individual's estate or of any person or partnership with which the individual or estate does not deal at arm's length immediately after that time;

(2) a share (other than one listed on a designated stock exchange) of the capital stock of a corporation with which the individual or the estate does not deal at arm's length or, in the case of a trust, with which the trust is affiliated immediately after that time;

(3) a beneficial interest of the individual or estate in a trust that:

(a) immediately after that time is affiliated with the individual or estate, or

(b) holds, immediately after that time, a non-qualifying security of the individual or estate, or held, before that time, a share described in (2), above, that is, after that time, held by the donee; or

(4) any other security (other than one listed on a designated stock exchange) issued by the individual or the estate or any person or partnership with which the individual or estate does not deal at arm's length or, in the case of a trust, with which the individual or the estate is affiliated immediately after that time.

A designated stock exchange is one listed in items (2) and (3) at ¶2618.

The concept of non-arm's length is considered in ¶812.

Excepted Gifts: Notwithstanding the definition above, a non-qualified security will not be subject to the restrictions described below if all the following conditions are met: (a) the security is a share; (b) the donee is not a private foundation; (c) the taxpayer deals at arm's length with the donee; and (d) where the donee is a charitable organization or a public foundation, the taxpayer deals at arm's length with each director, trustee, officer and like official of the donee.

Commentary on Bill C-29 Measures (Oct. 25, 2016)

Note: When Bill C-29, October 25, 2016, achieves Royal Assent, the commentary will be modified to read:

Excepted Gifts: Notwithstanding the definition above, a non-qualified security will not be subject to the restrictions described below if all the following conditions are met: (a) the security is a share; (b) the donee is not a private foundation; (c) the taxpayer deals at arm's length with the donee, or, for 2016 and subsequent taxation years, if the taxpayer is an individual's graduated rate estate, the individual dealt at arm's length with the donee immediately before death and the graduated rate estate deals at arm's length with the donee (without regard to 251(1)(*b*)); and (d) where the donee is a charitable organization or a public foundation, the taxpayer deals at arm's length with each director, trustee, officer and like official of the donee.

Gifts of a "non-qualifying security" (NQS) other than an excepted gift are ignored for purposes of all the charitable donation rules (but not the capital gain recognition rules) at ¶1267 to ¶1270; that is to say, no tax credit is permitted at the time the gift is made. However, if:

(1) the donee disposes of the NQS within five years after the gift is made, the gift is considered to be made at the time of that later disposition. The fair market value of the gift, if and when it is recognized, is the lesser of (i) the fair market value of the consideration received by the donee on its disposition (except, prior to March 22, 2011, to the extent that the consideration is another NQS of the same donor and, from March 22, 2011, another NQS of any other person), and (ii) the fair market value of the gift at the time it was originally contributed by the donor to the donee. In short, a gift of NQS will be recognized upon subsequent disposition by the recipient, and that subsequent disposition will fix the maximum (but not the minimum) value of the charitable donation. See also the anti-avoidance rules discussed below.

(2) the security ceases to be a non-qualified security within five years after the gift is made (presumably because, for example, the security becomes publicly traded or the non-arm's length relationship is severed), the gift is considered to be made at the time of that cessation of non-qualified status. The fair market value of the gift, if and when it is recognized, is the lesser of (i) the fair market value at the time of cessation of non-qualified status, and (ii) the fair market value of the gift at the time it was originally contributed by the donor to the donee.

Capital gains and losses are recognized at the time of the actual disposition, but a special reserve is allowed which defers recognition of any capital gain until the year in which a disposition by the recipient triggers recognition of the offsetting contribution, or the security ceases to be non-qualified, as the case may be, to a maximum of five years. As with most reserves, the non-qualified property reserve is optional; that is, you may claim as much as you wish up to the entire gain from the disposition in question. The reserve claimed at the end of each year is brought back into income the following year, and may be claimed again from year to year to the extent of the prior year reserve. That is, once you choose to forgo part or all of the reserve and recognize any portion of the gain for a year, you cannot claim a larger reserve in a subsequent year.

Where an individual makes an NQS gift and recognition of gain occurs in a later year, the addition to net income limitation of 25% of the capital gain discussed in ¶1270 and ¶1290 will apply in that later year. As well, the election described at ¶1269.10 can be made in that later year.

Where an individual makes an NQS gift and dies before the donee disposes of the NQS or the NQS status is eliminated within the five-year period, the individual's gift will be considered to have been made in the year of death rather than the time of the later disposition, so the appropriate gain and tax credit can be recognized on terminal returns.

The five-year period runs for 60 months from the day on which (literally from the particular time at which) the donor makes the original gift.

An anti-avoidance rule applies from March 22, 2011, where, as a result of a series of transactions, (i) a donor makes a gift of a particular property to a donee, (ii) a particular person holds an NQS of the donor, and (iii) the donee has acquired, directly or indirectly, an NQS of the particular person or of the donor. Where the rule applies, the fair market value of the gift of the particular property is reduced by the fair market value of the NQS acquired by the donee, and the donor is deemed to have made a gift of the NQS equal to the actual fair market value of the particular property in excess of the fair market value of the particular property after the above-noted reduction. The gift of the NQS will then be subject to the NQS rules described above. For example, if the fair market value of a gifted particular property is $120,000 and the fair market value of the NQS acquired by the qualified donee is $100,000, the donor will have made a gift of the particular property with a deemed fair market value of $20,000, and to have made a gift of an NQS with a fair market value of $100,000. The latter gift will be subject to the NQS rules, such that the gift will be deferred until such time as the donee has disposed of the NQS for consideration that is not, to any person, another NQS, if such disposition occurs within five years of the original gift.

There are also complex provisions to grind the value of a gift where through a series of loan-back or non-arm's length arrangements with a charity a taxpayer contrives a charitable deduction without having to forgo the use of the donated funds or property.

(ITA: 40(1.01); 118.1(13)–(20))

[¶1290g] GIFT OF INVENTORY OR SERVICES

As with capital property, a gift of inventory or other non-capital property is considered a disposition at fair market value. An exception applies to art inventory, as discussed at ¶1291.

The CRA says in Interpretation Bulletin IT-297R2 that the donation rules do not apply to donations of property where the cost has been or should be charged as a business expense. "For example," it says, "if a taxpayer transfers merchandise or supplies to a charity in consideration of a right, privilege, material benefit or advantage such as promotion or advertising for the taxpayer's business, then the transfer would not be a gift." Presumably, the same result is obtained by offsetting the value of the property transferred by the advantage conferred on the business.

A gift of services is not a gift of property and does not generate a donation credit. Where a taxpayer wants to provide services to a charity and appear as a donor, it can agree with the charity to bill for its services and give a cross cheque back as a charitable donation. Its income from the services (which must be recognized for tax purposes) will be offset by the donation (subject to the 75% income limitation). The transaction will normally be a wash for tax purposes.

(ITA: 69(1); IT-110R3 [Archived]; IT-297R2 [Archived])

[¶1290g.15] *Gift of Medicine in Inventory*

Special treatment is accorded *to corporations only* for gifts of medicine in inventory. See the companion Wolters Kluwer volume *Preparing Your Corporate Tax Returns* at ¶4047 of that book.

[¶1291] GIFT OF ARTIST'S INVENTORY

Artists who create works of art for sale must in general treat the works as inventory of a business. However, a special rule (¶789) allows them to value that inventory at nil, with the result that they can treat the costs incurred in creating the inventory as deductions from income as they are incurred. When the inventory is sold, the full price is income, since the offsetting costs have already been deducted. This is usually preferred to treating the costs as a cost of inventory, in which case the deductions can only be taken when the inventory is sold.

As with capital property, the general rule is that inventory donated to a charity, which may include a museum or art gallery if registered, is considered to be disposed of for proceeds equal to its fair market value. Accordingly, absent any other rules, a gift of artist's inventory would result in a wash transaction: the value of the property would be included in income and the tax payable would be offset by a charitable donation credit.

A technical problem would arise if the value of the property exceeded 75% of net income, for then the income would be wholly recognized in the year but the charitable donation would be limited, resulting in tax payable and a charitable donation carryover for use in future years. The problem can be resolved by the election noted below.

[¶1291.05] *Inventory That Does Not Qualify as Cultural Canadian Property*

An artist can elect, in the tax return for the year of the donation, to set an amount that is deemed to be both the proceeds of disposition of the donated art and its fair market value for the purposes of determining the eligible amount of the gift. The election is allowed if the fair market value of the art exceeds its cost amount (inventory value). The elected amount may not exceed the fair market value of the art and may not be less than the greater of the cost amount and any advantage in respect of the gift.

This provision applies only to works of art created by an individual donor that are inventory of the donor; i.e., the donor must be in the business of creating works of art. The artist (or his or her executor if the gift is by will) must designate the elected value in the tax return and obtain a charitable donation receipt acknowledging the gift.

[¶1291.10] *Inventory That Qualifies as Cultural Canadian Property*

An artist that makes a gift of inventory that qualifies as a gift of cultural property (¶1268) is deemed to have disposed of the art for proceeds equal to the greater of the cost amount of the art and the advantage, if any, received in respect of the gift. However, the amount of the gift that qualifies for the credit is still based on the eligible amount of the gift (the fair market value less any advantage).

Application for certification (which is usually made jointly by the donee and donor) is made to the:

Canadian Cultural Property Export Review Board
300 Slater Street
Ottawa, ON
K1A 0C8
Telephone: (613) 990-4161.

[¶1291.15] *Artist's Inventory on Death*

Where the charitable donation arises as a result of death prior to 2016, the donation is deemed to be made immediately before death, so that the above rules clearly apply to the year of death return rather than the estate. As well, where the art in question is transferred to a beneficiary under the "rights or things" rules in ¶1908, so that proceeds would be taxable to the beneficiary and not the deceased, the beneficiary can make the same donation with the same results for the beneficiary as if the artist had made the donation. Where death occurs after 2015, a donation made by the deceased's graduated rate estate can be reported either by the estate or as though it were made by the deceased. See Chapter 19.

[¶1291.20] *Property That is Not Inventory*

The donation by an artist, author or composer of property such as diaries or correspondence, or by an author or composer of original manuscripts or similar papers is generally considered to be a disposition of capital property, since it is not usually the business of the artist to sell such property. It is then subject to the rules at ¶1290.

(ITA: 118.1(1), (3), (7), (7.1); IT-288R2, para. 7 [Archived]; IT-504R2 [Archived])

[¶1292] GIFT OF A RESIDUAL INTEREST

A donation credit may be claimed for the gift of a residual interest of a trust or estate to a qualified donee. To be eligible, the gift must vest at the time it is given. The valuation of the residual interest will vary according to the type of gift, the interest retained, and the wording of the document that sets out the gift. The general approach is to value the life interest using the present fair market value of the property, current interest rates and the life expectancy of the life tenant, and to deduct this amount from the value of the total gift or bequest to arrive at the value of the residual interest.

In cases where the residual interest is not reasonably ascertainable, such as when the life tenant has a right to encroach on capital, no deduction will be allowed as a charitable donation.

For general information, see Interpretation Bulletin IT-226R, "Gift to a Charity of a Residual Interest in Real Property or an Equitable Interest in a Trust".

(ITA: 110(1)(*a*), (*b*); 118.1(1); IT-226R [Archived])

[¶1293] CRA COLLECTION OF 50% OF DISPUTED AMOUNTS IN TAX SHELTER DONATIONS

Generally, if an individual taxpayer objects to or appeals an assessment or reassessment, the CRA is prohibited from taking any collection actions in respect of the amount in dispute until the issue is ultimately resolved or the taxpayer abandons the objection or appeal. However, the CRA is authorized to collect half of the disputed tax, interest, or penalties, where the taxpayer has objected to or appealed the CRA's disallowance of a tax credit claimed in respect of a tax shelter (as defined in subsection 237.1(1)). This measure applies to 2013 and subsequent taxation years.

HOW TO CLAIM CHARITABLE DONATIONS

[¶1294] CHARITABLE DONATIONS

No schedule is provided to list your charitable donations, but you must complete Schedule 9 to determine the amount eligible for a charitable donation tax credit. You should total the amounts on your current year donation receipts, plus any amounts donated in the preceding five years (or, for ecological property, 10 years) for which you have not yet claimed donation credit, on line 1 of Schedule 9. Schedule 9 will compare the result to 75% of your net income as shown at line 236 of your T1 return, which is the usual limit for such gifts. If you made gifts of capital property, Schedule 9 will increase the 75% limit to offset any capital gain and/or recapture of capital cost allowance realized in the year on the gift, as described at ¶1270. The federal tax credit is calculated at different rates for the donations:

(1) 15% on the first $200 of donations;

(2) 33% on the lesser of

(i) excess of donations over $200 and

(ii) taxable income over $200,000; and

(3) 29% on excess of donations over $200 not subject to the 33% rate

Lines are provided on Schedule 9 for this calculation, following line 344.

IMPORTANT POINTS TO REMEMBER — CHARITABLE DONATIONS

[¶1295] IMPORTANT POINTS TO REMEMBER — CHARITABLE DONATIONS

- Three different rates must be used (15%, 29%, and 33%) to calculate the charitable donations tax credit of a taxpayer with a taxable income over $200,000 and a charitable donation over $200.
- Use Schedule 9 to determine the actual amount eligible for charitable donation credit.

- Attach your receipts in support of any charitable donations claimed if you paper-file your return, but keep copies for your records. If you are filing electronically, keep the receipts with your tax records so you can show them to the CRA on request.
- Although a list of charitable donations is not required, you may want to make your own list to ensure that all donations are recorded and properly totalled. Do not forget to take into consideration any donations made in the five immediately preceding taxation years (10 years for ecological gifts) to the extent that they were not deducted in those years.
- You may not deduct charitable donations in excess of 75% of your net income, except that gifts of capital property extend the 75% limit to cover another 25% of taxable capital gain and recapture of capital cost allowance arising in the year from the gifts (¶1270 and ¶1290). Deductions which are in excess of the limitation may be carried forward. A suggested format for listing donations and calculating the limitation is found at ¶1263.
- No capital gain is taxable on gifts of capital property consisting of publicly traded shares and bonds, and certain other investments are subject to a reduced capital gains tax when disposed of by gift to a qualified donee. If you have made gifts which qualify for this treatment, do not report the dispositions in the usual fashion on Schedule 3, but rather on form T1170, where the reduced gain is calculated and then carried to Schedule 3. See ¶1290d. Note that if you made a gift of publicly traded securities acquired with stock options exercised, comparable relief is available from the employment income inclusion on those shares. See ¶330.
- Gifts of securities (other than a publicly-traded securities) issued by the donor or anyone not at arm's length from the donor do not give rise to charitable donation credit unless and until they are disposed of by the recipient charity within five years of the gift; see ¶1290d.
- Certified cultural property is not subject to capital gains tax on the disposition of the property by gift to designated institutions, and the 75% income limit does not apply to such gifts; see ¶1268.
- Gifts of certified ecologically sensitive land and related rights are not subject to capital gains tax on the disposition of the property to specified recipients. See ¶1268d.
- If you took back consideration for a gift or the gift is subject to an anti-avoidance provision which reduces its value to you, you are obliged to disclose this to the donee before the receipt is issued. See ¶1261.
- Individuals who file Ontario returns are given the option on page 4 of contributing part or all of any tax refund to the Province of Ontario. If you designated such an amount on line 465 of your return for a year, that gift would be a gift eligible for credit for the next year (i.e., the year the refund is donated).

SPECIFIC QUESTIONS AND ANSWERS — CHARITABLE DONATIONS

[¶1298] SPECIFIC QUESTIONS AND ANSWERS

Pledges

During the year, I pledged $2,500 to my church's building fund payable over five years. I actually paid the first $500 on December 1. Is the full $2,500 eligible as a charitable donation for the year?

No. Only the $500 actually paid is eligible for claim. The balance may be deducted when it is actually paid.

Donations of Shares

I donated my publicly traded shares in a large Canadian company to McGill University. The stock had a market value at that date of $3,000 and my cost was $2,000. What amount is eligible as a charitable donation for the year?

Your tax credit will be based on a gift of $3,000. Assuming no other gifts, the federal credit (subject to the charitable donation limit) will be 15% of the first $200 and 29% of the remaining $2,800 if your taxable income is $200,000 or less. If your taxable income is in excess of $200,000, the lesser of: (1) the donation over $200 [$2,800]; and (2) the taxable income over $200,000 will be subject to a 33% tax credit rate. For additional information on this calculation, see ¶1263. Your gift will be considered a disposition at fair market value and give rise to a capital gain of $1,000, but as the shares are publicly traded, the inclusion rate on that gain will be nil. You must fill out form T1170 and follow the directions thereon about filing. Your charitable donation limit will be 75% of your net income for the year. In all likelihood, the limitation will permit you to claim the entire tax credit for the year, unless your income is extremely low. See ¶1290.

Donations of Merchandise

I operated an unincorporated retail appliance business during the year and I donated six table radios from my regular inventory to Toronto General Hospital. Will the value of these radios — $150 — be eligible as a charitable donation?

No. You cannot deduct the value of merchandise where its cost has been deducted in computing your income from a business unless you include the value of the merchandise in your income (¶1269).

Volunteer Workers

I worked as a volunteer canvasser for my church's building fund for a considerable length of time — one month in all — during the year. May I claim a charitable donation for the value of my services?

No. Only gifts in money or property are eligible and gifts in the form of free services do not qualify. Furthermore, you may not claim any expenses you incurred in connection with the canvassing work.

Gift of Property

On October 10, I sold a house to my church for $25,000. The fair market value of the house at that date was $50,000. May I claim the $25,000 difference as a charitable donation?

Yes, assuming your church is a registered charity. You may obtain a charitable donation credit for the fair market value ($50,000) less the advantage you received back ($25,000). Note, however, that there must be firm evidence of the fair market value of the house at the time of the gift. The CRA prefers a professional appraisal just prior to sale by an appraiser who is independent of both you and the charity. However, if you can document sales of similar properties in your neighbourhood at about the same time, that may suffice. If you take back value which is more than 80% of the value of the house, it almost certainly will not suffice, and an independent professional appraisal will be essential.

Worthy Causes

During the year, I contributed $300 towards the support of a needy child in our neighbourhood who was not related to me. May I claim the $300 as a charitable donation?

No. Private acts of benevolence do not qualify — no matter how worthy the cause. The contribution must be to a charitable organization.

Chapter 13

Other Personal Tax Credits

THESE POINTS ARE COVERED IN THIS CHAPTER

CRA REFERENCES RELATING TO THIS CHAPTER

T1 Lines and Schedules

- Line 115 — Other pensions and superannuation
- Line 129 — RRSP income (from all T4RSP slips)
- Line 222 — Deduction for CPP or QPP contributions on self-employment and other earnings
- Line 260 — Taxable income
- Line 421 — CPP contributions payable on self-employment and other earnings
- Line 448 — CPP overpayment
- Line 450 — Employment Insurance overpayment
- Line 459 — Children's fitness credit
- Federal Worksheet, Line 314 — Pension income amount

- Schedule 1, Line 308 — CPP or QPP contributions through employment from box 16 and box 17 on all T4 slips
- Schedule 1, Line 310 — CPP or QPP contributions on self-employment and other earnings
- Schedule 1, Line 312 — Employment Insurance premiums through employment from box 18 and box 55 on all T4 slips
- Schedule 1, Line 313 — Adoption expenses
- Schedule 1, Line 314 — Pension income amount
- Schedule 1, Line 317 — Employment Insurance premiums on self-employment and other eligible earnings
- Schedule 1, Line 319 — Interest paid on your student loans
- Schedule 1, Line 323 — Your tuition, education, and textbook amounts
- Schedule 1, Line 324 — Tuition, education, and textbook amounts transferred from a child
- Schedule 1, Line 326 — Amounts transferred from your spouse or common-law partner
- Schedule 1, Line 362 — Volunteer firefighters' amount
- Schedule 1, Line 363 — Canada employment amount
- Schedule 1, Line 364 — Public transit amount
- Schedule 1, Line 369 — Home buyers' amount
- Schedule 1, Line 370 — Children's arts amount
- Schedule 1, Line 395 — Search and rescue volunteer amount
- Schedule 2 — Federal amounts transferred from your spouse or common-law partner
- Schedule 8 — Canada Pension Plan contributions and overpayment for 2016
- Schedule 11 — Tuition, education, and textbook amounts
- Schedule 13 — Employment Insurance premiums on self-employment and other eligible earnings

CRA Guides

5000-G, "General Income Tax and Benefit Guide"; **5013-G**, "General Income Tax and Benefit Guide for Non-Residents and Deemed Residents of Canada"; **P105**, "Students and Income Tax"; **P119**, "When You Retire"; **RC190**, "Information for Educational Institutions Outside Canada"

CRA Forms

CPT20, "Election to Pay Canada Pension Plan Contributions"; **T4**, "Statement of Remuneration Paid"; **T4E**, "Statement of Employment Insurance and Other Benefits"; **T4EQ**, "Statement of Employment Insurance and Other Benefits [Quebec]"; **T4RIF**, "Statement of Income from a Registered Retirement Income Fund"; **T4RSP**, "Statement of RRSP Income"; **T451**, "Notice of Assessment"; **T491**, "Notice of Reassessment"; **T1032**, "Joint Election to Split Pension Income"; **T2202A**, "Tuition, Education and Textbook Amounts Certificate"; **T2204**, "Employee Overpayment of Canada Pension Plan Contributions and Employment Insurance Premiums"; **TL11A**, "Tuition, Education and Textbook Amounts Certificate — University Outside Canada"; **TL11B**, "Tuition, Education, and Textbook Amounts Certificate — Flying School or Club"; **TL11C**, "Tuition, Education, and Textbook Amounts Certificate — Commuter to the United States"; **TL11D**, "Tuition Fees Certificate — Educational Institutions Outside Canada For a Deemed Resident of Canada"

Income Tax Folios

S1-F2-C1, "Education and Textbook Tax Credits"

S1-F2-C2, "Tuition Tax Credit";

S1-F2-C3, "Scholarships, Research Grants and Other Education Assistance";

Interpretation Bulletins

IT-523, "Order of Provisions Applicable in Computing an Individual's Taxable Income and Tax Payable" (Archived by the CRA)

Information Circulars

75-23, "Tuition Fees and Charitable Donations Paid to Privately Supported Secular and Religious Schools"

Income Tax Technical News

No. 13, May 7, 1998, "Employer-Paid Educational Costs (Archived by the CRA)";

No. 22, January 11, 2002, "Employee Benefits — Question 9 (Archived by the CRA)"

WHAT YOU SHOULD KNOW ABOUT TAX CREDITS

RECENT CHANGES

Bill C-15

School Supplies Tax Credit

Effective for 2016 and subsequent taxation years, teachers may claim a school supplies tax credit. This provides a refundable credit of up to $150 per year for an eligible educator with respect to eligible supplies expenses incurred by that educator. See ¶1360b.

Children's Arts Tax Credit

The maximum eligible amount for the children's arts tax credit is reduced from $500 to $250 for the 2016 taxation year. The credit will be discontinued after 2016.

Children's Fitness Tax Credit

The maximum eligible amount for the refundable children's fitness tax credit is reduced from $1,000 to $500 for the 2016 taxation year. The credit will be discontinued after 2016.

Education and Textbook Credits

The education and textbook tax credits are repealed effective January 1, 2017. Unused amounts may be carried forward indefinitely.

Family Tax Cut Credit

The family tax credit was eliminated for 2016 and subsequent taxation years.

[¶1303] TAX CREDIT CONVERSION RATE

The non-refundable tax credits discussed in this chapter (and Chapters 11 and 12) are expressed on Schedule 1 of your tax return as amounts which are then converted to tax credits at line 338. The rate at which these amounts are converted to tax credits is generally (always, for the federal government) fixed at the lowest marginal income tax rate of 15%.

Personal amounts for provincial purposes are usually (except in Quebec) set at the lowest provincial marginal rate, as calculated on the provincial portion of your return (or on the separate Quebec return).

TAX CREDITS FOR CPP/QPP CONTRIBUTIONS AND EI PREMIUMS

[¶1305] TAX CREDIT FOR CANADA AND QUEBEC PENSION PLAN CONTRIBUTIONS

You are entitled to a tax credit equal to 15% of the Canada Pension Plan (CPP) and Quebec Pension Plan (QPP) contributions you should have paid in the year. To claim this credit, you enter the eligible contributions at line 308 and/or 310, as the case may be, and convert the total, together with other amounts eligible for credit, at line 338 by multiplying by 15%. Contrary to other personal amounts, eligible CPP and QPP contributions are not annually indexed and vary from year to year according to specific criteria.

[¶1305.05] *Employees' CPP/QPP Contributions*

These are your share as an employee of CPP/QPP contributions, which your employer or employers have withheld from your pay on account of this liability; this does not include amounts which your employer has been required to contribute on your behalf. For employees, these contributions are shown in box 16 of your T4 slip for the year (box 17 for QPP contributions). If you have had more than one employment, you may have overcontributed. This will be the case if the total of amounts from box 16 and/or box 17 of each T4 is greater than $2,544.30 for any employee outside Quebec and $2,737.05 for a Quebec employee. In this case, you are entitled to the CPP credit only for 15% of $2,544.30; you should enter $2,544.30 at line 308 of your T1 and claim a refund for any contribution in excess of $2,544.30 on line 448 of your T1 return if you are filing a return for a province other than Quebec. If you are filing a federal return for Quebec, you still claim the QPP credit to a maximum of $2,737.05 credit on line 308 of the federal return but claim your refund of any excess on line 452 of your Quebec provincial return.

Example

Donna Johnston had three jobs in the year, and her CPP contributions on her three T4 slips are:

$ 835.87
871.68
997.77
$2,705.32

Donna should enter $2,544.30 at line 308 and $2,705.32 - $2,544.30 = $161.02 at line 448.

If as an employee you did not contribute the full amount of $2,544.30, it is possible that you have contributed less than you are allowed. Common situations in which you might have employment earnings which have not been subjected to full CPP withholding are: you had more than one job in the year; you had income, such as tips, from which your employer did not have to withhold contributions (except in Quebec); or, you were in a type of employment not covered by CPP rules, such as casual employment.

If you contributed less than $2,544.30 and you had employment earnings which were not subject to CPP withholding, you have the option of paying 9.9% on any portion of your pensionable earnings that was not subject to contributions to bring the amount up to $2,544.30 (or whatever lesser amount is 9.9% of pensionable earnings). You would do this to increase your eventual CPP/QPP pension. The 9.9% represents your ordinary employee share of 4.95% plus the equal employer share which of course was not matched on the amount that was not, for whatever reason, withheld.

Pensionable earnings are (for 2016) earnings between $3,500 and $54,900. (The maximum 2016 employee contribution of $2,544.30 is 4.95% of [$54,900 - $3,500] = $51,400.) To make the additional contribution you must obtain form CPT20 from your Tax Services Office and submit it, together with payment of the additional contribution, by April 30, 2018. Technically, only payment is required by April 30, 2018; the form itself is not finally required until June 15, 2018. It follows that you may submit form CPT20 either with your return or separately. However, although form CPT20 includes the necessary calculations for determining the additional contribution you can make, it requires the use of Schedule 8 of your return for the year of contribution, so that you should file it currently where possible. See also ¶1491. Employees filing a federal T1 return for Quebec do not use form CPT20 for this purpose. Quebec provincial returns provide for optional additional contributions in a work chart for line 248, and federal T1 returns for Quebec have a slightly different version of Schedule 8, which is driven off the Quebec provincial return income numbers and provides for the optional contribution calculated for Quebec purposes.

[¶1305.10] *Self-Employment Contributions*

If you are self-employed (¶304 and ¶700) for all or part of the year, you are responsible, in effect, for the employer's as well as the employee's contributions to the Canada Pension Plan or Quebec Pension Plan. The total contribution must be calculated on Schedule 8 of your T1.

Since Schedule 8 is calculating CPP/QPP contributions on your self-employment income, it accumulates business income from lines 122 and 135 to 143 of your T1 return.

Contributions you (and your employer, if you were also employed at any time during the year) have already made for the year are backed out of the amount you are required to contribute on self-employment earnings (at line 9 of Schedule 8), and any remaining contribution is entered at line 421 as a special payment of tax (unless you are a resident of Quebec, in which case it is calculated and entered on the Quebec return). For 2016, your total carried from Schedule 8 to line 421 cannot exceed $5,089.

As with CPP/QPP on employment earnings, you get a tax credit for your self- employment contributions in calculating income tax. Half of the amount payable on self-employment earnings (the employer's half, as it were) is a deduction from income, entered on line 222 of your T1 return. The other half (the employee's half) is entered on line 310 of Schedule 1, along with your employee contributions if you also had employment income. Even if you are a Quebec resident, you can enter the self-employment contributions off (the Quebec version of) Schedule 8 on lines 222 and 310 of your federal return, since the federal treatment of the result of the QPP calculation is the same as for CPP.

[¶1305.15] *Where No Liability for CPP/QPP*

The various components of the CPP liability calculation (illustrated on Schedule 8, and consisting of pensionable earnings, basic exemption, maximum earnings) are prorated on a monthly basis to exclude months in the year:

- in which you are not yet 18 years of age (thus exclude the month in which you turn 18);
- throughout which you are 70 years of age or older (thus do not exclude the month in which you turn 70);
- for any part of which you are in receipt of (or entitled to receive) a CPP/QPP retirement or disability pension;
- for which you were a CPP working beneficiary and elected to stop paying CPP contributions; or
- which, in the year of death, follow the month of death.

If, because of any of these situations, you have overpaid your contribution, you would usually report the full amount paid (up to $2,544.30 for an employee outside Quebec and $2,737.05 for a Quebec employee) and allow the CRA's computers to prorate the contribution for periods of ineligibility based on your age or pension information slips and issue the appropriate refund. However, employees have the alternative of using form T2204, which permits you to calculate your overpayment, if any, and claim a refund at line 448. The form also corrects the employee's credit calculation at line 308.

Schedule 8 makes no allowance for such overpayments when calculating self-employment contributions, and the CRA provides no alternative calculations. Instead, you are asked to complete Schedule 8 and pay the full liability calculated (and claim credit thereon), and permit the CRA's computers to prorate your contribution for periods of ineligibility based on your age or pension information slips. The difference will be accounted for on your Notice of Assessment.

[¶1305.20] *General Comment*

Uniquely on the T1 return, it is essential to report both the dollars and cents you have contributed to CPP/QPP. That is, you should always calculate the exact amount in both dollars and cents and enter this at line 308 or 310, as the case may be. Failure to include the cents may impair your eventual pension amount.

Beginning January 1, 2012, you must make contributions to the CPP or the QPP if:

- you are at least 60 years of age but under 70;
- you are employed or self-employed; and
- you are receiving a CPP or QPP retirement pension.

However, if you are at least 65 years of age, but under 70, you can elect to stop contributing to the CPP or revoke an election made in a prior year.

- If you are employed, you must complete Form CPT30, Election to Stop Contributing to the Canada Pension Plan or Revocation of a Prior Election and submit the form to the CRA and your employer(s).
- If you are self-employed, you must complete the applicable part of Schedule 8, Canada Pension Plan Contributions and Overpayment. Indicate in box 372, the month you choose to start the election. Indicate in box 374, the month you choose to revoke the election.

- If you are both employed and self-employed, you must complete form CPT30. The form will apply to all income from pensionable earnings, including self-employment earnings as of the first day of the month after the date you gave the form to your employer. If you want to elect to stop CPP contributions on self-employment earnings on an earlier date, enter the month in Schedule 8 on box 372 or box 374 if you want to revoke an election. If you did not complete and submit form CPT30 for 2016 when you became employed, you cannot elect to stop CPP contribution payments or revoke a prior year election on your self-employment earnings for 2016 on Schedule 8.

(ITA: 118.7; T1 Guide)

[¶1307] TAX CREDIT FOR EMPLOYMENT INSURANCE PREMIUMS

The federal government has ceded some points of Employment Insurance (EI) premium to allow Quebec to operate for its residents a modified supplemental version of the EI plan called the Quebec Provincial Parental Insurance Plan (PPIP). Accordingly, instructions are different for Quebec residents and residents of other provinces, and Quebec residents with business and/or out-of-province employment income of $2,000 or more must use a Schedule 10 not provided to residents of other provinces.

On June 26, 2013, Bill C-48, *Technical Tax Amendments Act, 2012*, received Royal Assent, becoming S.C. 2013, c. 34. Bill C-48 enacts numerous technical amendments including the 2010 technical amendments to provide for a tax credit in respect of premiums paid under the Quebec Parental Insurance Plan ("QPIP").

On, September 9, 2013, the federal government froze the Employment Insurance (EI) premium rate for employees at the 2013 level of $1.88 per $100 of insurable earnings. This figure did not change for 2015 and 2016. For residents of Quebec, covered under the QPIP, the EI premium rate is $1.54 per $100 of insurable earnings in 2015 and $1.52 per $100 of insurable earnings in 2016.

On September 11, 2014, the Honourable Minister of Finance Joe Oliver announced the introduction of the Small Business Job Credit, applicable to any 2015 or 2016 payer of employer EI premiums of $15,000 or less. The mechanics of the credit are such that the CRA will automatically recalculate employer EI premiums from the 2015 and 2016 legislated rate of $1.88 to $1.60 per $100 of insurable earnings, with a refund of any amount past outstanding balances in payroll accounts. As well, an equivalent rate of $0.28 is to be applied to the EI premium in Quebec, owing to the different EI rates applicable under the Quebec Parental Insurance Plan. Parties are required to either record the credit as business income or treat it as a reduction of EI expense when filing a business return for the year in which the credit is received.

Contrary to other personal amounts, those eligible contributions are not annually indexed and vary from year to year according to specific criteria.

[¶1307.05] *Residents of All Provinces and Territories other than Quebec*

You are entitled to a tax credit equal to 15% of the Employment Insurance (EI) premiums you should have paid in the year. To claim this credit, you enter the eligible premiums at line 312 of Schedule 1 of your T1 and convert it, together with other amounts eligible for credit, at line 338 by multiplying by 15%.

EI premiums are shown in box 18 of your T4 slips. If you have had more than one job in the year and therefore have more than one T4, you should total the amounts in box 18 of each slip and enter the total at line 312.

If you were employed in Quebec during the year, you may also have Quebec PPIP amounts reported in box 55 of your T4 slips, and a Quebec RL-1 slip in respect of your Quebec income in addition to your T4 in respect of that income, even if you are a non-resident of Quebec at the end of the year. The box 55 amounts are also included in the total at line 312. You do not use the RL-1 slip in your federal calculations, but should file it along with your T4 with your federal return. As a non-resident of Quebec at the end of the year, you will not file a Quebec return for the year, but the federal government will take account of your PPIP premiums in determining your federal EI amounts.

The maximum earnings on which you as an employee could make EI contributions for 2016 was $50,800, and the contribution rate was 1.88%, so that any contributions in excess of $955.04 are on their face excessive and are refunded (on line 450 of the T1) rather than included on line 312. That is, do not enter more than $955.04 on line 312; if your total EI and PPIP contributions exceed that amount, enter $955.04 on line 312, deduct that amount from total contributions, and carry any balance to line 450.

It is possible to have an overpayment of EI contributions even if your contributions totalled $955.04 or less. The CRA's computers will normally adjust for this and refund any overpayment, but you have the option of computing it yourself on Part 2 of T2204 and claiming the refund on line 450 of your return.

If your total insurable earnings from box 24 of your T4 slips (or box 14 if box 24 is blank) is $2,000 or less, you are not liable for EI contributions and the CRA will refund them. In this case, you should not enter any EI premiums on line 312, but you claim the entire amount of premiums as a refund on line 450.

If total earnings are more than $2,000 but less than $2,038, contributions are refunded in part. In this case, the easy thing to do is enter the total EI premiums on line 312 and let the CRA calculate the actual amount and adjust your refund (or tax owing) accordingly. You are entitled, however, to calculate the refund yourself on form T2204, available from any Tax Services Office (¶287).

As well as the situation where your insurable earnings are less than $2,038, it is possible, indeed likely, where you have more than one employer in the year, that you have overpaid EI premiums even if you contributed less than the maximum. The CRA's computers are supposed to (and usually do) correctly calculate the overpayment and include it in your refund or assessment. If you want to calculate the overpayment yourself, you can do so on form T2204, available from any Tax Services Office or from the CRA website. See ¶287.

(ITA: 118.7; T1 Guide)

[¶1307.07] *Employment Insurance for Self-Employed*

Canadians who are self-employed are now able to register for the EI program on a voluntary basis which will provide them with maternity, parental, sickness, and compassionate care benefits, collectively referred to as special benefits. These special benefits will mirror those currently available to salaried employees under the EI program.

Self-employed residents of Quebec will continue to receive maternity and parental benefits through the Quebec

Parental Insurance Plan provided by the Government of Quebec (see ¶1307.10). In addition, they will now be eligible to take advantage of sickness and compassionate care benefits offered by the Government of Canada through the EI program.

For more information, visit www.servicecanada.gc.ca.

If you have entered into an agreement with the Canada Employment Insurance Commission through Service Canada to take advantage of the EI special benefits for the self-employed, you will have to complete Schedule 13, Employment Insurance Premiums on Self-Employment and Other Eligible Earnings, to determine the EI premiums payable.

Enter the amount from line 10 of Schedule 13 on line 317 of Schedule 1 and on line 430 of the return. Unlike the regular EI program, self-employed Canadians do not have to pay the employer's portion of the EI premium.

[¶1307.10] *Residents of Quebec*

If you were a resident of Quebec at the end of the year, you pay a lower EI contribution for the year, but more than make up for it with a required contribution to the QPIP (which the CRA refers to with the English acronym PPIP and Revenu Québec with the English acronym QPIP, and, in French, Régime québécois d'assurance parentale (RQAP)).

As with CPP/QPP, but unlike the federal EI contributions which apply only to employment income, Quebec levies QPIP contributions on self-employment as well as employment income. The self-employed (and employees with non-Quebec employment income) must use Schedule 10 (available only with the Quebec return) if self-employment income and/or non-Quebec employment income is $2,000 or more. Since Quebec levies QPIP on self-employment income, it follows the federal CPP/QPP example by allowing a portion of the QPIP contribution on self-employment earnings as a deduction from self-employment income. The federal government allows this deduction for federal purposes on line 223 of the Quebec version of the T1 return (which appears only on the Quebec version of the T1). Quebec allows the deduction for Quebec purposes on line 248 of the Quebec TP-1 tax return.

Whether you were an employee or self-employed in 2016, you are liable for PPIP contributions only if you were a resident of Quebec at the end of the year. If you were resident in another province at the end of the year, any PPIP contributions withheld in respect of your employment in Quebec during the year are credited to your federal EI, with any excess refunded through the federal machinery in ¶1307.05, above.

If you were a resident of Quebec at the end of the taxation year and worked only as an employee in Quebec during the taxation year, your EI and PPIP contributions should be adequately reported on (for federal purposes) your T4 slip(s). For EI purposes, you simply transfer the sum of your box 18 amounts to line 312, to a maximum of $772.16. Any excess over $772.16 should be entered on line 450 for refund. For PPIP purposes, you transfer the sum of box 55 entries from your T4 slips to line 375 of Schedule 1, to a maximum of $391.82. Line 375 appears only on the Quebec version of federal Schedule 1. Any excess over $391.82 is claimed on line 457 of your Quebec return, not on your federal return. As with federal EI contributions, you are not required to make QPIP contributions if your earnings subject to QPIP are less than $2,000. If this is the case, you do not enter any amount on line 375, and you claim any QPIP contributions withheld from your income on line 457 of your Quebec provincial return (not on the federal T1 return).

You must use Schedule 10 (available only with the Quebec version of the federal T1 return) to determine your PPIP premium amounts if you were resident in Quebec on December 31 of the taxation year and met one of the following conditions:

- The total of your net self-employment income (lines 135 to 143 of your return) and your net remuneration for a family-type resource or immediate resource is $2,000 or more.
- The total of your net self-employment income and employment income from within or outside Canada is $2,000 or more.
- You reported a province of employment other than Quebec in box 10 of a T4 and employment income from within or outside Canada of $2,000 or more.

Schedule 10 accumulates PPIP contributions on non-Quebec employment income and self-employment income, and you carry the totals to lines 376 and 378, respectively, of your federal Schedule 1.

The Quebec aspect of these rules is discussed at ¶1650d.10.

(ITA: 118.7; T1 Guide)

TAX CREDITS FOR PENSION INCOME

[¶1311] CREDIT FOR PENSION INCOME

You are allowed a non-refundable tax credit in respect of up to $2,000 of pension income. To compute your credit, you must first determine the amount of your eligible pension income. The lesser of this amount and $2,000 is then entered at line 314 of Schedule 1 of your T1 return, and converted to a credit by multiplying it, along with other creditable amounts accumulated at line 335, by a 15% conversion rate (¶1303).

Commentary on Legislative Proposals (Sept. 16, 2016)

Note: When Legislative Proposals, September 16, 2016, achieves Royal Assent, the commentary will be modified to read:

You are allowed a non-refundable tax credit in respect of up to $2,000 of pension income. The amount eligible for the credit is the lesser of:

(a) 2,000, and

(b) the total of

i. your eligible pension income for the taxation year (see below), and

ii. effective for 2015 and subsequent taxation years, the total of all payments you received in the year on account of a retirement income security benefit under the

> *Canadian Forces Members and Veterans Re-establishment and Compensation Act.*
>
> This amount is then entered at line 314 of Schedule 1 of your T1 return, and converted to a credit by multiplying it, along with other creditable amounts accumulated at line 335, by a 15% conversion rate (¶1303).

Contrary to various other personal amounts, the $2,000 pension amount is not subject to any annual indexation.

The amounts eligible for the pension income credit differ depending on whether you reached the age of 65 or older during the year.

Taxable benefits paid out of or under a PRPP (including variable benefits and payments from a PRPP qualifying annuity) are eligible for the pension credit and pension income splitting on amounts received after the taxpayer has attained 65 years of age.

(a) Amounts Eligible for Pension Deduction if You were 65 or Older in the Year ("Pension Income")

An individual who has attained the age of 65 years before the end of the year is entitled to credit for an amount equal to the lesser of $2,000 and the "pension income" the individual included in income in the year. "Pension income" is defined as follows:

(1) an annuity (not lump-sum) payment out of or under a superannuation or pension fund (other than a PRPP) or the Saskatchewan Pension Plan (referred to in the legislation as a "specified pension plan"). This includes foreign pension plans and foreign government plans, such as U.S. Social Security, to the extent the income is not otherwise deductible under a tax treaty (see ¶919, ¶921);

(2) an annuity payment out of a registered retirement savings plan (RRSP) or an "amended plan", or an annuity purchased with a refund of RRSP premiums received on the death of a spouse or common-law partner and on which a proper deduction was taken for the purchase of the annuity by a surviving spouse or common-law partner over 71;

(3) a payment out of or under a registered retirement income fund (RRIF);

(4) a payment (not already included in (1), above) payable on a periodic basis out of a money purchase pension plan; such plans are allowed to make payments in the same fashion as RRIFs without actually being converted to a RRIF;

(5) a payment out of or under a PRPP;

(6) an annuity payment out of a deferred profit sharing plan (DPSP) or a "revoked plan";

(7) an annuity payment purchased for the taxpayer by a DPSP trustee as a pay-out of the taxpayer's vested interest;

(8) the income element of annuity payments included in income under the accrual rules or otherwise. Note that the claim for pension credit for annuities on line 314 of the T1 form will affect the reporting of the income as interest or pension on page 2; see ¶480; and

(9) the income from an "income-averaging annuity contract" (¶480) is technically eligible for the pension income deduction for taxpayers 65 and over and for taxpayers under 65 to the extent permitted by the rule in (b)(3), below.

(b) Amounts Eligible for Pension Credit if You Had Not Yet Attained the Age of 65 in the Year ("Qualified Pension Income")

In this case, you may claim up to $2,000 as eligible for credit to the extent you have received income from the following sources:

(1) annuity payments from superannuation or pension plans, or the Saskatchewan Pension Plan (provided they are life annuity and not lump-sum payments or payments out of PRPPs);

(2) annuity payments arising by virtue of the death of your spouse or common-law spouse or partner (under the law as it stood at the time of death as discussed at ¶1113) under a registered retirement savings plan, registered retirement income fund, a money purchase pension plan,. a PRPP, a deferred profit sharing plan and other specified plans (including foreign government pension plans, e.g., U.S. Social Security); and

(3) the income portion of any annuity payment (not already included under (2), above) arising by virtue of the death of your spouse or common-law spouse or partner under the law as it stood at the time of death (as discussed at ¶1113).

You should note that the income described in (2) and (3), above, qualifies for the credit only where it is received as a consequence of the death of your spouse or common-law partner. If you receive this income on your own account, you must be at least 65 to claim the credit for it. The CRA is explicit that a former spouse (at the time of death) is not a spouse for these purposes. It is not explicit about someone who was not a common-law spouse or partner at the time of death, but would have been recognized as such under subsequent changes to the law. It is generally thought that these changing definitions are quite explicitly not retroactive in this respect, and so far no one has come forward to challenge that point of view.

The terms of some deferred profit sharing plans require payment to be made to the beneficiary under the plan on the basis of equal instalments over a period not exceeding 10 years. If, as a result of the death of your spouse (or common-law spouse as defined), you receive the unpaid instalments under such a plan, then these amounts are eligible for the pension income credit even if you are under 65.

[¶1311.05] Exclusions from Pension Income

For all purposes relating to the pension income credit, pension income does not include:

(1) amounts of pension or supplement under the *Old Age Security Act* or of any similar payment from a province;

(2) amounts under the *Canada Pension Plan* or the *Quebec Pension Plan*;

(3) a payment received out of or under a salary deferral arrangement (¶307), a retirement compensation arrangement (¶359.05), an employee benefit plan (¶359.10), or an employee trust (¶359);

(4) death benefits (¶925); and

(5) amounts for which a deduction has already been taken (for example, foreign pension income protected from Canadian tax by a tax treaty, which is reported as income and deducted again on line 256), other than a deduction by the transferor of amounts transferred to a spouse or common-law partner under the rules at ¶1311.15, below.

[¶1311.07] *Pension Income on the T1 Return*

Generally speaking, pension income is collected on line 115 of the T1 Return. Because line 115 collects gross amounts of pension income, some or all of which may be deducted at a later stage of the T1, not all amounts on line 115 are eligible for pension credit. Accordingly, you must do a supplementary calculation for line 314 on the federal worksheet which accompanies the T1 package.

[¶1311.10] *Spouse's Pension Income*

If your spouse or common-law partner receives pension income but has too little income overall to utilize the pension income credit, the unused portion can be transferred to you as described at ¶1361.

You may be able to create pension income for your spouse or common-law partner, if he/she is not yet 71, by contributing to a spouse or common-law partner RRSP out of your own earned income (see ¶2624.05). Your spouse or common-law partner's eventual pension income so created would be eligible for the pension credit.

(ITA: 60(*j*); 118(3), (7), (8); 147; 147.5)

[¶1315] TAX ISSUES ON RETIREMENT

When individuals retire, the following tax issues discussed in other chapters may arise for them:

(A) Types of Income You May Have

Old Age Security (OAS)	¶913
Canada/Quebec Pension Plan	¶915
Retiring allowances	¶923
Termination payments	¶923
Pensions	¶911
Foreign pensions	¶919
U.S. Social Security	¶921
Annuities	¶480
Investment income	Chapter 4
RRSP income	¶903
RRIF income	¶907; ¶2630
Rental income	Chapter 6
Capital gains (or losses)	Chapter 5

(B) Tax Offsets

RRSP contributions	¶2610.05
Special (rollover) RRSP contributions	¶2612.05
RRSP spousal contributions	¶2624.05
Age credit	¶1108
Pension credit	¶1311
Spouse's unused credits	¶1361
Medical expenses	¶1205
Attendant or nursing care	¶1207
Disability credit	¶1255

(C) Converting RRSP Savings to Retirement Income

See ¶2616.05.

(D) Instalment Requirements

When you retire and depend on investment and pension income, you may find that the amount withheld from this income on account of tax is less than your final tax liability. Employees in particular are often uncomfortably surprised to have to meet tax requirements out of cash received (and spent), since they have been accustomed to having full tax withheld by the employer. You are obliged to pay your full tax liability to the extent it has not been withheld, and further obliged to make quarterly payments on account of your projected tax liability where it is not adequately covered by withholding. See ¶227.

(E) Leaving Canada

See ¶115 to ¶117 and Chapter 21.

[¶1315.05] *Additional Information*

The CRA publishes a useful pamphlet called *When You Retire* (P119), available without charge from your Tax Services Office (¶287).

TAX CREDIT FOR FAMILY INCOME SPLITTING

[¶1317] CREDIT FOR FAMILY TAX CUT

The family tax cut credit was eliminated for 2016 and subsequent taxation years. The credit could be claimed for 2014 and 2015 by couples with at least one child under 18. The spouse or common-law partner with the higher income could transfer to the spouse or common-law partner with the lower income up to $50,000 of taxable income to realize combined tax savings not exceeding $2,000.

The information below is still relevant but only for the years 2014 and 2015.

On October 30, 2014 the federal government announced measures that would enable limited income-splitting via the "Family Tax Cut". A non-refundable federal tax credit intended for 2014 and subsequent taxation years, the Family Tax Cut credit would effectively enable a "qualifying individual" in certain situations (see below) to transfer up to $50,000 of taxable income to a spouse/partner in a lower tax bracket; the tax relief (i.e., the difference in tax before and after the effective transfer of income) received via this credit, however, would be capped at $2,000. The credit would be claimed when filing the relevant year's tax returns, e.g., in spring of 2015 when filing the 2014 tax returns.

A "qualifying individual" able to claim the credit must:

- at the end of the taxation year be a Canadian resident;

- not be confined to a prison/similar institution 90 or more days in the year;
- have an "eligible relation" for the year; and
- have a child under the age of 18 ordinarily reside throughout the taxation year with the individual or with the individual's "eligible relation".

An "eligible relation" of a qualifying individual must, in turn, be a spouse or common-law partner also resident in Canada at the end of a taxation year; the couple must also not be living separate and apart by reason of relationship breakdown at either the end of the year or for a period of 90 days commencing in the year. As well, the credit cannot be claimed for a year that either the qualifying individual or the eligible relation (a) fails to file an income tax return, (b) elects to split pension income, or (c) becomes bankrupt.

Where eligibility would be established per the above criteria, the credit could still be claimed if either a qualifying individual or the eligible relation died in the year. Similarly, the credit would be available in the year of birth, adoption, or death of a child (explicit wording precludes pro-rating of the credit in any of these situations). Per the Department of Finance's "backgrounder" information, it seems there may be joint or shared custody circumstances where the same child may be considered to "ordinarily reside" with two couples, e.g., when parents who have divorced/separated have subsequently remarried or entered into new common-law relationships and seek to claim the credit.

The family tax cut mechanism provides a deduction from tax for the higher income spouse. In particular, subsection 119.1(2) allows the qualifying individual to deduct from tax payable the lesser of (a) $2,000 and (b) the difference between the spouses' combined tax payable for the year before the transfer ("combined base tax payable") and their combined tax payable as a result of the transfer ("combined adjusted base tax payable").

The combined base tax payable is simply the total of the qualifying individual's "base tax payable" and the spouse's base tax payable for the year. The base tax payable for each individual is the tax otherwise payable for the year taking into account only the personal tax credits in sections 118 through 118.9 and no other credits in Division E.

The combined adjusted tax payable is the total of the qualifying individual's adjusted base tax payable and the spouse's adjusted base tax payable for the year. The adjusted base tax payable of each individual is the tax that would be payable on the individual's "split-adjusted income" for the year. The latter term is essentially the individual's taxable income otherwise determined plus (lower income spouse) or minus (higher income spouse, i.e. the qualifying individual) the lesser of $50,000 and the difference between the taxable income otherwise determined for the two parties. However, the only tax credits allowed in computing the adjusted base tax payable are the individual's "adjusted non-refundable tax credits amount" — see lines 11 and 12 on Schedule 1-A. For these purposes, the 2015 Federal Budget introduced changes that allow the transfer of tuition and education credits to calculate the family tax cut credit, but only for 2014 and 2015 — the family tax credit is eliminated after 2015, and the education and textbook credits are eliminated after 2016. As the Budget documents indicate

> Where personal income tax credits have been transferred from one spouse or common-law partner to the other, the Family Tax Cut suppresses the use of those credits in the transferee's hands. Instead, the personal income tax credits previously transferred are taken into consideration in the calculation of the transferor's adjusted tax payable. This prevents the double counting of these credits in the calculation of the Family Tax Cut.
>
> The previously-announced Family Tax Cut rules prevent transferred education-related amounts (Tuition, Education and Textbook Tax Credits) from being included in the Family Tax Cut calculation. Due to the rules for calculating these education-related credits, the double-counting issue described above is not present. This may therefore reduce the value of the Family Tax Cut for couples who transfer education-related amounts between themselves ... Budget 2015 proposes to revise the calculation of the Family Tax Cut for the 2014 and subsequent taxation years to ensure that couples claiming the Family Tax Cut and transferring education-related credits between themselves receive the appropriate value of the Family Tax Cut.

The calculation of the family tax cut, if any, is on Schedule 1-A. The reduction in tax for the qualifying individual is on line 423 on Schedule 1.

(ITA: 119.1(1))

STUDENTS' TUITION FEES AND EDUCATION/TEXTBOOK CREDITS

[¶1319] CREDITS FOR TUITION FEES AND EDUCATION/TEXTBOOK AMOUNT

Both the education and textbook credits are eliminated after 2016. All the information contained in ¶1319 to ¶1341 concerning these two credits remains valid for 2016 and the preceding taxation years.

You are entitled to a tax credit equal to 15% of the total of:

- your tuition fees at specified educational and training institutions;
- $400 per month for the number of months in the calendar year during any part of which you were a full-time student, plus a "textbook" credit of $65 for each month for which you were entitled to the $400 credit (effective January 1, 2017, the education and textbook credits are eliminated); and
- $120 for any month in which you were a part-time but not a full-time student, plus a "textbook" credit of $20 for each month for which you were entitled to the $120 credit (effective January 1, 2017, the education and textbook credits are eliminated).

Part-time students entitled to the disability credit or suffering from a milder but significant impairment may be entitled to the $400 per month amount; see ¶1337.10.

The meaning of specified institutions and full-time and part-time students is discussed at ¶1337.

To claim this credit, you enter the eligible fees and per month amounts at lines 320 to 322 of Schedule 11, which permits you to calculate the maximum amounts you can utilize on your return. These amounts are then carried to line 323 on Schedule 1 of your return (and converted to credit on line 338), and any excess amounts can (subject to the limit below) be transferred to either a spouse or a supporting parent or grandparent (which can include a spouse's parent or grandparent) or carried forward to future years.

Education and textbook amounts and eligible tuition fees qualify for transfer only to a spouse, parent, or grandparent, up to a total of $5,000 of fees and amounts (before conversion to the credit equivalent). A reconciliation of this transfer amount for transfers to supporting parents or grandparents is provided in a chart on the back of form T2202A. This transfer is discussed at ¶1339, below. Transfers to a spouse operate under different rules and are discussed at ¶1361. Unlike various other personal amounts, the above amounts of $400, $65, $120, $20, and $5,000 are not subject to any annual indexation.

Qualifying institutions and other criteria are not the same for the tuition fee and the education/textbook amount credits, although in most cases they will come to the same thing as a practical matter. Nevertheless, the rules for determining the tuition and education/textbook claims must be studied independently.

[¶1319.05] *Age and Course Limitations*

It is the intention of the government that the tuition credit should only be available for post-secondary (i.e., university and college) level courses and for programs certified as providing courses for occupational training. The following rules are intended to ensure this result. Under these rules, no credit will arise for the following tuition fees:

(1) tuition fees, paid to universities, colleges, and other educational institutions in Canada offering post-secondary courses, for courses that are not at post-secondary (post-high school) level; and

(2) tuition fees paid to certified institutions (offering job skills) as described at ¶1323(2) if:

- (a) the student had not attained the age of 16 before the end of the year in which the courses were taken, or
- (b) the purpose of the enrolment in the institution cannot reasonably be regarded as being to provide the student with new or enhanced skills in an occupation.

Students at certified institutions referred to in (2) must meet both age and purpose tests in (2). All the courses taken at a certified institution must meet the occupational skills test, so long as the general purpose of enrolment is to obtain such skills.

Where no credit arises for the student's tuition because of these rules, it follows that no transfer can be made to spouse, parents, or grandparents under the rules at ¶1339.

[¶1319.10] *CRA Publications for Students*

The CRA offers the pamphlet P105, *Students and Income Tax*, which students may find helpful. It does not offer any information not found in this book, but it is a concise summary of the provisions that are most likely to affect students.

Students from other countries studying in Canada may have particular problems determining not only whether to file but which returns to file. They may often be considered residents of Canada but not of a province and so, confusingly, be asked to file as non-residents. This is discussed in Chapter 1 of this book at ¶115, ¶116, and ¶117. The CRA offers a specific and reasonably detailed *General Income Tax and Benefit Guide for Non-Residents and Deemed Residents of Canada* (5013-G), and sometimes maintains a page on its website for international students, which can be accessed at www.cra-arc.gc.ca by searching for "international students".

The CRA guides and pamphlets are available free of charge on the CRA website.

[¶1319.15] *History of Education and Transfer Amounts*

The full amount of tuition fees is eligible for credit to the student, both for current use and carryforward to the extent not used or transferred, but there is a limit on the amount of education, textbook, and tuition amounts (the education and textbook credits are eliminated effective January 1, 2017) that can be transferred to a spouse or parent. Following is a table of this history of the transfer limit and the education amounts.

Year	*Education amount full/part-time*	*Transfer limit*
2006 to 2016	$465/$140[1]	$5,000
2001 to 2005	$400/$120	$5,000

[1] Includes "textbook amount" of $65/$20, which simply adds to the education amount.

(ITA: 118.5; 118.6; 118.8; 118.9)

[¶1321] TUITION FEE REQUIREMENTS

If you were enrolled at a qualified educational institution you can claim a credit as described at ¶1319 for your tuition fees provided they are over $100 and cover a period not exceeding 12 months. A course will qualify whether it is a full-time day course, night course, summer course or correspondence course. However, the educational institution must be in Canada except as noted at ¶1323 below. As well, where the educational institution is one certified as described at ¶1323(b), a student is entitled to claim the deduction only if enrolled to obtain skills or improve skills in an occupation. Thus, if you take a series of courses leading to an occupational skill, you could make a claim for all the fees involved, whereas if you took only an introductory course you might not be entitled to claim the fees. It must be said that this last distinction is virtually unenforceable in most cases, and is usually ignored as a practical matter, but you should know that it is the rule.

In CRA Document No. 2003-0000617, the CRA comments that in the case of a flight school, its auditors have required the student to provide a written statement from the flight school confirming the student's enrolment in a commercial licence program, of which the first stage may in fact be training for a private licence. Absent this, the tuition credit will be denied, but the CRA will go back and reassess the year if the student later goes on to train for a commercial licence. This of course assumes that the year is not statute-barred (¶268). Where a student really does intend to train for a commercial licence (or similarly build on particular courses in his or her field) as funds become available, which may go beyond the normal statute-barred period, the student should consider filing a waiver to keep the year open on this issue, as discussed in ¶277.

In addition to tuition fees, a student or an individual supporting him under certain circumstances may claim an education amount credit (see ¶1337).

(ITA: 118.5)

[¶1321.10] *Tuition Fees as Business Expense*

In *Setchell v. The Queen*, 2006 DTC 2279 (T.C.C.), the Court denied the tuition credit for very high fees paid to take a commercial computer course because the course could not be considered a university or post-secondary course. However, it was taken as part of an effort to commence a business, and the Court ruled that the business had actually begun when the course was taken, and the tuition was therefore deductible as a business expense. The case was heard under the informal procedure, so strictly speaking it has no precedent value. As well, it seems to be more a humane than a closely reasoned decision. However, it does suggest another avenue of argument where the strict tuition fee credit rules cannot be met.

[¶1321.15] *Tuition Fees as Employment Expense*

In *Auclair v. The Queen*, 2013 DTC 1199 (T.C.C.), the Court denied deduction of repaid flight school fees, where the taxpayer had claimed the deduction as "supplies consumed directly in the performance of the duties of the office or employment", i.e., as a subparagraph 8(1)(*i*)(iii) employee expense. In that case, the taxpayer had to take flight school training, but had left his employer within 24 months of the training's completion and was by contract required to pay his employer compensation because of his early departure. While the Court also considered if the training costs were to be classed as "supplies" under subparagraph 8(1)(*i*)(iii), the deciding factor was that the taxpayer's compensation-payment had been paid to his employer not under a contract of employment, but under a contract of termination.

[¶1323] WHICH EDUCATIONAL INSTITUTIONS WILL QUALIFY?

In order to obtain a credit for your tuition fees, the educational institution in Canada which you have attended must be one of the following:

(1) a university, college or other educational institution providing courses at a post-secondary school level; or

(2) an institution certified by the Minister of Employment and Social Development to provide courses, other than courses designed for university credit, that furnish a person with skills for, or improve a person's skills in, an occupation.

If you attended a university outside Canada you may also be entitled to a deduction (see ¶1335).

The CRA takes the view that if you are attending a school (other than a post-secondary institution or a designated educational institution) which teaches religion exclusively or operates in a dual capacity providing both secular (academic) and religious education, then a portion or all of the amounts paid to the school may be considered as a donation. The school you are attending should provide you with a receipt indicating which portion of your fees is a charitable donation and which portion is the tuition fee. If one of your parents paid your fees for attending such an institution, the portion considered as a donation would be claimed on your parent's return within the limits discussed in ¶1270. Since the institutions in question are typically primary or secondary (i.e., pre-college level) schools, the tuition fee portion generally would not qualify as eligible for credit.

(ITA: 118.5; IC 75-23 Tuition fees and charitable donations paid to privately supported secular and religious schools)

[¶1323.05] *Other Educational Institution*

In *Hillman v. The Queen*, 2007 DTC 81 (T.C.C.), the Court ruled that an organization providing a bar review course for Toronto students intending to take the New York bar examination was not an educational institution "in Canada" providing courses at the post-secondary level. The private organization offering the courses had no permanent premises in Canada; it merely rented a room in which students viewed videotapes and performed time-limited assignments. The fact that the CRA recognizes provincial bar associations in Canada as "other educational institutions" did not avail the appellant. Nor was the organization offering the course a foreign university under the rules at ¶1335.

On the other hand, in *Tarkowski v. The Queen*, 2007 DTC 1555 (T.C.C.), the Court found that a Toronto music school was an "other educational institution" offering courses at the post-secondary level (for the purposes of (1) in the description of qualifying educational institutions in ¶1323, above). Moreover, although the student whose fees were in issue was a high school student, he had already obtained grade 12 credit for music, so the courses he took thereafter at the music school were post-secondary courses even though he was not yet a high school graduate.

[¶1325] WHO CAN CLAIM THE CREDIT?

The student must claim the tuition fee credit (and for that matter, the education/textbook amount at ¶1337) to the extent necessary to eliminate tax; a spouse, parent or grandparent may claim the balance as described at ¶1339, below. The education and textbook credits are eliminated effective January 1, 2017.

(ITA: 118.8; 118.9)

[¶1327] WHAT FEES WILL QUALIFY?

The following items are considered as tuition fees: fees paid for admission, use of the library or laboratory, exemption, examination (including rereading), application, confirmation, certificate, diploma or degree, membership, or seminar fees specifically related to a program, mandatory computer service fees, and academic fees. If GST (and HST) is charged on an item, that too is included in the fee. Tuition fees — even if compulsory — do not include fees for a student association or property to be acquired by the student.

Examination Fees

Examination fees paid to an educational institution, professional association, provincial ministry, or other institution for an examination required to obtain a professional status recognized by federal or provincial statute, or to be licensed or certified to practice a trade or profession in Canada, are eligible for the tuition tax credit and apply to examinations taken in 2011 and subsequent taxation years.

The total of tuition and examination fees paid to the institution must exceed $100 to be eligible, so as to be consistent with the general rule for the existing tuition tax credit. An amount is considered to be paid in the year the examination is taken.

Fees for examinations taken to begin study in a profession or field, such as the law school admission test, do not apply. However, fees to write law bar exams and the chartered accountant exams (the UFE), as well as any other licensing exam, are eligible for the credit.

Ancillary Fees and Charges for Examinations

Mandatory ancillary fees and charges paid in respect of the individual's occupational, trade, or professional examination are also eligible. Ancillary fees could include the cost of examination materials used during the examination, such as identification cards that must be purchased for the examination day and certain prerequisite study materials. Non-mandatory ancillary fees and charges may not be included in computing the tuition fee credit to the extent that such fees and charges exceed $250. The mandatory ancillary fees eligible for the tuition fee credit apply to tuition fees paid for the 2011 and subsequent taxation years.

Effective for 2012 and subsequent taxation years, ancillary fees relating to the provision of financial assistance are excluded for the purposes of calculating the tuition tax credit. except to the extent that (i) the amount of the assistance is required to be included in computing the income of the individual, or (ii) the amount would be required to be included but for the scholarship exemption in subsection 56(3).

Eligible ancillary fees and charges do not include costs for travel, parking, equipment (items that have enduring value, such as calculators, computers, etc.), or other costs that are currently ineligible for the tuition tax credit.

A list of fees considered eligible and non-eligible as tuition fees can be found in Income Tax Folio S1-F2-C2, paragraphs 2.34 and 2.35.

Technically speaking, tuition fees are considered to include ancillary fees and charges that comply with the rules in ¶1319 to ¶1323, above, with two sets of exceptions, discussed below. It is not clear exactly what an ancillary fee is; as a matter of definition, "ancillary" merely means subordinate, which hardly helps. Presumably, an ancillary fee is ancillary whether or not it is identified as a separate charge, although some brave taxpayer may wish to challenge this. On the other hand, it is doubtful as a practical matter that costs buried in a flat non-itemized tuition fee can be identified as non-qualified in any event.

The first and more general exception disqualifies any ancillary fee from inclusion in tuition eligible for credit if the fee is not required of all full-time students (if the student making the claim is a full-time student) or all part-time students (if the student making the claim is a part-time student); however, this rule only disqualifies such fees to the extent that in the aggregate they exceed $250.

The second set of more specific rules disqualifies the following ancillary fees and charges even if they meet all other criteria:

(1) fees levied for a student association;

(2) fees for property to be acquired by the student (the CRA perhaps softens this by saying that it refers to goods of enduring value, such as equipment);

(3) services not ordinarily provided at educational institutions in Canada that offer post-secondary courses (certain charges levied by foreign universities as well as non-typical Canadian charges would seem to be the target of this);

(4) fees in respect of the provision of financial assistance to students, except to the extent that the assistance is included in income (or would be included but for the exemption for scholarships, etc., at ¶953) and is not offset by a deduction in computing taxable income; and

(5) fees for the construction, renovation or maintenance of any building or facility unless the building or facility is owned by the institution and is used to provide either post-secondary courses or services for which the fees or charges would be included in tuition under these rules (or would be included if charged to all students).

Other Fees

Again as a technical matter, all fees must be tested against the exclusions above. Some uncertainties remain. The CRA now asserts (in its pamphlet P105, *Students and Income Tax*) that the cost of books included in fees for a correspondence course are available for credit, presumably on the theory that they are not ancillary in the circumstances.

Tuition fees will qualify for a credit even though they were paid out of prizes, scholarships, bursaries or fellowships. Where such an award is made by the educational institution itself, however, a credit will be allowed only if the award is made out of trust funds, or the income therefrom, held by the educational institution.

Fees incurred in a certified institution as opposed to a university must be incurred to furnish or improve the student's occupational skills; see ¶1321.

The costs of ground school training and flying training incurred while a student is under instruction and enrolled in a course leading to a pilot's licence at a certified flying school or club will qualify as deductible tuition fees, although under the rules at ¶1321 the CRA says the fees will only qualify where the student is taking lessons in order to become a commercial pilot or professional instructor. Subject to this limitation, a deduction for tuition is permitted for time during which the student is under instruction and direct supervision. This includes the cost of dual and solo flying hours required to obtain specified flight licences or ratings to the minimum flight training requirements of the Department of Transport. This is currently 45 hours for a private pilot licence and 65 hours for a commercial pilot licence. Fees for ground school and flight simulators are eligible for the tuition tax credit but costs incurred by a student in flying a personal aircraft while taking a course at a flying training school or club are not eligible. Flying clubs should provide form TL11B to support your claim. Note that the form requires you to certify your intention to use your flying skills in a related occupation.

Classroom Fees

In CRA Document No. 2003-0000565, the CRA comments that the Ontario classroom fees of $10/day, introduced August 1, 2002 into Ontario's apprenticeship program, would qualify as a creditable tuition fee.

Occupational Skills Program

Only fees for post-secondary courses or courses for students 16 or older taken as part of a program of occupational skills are intended to qualify; see ¶1319.

(ITA: 118.5(3), (4); Income Tax Folio: S1-F2-C2 Tuition Tax Credit)

[¶1327.05] Where Fees Reimbursed or Assistance Received

Fees do not qualify for tuition credit to the extent that:

(1) you are or were entitled to receive reimbursement or any assistance *not included in your income* under a federal government program intended to facilitate entry or re-entry of workers into the workforce;

(2) the fees are paid on your behalf or you are entitled to reimbursement for them under a federal program designed to assist athletes and you are not required to include the amounts paid or reimbursed in your income.

(3) the fees are paid on your behalf or reimbursed to you by your employer and are not included in computing your income; or

(4) the fees were included as part of an allowance received by your parent on your behalf from an employer which your parent did not have to include in income (¶344).

See also limitations in ¶1319–¶1323 and ¶1328–¶1333.

(ITA: 118.5(1)(a))

[¶1327.10] *Fees for Auditing Courses*

In a technical opinion, the CRA considered the eligibility for the tuition credit of fees paid by students enrolled in a university course on an audit basis. Apparently the students would pay half the regular course fee to attend lectures and to receive the course material. However, they were not permitted to write the course exam, nor awarded a grade upon completion of the course. The CRA's view was that fees paid in respect of post-secondary level courses taken on an audit basis represent fees paid by the student for instruction and/or teaching, and as such would be considered eligible tuition fees for purposes of the tuition tax credit "provided the other requirements of the provision are satisfied".

The CRA would not comment on whether enrolment in these types of courses would qualify the student for the education and textbook tax credits in the absence of information as to whether the specific requirements, notably the hour requirements for those credits, would be met in any particular case. The education and textbook tax credits are eliminated effective January 1, 2017.

(CRA Document No.: Eligible Tuition Fees, *January 27, 2006*, CRA Document No. 2006-0167441E5)

[¶1328] THE $100 MINIMUM RULE

The tuition fees paid to each Canadian educational institution *in respect of* the year (¶1329) must total over $100 to qualify, but if the fees are over $100, the full amount will be eligible for credit. It does not matter if some individual fees paid to a qualifying Canadian institution are less than $100 as long as the total for the year for that institution year is *more than* $100. Thus, if you pay $50 for the year to one Canadian educational institution and $51 to another, it appears that no amount will be eligible for credit, whereas if each amount had been paid to the same institution, the entire $101 would be eligible for credit.

The $100 minimum per school per year also applies to tuition fees of a student commuting to the United States as described at ¶1335, but not to a student in full-time attendance at a U.S. or other foreign university who meets the three criteria described in items (1), (2) and (3) at ¶1335.

(ITA: 118.5; Income Tax Folio: S1-F2-C2 Tuition Tax Credit)

[¶1329] CALENDAR YEAR MUST BE USED TO CALCULATE TUITION FEES

You must claim a tuition fee credit on a calendar year basis. That is, you may claim all tuition fees paid in respect of the calendar year as being eligible for the credit. Note that it is the period for which the fees are paid that qualifies them, not when the fee is paid. If you paid in Year 1 for an academic year from September of Year 1 to May of Year 2, you would be able to claim for 4/9 of the payment in Year 1 and 5/9 in Year 2. If you paid in December of Year 1 for a course commencing in January of Year 2, you would not be able to claim the fees until you file your Year 2 return in Year 3.

Generally speaking, where the tuition is paid to a Canadian university or other qualifying Canadian institution, the school will issue a tax receipt (T2202A) showing the tuition applicable to a calendar year, and you may rely on that allocation.

(ITA: 118.5; Income Tax Folio: S1-F2-C2 Tuition Tax Credit)

[¶1331] WHAT SUPPORT IS REQUIRED?

All claims for tuition fee credits must be supported by formal receipts in your possession, but it is not necessary to submit the receipts with your return. This policy may change from year to year, so it is always advisable to check it against the T1 Guide directions for line 323 of the T1 return. Generally speaking, Canadian educational institutions will issue you form T2202A, which will show both tuition and course eligibility for the $400/$120 monthly education and $65/$20 textbook amounts, and so will support both claims. The content of form T2202, which was cancelled, is now reflected in revised form T2202A. The education and textbook tax credits are eliminated effective January 1, 2017.

If you attended a foreign university and qualify under the rules at ¶1335, you must have the foreign university fill out form TL11A, C or D as described at ¶1335.

If your tuition receipts and certificates are on an academic year basis, you may be in the position of claiming in one year fees based partly on a certificate for another year (¶1329). In general, when you receive a receipt that covers a period including two calendar years you should write on it the portion attributed to each year and keep a copy to file with each return. Thus, if you have a Year 1 receipt for the period of September of Year 1 to May of Year 2, you would note 4/9 to Year 1 and 5/9 to Year 2 on it, and keep one copy with your file copy of your Year 1 return and one with your file copy of your Year 2 return. You should of course make only the appropriate claim in each year. The CRA now tells you that you need not file the official receipt with your return, but you must keep it on hand should the CRA request to see it. In any event you should keep a clear record of the allocations with your receipt in your own tax return file.

(Income Tax Folio: S1-F2-C2, Tuition Tax Credit, para. 2.3)

[¶1333] TUITION FEES PAID BY YOUR EMPLOYER

If your employer paid tuition fees on your behalf you may not make a credit claim for them unless you have reported the amount paid by your employer as income.

CRA practice requires that tuition fees paid by an employer for a course that benefits the employee than the employer be reported as a taxable benefit of the employee. For more details, see ¶310. If your employer has done this, you should claim the fees on your income tax return if they are eligible for credit. If you are in doubt as to whether tuition fees paid by your employer have been included in your income, you should check with your employer.

Where your employer reimbursed you for tuition fees rather than paying them directly, you must include the reimbursement in income in the year received in order to be eligible for the credit.

The amount of a student's tuition fees must be reduced by the amount of any allowance received by the student's parent from his or her employer for costs of schooling his or her children in the family's official language while living away from the employee's domestic establishment and local schooling in that official language is not available. However, such benefits received from an employer are exempt from tax (¶344).

(ITA: 6(1)(*a*); 118.5)

[¶1335] EDUCATIONAL INSTITUTIONS OUTSIDE CANADA

Tuition fees paid to educational institutions outside Canada will normally be eligible for credit only if all of the following requirements are met:

(1) the educational institution must be a university;

(2) you must have been in full-time attendance in a course leading to a degree; and

(3) the course must have been at least three consecutive weeks in duration. Prior to 2011, the course must have been at least 13 weeks in duration.

The CRA will accept that a foreign educational institution is a university for purposes of (1), above, if it is recognized by an accrediting body that it is nationally accepted in its country as being an educational institution which confers degrees at least at the bachelor or equivalent level. For example, the CRA accepts as qualified U.S. universities those listed in the current edition of *Accredited Institutions of Post-Secondary Education* published by the American Council on Education and indicated therein as granting degrees at the B, M, D, or P level. CRA offices (¶287) should have a list of qualified schools. Schools not on the list may apply to the CRA's Individual Returns Directorate, as discussed in Income Tax Folio S1-F2-C2, *Tuition Tax Credit*, para. 2.13. The CRA confirmed in CRA Document No. 2008-0288251E5 that a Canadian student attending a state college in the United States would be eligible for the education tax credit since the college is considered a designated educational institution.

The fact that a school is not listed by the CRA is not definitive for purposes of the tuition credit. In *Dean v. The Queen*, 2005 DTC 322 (T.C.C.), a student was enrolled in a helicopter pilot program at a technical college in New Zealand. He did not earn a degree but left as soon as he had sufficient credits for a licence. The CRA contended the college was not a degree-granting institution, but the Court accepted the evidence of the school's literature that it granted a Bachelor of Commerce degree and the courses taken counted as credits to that degree. Accordingly the tuition credit was allowed. The education amount credit (¶1337) was denied because the school was not a designated institution for purposes of that credit.

If you meet the tests above and wish to claim tuition fees paid to a foreign university, you must complete form TL11A, which can be obtained from any Tax Services Office, and file it with your income tax return. The $100 minimum fee rule (¶1328) does not apply where the tests in (1), (2), and (3), above, are all met.

If you lived in Canada near the Canada–U.S. border and commuted to a post-secondary educational institution in the United States then the tuition fees will be eligible for credit even if they do not meet all of the above tests, provided they are in excess of $100. The type of post-secondary school eligible under this rule is broader than under the general rule; there is no all-inclusive list, but the criteria are discussed in Income Tax Folio S1-F2-C2, para. 2.10. You must file a completed form TL11C with your income tax return.

If you are deemed to be a resident in Canada throughout the year or during part of the year by virtue of the rule at ¶117, and are therefore taxable in Canada, you may claim tuition fees paid to an educational institution outside of Canada. You will be treated as if you were actually resident in Canada and the fees were paid to an educational institution in Canada. You must complete form TL11D, which can be obtained from any Tax Services Office, and file it with your income tax return.

(ITA: 118.5(1), (2); Income Tax Folio: S1-F2-C2 Tuition Tax Credit)

[¶1335.05] *Physical Attendance Required?*

For Canadian educational institutions, you are required to be "enrolled" to claim tuition credit, whereas for foreign universities you are required to be "in full-time attendance". It follows, in the CRA's view, that Canadian courses attended by correspondence or the internet may qualify for tuition credit if generally qualified, but foreign courses require physical presence at the foreign university to qualify.

In *Valente v. The Queen*, 2006 DTC 2685 (T.C.C.), the Court ruled squarely that tuition fees for a course in England provided essentially by CD and internet qualified for tuition credit. The Court reviewed earlier cases, and gave particular weight to *obiter* by the Tax Court's chief judge that "it is strongly arguable that full-time attendance at a foreign university can include full-time attendance through the internet or online as is the case here. That view conforms to common sense and to the reality of modern technology. If there continues to be doubt on the point Parliament should move to resolve that doubt." Accordingly, the Court held that "Parliament is certainly entitled to require a student's physical presence at a foreign university for purposes of the credit. The legislation does not clearly provide that requirement, however, and I do not think that it should be inferred from a narrow interpretation of the expression 'full-time attendance'". As an informal procedure case, the decision cannot set a binding precedent.

The same issue arose in the informal procedure case of *Kuwalek v. The Queen*, 2007 DTC 199 (T.C.C.). There the Tax Court reviewed various inconsistent prior cases and came down on the side of *Valente*. Apparently, the CRA took this to be the handwriting on the wall, and published an opinion (found in CRA Document No. 2007-0233661I7) stating:

> In light of recent jurisprudence, we have reconsidered our interpretation of paragraph 118.5(1)(*b*), such that a student enrolled at a university outside Canada and taking courses over the Internet may be able to claim a tuition tax credit for the related tuition fees, provided that the student is able to demonstrate that their attendance via Internet constituted "full-time attendance".
>
> Consistent with [our usual practice] ... the new position applies to tuition fees paid for the 2007 taxation year unless a notice of objection was filed and is still outstanding, or can still be filed for a prior period.

The fixed monthly education credit discussed below requires only enrolment in all cases, so that courses which meet the requirements for that credit do not necessarily require physical presence, whether within or outside of Canada. The credit was eliminated as of January 1, 2017.

In a technical opinion under the revised policy, the CRA commented on a case where a Canadian-resident general practitioner incurred tuition fees, as well as travel and living expenses, in the course of taking distance university courses via the internet. He was enrolled as a full-time student in a two-year medical master's program provided through the Internet by a foreign university listed in ¶1265 (although the relevance of this is not clear, except as adding substance to the legitimacy of the foreign university). Under that program, he was required to spend three one-week periods at the university every year, incurring travel and living expenses. The CRA confirmed that the taxpayer could claim the tuition fees but not the travel and living expenses as eligible for tuition credit, and could also claim education credit. The travel and living expenses could not be claimed as moving expenses, since the taxpayer did not change his residence. Nor could they be deducted from business income, since they would not be incurred for the purpose of earning business or property income (being more in the nature of a capital outlay). Accordingly, they would be subject to the general rule prohibiting the deduction of personal living expenses. In general, students enrolled in distance learning via the Internet may claim tuition credit provided they can demonstrate that the learning is equivalent to full-time attendance at a university and meets all other conditions to qualify for the credit. In particular, the definitions of "designated educational institution" and "qualifying educational program" must be considered. The CRA further noted, protecting itself as best it can, that the student would not qualify for the credit if he received any benefit or reimbursement of his tuition fees from a person not dealing at arm's length with him, if he received employment income during his courses, or if the training was related to his employment duties. The summary above is drawn from the English commentary in Wolters Kluwer's *Window on Canadian Tax* 9666, summarizing the French document in CRA Document No. 2008-0292531I7.

(Income Tax Folio: S1-F2-C2, Tuition Tax Credit, paras. 10–13; *Cleveland v. The Queen*, 2004 DTC 2199 (T.C.C.))

[¶1337] EDUCATION AND TEXTBOOK CREDIT AMOUNT

[¶1337.05] *Overview*

The education and textbook tax credits were eliminated effective January 1, 2017. Until then, a "full-time" student could claim a tax credit in respect of an amount equal to $400 times the number of months in the calendar year during which he or she was (1) enrolled as a full-time student at a designated educational institution, and (2) enrolled in a "qualifying educational program". The months in the year in which the program started and ended were included in the number of months in determining the amount of the credit. A "part-time" student could claim a tax credit in respect of an amount equal to $120 times the number of months in the calendar year during which he or she was (1) enrolled at a designated educational institution, and (2) enrolled in a "specified educational program". No amount could be claimed under the part-time rules for any month for which the student made a claim under the full-time rules.

Post-secondary students enrolled in distance education programs or correspondence courses could meet the full-time or part-time requirements if the course met the required standards.

Although the education and textbook credits are eliminated for 2017 and subsequent taxation years, credits claimed for years prior to 2017 remain available as carryforwards indefinitely.

[¶1337.07] *Textbook Amount*

The textbook credit, which was eliminated effective January 1, 2017, was $65 per month for each month in the year for which you were entitled to the $400 full-time student amount above, and $20 per month for each month in the year for which you were entitled to the $120 part-time student amount above.

[¶1337.10] *Students with Infirmity or Disability*

Until it was repealed January 1, 2017, the $400 full-time education amount could be claimed by students who were disabled regardless of whether they met the full-time attendance requirement. Disability could be assumed where a disability credit could be deducted for the student either by the student or a supporting person (¶1255).

Disability could also be shown by a certificate in writing from a medical doctor, or from an appropriate specialist qualified to issue certificates for certain conditions under the rules at ¶1209, to the effect that the student suffered in the year from a physical or mental impairment such that the student could not reasonably be expected to be enrolled as a full-time student while so impaired. For new claims, you had to submit a completed and certified form T2201, "Disability Tax Credit Certificate", to claim the full-time education amount.

[¶1337.15] *Full-Time Student (Qualifying Educational Program)*

The term "full-time student" is not defined. It is given some content by the requirements of a qualifying educational program, discussed below, but presumably goes beyond that. The CRA gives the term a fairly broad interpretation in S1-F2-C2, paras. 2.17-2.21. You are entitled to the education credit if you hold a full-time job and at the same time take a major course load that would qualify you as a full-time student at the educational institution you are attending. If you are participating in post-graduate studies on a regular basis and are registered for the regular academic year, you will be entitled to the education deduction even though the requirements for attendance in class for such studies are minimal. However, if you are in a program where you go to school for a certain period of the year and work at a related job for a certain period, you will not be entitled to any education amount for a period during which you worked and carried no significant course load.

While this definition has been amended as a consequence of the repeal of the education tax credit, for the time being a qualifying educational program for purposes of the full-time student education amount requirements generally means a program at a post-secondary level of not less than three consecutive weeks in duration that requires at least 10 hours per week on courses or work in the program. However, an exception is made for courses given by a designated Canadian institution described in the second item under the subheading "Designated Educational Institution", below; programs given by these schools will qualify even if they are not at post-secondary level, provided they meet the 3-week/10-hour requirements.

The 3-week/10-hour requirements must be met on a continuing basis, so that taking a cluster of courses for a three-week period but not for the entire semester would not qualify as a whole semester, although it might qualify for two months to be included in the period if it overlapped a month end.

A post-secondary program that consists principally of research is not a "qualifying education program", and, therefore, not eligible for the education tax credit unless the program leads to a diploma from college or CEGEP, or a bachelor, masters, or doctoral degree (or an equivalent degree). This means that post-doctoral fellowships are not subject to the scholarship exemption and therefore are taxable (see ¶953).

[¶1337.20] *Part-Time Student (Specified Educational Program)*

A student is qualified for the $120 per month education amount for months in which the student is enrolled at a designated educational institution (discussed below) in a specified educational program. A specified educational program is essentially a qualifying educational program except that it does not have a 10-hour per week course or work load requirement. That is, it is a program at the post-secondary level of not less than three consecutive weeks in duration. Courses given by a designated Canadian institution described in the second item under the subheading "Designated Educational Institution", below will qualify even if they are not at post-secondary level.

[¶1337.25] *Designated Educational Institution and Qualifying Student*

The definition of "designated educational institution" has been slightly amended as a consequence of the elimination of the education tax credit. For the time being, for the purposes of the education and textbook tax credits, a designated educational institution is:

(1) An educational institution in Canada that is a university, college, or other educational institution designated under the *Canada Student Loans Act*, the *Canada Student Financial Assistance Act*, or, in Quebec, *An Act respecting financial assistance for education expenses.*

(2) An educational institution in Canada that is designated by the Minister of Human Resources Development (formerly Employment and Immigration) as one which offers courses, other than courses designed for university credit, that will provide or improve the qualifications of a person for employment or for the carrying on of a business or profession.

(3) A university outside of Canada in which the student (as of January 1, 2017, a qualifying student) was enrolled for at least three consecutive weeks in a course leading to a Bachelor or equivalent level degree. Prior to 2011, the minimum course duration was 13 consecutive weeks.

(4) A U.S. college, university or other educational institution which provides courses at a post-secondary school level if the student (as of January 1, 2017, a qualifying student) lived throughout the year near the Canada–U.S. border and commuted to the U.S. institution.

Generally speaking, the school will know if it is qualified, since it must certify the student's attendance on form T2202A. The information is available to it from various government departments listed in Income Tax Folio S1-F2-C1, para. 1.13.

Effective for the 2017 taxation year, the newly defined term "qualifying student" is added to the definition of "designated educational institution". This addition was made to accommodate the repeal of the education tax credit. A qualifying student refers to an individual who:

(1) is enrolled for at least one month in the taxation year in a qualifying educational program as a full-time student at a designated educational institution, or

(2) is enrolled at a designated educational institution in a specified educational program (with not less than 12 hours in the month spent on courses in the program).

[¶1337.30] *Vocational Training*

Where the student is enrolled in an educational institution described in (2), above (essentially, a designated school that is not an academic college or university, but may be a vocational school or community college), the education credit is only available if the student is enrolled in a program to obtain skills for, or improve the individual's skills in, an occupation. Presumably the school itself will provide information as to which programs qualify.

Where the student is enrolled in an educational institution described in (2), above, the education credit will only be given if the student has reached the age of 16 before the end of the year for which credit is sought.

[¶1337.40] *Forms and Schedules*

If you are eligible for the education and/or textbook tax credits your school should provide you with form T2202A, which it has completed, confirming your enrolment in a qualifying program of a particular length. These need no longer be filed with the T1 return, but you should keep them on file with your tax information for the year in case the CRA should want to see them. These two credits were eliminated as of January 1, 2017.

This is true even if you are making declarations or transferring unused credits on form T2202A. If you are transferring unused credits to a parent/grandparent (as discussed at ¶1339) or to a spouse/common-law partner (as discussed at ¶1361), you should provide a completed copy of your entire form T2202A to the designated transferee, as well as retaining a completed copy of the entire form with your tax records. The transferee similarly retains his or her copy on hand, but should not file it with the return. Similarly, you should provide the transferee with a copy of your completed Schedule 11. You do file a copy of your own Schedule 11, but a transferee does not file a copy of your Schedule 11, but simply enters the amount you designated to the transferee on the appropriate line of the transferee's return.

Proceed as follows to claim the tuition, education, and textbook amounts:

- enter on line 320 of Schedule 11 the eligible tuition fees paid for the year;
- enter beside the amounts of $400 and $65 the number of months for which you qualified as a full-time student (i.e., number of months shown in column C of form T2202A) and report the product on Line 322 of Schedule 11;
- enter beside the amounts of $120 and $20 the number of months for which you qualified as a part-time student (i.e., number of months shown in column B of form T2202A) and report the product on Line 321 of Schedule 11.

You cannot make a claim for both the $400 and $120 amounts for any month; if there is a month in which you qualified for both, you must choose the $400 amount only.

The tuition, education, and textbook amounts for the year accumulated on Schedule 11, along with those carried forward from prior years (¶1341), are measured against your income and the amount needed to reduce your income to nil is carried to line 323 of the T1, and is converted, together with other amounts eligible for credit, at line 338. Up to $5,000 of any amount remaining on Schedule 11 may be designated by you for transfer to a spouse, parent or grandparent. Any amounts not so transferred are carried forward to reduce your tax in future years. The education and textbook amounts were eliminated effective January 1, 2017.

Example

> Albert Cox is enrolled as a full-time student at McGill University. He is taking a course leading to a commerce degree. The semester is eight months in duration. Albert may claim an education credit for 8 × $400 or $3,200, and a textbook credit of 8 × $65 or $520. The total of these amounts ($3,720) will be entered at line 322 of Schedule 11 and the related credit will be 15% × $3,720 = $558. If Albert attended from January 1 to May 15 and from September 15 to December 31, his credit would be based on nine months because the number of months includes the months during which a course begins and ends.

[¶1337.45] *Other Conditions*

No claim may be made if a student has received from a non-related person a benefit, grant or reimbursement of expenses in respect of that program. Examples of students disqualified under this rule would be nurses in training who receive board and lodging or an allowance, students in receipt of training allowances under government programs (but see below), and individuals who receive benefits from seminars and training programs because of their membership in a registered national arts service organization.

An award such as a scholarship, fellowship, bursary, or prize for achievement is not considered a benefit, grant, or reimbursement of expenses which disqualifies the student. Note that such benefits are taxable but eligible for a partial or full exemption, depending on the year of receipt and fulfillment of certain conditions; see ¶953–¶969. Similarly, any benefit granted under the *Canada Student Loans Act*, the *Canada Student Financial Assistance Act*, or (effective January 2, 2015) the *Apprentice Loans Act*, or, in Quebec, *An Act respecting financial assistance for education expenses*, is not considered a disqualifying benefit, grant, or reimbursement of expenses, nor is the non-repayable portion of a student loan.

You are entitled to claim the education tax credit even if you receive taxable assistance for post-secondary education under:

(1) Part II of the *Employment Insurance Act* or a similar provincial program as agreed with the federal government; and

(2) another prescribed training program or a program established under the authority of the Minister of Employment and Social Development as discussed under the subheading "Offsetting Deduction for Adult Education Training Tuition" in ¶971.

It is understood that, in addition to the programs described in (1), above, the following programs have in fact been determined by Employment and Social Development Canada as qualified under these rules:

- Employability Assistance for People with Disabilities (EAPD);
- Opportunities Fund for Persons with Disabilities (OF); and
- Fisheries Restructuring and Adjustment Measures.

Where you receive taxable amounts for tuition under such programs, you could claim offsetting tuition tax credit providing the educational program was otherwise eligible. See also ¶971.

(ITA: 118.6; 118.8; 118.9; Income Tax Folio: S1-F2-C1 Education and Textbook Tax Credits)

[¶1339] TRANSFER OF UNUSED TUITION, EDUCATION, AND TEXTBOOK CREDITS TO PARENT OR GRANDPARENT

The education and textbook credits were eliminated effective January 1, 2017, but the information below is still relevant for 2016 and preceding taxation years.

As discussed at ¶1319, the tuition, education (prior to 2017), and textbook (prior to 2017) credits generated in the current year which are not utilized by the student may be transferred to a parent or grandparent, as discussed here, or to a spouse as discussed at ¶1361, below. A spouse includes a common-law spouse within the definition at ¶1113.

The transfer to a parent or grandparent is only available where no credit is claimed by the student's spouse for either the married exemption credit (¶1114, line 303) or any of the spousal credit transfers (¶1361, line 326).

[¶1339.05] *Definition of "Parent or Grandparent"*

"Parent" is defined in the *Income Tax Act* by reference to the definition of child. The child of an individual is defined to include:

- a person of whom the individual is the legal parent whether the person was born within or outside marriage. This replaces the previous references in the Act to "the natural parent" and "an adopted child of the taxpayer";
- a person who is wholly dependent on the individual for support and of whom the individual has, or immediately before the person attained the age of 19 years had, in law or in fact, the custody and control (note that the CRA considers that this does not include a foster child, since a foster child is not "wholly dependent" on the foster parents because of the support payments received from an agency responsible for the child's care);
- a child of the individual's spouse or common-law partner; and
- a spouse or common-law partner of a child of the individual.

A parent is an individual who has a child within the above definition and includes a natural parent, a step-parent and an adoptive parent of the individual as well as a person on whom the individual is, or was, (if the individual is over 18) wholly dependent. The rules make it clear that a parent or grandparent includes a spouse's parent or grandparent. As well, in the case of a grandparent, the spouse of the spouse's grandparent is specified to be a grandparent (at the parent level this inclusion would be accomplished by the general rule).

[¶1339.10] *Amount Which Can Be Transferred (1): Designation to Parent*

The amount which can be transferred to a parent or grandparent is limited to the amount which the student designates in writing to transfer. The transferee parent or grandparent need not be the one to claim the student as a dependant, if anyone does make such a claim. However, any claim by a spouse for the student, as discussed above, will bar this transfer claim by a parent or grandparent.

If no spouse is making a claim for the student, the student can make the transfer by designating in writing one, and only one, recipient parent or grandparent. The student is also required to designate the amount to be transferred. The amount which can be designated in a particular year is limited by the calculation below to any excess (up to $5,000 of education (prior to 2017), textbook (prior to 2017), and tuition amounts before conversion to credit) after using the credits to wipe out the student's own tax, but the student may choose to designate less than the entire excess amount as available for transfer. This is because the student is given the option of carrying forward for his or her own use in future years (but not for transfer in future years) any excess credits that are not designated to others in the current year. Schedule 11 is required to deal with carryforward amounts, and should be used to ensure the correct calculation of transfer amounts even if the student does not have to file a return.

In practice, the student designates the amounts eligible for credits rather than the credits themselves, and these designations must be made on the chart on the back of form T2202A, which is usually the receipt given by the educational institution to support the credit claim.

Under these rules, it is possible for the student to overdesignate a transfer. In the first place, of course, the transfer cannot exceed the lesser of the student's combined education, textbook, and tuition amounts generated in the taxation year and $5,000, reduced by the student's income after personal amounts as specified under the next subheading below. However, even within this limit, the student could designate more than the parent/grandparent could utilize.

Example

Joan Hull had $7,500 worth of qualifying education, textbook, and tuition amounts (before conversion to credit). Joan herself had no taxable income, and she designated the maximum permissible $5,000 to her mother, who however only had enough income to use $4,500 of the amount. Joan can carry forward the $2,500 she could not designate, but technically no one seems able to use the $500 her mother could not use. Her mother cannot carry forward a transferred amount, and Joan cannot carry forward amounts she has designated to someone else. If Joan designates only $4,500, her mother uses the full amount designated to her and Joan carries forward $3,000, so no credit is lost. The CRA does not want to administer this rule harshly, and says in the T1 Guide that you should transfer no more than the transferee needs to reduce tax to zero. However, its systems may not be sophisticated enough to correct the transferred amounts.

[¶1339.15] *Amount Which Can Be Transferred (2): Calculation of Amount Transferable*

Technically, it is the actual credit which is transferred, and this is the lesser of (i) the conversion rate for the year (¶1303) multiplied by $5,000 and (ii) the total credits for tuition fees and education and textbook amounts combined, minus tax payable after claiming credits for personal amounts, CPP/QPP/QPIP/EI contributions, pension income amount, employment amount, adoption expenses, transit passes, child fitness expenses (after 2006 and before 2015), children's arts amount (for 2016 and prior years), first-time home buyers' amount, volunteer firefighters' amount, search and rescue volunteer amount, disability amounts, and education/tuition carryforwards claimed, but no other credits. Effective January 1, 2017, the education and textbook credits are repealed but remain available as carryforwards.

As a practical matter, it is the amounts eligible for credit rather than the credits themselves which are transferred on Schedule 11. The amount which can be designated by the student for transfer is limited to:

(1) the lesser of the student's total tuition fees and education and textbook amounts and $5,000

minus

(2) the excess of the student's taxable income (from line 260 of the student's return) over the total of amounts deducted on lines 1 to 24 (boxes 300 to 318, 362 to 365, 367, 369 to 370, and 395) of the Schedule 1 of the student's return.

If the student is not filing a return because he or she has no taxable income, then the amount in (1), above, will be the amount eligible for transfer. Note that (2) cannot be a negative amount; that is, the student's income (or tax) cannot be less than zero. If the student has any taxable income at all, however, Schedule 11 is essential to the correct calculation of the amount available for transfer even if the student need not file it because there is no tax owing (and no amount to be carried forward).

You need not attach to your T1 return a copy of the student's tuition fees receipt if you are claiming a transfer in respect of tuition fees, nor a copy of the student's form T2202A if you are claiming a transfer in respect of the monthly education amount. However, you should have the student fill out the back of the form T2202A to indicate the designation to you of the transferred amount. In the absence of these forms, you should have a copy of the official tuition receipt and a written designation signed by the student. Although you need not file these forms, you should have them available with your copy of the T1 return, since the CRA can demand them.

Example

Rocky Ceccetti, a bachelor, is 20 years old and attended the University of Calgary during eight months of the year. During the summer, Rocky was employed and earned net income of $13,700. Rocky paid tuition fees of $5,000, had CPP contributions of $505 and EI contributions of $258.

Rocky may designate in writing any parent or grandparent to claim the unused portion of the tuition and education amounts. Rocky will compute his tuition and education amounts as follows:

Tuition fee	$ 5,000
Education amount — 8 × $400	3,200
Textbook amount — 8 × $65	520
Basic amounts available for transfer	$ 8,720
Salary	$ 13,700
Taxable income	$ 13,700
Less — basic exemption amount	(11,474)
— CPP contribution	(505)
— EI premium	(258)
— Canada Employment amount	(1,161)
Taxable amount before tuition and education amounts	$ 302
Rocky can transfer:	
Tuition fees and education amount (maximum $5,000)	$ 5,000
Less — Rocky's taxable amount before claiming the tuition and education amounts	($ 302)
Net transferable claim	$ 4,698

In effect, Rocky has used as much of his tuition and education amounts as is necessary to wipe out his own income (tax) and can transfer the remaining amounts (credits).

To transfer any portion of the $4,517 to a parent or grandparent, Rocky must identify the recipient and the amount of transfer on his form T2202A from the university. He should also complete Schedule 11. He should ensure that the transferee can utilize the entire amount. If the entire transfer cannot be utilized, he should reduce the designation and claim any remaining balance amount as a carryforward on Schedule 11.

There is an explicit ordering provision in the statute (¶1365) which requires deduction of personal exemption credits — age credit, CPP/QPP and EI credits, pension credit, employment credit, adoption credit, transit credit, child fitness credit (after 2006 and before 2015), children's arts credit (for 2016 and prior years), first-time home buyers' credit, volunteer firefighter credit, search and rescue volunteer credit (beginning in 2014), disability credit, and tuition, education (prior to 2017), and textbook (prior to 2017) credits carried forward from prior years — before the current year tuition, education, and textbook credits. If the disability credit is also being transferred, and an amount of transferable disability credit survives these deductions, then no further deduction is made in arriving at the student's income in (2), above. In these circumstances the whole of (1) will be transferable, even if the transfer is not made to the same person. That is, a disability credit could apparently be transferred to a spouse and an education credit to a parent.

[¶1339.20] *Amount Which Can Be Transferred (3): Calculation of Carryforward Amounts*

The example below further illustrates the application of the rules relating to transfers of tuition and education amount credits.

Example

Mr. David Taylor has a daughter, Karen, who transferred tuition, education, and textbook amount credits to her father. Karen's tuition, education, and textbook amounts were calculated as follows:

Tuition fee	$ 29,800
Education amount — 8 × $400	3,200
Textbook amount — 8 × $65	520
Basic amounts available for transfer	$ 33,520

Karen had no taxable income and so the maximum allowable amount of $5,000 was transferred to David. Karen now has $28,520 ($33,520 - $5,000) in tuition credits available to be carried forward to future years.

As well, Mr. Taylor has a son, Mike, who transferred $3,172 to Mr. Taylor. The relatively small portion of Mike's tuition credits transferred reflects the fact that Mike's taxable income was much higher than Karen's. In Mike's case, the facts were as follows:

Tuition fee	$ 6,990
Education amount — 8 × $400	3,200
Textbook amount — 8 × $65	520
Basic amounts available for transfer	$ 10,710
Taxable income	$ 15,143
Less — basic exemption amount	(11,474)
— CPP contribution	(576)
— EI premium	(285)
— Canada Employment Amount	(1,161)
Taxable amount before tuition and education amounts	$ 1,647
Mike can transfer:	
Tuition fees and education amount (maximum)	$ 5,000
Less — Mike's taxable amount before claiming the tuition and education amounts	(1,647)
Net transferable claim	$ 3,353

(ITA: 118.5; 118.6; 118.61; 118.81; 118.9; Income Tax Folio: S1-F2-C1 Education and Textbook Tax Credits)

[¶1339.25] *Forms and Schedules*

If you have been designated as a transferee under these rules, the student should provide you with a completed copy of the form (typically T2202A) which reported the eligible amounts to the student, including the portion of the form on which an excess amount has been designated to you. The student should also provide you with a copy of the student's Schedule 11, showing the calculation of the transfer amounts. You should enter the amount transferred on line 324 of your Schedule 1, but you should not file the student's tuition slips or the student's Schedule 11 with your return. However, you should keep these copies with your tax records to support the claim should the CRA wish to verify it.

(ITA: 110.3; 118.5; 118.6; 118.9; 252)

[¶1341] CARRYFORWARD OF UNUSED TUITION, EDUCATION, AND TEXTBOOK CREDITS

The combined education, tuition, and textbook credits which arise in a year and which the student cannot deduct from tax in a year because he or she has insufficient tax to absorb them (and to the extent the student does not designate the current year excess to a spouse, parent or grandparent), will carry forward for future use by the student. The student (and only the student) must use these carryforwards in future years immediately as sufficient income arises to absorb them. Effective January 1, 2017, the education and textbook tax credits were eliminated; however, unused education and textbook credit amounts carried forward from years prior to 2017 will remain available to be claimed in 2017 and subsequent years.

The carryforward is calculated on Schedule 11.

Virtually the only complex feature of this carryforward concept is the ordering and timing of credits.

Where a student has a carryforward balance at the end of Year 1, the student *must* in Year 2 deduct the lesser of:

(1) the balance at the end of Year 1; and

(2) the amount that would be the student's tax payable for the year if no deduction were available for new credits generated in Year 2.

What this means is that carryforwards must be claimed in Year 2 before a new carryforward is calculated. It is a first-in first-out system in which old credits must be used before new ones, and any new credits so blocked are added to the carryforward.

The calculation of the carryforward itself consists of three steps, as follows:

(1) Begin with the balance carried forward from the end of the preceding year. Call this the Year 1 balance.

(2) To the Year 1 balance carried forward the student adds the excess of the total education/tuition/textbook credits generated in Year 2 over the lesser of (i) that total, and (ii) the student's Year 2 tax that would be payable if the only credits available were for unused tuition, education, and textbook amounts from Year 1, personal amounts in Chapter 11 (basic amount, spousal, age, dependants, etc.), CPP/EI credits, pension income credit, employment credit, adoption credit, transit credit, child fitness credit (after 2006 and before 2015), children's arts credit (for 2016 and prior years), first-time home buyers' credit, volunteer firefighter credit, search and rescue volunteer credit, and disability credit.

(3) From the subtotal in (2) of carryforwards plus current year credits in excess of notional tax payable, the student must then deduct the sum of the amount of the carryforward that the student can currently absorb against Year 2 tax payable plus any current tuition and education credits (education and textbook credits eliminated effective January 1, 2017) designated to be transferred for the current year. What remains is the Year 2 carryforward which is the starting point for Year 3 calculations. This step removes from the Year 2 carryforward balance any portion of the Year 1 carryfor-

ward which the student has sufficient tax to claim. It also removes any Year 2 amounts which are designated to a spouse, parent or grandparent. The amount designated is optional subject to the overall limits of the lesser of the amount eligible for Year 2 credit and $5,000. The student can designate only part of an amount eligible for transfer and keep on hand the balance for carryforward. For an example, see ¶1339.20. In theory, the student could overdesignate a transfer to the extent the transfer recipient also cannot use the credits; this is discussed at ¶1339 under the subheading "Amount Which Can Be Transferred (1): Designation to Parent". Although the calculations are expressed in terms of credits in the law, as a practical matter the calculations on Schedule 11, where the carryforward is determined, and T2202A, where designations to others are made, are carried out in eligible amounts before conversion to credit. This cannot distort the results, since for carryforwards to arise income must be so low that the distorting effects of higher income brackets cannot arise.

(ITA: 118.61; 118.81)

[¶1345] AMOUNT FOR INTEREST PAID ON STUDENT LOAN

You can claim credit (on line 319 of Schedule 1 of the T1 return) for interest paid in the year on your student loan. There is a five-year optional carryforward; that is, to the extent you cannot (because of insufficient tax to utilize the credit) or choose not to claim interest paid in the current year, you can claim it in any of the five subsequent years. You should keep track of these carryforwards yourself.

To be eligible for credit, interest must in fact have been paid (not merely due or payable). It is only the student (or former student) to whom the loan was made or who legally owes the interest who can claim the credit. However, the interest need not have been paid by the student; the student can claim the credit if the interest was paid by the student or anyone related to the student. For a discussion of related persons, see ¶1122.

To be eligible for credit, the interest must be on a loan made under the *Canada Student Loans Act*, the *Canada Student Financial Assistance Act*, the *Apprentice Loans Act* (effective January 2, 2015), or a law of a province governing the granting of financial assistance to students at post-secondary level. Since June 19, 2014, interest will also be eligible when paid on loans made under the *Apprentice Loans Act*. Personal or family loans will not qualify. As well, in the case of *Sandhu v. The Queen*, 2010 DTC 1165 (T.C.C.), the student loan tax credit was denied when the taxpayer could not prove that his bank loan was made under designated legislation.

In a technical opinion (CRA Document No. 9911706), the CRA has said that a consolidated bank loan which included student loans would not qualify, since payments would no longer be on a loan under one of the permitted statutes.

In the case of *Mueller v. The Queen*, 2013 DTC 1044 (T.C.C.), the Court found that interest on a student line of credit was not eligible for the student loan tax credit, as the line of credit did not constitute a loan/loans made under any eligible government program. The taxpayers had apparently sought to access the student loan tax credit by means of the line-of-credit, where because their parents' income was too high they did not qualify for student loans under the federal government student loan program.

In the rather odd case of *Napier v. The Queen*, 2007 DTC 362 (T.C.C.), a student loan was not a normal loan from the university, but rather a series of promissory notes to the university. The Court held that this was, in effect, financial assistance under the laws of a province, since the university had by its founding statute the ability to invest money as it saw fit. The case contains a useful review of cases in which interest did not fit the statutory requirements for credit eligibility.

The amount of interest paid is entered at line 319 and converted, along with other amounts, to credit at line 338. Receipts should be attached to the return (unless you are using EFILE or NETFILE, in which case you keep the receipts on file yourself).

(ITA: 118.62)

OTHER CREDITS

[¶1351] CANADA EMPLOYMENT CREDIT

For 2016, the amount eligible for employment tax credit is the lesser of $1,161 and the total of your employment income for the year (including taxable benefits) before employment deductions under section 8 of the *Income Tax Act* and the amounts received under the *Wage Earner Protection Program Act* (WEPP) under subparagraph 56(1)(*r*)(v). Section 8 deductions are, generally speaking, those identified in ¶365 to ¶379 inclusive.

The T1 Guide tells you to calculate the employment tax credit by adding all employment income from lines 101 and 104, and carrying to box 363 of Schedule 1 the lesser of that total and $1,161. Since employment deductions are generally claimed at 229 (or 231), this is in general a simple formula. In fact, it may in some circumstances be too simple, since the CRA does tell you to include some items in line 104 which are not, technically speaking, employment income. These are discussed at ¶308. You cannot be faulted for carrying out CRA instructions, although if you are claiming some items (such as royalties) as business income with offsetting deductions, the CRA may perhaps identify the discrepancy.

The amount eligible for the credit is carried to Schedule 1, box 363 (line 15 or, on the Quebec version, line 18), where, along with other amounts eligible for non-refundable credit, it is converted to credit at the conversion rate for the year (¶1303).

The credit is indexed in accordance with the rules at ¶1101. Values for preceding years and the following year are given in a chart preceding Chapter 1 at ¶65.

(ITA: 118(10))

[¶1353] TRANSIT PASS CREDIT

You can claim a non-refundable credit on Schedule 1 for the cost of eligible public transit passes used by (i) yourself, (ii) the person who was your spouse or common-law partner at any time in the year, and (iii) all your children who have not attained the age of 19 during the taxation year. "Child" has the extended meaning discussed at ¶1122.15.

An eligible transit pass is one which:

(1) entitles the holder to unlimited use on any day on which the transit company provides eligible services during an uninterrupted period of at least 28 days; generally speaking, these will be monthly or longer passes;

(2) is one of a series of unlimited passes, each valid for at least five days, which together provide for the use of public commuter transit services for at least 20 days in any 28-day period; the CRA interprets this as at least four consecutive weekly passes, where each weekly pass provides unlimited public transit use for an uninterrupted period of between five and seven days (the purpose is to allow taxpayers who cannot afford monthly passes to use a series of weekly passes);

(3) is an electronic payment card which you (or your family members) use for at least 32 one-way trips (so, 16 round trips) during a period of 31 days; the card must be issued by a public transit authority that records and provides a receipt for the cost and usage of the card — this appears to refer to cards which are good for a specific number or dollar amount of fares, and which can be topped up with additional funds needed for additional travel.

You are expected to keep the transit passes themselves and adequate receipts to document your claim. If your transit pass displays all of the following information, the pass itself will be sufficient to support a claim for the tax credit:

- an indication that it is a monthly (or longer duration) pass;
- the date or period for which the pass is valid;
- the name of the transit authority or organization issuing the pass;
- the amount paid for the pass; and,
- the identity of the rider, either by name or unique identifier.

If the pass does not have all of this information, you will need to keep receipts, cancelled cheques or credit card statements, along with your pass(es), to support your claim. The CRA will accept receipts (letters) generated by employers or Employer Pass Program Coordinators for employer transit pass programs. The receipt should note the purpose, exact amount received, date of payment, and name of the payee. Generally, the CRA does not consider a bank statement to be a valid receipt. However, if the statement clearly indicates the purpose of the debit (for example, Employee FareCard), the CRA will accept this as support for the claim.

In the case of electronic passes, it is the receipts supporting purchase of enough fares to meet the 32 one-way trip requirement that will be the chief evidence that the conditions are met. The CRA has issued no additional guidelines on this requirement.

Strictly speaking, the amount eligible for credit is the portion of the cost attributable to the use of public commuter transit services, which are defined as services:

- offered to the general public, ordinarily for a period of at least five days a week, of transporting individuals from one place in Canada to another in Canada by means of bus, ferry, subway, train or tram; and
- in respect of which it can reasonably be expected that those individuals would return daily to the place of their departure.

The company offering the services must be authorized under a federal or provincial law to carry on such a business through a permanent establishment in Canada.

The second item in this list is ambiguous. The most likely interpretation is that it is the services which are being described, so that if the pass is for a transit service which normally serves commuters, the cost qualifies. It is perhaps possible to interpret the requirement as one for the pass holder to be a regular commuter, and indeed to be required to apportion the cost of the pass between that use and other uses. So far, the CRA does not seem to have taken the latter view, and in the short run it is probably unlikely to try.

The amount eligible for the credit is the cost of each eligible pass for yourself, your spouse or common-law partner, and your eligible children in respect of travel in the taxation year. The eligible amounts are reduced by any reimbursements, allowances, or other assistance that anyone was entitled to receive in respect of those passes unless the reimbursements, etc., were included in income of the person entitled to them and were not deducted again in computing taxable income. In short, eligible cost is cost less any reimbursements from any source unless the reimbursements are fully taxable to the recipient.

Your claim in any taxation year is limited to travel for that year. Thus, if you paid for your Year 2 annual pass in Year 1, you will only be able to claim the tax credit on your Year 2 tax return, because no portion of the cost of the Year 2 annual pass was used for travel in Year 1. If you paid in Year 1 for a student annual pass for months in Year 1 and Year 2, you can claim the amount paid for the portion of travel that occurs in each taxation year. For the portion used in Year 1, you can claim the cost for travel on your Year 1 tax return. You can claim the portion of the cost of travel that occurs in Year 2 on your Year 2 tax return.

Where more than one person is eligible to claim the credit in respect of a particular pass, those eligible to make the claim must divide the credit between them in such a fashion that the total credit claimed does not exceed the amount that could have been claimed in the hands of one claimant. Where claimants cannot agree, the CRA may arbitrarily apportion the credit.

In general, since the credit for any pass is limited to the cost of the pass times the conversion rate for the year, which is the minimum marginal tax rate, the value of the credit is the same in the hands of any taxpayer, so long as the taxpayer has sufficient tax to absorb the credit.

The amount eligible for transit pass credit is reported in box 364 on Schedule 1. You should not submit your supporting documentation when you file your return, but you must keep it on hand with your tax documents for the year in case the Canada Revenue Agency (CRA) asks for it in verifying your claim.

(ITA: 118.02; Other Publications: CRA document *Public Transit amount*, at the time of writing was available on the CRA website at www.cra-arc.gc.ca/transitpass)

[¶1356] CHILD FITNESS CREDIT

Before 2014, an individual was entitled to claim a non-refundable child fitness tax credit calculated at the rate of 15% on up to $500 of eligible fitness expenses incurred for a child who was under 16 at the beginning of the year and was registered in a prescribed program of physical activity. If at least $100 of eligible fitness expenses were incurred for a child who was under 18 at the beginning of the year and qualified for the disability tax credit, the individual could claim an additional credit at the rate of 15% on $500.

Effective for 2014, the $500 maximum limit for the basic credit in respect of a non-disabled child was increased to

$1,000, but the limit for the additional credit in respect of a disabled child remained at $500.

Effective for 2015, the non-refundable child fitness tax credit became refundable. See ¶1497.

Refundable Child Fitness Tax Credit

Calculation

The refundable child fitness tax credit has two components:

- a basic credit of up to $75 [$500 × 15%] for a child under 16 at the beginning of the taxation year; and
- an additional credit of up to $75 [$500 × 15%] for a disabled child under 18 at the beginning of the year.

To qualify for the regular credit, the taxpayer must pay eligible fitness expenses for a qualifying child, pay them to a qualifying entity, and file an income tax return. To qualify for the additional credit, the taxpayer must also incur at least $100 of eligible fitness expenses for the regular credit.

Refundability

The child fitness tax credit is fully refundable (even if the taxpayer does not have enough tax payable to cover the full amount of the credit) and is calculated by reference to eligible fitness expenses incurred for children registered in prescribed programs of physical activity. There is no limit on the number of children for which the credit may be claimed.

Claim Period

A taxpayer must claim the credit in the year in which the eligible fitness expenses are paid to a qualifying entity, which is not necessarily the same year in which the child performs the related physical activities.

Multiple Claimants

If more than one person (e.g., two spouses) qualifies for the credit, they must share it between themselves. Otherwise, the CRA will allocate the credit. Under no circumstances, can the combined credit claimed by two persons exceed the one that could be claimed by one person.

Additional Information

For more information on the child fitness tax credit, see the Historical Information section below, since the calculations and considerations relevant for the non-refundable child fitness tax credit claimable before 2015 are also valid for the refundable child fitness tax credit claimable for 2015 and 2016.

Historical Information

You may claim the credit for any eligible expense paid by yourself or your spouse or common-law partner in respect of the children of either person who are under 16 at the beginning of the year. Where more than one person is eligible to claim the credit in respect of a particular expense (typically either parent could make the claim), those eligible to make the claim must divide the credit between themselves so that the total credit claimed does not exceed the amount that could have been claimed by a single claimant. Where claimants cannot agree, the CRA may arbitrarily apportion the credit.

For each of your children for which someone can claim a disability credit (¶1255) for the year, the age limit is raised to under 18 at the beginning of the year. As well, as long as you make a claim of at least $100 for the disabled child, you get an automatic additional credit of $500. That is, if you claim $90 of eligible expenses for the disabled child for the year, the amount eligible for credit is $90, but if you claim $100, the amount eligible for credit is $600 (the $100 actual amount and the $500 automatic amount). Expenditures for the disabled child of $500 or more command the maximum amount eligible for credit of $1,000.

The amount you can claim is reduced by any reimbursements, allowances, or other assistance that anyone was entitled to receive in respect of the expenses unless the reimbursements, etc., were included in income of the person entitled to them and were not deducted again in computing taxable income. In short, eligible cost is cost less any reimbursements from any source unless the reimbursements are fully taxable to the recipient.

In general, since the credit for any expense is limited to the lesser of (i) $500 and (ii) the amount paid, times the conversion rate for the year, which is the minimum marginal tax rate, the value of the credit is the same in the hands of any taxpayer, so long as the taxpayer has sufficient tax to absorb the credit. In short, it makes no sense to assign the credit to a parent whose income, after other credits (¶1365), is too low to make use of it.

An eligible fitness expense is a fee paid in respect of a child who is under 16 (18 if disability credit can be claimed) at the beginning of the year to a "qualifying entity" to the extent that the fee is attributable to the cost of registration or membership of the child in a "prescribed program of physical activity".

A fee is specifically said to be eligible to the extent that it represents the cost to the entity of the program for administration, instruction, rental of required facilities, and uniforms and equipment not available to the participant at less than fair market value (apparently this is meant to accommodate team jerseys and equipment used in common). A fee is not eligible to the extent it includes the cost of accommodation, travel, food or beverages, or amounts deductible as child care expenses. Presumably it is up to the organizations to determine eligible expenses and receipt them properly, although there is no compulsion to do this, creating, one imagines, an enforcement nightmare for the CRA.

A qualifying entity is merely one which offers one or more prescribed programs of physical activity. It need not be registered with the CRA, or, apparently, with anyone. You cannot deduct a fee paid to your spouse or common-law partner, or any individual who is under 18 at the time the payment is made. There seems to be nothing to prevent you from paying your older children to provide a prescribed program of physical activity to your younger children.

Obviously, the devil lurks in the details of what is a prescribed program of physical activity. Under current regulations, a prescribed program is a program *which is not part of a school's curriculum* and is:

(1) a weekly program of a duration of eight or more consecutive weeks in which all or substantially all of the activities include a significant amount of physical activity, as defined for these purposes;

(2) a program of a duration of five or more consecutive days of which more than 50% of the daily activities include a significant amount of "physical activity" (this would apply to summer and day camp programs);

(3) a program offered to children by a club, association, or similar organization (all described as "the organization", below) in circumstances where a participant in the program may select amongst a variety of activities if

(a) more than 50% of those activities offered to children by the organization are activities that include a significant amount of "physical activity", or

(b) more than 50% of the time scheduled for activities offered to children in the program is scheduled for activities that include a significant amount of "physical activity"; or

(4) a membership in an organization of a duration of eight or more consecutive weeks if more than 50% of all the activities offered to children by the organization include a significant amount of "physical activity".

"Physical activity" in the definition above means a supervised activity suitable for children other than an activity of which an essential component involves the child riding in or on a motorized vehicle. (This is intended to exclude snowmobiling but permit water skiing.) In general, it must be an activity that contributes to cardio-respiratory endurance, plus one or more of muscular strength, muscular endurance, flexibility, and balance. (Horseback riding is specifically defined to be such an activity.) However, in the case of a disabled child (one for whom a disability credit can be claimed), it is sufficient that the activity results in movement and an observable expenditure of energy in a recreational context.

Where a program is not a prescribed program of physical activity because it does not meet the 50% requirement set out in (3), above, a special rule allows you to claim a portion of the amount that is paid for the program. In such circumstances, a portion of the program is considered a prescribed program of physical activity. That portion is either:

- the percentage of those activities offered to children by the organization that are activities that include a significant amount of physical activity, or
- the percentage of the time scheduled for activities in the program that is scheduled for activities that include a significant amount of physical activity.

Example

Sabrina's mother pays $200 for the registration of her daughter at a community centre. The portion of the activities offered to children by the centre that qualify as physical activity for the purpose of the credit is 40%. Therefore, only 40% of the program will be considered a prescribed program of physical activity and Sabrina's mother may claim, as a child fitness amount, 40% of $200, i.e., $80.

Where a membership in an organization does not meet the 50% activities requirement in (4), above, the portion of the expense that will be an eligible amount for fitness credit purposes is the portion of the activities offered to children by the organization that are activities that include a significant amount of physical activity.

As well, the CRA has noticed that the same expenditure might qualify for both child care expense deduction (¶1049) and fitness credit. The T1 Guide says that such expenses should be attributed to child care first, with any excess eligible for fitness credit. There actually appears to be no such ordering provision in the *Income Tax Act*, but the CRA position would seem to be beneficial in most situations. However, it may be more accurate to say that the taxpayer can claim such expenses in the most beneficial way.

If an expense is eligible for the children's fitness amount, it is not eligible for the children's art amount.

Where there are two distinct prescribed programs, one eligible for the children's fitness amount and the other for the children's arts amount, there should be two receipts, or one receipt that indicated the amounts paid for each distinct program.

The children's fitness credit is now claimed in box 459 on page 4 of the T1 return.

[¶1356.05] *Eligible Expenses and Documentation*

The CRA provided taxpayers intending to claim a child fitness credit with the following Technical Interpretations concerning the expenses that would be eligible for the credit and the documentation that they would need to keep on file:

- Swimming lessons offered by a municipality to pre-school children to help them become more comfortable with water, rather than to teach them to swim, qualify for the credit provided the course is a weekly program of at least eight weeks or one of at least five consecutive days (No. 2008-0280121I7).
- Therapeutic horseback riding activities qualify for the credit provided the disabled child is under 18 (No. 2007-0240721I7).
- Lesson enrollment fees, rental charges for speed skates, mandatory affiliation fees to the Quebec Speed Skating Federation, and competition registration fees paid in connection with skating lessons qualify for the credit (No. 2007-0232041E5).
- The enrollment of ringette players in a fitness camp to prepare them for the next season could not qualify for the credit to the extent the camp was for less than five consecutive days (No. 2007-0241341E5).
- The receipt used by the taxpayer to support the credit must include the following information: name/address of organization, name of program or activity, amount received and portion eligible for the credit, full name of the payer, name and year of birth of the child, and authorized signature (No. 2007-0228551M4); this receipt does not need an authorized signature if it is produced electronically and generated from a computer system (No. 2008-0267001E5).

(ITA: 122.8; ITR: 9400 [Child Fitness Tax Credit])

[¶1356a] CHILDREN'S ARTS TAX CREDIT

For the 2011 to 2016 taxation years, you may claim the children's arts tax credit. This credit and its parameters, except for the definition of eligible activities, are similar to the children's fitness tax credit except for the fact that since 2015 the fitness credit is refundable and the arts credit is not. Where the children's fitness tax credit is for physical activities, the children's arts tax credit will be for programs that promote artistic, cultural, recreational, or developmental activities. Effective January 1, 2017, both the child fitness tax credit and children's arts tax credit are eliminated.

This credit allows parents to claim a 15% non-refundable tax credit based on an amount of up to $250 in eligible expenses paid per child in a taxation year (this amount was $500 for taxation years prior to 2016). The credit is available for the enrolment of a child under 16 years of age at the beginning of the year in an eligible program of artistic, cultural, recreational, or developmental activities. For a child under 18 years at the beginning of the year who is eligible for the disability tax credit, the 15% non-refundable tax credit may be claimed on an additional $500 disability supplement amount, when a minimum of $100 is paid for eligible expenses. That is, if you claim $90 of eligible expenses for the disabled child for the year, the amount eligible for credit is $90, but if you claim $100, the amount eligible for credit is $600 (the $100 actual amount and the $500 automatic amount). Expenditures for the disabled child of $500 or more command the maximum amount eligible of $750.

The amount you can claim is reduced by any reimbursements, allowances, or other assistance that anyone was entitled to receive in respect of the expenses, unless the reimbursements, etc., were included in the income of the person entitled to them and were not deducted again in computing taxable income. In short, eligible cost is cost less any reimbursements from any source, unless the reimbursements are fully taxable to the recipient.

An eligible expense is a fee paid in the taxation year to a qualifying entity if that fee is for the registration or membership of a child in an eligible program of artistic, cultural, recreational, or developmental activities. These fees may be paid for expenses for the operation and maintenance of the program, instruction, renting facilities, common equipment, and incidental supplies. Fees will not be eligible if they are used for purchase or rental of equipment for personal use, travel, meals, or accommodation. Expenses eligible for the child care expenses deduction or the children's fitness tax credit are also ineligible. Expenses claimed under other credits (e.g., the medical expense tax credit) will not qualify.

Where there are two distinct prescribed programs, one eligible for the children's fitness amount and the other for the children's arts amount, there should be two receipts, or one receipt that indicated the amounts paid for each distinct program.

A qualifying entity will be a person or partnership, not under the age of 18 years, which offers one or more eligible programs of artistic, cultural, recreational, or developmental activities. A qualifying entity cannot include the spouse or common-law partner of a person claiming the credit for his or her child.

An eligible activity is a supervised activity, suitable for children, that:

- contributes to the development of creative skills or expertise in an artistic or cultural activity (creative skills or expertise involved are those that improve a child's dexterity or coordination, or where a child acquires and applies knowledge in the pursuit of artistic and cultural activities. Artistic and cultural activities include the literary arts, visual arts, performing arts, music, media, languages, customs, and heritage);
- provides a substantial focus on the wilderness and the natural environment;
- helps develop and use particular intellectual skills;
- includes supervisors teaching or helping children develop interpersonal skills using structured interaction; or
- provides enrichment or tutoring in academic subjects.

An eligible program must be ongoing and include a significant amount of eligible activities. This means an eligible program must be either a weekly program that is a minimum of eight consecutive weeks or a children's camp that lasts a minimum of five consecutive days. The full cost of a child's membership in an organization will be eligible for the credit if more than 50% of the activities offered by the organization include a significant amount of eligible activities. Programs that are part of a school curriculum will be ineligible.

Either parent may claim the entire credit, or the credit can be shared between the parents if the total amount claimed is not more than the maximum amount that would be allowed if only one parent made the claim. In general, since the credit for any expense is limited to the lesser of (i) $250 and (ii) the amount paid, times the conversion rate for the year (which is the minimum marginal tax rate), the value of the credit is the same in the hands of any taxpayer, so long as the taxpayer has sufficient tax to absorb the credit. In short, it makes no sense to assign the credit to a parent whose income, after other credits (¶1365), is too low to make use of it.

The credit is claimed in box 370 of Schedule 1. You should not submit your supporting documentation when you file your return, but you must keep it on hand with your tax documents for the year in case the CRA asks for it in verifying your claim.

[¶1357] ADOPTION EXPENSE CREDIT

You are allowed in the year an adoption becomes permanent (the year of the end of the "adoption period" discussed below) to claim a non-refundable credit in respect of up to $15,453 of the accumulated adoption expenses incurred in the adoption period. The amount is indexed every year.

[¶1357.05] *Eligible Adoption Expenses*

Eligible adoption expenses must be incurred for the adoption of an eligible child, which means a child under the age of 18 at the time an adoption order is issued or recognized by a government in Canada in respect of the adoption of the child by you.

Eligible adoption expenses are the accumulated expenses for the "adoption period". The adoption period begins at the earlier of (i) for 2013 and subsequent years, the time when an application is made for registration with a provincial or territorial ministry responsible for adoption (or with an adoption agency licensed by a provincial or territorial government), and (ii) the time (if any) that an application related to your adoption is made to a Canadian court. The adoption period ends at the later of (iii) the time an adoption order is issued by, or recognized by, a government in Canada in respect of that child, and (iv) the time that the child first begins to reside permanently with you (the adopting individual).

The expenses which qualify for tax credit include any "amount paid in respect of the adoption of that child during the adoption period". This is an extremely broad definition, which one suspects the government may come to regret and to limit in future. The statute goes on to list items which are specifically included as qualifying, but eligible items are not limited to those on the list. The items which are specified as eligible expenses are:

(1) fees paid to an adoption agency licensed by a provincial government;

(2) court costs and legal and administrative expenses related to an adoption order in respect of that child;

(3) reasonable and necessary travel and living expenses of the child and the adoptive parents;

(4) document translation fees;

(5) mandatory fees paid to a foreign institution;

(6) mandatory expenses paid in respect of the immigration of that child; and

(7) any other reasonable expenses related to the adoption required by a provincial government or an adoption agency licensed by a provincial government.

[¶1357.10] *Calculation of Credit*

In your taxation year which includes the end of the adoption period, you may claim a tax credit for the lesser of

(i) $15,453, and (ii) the total of all eligible adoption expenses in respect of the eligible child minus any reimbursement or other assistance that you or any individual is or was entitled to receive in respect of an expense included in the claim. Reimbursements do not reduce the amount eligible for credit if they themselves included in your income and not deductible in calculating taxable income.

Reimbursements might come from employer programs which assist employees with adoption expenses. If the employer assistance is taxable to the employee, as probably it would be, and not offset by a deduction from taxable income, as also seems likely, it would be included in income and should not also reduce the expense eligible for credit.

The eligible amount calculated above will be accumulated with other non-refundable credits and, with them, be converted at the current minimum tax rate to a credit deductible from your tax payable.

The government recognizes that children are commonly adopted by couples. Where more than one person can claim adoption expense credit, they may divide the credit amount (which amounts to dividing the underlying expenses) in any manner so long as the amount divided does not exceed the amount that any one individual could claim if that individual were making the entire claim. Where individuals cannot agree on a division, the CRA has the authority to apportion the credit arbitrarily.

[¶1357.15] *Quebec*

The federal credit more or less follows the model of the Quebec adoption expense credit introduced in 1999 and discussed at ¶1684. There are, however, significant differences. The Quebec credit is refundable if it exceeds tax payable. The federal credit is non-refundable and limited to tax payable in the year the adoption is complete; there is no provision for carryover of unused credit, let alone a refund. The Quebec credit rate is considerably higher than the federal rate, and is capped at $20,000 of expense rather than the federal amount of $15,453. (However, the Quebec credit amount is not indexed, so the federal amount could conceivably catch up eventually.) The Quebec credit is limited to specified expenses, the federal credit is not. Generally speaking, expenses which qualify for the Quebec credit will qualify for the federal credit, but the reverse may not be true.

[¶1357.20] *Other Provinces*

Provinces and territories for which the federal government collects personal income taxes (all except Quebec) are not obliged to follow the federal lead in allowing an adoption credit, nor are they obliged to accept the federal credit determination. In general, those provinces which choose to give the credit may be expected to follow the federal determination of eligible amounts and apply their own credit conversion rates. A list of provinces which currently provide this credit is found at ¶1501.05.

(ITA: 118.01)

[¶1358] HOME ACCESSIBILITY CREDIT

[¶1358.05] *General*

Effective for 2016 and subsequent taxation years, an individual meeting certain conditions may claim a non-refundable home accessibility tax credit calculated at the rate of 15% of renovation expenditures incurred for the benefit of a senior person (i.e., who is 65 or older at year-end) or of a disabled person (i.e., who is entitled to claim the disability tax credit).

More specifically, the conditions are the following:

- the claimant is a qualifying or eligible individual;
- the expenditures are qualifying expenditures;
- the home being renovated is an eligible dwelling;
- the renovation undertaken is a qualifying renovation; and
- the credit is calculated on up to $10,000 of expenditures.

The terms "qualifying individual", "eligible individual", "qualifying expenditure", "eligible dwelling", and "qualifying renovation" are discussed at ¶1358.10, ¶1358.15, ¶1358.20, and ¶1358.25.

The formula used to calculate the credit is discussed at ¶1358.30.

If an expenditure qualifies for both the home accessibility and medical expense tax credits, both credits may be claimed by the qualifying or eligible individual. See discussion at ¶1358.35.

Even if both the qualifying and eligible individual can claim the credit, the total credit cannot exceed $1,500 (i.e., $10,000 × 15%). See discussion at ¶1358.35.

[¶1358.10] *Who Is Eligible to Claim the Credit?*

Only qualifying and eligible individuals may claim the credit for a particular taxation year.

Qualifying individual

An individual is a qualifying individual and may claim the credit for the year if:

- he/she is 65 or older at year-end; or
- he/she is disabled (i.e., eligible for section 118.3 disability tax credit) for that year.

An individual does not include a trust for the purpose of this definition.

Eligible individual

An individual is an eligible individual and may claim the credit for the year if he/she claimed one of the following personal amounts for the qualifying individual for the year:

- spouse or common-law partner amount;
- eligible dependant amount;
- caregiver amount; or
- infirm dependant amount.

Even if the individual could not claim one of the above amounts, he/she is still an eligible individual if he/she could have claimed one of the following:

- the spouse or common-law partner amount if the qualifying individual had no net income in the year;
- the eligible dependant amount if the qualifying individual had no spouse or common-law partner and had no net income in the year;
- the caregiver amount if the qualifying individual was over 17 and had no net income in the year; or

- the infirm dependant amount if the qualifying individual was over 17, had no net income in the year, and was dependent by reason of infirmity.

An eligible individual would normally include any of the following persons who could claim one of the above personal amounts for a qualifying individual:

- spouse or common-law partner of the qualifying individual; or
- parent, grandparent, child, grandchild, brother, sister, aunt, uncle, niece, or nephew of the qualifying individual or the qualifying individual's spouse or common-law partner.

Only qualifying expenditures incurred for the qualifying renovation of an eligible dwelling may be considered to calculate the home accessibility tax credit. The terms qualifying expenditure, qualifying renovation and eligible dwelling are discussed at ¶1358.15, ¶1358.20, and ¶1358.25.

[¶1358.15] *What Is an Eligible Dwelling?*

To be considered an eligible dwelling for the purpose of claiming the home accessibility credit in a particular taxation year, a home must meet all the following conditions:

- the home must be the principal residence of the qualifying or eligible individual at any time in the year;
- the home must be a housing unit located in Canada, including the subjacent land and one-half hectare of contiguous land;
- the qualifying or eligible individual must own jointly or otherwise the housing unit itself or a share in a cooperative housing corporation acquired to live in a housing unit owned by the corporation;
- if the qualifying individual owns the unit, he/she must ordinarily live in it at any time in the year; and
- if the eligible individual owns the unit and the qualifying individual does not own another unit at any time in the year, both of them must ordinarily live in the unit at any time in the year.

A trust of which the individual is a beneficiary may also own the unit or share of capital stock.

[¶1358.20] *What is a Qualifying Renovation?*

To be considered a qualifying renovation for the purpose of claiming the home accessibility tax credit in a particular taxation year, the renovation must be:

- related to the eligible dwelling owned by a qualifying or eligible individual;
- of an enduring nature (i.e., capital vs. current expenditures); and
- undertaken for one of the following reasons:
  - to improve the qualifying individual's mobility within the dwelling;
  - to improve the dwelling's accessibility and functionality for him/her; or
  - to reduce the risk of harm for him/her in living or accessing the dwelling.

[¶1358.25] *What is a Qualifying Expenditure?*

To be considered a qualifying expenditure for the purpose of claiming a home accessibility tax credit in a particular taxation year, the expenditure must be

- incurred during the year; and
- directly attributed to the qualifying renovation of the eligible dwelling of a qualifying or eligible individual (all those terms are defined above).

The cost of the following items is specifically included in the qualifying expenditures:

- goods and services received to complete the qualifying renovation;
- permits required for the renovation; and
- rental of equipment needed for the renovation.

The cost of the following items is specifically excluded from the qualifying expenditures:

- property for general improvement of the dwelling independently of the renovation;
- routine repairs and general maintenance of the dwelling;
- purchase of household appliances or electronic home-entertainment devices;
- housekeeping, security monitoring, gardening, or outdoor maintenance services;
- mortgage interest or other similar costs of financing the renovation.
- renovation of a portion of dwelling used to earn business or property income;
- goods or services provided by a person related to the qualifying or eligible individual, and not registered for GST/HST purposes; and
- expenses reimbursed by a person other than the government.

[¶1358.30] *How Do You Calculate the Credit?*

The home accessibility tax credit claimed for a particular taxation year cannot exceed $1,500 and is calculated at the rate of 15% on the lesser of two amounts:

- $10,000; and
- the qualifying expenditures incurred during the year.

Qualifying expenditures are expenditures incurred for the qualifying renovation of the eligible dwelling of a qualifying individual or eligible individual.

The terms "qualifying individual", "eligible individual", "qualifying expenditure", "eligible dwelling", and "qualifying renovation" are discussed at ¶1358.10, ¶1358.15, ¶1358.20, and ¶1358.25.

[¶1358.35] *Special Situations*

Total credit claimed by qualifying and eligible individuals limited to $1,500

If both the qualifying and eligible individuals are eligible to claim the home accessibility tax credit in respect of qualifying expenditures for a particular taxation year, they cannot double dip and claim the credit twice for that year. In this case, the maximum qualifying expenditures must be claimed by one of them or shared between themselves.

In case the qualifying and/or eligible individuals become bankrupt during the year, they will not be considered to have two taxation years in the year of bankruptcy for the purpose of calculating their combined home accessibility tax credit. This rule applies to calculate the bankrupt's taxable income before and after the date of bankruptcy but not to calculate the credit claimed by the qualifying and eligible individuals.

Both home accessibility and medical expense tax credits claimed for same expenditure

If a qualifying individual is eligible to claim the home accessibility and medical expense tax credits, the qualifying or eligible individual can claim both credits.

Credit eligibility in death or bankruptcy situations

A qualifying individual dying in a year in which he/she would have turned 65 will be deemed to be 65 at the beginning of the year for the purpose of determining his/her eligibility for the credit.

An individual becoming a qualifying individual and bankrupt in the same year is deemed to be a qualifying individual at the start of the year for the purpose of determining his/her eligibility for the credit. The same rule applies if the eligible individual, not the qualifying individual, becomes bankrupt in that year.

(ITA: 118.041)

[¶1359] FIRST-TIME HOME BUYER'S CREDIT

[¶1359.05] *General*

If you purchased a qualifying home and neither you nor your spouse or common-law partner owned and lived in another home in the year of purchase or any of the four preceding calendar years (i.e., you were a first-time home buyer), you may claim a non-refundable credit, the Home Buyer's Tax Credit, on line 369 of Schedule 1. This credit must be calculated at the lowest marginal tax rate of 15% on an amount of $5,000, for a maximum credit of $750. The $5,000 may be split between you and your spouse or common-law partner or between two individuals buying the qualifying home on a joint basis, but the combined amount claimed by both persons must not exceed $5,000 under any circumstances.

You do not have to attach to your tax return the purchase agreement or other documents supporting your transaction, but you should keep them in case of audit by the CRA.

[¶1359.10] *What Is a Qualifying Home?*

A qualifying home includes a single-family house, a semi-detached house, a townhouse, a mobile home, a condominium unit, an apartment in a duplex, a triplex, a fourplex, or an apartment building, or a share in a cooperative housing corporation (but only if the share gives you an equity interest, not only a right to tenancy in the housing unit), providing the following conditions are met:

- the home is located in Canada;
- the home is registered in your name and/or the name of your spouse or common-law partner; and
- you, your spouse or common-law partner, or the person eligible for the disability tax credit (see below) must intend to inhabit the qualifying home as a principal residence no later than one year after the date of purchase.

Homes eligible under the Home Buyers' Plan would also generally qualify for this credit, and both existing homes and homes under construction would be eligible.

[¶1359.15] *Special Treatment for Disabled Persons*

You may also claim the first time home buyer's tax credit for the acquisition of a qualifying home for the benefit of an individual entitled to claim the disability tax credit provided the home is acquired to enable the disabled person to live in a home that is more accessible or better suited for that person's personal needs and care. The person does not have to be a first-time home buyer to qualify for the credit but must intend to use the qualifying home as a principal residence no later than one year after the date of acquisition. If the credit is claimed by two or more taxpayers, the combined claim may not exceed the maximum credit available if only one taxpayer claimed the credit.

To qualify for this credit without being a first-time home buyer, the disabled person must be able to claim the disability amount (see ¶1255) for the year in which the agreement to purchase the qualifying home is signed, or would be able to claim that amount if the costs for attendant care or care in a nursing home were not claimed for the medical expense tax credit (see ¶1235).

(ITA: 118.05)

[¶1360] VOLUNTEER FIREFIGHTERS TAX CREDIT

You may claim the volunteer firefighters tax credit if you are an eligible volunteer firefighter. The credit is a 15% non-refundable tax credit based on an amount of $3,000.

A person eligible for this credit will be a volunteer firefighter who performs a minimum of 200 hours of volunteer firefighting services for one or more fire departments, which consist primarily of responding to and being on call for firefighting and related emergency calls, attending meetings held by the fire department, and participating in required training for the prevention or suppression of fires.

However, if you provided services to the same organization, other than as a volunteer, for the same or similar duties, you cannot include any hours related to that organization in determining if you have met the 200-hour threshold.

An individual claiming the credit will be required to provide written certification from the chief or a delegated official of the fire department, confirming the number of eligible volunteer firefighting hours performed. You should not submit your supporting documentation when you file your return, but you must keep it on hand with your tax documents for the year in case the CRA asks for it in verifying your claim.

If an individual performs services that are eligible for both the search and rescue and the volunteer firefighters credits, then the individual can claim either credit but not both. An individual claiming either of these two credits is ineligible for a tax exemption under subsection 81(4) for honoraria of up to $1,000 paid by a government, municipality or public authority.

(ITA: 118.06)

[¶1360a] SEARCH AND RESCUE VOLUNTEERS TAX CREDIT

Since 2014, an individual who volunteers to provide search and rescue services on the ground, in the air, or in water, may claim a non-refundable credit of 15% on an amount of $3,000.

The individual must volunteer at least 200 hours for search and rescue activities in a taxation year. Eligible and rescue activities include:

- responding to and being on call for search and rescue and related emergencies;
- attending meetings held by the search and rescue organization; and
- participating in training sessions related to search and rescue.

However, if you provided services to the same organization, other than as a volunteer, for the same or similar duties, you cannot include any hours related to that organization in determining if you have met the 200-hour threshold.

The individual claiming this tax credit may have to obtain a written certificate from a team president, or an individual with equivalent authority, to certify the number of hours of service completed. You should not submit your supporting documentation when you file your return, but you must keep it on hand with your tax documents for the year in case the CRA asks for it in verifying your claim.

If an individual performs services that are eligible for both the search and rescue and the volunteer firefighters credits, then the individual can claim either credit but not both. An individual claiming either of these two credits is ineligible for a tax exemption under subsection 81(4) for honoraria of up to $1,000 paid by a government, municipality or public authority.

Eligible search and rescue organizations include:

- Search and Rescue Volunteer Association of Canada;
- Civil Air Search and Rescue Association;
- The Canadian Coast Guard Auxiliary; or
- any other search and rescue organization that is recognized by a provincial, municipal or public authority.

(ITA: 118.07)

[¶1360b] SCHOOL SUPPLIES TAX CREDIT

Overview

Beginning in the 2016 taxation year, eligible educators can claim a 15% refundable tax credit for eligible supplies expenses incurred in the year. Maximum annual expenses of $1,000 are permitted, thus generating up to $150 in tax savings per year. The terms "eligible educator", "eligible supplies expense", and "teaching supplies" are discussed below.

Eligible Educator and Eligible Supplies Expense

You are considered to be an eligible educator if you:

(a) are employed in Canada as a teacher or early childhood educator at an elementary or secondary school, or a regulated child care facility; and

(b) hold a valid and recognized (in the province or territory in which you are employed)

(i) teaching certificate, licence, permit, or diploma; or

(ii) certificate or diploma in early childhood education.

The definition of eligible supplies expense is more complex. Eligible supplies expense refers to an amount paid by an eligible educator for teaching supplies to the extent that the teaching supplies were:

(i) purchased for the purpose of teaching or facilitating students' learning; and

(ii) were directly consumed or used in an elementary or secondary school or in a regulated child care facility in the performance of the individual's employment duties.

Expenses that were deducted from any person's (including your own) income or taxes payable in any taxation year are ineligible for the credit. Furthermore, expenses for which you are entitled to receive a reimbursement, allowance, or any other form of assistance (excluding amounts that are included in your income and are not deductible) are also ineligible for the credit.

The term "teaching supplies" means consumable supplies and prescribed durable goods. According to the Department of Finance, consumable supplies include:

- construction paper for activities;
- flashcards for activity centres;
- items for science experiments, such as seeds, potting soil, vinegar, baking soda, and stir sticks;
- art supplies such as paper, glue, and paint; and
- various stationary items, such as pens, pencils, posters, and charts.

"Prescribed durable goods" includes:

- games and puzzles;
- books for the classroom;
- containers such as plastic boxes or banker boxes; and
- educational support software.

Computers, tablets, and rugs for children to sit on are not eligible expenses as they are durable goods and are not specifically prescribed.

Computing the Credit

Since the credit is refundable, you are deemed to have paid the amount of the credit on the account of tax payable. The amount of the credit is computed by multiplying the appropriate percentage for the year (15%) by the lesser of:

(1) $1,000; and

(2) your total eligible supplies expenses incurred in the year.

However, if you fail to provide a certificate when the Minister requests it (see below), the credit is denied for the year in question.

Certification

It is crucial that you be able to produce a certificate with respect to the expenses if requested by the CRA. Upon request, you must provide a written certificate from your employer or a delegated official of the employer (e.g., the school principal). This certification must attest that the amounts were paid as eligible supplies expenses with respect to a taxation year, and that you are an eligible educator. According to the CRA's guidance pertaining to this compliance requirement, the certification should be a statement signed by the employer or official that provides and attests (to the best of their knowledge) to the amount paid for the eligible teaching supplies purchased in the year:

- by an eligible educator;
- for the purpose of teaching or facilitating students' learning;
- directly consumed or used in an elementary or secondary school or regulated child care facility in the performance of the individual's employment duties; and
- not reimbursable, not subject to an allowance or other assistance (unless the assistance is included in the individual's income and is not deductible), and not deducted or used in computing a deduction from any person's income for any taxation year.

The employer or official should take a reasonable approach regarding the fourth requirement. The CRA provides examples of ineligible expenses where:

- form T2200 allows a teacher to deduct the expenses from income because the contract of employment requires him or her to provide for and pay for supplies and the expenses; or
- an educator is entitled to a reimbursement from the employer, students or parents, or through fundraising activities.

As mentioned previously, where you fail to provide the certification with respect to a year that the Minister requests it, the amount of the credit will deemed to be nil.

Additional Rules

If you become bankrupt in a particular calendar year, the return for the last taxation year in that calendar year (i.e., the return for the taxation year that begins at the bankruptcy date and ends on December 31 of that calendar year) is the only return of income in which you may claim the credit.

You may not claim the school supplies tax credit for a taxation year in which you were not resident in Canada at any time during that year. However, you may still claim the credit if all or substantially all (at least 90%) of your income for that year was included in your taxable income earned in Canada for that year. Where you are resident in Canada for part of a taxation year, the credit is computed for two periods: the period of residency, and the period of non-residency. But the credit for the calendar year still may not exceed $150.

(ITA: 122.9)

TRANSFER OF SPOUSE'S OR COMMON-LAW PARTNER'S UNUSED CREDITS

[¶1361] TRANSFER OF YOUR SPOUSE'S OR COMMON-LAW PARTNER'S UNUSED CREDITS

All references to a spouse in the material below also include a reference to a common-law partner.

You are permitted to transfer to your return certain amounts eligible for tax credits which your spouse has available but does not require in order to reduce his or her tax payable to nil. Your spouse, for purposes of this transfer (and for all purposes related to personal exemption credits), is your legal spouse and/or your common-law partner (¶1113). The amounts eligible for credit which may be transferred are:

- tuition fee, education, and textbook amounts (up to a maximum of $5,000 of eligible fees and amounts; the education and textbook amounts were eliminated effective January 1, 2017, and the unused amounts generated in taxation years may be carried forward indefinitely to 2017 and subsequent taxation years), to the extent the student has designated them to the spouse on the back of form T2202A;
- the age credit (¶1108, line 301);
- the pension credit (¶1311, line 314);
- the disability credit (¶1255, line 316); and
- the credit for each child under 18 at the end of the year (but only for years before 2015; see ¶1124, line 367).

Note that the spouse receiving a transferred age amount is not subject to any reduction in the transferred credit where the receiving spouse's income exceeds $35,927 (¶1108). That is, the transferring spouse must grind the age amount according to the transferring spouse's income, but the result is not subject to any adjustment on the return of the transferee.

Technically, the amount which may be transferred is the excess of your spouse's credits eligible for transfer over your spouse's tax payable for the year before claiming any credits other than: the basic personal credit (for 2016, 15% of $11,474); credits for Employment Insurance premiums and Canada/Quebec Pension Plan contributions; credits for Quebec PPIP (Quebec residents only — ¶1307.10); volunteer firefighter credit; search and rescue volunteer credit; employment credit; public transit credit; child's fitness credit (prior to 2015); children's arts credit (prior to 2017); first-time home buyers' credit; adoption credit; and tuition, education (prior to 2017), and textbook (prior to 2017) carryforwards your spouse may have from his or her previous untransferred education/tuition amounts or amounts which would add to that balance in the current year. Put another way, your spouse must calculate tax payable and then deduct the basic personal amount, CPP/QPP and EI/PPIP credits; volunteer firefighter credit; search and rescue volunteer credit; employment credit; public transit credit; child's fitness credit (prior to 2015); children's arts credit (prior to 2017); first-time home buyers' credit; adoption credit; and tuition/education carryforward credits which arose in prior years, as well as tuition/education/textbook credits of the current year which your spouse has insufficient income to utilize in the current year and so would add to your spouse's tuition/education/textbook carryforward balance if not transferred to you; if your spouse has any tax remaining after these credits, your spouse's transferable credits must be used to eliminate that tax before the balance can be transferred to you.

Special considerations arise where your spouse has tuition, education, and textbook credits. First, you should know that only your spouse's current education/tuition/textbook amounts are available for transfer. You spouse's Schedule 11 handles this limitation accurately. However, as explained at ¶1341, it is theoretically possible for your spouse to misdesignate the amount and transfer more tuition/education/textbook credit than you can use to reduce your tax to zero. This is a waste of credit which could be carried forward by the student spouse. If the total amounts from lines 300 to 326 of your Schedule 1 of the T1 return are greater than your net income, you should reduce the tuition and education transfer on line 5 of your Schedule 2 until the amount carried from line 10 to line 326, plus the amounts from lines 300 to 324 of your Schedule 1 of the T1 return, are exactly equal to your net income. Your spouse should designate no more than your revised line 5 amount on form T2202A. This will maximize your spouse's carryforward.

If you have been designated as a transferee of part or all of your spouse's, etc., tuition/education/textbook amounts under these rules, the student should provide you with a completed copy of the form (typically T2202A) which reported the eligible amounts to the student, including the portion of the form on which an excess amount has been designated to you. The student should also provide you with a copy of the student's Schedule 11, showing the calculation of the transfer amounts. You should enter the amount transferred on line 360 of your Schedule 2, but you should not file the student's tuition slips or the student's Schedule 11 with your return. However, you should keep these copies with your tax records to support the claim should the CRA wish to verify it.

If you are also claiming medical expenses and/or charitable donations on your return, and it is these which reduce your tax to nil, the matter is somewhat more complex. You can adjust medical expense claims to defer some expenses to the following year, and you can defer charitable donation claims for up to five years. To the extent that you maximize these claims in the current year and so minimize the current year education/tuition credit transfer from your spouse, you will maximize your spouse's future credit. On the other hand, if it will be some years until your spouse has sufficient income to use the credit, it may be preferable to maximize the spousal transfer credit and utilize the deferred medical/charitable claims on your own return in the following year. Subject to the peculiar medical expense rules, the same overall credit should be available to you and your spouse, so that claiming total credit in the shortest possible time frame is the important issue.

Although the law deals with the actual tax and credits, Schedule 2 deals with the amounts of income on which the tax would be payable and the amounts eligible for credit before they are converted by multiplying by 15%. The result in either case should be the same.

Example

Sam and Evelyn are married. In 2016, Sam, age 66, had the following income: $700 of eligible dividends (before gross-up), $1,670 of bank interest, $3,000 of annuity payments from a registered retirement savings plan, and $6,677 from Old Age Security (OAS) pension.

(1) Calculate the amount by which Sam's taxable income exceeds the total of his or her basic personal exemption amount (see ¶1106), CPP/QPP contributions, EI/PPIP premiums, and education/tuition carryforwards. (This cannot be a negative amount.)

Sam's taxable income:	
Dividend income ($700 × 138%)	$ 966
Interest income	1,670
Annuity payments from an RRSP	3,000
Old Age Security pension	6,677
Taxable income	$ 12,313
Less: Basic personal exemption amount	11,474
CPP/QPP/EI contributions	0
Amount of calculation	$ 839

Note that on a tax basis, the calculation would show tax of 15% × $12,313 = $1,846 less credit of 15% × $11,474 = $1,721, for a basic federal tax of $125.

Sam's taxable income for the year is the income that would be shown at line 260 of his return, assuming he filed a return for the year. Sam should prepare a T1 return, even if it need not be filed. Evelyn would then use the necessary data from that return in her Schedule 2.

(2) Calculate the total of the applicable following amounts that are available to Sam:

- Sam's age amount (see ¶1108);
- Sam's tuition, education, and textbook amounts (see ¶1339);
- Sam's disability amount (see ¶1255); and
- Sam's pension income amount (see ¶1311).

(3) The amount of Sam's personal amounts transferable to Evelyn is then calculated as follows:

	Personal amount	*Tax credit value*
Transfers available to Evelyn:		
Age exemption amount	$ 7,125	$ 1,069
Pension income amount	2,000	300
Amount eligible for transfer	$ 9,125	$ 1,369
Less: Income (tax) to be absorbed by deductions (credits) before transfer (from (1), above)	839	126
Amount/credit available for transfer	$ 8,286	$ 1,243

Pension Transfer Considerations:

Note that the transferor in the example above (Sam), could have transferred up to half the $3,000 annuity payment to the recipient spouse (Evelyn) under the income transfer rules at ¶1311.15. The $3,000 in annuity payment is the only pension amount to be considered for pension-splitting in this example, since per (1) in ¶1311.05 Old Age Security is not eligible for pension splitting.

If Evelyn had less than $1,500 of pension income eligible for credit of her own, so that she could use her pension credit for all the transferred pension income, the result would be neutral. The same $1,500 is eligible for credit either way. If, however, Evelyn already has $2,000 of pension income, the result of a pension income transfer of more than $1,000 from Sam will be negative for Sam and Evelyn as a couple (at least in terms of pension credit), because (in receiving Sam's transferred pension credit on her Schedule 2) Evelyn obtains less total credit than Sam would have obtained in pension credit by retaining at least $2,000 in his own return.

See also the checklist of items of interest to pensioners at ¶1315.

(ITA: 118.8; 118.92; Income Tax Folio: S1-F2-C1 Education and Textbook Tax Credits; S1-F2-C2 Tuition Tax Credit)

[¶1365] ORDER OF CREDITS

The order in which you must claim your credits in calculating your tax is as follows:

(1) the married, equivalent-to-married, single, and dependant tax credits (see Chapter 11);

(2) the age credit (see ¶1108);

(3) the Employment Insurance credit and *Canada Pension Plan* and *Quebec Pension Plan* credits (see ¶1305 and ¶1307);

(4) pension credit (see ¶1311);

(5) employment credit (see ¶1351);

(6) adoption expense credit (see ¶1357);

(7) transit pass credit (see ¶1353);

(8) children's arts credit (after 2010 and before 2017 — see ¶1356a);

(9) home accessibility credit (2016 and later — see ¶1358);

(10) first-time home buyers' credit (see ¶1359);

(11) volunteer firefighters credit (2011 and later — see ¶1360);

(12) search and rescue volunteers credit (2014 and later — see ¶1360a);

(13) disability credit (see ¶1255);

(14) tuition/education/textbook credits carried forward from prior year (see ¶1341; the education and textbook credits were eliminated effective January 1, 2017, but are available as carryforwards);

(15) tuition fees credit (see ¶1319);

(16) education and textbook credit (see ¶1337; education and textbook credits were eliminated effective January 1, 2017);

(17) transfer of tuition, education, and textbook credits to parent (see ¶1339; education and textbook credits were eliminated effective January 1, 2017);

(18) transfer of spouse's or common-law partner's credits (see ¶1361);

(19) medical expenses credit (see ¶1205 to 1250);

(20) charitable donations credit (see ¶1261 to 1292);

(21) credit for interest paid on student loans (see ¶1345);

(22) family tax cut credit (see ¶1317; family tax cut credit is eliminated effective January 1, 2016); and

(23) dividend tax credit (¶1425).

This ordering of credits is relevant primarily in ensuring that spousal credit transfers work properly.

(ITA: 118.92; IT-523 Order of Provisions Applicable in Computing an Individual's Taxable Income and Tax Payable)

Chapter 14

How To Calculate Your Federal Tax

THESE POINTS ARE COVERED IN THIS CHAPTER

CRA REFERENCES RELATING TO THIS CHAPTER

T1 Lines and Schedules

- Line 232 — Other deductions (split income)
- Line 235 — Social benefits repayment
- Line 256 — Additional deductions
- Line 260 — Taxable income
- Line 420 — Net federal tax
- Line 421 — CPP contributions payable on self-employment and other earnings
- Line 422 — Social benefits repayment
- Line 430 — Employment insurance premiums on self-employment and other eligible earnings
- Line 437 — Total income tax deducted
- Line 440 — Refundable Quebec abatement
- Line 448 — CPP overpayment
- Line 450 — Employment Insurance overpayment
- Line 453 — Working Income Tax Benefit (WITB)
- Line 454 — Refund of investment tax credit
- Line 459 — Child Fitness Credit
- Line 469 — Eligible educator school supply tax credit
- Federal Worksheet, Line 235 — Social benefits repayment
- Federal Worksheet, Line 410 — Federal political contribution tax credit
- Schedule 1, Lines 36–43 — Tax calculation
- Schedule 1, Line 350 — Total federal non-refundable tax credits
- Schedule 1, Line 405 — Federal foreign tax credit
- Schedule 1, Line 406 — Federal tax
- Schedule 1, Line 409 — Total federal political contributions
- Schedule 1, Line 410 — Federal political contribution tax credit
- Schedule 1, Line 411 — Federally registered labour-sponsored funds — Net cost
- Schedule 1, Line 412 — Investment tax credit
- Schedule 1, Line 413 — Provincially registered labour-sponsored funds — Net cost
- Schedule 1, Line 414 — Provincially registered labour-sponsored funds — Allowable tax credit
- Schedule 1, Line 415 — Working income tax benefit (WITB) advance payments received
- Schedule 1, Line 419 — Federally registered labour-sponsored funds — Allowable tax credit
- Schedule 1, Line 420 — Net federal tax
- Schedule 1, Line 424 — Federal tax on split income
- Schedule 1, Line 425 — Federal dividend tax credit
- Schedule 1, Line 427 — Minimum tax carryover
- Schedule 1, Line 429 — Basic federal tax
- Schedule 6 — Working income tax benefit
- Schedule 8 — CPP contributions on self-employment and other earnings
- Schedule 13 — Employment insurance premiums on self-employment and other eligible earnings

CRA Guides

5000-G, "General Income Tax and Benefit Guide"; **RC4157**, "Deducting Income Tax on Pension and Other Income, and Filing the T4A Slip and Summary Form"; **T4088**, "Guide to Form T661 — Scientific Research and Experimental Development (SR&ED) Expenditures Claim"; **T4114**, "Canada Child Benefits (Including Related Federal, Provincial, and Territorial Programs)"

CRA Forms

CPT20, "Election to Pay Canada Pension Plan Contributions"; **RC65**, "Marital Status Change"; **RC66**, "Canada Child Benefits Application"; **RC210**, "Statement of working income tax benefit advance payments"; **T3**, "Statement of Trust Income Allocations and Designations"; **T4A**, "Statement of Pension, Retirement, Annuity and Other Income"; **T4A (OAS)**, "Statement of Old Age Security"; **T4E**, "Statement of Employment Insurance and Other Benefits"; **T4PS**, "Statement of Employee Profit-Sharing Plan Allocations and Payments"; **T5**, "Statement of Investment Income"; **T101**, "Statement of Resource Expenses"; **T661**, "Scientific Research and Experimental Development (SR&ED) Expenditures Claim"; **T691**, "Alternative Minimum Tax"; **T1198**, "Statement of Qualifying Retroactive Lump-Sum Payment"; **T1206**, "Tax on Split Income"; **T2036**, "Provincial or Territorial Foreign Tax Credit"; **T2038(IND)**, "Investment Tax Credit (Individuals)"; **T2201**, "Disability Tax Credit Certificate"; **T2203**, "Provincial and Territorial Taxes — Multiple Jurisdictions"; **T2204**, "Employee Overpayment of Canada Pension Plan Contributions and Employment Insurance Premiums"; **T2209**, "Federal Foreign Tax Credits"; **T5006**, "Statement of Registered Labour-Sponsored Venture Capital Corporation Class A Shares"; **T5013**, "Statement of Partnership Income"

Income Tax Folios

Income Tax Folio **S5-F2-C1**, "Foreign Tax Credit"

Interpretation Bulletins [Archived]

IT-67R3, "Taxable Dividends from Corporations Resident in Canada"; **IT-86R**, "Vow of Perpetual

Poverty"; **IT-106R3**, "Crown Corporation Employees Abroad"; **IT-497R4**, "Overseas Employment Tax Credit"; **IT-506**, "Foreign Income Taxes as a Deduction from Income"

Information Circulars

74-21R, "Payments out of Pension and Deferred Profit Sharing Plans–ITAR 40"; **75-2R8**, "Contributions to a Registered Party, a Registered Association or to a Candidate at a Federal Election"; **78-4R3**, "Investment Tax Credit Rates";

Income Tax Technical News

No. 31R2, May 16, 2006, "Social Security Taxes and the Foreign Tax Credit"

WHAT YOU SHOULD KNOW ABOUT CALCULATING YOUR FEDERAL TAX

RECENT CHANGES

Bill C-15 (Royal Assent June 22, 2016)

Canada Child Benefit

The former Canada Child Tax Benefit was replaced with the new Canada Child Benefit. The new benefit is designed to increase the amount that the average Canadian family receives. It is computed on the basis of the family's adjusted income and the number of children in that family. Bill C-15 will also repeal the National Child Benefit Supplement on July 1, 2017. With respect to the Child Disability Benefit, Bill C-15 increased the benefit amount and made minor changes to the income-tested phase-out amounts. The first payment of the new benefit amounts occurred on July 20, 2016. See ¶1498.

Credit for Family Tax Cut

Bill C-152 eliminated, for 2016 and subsequent taxation years, the non-refundable income splitting tax credit (Family Tax Cut) of up to $2,000 that was available for couples with children under the age of 18. See ¶1423.

Child Fitness Tax Credit

Bill C-15 phased out the child's fitness tax credit. Effective for the 2016 taxation year, the maximum amount per child is reduced to $500 from $1,000. The credit is eliminated for the 2017 and subsequent taxation years. See ¶1497.

Eligible Educator School Supply Tax Credit

Bill C-15 introduced an eligible educator school supply tax credit for 2016 and subsequent taxation years. This measure will allow an employee who is an eligible educator to claim a 15% refundable tax credit on up to $1,000 of eligible teaching supplies purchased by the employee in a taxation year. See ¶1497a

Mineral Exploration Tax Credit

Bill C-15 extended the 15% mineral exploration tax credit for an additional year, that is to flow-through share agreements entered into on or before March 31, 2017. See ¶1463.

Labour-sponsored Venture Capital Corporations Tax Credit

Bill C-15 restored the labour-sponsored venture capital corporation (LSVCC) tax credit to 15% for share purchases of provincially registered LSVCCs for 2016 and subsequent tax years. The tax credit for federally registered LSVCCs remains at 5% for 2016 and will be eliminated in 2017. See ¶1466.

[¶1405] GENERAL TAX CALCULATION

[¶1405.05] *Schedule 1 Calculations*

All taxpayers with taxable income must calculate tax on Schedule 1. On Schedule 1, you begin on page 1 with your applicable non-refundable (personal amount) tax credits, discussed in Chapters 11, 12, and 13. This is followed (at the top of page 2) by a calculation of initial tax based on current year tax rates, and application of the tax on split income on certain income of minor children (¶1490), with the resulting tax offset by the previously calculated non-refundable credits. Next comes a series of special purpose tax credits (which are non-refundable except for certain aspects of the investment tax credit), as follows:

- Federal dividend tax credit (¶1425)
- Minimum tax carryforward applied (¶2481)
- Foreign tax credit (¶1450)
- Federal political contribution tax credit (¶1462)
- Investment tax credit (¶1463): some (but not all) programs under this credit may create a refundable credit (¶1464); only the non-refundable portion is applied on Schedule 1 (line 412), the refundable portion is applied on page 4 of the T1 return at line 454
- Labour-sponsored funds tax credit (¶1466)
- Federal logging tax credit, which you are instructed to write in below line 55, as discussed at ¶1467
- Recapture of federal SR&ED investment tax credit, which form T2038(IND) instructs you to add to line 406. This is not actually the appropriate treatment, as the recapture should be subject to offset by non-refundable credits, as discussed at ¶1463.

You also enter on Schedule 1 the penalty tax on RESP income returned to contributors (¶2612.65), the tax on excess EPSP amounts (¶2626d), the tax related to the non-purchase of replacement shares in a Quebec labour-sponsored fund (¶1669.05), and advance payments received under the Working Income Tax Benefit (WITB) (¶1495).

[¶1405.10] *Page 4 Calculations*

Having completed the Schedule 1 calculations, you enter the results on page 4 of your T1 return and go on to enter a number of additional taxes and tax credits, as follows.

Additional taxes:

- CPP contributions on self-employment earnings (¶1305.10)
- EI premiums on self-employment and other eligible earnings (¶1307)
- Social benefits repayment (OAS/EI payments subject to clawback — ¶1419)

- Provincial taxes (Chapter 15), except Quebec, which collects its own income tax (Chapter 16)

Additional tax credits:

- Refundable Quebec abatement (¶1435)
- CPP overpayment (¶1305.05)
- Employment Insurance overpayment (¶1307)
- Refundable medical expense supplement (¶1237)
- Working income tax benefit (¶1495)
- Refundable investment tax credit (¶1464)
- Part XII.2 tax where trust allocations made to non-resident beneficiaries (¶460)
- Employee and Partner GST/HST rebates (¶363)
- Child fitness tax credit (¶1356)
- Eligible educator school supply tax credit (¶1497a)
- Provincial tax refunds and credits in excess of provincial tax (Chapter 15), except Quebec, which has its own tax and refunds system (Chapter 16)

In addition, you claim amounts withheld from income paid to you (generally employment income, but there is withholding on certain investment income as well), and amounts you pre-paid by instalment (¶227).

[¶1410] TAXABLE INCOME

Before beginning a calculation of your tax, you must determine your taxable income for the year. Taxable income is reported at the bottom of page 3 of the T1 return, at line 260. The calculation of taxable income is described in other chapters of this book.

Enter your taxable income from page 3, line 260, of your return in Step 2 at the top of Schedule 1, page 2.

[¶1415] FEDERAL INCOME TAX ON TAXABLE INCOME

Tax is calculated (in Step 2 of Schedule 1) by applying the federal income tax rates for the current year to the taxable income.

The rate brackets within which a specified rate applies are indexed annually (see ¶1101).

[¶1415.50] *Rate Schedule for 2017 Taxation Year*

Indexed rates for 2017 should be announced late in 2016. If available in time for publication, they will be found at ¶64 preceding Chapter 1.

[¶1415.52] *Rate Schedule for 2016 Taxation Year*

Taxable income	*Tax*
$45,282 or less	15%
In excess of	
$45,282	$6,792 + 20.5% on next $45,281
$90,563	$16,075 + 26% on next $49,825
$140,388	$29,030 + 29% on next $59,612
$200,000	$46,317 + 33% on remainder

[¶1415.54] *Rate Schedule for 2015 Taxation Year*

Taxable income	*Tax*
$44,701 or less	15%
In excess of	
$44,701	$6,705 + 22% on next $44,700
89,401	$16,539 + 26% on next $49,185
$138,586	$29,327 + 29% on remainder

[¶1415.56] *Rate Schedule for 2014 Taxation Year*

Taxable income	*Tax*
$43,953 or less	15%
In excess of	
$43,953	$ 6,593 + 22% on next $43,954
$87,907	$16,263 + 26% on next $48,363
$136,270	$28,837 + 29% on remainder

[¶1415.58] *Rate Schedule for 2013 Taxation Year*

Taxable income	*Tax*
$43,561 or less	15%
In excess of	
$43,561	$ 6,534 + 22% on next $43,562
$87,123	$16,118 + 26% on next $47,931
$135,054	$28,580 + 29% on remainder

[¶1415.60] *Rate Schedule for 2012 Taxation Year*

Taxable income	*Tax*
$42,707 or less	15%
In excess of	
$42,707	$ 6,406 + 22% on next $42,707
$85,414	$15,802 + 26% on next $46,992
$132,406	$28,020 + 29% on remainder

[¶1419] OLD AGE SECURITY AND EMPLOYMENT INSURANCE CLAWBACK TAX

[¶1419.05] *Employment Insurance Clawback — Lines 235 and 422*

Employment Insurance (EI) payments are subject to a special recovery if your income exceeds 125% of maximum insurable earnings under the program. For 2016, maximum insurable earnings for this purpose are $50,800; consequently, payments are recovered by the government ("clawed back" in current jargon) at a 30% rate to the extent that they exceed the threshold net income of 125% × $50,800 = $63,500. In effect, a special tax is imposed equal to the lesser of EI benefits received and 30% of income in excess of the $63,500 threshold. This tax is not imposed under the *Income Tax Act* but arises out of the *Employment Insurance Act* itself; the CRA is empowered to collect the recovery under the income tax administration provisions.

The EI authorities calculate the clawback rate based on their payment (and repayment) records under rules set out in the *Employment Insurance Act* and report the rate to you in box 7 of the T4E slip. The clawback calculation itself is found on the back of the T4E earnings slip; it is reproduced at ¶1419.35, below.

The EI clawback, together with the Old Age Security (OAS) clawback if applicable, are both deducted from income at line 235 and reported as tax at line 422 of your T1 return.

The technically-minded will note that the EI clawback is calculated by reference to net income before EI and OAS clawback (below).

(*Employment Insurance Act*: 144–149)

[¶1419.10] *Old Age Security Clawback*

A similar clawback tax (but with a different threshold amount) taxes back OAS benefits at a 15% rate if your income for 2016 exceeds $73,756, a limit which is indexed annually to inflation. A table of clawback thresholds for earlier years (and the immediately following year) is included in ¶65 preceding Chapter 1.

The OAS clawback tax is calculated on the worksheet chart for line 235 (worksheet charts are found on the *Federal Worksheet* page accompanying your T1 return). The tax is then entered both as a special tax at line 422 on page 4 of the T1 and as a deduction at line 235 on page 2. The deduction at line 235 prevents double taxation, as it results in the amount received but clawed back not being included in income.

Technically, the OAS clawback tax is the lesser of:

(1) the total of all payments included in your income as pension, supplement or spouse's allowance under the *Old Age Security Act* (reported on your T4A (OAS)), reduced by any overpayments you had to return during the year (¶1029); and

(2) 15% of your net income before the offsetting deduction for this tax in excess of (for 2016) $73,756. Net income for these purposes is net income after all deductions allowed to arrive at net income (including the deduction for the EI clawback), except the deduction of the OAS clawback itself. Net income excludes any capital gain realized on mortgage foreclosures or conditional sales repossessions (see ¶518), although these are rare enough that the chart worksheet calculation does not refer to them. Net income also excludes the Universal Child Care Benefit (UCCB) and repayments (see ¶935), and Registered Disability Savings Plan (RDSP) benefits and repayments (see ¶2529h); these adjustments are accounted for on the worksheet.

In the event that you receive OAS supplements (net federal supplements) in a year in which the clawback applies, those too are clawed back, subject to an ordering problem discussed at ¶1026.

(ITA: 60(v.1), (w); 180.2)

[¶1419.15] *Withholding Tax on (Prepayment of) the OAS Clawback — Line 437*

The system of clawing back Old Age Security payments extends to the application of withholding tax, so that where net income for a base period exceeds the current year clawback threshold, the potential clawback will be withheld from the OAS payments you receive. For OAS payments made in January–June of the current year, the withholding is based on your net income in second prior year return. For OAS payments in July–December of the current year, withholding is based on your net income in your prior year return. See ¶225. Amounts withheld from OAS payments should be shown in box 22 of your T4A(OAS) slip, and claimed, along with any other tax withheld on other income, at line 437 on page 4 of your T1 return.

[¶1419.20] *Application of OAS Clawback to Non-Residents of Canada*

The clawback system extends to non-residents.

The enforcement mechanism for non-residents is described in ¶225. Note that residents of a country with which Canada has a tax treaty may be protected from the application of the OAS clawback.

[¶1419.25] *The OAS Clawback Base and Treaty-Exempt Income*

Problems have arisen over time with the inclusion of amounts in the clawback base. These seem largely to involve payments from foreign pension or social security plans which are exempt from tax in Canada under tax treaties. It is the CRA's view that such payments are included in net income for purposes of the OAS clawback tax and so may increase the clawback even though the payments are themselves deducted in arriving at taxable income (¶990).

In the case of *Swantje v. The Queen*, 94 DTC 1359 (T.C.C.), the Tax Court of Canada made a detailed ruling that in the case of the OAS clawback in particular, the CRA's position was in error, but this ruling was overturned on appeal to the Federal Court of Appeal (94 DTC 6633; aff'd 96 DTC 6310 (S.C.C.)), which upheld the CRA's position. It follows that treaty-exempt income is included in net income in determining the clawback.

(Window on Canadian Tax: 2769, 2581; *The Queen v. Swantje*, 94 DTC 6633 (F.C.A.), aff'd 96 DTC 6310 (S.C.C.))

[¶1419.30] *OAS Benefits Clawback Chart*

OAS pension from line 113		$	1
Net federal supplements from line 146		+	2
Line (1) plus line (2)		$	3
Overpayment of OAS benefits recovered (from box 20 of your T4A(OAS))		-	4
Line (3) minus line (4) (if negative, enter "0")		$	5
Net income before adjustments from line 234		$	6
EI benefits repayment (if any) from line 4 of the chart on your T4E slip (or line (10) of the EI Benefits Clawback Chart below)	$ 7		
Universal Child Care Benefit (line 117 of your T1)	$ 8		
Registered Disability Savings Plan (RDSP) income (line 125 of your T1)	$ 9		
Total of line (7) plus line (8) plus line (9)		$	10

Line (6) minus line (10)	$	11
Universal Child Care Benefit repayment (line 213 of your return) $ ___ 12		
RDSP repayment (included in line 232 of your return, which may also contain other amounts) $ ___ 13		
Line (12) plus line (13)	$	14
Line (11) plus line (14)	$	15
Base amount	- 73,756	16
Line (15) minus line (16) (if negative, enter "0")	$	17
	x 15%	
Multiply line (17) by 15% and enter the result on this line	$	18
OAS pension and net federal supplements repayment: Enter either line (5) or line (18), whichever is less	$	19
EI benefits repayment (line (7), above) (if any)	+	20
Total social benefits repayment payable (line (19) plus line (20))	$	21

Enter the amount from line 21 on lines 235 and 422 of your return.

[¶1419.35] *Employment Insurance Benefits Clawback Chart*

Complete this repayment chart if the rate in box 7 of your T4E slip is 30% and, on your T1 return, the total of lines 213 and 234 plus the amount of registered disability savings plan (RDSP) income repayment included on line 232, minus the total of lines 117 and 125 is more than $63,500.

Chart 1

Enter the amount of benefits from box 15 if the repayment rate in box 7 is 30%		1
Enter the EI benefits you repaid from box 30	-	2
Line (1) minus line (2) (if negative, enter "0")	=	3
Enter the total of amounts from lines 213 plus 234 plus the amount of RDSP included on line 232 of your return		4
Enter the amount from line 117 plus the amount from line 125 of your return (if any)		5
Line (4) minus line (5) (if negative, enter "0")	=	6
Minus: Base amount	- 63,500	7
Line (6) minus line (7) (if negative, enter "0")	=	8
Enter the amount from line (3) or (8), whichever is less		9
	x 30%	
EI benefits repayment. Enter this amount on lines 235 and 422 of your return unless you received OAS benefits and your line 234 income exceeds $73,756. If you did receive OAS benefits and your line 234 income exceeds $73,756, enter the line (10) amount on line (7) of the OAS Benefits Clawback Chart above	=	10

[¶1422] NON-REFUNDABLE TAX CREDITS

These are the total credits calculated by reference to "personal amounts" on Schedule 1 of your T1 return. Each element of the credits is discussed in Chapters 11, 12, and 13.

(ITA: 118–118.95)

[¶1423] FAMILY TAX CUT — FORMER LINE 423

Budget 2016 eliminated, for 2016 and subsequent taxation years, the non-refundable income splitting tax credit (Family Tax Cut) of up to $2,000 that was available for couples with children under the age of 18.

The family tax cut mechanism provided a deduction from tax payable of the lesser of (a) $2,000 and (b) the difference between the spouses' combined tax payable for the year before the transfer and their combined tax payable as a result of the transfer. The calculation of the family tax cut was on Schedule 1-A. The reduction in tax was carried on line 423 on Schedule 1. See ¶1317.

(ITA: 119.1(2) Repealed)

[¶1425] DIVIDEND TAX CREDIT — LINE 425

There are two versions of the dividend tax credit available. The dividend tax credit for "eligible dividends" is more generous than the dividend tax credit for what are somewhat uncreatively called "other than eligible dividends" or "non-eligible dividends". Non-eligible dividends for this purpose are dividends notionally paid out of amounts subject to the lower small business tax rates in the Canadian corporations which paid them, or from investment income on which the corporation paid refundable tax. They do not include, for example, foreign dividends. Eligible dividends are those paid by Canadian corporations out of income subject to high rates of corporate tax; most dividends paid by large public Canadian companies will be in this category. It is possible for a company to have both kinds of income and to pay both kinds of dividends.

Fortunately for you, the onus of determining which kind of dividend you have falls entirely on the payer corporation. Your T5 slip from each company (or T3, T4PS or T5013 slip if the dividends have passed through a trust or partnership) will show both eligible and non-eligible dividends (as applicable), along with the associated "grossed up" (taxable) amount of the dividends and the associated dividend tax credit. The concept of the grossed-up amount is discussed in the context of reporting dividend income at ¶404.

You are permitted to deduct from your federal tax for 2016

- 15.02% of the taxable amount of *eligible* dividends from taxable Canadian corporations reported on line 120 of your T1 return, PLUS
- 10.52% of the taxable amount of *other* (i.e., *non-eligible*) dividends from taxable Canadian corporations (reported on line 180 of your T1 return).

The taxable amount of each type of dividend from a taxable Canadian corporation is totaled in the first section of Schedule 4, "Statement of Investment Income".

Note that the dividend tax credit claimed cannot exceed your total federal tax payable — i.e., it cannot create a refund. A dividend tax credit in excess of tax otherwise payable cannot be applied in earlier or later taxation years. Moreover, there is a required ordering of credits which puts the dividend tax credit after all the personal amount credits.

Example

Mildred Pierce has income of $10,600, consisting of interest of $8,200 and eligible dividends of $2,400. Her only personal credit amount (on Schedule 1) for 2016 is the basic personal amount of $11,474.

Actual income		$ 10,600
Taxable income		
Interest	$ 8,200	
Taxable amount of dividend from taxable Canadian corporations (dividend received ($2,400) plus 38% of $2,400)	3,312	$ 11,512
Federal tax on taxable income		$1,726
Less: Basic 2016 personal credit ([$11,474 × 15%])		1,721
Limitation on dividend tax credit		$ 5
Available dividend tax credit — 15.02% of taxable amount of dividends		$ 497

The dividend tax credit in this example is limited to $5 — her tax otherwise payable. The unused portion of the dividend tax credit is simply lost; there is no carryover provision.

Where there is an unused portion of the dividend tax credit it may be advantageous for your spouse to make the election to include the taxable dividends in the spouse's income (see ¶408).

Planning

In the above example there is no alternative to the lost credit if the spousal transfer is not available. This will often be the case in fact. However, where dividend tax credit is being wasted, the situation should be examined to see if any optional claims with carryovers can be foregone to use the credit. For example, the charitable donation credit has a carryforward period and could be omitted in the current year and used later. Capital cost allowances and reserves are optional deductions and could be reduced to bring income up to the level at which the credit is fully used. The other alternative is to bring income forward that would otherwise be reported in later years, where this is possible. Usually actions like these will reduce the overall tax burden over time, although those with a heavy dividend bias in their income over a long period may have no useful options. Even in this situation, changing the income mix by reinvesting from shares to bonds, if there is a benefit in yield and no severe capital gains penalty, should be considered.

History

Prior to 2016, the dividend tax credit for non-eligible dividends was 11.02% of the grossed-up dividends. The tax treatment of non-eligible dividends changed in 2016 to 10.52% of the grossed-up dividends; see ¶404.20.

(ITA: 82; 118.92; 121)

[¶1427] MINIMUM TAX CARRYOVER — LINE 427

As discussed at ¶2481, alternative minimum tax of prior years may be deducted (at line 427 of Schedule 1) from current year tax in excess of current year alternative minimum tax. This of course requires you to compute your current year alternative minimum tax on form T691 (Chapter 24) even if it is clearly not applicable for the year, to determine the current tax reduction.

[¶1429] BASIC FEDERAL TAX — LINE 429

Basic federal tax is not a term defined in the *Income Tax Act*. It is the amount on which provincial tax was computed at one time. It remains the amount on which Quebec abatement (¶1435) is computed (Quebec taxpayers compute provincial tax on a special provincial form; see Chapter 16). It is also used for some provincial calculations, as a step in the computation of foreign tax credit, and as the base for calculating non-resident surtax in lieu of provincial tax (¶1445).

Basic federal tax is the amount from line 429 of Schedule 1; that is, it is tax after claiming, non-refundable (personal amount) credits, the dividend tax credit (¶1425), and the credit for minimum tax carryforwards (¶2481), but before the federal foreign tax credit (¶1455) or any other tax credits.

[¶1435] ABATEMENT FOR QUEBEC INCOME TAX — LINE 440

You may deduct (at line 440 on page 4 of your T1 return) a refundable Quebec abatement if you resided in Quebec at the end of the year or carried on business in Quebec during the year.

The refundable Quebec abatement is 16.5% of basic federal tax on income earned in Quebec. Basic federal tax for this purpose is essentially the tax calculated at line 429 of Schedule 1 of the T1; see ¶1429.

If the Quebec tax abatement results in a negative amount of federal tax payable, the negative amount will be refunded to you.

Calculate your refundable Quebec abatement as follows:

(1) If you lived in Quebec on December 31, and have no income from a business establishment in another province, claim an abatement equal to 16.5% of your basic federal tax.

(2) If you lived in a province other than Quebec on December 31, and had income from a business with a permanent establishment in Quebec, you must allocate your business income between the province in which you resided at year end and Quebec. If part of your business income is allocated to the province of Quebec, claim 16.5% of the portion of the basic federal tax equal to the ratio of Quebec business income to your total net income. The method of allocating income is described below under Allocation of Income. See ¶1440. Form T2203 will assist you with the allocation.

Example 1

You were resident in Ontario on December 31 and had net income of $30,000 made up of net income of $25,000 from a business in Quebec, $1,000 from employment in Quebec and $4,000 from employment in Ontario. Your basic federal tax is $2,005.

Your refundable Quebec abatement is calculated as follows:

$$16.5\% \text{ of } \frac{\$25{,}000 \text{ (Quebec income)}}{\$30{,}000 \text{ (net income)}} \times \$2{,}005 = \$275.68$$

You are obliged in this situation to file a Quebec as well as a federal income tax return (Chapter 16) and Quebec form TP-25 (¶1607).

(3) If you lived in Quebec on December 31 and had income from a business with a permanent establishment in another province or country(ies), you must allocate your income between Quebec and the other provinces or countries in which you had permanent establishments of your business. You may claim an abatement for Quebec income taxes only on the portion of your basic federal tax equal to the ratio of income from Quebec to net income.

Example 2

For the year you had a net income of $30,000 including $5,000 from a permanent establishment of your business in the U.S. and $3,000 from a permanent establishment in Ontario. Your basic federal tax is $2,005. On December 31, you lived in Quebec.

Your refundable Quebec abatement is calculated as follows:

$$16.5\% \text{ of } \frac{\$22{,}000 \text{ (Quebec income)}}{\$30{,}000 \text{ (net income)}} \times \$2{,}005 = \$242.60$$

(4) If you lived in Canada during the year, but not on the last day of the year, and your province of residence was Quebec on the last day you resided in Canada, then your Canadian income (other than business income) is allocated to Quebec for purposes of the refundable Quebec abatement. Business income is allocated according to permanent establishments in the usual manner.

(5) If you were a non-resident of Canada who had employment income, or income from a business with a permanent establishment in Quebec, or capital gains on taxable Quebec property, your employment income is allocated to Quebec on a basis consistent with the amount of employment services performed in that province. Business income is allocated according to permanent establishments in the usual manner and the capital gain is allocated to Quebec. See ¶1602 and ¶1607.

(ITA: 115; 120; ITR: 2601–2603; 6401; QTA: 26)

[¶1440] ALLOCATION OF INCOME

If you had income from a business for the year, and if this business had a permanent establishment in a province other than that in which you resided at the end of the year, or in a foreign country, you must allocate your income. As only income earned in the year is allocated to a province, losses from a separate business are not allocated, but are applied to the province (or country — see ¶1445) of residence.

This income allocation is necessary in computing your refundable Quebec abatement. It is also used in the calculation of your provincial tax payable, and can be relevant in the calculation of a foreign tax credit.

CRA form T2203 will assist you with the allocation of income among provinces and outside Canada, if that is relevant.

(A) Permanent Establishment

Income is allocated to a province or foreign country in which you did not reside at the end of the year only if your business had a permanent establishment there at some time during the year (see also "Business Income" — ¶2030).

The term "permanent establishment" means a fixed place of business and includes an office, a branch, a mine, an oil well, a farm, a timberland, a factory, a workshop or a warehouse. You will also have a permanent establishment if:

(1) You have an *employee or agent* established in the province or country *and* the agent has general authority to contract for you or has a stock of your merchandise from which the agent regularly fills orders; or

(2) You made *use of substantial machinery or equipment* in the province or country at any time in the year. Your business need not own the machinery or equipment. The size, quantity and dollar value of machinery or equipment used in the particular place are some of the criteria to be considered in the determination of whether the use is "substantial". A comparison of the total or type of machinery or equipment used by the business as a whole with that used in the particular place is not relevant. Another factor that may be taken into account is whether the machinery or equipment contributes substantially to the generation of the gross income of the business earned at the particular place.

It is possible to carry on business in a province or country without having a permanent establishment there. For example, having salesmen in a place will not constitute a permanent establishment unless they have general authority to contract for you, or fill orders from a stock of merchandise. If they work from an office of your business, this office will be a permanent establishment; but if they merely work from their residences and do not advertise these in any way as an office of your business, you will probably not have a permanent establishment there. Also, you will generally not have a permanent establishment in a province if you maintain an office solely for the purchase of merchandise.

For a brief overview of case law on the meaning of the term "permanent establishment", see the Wolters Kluwer Newsletter *Tax Topics* No. 1737, dated June 23, 2005. For comment as to whether a website or Internet host server may be a permanent establishment in Canada, see CRA Document No. 2008-0279141E5, "Electronic commerce — Articles 7 and 12 tax treaties", dated June 23, 2008.

(B) Allocation

Allocate your business income as follows:

(1) Determine the provinces or countries in which you had permanent establishments in the year.

(2) Allocate net income by the percentage of the gross revenue of your business attributable to each permanent establishment for the year.

Gross revenue is attributed according to the following rules:

(a) To the province or country in which the customer is located, if your business has a permanent establishment there;

(b) To the province in which the permanent establishment negotiating the sale is located, if there is no permanent establishment in the province where the customer is located;

(c) To the province where the goods were manufactured or produced, if the sale is to a foreign country where no permanent establishment exists, irrespective of where the shipment is directed. Where the goods are manufactured or produced in more than one province, the gross revenue is attributed to the respective provinces based on the proportion that the salaries and wages paid to employees of the permanent establishment in the province is of the total salaries and wages paid in the year to employees of the permanent establishments where the goods are manufactured or produced;

(d) To the province or country where services were performed, if the revenue is from services and a permanent establishment was located there; and

(e) To the province or country in which the establishment negotiating a contract for services is located, if the services are performed in a place where no permanent establishment existed. If you are a bus or truck operator, you substitute for the percentage of gross revenues the proportion of the number of miles travelled by your vehicles in the province or country in the fiscal period ending in the year to the total number of miles travelled by your vehicles in that period in provinces in which you have a permanent establishment.

CRA Document No. 2013-0514921I7 reflects the CRA's position that certain volume rebates and government assistance are not included in determination of "gross revenue" (this position differs from earlier CRA Document No. 2010-0382161I7).

(3) Allocate net income by the percentage of salaries or wages paid to employees of each permanent establishment for the year in relation to total salaries and wages paid to employees.

(4) For each permanent establishment add the portions of net income allocated as calculated in (2) and (3), above, and compute one-half of this total. The resulting amounts are the income allocated to each permanent establishment.

(5) From your income for the year, deduct the business income allocated to provinces or countries in which you did not reside at the year end. The result will be the income allocated to your province of residence.

If you operate more than one business, a separate computation must be made for each. The amount of income for the year from carrying on business in a particular province is the sum of the amounts so determined for each business.

Your business income from all the provinces and countries other than Canada cannot exceed your income for the year. That is, the deduction for the allocation of business income cannot result in a loss in your province of residence.

Where land constitutes a permanent establishment in the particular province, the gross revenue which arises from leasing the land is attributable to that permanent establishment.

Example 1:

You live in Ontario and operate a business with its head office in Ontario and sales offices in Manitoba and Quebec. Your business income was $40,000, and you also received investment income of $6,000. Sales to customers in each of these provinces (there were no sales to customers outside these provinces) and salaries paid to employees in each province were as follows:

	Sales	*% × Business income (1)*	*Salaries*	*% × Business income (2)*
Ontario	$200,000	$20,000	$ 75,000	$24,000
Quebec	150,000	15,000	40,000	12,800
Manitoba	50,000	5,000	10,000	3,200
	$400,000	$ 40,000	$125,000	$ 40,000

Allocate your business income to the provinces as follows (allocation is equal to ½ of (1) + (2)):

Quebec	($15,000 + $12,800) ÷ 2 =	$13,900
Manitoba	($ 5,000 + $ 3,200) ÷ 2 =	4,100
		$18,000
Ontario	— $40,000 (net business income) minus $18,000 (net business income allocated to other provinces)	22,000
	— investment income	6,000
	Total income	$46,000

Example 2:

Your situation was the same as in Example 1, except that your business made sales to customers in New Brunswick and Nova Scotia totalling $10,000, and sales to customers in British Columbia of $15,000, in addition to the sales to Ontario, Manitoba and Quebec customers.

Sales to customers east of Quebec are negotiated by your Quebec sales office, but sales in British Columbia are negotiated by your Ontario office.

Allocate your business income as follows:

Calculate your business income allocation in proportion to sales and salaries by provinces in the following manner:

	Sales	*% × Business income (1)*	*Salaries*	*% × Business income (2)*
Ontario	$215,000	$20,235	$ 75,000	$24,000
Quebec	160,000	15,059	40,000	12,800
Manitoba	50,000	4,706	10,000	3,200
	$425,000	$ 40,000	$125,000	$ 40,000

Remember that sales and income are attributed only to provinces in which you have a permanent establishment. Sales to a province where there is no permanent establishment are usually attributed to the establishment negotiating the sale.

Allocate your income to the provinces as follows (allocation is equal to ½ of (1) + (2)):

Quebec	($15,059 + $12,800) ÷ 2 =	$13,900
Manitoba	($ 4,706 + $ 3,200) ÷ 2 =	3,953
		$17,883

Ontario	— $40,000 (net business income) minus $17,883 (net business income allocated to other provinces)	22,117
	— investment income	6,000
	Total income	$46,000

(ITR: 2600–2607)

[¶1445] SURTAX FOR INCOME NOT EARNED IN A PROVINCE

Where you have income which is not considered to be earned in a province, a 48% federal surtax applies instead of the provincial tax. For tax purposes, "province" includes Nunavut, the Yukon, and the Northwest Territories, so that income earned in those territories is subject to their tax regimes and not to the federal surtax.

The surtax of 48% of basic federal tax is levied on the following income:

(1) income earned by Canadian residents from a permanent establishment in a foreign country;

(2) income earned by persons who are deemed to be residents of Canada but who reside outside of Canada and therefore have no province of residence, such as members of the Canadian armed forces;

(3) income earned by persons who are deemed to be residents of Canada by virtue of having spent more than 183 days here without establishing actual residence; these persons are "deemed residents" (¶117) of Canada but are not deemed residents of a province unless 183 days were spent in Quebec, in which case they are effectively treated as Quebec residents; foreign students are often in this category (see ¶115, ¶117); and

(4) income earned by non-residents but taxable in Canada, as discussed in Chapter 20; this includes income from a business or employment in Canada, or income from scholarships, bursaries, and research grants (¶2024); it would also include income from dispositions of "taxable Canadian property" as described at ¶2040; note, however, that individuals who dispose of Quebec real estate or property used in Quebec in carrying on a business are liable to Quebec tax on these dispositions (¶1608) and federal surtax on the same gains is relieved under federal remission orders.

The 48% surtax applies to the basic federal tax as shown on Schedule 1. Since the surtax may apply only to certain income it may be necessary to allocate your income for the year between income earned in a province and income to which the surtax applies.

Example

You lived in Ontario and operated a business with its head office in Ontario, and sales offices in Alberta and the U.S. Your net business income was $40,000 and you also received investment income of $6,000. Your basic federal tax is $5,048. Allocation of income to both of the provinces and the U.S. based on sales and salaries paid were as follows:

	Sales	*% × Business income (1)*	*Salaries*	*% × Business income (2)*
Ontario	$200,000	$20,000	$ 75,000	$24,000
Alberta	150,000	15,000	40,000	12,800
U.S.	50,000	5,000	10,000	3,200
	$400,000	$ 40,000	$125,000	$ 40,000

Allocate your business income to the provinces as follows (allocation is equal to $^1/_2$ of (1) + (2)):

Alberta	($15,000 + $12,800) ÷ 2 =	$13,900
U.S.	($ 5,000 + $ 3,200) ÷ 2 =	4,100
		$18,000
Ontario	— $40,000 (net business income) minus $18,000 (net business income allocated to other provinces)	22,000
	— investment income	6,000
	Total income	$46,000

Calculate the 48% surtax as follows:

$$48\% \text{ of } \frac{\$4{,}100 \text{ (U.S. income)}}{\$46{,}000 \text{ (total income)}} \times \$5{,}048 = \quad \$216$$

The remaining allocation, $41,900/$46,000, will be subject to provincial tax. The allocations should be made on form T2203. In practice, you treat non-resident allocations as just one more jurisdiction in making the allocations for provincial surtax discussed at ¶1502.

If you are subject to alternative minimum tax (Chapter 24) in lieu of regular tax for the year, use basic federal tax from form T691 in computing the surtax, and make foreign and provincial surtax allocations on form T2203.

(ITA: 120; 250; ITR: 2601 Residents of Canada; IT-106R3 Crown Corporation Employees Abroad)

[¶1446] ALLOCATION OF BUSINESS INCOME TO A PROVINCE BY A NON-RESIDENT

A non-resident individual who carries on business in Canada must file an individual income tax return. However, where there is a treaty between Canada and the non-resident individual's country of residence, typically only income earned from a business with a "permanent establishment" in Canada will be subject to tax. A permanent establishment for this purpose will be defined by the treaty.

It appears, however, that Canada expects a non-resident who carries on a business in Canada but does not have a permanent establishment here under the relevant treaty to file a Canadian income tax return and report Canadian income, claiming an offset for treaty-protected income at line 256 of the T1. The logic of this position is that treaties protect non-residents from tax but not from compliance procedures. Although this may be technically correct, it appears that there is no penalty for failure to file a return if no tax is owed. There is a penalty for omitting information from a return, but it seems that this penalty only applies to omissions on returns actually filed; if no form is filed, the penalty is a percentage of tax owing, and if that is zero, there seems to be no penalty.

See ¶2030 for a discussion of what constitutes carrying on business in Canada and for comments on the Canada–U.S. Tax Treaty.

If you are a non-resident earning business income in Canada, for the purposes of determining the Quebec abatement and provincial tax payable, your business income must be allocated among the provinces. See ¶1440 for a discussion of how to determine where you have a permanent establishment for the purposes of those allocations, which may be somewhat different from treaty definitions of the same term, and an explanation of how this allocation is made.

The CRA provides a special T1 return package for *Non-residents and Deemed Residents*. This is available on-line and from Tax Services Offices (¶218), from the International Taxation Office (¶218), and from Canadian embassies and consulates abroad.

(ITA: 2; 110(1)(*f*)(i))

[¶1450] FOREIGN TAX CREDIT — LINE 405

You may deduct from your Basic Federal Tax a foreign tax credit for foreign income or profits taxes paid. To claim a credit for foreign taxes, you must use the detailed tax calculation on form T2209 and enter the foreign tax credit on line 405 of Schedule 1 of your return.

A separate foreign tax credit calculation must be made for each country for which you are claiming a credit. In addition, a separate computation is required for business income tax and non-business income tax for each country (see ¶1455). Both credits are calculated on form T2209. A credit for tax on foreign business income which cannot be utilized in the current year may be carried back three years and forward 10 years. A credit for tax on foreign investment income has no carryover, and moreover is limited to 15% of net income from foreign property (other than real estate), but excess credits may be deducted from income. These matters are discussed in more detail at ¶1455. Non-business income credits which cannot be claimed against federal tax may also be eligible for credit against provincial tax; see ¶1506. Except for Quebec (see ¶1670), there is no provincial tax credit for business income taxes.

Your foreign tax credit cannot exceed either the foreign taxes paid or the amount of Canadian federal tax payable for the year on the income from sources in that country. Foreign taxes paid do not include taxes on income which is exempt from tax in Canada by virtue of a tax treaty.

Non-Business Income Foreign Tax Credit

In calculating the foreign non-business tax credit, foreign taxes paid (for each country) are included in Canadian dollars at line 431 on form T2209, and the limitation is calculated on the succeeding lines as the proportion of "Basic Federal Tax" that "Net Foreign Non-Business Income" is of "Net Income". "Basic Federal Tax" in this calculation is the total of (i) Basic Federal Tax as calculated on Schedule 1, line 429, (ii) your dividend tax credit, and (iii) the surtax on income not earned in a province, less (v) the refundable Quebec abatement and (vi) the refundable First Nations abatement. "Net Income" is the total of the amount on line 236 of page 3 of your return and your split income at line 4 on form T1206 (see ¶1490), reduced by:

- net capital losses relating to other years claimed in the current year (line 253, see ¶1093);
- the deduction for certain members of the Canadian Forces and Canadian police services (line 244, see ¶385);
- the deduction for employee home relocation loans (line 248, see ¶409);
- the deduction in respect of the benefit included in the income of an employee in respect of qualifying stock options (line 249, see ¶330);
- the deduction for distributions of DPSP shares (line 249, see ¶917);
- the deduction for prospector's shares (line 249, see ¶776);
- the capital gains deduction (line 254, see ¶502);
- adult basic education tuition and treaty exemption claims (deducted at line 256, if included in net income, see ¶990); and
- social assistance or worker's compensation amounts (if included in net income, line 250, see ¶990).

For each country, foreign source income from that country for the non-business tax credit is income allocable to sources in that country reduced by amounts exempt by treaty and by amounts on which the capital gains deduction (¶502) has been claimed, and calculated as if the taxpayer (i) carried on no business in that country, (ii) had no employment income from that country to the extent the employment income was eligible for overseas employment tax credit, and (iii) had no deduction from dividend income from that country for amounts previously taxed as foreign accrual property income.

Non-business income taxes paid in respect of a participating interest in a foreign investment entity (FIE) in respect of which you have elected to account for tax under the FIE accrual method (discussed at ¶492), are excluded from the general foreign tax credit rules. The FIE rules for the accrual election carry instead a specified tax allocation deduction defined in those rules.

For example, if "Basic Federal Tax" is $1,026, the "Dividend Tax Credit" is $500, "Net Foreign Income" is $3,000, and "Net Income" is $20,000, the foreign tax credit deduction is limited to:

$$\frac{\$3,000}{\$20,000} \times \$1,526 = \$229$$

even if foreign tax paid was in excess of $229 (but see ¶1506). Insert the appropriate figures and make this calculation on form T2209.

The ordering of taxes and credits on Schedule 1 and page 4 of the T1 simplifies, although it does not distort, the calculation of the foreign tax credit limitation.

If excess non-business foreign tax remains unabsorbed after the federal claim, a further claim can be made against provincial tax on form T2036 (¶1506) or, for Quebec residents, on form TP-772V (¶1659).

Business Income Foreign Tax Credit

Form T2209 also must be used if you are calculating credit on tax paid on foreign business income.

The calculation parallels the one used in calculating your non-business tax credit. However, "Basic Federal Tax" for purposes of the business income credit is calculated as the total of (i) Basic Federal Tax as calculated on Schedule 1, line 429, and (ii) your dividend tax credit claimed. "Net Income" for purposes of the business income tax credit is calculated in the same manner as it is in claiming the non-business tax credit.

Foreign source business income from a country is income from business carried on there (except income which is treaty-exempt in Canada).

For calculation of the business tax credit limitation only, the portion of the surtax on income not earned in a province that applies to the foreign source income is added to prorated basic federal tax applicable to that income. Thus, the business tax credit is limited to the lesser of the foreign business income tax paid and the total of the basic federal tax and surtax that relates to that income.

Note that where Alternative Minimum Tax applies, a special foreign tax credit calculation may be made — see Chapter 24.

Unused business foreign taxes may be carried over (see ¶1455, item 3(B)); unused non-business foreign taxes may be eligible for provincial credit (¶1506). Taxes not creditable may be eligible for deduction; see ¶1455.

(ITA: 126; S5-F2-C1 Foreign Tax Credit)

[¶1452] RESTRICTIONS ON FOREIGN INCOME FOR FOREIGN TAX CREDIT

[¶1452.05] *General Foreign Tax Credit Limitations*

As discussed in ¶1450, there are in principle two limitations on both business and non-business foreign tax credits: first, the foreign taxes paid; and second, the limitation imposed by the formula:

$$\frac{\text{foreign source income}}{\text{world income}} \times \text{Canadian tax otherwise payable}$$

Each of these limitations applies separately to each of the business and non-business foreign tax credit calculations for each country to which taxes are paid.

Foreign tax on income which is exempt from tax in Canada by virtue of a tax treaty (literally, which is deductible from Canadian taxable income by virtue of the provision allowing a deduction for treaty-protected income) is not included in foreign taxes paid in the first limitation.

As well, income exempt (deductible) in Canada under a tax treaty is excluded from foreign source income in the numerator of the second limitation. Furthermore, in calculating non-business income only, there is also an exclusion from foreign source income for amounts on which you can claim the capital gains deduction.

Since a separate computation of foreign source income is required for each country, sourcing can be a complex issue. The sourcing rules, and general overall rules for computing foreign source income, are discussed in some detail under subheading (4) in ¶1455. The rules below impose some specific restrictions on foreign income which is exempt from local taxation.

[¶1452.10] *Restrictions on Foreign-Source Income Calculation*

The additional rules which follow deal with foreign income in the numerator of the foreign tax credit limitation only, and not the determination of foreign tax paid.

For these purposes, both foreign non-business income and foreign business income must exclude income that is exempt from both foreign and Canadian tax. To quantify the exclusion, you must calculate foreign source income for each of the business and non-business credit calculations for each country as "qualifying income" in excess of "qualifying loss".

Both qualifying income and qualifying loss are income and loss from the country excluding (i) any portion of income *deductible* from Canadian taxable income (at line 256; see ¶990) by virtue of a Canadian tax treaty and (ii) any income or loss from a source in that country if any of your income from that source would be "tax-exempt income". Tax-exempt income is income not subject to tax in the foreign country because *both* (i) you are entitled to an exemption from *all* income or profits taxes to which a Canadian tax treaty with that country applies, and (ii) no income or profits tax to which the treaty does not apply is imposed in any country other than Canada. For purposes of the non-business tax credit only, qualifying income and loss also exclude income against which you claimed the capital gains deduction.

The point of the double barrelled test of tax-exempt income is that it should not cover income which, although exempt from taxes covered by the treaty, may nevertheless be subject to non-Canadian taxes, typically imposed by a political subdivision of the foreign country. Such income should enter into the formula for the calculation of foreign tax credit.

Thus, only foreign source income both wholly exempt under a treaty and not otherwise taxed is caught by the tax-exempt rule. Income taxed at low rates or not taxable because of foreign deductions or credits is not affected. The benefit from this relief may be mitigated by the rules at ¶1453.

(ITA: 126(1), (2.1), (7), (9))

[¶1452.15] *Tax Treaty Countries*

A list of countries with which Canada has tax treaties is found at ¶2005.

[¶1453] FOREIGN TAX CREDIT RESTRICTIONS: LOW-YIELD PROPERTY; SHORT-TERM ACQUISITIONS; FOREIGN RESOURCE TAXES

The rules summarized below are intended to capture fairly elaborate tax planning schemes involving foreign tax credits. They probably apply more often to corporations than individuals; and rarely to individuals who simply hold foreign investments as part of a diversified portfolio. The short-term acquisition rules, for example, which seem at first blush to be of concern to the general investor, do not apply to capital property, that is, to property purchased as an investment rather than for speculation. In general, both sets of rules are aimed primarily at investments that depend on tax arbitrage to yield profit. That said, the rules are of general application and therefore of general concern.

In calculating business and non-business foreign taxes, specific limitations will apply to foreign tax paid on:

- non-capital shares or debt held for only one year or less
- non-capital property which at the time of acquisition would be expected to yield an economic return which is insubstantial in relation to associated foreign income and profits taxes

will be limited as discussed below.

[¶1453.05] *Short-Term Securities Acquisitions*

Where shares or debt acquired are held for one year or less, the amount of foreign tax relating thereto included in both the business and non-business income tax credit is calculated by applying a notional rate (see below) to the gross income from the security for the period for which it was held. This rule does not apply to capital property, or to a debt obligation having a term of one year or less that is issued to you and held to maturity. It is aimed at short-term acquisitions intended to generate a foreign tax liability giving rise to Canadian credit which can be used to shelter income from the same country which was taxed at low rates there.

This rule only applies to foreign withholding taxes on dividends and interest which would otherwise be included in business or non-business foreign tax for purposes of Canadian tax credit. The amount of such foreign tax which may be included in your creditable tax for Canadian purposes is limited to 25% (where the tax would be included in foreign business-income tax paid) or 28% (where the tax is included in foreign non-business income tax paid) of the total proceeds of disposition of the share or debt, plus interest and dividends received, minus the cost of the property and expenses of disposition. No deduction is allowed for carrying charges.

Where the ownership period of a year or less falls into more than one taxation year, the limited credit is apportioned between the years in the same proportion that would have applied if the limitation had not applied. That is, the foreign withholding tax on the property for a particular taxation year divided by the foreign withholding tax on the property for all taxation years in the ownership period is used to prorate the limited amount.

If a "synthetic disposition arrangement" is entered into in respect of a property owned by a taxpayer and the "synthetic disposition period" in respect of the synthetic disposition arrangement is at least 30 days, for the purpose of determining whether the one-year holding period is met, the period is deemed to begin at the earlier of (i) the time that the taxpayer disposes of the property, and (ii) the end of the synthetic disposition period. Effectively, you must own the property for at least a year after the end of the synthetic disposition period in order to meet the holding period test. Synthetic dispositions are discussed at ¶542a.

(ITA: 126(4.2), (7) "business income tax" and "non-business income tax")

[¶1453.10] *Insubstantial Profit*

Where it is reasonable to expect at the time of acquiring property that the economic profit on the property will be insubstantial relative to the total amount of foreign tax that is expected to be payable in respect of the property and related transactions, no amount may be included in business or non-business foreign taxes for any year for purposes of calculating your Canadian foreign tax credit.

Any credit denied under this rule may be available as a deduction from income, but only to the extent of income for the year attributable to the property or related transactions.

"Economic profit" is a defined term. It includes the business income attributable to the property or to related transactions. In calculating income attributable to the property or related transactions, only interest and financing expenses, income or profits taxes payable to a foreign government or political subdivision, and other expenses directly attributable to the acquisition, holding, or disposition of the property are deducted. General overhead expenses are not taken into account. Economic profit is calculated for the period of continuous ownership of the property from acquisition to disposition, and includes income attributable to the property for that period and income in respect of related transactions.

"Related transactions", also a defined term, simply means transactions you enter into as part of the arrangement under which the property was owned. Department of Finance Technical notes suggest that related transactions could include financing, hedging and insurance transactions, and counterparty arrangements contingent on the acquisition of the property.

The objective of these rules is to identify transactions which only make economic sense if you can use foreign tax credits to shield from Canadian tax other income from the country.

(ITA: 20(12.1); 126(4.1), (4.3), (7))

[¶1453.15] *Deemed Dispositions*

In applying both sets of rules above, certain rules which normally apply to deem an acquisition or disposition of property will not apply. These are: change in use rules (¶1450); immigration/emigration rules (Chapter 21); and several rules exclusive to corporations (discussed in the companion Wolters Kluwer volume *Preparing Your Corporate Tax Returns*). As well, several corporate reorganization provisions are considered not to create a disposition or acquisition, including some share conversions discussed at ¶536 and bond-for-bond exchanges discussed at ¶560c.

(ITA: 126(4.3))

[¶1453.20] *Foreign Resource Taxes*

Foreign tax credit limitations with respect to foreign resource exploitation are discussed in the context of the specialized resource industry rules in Chapter 22; see ¶2227.

[¶1454] FOREIGN TAX CREDIT RESTRICTION: "FOREIGN TAX CREDIT GENERATORS"

Foreign tax credit generators exploit situations where, under the foreign income tax law, the underlying foreign income is included to a lesser degree in the income of a Canadian partner than it would be for Canadian purposes. Effectively, the Canadian partner pays Canadian tax on a larger share of partnership income than is taxable in the foreign jurisdiction, but still qualifies for the foreign tax credit based on its share as determined for Canadian tax purposes.

Subsection 126(4.11) effectively eliminates these benefits of foreign tax credit generators, by providing that where a partner's direct or indirect share of the income from a partnership under the foreign income tax laws is less than the direct or indirect share thereof under the Canadian Act, the foreign tax paid in respect of that income is not business-income tax or non-business-income tax for purposes of the foreign tax credit. Although the provision appears to be aimed primarily at corporate taxpayers, it applies to all taxpayers, including individuals.

For the purposes of the provisions, you are not considered to have a lesser direct or indirect share of the income of a partnership under the relevant foreign tax law than for Canadian purposes solely because of one or more of the following (subsection 126(4.12)):

(1) a difference between the relevant foreign tax law and the Act in the manner of

(a) computing the income of the partnership, or

(b) allocating the income of the partnership because of the admission to, or withdrawal from, the partnership of any of its members;

(2) the treatment of the partnership as a corporation under the relevant foreign tax law; or

(3) for corporations only, the fact that a taxpayer is not treated as a corporation under the relevant foreign tax law.

[¶1455] FURTHER COMMENTS ON FOREIGN TAX CREDIT

The following points should be considered when applying the general rules described in ¶1450.

(1) Foreign Tax Paid

Foreign tax eligible for credit is the amount paid for the year even though part or all of the tax may be paid before or after the taxation year. Thus, where the tax paid by you to a foreign country is adjusted, your Canadian foreign tax credit may also require adjustment. The CRA should be informed so that the necessary adjustments can be made to ensure that the foreign tax credit corresponds to the actual foreign taxes paid for the year. Any amount of tax paid which will be refunded to you is not considered to be tax paid for the year.

The following amounts are excluded from *non-business income taxes* available for the credit:

(1) foreign taxes which were payable only because you were a citizen of the foreign country concerned, if such taxes cannot reasonably be attributed to income from a source outside Canada;

(2) the portion of foreign taxes attributable to capital gains on which a capital gains exemption (¶502) has been claimed, whether in the year or in another year and whether by you or by your spouse, which might be the case if the attribution rules apply (see ¶531);

(3) the foreign taxes paid by a person or a partnership which have been or are entitled to be repaid by the foreign jurisdiction to any other person or partnership (these qualify for a deduction from income rather than a foreign tax credit); and

(4) taxes on income which is exempt from tax in Canada by virtue of a tax treaty between Canada and the foreign country (see ¶2005).

Since the CRA has the exclusive treaty right to tax U.S. Social Security benefits received by Canadian residents, it will not give foreign tax credit for ordinary U.S. taxes which are paid on U.S. Social Security. On the other hand, it will allow Canadian foreign tax credit for U.S. Alternative Minimum Tax imposed on U.S. Social Security benefits; see ¶921.

Where you expect to be assessed or reassessed on income or profits tax by a foreign country and the limitation for reassessment by the Canadian tax authorities may expire before you receive the foreign assessment and pay the foreign tax, the CRA will accept, with a waiver (¶277) a request in writing for a refund of whatever amount may become claimable when the foreign tax has been paid.

(2) Currency Conversion

Any income tax paid to a foreign country in a foreign currency should be converted to Canadian dollars at the rate at which the income itself (other than capital gains) is converted. For business income, the conversion could be done monthly, quarterly, semi-annually or annually, using the average rate for the period, depending on your normal method of reporting the income. For investment income subject to withholding tax, the rate should be that of the date of receipt of the income, although the use of the average rate for the month or the mid-month rate is usually acceptable. For other types of income, such as salaries and wages, the average rate for the months in which they are earned is the most appropriate rate. For capital gains, the rate should approximate the rate at the time the gain was realized.

(Tables of yearly average conversion rates for several major currencies, and monthly averages for U.S. and U.K. currencies, are found at ¶95 and ¶90, respectively, preceding Chapter 1. The Bank of Canada website offers daily and average conversion rates for several years back.)

Where the tax is not paid until after the income has been earned, your actual cost in Canadian dollars of paying the tax may vary from the amount computed above. Where this occurs, the difference will be an exchange gain or loss (see ¶556). In this context, the actual cost of paying the tax is the Canadian dollar equivalent of the payment computed on the day of payment.

In the event that you have overpaid a foreign tax, the overpayment is not allowable as a foreign tax credit. The overpayment should be converted to Canadian dollars as above, and any difference between this figure and the Canadian dollar value of a refund of the overpayment, computed on the day of its receipt, will be an exchange gain or loss. See ¶556.

(3) Foreign Taxes Eligible for Credit

To be creditable, the foreign taxes must be income or profit taxes paid to the government of a foreign country or a political subdivision of such a country. Political subdivisions include states, provinces, counties or municipalities of a foreign country. In determining whether or not a particular foreign tax qualifies as an income or profits tax, the basic scheme under which the tax is applied is compared with that of the Canadian *Income Tax Act*. If the basis of taxation is substantially similar, the foreign tax is accepted as an income or profits tax. To be "substantially similar", the foreign tax must be levied on net income or profits (but not necessarily as would be computed for Canadian tax purposes) unless it is a tax similar to Canada's non-resident withholding tax. Since taxable capital gains are included in income for Canadian income tax purposes, a foreign tax on a capital gain is considered to be an income or profits tax for these purposes. If a particular tax imposed by a foreign country is specifically identified, in an "elimination of double tax" article of an income tax treaty between Canada and that country, as a tax for which Canada must grant a deduction from Canadian taxes on profits, income or gains which arose in that other country and which gave rise to the foreign tax in question, the foreign tax will qualify as an income or profits tax when applying Canadian foreign tax credit provisions in conjunction with that treaty article. (Income Tax Folio S5-F2-C1, "Foreign Tax Credit", paragraph 1.8). See, for example, the U.S. taxes referred to in paragraph 2(*a*) of Article XXIV of the *Canada-United States Income Tax Convention* dealing with US social security tax. Examples of taxes that do not qualify for purposes of the foreign tax credit provisions include the following:

(a) sales, commodity, consumption or turnover taxes;

(b) succession duties or inheritance taxes;

(c) property or real estate taxes;

(d) franchise or business taxes;

(e) customs or import duties;

(f) excise taxes or duties;

(g) gift taxes;

(h) capital or wealth taxes (capital tax presumably means a tax on business capital, as opposed to a tax on capital gains); and

(i) social security taxes other than U.S. Social Security, as discussed below.

A unitary tax of a state of the United States is not regarded as an income or profits tax if it is not computed on the basis of net business income. The following are instances where a unitary tax does not qualify as an income or profits tax (Income Tax Folio S5-F2-C1, "Foreign Tax Credit", paragraphs 1.10 – 1.11):

- The tax represents an annual minimum franchise tax.
- The tax is applicable even when there is no income.
- The calculation of the tax does not attempt to allocate income to the particular state.
- The tax is in the nature of a capital tax.

According to the CRA, a decision as to whether a particular state's unitary tax can be regarded as an income or profits tax for purposes of claiming a foreign tax credit can be made only after a review of the applicable state legislation. A unitary tax that does not qualify as an income or profits tax for purposes of claiming a foreign tax credit would likely be deductible in computing the taxpayer's income pursuant to subsection 9(1) as an expense for the purpose of earning income. See also paragraphs 1.18 and 1.38 of Income Tax Folio S5-F2-C1.

U.S. Social Security tax (FICA) is eligible for Canadian tax credit, but only to the extent it relates to U.S. source employment income. Thus a non-business income tax credit may be taken against U.S. source employment income; see Income Tax Folio S5-F2-C1, "Foreign Tax Credit", paragraph 1.8 and paragraph 2(a) of Article XXIV of the *Canada-United States Income Tax Convention*.

Social security taxes levied by other jurisdictions are not accepted as taxes on income and are therefore not available for credit. U.S. Social Security Taxes are specifically identified as creditable in the Canada-U.S. Tax Treaty (as noted above), which is why they qualify where other jurisdictions taxes don't. (For other aspects of the taxation of U.S. social security and other foreign social security, see ¶921 and ¶923, and ¶2111.)

However, in *Income Tax Technical News* No. 31R2 (now archived), the CRA accepted that a contribution by an employee resident in Canada to a foreign public pension plan will be considered as a non-business income tax for purposes of the foreign tax credit where the following two conditions apply: (1) the employee is compelled to make the contribution pursuant to the legislation of the foreign country; and (2) it is reasonable to conclude that the employee will not be eligible for any financial benefit from his or her contribution considering that the employment in the foreign country is temporary and for a short period of time.

Despite not qualifying as income or profits taxes, some tax treaties may specifically provide for a deduction in respect of such foreign taxes paid from Canadian taxes otherwise payable independently of the *Income Tax Act*. See, for example, paragraph 6 of Article XXIX B of the *Canada-United States Income Tax Convention*, which allows a deduction of U.S. estate taxes in computing Canadian income tax in the year of death (Income Tax Folio S5-F2-C1, paragraph 1.9). A similar provision is found paragraph 1(c) of Article 23 in the *Canada-France Income Tax Convention* regarding inheritance tax payable in France.

The CRA has indicated that the 10% additional tax in the United States for early withdrawals from an IRA is an income or profits tax and is eligible for the foreign non-business income tax credit (CRA Document No. 2011-0398741I7, April 19, 2011).

(A) Foreign business income tax credit

Creditable foreign business income taxes are those paid *for* the year in respect of a business carried on in a particular foreign country. Some foreign income or profits taxes that might otherwise be regarded as business-related can fall within the definition of non-business-income tax, as in the following examples:

- foreign tax paid in respect of a capital gain on the sale of a property used by you in carrying on a business in the foreign country, because a capital gain is not business income; and
- a foreign tax paid to the extent that it is in respect of a business (or a part of a business) that is carried on in Canada.

The amount paid *for* the year will not necessarily be the same amount as foreign taxes paid *in* the year. For example, if you operated a business in the U.S. in 2014 and incurred U.S. tax on the business income for 2014 which was not paid until 2015, this tax is a tax for the 2014 year and should be claimed as a credit on your 2014 Canadian income tax return. On the other hand, the foreign tax must actually have been paid. If payment has not been made by the time a Canadian return must be filed for the year, the credit is not technically available, and must be claimed by a subsequent request for adjustment to the return under the procedures at ¶221. If the foreign tax will not be assessed within the Canadian statutory time period for the year (¶268), a waiver (¶277) must be filed to keep the year open.

Only the foreign taxes actually paid which were properly payable may be claimed as a credit. If you overpay foreign tax, or if foreign tax is withheld from your income in error, you should claim a refund from the foreign country and not claim a foreign tax credit for the excess tax. The CRA is quite specific that any portion of a taxpayer's foreign tax which is paid but which subsequently is, or will be, refunded to the taxpayer is not considered to be tax "paid for the year". In other words, the foreign tax "paid for the year" for purposes of claiming a foreign tax credit cannot be more than the Canadian-dollar equivalent of the applicable foreign tax liability, as finally determined.

If you were a resident of Quebec, the business income tax paid to a foreign country entering in the calculation of your federal foreign business tax credit is multiplied by 55%. The remaining 45% of foreign business income tax paid will enter in the calculation of your Quebec foreign tax credit (see ¶1670).

(B) Foreign tax credit carryover for business taxes

If you carried on business in a foreign country, the foreign tax credit rules are slightly different from those which apply to employment and investment income. Foreign "business income" tax which is not absorbed as a foreign tax credit in the current year becomes an unused foreign tax credit. Your unused foreign business income tax credit generated in the year can be carried back three years and forward ten years for purposes of computing your business income tax credit.

The legislation provides that the amount of foreign business income tax credit claimed in a taxation year will be considered first to be in respect of foreign taxes paid for that year, and then in respect of carryover tax credits. Carryover tax credits will be considered to be used in the order in which they arose.

Example 1

Calculation of foreign business tax credit and carryover.

Your income from business carried on in a foreign country was $20,000 on which you paid foreign income taxes of $6,000. You are married and your net income was $30,000 which includes the foreign business income of $20,000. Your basic federal tax was $2,495, plus surtax on income not earned in a province of 48% of two-thirds (20,000/30,000) of basic federal tax, or $798.

Your federal foreign tax credit is calculated as follows:

Lesser of:

(a) $6,000 paid, or

(b) the aggregate of:

$20,000 (foreign business income) / $30,000 (net income)	× $2,495 =	$1,663
plus		
$20,000 (foreign business income) / $20,000 (income not earned in a province)	× $798 =	$798
		$2,461

You may claim $2,461 as a federal foreign tax credit against federal tax (this includes the 48% surtax on income not earned in a province) of $3,293, and you may carry over ($6,000 - $2,461) = $3,539 to be applied against federal tax arising from foreign business income in the past three years and next 10 years.

(C) Foreign non-business income tax credit

You are limited to 15% of the net amount of the income from the foreign property in calculating the amount of foreign non-business tax that is available to credit. However, this limitation does not apply to income derived from real property situated outside Canada. Foreign taxes paid in excess of the 15% limitation can be deducted in computing the income from the property. (See below, ¶407 and ¶435.) Also, there is no limitation on non-business income taxes paid on account of other sources of non-business income other than foreign property.

Example 2

Your non-business income from a foreign country was $400 on which you paid $125 in taxes. Your net income including the foreign non-business income after being adjusted for the foreign taxes paid in excess of 15% (as calculated below) was $11,270.

Your federal tax was $415.

Gross foreign non-business income	$400
Less: taxes paid in excess of 15%	65
Amount to be included in income	$ 335
Non-business income tax paid	$125
Less: amount allowed as a deduction in computing foreign non-business income	65
Amount available for foreign tax credit	$ 60

Foreign tax credit is lesser of:

(a) $60, or

(b) $335 (Foreign non-business income) / $11,270 (Net income) × $415 = $ 12

Allowable foreign tax credit .... $ 12

The excess foreign tax credit on non-business income of $48 ($60 - $12) may not be carried forward but may be claimed as a provincial foreign tax credit (see ¶1506) or as a deduction in arriving at net income (see below).

(D) Foreign tax deduction

As an alternative to claiming foreign tax credit for foreign non-business income taxes paid, you are allowed to deduct your foreign non-business taxes paid (provided they would be eligible for non-business income tax credit as described above) in computing income rather than claim a foreign tax credit. Generally, you will prefer to claim a foreign tax credit rather than a deduction. However, where the taxes exceed the limitation discussed at ¶1450, you will want to deduct the excess. Non-business income taxes so deducted reduce foreign taxes in calculating the allowable credit and credit limitation.

The deduction of foreign non-business tax paid from income is known in tax jargon as "the 20(12) deduction". Its rules can be intricate. The CRA (in CRA Document No. 2002-0144257, as interpreted in Wolters Kluwer *Tax Topics* No. 1599) gives the following example of the issues that can arise where income is recognized on an accrual basis but tax is paid in a lump sum:

Facts:

- in each of 1999 through 2001, the individual reported accrued interest income of $10,000;
- the individual's marginal tax rate for each year is 30% and tax of $3,000 was paid in each year for a total of $9,000;
- the individual receives the $30,000 of interest in 2001, net of $4,500 (15%) withholding tax.

Results:

The individual is only allowed to claim a foreign tax credit up to the amount of the Canadian tax paid with respect to foreign-source income for the year in which the withholding tax was actually exigible, that is, 2001. Thus, the individual is limited to a foreign tax credit of $3,000, which does not fully account for the $4,500 of withholding tax paid, even though the individual actually paid $9,000 in Canadian tax on the interest income.

The individual can deduct the whole of the remaining $1,500 of withholding tax (the "Excess Foreign Tax") as a 20(12) deduction in 2001. Subsection 20(12) refers to a deduction in computing income "for a taxation year... not exceeding the non-business income tax paid by the taxpayer for the year... in respect of that income". The income for Canadian tax purposes for 2001 is $10,000, and the amount of withholding tax paid in respect of that income is $1,500. Therefore, in computing his Canadian tax payable for 2001, the individual can claim a foreign tax credit of $3,000 and a 20(12) deduction of $1,500.

The individual's foreign tax credit for 2001 is limited by the Canadian tax applicable to the foreign source income that is reported in the year, $3,000 ($10,000 × 30%). The subsection 20(12) deduction is the balance of the foreign tax paid, $1,500. The 20(12) deduction is limited to the withholding tax that is applicable to the $10,000 of foreign source interest income for 2001 — here, $3,000.

The document notes that if the individual's marginal tax rate was 25%, there would be $500 of foreign tax that would not qualify for the deduction. The deduction would not change because it is limited to the foreign "tax paid ... for the year ... in respect of that income" — 15% of $10,000 = $1,500. However, the foreign tax credit would be $2,500 ($10,000 × 25%).

Non-business-income taxes paid in respect of employment income are not deductible under subsection 20(12), since subsection 8(2) restricts employment income deductions to those allowed under section 8 (Chapter 3). However, a non-business-income tax paid by a taxpayer resident in Canada on self-employment income, such as U.S. Social Security Tax, may be deducted to the extent it relates to business income.

In addition to the 20(12) deduction for, generally speaking, non-business taxes in excess of the amount eligible for foreign tax credit because of the foreign tax credit limitation, there is also a 20(11) deduction which is the only tax relief available for foreign non-business income tax on property other than real estate to the extent the tax is in excess of 15% of the gross income from the property. The 15% limit on foreign tax credit for such income is discussed in (C), above.

(4) Foreign Income or Profits

Foreign income or profit taxes which are creditable are those paid for the year. The determination of the source of income, however, may be difficult. All facts related to the income must be considered. In most cases, however, the following rules will apply to the determination of the source of *property* income:

- The source of dividend income is the country or political subdivision in which the paying corporation is resident. Determination of the payer's residence may depend on Canadian tax treaties.
- The source of interest income will be the country or political subdivision of residence of the debtor.
- The source of income derived from rental of tangible property (other than income from a business carried on in a foreign country) is determined to be as follows:
    - in the case of income from rental of real property, its source is the country where the property is located; and
    - in the case of income from rental of other tangible property, its source is the country where the property is used.
- Royalty payments have their geographical source in the country in which the related right is used or exploited. For example, a royalty received on the quantity of ore extracted from a mine is income from the country in which the mine is situated. A writer's copyright royalties are income from the country whose laws would otherwise have prohibited the reproduction of the writer's work by anyone else (i.e., the country from which the royalty payments are derived).

The source of *business* income will be the country or political subdivision in which the business is carried on. More detail is provided in Income Tax Folio S5-F2-C1, para. 1.53.

The source of *employment* income will be the country or political subdivision where the services are performed. Where those duties require you to spend a significant part of the time in a country other than Canada, you may be subject to tax in that foreign country on a portion of your remuneration. In such cases an apportionment of your regular salary or wages based on the number of working days spent in Canada, and in that other country, is usually considered appropriate in determining the foreign income from employment for purposes of the foreign tax credit calculation. Director's fees are generally considered to be earned where the director's meetings are held and commission income is earned in the country in which the effort was expended for the purposes of gaining such remuneration. Note, however, that the CRA is prepared to challenge the sourcing of employment income for U.S. citizens resident in Canada for Canadian foreign tax credit purposes to the extent income allocated to the United States is not the minimum amount consistent with the Canada–U.S. Tax Treaty as the CRA understands it; see ¶2173.

Your foreign income or profits for purposes of the numerator in calculating the foreign tax credit limitation must be computed in accordance with the Canadian rules and without regard to the method used in the foreign country of computing income. For example, one-half of capital gains and losses from a foreign country are excluded, as are expenses allowed by that country but not allowable in Canada, while other amounts may be included as income pursuant to Canadian rules that are excluded from income in the foreign country. Neither the tax treatment of the component items by the foreign jurisdiction nor any provision in a comprehensive tax treaty that prohibits taxation by the foreign country alters the calculations of income or net income for purposes of the credit.

Special restrictions apply to foreign income which is exempt from local taxation; see ¶1452. There are also anti-avoidance rules which can limit foreign tax credits on certain transactions; see ¶1453.

In arriving at your total net income, each permissible deduction is theoretically allocable in whole or in part to a geographical source of income (subject to the exceptions explained below). Ordinarily, such an allocation can be made on the basis of the factual relationship between a particular deduction and the gross income arising in a particular country. An allocation of expenses to geographical sources of gross income for financial statement purposes is normally accepted for purposes of computing the foreign tax credit. Once a basis of allocation has been established, future allocations are expected to be made on a consistent basis.

A number of deductions, including many of those discussed in Chapter 10 (child care expenses, attendant care expenses, etc.) are not to be allocated on a geographical basis. However, specific exceptions are provided. The most significant of these are transfer deductions to Canadian tax-deferred plans (such as RRSP refund of premium rollovers), the payments from which will ultimately be taxable in Canada. This is intended to allow an individual who pays foreign tax in respect of a transfer to such a plan to access to foreign tax credit for the year of transfer.

The other "Deductions from Total Income" on page 2 of your return need to be allocated between geographical sources of income only when your employment services are performed in more than one country or your business is carried on in more than one country. In such cases, each deduction claimed must be allocated on a reasonable basis to the geographical source or sources of income to which it can be said to apply.

The amount allocated in this manner to income arising in a particular foreign country must be used in calculating the net income from that country.

In determining the geographic source of a capital gain or capital loss on the sale of real property, the location of the property is usually the source of the gain or loss. In the case of capital property other than real property, the source of the capital gain or capital loss is usually the location at which the sale or disposition took place.

Where there has been a deemed disposition of property, for example on your departure from Canada (see ¶528), any capital gain or capital loss resulting therefrom is not from a foreign source, regardless of the geographic location of the property at that time.

Generally, the source of a capital gain or capital loss from the sale of a stock or bond is the securities or stock exchange where the sale occurs, regardless of the location of the issuer's transfer office.

(5) Foreign Business or Non-Business Income

Your foreign income must be calculated net of any expenses related to it, but before deducting the foreign tax. Amounts that could also be regarded as income from property are included as business income if such income arises in the course of carrying on business in the foreign country. In addition, income from a foreign source outside the particular foreign country is included as long as it is derived from the carrying on of a business in that country.

(6) Foreign Business and Non-Business Income Tax Credit

The calculation of the foreign tax credit for business income differs from the non-business income calculation. See ¶1450.

(7) Proof of Foreign Taxes Paid

When claiming a foreign tax credit, you must file with your return (or have available for audit, where your return is filed electronically) proof that the foreign taxes were paid. Where your foreign tax liability is settled by an amount withheld by the payer of the related income, a copy of the foreign tax information slip is usually satisfactory. In most other cases, a copy of the tax return filed with the foreign government is required, together with copies of receipts or documents establishing payment. A change in the amount of foreign tax paid as a result of an assessment or reassessment subsequent to the time of filing should be reported to the CRA, supported by a copy of the assessment notice involved and proof of payment of any additional tax.

Tax withheld from receipts or income and remitted to the foreign jurisdiction on your behalf is considered to have been paid by you at the time the amount was withheld.

(8) Apportionment of Foreign Taxes Paid

Where both you and your spouse are resident in Canada, have income from a foreign country, and have paid foreign tax on a community income basis (for example by filing a joint return in the United States), you and your spouse are, for the purpose of Canadian foreign tax credits, entitled to apportion the foreign taxes. The amount paid is apportioned based on the relationship of your respective foreign incomes that gave rise to the foreign tax, rather than the amount actually paid by each spouse.

(ITA: 20(11), (12); 122.3; 126; IT-506 [archived]; Income Tax Folio: S5-F2-C1 Foreign Tax Credit; ITTN: 31R2 No. 31R2)

[¶1455f] FOREIGN TAX CREDIT CARRIED BACK AGAINST DEPARTURE TAX

Where an individual ceasing Canadian residence pays departure tax on accrued gains on leaving Canada, and is later taxed again on an actual disposition of the same property by another country, Canada will in some circumstances permit credit against the original departure tax for the foreign tax paid, under specific rules discussed at ¶2153.

[¶1456] EMPLOYEES OF INTERNATIONAL ORGANIZATIONS

[¶1456.05] *Organizations Other Than the United Nations and its Affiliates*

A special tax credit is intended to offset Canadian tax on the employment income of Canadian taxpayers who are employees of certain specified international organizations. Different rules apply for employees of the United Nations and its affiliated agencies on the one hand, and employees of an organization recognized in section 2 of the *Foreign Missions and International Organizations Act* on the other. The latter (non-UN) agencies appear to include at least three separate organizations: the European Communities; the European Space Agency; and the Sinai Multinational Force and Observers.

For employees of these "Foreign Missions and International Organizations", the tax credit is designed only to offset levies in lieu of tax that the organization may require. (The *Foreign Missions and International Organizations Act* itself provides a tax exemption for foreign employees of certain international organizations as well as foreign diplomatic missions and the like, but those exemptions specifically do not apply to Canadian citizens normally resident in Canada. Credit against the special levies, however, is available to Canadians.) Special credit may be claimed by individuals resident in Canada at any time during the year. The credit is calculated as follows:

$$\frac{\text{employment income from int. organization}}{\text{total income for the year}} \times \text{tax otherwise payable}$$

Total income in the denominator is the total of net income (line 236) and any "split income" deducted under the anti-income-splitting rules at ¶1490, less deductions allowed in computing taxable income for your capital gains deduction, capital loss carryovers applied, the employee stock option deductions (¶330), treaty exemptions, prospector's shares (¶776), and DPSP special payments ¶917.

If you are a part-year resident, total income in the denominator is your taxable income for the period of Canadian residence, as calculated in Chapter 21, plus "taxable income earned in Canada" for the period of non-residence, calculated without the reductions referred to above.

Tax otherwise payable has the same meaning as for non-business income tax (¶1450).

The amount of the tax credit may not exceed that proportion of the amount you paid to the organization as a levy that (a) the employment income from the organization is of (b) employment income from the year assuming no part thereof is exempt income (per ¶991). The levy in question is typically one that the international organization itself charges in lieu of income tax.

(ITA: 126(3); Window on Canadian Tax: 4861; 8908)

[¶1456.10] *UN Employees*

Employees of the United Nations and its affiliates are not eligible for the foreign tax credit described at ¶1456.05. Instead their employment income is treated as if it were treaty-exempt; that is, it is reported but deducted from taxable income at line 256 of the T1 return.

Under articles 57 and 63 of the UN charter, the following are affiliates whose employees, together with those of the UN itself, would (if subject to tax in Canada under the rules in Chapter 1) be eligible for the deduction to offset employment income:

- Food and Agriculture Organization (FAO)
- International Atomic Energy Agency (IAEA)
- International Bank for Reconstruction and Development (IBRD — World Bank)
- International Centre for Settlement of Investment Disputes (ICSID) — World Bank)
- International Civil Aviation Organization (ICAO)
- International Development Association (IDA — World Bank)
- International Finance Corporation (IFC — World Bank)
- Multilateral Investment Guarantee Agency (MIGA — World Bank)
- International Fund for Agricultural Development (IFAD)
- Organisation for the Prohibition of Chemical Weapons (OPCW)
- World Trade Organization (WTO)
- World Tourism Organization (UNWTO)
- International Labour Organization (ILO)
- International Maritime Organization (IMO)
- International Monetary Fund (IMF)
- International Telecommunications Union (ITU)
- United Nations Development Programme (UNDP) (see CRA Document No. 2000-0004537)
- United Nations Educational, Scientific and Cultural Organization (UNESCO) — including the International Institute for Educational Planning, International Bureau of Education and Intergovernmental Committee for Physical Education and Sport
- United Nations Environment Programme (UNEP) (see CRA Document No. 2004-008586117, in French, summarized in English in Wolters Kluwer *Window on Canadian Tax*8430)
- United Nations Industrial Development Organization (UNIDO)
- Universal Postal Union (UPU)
- World Health Organization (WHO)
- World Intellectual Property Organization (WIPO)
- World Meteorological Organization (WMO)

(ITA: 110(1)(*f*)(iii); 126(3); ITR: 8900 International Organizations; Window on Canadian Tax: 4861; 8908)

[¶1456.15] *Prescribed International Organizations (IATA and ISAT)*

If you are employed in Canada with certain international organizations prescribed by regulation you are allowed to deduct that employment income in computing your taxable income (¶1000) provided you meet all of the following conditions:

(1) you were not at any time in the year a Canadian citizen;

(2) you were not a non-resident of Canada immediately before commencing that employment; and

(3) if a resident of Canada at all, you became resident in Canada solely for the purpose of that employment.

Prescribed organizations are the International Air Transport Association, the Société internationale de télécommunications aeronautiques (International Society of Aeronautical Telecommunications), and the World Anti-Doping Agency. The deduction is claimed on line 256 of the T1 return.

(ITA: 110(1)(*f*)(iv); ITR: 8900(2) International Non-governmental Organizations)

[¶1456.20] *Diplomats*

Officers and servants of foreign governments, and their families, are exempt from tax where the foreign government grants similar immunity to Canadians, provided the person is not a Canadian citizen and was not resident in Canada before taking up service with the foreign government.

As well, the *Vienna Convention on Diplomatic Relations* may exempt foreign diplomats and their families, and the Canadian *Foreign Missions and International Organizations Act* may extend that treatment to foreign representatives to UN Agencies operating in Canada, who thus might be exempt on items other than UN agency employment income. It is the CRA's view that capital gain on disposition of a principal residence in Canada by a foreign representative to the ICAO is not exempt under these rules.

(ITA: 149(1)(*a*), (*b*); CRA Document No.: Senior Official of the ICAO, *October 27, 2003*, CRA Document No. 2003-0034157; Representative of a Member State to the ICAO, *February 14, 2006*, CRA Document No. 2004-0096641I7)

[¶1458] OVERSEAS EMPLOYMENT TAX CREDIT — FORMER LINE 426

The Overseas Employment Tax Credit (OETC) was phased out in 2016. This credit was available if you were resident in Canada and working abroad for six consecutive months or longer in connection with a resource, construction, installation, agricultural or engineering project. To claim the credit, you had to fill out form T626 to calculate personal tax, and have your employer certify the period of employment.

The credit was equal to the lesser of:

(i) a specified maximum qualifying foreign employment income amount × # of days employed outside of Canada during the year / 365, and

(ii) a specified percentage of your net overseas employment income taxable in Canada

Divided by: total adjusted income taxable in Canada
Multiplied by: total tax otherwise payable for the year

History

The maximum specified qualifying foreign employment income level was $80,000 prior to 2013. It was reduced to $60,000 for 2013, $40,000 for 2014, $20,000 for 2015, and $0 for 2016.

The specified percentage was 80% prior to 2013. It was reduced to 60% for 2013, 40% for 2014, 20% for 2015, and 0% for 2016.

There was an exception to the phase-out rules that provided that qualifying foreign employment income for project commitments prior to March 29, 2012 would not have been subject to the sliding scale percentages and would have remained at 80% up to 2015. However, even for commitments prior to March 29, 2012, the OETC was eliminated in 2016.

[¶1460] FOREIGN INCOME FROM ESTATES, TRUSTS, AND SEGREGATED FUND LIFE INSURANCE POLICIES

If you are the beneficiary of an estate or trust that has received foreign income and paid foreign tax, you are entitled to claim a foreign tax credit for the tax paid on foreign income attributed to you, providing that the estate or trust has not claimed a deduction for those foreign taxes when filing its tax return (see ¶458). This is also the case if a segregated fund of a life insurance policy has received foreign income and paid foreign tax. As a policyholder, you will be entitled to claim a foreign tax credit for the tax paid on foreign income allocated to you (see ¶983).

(ITA: 104; 138.1)

[¶1462] POLITICAL CONTRIBUTIONS — LINES 409 AND 410

You may deduct from your federal income tax payable a portion of political contributions that you make to a federally registered political party, or to a federal election candidate or candidates, whether or not they are members of a registered federal political party, provided that the candidates are officially nominated to serve in the House of Commons. Federally registered parties are discussed below at ¶1462.10. The amount of the credit is discussed at ¶1462.05, below.

[¶1462.02] *Contribution Limits Imposed by (Non-Tax) Law*

The *Federal Accountability Act* imposes limits on the amounts that can be contributed to political parties and candidates. These limits are not directly related to tax credit contribution limits, although it is perhaps doubtful if a credit can be claimed for improper contributions. Under the limitations:

- You can make a political donation to registered political entities only if you are a citizen or permanent resident of Canada.
- You can give no more than $1,500 in each calendar year to each registered political party.
- You can give no more than $1,500 in total in any calendar year to the various entities of each registered political party (registered associations, nomination contestants, and candidates).
- You can give no more than $1,500 to each independent candidate for a particular election.
- You can give no more than $1,500 in total to the leadership contestants in a particular leadership contest.
- You cannot make a political contribution with money, property, or services given to you for that purpose.
- Corporations, trade unions, associations, and groups (which would seem to include partnerships) cannot make political contributions. However, your employer can give you a paid leave of absence during an election period to allow you to be a nomination contestant or a candidate without that leave being considered a contribution.
- If you are running as a nomination contestant, you can make an additional contribution up to $1,000 in total per election from your own funds to your own campaign. This increases to $5,000 if you are running as a candidate.
- If you are running as a party leadership contestant, you can make an additional contribution of up to $25,000 in total per contest from your own funds to your own campaign and up to $1,500 to the campaigns of other candidates.
- Tax credits are not available for donations to unregistered parties and their electoral district associations but contributions are allowed to independent candidates.

These limits are independent of the tax credit rules, which permit credit on only $1,275 of contributions in a year, no matter how much you actually give.

History

All of the limits imposed under *The Federal Accountability Act* are subject to adjustment. A history of the limits can be found at www.elections.ca.

[¶1462.05] *Tax Credit Limits — Line 410*

The political contribution tax credit is limited to:

(a) 75% of the first $400 contributed; plus

(b) 50% of the next $350 contributed; plus

(c) 33¹/₃% of the next $525 contributed.

The maximum credit that you will be able to claim in one taxation year under these limits is $650 and it is reached when $1,275 has been contributed.

Your claim must be supported by official receipts signed by the registered agent of the registered party or the official agent of the candidate. You are instructed to file the political contribution receipts supporting your claim with your return if you are filing a paper return. If you are filing electronically, you should keep the receipts on hand for at least six years. If you are claiming based on a partnership allocation on a T5013 slip, the slip is sufficient.

The amount of your political contribution credit will depend on the amount of your total eligible contributions made in a particular taxation year. Contributions must be made in cash or by way of a negotiable instrument (cheque, money order, draft, etc.) issued by you.

Most provinces permit deductions from provincial tax in respect of provincial political contributions. These are discussed by province in Chapter 15. Quebec permits a political contribution credit in respect of municipal elections only. This is discussed in Chapter 16.

(ITA: 127(3))

[¶1462.10] *General Rules*

The tax credit may be claimed only against the federal income tax payable in the year in which the political contribution was made. Political contribution tax credits in excess of the amount required to reduce federal tax payable to nil are not available for carryforward and do not result in a refund.

No credit is available for contributions in respect of which you have received, or are entitled to receive, any financial benefit from the government or other public authority (other than the political contribution credit itself). The political contribution credit is calculated on the value of the contribution "less the advantage to the contributor". The considerations are identical to those at ¶1261, including the rule that the contributor must, before a receipt is issued, notify the donee of any circumstance which lowers the value of the contribution below fair market value, or no contribution may be claimed.

You may claim a credit for a contribution made by your spouse or common law partner, so spouses/partners can aggregate their contributions to maximize the credit available (see T2 Guide 5013 to line 409). Contributions by a partnership can be allocated to the partners for credit purposes.

Although you can contribute money, goods or services to a political party or candidate, only contributions made in cash or by negotiable instrument qualify for credit.

A "registered party" is defined in the *Canada Elections Act*. Elections Canada maintains a list of registered parties at its website (www.elections.ca).

(ITA: 127(3)–(4.1); 248(30)–(33); IC 75-2R8 Contributions to a Registered Party, a Registered Association or to a Candidate at a Federal Election)

[¶1463] INVESTMENT TAX CREDIT

The following expenditures may generate an investment tax credit, which you can claim in calculating your tax payable:

- 25% of expenditures for eligible child care spaces created in the year (¶1463.83), maximum $10,000 per space;
- 10% of eligible expenditures under the apprenticeship tax credit program (¶1463.80), maximum $2,000 per apprentice;
- scientific research expenditures for research activities in Canada;
- expenditures for equipment for a variety of qualified activities if carried on in the four Atlantic provinces and the Gaspé Peninsula of Quebec; this credit is being phased out over a four-year period for qualified resource property acquired on or after March 29, 2012 but will continue to be available for expenditures on other qualified property (see ¶1463.15 and ¶1463.20);
- Canadian exploration expenses, incurred by corporations principally engaged in exploration and development of minerals or other natural resources, that are flowed out to individual shareholders holding "flow-through" shares of such corporations (see ¶248a and ¶2521.50); the expenditures must be incurred by the corporations in relation to mining exploration activities before 2018.

You may deduct an amount in respect of an "investment tax credit" from your federal income tax otherwise payable. The credit for the current year cannot exceed the lesser of (1) and (2), as follows:

(1) the aggregate of:

(a) your investment tax credit at the end of the year in respect of all property acquired, or expenditures made, before the end of the year, including unused and unexpired credits carried forward (the carryforward period is gradually being extended from 10 years by adding one year to the carry forward period for each taxation year ending after 1997, to a maximum period of 20 years; thus, credits generated from 2007 that cannot be used in the year carry forward for 20 years); and

(b) the lesser of:

(i) your unutilized tax credits carried back from the subsequent three years, and

(ii) the amount, if any, by which your tax otherwise payable for the year exceeds the amount, if any, determined under (a), above; and

(2) where alternative minimum tax is applicable for the year, the amount if any by which:

(a) your taxes payable after all adjustments and credits except the investment tax credit and the credit for alternative minimum tax carryover

exceeds

(b) your alternative minimum tax for the year.

Essentially, rule (1) limits your investment tax credit claim to your available credits, including all applicable carryovers. It also imposes, in clause (b), an ordering requiring current year credits and carryforwards to be used in the current year before carrybacks. This is in any event the most favourable ordering. Rule (2) imposes the further limitation that if alternative minimum tax (Chapter 24) applies, investment tax credits cannot be used to reduce ordinary tax liability below your minimum tax liability. The intention of this rule is to allow you to carry back or forward investment tax credits which cannot be used in the year due to AMT.

Your investment tax credits are calculated on form T2038 (IND).

Your investment tax credit at the end of the year is a pool that includes certain amounts carried over from other years, as discussed at ¶1463.10, below. The pool includes unexpired carryover amounts, and is in effect always on hand. Accordingly, the credit claimed in any given year is optional; any claim can be made up to the limits calculated for the year. Claims foregone in a year remain on hand until used or expired.

Specific rules govern the allocation of tax credits earned in a partnership. See ¶1821.

[¶1463.05] *All ITC Claims Must be Made within One Year of Filing Deadline*

All claims for investment tax credit must be filed in prescribed form (i.e., claimed on form T2038(IND)) on or before the day that is one year after the filing-due date for the particular year in which the expense was made or incurred. Since investment tax credits are normally incurred in connection with a business, an individual's 2016 investment tax credit claim must be filed by June 15, 2018, i.e., no more than one year following the normal June 15, 2017 filing-due date for 2016 returns (¶218). For investors in mining flow-through shares, however, unless they are otherwise carrying on a business, the normal April 30 filing deadline would apply, so a tax credit allocated in 2016 would have to be claimed by filing T2038(IND) by April 30, 2018.

While the CRA generally has the ability to waive the requirement that a particular filing be made by a fixed date, this discretionary power does not extend to the filing of the T661 Scientific Research and Experimental Development claim or the T2038 form. It is therefore vitally important that you file your investment tax credit claim on a timely basis.

(ITA: 127(9) "investment tax credit" (*m*); 220(2.1); (2.2))

[¶1463.10] *Investment Tax Credit Pool: Specified Rates*

The investment tax credit available at the end of the current year is calculated as follows:

(1) 25% of the eligible child care space expenses for the year to a maximum credit of $10,000 per child care space created (¶1463.83). This credit is not refundable.

(2) 10% of the eligible per apprentice expenses under the rules at ¶1463.80 to a maximum of $2,000 per apprentice. This credit is not refundable.

(3) 10% of your capital cost of qualified property and 5% of your capital cost of qualified resource property (see ¶1463.20) acquired for use in the four Atlantic provinces, the Gaspé Peninsula, and *related offshore areas*. This credit, whether calculated at 5% or 10%, is refundable.

(4) 15% of scientific research and experimental development expenditures as described at ¶1463.35. This credit is refundable.

(5) 15% of flow-through mining expenditures allocated to you on your flow-through mining shares, as described at ¶1463 above. This credit is not refundable.

No amount may be included as eligible for investment tax credit, either for your own business or under a tax shelter syndication, if any of the income from the business to which the expenditure relates will be exempt from income tax.

(ITA: 127(5), (9))

[¶1463.15] *Qualified Activities*

To qualify for the investment tax in (3) of the description at ¶1463.10, you must acquire qualified property or qualified resource property in the year. Only certain types of property are eligible; the list of such property is set out at ¶1463.20.

Furthermore, property is qualified only if it is acquired primarily for use in qualified activities. Two categories of qualified activities are identified: those for which eligible expenditures are qualified property, and those for which eligible expenditures are qualified resource property.

Qualified Property Activities

Activities for which eligible expenditures are "qualified property" are:

- manufacturing or processing of goods for sale or lease (specifically excluded is building construction and producing or processing electrical energy or steam for sale, but note that producing electrical energy and steam for own use in eligible areas may be an independently qualified activity as discussed below);
- logging;
- farming;
- fishing;
- storing grain; or
- harvesting peat moss.

Qualified Resource Property Activities

Activities for which eligible expenditures are "qualified resource property" are:

- operating an oil or gas well or extracting petroleum or natural gas from an accumulation thereof;
- processing heavy crude oil from a natural reservoir in Canada to a stage not beyond the crude oil stage or its equivalent;
- extracting minerals from a mineral resource;
- processing (i) ore (other than iron ore or tar sands ore) from a mineral resource to any stage not beyond prime metal stage, (ii) iron ore from a mineral resource to any stage that is not beyond the pellet stage, or (iii) tar sands ore from a mineral resource to any stage that is not beyond the crude oil stage;
- prospecting, exploring for, or developing a mineral resource;
- exploring or drilling for petroleum and natural gas;
- Canadian field processing; or
- producing industrial minerals.

The credit for the acquisition of property that falls under the definition of "qualified resource property" is being phased out over a four-year period for assets acquired on or after March 29, 2012. The credit was 10% for assets acquired before 2014, was reduced to 5% for assets acquired in 2014 and 2015, and was not available for assets acquired after 2015. Transitional relief existed where you acquired an asset under a written agreement entered into before March 29, 2012.

You may claim the investment tax credit for qualified property, if otherwise applicable, with respect to a commercial rental building provided the building qualifies in all other respects for the investment tax credit and the tenant (who is not an exempt taxpayer) uses the building for one of the purposes described above.

You generally cannot claim the investment tax credit for what would otherwise be qualified property with respect to equipment and machinery leased to others (although certain corporations can do so). However, if you lease a fishing vessel to a corporation you control in circumstances where the corporation carries on a fishing business in connection with one or more federal commercial fishing licences issued to you, you may claim the qualified property credit for the vessel, including its furniture, fittings and equipment.

Qualifying purposes do not include activities such as storing (other than grain); shipping; selling and leasing of finished goods; purchasing raw materials; administration functions; purchase and resale operations; data processing; or providing facilities for employees such as housing, cafeterias, clinics, or recreational facilities. However, the CRA has given an opinion (CRA Document No. 2007-0238901E5) that an otherwise qualified building used to store fishing gear and/or vessels would qualify as property used primarily in fishing and would not be disallowed as a storage activity.

Where a building is used partly for eligible activities and partly for non-eligible activities, the entire cost of the asset will be available for the credit under (3) at ¶1463.10, provided the primary use is an eligible activity.

History

The definition of "qualified resource property" was introduced for acquisitions after March 28, 2012. Prior to that date, all otherwise eligible property was simply "qualified property" and the related investment tax credit was 10% of the capital cost. The 10% rate continued to apply to both categories in 2012, but from 2013 the rate for expenditures of qualified resource property is 5% and only qualified property qualifies for the 10% rate.

(ITA: 127(5), (9), (11); ITR: 4600–4610)

[¶1463.20] *Qualified Property and Qualified Resource Property*

To qualify for the investment tax credit, property must be used in qualified activities as described at ¶1463.15. In addition, the property must also be of a prescribed type as described in the following list. (Refer to ¶898 for a description of properties by class.)

(1) a building or grain elevator erected on land owned or leased by you which is included in Class 1, 3, 6, 20, 24, or 27, or paragraph (*c*), (*d*), or (*e*) of Class 8, or paragraph (*g*) of Class 10 or that would be included in paragraph (*g*) of Class 10 if it were not for Class 28, Class 41, Class 41.1, or Class 41.2;

(2) machinery and equipment if it is depreciable property owned by you, and is:

(a) a property included in paragraph (*k*) of Class 1 or paragraph (*a*) of Class 2;

(b) an oil or water storage tank;

(c) a property included in Class 8 (other than railway rolling stock);

(d) a vessel, including the furniture, fittings and equipment attached thereto;

(e) a property included in paragraph (*a*) of Class 10, or Class 22 or 38 (other than a car or truck designed for use on highways or streets);

(f) notwithstanding (e), above, a logging truck acquired to be used in the activity of logging and having a weight, including the weight of property the capital cost of which is included in the capital cost of the truck at the time of its acquisition (but not including fuel), in excess of 16,000 pounds;

(g) a property included in any of paragraphs (*b*) to (*f*), (*h*), (*j*), (*k*), (*o*), (*r*), (*t*), or (*u*) of Class 10, or property included in paragraph (*b*) of Class 41 and that would otherwise be included in paragraph (*j*), (*k*), (*r*), (*t*), or (*u*) of Class 10;

(h) a property included in paragraph (*n*) of Class 10, or Class 15 (other than a roadway);

(i) a property included in any of the paragraphs (*a*) to (*f*) of Class 9;

(j) a property included in Class 28 or paragraph (*a*), (*a*.1), (*a*.2), or (*a*.3) of Class 41 or in Class 41.1 or Class 41.2 that would, but for that class, be included in paragraph (*k*) or (*r*) of Class 10;

(k) a property included in any of Classes 21, 24, 27, 29, 34, 39, 40, 43, 45, 46, 50, 52, or 53 in Schedule II;

(l) property included in Class 43.1 because of paragraph (*c*) of that class or in Class 43.2 because of paragraph (*a*) of that class;

(3) Energy generation and conservation property included in any of subparagraph (*a*.1)(i) of Class 17 and Classes 43.1, 43.2, and 48 of Schedule II effective March 29, 2012;

(4) Property to be used in Canada primarily for the purpose of producing or processing electrical energy or steam, provided all or substantially all of the energy or steam is used by the producer in its business or is sold, directly or indirectly, to a related person who so uses the energy or steam.

Property will qualify only if it is acquired for use in the Atlantic Provinces and the Gaspé Peninsula of Quebec. The expression "Gaspé Peninsula" is defined as the portion of the Gaspé area in Quebec that extends to the western border of Kamouraska County. The CRA has given an opinion (reported in Wolters Kluwer Window on Canadian Tax ¶8239) to the effect that the term "County" in that definition does not refer to the federal or provincial electoral district but to the Quebec administrative regions (County Regional Corporations (CRCs) or Municipalités Régionales de Comtés (MRCs) in French). The reference to the Kamouraska County in the definition is a reference to the Kamouraska CRC (Region No. 140 according to the classification of the Quebec regions). The Gaspé Peninsula region includes the Lower Saint-Lawrence Region No. 1 and the Gaspesia-Magdalen Islands Region No. 11, but would exclude the administrative regions of Montmagny and L'Islet included in Region No. 12.

Where qualified property is acquired to produce steam or electrical energy, 90% of the energy or steam ("all or substantially all") must be used by the taxpayer or related parties, but only 51% must be used in the Atlantic/Gaspé area. It would seem that the power can be sold to a provincial power grid provided essentially equivalent power is taken from the grid. This kind of activity is specifically excluded from the definition of manufacturing and processing, but is treated as an independently qualified activity when carried out in a prescribed region.

The cost of qualified property explicitly does not include any interest capitalized pursuant to section 21 (see ¶1073).

(ITA: 127(5), (9); ITR: 4600)

[¶1463.25] *When Property Acquired*

Qualified property and qualified resource property are deemed not to be acquired for investment tax credit purposes until they become available for use for capital cost allowance purposes (¶804b), so that the investment tax credit becomes claimable when the property is available for use. Acquisition for purposes of determining eligibility for credit (where that varies with a date of acquisition), as opposed to timing of when credit may be claimed, is governed by the actual acquisition date (¶804a) and not the available-for-use date.

(ITA: 127(5), (9), (11.2))

[¶1463.35] *Scientific Research — Lines 412 and 454*

You may claim an investment tax credit of 15% of non-capital expenditures you make in the year related to scientific research and experimental development (SR&ED). Eligible costs include those related to SR&ED you carry out yourself and 80% of the amount you pay to an arm's length third party (referred to as "contract payments") to have SR&ED activities performed on your behalf.

In general, SR&ED investment tax credits cannot be doubled up where one taxpayer makes payment to another to carry out the research. If the credit is available to the payer, the amount received by the Canadian payee is likely to be, or at any rate is intended to be, a "prescribed expenditure" by virtue of being a reimbursement. Thus, where a taxpayer (the payer) contracts out SR&ED work to another party (the performer), the current rules provide investment tax credits to the payer. This is changed in non-arm's length situations to put the credit in the hands of the performer, who may transfer them to the payer as payment is received for them.

The investment tax credit claimed reduces the deduction for scientific research expenditures (see ¶740).

Expenditures of a year will not qualify for the scientific research investment tax credit unless claims are identified on form T661 and form T2038 (IND) by the due date for the return for the year following the year in which the expenditure is incurred. The intention is that scientific research expenditures must be reported on forms T661 and T2038 (IND) filed no later than 12 months following the filing due date of the year the expenditure is incurred.

History

Capital SR&ED expenditures made prior to 2013 also qualified for the investment tax credit. 100% of SR&ED contract payments made prior to 2013 qualified as eligible for the investment tax credit. Prior to 2014, the investment tax credit was calculated as 20% of qualifying expenditures.

(ITA: 37; 127(5), (9) "contract payment", "qualified expenditure" (*f*), (11.1), (13)–(20); ITR: 2902; 4600–4602; IT-151R5 (Consolidated) [Archived])

[¶1463.40] *Unpaid Amounts Rule*

The unpaid remuneration rule at ¶746 can require deferral of a deduction for remuneration unpaid 180 days after year end. A similar rule provides that any other current expenditure for scientific research does not currently qualify for an investment tax credit claim if the amount remains unpaid on the day that is 180 days after the end of the taxation year. Instead, as with unpaid remuneration, the expenditure is recognized for investment tax credit purposes to the extent that it is actually paid in a later year.

Amounts deferred under these rules must nevertheless be identified on the T661 form for the year they are incurred rather than the year they are deductible.

(ITA: 127(26))

[¶1463.55] *Reduction of ITC Base for Other Cost Assistance*

The capital cost of all capital property for investment tax credit purposes, and the amount of a current scientific research expenditure eligible for credit, is the actual cost of the asset or the actual amount of the expenditure reduced by any government or non-government assistance in respect of the outlay which you have received, will receive, or may reasonably be expected to receive, at the time a tax return is filed for the year the expenditure was made. The tax credit itself does not reduce the cost of the property or the expenditures, although it does reduce the cost of depreciable property for capital cost allowance purposes in the year following the year in which credit is claimed, as discussed at ¶827. This reduction in cost applies to all capital property for which an investment tax credit may be claimed — child care spaces, qualified property, and qualified resource property — and is not limited to capital property used in SR&ED, the cost of which no longer qualifies for an investment tax credit in any event.

Government assistance means any assistance from a government, municipality or other public authority whether as a grant, subsidy, forgivable loan, deduction from tax, investment allowance or any other form of assistance, but does not include the investment tax credit itself. Non-government assistance is assistance, not included as government assistance under the rules above, as described in ¶729 under the heading "Statutory Rules: Inducements [etc.]", but not including any reference to the investment tax credit itself.

(ITA: 127(9), (11.1); ITR: 2900(4); IT-151R5 (Consolidated) [Archived])

[¶1463.60] *Recapture — Line 406*

Where an investment tax credit drives the related capital cost allowance pool negative, or the related cost is already fully deducted (as is typically the case with scientific research expenditures), the credit which cannot be accounted for as a reduction to cost must be taken into income.

The recapture of investment tax credits *under the scientific research rules* is discussed below.

Where the recapture rules on scientific research credits do not apply, to the extent the capital cost of the property has been reduced by the amount of the credit (¶827 and ¶740) it is possible that there could be a capital gain instead of recapture, since recapture of capital cost allowance will only occur up to the reduced cost base. Note that a capital gain is accounted for on a property-by-property basis and not a class basis, so that there may be a capital gain on the disposition of a particular depreciable property even though there is no recapture of capital cost allowance because of a balance in the related capital cost allowance pool.

The investment tax credit on property acquired in the year or any of the 10 preceding years which qualified for SR&ED will be recaptured if the property, or property which incorporates it, is converted to commercial use or otherwise disposed of. (Capital property qualified for SR&ED treatment prior to 2014.) You will have a recapture of an investment tax credit in a year when all of the following conditions are met:

- you acquired a property in any of the 10 preceding taxation years;
- you claimed the cost, or a portion of the cost (as in the case of shared-use property) as a qualified R&D expenditure on form T661, or could have claimed the cost as a qualified expenditure but for the unpaid amounts rule discussed under that subheading above;
- the cost of the property, or a portion of the cost (as in the case of shared-use property), was included (or would have been included but for the unpaid amounts rule discussed under that subheading above) in computing your investment tax credit or was the subject of a subcontracting agreement to transfer qualified expenditures (these subcontracting agreements typically involve corporations and are discussed in detail in the Wolters Kluwer companion volume on corporate income tax *Preparing Your Corporate Tax Returns* under the heading *Subcontracting Payments to Non-Arm's Length Parties* at ¶8525.55); and
- you disposed of the property or converted it to commercial use. This condition is also met if you disposed of or converted to commercial use a property which incorporates the property previously referred to.

Under the general rule, which operates if you have not transferred the credit under a subcontracting agreement, the recaptured amount is the lesser of:

(1) the original tax credit generated on the property, including amounts that would have been included in the original investment tax credit but for the unpaid amounts rule discussed under that subheading above; and

(2) the tax credit rate which originally applied to the property multiplied by

(a) if the property is disposed of and is first-term shared-use property and not second-term shared-use property, 25% of the proceeds, and if the property is second-term shared-use property, 50% of the proceeds; and

(b) if the property is converted and is first-term shared-use property, 25% of the fair market value, and if the property is second-term shared-use property, 50% of the fair market value.

If you have transferred the credit under a subcontracting agreement, there is a separate recapture formula, discussed in *Preparing Your Corporate Tax Returns*.

Once a recapture amount is determined, it is added to both tax payable and to the pool of deductible SR&ED expenditures, but that element of the pool is not eligible for further investment tax credit. Where new credits are being generated, they will of course shelter the recapture.

No specific provision is made on T1 returns (as there is on corporate T2 returns) for the recapture. The investment tax credit form itself (form T2038(IND)) directs you to add recapture amounts directly to line 406 of the T1 return.

This perhaps fails to address the proper ordering of the SR&ED recapture. There seems to be no obvious ordering provision; the recapture is simply added to Part I tax otherwise payable. The general rule is that in the absence of an ordering provision, you can choose the most favourable ordering. In most cases, one would assume that this would be to add the recapture to tax payable immediately after line 46 of Schedule 1, so that non-refundable credits could be claimed against it. It is true that the non-refundable credits have an internal ordering provision which applies among the credits themselves, but there is no obvious reason why those and all other credits should not apply to reduce the recapture. On the contrary, it seems reasonably clear in law (and the CRA is understood to accept in principle) that you can insist on the application of any remaining non-refundable credit to recaptured investment tax credit, and before the application of new refundable credits.

Where non-refundable credits are not fully absorbed by other Part I tax, the best option may be to attach a letter to your return showing the Schedule 1 calculation as if "SR&ED investment tax credits recaptured" (from form T2038(IND)) followed line 46 of Schedule 1. Add line 46 and the recapture amount (which must, of course, increase tax, even if you calculate it as a negative), and proceed to apply applicable tax credits. It is possible that the CRA's computer system will insist on the application of recapture after non-refundable tax credits rather than before them, but where non-refundable credits are not fully absorbed by other Part I tax payable, you should not simply accept this treatment without objection.

Where the recapture occurs in a partnership, the partnership allocates it to the partners for the fiscal period of the partnership that ends in the corporation's taxation year. There is a corresponding adjustment to the cost base of the partner's interest in the partnership.

Similar rules apply to the recapture of investment tax credits relating to child care spaces. See ¶1463.83.

(ITA: 12(1)(*t*); 127(27)–(35))

[¶1463.65] *Forms T2038 and T661*

Calculate your investment tax credit on form T2038(IND) and enter the amount of credit on page 2 of Schedule 1 at line 412. Scientific research claims *must* be supported by a detailed (and timely) form T661. The CRA will not process a claim unless and until this form is completed. Form T661 is accompanied by its own Guide (T4088). The CRA has also published several Information Circulars, "Guidelines" and "Application Policies" setting forth its views on specific elements of SR&ED tax credits (e.g., effect of provincial tax credits) and on the application of SR&ED tax credit rules in specialized areas (e.g., clinical research). These are available from the CRA website area devoted to SR&ED. If you have access to the Wolters Kluwer electronic database including the Canadian Tax Reports, you can find a list by opening the Commentary database, under the heading therein "Government and Agency Documents" and then the subheading "Scientific Research and Experimental Development", and the various subheadings under that.

Since audits of these claims are virtually certain, and the supporting documentation must go back to the inception of the project, it is clear that contemporaneous documentation must support not only the form T661 but the eventual audit review.

Unless your business so clearly involves scientific research that you consider the issue beyond dispute, professional tax advice is desirable in making these claims. The issues involved are typically contested by the CRA.

(ITA: 37(1); 125(5))

[¶1463.70] *Carryovers of Unused Credit*

Where any amount of the credit cannot be utilized or has not been refunded (see ¶1464) the credits can be carried over to other years to recover or offset federal taxes payable.

Investment tax credits generated on acquisitions or expenditures may be carried back for three taxation years and may be carried forward for 20 years. You should keep track of unutilized investment tax credits with regard to their year of origin in order to monitor the rules applicable to their application and carryover.

(ITA: 127(5), (9))

[¶1463.80] *Employer's Apprenticeship Job Creation Tax Credits*

"Apprenticeship expenditures" are eligible for tax credit under the investment tax credit rules.

An apprenticeship expenditure is, in respect of each eligible apprentice you employ during the year, the lesser of (i) $2,000 and (ii) 10% of "eligible salary and wages" paid by you in the year to the apprentice in the course of a business you carried on in Canada during the year.

An eligible apprentice is an individual employed in Canada, in a trade prescribed in respect of Canada or of a province, during the first 24 months of the individual's apprenticeship contract. The contract must be registered with Canada or a province under an apprenticeship program designed to certify or license individuals in the trade. Prescribed trades are those included as Red Seals trades under the Interprovincial Standards Red Seal Program (see www.red-seal.ca).

Eligible salary and wages are amounts you pay as an employer to the eligible apprentice in respect of the first 24 months of the apprenticeship. However, the rules specifically exclude most fringe benefits (by and large, benefits described in ¶309.05 through ¶328 and ¶330) and unpaid remuneration included in income under the rules at ¶746.10. Eligible salary and wages exclude a qualified expenditure so that when an amount is paid to an eligible apprentice and it is eligible to be included in salary and wages for purposes of the apprenticeship credit and as a qualified expenditure for purposes of that credit, it can only be included in one, not both.

A specific rule prevents doubling up the credit among related employers. Under this rule, eligible salary and wages paid by a particular employer are deemed to be nil if the apprentice is employed in a calendar year that includes the end of the employer's taxation year by any other employer related to the particular employer (including a partnership that has a member related to the employer). However, a group of related employers may designate "in prescribed form" one of their number to be the sole employer for the year for purposes of the credit. The concept of related persons is discussed in ¶812.05 and ¶812.10. No form has been prescribed, but form T2038(IND) requires an employer claiming the credit to certify the existence of a written agreement among related taxpayers under which no one else claims the credit. It appears that you are not required to file the agreement, but you should have it on hand.

As is typical of investment tax credits, the amount eligible for credit is reduced by any other government or non-government assistance you receive, are entitled to receive, or can reasonably be expected to receive in respect of an eligible expenditure (see ¶1463.55). On the other hand, where government or other assistance which reduced the credit is repaid, the credit is increased accordingly.

Although the apprenticeship job creation credits operate through the investment tax credit system, they are not eligible for the refundable credit treatment at ¶1464, below. However, they are eligible for 20-year carryforward and 3-year carryback.

In a technical opinion (Wolters Kluwer *Window on Canadian Tax* 9640, giving an English summary of a French document), the CRA confirmed that the maximum apprenticeship job creation tax credit amount that a taxpayer may claim is not reduced on a *pro rata* basis or otherwise if the taxation year has less than 53 weeks. Provided all the conditions concerning the credit are met, the taxpayer may claim the whole credit during a short taxation year.

(ITA: 127(5), (9), (11.1), (11.4); ITR: 7310)

[¶1463.83] *Employer's Child Care Space Tax Credit*

A tax credit is available for cost incurred in creating child care spaces. The spaces must be ancillary to one or more businesses you carry on in Canada in the taxation year that do not otherwise include the provision of child care spaces. The "ancillary" requirement is clearly intended to deny the credit to businesses which are primarily concerned with providing child care. How little business makes a business ancillary to another is not a matter for which the CRA has a clear benchmark. But the credit is clearly intended for businesses which provide child care spaces as an employee perquisite or incentive, although it is not forbidden for the child care facility to operate at a profit.

The amount of credit is the lesser of:

(1) $10,000 times the number of new child care spaces created during the taxation year in a licensed child care facility for the benefit of children of your employees, or of a combination of children of your employees and other children; and

(2) 25% of your eligible child care spaces expenditure for the taxation year. To be an "eligible child care space expenditure" for the taxation year, amounts must meet both of the following tests:

- the amounts must be incurred in the year for the sole purpose of the creation of one or more new child care spaces in a licensed child care facility operated for the benefit of children of your employees, or of a combination of children of your employees and other children; and
- the amounts must be either (i) incurred by you to acquire depreciable property of a prescribed class (other than a specified property) for use in the child care facility, or (ii) incurred by you to make a specified child care start-up expenditure in respect of the child care facility.

Two categories of specified depreciable property are excluded, the costs of which do not qualify for the child care spaces credit. First, it excludes from credit a motor vehicle, including any kind of motorized vehicle. Accordingly, the exclusion is not limited to a motor vehicle as defined for other purposes of the *Income Tax Act*, such as those in ¶738 or ¶810a. Second, it excludes from credit any property that is, or is located in or attached to, a residence of (i) the taxpayer making the claim, (ii) an employee of that taxpayer, (iii) a person who holds an interest in that taxpayer's business, or (iv) a person related to any person referred to in (i) to (iii).

Depreciable property eligible for the child care space credit may only be claimed when it becomes available for use under the rules at ¶804b.

Specified start-up expenditures, which qualify for credit, cannot include expenditures to acquire depreciable property (which qualify under rule (4)(i), above, subject to the specified property exclusions). Specified start-up expenditures are, subject to the depreciable property exclusion, defined as:

- landscaping costs incurred to create, at the child care facility, an outdoor play area for children;
- architectural fees for designing the child care facility, or fees for advice on planning, designing, and establishing the child care facility;
- costs of construction permits in respect of the child care facility;
- initial licensing or regulatory fees in respect of the child care facility, including fees for mandatory inspections;
- costs of educational materials for children; or
- similar amounts incurred for the sole purpose of the initial establishment of the child care facility.

These start-up expenses are only for the initial establishment of the child care space; it is not intended that the credit can be used for ongoing or operating expenses. On the other hand, it is intended that eligible depreciable property should include the costs or incremental costs of buildings housing the child care facility, as well as initial costs of furniture, appliances, computers and audio-visual equipment, and playground structures and equipment.

A special prepaid expense rule ensures that where start-up expenses are incurred in a year but can reasonably be considered to relate to a later year, they are eligible for credit only in that later year.

Since the specified property exclusions apply only with respect to depreciable property, start-up expenditures are eligible for credit if other requirements are met, even if you use your personal residence as the child care facility.

Where a child care spaces credit has been claimed and the property on which the claim is based is disposed of within 60 months of acquisition, or where a child care space in respect of which credit has been claimed ceases to be available within 60 months of its creation, the associated credit is recaptured. Cessation of spaces is deemed to occur in reverse order to their creation.

As is typical of investment tax credits, the amount eligible for credit is reduced by any other government or non-government assistance you receive, are entitled to receive, or can reasonably be expected to receive in respect of an eligible expenditure (see ¶1463.55). Where you have repaid any government or other assistance which reduced the credit, the credit is increased accordingly.

As is also typical of investment tax credits, the tax credit on depreciable property reduces the cost for capital cost allowance purposes in the year following the year in which the credit is claimed (see ¶827). Similarly, amounts of investment tax credit in relation to non-depreciable expenditures are added back to income in the year following the claim. The child care spaces credit is eligible for the 20-year carryforward and 3-year carryback.

(ITA: 12(1)(*t*); 18(9)(*f*); 127(5), (9), (11.1), (11.2), (27.1)–(30))

[¶1464] REFUNDABLE INVESTMENT TAX CREDITS — LINE 454

Investment tax credits generated on research and development expenditures or on acquisitions of qualified property or qualified resource property are available in part to be refunded in cash. The refund rules do not apply to the apprenticeship job creation tax credit, the child care spaces credit, or the Canadian mineral exploration credit available through the flow-through share mechanism.

The refund should not be confused with the refund which may be generated by carrying back current year credits against tax of prior years, which applies to all investment tax credits as described at ¶1463. The refund discussed here allows a recovery of current year credits in excess of current year tax.

The amount of the cash refund reduces the amount of the investment tax credit pool that you may deduct in subsequent years.

The refund is 40% of the unused refundable investment tax credits generated *in the year.* No refund is available for the return of a bankrupt individual or a special year of death return described in (3), (4), or (5) of ¶1901. Your refund should be calculated on form T2038(IND) and entered on line 454 of page 4 of your return. You need not claim the full refund to which you are entitled in a year, but you cannot carry a refund claim over to another year. Not claiming the refund allows you to use the credits for carryover. However, the value of the refund does not change so that generally it makes sense to claim the full refund in the year it arises.

The amount refundable for a year is deemed to have been paid by you on account of tax on the day on which your balance of taxes owing is due (April 30 except for deceased taxpayers). It will therefore offset any other liability you may have and interest thereon. Further, any refund for the year is considered to be a claim for investment tax credit and must be applied to reduce adjusted cost bases and other pools as appropriate (for example, see ¶740 or ¶827).

The refund is claimable once, on acquisitions or expenditures made in the year which are eligible for the investment tax credit. The refund percentage cannot be applied again to the same expenditures in a subsequent year. The refund applies only to current year expenditures.

(ITA: 127.1; IT-151R5 (Consolidated) [Archived])

[¶1466] LABOUR-SPONSORED VENTURE CAPITAL FUNDS — LINE 414 AND LINE 419

These are venture capital funds established and registered under specific federal or provincial legislation and managed by labour unions or employee groups.

If you invest in such a fund (that is, in shares of the labour-sponsored venture capital corporation (LSVCC)) through an irrevocable commitment within 60 days of year end to acquire LSVCC shares, you are entitled to a federal tax credit. The credit for 2016 is 5% of the "net cost" of the shares to a maximum credit of $250 for federally-registered LSVCCs and 15% of the "net cost" of the shares to a maximum credit of $750 for provincially-registered shares. If both types of shares are purchased in 2016, the dollar limit is calculated with a formula taking into account both the 5% and 15% rates. After 2016, the above credit may only be claimed for provincially-registered LSVCC shares. It follows that an investment of $5,000 will generate the maximum credit.

The credit is calculated on Schedule 1; at line 414 for the provincially-registered shares and at line 419 for federally-registered shares.

The credit is generated on contributions to federally registered plans or prescribed provincial plans. Provincial plans are discussed in detail by province in Chapter 15 (Chapter 16 for Quebec) and in ¶2522(2). The federal government will not give federal credits for purchases of shares in provincial plans which are prescribed but not federally registered unless the province also provides assistance in respect of the same shares. Generally speaking, each province provides LSVCC credits only to its residents and only for contributions to the plans it specifies, although this must be verified for each particular province.

History

In 2013, the government announced that the LSVCC regime would be phased out as follows for shares purchased in both provincially-registered and federally-registered LSVCCs: 10% rate and $500 limit for 2015, 5% rate and $250 limit for 2016, and no credit after 2016. As indicated above, the phasing out of the credit has now been restricted to shares purchased from federally-registered LSVCCs

(ITA: 127.4(1), (2), (5), (6); 204.8–204.87; ITR: 6701 [Prescribed labour-sponsored venture capital corporation]; 6708 [Prescribed wind-up rule])

[¶1466.05] *Contributions to RRSPs/TFSAs*

You may contribute cash to your own or to a spousal/common-law partner RRSP or to a TFSA to acquire federal or provincial LSVCC shares and claim the federal portion of the credit on your return. Such an investment can be made in the year or within the first 60 days following the year and generate a federal credit applicable in the year. Most provinces with LSVCC credit provisions will match this treatment; a summary of the provincial situation at the time of writing is found at ¶2522(2). Note that the cash contribution to an RRSP/TFSA followed by an RRSP/TFSA investment is the only formula that will formally maximize tax benefits. See ¶2522(2).

(ITA: 127.4(1) "qualifying trust", (2), (5), (6))

[¶1466.10] *Continuing Restrictions on Credits*

There are restrictions that deny LSVCC credit on a share where:

(1) the required information return issued to the investing individual by the LSVCC is not filed with your T1 return (except for the separate returns filed at death (¶1901) for "rights or things", partner or proprietor income, or income from a testamentary trust, and the trustee's return for a bankrupt);

(2) you die before the acquisition of the share;

(3) a refund has been made in respect of the disposition of the share (see or ¶1466.20); or

(4) a new LSVCC share has been acquired in exchange for another share.

(ITA: 127.4(6) Labour-sponsored funds tax credit)

[¶1466.15] *Matching Provincial Credits*

In addition to the federally registered LSVCCs, there are prescribed provincial LSVCCs. Where you contribute to an LSVCC of a province in which you reside which offers matching 15% credits (and sometimes more), you are entitled to claim the credit against your provincial income tax. Several (but not all) provinces offer matching credits; see details by province in Chapter 15 (Chapter 16 for Quebec). Some provinces also have plans which offer provincial but not federal credits; see the discussions for each province in Chapter 15.

For an overall summary of the federal and provincial rules, see ¶2522(2).

Note that if you do not reside in or pay income tax to the province, you will not be eligible for the provincial component of these credits.

You should receive an information slip from the fund to support this credit, and file that receipt with your return (or maintain it for review by the CRA if you file electronically). Quebec credits are claimed on line 424 of the Quebec TP-1 return. For other provinces which provide credits, the credits are found on the provincial portion of the return.

(ITA: 127.4; 204.8–204.87; ITR: 6701 [Prescribed labour-sponsored venture capital corporation])

[¶1466.20] *LSVCC Share Credits Recaptured*

Federal rules require that shares of federally registered LSVCCs must be locked in for at least eight years; that is, they cannot be redeemed for eight years after issue. Regulations also permit early redemption of the shares upon repayment of the related credit, to the extent of the redemption value of the shares. Where a provincial credit is also available on federally registered shares, the federal government will also recapture that credit unless its recapture is already provided for.

Provincial governments typically have similar restrictions on the premature redemption of provincially registered LSVCC shares. Federal legislation ensures that where provincial credits are repaid under provincial rules, the corresponding federal credit will necessarily be recaptured.

A recapture of credits will apply to premature redemptions whether or not the shares are held by an RRSP or TFSA. As well, normal rules provide (as for any other investment held by an RRSP) that where shares are purchased through an RRSP, withdrawal of them (or redemption of the shares in the RRSP followed by withdrawal of the funds) from the RRSP will entail the normal income inclusion on RRSP withdrawals (¶2615.15). Withdrawals from a TFSA are, of course, not taxable.

A withholding regime provides that the LSVCC may not acquire, cancel, or redeem a share or, in the case of unregistered (provincial) LSVCC shares, no shareholder may dispose of a share, without withholding on account of the shareholder's liability the full tax credit content potentially inherent in the share. Provincially registered LSVCCs will generally be subject to the same withholding requirement, but the federal rule makes allowance for differing provincial rules under which shares might be disposed of otherwise than back to the LSVCC; where this happens, you remain liable for the recapture tax even if it has not been withheld.

The credit recaptured under the eight-year look-back rules is calculated as the full federal credit given on federally-registered LSVCCs and the federal credit divided by provincial credit in the case of a provincial LSVCC. The amount subject to recapture (and usually to withholding on acquisition, cancellation or redemption by the LSVCC) is the full credit content implicit in the share regardless of the $5,000 limit. That is, the credit content of federal LSVCC shares is considered to be the credit rate that applied in the year of acquisition of the shares, as summarized at ¶1466. The same result should follow for provincial shares.

The recapture tax will not apply where:

(1) the disposition was a redemption of shares on which no credit was claimed as witnessed by the fact that the redemption request was accompanied by the original (unused) tax credit form issued by the LSVCC;

(2) the disposition was a redemption of shares permitted because an individual became disabled and permanently unfit for work or terminally ill;

(3) the disposition was a redemption of shares on which no credit was issued because it was purchased by someone intrinsically not entitled to credit (e.g., a non-RRSP trust or RRSP trust for someone other than the purchaser or spouse);

(4) the original acquisition of the shares was before March 6, 1996 and the disposition was more than 5 years after issue or, the disposition occurred more than two years after issue pursuant to the Articles of the LSVCC because an individual attained 65 year of age, retired, or ceased to be resident of Canada; or

(5) the taxpayer has engaged in a "qualifying exchange"; i.e., received a new Class A LSVCC share as the sole consideration for a different Class A LSVCC share with identical rights (these rights can differ with respect to the reserve).

Refunds must in general be applied for no later than two years after the end of the calendar year in which the disposition occurred.

The redemption rules recognize the identical nature of LSVCC shares and provide the CRA with the discretion to make certain assumptions in calculating the refund it will provide.

There is no recapture tax in respect of the redemption by a federally registered LSVCC of a share, if the redemption occurs on a day that is in February or on March 1st of a calendar year and that day is no more than 31 days before the day that is eight years after the day on which the share was issued. The purpose of these rules is to accommodate taxpayers wishing to acquire new LSVCC shares in the first 60 days of a year using the proceeds from the redemption of LSVCC shares.

The federal rules on recapture of the credit accommodate Quebec's regime, under which shares in its two provincially registered LSVCCs which are held in RRSPs can be redeemed to fund withdrawals under the RRSP Home Buyers' Plan and Lifelong Learning Plan. Details of the Quebec plan are found at the end of ¶1669. To this effect, these redemptions are not subject to the recapture of the related credit, no deduction is allowed on repurchases, and a federal tax will match the Quebec 15% recapture tax in the event that timely repurchases are not made. The federal government applies this treatment to prescribed provisions of provincial law, and this treatment is not extended to federally registered or other non-Quebec plans. The logic is that Quebec generally does not permit redemption from its plans before age 65, whereas the federal rules allow redemption after eight years.

(ITA: 204.81(1)(c)(v), (vi); 211.7(1)–211.82; ITR: 6706 [Prescribed condition]; 6709 [Prescribed provisions of a provincial law])

[¶1466.25] *General Rules*

The credit is neither refundable nor eligible for carryover, so that credit which is greater than tax payable will be lost. Certain other credits, such as the charitable donations credit and the medical expense credit, do provide some flexibility in leaving tax room to absorb otherwise unusable credit.

The provision for a commitment within 60 days puts these investments on a par with RRSP investments in terms of a deadline; typically an investment by March 1 (February 29 in a leap year) will qualify for credit on the return filed the same April.

Note that you need not actually have acquired the shares, which may not have been issued within the requisite 60 days. However, they must be original acquisition shares; that is, you must be the first holder of the shares other than a broker or dealer.

The "net cost" of the shares is their cost reduced by any form of government assistance other than federal or provincial tax credits on the share. These credits do not reduce net cost. The federal and provincial tax credits also do not reduce the adjusted cost base of these shares for calculating capital gains, although they do reduce capital losses which might arise on ultimate disposition of the shares (see ¶2522).

(ITA: 127.4(5.1))

[¶1467] LOGGING TAX CREDIT — BELOW LINE 54 OF SCHEDULE 1

If you paid logging tax to a province in respect of income for the year from logging operations in that province, you may deduct a portion of the logging tax paid in computing your federal income tax. Only British Columbia and Quebec levy logging tax.

The deduction is the lesser of 2/3 of the logging tax paid to a particular province for the year and 6 2/3% of your income from logging operations in that particular province. The deduction is computed separately with respect to each province to which you paid logging tax. The total deduction claimed by you in respect of all provinces cannot exceed 6 2/3% of your taxable income, or if you are a non-resident, your taxable income earned in the year in Canada. Taxable income for the purposes of this credit is the amount at line 260 of your return, adjusted by adding back deductions taken for alimony and maintenance payments (line 220, Chapter 23), RRSP contributions (line 208, Chapter 26), contributions to provincial pension plans (line 209, Saskatchewan only, ¶1028), moving expenses (line 219, ¶1039), child care expenses (line 214, ¶1049), and attendant care expenses (line 215).

If your logging operations are in only one province, your income for the year from logging operations is the aggregate of the following amounts:

(1) where you cut standing timber in the province or acquired logs cut from standing timber in the province and sold the logs in the province to a sawmill, pulp or paper plant or other place for processing logs, your income for the year from the sale (to the extent not previously included in income from logging operations in the province);

(2) where you sold standing timber in the province, or the right to cut standing timber in the province, your income for the year from the sale (to the extent not previously included in income from logging operations in the province);

(3) where you exported logs cut by you from standing timber in the province, or logs acquired by you which were cut from standing timber in the province, whether exported from the province (that is sold to a sawmill, pulp or paper plant or other place for processing logs in another province) or exported from Canada, income is determined by deducting from the value of the logs (as determined by the province) any related costs such as acquisition costs, cutting costs, selling costs, transportation costs; and

(4) where you operate in Canada a sawmill, pulp or paper plant or other place for processing logs cut by you from standing timber in the province, or logs acquired by you which were cut from standing timber in the province, your total income for the year from all sources less:

(a) your income from sources other than logging operations, and other than the processing and sale of logs, timber and products produced therefrom,

(b) any amounts described in (1), (2), or (3), above, and

(c) 8% of the original cost of properties described in ¶898 used by you in the processing of logs or products derived therefrom. If you qualify for this deduction, you are allowed as a minimum 35% of the income remaining after making the deductions in (a) and (b), above, and the maximum amount you can claim is 65% of the income remaining after making the deductions in (a) and (b), above.

If your logging operations are in more than one province, your income for the year from logging operations in a particular province is the aggregate of the following amounts:

(1) the amounts determined in respect of that province in accordance with (1), (2), and (3), above; and

(2) where you operate in Canada a sawmill, pulp or paper plant or other place for processing logs, an amount equal to the proportion of your income for the year from all sources minus the aggregate of the amounts determined under (4)(a), (b), and (c), above, that,

(a) the quantity of standing timber cut in the province in the year by the taxpayer and logs cut from standing timber in the province acquired by the taxpayer in the year,

is of

(b) the total quantity of standing timber cut and logs acquired in the year by the taxpayer.

The T1 Return does not provide space for the calculation of this tax credit. You should attach a schedule to the tax return (or maintain one for audit, if filing electronically) showing your calculation of the credit, and write in "Federal logging tax credit" on Schedule 1 below line 54 (57 for a Quebec resident). Subtract the amount from line 54 and use the net balance in the additional calculations leading up to net federal tax. If the result is negative, enter nil at line 61 of Schedule 1.

You are also permitted a deduction for logging tax from your provincial tax payable to Quebec or British Columbia. See ¶1519 and ¶1671.

(ITA: 127(1), (2); ITR: 700 Logging)

[¶1469] TIMELY FILING FOR CARRYBACK OF CREDITS

Certain credits — business foreign tax credits, investment tax credits, alternative minimum tax credit in the year of death — may be carried back to prior years to the extent they exceed current year's federal taxes. This is discussed in the context of these credits.

There is a technical requirement to the effect that the CRA is not required to accept requests for carrybacks unless the request is made by the filing deadline for the year in which the credit arose, although there is also adequate authority to accept carrybacks requested for any year which is not statute-barred (i.e., closed by the general six-year rule on carryback revisions unless otherwise extended — see ¶221 and ¶277). The CRA will normally allow credits to be carried back and to open any eligible years regardless of the technical filing requirement concerning the year the credit arose.

Presumably, if the CRA declined to honour its policy, you could achieve the same result by applying under the Taxpayer Relief provisions (see ¶268.25).

(ITA: 152(4), (6))

PENSION AVERAGING PROVISIONS

[¶1471] TYPES OF PAYMENTS WHICH QUALIFY FOR SPECIAL RATES

Pension payments and deferred profit sharing payments received from a plan which was in existence at December 31, 1971 and of which you were a member at that date will qualify for special tax treatment (see ¶1472) if they meet the criteria described below.

[¶1471.05] *Pension Payments*

Averaging can apply to single payments made under a superannuation or pension plan on:

- the death, withdrawal or retirement from employment of an employee or former employee; or
- the winding-up of the fund or plan in full satisfaction of all rights of the payee in the fund; or
- the amendment of the fund or plan even though the payee continues to be an employee to whom the plan is applicable.

[¶1471.10] *Deferred Profit Sharing Payments*

Averaging can apply to single payments pursuant to a deferred profit sharing plan on the death, withdrawal or retirement from employment of an employee or former employee to the extent that the payment would otherwise be included in the income of the payee.

(ITAR: 40(1)(*a*)(i), (iv), (7); IC 74-21R Payments out of pension and deferred profit sharing plans — ITAR 40)

[¶1472] AMOUNT ELIGIBLE FOR SPECIAL ELECTION

The lump-sum payment of a pension or DPSP amount is reported in boxes 18 and 110 of the T4A slip, and included in income at line 130 of the T1 return. The portion of the amount eligible for special election in ¶1471 is limited to amounts accrued to December 31, 1971. This portion should also be included in box 18 and in the "Other information" area; Code 110 should be entered and the amount of the payment eligible for the election should be reported. On the basis of this information, the CRA should compute the reduced tax for you; see ¶1476. Note that there may be limitations on the amount you might otherwise think eligible; see ¶1479 and ¶1480.

(RC4157 Deducting Income Tax on Pension and Other Income, and Filing the T4A Slip and Summary)

[¶1473] WHAT IS THE EFFECT OF THE ELECTION?

Where you make this election, the payments specified therein are deemed not to be income. This rule should be kept in mind when various non-refundable credits are being computed, the amount of which is related to the amount of your income for the year. In such instances, the payments which qualify for the election will be excluded from the amount of the income serving as the basis for computing the non-refundable credit. This may be the case, for example, when computing the non-refundable credit for charitable donations, medical expenses, losses, and the foreign tax credits. Analogous situations may arise when your deductions depend on the amount of income of other persons, such as your spouse or dependants.

(ITAR: 40(1), (7))

[¶1476] HOW TO REPORT INCOME ELIGIBLE FOR SPECIAL REDUCED TAX TREATMENT

There is no special form required to elect to be taxed at the special reduced rate.

The CRA's practice is to encourage you to report income eligible for the special election as ordinary income. The CRA's review of your T4A slip should identify the payment, and the CRA will then calculate the revised tax and include the tax reduction when processing your return. To the extent your tax liability has been fully paid, you should receive a refund of the reduction, together with a Notice of Assessment identifying the tax reduction with some such comment as "Your tax has been reduced by the application of the pension averaging provisions in section 40 of the *Income Tax Application Rules*".

The situation may be somewhat different if you are obliged to pay tax when you file your return. You cannot be required to overpay your tax and wait for a refund (although you can do that). If you wish to account for the special reduced tax treatment on lump-sum pension payments or deferred profit sharing plan payments on your return, you will have to make the calculation yourself and reflect the reduction in tax in your return. Given the complexity of the calculation, is it generally much easier to allow the CRA to do it and await your refund in due course.

Be sure to attach a copy of your special tax calculation to your return, if you prepare one.

[¶1478] EMPLOYEES NOT RESIDENT IN CANADA DURING THE WHOLE OF THE THREE TAXATION YEARS PRECEDING RECEIPT

If you were not resident in Canada throughout the whole three-year period on which the averaging calculation is based, and you receive a lump-sum payment eligible for this election, you are allowed to calculate the special tax as if you had been a resident of Canada and had derived your world income from Canadian sources in that period. It will be necessary for you to compute what your income would have been in each of the three years prior to the receipt of the special payment and what tax would have been payable by you in those years.

The amount of tax which you are required to pay will then be computed in the same way as in the case of an employee who was resident in Canada for those years.

To qualify for this optional tax treatment, you must file a return of your incomes for each of the three years in the averaging period in the same form and containing the same information as you would have been requested to file if you had been a resident of Canada during those years. You will not be required to pay the tax indicated for those years. That is, filing returns for years of non-residence does not subject to

Canadian tax any income which would normally not have been taxable because of your non-resident status in those years. The prior year returns filed on the hypothesis that you were a Canadian resident are merely used to measure the averaging entitlement for the eligible lump-sum payment.

(ITAR: 40(2))

[¶1479] AMOUNTS TO BE SUBTRACTED FROM PAYMENTS ELIGIBLE FOR SPECIAL REDUCED TAX TREATMENT

Qualifying lump-sum amounts you were entitled to in 1997 as pension payments and deferred profit sharing payments should not be subject to tax if they were transferred in 1997 directly into a registered pension fund or plan, a registered retirement savings plan or a deferred profit sharing plan, rather than being paid to you. See ¶1021.

Also, where pension payments or deferred profit sharing payments were payable on death and included as income of a beneficiary, a proportion of the amounts paid on account of provincial succession duties may be deducted from income. See also ¶1032.

Where either of the above deductions is made and you elect to pay the special tax, such election may be made only on the balance of the pension or other eligible payment, i.e., net of the deductions noted above.

(ITAR: 40(3))

[¶1480] LIMITATIONS ON THE AMOUNT ON WHICH AN ELECTION CAN BE MADE

The amount which you can elect to have taxed at the special reduced rate is limited, although as we move further away from 1971 the limitation is ever less likely to reduce the lump sum eligible for election. Nevertheless, it must be considered.

In the case of a payment or payments out of a pension fund or a deferred profit sharing plan the maximum amount on which an election may be made is the lesser of:

(1) the portion of the payment or payments which would have been payable at December 31, 1971 minus any amount subtracted as in ¶1479 above; or

(2) $1,500 times the number of consecutive 12-month periods that you were a member of the plan — if your employer has contributed thereto on your behalf. This amount is reduced by the amount of any payment made after April 26, 1965 under such a plan whereby your employer has contributed and on which an election has already been made.

In the case of a payment or payments made to a taxpayer on the death of an employee or former employee, the amount on which an election may be made is limited to the portion of the payment or payments which would have been payable at December 31, 1971, minus any amount subtracted as in ¶1479 above.

(ITAR: 40(5), (7))

SPLIT INCOME

[¶1490] TAX ON SPLIT INCOME — LINES 232 AND 424

The tax on split income is intended to prevent income splitting with minor children, which is typically accomplished by having children subscribe for shares in corporations owned and run by their parents, or invest in partnerships which, typically, provided management services to a parent's professional practice. Often, the property generating the income to be split is held by a trust of which the minor child is a beneficiary.

The benefit of such income splitting is eliminated by taxing all children at top marginal rates on (i) taxable dividends received on, or taxable benefits conferred in respect of, corporate shares not listed on a public stock exchange, (ii) partnership income which can be sourced to a business carried on by a relative of the child directly or through specified corporate structures, (iii) capital gains realized on a non-arm's length sale of shares, where dividends on the shares would be subject to the tax, (iv) trust income which is essentially a flow-through of the kinds of income described in (i) and (ii), and (v) trust or partnership income derived from services to arm's length parties where a person related to the minor is engaged in providing those services or has an interest in the partnership.

The income so taxed is deducted from net income (at line 232), so that it is not taxed twice, and taxed at the highest federal marginal tax rate (33% for 2016). The deduction from ordinary income requires addbacks in certain specified calculations, such as the foreign tax credit limitations.

(ITA: 120.4)

[¶1490.05] *Who is Subject to Tax on Split Income*

An individual can be subject to the tax on split income only in respect of years in which he or she:

(1) had not attained the age of 17 before the year (thus a child who turns 17 in the year is still subject to the tax);

(2) was at no time in the year a non-resident of Canada; and

(3) has a parent who is resident in Canada at any time in the year.

All three conditions must be met to be subject to the tax on split income. The concept of residence is discussed in Chapter 1, especially ¶115–¶117. The term "parent" has a rather broader definition than might be expected, as discussed at ¶1122.20, so that a child in the care and custody of a Canadian on whom the child was wholly dependent would have a Canadian parent even if both natural parents lived outside Canada. Technically, both natural parents and adoptive parents are parents, but it is an open question whether the CRA would push a case in which liability depends on the residence status of natural parents where a child has been legally adopted.

(ITA: 120.4(1); 252)

[¶1490.10] *Liability of Parents*

Although it is the child who is liable for the tax in the first instance, the government recognizes that pursuing children for tax liabilities is likely to be politically embarrassing, if not morally repugnant, and has made parents jointly and severally liable. Thus, the CRA can bring to bear its whole panoply of collection procedures on a parent, whether or not it tries to collect from the child, provided the parent:

- carried on a business that was provided with property or services by a partnership or trust all or a portion of the income of which partnership or trust is included in the split income of the child;
- was a specified shareholder (defined in (3)(a), below) of a corporation that was provided property or services by a partnership or trust all or a portion of the income of which the partnership or trust is directly or indirectly included in computing the split income of the child for the year;
- was a specified shareholder of a corporation dividends of which were directly or indirectly included in computing the child's split income for the year;
- was a shareholder of a professional corporation that was provided with property or services by a partnership or trust all or a portion of the income of which the partnership or trust is directly or indirectly included in split income of the child; or
- was a shareholder in a professional corporation dividends of which were directly or indirectly included in computing the child's split income for the year.

(ITA: 160(1.2))

[¶1490.15] *Definition of Split Income*

Split income includes:

(1) amounts required to be included in the income of the child in respect of taxable dividends on shares of stock of a corporation unless the shares are listed on a designated stock exchange (see ¶2618) or are shares in a Canadian mutual fund corporation (which by definition must be widely held);

(2) amounts required to be included in the income of the child by virtue of the ownership by anyone of shares not listed on a designated stock exchange under the rules at ¶409 and ¶409a including in income benefits conferred by a corporation on shareholders or their relatives;

(3) partnership income included in the child's income, to the extent that the source of the partnership income can reasonably be considered to be the provision of property or services by a partnership or trust to, or in support of, a business carried on by

(a) a person related to the child at any time in the year (for the definition of who is related, see ¶812)

(b) a corporation of which a person related to the child is a specified shareholder at any time in the year; a specified shareholder is essentially a shareholder who holds (directly or indirectly) 10% or more of the shares of the corporation, but the definition goes much further and deems a person to own shares held by non-arm's length persons, through a trust or partnership, and more;

(c) a professional corporation of which a person related to the child is a shareholder (of any shares at all);

(4) income of the child from a trust (other than a mutual fund trust) which can reasonably be considered to come through the trust from a source described above;

(5) capital gains realized from the disposition of shares to a person not dealing at arm's length with the minor child (except publicly listed shares or mutual fund shares); the capital gain is deemed to be a non-eligible taxable dividend;

(6) business or rental income paid/allocated to the child directly or indirectly from a trust or partnership, if a person related to the child

(a) is actively engaged on a regular basis in the partnership/trust's earning income from a business or the rental of property, or

(b) has an interest in the partnership, whether directly or indirectly through one or more other partnerships.

An example of the workings of this system is found in a CRA technical opinion, CRA Document No. 2003-0181705. There a father proposed to lend money to a trust for his children. The trust would pay prescribed interest to the father (which prevents the income attribution rules from applying), and on-lend the money to the father's corporation, which in turn would pay market interest to the trust. Under the "property or services" rule, the trust income taxed to the children is split income from the provision of property to the corporation. Under the "goods or services" rule, the CRA would have still argued it was split income from the provision of a financial service. Income not taxed to the children would, of course, be taxed in the trust at top marginal rates.

(ITA: 120.4(1); 251; 252)

History

Split income relating to capital gains, item (5) above, only arises where the shares are sold after March 21, 2011. Split income relating to third-party services, item (6) above, only applies to 2014 and subsequent years.

[¶1490.20] *Excluded Income*

The following items are specifically excluded from a child's split income:

- income from, *or the taxable capital gain from the disposition of*, a property acquired by or for the child on the death of a parent;
- income from, *or the taxable capital gain from the disposition of*, a property acquired by or for the child on the death of anyone if the child is a full-time student enrolled in a course at a post-secondary institution as defined for purposes of the life-long learning plan (¶2626a);
- income from, *or the taxable capital gain from the disposition of*, a property acquired by or for the child on the death of anyone if the child is one for whom anyone may claim a disability amount under the rules at ¶1255.

The addition to the definition of split income of certain services or property provided by third parties, seemingly still spares certain payments of such income to minors from the tax on split income where both: (a) those actively engaged on a regular basis in the income-earning activities are not related to the recipient minors; and (b) no person related to the recipient minors has a direct or indirect interest in a particular income-earning partnership. Practically, however, it may be difficult to structure such an arrangement.

(ITA: 120.4(1))

[¶1490.25] *Deduction from Income; Calculation of Tax*

The calculation of the tax on split income is a two-step process. The first calculates tax at the top federal marginal tax rate (33% for 2016) on the split income. This tax is entered at line 424 of Schedule 1. It adds to the tax on income not subject to the tax on split income entered at line 454. The result is entered at line 404. The second provides for a reduction of credits for the sum of:

(1) a dividend tax credit related to the split income; and

(2) a foreign tax credit calculated on the split income.

The amount so determined is compared to federal tax otherwise calculated, at line 406 of Schedule 1, reduced by your federal political contribution credit, investment tax credit, and labour-sponsored fund tax credit. If the tax on split income is greater, it overrides the regular tax amount and the tax on split income is entered directly at line 417.

[¶1490.30] *Form T1206*

The CRA provides form T1206 for calculating split income. The provinces also impose this tax and page 2 of form T1206 calculates the provincial tax (except, of course, for Quebec) and also the provincial dividend tax credit and provincial foreign tax credit, using provincial rates for these items.

Quebec imposes its own split income tax under essentially similar rules.

(ITA: 20(1)(ww); 120.4(2), (3); 248(1) "specified shareholder")

OTHER COMMENTS ON TAX PAYMENTS

[¶1491] CANADA PENSION PLAN — LINE 448

Most employees and self-employed persons are required to contribute to the Canada Pension Plan, or the Quebec Pension Plan. If you are an employee, these are deducted from your pay and reported on your T4 slip. It is possible, especially if you have held more than one job in the year, that the total CPP or QPP payments you have had withheld exceed your CPP/QPP liability.

Line 448 of the T1 return is used to claim a refund of contributions in excess of the maximum for the year - $2,544.30.

If you have paid less than the maximum but still more than required, the CRA automatically computes your overpayment and adjusts your tax liability or refund. However, you may compute the overpayment yourself using Schedule 8.

If as an employee you contributed less than the maximum and less than 4.95% of your earnings, you may be able to make an additional payment to increase your eventual CPP pension. You can do this using form CPT20 and Schedule 8; see ¶1305.

If you are self-employed you must complete Schedule 8, included with the T1 General return package; see ¶1305.

History

Canada Pension Plan maximum contributions were:

- $2,479.95 in 2015
- $2,425.50 in 2014
- $2,356.20 in 2013
- $2,306.70 in 2012

[¶1492] EMPLOYMENT INSURANCE PREMIUM OVERPAYMENT — LINE 450

Most employees are required to pay premiums for Employment Insurance. These are deducted from your pay and reported on your T4 slip. It is possible, especially if you have held more than one job in the year, that the total EI payments you have had withheld exceed your EI liability.

You may claim a refund of contributions in excess of the maximum required employee contribution (which, for 2016, is $955.04 for individuals not resident in Quebec, and $772.16 for individuals resident in Quebec on December 31). This is fully discussed at ¶1307. If you paid more than the maximum, your claim for overpayment should be entered at line 450 on page 4 of the return.

If you paid less than the applicable maximum, but still more than you were required, the CRA automatically computes your overpayment and adjusts your tax liability or refund. However, you may compute the overpayment yourself using form T2204.

History

Employment insurance maximum contributions were:

- $930.60 federally and $762.30 in Quebec in 2015
- $913.68 federally and $743.58 in Quebec in 2014
- $892.18 federally and $720.48 in Quebec in 2013
- $839.97 federally and $674.73 in Quebec in 2012
- $786.76 federally and $623.22 in Quebec in 2011

[¶1494] TAX PAYMENTS

After calculating your total tax payable for the year (see "Total Payable" on page 4 of your return) you should enter the amounts of tax you have paid for the taxation year of the return (either by instalments, at line 476, or through withholdings from your salary, at line 437) to the date of filing the return, and calculate the balance of tax payable or refundable. The rules for payment of tax are described in Chapter 2.

REFUNDABLE FEDERAL TAX CREDITS

[¶1495] WORKING INCOME TAX BENEFIT — LINE 453 AND SCHEDULE 6)

[¶1495.05] *Income Levels*

A low income individual or family may face a high marginal tax rate on its income, as the entitlement to means-tested support, such as the GST credit and the Canada Child Benefit, are eroded. To reduce the impact of the loss of these benefits, a refundable credit is provided to such taxpayers who earn employment or business income.

For single individuals, the working income tax benefit (WITB) is phased in beginning at a "working income" level of $3,000. In most provinces and territories it begins to erode in

2016 at a net income of $11,675, and is eliminated at a net income of $18,529.

For families (including single parents), the working income tax benefit becomes payable beginning at a "working income" level of $3,000. In most provinces and territories it begins to erode in 2016 at a net family income of $16,122, and is eliminated at a net family income of $28,576.

For individuals eligible for the disability tax credit (¶1255) in the taxation year (i.e., who have a valid form T2201 disability certificate) there is a separately calculated WITB "disability supplement" of, for 2016, $514. In most provinces, the supplement is phased in at an earned income level of $1,150 (regardless of whether income is below the $3,000 level at which the main benefit begins) and extends the upper limits of the credit to 2016 incomes of $21,958 for a single individual, $32,002 for a family where one spouse or common-law partner has a disability certificate, and $35,429 for a family where each spouse or common-law partner has a disability certificate. Like the WITB, in 2016 the WITB disability supplement in most provinces and territories begins to be phased out at an income level of $18,529 for a single individual and $28,576 for a family.

Commentary on Bill C-26 Measures (Oct. 6, 2016)

Note: When Bill C-26, October 6, 2016, achieves Royal Assent, the commentary will be modified to read:

For single individuals, the working income tax benefit (WITB) is phased in beginning at a "working income" level of $3,000. Effective January 1, 2019, in most provinces and territories it begins to erode at an indexed net income amount, and is eliminated at a net income over an indexed amount.

For families (including single parents), the working income tax benefit becomes payable beginning at a "working income" level of $3,000. Effective January 1, 2019, in most provinces and territories it begins to erode in 2016 at an indexed net family income amount, and is eliminated at an indexed net family income.

For individuals eligible for the disability tax credit (¶1255) in the taxation year (i.e., who have a valid form T2201 disability certificate) there is a separately calculated WITB "disability supplement" which, effective January 1, 2019, is indexed annually. In most provinces, the supplement is phased in at an earned income level of $1,150 (regardless of whether income is below the $3,000 level at which the main benefit begins) and extends the upper limits of the credit to 2019 indexed incomes. Like the WITB, in 2019 the WITB disability supplement in most provinces and territories begins to be phased out at an income level of $20,844 for a single individual and $32,491 for a family.

Where the disability supplement is claimed, the general WITB is also claimed if you qualify; that is, if your (family) working income is over $3,000 and below the upper limits for that benefit.

The $3,000/$1,150 thresholds are not indexed, but all other values in WITB calculations are indexed.

[¶1495.07] *Income Levels Vary for Some Provinces*

The WITB legislation includes provision for the Minister of Finance to enter into an agreement with a province or territory to modify the income level parameters of the program for residents of that province, presumably to harmonize with local support programs. Quebec, British Columbia, Alberta and Nunavut have entered into such agreements, and each has a version of Schedule 6 unique to the province or territory.

[¶1495.10] *Prepayment of Benefit*

A prepayment mechanism has been put in place for the WITB. The machinery is rather different from the GST/HST (¶1496) and Canada Child Benefit (CCB) (¶1498) refundable tax payment systems. In the GST and CCB systems, payments are based on known income numbers from preceding years and, unless those numbers change retrospectively, either through reassessment or change of circumstances (such as separation), there is unlikely to be a subsequent alteration of benefits. In short, they need not be trued up on a later return.

The WITB prepayment machinery is truly a prepayment of (half of) the benefit estimated to be payable for the current taxation year, and must be applied for each year on form RC201 and trued up on the return for that year. For example, if you made a timely application for prepayment of your 2016 WITB in 2015 and received prepayment(s) in 2015 (or early 2016), you will enter the total prepayment(s) received, as shown in box 10 of your RC210 slip, on line 415 on Schedule 1 of your 2016 T1 return, and you will calculate your actual 2016 WITB entitlement on Schedule 6, and enter the result on line 453 of your 2016 return. Thus, you are adding the prepayment back to tax and deducting the actual credit entitlement.

If you want to apply for prepayment of 2017 WITB, you must again file form RC201. The application for the 2017 advance payment must be made between January 1 and August 31, 2017.

If you apply for prepayment, the CRA can pay up to half the anticipated credit *before the end of January 2018*. It appears to be intended that, although the CRA is required to honour a valid prepayment request by making payment before the end of January 2018, it will, where possible (i.e., where there is sufficiently early application), include the prepayments in the GST credit cycle. Thus, a prepayment approved on application in May 2017 would be paid in three equal instalments, in July 2017, October 2017, and January 2018. (A prepayment approved before April 2017 would be paid in four equal instalments, the first on April 2017.) The reconciliation of these prepayments with actual entitlements would be made on the 2017 tax return filed in 2018.

The prepayment application should, in the case of a family, be made by the spouse or common-law partner with the higher anticipated *working* income, except that where one spouse or partner has a disability certificate, that person should make the application. Where both spouses/partners have a disability certificate, it is again the one with the higher anticipated working income that should apply.

(ITA: 122.7(6)–(8))

[¶1495.15] *Schedule 6 Required*

The credit is calculated on Schedule 6. The result is carried on line 453 of the return. The advanced payments received, if any, are considered in the calculation of the net federal tax on line 415 of Schedule 1.

[¶1495.20] *Definitions*

The basic definitions associated with the WITB are as follows.

"Working income" is the sum of:

(1) your employment income, including exempt amounts such as the non-taxable part of income earned on a reserve or of an allowance received as an emergency volunteer (¶338), before employment income deductions;

(2) your net business income from each business carried on in the year, other than income earned as a specified member of a partnership; generally speaking, a specified member of a partnership is a passive member, as defined at ¶1842.30; if one or more businesses carried on in the year have a net loss, those losses are not subtracted from the income of other businesses which have net income;

(3) your income from scholarships, bursaries, prizes for achievement, and artistic grants to the extent the income is not exempt under the rules at ¶953.10, from research grants net of deductible expenses (¶961), and financial assistance received under the *Wage Earner Protection Program Act* (¶975.03).

You are an "eligible individual" if you were resident in Canada throughout the year, and at the end of that year you were (i) 19 years of age or older, or (ii) the cohabiting spouse or common-law partner of another individual, or (iii) the parent of a child who lives with you. However, even if you meet these tests, you will not be an eligible individual if you are exempt from tax because you (i) are a full-time student at a designated (post-secondary) educational institution for more than 13 weeks in the taxation year, unless you have an eligible dependant, in which case you are not disqualified; (ii) were confined to prison or a similar institution for a period of at least 90 days in the taxation year, or (iii) are, or are a member of the family of, a servant of a foreign country (i.e., diplomats and their families).

An "eligible dependant" is a child of yours who, at the end of the taxation year, (i) resided with you, (ii) was under the age of 19, and (iii) was not an eligible individual (for example, because he or she has a child of his or her own).

An "eligible spouse" is a spouse or common-law partner who was resident in Canada throughout the year and who was, at the end of the year, a cohabiting spouse or partner. A cohabiting spouse or partner has the same definition as for Canada child benefit purposes; that is, it is a spouse or common-law partner who on December 31 was not living separate and apart from you by reason of a breakdown of the relationship which proved to have lasted for at least 90 days. By and large, as discussed at ¶1113, a common-law partnership breaks down on the same basis of a 90-day separation, so typically you will not have a common-law partner at all on December 31 if the 90-day test is met.

However, for some purposes, such as claiming the spousal amount, the issue is whether you had a common-law partner at any time during the year, and essentially it is that test which the CRA uses on page 1 of the T1. Thus, you could report a common-law partner for T1 purposes who would not be an eligible cohabiting spouse for WITB purposes. In this case, you claim the WITB as a single person.

The case of a legal spouse is somewhat different, at least in theory. Your legal spouse remains your spouse regardless of separation, so the definition imposes a cohabitation/separation requirement to deny the WITB where you are separated from your legal spouse.

If you have an *eligible spouse* for the taxation year in question, only one of you may make the ordinary WITB credit claim. If you both apply, the credit is reduced to nil. The prepayment mechanism requires a joint application by you and your eligible spouse, agreeing as to whom the prepayment will be made (in accordance with the rules in ¶1495.10, above). The spouse receiving the advance payment must be the one who trues it up on Schedule 6 of the T1 return.

Finally, "adjusted net income" is total net income (before taxable income adjustments), including (as with working income) the non-taxable part of income earned on a reserve or of an allowance received as an emergency volunteer, and including amounts normally deducted as repayments of universal child care benefits overpaid to you (¶935.10), but excluding amounts received as universal child care benefits (¶935), as disability payments under a registered disability savings plan (¶2529h), and capital gains arising on the repossession of property you obtained by foreclosing a mortgage (¶518).

(ITA: 122.7(1) Definitions)

[¶1495.25] *Basic WITB Calculation*

For residents of provinces or territories other than British Columbia, Quebec, Nunavut, and Alberta, the WITB becomes payable when your working income, and that of your eligible spouse, if any, exceeds $3,000. The credit is 25% of the amount by which your income (and that of your eligible spouse, if any) exceeds $3,000, to a maximum credit, in 2016, of $1,028 for a single individual and $1,868 for an individual with an eligible spouse or eligible dependant. For a single individual, the credit amount is reduced by 15% of your adjusted net income in 2016, in excess of $11,675. If you have an eligible spouse and/ or an eligible dependant, your credit amount is reduced by 15% of the joint 2016 income of you and your eligible spouse (but not your eligible dependant) in excess of $16,122

Commentary on Bill C-26 Measures (Oct. 6, 2016)

Note: When Bill C-26, October 6, 2016, achieves Royal Assent, the commentary will be modified to read:

For residents of provinces or territories other than British Columbia, Quebec, Nunavut, and Alberta, the WITB becomes payable when your working income, and that of your eligible spouse, if any, exceeds $3,000. Effective January 1, 2019, the credit is 26% of the amount by which your income (and that of your eligible spouse, if any) exceeds $3,000, to a maximum credit, in 2019, of $1,192 for a single individual and $2,165 for an individual with an eligible spouse or eligible dependant. For a single individual, the credit amount is reduced by 14% of your adjusted net income in 2019, in excess of $10,500. If you have an eligible spouse and/or an eligible dependant, your credit amount is reduced by 1% of the joint 2019 income of you and your eligible spouse (but not your eligible dependant) in excess of $14,500.

For residents of Quebec, British Columbia, Nunavut, and Alberta, see ¶1495.07 and the Schedule 6 for your jurisdiction.

[¶1495.30] *WITB Disability Supplement*

The disability supplement is a separate calculation governed by separate rules. The disability supplement must be claimed by the single individual or eligible spouse who is entitled to a disability tax credit for the year (¶1255) on his or her own account, and not as a transfer. If each eligible spouse is entitled to a disability credit on his or her own account, each files a T1 return and a Schedule 6 to make the Step 3 claim on Schedule 6. One — but only one — of them should also claim the general credit in Step 2 of Schedule 6.

The disability credit threshold is 25% of the disabled person's working income in excess of $1,150 (not indexed), to a maximum credit for 2016 of $514. Even if there is an eligible spouse, only the working income of the spouse entitled to his or her own disability credit in the year is counted in this calculation. The credit is reduced, in the case of a single person, by 15% of that person's 2016 adjusted net income in excess of $18,529. For a disabled person with an eligible spouse or eligible dependant, the credit is reduced by 15% of the combined 2016 adjusted net income of the disabled person and that person's eligible spouse (if any) but not eligible dependant, in excess of $28,576. However, if the disabled person's spouse is also disabled, each person claims the disability supplement and reduces his or her own disability credit by 7.5% of the combined adjusted net income in excess of $28,576.

Commentary on Bill C-26 Measures (Oct. 6, 2016)

Note: When Bill C-26, October 6, 2016, achieves Royal Assent, the commentary will be modified to read:

Effective January 1, 2019, the disability credit threshold is 26% of the disabled person's working income in excess of $1,150 (not indexed), to a indexed maximum credit. Even if there is an eligible spouse, only the working income of the spouse entitled to his or her own disability credit in the year is counted in this calculation. The credit is reduced, in the case of a single person, by 14% of that person's 2019 adjusted net income in excess of $20,844. For a disabled person with an eligible spouse or eligible dependant, the credit is reduced by 14% of the combined 2019 adjusted net income of the disabled person and that person's eligible spouse (if any) but not eligible dependant, in excess of $32,491. However, if the disabled person's spouse is also disabled, each person claims the disability supplement and reduces his or her own disability credit by 7% of the combined adjusted net income in excess of $32,491.

It might appear at first blush that there is a missing cog here, as there is no credit for a disabled eligible dependant. However, the eligible dependant is (presumably) covered by the Child Disability Benefit under the Canada Child Benefit program at ¶1498. In any event, the logic of this benefit, intended to offset the benefit cost of earning additional income, is in general not applicable to minors.

(ITA: 122.7)

[¶1495.50] *WITB Publications*

The CRA no longer publishes a separate pamphlet called *Working Income Tax Benefit*, RC4227. However, using the search feature on the CRA website at www.cra.gc.ca, typing in "RC4227" will result in useful information regarding the WITB. Form RC201, application for advance payment, is similarly available.

[¶1496] GST CREDIT

The GST credit is intended to offset the cost of the goods and services tax for lower-income individuals and families.

The introduction of the Harmonized Sales Tax increased the GST rate in the harmonizing provinces. Only Newfoundland and Labrador, Nova Scotia, and British Columbia offer a supplemental provincial credit designed to offset the impact of sales taxes on low income taxpayers; these are calculated by the CRA and incorporated into your GST credit payment. See Chapter 15 for the criteria used to assess eligibility for the provincial credits. The CRA has taken to referring to the whole thing as the GST/HST credit, although for most taxpayers it is in fact only a GST credit.

The GST credit was, when introduced, entirely novel in its form of payment. Its model is now followed in the Canada Child Benefit (¶1498). Traditionally, federal tax credits, including refundable credits, were calculated on your current return and fully applied (or refunded if a refundable credit exceeded your tax payable) as part of that return. The GST credit as calculated on your current return cannot be used to offset current taxes payable. Rather, it is paid out to you in instalments over the year following the due date of your return. These payments are to be made to you quarterly in July, October, January, and April following the timely filing of a return.

Thus, based on your 2016 return filed in April 2017, a tax credit would be determined, which does not reduce your tax payable but will be paid to you commencing in July 2017. Earlier 2017 payments to you (if any) will have been based on your 2015 return. Of course, if you leave taxes unpaid on your 2016 return, the CRA may apply your GST credit payments (when they become payable to you) to your taxes owing, but you will still be liable for interest and possible penalties and collection procedures for the interim period. You are not required to file a separate form to claim the GST/HST credit, as eligibility is automatically determined by the CRA based on the T1 information submitted.

Eligibility for the credit is responsive to changing family circumstances, such as the birth of a qualifying child. For example:

- following the birth of a child, a family will receive an additional GST/HST credit amount for that child included in the next quarterly payment;
- the GST credit is available to you in the next quarterly payment immediately following your 19th birthday (the implication is that if you turn 19 before April 1, 2018, and are otherwise eligible, you should apply for the credit on your 2016 return, which establishes the credits to be paid, if any, in July and October 2017 and January and April 2018);
- individuals who marry, or become separated or widowed, will have their credits adjusted in the quarter following their change in marital status to ensure that they receive the amount to which they are entitled;
- new or returning residents to Canada will be eligible for the credit in the next quarterly payment following their entry or return into Canada.

Under these rules, you have to be eligible at the beginning of each quarter to receive a particular amount, and the adjusted payment will show up in your quarterly payment. It follows that, if you claim this credit, the CRA requires information of changes in: marital/common-law status; the birth of a child; becoming resident or ceasing to be resident (for you and/or your spouse or common-law partner); and when a child for whom you are receiving credit is no longer in your care, stops living with you, becomes a spouse or common-law partner or a parent, or dies. You can do this by telephone, to 1-800-959-1953 or by filing form RC65 for a change of marital status or RC66 for children.

Two eligible individuals are permitted to claim the quarterly GST/HST credit for a qualified dependant. A "shared custody parent" is one of the two parents of the qualified dependant who is not a cohabiting spouse or common-law partner and resides with the qualified dependant on an equal or near equal basis. Where two people may be eligible to claim a person as a qualified dependent — or where two individuals are qualified relations of each other and would otherwise qualify for the GST/HST credit in a given month — the Minister will designate which eligible individual will receive the credit.

The CRA bases its GST credit payments for children on the data it has for Canada Child Benefits (CCB), so that if you claim GST credit but not CCB, your claim is likely to fail until you clarify the matter with the CRA.

If your GST credit is less than $50 per quarter, it should be paid to you in one lump sum in July (if your return is filed and assessed on time), with no further payments.

GST credits due to you may be applied by the CRA to any unpaid amounts you owe them. The law says that you must file a GST claim with your return to be entitled to the credits. You do this by checking the box on page 1 of your T1 return. On the other hand, you are allowed to file a return requesting a refund within three years from the end of the taxation year in issue. CRA officials have indicated informally that they will honour late requests for the GST credit, and the CRA does have discretion to honour late-filed requests for GST credit without any time limit.

(ITA: 122.5; 152(1.2)(*d*))

[¶1496.05] *Income Levels at Which GST Credit Expires (2015 Returns)*

The GST credit is income-tested, as discussed below. The CRA provides a table of the approximate income levels at which the credit applies on the CRA website: click on "Individuals and families", then on the next page, "Child and family benefits", and then "GST/HST credit". Generally speaking, the credit based on your 2015 return (to be paid in 2016 and 2017) will expire at a net income (line 236 of your T1) of $44,266 if you are single, or a joint income of you and your spouse or common-law partner of $46,886 for a couple. For a couple, add $2,900 for each child to this level. For a single parent with one child, the credit expires at 2015 income of $49,786; add $2,900 for each additional child. There is a calculation below at ¶1496.45 to help you decide if you qualify for the 2016 credit.

[¶1496.10] *Calendar Quarters*

Lest there be any doubt, references throughout this section to "quarter" or "calendar quarter" are always to the three-month periods beginning January 1, April 1, July 1, and October 1.

[¶1496.15] *Who May Claim the Credit*

As discussed above, your GST credit status is redetermined quarterly. When filing your 2016 return (for which GST credit payments will commence in July 2017), you will be eligible for the GST credit if, at the time your return is being filed, you are resident in Canada and you are:

(1) 19 years of age or older, or will turn 19 before April 1, 2017 (in which case you would qualify for the credit for the quarter beginning April 1, 2017, and should receive the credit for that quarter); or

(2) married or living with a common-law partner as defined at ¶1113; or

(3) the parent of a child, as defined at ¶1122.15.

The CRA's computers rely on the family information in your return, and your Canada Child Benefit information, and determine what credit, if any, to send you.

If you are married or living with a common-law partner when you file your return for the year, only one of you will receive the GST credit, although the credit so claimed will include credits for both spouses. The credit will be paid to the spouse or common-law partner whose return is assessed first.

You are not entitled to the GST credit for your spouse or common-law partner for a calendar quarter if on the first day of that quarter you were separated by reason of breakdown of the marriage or relationship. A breakdown must last for a period of 90 days under these rules to disqualify you from the spousal credit, but once it has lasted for 90 days, the disqualification goes back to the first day of the separation. The CRA is quite clear that they do not want you to report the separation until it has lasted for 90 days, but once the 90 days are up, the CRA will adjust your future benefits to deduct overpayments they have made during the 90-day period. Similarly, the other spouse or partner becomes eligible for an independent GST credit beginning with the first calendar quarter in which you were separated on the first day, although the separation cannot be proven until the 90-day period is up.

Once you have been married or living in a common-law relationship, or have had children, the age 19 limit no longer applies to you. You are entitled to your own credit, and this will prevent someone else from claiming you as a dependent child for GST purposes, even if you return to live in your parents' home.

[¶1496.20] *Eligible Children*

Eligible children are determined as of the first day of each calendar quarter. Each child is eligible for a particular quarter if on the first day of the first month of that quarter the child is an unmarried (or non-common-law partner per ¶1113) child (see the definition of child at ¶1122.15) of you and your spouse or common-law partner and (i) is under 19, (ii) is not a parent, and (iii) resided with you.

You are not entitled to the credit for a particular child unless you have registered the child for either Canada Child Benefit or GST Tax Credit purposes. Either is sufficient.

[¶1496.25] *When You Cannot Claim the Credit*

Notwithstanding the general rules above, there are specific circumstances in which you may not claim the GST credit for yourself or your dependants.

You may not receive the credit for a spouse or common-law partner if you are separated, as discussed above.

You are not entitled to the GST credit for a calendar quarter for yourself if you were, or for a dependant who was, confined to prison or a similar institution for a period of 90 days or more which included the first day of that quarter.

You are not entitled to credit for a person who died before the first day of the calendar quarter.

You are not entitled to credit for a person who was a non-resident on the first day of the calendar quarter, unless that person is the spouse or common-law partner of a person deemed resident in Canada throughout the year which includes the first day of the quarter, and was a resident of Canada at some previous time. What this rule seems to be trying to say is that you cannot receive the credit for yourself if you are a non-resident, but can if you are a deemed resident.

You cannot receive the credit for your non-resident spouse or partner (nor can that person) unless you are a deemed resident and your spouse or partner was at some time resident in Canada. Of course, the normal marriage breakdown rules apply.

No credit can be received by or for anyone who is exempt from tax in Canada by virtue of the rules at ¶120 (essentially, diplomatic status).

[¶1496.30] *Calculating the Basic Credit You Are Receiving (2015 Returns)*

When you file your return, the CRA will determine your eligibility and tell you if you are entitled to receive the GST credit. The CRA will determine your eligibility and calculate your credit based on the information in your and your spouse or partner's returns, and the number of dependent children from its Canada Child Benefit data bank. It follows that if the children are not registered for Canada Child Benefit, you will have to sort out their eligibility with the CRA.

Note that the amounts discussed below are annual amounts. The total credit you receive quarterly will be $^1/_4$ of the total payments described, calculated on the eligibility of you or your dependants on the first day of that quarter (i.e., of January, April, July, or October) or of the preceding quarter, if changes were not given to CRA in time for it to reprogram. Looked at another way, your quarterly credit will be normally $^1/_4$ of the amounts applicable to a particular quarter, but catch-up adjustments can occur where the facts change during the year.

The values below are based on 2015 returns: they are the amounts you should have received in the last half of 2016 and should be receiving in the first half of 2017. For values based on 2016 returns, see the chart at ¶1496.45.

For payments commencing July 2016, based on 2015 returns, the basic (adjusted) annual GST credit for an individual should have been $276. If you were 19 years of age or older at the end of 2015, and lived alone or with your parents or with unrelated persons, and had no dependent children, you were entitled to at least some part of an additional $145 supplement if your 2015 net income (from line 236 of your return) exceeded $8,948. The supplement is calculated as the balance remaining when $8,948 is subtracted from 2% of your net income, to a maximum of $145. Note that the $8,948 amount represents a figure that at one time was tied to the basic personal amount, but now stands on its own (and is indexed).

If you were married on the first day of a quarter, or party to a common-law relationship as described at ¶1113, and in either case not separated under the rules in the section "Who May Claim the Credit", above, you could claim a basic annual credit for 2016/2017 (based on your 2015 base year return) of $276 for yourself and $276 for your spouse or common-law partner. Neither of you could claim the extra $145 for low-income earners. Either one of you may file to claim the credit, but not both of you; one must file for both.

If you had no "cohabiting" spouse or common-law partner (¶1113) on the first day of a particular quarter, and you are entitled to claim the "eligible dependant" personal amount described at ¶1120, you could claim a quarterly share of $276 for the dependant you are so claiming on line 305 of your return. For payments commencing July 2016, if you are a shared custody parent (see ¶1498) you will be entitled to one half of this amount for a qualified dependant. You could not claim a further $143 GST credit for the same person as a dependant under the rules below. If the eligible dependant claim had been eliminated by the dependant's income, you could not claim the $276 GST credit for that dependant.

The basic credit for an eligible child as described above (referred to as a "qualified dependant") was $145 (for 2016/2017 based on 2015 returns) for each such child.

If you had no "cohabiting" spouse or common-law partner (¶1113) on the first day of a calendar quarter, but you do have qualified dependants for whom you are making claims above, you may also claim a quarterly share of the single parent supplement of an additional $145.

Your total credit based on the sum of your entitlements under the rules above was reduced by 5% of your "adjusted net income" in excess of (for 2016/2017 payments determined by 2015 returns) $35,926. Adjusted net income is explained below.

[¶1496.35] *Reducing the Basic Credit by "Adjusted Net Income" (2015 Returns)*

The total credit you may claim based on the sum of your entitlements under the rules above is reduced by 5% of your adjusted net income in excess of (for 2016/2017 payments determined by 2015 returns) $35,926. This $35,926 is known as the "threshold amount," and is indexed annually for inflation (¶1101).

Adjusted net income is essentially the net income of yourself and your "cohabiting spouse or common-law partner" as defined at ¶1498.10. Net income, in turn, is essentially income as reported at line 236. In particular it includes any treaty-exempt income (as discussed at ¶1103). However, you should exclude from line 236 net income (1) any amount included (on line 117) or deducted in respect of the universal child care benefit (¶935) and, (2) any capital gain realized on property you (or your spouse or partner) reacquired by foreclosing on a mortgage or repossessing property you (or your spouse) sold under a conditional sales contract (see ¶518).

Unlike the GST credit amounts, which can vary from quarter to quarter as circumstances change, adjusted net income is essentially set by the base year, although it should be adjusted to include the income of acquired new spouse or common-law partner or exclude the income of one from whom you are living separate and apart as of the first day of the first month of the calendar quarter on which you have (or have not) a spouse or common-law partner.

[¶1496.40] *Indexing*

The basic credit amounts and the threshold amount are indexed annually, based on changes in the Consumer Price Index (¶1101).

[¶1496.45] *GST Credit Calculation: 2015 Returns*

The following calculation shows the payments you should be entitled to receive in July and October 2016 and January and April 2017, based on your 2015 return.

Basic goods and services tax credit .... Claim $276		1
Calculation of single supplement — If you were not married or not living with your spouse or common-law spouse (¶1113) at the end of the year, and had no qualified dependants at the end of the year, you may claim this credit:		
Income from line 236 of your T1 return		2
Subtract base amount	$ 8,948	3

Income over base amount (if negative, enter zero)			4
Single (non-parent) supplement — Enter 2% of line (4), above, or $145, whichever is less			5
Credit for spouse or common-law partner	Claim $276		6
Qualified dependant credit — If you have no spouse or common-law partner and made an "eligible dependant" claim on line 305	Claim $276		7
Credit for qualified children — Do not include a child claimed on line (7): Number of qualified children ______ × $145			8
Single Parent Supplement — If you were not married or not living with your spouse or common-law partner (¶1113) at the end of the year but you claim any qualified dependants on line 7 or 8	Claim $145		9
Add line (1), (5), (6), (7), (8), and (9)			10
Income from line 236 of your T1 return			11
Income from line 236 of the T1 return of your spouse or common-law partner (even if your spouse or partner need not file)			12
Aggregate net income (total of lines (11) and (12))			13
Subtract base amount	$35,926		14
Income over base amount (if negative, enter zero)			15
Enter 5% of line (15)			16
Goods and services tax credit (line 10) minus line (16)) (if less than $1. enter zero			17
Enter 1/4 of line (17) — This amount will be paid to you in July 2016, October 2016, January 2017, and April 2017 unless you notify the CRA of a change in conditions			18

(If line (17) is less than $200, you will receive the entire amount as your first quarterly credit, and no further instalments.)

(ITA: 122.5; 152(4.2); 164(1.5))

[¶1497] CHILD FITNESS CREDIT — LINE 459

For taxation years 2015 and 2016, the refundable child fitness tax credit replaces the non-refundable child fitness credit, see ¶1356. The child fitness tax credit is discontinued after 2016.

Refundable Child Fitness Tax Credit

For 2016, an individual is entitled to claim a refundable child fitness tax credit calculated at the rate of 15 % on up to $500 ($1,000 for 2015) of eligible fitness expenses incurred for a child who was under 16 at the beginning of the year and was registered in a prescribed program of physical activity. If at least $100 of eligible fitness expenses were incurred for a child who was under 18 at the beginning of the year and qualified for the disability tax credit, the individual is entitled to claim an additional credit of $75, representing an additional $500 worth of expenses.

Calculation

The refundable child fitness tax credit has two components:

- a basic credit of up to $75 ($500 × 15%) for a child under 16 at the beginning of the taxation year;
- an additional credit of $75 for a disabled child under 18 at the beginning of the year for whom the eligible expenses are $100 or more.

Refundability

The child fitness tax credit is fully refundable (even if the taxpayer does not have enough tax payable to cover the full amount of the credit) and is calculated by reference to eligible fitness expenses incurred for children registered in prescribed programs of physical activity. There is no limit on the number of children for which the credit may be claimed.

Claim Period

A taxpayer must claim the credit in the year in which the eligible fitness expenses are paid to a qualifying entity, which is not necessarily the same year in which the child performs the related physical activities.

Multiple Claimants

If more than one person (e.g., two spouses) qualifies for the credit, they must share it between themselves. Otherwise, the CRA will allocate the credit. Under no circumstances, can the combined credit claimed by two persons exceed the one that could be claimed by one person.

Additional Information

The amount you can claim is reduced by any reimbursements, allowances, or other assistance that anyone was entitled to receive in respect of the expenses unless the reimbursements, etc., were included in income of the person entitled to them and were not deducted again in computing taxable income. In short, eligible cost is cost less any reimbursements from any source unless the reimbursements are fully taxable to the recipient.

An eligible fitness expense is a fee paid in respect of a child who is under 16 (18 if disability credit can be claimed) at the beginning of the year to a "qualifying entity" to the extent that the fee is attributable to the cost of registration or membership of the child in a "prescribed program of physical activity".

A fee is specifically said to be eligible to the extent that it represents the cost to the entity of the program for administration, instruction, rental of required facilities, and uniforms and equipment not available to the participant at less than fair market value (apparently this is meant to accommodate team jerseys and equipment used in common). A fee is not eligible to the extent it includes the cost of accommodation, travel, food or beverages, or amounts deductible as child care expenses. Presumably it is up to the organizations to determine eligible expenses and receipt them properly, although there is no compulsion to do this, creating, one imagines, an enforcement nightmare for the CRA.

A qualifying entity is merely one which offers one or more prescribed programs of physical activity. It need not be registered with the CRA, or, apparently, with anyone. You cannot deduct a fee paid to your spouse or common-law partner, or any individual who is under 18 at the time the payment is made. There seems to be nothing to prevent you from paying your older children to provide a prescribed program of physical activity to your younger children.

Obviously, the devil lurks in the details of what is a prescribed program of physical activity. Under current regulations, a prescribed program is a program which is not part of a school's curriculum and is:

1. a weekly program of a duration of eight or more consecutive weeks in which all or substantially all of the activities include a significant amount of physical activity, as defined for these purposes;
2. a program of a duration of five or more consecutive days of which more than 50% of the daily activities include a significant amount of "physical activity" (this would apply to summer and day camp programs);
3. a program offered to children by a club, association, or similar organization (all described as "the organization", below) in circumstances where a participant in the program may select amongst a variety of activities if
   a. more than 50% of those activities offered to children by the organization are activities that include a significant amount of "physical activity", or
   b. more than 50% of the time scheduled for activities offered to children in the program is scheduled for activities that include a significant amount of "physical activity"; or
   c. a membership in an organization of a duration of eight or more consecutive weeks if more than 50% of all the activities offered to children by the organization include a significant amount of "physical activity".

"Physical activity" in the definition above means a supervised activity suitable for children other than an activity of which an essential component involves the child riding in or on a motorized vehicle. (This is intended to exclude snowmobiling but permit water skiing.) In general, it must be an activity that contributes to cardio-respiratory endurance, plus one or more of muscular strength, muscular endurance, flexibility, and balance. (Horseback riding is specifically defined to be such an activity.) However, in the case of a disabled child (one for whom a disability credit can be claimed), it is sufficient that the activity results in movement and an observable expenditure of energy in a recreational context.

Where a program is not a prescribed program of physical activity because it does not meet the 50% requirement set out in (3), above, a special rule allows you to claim a portion of the amount that is paid for the program. In such circumstances, a portion of the program is considered a prescribed program of physical activity. That portion is either:

- the percentage of those activities offered to children by the organization that are activities that include a significant amount of physical activity, or
- the percentage of the time scheduled for activities in the program that is scheduled for activities that include a significant amount of physical activity.

Example

Sabrina's mother pays $200 for the registration of her daughter at a community centre. The portion of the activities offered to children by the centre that qualify as physical activity for the purpose of the credit is 40%. Therefore, only 40% of the program will be considered a prescribed program of physical activity and Sabrina's mother may claim, as a child fitness amount, 40% of $200, i.e., $80.

Where a membership in an organization does not meet the 50% activities requirement in (3), above, the portion of the expense that will be an eligible amount for fitness credit purposes is the portion of the activities offered to children by the organization that are activities that include a significant amount of physical activity.

As well, the CRA has noticed that the same expenditure might qualify for both child care expense deduction (¶1049) and fitness credit. The T1 Guide says that such expenses should be attributed to child care first, with any excess eligible for fitness credit. There actually appears to be no such ordering provision in the Income Tax Act, but the CRA position would seem to be beneficial in most situations. However, it may be more accurate to say that the taxpayer can claim such expenses in the most beneficial way.

If an expense is eligible for the children's fitness amount, it is not eligible for the children's art amount.

Where there are two distinct prescribed programs, one eligible for the children's fitness amount and the other for the children's arts amount, there should be two receipts, or one receipt that indicated the amounts paid for each distinct program.

(ITA: 122.8)

[¶1497a] ELIGIBLE EDUCATOR SCHOOL SUPPLY TAX CREDIT — LINE 469

Budget 2016 introduced a teacher and early childhood educator school supply tax credit for 2016 and subsequent taxation years. This measure will allow an employee who is an eligible educator to claim a 15% refundable tax credit based on an amount of up to $1,000 of purchases of eligible teaching supplies by the employee in a taxation year. Therefore, the maximum tax credit is $150 per year.

Eligible educator

You are considered an eligible educator if you were employed in Canada at any time during the taxation year as

- a teacher at an elementary or secondary school, or an early childhood educator at a regulated child care facility; and
- you held a certificate, license, permit or diploma in teaching or early childhood education, which was valid and recognized in the province or territory in which you were employed

Eligible supplies expenses

An eligible supplies expense is an amount that you paid during the taxation year for teaching supplies that meet all of the following conditions:

- you bought the teaching supplies for teaching or facilitating students' learning;
- the teaching supplies were directly consumed or used in an elementary or secondary school or in a regulated child care facility in the performance of your employment;

- you were not entitled to a reimbursement, allowance, or any other form of assistance for the expenses (other than an amount included in your income for any tax year which is not deductible in the calculation of your taxable income); and
- the eligible supplies expense was not deducted from any person's income for any year or included in calculating a deduction from any person's tax payable for any year.

Teaching supplies are consumable supplies and prescribed durable goods. Prescribed durable goods are:

- books, games and puzzles;
- containers (such as plastic boxes or banker boxes); and
- educational support software.

How to claim the credit

You must enter the total of the expenses for the eligible educator school supply tax credit on line 468. The refundable credit of 15% is entered on line 469 of the return.

Supporting documents must be kept in case the CRA ask to see them later. The CRA may also ask you at a later date to provide a written certificate from your employer, or a delegated official of the employer, attesting of the eligibility of the expenses.

(ITA: 122.9; ITR: 9600 Prescribed durable goods)

[¶1498] CANADA CHILD BENEFIT

Overview

The Canada Child Benefit ("CCB") provides a tax-free monthly payment to the custodial parent (usually the mother) of children (described as "qualified dependants") who are under the age of 18. Strictly speaking, the CCB is not really part of the income tax system at all, since any amounts received are not taxed as income. As well, income arising from CCB payments saved and invested in the name of the child or children is not subject to the income splitting rules described at ¶2529. The CCB is, however, income-tested so the family income you report on your tax returns is used to calculate the amount of the benefit.

The system operates on a time lag basis, so that the benefit payable for the first half of the year (i.e., January to June inclusive) is based on the adjusted income (defined at ¶1498.10) of the custodial parent and his or her spouse or common-law partner (the "parents") in the second preceding tax year (the base year), and the benefit payable in the months July through December is based on that income in the immediately preceding year. Therefore, in 2016, Canada child benefits payable for the months January through June 2016 were based on 2014 income. Payments for the months of July through December 2016 were based on 2015 income.

Eligibility

The CCB is only paid to an "eligible individual" with respect to one or more "qualified dependants." In order to be a qualified dependant, the child must be under the age of 18. An eligible individual must be a person who resides with the qualified dependant, is the parent of the qualified dependant who primarily fulfills the responsibility for care and upbringing, and is resident in Canada.

Generally, you must be a Canadian citizen to be considered an eligible individual. However, individuals granted a certain immigrant or refugee status are also eligible. Effective July 1, 2016, individuals who are considered Indians within the meaning of the *Indian Act* are eligible too; this provides child benefits to Indians who are not Canadian citizens.

An eligible individual also includes a shared custody parent, so two eligible individuals who primarily fulfill the responsibility for care and upbringing of a qualified dependant can each receive 50% of the CCB. A "shared custody parent" is one of the two parents of the qualified dependant who is not a cohabiting spouse or common-law partner and who resides with the qualified dependant on an equal or near equal basis.

Note that the CRA provided, at the time of writing, a useful guide called Canada Child Benefits (T4114) that describes the Quebec variations of child benefits, since the program is not uniform across the country. All provinces and territories except Quebec, Manitoba, and Saskatchewan provide more or less parallel child tax benefits administered by the CRA; these are described in Chapter 15. Quebec provides a far more complex program of family assistance payments through its own government agencies.

[¶1498.01] *Computing the CCB Amount*

The CCB is computed and paid on a monthly basis. It is actually the sum of three components each with its own base benefit and income-tested phase out limits: (1) the basic CCB amount, (2) the national child benefit supplement ("NCBS"), and (3) the Child Disability Benefit ("CDB"). When computing the total monthly entitlement, each component is calculated on an annual basis, aggregated, and the result is divided by 12 to arrive at the final amount payable for that month. Note that the CCB is a new amount, which replaced the Canada Child Tax Benefit ("CCTB"). Historical information on the computation of the CCTB can be found below at ¶1498.02. The CCB began in July 2016. Unlike the previous CCTB, the benefit and phase-out dollar amounts used in the computation of the CCB are not indexed to inflation.

Commentary on Bill C-29 Measures (Oct. 25, 2016)

Note: When Bill C-29, October 25, 2016, achieves Royal Assent, the commentary will be modified to read:

Applicable to the payment period beginning in July 2020, the base amounts and dollar limits used in computing the CCB are indexed to inflation.

The Basic CCB Amount

Determining the basic CCB amount is a two-step calculation. First, the base amount is calculated using the number of qualified dependants and their age. Second, the base amount is reduced by a phase-out amount that is dependent on the family's adjusted income. The base amount is the sum of:

$6,400 multiplied by the number of qualified dependants in respect of the eligible individual who have not yet reached the age of six at the beginning of the month; plus

$5,400 multiplied by the number of qualified dependants in respect of the eligible individual who do not fall into the previous category (i.e., dependants between the ages of six and 17).

To arrive at the CCB payment, the base amount is then reduced by the phase-out amount. The phase-out begins where adjusted income exceeds $30,000. The reduction equals the amount by which adjusted income exceeds $30,000 multiplied by a specified percentage. Another set of phase-out rates apply to the amount by which adjusted income exceeds $65,000. The phase-out rates also depend on the number of qualified dependants in the family. These phase-out rates are provided in the chart below.

Number of Qualified Dependants	Adjusted Income	
	$30,000 - $65,000	Over $65,000
1 child	7.0%	3.2%
2 children	13.5%	5.7%
3 children	19.0%	8.0%
4 or more children	23.0%	9.5%

Take for example, a family with an adjusted income of $60,000 and two children aged one and four. The base amount would be $12,800 ($6,400 × 2), but this amount would be reduced by a phase-out amount of $4,050 ((60,000 – 30,000) × 13.5%) resulting in an annual entitlement to a CCB of $8,750 which would be paid out as $729 per month.

National Child Benefit Supplement

This component was available in the years prior to the introduction of the CCB. After its final payment on June 20, 2017, the NCBS will be repealed. For its final payment period from July 2016 through June 2017, the annual benefit amounts are as follows:

(1) for one qualified dependant, the benefit is $2,308, reduced by 12.2% of the amount by which the adjusted income for 2015 exceeds $26,364;

(2) for two qualified dependants, the benefit is $2,308 for the first child plus $2,042 for the second child, reduced by 23% of the amount by which adjusted income for 2015 exceeds $26,364; and

(3) for three or more qualified dependants, the benefit is $2,308 for the first child, $2,042 for the second child, plus $1,943 for each additional child, reduced by 33.3% of the amount by which adjusted income for 2015 exceeds $26,364

Child Disability Benefit

The third component is the CDB, which has been available since July 2003. The CDB is paid for each qualified dependant that is eligible for the disability tax credit. Like the CCB, the CDB is subject to an income-tested phase-out where adjusted income exceeds specific dollar limit. The 2016 federal Budget amended these rates and dollar limits.

For the payment period from July 2016 through June 2017 and all subsequent periods, the CDB provides $2,730 per qualified dependant per year to the eligible individual. Where adjusted income for 2015 exceeds $65,000, the CDB is reduced by the excess income multiplied by the specified phase-out percentage. Where the CDB is claimed for a single qualified dependant, the phase-out rate is 3.2%. Where the eligible individual receives the CDB with respect to two or more qualified dependants, the phase-out rate is 5.7%.

As mentioned previously, once the CCB, NCBS, and CDB are individually computed, they are aggregated and the result is divided by 12 to arrive at the monthly payment amount.

Commentary on Bill C-29 Measures (Oct. 25, 2016)

Commentary on Bill C-29 Measures (Oct. 25, 2016)

Note: When Bill C-29, October 25, 2016, achieves Royal Assent, the commentary will be modified to read:

Applicable to the payment period beginning in July 2020, the base amounts and dollar limits used in computing the CDB are indexed to inflation.

[¶1498.02] *Historical Information — Canada Child Tax Benefit Amount*

The final CCTB payment occurred on June 20, 2016. For historical reference, computation information for the final payment period is provided here. These amounts were indexed annually to inflation. The annual CCTB basic benefit for the final period from July 2015 to June 2016 was equal to:

(A) the base amount, which was $1,471 per child for each of the first two children and an additional $103 for each of the third and subsequent children; minus

(B) the phase-out amount, which was 4% (or 2% in the case of only one child) of the amount by which adjusted income for 2014 exceeded $44,701. The NCBS and CDB (which remain effective and are discussed at ¶1498.01) were the second and third components and were paid in tandem with the CCTB.

(ITA: 122.6 Definitions)

[¶1498.04] *Applying for Benefits*

There are several methods to apply for the child benefits. First, you can apply using the online service "Apply for child benefits" under My Account on the CRA website. Second, you can complete and submit CRA Form RC66, Canada Child Benefits Application. Third, if you are the mother of a newborn and live in a province that offers the Automated Benefits Application Service, you may use this service to apply for all child-related benefits simultaneously. All the provinces are offering this service, but Yukon, Northwest Territories, and Nunavut are currently not participating. Within 80 calendar days, a notice will be issued to the applicant that confirms how much you will receive.

(RC66; T4114)

[¶1498.05] *Filing Requirements*

It is essential to the operation of this system that, unless the parent claiming the CCB is a single parent, both that parent and his or her spouse file tax returns for the year. This awkward formulation is necessary to cover the case of a spouse living with someone other than the other parent of the child. The definition of spouse for tax purposes includes a common-law partner as defined at ¶1113.

If your spouse or common-law partner is a non-resident of Canada during any part of the year, you must complete form CTB9, Canada Child Benefit — Statement of Income, for each year or part of a year that he or she is a non-resident of Canada.

The system deals with separation of the parents by providing that the custodial parent notify the CRA in prescribed form before the end of the first calendar month of separation. The prescribed form is RC65 — Marital Status Change. Separation is deemed to occur when the spouses commence living separate and apart by reason of marriage breakdown and the separation lasts at least 90 days. This rule applies equally to legal and common-law marriages. For this reason, the CCB rule that defines a "cohabiting spouse" is used elsewhere in the *Income Tax Act* where the drafters want to deal with the situation of *de facto* separations of legal as well as common-law marriages.

In cases of separation or divorce, both parents may share more or less equally in the care and upbringing of a child. In such shared custody situations, each parent is eligible to receive their half of the amount they are entitled to receive on a monthly basis.

The section of the Act which pertains to the CCB also allows individual provinces to modify, to an extent, the benefit paid to residents of that province, by modifying the amounts paid on the basis of the age or number, or both, of qualified dependants, as long as the modified amount is at least 85% of the amount which would otherwise have been paid. The provinces of Alberta and Quebec have elected to modify the payments, Alberta on the basis of age and Quebec on the basis of age and family size.

The legislation imposes on taxpayers a requirement to notify the CRA when a child becomes eligible or ceases to be eligible for the CCB. Where eligibility ceases only by reason of the fact that a child has turned 18, no special notification is required to terminate payments.

In the event of the death of a spouse or common-law partner, an election can be made to ignore the income of the deceased spouse for the purpose of computing the Canada Child Benefit in subsequent months. The CRA should be notified within one month of the date of death. A similar election is available where there is a marriage breakdown, and the spouses have lived separate and apart for a period of at least 90 days.

Where two taxpayers become cohabiting spouses, they may jointly elect to be so treated from the end of the relevant base taxation year.

(ITA: 122.61; 122.62; 257)

[¶1498.10] *Adjusted Income and Net Family Income*

The definition of "adjusted income" for purposes of the CCB calculation is increasingly used by other federal provisions and by provincial tax laws for a number of purposes. For example, the federal government uses it in the refundable medical expense supplement (¶1237), and Manitoba uses it in calculating tax credits for low-income families (¶1530). So an explanation may be useful.

The CRA and most provincial revenue authorities refer to adjusted income as "net family income", presumably because they find that this makes it clear that it may include the income of someone in addition to that of the person filing the return. We follow the statute here and use the term adjusted income, but net family income usually means exactly the same thing (unless the CRA or another authority has appropriated the term for a particular purpose).

Your adjusted income for a particular taxation year is the total of all income amounts for the year of both you and your "cohabiting spouse or common-law partner" provided you and your partner were cohabiting at the end of that taxation year. If you were not cohabiting at the end of the year, only your income is included in adjusted income.

A cohabiting spouse or common-law partner at any particular time is in turn defined as a person who is your spouse or common-law spouse or partner (as defined in ¶1113) at that time, and who is not living separate and apart from you at that time. A couple are only considered to be living separate and apart if the separation is due to a breakdown of the marriage (or relationship) for a period of at least 90 days that includes that time. It follows that you are considered to be living with your spouse at December 31 unless on that day you were separated by reason of a marriage breakdown which in fact lasted for at least 90 days.

Example

> Jim and Jeanne were living together for several years but separated on December 1, 2015. They reconciled and resumed living together on February 1, 2016. They are presumed to have been common-law partners on December 31, 2015, because the separation lasted less than 90 days. The same result would have obtained if they had been legally married and separated on December 1 but reconciled on February 1. It follows that the adjusted income of each of them for 2015 must include the income of both. If the separation had commenced December 1 and lasted at least 90 days, they would be considered separated on December 31, and neither would include the income of the other in adjusted income.

Income for these purposes is usually net income from line 236. Where one spouse (or both) need not file a return because no tax is payable, it is necessary to complete a return up to line 236 for the non-filing spouse to obtain the necessary information. For some purposes, such as the CCB, if the spouses are cohabiting it is essential for both to file completed returns to obtain the benefits. In other cases, such as the refundable medical expense supplement, it is only necessary for one spouse to file, but the return must contain accurate income information for the other cohabiting spouse as if a return for that spouse had been completed at least to line 236.

Although in most cases adjusted income is net income from line 236, there are exceptions:

- because the *Income Tax Act* distinguishes income from losses, negative income (loss) of one spouse does not reduce the income of the other;
- income does not include any amounts received under the former universal child care benefit (¶935), nor is it reduced by any required repayments of that benefit; and
- income does not include any gain in the year arising under the rules at ¶518 on property you (or your spouse, etc.) reacquired by foreclosing on a mortgage or repossessing property sold under a conditional sales contract.

In *Lawin v. The Queen*, 2006 DTC 2768 (T.C.C.), a spouse whose husband had a stroke and was confined to a long-term care facility took the position that they were no longer cohabiting spouses obliged to meld their net incomes. The Court had no difficulty in finding, on the facts of the case (which included daily visits by the spouse to her husband), that they were not separated by reason of marital breakdown but by reason of mental and physical impairment. The case, which was argued without counsel under informal procedure, stands for little beyond the fact that the CRA is taking the expected view of the nature of separation by reason of marital breakdown.

In *Thorpe v. The Queen*, 2007 DTC 1383 (T.C.C.), the Tax Court ruled that where a husband was resident in the U.S. throughout the year, his income was not included in net family income, even though he and his wife were not separated and he visited her regularly at her home in Canada. With respect, the result is not as obvious as it seemed to the Court. The case was heard under informal procedure rules, which means it is not binding on the CRA; nor is it likely to be accepted by the CRA. However, it is a precedent of sorts.

(ITA: 3; 122.6 "adjusted income")

[¶1498.11] *Applying for Retroactive Benefits*

Generally, notice to the Minister of one's eligibility, to be made within 11 months after the end of the first eligible month, is required before the CCB will be paid. However, the time period for making this notice can be extended, or the requirement waived altogether by the Minister. However, the 2016 federal Budget amended this deadline. Applicable to requests made after June 2016, the deadline for a retroactive request for the payment with respect to a specific month will be the day that is 10 years after that month began.

For example, a taxpayer would have been eligible for the CCTB for the month of September 2008 (among other months), but did not apply for benefits and hence did not receive them. In order to receive a retroactive payment, the taxpayer must apply by September 1, 2018.

[¶1498.15] *Informing the CRA of Changes*

As noted above, it is essential to the operation of the child benefit system that you inform the CRA as early as possible of relevant changes in your situation, as well as the date they happened or will happen. Relevant changes include:

- if a child for whom you were receiving the benefit is no longer in your care, stops living with you, or dies, call 1-800-387-1193 to inform the CRA;
- if you move, inform the CRA immediately. You can inform the CRA of a change of your address by using their online service, My Account, at www.cra.gc.ca/myaccount, calling 1-800-387-1193, or sending a letter to one of the taxation centres listed at ¶218 (preferably the one with which you filed your last return, but any one should be able to cope);
- if your marital status changes, complete form RC65, Marital Status Change, or tell the CRA in a letter of your new status and the date of the change. If you are now married or living common law, also include your spouse or common-law partner's name, address, and social insurance number. You and your spouse or common-law partner must sign the form or letter within one month of the date of change. Send the form or letter to one of the taxation centres listed at ¶218;
- if a CCTB recipient dies, the next of kin or the estate should inform the CRA as soon as possible. Someone else may be eligible to get the benefits for the child. Call 1-800-387-1193 or send a letter to one of the taxation centres listed at ¶218.

Chapter 15

How To Calculate Your Provincial Tax

THESE POINTS ARE COVERED IN THIS CHAPTER

CRA REFERENCES RELATING TO THIS CHAPTER

T1 Lines and Schedules

- Line 479 — Provincial or territorial credits

CRA Guides

5001-PC, "Information for Residents of Newfoundland and Labrador"; **5002-PC**, "Information for Residents of Prince Edward Island"; **5003-PC**, "Information for Residents of Nova Scotia"; **5004-PC**, "Information for Residents of New Brunswick"; **5006-PC**, "Information for Residents of Ontario"; **5007-PC**, "Information for Residents of Manitoba"; **5008-PC**, "Information for Residents of Saskatchewan"; **5009-PC**, "Information for Residents of Alberta"; **5010-PC**, "Information for Residents of British Columbia"; **5011-PC**, "Information for Residents of the Yukon"; **5012-PC**, "Information for Residents of the Northwest Territories"; **5014-PC**, "Information for Residents of Nunavut"; **T4114**, "Canada Child Benefits (including related federal, provincial, and territorial programs)"; **RC4210**, "GST/HST Credit (including related provincial credits and benefits)"

CRA Forms

AB428, "Alberta Tax and Credits"; **BC428**, "British Columbia Tax"; **BC479**, "British Columbia Credits"; **MB428**, "Manitoba Tax"; **MB428-A**, "Manitoba Family Tax Benefit"; **MB479**, "Manitoba Credits"; **NB428**, "New Brunswick Tax and Credits"; **NB (S12)**, "New Brunswick Seniors' Home Renovation Tax Credit"; **NL428**, "Newfoundland and Labrador Tax and Credits"; **NS428**, "Nova Scotia Tax and Credits"; **NT428**, "Northwest Territories Tax"; **NT479**, "Northwest Territories Credits"; **NU428**, "Nunavut Tax"; **NU479**, "Nunavut Credits"; **ON428**, "Ontario Tax"; **ON479**, "Ontario Credits"; **ON(S12)**, "Ontario Healthy Home Renovation Tax Credit"; **ON-BEN**, "Application for the Ontario Trillium Benefit and the Ontario Senior Homeowners' Property Tax Grant"; **PE428**, "Prince Edward Island Tax and Credits"; **RC360**, "Saskatchewan Graduate Retention Program"; **SK428**, "Saskatchewan Tax and Credits"; **T1 General**, "Income Tax and Benefit Return"; **T88**, "British Columbia Mining Exploration Tax Credit (Individuals)"; **T691**, "Alternative Minimum Tax"; **T1005**, "Manitoba Tuition Fee Income Tax Rebate"; **T1014**, "British Columbia Training Tax Credit (individuals)"; **T1014-1**, "British Columbia Training Tax Credit (employers)"; **T1014-2**, "British Columbia Shipbuilding and Ship Repair Industry Tax Credit (employers)"; **T1129**, "Newfoundland and Labrador Research and Development Tax Credit (Individuals)"; **T1206**, "Tax on Split Income"; **T1221**, "Ontario Focused Flow-Through Share Resource Expenses (Individuals)"; **T1231**, "British Columbia Mining Flow-Through Share Tax Credit"; **T1232**, "Yukon Research and Development Tax Credit (Individuals)"; **T1237**, "Saskatchewan Farm and Small Business Capital Gains Tax Credit"; **T1241**, "Manitoba Mineral Exploration Tax Credit"; **T1256**, "Manitoba Community Enterprise Development Tax Credit"; **T1256-1**, "Manitoba Small Business Venture Capital Tax Credit (Individuals)"; **T1256-2**, "Manitoba Employee Share Purchase Tax Credit"; **T1258**, "New Brunswick Small Business Investor Tax Credit"; **T1272**, "Newfoundland and Labrador Equity Tax Credit"; **T1284**, "Saskatchewan Employee's Tools Tax Credit"; **T1285**, "Nova Scotia Equity Tax Credit"; **T1297**, "Newfoundland and Labrador Resort Property Investment Tax Credit (Individuals)"; **T1299**, "Manitoba Book Publishing Tax Credit (Individuals)"; **T2036**, "Provincial or Territorial Foreign Tax Credit"; **T2038 (IND)**, "Investment Tax Credit (Individuals)"; **T2202**, "Education and Textbook Amounts Certificate"; **T2203**, "Provincial and Territorial Taxes — Multiple Jurisdictions";

T2209, "Federal Foreign Tax Credits"; **T4164**, "Manitoba Odour-Control Tax Credit (Individuals)"; **YT428**, "Yukon Tax"; **YT479**, "Yukon Credits"; **YT432**, "Yukon First Nations Tax"

Income Tax Folios

Income Tax Folio **S5-F1-C1**, "Determining an Individual's Residence Status"

WHAT YOU SHOULD KNOW ABOUT CALCULATING YOUR PROVINCIAL TAX

RECENT CHANGES

Alberta

In the 2016 budget, the government announced it is maintaining the dividend tax credit rate (¶1510.12) at 10% for eligible dividends, but for non-eligible dividends the rate will decrease to 2.2% in 2017 (this is a result of lowering the small business rate to 2%, effective January 1, 2017; the rate was previously 3.08%).

Beginning in July 2016, the refundable family employment tax credit (¶1511c) was enhanced: the rate at which benefits are phased in will increase from 8% to 11%, and the phase-out threshold will increase from $36,778 to $41,250.

The Alberta child benefit (¶1511d) is a new program that began in July 2016. The program provides families with an annual benefit of up to $1,100 for one child, with a further $550 for each additional child (for a maximum of $2,750, or four children per family). The benefit and related amounts are indexed annually.

To offset the impact of Alberta's new carbon levy, carbon rebates (¶1511e) will be provided to lower- and middle-income Albertans starting in 2017.

British Columbia

The sixth individual income tax rate has been eliminated effective 2016 (¶1518.05).

In 2016, the B.C. dividend tax credit for non-eligible dividends (¶1518.05) is 2.47% (down from 2.59%).

Effective for the 2016 tax year, the B.C. tax reduction credit (¶1518.10) phase-out threshold is increased to $19,400 from $19,000. The credit phase-out rate is also increased to 3.56% from 3.5%.

Effective February 17, 2016, a new non-refundable farmers' food donation tax credit (¶1522a) was introduced. The credit is available to individuals and corporations that carry on the business of farming and donate a qualifying agricultural product to a registered charity that provides food to those in need or helps to operate a school meal program. The credit is worth 25% of the fair market value of the qualifying agricultural product.

Effective for the 2016 tax year and thereafter, the B.C. seniors' home renovation tax credit (¶1521g) is expanded to include persons with disabilities who are eligible to claim the federal disability tax credit.

The B.C. mining flow-through share tax credit (¶1526) is extended to the end of 2016 and the mining exploration tax credit (¶1525) is extended for an additional three years to the end of 2019.

The B.C. training and education savings grant (¶1521m) has been extended to children born on or after January 1, 2006.

The B.C. overseas employment tax credit has been eliminated.

Manitoba

The seniors' school tax rebate (¶1531a) is now claimed through the income tax system rather than by direct application to Manitoba Finance.

The Manitoba overseas employment tax credit has been eliminated.

Rates were revised for certain components of the paid work experience tax credit (¶1537).

The small business venture capital tax credit (¶1535e) has been extended until December 31, 2019.

New Brunswick

New Brunswick's tax rate on taxable income over $150,000 has decreased to 20.3%. The sixth tax bracket for taxable income over $250,000 has been eliminated (¶1540.05).

Income levels for the lowest four tax brackets (¶1540.05), many personal, non-refundable credit amounts (¶52), and low-income tax reduction amounts (¶1540.10) have been indexed for 2016.

The small business investor tax credit (¶1543d) is available for investments in community economic development funds as of April 1, 2016.

New Brunswick's dividend tax credit rate (¶1540.07) for eligible dividends has increased to 13.5% and the rate for non-eligible dividends has decreased to 3.625% for dividends received in 2016.

New Brunswick introduced a new harmonized sales tax credit (¶1544a).

The New Brunswick overseas employment tax credit has been eliminated.

Newfoundland and Labrador

The income level tax brackets, most provincial non-refundable tax credits, and the low-income tax reduction have changed.

Personal income tax rates have increased for all income brackets (¶1545.05).

Newfoundland and Labrador introduced a temporary deficit reduction levy (¶1545.20), payable by all individuals with taxable income in excess of $50,000.

The dividend tax credit rate (¶1545.10) for non-eligible dividends decreased from 4.1% to 3.5% for dividends received after June 30, 2016.

The low income seniors' benefit (¶1548.10) increased from $1,063 per year to $1,313.

The Harmonized Sales Tax Credit (¶1548.05) has been renamed to the Newfoundland and Labrador income supplement and will now be paid on a quarterly basis.

Northwest Territories

While not effective until 2017, the Northwest Territories child benefit (¶1552k) will be enhanced, including different benefit amounts for children under and over the age of six.

The Northwest Territories overseas employment tax credit has been eliminated.

Nova Scotia

There is a new non-refundable food bank tax credit for farmers (¶1557) who donate agricultural products to eligible food banks.

Nova Scotia's dividend tax credit rate (¶1553.10) for non-eligible dividends was reduced from 3.5% to 3.33%.

The Nova Scotia overseas employment tax credit has been eliminated.

Nunavut

In 2016, the Nunavut dividend tax credit for non-eligible dividends is 2.91% (down from 3.05%).

The Nunavut overseas employment tax credit has been eliminated.

Ontario

Income thresholds for tax brackets (¶1564.05), surtax thresholds (¶1564.15), many personal non-refundable tax credits (¶52), Ontario tax reduction amounts (¶1565), the energy and property tax credit (¶1567.05), the northern Ontario energy credit (¶1567c), the sales tax credit (¶1568), and the children's activity credit (¶1568e) have all been indexed for 2016.

Ontario's dividend tax credit rate (¶1564.07) for non-eligible dividends was reduced from 4.5% to 4.2863%.

The Ontario overseas employment tax credit has been eliminated.

Prince Edward Island

The maximum PEI sales tax credit (¶1579c) increased from $200 to $220, effective July 1, 2016. The basic credit amount increased from $100 to $110 and the spouse or common-law partner, eligible dependant, and supplement amounts each increased from $50 to $55.

Several changes were made to the low income tax reduction (¶1577.20) for 2016 and subsequent years. The amounts for an individual and for a spouse, common law partner or eligible dependant each increased from $300 to $350, while the tax reduction amount for each dependent child increased from $250 to $300.

The following personal non-refundable tax credits (¶¶1577.07) were increased for 2016 and subsequent years: the basic personal exemption increased from $7,708 to $8,000; the spouse or common-law partner amount increased from $6,546 to $6,795; and the eligible dependant amount increased from $6,294 to $6,795.

P.E.I.'s dividend tax credit rate (¶1577.07) for non-eligible dividends was reduced from 3.2% to 3.05%.

The P.E.I. overseas employment tax credit has been eliminated.

Quebec

Quebec — see Chapter 16.

Saskatchewan

The Active Families Benefit (¶1584f) has been eliminated, effective January 1, 2016.

Saskatchewan's dividend tax credit rate (¶1581.10) for non-eligible dividends was reduced from 3.4% to 3.367%.

The Graduate Retention Program First Home Plan allows eligible graduates to borrow up to $10,000 of their future graduate tuition tax credits (¶1584) as an interest-free loan towards the down payment on their first home in Saskatchewan.

The Saskatchewan overseas employment tax credit has been eliminated.

Income thresholds for tax brackets (¶1581), personal non-refundable credit amounts (¶52), and low-income tax credit amounts (¶1591.10) have been indexed for 2016.

Yukon

The Premier announced that his government would maintain, for 2017 and beyond, the territorial portion of the children's fitness tax credit (¶1596g) and the children's arts tax credit (¶1596h), which were eliminated in the 2016 Federal Budget for taxation years after 2016.

In 2016, the Yukon dividend tax credit for non-eligible dividends is 3.14% (down slightly from 3.17%).

The Yukon overseas employment tax credit has been eliminated.

Beginning in 2016, the calculation of the Yukon political contribution tax credit has changed to match the federal calculation.

[¶1501] PROVINCIAL AND TERRITORIAL TAX SYSTEMS

With the exception of Quebec (Chapter 16), all provinces and territories of Canada have tax collection agreements with the federal government under which personal income taxes are collected by the federal government. This system has advantages for individual taxpayers, in that the calculation of income is the same throughout Canada, and only one set of annual tax return forms needs to be filed (except in Quebec).

Under this tax collection agreement system, each provincial government levies provincial taxes directly on taxable income determined under federal income tax rules (determined at line 260 of the T1 return). However, each province and territory sets its own tax brackets and tax rates for provincial or territorial income tax purposes. Moreover, each province or territory offers its own tax credits.

All provinces and territories offer select personal tax credits similar to the federal non-refundable credits. Although eligibility criteria for these credits often mirror federal requirements, provincial or territorial credit amounts generally differ from federal credit amounts, and are converted to tax credits at provincial tax rates. Many federal tax credits introduced in more recent years have only been picked up selectively by certain provinces and territories. Each jurisdiction also offers additional provincial- or territorial-specific credits, many of which are refundable.

With the exception of Quebec, provincial or territorial tax payable (or refundable) is calculated on schedules accompanying the annual T1 tax return. Tax is collected or administered by the CRA, along with federal income tax.

This provincial tax system has been dubbed TONI ("Tax on Net Income"). All provinces and territories except Quebec have adopted this system for determination and collection of personal income tax.

For a chart of current year provincial and territorial tax rates, see ¶50.

[¶1501.05] *Provincial and Territorial Tax Credits*

All provinces and territories offer select personal tax credits similar to federal personal non-refundable amounts, although actual credit amounts and rates differ across jurisdictions. (For a chart of current year credit amounts, see ¶52.)

All provinces and territories except Quebec that have entered into tax collection agreements with the federal government offer the personal tax credits package that was in effect in 1999, when the agreements were implemented. These include the following credits:

- basic personal amount;
- spouse or common-law partner amount;
- eligible dependant amount;
- disability amount and supplement;
- age amount;
- infirm dependant amount;
- caregiver amount;
- medical expense amount;
- pension income amount;
- CPP/QPP and EI contribution amounts;
- tuition and education amounts (the federal education and textbook credits are repealed effective January 1, 2017); and
- interest on student loan amount.

Federal credits introduced subsequent to this time have only selectively been picked up for provincial or territorial tax purposes. A summary of these credits and provincial tax applications (with the exception of Quebec) is as follows.

Adoption Credit

In 2005, the federal government introduced an adoption expenses credit (¶1357). In 2014, the government's Economic Action Plan increased this credit to a maximum of $15,000, indexed for subsequent years. The amount for 2016 is $15,453.

Alberta, Newfoundland and Labrador, and Ontario also adopted the credit in 2005. In 2006, Manitoba and the Yukon adopted the credit. British Columbia adopted the credit in 2007. These provinces and territories have adopted their own versions and maximums for this credit.

Transit Pass Credit

In 2006, the federal government introduced a transit pass credit (¶1353). Only the Yukon followed this initiative for 2006 and later years.

Employment Income Credit

In 2006, the federal government introduced a credit for the first $1,000 of employment income, indexed annually (¶1351). The amount for 2016 is $1,161. Only the Yukon followed this initiative for 2006 and later years.

Child Fitness Credit

In 2007, the federal government introduced a non-refundable child fitness credit (¶1356) which was changed to a refundable credit in 2015 (and will be discontinued after 2016). A number of provinces have adopted similar fitness credits, but with variation in credit terms and at differing effective dates. Manitoba and the Yukon adopted this credit for 2007 and later years, but only the Yukon adopted the federal change to a refundable credit in 2015. Unlike the federal government, the Yukon decided to maintain the credit after 2016. Saskatchewan provided a similar refundable active families benefit from 2009 to 2015 (¶1584f), but it has been eliminated. Similarly, Ontario offers a refundable children's activity credit, for 2010 to 2016 (¶1568e). Nova Scotia introduced its own version of such a credit back in 2005, prior to the adoption of the federal credit, but it was eliminated in 2015 (¶1554c). British Columbia introduced a children's fitness credit in 2012 and a children's fitness equipment amount and education coaching credit in 2015.

In 2014, the federal government doubled the amount of the credit to a maximum of $1,000. The limit on eligible expenses was decreased to $500 for the 2016 taxation year; it is eliminated for 2017 and thereafter. For 2016, the amount of the credit for disabled children under the age of 18 will be $1,000 as long as you paid at least $100 of eligible expenses in the year.

Credit for Each Child under 18

In 2007, the federal government introduced a new personal amount of $2,000 per child under 18 at the end of the year, indexed annually (¶1124). The Yukon followed this initiative from 2007 to 2015. Saskatchewan offers its own version of a dependent child credit. Nunavut has a personal non-refundable amount of $1,200 per child for children under six but no credit for children between six and 18.

Working Income Tax Benefit (WITB)

In 2007, the federal government introduced a refundable credit for low-income families (¶1495). Although strictly a federal payment, the WITB provisions allow the federal Minister of Finance to vary the terms of the benefit, by agreement with a province or territory, to better harmonize with a local benefit system. Where there is such an agreement, there will be a unique version of Schedule 6 included in the T1 package for residents of that jurisdiction.

First-Time Home Buyer's Tax Credit (FTHBTC)

In 2009, the federal government introduced a non-refundable income tax credit for first-time home buyers (¶1359). In 2012, British Columbia and Saskatchewan adopted similar first-time homebuyer credits. The B.C. credit has now expired.

Children's Arts Tax Credit

In 2011, the federal government introduced a non-refundable children's arts tax credit (¶1356a) (which is discontinued as of 2017). This initiative was followed by Manitoba for 2011 and the Yukon for 2012. Unlike the federal government, the Yukon decided to maintain the credit after 2016. Saskatchewan and Ontario already provided provincial versions of similar refundable credits: the Saskatchewan active families benefit, was effective from 2009 to 2016(¶1584f), and the Ontario children's activity credit, effective from 2010 to 2016 (¶1568e). British Columbia has adopted this credit for 2012 and later years.

Volunteer Firefighters Credit

In 2011, the federal government introduced a non-refundable volunteer firefighters credit (¶1360). This initiative was followed by Newfoundland and Labrador in 2011. Nova Scotia already provided a provincial version of a refundable tax credit for volunteer firefighters, effective from 2007

(¶1559). Prince Edward Island has adopted a refundable version of this credit for 2012 and later years (¶1579b). Nunavut provides a provincial version of a non-refundable volunteer firefighters tax credit (¶1562k). Manitoba adopted the volunteer firefighter tax credit in 2015 (¶1528.07).

Search and Rescue Volunteers Tax Credit

In 2014, the federal government introduced a non-refundable tax credit for search and rescue volunteers similar to the volunteer firefighters credit. This credit can only be claimed if the individual has performed at least 200 hours of qualifying volunteer work in the year and has not claimed the volunteer firefighters credit. To date, only Nova Scotia has a ground search and rescue credit, adopted in 2008, which is part of its firefighters credit. Quebec has adopted a credit similar to the federal credit. Manitoba adopted the volunteer search and rescue tax credit in 2015 (¶1528.07).

Home Accessibility Credit

Effective for 2016 and subsequent taxation years, the federal government introduced the non-refundable home accessibility tax credit. This credit can be claimed by persons:

- over 64 at year-end;
- qualifying for a disability tax credit for that year;
- claiming a spouse or common-law partner, eligible dependant, caregiver, or infirm dependant tax credit for one of the above persons for that year.

Since 2012, British Columbia has provided a refundable home renovation tax credit for seniors and, effective in 2016, for persons with disabilities.

Eligible Educator School Supply Tax Credit

Budget 2016 introduced a teacher and early childhood educator school supplies tax credit for 2016 and subsequent taxation years. This measure will allow an employee who is an eligible educator to claim a 15% refundable tax credit on up to $1,000 of eligible teaching supplies purchased by the employee in a taxation year. See ¶1497a. There is no such provincial credit except for Prince Edward Island, which has had its own teacher school supply tax credit since 2003.

[¶1502] PROVINCIAL OR TERRITORIAL TAX PAYABLE

You must add provincial tax payable to your federal tax payable to arrive at your total tax for the year. However, if all of your income is from Quebec you will not add any provincial tax payable on your tax return, but must instead file a Quebec income tax return and report the Quebec tax payable on that return. (Quebec taxpayers can claim an abatement of federal tax on the federal T1; see ¶1435.)

If you did not operate a business at any time during the year, your entire income is considered to have been derived from the province in which you resided on the last day of the year. You are required to enter this amount on page 1 of your T1 return.

If you operated a business, see the rules under Allocation of Income (¶1440) for allocating income to provinces. You must file a Quebec provincial income tax return in addition to your federal return to report business income earned in that province. You are also required to show the provinces in which you had a permanent establishment in the year on page 1 of your T1 return.

(ITR: 2601 Residents of Canada)

[¶1502.05] *Provincial Tax Forms*

Supplementary CRA forms are provided for each province or territory (except Quebec) as part of the tax return package for that province. These provincial tax forms are designated (in the upper right hand corner) with the postal abbreviation for the province (BC, ON, etc.) along with a form number.

The basic provincial tax calculation form is 428 (so for Ontario, for example, ON428). Provincial tax calculated on a 428 form will be carried to line 428 of the T1 return. Where a province offers tax credits beyond those incorporated in the basic provincial form (428), a tax credit form is usually provided, identified by the provincial postal code and the number 479 (e.g., ON479), indicating that the tax credits reported on that form will be carried to line 479 of the T1 return.

In addition, the CRA provides provincial tax worksheets for each province and provincial versions of Schedules 2 (Amounts Transferred from Your Spouse or Common-Law Partner) and 11 (Tuition, Education and Textbook Amounts; the education and textbook credits are repealed effective January 1, 2017). As well, selected provinces may have additional CRA return forms as administration of specific provincial credit or benefit programs may require. (For example, form ON-BEN, used to apply for certain Ontario refundable credits paid out as instalment benefit payments over the course of the following year.)

In the CRA printed forms packages (as opposed to computer generated forms), the provincial forms are readily recognized by their pink background.

Where Alternative Minimum Tax (AMT) is payable (or recoverable) federally (Chapter 24), supplementary provincial tax based on AMT is taken from the federal form T691, although the T691 lines on which the provincial tax is based may vary somewhat from province to province.

Where Split Income tax is payable federally (¶1490), provincial tax is calculated on federal form T1206.

Taxpayers who must allocate business income to more than one jurisdiction (¶1440) must also use form T2203.

Quebec residents (or deemed residents) use their forms package to accommodate the Quebec abatement, and must file a separate Quebec return (TP-1.D-V) to determine provincial tax. See Chapter 16.

[¶1504] PROVINCE OF RESIDENCE

Generally speaking, you must pay provincial tax to the province in which you were resident on December 31 of the taxation year in question. If you had residences in more than one province on December 31, the law says that you are considered a resident of the province which may reasonably be regarded as your principal place of residence. In cases where your province of residence is not self-evident, it is the policy of the CRA to apply essentially the same criteria in determining your "significant ties" with a particular place of residence that it uses in determining whether you are a factual resident of Canada or another country, as discussed in ¶115.

Normally, all your income is allocated to your province of residence as of December 31. There are several exceptions, of which the most common is earning business income which must be allocated to more than one province. This is discussed at ¶1505 and in more detail at ¶1440.

If you ceased residence in Canada during the taxation year, you must file a return for the province in which you resided immediately before departure; see ¶115 and Chapter 21.

If you were living in Canada for 183 days or more in a year but cannot be considered a "factual resident" as discussed in ¶115 in Chapter 1, you are nevertheless deemed to be resident in Canada (subject to the deemed non-resident rules in ¶116). If you were in Quebec for 183 days or more, you are also deemed resident in Quebec and file Quebec tax returns. If you were a deemed resident of Canada living in any other province, you are deemed to be a resident of Canada but not necessarily of the province. Business income earned in any province must be allocated to that province (¶1505). Other income will be taxed at the non-resident rate. Generally, you must file a non-resident return rather than a provincial return, unless all your reported income is business income from one province, in which case you may file a return for that province.

If you were a non-resident of Canada living in Canada for less than 183 days in the year but you earned employment or business income in one province in Canada, you may file a provincial return for that province. Otherwise you may file a non-resident return, following the directions in Chapter 20.

(ITA: 120(4); ITR: 2601 Residents of Canada; 2607 Dual Residence; Income Tax Folio: S5-F1-C1 Determining an Individual's Residence Status)

[¶1504.05] *Provincial Tax Rates*

Provincial tax rates are summarized in ¶50, and credits are summarized in ¶52, preceding Chapter 1.

[¶1505] BUSINESS INCOME EARNED IN MORE THAN ONE PROVINCE (FORM T2203)

If you have business income attributable to a permanent establishment in more than one province you must allocate your business income among those provinces on form T2203. The detailed rules as to when allocation is necessary and how it works are discussed at ¶1440. If you have a permanent establishment outside of Canada, see ¶1445 as well.

Form T2203 not only allocates income among provinces, but also provides detailed guidance to the completion of provincial schedules to accommodate these allocations. You must in all cases complete a schedule for your province of residence (unless you have no income allocated to that province). In most cases you must also complete, at least in part, provincial schedules for each other province to which you are allocating (business) income.

Once income is allocated to a province on form T2203, it follows that income tax, surtaxes, flat taxes, etc. will normally apply to the provincial allocation. On the other hand, some tax credits may be restricted to provincial residents only. Form T2203 also provides detailed guidance to carrying tax allocations to provincial forms for residents or non-residents of each jurisdiction.

If you are doing business in Quebec, you would allocate income to Quebec in the same way, but you would then have to report that allocation on a Quebec income tax return as described in Chapter 16; you can however claim federal abatement for Quebec tax on that amount (on line 440 of the T1 return).

Generally speaking, since only business income is allocated to provinces other than your province of residence, only your province of residence will permit provincial foreign tax credit on foreign investment income (since all investment income is allocated to the province of residence).

In general, for each province in which business income is earned, provincial tax is calculated on all income regardless of allocation, certain non-refundable tax credits are applied, and the tax is then prorated according to the income allocation rules. Essentially, each province is allowed a *pro rata* share of these credits. However, certain credits, including the provincial foreign tax credit and specific personal tax reduction credits, are given only by the province of residence.

Most provinces give no provincial tax credit to non-residents for dividends or pension income, but give 100% credit to residents for these credits. The concept is that since all investment, pension and employment income is allocated to the province of residence, that province only should give full credit to its residents — but not to others. Provinces that offer an adoption expense credit also tend to restrict this credit to provincial residents only.

Quebec has its own unique rules. Quebec gives prorated dividend and other non-refundable credits to residents of other provinces, and prorates those credits for its own residents.

[¶1506] PROVINCIAL FOREIGN TAX CREDIT

You may not have been able to deduct the entire amount of foreign taxes you have paid on foreign non-business income through the Federal Foreign Tax Credit. In this case, you will be allowed a deduction from Provincial Tax Payable for a portion of the excess foreign taxes paid on foreign non-business income.

The deduction from Provincial Tax will be the lesser of:

(1) foreign taxes paid on foreign non-business income but not claimed in the Federal Foreign Tax Credit; or

(2) the proportion of the provincial income tax with respect to the province in which you resided equal to the ratio of net foreign non-business income to the net income allocated to your province of residence. Net income, for this purpose, is subject to the same adjustments as for federal purposes in claiming the federal non-business foreign tax credit; see ¶1450.

Generally speaking, the provincial foreign tax credit is only available from your province of residence.

Form T2036 (Provincial or Territorial Foreign Tax Credit) should be obtained from your Tax Services Office and filed with your return if you claim a deduction from Provincial Tax for foreign taxes. This form is for use by individuals resident in a province other than Quebec on December 31. Typically you will also need form T2209 to complete T2036. All these forms are discussed at ¶1450.

The provincial foreign tax credit figure which is calculated on form T2036 is carried to the provincial form 428 that accompanies your T1 return. For Quebec, the provincial foreign tax credit is calculated on the Quebec form TP-772-V and entered on Schedule E; see ¶1670.

ALBERTA

[¶1510] BASIC TAX, PERSONAL AMOUNTS

[¶1510.05] *Basic Tax*

For 2016, the personal tax rates and income brackets are:

Taxable income	*Tax*
$125,000 or less	10.0%
In excess of	
$125,000	$12,500 + 12.0% on next $25,000
$150,000	$15,500 + 13.0% on next $50,000
$200,000	$22,000 + 14.0% on next $100,000
$300,000	$36,000 + 15.0% on remainder

Until 2015, Alberta had only one flat rate of tax under the TONI system: 10% of federal taxable income.

Effective October 1, 2015, the personal tax rates and income brackets were:

- $125,000 and below – 10%;
- $125,000-$150,000 – 12%;
- $150,000-$200,000 – 13%;
- $200,000-$300,000 – 14%; and
- $300,000 and above – 15%.

Considering the new rates only became effective on October 1, 2015, the 2015 average tax rates are:

Taxable income	*Tax*
$125,000 or less	10.0%
In excess of	
$125,000	$12,500 + 10.5% on next $25,000
$150,000	$15,125 + 10.75% on next $50,000
$200,000	$20,500 + 11.0% on next $100,000
$300,000	$31,500 + 11.25% on remainder

(APITA: 4; 5)

[¶1510.10] *Personal Amounts*

Alberta personal amounts are converted to non-refundable Alberta tax credits at the lowest Alberta tax rate of 10%. Most Alberta personal amounts differ from federal amounts, and must be computed on form AB428 and the Alberta worksheet. Amounts eligible (before conversion to credit) for CPP/QPP, EI, and student loan credit will be the same as on the federal return.

Even though it has only one rate of tax, Alberta makes an exception for the charitable donation credit, giving credit at its standard rate (10%) on the first $200 of donation (as does the federal government) and at an arbitrary higher rate on the balance. The rate on donations over $200 is 21%.

Where a student must calculate education/tuition tax credit amounts and/or transfers on federal Schedule 11, the student must make a parallel provincial calculation on AB(S11). Similarly, where you are claiming a transfer of personal amounts from your spouse or common-law partner on federal Schedule 2, you must make the parallel Alberta claim on AB(S2). The federal education credit (upon which the provincial credit is based) will be eliminated effective 2017. Legislative changes must be made if Alberta wishes to maintain the credit, but at this time no such action has been taken.

The TONI system requires the provinces to maintain the package of personal amounts that was in place in 1999, although not the dollar values of those amounts. It does not require the provinces to adopt later personal amount credits which the federal government may offer. Nevertheless, Alberta has chosen to adopt the federal adoption expense credit based on federal eligibility rules. It has not chosen to adopt other new federal credits, such as employment amount, transit pass, children under 18, first-time homebuyers, child arts, volunteer firefighters, search and rescue volunteers, and child fitness credits. Alberta has not matched the federal increase of the amount eligible for pension credit to $2,000, although it does index its $1,000 pension credit amount: $1,421 for 2016 based on its own Alberta Consumer Price Index, rather than the federal index.

The TONI system requires Alberta to impose its own tax or tax credits at the rate of its choosing on several items, which it has done as follows:

- dividend tax credit on eligible dividends is 10%, and on other Canadian dividends, 3.08% for 2014 to 2016, and 2.2% for 2017 and subsequent years (rates for other years are discussed at ¶1510.12);
- alternative minimum tax (for 2016, line 108 minus line 111 of form T691) at 35%;
- alternative minimum tax credit (Schedule 1 line 427) at 35%; and
- tax on split income (form T1206) at the top marginal rate for Alberta of 15% (11.25% for 2015).

The AMT tax/tax credit rate is essentially the old provincial tax-on-tax rate; its use takes a federally calculated tax/tax credit number and applies it for provincial purposes as a kind of shorthand, rather than working through the income calculation again and applying an appropriate provincial tax (or, with more difficulty, tax credit) to the income. The tax on split income, by contrast, imposes the top provincial rate on the actual split income as determined for federal purposes.

Basic personal amounts are shown on AB428 and the Alberta provincial worksheet which accompanies the T1 return package for Alberta.

(APITA: 7–27; 47; 48)

[¶1510.12] *Dividend Tax Credit*

The dividend tax credit on eligible dividends is 10% for 2009 and later taxation years. The dividend tax credit on other taxable dividends is 3.08% for 2014 to 2016 (the rate will be reduced to 2.2% effective in 2017). It was 3.5% for 2009 to 2013.

The dual rate dividend tax credit requires a special, if simple, calculation on the Alberta provincial worksheet provided with the Alberta T1 package. Where you have only eligible dividends in the year on federal line 120, you simply apply the current annual eligible dividend rate. Where you also have other dividends at federal line 180, you apply the lower rate to that amount, subtract the line 180 amount from the line 120 amount, and apply the higher rate to the balance.

Your Alberta credit is the sum of the two amounts thus computed.

(APITA: 21)

[¶1510.15] *Multi-Jurisdictional Taxpayers*

As discussed at ¶1505, taxpayers who must allocate business income between Alberta and another jurisdiction (on form T2203) are subject to the rule that residents of Alberta will get full credit from Alberta for dividend tax credit, pension income credit, and adoption expense credit, but non-residents of Alberta will get zero credit for these items.

[¶1511c] FAMILY EMPLOYMENT TAX CREDIT

The refundable family employment tax credit essentially replicates the former federal working income supplement at a somewhat higher income level. It is based on Canada Child Benefit criteria. Payments are made semi-annually, in January and July. They are issued by the CRA based on Canada Child Benefit information, but are issued as separate cheques.

As with the Canada Child Benefit at ¶1498, once you have registered a child you neither apply for nor calculate the Alberta supplement. It is simply sent to you based on your (and your spouse's) return for the year preceding the July payment. The program is administered by the CRA through the Canada Child Benefit program, so in addition to the usual rules at ¶1498 obliging you to inform the CRA of changes in marital status and number of children, you should inform them promptly of changes in your province of residence. Overpayments can be recovered through the usual assessment, penalty and interest rules discussed in Chapter 2.

To qualify for the supplement in any month, you must be resident in Alberta on the first day of the month and the last day of the preceding month. Your family net income for the previous calendar year must be less than $60,325 for families with one child, $77,675 for families with two children, $88,075 for families with three children, and $91,550 for families with four or more children. Rules regarding marriage, cohabitation, separation, and so on, are the same as federal rules at ¶1498. The rules concerning eligible dependants are precisely those which apply for Canada Child Benefit purposes, as are the rules for cohabiting spouse, filing of tax returns, and so on. In short, if you are an Alberta resident receiving Canada Child Benefits, you may receive the additional supplement, depending on your income.

Effective July 1, 2016, the maximum annual Alberta Family Employment Tax Credit is $763 per child or similar dependant for the first child, $1,457 for two children, $1,873 for three children, and $2,012 for four or more children. There is a further annual limit which ensures that the benefit is phased in only when net family working income exceeds $2,760, as discussed below.

Payments are made at six month intervals, in January and July.

The Alberta supplement will be calculated on a monthly basis for each eligible dependant, for each month of eligibility, as one-twelfth of the least of:

(1) the per child amount for each child eligible for Canada Child Benefits in Alberta;

(2) 11% of parents' earned income (i.e., income of taxpayer and spouse or cohabiting partner as determined for child tax care deduction purposes at ¶1055, regardless of whether child tax care expense is claimed) in excess of $2,760; and

(3) the cumulative amount for four children (for 2016, $2,012) reduced by 4% of parents' net income for the base year in excess of (for 2016) $41,250.

The per dependant amounts and the $41,250 threshold amount are indexed annually.

Details of the Alberta program should be available from 1-800-959-2809. See also the CRA booklet *Canada Child Benefits* (T4114), which includes extensive information on both federal and Alberta programs. It can be downloaded from the CRA website at www.cra-arc.gc.ca/forms, or ordered by phone from 1-800-959-2221. The CRA maintains a very useful website on Canada Child Benefits at www.cra-arc.gc.ca/benefits; information can also be had by phone from 1-800-387-1193.

(APITA: 28–35; T4114 Canada Child Benefits — Including related federal, provincial and territorial programs)

[¶1511d] ALBERTA CHILD BENEFIT

The Alberta Child Benefit is a new program that began in July 2016. The first payment was issued August 2016 and is paid separately from the Canadian Child Benefit and the Alberta family employment tax credit.

The program will provide families with an annual benefit of up to $1,100 for one child, with a further $550 for each additional child (for a maximum of $2,750 or four children per family). The benefit and related amounts are indexed annually.

Families with net income of up to $25,500 will receive the maximum benefit under this program. Benefits begin to phase out once family net income surpasses $25,500, and will be fully phased out once family net income reaches $41,220.

Enrollment is automatic if the individual is enrolled in the federal government's Canada Child Benefit and meets the following criteria:

- is a parent of one or more children under the age of 18;
- has a family net income that is less than $41,220 per year;
- is a resident of Alberta for at least one month prior to receiving the credit; and
- has filed a tax return.

(APITA: 30.1; 31–35)

[¶1511e] ALBERTA CLIMATE LEADERSHIP ADJUSTMENT REBATE

Starting January 1, 2017, Alberta's new carbon levy will be applied to fuels at a rate of $20/tonne; in 2018, the levy will increase to $30/tonne. To offset the impact of the levy, carbon rebates will be provided to lower- and middle-income Albertans. For 2017, the rebate will be:

- $200 for the first adult;
- $100 for a spouse or spouse equivalent; and
- $30 per child (for a maximum of four children).

Those amounts will increase for 2018 to:

- $300 for the first adult;
- $150 for a spouse or spouse equivalent; and
- $45 per child (for a maximum of four children).

Potential rebate recipients don't need to apply for the rebate, but must:

- be Alberta residents;
- file a 2015 (or later) tax return; and
- meet the income requirements.

The rebate will begin to phase out at $47,500 in net income for single persons, and $95,000 for couples and families. Payments will be made according to the amount the recipient is eligible to receive.

(APITA: 35.2–35.3)

[¶1511f] ALBERTA CENTENNIAL EDUCATION SAVINGS PLAN

For children born in or after 2006 to residents of Alberta, Alberta will provide a grant of $500 to an RESP if one has been opened for the child, and will also offer a matching grant of $100 for children born in or after 2006 and attending school in Alberta when at the age of 8, 11, or 14 years. However, the program has closed and the deadline for submitting a completed application to an RESP provider/Alberta Centennial Education Savings Plan promoter was July 31, 2015. The federal government has a similar program, but the federal program is limited to low-income families. Both programs are discussed in ¶2529d.

[¶1512] ROYALTY TAX CREDIT AND REBATE (FORM T79)

If you paid any royalties to the province of Alberta, the federal government, or any other provincial governments before 2007, you may be eligible for the Alberta Royalty Tax Credit and Alberta Royalty Tax Rebate (see ¶2270).

Alberta discontinued the royalty tax rebate program in 2007. Carryforwards of unused rebates remained available until December 31, 2013.

(APITA: 25)

[¶1513] POLITICAL CONTRIBUTION TAX CREDIT

You may deduct from your Alberta income taxes payable a tax credit for political contributions made in the year. Only contributions to

- registered Alberta political parties or registered Alberta constituency associations, or to registered candidates at an election to the Alberta Legislature; or
- registered Alberta political parties that have nominated a candidate under the Alberta *Senatorial Selection Act* in an Alberta senatorial election

are eligible for this credit.

A separate credit may be claimed for contributions made in respect of *each* of the elections above. Your Alberta political contribution receipt should indicate whether your contribution is in respect of a legislative election ("Annual Contribution") or a senatorial election ("Senatorial Selection Campaign Contribution").

The credit for each type of political contribution is calculated as follows:

(1) 75% of the first $200 of contributions;

(2) 50% of next $900 of contributions; and

(3) 33 1/3% of the next $1,200.

The maximum credit of $1,000 (for each of the elections referred to above) is reached when you have made eligible contributions totalling $2,300. Contributions in excess of $2,300 may not be carried forward to the following year. The credit claimed cannot exceed your Alberta income tax payable.

The Alberta Political Contribution Tax Credit can be calculated on the Alberta provincial worksheet and should be entered on form AB428, lines 51 through 55. Proof of payment, in the form of an official receipt signed by the chief financial officer of the registered party, constituency association, or candidate must be attached to the paper form. In the case of electronic filing, you should have the receipt on hand to provide to the CRA should they request it.

Application must be made with your return for the taxation year in which the contribution was made, or within 90 days from the mailing date on the notice of assessment or reassessment for that taxation year. If as a result of an assessment or reassessment of your tax payable for the taxation year, you have not claimed the maximum Alberta Political Contribution Tax Credit to which you are entitled, you may file a revised application for the credit in the prescribed form within 90 days from the date of the mailing of the notice of assessment or reassessment for that taxation year, but not afterwards.

(APITA: 24)

BRITISH COLUMBIA

[¶1518] BRITISH COLUMBIA INCOME TAX, BASIC CREDITS

[¶1518.05] *Basic Tax*

British Columbia uses the TONI system (¶1501). Accordingly, B.C. tax is based on federal taxable income from line 260 of the T1 return, to which British Columbia applies (for 2016) the following tax rates:

Taxable income	*Tax*
$38,210 or less	5.06%
In excess of	
$38,210	$1,933 + 7.7% on next $38,211
$76,421	$4,875 + 10.5% on next $11,320
$87,741	$6,064 + 12.29% on next $18,802
$106,543	$8,375 + 14.7% on remainder

For the 2014 and 2015 tax years, there was a temporary tax rate and tax bracket of 16.8% on taxable income over $150,000 ($151,050 for 2015).

Like the federal government, British Columbia gives tax credit at its lowest rate (for 2016, 5.06%) on personal amounts. Also similar to the federal government, British Columbia makes an exception for the charitable donation credit, giving credit at its lowest rate (5.06%) on the first $200 of donation and a second higher rate (14.7%) on the balance. Donation amounts should be taken from lines 345 and 347 of Schedule 9 of the federal return.

Except for CPP/QPP, EI, adoption expenses, child fitness (repealed effective January 1, 2017), child arts (repealed effective January 1, 2017), student loan interest, and charitable donation amounts, non-refundable credits are different from federal amounts and must be calculated on form BC428 and the British Columbia Provincial Worksheet which accompanies the return.

Where a student must calculate education/tuition tax credit amounts and/or transfers on federal Schedule 11, the student must make a parallel provincial calculation on BC(S11). Similarly, where you are claiming a transfer of personal amounts from your spouse or common-law partner on federal Schedule 2, you must make the parallel British Columbia claim on BC(S2). The federal education credit (upon which the provincial credit is based) will be eliminated effective 2017. Legislative changes must be made if British Columbia wishes to maintain the credit, but at this time no such action has been taken.

The TONI system requires the provinces to maintain the federal package of personal amounts that was in place in 1999, although not the dollar values of those amounts. It does not require the provinces to adopt later personal amount credits which the federal government may offer. British Columbia does offer the adoption expenses credit, the children's arts credit, and the children's fitness tax credit. So far, British Columbia does not offer credits parallel to the federal employment, public transit, children under 18, first-time home buyers (although there was a limited time First-Time New Home Buyers' Bonus until March 31, 2013; see ¶1521h), volunteer firefighters, or the new federal search and rescue volunteers credits, nor has it matched the federal increase in the amount eligible for pension income credit from $1,000 to $2,000.

The TONI system requires British Columbia to impose its own tax or tax credits, at the rate of its choosing, on several items, which it has done (for 2016) as follows:

- dividend tax credit is 10% on eligible dividends, and 2.47% for 2016 and subsequent years (2.59% for 2014 and 2015) on ineligible taxable Canadian dividends;
- tax on split income (form T1206) at 14.7%;
- alternative minimum tax from line 117 of form T691 at 33.7%; and
- alternative minimum tax credit (Schedule 1, line 427) at 33.7% (for 2016).

The AMT tax/tax credit rate is essentially the old provincial tax-on-tax rate adjusted to approximate current British Columbia tax levels. British Columbia has legislated a formula for determining this rate: it is the lowest provincial marginal rate (5.06% for 2016) divided by the lowest federal marginal rate (15% for 2016).

The tax on split income, by contrast, imposes the 14.7% provincial rate on the actual split income as determined for federal purposes.

(BCITA: 4.1–4.85)

[¶1518.10] *Low-Income Tax Reduction*

British Columbia offers a mechanical tax credit that reduces tax for individuals with income below (for 2016) $31,647. The 2016 tax reduction credit is $436 reduced by 3.56% of income in excess of $19,400. These amounts are indexed to provincial inflation for the 2017 and following years.

The reduction is calculated on lines 57 to 63 on form BC428.

(BCITA: 4.301; 4.52)

[¶1518a] RATE HISTORY

For 2015, the B.C. tax rate schedule was:

Taxable income	*Tax*
$37,869 or less	5.06%
In excess of	
$37,869	$1,916 + 7.7% on next $37,871
$75,740	$4,832 + 10.5% on next $11,218
$86,958	$6,010 + 12.29% on next $18,634
$105,592	$8,300 + 14.7% on next $45,458
$151,050	$14,982 + 16.8% on remainder

The dividend tax credit for 2015 was 10% on eligible dividends and 2.59% on other taxable Canadian dividends.

For 2014, the B.C. tax rate schedule was:

Taxable income	*Tax*
$37,606 or less	5.06%
In excess of	
$37,606	$1,903 + 7.7% on next $37,607
$75,213	$4,799 + 10.5% on next $11,141
$86,354	$5,968 + 12.29% on next $18,504
$104,858	$8,243 + 14.7% on next $45,142
$150,000	$14,878 + 16.8% on remainder

The dividend tax credit for 2014 was 10% on eligible dividends and 2.59% on other taxable Canadian dividends.

For 2013, the B.C. tax rate schedule was:

Taxable income	*Tax*
$37,568 or less	5.06%
In excess of	
$37,568	$1,901 + 7.7% on next $37,570
$75,138	$4,794 + 10.5% on next $11,130
$86,268	$5,963 + 12.29% on next $18,486
$104,754	$8,235 + 14.7% on remainder

The dividend tax credit for 2013 was 10% on eligible dividends and 3.4% on other taxable Canadian dividends.

For 2012, the B.C. tax rate schedule was:

Taxable income	*Tax*
$37,013 or less	5.06%
In excess of	
$37,013	$1,873 + 7.7% on next $37,015
$74,028	$4,723 + 10.5% on next $10,965
$84,993	$5,874 + 12.29% on next $18,212
$103,205	$8,112 + 14.7% on remainder

The dividend tax credit for 2012 was 10% on eligible dividends and 3.4% on other taxable Canadian dividends.

For 2011, the B.C. tax rate schedule was:

Taxable income	*Tax*
$36,146 or less	5.06%
In excess of	
$36,146	$1,829 + 7.7% on next $36,147
$72,293	$4,612 + 10.5% on next $10,708
$83,001	$5,736 + 12.29% on next $17,786
$100,787	$7,922 + 14.7% on remainder

The dividend tax credit for 2011 was 10.31% on eligible dividends and 3.4% on other taxable Canadian dividends.

[¶1519] LOGGING TAX CREDIT

You may deduct from the tax payable to British Columbia an amount equal to $^1/_3$ of any logging tax paid or payable to British Columbia for the year shown on FIN 542S or FIN 542P. For 2016, the credit is reported on line 65 on form BC428. The credit amount should be reported to you on a British Columbia FIN 542 slip, which you should file with your return (unless you EFILE, in which case you must keep it on file with your tax data for the year).

(BCITA: 19.1; Other Publications: BC Bulletin LTA 001, *Logging Tax*)

[¶1520] BRITISH COLUMBIA FIRST NATION INFORMATION

Parliament has ratified an agreement with the Nisga'a First Nation. Consequently, there is a unique version of the T1 return for British Columbia that differs from the common version in requiring information as to whether you were resident on Nisga'a lands and, if a resident of the lands, were you a citizen of the Nisga'a nation. The remainder of the B.C. T1 return makes no further mention of the tax consequences for such residents. The Canada Revenue Agency uses Nisga'a residency and citizenship information to administer the agreement for the First Nation, which entitles them to the benefits of the agreement.

Document T1-BC10 specifies that all individuals, including non-citizens who reside on Nisga'a lands, are required to identify themselves by ticking "Yes" in the residency information for tax administration agreements box on page 1 of the British Columbia T1 Income Tax and Benefit Return. Question 2 on page 1 of the T1 indicates that Nisga'a residents who are citizens of the Nisga'a First Nation should identify themselves by ticking "Yes" in the box provided.

If your residence status is in doubt because you maintain more than one residence, you should be guided by the same "residence in fact" criteria that determine national residence in ¶115.05.

(Income Tax Folio: S5-F1-C1 Determining an Individual's Residence Status)

[¶1521] REFUNDABLE SALES TAX CREDIT

In 2013, the government re-implemented the refundable Sales Tax Credit. The Sales Tax Credit has the same eligibility criteria and benefit calculation that existed prior to the short-lived HST regime.

The credit is essentially $75 each for you and your spouse or common-law partner (¶1113). The basic credit is reduced by 2% of adjusted family net income over $15,000 for singles and over $18,000 for families.

The reductions may decrease the joint net income number to zero but not below. The result of these reductions is that a family's income must reach $18,000 before the "grind" to the sales tax credit for family income begins to operate. Income from an RDSP is excluded from income for purposes of determining eligibility for the sales tax credit.

The reference to line 236 income is an oversimplification in cases where you were separated from your spouse or common-law partner at the end of the year or had gains from the repossession of mortgaged or conditional sale property; for more details see the discussion of adjusted income at ¶1498.

To qualify for the Sales Tax Credit, you must be a resident of British Columbia on December 31 of the tax year and:

- be 19 years of age or older; or
- have a spouse or common-law partner; or
- be a parent.

As with the GST credit, only one cohabiting spouse or common-law partner may claim the credit, although it may be either one. Simplicity will normally be served by having the spouse or common-law partner who claims the GST credit claim the B.C. credit, although technically the British Columbia and federal claims need not be made by the same person.

Eligible taxpayers will claim the Sales Tax Credit when they file their income tax return. The credit is refundable to the extent it exceeds income tax payable.

(BCITA: 8)

[¶1521a] REFUNDABLE LOW INCOME CLIMATE ACTION (GST) CREDIT

As a partial offset to its carbon tax, British Columbia introduced a Low Income Climate Action Tax Credit. The credit is essentially a B.C. add-on to the federal GST tax credit (¶1496). Accordingly, you are eligible for the B.C. credit if you are an eligible individual for GST credit purposes as described in ¶1496.15 *and* you were resident in British Columbia on the first day of a "specified month" and the first day of the preceding specified month. A specified month is July and October of the year following your taxation year and January and April of the second year following your taxation year. Thus, if you filed a 2015 tax return, and otherwise qualified for GST credit based on that return, you would receive the British Columbia supplement in July and October 2016 and January and April 2017, provided you were still resident in

British Columbia on the first day of each of those months. Similar to the federal GST credit, in 2016 the CRA will determine a taxpayer's eligibility for the credit and no application form will be required.

For payments starting July 2016 (and into 2017), the basic credit is $115.50 for an individual, $115.50 for a spouse or common-law partner, and $34.50 for each child ($115.50 for the first child in a single parent family). For single individuals with no children, the credit will be reduced by 2% of their net income over $32,737. For families, the credit will be reduced by 2% of their net income over $38,193.

The credit is combined with the GST credit into one payment issued every quarter.

As with the GST credit, changes to your status (address, marital status, children added to your household or departed from your household, and so on) should be promptly reported to the CRA at 1-800-959-8281.

For more information on the Low Income Climate Action Tax Credit, please visit the B.C. Ministry of Finance website or contact the Ministry of Finance by telephone at 1-877-387-3332 or via e-mail to ITBTaxQuestions@gov.bc.ca.

The CRA guide *GST/HST Credit* (RC4210) also contains a great deal of useful information, including a brief description of the B.C. Climate Action Tax Credit. You can download the guide from the CRA website at www.cra-arc.gc.ca, or order it by telephone at 1-800-959-2221.

(BCITA: 8.1)

[¶1521c] BRITISH COLUMBIA FAMILY BONUS AND EARNED INCOME BENEFIT

British Columbia provides a refundable "British Columbia Family Bonus", which essentially replicates the federal Canada Child Benefit (and the former working income supplement component of that benefit) for parents with a minimum earned income of $3,750. It is not a credit claimed on a tax return, but is based on Canada Child Benefit criteria, and is rolled into the federal Canada Child Benefit paid monthly by the CRA.

Both these amounts are administered by the federal government as part of the Canada Child Benefit program. You apply for them automatically with your application for the federal Canada Child Benefit at ¶1498. You do not calculate the British Columbia supplement. It is simply sent to you based on your (and your spouse's) returns for the preceding two years. The program is administered by the CRA through the Canada Child Benefit program; so in addition to the usual rules at ¶1498 obliging you to inform the CRA of changes in marital status and number of children, you should inform them promptly of changes in provincial residence. Overpayments can be recovered through the usual assessment, penalty, and interest rules discussed in Chapter 2.

To qualify for these amounts in any month, you must be resident in British Columbia on the first day of the month and the last day of the preceding month. Rules regarding marriage, cohabitation, separation, and so on, are the same as federal rules at ¶1498.

The B.C. Family Bonus rules are prescribed by British Columbia regulations; these are supposed to square with the interpretation of the CRA, which administers the program. The B.C. regulation (which in theory should govern) indicates a family bonus of $111 per year ($9.25 per month) per child, and the B.C. Family Bonus website states that the bonus provides "up to $111 per month *when combined with the National Child Benefit Supplement*" (emphasis added).

British Columbia also provides an earned income benefit which is phased in as earned income exceeds $3,750 and phased out as net family income exceeds $21,480. Currently, the Earned Income Benefit amount is zero.

Additional information, especially on registration and change of status, is available from the CRA's information line at 1-800-387-1193. There is also a brief description in the CRA guide *Canada Child Benefits* (T4114).

See details on the additional British Columbia Early Child Tax Benefit at ¶1521d. Payments of this new British Columbia Early Child Tax Benefit, the existing B.C. Family Bonus, and the Canada Child Benefit are combined into one monthly payment via the B.C. family bonus program.

(*Income Tax (BC Family Bonus) Regulation*; BCITA: 9–13; T4114 Canada Child Benefits — Including related federal, provincial and territorial programs)

[¶1521d] BRITISH COLUMBIA EARLY CHILDHOOD TAX BENEFIT

The B.C. early childhood tax benefit is a non-taxable amount of up to $55 per month paid to most families with children under the age of six. The amount of the benefit is based on the number of qualified children and the family's net income. The benefit is reduced when family net income exceeds $100,000 and is entirely eliminated when family income exceeds $150,000.

Eligibility for the tax benefit in the first year is based on your and your spouse's or common-law partner's personal tax return(s). There is no separate application for the new benefit. If your child is registered for the Canada Child Benefit then he or she is automatically registered for the new benefit. Payments of this new tax benefit, the existing B.C. Family Bonus, and the CCTB are combined into one monthly payment via the B.C. family bonus program.

(BCITA: 13.07–13.09)

[¶1521e] BRITISH COLUMBIA WORKING INCOME TAX BENEFIT (SCHEDULE 6)

The federal government has a refundable tax credit for low-income families, the Working Income Tax Benefit (¶1495). Although strictly a federal payment, its provisions allow the federal Minister of Finance to vary the terms of the benefit, by agreement with a province or territory, to better harmonize with a local benefit system. British Columbia has reached such an agreement, which is reflected in the unique version of federal Schedule 6 included in the British Columbia version of the T1 tax package.

[¶1521g] HOME RENOVATION TAX CREDIT FOR SENIORS AND PERSONS WITH DISABILITIES

The Home Renovation Tax Credit is a refundable credit meant to assist with the cost of permanent home renovations for individuals age 65 and over who are residents of British Columbia at the end of the tax year. The maximum credit is $1,000 annually, calculated as 10% of eligible expenditures up to $10,000. Effective for the 2016 tax year and thereafter, the credit is expanded to include persons with disabilities who are eligible to claim the federal disability tax credit. The expanded credit will be available in respect of eligible expenditures made on or after February 17, 2016.

The credit is available to individuals who incur eligible expenditures. The credit can be claimed by seniors (or disabled persons as of 2016), whether they own their home or rent, and by individuals (such as a child or grandchild) who share a home with the senior/disabled person. In addition, if someone not living with or not related to the senior/disabled person (such as a landlord) paid for the qualifying home renovation to the senior/disabled person's residence, the senior (or disabled person) can still claim the credit. A claim can also be filed on behalf of or in relation to a deceased person.

The home must be located in British Columbia and must also be the individual's "principal residence", which means his or her primary place of residence. A principal residence includes a residence the senior/disabled person may not currently occupy but expects to occupy within 24 months after the end of the taxation year. If the senior/disabled person occupied more than one principal residence at different times in the year, eligible expenses paid or incurred for one or more of those residences qualify for the credit.

A renovation to an individual's principal residence (or the land where the principal residence is located) will qualify for the credit if it:

- enables a senior/disabled person to gain access to, or to be mobile or functional within, the residence or the land, or reduce the risk of harm to a senior/disabled person;
- is of an enduring nature and is integral to the residence or the land, or relates to the purchase and installation of a modular or removable version of an item that can be installed as a permanent fixture to the residence or the land;
- is not for the principal purpose of increasing the value of the residence or the land; and
- would ordinarily be undertaken by, or on behalf of, a person who has an impairment to enable him or her to gain access to, or be mobile or functional within, his or her residence or land.

Examples of eligible renovations include:

- upgrades to improve accessibility (handrails, grab bars, walk-in bathtubs, and wheel-in showers);
- wheelchair ramps, lifts, and elevators;
- motion-activated lighting; and
- some renovations to allow first-floor occupancy or a second suite for a senior relative.

Eligible expenses are deemed to have been incurred on the earlier of the date they were invoiced or the date they were paid. Eligible expenses must be reduced by the amount of any government assistance received or expected to be received that relates to the eligible expenses. Other expenditures excluded from this credit include:

- general maintenance (roof repairs, windows, flooring, insulation, and painting);
- standard appliances;
- equipment for medical monitoring and home security; and
- services (home care, housekeeping, and gardening).

The expenses of a "do-it-yourself" renovation can be claimed, but your labour performed on these renovations is not an eligible expense.

If more than one individual is entitled to claim the credit in a taxation year for a residence of all of the individuals, the total amount of qualifying expenditures that may be claimed by all of the individuals cannot exceed $10,000 (the individuals can agree how to divide the credit, but if they cannot agree, the Minister of Finance will fix the portions). If at the end of the year, the senior/disabled person and his or her spouse or common-law partner occupied separate principal residences for medical reasons or because of a breakdown in their marriage or common-law relationship for a period of 90 days or more, each spouse or common-law partner can claim up to $10,000 of eligible expenses.

If an eligible expense also qualifies as a medical expense, you can claim both the medical expenses and the seniors/disabled persons' home renovation tax credit for that expense.

The information about the eligible expenses must be entered on Schedule BC(S12). The credit is claimed on line 14 of form BC479. If the senior/disabled person and his or her spouse occupied separate principal residences for medical reasons, tick box 6089 on Form BC479. Do not submit any documentation, such as receipts from suppliers and contractors, when you file your return, but retain them in case the CRA requests them to confirm your claim.

(BCITA: 141–148)

[¶1521h] FIRST-TIME NEW HOME BUYERS' BONUS

Effective from February 21, 2012 to March 31, 2013, the B.C. government offered a temporary First-Time New Home Buyers' Bonus. The deadline for filing an application for this bonus was March 31, 2015. This one-time bonus is a refundable income tax credit for first-time homebuyers who purchase a newly constructed or substantially renovated home. The credit may also be available for an owner-built home and to purchasers of a mobile or a floating home.

The bonus is 5% of the purchase price (not including HST — the purchase eligibility period was exclusively in the time period that HST applied) of the home, up to a maximum credit of either $10,000 or the amount of the B.C. HST New Housing Rebate (whichever is less). The credit is phased out at a rate of 20% of net income in excess of $150,000 for single individuals (and eliminated at incomes greater than $200,000), and 10% of family net income in excess of $150,000 for couples (and eliminated at family incomes greater than $250,000). Only one credit can be claimed per home.

The credit is available for purchases of newly constructed or substantially renovated housing where a written agreement of purchase and sale is entered into on or after February 21, 2012 and before April 1, 2013. Ownership or possession of the home must transfer before April 1, 2013. For owner-built homes, a written agreement of purchase and sale of the land where the home is to be built must be entered into on or after February 21, 2012, and construction of the home completed, or the home occupied, before April 1, 2013.

Other eligibility criteria for the credit include:

- the home must be located in British Columbia and newly constructed or substantially renovated (generally, 90% or more of the interior dwelling must be renovated);
- the home must be an individual's and, if applicable, his or her spouse or common-law partner's first home anywhere in the world — in cases where there are multiple buyers, each buyer must be a first-time homebuyer;

- the home must be intended as the individual's primary residence;
- HST (purchase eligibility period is exclusively in HST period) is payable on the home;
- the claimant was a B.C. resident on December 31 of the eligible tax year;
- the claimant is eligible for the B.C. HST New Housing Rebate;
- the claimant must file a B.C. resident personal income tax return for 2011, or if the claimant moves to British Columbia after December 31, 2011, must file a 2012 B.C. resident personal income tax return; and
- no one else can have claimed a bonus in respect of the home.

Individuals or families who moved to British Columbia after December 31, 2012, are not eligible for the credit.

You apply for the credit to the B.C. Commissioner of Income Tax using forms FIN 520, *Application for the BC First-Time New Home Buyers' Bonus*, and FIN 520A, *Schedule A — Certification BC First-Time New Home Buyers' Bonus*. The individual who claimed the B.C. HST New Housing Rebate must complete the FIN 520 application. In the case of multiple buyers of a new home, the other co-owners must complete FIN 520A. If the applicant is married or has a common-law partner, the applicant's spouse or partner must complete FIN 520A. You will also need to provide the following documentation with the application:

- a copy of your Notice of Assessment for the eligible tax year;
- a copy of your spouse or common-law partner's Notice of Assessment for that year;
- a complete copy of your form GST 190, GST/HST New Housing Rebate Application for Houses Purchased from a Builder, including the form RC7190 — BC, GST 190 British Columbia Rebate Schedule, or a copy of form GST 191, GST/HST New Housing Rebate Application for Owner-Built Houses, including the form RC7191 — BC, GST191 British Columbia Rebate Schedule; and
- a copy of the final, signed purchase and sale agreement for your eligible new home and/or the land.

For owner-built homes, keep receipts for all construction costs in case the Commissioner of Income Tax requests them.

The Commissioner of Income Tax pays any refundable part of the bonus directly to the applicant.

(BCITA: 151–167)

[¶1521i] CHILDREN'S FITNESS CREDIT

The Children's Fitness Credit for British Columbia is effective from 2012 to 2016. The federal government announced in the 2016 Budget that it will eliminate the child fitness credit (upon which the provincial credit is based) for the 2017 taxation year.

The Children's Fitness Credit for British Columbia is a non-refundable credit of 5.06% of eligible expenditures up to $500 for each child under 16 at the beginning of the year and under 18 if someone is entitled to claim the disability tax credit on behalf of the child. If at least $100 of eligible fitness expenses were incurred for a child who was under 18 and qualified for the disability tax credit, the individual is entitled to claim an additional credit representing an additional $500 worth of expenses. Therefore, the maximum benefit from the credit is $25.30 per child ($50.60 if disabled).

Only residents of British Columbia are eligible for this credit. You may claim this amount if the requirements are met for claiming the federal children's fitness credit (see ¶1356) on line 459 of the return. The credit is claimed on line 11 of form BC428.

(BCITA: 4.34)

[¶1521j] CHILDREN'S ARTS CREDIT

The Children's Arts Credit for British Columbia is effective from 2012 to 2016. Like the child fitness credit, the federal government announced in the 2016 Budget that it will eliminate the child arts credit for the 2017 taxation year.

The Children's Arts Credit is a non-refundable credit of 5.06% of eligible expenditures up to $500 for each child under 16 at the beginning of the year and under 18 if someone is entitled to claim the disability tax credit on behalf of the child. If at least $100 of eligible expenses were incurred for a child who was under 18 and qualified for the disability tax credit, the individual is entitled to claim an additional credit representing an additional $500 worth of expenses. Therefore, the maximum benefit from the credit is $25.30 per child ($50.60 if disabled). Only residents of British Columbia are eligible for this credit. You can claim this amount if the requirements are met for claiming the federal children's arts credit (see ¶1356a) on line 15 of the federal Schedule 1. The credit is claimed on line 13 of form BC428.

(BCITA: 4.35)

[¶1521k] CHILDREN'S FITNESS EQUIPMENT CREDIT

Effective beginning in the 2015 tax year, a non-refundable children's fitness equipment credit is available for fitness equipment purchased for a child. The credit is 50% of the B.C. children's fitness credit amount claimed on line 11 of form BC428, up to $12.65 per child ($25.30 if disabled). Since the children's fitness equipment credit is based on the Children's Fitness Credit (which has been eliminated), the province will need to take action to maintain the equipment credit. As of September 2016, no action has been taken.

The credit is claimed on line 12 of form BC428. Parents are not required to keep receipts.

(BCITA: 4.341)

[¶1521l] EDUCATION COACHING TAX CREDIT

Effective beginning in the 2015 tax year, a non-refundable education coaching tax credit is available to teachers and teaching assistants who carry out at least ten hours of extracurricular coaching activity in the tax year. The credit amount is $500, providing a tax benefit of up to $25.30 per eligible taxpayer.

An individual is eligible for the credit if he or she meets the following criteria:

- resident in British Columbia on the last day of the taxation year;
- carries out 10 or more hours of eligible coaching activities during the taxation year;
- meets any additional criteria established by regulation (none at this time); and
- if requested, provides information to establish eligibility.

The credit is claimed on line 14 of form BC428. It is available for the 2015, 2016, and 2017 tax years, at which time the credit will be reviewed.

(BCITA: 4.36)

[¶1521m] TRAINING AND EDUCATION SAVINGS GRANT

The B.C. Training and Education Savings Grant is a one-time $1,200 grant towards a B.C. resident child's Registered Education Savings Plan after the child turns six years old. Payments are made from the Children's Education Fund.

The basic criteria to apply for the grant are that:

- the child must have been born on or after January 1, 2006;
- the child must have an RESP in place; and
- the child and a parent/guardian must be residents of B.C.

Children are eligible for the grant on their 6th birthday up until the day before their 9th birthday. Since applications for the grant can only be submitted on or after August 15, 2015, for children who had their 6th birthday in 2013, 2014, or 2015, there is an extension until August 14, 2018, or the day before their ninth birthday, whichever is later, to apply for the grant. If the child was born in 2006, there is an extension until August 14, 2019, to get the grant.

Contact your financial institution to see if they are offering the B.C. Training and Education Savings Grant; if so, request an application form.

(*British Columbia Training and Education Savings Program Regulation*, B.C. Reg. 127/2014)

[¶1522] POLITICAL CONTRIBUTION TAX CREDIT

You may deduct from your British Columbia income taxes payable a tax credit for political contributions. To qualify for the credit you must have made a contribution to a recognized British Columbia political party or constituency association, or to a candidate for election to the British Columbia legislature.

The credit is calculated as follows:

- 75% of the first $100 contributed;
- plus 50% of contributions between $100 and $550;
- plus 33¹/₃% of contributions in excess of $550.

There is an annual ceiling on political contributions tax credits of $500, meaning that credits may be earned on a maximum of $1,150 of qualifying contributions in any one taxation year.

The political contribution credit is not refundable; it is limited to the amount of British Columbia tax payable before application of the credit and there are no carryforward or carryback provisions.

You must have obtained an official receipt for your contribution, and submit it with the T1 (or, if you are submitting your form electronically, retain the receipts in case the CRA asks to see them). The B.C. provincial worksheet in your forms package offers a format for calculating the credit, which is then carried to form BC428, line 69.

[¶1522.05] *General Information*

Questions on the British Columbia Political Contributions Tax Credit should be addressed to:

Income Taxation Branch
1802 Douglas Street
Victoria, British Columbia
V8T 4K6
Telephone: 1-877-387-3332

For information about the issuance of political donation receipts, please contact Elections B.C. at 1-250-387-5305 or see the Elections B.C. website at http://www.elections.bc.ca/.

(*Political Contributions Regulations*, B.C. Reg. 343/95; BCITA: 20)

[¶1522a] FARMERS' FOOD DONATION TAX CREDIT

Effective February 17, 2016, a non-refundable farmers' food donation tax credit is available for individuals (and corporations) that carry on the business of farming and donate a qualifying agricultural product to a registered charity that provides food to those in need or helps to operate a school meal program.

The credit is worth 25% of the fair market value of the qualifying agricultural product and must be claimed in the same year that a charitable donation tax credit or deduction is claimed for the donation.

You can claim this credit if you meet all of the following conditions:

- you were a resident of British Columbia at the end of the year, or you were not a resident of British Columbia on the last day of the year but you had earned farming income in British Columbia in the year;
- you or your spouse or common-law partner was a farmer in the year;
- you made a qualifying gift to an eligible charity in the year; and
- you have claimed the qualifying gift on line 340 of your federal Schedule 9 and on line 33 of your Form BC428 as a charitable donation or gift for the year.

An agricultural product includes meat products, eggs or dairy products, fish, seafood, fruits, vegetables, grains, pulses, herbs, honey, maple syrup, mushrooms, nuts, or other produce that has been grown, raised, or harvested on a farm in British Columbia and can legally be sold, distributed, or offered for sale at a place other than the producer's premises as food or drink in British Columbia. An item of any of these types that has been processed is an agricultural product if it was processed only to the extent necessary to be legally sold off the producer's premises as food or drink intended for human consumption. Items that have been processed beyond this point, such as pies, sausages, beef jerky, pickles, and preserves are not agricultural products.

An eligible charity is a registered charity under the federal *Income Tax Act* that meets one of the following conditions:

- it distributes food to the public without charge in British Columbia and does so to provide relief to the poor (food banks meet this condition); or
- it is engaged in providing meals or snacks to students in a qualifying school.

A qualifying gift is a gift of one or more agricultural products you produced in British Columbia and donated to an eligible charity in British Columbia after February 16, 2016.

The amount of qualifying donations can be split between spouses or common-law partners. However, the total amount of qualifying donations that can be claimed by spouses or common-law partners cannot be more than the total of the qualifying donations made in the tax year. If you are preparing a return for a person who died in 2016, you can claim this credit on the deceased person's final return. If you were bankrupt in 2016, claim your farmers' food donation tax credit on either the pre- or post-bankruptcy return you file for the tax year ending December 31, 2016, depending on when the qualifying donations were made. If qualifying donations are claimed on more than one return, the total amount of donations that can be claimed on all returns filed for the year cannot be more than the total qualifying donations made.

The credit is available for the 2016, 2017, and 2018 tax years, after which the credit will be reviewed. The credit must be claimed within five tax years of the donation of agricultural product being made. The credit is claimed on line 5898 of Form BC428.

(BCITA: 20.1 Farmers' food donation tax credit; 4.52; Farmers' Food Donation Tax Credit Regulation, B.C. Reg. 113/2016)

[¶1523] SMALL BUSINESS/VENTURE CAPITAL TAX CREDIT

Individuals (and corporations) who invest in eligible British Columbia small businesses may qualify for a venture capital tax credit. Individual investors will receive a credit against B.C. tax payable equal to 30% of their investment, to a maximum credit of $60,000 in any one year. Where your B.C. provincial tax payable is less than the credit received, you will receive a refund equal to the lesser of:

(1) the venture capital tax credit; or

(2) $60,000

minus the amount of tax otherwise payable.

Any remaining credit may be carried forward and applied against B.C. tax payable for four years.

There are two forms of investment which can generate the tax credit: Investment in B.C. registered venture capital corporations (VCCs), and investment directly in approved small business corporations. The overall credit limits are the same for all such investments. The difference is that VCCs will determine the eligibility of particular small businesses and make diversified investments in them. Investors who themselves invest directly in authorized small businesses must satisfy themselves as to the eligibility and suitability of a particular investment.

In either case, investments must be made in qualified small businesses substantially engaged in one of the following activities:

- manufacturing, processing, or export of value-added goods produced in British Columbia;
- British Columbia destination tourism;
- development of proprietary technology;
- development of interactive digital new media product;
- community diversification outside of the Greater Vancouver Regional District and the Capital Regional District; or
- manufacturing, processing, or research and development within British Columbia of technologies that increase energy efficiency and conservation, reduce greenhouse gas emissions, or reduce the environmental impact of energy production, generation, storage, transmission, delivery, provision, or conversion.

A certificate from the administrator of the Small Business Venture Capital Tax Program is required (Certificate SBVC 10) and must be filed with your T1 return in order to claim the credit (or retain the certificate if you are filing electronically). Enter the amount of the credit you are claiming on line 15 or line 16 (depending on when the purchase was made) of Form BC479, *British Columbia Credits*.

Investments made in the 60 days following year end can qualify for preceding year credit provided you elect to have the rule apply. You elect simply by claiming the credit on the prior year's return on the line provided for that purpose (i.e., line 16 on the prior year's form BC479). Thus, if you buy shares on, say, February 28, 2017, you can elect to claim the credit on your 2016 return. Should you fail to do so, you can claim it on your 2017 return. VCC credits should be reported on the certificate SBVC 10, which should show the "Investment date" on which you acquired the shares.

See also ¶2522.

[¶1523.05] *General Information*

Questions on B.C. Venture Capital Corporation (VCC) Investments should be addressed to:

Investment Capital Branch
7th Floor, 1810 Blanshard Street
PO Box 9800, Stn Prov Govt
Victoria, BC V8W 9W1
Telephone: (250) 952-0136
Toll free: 1-800-665-6597
Facsimile: (250) 952-0371
Email: ecp@tbc.gov.bc.ca
Website: http://www.jti.gov.bc.ca/icp/

(*Small Business Venture Capital Act*, R.S.B.C. 1996, c. 429; *Small Business Venture Capital Act Regulation*, B.C. Reg. 390/98; BCITA: 21)

[¶1524] EMPLOYEE INVESTMENT PLAN TAX CREDITS

Under the *B.C. Employee Investment Act*, a company may establish and register with the British Columbia government either an employee share ownership plan (ESOP) or an employee venture capital plan (EVCC). Either plan permits shareholder-employees to obtain provincial tax credit for shares purchased under the plan. The British Columbia credit is 20% on ESOP shares but 15% on EVCC shares.

Investments made in the year or within 60 days of year end generate provincial credit (15% for EVCC shares) or 20% for ESOP shares to an overall collective maximum of $2,000. There must be sufficient British Columbia tax payable to absorb the credit, as it is not refundable and may not be carried forward.

Under an employee share ownership plan, shares must be held for three years or the credit is recaptured at the time of disposition. Under an employee venture capital plan, the shares must be held for five years or the credit is recaptured on disposition.

EVCC30 slips issued in 2017 for the 2016 tax year should show the B.C. EVCC on your investments at the 15% rate to a maximum of $2,000. You carry this amount to line 72 of form BC428.

Eligible ESOP investments *must* be reported to you to claim the British Columbia credit. These credits (eligible for British Columbia but not federal credit) should be reported on form ESOP 20. On line 71 of form BC428, enter the "Tax credit amount" shown on ESOP 20.

See ¶1466 and ¶2522 for details about the federal labour-sponsored venture capital corporation rules. The federal credit is being phased out from 2014 to 2016.

(*Employee Investment Act*; *Employee Investment Regulation*; BCITA: 13.1)

[¶1524.05] *General Information*

Questions on British Columbia ESOP and EVCC Investments should be addressed to:

Investment Capital Branch
7th Floor, 1810 Blanshard Street
PO Box 9800, Stn Prov Govt
Victoria, BC V8W 9W1
Telephone: (250) 952-0136
Toll free: 1-800-665-6597
Facsimile: (250) 952-0371
Email: ecp@tbc.gov.bc.ca
Website: http://www.jti.gov.bc.ca/ICP/index_icp.htm

[¶1525] BRITISH COLUMBIA MINING EXPLORATION CREDIT (FORM T88)

British Columbia offers a 20% refundable credit for qualified mining exploration expenses incurred before January 1, 2020. Qualified expenses are those for the purpose of determining the existence, location, extent or quantity of a mineral resource in British Columbia, including expenses incurred in the tax credit period in the course of:

- prospecting;
- carrying out geological, geophysical or geochemical surveys;
- drilling by rotary, diamond, percussion or other methods; or
- trenching, digging test pits and preliminary sampling.

Qualified expenses must be for goods or services acquired by the taxpayer that are all or substantially all provided in British Columbia. Qualified expenses are reduced by "assistance" received in respect of the expenses. Assistance is defined by reference to the federal rules including inducements and reimbursements in income (paragraph 12(1)(*x*) — see ¶729), except that most of the offsetting reductions to assistance (i.e., for expenses which otherwise reduce income or cost base) do not reduce assistance for purposes of the credit.

Certain expenses are specifically excluded from qualified expenses, such as:

- expenses that may reasonably be considered related to a mine that has come into production in reasonable commercial quantities, or to the extension of such a mine;
- partnership expenses (unless the individual is an active member of the partnership);
- expenses incurred in drilling or completing an oil or gas well, in building a temporary access road to an oil or gas well or in preparing a site in respect of an oil or gas well;
- outlays for Canadian development expense;
- Canadian exploration and development overhead expenses;
- Canadian exploration expenses;
- seismic data expenses;
- certain other expenses renounced under an agreement;
- personal or living expenses; and
- expenses incurred in the year in earning tax-exempt income.

Individuals must be resident in British Columbia on December 31 of the taxation year to claim the credit. Application for the credit (on form T88) must be made within 36 months of the end of the taxation year in which it is earned for tax years ending on or before December 31, 2016. A taxpayer is not entitled to the credit in respect of a taxation year that ends on or after January 1, 2017, unless the taxpayer files an application for the credit within 18 months after the end of the taxation year.

The credit calculated on form T88 is carried to line 19 on the BC479 provincial tax credit form.

[¶1525.10] *Extra 10% Credit for Exploration in Prescribed Mountain Pine Beetle Affected Areas*

An enhanced rate of 30% (rather than 20%) is available for qualified mineral exploration undertaken in prescribed Mountain Pine Beetle affected areas. The regulation prescribing affected areas merely says that the prescribed area is outlined in heavy black and shaded grey on a map filed with the Corporate Information Services Branch of the Ministry of Agriculture and Lands with the file name MPB_Salvage_Area2_2006-12-14. Effective December 1, 2008, the prescribed areas were enlarged, and the new area is described on map MPB_Salvage_Area3_2008-6-25.

To view a map of the expanded qualifying Mountain Pine Beetle area, please see the overview map at http://www.sbr.gov.bc.ca/documents_library/shared_documents/METC/Compare_SalvageArea3_and_Area2_2008-10-28.pdf or the detailed area maps at http://www.sbr.gov.bc.ca/documents_library/shared_documents/METC/KEYMAP_MPB_Salvage_Area3_2008-06-25.pdf.

(*Mining Exploration Tax Credit Regulation,* B.C. Reg. 242/2007; BCITA: 25.1)

[¶1525.15] *Forms and Publications*

The British Columbia Ministry of Finance publishes Bulletin CIT 006, *Mining Exploration Tax Credit*, which offers detailed information about the program. That and other information should be available from:

Ministry of Finance
Income Taxation Branch
PO Box 9444 Stn Prov Govt
Victoria BC V8W 9W8
Telephone (Victoria): (250) 387-3332
Service BC (In Vancouver): (604) 660-2421
Service BC (Elsewhere in BC): 1-800-663-7867, 1-877-387-3332
Fax: (250) 356-9243
Email: ITBTaxQuestions@gov.bc.ca
Website: www.gov.bc.ca/fin

The federal government provides form T88, required to support the credit claim on individual T1 returns.

[¶1525c] QUALIFYING ENVIRONMENTAL TRUST TAX CREDIT

If you are the beneficiary of a qualifying environmental trust, you may be eligible for a tax credit. A "qualifying environmental trust" is defined in subsection 248(1) of the federal Act, and may generally be described as a trust with the sole purpose of funding the reclamation of a site in British Columbia that has been a quarry or a site used for mining or waste disposal. These operations, required by the government, would involve restoration after profitable activity has ceased. Certain trusts are excluded, as listed in paragraphs (*a*) to (*j*) of the definition of "qualifying environmental trust" in subsection 248(1).

Generally, the beneficiary may claim a tax credit for a particular taxation year not exceeding (A) the trust tax paid by the qualifying environmental trust multiplied by (B) the beneficiary's income and then divided by (C) the trust's income.

This credit is claimed in section BC428MJ of form T2203, *Provincial and Territorial Taxes — Multiple Jurisdictions*. For further information about the subsection 248(1) definition of "qualifying environmental trust", see the *Canadian Tax Reporter* commentary at ¶28,226b. For additional details about qualifying environmental trusts, see ¶2232.

(BCITA: 25)

[¶1526] BRITISH COLUMBIA MINING FLOW-THROUGH SHARE CREDIT (FORM T1231)

If you have invested in flow-through shares of a company carrying on mining exploration activities in British Columbia which qualify for the federal investment tax credit described at ¶1463, the qualifying expenses of the company incurred for British Columbia exploration are eligible for a 20% tax credit against British Columbia tax payable. The credit is not refundable if it exceeds British Columbia tax, but excess credit may be carried forward 10 years and back three years. In accordance with the rules at ¶1463.05 for investment tax credit claims, you must claim your British Columbia mining flow-through share credit no later than 12 months after your filing due date for the tax year for which you received an Information Slip T101 or T5013.

Eligible British Columbia expenditures should be noted in box 141 on your T101 slip or in box 197 on your T5013 slip (partnership income). Copies of these information forms, and the calculation form T1231, should be filed with your return (unless you are filing electronically, in which case you must keep them on file in your tax records for the year in the event that the CRA requires you to support your claim). Current year credits are carried (for 2016) to line 75 of the BC428 form. Requests for carryback of excess credit are also made on form T1231. Amended returns for earlier years should not be necessary.

The credit expires on December 31, 2016 for new expenditures. After 2016, the credit will exist in carryforward form only with December 31, 2025 as the last available carryforward utilization date.

(BCITA: 4.721; Other Publications: BC Bulletin PIT 001, *Mining Flow-Through Share Tax Credit*)

[¶1527] BRITISH COLUMBIA EMPLOYER/EMPLOYEE TRAINING CREDITS

The British Columbia Training Tax Credit Program provides refundable tax credits for employees and employers engaged in apprenticeship programs administered through the British Columbia Industry Training Authority (BCITA). The credits expire on January 1, 2018 (with the exception of the tax credit for shipbuilding and ship repair industry employers — see ¶1527.30 for details). An enhanced credit of 50% of the normal credit is available for First Nations individuals and people with disabilities. The credit is claimed in the year a level is completed and it must be claimed no later than 36 months after the end of the tax year in which the level was completed.

The British Columbia Training Tax Credit Program is intended to complement the federal government's training incentives for employees and for employers (under the federal investment tax credit program — see ¶1463.80). The federal incentives apply to the first two years' enrolment in the "Red Seal" apprenticeship programs. The B.C. program is primarily intended to provide similar incentives to B.C.-recognized (non-Red Seal) apprenticeship programs, although it will also provide enhanced or supplementary benefits to Red Seal programs in some circumstances.

[¶1527.05] *Terminology*

There are basically two kinds of programs that qualify for some level of B.C. training credit — eligible recognized programs and eligible training programs. Both are prescribed by a B.C. income tax regulation, the *Training Tax Credits Regulation*. Eligible recognized programs do not include, generally speaking, Red Seal programs. Eligible training programs do include some (but not all) Red Seal programs (Red Seal programs are established under an inter-provincial program to provide standardized national credentials for some trades). See Schedule 1 of the *Training Tax Credit Regulation* for a full list of eligible recognized programs, and Schedule 2 for a list of eligible training programs.

Additional information can be found at the B.C. Ministry of Finance website, www.gov.bc.ca/fin.

[¶1527.10] *Individual's Training Credit (Form T1014)*

A person cannot be eligible for a basic credit or other training credit in a year if he or she was still in primary or secondary school at any time while taking the program in that year.

The *basic credit* for an individual is $1,000 per year for each of the first two years of an eligible recognized program (i.e., a program prescribed in Schedule 1 of the *Training Tax Credits Regulation*). By and large, these do not include programs under the Red Seal apprenticeship program. The omission of Red Seal programs recognizes the federal grants available for those programs.

This *basic credit* is available to individuals who:

- were resident in British Columbia on December 31 of the taxation year;
- were registered in an eligible recognized program (Schedule 1) in the taxation year; and
- completed in the year either the level 1 or level 2 requirements of the British Columbia recognized program.

The *completion credit* is available to individuals who were resident in British Columbia on December 31 of the taxation year, were registered in an eligible training program (Schedule 2) in the taxation year, and completed in the year either the level 3 or level 4 (or higher) requirements of the eligible training program. The credit is $2,000 if level 3 was completed in the year. If one or more of the level 4 or higher requirements were completed in the year, the credit is $2,500 for each such requirement completed in the year.

The *certification credit* is available to individuals who:

- were resident in British Columbia on December 31 of the taxation year;
- were not registered in an eligible recognized program (Schedule 1) or an eligible training program (Schedule 2) in the taxation year; and
- received a Certificate of Qualification from the Industry Training Authority in the taxation year for completing an eligible recognized program or an eligible training program after passing a challenge exam, or for completing a prescribed eligible recognized program or a prescribed eligible training program.

If the individual completed one or more eligible recognized programs in the taxation year with level 1 or level 2 completion requirements, a credit of $1,000 for each of the programs completed may be claimed. If the individual completed one or more eligible training programs in the taxation year with level 3 completion requirements, the credit is $2,000 for each of those programs completed. Finally, if the individual completed one or more eligible training programs in the taxation year with level 4 or higher completion requirements, a $2,500 credit for each of those programs completed may be claimed.

There are also *enhanced credits* for First Nations individuals or persons with disabilities. Eligible First Nations individuals are those persons who hold Status Indian cards. Persons with disabilities are those eligible for the federal disability amount credit (¶1255) on their income tax return. As well as the First Nations or disability criteria, an individual must already be entitled to a basic, certification, or completion credit above *or* be an eligible apprentice described in ¶1463.80. Thus the enhanced credit is available to both apprentices eligible for ordinary British Columbia training credits for individuals and those who are enrolled in Red Seal programs and may be ineligible for British Columbia credits.

The enhanced credit (which is *in addition* to the other credits) is 50% of the basic, certification, or completion credits, or 50% of the federal apprenticeship incentive grant, for the taxation year.

[¶1527.15] *Employer's Training Credit (Form T1014-1)*

The employer's credit is divided into basic, completion, and enhanced components.

The *basic* 20%/$4,000 credit applies to salary and wages payable within 24 months after the date the employee entered into an industry training agreement (as defined in the *Industry Training Authority Act*), and payable after 2006.

The employee must be employed in a position in a business carried on by the employer in British Columbia, and in a position that relates to an eligible recognized program (Schedule 1) in which the employee is registered in the *employer's* taxation year.

The employer's *completion credit* for an employee registered in an eligible training program (Schedule 2) is earned for an employer's taxation year in which an employee completes level 3 or level 4 or higher requirements for the program. For a level 3 completion, the credit is 15% of salary and wages payable in an eligible period to a maximum of $2,500. For a level 4 (or higher) completion, the credit is 15% of salary and wages payable in an eligible period to a maximum of $3,000. An eligible period is the period that ends at any time in a month which includes the employee's completion date for the level and does not exceed 12 months.

The employee must be employed in a position in a business carried on by the employer in British Columbia that relates to an eligible training program (Schedule 2) in which the employee is registered in the *employer's* taxation year.

An employer's *enhanced credit* is available in respect of employees who are either First Nations individuals or persons with disabilities. Eligible First Nations individuals are those persons who hold Status Indian cards. Persons with disabilities are those eligible for the federal disability amount credit (¶1255) on their income tax return.

An employer's enhanced credit is an *additional* 50% of the employer's basic or completion credit for a First Nations or disabled employee for the employer's taxation year. Where no basic employer credit is available in respect of the First Nations or disabled employee, essentially because the employee is in a Red Seal program, the enhanced credit is 5.5% of salary and wages payable in an eligible period to a maximum of $1,000 (the employer must also be claiming the federal apprenticeship job creation tax credit). The eligible period is identical to that for the basic employer credit. An eligible apprentice for purposes of the employer's federal investment tax credit (see ¶1463.80) is also an eligible apprentice for the employer's enhanced training credit, except that the apprenticeship agreement must be under the auspices of the British Columbia *Industry Training Authority Act*.

An eligible employer for all credit purposes is an individual liable for B.C. income tax. Where there are multiple non-arm's length employers in respect of a particular period, the total employer credits cannot exceed the maximum that could be claimed by any one of them if that employer had made the only claim. An employee of a partnership will generate credit apportioned among the partners.

For all levels of credit, the employee's salary and wages do not include profits, bonuses, and most taxable benefits described in Chapter 3. Salary and wages do not include amounts deferred to the taxation year under the unpaid amounts rule (¶746.10). Salary and wages must be reduced by government and non-government assistance in respect of the salary and wages for the period that the employer has received or may reasonably be expected to receive.

[¶1527.20] *General Rules*

The tax credit is refundable to individuals or employers, as the case may be, to the extent it exceeds British Columbia tax payable. Individual claims must be supported by form T1014; employer's claims by form T1014-1 (form T1014-2 for claiming the shipbuilding credit). The amounts calculated on forms T1014, T1014-1 and T1014-2 are carried respectively on lines 23, 24, and 25 of form BC479.

Claims must be made within 36 months of the end of the taxation year to which they relate.

(Training Tax Credits Regulation, B.C. Reg. 243/2007; Training Tax Credits (Prescribed Requirements and Date) Regulation, B.C. Reg. 299/2010; BCITA: 116–126; BC-InfB: PIT 002 Training Tax Credits for Apprentices; CIT 013 Training Tax Credits for Employers)

[¶1527.30] *Tax Credits for Shipbuilding and Ship Repair Industry Employers (Form T1014-2)*

Effective October 1, 2012, eligible shipbuilding and ship repair industry employers may receive refundable basic, completion, and enhanced tax credits similar to other apprentice training tax credits. The shipbuilding and ship repair training tax credits will expire at the end of 2019. An "eligible employer" is an individual liable for B.C. income tax (or a corporation liable for B.C. tax and whose income is not exempt from federal or B.C. tax).

The *basic credit* is 20% of salary and wages (up to $5,250) paid to an apprentice in the tax year while the apprentice was within the first 24 months of an eligible recognized program (see Schedule 1 of the *Training Tax Credit Regulation*) or an accredited program as defined in the *Industry Training Authority Act*. Salary and wages paid before October 1, 2012 are not eligible for this credit. There is no requirement for the apprentice to complete any technical training or a set number of hours for the employer to claim the basic tax credit. The start of the apprenticeship is the date the apprentice is registered in an eligible program with the Industry Training Authority.

The *completion credit* is 20% of salary and wages (up to $5,250) paid to an apprentice in the 12-month period prior to the apprentice completing the requirements for level 3 or higher of an eligible training program (see Schedule 2 of the *Training Tax Credit Regulation*). The completion tax credit is claimed in the tax year the level is completed, so long as the level is completed after September 30, 2012. The 12-month salary and wage period can include some portion of a prior tax year and can also include time before October 1, 2012.

The *enhanced credit* is available to an employer if an apprentice qualifies for the federal disability tax credit or is a First Nations person registered as an Indian under the *Indian Act* (Canada). The enhanced credit is 50% in addition to the basic credit or the completion credit.

You will be eligible for this credit if you are an employer whose principal business is constructing, repairing, or converting ships. Ships are defined as seagoing vessels propelled by engine, but do not include vessels ordinarily used for personal or recreational purposes. Accordingly, if your principal business is to build boats, yachts, or other water crafts ordinarily used for personal or recreational purposes, you are not eligible for this credit.

An eligible apprentice is an employee who is registered as an apprentice with the Industry Training Authority and is enrolled in an eligible apprenticeship program.

Eligible salary and wages are the gross salary and wages payable by the employer to an eligible apprentice. This does not include remuneration based on profits, bonuses, and taxable benefits including stock options, and certain unpaid remuneration.

Unlike the other training credits, the shipbuilding and ship repair training tax credits will expire at the end of 2019. Eligible shipbuilding and ship repair industry employers that claim the new tax credits will not be eligible to claim training tax credits under the existing training tax credit program. Apprentices not eligible for the shipbuilding and ship repair training tax credits may be eligible for the regular apprentice training credits.

To claim this credit, complete form T1014-2, *British Columbia Shipbuilding and Ship Repair Industry Tax Credit (Employers)*. The amount calculated on form T1014-2 is carried on line 25 of form BC479.

(*Training Tax Credits Regulation*, B.C. Reg. 243/2007; *Training Tax Credits (Prescribed Requirements and Date) Regulation*, B.C. Reg. 299/2010)

MANITOBA

[¶1528] MANITOBA INCOME TAX, BASIC CREDITS, AND LOW-INCOME TAX REDUCTIONS

[¶1528.05] *Basic Tax Rates*

Manitoba tax is based on federal taxable income from line 260 of the T1 return, upon which Manitoba rates and brackets are applied to calculate provincial tax. Manitoba tax rates applicable for 2016 are:

Taxable income	*Tax*
$31,000 or less	10.8%
In excess of	
$31,000	$3,348 + 12.75% on next $36,000
$67,000	$7,938 + 17.4% on remainder

The 2016 Manitoba Budget announced that Manitoba tax brackets will be indexed for inflation, beginning with the 2017 taxation year. A recent Manitoba rate history is found at ¶1528a.

Like the federal government, Manitoba imposes its highest tax rate (17.4%) on tax on split income (form T1206). Manitoba also imposes alternative minimum tax (AMT) at a rate of 50% of federal AMT (form T691, line 108 minus line 111 of that form).

(MITA: 4.1; 4.4; 4.5)

[¶1528.07] *Basic Tax Credits*

Manitoba offers tax credits similar to most (but not all) federal personal non-refundable tax credits, although Manitoba credit amounts differ from federal amounts and are converted to tax credits at provincial tax rates. Manitoba personal non-refundable tax credits are claimed on form MB428.

Available Manitoba personal tax credits include: a basic personal credit, spouse or common-law partner credit, eligible dependant credit, caregiver credit, infirm dependant credit, age credit, EI premium and CPP contribution credits, pension income credit, disability credit and supplement, tuition and education credits (the federal education credit is repealed effective January 1, 2017), student loan interest credit, medical expense credit, charitable donations credit, fitness credit, children's arts and cultural activity credit, and adoption expense credit. Beginning in 2015, Manitoba also adopted the volunteer firefighters' tax credit and the search and rescue volunteers' tax credit. Manitoba has not adopted tax credits similar to the federal textbook credit (the federal textbook credit is repealed effective January 1, 2017) or public transit pass credit.

The Manitoba fitness credit, children's arts and cultural activity credit, adoption expense credit, volunteer firefighters' credit, search and rescue volunteers' credit, and pension income credit are available only to residents of the province. The Manitoba fitness credit differs from the federal credit in that it is available for children as well as young adults under the age of 25.

Like the federal government, Manitoba gives tax credit at its lowest rate (10.8%) on personal amounts. Also like the federal government, Manitoba makes an exception for charitable donation credit, giving credit at its lowest rate (10.8%) on the first $200 of donation and at its highest rate (17.4%) on the balance. Donation amounts should be taken from lines 345 and 347 of Schedule 9 of the federal return.

Most Manitoba credit amounts differ from the federal amounts. Personal amounts for CPP/QPP premiums, EI premiums, student loan interest credit, and the children's arts credit will be the same as on the federal Schedule 1. All other personal amounts require calculation on form MB428 and/or the Manitoba worksheet provided with the Manitoba T1 package. Although Manitoba does not index most of its credit amounts annually, select credit amounts are adjusted periodically. The 2016 provincial Budget announced that the basic personal amount will be indexed beginning in 2017. For a chart of Manitoba personal credit amounts for 2016, see ¶52 at the beginning of this book.

As well, where a student must calculate education/tuition tax credit amounts and/or transfers on federal Schedule 11, the student must make a parallel provincial calculation on MB(S11). Similarly, where you are claiming a transfer of personal amounts from your spouse or common-law partner on federal Schedule 2, you must make the parallel Manitoba claim on MB(S2).

Other Manitoba tax credits based on federal credits, but for which Manitoba imposes its own tax credit rates, include the following:

- dividend tax credit: for eligible dividends, 8%; for other taxable Canadian dividends, 0.7835%; and
- minimum tax carryover (from Schedule 1 line 427): at 50%.

(MITA: 4.1; 4.6–4.9)

[¶1528.10] *Manitoba Family Tax Benefit*

The Manitoba Family Tax Benefit is a set of personal amounts which convert to non-refundable tax credit. They supplement the general personal amount system but are means-tested, which is to say their value is reduced as income increases.

The Manitoba Family Benefit is calculated on form MB428-A and claimed on line 6147 of Form MB428. It consists of a personal amount of $2,065 for you, plus $2,065 if you were 65 or over. There is a further amount of $2,065 for your spouse or common-law or eligible dependant provided there was a positive amount (even $1) you could claim for that person on line 5812 or 5816 of form MB428.

You can claim an additional $2,065 if your spouse or common-law partner was 65 or over in the year *and* you claimed an amount on Manitoba Schedule MB(S2) (transfer of personal amounts from spouse or common-law partner) in respect of your spouse/partner. For you to have claimed such an amount, the CRA says, in effect, that your claim for your spouse/partner's age amount must exceed your spouse/partner's income as calculated for MB(S2) purposes. This follows from the Manitoba ordering provisions, which include specific ordering provisions for these credits.

You can claim an additional $2,752 if your spouse or common-law partner had a disability certificate (form T2201) valid for the year *and* you claimed an amount on Manitoba Schedule MB(S2) (transfer of personal amounts from spouse or common-law partner) in respect of your spouse/partner. For you to have claimed such an amount, the CRA says, in effect, that your total claim for your spouse/partner's disability amount plus the total claims at line 9 of MB(S2) must exceed your claim for your spouse/partner's tuition/education amounts on line 4. Presumably, this follows from the ordering provisions of the Manitoba statute.

There is a further $2,752 for each dependant who was 18 or younger at the end of the taxation year, and for whom you or your spouse or common-law partner could claim the Canada Child Benefit during the year, or could have made such a claim but for your family income. As between you and your spouse or common-law partner, only the person with the higher income can make this claim. You cannot make this claim for a child who you must claim as an eligible dependant or have claimed as an infirm dependant.

You may also claim $2,752 if you claimed a disability amount yourself, and for each dependant for whom you claimed a Manitoba disability credit. You may also make this claim for a disabled dependant of your spouse or common-law partner, but the higher income spouse or partner must make this claim.

The total of these accumulated amounts is then reduced by 9% of your own (but not your spouse's or common-law partner's) net income from line 236 of the federal return.

There are several overriding rules (some of which repeat rules mentioned above). These are:

- if two individuals who are spouses or common-law partners of each other may otherwise include an amount in respect of the same dependant for a taxation year, only the individual with the greater income for the year may include it;
- if two or more individuals who are not spouses or common-law partners of each other may otherwise include an amount in respect of the same dependant for a taxation year, only one of them may include the amount and, if they cannot agree as to who will include it, only the individual with the greater income for the year may include it;
- if an individual becomes bankrupt in a calendar year, the total of the amounts that may be claimed under the family tax benefit rules for the individual's taxation years ending in the calendar year must not exceed the total of the amounts that would have been included under that provision for the calendar year if the individual had not become bankrupt.

One conclusion from these rules is that in the case of a married or common-law couple, each spouse/partner can claim his or her own basic amount, age amount, and disability amount. Where amounts remain for spousal transfer after each return is complete, the spouse/partner receiving the transfer may also claim for age and disability amounts of the transferor, subject to the ordering provisions imposed. Where amounts are claimed in respect of common dependants, the higher income spouse/partner must make the claim (thus of course reducing its value, as the higher income will be used to grind the claim).

(MITA: 4.6(16.1), (16.2), (20)(*m*))

[¶1528.15] *Manitoba Personal Tax Credit*

Having given you non-refundable credit for yourself and your eligible dependants on forms MB428 and MB428-A, Manitoba then repeats the process by giving you a refundable credit on the MB479 for yourself and essentially the same set of dependants eligible under the first set of rules. The amounts differ from the MB428 and MB428-A amounts, and the rules differ slightly, as discussed at ¶1532.

(MITA: 5; 5.3; 5.7)

[¶1528a] RECENT RATE HISTORY

For 2011 through 2015, Manitoba rates were:

Taxable income	*Tax*
$31,000 or less	10.8%
In excess of	
$31,000	$3,348 + 12.75% on next $36,000
$67,000	$7,938 + 17.4% on remainder

The dividend tax credit rate was 8% for eligible dividends for 2012 through 2015, and 11% for 2011. For other Canadian dividends, the rate was 0.83% for 2014 and 2015, and 1.75% for 2011 to 2013.

[¶1530] REFUNDABLE CREDITS AND FAMILY INCOME

Among the various personal tax reductions and credits permitted by Manitoba, several are refundable if they exceed provincial tax payable. Among these refundable credits are the property tax credits discussed at ¶1531, the personal tax credit at ¶1532, the primary caregiver credit at ¶1533c, the fertility treatment tax credit at ¶1533e, and the advance tuition tax credit at ¶1533g.10. The property tax credit is subdivided into an education property tax credit (¶1531.05 through ¶1531.20) and a homeowner's school tax credit for those 55 or older (¶1531.25). If you are not required to file a return (see ¶200), for example, because you have no tax payable for the year, you should nevertheless file a return to obtain your Manitoba credits if you are eligible for them. As for federal purposes, you must ask for any refund due to you by filing a return within three years of December 31 of the year for which the refund is sought.

The refundable personal and property tax credits (except for the homeowner's school tax credit) are "means-tested". That is, for these credits, the amount otherwise determined is reduced by a percentage of your "family income". Family income is calculated on Schedule MB479 on which various credits are also calculated. Family income is simply the sum of your own net income from line 236 of your T1 form, and that of any cohabiting spouse or common-law partner (¶1113) as of December 31 of the year for which the return is filed. It appears that, in calculating family income, net income from line 236 of the return of anyone whose income is required to be included (whether that person must file a return or not) is included in full. However, any universal child care benefits (UCCB; see ¶935) included in the income of either you and your spouse or common-law partner are subtracted from family income for these purposes. Repayments of UCCB are added back. The taxable portion of withdrawals from registered disability savings plans is also excluded from family income.

The Manitoba statute specifies that a cohabiting spouse or common-law partner does not include (i) someone from whom you are living separate and apart on December 31 by reason of marital/partnership breakdown, provided the separation lasts for 90 days including December 31; or (ii) someone from whom you were living separate and apart on December 31 by reason of medical necessity. Your spouse's or common-law partner's net income should be calculated as discussed at ¶1103. The spouse (or common-law partner) is not required to file a return.

If you are a widow(er), separated, divorced, or single, your net income alone (net of UCCB and RDSP income) is family income.

Manitoba law provides fines and prison penalties for deliberately making a false claim or return to obtain a refund to which you are not entitled.

(MITA: 5.3)

[¶1531] REFUNDABLE EDUCATION PROPERTY TAX CREDIT/SCHOOL TAX CREDIT

The Manitoba property tax credit system has two components. First, there is an element of the credit based on occupancy cost of your principal place of residence, called the Education Property Tax Credit. This credit may be higher for taxpayers who have reached the age of 65 or older during the taxation year. Second, there is a School Tax Credit element which will offset some or all school taxes paid by property tax payers who have reached the age of 55 or older during the taxation year. The collective credit accumulated by these rules is reduced by any Manitoba Rent Assist benefits received, and is further reduced for Manitoba social assistance (welfare) recipients as described at ¶1533.

[¶1531.05] *Occupancy Costs*

The Manitoba education property tax credit computation commences with your "dwelling unit cost". Dwelling unit cost includes municipal tax paid, and 20% of rental payments paid in Manitoba for the taxation year in respect of a principal residence.

Rental payments must exclude any amounts on account of meals or board. If your principal residence is a personal care home, the rental cost includes 50% of the *per diem* charges that have not been claimed as a medical expense under the first rule discussed at ¶1207. In practice, a resident of such a home totals up the *per diem* charges for the year, deducts any portion *of those charges* claimed on line 330 of Schedule 1, and includes 50% of the balance in the box for "Total rent paid in Manitoba" (box 6110) on form MB479. A "personal care home" is not defined as such in the Manitoba tax rules, but is clearly intended to mean a nursing home which under Manitoba Health Department regulations charges a regulated *per diem* rate based on the resident's income.

If your principal residence is a mobile home, the municipal licence fee paid for the year is a dwelling unit cost.

If you have not paid any municipal tax or mobile home licence fee, but you paid a service charge for the year to the government, a local government district, or a person who manages and administers in your area services of the type normally managed and controlled by a municipal council, the service charge is a dwelling unit cost.

Your dwelling unit costs for the year are then reduced by $250 to arrive at "occupancy cost".

(MITA: 5.3)

[¶1531.10] *Principal Residence for Manitoba Credit*

A principal residence for purposes of the Manitoba education property tax credit includes premises owned or rented by you or your spouse or common-law partner in Manitoba and ordinarily inhabited by you or your spouse or common-law partner. It may include contiguous land which contributes to the enjoyment of the unit as a residence, excluding any land which is not assessed as residential property, is exempt from municipal tax, or is not the subject of a grant in lieu of municipal tax. This conforms to the federal rule at ¶554(5).

Only one residence at a time may be a principal residence. It would seem to follow that if you have more than one qualifying residence you ordinarily inhabit, you may choose any one for a particular year. On the other hand, if you moved during a year, or shifted your principal residence from one house you already own to a second house you already own, you may claim dwelling unit costs in respect of each principal residence in the proportion that the cost for each period is of the whole year.

Subject to the year of marriage/partnership rule below, you and your spouse or common-law partner may make only one claim for the property tax credit; you must decide which of you will make it. It should not matter who makes the claim, since the credit is refundable if it exceeds tax. The spouse or common-law partner who claims this credit must also claim the cost-of-living credit at ¶1532 and the School Tax Credit below. In the year of death the surviving spouse must make the claim (but if there is no surviving spouse it can be made on the final return for the year of death).

In the year in which you marry or become a common-law partner, if each spouse would otherwise have qualified to claim the property tax credit, each may claim the credit for the period prior to the marriage/partnership, but only one of you can make the claim for the remaining period of the year.

(MITA: 5.3)

[¶1531.15] *Education Property Tax Credit*

Your basic property tax credit is the lesser of your occupancy cost and $700. If you turned 65 or older in the year, the credit is the lesser of occupancy cost and $1,100 minus the lesser of $400 and 1% of family income. The credit is reduced by any Rent Assist benefits received. Form MB479 clearly directs you through these calculations.

These maximum credit thresholds of $700 for taxpayers other than seniors and $700 to $1,100 for senior taxpayers have been adjusted periodically. The maximum available credit for taxpayers other than seniors was $700 for 2011 through

2014. For senior taxpayers, the maximum available credit was $1,100 for 2013 and 2014, $1,025 for 2012, and $950 for 2011.

Family income is simply the income for the year of both you and your spouse or common-law partner, reduced by any UCCB inclusions and registered disability savings plan payments and increased by any UCCB repayments in the year, as discussed at ¶1530, above.

Most homeowners receive the base amount as a deduction on their municipal property tax statement. Tenants and homeowners who qualify for more than the minimum amount must claim the credit on form MB479.

(MITA: 5.3; 5.4)

[¶1531.20] *Property Tax Credit Denied*

The education property tax credit may be claimed by all individuals resident in Manitoba on December 31, *except*:

(1) persons under age 16 at the end of the year;

(2) a person living in the Manitoba principal residence of someone who claimed that person as a dependant for the taxation year in question;

(3) employees of foreign governments, and members of their family, who are exempt from income tax (¶120); and

(4) a non-Canadian citizen (and members of his or her family) on active service with foreign armed forces.

Taxpayers are not eligible for the education property tax credit while receiving social assistance payments. The credit is disallowed for the months in the year that social assistance payments were received. See ¶1533.

(*Manitoba Social Assistance Recipients' Tax Credit Eligibility Regulation*; MITA: 5.4)

[¶1531.25] *School Tax Credit*

A second form of property tax credit is provided if in the taxation year you: (i) turned 55 years or older, (ii) you or your cohabiting spouse or partner were the principal owner or a life tenant of a principal residence or had entered into an agreement to purchase a principal residence in the year, and (iii) you or your cohabiting spouse or partner paid school taxes in respect of that principal residence.

Your cohabiting spouse or partner is a spouse or common-law partner with whom you lived at any time during the year. It does not include someone from whom you were separated throughout the year by reason of breakdown of the relationship, or someone from whom you lived apart by reason of medical necessity.

If you have a spouse or common-law partner, only one of you can make this claim.

If you meet the above qualifications, you may claim additional property tax credit of the least of:

(1) $175 minus 2% of family income (¶1530) in excess of $15,100, which eliminates the credit at family income of $23,800; there is authority to simplify this calculation which Manitoba exercises through the chart which forms part of the Manitoba information sheet which is part of the Manitoba T1 return;

(2) municipal taxes imposed for school purposes in respect of your principal residence in excess of $160 (minus any seniors' school tax rebate received by you or your spouse or common-law partner); and

(3) occupancy cost in excess of the basic property tax credit for occupancy, as calculated under that heading above.

The credit is reduced by any Rent Assist benefits received. Form MB479 sets out this calculation.

Taxpayers are not eligible for the school tax credit while receiving social assistance payments. The credit is disallowed for the months in the year that social assistance payments were received. See ¶1533.

(MITA: 5.3; 5.5)

[¶1531a] SENIORS' SCHOOL TAX REBATE

The seniors' school tax rebate provides a refundable tax credit for eligible Manitobans age 65 or older who own their own home or are liable for the payment of school tax on their principal residence. The 2016 Manitoba Budget announced several changes to the rebate for 2016 and subsequent years, including the fact that it will now be administered by the CRA through the income tax system, rather than by direct application to Manitoba Finance as in past years.

You can claim this rebate if you or your spouse or common-law partner met all of the following conditions:

- you were 65 years of age or older at the end of the year;
- you own your home or you are liable for paying the school taxes on your principal residence;
- either you or your spouse or common-law partner lived at the property as your principal residence on the municipal property tax due date;
- you were a resident of Manitoba at the end of the year; and
- your family income is less than $63,500.

The rebate is calculated on Form MB479, lines 33 to 41. You start by entering the amount of school taxes assessed for Manitoba in box 6149. This includes any community revitalization levy amounts in lieu of school taxes. However, you should only include that portion which relates to your principal residence. For example, if you live in one side of a duplex and rent out the other side, you can only claim half of the school taxes. Then you subtract your education property tax credit (¶1531.15). The maximum rebate is $470, but this is reduced by 2% of net family income over $40,000. Partial rebates are available to seniors with a net family income of less than $63,500.

If you have a spouse or common-law partner, only one of you can claim the rebate. You and your spouse or common-law partner have to decide who will claim it.

The following rules apply in special situations.

- If you do not own the property, you may also be eligible if you, or your spouse or common-law partner, are identified on the municipal property tax statement as the person(s) responsible for paying the school tax, as of the municipal property tax due date.
- If you and your spouse or common-law partner are separated for medical reasons (e.g., one spouse living in a personal care home) or you and your spouse or common-law partner own more than one property, you may still be eligible.
- If you and your spouse moved to a new principal residence, your move will determine if you qualify for a rebate on your new residence. You are eligible to claim

the rebate if you own and live in the residence on the municipal property tax due date. If you take possession of your new residence before the municipal property tax due date, you are eligible to claim the rebate on your new residence. In this situation the previous owner would not be eligible. If you take possession of your new residence after the municipal property tax due date, you cannot claim the rebate on that property for that year, but you can claim with respect to your previous residence if you owned and lived at the property as of the municipal property tax due date.

- A person under age 65 can claim the rebate as long as they live with a spouse or common-law partner who is 65 or older.

(MITA: 5.5.1)

[¶1532] REFUNDABLE PERSONAL TAX CREDIT

The refundable personal tax credit is the sum of the specified amounts listed on page 1 of form MB479, reduced by 1% of family income as discussed at ¶1530 above. Eligibility for each item of the credit is described accurately in the CRA information sheet that accompanies MB479.

Couples (married or common-law partners) must choose which one of them is to claim the credit. Since the credit is refundable and should be the same whoever claims it, it does not matter which one makes the claim; however, if either spouse or common-law partner claims the refundable property tax credit at ¶1531, the same one must claim the refundable personal credit as well. In the year the marriage or common-law partnership commences, this means the person who claims the property tax credit for the period of marriage/partnership. This should work to your advantage, since claiming the credits separately could double up the family income reduction. If one spouse dies in the year, the other must claim the credits (whereas if you die without a spouse, the credits may be claimed on your final return for the year of death).

(MITA: 5; 5.1; 5.7)

[¶1532.05] *Where Deduction Denied*

According to the statute, the Manitoba refundable personal tax credit may be claimed by all individuals resident in Manitoba on December 31, except:

(1) persons under age 16 at the end of the year;

(2) persons under age 19 at the end of the year unless (i) married or a common-law partner, (ii) a parent, or (iii) eligible for property tax credit for the year;

(3) persons claimed as a dependant by another individual on any of line 303, 305, 306, 318, or 326 of the other individual's federal T1 return;

(4) persons whose age exemption or disability deduction (or any portion thereof) has been used by another individual on line 318 or 326 of the other individual's T1 return;

(5) a person who was on December 31 an inmate of a penitentiary, correctional institution or penal institution and had been an inmate of such a prison for six months or longer during the year;

(6) employees of foreign governments, and members of their family, who are exempt from income tax (¶120); and

(7) a non-Canadian citizen (and members of its family) on active service with foreign armed forces.

Taxpayers are not eligible for the personal tax credit while receiving social assistance payments. The personal tax credit is disallowed for the months in the year that social assistance payments were received. See ¶1533.

(MITA: 5.7)

[¶1533] SOCIAL ASSISTANCE RECIPIENTS AND PROPERTY/PERSONAL TAX CREDITS

Generally, social assistance (welfare) recipients are denied the credits discussed under ¶1531 and ¶1532 above. Instead, social assistance benefits themselves have been increased to give effect to the value of the credits. This is alleged to have several benefits: the recipients receive the sums monthly, rather than in a lump sum at the end of the year; tax discounters are not entitled to a share; and a complex tax return calculation can be avoided by those who file only to obtain credits.

These rules apply only if you or your spouse (at the end of the year as defined for purposes of the Canada Child Benefit at ¶1498) received provincial or municipal social assistance payments during the year. The combined refundable personal and property tax credits are disallowed for the months in the year that social assistance payments were received. This number is reported as a fraction in box 14 on the T5007 slip issued by Manitoba; the total credits (at line 58 of the MB479) are reduced by multiplying by this fraction (on line 6130 of the MB479). Federal or charitable social assistance payments should not put you offside; that is, these can be received without disqualifying you from receiving credit.

(*Social Assistance Recipients' Tax Credit Eligibility Regulation*; MITA: 5(2))

[¶1533c] PRIMARY CAREGIVER CREDIT

This refundable tax credit is intended to provide some recompense to a "primary caregiver" who provides care *without remuneration* (earned by either the taxpayer or the taxpayer's spouse or common-law partner) to a Manitoba Home Care recipient. There is no limitation on who may be a primary caregiver; it may be a spouse, relative, neighbour, or friend of the recipient. The recipient must be resident in Manitoba, eligible for Manitoba health insurance benefits, and assessed by Manitoba health care authorities as requiring Care Levels 2, 3, or 4 while living at home. Examples include those with a disability, people with life-threatening illnesses, and others needing care and supervision for periods of more than three months.

After a three-month qualifying period, the refundable credit is a maximum annual amount of $1,400 per care recipient of the primary caregiver. A caregiver may not claim the credit for more than three care recipients in a given month. This maximum amount per recipient was increased for 2015 and subsequent years; previously, the maximum annual credit per care recipient was $1,275.

The caregiver and the person receiving care must jointly complete a primary caregiver tax credit application and have it approved by their regional health authority or Manitoba Family Services before being eligible to claim the credit. Caregivers must use a log form to keep track of the number of days that care is provided for each care recipient since the credit is prorated on a daily basis. Additional information, including application and log forms, is available on the Manitoba Finance website at: www.gov.mb.ca/finance/tao/caregiver.html.

Technically, each of the credits to which the primary caregiver is entitled is $1,400 prorated by the number of days in the taxation year (of the caregiver) over 365 which, in relation to a particular care recipient,

(1) is within the caregiver's creditable period;

(2) does not fall within an interruption period;

(3) is not included in determining the caregiver's tax credit for the taxation year in respect of more than two other qualified home care recipients; and

(4) is not included in determining another individual's primary caregiver tax credit for the taxation year in respect of the care recipient.

That is, you prorate days in the year in a creditable period (but not in an interruption period) over 365. You may only count a particular day in respect of three care recipients, and you may not count a day for which someone else is claiming the primary caregiver credit.

A creditable period begins when the caregiver has already acted as primary caregiver for a period of 90 days, and ends when

(1) the caregiver ceases to provide care or supervision as the care recipient's primary caregiver,

(2) an interruption period in relation to the creditable period has lasted three years, or

(3) the care recipient permanently ceases to be a qualified home care client. It is the responsible regional health authority that determines who is a *primary* caregiver and when the periods commence and end.

An "interruption period" is a period of more than 14 consecutive days during which (a) the care recipient is hospitalized or temporarily residing in a personal care home or other institution; (b) the care recipient has temporarily ceased to be a qualified home care client, or (c) the caregiver has not provided care or supervision to the care recipient. Regulations may add to this definition.

The credit is claimed on line 6125 of form MB479. A worksheet at the bottom of that form is used to list the name of each qualifying care recipient and prorate the credit for the number of days of care provided to each recipient.

Program details for caregivers and their care recipients are available from regional health authorities (RHAs), Manitoba Health and Healthy Living, and through related community resources. Caregivers and their care recipients may obtain information from At Your Service Manitoba at 1-866-626-4862, or by emailing Manitoba Health and Healthy Living at ContinuingCareBranch@gov.mb.ca.

(MITA: 5.11)

[¶1533e] FERTILITY TREATMENT TAX CREDIT

Manitoba provides a refundable tax credit for medical costs associated with fertility treatments. The credit is available for 40% of eligible costs, up to a maximum annual tax credit amount of $8,000 on expenditures up to $20,000.

Eligible costs include expenditures incurred in the year for infertility treatment services provided at an accredited clinic in Manitoba, as well as prescription medication prescribed in relation to such services, net of any reimbursements, such as amounts provided by private health care coverage. To qualify for the Manitoba credit, these expenditures must also be eligible for the federal medical expense credit. Examples of qualifying services include *in vitro* fertilization, drug therapies, and insemination procedures.

To be eligible for the credit, you must have been resident in Manitoba on the last day of the taxation year. Where you have a spouse or common-law partner, the credit may be claimed either by you or your spouse or partner, but may not be split between you.

The credit is claimed at line 6146 of form MB479. Receipts in support of your claim should be filed with your paper return, or if you are filing electronically, should be retained.

(MITA: 5.13)

[¶1533g] MANITOBA TUITION TAX REBATE (FORM T1005)

This credit is in addition to the tuition and education amounts calculated on Schedule MB(S11) and claimed in box 5856 of form MB428. The credit is available for individuals that have graduated from an eligible post-secondary course. In addition, eligible post-secondary students may claim an advance rebate in the form of a refundable tax credit (see ¶1533g.10 below). To claim the credit or advance credit, you must have been resident in Manitoba at the end of the taxation year.

Eligible individuals may claim, as a tuition fee tax credit for the taxation year, an amount not exceeding the least of the following amounts:

(1) $2,500;

(2) 10% of the individual's "eligible tuition amount" at the end of the taxation year;

(3) the amount, if any, by which 60% of the individual's "eligible tuition amount" at the end of the taxation year exceeds the total of all amounts deducted in computing tax payable for the tuition fee tax credit in the preceding 19 taxation years and all amounts claimed as an advance tuition fee tax credit for a preceding taxation year. (Although the statute could be clearer, this must mean that the claim of any one year is limited to 60% of the entire accumulated tuition pool minus the total claims made in preceding 19 years. Thus, for example, if the tuition pool was $40,000, the cap is 60% of $40,000, or $24,000. If annual claims are $2,500, after nine years they will total $22,500, and the claim in the tenth year will be the $24,000 cap minus the $22,500 of accumulated claims, or $1,500);

(4) $25,000 minus the total of all amounts deducted for the tuition fee tax credit and claimed for the advance tuition fee tax credit for a preceding taxation year. The maximum lifetime rebate is $25,000 (equivalent to a 60% rebate on tuition fees of $41,667), payable over a period of six years; and

(5) Manitoba tax payable for the year after virtually all other non-refundable credits.

The "eligible tuition amount" (which is the subject of the annual limitations in (2) and (3), above) of an individual at the end of a particular taxation year is defined as the total of all amounts each of which is a tuition fee

- that was paid for a course that ended when the individual graduated or before that time;
- that was eligible for a federal tuition credit (¶1321–¶1335) not more than 19 years before the particular year; and
- in respect of which the individual first claimed an amount under this section within 10 years after his or her first graduation after completing the course.

The eligible tuition amount is therefore the whole pool of tuition accumulated in the course of higher education.

Unclaimed amounts, on a first-in first-out basis, expire after 19 years. Claims must commence within 10 years of graduation.

The mechanics of the 10% limitation and the 60% limitation mean that the allowable pool of tuition fees can be utilized in no less than six years.

The rebate will not affect bursaries and scholarships or existing tax credits for education and tuition fees.

The CRA provides form T1005 to calculate the amount you may claim for a year, which is then carried to line 6086 of form MB428. Documents in support of the credit should be retained if the return is filed electronically, or filed with the return if paper filed.

In the year of death, the $2,500 and 10% annual limits do not apply to a claim by the deceased taxpayer.

(MITA: 4.9.1)

[¶1533g.10] *Advance Tuition Tax Rebate*

Manitoba post-secondary students can claim an advance of the tuition fee tax rebate, in the form of a refundable tax credit.

The advance credit is available for 5% of fees paid, to a maximum credit amount of $500. In addition, the credit is subject to a lifetime cap of $5,000. Any advance credit amounts claimed will reduce available tax credit amounts that may be claimed after a student graduates, under the tuition tax rebate above.

To claim the advance credit, you must be resident in Manitoba at the end of the taxation year. You may not claim the credit if you are claiming the tuition rebate at line 6086 of form MB428. The advance credit is claimed at line 6145 of form MB479.

(MITA: 4.9.1; 5.12)

[¶1534] POLITICAL CONTRIBUTION TAX CREDIT

You may deduct from Manitoba income taxes otherwise payable a portion of contributions you made to recognized Manitoba political parties, and candidates for election to the Manitoba legislature. The Manitoba political contribution tax credit is the aggregate of:

(1) 75% of the first $400 of total contributions;

(2) 50% of the next $350 of total contributions (contributions over $400 but under $751); and

(3) 33.33% of the next $525 of total contributions (over $750 but not over $1,275).

The maximum allowable credit is $650, reached at a contribution level of $1,275. The credit can be calculated on the Provincial Worksheet and is claimed on line 55 of form MB428. Documents in support of the credit should be retained if the return is filed electronically, or filed with the return if paper-filed.

(MITA: 4.11)

[¶1535] LABOUR-SPONSORED FUNDS TAX CREDIT

Taxpayers who purchase qualifying shares in a labour-sponsored venture capital corporation may receive a Manitoba tax credit of 15% of invested amounts. For funds registered after July 1, 2006, the maximum credit is $1,800 (based on an investment of $12,000). Manitoba taxpayers can earn these credits by investing in one of the two companies currently registered under Manitoba's *Labour-Sponsored Venture Capital Corporations Act*: GrowthWorks Canadian Fund Ltd. and Golden Opportunities Fund Inc.

The Manitoba legislation provides that funds registered before July 1, 2006 are eligible for a maximum Manitoba credit of $750 based on a maximum eligible investment of $5,000. However, the only funds registered prior to that date were the Crocus Investment Fund (which went into receivership in 2005 and was subsequently liquidated) and the ENSIS Growth Fund (which subsequently merged with GrowthWorks Canadian Fund Ltd.).

Investments can be made through an RRSP, as discussed at ¶2522.

Manitoba credits are claimed on line 6080 of form MB428, and federal credits at line 414 on Schedule 1 of the federal T1 return. Manitoba credits are to be supported by form T2C(MAN.), which should be filed with the return where a paper return is filed. In other cases, it must be kept on hand in case the CRA questions the credit.

Note the federal redemption restrictions and potential credit recapture on these shares, discussed at ¶1466.

(MITA: 11.1–11.5)

[¶1535d] MANITOBA COMMUNITY ENTERPRISE DEVELOPMENT TAX CREDIT (FORM T1256)

This credit is available to individuals resident in Manitoba who invest in specifically approved "community enterprises or community development investment pools" within the taxation year or the first 60 days of the following calendar year.

Significant enhancements to this credit were implemented for investments made after June 11, 2014. Accordingly, the credit claimed by an investor will vary depending on the date of the investment, as explained below.

- Investments made after June 11, 2014 and before 2021 are eligible for a 45% refundable credit to a maximum of $27,000 (on a $60,000 investment). The refundable credit is claimed on line 6135 of form MB479.
- Investments made before June 12, 2014 were eligible for a 30% non-refundable credit, to a maximum of $9,000 (on a $30,000 investment). Unused credits may be carried forward 10 years and back three years and are claimed on line 6085 of form MB428.

The credit is calculated on form T1256, Manitoba Community Enterprise Development Tax Credit. If filing a paper return, T1256 should be attached, along with the investment receipt, Slip T2CEDTC (MAN). If filing electronically, these documents do not have to be remitted, but should be retained by the taxpayer.

Investments must remain in place for three years; to the extent they are transferred or redeemed before the three-year holding period is up, tax credits claimed are subject to recapture by Manitoba. Manitoba can prescribe circumstances in which earlier transfers or redemptions are permitted. Thus, early transfer is permitted in the case of death, where investments can be transferred to an estate or heirs. Early redemptions are permitted where the credit has not been claimed and the tax credit receipt returned to the issuer; where the holder of the investment has received it on the death of the investor; or where the individual to whom the CED tax credit receipt was issued in respect of the investment became disabled and permanently unfit for work, or terminally ill, after the investment was acquired.

Eligible community enterprises turn out to be partnerships or taxable Canadian corporations with assets not in excess of $25 million and net assets not in excess of $10 million. The enterprise must not have more than 200 employees; 25% of its employees must be employed in Manitoba; and 90% of the carrying value of its property must be attributable to property it uses in an active business (other than an ineligible business) it carries on.

Ineligible businesses are many. An ineligible business is a business the principal purpose of which is to derive income from one or more of the following:

(1) property, other than commercial property owned by a community development corporation or by a corporation controlled by a community development corporation;

(2) providing management, administrative, financial or other similar services;

(3) providing maintenance services, unless they are provided primarily to persons who deal at arm's length with the provider;

(4) farming, fishing, forestry, hunting, resource exploration or other similar activities;

(5) the performing arts, sports, amusement, gaming or recreational activities;

(6) an incorporated business that would be a personal services business as defined for federal purposes if that definition were read without reference to paragraphs (c) and (d) of the definition; that is, an incorporated employee regardless of the number of employees of the incorporated employee and regardless of whether the source of income is an associated corporation;

(7) providing seasonal facilities, services or activities, such as recreational parks or camps, hunting or fishing lodges or camps, or golf courses;

(8) providing professional services that are governed by an Act of the Legislature;

(9) providing educational, health care, social or other similar services, unless they are recognized by the minister as being eligible in the circumstances;

(10) any other activity that, in the opinion of the minister, (i) does not constitute or promote community economic development, or (ii) it would be contrary to public policy to support with public funds.

There are, of course, many other requirements to be complied with by the underlying business.

An investment corporation to invest in eligible businesses may itself be eligible.

A business plan and project application must be submitted to the CED Tax Credit Office for review and approval. Successful applicants will receive a letter of commitment pending final approval of an Offering Memorandum from the Manitoba Securities Commission. Once approval is received funds must be invested as per the conditions of issuance.

The program operates under the aegis of the Manitoba Department of Agriculture, Food and Rural Initiatives. Details of the program are available from:

Economic Development Initiatives Knowledge Centre
915–401 York Ave.
Winnipeg, MB R3C 0P8
Phone: (204) 945-2157
Fax: (204) 948-2362
Toll free: 1-800-567-7334 (Manitoba)
Email: ruralinits@gov.mb.ca

(Community Enterprise Development (CED) Tax Credit Regulation; MITA: 11.8–11.12)

[¶1535e] SMALL BUSINESS VENTURE CAPITAL TAX CREDIT (FORM T1256-1)

This credit provides a provincial non-refundable income tax credit for individuals and corporations in Manitoba who invest directly in emerging enterprises that require larger amounts of investment capital than community ownership can provide. The minimum investment amount by an investor is $20,000 and the lifetime limit on the amount that an investor can contribute to a qualifying investee corporation is $450,000. Securities do not qualify as registered savings plan investments.

Significant enhancements to this credit were implemented for investments made after June 11, 2014. Accordingly, the credit earned by an investor will vary depending on the date of the investment, as explained below.

- Investments made after June 11, 2014 and before 2020 earn a 45% credit to a maximum of $202,500 (on a $450,000 investment).
- Investments made before June 12, 2014 earned a 30% credit to a maximum of $135,000 (on a $450,000 investment).

The maximum annual credit that may be claimed in 2014 and subsequent years is $67,500 ($45,000 for prior years), even though the earned credit may be significantly higher. Any earned but unused credit amounts may be carried back three years and carried forward 10 years.

The credit is calculated on form T1256-1, Manitoba Small Business Venture Capital Tax Credit (Individuals), and claimed at field 6092 of form MB428. If filing a paper return, T1256-1 should be attached, along with the investment receipt, Slip T2SBVCTC (MAN). If filing electronically, these documents do not have to be remitted, but should be retained by the taxpayer.

There is a penalty tax if the investment is returned as a return of capital within three years.

An investor is not entitled to credit if the investor was, within the 24-month period preceding the issuance of shares to the investor, a specified shareholder of the issuer, an affiliate of the issuer, or a predecessor of any of them. There is, however, provision for an investor to make "a follow-on" investment free of this rule.

The entire legislation turns on the issuance of a receipt for an eligible investment. Receipts are issued by corporations that issue eligible shares. A corporation that wishes to issue shares as eligible investments must apply for and obtain the approval of the Department of Jobs and the Economy. Application forms and approval guidelines for corporate issuers are available for download on the Department website at http://www.gov.mb.ca/jec/busdev/financial/sbvctc/index.html.

An eligible investee corporation must meet a number of requirements. It must be a Canadian-controlled private corporation with a permanent establishment in Manitoba. All or substantially all of the carrying value of the assets of the corporation must be used, directly or through affiliates, principally in an active business carried on by the corporation or by an affiliate of the corporation. The revenue of the corporation and its affiliates for the most recently completed fiscal period must have been derived principally from one or more active businesses and not principally from property, ineligible activities, or any combination of them. (There is a substantial list of ineligible activities, including professional services, property development, mineral or oil and gas exploration, most primary industries, franchises, restaurants and bars (except brew pubs after July 31, 2015), performing arts, gaming and amusement, and certain other services.) The corporation's stated capital must be at least $25,000. Either (a) the corporation and its affiliates did not have, for the immediately preceding calendar year, more than 100 full-time equivalent employees (increased from 50, effective July 31, 2015), or (b) the gross revenue of the corporation and its affiliates (determined on a combined and consolidated basis, where applicable) for the most recently completed fiscal period is less than $15,000,000. At least 25% of the "full-time equivalent employees" of the corporation and its affiliates must be attributable to employees who are resident in Manitoba. "Full-time" is considered to be 40 hours per week. Full-time equivalent employees are (i) full-time employees for the whole year, plus (ii) part-year full-time employees prorated by the number of weeks of employment in the year, plus (iii) for part-time employees, if salary is determined as a fraction of the salary that would be paid to a full-time employee, that fraction, prorated by weeks of employment, or, if paid by the hour, paid hours of work in the year (excluding those falling within the weeks, if any, already taken into account) divided by 2,080.

Details of the rules are found in the statute and the *Small Business Venture Capital (SBVC) Tax Credit Regulation.*

(*Small Business Venture Capital (SBVC) Tax Credit Regulation*; MITA: 11.13–11.17)

[¶1535f] EMPLOYEE SHARE PURCHASE TAX CREDIT (FORM T1256-2)

Manitoba's Employee Share Purchase Tax Credit provides employees (including directors and officers) with a tax credit equal to 45% of the cost of shares purchased under a registered Employee Share Ownership Plan ("ESOP").

The maximum tax credit that may be earned in a year is:

- $202,500 (on a $450,000 investment) if the ESOP was established and registered to facilitate succession planning for a family business or to facilitate an employee buyout or takeover designed to create and maintain employment in Manitoba; or
- $27,000 (on a $60,000 investment) for shares acquired under any other registered ESOP.

The credit is partially refundable. There is a refundable credit of up to $27,000. Any credits earned in excess of that amount are non-refundable. An additional restriction provides that only $67,500 may be claimed as a credit in any one year. Excess credits can be carried forward 10 years or back three years.

Investments may also be made through an employee's RRSP or TFSA.

The credit is calculated on form T1256-2, Employee Share Purchase Tax Credit. The refundable portion is claimed on line 6137 of form MB479 and the non-refundable portion is claimed on line 6096 of form MB428. If filing a paper return, form T1256-2 should be attached, along with the ESOP receipts. If filing electronically, these documents do not have to be remitted, but should be retained by the taxpayer.

An eligible corporation must:

- be a Canadian-controlled private corporation with a permanent establishment in Manitoba;
- use all or substantially all of its assets in carrying on an active business;
- derive its revenue principally from an active business and not from property and/or prescribed activities;
- not have more than $25 million in gross assets and $10 million in net assets; and
- pay at least 25% of total wages and salaries to Manitoba residents.

The definition of "eligible corporation" also includes a corporation authorized to issue shares that qualify for a Community Enterprise Development Tax Credit or the Small Business Venture Capital Tax Credit.

The following corporations are not eligible:

- prescribed venture capital corporations (under Part LXVII of the federal *Income Tax Regulations*); and
- financial institutions.

In addition to banks, credit unions, and Caisses Populaires, the term "financial institution" is broadly defined to include a corporation that provides services as a trustee to the public; carries on the business of insurance; carries on business as a trader or dealer in securities; or whose principal business is any combination of lending money, cashing cheques, purchasing and collecting or selling debt obligations, or discounting tax refunds or rebates.

To claim the credit, employees must attach tax credit receipts to their income tax returns, unless filing electronically, in which case they must retain the receipts.

(MITA: 11.18–11.21)

[¶1535j] MANITOBA MINERAL EXPLORATION TAX CREDIT (FORM T1241)

As discussed at ¶1463, the federal government offers a non-refundable investment tax credit for Canadian exploration expenses (¶2210) incurred in mining exploration activities corporations principally engaged in exploration and development of mineral or other natural resources that are flowed out to individual shareholders holding "flow-through" shares of such corporations.

Where expenses eligible for the federal credit are incurred, Manitoba offers a supplemental non-refundable credit for those amounts which are directly attributable to expenditures that:

(1) were incurred for exploration in Manitoba for a mineral resource in Manitoba;

(2) are for goods or services or both most of which, if they were available in Manitoba, were provided in Manitoba;

(3) have been approved by the Minister responsible for the Manitoba *Mines and Minerals Act*; and

(4) are not expenditures for which this credit may be claimed by another person.

For flow-through share agreements entered into after March 31, 2010 and before April 1, 2018, the Manitoba credit rate is 30%. For agreements entered into after March 31, 2009 and before April 1, 2010, the Manitoba credit rate is 20%. For agreements made prior to April 2009, the rate is 10%.

To the extent the Manitoba credit exceeds Manitoba tax for a particular year, the excess will carry back three years and forward 10 years against Manitoba tax.

The credit is determined on form T1241 and carried to line 6083 of form MB428. Documents in support of the credit should be retained if the return is filed electronically, or filed with the return if paper-filed.

(MITA: 11.7)

[¶1537] MANITOBA PAID WORK EXPERIENCE TAX CREDIT

Variations of this refundable credit are available to an employer (including an unincorporated employer) that provides paid work experience to students and recent graduates of certain programs. There are several components of the credit, each of which is discussed below.

The credit is claimed on line 6131 of form MB479. Supporting documents do not have to be sent with the return, whether filing on paper or electronically, but should be retained in case they are requested later for verification. Prior to 2015, employers were required to obtain information slip T2CETC (MAN) from Manitoba Finance and attach it to the tax return. However, this "Proof of Credit Certificate" from Manitoba Finance is no longer required for 2015 or subsequent years.

A general partner may claim its *pro rata* share of the salary and wages paid by the partnership; that is, the partner may claim the amount determined at the partnership level under the rules above, prorated by the partner's share of the salary and wages paid for the placement over the total paid for the placement by the partnership.

Documents in support of the credit should be retained in case the CRA questions the credit.

[¶1537.05] *Co-op Student Hiring Incentive*

Under the co-op student hiring incentive, employers that provide qualifying work placements for students enrolled in an approved post-secondary co-operative education program are eligible to claim a credit equal to 15% of the salary or wages paid to the student, to a maximum of $5,000. For taxation years ending before January 1, 2016, the rate was 10% and the maximum credit was $1,000

Some useful information is available from the website of the Manitoba Department of Education and Advanced Learning at: http://www.edu.gov.mb.ca/ald/tax_credit/index.html.

[¶1537.10] *Co-op Graduate Hiring Incentive*

This program provides a refundable tax credit to an employer of 15% of wages and salaries paid to graduates of a cooperative program in each of the first two years of employment in a field related to the program, to a maximum of $2,500 for each year, where the employment commences within 18 months of graduation. For taxation years ending before January 1, 2016, the rate was 5%. In detail, a period of employment of a qualifying graduate qualifies for the credit if:

(1) the graduate is employed in a permanent position, and not in a position for a specified term or completion of a specified task or project;

(2) the employment is full-time (at least 35 hours per week);

(3) the work is to be performed primarily in Manitoba for an employer who is resident in Manitoba or has a permanent establishment in Manitoba;

(4) the work is closely related to the subject matter of the cooperative education program completed by the graduate, or requires skills and knowledge acquired in that program; and

(5) the period of employment begins at the beginning of a pay period that begins

(a) within 18 months after the graduate completed the cooperative education program, if the employer has not already claimed a credit under this provision for a previous period of employment in relation to that graduate, or

(b) immediately after the end of the previous period of employment for which the employer has claimed a credit under this provision in relation to that graduate.

Some useful information is available from the website of the Manitoba Department of Education and Advanced Learning at: http://www.edu.gov.mb.ca/ald/tax_credit/index.html.

[¶1537.15] *Journeyperson Hiring Incentive*

A refundable credit is also available for salary or wages paid by an employer for a period of qualifying employment of a qualifying journeyperson who first becomes certified in Canada as a journeyperson.

For 2015 and subsequent years, the credit is the lesser of (i) $5,000, and (ii) 15% of the amount by which the total salary and wages paid to the journeyperson for a period of qualifying employment that ended in the taxation year exceeds the amount of any other government assistance received or receivable by the taxpayer in respect of the salary and wages paid to the journeyperson for that period.

The credit is available to an employer who is or has been participating in one or more of the following ways in an apprenticeship program administered by the Manitoba government:

(1) by employing, in the taxation year, at least one apprentice who has completed his or her first year of apprenticeship with the taxpayer;

(2) by having employed, within the preceding five taxation years, at least one apprentice who completed at least two years of apprenticeship with the taxpayer during those years;

(3) by being an active member, in that taxation year, of an association

(a) that is recognized under the regulations under *The Apprenticeship and Trades Qualifications Act* as an employer under the apprenticeship program, and

(b) any member of which satisfies the requirement in clause (1) or (2).

A period of employment of a journeyperson qualifies for the purposes of the credit where:

(1) the journeyperson is employed in a permanent full-time position of at least 35 hours per week (and not in a position for a specified term or completion of a specified project);

(2) the work undertaken by the journeyperson is related to the trade in which he or she is certified, and that work is performed primarily in Manitoba, for an employer who is resident in Manitoba or has a permanent establishment in Manitoba;

(3) the period of employment begins within 18 months of the journeyperson receiving certification (or, where a

previously qualifying period has been claimed in relation to the journeyperson, immediately after the end of a period for which the employer has claimed the credit); and

(4) the period of employment comprises 12 consecutive months of continuous employment, during which the journeyperson is resident in Manitoba on December 31 (or, where there is a seasonal layoff, two periods of continuous employment before and after the layoff totalling 12 months).

The credit covers the first two 12-month periods of such employment. For a period of employment after this time, the credit must be specifically approved by the Minister of Finance.

Where an individual employed qualifies as either a qualifying graduate (¶1537.10, above) or a qualifying apprentice, the employer may choose which credit component to include the period of employment in, but cannot claim both.

[¶1537.20] *Apprentice Hiring Incentive*

This component of Manitoba's apprenticeship credit program was apparently introduced to supplement the federal credit available for the first two levels of an apprenticeship training program.

For 2015 and subsequent years, the apprenticeship hiring incentive is calculated at 15% of wages and salaries paid to an eligible apprentice, for a credit of up to $5,000 per training level completed. There is an additional 5% bonus, which increases the credit rate from 15% to 20%, for employers hiring early-level apprentices in rural or northern Manitoba. This applies to apprentices who normally reside outside Winnipeg and whose work, in the normal course of employment, is performed outside Winnipeg. For high school apprentices, this rate increased to 25%, effective for taxation years ending on or after January 1, 2016.

The credit is available for levels 1 through 5 of a qualifying apprenticeship training program and for high school apprentices. It may be claimed in the taxation year an apprentice completes a training level. There is no limit on the number of apprentices an employer may hire to earn the credit. To be eligible for the credit, wages paid to an apprentice must be at least at the level of minimum wage.

Prior to 2015, there were two separate components for apprentices. The advanced level apprentice hiring incentive provided a 10% credit to employers who hired level 3, 4, or 5 apprentices, with a maximum credit of $5,000 per apprentice. The early level apprentice hiring incentive provided a 15% credit, to a maximum of $3,000, for hiring level 1 or 2 apprentices or high-school apprentices. However, the rates for all levels of apprenticeship programs have been standardized for 2015 and subsequent years.

(MITA: 10.1)

[¶1537.25] *Youth Work Experience Hiring Incentive*

A youth work experience hiring incentive was introduced for 2015 and subsequent years. It is calculated at 25% of salary and wages, to a lifetime maximum credit of $5,000 per student. It will apply to a high school course or other training program approved by the Minister of Education and Advanced Learning for the purpose of this incentive. In introducing this incentive, the 2015 Budget stated that it was intended to apply to high school vocational programs such as health care, child care, business, and hospitality.

[¶1538] MANITOBA ODOUR-CONTROL TAX CREDIT (FORM T4164)

Manitoba offers a refundable 10% tax credit for depreciable property acquired primarily for the purpose of preventing, reducing, or eliminating odours that arise — or without the use of the property would arise — from organic waste used or created in the course of a corporation's or farmer's business in Manitoba.

Qualifying property must, in the case of an individual, be acquired (within the meaning in ¶804a) after March 6, 2006, and before 2018. The credit only becomes available in the year the property becomes available for use in accordance with the rules in ¶804b, and it must become available for use before 2018. The property must be new (not used or acquired for any use by anyone before the taxpayer), and must not be subject to any other Manitoba tax credit. The property may be acquired by a partnership or trust, and its characteristics flowed out *pro rata* to the partners or beneficiaries.

Eligible property includes straw cannons, sewage lagoon covers and seals, biofiltering units, storage tanks or containers, spraying equipment for aerobic or anaerobic treatment of organic waste, and soil injectors attached to manure spreaders. On the other hand, the following items are deemed not to be eligible for the purposes of the credit: equipment that is used for monitoring or testing for odours, equipment that is used to transmit or transport organic waste or odours (other than soil injection manure spreaders), or property that is used primarily to prevent, reduce, or eliminate air pollution or water pollution.

Other property may be certified by the Minister as qualifying property. The Minister is authorized to certify property if satisfied that it (a) is capable of being used, and is being or will be used, by the taxpayer primarily for the purpose of preventing, reducing, or eliminating odours that arise — or without the use of the property would arise — from organic waste used or created in the course of the taxpayer's business in Manitoba; and (b) is being, or will be, used by the taxpayer in a process that involves anaerobic or aerobic treatment, composting, drying or dehydration, or fermentation of organic waste.

Where the tax credit exceeds Manitoba tax payable in a year, a taxpayer in the business of farming may obtain a tax refund of the lesser of:

(1) the tax credit in excess of tax payable, and

(2) the property tax paid, for the calendar year that ended in that taxation year, on Manitoba farmland used by the taxpayer in the business of farming (net of any property tax refund, rebate, or other government assistance received or receivable in respect of that property tax).

The credit is calculated on form T4164 and claimed on MB479 at line 6134. Documents in support of the credit should be retained if the return is filed electronically, or filed with the return if paper-filed.

(MITA: 10.2)

[¶1538b] MANITOBA NUTRIENT MANAGEMENT TAX CREDIT

Farmers carrying on business in Manitoba can claim a refundable nutrient management tax credit, equal to 10% of the capital cost of prescribed nutrient management equipment for water quality protection. The credit is available for equipment acquired and available for use after April 17, 2012 and before 2019.

Eligible equipment must be used by the farmer for the purpose of eliminating or significantly reducing the risk that nutrients or pathogens in organic waste will be transported to a waterway. The following types of equipment are eligible: solid-liquid separation systems; anaerobic digesters; gravity settling tanks; manure treatment systems; and manure composting facilities. Storage tanks suitable for winter manure storage are also eligible for farmers with fewer than 300 animal units.

Costs eligible for the credit include expenditures associated with electrical installations, plumbing, pumps, piping, and groundwork required for installation of eligible systems that are included in the capital cost of equipment, as well as costs to acquire the system and make it operational, such as engineering, design, and installation costs. Borrowing costs are not eligible for the credit. The amount of the credit is reduced by any government or non-government assistance received or receivable.

Where the agricultural operations are owned by a partnership, the total tax credit is allocated among those partners who reside in Manitoba.

The credit may be claimed on line 6136 of form MB479. Receipts in support of credit claims should be retained if you are filing electronically, or filed with the return if you are filing a paper return.

(MITA: 10.2.1)

[¶1538d] MANITOBA GREEN ENERGY EQUIPMENT TAX CREDIT

Manitoba provides a refundable Green Energy Equipment Tax Credit for both manufacturers and purchasers of specified equipment. Unincorporated manufacturers and purchasers may claim the credit on Form MB479.

The program has two components: a manufacturer's credit and a purchaser's credit, described below. General rules under the legislation permit credits to flow through a partnership to the partners, or at least those partners who are eligible Manitoba taxpayers, and prohibit assignments of credit.

[¶1538d.05] *Purchaser's Credit*

The purchaser's component of the refundable Green Energy Equipment Tax Credit is available to any "eligible taxpayer" who purchases specified types of green energy equipment. An eligible taxpayer is either a corporation that has a permanent establishment in Manitoba in the year, or an individual who is resident in Manitoba at the end of the year.

There are three rates of credit in effect. A 7.5% credit rate is given on eligible purchases of geothermal heat pumps for which a manufacturer is eligible for the tax credit discussed at ¶1538d.15, below. This rate is applied to the sale price of the equipment (or to its fair market value in the case of a non-arm's length transaction). Such claims must be supported by a statement from the manufacturer of the heat pump setting out the manufacturer's name and address and confirming that the heat pump, if purchased for use in heating or cooling with geothermal energy in Manitoba, qualifies for the manufacturer's tax credit.

Taxpayers who purchase other types of geothermal energy equipment (for which a manufacturer is not eligible for a tax credit) are eligible for a 15% credit. This credit rate is applied to the capital cost of qualifying equipment. Capital cost includes the purchase price plus taxes and other related costs, such as delivery and installation, but does not include borrowing costs. Where government assistance is received for purchasing or installing the system, the tax credit is reduced by the amount of such assistance.

A 15% credit for purchasers of energy co-generation equipment, gasification equipment and clean air emission equipment came into effect on November 5, 2015. However, specific definitions and eligibility information for each type of equipment are to be set out in regulations, which have not been introduced as of the time of writing.

Taxpayers who purchase solar thermal energy equipment, as described in the schedule to *The Green Energy Equipment Tax Credit Regulation*, are eligible for a 10% credit, applicable to the capital cost of such equipment.

To be eligible for the credit, equipment must be designated as such in the regulation, must not be reconditioned or remanufactured, and must be purchased before July 1, 2023 by an eligible taxpayer.

Geothermal energy equipment is described in the schedule to the regulations as equipment that is or will be used primarily for heating an actively circulated liquid or gas, and is part of a ground source heat pump system that meets the standards set by the Canadian Standards Association for the design and installation of earth energy systems, including such equipment that consists of underground piping, energy conversion equipment, energy storage equipment, control equipment, and equipment designed to interface with other heating equipment; however, it does not include a building or part of a building, equipment used to heat water for use in a swimming pool, energy equipment that backs up equipment described above, equipment that distributes heated air or water in a building, or a heat pump with a full load coefficient of performance (as rated in accordance with the International Standards Organization standard 13256-1 for water-to-air and brine-to-air heat pumps, and standard 13256-2 for water-to-water and brine-to-water heat pumps) of less than 3.3 for a closed loop design, or less than 3.6 for an open loop design.

Solar thermal energy equipment is described as active solar heating equipment that is or will be used primarily for the purposes of heating a gas or liquid, including solar collectors that meet CSA standard F378-87 or an equivalent standard, solar energy conversion equipment, solar water heaters, control equipment, and equipment designed to interface solar heating equipment with other heating equipment. Similar to the restrictions for geothermal energy equipment described above, qualifying solar thermal energy equipment does not include a building or part of a building, equipment used to heat water for a swimming pool, or equipment that distributes heated air or water in a building.

Purchasers may claim the credit on line 6138 of form MB479 — *Manitoba Credits*. Receipts should be attached if filing a paper return. If filing electronically, the taxpayer should retain the receipts in case verification is requested. A worksheet to help calculate the credit for geothermal ground source heating systems is available on the Manitoba Finance website at: www.gov.mb.ca/finance/tao/green.html .

[¶1538d.15] *Manufacturer's Credit*

The manufacturer's component of the refundable Green Energy Equipment Tax Credit is available to manufacturers who are "eligible taxpayers" and whose primary business in Manitoba is manufacturing geothermal energy equipment or green energy transmission equipment. An eligible taxpayer is either a corporation that has a permanent establishment in Manitoba in the year, or an individual who is resident in Manitoba at the end of the year.

The manufacturer's tax credit was originally only available for geothermal heat pumps. Effective November 5, 2015, this credit is calculated at 7.5% of the manufacturer's "adjusted cost" (125% of the cost of manufacturing). Prior to that date, it was 7.5% of the price for which the heat pump was sold by the manufacturer, or, if the item was sold to a person with whom the manufacturer did not deal at arm's length, the lesser of the purchase price and the fair market value of the heat pump at the time of the sale.

Qualifying geothermal heat pumps for purposes of the manufacturer's credit must be:

(1) designated in the regulations as geothermal energy equipment;

(2) manufactured primarily in Manitoba by an eligible manufacturer after April 4, 2007; and

(3) sold by the manufacturer before July 1, 2023, for use in heating or cooling with geothermal energy (or for installation by a contractor or resale by a retailer for such purposes).

The manufacturer's tax credit claim must be supported by a statement signed by the purchaser, setting out the purchaser's name and address, and confirming that the heat pump is being purchased for an eligible use.

A credit is also available for manufacturers of green energy transmission equipment, which is defined as property "...that is related to the transmission of energy from a renewable resource, is designed to minimize the loss of energy through transmission and is designated in the regulations as green energy transmission equipment." This credit is equal to 8% of the "adjusted cost" of green energy transmission equipment, which is defined as 125% of the cost of manufacturing. The equipment must be manufactured primarily in Manitoba and sold to a purchaser for use in Manitoba. Although this credit was originally authorized by legislative amendments in force on June 16, 2011, details regarding the calculation and applicability of the credit were only brought into force on June 30, 2016.

Unincorporated manufacturers may claim the credit on line 6139 of form MB479 — *Manitoba Credits*. Receipts should be attached if filing a paper return. If filing electronically, the taxpayer should retain the receipts in case verification is requested.

(Green Energy Equipment Tax Credit Regulation; MITA: 10.3)

[¶1538g] MANITOBA BOOK PUBLISHING CREDIT (FORM T1299)

Manitoba offers a refundable tax credit for book publishers, available to both corporate and individual taxpayers. The credit is available for eligible book publishing expenses incurred after April 9, 2008 and before 2018.

There are two components to this tax credit. The first component is the lesser of (i) $100,000 and (ii) 40% of the sum of

(1) the total of the non-refundable monetary advances made in the taxation year by the publisher to authors of eligible books published, or to be published, by the publisher (subject to any limit prescribed by regulation, of which none were in evidence at the time of this writing); and

(2) the publisher's "book publishing labour costs" for the taxation year, prorated by (i) the total number of pages that make up the eligible books published by the publisher in the taxation year over (ii) the total number of pages of books published by the publisher in the taxation year (including electronic books, the number of pages for which is to be determined in accordance with regulations).

In 2011, this component of the tax credit was expanded to include non-refundable monetary advances and labour costs related to publishing electronic or digital versions of eligible literary works, applicable for expenses incurred and paid after April 12, 2011.

The second component of the credit provides an additional 15% credit on eligible printing costs incurred for books printed on paper with a minimum of 30% recycled content. This credit rate has been increased from 10%, effective for expenditures incurred after April 12, 2011. Eligible printing costs for this credit component include costs incurred in the year for printing, assembling, and binding eligible books, to the extent that those costs:

(1) are reasonable in the circumstances;

(2) are incurred after April 9, 2008 and before 2019;

(3) are incurred in relation to an eligible book in the year it is published or in the immediately following year;

(4) are paid by the publisher in the taxation year;

(5) relate to the publication of eligible books that are printed on paper having at least 30% recycled content comprised of post-consumer waste paper; and

(6) satisfy any other requirements prescribed by regulation (none at the time of writing).

To be eligible, a publisher must: be engaged primarily in the business of publishing books; have a permanent establishment or be resident in Manitoba; pay at least 25% of its wages and salaries to Manitoba residents; and have recently published at least two qualifying books. Qualifying books include Canadian-authored fiction, non-fiction, poetry, drama, biography, and children's books.

Unincorporated publishers can calculate the credit using form T1299, *Manitoba Book Publishing Tax Credit (Individuals)* and claim the credit on line 6143 of form MB479. Documents in support of the credit should be retained if the return is filed electronically, or filed with the return if paper-filed.

If more than one publisher claims to be the publisher of an eligible book, the book must be excluded in determining the tax credit of each of them, unless they file with the Minister an agreement signed by all of them that allocates among them the number of pages of the book that are to be included in determining their tax credits.

If it is subsequently determined that a tax credit paid or applied to reduce tax did not in fact qualify, it becomes a debt to the province.

(MITA: 10.4)

[¶1538h] CULTURAL INDUSTRIES PRINTING TAX CREDIT

Manitoba provides a refundable cultural industries printing tax credit for Manitoba printers. The credit is available to individuals resident in the province at the end of the taxation year, as well as to corporations, who in the course of carrying on business, print, assemble, and bind books.

The rate and calculation of the credit were amended for 2015 and subsequent taxation years. The credit is now calculated as 35% of salary or wages paid to Manitoba residents in respect of their employment in the printer's book printing division. However, this amount must be reduced by a fraction consisting of the printer's "eligible printing revenue" for the taxation year over the printer's total book printing revenue (other than revenue from the printing of yearbooks). Prior to these changes, the credit was simply calculated as 15% of eligible printing revenue for the year. Eligible printing revenue, which is capped at $200,000 per book title, includes amounts paid to the printer after April 12, 2011, and before 2019 by a non-related publisher resident in Canada for services provided in respect of printing, assembling, or binding an eligible book.

Eligible books include those eligible for the Manitoba book publishing tax credit, with the exception that the books do not have to be first editions. This includes books, substantially all of which have been written, adapted, or translated by a Canadian author, in the categories of fiction, non-fiction, poetry, biography, or children's books. Additional criteria also apply, including prescriptions for minimum length and print run. Certain types of books are specifically excluded from eligibility including directories, agendas, catalogues, maps, loose leaf publications, colouring or activity books, periodical publications, and publications containing advertising other than the publisher's own promotional material.

Additional restrictions on eligible books were introduced in the 2014 Manitoba Budget. Effective March 6, 2014:

- at least 90% of the book must be new material that has not been previously published;
- at least 65% of the book must be text, except in the case of a children's book; and
- the book must be sold through an established distributor.

The credit is claimed on line 6148 of form MB479. Documents in support of the credit should be retained if the return is filed electronically, or filed with the return if paper-filed.

(MITA: 10.4.1)

[¶1539] MANITOBA INFORMATION

If you have any questions about the Manitoba tax credit plans or if you need help in completing your application, you can contact your local CRA office (¶287) or:

Manitoba Tax Assistance Office
809–386 Broadway
Winnipeg MB R3C 3R6

In Winnipeg, telephone 948-2115. If you live outside Winnipeg, you may contact the information office by phoning the toll free number 1-800-782-0771. Outside Manitoba, you may call long distance, 1-204-948-2115. You can contact the office by email at TAO@gov.mb.ca.

NEW BRUNSWICK

[¶1540] TAX RATES, BASIC CREDITS, AND LOW-INCOME REDUCTION

[¶1540.05] *Basic Tax Rates*

New Brunswick tax is based on federal taxable income from line 260 of the T1 return, to which New Brunswick tax rates and brackets are applied. New Brunswick tax rates for 2016 are as follows:

Taxable income	*Tax*
$40,492 or less	9.68%
In excess of	
$40,492	$3,920 + 14.82% on next $40,493
$80,985	$9,921 + 16.52% on next $50,679
$131,664	$18,293 +17.84% on the next $18,336
$150,000	$21,564 + 20.3% on remainder

New Brunswick reduced the rate for taxable income over $150,000 to 20.3% for 2016 and subsequent years and eliminated a higher rate for income over $250,000. Threshold income levels for the four lowest tax brackets are indexed annually, and the highest tax bracket will be indexed beginning in 2017. Rates and brackets applicable to recent prior years are set out at ¶1540.20 below.

Like federal income tax, New Brunswick applies its highest tax rate (20.3%) to tax on split income (form T1206). New Brunswick also imposes alternative minimum tax ("AMT") at 57% of federal AMT (form T691, lines 108 minus 111).

Basic New Brunswick tax payable is calculated in Step 2 on form NB428. Tax on split income and AMT are calculated in Step 3.

(NBITA (2000): 14;45; 46)

[¶1540.07] *Basic Tax Credits*

New Brunswick offers provincial personal tax credits similar to most, but not all, federal personal non-refundable credits. Although eligibility for provincial credits largely mirrors federal credit rules, most credit amounts differ from federal amounts and are converted to credit at provincial tax rates.

Personal tax credits offered by New Brunswick include: a basic personal credit, spouse or common-law partner credit, eligible dependant credit, caregiver credit, infirm dependant credit, age credit, CPP contributions and EI premiums credits, pension income credits, disability credit and supplement, tuition and education credits (the federal education credit is repealed effective January 1, 2017), student loan interest credit, medical expense credit, and charitable donations credit. The New Brunswick pension income credit is available only to residents of the province. New Brunswick does not presently offer credits similar to the federal adoption tax credit, children's fitness and arts activities credits, textbook credit (the federal textbook credit is repealed effective January 1, 2017), public transit credit, or volunteer firefighters credit.

Like the federal government, New Brunswick gives credit for most personal amounts at its lowest rate (9.68%). An exception is the charitable donation credit, for which credit at its lowest rate (9.68%) on the first $200 of donation and a higher rate (17.95%) on the balance. Donation amounts are the same as those eligible for federal credit and should be taken from lines 345 and 347 of Schedule 9 of the federal return.

Most N.B. personal credit amounts differ from federal amounts, with the exception of certain credits such as CPP, EI, student loan interest and charitable donation credits, for which amounts are the same and may be picked up from the federal return. New Brunswick tax credit amounts are calculated on form NB428 and the Provincial Worksheet which accompanies the T1 return. Where a student must calculate education/tuition tax credit amounts and/or transfers on federal Schedule 11, the student must make a parallel provincial calculation on NB(S11). Similarly, where you are claiming a transfer of personal amounts from your spouse or common-law partner on federal Schedule 2, you must make the parallel NB claim on NB(S2).

Other New Brunswick basic credit rates are as follows:

- dividend tax credit: for eligible dividends, 13.5%; for other taxable Canadian dividends, 3.625%; and
- AMT credit (from Schedule 1 line 427): at 57%.

For a chart of basic N.B. credit amounts for the 2016 taxation year, see ¶52 at the beginning of this book.

(NBITA (2000): 17–36)

[¶1540.10] *Low-Income Tax Reduction*

New Brunswick offers a tax reduction intended to reduce or eliminate provincial tax payable for individuals and families with income below certain thresholds.

For 2016, the reduction provides a non-refundable credit amount of up to $632 for an individual, plus $632 for an individual's spouse, common-law partner, or eligible dependant for a maximum tax credit of $1,264. This credit amount is reduced by 3% of net family income over $16,285, and is eliminated at income over $37,352 for individuals and $58,419 for families.

Both the credit amounts and income thresholds are indexed annually.

The credit is available to individuals resident in New Brunswick at the end of the year (or who died in the year resident in New Brunswick). If you have a spouse or cohabiting partner, only one of you can claim the credit. However, any unused credit may be transferred to your spouse or partner.

If both you and your spouse or partner file tax returns, and the spouse or partner claiming the credit has excess credit (which would reduce tax below nil), the claimant partner should calculate the excess credit on the New Brunswick NB428 (the last item on page 3), and the non-claimant spouse or partner can then claim this excess amount. The non-claimant spouse or partner picks up this excess credit in box 6156 of his or her own return, using it to reduce tax to that point, but then omits the balance of the low-income reduction calculation (lines 53 to 69 on NB428), since it has already been claimed by the other spouse or partner. In these circumstances, it should not matter who makes the initial claim, since the dollar value of the two claims should come to the same amount.

The low-income tax reduction applies to tax payable after all tax credits except political contribution tax credit, LSVCC tax credit, and small business investor tax credit. Accordingly, those credits are lost where tax is reduced below levels which can absorb them.

Net family income for this purpose is calculated under the rules for federal GST credit, which is to say it is normally your income from line 236 of your federal return plus your spouse or common-law partner's income from line 236 of that person's return. However, if the income calculation (on either return or both) includes amounts on line 117 and/or line 125 of the T1 in respect of the former universal child care benefit (UCCB) and/or registered disability savings plan (RDSP) income, repayments of UCCB on line 213 and/or repayments of RDSP benefits included in line 232, and/or a gain from a disposition of property under foreclosure proceedings (as discussed in ¶518), that income (or income reduction) is not included in net family income.

(NBITA (2000): 16.1; 49.1)

[¶1540.15] *Low-Income Seniors' Benefit*

New Brunswick offers a non-tax benefit for seniors, resident in the province, who receive any one of the following federal benefits:

- Guaranteed Income Supplement (GIS) (65 years or older)
- Allowance for Survivor (between 60–64 years old)
- Federal Allowance (between 60–64 years old)

The benefit provides an annual payment of up to $400 for eligible seniors, and is obtained by application directly to the New Brunswick Department of Finance. Application forms may be found directly on the New Brunswick Finance website (http://www.gnb.ca/Finance) or by calling 1-800-669-7070.

(NBITA (2000): 52)

[¶1540.20] *New Brunswick Tax Rate History*

For 2015, New Brunswick rates were:

Taxable income	*Tax*
$39,973 or less	9.68%
In excess of	
$39,973	$3,869 + 14.82% on next $39,973
$79,946	$9,793 + 16.52% on next $50,029
$129,975	$18,058 +17.84% on the next $20,025
$150,000	$21,631 + 21% on the next $100,000
$250,000	$42,631 + 25.75% on remainder

For 2014, New Brunswick rates were:

Taxable income	*Tax*
$39,305 or less	9.68%
In excess of	
$39,305	$3,805 + 14.82% on next $39,304
$78,609	$9,630 + 16.52% on next $49,193
$127,802	$17,756 + 17.84% on remainder

For 2013, New Brunswick rates were:

Taxable income	*Tax*
$38,954 or less	9.39%
In excess of	
$38,954	$3,658 + 13.46% on next $38,954
$77,908	$8,901 + 14.46% on next $48,754
$126,662	$15,951 + 16.07% on remainder

For 2012, New Brunswick rates were:

Taxable income	*Tax*
$38,190 or less	9.1%
In excess of	
$38,190	$3,381 + 12.1% on next $38,190

Taxable income	Tax
$76,380	$8,096 + 12.4% on next $47,798
$124,178	$14,023 + 14.3% on remainder

For 2011, New Brunswick rates were:

Taxable income	Tax
$37,150 or less	9.1%
In excess of	
$37,150	$3,381+ 12.1% on next $37,150
$74,300	$7,876 + 12.4% on next $46,496
$120,796	$13,641 + 14.3% on remainder

[¶1540g] FORMER TUITION CASH BACK TAX CREDIT

The New Brunswick tuition rebate, also known as the tuition cash back tax credit, has been eliminated as of January 1, 2016. Applications with respect to the 2014 taxation year were accepted until December 31, 2015, but no applications will be accepted with respect to 2015 or subsequent years.

The credit provided a rebate of New Brunswick personal income taxes paid, in an amount of up to 50% of eligible tuition expenses. The maximum rebate that could be claimed was $4,000 per year, and the maximum lifetime rebate was $20,000. The credit was not claimed on the T1 return but required direct application to the New Brunswick Department of Finance.

Despite being called a "cash back" tuition credit, the credit was non-refundable, and was only paid to the extent of New Brunswick tax payable in the year for which the credit claim was made. In previous years, graduates were able to carry forward unused amounts to claim against future tax payable. However, since the program has been eliminated, accumulated credits cannot be carried forward after December 31, 2015.

(NBITA (2000): 30.1; *Tuition Tax Cash Back Credit Act*)

[¶1540k] HOME ENERGY ASSISTANCE PROGRAM

The New Brunswick Home Energy Assistance Program provides a $100 annual benefit payment for eligible low-income individuals and families. The benefit is obtained though application to the New Brunswick Department of Finance.

To receive the benefit, you must be resident in New Brunswick at the end of the year. Your total family income for the year (consisting of your income plus that of your spouse or common-law partner) must be $28,000 or less. You can also apply for the benefit if your expected income in the year of the benefit payment is anticipated to be below this amount. Only one individual per household may apply for the credit.

Application forms for the benefit are available on the New Brunswick Department of Finance website (http://www.gnb.ca/Finance). The benefit must be applied for annually. Application forms must be accompanied by a recent electricity bill or for renters, the name of your landlord. Applications must be filed by the end of June of the benefit payment year.

To receive the benefit, you must maintain a principal residence in the province and have filed a tax return for the benefit year.

Availability of this benefit has been extended through 2016. It is important to note that the deadline to apply for the 2016 benefit was June 30, 2016.

(NBITA (2000): 52.1)

[¶1541] POLITICAL CONTRIBUTION TAX CREDIT

If you contributed in the year to registered New Brunswick political parties, registered New Brunswick district associations, or registered New Brunswick independent candidates, you are entitled to claim a credit for such contributions as a credit against N. B. income tax.

The credit can be claimed on line 72 of form NB428. Claims must be supported by proof of payment in the form of an official receipt signed by the official representative of the registered political party, registered association or registered independent candidate. Receipts must be filed with a paper return, or retained if you are filing electronically.

The New Brunswick political contribution credit is calculated as 75% of the first $200 of contributions, 50% of the next $350, and 33.33% of the next $525, so that the maximum credit of $500 is reached on total contribution(s) of $1,075. This calculation is provided for on the New Brunswick Provincial Worksheet.

(NBITA (2000): 61)

[¶1542] SENIORS' HOME RENOVATION TAX CREDIT (SCHEDULE NB(S12))

New Brunswick introduced a refundable seniors' home renovation tax credit for 2015 and subsequent taxation years. It provides tax assistance to seniors and family members who live with them for renovations to their principal residence.

Credit Rate

The credit is calculated at 10% of eligible expenditures. Up to $10,000 of renovation expenditures may be eligible each year, resulting in a maximum tax credit of $1,000.

Eligible Taxpayers

The credit may be claimed by residents of New Brunswick who are either a senior (at least 65 years of age at the end of the taxation year) or a family member living with a senior. A family member includes a parent, step-parent, grandparent, in-law, sibling, spouse, common-law partner, aunt, uncle, great-aunt, great-uncle, child, step-child, grandchild, niece, and nephew.

If an individual and that individual's spouse or common-law partner are both entitled to claim the tax credit, the expenditure limit must be allocated between them (unless they are living separate and apart because of medical necessity or the breakdown of their marriage or common-law partnership). The expenditure limit must also be shared where more than one person is entitled to claim the tax credit in respect of a single residence.

Eligible Renovation Expenses

The credit is available for expenses paid, or billed for, during the relevant taxation year. However, expenses will not be eligible if they were made or incurred under the terms of an agreement entered into before January 1, 2015. The renovation or alteration must be of an enduring nature, and be designed to improve accessibility or to help a senior be more functional or mobile at home. A list of eligible expenses is provided in the CRA document "Information for Residents of New Brunswick", which is part of the T1 package. The amount of eligible expenses must be reduced by any related government assistance, other than tax credits, that the taxpayer received or expects to receive.

Claiming the Credit

The credit is calculated on Schedule NB(S12), which must be attached to the T1 return. It requires taxpayers to list all eligible expenses, including the amount, date, supplier, and a description. It also includes a box to check in the case of involuntary separation because of medical necessity. The amount calculated on Schedule NB(S12) must be entered on line 479 of the T1 return.

Documents to support the claim, including receipts from retailers, suppliers and contractors, do not have to be submitted with the return, but must be retained in case the Canada Revenue Agency asks for verification.

(NBITA (2000): 52.01)

[¶1543] LABOUR-SPONSORED VENTURE CAPITAL FUND TAX CREDIT

New Brunswick offers a provincial credit for investments in labour-sponsored venture capital corporations (LSVCCs).

The New Brunswick credit is calculated at 20% of eligible investments up to $10,000, for a maximum annual tax credit of $2,000. The credit is available for investments made in the year, or within 60 days following the end of the taxation year.

GrowthWorks Atlantic Venture Fund Ltd. is the only eligible fund in New Brunswick. Various other funds that had been active and eligible in New Brunswick in earlier years are no longer prescribed.

Credits are reported to you on form NB LSVC-1. If you are filing a paper return, you must attach the reporting slip to the return. In other cases, you must keep the slip on hand to substantiate your claim, should it be questioned.

Shares may be purchased through an RRSP. Recapture of the credit applies where LSVCC shares are disposed of within eight years of acquisition. Investors wishing to reinvest in LSVCC funds from their RRSPs following the eight-year hold period and qualify for the LSVCC tax credit may rollover their investments without cashing their RRSP.

New Brunswick credits are claimed in box 6167 of form NB428. The LSVCC credit is claimed next to last (before the Small Business Investor Tax Credit) in order among New Brunswick credits; that is, it is claimed after political contribution credits to the extent of any New Brunswick tax remaining. Credit may be wasted if there is insufficient remaining tax.

See also the discussion at ¶1466 concerning redemption restrictions and credit recapture and the discussion at ¶2522(2).

(NBITA (2000): 50; *Registered Labour-Sponsored Venture Capital Corporations Regulation*)

[¶1543d] NEW BRUNSWICK SMALL BUSINESS INVESTOR TAX CREDIT (FORM T1258)

The New Brunswick small business investor tax credit is available for investments in eligible shares of registered small business corporations or, effective April 1, 2016, community economic development corporations or associations ("CED Funds").

The credit rate for individual investors is :

- 50% of eligible investments made after March 31, 2015, up to $250,000, for a maximum annual tax credit of $125,000;
- 30% of eligible investments made prior to April 1, 2015, up to $250,000, for a maximum annual tax credit of $75,000.

Eligible investments are those made within the year, or within 60 days after the end of the year.

The rules contemplate that shares acquired by an RRSP will incur credit on behalf of the RRSP contributor, although of course contributions to an RRSP will be limited by the RRSP rules. RRSPs could presumably use funds already in the plan to acquire shares with credits. Presumably the shares would be qualified investments because the small business corporation is exclusively carrying on an active business, but the cautious investor will want to verify that shares acquired through an RRSP are indeed qualified RRSP investments.

Eligible shares must be newly issued, fully paid shares of either CED Funds or private corporations registered with the New Brunswick Department of Finance. To be eligible to register for the program, both private corporations and CED Funds must meet eligibility requirements set out in the legislation. Among other things, these require the corporation or CED Fund to be incorporated in or registered to carry on business in the province with total assets (including assets of any associated corporation) of less than $40 million. In addition, at least 75% of salaries and wages must be paid to residents of the province. However, if at least 50% of total revenue is derived from the sale of goods and services outside New Brunswick, only 50% of its wages and salaries must be paid to New Brunswick residents.

The shares are not redeemable or transferable until more than four years after issue. Earlier redemption or transfer may result in recapture of the original credit, except where the original purchaser (or RRSP contributor) has died.

The credits are non-refundable, but credits in excess of N.B. tax can be carried forward seven years and carried back three years. However, the maximum credit claimed in one year (including carryovers) cannot exceed $125,000 for 2015 or subsequent years ($75,000 for previous years).

Credits must be supported by a certificate, NB SBITC-1, issued by the N.B. Department of Finance. Certificates, together with form T1258, which calculates eligible credit for the year and any carryover amounts, are to be filed with your return, unless filing electronically, in which case you should simply keep them on file. The amount calculated on form T1258 must be entered on line 76 of form NB428.

(NBITA (2000): 61.1; *Small Business Investor Tax Credit Act*; Other Publications: New Brunswick Small Business Investor Tax Credit — Frequently asked questions)

[¶1544] CHILD BENEFIT SUPPLEMENT

The New Brunswick child tax benefit enhances the Canada Child Benefit program described at ¶1498. Available N.B. benefit amounts include a child benefit, working income supplement, and school supplement. Provincial benefit payments are issued along with federal payments.

The New Brunswick benefit adopts the federal standards of eligibility set out in ¶1498, and is administered by the CRA as part of the Canada Child Benefit program. However, benefits accumulate under the N.B. program only for each month in a base year in which the recipient of the benefit (typically the mother of an eligible child) was resident in N.B. for a period that commenced before and included the first day of the month.

The child benefit component of the N.B. benefit is $250 per year ($20.83 per month) per eligible child, reduced by 5% (2.5% where there is only one child) of the amount by which net family income (¶1498) exceeds $20,000. The working income supplement component is the lesser of $250 per year (or $20.83 per month, regardless of the number of children) and 4% of the amount by which family earned income (income of parent and parent's spouse if living together as defined for child care deduction purposes at ¶1055) exceeds $3,750, with the result (if any) further reduced by 5% of net family income in excess of $20,921. The school supplement amount is $100 per child between the ages of 5 and 17, paid annually in July.

Inquiries should be directed to 1-800-387-1193.

(NBITA (2000): 51; 51.01; T4114 Canada Child Benefits — Including related federal, provincial and territorial programs)

[¶1544a] HARMONIZED SALES TAX CREDIT

New Brunswick introduced a Harmonized Sales Tax (HST) Credit to help lessen the impact of the July 1, 2016 HST rate increase (from 13% to 15%) on lower-income families.

The HST credit is calculated at $300 for individuals; $300 for a spouse, common-law partner or eligible dependant; and $100 per child under the age of 19 (unless claimed as an eligible dependant). The credit is reduced where adjusted family income exceeds $35,000, at a rate of 2% of income above that threshold. Accordingly, the credit will be eliminated when income exceeds $50,000 for single individuals or $75,000 for a family of four.

New Brunswick has adopted the federal definition of "adjusted income". This is basically the individual's income and the income of a cohabiting spouse or common-law partner but does not include amounts received under the former Universal Child Care Benefit or a registered disability savings plan.

Eligibility requirements are the same as for the federal GST/HST Credit except that individuals must be resident in New Brunswick in order to claim the provincial credit.

Rather than being used to reduce income taxes payable, the HST credit is refunded to taxpayers in quarterly instalments along with the federal GST/HST credit. No application is required. The credit is administered by the CRA, which automatically determines a taxpayer's eligibility based on income reported on tax returns.

(NBITA (2000): 52.02; RC4210 GST/HST Credit)

NEWFOUNDLAND AND LABRADOR

Basic Newfoundland and Labrador tax payable is calculated in Step 2 on form NL428.

(NFITA: 7; 29; 30)

[¶1545] TAX RATES, BASIC CREDITS, AND LOW-INCOME REDUCTION

[¶1545.05] *Basic Tax Rates*

Newfoundland and Labrador tax is based on federal taxable income from line 260 of the T1 return, to which Newfoundland and Labrador tax rates and brackets are applied. Newfoundland and Labrador tax rates for 2016 are as follows:

Taxable income	*Tax*
$35,148 or less	8.2%
In excess of	
$35,148	$2,882 + 13.5% on next $35,147
$70,295	$7,627 + 14.55% on next $55,205
$125,500	$15,659 + 15.8% on next $50,200
$175,700	$23,591 + 16.8% on remainder

Rates for all tax brackets were increased in 2016 and are scheduled to increase further in 2017. The following is a list of rates for the 2017 taxation year (note that Newfoundland and Labrador tax brackets are indexed annually, so the 2016 brackets shown below will be adjusted for 2017).

- Income up to $35,148 — 8.7%
- $35,148 to $70,295 — 14.5%
- $70,295 to $125,500 — 15.8%
- $125,500 to $175,700 — 17.3%
- More than $175,700 — 18.3%

For a history of tax rates in recent years see ¶1545.85.

Like federal income tax, Newfoundland and Labrador imposes tax on split income (form T1206) at its highest tax rate (16.8% in 2016; 18.3% for 2017). The province also imposes alternative minimum tax ("AMT") at a rate of 54.7% of the federal AMT (from line 117 on form T691).

[¶1545.10] *Basic Tax Credits*

Newfoundland and Labrador offers personal tax credits similar to most (but not all) federal personal non-refundable credits. For provincial tax purposes, most credit amounts differ from federal amounts, and are converted to credit at provincial tax rates.

Basic personal amounts available for N.L. tax purposes include: a basic personal amount, spouse or common-law partner amount, eligible dependant credit, caregiver credit, infirm dependant credit, medical expense credit, age credit, pension income credit, CPP contribution and EI premium credit, disability credit and supplement, tuition and education credits (the federal education credit is repealed effective January 1, 2017), interest on student loans credit, adoption expense credit, charitable donations credit, and volunteer firefighters credits. Newfoundland and Labrador pension income and adoption expense credits are available only to residents of the province. Newfoundland and Labrador also offers a child care credit (¶1548.17) available for expenses claimed as a deduction for federal income tax purposes. The province does not currently offer any credits similar to the following federal credits: textbook credit (the federal textbook credit is repealed effective January 1, 2017), public transit pass credit, Canada employment credit, or children's fitness or arts activities credits.

Most N.L. personal amounts differ from federal amounts, and must be computed on NL428 and the N.L. worksheet, included in the provincial forms package. Amounts eligible (before conversion to credit) for CPP/QPP, EI, and student loan amounts will be the same as on the federal return.

Like the federal government, Newfoundland and Labrador gives credit for most personal amounts at its lowest tax rate (8.2% for 2016; 8.7% for 2017). An exception is for charitable donation credit, giving credit at its lowest rate (8.2% for 2016; 8.7% for 2017) on the first $200 of donation and at its highest rate (16.8% in 2016; 18.3% in 2017) on the balance. Donation amounts should be taken from lines 345 and 347 of Schedule 9.

Where a student must calculate education/tuition tax credit amounts and/or transfers on federal Schedule 11, the student must make a parallel provincial calculation on NL(S11). Similarly, where you are claiming a transfer of personal amounts from your spouse or common-law partner on federal Schedule 2, you must make the parallel N.L. claim on NL(S2).

Other N.L. credit rates include the following:

- dividend tax credit: 5.4% for eligible dividends, 4.1% for other Canadian dividends received before July 1, 2016 and 3.5% for other Canadian dividends received after June 30, 2016; and
- alternative minimum tax credit (from Schedule 1 line 427) at 54.7% for 2016.

The Newfoundland and Labrador AMT credit rate is determined by dividing its lowest personal tax rate by the lowest federal rate. Accordingly, it will increase to 58% in 2017.

For a chart of 2016 Newfoundland and Labrador basic credit amounts, see ¶52 at the beginning of this book. Most personal credit amounts are indexed annually.

(NFITA: 9–21)

[¶1545.15] *Low-Income Tax Reduction*

The N.L. low-income tax reduction reduces or eliminates tax for individuals and families with income below threshold amounts. For 2016, the reduction eliminates tax for individuals with income of up to $19,031 and families with income up to $32,180.

The credit is available to individuals resident in Newfoundland and Labrador at the end of year, or who died in the year resident in the province. Where an individual has a spouse or common-law partner, only one credit may be claimed for the family.

However, any unused credit can be transferred to the other spouse or partner. If you both file tax returns and the spouse or partner claiming the credit has excess credit (which would reduce tax below nil), the claimant partner should calculate the excess, and the non-claimant spouse or partner can claim the excess. The non-claimant spouse or partner picks up this excess in box 6186 of his or her own form NL428, uses it to reduce tax to that point, but then omits the balance of the low-income reduction calculation (lines 67 to 83 on NL428), since it has already been claimed by the other spouse or partner. In these circumstances, it should not matter who makes the initial claim, since the dollar value of the two claims should come to the same amount.

The low-income tax reduction applies to tax payable after all other tax credits. Accordingly, those credits are lost where tax is reduced below levels which can absorb them, subject to the spousal transfer discussed above.

For 2016, the basic reduction is $746, plus $415 if you have a qualified relation (cohabiting spouse or common-law partner) at the end of the taxation year or have claimed an eligible dependant for the year on line 5816 of form NL428. The definition of qualified relation is tied to the definition for federal GST credit (¶1496.15).

If you have no qualified relation or eligible dependant, your basic reduction of $746 is reduced by 16% of your adjusted net income for the year in excess of, for 2016, $19,031.

If you do have a qualified relation or eligible dependant, your basic reduction of $1,161 is reduced by 16% of your combined family net income (yourself and your spouse or common-law partner, but not your eligible dependant) in excess of (for 2016) $32,180.

Net family income for this purpose is your income from line 236 of your federal return plus your spouse or common-law partner's income from line 236 of that person's return. However, if the income calculation (on either return or both) includes amounts on line 117 [and/or line 125] of the T1 in respect of the former universal child care benefit (UCCB) [and/or registered disability savings plan (RDSP) income], repayments of UCCB on line 213 [and/or repayments of RDSP benefits included in line 232], and/or a gain from a disposition of property under foreclosure proceedings (as discussed in ¶518), that income (or income reduction) is not included in net family income.

The credit amounts and reductions are indexed annually.

(NFITA: 21.1)

[¶1545.20] *Temporary deficit reduction levy*

The 2016 Newfoundland and Labrador Budget introduced a temporary deficit reduction levy, payable by all individuals resident in the province with taxable income in excess of $50,000. The levy is scheduled to apply for the 2016 to 2019 taxation years inclusively. Levy amounts vary according to taxable income and are set out in a chart at the end of Form NL428. Because the levy took effect on July 1, 2016, there is a 50% reduction in the levy amount otherwise payable for the 2016 taxation year. The temporary reduction is calculated on Form NL428, lines 82 to 91.

(NFITA: 7.1 Temporary deficit reduction levy)

[¶1545.75] *Newfoundland and Labrador Inuit Information*

The Government of Canada has a tax administration agreement with the Nunatsiavut Government. Its impact on N.L. taxpayers generally is that there is a unique N.L. version of T1 return. It differs from the common version in requiring information on page 1 of the T1 as to whether you were resident in an Inuit community on December 31 of the taxation year. An information sheet with the N.L. T1 specifies that you should answer yes if you resided in the Labrador Inuit Lands or within the Inuit communities of Rigolet, Nain, Hopedale, Makkovik, or Postville. *All* residents of the Inuit lands and specified Inuit communities are to identify themselves, whether Inuit or not. All individuals not resident in those communities are to tick "No", whether Inuit or not. The CRA uses this to administer the Nunatsiavut agreement.

If your residence status is in doubt because you maintain more than one residence, you should be guided by the same "residence in fact" criteria that determine national residence in ¶115.05.

(Income Tax Folio: S5-F1-C1 Determining an Individual's Residence Status)

[¶1545.85] *Newfoundland and Labrador Tax Rates History*

For 2015, N.L. tax rates were:

Taxable income	*Tax*
$35,008 or less	7.7%
In excess of $35,008	$2,696 + 12.5% on next $35,007

Taxable income	*Tax*
$70,015	$7,071 + 13.3% on next $54,985
$125,000	$14,384 + 13.8% on next $50,000
$175,000	$21,284 + 14.3% on remainder

For 2014, N.L. tax rates were:

Taxable income	*Tax*
$34,254 or less	7.7%
In excess of	
$34,254	$2,638 + 12.5% on next $34,254
$68,508	$6,919 + 13.3% on remainder

For 2013, N.L. tax rates were:

Taxable income	*Tax*
$33,748 or less	7.7%
In excess of	
$33,748	$2,599 + 12.5% on next $33,748
$65,785	$6,817 + 13.3% on remainder

For 2012, N.L. tax rates were:

Taxable income	*Tax*
$32,893 or less	7.7%
In excess of	
$32,893	$2,533 + 12.5% on next $32,892
$65,785	$6,644 + 13.3% on remainder

For 2011, N.L. tax rates were:

Taxable income	*Tax*
$31,904 or less	7.7%
In excess of	
$31,904	$2,457 + 12.5% on next $31,903
$63,807	$6,444 + 13.3% on remainder

Newfoundland and Labrador's dividend tax credit rate for eligible dividends was 11% from 2011 until July 1, 2014, and 5.4% after July 1, 2014. For other Canadian dividends, the rate was 5% from 2011 until July 1, 2014, and 4.1% from July 1, 2014, to July 1, 2016, and 3.5% after July 1, 2016.

[¶1546] POLITICAL CONTRIBUTION TAX CREDIT

Newfoundland and Labrador provides a political contribution tax credit for contributions made in the taxation year to registered political parties or candidates in a provincial election.

The available credit is calculated as:

- 75% of the first $100 of contributions,
- 50% of the next $450 of contributions, and
- 33.33% of the next $600 of contributions.

The maximum credit of $500 is reached at a contribution level of $1,150.

Credits may be claimed only if supported by a valid tax credit receipt issued under the authority of N.L. law. The credit is calculated on the provincial worksheet provided with the N.L. T1 package and claimed on line 54 of NL428.

(NFITA: 47)

[¶1547] LSVCC CREDIT (EXPIRED)

Newfoundland and Labrador provided a non-refundable provincial tax credit for investment in registered labour-sponsored venture capital corporations, in addition to the federal credit. This has now expired and no provincial credit can be claimed for shares issued after December 31, 2014. The credit was equal to 20% of the cost of eligible investments up to $10,000, for a maximum annual credit of $2,000. Eligible investments include qualifying investments made in the taxation year, or 60 days after the end of the year.

Investors in N.L.'s LSVCC program are also eligible for the federal tax credit.

Investors must hold the shares for at least eight years. The money invested in the corporation will go into a pooled fund which is to be reinvested by the LSVCC into eligible Atlantic region businesses. For several years, there has been only one eligible fund, GrowthWorks Atlantic Venture Fund.

N.L. credits were claimed in box 6176 on form NL428. Credit amounts were shown on N.L. LSVC-1 certificates. However, references to the LSVCC credit have been removed from the 2015 version of form NL428 since the credit expired at the end of 2014 and there are no carryover provisions allowing taxpayers to claim unused credits from previous taxation years.

(NFITA: 45.1)

[¶1547b] VENTURE CAPITAL TAX CREDIT

Newfoundland and Labrador offers a non-refundable venture capital tax credit to individuals who invest in a qualifying venture capital fund that is registered with the provincial Minister of Finance. The credit is equal to 30% of investments made in the year or the first 60 days of the following year. However, the total tax credits that may be claimed by one investor are subject to a $75,000 lifetime limit.

The credit is claimed on line 6190 of NL428 based on the amount of eligible investments shown on certificate NL VCTC. The certificate must be attached if filing a paper income tax return, or retained by the taxpayer if filing electronically. The credit is non-refundable, but unused amounts can be carried forward for seven years or carried back three years (but not to a year prior to 2014). Amounts carried forward from a previous year are claimed on line 61. To carry-back amounts, you must request an adjustment to your prior year return.

The credit came into effect on January 1, 2014.

(NFITA: 46.2; *Venture Capital Tax Credit Regulations*, N.L. Reg. 37/15, s. 20-22)

[¶1547d] R&D TAX CREDIT (FORM T1129)

A business carrying out scientific research in Newfoundland and Labrador is eligible for a 15% refundable tax credit for eligible expenditures. In effect, an eligible expenditure is an expenditure made by a taxpayer with a permanent establishment (¶1440) in Newfoundland and Labrador for scientific research to be carried out in Newfoundland and Labrador, to the extent that the expenditure is eligible for federal scientific research investment tax credit on form T2038 (Ind.); see ¶1463.

Expenditures flowed through partnerships and trusts will also qualify.

Individuals eligible for the credit should calculate it on form T1129 and carry the eligible credit to line 479 of the T1 return.

(NFITA: 42)

[¶1547g] DIRECT EQUITY TAX CREDIT (FORM T1272)

The Direct Equity Tax Credit is available to individuals who invest in eligible small businesses and keep their investment in the business for five years.

The available credit is calculated as 20% of the cost of investments made in businesses in the Northeast Avalon area of the province or 35% of the cost of investments in businesses within the province but outside that area. The maximum credit per investor per year is $50,000.

Any Canadian-controlled private corporation with assets of under $20 million, fewer than 50 employees, a permanent establishment in Newfoundland and Labrador, and 75% of salaries and wages paid in Newfoundland and Labrador can register under this program and, if its application is approved, can issue eligible shares to investors. Eligible businesses are limited to certain areas of the economy (e.g., technology, aquaculture, manufacturing, export, tourism, R&D, forestry, agrifoods, processing, import replacement, cultural industries) and funds raised from the issuance of eligible shares can be used for start-up, modernization or expansion, but not to retire existing debt nor refinance existing operations.

Investors must be over 18 years of age and resident in Newfoundland and Labrador. Eligible investments can be made in the calendar year or within 60 days following the end of the year. The credit is not refundable, but to the extent that it exceeds tax payable for the year after all other credits are applied, it may be carried forward for seven years or back three years. Eligible shares must be held for five years or the related tax credits are recaptured.

The credit amount should be reported to you on form NFETC. That amount is entered on federal form T1272, which also allows for the calculation of carryovers. The T1272 calculation is carried to line 56 of form NL428.

Information on the program is available on the Newfoundland and Labrador Department of Finance website (http://www.fin.gov.nl.ca/fin/tax_programs_incentives/business/directequitytaxcredit.html) or by contacting:

Newfoundland and Labrador Department of Finance
Tax Policy Division
PO Box 8700
St. John's, NL
A1B 4J6
Telephone: (709) 729-3166

(NFITA: 46)

[¶1547j] RESORT PROPERTY INVESTMENT TAX CREDIT (FORM T1297)

This program provides a non-refundable provincial income tax credit of 45% of the purchase price of qualifying resort development property units of a qualifying resort development complex outside the North East Avalon.

The application deadline for developers to register for this program was January 1, 2013. However, developers that have already registered may sell units to qualifying investors for up to five years after the resort development property was first made available for sale.

A qualifying resort development complex includes a newly constructed tourism complex, a newly constructed expansion, or a property where at least 90% of the building area is rebuilt, containing a minimum of 50 units and including a variety of amenities and leisure facilities. The qualifying resort development property unit must be a minimum of 35 square metres (376 square feet). The credit is not available for units which have been on the market for more than five years.

A qualifying investor must be a corporation or an individual (other than a trust) who is at least 19 years of age. Regulations prohibiting non-arm's length investments were repealed and replaced with a requirement that the purchase price in a non-arm's length transaction must be the same price that would have been paid if the transaction had been at arm's length.

The qualifying investor must enter into a 20-year contract relating to the availability of the unit for the rental pool. The investor must not sell or transfer ownership of the property unit for a minimum of five years after the original sale of the unit. While the five-year holding period is mandated in regulations, there does not appear to be a penalty tax to recapture credits where it is violated.

The overall maximum credit available to any one investor is $150,000 (reached on a purchase price of $333,333). The maximum credit which may be claimed in a year is $50,000 (reached on an investment of $111,111). Credit which is unused in the year of investment, either because provincial tax is less than $50,000, or because the investment is greater than $111,111, can be carried forward seven years and back three years.

The tax credit mechanism requires a qualifying resort developer to apply to the provincial Minister of Finance on behalf of each qualifying investor for a tax credit receipt not more than 90 days after the sale of a qualifying unit. The Minister will verify the tax credit application and, when satisfied, will issue to the qualifying investor a tax credit receipt equal to the lesser of (i) 45% of the purchase price and (ii) $150,000.

The credit is claimed on form T1297 and line 58 of form NL428. Claims must be supported by an NL RPITC receipt, which should be filed with a paper return or retained if filing electronically.

Information on the program is available on the Newfoundland and Labrador Department of Finance website: http://www.fin.gov.nl.ca/fin/tax_programs_incentives/business/resortproperty.html. Additional information can also be obtained by contacting:

Newfoundland and Labrador Department of Finance
Tax Policy Division
PO Box 8700
St. John's, NL
A1B 4J6
Email: taxpolicy@gov.nl.ca
Telephone: (709) 729-3166

(*Resort Property Investment Tax Credit Regulations*; NFITA: 46.1)

[¶1547p] HOME HEATING REBATE (REPEALED)

The home heating rebate was eliminated in the 2016 Newfoundland and Labrador budget. Applicants had until September 30, 2016 to apply for a rebate of eligible heating costs incurred from September 2015 to April 2016. No further applications are being accepted after this date, and no rebates will be offered for future years.

The home heating rebate program was a benefit program administered by the Newfoundland and Labrador Department of Finance. Rebates were obtained directly by application to the Department of Finance. This program was not administered directly through the income tax system, and did not appear on T1 returns.

Although not an income tax program, the Home Heating Rebate used the concept of net family income, as defined for income tax purposes. It was available to residents of Newfoundland and Labrador whose household income was $40,000 or less, regardless of the primary source of heat. Household income is the net income of the applicant plus, if applicable, the income of that applicant's spouse or partner.

The maximum rebate amount was $250, regardless of what type of energy source is used to heat the home. In the case of those living in coastal Labrador communities, the maximum rebate amount was $500, to reflect the higher heating costs in the region. Individuals and families with adjusted family incomes of up to $35,000 received a full rebate, while the available amount gradually decreased as income levels rose to $40,000. The minimum rebate was $100.

[¶1548] HST, CHILD BENEFIT, AND SENIORS' TAX CREDITS

[¶1548.02] *Net Family Income*

For purposes of the Income Supplement and the Senior's Tax Benefit, net family income has the same meaning as for the federal GST/HST credit (¶1496). That is, it is the sum of your own income and that of your spouse or common-law partner (if any) who, at the beginning of October of the base year on which the benefit is being calculated, was your cohabiting spouse or common-law partner (as defined in ¶1498.10).

Income for these purposes is net income as computed for federal purposes, except that former universal child care benefits (UCCB) (¶935) received in the year and any repayments of those benefits deducted in a year are backed out of the calculation. Registered disability savings plan benefits and repayments should be similarly backed out. Also, any capital gain or loss arising by reason of you foreclosing on a mortgage under the rules at ¶518 is backed out of the calculation.

Net family income for provincial child benefit payments is virtually the same calculation, except that your cohabiting spouse or partner is determined at the end of the base year under the federal rules at ¶1498.

[¶1548.05] *Newfoundland and Labrador Income Supplement (formerly Harmonized Sales Tax Credit)*

The 2016 provincial Budget introduced a Newfoundland and Labrador Income Supplement to replace the former Harmonized Sales Tax (HST) Credit. Effective July 2016, the income supplement will be paid in quarterly instalments, along with the federal GST credit. However, for 2016, the payments due for July and October will be combined and paid in October 2016.

The calculation of the maximum annual supplement begins by adding any of the following amounts that may apply. The result is reduced by 9% of adjusted income over $40,000.

- basic amount - $220
- amount for a spouse - $60
- amount for eligible child - $200
- 4.6% of income above $15,000 - up to $230

An additional amount of $200 is available if the taxpayer or the taxpayer's cohabiting spouse or common-law partner is entitled to the disability tax credit. This amount is reduced by 1.4% of adjusted income over $29,402.

Examples of maximum benefit amounts are:

- for a single person - $450 annually ($112.50 quarterly);
- for a single person entitled to the disability tax credit - $650 annually ($162.50 quarterly)
- for a single parent with one child - $650 annually ($162.50 quarterly)
- for a couple with no children - $510 annually ($125.50 quarterly);
- for a couple with one child - $710 annually ($177.50 quarterly); and
- for a couple with two children - $910 annually ($227.50 quarterly);

Eligibility requirements are the same as for the federal GST credit except that individuals must be resident in Newfoundland and Labrador in order to claim the provincial income supplement. No application is required, although taxpayers must file an annual income tax return in order to receive the supplement.

Historical Notes

Prior to 2016, the Newfoundland and Labrador HST credit was $40 for the taxpayer, $40 for the spouse/ common-law spouse, and $60 for each qualified dependant; the total of these amounts was reduced by 5% of net family income for the year (per ¶1498) in excess of $15,000. Thus for a family of four the credit would be eliminated at a family income level of $19,400. Rather than quarterly instalments, the former HST credit was paid once a year along with the October GST payment.

(NFITA: 34 Income supplement; Income Supplement and Seniors' Benefit Regulations, NL Reg. 32/16; RC4210 GST/HST Credit)

[¶1548.10] *Seniors' Tax Benefit*

The Newfoundland and Labrador seniors' tax benefit is an addition to the income supplement described above. Effective July 2016, the seniors' tax benefit will be paid in quarterly instalments along with the federal GST credit payments (previously it was paid once a year along with the October GST credit payment). However, for 2016, the payments due for July and October will be combined and paid in October 2016.

If you and/or your spouse or common-law partner were 65 or older at any time in the year, you may receive a payment of up to $1,313 for 2016, regardless of whether you are single or living with a spouse or common-law partner. This amount was increased from $1,063 by the 2016 Newfoundland and Labrador Budget. This benefit amount is reduced by 11.66% of net family income in excess of $29,402. At this income threshold, the credit is eliminated entirely when net family income exceeds $40,663.

Benefit amounts are indexed annually. For 2015, the maximum benefit was $1,059, reduced by 11.66% of income in excess of $29,284, and eliminated for income over $38,366.

(NFITA: 34(3); Income Supplement and Seniors' Benefit Regulations, NL Reg. 32/16; RC4210 GST/HST Credit)

[¶1548.15] *Newfoundland and Labrador Child Benefit*

As with most provinces, Newfoundland and Labrador offers a child tax benefit harmonized with the federal Canada Child Benefit and administered by the CRA. Accordingly, where you receive the federal benefit, you should automatically receive any Newfoundland and Labrador supplement to which you are entitled.

The Newfoundland and Labrador Child Benefit is available for any month in which you were a Newfoundland and Labrador resident immediately before the first of the month and on the first day of the month.

For the period from July 2016 through June 2017, the benefit entitlement is $31.58 per month for the first child, $33.50 for the second child, $36.00 for the third child, and $38.58 for each additional child. Benefit payments are reduced where your net family income exceeds $17,397. Where income exceeds this threshold, the total credit for any given month is reduced by 1/12 of the annual amounts for dependants eligible in that month, reduced by 5.07% of net family income in excess of $17,397 where there is one child, 10.45% where there are two, 16.22% where there are three, and where there are more than three, the total of 16.22% and the product obtained by multiplying the number of qualified dependants in excess of three by 6.19%.

Net family income is essentially net income of yourself and your spouse, subject to the comments at ¶1498, since the federal definition of "adjusted income" discussed there is used for Newfoundland and Labrador purposes.

In addition, there is a $60 per month Mother Baby Nutrition Supplement (MBNS) for each child, beginning the month after the birth and lasting while the child is under the age of one (11 payments). It appears that you qualify for the full $60 payment if you qualify for any amount of the Newfoundland and Labrador Child Benefit, i.e., the payment is not ground down by family income so long as any amount of normal benefit is payable.

Historical Notes

Child benefit amounts are indexed annually. The Newfoundland and Labrador Child Benefit amounts for the period from July 2015 through June 2016 were $31.41 per month for the first child, $33.33 for the second child, $35.83 for the third child, and $38.41 for each additional child, reduced where your net family income exceeded $17,397.

(*Newfoundland and Labrador Child and Parental Benefits Regulations*; 38 Newfoundland and Labrador child tax benefit; T4114 Canada Child Benefits — Including related federal, provincial and territorial programs)

[¶1548.17] *Supplemental Child Care Credit*

Newfoundland and Labrador offers a non-refundable child care tax credit for child care expenses deductible for federal income tax purposes. This credit is in addition to the deduction already taken in the calculation of income.

The credit is calculated at the lowest Newfoundland and Labrador tax rate of 8.2% for 2016 (8.7% for 2017) applied to eligible expenses claimed for the federal deduction (line 214 of your federal return). The maximum amount of child care expenses eligible for the credit includes up to $8,000 for each child under the age of 7; $5,000 for each child aged 7 to 16; and $11,000 for each child for whom the disability credit can be claimed.

The child care amount is input on line 5831 of form NL428; enter the line you claimed on line 214 of your federal return, based on form T778.

(NFITA: 17.2)

[¶1548.20] *Additional Parental Benefits*

Newfoundland and Labrador offers additional parental benefit payments. The Progessive Family Growth Benefit and the Parental Support Benefit are not administered through the income tax system, but rather require direct application to the N.L. Department of Finance. Both of these benefits were eliminated effective April 15, 2016. However, eligible births and placements for adoption which took place on or before April 14, 2016 will remain eligible for the full benefit.

The Progressive Family Growth Benefit provides a $1,000 lump-sum payment to residents of the province who give birth to a baby or have a child placed with them for adoption before April 15, 2016.

The Parental Support Benefit (PSB) is a $100 monthly benefit available to residents of the province for the 12 months after the child's birth, or the 12 months after the adopted child is placed in the home. Children must be born or placed for adoption before April 15, 2016 to qualify for this benefit.

Where there are multiple births or adoptions, both benefits are available for each child.

These are non-taxable benefits and are universal in nature. A person's or family's income level or source is not a factor in determining eligibility.

Eligible individuals must apply for these benefits. Only one person per household may make such an application (one application form covers both benefits). Normally, the mother would make the application, unless legal custody is with the father who is not a cohabiting spouse. Parents are encouraged to submit applications as soon as possible after the birth, or after placement of the child in their home for adoption. A separate form should be submitted for each child. A copy of the long form birth certificate (for births) or a copy of the letter of placement from the Department of Health and Community Services (for adoptions) must accompany the application form.

Application forms for both benefits are available at www.fin.gov.nl.ca/fin/tax_programs_incentives/parental_support_benefit.html and should also be available at all Government Services Centres, obstetrical units, offices of family doctors, Newfoundland and Labrador Medical Care Plan (MCP) offices, and regional child, youth, and family services offices. The forms should also be included in all *You and Your New Baby* packages available through public health nurses.

Applications must be sent to:

Parental Benefits Program
Tax Administration Division
Department of Finance
PO Box 6010
32 Queensway
Grand Falls-Windsor, NL
A2A 0B9

Further information on both the Progressive Family Growth Benefit and the Parental Support Benefit can be obtained by calling 1-866-990-3444 or by email at parentalbenefits@gov.nl.ca.

(*Child and Parental Benefits Regulations*)

NORTHWEST TERRITORIES

[¶1549] NORTHWEST TERRITORIES TAX RATES AND CREDITS

The Northwest Territories follows the TONI system (¶1501). Accordingly, N.W.T. tax is based on federal taxable income from line 260 of the T1 return, to which Northwest Territories applies (for 2016) the following tax rates:

Taxable income	*Tax*
$41,011 or less	5.9%
In excess of	
$41,011	$ 2,420 + 8.6% on next $41,013
$82,024	$ 5,947 + 12.2% on next $51,329
$133,353	$12,209 + 14.05% on remainder

N.W.T. personal amounts and tax brackets differ from federal amounts and brackets. This requires N.W.T. taxpayers to recalculate these amounts on NT428 and the Territorial Worksheet which accompanies it.

Like the federal government, the Northwest Territories makes an exception for the charitable donation credit, giving credit at its lowest rate of 5.9% on the first $200 of donation and at its highest rate of 14.05% on the balance. Hence donation amounts should be taken from Schedule 9.

Where a student must calculate education/tuition tax credit amounts and/or transfers on federal Schedule 11, the student must make a parallel provincial calculation on NT(S11) (the federal education tax credits will be eliminated after December 31, 2016; in order for the education credit to continue in the Northwest Territories, legislative changes would have to be made, but these changes have not been made as of September 2016). Where you are claiming a transfer of personal amounts from your spouse or common-law partner on federal Schedule 2, you must make the parallel Northwest Territories claim on NT(S2).

The TONI system requires the provinces and territories to maintain the package of personal amounts that was in place in 1999, although not the dollar values of those amounts. It does not require the provinces and territories to adopt later personal amount credits which the federal government may offer, and the Northwest Territories has to date not chosen to adopt any of the subsequent credits discussed at ¶1501.05.

The TONI system requires the Northwest Territories to impose its own tax or tax credits at the rates of its choosing on several items, which it has done as follows:

- dividend tax credit on eligible dividends is 11.5%, and on other taxable Canadian dividends, the rate is 6%;
- tax on split income (from form T1206) at the top N.W.T. marginal rate of 14.05%;
- alternative minimum tax (from line 117 of form T691) at 45%; and
- alternative minimum tax credit (Schedule 1 line 427) at 45%.

The AMT tax/tax credit rate is essentially the old provincial tax-on-tax rate; its use takes a federally calculated tax/tax credit number and applies it for provincial purposes as a kind of shorthand, rather than working through the income calculation again and applying an appropriate provincial tax (or, with more difficulty, tax credit) to the income. The tax on split income, by contrast, imposes the top provincial rate on the actual split income as determined for federal purposes.

[¶1549.05] *N.W.T. Rate History*

For 2015, the tax rates were:

Taxable income	*Tax*
$40,484 or less	5.9%
In excess of	
$40,484	$ 2,389 + 8.6% on next $40,487
$ 80,971	$ 5,870 + 12.2% on next $50,670
$131,641	$12,052 + 14.05% on remainder

In 2015, the dividend tax credit on eligible dividends was 11.5%, and on other taxable Canadian dividends the rate was 6%.

For 2014, the tax rates were:

Taxable income	*Tax*
$39,808 or less	5.9%
In excess of	
$39,808	$2,349 + 8.6% on next $39,810
$79,618	$5,772 + 12.2% on next $49,823
$129,441	$11,851 + 14.05% on remainder

The dividend tax credit on eligible dividends was 11.5%, and on other taxable Canadian dividends the rate was 6%.

For 2013, the tax rates were:

Taxable income	*Tax*
$39,453 or less	5.9%
In excess of	
$39,453	$2,328 + 8.6% on next $39,455
$78,908	$5,721 + 12.2% on next $49,378
$128,286	$11,745 + 14.05% on remainder

The dividend tax credit on eligible dividends was 11.5%, and 6% on other taxable Canadian dividends.

For 2012, the tax rates were:

Taxable income	*Tax*
$38,679 or less	5.9%
In excess of	
$38,679	$2,282 + 8.6% on next $38,681
$77,360	$5,609 + 12.2% on next $48,411
$125,771	$11,515 + 14.05% on remainder

The dividend tax credit on eligible dividends was 11.5%, and on other taxable Canadian dividends, the rate was 6%.

For 2011, the tax rates were:

Taxable income	*Tax*
$37,626 or less	5.9%
In excess of	

Taxable income	*Tax*
$37,626	$2,189 + 8.6% on next $37,627
$75,253	$5,456 + 12.2% on next $47,092
$122,345	$11,201 + 14.05% on remainder

The dividend tax credit on eligible dividends was 11.5%, and on other taxable Canadian dividends, the rate was 6%.

(NTITA: 2–2.44)

[¶1550] COST OF LIVING CREDIT AND SUPPLEMENT

The Northwest Territories has a refundable cost-of-living credit against N.W.T. tax. The credit has two components, as discussed below. Both are available only to residents of the N.W.T. on December 31 of the taxation year. Neither is available to trusts or estates.

The basic credit is based on "adjusted net income", which is net income from line 236 of your return minus treaty-protected payments deducted at line 256 and the social assistance component, if any, of amounts deducted at line 250 and the Canadian Forces personnel and police deduction at line 244. Accordingly, although there is no age limitation on claiming the credit, you must have income to be entitled to basic credit.

The basic credit is 2.6% on the first $12,000 of adjusted net income, 1.25% on the next $36,000, and 1% on the next $18,000. The basic credit is thus capped at $942 on $66,000 of adjusted net income. The basic credit does not take any account of spousal income; each taxpayer computes it based on his or her income alone, regardless of marital status. The basic credit is calculated on the Territorial Worksheet and claimed on line 6 of form NT479.

The basic credit is supplemented (on NT479) by an additional refundable credit which is not based on income, but is only available to N.W.T. residents 18 years of age or over on the last day of the taxation year. You do not have to have income for the year to obtain the supplement. However, if you do have income, the supplement is reduced by the basic refundable cost of living credit of you and your spouse or common-law partner (if any), so the cost of living credit and the supplement cannot double up, and the maximum refund is always $942. The supplementary credit is $350 for yourself and $350 for your spouse or common-law partner, if you were living together at the end of the year and not separated by a breakdown of the relationship which proves to last longer than 90 days. Unlike the basic credit, which is claimed by each spouse/partner independently, one of you must claim the supplement for both. If you both file T1 returns, the basic credit from both returns must be used to reduce the supplemental credit. Since the supplement is refundable and not income-tested, it does not matter to household income which spouse or partner makes the claim. The credit supplement is calculated on the territorial worksheet and claimed on line 13 of Form NT479.

The statute does not contemplate the situation in which spouses or partners might be living apart not by reason of marriage breakdown but because, say, they are temporarily pursuing separate careers. If one spouse does not reside in the Northwest Territories and files a return elsewhere, there is no amount on that person's return to reduce that person's $350 credit. The statute seems clear that the $700 could be claimed anyway, but is perhaps ambiguous as to whether the $700 is reduced only by the N.W.T. resident's basic credit. Certainly that is not the intended result, and one could make a case that the statute requires the calculation for the non-resident spouse even if it then denies the basic credit. The matter is by no means certain, and the case would certainly be rare.

(NTITA: 4.1)

[¶1550b] NORTHWEST TERRITORIES FIRST NATION INFORMATION

Parliament has ratified an agreement with the "Tâîchô" First Nation. Among other things, that bill provided authority to negotiate tax administration agreements, which would probably replicate in principle the arrangements in place with Yukon First Nations discussed in ¶1596f, although details of the agreement do not have the same degree of certainty.

For 2004 and later years, there is a unique version of the T1 return for the Northwest Territories. It differs from the common version in requiring information as to whether you were resident on "Tâîchô" lands or in a specified "Tâîchô" community at December 31 of the taxation year. The remainder of the N.W.T. T1 return makes no further mention of the tax consequences for such residents. Information sheet T1-NT12, *Residency information for tax administration agreements*, is included in the N.W.T. T1 package, and says that a tax administration and sharing agreement has been reached in respect of personal income tax. No details of the agreement are provided; it is simply stated that the Canada Revenue Agency will use Tâîchô residency information to administer the agreement for the First Nation, and notes the geographical areas in which Tâîchô citizens may reside which entitle them to the presumed benefits of the agreement.

The CRA information sheet specifies that all individuals, including non-Tâîchô citizens, who reside on Tâîchô lands or in the Tâîchô communities of Behchokö (Rae-Edzo), Whati (Lac La Martre), Gamèti (Rae Lakes), or Wekweèti (Snare Lake) are required to identify themselves by ticking "Yes" in the "Residency information for tax administration agreements" box on page 1 of the Northwest Territories Income Tax and Benefit Return.

All individuals residing in the designated areas, whether Tâîchô citizens or not, are directed to identify themselves as Tâîchô residents. All N.W.T. residents who reside elsewhere are not to identify themselves as such, whether Tâîchô citizens or not.

If your residence status is in doubt because you maintain more than one residence, you should be guided by the same "residence in fact" criteria that determine national residence in ¶115.05

(Income Tax Folio: S5-F1-C1 Determining an Individual's Residence Status)

[¶1551] POLITICAL CONTRIBUTION TAX CREDIT

If you contributed in the year to candidates seeking election as members of the Northwest Territories Legislative Assembly, you may deduct a portion of your contribution(s) from your Northwest Territories income tax.

The credit is calculated on the N.W.T. worksheet and claimed on line 51 of form NT428.

The N.W.T. credit is somewhat different from those of other provinces and is calculated as follows:

- 100% credit on the first $100 contributed; and
- 50% credit on the next $800, for a maximum credit of $500 (reached when eligible contributions totalling $900 have been made).

The credit also differs from those of other provinces in making no provision for contributions to local political parties as such, presumably because candidates for the Assembly are considered to run without political affiliation.

Proof of contributions on which credit is claimed must be filed with your return in the form of an official receipt signed by the official agent of the candidate. If you are filing electronically, keep your documents in case the CRA asks to see them.

(NTITA: 5)

[¶1552] NORTHWEST TERRITORIES RISK CAPITAL INVESTMENT TAX CREDITS (EXPIRED)

When funded, this program encouraged investment in shares of northern businesses. The program offered non-refundable tax credits of 30% up to a maximum credit of $30,000 (reached on a maximum investment of $100,000) per year against N.W.T. tax for investors in eligible business or venture capital corporations. Credits in excess of N.W.T. tax may be carried back three years or forward seven, but no tax may be carried back to years preceding the enactment of the tax credit on September 25, 1998. The calculation and carryover requests were incorporated on form NT428. Since the program terminated in 2008, the carryforward period for unused credits expired December 31, 2014.

(*Risk Capital Investment Tax Credit Act*, S.N.W.T. 1998, c. 22; NTITA: 6.1)

[¶1552d] INQUIRIES

Questions concerning these credits should be addressed to:

Treasury, Financial Services
Department of Finance
Government of the Northwest Territories
3rd Floor YK Centre
Box 1320
Yellowknife, Northwest Territories
X1A 2L9
Telephone (867) 873-7500

[¶1552k] NORTHWEST TERRITORIES CHILD TAX BENEFITS

The Northwest Territories has implemented a child tax benefit supplement. If you are already receiving federal Canada Child Benefits (¶1498), you should automatically receive any N.W.T. supplement to which you are entitled.

The N.W.T. program replicates two elements of the federal program described at ¶1498, the basic per child amount and the (former) working income supplement.

The N.W.T. benefit adopts the federal standards of eligibility set out in ¶1498, and is administered by the CRA as part of the federal Canada Child Benefit program. The N.W.T. portion of the benefit, however, is paid only for a month in which the recipient of the benefit (typically the mother of an eligible child) was resident in the Northwest Territories for a period which included both the first day of the month and the last day of the preceding month.

The first component of the N.W.T. benefit is $330 per year ($27.50 per month) per eligible child. The second component — the Territorial Worker's Supplement — is $275 ($22.91 per month) for one child or $350 ($29.16 per month) if there is more than one child. The Territorial Worker's Supplement component only functions if the family has "earned income" (as defined for child care expense purposes at ¶1055) of more than $3,750, and is reduced by prorating it by ((the lesser of $10,000 and family earned income) minus $3,750) divided by $6,250. This formula means the Supplement component increases from zero at earned income of $3,751 to the full amount at earned income of $10,000 or more. The whole benefit (both components) is then reduced by 5% (3% where there is only one child) of the amount by which net family income exceeds $20,921.

In the fall of 2016, the Northwest Territories *Income Tax Act* will be amended to enhance the child benefit, including different benefit amounts for children under and over the age of six. The basic amount would be paid to all families with less than $30,000 in family income and gradually reduced as income increases. Families with income over $80,000 will not qualify for the benefit. The enhanced credit will be implemented in 2017. At the time this chapter was written, the legislation has not been passed.

Inquiries about the benefit should be directed to the CRA at 1-800-387-1193.

(NTITA: 3.1–3.4)

NOVA SCOTIA

[¶1553] TAX RATES AND BASIC CREDITS

[¶1553.05] *Basic Tax Rates*

Nova Scotia tax is based on federal taxable income from line 260 of the T1 return, to which Nova Scotia applies the following tax rates for 2016:

Taxable income	*Tax*
$29,590 or less	8.79%
In excess of	
$29,590	$2,601 + 14.95% on next $29,590
$59,180	$7,025 + 16.67% on next $33,820
$93,000	$12,662 + 17.5% on next $57,000
$150,000	$22,637 + 21.0% on remainder

These rates and brackets have been in effect since 2010. In 2010, Nova Scotia temporarily introduced a fifth personal income tax bracket, to remain in effect until the provincial budget is balanced. This increased Nova Scotia's highest income tax rate to 21%. While this high-income bracket remains in place, the Nova Scotia high-income surtax has been suspended.

Until the surtax was suspended in 2010, Nova Scotia imposed an additional surtax of 10% of Nova Scotia tax in excess of $10,000. This implied a taxable income of at least $80,841 before the surtax would apply, or higher if tax credits in excess of the basic personal credit applied.

Nova Scotia does not regularly index income thresholds for its brackets. Rather, tax brackets or rates have been periodically reset by statute. In 2011, the province announced that personal income tax brackets and certain credits would begin to be indexed by regulation. However, to date, no such regulations have been made. For a recent history of N.S. tax rates see ¶1553.15.

Like federal income tax, Nova Scotia applies its highest tax rate (21%) to tax on split income (form T1206). Nova Scotia also imposes AMT at 57.5% of federal AMT (line 117 of form T691).

(NSITA: 8; 22A; 33)

[¶1553.10] *Basic Tax Credits*

Nova Scotia offers provincial personal tax credits similar to most, but not all, federal personal non-refundable tax credits. However, most Nova Scotia personal amounts differ from federal amounts, and are converted to tax credits at Nova Scotia tax rates. Accordingly, Nova Scotia residents must for provincial purposes use the personal amounts computed on NS428 and the Nova Scotia worksheet.

Personal tax credits offered by Nova Scotia include: a basic personal credit, spouse or common-law partner credit, eligible dependant credit, caregiver credit, infirm dependant credit, age credit, CPP contributions and EI premiums credits, pension income credits, disability credit and supplement, tuition and education credits (the federal education credit is repealed effective January 1, 2017), student loan interest credit, medical expense credit, and charitable donations credit. The Nova Scotia pension income credit is available only to residents of the province. Nova Scotia offers its own version of a credit for young children (¶1554f), and volunteer firefighters' credit (¶1559). Nova Scotia does not presently offer credits similar to the federal adoption tax credit, children's fitness or arts credit, textbook credit (the federal textbook credit is repealed effective January 1, 2017), Canada employment credit, or public transit credit.

Most N.S. personal credit amounts differ from federal credit amounts. As exceptions, amounts eligible (before conversion to credit) for CPP/QPP, EI, and student loan interest will be the same as on the federal return. Other credits may be calculated on NS428 and the provincial worksheet. For a chart of 2016 N.S. tax credit amounts, see ¶52 at the beginning of this book.

Nova Scotia does not regularly index its personal credit amounts. Rather, certain credits are reset periodically by statute. In 2011, the province announced that certain personal non-refundable tax credits would begin to be indexed by regulation, but to date no such regulations have been made. In recent years, the basic personal amount, spouse or common-law partner credit, eligible dependant credit, disability credit, caregiver credit, age credit, pension income amount and infirm dependant credit have all been increased periodically. However, no increases in these credit amounts were affected for 2016.

Once the amounts eligible for non-refundable credit are determined, Nova Scotia, like the federal government, calculates the credit at its lowest tax rate (8.79%). Also like the federal government, Nova Scotia makes an exception for charitable donation credit, giving credit at its lowest rate (8.79%) on the first $200 of donation and at its highest rate (21%) on the balance. Donation amounts should be taken from lines 345 and 347 of Schedule 9.

Where a student must calculate education/tuition tax credit amounts and/or transfers on federal Schedule 11, the student must make a parallel provincial calculation on NS(S11). Similarly, where you are claiming a transfer of personal amounts from your spouse or common-law partner on federal Schedule 2, you must make the parallel Nova Scotia claim on form NS(S2).

Other Nova Scotia credit rates for tax credits based on federal credits include the following:

- dividend tax credit: 8.85% on eligible dividends, 3.33% on other taxable Canadian dividends; and
- alternative minimum tax credit (Schedule 1 line 427) at 57.5%.

The AMT tax/tax credit rate is essentially the old provincial tax-on-tax rate; its use takes a federally calculated tax/tax credit number and applies it for provincial purposes as a kind of shorthand, rather than working through the income calculation again and applying an appropriate provincial tax (or, with more difficulty, tax credit) to the income.

(NSITA: 8–32)

[¶1553.15] *Rate History*

For 2011 through 2015, Nova Scotia tax rates were:

Taxable income	*Tax*
$29,590 or less	8.79%
In excess of	
$29,590	$2,601 + 14.95% on next $29,590
$59,180	$7,025 + 16.67% on next $33,820
$93,000	$12,662 + 17.5% on next $57,000
$150,000	$22,637 + 21.0% on remainder

Nova Scotia dividend tax credit rates for 2011 to 2013 were 8.85% on eligible dividends and 7.7% on other taxable Canadian dividends. In 2014, the rates were 8.85% on eligible dividends and 5.87% on other taxable Canadian dividends. In 2015, the rates were 8.85% on eligible dividends and 3.5% on other taxable Canadian dividends.

(NSITA: 33)

[¶1554] LOW-INCOME TAX REDUCTION

Nova Scotia permits a low-income tax reduction of $300 for each of yourself and your spouse or a dependant claimed on line 305 (the eligible dependant amount, see ¶1120), and $165 for other dependent children as described below. This credit is reduced by 5% of your family income in excess of $15,000. This means that for a family of four, some reduction would apply below an income of $33,600.

The CRA provides an income calculation for the low-income reduction calculation on NS428, which starts with net income (from line 236 of the T1 return) of yourself and, if you had a spouse or common-law partner on December 31 of the taxation year, that person. It then provides adjustments to back out universal child care benefits (UCCB) received in the year, registered disability savings plan (RDSP) income, and UCCB and RDSP repayments deducted in a year.

Using net income from line 236 as the starting point for determining income for purposes of the low-income tax reduction is something of an oversimplification. You count your spouse or common-law partner at December 31 provided you were not separated at that time by virtue of breakdown of the relationship for a period which proved to last for 90 days. This definition also applies to determine eligibility for the $300 claim for your spouse. As well, net income at line 236 should not include income from a gain on repossession of property as described at ¶518.

To be a person eligible to claim the reduction, you must be an individual (other than a trust) resident in Nova Scotia on December 31 of the taxation year, or resident in Nova Scotia on the date of death if that occurred in the year.

There are additional criteria for eligibility, and these are that on December 31 of the taxation year you met one of the following criteria:

- you were 19 years of age or over;
- you had a spouse or common-law partner; or
- you were a parent.

A dependent child is essentially a child who:

(1) was under 19 on December 31;

(2) did not have a spouse or common-law partner;

(3) was not a parent; and

(4) lived with you on December 31 or was claimed as a dependant by you or your spouse or common-law partner and by no one else under Nova Scotia rules.

Only one person can claim the Nova Scotia tax reduction in respect of a particular child.

Where both spouses are eligible to claim the reduction, only one may do so. The reduction should be the same whoever claims it, so the important thing is that it should not be wasted if the credit is more than the tax.

The reduction cannot be claimed by someone who was confined to prison or a similar institution for a total of more than six months during the year.

Reduction amounts are not subject to annual indexation, but Nova Scotia has the authority to increase them by regulation.

(NSITA: 35)

[¶1554b] AGE TAX CREDIT FOR LOW-INCOME SENIORS

Beginning with the 2014 taxation year, Nova Scotia has introduced an additional non-refundable tax credit for low-income seniors.

The credit provides a non-refundable tax credit amount of $1,000 to seniors with taxable income below $24,000.

To be eligible for the credit, an individual must be at least 65 years of age by December 31 of the taxation year and must be resident in the province at the end of the year. Where the individual died during the year, the residency requirement is met where the individual was resident in the province on the day of death.

The credit is claimed on line 79 of form NS428.

(NSITA: 36B)

[¶1554c] SPORT AND RECREATIONAL EXPENSES FOR CHILDREN (HEALTHY LIVING TAX CREDIT) (REPEALED)

The healthy living tax credit, which provided a $500 non-refundable credit for children's sports and recreational activities, has been eliminated and cannot be claimed on 2015 or later tax returns.

Historical Notes

The Nova Scotia healthy living credit (also called the sport and recreational expenses for children credit) was similar to the federal child fitness credit. The maximum eligible amount for this non-refundable credit was $500 per child for registration in a designated sport or recreational activity. The credit was available for children under the age of 18 at the end of the year.

Where more than one individual was entitled to claim a credit in respect of the same child, the credit was apportioned so that the total amounts claimed did not exceed the maximum allowable credit amount. Qualifying sports and recreational activities had to be registered with the Nova Scotia Department of Health and Wellness before December 31 of the applicable taxation year.

(NSITA: 12A; *Sport and Recreation Activity Regulations*)

[¶1554f] AMOUNT FOR YOUNG CHILDREN (CHILD CARE BENEFIT TAX CREDIT)

Nova Scotia offers a credit originally designed to offset the former universal child care benefit (UCCB; see ¶935). Although the UCCB was eliminated in July 2016, the 2016-2017 Nova Scotia Budget announced that the provincial amount for young children will be maintained. The credit is available to parents and guardians of children under six years of age.

Under this credit program, you claim $100 per month for each child less than six years of age if all the following conditions are met:

- the child was less than six years old and living with you on the first day of the month;
- no one else claimed this amount for the child for the month;
- the child has not been claimed by you or anyone else as an eligible dependant on line 5816 of the NS428; and
- no one received a special allowance under the *Children's Special Allowances Act* for that child for that month.

If you have a spouse or common-law partner at the end of the year, only the person with the lower net income (including zero) can make the claim. In the case of spouses with equal incomes, you have to decide who claims the credit (this differs slightly with the UCCB income inclusion rules, which give the UCCB income inclusion to the recipient parent in the case of equal incomes).

Nova Scotia uses the criteria of spouse or common-law partner as it is used for purposes of the child tax credit in ¶1498.10, which imports the 90-day separation rule discussed there (the UCCB income inclusion simply refers to the spouse or common-law partner you were living with on the last day of the taxation year, which is not quite the same thing).

The credit amount is claimed on line 5823 of NB428. In addition, you must complete the "details of amounts claimed for young children" section of the form, setting out a list of the children for whom you are making the claim, giving the child's name, relationship to you, date of birth, and number of months you are claiming for each child.

(NSITA: 10(5)– 10(8))

[¶1554h] POST-SECONDARY GRADUATE RETENTION REBATE (REPEALED)

Nova Scotia has eliminated the graduate retention rebate. Post-secondary graduates could claim this rebate as a non-refundable credit on their 2013 tax returns, but no rebates are available for 2014 or subsequent years.

The rebate offered graduates with a university degree (including bachelor's, master's, and doctorate degrees) a tax credit of $2,500 per year, for a maximum of $12,500 over five years. College diploma and certificate graduates were eligible for a tax reduction of $1,250 per year, for a maximum of $6,250 over five years. Graduates could only claim this credit for one degree, diploma, or certificate, even if they graduated from more than one eligible program.

This non-refundable credit was only available for the year of graduation and each of the following four years, and Nova Scotia did not allow unused credits to be carried forward for use in subsequent years. Therefore, graduates who did not have sufficient taxable income in the years immediately following graduation did not receive the full benefit. This credit was claimed on Form NS428.

(NSITA: 36A)

[¶1554j] AFFORDABLE LIVING TAX CREDIT

The Nova Scotia Affordable Living Tax Credit is a refundable tax credit intended to offset the 2010 increase in the Nova Scotia HST rate, for low- to modest-income households. Credit payments are received quarterly along with federal GST/HST credits. No application is required for 2014 and subsequent years. The credit is administered by the CRA, which will automatically determine your eligibility based on income reported on your tax return.

For the 2016-2017 benefit year, qualifying individuals and families are entitled to receive a maximum credit of $255 per individual or couple, plus $60 per child under 19 years of age. These credit amounts are reduced by 5% of adjusted net family income over $30,000. Tax credit payments will be issued quarterly, from July 2016 through June 2017.

Credit amounts are indexed periodically, but have not increased since the 2012-2013 benefit year.

(*Nova Scotia Affordable Living Tax Credit Regulations*, NS Reg. 178/2013; NSITA: 80; RC4210 GST/HST Credit)

[¶1554k] POVERTY REDUCTION TAX CREDIT

The Poverty Reduction Credit provides tax-free benefit payments to individuals and couples receiving income assistance, with total annual income of $12,000 or less. The credit is not applied for on income tax returns, but rather administered by the Nova Scotia Department of Community Services.

Under this program, eligible individuals may be entitled to receive up to $250 in annual benefit payments, paid over a benefit year from July through June, through quarterly instalments of $62.50. Periodically, these annual benefit amounts have been adjusted for inflation.

To qualify, applicants must be 19 years of age with no dependants, receiving Social Assistance through the Income Assistance program as their main source of income, with a total annual income of $12,000 or less for the previous tax year. Social Assistance clients need not apply for this allowance — eligibility is determined by the Department of Community Services. Only one person of a married or common-law couple can receive the credit on behalf of the family.

Further information on this credit can be obtained from the Nova Scotia Department of Community Services website at www.novascotia.ca/coms/noteworthy/PovertyReduction-Credit.html.

(NSITA: 80)

[¶1555] POLITICAL CONTRIBUTION TAX CREDIT

If you contributed in the year to recognized Nova Scotia political parties or to candidates seeking election as members of the Nova Scotia House of Assembly, you are entitled to deduct from your Nova Scotia taxes (if any) a portion of such contributions. The credit is calculated as 75% of the contribution, to a maximum credit of $750 (reached on total contributions of $1,000). The credit is claimed on line 6210 of NS428.

Proof of payment in the form of an official receipt signed by the official agent of the recognized political party or the official agent of the candidate must be attached to your return, unless you are filing electronically, in which case you must keep the receipts on hand for possible review by the CRA.

If you have further questions concerning the Nova Scotia political contribution tax credit, you can contact: Office of the Chief Electoral Officer, PO Box 2246, Halifax, Nova Scotia B3J 3C8. Telephone: (902) 424-8584.

(NSITA: 50)

[¶1556] LABOUR-SPONSORED VENTURE CAPITAL TAX CREDIT

The Nova Scotia Labour-Sponsored Venture Capital Tax Credit is available for qualifying investments in registered LSVCCs. The credit is calculated at 20% of eligible investments made in the year, or within 60 days following the end of the year. The maximum annual credit is $2,000. Previously set to expire, this credit has been extended through February 2022.

The *Nova Scotia Equity Tax Credit Act* allows Nova Scotia to register for provincial purposes federally sponsored Labour-Sponsored Venture Capital Corporations (LSVCCs) which comply with Nova Scotia regulations (principally, agree to invest in Nova Scotia the large bulk of funds raised there). See ¶2522(2) for a list of LSVCCs which qualify at the time of writing. Note that investments in these funds are typically locked in for at least eight years, with some exceptions (see ¶1466).

The maximum annual tax credit that may be claimed is $2,000. The credit is calculated at a rate of 20% of the eligible investment, so the maximum $2,000 credit would be reached on an investment of $10,000. Investments may be eligible for both the provincial and federal credits.

N.S. law requires that the credit must be claimed in a return filed within seven years of the end of the year to which the credit pertains.

These investments are discussed in detail in Chapter 25, ¶2522(2). At the time of writing, only one plan (GrowthWorks Atlantic Venture Fund Limited) had successfully registered.

Note the federal redemption restrictions and potential credit recapture on these shares, discussed at ¶1466.

The N.S. LSVCC eligible investment amount is reported to you on form NSLSV, and the credit is claimed on line 6238 of form NS428. The NSLSV should be filed with your return, unless you are filing electronically, in which case it should be kept on hand with your tax records.

(*Equity Tax Credit Act; Equity Tax Credit Regulations;* NSITA: 38)

[¶1557] FOOD BANK TAX CREDIT FOR FARMERS

For 2016 and subsequent years, farmers in Nova Scotia, or their spouses or common-law partners, can claim a non-refundable 25% income tax credit for donating agricultural products to an “eligible food bank”. This is defined as a registered charity that distributes food in the province without charge for the relief of poverty as part of its mandate.

The credit is calculated as 25% of the fair market value of qualifying donations. Donations must be produced in Nova Scotia and must be claimed by the individual, in the same taxation year, for purposes of the charitable donation tax credit. Accordingly, donations are subject to the same receipt requirements as the charitable donation credit.

The credit is claimed on line 6098 of form NS428.

You can claim this credit if you meet all of the following conditions:

- you were a resident of Nova Scotia at the end of the year;
- you or your spouse or common-law partner was a farmer;
- you made a qualifying donation to an eligible food bank in the year; and
- you have claimed the qualifying donation on line 340 of your federal Schedule 9 and on line 29 of Form NS428 as a charitable donation or gift for the year.

The amount of qualifying donations can be split between spouses or common-law partners; however, the total amount of qualifying donations that can be claimed by spouses or common-law partners cannot be more than the total of the qualifying donations made in the tax year. If you are preparing a return for a person who died in 2016, you can claim this credit on the deceased person's final return. If you were bankrupt in 2016, claim your food bank tax credit for farmers on either the pre- or post-bankruptcy return you file for the tax year ending December 31, 2016, depending on when the qualifying donations were made. If qualifying donations are claimed on more than one return, the total amount of donations that can be claimed on all returns filed for the year cannot be more than the total qualifying donations made.

(NSITA: 50A)

[¶1558] EQUITY TAX CREDIT (FORM T1285)

The Nova Scotia Equity Tax Credit provides a 35% credit for eligible investments in shares of qualifying small businesses, co-operatives, and community development corporations. Previously set to expire, this credit has been extended through February 2022.

The credit is calculated as 35% of the cost of qualifying investments, to a maximum annual tax credit of $17,500, reached on a total annual investment of $50,000. The credit applies to investments made in the year or within 60 days following the end of the year.

An eligible company or co-op must be accepted by the Nova Scotia Department of Finance and Treasury Board for registration. On its face, any Nova Scotia company or marketing co-op with 25% of its payroll in Nova Scotia and assets of less than $25 million can qualify. Once registered, the company can issue qualifying shares for the purposes of the credit.

There must be at least three investors for an issue of shares. However, three related persons could go into business together and receive the credit, so long as their business intent is accepted as viable and not merely an effort to obtain the credit. A corporation must devote substantially all of its assets to an active business carried on in Canada as defined for federal corporation income tax purposes, and cannot be a specified investment business or incorporated employee as defined for those purposes.

Tax credits are non-refundable for investors. However, credits in excess of Nova Scotia tax may be carried back three years and forward seven years against Nova Scotia tax of those years. A return claiming the credit may be late-filed, but must be filed within three years after the end of the year to which the deduction pertains.

The credits are reported to the investor on form NSETC. Credits are calculated on form T1285 (which accounts for carryovers) and claimed at line 77 on form NS428 (which is part of the Nova Scotia T1 package). The T1285 and NSETC should be filed with your return, unless you are filing electronically, in which case they should be kept on hand with your tax documents.

Further information on this program, including application forms and guidelines for business registrations, is available on the Nova Scotia Depart of Finance website at http://www.novascotia.ca/finance/en/home/taxation/tax101/personalincometax/equitytaxcredit/default.aspx, or by contacting:

Nova Scotia Department of Finance and Treasury Board
Fiscal Policy Division
PO Box 187
Halifax, Nova Scotia
B3J 2N3
Telephone: (902) 424-8369

(*Equity Tax Credit Act*; *Equity Tax Credit Regulations*, NS Reg. 18/94; NSITA: 37)

[¶1559] VOLUNTEER FIREFIGHTERS AND GROUND SEARCH AND RESCUE TAX CREDIT

The Nova Scotia Volunteer Firefighters Tax Credit provides a refundable tax credit of up to $500, for qualifying volunteers meeting the conditions described below.

To be eligible for the tax credit you must:

(1) be an individual (not including a trust) resident in Nova Scotia on December 31 of the taxation year; an individual who died in a taxation year will meet this condition for the year of death return if resident in Nova Scotia at the time of death;

(2) have been a volunteer firefighter or volunteer ground search and rescue worker, for a minimum of six months in the calendar year for which the claim is made;

(3) not have received salary, wages, or compensation or anything in lieu of salary, wages, or compensation, other than reasonable reimbursement or allowance for expenses, in respect of the firefighting or ground search and rescue services provided during the taxation year for which you claim the deduction;

(4) be listed as a volunteer firefighter on a report filed by the fire chief of your volunteer fire department or as a volunteer ground search and rescue worker by a report filed by your team president.

The fire chief or rescue team president is required to file a report by January 31 of the year containing prescribed information. The report format is found on the Nova Scotia Finance website (www.novascotia.ca/finance/en/home/taxation/personalincometax/volunteerfirefighterstaxcredit.aspx).

A volunteer fire department is a fire department that the Fire Marshal recognizes as a volunteer fire department.

A volunteer firefighter must satisfy all of the following criteria during a taxation year:

(1) the individual provides fire services as a member of a volunteer fire department during the taxation year;

(2) the individual participates in at least 20% of each of the following activities during the taxation year:

(a) responses by the volunteer fire department to emergency calls,

(b) training sessions conducted by the volunteer fire department,

(c) meetings held by the volunteer fire department.

The credit is is claimed at the end of form NS428, in box 6228. This amount is then transferred to line 479 of the T1 return.

(*Volunteer Fire Fighter Tax Credit Regulations*; NSITA: 38A)

[¶1560t] NOVA SCOTIA CHILD TAX BENEFITS

Nova Scotia offers a provincial supplement to the Canada Child Benefit discussed at ¶1498. Eligibility for the benefit, apart from dollar amounts, is determined under the federal rules at ¶1498, and the CRA administers the program as part of the Canada Child Benefit program.

The Nova Scotia supplement is payable for each month for each qualified dependant (¶1498) resident in Nova Scotia on the first of the month. Accordingly, if you receive federal Canada Child Benefits and you show on CRA records as being resident in Nova Scotia, you should automatically receive any benefit you are entitled to. It is incumbent upon you to notify the CRA immediately if you change your province of residence. Several provinces have these supplementary programs, but the rates tend to be different for each. The CRA can recapture any benefits it pays to you in error.

For the 2016 benefit year, from July 2016 through June 2017, the annual benefit is $625 for your first child (or $52.08 per month), $825 for your second child (or $68.75 per month), and $900 for your third and subsequent children (or $75 per month). These benefit amounts are the same as for the 2015 benefit year.

The full Nova Scotia supplement is payable so long as your net family income (¶1498) of the preceding base-year (¶1498) used to measure the benefit is less than $18,000. Where net family income for the base period exceeds $18,000, the monthly benefit is reduced by formula, and is eliminated entirely when net family income exceeds $26,000.

Net family income is essentially net income of yourself and your spouse, subject to the comments at ¶1498, since the federal definition of adjusted income discussed there is used for Nova Scotia purposes.

For official information, call 1-800-387-1193.

(NSITA: 80(1); Other Publications: *Nova Scotia Child Benefit Regulations*)

NUNAVUT

[¶1562] NUNAVUT TAX RATES AND CREDITS

Nunavut uses the TONI system (¶1501) for 2001 and later years. Accordingly, Nunavut tax is based on federal taxable income from line 260 of the T1 return, to which Nunavut applies (for 2016) the following tax rates:

Taxable income	*Tax*
$43,176 or less	4%
In excess of	
$43,176	$1,727 + 7% on next $43,175
$86,351	$4,749 + 9% on next $54,037
$140,388	$9,613 + 11.5% on remainder

Most Nunavut personal amounts differ from federal amounts, and must be computed on form NU428, the territorial worksheet which accompanies the Nunavut T1 package. Amounts eligible (before conversion to credit) for CPP/QPP, EI, and student loan interest amounts will be the same as on the federal return.

Like the federal government, Nunavut gives tax credit at its lowest rate (4%) on personal amounts.

Like the federal government, Nunavut makes an exception for charitable donation credit, giving credit at its lowest rate (4%) on the first $200 of donation and at its highest rate (11.5%) on the balance. Donation amounts should be taken from lines 345 and 347 of Schedule 9.

The TONI system requires the provinces and territories to maintain the package of personal amounts that was in place in 1999, although not the dollar values of those amounts. It does not require the provinces and territories to adopt later personal amount credits which the federal government may offer, and Nunavut has to date not chosen to offer most of the additional federal credits described at ¶1501.05. It has, however, chosen to vary the Working Income Tax Benefit, requiring a unique federal Schedule 6 included with the Nunavut T1 package, and has adopted the federal increase to $2,000 in the amount eligible for pension credit.

The TONI system requires Nunavut to impose its own tax or tax credits, at the rate of its choosing, on several items, which it has done as follows:

- dividend tax credit on eligible dividends is 5.51%, and on other taxable Canadian dividends, the rate is 2.91% for 2016 and subsequent years (3.05% in 2014 and 2015);
- tax on split income (from form T1206) at 11.5%;
- alternative minimum tax (from line 117 of form T691) at 45%; and
- alternative minimum tax credit (from Schedule 1 line 427) at 45%.

The AMT tax/tax credit rate is essentially the old provincial tax-on-tax rate; its use takes a federally calculated tax/tax credit number and applies it for provincial purposes as a kind of shorthand, rather than working through the income calculation again and applying an appropriate provincial tax (or, with more difficulty, tax credit) to the income. The tax on split income, by contrast, imposes the top provincial rate on the actual split income as determined for federal purposes.

[¶1562.05] *Rate History*

The Nunavut tax rate schedule for 2015 was:

Taxable income	*Tax*
$42,622 or less	4%
In excess of	
$42,622	$1,705 + 7% on next $42,621
$85,243	$4,688 + 9% on next $53,343
$138,586	$9,489 + 11.5% on remainder

The dividend tax credit on eligible dividends was 5.51%, and on other taxable Canadian dividends the rate was 3.05%.

The Nunavut tax rate schedule for 2014 was:

Taxable income	*Tax*
$41,909 or less	4%
In excess of	
$41,909	$1,661 + 7% on next $41,909
$83,818	$4,610 + 9% on next $52,452
$136,270	$9,331 + 11.5% on remainder

The dividend tax credit on eligible dividends was 5.51%, and on other taxable Canadian dividends the rate was 3.05%.

The Nunavut tax rate schedule for 2013 was:

Taxable income	*Tax*
$41,535 or less	4%
In excess of	
$41,535	$1,661 + 7% on next $41,536
$83,071	$4,569 + 9% on next $51,983
$135,054	$9,247 + 11.5% on remainder

The dividend tax credit on eligible dividends was 5.51%, and on other taxable Canadian dividends, the rate was 4%.

The Nunavut tax rate schedule for 2012 was:

Taxable income	*Tax*
$40,721 or less	4%
In excess of	
$40,721	$1,629 + 7% on next $40,721
$81,442	$4,479 + 9% on next $50,964
$132,406	$9,066 + 11.5% on remainder

The dividend tax credit on eligible dividends was 5.51%, and on other taxable Canadian dividends, the rate was 4%.

The Nunavut tax rate schedule for 2011 was:

Taxable income	*Tax*
$39,612 or less	4%
In excess of	
$39,612	$1,584 + 7% on next $39,612
$78,130	$4,357 + 9% on next $49,576
$128,800	$8,697 + 11.5% on remainder

The dividend tax credit on eligible dividends was 5.82%, and on other taxable Canadian dividends, the rate was 4%.

(NUITA: 2–2.44)

[¶1562e] COST OF LIVING CREDIT

[¶1562e.05] *Adjusted Net Income for Cost of Living Credits*

Nunavut inherited the Northwest Territories' refundable cost of living credit. The credit is available only to residents of Nunavut on December 31 of the taxation year. It is not available to trusts or estates.

The credits discussed here are based on "adjusted net income", which is net income from line 236 of your return minus treaty-protected payments deducted at line 256 and minus the social assistance component, if any, of amounts deducted at line 250 and the Canadian Forces personnel and police deduction at line 244. Accordingly, although there is no age limitation on claiming the credit, you must have income to be entitled to basic credit.

The credit does not take any account of spousal income; each taxpayer computes it based on his or her income alone, regardless of marital status.

[¶1562e.10] *Basic Cost of Living Credit*

The basic cost of living credit is 2% of your adjusted net income to a maximum credit of $1,200. The $1,200 limit is reached at an adjusted income level of $60,000.

[¶1562e.15] *Cost of Living Supplement*

The cost of living supplement picks up where the basic credit leaves off, at $60,000, but is only available to a "single parent", defined as a person who, *at any time in the taxation year*:

(1) is unmarried and does not live in a common-law partnership, or is married or in a common-law partnership and is living separate and apart from the spouse or common-law partner by reason of a breakdown of their marriage or common-law partnership; *and*

(2) has, in law or in fact, the custody and control of a child, who has not attained the age of 18 years and who is wholly dependent for support on the individual, or who has attained the age of 18 years, but who is wholly dependent for support on the individual because of mental or physical infirmity.

Where custody and control of a child is shared, any individual who fulfils the responsibility for the care and upbringing of the child for at least 50% of the time qualifies as a single parent.

The credit itself is 2% of adjusted net income (as determined for purposes of the general cost of living credit above) in excess of $60,000, to a maximum of $255.12.

The credit is calculated and claimed on line 14 of form NU479.

(NUITA: 4.1)

[¶1562g] AMOUNT FOR YOUNG CHILDREN

For each qualifying child under the age of six at any time in the year, you may claim an amount of $1,200. The lowest Nunavut tax rate is applied to this amount, for a tax credit of $48 per child under six.

While the lower income spouse or common-law partner (if any) must make the claim initially, any credit not absorbed by that person's tax can be transferred to the other spouse/partner on Schedule NU(S2), *Territorial Amounts Transferred from Your Spouse or Common-Law Partner.*

Essentially, the credit is available for each child:

- who was under six at any time in the year;
- who lived with you at the end of the year (or on the date of death if the child died during the year); and
- for whom no special allowance under the *Children's Special Allowances Act* was received by anyone during the year.

You cannot make the claim if anyone has claimed the child as an eligible dependant on line 4 of the NU428.

The credit is claimed on line 6 of form NU428. You must file with your return a list of the children for whom you are making the claim, giving the child's name, relationship to you, date of birth, and social insurance number (if any). A chart is provided on the last page of the NU428 for this data.

(NUITA: 2.211)

[¶1562i] POLITICAL CONTRIBUTION TAX CREDIT

If you contributed in the year to candidates seeking election to the Nunavut government, you may deduct a portion of your contribution(s) from your Nunavut income tax.

The credit is is calculated at lines 15 to 20 of form NU479.

The Nunavut credit is somewhat different from those of most provinces, and provides:

- a 100% credit on the first $100 contributed; and
- a 50% credit on the next $800;

for a maximum credit of $500.

The credit also differs from those of other provinces in making no provision for contributions to local political parties as such, presumably because candidates for the Assembly are considered to run without political affiliation.

Proof of contributions on which credit is claimed must be filed with your return in the form of an official receipt signed by the official agent of the candidate. If you are filing electronically, keep these documents in case the CRA asks to see them.

(NUITA: 5)

[¶1562k] VOLUNTEER FIREFIGHTERS TAX CREDIT

Nunavut has a non-refundable tax credit for volunteer firefighters. For 2016, you can claim a credit of $570 ($563 for 2015) if you meet all of the following conditions:

(1) you are an individual resident in Nunavut on December 31 of the taxation year (an individual who died in a taxation year will meet this condition for the year of death return if resident in Nunavut at the time of death);

(2) you were a firefighter for a minimum of six months during the calendar year in which you claim the deduction;

(3) you were a member of a fire department established by a municipality;

(4) you have a letter signed by the Fire Marshal, or the chief or acting chief of the fire department, stating that you spent at least 200 hours:

(a) responding to emergency calls as a firefighter,

(b) being on call as a firefighter to respond to emergency calls,

(c) participating in training courses related to fire fighting or fire inspection, and

(d) attending meetings held by the fire department (according to the CRA's instructions for completing your Nunavut return, the requirement is that you completed a minimum of 200 hours of community service — including training — and were listed as a volunteer firefighter on the report filed by the fire chief of the volunteer fire department); and

(5) you have not received salary, wages, or compensation, other than reasonable reimbursement or allowance for expenses, in respect of firefighting services during the taxation year in which you claim the credit.

The fire chief is required to file a report by January 31 of the year and it must contain prescribed information. That at least is what is required for the Nova Scotia credit on which the Nunavut credit appears to be modelled. See ¶1559.

The credit is claimed on line 51 of form NU428.

Nunavut has not adopted a territorial version of the new federal search and rescue volunteer credit.

(NUITA: 6.2)

[¶1562n] NUNAVUT BUSINESS TRAINING TAX CREDIT (EXPIRED)

The Nunavut Business Training Tax Credit provided a refundable tax credit for eligible employers who pay for business training for eligible employees. The credit was 20% to 30% of business training tax expenses for eligible employees to a maximum of $10,000 for any 12-month period. The credit expired on April 1, 2014.

An employer providing business training to one or more employees had to apply for a business training tax credit certificate from the Deputy Minister of the Department of Finance. The certificate indicates the amount of the maximum business training tax credit to which the employer is entitled and the taxation year to which the credit applies.

(NUITA: 6.3)

[¶1562v] NUNAVUT WORKING INCOME TAX BENEFIT

The federal government has a refundable tax credit for low-income families, the Working Income Tax Benefit (¶1495). Although strictly a federal payment, its provisions allow the federal Minister of Finance to vary the terms of the benefit, by agreement with a province or territory, to better harmonize with a local benefit system. Nunavut has made such an agreement, which is reflected in the unique version of federal Schedule 6 included in the Nunavut version of the T1 tax package.

[¶1562x] NUNAVUT CHILD TAX BENEFITS

Nunavut inherited the N.W.T. Child Tax benefit provisions. If you are already receiving federal Canada Child Benefits (¶1498), you should automatically receive any Nunavut supplement to which you are entitled.

The Nunavut program replicates two elements of the federal program described at ¶1498, the basic per child amount and the (former) working income supplement.

The Nunavut benefit adopts the federal standards of eligibility set out in ¶1498, and is administered by the CRA as part of the federal Canada Child Benefit program. The Nunavut portion of the benefit, however, is paid only for a month in which the recipient of the benefit (typically the mother of an eligible child) was resident in Nunavut for a period which included both the first day of the month and the last day of the preceding month.

The first component of the Nunavut benefit is $330 per year ($27.50 per month) per eligible child. The second component — the Territorial Worker's Supplement — is $275 ($22.91 per month) for one child or $350 ($29.16 per month) if there is more than one child. The Territorial Worker's Supplement only functions if the family has "earned income" (as defined for child care expense purposes at ¶1055) of more than $3,750, and is reduced by prorating it by ((the lesser of $10,000 and family earned income) minus $3,750) divided by $6,250. This formula means that the Supplement component increases from zero at earned income of $3,751 to the full amount at earned income of $10,000 or more. The whole benefit (both components) is then reduced by 5% (3% where there is only one child) of the amount by which net family income exceeds $20,921.

Inquiries should be directed to the CRA at 1-800-387-1193.

(NUITA: 3.1–3.4)

ONTARIO

[¶1564] TAX RATES AND BASIC CREDITS

[¶1564.05] *Basic Tax Rates*

Ontario income tax is based on federal taxable income from line 260 of the T1 return, to which Ontario tax rates and brackets are applied to calculate provincial tax. For 2016, Ontario basic tax rates and brackets are as follows:

Taxable income	*Tax*
$41,536 or less	5.05%
In excess of	
$41,536	$2,098 + 9.15% on next $41,539
$83,075	$5,898 + 11.16% on next $66,925
$150,000	$13,367 + 12.16% on next $70,000
$220,000	$21,879 + 13.16% on remainder

Effective January 1, 2016, Ontario imposes its top marginal tax rate (20.53%) on split income (applied to the federal amount form T1206). This is a special rate that also applies to trusts and is not subject to the Ontario surtax (¶1564.15), which is already reflected in the rate. For 2015 and prior years, split income was taxed at the highest personal income tax rate (13.16%). Ontario also imposes AMT at 33.67% of the federal AMT amount from line 95 of form T691. In addition, Ontario imposes a surtax (¶1564.15) on gross tax payable above certain thresholds.

Income thresholds for the two highest brackets are not indexed for inflation, but thresholds for the lower three brackets are indexed annually. Rates and brackets applicable to prior years are set out at ¶1564.10, below.

(OTA: 3(1); 6(1); 11; 12; 16; 23)

[¶1564.07] *Basic Tax Credits*

Ontario offers tax credits similar to most (but not all) federal personal credits. Most Ontario personal tax credit amounts differ from federal amounts, and must be computed on form ON428 and the Ontario worksheet provided with the Ontario T1 package.

Available Ontario personal credits include: a basic personal amount, spouse or common-law partner amount, eligible dependant amount, caregiver amount, infirm dependant amount, age amount, EI and CPP contributions amounts, pension amount, disability amount and supplement, tuition and education amounts (Ontario tuition and education credits will be repealed in fall 2017; the federal education credit is also repealed effective January 1, 2017), medical expense amounts, charitable donations amounts, interest on student loans, and adoption expense amount. Ontario credits for adoption expenses and pension income are available only to residents of the province. Ontario also offers a refundable tax credit for children's fitness and arts activities, although this will be eliminated effective January 1, 2017 (¶1568e). Ontario does not offer tax credits similar to federal credits for transit passes, textbooks (the textbook credit is repealed effective January 1, 2017), Canada employment, or volunteer firefighters.

Most Ontario credit amounts differ from federal credit amounts (see the table at ¶52). However, amounts eligible (before conversion to credit) for CPP/QPP, EI, and student loans will be the same as federal amounts and can be taken from federal Schedule 1. For the purposes of the medical expense credit, Ontario still imposes a threshold on eligible medical expenses of other dependants (despite the federal threshold having been eliminated) and also thresholds on certain eligible expenses (see Chapter 12).

Following the federal model, Ontario gives tax credits at its lowest tax rate (5.05%) for most personal amounts. An exception (again following the federal model) is for charitable donations, for which Ontario provides credit at its lowest rate (5.05%) on the first $200 of donation and at a higher rate (11.16%) on the balance. Donation amounts eligible for this credit should be taken from lines 345 and 347 of Schedule 9.

Other credits for which Ontario imposes its rates include the dividend tax credit, calculated at credit rates of 10% for eligible dividends and 4.2863% for other taxable Canadian dividends.

For 2014 and subsequent years, Ontario has adjusted the method of calculating the dividend tax credit to eliminate the impact of Ontario surtax. The credit is now deducted on line 6152 of form ON428, after the calculation of the surtax. As a result, the credit will have the same value for all taxpayers regardless of their income level. For prior years, it was deducted before the calculation of surtax, meaning that higher income individuals received a greater benefit from the credit than lower income individuals.

Where a student must calculate education/tuition tax credit amounts and/or transfers on federal Schedule 11, the student must make a parallel Ontario calculation on form ON(S11). Similarly, where you are claiming a transfer of personal amounts from your spouse or common-law partner on federal Schedule 2, you must make the parallel Ontario claim on form ON(S2).

(OTA: 3(1); 9; 18; 20.1; 23)

[¶1564.10] *History of Rates*

Ontario tax rates and brackets for recent prior years are as follows.

For 2015, the Ontario basic rate schedule was:

Taxable income	*Tax*
$40,922 or less	5.05%
In excess of	
$40,922	$2,067 + 9.15% on next $40,925
$81,847	$5,811 + 11.16% on next $68,153
$150,000	$13,417 + 12.16% on next $70,000
$220,000	$21,929 + 13.16% on remainder

Ontario surtax rates were 20% of basic Ontario tax in excess of $4,418, plus 36% of basic Ontario tax in excess of $5,654. Ontario dividend tax credit rates were 10% for eligible dividends and 4.5% for other taxable Canadian dividends.

For 2014, the Ontario basic rate schedule was:

Taxable income	*Tax*
$40,120 or less	5.05%
In excess of	
$40,120	$2,026 + 9.15% on next $40,122
$80,242	$5,697 + 11.16% on next $69,758
$150,000	$13,482 + 12.16% on next $70,000
$220,000	$21,994 + 13.16% on remainder

Ontario surtax rates were 20% of basic Ontario tax in excess of $4,331, plus 36% of basic Ontario tax in excess of $5,543. Ontario dividend tax credit rates were 10% for eligible dividends and 4.5% for other taxable Canadian dividends.

For 2013, the Ontario basic rate schedule was:

Taxable income	*Tax*
$39,723 or less	5.05%
In excess of	

Taxable income	*Tax*
$39,723	$2,006 + 9.15% on next $39,725
$79,448	$5,641 + 11.16% on next $429,552
$509,000	$53,579 + 13.16% on remainder

Ontario surtax rates were 20% of basic Ontario tax in excess of $4,289, plus 36% of basic Ontario tax in excess of $5,489. Ontario dividend tax credit rates were 6.4% for eligible dividends and 4.5% for other taxable Canadian dividends.

For 2012, the Ontario basic rate schedule was:

Taxable income	*Tax*
$39,020 or less	5.05%
In excess of	
$39,020	$1,874 + 9.15% on next $37,776
$78,043	$5,541 + 11.16% on next $421,957
$500,000	$52,632 + 12.16% on remainder

Ontario surtax rates were 20% of basic Ontario tax in excess of $4,213, plus 36% of basic Ontario tax in excess of $5,392. Ontario dividend tax credit rates were 6.4% for eligible dividends and 4.5% for other taxable Canadian dividends.

For 2011, the Ontario basic rate schedule was:

Taxable income	*Tax*
$37,774 or less	5.05%
In excess of	
$37,774	$1,874 + 9.15% on next $37,776
$75,550	$5,364 + 11.16% on remainder

Ontario surtax rates were 20% of basic Ontario tax in excess of $4,078, plus 36% of basic Ontario tax in excess of $5,219. Ontario dividend tax credit rates were 6.4% for eligible dividends and 4.5% for other taxable Canadian dividends.

[¶1564.15] *Surtax*

Ontario also imposes a surtax, calculated on the "gross tax amount" of Ontario tax payable (i.e., before certain credits and adjustments), above certain threshold amounts. These threshold amounts, above which surtax applies, are indexed annually.

For 2016, applicable Ontario surtax rates are:

- 20% of basic Ontario tax in excess of $4,484; plus
- 36% of basic Ontario tax in excess of $5,739.

Effective for 2014 and subsequent years, Ontario has amended the calculation of surtax so that it is determined before deducting Ontario dividend tax credits from Ontario tax. This change is intended to eliminate the impact of Ontario surtax on dividend tax credit amounts.

Ontario surtax is calculated on lines 50 to 55 of form ON428.

For surtax rates in recent prior years see the history of Ontario rates at ¶1564.10.

(OTA: 16)

[¶1564.20] *Ontario Health Premium*

Ontario imposes a health care premium on individuals resident in the province, administered through the Ontario income tax system. The premium is in the form of a graduated tax applicable to taxable income in excess of $20,000. It applies directly to taxable income as calculated for federal purposes (line 260 of the T1 return). There are no applicable credits, and the premium is not deductible in any way, but it is not subject to surtax.

The Ontario Health Premium applies to taxpayers resident in Ontario on December 31 of the taxation year. In the case of dual residence, it applies if your principal place of residence is Ontario. Administratively, the CRA will determine principal residence in accordance with the principles laid out in Income Tax Folio S5-F1-C1 (see ¶115).

The premium operates to impose a graduated tax, in large income steps, subject to a diminishing phase-in amount with each step. The basic income ranges and premium steps are shown below, as set out on form ON428:

The basic premium steps are:

Ontario Health Premium

Enter your **taxable income** from line 31. ______ 1

Go to the line that corresponds to your taxable income.

- If there is an Ontario health premium amount on that line, enter that amount on line 73.
- Otherwise, enter your taxable income in the first box, complete the calculation, and enter the result on line 73.

Taxable income				Ontario health premium
not more than **$20,000**	▶	▶	▶	**$0**
more than **$20,000**, but not more than **$25,000**		☐ – $20,000 =	☐ × 6% =	☐
more than **$25,000**, but not more than **$36,000**	▶	▶	▶	**$300**
more than **$36,000**, but not more than **$38,500**	☐ – $36,000 =	☐ × 6% =	☐ + $300 =	☐
more than **$38,500**, but not more than **$48,000**	▶	▶	▶	**$450**
more than **$48,000**, but not more than **$48,600**	☐ – $48,000 =	☐ × 25% =	☐ + $450 =	☐
more than **$48,600**, but not more than **$72,000**	▶	▶	▶	**$600**
more than **$72,000**, but not more than **$72,600**	☐ – $72,000 =	☐ × 25% =	☐ + $600 =	☐
more than **$72,600**, but not more than **$200,000**	▶	▶	▶	**$750**
more than **$200,000**, but not more than **$200,600**	☐ – $200,000 =	☐ × 25% =	☐ + $750 =	☐
more than **$200,600**	▶	▶	▶	**$900**

See the privacy notice on your return.

The lines showing calculated premium amounts in the table above (e.g., from $20,000 to $25,000) represent the range over which the flat rate applicable to each step is phased in. The phase-in machinery for those gaps operates as follows:

- For the first step (income over $20,000), the premium is phased in over a range of $5,000 at a 6% rate. At an income level of $25,000, the tax at 6% reaches $300, the tax is fully phased in, and the flat rate of $300 applies until income reaches $36,000.
- For the second step (income over $36,000), the premium is phased over a range of $2,500 at a 6% rate. At an income level of $38,500, the tax at 6% reaches $150, which is added to the $300 from the first stage. The tax is now fully phased in and the flat rate of $450 applies until income reaches $36,000.
- For the remaining three steps (income over $48,000, $72,000 and $200,000), the premium is phased over a range of $600 at a 25% rate. In each case, when the tax on the first $600 at 25% reaches $150, this is added to the accumulated tax from lower brackets, the tax is now fully phased in for that step, and the flat rate applies until income reaches the next threshold. Above income of $200,600, the tax is simply $900.

The CRA includes a very clear calculation of the premium at the end of form ON428, as shown above.

In the case of death, the premium is paid only on the year of death return, and not on any of the special returns discussed in Chapter 19. Similarly, in a year of bankruptcy, you are deemed for purposes of the premiums to have a calendar taxation year which includes all you taxable income for that period. Trusts are not subject to the premium.

(OTA: 16(2); 24)

[¶1564.25] *Gifts to Ontario*

Ontario provides for voluntary donations to its deficit reduction program on the T1 tax return through the Ontario Opportunities Fund box at page 4 of the Ontario version of the T1 return. Completing this box permits you to gift all or any part of your total federal and provincial tax refund to the Province of Ontario, for the purposes of provincial debt reduction.

Where you filled out this box on your 2015 return, your gift will be a 2016 gift eligible (to the extent of 75% of 2016 net income) for tax credit on a 2016 return filed in 2017. Similarly, a gift you identify now on your 2016 return will be made in 2017 and claimed on your 2017 return.

The CRA specifies on the Ontario information sheet that donations under $2 will not be processed or, if the refund you have calculated is reduced by $2 or more when your return is assessed, it will not be processed.

Where you choose to donate all or part of your tax refund for the year to the Ontario Opportunities Fund, you will be issued a receipt for the purposes of claiming a tax credit on your next year's return.

(ITA: 161.4)

[¶1565] TAX REDUCTION

The Ontario Tax Reduction operates to reduce or eliminate Ontario tax payable for low-income individuals and families. If you were resident in Ontario on December 31, 2016, and if your Ontario tax payable for the year is $231 or less, the reduction will operate to eliminate your tax and no Ontario income tax will be payable. This reduction amount is increased if you have dependent children up to 18 years of age at the end of 2016 (i.e., children born in 1998 or later) or dependants 18 or over who were disabled. The Ontario Tax Reduction is phased out at higher income levels as tax payable increases. The tax reduction does not apply unless you are resident in Ontario on December 31 of the taxation year.

The Ontario Tax Reduction is calculated on Ontario tax payable (after deducting the non-refundable tax credits but before deducting Ontario refundable tax credits and foreign tax credits). Step 4 on form ON428 is provided for calculating the reduction. The basic reduction amount for a taxpayer for 2016 is $231.

To this basic reduction amount you may add a further $427 for each child to whom you or your cohabiting spouse or common-law partner (as discussed in ¶1566) are the parent (¶1122.20) and who was eligible for the child tax benefit in the year. Essentially, this means the child must be 18 years of age or younger at the end of the year, have lived with you in the year, and have been a resident of Canada. However, you may not make a claim for such a dependent child if anyone claims the child as a spouse or common-law partner or receives an amount for the child under the *Children's Special Allowances Act*.

In addition, you may claim $427 for each infirm or disabled dependant of yours or of your cohabiting spouse or common-law partner for whom you claimed any amount of federal personal amount credit on line 5816, 5820, 5840, or 5848 of form ON428. As well, you may add $427 for a disabled spouse or common-law partner if you are receiving a transfer of disability credit from that person on line 3 of Ontario Schedule ON(S2) (carried to line 5864 of the Ontario form ON428). For dependants other than a spouse or common-law partner, you may double up the child-18-or-under claim with the disability claim; that is, you may claim a total of $854 for a disabled or infirm child of yours as described above, $427 on each of lines 6269 and 6097 of ON428.

In all cases of "cohabiting" spouses or common-law partners (as defined under a separate heading under ¶1566.15, below) who are residing together on December 31 of the taxation year, the spouse with the higher income must make all claims under the tax reduction provision.

Once Ontario reduction amounts for yourself, your minor dependants, and your disabled dependants are determined and totalled, the total is compared to twice the Ontario tax payable after the application of personal amount credits, dividend and minimum tax credits, but before reduction for Ontario foreign tax credit, if any, and before application of other refundable Ontario tax credits. It follows that when Ontario tax reaches 200% of total Ontario reduction amounts, the reduction disappears.

You may not claim any tax reduction if you are subject to AMT in the year (Chapter 24), even if the Ontario tax based on AMT is less than Ontario reduction amounts. You cannot claim any reduction if you were a non-resident of Canada at the beginning of the taxation year. As well, the reduction may not be claimed on returns filed by trustees for bankrupt individuals. Trusts are also not eligible for the credit.

The CRA information sheet for Ontario states, however, that you can claim the tax reduction on the year of death return for a deceased taxpayer.

The Ontario tax reduction amounts are indexed annually by the Ontario cost of living. Amounts in recent previous years were as follows:

Year	*Basic personal reduction*	*Each dependant*
2015	$228	$421
2014	$223	$413
2013	$221	$409
2012	$217	$401
2011	$210	$389

(OTA: 20)

[¶1566] PROVINCE-SPECIFIC TAX CREDITS

In addition to personal credit amounts (¶1564.07), the Province of Ontario offers a number of other provincial tax credits, deductible in computing Ontario tax payable. These include the following credits:

- Ontario energy and property tax credit (see ¶1567);
- northern Ontario energy credit (see ¶1567c);
- Ontario sales tax credit (see ¶1568);
- senior homeowners' property tax grant (see ¶1567f);
- healthy homes renovation tax credit (see ¶1567h);
- children's activity tax credit (see ¶1568e);
- political contribution tax credit (see ¶1569);
- Ontario focused flow-through share tax credit (mining exploration investment tax credit) (see ¶1571j);
- apprenticeship training tax credit (see ¶1572.05); and
- cooperative education tax credit (see ¶1572.10).

Three of the above credits — the Ontario energy and property tax credit, the northern Ontario energy credit, and the Ontario sales tax credit — form the Ontario Trillium Benefit (see ¶1567). This benefit, along with the senior homeowners' property tax grant, are applied for on the individuals' annual tax returns, and subsequently paid out to qualifying individuals as tax benefit payments.

The apprenticeship training and cooperative education credits are available to individuals carrying on unincorporated businesses.

All the above credits are refundable to the extent that they exceed Ontario tax payable. Accordingly, it may be beneficial to file a return to obtain such a refund, even where no income tax is payable for the year.

Ontario rules generally provide that its tax credits are only available to individuals resident in the province on December 31 of the taxation year; it follows that multi-jurisdictional taxpayers resident outside Ontario may not claim the credits (¶1504). Neither can emigrants who have left the province in the course of the year to move to another province or country but must file Ontario returns for the year of departure.

Foreign students admitted as visitors to Canada are entitled to Ontario tax credits on the same basis as other Ontario taxpayers, provided that they are considered factual rather than deemed residents of Canada (see ¶115 and ¶117). The visa issued has no bearing on residence status for tax purposes; rather a factual test discussed in Chapter 1 determines each case.

[¶1566.05] *Adjusted Income for Ontario Tax Credit Calculations*

The Ontario energy and property tax credit, sales tax credit, senior homeowners' property tax grant, and northern Ontario energy credit are all "means-tested"; that is, they are reduced to the extent your "adjusted net family income" exceeds a certain level. Your adjusted net family income for Ontario tax credit purposes is the same as your income level determined for federal GST/HST tax credit purposes. This family income amount basically includes your income and the income of your cohabiting spouse or common-law partner (see ¶1566.15, below), adjusted to exclude certain amounts including amounts related to the federal Universal Child Care Benefit and *Canada Disability Savings Act*.

Your adjusted net family income includes the income of your spouse or common-law partner, provided that you were living together at the end of the year. If you and your spouse or common-law partner are divorced or separated at the end of the year (as discussed at ¶1566.15, below), you may each claim the above-listed credits individually, and your income is counted separately for the purposes of determining credit eligibility. If you and your spouse or common-law partner are living in separate residences at the end of the year by virtue of medical reasons, you are considered "involuntarily separated" and may choose to apply for certain credits (including those listed above, with the exception of the sales tax credit) individually or as a couple. (If applying separately, you must check box 6108 on form ON-BEN.) Note that information on your marital status and spouse or common-law partner's net income is required to be filled in on page 1 of your T1 return.

You do not have to calculate your adjusted family net income on your Ontario forms, as the CRA will automatically make this calculation based on information provided in your return. For the purposes of determining your eligible amount for the credits listed above, threshold income amounts applicable to each credit are subtracted from your adjusted net family income amount. Net family income in excess of these threshold income levels reduce the amount of the claim to which you are entitled for each credit and effectively eliminate credit entitlements as certain net income levels are reached. For taxpayers with net family income below the applicable thresholds, entitlements are to full credit amounts. Through this credit calculation process, the assistance provided by these credits is directed to low- to moderate-income taxpayers.

Income thresholds for the purposes of these credits generally vary for single individuals and families (including couples and single parents), and for seniors (age 65 or older) and senior families. One purpose of the special thresholds for seniors and senior families is to enable them to receive the full benefit of guaranteed minimum income support payments, including federal Old Age Security and Guaranteed Income Supplement, and the provincial Guaranteed Annual Income System, without grinding down the value of these tax credits. Applicable income thresholds for the calculation of individual tax credits are discussed at relevant paragraphs below detailing each credit.

[¶1566.10] *Dependent Children*

Ontario uses the concept of "qualified dependant" similar to the Canada Child Benefit and GST/HST credit rules (¶1498) as the appropriate definition of dependent child for many of its tax credit (and tax reduction) purposes.

Generally, a child is your dependent child for Ontario tax purposes if you or your cohabiting spouse or common-law partner is the parent (¶1122) and the child was eligible for the Canada Child Benefit in the year. Essentially, this means the child must:

(1) be 18 years of age or younger at the end of the year;

(2) have lived with you at some time in the year; and

(3) have been a resident of Canada at some time in the year.

In addition, the child must *not* be a person:

(1) for whom anyone claims a personal amount as a spouse or common-law spouse; or

(2) for whom anyone receives an amount under the *Children's Special Allowances Act*.

[¶1566.15] *Spouses or Common-Law Partners*

Ontario uses the concept of a "qualified relation" or "cohabiting spouse or common-law partner" similar to the Canada Child Benefit rules (¶1498) or GST/HST tax credit rules for many of its tax credit (and tax reduction) purposes. A qualifying spouse or common-law partner is defined (under the federal rules) at any particular time as an individual's cohabiting spouse or common-law spouse or partner (under the rules at ¶1113) who is not at the time living separate and apart from the individual by reason of marriage breakdown for a period of a least 90 days that includes the time. The relevant time for determining if the spouses are separated for purposes of the joint income calculation is December 31 of the taxation year.

The use of this definition has the advantage of applying the 90-day *de facto* separation test to both legal and common-law partners. It also makes it reasonably clear where there is both a legal spouse and a different common-law partner with whom you are living, "qualifying spouse" refers to the spouse with whom you are living. If there is more than one of those, the statute provides no guidance.

In many cases only one spouse or common-law partner in a couple may claim a tax credit. Form ON-BEN notes that the same spouse or partner must apply for the senior homeowners' tax grant, energy and property tax credit, and northern Ontario energy credit.

[¶1566.17] *Couples Not Living Together at December 31*

If on December 31 you are divorced or separated as discussed at ¶1566.15, you can each claim tax credits and ignore each other's income in calculating total income.

If you have shown your marital status on your return as married or living with a common-law partner but you and your spouse or common-law partner have been occupying separate residences for all or part of the year for medical reasons, you are considered to be "involuntarily separated" for the portion of the year which you did not reside together. If you and your spouse or common-law partner are involuntarily separated on December 31 of the year by medical reasons, both you and your spouse have the option to claim the Ontario energy and property tax credit, northern Ontario energy credit, and senior homeowners' property tax grant individually, and you are not required to include each other's income in calculating total income for the purposes of the credits. If you choose to claim these credits separately, you must check box 6108 in Part A of form ON-BEN.

(OTA: 98(6))

[¶1566.20] *Seniors (65 and older)*

Persons 65 and older are entitled to claim Ontario tax credits for seniors, including an enhanced amount for the Ontario energy and property tax credit (¶1567), the Ontario senior homeowners' property tax grant (¶1567f), and healthy homes renovation tax credit (¶1567h).

Persons age 64 or older at December 31, 2016 may apply on their 2016 tax returns to receive payments under the enhanced Ontario energy and property tax credit (¶1567) and the Ontario senior homeowners' property tax grant (¶1567f) for the 2017 benefit year. For couples, where one spouse or common-law partner is 64 years of age or older at the end of the year, that person must apply for the credits (this is beneficial to receive the enhanced amounts). According to form ON-BEN, the same spouse must apply for all of the senior homeowners' property tax grant, energy and property tax credit, and northern Ontario energy tax credit, as applicable.

(OTA: 103.4; 104.1)

[¶1566.25] *Deceased Taxpayers*

The Ontario energy and property tax credit may not be claimed on the final return for a person who has died in the year. In addition, application may not be made for payments under the senior homeowner's property tax grant or northern energy credit. However, the following Ontario credits may be claimed in the year of death: the children's activity credit, political contributions credit, focused flow-through share tax credit, healthy homes renovation tax credit, and tax credits for self-employed individuals (apprenticeship training tax credit and cooperative education tax credit).

[¶1567] ONTARIO TRILLIUM BENEFIT

The Ontario Trillium Benefit ("OTB") combines payments of the following refundable Ontario tax credits: the Ontario energy and property tax credit (¶1657.05), northern Ontario energy credit (¶1567c), and Ontario sales tax credit (¶1568). Payments related to these credits are issued as one consolidated OTB payment, either in monthly instalments or as a lump-sum amount, over the course of a benefit year from July through June.

The OTB is applied for on form ON-BEN as part of your annual tax return. Application is made for the following benefit year, so that, on your 2016 return, you will apply for 2017 benefit payments. Each credit is applied for individually, by checking the appropriate box (box 6118 for the Ontario energy and property tax credit and box 6119 for the northern Ontario energy credit). No application is required for the Ontario sales tax credit for 2014 and subsequent years. The CRA will automatically determine eligibility based on income reported on your tax return.

For benefit entitlements over $360, payment amounts are issued in monthly instalments over the benefit year from June through July, unless you elect to receive payment as one lump-sum amount at the end of the benefit year. For example, benefit entitlements applied for on a taxpayer's 2016 return will be paid out in monthly instalments from July 2017 through June 2018, unless the taxpayer elects to have the full benefit entitlement paid in June 2018. The election to receive benefits as one lump-sum payment is made by checking box 6109 on form ON-BEN. For small benefit entitlements, where the total entitlement for the year is $360 or less, payment will be issued at the beginning of the benefit year in July. Regardless of whether benefits are paid monthly or annually, total entitlements will be the same.

Eligibility criteria and payment amounts vary for each available credit. Details of each credit are set out in the commentary below, under headings for the individual credits.

For couples living together, only one spouse or common-law partner may receive the OTB. Where one spouse or common-law partner receives an amount in respect of the northern Ontario energy credit, only that individual may receive the Ontario energy and property tax credit. For senior couples, if one spouse or common-law partner receives an Ontario senior homeowners' property tax grant, only that individual may receive the Ontario energy and property tax credit and northern Ontario energy credit. Hence, the same spouse must apply for the Ontario energy and property tax credit, northern Ontario energy credit, and Ontario senior homeowners' property tax grant.

To be eligible to receive an OTB payment, an individual must be resident in Ontario at the beginning of the payment month; additional eligibility criteria may also apply, varying by credit. Where credit entitlement is less than $2, no benefit payment will be issued.

(Ontario Regulation 468/11; OTA: 103.2–103.17)

[¶1567.05] *Ontario Energy and Property Tax Credit*

The Ontario energy and property tax credit is a refundable tax credit designed to provide tax relief for property taxes and sales tax on energy costs paid by low- to middle-income taxpayers who own or rent their own home. The credit is means-tested, with income thresholds varying for individuals, families, and seniors. Enhanced credit amounts are available for seniors. This credit forms part of the OTB (discussed at ¶1567), so that credit amounts are issued as part of a combined benefit payment for a benefit year from July through June. To receive these payments, the credit must be applied for on form ON-BEN, filed with your annual tax return.

For the 2016 benefit year, eligible individuals other than seniors may receive a total Ontario property and energy tax credit amount of up to $1,008, consisting of an energy amount of up to $224, plus a property tax amount of up to $784. The credit amount is reduced by 2% of adjusted net family income (see ¶1566.05, above) in excess of $22,388 for single individuals or $27,985 for families (including couples and single parents). The credit becomes fully phased out for income over $72,788 for individuals and $78,385 for families.

Eligible seniors are entitled to claim an enhanced credit amount of up to $1,148 for 2016, consisting of an energy amount of up to up to $224, plus a property tax amount of up to $924. The credit amount for seniors is reduced by 2% of adjusted net family income in excess of $27,985 for single seniors or $33,582 for senior couples. In addition, the credit is reduced where the amount of the credit, together with any senior homeowners' property tax grant received (see ¶1567f, below), exceeds occupancy cost for the year. The credit for seniors becomes fully phased out for income over $85,385 for single seniors and $90,982 for senior families.

Credit amounts and income thresholds are indexed annually for inflation. In addition, amounts related to the seniors' credit are indexed for annual increases in federal Old Age Security and Ontario Guaranteed Annual Income payments. For 2015, for individuals other than seniors, the maximum credit amount was $993, reduced by 2% of adjusted net family income in excess of $22,057 for single individuals or $27,571 for families. For seniors, the maximum credit was $1,131, reduced by 2% of adjusted net family income in excess of $27,571 for single seniors or $33,086 for senior couples.

Individuals eligible to apply for the credit include those persons resident in Ontario at the end of the taxation year who will be 18 years of age or older in the benefit year or, if under 18 years of age, who have a spouse or common-law partner at the end of the taxation year or are the parent of a child with whom they reside at the beginning of a benefit payment month. Individuals who paid (or had paid for them) rent or property taxes on a principal residence in Ontario are eligible for both the property tax and energy components of the credit. In addition, individuals who lived in a designated school residence in Ontario are eligible for the property tax component of the credit. Individuals who paid accommodation charges for living in a public long-term care home in Ontario, and individuals who lived on a reserve in Ontario and paid home energy costs are eligible for the energy component of the credit. Persons who will be 65 years of age or older in the benefit year may be eligible to receive the seniors' credit amount.

In applying for the credit, you must designate your principal residence(s) for the year on your return form by filling out the declaration in Part B on page 2 of form ON-BEN. In general terms, your principal residence is a housing unit in Ontario usually occupied by you during the year, such as a house, apartment, condominium, hotel or motel room, mobile or modular home, or rooming house. If you moved during the year, all such residences you inhabited qualify for the credit. If you have more than one residence in Ontario, your principal residence is your "primary" place of residence.

Calculation of the credit amounts is dependent on your "occupancy cost" for the year. If you owned your home (or it was held in trust), your occupancy cost includes total property taxes paid by you or your cohabiting spouse or common-law partner in respect of your designated principal residence. This amount is entered on line 6112 of form ON-BEN. If you rented your home, occupancy cost is 20% of rent paid in the year by you or your cohabiting spouse or common-law partner for your designated principal residence. The total amount of rent paid for the year (not the 20% amount) is entered on line 6110 of form ON-BEN.

For certain situations, specific rules apply to determine your qualifying occupancy cost amount. For homes held under a life lease (having a term of 10 years or more), occupancy cost is the amount of property tax that is reasonably attributable to the residence for the year. If you were a farmer, occupancy cost includes property tax or rent paid for your principal residence plus one acre of land. If you owned a mobile or modular home, your occupancy cost includes property tax paid in the year in respect of the home by you or your spouse or common-law partner, plus property tax paid by the owner of the land in respect of the lot on which the home is located. (If a property tax assessment for the individual lot is unavailable, property tax paid on the lot can be estimated based on a portion of the fees paid to the owner; the CRA's T1 guide suggests that 20% of fees would be a reasonable allocation.) If you lived in a private long-term care facility that was subject to full municipal and school taxes, your occupancy cost includes your rent paid. If you lived in a public long-term care home that was not subject to full municipal and school taxes, you may claim your accommodation costs as your occupancy cost (on line 6123). If your long-term care home does not break down separate charges for room and board, you may claim up to 75% of payments made as rent or accommodation costs. If you lived in a designated student residence (indicated by checking box 6114), a deemed occupancy cost of $25 will be allocated to the portion of the year that you lived in residence.

Where two or more individuals who are not part of a couple inhabit the same principle residence, occupancy cost must be allocated according to beneficial ownership or rent paid by each individual. Note that occupancy cost may not include property tax or rent paid in respect of a secondary residence (such as a cottage that is not your primary place of residence), a portion of your residence that is used for business or rental purposes, or a principal residence which is not subject to municipal or school taxes (for example, certain public housing units, nursing homes, charitable organizations, or similar institutions). Occupancy cost also may not include payments made to relatives or friends who are not reporting the payments as rental income.

For cohabiting spouses or common-law partners, only one person may claim the credit. Your occupancy cost, however, may include eligible amounts paid by either spouse or common-law partner, including amounts paid during a period of separation. If you and your spouse or common-law partner separated or divorced during the year and were living apart at the end of the year, you may each claim the credit, based on your respective shares of occupancy cost prior to separation, plus each individual's occupancy cost after separation. You and your spouse or common-law partner will also be considered to have been "involuntarily separated" during the year where you were living separate and apart for all or part of the year due to medical reasons, in which case, each person has the option to claim an individual credit. Where claiming separate credits due to involuntary separation, you must check box 6108 and complete Part C of form ON-BEN.

Note that the same spouse or common-law partner that applies for the Ontario energy and property tax credit must also apply for the northern Ontario energy credit and Ontario senior homeowners' property tax grant. Where only one spouse will be 65 years of age or older in the benefit year, that spouse must apply for all three credits.

The Ontario energy and property tax credit is applied for by checking box 6118 on form ON-BEN, in respect of credit instalment payments to be made in the following year. So, for 2016 returns, form ON-BEN is completed to apply for 2017 benefit payments, to be issued over the benefit year from July 2017 through June 2018. Credit instalment payments are made as part of the OTB (¶1567), paid monthly or, if elected by checking box 6109, in one lump sum at the end of the benefit year. To receive a payment, individuals must meet the eligibility criteria for the credit (including being resident in Ontario and 18 years of age or older) at the beginning of each benefit payment month. Note that if you will be 18 years of age or older before June 1, 2018, you should apply for the credit on your 2016 return if you are otherwise eligible to receive the credit, as you may be eligible to receive 2017 credit payments upon turning 18 in the benefit payment year.

(OTAR: 2; OTA: 103.9–103.11; 104.35–104.41)

[¶1567c] NORTHERN ONTARIO ENERGY CREDIT

The northern Ontario energy credit is a refundable tax credit designed to assist low- to moderate-income individuals resident in northern Ontario with higher than average energy costs. This credit is available to eligible individuals in addition to the Ontario property and energy tax credit described above. The credit is means-tested, with income thresholds varying for individuals and families. This credit forms part of the OTB (discussed at ¶1567) so that credit refunds are issued as benefit instalment payments over a benefit year from July through June. To receive these payments, the credit must be applied for on form ON-BEN, filed with your annual tax return.

For the July 2016 to June 2017 benefit year, eligible individuals may be entitled to receive a total credit amount up to $146 for single individuals or $224 for families (including both couples and single parent families). This amount is reduced by 1% of adjusted net family income (see ¶1566.05) in excess of $39,179 for single individuals and $50,373 for families. The credit becomes fully phased out for income over $53,779 for individuals and $72,773 for families.

These credit amounts and income thresholds are indexed annually. For 2015, the credit provided up to $143 for single individuals and up to $221 for families, reduced by 1% of adjusted net income in excess of $38,600 for single individuals and $49,628 for families.

Individuals eligible to receive the credit include persons who reside in the districts of Algoma, Cochrane, Kenora, Manitoulin, Nipissing, Parry Sound, Rainy River, Sudbury, Thunder Bay, or Timiskaming. In addition, you must be at least 18 years of age in the benefit year, or if under 18, you must have had a spouse or common-law partner at the end of the taxation year or be the parent of a child with whom you resided at the beginning of a benefit payment month. As well, eligible individuals must have paid rent or property taxes for a designated principal residence in northern Ontario in the year. (Qualifying rent or property tax amounts include those eligible as "occupancy costs" for the Ontario energy and property tax credit described above.) Individuals who lived on a reserve in Ontario and who paid home energy costs in the year and individuals who lived in a public long-term care home in Ontario and who paid accommodation fees may also apply to receive the credit.

The credit is applied for by checking box 6119 on form ON-BEN, filed with your annual tax return, for benefit payments to be received starting in July of the following year so that, on your 2016 return, you will apply for 2017 benefit payments. In addition, you must complete Part A of the form by filling in your rent, property tax, or other qualifying amount paid in the year, and Part B of the form, designating your eligible principal residence.

If you have a spouse or common-law partner at the end of the year, only one person may apply for the credit. Note that the same spouse or partner must apply for the energy and property tax credit, northern Ontario energy credit, and senior homeowners' property tax grant. If one spouse or partner has attained at least 64 years of age by the end of the taxation year, that spouse must apply for these credits. If you and your spouse or common-law partner separated or divorced during the year and were living separate and apart at the end of the taxation year, each person may claim the credit. If you and your spouse or common-law partner were living separate and apart at the end of the year due to medical reasons, you will be considered to have been "involuntarily separated" during the year and have the option of each claiming the credit individually. When claiming credits separately due to involuntary separation, you must check box 6108 and complete Part C of form ON-BEN.

Credit entitlements are paid in monthly instalments as part of the OTB (¶1567), over a benefit year from June through July. Payments are issued in monthly instalments, unless a taxpayer elects to receive a lump-sum payment at the end of the benefit year in June by checking box 6109, or the taxpayer is entitled to receive only a small benefit amount which is paid out at the beginning of the benefit year in July. To receive a benefit payment in a given month, eligibility requirements (including the requirements to be resident in northern Ontario and 18 years of age or older) must be met at the beginning of the payment month. Note that, since credits applied for on current year returns are paid out as benefit payments beginning in the following year, individuals attaining 18 years of age in the first half of the following year may be eligible to receive a credit payment — for example, if you will reach 18 years of age by June 1, 2018, you may be eligible to receive 2017 credit payments if you apply on your 2016 return, assuming you are otherwise eligible to receive the credit.

(OTA: 103.12; 104.19–104.34)

[¶1567f] SENIOR HOMEOWNERS' PROPERTY TAX GRANT

The Ontario senior homeowners' property tax grant is administered through the income tax system as a refundable tax credit and is designed to help offset property taxes for low- to moderate-income seniors who own their own homes. The grant is available in addition to the Ontario energy and property tax credit (see ¶1567.05) for eligible seniors age 65 or older in the payment year. The grant is means-tested, with income thresholds varying for senior individuals and couples. To receive the grant, it must be applied for on form ON-BEN, filed with your annual tax return, in respect of benefit payments issued in the following year.

For 2017 grants (applied for on 2016 returns), eligible individuals may be entitled to receive a grant in the amount of property taxes paid in the year, up to a maximum grant amount of $500. The amount of the grant is reduced by 3.33% of adjusted net family income (see ¶1566.05) over $35,000 for single individuals or $45,000 for senior couples. The grant is eliminated at income over $49,985 for individuals and $59,985 for senior couples. These rates also applied for grants applied for on 2010 through 2015 returns.

For the purposes of the grant, property taxes paid include municipal tax paid by the individual or the individual's spouse or common-law partner in respect of a designated principal residence owned (or held in trust for) and occupied by the individual or the individual's spouse or common-law partner. If you lived in a mobile home, property tax includes municipal tax paid in respect of the home as well as an amount of tax reasonably attributable to the land on which the home is situated. If you owned your home under a long-term lease (being 10 years or more), your property tax paid includes an amount of municipal tax reasonably attributable to the residence for the year.

Individuals entitled to apply for the grant include seniors aged 64 or older at the end of the taxation year (and who will, therefore, be 65 years or age or older in the year of grant payment) who are resident in the province at the end of the taxation year. In addition, you or your cohabiting spouse or common-law partner must have paid (or had paid for you) property tax in the year in respect of a designated principal residence that you or your spouse or common-law partner owned and occupied.

Only one cohabiting spouse or common-law partner may apply for the grant. Note that the same spouse or common-law partner must apply for the senior homeowners' property tax grant, the Ontario energy and property tax grant, and the northern Ontario energy credit. Where only one spouse or partner has attained 64 years of age by the end of the taxation year, that person must claim these credits.

If you and your spouse or common-law partner were separated or divorced during the year and were living separate and apart at the end of the taxation year, each of you may claim the grant as separate individuals. In addition, if you and your spouse or common-law partner were living separate and apart due to medical reasons at the end of the taxation year, you will be considered to have been "involuntarily separated" and will have the option of applying for the credit individually. Where a senior dies after having applied for a grant but before receiving it, a surviving cohabiting spouse or common-law partner may receive the grant, but if there is no such person, no one may receive the grant.

To receive the grant, you must apply for it on form ON-BEN, filed with your annual tax return. You may apply for the 2017 grant on your 2016 return by checking box 6113 on form ON-BEN. In addition, you must fill in box 6112 setting out your total property tax paid in the year, and designate your principal residence(s) for the year in Part B of form ON-BEN. If you and your spouse or common-law partner are applying for separate grants due to involuntary separation, you must also check box 6108 and complete Part C of form ON-BEN. Grant amounts are paid following the filing of your annual tax returns, generally within four to eight weeks after receiving your notice of assessment for the taxation year.

(OTA: 104.1; Other Publications: Ontario Information Bulletin: Senior Homeowners' Property Tax Grant)

[¶1567h] HEALTHY HOMES RENOVATION TAX CREDIT

The Healthy Homes Renovation Tax Credit will be eliminated for 2017 and subsequent taxation years. However, it can still be claimed on 2016 returns.

The Ontario Healthy Homes Renovation Tax Credit is available to seniors and specified family members living with seniors. This 15% refundable tax credit provides a maximum annual tax credit of $1,500, on annual eligible expenditures of up to $10,000. Expenditures eligible for the credit include expenses related to qualifying home renovations made for the purposes of improving the accessibility, functionality, or safety of a principal residence for a senior. The credit is claimed on line 4 of form ON479 and Schedule ON(S12).

Qualifying home renovations for the purposes of the credit include permanent improvements made to a senior's principal residence that are designed to improve the accessibility, functionality, or safety of the residence to the senior individual. For the purposes of the credit, a senior's or other qualifying family member's principal residence includes an Ontario residence that the senior ordinarily occupies, or can reasonably be expected to occupy, within 24 months after the end of the taxation year. Renovations must be of kinds that are ordinarily undertaken by a person with an impairment. The improvements must be enduring and integral to the residence, or be in the nature of permanent fixtures. Renovations undertaken for the primary purpose of increasing the value of a residence are not eligible for the credit.

Examples of eligible renovations include renovations to permit first-floor occupancy or secondary suite for a senior; installation of wheelchair ramps, stair lifts, and elevators; widening of doorways and installation of corridor handrails; installation of bathroom grab bars, walk-in bathtubs, wheel-in showers, hand-held showers, non-slip flooring, and levered or hands-free taps; modifications to counters and cupboards such as lowering of fixtures, installation of adjustable fixtures, pull-out shelves, and touch-and-release doors or drawers; and modifications to lighting, outlets, and doors, such as installation of motion activated lighting, additional lighting, placement of accessible switches and outlets, and installation of easy operation handles and locks.

Expenditures eligible for the credit include expenses directly related to qualifying renovations, including outlays for equipment rentals and permits. Eligible expenses are to be reduced by any amount of government assistance received. However, expenses may be eligible for both the home renovation credit and the medical expense credit, assuming eligibility criteria for both credits are met. Expenses not eligible for the credit include expenditures for routine maintenance, acquisition of household appliances, and financing costs. Expenditures incurred for the purpose of gaining or producing income will not be eligible for the credit.

Examples of non-eligible expenses include general home maintenance expenses such as for roof, plumbing, electrical, or heating repairs; aesthetic enhancements; expenditures for devices and equipment such as wheelchairs or medical monitoring equipment; and expenses for services such as home care, security, medical monitoring, or housekeeping services. For individuals performing work themselves, eligible expenses will include direct costs such as building materials, tool rentals, and permit fees, but no amount related to self-supplied labour or tools.

Individuals entitled to claim the credit include senior homeowners and tenants, age 65 or older at the end of the taxation year, as well as specified family members living with a senior. Examples of eligible family members living with a senior include a senior's spouse or common-law partner, children and grandchildren, nieces and nephews, siblings, and in-laws (as defined under federal legislation). Landlords simply renting homes to seniors are not eligible to claim the credit. Individuals must be resident in Ontario at the end of the taxation year to receive the credit.

Amounts eligible for the credit must be incurred in the year. For the purposes of the credit, expenditures will be deemed to have been paid on the earlier of the date on which the expenditure was paid or became payable. If payments are made in instalments, the total of all instalments will be deemed to be paid on the earlier of the date on which the last instalment was paid or payable.

If more than one individual is entitled to claim the credit in respect of the same principal residence, the total amount of expenditures claimed by all individuals may not exceed the annual limit of $10,000. For spouses or common-law partners who may both be eligible to claim the credit, the total amount claimed by both individuals in a year cannot exceed the $10,000 yearly limit. However, couples living separate and apart because of marriage breakdown or medical necessity (known as "involuntary separation") may each claim a credit up to the $10,000 limit. If a taxpayer moves residences during the year, eligible expenditures may include qualifying expenses incurred in relation to both residences, up to a maximum of the $10,000 combined.

The credit may be claimed in the year of death or bankruptcy. It may not be claimed by trusts. However, expenditures made on an individual's behalf by a trust or by a housing or condominium corporation may be eligible, to the extent that they can reasonably be attributed to the individual.

The credit is claimed on line 4 of form ON479. In addition, you must complete Schedule ON(S12) listing details of eligible expenditures. Qualifying expenditures should be supported by receipts. Receipts do not need to be filed with returns, but should be retained by taxpayers claiming the credit. If you and your spouse or common-law partner are involuntarily separated and each claiming separate credits, you must also enter your spouse or common-law partner's address beside box 6089 on Schedule ON(S12).

(OTA: 103.1.1; News Releases: Helping Seniors Stay at Home Safely; Healthy Homes Renovation Tax Credit)

[¶1568] SALES TAX CREDIT

The Ontario sales tax credit is a refundable tax credit designed to provide tax relief to low- to moderate-income taxpayers for sales tax paid on consumer purchases. The credit is means-tested, with varying income thresholds for individuals and families, and cumulative amounts are available for an individual and his or her qualifying spouse or common-law partner and dependants. This credit forms part of the OTB (discussed at ¶1567), so that credit amounts are issued as benefit payments over a benefit year from July through June.

For 2016, eligible individuals who apply for the credit will be entitled to receive up to $291 for each of themselves, their cohabiting spouse or common-law partner, and any qualifying dependants under 19 years of age. The resulting credit amount is reduced by 4% of adjusted net family income (see ¶1566.05) in excess of $22,388 for individuals and $27,985 for families, including single parents. The credit is fully phased out for individuals with income over $29,663, and at varying thresholds for families, dependent on family size, starting at $42,535 for two-person families.

These credit amounts and income thresholds are indexed annually. For 2015, the maximum credit entitlement was $287 for each of: the individual, the individual's spouse or partner, and each qualifying dependant, reduced by 4% of adjusted family net income in excess of $22,057 for individuals and $27,571 for families.

Individuals eligible to receive the credit include persons resident in Ontario at the beginning of a payment month who are at least 19 years of age or, if under 19 years of age, are the parent of a child with whom they reside or are a spouse or common-law partner of another individual. If you are married or have a common-law partner, only one of you may apply for and receive the credit.

Only one person may receive a credit for a dependent child. Amounts may not be claimed in respect of a person for whom another person receives a child benefit allowance. For shared custody arrangements, credit amounts are split between parents.

Persons who have died in the year are not eligible for the credit.

For 2014 and subsequent years, no application is required. The CRA will automatically determine eligibility based on income amounts reported on your tax return. Payments based on 2016 returns will be made as part of the OTB (¶1567) monthly payments from July 2017 until June 2018, unless a taxpayer elects to receive a lump-sum payment by checking box 6109 on form ON-BEN, so that one payment is received at the end of the benefit year in June 2018. Alternatively, if the taxpayer's benefit entitlement is small, the amount may be paid out at the beginning of the benefit year in July 2017.

To receive the benefit payment, you must meet eligibility criteria at the beginning of the payment month (including being resident in Ontario). Note that since credits applied for on returns are paid out during the following benefit year, individuals otherwise eligible for the credit who will become 19 years of age during the benefit year should apply for the credit. For example, if you will reach 19 years of age by June 1, 2018, you may be eligible to receive 2017 credit payments if you apply on your 2016 return, assuming you are otherwise eligible to receive the credit.

(OTA: 98; 99; 100; 101; 103.9; 104.11; RC4210 GST/HST Credit)

[¶1568e] CHILDREN'S ACTIVITY TAX CREDIT

The Ontario children's activity tax credit will be eliminated for 2017 and subsequent taxation years. However, it can still be claimed on 2016 returns.

The Ontario children's activity tax credit is a refundable tax credit available for fees paid in the year to register children in qualifying activity programs (including both eligible fitness and non-fitness activities). This credit is similar to the federal child fitness and arts activities credits, except that it is refundable.

For 2016, eligible parents and guardians may claim a 10% tax credit for up to $560 of qualifying expenses per child, for a maximum annual tax credit of up to $56 per child under 16 years of age. For children with disabilities under 18 years of age (who are eligible for the disability amount), you can claim an additional $560 as long as you paid at least $100 of eligible expenses in the year, for a maximum annual tax credit of $112 per child with a disability.

These maximum credit amounts are indexed annually. For 2015, qualifying individuals were entitled to claim a credit amount of up to $551 per child (or a tax credit of up to $55 per child) and an additional amount of up to $551 per disabled child (or a tax credit of up to $110 per disabled child).

Expenditures qualifying for the credit include eligible expenses incurred in the year for enrolment of a child in a qualifying activity. Eligible expenses include registration and membership fees, as well as fees paid to cover the cost of uniforms, equipment used in common, incidental supplies, facility rentals, referees and judges, instruction, and administration. The following expenses are not eligible for the credit: fees paid to cover costs of accommodation, travel, food and beverages; expenditures for the purchase or rental of equipment for exclusive personal use; or fees paid to an individual's spouse or common-law partner or directly to anyone under 18 years of age. Eligible fees are reduced by any amount of reimbursement you received (unless such reimbursement has been included in your income, such as a benefit on your T4 slip) and may only be claimed by one individual.

Expenses eligible for this credit may also be eligible for the federal child care expense deduction (at line 214). Where this occurs, you must first claim the eligible amount under the child care expense deduction, and any remaining unused amount may then be claimed for the activity credit. Amounts eligible for the charitable donations credit (at lines 345 or 347 of Schedule 9) or the political contributions credit (at line 48 of Schedule 1 or box 6310 and line 6 of ON479) may not be claimed under the activity credit.

Activities eligible for the Ontario credit include fitness activities, as well as certain non-fitness activities, designed for children. Fitness activities eligible for the credit include those eligible for the federal credit (see ¶1356). Examples of eligible fitness activities include aerobics, badminton, ball hockey, baseball, basketball, biking, curling, dodgeball, figure skating, floor hockey, football, golf, gymnastics, hockey, horseback riding, ice skating, karate, kickboxing, lacrosse, running, skiing, soccer, snowboarding, squash, swimming, tennis, track and field, volleyball, water polo, and similar activities adapted for children with disabilities. Non-fitness activities eligible for the credit include instruction in music, dramatic arts, dance, and visual arts; language instruction; wilderness and natural environment activities; activities designed to teach children interpersonal skills; and tutoring in academic subjects. Examples of eligible non-fitness activities include after-school extracurricular activities, cadets, chess, choir, cooking, CPR training, crafts, dance, drama, drawing, first aid, gardening, girl guides, languages, leadership development, lifeguarding, music, non-medical therapeutic activities for children with a disability, painting, photography, pottery, public speaking, scouts, sculpture, sewing, tutoring, and voice lessons.

Activities that are not eligible for the credit include activities that are unsupervised or not suitable for children, activities that are part of a school curriculum, and activities that do not meet federal duration requirements (see ¶1356).

The credit may be claimed for eligible fees paid to register your child or the child of your spouse or common-law partner in a qualifying activity. To receive the credit, you must be resident in Ontario on the last day of the taxation year. If more than one individual is eligible to claim the credit in respect of the same child, the total of amounts claimed by each individual may not exceed the maximum credit amount.

The Ontario credit is claimed at box 6309 and line 3 of form ON479. Receipts do not need to be filed but should be retained to support the credit claim.

(OTA: 103.1; Other Publications: Ontario News Release, Ontario Children's Activity Tax Credit, September 6, 2010)

[¶1569] POLITICAL CONTRIBUTION TAX CREDIT

The Ontario political contributions tax credit is available for political contributions made in the year to registered Ontario political parties, constituency associations, or candidates in an Ontario election. This refundable tax credit is available up to threshold contribution amounts and must be supported by official receipts.

To be eligible to claim this credit, you must be resident in Ontario on the last day of the taxation year and have made an eligible contribution in the year. Only contributions to political parties and constituency associations registered under the Ontario *Election Finances Act* or to registered candidates who stand for election to serve in the Ontario Legislative Assembly are eligible for this credit. Eligible contributions must be supported by official receipts.

For 2016, credit rates are as follows:

(1) 75% of first $399 of contributions;

(2) 50% of next $931 of contributions; and

(3) 33.33% of the next $1,696 of contributions.

The maximum annual credit is $1,330, which is reached when you have made eligible contributions totalling $3,026. Only contributions made in the year are eligible for the credit. These credit rates and thresholds are effective for taxation years from 2014 through 2018.

These credit limits and contribution thresholds are indexed every five years. From 2005 through 2013, the available tax credit was calculated as 75% of the first $372 of contributions, plus 50% of the next $868 of contributions, plus $33^1/_3$% of the next $1,581 of contributions. The maximum annual credit was $1,240, reached at contributions totalling $2,821.

If you have a spouse or common-law partner, Ontario administrative policy is to allow the credit to be claimed by either spouse or common-law partner regardless of to whom the receipt is issued. However, a single contribution for which an official receipt is issued cannot be divided between spouses.

The credit is claimed on line 6 of form ON479, filed with your annual tax return. Total contributions for the year are entered on line 6310 of form ON479. Your total credit may be calculated on the Ontario Provincial Worksheet. Receipts are to be filed with paper returns or kept on hand for support for electronically filed returns.

(OTA: 84(1); 102; Other Publications: Ontario Ministry of Revenue Information Bulletin 6304, *Political Contribution Tax Credit*)

[¶1570] COMMUNITY FOOD PROGRAM DONATION TAX CREDIT FOR FARMERS

Ontario farmers can now take advantage of a provincial tax credit for food donations to eligible community food programs such as food banks, soup kitchens, and school breakfast programs. This non-refundable credit is calculated at 25% of the fair market value of donated agricultural products. The credit may be claimed by farmers who are resident in Ontario at the end of the year or their spouses or common-law partners.

To qualify for the credit, donations of agricultural products must be made to an "eligible community food program". This is defined as a person or entity that is registered as a charity under the federal *Income Tax Act* and is engaged in the distribution of food to the public without charge in Ontario. The definition specifically includes food banks, but is not limited to such entities. Additionally, community food programs must satisfy at least one of the following prescribed conditions:

- the primary purpose for which the person or entity distributes food to the public without charge is to provide relief to persons who are destitute or who are lacking essential amenities available to the general public; or
- the person or entity either provides meals or snacks to pupils enrolled in an elementary school, secondary school, or supervised alternative learning program, or oversees the administration of such a program.

The definition of an "agricultural product" includes meat or meat by-products, eggs, dairy products, fish, fruit, vegetables, grains, pulses, herbs, honey, maple syrup, mushrooms, nuts, and anything else that is grown, raised, or harvested on a farm. However, products are not eligible if they have been processed more than to the extent necessary to allow them to be legally sold from the producer's premises as food or drink for human consumption. Therefore, items such as pickles, preserves, and sausages are not eligible. Donations of live food animals will be eligible for the credit if suitable for and intended to be processed as food.

In order to claim the credit, farmers will require a donation receipt from the recipient charity. The legislation does not set out separate receipt requirements for the food donation credit. Instead, it incorporates existing federal requirements for in-kind donations to registered charities, since food program donations must be eligible for the charitable donation tax credit. As with any non-cash donation, community food programs will be required to determine the fair market value of donated goods and record that value on donation receipts.

The credit is claimed on Form ON428. The amount of qualifying donations must be entered in box 6098. Note that these amounts must also be claimed as a charitable donation on line 340 of your federal Schedule 9 and line 29 of ON428. This amount is then multiplied by 25% and the result entered on line 72 of ON428. The credit can be split between spouses or common-law partners and can be claimed on a deceased person's final return.

(*Community Food Program Donation Tax Credit for Farmers Regulation*, O. Reg. 153/14; OTA: 103.1.2)

[¶1571] ONTARIO FOCUSED FLOW-THROUGH SHARE CREDIT (MINING EXPLORATION INCENTIVE)

As discussed at ¶1463, the federal government offers a 15% (non-refundable) investment tax credit for Canadian exploration expenses (¶2210) incurred (or deemed to have been incurred) in mining exploration activities after October 17, 2000 by corporations principally engaged in exploration and development of mineral or other natural resources that are flowed out to individual shareholders holding "flow-through" shares of such corporations.

Ontario offers a supplemental *refundable* credit of 5% of eligible *Ontario* mining exploration expenses allocated to you on mining flow-through shares eligible for the federal investment tax credit on such shares. The Ontario credit is tied to a modified federal definition of flow-through mining expenditure, and not to the federal credit itself, so that it does not expire with the federal credit.

Essentially, Ontario mining exploration expenses are Canadian exploration expenses (¶2210) if that definition were read with the references to Canada replaced by references to Ontario. The federal and provincial allocations of these expenditures should be reported to you on form T1221. When you invest in such shares, you should be informed of the probable eligibility for various tax credits of expenditures attached to the particular shares.

The Ontario credit is only available to an individual (other than a trust) resident in Ontario on the last day of the taxation year and subject to Ontario tax throughout the year. It is refundable to the extent it exceeds Ontario tax payable.

Claim for the Ontario credit requires the use of federal form T1221, which should be submitted with your tax return, together with the T101 or T5013 form which supports the claim (see Chapter 22). If you are filing electronically, you do not submit these documents at the time of filing, but you must keep them on hand for possible future verification. The expenses must be entered in box 6266. The credit is claimed on line 7 of form ON479.

(OTA: 103; Ont-InfB: 6315 Ontario Focused Flow-Through Share Tax Credit)

[¶1572] ONTARIO BUSINESS TAX CREDITS

[¶1572.05] *Apprenticeship Training Tax Credit (ATTC)*

Both corporations and unincorporated businesses are eligible for a refundable tax credit on wages and salaries paid to eligible apprentices in qualifying skilled trades, hired under qualifying apprenticeship programs. If you operated an unincorporated business and employed eligible apprentices in the year at a permanent establishment in Ontario, you may be eligible to claim this credit on your individual tax return.

The 2015 Ontario Budget announced reductions in this credit. Accordingly, the credit rates vary depending on when each apprentice began his or her apprenticeship program. Rates also vary depending on the total salaries and wages paid by your business in the previous tax year. If total payroll costs were:

- $600,000 or more, the credit is 25% of eligible expenditures for each apprentice who started an apprenticeship program after April 23, 2015, and 35% for each apprentice who started before April 24, 2015;
- not more than $400,000, the credit is 30% of eligible expenditures for each apprentice who started an apprenticeship program after April 23, 2015, and 45% for each apprentice who started before April 24, 2015;
- more than $400,000 but less than $600,000, the credit rate is prorated using the calculation for line 9 on the Provincial Worksheet.

The maximum annual credit was also reduced to $5,000 for each apprentice who started an apprenticeship program after April 23, 2015, but remains at $10,000 for each apprentice who started on or before that date. If an apprentice was only employed for part of the year, the maximum credit must be prorated by multiplying the maximum credit amount by the number of days that the apprentice was employed and then dividing by the number of days in the year.

Eligible expenditures are salaries and wages, including taxable benefits (i.e., amounts reported on the apprentice's T4 slip) paid or payable to an apprentice in a qualifying skilled trade for services performed by the apprentice for the business. Eligible expenditures also include fees paid or payable to an employment agency by a corporation or unincorporated business for services performed by the apprentice in a qualifying apprenticeship. Expenditures eligible for the credit are reduced by amounts of government assistance received. If this assistance is subsequently repaid, repaid amounts are eligible for the credit in the year these expenditures are made. Expenditures made for salaries and wages must be provided for services rendered by the apprentice under a registered apprenticeship contract or agreement, and attributable to a permanent establishment in Ontario.

Eligible apprentices include those apprentices in their first 36 months of a registered apprenticeship training program in a qualifying skilled trade (48 months for apprentices who started an apprenticeship program before April 24, 2015). Qualifying skilled trades include designated trades in construction, industrial, motive power, and service industries. See the Ministry of Finance website, or its publication entitled Apprenticeship Training Tax Credit — General Guidelines, for a full list of designated trades eligible for the credit. In the 2013 Ontario Budget, it was announced that designated trades in information technology contact centres would no longer be eligible for credit, effective for expenditures incurred after March 31, 2014. Alternative support programs will be available for employers of eligible apprentices hired into the three affected trades before these trades became ineligible for the credit for the first 24 months from the date of hire.

In the 2014 Ontario Budget it was announced that the apprenticeship training tax credit program would be reviewed, with the intent of making this tax credit non-refundable for larger businesses. This change would limit credit claims by these businesses to the amount of Ontario tax payable. Tax credits claimed by smaller businesses would continue to be refundable over and above Ontario tax payable. No further details of this change, such as a proposed effective date, have yet been announced.

The credit is calculated on the Provincial Worksheet and claimed on line 6322 of form ON479.

(OTA: 84(1); 89)

[¶1572.10] *Cooperative Education Tax Credit (CETC)*

If you are in business (self-employed) and provide qualifying work placements for co-op students, Ontario offers a refundable tax credit for eligible expenditures incurred in providing such placements for post-secondary co-op students.

The tax credit rates for qualifying expenditures are as follows:

- 25% of eligible expenditures if the total of salaries or wages paid by the employer in the previous taxation year was $600,000 or more;
- 30% of eligible expenditures if the total of salaries or wages paid by the employer in the previous taxation year was $400,000 or less;
- if the total of salaries or wages paid by the employer in the previous taxation year was more than $400,000 but less than $600,000, the credit rate is prorated. (The Ontario Provincial Worksheet provides a convenient chart for calculating your eligible credit amount in these circumstances.)

The credit cannot exceed $3,000 for each work placement (regardless of the rate of credit). However, where a program lasts more than four months, it may, in some circumstances, qualify for multiple successive placements.

Qualifying expenditures are reduced by all related government assistance received or expected, but increased as that assistance is repaid. Government assistance includes grants, subsidies, forgivable loans, deductions from tax, and investment allowances, but does not for these purposes include federal investment tax credits (¶1463) or the Ontario R&D credit.

Details of the program are described in Corporations Tax Information Bulletin 4014. Eligible employers are individuals who, alone or as a member of a partnership, carry on business during the taxation year through a permanent establishment in Ontario and are not exempt from Ontario tax.

Eligible expenditures are salaries, wages, and other remuneration paid to a student in a qualifying work placement and allocated to an Ontario permanent establishment for purposes of calculating provincial income allocations (¶1440). Fees paid to an eligible educational institution or to an employment agency for the student's services will also qualify. Finally, repayment of government assistance made by the employer during the taxation year will qualify as eligible expenditures to the extent that they do not exceed either the amount of the original assistance that has not been repaid in a prior year or the amount that can reasonable be considered to have reduced the co-op credit that would otherwise have been allowed.

A qualifying *co-op* work placement must be a co-op work program that earns credits towards completion of a post-secondary co-op education program offered by: a university, or college of applied arts and technology funded in part by per-student operating grants from Ontario; an agricultural college in Ontario administered by the Ontario government; the Michener Institute of Applied Health Sciences; and the Ontario College of Art and Design. The definition of a co-op program is based on the Canadian Association for Co-operative Education definition of cooperative education program. The college or university must certify that the placement is a qualifying co-op work placement.

The credit is claimed on line 6320 of form ON479.

(OTA: 84(1); 88)

[¶1573] ONTARIO CHILD BENEFITS

[¶1573.10] *Ontario Child Benefit (OCB)*

The Ontario Child Benefit (OCB) program provides monthly benefit payments to low- to moderate-income families with children under age 18.

For the 2016 benefit year, running from July 2016 through June 2017, the OCB provides an annual benefit amount of up to $1,356 per child, reduced by 8% of adjusted net family income over $20,706. Net family income is the income of you and your spouse or common-law partner as determined under the rules for the federal Canada Child Benefit, discussed at ¶1498.10.

Both the annual benefit amount and the income threshold at which the benefit begins to be reduced are indexed annually, starting in July 2015.

The annual benefit was $1,336 from July 2015 to June 2016.

Since the program is intended to be completely integrated with the Canada Child Benefit discussed at ¶1498, all definitions as to who is eligible to claim the credit and for which dependants it can be claimed are the same as for the federal program. If you (and your spouse or common-law partner, if any) have filed annual tax returns and registered for the federal benefit for your eligible children, the additional Ontario benefit amount should come to you automatically with your federal payments.

(OTA: 104; T4114 Canada Child Benefits — Including related federal, provincial and territorial programs)

[¶1575] GENERAL INFORMATION ON CREDITS

Ontario's personal amount credits, tax reduction credit, and foreign tax credit are claimed on form ON428. Other refundable credits, including the children's activity credit, political contributions tax credit, focused flow-through share tax credit, healthy homes renovation tax credit, and tax credits for self-employed individuals (including the apprenticeship training tax credit and cooperative education tax credit) are claimed by completing form ON479. Form ON-BEN is used to apply for 2017 credit (or benefit) payments determined based on 2016 return information, including the senior homeowners' property tax grant and OTB (consisting of the energy and property tax credit, northern Ontario energy credit, and sales tax credit).

Generally speaking, taxpayers filing returns electronically do not need to file receipts, but should maintain this supporting documentation on hand in case verification is demanded.

The tax credits claimed on these forms are carried to page 4 of your T1 return, and accordingly the information on them is incorporated into the information you certify to be accurate when signing page 4.

You may obtain additional information on the Ontario Tax Credits by calling the Ontario Ministry of Finance information centre. The information centre can be reached free of charge, from anywhere in the Province:

Toll-free:
1-866-ONT-TAXS (1-866-668-8297)
Outside North America:
905-433-6000
Teletypewriter (TTY) device for the deaf:
1-800-263-7776

Fax inquiries may be directed to 1-866-888-3850.

The website is www.fin.gov.on.ca.

If you wish to write for tax credit information, the address is:

Ontario Ministry of Finance
PO Box 627
33 King Street West
Oshawa, Ontario
L1H 8H5

PRINCE EDWARD ISLAND

[¶1577] TAX RATES, BASIC CREDITS, AND LOW-INCOME TAX REDUCTION

[¶1577.05] *Basic Tax Rates*

Prince Edward Island tax is based on federal taxable income from line 260 of the T1 return, to which Prince Edward Island applies the following tax rates for 2016:

Taxable income	*Tax*
$31,984 or less	9.8%
In excess of	
$31,984	$3,134 + 13.8% on next $31,985
$63,969	$7,548 + 16.7% on remainder

These tax rates and brackets have been in effect since 2008. Unlike most other jurisdictions, Prince Edward Island does not index its tax brackets annually, but rather implements changes periodically by statute.

Like the federal government, Prince Edward Island imposes its highest tax rate (16.7%) on split income (form T1206). As well, Prince Edward Island imposes AMT at 57.5% of federal AMT (line 117 on form T691).

(PEIITA: 7; 29; 30)

[¶1577.07] *Basic Tax Credits*

Prince Edward Island provides personal credits similar to most, but not all, federal personal non-refundable credits. However, most P.E.I. personal credit amounts differ from federal amounts, and are converted to tax credit at provincial tax rates.

Personal non-refundable tax credits offered by Prince Edward Island include: a basic personal amount, spouse or common-law partner credit, eligible dependant credit, caregiver credit, infirm dependant credit, age credit, CPP contributions and EI premiums credits, pension income credit, disability credit and supplement, tuition and education credits (the federal education credit is repealed effective January 1, 2017), credit for interest on student loans, medical expense credit, and charitable donations credit. Prince Edward Island also offers a refundable volunteer firefighters tax credit (¶1579b) and a young child tax credit (¶1577.30). Prince Edward Island does not currently offer provincial credits similar to the following federal credits: adoption credit, children's fitness or arts credits, Canada employment credit, textbook credit (the federal textbook credit is repealed effective January 1, 2017), or public transit credit. The P.E.I. pension income credit is available only to residents of the province.

Most P.E.I. personal amounts differ from federal amounts, and must be computed on form PE428 and the Prince Edward Island provincial worksheet. Amounts eligible (before conversion to credit) for CPP/QPP, EI, and student loan amounts will be the same as on the federal return. For a chart of 2016 P.E.I. tax credit amounts see ¶52 at the beginning of this book.

Once the amounts eligible for non-refundable credit are determined, Prince Edward Island, like the federal government, calculates the credit at its lowest tax rate (9.8%). Also like the federal government, Prince Edward Island makes an exception for charitable donation credit, giving credit at its lowest rate (9.8%) on the first $200 of donation and at its highest rate (16.7%) on the balance. Hence donation amounts should be taken from lines 345 and 347 of Schedule 9.

Where a student must calculate education/tuition tax credit amounts and/or transfers on federal Schedule 11, the student must make a parallel provincial calculation on PE(S11). Similarly, where you are claiming a transfer of personal amounts from your spouse or common-law partner on federal Schedule 2, you must make the parallel P.E.I. claim on PE(S2).

Other P.E.I. credit rates for amounts that follow federal credits are:

- dividend tax credit: on eligible dividends, 10.5%; on other taxable Canadian dividends, 3.05%; and
- AMT credit (from Schedule 1 line 427): at 57.5%.

(PEIITA: 9–20)

[¶1577.15] *Surtax*

Prince Edward Island imposes a surtax of 10% on P.E.I. tax in excess of $12,500. With this threshold and the current tax rate schedule, the surtax applies to incomes above $98,317 — higher if there are personal amount or dividend tax credits in addition to basic credit, but not taking account of alternative minimum tax. The surtax is calculated on line 50 of form PE428.

(PEIITA: 31)

[¶1577.20] *Tax Reduction*

Prince Edward Island offers a tax reduction for low income taxpayers. For 2016 and subsequent years, the reduction is equal to the sum of:

- $350 for the taxpayer;
- $350 for the taxpayer's spouse, common-law partner, or an eligible dependant;
- $300 for each dependent child aged 18 or younger at the end of the year (unless claimed as an eligible dependant); and

- $250 if the taxpayer is at least 65 years of age before the end of the year, and
- $250 if the taxpayer's spouse or common-law partner is at least 65 years of age before the end of the year.

reduced by

- 5% of adjusted family income in excess of $17,000.

The tax reduction is available to individuals resident in Prince Edward Island on December 31 of the taxation year (and therefore it is not available on business income allocations to Prince Edward Island by non-residents of Prince Edward Island).

A dependent child must either live with you or be claimed as a dependant by you or your spouse or common-law partner (and no one else). A dependent child who is a parent, spouse or common-law partner cannot be claimed.

The CRA provides an income calculation for the low-income reduction calculation at lines 54 to 73 on form PE428 which starts with net income (from line 236 of the T1 return) of yourself and, if you had a spouse or common-law partner on December 31 of the taxation year, that person. It then provides adjustments to back out both universal child care benefits (UCCB) received in the year and UCCB repayments deducted in a year. As well, net income at line 236 should not include income from a gain on repossession of property as described at ¶518. The definition of net family income is in fact the same as that discussed at ¶1498.

If you were divorced or separated at December 31 by virtue of breakdown of the relationship for a period which proved to last for 90 days, you should not claim a reduction for your spouse or partner, and do not need to include his or her income in your net family income calculation.

To be eligible to claim the credit, you must be an individual, other than a trust, who is resident in Prince Edward Island on December 31 of that year, and who is (i) married or in a common-law partnership, (ii) a parent of a child, or (iii) 19 years of age or over. The credit cannot be claimed for a deceased person.

Either you or your spouse or common-law partner may make the initial claim; if the tax reduction exceeds the P.E.I. tax of the person who makes the initial claim, the excess can be transferred to the spouse or common-law partner. Form PE428 provides for this transfer. Since the transferor has already calculated the credit, the transferee makes no further low-income reduction claim after entering the transferred amount on line 52 of form PE428.

Example

An example of the credit calculation for a qualifying taxpayer with a spouse, three dependent children, and an annual income of $30,000 is as follows:

Individual Reduction		$350
Qualified Relation (spouse)		$350
Dependent Children	$300 × 3	$900
Total Reduction		$1,600
Reduced by	($30,000 - $17,000) × 5%	($650)
Total Reduction Claimable		$950

Historical Notes

In 2015, the reduction was equal to $300 for the taxpayer, plus $300 for the taxpayer's spouse, common-law partner or an eligible dependant, plus an additional $250 for each dependent child and $250 if the taxpayer was at least 65 years of age. The total of these amounts was reduced by 5% of the taxpayer's adjusted family income in excess of $17,000.

Prior to 2015, the reduction was equal to $250 for the taxpayer, plus $250 for the taxpayer's spouse, common-law partner or an eligible dependant, plus an additional $200 for each dependent child. There was no additional amount available for seniors. The total of these amounts was reduced by 5% of the taxpayer's adjusted family income in excess of $15,000.

(PEIITA: 32)

[¶1577.30] *Amount for Young Children (line 5823)*

Prince Edward Island provides a non-refundable tax credit originally designed to offset the income inclusion of the universal child care benefit (UCCB — see ¶935). Although the UCCB was eliminated in July 2016, P.E.I. has not yet made any changes to the amount for young children.

The credit is calculated at $100 per month per child who was both under six and living with you at the beginning of the month.

The credit can only be claimed by one person for each month. Where you are living with a spouse or common-law partner at the end of the taxation year, the person with the lower net income must claim the credit. Where incomes are exactly equal, you may choose which of you claims the credit.

The P.E.I. credit rules differ from those for some other provinces which are offering a similar credit. For example, there is no exclusion for children claimed as eligible dependants on line 5816. On the other hand, it is common ground that no amount can be claimed for a month for which anyone received a special allowance under the *Children's Special Allowance Act* (i.e., foster care payments).

The credit is claimed on line 5823 of PE428. In addition, at the end of form PE428 you must fill in detailed information for each child for whom you are making the claim, including the name of the child, his or her relationship to you, the child's birth date, and the number of months for which you are claiming the credit.

(PEIITA: 9(5))

[¶1577f] TEACHER SCHOOL SUPPLY TAX CREDIT (LINE 5850)

Prince Edward Island provides a teacher school supply tax credit, which allows a teacher to claim credit against P.E.I. tax for amounts paid personally for specified school supplies. The credit is available for up to $500 per year in eligible expenditures. This amount is multiplied by the lowest provincial tax rate of 9.8%, resulting in a maximum tax credit of $49.

A teacher includes a teacher as defined in the P.E.I. *Education Act*, as well as a member of staff of a child care facility, or a supervisor as defined in the P.E.I. *Child Care Facilities Act*.

The P.E.I. Department of Education has issued "Guidelines" and a Prince Edward Island Teacher School Supply Tax Credit Form to schools and child care facilities, and teachers who incur expenses eligible under the guidelines should submit the form to the school principal (or child care facility administrator), who is specifically charged to verify that the supplies purchased fit the description and conditions of the allowable supplies given in the guidelines, and if so to sign the approval form and return the approval form and receipts to the eligible individual who submitted them. Documentation and receipts do not need to be filed, but should be retained to substantiate your claim. The credit is claimed on line 5850 of form PE428.

Although PEI has had a teacher school supply tax credit since 2003, the federal government introduced its own teacher and early childhood educator school supplies tax credit only for 2016 and subsequent taxation years. The federal credit is available for up to $1000 per year in eligible expenditures. This amount is multiplied by the lowest federal tax rate. See ¶1497a.

(*Income Tax Act Regulations* 1(1)(c.1), 12; PEIITA: 15.1)

[¶1578c] SPECIALIZED LABOUR TAX CREDIT

The specialized labour tax credit provides a tax rebate to individuals working in certain sectors with specialized skills or knowledge. The 17% tax rebate applies to eligible income earned by the worker for a maximum period of one year. The credit is not claimed on the T1 tax return, but rather obtained by application to Innovation P.E.I.

The credit is available to individuals with special skills who move to Prince Edward Island to work in any of six strategic sectors: aerospace; bio-science; interactive, information and communications technology; renewable energy; financial services (except share purchase); and export focused manufacturing and processing. The rebate is available only when the skills of specialized workers are not available locally and are needed to fill a specific, identified position of the employer.

This credit is issued by the provincial government directly, and not through the income tax system. The process is that an employer seeking to recruit an individual for employment in an area requiring specialty knowledge or expertise applies to Innovation P.E.I. for a Specialized Labour Tax Credit Certificate. The application will be reviewed along with any evidence that efforts were made to identify a capable person from within the existing labour force. If approved, an evidence of credit will be issued to the employer, who will provide a certificate to the eligible individual. The individual then submits the credit certificate to the Department which issued the credit to the employer, along with the employee's T4 for the eligible employment and notice of assessment, to receive the rebate.

Additional information on the specialized labour credit, including application forms and guidelines, are available on the Innovation P.E.I. website (http://www.innovationpei.com).

(Other Publications: Program Summary: Specialized Labour Tax Credit)

[¶1578e] SHARE PURCHASE TAX CREDIT

The share purchase tax credit provides a tax rebate for eligible investments made in shares of qualifying companies operating in certain strategic sectors. The credit is not claimed on the T1 tax return, but rather obtained by application to Innovation P.E.I.

The credit is calculated at 35% of the value of eligible investments made in qualifying P.E.I. companies which are active in a strategic sector. The six strategic sectors benefiting from this incentive are: aerospace; life sciences; interactive, information and communications technology; renewable energy; and export-focused manufacturing and processing. The rebate is capped at $35,000 a year.

Eligible companies may apply for the certificate which, if approved, is passed to the investor. To be eligible for the credit, a company must maintain a permanent establishment in the province and pay at least 75% of total payroll to employees resident in the province. Publicly traded companies are not eligible to apply. To claim the rebate, investors must be at least 19 years of age, and resident in the province at the time the investment is made.

This program is not administered through the income tax system. Rather, the company which considers itself to be an eligible corporation, and has identified eligible investors, may make an application to Innovation P.E.I. for a Share Purchase Tax Credit certificate. The department will review the application and, if it is found to meet the criteria, will issue a Share Purchase Tax Credit certificate to the company. The certificate will set out the cost of the qualified share, the name of the eligible corporation and the name of the eligible investor as well as certain other information. The company will deliver the certificate to the individual upon receipt of compensation for the share, at which time the company and the investor are required to provide to government a signed receipt to confirm that the transaction has occurred. To receive the tax rebate, the investor will submit the Share Purchase Tax Credit certificate with the investor's income tax return for the applicable taxation year to Innovation P.E.I.

Additional information on the share purchase tax credit, including application forms and guidelines, are available on the Innovation P.E.I. website (http://www.innovationpei.com).

(Other Publications: Program Summary: Share Purchase Tax Credit)

[¶1579] POLITICAL CONTRIBUTION CREDIT

If you contributed in the year to recognized P.E.I. political parties or candidates seeking election as members of the P.E.I. Legislative Assembly, you may claim a portion of your contribution as a credit against your P.E.I. income tax (if any). The credit is calculated on the P.E.I. provincial worksheet and claimed on line 78 of form PE428. Proof of payment in the form of an official receipt signed by the official agent of the party or candidate must be attached to your return, unless you are filing electronically, in which case you must keep it on file should the CRA ask you to verify the claim.

The P.E.I. credit is limited to 75% of the first $100 of qualifying contributions made in a taxation year, 50% of the next $450, 33.33% of the next $600, so that the maximum credit of $500 is reached on total contribution(s) of $1,150.

(PEIITA: 42)

[¶1579a] EQUITY TAX CREDIT

The P.E.I. equity tax credit is available for eligible investments made in local businesses registered as community economic development businesses. Where an eligible investment has been made, the investor will receive a PE-ETC certificate showing the amount of credit that may be claimed.

The credit is calculated at 35% of eligible investments up to $20,000 annually, for a maximum annual tax credit of $7,000 (including any carryovers). Eligible investments must be made in the year, or within 60 days following the end of the year.

Businesses issuing eligible shares must be registered with the P.E.I. Department of Finance as a community economic development business. Qualifying businesses include companies and cooperative associations formed under the laws of Prince Edward Island, with total assets or revenues under $3 million (including those of affiliated businesses) and at least 75% of salaries and wages paid in Prince Edward Island. Additional criteria apply, including restrictions on the use of funds raised by eligible shares. Professional practices are not eligible for registration.

To claim the credit, investors must be at least 19 years of age and resident in the province. An investor is required to hold the eligible investment for at least five years. If investments are disposed of prior to the end of this holding period, the credit is subject to repayment.

The credit is non-refundable, claimable only up to the extent of P.E.I. income tax. However, unused credits may be carried forward for up to seven years or carried back for up to three years, but no credit may be carried back prior to 2011. Unused tax credit amounts claimed in a subsequent year are entered on line 82 of form PE428; credits may be carried back by requesting an adjustment to a prior year return.

A credit for the current year is claimed on line 6350 of form PE428. Claims must be supported by a PE-ETC certificate. If you are filing a paper return, this certificate should be attached; if you are filing electronically, this certificate should be retained.

This credit is available from 2011 through February 2021.

Additional information on this credit, including guidelines and application forms for registration of a community economic development business, is available in the Community Economic Business Development website of the P.E.I. Department of Finance (http://www.gov.pe.ca/cedb/).

(*Community Development Equity Tax Credit Act*; PEIITA: 36.1; Other Publications: Guide to Starting a CEBD)

[¶1579b] VOLUNTEER FIREFIGHTERS TAX CREDIT

If you claimed the federal volunteer firefighters tax credit on line 362 of federal Schedule 1, you can also claim a volunteer firefighters tax credit for P.E.I. tax purposes. The P.E.I. tax credit amount is $500. Unlike the federal credit, the P.E.I. credit is refundable.

The P.E.I. credit is available to individuals, resident in the province at the end of the year, who are entitled to claim the federal credit. This includes individuals who have completed at least 200 hours of eligible volunteer services within the year. The credit also may be claimed on a return for a person who died in the year while resident in the province.

The credit is claimed on line 6351 of form PE428.

The P.E.I. volunteer firefighters tax credit is available for 2012 and subsequent taxation years.

(PEIITA: 36.2)

[¶1579c] PRINCE EDWARD ISLAND SALES TAX CREDIT

Prince Edward Island adopted the Harmonized Sales Tax ("HST") on April 1, 2013. In order to protect low- and modest-income taxpayers from any negative impacts of this tax, the provincial government introduced a sales tax credit, which provides taxpayers with a refundable income tax credit of up to $220 per year. Rather than being used to reduce income taxes payable, the sales tax credit is refunded to taxpayers in quarterly instalments along with the federal GST credit.

Effective July 1, 2016, the base credit amount is $110. An extra $55 is available where the individual has a cohabiting spouse or common-law partner, or is entitled to claim the eligible dependant credit. An additional amount of up to $55 is available where the taxpayer's "adjusted income" is above $30,000 (calculated as 0.5% of the amount by which adjusted income exceeds $30,000). The total credit is reduced by 2% of the amount by which the taxpayer's adjusted income exceeds $50,000.

Prince Edward Island has adopted the federal definition of adjusted income. This is basically the individual's income and the income of a cohabiting spouse or common-law partner but does not include amounts received under the former Universal Child Care Benefit or a registered disability savings plan.

Eligibility requirements are the same as for the federal Goods and Services ("GST") credit except that individuals must be resident in Prince Edward Island on December 31 in order to claim the provincial credit. No application is required for the credit. Instead, the CRA will automatically determine eligibility based on income reported on annual income tax returns.

Prior to July 1, 2016, the maximum credit was $200, consisting of a base credit amount of $100 with $50 amounts for a spouse, common-law partner or eligible dependant and an additional amount of up to $50 where the taxpayer's adjusted income was above $30,000.

(PEIITA: 36.3; RC4210 GST/HST Credit)

SASKATCHEWAN

[¶1581] SASKATCHEWAN INCOME TAX

[¶1581.05] *Basic Tax Rates*

Saskatchewan tax is based on federal taxable income from line 260 of the T1 return, to which Saskatchewan applies its own provincial tax rates. For 2016, Saskatchewan tax rates and brackets are as follows:

Taxable income	*Tax*
$44,601 or less	11%
In excess of	
$44,601	$4,906 + 13% on next $82,829
$127,430	$15,674 + 15% on remainder

Income thresholds for Saskatchewan tax brackets are indexed annually. For a recent history of Saskatchewan tax rates and brackets see ¶1582 below.

Like the federal government, Saskatchewan imposes its highest tax rate (15%) on tax on split income (form T1206). Saskatchewan also imposes AMT, calculated at 50% of federal AMT (form T691, line 108 minus line 111 from that form).

(SITA: 7–9; 47; 48)

[¶1581.10] *Basic Tax Credits*

Saskatchewan offers tax credits similar to most (but not all) federal personal credits, although provincial credit amounts differ from federal amounts and are converted to tax credits at Saskatchewan tax rates. Saskatchewan personal non-refundable tax credits are claimed on form SK428.

Available Saskatchewan personal credits include: a basic personal credit, spouse or common-law partner credit, eligible dependant credit, caregiver credit, infirm dependant credit, age credit, EI premium and CPP contribution credits, pension income credit, disability credit and supplement, tuition and education credit (the federal education credit is repealed effective January 1, 2017), student loan interest credit, medical expense credit, charitable donations credit, dependent child credit, and first-time homebuyers credit. In addition to the age credit, Saskatchewan also offers an additional senior supplementary amount for those aged 65 or older. Saskatchewan does not currently offer tax credits similar to any of the following federal credits: adoption expense credit, textbook tax credit (the federal textbook credit is repealed effective January 1, 2017), public transit pass credit, or volunteer fire fighters tax credit. The Saskatchewan pension income credit is available only to residents of the province.

Most Saskatchewan personal amounts differ from federal amounts, and must be computed on form SK428 and the provincial worksheet which accompanies the Saskatchewan T1 package. Amounts eligible (before conversion to credit) for CPP/QPP, EI, and student loans are the same as on the federal return. For a chart of 2016 Saskatchewan credit amounts see ¶52 at the beginning of this book.

Once the amounts eligible for non-refundable credit are determined, Saskatchewan, like the federal government, calculates the credit at its lowest tax rate (11%). Also like the federal government, Saskatchewan makes an exception for charitable donation credit, giving credit at its lowest rate (11%) on the first $200 of donation and at its highest rate (15%) on the balance. Hence donation amounts should be taken from lines 345 and 347 of Schedule 9.

Where a student must calculate education/tuition tax credit amounts and/or transfers on federal Schedule 11, the student must make a parallel provincial calculation on SK(S11). Similarly, where you are claiming a transfer of personal amounts from your spouse or common-law partner on federal Schedule 2, you must make the parallel Saskatchewan claim on SK(S2).

Other items for which Saskatchewan imposes its own tax credit rates include:

- dividend tax credit: on eligible dividends, 11%; on other taxable Canadian dividends, 3.367%; and
- minimum tax carryover (from Schedule 1 line 427): at 50%.

The AMT tax/tax credit rate is essentially the old provincial tax-on-tax rate; its use takes a federally calculated tax/tax credit number and applies it for provincial purposes as a kind of shorthand, rather than working through the income calculation again and applying an appropriate provincial tax (or, with more difficulty, tax credit) to the income.

(SITA: 8–29; 32; 37)

[¶1581.20] *First-Time Home Buyers' Tax Credit*

Saskatchewan offers a non-refundable tax credit for eligible first-time homebuyers, effective for 2012 and subsequent taxation years. The credit is calculated at 11% of up to $10,000 of eligible costs, for a tax credit of $1,100, claimable against Saskatchewan income tax payable.

The credit is available to persons claiming the federal home buyers' amount at line 369 of federal Schedule 1, who have purchased a home located in Saskatchewan, with a closing date after 2011. The qualifying home must be registered in your or your spouse's or common-law partner's name.

The credit may be split between you and your spouse or common-law partner, and may be claimed by more than one individual where more than one person purchases the home. However, in no case may the total credit related to a single purchase total be more than the maximum $10,000 credit amount.

In addition to first-time homebuyers, the credit is available to allow persons with a disability to qualify for the purchase of more accessible homes.

The credit cannot be claimed by individuals who have borrowed for a down payment under the Graduate Retention Program First Home Plan (¶1584).

The credit is claimed on line 5837 of form SK428.

(SITA: 19.2)

[¶1582] RECENT RATE HISTORY

The following rates were in effect for 2015:

Taxable income	*Tax*
$44,028 or less	11%
In excess of	
$44,028	$4,843 + 13% on next $81,767
$125,795	$15,473 + 15% on remainder

The following rates were in effect for 2014:

Taxable income	*Tax*
$43,292 or less	11%
In excess of	
$43,292	$4,762 + 13% on next $80,400
$123,692	$15,214 + 15% on remainder

The following rates were in effect for 2013:

Taxable income	*Tax*
$42,906 or less	11%
In excess of	
$42,906	$4,720 + 13% on next $79,683
$122,589	$15,078 + 15% on remainder

The following rates were in effect for 2012:

Taxable income	*Tax*
$42,065 or less	11%
In excess of	
$42,065	$4,501 + 13% on next $78,120
$120,185	$14,783 + 15% on remainder

The following rates were in effect for 2011:

Taxable income	*Tax*
$40,919 or less	11%
In excess of	
$40,919	$4,501 + 13% on next $75,992
$116,911	$14,380 + 15% on remainder

Saskatchewan's dividend tax credit rate for eligible dividends has been 11% since 2011. The rate for other Canadian dividends was 5% for 2011, 4% for 2012 and 2013, and 3.4% for 2014 and 2015.

[¶1584] GRADUATE TUITION TAX CREDIT

Saskatchewan's Graduate Retention Program (GRP) provides graduates of eligible post-secondary institutions, who are living and working in Saskatchewan, with a tax credit for qualifying tuition fees paid. The overall available credit amount is claimed over a period of at least seven years, beginning with the year of graduation, based on eligible tuition fees up to specified thresholds. In any one taxation year, the maximum annual credit that may be claimed is calculated as:

- 10% of your total eligible tuition amount for the year of graduation and each of the subsequent three years; and
- 20% of your total eligible tuition amount in each of the remaining three taxation years.

The credit is non-refundable for 2015 and subsequent years; therefore, any credit amount that cannot be applied against taxes payable will be carried forward and added to the next year's credit amount. Graduates will be allowed up to 10 years to claim their full tuition credit. Once you claim the credit for your first year of eligibility, the amount of credit available for each subsequent year will be shown on the previous year's notice of assessment or reassessment. This will include the annual credit allowed for that year, plus any unused credits carried over from previous years. To receive the credit in each eligible year, you must continue to be resident in Saskatchewan and file an annual tax return.

Eligible tuition fees

Maximum eligible tuition fee amounts vary with programs of study as follows:

- graduates of certificate and diploma programs, including journeypersons, requiring less than two years of study will be eligible for credits up to $3,000;
- graduates of two-year certificate and diploma programs will be eligible for credits up to $6,400;
- graduates of three-year undergraduate degree programs will be eligible for credits up to $15,000; and
- graduates of four-year undergraduate degree programs will be eligible for credits up to $20,000.

Approved programs must either (i) be equivalent to at least six months of full-time study and result in a certificate, diploma, or undergraduate degree, or (ii) provide journeypersons certification. Saskatchewan does not provide this credit for master's or doctorate degrees. Graduates who opt to continue their post-secondary education in another program will be eligible for additional tuition credits, subject to the lifetime credit limit of $20,000 per graduate.

Claiming the credit

To be eligible to claim the credit, you must receive a GRP Eligibility Certificate from the Saskatchewan Ministry of Advanced Education. Your educational institution can apply for this certification for you, or if it doesn't offer this service you can apply directly to the Saskatchewan Ministry. Application forms are available directly on the Saskatchewan website for this program at www.saskatchewan.ca/residents/education-and-learning/graduate-retention-program.

The credit is calculated on Form RC360, Saskatchewan Graduate Retention Program, and transferred to line 6364 of SK428. Form RC360 and the eligibility certificate must be attached to the T1 income tax return for those filing a paper return. If filing electronically, the documents must be retained in case the Canada Revenue Agency asks to see them at a later date.

RC360 can only be used to record eligibility certificates received in the current taxation year. If you received an eligibility certificate for a previous year but did not claim the tax credit for the year shown on the certificate, you must send an adjustment request to the CRA in order to determine your tax credit eligibility for each year.

GRP First Home Plan

Effective May 1, 2016, the GRP First Home Plan allows eligible graduates to borrow up to $10,000 of their future GRP tax credits as an interest-free loan towards the down payment on their first home in Saskatchewan. Details are available on the GRP website.

Historical Notes

Prior to 2015, the credit was refundable, although an unusual system was used for 2012 to 2014, which involved claiming a non-refundable graduate tuition tax credit and then an additional refundable credit for graduates who were not able to apply the full amount of the non-refundable credit against taxes payable. The refundable portion of the credit was calculated on form RC360 and claimed on form SK 479.

(*The Graduate Retention Program Act; The Graduate Retention Program Regulations;* SITA: 37.1; 37.2; 39.1; 39.11)

[¶1584c] SASKATCHEWAN EMPLOYEE'S TOOLS CREDIT (FORM T1284)

Saskatchewan provides a personal income tax credit designed to recognize the costs associated with purchasing, replacing, and upgrading eligible tools required by qualifying employees as a condition of their employment. The tax credit consists of two components: a one-time trade entry amount and an annual maintenance amount.

One-time trade entry amount

The one-time trade entry amount is intended to recognize the high initial cost of tools that are required to be purchased by employees to enter their trade. It may only be claimed in the year in which the individual commences employment in a particular trade, and can only be earned once in a lifetime. Individuals who are not able to use the entire trade entry amount in their first year of employment can carry forward the unused portion for two taxation years. The amount of the credit is dependent upon the trade group that is the individual's primary source of income. To be eligible, the actual cost of the tools purchased in the year in which the tradesperson commences employment must exceed the credit amount specified below for the employee's trade group. Once that threshold is reached, the tax credit is 11% of the specified credit amounts listed below. It is *not* 11% of the actual expenditure, which is only relevant to determine if the threshold is reached.

- GROUP 1 (hairstylist, bricklayer, drywaller, roofer, insulator, glazier, painter, or floor covering installer): $1,350
- GROUP 2 (plumber, pipefitter, gas fitter, carpenter, electrician, sheet metal worker, boilermaker, ironworker, auto body repairer, refrigeration mechanic, or machinist): $5,000

- GROUP 3 (vehicle mechanic, cabinet maker, or millwright): $9,000
- GROUP 4 (heavy-duty mechanic): $12,500

Annual maintenance amount

The annual maintenance amount is intended to recognize the ongoing cost to a tradesperson of maintaining his or her tools. There is no carryforward permitted for unused amounts. You cannot claim this amount in a year in which you claim the one-time entry amount, but the Saskatchewan government apparently intends that the rule against double-ups only applies in that initial entry year. In the following year, you can claim the annual amount even if you are also carrying forward an unused initial year credit.

For this component, there is no minimum expenditure; so long as you earn your primary income from the relevant trade, the tax credit is calculated as 11% of the eligible amounts listed below:

- GROUP 1 — $300
- GROUP 2 — $1,000
- GROUP 3 — $1,500
- GROUP 4 — $2,500

Claiming the Credit

The credit is claimed on form SK428 at lines 63 to 67, based on amounts calculated on form T1284, Saskatchewan Employee's Tools Tax Credit. Form T1284 must be signed by both the employee and employer, declaring that the individual is an eligible employee performing a designated task and that the tools were required as a condition of employment. T1284 should be attached to the employee's tax return, along with a list of eligible tools acquired in the year, if filing a paper tax return. If filing electronically, the taxpayer must retain these documents in case the CRA asks to see them at a later date.

(*The Employee's Tools Credit Regulations*; SITA: 34.2)

[¶1584f] ACTIVE FAMILIES BENEFIT (REPEALED)

Saskatchewan's active families benefit has been eliminated for 2016 and subsequent years. This program provided a refundable tax credit for eligible expenses paid to register children in cultural, recreational, or sports activities. The credit was available for eligible expenditures of up to $150 per child under 19 years of age at the end of the taxation year. For the 2015 taxation year, the credit was income tested and only available to families with adjusted family income of up to $60,000.

Eligible activities included cultural, recreational, and sports activities which met criteria set out under regulation. The activities had to: be offered by a service provider in Saskatchewan; require active participation by children; involve instruction and supervision; and be suitable for children. Activities provided as part of a school curriculum or child care services by a child care facility were not eligible for the credit.

The credit was claimed on form SK479, which was also eliminated in 2016. For prior years, the form included an area to record the name of each eligible child, along with their date of birth and the amount paid for eligible activities. Adjusted family income was also calculated on form SK479.

(*The Active Families Benefit Act; The Active Families Benefit Regulations*; SITA: 39.2)

[¶1585] SASKATCHEWAN FARM AND SMALL BUSINESS CAPITAL GAINS TAX CREDIT

Saskatchewan offers a non-refundable farm and small business capital gains tax credit, which allows taxable capital gains on qualified farm property and small business shares (exceeding the lifetime capital gains exemption) to be taxed at the lowest provincial income tax rate.

You must be resident in Saskatchewan on the last day of the taxation year to claim this credit.

Obviously this rule creates an incentive to maintain the qualified status of farm property or small business shares even if your lifetime exemption limit has been used.

Saskatchewan tax can be revised to apply this rule on federal form T1237, and the resulting credit is carried to line 6355 of SK428.

(*Farm and Small Business Capital Gains Credit Regulations*, c. I-2.01, Reg. 2; SITA: 31)

[¶1586] LABOUR-SPONSORED VENTURE CAPITAL TAX CREDIT

Investments in Saskatchewan labour-sponsored venture capital funds are eligible for a credit against Saskatchewan tax which can be matched by a federal credit (see ¶1466). Saskatchewan LSVCC credits for individuals are only available to taxpayers resident in Saskatchewan on December 31 of the taxation year. The credit is claimed on form SK428 at line 58 (for provincially registered funds) or line 59 (for federally registered funds), based on amounts shown on Slip T2C (Sask).

The Saskatchewan credit is calculated at 20% of an eligible investment, up to a maximum credit of $1,000 on a $5,000 investment.

Eligible funds

There are two types of funds that can be registered under Saskatchewan's *Labour-Sponsored Venture Capital Corporations Act*. Type A funds are broad-based pool funds that make equity investments in small and medium-sized Saskatchewan businesses and can sell shares to any Saskatchewan resident. Such funds include: SaskWorks Venture Fund Inc., and Golden Opportunities Fund Inc.

Type B funds under the Employee Investment Program allow employees to set up a fund to invest in the company that employs them. Eligible companies must be corporations or co-operatives with between five and 500 employees who reside in Saskatchewan, and must have at least 25% of salaries paid to employees in Saskatchewan.

The provincial tax credit is also available for investments in federally registered LSVCCs. See also ¶1466 for a discussion of federal redemption restrictions and potential credit recapture on these shares, and ¶2522 (2) for a list of federal plans eligible for investment by the Saskatchewan public.

Additional Information

Additional information on LSVCCs can also be found on the Saskatchewan Ministry of Economy website at http://economy.gov.sk.ca/investinsaskatchewan, or by contacting the Ministry by email at invest@economy.gov.sk.ca or by telephone 306-798-1278.

(*The Labour-Sponsored Venture Capital Corporations Act*; SITA: 34)

[¶1588] SASKATCHEWAN MINERAL EXPLORATION CREDIT

Saskatchewan provides a 10% non-refundable mineral exploration tax credit for individuals who purchase flow-through shares of eligible mineral exploration companies. The Saskatchewan credit parallels the federal investment tax credit for flow-through mining expenditures (¶1463), and follows the federal eligibility rules. However, the provincial credit is only available for eligible flow-through exploration funds slated for expenditure within Saskatchewan.

The credit is calculated at 10% of a taxpayer's eligible flow-through mining expenditures. These are exploration expenditures that are allocated by a mining corporation to the taxpayer. Eligible amounts will be listed on Information Slip SK-METC, Mineral Exploration Tax Credit Certificate, which the corporation will send to investors. To claim the credit, an investor must report amounts from the SK-METC slip at line 6360 of form SK428. SK-METC slips should be attached if filing a paper return. If filing electronically, the taxpayer should retain the slips.

The credit is non-refundable, but unused credits may be carried back three years and forward 10 years. Unused credits will be shown on your notice of assessment from the previous year and can be claimed on line 70 of form SK428. To request a carryback of unused credits to a previous year, complete lines 75 to 80 of SK428.

(*Mineral Resources Act, 1985*, s. 10.1; *The Mineral Exploration Tax Credit Regulations, 2014*; SITA: 34.1)

[¶1590] POLITICAL CONTRIBUTION CREDIT

The Saskatchewan political contribution credit is given for amounts contributed to a registered Saskatchewan political party; to an independent candidate in a Saskatchewan provincial election during a campaign period; and, to amounts paid to a registered Saskatchewan political party as a membership fee. Contributions must be in cash or by negotiable instrument.

The credit is 75% on the first $400 contributed, 50% on the next $350, and 33.33% on the next $525. The maximum credit of $650 is reached on annual contributions of $1,275.

The credit is claimed on line 56 of form SK428, and may be calculated on the Provincial Worksheet that accompanies the Saskatchewan T1 package. Receipts must be attached to your return if you are filing a paper return; if filing electronically, receipts should be retained to support amounts reported.

(*The Political Contributions Tax Credit Act*; SITA: 67.1)

[¶1591] NON-RETURN CREDITS

[¶1591.10] *Low-Income Tax Credit*

Saskatchewan offers a credit parallel to and paid with the quarterly GST credit. No application is required. The credit is administered by the CRA, which will automatically determine your eligibility based on income reported on your tax return.

For the 2016 benefit year (from July 2016 through June 2017), the Saskatchewan low-income tax credit provides an annual tax credit of up to $246 for an individual, $246 for a spouse or common-law partner (or for an eligible dependant), and $96 per child (maximum of two children), for an annual credit of up to $684 per family. The credit starts to be reduced once adjusted family net income is more than $32,301. Families with net income between $32,301 and $66,500 may get part of the credit. These amounts and income thresholds are indexed annually for inflation.

(SITA: 39; *GST/HST Credit* Guide (RC4210))

[¶1591.20] *Saskatchewan Health Benefits*

This is not a tax program as such. However, Saskatchewan administers a Family Health Benefits program that gives health coverage to low-income families. Saskatchewan Social Services can nominate you for Family Health Benefits if you qualify based on the income you reported on your income tax return. However, the CRA by law requires a taxpayer's consent before it can inform Saskatchewan Social Services that you qualify. Consent can be given on CRA form RC116. The CRA says that this consent will be used only for Saskatchewan Family Health Benefits.

Information about Saskatchewan Family Health Benefits should be available from 1-888-488-6385 (toll free, at least in Saskatchewan). In Regina, call 306-787-4723.

YUKON TERRITORY

[¶1595] YUKON TAX RATES AND CREDITS

The Yukon uses the TONI system (¶1501). Effective January 1, 2003, the Yukon introduced an entirely new *Income Tax Act*.

Yukon tax is based on federal taxable income from line 260 of the T1 return, to which the Yukon applies (for 2016) the following tax rates:

Taxable income	*Tax*
$45,282 or less	6.4%
In excess of $45,282	$2,898 + 9.0% on next $45,281
$90,563	$6,973 + 10.9% on next $49,825
$140,388	$12,404 + 12.8% on next $359,612
$500,000	$58,435 + 15.0% on remainder

Most non-refundable credits are the same as on the federal Schedule 1 and these amounts are carried to form YT428.

Where a student must calculate education/tuition tax credit amounts and/or transfers on federal Schedule 11, the student must make a parallel provincial calculation on YT(S11) (the federal education and textbook tax credits will be eliminated after December 31, 2016; in order for the credits to continue in the Yukon, legislative changes would have to be made — these changes have not been made as of September 2016). Where you are claiming a transfer of personal amounts from your spouse or common-law partner on federal Schedule 2, you must make the parallel Yukon claim on YT(S2).

The TONI system requires the provinces and territories to maintain the package of personal amounts that was in place in 1999, although not the dollar values of those amounts. It does not require the provinces and territories to adopt later personal amount credits which the federal government may offer. The Yukon matched the federal adoption expenses credit; it does include the amount eligible for federal credit (¶1357) in its own non-refundable credits. As well, the Yukon adopted the federal credits for the Canada employment amount (¶1351), and for public transit passes (¶1353), in both cases using the amount eligible for federal credit as the base for its own non-refundable credit. It also followed the federal initiative to increase the amount eligible for pension credit from $1,000 to $2,000 (¶1311). The Yukon adopted the federal personal amounts for a spouse or common-law partner or eligible dependant (Chapter 11), the $2,000 personal amount for each child under 18 until it was eliminated by the Yukon in 2015 (¶1124), and the federal child fitness credit (¶1356) (eliminated federally for 2017 and following years but maintained by the Yukon) using the total per child amount available for federal purposes, but apparently allowing parents to divide it differently from federal claims if they choose. The Yukon adopted the federal children's arts tax credit (¶1356a), which was also eliminated federally for 2017 but is maintained by the Yukon.

Like the federal government, the Yukon gives tax credit at its lowest rate (6.4%) on personal amounts. Also like the federal government, the Yukon makes an exception for the charitable donation credit, giving credit at its lowest rate (6.4%) on the first $200 of donation and at its "highest" rate (12.8%, regardless of the 15% rate for income over $500,00) on the balance. Hence donation amounts should be taken from lines 345 and 347 of Schedule 9 of the federal return.

The TONI system requires the Yukon to impose its own tax or tax credits, at the rate of its choosing, on several items as follows:

- dividend tax credit on eligible dividends is 15% for 2015 and subsequent years, and on other taxable Canadian dividends 3.14% for 2016 and subsequent years;
- tax on split income (form T1206) at 15.00%;
- alternative minimum tax (from line 117 of form T691) at 42.67%; and
- alternative minimum tax credit (Schedule 1 line 427) at 42.67%.

The AMT tax/tax credit rate is essentially the old provincial tax-on-tax rate; its use takes a federally calculated tax/tax credit number and applies it for provincial purposes as a kind of shorthand, rather than working through the income calculation again and applying an appropriate provincial tax (or, with more difficulty, tax credit) to the income. The tax on split income, by contrast, imposes the top provincial rate on the actual split income as determined for federal purposes.

[¶1595.05] *Continuing Surtax (Repealed)*

The Yukon also had a surtax of 5% of the basic Yukon tax (after deducting personal amount credits and adjusting for the other credits and surtaxes above) in excess of $6,000. The surtax was repealed effective for 2015 and subsequent years.

[¶1595.10] *Rate History*

For 2015, the Yukon rate structure was:

Taxable income	*Tax*
$44,701 or less	6.4%
In excess of	
$44,701	$2,861 + 9.0% on next $44,700
$89,401	$6,884 + 10.9% on next $49,185
$138,586	$12,245 + 12.8% on next $361,414
$500,000	$58,506 + 15.0% on remainder

The dividend tax credit on eligible dividends for 2015 was 15.00%, and on other taxable Canadian dividends 3.17%.

For 2014, the rate structure was:

Taxable income	*Tax*
$ 43,953 or less	7.04%
In excess of	
$ 43,953	$ 3,094 + 9.68% on next $43,954
$ 87,907	$ 7,349 + 11.44% on next $48,363
$136,270	$12,882 + 12.76% on remainder

The dividend tax credit on eligible dividends was 15.08%, and on other taxable Canadian dividends 4.03%.

For 2013, the rate structure was:

Taxable income	*Tax*
$ 43,561 or less	7.04%
In excess of	
$ 43,561	$ 3,067 + 9.68% on next $43,562
$ 87,123	$ 7,283 + 11.44% on next $47,931
$135,054	$12,767 + 12.76% on remainder

The dividend tax credit on eligible dividends was 15.08% and 4.51% on other taxable Canadian dividends.

For 2012, the rate structure was:

Taxable income	*Tax*
$ 42,707 or less	7.04%
In excess of	
$ 42,707	$ 3,007 + 9.68% on next $42,707
$ 85,414	$ 7,141 + 11.44% on next $46,992
$132,406	$12,516 + 12.76% on remainder

The dividend tax credit on eligible dividends was 15.08% and 4.51% on other taxable Canadian dividends.

For 2011, the rate structure was:

Taxable income	*Tax*
$ 41,544 or less	7.04%
In excess of	
$ 41,544	$ 2,884 + 9.68% on next $41,544
$ 83,088	$ 6,946 + 11.44% on next $45,712
$128,800	$12,176 + 12.76% on remainder

The dividend tax credit on eligible dividends was 15.08%, and 4.45% on other taxable Canadian dividends.

(YITA: 3–7)

[¶1595d] LOW-INCOME FAMILY TAX CREDIT (REPEALED)

Until this credit was repealed in 2015, the Yukon permitted a reduction of tax if your income was below $25,000. If you have a "cohabiting spouse" (or cohabiting common-law partner) at the end of the year, as determined under the rules at ¶1498.10, only the spouse with the higher income could claim the credit. If both net incomes were exactly the same, only one spouse could elect to claim the credit; presumably this was done by simply having one spouse make the claim.

The credit was the lesser of the following two amounts:

- $300, reduced by 3% of net income in excess of $15,000 — the mechanics of this calculation meant that the full credit was available if your income was less than $15,000 and no credit was available if your income was $25,000 or more; and
- the alternative limitation was 80% of your Yukon tax payable before other tax credits.

Uniquely among provisions of this kind, net income for the year was simply income from line 236 of the federal T1 return, reduced by the former Universal Child Care Benefit. Net income was also increased by deductions of UCCB benefits you have repaid and deducted. Form YT428 provided for this calculation.

(YITA: 8)

[¶1596] POLITICAL CONTRIBUTION TAX CREDIT

If you contributed in the year to recognized Yukon political parties or to candidates seeking election as members of the Council of the Yukon Territory, you are entitled to claim a credit on a portion of such contributions against Yukon income tax (if any). The credit is calculated in a box provided in the Territorial Worksheet which accompanies Yukon provincial tax forms included in the T1 return package, and is claimed on line 56 on form YT479. Proof of payment in the form of an official receipt signed by the official representative of the recognized political party, or an official agent of the candidate must be attached to paper form YT479 (but if you file electronically, then keep them with your tax records).

For amounts contributed after 2015, the Yukon political contribution credit is:

- 75% of the first $400 of qualifying contributions made in a taxation year;
- 50% of the next $350; and
- 33¹/₃% of the next $525.

The maximum credit of $650 is reached on total contribution(s) of $1,275.

For amounts contributed in 2015, the credit is calculated as:

- 75% of the first $100 of contributions;
- 50% of the next $450 of contributions; and
- 33 1/3% of the next $600 of contributions.

The maximum credit is $500, reached on total contributions of $1,150.

If you have any questions concerning the Yukon Territory Political contribution tax credit you can contact:

Government of Yukon, Department of Finance
PO Box 2703
Whitehorse, Yukon Y1A 2C6
Telephone: 1-867-667-5343

(YITA: 11)

[¶1596b] YUKON LSVCC CREDIT

The Yukon has a labour-sponsored venture capital fund tax credit, provided only for investments in the Fireweed Fund Corporation by individuals resident in the Yukon on December 31 of the taxation year. The credit is 25% of your annual investment to a maximum credit of $1,250, which would be reached on an investment of $5,000.

The federal government offers a matching credit (see ¶1466) of 15% to a maximum of $750, also reached on a $5,000 investment, so that the combined credit is 40% to an annual maximum of $2,000. As a tax planning item, the federal LSVCC credit is being phased out in the 2014 to 2016 period. The federal credit is 15% in 2014, 10% in 2015, 5% in 2016, and nil thereafter.

Unlike most LSVCC credits, including the federal credit, Yukon LSVCC credit generated in a particular year in excess of Yukon tax otherwise payable for that year is eligible for seven-year carryforward and three-year carryback.

Your investment and the credit it generates should be reported to you on a certificate issued by the Fund; you claim the credit on line 16 of form YT479 and attach the certificate to your return (unless you are filing electronically, in which case you must keep it on file in case the CRA asks for it).

LSVCC credits are discussed in greater detail in ¶2522(2).

(YITA: 14)

[¶1596c] SMALL BUSINESS INVESTMENT TAX CREDIT

The small business investment tax credit is available to arm's length individuals who invest in qualified Yukon companies. To claim the credit, investors must be both 19 years of age (or older) and resident in the Yukon on the last day of the taxation year. The credit is 25% of the cost of qualified investments acquired in the taxation year or within 60 days after the taxation year. The maximum credit which can be claimed in any year is $25,000. Where you have made eligible investments in the year which accumulate credits in excess of the lesser of your Yukon tax payable and $25,000, the unused credit is available for three-year carryback and seven-year carryforward.

The law provides that the investment can be made by an individual through an RRSP of which the individual or the individual's spouse is the annuitant. In this case, the credits flow directly to the individual. The purchase, ownership, or disposition of the security is attributed to the individual for all purposes related to the credit. The rules do not provide for credits to flow through a RRIF, although once the credits have flowed through and there is no concern about disqualifying the investment, there should be no problem rolling over the investments to a RRIF. If the omission of a RRIF is intentional, it may be meant to restrict those on a retirement income from making what are likely to be high risk investments with their retirement funds.

Qualifying investments are, essentially, investments in common shares or subordinated/unsecured debt of private corporations or co-ops with less than $25 million in assets, a Yukon permanent establishment, and at least 50% of assets and payroll in the Yukon. Professional corporations will not qualify. The shares or debt must be paid for in currency, not in kind. The corporation must not provide a form of financial assistance to the investor for the acquisition. The corporation cannot redeem the shares or repay the debt within one year. The corporation and the investor must deal at arm's length immediately after the acquisition (but for no particular time thereafter). The corporation must use the funds invested in an active business in the Yukon, and not to lend, pay down debt or pay dividends, redeem shares, and so on.

Only qualified corporations that register under the program and have received the approval of the Minister of Economic Development can issue specified shares or debt to individual investors permitting the investors to claim the non-refundable credit. The corporations are also responsible for issuing the small business investment tax credit certificate (YSBITC-1), which you must submit with your return to claim the credit (but if you are filing electronically, you must instead keep the certificate on file with your tax records).

The credit is claimed on line 6 of form YT479.

(YITA: 13)

[¶1596f] YUKON FIRST NATIONS TAX CREDIT

Effective January 1, 1999, new federal agreements came into effect which provide for tax sharing with seven "self-governing Yukon First Nations" (11 agreements as of September 2016). In consequence of these agreements both the federal and Yukon governments provide a substantial abatement of tax to residents of specified Yukon First Nation settlement lands. Under these rules the federal government rebates to these residents 75% or 95% of basic federal tax and the Yukon government remits 95% of Yukon tax payable net of Yukon tax credits, and these amounts become tax allocated to the settlement territory in which the resident lives.

This system requires a special T1 return for the Yukon, distinguished by:

- the provision on page 1 of an area indicating residence on December 31 in one of the Yukon First Nation settlement lands, including the name and code number found on form YT432 which accompanies Yukon returns;
- the provision on line 432, for the allocation of Yukon First Nations tax (calculated on YT432); and
- the provision on line 441, for the refundable abatement of the federal portion only of tax allocated to the First Nation settlement (also calculated on form YT432).

The form YT432 provides (on line 8) for the refundable abatement of Yukon tax, which is carried to form YT479 and from there, with other applicable Yukon tax credits, to line 479 of the T1 return. All this is reconciled on form YT432, provided with the Yukon tax return package, which calculates the rebates, allocates the federal rebate to line 441 of the T1 and the Yukon rebate to line 22 of the YT479 and transfers both amounts to line 432 of the T1 return as tax allocated to the appropriate First Nation.

(*First Nation Income Tax Credit Regulation*, O.I.C. 1999/184, s. 1; YITA: 12)

[¶1596g] YUKON CHILD FITNESS TAX CREDIT

For individuals resident in the Yukon on the last day of the taxation year who file an income tax return, the territory offers a child fitness tax credit that, starting in 2015, is refundable. It's based on the federal child fitness tax credit rules and provides a credit equal to 6.4% of the eligible fees from line 458 of your T1, resulting in a maximum tax credit of $64 per child ($96 per child with a disability). The credit is calculated on line 1 of form YT479.

In Yukon Budget 2016, the Premier announced that his government will maintain, for 2017 and beyond, the territorial portion of the children's fitness tax credit (and the children's arts tax credit), which were eliminated in the 2016 Federal Budget for taxation years after 2016. Yukon legislation has been amended accordingly.

(YITA: 9.01)

[¶1596h] CHILDREN'S ARTS CREDIT

For individuals resident in the Yukon, the Yukon offers a children's arts credit of up to $500 per child for 2016 ($1,000 per child with a disability) for individuals entitled to claim the federal credit pursuant to s. 118.031 of the federal *Income Tax Act*. The actual non-refundable credit is calculated by multiplying the eligible expenses by the Yukon personal income tax rate of 6.40%, resulting in a maximum tax credit of $32 per child ($64 per child with a disability). The credit is claimed on line 13 of Form YT428.

In Yukon Budget 2016, the Premier announced that his government will maintain the territorial portion of the children's fitness tax credit and the children's arts tax credit, which were eliminated for 2017 and beyond in the 2016 Federal Budget.

(YITA: 6(29)(ii))

[¶1596p] YUKON R&D TAX CREDIT

Expenditures for scientific research and experimental development ("SR&ED") made by corporations and by individuals resident in the Yukon qualify for a 15% refundable tax credit for scientific research expenditures attributable to the Yukon; an additional 5% is available in respect of qualified SR&ED expenditures made to the Yukon College.

Eligible expenditures are those which qualify for federal SR&ED tax credit and are incurred in respect of SR&ED carried on in the Yukon through a business with a permanent establishment there.

A claim for credit must be supported by the calculations on form T1232, available from the CRA (¶287). Form T1232 should accompany your tax return (unless you file electronically, in which case you must keep form T1232 with your tax records to show the CRA should they ask). The amount calculated on form T1232 is carried on line 20 of form YT479.

(YITA: 15)

[¶1597] YUKON CHILD BENEFIT

As of July 1, 2015, the Yukon provides a child benefit of $820 annually ($68.33 per month) for each dependent child, less:

- 2.5% of family net income in excess of $35,000 for families with one child; or
- 5.0% of family net income in excess of $35,000 for families with more than one child.

Net family income is the same as for federal child care benefits (¶1498).

Prior to July 1, 2015, the benefit was $690 per month per child, reduced where net family income exceeded $30,000. The benefit is reduced to 2.5% of net family income in excess of $30,000 if there is one child, and 5% if there are two or more children.

The Yukon benefit is payable to a Yukon parent (typically the mother) for any month in which the parent was resident in the Yukon immediately before and on the first day of the month. Parents who share custody of a child may share the benefit.

The Yukon child benefit program is integrated into the federal child care benefit program discussed at ¶1498, and is administered by the CRA. It follows that if you were already receiving federal child care benefits, you should automatically receive the Yukon supplement to which you are entitled. Applications for new children are made on federal form RC66, and changes of status (marriage, separation, change of province of residence) which may affect your credit should be reported immediately to the CRA at 1-800-387-1193.

(YITA: 9)

Chapter 16

Quebec Income Tax

THESE POINTS ARE COVERED IN THIS CHAPTER

WHAT YOU SHOULD KNOW ABOUT QUEBEC INCOME TAX

WHO MUST PAY QUEBEC INCOME TAX?

RECENT CHANGES

Quebec primarily mirrors the federal changes noted throughout this book. The following summary is devoted primarily to situations where Quebec has its own unique rules.

Quebec

Some of the following changes, which were announced in 2016 or previously may not, as of the date of writing, been enacted into law:

- In the October 2016 update of the Quebec Economic Plan, the government announced the complete elimination of the health contribution as of January 1, 2017. In addition, in 2016, there was a reduction to the premiums for almost all taxpayers.
- The RénoVert tax credit is a new temporary refundable tax credit for eco-friendly renovation work carried out on eligible dwellings owned by individuals. The credit applies to agreements entered into after March 17, 2016 and before April 1, 2017.
- The refundable tax credit respecting a work premium has been enhanced by 2% in 2016 for households without children in order to increase the incentive for them to work.
- The tax shield refundable credit for low to middle income households is a new credit announced in the 2015 budget for 2016 and further enhanced in the 2016 Budget.

- The tax treatment of gifts to charitable organizations and organizations dedicated to amateur sports and culture and communications were enhanced.
- The distance standard imposed for certain tax credits related to obtaining medical care was reduced.
- The eligibility age for the tax credit for experienced workers will be gradually lowered from 64 in 2016 to 62 in 2018.
- The additional subsidized child care contribution in respect of a second child has been reduced by 50% retroactively to April 22, 2015.
- An income averaging mechanism for forest producers was introduced in 2016.
- The eligible amount of donated food products made to an eligible donee after March 17, 2016 by a taxpayer carrying on a food processing business may be raised by 50% for the purposes of calculating the non-refundable tax credit for gifts.
- The exemption threshold for the tax on logging operations was raised from $10,000 to $65,000.
- The tax credit for the acquisition of a class "A" or class "B" shares issued by Fondaction will be maintained at 20% for an additional two years.

[¶1601] BASIC INFORMATION ABOUT THE QUEBEC INCOME TAX

The information to be reported on the Quebec income tax return and the method of calculating the Quebec taxable income are similar, and in most respects identical, to those on the federal return. However, there are certain differences and this chapter will outline the more important differences between the two systems. We suggest that you refer to the other chapters of this book when a particular point is not discussed in this chapter.

[¶1601.05] *Declaratory Amendments*

From time to time, Quebec will announce, in a Budget or other policy statement, that a particular amendment will be "declaratory". This means that the change will be declared always to have represented the correct interpretation of the law, so that all taxation years not statute-barred, and all pending litigation, are bound by the declaratory interpretation. In explaining one such example, Quebec Finance released a statement which explains in some degree the logic of a declaratory amendment:

> ... the decision to make a declaratory amendment is never reached lightly and is always tightly framed. In the great majority of cases, the amendments made to the tax legislation are not retroactive. When they are, either they are to the advantage of the taxpayers concerned or the rights of those who contested the amended legislative provisions are protected. In exceptional situations, as is the case today, amendments to the tax legislation are declaratory, i.e., they apply retroactively, even regarding cases pending before the courts and notices of objection. However, such cases are extremely rare and in every case they are justified by an approach designed to secure compliance with a fiscal policy that is clear and applied from the outset.

Declaratory amendments are sometimes (but not always) framed with exceptions, so that they may be declaratory from a certain date, or declaratory except for cases already before the courts.

(Quebec *Interpretation Act*, s. 50; Other Publications: Quebec Finance News Release on QST, June 27, 2002)

[¶1602] WHEN SUBJECT TO QUEBEC TAXES

The following persons are subject to Quebec taxes for the year:

(1) Factual residents (¶1605) of Quebec on the last day of the year who:
   - have sufficient taxable income to have tax liability;
   - have sufficient income to have additional subsidized child care contribution liability;
   - have sufficient income not subject to withholding (usually self-employment income) to have *Quebec Pension Plan* liability;
   - have sufficient income to have Quebec Parental Insurance Plan liability;
   - have sufficient income (primarily self-employment income) to have Health Services Plan liability;
   - have sufficient income to have a Health Contribution liability;
   - have sufficient net income to have Prescription Drug Plan liability;
   - disposed of capital property in the current year;
   - claimed a capital gains reserve in the previous year; or
   - worked in the restaurant and hotel sector and received tips.

(2) Residents of Quebec on the last day before ceasing to reside in Canada.

(3) Residents of some other part of Canada who carried on a business through an establishment in Quebec at any time during the year (see ¶1607, ¶1445).

(4) Residents of some other part of Canada who had Quebec health insurance and therefore have a liability for the Quebec Prescription Drug Plan Premium (¶1663).

(5) Beneficiaries of a designated trust.

(6) Individuals who have had no Quebec tax payable in the year because of the application of Quebec loss carryforwards.

(7) Non-residents of Canada are subject to Quebec tax on income from employment performed in Quebec, from a business carried on through an establishment (¶1607) in Quebec, and on dispositions of taxable Quebec property. The employment income rules are essentially similar to the federal rules at ¶2020–¶2024; the business income rules parallel to the federal rules at ¶2030. Taxable Quebec property is described at ¶1608. As well, employees, students and professors who were resident in Quebec before becoming non-residents of Canada will be subject to Quebec tax rather than federal non-resident surtax on such items as income paid from Canada in respect of Canadian employment (unless taxed in a foreign country) and Canadian source scholarships and research grants. The rules for all non-resident situations are essentially the same as described for the non-resident period of a part-year resident; for greater detail see ¶1606.

(8) Trusts and estates which come within the above provisions.

(9) Individuals who are splitting retirement income with their spouses.

(10) A sole proprietor required to pay an annual registration fee for the enterprise register.

(11) An individual who wants to receive the child assistance payment.

(12) An individual who wants to receive the shelter allowance.

(13) An individual who received advance payments of the tax credit for child care expenses, one of the tax credits respecting the work premium (work premium, adapted work premium, supplement to the work premium), the tax credit for the treatment of infertility, or the tax credit for home-support services for seniors.

(14) Individuals who wish to transfer the unused portion of their non-refundable tax credits to their spouses, an amount as children 18 or over enrolled in post-secondary studies to their father or mother, or a portion of their tuition or examination fees (paid for the current taxation year) to a parent or grandparent.

(15) An individual who wishes to claim the solidarity tax credit (¶1681), the tax credit for child care expenses, one of the work premium credits or the work premium supplement, the tax credit for home-support services for seniors, the QST rebate for employees and partners, the property tax refund for forest producers, the tax shield credit, or other credits or refunds covered on line 462.

(16) Individuals who owe no income tax as a result of the transfer of non-refundable tax credits from their spouses.

(17) The spouse of an individual who wants to receive the child assistance payment or who wishes to claim the solidarity tax credit (¶1681).

(QTA: 22–27; 1000; 1087–1093)

[¶1602.05] *Where Quebec Tax Paid by Resident of Another Province*

Since residence on December 31 determines (for Canadian residents) which province has jurisdiction to apply provincial tax for the entire year, it follows that if you have moved into or out of Quebec in the year, part of the tax withheld from your income may have been withheld by or for the wrong province. Since the federal government collects tax for all provinces except Quebec, this creates no problem for moves among other provinces. For withholding issues on moves to or from Quebec, see ¶1692.

A similar problem can arise where you are employed in Quebec but resident in another province. Your employer typically would have withheld Quebec tax rather than that of your province of residence; where this arises, see ¶1692.

If you earn business income in Quebec and another province, see ¶1607.

[¶1602.10] *Penalties*

The penalties for failing to file Quebec returns are similar, at least in principle, to those for federal returns at ¶242, ¶245 and ¶251, although there are differences of detail and amount. Interest on under- and overpayments and on penalties is provided for under the *Tax Administration Act*; instalment requirements and interest thereon under the *Taxation Act* (see ¶1691). If you are not liable for Quebec tax by reason of low income, or if instalments or withholdings are greater than tax owing, there is no cash penalty to a failure to file. However, failure to file timely returns may bar you from claiming certain optional exemptions or deductions. Failure to file within one year of its due date will deny you access to the capital gains exemption.

(QTA: 1045; 1049)

[¶1603] SAME-SEX SPOUSES

Quebec legislation defines a spouse for purposes of the Quebec *Taxation Act* (among other things) to include same-sex couples living in a conjugal relationship for a period of 12 months or more. The considerations for same-sex couples are exactly the same as those discussed in ¶1113 for opposite-sex couples.

(QTA: 1 "child"; 2.2.1)

[¶1605] RESIDENCE

[¶1605.05] *Residence in Fact*

The general factors determining whether an individual is a factual resident of Quebec are in theory the same as those discussed for federal purposes at ¶115. However, Revenu Québec attempts to outline a somewhat more restrictive view of when a person has severed ties with Quebec than the CRA does for Canada. Although Revenu Québec follows the same general principles outlined by the CRA in Income Tax Folio S5-F1-C1, Revenu Québec insists in Quebec bulletin IMP.22-3/R1 that, "Where an individual leaves Canada, even for a period of two years or more, and the facts prove that return to Quebec is anticipated at the end of the stay away from Canada, this factor together with other existent residential ties must be examined". Although Quebec courts might be expected to follow federal precedent in the determination of residence, the Quebec revenue authorities seem to be affirming an intention to impose more rigorous administrative standards for review than federal authorities.

[¶1605.10] *Deemed Residents*

The following are deemed to be residents of Quebec during the whole year:

(1) Individuals who sojourned in the province for a period or periods totalling 183 days or more during the year, and were ordinarily resident outside Canada. This rule is identical to the federal sojourning rule at ¶117.

(2) Individuals who are members of the Canadian Forces and were resident in Quebec immediately prior to their departure from Canada to perform their military service in a foreign country.

(3) Individuals who were, at any time in the year, an ambassador, minister, high commissioner, officer or servant of Canada; or an agent-general, officer or servant of a province; residing outside of Canada but who were resident in Quebec immediately prior to their appointment or employment, or received representation allowances in respect of the year. A member of the House of Commons who resided in Quebec prior to election or appointment will be deemed to be a Quebec resident regardless of the actual place of residency.

(4) Individuals who were resident in Quebec at any time in the six months preceding the day on which they commenced performing services outside Canada under a prescribed international development assistance program of the government of Canada or Quebec.

(5) Dependent children of an individual contemplated in paragraph (2), (3), or (4), provided the child's income did not exceed:

- $7,610 for 2016,
- $7,530 for 2015,
- $7,450 for 2014,
- $7,380 for 2013, and
- $7,200 for 2012.

(6) An individual who was at any time in the year, under a tax agreement with one or more other countries, entitled to an exemption from an income tax otherwise payable in any of those countries in respect of income from any source, unless all or substantially all of the individual's income from all sources was not so exempt, because at that time the individual was related to or a member of the family of a particular individual, other than a trust, who was resident in Quebec.

Individuals who reside in more than one province on the last day of a taxation year shall be deemed for Quebec income tax purposes to be residing on that last day in that province which may reasonably be regarded as their principal place of residence.

The rules in (2) to (6), above, are similar but not in all cases identical to the federal deemed residence rules in ¶117. Note in particular the six-month rule in (4), above, which is three months for federal purposes, and the apparent omission of a Quebec rule similar to the federal rule for overseas Canadian forces school staff.

Individuals who are residents of Quebec and who are also residents in another country will have to refer to any tax treaty between Canada and that country. Quebec does accept the authority of such treaties.

An individual can, upon application, request Revenu Québec to rule on his or her tax status during the time he or she is absent from Quebec.

(QTA: 8; 8.2)

[¶1605.15] *Deemed Non-Residents*

Quebec does not follow the federal rules at ¶116 compelling immigrants/emigrants to abide by tax treaty rules determining Canadian residence.

A special non-refundable credit may apply to certain deemed residents of Quebec, so as to avoid the possibility of double taxation on certain office or employment income (see ¶1670.05).

[¶1606] RESIDENT IN CANADA FOR PART OF THE YEAR ONLY

[¶1606.05] *Period of Residence*

If you were a resident of Quebec immediately before taking up residence in a foreign country during the year, the day you left Canada is considered the last day of your taxation year for Quebec. The rules are comparable to the federal rules in ¶2103: you will be subject to Quebec income taxes on the income earned while you resided in Canada and you must file a Quebec income tax return as if your period of residence in Quebec constituted a whole taxation year. As with federal credits at ¶2107, most Quebec personal amount tax credits (¶1649) will be prorated on the basis of the number of days of residence in Canada. Credits for charitable donations, medical expenses, union and professional dues, student loan interest, and tuition or examination fees will be allowed to the extent they are wholly applicable to the period of residence in Canada.

The same rules apply if you take up residence in Canada part way through a taxation year and are resident in Quebec on December 31 of that year.

(QTA: 23; 24; 752.0.24)

[¶1606.10] *Period of Non-Residence*

There are several sets of rules concerning the period of non-residence. Since the non-resident period of a part year resident is treated as if it were a whole year of non-residence, these rules apply to complete year non-residents as well.

Regardless of previous Quebec residence, the non-resident of Canada is taxed in Quebec on income from employment performed in Quebec, business carried on in Quebec, and dispositions of taxable Quebec property. The employment and business rules parallel the federal rules in ¶2020–¶2030; the taxable Quebec property rules are discussed at ¶1608. Such non-residents file ordinary federal and Quebec returns, as described at ¶115.

A non-resident of Canada who was resident in Quebec at some time prior to Canadian emigration and is a student or professor or has been a Canadian employee is also taxable by Quebec on certain income. Essentially, Quebec wants federal abatement and its taxes, rather than federal non-resident surtax, to apply to its share of the taxation imposed on its former residents at the federal level under ¶2022 and ¶2024. Quebec statutory language seems to suggest that Quebec wants its share from any former Canadian employee regardless of connection to Quebec, and any former student or professor who ever resided in Quebec. However, the federal *Income of Individuals Earned in Quebec Remission Order*, which seems in fact to govern these allocations, is clear in that the income which can be reached by Quebec under these rules is limited to amounts paid directly or indirectly by (1) the Province of Quebec or any corporation, commission, association, or subsidiary thereof the shares, capital or property of which were at least 90% owned by the Province of Quebec, or (2) a Quebec university, school or health or social services institution (other than an institution of the Government of Canada). These non-residents should file a federal T1 General Return for Non-Residents and Deemed Residents and provincial returns for Quebec and attach a note to the federal return explaining that a Quebec return is also filed. Quebec has no publications outlining its position, and advises the non-resident to follow the instructions in the federal guide.

If the situations calling for ordinary and non-resident federal returns both apply, use ordinary federal returns.

Although Quebec does attempt to collect its share of ordinary income tax from its former residents who have become non-residents of Canada, it does not attempt to match federal withholding rules on pensions, interest, etc., described in ¶2080.

(QTA: 23; 24; 26; 752.0.25; 1089–1093)

[¶1607] BUSINESS ESTABLISHMENT IN QUEBEC AND ANOTHER PROVINCE

[¶1607.05] *Canadians Outside Quebec Allocating Income to Quebec*

If you are resident in another province of Canada and carry on a business at an establishment in the province of Quebec, you must file a Quebec as well as a federal income tax return and pay Quebec tax on the income attributable to that establishment. The meaning of Quebec's term "establishment" is essentially the same as the term "permanent establishment" for federal tax purposes, discussed at ¶1440, and the allocation formula, although governed by Quebec law and regulation, is in practice identical to that for other provinces as illustrated at ¶1440. That is, your Quebec tax is equal to the proportion of the tax which would be payable if you were a resident of Quebec that the income earned in Quebec is of net income. Note that the tax should not exceed the amount that would be payable if you were a resident of Quebec.

Federal form T2203 governs the allocation of business income among provinces; see ¶1440. If as a Canadian not resident in Quebec, you are allocating income to Quebec, form T2203 will perform the allocation and calculate a Quebec abatement on line 440 of your federal return, as illustrated at ¶1435.

On your Quebec return, report your entire income (as on the federal return but making any necessary allowances for Quebec rules) and claim deductions from income (such as RRSP) in order to obtain net income in Quebec on line 275, taxable income at line 299, and tax at line 401. Then, refer to Quebec form TP-25-V, which takes the income allocations otherwise determined on form T2203 and redetermines income earned in Quebec, which may differ from form T2203 income if deductions from taxable income have been made for capital gains exemption for resource property or certain employment income exemptions. Form TP-25-V then adjusts basic Quebec tax for permissible non-refundable credits and prorates the resulting tax by the Quebec income allocation.

The result is similar to the result which would be achieved on federal form T2203 if it applied to Quebec, although it will not in all cases be identical. The resulting Quebec tax is then transferred to the Quebec form at line 432.

(QTA: 12–16.1.2; 24; 25; 1088)

[¶1607.10] *Quebec Residents Allocating Income Outside Quebec*

If you are resident in Quebec and carry on a business through a permanent establishment in another province, you must file a Quebec as well as a federal income tax return. You must allocate business income among provinces on federal form T2203, and determine your federal abatement for Quebec taxes (¶1435) and the amount you must pay with your federal return for income tax allocated to other provinces. The meaning of Quebec's term "establishment" is essentially the same as the term "permanent establishment" for federal tax purposes, discussed at ¶1440, and the allocation formula, although governed by Quebec law and regulation, is in practice identical to that for other provinces as illustrated at ¶1440. Quebec then prorates your Quebec tax to allow for the non-Quebec allocation.

On your Quebec return, you report your entire income (including the portion allocated elsewhere) and claim deductions from income to come to net income at Quebec line 275, taxable income at line 299, and tax at line 401. At this point you must turn to Quebec form TP-22-V, which takes the income allocations otherwise determined on form T2203 and re-determines income earned in Quebec, which may differ from form T2203 income if deductions from taxable income have been made for capital gains exemption for resource property or certain employment income exemptions. Form TP-22-V then adjusts basic Quebec tax for permissible non-refundable credits and prorates the resulting tax by the Quebec income allocation.

The result is then fed back into the Quebec form at line 432 and subjected to further credits.

(QTA: 12–16.1.2; 22–24)

[¶1608] TAXABLE QUEBEC PROPERTY

The term "taxable Quebec property" generally has the same meaning as "taxable Canadian property" discussed at ¶2040 except that the word "Quebec" must be substituted for the word "Canada" or "Canadian". In general, Quebec has followed federal changes to these rules.

Since the tax imposed by the federal government on capital gains realized on dispositions of taxable Canadian property is essentially imposed on non-residents and assumes no provincial *situs* for the property, it does not harmonize with the Quebec tax on taxable Quebec property. The difficulties are resolved to some extent by the fact that Quebec, by regulation, limits the concept of taxable Quebec property in practice to real property situated in Quebec and capital property used in Quebec in carrying on a business. (Insurance businesses have special rules.) Where a non-resident disposes of Quebec real estate or business property, there is theoretically double taxation, alleviated in practice by periodic federal remission orders which remit the amount of federal tax that would have been payable if federal regulations had provided that the gains were earned in Quebec.

Non-residents of Canada disposing of Quebec real or business property must follow a double set of compliance procedures, as Quebec imposes requirements similar to those at ¶2042.

Income of non-residents of Canada which arises from dispositions of Quebec resource properties, Quebec timber resource properties, an income interest in a trust resident in Quebec, and a right to share in the income or loss of a partnership having an establishment in Quebec under an agreement to allocate such a share to a retired partner or his or her estate, is accorded similar treatment.

Where a non-resident disposes of property used in a business at the time of disposition, any recapture of Quebec capital cost allowance would be business income allocated to Quebec. A taxpayer who disposed of a leased building would presumably have property income, and recapture would not be allocated to Quebec, although the capital gain would be.

Quebec residents purchasing taxable Quebec property from non-residents have a withholding obligation; see the discussion below and also at ¶1693.

(QTA: 1; 26; 1089; 1094; 1097–1102.3; QTAR: 1089R17)

[¶1608.05] *Dispositions of Taxable Quebec Property*

This book is concerned only with annual tax returns, and dispositions of taxable Quebec property can have an impact on filing requirements as discussed immediately above. Taxpayers should also note that Quebec rules can require contemporaneous filings and/or withholding of tax at the time a non-resident disposes of taxable Quebec property. These rules are similar to the federal rules at ¶2042, but not in all cases identical.

When a non-resident of Canada disposes of taxable Quebec property, section 1101 of the Quebec *Taxation Act* provides that the purchaser can be liable to pay an amount of up to 12% of the purchase price, unless a clearance certificate relating to the proposed disposition has been obtained from Revenu Quebec, unless after reasonable inquiry the purchaser had no reason to believe that the non-resident was not a resident of Canada, or, for dispositions after 2008, unless the property is "treaty-protected" property (see ¶2042.50). As on the federal level, the gain may be tax exempt due to the application of an income tax convention. The definition of taxable Quebec property is broadly similar to the federal definition of taxable Canadian property, with certain important technical differences that should be considered before deciding whether to apply for such a certificate. For example, paragraph 1094(*c*) includes in the definition of taxable Quebec property shares of a corporation residing in Quebec other than a public corporation. While the *Taxation Act* contains a specific definition of a Canadian resident corporation, and provides mechanisms by which non-Quebec resident corporations can be subject to Quebec income tax, there is no specific definition of a corporation resident in Quebec. For the purposes of paragraph 1094(*c*), a corporation is deemed resident in Quebec if the central management and control is, according to the facts, situated in Quebec. If the head office of the corporation is outside Quebec, if it is not incorporated under the Quebec *Companies Act*, if the majority of the directors are outside of Quebec, and if the governing minds are as well outside the province, then the corporation is generally not considered to be resident in Quebec, and as a result, the disposition of its shares by a non-resident would not require a Quebec clearance certificate. If there is some doubt as to residency, then the purchaser should request on a Quebec clearance certificate to avoid liability.

One key difference is that under section 1097 of the Quebec *Taxation Act*, if the non-resident vendor is an individual instead of a corporation then a Quebec clearance certificate is only required if the taxable Quebec property is real estate, or any other form of real property used in the province in an enterprise. If the non-resident vendor is a corporation, then a clearance certificate is required regardless of the type of taxable Quebec property, such as shares of a private Quebec company.

Another important difference from the federal level is that a federal section 116 certificate is not required for property that is transferred or distributed on or after death and as a consequence thereof. Thus, if the non-resident dies, and taxable Canadian property passes to his or her heirs, then no federal certificate is required. The same is not true at the Quebec provincial level, where Interpretation Bulletin 1097-1/R1, January 31, 1995, explains that a Quebec clearance certificate is required upon a deemed transfer, such as which occurs upon the death of a non-resident individual. Projecting this broad wording, a Quebec clearance certificate might also be required when the taxable Quebec property is transferred from the estate to the heirs.

Thus, when applying for a federal section 116 certificate relating to property in Quebec such as shares or real estate, you should always inquire whether a Quebec clearance certificate is needed as well.

(QTA: 1102.4; 1102.5; Other Publications: Article provided to CCH Quebec Tax Reporter Newsletter No. 445 (September 15, 1999) by Fred Purkey, BCL, LLB, currently of Davies Ward Phillips and Vineberg LLP, with additional material provided by Mr. Purkey; 2001 Quebec Budget, *Additional Information on the Budgetary Measures*, 4.2; 2008 Quebec Budget, *Additional Information on the Budgetary Measures*, 4)

[¶1609] REPRESENTATIVES OF FOREIGN COUNTRIES

Representatives of foreign countries (typically diplomats) required by their duties to reside in Canada are not subject to Quebec income taxes provided they meet the following conditions:

(1) the foreign country grants reciprocal immunity to representatives of Canada or Quebec;

(2) the representative does not engage in business in Canada nor in an office or employment in Canada other than as representative of a foreign country; and

(3) the representative resided outside Canada immediately before taking up his or her duties in Canada.

Members of the family of such representatives are similarly exempt from Quebec tax if:

(1) the foreign country grants reciprocal immunity to families of representatives of Canada or Quebec;

(2) the family member has not been admitted to Canada as a permanent resident;

(3) the family member does not engage in business in Canada nor in an office or employment in Canada;

(4) neither the family member nor the representative is a citizen of Canada; and

(5) the representative resided outside Canada before assuming his or her duties and has not subsequently been engaged in a business or employed in Canada except as an exempt representative.

(QTA: 982, 983)

[¶1609c] EMPLOYEES OF INTERNATIONAL ORGANIZATIONS

Quebec essentially follows the federal rules at ¶1456 for international "governmental" organizations, as opposed to non-governmental organizations such as IATA, for which Quebec has its own list of organizations as described at ¶1609f. For governmental organizations, Quebec accepts the distinction at ¶1456 between the U.N. and other organizations and the federal determination of which are which. As with federal rules, a tax credit is provided for quasi-tax contributions paid to international organizations by Canadian employees covered by the *Foreign Missions and International Organizations Act*, and a deduction from taxable income ¶1641 is provided for employees of the U.N. and related organizations.

However, Quebec expects employees of the U.N. and related organizations working at a permanent establishment of the organization in Quebec to be exempt on employment income earned in Quebec only where the organization has signed an agreement with Quebec.

(QTA: 725(*d*); 771.11)

[¶1609f] EMPLOYEES OF INTERNATIONAL NON-GOVERNMENTAL ORGANIZATIONS

Employees of the following "international non-governmental organizations" (INGOs) (which have signed an agreement with Quebec):

- Association des universités partiellement ou entièrement de langue française (AUPELF);
- Electronic Commerce World Institute;
- International Air Transport Association (IATA);
- International Business Aviation Council (IBAC);
- International Council on Social Welfare (ICSW);
- International Organization of Securities Commissions (IOSCO);
- International Union of Psychological Science (IUPsyS);
- Société internationale de télécommunications aéronautiques (SITA); or
- World Conservation Union (IUCN)

are exempt from Quebec tax if the employee:

(1) registers with Revenu Québec;

(2) is not a Canadian citizen;

(3) is required to reside in Canada owing to his or her duties;

(4) immediately before taking up his or her duties with the organization, either resided outside Canada or was assuming functions with another international organization prescribed under subparagraph *b* of the first paragraph of section 96 of *An Act respecting the Ministère du Revenu*; or

(5) does not operate a business in Canada and does not have any position or employment in Canada other than his or her duties to the INGO.

The spouse (but not other family members) of such an employee will similarly be exempt if the spouse meets conditions (1), (2), and (5), above. Other family members will similarly be exempt if they meet conditions (1), (2), and (5) and are residing with the employee.

Where INGOs are added to this Quebec list after May 9, 1996, there is an additional requirement to those listed in (1) to (5), above, namely that the employee is not a permanent resident of Canada. As before, the spouse of such an employee will similarly be exempt if the spouse meets conditions (1), (2), and (5), above, and the non-permanent resident criteria. Other family members will similarly be exempt if they meet the spousal condition and are residing with the employee.

The following organizations qualified under this rule:

- International Confederation of Free Trade Unions;
- International Federation of Air Traffic Controllers' Associations (IFATCA); and
- World Anti-Doping Agency.

(Tax Administration Act: 9; An Act respecting the Ministère du Revenu: 96(*b*); Other Publications: Quebec Regulation respecting tax exemptions granted to certain international non-governmental organizations and to certain employees of such organizations and to members of their families, c. M-31, r.3.01, available by searching the Quebec website under Laws and Regulations for M-31)

[¶1611] TRUSTS

An estate or trust must file a Quebec TP-646-V return if the trust is resident in Quebec, or if the trust is resident anywhere in Canada and operates a business in Quebec. A trust is usually considered resident where the trustee or the management and control of the trust is resident.

A return is required only if the trust:

(1) has income tax payable;

(2) is required to report a death benefit payable under the *Quebec Pension Plan* or the *Canada Pension Plan*, unless the succession has no other income and the death benefit is included in the income of a beneficiary;

(3) has no income tax payable for the year only because it is deducting a loss from a previous year;

(4) disposes of capital property;

(5) allocates a benefit of more than $100 to a beneficiary;

(6) is resident in Quebec on the last day of the taxation year and the total of the cost amounts of property it owns at some time of the year exceeds $250,000, or if not resident in Quebec, the total cost amounts of property that it owns at some time of the year and uses in carrying on a business in Quebec exceeds $250,000; or

(7) is an amateur athlete trust.

A trust return need not be filed for an estate if the property is distributed immediately after death, or if no income is earned by the estate before the property is distributed, although the estate must provide a statement to the beneficiaries.

The income of trusts is not taxable if they are established solely in connection with, or for the administration of, the following:

- a registered pension plan;
- a profit sharing plan;
- a deferred profit sharing plan;
- a registered education savings plan;
- a registered retirement savings plan;
- a registered disability savings plan;
- a tax-free savings account;
- a registered retirement income fund;
- a registered supplementary unemployment benefit plan;
- a trust governed by a pooled registered pension plan;
- an insurer that is not engaged in any business other than insurance if at least 20% of the total of the gross premium income earned by the insurer and, where the insurer is not a prescribed insurer, is in respect of insurance of property used in farming or fishing;
- a trust established in accordance with a law of Canada or of a province in order to provide funds out of which to compensate persons for claims against the owner of a business;
- a retirement compensation arrangement;
- vacation pay under a collective agreement;
- an amateur athlete trust;
- an environmental trust;
- a trust established under subsection 9(1) of the *Nuclear Fuel Waste Act* (Statutes of Canada, 2002, chapter 23);
- a trust established under section 56 of the *Environmental Quality Act* (chapter Q-2);
- an eligible funeral arrangement;
- an RCA trust; or
- a cemetery care trust.

The exemption is applicable only while the trust is governed by such a plan.

(QTA: 998(*d*)–(*q*); TP-646.G-V Guide to Filing the Trust Income Tax Return (2015-10))

[¶1613] HOW TO REPORT YOUR INCOME IN QUEBEC

If you are liable to pay Quebec tax for the year, you must file a prescribed Quebec tax return. The standard Quebec Income Tax Return for individuals is TP-1.D-V.

As with the federal government (see ¶219), Quebec encourages both EFILE returns and direct Internet filing of personal tax returns. If you file directly via the Internet, you require an authorized software program. The Revenu Québec website (www.revenuquebec.ca) has a section devoted to Internet filing.

Tax return preparers who file more than 10 tax returns per year must file online with Revenue Quebec. This applies to individuals, partnerships, and corporations. This provision is identical to the federal provisions.

The tax return comes as a package which includes a guide, numerous work charts which provide supporting calculations for various lines of the form (such as income tax, surtax, medical expenses, and so on), and the following Schedules:

Schedule A:	Amount for Dependants and Amount Transferred by a Child Pursuing Studies
Schedule B:	Tax Relief Measures
Schedule C:	Tax Credit for Childcare Expenses
Schedule D:	Solidarity Tax Credit
Schedule E:	Tax Adjustments and Credits
Schedule F:	Contribution to the Health Services Fund
Schedule G:	Capital Gains and Losses
Schedule H:	Tax Credit for Caregivers
Schedule I:	Additional Subsidized Educational Childcare Contribution
Schedule J:	Tax Credit for Home-Support Services for Seniors
Schedule K:	Premium Payable Under the Quebec Prescription Drug Insurance Plan
Schedule L:	Business Income
Schedule M:	Interest Paid on a Student Loan
Schedule N:	Adjustment of Investment Expenses
Schedule O:	Tax Credit for Respite of Caregivers (not included in the package; the individual must order Schedule O from Revenu Québec either by phone or by accessing the Revenu Québec website.)
Schedule P:	Tax Credits Respecting the Work Premium
Schedule Q:	Retirement Income Transferred to Your Spouse
Schedule R:	Quebec Parental Insurance Plan (QPIP) Premium
Schedule S:	Amount Transferred by a Child 18 or Over Enrolled in Post-Secondary Studies
Schedule T:	Tax Credit for Tuition or Examination Fees (Claiming or Transferring the Credit)
Schedule V:	Tax Credit for Donations and Gifts (not included in the package; the individual must order Schedule O from Revenu Québec either by phone or by accessing the Revenu Québec website.)

The Quebec Income Tax Return Guide (TP-1.G-V) is an essential document in preparing a Quebec return. It sets out numerous Revenu Québec policies, and in the case of new measures announced in the current year is often the only authoritative source of practical information.

[¶1617] GENERAL INFORMATION

You should begin to prepare your Quebec return by answering the general questions concerning name, address, social insurance number, marital status, etc. These questions are substantially the same as on the federal return.

CALCULATION OF NET INCOME

[¶1621] OVERVIEW OF INCOME CALCULATION

Broadly speaking, the Quebec income tax return follows the outline of the federal form, in that it begins with income inclusions from employment, pension, investment, rental, capital gains and business income, and some miscellaneous inclusions, goes on to permit certain deductions allowed in computing net income, and then moves on to further deductions allowed in computing taxable income.

As with the federal return, the two stage net income/ taxable income computation allows an income measurement for the purpose of computing certain tax and social benefits before some deductions are allowed. As with the federal form, the Quebec return then moves on to calculation of personal amount credits, additional tax credits, and amount owing. The return is therefore familiar in outline once the federal return is done.

At each stage, Quebec's rules differ in greater or lesser degree from federal rules. These differences multiply as the form progresses; income inclusions are broadly the same as federal income inclusions, although in each category there may be the odd difference. Similarly, deductions to arrive at net income are broadly the same. Greater divergences start to appear at the taxable income stage, and become very broad at the tax credit stage, where Quebec chooses to offer a broad range of economic incentives through the tax system which the federal government and other provinces do not match.

By and large, the descriptions below concentrate on differences from federal rules; in the absence of differences, it is likely that Quebec mirrors the federal rules described in the rest of this book.

[¶1623] EMPLOYMENT INCOME

Quebec has its own equivalent of the federal "Employment Expenses Tax Guide" (T4044); the Quebec version is "Employment Expenses" (IN-118-V). An overview of Quebec employment income rules is found in the Quebec booklet "Employment and Other Income: Guide to filing the RL-1 slip" (RL-1.G-V). Although that booklet sets out Quebec positions in detail, it ignores the existence of federal rules which are, in most instances, identical. In general, the rules in Chapter 3 apply for Quebec as well as federal purposes. Some of the differences are:

[¶1623.05] *Tips*

Quebec has a system to compel the reporting of tips received by employees. Employees in Quebec in businesses in which tipping is expected (hotels, restaurants, bars, trains, and the like) who are designated "tippable employees" are required to report tips to their employer.

Tippable employees must complete and submit to their employer form TP-1029.4.V Register and Statement of Tips or an equivalent document at the end of each pay period. Employers use this information to file form TP-1086.R.1.V Employer's Statement of Tips and Tippable Sales to allocate tips, where applicable, and calculate their source deductions and employer contributions. Where the amount of tips reported by an employee is less than 8% of the employee's sales, the employer is required to allocate an amount as tips to the employee representing the amount needed to bring the total tips reported to a minimum of tip rate of 8%. The 8% allocation rate may be reduced further to a request from the employer under certain circumstances. For federal purposes there is no top-up, although not surprisingly the employer has a duty to report and withhold on actual tips allocated to the employee.

Employers are to be compensated for additional payroll taxes incurred because of the higher tip reporting through a refundable tax credit calculated on form TP-1029.8.33.13-V. See ¶1687.

(QTA: 42.6–42.14; Other Publications: IN-250-V Tax Measures Respecting Tips (2016-10); IN-251-V Questions About Tips — Employees (2013-09); IN-252-V Questions about Tips — Employers (2012-10))

[¶1623.10] *Automobile Standby Charge Logbooks*

Quebec follows the federal standby charge rules at ¶326 attributing a taxable employment benefit for personal use of an employer automobile. This requires, as with federal purposes, a determination of mileage attributable to personal use as distinct from use in the employer's business, which in turn typically requires the employee to maintain a mileage log on which the employer can base the proper reporting of the employment benefit. Quebec has legislated, for 2005 and later taxation years, the employee's obligation to maintain such a log, which must be provided to the employer no later than the tenth day after the end of the taxation year, or (if earlier) the tenth day after the end of the period during which the automobile was made available. The employee who does not comply is liable to a $200 penalty.

The log must provide:

(1) the total number of days in the year during which the employer or a person to whom the employer is related made the automobile available to the individual or to a person related to the individual;

(2) on a daily, weekly or monthly basis, the total number of kilometres travelled by the automobile during the total number of days referred to in (1), above; and

(3) on a daily basis, for each trip made with the automobile in connection with or in the course of the office or employment of the individual, the identification of the place of departure and the place of destination, the number of kilometres travelled by the automobile between those two places, and any information necessary to establish that the trip was made in connection or in the course of the office or employment of the individual.

However, if the kilometres travelled by the automobile during the total number of days referred to in (1), above, are kilometres exclusively travelled by the automobile otherwise than in connection with or in the course of the office or employment of the individual, the information to be provided is:

(1) the total number of days in the year during which the employer or a person to whom the employer is related made the automobile available to the individual or to a person related to the individual; and

(2) the kilometres registered on the odometer of the automobile at the beginning and end of each period, within the year, during which the automobile was made available, on a continuous basis, to the individual or a person to whom the individual is related by the employer or a person related to the employer.

(QTA: 41.1.4; 41.1.5)

[¶1623.15] *Meal and Transportation Allowances in Respect of Overtime*

Generally speaking, Quebec follows the federal rules in Chapter 3 (including those for rail and transport employees).

For Quebec purposes, an individual must include, in calculating income from an office or employment, the value of any indemnity for meals or transportation between the ordinary place of residence and the place of work that is paid under any form whatever, in particular as an allowance or refund, for overtime worked in the course of the duties of office or employment. Similarly, an individual must include, in calculating income from an office or employment, any amount corresponding to the excess of the value of a meal or transportation service supplied for overtime worked in the course of the duties of such office or of such employment over any amount paid by the employee in relation to such meal or such service.

However, some moderation of this policy is allowed, both for overtime meals and transportation.

As to meals, when because of overtime worked by an individual in the course of the duties of his or her office or employment, an indemnity for meals is paid or a meal is supplied, no amount need be included in calculating the employee's income from the office or employment in relation to such indemnity or such meal if the following conditions are satisfied:

- the overtime is worked at the request of the employer for a scheduled period of at least three consecutive hours;
- the overtime is infrequent or occasional in nature;
- the meal indemnity, if any, consists of a full or partial refund, upon submission of vouchers, of the meal expenses incurred by the individual because of the overtime; and
- the meal expenses thus indemnified or the value of the meal supplied, as the case may be, are reasonable.

As to transportation, if because of overtime worked by an individual in the course of the duties of office or employment, he or she receives an indemnity for transportation or transportation service, for travel between the employee's place of residence and place of work, no amount need be included in calculating income from the office or the employment in relation to such indemnity or such service if the following conditions are satisfied:

- the overtime is worked at the request of the employer for a scheduled period of at least three consecutive hours;
- the overtime is infrequent or occasional in nature;
- the transportation indemnity, if any, consists of a full or partial refund, upon submission of vouchers, of the taxi transportation expenses the individual incurred, because of the overtime, to travel between the place of residence and the place of work; and
- public transit service is not available or it is reasonable to consider, in view of the circumstances, that the individual's security will be threatened because of the time at which the employee is travelling.

In addition, like allowances for travel expenses, personal expenses, living expenses or representation expenses set by government order-in-council or a decision of the Conseil du trésor, any refund obtained by an individual in relation to such expenses or any payment of them on his or her behalf will result in no inclusion in the calculation of income from an office or employment, if such refund or such payment, as the case may be, is made under a government order-in-council or a decision of the Conseil du trésor or has been authorized in accordance with such order-in-council or such decision.

(QTA: 37.0.3; 39(*g*); QTAR: 39R1; Other Publications: Quebec Finance Information Bulletin 2001-13, December 20, 2001, item 1.1)

[¶1623.20] *Gifts from Employer*

Generally, Quebec follows the federal rules at ¶315. Quebec specifically excludes from employment income the following amounts:

- for all gifts received from an employer in the year for special occasions, such as Christmas, a birthday or marriage, the lesser of the aggregate value of such gifts and $500; and
- for all awards received from an employer in the year in recognition of certain achievements, such as reaching a certain number of years of service, meeting or exceeding safety requirements or reaching other similar objectives, the lesser of the aggregate value of such awards and $500.

This measure does not apply to gifts or rewards in cash or that can be easily converted into cash, nor to the payment by the employer of a person's insurance premiums. However, gift certificates (gift cheques), including smart cards, that must be used to purchase a good or service at one or more identified merchants, will not be considered gifts or rewards easily converted into cash. Also excluded is any amount that constitutes a benefit that is referred to in another special provision governing employment income inclusions, or that may reasonably be considered to be a benefit received or enjoyed by the individual as consideration for the individual's performance of work.

The cost of goods and rewards covered by this measure are fully deductible in calculating the income of the employer, provided it is reasonable in the circumstances.

(QTA: 37.1.5; 134; 142.2; Other Publications: Quebec Finance Information Bulletin 2001-13, December 20, 2001, item 1.2)

[¶1623.25] *Moving Allowance*

Allowances for (as opposed to reimbursements of) moving expenses incidental to a change in the location of employment are not included in an employee's income to the extent the allowance does not exceed two weeks of salary at the new place of employment. An allowance is an arbitrary amount which the employee does not have to account for.

In all other respects, Quebec follows the federal rules for both reimbursement of specific moving expenses by your employer (¶356) and deduction of moving expenses not reimbursed by your employer (¶1039 *et seq.*).

(QTA: 39(*f*.2))

[¶1623.30] *Taxable Benefits from Multi-Employer Insurance Plans*

Quebec encourages industry wide insurance plans, usually supplemental private health insurance and dental plans, whether under collective agreements or otherwise. Its rules provide for the plan administrator to calculate any taxable benefit arising from the plan and report it directly to the employee on a RL-22 slip. This becomes additional employment income, requiring a workchart calculation to support an entry on line 105 of the Quebec return. The rules determining the amounts reported to you on RL-22 are set out in the Quebec *RL-22 Guide.*

(QTA: 37.0.1.1; 43.1–43.3)

[¶1623.35] *Stock Option Benefits*

Quebec follows the federal rules at ¶330, except that the offsetting deduction for stock option benefits is reduced to 25%. For options issued by certain R&D companies after March 13, 2008, a 50% offset may be available, as discussed later in this subsection. The offsetting deduction is a deduction from taxable income (¶1641.10).

Where shares are acquired and donated to charity, the rules at ¶330.50 apply in principle, but the offsetting deduction is limited to 50% of income inclusions for gifts made after May 1, 2006 (25% for earlier donations).

Where non-CCPC stock options are exercised and you elect for federal purposes to defer taxation to the year of disposition, the same election will be deemed to have been made for Quebec purposes. Also, despite the election, you will have a current tax benefit in the year of exercise of the option for purposes of health insurance premiums, QPP, and manpower training and labour standards rules.

Stock options which a Quebec "SME" (small and medium enterprise) corporation has agreed, after March 13, 2008, to sell or issue to an employee, qualify for an offsetting deduction of 50% on disposition. The shares may be shares of the SME itself or of a non-arm's length corporation, and must be issued to an employee of the SME or of a non-arm's length corporation. The SME must be engaged in "carrying out innovative activities for the calendar year" in which the share is issued, but it appears that it will be considered to meet this criterion if it was granted a Quebec R&D credit for the taxation year ending in the calendar year or in any of the three preceding years. (A Quebec R&D credit includes the refundable tax credit for R&D salary; the refundable tax credit for fees or contributions paid to an eligible research consortium; the refundable tax credit for university R&D; the refundable tax credit for pre-competition research; and the refundable tax credit for private partnership pre-competition research.) A company qualifies as an SME if its shareholder financial statements at the beginning of the taxation year ending in the calendar year indicate assets (as calculated for R&D credit purposes) of less than $50 million. As well, the corporation must carry on business and have a permanent establishment in Quebec in the calendar year in which the options are issued.

(QTA: 47.18–58.0.7; 725.2–725.3; Other Publications: June 12, 2003 Quebec Budget, *Additional Information on the Fiscal Measures* 1.3.17; 2004 Quebec Budget, *Additional Information on the Budgetary Measures* 1.12; 2008 Quebec Budget, *Additional Information on the Budgetary Measures* 1.6)

[¶1623.40] *Employee Loans*

For Quebec purposes, the rules relating to interest-free or low-interest-bearing loans are similar to the existing federal rules (see ¶353).

Quebec has adopted the federal rules that allow a reduction of the taxable benefit to an employee relating to the interest on a housing loan received from the employer on the first $25,000 of the loan.

Quebec also follows the federal rule that deemed interest which is taxable is also considered to be interest paid, so that it will be deductible to the extent the loan was used for an income earning purpose.

(QITR: 487.2R1; 487.2R2; QTA: 487.1–487.6; 725.6)

[¶1623.45] *Amounts Excluded from Employment Income*

If an amount is specifically excluded from income for federal purposes, it may also be excluded for Quebec purposes. However, certain amounts are included in income at the federal level but are excluded for Quebec purposes. In general, the employer will exclude these amounts from income in preparing the Quebec RL-1 slip, which may thus differ from the federal T4 slip. Some of these amounts are:

- Reimbursements for, or the value of, public transportation or paratransportation passes provided by employers to employees primarily for the employees to commute to and from work. (The federal government offers a rather different benefit, consisting of a tax credit for transit pass holders themselves; see ¶1353.) The Quebec rules exclude from employee income the value of a benefit which qualifies for the 200% deduction to the employer for providing a pass itself or full or partial reimbursement for a pass acquired by the employee. Details of that deduction are discussed at ¶1631.50.
- Quebec excludes from employment income a reasonable allowance made to an employee for the acquisition and upkeep of distinctive clothing the employee is required under an employment contract to obtain to carry on the duties of employment.
- A special allowance granted by the Province of Quebec to one of its officers pursuing studies in a teaching institution outside Canada. Quebec also offers a number of income exclusions or tax holidays by permitting offsetting deductions from taxable income; see ¶1641.

(QTA: 38.1; 39(1))

[¶1623.47] *Volunteer Emergency Workers Deduction*

Prior to 2009, Quebec matched the federal income exclusion described at ¶338 for the first $1,000 of employment income or benefits received from a government, municipality, or public authority by volunteer firefighters, ambulance technicians, and search and rescue personnel. For 2009 and later years, the limit is indexed annually for Quebec purposes under the rules at ¶1661.05.

The Quebec exclusion amount is:

- $1,130 for 2016;
- $1,120 for 2015;
- $1,110 for 2014 ;
- $1,100 for 2013; and
- $1,075 for 2012.

A Quebec tax credit for volunteer firefighters was also introduced in 2011 and extended to volunteers participating in search and rescue activities for 2014 and beyond (see ¶1655). Under certain conditions, the taxpayer can claim this non-refundable tax credit of $480 at line 390 instead of claiming the Volunteer Emergency Workers deduction discussed here.

The amount is deducted on line 201 of the return.

(QTA: 39.6; 78.7; Other Publications: March 13, 2008 Quebec Budget, *Additional Information on the Budgetary Measures,* Revenue Measures, 1.5; Quebec Finance Information Bulletin 2011-3, *Harmonization with certain measures of the June 6, 2011 federal budget and other fiscal measures,* Item 1.1)

[¶1623.48] *Indemnity Paid to a Research Subject*

Since 2010, the income from indemnities paid to a research subject who participates in a clinical trial carried out by another person in accordance with the standards set by the Food and Drug Regulations adopted under the *Food and Drugs Act* is not taxable up to a limit of $1,500 per year.

(QTA: 358.0.4; 1029.8.0.0.2; Other Publications: 2010 Quebec Budget, *Additional Information on the Budgetary Measures, Revenue Measures,* item 2.7.1)

[¶1623.50] *Travelling Expenses of Member of Board or Committee*

Quebec permits an individual who is elected or appointed as a representative to fill an office (such as director) in a corporation, association or other organization to exclude from income amounts received from that body in the form of an allowance for travelling expenses or a reimbursement of such expenses to attend the meetings of the board or committee on which the individual sits, to the extent that the amount does not exceed a reasonable amount.

However, to benefit from this exemption, the following conditions must be met:

- the individual must be dealing at arm's length with the body;
- the expenses must not be incurred to travel in the performance of the individual's duties;
- the meeting must be held at a location not less than 80 kilometres from the ordinary place of residence of the individual, in a place that can reasonably be regarded as consistent with the territorial scope of the body's activities when it is a not-for-profit organization, or that is within the local municipal territory or, if applicable, the metropolitan area where the head office or main place of business of the body is located, in all other cases.

(QTA: 39.4.1; Other Publications: 2000 Quebec Budget, *Additional Information on the Budgetary Measures,* Revenue Measures 1.11)

[¶1623.75] *Employment Income Guides*

Revenu Québec offers guides to employment income. "Taxable Benefits", IN-253-V, is perhaps a more thorough discussion of employment income, benefits and exclusions. The "Guide to Filing the RL-1 Slip", RL-1G-V, is as its title suggests aimed at employers filing information slips for their employees.

[¶1624] DEDUCTIONS FROM EMPLOYMENT INCOME

These deductions are essentially the same as for federal purposes. For example, salespeople's expenses and employees' travelling expenses can be deducted from their income on a basis similar to the federal deduction (see ¶368, ¶369). The Quebec equivalent of the employer's certification on federal form T2200 is TP-64.3-V.

Quebec publishes its own guide to employment expenses (IN-118-V), which is useful in ensuring that federal treatment of a particular issue can be assumed to apply in Quebec as well. Although this will generally be true, there may be minor policy discrepancies.

[¶1624.05] *General Deduction for Workers*

Quebec currently allows individuals to deduct from income an amount equal to 6% of their "eligible earned income" for the year, up to a maximum deduction of:

- $1,130 for 2016;
- $1,120 for 2015;
- $1,110 for 2014;
- $1,100 for 2013; and
- $1,075 for 2012.

The limit will be reached at an eligible income level of:

- $18,833 in 2016;
- $18,667 in 2015;
- $18,500 for 2014;
- $18,333 for 2013; and
- $17,917 for 2012.

Generally speaking, eligible income is employment income not otherwise eligible for exemption or preferential allowances and business income net of business loss.

The maximum amount is indexed for 2009 and subsequent taxation years under the rules at ¶1661.05.

Strictly speaking, an individual's eligible earned income for a given taxation year is the aggregate of the following amounts:

- the salaries, wages and other remuneration, including tips actual or attributed (see ¶1623), included in the calculation of the individual's income for the year from an office or employment, other than an office or employment held as a member of a municipal or school body or as a member of the National Assembly, of the House of Commons, of the Senate or the Legislature of another province; a member of a municipal or school body should include an elected member of a municipal council, a member of the council or executive committee of an urban community, regional county municipality or other similar body established under an act of the Parliament of Quebec, a member of a municipal utilities commission or corporation or any other similar body administering such a service or a member of a public or separate school board or any other similar body administering a school district;
- if the employment remuneration for the year described above comprises solely the value of benefits received by reason of a previous year's office or employment, it is not included in eligible earned income; this amount figures at box 211 of the RL-1 slip (examples would be a retiree's medical insurance coverage, securities options, or low-interest loans);
- the amount by which the individual's income for the year from businesses carried on alone or as a partner actively engaged in the businesses exceeds the individual's losses for the year from the businesses;
- amounts received as part of a work incentive program; technically, any amount included in the calculation of the individual's income for the year as earnings supplements (other than amounts attributable to child care expenses) received under a project sponsored by a government or government agency in Canada, and aimed at encouraging an individual to find or keep a job or to carry on a business alone or as a partner actively engaged in the business; and
- net research grants; technically, any amount included in the calculation of the individual's income for the year as a grant awarded to undertake research or similar work; the income inclusion would be net of deducted expenses

Indians are not able to include income situated on a reserve or premises in the calculation of their eligible earned income.

(QTA: 358.0.3; Other Publications: March 13, 2008 Quebec Budget, *Additional Information on the Budgetary Measures,* Revenue Measures, 1.5)

[¶1624.10] *Automobile Expense Limitations*

Automobile expense limitations are essentially identical to the federal rules at ¶370; on Quebec returns automobile expenses are claimed on TP-64.3-V.

[¶1624.15] *Employees Working on a Commission Basis*

Employees engaged in sales or contract negotiations and remunerated in whole or in part on a commission basis may deduct expenses essentially on the same basis as under federal rules (¶368).

As with federal rules on the deduction of meal and entertainment expenses, Quebec imposes an overriding limitation that only 50% of such expenses may be deducted.

(QTA: 62; 65; Other Publications: 2008 Quebec Budget, *Additional Information on the Budgetary Measures,* Revenue Measures, 1.7)

[¶1624.20] *50% Meal and Entertainment Disallowance*

At present the rules are harmonized with federal rules (e.g., ¶369 and ¶374). The additional Quebec limitation related to sales applies only to Quebec business and property income (see ¶1631.30) and has no bearing one way or the other on the 50% disallowance for employment income purposes.

[¶1624.25] *Professional Dues and Fees*

Quebec does not permit the deduction of professional dues (except for the portion that covers professional liability insurance, which remains deductible) nor union dues. Similarly, no deduction from employment income is allowed for dues to a professions board, parity or advisory committee. Compare the federal rules at ¶372(1), (2), and (6). The amounts disallowed as a deduction in Quebec are converted to non-refundable tax credits, as described at ¶1651. Note that where a fee includes a portion dedicated to a retirement or insurance plan, the amount may be deductible under other rules rather than eligible for credit.

(QTA: 59; 75.1; 752.0.3; 752.0.7)

[¶1624.35] *QPP, QPIP, CPP, EI, and Salary Repayments*

Quebec essentially follows the federal rules at ¶1029 permitting a deduction where certain kinds of benefits previously included in income are repaid. However, where the repayments are related to QPP, QPIP, CPP, or EI benefits, and occur in a later year than the payments they offset, Quebec (uniquely) gives you the option to take a refundable tax credit in place of the deduction; see ¶1676d.

(QTA: 78.1; 336(*d*), (*d.1*); 736.3)

[¶1624.40] *Amounts under Industrial Accident and Occupational Disease Legislation*

A Quebec worker is generally entitled to wages for the first five days off work "following a preventive withdrawal from work" and thereafter to wage-loss compensation. The wage loss compensation is subject to an offsetting deduction.

(Other Publications: Quebec Finance Information Bulletin No. 99-1, item 1.2.3)

[¶1625] PENSION AND INVESTMENT INCOME

Quebec has essentially the same pension/investment income inclusions as the federal government. Quebec does offer offsetting tax deductions for a number of specified Quebec "strategic" (i.e., sanctioned tax shelter) investments; these are deductions from taxable income discussed at ¶1642 through ¶1642a. For Quebec dividend tax credit, see ¶1666.

Quebec does limit some deductions which the federal government permits in calculating investment income. See especially Quebec's limitations at ¶1635.

Quebec does not permit the deduction of costs of publications and journals relating to investments nor the deduction of safety deposit box fees. On the other hand, custodial fees paid to a broker for safekeeping of securities should be deductible.

Quebec does essentially match the federal rules at ¶1311.15 permitting a taxpayer to split pension income with a spouse or common-law partner, provided the partner whose pension income is being split is of the age of 65 by the end of the year. Quebec Schedule Q is the equivalent of federal form T1032. For Quebec Split Retirement Income Rules, see ¶1626.

(QTA: 135.3.2; 336.8–336.13)

[¶1626] QUEBEC SPLIT RETIREMENT INCOME RULES (SCHEDULE Q)

Quebec has adopted the federal pension income splitting rules as set out in ¶1311.15, with the same implementation dates. Quebec provides Schedule Q as its equivalent of federal form T1032. However, as opposed to what occurs at the federal level, no proration will be applied to pension income eligible for the Quebec split when there is union in the year or when the pension transferee deceased in the year. Furthermore, Schedule Q bears no signature. The agreement of both parties is implicitly obtained by the signature of the taxpayer and spouse on their respective tax return. Also, the Quebec instalments must be calculated as if the pension income transfer had not occurred.

Income splitting for Quebec purposes is allowed only to persons who meet the Quebec definition of "eligible spouse" in ¶1650. As with federal rules, income may be split only if both spouses are resident in Canada. As well, for 2014 and beyond, the qualifying pension income can only be split among spouses if the spouse whose income is being split is at least 65 years old by the end of the taxation year.

Where both spouses reside in Quebec at the end of the taxation year, they may elect to transfer any amount up to the 50% limit regardless of whether an election has been made for federal purposes and regardless of the amount (if any) of a federal election. The rules and general considerations regarding such transfers are the same as for federal purposes at ¶1311.15 (although the general considerations must make allowance for differing Quebec amounts eligible for retirement income credit).

Where one of the eligible spouses resides in another province at the end of a given taxation year, the amount (if any) elected for federal purposes must be the amount used for Quebec purposes. That is, if the transferor spouse is the one resident in Quebec, he or she must deduct on Quebec line 245 (line 250 before 2014) the amount deducted on federal line 210 in respect of the federal election. If the transferee spouse is the one residing in Quebec, the transferee's income inclusion (on Quebec line 123) must be the amount deducted by the transferor on (line 116 of) the transferor's federal return.

(QTA: 336.8–336.13; Other Publications: 2014 Quebec Budget, *Additional Information on the Budgetary Measures* Other Measures, item 4.1; Quebec Finance Information Bulletin 2006-6, item 4.3, pages 35 to 38)

[¶1627] CAPITAL GAINS

Quebec publishes a useful and detailed guide to capital gains and losses, IN-120-V.

The treatment of capital gains for Quebec purposes (calculated on Schedule G, the equivalent of federal Schedule 3) is virtually identical to that described in Chapter 5 for federal purposes. In addition to the capital gains exemption on ecological gifts and gifts of publicly listed securities, gifts of musical instruments donated to recognized educational institutions are also exempt for Quebec purposes. Quebec follows the federal rules (¶1290d) on the tax exemption for capital gains realized on the donation of listed securities to a private foundation, as well as donations of exchangeable securities.

Quebec also paralleled the federal lifetime capital gains exemption and the withdrawal rules and election rules. As with federal rules, the exemption for eligible farm or fishing property (¶502f) and small business share (¶502i) rules remain. However, Quebec has a modified CNIL account (¶502q) calculation (carried out on TP-726.6-V) intended to exclude Quebec strategic investments allowed special treatment on form TP-965.32-V (Schedule D prior to the 2007 taxation year). Thus, the Quebec cumulative net investment loss calculation will not include:

- the additional deduction for Quebec exploration expenses or certified Quebec films;
- 100% depreciation on certified Quebec films;
- deductions for the purchase of qualifying securities for CIPs, and SPEQs (also called QBICs); and
- the additional $^1/_3$ and $^2/_3$ write-offs for scientific research.

Quebec offers a unique capital gains exemption on the disposition of Quebec flow-through resource shares. These shares are a "Quebec strategic investment" (¶1697); 75% of certain mining, oil and gas exploration expenses incurred in Quebec by the issuing company can incur a 25% or 75% deduction in addition to the normal 100% deduction permitted by Quebec, although this superdeduction is reduced as discussed below under the heading *Resource Deductions* in ¶1629.25. The expenses which incur the extra deduction also go into a notional account and the deemed capital gain on disposition (the gain from zero to cost) can be reduced by the lesser of 75% of the gain and the balance of the account. Any gain on the shares above real cost remains taxable and cannot be offset by the special account. Losses on such shares are not deductible. The exemption is claimed on Quebec form TP-726.20.2-V.

(QTA: 28; 231–247.6; 726.7–726.20.4; Other Publications: June 12, 2003 Quebec *Additional Information on the Fiscal Measures* 1.5.5; 2004 Quebec *Additional Information on the Budgetary Measures* 2.3.2)

[¶1627.05] *Rollovers*

Quebec parallels most of the rollovers provided by the federal government; see ¶585 and the other paragraphs cited therein. Quebec also has a string of anti-avoidance procedures which by and large assure that the same elections must be made using the same values as for federal purposes. There are a string of exceptions to the anti-avoidance rules, of which the broadest is that they do not apply where all parties are doing at least 90% of their business in Quebec, in which case an independent Quebec election can be made. The exceptions are set out and expanded in Quebec Finance Information Bulletin 2000-10. A summary will be found in ¶12,243 of the CCH companion volume *Preparing Your Corporate Tax Returns.*

(QTA: 521.2; 522; Other Publications: Quebec Finance Information Bulletin 2000-10, dated December 21, 2000, item 1.2)

[¶1628] INCOME ALLOCATED FROM A TRUST

In general, income allocated from a trust is included in Quebec income on the same basis as for federal purposes (Chapter 4).

Under federal rules, a Canadian trust normally deducts, from its own income, distributions of income or capital gain paid or payable to beneficiaries, and those distributions are included in the beneficiaries' incomes. However, there is provision under federal *Income Tax Act* subsections 104(13.1) and (13.2) for a Canadian resident trust to elect to include such paid or payable amounts of income or capital gain in its own income, in which case it is not taxed to the beneficiaries. This is normally done to allow the trust to utilize losses or capital losses on hand in the trust. Effective for 2016 and subsequent years, the designations under subsections 104(13.1) and (13.2) have been severely restricted. The designations will now be invalid if the trust's taxable income for the year is greater than nil. Basically, this means that the designations will be allowed only to the extent that they are offset by loss carryovers that are deductible in computing taxable income.

Quebec has traditionally accepted such a federal election made by a Canadian non-Quebec trust as eliminating the elected allocations from the income of Quebec beneficiaries. However, where a non-Quebec Canadian trust makes this election, it may be removing income distributed to Quebec resident beneficiaries from the Quebec tax base, and perhaps subjecting the income to lesser provincial rates in other jurisdictions.

Quebec no longer allows the reduction of income of "designated" Quebec beneficiaries where a "designated trust" makes a federal 104(13.1) or (13.2) election. Rather, the Quebec resident designated beneficiary must include in the calculation of its income, for a taxation year, the amounts attributed to the designated beneficiary by a designated trust for that year, notwithstanding the federal 104(13.1) and (13.2) election.

A "designated trust" is a trust resident in Canada but outside Quebec, with the exception of a unit trust and a trust for which (federal) tax legislation specifically stipulates that the federal section 104(13.1) and (13.2) election cannot be made. Non-resident (of Canada) trusts and trusts exempt from federal income tax (under federal section 149(1)) are prohibited from making the federal election.

A "designated beneficiary" of a trust which makes the election is, for a taxation year of the trust, a trust beneficiary having, for such year, either a $5,000 or more share of the aggregate of income interests of the designated trust, or a 10% or more share of the aggregate of capital interests or of the aggregate of income interests of the trust.

The Quebec beneficiary must include with his or her income tax return form TP-671.9-V, *Information Return to be Completed by the Beneficiary of a Designated Trust.* The amount of provincial tax paid by the designated trust that relates to the amounts that were attributed to the designated beneficiary by reason of the federal 104(13.1) and (13.2) election must be included on TP-671.9. This rather neatly offloads on the beneficiary the problem of obtaining compliance from a trust which by hypothesis is not subject to Quebec jurisdiction. Presumably the trustee cannot, given its necessary concern for the best interests of the beneficiaries, readily refuse to provide the information. These amounts must be included in the calculation of income for the year. A Quebec designated beneficiary who fails to include such amounts in income will be subject to a penalty of the greater of $100 or 25% of the extra tax that should have been paid but for the omission.

To prevent double taxation of such amounts in Quebec and the province of residence of the trust, Quebec will allow the Quebec resident beneficiary to claim a non-refundable tax credit for a taxation year for the amount of tax paid by the designated trust to a province other than Quebec that relates to the amount attributed to such beneficiary for the year and that was covered by a federal 104(13.1) and/or (13.2) election. However, the non-refundable credit may not exceed the amount of tax the trust would have paid under Quebec's tax legislation had it been a resident of Quebec. The non-refundable tax credit is calculated on TP-671.9, with the resulting amount entered on the beneficiary's income tax return (line 411 of Schedule E of the personal return or line 128 of the trust return).

For greater certainty, the Quebec announcement does specify that these changes will not apply in regard to a trust resident in Quebec. Accordingly, beneficiaries of such a trust resident in Quebec that makes the federal 104(13.1) and/or (13.2) election will not have to include amounts subject to the election in Quebec income.

Quebec has agreed to harmonize its tax laws respecting the taxation of trusts after 2015 with those of the federal government.

[¶1628.05] *Cost Base of Shares*

Under federal rules, an amount designated under subsection 104(13.1) or (13.2) for a beneficiary by a *commercial trust* (but not by a personal trust), except to the extent it was paid or payable to the beneficiary as proceeds of disposition of all or part of his or her interest in the trust, will reduce the adjusted cost base of the beneficiary's (purchased) interest in the trust. On a later disposition by the beneficiary of his or her interest, he or she will incur an increased capital gain, as a result of the reduction in the adjusted cost base (federal subclause 53(2)(*h*)(i.1)(B)(I)).

Quebec attempts to maintain parity with federal tax legislation in relation to the tax attributes of the beneficiary's interest in the trust. Specifically, when a designated beneficiary receives a non-refundable tax credit relating to the tax paid by the trust to a province other than Quebec, the adjusted cost base of the beneficiary's interest in the trust is reduced, if applicable, by an amount equivalent to such non-refundable tax credit.

[¶1628.10] *Return Required from Quebec Beneficiary Even If Not Designated*

To build a tax base of information and assist in the collection of the tax, and perhaps to alert the Quebec taxpayer to the issue, Quebec requires all Quebec taxpayers who are beneficiaries of a trust which has made the federal 104(13.1) or (13.2) election during its taxation year to declare in their Quebec tax return for that taxation year the name of the trust, the name and address of the trustee of the trust, and the date from which the taxpayer has been a beneficiary of the trust. Note that this will be required whether or not the beneficiary is a designated beneficiary i.e., has a large enough interest in the trust to be subject to the tax.

It is worth noting that the beneficiary would not, under current federal rules, necessarily be aware of an election by the trust, and the trust, not being a Quebec taxpayer, might not be aware of the Quebec rule, particularly if the trust has relatively minor and obscure Quebec beneficiaries. It remains to be seen whether the federal government will accommodate Quebec by adapting its T3 slip for this information.

In addition to this information, a taxpayer who is a designated beneficiary of such a trust, during a taxation year, must also declare, on form TP-671.9-V, any change during the last five years of the trustee or of the address of the trust, together with the preceding trustee name and/or address, as the case may be. It appears that the same declaration will be used by the designated beneficiary to report all the amounts paid or that became payable in the year and regarding which the trustee made the federal 104(13.1) or (13.2) election. Failure to file a required declaration with a tax return appears to incur a standard failure to file penalty of $100 for each item omitted. This penalty may be assessed at any time.

The 2010 Quebec Budget introduced an alleviation to the obligation to declare information about such a trust. Beneficiaries of a designated trust for a given taxation year ending after March 30, 2010, of such trust are required to enclose with their tax returns, which they must file for their taxation year in which the given year ends, or that they would have to file if they had tax payable for their taxation year in which the given year ends, an information return on a prescribed form containing the prescribed information only if, in the case of an individual, such individual resides in Quebec the last day of their taxation year or, in the case of a corporation, such corporation has an establishment in Quebec at any time of taxation year.

(QTA: 257(p.1); 663.1; 663.2; 671.5–671.10; 772.14–772.16; Other Publications: Quebec Finance Information Bulletin 2010-6, item 2.5; Quebec Finance Information Bulletin 2002-8, item 3.1)

[¶1629] MISCELLANEOUS INCOME INCLUSIONS, EXCLUSIONS, AND DEDUCTIONS

[¶1629.05] *Scholarships, Bursaries, Prizes*

Virtually all scholarships, bursaries and prizes for achievement in your field of endeavour are included in income but deducted from taxable income, as discussed at ¶1641. This would appear to include prizes exempt for federal purposes as discussed at ¶960. Prizes which constitute business or employment income will of course continue to be taxed as such, as under the federal rules at ¶953.

Registered Education Savings Plan (RESP) disbursements continue to be taxed under the RESP regime and were not and are not affected by these rules.

Certain items, however, remain excluded from income in the first place. These are:

- A bursary received from a school board under the *Education Act for Cree, Inuit and Naskapi Native Persons* which relates to the actual costs of periodic transportation which you or a member of your household incurred.
- A bursary received from the Ministry of Education under the allocation program for the special needs of students with a major functional impairment.

(QTA: 312(*g*); Other Publications: 2001 Quebec Budget, *Additional Information of Budgetary Measures* 1.3)

[¶1629.10] *Income Averaging Annuity Contracts for Artists*

Quebec allows artists to average their artistic income, for a taxation year in excess of a specified amount of $25,000, over a period of up to seven years. The averaging is accomplished by allowing the artist to purchase an income averaging annuity contract (IAAC) to the extent of artistic income earned in the year in excess of the specified amount and deduct the cost from income of the year. The IAAC will return the money (plus any accumulated income) to the artist in equal instalments over the seven subsequent years.

The IAAC may be purchased in the course of the year for which the deduction is to be taken or within 60 days following the year end. It follows that the artist must have a good grasp of income for the year within that 60-day period to correctly judge the amount to be sheltered in an IAAC. The IAAC will then pay out the amount sheltered (plus any income earned under the contract) in equal annual instalments commencing no later than 10 months after the contract is entered into. It follows that the income flow will commence in the year following the year being sheltered. There appears to be nothing to prevent the sheltering of income over several successive years in this way, although if income is always subject to top marginal rates, there is also little to gain.

Amounts deductible from income for Quebec income tax purposes on the purchase of an IAAC will also be deductible from income subject to the Health Services Contribution, provided of course that the income itself is included in the computation.

To be a "recognized artist" qualified to obtain an IAAC, an individual must be a professional artist within the meaning of the Quebec *Act respecting the professional status of artists in the visual arts, arts and crafts and literature, and their contracts with promoters* or the Quebec *Act respecting the professional status and conditions of engagement of performing, recording and film artists*. In theory, at least, an artist can meet the definition without actually belonging to a recognized artist's association.

The amount of a recognized artist's income eligible for averaging for a given taxation year will be the amount by which the part of the artist's income for the year that may reasonably be considered attributable to the artistic activities for which he or she is a recognized artist exceeds the aggregate of $25,000 plus, where applicable, the amount of the deduction for copyright income (see "Artists' Royalties" in ¶1641.25) to which he or she is entitled for the year. Apparently this means that only income from artistic endeavours, and indeed only from artistic endeavours in the field in which the artist is recognized, is used in calculating the amount eligible for IAAC treatment, and only that portion of such income in excess of $25,000.

The logic of the IAAC is that current income which in general would be taxed at the highest Quebec rate is reduced, and recognized in future years when it may be taxed only at a lower rate (or indeed nil, if income is low enough). The federal government has not bought into this program, and so the only savings are against Quebec rates.

Note that the dollar limit, after its reduction to $25,000, is less than the limit at which the lowest marginal rate begins (¶1661). This means it is possible to reduce a certain amount of income which would not be taxed in any event, as well as income otherwise taxed at the 16%, 20%,or 24% rate rather than the 25.75% top marginal Quebec rate, with the corresponding possibility that income deducted from a low rate could be taxed at a higher rate in future if income increases rather than decreases. The result is accentuated because the $25,000 limit is not indexed, whereas rate brackets are. In short, estimates of current year and future income must be made with care. It can never be beneficial, for example, to average income below the lowest marginal rate. And the deferral benefit of averaging income otherwise subject to tax can be more than offset if taxed at higher rates in future. On the other hand, where income will in any event be taxed at the highest rate, deferral itself is perhaps a benefit.

There is a peculiar anti-avoidance measure associated with this IAAC rule. When the annual payment (or a commutation payment) is made, it is subject to a special 25.75% (24% for years prior to 2013) withholding tax, which is refunded when the income is reported. Accordingly, at the end of the day payments out of the IAAC are included in income and taxed at marginal Quebec rates, but the benefit (if any) will show up as a refundable tax credit upon filing a return.

IAACs are in general not subject to the special rules for annuities regarding mixed payments of capital and income (see ¶480 for the federal equivalent). The IAAC may name a successor or beneficiary, and payments made after death will retain their IAAC characteristics in the hands of that beneficiary. The IAAC is not subject to deemed disposition if the holder becomes a non-resident of Canada.

All these rules are very well for Quebec purposes, but do not automatically follow for federal purposes. The federal *Income Tax Act* still has statutory provisions covering the federal IAAC program which operated from 1972 through 1981, with payments continuing through 1996, but the Quebec IAACs will not meet the federal definition. It seems to follow not only that the payments will not be deductible for federal purposes, but that the repayments will be blended payments of capital and interest (¶480). It follows that the IAAC issuers will prepare very different income amounts for federal and Quebec purposes. Presumably the issuers of Quebec artists' IAACs will be familiar with determining the income and capital elements of periodic payments, which will be fixed by the contract.

It appears that anyone who has the permission of the Quebec Minister of Revenue may issue an IAAC; one would expect that trust companies and perhaps other financial institutions would enter this market, perhaps in conjunction with artistic organizations.

If money is borrowed to fund the purchase of an IAAC, the interest will not be deductible for Quebec purposes. It is not clear whether it would be deductible for federal purposes, although it would not be unreasonable to suggest that it would, so long as some income is earned on the investment.

Where amounts from an income-averaging annuity for artists were included in income and income tax was withheld from the annuity, the taxpayer may be entitled to a refundable tax credit. The amount is shown in box C-9 of RL-2 slip. The credit is claimed on line 462 of the return, item 19.

(QTA: 346.0.1; 346.0.4; 669.5; Other Publications: 2004 Quebec Budget, *Additional Information on the Budgetary Measures* 1.8)

[¶1629.20] *Amounts Excluded from Quebec Income*

The following items are not included in income for Quebec purposes:

- An amount received from the Quebec Housing Authority to reduce monthly interest payments.
- Scholarships provided to severely disabled students for eligible expenses (see subheading "Scholarships, Bursaries, Prizes", above; see also ¶1641 for other scholarship exemptions).
- Most payments to foster parents and to most family-type lodging resources, provided in the latter case there are not more than nine persons lodged there by Quebec authorities.
- Transportation assistance provided through specified school boards to assist students from northern villages who must live away from home in order to pursue their studies (see subheading "Scholarships, Bursaries, Prizes", above).
- Amounts received on account of child care expenses under (i) federal or provincial income support or employment supplement programs, (ii) Part II of the federal *Employment Insurance Act* or similar programs, or (iii) Emploi-Quebec programs. Note that for Quebec purposes, "split income" taxed to minor children is deducted from taxable income rather than (as with the federal rules) net income; see ¶1641.

(QTA: 489–496; Other Publications: 2000 Quebec Budget, Additional Information, Revenue Measures 1.6.1; Quebec Finance Information Bulletin 2000-4, June 29, 2000, item 1.2.2, 1.2.3)

[¶1629.25] *Resource Deductions*

Quebec essentially runs two separate schemes for allowing tax shelter resource investments. It allows essentially the same deductions allowed for federal purposes under ¶2521.50; that is, typically 100% of certain exploration expenditures flow out. These deductions from *income*, where the investments are not made in Quebec, are claimed on line 241 of the Quebec return. However, where qualifying investments are made in Quebec oil, gas or mining exploration, the flow-through regime also stipulates two additional deductions. The basic 100% deduction from income for exploration expenditures flowed out to investors is claimed on Quebec line 250 (not 241), with the additional deduction from *taxable income* claimed on line 287; these expenditures also give rise to a potential capital gains exemption on the cost of the investment, as described at ¶1627, above.

For shares issued after June 4, 2014, where exploration expenses are incurred in Quebec, the shareholder may claim an additional deduction of 10%. Furthermore, he or she may claim another additional deduction of 10% where the expenses incurred are surface mining exploration or oil and gas exploration expenses incurred in Quebec. Accordingly, for flow-through shares issued after June 4, 2014, the deduction an individual may claim will be equal to 110% or 120%, as the case may be, for mining, oil or gas exploration expenses incurred in Quebec.

For shares issued before June 5, 2014, the deduction rate for each additional deduction was 25%. Thus, the deduction could be 125% or 150%.

Quebec also provides an additional deduction of 12% for certain issue expenses. For shares issued before June 5, 2014, this deduction was 15%.

(QTA: 147; 359.1–359.8; 368; 726.4.9–726.4.17.25; Other Publications: 2001 Quebec Budget, *Additional Information on the Budgetary Measures* 2.1.5; Quebec Finance Information Bulletin 2001-9; March 11, 2003 Quebec Budget, *Additional Information on the Budgetary Measures* 2.4; June 12, 2003 Quebec Budget, *Additional Information on the Fiscal Measures* 1.3.16, 1.5.5, 3.2.4; 2004 Quebec Budget, *Additional Information on the Budgetary Measures* 2.3 ; 2014 Quebec Budget, *Additional Information on the Budgetary Measures* 3.1.8)

[¶1629.30] *Miscellaneous Amounts Deductible from Quebec Income*

Generally speaking, miscellaneous deductions from federal income are also deductible from Quebec income. Note the following:

(1) Legal expenses incurred for the establishment of the initial right to receive support payments, the collection or the review of the amount of alimony following an order or judgment of a competent tribunal are deductible for Quebec purposes. Collection expenses are allowed for federal purposes as well, but allowing deduction of the legal expenses of obtaining the initial right or a review of an amount are more generous than the federal position at ¶2355. As with the federal government, the initial legal costs of obtaining separation or divorce are not deductible.

(2) Repayments of interest and principal on loans under prescribed Quebec programs are deductible; at present

training loans under the subsidy and loan program for workers (SPRINT) is prescribed. The federal government apparently achieves a similar result by treating the loan as a scholarship (eligible for $500 exemption) and the repayment of amounts previously included in income (in excess of the $500) as a deduction.

(Former QTAR: 336R16; 488R1(*y*); QTA: 334; 336(*k*); 336.0.5; CRA Document No.: Subvention de formation, *September 30, 1992*, CRA Document No. 9221855)

[¶1631] BUSINESS INCOME

The general rules for computing business or self-employment income are the same as the federal rules in Chapters 7 and 8 and the interest deduction rules in Chapter 10. However, there are numerous instances where Quebec imposes additional rules. These may be restrictive, as in the case of office-in-home expenses, or generous, as in the case of certain capital cost allowance rules. Quebec business or professional income is in general calculated on form TP-80-V and carried to Schedule L. Quebec also publishes an extensive *Business and Professional Income Guide* (IN-155-V). Some of the divergences from federal rules are outlined below.

[¶1631.10] *Automobile Expenses*

Quebec imposes the same rules as the federal government (¶738 and ¶810a). Moreover, Quebec has so far followed federal adjustments to limitation amounts, so that the calculations should be identical to federal amounts.

(Former Regulation Respecting the Taxation Act: 421.5R1–421.6R3; QTA: 421.5–421.7; Other Publications: IN-155-V Business and Professional Income (2015-10))

[¶1631.15] *Deduction for QPP/CPP and QPIP Premiums on Self-Employment Income*

Quebec permits 50% of CPP/QPP premiums *in respect of self-employment earnings and net remuneration for family-type resources* to qualify for a deduction from income. (The other 50% continues to qualify for non-refundable tax credit, as discussed at ¶1650d.) The concept is that this equates the premiums on self-employed earnings to the treatment that would be available if they were employment earnings: the employer's share would be deductible and the employee's share creditable. Work Chart 445 is used to determine the amount deductible if the QPP/CPP contribution entered on line 98 is less than the yearly maximum of:

- $2,737.05 in 2016,
- $2,630.25 in 2015,
- $2,535.75 in 2014,
- $2,427.60 in 2013, and
- $2,341.65 in 2012.

The half share which is deductible from income is also deductible in determining the Health Services Fund contribution (¶1663). In fact, the deduction will apparently reduce income for virtually all measurement purposes.

Quebec also permits a portion of QPIP premiums in respect of self-employment earnings and net retribution for family-type resources to qualify for a deduction from income. Use Schedule R to determine the amount deductible if the QPIP contribution entered on line 97 is less than the annual maximum:

- $695.70 in 2016,
- $695.10 in 2015,
- $685.17 in 2014,
- $670.28 in 2013, and
- $655.38 in 2012.

(QTA: 339(*i.1*), (*j*))

[¶1631.20] *Office-in-Home Expenses*

Quebec imposes the same restrictions as the federal government (¶742). In addition, however, where expenses pertain to the household generally (usually this will be true for electricity, water, heat, insurance, and so on, although in some cases the expense might be isolated if, for example, there is a separate electric meter for the office) Quebec imposes a further restriction. After the expense is calculated and a portion allocated to the office (usually based on floor space), 50% of the common expense deduction so allocated to the office is disallowed. Note that there is no comparable 50% restriction on employees, where Quebec follows the federal home office rules (¶373) without alteration.

The 50% disallowance does not apply to expenses relating to the portion of a residence used in connection with the operation of licensed (under the *Tourist Establishments Act*) tourist home, bed and breakfast, or hospitality village accommodation. The 50% disallowance does not apply to expenses relating to the portion of a residence used for the business of private receptions.

In addition, the 50% disallowance does not apply to expenses that are specifically related to the use of the office (in particular, the cost of heating and lighting), provided that the basic tests permitting the deduction are met.

(QTA: 175.4–175.6; Other Publications: IN-155-V Business and Professional Income (2015-10))

[¶1631.25] *Professional Dues and Fees*

Quebec does not permit the deduction of professional dues (except for the portion that covers professional liability insurance, which remains deductible), fees paid to a recognized artistic association, or dues paid to a recognized association as a home child care provider. Rather, these amounts are converted to non-refundable tax credits, as described at ¶1651. To the extent dues represent payment toward a retirement plan, annuity, insurance or similar benefit, or for any other purpose not related to the operating expenses of the entity to which they are paid, their deduction is not prohibited *by virtue of this provision.*

(QTA: 134.1–134.3)

[¶1631.27] *Political Contributions*

The Court of Appeal of Quebec had ruled, in a 2007 decision, that reimbursement by an employer of political contributions made by its employees constituted a deductible business expense in calculating its income under Quebec tax legislation. Considering that under the *Election Act*, a political contribution must be made directly by the elector out of the elector's own property, that such a contribution must be made voluntarily, without compensation and for no consideration, and that a political contribution may not be reimbursed in any way, it was announced in the 2016 Quebec Budget that tax legislation will be amended to stipulate that political contributions, made illegally or otherwise, will not be deductible in calculating a taxpayer's business or property income. This amendment applies to political contributions made after March 17, 2016.

(Other Publications: 2016 Quebec Budget, *Additional Information*, item 2.12)

[¶1631.30] *Meals and Entertainment Expenses*

In general, Quebec has harmonized its rules with the 50% disallowance provided under federal rules (¶734). (This includes the special disallowance rates for long haul truck drivers.)

In addition to the exemptions from 50% disallowance under federal rules, Quebec also exempts from the 50% cap the cost of any subscription to cultural events if the subscription includes at least three such events held in Quebec. Cultural events eligible under the subscription rule are defined as: concerts of a symphony orchestra or a classical music or jazz ensemble; operas; dance performances; theatre performances; vocal performances (unless given in sports arenas); or performing arts variety shows or museum exhibits. "Performing arts variety shows" are meant to include such things as comedies and musical comedies, which are apparently not included in the French concept of theatre. *My Fair Lady*, for example, was apparently denied the status of theatre, but would qualify as a performing arts variety show.

The eligible cost of a subscription does not include amounts payable in respect of beverages and meals. As well, purchases of all or substantially all the tickets for a performance in an eligible discipline (and, for vocal performances, venue) are not subject to the application of the 50% limit.

The reference to "a subscription" is not intended to suggest that only one subscription per taxpayer will be eligible.

In addition to the 50% disallowance, deductions for meal, beverage and entertainment expenses may not exceed:

- where gross sales are $32,500 or less, 2% of such sales;
- where gross sales are between $32,500 and $52,000, $650; and
- where gross sales are $52,000 or more, 1.25% of such sales.

The expenses exempted from the 50% disallowance will be similarly exempt from this rule.

Where the taxpayer carries on more than one business, the applicable limit must be calculated for each business. Where business is carried on through a partnership, the limit will apply to gross revenue of the partnership for its fiscal period.

The additional limitation based on sales does not apply to expenses for food and beverages consumed in the course of business activities that take place more than 40 kilometres from the taxpayer's place of business provided that the business activities are normally incurred at a distance more than 40 kilometres from the taxpayer's place of business. The object of this exception is to avoid penalizing businesses where travel is a necessity of the business, but not to encourage people to simply travel a long distance for lunch. While the intention is clear, one can imagine that the enforcement will be difficult.

Sales agencies specializing in the sales of inventories (typically for manufacturers) will calculate the overall limitation based on the amount of commissions divided by the rate (percentage) of commission. The objective of this exception is to equate the limit for sales agencies which specialize in selling the inventories of other business with the limit on those businesses which sell (or wholesale) their inventory directly. Thus it is not intended that real estate agents, for example, will be able to use the percentage commission method even though they receive commission income.

Various adjustments are required for short fiscal periods. These are discussed in the Quebec Guide for *Business and Professional Income* (IN-155-V).

(QTA: 175.6.1; 421.1–421.4.1; Other Publications: June 12, 2003 Quebec Budget, *Additional Information on the Fiscal Measures* 1.8.4; 2004 Quebec Budget, *Additional Information on the Budgetary Measures* 2.12; 2005 Quebec Budget, *Additional Information on the Budgetary Measures* 2.6.3)

[¶1631.35] *Fines and Penalties*

Quebec has adopted the federal rules on the non-deductibility of fines and penalties (¶763), but does not match the federal exceptions for penalty interest imposed under the *Excise Act*, the *Air Travellers Security Charge Act*, and the GST/HST portions of the *Excise Tax Act*.

(QTA: 421.9; Other Publications: 2004 Quebec Budget, *Additional Information on the Budgetary Measures* 5.1.1; Quebec Finance Information Bulletin 2004-6, item 2.2)

[¶1631.40] *Capital Cost Allowance*

See ¶1633.

[¶1631.45] *Building Modifications for Persons with Disabilities*

Quebec has measures in place identical to the federal measures described in ¶765(5) permitting the deduction of prescribed renovations or alterations to a building that are made to enable individuals who have a mobility impairment to gain access to the building or be mobile within it. The building must be used by the taxpayer primarily for the purpose of gaining or producing income from the property or from a business. (The Quebec provision also extends to prescribed disability-specific devices or equipment described in ¶765(5).) In the absence of these provisions, such expenditures would typically be capital improvements depreciated through the capital cost allowance system.

The prescribed renovations or alterations do not include many items in the Quebec *Construction Code* which are considered accessibility measures, such as obstacle-free areas, parking spaces, elevators and lifting apparatus, as well as adaptability measures applicable to a certain percentage of hotel rooms. For renovation or alteration expenditures, a taxpayer may deduct, in calculating his or her income from a business or property, the portion of the amount he or she paid during the year for renovations or alterations made to a building he or she uses mainly to earn such income, and regarding which he or she holds eligibility certificate TP-157, "Eligibility Certificate for Renovation or Alteration Expenses", signed by an architect, an engineer, or a professional technologist, certifying that the renovations or alterations incorporate the obstacle-free design standards set out in the *Construction Code*.

Certificate TP-157 must specify the types of specialized or adapted equipment installed during such renovations or alterations (for example, a specialized sign device, adapted chairs, or a telecommunications system) and the portion, in per cent, of the renovations or alterations made to the building reasonably attributable to the execution of the obstacle-free design (for example, to adapt the height of switches or widen access points).

Certificate TP-157 does not need to be completed if an eligibility certificate has already been obtained from the Régie du bâtiment du Quebec (a requirement under the earlier rule) or an authorized professional completed the form entitled "Attestation d'admissibilité", even if it was not submitted in order to obtain the eligibility certificate.

(QTA: 157(*h*.1), (*h*.1.1); Other Publications: March 23, 2006 Quebec Budget, *Additional Information on the Budgetary Measures*, Revenue Measures 2.9; IN-155-V Business and Professional Income (2015-10))

[¶1631.50] *Transit Passes for Employees*

Employers have generally been entitled to deduct the cost of providing transportation passes to employees as a cost of doing business. Employers may in effect deduct 200% of the cost of specified transportation passes which they either provide to employees or for which they reimburse employees. Where the employer provides an eligible transit pass or paratransit pass primarily for an employee to commute between the employee's residence and place of work, the cost is eligible for the additional 100% deduction to the employer. An eligible transit pass is one which enables the employee to use a public transport service provided by an authorized public entity, other than a paratransit pass. A paratransit pass is one which enables the employee to use a paratransit service provided by an authorized public entity. Paratransit apparently means transportation services provided for persons with disabilities.

Where the employer does not provide the actual pass but rather provides a reimbursement to the employee for part or all of the cost of the pass, and provided the employee acquired the pass "with a view to allowing the employee to commute between its residence and place of work", the reimbursement qualifies for the additional 100% deduction provided (in the case of a transit pass, but not a paratransit pass) the pass is valid for a minimum period of one month.

The employee is not required to include in income any benefit with respect to transit pass benefits eligible for the 200% deduction, something the employer generally must take account of in preparing employee benefit slips.

Only employee passes qualify for this treatment; the self-employed business person receives no extra deduction for his or her own transit pass costs.

(QTA: 156.8, 156.9; Other Publications: Quebec Finance Information Bulletin 2010-8, Changes to various fiscal measures, item 1.1; March 23, 2006 Quebec Budget, *Additional Information on the Budgetary Measures*, Revenue Measures 1.3)

[¶1631.75] *Updating the Quebec Enterprise Register*

If you are registered with the Quebec enterprise register pursuant to the Quebec Act respecting the legal publicity of enterprises, you must update the information annually. Registered individual taxpayers are expected to verify that their registration information is correct as it appears online at www.registreentreprises.gouv.qc.ca. If it is correct, the taxpayer must check "Yes" on line 436. If it is not correct, he/she must check "No" on line 436 and also update the information online at the above-mentioned website.

The Act referred to above also requires an annual fee (indexed yearly starting in 2012), collected at line 438 of the Quebec return for sole proprietorships. You may consult the website of the Quebec enterprise register at www.registreentreprises.gouv.qc.ca for fees applicable to different situations. As of January 2016, the fee was $34 for a sole proprietorship, and $52 for a partnership. It is not required for the year following registration (presumably, because an initial fee has already been charged). A partnership must pay the fee online on the register website using direct payment.

The following are obliged to register under the legislation:

- Individuals operating a sole proprietorship in Quebec under a name that does not include both their first and last name. However, natural persons who operate a retail establishment that sells tobacco products, under a name that includes their surname and first name, are required to register;
- General and limited partnerships formed in Quebec;
- Partnerships not formed in Quebec but active there, which includes operating an enterprise or possessing property rights other than a prior claim or mortgage;
- Legal persons established for private interests and incorporated under Quebec law;
- Legal persons established for private interests and incorporated outside of Quebec (federal, other provinces/territories or countries), yet domiciled (have an office) in Quebec, active including operation of an enterprise in Quebec, or possess real property rights other than a prior claim or mortgage in Quebec.

The following are exempt from mandatory registration, although they may register voluntarily in some circumstances:

- Individuals operating a sole proprietorship under a name that includes their first and last name. However, natural persons who operate a retail establishment that sells tobacco products, under a name that includes their surname and first name, are required to register;
- Unincorporated non-profit organizations;
- Public authorities.

The Registraire des enterprises du Quebec maintains an informative website in both official languages.

(Act respecting the legal publicity of enterprises: 79)

[¶1633] CAPITAL COST ALLOWANCE

In general, Quebec capital cost allowance rules and classes are identical to those for federal purposes in Chapter 8. However, computers and manufacturing and processing equipment are eligible for special accelerated depreciation, as discussed immediately below. Also, the Quebec rules for computers and office equipment differ slightly, as discussed under that subheading below.

[¶1633.35] *Computers and Office Equipment*

Quebec has adopted the federal Budget changes related to capital cost allowance rates for computers, systems software, and ancillary data processing equipment, discussed at ¶886t, including:

- Class 10 equipment acquired before March 23, 2004 at a rate of 30%;
- Class 45 equipment acquired after March 22, 2004 but before March 19, 2007 at a rate of 45%;
- Class 50 equipment acquired after March 18, 2007 and before January 28, 2009 at a rate of 55%;
- Class 52 equipment acquired after January 27, 2009 but before February 1, 2011 at a rate of 100%, provided the conditions outlined in ¶886t.05 are met (note that the half-year rule does not apply to Class 52 property).

(Former Regulation Respecting the Taxation Act: 130R119; 130R198; Other Publications: 2007 Quebec Budget, Additional Information on the Budgetary Measures, item 5.1; IN-155-V Business and Professional Income (2015-10))

[¶1633.40] *Separate Class for Manufacturing Equipment Items*

Quebec has picked up the temporary federal accelerated CCA incentives for eligible manufacturing and processing machinery and equipment acquired on or after March 19, 2007 and before 2016, discussed at ¶878. Such property qualifying for Class 29 inclusion (normally included in Class 43) is eligible for capital cost allowance on a 50/50 straight-line basis, subject to the half-year rule. After 2015 and before 2026, such equipment will be included in a new class 53.

Class 43 equipment includes, among other things, newly acquired (but not necessarily new) equipment acquired for manufacturing and processing; for a more specific definition, see ¶898. For each item of Class 43 manufacturing and processing property acquired after February 27, 2000 that costs more than $1,000, the federal government will permit the taxpayer to establish a separate Class 43. Presumably, as with the special class rules for computer and office equipment, more than one qualifying property can be placed in the same separate class, or a separate class can be established for each, so long as the $1,000 threshold is met for each property.

Quebec follows the federal rule in principle for property acquired after February 27, 2000, but it imposes a threshold cost of only $400 on each property, and exempts the special class(es) from the half-year rule.

The purpose of the special class election under federal rules is not to provide accelerated depreciation but to permit terminal losses to be claimed where the equipment proves to have in fact a short operating life. However, under the Quebec rules, there is now the added advantage of escaping the half-year rule on acquisition.

As with the federal rules, Quebec rules provide that where a particular special Class 43 is in place for more than five years, the property reverts to the general Class 43 under the general Class transfer rules at ¶873.

(Former Regulation Respecting the Taxation Act: 130R119; 130R199; Other Publications: 2000 Quebec Budget, *Additional Information, Revenue Measures* 2.13.2)

[¶1633.45] *Government Grants*

For Quebec income tax purposes a government grant does not reduce the capital cost of property for capital cost allowance purposes if received under a plan prescribed in Regulation 101.1R1. Government and non-government assistance received in connection with scientific research expenditures are prescribed. So are many other programs, but most of the programs are obsolete. Occasionally, something of recent vintage is added. Given the length of time it takes Quebec to amend regulations, it is best to check with authorities on the status of a particular grant.

(Former Regulation Respecting the Taxation Act: 101R1; QTA: 101)

[¶1633.50] *Federal R&D Tax Credits*

Federal tax credits related to R&D expenditures for property made after May 9, 1996 reduce the capital cost of property. It would appear, however, that Quebec R&D credits do not have this result.

(Former Regulation Respecting the Taxation Act: 87R4; QTA: 87(w); 101.6)

[¶1633.55] *Works of Art*

In general, Quebec follows the federal rules at ¶891 which deny capital cost allowance on works of art except specified kinds of art by Canadian artists. For Canadian art acquired after April 22, 2005, Quebec will permit a 33 1/3% depreciation rate (see Class 8.1).

To encourage Quebec citizens to donate public works of art to be displayed in public places or educational institutions, the government increased the eligible amount of a donation of public art donated to the province, a municipality in Quebec, or an educational institution, including school boards.

Traditionally, public art includes art of a permanent nature, often large in size, or of an environmental nature, usually installed in a public place or in an environment or space accessible to the public or of the type which is integrated into the architecture of public buildings and sites.

The eligible amount of a donation of public art to a municipality or the province was increased by 25%, and for such donations to educational institutions, including schools, the amount was increased to 50%. The increase will apply to the fair market value of the art (other than cultural property) as certified by the Minister of Culture and Communications (the "Ministry"). To support the increased credit amount, the taxpayer must attach a certificate issued by the Ministry, supporting the value of the donated work. The Ministry reserves the right to reset the value of the public art at any time and issue a new certificate a copy of which will be sent to the donee and the Minister of Revenue. A reassessment in such circumstances would be issued in due course, and penalties and interest could apply. A determination of value or redetermination may be appealed to the Court of Quebec.

This enhanced credit is available to donations of public art after July 3, 2013. See ¶1657.65.

(QTA: 752.0.10.15; Former Regulation Respecting the Taxation Act 130R2(8)(*a*); 130R205(*i*); Other Publications: April 21, 2005 Quebec Budget, *Additional Information on the Budgetary Measures,* Revenue Measures, 2.6.2; Quebec Information Bulletin 2013-6 New Fiscal Measures to Encourage Cultural Philanthropy)

[¶1633.60] *Trucks and Tractors Designed for Hauling Freight*

Quebec's tax regulations allow a capital cost allowance rate of 60%, according to the diminishing balance method, and is applicable to property consisting of a truck or a tractor designed for hauling freight, and that is primarily so used by the taxpayer, or a person with whom he or she does not deal at arm's length, in a business that includes hauling freight, where the gross vehicle weight rating exceeds 11,788 kilograms.

This 60% capital cost allowance rate also applies to additions and modifications made to such a truck or tractor to enable such truck or tractor to run on LNG. The half-year rule will apply to the property covered by this increase in the capital cost allowance rate.

Furthermore, Quebec's tax legislation and regulations have been amended to enable a taxpayer to claim an additional deduction of 85% of the amount deducted in calculating its income for the year on account of capital cost allowance in respect of a truck or tractor designed for hauling freight and covered by the 60% capital cost allowance where such truck or tractor is fuelled by LNG. This additional 85% deduction is a temporary measure applied to acquisitions after March 30, 2010 but before January 2016. A separate class will be stipulated for all property of a taxpayer giving rise to this additional deduction. Such additional deduction will not be recaptured following the alienation of the property.

(QTA: 156.7.1; Other Publications: 2010 Quebec Budget, *Additional Information on the Budgetary Measures, Revenue Measures,* item 2.11)

[¶1635] INVESTMENT INCOME AND DEDUCTIONS (SCHEDULE N)

In general, Quebec adopts the federal rules in ¶1064 limiting interest deductions on money borrowed to make tax favoured investments, and the federal rules in ¶502q reducing the capital gains exemption by cumulative net investment losses (CNIL).

Quebec has its own regime limiting investment expenses deductible in a year to investment income for the year, with a three-year carryback and unlimited carryforward of excess expenses against investment income. This is not entirely dissimilar in result to the federal approach, but is a much more mechanical system, not dependent on the vagaries of judicial determinations of when there is a reasonable expectation of profit. The concept will be familiar to those who are accustomed to the cumulative net investment loss calculation.

Unlike the federal counterpart rules, the Quebec investment deduction limitation does not apply to business income nor to rental income. The types of investment income included in the calculation of the limitation will include only the following items "that would otherwise be included in the calculation of the cumulative net investment loss, were it not for this limitation":

- taxable dividends of taxable Canadian corporations;
- interest from Canadian sources;
- the share of the income of a partnership of which the individual is a specified member (as defined in ¶1842);
- gross foreign investment income;
- taxable capital gains not eligible for the exemption on taxable capital gains;
- benefits received as a shareholder of a corporation;
- royalties from Canadian sources (presumably being royalties which are treated as investment income and not business income per ¶490, although this is certainly not clear in Budget documents);
- accumulated income of a life insurance policy;
- income from a trust (presumably trust income which is flowed out with specific characteristics such as dividend, capital gain, or foreign business income characteristics, will retain that character and be included only to the extent provided in the rules above, although this is certainly not specified in the Budget documents; nor is it clear if business income from an income trust as discussed under that subheading in ¶491 is swept into income, although one might well assume that this is precisely what is intended);
- income from property attributed to shareholders;
- per Quebec Finance Information Bulletin 2005-3, dated March 11, 2005, notwithstanding the wording otherwise included in the CNIL calculation, income subject to these rules is (retroactive to March 30, 2004) to include taxable net capital gains attributed by a trust to a beneficiary of such trust that are not otherwise taxable capital gains eligible for the capital gains exemption, and to include the taxable portion of capital gains eligible for the capital gain exemption that exceed the exemption threshold;
- per Quebec Finance Information Bulletin 2005-3, 50% of exploration expenses and development expenses incurred in Canada (other than in Quebec) that have been foregone in favour of an investor under the flow-through share system; however, this rule applies only to flow-through shares issued either after a placement made no later than March 11, 2005 or following an application for a preliminary prospectus certificate or prospectus exemption, as the case may be, filed no later than such date; and
- bad debt deducted by an individual in calculating his or her property income must not be considered for taxation years after 2008.

The expenses the aggregate of which can be deducted only to the extent of aggregate investment income of the year include the following expenses "that would otherwise be considered in calculating the cumulative net investment loss, were it not for this limitation":

- investment administration or management expenses;
- stock or securities custody expenses;
- fees paid to investment advisers;
- interest paid on borrowings contracted to acquire bonds, stock, or units of mutual fund trust;
- the portion of the loss of a partnership of which the individual is a specified member.

One may infer from the references to items which "would otherwise be included in calculating the cumulative net investment loss, were it not for this limitation" that amounts which go into this calculation do not also go into the cumulative net investment loss calculation. While this is perhaps not beyond doubt, it seems likely.

Unapplied carryovers on hand in the year of death may be applied in full to the year of death return or the return for the preceding year.

(Other Publications: 2004 Quebec Budget, *Additional Information on the Budgetary Measures* 2.16; Quebec Finance Information Bulletin, 2005-3; 2010 Quebec Budget, *Additional Information on the Budgetary Measures, Revenue Measures,* item 2.14)

CALCULATION OF TAXABLE INCOME

[¶1639] ADDITIONS TO TAXABLE INCOME

Generally speaking, Quebec follows federal rules at ¶1077 in separating income and taxable income. However, Quebec will sometimes move to taxable income items which the federal government includes in ordinary income. For example, the former federal Universal Child Care Benefit (UCCB — see ¶935), which the federal government includes in income at line 117 of the T1 return, Quebec instead includes in taxable income. The purpose for Quebec is that this is a simple way of removing the benefit from the calculation of net family income which is used to grind a number of Quebec tax credits and transfer program amounts. The federal government and some other provinces achieve the same result by providing for the specific deduction of the UCCB from net family income.

[¶1641] DEDUCTIONS FROM NET INCOME TO ARRIVE AT TAXABLE INCOME

In general, the deductions from net income for Quebec purposes parallel those listed at ¶1077 for federal purposes. The notable exceptions include:

- Quebec does not offer a vow of perpetual poverty deduction to members of religious orders; rather, provided the order is a qualified charity, the charitable donation credit will offset the tax where income is donated back; see ¶1657.
- Quebec's equivalent to the federal deductions for northern residents (¶361a) is not a deduction from

taxable income but rather a deduction from net income, thus reducing the net income and increasing various benefits and credits reduced by net income; however, in calculating the amount you may claim for dependants, the reduction must be added back to the dependant's income, thus reducing the potential claim for that dependant (or at least restoring it to the lesser value it would have if the deduction had remained a deduction from taxable income).

- Quebec offers a series of full or partial tax holiday incentives to workers in specialized areas, geographical or industrial (or both) it wishes to encourage. Typically these tax holidays are for a five-year period for foreign specialists brought in to bring their expertise to bear on high-tech or specialized financial markets, although in a few cases, local residents may benefit from a tax incentive aimed at foreign markets (international financial centres) or newly arrived industries (electronic markets for financial derivatives). These incentives, given by way of a deduction from taxable income, are discussed at ¶1646 to ¶1646t, below.
- Quebec offers special deductions for "strategic investments", which are those discussed at ¶1642–¶1642a, below. Note that other investment incentives are given by way of tax credits (see ¶1669, ¶1669c) or, in the case of flow-through shares, deductions from income (¶1629).
- Quebec's deduction for employees of non-governmental organizations does not necessarily cover the same organizations as does the federal deduction. Compare ¶1456 and ¶1609f. Since both governments list organizations in regulations which are often years late, it may be wise to check with the appropriate government to ensure that apparent discrepancies are indeed real.

Other, perhaps more significant departures from federal principles are itemized under separate subheadings below.

[¶1641.05] *Scholarships, Bursaries, and Prizes*

In Quebec, the entire amount of a scholarship, bursary or prize which would under federal rules be eligible for the $500 exemption must be added to income, but the entire amount so added may then be deducted from taxable income. The deduction also applies for purposes of calculating the amount subject to the Health Services Fund Contribution (¶1663).

This does not extend to research grants, which continue to be taxed under rules which parallel the federal rules at ¶961.

Note that Quebec also makes special exceptions for bursaries it provides for disabled students and for transportation costs for native persons in the north. These bursaries are excluded from income altogether. See ¶1631.

Prizes which would not be eligible for the $500 exemption (¶959) will continue to be fully taxable; that is, they are included in income and not entitled to the offsetting deduction from taxable income. Similarly, distributions under registered education savings funds are taxed under rules which mirror those at ¶2529d.

In general, the moving expense deduction for students (¶1047) only applies to the extent of scholarships etc. included in income. Where the deduction from taxable income reduces scholarships, etc. to nil, no moving expenses can be claimed on the Quebec return. On the other hand, moving expenses can still be claimed by students (moving 40 kilometres or more) to the extent of research grants included in income.

Quebec's refundable child care tax credit (¶1677) ignores the deduction for taxable income for scholarships, etc. That is, the amounts included in income continue to be included in the student's earned income base in calculating child care credit, notwithstanding the deduction from taxable income.

(QTA: 312(g), 312(h); 725(c.0.1), 725(c.1); Other Publications: 2001 Quebec Budget, *Additional Information on the Budgetary Measures*, item 1.3)

[¶1641.10] *Employee Stock Options*

Quebec has traditionally followed the federal rules and timing at ¶330 for including stock option benefits in income and permitting an offsetting deduction from taxable income; the income inclusion side of the Quebec rules is discussed above under the subheading "Employee Stock Options" in ¶1623.35.

Although the capital gains tax rate remains at 50%, the Quebec (but not federal) deduction for stock option benefits is to be reduced to 25%. The deduction is equal to the amount shown in box L-9 and L-10 of the RL-1 slip. However, if the security option rights are cashed without acquiring securities, the deduction is allowed provided an amount is shown in box L-8 of the RL-1 slip, or in box 86 of the T4 slip.

Stock options from a "small and medium enterprise" (generally a corporation with less than $50 million of assets) with a permanent establishment in Quebec and an entitlement to Quebec R&D credits can carry a 50% offsetting deduction. This is discussed in more detail at ¶1623.35.

Quebec tax legislation and regulations incorporate the federal measures relating to the temporary relief allowed to individuals who elected to defer taxation of a benefit arising from the exercise of a stock option granted to an employee of a corporation, other than a CCPC, or a mutual fund trust subject to the specific features described in the 2010 Quebec Budget, *Additional Information on the Budgetary Measures*:

> Where an individual, during a given taxation year and before 2015, disposes of securities regarding which a valid election to defer taxation of the benefit attributable to their acquisition was made for the purposes of paragraph 8 of section 7 of the *Income Tax Act* and he or she made the election, on the prescribed form, to claim preferential tax treatment for the given year, the following rules will apply:
>
> - the rate of the deduction relating to the employee stock options will rise, regarding securities covered by these elections, from 50% to 100% if the securities were alienated or exchanged before June 13, 2003, or if they were acquired under a stock option granted after March 13, 2008, by a small or medium-size enterprise carrying out innovation activities, from 37.5% to 87.5% if the securities were alienated or exchanged after June 12, 2003, and before March 31, 2004, and from 25% to 75% if the securities were alienated or exchanged after March 30, 2004;
> - an amount equal to 50% of the lesser of the value of the taxable benefit attributable to the acquisition of such securities and the capital loss resulting from their alienation will be included, on account of taxable capital gain, in the calculation of the individual's income for the given year;
> - a special tax, equal to 50% of the proceeds of alienation of the securities must be paid by the individual for the given year.

An individual may, for purposes of Quebec's tax system, make an election separate from the one he or she made for the purposes of the federal tax system concerning preferential tax treatment.

(QTA: 47.18–58.0.7; 725.2–725.3; Other Publications: June 12, 2003 Quebec *Additional Information on the Fiscal Measures*, item 1.3.17; 2004 Quebec *Additional Information on the Budgetary Measures*, item 1.12; 2008 Quebec *Additional Information on the Budgetary Measures*, item 1.6; 2010 Quebec Budget, *Additional Information on the Budgetary Measures, Revenue Measures*, item 5.1)

[¶1641.15] *Federal Supplements*

Quebec allows deductions for repayments in the current year of previous overpayments of OAS spouse allowance or supplement. The deduction from taxable income for OAS spouse allowance and supplement benefits is reduced by any recapture tax where income exceeds the deduction already permitted for recapture tax on income over the OAS clawback threshold (see ¶1419).

(QTA: 317; 725(c); Other Publications: Quebec Finance Information Bulletin No. 99-1, items 1.2.4 and 1.2.5)

[¶1641.25] *Artists' Royalties*

An artist reporting income from copyrights of which he or she is the first holder may claim a deduction in computing taxable income of the lesser of such income and $15,000. The deduction will be reduced by 0.5 times the artist's entire income from such first-holder copyrights in excess of $30,000. This will eliminate the deduction where such income reaches $60,000.

Income eligible for this deduction includes the artist's income from public lending rights as well as income from first-holder copyrights.

To be eligible, the artist must meet the definition of artist in either the Quebec:

- *Act respecting the professional status of artists in the visual arts, arts and crafts and literature, and their contracts with promoters*; or
- *Act respecting the professional status and conditions of engagement of performing, recording and film artists.*

Contrary to the original announcement, the artist will not actually have to be a member of an association recognized under those statutes.

The deduction is not available for income earned from performances by a performing artist, but the following income will qualify for the copyright deduction under the general rules set out above:

- copyright income derived from a performer's copyright in his or her performance; a performance copyright includes the exclusive right to authorize or prohibit the fixation of the performance in any material form and the renting out of the sound recording;
- copyright income from remuneration under the *Copyright Act* for the performance in public or communication to the public by telecommunication or recording of a performer's performance; generally speaking it seems that these amounts would be distributions by the Copyright Board of Canada of royalties for the radio play of music;
- copyright income for the private copying of sound recordings or performances of musical work; again, this seems intended to allow deduction of distributions received by performers of royalties collected by the Copyright Board of Canada from manufacturers and importers of blank audio media.

This deduction reduces the amount eligible for the income averaging provision available to artists, described at ¶1629.10.

(QTA: 726.26; Other Publications: Quebec Finance Information Bulletin 95-4 of July 5, 1995; 2001 Quebec *Additional Information on the Budgetary Measures* 1.9; 2004 Quebec *Additional Information on the Budgetary Measures* 1.7)

[¶1641.30] *Quebec Tax on Split Income*

Quebec follows the federal government in imposing a "Kiddie Tax" on income split with minor children (¶1490), but income subject to the special tax is treated as a deduction from Quebec taxable income rather than from net income as under federal rules. Quebec's purpose is to have a higher net income for the child, and so reduce various tax credits for dependants which are reduced by the dependant's income.

(Other Publications: Quebec Finance Information Bulletin 2000-4, June 29, 2000, item 1.4; Quebec Finance Information Bulletin 2011-3, *Harmonization with certain measures of the June 6, 2011 federal budget and other fiscal measures*, Item 1.1)

[¶1641.40] *Forest Producers Income Averaging Mechanism*

The 2016 Quebec Budget introduced a temporary income-averaging mechanism for forest producers. This mechanism will, for the purposes of income tax and the individual contribution to the health services fund, make it possible to average a portion of income generated by non-retail sales of timber produced in a private forest and sold to a buyer having an establishment in Quebec for a period not exceeding seven years.

This mechanism will apply to an eligible individual, at the end of a particular taxation year ending after March 17, 2016, but before January 1, 2021, who is either a certified forest producer in respect of a private forest or a member of a qualified partnership that is a certified forest producer in respect of a private forest at the end of the partnership's fiscal period ending in the year. An individual will be considered an eligible individual for a particular taxation year if the individual resides in Quebec at the end of that year.

An individual will be considered to be a certified forest producer at any time in respect of a private forest if the individual at that time holds a certificate as a certified forest producer issued under the *Sustainable Forest Development Act* in respect of that private forest.

Income-averaging mechanism for the purposes of calculating income tax

The new rules allow an eligible individual to deduct, in calculating taxable income for the year, an amount not exceeding 85% of the lesser of the following amounts:

(i) $200,000; or

(ii) the income earned from certified commercial activities in respect of a private forest minus the losses resulting from these activities.

An individual that has deducted, in calculating the taxable income for a particular taxation year, an amount from certified commercial activities in respect of a private forest will be required to include in calculating taxable income:

- for each of the six taxation years following the particular taxation year, an amount that cannot be less than 10% of the amount so deducted, up to the amount by which the amount so deducted exceeds the aggregate of the amounts each of which is an amount included in the calculation of the taxable income for a previous taxation year in respect of the amount so deducted;

- for the seventh year following the particular year, an amount equal to the amount by which the amount so deducted exceeds the aggregate of the amounts each of which is an amount included in the calculation of the taxable income for a previous taxation year in respect of the amount so deducted.

To calculate and claim the amount, you must complete and file form TP-726.30, *Income-Averaging for Forest Producers*. A copy of the certificate as a certified forest producer issued under the *Sustainable Forest Development Act* must also be filed with the return. The amount is claimed on line 297, item 21 of the return.

Income-averaging mechanism for the purposes of calculating the contribution to the Health Services Fund

For many individuals who are private forest owners, earning income from the sale of timber may result in a requirement to pay a substantial contribution to the Health Services Fund. To address this, measures will be put in place to enable an individual who resorts to the income-averaging mechanism for forest producers to average a portion of his or her income from the sale of timber for the purposes of calculating his or her contribution to the Health Services Fund. See ¶1663.10.

(Other Publications: 2016 Quebec Budget, *Additional Information*, item 2.4)

[¶1642] QUEBEC STOCK SAVINGS PLANS

[¶1642.02] *Quebec Stock Savings Plan II (formerly SME Growth Stock Plan)*

No QSSP deduction is available for 2015 and beyond. The following commentary relates only to previous years.

The 2009 Budget announced that, effective March 20, 2009, the SME Growth Stock Plan, also known as the "Accro PME plan" would be renamed the "Quebec Stock Savings Plan II" (QSSP II). This name change reflects a shift back to the original incarnation of the plan, (the "Quebec Stock Savings Plan"), which was replaced in 2005 by the SME Growth Stock Plan with the intention of focusing assistance on smaller sized corporations. As with its predecessor, the QSSP II provides a deduction from taxable income for qualified investments in small and medium-sized enterprises.

The QSSP II plan permits a taxpayer to establish a plan with a stock broker or acquire eligible investments through an investment fund. The "adjusted cost" of eligible securities acquired under the plan will be deductible from taxable income. Adjusted cost in the case of a qualifying share is the cost of the share, but does not include borrowing, brokerage, custody, or other similar expenses. In the case of an adjusted security (as opposed to share), which is essentially a security issued by an investment fund that has a favourable tax ruling on eligibility, the adjusted cost is further prorated by a percentage disclosed in the prospectus.

Under the QSSP II, an individual may deduct, in the calculation of his or her taxable income for the year, 150% of the acquisition cost of qualifying shares and valid shares acquired after March 19, 2009, and before January 1, 2011, and included in the plan no later than January 31 following the year of their acquisition. Qualifying shares and valid shares acquired after December 31, 2010, and before January 1, 2015, and included in the plan no later than January 31 following the year of their acquisition, qualify for a deduction of 100% of the acquisition cost. The deduction may not exceed 10% of the individual's total income for the year.

The QSSP II deduction is calculated on form TP-965.55-V.

(QTA: 965.55–965.133; Other Publications: 2009 Quebec Budget, *Additional Information on the Budgetary Measures, Revenue Measures*, item 3.2; Quebec Finance Information Bulletin 2009-4, item 5)

[¶1642a] COOPERATIVE INVESTMENT INCENTIVES

[¶1642a.05] *Cooperative Investment Plan*

Cooperatives which obtain an eligibility certificate under the revised plan ("2004 CIP") after March 30, 2004 may issue eligible securities to qualified individuals (not including trusts) which will allow the individual to deduct, in effect, 125% of the cost of the security. The deduction taken in any one year may not exceed 30% of the individual's "total income" for the year. However, any unused portion of the deduction may be claimed in any of the following four years. Early redemption or repayments are subject to special taxes applicable to the cooperative and to a holder of securities (see ¶1642a.07). Generally, individuals holding the security (including individuals to whom the security was passed on through death or a trust governed by an RRSP or RRIF) immediately before the early redemption or repayment by the cooperative (unless the redemption is part of a process of block redemption of certain securities) will have the special tax withheld at the time the security was redeemed or repaid.

Total income for purposes of the 30% limit excludes income replacement indemnities and, apparently, exempt capital gains, although the precise meaning of the Budget in this regard is obscure.

A self-directed RRSP may hold the security on behalf of an eligible individual, and the deduction will continue to accrue to the individual. In certain circumstances, the tax benefit may flow through a partnership to an eligible partner.

Eligible individuals who may obtain the 125% deduction for the acquisition of eligible securities are in the first instance members and employees of the eligible cooperative or federation of cooperatives. However, there are extensive and complex rules which allow eligibility to flow through partnerships and even corporations which are members or subsidiaries of the cooperative or federation.

The CIP deduction is calculated on form TP-965.39.4-V (formerly TP-965.32-V). The deduction is claimed on line 287 of the return.

(QTA: 965.35; Other Publications: 2004 Quebec Budget, *Additional Information on the Budgetary Measures*, item 2.2.3; Quebec Finance Information Bulletin 2004-6, item 1.2; Quebec Finance Information Bulletin 2004-11, item 1.2; Quebec Finance Information Bulletin 2009-4, item 6)

[¶1642a.20] *Deduction for Cooperative Rebate Units*

As discussed at ¶413, patronage dividends (called "rebates" in Quebec taxspeak) issued by cooperatives to members, other than a rebate relating to goods or services whose cost cannot be deducted in calculating business or property income, must be included in income. This is true regardless of whether the rebate (or patronage dividend) is issued in the form of cash payments, acknowledgment of debt or a preferred unit of the cooperative. Such "dividends" are not eligible for dividend gross-up and credit. The rule traditionally has been the same for both federal and Quebec purposes.

Patronage dividends from eligible cooperatives which must be included in income (that is, which are not already exempt under the rule above) are subject to an offsetting deduction from Quebec *taxable* income provided the dividend is issued in the form of a "preferred unit". Quebec refers to this as a deferral of income recognition, since the deduction will be recaptured on alienation of the share, whether by sale, redemption by the cooperative, or, presumably, death.

Initially, the offsetting deduction was allowed for eligible rebates received after February 21, 2002 and no later than December 31, 2012. The 2012 Budget announced that this patronage dividend tax deferral mechanism will be renewed for an additional period of ten years. Thus, the offsetting deduction will be allowed for eligible rebates received no later than December 31, 2022.

The cooperative should indicate in box O-2 of the R1 slip issued to the taxpayer the amount of patronage dividend (or "rebate") eligible for this deduction. The deduction is claimed at line 297 of the return, item 22.

An eligible cooperative for a taxation year is one that has received a certificate from the Minister of Economic and Regional Development and Research for that year to the effect that it has met specified conditions. Those conditions change somewhat for taxation years of cooperatives which end after March 30, 2004. The changes require eligible cooperatives to conform to the same standards for purposes of this tax deferral as for purposes of the 125% deduction under the first subheading above.

The eventual inclusion in the calculation of a member's taxable income of the amount of the deduction for an eligible rebate previously allowed will not affect the tax consequences of the alienation of such unit.

There will be a FIFO (first-in, first-out) presumption, so that where over time a member acquires many preferred units of the same cooperative and such units are identical assets, the member shall be deemed to have alienated such units in the order in which they were acquired.

When a cooperative redeems a preferred unit, previously issued as an eligible rebate, the cooperative must forward to Revenu Québec, the prescribed form showing the member's name from whom the preferred unit has been redeemed and the amount paid in this regard. For greater clarity, the presumption described above, stating that the order in which alienation of the preferred units which are identical assets are considered, also apply in order to determine if a specific preferred unit has, whether or not, been issued as an eligible rebate.

Quebec has asked the federal government (and by implication other provinces) to buy into this scheme by providing a corresponding federal deduction for Canadian cooperatives. The federal government has responded with a plan similar in concept if not in detail; see ¶413.05.

(QTA: 726.27–726.29; Other Publications: Quebec Finance Information Bulletin 2002-2, February 21, 2002; Quebec Finance Information Bulletin 2002-13, December 19, 2002, item 2.8; 2004 Quebec *Additional Information on the Budgetary Measures*, item 2.2.4; 2012 Quebec *Additional Information on the Budgetary Measures*, item 7.2)

[¶1642a.25] *Tax Credit for Investment in Capital Régional et Cooperative Desjardins*

See ¶1669c.

[¶1644] OVERSEAS EMPLOYMENT TAX CREDIT

Quebec did not offer a tax credit to its residents employed abroad comparable to the former federal credit at ¶1458. It did, however, permit a deduction for an out-of-Canada living allowance for employees in essentially the same employment for which the federal credit was given, as well as some other employment circumstances.

As part of the initiative to harmonize the effects of federal Budgets, Quebec has gradually eliminated the deduction for overseas employment income. This elimination began in 2013 and the deduction is fully eliminated by the year 2016. For 2013, the allowable deduction was 75% of the amount otherwise calculated. This percentage was reduced to 50% for 2014 and to 25% for 2015. However, the full allowable deduction was available for the years 2013 through to the end of 2015 in respect of commitments made by the employer prior to January 1, 2013. No overseas employment income deduction will be available for anyone after December 31, 2015.

The deduction for working outside Canada was a deduction from taxable income, so that it will had to be recognized in calculating any tax benefits (such as Quebec refundable credits) to which the taxpayer was entitled.

Quebec residents who worked outside Canada for a period of at least 30 consecutive days could have deducted part of their income earned while working abroad. In order to qualify for this deduction, you must have worked for a Canadian employer and your duties must have related to a contract under which the Canadian employer operated a qualifying business in a foreign country. Qualifying businesses included oil and gas exploration, drilling and development, mining exploration and development, agriculture and engineering, installation of data processing, office automation or teleprocessing systems (if such installation was the principal purpose of the contract), scientific or technical services, and providing management and administrative services to other qualifying businesses. If you were working abroad, your wages were exempted from a portion of tax on your income earned abroad in proportion to the number of full months that you worked abroad, so that after 12 months you became completely exempt from paying tax on that income. Out-of-Canada living allowances for working in other countries was totally exempt if they amounted to less than half of the basic remuneration. The excess was treated as wages earned abroad.

The deduction for work outside Canada did not apply to individuals who work for:

- a government (federal, provincial, municipal);
- a school board; and
- an educational institution or an establishment providing health or social services that receives financial governmental assistance.

The deductible amount was reported to the Quebec employee by the employer in box A of the RL-17 slip; the deduction was claimed at line 297, former item 15.

(Former Regulation Respecting the Taxation Act: 737.25R1; QTA: 737.24–737.26; Other Publications: Quebec Finance Information Bulletin 2012-5, item 10)

[¶1644.05] *Sailors on International Freighters*

Sailors assigned to international freighters owned by eligible Canadian ship owners for at least 10 consecutive days may offset their Quebec employment income from these periods of employment with a deduction from taxable income. The deduction will be 75% of qualified income. An eligible ship owner is a person resident in Canada, a corporate foreign affiliate of a Canadian resident, or a partnership whose Canadian members have a more than 10% interest in the value of the partnership. The amount of the deduction should be reported to the Quebec employee by the employer in box A-6 of the RL-1 slip; the deduction is claimed at line 297 of the return, item 8.

(QTA: 737.27–737.28.1; June 12, 2003 Quebec Budget, *Additional Information on the Fiscal Measures*, item 1.3.19)

[¶1646] TAX HOLIDAY: EMPLOYEE OF AN INTERNATIONAL FINANCIAL CENTRE

An employee of an International Financial Centre recruited from abroad is entitled to the following deduction:

- First, the tax holiday period runs for a continuous five-year period beginning on the day the eligible employee commences an eligible employment. The employee can still change from one eligible employment to another, but any gap between such employments is included in the five-year period, even though no deduction is allowed for any unqualified employment income earned in the period between eligible employments. In short, while mobility between eligible employments is allowed, the five-year eligibility period is an absolute limit that commences the first day of the first eligible employment.

- Second, the amount which may be deducted during the continuous five-year period is 100% of eligible income for the first and second years of the period, 75% for the third year, 50% for the fourth year, and (for employees of International Financial Centres) 37.5% for the fifth year. (Most other tax holiday employees would get only a 25% deduction in the fifth year.)

The five-year period is continuous from its start, and the applicable rate ticks over on the anniversary of that starting date regardless of intervening circumstances.

The amount of the deduction should be reported to the Quebec employee by the employer in box A-14 of the RL-1 slip; the deduction is claimed at line 297 of the return, item 9.

(*Act respecting international financial centres*: 65-73; Government and Agency Documents: 2004 Quebec Budget, *Additional Information on the Budgetary Measures*, item 2.6)

[¶1646.10] *Stock Options*

Employees may receive and exercise stock options during a tax holiday period which result in a taxable event either on exercise of the option or sale of the acquired shares (¶330).

If both the receipt of options and the taxable event occur in the tax holiday period, and the employee is eligible for a deduction of IFC remuneration, the stock option benefit will also be eligible for deduction from taxable income. There will, in the circumstances, presumably be no extra deduction to reduce the tax benefit to capital gain rates.

If you cashed out your security option rights without acquiring securities, you are still entitled to the security option deduction, provided an amount is shown in box L-8 of your RL-1 slip, or in box 86 of your T4 slip (if you did not receive an RL-1 slip). If you are entitled to the deduction, enter the amount shown in box L-9 of your RL-1 slip, or on your T4 slip if you did not receive an RL-1 slip, on line 297 of the return, item 2 . If you did not receive an RL-1 slip, enclose a copy of your T4 slip with your return.

(Other Publications: Quebec Finance Information Bulletin 2000-4, June 29, 2000, item 2.9.2)

[¶1646.15] *Transition Rules Regarding the Replacement of the International Financial Centres (IFC) Regime with a Refundable Tax Credit*

An IFC employee, other than a foreign specialist, could claim a deduction in the calculation of taxable income of up to $50,000 per year. This deduction was eliminated effective for years after 2013.

More specifically, the deduction such an IFC employee could claim for a taxation year covered by the transition period was limited by the following parameters:

- 2010: 37.5% of the income from the IFC, to a maximum of $50,000 on an annual basis;
- 2011: 30.0% of the income from the IFC, to a maximum of $40,000 on an annual basis;
- 2012: 20.0% of the income from the IFC, to a maximum of $26,667 on an annual basis; and
- 2013: 10.0% of the income from the IFC, to a maximum of $13,333 on an annual basis.

(*Act respecting international financial centres*: 71-73; QTA: 1129.45.41.19–1129.45.41.22; Government and Agency Documents: 2010 Quebec Budget, *Additional Information on the Budgetary Measures, Revenue Measures*, item 2.2)

[¶1646c] TAX HOLIDAY: FOREIGN SPECIALISTS EMPLOYED BY QUEBEC STOCK EXCHANGE OR CLEARING HOUSE

Quebec provided a tax holiday for foreign specialists employed by securities stock exchanges and securities clearing-house corporations in Montreal. The definition of foreign specialist at s. 737.18.29 of the *Taxation Act* provided that if the foreign specialist entered employment after April 26, 2000 but before January 1, 2011 he or she could benefit from a deduction in the calculation of his or her taxable income for a period of 5 years. This period ended December 2015. Therefore, no deduction is allowed after 2015. An eligible employer is a corporation which, during a taxation year, carries on a stock exchange business or a securities clearing-house corporation in Quebec, performs eligible activities in an establishment located within the territory of the City of Montreal, and more than half of whose salaries paid to employees of the corporation are paid to employees of an establishment located in Quebec.

In general, the application details of this tax holiday were similar to those of the tax holiday available to foreign specialists employed by an IFC.

The employer could take the tax holiday into account for the purposes of calculating tax withholdings.

A qualified "foreign expert" of an eligible corporation for a year means an individual who satisfied the following conditions:

- he or she was an employee of the stock exchange business or securities clearing-house business carried on within the territory of the City of Montreal by the eligible corporation;
- immediately prior to the conclusion of his or her employment contract or to the start of the employment as an employee of the eligible corporation, he or she did not reside in Canada;
- he or she worked exclusively or almost exclusively for the eligible corporation;
- the Minister of Finance had issued an eligibility certificate for the employee, for such year.

The eligible corporation must have applied for an eligibility certificate for such individual no later than February 28 of the year following the one for which the individual benefitted from the tax holiday. The certificate stated that, for the entire period covered by the certificate, the individual satisfied the following conditions:

- the employee held a full-time job, involving a minimum of 26 hours of work a week, for a planned minimum of 40 weeks;
- almost all duties consisted of carrying out, supervising or directly supporting the work relating to the eligible activities of the corporation;

- the employee carried out the duties either at the establishment of the eligible corporation where the stock exchange business or the securities clearing-house business was carried on within the territory of the City of Montreal, or elsewhere but in relation with the employment at such establishment of the eligible corporation. If duties were carried out elsewhere, the employee must have had a space for his or her use in the establishment of the eligible corporation where the stock exchange business or securities clearing house business was carried on within the territory of the City of Montreal, and such space must have been of reasonable size.

The Minister of Finance may have issued an eligibility certificate for a portion of a taxation year of the individual, in which case the eligibility certificate indicated the eligibility period of the individual.

The parameters of the tax holiday were as follows:

- First, the tax holiday period had to run for a continuous five-year period beginning on the day the eligible employee commenced an eligible employment. The employee could change from one eligible employment to another, but any gap between such employments was included in the five-year period, even though no deduction was allowed for any unqualified employment income earned in the period between eligible employments. In short, while mobility between eligible employments was still allowed, the five-year eligibility period was an absolute limit that commenced the first day of the first eligible employment.

- Second, the amount which could be deducted during the continuous five-year period was 100% of eligible income for the first and second years of the period, 75% for the third year, 50% for the fourth year, and (for employees of a securities exchange or securities clearing house) 37.5% for the fifth year. (Most other tax holiday employees would get only a 25% deduction in the fifth year.)

The five-year period was continuous from its start, and the applicable rate ticked over on the anniversary of that starting date regardless of intervening circumstances. The amount of the deduction was equal to the eligible income multiplied by the exemption rate shown in box A-14 of the RL-1 slip. The deduction was claimed at line 297 of the return, former item 18.

(QTA: 737.18.29–737.18.35; Other Publications: June 12, 2003 Quebec Budget, *Additional Information on the Fiscal Measures*, item 1.3.18; 2004 Quebec Budget, *Additional Information on the Budgetary Measures*, item 2.6)

[¶1646h] TAX HOLIDAY: SCIENTIFIC RESEARCH EMPLOYEES FROM ABROAD

A tax holiday is available on research employment income of foreign researchers for a period of up to 60 months of research activity with a company conducting research in Quebec. The foreign researcher must reside outside of Canada immediately before signing his or her contract or taking up his or her duties with the R&D company, and be a specialist in the field of pure or applied science or a related field and hold at least a Master's degree recognized by a Quebec university, or its equivalent. The employer must obtain a certificate from the Conseil de la science et de la technologie. The tax holiday will not apply to employees of Quebec universities or government or municipal agencies or corporations.

Stock options qualify for the tax holiday.

The parameters of the tax holiday are:

- First, the tax holiday period runs for a continuous five-year period beginning on the day the eligible employee commences an eligible employment. The employee can change from one eligible employment to another, but any gap between such employments is included in the five-year period, even though no deduction is allowed for any unqualified employment income earned in the period between eligible employments. In short, while mobility between eligible employments is still allowed, the five-year eligibility period is an absolute limit that commences the first day of the first eligible employment.

- Second, the amount which may be deducted during the continuous five-year period is 100% of eligible income for the first and second years of the period, 75% for the third year, 50% for the fourth year, and 25% for the fifth year.

The five-year period is continuous from its start, and the applicable rate ticks over on the anniversary of that starting date regardless of intervening circumstances.

The deduction is equal to the following result: Add the total deductions claimed at line 105, *Correction of employment income*, line 205, *QPP deduction*, and line 207, *Employment expenses and deductions* related to the income entitling the deduction for foreign researchers. Multiply the total by the exemption rate shown in box A-14 of the RL-1 slip. Subtract the result from the amount shown in box A-10 of the RL-1 slip. The deduction is claimed at line 297, item 3.

(QTA: 737.19–737.21; Other Publications: 2004 Quebec *Additional Information on the Budgetary Measures* 2.6)

[¶1646h.10] *Post-Doctoral Interns*

The tax holiday for foreign researchers, i.e., the deduction of 100%/75% of R&D employment income from taxable income for a 60-month period, was extended to include foreign post-doctoral interns who conclude employment agreements with eligible universities and public research centres, where the institutions can obtain a certificate from the Quebec Ministry of Education certifying that the employee has a doctorate and is specializing in pure or applied sciences or in a related field. The employee must not reside in Canada immediately before the conclusion of the contract or assumption of duties and must work continuously and almost exclusively for the eligible employer. Employment duties must consist almost exclusively in carrying out of R&D activities.

The revised parameters as outlined in ¶1646h apply to this tax holiday.

The deduction is equal to the following result: Add the total deductions claimed at line 105, *Correction of employment income*, line 205, *QPP deduction*, and line 207, *Employment expenses and deductions* related to the income entitled to the deduction for foreign researchers on a post-doctoral internship. Multiply the total by the exemption rate shown in box A-14 of the RL-1 slip. Subtract the result from the amount shown in box A-11 of the RL-1 slip. The deduction is claimed at line 297, item 5.

(QTA: 737.22.0.0.1–737.22.0.0.4; Other Publications: June 12, 2003 Quebec Budget, *Additional Information on the Fiscal Measures*, item 1.3.18)

[¶1646h.15] *Technology Commercialization Experts*

The five-year 100%/75% tax holiday for foreign researchers of Quebec R&D employers extends to employees who are experts in management or financing of innovation activities, or foreign commercialization or transfer of leading edge technology. To qualify for the tax holiday, the employee must be certified by Quebec authorities (on application of the R&D employer), must take up the employment duties, must not have resided in Canada immediately prior to concluding the contract or immediately before taking up the employment.

The employee must work almost exclusively for the employer on a continuous basis as part of an R&D project.

The revised parameters outlined in ¶1646h apply to this holiday.

The deduction is equal to the following result: Add the total deductions claimed at line 105, *Correction of employment income*, line 205, *QPP deduction*, and line 207, *Employment expenses and deductions* related to the income entitling the deduction for foreign experts. Multiply the total by the exemption rate shown in box A-14 of the RL-1 slip. Subtract the result from the amount shown in box A-12 of the RL-1 slip. The deduction is claimed at line 297, item 4.

(QTA: 737.22.0.0.5–737.22.0.0.8; Other Publications: June 12, 2003 Quebec *Additional Information on the Fiscal Measures*, item 1.3.18)

[¶1646h.20] *Change of Tax Holiday Employment*

It is a general rule with tax holiday employment that the employee may change jobs from one employment to another which qualifies for the same type of credit, or may leave the job and return abroad and then return to another job under the same type of credit, but the total period of exemption for all such occasions together may not exceed the applicable tax holiday period. The employee may also change from one type of tax holiday job to another (e.g., from post-doctoral intern to research employee, or to ¶1646k or ¶1646m tax holiday) subject to the same rule that the total period of exemption for all such occasions together may not exceed the applicable tax holiday period.

(Other Publications: Quebec Budget of November 1, 2001: Revenue Measures, item 1.12; June 12, 2003 Quebec Budget, *Additional Information on the Fiscal Measures*, item 1.3.18)

[¶1646k] TAX HOLIDAY: FOREIGN PROFESSORS AT QUEBEC UNIVERSITIES

Quebec provides a five-year tax holiday for scientific research employees (¶1646h) to foreign professors who take up positions in Quebec universities in certain fields of science, technology or finance. A foreign professor employed by a Quebec university may, for a period of five years, deduct from taxable income (¶1641) 100% of qualifying employment income (typically the salary paid by the Quebec university).

The tax holiday applies to an individual who takes up the duties of an employee at a Quebec university pursuant to an employment contract. The tax holiday is conditional on the Quebec university obtaining a certificate from the Ministère de l'Éducation et de l'Enseignement supérieur attesting that the individual is a specialist in science, engineering, finance, health or new information and communications technologies, and possesses a doctorate.

To qualify, the individual must:

- not have resided in Canada immediately prior to the conclusion of the employment contract or immediately prior to taking up his or her duties;
- work almost exclusively and continuously for a Quebec university; and
- have duties which consist almost exclusively of engaging, as an employee, in activities in the realms of the sciences, engineering, health or new information and communications technologies.

The conditions governing the tax holiday for a foreign researcher or expert, especially in regard to the renewal of an employment contract, will apply in principle to the tax holiday for a foreign professor.

It is a general rule with tax holiday employment that the employee may change jobs from one employment to another which qualifies for the same type of credit, or may leave the job and return abroad and then return to another job under the same type of credit, but the total period of exemption for all such occasions together may not exceed the applicable tax holiday period. The employee may also change from one type of tax holiday job to another (e.g., from foreign professor to research employee, or to ¶1646m tax holiday) subject to the same rule that the total period of exemption for all such occasions together may not exceed the applicable tax holiday period.

Particulars of the tax holiday are:

- First, the tax holiday period runs for a continuous five-year period beginning on the day the eligible employee commences an eligible employment. The employee can change from one eligible employment to another, but any gap between such employments is included in the five-year period, even though no deduction is allowed for any unqualified employment income earned in the period between eligible employments. In short, while mobility between eligible employments is still allowed, the five-year eligibility period is an absolute limit that commences the first day of the first eligible employment.
- Second, the amount which may be deducted during the continuous five-year period is 100% of eligible income for the first and second years of the period, 75% for the third year, 50% for the fourth year, and 25% for the fifth year.

The five-year period is continuous from its start, and the applicable rate ticks over on the anniversary of that starting date regardless of intervening circumstances.

The deduction is equal to the following result: Add the total deductions claimed at line 105, *Correction of employment income*, line 205, *QPP deduction*, and line 207, *Employment expenses and deductions* related to the income entitling the deduction for foreign professors. Multiply the total by the exemption rate shown in box A-14 of the RL-1 slip. Subtract the result from the amount shown in box A-13 of the RL-1 slip. The deduction is claimed at line 297, item 19.

(QTA: 737.22.0.5–737.22.0.8; Other Publications: June 12, 2003 Quebec Budget, *Additional Information on the Fiscal Measures*, item 1.3.18; 2004 Quebec Budget, *Additional Information on the Budgetary Measures*, item 2.6)

[¶1646m] TAX HOLIDAY: FOREIGN INSTRUCTORS AT INFORMATION TECHNOLOGY DEVELOPMENT CENTRES; FOREIGN SPECIALISTS AT DESIGNATED INNOVATION SITES

[¶1646m.05] *Tax Holiday for New Employment of Biotechnology Workers*

The parameters of the tax holiday are:

- First, the tax holiday period runs for a continuous five-year period beginning on the day the eligible employee commences an eligible employment. The employee can change from one eligible employment to another, but any gap between such employments is included in the five-year period, even though no deduction is allowed for any unqualified employment income earned in the period between eligible employments. In short, while mobility between eligible employments is still allowed, the five-year eligibility period is an absolute limit that commences the first day of the first eligible employment.

- Second, the amount which may be deducted during the continuous five-year period is 100% of eligible income for the first and second years of the period, 75% for the third year, 50% for the fourth year, and 25% for the fifth year.

The five-year period is continuous from its start, and the applicable rate ticks over on the anniversary of that starting date regardless of intervening circumstances.

(QTA: 737.22.0.1–737.22.0.4; Other Publications: June 12, 2003 Quebec Budget, *Additional Information on the Fiscal Measures*, items 1.2.1, 1.2.11, 1.3.18; 2004 Quebec Budget, *Additional Information on the Budgetary Measures*, item 2.6)

[¶1646m.10] *Foreign Instructors at Information Technology Development Centres*

Quebec established Information Technology Development Centres (ITDCs, sometimes called by the French acronym, CDTIs) to house companies newly established to engage in research and development of high value-added products or services. The companies can obtain substantial tax advantages, and if they employ training instructors from abroad, those employees may be eligible for a two-year tax holiday in respect of the income from that employment.

The exemption consists of a deduction from taxable income, so that the foreign instructor must report income as otherwise required under Quebec rules, but may then claim an offsetting deduction equal to income and benefits received from the employer and attributable to the tax holiday period.

The tax holiday period commences when the qualifying instructor assumes duties as an employee of an eligible employer and extends to five years following the date of hire. It flows through a transfer of employment to a controlling, subsidiary or successor corporation.

A qualifying instructor must not have been resident in Canada immediately before entering into the employment contract or assuming duties with the ITDC employer and, from the time of assuming duties for the employer, must work almost exclusively and without interruption for that employer (subject to the related company transfers above), and must perform duties which consist *almost exclusively* of providing instruction.

The exemption is only available if a certificate is obtained by the employer from the Ministry of Finance within 30 days of the later of the contract or assumption of duties. There must be an employment contract entered into. The contract may initially be for less than two years and may be extended without compromising the instructor's tax holiday period.

Foreign tax holiday employees are allowed to change from one employer to another and continue the tax holiday, so long (presumably) as the employment itself qualifies in the new position. The five years cannot be extended by this means.

(QTA: 737.22.0.1–737.22.0.4, 771.12; Other Publications: Quebec Budget of March 9, 1999: *Revenue Measures*, item 2.1.10; Quebec Budget of March 29, 2001: *Revenue Measures*, item 2.2.5)

[¶1646m.15] *Tax Holiday: Foreign Specialists at Designated Innovation Sites*

Subsequent to the IDTC program discussed above, Quebec has added a plethora of programs which depend on designated locations where certain innovative and high value added businesses can, with the approval of the Quebec authorities, locate together and obtain tax benefits. The tax benefits are typically tax credits related to payroll, sometimes related to payroll increases in a particular area, granted to a particular corporation in a particular business in a particular location or region. These tax benefits are generally available only to corporations; they are itemized in the companion volume for corporations, *Preparing Your Corporate Tax Returns*.

Although most of these tax benefits go to corporations, the granting of a five-year tax holiday to foreign specialists employed by qualified businesses at these sites has become an increasingly common feature of Quebec taxation. Essentially these tax holiday programs are shaped by the same cookie-cutter. The main differences relate to the defined field of expertise of the foreign specialist, the location of the designated site, and the implementation, extension, and termination dates of the tax holiday program. In all cases the appropriate arm of the Quebec government (usually Investissement Quebec) must certify that the employer's business meets the required definitions and that the foreign specialist has been hired in compliance with program provisions. Accordingly, there is typically advance negotiation between the employer and the Quebec government to ensure that a particular foreign specialist has been hired under applicable tax holiday provisions, and the foreign specialist will be offered this inducement when hired. The employer must obtain a certificate from Quebec Finance for each foreign specialist and typically must provide a copy of the certificate to the employee, who in turn must file it with his or her tax return.

The foreign tax holiday typically runs for five full years from the date employment commences, although it may be terminated by the government for non-compliance of the employer, or by the employee leaving a tax holiday employment. The foreign specialist must not have been resident in Canada immediately before entering into the employment contract or immediately before taking up employment with the eligible employer.

The tax holiday employee must file a (federal and) Quebec tax return showing all employment income and, normally, all other income which must be reported by a Quebec resident. From this, the employee may deduct, in computing Quebec (but not federal) taxable income (at line 297 of the Quebec return), pretty well all benefits and remuneration received from the employer during the tax holiday period. Where the tax holiday period ends during a year, only the portion of income related to the holiday is deductible. Normally it is the employer's task to calculate the appropriate deduction and report it on the RL-1 slip.

Foreign specialists eligible for a tax holiday may be certified under the following programs:

- Cité du multimédia; program supports information technology and multimedia, in particular as applied to arts and culture;
- Centre national des nouvelles technologies de Quebec (CNNTQ);
- Carrefours de la nouvelle économie (CNEs) (also called Marketplace for the New Economy (MNE); program supports ITDC and multimedia centres in various locations;
- Cité du commerce électronique; supports the development and supply of products and services relating to E-business (consulting and technology), and the operation of E-business solutions, such as management, operation, maintenance and development of systems, applications and infrastructures;
- biotechnology development centres; (original centre in Laval, now extended to other locations);
- nutraceuticals (compounds which reduce the risk or effects of chronic illness) and functional foods (which have a direct and measurable effect on health beyond nutrition).

Generally speaking, the duties of the foreign specialist must be attributable almost exclusively to eligible activities of the corporation, and must consist almost exclusively of:

- training;
- research and development;
- specialized management tasks in the field of innovations, commercialization, technology transfer or innovation financing; or
- any combination of the above items;

although some details will vary from one business to another.

A general summary of the various credits and their conditions is found in the Quebec *Guide to Filing the RL-1 Slip* (RL-1.G-V).

(QTA: 737.22.0.1–737.22.0.4; Other Publications: 2000 Quebec Budget, *Additional Information, Revenue Measures,* item 2.8.1; Quebec Finance Information Bulletin 2000-3, May 11, 2000; 2001 Quebec Budget, *Additional Information, Revenue Measures,* item 2.2.5; Quebec Finance Information Bulletin 2001-13, December 20, 2001; 2002 Quebec Budget, *Additional Information, Revenue Measures,* items 2.2.1 through 2.2.5)

[¶1646m.20] *Change of Tax Holiday Employment*

It is a general rule with tax holiday employment that the employee may change jobs from one employment to another which qualifies for the same type of credit, or may leave the job and return abroad and then return to another job under the same type of credit, but the total period of exemption for all such occasions together may not exceed the applicable tax holiday period. The employee may also change from one type of tax holiday job to another (e.g., from post-doctoral intern to research employee, or to ¶1646k or ¶1646m tax holiday) subject to the same rule that the total period of exemption for all such occasions together may not exceed the applicable tax holiday period.

(Other Publications: Quebec Budget, 2001: *Revenue Measures,* item 1.12)

[¶1646s] TAX HOLIDAY FOR FOREIGN FARM WORKERS

A 50% deduction from Quebec taxable income is available to an individual who did not "in fact" reside in Canada at any time in the taxation year and who had a valid Canadian federal work permit exclusively for seasonal farm work under one of the following programs:

- the Seasonal Agricultural Worker Program;
- the Agricultural Stream.

Although these workers cannot be resident in fact to qualify for the partial tax holiday, they may be taxed as deemed residents if they sojourn in Canada for more than 182 days (see ¶117). In this case, the 50% deduction will apply to net Quebec remuneration received under the employment program for which the visa was issued (that is, 50% of remuneration received on account of the employment in Quebec net of permitted deductions in respect of that employment income). Where the employee is not a deemed resident, and so a non-resident, the deduction will be reflected in the calculation of non-resident taxable income earned in Quebec and in Canada. The deduction is to be reflected in the employer's source deductions, since many such employees would probably not file tax returns. The deduction is claimed on line 297, item 20.

(QTA: 737.22.0.12–737.22.0.14; Other Publications: Quebec Finance Information Bulletin 2015-4, item 2.6)

[¶1646t] TAX HOLIDAY FOR FOREIGN SPECIALISTS EMPLOYED BY A NEW FINANCIAL SERVICES CORPORATION

The March 20, 2012 Budget introduced a new tax holiday to foreign specialists hired by a new financial services corporation and to whom the Minister of Finance has issued a certificate. The certificate will certify that the specialist has the required level of expertise required to carry out the duties as spelled out in his or her employer's qualification certificate, which it obtained for the purpose of qualifying for the tax credit for hiring employees.

Such a qualified taxpayer will be able to deduct 100% of the income earned in the first and second years, 75% in the third year, 50% in the fourth year, and 25% in the fifth. The starting date for this deduction is the day that he or she starts employment after the budget date of March 20, 2012. Certain other conditions must be met, namely that the employee must be not have been a resident of Canada prior to commencing work for the new corporation or another qualified corporation.

(QTA: 737.22.0.4.1–737.22.0.4.8; Other Publications: 2012 Quebec Budget: *Additional Information on the Fiscal Measures of the Budget,* item 3.7.3)

PERSONAL AMOUNT TAX CREDITS

[¶1649] PERSONAL AMOUNT TAX CREDITS

Quebec personal amounts are considerably different from federal amounts in several respects, not only as to the actual dollar amount but also as to situations covered, conversion rate and indexing amount. Quebec views its personal amount system as an integrated part of an elaborate family support system comprising income-measured benefits as well as tax relief. Quebec revised its family support and personal amount credit systems in 2005 and eliminated most personal amounts for children under 18 at the end of the taxation year, although if you have children under 18 engaged in secondary vocational training (or post-secondary studies), you will qualify for a per semester training credit. While this brings the Quebec system more closely into alignment with the federal system in principle, the details of personal amount credits will still be substantially different from the federal personal amount system.

Another point of difference from federal rules is that Quebec offers personal amount credits instead of deductions for several items, such as union or professional dues.

In general, Quebec has converted its personal amounts to tax credit at the middle bracket rate (rather than the low rate, as with federal conversions). It is to follow this practice for 2016, so that the 2016 conversion rate is 20% (with some exceptions).

In any event, Quebec credits are more valuable than deductions for taxpayers in the lowest income bracket, (roughly) equivalent in the middle bracket, and less valuable at the top marginal rate.

Quebec annually indexes the personal amounts in (a) to (i), below. Indexing is based on the change in the Quebec consumer price index for the 12 months ending the preceding September 30th, with the indexed personal amount rounded to the nearest $5 (rounded up if equidistant between two $5 amounts). For tax indexing purposes, the cost of alcohol and tobacco products is removed from the Quebec consumer price index.

(QTA: 750.1–750.3)

[¶1649.01] *2016 Personal Amounts*

The following amounts, to the extent you are entitled to them, are converted to 2016 non-refundable tax credits at a conversion rate of 20%.

	2016 $
(a) Basic amount (line 350; see also ¶1106)	11,550
(b) Transfer of spouse's unused personal amount at line 431; see ¶1650.	
(c) Amount for person living alone, or with persons under 18, or with children 18 or over who were pursuing full-time post-secondary vocational or other studies (line 361 and Schedule B line 20)[1]	1,355
(d) Additional amount for single parent of a child 18 or over at the end of the year and either in full-time post-secondary studies or vocational studies at secondary level (line 361 and Schedule B line 21)[2]	1,675
(e) For each child (but not other dependant) who is not yet 18 years of age at the end of the year and is in full-time attendance in a secondary vocational training or a post-secondary level school, per semester (not exceeding two) (line 367 and Schedule A, Part A, line 7)[3]	2,130
(f) Other children and dependants, who are 18 years of age or older at the end of the taxation year and usually residing with the claimant, in respect of whom no deduction under (d) is made (line 367 and Schedule A, Part C, line 37). Note that parents, grandparents, aunts, and uncles as well as older, non-student children may qualify under this provision.	3,100
(g) Age amount[1]	2,485
(h) Physical or mental impairment amount	2,625
(i) Retirement income amount[1]	up to $2,210

[1] This amount is reduced by 15% of "family income" over $33,505.

[2] This amount is reduced by 1/12 for each month for which the parent received child assistance payments from the Régie des rentes du Quebec.

[3] Reduced by 80% of the child's income for the year net of scholarships, bursaries, fellowships, prizes for achievement, or, if applicable, the deduction for residents of a designated remote area.

[¶1649.02] *2015 Personal Amounts*

The following amounts, to the extent you are entitled to them, are converted to 2015 non-refundable tax credits at a conversion rate of 20%.

	2015 $
(a) Basic amount (line 350; see also ¶1106)	11,425
(b) Transfer of spouse's unused personal amount at line 431; see ¶1650.	
(c) Amount for person living alone, or with persons under 18, or with children 18 or over who were pursuing full-time post-secondary vocational or other studies (line 361 and Schedule B line 20)[1]	1,340
(d) Additional amount for single parent of a child 18 or over at the end of the year and either in full-time post-secondary studies or vocational studies at secondary level (line 361 and Schedule B line 21)[2]	1,655
(e) For each child (but not other dependant) who is not yet 18 years of age at the end of the year and is in full-time attendance in a secondary vocational training or a post-secondary level school, per semester (not exceeding two) (line 367 and Schedule A, Part A, line 7)[3]	2,105
(f) Other children and dependants, who are 18 years of age or older at the end of the taxation year and usually residing with the claimant, in respect of whom no deduction under (d) is made (line 367 and Schedule A, Part C, line 37). Note that parents, grandparents, aunts, and uncles as well as older, non-student children may qualify under this provision.	3,065
(g) Age amount[1]	2,460
(h) Physical or mental impairment amount	2,595
(i) Retirement income amount[1]	up to $2,185

[1] This amount is reduced by 15% of "family income" over $33,145.

[2] This amount is reduced by 1/12 for each month for which the parent received child assistance payments from the Régie des rentes du Quebec.

[3] Reduced by 80% of the child's income for the year net of scholarships, bursaries, fellowships, prizes for achievement, or, if applicable, the deduction for residents of a designated remote area.

[¶1649.03] *2014 Personal Amounts*

The following amounts, to the extent you are entitled to them, are converted to 2014 non-refundable tax credits at a conversion rate of 20%.

	2014 $
(a) Basic amount (line 350; see also ¶1106)	11,305
(b) Transfer of spouse's unused personal amount at line 431; see ¶1650.	
(c) Amount for person living alone, or with persons under 18, or with children 18 or over who were pursuing full-time post-secondary vocational or other studies (line 361 and Schedule B line 20)[1]	1,325
(d) Additional amount for single parent of a child 18 or over at the end of the year and either in full-time post-secondary studies or vocational studies at secondary level (line 361 and Schedule B line 21)[2]	1,640

(e) For each child (but not other dependant) who is not yet 18 years of age at the end of the year and is in full-time attendance in a secondary vocational training or a post-secondary level school, per semester (not exceeding two) (line 367 and Schedule A, Part A, line 7)[3] 2,085

(f) Other children and dependants, who are 18 years of age or older at the end of the taxation year and usually residing with the claimant, in respect of whom no deduction under (d) is made (line 367 and Schedule A, Part C, line 37). Note that parents, grandparents, aunts, and uncles as well as older, non-student children may qualify under this provision. 3,035

(g) Age amount[1] 2,435

(h) Physical or mental impairment amount 2,570

(i) Retirement income amount[1] .... up to $2,160

[1] This amount is reduced by 15% of "family income" over $32,795.

[2] This amount is reduced by 1/12 for each month for which the parent received child assistance payments from the Régie des rentes du Quebec.

[3] Reduced by 80% of the child's income for the year net of scholarships, bursaries, fellowships, prizes for achievement, or, if applicable, the deduction for residents of a designated remote area.

[¶1649.04] *2013 Personal Amounts*

The following amounts, to the extent you are entitled to them, are converted to 2013 non-refundable tax credits at a conversion rate of 20%.

2013
$

(a) Basic amount (line 350; see also ¶1106) 11,195

(b) Transfer of spouse's unused personal amount at line 431; see ¶1650.

(c) Amount for person living alone, or with persons under 18, or with children 18 or over who were pursuing full-time post-secondary vocational or other studies (line 361 and Schedule B line 20)[1] 1,310

(d) Additional amount for single parent of a child 18 or over at the end of the year and either in full-time post-secondary studies or vocational studies at secondary level (line 361 and Schedule B line 21)[2] 1,625

(e) For each child (but not other dependant) who is not yet 18 years of age at the end of the year and is in full-time attendance in a secondary vocational training or a post-secondary level school, per semester (not exceeding two) (line 367 and Schedule A, Part A, line 7)[3] 2,065

(f) Other children and dependants, who are 18 years of age or older at the end of the taxation year and usually residing with the claimant, in respect of whom no deduction under (d) is made (line 367 and Schedule A, Part C, line 37). Note that parents, grandparents, aunts, and uncles as well as older, non-student children may qualify under this provision. 3,005

2013
$

(g) Age amount[1] 2,410

(h) Physical or mental impairment amount 2,545

(i) Retirement income amount[1] .... up to $2,140

[1] This amount is reduced by 15% of "family income" over $32,795.

[2] This amount is reduced by 1/12 for each month for which the parent received child assistance payments from the Régie des rentes du Quebec.

[3] Reduced by 80% of the child's income for the year net of scholarships, bursaries, fellowships, prizes for achievement, or, if applicable, the deduction for residents of a designated remote area.

[¶1649.05] *2012 Personal Amounts*

The following amounts, to the extent you are entitled to them, are converted to 2012 non-refundable tax credits at a conversion rate of 20%.

2012
$

(a) Basic amount (line 350; see also ¶1106) 10,925

(b) Transfer of spouse's unused personal amount at line 431; see ¶1650.

(c) Amount for person living alone, or with persons under 18, or with children 18 or over who were pursuing full-time post-secondary vocational or other studies (line 361 and Schedule B line 20)[1] 1,280

(d) Additional amount for single parent of a child 18 or over at the end of the year and either in full-time post-secondary studies or vocational studies at secondary level (line 361 and Schedule B line 21)[2] 1,585

(e) For each child (but not other dependant) who is not yet 18 years of age at the end of the year and is in full-time attendance in a secondary vocational training or a post-secondary level school, per semester (not exceeding two) (line 367 and Schedule A, Part A, line 7)[3] 2,015

(f) Other children and dependants, who are 18 years of age or older at the end of the taxation year and usually residing with the claimant, in respect of whom no deduction under (d) is made (line 367 and Schedule A, Part C, line 37). Note that parents, grandparents, aunts, and uncles as well as older non-student children may qualify under this provision 2,930

(g) Age amount[1] 2,350

(h) Physical or mental impairment amount 2,485

(i) Retirement income amount[1] .... up to $2,090

[1] This amount is reduced by 15% of "family income" over $31,695.

[2] This amount is reduced by 1/12 for each month for which the parent received child assistance payments from the Régie des rentes du Quebec.

[3] Reduced by 80% of the child's income for the year net of scholarships, bursaries, fellowships, prizes for achievement, or, if applicable, the deduction for residents of a designated remote area.

[¶1649.32] *Basic Personal Amount*

The basic personal amount for 2016 is $11,550 ($11,425 for 2015, $11,305 for 2014, $11,195 for 2013, and $10,925 for 2012).

The amount is claimed on line 350 of the return.

(QTA: 750.2; 752.0.0.1)

[¶1649.40] *Person Living Alone or With Dependant*

There is a special amount (in (c), above) for a person living alone or with a child or dependant in a self-contained domestic establishment (as defined at ¶1122). To qualify, you must have lived in the self-contained domestic establishment throughout the entire year and no one other than one or more children, grandchildren, sisters, brothers, nieces or nephews of you or your spouse who are under 18 or, if older, in full-time attendance at a school or university, which qualifies them for an education amount reported in box A on a Quebec RL-8 slip, may have lived there at any time in the year. If you have a spouse who did not live with you at any time in the year and whom you did not support (except through support payments described in Chapter 23), this will not disqualify you.

You must support this claim with proof that you maintained a self-contained domestic establishment (school and municipal tax bills, RL-31, lease, home insurance policy, telephone and utility bills, etc.).

The amount of this credit, $1,355 for 2016 ($1,340 for 2015) is reduced by 15% of your "family income" in excess of $33,505 for 2016. This amount is indexed for the Quebec cost of living, under the same formula described for personal amounts.

- For 2015, the amount was $33,145.
- For 2014, the amount was $32,795.
- For 2013, the amount was $32,480.
- For 2012, the amount was $31,695.

Family income is the income from line 275 of the Quebec return. Technically it includes the income of both the taxpayer and his/her "eligible" spouse (¶1650.03); but since you must in general be single or separated for this particular credit to apply, that should not be relevant to this claim.

The credit is available to a taxpayer who lived in a self-contained domestic establishment in a year from January 1 to the date of death alone or with only qualified dependants. Once the deduction is made for family income the remaining credit may be spread among the various Quebec death returns that may be filed (see ¶1901).

Note that a supplemental amount (in (d), above) of $1,675 for 2016 ($1,655 for 2015) is available for eligible single-parent families.

The amount is calculated on Schedule B at part B and claimed on line 361 of the return.

(QTA: 750.2–750.3; 752.0.7.1–752.0.10.0.1)

[¶1649.55] *Post-Secondary and Vocational Studies 1: Children 17 and Under Throughout the Year*

In addition to the basic non-refundable credits for dependants, Quebec offers a personal amount of $2,130 for 2016 ($2,105 for 2015) for each dependent child for each completed term of post-secondary studies at an eligible educational institution, to a maximum of two terms per year ($4,260). The personal amount is converted to non-refundable tax credit at standard Quebec rates for the year. The dependant must be engaged in full-time studies, which is to say must have a course or required work load of at least nine hours a week. Students with "a major functional deficiency" (as defined in regulations under the Quebec *Act respecting financial assistance for educational expenses*), will be considered full-time students if enrolled in a recognized program involving at least 20 hours of instruction per month.

This Quebec education amount is reduced by 80% of the child's income specifically excluding scholarships, fellowships, and awards received in the year and deductible in calculating taxable income. In addition, the credit is not available to a child who has a spouse who claimed a transfer of any unused credits from the child.

The credit is available for each completed term (up to two):

- in an educational institution in Quebec designated by the Minister of Education in an authorized program of full-time studies in vocational training at the secondary level or full-time studies at the post-secondary level; or
- in an educational institution outside Quebec and designated by the Minister of Education in a course of study at the college or university level or an equivalent level.

It is essentially the responsibility of the school to know which courses are qualified and issue an RL-8 slip allowing the parent to make the claim. In general, colleges and universities outside Quebec which qualify for federal tuition tax credit should also qualify for this credit.

The amount is calculated on Schedule A at part A and claimed on line 367 of the return.

(QTA: 752.0.1(d)–752.0.4)

[¶1649.57] *Post-Secondary and Vocational Studies 2: Children 18 and Over During the Year*

There is a transfer system which is similar but not identical to the transfer of federal education amounts. The similarity is that the student can transfer (on the student's Schedule S) an amount in excess of the amount that would, more or less, reduce the student's income to nil. The difference is that the student cannot actually utilize the education amount for his or her own taxes; the student can only transfer the notional surplus.

The amount eligible for transfer is, in the first instance, the Quebec basic personal amount without the "complementary amount" component, even after those two amounts are rolled into one for most purposes. This amount is $7,610 for 2016 ($7,530 for 2015). It is available if the student has completed, in the calendar year, two semesters of qualified vocational or post-secondary education. If only one semester has been completed, the amount initially available for transfer is reduced by the education amount (¶1649.55) of $2,130 for 2016 ($2,105 for 2015), so the amount would be $5,480 for 2016 ($5,425 for 2015).

Schedule S, on which the transfer is calculated, simplifies this calculation by starting with $3,350 for 2016, which is the $7,610 basic amount, reduced by the education amount for two semesters ($4,260). To this the student adds the per semester amount ($2,130) for each semester of school attendance in the year.

As before, this amount must be adjusted in the year the child turns 18 to recognize months in which the parents were eligible for Quebec child assistance payments. In that year, the basic amount of $7,610 for 2016, net of the maximum credit ($4,260), or $3,350, is prorated by the number of months in the year following the month in which the child turns 18, divided by 12. In 2016, the calculation appears in the Guide description of line 367. Again, Revenu Québec stands the technical rule on its head and has you subtract the monthly amount

($3,350 / 12 = $279.16) for each month the child was less than 18, including the month in which the child turned 18.

The amount must also be reduced by five times the amount of the Solidarity Tax Credit received by the student during the taxation year.

Finally, the amount eligible for transfer is reduced by 80% of the student's Quebec taxable income. The amount remaining (if any) may be transferred to either the student's mother or father, as the student designates.

For these purposes, a mother or father means the person with whom the taxpayer is related by "filiation"; the person who is the spouse of the taxpayer's father or mother; the person who is the father or mother of the taxpayer's spouse; or the person on whom the taxpayer depends to provide for his or her support and who has the custody and control of the individual, in law or in fact, or had such custody and control immediately before the taxpayer attained the age of 19, including a person who has already satisfied these conditions.

A parent who receives a transfer under these rules cannot also claim, for the same child, the credit for other dependants 18 years of age or older (¶1649.59).

A student whose parent deducts an education amount transferred from the student will not be eligible for the refundable work premium credits (¶1677f).

Any amount paid to a student in respect of the solidarity tax credit (¶1681) must be taken into account to determine the amount the student may transfer to his or her parent in respect of the recognized parental contribution.

Note that the first child amount of $1,675 for 2016 ($1,655 for 2015) for a single parent remains available to the transferee of a student education amount.

A student may not transfer to his or her spouse any amount designated to a parent under these rules.

The transfer requires the student to have an RL-8 slip. Qualifying Quebec post-secondary institutions should issue this automatically. For students at non-Quebec institutions unfamiliar with this system, the student must obtain an RL-8 from Revenu Québec and have it completed by the registrar of the institution.

The amount of the transfer is calculated on the student's Schedule S. The result is entered on the parent's Schedule A at part B. The amount is claimed on line 367 of the parent's return.

(QTA: 776.41.12–776.41.20; Other Publications: May 24, 2007 Quebec Budget, *Additional Information on the Budgetary Measures*, Revenue Measures, Section A, Appendix, 1.2.2; 2010 Quebec Budget, *Additional Information on the Budgetary Measures, Revenue Measures*, item 1.2.6; Quebec Finance Information Bulletin 2010-8, *Changes to various fiscal measures, item 1.5*)

[¶1649.59] *Other Dependants*

Quebec uses the term "other dependants" to refer to any person (other than a spouse) related to the claimant by blood, marriage, or adoption or to the claimant's common-law spouse by blood or adoption. In general this group includes those who would be dependent children in the definition above but for age or school attendance, as well as parents, grandparents, aunts, uncles, nephews, nieces, brothers, or sisters of the claimant or the claimant's legal spouse.

The amount you can claim (on Part C of Schedule A) for 2016 is $3,100 ($3,065 for 2015) for each "other dependant", reduced by 80% of his or her income excluding scholarships, fellowships, and awards received in the year and deductible in calculating taxable income.

This amount must also be adjusted in the year the child turns 18 by subtracting $258.33 for each month the dependant was less than 18, including the month in which the child turned 18. This calculation appears in the Guide description of line 367.

The amount is calculated on Schedule A at part C and claimed on line 367 of the return.

[¶1649.60] *Impairment Amount*

There is a personal amount for persons with a severe and prolonged impairment of physical or mental function. Essentially, this is the Quebec equivalent to the federal amount discussed at ¶1255, and its terms are virtually identical. One point on which Quebec purports to differ is the criterion that you are entitled to the disability amount if you (or the disabled person) must devote at least 14 hours per week to prescribed therapy essential to maintaining vital functions. Quebec counts post-treatment recovery time in the 14 hours, which it says the federal government does not.

The unused portion of this credit is transferable to a spouse. However, the amount is not transferable to other relatives, as it was for earlier years. The transfer has been replaced with a refundable caregiver credit discussed at ¶1679a.

The impairment amount of $2,625 for 2016 must be reduced if another person received the supplement for handicapped children with regard to you. This supplement is included in the child assistance payment from the Régie des rentes du Quebec. For each such month the $2,625 impairment amount is reduced by one-twelfth (for 2016, $218.75/month).

The impairment amount, indexed annually, was $2,595 for 2015, $2,570 for 2014, $2,545 for 2013, and $2,485 for 2012.

Enclose form TP-752.0.14-V with your return if you are claiming this amount for the first time. You may also send a copy of federal form T2201, *Disability Tax Credit Certificate*. However, form TP-752.0.14-V must be used if the taxpayer is required to provide a certificate confirming that the impairment is considered severe because of the time spent undergoing therapy that is essential to sustain a vital function.

The amount is claimed on line 376 of the return.

(QTA: 752.0.14–752.0.18; Other Publications: 2001 Quebec Budget, *Additional Information on the Budgetary Measures*, item 1.6; April 21, 2005 Quebec Budget, *Additional Information on the Budgetary Measures*, item 1.2)

[¶1649.70] *Age Amount*

Commencing in 2016, the age at which you become entitled to receive the age amount will increase to 66 years (prior to 2016 the age requirement was 65 years). The age requirement will increase by one year each year thereafter until it reaches age 70 in 2020. Hence, the age requirement will be 67 in 2017, 68 in 2018, 69 in 2019, and 70 in 2020 and subsequent years.

The age amount is calculated in Part B of Schedule B. If you turned 66 or older in 2016, you enter $2,485 and, if your spouse turned 66 or older in the year, you enter another $2,485 for that person.

The age amount is indexed annually. For 2015, the amount was $2,460; for 2014, the amount was $2,435; for 2013, the amount was $2,410; for 2012, the amount was $2,350. You deduct from the total (and from the other claims on Part B of Schedule B) 15% of net family income in excess of $33,505 for 2016 ($33,145 for 2015, $32,795 for 2014, $32,480 for 2013, and $31,695 for 2012), and you then deduct the claim your spouse makes on his or her own behalf, a step which of course prevents you and your spouse both from claiming the same amount.

Family income for this purpose is simply the income of both you and your "eligible" spouse as calculated on line 275 of the return each of you files or would file if required. Your eligible spouse for Quebec purposes (also referred to by Revenu Quebec as "your spouse as of December 31") is discussed at ¶1650.03.

Revenu Québec presumes that if you are 65 or older, you are receiving Canadian Old Age Security (OAS) Pension, and will look for it on your return. If for some reason you are not receiving OAS, you must send Revenu Québec an explanation and confirmation from Human Resources Development Canada or a Canadian entry visa which accounts on its face for the absence of OAS (because you have not resided in Canada long enough to claim it). Failure to provide these documents will result in the OAS being automatically added to your income.

The amount is calculated on Schedule B at part B and claimed on line 361 of the return.

(QTA: 750.2–750.3; 752.0.7.1–752.0.7.10.0.1; Other Publications: Quebec Guide information for line 361; 2015 Quebec Budget, *Additional Information*, item 1.4; March 13, 2008 Quebec Budget, *Additional Information on the Budgetary Measures*, Revenue Measures, item 1.2; 2015 Quebec Budget, *Additional Information*, item 1.4)

[¶1649.75] *Retirement Income Amount*

You may claim a non-refundable credit on Quebec returns for up to $2,210 of pension income for 2016. This is essentially the same pension income which qualifies for federal pension income credit purposes at line 314 of your federal return (¶1311). That is, Quebec follows the same rules in determining eligible pension income. In 2015 the limit was $2,185, in 2014 the limit was $2,160, in 2013 the limit was $2,140, and in 2012 the limit was $2,090. The amount is indexed annually. (The federal limit on pension income eligible for credit, is $2,000.)

You may also claim your spouse's eligible pension income amount. The offsetting deduction at line 33 of Schedule B ensures that you and your spouse cannot both claim the same amounts.

Unlike the federal pension income amount eligible for credit, the Quebec amount is subject to a "grind" where your family income exceeds $33,505 for 2016 ($33,145 for 2015). (The family income threshold for earlier years is the same as that in ¶1649.70, above.) That is, you deduct $33,505 from family income (on line 14 of Schedule B) and multiply the result (if more than nil) by 15%; this amount reduces the retirement income amount after applying the $2,210 maximum limitation. Family income for this purpose is simply the income of both you and your "eligible" spouse as calculated on line 275 of the return each of you files or would file if required. Your eligible spouse for Quebec purposes (also referred to by Revenu Quebec as "your spouse as of December 31") is discussed at ¶1650.03.

The amount is calculated on Schedule B at part B and claimed on line 361 of the return.

(QTA: 750.2–750.3; 752.0.7.1–752.0.10.0.1; Other Publications: March 13, 2008 Quebec Budget, *Additional Information on the Budgetary Measures*, Revenue Measures, item 1.2)

[¶1649.80] *Other Differences from Federal Rules*

In addition, the Quebec rules differ in the following significant respects from the federal rules on personal amounts:

- Charitable donations: Generally speaking, Quebec follows federal rules for calculating charitable donation credit, although Quebec allowances for capital gain and recapture on gifts of capital property are more restrictive than federal rules. As well, most gifts eligible for federal credit will be eligible for Quebec credit. That said, Quebec has a number of unique rules on gifts eligible for credit. Quebec charitable donation rules are discussed in detail at ¶1657.
- Quebec has a somewhat different system of computing the limitations on credit for medical expenses; see ¶1652.
- There is no Quebec equivalent to the federal eligible dependant exemption (formerly the "equivalent-to-married" exemption) at ¶1120.
- Quebec allows a non-refundable credit based on the amount levied on business and investment income as a Health Services Fund "contribution" (¶1663).
- Quebec has no family tax cut credit.

(QTA: 752.0.1–752.0.22)

[¶1649d] INCOME REPLACEMENT INDEMNITIES

Quebec by and large excludes from income the same items as those excluded by the federal government under the federal rules at ¶991. Traditionally these non-income items have included such things as income replacement indemnities paid by the Commission des normes, de l'équité, de la santé et de la sécurité du travail following an industrial accident or an occupational disease, and the income replacement indemnities paid by the Société de l'assurance automobile du Quebec following an accident caused by an automobile.

[¶1649d.05] *Indemnity Payments Subject to Quebec Adjustments*

The payments subject to the rules below are income replacement indemnities paid or determined under the following Acts:

- *the Act respecting industrial accidents and occupational diseases*, the *Workers' Compensation Act*, the *Act respecting indemnities for victims of asbestosis and silicosis in mines and quarries*, or a similar law of Canada or another province respecting industrial accidents, in the wake of injury, disability or death;
- the *Act respecting occupational health and safety*;
- the *Automobile Insurance Act* or a similar law of another province;
- the *Crime Victims Compensation Act* or a similar law of another province;
- the *Act to promote good citizenship*.

[¶1649d.15] *Adjustment to Quebec Basic Personal Amount*

An individual who is resident in Quebec at the end of a given taxation year, and who received during the year an indemnity listed above, will have to make an adjustment to the Quebec basic personal amount used in calculating non-refundable personal amount credits for the year.

The actual reduction to personal amounts appears on line 358 of the Quebec return. Where the indemnities have been provided by specified Quebec authorities (the Commission des normes, de l'équité, de la santé et de la sécurité du travail (CNESST) or the Société de l'assurance automobile du Quebec (SAAQ)), those authorities have performed the necessary calculations and simply report the reduction in box M of the RL-5 slip. If the indemnities come from a non-Quebec source, there is a calculation provided on form TP-752.0.0.6-V. In its Bulletin 2010-6 dated June 2010, the Quebec Ministry of Finance announced changes to the already complex formula used to determine the reduction. Those seeking to anticipate or verify the reduction calculation must consult that document.

(QTA: 752.0.0.3–752.0.0.6; Other Publications: 2004 Quebec Budget, *Additional Information on the Budgetary Matters*, item 1.11; Quebec Finance Information Bulletin 2004-9; Quebec Finance Information Bulletin 2010-6, June 29, 2010, item 1.4)

[¶1650] TRANSFER OF PERSONAL AMOUNTS FROM SPOUSE OR COMMON-LAW PARTNER

Virtually all personal amounts, and several other non-refundable credits (political contribution credit, dividend tax credit, and certain specified investment credits such as the labour-sponsored fund contribution credit) are accumulated for each spouse and, to the extent the total for one spouse exceeds that spouse's tax payable, the remainder (except for amounts attributable to the deduction for Quebec alternative minimum tax (AMT) carried forward) is transferable to the other spouse. The transfer as a practical matter arises if you have a negative amount at line 430, which can be transferred to your spouse's return at the highlighted line 431.

[¶1650.03] *Quebec Definition of Spouse and Eligible Spouse*

Quebec uses the term "spouse" in the same sense that the federal government uses the term "spouse or common-law partner" (¶1113 and ¶1603). Your spouse is your legal spouse or your common-law partner, essentially as the term common-law partner is determined for federal purposes. It is this broadened definition of spouse that is used throughout the discussion of "eligible spouse" below.

For purpose of the transfer of Quebec credits between spouses, an individual's "eligible spouse" for a given taxation year refers to any of the following persons:

- the person who is the individual's spouse at the end of the year and who, at that time, is not living apart from the individual;
- in the case of an individual who does not have a spouse at the end of the year, the last person to be the individual's spouse during the year, where that person dies during the year and, at the time of his or her death, is the individual's spouse and is not living apart from the individual;
- in the case of an individual who dies during the year, the person who is his or her spouse at the time of the individual's death, unless that person is living apart from the individual at the time or is the spouse of another individual at the end of the year or, where that person dies in the year, at the time of his or her death;
- in the case of an individual who dies during the year and who does not have a spouse at the time of his or her death, the last person to be the individual's spouse during the year, where that person dies during the year and, at the time of his or her death, is the individual's spouse and is not living apart from the individual.

A person will be considered to be living apart from an individual at a given time in a taxation year only if he or she is living apart from the individual at that time because of the breakdown of their union and if the separation lasts for a period of at least 90 days that includes that time.

The upshot of all this is that the Quebec definition of eligible spouse is essentially the same as the federal definition of cohabiting spouse for child tax credit purposes (¶1498.10).

In addition, the spousal transfer mechanism has finally obliged Quebec to address the issue that the definition of "spouse" (federally, spouse or common-law partner) for tax legislation purposes permits an individual to have two spouses at the same time, since "spouse" refers to both legally married and common-law spouses. For purposes of the transfer mechanism at least, an individual is presumed to have only one eligible spouse for a given taxation year, and to be the eligible spouse of that person alone for that year. Should more than one individual take advantage of the transfer mechanism regarding the same person for a given taxation year, the Minister of Revenue has the authority to designate which of the individuals is the person's eligible spouse.

(QTA: 776.41.1–776.41.4)

[¶1650.05] *Uses of the Definition of "Eligible Spouse"*

The concept of "eligible spouse" above will, in addition to applying for purposes of the transfer of tax credits from one spouse to the other, also be used to determine family income in applying the following Quebec provisions:

- the tax credits for a person living alone, with respect to age and for retirement income (Schedule B);
- the tax credits for medical expenses (Schedule B);
- the independent living tax credit for seniors (Schedule B);
- the tax credit for child care expenses (Schedule C);
- the solidarity tax credit (Schedule D);
- the additional subsidized childcare contribution (Schedule I);
- the tax credit for home-support services for seniors (Schedule J);
- the tax credit for respite of caregivers (Schedule O);
- the tax credits respecting the work premium (Schedule P);
- the tax shield credit (line 460).

The definition will also apply to the calculation of the premium payable under the Quebec prescription drug insurance plan.

[¶1650.10] *Order of Application of Non-Refundable Credits*

Individuals will be able to claim the deduction for the transfer of non-refundable credits from one spouse to the other once all other non-refundable credits, excepting the deduction for AMT carried forward, have been taken into account in the calculation of their income tax otherwise payable. This applies to both the general rule above and the special cases below.

[¶1650.15] *Spouse's Personal Amounts on Death*

The portion of credits unused by a spouse deceased during the year (to the extent not attributable to the deduction for alternative minimum tax (AMT) carried forward) on the deceased spouse's principal (year of death) return only can be used on the surviving spouse's return for the year.

Similarly, excess non-refundable tax credits of the surviving spouse may be claimed only on the principal (year of death) return of the deceased spouse.

[¶1650.20] *Individuals Residing Outside Canada Throughout the Year*

Individuals who do not reside in Canada at any time during a taxation year and who, during that year or a previous taxation year, are, among other things, employed in Quebec or carry on a business there, will be able to claim the deduction respecting the transfer of non-refundable tax credits from one spouse to the other, provided all or almost all of their income for the year is included in the calculation of their taxable income earned in Canada for that year.

Individuals who meet the all or substantially all test condition will be able to deduct, in the calculation of their income tax otherwise payable for the year, the portion of the deduction respecting the transfer of non-refundable tax credits from one spouse to the other, as represented by the ratio (to a maximum of 1) of income earned in Quebec to income earned in Canada for the year.

[¶1650.25] *Individuals Who Reside in Canada for Part of a Year*

The following rules will determine the transfer amount for individuals who reside in Canada for only part of a taxation year:

- For any period throughout which an individual resides in Canada during a year, the individual may claim an amount equal to the portion of the non-refundable tax credits (other than that attributable to the deduction for AMT carried forward) which cannot be used to reduce the income tax otherwise payable by the individual's eligible spouse for the year, prorated by the number of days in the period over the number of days in the year.
- For a period in the year during which the individual resides outside Canada, the deductible amount must be calculated as if the period represented an entire taxation year.

However, the amount that the individual may deduct for the year cannot exceed the amount that would be deductible in this regard were the individual to reside in Canada throughout the year.

[¶1650.30] *Individuals Residing in Canada Who Allocate Income between Quebec and other Canadian Jurisdictions*

Individuals who reside in Quebec and who carry on a business in Canada, outside Quebec, as well as those who reside in Canada, outside Quebec, and who carry on a business in Quebec, must allocate income to determine tax payable, as discussed at ¶1440.

For the purpose of calculating the transfer of non-refundable tax credits from one spouse to the other, such individuals must apply to the portion of the non-refundable tax credits (other than that attributable to the deduction for AMT carried forward) which cannot be used to reduce the income tax otherwise payable by their eligible spouse for a given taxation year, the same ratio used to determine their income tax payable for the year.

[¶1650.35] *Individuals Who Go Bankrupt During a Year*

Individuals who go bankrupt during a calendar year are deemed to have two taxation years during that calendar year: the first one extending from January 1 to the day before the bankruptcy, and the second from the day of the bankruptcy to December 31 (compare essentially the same federal rule at ¶286).

For purposes of the transfer of non-refundable tax credits from one spouse to the other, individuals whose eligible spouse goes bankrupt during a calendar year will be able to take into account all of the portion of the non-refundable tax credits (other than that attributable to the deduction for AMT carried forward) which cannot be used to reduce the income tax otherwise payable by their spouse for each of the taxation years included in the calendar year.

Individuals who go bankrupt during a calendar year will be able to claim the deduction respecting the transfer of non-refundable tax credits from one spouse to the other only in the calculation of their income tax otherwise payable for the taxation year beginning on the day of their bankruptcy.

[¶1650.40] *Alternative Minimum Tax*

The alternative minimum tax applicable to an individual for a taxation year is equal to the difference between an amount representing 16% of the portion of his or her adjusted taxable income in excess of $40,000, and his or her basic minimum tax deduction (see ¶1698).

In general, the basic minimum tax deduction takes into account all personal tax credits other than the transfer of the unused portion of the tax credit for a spouse's impairment.

The deduction for transfer of non-refundable tax credits from one spouse to the other will not be taken into account in the calculation of the basic minimum tax deduction.

Alternative minimum tax is calculated on Form TP-776.42-V and entered on line 15 of Schedule E.

[¶1650d] CPP, QPP, EI, AND PARENTAL INSURANCE PLAN CREDITS

Unlike the federal rules, Quebec does not allow any non-refundable tax credit for CPP/QPP premiums. However, as with the federal rules, 50% of CPP/QPP premiums in respect of self-employment earnings and the net retribution for family-type resources (essentially the self-employment component of the premiums) qualifies for a deduction from income (see ¶798 and ¶1305). (The federal government in fact adopted this policy from Quebec.)

The half share that is deductible from Quebec income (on line 248 of the Quebec return) will also be deductible in determining the Health Services Fund contribution (¶1663). In fact, the deduction will reduce income for virtually all measurement purposes.

There is also a deduction at line 248 for certain QPIP premiums on self-employed income. This deduction requires a calculation on Schedule R. It is not available in respect of various forms of income eligible for offsetting deductions from taxable income, such as treaty exempt income, various forms of foreign specialist income, and the like.

(QTA: 339(*i.1*), (*j*); 752.0.0.1)

[¶1650d.10] *Quebec Parental Insurance Plan (QPIP)*

Quebec provides a parental insurance plan (QPIP) under which eligible workers are entitled to benefits when they take maternity, paternity, adoption or parental leave. In effect, Quebec controls the collection of premiums and provides its own benefit rules for a program previously administered by the federal government under the Employment Insurance (EI) program. The concept is similar to the CPP/QPP relationship, under which Quebec credits and benefits are supposed to be interchangeable with federal benefits as workers move back and forth between federal and provincial plans, and benefits are harmonized, at least up to a minimum standard. The federal contribution to this program takes the form of reduced federal EI contributions for employees and employers subject to the Quebec plan.

QPIP is, like EI, funded by employer and employee (and self-employment) contributions. Employee contributions are personal amounts eligible for Quebec (and federal) personal amount credit. Employer contributions are deductible from income. Employees who can deduct the salary of a substitute or assistant can similarly deduct contributions paid on behalf of that person.

As with CPP/QPP, self-employed workers may pay both employee and employer premiums. The employer's portion is deductible from income for both income tax and Health Services Fund purposes.

Benefits are taxable, both by Canada and Quebec.

QPIP contributions are generally part of the Quebec withholding system and are simply reported to employees. The self-employed, and employees who work outside Quebec but are resident in Quebec at December 31, must calculate QPIP contributions on Schedule R.

The federal government refers to QPIP as PPIP (Provincial Parental Insurance Plan), presumably to indicate that any province might strike such a deal. Federal treatment of PPIP contributions is discussed at ¶1307.

(Other Publications: April 21, 2005 Quebec Budget, *Additional Information on the Budgetary Measures, Revenue Measures,* item 1.5; (Federal) Department of Finance News Release 2005-050, July 19, 2005)

[¶1651] UNION OR PROFESSIONAL DUES

Neither employees nor the self-employed are permitted to deduct professional dues, union dues or dues to maintain a membership in an artistic organization. Rather, the amounts paid are converted to a non-refundable tax credit at the rate of 10% (20% for taxation years prior to 2015). However, the portion of professional dues relating to professional liability insurance will continue to be allowed as a deduction. Similarly, professional or artistic dues that are in effect levied under a retirement plan, plan for annuities, insurance or similar benefits, or any other purpose not related to the ordinary operating expenses of the professional or artistic organization are deductible. Quebec sales tax on the deductible element of dues is also deductible, although presumably it may be offset by input tax credits if the tax is recovered.

Professional dues are those necessary to maintain a professional status recognized by statute (including dues required from home child care providers for representation by a recognized association); artistic organization dues are those necessary to maintain membership in an artists' association recognized by the Quebec Minister of Culture and Communications.

Where a partnership pays the dues, they are allocated to members who are partners at the end of the partnership fiscal period. Corporate partners may deduct their share and individuals may claim credit on their share in computing income or tax for the taxation year in which the fiscal period ends. If a partnership is a member of another partnership at the end of a fiscal period, dues flow through to that partnership and are in turn allocated at the end of its fiscal period.

Dues borne by an employer will be a taxable benefit for the employee regardless of whether the employer pays the dues or reimburses the employee, but the employee can then claim the credit for the benefit.

Generally speaking, GST/QST on dues is not eligible for credit, the assumption being that the professional can obtain input tax credit to recover the tax, whether self-employed or an employee. Where an employee's dues are paid or refunded by the employer and a taxable benefit is imputed which includes QST/GST on the dues, and the employee cannot recover the tax through the input tax credit system, the tax will be eligible for the professional dues tax credit.

If the income against which the dues would normally be deducted is in effect exempt because it is subject to offsetting deductions in computing taxable income, no tax credit is permitted.

The credit is claimed at line 397 of the return (line 373 for taxation years prior to 2015).

(QTA: 134.1–134.3; 752.0.18.3–752.0.18.9; Other Publications: Quebec Finance Information Bulletin 2000-4, June 29, 2000, item 1.4; Quebec Finance Information Bulletin 2014-11, item 2.5)

[¶1652] MEDICAL EXPENSES

By and large, medical expenses which are eligible for federal medical expense credit are also eligible for Quebec credit. However, there are some (usually minor) differences of detail and interpretation. Qualifying expenses are discussed in further detail below. Quebec's basic reduction to medical expenses, however, can be significantly higher than the federal reduction.

[¶1652.05] *Quebec Reduction*

Medical expenses eligible for Quebec credit must be reduced (on Schedule B) by 3% of family income. Family income is the income of yourself and, if any, of your spouse. Essentially, this means income from line 275 of your Quebec return and that of your spouse, or what would be the income as calculated for Quebec purposes of each of you if you were both obliged to file a return. Your spouse's income need not be included provided the spouse was not living with you on December 31 of the taxation year due to a breakdown of the relationship that lasted for a period of at least 90 days.

Note that for Quebec purposes there is no maximum amount which will limit the grind of eligible medical expenses by 3% of family income.

Quebec's version of the refundable medical expense supplement is reduced by 5% of family income in excess of \$22,560 for 2016 (\$22,315 for 2015), as compared to the federal amount (see ¶1678).

The amount is calculated on Schedule B at part C and claimed on line 381 of the return.

[¶1652.10] *Eligible Medical Expenses*

As with federal rules, eligible medical expenses include those of a spouse and those of a child. However, Quebec rules differ when it comes to other dependants. For Quebec purposes, you may claim medical expenses for any person for whom you or your spouse paid the expenses and who (i) was dependent on you for support and either (ii) ordinarily lived with you or (iii) was dependent on you by reason of infirmity.

In the case of an infirm dependent (other than the child or grandchild of you or your spouse) not living with you, the person must have been resident at some time in the year. The dependants (in addition to your children) who qualify under this rule appear to be identical to those for whom you can claim the federal credit at ¶1126, or could claim it if the dependant were 18 or over. Quebec imposes no age limit on this claim, and there is no equivalent of the federal restriction to $10,000 of expense per dependant.

Quebec generally follows the federal rules in ¶1205 (¶1235 with respect to the $2,237 limitation) with respect to the nature of eligible medical expenses and accumulating medical expenses for any 12-month period ending in the year. No medical expense, of course, can be claimed more than once for each jurisdiction. Quebec does require you to reduce total medical expenses by 3% of net family income, as contrasted with the federal system where you use 3% of your own net income only.

Note that the medical expenses already considered in the calculation of another refundable or non-refundable credit (e.g., the credit for home-support services for seniors, the credit for the cost of equipment purchased or leased by seniors to help maintain their autonomy) cannot be used also as medical expenses.

(QTA: 752.0.11–752.0.13.0.1; CRA Document No.: Régime D'assurance Médicaments du Québec, *April 27, 1998,* CRA Document No. 9804307; Régime général d'assurance — Médicaments du Québec, *March 19, 1998,* CRA Document No. 9719165; Other Publications: 1999 Quebec Guide for line 381; 2000 Quebec Budget, *Additional Information, Revenue Measures,* item 4.2)

[¶1652.15] *Medical Expenses Denied by Quebec*

Expenses incurred for purely cosmetic purposes will not be considered eligible for medical expense credit. Examples of cosmetic services subject to this disallowance include liposuction, facelifts, botox injections, and teeth whitening. The transportation, travel or accommodation expenses for such services will similarly be disallowed.

Similarly, expenses incurred for eyeglass frames are limited to $200 per person for whom you claim medical expenses. The $200 limit will apply for each person for each period (typically each 12-month period ending in the year) for which medical expenses are claimed.

Specified infertility treatments are eligible for the tax credit at ¶1684c and not for the medical expense credit discussed here.

(QTA: 752.0.11.3–752.0.12.1; Other Publications: April 21, 2005 Quebec Budget, *Additional Information on the Budgetary Measures,* item 1.4.1)

[¶1652.17] *Interplay of Medical Expense Credit and Home Support Credit*

See the discussion under the subheading "Medical Expense Credit" in ¶1679d.

[¶1652.20] *Medical Expenses Specifically Allowed by Quebec*

There are some expenses not currently allowed by the federal government which Quebec will recognize.

Quebec includes in its definition plans which afford moderate coverage of expenses not eligible for medical expense credit so long as the main purpose of the plan is to cover eligible expenses. The fact that a private plan continued to provide for this would not automatically disqualify its premiums as a medical expense. Since the federal definition of eligible medical services may be broader than that in Quebec, it may be that in practice private health services plans will be the same under both sets of rules. However, so long as the definition differs for federal and Quebec purposes, the possibility exists that a plan will qualify for one jurisdiction but not the other.

Amounts paid for hyperbaric (high pressure) oxygen therapy will be eligible medical expenses if the therapy is provided to an individual with a severe and prolonged neurological disorder as certified for purposes of the (Quebec) disability credit. It is not clear that the federal government would deny the expense as eligible in these circumstances; the matter may arise in respect of a purely Quebec ruling on the issue.

Quebec has revised its own criteria as to who is a medical practitioner. Since the federal government generally relies on provincial criteria, this should not open up a difference between federal and Quebec standards, although the same services offered in other provinces may not qualify for federal purposes. Generally speaking, it is where the services are provided that determines whose rules apply for both federal and Quebec purposes.

Quebec's revised definition includes a person whose profession is one in which virtually all services provided are eligible health-related care and treatment. Qualified practitioners under this rule include: acupuncturist, audiologist, chiropractor, dental hygienist, dentist, dietitian, midwife, nurse, occupational therapist, optometrist, physician, physiotherapist, podiatrist, respiratory therapist or speech therapist. For certain practitioners, only certain services provided are eligible, and their services only qualify to the extent they are eligible. Such limited practitioners include:

- the profession of psychologist, in regard to therapy and rehabilitation services;
- the profession of social worker, in regard to psychotherapy and rehabilitation services for accident victims and people suffering from illness or a handicap;
- the profession of guidance counsellor or psychoeducator, in regard to psychotherapy services, where the person carrying on the profession is a psychotherapist duly certified by the Ordre des conseillers et conseillères d'orientation et des psychoéducateurs et psychoéducatrices du Quebec;
- the profession of marital and family therapist, in regard to therapy services.

Finally, Quebec will recognize certain practitioners under a separate heading of the definition. These will include:

- the profession of homeopath, naturopath, osteopath and physiotherapist;
- the profession of psychoanalyst, in regard to therapy services;
- the profession of psychotherapist, in regard to therapy and rehabilitation services;
- the profession of sexologist, in regard to therapy services.

(Other Publications: April 21, 2005 Quebec Budget, *Additional Information on the Budgetary Measures,* item 1.4.1)

[¶1652.25] *Travel and Moving Expenses Allowed as Medical Expenses by Quebec (line 378)*

Since Quebec matches federal rules on eligible medical expenses, it provides that travel expenses are allowable medical expenses if travel of at least 80 kilometres from the patient's home locality is required; travel expenses can include lodging if it is essential rather than merely convenient; see ¶1205. Quebec also offers an alternative tax credit claim for travel and lodging expenses for an individual (and accompanying person if the individual is a minor or unable to travel unassisted) who must travel 200 kilometres or more (250 km before July 1, 2016) from home to obtain medical care *in Quebec* which is unavailable at a closer location. A medical certificate (form TP-752.0.13.1-V) is required to show that the specialized care is not otherwise available in Quebec and, if applicable, that the patient cannot travel alone. This claim cannot be made if the expense is otherwise claimed under general medical expense rules or the travel allowances for residents of remote locations rules; the latter claim may be preferable if available. The advantage of this claim is that it is not subject to the 3% of family income reduction.

Quebec also offers a special tax credit claim for moving expenses for an individual who moves to another residence if the new residence is within 80 kilometres of a health establishment in Quebec which offers medical care which was not available in Quebec within 200 kilometres (250 km as of July 1, 2016) of the old residence. Again, this claim is not subject to the 3% of family income reduction. Eligible moving expenses are those for which a deduction would be allowed under ¶1041 if the taxpayer met the criteria for claiming a deduction for moving expenses. If you meet the criteria for both the medical expense moving credit and the ordinary moving expense deduction, you may choose whichever produces the most favourable tax result.

The minimum distance standard has been reduced from 250 km to 200 km with respect to travel, lodging, and moving expenses that are incurred after July 1, 2016, as per Quebec Finance Information Bulletin 2016-7, Changes to Various Measures of a Fiscal Nature.

Since these expenses are not subject to the 3% grind, they are reported on line 378 rather than with other medical expenses on line 381.

(QTA: 752.0.13.1–752.0.13.3; Other Publications: Quebec Information Bulletin 2016-7, *Changes to Various Measures of a Fiscal Nature*, item 1)

[¶1653] TUITION FEES

Tuition fees must exceed $100 per educational institution to be eligible for the federal credit (¶1321). Tuition fees must exceed $100 as a total to be eligible for a Quebec non-refundable tax credit. Eligible fees are essentially those eligible for federal tuition credit at ¶1327, except that Quebec also permits inclusion of professional examination fees charged separately by a recognized profession under the Quebec *Professional Code*. As well, Quebec ensures that fees paid to an eligible institution in connection with financial assistance will be qualified ancillary fees even if the assistance is not itself taxable. The issue appears to arise because Quebec offers a broader category of non-taxable assistance than does the federal government (see ¶1629).

Fees paid by an employer of the student or the student's parents are typically included in income of the student or parents; they are eligible for the student's credit to the extent they have been included in income of the student or parents.

Quebec's transfer system is very similar to the federal system, in that the student must use applicable tuition credits for the year to reduce the student's Quebec tax to zero, and any current-year balance unused may, to the extent the student chooses, be transferred to one (but only one) parent or grandparent the student designates. In reviewing the required ordering of credits to be applied to a student's tax (see ¶1659), the tuition credit thus comes well down the list of credits the student is likely to have, thus maximizing the remainder to be transferred.

To the extent the student's tuition credit is greater than the student's Quebec tax payable, the unused credit amount not transferred to a spouse, parent, or grandparent is carried forward to future years. The student has complete discretion to forgo making the claim in any particular year and make it instead in any subsequent year. This is more flexible than the federal rule, which requires carryforward to be used as soon as tax is available to absorb it. The only restrictions are that you cannot, of course, claim a carryforward twice, and that you cannot apply a credit in Quebec for tuition claimed in a prior year on federal returns at a time when you were not liable to Quebec tax. That is, if you were resident in, say, New Brunswick in Year 1 and Quebec in Year 2, you cannot claim for Quebec purposes in Year 2 tuition paid in Year 1 and claimed on Year 1 federal returns by you, your parent or spouse. However, it seems to follow that to the extent you have unused federal carryforward arising outside Quebec and you move to Quebec or carry on business in Quebec, you can claim the carryforward against Quebec tax. Note that the Quebec tuition credit comes much later in the required ordering of credits than its federal counterpart, so that carryover amounts for Quebec may well differ from federal amounts even if tuition and income are the same; see ¶1659.

In 2013 the rate applicable to the conversion of tuition fees and examination fees into a tax credit was changed from 20% to 8% unless such fees were paid for 2013 and were:

- tuition fees paid to a university or college, or a post-secondary institution for a study session the individual started before March 28, 2013; or
- tuition fees paid to an educational institution recognized by the Minister of Revenue for training, other than training that is part of an institutional program at the post-secondary school level, in which the individual enrolled no later than March 28, 2013; or
- examination fees paid for an examination the individual took before May 1, 2013; or
- unused fees paid for prior years (1997 to 2012).

The tuition fees and examination fees to which the 8% rate will apply will be, when carried forward to a subsequent year, converted into a tax credit at the rate of 8%. The 20% rate will continue to apply to the conversion into a tax credit of tuition fees and examination fees carried forward to a subsequent taxation year provided such fees were paid for a taxation year prior to the 2013 taxation year, or if they were paid for the 2013 taxation year and the 20% rate applied to such fees.

To make matters easier for individuals who elect to carry forward to a subsequent year all or part of their tuition fees or examination fees paid for a given taxation year, Revenu Quebec will indicate, on the notice of assessment or of reassessment sent to them for a taxation year following 2012, the unused portion of their tuition fees and examination fees that may subsequently be converted into a non-refundable tax credit at the rate of 20% and such portion that may be so converted at the rate of 8%.

Quebec also differs from the federal government in the way it provides tax benefits for students in addition to tuition credits. Quebec provides no "education amounts" to the student equivalent to the federal amount at ¶1337. Rather, the supporting person of a child under 18 years of age can claim a flat per semester amount on Schedule A; the student (if 18 or over) assigns the amount to a parent; see ¶1649.55 and ¶1649.57.

The amount of the tax credit for tuition and examination fees is calculated on the student's Schedule T at part A and is claimed on line 398 of the student's return. The amount of the transfer to a parent is calculated on the student's Schedule T at part B. The result is entered on the parent's Schedule A at part D. The amount is claimed on line 398.1 of the parent's return.

(QTA: 752.0.18.10–752.0.18.14; Other Publications: Quebec Finance Information Bulletin 2005-7, item 1.3; 2007 Quebec Budget, *Additional Information on the Budgetary Measures*, item 5.2; Quebec Finance Information Bulletin 2013-3, Item 1; Quebec Interpretation Bulletin IMP. 752.0.18.10-1)

[¶1654] INTEREST ON STUDENT LOANS

Quebec allows a non-refundable credit for the interest paid in the year on student loans (¶1345). Quebec's credit is at its general credit rate of 20% of the interest repaid. For Quebec purposes, interest eligible for credit but unclaimed in a particular year will carry forward indefinitely, whereas for federal purposes it carries forward for five years only. You need not claim the maximum possible credit sufficient to eliminate tax in a year. You may claim as much or as little eligible interest as you wish and carry forward the balance.

The amount is calculated on Schedule M and claimed on line 385 of the return.

(QTA: 752.0.18.15)

[¶1655] VOLUNTEER FIREFIGHTERS CREDIT AND VOLUNTEERS PARTICIPATING IN SEARCH AND RESCUE ACTIVITIES CREDIT

A Quebec taxpayer who is a volunteer firefighter and who performed at least 200 hours of eligible services as a volunteer firefighter during the year can claim a non-refundable credit of $480 (16% of $3,000).

For 2014 and beyond, the former Volunteer Firefighters Credit, which was introduced in 2011, was extended to include volunteers participating in search and rescue activities.

Eligible services consist of:

- responding to calls and being on call for firefighting, search and rescue activities, or emergency related calls;
- attending meetings held by fire departments or eligible rescue associations; and
- participating in required training related to the prevention or suppression of fires, or search and rescue activities.

If a volunteer performed other duties in a capacity other than as a volunteer for a fire department or rescue association, the hours for those services do not count towards the 200 hours required to qualify for the credit.

If the volunteer chooses not to include in income any tax-exempt remuneration received from a municipality, government, or other public authority (maximum tax-exempt remuneration amount is $1,130 for 2016 and $1,120 for 2015; see ¶1623.47), he or she cannot claim the $480 credit for volunteer firefighters and search and rescue volunteers.

The volunteer may have to provide a certificate attesting the hours of volunteer service from the fire chief of each fire department or from the rescue association that the volunteer worked for.

The amount is claimed on line 390 of the return.

(QTA: 752.0.10.0.4–752.0.10.0.5; Quebec Guide TP-1.G, *Guide to the Income Tax Return*; Other Publications: 2014 Quebec Budget, *Additional Information on the Fiscal Measures of the Budgetary Measures*, item 5.1 Harmonization with certain measures of the federal Budget of February 11, 2014, item 2)

[¶1656] EXPERIENCED WORKERS CREDIT

Quebec introduced a credit in 2012 to mitigate the loss of skilled workers who are expected to retire over the next few years. To encourage individuals who live in Quebec and are 65 and over to remain in or return to the labour market, a tax credit was introduced to eliminate the income tax that these individuals would have to pay on part of their eligible work income in excess of $5,000. To encourage experienced workers to remain in or re-enter the workforce in 2015 and 2016, Quebec Budgets have enhanced the credit by lowering the eligibility age and increasing the maximum amount of eligible work income.

The eligibility age has been reduced and the eligible work income amount has been increased as follows:

	Maximum Eligible Work Income			
Age	*2015*	*2016*	*2017*	*2018 and later*
65 and over	$4,000	$6,000	$8,000	$10,000
64		$4,000	$6,000	$8,000
63			$4,000	$6,000
62				$4,000

If you were 65 or over as of December 31, 2016, the maximum tax credit is $902.40 calculated as follows:

Eligible work income that exceeds $5,000 to a maximum of $6,000 multiplied by 15.04%

If you were 64 as of December 31, 2016, the maximum tax credit is $601.60 calculated as follows:

Eligible work income that exceeds $5,000 to a maximum of $4,000 multiplied by 15.04% less 5% of the eligible work income in excess of $33,505.

15.04% is the rate applicable to the first taxable income bracket (16%) multiplied by (1.06) where .06 is the rate of the general tax deduction from work.

Beginning in 2016, the credit is reduced by 5% of your working income in excess of $33,505. However, in order to provide a credit not lower than the one that you would have benefited from under the rules effective prior to 2016, this reduction does not apply if you were at least at the age of 65 as of December 31, 2016, and your credit otherwise calculated does not exceed $601.60.

Eligible work income is the same as defined for the purpose of the general deduction from work income (see ¶1624.05) but excluding income earned before the eligibility age.

Any unused portion of the tax credit may not be carried forward or transferred to the individual's spouse.

Individuals qualifying for this credit who expect to earn more than $5,000 in eligible work income may ask his or her employer, on a prescribed form, to reduce the source deductions in order to take into account this new tax credit.

The TP1 Guide provides a workchart for the calculation of the credit, which is claimed on line 391 of the return.

(QTA: 752.0.10.0.2–752.0.10.0.3; Other Publications: 2016 Quebec Budget, *Additional Information*, item 1.6; 2015 Quebec Budget, *Additional Information*, item 1.2; 2014 Quebec Budget, *Additional Information on the Fiscal Measures of the Budget*, item 2.1; 2011 Quebec Budget, *Additional Information on the Fiscal Measures of the Budget*, item 1.1)

[¶1656a] NON-REFUNDABLE CREDIT FOR NEW GRADUATES WORKING IN REMOTE REGIONS

Essentially, this non-refundable tax credit allows recent graduates to reduce their income tax payable by up to $3,000 a year, to a cumulative amount of $10,000 (or $8,000 in certain situations explained below), as long as they reside continuously in a remote resource region and hold in that region a job related to their field of specialization. The amount of the credit cannot be higher than 40% of the recent graduate's eligible wages.

"Remote resource regions" for purposes of this credit means the territories included in the following administrative regions, regional county municipalities (RCMs), and urban agglomeration:

- Bas-Saint-Laurent (region 01);
- Saguenay-Lac-Saint-Jean (region 02);
- Abitibi-Témiscamingue (region 08);
- Côte-Nord (region 09);
- Nord-du-Quebec (region 10);
- Gaspésie-Îles-de-la-Madeleine (region 11);
- Antoine-Labelle RCM;
- La Vallée-de-la-Gatineau RCM;
- the Mékinac RCM;
- Pontiac RCM; and
- the urban agglomeration of La Tuque.

To claim the non-refundable tax credit for a given taxation year, an individual must reside in a remote resource region at the end of the year and be in one of the following situations:

(1) the individual started an "eligible job" in the taxation year, at any time during the 24-month period following the date on which the training course leading to a recognized diploma was successfully completed, or obtained a recognized graduate degree in an educational program requiring an essay, dissertation, or thesis to be written; recognized diplomas include a Diploma of Vocational Studies (DVS), an Attestation of Vocational Specialization (AVS), an Attestation of Vocational Education (AVE), a Diploma of College Studies (DCS) in technical training, an Attestation of College Studies (ACS) in technical training, a university diploma sanctioning a course of studies at the under-graduate or graduate level, and certain attestations sanctioning a specialized post-secondary program; for greater certainly, training means courses and training periods, but excludes a period during which a student writes an essay, a dissertation, or a thesis;

(2) the individual held an "eligible job" in the taxation year and resided in a remote resource region throughout the period beginning at the end of the last year of eligibility for the refundable or non-refundable tax credit for new graduates and ending at the end of the taxation year.

The term "eligible job" means, with respect to individuals, an office or employment the duties of which are ordinarily performed in a remote resource region, where the duties are related to a business carried on by the employer in the region, and to the knowledge and skills acquired by an individual in the training course or the program having led to a recognized diploma.

To allow for the fact that some employers hire employees to perform duties related to a business they carry on in a remote resource region, without actually having an establishment in the region the duties of the new graduate's office or employment are required to be ordinarily performed in a remote resource region and related to a business carried on by the employer in that region.

The amount an individual may deduct in the calculation of the income tax otherwise payable for a given taxation year will be equal to the lowest of the following amounts:

- the income tax otherwise payable by the individual for the year;
- 40% of the salary or wages from an eligible job for the year;
- $3,000;
- for the individuals who begin to hold an eligible job after March 20, 2012 and within the 24 months following the date on which they either successfully completed training leading to a recognized post-secondary diploma or obtained a recognized master's or doctoral degree under a program of instruction stipulating the writing of an essay, a dissertation or a thesis, the amount by which $10,000 ($8,000 for 2011 and prior years) exceeds the aggregate of the amounts obtained by the individual as the refundable or non-refundable tax credit for new graduates working in the resource regions for a taxation year prior to the given taxation year;
- for the individuals who begin to hold an eligible job within the 24 months following the date on which they completed training leading to a recognized secondary level diploma, the amount by which $8,000 exceeds the aggregate of the amounts obtained by the individual as the refundable or non-refundable tax credit for new graduates working in the resource regions for a taxation year prior to the given taxation year.

An individual who was residing in Quebec in a remote resource region immediately prior to death will be deemed to have been residing in Quebec in such a region at the end of December 31 of the year of death. Thus, the legal representative of a deceased person will be able to claim the non-refundable tax credit for new graduates working in the resource regions in the income tax return to be filed on behalf of the deceased for the year of death.

For the calendar year during which an individual goes bankrupt, the non-refundable tax credit for new graduates working in the resource regions may be claimed only in the post-bankruptcy tax. For the purpose of calculating the tax credit, the full amount of the salary or wages received during the calendar year must be taken into account.

A presumption has been established to enable an individual who is living in Quebec outside a remote resource region at the end of a given taxation year and who received, in the year, a salary or wages for an eligible job held in the previous taxation year to deduct, in the calculation of the income tax otherwise payable for the year, the additional amount that would have been deductible for the purposes of the tax credit had the salary or wages been received during the previous taxation year. The intention is to provide for individuals who cease to hold an eligible job in the last few days of a year and who, at the beginning of the following year, receive a salary or wages attributable to that job.

This credit is claimed on line 392 of the return. Individuals must enclose form TP-776.1.ND-V with their return.

(QTA: 776.1.5.0.16–776.1.5.0.19; Other Publications: March 23, 2006 Quebec Budget, *Additional Information on the Budgetary Measures, Revenue Measures*, item 1.9; 2012 Quebec Budget, *Additional Information on the Budgetary Measures, Revenue Measures*, item 3.3)

[¶1657] CHARITABLE CONTRIBUTION DONATIONS

Speaking generally, Quebec follows federal rules in permitting the donation credit to be claimed in the year of the gift or the following five years, and, prior to 2016, imposing a limitation that gifts can only be claimed to the extent of 75% of net (Quebec) income for a particular year, with certain additions for capital or depreciable gifts. Unused donation amounts must be carried forward within the five-year carryforward period. As announced in the 2016 Budget, commencing in 2016 the 75% income-related limit for the purpose of calculating the donation tax credit has been eliminated and donors will now be able to claim a tax credit of up to 100% of their income. Unused donation amounts may still be carried forward for up to five years.

Quebec has not mirrored the new federal first-time donor super credit, but has instead created enhanced donation credits aimed at fostering cultural philanthropy. These enhanced credits are explained in greater detail in ¶1657.65.

As you might expect, to the extent you claimed federal credit for a donation during a period in which you were not subject to Quebec tax, the credit is considered to have been claimed for Quebec purposes and does not form part of the carryforward pool.

After these general similarities, however, Quebec rules exhibit several unique features.

Schedule V has been introduced in 2013 to facilitate the calculation of the different components of the credit:

- credit for charitable donations and gifts;
- credit for gifts of cultural property, ecological gifts and gifts of musical instruments;
- additional credit for a large cultural donation; and
- credit for cultural patronage.

A workchart is supplied for the calculation of the credit at line 395 of the return. The workchart must be used only when donations were made in cash and during the current year. Otherwise, Schedule V must be completed. The individual must order Schedule V from Revenu Québec either by phone or by accessing the Revenu Québec Website.

(Other Publications: 2016 Quebec Budget, Additional Information, item 1.5)

[¶1657.05] *Rates Used to Calculate Quebec Tax Credit for Gifts*

For taxation years prior to 2017 Quebec provided a credit for the first $200 of charitable donations at its middle tax bracket rate of 20%, and a credit for the balance at a rate of 24%.

The 20% credit rate is consistent with Quebec practice for converting personal amounts to tax credits. Quebec practice in regard to the 20% rate is more favourable than federal practice, which gives credit on the first $200 only at the lowest tax bracket rate (compare ¶1263).

As announced in the 2016 Budget, commencing in 2017 the rates used for calculating the donation tax credit will be increased to 25.75% for individuals whose marginal tax rate is higher than 24%. Specifically, the credit will be calculated as follows:

- 20% of the lesser of $200 or the individual's total eligible gifts for the year;
- 25.75% of the lesser of the following amounts:
  - the amount by which the individual's total eligible gifts for the year exceeds $200, or
  - the amount by which the individual's taxable income for the year exceeds the threshold for the year of the fourth tax bracket of the personal income tax table;
- 24% of the amount by which the individual's total eligible gifts for the year exceeds the aggregate of $200 and the amount of such gifts to which the rate of 25.75% applies.

As with the federal rules, there appears to be no obstacle to accumulating credits for several years in order to exceed the $200 limit, although at the cost of deferring use of the credit to a future year, one might be skeptical of the merit of this plan.

(Other Publications: 2016 Quebec Budget, Additional Information, item 1.5)

[¶1657.15] *75% of Income Limitation*

Prior to 2016 charitable donations qualified for the credit in a particular year only to the extent that they did not exceed 75% of Quebec income on line 275 of your Quebec return. Unused amounts could generally be carried forward for five years. However, for donations of ecological gifts made after February 10, 2014, the amounts may be carried forward for ten years. As announced in the 2016 Budget, commencing in 2016 the 75% income-related limit for the purpose of calculating the donation tax credit has been eliminated and donors will now be allowed to claim a tax credit of up to 100% of their income.

Prior to 2016 where a gift of property was made to a recognized charity or to the Crown and the gift was considered to be in furtherance of the donee's mission, regardless of whether the gift was in furtherance of the donee's mission, the donor's credit limit of 75% of income in respect of the gift was supplemented by an additional limit of 25% of the sum of following amounts:

(1) the lesser of (i) the amount of recapture of (Quebec) capital cost allowance included in the donor's income for the year with respect to a class that included the property, and (ii) for each gift included in that class, the lower of the capital cost of the gift or fair market value (less any outlays or expenses relating to the disposition) of the gift; and

(2) the amount of taxable capital gain included in the donor's income for the year on account of the gift.

In addition, prior to 2016 Quebec matched the federal rule that gifts could be claimed to the extent of 100% in the year of death and the preceding year.

(Other Publications: 2014 Quebec Budget, *Additional Information on the Fiscal Measures of the Budgetary Measures*, item 5.1 Harmonization with certain measures of the federal Budget of February 11, 2014, item 8.; 2016 Quebec Budget, Additional Information, item 1.5)

[¶1657.20] *Vow of Perpetual Poverty*

Members of a religious order who have taken a vow of perpetual poverty may claim a deduction of up to 100% of their charitable contributions. The result will be a complete offset of taxable income by charitable contribution for income donated back to (or held back by) the religious order *provided the religious order is an approved charity*.

Prior to 2016, if the charitable contributions made to the religious order (and as other gifts or donations) exceeded 75% of income, certificate TP-752.0.1.I-V had to be enclosed with the return. The certificate had to be completed by an authorized representative of the religious order certifying that the individual specified on the certificate was a member of the order during the taxation year in question and had taken vows of perpetual poverty. If the certificate had already been completed with a previous return, it did not have to be filed again as long as the individual had not left or changed religious orders. Commencing in 2016, the 75% income related limit has been eliminated, thus this special credit is no longer applicable.

[¶1657.25] *Qualifying Charities, etc.*

Amounts which qualify for federal charitable donation credits (¶1265) qualify for Quebec purposes as well. Quebec also allows as charitable donations contributions to artistic organizations sanctioned by the Quebec Minister of Culture and Communications.

Quebec amateur athletic associations meeting the criteria are eligible to issue donation receipts. This, in effect, includes these contributions in charitable contributions for Quebec purposes, subject to the general rules and limitations on all charitable contributions.

Similarly, Quebec will recognize as charitable donations contributions to the Organisation internationale de la Francophonie and its subsidiary bodies. Such contributions are presumably analogous to contributions to the United Nations and its subsidiaries, but unlike UN contributions will be eligible for charitable donation credit for Quebec but not federal purposes.

Quebec follows federal rules (at ¶1285) with respect to donations to U.S. organizations, and with respect to artist's inventory (¶1291).

Quebec accepts federal rules with respect to federally certified cultural property (¶1268), but also includes as eligible recipients of cultural property gifts a certified archival centre or recognized museum where the gift is cultural property certified by Quebec. Similarly, Quebec has its own ecological property rules parallel to the federal rules at ¶1268d. For Quebec purposes, land must be certified by the Quebec Minister of Sustainable Development, Environment and Parks.

The Quebec Income Tax Return Guide includes three useful workcharts that help understand the tax treatment of the different types of donations.

(QTA: 752.0.10.1)

[¶1657.30] *Donations of Works of Art: (1) Extra Benefit for Donation to Museum*

For gifts of works of art donated to a Quebec museum, Quebec allows a tax credit based on 125% of the eligible amount of the gift, or of the deemed fair market value where a lesser value is elected. The rule applies regardless of whether the property qualifies under the certified cultural property rules. The eligible amount of the gift is defined as the amount by which the fair market value of the property exceeds the amount of the advantage, if any, derived from the gift or contribution.

A "Quebec museum" includes any museum located in Quebec, and any other institution that at the time of the gift was a museum recognized by the Minister of Culture and Communications.

(QTA: 752.0.10.15.1)

[¶1657.35] *Donations of Works of Art: (2) Limitation for Works Not Used by the Donee in its "Primary Mission"*

Quebec limits the charitable donation credit for gifts of a "work of art" to gifts to registered charities, registered amateur athletic associations, exempt housing corporations, the UN or its agencies, foreign universities, Quebec amateur athletic associations, and the Organisation internationale de la Francophonie. Thus, the limitation does not apply to: gifts under federal or Quebec cultural property rules; gifts to the Crown; gifts to artistic organizations or Canadian municipalities; and gifts of ecological property. Rather, it is aimed at gifts of works of art (which are intrinsically difficult to value) given to charities which may be expected to sell the work to further the charitable cause. Accordingly, even where a work of art is acquired by a charitable organization otherwise subject to these rules, if the acquisition by the charity is connected with the charity's "primary mission", such as a painting given to an art museum for display, the limitation will not apply. In all other cases, where a gift of cultural property is made to a charity, the charity cannot issue a tax receipt for a work of art until the work has been sold (which must occur by December 31st of the fifth year following the year in which the gift was made), and the value on the receipt may not exceed the lesser of fair market value and the actual selling price of the work. A work of art for this purpose will include a print, etching, sculpture, painting or other work of a similar nature, tapestry or handwoven carpet or handmade appliqué, lithograph, rare folio, rare manuscript or book, stamp or coin.

It would seem that a deemed disposition occurs in the year a gift of a work of art is made notwithstanding that no credit may be allowed. Accordingly, there may be capital gain on the estimated fair market value. It would seem that since the taxpayer is deemed not to have made a gift for all purposes of the gift credit, the taxpayer could not elect (under Quebec section 752.0.10.12) to value the property at adjusted cost base (assuming fair market value was not less) under the rules equivalent to those described in "The Alternative Solution" at ¶1290. Given the uncertainty of value which is the basis for this provision, it would seem possible for the taxpayer to low-ball the fair market value (unless steps have been taken to ascertain it) and claim no gain or even a loss. If the charity does dispose of the gift within the requisite five-year period, the taxpayer is entitled to refile for the year of gift to give effect to the charitable donation and the now established fair market value. It would be open to Revenu Quebec to dispute the fair market value (FMV) in the year of gift regardless of subsequent events; it is less clear what penalties might run if subsequent events establish a high FMV but the taxpayer is entitled to refile for the year to give effect to the credit and, presumably, the valuation election. A rather obscure provision relating to interest suggests that where income is increased by reason of a subsequent year's disposition by the donee, interest is not computed on the increased income, but if tax after the application of credit is increased, interest on the increased tax runs only from the filing due-date of the year of subsequent disposition.

(QTA: 752.0.10.11.1)

[¶1657.40] *Gifts of Art or Cultural Property Subject to a Right of Continued Use*

To encourage more taxpayers to enrich the collections of museums and other museum-related institutions, Quebec modified its tax system so that, subject to some very detailed conditions and limitations, at least a portion of the tax benefits that apply to outright gifts of specified cultural property or works of art also apply to gifts of such property, other than immovable property, made with reserve of usufruct or usage.

Under these rules, a donation made by a taxpayer is considered a "recognized donation with reserve of usufruct or usage", provided it is the donation of an "eligible object", i.e., a work of art or specified cultural property, other than immovable property, and the conditions below are satisfied. The "specified cultural property" includes property (other than immovable, i.e., real, property), in the following three categories:

- Canadian cultural property, i.e., objects that, according to the Canadian Cultural Property Export Review Board, satisfy the significance and importance criteria stated in the (federal) *Cultural Property Export and Import Act* and are alienated in favour of an entity specified under the Act (see ¶1268);
- Quebec cultural property, i.e., objects that are recognized or classified in accordance with the (Quebec) *Cultural Property Act* and are alienated in favour of an entity specified in the (federal) *Cultural Property Export and Import Act*;
- recognized cultural property, i.e., property covered by a certificate issued by the Conseil du patrimoine culturel du Quebec indicating that it has been acquired by a certified archival centre or accredited museum-related institution, in accordance with its acquisition and conservation policy and the directives of the Ministère de la Culture et des Communications.

The donation of an eligible object will be considered a recognized donation with reserve of usufruct or usage if it complies with the following conditions:

- the bare ownership of the eligible object was alienated by the taxpayer by means of a donation *inter vivos* under whose terms he or she reserves the usufruct or usage of the object;
- the donation *inter vivos* was made either, when the eligible object is specified cultural property, to a donee currently recognized regarding such type of property, or, when the eligible object is a work of art that is not specified cultural property, to a Quebec museum-related institution recognized for the purposes of the tax credit for charitable gifts;
- the usufruct or usage was established for the sole benefit of the taxpayer, being neither successive nor joint;
- the usufruct or usage was established either for the lifetime of the taxpayer, or for not more than 30 years;
- the taxpayer was the sole owner of the eligible object immediately prior to donating the bare ownership;
- the deed of gift includes a series of imperative clauses covering the alienation of the usufruct or usage, custody of the eligible object, purchase of insurance, as well as the deterioration or disappearance of the eligible object. More specifically, the deed of gift must include an undertaking by the taxpayer not to alienate his or her usufruct or usage over the eligible object without first obtaining the authorization of the donee. Furthermore, such deed must include the obligation, on the taxpayer, to keep the eligible object in a designated place, any removal of the object from such place being authorized only with the consent of the donee and under terms and conditions set by the donee.

The deed of gift must also specify that the taxpayer be required to insure the eligible object against the usual risks, such as theft or fire, and pay the premiums for such insurance during the length of the usufruct or usage. Such obligation must be accompanied by the taxpayer's undertaking to inform the donee without delay of the deterioration or disappearance of the eligible object.

Should the object become deteriorated, the deed of gift must stipulate that the decision whether or not to restore the object lies with the donee. Restoration of the object, as the case may be, may only be carried out by a person designated by the donee, and the taxpayer must undertake to use the insurance indemnity for such purpose. Should the donee decide not to restore the object, it must be specified that the taxpayer must remit to him or her the insurance indemnity within 10 days of receiving written confirmation of this decision.

In the event the eligible object disappears, the deed of gift must stipulate that the usufruct or usage terminates and that the insurance indemnity is payable to the donee.

Notwithstanding all these requirements, the deed of gift may include any stipulation that is not incompatible with the required clauses.

Finally, the alienation (disposition) by the donee of its (bare ownership) rights to an eligible object may entail application of the special tax payable by a donee recognized for the purposes of the cultural property regime when it alienates, during a specified holding period, specified cultural property in favour of a non-recognized donee.

[¶1657.45] Value for Tax Credit Purposes of a Donation Subject to a Reserve

For the purposes of the provisions relating to gifts and capital gains, the fair market value of a recognized donation with reserve of usufruct or usage of an eligible object shall be deemed equal to the product obtained by multiplying the amount of the fair market value of the eligible object otherwise determined by the "determined percentage of the value of the bare ownership".

If the usufruct or usage the donor reserves for himself on the eligible object is for life, the determined percentage is the percentage attributed to the value of the (donee's) bare ownership on the basis of the donor's age, as indicated in the following table.

Determined Percentage

Donor's age	*Value of bare ownership*
Under 25	25%
25 or over	31%
30 or over	38%
35 or over	44%
40 or over	50%
45 or over	56%
50 or over	62%
55 or over	68%
60 or over	73%
65 or over	78%
70 or over	83%
75 or over	87%
80 or over	91%

If the usufruct or usage is constituted for a fixed length of time, the determined percentage of the value of the bare ownership shall be, with no fraction and regardless of the donor's age, equal to:

- 87% if the fixed length of time is 10 years or less;
- 74% if the fixed length of time is greater than 10 years and less than or equal to 20 years;
- 61% otherwise.

Where the object donated under these rules would qualify for the 125% deduction for donations to museums, the fair market value of the donation for purposes of these rules shall be grossed up by 25%.

(QTA: 752.0.10.4.2–752.0.10.4.3)

[¶1657.50] *Donations of Securities*

For gifts of publicly traded (and certain other) securities, Quebec matches the federal rules at ¶1290d.05. Thus, Quebec applies a zero capital gains rate to such gifts.

For gifts of employee stock option proceeds, Quebec allows only a 50% deduction from the related employment income (see ¶330.50 for federal rules, ¶1623.35 for Quebec rules).

Quebec has adopted the federal rules on non-qualified securities (¶1290d.15).

(QTA: 231.2; 725.2.3)

[¶1657.55] *Gifts of Musical Instruments to Quebec Educational Institutions*

Gifts of musical instruments made to Quebec educational institutions will not incur Quebec capital gains tax and will be eligible for full recognition from Quebec as a charitable donation. Eligible Quebec educational institutions include Quebec primary and secondary schools, vocational colleges, universities, and institutions providing instruction in music that are part of the network of the Conservatoire de musique et d'art dramatique du Quebec.

(QTA: 752.0.10.1; 752.0.10.3; 752.0.10.5.1; 752.0.10.6; Other Publications: Quebec Finance Information Bulletin 2013-6; 2015 Quebec Budget, Additional Information, item 5.2; 2016 Quebec Budget, Additional Information, item 1.5; 2016 Quebec Budget, Additional Information, item 2.13)

[¶1657.65] *Additional Tax Credits to Promote Cultural Philanthropy*

Additional credit of 25% for an initial large cultural donation

In addition to the tax credit for donations currently allowed, the Quebec government will allow a new non-refundable credit equal to 25% of the initial eligible amount of large donations to charities, museums, or other registered cultural organizations operating in Quebec, of between $5,000 and $25,000 in the year. The donation must be a donation of money, and made after July 3, 2013 and before January 1, 2018. Other normal deductibility rules apply, hence, commencing in 2016, the 75% income related limit has been eliminated. Each member of a couple may claim the additional credit, however, unused portions may not be transferred between spouses. Any unused portion of such a credit may be carried forward for a period of four years.

Additional 30% tax credit for cultural patronage

In order to recognize the important role a patron of the arts plays in the creation of culture, a new credit is created at a rate of 30% for substantial donations of money. This non-refundable credit will be for large donations in excess of $250,000 paid to charities, museums, or other registered cultural organizations operating in Quebec. The amount must be paid during the year or promised to be paid in instalments of at least $25,000 per year, over a period not exceeding 10 years.

This is not an additional credit, but rather a separate credit that replaces the tax credit for donations and the new additional tax credit for an initial large cultural donation. Other normal deductibility rules apply, hence, commencing in 2016, the 75% income related limit has been eliminated. As with the credit for an initial large cultural donation, the credit for cultural patronage is only granted where the donation is made by cash, cheque, credit card, postal money order, wire transfer, or electronic transfer, and applies to such donations made, or promised to be made, after July 3, 2013 and before January 1, 2018. For the purpose of this credit, any unused portion can be transferred between spouses.

Increase of 25%–50% in the eligible amount of a donation of a public work of art

To encourage Quebec citizens to donate public art work to be displayed in public places or in educational institutions, the government will increase the eligible amount of a donation of public art donated to the province, a municipality in Quebec, or an educational institution including school boards. Traditionally public art includes art of a permanent nature, often large in size, or of an environmental nature, usually installed in a public place or in an environment or space accessible to the public or of the type which is integrated into the architecture of public buildings and sites.

The eligible amount of a donation of public art to a municipality or the province will be increased by 25% and for such donations to educational institutions including schools, the increased amount will be 50%. The increase will be applied to the fair market value of the art (other than cultural property) as certified by the Minister of Culture and Communications (the "Ministry"). To support the increased credit amount, the taxpayer must attach a certificate issued by the Ministry, supporting the value of the donated work.

The Ministry reserves the right to reset the value of the public art at any time and issue a new certificate a copy of which will be sent to the donee and the Minister of Revenue. A reassessment in such circumstances would be issued in due course and penalties and interest could apply. A determination of value or redetermination may be appealed to the Court of Quebec.

This enhanced credit is available to donations of public art made after July 3, 2013.

Increase of 25% of the eligible amount of a gift of an immovable for cultural purposes

So as to promote the donation of housing for artists and generally to give a "roof to culture", the government will allow a 25% increase in the value of a gift of an "eligible immovable" (the value of which has been certified by the Ministry, for the purpose of calculating the tax credit for the donation).

An eligible immovable would include a building capable of housing an artist's studio or one or more cultural organizations, including the land on which it is located and for which the Ministry has issued a qualifying certificate. The property must be donated to a municipal or public body performing a function for the Government of Quebec; a registered charity operating in Quebec for the benefit of the community or operating in the field of arts and culture; a registered cultural or communications organization; or to a museum. The building must meet certain requirements and be in an appropriate geographic location, so not all buildings, that would otherwise be suitable, would qualify.

To qualify for the enhanced credit amount, the donee will be required to attach a copy of the qualifying certificate issued by the Ministry to his or her tax return for the year. The Ministry must provide such a certificate to the donee within 90 days of making a request for a certificate. The Ministry, however, reserves the right to reset the value of the immovable at any time and such reset value will become the value for the purpose of this enhanced credit and issue a new certificate, a copy of which will be sent to the donee and the Minister of Revenue. A reassessment in such circumstances would be issued in due course and penalties and interest could apply. A determination of value or redetermination may be appealed to the Court of Quebec.

This enhanced credit for the donation of an eligible immovable will apply to the donation of such property made after July 3, 2013.

[¶1657.68] *Additional Tax Credit to Promote Food Donations by Farming Businesses and Food Processing Businesses*

The eligible amount for a donation of eligible agricultural products that is made after March 26, 2015, by a recognized farm producer to a registered charity that is either the Food Banks of Quebec or a Moisson member can be increased by 50% for purposes of calculating the deduction for donations and gifts or the non-refundable tax credit for donations and gifts, as the case may be. The 2016 Quebec Budget enhanced this non-refundable credit to include registered charites that are Associate Moisson Members as eligible donees and to include food processors as eligible donors. These enhancements apply to eligible donations made after March 17, 2016.

A recognized farm producer is an individual or a corporation that carries on a business registered as an agricultural operation with the Ministère de l'Agriculture, des Pêcheries et de l'Alimentation or that is a member of a partnership carrying on such a business at the end of its fiscal period. A recognized food processor is a corporation, partnership, or individual that carries on a food processing business.

For the purpose of this credit, the following products are considered eligible agricultural products (this is not an extensive list):

- meat and meat by-products;
- eggs and dairy products;
- fish;
- fruit;
- vegetables;
- grain;
- legumes;
- *fines herbes*;
- honey;
- maple syrup;
- mushrooms;
- nuts; and
- any other product grown, raised or harvested by a registered agricultural operation, provided the product can be legally sold, distributed or offered for sale — at a place other than where it was produced — as a food or beverage intended for human consumption.

For the purpose of this credit, the following products are considered eligible processed food products (this is not an extensive list):

- oil;
- flour;
- sugar;
- deep frozen fruits and vegetables;
- pasta;
- prepared meals;
- baby food; and
- infant formula.

(Other Publications: Quebec Finance Information Bulletin 2013-6; 2015 Quebec Budget, Additional Information 2015-2016, Item 5.2; 2016 Quebec Budget, Additional Information, item 2.13)

[¶1659] ORDERING OF NON-REFUNDABLE CREDITS

The Quebec personal amounts claimed under the rules in ¶1649–¶1657 must be claimed in the following order:

(1) Basic personal tax credit (¶1649.32);

(2) Child under the age of 18 in school (¶1649.55);

(3) Other dependant over the age of 18 (¶1649.59);

(4) Transfer of the unused basic personal tax credit of a student (¶1649.57);

(5) Person living alone or as a single parent (¶1649.40);

(6) Retirement amount (¶1649.75);

(7) Age amount (¶1649.70);

(8) Experienced Workers Credit (¶1656);

(9) Professional or union dues of an employee (¶1651);

(10) Professional dues of a self-employed individual (¶1651);

(11) Credit for new graduates working in remote resource regions (¶1656a);

(12) Eligible amounts in relation to 11 (above) received in the following year (¶1656a);

(13) Volunteer Firefighter and Volunteers Participating in Search and Rescue Activities Credit (¶1655);

(14) Credit for severe and prolonged impairment in physical or mental functions (¶1649.60);

(15) Medical expenses credit (¶1652);

(16) Transfer of tuition/examination fees credit amount (¶1653);

(17) Charitable contributions credit (¶1657);

(18) Credit for tuition/examination fees (¶1653);

(19) Credit for interest paid on student loans (¶1654);

(20) Dividend tax credit (¶1666); and

(21) Transfer of spouse's credits (¶1650).

Note that this ordering of credits varies considerably from the federal ordering in ¶1365. Where there is insufficient tax to absorb all credits, this may vary the claims for amounts which might otherwise be similar, such as medical expenses credit and tuition fees credit.

(QTA: 752.0.22)

INCOME TAX CALCULATION AND APPLICATION OF NON-REFUNDABLE CREDITS

[¶1661] INCOME TAX ON TAXABLE INCOME

Quebec provides workchart 401 with its forms package to calculate the tax payable on your taxable income determined at line 299. The applicable rates for 2016 are:

[¶1661.05] *Rate Table — 2016*

Taxable income		*Tax*
$42,390 or less		16%
$42,391 to $84,780	$6,782.40 +	20% on excess over $42,390
$84,781 to $103,150	$15,260.40 +	24% on excess over $84,780
over $103,150	$19,669.20 +	25.75% on excess over $103,150

(QTA: 750–750.3)

[¶1661.10] *Quebec Indexing*

The rate brackets (currently shown as $42,390, $84,780, and $103,150) are indexed every year by the annual percentage change in the Quebec consumer price index at the preceding September 30. In adjusting the rate brackets, alcohol and tobacco prices are removed from the index, intended to result in a lower index amount to the extent of increases based on alcohol and tobacco taxes. The same indexing applies to family income brackets used to calculate the refundable child tax credit, and to a number of the personal amounts at ¶1649 and to certain refundable tax credits discussed at ¶1675 *et seq.*

Although the indexing numbers are to be published shortly after September 30, one must wait until the Quebec Budget of the following spring to be confident that rates or brackets will not change.

The Quebec rate for converting personal amounts to non-refundable tax credits (at line 388) is 20% (with some exceptions).

(QTA: 750.1–750.3)

[¶1661.15] *Application of Non-Refundable Credits*

Having calculated tax on taxable income, non-refundable credits and tax adjustments are applied. The Quebec return mandates the following order, although this is not necessarily directed by the statute. Unless carryovers are permitted, ordering is not important. Use of alternative minimum tax carryforward is optional, and normally will not be used except to reduce tax after the application of other non-refundable credits.

(1) Tax adjustment, if any (¶1665);

(2) Personal amount credits from line 399 (¶1649–¶1657) in the order discussed in ¶1659; usually these will be entered directly at line 406; however, if tax adjustments or foreign tax credits are claimed, the personal amount credits are taken to Schedule E and the resulting tax to line 412;

(3) Foreign tax credit (use Schedule E, ¶1670);

(4) The tax credit for the Beneficiary of a Designated Trust (¶1628);

(5) Political contribution tax credit (use workchart 414, ¶1667);

(6) Dividend tax credit (¶1666);

(7) Labour-Sponsored Venture Capital Fund (LSVCC) credit (¶1669);

(8) Capital régional et coopératif Desjardins Share Tax Credit (¶1669c);

(9) Alternative Minimum Tax (use form TP-776.42-V and Schedule E, ¶1697);

(10) Deduction for logging tax (use Schedule E, ¶1671).

[¶1661.20] *Application of Additional Taxes*

In addition to its income tax, Quebec imposes several additional taxes, either as surtax or special levies. These are discussed at ¶1663.

[¶1662] TAX RATES PRIOR TO 2016

[¶1662.21] *Rate Table — 2015*

Taxable income		*Tax*
$41,935 or less		16%
$41,936 to $83,865	$6,709.60 +	20% on excess over $41,935
$83,866 to $102,040	$15,095.60 +	24% on excess over $83,865
over $102,040	$19,457.60 +	25.75% on excess over $102,040

[¶1662.22] *Rate Table — 2014*

Taxable income		*Tax*
$41,495 or less		16%
$41,496 to $82,985	$6,639.20 +	20% on excess over $41,495
$82,986 to $100,970	$14,937.20 +	24% on excess over $82,985
over $100,970	$19,253.60 +	25.75% on excess over $100,970

[¶1662.23] *Rate Table — 2013*

Taxable income		*Tax*
$41,095 or less		16%
$41,095 to $82,190	$6,575.20 +	20% on excess over $41,095
$82,190 to $100,000	$14,794.20 +	24% on excess over $82,190
over $100,000	$19,068.60 +	25.75% on excess over $100,000

[¶1662.24] *Rate Table — 2012*

Taxable income		*Tax*
$40,100 or less		16%
$40,101 to $80,200	$6,416.00 +	20% on excess over $40,100
over $80,200	$14,436.00 +	24% on excess over $80,200

[¶1663] ADDITIONAL TAXES

[¶1663.05] *Quebec Pension Plan (QPP) Self-Employment Contribution*

Quebec requires self-employed individuals to make QPP contributions in a similar manner as the federal government requires for *Canada Pension Plan* (CPP). As with CPP, Quebec also permits employees to top up QPP contributions where less than the permitted maximum has been withheld. See ¶1305 and ¶1491. The Quebec calculations are made on a workchart for line 445. QPP overpayments are refunded as described at ¶1676.

[¶1663.07] *Quebec Parental Insurance Plan (QPIP) Self-Employment or Employment Outside Quebec Contribution*

Quebec requires self-employed individuals and individuals who work outside of Quebec, whether in Canada or in another country, to pay QPIP premiums if their total net business income and employment income (that is subject to the QPIP premium) is $2,000 or over. In either situation, Schedule R is used to calculate the amount payable.

[¶1663.10] *Health Services Fund Contribution (Schedule F)*

Quebec adds a Health Services Fund contribution tax designed to supplement the employer payroll tax which funds provincial health insurance. The tax is actually imposed under the *Act Respecting the Régie de l'assurance maladie du Quebec*. The tax is calculated on Schedule F of the Quebec return.

The tax is calculated on the general income base before most deductions, from which you are then allowed to back out employment income, certain profit-sharing plan allocations, dividend gross-up amounts, Old Age Security (OAS) pension payments received, taxable support payments received, social assistance payments and the like, income replacement indemnities and federal supplements, scholarships and bursaries deductible from Quebec taxable income, RRSP income attributed to you on early withdrawal of spousal RRSP contributions, government payments received under Quebec's *Action emploi* programs, transitional income supplements for employment assistance recipients entering employment or business, and recaptures of Quebec stock savings plan deductions for early withdrawal of funds. You may then further reduce income by some of the usual deductions, such as eligible business losses, expenditures made to earn business income, deductible interest and carrying charges, and some other itemized items.

The table is indexed annually by the Quebec indexing factor.

For 2016, the resulting income is taxed at the following rates:

HSF tax base	*Tax*
$14,440 or less	nil
$14,441 to $50,200	1% of the amount over $14,440 to a maximum of $150
$50,201 to $135,200	$150 + 1% on the amount over $50,200 to a maximum of $1,000
over $135,200	$1,000

For 2015, the resulting income is taxed at the following rates:

HSF tax base	*Tax*
$14,285 or less	nil
$14,286 to $49,660	1% of the amount over $14,285 to a maximum of $150
$49,661 to $134,660	$150 + 1% on the amount over $49,660 to a maximum of $1,000
over $134,660	$1,000

For 2014, the resulting income is taxed at the following rates:

HSF tax base	*Tax*
$14,135 or less	nil
$14,135 to $49,140	1% of the amount over $14,135 to a maximum of $150
$49,140 to $134,140	$150 + 1% on the amount over $49,140 to a maximum of $1,000
over $134,140	$1,000

For 2013, the resulting income is taxed at the following rates:

HSF tax base	*Tax*
$14,000 or less	nil
$14,001 to $29,000	1% of the amount over $14,000
$29,001 to $48,670	$150
$48,671 to $133,670	$150 + 1% on the amount over $48,670
over $133,670	$1,000

For 2012, the resulting income is taxed at the following rates:

HSF tax base	*Tax*
$13,660 or less	nil
$13,660 to $28,660	1% of the amount over $13,660
$28,661 to $47,490	$150

HSF tax base	*Tax*
$47,491 to $132,490	$150 + 1% on the amount over $47,490
over $132,490	$1,000

Forest producers Income-averaging mechanism

The 2016 Quebec Budget introduced a temporary income-averaging mechanism for forest producers (see ¶1641.40). To take into account the fact that, for many individuals who are private forest owners, earning income from the sale of timber may result in a requirement to pay a substantial contribution to the Health Services Fund, measures will be put in place to enable an individual who resorts to the income-averaging mechanism for forest producers to average a portion of his income from the sale of timber for the purposes of calculating his or her contribution to the Health Services Fund.

The individual may deduct, in calculating his or her total income for a particular year, an amount equal to the amount that he or she deducted for the purpose of calculating his or her taxable income for the year under the income-averaging mechanism for forest producers. That being said, an individual who uses this deduction will be required to include, in calculating total income for each of the seven years following the particular year, an amount equal to the amount that was included in calculating his or her taxable income for that year under the income-averaging mechanism for forest producers.

(*Act respecting the Régie de l'assurance maladie du Quebec*, ss. 34.1.1 to 34.1.7; 2016 Quebec Budget, Additional Information, item 2.4; QTA: 752.0.13.4; 752.0.13.5)

[¶1663.15] *Quebec Prescription Drug Plan Premium*

Prescription drug insurance is compulsory for all Quebec residents. Those not covered by a private plan (i.e., group insurance or employee benefits plans) must register for the public plan, administered by the Régie de l'assurance maladie du Quebec (RAMQ). Generally, all persons whose coverage is provided by RAMQ must pay a premium when filing their Quebec income tax return. From July 1, 2015 to June 30, 2016, the maximum annual premium was $640 per adult. From July 1, 2016, to June 30, 2017, the maximum annual premium increases to $660 per adult, for an overall maximum annual amount payable for the 2016 taxation year of $650. The amount is dependent upon the net family income. The premium calculated on Schedule K is reported on line 447 of the return.

The annual amount was $625.50 for 2015, $609 for 2014, $593 for 2013, and $571 for 2012.

Essentially the following are exempt from paying the premium:

- Persons receiving social assistance payments;
- Persons aged under 18;
- Persons who are registered Indians or were recognized as an Inuk;
- Persons aged 65 or over receiving 94% to 100% of the federal Guaranteed Income Supplement;
- Children of insured persons under the age of 18 or between 18 to 25 who are full-time students with no spouse and are living with their parents; and
- Persons residing in a long-term care centre governed by the *Act respecting health services and social services.*

For the treatment of this premium as a medical expense, see ¶1652.

(*Act respecting the Régie de l'assurance maladie du Quebec*, ss. 37.1 to 37.15; Other Publications: Quebec Finance Information Bulletin 2002-8, item 1.5; Revenu Québec publication IN-113-V, "Provisions of the Public Prescription Drug Insurance Plan"; *Gazette officielle du Quebec*, June 19, 2009)

[¶1663.17] *Health Contribution*

Beginning July 1, 2010, individuals resident in Quebec 18 years of age or older are required to pay a "health contribution". The requirements of this contribution, outlined below, are similar to those concerning the public prescription drug insurance plan.

Commencing January 1, 2013 the premium for the health contribution was changed from a flat rate health contribution tax to a progressive tax that ranges in 2016 from $50 to $1,000 per adult, depending on income ($100 to $1,000 per adult for 2015, 2014, and 2013). The parameters of the contribution are subject to yearly indexation. Those individuals who were exempt from paying this tax under the old system will remain exempt under this new system. While announced in the 2016 Budget to be eliminated in 2017 for lower income earners, and completely eliminated in 2018 for all other taxpayers, the October 2016 update to the Quebec Economic Plan announced the complete elimination of the health contribution as of January 2017. In addition, the 2016 Budget also announced reductions to the 2016 contribution rates.

For 2016, the reduced contribution rates are as follows:

- for those adults earning between $18,570 and $41,265, the rate is the lesser of 5% of income or $50;
- for those adults earning between $41,265 and $134,095, the rate is the lesser of $50 plus 5% of the income over $41,265 or $175;
- for those adults earning between $134,095 and $154,720, the rate is $175 plus 4% of the income over $134,095; and
- for income over $154,720 the rate is $1,000.
- individuals over the age of 18 earning less than $18,570 will not have to pay any contribution tax;

For 2015, the contribution rates were as follows:

- individuals over the age of 18 earning less than $18,370 will not have to pay any contribution tax;
- for those adults earning between $18,370 and $40,820, the rate is the lesser of 5% of income or $100;
- for those adults earning between $40,820 and $132,650, the rate is the lesser of $100 plus 5% of the income over $40,820 or $200;
- for those adults earning between $132,650 and $152,650, the rate is $200 plus 4% of the income over $132,650; and
- for income over $152,650 the rate is $1,000.

The contribution is payable no later than April 30 of the year following the year the contribution is due. Individuals required to make income tax instalment payments were required to make instalment payments on their health contribution. Individuals could request that the health contribution be included in their source deductions.

Where an individual goes bankrupt, the family income of the post-bankruptcy period only must be considered.

Note that the health contribution is not considered as a medical expense.

(LRAMQ: 37.4, 37.16–37.18, 37.21–37.21.1; Other Publications: 2010 Quebec Budget, *Additional Information on the Budgetary Measures, Revenue Measures*, item 1.1; 2010 Quebec Finance Bulletin 2010-7, item 1; 2012 Quebec Budget, *Additional Information on the Budgetary Measures*, item 1.1; 2013–2014 Quebec Budget, *Additional Information on the Fiscal Measures*, item 1.1; 2015 Quebec Budget, *Additional Information*, item 1.1; 2016 Quebec Budget, *Additional Information*, item 1.1; Quebec Economic Plan October 2016 Update, Section A, item 2.2)

[¶1663.20] *Additional Subsidized Child Care Contribution*

To ensure the sustainability of Quebec's educational child care network, the government announced certain changes to the subsidized educational child care program on November 20, 2014. One such change is a revision of the contribution paid for a child who occupies a subsidized child care space.

For 2016, subsidized child care fees include a basic contribution of $7.55 per day ($7.30 per day effective April 22, 2015 to December 31, 2015), per child, and an additional contribution adjusted to family income. Both the basic and additional contributions will be indexed every year starting on January 1, 2016.

In 2016 an additional contribution of up to $13.15 per day per child ($12.70 in 2015) is paid to Revenu Québec for subsidized child care services with the contribution based on family income. This contribution is required for the taxpayer's first and second child but is not required for their third and subsequent children. The 2016 Budget announced that the additional contribution in respect of the second child will be reduced by 50% retroactive to April 22, 2015.

The basic contribution will continue to be paid to the child care service provider. The additional contribution will be paid by parents when they file their income tax return.

There is no additional contribution to pay in the case of child care services provided at school by a school board or private educational institution, or as part of a day camp or vacation camp.

To help them determine the amount of the additional contribution to pay in their income tax return, all parents who have signed a subsidized child care services agreement will receive, by February 28, 2017, an RL-30 slip issued by one of the following:

- a child care centre,
- a subsidized daycare centre, or
- a home child care coordinating office, in the case of a home child care provider.

The amount of the additional subsidized child care contribution will be calculated in Schedule I of the income tax return of every parent who signed a subsidized child care agreement for services received after April 21, 2015. The result will be reported on line 434 of the tax return.

The amount of the additional contribution is based on the following:

- your family income for the previous taxation year (line 275),
- the number of children who received subsidized childcare (as indicated on the RL-30 slip), and
- the number of days of care received by each child for whom you must pay the additional contribution (as indicated on the RL-30 slip).

If your family income for either 2015 or 2016 is $50,545 or less, you do not have to pay the additional contribution for 2016. For 2015, you did not have to pay the additional contribution if your family income for either 2014 or 2015 was $50,000 or less.

The additional contribution must be paid for no more than two children, with the rate for the second child being reduced by 50%. If three children or more occupied a subsidized child care space, the additional contribution must be paid only for the two children for whom the total days indicated in box B of the RL-30 are the higher. The case being, if the number of days is the same for two children, you must take in account the number of days of the older of the children.

The amount of the additional contribution for 2016 is based on your family income for 2015 — that is, your net income for 2015 plus the net income for 2015 of your spouse on December 31, 2016.

The amount of the additional contribution for 2016 is as follows:

Family income for 2015	Additional contribution (for the 1st child, 50% of the calculated amount for the 2nd child)
More than $50,545 but not more than $75,820	$0.70 per day, per child
More than $75,820 but not more than $158,820	$0.70 to $13.15 per day, per child, that is, 3.9% of the excess of the family income over $75,820, divided by 260 days (52 weeks × 5 days) plus $0.70
More than $158,820	$13.15 per day, per child

The amount of the additional contribution for 2015 was as follows:

Family income for 2014	Additional contribution (for the 1st child, 50% of the calculated amount for the 2nd child)
More than $50,000 but not more than $75,000	$0.70 per day, per child
More than $75,000 but not more than $155,000	$0.70 to $12.70 per day, per child, that is, 3.9% of the excess of the family income over $75,000, divided by 260 days (52 weeks × 5 days) plus $0.70
More than $155,000	$12.70 per day, per child

The Ministère des Finances offers a tool on its Website to help you estimate the amount of the additional subsidized child care contribution you will have to pay when filing your income tax return (http://www.budget.finances.gouv.qc.ca/budget/outils/index_en.asp).

If you would like to add that amount to your source deductions of income tax, you must complete one of the following forms and give it to your employer:

- *Request to Have Additional Income Tax Withheld at Source* (TP-1017-V);
- *Source Deductions Return* (TP-1015.3-V).

The contribution is calculated on Schedule I and reported on line 434 of the return.

(Loi sur les services de garde éducatifs à l'enfance, art 81.3 - 88.14; Other Publications: Guide to Filing the RL-30 Slip: Subsidized Educational Childcare; 2016 Quebec Budget, The Quebec Economic Plan, item 3.1)

[¶1664] QUEBEC FAMILY ALLOWANCES

[¶1664.05] *Prepayments of Child Care, Work Premium*

Quebec's revised child assistance payments include components which are prepayments of the work premium credits (line 456, Schedule P) and the Child Care Expenses Credit (line 455, Schedule C). These monthly prepayments must be trued up against actual credit entitlements as determined on the relevant schedules. Accordingly, they are included in tax payable at line 441 and the appropriate credits are calculated on the schedules and claimed at lines 455 and 456.

(QTA: 1029.8.80.2; 1029.8.116.9; Other Publications: 2010 Quebec Budget, *Additional Information on the Budgetary Measures, Revenue Measures*, item 1.5)

[¶1664.10] *Other Social Assistance*

Generally speaking, social assistance other than child assistance is taxable in Quebec, although the offsetting deductions from taxable income are provided for the same programs as for federal purposes. Quebec's "Last Resort Assistance" is taxable except for certain amounts related to children.

[¶1665] TAX ADJUSTMENTS

[¶1665.05] *Lump-Sum Payments from RPP/DPSP*

The federal rules with respect to the items outlined in ¶1471 are also applicable for Quebec income tax purposes. The adjustment is entered at line 402 on Schedule E and, after application of personal amount credits, carried to line 412 of the Quebec return.

[¶1665.10] *Retroactive Payments (Payments Related to an Earlier Year)*

Quebec permits taxpayers to elect to deduct from taxable income certain amounts received in the year but related to prior years, provided the aggregate of such qualifying receipts in the year exceeds $300. The offset is a tax inclusion of the amount of tax which would have been payable in the prior year or years to which the payment relates had it been received in that year. Clearly, the greatest benefit will arise where a payment can be spread over several prior years, resulting in application of a lower marginal rate. The election must be weighed carefully; it will not confer a benefit in all cases.

Following an announcement in Quebec Finance Information Bulletin 2012-6, the tax legislation will be amended to stipulate that, where an addition must be made in the tax otherwise payable of an individual for a given taxation year after the 2012 taxation year, further to the application of the averaging mechanism for lump-sum payments or the retrospective determination of a benefit under a public compensation plan, such addition must be made after all the amounts allowed the individual to reduce his or her tax otherwise payable for the year have been deducted.

Consequently, beginning in 2013, the tax adjustment is entered at line 443 of the return (prior to 2013, the adjustment was entered on line 402 of the Schedule E).

The types of income which now qualify under this rule include:

(1) employment income received as a result of a judgment, arbitration award or agreement terminating a lawsuit;

(2) QPP or CPP benefits, parental insurance benefits, Employment Insurance benefits, old age security pension, payments from a pension plan, RRSP, RRIF, DPSP, or annuities, social assistance payments, labour adjustment benefits, income assistance payments, or Universal Child Care Benefits;

(3) interest on a retroactive interest or other investment income payment;

(4) support payments received;

(5) a wage loss insurance benefit;

(6) amounts paid to plan members (or, if deceased, their spouses) under a distribution plan ordered by the Superior Court of Quebec on December 4, 1995, with respect to the pension fund surplus of Singer Company of Canada; or

(7) any payment in respect of prior years which in the opinion of Revenu Québec imposes an undue burden if taxed in the year of receipt. Presumably, an undue tax burden arises if the income is taxed at a higher marginal rate in the year of receipt than if shifted to the year in which it notionally belongs.

See also the rules at ¶1676d where you are required to repay certain amounts previously included in income.

(QTA: 36.1 (repealed); 725.1.2–766.2; Other Publications: Form TP-766.2-V, "Averaging of a Retroactive Payment, Support Payment Arrears or a Repayment of Support"; Quebec Finance Information Bulletin 2012-6, item 1.4; Quebec Finance Information Bulletin 2015-4, item 2.3)

[¶1666] DIVIDEND TAX CREDIT

You are allowed a deduction from tax with respect to "dividends received from taxable Canadian corporations". This is similar to the federal dividend tax credit and the amount of dividends upon which the credit is calculated.

Quebec has adopted the federal system of separate dividend gross-up and dividend tax credit rates for dividends paid out of corporate earnings subject to small business rates and dividends paid out of corporate earnings taxed at higher rates (the federal system is described at ¶404). In both the federal and Quebec systems, corporate income taxed at small business rates will require an individual receiving the dividend to report 117% of the actual dividend as taxable income. The Quebec dividend tax credit on these "other" (as the federal government says) or "ordinary" (as Quebec says) dividends is 7.05% of the 117% grossed-up amount, or 8.2485% of the actual amount, of the dividends. Currently, "eligible" dividends (as both governments call them) paid out of earnings subject to the general rate of corporate tax are grossed up, in both systems, by 138% of the actual dividend, and the Quebec credit is 11.9% of the grossed-up amount or 16.422% of the actual dividend. Quebec has also adopted the 2008 federal Budget adjustments to the gross-up rates of eligible dividends. The gross-up rate was reduced from 45% in 2009 to 44% in 2010, further reduced to 41% in 2011, and finally to 38% in 2012 and subsequent years.

The amounts eligible for the small business and eligible dividends rates should in most cases be the same for federal and Quebec purposes, although it is conceivable, especially where Quebec corporations eligible for the Quebec small business rate are concerned, that Quebec will assess the corporate pools differently.

The taxable amount of dividends from taxable Canadian corporations is the total of the following amounts:

- the amount from box B of your RL-3 slip;
- the amount from box I of your RL-16 slip;
- the amount from box F of your RL-25 slip; and
- the amounts from boxes 6-1 to 6-3 of your RL-15 slip.

The tax credit for dividends from taxable Canadian corporations, is the total of the following amounts:

- the amount from box C of your RL-3 slip;
- the amount from box J of your RL-16 slip;
- the amount from box 44 of your RL-25 slip; and
- the amounts from box G of your RL-15 slip.

If you did not receive one or more of the above-mentioned RL slips, the amounts are shown on your T3, T4PS, T5, and T5013 slips.

You may not claim credit for dividends not included in computing your Quebec income.

The amount is claimed on line 415 of the return.

(QTA: 497; 767; Other Publications: Quebec Finance Information Bulletin 2006-2, June 29, 2006)

[¶1667] POLITICAL CONTRIBUTION CREDIT

Commencing in 2013 you may deduct from your Quebec income tax otherwise payable (i.e., claim a non-refundable tax credit) with respect to amounts contributed only for contributions in respect of municipal elections. Prior to 2013 you could also claim amounts contributed to a Quebec political party. However, considering that the *Election Act* allows, in certain circumstances, for a leadership candidate of a provincial party to receive contributions up to 36 months after the leadership vote (i.e., the candidates to the Liberal leadership vote of January 2013 could receive contributions up to March 17, 2016), such contributions will still give rise to the credit.

Contributions to the official representative of a municipal party or independent candidate authorized to receive contributions under the *Act respecting elections and referendums in municipalities*, the credit is the total of:

(1) 85% of the lesser of $50 and the total amount of all such contributions, and

(2) 75% of the amount by which $50 is exceeded by the lesser of $200 and the total amount of such contributions.

For 2012 and prior taxation years, contributions for the benefit of a political party, party authority, independent member, or independent candidate authorized to receive contributions under the *Election Act*, the credit was the total of:

(1) 85% of the lesser of $100 and the total amount of such contributions, and

(2) 75% of the amount by which $100 is exceeded by the lesser of $400 and the total amount of such contributions.

The maximum annual credit after 2012 is $155. The maximum annual credit for 2012 and 2011 was $465 ($310 + $155). The credit is calculated on the Quebec workchart for line 414.

(QTA: 776; Election Act 127.15)

[¶1669] QUEBEC LABOUR-SPONSORED FUNDS CREDIT

These funds are the Quebec version of Labour-Sponsored Venture Capital Funds (LSVCCs — see ¶1466), and investments in them qualify for both federal and provincial tax credits.

A Quebec taxpayer can claim a non-refundable tax credit for certain investments in labour-sponsored funds.

The purchaser must purchase new shares of:

- class A shares in the Fonds de solidarité des travailleurs du Quebec ("FTQ"); or
- class A or class B shares in the Fonds de développement de la Confédération des syndicats nationaux pour la coopération et l'emploi ("Fondaction").

The credit applies to the cost of shares bought during the year (or the first 60 days of the following year) up to a maximum purchase limit of $5,000.

For FTQ, the credit rate is 15% of the cost of shares, for a maximum credit of $750. For Fondaction, the credit rate depends on when the shares were purchased, as shown below:

- 25% for shares issued after May 31, 2009 and before June 1, 2015, for a maximum credit of $1,250;
- 20% for shares issued after May 31, 2015 and before June 1, 2016, for a maximum credit of $1,000 (announced in the 2015 Quebec Budget);
- 20% for shares issued after May 31, 2016 and before June 1, 2018, for a maximum credit of $1,000 (announced in the 2016 Quebec Budget); and
- 15% for shares issued after May 31, 2018 or before June 1, 2009, for a maximum credit of $750.

You may carry forward for Quebec (but not for federal) purposes any remaining undeducted balance as a deduction against your Quebec income taxes payable for future taxation years, subject to an overall limitation that no more than $750 may be deducted in any one year ($1,000 if subject to the temporary increase of this credit to 20% applicable to any share of Fondaction acquired after May 31, 2015, and before June 1, 2018).

You can invest in these funds either directly or through an RRSP of which you are the annuitant or an RRSP of which your spouse is the annuitant and utilize the credit yourself. These rules are discussed in detail in ¶2522(2).

You do not qualify for this deduction if:

(1) you reached 45 years of age or more and were retired or on pre-retirement leave in the taxation year for which your Quebec return is being filed; however, if you earned employment income or carried on a business or practised a profession in the year, Revenu Québec will apparently permit the credit under certain conditions; it is understood that these conditions (which you may want to verify with the CRA) are:

(a) you must have employment, business or professional income in excess of $3,500 for the year, and

(b) you must not have disposed of any shares in the fund during the year;

(2) where the credit is acquired through an RRSP or RRIF of which your spouse is the annuitant, your spouse reached 45 years of age or more and was retired or on pre-retirement leave in the taxation year (presumably subject to the same relief as in (1));

(3) you reached the age of 65 years or more in the taxation year for which your Quebec return is being filed;

(4) where the credit is acquired through an RRSP or RRIF of which your spouse is the annuitant, your spouse reached 65 years of age or more in the taxation year; or

(5) you requested a redemption of the shares in the year of purchase or within 120 days following the year of purchase (the Quebec Guide says if you redeem a share within 60 days of purchase; the Guide is apparently based on the Quebec LSVCC legislation which permits you to change your mind about a purchase within 60 days but restricts redemption thereafter; essentially the two rules are the same, since the 120-day rule embraces a redemption 60 days after a purchase 60 days after year end).

See Quebec Information Bulletin 2009-6 for situations in which a person will be considered to have opted for retirement or early retirement for the purposes of this credit.

The amount is claimed on line 424 of the return.

(QTA: 776.1.1–776.1.5; Other Publications: 2016 Quebec Budget, Additional Information, item 3.3; Quebec Finance Information Bulletin 2008-8, 1.3; Quebec Finance Information Bulletin 2009-6, item 7; Quebec Finance Information Bulletin 2010-6, *Fiscal Measures Relating to Individuals and Businesses and Pertaining to Consumption Taxes;* 2015 Quebec Budget, Additional Information, item 2.7)

[¶1669.05] *Share Redemptions for Home Purchase and Further Education*

Investors in Quebec LSVCCs are able to redeem their shares if they meet RRSP criteria for HBP or LLP borrowing, but must buy back the shares at the redemption price over the same period that applies for RRSP repayment purposes. A special tax will be imposed on any repurchase shortfall, unless the taxpayer could as of right redeem shares before the end of the period on which a particular repayment is due. The federal government matches this policy, ensuring that Quebec LSVCC investors will not suffer federal or Quebec recapture of LSVCC credits where they redeem shares in conformity with these rules.

The special tax related to the non-purchase of replacement shares is indicated on a RL-10 slip box F at line 1 for the 15% tax or at line 2 for the 25% tax. The amount is entered on line 443 of the tax return.

(QTA: 776.1.5.0.1–776.1.5.0.10)

[¶1669.10] *Cost of Share*

Quebec only allows the issue price of the shares to be used as the "amount paid for the purchase of a share", which gives entitlement to the LSVCC credit. The issue price will thus not include expenses associated with the purchase, such as the cost of opening an account.

(Other Publications: June 12, 2003 Quebec Budget, *Additional Information on the Fiscal Measures,* item 1.8.1)

[¶1669.15] *Interest on Money Borrowed To Buy LSVCC Shares*

No deduction is permitted for interest on money borrowed to acquire shares which carry the Quebec LSVCC tax credit. Note that this was always true where shares were contributed to an RRSP, under rules comparable to those at ¶1064.

(Other Publications: June 12, 2003 Quebec *Additional Information on the Fiscal Measures,* item 1.8.1)

[¶1669.20] *Limitations on Share Availability and Return*

Effective June 13, 2003, Quebec's LSVCCs became subject to provincial income tax. While this has no direct effect on investors, it affects the potential funds on hand in the corporation and accordingly the expectation of return on the investment.

As well, the funds the LSVCCs are allowed to raise will be limited to specified annual amounts, which may affect the availability of shares.

(Other Publications: June 12, 2003 Quebec Budget, *Additional Information on the Fiscal Measures,* item 1.8.1; 2004 Quebec *Additional Information on the Budgetary Measures,* item 2.7)

[¶1669c] CAPITAL RÉGIONAL ET COOPÉRATIF DESJARDINS SHARE TAX CREDIT

To encourage taxpayers to participate in economic development of resource regions and the growth of cooperatives in Quebec, a non-refundable tax credit is available for share investments in Capital régional et coopératif Desjardins.

The credit is claimed on line 422 and must be supported by an RL-26 slip. There is no carryforward of unused credits.

An individual (other than a broker acting in his or her capacity as intermediary or firm underwriter) may deduct, in calculating tax otherwise payable for a taxation year:

- for shares acquired before March 24, 2006, 50% of all the amounts, up to $2,500, paid during the investment year;
- for shares acquired after March 23, 2006, and before November 10, 2007, 35% of all the amounts, up to $2,500, paid during the investment year;
- for shares acquired after November 9, 2007 and before March 1, 2014, 50% of all the amounts, up to $5,000, paid during the investment year;
- for shares acquired after February 28, 2014, 45% of all amounts, up to $5,000, paid during the investment year;
- for shares acquired after February 29, 2016, 40% of all amounts, up to $5,000, paid during the investment year.

For a given taxation year, an individual may claim the appropriate credit for all shares purchased at any time during a period beginning on March 1 of such given taxation year and ending on the last day of February of the following taxation year, to purchase, as first acquirer, a share of Capital régional et coopératif Desjardins.

In the event that the acquisition period applicable for a given taxation year ends on a public holiday, it shall be deemed, for the purposes of this tax credit, to end on the preceding day.

This tax credit is only available to an individual residing in Quebec on December 31 of the taxation year for which the credit may be claimed, but is available whether the individual files a tax return under the general or simplified tax system.

The tax credit may not be claimed for a share if a request to redeem it has been made in writing within 30 days of its subscription, nor if the subject shares are subject to redemption or purchase by Capital régional et coopératif Desjardins prior to March 1 of the taxation year following the year for which the credit is claimed. The tax credit is not available against Quebec alternative minimum tax or child split income tax.

To the extent shares are not held for at least seven years from the date of issue, a recapture tax will tax back credits *pro rata* to the number of days short of seven years (specified as 2,556 days) the shares have been held. The actual recapture formula will be (2,556 - A × B) ÷ 2,556, where:

- A represents the number of days during which the share is held by the holder and, if applicable, by the person who received such share by inheritance; and
- B is the lesser of 35% of the amount paid by the holder to acquire the share and the price paid for its redemption or purchase by agreement.

The following table summarizes certain effects of the redemption or purchase by agreement of a share of Capital régional et coopératif Desjardins.

EFFECTS OF THE REDEMPTION OR PURCHASE BY AGREEMENT OF A SHARE

Reason for the redemption or purchase by agreement	Possibility of subsequent subscription by the holder	Liability for special tax
REDEMPTION		
— after holding seven years	NO	NO
— because of disability	NO	YES
— because of death	—	YES[1]
— within 30 days of purchase	YES	NO
PURCHASE BY AGREEMENT		
— because of lack of tax assistance	YES	NO
— because of emigration	NO	YES[2]
— because of terminal illness	NO	YES
— because of urgent need for cash	NO	YES

[1] Except for shares acquired in the year of death.

[2] Except for shares acquired in the year of emigration.

The tax credit will not reduce adjusted cost base of Capital régional et coopératif Desjardins shares acquired for the purposes of determining the (at least Quebec) capital gain on the disposition of such shares. However, in the event of capital loss on disposition, the loss will be reduced by the excess of the tax credit obtained over any recapture tax paid on the redemption of the share.

(QTA: 776.1.5.0.11–776.1.5.0.15; Other Publications: 2016 Quebec Budget, Additional Information 2016-2017, item 3.2; 2014 Quebec Budget, *Additional Information on the Fiscal Measures of the Budget*, item 4.4; March 23, 2006, Quebec Budget, *Additional Information on the Budgetary Measures*, Revenue Measures, item 4.2; Quebec Finance Information Bulletin 2007-8)

[¶1669c.05] *Cost of Share*

Quebec only allows the issue price of the shares to be used as the "amount paid for the purchase of a share", which gives entitlement to the credit. As such, the cost of the shares will not include expenses associated with the purchase.

(QTA: 776.1.5.0.15)

[¶1669c.10] *Interest on Money Borrowed To Buy Shares*

No deduction will be permitted for interest on money borrowed to acquire shares which carry the Capital régional et coopératif Desjardins tax credit. Note that this would always have been true where shares are contributed to an RRSP, under rules comparable to those at ¶1064.

(QTA: 175.2– 175.2.1)

[¶1669c.15] *Limitations on Share Availability and Return*

The Capital régional et coopératif Desjardins is subject to provincial income tax. While this has no direct effect on investors, it will of course affect the potential funds on hand in the corporation and accordingly the expectation of return on the investment.

As well, the funds the organization is allowed to raise will be limited to a specified annual amount, which may affect the availability of shares.

(Other Publications: June 12, 2003 Quebec Budget, *Additional Information on the Fiscal Measures*, item 1.8.1; 2004 Quebec Budget, *Additional Information on the Budgetary Measures*, item 2.7)

[¶1670] CREDIT FOR FOREIGN INCOME TAXES

You are allowed a credit for income taxes paid to a foreign country, to a political subdivision of a foreign country and for an income tax or contribution of the same nature as income taxes under the Quebec *Taxation Act* paid to a prescribed international organization.

The Quebec foreign tax credits are calculated on form TP-772-V and entered on Schedule E (line 409).

Essentially, you may claim a foreign tax credit on your business or non-business income if you meet both of the following conditions:

- You were resident in Quebec on December 31 of the taxation year, or on the date on which you ceased to reside in Canada during the taxation year.
- You paid income tax on the income in question to the government of a foreign country or of a political subdivision of a foreign country, or you paid a similar contribution on the income in question to certain international organizations.

Your foreign tax credit on non-business income cannot be higher than the result of the following calculation: the total foreign income tax paid on your non-business income, minus the foreign tax credit granted by the Canada Revenue Agency on this income.

You must calculate foreign tax credits separately for each country to which you pay foreign tax. You should submit a separate form TP-772-V for each country; the form permits you to calculate both business and non-business tax credit for that country.

The credit with respect to foreign *business* income will be, for each country, the least of:

(1) 45% of the foreign income taxes paid for your Canadian taxation year to the particular foreign country, or to a political subdivision of that foreign country, plus your unused Quebec foreign tax credit in respect of that country for the ten taxation years preceding the year and the three taxation years following the year; (that is, there is a ten-year carryforward and three-year carryback of unused business foreign tax credits);

(2) the proportion of the Quebec income taxes payable before the dividend tax credit and logging tax credit that net foreign business income is of net income for the year less the deduction permitted for net capital losses incurred in prior years or in a subsequent year; or

(3) the Quebec income taxes payable before the dividend tax credit and logging tax credit less the foreign tax credits claimed on foreign non-business income.

The credit for foreign *non-business* income will be the lesser of:

(1) foreign taxes paid to a foreign country, or to a political subdivision of a foreign country, on foreign non-business income but not allowed in the federal foreign tax credit; or

(2) the proportion of the Quebec income taxes payable before the dividend tax credit and logging tax credit that net foreign non-business income is of the net income for the year less the deduction permitted for net capital losses incurred in prior years or in a subsequent year.

If foreign tax paid on foreign income from a property other than an immovable exceeds 15% of the foreign income, the foreign taxes eligible for the foreign tax credit will be limited to the 15% amount. You may deduct the foreign taxes in excess of 15% in computing your income from the property. If you claim such a deduction you must enter the amount as carrying charges on line 231 of your return.

Where an individual employed by an international organization has paid to such organization a levy computed in a manner similar to the manner in which income tax is computed, to defray the expenses of such organization, he or she may claim as a credit in addition to the foreign tax credits on foreign business and non-business income, the least of:

(1) the amount by which the levy exceeds the amount allowed as a credit for federal foreign tax credit purposes;

(2) the proportion of the Quebec income taxes payable before the dividend tax credit and logging tax credit that the amount included in his or her income for the year as remuneration, in respect of which the levy was computed, is of his or her net income for the year; or

(3) the proportion of the levy that the amount included in income for the year as remuneration is of the amount that would be included in computing income for the year from employment with the organization if a portion was not exempt.

Foreign income can include investment income, rental income, business income or employment income. The facts determining the source of income are discussed at ¶1455. In all cases, the foreign income should be calculated before deducting any foreign taxes withheld and after deduction of related expenses.

(QTA: 772.2–772.13)

[¶1670.05] *Credit for Tax Paid in Another Province by Deemed Residents of Quebec*

In 2011 Quebec introduced a non-refundable tax credit available to deemed residents of Quebec who may be subject to double taxation by virtue of the Federal tax rules regarding the taxation of income earned by a resident of another country with which Canada has a tax treaty. In certain situations, such individuals may end up having to pay tax to both Quebec and another province by virtue of the federal tax rules.

This credit applies to income earned from an office or employment and will work so as to ensure that the total taxes paid at the provincial level is not greater than the tax paid at the Quebec level on the total of such income, should the individual be deemed to be a resident of Quebec. Basically it will allow a credit for the taxes paid or payable to another province on that income, as Quebec's marginal tax rate is generally higher than those in other provinces.

In order to be able to claim this credit the individual must be able to meet the following conditions:

- be deemed to be a resident of Quebec by virtue of having sojourned in the province for one or more periods during the year, totaling more than 183 days;
- be otherwise a resident of a country with which Canada has a tax treaty and by virtue of such a treaty, is deemed not to be a resident of Canada and subject to federal tax.

In calculating the credit, the tax payable in Quebec is calculated before deducting the following:

- tax adjustment for certain retroactive payments such as repayment of income and benefits received and taxed in other years;
- dividend tax credit;
- tax credit for investments in a labour fund;
- tax credit for the purchase of shares of Capital regional et cooperative Desjardins;
- political contribution tax credit;
- credit for graduates working in the resource regions;
- credit received for an investment in an environmental trust;
- the deduction for logging taxes paid;
- foreign tax credit;
- credit for income from a designated trust.

The tax credit so calculated, if not fully deductible in the year, may not be carried forward to other years, but does however qualify to be transferred to a taxpayer's spouse under the spousal transfer rules (see ¶1650).

In the year of death, the credit can only be claimed by the deceased taxpayer on the principal return.

(QTA: 772.13.1–772.13.3)

[¶1670.10] *Credit for U.S. Social Security Contributions*

Generally speaking, the Quebec foreign tax credit rules as to what qualifies as foreign tax eligible for credit are identical to the federal rules at ¶1455, so that foreign tax eligible for federal credit will be eligible for Quebec credit. However, differences of interpretation are always possible. In particular, Quebec does not consider itself bound by federal tax treaties, which gave rise, for a time, to a different Quebec treatment of foreign tax credit for contributions to U.S. Social Security (known to the tax literati as "FICA" — for U.S. *Federal Insurance Contributions Act* — contributions.

The general position, shared by Quebec and federal authorities, is that contributions to foreign social security systems are not taxes eligible for foreign tax credit (there may be an exception where the contributions are for temporary foreign employment and no benefits will be derived from the contributions). See the discussion at ¶1455(3). However, by virtue of the Canada–U.S. Tax Treaty, the federal government must recognize FICA contributions as eligible for federal foreign tax credit (at least to the extent they are related to U.S.-source income, which would normally be the case).

(QTA: 772.2–772.13; Other Publications: March 13, 2008 Quebec Budget, *Additional Information on the Budgetary Measures,* Revenue Measures, item 1.8)

[¶1671] LOGGING TAX DEDUCTION

If you have a logging business which is subject to logging tax under Part VII of the *Taxation Act*, you may claim a deduction from your income of up to one-third of the Quebec logging tax paid or payable for the year to a maximum of Quebec income tax payable.

The logging tax that an individual must pay is equal to 10% of their total logging income, provided the logging income is in excess of $10,000 for the year. As announced in the 2016 Quebec Budget, the exemption threshold for tax on logging operations has been increased from $10,000 to $65,000 for taxation years that begin after March 17, 2016.

Complete line 17 of Schedule E (line 432) based on logging tax calculated on form TPZ-1179-V. This credit should not be confused with the property tax refund for forest producers (¶1683), calculated on Schedule E at part C.

(QTA: 1183; Other Publications: 2016 Quebec Budget, Additional Information, item 3.7)

REFUNDS AND REFUNDABLE CREDITS

[¶1675] REFUNDS AND REFUNDABLE CREDITS

Quebec provides the standard tax return refunds for CPP/QPP excess withholdings, as well as excess withholdings on account of employment or investment income and excess instalment payments.

Quebec has an inordinate number of refundable tax credits, for everything from adoption expenses to taxi permits. Presumably, this indicates a more interventionist fiscal policy than is common in the other Canadian provinces, or (arguably) a more finely tuned one. In any event, Quebec has a tendency to try to assimilate all aspects of Quebec life into a grand fiscal design. However admirable this may be as an intellectual construct, it makes for a singularly complex tax system.

Quebec refundable credits, like their relatively limited federal counterparts, are deemed to be payments made on account of tax. It follows that tax payable normally describes taxes before the application of refundable credits.

[¶1676] QUEBEC PENSION PLAN REFUND

Usually, an overpayment of contributions to the *Quebec Pension Plan* will arise if you were employed for less than the full year or if you changed jobs during the year.

If you were resident in the Province of Quebec on December 31, and are entitled to a refund on account of an overpayment under either the *Canada Pension Plan* ("CPP") or *Quebec Pension Plan* ("QPP"), or both plans, your claim for refund must be entered on line 452 of the Quebec Income Tax return. If you were resident in another province of Canada on December 31, but have made contributions to the QPP and wish to claim refund for an overpayment, you should follow the instructions on CPP or QPP contributions in your T1 Tax Guide, and report QPP contributions as if they were contributions to CPP.

The amount of the overpayment to be refunded must be taken into account in determining the allowable deduction for QPP contributions.

Although the Quebec rules on QPP liability at age 18 and 70, and on disability and death are virtually identical to the federal rules at ¶1305, as are the optional employment contribution requirements and the mandatory self-employment contribution requirements (calculated on form LE-35-V accompanying the Quebec return) the contribution rates and refund calculations for Quebec tax purposes differ from the federal rates and calculations.

[¶1676a] QUEBEC PARENTAL INSURANCE PLAN REFUND

If you are entitled to a refund on account of an overpayment under the Quebec Parental Insurance Plan, enter the amount on line 457.

[¶1676d] CREDIT FOR THE REPAYMENT OF BENEFITS

[¶1676d.05] *QPP/CPP/QPIP/EI Repayments*

If you are required in a year to repay benefits under the *Quebec Pension Plan*, *Quebec Parental Insurance Plan*, *Canada Pension Plan*, or federal *Employment Insurance Act* which were received by you and included in your income in the year or a preceding year, you may deduct these repayments from Quebec income of the year of repayment under rules identical to the federal rules at ¶1029. The comparable Quebec deduction is discussed in ¶1624.

However, where the payments relate to amounts included in income of a preceding year, you have the option of foregoing the deduction and choosing instead to take a refundable tax credit. This may be preferable if in the year of repayment you have low or no income.

The refundable tax credit is based on the tax that would have been payable in the year or years in which the payments were made had they been excluded from income in those years. The notional excess tax attributable to the original payments becomes a refundable credit for the year of repayment.

The mechanism is to take the deduction on line 246 of the Quebec return and enter the code 08 in box 461 of the return (you must not enter any amount on line 462). By indicating the code 08, you are asking Revenu Québec to determine whether it would be to your advantage to take a credit at line 462 rather than a deduction at line 246. Revenu Québec will assess accordingly. Note that you cannot efile the return, you must paper file the return and any supporting documents.

[¶1676d.10] *Repayments of Salary or Wages Included in Earlier Year Income*

A deduction from income is allowed for all qualified repayments of amounts included in an earlier year as salary or wages for a period of non-performance of employment duties (essentially, wage loss replacement plans, typically workers' compensation other than top-up payments, as described under the heading "QPP, EI and Salary Repayments" at ¶1624 and, for comparable federal rules, at "Repayment of Salary or Wages" at ¶362), regardless of the prior year to which they relate.

As a general rule, a non-capital loss resulting from the deduction in the year of benefits repaid can be carried back over three taxation years preceding the year of its realization and carried forward over the subsequent 20 taxation years. Since it can happen that the rights to covered benefits be recognized more than three years after an accident, employment injury, bodily injury or death, certain individuals may not be able to fully benefit from the carryback of the loss. The tax legislation stipulates that, where an amount is paid, during a given taxation year, on account of reimbursement of an amount included in the calculation of the individual's income for a taxation year prior to the given year, and that such reimbursement is related to the fact that covered benefits attributable to such prior year have been determined in the given year, the individual may deduct, in calculating his or her taxable income for the prior year, an amount in respect of a non-capital loss that he or she realized in the given year, provided such amount can reasonably be attributed to such reimbursement.

The amendments will apply regarding the reimbursement of an amount received while waiting for recognition of the right to covered benefits.

(QTA: 78.1; 336(*d*), (*d.1*); 1029.8.50; 1029.8.50.1 (repealed); Other Publications: 2004 Quebec Budget, *Additional Information on Budgetary Measures*, item 1.10; Quebec Finance Information Bulletin 2010-6, item 1.4)

[¶1677] REFUNDABLE CREDIT FOR CHILD CARE EXPENSES (SCHEDULE C)

The Quebec tax relief for child care expenses is, with some minor exceptions, identical to the federal rules at ¶1051 in the determination of actual child care expenses and the federal rules in ¶1051.05 as to the purposes for which the expenses must be incurred. Quebec differs from federal rules in permitting allowable child care expenses to include expenses incurred to allow a taxpayer to actively seek employment.

Quebec has abandoned the earned income limitation. Even more significantly, Quebec abandoned the complex machinery of requiring the expenses to be claimed by the lower-income supporting person except in specified circumstances. Instead, child care expenses incurred by a taxpayer or the taxpayer's "eligible spouse" (¶1650.03) may be claimed by either party or divided between them as they see fit, in accordance with Quebec's general spousal transfer rules at ¶1650.

The upshot is that either spouse may claim child care expenses. The expenses are essentially those recognized for federal purposes, i.e., expenses for child care services for an eligible child of the taxpayer, including babysitting, day nursery services, or services provided at a boarding school or camp. The expenses must enable one partner or the other who resides with the child at the time the expenses are incurred to perform the duties of an office or employment, carry on a business (either alone or as a partner actively engaged in the business), carry on research or any similar work for which he or she received a grant, pursue studies in a qualified educational institution, or actively seek employment. These activities include those which qualify for federal purposes (plus the actively seeking work criterion). The new Quebec rules enable the use of expenses of a spouse who works in the family business without pay, or those of a spouse who works in a business with a loss for the year.

Eligible child care expenses include those incurred for child care services during a period in which an individual (or his or her spouse) received Quebec Parental Insurance Plan benefits, federal Employment Insurance plan birth- or adoption-related benefits, or benefits under a plan established in another province.

The rules disqualifying certain payments are almost but perhaps not always identical to federal rules at ¶1051.15. The Quebec rules specify that payments to the following are not expenses eligible for Quebec credit:

- the child's father or mother;
- a person with whom the individual is living in a conjugal relationship;
- a person who is residing with the individual and for whom the child in respect of whom the child care expenses are incurred is an eligible child;
- a person under 18 years of age related to the individual or to the person with whom the individual is living in a conjugal relationship;
- a person in regard to whom either the individual, or a person who is residing with the individual and for whom the child in respect of whom the expenses are incurred is an eligible child, deducts, in the calculation of his or her income tax otherwise payable for the year, an amount as a tax credit respecting a dependant or an amount for the purposes of the transfer of the recognized parental contribution.

The annual per child dollar limitations on eligible child care expenses for Quebec purposes, $11,000/$9,000/$5,000, (prior to 2015, the limits were $10,000/$9,000/$4,000) are dependent on the age or, where applicable, impairment of the eligible child annually. This limitation is $11,000 for any eligible child who has a severe and prolonged mental or physical impairment certified as such by a physician or in the case of sight impairment by an optometrist, regardless of age; plus $9,000 for any other eligible child that had not reached 7 years of age at the end of the year; plus $5,000 for any other eligible child under the age of 17 at any time in the year.

In addition, the federal per week limitations of $250 for impaired children, $175 for children under 7 at the end of the year, and $100 for children over 6 but not yet 17 at the end of the year will apply to payments made to a boarding school or a camp.

As before, Quebec will not allow as child care expenses the $7.55 per day fee paid to a Quebec subsidized child care centre, a home daycare centre or a daycare centre, or for basic school daycare services. However, since they will not be prescribed, expenses for basic services provided through subsidized child care at school for spring break will continue to be qualified expenses for the purposes of the tax credit for childcare expenses. (Note that these amounts may qualify for federal purposes; see ¶1051.20.)

To ensure the sustainability of Quebec's educational child care network, the government announced certain changes to the subsidized educational child care program on November 20, 2014. One such change is a revision of the contribution paid for a child who occupies a subsidized child care space.

Effective April 22, 2015, subsidized childcare fees include a basic contribution of $7.55 per day, per child, and an additional contribution adjusted to family income. Both the basic and additional contributions will be indexed every year starting on January 1, 2016 (see ¶1663.20).

The basic contribution will continue to be paid to the child care service provider. The additional contribution will be paid by parents when they file their 2016 income tax return (see ¶1663.20).

Tax Shield Credit

If you resided in Quebec on December 31, 2016, and if in 2016 you or your spouse were eligible for one of the refundable work premium credits or for the child care expense credit, you could benefit from the tax shield credit (¶1681a) if you meet the following two conditions:

- your family income (line 275) for 2016 is higher than that of 2015;
- your working income for 2016 is higher than that of 2015.

The portion of the tax shield respecting the work premium tax credit can be as much as $225 for an individual and $450 for a couple. The part of the tax shield respecting the tax credit for child care expenses can represent an increase of a few percentage points in the tax credit rate for child care expenses.

To claim the tax shield credit you must check box 99 on Schedule C (Tax Credit for Childcare Expenses) or box 5 on Schedule P (Tax Credits Respecting the Work Premium). However, if you want to calculate the amount of the credit yourself, you must complete Form TP-1029.BF (Tax Shield Credit). The credit is claimed on line 460 of the tax return.

(QTA: 1029.8.67–1029.8.81; Other Publications: Quebec Finance Information Bulletin 2015-5)

[¶1677.10] *Residence Requirements*

The Quebec child care expense credit is, in the first instance, available to an individual resident in Quebec at the end of the taxation year.

The following Quebec residence rules apply:

(1) Where an individual is resident in Canada outside Quebec at the end of a given taxation year but carried on a business in Quebec during the year (¶1607) and has an eligible spouse resident in Quebec at the end of the year, the individual may claim the refundable tax credit for qualified child care expenses. The tax credit will be calculated as if the individual were resident in Quebec at the end of the year.

(2) Where an individual is resident in Canada outside Quebec, carried on a business in Quebec (¶1607), and whose eligible spouse (if any) is not resident in Quebec at the end of the taxation year, the flexible credit rate discussed below (¶1677.15) will be replaced by the highest applicable Quebec income tax rate (¶1661.05), currently 25.75%, and the allocation rules will apply as follows:

(a) Where an individual is resident in Canada outside Quebec at the end of a given taxation year, carried on a business in Quebec during the year and who either did not have an eligible spouse or whose eligible spouse is neither (i) a person resident in Quebec at the end of the year, nor (ii) a person resident in Canada outside Quebec at the end of the year who carried on a business in Quebec during the year, he or she may claim a refundable child care expense credit equal to the product obtained by multiplying, by the ratio used to determine his or her income tax payable for the year, the amount obtained by applying to his or her qualified child care expenses for the year a flat rate which is the lowest applicable child tax credit rate (currently 26%). This appears to mean the flat credit rate of 26% is prorated by the Quebec income allocation (determined on federal form T2203 as described at ¶1440, and reported on Quebec form TP-25-V) over total income.

(b) For an individual who is resident in Canada outside Quebec at the end of a given taxation year, carried on a business in Quebec during the year, and has an eligible spouse for the year who is also an person resident in Canada outside Quebec at the end of the year who carried on a business in Quebec during the year, the individual's Quebec child care expense credit claim is "the product obtained by multiplying, by the average of the ratios used to determine the income tax payable for the year by the individual and by his or her eligible spouse for the year, the amount obtained by applying to his or her qualified child care expenses for the year a rate equal to the tax rate applicable to the last income tax bracket of the tax table". This appears to mean the flat credit rate of 26% is prorated by the average of the Quebec income allocation of each spouse (determined on federal form T2203 as described at ¶1440, and reported on Quebec form TP-25-V) over the total income of that spouse.

The federal rules for commuters to the United States and for residents absent from Canada (read Quebec) in ¶1051.10 apply equally for the Quebec credit.

[¶1677.15] *Quebec Credit Rates*

The most significant difference between federal and Quebec treatment of child care expenses generally is that Quebec has replaced a deduction from income with a refundable child care expense tax credit. Essentially, the Quebec credit takes the eligible expenses (which are generally the expenses eligible for federal deduction purposes), applies its own earned income and dollar limit rules, and converts the resulting "eligible expenses" to refundable tax credits at a rate that varies from 26% to 75% of the amount. The rate of credit falls as family income rises. "Family income" includes the joint income of you and your spouse (if any). This is simply the income from line 275 of each return. As with other definitions of family income in the Quebec tax credit field, your spouse, does not include a spouse from whom you were separated on December 31, provided the separation was due to a breakdown of the relationship which proved to last for at least 90 days.

[¶1677.20] *Comparative Benefits of Quebec Credit*

Generally speaking, the Quebec credit is more valuable than the federal deduction. First, of course, it is refundable, and cannot only eliminate tax but can generate payments to low-income families. Second, the complex earned income limitations and rules generally confining the benefit to the income of the lower-income spouse no longer apply to the Quebec credit.

[¶1677.22] *Prepayments of Credit*

To permit parents to finance child care expenses during the year, Quebec allows parents to file for prepayment of anticipated credits. Advance payments of the child care expenses credit will be made, on a monthly basis. Advance payments are available only to applicants willing to accept direct deposit of the prepayments.

Prepayments are trued up on your annual return. The prepayments (reported to you on an RL-19 slip) must be included on line 441 of your return.

To receive advance payments of the tax credit for child care expenses, you are required to complete form TPZ-1029.8.F-V, "Tax Credit for Child-Care Expenses: Application for Advance Payments", and have the person who provides the child care services complete form TPZ-1029.8.F.A-V, "Child-Care Expenses Giving Entitlement to the Tax Credit". You then send both these forms to Revenu Québec.

To qualify for the advance payments, you must:

- be the father or mother of a child with whom you are living at the time of your application;
- be resident in Quebec at the time of your application;
- estimate that, for the taxation year concerned, you are entitled to an amount of more than $1,000 as a tax credit for child care expenses (this condition does not

apply if you estimate that you will also be entitled to a work premium of at least $500).

If you and your spouse both expect to be entitled to the tax credit for child care expenses, only one of you may apply for advance payments.

You must inform Revenu Québec of any change in your personal or family situation that could affect the amount of your advance payments of the tax credit. For example, you must notify Revenu Québec if your child care expenses are lower than expected or if for some reason they cease to qualify for the credit (for example, if you commence living in a conjugal relationship with the caregiver).

(QTA: 1029.8.80.2; Other Publications: 2010 Quebec Budget, *Additional Information on the Budgetary Measures, Revenue Measures,* item 1.4)

[¶1677.30] *Schedule and Guide*

The Quebec child care credit has complex rules, and differs in significant detail from the federal version. Quebec's annual tax return guide provides much necessary explanation in its discussion of line 455. Schedule C facilitates the calculation, and provides the essential table which converts family income to an applicable credit rate.

(QTA: 1029.8.67–1029.8.81; Other Publications: 2007 Quebec Budget, *Additional Information on the Budgetary Measures,* Section A, Appendix, 1.5; 2009 Quebec Budget, *Additional Information on the Budgetary Measures,* item 1)

[¶1677f] REFUNDABLE CREDITS IN RESPECT OF WORK PREMIUM (SCHEDULE P)

The work premium, a refundable tax credit aimed at low- and middle-income families, includes a supplement for long-term recipients, providing a last-resort financial assistance, as well as a work premium specifically adapted to persons with severely limited capacity for employment (the "Adapted Work Premium"). Note that individuals entitled to both the work premium and the adapted work premium may claim only one. If an individual applies for the adapted work premium, his or her spouse cannot apply for the work premium. Individuals in prison (or a similar institution) at the end of the taxation year and whose confinement lasted more than six months may not claim a work premium tax credit.

Since 2015, similar to the federal provision, an individual who is a full-time student is no longer considered to be an eligible individual for the purposes of the refundable tax credits to increase the incentive to work, unless, at the end of December 31 of that year or, on the date of the individual's death, the individual is the father or the mother of a child with whom he or she lives.

[¶1677f.05] *Work Premium*

To claim the work premium, an individual who has a spouse must have at least $3,600 a year in earned income; an individual who does not have a spouse must have at least $2,400 a year in earned income. Earned income is, essentially, aggregate of income for the year from an office or employment and net business income. If employment income for the year consists only of the value of benefits received by reason of a previous year's office or employment, it is not included in eligible earned income; examples would be a retiree's medical insurance coverage, securities options, or low-interest loans. Moreover, business income is limited to income from a business carried on alone or as a partner actively engaged in the business; passive partnership income no longer qualifies.

The work premium supplements work income earned by an individual and his or her spouse vary according to type of household. The types of households are (1) a person living alone; (2) a couple without children; (3) a single-parent family; (4) a couple with at least one child. For the purposes of this credit, a child may be designated as a "dependent child". See line 456 of the guide for the definition of "designated dependent child".

The premium amount is reduced when the household's family income exceeds a certain threshold. The reduction rate is 10% for each dollar of family income in excess of the applicable reduction threshold.

The credit, fully described in the Revenu Quebec Income Tax Return Guide for line 456 of the return, is calculated on Schedule P.

Advance payments of the work premium are made on a monthly basis.

Prepayments of the credit may be included with your Quebec child assistance benefit. Prepayments are available to households without children. Where prepayments are made, they are added back to tax on line 441 of the Quebec return and the proper credit is calculated on Schedule P.

Last-resort financial assistance benefits (the Social Solidarity Program and the Social Assistance Program) are indexed at the rate used for the personal income tax system (1.09% for 2016, 1.06% for 2015, 0.97% for 2014, 2.48% for 2013, and 2.66% for 2012). This also raises the amounts paid for Child Assistance and the Work Premium, both of which are integrated into the last-resort assistance program.

The 2016 Quebec Budget announced a 2% enhancement to the basic and adaptive work premiums commencing in 2016 for households without children.

The following chart lists the parameters used for determining the maximum work premium in taxation year 2016:

MAIN PARAMETERS OF THE WORK PREMIUM FOR 2016

	Single person	*Childless couple*	*Single parent family*	*Couple with children*
Specified rate	9%	9%	30%	25%
Excluded labour income	$2,400.00	$3,600.00	$2,400.00	$3,600.00
Reduction threshold	$10,464.00	$16,190.00	$10,464.00	$16,190.00
Reduction rate	10%	10%	10%	10%
Maximum work premium	$725.76	$1,133.10	$2,419.20	$3,147.50

The following chart lists the parameters used for determining the maximum work premium in taxation year 2015:

MAIN PARAMETERS OF THE WORK PREMIUM FOR 2015

	Single person	*Childless couple*	*Single parent family*	*Couple with children*
Specified rate	7%	7%	30%	25%
Excluded labour income	$2,400.00	$3,600.00	$2,400.00	$3,600.00
Reduction threshold	$10,370.00	$16,056.00	$10,370.00	$16,056.00
Reduction rate	10%	10%	10%	10%
Maximum work premium	$557.90	$871.92	$2,391.00	$3,114.00

(QTA: 1029.8.116.9; Other Publications: 2010 Quebec Budget, *Additional Information on the Budgetary Measures, Revenue Measures,* item 1.4)

[¶1677f.10] *Adapted Work Premium*

This premium is specially adapted from the work premium to apply to individuals with a severely limited capacity for employment. Individuals who are part of a household that includes an adult with a severely limited capacity for employment and who meet the conditions for the work premium will qualify for this adapted work premium. Individuals may claim only one of the two premiums in a given year. Moreover, if an individual claims the adapted work premium, his or her spouse cannot claim the work premium. The 2016 Quebec Budget announced a 2% enhancement to the adaptive work premiums commencing in 2016 for households without children.

To be considered eligible, an individual or, if applicable, his or her spouse, must:

- have received in 2016 or during one of the five preceding years a social solidarity allowance or a severely limited capacity for employment allowance; or

- qualify to receive the credit for severe and prolonged impairment in mental or physical functions.

The following chart sets out the parameters used in the calculation of the adapted work premium for taxation year 2016:

MAIN PARAMETERS OF THE ADAPTED WORK PREMIUM FOR 2016

	Single person	*Childless couple*	*Single parent family*	*Couple with children*
Excluded work income	$1,200.00	$1,200.00	$1,200.00	$1,200.00
Rate of tax credit	11%	11%	25%	20%
Reduction threshold	$13,366.00	$19,444.00	$13,366.00	$19,444.00
Reduction rate	10%	10%	10%	10%
Maximum adapted work premium	$1,338.26	$2,006.84	$3,041.50	$3,648.80
Cut-off threshold	$26,748.60	$39,512.40	$43,781.00	$55,932.00

The following chart sets out the parameters used in the calculation of the adapted work premium for taxation year 2015:

MAIN PARAMETERS OF THE ADAPTED WORK PREMIUM FOR 2015

	Single person	*Childless couple*	*Single parent family*	*Couple with children*
Excluded work income	$1,200.00	$1,200.00	$1,200.00	$1,200.00
Rate of tax credit	9%	9%	25%	20%
Reduction threshold	$13,232.00	$19,242.00	$13,232.00	$19,242.00
Reduction rate	10%	10%	10%	10%
Maximum adapted work premium	$1,082.88	$1,623.78	$3,008.00	$3,608.40
Cut-off threshold	$24,060.80	$35,479.80	$43,312.00	$55,326.00

[¶1677f.15] *Supplement*

A supplement to the Work Premium or the Adapted Work Premium is available to long-term recipients of last-resort financial assistance who were no longer eligible for such assistance because of work income earned by the individual or his or her spouse. This supplement, intended to assist in costs related to the transition to the labour market, is $200 per month (for a maximum of 12 consecutive months) for each month in which the ex-recipient earns work income of at least $200. In this context, the term "work income" is the total of both gross income from employment (including tips) and net income from any business carried on alone or with a partner actively engaged in the business.

In additional to being resident in Quebec, individuals must meet the following qualifications to be considered eligible for the supplement:

- they are not in prison (or a similar institution) on December 31 of the year the application is made, and did not spend more than six months there in the year;

- their work income is at least $200 in the month for which he or she is claiming the supplement;
- they received last-resort financial assistance during at least 36 of the 42 months preceding the month they ceased to receive the assistance because they, or their spouses, earned work income;
- in the first month of ineligibility (for the Social Assistance Program or the Social Solidarity Program), they held a claim booklet issued by the Ministère du travail de l'Emploi et de la Solidarité sociale that entitled them to certain dental and pharmaceutical services.

Individuals claim the work premium supplement on their tax return using Schedule P, "Tax Credits Respecting the Work Premium". An individual may request that part of the premium be paid in advance. Advance payments of the Work Premium supplement are made on a monthly basis.

To receive such advance payments, an individual must complete Form TPZ-1029.8.PS-V, "Supplement to the Work Premium: Application for Advance Payments".

Tax Shield Credit

If you resided in Quebec on December 31, 2016 and if in 2016 you or your spouse were eligible for one of the refundable work premium credits or for the child care expense credit, you could benefit from the tax shield credit (¶1681a) if you meet the following two conditions:

- your family income (line 275) for 2016 is higher than that of 2015;
- your working income for 2016 is higher than that of 2015.

The portion of the tax shield respecting the work premium tax credit can be as much as $225 for an individual and $450 for a couple. The part of the tax shield respecting the tax credit for child care expenses can represent an increase of a few percentage points in the tax credit rate for child care expenses.

To claim the tax shield credit, you must check box 99 on Schedule C (Tax Credit for Childcare Expenses) or box 5 on Schedule P (Tax Credits Respecting the Work Premium). However, if you want to calculate the amount of the credit yourself, you must complete Form TP-1029.BF (Tax Shield Credit). The credit is claimed on line 460 of the tax return.

(QTA: 1029.8.116.1–1029.8.116.11; Other Publications: 2008 Quebec Budget, *Additional Information on the Budgetary Measures*, Revenue Measures, item 1.4; 2010 Quebec Budget, *Additional Information on the Budgetary Measures, Revenue Measures*, item 1.4; Quebec Finance Information Bulletin, 2014-11, item 2.6)

[¶1678] REFUNDABLE CREDIT FOR MEDICAL EXPENSES (SCHEDULE B, PART D)

Quebec, like the federal government (see ¶1237), offers a refundable medical expense credit.

As with the federal credit, you must have a minimum income from business and/or employment. For Quebec, this minimum is $2,985 for 2016. (The amount was $2,955 in 2015, $2,925 in 2014, $2,895 in 2013, and $2,825 in 2012.)

Quebec provides a workchart to calculate qualifying employment and business income in the Quebec Guide discussion of line 462, item 1.

If your spouse did not reside in Canada throughout the year, you must nevertheless take into account, in calculating your family income (Part A of Schedule B), all of your spouse's income, including the income your spouse earned while he or she was not resident in Canada.

Business income is limited to income from a business carried on alone or as a partner actively engaged in the business; passive partnership income does not qualify. If employment remuneration for the year described above comprises solely the value of benefits received by reason of a previous year's office or employment, it is not included in eligible earned income; examples would be a retiree's medical insurance coverage, securities options, or low-interest loans.

You must also be at least 18 years old and resident in Quebec on December 31 of the taxation year, and resident in Canada throughout that year.

The credit is calculated on Schedule B at part D, and claimed on line 462 of the return, item 1.

The credit is 25% of the medical expenses eligible for non-refundable credit (after the Quebec reduction for 3% of family income; see ¶1652) to a maximum of $1,166 for 2016, reduced by 5% of family income in excess of $22,560.

The amounts of $1,153 and $22,315 were applicable in 2015, $1,141 and $22,080 were applicable in 2014, $1,131 and $21,870 were applicable in 2013, and $1,103 and $21,340 in 2012. These amounts are indexed annually for changes in the Quebec consumer price index in the 12-month period ending September 30 of the preceding year. In general, the indexed amount is rounded to the nearest $5; rounded up in case of a tie.

(QTA: 1029.8.117–1029.8.118; Other Publications: 2005 Quebec Budget, *Additional Information, Revenue Measures*, 1.4.2)

[¶1678b] INDEPENDENT LIVING TAX CREDIT FOR SENIORS (SCHEDULE B, PART E)

This credit consists of two components: a credit on the cost of certain equipment, as well as a credit on the cost of a stay in a Functional Rehabilitation Transition Unit.

Cost of Equipment

A senior over the age of 70 is allowed to claim a refundable credit equal to 20% of an amount in excess of $500 representing the cost of equipment purchased or leased, that will assist such seniors to live independently at home.

The following equipment will qualify for this credit:

- a person-focused remote monitoring device, such as an emergency call device ("panic button"), a device for remotely measuring physiological parameters, or a device for remotely supervising the taking of medication;
- a GPS device for tracking a person;
- a device designed to assist a person to get on or off a toilet, or into or out of a bathtub or shower;
- a walk-in bathtub or a walk-in shower;
- a mechanized, rail-mounted chair lift designed solely to carry a person up or down a stairway; and
- a hospital bed.

Such equipment must be installed in their principal place of residence. The qualifying cost includes the cost of installation. Amounts that have been used in the calculation of other refundable or non-refundable credits are not also eligible for this credit.

Cost of a stay in a functional rehabilitation transition unit

Seniors age 70 or over are also allowed to claim a credit for the costs associated with a rehabilitative stay in a functional rehabilitation transition unit following surgery. The credit is equal to 20% of the costs of such a stay, for a maximum stay of 60 days, commenced in the year or the previous year.

For the purpose of this credit, a functional rehabilitation transition unit is defined as a public or private resource offering accommodation and services focusing on re-education and rehabilitation for persons experiencing a loss of autonomy, who are elderly (70 or over), and present a potential for recovery with a view of returning home following hospitalization.

If the amount for such a stay is claimed as a non-refundable medical expense credit it cannot also be used for the purpose of this new credit.

The credit is calculated on Schedule B at part E, and claimed on line 462 of the return, item 24.

(QTA: 1029.8.61.97–1029.8.61.102; Other Publications: 2012 Quebec Budget, *Additional Information on the Fiscal Measures of the Budget*, item 1.3)

[¶1679a] CREDIT FOR CAREGIVERS (SCHEDULE H)

The Tax Credit for Caregivers is divided into three components to provide for wider eligibility. The first component concerns caregivers of a spouse 70 or older who is unable to live alone; the second concerns caregivers housing an eligible relative; and the third concerns caregivers cohabiting with an eligible relative who is unable to live alone.

[¶1679a.05] *Tax Credit for Caregivers of a Spouse*

The caregiver can claim a refundable tax credit of $1,000 in 2016 ($925 in 2015, $850 in 2014, $775 in 2013, and $700 in 2012) if:

- the spouse was 70 or older at the end of 2016 and had a severe and prolonged impairment in mental or physical functions that rendered him/her unable to live alone, as certified by a physician;
- the spouse lived with the caregiver in Canada for at least 365 consecutive days, including at least 183 days in 2016. The caregiver and spouse must have lived together in a dwelling that is not located in a senior citizens' residence. The caregiver or the spouse or both of them, independently or with another person, must have owned, rented, or sublet the dwelling. The period of 365 consecutive days must have begun in 2015 or 2016. If it began in 2016, it may end in 2017.

You cannot claim the tax credit as a caregiver of a spouse if another person is claiming, with respect to the caregiver or his or her spouse, the tax credit as a caregiver housing an eligible relative or as a caregiver cohabiting with an eligible relative.

The credit for caregivers caring for an elderly spouse has increased $75 annually to $1,000 in 2016. This amount will be automatically indexed each year as of January 1, 2017.

(QTA: 1029.8.61.91–1029.8.61.96; Other Publications: 2012 Quebec Budget, *Additional Information on the Fiscal Measures of the Budget*, item 1.2)

[¶1679a.10] *Tax Credit for Caregivers Housing an Eligible Relative*

The caregiver can claim a refundable tax credit in 2016 of up to $1,167 ($1,154 in 2015, $1,142 in 2014, $1,131 in 2013, and $1,104 in 2012) for each eligible relative living with him or her in Canada in a dwelling, provided the caregiver or his or her spouse or both of them, independently or with another person (other than the eligible relative), owned, rented, or sublet the dwelling.

An eligible relative is a person other than the spouse who

- is 70 years old or older and lived with the caregiver for a period of at least 365 consecutive days, including at least 183 days in 2016; or
- has a severe and prolonged impairment in mental or physical functions, lived with the caregiver for a period of at least 365 consecutive days (including at least 183 days in 2016), and was at least 18 years of age at some time in the housing period in 2016. The person may have lived in the caregiver's home and in the home of another person of whom he or she is also an eligible relative.

An eligible relative who is 70 years old or older can be:

- the caregiver or his or her spouse's father, mother, grandfather, grandmother, or any other of the caregiver or his or her spouse's direct ascendants; or
- the caregiver or his or her spouse's uncle, aunt, great-uncle, or great aunt.

An eligible relative with a severe and prolonged impairment in mental or physical functions can be

- the caregiver or his or her spouse's father, mother, grandfather, grandmother, or any other of the caregiver or spouse's direct ascendants;
- the caregiver or his or her spouse's child, grandchild, nephew, niece, brother, or sister; or
- the caregiver or his or her spouse's uncle, aunt, great-uncle, or great-aunt.

The period of 365 consecutive days must have begun in 2015 or 2016. If it began in 2016, it may end in 2017.

Special rules apply if the eligible relative is housed by more than one person or if the eligible relative reached the age of 18 in 2016. The reader seeking more information should refer to the Quebec TP1 Guide, item 2 of line 462.

(QTA: 1029.8.61.61–1029.8.61.70)

[¶1679a.15] *Tax Credit for Caregivers Cohabiting with an Eligible Relative*

A caregiver can claim a refundable tax credit of up to $1,167 in 2016 ($1,154 in 2015, $1,142 in 2014, $1,131 in 2013, and $1,104 in 2012) for each eligible relative with whom he or she cohabited in Canada in a dwelling, provided the relative, the relative's spouse, or both of them, independently or with one or more other persons, owned, rented, or sublet the dwelling.

An eligible relative is a person other than the caregiver's spouse

- with whom the caregiver cohabited for a period of at least 365 consecutive days (including at least 183 days in 2016);
- who was at least 18 years of age at some time during the cohabitation period in 2016 and had a severe and prolonged impairment in mental or physical functions that rendered him/her unable to live alone as certified by a physician.

The relative can be

- the caregiver or his or her spouse's father, mother, grandfather, grandmother, or any other of the caregiver or his or her spouse's direct ascendants;

- the caregiver or his or her spouse's child, grandchild, nephew, niece, brother, or sister; or
- the caregiver or his or her spouse's uncle, aunt, great-uncle, or great-aunt.

The period of 365 consecutive days must have begun in 2015 or 2016. If it began in 2016, it may end in 2017.

If the caregiver and another person living with the eligible relative both meet the conditions for claiming the tax credit for caregivers cohabiting with an eligible relative, only the person who is the relative's primary caregiver is eligible to claim the credit.

Special rules apply if the eligible relative reached the age of 18 in 2016.

The amounts, for each of the three components of the credit, are calculated on Schedule H and claimed on line 462 of the return, item 2.

(QTA: 1029.8.61.61–1029.8.61.70; 1029.8.61.83–1029.8.61.90; Other Publications: April 21, 2005 Quebec *Additional Information on the Budgetary Measures* 1.3.2)

[¶1679c] REFUNDABLE CREDIT FOR RESPITE FOR CAREGIVERS

[¶1679c.05] *(1) Credit for Persons Providing Respite to Informal Caregivers (Volunteer Assistance)*

Note that this credit is restricted to persons who assist a primary caregiver for at least 400 hours in a year on a volunteer (unpaid) basis. The primary caregiver must assign the credit to the volunteer. There is a separate credit (discussed at ¶1679c.10) for primary caregivers who require professional assistance for respite.

The concept of this credit is to benefit those who help out caregivers ("eligible persons") by providing the services normally provided by the normal caregiver, or by providing services which enable the normal caregiver to provide care. The normal caregiver, referred to in Quebec Budget papers as the "informal caregiver", controls the credit and can assign up to $500 to any particular "eligible person". The normal or informal caregiver can assign a total of $1,000 per year, which can be divided up among eligible persons in any fashion, so long as no single assignment exceeds $500.

There are, in effect, three parties in play in determining the credit. There must be a "care recipient" (the person cared for), the "informal caregiver" (who normally cares for the care recipient), and the "eligible person" who provides relief ("respite") to the informal caregiver.

The care recipient must be an individual with a long-term significant disability. For care recipients 18 years of age or over, this means a severe and prolonged impairment in mental or physical functions, the same test as for the non-refundable disability credit at ¶1649.60, which in turn is essentially the same test as for federal purposes at ¶1209.05. For care recipients under 18, the care recipient must be someone for whom Quebec's supplement for handicapped children is paid. In addition, the care recipient, whether adult or minor, must have an intervention plan or individualized service plan established by a Quebec health and social services centre.

The informal caregiver who controls the credit must be a person who lives with the care recipient throughout the period during which volunteer respite services are provided by the eligible individual, and who is the care recipient's spouse or a person in respect of whom the care recipient is an eligible relative, within the meaning of that term for the purposes of the refundable tax credit for informal caregivers of adults (¶1679a). If, for a given year, more than one individual may be considered an informal caregiver of the care recipient, only the individual who is the principal person providing support to the care recipient will be considered the caregiver.

Note that although the informal caregiver will ordinarily be entitled to the refundable credit at ¶1679a, the Budget papers setting out the respite credit go to some lengths not to make this a requirement.

Finally, the eligible person, who is providing respite to the informal caregiver, (i) must not be an excluded person, and (ii) must, during a given calendar year, provide a total of at least 400 hours of "volunteer respite services" in Quebec to the informal caregiver of the person recognized as the care recipient. The care recipient's father, mother, child, brother or sister, and their spouse, where applicable, are excluded persons for the purposes of this definition. When volunteer respite services are provided to more than one care recipient in the same place, the hours of services provided must be divided equally between each recipient in the calculation of the number of hours of services provided. The 400-hour requirement seems to be formidable; it amounts to 50 × 8-hour days, $33^1/_3$ × 12-hour days. It is not clear if 17 × 24-hour days would qualify.

"Volunteer respite services" are non-remunerated services provided by an individual at the home of a person recognized as a care recipient. The services must consist of providing care to the recipient, performing tasks normally carried out by the informal caregiver with respect to the recipient, taking over certain daily tasks of the informal caregiver so that the latter can be with the care recipient at all times, or providing any similar service that gives the caregiver a break.

An informal caregiver can assign $1,000 per year with regard to each care recipient of whom he or she is an informal caregiver during the year. The informal caregiver may use that amount to allocate a maximum of $500 of refundable credit to any person who provides them with at least 400 hours of volunteer respite services in the year regarding a given care recipient.

Informal caregivers allocate amounts to eligible individuals by filing an information return (RL-23 Summary) with the Minister of Revenue no later than the last day of February following the year for which a credit is allocated. The information return must specify, for each individual to whom an amount is allocated regarding a given care recipient, the amount allocated, as well as the name of the individual, care recipient, and informal caregiver. The informal caregiver must then prepare for each individual to whom a credit amount is allocated an RL-23 slip, copies of which are given to the individual and filed with the Summary.

The amount is claimed on line 462 of the return, item 20.

(QTA: 1029.8.61.71–1029.8.61.75; Other Publications: May 24, 2007 Quebec Budget, *Additional Information on the Budgetary Measures*, Section A, Appendix, item 1.4; March 13, 2008 Quebec Budget, *Additional Information on the Budgetary Measures*, Revenue Measures, item 2.1.7)

[¶1679c.10] *(2) Credit for Respite Expenses of Informal Caregivers (Professional Assistance) (Schedule O)*

An informal caregiver who is resident in Quebec at the end of a given year may claim a refundable tax credit for that year equal to 30% of the total expenses the caregiver paid in the year, to a maximum of $5,200, for specialized respite services respecting the care and supervision of a person who, at the time the expenses were incurred, ordinarily lived with the caregiver and had a significant disability. The maximum dollar value of the credit is 30% of $5,200 = $1,560.

The credit is means tested; that is, the maximum amount of the tax credit is reduced by 3% of the caregiver's net family income in excess of, for 2016, $56,515 ($55,905 for 2015,

$55,320 for 2014, $54,790 for 2013, and $53,465 for 2012). This amount is indexed annually. Net family income is the line 275 income of the caregiver and the caregiver's eligible spouse, as defined for Quebec purposes at ¶1650.03.

If more than one individual living with the disabled person may be considered the informal caregiver, only the individual who is the principal person providing support to the care recipient will be considered the informal caregiver.

Person with a Significant Disability

A person will be considered to have a significant disability if, at the time the expenses for specialized respite services are incurred by an informal caregiver, the person is at least 18 years old, cannot, because of the disability, be left without supervision, and meets the following conditions:

- the person is the informal caregiver's spouse, or the child, grandchild, nephew, niece, brother, sister, father, mother, uncle, aunt, grandfather, grandmother, great-uncle, great-aunt, or another direct ascendant of the informal caregiver or the informal caregiver's spouse;
- the person has a severe and prolonged impairment in physical or mental functions such that he or she qualifies for the Quebec disability credit, or is receiving palliative care.

Specialized Respite Services

Specialized respite services are services which replace those of the informal caregiver in order to provide home care to the person with a significant disability. The services must be provided by an individual who holds at least one of the following recognized diplomas or degrees:

- a Diploma of Vocational Studies (DVS) in Home Care and Family and Social Assistance or its replacement "Home Care Assistance" program;
- a Diploma of Vocational Studies (DVS) in Assistance to Patients or Residents in Health Care Establishments or its replacement "Assistance in Health Care Establishments" program;
- a Diploma of Vocational Studies (DVS) in Health, Assistance and Nursing;
- a Diploma of College Studies (DCS) in Nursing;
- a Bachelor's degree (B.A.) in Nursing;
- any other diploma or degree enabling an individual to be a visiting homemaker, home support worker, family and social auxiliary, nursing attendant, health care aide, beneficiary care attendant, nursing assistant, or nurse.

An individual who supplies home care services to a person with a significant disability will be deemed to hold a recognized diploma where he or she

- is an individual whose services are already retained by the direct allowance and provides the informal caregiver with services in addition to those paid through direct allowance; or
- acts as an employee of a social economy business, or other entity that is one of those proposed to supply home care services, by the institution that developed a service plan.

General Restrictions

Expenses paid for specialized respite services do not qualify for credit to the extent that they are taken into account in the calculation of eligible costs or expenses for the purposes of the application of another refundable or non-refundable tax credit claimed by an informal caregiver or any other person. Thus, for example, expenses claimed by anyone for purposes of the refundable tax credit for child care expenses, the refundable tax credit for home support for elderly persons (¶1679d), or the non-refundable tax credit for medical expenses do not qualify for this credit as well.

Similarly, no tax credit can be claimed with respect to expenses for which a taxpayer is or was entitled to a refund or other form of assistance, unless the expenses must be included in the calculation of the taxpayer's income and are not deductible in the calculation of the taxpayer's income or taxable income.

Although the matter could be clearer, the Budget wording seems to allow for the same caregiver to claim the caregiver credits here and at ¶1679a, and to allocate the credits at ¶1679c.05. The logic is that those credits do not involve expense claims, so there is no duplication of claims for the same expense.

Documentation

It is a condition of the credit for each taxation year that the informal caregiver must enclose with his or her Quebec income tax return for the year one or more receipts issued by the service provider and indicating the provider's social insurance number if the provider is an individual. The individual must order Schedule O from Revenu Québec either by phone or by accessing the Revenu Québec website.

The credit calculated on Schedule O is claimed on line 462 of the return, item 21.

(QTA: 1029.8.61.76–1029.8.61.82; Other Publications: March 13, 2008 Quebec Budget, *Additional Information on the Budgetary Measures*, Revenue Measures, item 1.3; Quebec Finance Information Bulletin 2008-8)

[¶1679d] REFUNDABLE CREDIT FOR HOME SUPPORT SERVICES FOR SENIORS (SCHEDULE J)

Age Criterion

The credit is available to an eligible individual. This is an individual resident in Quebec at the end of the taxation year and who has reached 70 years of age by the end of the year. In the year in which you turn 70, eligible expenses are those incurred on or after the day you turn 70.

Credit Amount

An eligible individual is entitled to a refundable tax credit at a rate of 34% for 2016 (33% for 2015, 32% for 2014, 31% for 2013, 30% for 2008 to 2012). The rate of the credit will rise to 35% for 2017 and later years. The maximum credit is:

- in general, $19,500 ($15,600 for 2012 and prior years) of annual eligible expenditures; accordingly, the maximum credit for 2016 is 34% of $19,500 = $6,630;
- for "dependent seniors", $25,500 of annual eligible expenditures in years 2016, 2015, 2014, and 2013 ($21,600 for 2012 and prior years); accordingly, the maximum credit for 2016 for a dependent senior is 34% of $25,500 = $8,670.

Dependent Senior

A "dependent senior" is a person 70 years of age or older who either:

(1) depends and will continue to permanently depend, for a prolonged and indefinite period, on other people

for most of his or her needs and personal care (personal hygiene, dressing, eating and drinking, personal mobility and transfers); or

(2) requires constant supervision because of a serious mental disorder characterized by an irreversible breakdown in thought activity.

Revenu Québec says that written certification from a physician confirming the senior's condition "may be requested". Seniors required to provide written certification that they are a dependent senior must have a physician complete from TPZ-1029.MD.A-V. Note that although the criteria for a dependent senior appear to be much the same as for a disability credit for federal and Quebec purposes, they do not appear to be identical. The disability criteria must last for a period of at least 12 months, whereas the dependent senior criteria refer to "permanent" dependence. The dependent senior criteria seem more focused on the need for care than the condition of the individual, which makes sense after a fashion.

Reduction for Excess Income

The credit to which an individual is entitled is reduced by 3% of family income in excess of $56,515 for 2016, ($55,905 for 2015, $55,320 for 2014, $54,790 for 2013, and $53,465 for 2012), indexed annually thereafter. Family income is income for yourself and your spouse as it appears on line 275 of the Quebec return for each of you.

Eligible Expenses

Eligible expenses are, very generally speaking, support services that allow an elderly person to continue living at home or in a residence for elderly persons.

Eligible expenses are closely related to the kind of home you live in. There are different regimes for the expenses of senior citizens depending on whether they live in a residence for the elderly, an apartment, a condominium, or a personal home.

Expenses if You Live in a Private Seniors' Residence

For persons living in private seniors' residences, there are very specific rules as to how rental payments may be allocated to various eligible services (a basic component, laundry service, housekeeping, food service, nursing service, and personal care service). These services must be included in the lease or the schedule to the lease. In general, no more than 65% of rent can be attributed to eligible support services; this rises to 75% for dependent seniors. If eligible expenses total less than the 65%/75% limit, it is the lower amount which is eligible. Amounts are calculated using calculation tables applicable for each service included in the rent. If no eligible service is included in the lease or schedule, an individual may still receive the basic amount.

On the other hand, where the amount paid to a private seniors' residence and allocated under your lease for eligible services does not reach the credit limit available to you, you may also claim (i) additional amounts paid (presumably other than under the lease allocation) to the residence for nursing or personal care services, or (ii) amounts paid to a service provider (not to a related person) for nursing service, personal care service, meal preparation (if paid for assistance in meal preparation at home provided by, or for meals delivered by, a not-for profit organization), or housekeeping service for living areas (including laundry). However, no other additional service payments will qualify. Personal care service is to be defined as limited to services which relate only to personal hygiene, dressing, eating, and mobility for individuals who because of their condition are unable to care for themselves fully in these respects.

For purposes of these rules, a residence for elderly persons is "a congregate residential facility where dwelling units (rooms, studios or apartments) intended for elderly persons are offered for rent along with a varied range of services relating, in particular, to security, housekeeping assistance and assistance with social activities", except for facilities maintained under specified aspects of the *Act respecting health services and social services.*

For a senior to be able to deduct a portion of the rent paid to such a facility, the operator of the facility must hold a temporary certificate of compliance or a certificate of compliance issued by the health and social services agency of the region where the facility is located. Transitional rules to tighten up the certification rules apply. Residences that were a residence for elderly persons for the purpose of the credit, but were not registered by December 1, 2012, will still be considered to be a private seniors' residence until June 30, 2013, unless the facility receives a notification that it does not qualify. If that is the case, then it would cease to qualify as a private seniors' residence on the date that such notice was issued. This transitional rule extends the time for such qualified residences to become registered.

Expenses if You Live in an Apartment, Condo, or Personal Home

If you live in an apartment, you can include as an eligible expense 5% of the monthly cost of rent on your lease to a maximum monthly rent of $600 per month. Thus, if you pay $800 rent per month, you can claim as an eligible expense 5% of $600 = $30 per month, yielding a credit of $9.90 per month for 2016. Presumably, this is rough justice recognition of the services provided by the building. If you live with one or more co-tenants (other than your spouse), the monthly amount eligible for the tax credit is calculated by dividing the monthly cost of rent by the number of co-tenants. A co-tenant is a person with whom you live and who pays his or her share of the rent. His or her name appears on the lease. If you live with your spouse only, you are not considered co-tenants.

If you live in a condominium unit, the condominium fees you pay may cover certain services eligible for the tax credit. The condominium's administrators are obliged to evaluate the total cost of home support services eligible for the tax credit that are covered by condominium fees (the administrators are not required to assign a cost to each individual service offered). The work chart on form TPZ-1029.MD5.C-V, "Cost of Eligible Services Included in Condominium Fees: Tax Credit for Home-Support Services for Seniors", should be used to evaluate the total cost of services. After the calculations are complete, the condominium's administrators must complete the information return TPZ-1029.MD.5-V, two copies of which are to be provided to the senior citizen and one copy to Revenu Quebec no later than the last day of February of the following year for which the senior requested it. It is essential that you let the condominium's administrators (the syndicate of co-owners) know that you (or the person with whom you share the dwelling) are 70 or older, or will turn 70 during the year. There is a penalty of $25 for each day the form is late, to a maximum penalty of $2,500.

There is no basic expense claim related to a personal house.

Whether you live in an apartment, a condo, or your own house, you can include in eligible expenses a long list of amounts, discussed below.

Qualifying expenses are subject to the general limitations that they must be rendered in Quebec to the eligible individual by a person or a service provider who is *not* (i) the spouse of the eligible individual, (ii) a dependant of the eligible individual, or (iii) a person who claims (or whose spouse claims) the eligible individual under the credit for adults housing their parents.

That said, qualifying expenses are of two kinds. First, there are personal support services which enable an eligible individual to remain at home. Technically, personal support services include:

(1) a non-professional assistance service to enable the individual to perform an activity of daily living (limited to services related to personal hygiene, dressing, eating, and mobility or transfers);

(2) a meal preparation or delivery service (but not including the cost of the food itself), if provided by a not-for-profit organization;

(3) a non-specialized supervision service (e.g., night supervision, companion sitting service);

(4) a person-centered remote monitoring service;

(5) a service related to the use of a personal GPS locator;

(6) a support service to enable the individual to fulfil the individual's duties or civic obligations (e.g., budget management, assistance in filling out forms other than tax forms, except for the tax form for advance payment of this credit); and

(7) a service rendered, or to be rendered, by a person who is a member of the Ordre des infirmières et infirmiers du Quebec or of the Ordre des infirmières et infirmiers auxiliaires du Quebec. The prescribed frequency for nursing services to be eligible is at least seven hours' presence a day to a period of at least three hours' presence a day.

The second category of qualifying expenses consists of maintenance or supply services. These must be rendered in respect of a dwelling unit or a residential unit. A dwelling unit must be the eligible individual's principal place of residence and must be either self-contained domestic establishment or a room leased by the eligible person or the person's spouse in a residence for the elderly, or a room leased for at least 60 days in a hotel or boarding house. It may not be a room in the household of a person (or person's spouse) who claims the eligible individual under the credit for adults housing their parents.

Maintenance or supply services include:

(1) a housekeeping service (e.g., housekeeping of living areas, maintenance of appliances, cleaning of rugs and upholstery). (The prescribed frequency for housekeeping services to be eligible is at least once a week to at least once every two weeks);

(2) laundry services (but not including service provided by an entrepreneur whose principal business is providing dry cleaning, laundering, pressing and related services, except where the service is provided in the context of a senior citizens' residence);

(3) a maintenance service consisting of minor maintenance work performed outside, including work to be performed usually at about the same date each year because of the change in seasons;

(4) a maintenance service consisting of minor maintenance work on a facility that is inside the self-contained domestic establishment or, as the case may be, the building in which the self-contained domestic establishment or the room is situated, and that could have been outside, by reason of its nature or intended use; and

(5) an everyday necessities supply service (e.g., a grocery delivery service).

Expenses incurred for home support services are not eligible if they are reimbursed or reimbursable to the recipient of the services (or to the recipient's spouse). For example, expenses related to home support services are not eligible for the credit if they are reimbursed through compensation, indemnities, or financial assistance received from the Commission de la santé et de la sécurité du travail (CSST), the Société de l'assurance automobile du Quebec (SAAQ), the Régie de l'assurance maladie du Quebec (RAMQ) (under the Financial Assistance Program for Domestic Help Services), or Veterans Affairs Canada.

The credit depends heavily on maintaining proper receipts for qualified expenses. In the circumstances, it is perhaps fortunate, even essential, that personal services include a support service to enable the individual to fulfill the individual's duties or civic obligations, which one trusts would include assistance in applying for and keeping records for the credit itself.

The Revenu Québec publication, *Overview of the Tax Credit for Home-support Services for Seniors* (IN-151-V) interprets this list in practical terms.

Expenses Incurred by Spouse

Revenu Québec has, as a matter of policy, accepted that an expense for a spouse 70 or older but paid in fact by the other spouse is a valid eligible expense for the spouse over 70. This is true regardless of the age of the payer spouse. This principle is now to be enshrined in law. In addition, where two spouses are both 70 or older in the year (and they are not living separate and apart at the end of the year except on account of death), only one of them may claim the eligible expenses, but that spouse may claim the expenses for each of them, and the annual limit of each spouse otherwise applicable will be aggregated.

Advance Payments

The credit is claimed after the fact on the tax return for the year (using Schedule J), but permits a prepayment option.

To apply for advance payments,

- if you live in a senior citizens' residence, or an apartment, so that you are applying for eligible expenses included in the total cost of your monthly rent, complete form TPZ-1029.MD.7.P-V, "Application for Advance Payments Based on Rent and Services Included in Rent";
- for eligible expenses included in condominium fees (for seniors living in condominiums), complete form TPZ-1029.MD.P.8-V, "Application for Advance Payments for Services Included in Condominium Fees";
- for all other eligible expenses, complete form TPZ-1029.MD.9.P-V, "Application for Advance Payments for Occasional Services"; you may file this form in addition to one of the two forms above if you have eligible payments in addition to those included in rent or condominium fees.

Note that you may accumulate several invoices, receipts, and service contracts before sending the application for advance payments. You are not required to complete a separate application for each expense when it is incurred. You have until December 1st of the year in which an expense is incurred to send Revenu Québec the application for advance payments.

At the end of the year, you will receive an RL-19 slip stating the total of the amounts received as advance payments. This amount must be entered on your return. Revenu Quebec will verify that the advance payment amounts were related to eligible expenses and that all other conditions have been met. Overpayments must be reimbursed.

Medical Expense Credit

To prevent overlapping credit claims, you will not be permitted to claim medical expense credit for expenses for remuneration for attendant care under the Quebec equivalent of the $10,000/$20,000 attendant care medical expense described as the *fourth rule* in ¶1207 (see also ¶1255.05) if you or your spouse is entitled, at the time the attendant care remuneration is paid, to the home support credit "with respect to the expenses". The full import of this rule is ambiguous. It is clear that if you accept the home support credit, you cannot also claim the medical expense credit for full-time attendant care. It is not clear, however, that if you have expenses which might qualify for either credit, you cannot claim the more beneficial treatment. The Quebec home support services guide (IN-102-V, discussed below) does not fully resolve the uncertainty. Having said that, some expenses may in principle qualify for either credit, the guide goes on to say:

> If you receive the tax credit for home-support services for seniors for certain services eligible for the tax credit for medical expenses, you cannot claim the tax credit for medical expenses. *In the rare cases where services are eligible for both tax credits, you must examine your situation to choose the tax credit that is most beneficial for you.* [emphasis added]
>
> Note that if you pay for the services of a personal care attendant offered on a part time basis and the expense is also eligible for the tax credit for medical expenses, under no circumstances may you include the remuneration so paid in the calculation of your medical expenses. The expense may only be considered in the calculation of the tax credit for home support services for seniors.
>
> As a general rule, if you live in a senior citizens' residence, no portion of the rent paid may be considered a medical expense for the purposes of the tax credit for medical expenses.

Quebec also matches the federal credit described under the *fifth rule* in ¶1207 (amounts paid for care and training at a school, institution, or other specialized place for a handicapped person required to stay there to receive the services). Quebec courts have extended the Quebec version of this rule to permit the full amount of rent paid to a residence for the elderly to qualify for this medical expense credit for persons who otherwise meet the requirements for that medical expense credit. Quebec does not like this result, and has said that amounts paid "for the care, or the care and training, at a school, institution or other place, of a particular person will not include amounts paid to a residence for elderly persons".

Generally speaking, Quebec follows the federal rules regarding medical expense credits, although there are a few specific policy differences (discussed at ¶1652).

The amount calculated on Schedule J is claimed on line 458 of the return.

(QTA: 1029.8.61.1–1029.8.61.7.1; 1086.9–1086.12; Other Publications: March 13, 2008 Quebec Budget, *Additional Information on the Budgetary Measures, Revenue Measures,* item 1.1; 2010 Quebec Budget, *Additional Information on the Budgetary Measures, Revenue Measures,* item 1.3; Quebec Finance Information Bulletin 2002-8, July 11, 2002, item 1.1; 2008-6, June 20, 2008, item 6; 2008-5, June 5, 2008)

[¶1679d.05] *Forms and Guide*

This credit is calculated on Schedule J. The claim is discussed in the line 458 information in the Revenu Québec "Income Tax Return Guide".

Revenu Québec also produces a publication, "Overview of the Tax Credit for Home-support Services for Seniors" (IN-151-V). The document is clear and reasonably detailed, especially as to which expenses qualify and which do not, and should always be consulted in preparing home support credit claims.

Note also the application forms for advance payment of credit, discussed above.

[¶1680] QUEBEC SALES TAX REBATE

This rebate is intended to reimburse the Quebec portion of QST to employees (and partners in business partnerships) of entities registered under the Quebec QST rules who incur QST taxable expenses in the course of employment (or partnership business) which are not reimbursed explicitly or through an allowance and which are *deductible under income tax rules* by the employee or partner. The rebate is given on capital cost deducted on vehicles, musical instruments or aircraft. It is also given on other deductible expenditures to the extent of Quebec sales tax thereon, including amounts for the lease, licence, etc. of vehicles, musical instruments or aircraft. The rebate is claimed on the income tax return (line 459) and reported as income the following year (line 107 for employees, or at Section 7 of form TP-80-V Business or Professional Income and Expenses for partners), except that the portion of the rebate related to capital cost allowance is a reduction to capital cost eligible for allowance in the following years. The examples at ¶363 illustrate these principles.

The required calculations are set out clearly on form VD-358-V. The amount calculated on form VD-358-V is claimed on line 459 of the return.

(Quebec *Sales Tax Act*: 358)

[¶1681] SOLIDARITY TAX CREDIT

The Quebec tax system provides for various measures to help low- and middle-income households, including, until 2010, the refundable tax credit for the QST, the property tax refund, and the refundable tax credit for individuals living in a northern village.

These tax measures were grouped into a single refundable tax credit to form the solidarity tax credit with each measure being indexed annually, and will be reduced on the basis of family income over a certain threshold.

General eligibility conditions:

- Be at least 18 years of age (subject to certain exceptions);
- Be a resident of Quebec;
- Hold a recognized status (e.g., Canadian citizen, permanent resident, refugee); and
- Not be confined to prison.

The tax credit is claimed by completing Schedule D of the income tax return in all cases where the individual was living in Quebec on December 31 of the year preceding the year for which the tax credit is claimed. In all other cases, the tax credit must be claimed on form TP-1029.CS.1 *Demande du credit d'impôt pour solidarité pour un nouveau résident du Québec.*

The credit is paid monthly from July to June of the following year. The 2015 Budget included changes to the credit, which took effect in July 2016. From July 2016 and onwards, the credit is paid as follows: monthly for annual credits of $800 or more, quarterly for annual credits that are between $241 and $799, and yearly for annual credits of $240 or less.

The individual who claims the credit must agree to have the payments made by direct deposit. When there is a spouse, only one member of the couple may claim the credit. Further to an announcement in the 2015-2016 Budget, starting with the payment for the month of July 2016, in general, the eligibility conditions are to be met at the end of the previous year. Changes in the individual's situation during the year should not affect the value of the credit, and there is no requirement for Revenue Quebec to be notified, except in the following situations:

- The individual dies
- The individual is confined to a prison or similar institution
- The individual cease to be a resident of Quebec

Individuals will not be entitled to receive the solidarity credit in the following month where the above situations apply.

For payments prior to July 2016, individuals were required to notify the Minister of Revenue of any change in their situation of a nature to modify their right to receive an amount in respect of the tax credit for any given month.

Given that the QST and northern villages components were incorporated into the solidarity tax credit beginning in July 2011 and the lodging component was incorporated into the solidarity tax credit beginning in 2012, the monthly payments of the solidarity tax credit for 2011 were determined according to parameters different from the ones used as of 2012 and subsequent years. The credit is made of three components:

- QST component;
- Housing component; and
- Individuals living in a northern village component.

The 2016 solidarity credit payments are as follows:

QST Component	January 2016 to June 2016	July 2016 to June 2017
Basic amount	$281	$283
Additional amount for spouse	$281	$283
Additional amount for living alone	$134	$135
Housing Component	**January 2016 to June 2016**	**July 2016 to June 2017**
Basic amount for an individual without a spouse	$545	$548
Basic amount for an individual with a spouse	$661	$665
Basic amount for a shared dwelling (to be divided between the tenants)	$661	$665
Additional amount per dependent child	$116	$117
Individuals Living in a Northern Village Component	**January 2016 to June 2016**	**July 2016 to June 2017**
Basic amount	$1,655	$1,664
Additional amount for spouse	$1,655	$1,664
Additional amount per dependent child	$358	$360

The 2015 and 2014 solidarity credit payments were as follows:

QST Component	January 2014	January 2015
Basic amount	$275	$278
Additional amount for spouse	$275	$278
Additional amount for living alone	$132	$133
Housing Component	**January 2014**	**January 2015**
Basic amount for an individual without a spouse	$533	$539
Basic amount for an individual with a spouse	$647	$654
Basic amount for a shared dwelling (To be divided between the tenants)	$647	$654
Additional amount per dependent child	$114	$115
Individuals Living in a Northern Village Component	**January 2014**	**January 2015**
Basic amount	$1,620	$1,637
Additional amount for spouse	$1,620	$1,637
Additional amount per dependent child	$350	$354

The credit is reduced on the basis of family income. The reduction rate is equal to 6%, unless the individual is entitled to only one of the three components of the solidarity tax credit, in which case the reduction rate is equal to 3%. However, as a result of applying this calculation method, it is possible that some individuals whose family income exceeds the applicable reduction threshold may be entitled, if they avail themselves of both the Quebec sales tax component and the housing component, to tax assistance less than they would have received had they availed themselves only of the Quebec sales tax component. So that the method used to calculate the solidarity tax credit gives the best result, Quebec Finance Information Bulletin 2011-2 announced that the tax legislation will be amended to stipulate that the amount of the solidarity tax credit will be equal to the greater of the following amounts:

(1) the amount determined pursuant to the existing calculation method; or

(2) the amount that would have been determined pursuant to the existing calculation method had the individual been entitled only to the Quebec sales tax component of the tax credit.

The reduction threshold for the taxation year that includes the given month is equal to $33,505 from January 1, 2016 to June 30, 2016, and $33,685 from July 1, 2016, to June 30, 2017 ($33,145 for 2015, $32,795 for 2014, $32,480 for 2013, and $31,695 for 2012).

All of the parameters of the solidarity tax credit, with the exception of the reduction rates, are indexed annually.

For the purposes of the solidarity tax credit, where an individual goes bankrupt, the rule under which the bankrupt's taxation year is deemed to begin on the date of the bankruptcy and the current taxation year is deemed to end the day before that date will not apply for the purpose of determining the individual's family income for the year. Where an individual does not reside in Canada throughout a given taxation year, the individual's income for that year will be deemed to be equal to the income that would have been determined in his or her regard had he or she resided in Quebec and Canada throughout the year or, if the individual dies during the year, throughout the period of the year preceding his or her death.

To claim the credit, the individual must complete Schedule D *Solidarity Tax Credit* when filing his/her tax return. Furthermore, to claim the housing component, individuals are required to enter the cadastral designation indicated on their municipal tax account or the sequential number indicated in box A of the RL-31 transmitted to them by the owner, as applicable.

(QTA: 1029.8.109.2–1029.8.109.6; 1029.8.114; 1029.8.116.12–1029.8.116.35; 1029.8.116.16; 1029.8.116.17.1; 1029.8.116.20; Other Publications: 2010 Quebec Budget, *Additional Information on the Budgetary Measures, Revenue Measures*, item 1.2; Quebec Finance Information Bulletin 2013–13, December 4, 2013; Quebec Finance Information Bulletin 2011-2, *Clarification relating to certain application details of the refundable tax credit for solidarity*; 2015 Quebec Budget, Additional Information, item 1.5)

[¶1681a] TAX SHIELD CREDIT

The Tax Shield credit applicable to 2016 was introduced in the 2015 Budget. Beginning in 2016 a refundable credit is provided to low income individuals to offset, in part, a reduction in the refundable work premium credits (see ¶1677f) or in the refundable credit for child care expenses (see ¶1677) experienced as a result of an increase in income. Such individuals are often subject to higher marginal tax rates on additional income they earn as their entitlement to these refundable credits is eroded.

If you resided in Quebec on December 31, 2016 and if in 2016 you or your spouse were eligible to one of the refundable work premium credits or to the child care expense credit, you could benefit from the tax shield credit if you meet the following two conditions:

- your family income (line 275) for 2016 is higher than that for 2015;
- your working income for 2016 is higher than that for 2015.

The tax shield credit is the excess of the sum of the individual's work premium credits and child care expenses credit, calculated on a notional amount (referred to as "total modified income"), over the sum of the actual credits.

Total modified income is a measure of the increase in the individual's income for the year. The calculation is quite complex but will generally allow the individual to calculate the credits as though he or she had not realized up to 75% of the actual increase in income. The maximum increase of $2,500 in eligible work income relative to the previous year for each member of a household previously announced in the 2015 Budget has been enhanced to $3,000 in the 2016 Budget.

The portion of the tax shield respecting a work premium tax credit can be as much as $225 for an individual and $450 for a couple. The part of the tax shield respecting the tax credit for child care expenses can represent an increase of a few percentage points in the tax credit rate for child care expenses.

If you and your spouse both claim the tax shield, the total amount to which you are entitled will be shared equally between you.

To claim the credit, you must check box 99 on Schedule C (Tax Credit for Childcare Expenses) or box 5 on Schedule P (Tax Credits Respecting the Work Premium). However, if you want to calculate the amount of the credit yourself, you must complete Form TP-1029.BF (Tax Shield Credit). The credit is claimed on line 460 of the tax return.

(Other Publications: 2015 Quebec Budget, Additional Information, item 1.1; 2016 Quebec Budget, Additional Information, item 1.4; Form TP-1029.BF-V Tax Shield)

[¶1681b] CHILD ASSISTANCE PAYMENT

The refundable tax credit is paid by the Quebec Government to all families with one or more dependent children under the age of 18. This payment replaces the old family benefits, the non-refundable tax credit respecting dependent children, and the tax reduction for families.

The amount of assistance payment is dependent upon the:

- number of children under the age of 18 living with the beneficiary;
- number of children in shared custody;
- family income; and
- type of family (single-parent or two-parent).

The amounts are recalculated in July of each year based on the changes in family income and dynamics. Child assistance amounts are indexed each January. Recipients must file an annual income tax declaration in order to qualify. The amounts received are not taxable. The payments are made by Retraite Quebec.

To be eligible for the program, a person must:

- be responsible for the care and education of a child under the age of 18;
- live with the child, or, if the child has been placed elsewhere by a youth center, retain responsibility for paying the costs of caring for that child to the center;
- live in Quebec;
- be — or have a spouse that is — one of the following:
  - a Canadian citizen;
  - a permanent resident;
  - a temporary resident living in Canada at least 18 months; or
  - a protected person.

To be eligible for the program both spouses must have filed a Quebec tax return.

There is no entitlement to payments for:

- the child's foster family;
- a person who is exempt from paying Quebec income tax;
- a person who is waiting for protected status (refugee claimant); or
- a child who is married or in a common-law relationship and the other partner is entitled to a transfer from one spouse to the other.

When a birth is declared to the Registrar of Civil Status, the child is automatically enrolled.

Payments are made quarterly, but they can be paid monthly if an application is made.

The level of payment varies depending on several factors. The minimum and maximum amounts are as follows:

MAIN CHARACTERISTICS OF CHILD ASSISTANCE PAYMENTS

Characteristic	Amount				
	2016	2015	2014	2013	2012
Maximum Assistance					
First child	$2,392	$2,366	$2,341	$2,319	$2,263
Second child	$1,195	$1,182	$1,170	$1,159	$1,131
Third child	$1,195	$1,182	$1,170	$1,159	$1,131
Fourth child (and each subsequent child)	$1,793	$1,774	$1,755	$1,738	$1,696

Characteristic	Amount				
	2016	2015	2014	2013	2012
Single-parent family	+$839	+$830	+$821	+$813	+$793
Minimum Assistance					
First child	$671	$664	$657	$651	$635
Second child	$620	$613	$607	$601	$586
Single-parent family	+$335	+$331	+$328	+$325	+$317
Monthly amount for a handicapped child	+$189	+$187	+$185	+$183	+$179
Monthly amount for a handicapped child with exceptional needs (commences April 1, 2016)	+$947				

Supplement for Handicapped Children

One of the **components** of the child assistance payment is the **supplement for handicapped children**. This supplement is granted to individuals who are primarily responsible for the care and education of a handicapped child with whom they ordinarily live. To be considered eligible, the child must be under 18 and have an impairment or a developmental disorder which considerably restricts his or her daily activities.

This supplement is also not taxable and is not reduced on the basis of family income. This supplement is also indexed annually.

Additional Supplement for Handicapped Children with Exceptional Care Needs

As announced in Information Bulletin 2016-6, an additional component of the child assistance payment called the **additional supplement for handicapped children with exceptional care needs** was introduced. This additional supplement came in effect on April 1, 2016 and is granted to individuals who are primarily responsible for the care and education of a handicapped child with exceptional care needs with whom they ordinarily live. To be considered eligible, the child must be under 18 and for a foreseeable period of at least one year is:

(A) a child who has impairments or a designated mental function disability causing severe, multiple disabilities which, according to the prescribed rules, prevent the child from performing the life habits of a child of his or her age without assistance; or

(B) a child whose health condition requires specified complex medical care at home that is provided by the child's father or mother, who received prior training at a specialized centre in order to learn the specific techniques for using the required equipment and be able to respond to any potentially life-threatening change in the child's clinical condition.

For an amount to be granted as the additional supplement for handicapped children with exceptional care needs, an application, along with multidisciplinary reports prepared in respect of the child, must be submitted to Retraite Quebec.

This supplement is also not taxable and is not reduced on the basis of family income. This supplement is granted in addition to the supplement for handicapped children and are both indexed annually.

(QTA: 334 Deductions allowed; 336 Amounts included; 1029.8.61.8–1029.8.61.60; Other Publications: Quebec Form LPF-800A; Quebec Information Bulletin 2016-6)

[¶1682] RESEARCH AND DEVELOPMENT TAX CREDIT

A Quebec taxpayer may be entitled to a refundable tax credit if the taxpayer or a partnership of which he or she was a partner, operated a business and carried out scientific research and experimental development, or had such activities carried out on their behalf.

The effective rate for all R&D credits would be 30% for all qualifying R&D work for SMEs with assets less than $50 million and 14% for all SMEs with assets greater than $75 million. The rate decreases linearly for SMEs with assets between $50 million and $75 million.

In 2014, the Quebec government imposed a threshold for all R&D expenses. Effective for taxation years that begin after December 2, 2014 and for R&D work carried out after December 2, 2014, the first $50,000 of expenses will be excluded from the credit calculation for all SMEs with assets of $50 million or less. This amount will increase to $225,000 for enterprises with assets of $75 million or more. The amount of the threshold will increase linearly from $50,000 to $225,000 for enterprises with assets between $50 million and $75 million.

Where amounts which have generated credits (wages, contract payments, research contract payments) are subsequently refunded to the taxpayer, the associated credits are recaptured by an offsetting tax.

The taxpayer must file Form RD-1029.7-V to claim the credit. The credit calculated on form RD-1029.7V is claimed at line 462 of the return, item 15.

(QTA: 222–230.0.0.6; 1029.6.4–1029.8.16.1.9; Other Publications: 2014 Quebec Budget, *Additional Information on the Fiscal Measures of the Budget*, item 3.2.1; Quebec Finance Information Bulletin 2014-11, item 2.3)

[¶1683] FOREST PRODUCERS' PROPERTY TAX REFUND

Taxpayers who in the year hold a forest producers' certificate under the *Sustainable Forest Development Act* and are further certified by the Minister of Natural Resources to be actively engaged in developing their woodlots, are entitled to a refund of a portion of real estate taxes paid under *An Act respecting municipal taxation*. To receive the refund you must have a report described in the *Sustainable Forest Development Act* from a forest engineer which sets out your eligible development work expenses for the year. These expenses must equal or exceed the real estate taxes on which the refund is claimed. Eligible work expenses not claimed in the current year may be carried forward ten years if greater than real estate taxes paid, but only five years if less than real estate taxes (for expenses prior to 2014, the carry forward period was two years).

The refund applies to each "assessment unit" listed on the woodlots certificate; for each unit the refund is 85% of the product of real estate taxes not otherwise reimbursed times the ratio of the value of the land over the value of the assessment unit as listed on the assessment rolls.

The refund calculated on Schedule E at part C is claimed on line 462 of the return, item 5.

(Quebec *An Act respecting municipal taxation*, ss. 220.2–220.13; *Sustainable Forest Development Act* s. 120; Other Publications: Gazette Officielle du Quebec, Partie 2-Lois et règlements, No.2 December 4, 2013)

[¶1684] REFUNDABLE CREDIT FOR ADOPTION EXPENSES

If in the year a Quebec court handed down a final adoption order, or you have received or been issued a qualifying international adoption certificate under the *Convention on Protection of Children and Co-operation in Respect of Intercountry Adoption* (unless the certificate has been referred to the

Quebec courts by the Quebec Ministry of Health and Social Services), you are entitled to a refundable credit for adoption expenses for the year.

The credit may be claimed in the year in which a qualifying decision is made. A qualifying decision includes:

- a judgment rendered by a court having jurisdiction in Quebec in recognition of a decision rendered outside Quebec authorizing the adoption of the child by the individual;
- a judgment authorizing adoption of the child by the individual by a court having jurisdiction in Quebec, other than a judgment approving the proposed adoption of a child domiciled in the People's Republic of China;
- where the application for adoption was submitted before February 1, 2006, in respect of a child domiciled in the People's Republic of China, the certificate of registration, issued by the clerk of the Court of Quebec, of the adoption of the child by the individual; and
- the certificate of compliance with the Convention issued by the competent authority of the State in which the adoption of the child by the individual took place, unless the Minister of Health and Social Services has referred it to the courts.

If the order or certificate is issued during the year, the credit is 50% of specified adoption expenses, to a maximum credit of $10,000 (representing $20,000 of qualified expenses).

Specified adoption expenses are expenses paid at the earlier of the time that an application is made for registration with a provincial ministry responsible for adoption (or with an adoption agency licensed by a provincial government) and the time, if any, that an application related to the adoption is made to a Canadian court. Such expenses include:

- judicial, extrajudicial, or administrative expenses incurred to obtain a qualifying certificate or a qualifying judgment, as the case may be, in respect of the adoption of the person by an individual (generally speaking, court and legal fees paid to obtain the final adoption order in Quebec or a foreign country); for 2006 and later years, this concept was broadened by the addition of reference to administrative expenses; the change was retroactive in that Revenu Québec could apply the new definition to earlier years not statute-barred. For 2013 and subsequent years the concept was expanded to include allowable expenses incurred prior to the time that the child is matched with the parents. Such expenses would include those incurred to match a child to a parent. This change is identical to the change brought forth at the federal level by the March 21, 2013 federal Budget;
- travel expenses of the escort as well as of the child when the adoptive parents are not required to (and do not) travel to bring back their child;
- travel and accommodation expenses of the adoptive parents and the child when the adoptive parents travel to a foreign country to bring back their child;
- travel and accommodation expenses paid by parents to pick up an adopted child escorted only as far as a major urban centre in Quebec;
- the travel and living expenses, in respect of the adoption of the child by the individual, of the individual and, where applicable, the individual's spouse, to the extent that the travel is necessary. This rule replaced two older rules. It appears to be intended that this provision will extend the eligibility of travel expenses to trips within Canada, and to trips to familiarize the child with the adoptive parents, as well as trips to bring the child to its new Quebec home. Although the change applies for 2006 and later, Revenu Québec is authorized to apply it retroactively to taxation years which are not statute barred. The eligibility of travel and living expenses remains conditional on the payment of such expenses after the opening, by the Minister of Health and Social Services or a certified agency, of the file relating to the adoption of a child, and the requirements that they be reasonable under the circumstances and that they do not give rise to a refund;
- expenses relating to the translation of documents pertaining to the adoption, where necessary;
- fees charged by agencies approved by the Ministère de la Santé et des Services sociaux;
- repayment of fees charged by a certified foreign institution that took care of the child;
- expenses related to the psychosocial evaluation of the child as required under the Quebec *Youth Protection Act*; and
- expenses that result from a requirement imposed by a government authority in respect of the adoption.

The claim for this credit must be supported by Quebec form TP-1029.8.63-V and by a copy of the final adoption order or proof of its registration with the Court of Quebec. The amount calculated on form TP-1029.8.63-V is claimed on line 462 of the return, item 6.

(QTA: 1029.8.62–1029.8.66; Other Publications: 2008 Quebec Budget, *Additional Information, Revenue Measures,* item 1.10; The federal Budget, March 21, 2013, resolution 1; Quebec Finance Information Bulletin 2013-7, item 1.1)

[¶1684c] TREATMENT OF INFERTILITY TAX CREDIT

Amounts paid to a physician or licensed hospital or for prescription drugs in connection with *in vitro* fertilization may be eligible for the infertility tax credit.

For expenses incurred after November 10, 2015, the credit calculation has changed and is now 80% of eligible expenses for couples with combined income of $50,000 or less and is reduced to 20% of eligible expenses for couples with combined income of $120,000 or more. The credit is reduced proportionately for family income between $50,000 and $120,000. For single parents the income level for 80% is $25,000 and for 20% it is $60,000. These income levels will be adjusted annually for inflation. The changes to this credit were outlined in Quebec Finance Information Bulletin 2015-6, *Changes to the List of Expenses Eligible for Tax Assistance for the Treatment of Infertility Following Assent to Bill 20.*

The maximum amount of eligible expenses paid by the taxpayer and their spouse is $20,000 per year. Expenses must be attributable to a single in vitro fertilization cycle, in the case of a woman 36 years of age or under, or no more than two in vitro fertilization cycles, in the case of a woman 37 years of age or over.

Prior to November 11, 2015, the credit was equal to 50% of eligible expenses incurred up to a maximum of $20,000 of eligible expenses.

Where more than one person is entitled to the credit, each may claim a part of the credit up to the maximum. The total credit cannot exceed the amount each would have claimed if only one made a claim.

To be eligible for the credit, the taxpayer and his or her spouse must:

- be a resident of Quebec on December 31 of the taxation year;
- pay for eligible in vitro expenses during the taxation year. If expenses are reimbursed to the taxpayer or the spouse, they do not qualify for the credit unless the amount reimbursed is included in the taxpayer's or spouse's income; and

- not have any existing children before the start of the in vitro treatment, and a physician must certify that neither the taxpayer nor their spouse have previously undergone surgical sterilization (i.e., vasectomy or tubal ligation) other than for strictly medical reasons. This condition only applies for expenses incurred after November 10, 2015.

Expenses related to an in vitro fertilization treatment are considered eligible expenses only if the treatment:

- is not covered by a health insurance plan;
- is carried out in a centre for assisted procreation that holds a licence issued in accordance with the *Regulation respecting clinical activities related to assisted procreation*;
- involves the expected transfer of a single embryo or, in accordance with a decision made by a physician:
  - a maximum of two embryos, in the case of a woman 36 years of age or younger, or a maximum of three embryos, in the case of a woman 37 years of age or older, if the transfer is carried out before November 11, 2015; or
  - a maximum of two embryos, in the case of a woman 37 years of age or older, if the transfer is carried out after November 10, 2015.

Eligible expenses include, in particular, the following expenses, provided that they have not been reimbursed and do not qualify for reimbursement:

- expenses paid for an *in vitro* fertilization activity provided by a physician;
- expenses paid for an assessment carried out by a member of the Ordre des psychologues du Quebec or the Ordre des travailleurs sociaux et des thérapeutes conjugaux et familiaux du Quebec;
- expenses paid for prescribed medications, the purchase of which is recorded by a pharmacist, and that are not covered by the Quebec prescription drug insurance plan;
- transportation expenses paid to a business for the taxpayer to undergo an in vitro fertilization treatment at a centre located at least 40 kilometres away, if treatment is not offered in the taxpayer's locality; and
- travel expenses incurred for the taxpayer to undergo an in vitro fertilization treatment at a centre located at least 80 kilometres away, if treatment is not offered in the taxpayer's locality.

Eligible expenses also include travel and lodging expenses incurred in order to obtain medical services that are not available in Quebec within 250 kilometres (200 km as of July 1, 2016) of the locality in which the person undergoing treatment resides. The minimum distance standard has been reduced from 250 km to 200 km with respect to travel and lodging expenses that are incurred after July 1, 2016, as per Quebec Finance Information Bulletin 2016-7, *Changes to Various Measures of a Fiscal Nature*.

Certain medical expenses relating to *in vitro* fertilization activity will be excluded from the list of qualifying medical expenses for the purpose of the medical expense credit, where:

- *in vitro* fertilization activities are carried out where more than the allowable number of embryos are transferred as set out in the criteria above; and
- *in vitro* fertilization activities are carried out in a Quebec clinic that does not have the proper licence issued in compliance with the *Act respecting clinical and research activities relating to assisted procreation.*

The claim for this credit must be supported by Quebec form TP-1029.8.66.2-V, and documents specified therein, filed with your return. The amount calculated on form TP-1029.8.66.2-V is claimed on line 462 of the return, item 11.

Advance payments of the tax credit for the treatment of infertility will be available to applicants willing to accept direct deposit of the prepayments. The prepayments (reported on an RL-19 slip, box G) must be included on line 441 of the tax return.

(QTA: 1029.8.66.1–1029.8.66.5; Other Publications: Quebec Finance Information Bulletin 2010-8, *Changes to Various Fiscal Measures;* 2008 Quebec Budget, *Additional Information, Revenue Measures,* item 1.10; May 24, 2007 Quebec *Additional Information on the Budgetary Measures,* Section A, Appendix, 1.6; Quebec Finance Information Bulletin 2014-10, item 1; Quebec Information Bulletin 2015-6, *Changes to the List of Expenses Eligible for Tax Assistance for the Treatment of Infertility Following Assent to Bill 20;* Quebec Information Bulletin 2016-7, *Changes to Various Measures of a Fiscal Nature,* item 1)

[¶1685] REFUNDABLE TAX CREDIT FOR CHILDREN'S ACTIVITIES

Families may receive a refundable tax credit for certain expenses incurred to foster development of a child's aptitude and skills.

The parameters of this program are as follows:

- the rate of the credit is 20% of eligible expenses up to a maximum of $400 in expenses in 2016 ($300 in 2015), increasing at the rate of $100 per year to a maximum of $500 in the year 2017;
- the credit applies to each child who at the beginning of the year is not yet 16. If a child has a severe or prolonged impairment in mental or physical functions, the age limit is extended to those who are not yet 18 at the beginning of the year;
- the limit for a child with a severe or prolonged impairment in mental or physical function is doubled. The credit for 2016 will be $800 ($600 in 2015) increasing to $1,000 by 2017;
- this credit applies to eligible expenses for physical, cultural and artistic activities within guidelines that mirror those of the federal children's fitness and arts tax credits;
- the credit can be claimed by either spouse, provided the family income does not exceed $134,095 in 2016 ($132,650 in 2015);
- the credit is a refundable credit, unlike the similar federal credit which is non-refundable.

The credit is claimed on line 462 of the return, item 25.

(QTA: 1029.8.66.6–1029.8.66.10; Other Publications: 2013 Quebec Budget, *Additional Information on the Fiscal Measures,* item 2)

[¶1685a] REFUNDABLE TAX CREDIT FOR SENIORS' ACTIVITIES

The June 4, 2014 Budget introduced a refundable tax credit that grants to seniors — aged 70 or over at the end of a tax year — a credit equal to 20% of qualified expenses paid in the year for a recognized activity program or programs. The credit is limited to 20% of $200, that is, $40. The credit is also limited to those individuals with an annual individual net income (line 275) of $40,865 or less in 2016 ($40,425 in 2015), subject to yearly indexation.

To qualify, an activity must generally be:

- engaged in weekly for at least eight consecutive weeks;
- structured, that is, it must enable seniors to participate in an activity in a specific setting.

A physical activity must also enable seniors to develop or maintain their cardiorespiratory endurance, their muscular strength or endurance, their flexibility or their balance. An artistic, cultural or recreational activity must enhance senior's ability to develop or improve their dexterity, coordination, cognitive skills, social integration or psychological well-being.

The credit will apply to qualified amounts paid during 2016.

The credit is claimed on line 462 of the return, item 28.

(Other Publications: 2014 Quebec Budget, *Additional Information on the Fiscal Measures of the Budget*, item 2.2)

[¶1686] ENVIRONMENTAL TRUST CREDIT

Quebec parallels the federal rules at ¶2232 permitting deduction of contributions to qualifying environmental trusts. These trusts accumulate funds from contributions by beneficiaries with an obligation to rehabilitate mine sites, waste disposal sites and quarries after operations are complete. When funds are paid to beneficiaries they are taxable, but offset by restoration expenses. While funds sit in the trust, the government taxes investment income of the trust, which income is nevertheless allocated to beneficiaries along with a tax credit for tax paid by the trust. The credit claimed here is part of that machinery.

The claim must be supported by Quebec form CO-1029.8.36.53 and documents specified therein, and filed with your return. The credit is claimed on line 462 of the return, item 9.

(QTA: 87(*z*), (*z*.1); 692.1–692.4; 998(*p*); 998(*q*); 1029.8.36.52–1029.8.36.53; 1129.51–1129.54)

[¶1687] TIP REPORTING CREDIT

Quebec has embarked on a complex program to ensure the taxation of tips received by service industry workers by, in effect, requiring employees (in theory) to turn over tips to their employer and having the employer redistribute them to employees as wages, with a minimum tip rate which must be allocated by the employers if not recovered from employees. Since the incomes of employees presumably increase under this scheme, the employers will suffer new payroll taxes on the newly reported income. Additional payroll taxes incurred by employers pursuant to this scheme are in theory offset by a refundable tax credit. On the expense side, everything operates through the payroll deduction system. On the credit side, tax credits are calculated and claimed on form TP-1029.8.33.13-V.

Generally speaking, the tax credit a taxpayer may claim for a given taxation year is equal to all his or her qualified expenditures for the taxation year or, if the qualified expenditures are borne by a partnership, to the taxpayer's share of the qualified expenditures of the partnership for its fiscal year ending in his or her taxation year.

Essentially, the qualified expenditures regarding an employer for a taxation year (or a fiscal year) correspond:

- to the portion of employer contributions which is attributable to tips — i.e., the contributions to the *Quebec Pension Plan*, to the HSF, to employment insurance, parental insurance, to the Commission des normes du travail and to the Commission de la santé et de la sécurité du travail — and which was paid for the calendar year ending in the taxation year or the fiscal year, as the case may be;
- to the portion of the annual vacation benefit of an employee that is attributable to tips and that was received or is receivable for the taxation year or the fiscal year, as the case may be, as well as to the employer contributions payable in relation to such portion of the vacation benefit.

A taxpayer who is required to pay qualified expenditures regarding a taxation year (or a fiscal year if the employer is a partnership) may claim a tax credit whose amount will be limited to 75% of all his or her qualified expenditures for the year.

Similarly, where a partnership is required to pay qualified expenditures for a fiscal year, the amount of the tax credit each taxpayer who is a member of such partnership at the end of such fiscal year may claim for his or her taxation year in which such fiscal year of the partnership ends will be limited to 75% of an amount representing his or her share of all the qualified expenditures of the partnership for the fiscal year.

The credit is claimed on line 462 of the return, item 10.

(QTA: 1029.8.33.12–1029.8.33.19; Other Publications: June 12, 2003 Quebec Budget, *Additional Information on the Fiscal Measures*, item 1.3.11; Quebec Finance Information Bulletin, 2000-4, June 29, 2000, item 2.11)

[¶1688] ON-THE-JOB TRAINING CREDIT

This program is designed to allow tax credits for on-the-job training periods provided by employers to apprentices, secondary school students in vocational training, college students in technical training, and university students in certain courses and cooperative programs. The credit is generated by salaries paid to eligible supervisors and eligible trainees under the program. For qualifying expenses paid prior to June 5, 2014 in relation to an eligible training period commenced before that date, the rate was 15% for unincorporated employers. In 2015 this rate was increased to 20% for training periods beginning after March 26, 2015, but only if:

- the trainee is enrolled as a full-time student;
- this is the third consecutive year that the employer has hired student trainees; and
- the employer has incurred at least $2,500 in qualified expenditures for each of the past three years.

The credit is calculated as a percentage of eligible wages paid to:

- apprentices;
- secondary school students in vocational training;
- college students in technical training; and
- university students in certain courses and cooperative programs.

Salaries paid to eligible supervisors up to a maximum of 20 hours per week per trainee for some programs qualify for the credit.

In general, the maximum number of hours of supervision provided by an eligible supervisor that an employer may consider regarding an eligible trainee is 20 hours per week, if the eligible trainee is an individual enrolled as a full-time student in a prescribed program; and 10 hours per week for any other eligible trainee. For a handicapped person (but not, apparently, for an immigrant), these maximum numbers are raised to 40 and 20, respectively.

In general, the cap on the eligible expenditure that applies regarding an eligible trainee is:

- $750 per week, if the eligible trainee is an individual enrolled as a full-time student in a prescribed program;
- $600 per week for any other eligible trainee.

The credit calculated on form TP-1029.8.33.6-V is claimed on line 462 of the return, item 7.

This credit is part of a larger Quebec training initiative which will also impose a 1% payroll tax on employers with payrolls in excess of $2 million ($1 million before 2015) who fail to make sufficient eligible expenditures on training.

[¶1688.10] *Enhanced Credit for Immigrants and the Handicapped*

Enhanced credits are available for trainees who are immigrants or are disabled. Essentially, for such trainees, five points will be added to the credit; and, for handicapped persons, the maximum hours of support for which credit can be claimed is increased, and the weekly limit on eligible expenses is increased.

Enhanced credits are available for trainees who are also immigrants or individuals who are handicapped. The June 4, 2014 Budget reduced the enhanced rate to 16% for individuals who are employers of eligible trainees who are either immigrants or handicapped persons (for a training period that began before June 5, 2014, the rate for unincorporated employers was 20%). This rate was increased to 25% for training periods beginning after March 26, 2015, but only if:

- the trainee is enrolled as a full-time student;
- this is the third consecutive year that the employer has hired student trainees; and
- the employer has incurred at least $2,500 in qualified expenditures for each of the past three years.

Also for handicapped persons, the maximum hours of support for which credit can be claimed is increased to 40 hours if they are also an apprentice or an individual enrolled as a full-time student in a secondary, college, or university-level education program or a prescribed program offered by a recognized educational institution and to 20 hours for any other eligible disabled trainee.

A handicapped person for purposes of the enhanced credit is a person who, at such time, is entitled to the tax credit for severe and prolonged impairment in physical or mental functions.

An immigrant for the purposes of the enhanced credit is:

- a person who, at such time, holds one of the following statuses, within the meaning of the *Canadian Immigration and Refugee Protection Act*;
- protected person;
- permanent resident; or
- temporary resident or holder of a temporary resident permit, who resided in Canada during the 18-month period preceding such time.

In general, the maximum number of hours of supervision provided by an eligible supervisor that an employer may consider regarding an eligible trainee is 20 hours per week, if the eligible trainee is an individual enrolled as a full-time student in a prescribed program; and 10 hours per week for any other eligible trainee. For a handicapped person (but not, apparently, for an immigrant), these maximum numbers are raised to 40 hours per week and 20 hours per week, respectively.

In general, the cap on the eligible expenditure that applies regarding an eligible trainee is:

- $750 per week, if the eligible trainee is an individual enrolled as a full-time student in a prescribed program;
- $600 per week for any other eligible trainee.

For a handicapped person (but not for an immigrant) these limits will be raised to:

- $1,050 per week, if the eligible trainee is an individual enrolled as a full-time student in a prescribed program;
- $750 per week for any other eligible trainee.

[¶1688.20] *Forms*

Revenu Québec provides form TP-1029.8.33.6-V for individual employers claiming this credit. The form summarizes many of the details of the credit, including details of the certificates which must be provided by the educational institution or the Ministère du Travail, de l'Emploi et de la Solidarité sociale (or the Kativik Regional Government, where applicable) to corroborate the eligibility of the trainees.

(QTA: 1029.8.33.2–1029.8.33.10; Other Publications: 2004 Quebec Budget, *Additional Information on the Budgetary Measures*, item 2.2.2; 2008 Quebec Budget, *Additional Information on the Budgetary Measures, Revenue Measures*, item 2.5; 2014 Quebec Budget, *Additional Information on the Budgetary Measures*, item 3.1.21; 2015 Quebec Budget, Additional Information on the Budgetary Measures, item 2.4)

[¶1689] OTHER CREDITS

[¶1689.05] *Taxi Driver/Owner Tax Credit*

This refundable credit applies in every region of Quebec, and is generally being paid directly to taxi drivers rather than to permit holders. The credit consists of two elements. The first is intended for taxpayers who hold a taxi driver's permit but do not hold a taxi owner's permit, while the second is intended for taxpayers who hold one or more taxi owner's permits, whether or not they hold a taxi driver's permit.

If the vehicles attached to a taxi permit are used by one or more drivers who assume all or part of the cost of fuel to keep the vehicles in service, the holder of the taxi permit has to turn over to each of the drivers, within the 12 months following the end of his or her taxation year, the portion of the tax credit attributable to him or her based on the mileage covered.

The *taxi driver's credit* applies to a taxpayer who, at any time of a given taxation year, holds a *taxi driver's permit*, was on December 31 of such taxation year a resident of Quebec, and does not hold a taxi owner's permit. The credit is available to a taxi driver who dies during the year and was resident in Quebec at the time of death.

The credit allowed in this situation is the lesser of, for 2016, $565 ($559 for 2015, $553 for 2014, $548 for 2013, and $535 for 2012) and 2% of the sum of the following amounts:

- the gross income for the taxation year from employment as a taxi driver (i.e., income before deductions attributed to this source);
- the gross income for the taxation year from the taxi service business; or
- the gross income for the taxation year from renting the automobile attached to a taxi owner's permit which is held by the taxpayer.

The holder of a *taxi owner's permit* on December 31 of a taxation year must claim under the following rules. The credit is only available if you held at least one such permit on December 31 of the taxation year for which the credit is claimed and, during the portion of the year you held the permit, you bore at least 90% of the fuel costs for the taxi covered by the permit. In these circumstances, you may claim a refundable tax credit equal to the lesser of the following amounts:

- an amount representing 2% of all the following amounts:
  - gross income for the taxation year from employment as a taxi driver (i.e., income before deductions attributed to this source);
  - gross income for the taxation year from the taxi service business; or
  - the gross income for the taxation year from renting the automobile attached to a taxi owner's permit which is held by the taxpayer;
- an amount equal to the product obtained when, for 2016, \$565 (\$559 for 2015, \$553 for 2014, \$548 for 2013, and \$535 for 2012) is multiplied by the number of each such permit the taxpayer held at this date if, during the taxation year, the taxpayer covered all or almost all the cost of fuel to keep any automobile attached to such permit in service. This limit is indexed annually under the rules at ¶1661.05.

For the purposes of this measure, the expression "taxi owner's permit" means a taxi permit covered by the *Act respecting transportation services by taxi*, including a limousine permit or other specialized taxi permit covered by the Act. The expression "holder" of a taxi owner's permit means the person in whose name the taxi owner's permit is issued or, if the permit is issued in the name of a number of persons, the person they designate from among themselves.

To avoid reducing the tax assistance granted, the taxi refundable tax credit will not be taxable.

The credit calculated on form TP-1029.9-V is claimed on line 462 of the return, item 3.

(Former QTAR: 1029.9R1; QTA: 1029.9–1029.9.4; Other Publications: 2008 Quebec Budget, Additional Information on the Budgetary Measures, item 1.5; Quebec Finance Information Bulletin 2002-8, July 11, 2002, item 1.6)

[¶1689.10] *Top-Level Athletes' Tax Credit*

Athletes who achieve the performance levels designated "Excellence", "Elite" or "Relève", as determined by the Quebec sport federation to which they belong, are eligible for special refundable tax credits. Athletes resident in Quebec at the end of the year will qualify for the credit. You cannot claim this credit if you are exempt from tax.

The basic credit is \$4,000 at the Excellence and Elite levels in individual sports, and \$2,000 at the Relève level in individual sports. For team sports, the credits are halved (\$2,000 at Excellence and Elite, \$1,000 at Relève). The actual credit is the basic amount prorated for the number of days in the year that the athlete is certified at a particular level by the sport federation. Thus, if the athlete is certified at Relève level in a team sport for 165 days, the credit will be 165/365 × \$2,000 = \$904. If the same athlete also qualified at the Elite level for the remaining 200 days, there would be additional credit of \$2,192, for a total of \$3,096. In leap years, 366 days are included in the denominator, and may be included in the numerator if qualified.

An athlete may only qualify for a particular day in one sport at one level, and must include with his or her tax return an attestation issued by the Ministère de l'Éducation et de l'Enseignement supérieur, which will be based on information supplied by the sporting federation. The Ministère will lay down rules as to the number of athletes who can be certified in a particular sport.

The credit is claimed on line 462 of the return, item 18.

(QTA: 1029.8.119–1029.8.121; Other Publications: 2000 Quebec Budget, *Additional Information, Revenue Measures,* item 1.8)

[¶1689.15] *ÉcoRénov Tax Credit (2013–2014 only)*

To stimulate the economy in the short term by supporting employment in the residential renovation sector and to promote sustainable development, a refundable tax credit for eco-friendly residential renovation work was introduced on a temporary basis.

This tax credit targeted individuals who had a qualified contractor carry out eco-friendly renovation work on their principal place of residence or their cottage under a contract entered after October 7, 2013, and before November 1, 2014.

To be entitled to the tax credit, the work done must have had a positive impact on the environment or energy impact and satisfy recognized standards in this field.

The ÉcoRénov tax credit maximum amount of \$10,000 per eligible dwelling corresponded to 20% of the portion of an individual's eligible expenditures that exceeded \$2,500.

Determination of the tax credit

An individual who resided in Quebec at the end of the year may have received, for such year, a refundable tax credit for an amount equal to:

- where the given taxation year was 2013, the lower of \$10,000 or 20% of the excess, over \$2,500, of all the individual's eligible expenditures for the year regarding the eligible dwelling;
- where the given taxation year was 2014, the lower of the following amounts:
  - 20% of excess of all the individual's eligible expenditures for the year regarding the eligible dwelling over the lower of \$2,500 or the excess of \$2,500 over all the individual's eligible expenditures for the 2013 taxation year regarding the eligible dwelling;
  - the excess of \$10,000 over all the amounts that, regarding the eligible dwelling, were obtained on account of the ÉcoRénov tax credit for the 2013 taxation year by the individual or by any other person with whom he or she owned the dwelling.

To receive this tax credit, an individual must have completed an information return, using the prescribed form (TP-1029ER).

Eligible dwelling

Generally, an individual's eligible dwelling was defined as a dwelling located in Quebec whose construction was completed before January 1, 2013, and of which the individual was the owner. The dwelling must have constituted the individual's principal place of residence or a cottage that was habitable year round and normally occupied by the individual.

Recognized eco-friendly renovation work

Briefly, recognized eco-friendly renovation work included work related to insulation, air or waterproof sealing, heating, air conditioning, water heating and ventilation systems, as well as water and soil quality work, provided such work related to existing parts of the individual's eligible dwelling. Quebec Finance Information Bulletin 2013-10, item 1 must be referred to for the complete list of recognized eco-friendly renovation work.

Furthermore, the eco-friendly renovation work was recognized only if such work was awarded to a contractor under the terms of an agreement entered into after October 7, 2013 and before November 1, 2014.

Eligible expenditures

Eligible expenditures for a given taxation year were equal to all of the expenditures attributable to the execution of recognized eco-friendly renovation work stipulated in a renovation agreement regarding the dwelling, provided such expenditures were paid for in the qualified period of 2013, 2014, or the first 120 days of 2015.

Refund or other form of assistance

Eligible expenditures were reduced by the amount of any government assistance other than the assistance allowed under the Rénoclimat program, any non-governmental assistance, any refund, or other form of assistance including an indemnity paid under an insurance contract that the individual received or was entitled to receive in relation to the execution of recognized work.

The credit was claimed on line 462 of the return, item 26.

(QTA: 1029.8.153–1029.8.158; Other Publications: Quebec Finance Information Bulletin 2013-10, item 1)

[¶1689.20] *LogiRénov Tax Credit (2014 and 2015 only)*

On April 24, 2014, the Quebec government introduced a new stimulus tax credit (the "LogiRénov Tax Credit") aimed at assisting economic recovery while improving the quality of life for Quebec homeowners.

The credit was equal to 20% of renovation work performed in excess of $3,000 on the taxpayer's principal place of residence in Quebec, to a maximum credit of $2,500. The credit applied to most renovation work contracted to be done after April 24, 2014, and before July 1, 2015, on a Quebec taxpayer's principal place of residence, whether it was a house, a condominium townhouse, a high-rise condo, or a fixed mobile home, provided that construction of such residence was completed before January 1, 2014.

For the purpose of this credit, land adjoining the residence and contributing to the use and enjoyment of the house was considered part of the "dwelling". This did not, however, include entrances to parking areas, walkways, or retaining walls and other structures that were only there for landscaping purposes.

It should also be noted that work that was undertaken in accordance with the former ÉcoRénov Tax Credit [¶1689.15], which applied to specific renovations undertaken before November 1, 2014, would also be allowed to qualify for the LogiRénov Tax Credit.

For the work to qualify it must have been carried out by a contractor who was registered under the *Act respecting the Quebec sales tax*, or by a contractor that supplied a valid business number or social insurance number. Where there was more than one owner of a residence, the total amount of the credit claimed by each could not be more than what a single owner would be eligible to claim.

The credit calculated on form TP-1029.LR-V was claimed on line 462 of the return, item 27.

For a detailed list of the renovation work that was recognized for the LogiRénov Tax Credit, see Quebec Finance Information Bulletin 2014-6.

(QTA: 1029.8.159–1029.8.166; Other Publications: Quebec Finance Information Bulletin 2014-6)

[¶1689.22] *RénoVert Tax Credit (2016–2017 only)*

On March 17, 2016, Quebec introduced a temporary refundable tax credit to help stimulate the economy by implementing an eco-friendly home renovation credit. The tax credit will apply to eco-friendly renovation work carried out on a taxpayer's principal residence or cottage through contracts with a qualified contractor entered into between the period of March 18, 2016, and March 31, 2017. In order to qualify for the credit, eligible eco-friendly expenditures must be paid by an individual before October 1, 2017.

To be eligible for the credit in 2016, your expenses must have been paid after March 17, 2016, and before January 1, 2017. To be eligible for the credit in 2017, your expenses must have been paid after December 31, 2016, and before October 1, 2017.

The tax credit will apply at the rate of 20% of the portion of the eligible expenditures that exceed $2,500 up to a maximum credit of $10,000. The maximum credit is achieved at renovation expenses totalling $52,500 or more.

To be entitled to the tax credit, the work done must have a positive environmental or energy impact and satisfy recognized standards in this field.

Determination of the tax credit:

An individual who resides in Quebec at the end of December 31 of a given taxation year before the 2018 taxation year may receive, for such year, a refundable tax credit for an amount equal to:

- where the given taxation year is the 2016 taxation year, the lesser of $10,000 and 20% of the individual's aggregate eligible expenditures for the year that exceeds $2,500;
- where the given taxation year is the 2017 taxation year, the lesser of the following amounts:
  - 20% of the individual's aggregate eligible expenditures for the year that exceeds the lessor of $2,500 and the amount by which $2,500 exceeds the aggregate of individual's eligible expenditures for the 2016 taxation year;
  - the amount by which $10,000 exceeds the aggregate of the amount obtained on account of the RénoVert tax credit for the 2016 taxation year by the individual or by any other person with whom the individual owned the dwelling.

To claim the credit, you must:

- enclose form TP-1029.RV-V, RénoVert Tax Credit, with your income tax return for the year;
- have the contractor that did the work complete and sign a Certificate of Compliance with Energy and Environmental Standards (form TP-1029.RV.A-V).

The credit calculated on form TP-1029.RV-V is claimed on line 462 of the return, item 32.

In the case of an eligible dwelling located in a condominium building, eligible expenses include those paid by the syndicate of co-owners, up to your unit's share of the expenses. The syndicate of co-owners must provide you with information concerning the work done and the amount of your unit's share of the expenses by giving you a copy of form TP-1029.RV.D-V, Information Return: RénoVert Tax Credit.

You must keep your supporting documents (estimates, invoices, etc.) for six years in case Revenu Québec asks for them.

Eligible dwelling:

Generally, an eligible dwelling of an individual means an immovable or permanently installed dwelling located in Quebec whose construction was completed before January 1, 2016, and of which the individual is the owner at the time the eco-friendly renovation expenses are incurred and that constitutes either his or her principal place of residence, or a cottage habitable year round that is normally occupied by the individual.

Recognized eco-friendly renovation work:

Briefly, the eco-friendly renovation work that will be recognized will be work related to insulation, air or waterproof sealing, installation of doors and windows, heating and air conditioning, water heating and ventilation systems, as well as work related to water and soil quality.

Eligible expenditures:

Eligible expenditures for a given taxation year will be equal to all of the expenditures attributable to the execution of recognized eco-friendly renovation work stipulated in a renovation agreement regarding the dwelling, provided such expenditures were paid after March 17, 2016, and before January 1, 2017, for the 2016 taxation year, and paid after December 31, 2016, and before October 1, 2017, for the 2017 taxation year.

Refund or other form of assistance:

Eligible expenditures must be reduced by the amount of any government assistance other than the assistance allowed under the Rénoclimat program, any non-governmental assistance, any refund or other form of assistance including an indemnity paid under an insurance contract that the individual received or is entitled to receive in relation to the execution of recognized work.

(Other Publications: 2016 Quebec Budget, Additional Information on the Budgetary Measures, item 1.2)

[¶1689.25] *Assistance for seniors regarding an increase in municipal tax*

2015-2016 Quebec Budget, introduced, as of January 1 2016, an assistance program to support seniors coping with important increases in their property taxes.

The *Act respecting municipal taxation* will be amended to provide that seniors who are long-time homeowners can, provided certain conditions are met, receive a grant to partially offset the municipal taxes payable on their residence following an increase in its value if the increase significantly exceeds the average increase for certain residential immovables for the municipal territory as a whole.

To simplify the calculation of the amount of the grant to which individuals may be entitled for a year, municipalities will indicate, on the tax account or on the Quebec form FM-210.1-V Amount of the Potential Grant to Offset a Municipal Tax Increase sent for a particular fiscal year, the amount of the potential grant attributable to the increase in a unit's property value where, pursuant to a new assessment roll applicable to the fiscal year, the increase in the unit's value exceeds the average increase by 7.5%.

An individual may receive a grant regarding his municipal taxes for a particular year if the following conditions are met:

- at the end of the preceding year, the individual was resident in Quebec, was 65 or older, and had been the owner of the specified assessment unit for at least 15 consecutive years;
- the individual is a person to whom the tax account for the specified assessment unit was sent for the year;
- the specified assessment unit is the individual's principal place of residence;
- the individual's family income for the preceding year does not exceed $50,400 ($50,000 for 2015, subject to yearly indexation).

The grant for 2017 claimed in the 2016 tax return is calculated on Form TP-1029. TM Grant for Seniors Regarding an Increase in Municipal Tax. The credit is entered at line 462 of the tax return, item 29.

(Other Publications: 2015 Quebec Budget, Additional information on the Budget 2015-2016, item 1.6)

[¶1689.30] *Refundable credit respecting the seller-lender formula*

In its Economic Statement issued on December 2, 2014, the Quebec government introduced a temporary tax credit that will allow a buyer of farm property to claim a credit equal to 40% of the interest payable to a seller on a loan under the La Financière agricole du Québec (FADQ) program called the "seller-lender formula". The credit will apply to interest paid by the buyer under such a program commencing on January 1, 2015. The financing agreement must have been entered into under the seller-lender formula, after December 2, 2014 and before January 1, 2020. No maximum credit amount was announced.

The credit calculated on form CO-1029.8.36-V is claimed on line 462 of the return, item 30.

(Other Publications: Quebec Finance Information Bulletin 2014-11, Fiscal Measures Announced in The Update on Quebec's Economic and Financial Situation, item 1.4)

PAYMENT OF TAX, ASSESSMENT, APPEALS

[¶1691] PAYMENTS OF TAX, WITHHOLDING TAX, AND TAX INSTALMENTS

Withholding and instalment requirements for Quebec are similar to the federal requirements. If you are an employee, tax will be withheld from your salary or wages and remitted by your employer to the Quebec government. You will be given an RL-1 slip by your employer showing the total of your salary or wages and other benefits received, and the amount of Quebec tax withheld. The tax withheld should be shown on the Quebec tax return, and any balance of tax payable should be remitted by April 30.

Quebec has adopted the federal instalment rules described at ¶227, although the Quebec threshold amount differs from the federal amount. Instalment payments for 2016 are required only if you estimate that your net income tax payable for the year will be over $1,800 and if, for either 2014 or 2015, your net income tax payable was over $1,800 (do not take into account any amounts included or deducted for retirement income-splitting purposes, the property tax refund, the QST rebate, the property tax refund for forest producers, the tax credit for home-support services for seniors, or any transfer of income tax withheld from retirement income). The federal threshold amount for 2016 is $3,000. The Quebec threshold of $1,800 applied for the years 2008 and beyond, as did the federal threshold of $3,000. Once your liability for tax is established under these rules, you must pay instalments to cover the Health Contribution, QPP, health services fund, Quebec parental insurance plan premiums, and prescription drug insurance liabilities.

Quebec has an instalment notice system similar to the federal system; two notices (on form TPZ-1026.A-V) are usually sent each year if instalment liability is indicated, each showing instalments due for each of the following two quarters. As with federal rules, payment of the amounts indicated is generally sufficient to escape penalty and interest, although it appears that Quebec may issue notices in blank which require you to calculate your own liability unless the form clearly states that you are not required to pay instalments. Quebec also provides form TP-1026-V to help you calculate instalments if you do not want to follow the Quebec safe-haven notices, or if you are not required to make instalments but anticipate a current tax liability which you want to prepay. The considerations are essentially the same as in ¶227.

Quebec publishes a document, *Instalment Payments*, IN-105-V, to describe these rules.

Quebec farmers and fishermen are subject to special instalment rules identical to the federal rules at ¶1758.

Where estimated instalments are less than both the applicable prior year Quebec instalment base and tax owing, interest at substantial rates will be applied.

Where proper instalments leave a balance of tax owing for the year, you must pay any balance of tax owing by the normal tax deadline of April 30.

(QTA: 1026; 1026.1; 1040)

[¶1691.05] *Interest*

The interest rates on amounts payable to Quebec are by regulation set quarterly to reflect the financial market rates. Quarterly prescribed rates on unpaid taxes over the past few years are as follows:

Quarter	*1st*	*2nd*	*3rd*	*4th*
2007	9	9	9	9
2008	9	9	8	8
2009	7	6	5	5
2010	5	5	5	6
2011	6	6	6	6
2012	6	6	6	6
2013	6	6	6	6
2014	6	6	6	6
2015	6	6	6	6
2016	6	6	6	

Interest on insufficient instalments will be the same as the above rates plus an additional 10% to the extent the instalment actually paid (if any) was less than 75% of the amount due. However, this additional penalty interest on instalments is subject to an overriding contra-interest provision (compare with ¶227) which deems 5% offsetting interest to accrue on any amount of instalments actually paid for the period from the date of payment to the balance due date. Interest charged (or contra-interest allowed) by the Quebec government is compound interest, calculated on a daily basis.

The notices of assessment will fix a date for payment of the amounts stated therein, and no additional interest or penalty will run until the date fixed in the notice. However, the choice of that date is at the discretion of Revenu Québec.

Quebec does not pay the same interest on refunds that it charges on overdue taxes or instalments. Refund interest is set quarterly at the interest rate then payable on Quebec Savings Bonds. Over the past years they have been set as follows:

July 1, 2007	3.50%
October 1, 2007	3.75%
July 1, 2008	2.75%
July 1, 2009	1.15%
July 1, 2010	1.25%
October 1, 2010	1.25%
January 1, 2011	1.25%
April 1, 2011	1.25%
July 1, 2011	1.50%
October 1, 2011	1.50%
January 1, 2012	1.50%
April 1, 2012	1.50%
July 1, 2012	1.30%
October 1, 2012	1.30%
January 1, 2013	1.30%
April 1, 2013	1.30%
July 1, 2013	1.25%
October 1, 2013	1.25%
January 1, 2014	1.25%
April 1, 2014	1.25%
July 1, 2014	1.40%
October 1, 2014	1.40%
January 1, 2015	1.40%
April 1, 2015	1.40%
July 1, 2015	1.10%
October 1, 2015	1.10%
January 1, 2016	1.10%
April 1, 2016	1.10%
July 1, 2016	1.10%
October 1, 2016	1.10%

Interest on refunds is computed to the date of refund from the latest of:

(1) the date of overpayment made pursuant to a notice of assessment;

(2) the 46th day following the date of overpayment made otherwise than pursuant to a notice of assessment;

(3) the 46th day following receipt of the tax return filed;

(4) the 46th day following the day the tax return giving rise to the overpayment was required to be filed; or

(5) the 46th day following the day information is received from the federal government or another province, or (if earlier) from the taxpayer.

Where the taxpayer requests the carryforward of a loss, interest on the resulting overpayment will be made from the 46th day after the request is made to the date of refund.

(Regulation Respecting Fiscal Administration: 28R2; QTA: 1037–1040.1; 1052; 1053; Other Publications: 2004 Quebec Budget, *Additional Information on the Budgetary Measures*, item 4.1; 2002-4, May 4, 2002, item 1.1)

[¶1692] TAX WITHHELD IN OR FOR ANOTHER PROVINCE

[¶1692.05] *Quebec Residents Subject to Withholding in Another Province*

It is possible for tax to be withheld from an employee resident in Quebec on account of some other province. For example, if you resided in Ontario for part of the year and then moved to Quebec you will be taxable by Quebec on all of your income for the year, but no tax would have been remitted to Quebec for the period you lived in Ontario. Your tax for this period would have been remitted to the federal government for credit to Ontario.

You may consider tax withheld for some other province in these circumstances as a payment of Quebec tax and include it as tax paid on your Quebec return. Forty-five per cent of the total income taxes withheld by an employer in a province other than Quebec can be considered as Quebec income tax paid. That is, you have the option of electing any portion of the tax withheld in another province up to 45% for this treatment. Since the federal government will refund any excess non-Quebec tax you owe, and you will owe the federal and Quebec governments their share of tax regardless, precision is not essential. Your objective is to minimize the amount of Quebec tax you must otherwise pay out of pocket while awaiting a federal refund of other provincial tax withheld. If you are overwithheld in total, so that your withholding will exceed both federal and provincial tax, it doesn't much matter where you attribute the excess withholding. Calculate the amount you wish to transfer (up to the 45% limit) and insert it on both line 438 of the federal T1 return and line 454 of your Quebec income tax return. You should attach a copy of the T4 slips indicating the amount withheld with each of your federal and Quebec income tax returns. If you claim 45% of the amount withheld on your Quebec return, you will of course claim only the remaining 55% as a reduction of tax on your federal return.

(ITA: 154; ITR: 3300 [Prescribed rate]; QTA: 1020; 1022; Other Publications: T1 Guide re line 438; Quebec Guide re line 454)

[¶1692.10] *Taxpayers Resident in Another Province Who Have Been Subject to Quebec Withholding*

If you are resident in Canada, resided in a province other than the Province of Quebec at December 31 of the taxation year, and did not have an establishment of business in Quebec at any time during that year, you will not be liable for Quebec income tax. However, you may have had Quebec income tax withheld from your income during that year, for example:

(1) If you resided in Quebec during the year but moved to another province before December 31, Quebec income tax would be withheld on salary or wages paid to you while you were employed in Quebec.

(2) If you did not reside in Quebec during the year but were employed in that province, Quebec income tax would be withheld on salary or wages paid to you while you were employed in Quebec.

In the above instances, you should not file a Quebec income tax return for the year. You cannot file such a return to claim a refund from the Province of Quebec for income tax withheld.

Instead, you should show this tax on your federal return for the year as a payment on account of taxes administered by the federal government (i.e., enter it with other withholdings on line 437 of your federal return). To support this claim you must attach to the federal return a copy of the RL-1 slip showing the Quebec tax withheld.

Taxpayers carrying on a business in Quebec at any time during the year must file a Quebec income tax return (see ¶1607).

(ITA: 154(1), 154(4); QTA: 26; 1023–1024; Other Publications: T1 Guide re line 437)

[¶1693] PURCHASING PROPERTY FROM A NON-RESIDENT

If you are about to purchase any taxable Quebec property from a non-resident person, you should be aware of your obligation (subject to certain exceptions; see ¶1608) to withhold 12% of the purchase price, if no certificate was issued by the Minister in connection with the sale or, if there is a certificate, 12% of any excess of the purchase price over the amount mentioned in the certificate, and remit this amount to the Quebec tax authorities. If you have not withheld the amount required, you are personally liable to pay it and then you may attempt to recover the amount from the non-resident.

The Quebec compliance procedures for disposition of taxable Quebec property are similar to the federal procedures outlined at ¶2042 and 12% of the estimated capital gain must be paid to Quebec tax authorities. See also ¶1608.

(QTA: 1094–1102.5)

[¶1694] ASSESSMENTS, OBJECTIONS, APPEALS

After your return has been reviewed, you should receive an assessment, and there are provisions similar to those in the federal law for objecting to assessments and taking your objections to the Courts if your objection is not accepted.

(QTA: 1005–1014)

[¶1694c] FILING DATE

The Quebec income tax return filing-due dates are the same as the federal dates. In general, returns must be filed by April 30 of the year following the taxation year, except that returns for individuals reporting business income and their spouses (¶218) are not due until June 15. If June 15 falls on a Sunday, the filing day is extended to the next working day, that is, June 16. As for the federal return, the extended filing deadline does not extend the balance-due day for actually paying taxes owing, which remains April 30 for all living taxpayers.

A 5% penalty applies to the balance payable if your return is filed after April 30. The taxpayer is liable for a further penalty of 1% of such unpaid tax times the number of months the return is not filed to a maximum of 12%.

The 5% late-filing penalty will be assessed on the final balance owing by the taxpayer, rather than on the unpaid tax computed on the tax return. The unpaid balance does not take into account certain refund amounts to which the taxpayer may be entitled, and consequently may not reflect true liability. The rule is supposed to more accurately reflect true liability at the time.

The TP-646 return of a trust or estate is due within 90 days after the end of its taxation year. Year-of-death returns are due on the same dates as federal rules; see ¶1901.

Revenu Québec has the authority to extend any deadline for the filing of returns.

(QTA: 1000; 1045; 1045.0.2 (repealed); 1052; Other Publications: 2004 Quebec Budget, *Additional Information on the Budgetary Measures*, item 4.1)

[¶1694f] SPECIAL FILING REQUIREMENT IN RESPECT OF RENOVATIONS AND REPAIRS

Quebec has a unique requirement applicable to a person (unless tax exempt) or partnership that incurs expenses for the renovation, improvement, maintenance or repair of a building, structure or land situated in Quebec and used in the course of a business or to derive an income. That is, the rule applies to all payers of construction or repair expenses in connection with business or rental property, whether owned or leased. The person or partnership making the expenditure is required to include with its tax return a prescribed form (TP-1086.R.23.12-V) identifying the persons who carried out renovation, improvement, maintenance or repair work during the year on the building or the lot on which it stands. The form requires Social Insurance Numbers or QST registration numbers of the persons who carried out the work, and the amounts paid. The objective, clearly, is to identify workers not reporting construction or casual income. The requirement does not apply to work done by your own employees (already covered by reporting requirements), or in respect of work carried out by operators of gas, electricity, and telecommunication networks, and government agencies.

The *Quebec Revenue Act* provides a penalty of $200 for each person in respect of whom information is not provided. The penalty does not apply where you fail to provide someone's Social Insurance Number because you could not obtain it despite reasonable effort to do so, or because the person had applied for but not yet obtained such a number.

This rule was originally introduced for those who declare rental income or loss on a building in Quebec, to lessors or lessees of commercial premises in Quebec.

(*Quebec Revenue Act*: 59.0.2; Former QTAR: 1086R23.12; QTA: 1086)

[¶1694i] PENALTIES

Quebec has numerous late-filing and other penalties similar in principle, if not in amount, to those in Chapter 2.

[¶1694l] ADMINISTRATION

Revenu Québec maintains district offices in Montreal (2), Quebec City (2), Gatineau, Laval, Longueuil, Saint-Laurent, Jonquière, Rimouski, Rouyn-Noranda, Saint-Jean-sur-Richelieu, Sept-Îles, Sherbrooke, Sorel-Tracy, and Trois-Rivières.

The Province of Quebec also maintains an information office, which includes an office of Revenu Quebec, in Toronto. The address there is 20 Queen St. West, Suite 1504, P.O. Box 13, Toronto, Ontario M5H 3S3. Forms can be obtained from the Toronto office provided you are armed with a form number. The telephone number of the Toronto office is (416) 977-6060. For other information, contact Quebec's main bilingual information centre at 1-800-267-6299.

The Revenu Québec website is www.revenuquebec.ca.

QUEBEC TAX SHELTER INVESTMENTS AND QUEBEC MINIMUM TAX

[¶1697] QUEBEC STRATEGIC ECONOMIC INVESTMENTS

Quebec has identified a number of "strategic economic investments" for the Quebec economy which continue to be supported by income tax incentives available to the Quebec taxpayer. These have either no counterpart in federal rules or the Quebec rules are more generous than federal rules. Generally, these Quebec tax incentives are in the form of deductions from Quebec taxable income for the investments made by the taxpayer. Usually, the deduction is 100% of the investment, but in some cases, such as certain Quebec films and resource exploration, it may be greater. The following items are eligible for such tax incentives:

- certified Quebec films;
- Quebec resource exploration expenses; and
- Quebec Cooperative Investment Plans.

CIP investments must be accounted for on form TP-965.39.4-V (formerly TP-965.32-V). Excessive investments in these shelters can trigger the application of Quebec minimum tax. The details of these investments can be complex and their economic returns highly speculative (i.e., the investment may simply be lost). The investor should have personal expertise or competent independent advice as to both the probable tax and economic consequences before making such investments.

Some of these investments are discussed in greater detail in ¶1642 and ¶1642a.

[¶1698] QUEBEC MINIMUM TAX

Quebec imposes a minimum tax (QMT) similar in outline to the federal Alternative Minimum Tax (AMT) discussed at Chapter 24. However, given the plethora of special incentives Quebec offers, the computation is rather different, and incentives peculiar to Quebec can trigger the Quebec minimum tax even when the federal version does not apply.

The principal differences from federal rules (AMT) in Chapter 24 are:

- QMT rate is 16%.
- The Quebec deduction for stock option benefits is not added back to the Quebec AMT base.
- The unique Quebec deductions for foreign trainers, researchers, and the like are not added back to the QMT base.
- Inclusion of many specific Quebec tax credits and deductions.

The basic exemption used in calculating Quebec minimum tax is $40,000, which matches the federal exemption. Liability for Quebec minimum tax is tested on the checklist at line 432 of the Quebec Guide and in greater detail in a workchart for line 432 which is part of the Quebec tax return package. If liability is indicated, you must complete form TP-776.42-V.

(QTA: 776.42– 776.64; Other Publications: 2001 Quebec Budget, *Additional Information on the Budgetary Measures*, item 1.2; Quebec Finance Information Bulletin 2000-6, item 1.1)

[¶1698.05] *Anti-Avoidance Rules*

Quebec has enacted a general anti-avoidance rule (GAAR) similar to that adopted by the federal government. It provides that, where a transaction or series of transactions achieves a reduction, avoidance, or deferral of tax and is not primarily for other *bona fide* purposes other than to obtain the tax benefit, the intended tax benefit may be ignored in computing tax. An avoidance transaction must involve a misuse or abuse of the provisions of the *Taxation Act*. The Quebec rule applies to both income and capital tax imposed by the Quebec *Taxation Act*.

The Quebec tax administration targeted a number of tax avoidance schemes in recent years, including the "Quebec shuffle" and the "Quebec truffle". The Quebec government believed that these schemes eroded the provincial tax base and created inequality among Quebec taxpayers. As a consequence, on January 30, 2009 the Minister of Finance released a discussion paper entitled *Working Paper: Aggressive Tax Planning 2009*. Essentially, the measures are intended to require taxpayers to report or disclose aggressive tax planning and shift the burden of the government from seeking out schemes that it considers to be avoidance transactions. The Minister of

Finance initiated a public consultation soon thereafter on the proposed measures.

Following the public consultation, the Ministry of Finance released Information Bulletin 2009-5, *Fighting Aggressive Tax Planning*, in October 2009. This bulletin describes an aggressive tax plan (ATP) as a transaction that complies with the law, but is an abuse of the spirit of the law. ATP schemes involve a series of sophisticated steps to exploit inadequacies in certain tax jurisdictions by using complicated techniques, a range of different entities, and complex financial instruments.

The Bulletin also describes the measures to be adopted by the Quebec government to fight aggressive tax planning schemes, specifying mandatory and preventive disclosure rules. Key measures in the bulletin include:

- mandatory disclosure of arrangements between a taxpayer and an adviser that result in a tax benefit and that are confidential transactions or are specified transactions with conditional remuneration;
- clarification of "*bona fide* purpose" under GAAR, to be more consistent with other provincial GAARs;
- a three-year extension of the limitation period where GAAR applies, unless there has been mandatory or preventive disclosure; and
- a number of penalties applicable to taxpayers and promoters where GAAR applies, unless there has been mandatory or preventive disclosure.

The increased detail required for mandatory and preventive disclosure is not a simple exercise and will provide Revenu Québec with an improved platform for raising issues on transactions that would not normally be offensive under GAAR.

Mandatory Disclosure

Under the new mandatory disclosure rules, applicable for any transactions incurred after October 14, 2009, a taxpayer must disclose a confidential transaction to Revenu Quebec under the following circumstances:

- the transaction results directly or indirectly in a tax benefit of $25,000 or more for the taxpayer;
- the transaction results directly or indirectly in an income reduction of $100,000 or more for the taxpayer or the partnership of which he or she is a member and the taxpayer/partnership retained the services of an adviser concerning the transaction; and
- the contract between the taxpayer/partnership and the adviser includes a confidentiality clause towards other persons or the tax administration or the remuneration of the adviser is contingent upon the success of the transaction.

The mandatory disclosure form, TP-1079.DI, *Mandatory or Preventative Disclosure of a Tax Plan*, is due on the taxpayer's filing-due date. If filed late, the penalty is $10,000 for the first day plus an additional $1,000 for each subsequent day, up to a maximum of $100,000. If the mandatory disclosure is not made, Revenu Québec will be allowed to reassess the taxpayer or any person associated/related to the taxpayer at any time until the disclosure is made. If the mandatory disclosure is made, Revenu Québec will deem the disclosure complete if it does not request additional information within 120 days. In the event that a taxpayer has failed to meet the mandatory disclosure requirements, he or she can still satisfy the requirements of the voluntary preventive disclosure policy in order to mitigate any penalties.

A grace period was announced in Quebec Finance Information Bulletin 2010-4, *Aggressive Tax Planning: Easing related to Certain Confidentiality Undertakings* for any general application service contract entered into before March 1, 2010 that includes a confidentiality clause between an adviser and a taxpayer/partnership. Where the parties terminate the confidentiality clause before April 15, 2010 and enter into a new written contract without a confidentiality clause, the confidentiality clause will be deemed to have never existed. The absence of a confidentiality clause between the parties may result in not having to file mandatory disclosure forms.

Preventive Disclosure

Preventive disclosure involves filling out form TP-1079.DI, *Mandatory or Preventative Disclosure of a Tax Plan*, and then following the procedures similar to mandatory disclosure. A taxpayer will be able to avoid the extension of the limitation period discussed below and the application of GAAR penalties.

Bona Fide Purpose

Under GAAR, an avoidance transaction excludes a transaction that is incurred for *bona fide* purposes other than to obtain a tax benefit. The definition was modified so that the following will be excluded as a *bona fide* purpose:

- obtaining a tax benefit under the *Taxation Act*;
- the reduction, avoidance, or deferral of tax or other amount payable under a Quebec law other than the *Taxation Act* or another province's law or federal law;
- the increase in a tax refund or another amount under Quebec law other than the *Taxation Act* or another province's law or federal law; or
- any combination of the above.

The change in definition will apply to the 2009 and subsequent taxation years, as well as to earlier taxation years where the Minister reassesses or makes an additional assessment. The change also applies for taxation years covered by an objection or an appeal on or after October 15, 2009.

Extension of GAAR Assessment Period

In order to allow the tax administration more time to identify ATP schemes and change the risk/reward ratio that currently favours the taxpayer, the limitation period that applies to any taxation year to permit a GAAR-based reassessment is increased by three years, making the limitation period up to six or seven years. The three-year extension will not apply if the three-year period has already been added to the normal limitation period or if mandatory or preventive disclosure has already been made. These rules apply to a taxation year that ends after October 15, 2009. The application of these rules will not apply to transactions which are part of a series of transactions that began before October 15, 2009 and are completed before January 1, 2010.

GAAR Penalties

Aside from the mandatory disclosure penalties described above, additional penalties will be levied on a taxpayer and a promoter of a transaction to which GAAR applies. These penalties are unique to Quebec and are on top of the additional tax and interest. Taxpayers will be charged a penalty of 25% of any additional tax or tax refund reduction and of any other amounts payable under the *Taxation Act*. A promoter, who is a person/partnership that marketed the avoidance transaction or encouraged interest in it, received or is entitled to receive a benefit for encouraging the transaction, and has a substantial role in promoting the transaction will be subject to a penalty of 12.5% of any fees received or receivable related to the transaction.

The GAAR penalty can be avoided by a taxpayer who successfully raises a due diligence defence or who complies with mandatory and preventive disclosure rules. Quebec case law, including case law dealing with directors' liability, will be used to constitute an adequate defence of due diligence.

The penalties apply to transactions incurred after October 14, 2009, except for those transactions which are part of a series of transactions which began before October 15, 2009 and are completed before January 1, 2010.

(QTA: 1079.8.1–1079.15.1; Other Publications: Quebec Finance Information Bulletin 2010-4, *Aggressive Tax Planning: Easing related to Certain Confidentiality Undertakings*; Information Bulletin 2009-5, *Fighting Aggressive Tax Planning; Working Paper: Aggressive Tax Planning 2009*)

Chapter 17

Farming and Fishing

THESE POINTS ARE COVERED IN THIS CHAPTER

CRA REFERENCES RELATING TO THIS CHAPTER

T1 Lines

- Line 130 — Other income
- Line 141 — Farming income (Net)
- Line 143 — Fishing income (Net)
- Line 168 — Farming income (Gross)
- Line 170 — Fishing income (Gross)
- Line 232 — Other deductions

CRA Guides

RC4060, "Farming Income and the AgriStability and AgriInvest Programs Guide — Joint Forms and Guide"; **RC4408**, "Farming Income and the AgriStability and AgriInvest Programs Harmonized Guide"; **T4003**, "Farming Income — Includes Form T2042"; **T4004**, "Fishing Income — Includes Form T2121"; **T4005**, "Fishers and Employment Insurance"

CRA Forms

AGR-1, "Statement of Farm Support Payments"; **T1163**, "Statement A — AgriStability and AgriInvest Programs Information and Statement of Farming Activities for Individuals"; **T1164**, "Statement B — AgriStability and AgriInvest Programs Information and Statement of Farming Activities for Additional Farming Operations"; **T1175**, "Farming — Calculation of Capital Cost Allowance (CCA) and Business-Use-of-Home Expenses"; **T1273**, "Statement A — Harmonized AgriStability and AgriInvest

Programs Information and Statement of Farming Activities for Individuals"; **T1274**, "Statement B — Harmonized AgriStability and AgriInvest Programs Information and Statement of Farming Activities for Additional Farming Operations"; **T2034**, "Election to Establish Inventory Unit Prices for Animals"; **T2042**, "Statement of Farming Activities"; **T2121**, "Statement of Fishing Activities"

Income Tax Folios

S4-F11-C1, "Meaning of Farming and Farming Business"

Interpretation Bulletins

[Interpretation Bulletins (ITs) are gradually being replaced by Income Tax Folios. Although the following ITs have not yet been replaced, the Canada Revenue Agency (CRA) has added an "Archived Content" disclaimer on its website to all ITs. According to the CRA website, the notice has no effect on the status or reliability of the ITs. They are current up to the effective date stated in each publication. The notice confirms that the content will not be altered or updated and each IT will be cancelled when it is replaced by an Income Tax Folio.]

IT-184R, "Deferred Cash Purchase Tickets Issued for Grain"; **IT-200**, "Surface Rentals and Farming Operations"; **IT-234**, "Income of Deceased Persons — Farm Crops"; **IT-268R4**, "Inter Vivos Transfer of Farm Property to Child"; **IT-273R2**, "Government Assistance — General Comments"; **IT-349R3**, "Intergenerational Transfers of Farm Property on Death"; **IT-425**, "Miscellaneous Farm Income"; **IT-427R**, "Livestock of Farmers"; **IT-462**, "Payments Based on Production or Use"; **IT-481 (Consolidated)**, "Timber Resource Property and Timber Limits"; **IT-501**, "Capital Cost Allowance — Logging Assets"; **IT-521R**, "Motor Vehicle Expenses Claimed by Self-Employed Individuals"; **IT-526**, "Farming — Cash Method Inventory Adjustments"

WHAT YOU SHOULD KNOW ABOUT FARMERS' AND FISHERS' RETURNS

RECENT CHANGES

Bill C-15 (Royal Assent June 22, 2016)

Canadian Wheat Board

Applicable as of July 1, 2015, Bill C-15 enacted a set of tax rules that apply to farmers with ownership in the reorganized Canadian Wheat Board (CWB). On July 30, 2015, the CWB was continued as "G3 Canada Limited", with a joint venture known as the "G3 Global Grain Group" acquiring a 50.1% majority of the common shares. The remaining 49.9% of the shares are held in trust for participating farmers. The new tax rules applicable to farmers' units in the trust are explained at ¶1788.

Bill C-29 (Introduced October 25, 2016)

Eligible Capital Property (Farm Quotas) (¶1717)

The 2016 Federal Budget has repealed the eligible capital property (ECP) rules. Effective January 1, 2017, the ECP rules have been replaced with a new capital cost allowance Class 14.1 for depreciable property. Class 14.1 is found in Schedule II of the Regulations. Intangible property, such as goodwill and farm quotas that used to be ECP, is now depreciable property. See ¶880a for a discussion of the new rules.

2015 Federal Budget

Lifetime Capital Gains Exemption (LCGE)

An individual may claim a cumulative lifetime exemption for capital gains from "qualified farm or fishing property" ("qualified farm property" prior to 2014). Budget 2015 increased the lifetime limit for dispositions after April 20, 2015 to the greater of $1 million and the indexed lifetime limit applicable to qualified small business corporation shares (QSBCS), which is $824,177 for 2016 and indexed for subsequent taxation years to the Consumer Price Index (CPI). The $1 million is not indexed, and eventually this additional lifetime limit applicable to qualified farm or fishing property will be eliminated unless it is also indexed in the future (¶1759(B)).

Changes Reported Elsewhere

Remember that many of the general rules affecting businesses as described in Chapters 7 and 8, and investment tax credits at ¶1463, affect farmers and fishers as well. The same is true of the general rules affecting all taxpayers, the rules in Chapters 10 to 13, for example, and the RRSP rules in Chapter 26.

[¶1700] APPLICATION OF RULES IN OTHER CHAPTERS

In many respects the tax of a person engaged in farming or fishing will be calculated in the same manner as for other individuals. The other chapters in this book should therefore be consulted. However, there are some important differences in the calculation of tax by a farmer or fisher, and this chapter describes these differences.

It is very important for farmers or fishers who are in partnership to read Chapter 18 since there are many additional rules which must be considered in determining income from a partnership.

[¶1701] MEANING OF "FARMING" AND "FISHING"

(1) Farming

"Farming" includes:

- Tillage of the soil
- Livestock raising or exhibiting
- Maintaining of horses for racing
- Raising of poultry
- Fur farming
- Dairy farming
- Fruit growing
- Bee keeping

This list is not exhaustive, and farming would also include tree farming and the operation of a wild game reserve. Depending upon the circumstances, farming may also include raising fish, market gardening, the operation of nurseries and greenhouses, and the operation of a chicken hatchery. However, farming does not include trapping. In CRA Document No. 2011-0405411E5, the CRA was asked whether the business of raising earthworms would meet the definition of farming. Their comments indicated that "the activities of keeping, maintaining, and breeding earthworms in a controlled environment for the purposes of harvesting worm castings for sale at a profit ... generally would qualify as farming provided the activities in relation thereto are substantial and extensive".

An individual *employed by* a person engaged in the business of farming is not considered to be "farming" by virtue of that employment.

(2) Fishing

"Fishing" includes the fishing for or catching of fish, shellfish, crustaceans, and marine animals.

As with farming, an individual *employed by* a person engaged in the business of fishing is not considered to be "fishing" by virtue of that employment.

(ITA: 248(1) "farming" and "fishing"; Income Tax Folio: S4-F11-C1)

[¶1702] FEEDLOT OPERATION

A feedlot is now defined (in the CRA's view) as a confined space (such as a pen, corral or barn) where livestock are fed a concentrated diet for the purposes of producing a marketable animal. Although farming includes livestock raising, whether or not a feedlot operator is raising livestock and therefore farming remains a question of fact. To be considered farming, a feedlot operator must make an appreciable contribution to the growth and maturity of the livestock. In the case of a feedlot operation for cattle, an appreciable contribution will be assumed if:

(1) the animals are held in the feedlot for an average of at least 60 days; or

(2) the animals gain an average of at least 90 kilograms (200 pounds) in weight.

The feed may be grown by the feedlot operator, or it may be purchased. The fact that a feedlot is on a small acreage does not disqualify it as a farming operation. A feedlot owner may own all, some, or none of the livestock on the feedlot; this is irrelevant to the determination of farming.

The following types of operations, although they may involve the feeding of livestock, are not considered to be farming:

- acting as agent or broker for the sale of livestock;
- buying livestock for resale as quickly as a favourable opportunity presents itself; and
- assembling livestock for shipment.

Note that the last time CRA released a revised bulletin on feedlot operations was in January 1990, which contained much more specific guidelines in a number of areas than did the older version. There were also some very distinct policy changes; for example, the CRA no longer considers that most of the animals in a feedlot must be owned by the operator for the lot to qualify as a farming business, and the average holding period is reduced from three months to 60 days. As well, fattening or stuffing livestock is no longer considered a disqualified activity.

Support for the positions above was at one time found in Interpretation Bulletin IT-156R. That Bulletin was archived (¶283) in 2004 and cancelled in 2012. Therefore, it can no longer be relied on as policy.

(CRA Document No.: Feedlot Operators, *May 28, 1990,* CRA Document No. ACC9023)

[¶1705] CASH METHOD AND ACCRUAL METHOD OF COMPUTING INCOME

Farming or fishing is considered to be a business. Individuals engaged in other types of business are required to calculate income for tax purposes using the accrual method (see ¶714). In general the accrual method requires accounts receivable at the end of the year to be included in income, permits accounts payable to be deducted from income, and requires inventory fluctuations to be taken into account.

A farmer or fisher may use the accrual method, but has the option of using the cash method. Under the cash method of computing income, amounts are included in income in the year *received*, expenses are deducted from income in the year *paid*, and inventories are not taken into account. Inventories may be taken into account by cash method farmers (see ¶1723).

If you have previously been using the accrual method you may elect to change to the cash method at any time. However, if you are using the cash method, permission must be obtained from your tax services office before changing to the accrual method. Members of a partnership must all use the same method.

If you have been using the cash method and, on or after ceasing to carry on or disposing of all or part of your business, you have ceased to be a resident in Canada, you must include the following items in income for your last Canadian taxation year:

(1) the value of inventory of your business which is your property at the time you became non-resident; and

(2) accounts receivable owing to you at the time you became non-resident, to the extent they would have been included in income if they had been received while you were a Canadian resident.

If you cease to be resident in Canada but continue to carry on your business, the inventory and receivables do not have to be included in income until sold or collected.

A similar provision applies to accounts receivable which are collected after you have disposed of or ceased to carry on your farming or fishing business. Such amounts must be included in income in *the year received*, to the extent they would have been if the business were still being carried on.

There are several advantages of using the cash method of computing income:

(1) If records are maintained chiefly for tax purposes, this task is simplified by use of the cash method. Calculations at the year end of accounts receivable, accounts payable, and inventories are not necessary.

(2) Tax payments may be deferred, since income is taxed in the year payment is received, rather than in the year sales are made.

(3) Inventory of livestock may be calculated on a very general basis, permitting generous adjustments of income. See ¶1723.

Notwithstanding the general rule of the cash method, that amounts are recorded as income or expense of the year received or paid, there are several exceptions. The rules seek to ensure that for both cash-basis farmers and fishers the income inclusions for recaptured depreciation and recaptured deductions in respect of eligible capital property, and the income deductions for capital cost allowance (including terminal losses) in respect of depreciable property and the write-off for eligible capital property, are reflected in the calculation of farming or fishing income or loss.

Commentary on Bill C-29 Measures (Oct. 25, 2016)

Note: When Bill C-29, October 25, 2016, achieves Royal Assent, the commentary will be modified to read:

Notwithstanding the general rule of the cash method, that amounts are recorded as income or expense of the year received or paid, there are several exceptions. The rules seek to ensure that for both cash-basis farmers and fishers the income inclusions for recaptured depreciation and recaptured deductions in respect of eligible capital property, and the income deductions for capital cost allowance (including terminal losses) in respect of depreciable property and the write-off for eligible capital property, are reflected in the calculation of farming or fishing income or loss. With the repeal of the eligible property rules, recaptured deductions in respect of eligible capital property and the write-off for eligible capital property are no longer part of the calculation after January 1, 2017. See ¶880a for the revised rules and transitional rules.

[¶1705.05] *Prepaid Expenses*

Effective for amounts paid after April 26, 1995, other than amounts paid pursuant to a written agreement entered into on or before that date, a limitation on the deduction of prepayments is introduced. Prepaid expenses of a farming or fishing business will not be deductible in the year of payment to the extent that they relate to a taxation year later than the year of payment or the immediately following year. To the extent prepayments relate to the second following year or later, deduction must be deferred to the year in which deduction would be permitted under normal accrual rules (typically the prepayment rules at ¶753). Thus, for example, suppose payments are made in Year 1 for, say, rent for Years 1, 2 and 3. The rent applicable to Years 1 and 2 would be deductible in Year 1, but the rent applicable to Year 3 would be deductible only in Year 3. The prepayment limitation does not apply to nor affect deductions for inventory of a farming business.

(ITA: 28; Income Tax Folio: S4-F11-C1)

[¶1705.10] *Prepaid Expenses and Leased Automobiles*

The CRA has given the following example (which has been updated but not materially altered here) of the interaction of the prepaid expense limitation at ¶1705.05, above, and the automobile leasing limitations at ¶738:

Example

Assume that an individual computes income from a farming or fishing business using the "cash method" described in section 28 and, on January 1, 2015, the individual leases a passenger vehicle for three years, makes a payment of $3,000 on that date, and agrees to pay $800 per month for 2015, 2016, and 2017.

The application of the prepaid expense limitations would produce the following amounts:

- 2015: $11,600 [($800 × 12 months) + $2,000]
- 2016: $9,600 [$800 × 12 months]
- 2017: $10,600 [($800 × 12 months) + $1,000]

The leasing limitation rules will then apply to limit deductions to $9,600 per year for 2015, 2016, and 2017.

(ITA: 28(1)(e), (e.1); 67.3; IT-521R, para. 11)

[¶1707] AMOUNTS TO BE INCLUDED IN FARMING OR FISHING INCOME

In general, all amounts realized from the sale of products of your farming or fishing operations must be included in income. This will include such things as patronage dividends, certain government subsidies and grants (except in respect of capital assets), amounts received for rental, severance and inconvenience under petroleum and natural gas surface rentals (however, in some cases a portion of a lump sum receipt in the first year may be considered on account of capital), the value of tickets received upon the delivery of grain to elevators (but not storage tickets where payment is not due until the next year, see ¶1709), the cost of products which you take for personal use or consumption, gasoline tax rebates, and the value of products given others as consideration for purchases or other liabilities you have incurred.

Rentals received for the use of your farming property, whether collected in cash or on a share crop basis, should be reported as rental income (see Chapter 6) and not as farming income.

Where you are actively engaged in the business of farming, amounts received from the sale of soil, sod, sand, gravel or stone must be included in your farming income.

If you are a farmer and receive payments from another farmer for use of your marketing quotas, these payments are considered to be farming income. If you sell the quotas, you may realize a gain on the sale of an eligible capital property. See ¶766.

Commentary on Bill C-29 Measures (Oct. 25, 2016)

Note: When Bill C-29, October 25, 2016, achieves Royal Assent, the commentary will be modified to read:

> If you are a farmer and receive payments from another farmer for use of your marketing quotas, these payments are considered to be farming income. If you sell the quotas, you may realize a gain on the sale of an eligible capital property prior to 2017 or recapture and/or a capital gain on the disposition of Class 14.1 depreciable property after 2016. See ¶766.

If you sell a portion of the farm or fishing property itself you may realize a capital gain (see Chapter 5) rather than ordinary income. See ¶1759.

If you operate or periodically harvest a woodlot as part of your farming operation, the proceeds from the sale of trees, lumber, logs, poles or firewood, cut by you or for you, form part of your farm income. On the other hand, amounts you receive, in an isolated transaction, for permitting other persons to remove standing timber from your woodlot, will normally be considered to be capital receipts and a taxable capital gain or allowable capital loss may result. See Chapter 5.

A profit realized on the sale of depreciable assets is not taxable as ordinary income if you have been using the Part XVII method of computing capital cost allowances (see ¶1712). Such a profit may, however, be subject to tax as a capital gain (see Chapter 5) if the assets are sold for more than both their original cost and their value on December 31, 1971.

Recapture of capital cost allowance arising on the sale of assets depreciated for tax purposes under Part XI (see ¶1712) is included in income. Under certain circumstances, recapture and capital gains may be deferred if a replacement property is purchased within a prescribed period after the disposition. See also ¶523 and ¶843.

If you realize a capital gain on the sale of a home located on farming land used by you, refer to ¶553 which outlines a special optional method of calculating the tax free portion of the gain.

Insurance proceeds are income if they substitute for amounts you might otherwise have realized from the sale of crops, livestock, etc. See also ¶1705.

The rules regarding settlement of debt (¶565) in theory apply to farmers and fishers. Briefly, the rules say that where a commercial debt owed by the taxpayer is settled for less than its face amount, the difference is applied first to reduce the taxpayer's losses and other tax accounts, and then a specified percentage (being your capital gains inclusion rate for the year) — 50% for 2016 — of the remainder may be included in income. In theory, these rules apply to cash basis taxpayers, and indeed the rules are amended to make sure they do apply. However, the definition of a commercial debt subject to these rules specifically excludes a debt related to an amount unpaid by a cash basis taxpayer that is recognized for tax purposes only when it is paid. This would seem to cover most debt related to the business of a cash basis taxpayer.

A list of typical income items is included on the Statement of Income and Expenses in the guides. Other amounts which are not taxable are described at ¶991.

[¶1707.05] *Payments Under Federal Programs*

Generally speaking, farm support program payments are reported to you on an AGR-1 Supplementary slip, and the current *Farming Income* guide, as well as directions on the back of the AGR-1, provides the best current directions on reporting these amounts. AGR-1 does not report total payments of less than $100; these are nevertheless income which should be reported.

If the AGR-1 payments cover a period which differs from the taxation year of your farming business, you should report only the portion which relates to the taxation year. It is probably wise to attach a note to your return reconciling the AGR-1 slip to the amount you reported. In the following year you must report the balance, and should again include a copy of the reconciliation.

Your AGR-1 may report NISA amounts, which are on income account in box 18. Positive amounts are reported on line 130 of your T1 return, and negative amounts deducted on line 232.

NISA apart, payments you received from federal or provincial disaster assistance programs are taxable as farm income (subject to the comments on certain provincial programs below). For example, payments under the Agricultural Income Disaster Assistance (AIDA) Program and the Canadian Farm Income Program (CFIP) are taxable as farm income. These programs apparently operate in Saskatchewan, Manitoba, Nova Scotia, Newfoundland and Labrador, New Brunswick, Prince Edward Island, and Quebec. Administrative fees under these programs, if any, should be deductible.

You may pay some of your expenses by having them deducted from your cash grain tickets or grain stabilization payments. These expenses typically include seed, feed, sprays, or fertilizers. You can deduct these expenses if you include in your income the gross amount of the grain sale or stabilization payment.

Under the *Agricultural Marketing Programs Act*, you may be able to get advances for crops that someone stores in your name. CRA's position is that these advances are loans rather than income, and tax may be deferred accordingly. In short, you do not include these payments in your income until the crops are sold. However, for the tax year in which the sale occurs, you must include the full amount from the sale of your crops in your income.

If you receive compensation for livestock destroyed under statutory authority, or for breeding animals (and breeding bees for 2014 and subsequent years) sold in a prescribed drought year (or for 2008 and subsequent taxation years, prescribed flood/excessive moisture year), the compensation must be included in income. You are allowed to defer recognition of the income, if you wish, for one taxation year from the year it is received or becomes receivable (depending on the reporting method you follow). See ¶1723a.

(ITA: 12; 13; 20; 76; 135; Window on Canadian Tax: 2658; *Farming Income* guide (T4003); *Fishing Income* guide (T4004); IT-200 Surface rentals and farming operations; IT-273R2 Government Assistance — General Comments; IT-425 Miscellaneous farm income; Income Tax Folio: S4-F11-C1)

[¶1707.10] *Payments Under Ontario Programs*

Payments under the Ontario Whole Farm Relief Program (OWFRP) and the Ontario Farm Income Disaster Program (OFIDP) are taxable as farm income.

A 1993 technical interpretation from the CRA summarizes its interpretation of the tax consequences of various incentive programs administered under the Ontario Ministry of Agriculture. Many of these programs may now be obsolete, but some may still function. The statement that "12(1)(*x*) would apply" refers to the rule at ¶729 that inducements received in the course of a business are included in income to the extent they do not reduce the cost of related capital property of the taxpayer.

PROGRAM	COMMENTS
Artificial Insemination of Livestock Act	12(1)(*x*) would apply; however, as the payments are made to breeder associations, these organizations would likely qualify for an exemption under paragraph 149(1)(*l*)
Compensation for Livestock Killed by Bears	12(1)(*x*) would apply
Livestock, Poultry and Honey Bee Protection Act	12(1)(*x*) would apply
Grants in lieu of taxes	These amounts are paid to municipalities which are exempt from tax
Grants to Local Poultry Associations	Included in income to the extent they do not reduce expenses
Hunter Damage Compensation Act	Amounts received in respect of livestock would be regular farm income, amounts received for machinery or equipment would be treated as proceeds of disposition or in the case of repairs would reduce the expense
Ontario Farm-Start	12(1)(*x*) would apply
Ontario Farm Tax Rebate Program	12(1)(*x*) would apply where the amount received was not applied to reduce otherwise deductible taxes
The Ontario Establishment Loan Act	No tax consequences to low interest rate loans
Ontario Private Mortgage Guarantee Program	No tax consequences to the guarantee, section 80 [¶565] could apply if there is a settlement for less than the principal amount
Professional Services Assistance Program	Receipts by the professional receiving the payment would be income, no tax consequences to the farmer receiving the assistance
Pure Bred Livestock Sales Assistance Programs	Included in income of the club receiving the payment
Rabies Indemnification Program	12(1)(*x*) would apply
Sheep & Bull Indemnification Program	12(1)(*x*) would apply
Transportation of Livestock Exhibits Assistance Program (Livestock Exhibits Outside Ontario)	Included in income of the association to the extent that the amounts are not offset against expenses

The CRA also indicated that "T-slips" were required to be issued in respect of those payments where the amount was income, a reduction of expenses, or where paragraph 12(1)(*x*) applied, unless the payment under the program was less than $100. Payments under separate programs of less than $100 each but which in total exceeded $100 paid to a single individual or organization would not require the preparation of an information slip.

In a separate technical interpretation, the CRA confirmed that payments under the Big Game Damage Compensation Program would be included in income or, alternatively, paragraph 12(1)(*x*) would apply.

(Window on Canadian Tax: 2741)

[¶1707.15] Payments under Alberta and Saskatchewan Programs

Payments under the Farm Income Disaster Program (FIDP) in Alberta are taxable as farming income. Similarly, payments under the Agricultural Income Disaster Assistance (AIDA) Program and the Canadian Farm Income Program (CFIP), which operate in Saskatchewan (and other provinces) are taxable as farm income.

A 1993 technical interpretation from the CRA summarizes its interpretation of the tax consequences of various incentive programs administered by Alberta or Saskatchewan. Further 1995 and 1996 interpretations dealt with some subsequent programs. Some of these programs may now be obsolete.

The statement below that "12(1)(*x*) would apply" refers to the rule at ¶729 that inducements received in the course of a business are included in income to the extent they do not reduce the cost of related capital property of the taxpayer. "Included in income under section 9" means included in income from a business.

PROGRAM	COMMENTS
	ALBERTA
Alberta Crow Benefit Offset Program	Included in the taxpayer's income under section 9, either as revenue or a reduction in expenses; 12(1)(*x*) would apply to the extent the receipt was not otherwise included in income
Alberta Bipartite White Veal Stabilization Program	Included in business income, for cash basis taxpayers this may be accomplished through recording net receipts
Alberta Farm Credit Stability Program	Section 80 (¶565) may apply where a loan is settled for less than the principal amount; 12(1)(*x*) may apply to any portion of the loan which is forgivable to the extent the lender is committed to forgiving the loan
1990 Southeastern Alberta Disaster Assistance Program	The comments in IT-182 [now found in IT-273R2, paragraphs 1 and 2] would apply where the loss is a business loss, the compensation would be included in income or treated as proceeds of disposition of property; where the compensation was for a personal loss there would be no tax consequences

PROGRAM	*COMMENTS*
1995 Southern Alberta Disaster Recovery Program	Payments relating to crop losses represent regular farm income; payments relating to restoration of farmland, fence repairs and clean-up would generally reduce the related expense; payments related to farm buildings and equipment are proceeds of disposition if for replacement or income if related to repairs
Alberta Private Irrigation Development Assistance Program	To the extent that the grant is in respect of the acquisition of depreciable property, subsection 13(7.1) would apply to reduce capital cost; where the grant is in respect of non-depreciable property, paragraph 53(2)(*k*) would be applicable to reduce ACB [¶506(6)]; otherwise, the grant would be included in income under 12(1)(*x*)
On-Farm Demonstration Program	12(1)(*x*) would apply, a deduction would be available under paragraph 20(1)(*hh*) [¶729] where amounts were repaid
Surface Rights Compensation	Where the operator was unconditionally obligated to repay the "debt" arising under the compensation arrangement, the amount would not be a farm support payment
Alberta Horse Improvement Program	If the prize is received in the course of operating a business, then the amount would be included in income under subsection 9(1) if not received in the course of a business or employment, to the extent that it exceeds $500, it would be included in income under paragraph 56(1)(*n*) [¶953]
SASKATCHEWAN	
Capital and Production Loan Programs and Livestock Cash Advances	Except for grandfathered loans, 12(1)(*x*) would include the forgivable portion of the loan in the taxpayer's income; paragraph 20(1)(*hh*) [¶729] would provide a deduction for any portion of the loan subsequently repaid
The Interim Red Meat Production Equalization Program	Included in income under section 9, alternatively 12(1)(*x*) would apply
Feed Grain Adjustment Program	Included in income under section 9, alternatively 12(1)(*x*) would apply
Production Associations Loan Guarantee Program	The guarantee or the honouring of a guarantee would generally not have any tax consequences; subsection 80(1) [¶565] could apply if any portion of the debt were settled for less than the principal amount
Farm Land Leaseback Program	Assistance included in lender's income under subsection 9(1); 12(1)(*x*) would apply to the extent that the amount was not otherwise included in income
Farm Purchase Program	Included in income under section 9, alternatively 12(1)(*x*) would apply
Saskatchewan Enhanced NISA Program	Amounts paid out of NISA fund No. 2 or transferred to the No. 1 account are taxable
Crops Sector Companion Program	Payments are either income or a reduction of expenses or other costs
Agri-Food Innovation Program	Payments from the Agri-Food Innovation Fund to producers would have to be reported as either income or a reduction of expenses or other costs

(Window on Canadian Tax: 2792; 3967; 4207)

[¶1707.20] *Payments under B.C. Programs*

Payments under the Whole Farm Insurance Pilot (WFIP) Program in British Columbia are taxable as farm income.

[¶1709] CASH PURCHASE TICKETS

Where you deliver grain to a licensed public elevator or process elevator, you may receive a "storage ticket", a "cash purchase ticket", or a "deferred cash purchase ticket". A cash purchase ticket indicates that a final sale has occurred and you must include the value of the ticket as income at the time you receive it. A storage ticket is precisely the opposite: no sale has taken place and no income inclusion arises at that time.

Where you receive a post-dated (deferred) cash purchase ticket under the following conditions:

(1) the ticket is issued by a primary elevator or process elevator for grain (wheat, oats, barley, rye, flaxseed, rapeseed, and canola) produced in Canada, and

(2) you are entitled to payment by the elevator operator of the amount stated therein, without interest, at a date that is after the end of the taxation year in which the grain is delivered

you must exclude the amount stated on the ticket from the income of the taxation year in which the grain was delivered and include the amount in the income of the immediately following taxation year. Note that "canola" was added to the definition of "grain" and the restriction of "designated areas" was removed. These changes were effective for cash purchase tickets and other forms of settlement issued after December 14, 2011.

If you pledge a cash purchase ticket as security against a business or personal loan or sell it before its maturity you do not lose the right you would otherwise have had to defer the reporting of the proceeds of the ticket. On disposition of a cash purchase ticket for less than face value, the resulting discount is treated as a separate transaction in the fiscal period in which the discount is incurred. Whether the discount is deductible from income is determined in accordance with the facts of the particular situation.

The terms used in the above discussion are defined in accordance with the definitions contained in the *Canada Grain Act*. The following definitions are relevant:

(1) *"Cash Purchase Ticket"* — A document in prescribed form issued in respect of grain delivered to a primary elevator, process elevator, or grain dealer as evidence of the purchase of the grain by the operator of the elevator or the grain dealer and entitling the holder of the document to payment by the operator or grain dealer of the purchase price stated in the document.

(2) *"Primary Elevator"* — An elevator whose principal use is the receiving of grain directly from producers for storage or forwarding, or both.

(3) *"Process Elevator"* — An elevator whose principal use is the receiving and storing of grain for direct manufacture or processing into other products.

(4) *"Designated Area"* — The provinces of Manitoba, Saskatchewan and Alberta, and those parts of the Province of British Columbia known as the Peace River District and the Creston-Wynndel areas, and such other parts of the Province of British Columbia and such parts of the Province of Ontario lying in the Western Division as the Board may from time to time designate. Note, this definition has been removed from the *Canada Grain Act*. Therefore, there is no longer a geographical restriction for cash purchase tickets and other forms of settlement issued after December 14, 2011.

(ITA: 76; IT-184R Deferred cash purchase tickets issued for grain)

[¶1710] DEDUCTIBLE EXPENSES

In general, the expenses of earning your farming or fishing income are deductible, unless they are of a capital nature. You will be allowed to deduct capital cost allowances (see ¶1712) on most (but not all) capital expenditures.

Some specific expenses which you can deduct currently are:

(1) *Expenses listed on the Statements of Income and Expenses* (forms T2042 and T2121).

(2) *Board and lodging for employees:* The cost of providing board and lodging to employees is a deductible expense. It must also be reported as income by the employees (unless the employees qualify for the special treatment outlined in ¶360). Expenses which apply only partially to employees, and are partly your own personal and living expenses should be allocated on a reasonable basis. In general, the cost of providing meals to your employees is likely to come under one of the exceptions to the general rule that only 50% of meal costs are deductible (¶734). The applicable exceptions would be for meals which are a taxable benefit to the employee or for meals generally available to all employees at a particular location.

(3) *Provisioning offshore boats:* The cost of food used to provision offshore fishing boats is a deductible expense to self-employed fishers when purchased for consumption while at sea.

(4) *Wages to your children*, if:

(a) they were actually paid during the year;

(b) they were for services necessary to earn income from the business; and

(c) the amount is reasonable, considering the age of the child and the amount you would pay to an outside employee for the same work.

Note that wages you pay to your children are income to them, and may reduce the tax credits you can claim for them (Chapter 13). If sufficient, such wages require them to file their own returns, and you must consider whether income tax, CPP and EI withholdings are required.

The value of board supplied to dependent children is not deductible.

(5) *Wages to your spouse (or common-law partner):* Wages paid to your spouse or common-law partner are deductible expenses provided they meet the same general conditions as outlined with respect to wages paid to children. Where a claim is made you must indicate the amount paid to your spouse or common-law partner as a separate item in your statement of farming and fishing income and expenses. If you are in a business partnership with your spouse or common-law partner, you cannot deduct amounts paid from the business to the spouse or common-law partner, since the spouse's or common-law partner's income is business income from the partnership and not wages. See also ¶1808.

Note that wages you pay to your spouse or common-law partner are income to that person, and may reduce the dependant credits you can claim for that person (Chapter 11). If sufficient, such wages require your spouse or common-law partner to file his or her own return, and you must consider whether income tax, CPP and EI withholdings are required. See ¶741.

(6) *Farm home expenses* if the home is located on the farm and is used to earn income. The deduction is limited to a portion of house expenses (light, power, taxes, telephone, fire insurance and repairs) which is reasonable in relation to the business use of your house (unless the house is rented to a tenant or used entirely to lodge hired help, in which cases all expenses may be deducted to the extent they are not paid by the tenant or hired help). Note that the general limitations at ¶742 apply to farmers. If you own the home, capital cost allowance may also be claimed (see ¶742 and ¶1712), but you must consider the impact this will have on your principal residence exemption (¶742). If your home is located off the farm, you may be able to claim a portion of the expenses relating to it if one or more rooms is used solely for earning business income, again subject to the limitations at ¶742.

(7) *Automobile expenses, including capital cost allowance* (see ¶1712), to the extent they were spent to earn income rather than for personal use, and within the limitations as to leasing or interest cost (¶738) and capital cost allowance (¶810a).

(8) *Cost of meals and entertainment expenses:* To the extent that your expenses (other than those in (2) above) include meals and entertainment, you will be limited to deducting 50% of the expenses by the rules at ¶734.

(9) *Small tools:* You may claim capital cost allowance of 100% on tools purchased after May 2, 2006 which cost less than $500.

(10) *Cost of drilling or digging water wells:* However, you must capitalize the cost of casing and cribwork and the cost of the water distribution system, including the pump and its installation, the piping and the trenching.

(11) *Cost of replacing trees or bushes* if these produce income. The cost of commencing or extending tree-farming operations is not deductible.

(12) *Payments for utilities installations* if they remain the property of the public utility.

(13) *Cost of clearing or levelling land, tile drainage, or constructing an unpaved road* on a farm property. The cost of constructing a paved road must be capitalized; however, capital cost allowance may be claimed thereon. See ¶1712.

Some expenses you cannot deduct are:

(1) Replacement or improvements of capital assets (add to capital cost for capital cost allowance purposes if depreciable property);

(2) Cost of fisher's nets or traps (these must be capitalized or inventoried);

(3) Principal payments on borrowed money;

(4) Value of seed or feed grown by you;

(5) Value of animals which have died during the year;

(6) Value of your own time spent on farming or fishing; and

(7) Cost of produce consumed by yourself or your family, if such costs are included in your business expenses.

(ITA: 18; 30; *Farming Income* guide (T4003); *Fishing Income* guide (T4004))

[¶1711] WOODLOT OPERATIONS

[¶1711.05] *Is a Commercial Woodlot a Farm?*

If a commercial woodlot falls within the definition of farming, it has several advantages, notably the current ability to utilize the cash method of computing income (¶705), the ability to rollover the property to children (¶1759) and access to the capital gain exemption ($824,177 for 2016 and indexed annually) on disposition (¶1759). On the other hand, it may be subject to the loss restrictions if farming is not a chief source of income (¶1750). If a commercial woodlot does not constitute farming, none of these rules apply. If a woodlot is not commercial at all, but is merely a hobby conducted without a reasonable expectation of profit, income or loss rules do not apply at all.

It is the CRA's view that if the main focus of the woodlot business is not lumbering or logging, but is planting, nurturing and harvesting trees pursuant to a forestry management or other similar resource plan and significant attention is paid to manage the growth, health, quality and composition of the stands, it is generally considered a farming business (a commercial farm woodlot). If the main focus of a business is logging (a commercial non-farm woodlot), and is not growing, nurturing and harvesting trees, the fact that reforestation activities are carried out would not transform that business into a farming operation.

[¶1711.10] *Christmas Tree Growers*

The planting, caring for and harvesting of Christmas trees by a taxpayer who grows and nurtures evergreens to sell as Christmas trees, or who buys land so planted to tend and harvest the trees, is regarded as a farming business regardless of whether the taxpayer is carrying on any other type of farming operation, provided the operations are carried on with a reasonable expectation of profit. Where a taxpayer relies on naturally seeded regeneration, whether particular business will be a farming business will depend upon the focus of the business and how the trees are nurtured.

A stand of Christmas trees is not viewed as a timber limit since the output is trees, not timber or similar products, and the depletion allowance for timber limits (¶881) is not applicable.

[¶1711.15] *If it is a Farm*

Where a taxpayer is operating a commercial woodlot as a farm, the following rules will (subject to the general restrictions that expenses must be laid out to earn income and the farm loss restrictions) apply:

(1) the taxpayer is entitled to report the income from that operation in accordance with the cash method if an election is made (¶1705). The taxpayer may instead choose to report this income in accordance with the accrual method;

(2) the costs of purchasing and planting the trees are deductible in the year if the taxpayer is reporting the income from the operation under the cash method. The optional and mandatory inventory adjustments at ¶1723 apply to a taxpayer using the cash method to compute income from a farming business. Where a taxpayer buys land that is already planted with trees, the trees would not generally be inventory. However, where trees are purchased as inventory separately from the land on which they stand, the cost of purchasing the trees is added to inventory. Seeds or seedlings that have been planted are not considered purchased inventory on hand at the end of the year for purposes of the mandatory inventory adjustment;

(3) generally, under the cash method, recurring expenses directly related to the commercial activity are deductible in the year in which they are paid. Whether a particular planting, pruning, thinning, fertilizing, cultivating, and property tax expenditure is a recurring expense will depend on the particular circumstances. If land is not used in the business in a particular year, the rules at ¶655 may restrict the deductibility of interest and property taxes;

(4) capital cost allowance may be available in respect of the cost to the taxpayer of the woodlot; see ¶881 and ¶882 and IT-481; and

(5) certain assets used in a woodlot (roads, drainage systems, etc.) may be written off as current expenses or must be depreciated in accordance with the Act and the regulations. The appropriate income tax treatment is described in IT-501 (Archived).

Capital cost allowance is only available if an asset was acquired for the purpose of gaining or producing income.

[¶1711.20] *Woodlots and the Capital Gains Exemption*

A commercial farm woodlot may be a qualified farm or fishing property (qualified farm property prior to 2014) for the purpose of this definition if it is a "real property" at law.

For example, the capital gains deduction may be available where an individual sells a fee simple in treed land, since it is a real property. However, since the capital gains deduction is not available when "personal property" is sold, the capital gains deduction cannot be claimed on the sale of timber, or on the sale of a licence to cut and take timber. Where an individual sells property that is a right to cut and take timber, which is a real property (a *profit à prendre*), the capital gains exemption will not be available where the disposition was taxed on income account under the rules taxing as income proceeds of disposition which are dependent on the production or use of the property (¶490 and IT-462). (See *Berkheiser v. Berkheiser and Glaister*, [1957] S.C.R. 387; *Laidlaw v. Vaughan Rhys*, [1911] 44 S.C.R 458; *Lisafield v. M.N.R.*, 91 DTC 1197 and *Gillies Bros. Ltd. v. The King* (1947), 2 D.L.R. 769 for a discussion of the distinction between a licence and a *profit à prendre*.)

The capital gains deduction is not available on a disposition of a "timber resource property", which is defined in subsection 13(21) and explained in IT-481, "Timber Resource Property and Timber Limits", or on a disposition of treed land to the extent that the trees on the land are inventory since dispositions of timber resource properties and inventory are taxable on income, not capital, account.

In addition to the requirement that the property disposed of must be a real property, certain other requirements, such as a use test and a profits test, must be satisfied to qualify for this capital gains deduction. For property acquired on or before June 17, 1987, real property may qualify if the property has been used principally in the course of carrying on the business of farming in Canada by any of the taxpayers described in subparagraphs 110.6(1)(*a*)(i) to (v) of the definition of "qualified farm or fishing property" ("qualified farm property" for dispositions prior to 2014) in the year of its disposition, or if it was used principally in the business of farming or fishing for at least five years during which it was owned by any of the taxpayers described in subparagraphs 110.6(1)(*a*)(i) to (iii) and (v). See ¶502f. When reference is made to an asset being used "principally" in the business of farming or fishing, the asset will meet this test where more than 50% of the asset's use is in the business of farming or fishing. Whether or not particular assets are "used principally in the business of farming or fishing" is a question of fact to be determined on a property by property basis (i.e., this test would have to be satisfied for each legal parcel of land). A property that is a right to cut and take trees that is considered a *profit à prendre* would not qualify where paragraph 12(1)(*g*) applied (¶490) or where the *profit à prendre* itself (as opposed to the trees themselves) had not been used in carrying on a farming or fishing business.

For property acquired after June 17, 1987, a gross revenue test must be satisfied for a particular farm property to be qualified farm property for the purposes of the enhanced capital gains deduction.

The filing, in and of itself, of the capital gains election in respect of land on which timber grows will not cause income from subsequent sales of timber to be treated as on capital account.

(Income Tax Folio: S4-F11-C1)

[¶1711.25] *Transferring Woodlots to Children/ Grandchildren*

As discussed at ¶1759(A), a taxpayer may make an intergenerational transfer of farm property in Canada on an income tax-deferred ("rollover") basis, if the property was principally used in a farming business in which the taxpayer or a family member was actively engaged on a regular and continuous basis. Similar rules apply to intergenerational transfers of shares of family farm corporations and interests in family farm partnerships. Note all references to farm property, farming business, family farm corporations, and family farm partnerships are replaced with the combination term farm or fishing property, farming or fishing business, family farm or fishing corporations, and family farm or fishing partnerships, effective for 2014 and subsequent taxation years.

The operation of a commercial woodlot may or may not constitute a farming business. Even where it does, however, the intergenerational rollovers were generally not available for commercial woodlots because, aside from monitoring, the management of a woodlot may not demand regular and continuous activity as the transfer of farm property rules require.

Effective December 10, 2001, the intergenerational rollover rules were modified when they apply to intergenerational rollovers of commercial woodlot operations *that are farming businesses*. Where the regular and continuous activity test set out in the existing rollover rules cannot be met, a special test applies strictly for the purpose of applying those rules to commercial woodlot operations. The test will allow an intergenerational rollover where the conditions of the existing rollover rules are otherwise met and the transferor or a family member is involved in the management of the woodlot "to the extent required by a prescribed forest management plan in respect of that woodlot". A family member includes a spouse or common-law partner or any child of the transferor. This measure applies to transfers that occur after December 10, 2001.

Regulation 7400 sets out the criteria for a prescribed forest management plan applicable to transfers of woodlots that occur after 2007.

This rollover applies where the woodlot is operated through a partnership or family farm corporation, as discussed at ¶1759.

(ITA: 70(9)–(10); 73(3); ITR: 7400 [Prescribed forest management plan])

[¶1712] CAPITAL COST ALLOWANCE

The meaning of "capital cost allowance", and its usual method of calculation, are described in Chapter 8.

The method described in Chapter 8 is known as the "Part XI" method and is now to be used by all taxpayers, including farmers and fishers. For an alphabetical list of assets by capital cost class and depreciation rate, see ¶899.

Farmers or fishers were, prior to 1972, entitled to elect an optional method of calculating capital cost allowances and if they elected to use this optional method in those years, they may continue to use it now, but only for the assets which they acquired prior to January 1, 1972. This optional method is known as the "Part XVII" method. If the Part XVII method was adopted originally, a change can be made to the Part XI method at any time in a subsequent year.

The major features of the "Part XVII" method of computing capital cost allowances, and differences from the

"Part XI" method, including a table of rates, can be found in prior editions of this book.

Both the Part XI and Part XVII methods are modified somewhat when a taxpayer is a member of a partnership. Farmers and fishers who are members of a partnership should consult Chapter 18 to determine how capital cost allowances are to be computed on assets owned by the partnership. Where assets are owned by an individual partner, however, the general rules outlined following and in Chapter 8 will apply with respect to these assets.

NOTE: As an alternative to capital cost allowance on nets, the loss in value may be claimed as an expense, as shown in the following example:

Value of nets, traps, twine, etc., on hand at beginning of period			$ 750
Add:	Cost of nets and traps purchased	$200	
	Cost of twine and other net and trap materials purchased	125	325
Subtotal			$1,075
Deduct:	Value of nets, traps, twine, etc., on hand at end of period	$700	
	Proceeds from sale and insurance of nets, traps, twine, etc.	150	850
Loss on nets and traps claimed as expense			$ 225

Under both methods, capital cost allowance is an optional deduction — any amount up to the maximum allowance may be claimed; deferral of claims will leave a larger pool for future calculations (see ¶802).

(ITA: 20; 30; ITR: 1100–1102; 1700–1704; *Farming Income* guide (T4003); *Fishing Income* guide (T4004))

[¶1715] INVESTMENT TAX CREDIT

If you have purchased certain qualified buildings or equipment for use in the Atlantic provinces or the Gaspé region of Quebec, you may be entitled to an investment tax credit, which is a deduction from federal income taxes otherwise payable. From time to time, credits are available for other regions. Facilities used in farming, fishing and storing grains may qualify.

See ¶1463 for rates and details of how to calculate your investment tax credit.

You should also check the tax credit programs discussed in Chapter 15 for your province.

(ITA: 127)

[¶1715.10] *Investment Tax Credit for Storage of Fishing Gear*

The CRA has given an opinion (CRA Document No. 2007-0238901E5) that an otherwise qualified building used to store fishing gear and/or vessels would qualify as property used primarily in fishing; it would not be disallowed as a storage activity.

[¶1716] PROPERTY NOT ELIGIBLE FOR CAPITAL COST ALLOWANCES

You may not claim capital cost allowances on property described in ¶809. You may not claim such allowances for land, animals, trees, shrubs, herbs or similar growing things (except the expense of maintenance and replacement — see ¶1710, item (11)), and, in general, for any assets which do not fit into a capital cost allowance class.

[¶1717] ELIGIBLE CAPITAL PROPERTY (FARM QUOTAS)

Certain intangible property, such as goodwill and government rights, are not eligible for capital cost allowance but are in effect depreciated under a similar system called "eligible capital property". Like the capital cost allowance system, the disposition of such property can result in a recapture of previous deductions and, where proceeds exceed amounts depreciated, a taxable capital gain which may be eligible for the capital gains exemption (currently $824,177 for 2016 and indexed annually). See ¶766–¶770 for a description of the eligible capital property system, and ¶502 for the applicable capital gains exemption.

Commentary on Bill C-29 Measures (Oct. 25, 2016)

Note: When Bill C-29, October 25, 2016, achieves Royal Assent, the commentary will be modified to read:

The eligible capital property (ECP) rules have been repealed. Effective January 1, 2017 the ECP rules have been replaced with a new capital cost allowance Class 14.1 for depreciable property. Class 14.1 is found in Schedule II of the Regulations. Intangible property listed above that used to be ECP is now depreciable property. See ¶880a for a complete discussion of the new rules and transitional rules.

[¶1718] FISHING VESSELS

Some fishing vessels or conversion costs may qualify for the special capital cost allowance of $33^1/_3$% of original cost (see ¶884). This special capital cost allowance is provided under Part XI.

(*Fishing Income* guide (T4004))

[¶1720] LOSSES

In general, if farming or fishing is your chief source of income, your losses may be carried back three years or carried forward 20 years as a deduction against other income (if they have not been deducted in a previous year). See Chapter 10 for a further discussion of such losses.

If farming is not your chief source of income, loss restrictions discussed at ¶1750 may apply.

Losses from limited partnerships are subject to elaborate restrictions for partnership fiscal periods ending after February 25, 1986. See ¶1818.

(ITA: 111; 119)

[¶1722] INVENTORY VALUATION FOR THE ACCRUAL BASIS TAXPAYER

If the accrual method of computing income is used (see ¶1705), inventory must be calculated as of the end of each year.

A farmer or fisher who chooses the accrual basis may use any one of the following methods for valuing inventories, which are also those used by other taxpayers:

(1) All items valued at fair market value;

(2) Individual items valued at the lower of cost or fair market value.

Once you have chosen an inventory method, you are bound to continue using that method for tax purposes unless the Minister of National Revenue consents to a change. Generally speaking, you will use the "lower of cost or market" method. These methods are discussed at ¶758.

A third method of valuation is available only to breeders and raisers of animals, and is known as the "unit price basis". Use of this method requires election form T2034 (Election to Establish Inventory Unit Prices for Animals) to be filed. Under this method, each animal included in inventory is valued at a unit price based on the value placed on animals of that class at the end of the year preceding the first year an election is made. The value of all animals of a particular class in inventory at the end of that preceding year is divided by the number of animals of the class at that time to arrive at an average price which becomes the unit price for subsequent years. The unit price therefore remains constant each year, regardless of changes in the actual cost of animals.

If no animals of a particular class were on hand at the end of the year preceding the first year of election, the CRA will determine the unit price for animals of that class.

The unit price basis may not be used for:

(1) registered animals;

(2) animals purchased for feedlot or similar operations; or

(3) animals purchased by a drover or like person for resale.

If the aggregate value of a particular class of animal on the unit price basis exceeds market value, the animals may be valued at fair market value.

An election, once filed, is effective until you revoke it in writing. However, once the election is revoked, you cannot again make such an election without the CRA's approval.

Form T2034 includes reasonably detailed instructions on the calculation of unit prices.

(ITA: 10; ITR: 1800–1802; *Farming Income* guide (T4003))

[¶1723] LIVESTOCK AND OTHER INVENTORY OF THE CASH BASIS TAXPAYER

Note that the Farming Income Guide T4003 contains elaborate and valuable descriptions of the inventory adjustments. A series of extremely useful workcharts for determining the required income adjustments is provided.

[¶1723.10] *Rules for Cash Basis Farmers and Fishers*

The definition of inventory includes anything that would be inventory if the taxpayer were on an accrual basis. The definition is:

> . . . "inventory" means a description of property the cost or value of which is relevant in computing a taxpayer's income from a business for a taxation year or would have been so relevant if the income from the business had not been computed in accordance with the cash method and, with respect to a farming business, includes all of the livestock held in the course of carrying on the business.

This definition is clearly very broad, and it is perhaps not really clear what is included in addition to livestock. The CRA (in the *Farming Income* Guide) explains that inventory is the group of items your business holds that it intends either to consume or sell to its customers. It goes on to elucidate that, in its view, farm inventory is tangible property that is:

- held for sale, such as harvested grain;
- used in the production of saleable goods, such as seed and feed; or
- in the process of being produced, such as standing crops or feeder livestock.

The significance of inventory, generally speaking, is that income is recognized and related expenses are deducted only as the products in inventory are sold. Consequently it typically has no meaning for a cash basis taxpayer. However, the farm inventory rules limit the deduction of purchased inventory-type items to prevent them from creating or increasing a loss to a cash basis farmer (but not fisher) where the related products have not been sold in the year. Thus they will always become relevant to the cash basis farmer in a loss year.

In non-loss years, the closing value of not only livestock but all other "inventory" of cash basis farmers (but not fishers) may be added back to income on the optional basis. That is, you may add to income any amount up to the fair market value of your *total* (purchased and other) inventory at the end of the year to income (although in a loss year you will have to make an offsetting deduction for the value of *purchased* inventory under the mandatory adjustment rules). The amount added will be deducted again in the following year, permitting you to average current bad years against future good years (or so you hope). This right to elect to include in income any amount up to the fair market value of all inventory-type items on hand at the end of the taxation year is called the "optional inventory adjustment".

These rules ensure that for both cash basis farmers and fishers the income inclusions for recaptured depreciation and recaptured deductions in respect of eligible capital property, and the income deductions for capital cost allowance (including terminal losses) in respect of depreciable property and the write-off for eligible capital property, as applicable, are reflected in the calculation of farming or fishing income or loss.

Cash basis farmers who are or become non-resident and/or who move inventory out of Canada may be deemed to have disposed of inventory for fair market value, resulting in a full income inclusion. Accounts receivable will also have to be included in income where these rules apply.

[¶1723.15] *Calculation of Inventory Item Deductions in Loss Years (Farmers only)*

The rules for cash basis taxpayers provide for a "mandatory inventory adjustment" for farmers, in loss years only, in respect of *purchased* inventory on hand at the end of the year. This adjustment applies only in loss years. It requires an addition to income in a loss year of the lesser of the amount of the loss and the value of purchased inventory on hand at the end of the year. As with the optional inventory election, any amount required to be included in income in a year is deducted in the following year.

The following rules are provided for the manner in which a farmer's inventory is to be valued for the purposes of the mandatory inventory adjustment. Generally, inventory will be valued at the lower of its original purchase price and its fair market value. A "specified animal", however, will be valued at its original purchase price less 30% per year on a diminishing balance basis unless the taxpayer chooses to value the animal at a greater amount (not exceeding its original cost). For the purposes of this special rule, all horses are to be regarded as specified animals. A bovine animal registered under the *Animal Pedigree Act* may be treated as a specified animal at the option of a taxpayer.

Special rules apply to the valuation of specified animals in taxation years which are less than 51 weeks, and provide a formula for prorating the allowable 30% inventory value reduction for such animals. Thus, for example, where the taxation year is six months, the value of a specified animal could not be reduced below 85% of its value at the end of the preceding year — 85% being determined by the formula, $100 - (30 \times 183/365)$.

[¶1723a] LIVESTOCK INCOME WHERE FORCED DESTRUCTION OR DROUGHT, FLOOD, OR EXCESSIVE MOISTURE SALES

You can defer income recognition from livestock dispositions in specific situations.

[¶1723a.05] *Forced Destruction of Livestock*

First, to the extent the amount was included in income from a farming business in respect of the forced destruction of livestock under statutory authority in the taxation year, you may deduct such amount as you claim up to the full income inclusion. However, this is merely a deferral, as the amount deducted must be included in income of the following year. It does permit averaging of income recognition over two years at the discretion of the taxpayer, and replaces a somewhat less flexible rule in place for earlier years.

[¶1723a.10] *Drought-Induced Sales of Breeding Animals*

Second, if you carry on a farming business in a region that is a prescribed drought region at any time in the taxation year and your breeding herd has been reduced by at least 15% in the drought year, you may obtain a partial income deferral until the year following the drought year (or following a series of drought years).

The deferral consists of a deduction from proceeds of sale of breeding animals. 30% of proceeds may be deducted if the breeding herd has been reduced by at least 15% but less than 30% in the year, and 90% if the breeding herd has been reduced by 30% or more in the year. The proceeds of sale to which the reduction applies is net of amounts paid to acquire breeding animals in the year and does not include any amount which has been deducted as a reserve for proceeds of sale not due until a later year.

A breeding herd is the number of deer, elk, and other similar ungulates, bovine cattle, bison, goats, and sheep owned by a taxpayer that are over 12 months of age and that are held for the purposes of breeding. A cattle herd may not include heifers in excess of 50% of the number of cows included in the herd. Horses that are over 12 months of age and are kept for breeding purposes in the commercial production of pregnant mares' urine may qualify as breeding animals. Effective for 2014 and subsequent taxation years, the definition of "breeding animals" is expanded to include all horses that are over 12 months of age and the restriction that indicates that the horse must be used in the commercial production of pregnant mares' urine is removed.

Drought regions are prescribed in Regulation 7305. As a practical matter, however, prescribed drought regions are announced by Agriculture and Agri-Food Canada, with changes to the regulation lagging years behind. The 2012 designated regions are detailed in Regulation 7305. There were no designated regions for 2013. For 2014, there were designated regions in British Columbia and Alberta. For 2015, there were designated regions in British Columbia, Alberta, Saskatchewan, and Manitoba. For 2016, there were no regions designated at time of publication. The areas are usually announced later in the year or even early the following year. Information on current year eligibility is available from the Agriculture and Agri-Food Canada website under "Drought Watch".

[¶1723a.12] *Flood- or Excessive Moisture-Induced Sales of Breeding Animals*

Third, for 2008 and subsequent taxation years, the relief available for farmers in prescribed drought regions was extended to farmers who dispose of breeding livestock because of flood or excessive moisture. Therefore, if you carry on a farming business in a region that is a prescribed flood or excessive moisture region at any time in the taxation year and your breeding herd has been reduced by at least 15% in the flood or excessive moisture year, you may obtain a partial income deferral until the year following the flood/excessive moisture year (or following a series of these years).

The deferral is the same as that outlined above for prescribed drought regions, and consists of a deduction from proceeds of sale of breeding animals. If the breeding herd has been reduced by at least 15% but less than 30% in the year, 30% of proceeds may be deducted, and 90% may be deducted if the breeding herd has been reduced by 30% or more in the year. The proceeds of sale to which the reduction applies is net of amounts paid to acquire breeding animals in the year and does not include any amount that has been deducted as a reserve for proceeds of sale not due until a later year.

Flood and excessive moisture regions are prescribed in Regulation 7305.02. Prescribed flood/excessive moisture regions are also announced by Agriculture and Agri-Food

Canada, and the timing of these announcements is similar to the timing outlined above for announcements of drought regions. For 2012, 2013, and 2015, there were no designated regions. For 2014, there were designated regions in Saskatchewan and Manitoba. For 2016, there were no designated regions at the time of publication. The detailed regions can be found in Regulation 7305.02 or on the Agriculture and Agri-Food Canada website at www.agr.gc.ca.

[¶1723a.13] *Drought or Flood/Excessive Moisture-Induced Sales of Breeding Bees*

For 2014 and subsequent taxation years, the relief described in ¶1723a.10 and ¶1723a.12 available for farmers who dispose of breeding livestock is expanded to include farmers who dispose of breeding bee stock.

If you carry on a farming business in a region that is a prescribed drought region or prescribed flood/excessive moisture region at any time in the taxation year and your breeding bee stock has been reduced by at least 15% in the drought, flood, or excessive moisture year, you may obtain a partial income deferral until the year following the drought or flood/excessive moisture year (or following a series of these years).

The deferral is the same as that outlined above for breeding livestock. If the breeding bee stock has been reduced by at least 15% but less than 30% in the year, 30% of proceeds may be deducted, and 90% may be deducted if the breeding bee stock has been reduced by 30% or more in the year. The proceeds of sale to which the reduction applies is net of amounts paid to acquire breeding bees in the year and does not include any amount that has been deducted as a reserve for proceeds of sale not due until a later year.

Breeding bee stock is a reasonable estimate of the number of bees held at the time in the course of carrying on a farming business using an accepted industry standard as the unit of measurement. The same unit of measurement must be used by the farmer for calculating their breeding bee stock at the beginning and end of the year. The breeding bees that qualify under this provision are not used principally to pollinate plants in greenhouses and larvae of such bees.

[¶1723a.15] *General*

None of the above deferral rules can be applied (i) for a year at the end of which the taxpayer is a non-resident, unless the taxpayer carried on the business throughout the year in Canada, or (ii) for a year which a taxpayer dies.

The deferrals described here apply regardless of whether the farm income is computed on a cash or accrual basis. However, the forced destruction deferral applies only to income recognized in the same year the destruction occurs, and the drought or flood/excessive moisture relief deferral applies only to proceeds recognized in a taxation year from herd/bee stock reductions for the taxation year where the taxation year includes a prescribed drought or flood/excessive moisture period.

(ITA: 80.3; ITR: 7305 [Prescribed drought regions]; 7305.02 [Prescribed flood regions])

[¶1750] FARMING NOT CHIEF SOURCE OF INCOME

Many individuals operate a farm as a secondary source of income and obtain most or all of their income from other sources. The deductions from other income of farm losses of an individual whose chief source of income is not farming, nor a combination of farming and some other source of income (that is a subordinate source of income for the taxpayer), is restricted.

Budget 2013 introduced the addition of the clause "that is a subordinate source of income for the taxpayer" in response to the Supreme Court of Canada decision in *Craig v. The Queen* (2012 DTC 5115). The amendment codifies the Supreme Court's decision in *Moldowan* (77 DTC 5213) that the restricted farm loss rules will apply where the other source of income of the taxpayer is greater than income from farming. The details regarding the progression of court cases is detailed below. Essentially, the revised wording provides that if your chief source of income is not farming, then the restricted farm loss rules apply (subject to the exception in amended subsection 31(2) described below). Farm losses of such an individual may reduce income from other sources for the year only to the extent of the lesser of:

(1) the farming loss for the year; or

(2) $2,500 plus the lesser of:

(a) one half of the amount by which the farming loss for the year exceeds $2,500, and

(b) $15,000 ($6,250 for taxation years that end prior to March 20, 2013).

The deduction for the farm loss for a year is therefore limited to a maximum of $17,500 ($8,750 for taxation years that end prior to March 20, 2013), representing an actual loss of $32,500 ($15,000). If income in the current year in not sufficient to absorb the allowable portion of the farming loss, the unapplied portion forms part of the taxpayer's non-capital loss for the year (see ¶1085). Also applicable to taxation years that end after March 20, 2013, subsection 31(2) was amended to provide that the restriction on farm losses in subsection 31(1) does not apply if the taxpayer's chief source of income is a combination of farming and manufacturing or processing in Canada where all or substantially all of the output from the taxpayer's farming business is used in the manufacturing or processing business.

Note that the part-time farmer who incurs a scientific research expenditure in his farming activities does not include that expenditure in his farming loss in (1) above, but may claim it as an additional unrestricted farming loss provided it meets the criteria discussed at ¶740.

A farm loss for a year in excess of what may be deducted that year (termed a "restricted farm loss") may be carried back and deducted from farm income of the preceding three years or carried forward and deducted from farm income (but not other income) of subsequent years. The carryforward of restricted farm losses is limited to:

- for losses arising in 2005 and earlier taxation years, the 10 years following the year in which the loss was incurred (see ¶1089);
- for losses arising in 2006 and later taxation years, the 20 years following the year in which the loss was incurred (see ¶1089).

No farm loss is deductible unless the farm is being operated as a serious attempt to earn income. Losses resulting from farms operated as a hobby for the pleasure of the owner only are not allowed as deductions.

The determination whether farming constitutes a taxpayer's chief source of income has been the subject of numerous court cases. A simple comparison of net income from each source is not sufficient. Gross income, net income, capital investment, cash flow, personal involvement and other factors are relevant considerations. It is possible for a person who expends a substantial portion of his time in farming to be limited in his deduction for farm losses. However, some cases indicate where losses are incurred in a *bona fide* effort to establish a viable farming operation the losses may be allowed as an unrestricted deduction against other sources of income in the period during which the farming operation is being established. The determination of whether the deduction for farm losses is restricted will depend on each taxpayer's particular circumstances.

The original leading case on when the farm loss limitation rules apply was the Supreme Court decision in *Moldowan v. The Queen*, 77 DTC 5213 (S.C.C.). That case established that where farming is combined with some other source of income, the farming element must predominate if the taxpayer is to escape the farm loss limitation. Some considerable doubt was cast on this interpretation of *Moldowan* in *Gunn v. The Queen*, 2006 DTC 6544, where the Federal Court of Appeal, in a carefully reasoned decision, suggested (at paragraph 83) that:

> ... the combination question should be interpreted to require only an examination of the cumulative effect of the aggregate of the capital invested in farming and a second source of income, the aggregate of the income derived from farming and a second source of income, and the aggregate of the time spent on farming and on the second source of income, considered in the light of the taxpayer's ordinary mode of living, farming history, and future intentions and expectations. This would avoid the judge-made test that requires farming to be the predominant element in the combination of farming with the second source of income, which in my view is a test that cannot stand with subsequent jurisprudence. *It would result in a positive answer to the combination question if, for example, the taxpayer has invested significant capital in a farming enterprise, the taxpayer spends virtually all of his or her working time on a combination of farming and the other principal income earning activity, and the taxpayer's day to day activities are a combination of farming and the other income earning activity, in which the time spent in each is significant.*

The *Gunn* case was not appealed, and became the new standard and provided a clear interpretation of what constitutes "a combination of farming and some other source of income" in the context of the section 31 analysis.

The *Gunn* decision was followed in *Craig v. The Queen*, 2010 DTC 1032 (T.C.C.), aff'd by 2011 DTC 5047 (F.C.A.). In the *Craig* case, the courts held that the taxpayer's chief source of income was a combination of his law practice and his farming business and so his losses were not restricted. The Crown appealed the *Craig* decision to the Supreme Court of Canada. The Supreme Court (2012 DTC 5115) dismissed the Minister's appeal and affirmed the lower courts' decisions that the taxpayer's chief source of income was a combination of his law practice and his farming business and thus his farming losses were not restricted. The Supreme Court also overruled its previous decision in *Moldowan v. The Queen* (77 DTC 5213). The *Craig* decision was a major win for the taxpayer.

In Budget 2013, the addition of the term "that is a subordinate source of income for the taxpayer" to the restricted farm loss rules is Finance signalling its dissatisfaction with the *Craig* decision and reverting to the interpretation of the Supreme Court in the *Moldowan* decision from 1977. See *Tax Topics* No. 2156, dated July 4, 2013, for a comprehensive analysis of the revision introduced in Budget 2013.

Where restricted farm losses are created or increased by the payment of property taxes or interest related to acquisition of the property and are not deducted in computing income of a later year, the interest and taxes may under certain circumstances be added to the cost of the farming land for purposes of calculating future capital gains (see ¶508). These adjustments to cost base may reduce future capital gains but are limited so that they cannot create capital losses. Land not used in a farming business or primarily to produce income is subject to deduction restrictions described at ¶665.

When a restricted farm loss carryforward reaches the 10-year (or, for losses arising after 2005, the 20-year) limitation and will be lost unless there is sufficient farming income in the current year, if you are on the accrual basis you may find it advantageous to value your inventory at market if it has increased in value (see ¶757 and ¶759). This creates additional income against which to offset a loss carryforward which is due to expire.

Alternatively, if you are on the cash basis, you may consider increasing your income using the optional inclusion of value of livestock on hand (see ¶1723).

For a further discussion of losses generally see Chapter 10.

(ITA: 31; 53; 111; Income Tax Folio: S4-F11-C1)

[¶1750.05] *Disposition by Partnership of Farm Land Where Income Previously Restricted*

Where a partnership is engaged in the business of farming or fishing, it may utilize the cash method of computing partnership income provided all the partners jointly elect to do so. Farming or fishing income (or loss) will be computed at the partnership level and allocated in whole to the partners, as discussed in Chapter 18.

The CRA has traditionally taken the position that if there is a loss allocation, the restricted farm loss rules of section 31 apply at the partner level and not the partnership level. That is, the entire loss is allocated to the partners, and each partner must determine whether his or her share of the loss is deductible under the restricted farm loss rules above. This is a sensible result, if perhaps not an obvious one. The CRA position was for many years set out in Interpretation Bulletin IT-138R, paragraph 3. That Bulletin was withdrawn in 2002 for reasons primarily related to the notion of salaries paid to partners, as discussed at ¶1802. There is no suggestion that the CRA position on section 31 loss allocations has changed, but there is no longer any formal support for the position.

The possible application of the limited farm loss rules to a partner's share of partnership income can create an anomaly *vis-à-vis* cost base calculation which the partnership rules try to alleviate. The result of these provisions is to transfer restricted (undeducted) farm losses from an increase to farm property adjusted cost base to an increase to partnership adjusted cost base.

Where the taxpayer is not a partnership, this non-deductible portion of the farm loss, to the extent it represents expenses for property taxes and interest applicable to the land, can be added to the adjusted cost base of the farm land. The non-deductible loss therefore would reduce any capital gain realized on sale of the land.

However, in the case of a partnership, a partner is permitted to deduct his or her share of the annual farm loss from his or her adjusted cost base (but not for the computation of his or her share of the annual income of the partnership for tax purposes) without reference to the farm loss limitations. A compensating rule (in paragraph 96(1)(*e*)) requires that the gain of the partnership from disposal of farm land must be computed without reference to the general cost base adjustment for individuals; that is, the non-deductible losses cannot be added to the cost of the farm land owned by the partnership. The partner's share of the gain from disposal of the farm land by the partnership is also determined without reference to this addition in computing his or her adjusted cost base.

To compensate the partner for not being permitted to use this addition, section 101 permits the partner a deduction in computing his or her income for a taxation year in which the partnership realized a gain on disposal of farm land. This deduction is, in effect, the taxpayer's capital gains inclusion rate (¶500a) for the fiscal period in which the taxpayer recognizes the disposition times the aggregate of the partner's share of the farm loss for all taxation years subsequent to 1971 (including the year of sale of the land) to the extent that such loss:

(1) was not deductible because of section 31 in calculating the partner's income;

(2) was not deducted in calculating the partner's taxable income for the taxation year in which the taxation year of the partnership (in which the loss was sustained), ended or for a previous taxation year;

(3) did not exceed the partner's share of property taxes and interest paid by the partnership and applicable to the land sold; and

(4) did not exceed the remainder obtained when the aggregate of these losses is deducted from the reciprocal of the capital gains inclusion rate above times the amount of the taxable gain from the disposition of the land.

The result is that the partner is permitted a maximum deduction for the portion of farm loss not deductible because of the chief source of income restrictions equal to his or her share of the capital gain realized by the partnership on sale of the farm land. His or her share of the gain would be included in his or her income under normal partnership rules.

(ITA: 28(2); 96(1)(e); 101)

[¶1756] RECORDS REQUIRED

You must maintain records sufficient to enable the proper tax liability to be determined. The exact form of such records is not prescribed by law. However, as a minimum, you will need to keep the following records:

(1) A record of cash received, indicating amounts, dates, and sources.

(2) A record of expenses, indicating dates paid, to whom paid, and the items or services purchased.

(3) A list of assets upon which you are claiming Capital Cost Allowances, indicating the individual asset descriptions, the month and year acquired, the cost, the total of allowances claimed, the date of disposal, and the amount of proceeds received on disposition. The capital cost allowance schedule can be used for this purpose.

Invoices, cheques, bank statements, and other documents relating to farm or fishing operations should be retained on file.

See ¶796 for rules relating to the destruction of records used to prepare your tax returns.

[¶1758] PAYMENT OF TAX

As with other individuals who are not subject to withholding tax on most income payments they receive, farmers and fishers are required to pay periodic instalments on account of income tax due for the current year. However, if your chief source of income (¶1750) in a year is farming or fishing, you need not pay instalments on the same schedule that applies to other individuals (¶227).

Payment due dates for farmers or fishers are as follows:

(1) On or before December 31 of the taxation year, two-thirds of:

(a) the estimated tax for the year, calculated by applying the appropriate tax rates for the year to the estimated taxable income for the year; or

(b) the actual taxes payable for the preceding year.

If the "net tax owing" for the taxation year or either of the two preceding years is less than the "threshold amount", no December payment need be made and only the payment in (2), below, is required. For a farmer or fisher not resident in Quebec, net tax owing includes all federal income tax (but not clawback taxes at ¶1419), and all provincial income taxes, including surtax, flat tax, and so on, minus all taxes withheld directly by the payer (such as withholding on employment income); and the threshold amount will be, in calculating instalment requirements for December 2008, and later years, $3,000. For a farmer or fisher resident in Quebec, net tax owing includes only federal income tax and surtax after the Quebec abatement, and the threshold amount will be, in calculating instalment requirements for December 2008, and later years, $1,800.

Thus, for example, if a farmer resident in Ontario at the end of 2017 has federal and provincial tax owing of $3,000 or less in either 2016 or 2015, or expects to have such tax owing of less than $3,000 in 2017, no instalment is required in December 2017. If the exemption is based on estimated tax for the current year and the estimate proves wrong, interest will run on the entire amount which should have been paid from January 1 until final payment. It would appear that if you move to or from Quebec, you look to the rules for the province in which you resided on December 31 of a year to apply the test for that year. That is, if you were resident in Quebec in 2015, elsewhere in 2016, and in Quebec again in 2017, you determine your liability for 2017 instalments using the $1,800 limit for 2015, the $3,000 limit for 2016, and the $1,800 limit for 2017. And *vice versa*.

The instalment notice system described at ¶227 should operate for farmers and fishers, adjusted for their instalment system of one December payment only. Accordingly, as discussed at ¶227, paying the amount stated on such a notice will always assure that adequate payment is made (although it can be an overpayment), and it should be true (provided timely returns have been filed) that the absence of a notice will mean that no December instalment need be paid, although this premise might not hold for abusive cases.

(2) On or before April 30, of the next year, the balance of tax actually payable for the year must be paid.

The CRA provides a worksheet for calculating instalment payments. The most recent version is available on the CRA website (www.cra-arc.gc.ca), by searching "tax instalments" and selecting "Do you have to pay tax by instalments?" There is a link to the chart in the section "Net tax owing".

As an alternative to paying an instalment as outlined above, if you are a fisher, you may elect to have taxes withheld from the proceeds of your catches. The prescribed rate of withholding is 20%. You may make this election by completing and filing form TD3F with the payer and your Tax Services Office.

As self-employed persons, farmers and fishers are required to contribute to the Canada Pension Plan, or the Quebec Pension Plan. Payments can be made when filing your tax return. See ¶1491.

(ITA: 153; 155; 156.1; 161(4); ITR: 105.1 Fishermen's Election)

[¶1759] TRANSFER OF FARM OR FISHING PROPERTY: CAPITAL GAINS EXCEPTIONS (TRANSFER OF FARM PROPERTY FOR DISPOSITIONS PRIOR TO 2014)

For purposes of the rules outlined in ¶1759 for farming, and in ¶1785 for fishing, a new definition was introduced in the 2014 Budget for taxpayers who are involved in a combination of both farming and fishing. This new definition (found in subsection 248(29)) indicates that property used principally in a combination of farming and fishing will be deemed to be used at that time principally in the course of carrying on a farming or fishing business for the transfer/rollover rules and capital gains exemption rules.

Subsection 110.6(2) formerly discussed qualified farm property and has been amended to reflect qualified farm or fishing property. Therefore, the references in this section are now "farm or fishing" and "farm" only in (brackets) for dispositions and transfers prior to 2014. The rules in ¶1785 are for fishing only prior to 2014.

(A) Rollover at Cost Base to Children

Where farm or fishing property (farm property) is transferred to your child during your lifetime, special rules allow you to defer any tax on capital gains or recapture which would otherwise arise. Child is defined very broadly, as discussed at ¶1122.15. As well, a special applicable definition extends the meaning of child to include grandchild or great-grandchild using, it would seem, the extended definition of child in those terms.

This deferral is available only if all of the following conditions are met.

(1) The farm or fishing property (farm property) must be situated in Canada.

(2) The child must be resident in Canada immediately before the transfer.

(3) For dispositions before May 2, 2006, the property must have been, before the transfer, used principally in the business of farming in which you, your spouse or common-law partner (¶1113), or any of your children, were actively engaged on a regular and continuous basis. (Note that the "actively engaged" criterion is modified for woodlots, as discussed at ¶1711.25.)

(4) For dispositions after May 1, 2006 and before 2014, the property must be land, depreciable property of a prescribed class, or eligible capital property, which was, before the transfer, used principally in the business of farming (the business of farming or fishing in 2014 and subsequent years) in which you, your spouse or common-law partner (¶1113), any of your children, *or your parent* were actively engaged on a regular and continuous basis. A technical amendment originally issued November 5, 2010 and passed in 2013 deleted the word "immediately" from the conditions of the rollover. Therefore, in order to qualify for the rollover, the property does not need to be used in the business of farming immediately before the transfer. This amendment applies for transfers after May 1, 2006. (Note that the "actively engaged" criterion is modified for woodlots, as discussed at ¶1711.25.) The changes highlighted here, and a slight change to the rules for depreciable property, are generally effective for transactions after May 1, 2006. However, where a transaction occurs before 2007 and the disposing taxpayer elects in writing in the taxpayer's return for the taxation year of the disposition, the old rules apply to the transaction.

Commentary on Bill C-29 Measures (Oct. 25, 2016)

Note: When Bill C-29, October 25, 2016, achieves Royal Assent, the commentary will be modified to read:

(4) For dispositions after January 1, 2017, the rules are amended to provide that the property must be land or depreciable property in Canada of a prescribed class. Eligible capital property has been removed with the repeal of the eligible capital property rules. Eligible capital property is now considered depreciable property and is included in the new Class 14.1 under the capital cost allowance regulations.

Where the above conditions exist, and provided that the sale price is less than the lesser of the fair market value and the tax value of the property immediately before the transfer, the proceeds will be deemed to be equal to that lesser amount, and no capital gain, recapture of depreciation, or other income event will occur. The tax value is, essentially, (a) for capital property, the adjusted cost base — see ¶506; (b) for depreciable capital property, *the lesser of capital cost and* the undepreciated capital cost — see ¶843; and (c) for eligible capital property for transfers prior to January 1, 2017, $^4/_3$ multiplied by the cumulative eligible capital — see ¶766.

Where the disposing parent receives proceeds of disposition which are higher than the lesser of fair market value or tax value for any particular item, specific rules as outlined in ¶510 will establish proceeds of disposition.

Where a child who has received farm or fishing property (farm property) under these rules (or the rules below for shares or partnership interests in a farm or fishing business (farm business) dies, the property may revert to the parent on the same rollover basis.

Any capital gain or recaptured depreciation deferred in this manner will be taxable to the child when the property is actually disposed of to an arm's length person, as long as the child has attained the age of 18 years in the year of disposition. Otherwise, taxable income arising on disposition will be attributed to the original transferor.

Similar rules apply to family farming or fishing (family farming) corporations and partnership interests. A family farm or fishing corporation or partnership (family farm corporation or partnership) is defined to be a corporation or partnership carrying on the business of farming or fishing (business of farming) in Canada in which it uses all or substantially all of its property and in which business either the transferor, his or her spouse or common-law partner, child, or parent is actively engaged on a regular and continuous basis. The definition is broad enough to include shares of a holding corporation where all or substantially all of the property of the corporation is shares or debt obligations of one or more farm or fishing corporations (farm corporations) as defined above. Note that where a family farm corporation or partnership engages in a business other than farming (even if related to it) the benefit of this transfer may be lost. However, if the other business is fishing, then for 2014 and subsequent years the benefit of this transfer will not be lost with the revised legislation. It may be beneficial to organize one entity to farm and another for the second business to ensure qualification.

Shares owned by the transferor also qualify if substantially all of the fair market value of the property owned by the corporation immediately preceding the time of transfer has been used by the corporation or any other corporation which was the family farm or fishing corporation (family farm corporation) of the deceased or a spouse or common-law partner, child, or parent of the deceased principally in the course of carrying on the business of farming or fishing (business of farming) in Canada in which the deceased, spouse or common-law partner, child or parent was actively engaged on a regular and continuous basis. The definition further includes shares of the transferor if substantially all the fair market value of the property owned by the corporation immediately preceding the time of transfer has been used by the corporation or any related corporation principally in the course of carrying on the business of farming or fishing (business of farming) in Canada in which the transferor, spouse or common-law partner, child or parent was actively engaged on a regular and continuous basis.

The holding company rule includes capital stock of or indebtedness of one or more corporations substantially all of the assets of which are a family farm or fishing corporation (family farm corporation) of the family or a holding company thereof. This qualifies a family farm or fishing corporation (family farm corporation) where the property is not being used in farming or fishing (farming) at the time of transfer provided substantially all the property qualified at some time. It also adds a parent as a qualifying person, and broadens the scope of qualifying related corporations.

A similar definition exists for an interest in a family farm or fishing partnership (interest in a family farm partnership).

Transfers under these rules involve complex considerations and should not be undertaken without professional advice.

The tax-free transfer rules apply to property leased by a farmer to a family farm corporation or partnership owned by the farmer, his or her spouse, his or her child, or, for dispositions after May 1, 2006, his or her parent.

As an alternative to making a tax-free transfer, as outlined above, you may consider using the special rules which permit a deferral of tax on capital gains if the full proceeds of disposition have not been received. A minimum of 1/10 of the taxable capital gain must be recognized in each year (see ¶581). Where you dispose of farm or fishing property (farm property) or shares to a person other than your child and the full proceeds have not yet been received, a minimum of 1/5 of the taxable capital gain must be included in your income in each year (see ¶581).

Where the transfer is made for proceeds which are less than both fair market value and tax value, or less than fair market value but greater than tax value, the general rule that property transferred to a child is considered to have been disposed of by the transferor at fair market value, so that the transferor is taxed on any capital gain inherent in the property, does not apply. However, an anti-avoidance rule does apply to ensure that where the transaction is part of a series of transactions to reduce tax on a subsequent disposition arranged within three years, the original disposition is deemed to have occurred at fair market value.

(B) Lifetime Capital Gains Exemption (LCGE)

An individual may claim a cumulative lifetime exemption for capital gains from "qualified farm or fishing property" ("qualified farm property" prior to 2014). Budget 2015 increased the lifetime limit for dispositions after April 20, 2015 to the greater of $1 million and the indexed lifetime limit applicable to qualified small business corporation shares (QSBCS), which is $824,177 for 2016 and indexed for subsequent taxation years to the Consumer Price Index (CPI). The $1 million is not indexed, and eventually this additional lifetime limit applicable to qualified farm or fishing property will be eliminated unless it is also indexed in the future. If you take a reserve on a property that is eligible for a capital gains deduction, you can only claim the LCGE that was applicable for the year of disposition, not the LCGE for the year the reserve is taken into income. Budget 2013 included the following example in the explanatory notes.

Example

In 2013, Ben has a taxable capital gain of $50,000 from a disposition of qualified farm property. At the time, Ben has already used $350,000 of the existing $375,000 LCGE limit. As a result of unpaid balance of proceeds of disposition, he claims a reserve of $25,000 under subparagraph 40(1)(*a*)(iii) for 2013 and includes the remaining $25,000 in income. Ben also claims a $25,000 capital gains deduction.

For 2014, Ben includes the $25,000 capital gains reserve carried forward from 2013 in income, and does not claim a new reserve. Because of the $400,000 LGCE limit for 2014, Ben would, absent subsection 110.6(31), be able to claim a $25,000 capital gains deduction to offset the income inclusion. However, the potential $25,000 capital gains deduction is reduced by the amount determined by the formula (A - B) in subsection 110.6(31) where:

A is the total of all amounts each of which is an amount deductible as a capital gains deduction for the year or a preceding taxation year, computed without reference to this rule. This amount is $400,000. Ben deducted a total of $375,000 for taxation years before 2014, and had another $25,000 available for the 2014 taxation year.

B is the total of amounts that would have be deductible as capital gains deductions for the year or a preceding taxation year if the individual

- had not, for any preceding taxation year, claimed a capital gains reserve, and
- had claimed, for each preceding taxation year, the capital gains deduction that would have been deductible.

This amount is $375,000. If Ben had not claimed a $25,000 reserve for 2013, there would be no taxable capital gain to apply against the increased LCGE limit of $400,000.

Ben's available capital gains deduction is reduced by $400,000 – $375,000 = $25,000. Therefore, the capital gains deduction that Ben can claim for 2014 is nil (i.e., the capital gains deduction otherwise available of $25,000 less the amount determined under subsection 110.6(31) of $25,000).

For dispositions before March 19, 2007, the exemption applied to $500,000 of lifetime cumulative gains. For dispositions after March 18, 2007 and before 2014, the exemption applied to $750,000 of cumulative lifetime gains. In 2014, the exemption was increased to $800,000 and is now indexed annually for subsequent taxation years. Where part of the exemption has been claimed in earlier years, or if part or all of the now defunct $100,000 general capital gains exemption was claimed on dispositions in any earlier year, those claims reduce the current balance available. If you had used the entire $500,000 exemption on dispositions before March 19, 2007, you have a new balance to shelter later gains, but you cannot use the additional amount on any proceeds received after March 18, 2007 in respect of earlier dispositions.

"Qualified farm property" is a carefully defined term; the definition is discussed at ¶502f. Note that it has been subject to periodic revision and was repealed in Budget 2014 and replaced with "qualified farm or fishing property".

The permitted deduction in respect of qualified farm or fishing property (qualified farm property) is equal to the least of four amounts:

(1) The individual's unused lifetime exemption limit for the year in respect of post-1984 net taxable capital gains on qualified farm property (farm or fishing property after 2013). This amount is (after April 20, 2015)

equal to the amount by which the greater of: i) $500,000 (representing $1 million of actual gain) and ii) the lifetime limit for QSBCS ($412,089 for 2016 representing $824,177 of actual gain) — therefore, $500,000 — exceeds the total deductions claimed under this provision in respect of qualified farm or fishing properties (qualified farm properties prior to 2014) in all prior years. The amount in i) ($1 million) does not change, the amount in ii) is indexed to the CPI for subsequent taxation years. This amount is (for 2015) equal to the amount by which $406,800 (representing $813,600 of actual gain) exceeds the total deductions claimed under this provision in respect of qualified farm or fishing properties (qualified farm properties) in all prior years. This amount is (for 2014) equal to the amount by which $400,000 (representing $800,000 of actual gain) exceeds the total deductions claimed under this provision in respect of qualified farm or fishing properties (qualified farm properties) in all prior years. This amount is (after 2007 and before 2014) equal to the amount by which $375,000 (representing $750,000 of actual gain) exceeds the total deductions claimed under this provision in respect of qualified farm properties in all prior years. For 2006 and earlier years, the $375,000 amount was $250,000. Dispositions in 2007 are governed by the $250,000 limit and a specific transitional rule allowing another $125,000 on post-March 18 dispositions; see the discussion at ¶502f.06.

(2) The individual's "cumulative gains limit" at the end of the year. This amount is discussed at ¶502q.

(3) The individual's "annual gains limit" for the year. This amount is defined and discussed at ¶502m.

(4) The individual's net taxable capital gains for the year from the disposition of qualified farm property after 1984. This amount would include taxable capital gains from previous years included in income under the capital gains reserve mechanism provided such reserve relates to a disposition of qualified farm property after 1984. The individual's taxable capital gains would be computed, however, without taking into account capital gains reserve inclusions and deductions that relate to dispositions of qualified farm property before 1985.

For more detail, see ¶502f.

(ITA: 40; 69(11); 70; 73; 75.1; 110.6(2); 110.6(2.2); 110.6(2.3); 110.6(31); 110.6(32); 146; IT-268R4 Inter Vivos Transfer of Farm Property to Child; IT-349R3 Intergenerational Transfers of Farm Property on Death; *Farming Income* guide (T4003))

[¶1760] DECEASED FARMERS

Special rules apply for the final tax return of a farmer who died when farm property is left to a spouse or common-law partner trust, child, grandchild or great-grandchild. For a complete discussion, see ¶1923.

There are also special rules for treatment of the value of an interest in a crop that is sown but not harvested at the time of death. Where a taxpayer dies having such an interest the executors have the following options:

(1) the value of the unharvested crop can be included in the income of the deceased in a separate income tax return for "rights and things" existing at the time of death (see ¶1908); or

(2) the ultimate proceeds may be left to be taxed in the hands of the estate or the beneficiaries when the crop is harvested and sold.

In the event that the land is sold before the crop is harvested no amount in respect of the crop is included in the income of the deceased or his estate or beneficiaries unless the agreement of sale specifies the crop's selling price.

Livestock owned by a cash-basis farmer constitutes a "right or thing", and any value up to the fair market value of the livestock may be included in income on the separate tax return for "rights and things" (see ¶1908).

The *optional inventory adjustment* and *mandatory income adjustment* required by the inventory rules at ¶1723 will not apply in the year of death. This is intended to ensure that the "rights and things" rules operate as intended.

NISA Fund No. 2 amounts are deemed paid to the holder immediately before death, unless they are transferred to a spouse or spouse trust on death and vest within 36 months (longer on application). In the event of a spouse or spouse trust transfer, the legal representative of the deceased may elect to recognize the NISA fund as income of the deceased prior to death rather than as a transfer to the spouse; see ¶1922. Income so recognized would reduce the spouse's (or spouse trust's) income on later receipts out of the NISA Fund No. 2.

(ITA: 70; IT-234 Income of Deceased Persons — Farm Crops; IT-427R Livestock of Farmers)

[¶1770] REVISED INCOME STABILIZATION PROGRAMS: 2007 AND LATER YEARS

[¶1770.05] *Overview*

For many years, programs have been available to farmers to hedge against income fluctuations from year to year. Since the programs depend on measuring income fluctuations, they have been administered using the income tax system to measure income. Participants typically file a specialized set of income tax returns "harmonized" with the risk management program. For the 2004 through 2006 taxation years, the primary risk management program was known as the Canadian Agricultural Income Stabilization (CAIS) program. In the course of 2007, federal and provincial agriculture ministries announced a revised set of risk management programs, under which CAIS was apparently divided up into two programs, AgriInvest for minor income variations and AgriStability where income falls below 85% of reference income. Details of the risk management programs are beyond the scope of this book; general summaries are given below.

The federal, provincial and territorial Ministers of Agriculture reached agreement on a policy framework called the five-year Growing Forward 2 Agreement. Under this agreement, changes to the AgriInvest and AgriStability programs will be in effect for the 2013 program year.

The AgriStability and AgriInvest programs are two of four programs known as the Business Risk Management Programs or sometimes the Business Risk Management Suite. Brief outlines of the four programs follow.

[¶1770.10] *AgriInvest*

AgriInvest replaces the coverage for the top 15% of farm income covered previously by the Canadian Agricultural Income Stabilization (CAIS) program. The intent of the program is to help producers protect their margin from small declines. Producers have the flexibility to use the funds for risk mitigation and other investments. In theory at least, producers should be able to easily predict the government contribution to their account each year.

The program is open to individuals, partners in a partnership (except in Quebec), cooperatives, corporations, estates, trusts, limited partnerships (except in Quebec), and landlords in a joint venture. To be eligible, you must have:

- reported farming income (or loss) for tax purposes; and
- been engaged in the business of farming in the program year.

Status Indians farming on reserves in Canada who do not file a tax return are also eligible to participate in AgriInvest.

Under the AgriInvest program, producers can deposit a percentage of their "Allowable Net Sales" (ANS) into an AgriInvest account each year and receive a matching government contribution on a portion of it. Starting with the 2013 program year, producers can deposit up to 1% of their "Allowable Net Sales" (ANS) and receive a matching government contribution. The limit on the matching government contribution is $15,000. Prior to 2013, a producer with $100,000 in ANS could deposit up to $1,500 (1.5%) and federal and provincial governments would make a matching contribution totalling $1,500, up to a maximum of $22,500. ANS are the net sales of commodities allowable under AgriInvest. Allowable commodities include most primary agricultural commodities except those covered under supply management (dairy, poultry, and eggs).

Money is deposited to two funds within a producer's account. Producer deposits are held in fund 1 and government contributions are held in fund 2. Because fund 1 holds producer after-tax deposits, withdrawals from fund 1 are not taxable. Government contributions (fund 2) and interest earned on both funds are not taxable until withdrawn, and are taxed as investment income. For 2008 and subsequent program years withdrawals can be made at any time.

Prior to 2008, there was no limit on how much money can be held in an account. For 2008, limits were based on 25% of the average of 2007 and 2008 data. After 2008, accounts are limited to 25% of a producer's ANS for the program year and the two preceding program years. If ANS were not calculated for one or more of these years, the limit will be calculated based on the average of years available. Starting in 2013, producers will be able to contribute up to 100% of their ANS.

Participation in AgriInvest is (for individuals) harmonized with income tax forms in most provinces. The two available tax form groups are discussed at ¶1770.30, below. In Quebec and for corporations, the application will be harmonized with the AgriStability application.

[¶1770.15] *AgriStability*

AgriStability, together with AgriInvest, replaces the coverage previously provided under the Canadian Agricultural Income Stabilization (CAIS) program.

You receive an AgriStability payment when your current year "program margin" falls below 70% (85% prior to the 2013 program year) of your "reference margin". AgriStability is based on margins:

- Your "program margin" is your allowable income minus your allowable expenses in a given year, with adjustments for changes in receivables, payables, and inventory. These adjustments are made based on information you submit on the AgriStability harmonized form.
- Your "reference margin" is your average program margin for three of the past five years (the lowest and highest margins are dropped from the calculation).

Should your program margin fall below 70% (85% prior to 2013) of your reference margin in a given year, you will receive a program payment.

For 2013 and later years, payments will be based on the lower of your "reference margin" or the average allowable expenses reported in previous years. Therefore, should your program margin fall below 70% of your reference margins, producers will receive an AgriStability payment. The AgriStability fee will be adjusted and reduced accordingly to make the program less expensive for producers.

AgriStability is delivered in Manitoba, New Brunswick, Nova Scotia, Newfoundland and Labrador, and the Yukon by the federal government. Guides and forms for farm businesses in those provinces are available by telephone at 1-866-367-8506 and for download from the Agriculture and Agri-Food website (www.agr.gc.ca).

In British Columbia, Alberta, Saskatchewan, Ontario, Quebec, and Prince Edward Island, AgriStability is delivered provincially, and information for participants must be obtained from provincial agriculture authorities and the CRA information discussed at ¶1770.30.

[¶1770.20] *AgriInsurance*

AgriInsurance is an existing program which includes insurance against production losses related to specified crops or commodities caused by natural hazards such as hail, drought, flooding, and disease. AgriInsurance is delivered provincially, either by a provincial Crown Corporation or a branch of the provincial agriculture department, depending on the province. Some general information is available from the federal Agriculture and Agri-Food website (www.agr.gc.ca) or from its Business and Risk Management Division at 1-613-773-2600.

[¶1770.25] *AgriRecovery*

AgriRecovery is less a program than an agreement among federal and provincial governments to provide a process for the relevant governments to quickly determine whether or not further assistance beyond existing programming (e.g., CFIA, AgriStability, AgriInvest, AgriInsurance) is warranted, and, if so, what form that assistance should take. Where federal and provincial governments agree that assistance is warranted, the form of assistance will be unique to the specific disaster situation.

[¶1770.30] *Guides and Forms Available to Program Participants*

Two of the programs discussed above, AgriInvest and AgriStability, replace aspects of the CAIS program that was phased out after 2007. Participation in these programs appears to be voluntary, but for those who choose to participate, participation is harmonized with tax return preparation so that you must use specific tax return guides and forms dedicated to program participants rather than the general *Farming Income* guide (T4003) and the general *Statement of Farming Activities* form (T2142). Not surprisingly, there is a lack of uniformity among the provinces, so that (for 2015 at least) guides and forms for program participants fell into three distinct groups:

Alberta, Saskatchewan, Ontario, and Prince Edward Island

Use Guide RC4060, *Farming Income and the AgriStability and AgriInvest Programs,* and forms T1163, T1164, and T1175, RC322.

British Columbia, Manitoba, New Brunswick, Nova Scotia, Newfoundland and Labrador, and the Yukon

Use Guide RC4408, *Farming Income and the AgriStability and AgriInvest Programs*, and forms package T1273, T1274, T1275, and T1175.

Quebec

AgriStability and AgriInvest programs participants from Quebec will continue to use guide T4003, *Farming Income*. For forms and information on participation in the Quebec program, contact:

La Financiére agricole du Québec
Telephone: 1-800-749-3646
Website: www.fadq.qc.ca/accueil/

[¶1785] TRANSFER OF FISHING PROPERTY: CAPITAL GAINS EXCEPTIONS (FOR TRANSFERS PRIOR TO 2014)

A new definition was introduced in the 2014 Budget to accommodate taxpayers who are involved in a combination of both farming and fishing. This new definition (found in subsection 248(29) of the *Income Tax Act)* indicates that property used principally in a combination of farming and fishing will be deemed to be used at that time principally in the course of carrying on a farming or fishing business for the transfer/rollover rules and capital gains exemption rules. The new terms apply to dispositions and transfers in 2014 and subsequent taxation years.

Therefore, this section applies to transfers and dispositions of fishing property only prior to 2014. Please refer to ¶1759 for dispositions of farm or fishing property in 2014 and subsequent taxation years.

(A) Rollover at Cost Base to Children

Where land, depreciable property, or, prior to 2017, eligible capital property, that you use in a fishing business which you carry on in Canada ("fishing property") is transferred to your child during your lifetime, special rules allow you to defer any tax on capital gains or recapture which would otherwise arise. "Child" is defined very broadly, as discussed at ¶1122.15. As well, a special applicable definition extends the meaning of child to include grandchild or great-grandchild using, it would seem, the extended definition of child in those terms.

This deferral is available only if all of the following conditions are met:

(1) The property must be situated in Canada.

(2) The child must be resident in Canada immediately before the transfer.

(3) The property must be land, depreciable property of a prescribed class, or, prior to 2017, eligible capital property which was, before the transfer, used principally in the business of fishing in which you, your spouse or common-law partner (¶1113), any of your children, or your parent were actively engaged on a regular and continuous basis. A technical amendment originally issued November 5, 2010 and passed into legislation in 2013 deleted the word "immediately" from the conditions of the rollover. Therefore, in order to qualify for the rollover, the property does not need to be used in the business of fishing immediately before the transfer. This amendment applies for transfers after May 1, 2006.

(4) The disposition must occur after May 1, 2006.

Where the above conditions exist, and provided that the sale price is less than the lesser of the fair market value and the tax value of the property immediately before the transfer, the proceeds will be deemed to be equal to the lesser of those amounts, and no capital gain, recapture of depreciation, or other income event will occur. The tax value is, essentially, (a) for capital property, the adjusted cost base — see ¶506; (b) for depreciable capital property, the lesser of capital cost and the undepreciated capital cost — see ¶843; and (c) for eligible capital property, $^4/_3$ times the cumulative eligible capital — see ¶766.

Where the disposing parent receives proceeds of disposition which are higher than the lesser of fair market value or tax value for any particular item, specific rules kick in to establish proceeds of disposition.

Where a child who has received fishing property under these rules (or the rules below for shares or partnership interests in a fishing business) dies, the property may revert to the parent on the same rollover basis.

Any capital gain or recaptured depreciation deferred in this manner will be taxable to the child when the property is actually disposed of to an arm's length person, as long as the child has attained the age of 18 years in the year of disposition. Otherwise, taxable income arising on disposition will be attributed to the original transferor.

Similar rules apply to family fishing corporations and partnership interests. A family fishing corporation or partnership is defined to be a corporation or partnership carrying on the business of fishing in Canada in which it uses all or substantially all of its property and in which business either the transferor, his or her spouse or common-law partner, parent, or child is actively engaged on a regular and continuous basis. The definition is broad enough to include shares of a holding corporation where all or substantially all of the property of the corporation is shares or debt obligations of one or more fishing corporations as defined above. Note that where a family fishing corporation or partnership engages in a business other than fishing (even if related to it) the benefit of this transfer may be lost. It may be beneficial to organize one entity to fish and another for the second business to ensure qualification.

Shares owned by the transferor also qualify if substantially all the fair market value of the property owned by the corporation immediately preceding the time of transfer *has been used by* the corporation or any other corporation which was the family fishing corporation of the deceased or a spouse or common-law partner, child, or parent of the deceased principally in the course of carrying on the business of fishing in Canada in which the deceased, spouse or common-law partner, child, or parent was actively engaged on a regular and continuous basis. The definition further includes shares of the transferor if substantially all the fair market value of the property owned by the corporation immediately preceding the time of transfer has been used by the corporation principally in the course of carrying on the business of fishing in Canada in which the transferor, spouse or common-law partner, child, or parent was actively engaged on a regular and continuous basis.

The holding company rule includes capital stock of, or indebtedness of, one or more corporations substantially all of the assets of which are a family fishing corporation of the family or a holding company thereof. This qualifies a family fishing corporation where the property is not being used in fishing at the time of transfer, provided substantially all the property qualified at some time. It also adds a parent as a qualifying person, and broadens the scope of qualifying related corporations.

A similar definition exists for an interest in a family fishing partnership.

Transfers under these rules involve complex considerations and should not be undertaken without professional advice.

The tax-free transfer rules apply to property leased by a fisher to a family fishing corporation or partnership owned by the fisher, a spouse, a parent, or a child.

As an alternative to making a tax-free transfer, as outlined above, you may consider using the special rules which permit a deferral of tax on capital gains if the full proceeds of disposition have not been received. A minimum of 1/10 of the taxable capital gain must be recognized in each year (see ¶581). Where you dispose of fishing property or shares to a person other than your child and the full proceeds have not yet been received, a minimum of 1/5 of the taxable capital gain must be included in your income in each year (see ¶581).

Where the transfer is made for proceeds which are less than both fair market value and tax value, the usual rule that property transferred to a child is considered to have been disposed of by the transferor at fair market value, so that the transferor is taxed on any capital gain inherent in the property, does not apply. This is also true if fair market value exceeds tax value and proceeds are between the two. However, an anti-avoidance rule does apply to ensure that where the transaction is part of a series of transactions to reduce tax on a subsequent disposition arranged within three years, the original disposition is deemed to have occurred at fair market value.

(B) Lifetime Capital Gains Exemption (LCGE)

An individual may claim a cumulative lifetime exemption for capital gains from "qualified fishing property". For dispositions after May 1, 2006 and before March 19, 2007, the exemption applied to $500,000 of lifetime cumulative gains. For dispositions after March 18, 2007 and before 2014, the exemption applied to $750,000 of cumulative lifetime gains. Where part of the exemption has been before March 19, 2007, or if part or all of the now defunct $100,000 general capital gains exemption was claimed on dispositions in any earlier year, those claims reduce the maximum balance available. If you had used the entire $500,000 exemption on dispositions before March 19, 2007, you have a balance of $250,000 to shelter gains on any proceeds received before January 1, 2014 in respect of earlier dispositions. If you take a reserve on a property that is eligible for a capital gains deduction, you can only claim the LCGE that was applicable for the year of disposition, not the LCGE for the year the reserve is taken into income. Budget 2013 included an example in the explanatory notes that is reproduced at¶1759.

"Qualified fishing property" was a carefully defined term; this definition was repealed in Budget 2014 and replaced with the definition "qualified farm or fishing property". See ¶502f.10.

The permitted deduction in respect of qualified fishing property is equal to the least of four amounts:

(1) The individual's unused lifetime exemption limit for the year in respect of post-1984 net taxable capital gains on qualified fishing property. This amount is (after 2007 and before 2014) equal to the amount by which $375,000 (representing $750,000 of actual gain) exceeds the total deductions claimed under this provision in respect of qualified fishing properties in all prior years. For 2006, the $375,000 amount was $250,000. Dispositions in 2007 are governed by the $250,000 limits and a specific transitional rule allowing another $125,000 on post-March 18 dispositions.

(2) The individual's "cumulative gains limit" at the end of the year. This amount is discussed at ¶502q.

(3) The individual's "annual gains limit" for the year. This amount is defined and discussed at ¶502m.

(4) The individual's net taxable capital gains for the year from the disposition of qualified fishing property after May 1, 2006. This amount would include taxable capital gains from previous years included in income under the capital gains reserve mechanism provided the reserve relates to a disposition of qualified fishing property after May 1, 2006. The individual's taxable capital gains would be computed, however, without taking into account capital gains reserve inclusions and deductions that relate to dispositions of qualified fishing property before May 2, 2006.

(ITA: 40; 69(11); 70; 73; 75.1; 110.6(2), 110.6(31), 110.6(32); 146; IT-268R4 Inter Vivos Transfer of Farm Property to Child; IT-349R3 [note that bulletins relate to farming income; the rules for fishing income are largely the same]; *Fishing Income* guide (T4004))

[¶1788] SHARES OF FORMER CANADIAN WHEAT BOARD (G3 CANADA LIMITED)

[¶1788.01] *Overview*

Changes to the Canadian Wheat Board

The previous Canadian Wheat Board (CWB) was a "single desk" through which Canadian farmers sold their wheat and barley products. In 2011, the federal government announced that it would be replacing the CWB single desk with an entity based more on free market principles. On July 30, 2015, the CWB was continued as "G3 Canada Limited", with a joint venture known as the "G3 Global Grain Group" acquiring a 50.1% majority of the common shares. The remaining 49.9% of the shares are held in trust for participating farmers. Participating by farmers is voluntary and not mandatory.

The G3 Farmers Equity Plan

The following is a brief synopsis of how participants receive shares. It is provided to supplement the understanding of the tax rules applicable to the shares and should not be relied upon to determine how many shares you may be entitled to. To determine whether you are eligible for shares as a participant, please contact G3 Canada Limited.

The G3 Farmers Equity Plan provides farmers the opportunity to share in the profits of G3 Canada by granting farmers an ownership share in the corporation. 49.9% of the

CWB share have been transferred to a trust of which farmers will receive units. The number of units which a farmer is entitled to is based on the following variables:

(a) the amount of grain the farmer delivers to G3 Canada;

(b) the valuation of units (determined by the trustees periodically); and

(c) the incentive rate per metric tonne of grain delivered (determined by G3 Canada periodically).

The timing of the issuance of units is completely up to the trustees' discretion. At the time of issuance, the trustees must estimate the value of those units based on the value of the CWB shares held by the trust. Participating farmers do not have to pay tax with respect to the units until they receive a benefit from them. Units must be held until the participating farmer dies or reaches the age of 75. Alternatively, participating farmers can transfer their units to a "Permitted Transferee".

For further information, see "Farmers Equity Plan" at www.g3.ca. The discussion below deals strictly with the taxation of the units held by participating farmers. Separate tax rules apply solely to the trust and G3 Canada, but they are not discussed in this publication.

[¶1788.02] *Tax Treatment of Participating Farmers*

A participating farmer can be a person (including a corporation) or a partnership who is eligible to receive units of the trust and who is engaged in the production of grain or is a creditor of a grain producer who is entitled to that producer's grain. Where you acquire an eligible unit in the trust, you do not have to include any amount in your income at the time of acquisition. Moreover, your cost amount of the units is deemed to be nil.

When a unit is disposed of, the gain is fully included in income and is not a capital gain. Similarly, a loss is fully deducted and is not a capital loss. As a result, an eligible unit is not considered capital property. If you dispose of an eligible unit (otherwise than by death, eligible wind-up distribution, or the trust ceasing to be an eligible trust — see below), you are deemed to have received proceeds of disposition equal to the fair market value of the unit immediately before the disposition. If you own shares of a Canadian-controlled private corporation that is the holder of eligible units, such a gain is deemed to be income from an active business and thus may be eligible for the small business deduction.

(ITA: 104(6) Deduction in computing income of trust; 135.2(1) participating farmer; 135.2(5) Participating farmer — acquisition of eligible unit; 135.2(7) Eligible unit — gain (loss); 135.2(9) Participating farmer — disposition of eligible unit)

[¶1788.03] *Death of a Farmer*

Where an individual participating farmer dies while owning an eligible unit, there is a deemed disposition of the unit immediately before death. Unless there is a spousal rollover (as described below), the individual's proceeds of disposition are deemed to be equal to the fair market value of the unit, and the person who acquires the unit as a consequence of the death acquires the unit at a cost equal to that fair market value.

Assuming the deemed disposition results in a gain, the entire gain is included in the deceased's income. The legal representative of the deceased's estate can elect to allow the payment of the resulting tax in up to 10 annual instalments (see ¶1926). However, if the spousal rollover applies upon the individual participating farmer's death, the deceased has a nil gain on the deemed disposition of the unit. The spousal rollover applies if the following conditions are met:

- the individual is resident in Canada;
- the eligible unit is acquired by the individual's graduated rate estate (GRE) as a consequence of the death;
- the individual's legal representative makes an election in the deceased's tax return for the year of death; and
- the GRE distributes the eligible unit to a spouse or common-law partner of the deceased while it is a GRE (it can qualify as a GRE for up to 36 months after the death).

Where the rollover applies, the cost amount of the eligible unit for the estate is nil and it remains nil for the spouse or common-law partner. Effectively, any accrued gain is deferred until the spouse or common-law partner disposes of the unit.

If a participating farmer dies without receiving an eligible unit which he or she was entitled to receive, and the eligible trust then issues the eligible unit to the farmer's estate, the deceased farmer and the estate are deemed to be in the same position as they would have been had the farmer owned the unit immediately before death and the estate acquired the unit as a consequence of the death.

(ITA: 135.2(8) Death of a participating farmer)

[¶1788.04] *Taxation of Future Potential Changes to the CWB*

Eligible Wind-up Distribution

An "eligible wind-up distribution" occurs where shares in the CWB listed on a designated stock exchange are distributed by the trust to a person (the distribution can also include cash in Canadian dollars) in satisfaction of the person's interest (the eligible units) as a beneficiary in the trust, and the trust ceases to exist immediately after the distribution (or the last distribution if there is a series of eligible wind-up distributions). At the time of writing, CWB shares are not listed on a designated stock exchange, so that an eligible wind-up distribution appears to contemplate a wind-up in connection with a public offering or other event under which CWB shares become listed.

With respect to your units in the trust, you would be deemed to have disposed of the units at their cost amount, which results in no gain or loss on that disposition. You are also deemed to acquire the property (shares or cash) for fair market value proceeds. Since the trust is distributing the shares to its beneficiaries, the trust is deemed to have disposed of the shares at fair market value. If this deemed disposition results in a gain in the hands of the trust, the gain is deemed to have been "flowed out" to you and therefore you must report the gain as income.

Ceasing to be an Eligible Trust

If for some reason the trust ceases to be an "eligible trust" as defined in the Act, special tax rules apply to the trust and its unitholders. Each participating farmer who holds an eligible unit in the trust at the particular time is deemed to have disposed of the unit at its cost amount immediately before that time (such that no gain results), and to have reacquired the unit at a cost equal to its fair market value.

Reorganization of Capital of the CWB

If the CWB undergoes a reorganization of capital and meets certain requirements, the trust will have a tax-free rollover in respect of the exchange of its old shares in the CWB for new shares in the CWB in the course of the reorganization. Although certain conditions must be met for the trust to achieve a tax-free rollover, there are no requirements or tax implications imposed on participating farmers.

(ITA: 135.2(10) Eligible wind-up distribution; 135.2(11) Ceasing to be an eligible trust; 135.2(14) Rollover of shares on reorganization)

HOW TO REPORT INCOME FROM FARMING AND FISHING

[¶1795] HOW TO REPORT INCOME FROM FARMING AND FISHING

There are essentially two alternative income tax reporting regimes in place for farmers. If you want to participate in the AgriInvest or AgriStability income stabilization programs, you have to use one of the two specialized farming income guides, depending on your province of residence (see ¶1770.30), except that for Quebec you use the general federal farming guide and forms and specialized Quebec program forms. If you are not participating in the income stabilization programs (or are a Quebec resident), you use the *Farming Income* guide (T4003) and report your income on form T2042.

Fishers should use the *Fishing Income* guide (T4004) and calculate fishing income on form T2121. Note also the *Fishers and Employment Insurance* guide, T4005, which is to be completed by employers; it explains the meaning of a designated employer of fishers, the responsibilities of a designated employer, and how to calculate the insurable earnings of a fisher.

Although the CRA encourages you to use form T2042 or T2121, as the case may be, they will accept other forms of financial statements so long as you present adequate information in a reasonable format. It seems that AgriInvest and/or AgriStability participants must use the specific forms provided.

After computing your farming or fishing income on the above statements, enter the amounts of gross and net income or loss in boxes 168 and 141 (farming) or 170 and 143 (fishing) on (for 2016) page 2 of the T1 return.

Also enter any income or expenses not related to farming or fishing at the appropriate places on the T1 form. Such items should not be included in farming or fishing income.

In general, an income tax return must be filed if the farmer or fisher:

- Has taxable income for the year,
- Has self-employed earnings or both self-employed earnings and pensionable wages of more than $3,500,
- Disposed of capital property at a gain or loss (Chapter 5),
- Receives a demand to file an income tax return from the CRA, or
- For farmers only, wants to participate in the AgriInvest and/or AgriStability programs described above;

or if he or she wishes to obtain refundable:

- Canada Child Benefits (for self or spouse) (¶1498),
- Goods and services tax credit (¶1496),
- Working income tax benefit (¶1495), and/or
- Provincial income tax credits (if available; see Chapter 15).

A more complete list of the circumstances in which anyone must file a return is found in ¶200.

As in the case of other individuals operating businesses, the income tax return is due on or before June 15 of the year following the taxation year, but taxes must be paid in full by April 30 to avoid interest charges (see ¶218). Note that this is true for AgriInvest and AgriStability participants as well, although they may have a longer time to make other decisions about those programs.

The guides and forms referred to above are available from your local Tax Services Office, or may be viewed and downloaded from the CRA's website at www.cra-arc.gc.ca. You should obtain the appropriate guide before preparing your return.

Chapter 18

Partnerships

THESE POINTS ARE COVERED IN THIS CHAPTER

CRA REFERENCES RELATING TO THIS CHAPTER

CRA Guides

T4001, "Employers' Guide — Payroll Deductions and Remittances"; **T4002**, "Business and Professional Income"; **T4068**, "Guide for the Partnership Information Return (T5013 Forms)"; **T5013 Instructions**, "Statement of partnership income — Instructions for Recipient"

CRA Forms

T106, "Information Return of Non-Arm's Length Transactions with Non-Residents"; **T661**, "Scientific Research and Experimental Development (SR&ED) Expenditures Claim"; **T1134**, "Information Return Relating To Controlled and Not-Controlled Foreign Affiliates (2011 and later taxation years)"; **T1135**,

"Foreign Income Verification Statement"; **T1141**, "Information Return in Respect of Transfers or Loans to a Non-Resident Trust"; **T1142**, "Information Return in Respect of Distributions from and Indebtedness to a Non-Resident Trust"; **T2125**, "Statement of Business or Professional Activities"; **T5013**, "Statement of Partnership Income"

Interpretation Bulletins

IT-63R5, "Benefits, Including Standby Charge for an Automobile, from the Personal Use of a Motor Vehicle Supplied by an Employer"; **IT-151R5 (Consolidated)**, "Scientific Research and Experimental Development Expenditures" (Cancelled by the CRA and replaced by a series of policy documents on SR&ED expenditures and the calculation of SR&ED investment tax credits); **IT-153R3**, "Land Developers — Subdivision and Development Costs and Carrying Charges on Land"; **IT-195R4**, "Rental Property — Capital Cost Allowance Restrictions"; **IT-242R**, "Retired Partners"; **IT-413R**, "Election by Members of a Partnership Under Subsection 97(2)"; **IT-457R**, "Election by Professionals to Exclude Work in Progress from Income"; **IT-473R**, "Inventory Valuation"

Income Tax Folios

S4-F16-C1, "Price Adjustment Clauses"

Information Circulars

73-13, "Investment Clubs"; **89-4**, "Tax Shelter Reporting"

Income Tax Technical News

No. 5, July 28, 1995, "Adjusted Cost Base of Partnership Interest" (Archived by the CRA); **No. 6**, January 5, 1996, "Expenses Personally Paid by Partner" (Archived by the CRA); **No. 9**, February 10, 1997, "Calculation of the Adjusted Cost Base of a Partnership Interest" (Archived by the CRA); **No. 25**, October 30, 2002, "Partnership Issues"; **No. 38**, September 22, 2008, "SIFT Rules — Transitional Normal Growth; SIFT Entities — Definition of 'Real Estate Investment Trust' in Section 122.1"

WHAT YOU SHOULD KNOW ABOUT PARTNERSHIP INCOME

RECENT CHANGES

2016 Amendments

Draft legislation released on September 16, 2016 proposes an amendment to the adjusted cost base rules for interests in partnerships in respect of certain dividends received on shares that are not on capital account. In addition, Bill C-29 amends the calculation of the adjusted cost base of an interest in a partnership for certain life insurance proceeds received. See ¶1844.10.

Income Tax Folio

Effective May 5, 2015, The Canada Revenue Agency (CRA) released Income Tax Folio S4-F16-C1 "What is a Partnership?", which replaces and cancels Interpretation Bulletin IT-90.

Filing Requirements for Partnerships

Regulation 229 under the *Income Tax Act* requires that a partnership file an annual information return containing certain information concerning the partnership; the form is T5013. See ¶1880.15.

For 2015 fiscal periods, the CRA exempted family farm partnerships formed only of individuals from filing the T5013 form. However, a farm partnership that includes a trust or a corporation is still required to file a T5013 return. At the time of writing, the CRA stated on its website that a decision regarding the T5013 return filing requirements for farm partnerships for 2016 and later fiscal years would be made after consulting with stakeholders.

[¶1800] GENERAL RULES

[¶1800.05] *What is a Partnership?*

It is a question of fact and law as to whether a partnership exists. A partnership is not a separate legal entity, but rather a relationship between persons carrying on a business. More particularly, the courts have established the following general criteria when determining whether a partnership exists: (i) there must be a business (ii) carried on by two or more persons (iii) with a view to profit. The criteria are based on provincial partnership statutory laws and the case law interpreting those laws.

What constitutes sufficient activity to create a partnership can in marginal cases (and particularly in loss utilization transactions) be a vexed question. The poles are established by Supreme Court of Canada decisions in *Continental Bank Leasing Corporation v. The Queen*, 98 DTC 6505 (S.C.C.), and *Spire Freezers Ltd. v. The Queen*, 2001 DTC 5158 (S.C.C.), on the one hand, and *Backman v. The Queen*, 2001 DTC 5149 (S.C.C), on the other. *Spire* and *Backman* involved similar situations in which a Canadian partnership took over a U.S. apartment complex primarily for the tax losses involved. In *Spire*, the partners exercised themselves to manage and turn around the business to a profitable level. In *Backman*, by contrast, the Court found that the sole motivation of the "partnership" was to utilize losses; there was never an intention to operate a business with a view to profit, and therefore an essential ingredient of the partnership definition was missing. "The question at this stage is whether the taxpayer can establish an intention to make a profit, whether or not he was motivated by tax considerations." The CRA has commented that the "view to profit" test has been held by the courts to be a different and less onerous test than the "reasonable expectation of profit" test at ¶704. The view-to-profit test looks at the taxpayer's intention in each case, rather than trying to establish objective criteria as to whether the intention was realistic.

In its Income Tax Folio S4-F16-C1, "What is a Partnership?", the CRA summarizes some of the elements of a partnership as set out by the Supreme Court in the *Continental Bank* case:

- the contribution by the parties of money, property, effort, knowledge, skill or other assets to a common undertaking;
- a joint property interest in the subject matter of the adventure;
- the sharing of profits and losses;
- a mutual right of control or management of the enterprise;
- the filing of income tax returns as a partnership;
- joint bank accounts; and
- correspondence with third parties.

In *Income Tax Technical News* No. 25, the CRA comments on whether certain entities created under U.S. (state) laws constitute partnerships for Canadian purposes. It finds that partnerships created under laws such as the Delaware *Revised Uniform Partnerships Act* (DRUPA) in general have the attributes of a Canadian general partnership. However, where an entity is created under DRUPA for non-profit purposes, as that statute permits, it is the CRA's view, since entities not created to carry on business with a view to a profit under common law principles would not resemble Canadian partnerships, that such entities would not be considered partnerships for Canadian tax purposes. By contrast, where legislation in the U.S. allows for the creation of Limited Liability Companies to operate as separate legal entities and allows business profits (losses) to be allocated and taxed in the hands of the members, it is the CRA's view that the entities more closely resemble corporations and will be treated as such for Canadian tax purposes. At the Canadian Tax Foundation's Annual Conference in November 2009, the CRA reaffirmed its position that a Limited Liability Company is considered a corporation under Canadian domestic tax law. Furthermore, legislation first introduced on July 12, 2013 and now passed into law clarifies that US limited liability companies are considered corporations for Canadian tax purposes. The provisions are found in section 93.2 of the *Income Tax Act* (Act).

The CRA has offered other comments on foreign entities which it considers to be corporations or partnerships. See, for example, *Income Tax Technical News* No. 38, pages 9 and 10. More recently, in paragraph 1.3 of Income Tax Folio S4-F16-C1, the CRA states:

> "In the case of a foreign entity or arrangement, the CRA takes the following two-step approach to determine whether such entity or arrangement should be treated as a partnership for Canadian tax purposes:
>
> i. Determine the characteristics of the foreign business entity or arrangement by reference to any relevant foreign law and the terms of any relevant agreements relating to the entity or arrangement; and
>
> ii. Compare the characteristics of the foreign business entity or arrangement to the characteristics of business entities or arrangements under Canadian law in order to see which Canadian entity or arrangement it most fundamentally resembles.
>
> If the foreign entity or arrangement more fundamentally resembles a partnership arrangement under Canadian law than a corporation, trust or co-ownership, it will be treated as a partnership for Canadian tax purposes."

As for joint ventures, which are not necessarily partnerships, see paragraphs 1.19 through 1.22 of Income Tax Folio S4-F16-C1. A joint venture that is not a partnership is not required to file the T5013 partnership return.

[¶1800.10] *General Rules for Computing and Reporting Partnership Income*

For the purpose of computing income of a member of a partnership, a partnership is treated as a separate person whose taxation year is the fiscal period of the partnership. The income of the partnership includes taxable capital gains less allowable capital losses from the disposition of partnership property (see Chapter 5), and the amount of any income or loss of the partnership from any other source. In general, the rules in Chapters 6, 7, and 8 will provide the basis for the income computation of a partnership.

These amounts, as calculated for the partnership, are shared by the partners in the manner agreed on by them in their partnership agreement and each partner declares his or her share in his or her tax return for the taxation year in which the partnership's fiscal period ends under the general partnership income allocation rules of paragraph 96(1)(*a*). The income that flows through to the partner retains its characteristics as to source and nature and is combined on the partner's tax return with the partner's non-partnership income and losses.

A partner's share of partnership business income or loss is reported as self-employment income or loss on the T1 return, on one or more of lines 135–143, as applicable. You should also file the appropriate income statement, such as Form T2125 for most forms of professional or business income, Form T2121 for fishing income, or Form T2042 for farming income. However, in the case of income as a limited partner, the net income or loss is reported on line 122 of the T1 and also on Schedule 4. In the case of rental income from property, the reporting is on line 126 of the T1. If you receive the T5013 slip from the partnership (see ¶1880.05), the various amounts or losses should be reported in the appropriate boxes on the slip.

Certain elections may be available for computing income from a partnership activity. Generally these elections permit the partnership to elect in the same way an individual could elect in similar circumstances. Elections may be made by a partnership when dealing with:

- work in progress of professionals (¶1876),
- sale of accounts receivable (¶755),
- option to have a non-calendar year end (¶1804),
- exchanges of capital property (¶523 through ¶525), prior to 2017, eligible capital property (¶769), and depreciable property (¶846),
- sale of certain vessels, representation expenses (¶809),
- capitalization of interest (¶1073),
- optional "proxy amount" calculation for deductions and investment tax credits on scientific research expenditures (¶740),
- property acquired from a partner by a Canadian partnership (¶1866),
- treatment of investments as small business bonds,
- choosing or revoking a non-calendar fiscal period (¶1804),

- the optional reduction of a basic herd,
- the election to have the foreign spin-off rules apply to an exchange of shares (¶536c), and the related foreign affiliate election,
- elections under the demutualization rules (¶420),
- the election when disposing of eligible capital property after February 27, 2000 and before 2017, to withdraw the property from the pool of eligible properties and so realize a capital loss on the disposition (¶768),
- the election under the foreign investment entity (FIE) rules to treat an affiliate as a controlled foreign affiliate (¶492), and
- the election to use alternative methods of calculating income under the FIE rules (¶492).

In order to make one of these elections, all of the partners must agree. The election is made by one or more of the partners who has authority to act for the partnership. If the partnership as a whole does not make these elections, individual partners cannot make them independently in computing partnership income.

Note that the guaranteed capital gains election (¶501) is not one of the elections made at the partnership level. Accordingly, each partner's gain or loss from the disposition thereafter of his or her share of a Canadian security held by a partnership will now depend on whether the partner has personally elected under the guaranteed capital gain provision.

The partnership, rather than each partner, claims capital cost allowance on depreciable property of the partnership (see Chapter 8). Prior to 2017, the partnership also claims the allowance on eligible capital property, that is, goodwill or certain other intangibles (see ¶766), and computes its own capital gains and losses on dispositions of partnership property (see Chapter 5). When calculating the deemed cost of capital property which it owned on December 31, 1971, a partnership must always use the tax-free zone method (¶591); it is not eligible to elect the Valuation Day value method (¶590).

The calculation of partnership income excludes proceeds from the disposition of resource properties or deductions for Canadian oil and gas property expenses, depletion allowances or exploration and development expenses, and the income inclusion for 25% of a prescribed resource loss that applied prior to 2007. See Chapter 22. Where these items arise through a partnership activity, they are allocated directly to the partners, and may be claimed by the partners with similar items, if any, arising from their non-partnership activities (see Chapter 22). On the income side, resource allowances in respect of oil, gas, and mineral resources are also subject to the rule that they are claimed by the partners rather than by the partnership. Taxpayers may elect to forgo their share of Canadian development expense or Canadian oil and gas property expense (see Chapter 22) and have that amount added to their partnership adjusted cost base (ACB) (¶1844).

[¶1800.15] *Forms Required*

The partnership return is technically an information return only. It is not an income tax return and tax is not paid at the partnership level. However, the CRA has the authority to assess partnership returns and issue a determination of income or loss for the partnership as a whole, the consequences of which will be binding on the partners even if they are not personally served with the notice. Partnership returns are discussed at ¶1880. Partnership determinations and assessments are discussed at ¶1881.

(ITA: 96)

[¶1801] TAX TREATMENT OF PARTNERS

Income earned by the partnership flows through to the partners in their agreed proportions. Since each source of income retains its nature on the flow through, certain rules relating to different sources of income apply to each partner. For example, a partner's share of a partnership's:

- dividends received from taxable Canadian corporations must be grossed up in computing the partner's income (see ¶404). An individual partner can claim the dividend tax credit in computing personal tax (see ¶1425);
- foreign income and foreign tax paid can be used in computing a foreign tax credit (see ¶1450);
- taxable capital gains in excess of allowable capital losses can be reduced by a partner's personal allowable capital losses and capital gains exemption (see Chapter 5);
- allowable capital losses in excess of taxable capital gains can be used to reduce the partner's personal taxable capital gains in the year. Any remaining losses can be carried back or forward (see Chapter 5);
- donations can be claimed by the partner in computing his charitable donation credit (see ¶1270);
- investment tax credits earned in its fiscal period by the partnership on partnership expenditures are added to the partner's investment tax credit at the end of the partner's taxation year (subject to the limitations at ¶1819 and ¶1821; see also ¶1822 for effect on partnership cost of related property); and
- compensation payments that the partnership paid or received for earning dividend income from dividend rental arrangements (¶422 and ¶423).

Federal law does not permit a partnership to make a political contribution. If one is made by a partnership, there is no provision to allow it to flow through to the partners.

Special rules apply to the allocation of expenses on scientific research and related investment tax credits; see ¶1821.

There is an exception to the general rule that income retains its source characteristics for purposes of the attribution rules; see ¶1806.

(ITA: 96; 118.1(8); 127(4.2), (8))

[¶1801.01] *Shareholder Benefits and Loans*

As discussed in Chapter 4 (¶409a), certain benefits conferred by a corporation on a person who is a shareholder or on a person in contemplation of the person becoming a shareholder in the corporation are included in the person's income under subsection 15(1). Under amendments passed into law on June 26, 2013, subsection 15(1) "is clarified" to apply to a benefit conferred by a corporation on a member of a partnership that is a shareholder, or to a partnership or a member of a partnership in contemplation of the partnership becoming a shareholder of the corporation. The amendments apply in respect of benefits conferred on or after October 31, 2011.

Subsection 15(2) includes certain loans and indebtedness in the income of a person or partnership who is a shareholder in or connected to a shareholder in a corporation to whom the indebtedness is owed. The amendments noted above clarify that a partnership can be connected with a shareholder of a particular corporation if that partnership does not deal at arm's length with, or is affiliated with, the shareholder. A similar amendment applies to partnerships subject to the deemed interest provisions of subsection 80.4(2). These amendments apply in respect of loans made and indebtedness arising after October 31, 2011.

[¶1801.05] *Farm Losses Restricted Where Farming Not Chief Source of Income*

This issue is discussed at ¶1750.

[¶1801.10] *Partners and Their Automobiles*

Individuals who are partners or who are employees of a partner (as opposed to employees of the partnership) and have an automobile made available to them or to a person related to them in the year are subject to standby charges included in income in respect of the capital cost or lease cost of the automobile. These standby charges are calculated exactly as for employees (¶326). In the case of employees of the individual partner, this merely corrects an anomaly; through this rule the employee of a partner is put on an equal footing with other employees and is subject to tax on fringe benefits for both the value of the car (¶326) and its operating expenses (¶324).

Partners who have an automobile made available to them are subject to a standby benefit in respect of the value of the car made available to them by the partnership under the rules at ¶326. However, there is no income inclusion in respect of operating expenses paid by the partnership; presumably this is regarded as part of the allocation of partnership income and expense. The reporting of this benefit for partners is likely to be obscure. Where a partnership is subject to reporting rules at ¶1880, it appears that the benefit should be included in box 114 ("other income") of the partner's T5013 slip. It should appear as a reconciliation item on the T5013 Summary, reconciling financial statement income to tax allocations. In other cases it is presumably the responsibility of individual partners to ensure correct self-reporting.

Where individuals who are partners use their own automobiles (whether owned or leased) in the course of partnership business, expenses can be claimed at the individual level (see ¶1803). The GST/HST rebate rules for automobiles apply to non-registered individual partners of a GST-registered partnership. The calculation is identical to that for employees; see ¶363.

(ITA: 12(1)(y); "Guide for the Partnership Information Return (T5013 Forms)" (T4068); IT-63R5, para. 17 [Archived])

[¶1802] ALLOCATION OF PROFITS

A partnership is not taxable as such but the individual partners must include in their income their proportionate shares of the partnership's income — regardless of whether or not the partners have actually withdrawn the income, in cash, from the partnership.

Partners are entitled to claim certain deductions from their income for the purpose of computing their taxable income, as described at ¶1077. In determining the taxable income of a partner, it is the income rather than the taxable income of the partnership which is allocated among the partners.

Similarly, tax is not computed at the partnership level, so that charitable donations are not deductible by the partnership but are included in the eligible donations of each partner. In determining the credit to which each partner is entitled, donations made by the partnership are ordinarily apportioned in accordance with the respective interests of the partners in the partnership.

Partnership agreements will often divide profits and losses among the partners on a combination formula, incorporating provisions for interest on partners' capital and salaries to partners with the remainder being divided in a particular ratio. No deduction may be claimed for tax purposes, in the partnership's accounts, for partners' salaries or interest on their capital. Such items must be added to the partners' shares of profits and thus included in their income from the partnership. Drawings of partners should be ignored in determining partnership profits.

Life insurance premiums paid through the partnership are generally not deductible in arriving at partnership profits. If the policy proceeds are payable to an individual partner's estate or beneficiaries, the premiums should be added to that partner's share of income. If the policy proceeds are payable to the partnership, the premiums should be divided among the partners — in the profit and loss ratio — and added to their shares of income.

A partnership agreement may call for "salaries" to partners but the partnership profit for a year may be insufficient to meet these resulting in a "loss". Interpretation Bulletin IT-138R, now withdrawn, said that if a partner suffered a loss in his capital account due to such arrangements, the loss was a business loss deductible from other income for the year and available for carryback or carryforward. It has been suggested that the CRA had second thoughts about the sense of this comment, which may have been one reason for withdrawing it. In CRA *Technical News* No. 25, the CRA elaborated on this change of heart, saying:

> The CRA is of the view that salaries paid to individual partners are not deductible in computing the partnership's income for income tax purposes. This concept is an extension of the general criteria established under the provincial Partnership Acts. As an example, section 24, paragraph 6 of the *Partnership Act* of Ontario specifically states "no partner is entitled to remuneration for acting in the partnership business". Consequently, any amounts paid and deducted as such in the financial statements of the partnership as such must be added back when computing partnership income.

However, rent paid to a partner is an expense of the partnership and personal income of the particular partner. It is not an allocation of partnership income.

In comments at the CRA Round Table at the 2003 Canadian Tax Foundation Annual Conference, published in *Income Tax Technical News* No. 30 on May 23, 2004, the CRA elaborated somewhat on amounts which a partnership can pay to partners other than as an allocation of profit. It began by reiterating its general rule that remuneration paid to a partner is an allocation of profit not deductible by the partnership. An exception to this general rule would occur if the partner is providing a separate service in a business that is not provided by the partnership. Examples of this would include providing accounting services, equipment rental, or engineering services, if these were not the business of the partnership. The CRA gave a favourable ruling on this issue with respect to management fees (CRA Document No. 9711923). In the CRA's view, an agreement with the partnership to pay a salary to a partner is not valid. The CRA does not consider that there is any legal impediment to a partnership issuing preference units that entitle the holder to a preferential share of profits or losses in the partnership. However, the CRA warned that the reallocation provision in section 103 of the Act should be kept in mind. Section 103 may require that the allocation among partners be revised where it is determined that the principal reason for the allocation is to reduce or postpone the partners' income tax. See CCH Newsletter *Tax Topics* No. 1657, dated December 11, 2003, for a lawyer's argument that the CRA has pushed the general rule further than provincial partnership law permits, and that there will be further litigation on the issue.

Members of a partnership are permitted to enter into an agreement under which continuing income or losses of the partnership can be allocated to a retired partner, or to his spouse or common-law partner, estate, heirs, or other persons who have acquired the retired partner's rights under the agreement. The person to whom such income or losses are allocated is treated for tax purposes as a member of the partnership. See ¶1867.

(ITA: 96; *The Queen v. Gelber*, 83 DTC 5385 (F.C.A.); *Signum Communications Inc. v. The Queen*, 88 DTC 6427 (F.C.T.D.), aff'd by 91 DTC 5360 (F.C.A.))

[¶1802.25] *Unreasonable Allocations*

Where a partnership agreement allocates income or loss, or the elements which contribute to income or loss, in such a fashion that the principal reason for the allocation may reasonably be considered to be the reduction or postponement of tax, the CRA may reallocate to achieve a "reasonable" result. (A more specific rule applies in the case of non-arm's length partners; see ¶1810.)

The CRA has attacked some complex tax planning efforts using partnerships, and at times has succeeded in persuading the courts that allocations were unreasonable. See *XCO Investments Limited et al. v. The Queen*, 2007 DTC 5146 (F.C.A.), aff'g 2005 DTC 1731 (T.C.C.), and *Penn West Petroleum Ltd. et al. v. The Queen*, 2007 DTC 715 (T.C.C.). Discussions of these cases can be found in the CCH Newsletter *Tax Topics* Nos. 1740 (June 14, 2007) and 1841 (June 21, 2007).

These cases have led to some comment in the tax community that it may be easier for the CRA to prevail in its anti-avoidance cases using specific rules, such as the unreasonable allocation rule for partnerships, rather than the general anti-avoidance rule at ¶285, where its success has been mixed.

(ITA: 103)

[¶1803] PARTNERS' EXPENSES

A partnership agreement may require that certain expenses incurred by a member of the partnership, such as automobile expenses and advertising expenses, be paid by each member personally. The member may deduct such expenses to the extent that they are incurred in earning the partnership income.

If the partnership's fiscal period does not coincide with the calendar year, a partner who is an individual may deduct, in computing his or her income for a calendar year, those expenses otherwise allowable which were incurred during the fiscal period of the partnership ending in the calendar year (see the CRA's *Income Tax Technical News* No. 6). It would seem that an interest expense incurred to acquire an interest in a partnership remains deductible only on a calendar year basis.

There are certain restrictions on the amount of interest expenses and property taxes that owners of undeveloped land can deduct when computing their income for tax purposes. (See ¶665.) If a partner has borrowed money to assist (directly or indirectly) in the partnership's acquisition of land subject to these restrictions, the partner's interest deduction is restricted by these rules *provided the partner's share of partnership income or loss is 10% or more.* A less than 10% partner may deduct the interest expense; a 10%-or-more partner must forgo the deduction and add the interest to the partner's ACB of the partnership.

For automobile expenses, see ¶1801 concerning GST/HST rebate.

(ITA: 18(2), (2.1); 53(1)(e)(xi); IT-153R3 [Archived])

[¶1804] FISCAL PERIOD OF A PARTNERSHIP

The taxation year for individuals is always the calendar year. A partner's income from a partnership will be his or her share of the income from the partnership for the fiscal period ended in the calendar year. The fiscal period of a partnership is the period for which the accounts have been ordinarily made up.

Prior to 1995, the partners could initially choose any date for the fiscal year end of a new partnership; however, once adopted, it could not be changed without the concurrence of the Minister. No fiscal period can exceed 12 months. Essentially, these rules remain in place, except that current rules provide that, for taxation years commencing in or after 1995, a (revocable) election is required to maintain a non-calendar fiscal period, as discussed below. That election must be made for the partnership as a whole (see ¶1801).

Under the current rules, where a new partner joins a partnership of individuals and the partnership has a non-calendar fiscal period, the partner will be deemed to have made the Alternative Election discussed at ¶705. Although there may be no serious consequence in the year of admission, the new partner will then be faced in effect with double taxation in the following year . This is avoided by making a voluntary payment in the first year (and every year thereafter) which has the effect of averaging the double income inclusion. See the discussion in ¶705 and ¶707. Partners who were admitted before 1995 were allowed a special reserve, discussed below at ¶1804.05.

Where a partnership ceases to exist, except for the incomplete distribution of partnership assets, the fiscal period is deemed to end at that time.

An individual who was a member of a partnership that ceased to exist may make an election to treat the fiscal period of the partnership as ending at the time when it normally would have ended had the partnership not ceased to exist *unless the partnership has made the alternative election at ¶705.* This in fact pretty well vitiates the point of deferring the final year end in most cases; see the discussion at ¶707.

In the 2011 federal Budget, the government announced similar rules to corporate partners with off-calendar taxation year ends. These rules effectively limit the deferral of tax by a corporation that has a significant interest in a partnership having a fiscal period different from the corporation's taxation year. The rules, which apply to corporate partners but not individual partners, are discussed in more detail in the companion book *Preparing Your Corporate Tax Returns*, also published by Wolters Kluwer. The measures apply to taxation years of a corporation that end after March 22, 2011.

(ITA: 96; 99)

[¶1804.05] *Election to Maintain Non-Calendar Fiscal Period*

As discussed in detail at ¶705, a non-calendar fiscal period for any business of an individual, including a partnership, has always implied an element of tax deferral on increasing incomes. For 1995 and later years, the government decided to put a stop to this by requiring prepayment of the implicit tax deferral.

Initially, the government determined to do this by requiring all proprietorships, and all partnerships which included as partners any individuals (other than testamentary trusts or exempt individuals), professional corporations, or other partnerships, to convert to a calendar year end on December 31, 1995. This entailed two 1995 fiscal periods reporting income in the same year, and a reserve is allowed to permit gradual recognition of the second period income over a 10-year period.

On second thought, the government agreed, as an alternative, to permit non-calendar fiscal periods to continue provided an election is made and a prepayment is made of the tax deferral for the period which does not end at December 31. Where this election was made for 1995, the prepayment required as the new system commenced in 1995 need only be recognized over a 10-year period.

In the end, the general partnership fiscal period rule (for fiscal periods commencing after 1994) is that a fiscal period must end on December 31 (unless the alternative election is made) if any of the following are members of the partnership:

(1) an individual (other than a testamentary trust or a tax-exempt individual, which would typically also be a trust);

(2) a professional corporation (that is, a corporation which carries on the professional practice of an accountant, dentist, lawyer, medical doctor, veterinarian, or chiropractor); or

(3) a partnership described in (1) or (2).

There are exceptions. A person or partnership who joins the partnership in a fiscal period but after December 31 does not put the partnership offside for that fiscal period (but would for the next one). A person or partnership that would not have a share of partnership income or loss for a fiscal period of a partnership if that fiscal period ended at December 31 is deemed not to be a member of the partnership for that fiscal period. The calendar year end rule does not apply to the fiscal period of a business not carried on in Canada.

Once a fiscal period is established or converted to a calendar year basis, no change can be made without the permission of the CRA.

A partnership otherwise compelled to have a calendar year fiscal period may elect to maintain a non-calendar fiscal period provided that (i) each member of the partnership is an individual (which can include a trust), and (ii) the partnership is not a member of another partnership. It follows that a partnership with both corporate and individual members cannot make this election.

The alternative election to have a non-calendar fiscal period cannot be made by a partnership whose primary expenditures are for registered tax shelters (¶2521).

In general, the election must be made (on form T1139) with a timely return filed by the authorized partner by that partner's tax-due date, which will normally be June 15 of the year following the year in which the fiscal period commences. Where a testamentary trust is a partner, the election must be filed by the earliest filing due-date of any member of the partnership for the taxation year that includes the first day of the fiscal period; that is, it must be filed with the first trust return due among the partners (if any) before June 15.

The election must be made by the partnership as a whole, and is binding on the partners, including new partners who may be admitted later. Where the election is made, each of the partners admitted before 1995 was compelled in 1995 to make the tax prepayments described in ¶705. For partners admitted after 1994, the prepayment rules will not apply in the year of admission but double taxation may result in the following year if a voluntary payment for the first year is not made; see ¶705.

The election may be revoked by a similar election.

(ITA: 96(1)(*d*), (1.6), (3); 249.1)

[¶1806] PARTNERSHIP INCOME FOR PURPOSES OF THE ATTRIBUTION RULES

A special purpose rule contradicts the general rule that partnership income retains its usual characteristics in the hands of the partners. For purposes of the attribution rules only (¶977), a partner who is:

(1) a limited partner; or

(2) a partner neither actively engaged in partnership activities other than financing activities, nor carrying on a business similar to that of the partnership on a regular, continuous and substantial basis

is considered to have property income from the partnership. The purpose of this rule is to prevent the circumvention of attribution rules through the use of partnership investments, where the income for ordinary purposes would be considered business income and therefore not subject to attribution. In other words, even if the income earned by the partnership and allocated to the limited/passive partner is otherwise considered business income, it will be deemed to be income from property for the purposes of the income attribution rules.

(ITA: 96(1.8))

[¶1808] SPOUSE OR COMMON-LAW PARTNER AS EMPLOYEE OF A PARTNERSHIP

Remuneration paid by a partnership to a partner's spouse or common-law partner is fully deducted from partnership income if such remuneration is reasonable in the circumstances. As an employer, the partnership must withhold the proper tax, Canada Pension Plan premiums and Employment Insurance premiums from the spouse's salary and must file with the CRA a T4 information slip reporting the tax, CPP and EI payments. Note that CPP is withheld on payments deductible for tax purposes, i.e., those considered reasonable for the work done. EI is not withheld on non-arm's length payments unless the payment arrangements are similar to what they would be in an arm's length contract. It is not clear how this standard differs in practice from the CPP standard. Perhaps the EI rule anticipates periodic payments of set amounts based on time or work done, while the income tax/CPP standard is only concerned with the reasonableness of the amount paid in relation to the work, and not the systematic payment (although unpaid amounts are subject to the rules in ¶746). As a practical matter, only the CRA can rule on the proper withholding on a particular set of facts. Where payments are made to the child of a partner, the income tax rule would be the same (must be reasonable), the CPP rule appears to be that you must withhold from cash remuneration regardless, and the EI rule is the same non-arm's length rule as for a spouse. The withholding rules are summarized in the CRA's *Employers' Guide - Payroll Deductions and Remittances* (T4001).

(ITA: 18; 103)

[¶1810] NON-ARM'S LENGTH PARTNERS

Certain rules apply to "non-arm's length" (see ¶812) partners. These rules require that allocations of income, losses or any amounts relevant in computing the income or taxable income of a partner, or between partners who do not deal with each other at arm's length, must be "reasonable" in the circumstances. Factors such as capital invested, work performed and other relevant factors are considered in this assessment of reasonableness. The Minister may redirect income between non-arm's length partners where allocations are not considered reasonable. Note that this test does not require that the principal purpose of the allocation be to reduce or postpone tax, as is the case where partners deal at arm's length (see ¶1816).

In addition to the non-arm's length rules, there are more specific rules, usually deferring loss recognition, on transactions with "affiliated" persons or partnerships; see ¶852.

(ITA: 103)

[¶1812] RENTAL PROPERTIES

A partnership's rental buildings are held in the appropriate prescribed class or classes, and capital cost allowance (see Chapter 8) is limited, as usual, to the prescribed rates.

However, there is an additional limitation that a partnership cannot create or increase a rental loss through capital cost allowance claims on certain rental buildings (see ¶630). For this purpose, a partnership's rental buildings are grouped together and the total amount of capital cost allowance which may be claimed by the partnership for the year on these buildings cannot exceed the total rental income, if any, after expenses but before capital cost allowance on the buildings.

Keeping in mind the above-mentioned limitation, the net rental income or loss from the partnership is allocated among the partners according to the partnership agreement, and then declared in the partners' returns.

In the case of a partner who also holds rental property as a proprietor, that is, not in partnership, the capital cost allowance restriction will apply in a similar way to his or her own rental buildings. The partner's share of partnership rental income or loss (see Chapter 6) allocated to him or her (which may be after some capital cost allowance claimed by the partnership) should be added to the total rental income or loss after expenses, but before the claim for capital cost allowances on the partner's own rental buildings. The partner may claim capital cost allowance on his or her own rental buildings at the prescribed rates only to the extent of the aggregated income from rentals, if any, as described above (see ¶630).

Example

Allen Baker and Carol Jones are equal partners of A.C. Widget Distributors which earned rental income from a building. Allen also owns a rental building personally. The undepreciated capital cost, before claiming the Year 1 capital cost allowance, of the partnership building is $40,000 and of Allen's building is $60,000, and both buildings are Class 6 property (maximum rate of capital cost allowance is 10%). The partnership's rental income and Allen's rental income from the building owned personally are computed as follows:

	Year 1	*Year 2*
A.C. Widget:		
Rental revenue	$22,000	$25,000
Expenses	$12,000	$23,000
Net rental income before claiming capital cost allowance	$10,000	$ 2,000
Capital cost allowance (Year 1 — 10% of $40,000; Year 2 — see below)	$4,000	$2,000
Net rental income	$ 6,000	$ Nil
Allen:		
Allen's share of net rental income from partnership (50%)	$ 3,000	$ Nil
Allen's own rental (loss) income before claiming capital cost allowance	$(5,000)	$10,000
Combined rental (loss) income	$ (2,000)	$10,000
Capital cost allowance on Allen's building (Year 1 — see below; Year 2 — 10% of $60,000)	None allowed	$6,000
Allen's rental income (loss)	$ (2,000)	$ 4,000

Although in Year 1 the capital cost allowance available to Allen is $6,000 (10% × $60,000), he is restricted to claiming none since the combined rental operations, after claiming capital cost allowance in the partnership, result in a loss. In Year 2, the partnership is restricted to claiming only $2,000 of capital cost allowance although it has available $3,600 (10% × ($40,000 - $4,000)). Allen, in Year 2, can claim the full capital cost available (10% × $60,000 = $6,000) on his own building since the claim does not create a combined rental loss.

As described in ¶872, where a person, including a partnership, acquires a rental building costing $50,000 or more, this building must be recorded in a separate capital cost allowance class instead of being combined with similar buildings in one class.

Regulations include in gross revenue from rental buildings and leasing properties the income from occupancy rights and from services ancillary to the use of the properties. The apparent intent is to extend the capital cost allowance restrictions to what would otherwise be related business income. The rules are intended to apply only to passive individual ("tax shelter") investors, although an exception in regulation 1100(14.2)(*c*) would allow these investors up to a one-third stake in restricted partnership ventures.

(ITR: 1100(11)– (14.2); IT-195R4 [Archived])

[¶1813] LEASING PROPERTIES

Partnerships cannot claim capital cost allowances to create or increase a loss on leasing properties (see ¶873). The limitation works in the same manner as the restriction on rental properties (see ¶1812 and ¶630). Corporate partnerships where the sales or sales/leasing income of the partners amounts to at least 90% of total revenue are exempt from this provision.

(ITR: 1100(15)– (20))

[¶1816] PARTNERSHIP AGREEMENT

If members of a partnership have agreed to share any income, loss or other amounts of the partnership in a particular manner and the principal reason for the agreement may reasonably be considered to be the reduction or postponement of tax that might otherwise have been payable by a partner, the partners' arrangement for sharing these amounts can be considered invalid for tax purposes. In this case, the tax authorities will apportion the amounts to the partners in a manner which is reasonable in these circumstances.

For example, if members of a partnership agreed to allocate all of the partnership's foreign source income and foreign tax to one member of the partnership because he or she could claim the greatest foreign tax credit, the tax authorities might require these amounts to be reallocated among all the partners in proportion to their normal profit sharing ratio.

See also ¶1810 for rules concerning non-arm's length partners.

(ITA: 103)

[¶1817] LOSS CARRYOVERS

Since a partnership's incomes and losses from each source and its taxable capital gains and allowable capital losses are allocated to the partners at the end of each fiscal period of the partnership, the loss carryover provisions are not relevant to the partnership itself. Instead, each partner will report on his or her own return his or her share of partnership losses, if any, and losses from other sources and will make his or her own determination of any non-capital loss, net capital loss, or restricted farm loss that may be carried over to other years. (See Chapter 13.) However, special rules exist for "limited partnerships" as defined at ¶1818, below, and losses created by scientific research expenditures (¶1821).

(ITA: 96)

[¶1818] LIMITED PARTNERSHIP LOSSES

(Note that the general rules for losses involving partnerships without limited partners are discussed above at ¶1802 and ¶1817.)

[¶1818.05] *Background*

Because of their flow-through characteristics, partnerships have been used extensively as a vehicle for tax shelter investments. By limiting or guaranteeing the liability of passive investors, the investors obtain security against partnership creditors comparable to that of corporate shares, and can participate in the tax benefits which accrue to deductibility of initial start-up costs of a business venture.

The CRA accepts the legitimacy of limited partnership ventures as long as they have some reasonable expectation of profit (see *D'Amato and Ion v. The Queen*, 95 DTC 622 (T.C.C.), aff'd 96 DTC 6543 (F.C.A.)). The propriety of the reasonable expectation of profit test is perhaps undermined for partnerships as for sole proprietors and property owners by the *Walls* and *Stewart* cases discussed at ¶704 and ¶690 respectively. In any event, even where it accepted the legitimacy of the partnership venture, the statutory rules now limit the deductions of passive investors to their "at-risk amount" (¶1818.25)— essentially the partnership ACB (¶1843, ¶1844) plus any capital contributions the limited partner has agreed to pay.

These rules form only one prong of a multiple attack on tax shelters. Other initiatives include classifying business income as rental or leasing income from underlying property, thereby limiting related capital cost allowance to the income generated and preventing claims against unrelated income (see ¶630 and ¶873), restrictions on limited partnership investment tax credits (¶1819), special rules for general partnership scientific research expenditures (¶1821), and alternative minimum tax (Chapter 24). The negative ACB rules at ¶1842 and the limited recourse debt rules discussed below illustrate that imaginative taxpayers continue to find ways to syndicate tax losses and the government continues to develop new rules to oppose them. The risk that genuine entrepreneurial start-up costs will be denied as casualties of this battle becomes more commonplace as the battle continues.

[¶1818.10] *Limited Recourse Debt*

The government took several successive new steps against tax shelters in 1994 (see ¶2521 for the context of these and later sets of restrictions). Part of this effort involves the taxation of negative partnership cost base and the reduction of cost base for non-recourse financing associated with the acquisition of the partnership interest. This is discussed at ¶1842. A special definition of a limited partner is added there to accommodate those changes.

On December 1, 1994, the federal government announced that it would mount yet a further attack on tax shelters. Under these limited recourse rules, still in effect, the unpaid principal amount of any indebtedness on which recourse is limited, either immediately or in the future and either contingently or absolutely, is treated as a reduction of the expenditure to which it relates (see ¶835). Should an unpaid amount be paid in fact, it is treated as an expenditure or payment made at the time of payment. This rule applies to reduce (or increase on actual payment) the cost for tax purposes of limited partnership interests. That is, for expenditures on limited partnership interests after November 30, 1994, this rule adjusts the opening partnership ACB before the limited partnership "at-risk" rules come into play to further limit partnership loss claims. Since the partnership ACB rules also restrict the ACB of a limited partnership interest for limited recourse financing deductions (¶1844), a rule has been added to prevent a double-counting of the restriction. The general limited recourse rule will take precedence and its cost base reductions are not then to be replicated in the limited partnership at-risk amount.

The general limited recourse rule at ¶835 confuses matters by introducing its own "at-risk adjustment", which is similar to the negative elements of the "at-risk amount" in the limited partnership rules. An at-risk adjustment also reduces cost base under the new rules. However, it appears that it will not reduce the cost of a partnership interest if the at-risk amount rules of the limited partnership loss rules below apply to that partnership interest. Presumably, this is at least intended to prevent a double-up of the same restrictions. It is not entirely clear that no gap is left to the taxpayer to slide out of the new rules because the limited partnership rules apply and then have the limited partnership rules fail to make a restricting adjustment, although surely the borderline of the rules is intended to be seamless.

These changes have some impact on the limited partnership rules, as discussed in context below.

[¶1818.15] *Who is a Limited Partner?*

Generally speaking, a limited partnership is one registered under a provincial statute providing limited liability for the limited (as opposed to the general) partners.

However, in an effort to prevent simple tax avoidance techniques, the Act provides a specific and considerably extended definition of a limited partner for the purposes of restrictions on partnership investment tax credits and losses. A partner is considered to be a limited partner of a partnership at a particular time where, at that time or within three years thereafter,

(1) the partner's exposure in respect of his partnership interest is limited by operation of law (typically provincial partnership law, but this provision does not apply to a partner whose liability is limited by operation of a statute of Canada or a province that limits liability only for debts, obligations and liabilities of the partnership

or any member arising from negligent acts or omissions committed in the course of the business. In short, the rules do not apply to partners operating under limited liability statutes applicable to professional partnerships, as discussed at ¶1842);

(2) the partner (or a non-arm's length person) is entitled either immediately or in future and either absolutely or contingently to receive an amount or obtain a benefit which reduces the at-risk amount described below (assuming those benefits did not exclude amounts not included in the at-risk rules in the first place);

(3) one of the reasons for the existence of the partner (i) can reasonably be considered to be to limit the liability of anyone else, and (ii) cannot be considered to be to carry on that person's business (other than an investment business) in the most effective manner; for example, a shell corporation or, perhaps, a trust formed only to hold the partnership interest; or

(4) there is an agreement to wind up the partnership or to dispose of his partnership interest and one of the main reasons for the agreement may reasonably be considered to be to circumvent the definition of limited partner.

In the third case involving "shell" corporations or, possibly, trusts, the partner will not be considered to be a limited partner where one of the reasons for its existence is to permit those persons who have invested in the partner to carry on their ordinary business in the most effective manner. A person is not considered to be a limited partner in respect of an "exempt interest", that is, an interest protected under the transitional rules discussed below.

[¶1818.20] *Losses of Limited Partner Restricted*

The losses of a partnership allocated to a limited partner in his taxation year are deductible by the partner only to the extent of the partner's at-risk amount as at the end of the fiscal period of the partnership ending in that year. Where investment tax credits have also been allocated to the limited partner, these credits will reduce the partner's remaining at-risk amount for the purpose of determining the amount of the losses that are deductible by the partner. These provisions apply to losses of the partnership from business or property. No restriction is applied, however, in respect of capital losses or farm losses (although the farm losses may be restricted as described at ¶1750). These other losses will, however, reduce the at-risk amount of the limited partner for the purposes of determining the extent to which those losses subject to the new rules may be deducted. Losses rendered non-deductible by the new rules are designated as limited partnership losses and as such are eligible for an indefinite carryforward against future income from the partnership which generated the losses, generally to the extent of the partner's at-risk amount in the future year. As such, limited partnership losses may be deducted in future years where the taxpayer's at-risk amount in respect of the partnership increases — for example, by way of an increased investment in the partnership.

The "at-risk" rules also apply to restrict the deductibility of resource expenditures allocated to a limited partner. The rules limit the deduction by a limited partner of Canadian exploration expenses, Canadian development expenses and Canadian oil and gas property expenses incurred by the limited partnerships which otherwise are treated as expenses incurred by the limited partners (¶1800).

[¶1818.25] *"At-Risk Amount" Defined*

This at-risk amount at any particular time is calculated as follows:

(1) the partner's ACB of his partnership interest;

plus

(2) when computed at the end of the partnership's fiscal period, the partner's share of the current year's income and of proceeds of disposition of resource property which may be added to the partner's ACB of the partnership interest for the year;

minus

(3) all amounts owing by the partner (or a person not dealing at arm's length with the partner) to the partnership (or a person not dealing at arm's length with the partnership) and any amount or benefit to which the partner (or a person not dealing at arm's length with the partner) is entitled, where the amount or benefit is intended to protect him from the loss of his investment.

With the introduction of new negative ACB rules for limited partners (¶1842), certain non-recourse financing of the partner's partnership interest will reduce the cost base of the partner and potentially create income. Where the adjustment is made to partnership ACB, it does not also reduce the at-risk-amount under (3) above. Similarly, where the cost of a partnership interest is reduced by a loan to the partnership under the non-recourse financing rules at ¶2521, the at-risk amount here is not reduced again.

For the purpose of the reduction of the at-risk amount in respect of amounts owing to the partnership, loans between persons dealing not at arm's length with the partner or the partnership are taken into account. Thus, for example, where a general partner of a partnership has lent money to a limited partner in order to fund that limited partner's contribution to the partnership, the amount of that loan will reduce the limited partner's at-risk amount. Similarly, where an amount or benefit is made available to a person with whom the limited partner does not deal at arm's length, a reduction of the limited partner's at-risk amount will be required. A limited partner's at-risk amount is not reduced by protection from a loss on his investment that takes the form of:

(1) normal liability insurance protection;

(2) agreements to purchase the partnership interest at any time at its fair market value at that time; or

(3) a buy-sell agreement relating to the partnership interest that applies in the event of the death of the owner thereof.

For partnership interests acquired before April 27, 1995, revenue guarantees in respect of the gross revenues of a partnership did not reduce the at-risk amount except where the revenue guarantee ensures the partner of the return of a portion of his investment. As well, a specific provision excluded from reductions to the at-risk amount prescribed revenue guarantees in respect of certified film productions granted before February 28, 1995 or, in more limited circumstances, after that date but before 1996, in recognition of other rules applicable to such guarantees (see ¶874 and ¶2521).

Where a limited partner or a non-arm's length person has a right to exchange the partnership interest for some other property, the partner (or person) is considered to be entitled to an amount or benefit protecting the partner from loss to the extent of the fair market value of the other property at the time at which the at-risk amount is being computed. Similarly, where the partner's (or a non-arm's length person's) borrowings are guaranteed by the partnership or any person, an at-risk reduction is required in respect of the outstanding balance of the borrowings.

Where a limited partnership interest is acquired by a second or subsequent owner, a special rule provides for the determination of the amount to be used as a limited partner's cost of his partnership interest. If the limited partner is not the first person to acquire the interest, the cost of the interest, for the purposes only of the at-risk rules, is the lesser of its actual cost and the ACB of the taxpayer from whom it was acquired (but not less than zero).

Anti-avoidance provisions attempt to prevent artificial increases in the at-risk amount of a limited partner by way of a series of payments or loans and repayments between the partner and the partnership.

For special adjustments to at-risk amounts in the case of resource expenditures flowing through a limited partnership, see ¶2229.

[¶1818.35] *Grandfathering I: Exempt Amounts*

As stated in the definition of limited partner above, transitional or "grandfather" protection is provided in respect of interests in a partnership which existed on February 25, 1986 (June 17, 1987 for resource expenses). If his partnership interest is an exempt interest, a person who would otherwise be considered to be a limited partner will not be subject to the new rules. In general, an exempt interest is defined as at a particular time and means an interest in a partnership that was carrying on business or earning income from the rental or leasing of property on a regular and continuous basis on February 25, 1986 (June 17, 1987 for resource expenses) and continuously thereafter until that particular time. Nevertheless, a partnership interest can lose exempt status where, after February 25, 1986 (June 17, 1987 for resource expenses), there has been a substantial contribution of capital to the partnership or substantial partnership borrowings. The rules allow three circumstances where such contributions or borrowings will not be considered substantial. These circumstances are:

(1) where the funds are required to fulfill contractual obligations entered into by the partnership before February 26, 1986 (June 18, 1987 for resource expenses);

(2) where the funds are raised pursuant to a prospectus, preliminary prospectus or registration statement filed with the appropriate securities authority before February 26, 1986 (for resource expenses, add "offering memorandum or notice required to be filed before any distribution of securities may commence" and change the date to June 18, 1987); or

(3) where the use of the funds was for the day-to-day operation or maintenance of the activity as it existed on February 25, 1986 (June 17, 1987 for resource expenses).

For the purposes of these rules a partnership, in respect of which funds have been raised pursuant to a prospectus filed with an appropriate authority before February 26, 1986 (June 18, 1987 for resource expenses), will be considered to have been carrying on business on a regular and continuous basis on February 25, 1986 (June 17, 1987 for resource expenses) and continuously thereafter until the closing date stipulated in the prospectus or January 1, 1987 (January 1, 1988 for resource expenses), whichever is the earlier date.

Funds will be considered to have been *required* to fulfill a contractual obligation to make an expenditure entered into before February 26, 1986 (June 18, 1987 for resource expenses) if the obligation is unconditional, or if a condition is applicable after June 11, 1986 (June 17, 1987 for resource expenses), the condition does not relate to any proposed or actual change in the tax consequences of the expenditure under the Act. Accordingly, for the purposes of the definition of "exempt interest" an obligation conditional upon entitlement to transitional relief or grandfather protection from these budget proposals would not be considered to have been *required* to have been made.

[¶1818.40] *Grandfathering II: Transitional Rules*

In addition to the protection offered by the exempt amount rules, the enacting legislation somewhat broadens the at-risk rule for partnership interests acquired before 1987 pursuant to:

(1) a prospectus or similar offering document filed before June 12, 1986 and accepted (if required) by a public securities authority;

(2) an offering memorandum used for solicitation after February 25 and before June 12, 1986 which was, if required by law, filed with securities authorities; and

(3) an issue of partnership interests in a film production where expenditures had to be made by the partnership or film producer under an agreement entered into before June 12, 1986.

For agreements qualifying under these rules, the at-risk amount is reduced by reimbursements, revenue guarantees, etc. given "pursuant to an undertaking ... to indemnify the taxpayer with respect to any liability" rather than the broader phrase "for the purpose of reducing the impact ... of any loss the taxpayer may sustain".

This rule has no parallel in the resource expense rules.

(ITA: 66.8; 96(2.1)– (2.7))

[¶1819] LIMITED PARTNERSHIP INVESTMENT TAX CREDITS

In general, partnerships which generate investment tax credit (¶1463) on expenditures apportion those credits to the partners in accordance with each member's reasonable share. Allocations are made at the end of each partnership fiscal period. A partner's ACB is reduced by such credits allocated (¶1844). The capital cost of depreciable property (or the cost of research expenditures) of the partnership is reduced by credits allocated to members.

As part of its policy of limiting the tax shelter benefits of limited partnerships, rules have been introduced to bring the investment tax credits allocated to limited partners within the "at-risk" limitations for partnership losses.

[¶1819.05] *Limitation on Investment Tax Credit (ITC)*

In these rules, both "limited partner" and "at-risk amount" are defined by reference to the limited partner loss rules at ¶1818. The rules restrict the amount of investment tax credits that may be allocated by a partnership at the end of its fiscal period to a limited partner to the lesser of the following two amounts:

(1) the portion of the ITC that would have been allowable to the limited partner if the at-risk rules had not applied to any partner of the partnership and that may be considered to have been earned by the partnership in respect of its expenditure in that period of an amount equal to the limited partner's expenditure base for the year (as defined below); and

(2) the limited partner's at-risk amount in respect of the partnership at the end of the period.

In determining those ITCs that were earned by a partnership in respect of the expenditure by it of an amount equal to the expenditure bases of its limited partners, a partnership is entitled to allocate the high ITC rate expenditures in favour of limited partners. Thus, for example, if the expenditure base of the limited partners were $100,000 for a year in which the partnership acquired $150,000 of property qualifying for ITCs at the 40% rate and a further $50,000 of property qualifying for ITCs at the rate of 10%, the partnership could allocate a maximum of $40,000 (that is, 40% of $100,000) of investment tax credits to the limited partners for that year.

[¶1819.10] *Definition of Expenditure Base*

A limited partner's expenditure base for a taxation year of the partnership (its fiscal period) is defined as at the end of a partnership taxation year and means:

(1) the limited partner's at-risk amount in respect of his or her partnership interest at the time he or she last became a member of the partnership; plus

(2) any subsequent contributions to the partnership before the end of the year; plus

(3) the limited partner's share of the income net of losses from the partnership for the year and preceding years; *minus*

(4) all distributions to the limited partner before the end of the year from the partnership; and

(5) any amount previously considered to have been an expenditure by the partnership of funds in respect of the limited partner's expenditure base.

However, in no event can a limited partner's expenditure base exceed his proportionate share of the aggregate expenditure base of all limited partners of the partnership. In determining the proportionate share, the partnership's apprenticeship tax credit is limited to the lesser of $20,000 and actual apprenticeship salaries and wages paid by the partnership, and the partnership's child care expense tax credit is limited to the lesser of $40,000 and actual costs of creating the child care space.

[¶1819.15] *Allocation of Restricted Credits*

Given that the partnership may be restricted from allocating investment tax credits to limited partners, excess unallocated credits may remain. In such circumstances the remaining investment tax credit may be allocated to those non-limited partners — that is, the general partner or partners — who were members of the partnership throughout the fiscal period of the partnership, in proportion to their investment (whether by debt or equity) in the partnership. For those general partners who were not partners throughout the fiscal period of the partnership, the normal rules allocating investment tax credits according to equity participation would apply. Nevertheless, there may be situations where the general partners would rather have the remaining investment tax credits extinguished than to have them allocated. This could happen, for example, in those circumstances where the general partner is not in a position to use the credits. Accordingly, there is an election under which a general partner who has been allocated investment tax credits may renounce the credits allocated to him. In such circumstances, the investment tax credits are extinguished and a cost base reduction of partnership property is not required.

Note, however, that limited partners are also specified members of a partnership, and as such have additional limitations on the allocation of investment tax credits arising from scientific research. Those credits are denied to the limited partner and could not, prior to taxation years ending before May 2, 2006, be reallocated to active partners. See ¶1821.

(ITA: 127(8)–(8.4); IT-151R5 (Consolidated 2002) [Archived])

[¶1821] PARTNERSHIPS DOING SCIENTIFIC RESEARCH: HISTORY AND SUMMARY

A partnership must deduct all its eligible scientific research expenditures in the year incurred. Technically it is the entire pool described at ¶740 which is deducted. If a loss results from claiming this deduction, the loss from this source cannot be allocated to any partner who is a limited partner (as defined at ¶1819) of the partnership at any time in the year. Note that this definition for loss purposes is not as broad as the definition of "specified member" of a partnership which restricts investment tax credit allocations. A "specified member" includes not only a limited partner, but also a partner who is not actively engaged in the partnership business activities (which do not for this purpose include its financing), or a partner who is not actively carrying on a business similar to the partnership business but outside a partnership. A specified member is also denied investment tax credits arising from scientific research. For taxation years ending before May 2, 2006, there was no mechanism to reallocate the denied losses or credits, although arguably there is no specific mechanism to prevent a partnership agreement from allocating losses or credits in the most beneficial fashion (i.e., to those who can use them). Professional advice should be sought on the possible application of various anti-avoidance rules. Investment tax credits which cannot be allocated under these rules should not reduce the R&D expenditure pool of the partnership. For allocation rules after May 1, 2006, see ¶1821.15, below.

The purpose of this rule would seem to be to prevent the syndication of research by denying the tax benefits to partnership investors. Deliberately or otherwise, the rules also deny the indefinite carryforward of undeducted R&D expenses to all partners of all partnerships. The partnership R&D expense pool becomes an ordinary loss of the year to all the partners who are not denied the loss altogether. It therefore operates through each partner's loss carryover pool, rather than as an R&D expense pool.

These restrictions apply only to fiscal periods of partnerships ending after December 15, 1987, and only to expenses incurred after that date. They do not apply to "grandfathered partners" in respect of expenditures made by the partnership before January 1, 1989 pursuant to a written obligation of the partnership entered into before December 16, 1987, the terms of a prospectus or other offering document filed with a public authority in Canada before that date or an offering memorandum described below in respect of grandfathered partners. A grandfathered partner is a partner who acquired the partnership interest before December 16, 1987, or after December 15, 1987 pursuant to (a) a prior written agreement, (b) a prospectus or other offering document filed with a public authority in Canada by that date, or (c) the terms of a detailed offering memorandum distributed by that date as part of an offering of securities, provided solicitations for sales occurred by the date and the securities sales were made as projected.

Note that a partnership may have both grandfathered and specified member partners, so that it may have to claim R&D pool expenses *vis-à-vis* some partners and not others.

(ITA: 96(1)(e.1), (g); 127(8), (12.1))

[¶1821.15] *Allocation of Restricted R&D Credits: Current Rules*

As discussed above, investment tax credits (ITCs) arising from research and development (SR&ED, or, here, R&D) cannot be allocated to specified partners, i.e., limited partners or inactive partners (see definition at ¶1821 above). For taxation years ending before May 2, 2006, there was no mechanism to allocate those denied credits to active partners.

For taxation years ending after May 1, 2006 (and therefore applicable to 2006 and later returns of individuals), the denial of reallocation, at least so far as investment tax credits are concerned, is rescinded. ITCs arising from R&D continue to be denied to specified partners, but the credits which have been denied to specified shareholders can be reallocated to active general partners.

The new rule puts these credits on a par with other investment tax credits which are denied to limited partners (but not other specified partners) because they exceed the limited partner's at-risk amount under the rules at ¶1819. Those credits, other than R&D credits, could always be reallocated.

It remains a condition for reallocation that the amount can only be reallocated to an active general partner who was a member of the partnership throughout the fiscal period for which the partnership ITCs are being determined, and must be reasonable in the circumstances, having regard to the partner's investment in the partnership, in equity or debt, of each such active general member throughout the fiscal period.

As with the limited partner reallocations at ¶1819.15, partners entitled to a reallocation can elect to refuse it.

(ITA: 127(8)– (8.4); IT-151R5 (Consolidated 2002) [Archived])

CAPITAL COST ALLOWANCE ON DEPRECIABLE PROPERTY OF A PARTNERSHIP

[¶1822] GENERAL RULES

Capital cost allowance on depreciable property of a partnership is claimed by the partnership itself rather than by each partner.

If a partner uses property of his or her own, such as an automobile, in the partnership business, he or she will still be able to claim capital cost allowances personally. Generally, the partnership agreement will determine whether an asset is owned by the partnership or by the individual partners.

[¶1822.05] *Effect of Investment Tax Credits*

Investment tax credits earned by a partnership on expenditures in its fiscal period are allocated to partners to the extent that "may reasonably be considered" to represent the partners' shares. The investment tax credits so earned reduce the capital cost of related property in the partnership at the end of the fiscal period in which they are earned regardless of when, if ever, they are used by the partners. The reduction occurs as if the credits were "government assistance" rather than investment tax credit; it appears to follow that there is no one year time lag in making the adjustment to property cost as there is for credits earned directly by individuals. That is, the cost reduction occurs in the partnership fiscal period in which the expenditures are incurred. Similar rules apply to the notional capital cost pool of depreciable property acquired for scientific research. See also the special rules for resource expenditures, which are claimed outside the partnership (¶1801), limited partnerships (¶1819), and scientific research expenditures (¶1821).

(ITA: 96; 127(8)– (8.5), (12), (12.1))

WHERE PARTNERSHIP DEPRECIABLE PROPERTY ACQUIRED BEFORE 1972

[¶1823] TRANSITION FROM 1971 RULES TO 1972 RULES

The rules set out in ¶1823.05 to ¶1823.35 were applicable to the 1972 fiscal year of a partnership. Normally, a partnership will have already made its calculation of the capital cost and undepreciated capital cost of depreciable property of the partnership owned at the commencement of its 1972 fiscal year. This calculation does not need to be done a second time. For those partnerships which have not made this calculation the rules are set out in the following paragraphs.

(ITAR: 20)

[¶1823.05] *Capital Cost of Depreciable Property Owned on December 31, 1971*

Since the post 1971 law requires that capital cost allowances on depreciable property owned by a partnership be claimed at the partnership level and not by each partner, detailed rules exist to compute the capital cost and undepreciated capital cost to a partnership of depreciable assets of a prescribed class (see ¶1823.10 and ¶1823.15) owned by a partnership at December 31, 1971. The rules are necessary because under the rules in force prior to 1972, partnership assets may have had differing balances of capital cost and undepreciated capital cost in the hands of the partners, and therefore it was necessary to provide a starting point for capital cost allowances to be claimed by the partnership for 1972 and future fiscal years.

The starting point was also necessary to permit calculation of the following amounts:

(1) capital gains on disposal of depreciable partnership property after 1971;

(2) recapture of capital cost allowance on disposal of depreciable partnership property after 1971; and

(3) terminal losses on disposal of depreciable partnership property after 1971.

It is not necessary to apply the following rules if at the start of the partnership's 1972 taxation year, the partnership had been claiming capital cost allowances and using its own schedules and the partners did not make a separate calculation of capital cost allowance on the partnership property. In this case, the partnership continued using its own capital cost allowance schedules as it had in the past. However, situations may exist where if the following rules are used, the deemed capital cost or undepreciated capital cost of the partnership property would differ from the amount shown on the partnership's schedules. This might happen if a partner was admitted after the commencement of a partnership. If you are a member of a partnership which has its own capital cost allowance schedule, you may nonetheless wish to consider using the detailed calculations which are discussed in the following paragraphs if this allows a special deduction in 1972 or reduces the amount of potential recapture of depreciation.

(ITAR: 20)

[¶1823.10] *Capital Cost*

The partnership's capital cost of all properties of a capital cost allowance class was deemed to be the lowest amount which resulted when the following formula was applied for each partner who was a member of the partnership on June 18, 1971, or in the case of a new partnership formed after June 18, 1971, on the date the partnership was formed, and who remained a partner until December 31, 1971:

$$\text{Partner's "acquisition cost" of property of the class} \times \frac{100\%}{\text{Partner's percentage share of the partnership property of the class}}$$

The deemed capital cost of each class of property of the partnership was then prorated over all the properties in the class on the basis of their relative fair market value on December 31, 1971 to determine the deemed capital cost of each separate property in the class.

The acquisition cost to a partner of property of a prescribed class in which he or she had an interest was the total of his or her share of the undepreciated capital cost of the partnership's property of that class at December 31, 1971, plus the depreciation claimed by the partner before 1972 on property of that class, or the partner's share of any such depreciation computed by the partnership. Depreciation presumably meant capital cost allowances claimed since 1949 (when the capital cost allowance system commenced).

The "partner's percentage share" mentioned in the formula above means his interest in property of the class expressed as a percentage of the interest of all partners in property of that class on December 31, 1971. Presumably the partnership agreement will govern in determining what these interests were. If a partner has no interest in property of a particular class, do not make a calculation for him or her in respect of that class.

[¶1823.15] *Undepreciated Capital Cost*

For purposes of claiming capital cost allowance in 1972 and later years, or for computing any recapture of capital cost allowances, the undepreciated capital cost of a particular class of assets of the partnership was computed by taking the lowest amount which resulted from applying the following formula in respect of each partner who was a member of the partnership on the later of June 18, 1971 or the date on which the partnership was formed and who remained a partner until December 31, 1971:

$$(A - B)/C \times 100$$

A — is the partner's actual undepreciated capital cost of partnership property of the class at December 31, 1971.

B — is the lesser of:

(1) the amount by which the partner's actual capital cost of all property of the class at December 31, 1971 exceeds his share of the partnership's deemed capital cost of all property of the class at December 31, 1971 (¶1823.10), or

(2) A (as above).

C — is the partner's percentage share of the partnership property of the class.

It seems that if a partner had an interest in partnership property of a prescribed class and also owned personally some property used in the partnership business and therefore included in that class, the partner would include the personally owned property for the purposes of calculation of the acquisition cost (¶1823.10) and undepreciated capital cost of that class. If the partner's personal assets related to a different business than that of the partnership, then he or she would not include personally owned assets because similar assets must be placed in separate classes if they are used in separate businesses.

The excess of the deemed capital cost to the partnership of property in the class (¶1823.10) over its deemed undepreciated capital cost determined as above is considered to have been claimed by the partnership as capital cost allowance in prior years.

(ITAR: 20)

[¶1823.20] *Non-December Year Ends*

A partner's undepreciated capital cost of depreciable assets of a prescribed class where the partnership has a fiscal year end other than December 31, 1971 was calculated by adding to the undepreciated capital cost of his interest in the partnership assets at the end of its 1971 fiscal year, his share of the cost of acquisitions of property of that class after the 1971 year end and before January 1, 1972 and by subtracting the proceeds of disposition (to the extent the proceeds do not exceed the original cost of the asset or undepreciated capital cost of the pool) for the same "stub period". No capital cost allowance, whether prorated or otherwise, may be claimed for this period.

This "actual" undepreciated capital cost is the starting point for determining "acquisition cost" (¶1823.10) and the partnership's deemed undepreciated capital cost (¶1823.15).

[¶1823.30] *Depreciable Property Other Than Depreciable Property of a Prescribed Class for Farmers and Fishers*

Depreciable property owned by a partnership which is engaged in farming or fishing may have been depreciated under the Part XVII method of capital cost allowances (see ¶1712). Under this method, the depreciable property was not included in prescribed classes.

As was the case with other partnerships, special rules are available to compute a deemed capital cost and a deemed undepreciated capital cost to the partnership in order to commence claiming capital cost allowance at the partnership level, and to claim the special deduction allowed to partners (see ¶1823.35).

(ITAR: 20)

[¶1823.35] *Determination of Capital Cost and Undepreciated Capital Cost to the Partnership and Special Deduction to the Partners — Farmers and Fishers*

The capital cost of each depreciable property to the partnership is calculated by taking the lowest of the resulting amounts when the following calculation is made for each person who was a partner on the later of June 18, 1971, or the day the partnership was created and who remained a partner until December 31, 1971:

$$\text{Actual capital cost of the depreciable property to the partner} \times \frac{100\%}{\text{Partner's percentage share of the partnership property}}$$

The deemed undepreciated capital cost of each property of the partnership is the lowest of the amounts resulting from the application of the following formula to each partner who had an interest in the property on December 31, 1971:

$$\text{Undepreciated balance of the property to the partner at December 31, 1971} \times \frac{100\%}{\text{Partner's percentage share of the partnership property}}$$

A partner is allowed to claim as a deduction the amount of the excess, if any, of his actual undepreciated balance of a property as at December 31, 1971 over his portion of the partnership's deemed undepreciated capital cost of the property. As in the case of members of other partnerships, the partner may claim this deduction fully in 1972 or it may be spread over any number of years after 1971 as the taxpayer chooses. The 10% rule does not apply to a person who became a member of a partnership engaged in farming or fishing in 1971, but after June 18, where the special deduction relates to property depreciated under the Part XVII method.

Note that these calculations must be done separately for each partner and for each piece of property. If a farming partnership had four members and 25 items of depreciable property, 200 calculations would be required (2 × 4 × 25 = 200).

ACQUISITION OR DISPOSITION OF A PARTNERSHIP INTEREST

[¶1838] WHAT IS A PARTNERSHIP INTEREST?

For most purposes of the Act, property of a partnership is considered to be owned by the partnership itself and not by the partners. Therefore, for example, gains or losses on dispositions of partnership property are calculated as though the partnership were a separate person.

A partner's total rights and obligations under the partnership agreement (which may be written or verbal) are referred to as his or her "partnership interest". A partnership interest is acquired and sold by a partner personally. A person acquires a partnership interest by becoming a member of a partnership or increasing his or her interest in the partnership. A partnership interest is considered to be disposed of when the partner withdraws from the partnership and all of the partner's rights to receive partnership property have been satisfied (¶1841), or when the partner reduces his or her interest in the partnership. Alternatively, a partnership interest can be acquired from or disposed of to a third party.

An interest in a partnership is considered capital property (except for a person who trades in partnership interests as a business), and any gain or loss on disposal of a partnership interest is taxed in the partner's hands under the capital gain provisions (see Chapter 5).

The gain or loss on sale of a partnership interest is measured by subtracting from the proceeds of disposition of the partnership interest the partner's ACB of that interest and any selling expenses or other costs relating to the disposition.

Example

Mr. Axel sold a partnership interest for $10,000. His ACB of the interest in the partnership was $6,000 and legal fees for drawing up the sale agreement amounted to $300. Mr. Axel has realized a capital gain of $3,700 and must include in his income half (¶500a) of this amount as a taxable capital gain.

(ITA: 96; 98)

[¶1838.05] *Sale to Tax-Exempt Entity or Non-Resident Person*

If you dispose of a partnership interest to a tax-exempt entity, special rules in subsection 100(1) of the Act will recapture in full the portion of proceeds of disposition that represents the gain, if any, in respect of the partnership's depreciable property. The point is to ensure recapture of inherent capital cost allowance, which cannot be recaptured from the tax exempt entity on its dispositions. Where the value of depreciable property is difficult to assign, it may be preferable to sell it in advance of the disposition to a tax exempt entity if possible; at any rate, the implications of this rule must be considered in advance.

Subsection 100(1) was extended to sales of partnership interests to non-resident persons, effective for dispositions after March 28, 2012, with grandfathering for dispositions to arm's length persons before 2013 made under a written agreement entered into before March 29, 2012. An exception is made where the partnership carries on business through a permanent establishment in Canada and at least 90% of its assets (value basis) are used in that business.

Subsection 100(1) is extended further, generally after August 14, 2012, to sales of a partnership interest to another partnership in which a tax-exempt or non-resident person has an indirect interest through one or more partnerships. There are also look-through rules that apply where the interest is acquired by a partnership and a trust resident in Canada holds the interest indirectly through one or more partnerships, and a beneficiary of the trust, either directly or indirectly through one or more partnerships, is a tax-exempt person or a trust (but only if the total fair market value of the interests of such beneficiaries exceeds 10% of the total fair market value of all interests as beneficiaries). The rules also extend the application of subsection 100(1) to sales of a partnership interest to a trust resident in Canada with a beneficiary that is exempt from tax, a partnership in which an interest is held directly or indirectly by a tax-exempt person or a trust (generally, the value of the interest must exceed 10% of the value of all interests in the partnership), or another trust if a beneficiary is a tax-exempt person or a partnership or trust (generally, the value of the interest in the other trust as beneficiary must exceed 10% of the value of all interests of beneficiaries in the trust).

(ITA: 100(1))

[¶1841] TERMINATION OF A PARTNERSHIP

For the purposes of computing capital gains or losses, an interest in a partnership is deemed to be disposed of when the partnership is terminated. Under the various laws which govern partnerships, the termination of a partnership may occur for a number of reasons, including the withdrawal or death of a partner. However, the Act provides that a partnership will not be considered terminated, and therefore a partnership interest not disposed of, until all of the partner's rights to receive partnership property have been satisfied.

Where a taxpayer withdraws from a partnership, but retains for a period of time thereafter a right to receive property of the partnership in satisfaction of his interest therein, he is described as having a residual interest in the partnership. The residual interest is deemed to be an interest in the partnership (see ¶1842 and ¶1867).

(ITA: 98; IT-242R [Archived])

[¶1842] NEGATIVE ADJUSTED COST BASE OF AN INTEREST IN A PARTNERSHIP

Generally, for the purposes of calculating capital gains, when the ACB of a capital property is a negative amount, the negative amount is considered to be a capital gain (see Chapter 5). However, if the ACB of an interest in a partnership is negative, no capital gain will arise.

The exceptions to this rule are as follows:

(1) If a partner disposes of all or part of his interest in a partnership when the ACB of the interest is a negative amount, he must report a capital gain equal to his proceeds of disposition plus the negative ACB of his interest in the partnership or the part of the interest which is sold.

(2) Where the partner's residual interest (¶1841) is satisfied in full in the partnership's fiscal year in which he withdraws, it is deemed not to have been disposed of until the end of the fiscal period of the partnership. This provision allows time for any adjustments to be made in respect of the partner's last fiscal year before the deemed disposition occurs. Where the ACB of the residual interest becomes negative at the fiscal year end of the partnership, the negative amount is deemed to be a capital gain.

(3) Where a partnership ceases to exist but all of the partnership property has not been distributed, each person who was a partner is deemed not to have ceased to be a partner and the right of each such person to share in the partnership property is deemed to be an interest in the partnership. If the ACB of such a partnership interest is a negative amount at the end of a fiscal period of the partnership, the partner will be deemed to have a capital gain in that year equal to the negative amount.

(ITA: 98; 100)

[¶1842.05] *Negative Partnership ACB of Limited Partner*

As explained above, because of its unique characteristics and numerous adjustments, the ACB of a partnership is generally exempt from the rule that a negative ACB at the end of the year results in a deemed capital gain. However, where the partnership ACB of a "limited partner" or "specified member" of a partnership (¶1842.25 and ¶1842.30) is negative at the end of a particular fiscal period of the partnership, the amount of negative ACB is a deemed capital gain and the ACB itself is reset to nil. The purpose of this exercise is to prevent the passive investor from claiming deductible losses and receiving cash distributions which exceed the amount invested. These rules will allow a partner's subsequent positive ACB at the end of a partnership fiscal period to be claimed as a capital loss (and presumably carried back to offset the gain where timing permits) to the extent of prior deemed gains.

These deemed capital gain and loss rules operate independently of the limited partnership loss restriction rules at ¶1818. Those restrictions defer the claim of partnership losses flowed out to partners. Where it is those losses that drive a partner's ACB negative, those limitations would in most cases prevent their use to offset capital gains arising from the negative ACB.

The rules will apply only where at the end of the fiscal period of the partnership you are a limited partner as defined below or a specified member of a partnership as defined below who was a specified member at all times since becoming a member.

These rules do not apply where the partner held the partnership interest on February 22, 1994, and the partnership has been carrying on an active business, or earning income from a property owned continuously on and after that date. However, the exception will cease where there is a substantial contribution of capital to or substantial increase in the indebtedness of the partnership. Added capital or debt is permitted to finance an activity carried on February 22, 1994, but not to finance a significant expansion of the activity.

Elaborate grandfathering rules will protect some partnership interests acquired up to and including December 31, 1994. The most general rule will qualify such investments made before 1995 pursuant to the terms of a prospectus, preliminary prospectus or registration statement filed before February 22, 1994 with a public authority in Canada under securities legislation and, where required by law, accepted for filing by the authority, provided the investment is expended by the partnership in accordance with the filing before 1995.

For film production deals in process before February 22, 1994, investments in the partnership before January 1, 1995 may also be protected if numerous specific conditions are met as to funding commitments or prior agreements by the producer and rapid completion of the film. Only detailed study of the rules themselves can determine whether they apply in specific cases.

Similarly, 1994 film tax shelters established after February 21, 1994, could be viable if the investments were made in 1994 and specified 1995 completion dates are met. In these circumstances, deemed capital gain may arise only where there is a negative ACB at the end of the partnership's fifth fiscal period ending after 1994.

[¶1842.10] *Exception for Professional Partnerships*

Several provinces have introduced legislation to allow professionals to carry on their practice as a limited liability partnership (LLP) if all partners agree, professional standards permit, and professional liability insurance is carried. These rules are unlike the ordinary provincial limited liability partnership laws, in that under the professional LLP rules partners remain liable for the general debts and obligations of the partnership. The benefit under the professional LLP rules is that in a claim by a client for negligence, only the assets of the partner providing advice would be available to the claimant, and not the assets of all the partners.

The Act provides that the rule taxing negative ACB of a limited liability partner will not apply where the limited liability arises from a statutory provision providing only the kinds of limitations found in professional LLP statutes. Specifically, a limited partner will not include a partner whose liability is limited by operation of a statute of Canada or a province that limits the partner's liability only for debts, obligations and liabilities of the partnership or any member arising from negligent acts or omissions, misconduct or fault committed in the course of the business. The addition of fault, effective June 21, 2001, accommodates the addition of this civil law concept in the Quebec LLP statute.

In a comfort letter dated July 11, 2003, Finance discusses the situation where an LLP operates under a general partnership limited liability law (referred to as a "full shield professional LLP") rather than under the specific laws for professional partnerships. While refusing to extend the exception to such full shield LLPs, the letter does promise to recommend that in applying the negative ACB rule to a full shield LLP, an amendment will be introduced "to provide that the ACB of a full shield professional LLP be adjusted at the end of the fiscal period of the LLP to reflect income (loss) allocations made by the LLP at that time [rather than immediately after the end as at present]. If enacted, we would anticipate that such a change would apply to allocations of income (loss) made by full shield LLPs on or after December 1, 2001." The proposed amendment was first published in draft technical amendments released on November 5, 2010 and has now been passed into law.

[¶1842.15] *Negative ACB and Timing of Partnership Income*

The CRA takes the position that ACB at the end of a fiscal period does not include income or loss for that period for fiscal periods ending after February 20, 1995 (subject to the amendments regarding full-shield professional LLPs discussed above). Rather, the adjustment is made immediately at the commencement of the next fiscal period. This change creates a particular problem in the context of negative ACBs, since even a partnership which might normally be thought active (such as a partnership offering management services to professional practices, where the members are likely to be specified members) is likely to have little capitalization and would normally pay out income during the year as it is earned. These draws can easily drive ACB negative, while the offsetting income, although realized in cash, is not recognized until the subsequent year. Several solutions have been suggested to this. One is to simply contribute capital or let income accumulate for a year without draws to get ahead of game. Another is to characterize funds taken out as advances rather than draws, although this seems to some a rather cavalier solution which will appeal primarily to the brave or the desperate. Yet another, perhaps more plausible, version of recharacterization is to have the partners (in a fully documented transaction before year end) personally assume the liabilities of the partnership for the amounts owing, which in theory amounts to a contribution of capital for these amounts. The validity of these recharacterization measures may not be beyond challenge, and they should not be tried without competent tax advice and understanding of the risk of challenge by the CRA.

Note that the CRA's position on recognition of current fiscal period income or loss is slightly softened by a willingness to modify the position pursuant to a ruling request to avoid double taxation in cases such as death and withdrawal from the partnership.

(ITTN: Nos 5 and 9; CRA Document No.: Grandfather calculation — Partnership interest — Adjusted cost base, *October 31, 1996*, CRA Document No. 9613835)

[¶1842.20] *Limited Partner's Non-Recourse Financing*

A substantial extension of these rules applies where the partnership interest of a limited partner or a specified member (both terms as defined below) is financed with non-recourse debt after September 26, 1994. (There is an exception for debt entered into pursuant to an agreement in writing entered into by the taxpayer before September 27, 1994.) The heart of this rule is actually in the adjustments to cost base, where it is now provided that for a limited partner or specified member only, ACB as described at ¶1844 is further reduced by the unpaid principal amount of any debt of the partner in respect of which recourse against the partner is limited, either absolutely or contingently, and that can reasonably be considered to have been used to acquire the property. The intent is clearly to limit tax shelter investors to deductions based on cash invested plus money borrowed and fully at risk.

This specific rule has been to some extent overtaken by the more general limited recourse debt rules applicable to "tax shelter investments", which are effective December 1, 1994 and discussed at ¶835. The general rule at ¶835 would (where its provisions come into play) in the first instance reduce the cost and therefore the ACB of the partnership interest and as a result create the same negative ACB to the extent of limited recourse financing as the specific partnership rule. The specific partnership rule adjusting ACB for limited recourse debt as it defines it only comes into play for investments not covered by the general limited recourse debt rules at ¶835. The general rule has its own grandfathering provisions (see ¶835).

[¶1842.25] *Limited Partner*

The term limited partner for purposes of these rules is virtually identical to the definition of limited partner at ¶1818 (subject to grandfathering differences discussed below). Minor discrepancies which existed for fiscal periods ending prior to December 1, 1994, seem to be matters of drafting style rather than substance. Note, however, that the negative partnership ACB rules apply also to specified members of a partnership who are not necessarily limited partners.

[¶1842.30] *Specified Member of a Partnership*

A specified member of a partnership is either a limited partner under the definition at ¶1818, or any member of a partnership who is not:

(1) actively engaged in activities of the partnership business other than financing; or

(2) carrying on a similar business outside the partnership as that carried on by the partnership

on a regular, continuous and substantial basis throughout that part of the period or year during which the business of the partnership is ordinarily carried on and during which the member is a member of the partnership. The negative ACB rules discussed above apply to a member of the partnership who was a specified member of the partnership at all times since becoming a member of the partnership.

The intention of the definition is in general to include any passive partner.

(ITA: 40(3), (3.1)– (3.19), (3.2); 53(2)(c)(i.3); 143.2; 248(1) "specified member")

[¶1843] "COST" OF A PARTNERSHIP INTEREST

Where a partnership interest has been acquired after December 31, 1971, the word "cost" has its usual meaning in that it is the value of any payment by the partner, either in cash or other consideration, to acquire his partnership interest.

If you were a member of a partnership on December 31, 1971, your determination of "cost" for tax purposes requires a special calculation. This calculation is described in ¶1848.

(ITA: 54; ITAR: 26)

[¶1843.05] *Expense Restriction*

In *Alcatel Canada Inc. v. The Queen*, 2005 DTC 387 (T.C.C.), the Tax Court ruled that a stock option benefit granted the employees of an R&D corporation constituted an R&D expenditure eligible for deduction and investment tax credit, even though the corporation had not actually laid out any expenditure in granting the options. On November 17, 2005, the Department of Finance responded with legislation to reverse that decision. Although the matter is largely a corporate one, the new legislation sweeps in partnerships or any taxpayer who contrives to issue an option or interest in itself. Effective on or after November 17, 2005, the issuance of an option does not, in itself, create any amount of an expenditure. In the case of the issuance of an interest in a taxpayer or partnership, the taxpayer's or partnership's expenditure as a result of the issuance is reduced by the amount by which the fair market value of the interest exceeds the fair market value of the consideration provided for the interest (or, in the case of certain rollovers such as subsection 97(2) (see ¶1866), the deemed cost of the consideration to the taxpayer or partnership). Although aimed at the R&D situation, the rule is a general one.

(ITA: 143.3)

[¶1844] ADJUSTED COST BASE OF PARTNERSHIP INTEREST

The ACB of a partnership interest is the measure against which capital gain or loss is determined on disposition (Chapter 5) or in some cases deemed disposition when ACB is negative (¶1842).

[¶1844.05] *Limited Recourse Financing*

For calculations of the ACB of a partner's partnership interest, there can be an initial reduction to cost before the adjustments listed below. This adjustment may apply to all the partners in any partnership in which any interest is financed in such a way that its costs to any partner exceed its short-term expectation of profit, so that it runs afoul of the limited recourse "tax shelter" rules at ¶835. The rules at ¶835, although covered in the chapter on capital cost allowance, in fact apply to reduce cost for all purposes of the Act once they come into play. The rules are especially troublesome for partnerships because any tainted partnership interest will taint all the other interests. Moreover, where a tax shelter itself invests in a partnership it can taint the partnership based solely on the projected economic return from the target partnership, without the usual shield of being able to argue that the target partnership made no tax shelter representations to it.

As discussed at ¶1842.20, limited and specified (passive) partners may be subject to ACB reductions on limited recourse financing under rules specific to those types of partnerships, although it is intended that those reductions not apply where cost is already reduced under the general rule at ¶835. See also ¶1818.

(ITA: 53(2)(c)(i.3))

[¶1844.10] *Adjustments to Arrive at ACB*

As previously described, the ACB of the interest at any time is arrived at by adding or subtracting various adjustments to the "cost" of the interest. These adjustments are:

ADDITIONS:

- The partner's share of any income of the partnership for each fiscal year ending after 1971 and before that time, excluding income allocated to a retired partner who is deemed to be a member of the partnership (see ¶1867.05). In this computation, income is calculated under the normal income tax rules except:
  - 100% instead of 50% (or the applicable percentage for the year, ¶500a) of capital gains on the disposal of partnership capital properties are included. Note that gains from the disposition of certified cultural property (¶1268) are by definition not capital gains and do not add to ACB; however, for dispositions after 2003, the exempt gain from a disposition of certified cultural property is added to the ACB of a partnership interest, unless the property is related to a tax shelter gifting arrangement. In a similar vein, the partner's share of the gains from the donations of publicly listed securities or ecological gifts to qualified donees are added to the ACB of the interest, notwithstanding that they generate nil taxable capital gains;
  - the actual amount of any income or expense relating to eligible capital property (¶766) is included, not the percentage added to (or recaptured from) the depreciation pool at ¶768;

Commentary on Bill C-29 Measures (October 25, 2016)

Note: When Bill C-29, October 25, 2016, achieves Royal Assent, the commentary will be modified to read:

- for eligible capital property prior to 2017, the actual amount of any income or expense relating to the property (¶766) is included, not the percentage added to (or recaptured from) the depreciation pool at ¶768;

  - exempt income from a new mine is included;
  - the "gross-up" of taxable dividends received from taxable Canadian corporations (¶457) is excluded;
  - royalties payable or receivable pursuant to a federal statute in respect of resource property or production (¶2223) are excluded;
  - the deduction for the cost of a basic herd of farm animals is excluded;
  - deemed fair market value rules as they apply to the trading of resources with governments (¶2223) are excluded from consideration;
  - any capital gain on farm land is computed without the increase in its ACB otherwise allowed for hobby farm losses (¶508); and
  - capital gains and losses are computed without reference to any artificial reduction in capital gains as calculated by the CRA (¶582).

- The partner's share of the proceeds of any life insurance policy received by the partnership after December 31, 1971, as a result of death of the insured, less the adjusted cost basis of the policy immediately before the death of the insured.

Commentary on Bill C-29 Measures (Oct. 25, 2016)

Note: When Bill C-29, October 25, 2016, achieves Royal Assent, the commentary will be modified to read:

- The partner's share of the proceeds of any life insurance policy received as a result of death of the insured, less the adjusted cost basis of the policy immediately before the death of the insured. This rule extends to proceeds received in respect of deaths after March 21, 2016, regardless of whether the partnership is the policyholder. One subtracts from the proceeds of disposition for these purposes the amount that the fair market value of consideration given in respect of the disposition exceeds the greater of the cash surrender value of the policy and the adjusted cost base of the interest in the policy, if the death occurs after March 21, 2016, and the disposition was after 1999 and before March 22, 2016.

- The partner's contributions of capital to the partnership after December 31, 1971. A contribution of capital does not include a loan by the partner to the partnership, or any portion of a contribution which can be considered as a benefit conferred on (read "gift to" for contributions prior to July 1, 1988) another partner who is related to the contributor by blood, marriage or adoption.

- The partner's share of any capital dividend or life insurance capital dividend received by the partnership. For an explanation of a capital dividend, see ¶415.

- The amount of any superficial loss relating to a transaction by the partner involving an interest in the partnership (¶579).

- The amount of any negative ACB which has been considered as a capital gain to the partner (¶1842).

- Amounts included in income in respect of the partnership as a result of the partner's death (other than the value of rights to future partnership income) (¶1910).

- The partner's share of proceeds on the disposition of Canadian exploration expenses, Canadian development expenses, Canadian exploration and development expenses or Canadian oil and gas property expense amounts incurred by the partnership after 1971 (see Chapter 22).

- The partner's Canadian development expenses or Canadian exploration and development expenses renounced to the partnership (¶1800). This addition offsets the automatic ACB reduction for these amounts where the taxpayer has elected not to claim the deductions.

- Non-taxable partnership income arising from the disposition of resource properties owned on December 31, 1971. This addition is only available for disposition in taxation years prior to 1980.

- The partner's share of any government assistance received after 1971 in respect of a Canadian resource property or an exploration or development expense incurred in Canada, reduced (for calculations made after January 31, 1990) by any repayments of such amounts, whenever made.

- Amounts required to be added to the ACB on a transfer of property from a partner, see ¶1866.

- For partners with a 10% or more share of income or loss at any particular time, any amount of interest or tax on vacant land or construction soft costs (¶771) denied to them for years commencing before that time.

- Where a limited or passive partner has a negative partnership ACB included in income under the rules in ¶1842, the income inclusion is added to the partner's partnership ACB to return it to zero.

- Where an election is made to have a deemed disposition of the partnership interest on February 22, 1994, no increase in partnership ACB occurs as a result because the capitalized value goes instead to the exempt capital gains balance; however, in calculating ACB to make the election, the normal addition to ACB for income is prorated for the period of the year before February 23, 1994. This limited purpose addition does not permanently affect ACB; it exists only for calculating election values.

- Where an election was made to have a deemed disposition of the partnership interest on February 22, 1994, and an exempt capital gains balance resulted, and some portion of the balance remains on hand unused at the end of 2004, that portion is added to the ACB.

- Where an election was made to have a deemed disposition of the partnership interest on February 22, 1994, and an exempt capital gains balance resulted, and there is a final disposition of the partnership interest before the exempt capital gains balance expires immediately after 2004, the unused balance is not claimed on any resulting gain but rather is added to the cost base of your partnership interest, so that if there is a final loss rather than a final gain, there is an increased capital loss.

- Where a taxpayer reimburses another person for specified non-deductible resource crown charges, resource rules provide for the transfer of those charges and associated resource allowance to the taxpayer, subject to certain adjustments which may deny elements of deduction. If the taxpayer reimbursed the partnership for such amounts that were not deductible to the taxpayer, they were added to the taxpayer's ACB of the interest, generally for fiscal periods of the partnership beginning before 2007.

- Where a partnership disposes of a foreign resource property after 2000, the partners' shares of proceeds are included in their income, and, as a result of a recent technical amendment, there is a corresponding increase in partnership ACB, retroactive to fiscal periods commencing after 2000.

DEDUCTIONS:

- The partner's share of any loss of the partnership for each fiscal period ending after 1971 and before that time, excluding however, losses allocated to a taxpayer who is deemed to be a member of a partnership (¶1867). Note that losses *allocated* must be deducted from the ACB, regardless of whether the loss is utilized by the partner at that time. Limited partnership losses (that is, the excess of loss over at-risk amount as described at ¶1818) are not subject to this rule, but are deducted from the ACB only when deducted from the partner's taxable income. In general, a partnership loss deducted from the ACB is to be calculated under the normal income tax rules except:

- 100% rather than 50% (or the applicable percentage for the year, ¶500a) of losses on capital property of the partnership are included;
- a capital loss from disposition of a debt will be included, even if it is not otherwise deductible for tax purposes (see ¶563);
- a loss on the disposition of corporate shares is computed without the loss reduction for capital dividends received by partnership (see ¶580d);

Commentary on Legislative Proposals (Sept. 16, 2016)

Note: When Legislative Proposals, September 16, 2016, achieves Royal Assent, the commentary will be modified to read:

- effective September 16, 2016, a loss from the disposition of corporate shares that are inventory is similarly computed without the stop-loss rules of subsection 112(4);

- a loss from the disposition of personal use property other than listed personal property is included;
- prior to 2017, the actual amount of any income or expense relating to eligible capital property (¶766) is included, not the percentage added to or recaptured from the depreciation pool at ¶767;
- the full amount of a restricted farm loss is included (¶1750);
- a superficial loss on capital property (¶579) is included;
- royalties payable or receivable pursuant to a federal statute in respect of resource property or production (¶2223) are excluded;
- deemed fair market value rules as they apply to the trading of resources with governments (¶2223) are excluded from consideration; and
- the previous deduction for the 25% resource allowance (see Chapter 22) is excluded.

- The partner's share of the eligible amount (¶1261) of any charitable donations made by the partnership.
- The partner's share in the eligible amount (¶1462) of political contributions that was eligible for the tax credit (¶1801).
- The partner's share of any amounts which would have been deductible by the partnership in fiscal years ending after 1971 in respect of exploration and development expenses incurred prior to 1972 if the partnership were entitled to claim a deduction for those items (see Chapter 22).
- The partner's share of any Canadian exploration expenses, Canadian development expenses, Canadian exploration and development expenses, foreign exploration and development expenses (¶2225) or Canadian oil and gas property expense amounts (¶2223) incurred by the partnership after 1971.
- The taxpayer's share of the resource-related deductions and expenses incurred in a fiscal period after the fiscal period in which he ceases to be a partner do not reduce the ACB of his partnership interest.
- The partner's drawings after December 31, 1971 of his share of the partnership's income or capital. Any expenses incurred at the partnership level that were not allowed in computing the partnership income and that were personal expenses of a partner represent payments on behalf of that partner and should be treated as drawings on account of income or capital.
- Where there has been a partial disposition of an interest in the partnership after December 31, 1971, the ACB at the time of disposition of the part so disposed of (¶1846).
- Any amount which is required to be deducted because of settlement of a debt by the partner for less than its principal amount to the extent required by regulation (¶565).
- Any grant, subsidy or other government assistance (net of repayments) received by the partner in connection with his acquisition after November 18, 1974 of the partnership interest.
- Any amount received by a retired partner or any beneficiary as payment on account of his residual interest (¶1841).
- The amount of any investment tax credit, claimed by the partner after 1981, which was allocated to the partner from the partnership.
- The amount of any share-purchase tax credit allocated to him by the partnership. This applies for the 1983 and subsequent taxation years.
- The amount of the partner's share in any scientific research tax credit of the partnership passed through to the partner in 1983 and thereafter.
- The partner's share of any refundable investment tax credit allocated to him (see ¶1464).
- The partner's share of undeducted financing costs described at ¶764 which have ceased to be deductible to the partnership by virtue of its termination.
- Where a limited or passive partner has financed the acquisition of a partnership interest or an investment in the partnership with non-recourse debt described at ¶1842, the ACB of the partner's partnership interest (which on its face would include the amount so financed) is reduced by the non-recourse debt, unless the non-recourse debt is already dealt with under the tax shelter rules at ¶835.
- Where a negative partnership ACB has been included in a partner's capital gains under the rules at ¶1842, a subsequent increase in ACB may be treated as a capital loss at the election of the partner, offsetting prior gains. Where this election is made, the loss reduces the partner's ACB.

- Only for the purpose of calculating partnership ACB in making an election to have a deemed disposition of the partnership interest on February 22, 1994, the normal reduction to ACB for current year losses is prorated for the period of the year before February 23, 1994. This limited purpose reduction does not permanently affect ACB; it exists only for calculating election values.

(ITA: 53; Tax Topics: CCH Tax Topics No. 1269, July 5, 1996; IT-353R2 [Cancelled]; ITTN: Nos 5 and 9)

[¶1845] ADMISSION OR RETIREMENT OF A PARTNER

The admission or retirement of a partner may result in an addition or deduction to the ACB of the partnership interests of the existing or continuing partners depending upon whether by partnership law, agreement, or the Act, there is a disposition of all or part of an existing partnership interest or a further acquisition by a continuing partner.

When the applicable provincial laws and partnership agreements provide for a continuation of an existing partnership on the admission of a new partner, the effect on the existing partners' ACBs will depend on whether the new partner made a direct contribution to the partnership or whether he or she purchased his or her partnership interest from one or more of the existing partners. If a new arm's length partner makes a direct contribution of capital, and there is no corresponding withdrawal by any of the other partners, there is no adjustment made to the existing ACBs, and the new partner's ACB is equivalent to the value contributed. However, where the new partner buys his or her interest from an existing partner(s), the ACB of the existing partner's partnership interest is reduced by the ACB to the partner of the part so disposed of. Where a new contribution of capital is followed by a withdrawal by one or more other partners, this may be viewed as a capital transaction with consequent cost base adjustments.

Where the old partnership terminates on admission of a new partner, rollovers provided under the Act may in effect achieve the same position.

Where a partner retires and the partnership otherwise continues with the same partners and property (other than that of the retired partner), the Act may provide for a continuation even if there is a notional termination of the partnership at law. However, if the rollover conditions are not met, there may be a disposition of all partnership interests and a rollover to a new partnership, and some tax recognitions (such as negative ACB) may be involved. For a discussion of the tax treatment to the retiring partner, see ¶1867.10.

When a capital payment equal to a retiring partner's capital account is made to a retiring partner by the partnership and the partnership continues to exist pursuant to partnership laws/agreements, there is no adjustment to the continuing partners' partnership interests. However, when the amount paid for the retiring partner's capital interest exceeds the capital account and the excess is debited to the capital accounts of the remaining partners, these partners are considered to have purchased a partnership interest from the retiring partner. Under these circumstances, since the excess that is debited to the remaining partners' capital accounts is considered to be a withdrawal from the partnership of the purchase price and would decrease the ACB of their partnership interests by an amount equal to the increase in ACB arising from interests purchased, there is no net change.

A payment made by the remaining partners to a retiring partner may include an amount of the retiring partner's share of the partnership's goodwill or other property such as work in progress whose value has been excluded from income (¶1876). The CRA views such a payment as representing an increase in the cost of the remaining partners' partnership interests and no part of the payment is considered an eligible capital expenditure (prior to 2017) or addition to the cost of other property. The total payment is considered part of the proceeds of disposition of retiring partner's partnership interest.

Certain expenses incurred by the partnership in the course of issuing interests in the partnership are deductible from partnership income. This includes commissions or fees paid to a salesman or agent; legal, accounting, audit or filing fees related to the preparation of a prospectus and registrar's or transfer agent's fees.

Where a partnership continues to allocate income or loss to a retired partner, specific provisions usually treat that allocation as income or loss of the retired partner notwithstanding that there may no longer be a partnership interest. See ¶1867.05.

Technical amendments, in general retroactive to 1995, clarify that, although a taxpayer may have ceased to be a member of a partnership before the end of the partnership's fiscal period, an amount of the income or loss of the partnership is allocable at the end of the fiscal period to the taxpayer under the partnership allocation rules. In addition, an income or loss allocation for the "stub period" during which the taxpayer was a member is included in the calculation of the ACB of the partnership interest at the time the former member disposes of the interest or a residual interest. These provisions are intended to ameliorate situations where, under the earlier provisions of the Act, a former member may have been required to report a capital gain in the year that the person left the partnership, only to be offset by a capital loss in a subsequent year. Although these changes are applicable to retirements for 1995 and later years, they are also applicable for 2003 and later years where a partner ceases to be a partner on death. A useful example is found in the Department of Finance Technical Notes of October 24, 2012 to subsection 96(1.01) of the Act, reproduced in ¶1867.10.

(ITA: 97; 98; Window on Canadian Tax: 9641; *De Lasalle v. The Queen*, 85 DTC 5613 (F.C.T.D.); *Stursberg v. The Queen*, 93 DTC 5271 (F.C.A.))

[¶1846] PARTIAL DISPOSITIONS

The Act provides that on the partial disposition of a partner's interest, the ACB of the portion of the interest which was disposed of is the portion of the total ACB of his interest immediately before the transaction that can be reasonably attributed to it.

Example

> Stewart Learner had an interest in a partnership with an ACB of $10,000. This figure was computed immediately before he sold 25% of his interest for $30,000. Stewart is considered to have realized a capital gain in the amount of $27,500 being the difference between the sale price of $30,000 and 25% of $10,000.

(ITA: 43)

[¶1848] "COST" OF A PARTNERSHIP INTEREST OWNED ON DECEMBER 31, 1971

A special formula exists for determination of the "cost" of a partnership interest where a taxpayer has been a partner continuously since December 31, 1971. In this case, the cost of his interest in the partnership is deemed to be the middle value of the three following amounts:

(1) actual cost;

(2) adjusted fair market value; and

(3) tax equity value.

The intended effect of this formula is to achieve a result similar to that arrived at for other capital properties under the "tax-free zone" rule (¶591). However, this intended effect is not always achieved.

The three values which are used in the computation of the deemed cost of a partnership interest which was owned on December 31, 1971 cannot be computed in advance of the time when you are required to know the adjusted cost base of your interest in a partnership. This is because the computation takes into account events that occur up to the time of the calculation. Each computation contains adjustments to move the amounts forward or back in time so that each of the three values is comparable. The computation must be made separately by each partner.

The CRA provides form T2065 for this computation, which is to be included with your return for the year of disposition.

(ITAR: 26)

[¶1866] PROPERTY ROLLOVERS AND PARTNERSHIP DISSOLUTION

With respect to dispositions of property between a partnership and its members, the general rule in income tax law is that these transactions are deemed to take place at the fair market value of the property involved.

However, since this could result in taxation where there was no economic exchange or realization, special rules are provided whereby, in certain circumstances, all or part of the gain can be deferred. The intent of these provisions is to permit a taxpayer to change the method in which he or she holds property, such as through a corporation, a partnership or personally, without bringing accrued gains into income at the time of transfer. However, the special rules do not apply to all situations where there is no economic realization.

In general terms, the circumstances where these special rules may apply are:

(1) Where property is transferred from a partnership to a corporation and the consideration includes shares of the corporation;

(2) Where a partnership is wound up after transferring property to a corporation as in (1);

(3) Where property is transferred to a partnership by a partner or by a person who is about to become a partner;

(4) Where property of a partnership is transferred to one of the partners who then carries on the business as a sole proprietor;

(5) Where all of the property of a partnership is distributed to the partners who then become joint owners of the property.

The following properties can be transferred using the "rollover" provisions:

- capital property;
- certain resource properties;
- eligible capital property (prior to 2017); and
- inventory.

In addition, many of the rules with respect to "rollovers" of property to a corporation apply to "rollovers" of property to partnerships. These rules determine the transferor's proceeds of disposition, the partnership's cost of the property and the cost to the transferor of property received as consideration for the transfer. These rules apply to transfers where immediately after the transfer all of the partners are Canadian residents. In general, transfers must be made for tax purposes at any value between cost and fair market value. Any partnership interest received as consideration for the transfer is deemed to constitute taxable Canadian property where the transferred property was itself taxable Canadian property. "Taxable Canadian property" is a technical expression and generally means capital property any gain on which would be taxable under the Act if it were disposed of by a non-resident. See Chapter 20.

In computing the ACB to the partner of his partnership interest immediately after a disposition of property to the partnership, the following adjustments are required:

(1) If the partner's proceeds of disposition exceed the fair market value of the consideration received (other than an interest in the partnership) this excess is added to the ACB of his or her partnership interest.

(2) If the fair market value of the consideration received (other than an interest in the partnership) exceeds the fair value of the property transferred, this difference is deducted from the ACB of the partnership interest.

The mechanics of these rules are complex and are beyond the scope of this book. It is suggested that you seek professional tax advice if you wish to use one of these special elections.

Where special election forms are required to be filed in any of the above circumstances, these forms must be filed within specified time deadlines to avoid possible penalty situations and to ensure that the desired elections are not overruled by the fair market value rules. Elections may be filed up to three years late if prescribed penalties are paid.

The Minister of National Revenue *may* accept elections after the expiry of the three-year late-filing period where in his opinion it would be just and equitable and if applicable penalties are paid.

[¶1866.05] *Stop-Loss Rules*

The stop-loss rules for transfers between "affiliated persons" are described at ¶579 and ¶852. The affiliated person rules should be consulted in any potential transaction between a partnership and someone who might be regarded as a non-arm's length person. The definition of "affiliated persons", as it relates to partnerships, is discussed at ¶852.25 through ¶852.40.

(ITA: 85; 97; 98; IT-338R2 [Cancelled]; IT-413R [Archived])

[¶1867] RETIRING AND WITHDRAWING PARTNERS

[¶1867.05] *Income Allocations to Retired Partner*

Under subsection 96(1.1) of the Act, members of a partnership whose principal activity is carrying on a business in Canada are permitted to enter into an agreement under which continuing income or losses of the partnership can be allocated to a retired partner, or to his or her spouse or common-law partner, estate, heirs, or other persons who have acquired the retired partner's rights. The person to whom such income or losses are allocated is deemed to be a member of the partnership for the purposes of the partnership income allocation rules of subsection 96(1), and he or she will include such income or loss in respect of a partnership fiscal period in the taxation year in which the fiscal period ends.

The right to a share of the income or loss of the partnership of such person is deemed not to be a capital property. If the right to receive income is disposed of, the proceeds are included in the vendor's income, offset by the vendor's cost of the right, if any. This provision gives partnerships an alternative to the use of consulting agreements, where the retiring partner continues to provide services, or annuity agreements for retired partners.

[¶1867.10] *Residual Interest of Retired Partner*

Where a taxpayer retires from or otherwise ceases to be a member of a partnership, the taxpayer is deemed to have a "residual interest" in the partnership until all of the taxpayer's rights to receive property of the partnership in satisfaction of his or her interest are satisfied in full. Until that time, the residual interest is deemed for most purposes of the Act not to have been disposed of by the taxpayer. The residual interest is deemed to be an interest in the partnership and subject to the various additions and deductions to its ACB provided in the Act. When all of the taxpayer's rights have been satisfied in full before the end of a partnership's fiscal period, the taxpayer is deemed not to have disposed of the interest until the end of the fiscal period. Furthermore, if the taxpayer has a negative ACB in the residual interest at the end of a fiscal period of the partnership, the taxpayer will have a deemed capital gain equal to the negative amount.

These rules previously could result in undesirable consequences at the end of a partnership's fiscal period, since ACB adjustments to the taxpayer's interest did not include the taxpayer's share of income up to the time at which the taxpayer ceased to be a partner ("stub period"). To alleviate this potential problem, technical amendments allow an ACB adjustment reflecting the taxpayer's share of partnership income up to the end of the stub period. The amendments are retroactive to 1995 and subsequent years, except that where the taxpayer ceased to be a partner by virtue of his or her death, in which case the amendments are effective for 2003 and subsequent years. The CRA provides the following example of the amendments (new subsection 96(1.01)) in its explanatory notes to the provisions.

Example

Ms. Brown was a partner in XYZ Partnership until June 30. The fiscal period of the partnership ends December 31. The ACB of her partnership interest on January 1 was Nil. From January to June 30 she withdrew $16,000 in capital.

Just before the end of the partnership's fiscal period, all the partners agree that Ms. Brown's share of income for the [stub] period was $20,000. On December 30 she was paid $4,000 in satisfaction of her residual interest.

In the result, Ms. Brown is allocated $20,000 income under subsection 96(1.01). The ACB of her interest immediately before she retired on June 30 was $4,000 [i.e., the $20,000 stub period income less the $16,000 of capital withdrawals]. She is deemed by paragraph 98.1(1)(*b*) to have disposed of her residual interest on December 31 for proceeds of disposition of $4,000, such that she has no capital gain or loss on the disposition.

Although the residual interest is deemed to be an interest in a partnership, the taxpayer with the interest is deemed not to be a member of the partnership except for certain purposes such as claiming the taxpayer's share of the partnership's charitable donations, and the allocation of the taxpayer's income from the partnership for the fiscal period ending after the withdrawal from the partnership (subsection 98.1(1); paragraph 96(1.01)(*a*)).

Where a taxpayer has acquired a residual interest in a partnership by virtue of the death of an individual, he or she is deemed to have acquired a right to receive partnership property and not an interest in a partnership. The cost of the right to the taxpayer is the deemed proceeds of disposition to the deceased individual of his or her interest in the partnership. Any receipts from the partnership in satisfaction of this right to receive partnership property reduce the ACB of this right. If this ACB becomes negative, the negative amount is taxed under the capital gains rules.

These rules extend to taxpayers who acquire, by virtue of the death of an individual, a partnership interest other than a residual interest if the acquiring taxpayer is not a member of the partnership and does not become a member by virtue of the acquisition.

See also ¶1845.

Where a limited or passive partner has financed the acquisition of a partnership interest or an investment in the partnership with non-recourse debt as described at ¶1842, the ACB of the partner's partnership interest (which on its face would include the amount so financed) is reduced by the non-recourse debt, unless the non-recourse debt is already dealt with under the tax shelter rules at ¶835.

There may be circumstances under which a former member of a partnership or an heir of a deceased member is required to pay an amount to the partnership to cover a deficit in the former member's equity account. A technical amendment retroactive to 1995, deems a taxpayer to have a capital loss from the payment by the taxpayer of an amount after the time of disposition of the partnership interest, if that amount would have been a capital contribution to the partnership if the taxpayer had still been a member at the time of the payment. The loss is available to the former member or to an heir who has been deemed to have acquired a right to acquire partnership property. (Generally speaking, it is intended that the capital loss will offset a previous capital gain realized by virtue of the deficit.) A useful example is found in the Department of Finance Technical Notes (dated October 24, 2012) to subsection 100(5) of the *Income Tax Act*.

(ITA: 96; 98; IT-242R [Archived])

[¶1867.15] *Provincial Allocations*

Where a share of the income of the partnership is allocated to a retired partner, the amount so allocated must be apportioned on the retired partner's return among each of the provinces in which that partnership carried on business through a permanent establishment, in accordance with the rules at ¶1440.

(IT-242R, para. 14 [Archived])

PROFESSIONAL PARTNERSHIPS

[¶1868] GENERAL RULES

Professional taxpayers, such as accountants, lawyers, engineers, doctors and dentists, cannot calculate their income for tax purposes under the "cash" basis. The cash basis method for computing income is one where only amounts actually received during the fiscal period for services rendered are included in income for the year, notwithstanding when the services were rendered or when the bills for services were issued. As far as expenses are concerned, the cash basis method takes into account only amounts actually paid during the fiscal period regardless of when the expense was incurred.

The method to be used is similar to the "accrual method" of accounting. See ¶778 to ¶781 for a further description of how this method works.

(ITA: 34)

[¶1876] WORK IN PROGRESS

In the calculation of income using the accrual method, a professional taxpayer may elect not to include in income his or her work in progress at the end of a year (¶780). If the professional business is carried on in partnership with others, a similar election may be made on behalf of the partnership. If this election is made, the election is binding for subsequent years and cannot be changed without the concurrence of the CRA.

In order to make such an election for a partnership, all of the partners must agree to it. The election is then made in the tax return by one or more of the partners who has authority to act for the partnership, and becomes binding on all of the partners.

Accountants, dentists, lawyers, Quebec notaries, medical doctors, veterinarians, or chiropractors may use this election. For other professionals (such as engineers and architects), the entire value of year-end work in progress must be inventoried for tax purposes.

The valuation of work in progress, more specifically the proper components of "cost", is the subject of ongoing review and consideration by the CRA. It is clear that direct labour cost would exclude the cost of partners' or proprietors' time, as well as non-professional staff's time, e.g., secretaries. Corporate owner's time, in the case of a professional corporation, is to be included, but bonuses to such owners may be excluded if they are determined with respect to something other than work in progress. For example, a bonus computed with respect to gross revenue would not be included as part of the cost of corporate owners' time, but if the bonus was computed in relation to the number of files worked on it would be included in the cost of corporate owners' time.

(ITA: 10; 34; IT-457R [Archived]; IT-473R [Archived])

OTHER MATTERS

[¶1880] TAX FORMS, RETURNS, AND CALCULATIONS

A partnership is not required to file an income tax return, but most partnerships must file a T5013 information return annually and must provide each partner with specified information on a T5013 slip. As discussed below, the prerequisites for filing the return were changed, effective for 2011 and subsequent years.

Where a T5013 form is not required, financial statements and tax calculations relating to the partnership must be included in the income tax return of each partner, or retained for examination if the return is filed electronically.

[¶1880.05] *Partnership Information Returns*

Regulation 229 under the Act provides that a partnership that carries on a business in Canada, or a Canadian partnership or a SIFT partnership (¶1889) must file a T5013 form for each fiscal period ending in the year. However, the CRA has a general authority to waive filing requirements, and it uses this authority to waive the general partnership filing requirement in certain cases. These have changed from time to time. Usually, the most reliable authority for a particular year is the CRA's "Guide for the Partnership Information Return (T5013 Forms)" (T4068).

Under the CRA's current policy, a partnership that carries on a business in Canada, or a Canadian partnership with Canadian or foreign operations or investments, must file the T5013 form for each fiscal period of the partnership, if

- at the end of the fiscal period,
  - the partnership has an "absolute value" of revenues plus an absolute value of expenses of more than $2 million, or has more than $5 million in assets, **or**
- at any time during the fiscal period,
  - the partnership is a tiered partnership (has another partnership as a partner or is itself a partner in another partnership),
  - the partnership has a corporation or a trust as a partner,
  - the partnership invested in flow-through shares of a principal business corporation that incurred Canadian resource expenses and renounced those expenses to the partnership, or
  - the Minister of National Revenue requests one in writing.

For the above purposes, the "absolute value" of the revenues and expenses means the sum of those amounts without regard to the negative or positive nature of those amounts. For example, a partnership with revenues of $1.5 million and expenses of $1.25 million would have an absolute value of revenues and expenses of $2.75 million ($1.5 million plus $1.25 million), and therefore would be required to file the return. The revenues and expenses details should come from the financial statements. Revenues for these purposes are revenues that have not been netted. Expenses include both current costs and the amortization of capital costs — depreciation and amortization.

In terms of the $5 million asset threshold, the CRA provides that the partnership should use the "cost figure of all assets, both tangible and intangible, without taking into account the depreciated amount".

The CRA provides an updated form T5013 and a tax guide for partnerships, Guide T4068.

Investment clubs on the modified partnership basis are now required to file a partnership return if they meet any of the above criteria.

If all of the partners are individuals, trusts, or professional corporations, the T5013 return must be filed by March 31 of the calendar year following the year in which the fiscal period ended. If the partners are all corporations, the return must be filed by five months after the end of the fiscal period. In the case of any other partnership, the return must be filed no later than five months after the end of the fiscal period, if that is earlier than the following March 31. If the partnership ends its business or investment activity, it must file any outstanding T5013 return on or before the earlier of the day that is 90 days after the date the partnership, the business, or activity ends, and the date the return is otherwise required to be filed as noted above.

The rules allow one partner designated by the partnership to file the T5013 Summary. That return is considered to be filed by all the partners.

(ITA: 220(2.1); 221; ITR: 229 Partnership Return)

[¶1880.06] *Non-Resident Member with Canadian Investment Service Providers*

As noted above, regulation 229 generally requires that every member of a partnership that carries on a business in Canada must file a partnership return. An exception from the filing requirement is provided to a member of a partnership where, because of subsection 115.2(2) of the Act (non-resident providing designated investment services), the member is considered not to be carrying on business in Canada.

[¶1880.07] *Status Indians on Reserves*

The CRA provides that where all members of a partnership are status Indians, and the partnership earns all its income at its permanent establishment on a reserve, the partnership does not have to file a partnership information return. However, if the partnership has any income earned off the reserve and the income is not exempt from tax, the partnership may have to file a return based on the criteria noted above.

[¶1880.08] *Family Farm Partnerships*

For the 2013, 2014, and 2015 fiscal periods, the CRA exempts family farm partnerships that are formed of individuals from filing the T5013 partnership information return. However, a farm partnership that includes a trust or a corporation is still required to file a T5013 return. At the time of writing, the CRA had not indicated whether the same exemption would apply to 2016 and subsequent years.

[¶1880.10] *Partnership Identification Number*

Each partnership which is not exempt must obtain a partnership identification number. The current practice is that new non-exempt partnerships simply obtain and file the T5013, and the CRA issues a partnership number on receipt of the return, typically informing the partnership in about three weeks. The partnership number should thereafter be used on all forms and in all correspondence with the CRA related to the partnership.

If the partnership needs or wants to be assigned a partnership identification number before filing its first return, it should apply to the CRA on form T5011.

[¶1880.15] *Required Forms*

For fiscal periods ending after 2010, the returns, forms, and schedules that make up the partnership information return have been revised and some new forms and schedules have been introduced. As of January 2014, the T5013 Partnership Information Return can be filed electronically.

According to the CRA (see their website), the changes and updates to the partnership information return are intended to more closely align it with the T2, Corporation Income Tax Return, to facilitate better information processing, and to take into account the new filing requirements for partnerships. The new partnership information return (T5013 forms) includes the following forms:

- T5013 FIN, Partnership Financial Return, including the various schedules;
- T5013 SUM, Summary of Partnership Income; and
- Information slip T5013, Statement of Partnership Income, which now includes information previously provided on former T5013A, Statement of Partnership Income for Tax Shelters and Renounced Resource Expenses.

Schedules relating to the T5013 FIN, Partnership Financial Return include the following:

- T5013 SCH 1, Partnership's Net Income (Loss) for Income Tax Purposes — replaces the sample format of the Reconciliation of Partnership's Net Income (Loss) for Income Tax Purposes previously located in the guide. The older version is obsolete, and the CRA will no longer accept it.
- T5013 SCH 2, Charitable Donations, Gifts, and Political Contributions.
- T5013 SCH 5, Allocation of Salaries and Wages, and Gross Revenue for Multiple Jurisdictions (Schedule 5) — This schedule provides information about salaries and wages and gross revenues when the partnership operates in multiple jurisdictions (different provinces, territories, and other countries).
- T5013 SCH 6, Summary of Dispositions of Capital Property.
- T5013 SCH 8, Capital Cost Allowance (CCA) — replaces obsolete prescribed Form T5014, which the CRA will no longer accept.
- T5013 SCH 9, List of Partnerships — The new prescribed Schedule 9 provides information about your partnership's affiliations with corporations, majority interest partners of your partnership, other partnerships, or trusts.
- T5013 SCH 10, Calculation Relating to Cumulative Eligible Capital — replaces obsolete prescribed Form T5017, which the CRA will no longer accept.
- T5013 SCH 12, Resource-Related Deductions — provides additional information about resource claims. The partnership must provide this information to the partners on their T5013 information slips.

- T5013 SCH 50, Partner's Ownership and Account Activity — replaces obsolete prescribed Form T5015, which the CRA will no longer accept.
- T5013 SCH 52, Summary Information for Partnerships that Allocated Renounced Resource Expenses to their Members — replaces obsolete prescribed Form T5016, which the CRA will no longer accept. Information for tax shelters formerly on T5016 is now included in the T5013 Summary.
- T5013 SCH 100, Balance Sheet Information — replaces part of Section C of the obsolete T5013 Summary.
- T5013 SCH 125, Income Statement Information — replaces part of Section C and Section D of the obsolete T5013 Summary.
- T5013 SCH 141, Financial Statement Notes Checklist.

The partnership information return no longer requires the following forms:

- T5013 Summary, Information Return of Partnership Income — This obsolete form is replaced by new forms T5013 FIN, Partnership Financial Return, and T5013 SUM, Summary of Partnership Income. Form T5013 FIN replaces Sections A, B, D, E, and F, and Form T5013 SUM replaces Section C of the former T5013 Summary, Information Return of Partnership Income.
- Schedules T5013 SCH 19, Non Resident Member Information, and T5013 SCH 25, Investment in Foreign Affiliates — The information requested on these two obsolete schedules is now required to be made available to the CRA on the new T5013 SCH 9, List of Partnerships, and the revised T5013 SCH 50, Partner's Ownership and Account Activity.

The filing requirements can be found on the CRA website under Businesses > Sole proprietorships and partnerships.

[¶1880.20] *Guide Available*

The CRA provides a "Guide for the Partnership Information Return (T5013 Forms)" (T4068) which is essential to filing a partnership return correctly.

You need to obtain the T5013 Forms and Schedules Package and the T5013 information slip from the CRA. They can be downloaded from the CRA website "Forms and Publications" page, or ordered by phone at 1-800-959-5525.

[¶1880.25] *Where to File*

Paper partnership returns should be filed with the following office, depending on the province:

- Partnerships served by tax services offices in Newfoundland and Labrador, Prince Edward Island, Nova Scotia, New Brunswick, Quebec, Ontario, and Nunavut: Summerside Tax Centre, 275 Pope Road, Summerside, PEI C1N 6A2; and
- Partnerships served by tax services offices in Manitoba, Saskatchewan, Alberta, Northwest Territories, British Columbia, and Yukon: Surrey Tax Centre, 9755 King George Boulevard, Surrey, BC V3T 5E1.

For electronic filing, on its website the CRA states the following (see Businesses > Sole proprietorships and partnerships > Partnership Electronic filing for T5013 > Electronic filing methods for T5013 Partnership Information Return):

My Business Account or Represent a Client

"Using tax preparation software, you can file your return in extensible markup language (XML). Electronic filing, without a web access code, for the partnership information return in XML format is available to business owners using the "File a return" service in My Business Account and to authorized representatives and employees through Represent a Client. Original and amended returns are accepted for fiscal periods ending in 2013 and later years.

If you have to file a form T661, *Scientific Research and Experimental Development (SR&ED) Expenditures Claim*, an election, or any other paper form with your return and you are filing your partnership information return electronically, unless otherwise specified, send the document(s) to your tax centre. Clearly identify your partnership's name, account number, and the applicable fiscal period end on the documents."

Internet file transfer

"Internet file transfer allows you to transmit an original or amended Form T5013-FIN, Partnership Financial Return, the related schedules, and the T5013 summary and slips with a maximum file size of 150MB. Original and amended returns are accepted for fiscal periods ending in 2013 and later years. All you need is a web browser to connect to the Internet, and your software will create, print, and save your electronic information return in XML format."

Web Forms

"Our Web Forms application is free and secure. To use it, you need access to the Internet. You can fill out an information return for the T5013 summary and slips easily with Web Forms, following the step-by-step instructions.

After you submit your information return for the T5013 summary and slips, you will receive a confirmation number that will be your proof that we received it."

[¶1880.30] *Forms Available to Partners*

The calculation of the ACB of a partnership interest is necessary for reporting any capital gain or loss when a partnership interest is disposed of (¶1838). It is also necessary to determine the deduction allowed for a reserve in respect of 1971 accounts receivable where a professional is a member of a partnership. This calculation is made separately by each partner.

You should compute your partnership income on form T2125, which provides a page with a very simple allocation reconciliation. The form is included with the booklet *T1 Tax Guide for Income from a Business or Profession*, available from CRA Tax Services Offices (¶287), and is also available on the CRA website. In general, a partnership of individuals will calculate its income under the general rules in Chapters 5, 6, 7, and 8 of this book.

[¶1880.35] *Tax Shelter Reporting*

Partnerships which are considered tax shelter investments are subject to special additional reporting requirements. The criteria for tax shelters and the filing requirements are discussed at ¶2521.

(ITA: 237.1; ITR: 231; IC 89-4 Tax shelter reporting)

[¶1881] ASSESSMENTS OF PARTNERSHIPS

The CRA has the authority to assess partnership returns and issue a determination of income or loss for the partnership as a whole, the consequences of which will be binding on the partners even if they are not personally served with the notice. The Minister has the authority to issue a determination even where the partnership is excused from filing a return under the rules at ¶1880 above.

This procedure does not relieve each partner from filing their own personal return declaring partnership income and its attached attributes; rather, it gives the CRA the right to compel all partners to take the same positions *vis-à-vis* partnership income and its attributes.

Strictly speaking, the CRA has three years from the later of the day on which the partnership return is due or is filed to issue a determination of income or loss. If no return is due because the partnership is excused from filing (see ¶1880.05), the CRA has three years from the later of the date the return would have been due had the partnership not been excused and the actual date of filing. Since there will presumably be no filing unless there is a demand, this seems to leave the determination period open forever for partnerships exempt from filing.

The determination is binding on the CRA and each partner for the purposes of calculating the partner's income, taxable income, taxable income earned in Canada, and tax or other amounts payable or refundable or paid or overpaid. A notice of objection may be filed only by one partner designated or authorized by the partnership. The usual rights of objection and appeal attach to the authorized partner, and the consequences are binding on all.

Subsection 152(1.9) provides that a designated partner of a partnership may waive, on behalf of all of the partners, the three-year time limit that applies to the CRA for making a determination. The designated member of the partnership will be the member that is designated for that purpose in the information return, or if the return is not filed, the member that is otherwise expressly authorized by the partnership to so act. The provision applies on Royal Assent, being June 29, 2012.

In the event that, following a partnership determination, a purported partner is found not to have been a partner or the partnership not to have existed, the CRA has one year from that finding to reassess the non-partner in respect of the same issues notwithstanding the usual statutory limitations on assessment periods.

The partnership assessment procedure is not mandatory, and it is not clear whether it will become standard practice. Presumably, if no determination is issued, each partner stands on its own in matters of determining income or loss, etc., from the partnership, as is the case at present.

(ITA: 152(1.4)– (1.8); 165(1.15))

[¶1882] BECOMING A NON-RESIDENT

A partner becoming a non-resident will continue to have partnership income from carrying on a business in Canada, and may have to continue filing a Canadian tax return. However, many problems that used to plague the departing Canadian partner in the year of departure have been resolved by changes effective for 1992 and later years. As a result of these changes, the departing partner does become a non-resident on departure, and is no longer deemed to continue Canadian residence until the end of the departure year by virtue of the Canadian partnership interest. On the other hand, a departing partner may cause problems for the partnership if it endeavours to use the rollover rules on dissolution, since the partnership is not a Canadian partnership if it has a non-resident partner.

(ITA: 2; 98; 114)

[¶1885] DEALINGS WITH NON-RESIDENTS

Partnerships are considered reporting entities for purposes of filing:

- Form T1134, if the partnership has a foreign affiliate at any time in the year; where there are related corporate partners, only the lowest tier Canadian corporation has to file, but each partner with a direct equity percentage in the foreign affiliate must also file; see ¶493 and ¶495.
- Form T1135, where the partnership holds more than $100,000 of non-business foreign property, provided the income or loss of non-resident partners is less than 90% of the partnership income or loss for the fiscal period; if income is nil, the allocation must be made as if there were $1 million income; see also ¶496.
- Form T1142, where the partnership has received a distribution in the year from, or had a debt at any time in the year to, a non-resident trust in which it had a beneficial interest at any time in the year, provided that income or loss of non-resident partners is less than 90% of the partnership income or loss for the fiscal period; if income is nil, the allocation must be made as if there were $1 million income.

Where a partnership is liable to file these forms, its fiscal period is treated as if it were a taxation year. The filing deadline for form T1134 is 15 months after the end of that year, and the late-filing penalties discussed at ¶495 apply based on that deadline. The filing deadline for form T1142 is the filing deadline for form T5013 (¶1880), whether or not form T5013 is itself required. That is to say, the T1142 return must be filed by March 31 of the calendar year following the year in which the fiscal period ended. If there are any partners other than individuals (e.g., trusts, corporations, or other partnerships) the return must be filed no later than five months after the end of the fiscal period, if that is earlier than the following March 31. Late-filing penalties discussed at ¶496 will be based on that filing due date.

Form T1141, "Information Return in Respect of Transfers or Loans to a Non-Resident Trust", is not filed by partnerships but any such distribution or loan is considered to have been made by each member of the partnership, so that the determination of filing liability under ¶496 must be made by each partner; note that an election can be made to have one partner file for all; such an election must be in writing and each partner will be liable for any penalties which arise from late filing, errors and omissions.

(ITA: 233.2–233.7)

[¶1885.05] *Transfer Pricing Returns (Form T106)*

The requirement to file the transfer pricing form T106 applies to corporations, individuals and partnerships engaged in certain transactions with non-residents. Every partnership which has a Canadian resident partner or carries on a business in Canada in a fiscal period will be required to file the return in respect of each non-resident person with whom the partnership, or any partner, does not deal at arm's length in the fiscal period. For a year in which the partnership has no resident partners, it may nevertheless be required to file in respect of a series of transactions of the year or a prior year if it carried on business in Canada in a preceding year.

There is a $1 million *de minimis* exception which excuses a partnership from filing if the total fair market value of the property and services involved in reportable transactions with all non-arm's length non-residents (and partnerships of which non-arm's length non-residents are members) does not exceed $1 million. That is, no filing is required so long as the aggregate of all reportable transactions with all related non-residents is $1 million or less.

Once the $1 million threshold is met, the rules seem to contemplate a separate T106 filing for each non-resident with which there are reportable transactions.

The filing deadline for this return is the same as for form T5013, whether or not T5013 is also required; see ¶1880.

Whether or not form T106 is required, transactions with non-residents are subject to penalties where arm's length pricing standards are not only observed but documented at the time of the transaction. See the discussion at ¶796.

The purpose and parameters of this return are discussed in more detail at a partnership the partnership interests in which are, at that time, listed on a prescribed stock exchange in Canada if, at that time, the partnership carries on a business in Canada or is a Canadian partnership.

(ITA: 227; 233.1)

[¶1888] REPORTING BY PUBLIC PARTNERSHIPS

For fiscal periods of "public partnerships", additional information reporting requirements apply.

A public partnership is defined to be a partnership the partnership interests in which are listed on a designated stock exchange in Canada if the partnership carries on a business in Canada or is a Canadian partnership. The concept is obviously related to, though does not completely overlap with, the SIFT partnership concept discussed at ¶1889.

The purpose of separate filing requirements is to ensure the disclosure by publicly traded trusts and partnerships of information enabling investment managers to prepare the tax information slips that they are required to issue to investors. Disclosure is made through posting the required information on the website for CDS Innovations Inc. (a subsidiary of the Canadian Depository for Securities Limited), a website that is designed to provide this type of information to investment managers. The partnership is also required to inform the CRA in writing when a posting is made.

Regulations require publicly traded trusts and partnerships to disclose information concerning distributions and allocations of income and capital made in respect of each of their units. In general, the disclosure must be made on or before the day that is the earlier of (i) 60 days after the end of the calendar year in which the partnership fiscal period ends, or (ii) four months after the end of the fiscal period. An overriding rule requires "public investment partnerships" to make the disclosures on or before the day that is 67 days after the end of the calendar year to which the information relates. Public investment partnerships are public partnerships all or substantially all of the fair market value of which is attributable to investments in other publicly traded trusts, partnerships, or corporations.

Investment managers are expected to use this information to prepare the information slips that are required to be issued to their investors within 90 days of the end of the year. The taxation year and fiscal period of publicly traded trusts and partnerships normally end on December 31 of each calendar year. In the case of publicly traded trusts, a December 15 year end can be used upon election.

(ITA: 221(1)(*d.2*); ITR: 229.1 Definitions)

[¶1889] SIFT PARTNERSHIPS

A new tax regime, applicable to publicly traded income trusts and public partnerships, took effect from October 31, 2006. In respect of the latter, tax is imposed under Part IX.1 on the taxable non-portfolio earnings of a SIFT partnership (being a specified investment flow-through partnership) at a rate that approximates the general corporate tax rate. The Part IX.1 tax is imposed at the partnership level and is meant to parallel the general corporate tax payable by public corporations. The amount of the partnership's taxable non-portfolio earnings, net of the Part IX.1 tax, is deemed to be a taxable dividend received by the partnership and is flowed out to the partners under the regular partnership rules in subsection 96(1). As a result, a SIFT partnership and its partners are taxed, in respect of the partnership's taxable non-portfolio earnings, in a manner that replicates the taxation of a public corporation and its shareholders on its income that is distributed as taxable dividends.

The provisions of Part IX.1 came into force on October 31, 2006. However, owing to the application of the definition of SIFT partnership, the earliest the Part IX.1 tax can apply is to a partnership's taxation year ending after 2006. (The taxation year of a SIFT partnership is its fiscal period.) Furthermore, owing to grandfathering rules that apply to partnerships that otherwise would have been considered SIFT partnerships on October 31, 2006 (had the definition been applicable on that date), the Part IX.1 tax cannot apply to such partnerships until the 2011 taxation year, provided they do not exceed certain "normal growth" guidelines issued by the Department of Finance and reproduced in the commentary below.

A SIFT partnership for a taxation year is defined in subsection 197(1) as a partnership that meets the following conditions at any time during the taxation year (the partnership's fiscal period):

(1) the partnership is a "Canadian resident partnership", which is defined as a Canadian partnership, a partnership that would, if it were a corporation, be resident in Canada (including a partnership whose central management and control is located in Canada), or a partnership that was formed under the laws of a province;

(2) investments in the partnership are listed or traded on a stock exchange or other public market; and

(3) the partnership holds one or more non-portfolio properties.

An investment for these purposes is defined in subsection 122.1(1) to mean a "security" in the partnership (security is defined broadly to mean any right, whether absolute or contingent, to receive any of the capital, revenue, or income of the partnership, or interest payable by the partnership); a liability of the partnership; an interest as a member of the partnership; and any right to acquire any such right or interest or liability. Furthermore, "investment" is defined to also mean a right that may reasonably be considered to replicate a return on, or the value of, a security of the partnership, such that a derivative instrument that is listed or traded on a stock exchange or public market may result in the partnership being a SIFT partnership, notwithstanding that other interests or securities in the partnership are not so listed or traded.

A "public market" is defined in subsection 122.1(1), and its definition encompasses trading systems beyond stock exchanges that are prescribed for purposes of the Act. A public market includes any trading system or organized quotation facility on which securities that are qualified for public distribution are listed or traded, and will include, therefore, an organized quotation system that supports over-the-counter trading. Specifically excluded from the definition of "public market" is any facility that is operated solely to carry out the issuance of a security or its redemption, acquisition, or cancellation by its issuer.

"Non-portfolio property" of a partnership, which is defined in subsection 122.1(1), is:

- a security in a subject entity if the partnership owns securities in the subject entity that have a total fair market value that is greater than 10% of the subject entity's equity value (a "subject entity" generally means a Canadian-resident corporation or trust, a Canadian-resident partnership, or a non-resident corporation or trust or a partnership other than a Canadian-resident partnership if its principal source of income is in Canada; a security for these purposes is defined in the manner discussed above; an entity's equity value is the total fair market value of all of the issued and outstanding shares or interests in the entity);
- a security of a subject entity if the partnership holds securities of the subject entity or its affiliated subject entities that have a total fair market value that is greater than 50% of the partnership's equity value;
- Canadian real, immovable or resource property, which includes Canadian resource property, timber resource property, real property situated in Canada, or a share in a corporation or interest in a trust or partnership if the value of the share or interest is derived principally from any such properties, if the total fair market value of the Canadian real, immovable, or resource property held by the partnership is greater than 50% of the partnership's equity value; or
- property used by the partnership or a non-arm's length person or partnership in the course of carrying on a business in Canada.

Specifically excluded from the definition of SIFT partnership for a taxation year is an "excluded subsidiary entity" for a taxation year. An excluded subsidiary entity, in terms of a partnership, is a partnership none of the equity of which is at any time in the taxation year (a) listed or traded on a stock exchange or other public market; nor (b) held by any person or partnership other than a real estate investment trust, a taxable Canadian corporation, a SIFT trust, a SIFT partnership, or another excluded subsidiary entity for the taxation year. For these purposes, "equity" generally means an interest as a member of the partnership; and a liability of the partnership if the liability is convertible into, or exchangeable for, equity of the partnership or another entity, or an amount paid or payable under the liability is contingent or dependent upon the use of, or production from, property, or is computed by reference to revenue, profit, cash flow, commodity price, or any other similar criterion. The definition "excluded subsidiary entity" was amended to expand the range of qualifying interest holders in such an entity. The expanded list would include a person or partnership that does not have any security or right, in the entity, that is, or includes a right to acquire, directly or indirectly either any security of any entity that is listed or traded on a stock exchange or other public market, or any property the amount, or fair market value, of which is determined primarily by reference to any security that is listed or traded on a stock exchange or other public market. This amendment is deemed to have come into force on October 31, 2006. However, an entity that would, only because of this amendment, be an excluded subsidiary entity for a taxation year that begins on or before July 20, 2011, is able to elect to have this change apply to it only for taxation years that begin after July 20, 2011.

The same amendments take aim at certain "stapled securities" of an entity that is a trust, corporation, or partnership, if one or more of the stapled securities is listed or traded on a stock exchange or other public market and either the stapled securities are both issued by the entity, one of the stapled securities is issued by the entity and the other by a subsidiary of the entity, or one of the stapled securities is issued by a REIT (real estate investment trust) or the subsidiary of a REIT. Apparently, some trusts, partnerships, and corporations introduced these stapled security structures into their capital structures, which provided tax advantages similar to those associated with earlier income trust structures, that is, prior to the introduction of the new SIFT rules. Under the amendments, interest that is paid or payable on the debt portion of such a stapled security is not deductible in computing the income of the payer for income tax purposes. In the case of such structures involving REITs and another entity, any amount that is paid or payable by the other entity (or its subsidiaries) to the REIT (or its subsidiaries, and including "back-to-back" intermediary arrangements) is not deductible in computing the income of the payer for income tax purposes. These amendments apply to an entity in respect of an amount that is paid or becomes payable on or after July 20, 2011, with some grandfathering relief if stapled securities of the entity were issued and outstanding on the day immediately before that day.

As noted, the Part IX.1 tax is imposed on the taxable non-portfolio earnings of a partnership that is a SIFT partnership for a taxation year. The taxation year of a SIFT partnership for these purposes is its fiscal period (paragraph 249(1)(*a*)).

The amount of Part IX.1 tax is meant to approximately equal the combined federal and provincial general corporate tax that applies to a public corporation. In particular, the tax rate equals the "net corporate income tax rate" in respect of the SIFT partnership for the year, which equals the general corporate rate under subsection 123(1) net of the general rate reduction under section 123.4 and the provincial abatement, plus the "provincial SIFT tax rate" for the year. The provincial SIFT tax rate was originally 13%, meant to be an approximate average of all provincial general corporate tax rates. However, beginning in 2009, the provincial SIFT tax rate reflects the actual general corporate tax rate for the relevant province (or provinces, if the partnership has a permanent establishment in more than one province), and is the amount of the tax rate prescribed under regulation 414(3). Although the new provincial SIFT tax rate applies beginning in 2009, a SIFT partnership can elect to have it apply to 2007 and 2008 in its 2007 Part IX.1 return or to 2008 in its 2008 return.

A SIFT partnership's "taxable non-portfolio earnings" for a taxation year are defined (in subsection 197(1)) as the lesser of:

(1) the amount that would, if the SIFT partnership were a taxpayer for the purposes of Part I, be its income for the year as determined under section 3 of the Act (but without regard to paragraph 96(1)(*d*)); and

(2) the partnership's non-portfolio earnings for the year.

The "non-portfolio earnings" of a SIFT partnership for a taxation year are defined (in subsection 197(1)) to mean the total of:

(1) the SIFT partnership's income from a business it carries on in Canada and its income from a non-portfolio property in the year other than taxable dividends, net of losses from any business it carries on in Canada and from its non-portfolio property in the year; and

(2) its taxable capital gains in excess of allowable capital losses from its dispositions of non-portfolio property in the year.

If Part IX.1 tax is payable by a SIFT partnership in a taxation year, subsection 96(1.11) provides that the partnership is deemed to have received a taxable dividend in the year from a taxable Canadian corporation equal to the amount by which the partnership's taxable non-portfolio earnings for the year exceeds the partnership's Part IX.1 tax payable for the year. In other words, the partnership's taxable non-portfolio earnings, net of the Part IX.1 tax, are treated as a deemed taxable dividend, which is included in the Part I income of the partners pursuant to the general partnership rules of subsection 96(1). The dividend is considered an "eligible dividend", such that individual partners are eligible for the enhanced dividend tax credit.

If the Part IX.1 tax is payable by a SIFT partnership in a taxation year, every member of the partnership is required to file a return in prescribed form containing an estimate of the Part IX.1 tax payable for the year. However, if a member of the partnership who has authority to act for the partnership files the return, each other member is deemed to have filed the return such that only the first such return needs to be filed. The return is required to be filed and the Part IX.1 tax is required to be paid on or before the day on which the partnership information return is required to be filed under section 229 of the Income Tax Regulations (see ¶1880.05).

In terms of tax instalments, SIFTs have been subject to the rules that apply to individuals. However, in the Department of Finance News Release 2011-058, dated July 20, 2011, it was announced that SIFTs will be subject to the same monthly instalment rules that apply to public corporations. This amendment applies to taxation years that begin after July 20, 2011.

Grandfathered SIFT partnerships

As noted, although the new SIFT tax applies after 2006, for partnerships that otherwise would have been considered SIFT partnerships on October 31, 2006 (had the definition been applicable on that date), the definition does not apply to a taxation year that ends before the earlier of 2011 and the first day after December 15, 2006 on which the partnership exceeds the "normal growth" guidelines issued by the Department of Finance on December 15, 2006, as amended from time to time. As such, if such a partnership does not exceed these normal growth guidelines, the partnership will not be considered a SIFT partnership before its 2011 taxation year.

The guidelines issued by the Department are reproduced below. Also reproduced immediately following the guidelines is an extract from the February 25, 2009 Explanatory Notes relating to Bill C-10, *Budget Implementation Act, 2009*, S.C. 2009, c. 2. Although there was no amendment to subsection 122.1(2), the Department of Finance has used this explanatory note to provide notification that the normal growth guidelines described in News Release No. 2006-082 have been revised.

Department of Finance News Release No. 2006-082, released December 15, 2006, explaining the "normal growth" condition of deferral for the Distribution Tax mentioned in the Tax Fairness Plan of October 31, 2006, relating to income trusts:

> Following the close of financial markets today, the Department of Finance provided further guidance on "normal growth" in respect of the tax measures announced on October 31, 2006 regarding income trusts and other flow-through entities.
>
> On October 31, 2006, the Minister of Finance, the Honourable Jim Flaherty, announced a Tax Fairness Plan. The Plan includes a Distribution Tax on certain amounts distributed by a "specified investment flow-through" (SIFT) trust or SIFT partnership. This new tax applies as of 2007 to new entities, but is deferred until 2011 for SIFTs that were publicly traded as of October 31, 2006.
>
> The deferred application of these measures is, however, conditional on existing SIFTs respecting the policy objectives of the proposals. Materials released with the Minister's announcement indicated that, for example, the undue expansion of an existing SIFT might cause the deferral to be rescinded. On the other hand, the continuation of the normal growth of a SIFT would not raise concerns.
>
> This document provides existing SIFTs with more detail as to what is meant by "normal growth" in this context. The Department's guidance has been prepared following consultations with many publicly-traded trusts and partnerships, and is based on its observations as to the range of growth arising in the normal course of business.
>
> Specifically, the Department will not recommend any change to the 2011 date in respect of any SIFT whose equity capital grows as a result of issuances of new equity, in any of the intervening periods described below, by an amount that does not exceed the greater of $50 million and an objective "safe harbour" described below.
>
> The safe harbour amount will be measured by reference to a SIFT's market capitalization as of the end of trading on October 31, 2006. Market capitalization is to be measured in terms of the value of a SIFT's issued and outstanding publicly-traded units. For this purpose, it would not include debt (whether or not that debt carried a conversion right or was itself publicly-traded), options or other interests that were convertible into units of the SIFT.
>
> For the period from November 1, 2006 to the end of 2007, a SIFT's safe harbour will be 40 percent of that October 31, 2006 benchmark. A SIFT's safe harbour for each of the 2008 through 2010 calendar years will be 20 percent of that benchmark, together allowing growth of up to 100 percent over the four-year transition period.
>
> The following are additional details of the Department's approach:
>
> - The annual safe harbour amounts are cumulative: for example, a SIFT that issues no new equity in 2007 will as a result enjoy a greater safe harbour amount in 2008. The $50 million amounts, in contrast, are not cumulative.
> - New equity for these purposes includes units and debt that is convertible into units; if attempts are made to develop other such substitutes for equity, those may be included as well.
> - Replacing debt that was outstanding as of October 31, 2006 with new equity, whether through a debenture conversion or otherwise, will not be considered growth for these purposes. New, non-convertible debt can also be issued without affecting the safe harbour;

however, the replacement of that new debt with equity will be counted as growth.

- An issuance by a SIFT of new equity will not be considered growth to the extent that the issuance is made in satisfaction of the exercise by another person or partnership of a right in place on October 31, 2006 to exchange an interest in a partnership, or a share of a corporation, into that new equity.
- The merger of two or more SIFTs each of which was publicly-traded on October 31, 2006, or a reorganization of such a SIFT, will not be considered growth to the extent that there is no net addition to equity as a result of the merger or reorganization.

Consistent with the objectives of Tax Fairness Plan, the Department of Finance will monitor developments in the market and will take action accordingly to ensure that this guidance is respected.

Extract from the February 25, 2009 Explanatory Notes relating to Bill C-10, *Budget Implementation Act, 2009*, S.C. 2009, c. 2.

Subsection 122.1(2) of the Act limits the application of the definition "SIFT trust" in subsection (1) for the 2007 to 2010 taxation years. Where a trust (in this commentary referred to as a "transitional SIFT") would, under the text of that definition, be a SIFT trust on October 31, 2006, subsection 122.1(2) provides that the SIFT trust definition will not apply until the earlier of the trust's 2011 taxation year or the taxation year in which the trust exceeds its normal growth (as determined by guidelines issued by the Department of Finance on December 15, 2006), unless that excess arose as a result of a prescribed transaction.

For this purpose, the normal growth guidelines set the maximum growth from November 2006 to December 2010. Specifically, during each of the staging periods described below the maximum growth is the greater of $50 million and a safe harbour amount. That safe harbour amount is measured with respect to the transitional SIFT's market capitalization on October 31, 2006 and is staged as follows: 40% for Nov 2006–Dec 2007; 20% for 2008; 20% for 2009; and 20% for 2010. These percentages are cumulative (in contrast, the $50 million "*de minimis*" amounts cannot be carried forward from one staging period to the next) such that a transitional SIFT will have been able to issue, as of January 2010, new equity of up to 100% of its October 31, 2006 market capitalization.

This note is included to serve as notification that the Department's normal growth guidelines are revised, effective December 4, 2008.

The first revision applies to certain situations involving a transitional SIFT, units of which are publicly traded, that holds securities in another transitional SIFT (whether a trust or partnership and referred to in this commentary as the "second transitional SIFT") the units of which are not publicly traded. If the transitional SIFT's securities in the second transitional SIFT are non-portfolio property of the transitional SIFT (determined for purposes of this revision to the guidelines as through the definition "non-portfolio property" in subsection 122.1(1) of the Act were read without reference to its paragraphs (*b*) and (*c*) and as though a reference to "10%" in its paragraph (*a*) were a reference to "25%"), then new equity issued by the second transitional SIFT will count towards the growth of the transitional SIFT and not the second transitional SIFT, provided both of two conditions are met. Those conditions are:

- that the new equity is convertible into the equity of the transitional SIFT; and
- that the new equity can reasonably be regarded to be funded by the issuance of new equity in the transitional SIFT.

This revision of the normal growth guidelines is intended to prevent, in the particular circumstances described, an inappropriate duplication of growth as between the transitional SIFT and the second transitional SIFT where there is a sufficient level of non-arm's length relations between the two entities.

The normal growth guidelines are also being revised to accelerate the remaining growth room for transitional SIFTs by making the safe harbour, and the $50M *de minimis* amounts, for each of 2009 and 2010 available on and after December 4, 2008. This change does not affect the maximum available growth of a transitional SIFT, but allows it to use all of its remaining growth room in a single year, rather than staging it (i.e., at the greater of 20% and $50M per year) over the 2009 and 2010 years. In effect, the revision preserves the original 2008 staging period, and combines the 2009 and 2010 staging periods into a single period that starts on December 4, 2008.

The following three examples illustrate the application of this second revision to the normal growth guidelines.

Example 1

SIFT A is a transitional SIFT with a $2 billion October 31, 2006 market capitalization. For the period from November 1, 2006 to December 3, 2008, SIFT A's only issuance of new equity was on July 23, 2008 in the amount of $1.2 billion (60% of its benchmark market capitalization). The revised guidelines allow SIFT A to issue as of December 4, 2008 up to $800 million (i.e., the greater of 40% of its October 31, 2006 market capitalization and $100 million) in additional new equity during the remaining transition period. Because SIFT A had already maximized its growth limits for the original 2008 staging period, the revisions apply only to combine its 2009 and 2010 staging periods into a single period that starts on December 4, 2008.

Example 2

SIFT B is a transitional SIFT with a $90 million October 31, 2006 market capitalization. For the period from November 1, 2006 to December 3, 2008, SIFT B issued no new equity. The revised guidelines allow SIFT B to issue as of December 4, 2008 up to $150 million (i.e., the greater of 100% of its October 31, 2006 market capitalization and the total of its unused 2008, 2009 and 2010 *de minimis* amounts, being $150 million) in additional new equity in 2008. In effect, SIFT B has available to it both its $50 million growth from its original 2008 staging period, as well as the $100 million in growth from its combined 2009 and 2010 staging periods that starts on December 4, 2008. If SIFT B issues no new equity in 2008 (i.e., in the period from December 4 to December 31, 2008), the revised guidelines allow SIFT B to issue after 2008 up to $100 million (i.e., the greater of 100% of its October 31, 2006 market capitalization and the total of its unused 2009 and 2010 *de minimis* amounts, being $100 million) in additional new equity.

Example 3

SIFT C is a transitional SIFT with a $2 billion October 31, 2006 market capitalization. For the period from November 1, 2006 to December 3, 2008, SIFT C's only issuances of new equity were on October 1, 2007 in the amount of $200 million and on September 1, 2008 in the amount of $300 million. The revised guidelines allow SIFT C to issue as of December 4, 2008 up to $1.5 billion (i.e., the greater of 75% of its October 31, 2006 market capitalization and $100 million) in additional new equity during the remaining transition period. If SIFT C issued $1.5 billion of new equity on December 22, 2008 it will have maximized its available growth room and the issuance by it of additional new equity before 2011 will cause it to lose its status as a transitional SIFT.

Rollover on reorganization of SIFT partnership into corporate form

Special rules allow a tax-free rollover for taxpayers holding interests in a SIFT partnership that are disposed of to a taxable Canadian corporation in exchange for shares of a class in the corporation (subsections 85.1(7) and (8)). The new rules, generally applicable to dispositions occurring after July, 2008 and before 2013, are meant to facilitate the "reorganization" of a SIFT partnership into a corporate form. Where the rules apply, the taxpayer's proceeds of disposition of the partnership interest (or unit) and the cost of the taxpayer's share received on the disposition are deemed to be equal to the taxpayer's cost amount of the interest immediately before the disposition.

(ITA: 96(1.11); 122.1; 197)

Chapter 19

Final Returns of Deceased Taxpayers

THESE POINTS ARE COVERED IN THIS CHAPTER

CRA REFERENCES RELATING TO THIS CHAPTER

T1 Lines and Schedules

- Line 130 — Other income
- Schedule 1, Line 300 — Basic personal amount
- Schedule 1, Line 301 — Age amount
- Schedule 1, Line 303 — Spouse or common-law partner amount
- Schedule 1, Line 305 — Amount for an eligible dependant
- Schedule 1, Line 306 — Amount for infirm dependants age 18 or older
- Schedule 8, Line 448 — Canada Pension Plan Contributions

CRA Guides

RC4111, "Canada Revenue Agency — What to Do Following a Death"; **RC4177**, "Death of an RRSP Annuitant"; **RC4178**, "Death of a RRIF Annuitant";

T4011, "Preparing Returns for Deceased Persons"; **T4013**, "T3 Trust Guide"; **T4040**, "RRSPs and Other Registered Plans for Retirement"; **T4079**, "T4RSP and T4RIF Guide"

CRA Forms

RC4111, "What to Do Following a Death — Request for the CRA to Update Records"; **T1A**, "Request for Loss Carryback"; **T4RIF**, "Statement of Income from a Registered Retirement Income Fund"; **T4RSP**, "Statement of Registered Retirements Savings Plan Income"; **T1090**, "Death of a RRIF Annuitant — Designated Benefit"; **T2019**, "Death of an RRSP Annuitant — Refund of Premiums or Joint Designation on the Death of a PRPP Member"; **T2069**, "Election in Respect of Amounts Not Deductible as Reserves for the Year of Death"; **T2075**, "Election to Defer Payment of Income Tax, Under Subsection 159(5) of the *Income Tax Act* by a Deceased Taxpayer's Legal Representative or Trustee"; **T2204**, "Employee Overpayment of Employment Insurance Premiums"

Income Tax Folios

S1-F1-C1, "Medical Expense Tax Credit"; **S1-F1-C2**, "Disability Tax Credit" (updated June 21 and July 20, 2016); **S1-F1-C3**, "Disability Supports Deduction" (updated January 20, 2016)

Interpretation Bulletins

IT-125R4, "Dispositions of Resource Properties"; **IT-210R2**, "Income of Deceased Persons — Periodic Payments and Investment Tax Credit"; **IT-212R3**, "Income of Deceased Persons — Rights or Things"; **IT-278R2**, "Death of a Partner or of a Retired Partner"; **IT-305R4**, "Testamentary Spouse Trusts"; **IT-307R4**, "Spousal or Common-Law Partner Registered Retirement Savings Plans"; **IT-313R2**, "Eligible Capital Property — Rules Where a Taxpayer Has Ceased Carrying on a Business or Has Died"; **IT-326R3**, "Returns of Deceased Persons as 'Another Person'"; **IT-349R3**, "Intergenerational Transfers of Farm Property on Death"; **IT-500R**, "Registered Retirement Savings Plans — Death of an Annuitant"

WHAT YOU SHOULD KNOW ABOUT TAX IMPLICATIONS OF DEATH

RECENT CHANGES

Effective for deaths occurring after 2015, new charitable donation rules provide more flexibility relative to the former rules. See ¶1931.

Draft legislation released on September 16, 2016 proposes an amendment to the taxation of unexercised employee stock options held at the time of death. See ¶1925.

Bill C-29 was introduced on October 25, 2016. In this bill, effective January 1, 2017, the eligible capital property rules have been repealed and replaced by a new Class 14.1 of depreciable property. Property that previously was eligible capital property is now depreciable capital property and expenditures and receipts that previously were accounted for under the eligible capital property rules are now accounted for under the rules for depreciable property and capital property.

RETURNS AND PAYMENT OF TAX

[¶1901] RETURNS

The death of a taxpayer may involve the filing of more than one tax return. The following returns may be required:

(1) Prior year returns: Returns which were required but not filed for any earlier year (and are in effect overdue) should be filed as promptly as possible to avoid continuing interest on unpaid amounts; however, returns for a taxation year where death occurred in the period commencing November 1 and ending either April 30 or, if the deceased would have qualified for the extension for the self-employed and their spouses or common-law partners, June 15, are due on the later of six months after the date of death and the April 30 or June 15 date otherwise applicable. Note that the payment date (as opposed to the return filing date) operates under a different rule and can be earlier (as discussed below). If the deceased person had filed a return for the year (as might have happened if death occurred in, say, the following April) the legal representative still has up to six months from the date of death to refile as of right. Essentially, these rules provide an extension for the year of death return where death occurs in November or December, and an extension of the prior year return where death occurs in a year and before the filing deadline for the prior year. Payment dates and filing dates are not the same, and where death occurs in November or December, the payment date is six months following the date of death regardless of the (June 15) filing deadline; similarly, where death occurs in January to April inclusive (but not to June 15), the payment deadline for the prior year return is six months after the date of death.

(2) A return for the period from January 1 of the year of death to the date of death ("final return" or "terminal return") must be filed by the later of six months after the date of death and the normal filing date for the deceased for the year of death (normally April 30 of the year following death, but June 15 if the deceased or a "cohabiting spouse or common-law partner" of the deceased had business income for the year of death; a cohabiting spouse or common-law partner has the meaning given in ¶1498; essentially here this means a

spouse or common-law partner unless separated throughout the year). Notwithstanding the filing deadline, the payment date normally remains April 30 of the year following the year of death, except that under rule (1), above, where death occurs in November or December the payment date for the final return is six months after the date of death (and not June 15 if June 15 is later). Where there is a spouse (or common-law partner) trust which is "tainted" by a requirement for payment of debts of the deceased out of trust property (see ¶1922), there is provision for an extension to 18 months after the date of death.

(3) Where a taxpayer had rights or things (see ¶1908) at the time of death, the value of which would be included in his income for the year of death, the representative of the deceased taxpayer may elect to file a separate return for the value of the rights or things owned by the decedent at the time of death. This return must be filed by the later of:

(a) one year from the date of death; or

(b) 90 days after the assessment date of the ordinary return for the year of death.

(4) If a taxpayer died after the close of the fiscal period of his or her proprietorship or partnership business and before the end of the calendar year in which that fiscal period of the business closed (and had income in that period from the business), the representative may file, within the deadlines in (2) above, that is, by the later of six months after death or June 15 of the year following death, a separate T1 return which includes the business income of the stub period. If the deceased taxpayer was carrying forward a transitional reserve, the legal representative may elect to claim a reserve in the ordinary year of death return and recognize the income (with no further reserve) on this separate return (see ¶1910), even though there is no stub period. If this election is made, the separate return is mandatory. As well, where the taxpayer is operating on the non-calendar year "alternative method" described at ¶705 and died in the year after the close of the normal fiscal period of the business, causing a second fiscal period to end at the date of death, a separate return may be filed within these time limits for the income from the business pertaining to the period from the close of the fiscal year to the time of death. If the election is made, a prescribed addition to income (described in ¶1910) under the alternative method must be added to the year of death return, but is then deducted on the separate return. The result is that the year of death return will reflect both a deduction for the prior year additional income and an addition which is then deducted in the separate return. Timing of the separate return and payment appears to be governed by normal deceased person rules.

(5) Where a taxpayer died after the fiscal year end of a testamentary trust from which he had income, the income received by the taxpayer for the period between the fiscal year end of the testamentary trust and the date of death may be included in a separate return. The filing and payment deadlines in (2) above should apply.

Example of General Filing Time Limits:

Assume that Ms. A dies on March 15 of Year 3. She did not file income tax returns for Year 1 and Year 2. There is no extension in the filing requirement for Year 1; the return was due April 30 of Year 2, and interest and penalty will continue to run on any shortfall of tax paid. The Year 2 return deadline (and payment date for any balance owing) is deferred to September 15 of Year 3 (six months after the date of death). The terminal return for Year 3 for the period January 1 to March 15 of Year 3, would not be due until April 30 of Year 4 (June 15 of Year 4, if Mrs. A or her cohabiting spouse had self-employment income for Year 3, although payment would still be due April 30 of Year 4).

[¶1901.05] *Overall Limitations on Separate Returns*

Where separate returns (returns under (3), (4), and (5) above are referred to as "separate returns filed as another person", or separate returns) are filed, the following items can be claimed in full on each return:

- the basic personal amount (line 300);
- the age amount (line 301);
- the spouse or common-law partner amount (line 303);
- the amount for an eligible dependant (line 305);
- the family caregiver amount for children under 18 years of age (line 367);
- the amount for infirm dependants age 18 or older (line 306); and
- the caregiver amount (line 315).

Each of the following credits can be split among the various separate returns as you choose; however, the aggregate credit for each item from all separate returns cannot exceed the amount that could be claimed with respect to the deceased taxpayer if only the year of death return were filed. The credits and deductions to which this rule applies are:

- adoption expense credit (¶1357);
- the disability amount (¶1255), including credits transferred from a dependant but not credits transferred from a spouse or common-law partner;
- interest paid on certain student loans (¶1345);
- the education, textbook (¶1337; the education and textbook credits are repealed effective January 1, 2017), and tuition fees (¶1331) credits, including credits transferred from a child or grandchild (¶1339) but not credits transferred from a spouse or common-law partner;
- the charitable donations credit (¶1263), but donations for which credit is claimed on each return cannot exceed net income reported on that return;
- credit for cultural (¶1268) and ecological (¶1268d) gifts, where carryforward is still available; these items are not subject to the limitation that the donations for which credit is claimed on a particular return cannot exceed income on that return, but still cannot exceed the amount that could be claimed if only the year of death return were filed;
- public transit passes amount (¶1353);
- the refundable children's fitness credit or non-refundable children's arts credit (for taxation years before 2017);
- the first-time home buyers' credit; and
- the medical expenses credit (¶1215), which you can split any way you want between the final return and any optional returns; however, you have to reduce the total expenses by the lower of (for 2016) $2,237 or 3% of the total net income you report on all returns (note that the monetary amount may be slightly different on pro-

vincial returns, many of which use personal amount values which differ from federal values).

The following deductions and credits can be claimed only on the return on which you report the related income:

- the deductions for employees' stock options, prospectors' shares, and DPSP share distributions claimed on line 249 of the T1 return;
- the deduction for employee home relocation loans claimed on line 248 of the T1 return;
- the deduction for Employment Insurance repayments claimed on line 250 of the T1 return;
- the pension income credit (¶1311);
- the vow of perpetual poverty deduction (¶1080);
- CPP/QPP/EI credits (¶1305, ¶1307);
- the dividend tax credit (¶404);
- the Canada employment credit (¶1351); and
- the offsetting deductions discussed at ¶990 if those items are included in income.

(CRA Guide *Preparing Returns for Deceased Persons* (T4011))

[¶1901.10] *Restrictions on Separate Returns*

The following items can be claimed only on the year of death final or terminal return (in (2) above) and not on any of the separate returns ((3) through (5)):

- registered pension plan (¶365) and RRSP (¶2603) deductions;
- annual union, professional, or similar dues (¶1311);
- other employment expenses (Chapter 3);
- carrying charges (¶445) and interest expense (¶1063);
- child care expenses;
- disability supports deduction (¶1036);
- capital gains deduction;
- northern residents deduction;
- losses from other years;
- amounts transferred from a spouse or common-law partner;
- refundable GST credit;
- refundable Canada child benefit;
- refundable medical expense supplement;
- working income tax benefit (WITB);
- refundable investment tax credit;
- election to renounce investment tax credits allocated as a partner;
- forward averaging inclusions; and
- minimum tax liability or carryovers.

However, the clawback of Old Age Security benefits (¶1419) is applied separately to each tax return filed on behalf of the deceased, based on the liability in that return.

(IT-326R3 Returns of Deceased Persons as "Another Person")

[¶1901.15] *Amended Prior Year Returns*

A prior year return may need amendments for losses carried back to that year in the situation where non-capital or capital losses exceed other income in the year of death. This may be readily accomplished by filing a form T1A — "Request for Loss-Carryback". This form may be obtained from any Tax Services Office, and it will eliminate the necessity of filing amended returns. (See ¶1910 and ¶1933.) A prior year return may also need amendment for the carryback of excess charitable donations made in the year of death (see ¶1931).

[¶1901.20] *General*

Completed returns signed by the executor or other legal representative of the deceased person should be filed at the Tax Services Office which services the region where the deceased person resided.

The CRA publishes annually a very useful guide to *Preparing Returns for Deceased Persons* (T4011) as well as a guide for estate return filers, the *T3 Trust* guide (T4013). These may be downloaded from the CRA website; see ¶287.

In addition to guidance in respect of the particular forms discussed in this chapter, the CRA also publishes a useful information sheet, "What to do following a death" (RC4111), with directions on how to deal with the period immediately following death, including advice on instalments unpaid at the time of death (pay them if already due, but do not make payments due after death), GST/HST credit (inform the CRA), and so on.

(ITA: 70(2), (7)(*a*); 104(23)(*d*); 114.2; 118.93; 150(1)(*b*), (*d*), (4); 248(1) "balance-due day"; IT-326R3 Returns of Deceased Persons as "Another Person")

[¶1903] PAYMENT OF TAX

Any tax owing for the year of death is payable on April 30 following the year of death, except that where death occurs in November or December, the tax is due six months after the date of death. Where the death occurs in the period January through April inclusive, payment for the prior year is due six months following the date of death, and payment for the year of death is due on the following April 30 (see ¶1901).

The CRA also may assess interest and penalty on any tax unpaid from the time the tax is due until it is paid. For example, there is an extension to 18 months after the date of death for the filing of a return where there is a spouse or common-law partner trust, but interest may be assessed on any tax unpaid from the later of April 30 of the year following the year of death or six months after the date of death.

Further exceptions to the general rule are outlined at ¶1926. For example, any tax owing in respect of rights and things can normally be paid in annual instalments, not exceeding ten years.

(ITA: 70(7)(*a*); 156.1(4); 161(1); 248(1) "balance-due day")

COMPUTATION OF INCOME

[¶1905] GENERAL

Income of a deceased person is computed in the same manner as for other taxpayers except that only income earned to the date of death is recognized. However, there are a number of special rules which prescribe how income earned to the date of death is to be computed. These rules are discussed in the following paragraphs.

If, after taking into account all of the special rules outlined in this Chapter, it is determined that the deceased person has suffered a non-capital loss you should refer to Chapter 10 since it may be possible to recover all or a portion of the taxes paid in the three previous years. The carryback period for losses is three years (see ¶1311–¶1325). This may necessitate the amendment of a prior year return for this carryback period. This may be readily accomplished by filing a form T1A — "Request for Loss-Carryback". Net capital losses in the year of death are discussed at ¶1933.

(ITA: 70(1); 111(1)(*a*))

[¶1907] PERIODIC PAYMENTS

There must be included in income all amounts payable on a periodic basis that were accruing, but not due or received, on the date of death. These amounts should be reported in the deceased person's final return for the period ending with his death.

Some items of this nature are rents, interest, royalties, annuities and remuneration from an office or employment representing the amount accrued from the beginning of the pay period in which the employee died to the date of death. Amounts due and unpaid in respect of prior periods are also included in income up to the date of death, although these amounts are eligible to be treated as "rights or things" (see ¶1908).

If the accrual basis of computing income has been used, such items will already have been taken into account. If the cash basis has been used, the following rules apply.

Amounts payable on a periodic basis (e.g., weekly or monthly) but not due for payment on the date of death must be included in income. For example, if a deceased person owned bonds, interest received up to the date of death would be included in income in the normal manner, and interest accrued from the last interest date preceding death but not yet received would be included as an item of accrued income.

Amounts such as these are considered to accrue on a daily basis and are included in income based on the number of days from the date the last payment was due to and including the date of death. For example, if an employee died on June 15 and her salary was payable on the last day of the month, half of the June salary would be included in her income in the year of death.

Expenses (e.g., interest or property taxes) which relate specifically to accrued income may also be accrued on a daily basis, even though the payment was not actually made by the date of death.

Where, as a result of accruing expenses, a loss from a particular source arises, the loss may be offset against other income of the taxpayer.

(ITA: 70(1), (2); IT-210R2 Income of Deceased Persons — Periodic Payments and Investment Tax Credit)

[¶1908] RIGHTS OR THINGS

Where a person dies owning "rights or things" which, if they had been sold or otherwise realized during his lifetime, would have been included in income, the value of these items must be included in income in the final return (see exceptions below). Some examples of such "rights or things" are (a full list can be found in Interpretation Bulletin IT-212R3, "Income of Deceased Persons — Rights or Things"):

- Matured but unclipped bond coupons;
- Dividends declared but unpaid as of the date of death;
- Salaries, bonuses, commissions, and vacation pay owing but unpaid (that is, owing for a pay period which ended prior to death);
- Accounts receivable where the deceased person used the cash method of computing income; and
- Inventories of stock-in-trade (including operating supplies) where the deceased person used the cash method of computing income.

As indicated above, remuneration such as salary or bonuses owing in respect of a prior pay period but unpaid at the time of death are rights and things and are eligible for the separate return. However, the CRA takes the position that where "the employer has a contractual obligation to pay an annual bonus or on some other basis, but the bonus had not been declared at the time of death, the amount is remuneration 'payable periodically' as described in paragraph 70(1)(*a*)" (paragraph 19.1 of IT-212R3, and confirmed at the 2012 STEP Annual Conference). Such a bonus would not be a right or thing.

Farmers, being cash basis taxpayers with, in effect, inventories, are particularly likely to have rights or things in the form of a "trading herd" or harvested grain. Professionals, at least those who are sole proprietors, who have elected to exclude work in progress will have a right or thing. An artist's inventory valued at nil for tax purposes is a right or thing.

Certain income items are not considered "rights or things". These include eligible capital property prior to 2017, resource properties, land inventory and any amount which accrues periodically. [Also excluded from the rights or things category is property which is a participating interest in a foreign investment entity (FIE — see ¶492) on which interest the election to use the mark-to-market method applies in the year of death, unless a special mark-to-market rule (94.2(20)) forcing capital gain reporting does apply.] Items excluded by virtue of this paragraph are generally covered in ¶1909.

Any disagreement about whether the nature of income earned before a taxpayer's death is a periodic payment under ¶1907 or a "right or thing" is generally resolved in favour of the taxpayer.

On death, an income-averaging annuity contract is not a "right or thing". Any amount paid out of an income-averaging annuity contract subsequent to the death of the original annuitant is deemed to be a payment out of an income-averaging annuity contract and will therefore be included in the income of the recipient with no deduction for any capital element. Specific rules also provide that a life insurance contract, other than an annuity contract acquired on a rollover of RRSP or RRIF refund of premiums (¶903 and ¶907) or of Saskatchewan Pension Plan benefits (¶2612.35), is not a right or thing. For life insurance, see ¶1917.

It is important to note that only the "value" of the "rights or things" must be included in income. If, for example, accounts receivable included worthless accounts, such accounts would not be included in income since they have no value. In calculating value, there may be deducted from it related amounts incurred but unpaid at the date of death. These amounts must be of a kind that would have been deductible from the income had it been realized. Related but unpaid interest, property taxes or insurance premiums, for example, would offset value. Where the aggregate offset on particular rights or things exceeds their value, the excess is deductible from other income. However, where the aggregate value of all rights or things is negative, no separate return (¶1941) for rights or things is available. In this situation, the rights or things may be reported on the general year-of-death return.

In general, there are three choices for the reporting of rights or things on death:

(1) Where rights or things which would otherwise be included in income are transferred to beneficiaries within one year of death, or within 90 days after assessment of the deceased person's final return, whichever is the later date, the value of the "rights or things" transferred to beneficiaries must be included in their income (when realized) and will be excluded from income of the deceased person. The value to be included in the income of the beneficiary will be the amount eventually received by the beneficiary with respect to the right or thing minus its cost to the deceased to the extent not deducted in computing the income of the deceased and also minus any expenditures the recipient incurred to acquire the asset.

(2) If "rights or things" are included in the income of the deceased person rather than a beneficiary, it can be reported in the ordinary year-of-death return.

(3) If "rights or things" are included in the income of the deceased person rather than a beneficiary, a special election can be made to report such income on a separate return; this can substantially reduce the tax burden (see ¶1901 at item (3), ¶1901.05, and ¶1941).

(ITA: 61.1(2); 69(1.1); 70(2), (3), (3.1); IT-210R2 Income of Deceased Persons — Periodic Payments and Investment Tax Credit; IT-212R3 Income of Deceased Persons — Rights or Things)

[¶1908.05] *Individual Retirement Accounts as Rights or Things*

United States tax law provides rules for Individual Retirement Accounts (IRAs) that are similar to Canadian RRSP rules. In general, these plans are trusteed or depositary plans under which the owner can request payment of the full amount held in the plan at any time. However, where the owner turns 70½ years old (the Maturity Date), he or she must choose by the next April 1 to take either the whole balance or periodic distributions. Payments out of such plans in life are taxable to a Canadian resident recipient, subject to rollover rules at ¶919. It is the CRA's view that, where the Canadian resident owner of such an IRA dies before the plan's maturity date and the property in the plan was not used to acquire an irrevocable annuity, the value of such plans is a "right or thing". Accordingly, it is subject to the three possible treatments as outlined above. In the case of an IRA these would be:

(1) The total value of the IRA may be included in the deceased's income in the year of death. In a 1993 ruling, the CRA said that if the amount can be considered exempt under U.S. rules, an offsetting deduction may be claimed under Article XVIII of the Canada–U.S. Tax Treaty; in a 1997 ruling it says flatly that there would be no offsetting treaty deduction; presumably the original statement is correct and the revised statement amounts to saying there is no such exemption under U.S. law. However, a 2004 CRA interpretation (CRA Document No. 2003-0046111E5, April 16, 2004) provides that an amount would not be required to be included in computing the income of the deceased as a right or thing if such amount, had it been realized or disposed of before the owner's death, represented a payment out of or under an IRA and would not have been required to be included in computing the income of the owner under clause 56(1)(*a*)(i)(C.1) (which provides an exception for the payment essentially if it would not be subject to taxation in the United States if the taxpayer were resident in the United States).

(2) The total value of the IRA may be included in a separate rights and things return of the deceased; the comments in (1), above, concerning treaty exemption apply equally here.

(3) If the rights to amounts in the IRA are transferred to one or more beneficiaries of the decedent within the normal time limits under Canadian rules (the later of one year after death or 90 days after assessment of the final return of the deceased), the amounts received out of the IRA will be taxed in the recipient beneficiary's hands in the year of receipt. If the beneficiary is resident in Canada, those benefits will in fact be taxed when received. However, if the beneficiary is entitled to deduct US estate taxes payable in the United States in respect of the IRA under section 691(c) of the US Code, the same deduction is allowed for Canadian income tax purposes, owing to the Canada-US tax treaty (CRA document no. 2009-0313171E5, August 23, 2010; CRA document no. 2008-0304421I7, May 20, 2010). If the beneficiary is non-resident, Canada has no power to tax the beneficiary.

Where either alternative (1) or (2) is chosen, amounts later received by the Canadian resident beneficiary would seem to be taxable under the IRA rules at ¶919, which tax payments out of foreign retirement arrangements regardless of ACB adjustments under the rights or things rules, unless exempt under U.S. rules. Or so says the CRA's earlier opinion letter. Since the U.S. would also tax such receipts, it would seem that normal offsetting tax credit mechanisms would apply and treaty exemption would not apply.

Where an IRA owner dies after the plan's maturity date and he or she has begun to receive periodic distributions, the owner's interest in the IRA would not constitute a right or thing. In this case, the named beneficiary would receive the remaining distributions under the terms of the contract. Since there is no provision in this case requiring the inclusion of the amounts held in the IRA on the decedent's death, the beneficiary, if resident in Canada, would have to include the remaining distributions in income.

(CRA Document No.: Taxation of U.S. IRA on Death of Annuitant, *November 26, 1993,* CRA Document No. 9322935; Individual retirement account (IRA) & Death — Right or thing, *July 10, 1997,* CRA Document No. 9713295; Taxation of IRA Upon Death, *April 16, 2004,* CRA Document No. 2003-0046111E5)

[¶1908.10] *Inventory of an Artist*

Where an artist makes a charitable donation of inventory, special rules discussed at ¶789 mitigate the ordinary charitable donation limitations. Where the donation is made as a result of death, the donation is deemed to be made immediately before death, so that the rules clearly apply to the year of death return rather than the estate. As well, where the art in question is transferred to a beneficiary under the "rights or things" rules, so that proceeds are taxable to the beneficiary and not the deceased, the beneficiary can make the same donation with the same results for the beneficiary as if the artist had made the donation. See ¶789.

(ITA: 118.1(4), (7), (7.1))

[¶1909] GOODWILL, RESOURCE PROPERTIES, AND LAND INVENTORY

"Rights or things" of a deceased person passing on death do not include an interest in a life insurance policy (other than an annuity contract the purchase of which was funded by a refund of premiums for an RRSP (see ¶903), RRIF (¶907), or Saskatchewan Pension Plan lump-sum payment (¶2612.35)), eligible capital property prior to 2017 (see ¶766), resource properties (see ¶2044), periodic payments (see ¶1907) and land held as inventory.

Eligible capital property transferred to a person (or persons) other than the spouse or common-law partner or controlled corporation of the deceased person will be deemed to have been sold immediately prior to death. However, disposition is not deemed to have occurred at fair market value, but rather at a rollover value. The deemed proceeds to the deceased will be equal to $4/3$ of the cumulative eligible capital account. These proceeds are allocated to each eligible capital property based on its *pro rata* share of the fair market value of all eligible capital property immediately before death. (Where death occurred before the commencement of the first fiscal period of the deceased's business commencing after 1987, this was twice the amount; see ¶768.) When this value is pushed through the eligible capital property disposition rules at ¶768, there should be no income inclusion as a result of the eligible property disposition.

(Where this rule applies on a disposition at death, i.e., property is passed to a beneficiary other than the spouse or common-law partner or controlled corporation of the deceased, the normal rules at ¶770 for eligible capital property on ceasing to carry on business do not apply. Where eligible capital property passes to a spouse or common-law partner or controlled corporation, the rollover rules at ¶770 for such situations do apply.)

In situations where the property passes to a transferee (other than the spouse or common-law partner or controlled corporation) who does not continue to carry on the business of the transferor, the transferee is deemed to have acquired a capital property at a cost equal to the deemed proceeds to the deceased, and any subsequent gain or loss on disposition will be treated as a capital gain or loss in the transferee's hands (see ¶500).

Where the transferee continues to carry on the business, the transferee is considered to have acquired eligible capital property at a cost equal to the proceeds of disposition to the deceased plus $4/3$ of his or her share of any previous tax depreciation taken by the deceased which is not recaptured on death. A further adjustment then provides that $3/4$ of this unrecaptured depreciation (that is, of the $4/3$ amount included as cost) will be deemed to have been deducted by the transferee from the transferee's cumulative eligible capital pool. Finally, when the transferee does dispose of the property, capital gain or recapture will be adjusted to take account of old system (pre-1988) claims of the transferor. The result is intended to put the transferee in exactly the same position as the deceased with respect to amounts eligible for tax depreciation (¶767) and eventual recapture on disposition.

Eligible capital property may be transferred to more than one beneficiary, with *pro rata* proceeds to the deceased and *pro rata* acquisitions by the beneficiaries. Thus, for example, where property is left to a spouse or common-law partner and child, the portion left to the spouse or common-law partner would transfer under the spouse or common-law partner rules below, with no proceeds to the deceased on the proportion of fair market value (immediately before death) of the eligible capital property transferred to the spouse or common-law partner. The portion left to the child would create deemed proceeds according to its *pro rata* share of fair market value immediately before death, and the child would deal with its share of cumulative eligible capital according to that *pro rata* distribution.

Where eligible capital property passes through a testamentary trust which claims a depreciation deduction on the property, the beneficiary will not take over the position of the deceased where the eligible capital property is distributed to the beneficiary. It would seem that the trust will pick up the initial rollover, and distribute to the beneficiaries in accordance with trust rules.

Commentary on Bill C-29 Measures (Oct. 25, 2016)

Note: When Bill C-29, October 25, 2016, achieves Royal Assent, the commentary will be modified to read:

Beginning in 2017, property that was formerly eligible capital property will be considered depreciable property of a new Class 14.1. For deaths occurring after 2016, similar rollovers to those discussed above will continue to apply.

Resource properties transferred to a person other than a spouse or common-law partner or a spouse or common-law partner trust will be deemed to have been disposed of immediately prior to death at fair market value. This may cause an inclusion in income of the deceased taxpayer by way of a reversal of the cumulative Canadian oil and gas property expense (see ¶2223) or cumulative Canadian development expense (see ¶2217). The acquisition cost of these properties to such persons will be deemed to be the amount included in the deceased person's income, with a carryover of the transitional provisions in the case of transfers to a related person. Undeducted resource expenses that are not used in the deceased's final return are lost as there is no carry-over of these accounts to the estate or beneficiaries.

Land held as inventory transferred to a person other than a spouse or common-law partner or a spouse or common-law partner trust will be deemed to have been disposed of immediately prior to death at fair market value, with a corresponding acquisition cost to the transferee.

Upon his or her death, a person may transfer eligible capital property (prior to 2017), resource properties and land held as inventory to a spouse or common-law partner or spouse or common-law partner trust with no immediate tax consequences.

Resource properties transferred to a spouse or common-law partner or spouse or common-law partner trust may be elected to be disposed of for such an amount as is specified by the deceased's legal representatives in his final return. This amount may not exceed the fair market value of the resource property immediately before death. The property must "vest indefeasibly" (see commentary below) in the spouse or common-law partner or trust not later than 36 months after the deceased's death.

Similarly, land inventory of a business is transferred to a spouse or common-law partner or a spouse or common-law partner trust at cost if the property "vests indefeasibly" in the spouse or common-law partner or trust not later than 36 months after the death of the taxpayer.

(ITA: 24(2); 70(3.1), (5.1), (5.2), (6); IT-125R4 Dispositions of Resource Properties; IT-313R2 Eligible Capital Property — Rules Where a Taxpayer Has Ceased Carrying on a Business or Has Died)

[¶1909.05] *Meaning of "Vested Indefeasibly"*

In general, "vested indefeasibly", as it is used above and later in this chapter, has a technical legal meaning not provided by the *Income Tax Act*. In general, it is the CRA's view that a property vests indefeasibly in a spouse or common-law partner or child when such person obtains a right to absolute ownership of the property in such a manner that the right cannot be defeated by any further event, even though the person may not be immediately entitled to all the benefits of the property. (At any rate, this was the view propounded in Interpretation Bulletin IT-449R, which was archived in 2003, and there is no indication that it has changed.) However, there are some overriding statutory rules which prevent vesting where the intended beneficiary dies before it occurs. Under these rules, property will not be considered vested indefeasibly in a trust created by a taxpayer's will in which the spouse or common-law partner is a beneficiary unless the property became vested indefeasibly in the trust before the death of the beneficiary spouse or common-law partner. Similarly, property will not be considered vested indefeasibly in an individual unless it became so vested before the death of the recipient individual. These rules are said to ensure that a rollover only applies where appropriate gains will be recognized on the death of the qualifying beneficiary.

(ITA: 248(9.2))

[¶1910] BUSINESS INCOME

Business income for fiscal periods ending in the part of the year during which the person was living will be included in income in the deceased person's final return. For fiscal periods ending after death but in the calendar year, income may be included in the final return or a separate return, as discussed at ¶1901.

When an individual dies, the fiscal year of his business is considered to be terminated and the profit for this abbreviated period must be included in income. Similarly, a deceased partner would be required to include his profit for the abbreviated period in income.

The rules governing the computation of business income and losses for abbreviated fiscal periods are generally the same as those discussed in Chapter 7. Differences which arise include:

- Generally no deduction is permitted for the reserves listed in ¶1918. Deductions may be claimed for reserves for doubtful accounts receivable and for reserves against prepaid rents and amounts received in advance of delivery of goods or performance of services (see ¶732);
- Inventories and accounts receivable of cash basis taxpayers are handled as outlined in ¶1908;
- No deduction may be claimed for capital cost allowance if an individual operates as a sole proprietor except if a terminal loss results from the deemed disposition of depreciable property (see ¶1920); and
- If the investment tax credit is claimed in the year of death, the cost base reduction for related property or income inclusion for related expenditures must be recognized in the year of death, and not the following year as is otherwise the case.

If business profits for an abbreviated fiscal period are included in income a special election is available and is discussed in ¶1942.

If a business loss arises it is deducted first against other income in the year of death and the remainder may be carried back and applied to the three preceding years' income (¶1311).

Where the death of a partner causes the fiscal year of the partnership to end, the profits for the abbreviated fiscal period are included in income with the special election (discussed in ¶1941) available. However, where the death of a partner does not result in a fiscal year end of the partnership, the profits of the abbreviated fiscal period are considered rights or things (see ¶1908) and are available for the special election discussed in ¶1941.

(ITA: 20(1)(*l*), (*m*); 70(5); 72(1); 111(1)(*a*); 150(4); ITAR: 23(4)(*a*); IT-212R3 Income of Deceased Persons — Rights or Things; IT-278R2 Death of a Partner or of a Retired Partner)

[¶1910.10] *Investment Tax Credits*

Investment tax credits claimed in the year of death or a preceding year must be included in income for the year of death to the extent that the amount was not included in income for a previous year or used to adjust the tax cost of related expenditures (for example, by reducing the capital cost of depreciable property or increasing adjusted cost base of other capital property).

(ITA: 12(1)(*t*); 70(1)(*b*); IT-210R2, para. 7)

[¶1910.20] *If Business Has Non-Calendar Year End*

If the business of the deceased taxpayer had a non-calendar year end, it will be because there was an election under the rules at ¶705, from which it follows that the taxpayer is carrying forward a deduction from the prior year representing prior year stub period income (to the end of the preceding calendar year) on which tax has already been paid. Where the taxpayer dies in a calendar year but before the end of the business taxation year, that deduction may be made but no new income inclusion is required.

If the taxpayer dies in the calendar year, but after the end of the business taxation year, and there is a second fiscal period end (creating a stub period) due to the death, the legal representative may elect to have an income inclusion in the ordinary year of death return and claim the corresponding deduction on a separate return for the stub period.

The income inclusion must be the income for the full taxation year which ended in the year, minus the lesser of (a) any deemed taxable capital gain eligible for the capital gains exemption (which could arise on the deemed disposition of eligible capital property of a farming or fishing operation prior to 2017), and (b) all amounts on which capital gains exemption was claimed for the year (also necessarily on a disposition of farming or fishing property). The 2015 capital gains exemption amount is $813,600 for a taxation year ending before April 21, 2015 and $1 million for a taxation year ending after April 20, 2015. The amount is then prorated by days in the stub period divided by days in the earlier fiscal period ending in the year.

If this election is made, the representative must also file a separate return for the stub period under the rules at ¶1901(4), reporting stub period income and deducting the inclusion for the prior period. Conversely, if the representative elects to file a separate stub period return to report stub period income, this adjustment becomes mandatory.

(ITA: 34.1(8)(*a*), (9); 150(1)(*d*))

[¶1912] INCOME FROM TRUSTS

Where a deceased individual was a beneficiary under a trust all trust income paid or payable to the deceased person for the last fiscal period of the trust ending in the year of death must be included in income in the normal manner. Trust income which is paid or payable to the deceased person after the last fiscal period has ended and up to the date of death must also be included in income.

If the trust is a testamentary trust that was created on the death of another person the income of the deceased beneficiary for this second period (from the end of the trust's last fiscal period to the date of death of the beneficiary) may be excluded from income reported in the final return of the deceased beneficiary and may be included as the only item of income in a separate return. The separate return is prepared in the same manner as outlined in ¶1901. This provision is applicable only where the trust has a non-calendar year. Beginning in 2016, this provision will only apply where the trust is a graduated rate estate, since only such testamentary trusts will be permitted to have an off-calendar taxation year.

If the trust is not a testamentary trust, the income for the second period must be included in the regular return; no separate return is permitted with respect to this income.

(ITA: 70(1); 104(13), (23)(*d*))

[¶1913] PENSION PLAN BENEFITS AND DEATH BENEFITS

Pension payments prior to death are included in the deceased taxpayer's return under the rules in ¶1907. Lump-sum payments after death will normally be taxed in the hands of the recipient, who may be either a beneficiary (e.g., spouse, common-law partner, child) or the estate. An individual recipient may in certain circumstances "roll over" these payments into an RRSP to defer current tax (see ¶1021).

Payments to beneficiaries may also qualify as "death benefits" as described at ¶925. These payments would be income of the recipient and not the deceased.

(ITA: 56(1)(*a*); 70(1); 248(1) "death benefit"; IT-212R3 Income of Deceased Persons — Rights or Things)

[¶1913c] DEDUCTION FOR PAST SERVICE CONTRIBUTIONS TO PENSION PLAN

Rules enacted in 1998 but retroactive for deaths occurring in 1993 or later years remove the old annual $3,500 deduction limit for both the year of death and the year preceding the year of death. This does not change the cumulative limit of $3,500 times years of pre-1990 service which applies to years in which the deceased was not a contributor to a registered pension plan.

(ITA: 147.2(6))

[¶1914] REGISTERED RETIREMENT SAVINGS PLAN

[¶1914.10] *Where RRSP Matured before Death*

Where a plan has matured (i.e., commenced to pay retirement income; see ¶2616.05) and the taxpayer died after maturity, and by terms of the plan the surviving spouse or common-law partner becomes the successor annuitant (i.e., receives all retirement income under the plan), there is no tax consequence to the deceased and the surviving spouse or common-law partner is taxed on the retirement income as it is received. In effect, the surviving spouse or common-law partner becomes the annuitant for all further purposes of that RRSP. The surviving spouse or common-law partner is entitled to commute the plan and roll over the proceeds to an RRSP (where the surviving spouse or common-law partner has not passed the age of 71 in the year), RRIF or guaranteed annuity to age 90. To the extent the proceeds of an RRSP are payable to the estate for the benefit of the surviving spouse or common-law partner, the surviving spouse or common-law partner and the executor can jointly elect to treat the surviving spouse or common-law partner as the annuitant; again, in these circumstances, the surviving spouse or common-law partner (and not the deceased) is deemed to have become the annuitant of the plan as a consequence of the death and to be taxable on all payments received by the estate in consequence of the death. To the extent these are commutation payments (as for the most part they will be), the surviving spouse or common-law partner may roll over receipts to an RRSP, etc. In its Guide RC4177, the CRA states: "To make this election, the legal representative and the spouse or common-law partner need only to write a letter explaining their intention. A copy of the letter must be provided to the payer of the annuity and another copy attached to the spouse's or common-law partner's income tax and benefit return."

Absent a surviving spouse or common-law partner who becomes the successor annuitant, the value of a matured plan is included in the income of the deceased "immediately before death". However, if there is no surviving spouse or common-law partner but there are dependent children or grandchildren of the deceased, RRSP payments for their benefit can be paid and taxed to them rather than the deceased under the "refund of premium" rules discussed below. Dependent children or grandchildren cannot be successor annuitants and therefore, it would seem, must receive and may (in some cases) roll over the commuted value of the RRSP rather than receiving continuing payments.

(ITA: 60(*l*); 146(8.91); IT-500R Registered Retirement Savings Plans — Death of an Annuitant)

[¶1914.15] *Refund of Premium Rules*

If the annuitant dies prior to the maturity date of the plan (¶2616.05), and a person other than (i) the spouse or common-law partner of the deceased, or (ii) a child who was financially dependent on the deceased becomes entitled to an amount from the RRSP, the value of the amount is to be included in the income of the deceased immediately prior to his or her death.

Where the deceased's spouse or common-law partner becomes entitled to an amount from his or her RRSP, the amount is included in the income of the spouse or common-law partner rather than the deceased, and the spouse or common-law partner may transfer the funds to his or her own RRSP, pooled registered pension plan (PRPP), or Saskatchewan pension plan (SPP), or make an alternative permitted investment described at ¶903 and get a corresponding deduction. A spouse or common-law partner who cannot transfer funds to an RRSP by reason of age (¶2616.05) will be permitted to average a refund of premiums through the purchase of a special annuity or RRIF; see ¶903.

Where an amount is paid from the RRSP after the death to a child or grandchild who was financially dependent on the deceased, the amount (received as a "refund of premiums", per ¶903) will be included in the child or grandchild's income instead of in the deceased's. This can include any amount from the RRSP received by the dependent child or grandchild on the death of the parent or grandparent, regardless of whether the RRSP was "matured" (i.e., annuitized) at the time of death, although it would be rare in practice for a mature RRSP to provide for such payments. For amounts paid to a dependent child or grandchild, any such amount must be taxed to the dependent child or grandchild rather than the parent or grandparent, regardless of the child's age or the reason for dependency.

It is presumed in the first instance that a child/grandchild was not financially dependent if its income in the year preceding the death exceeded a specified amount. That presumption can be rebutted by factual evidence. The point is that the specified amount test only comes into play *vis-à-vis* a parent or grandparent on whom the child was in fact dependent. The CRA discusses financial dependency in CRA Document No. 9926947. There it states, among other things, that the CRA "would not normally accept that a grandchild was financially dependent on a grandparent where the grandchild lived with his or her parent(s) and the parent(s) could adequately provide for the grandchild's well being". On the other hand, in CRA Document No. 2001-0114425, the CRA says that it would generally accept that in the case of separation or divorce, where a child with no independent income lives with one parent and the other pays child support under a Court Order or Separation Agreement, the child is dependent on the parent paying child support. All CRA opinions on financial dependence stress that it is an issue of fact in each case, and should generally be decided at local Tax Services Office level.

The specified amount at which the presumption against dependence comes into play is the basic personal amount (¶1106) for the year preceding death, which amount is indexed for inflation. Thus, for a death in 2016, the child is presumed not to have been dependent on the deceased where the child's 2015 income exceeded the basic personal amount of $11,327.

Where the child/grandchild was dependent by reason of mental or physical infirmity on a supporting parent/grandparent, the preceding year basic personal amount used as a benchmark in the presumption of dependency is supplemented by the preceding year disability amount (both as indexed). Thus, where the death occurred in 2016 and the child/grandchild was dependent by reason of physical or mental infirmity, the dependency threshold is determined under the 2015 amounts of $11,327 + $7,899.

Infirmity for the purposes of these rules is discussed under the subheading "Infirmity Test" toward the end of ¶1209.

A dependent child who is under 18 can make a tax-deferred transfer of a refund of premiums to an annuity to age 18. The amount received will then be taxed as the annuity payments are received. The annuity must be acquired within 60 days of the end of the year of receipt of the refund of premiums. The recipient child is required to "designate" the amount transferred to the annuity on its tax return. No form is provided for such designation, and usually the annuity receipt is sufficient, although a short letter filed with the form stating that the filer "designates $ ... as an amount pursuant to paragraph 60(*l*) of the *Income Tax Act*" might make certainty more sure. It is also possible for a child under 18 to have the refund of premium proceeds contributed to a trust which acquires an annuity to age 18 for the child. The trust must conform to standards described below at ¶1914.16.

A child or grandchild who, regardless of age, was dependent on the deceased parent or grandparent by reason of physical or mental infirmity and who receives RRSP payments on the death of the parent or grandparent may defer tax by making any of the permitted investments described at ¶903 with a corresponding deduction. This includes transfer to an RRSP, SPP, PRP, RRIF, eligible annuity, or annuity to age 18. The transfer contribution must be made or the annuity must be purchased within 60 days of year end; see ¶903. Transfers to an RRSP or other plan are designated on line 14 of Schedule 7; annuities are designated as described for other children above. Furthermore, as discussed at ¶1914.17, the 2010 federal Budget introduced a rule that qualifying deductible transfers for these purposes will be allowed to the child's or grandchild's RDSP.

Where an individual has died whether before or after the maturity of his RRSP and the proceeds are to be paid to his estate, the spouse or common-law partner, or the financially dependent children of the deceased, may elect to file a joint election (form T2019) with the legal representative of the deceased to treat the proceeds as being paid directly to the spouse or common-law partner or to the financially dependent children as a refund of premiums. This would allow the amount to be taxed in the hands of the spouse or common-law partner (or financially dependent children), rather than the deceased, and enable a tax deferral to occur through contributions to an RRSP or purchase of an annuity (as discussed above).

As with the rule where an RRSP amount is paid directly to a spouse or common-law partner or dependent child, the rule where an amount is paid first to the estate and then passed on to the spouse or common-law partner or dependent child permits dependent children to take advantage of the rule regardless of whether there is also a surviving spouse or common-law partner.

These elections should be made where they reduce or defer the overall tax liability of the recipient and the estate. They allow the spouse, common-law partner, or children to utilize the RRSP transfer provisions, for example, where the estate is the beneficiary of the plan, rather than the spouse, common-law partner, or children.

It is the CRA's view that where a taxpayer has died during the year, his or her executors or legal representatives may make an RRSP contribution for the year to a spousal RRSP subject to the usual constraints as to the amount (¶2624.05) and provided that the contribution is made in the year of death or within 60 days following that year, as discussed further below.

For more information about taxation of RRSP benefits, see also ¶903 and Chapter 26.

(ITA: 60(*l*); 146(1) "refund of premiums", (1.1), (2)(c.2), (8), (8.1), (8.8); IT-307R4 *Spousal or Common-Law Partner Registered Retirement Savings Plans*; IT-500R *Registered Retirement Savings Plans — Death of an Annuitant*)

[¶1914.16] *Rollover for Annuities Acquired By Trust*

As discussed above and at ¶903.15, where a taxpayer dies and the taxpayer's spouse or common-law partner or financially dependent child or grandchild ("beneficiary") receives an amount from the RRSP as a consequence of the death, the beneficiary includes the amount in income but is allowed an offsetting deduction to the extent that the amount is used to acquire a qualifying annuity in the year of death or within 60 days thereafter. (Similar rules apply to receipts of eligible amounts from an RRIF of the deceased.) For spouses and common-law partners and children who were financially dependent by reason of physical or mental infirmity, the annuity can generally be a life annuity or a term annuity to age 90. For minor children who were not physically or mentally infirm but were dependent upon the deceased, a term annuity is allowed generally to age 18 if the child or a trust under which the child is the sole beneficiary is the annuitant.

Recent amendments refine the minor trust rule described above, and further provide that certain other trusts may acquire the annuity without affecting the offsetting rollover deduction for the spouse or common-law partner, or child or grandchild, as the case may be. These trusts are summarized below.

For annuities payable to age 18 for the benefit of minors, the rollover can apply if the annuitant is a trust under which the taxpayer (the minor) is the sole beneficiary (determined without regard to any right of a person to receive amounts from the trust only on or after the death of the taxpayer). For annuities acquired after 2005, the annuity must require that, in the event of the death of the taxpayer during the term of the annuity, amounts otherwise payable after the death be commuted into a single payment.

For annuities acquired after 2005, the rollover can apply if the annuitant is a personal trust under which the taxpayer, namely, the surviving spouse or common-law partner, or financially dependent infirm child or grandchild, is the sole beneficiary during the taxpayer's lifetime (in particular, no one else may receive any of the trust capital or income during the taxpayer's lifetime). The annuity in this case must be either for the life of the taxpayer or for a fixed term to the age of 90 of the taxpayer. If the annuity is guaranteed or for a fixed term, it must require that in the event of the death of the taxpayer during the term of the annuity, amounts otherwise payable after the death will be commuted into a single payment. The taxpayer must be mentally infirm. For annuities acquired after 2000 and before 2006, the rollover can apply if the annuitant is a trust under which the taxpayer is the sole beneficiary (determined without regard to any right of a person to receive amounts from the trust only on or after the death of the taxpayer); the annuity must be for the life of the beneficiary or to the age of 90 of the beneficiary; for annuities acquired in 2001 through 2004, the taxpayer must be mentally or physically infirm; and for annuities acquired in 2005, the taxpayer must be mentally infirm.

(ITA: 60(*l*); 60.011)

[¶1914.17] *Refund of Premiums and Similar Amounts Rolled Over to Registered Disability Savings Plan (RDSP)*

In the 2010 federal Budget, the government announced a similar rollover (inclusion followed by off-setting deduction) for RRSP refunds of premiums (and RRIF eligible amounts and lump-sum payments out of an RPP) that are paid to an RDSP under which a child or grandchild was financially dependent upon the deceased by reason of physical or mental infirmity. (The deceased does not normally include the amounts in income.) The rollover is currently found in section 60.02. The new rule applies to amounts received by the child or grandchild as a refund of premiums out of an RRSP or an eligible amount out of a RRIF or a lump sum from an RPP ("eligible proceeds") as consequence of the death of the annuitant or plan holder after March 3, 2010, where the contribution is made to the RDSP after June 2011. In order to claim the deduction, the contribution must be made in the year in which the amounts are included in the child's or grandchild's income or within 60 days after the year, or any longer period that is acceptable to the Minister. The qualifying amount of the contribution, referred to as the "specified RDSP payment", qualifies for the rollover only to the extent that there is room under the $200,000 limit on contributions to RDSPs under which the eligible individual is a beneficiary.

A recent amendment allows the same rollover for lump-sum death benefits paid out of the Saskatchewan Pension Plan to the child or grandchild that are transferred to the RDSP. This amendment applies to "specified RDSP payment" (as defined in subsection 60.02(1)) made after June 2011. Similarly, an amendment in force as of December 14, 2012 provides that the rollover can apply to payments received out of the deceased's PRPP.

Additionally, "transitional eligible proceeds" can be contributed to the RDSP by the infirm child or grandchild, the surviving spouse or common-law partner, or a person who was a beneficiary of the deceased's estate or otherwise received the proceeds as a consequence of the deceased's death, where a person (typically either the recipient or the deceased) is required to include such proceeds in income. Basically, these are amounts received by a person as a consequence of the death of the annuitant after 2007 and before 2011 (before March 4, 2010 in the case of the child or grandchild) out of the deceased annuitant's RRSP (or RRIF or as a lump-sum pension plan payment); or amounts withdrawn from the person's RRSP or RRIF where the person was the deceased's spouse or common-law partner or child or grandchild who rolled such amounts into the RRSP or RRIF under the rules described above at ¶903.15 and ¶1914.15 upon the death of the deceased. In order to qualify for the deduction as a specified RDSP payment, the amount of the transitional eligible proceeds must be contributed to the RDSP of the child or grandchild of the deceased after June 2011 and before 2012.

The following examples of "transitional eligible proceeds" were provided by the Department of Finance in its explanatory notes to the amendments:

> *Example 1:*
>
> Henri died in February 2010. In September 2010, the executor of Henri's estate made a cash payment of $25,000 from Henri's RRSP to Henri's adult son Patrick, who has a disability. At the time of Henri's death, Patrick was "infirm" and dependent on Henri for financial support. Patrick does not transfer the payment to an RRSP and so must include the amount in his taxable income for 2010 as a refund of premiums. In July 2011, Patrick decides to establish an RDSP for himself and he makes a $40,000 deposit to the RDSP. Patrick can designate $25,000 of that amount as a "specified RDSP payment" and he can claim a $25,000 deduction for tax year 2010, the year in which the $25,000 bequest from Henri was included in Patrick's income. The remaining $15,000 out of the $40,000 deposit to the RDSP is a regular non-deductible contribution to the RDSP.
>
> *Example 2:*
>
> Michael and Mary are Jordan's parents. Jordan is an adult who is "infirm" and dependent on his parents for financial support. Before his death in April 2009, Michael had contributed a total of $120,000 to an RDSP under which Jordan is the beneficiary. Michael was the sole contributor to Jordan's RDSP. In December 2009, $150,000 is transferred from Michael's RRSP to Mary's RRSP on a rollover basis. That is, Mary was able to offset the income inclusion from a "refund of premiums" under section 146 of the Act by a deduction that she claimed under paragraph 60(*l*).
>
> In August 2011, Mary withdraws $50,000 from her RRSP and contributes $50,000 to the Jordan's RDSP. (Based on the prior $120,000 of RDSP contributions from Michael, Mary could contribute up to $80,000 to the RDSP before it reached the $200,000 contribution limit.) Mary must include the $50,000 RRSP withdrawal in her taxable income for 2011, but she may claim an offsetting deduction under new

paragraph 60(*m*) for the contribution to Jordan's RDSP.

Example 3:

When Jane died in February 2010, her "infirm" financially dependent daughter Caitlyn benefited from a tax-free rollover of $70,000 from Jane's RRSP to Caitlyn's RRSP. Jane's daughters Caitlyn and Jessica were the beneficiaries of the death benefit payable from the registered pension plan (RPP) sponsored by Jane's employer. In May 2010, the administrator of the RPP paid a $20,000 death benefit to Jessica, who included that amount in her taxable income for 2009 because of paragraph 56(1)(*a*). After becoming aware of the 2010 Budget measure for rollovers to RDSP, Jessica decides to make a $20,000 contribution in July 2011 to an RDSP under which her sister Caitlyn is the beneficiary. Under new paragraph 60(*m*) and new subsection 60.02(4), Jessica can claim a $20,000 deduction for tax year 2010, the year in which she had included the RPP death benefit proceeds in her income. In December 2011, Caitlyn decides to deposit her share of the RPP death benefit ($20,000) to her RDSP. Caitlyn can also claim a $20,000 deduction for tax year 2010 to offset the income inclusion under paragraph 56(1)(*a*).

The deceased taxpayer will not normally include in income the amounts of the RRSP, RRIF, or lump-sum RPP amounts that are received by the surviving spouse or common-law partner or financially dependent child or grandchild upon the death. However, under the "transitional eligible proceeds" scenarios described above, another person could receive such RRSP or RRIF proceeds (e.g., an independent adult child, who could then contribute the amounts to an RDSP of a disabled child or grandchild of the deceased), such that the deceased would be subject to an income inclusion at death (because there would be no refund of premiums of the RRSP or designated benefit of the RRIF). In such case, there may be deducted in computing the deceased taxpayer's income for the year of death, an amount not exceeding the lesser of the amount so included in the deceased's taxpayer's income in the year of death and the total contributions made by that other person to the RDSP after June 2011 and before 2012. The amount must be "approved by the Minister".

(ITA: 60(*l*), 60(*m*), 60.02)

[¶1914.20] *Refund of Premium Adjustments; Increase in Plan Value after Death*

In general, these adjustment rules are relieving rules which alter the calculation of amounts included in the income of the deceased. Thus, the representatives of the deceased may elect to treat less than the full amount eligible for refund of premium treatment as taxable to the qualified beneficiary rather than the deceased where this gives a better result. It would appear that the refund of premium retains its character in the hands of the beneficiary, but to the extent elected taxability returns to the deceased.

As well, the rules are amended to minimize the effect of growth of RRSP assets after the death of the annuitant by allowing amounts accrued in the plan after death to be taxed to (and in the case of a spouse or common-law partner or infirm child rolled over by them to) the survivors rather than the deceased. Under these rules, the amount eligible for refund of premium treatment is the value of the plan at death plus a specified fraction of post-death growth. For this purpose, the total growth in the RRSP assets after the death of the annuitant is considered to be the amount, if positive, equal to:

(1) the total payments (referred to as the "relevant payments") out of or under the RRSP after the annuitant's death and before the later of the end of the first calendar year commencing after the death and the time immediately after the distribution of all refunds of premiums,

PLUS

(2) the fair market value of property of the RRSP at the later of the two times described in (1) (called the "residual value" and usually nil),

MINUS

(3) the fair market value of all the property of the RRSP at the time of death.

The specified fraction of that growth eligible for refund of premium treatment is the total of such refunds divided by the sum of the relevant payments in (1) and the residual value in (2).

The Department of Finance provided the following example of this machinery.

Example 1

Paul died in 1993. He had an unmatured RRSP, with assets having a fair market value of $40,000 at the time of his death. One year after his death, the RRSP assets (now having a fair market value of $50,000) are paid to Paul's estate. Paul's widow and the legal representative of the estate made an election to treat $30,000 of this amount as a refund of premiums for Paul's widow. The legal representative of the estate claimed the maximum deduction from Paul's income.

Result:

(1) The income inclusion for Paul for the taxation year of his death was $16,000 ($40,000 - ($30,000 (1 - ($50,000 - $40,000) / $50,000)).

(2) Paul's widow had an income inclusion of $30,000, although this income inclusion may be offset by virtue of a transfer of funds under the rules at ¶903.

(3) The estate had an income inclusion of $4,000 ($50,000 - $16,000 - $30,000).

(4) If the law were not amended, the income inclusions for Paul, Paul's widow and the estate would be $10,000, $30,000 and $10,000, respectively. The amendments thus have the effect of reallocating income inclusions on death and do not increase the total amounts included in computing income.

Comment:

It appears to be intended that, had the estate paid $46,000 (or $50,000) to the spouse and elected, $46,000 could be treated as a refund of premiums. It must be said that this interpretation depends on a comment in Department of Finance Technical Notes and not on the completely opaque words of the statute. It would be as well to verify this with the CRA.

Also for deaths occurring in 1993 or later, rules were introduced to attempt to ensure that where the RRSP funds are distributed to both qualifying and non-qualifying beneficiaries, any post-death accumulations in the RRSP could not be sheltered from tax in the hands of the deceased to the extent they represented distributions to non-qualified beneficiaries. Technical amendments issued on April 26, 1995, refine the rules on post-death accumulations and harmonize them with the rules under which RRSP trusts become taxable beginning with the year following the year of death. In particular, the rules provide that commencing in 1995, distributions of RRSP funds of a deceased taxpayer representing post-death accumulations will bear some measure of taxation in the year-of-death return of the deceased even when all distributions are made to a surviving spouse or other qualified beneficiaries. Identical rules apply to RRIF plans of the deceased.

For deaths occurring in and after 1993, where the RRSP is divided between a surviving spouse or common-law partner (as from time to time defined in ¶1113) and another beneficiary, the offset of the value included in the deceased's year of death return is fixed as the percentage of total distribution paid out to refund of premium beneficiaries. The refund of premium beneficiary takes all receipts (including post-death growth in the trust) except those arising after January 1 following the year of death as a refund of premiums. Other beneficiaries receive taxable amounts. To the extent the estate elects to be taxable on post-death growth, the recipients will not be taxable.

For 1995 and later years, and only in respect of deaths occurring in or after 1993, there is an exclusion from the refund of premiums representing the surviving spouse's (or common-law partner's) share of the increase in value of the plan from January 1 of the year following the year of death. This amount is taxed either in the RRSP trust (since that becomes taxable in the year following death) or in the hands of the recipient beneficiary if paid to the beneficiary in the year; in either case the amount does not qualify for refund of premium treatment.

The Department of Finance has provided the following examples of the operation of these rules:

Example 1:

Mary died in 1993. Her unmatured trusteed RRSP at the time of her death was $100,000. It was worth $120,000 on January 1, 1995 and $125,000 at the time of its distribution in July 1996. Mary's widower John received the entire distribution.

Result:

(1) Mary's legal representatives are entitled to an offset of $100,000 against the income inclusion otherwise arising for Mary on her death. Assuming the full offset is claimed, the income inclusion for John is equal to $125,000, of which $120,000 counts as a "refund of premiums" because the $5,000 paid out in respect of growth after 1995 is a "tax-paid amount". John is entitled to claim a deduction of $120,000 if it is transferred on a tax-deferred basis (¶903).

(2) More specifically, Mary's $100,000 offset is determined as follows. First, add the amount of the "refund of premiums" ($120,000) paid to John and the "tax-paid amounts" ($5,000) paid to John. This total is multiplied by a fraction ($^4/_5$), which is derived from the formula (1 - (B + C - D) / (B + C)) (essentially this is the formula preceding the last example). In this example, the values of the variables in this formula are:

- B is nil, as it will be in every case where nothing remains in an RRSP after the distribution of a "refund of premiums";
- C is equal to $125,000, representing the total RRSP distributions; and
- D is $100,000, representing the RRSP value at the time of death.

Example 2:

Same as Example 1, except that $70,000 was distributed to John and $55,000 was distributed to Mary's daughter, Karen.

Result:

(1) John is a 56% beneficiary and Karen is a 44% beneficiary of Mary's RRSP. Consequently, the "tax-paid amount" for John is equal to $2,800 (56% of $5,000) and the remaining $67,200 received by John counts as a "refund of premiums" that can be transferred by John under the rules at ¶903.

(2) Mary's legal representatives are entitled to offset $56,000 against the $100,000 income inclusion otherwise arising for Mary. This offset is determined by multiplying the distributions made to John ($70,000) by the specified fraction ($^4/_5$), which is calculated in the same way as in Example 1.

(3) Assuming the entire $56,000 offset is claimed by Mary's legal representatives, the income inclusion for Mary is equal to $44,000 ($100,000 - $56,000). As a consequence, Karen receives $44,000 of her $55,000 RRSP distribution on a tax-free basis, because the $44,000 received by Karen is not an RRSP "benefit" as defined.

(4) In summary, $44,000 of the total $125,000 RRSP value at the time of distribution is included in computing Mary's income, $11,000 is included in computing Karen's income and the remaining $70,000 is included in computing John's income ($67,200 of which he can transfer on a tax-deferred basis under ¶903).

(ITA: 146(8.8), (8.9); IT-500R Registered Retirement Savings Plans — Death of an Annuitant; Other Publications: Department of Finance Technical Notes of August 30, 1993; Department of Finance Technical Notes of April 26, 1995)

[¶1914.22] *Decrease in Plan Value after Death*

Previous legislation did not address the situation where an annuitant dies before the maturity of an RRSP plan and the value of the RRSP declines subsequent to the date of death of the plan holder and prior to the distribution of the plan to the beneficiaries. This was particularly relevant after the 2008 financial market meltdown. The government addressed this issue by implementing new legislation that allows RRSP losses incurred subsequent to the plan holder's death to be carried back and deducted against the fair market amount of the RRSP included in the deceased's year of death return. This deduction is available if the RRSP is wound up by the end of the year following the year of death of the last annuitant and the RRSP held only qualifying investments. Where either of these conditions is not met, the Minister of National Revenue may allow the deduction of all or a portion of the amount upon written request from the legal representative of the deceased plan holder. For example, a taxpayer dies in June 2008 and is the last annuitant under an RRSP. The fair market value of the RRSP at date of death is $100,000 and is included in the deceased's income for 2008. In November 2009, the estate distributes $80,000 to the beneficiaries and the executor winds up the RRSP. Now the deceased's 2008 tax return can be amended to claim a deduction of $20,000 against the deceased's income for 2008 ($100,000 - $80,000).

(ITA: 146(8.92), (8.93))

[¶1914.25] *Further Guidance: Form T2019; Form T1090; Interpretation Bulletin IT-500R; Worksheets RC4177 and RC4178*

Where there is a surviving spouse or common-law partner who is or elects to be the successor annuitant of deceased's matured RRSP, the rules are fairly simple (everything after death is the spouse's or common-law partner's income and is so taxed). Similarly, where there is no surviving spouse or common-law partner or dependent children, the value of an RRSP is simply taxed to the annuitant. Where the refund of premium rules enter in, however, taxpayers may be forgiven for finding the rules somewhat confusing. They can find some comfort in form T2019, which can be used to calculate the amount reported as income of the beneficiaries and the deceased. It can be downloaded from the CRA website, www.cra-arc.gc.ca.

Form T2019 *must* be used to designate an amount as a refund of premiums, except where a transfer has been made directly to the RRSP (or other eligible tax-deferred investment) of a spouse or common-law partner or financially dependent child or grandchild. That is, it must be used where an unmatured RRSP has become part of the estate of the annuitant and part or all of it is being transferred to a surviving spouse or common-law partner or where proceeds of a matured or unmatured RRSP are being transferred to a financially dependent child or grandchild. Form T2019 is filed jointly by the legal representative of the deceased and the beneficiary.

The student of these problems will also find guidance in Interpretation Bulletin IT-500R. The CRA has also issued two extensive "Worksheets": "Death of an RRSP Annuitant" (RC4177) and "Death of a RRIF Annuitant" (RC4178), which contain extremely helpful charts which simplify (and interpret) the refund of premium rules for RRSPs and designated benefit rules for RRIFs as lucidly as it can be done.

[¶1914.30] *Deduction for Final Contribution to Spousal Plan*

A final contribution may be made to a spousal RRSP (where there is a surviving eligible spouse or common-law partner, as defined from time to time at ¶1113) to utilize unused contribution room of the deceased. The contribution is made in fact by the legal representative of the deceased, and must be made within normal time limits, that is, within 60 days after the end of the calendar year in which the death occurred.

The deductible amount available for such contribution to a spousal plan is the unused contribution room at the start of the year as generated by earned income of the preceding year (subject to the RRSP monetary limit for the year of death), plus any unused contribution room carried forward from earlier years (¶2610.15).

Because of the time lag in generating RRSP room (¶2604), ordinary earnings in the year of death do not give rise to RRSP room which can be utilized.

A deductible payment to a spousal RRSP for a year is allowed where the contributor dies in the stub period of 60 days following the year end. In this case, a deductible spousal plan contribution can apparently be made within the 60-day stub period and deducted for the year preceding death. Such a contribution would still not include ordinary earnings for the year preceding death, but earnings of the year preceding a stub period death could be contributed and deducted in the year of death. It is also possible in the case of a stub period death to ignore the stub period and make a year-of-death spousal plan contribution under the general rule.

Example

James died in January 2016. His legal representative can make a spousal plan contribution for his spouse or common-law partner by March 1, 2016, based on James' 2014 earned income and carryforwards (namely, his 2015 contribution limit). This will be deductible in the 2015 taxation year. A further contribution based on remaining 2016 contribution limits (generated by 2015 earned income) can be deducted in 2016.

See also ¶2624.05.

(ITA: 146(5.1); T4011, *Preparing Returns for Deceased Persons*)

[¶1916] REGISTERED RETIREMENT INCOME FUND

If a plan holder dies, and the property in the plan passes to a person other than his spouse or common-law partner or a qualified child or grandchild of the deceased, the fair market value of the property in the plan immediately before his death must be included in the plan holder's income. The person receiving the property will only be taxed on any increase in value after the date of death of the plan holder.

Previous legislation did not address the situation where an annuitant dies and the value of the RRIF declines subsequent to the date of death of the plan holder and prior to the distribution of the plan to the beneficiaries. This was particularly relevant after the 2008 financial market meltdown. The government addressed this issue by implementing new legislation that allows RRIF losses incurred subsequent to the plan holder's death to be carried back and deducted against the fair market amount of the RRIF included in the deceased's year of death return. This deduction is available if the RRIF is wound up by the end of the year following the year of death of the last annuitant and the RRIF holds only qualifying investments. Where either of these conditions is not met, the Minister of National Revenue may allow the deduction of all or a portion of the amount upon written request from the legal representative of the deceased plan holder. For example, assume a taxpayer died in June of Year 1 and is the last annuitant under a RRIF. The fair market value of the RRIF at date of death is $100,000 and is included in the deceased's income for Year 1. In November of Year 2, the estate distributes $80,000 to the beneficiaries and the executor winds up the RRIF. Now the deceased's Year 1 tax return can be amended to claim a deduction of $20,000 against the deceased's income for Year 1 ($100,000 - $80,000).

Very often a RRIF plan holder (annuitant) names the annuitant's spouse or common-law partner a successor annuitant; in this case the RRIF payments continue to be made to the surviving spouse or common-law partner and the amounts paid after the date of death are taxed to the surviving spouse or common-law partner.

If the plan holder (annuitant) dies and no election has been made, and the RRIF property passes to the estate for the benefit of a surviving spouse or common-law partner, the spouse or common-law partner and estate may jointly elect for the spouse or common-law partner to become a successor annuitant.

If the plan holder dies and some or all of the RRIF property passes to the spouse or common-law partner, and no election had been made before or after the death to treat the surviving spouse or common-law partner as a successor annuitant, the lump-sum payment to the spouse or common-law partner is income of the spouse or common-law partner in the year received, is called a "designated benefit" and is taxed to the surviving spouse or common-law partner rather than included in the final return of the deceased; however, the surviving spouse or common-law partner may "roll over" the payment under the "eligible amount" rules, which are virtually identical to the RRSP refund of premium rules (see ¶1914 and ¶903). Where the property passes to the estate but there is a surviving spouse or common-law partner, the estate and the spouse or common-law partner may jointly elect to treat the value, or such amount of it as they elect, as an eligible amount. An eligible amount is the amount of the RRIF passing to the spouse or common-law partner reduced by that proportion that any unpaid minimum RRIF amount for the year of death is of the total RRIF amount paid to the spouse or common-law partner. It seems to be intended that this residual minimum amount, representing the minimum withdrawal required from the RRIF under ordinary RRIF rules for the year in excess of the amount actually withdrawn and taxed to the deceased, should be taxed to the surviving spouse or common-law partner.

If the recipient is the child or grandchild of the deceased who was financially dependent on the deceased, amounts received by the child or grandchild from the registered retirement income fund will be included in the income of the recipient as a "designated benefit".

It is presumed in the first instance that a child/grandchild was not financially dependent if its income in the year preceding the death exceeded a specified amount. That presumption can be rebutted by factual evidence. The point is that the specified amount test only comes into play *vis-à-vis* a parent or grandparent on whom the child was in fact dependent. The CRA discusses financial dependency in CRA Document No. 9926947. There it states, among other things, that the CRA "would not normally accept that a grandchild was financially dependent on a grandparent where the grandchild lived with his or her parent(s) and the parent(s) could adequately provide for the grandchild's well being". On the other hand, in CRA Document No. 2001-0114425, the CRA says that it would generally accept that in the case of separation or divorce, where a child with no independent income lives with one parent and the other pays child support under a Court Order or Separation Agreement, the child is dependent on the parent paying child support. All CRA opinions on financial dependence stress that it is an issue of fact in each case, and should generally be decided at local Tax Services Office level.

As with the refund of premium rules (¶1914.15), the specified amount at which the presumption against dependence comes into play is the basic personal amount (¶1106) for the year preceding death, which amount is indexed for inflation.

Where the child/grandchild was dependent by reason of mental or physical infirmity on a deceased supporting parent/grandparent, the preceding year basic personal amount used as a benchmark in the presumption of dependency is supplemented by the preceding year disability amount (both as indexed).

Infirmity for the purposes of these rules is discussed under the subheading "Infirmity Test" toward the end of ¶1209.

Where amounts are paid to a child or grandchild established to be a dependant under the rules above, any such amount must be taxed to the dependent child rather than the parent or grandparent, regardless of the child's age or the reason for dependency. These amounts (called "designated benefits") are calculated on form T1090 and reported on line 130 of the T1 return, and are treated exactly as if they were paid under the refund of premium rules for an RRSP. That is, a dependent child who is under 18 can make a tax-deferred transfer of a designated benefit to an annuity to age 18. The amount received will then be taxed as the annuity payments are received. The annuity must be acquired within 60 days of the end of the year of receipt of the refund of premiums. The recipient child who does roll over an amount to an annuity is in turn required to "designate" the amount transferred to the annuity on its tax return. Unlike the designation for contributions to an RRSP, done on Schedule 7, no form was provided at the time of writing for designation of a contribution to an annuity, and usually the annuity receipt is sufficient, although a short letter filed with the tax return stating that the filer "designates $ ... as an amount pursuant to paragraph 60(*l*) of the *Income Tax Act*" might make certainty more sure. It is also possible for a child under 18 to have the refund of premium proceeds contributed to a trust which acquires an annuity to age 18 for the child. The trust must conform to standards described in ¶1914.16.

Where the RRIF amounts pass through an estate to the dependent child or children, the estate and recipient(s) may jointly elect on form T1090 to treat the amounts as a designated benefit under a RRIF. For deaths occurring after 1998, there is no surviving spouse or common-law partner limitation, and for deaths after 1995 there is no surviving spouse or common-law partner limitation where an election is made which is identical to the one for direct payments above.

A child or grandchild who was dependent on the deceased parent or grandparent by reason of physical or mental infirmity and who receives RRIF payments on the death of the parent or grandparent may defer tax by making any of the permitted investments described at ¶903. This includes transfer to an RRSP, RRIF, SPP, PRPP, eligible annuity, or an annuity to age 18. The transfer contribution must be made or the annuity must be purchased within 60 days of year end; see ¶903. Furthermore, as discussed at ¶1914.17, the 2010 federal Budget announced that qualifying deductible transfers for these purposes will be allowed to the child's or grandchild's RDSP. Transfers to an RRSP, etc., are designated on line 14 of Schedule 7; annuities are designated as described for other children above. For receipts based on a death occurring in 1993 and later years, it appears that only the "eligible amount" calculated on form T1090 will qualify for rollover; that proportion of the infirm child's designated benefit that represents the RRIF minimum amount for the year of death not withdrawn and taxed to the deceased will be taxed to the child currently and is not eligible for deferral.

Where benefits are included in the estate, an election is available to allow dependent children to be treated as beneficiaries to reduce the estate liability within the limits set out above and in the case of infirmity permit rollover to an annuity. See ¶1914.

As with RRSP refund of premium rules, it is open to the legal representative of the deceased to forgo any amount of the deduction available to the deceased for amounts treated as designated benefits. To the extent the designated benefit is thus taxed in the hands of the deceased, it is not taxed to the recipient. It would appear to remain eligible for rollover to the extent permitted above, although the combination of taxing the deceased and rolling over the same amount to a tax-deferred plan is likely to create unnecessary tax. However, where the recipient cannot (as in the case of an able adult child) or does not wish to fully contribute to a tax-deferred plan, the flexibility to create income for the deceased rather than the beneficiary will be useful.

Also as with the refund of premium rules at ¶1914, for 1993 and later years the rules are amended to minimize the effect of growth of RRSP assets after the death of the annuitant by allowing amounts accrued in the plan after death to be taxed to (and in the case of a spouse or common-law partner or infirm child rolled over by) the survivors rather than the deceased. The amounts of post-death growth in RRIF asset values are calculated under rules identical to those for RRSPs at ¶1914.

For a more general discussion of registered retirement income funds, see Chapter 26, ¶2616.05 *et seq.*

(ITA: 60(*l*); 146(1) "refund of premiums"; 146.3(1) "designated benefit", (5)(a), (6), (6.1), (6.11), (6.2), (6.3), (6.4))

[¶1916.05] *Forms*

Form T1090 is used to calculate the "designated benefit" included in the income of a survivor and the "eligible amount" which may be rolled over to a tax-deferred plan of a qualified survivor. It is not necessary if the spouse or common-law partner is the successor annuitant of the plan, or where a transfer has been made directly to the RRSP (or other eligible tax-deferred investment) of a spouse or common-law partner. It is filed jointly by the legal representative of the deceased and the beneficiary. It should be used to calculate the amounts reported as income of the deceased as well as the beneficiaries.

If you are transferring the eligible amount to your RRSP and claiming the offsetting deduction, you also have to complete Schedule 7, *RRSP Unused Contributions, Transfers, and HBP or LLP Activities* and file it with your return.

The CRA has also issued an extensive "Worksheet", *Death of a RRIF Annuitant* (RC4178), which contains extremely helpful charts which simplify (and interpret) the refund of premium rules for RRIFs.

These items are available from all CRA offices (¶287), and may be downloaded from the CRA website at www.cra-arc.gc.ca.

[¶1916.10] *Rollover for Annuities Acquired by Trust*

As discussed above and at ¶903.15, where a taxpayer dies and the taxpayer's spouse or common-law partner or financially dependent child or grandchild ("beneficiary") receives an amount from the deceased's RRSP as a consequence of the death, or an eligible amount from the deceased's RRIF, the beneficiary includes the amount in income but is allowed an offsetting deduction to the extent that the amount is used to acquire a qualifying annuity in the year of the inclusion or within 60 days thereafter. For minor children who were not physically or mentally infirm but were dependent upon the deceased, a term annuity is allowed generally to age 18 if the child or a trust under which the child is the sole beneficiary is the annuitant. Draft technical amendments to the Act, released on July 16, 2010 and now passed into law, refine the minor trust rule described above, and further provide that certain other trusts may acquire the annuity without affecting the offsetting rollover deduction for the spouse or common-law partner, or child or grandchild, as the case may be. These rules are discussed at ¶1914.16.

[¶1916.15] *Refund of Premiums and Designated Benefits Rolled Over to Registered Disability Savings Plan (RDSP)*

In the 2010 federal Budget, the government announced a rollover similar to those discussed above (inclusion for beneficiary followed by offsetting deduction) for RRSP refunds of premiums, RRIF eligible amounts, and lump-sum payments out of an RPP upon the death of the annuitant or plan holder and that are paid to an RDSP under which a child or grandchild is financially dependent upon the deceased by reason of physical or mental infirmity. The rollover is discussed at ¶1914.17.

[¶1916f] TAX-FREE SAVINGS ACCOUNTS (TFSAS)

TFSAs are discussed in ¶2532c. Briefly, they are registered plans to which an individual resident in Canada can make non-deductible contributions (within specified limits) which must be invested in qualified investments. The investment income of the plan is tax free, and amounts can be withdrawn at any time without tax consequences. Where specified contribution limits are exceeded, the excess is subject to a monthly penalty tax.

[¶1916f.10] *Treatment of Survivor*

Where an individual has a TFSA at the time of death, the tax-free nature of the plan ceases immediately before death, subject to the comments in ¶1916f.20 below. There is no income inclusion for the deceased, but future earnings in the plan become taxable from the time of death. However, provision is made for the "survivor" (the person who was the spouse or common-law partner of the deceased at the time of death) to become a successor plan holder, in which case the plan does not cease at the time of death of the deceased. Technical amendments published on November 5, 2010 and now passed into law allow the survivor holder's survivor (i.e., the surviving person's spouse or common-law partner, if any), to become a successor plan holder, so that the plan can continue as a tax-exempt TFSA upon the death of the survivor. The amendments are retroactive to the 2009 year, when TFSAs became available.

Where a successor plan holder acquires a TFSA that was subject to the excess contributions tax, the survivor's own TFSA room can be used to soak up the excess, but any remaining excess will be subject to the monthly penalty tax.

While the consequences intended by the federal government to apply where there is a successor plan holder are clear and unexceptionable, it is not clear that provincial succession law will in all (or any) cases allow the designation of a successor plan holder unless the designation is specified in the will of the deceased. Provinces generally make a specific exception to such a rule for RRSPs, so that the designation in the plan itself will suffice. Presumably, a similar exception will be created, in the fullness of time, for TFSAs, although the pragmatic investor may want to take legal advice on the issue, especially once plan contribution room reaches significant levels.

If the survivor does not become a successor plan holder, the survivor may contribute to his or her own plan amounts received from the TFSA of the deceased by the end of the calendar year following the year of death free of the normal contribution room limits which would ordinarily apply to the survivor.

In particular, if the survivor (as defined above) has not been designated as a successor plan holder, the survivor may make an "exempt contribution" to a TFSA of the survivor if the following conditions are met:

(1) the contribution has been made during the "rollover period", i.e., the period that begins when the individual dies and that ends at the end of the first calendar year following the individual's death — the CRA may, on a discretionary basis, approve a later date for the end of the rollover period in a particular instance;

(2) a payment (the "survivor payment") has been made, as a consequence of the individual's death, to the sur-

vivor during the rollover period from an arrangement that ceased to be a TFSA because of the individual's death (i.e., excluding a TFSA of which a survivor of the individual became the holder) — such a payment may have been made either directly to the survivor or indirectly (e.g., a payment made indirectly to the survivor as a beneficiary of the individual's estate);

(3) the survivor "designates in prescribed form" the contribution as a survivor's exempt contribution [within 30 days after the day the contribution is made]; and

(4) the amount of the contribution does not exceed the least of the following three amounts:

(a) the excess of the particular survivor payment over the total of all other contributions designated by the survivor in relation to the particular payment; for example, if the particular payment was $20,000 and the survivor had already designated a $15,000 contribution in relation to the payment, the survivor could designate only an additional $5,000 contribution in relation to the particular payment;

(b) the excess of the fair market value of the assets of the deceased's plan immediately before death over the total of all other exempt contributions made by the survivor in relation to that arrangement; thus, for example, if the value of assets held by a trust that had been governed by a TFSA grows from $100,000 to $120,000 following the death of the holder and the $120,000 is paid entirely to the holder's survivor in two equal instalments, the amount of contributions that the survivor is permitted to designate in relation to the survivor payments cannot exceed $100,000; and

(c) nil, if the deceased had an excess TFSA amount (i.e., an overcontribution subject to penalty tax) immediately before death, or if survivor payments are made in the rollover period to more than one survivor of the individual (as might be the case if, immediately before death, the individual had both a legal spouse from whom the individual was separated and a common-law partner); however, the CRA has discretion to approve an exempt contribution in these circumstances — one might hope that the CRA will develop a policy to systematically approve contributions once the excess contributions have been dealt with in such fashion as it deems appropriate, or where the competing survivors can agree or be persuaded to each make an appropriate contribution.

Form RC240 must be used to make and designate TFSA exempt contributions.

[¶1916f.20] *Treatment of Deceased (and of TFSA Trust)*

Where a taxpayer dies possessed of a TFSA trust, and there is no successor plan holder (i.e., there no longer is a holder under the plan), the general rule is that the plan ceases at death. However, as an administrative convenience, the plan is allowed to continue for specific purposes until the earlier of (i) the time the trust ceases to exist, and (ii) the end of the first calendar year that begins after the death of the holder, referred to as the "exemption-end time".

The purposes for which the plan continues are primarily the tax-free status rules for the trust itself (and not for the deceased and his or her beneficiaries). That is, the trust continues to maintain its tax-exempt status until the end of the year following the year in which the holder dies. If it is still in existence at the beginning of the second year following the holder's death, the general rules applicable on the cessation of a plan come into effect at that time. These are:

(1) the trust becomes a taxable trust on the expiration of the extension period;

(2) the trust is treated as having disposed of, and reacquired, its property for its fair market value immediately before that time; and

(3) the trust has a deemed year-end immediately before that time and a new taxation year (as a taxable entity) begins immediately thereafter.

Any payments made from the trust during the exempt period (from the time of death to the beginning of the second calendar year thereafter) in full or partial satisfaction of a taxpayer's beneficial interest in the trust must be included in the recipient taxpayer's income for the year of receipt, except to the extent designated by the trust as being attributable to the fair market value of the TFSA at death. In other words, to the extent that the payment represents the distribution of income earned on, or appreciation in the value of, the trust's property during the exempt period, that amount will be included in the taxpayer's income. As with RRSPs, there are no specific rules in the Act for the trust to follow in determining the extent to which any given payment made following the death of the TFSA holder is attributable to post-death income or appreciation in value. The only constraint imposed on the trust is that the total amounts designated as being non-taxable cannot exceed the fair market value of the trust's assets at death.

The income inclusion determined immediately above must be included in determining the taxpayer's income from property. Note that it is only income earned after death that is the subject here. There should be no impact on the provision allowing a survivor to contribute earlier earnings to the survivor's TFSA.

With the exception of payments to non-residents, there is no requirement for the issuer to withhold tax on the payments.

If the trust continues to exist after the end of the exempt period, it must include in its income for its first taxable year any post-death exempt period income or appreciation that was not paid out during the exempt period. This amount is to be included in the trust's income as income from property, which may be flowed out to the beneficiaries of the trust under regular trust taxation rules.

(ITA: 12(1)(z.5); 146.2; 207.01; 248(1) "TFSA")

[¶1916g] REGISTERED DISABILITY SAVINGS PLAN

If the deceased was a beneficiary under a registered disability savings plan ("RDSP"), all amounts remaining in the plan after any required repayment of government grants and bonds must be paid to the beneficiary's estate by December 31 following the calendar year in which the beneficiary dies. The taxable portion of the payments must be included in the income of the beneficiary's estate's taxation year in which the payment is made, and, therefore, is not reported on the deceased's terminal return. (Payments made to the deceased while the person was alive are included in the deceased's income.) The taxable portion is the amount of the payment in excess of the "non-taxable portion", the latter of which is essentially a fraction of the payment equalling the amounts of contributions formerly made to the plan or other plans of the beneficiary (net of non-taxable portions paid out previously) divided by the fair market value of the property held by the plan immediately before the payments (subsections 146.4(6) and (7)).

In the 2011 federal Budget, the government introduced a new election available to a beneficiary of an RDSP with a shortened life expectancy, generally where a medical doctor certifies that the individual beneficiary is not expected to survive more than five years. Under the changes, withdrawals by the beneficiary made at any time following an election will not trigger the repayment of the government CDSGs and CDSBs (grants and bonds), provided that the total of the taxable portions of the withdrawals does not exceed $10,000 annually. The provision is applicable to the 2011 and subsequent taxation years, except that no election may be made before June 26, 2011 (the Royal Assent date). However, as a transitional rule, beneficiaries making an election under this measure will be permitted to utilize their 2011 withdrawal limit in 2012, provided that the required medical certification was obtained before 2012. Upon the death of the beneficiary, any CDSGs and CDSBs remaining in the plan and that were received by the plan within the preceding 10 years must be repaid.

[¶1917] SETTLEMENT OF DEBT

It is possible for the settlement of debt rules at ¶353, ¶409, or ¶565 to apply where debts owed by the deceased are cancelled or forgiven at death.

The forgiveness rules deem a settlement of commercial debt to occur at the beginning of the day of death provided the settlement occurs within six months of death (or longer if acceptable to the estate and the CRA). Amounts paid in satisfaction of principal by the estate reduce the forgiven amount. Commercial debt is debt the interest on which may be deducted, and it is this debt to which the rules at ¶565 apply. The intention of those rules is to allow forgiven amounts to be applied against the tax attributes of the deceased under those rules. Any income inclusion resulting from insufficient tax attributes to absorb the forgiveness is subject to the reserve described at ¶565 in the terminal return.

Where an obligation subject to the settlement of debt rules is not settled within six months of death (or longer if acceptable to the estate and the CRA), the settlement rules apply to the estate rather than the deceased. In these circumstances, interest accruing after death is ignored in computing the forgiven amount.

Where any debt settlement of an employee or shareholder is included in income under the rules at ¶353 or ¶409, the income inclusion is not reduced by tax attributes. This seems to be true regardless of whether the debt was a commercial debt.

Where debts owing to the deceased are settled by bequest or inheritance, the rules on the settlement of commercial debt do not apply. Accordingly, the beneficiary is not subject to tax attributes or income adjustments. For the deceased, a debt owed to him or her may be a capital property subject to deemed disposition rules. Debts forgiven by will may be rights or things included in the deceased's income unless transferred to the beneficiary (¶1908).

(ITA: 6(15), (15.1); 15(1), (1.2), (1.21); 80(2)(*a*), (*p*), (*q*); Other Publications: Department of Finance Technical Notes, December 20, 1994)

[¶1917.05] *Settlement of Debt — Life Insurance*

Proceeds from the disposition of an interest in a life insurance policy may be required to be brought into income (see ¶981).

Life insurance proceeds arising on death from a policy issued after December 1, 1982 may be subject to taxation if the policy is other than an exempt policy (see ¶981). Your insurance company should advise you as to whether or not your policy is exempt.

Special rules apply where a private corporation is the beneficiary of a life insurance policy. The proceeds received by the corporation go into a special account out of which tax-free dividends may be paid. This is typically part of a plan to provide for the buy-out of the corporation at the death of a significant shareholder. The rules governing these transactions were extensively modified after April 26, 1995, although extensive grandfathering provisions were later added where insurance was in place at that time. These rules require professional advice; they are beyond the scope of this book.

Where a partnership is the beneficiary, proceeds of a life insurance policy may add to the partnership adjusted cost base. A similar result may arise where a corporation or partnership has taken out life insurance on a key owner/manager to pay off debts to creditors in the event of death.

Where the life of a debtor (or a principal shareholder or officer of a debtor corporation or a partner of a debtor partnership) is insured and the cost is borne by the creditor without being passed on to the debtor, proceeds received on death that are applied to extinguish or reduce the debtor's commercial obligation are subject to the settlement of debt rules.

(ITA: 80; 148(2), (9); IT-430R3)

[¶1918] DEDUCTIONS AND RESERVES

The normal deductions for allowable amounts paid before death are permitted plus deductions for accrued amounts as outlined in ¶1907 and ¶1908.

Where multiple returns are filed under the special elections below, certain deductions from income to arrive at taxable income are limited so that they cannot be claimed on each separate return in amounts that total more than if all income were included in one return on which the whole deductions were claimed. See ¶1901.

Generally, no deductions may be claimed for reserves against:

(1) capital gains (see ¶581);

(2) proceeds of sale of resource properties;

(3) profits on sale of other types of property, generally inventory (see ¶732.45 and ¶732.50); and

(4) commission income of insurance agents or brokers (see ¶732),

unless (i) the related right to receive the amount is transferred to the deceased's spouse or common-law partner or to a special trust for that spouse or common-law partner, (ii) the spouse, common-law partner and/or the trust are resident in Canada, and (iii) an election on form T2069, "Election in Respect of Amounts Not Deductible as Reserves For The Year of Death", is filed. Where these conditions have been satisfied, subsection 72(2) provides that the applicable reserve may be claimed by the deceased in the terminal year. The amount so claimed is included in the income of the spouse, common-law partner or spouse trust for the first taxation year ending after the death, and the spouse, common-law partner or trust, as the case may be, may in effect carry on with the reserve treatment from year to year in the same manner as the deceased would have been entitled to do had he lived. If it appears that use may be made of this provision, it is suggested that professional advice be obtained.

(ITA: 72(1), (2))

DEEMED DISPOSITIONS OF CAPITAL PROPERTY

[¶1920] GENERAL

An individual who dies is deemed to have disposed of each capital property (including depreciable property and partnership interests) owned by him immediately before his death.

The capital property is deemed to have been sold for proceeds equal to its fair market value on the date of death (except as described in ¶1922 and ¶1923) and gains or losses are aggregated with gains or losses which were actually realized in the year while the taxpayer was living. If the total realized and deemed allowable capital losses for the year exceeds realized and deemed taxable capital gains for the year, the net capital losses may be deducted in full, first against taxable income of the year of death and next against taxable income of the preceding year. For details, see ¶578.

Where depreciable property (¶557) is held at the time of death, no capital cost allowance is permitted in the year of death with the exception of a terminal loss arising under the deemed disposition rule.

In general, the person who acquires the property of the deceased under these rules (as opposed to the rules at ¶1922 and ¶1923) will acquire it at fair market value immediately before the death. This is true also of depreciable property, but having said that, special rules will redetermine the capital cost for purposes of determining recapture/terminal loss to the deceased and capital cost allowance/potential recapture to the recipient. These rules are discussed under a separate heading below.

Where the property deemed to be disposed of in accordance with these rules was owned on December 31, 1971, the transitional rules discussed in Chapter 5 and ¶844 apply in determining the amount of any taxable capital gain or allowable capital loss. If the deceased person has not previously made the "V-Day" election referred to in ¶590, his executors or other legal representatives are empowered to do so on his behalf when the final return is submitted.

Where the property owned by the deceased person was a qualified small business corporation share, or qualified farm or fishing property, a resulting taxable capital gain may be offset by the deceased's remaining capital gains exemption, if any. See the discussion at ¶502.

Specific rules deal with the termination of a life estate in real estate on death, although the full interaction of those rules with the rules at death was not clear at the time of writing. See ¶541.

[¶1920.05] *Depreciable Property: Capital Cost*

In general, when a depreciable property is disposed of at fair market value, there will be recapture or terminal loss to the deceased based on "capital cost" (¶811–¶835) to the deceased. The recipient (inheritor) of the property will take over a property deemed acquired at fair market value and therefore eligible for capital cost on that amount. However, several special rules vary this result.

First, the capital cost of the deceased taxpayer is readjusted to ignore certain previous adjustments made in the hands of the deceased. These are:

(1) where the deceased acquired the property in a non-arm's length transaction, the adjustments in ¶813 are not applied to reduce the cost for these purposes;

(2) where the deceased suffered an adjustment under ¶823 because the proportion of business use of an asset used both for business and personal purposes changed, all the adjustments so made are ignored except that where business use increased, the proportion of increase is taken into account as if the only applicable rule were the one which prorates the increase according to the fair market value at the time of change by the increase in use; and

(3) where the deceased had commenced to use property originally acquired entirely for non-income producing use for an income purpose, the adjustment required by ¶823 is computed as if only the proportion of the fair market value at the time of change were required to be considered.

Essentially, then, capital cost may be increased as prior reductions are reversed, leading, it would seem, to possibly higher recapture/terminal loss and lower capital gain (since for depreciable property, adjusted cost base is capital cost).

These adjustments must also be made in the hands of the recipient of the depreciable property, who must take over not simply the fair market value of the property as cost, but also the capital cost of the deceased. Where there are no adjustments under the rules above and fair market value is equal to or less than capital cost (typically acquisition cost less adjustments for investment tax credit), there is presumably recapture or terminal loss to the deceased and capital cost equal to fair market value becomes capital cost to the recipient. Since no depreciation has been taken or deemed taken by the recipient, undepreciated capital cost (UCC) equals cost.

Where, however, the capital cost of a depreciable property to the deceased exceeds its fair market value immediately before the time of death, the recipient must take over the capital cost position of the deceased, with the difference decrease in value from cost to fair market value accounted for as capital cost allowance previously taken by the recipient.

Example

> Joe died owning a depreciable property which cost $120, had been subject to $20 of CCA and therefore had a UCC of $100, but was worth $105. The excess of cost over fair market value is therefore $15. He left the property to his friend, Harry, who could use it in his business. Joe has recapture of $5. Harry would seem to acquire the property at a cost of $120 less $15 of prior capital cost allowance and therefore a UCC of $105, but would have a deemed capital cost of $120. There is at least symmetry here. Joe has had the proper recapture at the time of death, and Harry is liable for potential recapture if he sells the property for proceeds between $105 and $120. There is potential capital gain above $120 and potential terminal loss below $105.

There is an exception to the rule immediately above where ¶859 rule operates to redetermine the proceeds of disposition to the deceased on a disposition of land and building. Where a building had a capital cost to the deceased taxpayer that exceeds the deceased taxpayer's redetermined proceeds, the capital cost to the inheritor is treated as being the amount that was the capital cost of the building to the deceased (as before). The amount by which the deceased's capital cost of the building exceeds the deceased's proceeds, rather than the cost of the building to the inheritor, is deemed to have been deducted by the inheritor as prior capital cost allowance. Finally the cost to the inheritor of the land is deemed to be the amount that was the deceased's redetermined proceeds of disposition on the land.

[¶1922] BEQUESTS TO SPOUSE, COMMON-LAW PARTNER, OR QUALIFYING TRUST

Where non-depreciable capital property of a deceased person (who was a resident of Canada immediately before death) passes to a Canadian resident spouse or common-law partner (as defined from time to time under the rules in ¶1113), or to a special trust for a spouse or common-law partner created by the deceased's will, the property is deemed to be disposed of at the deceased's adjusted cost base and the spouse, common-law partner, or trust receiving the property acquires the deceased person's adjusted cost base of the property for purposes of computing future gains or losses (see ¶1910). This will also apply if the transfer is the result of a disclaimer or renunciation by a beneficiary.

In order to obtain tax deferral benefits on transfers to a spouse or common-law partner trust, the property transferred or distributed must indefeasibly vest in the trust within 36 months of the death of the person (see ¶1909) and the trust must be resident in Canada immediately after the vesting. A trust will be considered a valid spouse or common-law partner trust if it is created by the deceased's will, or by court order.

In the case of depreciable property, the disposition is considered to take place at the lesser of "capital cost" or "cost amount". Capital cost for these purposes is capital cost as determined in ¶811 to ¶835 inclusive, except that:

(1) where the deceased acquired the property in a non-arm's length transaction, the adjustments in ¶813 are not applied to reduce the cost for these purposes;

(2) where the deceased suffered an adjustment under ¶823 because the proportion of business use of an asset used both for business and personal purposes changed, all the adjustments so made are ignored except that where business use increased, the proportion of increase is taken into account as if the only applicable rule were the one which prorates the increase according to the fair market value at the time of change by the increase in use; and

(3) where the deceased had commenced to use property originally acquired entirely for non-income producing use for an income purpose, the adjustment required by ¶823 is computed as if only the proportion of fair market value at the time of change were required to be considered.

These rules operate only to determine rollover values at death, and not any capital cost allowance claims of the deceased.

Cost amount is the proportion of undepreciated capital cost that capital cost to the deceased taxpayer (as adjusted making the same adjustments described in the preceding paragraph) of the property of a class passing under this rule is of all property of the class.

Since disposition effectively occurs at the lesser of cost or *pro rata* UCC, there should be no possibility of recapture or capital gain.

The surviving spouse, common-law partner, or trust will acquire the property at a cost deemed to be equal to the proceeds of disposition to the deceased under the rules above. The other characteristic required to determine capital cost allowance of the surviving spouse, common-law partner, or trust, namely undepreciated capital cost, is determined under the same rules which apply at ¶1920 except that references there to cost to the deceased will mean cost under these rules. That is, where the cost to the deceased (capital cost) exceeded proceeds of disposition (lesser of cost and UCC), the difference is considered prior capital cost allowance to the recipient spouse, etc. This merely means that the recipient spouse, etc. under these rules also takes over the prior depreciation of the deceased where, as is usually the case, cost exceeds undepreciated capital cost. The rule merely ensures an inheritance by the recipient of ordinary tax characteristics, including potential recapture where capital cost to the deceased exceeded UCC, as it normally does.

An ordering provision allows the legal representative of the deceased to select the order in which various depreciable properties of a prescribed class are considered to have been disposed of.

If the deceased person owned the depreciable property on December 31, 1971, the spouse, common-law partner, or trust may compute future capital gains as if they had owned the property on that date; only increases in value over the Valuation Day value will be taxed when the property is sold.

The legal representative of the deceased taxpayer can elect, on an asset by asset basis, not to have the "rollover" rules to a spouse or common-law partner or spouse trust apply; this could be done to trigger capital losses, ensure full utilization of the deceased's capital losses, and utilize the deceased's remaining capital gains exemption, if any. The election must be made in the return for the deceased's year of death. For these purposes, each share of a corporation is a separate property, such that the legal representative could elect that the rollover apply to some shares but not others of the same corporation. However, the CRA takes the position that a single share represents one property such that the legal representative cannot elect in respect of a fraction of that single share (2012 STEP Annual Conference, question 9). The same rationale would apply to the deceased's interest in a partnership.

For a bequest to a trust to qualify as one which permits the tax-free transfer of property the trust must provide that:

(1) the spouse or common-law partner of the deceased is entitled to receive all of the income of the trust during his or her lifetime; and

(2) no person except the spouse or common-law partner may, before the spouse's or common-law partner's death, receive or otherwise obtain the use of any of the income or capital of the trust.

If the trust provides that debts of the deceased are to be paid using trust property, bequests to the trust will not qualify for tax-free transfer unless special elections are made. However, the provisions for payments of debts of the deceased out of the trust does not automatically disqualify the trust from being a "spouse or common-law partner trust", if the proper elections are made.

Because of the deemed disposition rules, the CRA requests that a list of property owned by the taxpayer at death be supplied when the final return is filed.

(ITA: 70(6), (6.1), (6.2), (7), (12), (13); ITAR: 20(1.1); IT-305R4 Testamentary Spouse Trusts)

[¶1922.02] *Spouse or Common-Law Partner Trust — Deemed Income Inclusion for Beneficiary upon Beneficiary's Death after 2015*

Changes announced in the 2014 federal Budget affect the taxation of testamentary trusts. Perhaps most significantly, starting in the 2016 taxation year, testamentary trusts other than graduated rate estates and qualified disability trusts will be subject to a flat tax at the highest marginal rate. Testamentary trusts other than graduated rate estates will be required to have a calendar year taxation year.

Included with the changes is the deemed disposition rule for spousal or common-law partner trusts described in ¶1922. Under current rules, there is a deemed disposition by the trust of capital properties and certain other properties upon the death of the beneficiary spouse (common-law partner). Beginning in 2016, the deemed disposition rule will continue, but an election will be available for certain testamentary trusts (for deaths before 2017) under which the income or gains resulting from the deemed disposition will be deemed to be payable to the beneficiary, who will then include such amounts in income (rather than the trust).

[¶1922.05] *Partition of Matrimonial Property on Death*

Partition usually refers to a situation in which property subject to joint ownership is divided (see ¶2327). Typically the partition occurs under provincial laws that provide for the sharing of assets owned or acquired by a spouse during marriage and, in recent years, by a common-law couple during the period of the relationship). These laws include laws dealing with matrimonial regimes and those that provide for the sharing of property used by spouses, etc. during a marriage, etc. Tax legislation essentially provides that the partition rules at ¶2327 do not apply on death; rather property which transfers to the estate of the deceased spouse or common-law partner is deemed to transfer immediately before death, so that it transfers under the spousal rollover rules (¶531 and ¶532). If property transfers to the surviving spouse or common-law partner, there is a deemed transfer at death so the property transfers under normal death rules (¶1922).

(ITA: 248(23), (23.1))

[¶1922.10] *Bequest of Life Interest to Spouse*

In CRA Document No. 2002-0154725, the CRA addressed a situation where Mrs. X left a life interest in a real estate property to her husband with the remainder to her child. The life interest had to be valued at the time of death, and (absent an election) would pass to the husband at Mrs. X's adjusted cost base. The remainder would pass to the child at fair market value, establishing gain for Mrs. X and a cost base for the child. On Mr. X's later death, there would be a deemed disposition of the life interest immediately before death. The CRA assumed there would be a capital loss, and that it would be deemed to be nil because the property was a personal use property to Mr. X. There would be no adjustment to the cost base of the child resulting from the death of Mr. X. A somewhat different view of what happens to a life interest on death occurred in an earlier ruling, CRA Document No. 9330105, where it said that a life interest merely expired on death with no disposition. Presumably the later view is the better one.

[¶1923] BEQUESTS OF FARM PROPERTY

Rules first announced in the 2014 federal Budget effectively combine the relevant definitions of farming and fishing property that qualify for these rollovers. The combined definitions and provisions are relieving in nature, in that the previous tests regarding the principal use of the property referred to use in a farm or fishing business, but not in combination with each other. Beginning in 2014, the test can be met where the principal use is in either business or in a combination of the two businesses.

Special rules apply to farm property passing to a beneficiary who is a child, grandchild or great-grandchild of a deceased person. There are, in fact, two definitions of child which seem to apply. One is the definition at ¶1122.15. The second is part of the specific rule governing these transfers at death, and provides that a child "includes" a grandchild or great-grandchild, and also includes a person who was, at any time before he attained the age of 19 years, wholly dependent on the taxpayer and under the taxpayer's custody and control.

The rules apply if all the following conditions exist:

(1) the farm must be in Canada;

(2) the beneficiary must have been resident in Canada immediately before the death of the person;

(3) the property must be land or depreciable property (eligible capital property passing to a child on death automatically passes under the rollover rules described at ¶1909);

(4) the property must have been used before death principally in a farming business carried on in Canada in which the deceased, his or her spouse or common-law partner, *his or her parent*, or any of his or her children, grandchildren, or great-grandchildren was actively engaged on a regular and continuous basis (or, if the property is a woodlot, was engaged to the extent required by a prescribed forest management plan, as described at ¶1711.25). As noted above, beginning in 2014, the relevant test is that property must have been used principally in a farming or fishing business or a combination of the two; and

(5) the property must vest indefeasibly in the beneficiary within 36 months after the death of the person, or a longer period if reasonable in the circumstances (see ¶1909.05).

Property leased by a taxpayer to his or her family farm corporation or to a family farm corporation or partnership of his or her spouse or common-law partner, child, or parent qualifies for the tax-free transfer if the property is used principally in the course of carrying on the business of farming in Canada by any such family farm corporation or partnership at the time of the transfer.

Where all of these conditions exist, the following special rules apply:

(1) Land is deemed to be disposed of at the deceased's adjusted cost base, and acquired by the beneficiary at this same amount (see ¶506). Therefore, no capital gain or loss will arise; and

(2) Depreciable farm property (other than property being depreciated under Part XVII — see ¶1712) is deemed to be disposed of at the lesser of the deceased's "capital cost" and "cost amount", and acquired by the beneficiary at the same applicable value. For the meaning of these terms, see ¶1922. The intention is that there will be no recapture by the deceased (see ¶843) or capital gain or loss. The beneficiary may be subject to this recapture on a subsequent sale. It is not necessary that the beneficiary use the inherited farm property in the business of farming to maintain this rollover advantage.

Where land is transferred under these rules which would be treated as a depreciable property on disposition with respect to rental payments made prior to purchase (see ¶833), the rules should ensure that there will be a proper rollover of all characteristics.

Land or depreciable farm property of a prescribed class which was owned by the deceased on December 31, 1971 is eligible for tax-free zone treatment on a subsequent sale by the beneficiary (see ¶591). To be eligible for this treatment, certain elections must be made with the Minister of National Revenue within specified time limits (see ¶1909).

Where the farm property has been transferred to a spouse or common-law partner trust created on the death of the person (see ¶1922) or during his or her lifetime which provides that, on the death of the spouse or common-law partner, the property will pass to a child beneficiary described above, and if the above mentioned conditions are otherwise met at the time of the spouse's or common-law partner's death, then the special rules also apply, modified so that the trust's adjusted cost base and undepreciated capital cost flow through to the beneficiary. This will also be the case where the property distributed to the child is replacement property (in respect of which the trust has made certain elections) for the property originally transferred to the trust.

The legal representative of the deceased taxpayer or the spousal trust is permitted to elect to transfer: (a) land at any amount between the adjusted cost base to the deceased or the spousal or common-law partner trust and the fair market value of the property at the time of death of the taxpayer, or in the case of the trust, the death of the taxpayer's spouse or common-law partner, and (b) depreciable farm property (other than property being depreciated under Part XVII — see ¶1712) at any amount between the undepreciated capital cost to the taxpayer or the spousal or common-law partner trust and the fair market value of the property at the time of death of the taxpayer, or in the case of the spousal or common-law partner trust, the death of the taxpayer's spouse or common-law partner. These elections permit utilization of accumulated losses and the capital gains exemption (¶502), allowing an increased cost base to the beneficiaries. For deaths occurring after 1992, the rules ensure that where the legal representative elects not to have the rollover apply to land, the post-1992 rules at ¶1920 will apply, including the rules that provide for redetermination of proceeds on disposition of land and building.

These special rules on the disposition of farming property apply to the disposition of a share of a family farm (or fishing) corporation or an interest in a family farm (or fishing) partnership when the share of the corporation or interest in the partnership is transferred to a child, grandchild, or great-grandchild of the deceased. The definition of a "share of capital stock of a family farm (or fishing) corporation" is intended to include corporation shares owned by the deceased if substantially all the fair market value of the property owned by the corporation immediately preceding the time of death has been used principally in the course of carrying on a farming business in Canada in which the deceased, his or her spouse or common-law partner, or his or her child or parent was actively engaged on a regular and continuous basis (or, if the property is a woodlot, was engaged to the extent required by a prescribed forest management plan, as described at ¶1711.25). Beginning with the 2014 year, the "used principally" test refers to property used principally in a farming or fishing business or a combination of the two. Holding companies of such corporations qualify, as do corporations using the farm assets through partnerships, and so on. The definition is very technical and care must be taken in estate planning to ensure that corporations do qualify. The intention, at least, is that the holding structure should not matter unduly so long as the actual farm property is used by the deceased or specified family members in a Canadian farming business.

In order to qualify as a recipient of the property under these rules, the child, grandchild or great-grandchild must be a resident of Canada immediately before the death of the taxpayer and the property must vest indefeasibly with the child, grandchild or great-grandchild not later than 36 months after the death (see ¶1909.05).

A similar definition exists, and was similarly modified, for an interest in a family farm partnership.

The legal representative of the deceased taxpayer or the spousal or common-law partner trust is permitted to elect to transfer the share or partnership interest at any amount between the adjusted cost base to the deceased or the spousal or common-law partner trust and the fair market value of the property at the time of death of the taxpayer, or in the case of the spousal trust, the death of the taxpayer's spouse or common-law partner.

A transfer of farm property, including a share of a family farm corporation or an interest in a family farm partnership from a child to a parent may be accomplished under the rules described above. The rules apply to farm property received by the child as a result of the death of his or her parent or by *inter vivos* transfer from his or her parent. Such property can be transferred back to either parent for proceeds equal to an elected amount between the adjusted cost base and the fair market value of the property at the time of the child's death. The cost to the parent will be equal to the elected amount.

(ITA: 70(5)(*a*), (9), (9.1), (9.2), (9.3), (9.6), (9.8), (10); 252(1); ITAR: 20(2); 26(18); IT-349R3 Intergenerational Transfers of Farm Property on Death)

[¶1923d] BEQUESTS OF FISHING PROPERTY

Rules first announced in the 2014 federal Budget effectively combine the relevant definitions of farming and fishing property that qualify for these rollovers. The combined definitions and provisions are relieving in nature, in that the previous tests regarding the principal use of the property referred to use in a farm or fishing business, but not in combination with each other. Beginning in 2014, the test can be met where the principal use is in either business or in a combination of the two businesses.

Special rules apply to fishing property passing after May 1, 2006, to a beneficiary who is a child, grandchild, or great-grandchild of a deceased person. There are, in fact, two definitions of child which seem to apply. One is the definition at ¶1122.15. The second is part of the specific rule governing these transfers at death, and provides that a child "includes" a grandchild or great-grandchild, and also includes a person who was, at any time before he attained the age of 19 years, wholly dependent on the taxpayer and under the taxpayer's custody and control. It would seem that the specific definition is meant to be inclusive, and to add to, rather than derogate from, the definition at ¶1122.15.

The rules apply if all the following conditions exist:

(1) the fishing property must be in Canada;

(2) the beneficiary must have been resident in Canada immediately before the day of death of the deceased;

(3) the property must be land or depreciable property of a prescribed class (eligible capital property passing to a child on death automatically passes under the rollover rules described at ¶1909);

(4) the property must have been principally used by the deceased, his spouse or common-law partner, his parent (see ¶1122 again), or any of his children, grandchildren, or great-grandchildren in carrying on a fishing business in Canada before his death. As noted at ¶1923, beginning in 2014, the test is that property must have been used principally in a farming or fishing business or a combination of the two; and

(5) the property must vest indefeasibly in the beneficiary within 36 months after the death of the person, or a longer period if reasonable in the circumstances (see ¶1909.05).

Property leased by a taxpayer to his family fishing corporation or to a family fishing corporation or partnership of his spouse or common-law partner, or parent or child, qualifies for the tax-free transfer if the property is used principally in the business of fishing by any such family fishing corporation or partnership at the time of the transfer.

Where all of these conditions exist, the following special rules apply:

(1) Land is deemed to be disposed of at the deceased's adjusted cost base, and acquired by the beneficiary at this same amount (see ¶506). Therefore, no capital gain or loss will arise.

(2) Depreciable fishing property (other than pre-1972 property being depreciated under Part XVII — see ¶1712) is deemed to be disposed of at the lesser of the deceased's "cost amount" (undepreciated capital cost (UCC) — for each depreciable property this is apportioned from the UCC pool *pro rata* to the cost of the property over the cost of all property in the pool before death) and "capital cost", and acquired by the beneficiary at the same applicable value. The meaning of "capital cost" here is modified as described in ¶1922. The intention is that there will be no recapture by the deceased (see ¶843) or capital gain or loss. The beneficiary may be subject to this recapture on a subsequent sale. It is not necessary that the beneficiary use the inherited fishing property in the business of fishing to maintain this rollover advantage.

Where land is transferred under these rules which would be treated as a depreciable property on disposition with respect to rental payments made prior to purchase (see ¶833), the rules provide that the transfer will occur under the depreciable property rules, so there will be a proper rollover of all characteristics.

Land or depreciable fishing property of a prescribed class which was owned by the deceased on December 31, 1971, is eligible for tax-free zone treatment on a subsequent sale by the beneficiary (see ¶591). To be eligible for this treatment, certain elections must be made with the Minister of National Revenue within specified time limits (see ¶1909).

Fishing property being depreciated under the Part XVII method (see ¶1712) is not subject to the rule in (2) above. These assets would be deemed to be disposed of by the deceased at fair market value and acquired by the beneficiary at that value. There is no recapture by the deceased if fair market value is more than the undepreciated value, but a capital gain may occur (see Chapter 5). Note that the beneficiary may not use the Part XVII method in respect of these assets since they will have been acquired by him after 1971 (see ¶1712).

Where the fishing property has been transferred to a spouse or common-law partner trust, created on the death of the person (see ¶1922) or during his lifetime, which provides that, on the death of the spouse or common-law partner, the property will pass to a child beneficiary described above, and if the above mentioned conditions are otherwise met at the time of the spouse's or common-law partner's death, then the special rules also apply, modified so that the trust's adjusted cost base and undepreciated capital cost flow through to the beneficiary. This will also be the case where the property distributed to the child is replacement property (in respect of which the trust has made certain elections) for the property originally transferred to the trust.

The legal representative of the deceased taxpayer or the spousal trust is permitted to elect to transfer: (a) land at any amount between the adjusted cost base to the deceased or the spousal or common-law partner trust and the fair market value of the property at the time of death of the taxpayer, or in the case of the trust, the death of the taxpayer's spouse or common-law partner, and (b) depreciable fishing property (other than property being depreciated under Part XVII — see ¶1712) at any amount between the undepreciated capital cost to the taxpayer or the spousal or common-law partner trust and the fair market value of the property at the time of death of the taxpayer, or in the case of the spousal or common-law partner trust, the death of the taxpayer's spouse or common-law partner. These elections permit utilization of accumulated losses and the capital gains exemption (¶502), allowing an increased cost base to the beneficiaries.

These special rules on the disposition of fishing property apply to the disposition of a share of a family (farm or) fishing corporation or an interest in a family (farm or) fishing partnership when the share of the corporation or interest in the partnership is transferred to a child, grandchild, or great-grandchild of the deceased. The definition of a "share of capital stock of a family (farm or) fishing corporation" is intended to include corporation shares owned by the deceased if substantially all the fair market value of the property owned by the corporation immediately preceding the time of death has been used principally in the course of carrying on a fishing business in Canada, in which the deceased, his or her spouse or common-law partner, or his or her child or parent was actively engaged on a regular and continuous basis. Beginning with the 2014 year, the "used principally" test refers to property used principally in a farming or fishing business or a combination of the two. Holding companies of such corporations qualify, as do corporations using the farm assets through partnerships, and so on. The definition is very technical and care must be taken in estate planning to ensure that corporations do qualify. The intention, at least, is that the holding structure should not matter unduly so long as the actual fishing property is used by the deceased or specified family members in a Canadian fishing business.

A similar definition exists for an interest in a family farm partnership.

The legal representative of the deceased taxpayer or the spousal or common-law partner trust is permitted to elect to transfer the share or partnership interest at any amount between the adjusted cost base to the deceased or the spousal or common-law partner trust and the fair market value of the property at the time of death of the taxpayer, or, in the case of the spousal trust, the death of the taxpayer's spouse or common-law partner.

A transfer of fishing property, including a share of a family fishing corporation or an interest in a family fishing partnership from a child to a parent may be accomplished under the rules described above. The rules apply to fishing property received by the child as a result of the death of his or her parent or by *inter vivos* transfer from his or her parent. Such property can be transferred back to either parent for proceeds equal to an elected amount between the adjusted cost base and the fair market value of the property at the time of the child's death. The cost to the parent will be equal to the elected amount.

(ITA: 70(5)(*a*), (9), (9.1), (9.2), (9.3), (9.6), (9.8), (10); 252(1); ITAR: 20(2); 26(18); IT-349R3 Intergenerational Transfers of Farm Property on Death)

[¶1924] SMALL BUSINESS CORPORATION

Currently, any remaining capital gains exemption of the deceased can be deducted in computing taxable income in the year of death (with certain restrictions), to the extent of the deceased's taxable capital gains on the disposition of a qualified small business corporation share or qualified farm or fishing property in the year of death, including those resulting from the deemed disposition rules discussed at ¶1920; see ¶502 for a discussion of the capital gains exemption.

(ITA: 70(9.4); 70(9.5) (repealed); 70(11))

[¶1925] EMPLOYEE STOCK AND MUTUAL FUND OPTIONS

The general rules applicable to stock (and mutual fund) option benefits are discussed at ¶330.

There are now two rules governing the taxation of employee stock options on death. Where mutual fund unit options are subject to the rules in ¶330, they are equally subject to these rules.

Income Inclusion on Death

If a taxpayer dies owning an unexercised employee stock option, the taxpayer will include in the year of death the amount by which the value of the option immediately after death exceeds the amount, if any, paid by the taxpayer to acquire the option. In many cases, the taxpayer will be eligible for the deduction in computing taxable income that generally applies to employee stock option benefits (see ¶330 *et seq.*).

Commentary on Legislative Proposals (Sept. 16, 2016)

Note: When Legislative Proposals, September 16, 2016, achieves Royal Assent, the commentary will be modified to read:

If a taxpayer dies owning an unexercised employee stock option, the deceased taxpayer will include in the year of death the amount by which the value of the option immediately after death exceeds the amount, if any, paid by the taxpayer to acquire the option (paragraph 7(1)(*e*)). In some cases, the taxpayer will be eligible for the one-half deduction under paragraph 110(1)(*d*) in computing taxable income that generally applies to employee stock option benefits (see ¶330 *et seq.*). The one-half deduction will apply only if the option is exercised and the shares acquired within the first taxation year of the deceased's estate by the graduated rate estate of the taxpayer, a beneficiary of the graduated rate estate, or a person in whom the option under the agreement has vested as a result of the death. For taxation years ending before 2016, "graduated rate estate" is to be read as "estate".

Possible Deduction Where Value of Option Declines

It may happen that after the employee dies, the value of the shares subject to the option declines. In this situation, the employee has in effect been taxed on the value at death (subject to the offsetting deduction) but the estate, if it exercises the option, will receive shares of a lesser value. Subsection 164(6.1) solves this problem by allowing the estate to treat the reduction in value as a loss from employment for the year in which the deceased died. Beginning in 2016, the estate must be a "graduated rate estate" to make the election.

The loss carryback amount will be fixed by the value of the options when they are exercised, disposed of, or allowed to expire by the estate, but the loss will only arise if this occurs within the first taxation year of the estate. The loss carryback will be equal to the original income inclusion minus the exercise or disposition value and minus any taxable income deduction claimed in respect of the original income inclusion.

The representative of the estate is authorized to file an amended year-of-death return to give effect to this provision at the later of the last day the legal representative is required to have elected to file the year-of-death return, or the day the return of income for the first taxation year of the estate is due.

Example

A deceased taxpayer was required to include in income $10,000 under paragraph 7(1)(*e*) in the year of death; the value of the taxpayer's employee stock option was $10,000, and she paid nothing to acquire the option. The deceased claimed a 1/2 deduction under paragraph 110(1)(*d*) in respect of the benefit.

The deceased's estate disposes of the option in the estate's first taxation year for proceeds equal to $8,000.

If the subsection 164(6.1) election is made, 1/2 of the loss ($10,000 - $8,000), or $1,000, is deemed to be a loss from employment for the deceased in the terminal year. (As noted above, only 1/2 of the loss is carried back because the deceased claimed the 1/2 deduction under paragraph 110(1)(*d*).) The entire loss of $2,000 is subtracted from the estate's adjusted cost base of the option, such that its capital gain or loss from the disposition of the option is nil ($8,000 proceeds - $8,000 adjusted cost base).

(Technical notes of December 20, 1991; ITA: 7(1)(*e*); 164(6.1); ITR: 1000(2))

[¶1925.15] *Where Right Transferred in Non-Arm's Length Transaction*

Where employee stock options have been transferred in a non-arm's length transaction, they are normally taxed to the employee when exercised. However, if the employee has died when an option is exercised by a non-arm's length transferee, the benefit is taxed to the transferee as if it were employment income for the year of exercise earned in the country in which the employee primarily performed the duties of his or her employment. The result is that the transferee will be taxed, and a non-resident transferee may be liable for Canadian tax on the exercise.

(ITA: 7(1)(*c*), (*d*))

[¶1925a] TAXATION OF FLOW-THROUGH SHARES AT DEATH

Flow-through shares are a financing vehicle used in the oil and gas and mining industries and are issued by companies that need cash but do not need tax deductions. Instead, the investors in these issues receive the tax deductions. The investors can use the deductions to offset against other income. Because investors receive tax deductions, the shares acquired are deemed to have a cost base of nil. In the event of death, there is no provision in the Act to pass unused deductions on to the deceased's estate or beneficiaries. At the time of death, the shares are deemed to be sold for fair market value unless they are bequeathed to the spouse or common-law partner.

In a 2007 opinion (CRA Document No. 2006-0177471E5), the CRA commented that where a deceased taxpayer had held in interest in a limited partnership which in turn held flow-through shares, and died before the year end of the partnership, there could be no flow-out of CEE to the deceased, since he could not be a partner after death. However, in CRA Document No. 2006-0216201E5, the deceased held an interest in a limited partnership which in turn held flow-through shares. The partnership interest passed to the estate of the deceased, and the CRA said that the CEE flowing through the limited partnership would, subject to the limitations imposed by the limited partnership rules, be deductible to the estate. This would seem to be based on an earlier opinion (CRA Document No. 2000-0059517) in which the CRA said an interest in a partnership, the underlying property of which is a Canadian resource property, is not a Canadian resource property itself. That ruling comments on the situation where a child inherits a resource property interest from a deceased parent.

(ITA: 66(12.6); 66.1; 66.2; 66.3; 66.4)

[¶1926] PAYMENT OF TAXES

A special instalment method for payment of taxes may be used, by election, with respect to the tax attributable to certain items of income in the final return(s) of a deceased person. The income items which qualify for this instalment basis are:

(a) recapture of capital cost allowance (net of any terminal losses) arising from a deemed disposition of depreciable property upon death (¶1920);

(b) capital gains (net of any capital losses) arising from a deemed disposition of capital property upon death (¶1920);

(c) rights or things included in income of the deceased (¶1908), whether or not a special election has been made for them (¶1941); and

(d) gains arising from a deemed disposition of resource properties or land held as inventory.

To calculate the amount of tax which qualifies for payment on the instalment basis:

(1) Determine the tax payable as shown by the final return(s) of the deceased.

(2) Calculate the tax that would have been payable if the qualifying recapture, capital gains, rights and things and 1971 receivable reserve had not been included in the deceased's income.

(3) Subtract (2) from (1). The result is the maximum amount of tax which may be paid by instalments. You may use the instalment basis of payment for all or any portion of this maximum amount.

If the instalment basis is chosen, adequate security for payment must be provided with the Minister of National Revenue and taxes, in any number of equal instalments not exceeding ten, are payable according to the following schedule:

(1) The first payment is due at the same time as the deceased taxpayer's return is due (see ¶1901); and

(2) The remaining nine (or fewer) payments are due at one-year intervals following the date in (1), above.

If you wish to use the instalment method, you must complete and file form T2075, "Election to Defer Payment of Income Tax, Under Subsection 159(5) of the *Income Tax Act*, by a Deceased Taxpayer's Legal Representative or Trustee", with the Tax Services Office on or before the date when the first instalment payment is due. Interest will be charged at the rate prescribed by the government (at the rate for amounts owing to the Receiver General, so the prescribed rate plus four percentage points) and security will be required. A table of prescribed rates for past years (including the four percentage point addition) is found in a table at ¶80 preceding Chapter 1. Interest is subject to daily compounding.

(ITA: 70(2), (5), (5.2); 159(5), (5.1); ITR: 1001 Annual Instalments)

EXEMPTIONS, DEDUCTIONS, AND PERSONAL AMOUNT TAX CREDITS

[¶1930] PERSONAL AMOUNT CREDITS

Full personal amounts (described in Chapters 11 to 13) may be claimed even though the taxpayer did not live for a full calendar year.

For purposes of determining the amount claimed for a spouse or common-law partner in the return of a deceased taxpayer, the income of the spouse or common-law partner for the entire year must be taken into account to reduce the spousal or common-law partner amount (¶1114). Similarly, for all other dependants, personal amounts are determined by reference to the dependant's income for the full year.

Where there are separate returns for the year of death, some credits may be claimed repeatedly on each return and others must be allocated among returns; this is described at ¶1901.

(ITA: 118; CRA Guide *Preparing Returns for Deceased Persons* (T4011); IT-326R3 Returns of Deceased Persons as "Another Person")

[¶1931] DONATIONS

The legal representative of the deceased may claim, on the sundry returns which may be filed under the rules at ¶1901, tax credits for donations made during lifetime and bequests contained in the will of the deceased in accordance with the charitable donation rules discussed in Chapter 12. Prior to 2016, bequests not contained in the will were not allowable in the deceased's return(s). Beginning in 2016, gifts made by the deceased's estate may be claimed by the deceased or by the estate. See ¶1931.10 below.

Normally, the total of all donations eligible for the charitable tax credit generally may not exceed 75% of net income for the year. The exceptions available to taxpayers are described at ¶1268, ¶1270, ¶1290, and ¶1291. However, qualifying donations (including carryforwards from the preceding five years) up to 100% of net income are eligible for credit in the year of death; as well, the return for the year preceding death may be reopened (or filed, if it has not been) to treat donations made in or carried to that preceding year as eligible for credit to the extent of 100% of net income. Credits may be carried back from the year of death to the preceding year to the extent the taxpayer's representative does not or cannot utilize them in the year of death. The 100% of net income limitation in the year preceding death applies for that year to these carrybacks, any amounts carried forward to that year, and any amounts generated in the year itself.

For gifts of artist's inventory, see ¶1908.

(ITA: 118.1)

[¶1931.05] *Donations at Death Including RRSPs, RRIFs, TFSAs, and Life Insurance Proceeds: Deaths before 2016*

A charitable gift made by will is deemed to have been made by the deceased immediately before death and therefore gives rise to charitable donation tax credit in the year of death. If an RRSP or a RRIF names the estate of the deceased as beneficiary, the value of the RRSP etc. is included in income of the deceased immediately before death, and if the proceeds are then donated to charity under the will, there is a correct offset of income by charitable donation credit. A donation credit is permitted on the year of death return of the deceased where a charity is named as the beneficiary of an RRSP, a RRIF, or a life insurance policy. The actual transfer of funds must arise within 36 months (longer if there are extenuating circumstances). In the case of a life insurance policy, the deceased had to have, immediately before death, a right of consent to a change of beneficiary, and the charity must not have already been a policyholder or assignee of the policy. This is to prevent a double donation where credit has already been given on assignment of the policy. In the case of a RRIF or RRSP, the deceased must have been the annuitant immediately before death. Effective for the 2009 taxation year, these rules also apply to a charitable gift by will for a TFSA.

(ITA: 118.1(4), (5)–(5.3); CRA Document No.: Gift of Life Insurance Policy, *October 11, 1994*, CRA Document No. 9416675; 9611055 (decisions prior to 1999))

[¶1931.10] *Donations for Deaths After 2015*

Beginning in 2016, the rules provide that a gift made by a deceased individual's will or estate, or by a direct designation under the individual's life insurance policy, RRSP, RRIF, or TFSA (see above), is deemed to be a gift made by the individual's estate at the time the property that is the subject of the gift is transferred to the donee. If the gift is made while the estate is a graduated rate estate (GRE), the individual can claim the credit in respect of the gift in the year of death or in the immediately preceding year. Alternatively, the GRE can claim the credit in the year that the gift is made or a preceding year of the estate. In either case, the gifted property (or property for which it was substituted) must have been acquired by the estate as a consequence of the individual's death. If the gift is by way of a direct designation of a life insurance policy, RRSP, RRIF, or TFSA, the transfer to the donee must be made as a consequence of the individual's death. The credit can be shared or allocated between the individual and the GRE for these purposes, but the credit cannot be doubled up. The individual's surviving spouse or common-law partner cannot claim the credit for a gift made by the individual's will or otherwise by the individual's GRE.

Commentary on Bill C-29 Measures (Oct. 25, 2016)

Note: When Bill C-29, October 25, 2016, achieves Royal Assent, the commentary will be modified to read:

In general terms, an estate can qualify as a GRE for up to 36 months after the individual's death. Furthermore, gifts made by the individual's estate within 60 months after the death will qualify for the deceased's credit in the year of death or the immediately preceding year as long as the estate would qualify as a GRE but for the fact that more than 36 months have passed since the individual's death. Interestingly, this 24-month time extension does not apply for the purposes of the estate's credit in a preceding year of the estate, such that the estate must be a GRE in order to claim the credit in a preceding year. Otherwise, if the estate is not a GRE, the estate can claim the credit in the year of the gift or any of the five following years.

For a summary of the former rules and new rules beginning in 2016, see also the lead article in Tax Topics No. 2297, March 17, 2016.

[¶1932] MEDICAL EXPENSES

The general rule (¶1250) is that medical expenses may be claimed for any 12-month period ending in the year, to the extent the medical expenses exceed (for 2016) the lesser of $2,237 or 3% of the taxpayer's net income.

In the case of death, the legal representatives of the deceased taxpayer may claim, for the year of death, medical expenses paid by the taxpayer or his legal representatives within any 24-month period which includes the date of death. The same expense may not be claimed more than once; that is, if it was claimed by a taxpayer for a year on an earlier return, it may not be claimed again under this rule. There will be the usual deduction for 3% of net income up to the maximum dollar limit for the year of death.

If medical expenses are paid after the due date for filing the return but within a 24-month period including the date of death, an amended return should be filed claiming the medical expenses paid at the later date.

The refundable medical expense supplement is available in the year of death provided all other conditions of eligibility are met; see ¶1237.

Where the deceased was 18 or older and dependent on someone else for support, within the definition of dependant at ¶1122.35, and that supporting person paid medical expenses for the deceased, the medical expenses so paid in a 24-month period that includes the date of death should be assigned to the supporting person rather than the deceased. In general, the person who paid the expenses should always be the one to claim the credit. See ¶1225.

(ITA: 118.2; 122.51; S1-F1-C1 Medical Expense Tax Credit)

[¶1933] NET CAPITAL LOSSES

The limitations on deduction of allowable capital losses incurred in prior years as discussed in ¶1087 is removed in the year of death, and in the immediately preceding year. All allowable capital losses and net capital loss carryforwards may be deducted in computing taxable income in the year of death and the year preceding death, subject to complex ordering rules. See ¶578 for details.

As losses generally may be carried back three years, returns of prior years may require amendment (see Chapter 10).

As a consequence of the capital gains exemption (¶502), the net capital loss rule operates to reduce the losses which may be applied by total amounts claimed under the exemption (¶578).

(ITA: 111(2))

[¶1934] RRSP CONTRIBUTIONS

Deductions for RRSP contributions in the year of death are discussed at ¶1914.30.

[¶1935] OTHER DEDUCTIONS AND CREDITS

It should be noted that the deductions claimed for registered pension plan contributions, pooled registered pension plan contributions, registered retirement savings plan contributions, union dues, and professional fees are examples of some of the deductions that can only be claimed in the final return discussed in (2) of ¶1901. These deductions cannot be claimed in the special returns of deceased taxpayers discussed at ¶1941, ¶1942, and ¶1944, below. However, "personal amounts" and deductions from net income to arrive at taxable income (¶1077) can be claimed, if applicable, in any or all of the deceased's returns, subject to overall limitations (see ¶1901).

(IT-326R3 Returns of Deceased Persons as "Another Person")

[¶1937] CPP/QPP CONTRIBUTIONS

A taxpayer is not liable for Canada Pension Plan or Quebec Pension Plan contributions for the months in a year following the month of death. Moreover, the various contribution limits are apparently prorated in the year of death to include only the months up to and including the month of death. The CRA will normally process these adjustments automatically, although for employment income some adjustments can be made on Schedule 8 of Form T1. See ¶1305.

SPECIAL ELECTIONS

[¶1941] RIGHTS OR THINGS

Income items discussed in ¶1908 may, if not transferred to beneficiaries within the time limit outlined in that paragraph, be reported by filing a separate return, including only the value of rights or things in income. If this method is used these amounts are excluded from the final return. The separate return is prepared as if it were the return of another person and full personal exemptions may be claimed in both the rights and things return and the final return, as well as certain other deductions (see ¶1901 and ¶1935).

This election may be made within one year of the date of death or within 90 days from assessment of the regular return, whichever is later. Any tax payable calculated in the separate return is due at the same time as the tax return is due or, if so elected, may be paid on the instalment basis in the same manner as outlined in ¶1926.

(ITA: 70(2); IT-326R3 Returns of Deceased Persons as "Another Person")

[¶1942] BUSINESS INCOME

In ¶1910 it was stated that, when an individual dies prior to the end of the normal fiscal period of a business, the fiscal year is deemed to terminate and the income for the abbreviated fiscal period must be recognized as income of the year of death. Where an individual dies after the end of a fiscal period but before the end of the calendar year, the income from the second fiscal period may be included in the year of death return, or a separate tax return may be filed including in income only the business profits earned between the close of the last complete fiscal period and the date of death (see ¶1901).

This return is in addition to any other return filed, and, as outlined in ¶1941, separate claims for personal exemptions, etc., may be made. For more detail, see ¶1901.

(ITA: 150(4); IT-326R3 Returns of Deceased Persons as "Another Person")

[¶1944] TRUST INCOME

A separate return may be filed in respect of certain trust income from a testamentary trust. See ¶1912.

(ITA: 104(23)(*d*))

[¶1946] SUBSEQUENT LOSSES

The legal representative of an estate which realizes any net capital losses or terminal losses in its first taxation year may elect to have any part of the capital loss on any assets and any part of the terminal loss transferred to the year of death return of the deceased. Beginning in 2016, the estate must qualify as a "graduated rate estate".

The representative must file an amended year of death return for the deceased giving effect to the election, and must file the election "in prescribed manner and within a prescribed time" with the estate return. Regulations prescribing the manner and time of the election require the legal representative to file a letter with the Minister setting out:

(1) the amount of net capital loss elected to be carried back to the year of death; if this election is made, the letter must be accompanied by a schedule of all capital gains and losses of the estate in its first taxation year; and

(2) the amount of terminal losses elected to be carried back to the year of death; if this election is made, the letter must be accompanied by:

(a) a schedule of the amounts of undepreciated capital cost (UCC) of CCA classes closed out by the estate,

(b) a statement of the amount that but for the election would be the non-capital loss of the estate for its first taxation year, and

(c) a statement of the amount that but for the election would be the farm loss of the estate for its first taxation year.

This letter must be filed by the later of:

(1) the last day the legal representative is required or has elected to file for the taxation year in which the taxpayer died; or

(2) the day the return for the first taxation year of the deceased's estate is required.

The CRA is authorized (but not required) to accept late-filed elections under the rules discussed at ¶268.

Because of the complexity of the calculations required, it is suggested that the assistance of professional advisers be obtained whenever this election is considered.

For a discussion of the similar carryback of losses on unexercised employee stock options held at death, see ¶1925.

(ITA: 164(6); ITR: 1000 Property Dispositions)

[¶1955] ALTERNATIVE MINIMUM TAX

Under the alternative minimum tax (AMT) rules as they apply in the year of death, no AMT will arise on any returns filed for the year of death. Previous AMT may be applied to reduce ordinary tax in excess of the AMT which would normally be payable (but for the death) on the main year-of-death return only under the general rules at ¶2481. This reduction cannot be applied to any of the special returns described at ¶1941 to ¶1944 above. See ¶2485.

(ITA: 127.55)

[¶1960] ELECTION TO SPLIT PENSION INCOME ON DEATH

As discussed in ¶1311.15, an individual who receives eligible pension income in a year can jointly elect with a spouse or common-law partner to assign up to 50% of that income to the spouse or partner. The actual provision for the amount that can be transferred is half the pensioner's pension income prorated by: (i) the number of months in which (at any time in the month) the pensioner was married to, or in a common-law relationship with, the transfer recipient, over (ii) the number of months in the pensioner's taxation year.

The provisions clearly contemplate that the election can be made in the year of death of either party by joint election with the legal representative of the deceased, provided the deceased was resident in Canada immediately before death.

The CRA makes it clear in a technical opinion (CRA Document No. 2008-0275731E5) that a marriage or common-law partnership terminates at the death of either party. Thus, if a spouse died in February and the survivor wanted to assign pension income to the deceased (and the survivor lived to the end of the calendar year), the limitation on the amount to be transferred would be $^2/_{12}$ of one half of the survivor's pension income. The "2" in the numerator is the number of months during which they were married at any time in the month, and the "12" is the number of months in the transferor's taxation year.

[¶1960.10] *Length of Taxation Year of Deceased*

Where the survivor does not survive until December 31, or where the transfer operates in the other direction (that is, from the deceased to the survivor), the question arises as to the length of the taxation year of the deceased. That is, does the taxation year of a decedent terminate on the date of death or at the end of the calendar year? The year of death return, although clearly including only income to the date of death, does not answer this question because it merely provides a specific calculation rule for that return.

The argument arises because the definition of "taxation year" specifies that, for an individual, it is a calendar year, period. Nevertheless, the CRA has opined (in a 1991 document) that "we are satisfied that the taxation year of a taxpayer who dies in a taxation year ends on the date of his death, although it would obviously not be a twelve-month period". The opinion cites *Katz Estate v. M.N.R.*, 76 DTC 6377 (F.C.T.D.), where the Court says (in *obiter*):

> Notwithstanding that both counsel seem to share this view, I am not prepared to hold that, in the absence of a more express provision to that effect, a deceased taxpayer is, for taxation purposes, deemed to have a taxation year which ends at the end of the calendar year of his decease and, therefore, at a time when he no longer exists. It would seem more logical to conclude that, where section 249 refers to an individual, it must be taken to refer to an individual who is alive and that the deceased taxpayer's taxation year would end at the date of his death although it would obviously not be a twelve-month period. Be that as it may, it is not in my view necessary to decide this issue in the present case ...

One could also infer from the fact that the statutory formula for the amount of pension income which can be split refers to a denominator of the "taxation year" of a deceased transferor or transferee that the year must be something other than a 12-month period, which would have been easy enough to say if intended.

It would seem to follow that where a transfer is from the deceased to the survivor, the amount that can be transferred is half the pension income received (or accrued) to the date of death. There should be no proration because the period of marriage or partnership and the period of the taxation year would be the same.

Similarly, where the survivor transfers an amount to the deceased but the survivor dies before the end of the year, the numerator of the pension proration would be the number of months of the marriage/partnership and the denominator would be the number of months to (and presumably including) the month of death.

[¶1960.20] *Rights or Things*

In the opinion referred to above, the CRA says that where the survivor transferred pension income to the deceased, it is not a right or thing eligible for separate return treatment. There is no explanation, although the conclusion seems reasonable on its face. The result would presumably be the same if the deceased transferred pension income to a survivor who died later in the calendar year.

(ITA: 60.03; 249(1))

Chapter 20

Non-Residents

THESE POINTS ARE COVERED IN THIS CHAPTER

CRA REFERENCES RELATING TO THIS CHAPTER

T1 Return and Schedules

- T1 General, Income Tax and Benefit Return for Non-Residents and Deemed Residents of Canada
- T1, Federal Worksheet
- Schedule 1, Federal Tax
- Schedule 2, Federal Amounts Transferred from Your Spouse or Common-law Partner
- Schedule 3, Capital Gains (or Losses)
- Schedule 4, Statement of Investment Income
- Schedule 5, Details of Dependant
- Schedule 7, RRSP Unused Contributions, Transfers, and HBP or LLP Activities
- Schedule 8, CPP Contributions on Self-Employment and Other Earnings
- Schedule 9, Donations and Gifts
- Schedule 10, Employment Insurance (EI) and Provincial Parental Insurance Plan (PPIP) Premiums
- Schedule 11, Tuition, Education, and Textbook Amounts
- Schedule 13, Employment Insurance Premiums on Self-Employment and Other Eligible Earnings
- Schedule A, Statement of World Income
- Schedule B, Allowable Amount of Non-Refundable Tax Credits
- Schedule C, Electing Under Section 217 of the *Income Tax Act*

CRA Guides

5013-G, "General Income Tax and Benefit Guide for Non-Residents and Deemed Residents of Canada"; **RC4004**, "Seasonal Agricultural Workers Program"; **RC4445**, "T4A-NR — Payments to Non-Residents for Services Provided in Canada"; **T4016**, "Exempt U.S. Organizations — Under Article XXI of the Canada–United States Tax Convention"; **T4055**, "Newcomers to Canada"; **T4058**, "Non-Residents and Income Tax"; **T4061**, "NR4 — Non-Resident Tax Withholding, Remitting, and Reporting"; **T4144**, "Income Tax Guide for Electing Under Section 216"; **T4145**, "Electing Under Section 217 of the *Income Tax Act*"; **T4155**, "Old Age Security Return of Income Guide for Non-Residents"

CRA Forms

5013-R, "T1 General — Income Tax and Benefit Return for Non-Residents and Deemed Residents of Canada"; **NR4**, "Statement of Amounts Paid or Credited to Non-Residents of Canada"; **NR4(OAS)**, "Statement of Old Age Security Pension Paid or Credited to Non-Residents of Canada"; **NR5**, "Application by a Non-Resident of Canada for a Reduction in the Amount of Non-Resident Tax Required to be Withheld"; **NR6**, "Undertaking to File an Income Tax Return by a Non-Resident Receiving Rent from Real Property or Receiving a Timber Royalty"; **NR7-R**, "Application for Refund of Non-Resident Part XIII Tax Withheld"; **NR73**, "Determination of Residency Status (Leaving Canada)"; **NR74**, "Determination of Residency Status (Entering Canada)"; **NR601**, "Non-Resident Ownership Certificate (Withholding Tax)"; **NR602**, "Non-Resident Ownership Certificate (No Withholding Tax)"; **NR603**, "Remittance of Non-Resident Tax on Income from Film or Video Acting Services"; **NRTA1**, "Authorization for Non-Resident Tax Exemption"; **R105**, "Regulation 105 Waiver Application"; **R106**, "Regulation 102 Waiver Application — Film Industry"; **R107**, "Regulation 105 Waiver Application — Film Industry"; **T4A-NR**, "Statement of Fees, Commissions or Other Amounts Paid to Non-Residents for Services Rendered in Canada"; **T106**, "Information Return of Non-Arm's Length Transactions with Non-Residents"; **NR301**, **NR302**; **T1136**, "Old Age Security Return of Income"; **T1141**, "Information Return in Respect of Transfers or Loans to a Non-Resident Trust"; **T1142**, "Information Return in Respect of Distributions from and Indebtedness to a Non-Resident Trust"; **T1159**, "Income Tax Return for Electing Under Section 216"; **T1161**, "List of Properties by an Emigrant of Canada"; **T1198**, "Statement of Qualifying Retroactive Lump-Sum Payment"; **T1234**, "Schedule B — Allowable Amounts of Non-Refundable Tax Credits"; **T1243**, "Deemed Disposition of Property by an Emigrant of Canada"; **T1244**, "Election Under Subsection 220(4.5) of the *Income Tax Act*, to Defer the Payment of Tax on Income Relating to the Deemed Disposition of Property"; **T1248**, "Schedule D — Information About Your Residency Status"; **T1261**, "Application for a CRA Individual Tax Number (ITN) for Non-Residents"; **T1287**, "Application by a Non-Resident of Canada (Individual) for a Reduction in the Amount of Non-Resident Tax Required to Be Withheld on Income Earned from Acting in a Film or Video Production"; **T2062**, "Request by a Non-Resident of Canada for a Certificate of Compliance Related to the Disposition of Taxable Canadian Property"; **T2062A**, "Request by a Non-resident of Canada for a Certificate of Compliance Related to the Disposition of Canadian Resource or Timber Resource Property, Canadian Real Property (Other Than Capital Property), or Depreciable Taxable Canadian Property"; **T2062B**, "Notice of Disposition of a Life Insurance Policy in Canada by a Non-Resident of Canada"; **T2203**, "Provincial and Territorial Taxes — Multiple Jurisdictions"

Income Tax Folios

S5-F1-C1, "Determining an Individual's Residence Status"; **S5-F2-C1**, "Foreign Tax Credit"; **S6-F1-C1**, "Residence of a Trust or Estate"

Interpretation Bulletins

IT-76R2, "Exempt Portion of Pension When Employee Has Been a Non-Resident"; **IT-88R2**, "Stock Dividends"; **IT-113R4**, "Benefits to Employees — Stock Options"; **IT-125R4**, "Dispositions of Resource Properties"; **IT-155R3**, "Exemption from Non-Resident Tax on Interest Payable on Certain Bonds, Debentures, Notes, Hypothecs or Similar Obligations"; **IT-176R2**, "Taxable Canadian Property — Interests in and Options on Real Property and Shares"; **IT-262R2**, "Losses of Non-Residents and Part-Year Residents"; **IT-303**, "Know-how and Similar Payments to Non-Residents"; **IT-342R**, "Trusts — Income Payable to Beneficiaries"; **IT-361R3**, "Exemption from Part XIII Tax on Interest Payments to Non-Residents"; **IT-393R2**, "Election Re: Tax on Rents and Timber Royalties — Non-Residents"; **IT-420R3**, "Non-Residents — Income Earned in Canada"; **IT-421R2**, "Benefits to Individuals, Corporations and Shareholders from Loans or Debt"; **IT-434R**, "Rental of Real Property by Individual"; **IT-438R2**, "Crown Charges — Resource Properties in Canada"; **IT-451R**, "Deemed Disposition and Acquisition on Ceasing to Be or Becoming Resident in Canada"; **IT-465R**, "Non-Resident Beneficiaries of Trusts"; **IT-468R**, "Management or Administration Fees Paid to Non-Residents"; **IT-494**, "Hire of Ships and Aircraft from Non-Residents"; **IT-500R**, "Registered Retirement Savings Plans — Death of an Annuitant"; **IT-510**, "Transfers and Loans of Property Made After May 22, 1985 to a Related Minor"; **IT-511R**, "Interspousal and Certain Other Transfers and Loans of Property"

Information Circulars

71-17R5, "Guidance on Competent Authority Assistance Under Canada's Tax Conventions"; **72-17R6**, "Procedures Concerning the Disposition of Taxable Canadian Property by Non-Residents of Canada — Section 116"; **75-6R2**, "Required Withholding from Amounts Paid to Non-Residents Providing Services in Canada"; **76-12R6**, "Applicable Rate of Part XIII tax on Amounts Paid or Credited to Persons in Countries with Which Canada Has a Tax Convention"; **77-16R4**, "Non-Resident Income Tax"; **07-1**, "Taxpayer Relief Provisions"

Income Tax Technical News

No. 9, February 10, 1997 "Exemption from Withholding Tax on Interest — Clause 212(1)(b)(vii)(C)" (Archived by the CRA); **No. 14**, December 9, 1998 "Meaning of 'Credited' for the Purpose of Part XIII Withholding Tax" (Archived by the CRA); **No. 22**, January 11, 2002, "International Taxation"; **No. 23**, June 18, 2002, "Computer Software"; **No. 30**, May 21, 2004, "Withholding Tax on Interest"; **No. 35**, February 26, 2007, "Treaty Residence — Resident of Convenience"

WHAT YOU SHOULD KNOW ABOUT TAXATION OF NON-RESIDENTS

RECENT CHANGES

Bill C-15 (Royal Assent, June 22, 2016)

The 2015 Federal Budget proposed changes under which certain non-resident individuals earning employment income in Canada would not be subject to Canadian withholding tax. The changes were subsequently passed into law on June 22, 2016, and apply to payments made after 2015. See ¶2020.10 and ¶2080b.

Bill C-29 (Introduced October 25, 2016)

The 2016 Federal Budget proposed amendments to ensure that the back-to-back rules that apply to cross-border interest payments for Part XIII withholding tax purposes will apply to arrangements that involve multiple intermediaries. See ¶2080.01. The Budget also proposed to extend the back-to-back rules to cross-border rent and royalty payments, and certain "character substitution" arrangements. These proposals were subsequently introduced in Bill C-29. See ¶2080.05.

On April 15, 2016, the Department of Finance released draft legislative proposals to implement the Common Reporting Standard ("CRS"), which "will ensure tax fairness and improve Canada's ability to detect and address tax evasion. Canada is one of the more than 90 jurisdictions that have committed to implement the CRS, which was developed by the Organisation for Economic Co-operation and Development." The CRS is scheduled to begin on July 1, 2017. The CRA stated that, as of that date, Canadian financial institutions would be required to have procedures in place to identify accounts held by non-residents and to report the required information to the CRA. The Department of Finance invited interested parties to provide comments on the draft proposals, which remain in draft form at the time of writing. These proposals were subsequently introduced in Bill C-29.

Legislative Proposals (September 16, 2016)

Technical amendments released on September 16, 2016 "clarify" that where the adjusted cost base of a non-resident taxpayer's taxable Canadian property becomes negative, such that there is deemed disposition and deemed capital gain (see ¶535), the non-resident taxpayer will be required to file a tax return. See ¶2040. The technical amendments also provide an exemption from Part XIII withholding tax for certain transfers of pension benefits to the Saskatchewan Pension Plan. See ¶2080.04.

Notice of Ways and Means Motion (October 3, 2016)

Draft legislation released on October 3, 2016 tightens up the circumstances in which the principal residence exemption may be claimed. See ¶2040 under "Principal Residence Exemption".

Tax Treaty Negotiations

Canada's tax treaties continue to be renegotiated, revised, and ratified, and new negotiations are commenced to cover new countries. The list of treaties is updated accordingly and can be found on the CRA website under "Individuals and families / Individuals / Leaving or entering Canada and non-residents".

[¶2000] NON-RESIDENTS WHO ARE TAXABLE

If you are a non-resident of Canada (residence is discussed in ¶115) you may be subject to federal Canadian taxes if you:

(1) received in the year income from employment in Canada at any time in the year or a preceding year (¶2020);

(2) received employment income in the year relating to employment outside Canada while you were a Canadian resident (¶2020);

(3) were employed in Canada in a previous year and received employment income in the current year from a source in Canada (¶2022); but this rule only applies if you were exempt from tax in your country of foreign residence by virtue of a treaty between that country and Canada;

(4) exercised a stock option granted either to you or to someone from whom you received it in a non-arm's length transaction and who is now deceased, if the option related primarily to employment in Canada (¶2021);

(5) received a Canadian-source grant, scholarship, prize for achievement, or RESP payment in the year (¶2024);

(6) carried on business in Canada at any time in the year;

(7) disposed of taxable Canadian property (¶2040 and ¶2042);

(8) received income in the form of recaptured capital cost allowance to the extent that it was not included in computing income from a business (this would include, for example, recapture on disposition of a rental property);

(9) received income resulting in a negative balance of cumulative Canadian exploration and development expenses, less any portion that was included in computing income from a business in Canada;

(10) received proceeds of disposal of a right to share in the income or loss of a partnership in excess of the unrecovered cost of such right ordinarily deductible by residents of Canada;

(11) received proceeds of disposition of an income interest in a trust resident in Canada in excess of any portion that would be ordinarily deductible by residents of Canada; or

(12) received income of certain types from Canada, such as dividends, interest, rents, pensions and other passive income (see ¶2080).

Generally, as a non-resident receiving Canadian source income as described in (1) to (11), above, you will be subject to Canadian income tax on this income and be required to file a T1 return. Canada will tax you by applying the basic rules of the Act for computing income as if your only income was from the Canadian sources referred to in (1) to (11), above. (In CRA Document No. 2007-0228561E5, the CRA gave its opinion that where a Canadian resident left his employment under an agreement which continued his salary for two years, and then moved to the United States, the continuing remuneration was subject to ordinary employee withholding tax.)

In computing the income referred to in (1) to (11), you will generally be allowed to claim all deductions to arrive at the net income from those sources which you would have been allowed to deduct as a Canadian resident.

A non-resident may claim the deductions and credits discussed in Chapters 10, 11, 12 and 13 (deductions from income to arrive at taxable income and personal exemption credits) to the extent discussed in ¶2050–¶2069.

Even though a partnership is considered as a separate person resident in Canada for purposes of computing the income of its members (Chapter 18), this does not change the general rules relating to the taxation of its members. If you are a non-resident member of a partnership operating in Canada you must refer to your share of the partnership income from *each source* to determine whether and to what extent you are subject to Canadian tax.

Example

Jones and Smith is a partnership which carries on business in the United States and Canada. Bill Jones, who has a 50% interest in this partnership, is a resident of the United States. The partnership's income for the year was:

Business income attributable to the Canadian permanent establishment	$15,000
Business income attributable to the United States permanent establishment	$20,000
Total income	$35,000

Mr. Jones must file a Canadian income tax return reporting $7,500 of business income earned in Canada. He does not report his share of the U.S. business income because he is not subject to Canadian tax on that amount.

Any or all of the above circumstances numbered (1) to (11) may subject you to Quebec income taxes. See Chapter 16.

Although the income described in (12) above is subject to Canadian tax, it is treated differently than income from employment, business or the disposition of taxable Canadian property. Since the non-resident receiving payment is not required to file any Canadian return with respect to the income, the tax is paid on behalf of the non-resident by the Canadian payer, who is required to withhold and remit the appropriate tax to the Canadian government. The Canadian payer will withhold the amount of the Canadian tax from the payment and remit only the net amount to the non-resident. On the other hand, the non-resident taxpayer may obtain more favourable treatment on rent by electing to file a Canadian return on form T1159, as discussed at ¶2080.05. Similarly, non-residents in receipt of Canadian retirement income may benefit from filing a Canadian return under the rules at ¶2086, and non-resident recipients of Canadian Old Age Security benefits may (depending on country of residence) have to file a statement of world income to receive OAS benefits at all (¶2076).

(ITA: 2(3); 3; 96(1)(*a*), (*f*), (*g*); 115(1); 150; 212; 215; IT-420R3 [Archived])

[¶2005] TAX AGREEMENTS

The comments in this chapter are subject to modification if they are affected by the provisions of Tax Agreements which Canada has entered into with certain other countries. The terms of these agreements overrule the normal provisions of Canadian law regarding taxation where there is a conflict. In general, these agreements affect persons who are residents of, or citizens of, or have income from, Canada or the country with which an agreement has been signed; and provide special rules for determining whether a person is taxable in a particular country, upon what income he will be taxable, the rates of taxation, and the special treatment to be given various specific items. A full list of treaties that are in force, those signed but not in force, and those under negotiation can be found on the Department of Finance website, under the subheading "Activities and Issues / Status of International Tax Treaty Negotiations". Alternatively, see the CRA website under "Individuals and families / Individuals / Leaving or entering Canada and non-residents / Tax Treaties".

[¶2005.10] *U.S. Treaty Changes from 5th Protocol*

On September 21, 2007, Canada and the United States signed the Fifth Protocol to the 1980 Canada–U.S. Tax Treaty.

The Protocol received final ratification and came into force on December 15, 2008. Generally speaking, the Protocol is effective in respect of taxes withheld at source on February 1, 2009, and in respect of other taxes for taxation years beginning on or after January 1, 2009. However, different effective dates apply to certain other provisions of the Protocol, notably interest payments, as discussed below.

Some of the Fifth Protocol changes include:

Withholding Tax on Interest

Elimination of withholding tax on most forms of interest payments to unrelated parties is effective retroactively to January 1, 2008.

Interest on payments to related parties (e.g., a subsidiary company and its parent company) was reduced to 7% for interest payments to related persons, effective retroactively to January 1, 2008.

The withholding tax rate applicable to related person interest payments was 4% in calendar year 2009 and is nil in and after 2010 for most types of interest. Related persons are not defined in the treaty, and the phrase therefore has the meaning generally assigned by governing income tax law, although there is a deeming provision in Article IX(2) (not affected by the Fifth Protocol) which extends the common meaning in corporate situations defined for Protocol purposes.

Taxpayer Migration

If, on ceasing to be a resident of one country and becoming a resident of the other, an individual is treated by the first country as having disposed of a property, the individual can choose to be treated also in the second country (the new home country) as having disposed of and reacquired the property at the time of changing residence. In effect, this gives substance to the assurance given on September 18, 2000, when Canada announced that it had persuaded the United States in principle to amend the Canada–U.S. Tax Treaty to permit Canadian residents who move to the U.S. and suffer Canadian departure tax (¶2153) on their assets to elect for U.S. purposes to get a step-up in cost base. This provision is retroactive to changes in residence which occurred after September 17, 2000.

Independent Contractors

Article XIV of the former treaty (independent personal services) was deleted on the coming into force of the Protocol. That article provided that an independent contractor could be taxed in the country where services were provided to the extent the contractor had a "fixed base" in the country. *The Queen v. Dudney*, 2000 DTC 6169 (F.C.A.), affirming 99 DTC 147 (T.C.C.), the Court severely limited Canada's ability to tax independent contractors by limiting the concept of a fixed base. By withdrawing Article XIV, the concept of fixed base becomes irrelevant and the question becomes whether the U.S. independent contractor carries on business through a permanent establishment in Canada. The definition of "permanent establishment" has been amended to impose a permanent establishment in Canada

(1) where services are provided over periods aggregating 183 days or more in any 12-month period, if 50% of gross revenues are derived from those services during those periods, or

(2) if services are provided in Canada for an aggregate of 183 days or more in a 12-month period in respect of the same or a connected project for customers resident in Canada, or who maintain a permanent establishment in Canada in respect of which the services are provided.

The provision is reciprocal, but the matter seems to be primarily a Canadian concern. These tests may raise a number of new concerns beyond those of the single independent contractor, for example where a U.S. firm provides multiple short term employees to a Canadian customer. The issues are identified in an article in the CCH Newsletter *Tax Topics* No. 1859, dated October 25, 2007. They may or may not be resolved in some degree in the U.S. treaty explanation document.

Pensions and Other Registered Plans

This provision is intended to affect individuals residing in one country and working in the other who contribute to a pension plan (or any of certain other employment-related retirement arrangements) in the country where they work, as well as individuals who move from one country to the other on short-term (up to five years) work assignments, and continue to contribute to a plan or arrangement in the first country. In certain cases, such persons' employers may also benefit. Provided certain conditions are met, these "cross-border commuters" may deduct, for residence country tax purposes, the contributions they make to a plan or arrangement in the country where they work. Similarly, those who move for work and meet certain conditions can deduct, for source country tax purposes, their contributions to a plan or arrangement in the other country, for up to five years. In both cases, accruing benefits are not taxable. For example, consider a resident of Canada who is employed in the U.S., and contributes to an employer-sponsored pension plan there. The employee's contributions to the plan (up to the employee's remaining RRSP deduction room) will be deductible for Canadian tax purposes. Another example given by the Department of Finance is that of an employee of a Canadian company assigned for three years to a related U.S. company. The employee keeps contributing to the employee pension plan of the Canadian company. For U.S. tax purposes, both the employee and the U.S. company will be able to deduct the contributions.

Stock Options

This rule affects employees who are granted employee stock options while employed in one country, and who then work for the same or a related employer in the other country before exercising or disposing of the option (or disposing of the share). Under the Protocol, the income in question (the stock option benefit) will generally be considered to have been derived in a country to the extent that the individual's principal place of employment was in that country during the time between the granting of the option and its exercise (or the disposition of the share). For example, assume an employee of a United States company is granted a stock option on January 1, 2009. On January 1, 2010, the employee is moved from the company's U.S. head office to its Canadian subsidiary. On December 31, 2011 (i.e., two years after the move to Canada), the employee disposes of the option, giving rise to an income inclusion. Unless the revenue authorities agree that the circumstances warrant departing from the usual rule, one third of the income will be treated as having arisen in the U.S., and two thirds in Canada. As a set of detailed technical rules, this proposal is included in an exchange of diplomatic notes, rather than in the Protocol itself.

Limited Liability Companies (LLCs) and Other Hybrid Entities

The Protocol includes new rules to deal with entities that are treated as corporations under the law of one country, but are treated as partnerships (or "pass-through vehicles") in the other country. Absent the Protocol, there is no specific accommodation of these hybrid entities. To benefit from the tax treaty (reduced withholding taxes, etc.), an entity must be resident in (i.e., taxable in) one of the treaty countries. If an entity is a pass-through vehicle in its home country, it is not taxable there; instead, its investors are taxed directly as it earns income. But if the other country sees the entity as a corporation, that other country will apply the residence test (taxability) to the entity itself, and the entity will fail. Under the Protocol rules, income that the residents of one country earn through a hybrid entity will in certain cases be treated by the other country (the source country) as having been earned by a resident of the residence country. On the other hand, a corollary rule provides that if a hybrid entity's income is not taxed directly in the hands of its investors, it will be treated as not having been earned by a resident. For example, assume U.S. investors use a U.S. LLC to invest in Canada. The LLC (which Canada views as a corporation but is a flow-through vehicle in the U.S.) earns Canadian-source investment income. Provided the U.S. investors are taxed in the U.S. on the income in the same way as they would be if they had earned it directly, Canada will treat the income as having been paid to a U.S. resident. The reduced withholding tax rates provided in the tax treaty will apply. The basic rule is to apply for withholding tax purposes as of February 2009. The corollary rule applies as of January 2010.

Mandatory Arbitration

At present, the treaty provides that if, notwithstanding its provisions, double taxation arises, the competent authorities of each country are to attempt to agree on a resolution to eliminate the double taxation. There is no provision which actually compels them to agree; they may simply fail to resolve the issue. The Protocol provides that a taxpayer subject to double taxation can demand that the competent authorities send the dispute to binding arbitration. Details of the arbitration process are set out in an exchange of diplomatic notes (Annex A to the Protocol).

[¶2005.15] *Other Treaty Changes*

The Department of Finance website, under the sub-heading "Activities and Issues / Status of International Tax Treaty Negotiations", lists all of the current year's tax treaty developments, as well as a full list of treaties that are in force, those signed but not in force, and those under negotiation.

[¶2005.25] *Signed Treaties Not in Force and Treaties under Negotiation*

The Government of Canada continually negotiates, and enters into new or amended tax treaties, with various countries. A full list of treaties that are signed but not in force, and those under negotiation, can be found on the Department of Finance website, under the subheading "Activities and Issues / Status of International Tax Treaty Negotiations".

[¶2005.35] *Competent Authority Referrals*

Where serious disagreements arise as to whether Canada or another country should be entitled to tax a particular amount of a particular taxpayer, most treaties provide for a "competent authority" resolution. That is, revenue authorities of the two countries will review the situation and endeavour to find a mutually satisfactory solution which avoids double taxation to the taxpayer. This is, as you may imagine, a lengthy and convoluted project. To avoid the payment of double tax while waiting the many years that a competent authority resolution usually requires, statutory rules give the CRA the discretion to negotiate details of payment of tax under any treaty provision notwithstanding general tax rules. Although less than crystal clear, it appears that this provision is intended to authorize deferral of tax (and perhaps interest) while the competent authority mechanism grinds on.

Requests for competent authority consideration are described in Information Circular 71-17R5.

(ITA: 115.1; Other Publications: Department of Finance website section devoted to treaties. At the time of writing, the treaty page could be found from the Finance main page by clicking on "Tax Treaties" on the right-hand side of the page. Or, it could be found directly at www.fin.gc.ca/treaties-conventions/treatystatus_-eng.asp. At the time of writing, it was being updated regularly, and consequently should be the most up-to-date source of the status of a particular treaty)

[¶2007] TAX TREATIES AND THE DETERMINATION OF RESIDENCE

It is possible under the laws of most countries, including Canada, for a person to be resident in two or more countries at once for tax purposes. Tax treaties generally attempt to resolve the double taxation issues that might result. If you are resident under general rules in both Canada and another country with which Canada has a tax treaty, that treaty probably contains "tie-breaker" rules which attempt to determine in which of the two treaty countries you are resident for tax purposes. The general model for tie-breaker rules is as follows:

If an individual is a resident of both treaty countries

(1) he or she shall be deemed to be a resident only of the country in which he or she has a permanent home available to him or her; if he or she has a permanent home in both, he or she shall be deemed to be a resident only of the country with which his or her personal and economic relations are closer (the centre of vital interests test);

(2) if the centre of vital interests cannot be determined, or if he or she has not a permanent home available to him or her in either country, he or she shall be deemed to a resident only of the country in which he or she has a habitual abode;

(3) if he or she has a habitual abode in both countries or neither, he or she shall be deemed a resident only of the country of which he or she is a national (in some treaties, citizen); if he or she is a national (citizen) of both countries or neither, the Competent Authorities of the countries shall settle the question by mutual agreement.

The wording above is adopted from the OECD Model Tax Convention. It is used in most treaties. The Canada–U.S. treaty uses essentially this wording, substituting "citizen" for "national".

If you are a factual resident of Canada and a country with which Canada has a tax treaty, Canada will automatically deem you to be a resident of the country to which treaty rules would assign you (see subsection 250(5) of the Act). Accordingly, you may become a deemed non-resident of Canada, and face departure tax. Deemed non-residence is discussed in detail at ¶116; departure tax is discussed at ¶2153.

Under the terms of many of Canada's tax agreements, certain residents of Canada may be exempt from Canadian tax. For instance, an individual who is resident in Canada only because he or she is employed by a foreign government in an official or quasi-official capacity may be exempt from taxation in Canada. This may include employees of a foreign embassy for instance.

[¶2007.10] *Treaty Shopping and Residence of Convenience*

Although more commonly an issue with corporations and commercial entities than with individuals, the CRA is concerned in all cases where a taxpayer appears to take up residence in a particular jurisdiction to benefit from particular tax treaty provisions (treaty shopping). Of course, a genuine resident is entitled to treaty protection, but the CRA can question whether residence is *bona fide* in particular circumstances. Especially where a taxpayer claims residence in a country where it is subject to a special beneficial tax regime, the CRA may call into question whether the taxpayer is truly resident for treaty purposes. Thus, it has been a long-standing position of the CRA that, to be considered "liable to tax" for the purposes of treaty residence articles, a person must be subject to the most comprehensive form of taxation as exists in the relevant country. In the CRA's view, this generally means full tax liability on worldwide income. It considers this position supported by the comments found in the Supreme Court decision *The Queen v. Crown Forest Industries Ltd. et al.*, 95 DTC 5389 (S.C.C.), as well as the commentary to the OECD Model Treaty.

In *Income Tax Technical News* No. 35, February 26, 2007, the CRA withdrew somewhat from the rigidity of its position:

> It remains CRA's position that, to be considered "liable to tax" for the purposes of the residence article of Canada's tax treaties, a person must generally be subject to the most comprehensive form of taxation as exists in the relevant country. This, however, does not necessarily mean that a person must pay tax to a particular jurisdiction. There may be situations where a person's worldwide income is subject to a contracting state's full taxing jurisdiction but that state's domestic law does not levy tax on a person's taxable income or taxes it at low rates. In these cases, the CRA will generally accept that the person is a resident of the other Contracting State unless the arrangement is abusive (e.g. treaty shopping where the person is in fact only a "resident of convenience"). Such could be the case, for example, where a person is placed within the taxing jurisdiction of a Contracting State in order to gain treaty benefits in a manner that does not create any material economic nexus to that State.
>
> As confirmed by the Supreme Court in *The Queen v. Crown Forest Industries Ltd. et al.* (95 DTC 5389), reviewing the intention of the parties of a tax treaty is a very important element in delineating the scope of the application of the treaty. Accordingly, the determination of residency for the purposes of a tax treaty remains a question of fact, and each case will be decided on its own facts with an eye to the intention of the parties of the particular convention and the purpose of international tax treaties.

[¶2010] RETURNS TO BE FILED

If you are taxable on Canadian employment or business income, or income arising from disposition of taxable Canadian properties, you must file a T1 income tax return. Even if not taxable on these amounts, you will wish to file a T1 return if you have had any Canadian tax withheld from such amounts, in order to obtain a refund of this Canadian tax. Only the income from Canadian sources should be reported on this return.

The CRA provides a special version of the T1 return for non-residents, called the *T1 General for Non-Residents and Deemed Residents.* It is accompanied by a special version of the T1 Guide (5013G). There are also the following guides aimed at non-residents and published by the CRA:

- *Non-Residents and Income Tax* (T4058) — generally for non-residents who were employed or carried on business in Canada or disposed of taxable Canadian property (¶2040) in the taxation year, but also helpful for all non-residents taxable in Canada;
- *Electing under Section 217 of the Income Tax Act* (T4145)) — for non-residents receiving Canadian source pension income (see ¶2086); and
- *Income Tax Guide for Electing under Section 216* (T4144) — for non-residents receiving Canadian rental income (see ¶2080.05).

These are available from the CRA's website: www.cra-arc.gc.ca.

You should use the T1 *General for Non-Residents and Deemed Residents* if you were a non-resident of Canada throughout the year and you are reporting Canadian-source income **other** than from employment in Canada, from a business with a permanent establishment in Canada, from rental income from real property located in Canada, or from timber royalties on a timber resource property or a timber limit in Canada. The same return should be used if you were a non-resident of Canada throughout the year and are filing a return under the elective provision of section 217 (¶2086) or 216.1 (¶2078).

If you were a non-resident of Canada throughout the year and you are reporting **only** income from employment in Canada, or from a business or partnership with a permanent establishment in Canada, you should use the tax package for the province or territory in which you earned the income. The Guide T4058, *Non-Residents and Income Tax*, is also helpful. If you are also reporting other types of Canadian-source income (such as taxable scholarships, fellowships, bursaries, research grants, or taxable capital gains from disposing of taxable Canadian property), the CRA indicates that you will need Form T2203, *Provincial and Territorial Taxes — Multiple Jurisdictions*, to calculate your tax payable.

If you emigrated from Canada during the year, you should use the tax package for the province or territory where you resided on the day you left Canada. See also Chapter 21, which discusses the taxation of Canadian emigrants.

If you are non-resident throughout the year, no Canadian return is required to be filed if your only income from Canada is dividends, interest, pensions, or other income which is only subject to Canadian Part XIII non-resident withholding tax. On the other hand, it may be beneficial to file a Canadian return if you do have Canadian source pension income (¶2086) or real estate rental income (¶2080.05).

(ITA: 115; 150(1); 212(1); 216; 217)

NET INCOME TO BE REPORTED BY FILING AN INCOME TAX RETURN

INCOME FROM EMPLOYMENT IN CANADA

[¶2020] EMPLOYMENT INCOME

If you received income in a taxation year in respect of employment in Canada you are taxable on that income. This rule applies even if the income relates to employment in Canada in a previous year.

If you performed duties in the service of another individual or company, or held a position entitling you to a fixed or ascertainable remuneration, including such positions as a corporation director, you were "employed". If the duties were performed while you were physically present in Canada you were "employed in Canada" for the period you were present here.

Note that generally your performance as a non-resident of Canada of such duties in a foreign country, as an employee or officer of a Canadian individual or company, does not constitute employment in Canada. However, see ¶2022 for exceptions.

You are also subject to Canadian tax on income earned while you were a resident of Canada but employed outside Canada. This rule will generally apply if you were resident in Canada but employed outside Canada in a preceding year, have since become non-resident, and receive employment income in the current year from that earlier employment.

If as a non-resident you are employed in Canada for part of the year and are employed in another country at other times in the year, it is necessary to allocate your total income between duties performed in Canada and those performed abroad. If remuneration attributable to each source can be specifically identified, this method should be used. Otherwise, the Canadian tax authorities will normally accept an allocation based on the time spent by you in each country performing the duties of your employment. For example, if you received a salary of $36,000 for the year and worked 80 days in Canada and 160 days in other countries during the year, your employment income from duties performed in Canada will be considered as

$$80/240 \times \$36,000 = \$12,000$$

The Canadian tax authorities will accept the allocation based on 240 business days in the year, which excludes weekends and holidays from the 365 days in the calendar year.

If you are employed in the transportation of passengers or goods by rail, bus, truck or aircraft you may allocate your income between Canada and other countries either on a time basis as above, or on the proportion of your mileage in Canada to your total mileage.

Employment income earned in Canada by a non-resident is subject to provincial tax in the province in which it is earned. If you earned employment income in only one province, you file the form 428 that comes with the federal T1 return for that province (or a Quebec return if the province was Quebec). If you earned employment income in more than one province, regulations provide that you allocate income in accordance with duties performed in each province. The CRA tells you (in its publication T4058) to use form T2203 for this purpose, although that form is primarily directed to businesses carried on in more than one province (see ¶1446 and ¶1505). The practical answer seems to be that you apportion employment income to the province in which it was earned, and then use T2203 to calculate the appropriate tax for each province (except Quebec, where you must file a separate return reporting the Quebec allocation).

Under the Canada–U.S. income tax treaty, a resident employee of one of the Contracting States who receives employment income for services performed in the other Contracting State (the source State) will be exempt from tax in the source State if either of the following two conditions are met:

(1) The remuneration for the employment performed in the source State does not exceed $10,000 in the currency of the source State; or

(2) The employee has not been present in the source State for more than 183 days in any 12-month period commencing or ending in the relevant fiscal year and his or her remuneration is not borne by a person who is a resident of the source State or by a permanent establishment in the source State.

Similar exemptions are provided for residents of the other countries with which Tax Agreements have been concluded. The requirements for exemption differ in each case but the requirement that time spent in Canada not exceed 183 days is common to most.

If any or all of your employment income is exempt from Canadian tax under a treaty, you claim the exempt amount on line 256 of the return.

The Canada–U.S. Tax Convention also provides specific rules for the taxation of income of non-resident entertainers, musicians and athletes (except the income of an athlete employed with a team which participates in a league with regularly scheduled games in both Canada and the United States). Income earned in Canada from the personal activities of these individuals is exempt from tax provided the gross income (including expenses reimbursed or paid on their behalf) does not exceed $15,000 in Canadian currency. However, the Canadian source income of entertainers or athletes will be fully taxed in Canada if the income accrues, not to the athlete or entertainer but to another person, except where the athlete or entertainer (or persons related thereto) does not participate, directly or indirectly in the profits of that other person.

See also ¶2022 below, regarding other remuneration that may be subject to tax in Canada.

As noted under "Recent Changes" at the beginning of this chapter, the 2015 federal Budget introduced an exemption from withholding tax for remuneration paid by a qualifying non-resident employer to a qualifying non-resident employee. This exemption begins with payments made after 2015.

(ITA: 114; 115(1), (2); 248(1); ITR: 2602 Non-Residents; *Non-Residents and Income Tax* Guide (T4058); T1 Guide for Non-Residents and Deemed Residents of Canada; IT-171R2 [Archived]; IT-420R3 [Archived]; IT-421R2, para. 26 [Archived]; Other Publications: 1980 Canada–U.S. Tax Convention, Art. XIV, XV, XVI, XVII, XXX)

[¶2020.05] *Non-Resident Pilots Employed by Canadian Airlines*

An amendment effective for 2013 (subsection 115(3)) provides allocation rules for employment income earned by non-resident pilots who received employment income from Canadian-resident persons. Income is to be attributed to employment carried on in Canada in these proportions:

(1) all of the income attributable to the flight if the flight departs from a location in Canada and arrives at a location in Canada;

(2) one-half of the income attributable to the flight if the flight departs from a location in Canada and arrives at a location outside Canada;

(3) one-half of the income attributable to the flight if the flight departs from a location outside Canada and arrives at a location in Canada; and

(4) none of the income attributable to the flight if the flight departs from a location outside Canada and arrives at a location outside Canada.

[¶2020.10] *Waiver of Withholding Tax for Short-term Employment in Canada*

A non-resident employee who earns employment income in Canada is subject to Canadian income tax on that income, even if the employee's remuneration is paid by a non-resident employer. Furthermore, the withholding tax requirements of subsection 153(1) normally apply to the payment of such remuneration.

Recent amendments provide a blanket exemption from withholding for remuneration paid by a "qualifying non-resident employer" to a "qualifying non-resident employee".

A qualifying non-resident employee must be resident in a country with which Canada has a tax treaty, exempt from Part I tax in respect of the payment because of that tax treaty, and either (i) not present in Canada for 90 or more days in any 12-month period that includes the time of the payment or (ii) working in Canada for less than 45 days in the year that includes the time of payment.

A qualifying non-resident employer must be resident in a country with which Canada has a tax treaty. However, in general, where an employer is a partnership, members of the partnership who are resident in a treaty country must have an aggregate share of at least 90% of the partnership's income for the fiscal period that includes the time of the remuneration payment. In either case, the employer must be certified by the CRA. It is incumbent upon the employer to apply to the CRA for certification. The application form is RC473, "Application for Non-Resident Employer Certification."

This change applies to payments made after 2015. See also ¶2080b.

(ITA: 153(1) Withholding; 153(6) Definitions)

[¶2021] EXERCISE OF EMPLOYEE STOCK OPTIONS

If you were granted stock options in respect of employment in Canada by your employer or a company related to your employer to acquire shares of your employer or a related company, and you later exercise those options, you will be taxable on the difference between any amount you paid for the options and on the exercise and the value of the stock you acquired on exercise. This income is considered to be employment income earned in Canada in the year of exercise (or, in the case of CCPC stock options, when you later dispose of the shares) even if you are no longer an employee of that employer and/or you have since left Canada. For the general rules on employee stock options, see ¶330.

If you received such stock options in a non-arm's length transaction (or series) from the employee to whom they were granted, the benefit is normally taxable to the employee when you exercise the option. However, if the employee has since died, you will be taxable on the benefit even if you are a non-resident, so long as the options related primarily to a period of employment in Canada.

A non-resident who has a benefit under any of these rules is considered to have employment income from Canada during the year and must file a T1 return accordingly. The deduction from taxable income which offsets half of the employment income may be claimed if the requisite criteria are met (¶2066, ¶330).

See also ¶2005.10 below, regarding changes under the Fifth Protocol to the Canada–U.S. treaty that affect the current treatment of employee stock options.

Certain technical problems can arise where the non-resident exercises stock options arising from Canadian employment. First, there is a question as to whether the proper return to be filed is the T1 for non-residents or residents of a particular province. The CRA appears to take the view that the income is sourced to the province in which the employment occurred, and requires a resident return. This is arguably correct, although the point is not beyond dispute. It does appear to conform to the CRA's assessment policy, although reassessment does not always follow where a non-resident return is filed. A more esoteric problem can arise if the Canadian employment income arising from the stock option is treaty-protected. For example, if a Canadian employee of a Canadian subsidiary is given foreign company stock options for the Canadian employment which are later exercised while a foreign resident, it may be that the Canadian company cannot be said to bear the cost of the remuneration (a question of fact) and, if the employee was resident less than 183 days in a particular year, the remuneration could be treaty-exempt. On this fact situation, see the CRA's ruling No. 9333306 of December 2, 1993. A situation in which stock options were exercised by a wholly non-resident director of a Canadian company could still result in apportioned Canadian liability; see ruling no. ACC9961 dated September 12, 1990. See also ¶2021.10 below, regarding relevant provisions of the Canada-US tax treaty.

Where the employment in respect of the stock option is exercised in Canada and another country, the CRA follows the guidelines set out in paragraphs 12 to 12.15 of the Commentary on Article 15 of the OECD Model Income Tax Convention. Under those guidelines, a stock option benefit is apportioned to each source country based on the number of days of employment exercised in that country over the total number of days in the period during which the employment services from which the stock option is derived are exercised. In making this determination, a stock option benefit is generally presumed to relate to the period of employment that is required as a condition for the employee to acquire the right to exercise the option (the "vesting period"). Further, a stock option benefit is generally presumed not to relate to past services, unless there is evidence to indicate that past services are relevant in the particular circumstances. However, where the terms of the option agreement are such that the grant of the option is treated as a transfer of ownership of the securities (e.g., because the options were in-the-money or not subject to a substantial vesting period), the CRA may attribute the benefit accordingly (CRA document no. 2012-0459411C6).

If you die as a non-resident, and in consequence have employment income from your own employee stock options, and if your estate subsequently suffers a loss on those options, the carryback rules provided for in ¶1925 will apply.

(ITA: 7; 115(1); ITR: 2602(1)(a); IT-113R4, para. 22 [Archived]; IT-420R3, para. 6, 7 [Archived]; *Hurd v. The Queen*, 81 DTC 5140 (F.C.A.))

[¶2021.10] *Canada–U.S. Treaty Provisions*

The Fifth Protocol to the 1980 Canada–U.S. Tax Treaty implements a rule governing employees who are granted employee stock options while employed in one country, and who then work for the same or a related employer in the other country before exercising or disposing of the option. Under the Protocol, the income in question (the stock option benefit) will generally be considered to have been derived in a country to the extent that the individual's principal place of employment was in that country during the time between the granting of the option and its exercise or disposition.

For example, assume an employee of a U.S. company is granted a stock option on January 1, 2011. On January 1, 2012, the employee is moved from the company's U.S. head office to its Canadian subsidiary. On December 31, 2013, the employee disposes of the option, giving rise to an income inclusion. Unless the revenue authorities agree that the circumstances warrant departing from the usual rule, one third of the income will be treated as having arisen in the U.S., and two thirds in Canada. As a set of detailed, technical rules, this proposal is included in an exchange of diplomatic notes, rather than in the Protocol itself. See also ¶2005.10.

(Other Publications: Fifth Protocol to Canada–U.S. Tax Convention, dated September 21, 2007, Annex B, item 6)

[¶2022] REMUNERATION FROM A CANADIAN SOURCE: OTHER RULES

If you ceased in the year or a previous year to be resident in Canada, and you received in the year any salary, wages, or other remuneration from employment that was paid to you directly or indirectly by an entity resident in Canada, that income will be subject to tax in Canada if that income is entitled to an exemption from income tax otherwise payable in another country by virtue of an agreement or tax treaty with one or more countries to which Canada is a party.

Tax treaties are discussed in ¶2005. Other agreements which might produce this result are agreements covering the treatment of diplomatic personnel, visiting armed forces, and similar Canadian personnel.

Note that it is sufficient that a treaty would render the income exempt in the other country if invoked. It therefore operates whether or not the foreign exemption is actually claimed.

If you are a non-resident and receive income from employment for work performed outside of Canada, you may be subject to tax by Canada on this employment income if it is paid to you, directly or indirectly, by an entity in Canada. You will also be subject to tax in Canada on amounts received under a contract as consideration for entering into a contract of service or an agreement to perform a service in Canada or as remuneration for the duties of an office or employment. This rule may apply if you were resident in Canada in any previous year, or if you are a student in full-time attendance at a university or other post-secondary educational institution in Canada even though you have never been resident in Canada.

Such employment income paid to a person directly or indirectly by an entity resident in Canada is subject to tax in Canada unless it is subject to income tax imposed by a country other than Canada, or unless it is paid in connection with the selling of property, the negotiating of contracts, or the rendering of services for, and in the ordinary course of business of, the Canadian payer or another company or entity with whom the payer does not deal at arm's length.

The income is considered as subject to income tax in a country other than Canada if it falls within the taxing jurisdiction of the foreign country, even though the recipient may pay no tax on it because of claiming personal allowances and similar deductions to which a resident of that country would normally be entitled. However, it will not be considered as subject to income tax in a foreign country if that country imposes no income tax, if the income is exempt under an international tax agreement, or if the income is exempt under any agreement between the employer and the foreign government.

If you would otherwise be taxable under this rule except that you meet one of the exemptions (e.g., income taxed in a foreign country, or service performed abroad in ordinary course of your employer's business), the Canadian payer may be able to eliminate the Canadian tax deductions at source. If you think this may apply to your situation consider checking with your employer.

(ITA: 115(2); ITR: 104(2))

[¶2024] SCHOLARSHIPS, BURSARIES, AND RESEARCH GRANTS

[¶2024.05] *Canadian Source Funds Received by Non-Residents*

Many scholarships, fellowships, bursaries, and prizes for achievements in a field of endeavour are now exempt from tax for both residents and non-residents (see ¶953). However, a research grant, or payments from a registered education savings plan from a source in Canada may be subject to Canadian tax on that amount if he or she is:

(1) a student in full-time attendance at a Canadian university, college or other educational institution providing courses at a post-secondary school level;

(2) a student or teacher at a foreign university, college or other educational institution providing courses at a post-secondary school level, if he or she had previously been resident in Canada and emigrated from Canada to attend or teach at that institution; or

(3) a person who had previously been resident in Canada but emigrated from Canada in order to carry on research under a grant.

The taxable non-resident will generally be liable to non-resident surtax (¶1445). However, where the non-resident was a resident of Quebec immediately before leaving Canada, Quebec tax may apply instead of non-resident surtax.

The deduction for research expenses which could be claimed by a Canadian resident in respect of this income may also be claimed by a non-resident.

Additionally, a scholarship, fellowship, bursary, or prize for achievement in your field of endeavour is includible in income to the extent that it exceeds $500 if it is **not** in connection with a program that entitles you to an education amount credit (¶953).

A non-resident student who is taxable in Canada under this provision may claim a deduction for specified moving expenses (¶1047).

Many of the tax agreements which Canada has with other countries may override this rule and prevent Canada from taxing this income.

(ITA: 56(1)(*n*); 56(3); 115(2); QTA: 1093; IT-420R3 [Archived]; *Non-Residents and Income Tax Guide* (T4058))

[¶2024.10] *Students' Treaty Exemption (Foreign Source Funds Received in Canada; Canadian Funds Received Abroad)*

Most Canadian tax treaties (¶2005) follow in substance Article XX of the OECD Model Tax Convention in that Canadian treaties generally exempt from Canadian tax foreign payments for maintenance or education received by a student or business apprentice who is present in Canada solely for the purpose of education or training and was resident in the other treaty state immediately before coming to Canada. It does not matter if the student is a deemed or factual resident of Canada, but a landed immigrant would have difficulty meeting the sole purpose test. See ¶117. Where such a treaty is in place, Canadians studying abroad will have the same exemption on their Canadian source income, which remains taxable in Canada as discussed above.

[¶2028] VISITING ARMED FORCES

Members of a visiting armed force of a "designated state" are exempt from Canadian tax on their service pay, as are designated civilian personnel accompanying and employed by a visiting force of a designated state. The most recent lists of designated states and designated civilian personnel can be found in the regulations to the Visiting Forces Act, on the Department of Justice website, at http://laws-lois.justice.gc.ca/eng/acts/V-2.

INCOME FROM BUSINESS IN CANADA

[¶2030] BUSINESS INCOME

If you are a non-resident carrying on business in Canada, you are (in the absence of a tax treaty which limits your liability) liable for Canadian tax on any income from that business.

A business includes a profession, calling, trade, manufacture or any other kind of undertaking. It does not include office or employment income as described in ¶2020, nor the mere ownership of property.

If you produced, grew, mined, created, manufactured, fabricated, improved, packed, preserved, or constructed anything in Canada, you were carrying on business in Canada.

If you solicited orders or offered anything for sale in Canada through an agent or employee you were carrying on business in Canada.

Examples:

(1) A sale of goods by a non-resident to a Canadian is not carrying on business in Canada if there is no agent or employee in Canada.

(2) The mere purchase of goods in Canada is not carrying on business in Canada unless further work is done in Canada on the goods.

(3) The sale of machinery in Canada, and the giving of subsequent advice and installation supervision by employees in Canada, is not, in itself, carrying on business in Canada.

If all operations of a business are carried on in Canada, then all of its income arises from Canadian sources and is taxable by Canada. If not all operations are carried on in Canada, the business income must be apportioned. There is no method specifically provided in law for allocating such income, except that a reasonable allocation should be made. Where practical, separate accounts should be maintained for the Canadian portion of the business, in which revenue and expenses directly attributable to it would be recorded. Some expenses may require proration, on a reasonable basis, between Canada and the other country. If the business sells products manufactured by the business in some other country, the fair market value of these products should be deducted from Canadian income. Fair market value in these instances would usually be the estimated price which an outside party, at the Canadian business trade level, would pay for the products. Both the manufacturing part of the business and the sales part are entitled to a part of any profit (or loss) on sales.

Where separate accounts are not maintained, income might be allocated on some other basis. For instance, the ratio of Canadian sales to total sales, or of Canadian costs to total costs, might be appropriate.

Only the portion of the business income allocated to Canada is taxable by Canada. Business income is subject to provincial tax in the province in which it is earned (see ¶1446).

Most if not all tax treaties between Canada and another country provide that a resident of that other country is liable for Canadian tax on business carried on in Canada only if the business is carried on through a "permanent establishment" in Canada. Permanent establishment is a term of art. The definition used for purposes of allocating income among Canadian jurisdictions, discussed in ¶1440, gives some flavour of the concept of permanent establishment for international purposes as well, but there is a great deal of interpretive literature on the meaning of the phrase for international purposes which does not necessarily find its way into a Canadian internal context. The OECD model treaty and commentary is a basic tool for purposes of international interpretation. Some treaties, notably the Canada–U.S. treaty, include their own definitions and interpretive commentary. For a brief overview of case law on the meaning of the term "permanent establishment" see the CCH Newsletter *Tax Topics* No. 1737, dated June 23, 2005.

The Canada–U.S. Tax Convention permits Canada to tax a U.S. resident on Canadian "business profits" only to the extent they are attributable to a permanent establishment in Canada. "Business profits" explicitly includes rentals, royalties, interest, capital gains and other income attributable to the permanent establishment. However, as before, where these amounts are not subject to income tax, they may be subject to gross withholding tax (see ¶2080). No profits will be attributable to a permanent establishment where the permanent establishment was used solely for the purchase of goods or solely for the provision of executive, managerial or administrative services.

Where you are carrying on business in Canada through an employee or agent established there, who has general authority to contract for you or has a stock of merchandise from which he or she regularly fills orders which he or she receives, you will be deemed to have a permanent establishment.

Example

A U.S. enterprise employs salespeople who live in Canada but do not have any kind of office or other permanent establishment in Canada. They visit Canadian customers, who then order from the U.S. enterprise, and receive the goods directly from the U.S. part of the business.

Although the U.S. enterprise is soliciting orders through employees in Canada, it may not have a permanent establishment in Canada and therefore may not be taxable by Canada.

All tax agreements now in effect contain similar exemptions.

The Canada–U.S. Tax Convention expands the definition of a permanent establishment to specifically include a place of management, a gas well, a quarry or other place of extraction of natural resources, a building site (if it lasts more than 12 months), the use of a person (other than an independent agent acting in the normal course of business) who habitually exercises authority to conclude contracts, or the use of a drilling rig, ship or installation exploring for natural resources for more than three months in any 12-month period. The Convention also provides that a permanent establishment does not include a fixed place of business used in one country by a resident of the other solely for:

(1) storage, display or delivery of goods belonging to the resident;

(2) maintaining a stock of goods belonging to the resident for the purpose of storage, display, delivery or for processing by another person;

(3) purchase of goods or the collection of information for the resident; or

(4) advertising, supply of information, scientific research, etc. which have an auxiliary character for the resident.

Generally, the Canada–U.S. Tax Convention continues to exempt from Canadian tax the profits (including rentals) of ships, aircraft and motor vehicles used in international traffic. However, profits from the voyage of a ship which has the principal purpose of transporting passengers or property within Canada may be taxed in Canada.

Where a non-resident person carries on any of the following businesses, namely:

(1) production, refining or marketing of petroleum, petroleum products or natural gas, or exploring or drilling for petroleum or natural gas;

(2) mining or exploring for minerals;

(3) processing mineral ores in connection with metal recovery and processing of the recovered metals;

(4) fabricating metals;

(5) operating a pipeline for the transmission of oil or natural gas; or

(6) producing, marketing or processing sodium chloride or potash,

all amounts, such as royalties or proceeds on disposal of royalties, that would be required to be included in income if the non-resident were resident in Canada, are taxed as income to the extent the amount has not been included in computing income from a business in Canada or from the disposition of taxable Canadian properly, subject to whatever treaty protection may be available under the agreements at ¶2005.

(ITA: 115(1)(*a*); 248(1) "business"; 253; IT-420R3 [Archived]; Other Publications: *International Harvester Co. of Canada Ltd. v. Provincial Tax Commission* [1949] A.C. 36; 1980 Canada–U.S. Tax Convention, Art. V, VII, VIII)

[¶2030.05] *Section 105 Withholding*

A fee or commission or other amount paid to a non-resident not regularly employed by the payer, for services rendered in Canada, is subject to a 15% withholding tax at source. This is not equivalent to the Part XIII withholding tax on items such as dividends and interest (¶2080), which represents a final settlement of liability, but is merely a payment on account of the non-resident's final Part I tax liability, if any. Where, for example, the non-resident claims that services provided are subject to treaty protection, the claim must be made by filing a Canadian return on which the amount withheld is claimed as an overpayment of tax. (Employees performing services in Canada are subject to ordinary employee withholding required of employers.)

Waiver of the withholding requirement may be obtained from the CRA under limited circumstances described in Information Circular 75-6R2.

For details on the reporting of section 105 withholding, see ¶2070.

For special treatment of payments to actors, see ¶2078.

(ITA: 150(1); ITR: 105 Non-Residents)

[¶2034] NON-RESIDENTS USING CANADIAN ADVISERS

As discussed, Canada taxes non-residents on their income from sources in Canada, including income from carrying on a business in Canada. Section 115.2 of the *Income Tax Act* provides an interpretive rule. This rule is primarily intended to ensure that a non-resident will not be considered to be carrying on business in Canada (and therefore potentially subject to Canadian tax) merely by engaging Canadian advisers to provide certain investment management, advisory, and administration functions. The provision was added to the Act to place Canadian service providers to foreign investment funds on an equal footing with service providers in several other jurisdictions, including the United States and United Kingdom. The provision provides assurance that a foreign investment fund which retains a Canadian service provider will not be carrying on business in Canada if certain conditions are met.

In general, section 115.2 provides that, for purposes of computing taxable income earned in Canada (and for the purpose of computing reserves of an insurance company), a non-resident is not considered to be carrying on business in Canada at any particular time solely because the non-resident (or a partnership of which the non-resident is a member) is provided with "designated investment services" by a "Canadian service provider". Designated investment services are defined generally as investment management and advice with respect to qualified investments, purchasing and selling qualified investments, investment administration services, and, in the case of a corporation, trust, or partnership, the only undertaking of which is the investment of its funds in qualified investments, marketing investments in the corporation, trust, or partnership to non-residents. Qualified investments are generally defined to include most types of investments.

A Canadian service provider is defined as a corporation or trust resident in Canada or a partnership all of the partners of which are Canadian residents.

In addition, a non-resident which is provided with designated investment services by a Canadian service provider is not required to file Canadian tax returns.

If the non-resident is an individual (other than a trust), the provision applies only if the non-resident is not affiliated (¶852) with the Canadian service provider.

In the case of a non-resident corporation or trust, the provision will apply only if:

- the non-resident did not (directly or through agents) (i) direct the promotion of investments in itself principally to "Canadian investors" (defined as persons that the non-resident knew or ought after reasonable inquiry to have known were Canadian residents), or (ii) sell an investment in itself to a person who was a Canadian investor at the time of the sale and remains a Canadian investor at the time the rule is being invoked;
- the non-resident did not make a filing under Canadian or provincial securities legislation to distribute its interests to Canadian residents; and
- where the non-resident was in existence more than one year, not more than 25% of the fair market value of investments in it are owned by persons and partnerships that are affiliated with the Canadian service provider.

In the case of services provided to a partnership of which the non-resident is a member, the provision will apply only if, where the partnership has been in existence more than one year, a non-resident member of the partnership is, or is affiliated (¶852) with, a person that is affiliated with a Canadian service provider or is owned more than 25% by a person or partnership affiliated with the Canadian service provider (an "unqualified person") and, either alone or together with other unqualified persons, owns more than 25% of the fair market value of all interests in the partnership. It should be noted that this test was enacted in 2013 but applies to taxation years that end after 2001, and the taxpayer can elect before the filing-due date of its taxation year that includes October 31, 2011 that the previous rules relating to partnerships will apply. The previous rule for partnerships dealt with independence between the non-resident and the Canadian service provider at the partnership level as opposed to the present test, which is at the partner level.

Note that even where these conditions are not met, it does not automatically follow that a business is being carried on in Canada by the non-resident. Conversely, where the conditions are met, it is possible that the non-resident is carrying on business in Canada through activities other than receiving designated investment services.

(ITA: 115.2)

DISPOSITION OF TAXABLE CANADIAN PROPERTY

[¶2040] TAXABLE CANADIAN PROPERTY

A non-resident of Canada is subject to Canadian income tax on dispositions of "taxable Canadian property". Essentially, this is property which by its nature and its relation to Canada is in some way attachable by the Canadian government in the event of failure to pay the tax. Real property located in Canada is the most obvious example. Since the government can enforce the tax against the property itself but cannot necessarily reach the non-resident vendor, the purchaser is obliged to collect the tax unless the vendor has committed itself to the compliance procedures discussed in ¶2042 or ¶2044.

The concept of taxable Canadian property serves two slightly different purposes in the *Income Tax Act*, and the definition is broader for the second purpose than the first.

For the first purpose, "taxable Canadian property" is defined for purposes of determining capital gain or loss and levying the resulting tax on the property itself (if necessary), whether in the hands of the person who acquires it or disposes of it. The definition applies on the disposition by a non-resident of property which gives rise to capital gain or loss (Chapter 5), and subjects the transaction to the compliance procedures in ¶2042.

The definition provides that "taxable Canadian property" of a non-resident taxpayer at any particular time includes:

(a) real or immovable property situated in Canada;

(b) property used or held in, eligible capital property in respect of and inventory in, a business carried on in Canada (with certain exceptions for insurance businesses and ships and aircraft used principally in international traffic);

> **Commentary on Bill C-29 Measures (Oct. 25, 2016)**
>
> Note: When Bill C-29, October 25, 2016, achieves Royal Assent, the commentary will be modified to read:
>
> (b) property used or held in, prior to 2017 eligible capital property and subsequent to 2016 property included in Class 14.1 in respect of and inventory in a business carried on in Canada (with certain exceptions for insurance businesses and ships and aircraft used principally in international traffic);

(c) designated insurance property of an insurer;

(d) a share of a corporation (other than a mutual fund corporation) that is not listed on a designated stock exchange, an interest in a partnership, or an interest in a trust (other than a mutual fund trust or an income interest in a resident trust), if at any time during the 60-month period that ends at that time, more than 50% of the fair market value of the share or interest was derived directly or indirectly from one or any combination of (i) real or immovable property situated in Canada, (ii) Canadian resources properties, (iii) timber resource properties, and (iv) interests or options in respect of such properties. (In determining whether the fair market value of the share or interest is derived from such properties, one does not count any value derived through a corporation, partnership, or trust the shares or interests in which were not themselves taxable Canadian property);

(e) a share of the capital stock of a corporation that is listed on a designated stock exchange, a share of the capital stock of a mutual fund corporation, or a unit of a mutual fund trust, if, at any time during the 60-month period that ends at that time, (i) 25% or more of the issued shares of any class of the capital stock of the corporation, or 25% or more of the issued units of the trust, were owned by one or any combination of the taxpayer and persons with whom the taxpayer did not deal at arm's length (and after July 11, 2013, any partnership in which such persons were members, directly or indirectly), **and** (ii) more than 50% fair market value of the share or unit was derived directly or indirectly from one or any combination of properties described under items (d)(i) to (iv) above; or

(f) an option or interest in any of the above properties.

A non-resident is entitled to use the same rules as a Canadian resident in determining taxable capital gains and allowable capital losses (see Chapter 5), including the Valuation Day rules which apply to property owned on December 31, 1971, except that the non-resident is not permitted to claim a reserve for proceeds of disposition that are not due until after the end of the year. The lifetime capital gains exemption for individuals (¶502) is not allowed to non-residents (but note the special definition of non-resident at ¶502).

Despite the broad definition of taxable Canadian property, under most of its income tax treaties, Canada's authority to tax capital gains of non-residents is generally restricted to gains from dispositions of real estate in Canada, shares in corporations or interests in partnerships or trusts the value of which is primarily attributable to real estate in Canada, and sometimes resource properties. Some treaties also allow Canada to tax gains on dispositions of other properties of non-resident individuals who were previously resident in Canada for a specified period of time prior to the disposition (e.g., under the Canada–U.S. treaty, if the taxpayer was resident for at least 120 months during any period of 20 consecutive years preceding the disposition of the property).

The second set of "taxable Canadian property" is defined as such for purposes of the immigration (as well as emigration) rules, the requirement to file Canadian tax return rules, and certain rollover provisions. These properties (numbers (14) to (18) below) are generally not treated as capital properties under the *Income Tax Act*; rather, income or loss resulting from the disposition of any of these properties (whether by residents or non-residents) is ordinary income or loss which must be entirely included in calculating net income for Canadian tax return purposes. Profit on disposition of these properties is subject to tax and to the withholding tax and compliance procedures as discussed at ¶2044. These properties are:

(14) A Canadian resource property (¶2044).

(15) A timber resource property (¶881).

(16) An income interest in a trust resident in Canada (¶451).

(17) A retired partner's right to a share of the income or loss of a partnership (¶1867).

(18) A life insurance policy in Canada (but note that not every life insurance policy may rise to income on disposition; see ¶981.

Commentary on Legislative Proposals (Sept. 16, 2016)

Note: When Legislative Proposals, September 16, 2016, achieves Royal Assent, the commentary will be modified to read:

Where the adjusted cost base of a non-resident taxpayer's taxable Canadian property becomes negative, such that there is deemed disposition and capital gain (see ¶535), the taxpayer will be required to file a tax return. This applies to deemed dispositions occurring on or after September 16, 2016.

Non-residents are not, in general, subject to provincial taxes in respect of dispositions of taxable Canadian property. However, they are subject to 48% federal surtax for income not earned in a province (see ¶1445). Non-residents who dispose of Quebec real estate or business property are subject to a parallel Quebec tax on these dispositions; see ¶1608.

The Canada–U.S. Tax Convention allows the country where real property or resource property is situated to levy tax regardless of the residence status of the vendor. See ¶2115 for a more detailed discussion of those rules.

In many of the older tax agreements Canada negotiated with other countries, Canada agreed not to tax capital gains realized in Canada by citizens or residents of the other country. In more modern treaties, notably the U.S. Tax Treaty, there may be special provisions to harmonize at least some of the intricacies of the tax provisions and deferrals which may be available. Because the provisions of these international tax agreements override any conflicting provisions in the Canadian tax law, residents of those countries will be exempt from Canadian tax on gains from taxable Canadian property if they can fit within an exempting provision of the relevant tax agreement.

Commentary on Legislative Proposals (Oct. 3, 2016)

Note: When the Notice of Ways and Means Motion, October 3, 2016, achieves Royal Assent, the commentary will be modified to read:

Principal Residence Exemption

A taxpayer may designate a home under the principal residence exemption if the taxpayer is resident in Canada. The exemption can serve to exempt from tax part or all of the gain on the disposition from the home. There is a "plus one" rule that adds to the number of years one can designate a home as a principal residence. However, the plus one rule applies only if the taxpayer acquires the home in a year in which the taxpayer was resident in Canada, effective for dispositions after October 2, 2016. Prior to this date, all taxpayers had access to the plus one rule regardless of their residency status. See ¶553 for details.

Only certain types of trust can qualify for the principal residence exemption. Effective for taxation years beginning after 2016, the types of trusts that qualify for the exemption are further restricted. In general terms, only the following types of personal trusts resident in Canada will be able to designate a home as a principal residence:

- Certain spousal or common-law partner trusts, joint spousal or common-law partner trusts, *alter ego* trusts, and certain types of self-benefit trusts. These trusts provide that the relevant beneficiary must be entitled to all of the income of the trust and that no one else may use the capital of the trust during their lifetime;
- A qualified disability trust. This type of trust must have a beneficiary who is eligible for the disability credit, among other conditions; and
- A trust where the beneficiary is under the age of 18, whose parents are both deceased, and one of the parents was a settlor of the trust.

In each case, the relevant beneficiary under the trust must be resident in Canada in the year in which the trust designates the home as its principal residence. For tax years beginning before 2017, the beneficiary did not have to be resident in Canada, though the trust was required to be resident.

Historical Information: Dispositions of Taxable Canadian Property before March 5, 2010

Prior to March 5, 2010, the following property was taxable Canadian property when disposed of by a non-resident if it would give rise to capital gain or loss:

(1) Real property (e.g., land and buildings) situated in Canada. Mortgages are not considered to be an interest in real property.

(2) After December 23, 1998, all property used or held by a taxpayer in, eligible capital property (prior to 2017) in respect of, and inventory of, a business carried on in Canada, other than an insurance business, but not including ships and aircraft of a non-resident used principally in international traffic and personal property pertaining to their operations if the country in which the non-resident resides grants similar relief to Canadian residents. Prior to December 24, 1998, only *capital property* used by a non-resident in carrying on a business in Canada was TCP, with the same exceptions for insurers, ships and aircraft. See also ¶2153. Where a non-resident has been using capital property in a business in Canada and begins to use it in a business outside Canada (or *vice versa* (after October 1, 1996), it is deemed to have been disposed of at fair market value at that time under the change of use rules for capital property (¶513).

(3) Designated insurance property (defined in section 138(12) of the *Income Tax Act*) of an insurer used in carrying on an insurance business in Canada. Generally speaking, this is property used by any insurer (other than a Canadian resident insurer not in the life insurance business) in carrying on an insurance business in Canada. Before October 2, 1996, only capital property of a non-resident insurer carrying on business in Canada was TCP.

(4) For dispositions of shares after April 26, 1995, subject to transitional rules described below, shares of a corporation resident in Canada (other than a mutual fund corporation) which do not belong to a class that is listed on a prescribed Canadian or foreign stock exchange (Regulations 3200, 3201); note that this would make unlisted shares of a public corporation taxable Canadian property; for earlier or grandfathered dispositions, shares of a corporation which is resident or deemed to be resident in Canada and is not a "public corporation" under the income tax rules. There continues to be an exception for shares of a non-resident-owned investment corporation if, on the first day of the year, the corporation owns neither taxable Canadian property in this list nor items (13) to (16) in the following list.

(5) For dispositions after April 26, 1995, subject to transitional rules below, shares of a non-resident corporation which are not listed on a prescribed Canadian or foreign stock exchange (Regulations 3200, 3201), if at any time during the 60-month period (before October 2, 1996, read "12-month period") preceding the time at which taxable Canadian property status must be determined (usually the time of disposition or deemed disposition):

(a) more than 50% of the fair market value of all the property of the non-resident corporation was made up of properties listed in (1) to (16) in this list or interests or options in such properties (whether or not the property exists); and

(b) more than 50% of the fair market value of the share(s) disposed of is derived directly or indirectly from one or any combination of items (1), (14), and (15).

There continues to be an exception for shares of a non-resident-owned investment corporation if, on the first day of the year, the corporation owns neither taxable Canadian property in this list nor items (13) to (16) in the following list. There is also an exception for U.S. residents; see subheading U.S. Treaty Protocol below.

(6) For dispositions after April 26, 1995, subject to transitional rules below, shares otherwise described in (4) or (5), above, or shares of a Canadian mutual fund corporation, or for earlier dispositions, shares of a public corporation, if in either case, at any time during the 60-month period immediately preceding the time at which taxable Canadian property status must be determined (usually the time of disposition or deemed disposition), the non-resident and/or persons with whom the non-resident did not deal at arm's length owned 25% or more of the issued shares of any class of its capital stock. U.S. residents have treaty protection on this rule; see subheading "U.S. Treaty Protocol" below.

(7) An interest in a partnership if, at any time in the 60-month period (before October 2, 1996, read "12-month period") before the time at which taxable Canadian property status must be determined (usually the time of disposition or deemed disposition), 50% or more in value of the partnership property was taxable Canadian property, a Canadian resource property, timber resource property, an income interest in a trust resident in Canada, or an interest or option in any such property whether or not the property exists. The "whether or not the property exists" is added for dispositions after April 26, 1996, subject to transitional rules.

(8) A capital interest in a trust (other than a unit trust) resident in Canada.

(9) A unit of a unit trust resident in Canada (other than a mutual fund trust).

(10) A unit of a mutual fund trust if, at any time during the 60-month period immediately preceding the time at which taxable Canadian property status must be determined (usually the time of disposition or deemed disposition), the non-resident and/or persons with whom the non-resident does not deal at arm's length owned 25% or more of the issued units of the trust.

(11) For dispositions after April 26, 1995, subject to transitional rules below, an interest in a non-resident trust if, at any time in the 60-month period (before October 2, 1996, read "12-month period") before disposition:

(a) more than 50% of the fair market value of all the property of the non-resident trust was made up of properties listed in (1) to (16) in this list or interests or options in such properties (whether or not the property exists); and

(b) more than 50% of the fair market value of the share(s) disposed of is derived directly or indirectly from one or any combination of items (1), (14), and (15).

(12) Prior to October 2, 1996, property deemed by other tax rules to be taxable Canadian property. (This provision is considered superfluous under the taxpayer migration rules, and so has been withdrawn effective October 2, 1996.)

(13) An interest in or option in respect of taxable Canadian property described in (1) to (12) is deemed to be taxable Canadian property, whether or not the underlying property exists.

(ITA: 39(1); 40(2)(*a*); 96(1.4); 106(2); 115(1), (3); 248(1) "taxable Canadian property"; IT-176R2 [Archived]; IT-420R3 [Archived]; Other Publications: 1980 Canada–U.S. Tax Convention, Art. XIII)

[¶2042] COMPLIANCE PROCEDURES FOR DISPOSITION OF TAXABLE CANADIAN PROPERTY (SECTION 116 CERTIFICATES)

The *Income Tax Act* contains rules which are intended to ensure compliance by non-residents who dispose of taxable Canadian property. These rules constitute a prepayment on account of tax to be calculated on a Canadian T1 return for the year, calculated in accordance with the rules at ¶2050–¶2069.

Generally, any person (including another non-resident) who is purchasing a taxable Canadian property from a non-resident (other than "excluded property" described in ¶2042.50 or treaty-protected property in respect of which the notice described in ¶2042.50(c) has been provided to the CRA) is required to withhold 25% of the purchase price and remit this to the Canadian tax authorities to apply on account of the non-resident vendor's tax liability, unless the vendor has reported the transaction to the CRA and has either paid an amount equal to 25% of the estimated capital gain or else has posted security for payment of the tax liability.

Revisions to the taxable Canadian property (TCP) rules effective October 2, 1996 included inventory of a Canadian business in TCP; a corresponding change to the withholding rules excludes it again unless is inventory that is real property in Canada, Canadian resource property or Canadian timber property.

If the sale of taxable Canadian property is not reported in advance of the transaction, you, the non-resident vendor, are *required* to report it within 10 days after the date of sale.

The form to be filed by a non-resident vendor to report a proposed or completed sale of taxable Canadian property is form T2062 which is available at any Tax Services Office. The form requires the vendor to state the name and address of the purchaser or intended purchaser, the date or proposed date of the transaction, a description of the taxable Canadian property, the sale price or proposed sale price, and the vendor's adjusted cost base of the property. The form implies that you, the non-resident vendor, must make a payment on account of your tax equal to 25% of the estimated capital gain. Payment of this amount is not mandatory, but if it is not paid or if security is not provided, the purchaser will be obligated to withhold the same percentage from the gross purchase price and pay this amount to the tax authorities within 30 days after the end of the month in which the purchase occurred. Since 25% of the gain will normally be less than 25% of the total sales price, it will normally be to your advantage to pay the former amount.

If you, a non-resident vendor, file form T2062 in advance of a proposed sale of taxable Canadian property, and pay an amount equal to 25% of the estimated capital gain or provide acceptable security, the CRA will issue to you and to the proposed purchaser a "certificate" on form T2064. This certificate will set out an amount called a "certificate limit". If the actual purchase price does not exceed the certificate limit, the purchaser is not required to withhold and remit the 25% (or applicable rate of) tax. If the purchaser receives a certificate but the actual purchase price exceeds the certificate limit, the purchaser must withhold 25% of the amount by which the actual purchase price exceeds the certificate limit.

Filing of form T2062 in advance of a proposed transaction is optional. However, the form must be filed within 10 days after any sale of taxable Canadian property unless it was filed in advance and:

(1) the purchaser was the same person as that named as proposed purchaser in the form;

(2) the actual sales price was not greater than the amount estimated in the form; and

(3) the actual adjusted cost base was not less than the amount estimated in the form.

If a form T2062 is filed after the transaction is completed and you, the non-resident vendor, pay an amount equal to 25% of your capital gain or deposit acceptable security, the CRA will issue to you and the purchaser a certificate on form T2068. Upon receipt of this certificate, the liability of the purchaser to pay 25% of the purchase price to the Canadian tax authorities ceases.

Even though form T2062 is filed and a tax payment is made by you, the non-resident vendor, or by the purchaser, you are still required to file a Canadian income tax return after the end of the year to report your income taxable in Canada, and compute the tax thereon. Any overpayment of tax will be refunded to you or any balance of tax owing must be paid by April 30.

Some non-residents who are selling taxable Canadian property may be exempt from Canadian tax on capital gains because of the provisions of an international tax agreement. In these circumstances, the Canadian tax authorities will often waive the requirement for payment by the non-resident of 25% of the estimated capital gain, or deposit of acceptable security, and will issue a certificate to the purchaser provided the non-resident gives a written undertaking to file a Canadian tax return after the end of the year. Such arrangements should be negotiated in advance with the Non-Resident Section of the Tax Services Office for the district in which the property being sold is located.

Form T2062 is to be filed with the Tax Services Office for the district in which the property being sold is located (see ¶287).

(ITA: 116; 150(1); 248(1) "recognized stock exchange"; ITR: 3200; 3201; IC 72-17R6 Procedures concerning the disposition of taxable Canadian property by non-residents of Canada – Section 116)

[¶2042.05] *Real, Depreciable, and Resource Property*

Where a non-resident disposes or proposes to dispose of a property (other than capital property) that is real property situated in Canada, a Canadian resource property, a timber resource property, a depreciable property that is a taxable Canadian property, or any interest in or option in respect of these properties, the proposed or actual sale is reported on form T2062A rather than form T2062. In some cases, vendors may have to file both form T2062 and form T2062A for one disposition. When vendors dispose of depreciable taxable Canadian property, they should use form T2062 to declare the gain or loss. The recapture of capital cost allowance or terminal loss should be reported on form T2062A. Depreciable property is property for which a taxpayer is entitled to claim capital cost allowance, which is deductible when calculating income from business or property. Form T2062A should be filed even if capital cost allowance has not been claimed on a depreciable property. In these instances two certificates of compliance can be issued.

Where the vendor fails to apply for a certificate of compliance in advance of the disposition, or the certificate is less than the purchase price, the purchaser is liable to withhold and remit to Canada 50% of the uncertified amount in respect of these properties. See also ¶2044.05 and ¶2044.10 in respect of withholding on sales of Canadian resource property and timber resource property.

(ITA: 116; esp. 116(5.2), (5.3); 150(1); IC 72-17R6, esp. paras. 4, 15)

[¶2042.10] *Canadian Resource Property and Timber Limit*

In the case of a disposition by a non-resident of resource property (¶2044) or a timber limit (¶881), the reporting and withholding requirements are identical to those for depreciable property, etc., above. The purchaser of the property is responsible for withholding 50% of the total proceeds on sale and remitting the amount to the CRA within 30 days unless the CRA has issued the appropriate certificate to the non-resident vendor. This certificate will be granted only upon filing by the non-resident of forms T2062 and/or form T2062A (where recapture is involved) and payment of the tax liability arising on the disposition. The amount of tax to be paid will be dependent upon the amount of recapture, subject to full tax rates, and the amount of taxable capital gain, if any.

Vendors of Canadian resource property should use Form T2062A Schedule 1, Disposition of Canadian Resource Property by Non-Residents to determine the balances in the various "pools" and the payment on account of tax (if any) when they dispose of Canadian resource properties. To support the amounts reported, vendors should also submit form T2062A along with any other supporting documents. Vendors cannot use unrelated outlays and expenses and losses carried forward from previous years to reduce the balance in the "pools" and thus lower the amount subject to payment on account of tax under section 116.

(ITA: 116; esp. 116(5.2), (5.3); 150(1); IC 72-17R6, esp. paras. 4, 16)

[¶2042.15] *Life Insurance Policies*

See ¶2044.

[¶2042.20] *Quebec Compliance Rules*

Where a non-resident is disposing of Quebec real estate, business property, or resource property, Quebec has compliance procedures similar but not identical to the federal procedures. Speaking very generally, Quebec has a similar certificate procedure (form TP-1097). Although double tax may be avoided by federal remission order, it seems that double prepayment may be required. See ¶1608.

[¶2042.40] *Vendor's Obligation to File Canadian Return*

As noted in ¶2000, a non-resident individual is in general required to file a Canadian tax return if the non-resident has a taxable capital gain or disposes of taxable Canadian property in the year. For dispositions after 2008, the filing requirement is waived where the disposition is an "excluded disposition". A disposition is excluded if:

- the taxpayer is non-resident at the time of the disposition;
- no ordinary (Part I) income tax is payable by the taxpayer for the taxation year;
- the taxpayer is, at the time of the disposition, not liable to pay any amount on account of ordinary income tax in respect of any previous taxation year (other than an amount for which the CRA has accepted, and holds, adequate security); and
- each taxable Canadian property disposed of by the taxpayer in the taxation year is either (i) excluded property as discussed in ¶2042.50, below, or (ii) a property in respect of the disposition of which the Minister has issued to the taxpayer a certificate as discussed in ¶2042 above or ¶2044 below.

[¶2042.50] *Purchaser's Obligation to Withhold: Exceptions*

As discussed above, a Canadian purchaser of taxable Canadian property from a non-resident is required to withhold from the purchase price 25% of the cost in excess of the amount covered by a pre-transaction clearance certificate. The withholding is 50% of the excess where the properties described at ¶2042.05 and ¶2042.10 are the subject of the sale.

There are two protections against this liability. First there is a so-called "safe haven" protection. The purchaser is not required to withhold if, *after reasonable inquiry*, the purchaser has no reason to believe the vendor is a non-resident.

The safe-haven protection is extended where the property which is the subject of the transaction is "treaty-protected" property. Treaty-protected property at any particular time is, as you might expect, property the income or gain from which would be exempt from ordinary income tax by virtue of a Canadian tax treaty. That is, where the vendor's gain on the property would not be taxable by virtue of a tax treaty, the property is treaty-protected.

The safe-haven protection applies where the purchaser meets all the following conditions:

(a) the purchaser concludes after reasonable inquiry that the non-resident person is, under a tax treaty that

Canada has with a particular country, resident in the particular country;

(b) the property would be treaty-protected property of the non-resident person if the non-resident person were, under the tax treaty referred to in (a), resident in the particular country;

(c) the purchaser provides notice to the CRA under subsection 116(5.02) in respect of the acquisition, on or before the day that is 30 days after the date of the acquisition, setting out (i) the date of the acquisition, (ii) the name and address of the non-resident person, (iii) a description of the property sufficient to identify it, (iv) the amount paid or payable, as the case may be, by the purchaser for the property, and (v) the name of the country with which Canada has concluded a tax treaty under which the property is a treaty-protected property for the purposes of these rules.

It is important to note that requirements (a) and (b) are different in kind. Although the purchaser's conclusion as to the vendor's country of residence (in (a)) will usually be correct as a matter of fact, that is not strictly necessary. What is necessary is that the purchaser conclude, based on the results of a reasonable inquiry, that the non-resident is resident in a particular tax-treaty country. By contrast, the treaty effects of being resident in that particular country are not a matter of reasonable inquiry by the purchaser, but rather of the actual effect of the treaty. The purchaser's reading of the treaty must be correct in fact (or in law).

The second form of protection (after the safe-haven rules) for the purchaser from the obligation to withhold is found in the "excluded property rules". Excluded property is not subject to either withholding requirements by the purchaser or compliance procedures by the vendor. Excluded property includes:

(1) property that is taxable Canadian property solely because a provision of the *Income Tax Act* deems it to be taxable Canadian property, as opposed to being included in the definition of taxable Canadian property at ¶2040. Thus, for example, an interest in a partnership that is deemed to be taxable Canadian property under paragraph 97(2)(*c*) and that would not otherwise be a taxable Canadian property under the definition in subsection 248(1) would be excluded property for purposes of this rule;

(2) property that is inventory in a business carried on in Canada, other than real property, Canadian resource property or a timber resource property;

(3) a share of a corporation listed on a recognized Canadian or foreign stock exchange; a recognized stock exchange includes a designated stock exchange (¶2618) and any other stock exchange located in Canada or in a country that is a member of the Organization for Economic Cooperation and Development and that has a tax treaty with Canada;

(4) a unit of a mutual fund trust;

(5) most types of debt instruments (a bond, debenture, bill, note, hypothecary claim, or similar obligation);

(6) property of licensed non-resident insurers that carry on business in Canada;

(7) property of an authorized foreign bank that is used or held in the course of the bank's Canadian banking business;

(8) an option in respect of property referred to above;

(9) an interest in any property referred to above; and

(10) for dispositions after 2008, property that is at the time of disposition treaty-protected property in respect of which *if the purchaser and the vendor are related at the time of the disposition* the notice referred to in (c), above, has been provided to the CRA. If they are not related, the notice is not required.

[¶2042.55] *Refunds of Amounts Withheld Under Section 116*

In the 2010 federal Budget, the Department of Finance indicated a "unique problem" affecting non-residents in respect of whom an amount of tax was withheld pursuant to section 116 (or regulation 105 regarding services rendered in Canada by a non-resident). That is, there is no deadline for the CRA to assess the person required to withhold such amounts in respect of the failure to withhold the taxes, such that there could be cases where the non-resident vendor of taxable Canadian property (or similar property) could not claim a refund (e.g., where the non-resident is subject to treaty protection) under the regular refund limitation periods. As a result, the taxpayer relief provisions of subsection 164(1.5) were amended. For an overpayment in respect of which an application for a refund is made by a taxpayer after March 4, 2010, paragraph 164(1.5)(*c*) allows the CRA to make the refund to the extent that the overpayment for the relevant taxation year relates to another assessment of another taxpayer under subsection 227(10) or (10.1) (failure to withhold or remit taxes, etc.). The taxpayer's tax return for the taxation year must be filed on or before the day that is two years after the date of the other assessment of the other taxpayer. In the case of an amount assessed under subsection 227(10.1), the other assessment must relate to an amount payable under subsection 116(5) or (5.3) in respect of a disposition of property by the taxpayer — namely, an amount withheld on account of the non-resident's tax for dispositions of taxable Canadian property, Canadian resource property, real property situated in Canada, a timber resource property, or depreciable property as discussed above.

[¶2044] SALE OF A CANADIAN RESOURCE PROPERTY AND DISPOSITIONS OF OTHER TAXABLE CANADIAN PROPERTY

As discussed in ¶2040, the properties listed in items (14) to (18) are treated as non-capital properties on dispositions for Canadian as well as non-resident purposes. However, they are in principle subject to taxation on dispositions by non-residents, which can be enforced on the property against the acquiror.

[¶2044.05] *Canadian Resource Property*

The Canadian system of taxation of resource properties and allowances for resource investments is discussed in Chapter 22. A non-resident who sells a Canadian resource property will be subject to Canadian tax.

A Canadian resource property generally means any property that is:

(1) a right, licence, or privilege to explore for, drill for, or take petroleum, natural gas, or other related hydrocarbons in Canada, or to store those things underground;

(2) a right, licence, or privilege to prospect, explore, drill, or mine for minerals in Canada other than bituminous sands or oil shale deposits;

(3) any oil or gas well situated in Canada, or any real property in Canada the principal value of which depends on its petroleum or natural gas content but not including any depreciable property;

(4) any rental or royalty computed by reference to the amount or value of production from an oil or gas well or from a natural accumulation of petroleum or natural gas in Canada, if the payer of the rental or royalty has an interest or right in the well or accumulation, as the case may be, and 90% or more of the rental or royalty is payable out of, or from proceeds of, the production from the well or accumulation;

(5) any rental or royalty computed by reference to the amount or value of production from a mineral resource in Canada, other than a bituminous sands deposit or an oil shale deposit, if the payer of the rental or royalty has an interest in or right in the mineral resource, and 90% or more of the rental or royalty is payable out of, or from proceeds of, the production from the mineral resource;

(6) a real property situated in Canada but not including any depreciable property, if its principal value depends upon its mineral resource content other than where the mineral resource is a bituminous sands deposit or an oil shale deposit; or

(7) a right to or interest in any property (other than a right or interest that a taxpayer has because the taxpayer is a beneficiary under a trust or a member of a partnership) described above (including a right to receive proceeds of disposition in respect of a disposition thereof).

Only the proceeds from the sale of a Canadian resource property receivable in the year need be included in computing a non-resident's income.

Where a non-resident ceases to carry on a business (as listed in ¶2030) at a fixed place of business in Canada, and does not commence after that time and during the year to carry on any such business at a fixed place of business in Canada, the taxation year of the person will be deemed to have ended and he or she will be deemed to have disposed of his or her Canadian resource property at fair market value at that time and reacquired it immediately thereafter at fair market value.

The compliance procedures for a proposed disposition of a Canadian resource property are the same as for a disposition of taxable Canadian property (¶2040), except that the purchaser of the property is responsible for withholding 50% of the total proceeds on sale and remitting the amount to the CRA within 30 days unless the CRA has issued the appropriate certificate to the non-resident vendor. This certificate will be granted only upon the filing by the non-resident of forms T2062A, T2062A, Schedule 1, and payment of the potential tax liability arising on the disposition. However, the potential tax liability to be posted by the non-resident is an amount acceptable to the Minister, presumably equal to the tax applicable to this transaction, in order to take into account the fact that the disposition of such property could give rise to a full inclusion in income rather than a capital gain. Non-residents who dispose of taxable Canadian property, such as Canadian resource properties, are also required to obtain an identification number, such as an individual Tax Number, by completing form T1261.

(ITA: 66(15), 115(1), (4); 116; 248(1); IC 72-17R6 Procedures concerning the disposition of taxable Canadian property by non-residents of Canada – Section 116; IT-125R4 (Archived); IT-420R3 (Archived))

[¶2044.10] *Timber Resource Property (and Recapture of CCA Generally)*

Gains on disposition of timber resource property (¶881), as well as recapture of capital cost allowance on such dispositions, are taxed in effect as part of the tax from carrying on business in Canada.

In fact, all recapture of capital cost allowance on dispositions of depreciable property used in carrying on business in Canada, and of CCDE resource allowances on dispositions of resource property, is subject to tax in the hands of a non-resident under similar provisions. Form T2062A is used for recapture purposes.

(ITA: 115(1)(*a*)(iii.2); 248(1); IC 72-17R6 Procedures concerning the disposition of taxable Canadian property by non-residents of Canada – Section 116; IT-420R3 (Archived))

[¶2044.15] *Income Interest in a Trust*

Proceeds received by a non-resident from sale of an income interest in a trust which is resident in Canada are subject to Canadian tax. The non-resident will be allowed to deduct such portion of his cost, if any, of acquiring that interest in the trust as would have been deductible if he were resident in Canada (¶451). It appears that the compliance procedures described at ¶2042 would apply to this disposition.

(ITA: 115(1)(*a*)(iv); 248(1); IC 72-17R6 Procedures concerning the disposition of taxable Canadian property by non-residents of Canada – Section 116; IT-420R3 (Archived))

[¶2044.20] *Retired Partner's Income Interest*

A non-resident retired partner who has a continuing income interest described at ¶1867 is subject to taxation on the full profit from disposition of that interest.

(ITA: 115(1)(*a*)(iv.1); 248(1); IC 72-17R6 Procedures concerning the disposition of taxable Canadian property by non-residents of Canada – Section 116; IT-420R3 (Archived))

[¶2044.25] *Proceeds of Life Insurance Disposition*

A non-resident of Canada is taxable in Canada on his proceeds in excess of the adjusted cost base of the policy on the disposition or deemed disposition of a life insurance policy in Canada after November 12, 1981. See ¶981. The non-resident is required to notify the CRA of this disposition, by filing form T2062, either prior to the disposition or within 10 days thereafter. The insurer must ensure payment of tax out of proceeds, using form T2062B and form T2062B Schedule 1, Certification and Remittance Notice.

(ITA: 115(1)(*a*)(vi); 248(1); IC 72-17R6 Procedures concerning the disposition of taxable Canadian property by non-residents of Canada – Section 116; IT-420R3 (Archived))

[¶2046] FORMER RESIDENTS OF CANADA

If you emigrate from Canada, you are deemed to have disposed of certain property immediately prior to your emigration (see Chapter 21). The deemed disposition may result in net taxable capital gains or other income, and if so, the tax on those gains or income can be deferred until the property is actually disposed of; see ¶2153.10 and the ensuing commentary.

(ITA: 3(*e*); 128.1)

[¶2048] FOREIGN TAX CREDIT AVAILABLE TO FORMER RESIDENTS OF CANADA

[¶2048.05] *Credit against Departure Tax*

Taxpayers leaving Canada are taxable on deemed dispositions of certain types of taxable Canadian property. Where they are also taxable by their new country of residence on a later actual disposition of the same property, Canada may give a credit against the departure tax previously paid. These rules are discussed under the subheading "Double Taxation and the Special Foreign Tax Credit" at ¶2153.

(ITA: 126(2.21); Income Tax Folio: S5-F2-C1 Foreign Tax Credit)

DEDUCTIONS AND LOSSES

[¶2050] DEDUCTIONS ALLOWED IN COMPUTING INCOME

A non-resident subject to Canadian tax on Canadian source employment income, business income or income from the disposition of taxable Canadian property is generally allowed to claim all deductions to arrive at net income from those sources which could be claimed by a Canadian resident. In order to be deductible, such items must strictly meet the criteria laid down in the *Income Tax Act*.

In addition to the deductions related to a source of income, for example capital cost allowance related to business income, or deductible employment expenses, which may be claimed to the extent related income is subject to tax, there are some expenses of a more general nature which may or may not be deductible. For example, non-residents are subject to special restrictions on the moving expense deduction (these are described in ¶1039 and, for students, ¶1047), the child care expense deduction (¶1051), and the deduction for foreign exploration and development expenses (¶2227).

Similarly, some amounts are deductible only where income is reported under the general rule and not under the rules for withholding on royalties, dividends, and the like at ¶2080. Thus, the deduction for the capital portion of annuity payments (¶481) is not permitted where the income is subject to non-resident withholding.

(ITA: 3; 115(1); IT-420R3 [Archived])

[¶2055] LOSSES OF THE YEAR (SEE ALSO CHAPTER 10)

[¶2055.05] *Business Losses*

Losses incurred in a taxation year from businesses carried on in Canada during the year are deductible from income subject to tax in Canada for the year. However, business losses from "treaty-protected" businesses carried on in Canada are not included in deductible loses. A treaty-protected business is one the income of which, had there been any for the period, would have been exempt from Canadian income tax under a Canadian tax treaty (¶2005). Typically, these will be businesses carried on in Canada by a resident of a foreign treaty country, but carried on without a permanent establishment in Canada as defined in the treaty.

Losses incurred in the year by a non-resident from businesses carried on outside Canada, or from property (e.g., rental losses), whether inside or outside Canada, are not deductible.

[¶2055.10] *Employment Losses*

Losses incurred in a year from duties of an office or employment performed in Canada are deductible from income subject to tax in Canada for the year. Losses from employment are rare. In any event, the provision for employment losses is fair in principle if remote in practice.

[¶2055.15] *Allowable Business Investment Losses*

Allowable business investment losses (¶580) incurred in the year can be deducted from income subject to tax in Canada if the property giving rise to the allowable business investment loss would have given rise to income subject to Canadian tax if disposed of at a gain during the year. This appears to mean that allowable business investment losses arising in the year on taxable Canadian property (¶2040) may be deducted from Canadian income of a non-resident for the year.

The rules which deny capital losses arising on treaty-protected property (discussed below) mean that allowable business investment losses arising on treaty-protected property are not deductible.

[¶2055.20] *Capital Losses*

In the first instance, the non-resident taxpayer computes each capital gain and capital loss in the ordinary way, as discussed in Chapter 5, and then reduces it to a "taxable capital gain" (1/2 of the capital gain) or "allowable capital loss" (1/2 of the capital loss).

For non-residents, allowable capital losses arising from disposition in a year of taxable Canadian property (excluding personal property and listed personal property losses) are deductible from the taxpayer's taxable capital gains from the disposition of such property for the year. However, gains and losses from "treaty-protected property" are not included in this netting calculation. Treaty-protected property is property the gain on which would be exempt from Canadian tax to the non-resident disposer by virtue of a Canadian tax treaty between Canada and the disposer's country of residence, had there been a gain instead of a loss on the treaty. Clearly the gains would have been exempt in any case; the point of the change is to remove from the netting calculation losses on treaty-protected property.

To the extent that such allowable capital losses incurred by a non-resident taxpayer from the disposition of taxable Canadian property (other than property denied tax recognition as discussed above) exceed taxable capital gains from such property, that amount becomes a "net capital loss" which may be carried to other years (see ¶2061 below) to reduce taxable capital gains of those other years from the disposition of such property.

For deduction of losses from other years generally, see ¶2061.

(ITA: 111(8), (9); 115(1)(*b*), (*c*); 248(1) "taxable Canadian property", "treaty-protected business", "treaty-protected property"; IT-171R2 [Archived]; IT-262R2 [Archived])

CALCULATION OF TAXABLE INCOME AND TAX CREDITS

[¶2060] GENERAL INFORMATION

If you are a non-resident whose income from Canada is entirely in the form of dividends, interest or other similar amounts discussed under "other income" (¶2080), you are generally not permitted to file a Canadian tax return on which you report the income, since you are taxed on the gross amount received from Canada. However, where you elect to use the alternate method for pensions and similar benefits (see ¶2086) or for rents and timber royalties (see ¶2080.05), you are required to file a Canadian tax return claiming the appropriate deductions as outlined where these alternative methods are discussed.

If you are a non-resident with Canadian employment income, business income or taxable gains from the disposition of taxable Canadian properties, you are required to file a tax return on which you may claim the appropriate deductions and tax credits as outlined below. In all cases, the deductions and credits claimed must be reasonable.

(ITA: 67; 115; 150(1); 212; 216; 217)

[¶2061] LOSSES CARRIED OVER (SEE ALSO CHAPTER 10)

For deductions of current year losses against current year Canadian income of a non-resident, see ¶2055. For part-year residents, see also ¶2103.

Where losses from years of non-residence are carried to other years of non-residence, the limitations on income taxable in Canada provide sufficient limitation on the loss which may be claimed. That is, there are no special rules.

Where losses were generated in a year when you were not resident but are applied in a year when you are a resident of Canada, the rule is that losses for a year of non-residence must be determined as if you had no gains or losses other than those that would have been accounted for in a Canadian non-resident return for the year if one were filed for the year to which the losses are carried. That is, the losses generated in a non-resident year but applied in a resident year are only allowed to the extent of Canadian-source business and employment income and loss for the year, allowable business investment loss for the year, and gains and losses from taxable Canadian property. In calculating the limited Canadian income to which losses generated as a non-resident can be applied, you cannot include capital or allowable capital losses on "treaty-protected property" or business losses from "treaty-protected businesses". Treaty-protected property is property the gain on which would be exempt from Canadian tax to the non-resident vendor by virtue of a tax treaty between Canada and the vendor's country of residence, had there been a gain instead of a loss on the treaty. A treaty-protected business is one the income of which, had there been any for the period, would have been exempt from Canadian income tax to the non-resident under a tax treaty (¶2005). Typically, these will be businesses carried on in Canada by a resident of a foreign treaty country, but carried on without a permanent establishment in Canada as defined in the treaty.

Given these rules, matters seem to work themselves out as follows.

Losses of a non-resident from employment performed in Canada are included in loss carryovers available to the non-resident. A non-Canadian employment loss from a year of residence cannot be applied in a year of non-residence. It would appear that a Canadian employment loss in excess of income subject to Canadian tax in a year of non-residence can be applied in a year of residence.

A loss incurred in another year from a business carried on in Canada while you were not resident, and which was not deductible in that year due to insufficient Canadian income, is deductible in the current year under carryover rules identical to those for Canadian residents, except that the amount of loss is based strictly on income and loss calculations from Canadian sources. This allows the application of losses incurred when you are resident of Canada from a business carried on in Canada against income earned from a business carried on in Canada after you become a non-resident. Presumably, the reverse is also true. A loss incurred in another year from a business carried on outside Canada during a period when you were not resident is not deductible in computing the taxable income earned in Canada for a taxation year.

The only net capital losses incurred when you were not resident in Canada which are deductible in computing the taxable income earned in Canada as a non-resident are allowable capital losses from dispositions of taxable Canadian property.

Allowable business investment losses arising on taxable Canadian property during a year of non-residence in excess of Canadian source income for the year may be carried over against Canadian source income of other years of non-residence, and may apparently also be applied under normal carryback/carryforward provisions and applied to years of residence.

(ITA: 111(8), (9); 115(1)(*b*), (*c*); IT-171R2 [Archived]; IT-262R2 [Archived]; CRA Document No.: S. 115(1)(e), *March 10, 1995*, CRA Document No. 9501456; Application of losses by a non-resident, *January 29, 1996*, CRA Document No. 9510375)

[¶2062] DEDUCTIONS IN COMPUTING TAXABLE INCOME

If you are a non-resident with Canadian employment or business income or taxable Canadian capital gains you may generally claim deductions only for the following:

- qualifying employee stock option benefits (¶2123);
- Employment Insurance repayments (¶941);
- prospectors' exemptions (¶776);
- treaty-protected amounts;
- Canadian Workers' Compensation or social assistance (although it is difficult to imagine a non-resident being entitled to these); and
- applicable loss carryovers (¶2061).

Non-residents are barred from claiming the capital gains deduction (but see ¶502 as to who is considered a non-resident).

[¶2062.05] *90% Rule*

In addition, if all or substantially all (considered by the CRA to be 90% and referred to as "the 90% rule") of your income as a non-resident for the year is from employment in Canada or from carrying on a business in Canada, or is a scholarship, bursary, or research grants received as a former Canadian resident, you will be allowed any of the other deductions listed in ¶1077 which "may reasonably be considered wholly applicable". These could include the deductions for home relocation loans (¶2067).

(ITA: 110.6(2), (2.1), (3), (5); 115(1)(*d*), (*e*), (*f*))

[¶2062a] PERSONAL AMOUNTS ELIGIBLE FOR TAX CREDITS

If you are a non-resident with Canadian employment or business income or taxable Canadian capital gains you may claim only the following personal amounts eligible for credit (as discussed in Chapters 11, 12, and 13):

- charitable donations (¶1265);
- gifts of cultural property (¶1267);
- the disability credit (¶1255), but only for yourself and not for transfers to those who may claim a disabled person as a dependant;
- tuition fee credits (¶1319) but only for yourself, i.e., not including credits taken as transfers from the actual student; only tuition and not the per month education amounts (¶1337) can be claimed as of right by the student in all cases (effective January 1, 2017, the education and textbook tax credits were repealed); and
- Canada Pension Plan and Employment Insurance tax credits (¶1305).

[¶2062a.05] *90% Rule*

In addition, if all or substantially all (considered by the CRA to be 90% and referred to as "the 90% rule") of your income as a non-resident for the year is included in your taxable income earned in Canada for the year, you may deduct all the other credits discussed in Chapters 11, 12, and 13. These include credits for personal amounts, medical expenses and education/tuition amounts (the education and textbook credits were repealed effective January 1, 2017). Amounts are considered included in taxable income for purposes of the 90% rule even if they are subject to offsetting deductions, such as the treaty protection deduction (¶990) or the stock option deduction. The CRA makes this clear in its policy guidelines by saying that if 90% of your world income is reported on your Canadian return, you may claim full personal amount credits.

[¶2062a.10] *Schedules A and B*

The T1 General Return for Non-Residents and Deemed Residents of Canada includes two schedules not found with versions of the return aimed at use by residents. These schedules, A and B, facilitate the calculation of credits by non-residents.

(ITA: 115(1)(*d*), (*e*), (*f*); 118.94)

[¶2063] SPOUSE'S UNUSED PERSONAL AMOUNTS (SEE CHAPTER 13)

Provided you meet the 90% test yourself, you may deduct, in computing your Canadian tax, a credit for the unused portion of your spouse's or common-law partner's personal amounts for age, education (effective January 1, 2017, the education and textbook tax credits were repealed), or disability (see ¶1361). Your deduction is the amount transferable had your spouse or common-law partner filed a Canadian tax return. Your spouse's (partner's) unused amounts will not be usable by you unless all or substantially all of your income is from Canadian employment, business or grants (see ¶2062a).

The transfer of your spouse's, etc. unused pension income amount is not normally allowed as it applies to sources of income not requiring the filing of a tax return by a non-resident (there is an exception with respect to qualified pension income as discussed in ¶2086).

(ITA: 115(1)(*f*); 118.94)

[¶2064] CHARITABLE DONATIONS (SEE CHAPTER 12)

You do not have to meet the 90% test to claim donations to Canadian charitable organizations or governments, and certain foreign charities; these are fully eligible for tax credit except to the extent they exceed 75% of your Canadian net income. The five-year carryforward of unused amounts is permitted. Donations to most foreign charities are not creditable. However, there is a provision which allows non-residents a cost base adjustment (and tax-free disposition) for certain gifts of Canadian real property to prescribed non-resident charities. Friends of the Nature Conservancy of Canada, Inc., the Nature Conservancy, and American Friends of Canadian Land Trusts (all U.S. charities) are the only prescribed non-resident charities at the time of writing. See ¶1290.

The so-called first-time super donor's credit may also be claimed by non-residents. See ¶1264.

(ITA: 110(1)(*a*), (*b*), (2.1); 115(1)(*d*); 118.1(6); 118.94; ITR: 3504 [Prescribed Donees])

[¶2065] MEDICAL EXPENSES (SEE CHAPTER 12)

If all or substantially all of your income is included in computing your taxable income in Canada (see ¶2020 to ¶2055), you may claim credit for the excess of your medical expenses (including family medical expenses, as discussed in Chapter 12) whether incurred outside or inside Canada, over the lesser of the indexed annual amount (¶1235) and 3% of the net income reported on your Canadian return.

The refundable medical expense supplement (¶1237) is only available to individuals resident in Canada throughout the year.

(ITA: 115(1)(*f*); 118.94)

[¶2066] DEDUCTION FOR EMPLOYEE STOCK OPTION BENEFITS

A non-resident is allowed to deduct one-half of the stock option benefit deemed received during the year if the conditions relating to the terms of the shares, the exercise price under the option and the absence of non-arm's length dealings are met (¶330). The deduction may be claimed whether or not all or substantially all of your income is from Canadian sources. See subheading "Stock Options and Non-Residents" at ¶330.105. See also ¶2021 of this chapter.

Commentary on Legislative Proposals (Sept. 16, 2016)

Note: When Legislative Proposals, September 16, 2016, achieves Royal Assent, the commentary will be modified to read:

A non-resident is allowed to deduct one-half of the stock option benefit deemed received during the year if the conditions are met relating to the terms of the shares, the exercise price under the option, and the absence of non-arm's length dealings. If a deceased non-resident owned the right to acquire securities at the time of death, the deduction may apply if specific requirements are satisfied (¶330). The deduction may be claimed whether or not all or substantially all of your income is from Canadian sources. See subheading "Stock Options and Non-Residents" at ¶330.105. See also ¶2021 of this chapter.

(ITA: 110(1)(*d*); 115(1)(*d*); IT-171R2 [Archived])

[¶2067] HOME RELOCATION LOANS

If as a non-resident you are subject to tax on business, employment or grant income and you have a home relocation loan benefit included in income but eligible for the offsetting deduction from taxable income (¶353), that deduction is available on the Canadian return only if the 90% test (¶2062a) is met. A home relocation loan would only rarely be available to a non-resident, since it is only available to employees for relocation to a work place in Canada. However, nothing appears to terminate the validity of such a loan, once established, if you later become non-resident, although the tax benefit terminates after five years in any event.

(ITA: 110(1)(*j*); 115(1)(*d*))

[¶2068] DISABILITY CREDIT

If you are a non-resident you may claim the full disability credit for yourself regardless of the 90% rule (¶2062a). However, the claim for transfer of the credit from a spouse, common-law partner or dependant may be made only if all or substantially all of your income is included in computing your taxable income earned in Canada. As well, the dependant must independently meet the tests for dependants eligible to transfer the credit. In the case of a spouse or common-law partner, these are discussed at ¶2063. In the case of any other dependant, the transfer criteria are discussed at ¶1255, and include the requirement that the dependant be resident in Canada at some time in the year.

(ITA: 115(1)(*d*), (*f*); 118.3; 118.8; 118.94)

[¶2069] PENSION INCOME CREDIT

Normally, the non-refundable tax credit for $2,000 of pension income (¶1311) is not available if you are a non-resident since pension income arising in Canada is subject to the general withholding provisions and you would not report the income on a Canadian return. There is an exception if the "section 217 election" described at ¶2086 is made.

Foreign pension income not taxed in Canada at all does not give rise to pension credit by virtue of the definition of eligible pension income.

(ITA: 115(1)(*f*); 118(3), (7); 118.94)

PAYMENT OF PART I TAX AND REFUNDS

[¶2070] TAX PAYMENTS AND REFUNDS

Tax on employment income and business income should be paid as described in Chapter 2. However, a non-resident is liable for an additional tax on income not attributable to a province. The additional tax is calculated as 48% of the proportion of taxes otherwise payable (but before certain tax credits) that the income for the year not attributable to a province is of taxable income for the year (as calculated, but without reference to losses from businesses in Canada). See ¶1445.

Under regulation 105, a fee or commission or other amount paid to a non-resident not regularly employed by the payer, for services rendered in Canada, is subject to a 15% withholding tax at source. This is not equivalent to the withholding tax on items such as dividends and interest, but is merely a payment on account of the non-resident's final tax liability.

Canadian residents who make payments to a non-resident for fees, commissions or other amounts on which a 15% withholding tax is applicable must report such payments on form T4A-NR. Where the withholding is likely to be greater than the eventual tax liability, whether because of treaty protection or otherwise, the Source Deductions section of the Tax Services Office may grant a waiver if application is made prior to the payment from which the withholding is required. The procedure and form for applying for the waiver can be found on the CRA website; see "Home/International and Non-resident taxes/Common Topics/Rendering services in Canada/Guidelines for Treaty-Based Waivers Involving Regulation 105 Withholding".

In the 2010 federal Budget, the Department of Finance indicated a "unique problem" affecting non-residents in respect of whom the 15% tax was withheld pursuant to regulation 105. This problem was remedied by legislative amendment, see ¶2042.55.

Refunds of tax on employment and business income, pensions and similar benefits, and dispositions of taxable Canadian property are claimed on the T1 return.

A T1 return designed for non-residents is available on the CRA website (see "International and Non-resident" section).

(ITA: 115(1); 120(1); 150(1); ITR: 105 Non-Residents)

INCOME SUBJECT TO NON-RESIDENT WITHHOLDING TAX

[¶2076] OLD AGE SECURITY PENSION

Old Age Security (OAS) income payments are subject to Part XIII non-resident withholding tax of 25% (¶2080.04) or whatever lower rate may be specified in a treaty with the country of residence of the recipient (see ¶2005).

Under some of the treaties, the tax is limited to 15%. Under the Canada–U.S. tax treaty, the country of residence has exclusive right to tax social security benefits. Therefore, the Canadian withholding tax does not apply to OAS or CPP payments made to U.S. residents; see ¶2178.50.

In addition, the OAS clawback tax (¶1419) provides for additional withholding from OAS payments to non-residents to satisfy that tax. The OAS clawback withholding will apply unless a return is filed to substantiate that world income is low enough (see ¶913.10 for the threshold) so that the clawback should not be applied. Withholding is based on previous base years, and returns must be filed for those base years to avoid withholding.

It is evident that this system requires non-residents to file what is in effect a return of world income in order to qualify for OAS payments. That return is designated T1136, and called an Old Age Security Return of Income. Where Canadian tax treaties (¶2005) limit the amount of tax that Canada can impose on OAS payments, this generally overrides the withholding requirement, and the CRA somewhat grudgingly accepts this in the *Old Age Return of Income Guide* (T4155) to form T1136, as discussed at ¶225. Residents of the United States in particular, as well as many other treaty countries, are exempt from this requirement and do not have to file the T1136. The current list of these treaty countries can be found in the T4155 Guide.

Form T1136, along with the CRA guide to these rules, should be sent automatically to all taxpayers whom the CRA identifies as non-residents in receipt of OAS payments who live in countries where they are not treaty-protected. However, the vast majority of non-resident OAS recipients are residents of the United States and so are protected from these rules.

The rate of OAS clawback tax, if applicable, is reduced by the rate of Part XIII withholding tax applicable to the payment. Thus, if Part XIII tax of 25% was payable on the OAS benefits, the clawback tax would be reduced to 75% of the amount otherwise determined.

It appears that form T1136 is not generally available from the CRA offices or from Canadian embassies and consulates abroad. Where the non-resident does not receive the form but is aware of a liability to file, or is subject to improper withholding to be recovered, the remedy seems to be to file the T1 General for Non-Residents in lieu of T1136, or to contact the International Office of the CRA (¶287) and explain the situation.

Both the T1136 and the accompanying guide, *Old Age Security Return of Income — Guide for Non-Residents* (T4155) are available on the CRA website.

Where T1136 is filed, additional non-resident withholding for the period January–June is to be calculated on the basis of second prior year returns, and for July–December on prior year returns. These returns may be either T1s where the taxpayer was a full year resident in the base year or T1136s where the taxpayer was a part-year resident or non-resident in the base year. Where the return is filed for a base year, withholding will be calculated allowing for the withholding already applied to non-resident OAS payments, so that the total withheld should true up to the applicable ordinary withholding rate and the additional amount required to account for OAS clawback.

For more details, see ¶225.

Non-residents, especially temporary ones, concerned with social security contributions and benefits should also consider the totalization agreements at ¶2111 and, for the United States, the rules at ¶2183.

(ITA: 180.2)

[¶2078] ACTING SERVICES

A special withholding tax of 23% is imposed on the gross amount paid, credited or provided as a benefit to a non-resident person (either an individual non-resident actor or a corporation related to such an actor) in respect of film and video acting services provided by the non-resident person in Canada. The Department of Finance, in its technical notes describing these provisions, refers to them as "acting services payments". Acting services payments include payments for non-resident actors in film or video production, such as feature films, movies of the week, television series, documentaries, video productions, and commercials. These rules do not apply to other income earned in Canada (for services as a producer or director, for example), nor to behind-the-scenes personnel, nor to other sectors of the entertainment industry, such as musical performers or international speakers. These continue to be subject to the old rules, as follows.

Prior to the implementation of this system, acting services performed in Canada by a non-resident were usually subject to 15% withholding on gross income under Regulation 105 (¶2030) if paid to an independent contractor, or under the employee withholding rules if paid to an employee. That liability, however, was an interim withholding on account of tax, and the non-resident recipient was required to file a Canadian tax return and account for net income for services performed in Canada at full Canadian marginal rates.

Gross payments for acting services of non-residents are subject to 23% withholding, but the requirement for the non-resident payee to file a Canadian return has become optional. The non-resident recipient of the payments may, if beneficial, choose to file a Canadian tax return and pay tax on net income at the Canadian marginal rates; or can accept the 23% as a final settlement of Canadian tax liability. The option to file a Canadian return must be made for all acting services payments received in a particular taxation year, and must be made by filing a Canadian return specifying an election under section 216.1 by the normal Canadian filing due-date for the taxation year.

That is, if the recipient elects to file a Canadian return, acting services payments are included as Canadian-source business or employment income, as the case may be, in computing the recipient's taxable income earned in Canada under the ordinary rules for non-residents (¶2030 or ¶2020). The recipient may thus apply the deductions and tax credits that are available to non-residents in respect of such income. If the recipient does not choose ordinary Canadian taxation, no return need be filed (unless the recipient has other income subject to ordinary Part I tax), and the 23% withheld is the final amount of tax payable in respect of the acting services payment.

If the recipient is a corporation related to the actor, there may be two acting services payments: one to the corporation, and a second from the corporation to the actor. In this case, special rules apply. If the corporation chooses to have the payment to it (the "corporation payment") taxed under Part I, the actor is treated as also having chosen to have the corporation's payment to the actor (the "actor payment") taxed under Part I. If the corporation does not choose to have the corporation payment taxed under Part I, but instead treats the 23% withholding tax as final, the actor payment is not subject to the 23% withholding tax, except to the extent it exceeds the corporation payment. Note, however, that if the corporation makes the actor payment before the corporation's filing-due date, meaning that the corporation's choice is not known, the corporation is still required to withhold and remit the 23% from the actor payment. The amount withheld and remitted will be refundable to the actor (or applied against another liability of the actor) once the corporation's filing-due date has passed without the corporation having chosen Part I taxation.

If a corporation payment arising in one taxation year is taxed under the 23% withholding rule and not the section 216.1 election rule, and the corporation makes an actor payment in a subsequent taxation year, the actor payment is neither deductible in computing the corporation's income for any year nor included in computing the actor's taxable income earned in Canada for any year.

If you intend to elect under section 216.1, the CRA states

> you can apply to us for a reduction in the required amount of non-resident tax withheld on amounts paid, credited, or provided as a benefit to you for film and video acting services rendered in Canada. You have to apply **before** you provide the acting services in Canada. To apply complete and send us Form T1287, Application by a Non-Resident of Canada (individual) for a Reduction in the Amount of Non-Resident Tax Required to be Withheld on Income Earned from Acting in a Film or Video Production, or Form T1288, Application by a Non-Resident of Canada (corporation) for a Reduction in the Amount of Non-Resident Tax Required to be Withheld on Income Earned from Acting in a Film or Video Production. For more information, go to Film and Media Credits.

(ITA: 212(5.1)– (5.3), (13.1); 215(1); 216.1; ITR: 102 Periodic Payments; 105 Non-Residents)

[¶2080] PASSIVE INCOME

Certain amounts paid or credited to non-residents by Canadian residents are subject to Canadian tax, although they are not from employment in Canada or Canadian business operations. Such amounts are treated differently from employment or business income, since the non-resident receiving payment is not generally permitted to file any Canadian return with respect to the income, and tax is paid on behalf of the non-resident by the Canadian payer who is required to remit the appropriate tax to the Canadian government. The Canadian resident will withhold the amount of the Canadian tax from the payment and remit only the net amount to the non-resident. This withholding tax is imposed at a flat rate, usually 25%, on the gross amount of the payments, and no deductions are permitted for expenses or other reasons. An exception may be applicable for pension and similar benefits and rents or timber royalties, as described below.

The 25% rate specified in the *Income Tax Act* (and used throughout this section) is often reduced in tax agreements (tax treaties) with other countries. See ¶2005. Often, the reduced rate is 10% or 15%, but it varies in different treaties for different types of income. See also ¶2080a regarding treaty forms that may be used to benefit from reduced treaty rates.

Where a payment made to a non-resident is of a type that would normally be subject to withholding tax but it is being taxed as income of a Canadian resident because it is income on property transferred to a spouse, common-law partner or child or a transferred right to income (¶977), the non-resident is exempt from the withholding tax which would otherwise apply.

A partnership that pays or credits an amount to non-resident persons is considered as a person resident in Canada and must withhold tax on the amount to the extent that it is deductible in computing the partnership's income from a Canadian source.

The types of payment subject to tax in the above manner, and the rates of tax are as summarized below.

[¶2080.01] *(A) Interest: Nil or Treaty Rate or 25%*

For amounts paid or credited to a non-resident in 2008 and later years, there is no withholding tax on amounts paid or credited to persons dealing at arm's length with the payer, unless the interest is "participating debt interest". However, a recent amendment provides that interest (other than fully exempt interest — see below) is subject to withholding if it is paid to a non-resident (whether arm's length or not) on a debt owed to a non-resident that does not deal at arm's length with the payer. This amendment applies to arrangements put in place on or after March 16, 2011.

The concept of non-arm's length is discussed at ¶812.

Participating debt interest, which is always subject to withholding, means interest (other than interest described in any of paragraphs (2) to (4) of the definition "fully exempt interest", discussed in detail below) that is paid or payable on an obligation, other than a prescribed obligation, all or any portion of which interest is contingent or dependent on the use of or production from property in Canada or is computed by reference to revenue, profit, cash flow, commodity price, or any other similar criterion, or by reference to dividends paid or payable to shareholders of any class of shares of the capital stock of a corporation. This interest is seen by the Department of Finance as, in effect, a distribution of profit rather than a payment of interest. Note, however, that even interest which could be considered participating debt interest may be exempt in both arm's length and non-arm's length situations if it is "fully exempt interest" (items (2) to (4), but (1) is probably unlikely to be participating debt interest in any event).

As well as the general exemption for arm's-length interest payments, there is also an exception for amounts paid or credited to non-arm's length persons on account of "fully exempt interest". There are four categories of fully exempt interest:

(1) interest that is paid or payable on a bond, debenture, note, mortgage, hypothecary claim, or similar debt obligation

   (a) of, or guaranteed (otherwise than by being insured by the Canada Deposit Insurance Corporation) by, the Government of Canada,

   (b) of the government of a province,

   (c) of an agent of a province,

   (d) of a municipality in Canada or a municipal or public body performing a function of government in Canada,

   (e) of a corporation, commission, or association to which any of *Income Tax Act* paragraphs 149(1)(*d*) to (*d*.6) applies (generally speaking, these are federal or provincial Crown corporations and their subsidiaries, corporations 90% or more owned by the federal or provincial Crown, and most municipal corporations operating within the boundaries of the municipality),

   (f) of an educational institution or a hospital if repayment of the principal amount of the obligation and payment of the interest is to be made, or is guaranteed, assured or otherwise specifically provided for or secured, by the government of a province;

(2) interest that is paid or payable on a mortgage, hypothecary claim, or similar debt obligation secured by, or on an agreement for sale or similar obligation with respect to, real property situated outside Canada or an interest in any such real property, or to immovables situated outside Canada or a real right in any such immovable, except to the extent that the interest payable on the obligation is deductible for general income tax purposes in computing the income of the

payer from a business carried on by the payer in Canada or from property other than real or immovable property situated outside Canada;

(3) interest that is paid or payable to a prescribed international organization or agency; prescribed organizations and agencies for purposes of this exemption have been and presumably continue to be: the Bank for International Settlements and the European Bank for Reconstruction and Development;

(4) an amount paid or payable or credited under a securities lending arrangement (see ¶422) that is deemed by subparagraph 260(8)(*a*)(i) of the *Income Tax Act* to be a payment made by a borrower to a lender of interest, if

(a) the securities lending arrangement was entered into by the borrower in the course of carrying on a business outside Canada, and

(b) the security that is transferred or lent to the borrower under the securities lending arrangement is described in paragraph (*b*) or (*c*) of the definition "qualified security" in *Income Tax Act* subsection 260(1) and issued by a non-resident issuer.

Standby charges and guarantee fees are deemed to be interest and are therefore subject to withholding tax if paid to a non-resident in circumstances in which the tax would be applicable on interest payments. Standby charges and commitment fees paid under an agreement to lend money are exempt from non-resident withholding tax where interest payable on any obligation issued under the agreement would be exempt.

Back-to-Back Loans: Anti-Avoidance Rule

In the 2014 federal Budget, the government introduced measures "to address back-to-back loan arrangements by adding a specific anti-avoidance rule in respect of withholding tax on interest payments". Although the rule is aimed primarily at Canadian corporate debtors and non-resident creditors (and was introduced in conjunction with a similar anti-avoidance rule that applies to the corporate thin capitalization rules), it can apply to individuals and is therefore summarized here. Basically, the new rule ensures that the Part XIII withholding tax cannot be avoided by interposing an arm's length intermediary between a resident payer of interest and a non-resident that does not deal at arm's length with the payer. In general terms, the rule applies to amounts paid or credited after 2014 where the following conditions are met (subsection 212(3.1)):

- a taxpayer pays a particular amount of interest on a particular debt or obligation owing to an intermediary that deals at arm's length with the taxpayer or is non-resident;
- the intermediary or any person that does not deal at arm's length with the intermediary (i) owes a debt or other amount (intermediary debt) to a non-resident person for which recourse is limited, or that was owing or remained outstanding because the particular debt or obligation became owing to the taxpayer, or (ii) is granted security (a "specified right") in respect of a property by a non-resident person;
- the withholding tax that would have been payable if the interest on the particular amount had been paid directly to the non-resident person was higher than the withholding tax that applied, if any, to the interest paid to the intermediary; and
- the amount of the intermediary debt and fair market value of the secured property is at least 25% of the particular debt or obligation.

Where the rule applies, the Part XIII withholding tax will equal the amount referred to in the third point above (basically, the withholding tax that was avoided) with some adjustments. The non-resident person and the taxpayer are jointly and severally liable for the withholding tax. The rule applies to amounts paid or credited after 2014.

Commentary on Bill C-29 Measures (Oct. 25, 2016)

Note: When Bill C-29, October 25, 2016, achieves Royal Assent, the commentary will be modified to read:

The back-to-back rules were amended to ensure that they apply to arrangements that involve multiple intermediaries. In its explanatory notes, the Department of Finance stated that existing back-to-back provisions can apply to multiple-intermediary arrangements — that is, arrangements that include two or more intermediaries — but the manner in which the existing rules apply to multiple-intermediary arrangements may not be entirely clear in all cases. Thus the reason for the amendments was to "clarify" the manner in which they apply to multiple-intermediary arrangements. In general terms, the references to "intermediary" extends to one or more "immediate funders" or "relevant funders", who, in general terms are any of the intermediary funders under the arrangement. The non-resident person referred to above will be the "ultimate funder". The ultimate funder is basically the original source of funding that funds, directly or indirectly, the particular debt or obligation. These amendments apply to payments made after 2016, and therefore will not affect individual's 2016 taxation year.

See also ¶2080.05 regarding the addition of "character substitution" rules to the existing back-to-back rules to capture economically similar arrangements.

The back-to-back rules were extended to apply to rents and royalties, and to the existing shareholder loan rules.

(ITA: 212(1)(*b*), (3); 214; ITR: 806 International Organizations and Agencies)

[¶2080.03] *(B) Dividends (Including Deemed Dividends, Capital Dividends, Patronage Dividends, and Stock Dividends)*

For a detailed discussion of dividends (including deemed dividends and patronage dividends) see ¶416 and ¶413 and of stock dividends see ¶406.

The rate of tax to be withheld from a dividend is 25%; if there is an applicable tax treaty (¶2005) it will in most cases reduce withholding on dividends 15% for general investors, often less for corporate investors holding a substantial interest in the shares on which the dividends are paid.

This tax does not apply to dividends which are paid from "pre-1972 capital surplus on hand" on wind-up of the payer corporation nor to a capital gains dividend paid by a mutual fund corporation, a mortgage investment corporation (¶418), or a non-resident owned investment corporation. An exemption also exists for dividends received from a foreign business corporation which derives 90% or more of its income from operation of a public utility or from mining or processing ore in the country of residence of the non-resident.

Commentary on Bill C-29 Measures (Oct. 25, 2016)

Note: When Bill C-29, October 25, 2016, achieves Royal Assent, the commentary will be modified to read:

This tax does not apply to dividends which are paid from "pre-1972 capital surplus on hand" on wind-up of the payer corporation nor to a capital gains dividend paid by a mutual fund corporation, or a mortgage investment corporation (¶418). An exemption also exists for dividends received from a foreign business corporation which derives 90% or more of its income from operation of a public utility or from mining or processing ore in the country of residence of the non-resident.

Note that dividends paid out of a capital dividend account *are* subject to withholding tax. See ¶415.

Stock dividends are subject to withholding tax, but shares resulting from a stock split are not.

A non-resident is prevented from avoiding non-resident withholding tax on dividends by means of a non-arm's length sale of shares of a Canadian corporation to another Canadian corporation. When a non-resident disposes of shares of a Canadian corporation to another Canadian corporation, which does not deal at arm's length with the non-resident and which, immediately after the disposition is connected with (i.e., has more than a 10% interest in) the acquired Canadian corporation, the excess of the proceeds over the paid-up capital of the shares sold will be taxable as a dividend either immediately or eventually by means of a deduction in computing the paid-up capital of the purchasing corporation.

The rules for demutualization of life insurance companies (¶537d) provide rules to discourage the extraction of corporate surplus to non-residents by deeming a dividend on the disposition of shares to Canadian residents or partnerships as part of such a transaction.

Interest (or other income) paid to a non-resident but attributed to a Canadian resident under the "attribution rules" described at ¶977 is not subject to withholding tax. If withholding has been applied and the amount is taxed to a resident Canadian, a claim for refund of withholding should be made.

Loans to shareholders which are outstanding for more than a year are included in the shareholder's income, subject to certain specific exceptions. These rules are discussed at ¶407. Where a loan which would be included in the income of a Canadian resident under the rules at ¶409 is held by a non-resident, the amount is deemed to be a dividend paid at the time it would have been included in the income of a resident. At that point, it becomes subject to withholding by the payer company, which must make a remittance on behalf of the non-resident. In the case of a resident, repayment results in an offsetting deduction (unless it is part of a series of loans and repayments). A refund of tax withheld is similarly allowed to a non-resident upon the repayment of such loans. Where only a portion of the loan is repaid, the refund is the lesser of the tax originally paid in respect of the amount repaid and the tax that would be payable at the time of repayment if a dividend equal to that amount were paid at that time. This rule seems to deal with potential changes in the withholding rate, so that if the rate has fallen (for example, because a revised tax treaty has intervened), it is the rate at the time of repayment that will govern. In order to obtain the refund, application must be made to the CRA within two years after the end of the calendar year in which this repayment is made. Refunds are claimed on form NR7-R.

Securities lending arrangements are transfers of securities (usually to facilitate short term market liquidity) to an arm's length person who is expected to return the same or identical securities to the lender and to compensate the lender for any dividends paid during the loan. See ¶422 for more detail. Providing there is not a tax deferral motive, special tax rules facilitate securities lending arrangements by ensuring that a number of ordinary tax consequences do not apply. These include exemptions from the withholding provisions that might otherwise apply to interest or to be dividends deemed to have been paid on borrowed shares.

(ITA: 212(2), (2.1); 212.1; 214(3)(*a*), (3.1); 215; 227(6.1); Window on Canadian Tax: 4873)

[¶2080.04] *(C) Pensions, Retirement Payments; Payments out of Deferred Income or Government Benefit Programs; and Miscellaneous Benefits (25% or Treaty Rate)*

The following amounts are subject to 25% tax (subject to extensive treaty variations):

(1) superannuation and pension benefits *except for the following items*:

(a) the portion of a benefit reasonably attributable to services rendered by a person in a year when that person was at no time resident in Canada and throughout which the person was not employed, or was only occasionally employed, in Canada (see IT-76R2, but note that the phrase "only occasionally employed" was construed in *Nanne et al. v. The Queen*, 2000 DTC 1653 (T.C.C.), and that the CRA has said (in CRA Document No. 2003-0182715) that it will revise Interpretation Bulletin IT-76R2 to accommodate that decision);

(b) the portion of a benefit transferred (using prescribed form NRTA1) on behalf of the non-resident to a registered pension plan, PRPP, RRSP, or RRIF in circumstances in which the transfer would be non-taxable or deductible under the RPP direct transfer rules at ¶1021 and ¶2612.35 or the rollover rules for unregistered plans at ¶2612.05;

Commentary on Legislative Proposals (Sept. 16, 2016)

Note: When Legislative Proposals, September 16, 2016, achieves Royal Assent, the commentary will be modified to read:

(b) the portion of a benefit transferred (using prescribed form NRTA1) on behalf of the non-resident to a registered pension plan, PRPP, RRSP or RRIF in circumstances in which the transfer would be non-taxable or deductible under the RPP direct transfer rules at ¶1021 and ¶2612.35 or the rollover rules for unregistered plans at ¶2612.05. Benefits transferred to a specified pension plan (the Saskatchewan Pension Plan) after January 1, 2010 are also exempt;

(c) pension benefits which would not be included in income if received by a Canadian resident (e.g., War Veterans Allowances, see ¶991);

(d) pension benefits that are attributable to services rendered outside Canada (see IT-76R2);

(e) amounts which would have been treaty-protected to Canadian residents;

(f) Old Age Security pensions paid by the federal government or any similar pension paid by a province, subject to protection under a treaty and subject to withholding for OAS clawback tax as discussed at ¶2076; and

(g) benefits under the Canada Pension Plan or Quebec Pension Plan, subject to whatever protection a particular tax treaty may provide;

(2) deferred profit sharing plan payments (other than the portion transferred to a registered pension plan or RRSP for that non-resident under rollover rules that would have made the transfers non-taxable or deductible to a Canadian resident);

(3) registered retirement savings plan (RRSP) benefits (other than the portion transferred to another RRSP, a RRIF or an eligible annuity for that non-resident under rollover rules that would have made the transfers non-taxable or deductible to a Canadian resident — see ¶2612.05–¶2612.35 and IT-500R);

(4) registered retirement income fund (RRIF) benefits (other than the portion transferred to an RRSP, another RRIF or an eligible annuity for that non-resident under rollover rules that would have made the transfers non-taxable or deductible to a Canadian resident);

(5) a retiring allowance (which may include a termination payment — see ¶923 and IT-337R4), other than:

(a) the portion reasonably attributable to services rendered by a person in a year when that person was at no time resident in Canada and throughout which the person was not employed, or was only occasionally employed, in Canada;

(b) the portion transferred (in prescribed form) on behalf of the non-resident to a registered pension plan or RRSP in circumstances in which the transfer would be non-taxable or deductible under rollover rules if the taxpayer were resident in Canada; and

(c) retiring allowances out of or under an employee benefit plan (¶359), a salary deferral arrangement (¶307), or an RCA (but see (6) following);

(6) payments out of a Retirement Compensation Arrangement (RCA — ¶359) to the extent they would be taxable if received by a Canadian resident or if received by someone other than the recipient but taxed to the recipient; also, payments made as the purchase price of an interest in an RCA; an exception effective for 1996 and later years will exempt transfers from one RCA to another if made under statutory rollover rules;

(7) death benefits (¶925);

(8) (Un)Employment Insurance payments (¶941);

(9) benefits from a supplementary unemployment plan (¶737, ¶943);

(10) assistance payments in respect of the Canada–U.S. Auto Pact (¶973), and prescribed benefits under government assistance programs (¶975), grants for home insulation or energy conversion (¶988);

(11) an annuity payment to the extent it would be taxable if received by a Canadian resident, other than an amount paid or credited under an annuity issued in the course of carrying on a life insurance business outside Canada;

(12) payments under an income averaging annuity contract (including any amount received upon surrender, cancellation, redemption, sale or other disposition of an income averaging annuity contract);

(13) the portion of a payment in respect of a registered education savings plan, or in respect of an annuity which would have been taxable if received by a Canadian resident;

(14) grants under a prescribed program of the government of Canada relating to home insulation or energy conservation;

(15) payments (typically to farmers) out of a NISA Fund No. 2 to the extent they would be taxable to a Canadian resident;

(16) payments in respect of an amateur athlete trust (¶777) to the extent they would be taxable to a Canadian resident;

(17) payments by the custodian of an eligible funeral trust (¶984) to the extent they would be taxable to a Canadian resident;

(18) [payments treated as income by the recipient under the restrictive covenant rules (¶929); note that it is only income amounts under the general rule for restrictive covenants or the recovery of bad debts deducted from employment or covenant income in respect of restrictive covenants that is captured here; amounts treated as employment income or governed by one of the alternative elections are not covered *by this rule*, although they may be covered by other rules, for example the withholding rules which apply to employment income generally or to a business carried on in Canada. On the other hand, covenant payments which might also be considered royalties are specifically covered by this rule and not the royalty rule, presumably preventing treaty rates and exceptions for royalties from applying to covenant payments]; and

(19) payments from a former TFSA, after the death of the holder, that would have been included under paragraph 12(1)(*z*.5) if the recipient were resident.

Withholding tax also applies where *a non-resident pays or credits to another non-resident* an amount as payment of an amount which would be taxable under (2), (3), (4), (9), (12), (17), or (in some circumstances) (18), above. See also item ¶2080.09 below for more on this subject. Withholding tax also applies where a non-resident pays or credits to another non-resident a payment of a superannuation or pension benefit under a registered pension plan or a distribution out of a retirement compensation arrangement, or a payment of a retiring allowance or death benefit to the extent that the retiring allowance or death benefit is deductible in computing the payer's taxable income earned in Canada.

Some treaties provide that pensions — especially government pensions — may be taxed in their country of origin but not in the country where they are received. See, for example, the Canada–India treaty. On the other hand, the Canada–Germany treaty provides for taxation in the country of residence but also permits taxation by the country of origin for pension payments where tax deductions could be claimed against that country for the original pension contributions. The possibility and the details of treaty-protection should always be considered in dealing with cross-border pension payments. Information Circular IC 76-12R6 contains a helpful summary of withholding rates, although it should always be verified against the relevant treaty, which may provide exceptions to the general rules, or have been updated after the summary in the Information Circular was published in November 2007.

Under the Canada–U.S. tax treaty, the country of residence has the exclusive right to tax social security benefits. Therefore, the 25% Canadian withholding tax does not apply to OAS or CPP payments made to U.S. residents. See ¶2178.50.

Note that Social Security benefits and taxes may also be affected by treaties discussed at ¶2111.

If you are ordinarily resident in Canada but will temporarily have a mailing address outside Canada, you may obtain a certificate from the local Tax Services Office that you are a resident of Canada. This certificate will authorize the payer of your pension, annuity or similar benefit to send it to your mailing address, outside Canada without any non-resident tax being withheld.

If you are receiving a pension from a Canadian source and part of that pension was earned at a time when you were neither resident nor employed in Canada, that part of the pension is exempt from Canadian tax. The CRA issued Interpretation Bulletin IT-76R2 (now archived) which outlined their interpretation of how this exempt portion of such a pension should be calculated.

You may also elect to file a Canadian income tax return on certain pension income as discussed in ¶2086.

(ITA: 212(1)(*h*)–(*v*); IC 76-12R6 Applicable Rate of Part XIII Tax on Amounts Paid or Credited to Persons in Countries with which Canada has a Tax Convention [Please see pending updates from April 2011 at the end of this document.]; IC 77-16R4 Non-Resident Income Tax)

[¶2080.05] *(D) Rents, Royalties (Including Timber Royalties) and Similar Payments (25% or Treaty Rate)*

Withholding tax is imposed on the gross amount (without deduction of any expenses) of rent, royalties or similar payments paid or credited to non-residents for the use of property in Canada. The term "similar payments" would include, for example, payments made for obtaining exclusive Canadian rights to designs, payments for use of a non-resident's "know-how", patents, trademarks, etc.

Rents for the use in Canada of property, or timber royalties in respect of timber resource property or timber limits in Canada, paid by a non-resident to another non-resident are also subject to withholding tax.

Royalty or similar payments in respect of copyrights in respect of the production or reproduction of any literary, dramatic, musical or artistic work are exempt from withholding tax.

Payments under *bona fide* R&D cost sharing arrangements where the payer obtains an interest in the resulting property or other value are exempt from withholding tax.

Arm's length payments, to the extent deductible from Canadian income tax on a business carried on outside Canada, are exempt from withholding tax.

Rental payments for the right to use corporeal property outside Canada are exempt from withholding.

There are several specific exemptions related to arm's length payments for the use of aircraft and aircraft equipment or parts, air navigation equipment utilized in the provision of services under the *Civil Air Navigation Services Commercialization Act*, or related to computer software that is necessary to the operation of that equipment that is used by the payer for no other purpose and for limited period use of railway rolling stock.

The Canada–U.S. tax treaty provides for a 10% withholding tax on royalty payments. Royalties for treaty purposes include amounts received for the use of, or for the rights to use, tangible personal property, copyright patents, trademarks, etc. No withholding tax applies to royalties paid with respect to the production or reproduction of any literary, dramatic, musical or artistic work other than motion picture films or films or tapes for television use.

The treaty provides exemptions from withholding for payment for literary, dramatic, musical, or artistic work, other than motion picture films or films or tapes for television use, and for payments for the use of, or for the rights to use, computer software, patents, and information concerning industrial, commercial or scientific experience (which information "know-how" presumably includes designs, models, secret processes or formulae, but specifically excludes information provided in respect of a rental or franchise agreement).

The withholding rules make special provision for withholding on payments to non-residents for a right to use or the use of: (i) motion picture film; or (ii) film, videotape or other means of reproduction for use in connection with television other than solely in connection with and as part of a news program produced in Canada, provided in both (i) and (ii) that the film, videotape, etc. has been or is to be used or reproduced in Canada to the extent that the amount relates to that use or reproduction. Technical amendments effective for 2000 and later taxation years add the last qualification, to ensure that withholding does not apply to use or reproduction outside Canada.

The withholding rule for rents, royalties, etc. is specifically subordinated to the withholding rule for payments made for restrictive covenants (see ¶929) where both might apply. Presumably, the intent is to prevent the application of treaty rates or exclusions provided for royalties to payments under restrictive covenants.

Commentary on Bill C-29 Measures (Oct. 25, 2016)

Note: When Bill C-29, October 25, 2016, achieves Royal Assent, the commentary will be modified to read:

Back-to-Back Anti-Avoidance Rules

In the 2016 Federal Budget, the Department of Finance created new back-to-back rules similar to those in place in respect of interest payments (¶2080.01) that apply to rents, royalties and similar payments. In its explanatory notes, the Department explained that the "amendments are intended to ensure that non-resident withholding tax is not avoided in respect of payments subject to paragraph 212(1)(*d*), by an arrangement in which an intermediary entity is interposed between a Canadian-resident payor and a non-resident payee. These new rules may apply, for example, where a Canadian resident makes a royalty payment to a non-resident person (referred to as the "immediate licensor") and another non-resident (referred to as an "ultimate licensor") receives a payment from the immediate licensor under a sufficiently connected license agreement (referred to as a "relevant royalty arrangement"). The new rules apply only if the back-to-back arrangement results in a reduction of the non-resident withholding tax that would be payable if the payment were made directly to the ultimate licensor instead of the immediate licensor."

More particularly, subsection 212(3.9) provides that the back-to-back rules will apply where:

(a) a taxpayer pays or credits a particular amount of rent, royalty or similar payment, in respect of a particular lease, licence or similar agreement, to a non-resident person or a partnership any member of which is a non-resident person (the "immediate licensor");

(b) at any time at or after the time when the particular lease, licence or similar agreement was entered into, the immediate licensor or other "relevant licensor" (basically, the immediate licensor or any other intermediary licensor in the entire arrangement) in respect of a "particular relevant royalty arrangement" has an obligation to pay or credit an amount, either immediately or in the future and either absolutely or contingently, to a person or partnership, in respect of a "specified royalty arrangement", and any of the following additional conditions is met:

(i) the amount to be paid or credited by the relevant licensor is determined, in whole or in part, by reference to

(A) an amount paid or credited, or an obligation to pay or credit an amount, in respect of a royalty arrangement, or

(B) one or more of the fair market value of, any revenue, profits, income, or cash flow from, or any other similar criteria in respect of, a particular property, if a right in respect of the property is granted under the particular lease, licence or similar agreement, or

(ii) it can reasonably be concluded that the particular relevant royalty arrangement was entered into, or was permitted to remain in effect, because

(A) the specified royalty arrangement was entered into or was permitted to remain in effect, or

(B) it was anticipated that the specified royalty arrangement would be entered into or remain in effect;

and

(c) the withholding tax that would have been payable under Part XIII in respect of the particular amount, if it had been paid or credited to an "ultimate licensor" (basically, the "end" licensor, i.e., not any of the intermediaries) rather than the immediate licensor, is greater than the tax payable under Part XIII in respect of the particular amount.

Generally, by virtue of subsection 112(9.31), the total amount of withholding tax with respect to the particular amount is levied as if the particular amount were paid directly to the ultimate licensor (or ultimate licensors if more than one). In other words, the provision prevents the avoidance of withholding tax through the use of the intermediary party licensors.

These changes apply to payments made after 2016, so they will not affect individuals' 2016 taxation years.

Furthermore, Budget 2016 created back-to-back "character substitution" rules. In general terms, these rules are meant to apply where one type of payment (say interest) is paid by a Canadian resident to an intermediary who in turn is obligated to pay another type of payment (say a royalty) to a non-resident, the effect of which is to avoid or reduce Part XIII withholding tax. Where they apply, generally the back-to-back interest rules (¶2080.01) or the back-to-back rent or royalty rules (above) apply, with modifications as necessary.

In general terms, the character substitution back-to-back rules will apply where:

(1) interest is paid by a Canadian resident to an intermediary where there is an agreement obligating the intermediary to make royalty payments to another non-resident;

(2) royalties are paid by a Canadian resident to an intermediary where there is a loan between the intermediary and another non-resident; or

(3) interest or royalties are paid by a Canadian resident to an intermediary and another non-resident holds shares of the intermediary that includes obligations to pay certain dividends or that are redeemable or cancellable.

Generally, where the rules apply, the Canadian resident will be deemed to have made an additional payment to the other non-resident of the same nature as paid to the intermediary. This should result in the same amount of Part XIII withholding tax that would have been payable, had that payment actually been made directly to the non-resident. These rules are in effect for payments made after 2016.

Alternative Method under Part I of Act ("Section 216 Election" — Form T1159)

An alternative method of tax payment is provided for nonresidents receiving payment of rent on real property in Canada, income from timber resource properties, and income from a non-resident's share of partnership income from real property, timber resources and timber limits in Canada.

The non-resident may file an income tax return on form T1159 and report his rental or timber royalty receipts from Canada thereon. From this revenue, the non-resident can deduct all expenses of earning this income, including capital cost allowances, to arrive at a net income figure. None of the deductions normally made from "net income" to arrive at "taxable income" are allowed (see ¶1077). Tax is calculated on the net income figure in the usual manner, as if the non-resident taxpayer were a Canadian resident, whose only income was from the rents and timber royalties. The tax is levied using the graduated tax rates under Part I of the Act that applies to residents. However, no tax credits may be claimed for "personal amounts" discussed in Chapters 11, 12, and 13.

No deduction from income or tax may be made for extraneous expenses or allowances specifically denied to non-residents under the general provisions of the Act. This would apply mainly to certain trust distributions, and to the Canadian foreign tax credit.

The tax so calculated should be remitted to the Receiver General of Canada, less any tax previously withheld from payments to him. An overpayment can be claimed as a refund.

If capital cost allowances are claimed, and the property is subsequently disposed of, any recapture (see ¶843) must be reported for the year of disposal and tax paid, if applicable. Reporting may be done on form T1159, or on a T1 return if a T1159 election is not filed for that year.

The alternative method is optional, and can only be used if the non-resident has filed form T1159 within two years from the end of the taxation year in which the rents or timber royalties were received.

Note that filing form T1159 does not change the requirement that the Canadian resident must withhold 25% of any rent or royalty payments. It merely enables the non-resident to obtain a refund if his tax as calculated on the return is less than the tax withheld. However, there is an exception where amounts are paid to an agent or other person on behalf of the non-resident, and the non-resident has filed an undertaking on form NR6, to file form T1159 within six months after the end of the taxation year. If there is recapture of capital cost allowance for a year, an individual's return is due by April 30 of the year following disposition whether or not you have filed the NR6 undertaking. Form NR6 must be filed on or before January 1 of the taxation year or when the first payment of non-resident tax is due. In this case, 25% of the net rents or royalties available for remittance will be withheld. The CRA notes in its Guide T4058 that your agent must continue to withhold non-resident tax on the **gross** rental income until the CRA approves, in writing, your Form NR6.

If no such undertaking was filed, and no withholding tax has been deducted before the agent or other person receives the amounts, the agent or other person is required to remit the 25% tax on the gross receipts. However, where the undertaking has been filed, the agent or other person need only remit the 25% tax on the net amount available for payment to the non-resident. This would be significant, for example, when a non-resident uses an agent in Canada to collect rents from building tenants, and to pay building expenses out of the proceeds. The agent might receive $1,000 in rents for a month, out of which he pays expenses of $800. If no undertakings were filed, the agent would be required to remit tax of $250 (25% of $1,000) to the government. If an undertaking had been filed, the agent need only remit tax of $50 (25% of $200). Should the undertaking on form NR6 be filed, but the return on form T1 is not submitted within six months after the end of the taxation year, the agent is required to pay the full tax which would have been remitted if form NR6 had not been filed.

The CRA publishes an *Income Tax Guide for Non-Residents Electing under Section 216* (T4144) which provides more detail on this election and the form T1159 on which it is made.

(ITA: 212(1)(*d*), (*e*), (5); 216; *Income Tax Guide for Electing Under Section 216* (T4144); IT-303 [Archived]; IT-438R2 [Archived]; IT-494 [Archived]; IT-393R2 [Archived])

[¶2080.06] *(E) Alimony Payments*

As part of the changes to the taxability of support payments effective May 1, 1997, discussed in Chapter 23, the government abolished withholding on all alimony and maintenance payments effective for amounts paid or credited after April 1997. This would appear to be true even if subsequent payments are deductible, and even if they are on account of earlier obligations.

Of course, Canadian residents receiving alimony or other support payments from abroad may be subject to withholding by the country from which payments are made, depending on the laws of that country.

(ITA: 212(1)(*f*))

[¶2080.07] *(F) Estate or Trust Income (25% or Treaty Rate)*

Regular Withholding under Part XIII

Withholding tax is in general applicable to the full amount accruing to non-resident beneficiaries of a Canadian estate or trust including any amounts paid or credited (except on a distribution of capital or certain amounts going through a trust which would be exempt if paid directly) regardless of the source from which the estate or trust derived the income.

For withholding purposes, the amount payable to the non-resident beneficiary is deemed to be paid to the beneficiary on the earliest of the day on which the amount was paid or credited, the day that is 90 days after the end of the taxation year, and, if the Canadian trust becomes non-resident after July 25, 2012, the time that is immediately before it has a deemed year end as a result of becoming non-resident.

An exemption from this non-resident tax on trust or estate income is applicable if the beneficiaries are all residents in one foreign country, the total income of the trust comes from that country, and the trust was set up before 1949.

Withholding tax will not apply to that portion of the non-resident beneficiary's taxable capital gain which was designated by a mutual fund trust to be a deemed gain of the beneficiary (but see ¶2083, below).

Payments out of income of the trust or estate derived from a non-resident owned investment corporation or from certain copyrights and royalties are exempt if they would have been exempt if paid directly by the person making the payments.

A resident of the United States is exempt from Canadian tax on amounts received from a Canadian trust or estate which were out of income from sources outside Canada, under the terms of the Canada–U.S. Tax Convention. However, the Convention permits a maximum withholding tax of 15% on payments of Canadian source income from a trust.

See also Interpretation Bulletin IT-465R, now archived, which deals with trust withholding requirements.

Part XII.2 Tax

In some cases, the trust is subject to a special "Part XII.2" income tax on the kind of income (designated income; subsection 210(1)) that would normally be subject to tax in the hands of non-residents under ordinary, as opposed to Part XIII withholding, tax rules. This designated includes income from:

(1) real property situated in Canada;

(2) timber resource properties;

(3) Canadian resource properties;

(4) businesses carried on by the trust in Canada;

(5) capital gains from the disposition of property that would have been taxable Canadian property if the trust was not resident in Canada; and

(6) capital gains from the disposition after December 20, 2002 of specified transferred property

reduced by

(7) losses from those sources.

Specified transferred property in (5) (and, in effect, in (6)) is property that was transferred to a particular trust in circumstances in which subsection 73(1) or 107.4(3) of the Act applied; that is, where the *inter vivos* rollover rules to a spouse or common-law partner or to a spouse etc. trust or to an alter ego trust apply, or where the rollover for trusts where there is no beneficial change in ownership applies. This condition will be met whether the particular trust is the trust in respect of which income is being determined under these rules, or any other trust to which the transferred property was transferred in circumstances in which subsection 73(1) or 107.4(3) applied and that subsequently transferred, directly or indirectly, the property to the trust in respect of which the income is being determined under these rules. In addition, for gains to be caught by these rules:

- it must be reasonable to conclude that the transferred property was, at a particular time, transferred to the particular trust in anticipation of the emigration of a person beneficially interested at the particular time in the particular trust and that a person (whether the anticipated person or another) beneficially interested at that time in the particular trust subsequently ceases to reside in Canada; or
- at the particular time that the transferred property was transferred to the particular trust, that the terms of the particular trust satisfy the conditions in subparagraph 73(1.01)(*c*)(i) or (iii) of the Act and that it is reasonable to conclude that the transfer was made in connection with the cessation of residence, on or before that time, of a person who was, at that time, beneficially interested in the particular trust and a spouse or common-law partner, as the case may be, of the transferor of the transferred property to the particular trust.

This tax is creditable to residents but not non-residents on distribution (see ¶460). To the extent such income has already borne tax in Canada, it will not be subject to withholding tax on distribution providing the trust makes the requisite designations.

(ITA: 212(1)(*c*), (10), (11); IT-342R [Archived]; IT-465R [Archived])

[¶2080.08] *(G) Management or Administration Fee or Charge (25% or Treaty Rate)*

This term does *not* include reasonable amounts representing the following:

(1) payments for services in the ordinary course of business of a non-resident who is dealing at arm's length with the payer; and

(2) reimbursements of specific expenses incurred by the non-resident for services that were for the benefit of the payer, even if not dealing at arm's length.

(ITA: 212(1)(*a*), (4); IT-468R [Archived])

[¶2080.09] *(H) Registered Securities Dealers*

As discussed under ¶2080.03 above, securities lending arrangements are transfers of securities (usually to facilitate short term market liquidity) to an arm's length person who is expected to return the same or identical securities to the lender and to compensate the lender for any dividends paid during the loan. Providing there is not a tax deferral motive, special tax rules facilitate securities lending arrangements by ensuring that a number of ordinary tax consequences do not apply (see ¶422). Technical amendments retroactive to securities lending arrangements entered into after May 1995 ensure that compensation payments deemed to be dividends under the securities lending rules are exempt from withholding if (1) the arrangement was made by the borrower in the course of carrying on a business outside Canada, and (2) the securities lent were issued by a non-resident of Canada.

Certain payments to registered Canadian securities dealers by or on behalf of non-residents as collateral or compensation for securities lent in some but not all securities lending arrangements are subject to a sort of daily tax in lieu of withholding, payable by the dealer. Certain interest paid under securities lending arrangements is exempt.

(ITA: 212(2.1) Exempt dividends; 212(19) Tax on registered securities dealers; 212(20) Designated SLA)

[¶2080.10] *(I) Payments from One Non-Resident to Another*

As discussed in item ¶2080.04, above, there are a number of types of payments subject to withholding where the payer is deemed to be resident in Canada and therefore must apply withholding in making payments to other non-residents. To recapitulate, this is true for amounts paid or credited in respect of:

- rent for the use in Canada of property (other than property that is rolling stock as defined in section 2 of the *Railway Act*; note that certain short term rentals of rolling stock carry their own exemption, which would apply here)
- a timber royalty in respect of a timber resource property or a timber limit in Canada,
- a payment of a superannuation or pension benefit under a registered pension plan or of a distribution to one or more persons out of or under a retirement compensation arrangement,
- a payment of a retiring allowance or a death benefit to the extent that the payment is deductible in computing the payer's taxable income earned in Canada,
- a payment described in any of paragraphs (2), (3), (4) (9), (12), or (17) in ¶2080.04, above, as discussed there,
- interest on any mortgage, hypothecary claim or other indebtedness secured by real property situated in Canada or an interest therein to the extent that the amount so paid or credited is deductible in computing the non-resident person's taxable income earned in

Canada or the amount on which the non-resident person is liable to pay tax under Part I, or

- amounts which must be included in income of the recipient under the restrictive covenant rules at ¶929; note that it is only income amount under the general rule for restrictive covenants or the recovery of bad debts deducted from employment or covenant income in respect of restrictive covenants that is captured here; amounts treated as employment income or governed by one of the alternative elections is not covered; in addition, the rule forcing withholding on covenant payments made *by* non-residents only applies if the amount paid or credited by the non-resident is intended to affect
  (1) the acquisition or provision of property or services in Canada,
  (2) the acquisition or provision of property or services outside Canada by a person resident in Canada, or
  (3) the acquisition or provision outside Canada of a taxable Canadian property.

For amounts paid or credited under obligations entered into before December 21, 2002, a non-resident whose business is principally carried on in Canada or, who manufactures or processes goods, operates an oil or gas well in Canada, or extracts minerals from a mineral resource in Canada and, who pays or credits amounts to another non-resident person that are deductible in determining the payer's Canadian source income, will be deemed to be a resident for withholding tax purposes.

For amounts paid or credited under obligations entered into after December 20, 2002, any non-resident who pays or credits an amount to another non-resident is deemed to be a person resident in Canada in respect of the portion of the amount that is deductible in computing the non-resident's taxable income earned in Canada for any taxation year from a source that is neither a treaty-protected business or a treaty-protected property (subsection 212(13.2)). A treaty-protected business is, as you might expect, one the taxpayer's income from which is exempt from ordinary Canadian income tax under a tax treaty. Similarly treaty-protected property is property which is exempt from Canadian income tax on disposition by virtue of a Canadian tax treaty.

(ITA: 212(1)(s)–(v), (13.1), (13.2); 227(6.1))

[¶2080a] FORMS FOR NON-RESIDENT TAXPAYERS ELIGIBLE FOR TREATY RELIEF

The CRA provides Form NR301, *"Declaration of Benefits Under a Tax Treaty for a Non-Resident Taxpayer"*, which allows non-resident taxpayers receiving certain types of treaty-eligible income to apply for lower withholding tax rates as applicable under the relevant treaty. You should use the form if you are a non-resident taxpayer resident in a country with which Canada has a tax treaty and you are eligible to receive the reduced rate of tax or exemption provided by the treaty on all or certain income and you:

- receive income subject to Part XIII withholding tax, such as investment income, pension income, annuities, royalties, and estate or trust income, and the withholding tax rate is reduced by the tax treaty, or
- are completing T2062 forms regarding the disposition of taxable Canadian property and other properties for which section 116 certificates are required (see ¶2040).

The form states that it should be sent to the following persons:

- If you receive income subject to Part XIII tax (directly from a Canadian payer), send this form to your Canadian payer, to reduce the Part XIII withholding tax on income being paid or credited to you.
- If you derive income through a partnership or hybrid entity, and that partnership or hybrid entity asked you to complete form NR301, send it to that partnership or hybrid entity.
- If you are requesting a certificate of compliance for the disposition of treaty protected property, send the form, along with forms T2062 or T2062A, to the CRA according to the instructions on those forms.

For Part XIII tax withholding purposes, the form NR301 expires when there is a change in the non-resident taxpayer's eligibility for the declared treaty benefits, or three years from the end of the calendar year in which the form is signed and dated, whichever is earlier.

The form is not mandatory. However, if a non-resident does not provide the form or otherwise refuses to provide certification of beneficial ownership, residency, or eligibility for treaty benefits on request by a payer, the payer will likely (and should) withhold the full statutory rate rather than the reduced treaty rate. In that event, the payer will have withheld more tax than was necessary under the treaty. You can ask the CRA for a refund of the excess tax withheld by completing form NR7-R, Application for Refund of Part XIII Tax Withheld. The CRA generally will refund excess non-resident tax withheld if you complete and send the Form NR7-R within two years after the end of the calendar year in which the payer sent the withheld tax.

For treaty rates and instructions for payers including the due diligence expected of payers, see Information Circular 76-12R6"Applicable rate of Part XIII tax on amounts paid or credited to persons in countries with which Canada has a tax convention", and pending updates to Information Circular 76-12, *"Applicable rate of Part XIII tax on amounts paid or credited to persons in countries with which Canada has a tax convention related to forms NR301, NR302, and NR303"* (CRA website at www.cra-arc.gc.ca/formspubs/frms/ic76-12r6-eng.html).

The CRA provides similar forms for non-resident partners of a partnership (NR302, *"Declaration of Benefits Under a Tax Treaty for a Partnership with Non-Resident Partners"*), and for hybrid entities (NR303, *"Declaration of Benefits Under a Tax Treaty for a Hybrid Entity"*).

[¶2080b] SALARY PAID FROM NON-RESIDENT EMPLOYERS TO NON-RESIDENT EMPLOYEES

Note: The withholding exemption discussed here is not with respect to the non-resident withholding tax on investment income under Part XIII discussed above at ¶2080. The exemption here relates to withholding under Part I on employment income earned in Canada; see ¶2020. However, it is produced here for convenience.

Employment income earned in Canada by a non-resident employee is generally subject to Canadian income tax and thus an employer (including a non-resident employer) is required to withhold and remit tax from the remuneration. However, under some of Canada's income tax treaties (e.g., the Canada–U.S. treaty), the non-resident's employment income may be exempt from Canadian taxation in these situations.

Regardless of the fact that the non-resident employee is exempt from tax under a treaty, the employer is not exempt from its obligation to withhold tax. The CRA used to accept applications and issue withholding tax exemption waivers with respect to each individual employee for limited time periods.

However, Budget 2015 simplified the process. Applicable to payments made after 2015, a "qualifying non-resident employer" can receive a blanket withholding tax exemption with respect to remuneration paid to all of its "qualifying non-resident employees." These terms are defined below.

Qualifying Non-Resident Employee

An employee is considered a qualifying non-resident employee if he or she meets all of the following conditions:

(a) at the time of the payment, the employee is a resident in a country with which Canada has a tax treaty;

(b) the employee is not liable to pay Part I tax in respect of the payment because of that treaty; and

(c) the employee either

(i) works in Canada for less than 45 days in the calendar year that includes the time of the payment; or

(ii) is present in Canada for less than 90 days in any 12-month period that includes the time of the payment.

Days worked in Canada exclude weekends, days off, and holidays.

Qualifying Non-Resident Employer

An employer is considered a qualifying non-resident employer where it has been certified by the Minister (see "Certification Requirement" below) and:

(A) it is resident in a country with which Canada has a tax treaty; or

(B) it is a corporation that does not satisfy (A), but would be a resident of the country with which Canada has a tax treaty if it was treated as body corporate for the purpose of income tax in that country (e.g., flow-through entities in the United States).

Where the employer is a partnership, it is considered a qualifying non-resident employer where it is certified by the Minister and at least 90% of its income or loss for the fiscal period is allocated to members that fall under category (A) or (B) above.

Thus, provided that the employer is a qualifying non-resident employer and the employee is a qualifying non-resident employee, the employer can pay salary, wages, and other remuneration to the employee without withholding and remitting tax from payments. This rule applies to payment made after 2015.

Certification Requirement

An employer must be certified by the Minister to be considered a qualifying non-resident employer. The CRA requires that employers submit form RC473 to obtain certification. The instructions on the form recommend sending the application at least 30 days before the qualifying non-resident employer begins providing services in Canada. An employer can only be certified by the CRA for up to two calendar years, so it is important that an employer submit another RC473 as the end of the second calendar year of certification nears its end. Only one certification is required, so employers need not submit multiple applications for multiple employees. Moreover, the instructions on RC473 stipulate various compliance obligations which employers must adhere to in order to maintain their certified status.

[¶2083] MUTUAL FUND DISTRIBUTIONS

Canada imposes tax on capital gains realized by non-residents disposing of taxable Canadian property, as described at ¶2040. In general, there are restrictions on mutual funds to prevent them from being used by non-residents to avoid that tax, since (subject to the rules below) non-residents are not generally taxed on capital gain distributions from mutual funds. Those restrictions cause a Canadian mutual fund to lose its status if more than 10% of its property consists of taxable Canadian property and the fund is established or maintained primarily for the benefit of non-residents. Proposals in the 2004 Federal Budget would have extended these restrictions to mutual fund investments in Canadian resource properties and timber limits, but the government announced in 2004 that "Further discussions will be pursued with the private sector concerning the appropriate Canadian tax treatment of non-residents investing in resource property through mutual funds."

The rules below deal with gains on taxable Canadian property flowed out to non-residents from mutual funds which are not so non-resident oriented as to fail the status tests.

Mutual Fund Capital Gain Distributions

Where a Canadian mutual fund corporation or trust (which would include an income trust operating under Canadian mutual fund trust laws) realizes gains on taxable Canadian property (¶2040), it must keep a running account of its net gains and losses on such property, its "TCP gains balance". All capital gain distributions from the mutual fund are deemed to be made up in part of TCP gains balance distributions, in proportion to the general distribution.

Distributions out of the TCP gains balance of a mutual fund corporation should have no effect on Canadian residents, but non-resident recipients of capital gain distributions will be subject to withholding to the extent their share of the distribution comes from the TCP balance pool. The TCP gains distribution element is deemed to be an ordinary dividend, and withholding is required at the normal dividend rate for the recipient's country of residence.

Essentially the same result occurs on distributions from Canadian mutual fund trusts, except that twice the non-resident's share of the fund's TCP distribution is deemed to be taxable capital gain subject to withholding as trust income. Grossing up the distribution compensates for the fact that the distribution is stepped down to taxable capital gain under the trust election to distribute taxable capital gain; the amount subject to withholding is grossed up the whole capital gain, which is then subject to 25% withholding or the applicable treaty rate for trust distributions (generally 15%).

The withholding requirement does not apply to mutual fund distributions (from corporations or trusts) where 5% or less of the distribution recipients are non-residents. Such non-residents would normally escape Canadian tax on these distributions altogether.

(ITA: 104(21); 131(5.1)–(6); 132(4), (5.1), (5.2))

[¶2083.05] Distributions Derived from Underlying Canadian Real Estate, Resource Properties and Timber Limits

Apparently the government foresees situations in which the rules above will not capture some distributions to non-residents from mutual funds investing primarily in Canadian real estate, resource properties and timber limits, presumably because the gains in those funds will not be on capital account, although in effect derived from property values. In any event, an additional set of rules taxes all distributions by Canadian mutual funds to non-resident investors if those distributions are not already subject to tax under either general income tax or withholding tax rules (including the withholding rules immediately above). Distributions otherwise taxed by Canada are not subject to the following rules.

A 15% withholding tax is imposed under special rules on distributions to non-resident investors by mutual funds that both (i) are listed on a prescribed Canadian or foreign stock exchange (¶2618) and (ii) derive more than 50% of their value from one or more properties each of which is real property in Canada, a Canadian resource property, or a timber resource property.

The 15% withholding may be considered a final tax by the investor, who is not required to file a Canadian tax return or adjust the cost base of the share to reflect the distribution. However, if a non-resident realizes a loss on the disposition of a unit or share in respect of which the tax has been withheld, the non-resident can elect to file a Canadian income tax return in the year of disposition. To the extent the loss does not exceed the total of the distributions taxed in respect of the unit or share, the non-resident can apply the loss to offset those distributions, or to reduce tax on distributions on other shares or units which have been subjected to this tax. To the extent the loss exceeds current year distributions on the share or unit which generated it, it may be carried back three years to claim a refund of taxes withheld under this rule, and carried forward indefinitely against future withholdings under this rule (which will require Canadian tax returns in the future years in which the losses are utilized). Tax returns claiming loss utilization must be filed in the year in which the loss occurs and (if applicable) the future year in which it is claimed by the filing due date for that taxation year, typically for individuals which is April 30 of the following year. For a partnership, the filing due date is calculated as if the partnership were a corporation and its fiscal period were its corporate taxation year. Generally this will mean filing within six months of the end of its fiscal period.

(ITA: 218.3)

[¶2086] ELECTION BY NON-RESIDENT TO FILE CANADIAN TAX RETURN (SECTION 217 ELECTION)

An election under section 217 (commonly called a "217 election") is available to non-resident taxpayers who receive "Canadian benefits", as described below. Typically, these receipts have been subjected to Canadian non-resident withholding tax withheld by the Canadian payer, which applies at a flat rate of 25% unless reduced by a tax treaty with the country in which the recipient is resident. Where the non-resident's hypothetical Canadian tax on world income (including Canadian income), to the extent it has not already been taxed abroad at Canadian rates, and after applying the various (limited) personal amount and other miscellaneous deductions and tax credits which might apply, is less than the flat rate tax already withheld, it will be in the non-resident's interest to make a section 217 election. That election in effect consists of a Canadian tax return reporting only the amounts described (but all of them), and taxing them as if they were earned by a resident, albeit with some variations. The section 217 election is made on the T1 *General Return for Non-Residents and Deemed Residents of Canada,* which includes Schedules A, B and C to assist in the calculation, and a unique version of Schedule 1 on which the elected amount is reported (at line 445). The withholding tax already paid is claimed as a tax credit at line 437 of page 4 of the T1 return. The election is described in the CRA Guide for that version of the T1, and also in a separate Guide *Electing under Section 217 of the Income Tax Act* (T4145).

Schedule C provides a page designed to simplify the calculation by providing a format for reporting the elements subject to tax on the return. Schedule C also includes a section designed to indicate the correct withholding tax which should have been applied to the amounts subject to the election. The point is that a section 217 election is not always beneficial; comparison with the correct withholding tax allows the CRA to assess the withholding tax if it is less than the 217 tax. Note, however, that while the CRA can assess withholding tax in place of section 217 if the result is beneficial for the taxpayer, it has no authority to assess section 217 tax in place of withholding tax, even if more beneficial, if you do not make the section 217 election in a timely return as described below.

If you were non-resident throughout the year, you will file your 217 election on the *T1 General Return for Non-Residents and Deemed Residents of Canada*, and Schedules A, B and C will assist you in these calculations. If you were a part-year resident, see the subheading "Forms and Guides" below.

The starting point for the current rules is the determination of amounts eligible for a section 217 election. These are now called "Canadian benefits". A non-resident's Canadian benefits consist of the total of all amounts paid or credited to the non-resident in the year which (absent these rules) would be subject to non-resident withholding tax:

(1) pension or superannuation benefits, including OAS, CPP, and QPP benefits (¶911–¶915);

(2) registered retirement savings plan payments (Chapter 26);

(3) registered retirement income fund payments (Chapter 26);

(4) death benefits (¶925);

(5) benefits under the *Employment Insurance Act* (¶941);

(6) retiring allowances (including most termination payments — see ¶923);

(7) supplementary unemployment plan benefits (¶737, ¶943);

(8) deferred profit sharing plan payments (¶917);

(9) retirement compensation arrangement benefits, which in some cases can include benefits received by someone other than the recipient but taxed to the recipient (¶1030); and

(10) assistance payments in respect of the Canada–U.S. Auto Pact (¶973), and prescribed benefits under government assistance programs (¶975).

Note that in general these items are subject to withholding tax only to the extent they would be taxable if received by a Canadian resident and not subject to a tax-free rollover or offsetting deduction (see ¶2080.04). Presumably, receipts not subject to withholding are not Canadian benefits, but neither are they income for any other purpose under these rules.

If you were a non-resident of Canada for all or part (¶2103) of a year and had Canadian benefits described above, you may elect to have section 217 apply *provided you file a Canadian income tax return under the rules applicable to residents within six months of the end of the taxation year* for which you are making the election. This does not extend the normal filing and payment deadlines (¶218) for returns claiming a 217 election to June 30; rather, it requires you to file by June 30 or lose the right to elect at all. That is, you have no right to make a late-filed election after June 30 following the taxation year. It is far from clear that the CRA even has the discretion to make an assessment on a late-filed return after that time under the so-called "taxpayer relief provisions", described in Information Circular 07-1; on balance it seems likely they cannot do so. On the other hand, where the taxpayer has filed a return for a period under the ordinary resident tax rules which has been accepted and assessed, there seems to be a better case that the return can be amended to take account of a 217 election not made in the original return.

Where a timely election is made, a special calculation of "ordinary" income tax is required. That calculation has several steps (they are also summarized in the CRA T4145 Guide, and Guide 5013G under "Electing under section 217"):

STEP 1: Calculate taxable income earned in Canada plus Canadian benefits (on pages 2 and 3 of the Non-Residents T1 Return).

Calculate "taxable income earned in Canada" (if any) under the rules at ¶2010 to ¶2062, ¶2066 and ¶2067 for the year (or period of non-residence). This is the employment and business income and Canadian-source capital gains (on taxable Canadian property) for which you must file a Canadian tax return if you are a non-resident whether or not you are making the section 217 election; very often there will be no such income. In calculating this income, you can claim deductions for income or capital losses carried over from other years to the extent permitted by ¶1061. However, you may not deduct other amounts which reduce net income (line 236) to arrive at taxable income (line 260, ¶1077) unless these amounts may reasonably be considered to relate wholly to income amounts and not to gains on taxable Canadian property. Presumably, capital loss carryovers and the capital gains exemption are excluded by this rule.

To the income so calculated you add your Canadian benefits, as defined above. Note that if tax has in fact been withheld from the benefits, you must add the tax back to the payment you actually received to arrive at the actual benefit before withholding, which is the correct income amount. See the example in ¶2080.06, which has a comparable calculation. The tax component you add back here will be reversed out of your tax payable in Step 6.

STEP 2: Calculate world income (on Schedule A of the Non-Residents T1 Return).

Calculate your world income, including Canadian income, for the year (or period of non-residence), deducting ordinarily deductible items. Schedule A will assist you in making this calculation. However, you may not deduct amounts which reduce net income (line 236) to arrive at taxable income (line 260, ¶1077) unless these amounts may reasonably be considered to relate wholly to income amounts included in Step 1 (not including Canadian benefits).

STEP 3: Pick the greater of the Step 1 or Step 2 amounts and apply tax credits if 90% of your income is Canadian source.

Select the larger of the two amounts calculated as Step 1 and Step 2 above. This is your taxable income earned in Canada for purposes of the 217 election, and you calculate Canadian tax on this amount per Schedule 1 of (presumably) the *T1 General for Non-Residents and Deemed Residents of Canada*. You may not (at this stage) claim any page 3 tax credits (personal amount credits and the like discussed from Chapters 11–13) unless 90% of your income for the year is (i) included in your return for the period of non-residence if you were a part-year non-resident or (ii) included in Step 1 if you were a full year non-resident.

STEP 4: Calculate non-refundable tax credits if less than 90% of your income is Canadian source.

If you could not deduct page 3 tax credits under Step 3 (because of the 90% rule), you then follow the calculation in Box B of Schedule B to calculate on account of such credits the total of:

(1) the following credits calculated under ordinary rules (as if you were resident in Canada):

- all personal amount credits (i.e., for yourself (¶1106), your spouse or common-law partner (¶1114) or dependant qualified for the eligible dependant amount (¶1120), your infirm dependants over 18 (¶1126) and (¶1127), and your caregiver credits (¶1140));
- age (¶1108) and pension (¶1311) credit amounts;
- charitable donations, gifts to the Crown, etc., as discussed in Chapter 12;
- credit for your own physical or mental impairment but not that of a dependant (¶1255);
- credit for CPP/QPP contributions (¶1305) and Employment Insurance premiums (¶1307); and
- tuition tax credit (¶1321) but not education tax credit or education/tuition credits transferred from others (the education and textbook tax credits were repealed effective January 1, 2017);

and

(2) the following credits only if they "can reasonably be considered wholly applicable":

- medical expenses (Chapter 12);
- credit for the physical or mental impairment of a dependant (¶1255);
- education amount credit (¶1337; effective January 1, 2017, the education credit was repealed);
- education (repealed January 1, 2017) and tuition credits transferred from children or grandchildren (¶1339); and
- all credits transferred from a spouse or common-law partner on Schedule 2 (¶1361).

However, you may only claim the lesser of the credits calculated in (1) plus (2) and the annual tax credit conversion rate (see ¶1303 — currently 15%) multiplied by your Canadian benefits. That is, 15% of your Canadian benefits is an absolute cap on the credit claim under Step 4. The above amounts are listed in section 217(5) of the Act.

Note that certain personal amount credits are not included in the list above. These include the credits for student loan interest, adoption expenses, transit passes, the children's arts amount, the volunteer firefighters' and search and rescue volunteers' amount, and the home buyers' amount.

Your tax at this point is the tax calculated in Step 3 less the credits calculated in Step 3 or Step 4, as the case may be.

STEP 5: Back out the proportion of tax allocated to foreign income (calculated in Part 2 (formerly Part 3) of Schedule C of the Non-Residents T1 Return).

The penultimate step is to deduct a tax credit which represents that proportion of the tax calculated so far that your foreign-source income (and Canadian-source income which remains subject to withholding, such as dividends from Canadian sources) is of your total world income. The intention of the credit is to exclude foreign-source income (and Canadian income not taxed under the rules for residents) from Canadian tax, while applying the effective tax rate on the whole amount to your Canadian benefits and, incidentally, any other income (such as employment or business income or Canadian-source capital gains) on which you must in any event pay tax as if you were resident.

Technically, you claim a tax credit here equal to the tax calculated at the end of Step 4 prorated by:

World income from Step 2 – Canadian-source income from Step 1

World income from Step 2

STEP 6: Pay the tax calculated and claim credit for any amounts withheld on Canadian benefits.

If your tax liability at this point, after deducting any credits for amounts withheld on Canadian benefits paid or credited in the year, is less than the amount of withholding liability plus any amount you would pay on a T1 return you would otherwise have to file for the year to report Canadian business, employment income and capital gains, you will benefit from the election and will want to make a section 217 election by filing your non-resident T1 return on this basis.

STEP 7: Add federal surtax or provincial tax.

The tax calculated in Step 6, along with any tax on other Canadian source income (for example, from dispositions of Canadian real estate), is included in the tax subject to federal surtax in lieu of provincial tax (¶1445) if you were a non-resident for the entire year or provincial tax (Chapter 15) if you were a part-year resident.

[¶2086.05] *Forms and Guides*

If you were a non-resident of Canada throughout the taxation year and have no Canadian employment or business income, file the section 217 election on the *T1 General Return for Non-Residents and Deemed Residents of Canada*. Write "section 217" at the top of page 1 and enter "other" on the line where you identify your province or territory of residence. Schedules A and B, provided only with that version of the T1 return, assist you in the calculation of allowable credits. The CRA also provides a special guide, *Electing under Section 217 of the Income Tax Act* (T4145), to assist you.

If you left Canada to become a non-resident during the taxation year, you must file a T1 General return for the province in which you were resident on the day you left. You must include income for both resident and non-resident periods on the return, as well as the section 217 results.

If you became a resident of Canada during the taxation year, you must file a T1 General return for the province in which you were resident on December 31. You must include income for both resident and non-resident periods on the return, as well as the section 217 results. The CRA offers guidance in its Guide *Newcomers to Canada* (T4055).

If you were non-resident throughout the year but had, in addition to your section 217 income, income from employment in Canada or from a business with a permanent establishment in Canada, you must file a T1 General return for the province in which you were employed or had the establishment. In these circumstances, your problem is not so much electing into section 217, since you can merely report your retirement income on the T1 return, as it is electing out if you prefer to pay the flat tax. Presumably you do this by only reporting your business or employment income (and gains on the disposition of taxable Canadian property), and claiming no credit for withholding taxes paid on those items. If you are making a section 217 election on a return with Canadian business or employment income, you obviously include the income on the return. Calculating the correct non-refundable tax credits is tricky if you fail the 90% of world income test. Presumably, you calculate refundable credits twice, once as indicated in Box A of Schedule B, and once as indicated in Box B. Certain credits, such as disability and charitable donations, would double up in these calculations. This does not appear to be prohibited. Note that the CRA provides a nice example, shown below, in its Guide *Electing under Section 217 of the Income Tax Act* (T4145), but it does not deal with the more complex credit issues.

[¶2086.10] *Examples*

Example 1

Dave is a resident of the United States. In the relevant taxation year, he received the following income:

- $18,000 from a pension plan in Canada;
- $500 interest from a savings account in Canada; and
- $500 interest from a savings account in the U.S.

Dave elects to file a return under section 217 to have his pension income taxed at a lower rate. On the return, he includes the $18,000 pension he received (eligible income for section 217). His taxable income on line 260 of his return is $18,000.

He does not report any bank interest on the return as the U.S. interest is not subject to tax in Canada and the Canadian interest is subject to non-resident withholding tax at source and not eligible for the section 217 election, so his Canadian withholding is his final Canadian tax liability on that income. However, he must use both interest amounts in calculating his net world income on Schedule A.

Dave determines that he has included more than 90% of his net world income on his return, as follows:

$18,000 (the net income on his return)	= 95%
$19,000 (his net world income)	

As a result, he can claim all of the non-refundable tax credits that would have applied to him if he had been resident in Canada throughout the taxation year.

Example 2

If Dave also earned $12,000 interest on U.S. treasury bonds, he would not meet the 90% rule, calculated as follows:

$18,000 (the net income on his return)	= 58%
$31,000 (his net world income)	

Since Dave has not included at least 90% of his net world income on his return, his allowable non-refundable tax credits are limited to the lesser of $2,700 (15% of his $18,000 section 217 income) or the amount at line 350 of his Schedule 1.

[¶2086.15] *Alleviation of Withholding on Canadian Benefits*

You can at any time request the CRA to determine if, on the basis of your estimated Canadian and world tax liability, you will benefit from a 217 election for the current or coming year. If the CRA determines that you will benefit, it will authorize the payers of your Canadian benefits to reduce or eliminate withholding to match your estimated liability under the election. Form NR5 is designated for this purpose.

The CRA provides that only one form NR5 will have to be filed for every five tax years, if approved. On its website, in the "International and non-resident taxes" section, the CRA indicates that, when an NR5 application is approved:

- It will always cover a period of five tax years.
- The CRA will advise each relevant Canadian payer of the reduced rate of non-resident tax to deduct from the qualifying Canadian benefit income for the entire approval period.
- The reduced rate of tax withholding will be maintained throughout the entire approval period, unless the CRA has been informed of changes to the information provided on your most recently approved NR5 application.
- You are not required to file an amended form NR5 to inform the CRA of yearly increases to your pension payments due to a cost of living increase (indexing), because these changes are taken into account during the initial processing of your application.
- You will still have to file an income tax return under section 217 as indicated above, within six months from the end of each tax year covered by the approval period.

(ITA: 217)

[¶2090] TAX PAYMENTS AND REFUNDS

As previously described, tax on other income such as dividends, royalties, rent, etc., should be withheld at source by the payer and remitted by the 15th day of the following month to the government.

Refunds of excess tax withheld from other income, such as dividends or royalties, are claimed by applying to the CRA within two years after the end of the calendar year in which the tax was paid to the government. Form NR7-R is provided for making such claims, and is obtainable from CRA offices and on its website. In its Guide T4058, the CRA states:

> Generally, we can only refund excess non-resident tax withheld if you complete and send us Form NR7-R no later than two years after the end of the calendar year in which the payer sent us the tax. For example, if the payer sent us more than the required amount of tax in 2013, you have to send us Form NR7-R by December 31, 2015. Depending on the tax treaty Canada has signed with your country of residence, the period during which you can get a refund may be longer.

(ITA: 227(6))

HOW TO REPORT INCOME IF YOU ARE A NON-RESIDENT OF CANADA

[¶2091] HOW TO REPORT INCOME IF YOU ARE A NON-RESIDENT OF CANADA

If you were a non-resident of Canada throughout the year and are reporting income from employment in Canada or from a business carried on through a permanent establishment in Canada, the CRA requires you to use the T1 return for the province of employment or business. You will be subject to restrictions on your personal amount claims, and can use Schedules A and B below to assist you, although they are not part of the Canadian return you are using.

If you were an immigrant or emigrant in the taxation year, use the form for your province of residence while resident (if an emigrant, province of residence on the last day of residence; if an immigrant, province of residence on December 31), and see Chapter 21 rather than this chapter. You will be subject to restrictions on your personal amount claims for the period of non-residence, as explained in the Canada Revenue Agency (CRA) guide *Newcomers to Canada* (T4055). Even though you will not be using the non-resident version of the T1 return, you may want to obtain a copy so that you can use Schedules A and B below to assist you. Copies of these Schedules are also reproduced on the following pages.

If you were a non-resident throughout the year and are reporting income from a business carried on in Canada without a permanent establishment in Canada, or income from the disposition of taxable Canadian property (¶2040), use the T1 General Return for Non-Residents and Deemed Residents of Canada. Note that this includes Schedules A and B, not found with domestic versions of the T1 return, to assist you in the calculation of personal amount credits which you may claim against business and employment income.

If you were a non-resident for part or all of the year and you had retirement income subject to Canadian withholding tax, you may want to file a section 217 election to pay ordinary Canadian tax, which allows lower rates on lower incomes and certain personal amount credits, rather than the flat rate of withholding tax. If you were a non-resident throughout the year, you file a section 217 election on the *T1 General Return for Non-Residents and Deemed Residents of Canada*; see ¶2086. If you were a part year resident, file a T1 General return for your province of residence (see above) and see the directions in the CRA's guides for these situations (listed above), as well as the explanation at ¶2086. Schedule C is provided as part of *T1 General Return for Non-Residents and Deemed Residents of Canada* to assist in the section 217 election calculation. Although it is found only with the non-resident version of the T1, you will find it convenient no matter which version of the T1 return you must use. A copy of Schedule C is also reproduced in the following pages. The CRA also publishes a dedicated pamphlet called *Electing Under Section 217 of the Income Tax Act* (T4145). You should also consider filing the form NR5 to authorize payers of the amounts to reduce or eliminate any withholding tax; see ¶2086.15.

If you received rental income as a non-resident of Canada, you have an option to file a Canadian return (form T1159) and pay Canadian tax at marginal rates after related expenses rather than the flat rate withholding tax on gross rentals; see ¶2080.05, and the CRA *Income Tax Guide for Electing Under Section 216* (T4144).

If you receive income subject to Part XIII withholding tax, such as dividend income, pension, annuities, royalties, and estate or trust income, and the withholding tax rate is reduced by the tax treaty, you should consider filing the form NR301 or NR302 so that the payer of the amounts will withhold at the reduced treaty rates; see ¶2080a.

The CRA publishes a guide called *Non-Residents and Income Tax* (T4058) which explains the situations in which non-residents are liable for Canadian tax and the alternative filings available.

If you are filing the *T1 General Return for Non-Residents and Deemed Residents of Canada* for any of the reasons discussed above, you should note that there is a separate non-resident version of the standard T1 Guide which accompanies all domestic Canadian T1 returns. The non-resident version is called the *General Income Tax and Benefit Guide for Non-Residents and Deemed Residents of Canada* (5013-G).

SPECIFIC QUESTIONS AND ANSWERS

[¶2098] SPECIFIC QUESTIONS AND ANSWERS

Retirement Income Received Abroad

I am 67 and live abroad with my spouse. I receive about $10,000 a year from my Canadian retirement income, and I earn the equivalent of about $10,000 (Canadian) locally from various activities. Last year, $2,500 was withheld from my RRIF. Should I file a section 217 election?

It really depends on your circumstances. If you live in a non-treaty country, so that the Canadian withholding rate is 25% on this income, and given your income level, yes, it would make sense. You will not be taxed by Canada on your local (non-resident) income, and so long as your world income is less than (for 2016) $45,252, the lowest Canadian marginal rate bracket (about 22%) will apply to your Canadian source income, and with personal amount credits should at least bring your Canadian tax below the 25% which would otherwise apply. If the withholding rate on your Canadian source income is 15% or less, as would be normal if you live in a treaty country, you really have to do the calculation to see if you benefit.

In either case, as your world income increases beyond the upper limit for the lowest bracket, the higher Canadian marginal tax rates on your Canadian source income will rapidly offset your personal amount tax credits, and making the election would yield higher tax than simply accepting withholding rates. As your tax exceeds this line, there is no longer an easy rule of thumb to guide you. You will benefit from the election, at least in theory, only if the Canadian tax you would have paid on your world income (if your entire world income (including your retirement income) were subject to Canadian tax) would be less than the amounts withheld from your retirement income. To be sure whether this is the case, you must complete a return for the section 217 election and compare your withholding tax on the 217 income plus any tax payable on other Canadian source income for the year (none in your case, but if you had Canadian employment, business or capital gain income you would have to consider that).

Chapter 21

Immigrants and Emigrants, U.S. Citizens in Canada

THESE POINTS ARE COVERED IN THIS CHAPTER

CRA REFERENCES RELATING TO THIS CHAPTER

T1 Return and Schedules

- T1 General, Income Tax and Benefit Return for Non-Residents and Deemed Residents of Canada
- T1, Federal Worksheet
- Schedule 1, Federal Tax
- Schedule 2, Federal Amounts Transferred From Your Spouse or Common-law Partner
- Schedule 3, Capital Gains (or Losses)
- Schedule 4, Statement of Investment Income
- Schedule 5, Amounts for Spouse or Common-Law Partner and Dependants
- Schedule 7, RRSP and PRPP Unused Contributions, Transfers, and HBP or LLP Activities
- Schedule 8, Canada Pension Plan Contributions and Overpayment
- Schedule 9, Donations and Gifts
- Schedule 11, Tuition, Education, and Textbook Amounts
- Schedule A, Statement of World Income
- Schedule B, Allowable Amount of Non-Refundable Tax Credits
- Schedule C, Electing Under Section 217 of the *Income Tax Act*

CRA Guides

5013-G, "General Income Tax and Benefit Guide for Non-Residents and Deemed Residents of Canada"; **T4055**, "Newcomers to Canada"; **T4058**, "Non-Residents and Income Tax"; **T4061**, "NR4 — Non-Resident Tax Withholding, Remitting, and Reporting"; **T4144**, "Income Tax Guide for Electing Under Section 216"; **T4145**, "Electing Under Section 217 of the *Income Tax Act*"

CRA Forms

5013-R, "T1 General — Income Tax and Benefit Return for Non-Residents and Deemed Residents of Canada"; **CPT56**, "Certificate of Coverage Under the Canada Pension Plan Pursuant to Article V of the Agreement on Social Security Between Canada and the United States"; **NR4**, "Statement of Amounts Paid or Credited to Non-Residents of Canada"; **NR5**, "Application by a Non-Resident of Canada for a Reduction in the Amount of Non-Resident Tax Required to be Withheld"; **NR6**, "Undertaking to File an Income Tax Return by a Non-Resident Receiving Rent from Real Property or Receiving a Timber Royalty"; **NR7-R**, "Application for Refund Part XIII Tax Withheld"; **NR73**, "Determination of Residency Status (Leaving Canada)"; **NR74**, "Determination of Residency Status (Entering Canada)"; **NR301**, "Declaration of Eligibility for Benefits (Reduced Tax) under a Tax Treaty for a Non-Resident Person"; **RC269**, "Employee Contributions to a Foreign Pension Plan or Social Security Arrangement for 2016 — Non-United States Plans or Arrangements"; **T1159**, "Income Tax Return for Electing Under Section 216"; **T1161**, "List of Properties by an Emigrant of Canada"; **T1234**, Schedule B, Allowable Amounts of Non-Refundable Tax Credits; **T1243**, "Deemed Disposition of Property by an Emigrant of Canada"; **T1244**, "Election Under Section 220(4.5) of the *Income Tax Act*, to Defer the Payment of Tax on Income Relating to the Deemed Disposition of Property"; **T1248**, Schedule D, Information About Your Residency Status; **T2062**, "Request by a Non-Resident of Canada for a Certificate of Compliance Related to the Disposition of Taxable Canadian Property"; **T2062A**, "Request by a Non-Resident of Canada for a Certificate of Compliance Related to the Disposition of Canadian Resource or Timber Resource Property, Canadian Real Property (Other Than Capital Property), or Depreciable Taxable Canadian Property"

Income Tax Folios

S1-F3-C4, "Moving Expenses"; **S2-F3-C2**, "Benefits and Allowances Received from Employment"; **S5-F1-C1**, "Determining an Individual's Residence Status"; **S5-F2-C1**, "Foreign Tax Credit"; **S6-F1-C1**, "Residence of a Trust or Estate"

Interpretation Bulletins [Archived]

IT-91R4, "Employment at Special Work Sites or Remote Work Locations"; **IT-262R2**, "Losses of Non-Residents and Part-Year Residents"; **IT-393R2**, "Election Re: Tax on Rents and Timber Royalties — Non-Residents"; **IT-420R3**, "Non-Residents — Income Earned in Canada"; **IT-434R**, "Rental of Real Property by Individual"; **IT-451R**, "Deemed Disposition and Acquisition on Ceasing To Be or Becoming Resident in Canada"; **IT-497R4**, "Overseas Employment Tax Credit"

Information Circulars

72-17R6, "Procedures Concerning the Disposition of Taxable Canadian Property by Non-Residents of Canada — Section 116"; **76-12R6**, "Applicable Rate of Part XIII Tax on Amounts Paid or Credited to Persons in Countries With Which Canada Has a Tax Convention"; **77-16R4**, "Non-Resident Income Tax"; **84-6**, "Canada-United States Social Security Agreement"

Income Tax Technical News

No. 31R2, May 16, 2006, "Social Security Taxes and the Foreign Tax Credit"; **No. 35**, February 26, 2007, "Treaty Residence — Resident of Convenience"; **No. 38**, September 22, 2008, "Anti-Discrimination Provisions"

RECENT CHANGES

2016 Announcements and Changes

Historically, employment income paid to non-resident employees physically working in Canada was subject to the same income tax withholding rules as Canadian-resident employees, even if the employees were ultimately exempt from Canadian tax under a tax treaty. In many instances, the non-resident employees would still be required to file a personal Canadian tax return to obtain a refund of the excess income tax withholding if their employer did not properly apply for a tax withholding waiver with the Canada Revenue Agency (CRA). The 2015 Federal Budget proposed an exemption from these withholding requirements for payments made by "qualifying non-resident employers". The 2016 Budget confirmed the proposal, and the exemption was passed into law under Bill C-15 on June 22, 2016. The withholding exemption applies to payments made after 2015. See ¶2020.

Several measures intended to catch taxpayers hiding assets and income internationally may, in the near future, increase the audit risk of taxpayers with offshore transactions and assets. Effective January 1, 2015, the CRA launched its Electronic Funds Transfer Initiative, requiring banks to report transactions in excess of C$10,000 to/from international sources. An intergovernmental agreement for the sharing of various tax-related information is in the process of being negotiated between Canada and the United States, but is currently subject to legal challenges in both countries. In this regard, in the 2016 Federal Budget, the Canadian government confirmed that it will be implementing the G20/OECD common reporting standards, which will ensure tax fairness and improve Canada's ability to address tax evasion. On April 15, 2016, the Department of Finance released legislative proposals to implement the "Common Reporting Standard" ("CSR"), and invited interested parties to provide comments or submissions. Canada intends to implement the CSR starting on July 1, 2017.

WHAT IMMIGRANTS AND EMIGRANTS SHOULD KNOW

[¶2100] INTRODUCTION

The CRA publishes a pamphlet entitled "Newcomers to Canada" (T4055). This guide is helpful to part-year residents, especially in calculating personal amounts. It is available on the CRA website under "Forms and Publications / Tax Guides and Pamphlets". Former Guide T4056, "Emigrants and Income Tax" has been eliminated by the CRA, and is replaced by a website providing similar information (http://www.cra-arc.gc.ca/tx/nnrsdnts/ndvdls/lvng-eng.html).

PART-YEAR RESIDENTS (IMMIGRANTS AND EMIGRANTS)

[¶2103] PART-YEAR RESIDENTS: TAXABLE INCOME

Persons taking up permanent residence in Canada during a year, or giving up their Canadian residence to move to another country, are part-time residents of Canada for the year this change occurs.

[¶2103.05] *Income and Loss Calculation for the Year*

There is only one taxation year for the year of emigration or immigration (i.e., a full calendar year). Worldwide income is calculated under normal rules for the period of Canadian residency, and for the period of non-residency, the only income or losses included are those from a Canadian source (¶2000 to ¶2040). Although this formulation preserves separate calculations for periods of residency and non-residency, losses can offset income and capital gains for the year regardless of the period in which they arise. The non-resident rules themselves will eliminate non-resident foreign-source and treaty-protected losses from this calculation. However, none of the rules which limit loss carryovers between years of residency and non-residency should apply in offsetting the losses which arise within the calendar year of immigration or emigration.

If losses of any kind are left over from the netting for the part-year resident, it then becomes important to decide in which part of the year they arise, because those arising in a period of non-residency will be limited to Canadian-source income as discussed at ¶2061.

(ITA: 111(8), (9); 114; 115(1)(b), (c), (e); IT-262R2 [Archived])

[¶2103.10] *Deductions in Arriving at Taxable Income*

Loss carryovers from years of residency are applied in full against the income for the whole year determined under the rules above. If the losses carried over come from years of residency, they are usable in full; if they come from years of non-residency, they are restricted by the Canadian-source income limitations for the year in which they arose.

In arriving at taxable income, you are also allowed to deduct the following amounts *to the extent they relate to amounts included in computing income* for the year.

- stock and mutual fund options when the employment benefit is included in income (¶330);
- prospector's and grubstaker's shares when sold (¶776);
- social assistance payments (¶990);
- treaty-exempt income (¶990); and
- UN, ISAT, and IATA employees (¶1456).

With respect to all other deductions from taxable income (see the list at ¶1077), you may deduct them if you meet either of the following tests:

(1) the deduction can reasonably be considered applicable to the part of the year throughout which you were resident; or

(2) if the deduction can reasonably be considered applicable to the part of the year throughout which you were a non-resident, all or substantially all (usually interpreted as 90%) of your income for the part of the year you were non-resident is included in income and subject to tax in Canada.

(ITA: 2; 111(9); 114; 115(1))

[¶2107] TAX CREDITS FOR "PERSONAL AMOUNTS"

In order to determine the amount of personal credits you are entitled to, you first are required to make a notional computation of the personal amounts which would be available to you as a non-resident, as if your period of non-residency were a complete taxation year. Next, you would make a separate computation of the amounts available for the period of residence (under specific rules for that purpose). Finally, you would add the two together, subject to the overriding limitation that the total for each specific personal amount may not exceed the amount that would have been available had the taxpayer been resident throughout the year. The federal credits are claimed on Schedule 1.

(ITA: 118.91)

[¶2107.05] *Period of Non-Residency*

The following personal amounts are wholly available for the period of non-residency to the extent they are related to that period:

- charitable donations (which qualify under Canadian rules, ¶1265);
- tuition fees (but not the education amounts; effective January 1, 2017, the education and textbook tax credits are repealed) for yourself, if qualified under Canadian rules (line 323, ¶1319–¶1335);
- disability amount for yourself (line 316, ¶1255);
- Canada or Quebec Pension Plan contributions (line 308, ¶1305);
- Canadian Employment Insurance premiums (line 312, ¶1307);
- interest paid in the year on loans for post-secondary education (line 319, ¶1345); and
- social security arrangement contributions (use Form RC269, "Employee Contributions to a Foreign Pension Plan or Social Security Arrangement for 2016 – Non-United States Plans or Arrangements").

All other personal amounts may be deducted only if all or substantially all (usually considered at least 90%) of world income for the calendar year is included on the return, no matter how long the period of non-residency. In this regard, in its Guide T4005, "Guide for Newcomers to Canada", the CRA states:

> If you are claiming full federal non-refundable tax credits, attach a note to your tax return stating your net world income (in Canadian dollars) for the part of the year that you were not a resident of Canada.
>
> Show separately the net income you received from sources inside and outside Canada for that part of the year. We cannot allow the full amount of these federal credits without this note.
>
> If you are filing your return electronically, follow the instructions on claiming these credits and providing your income in your NETFILE certified software or provided by your EFILE service provider.

See also ¶2062a.

[¶2107.10] *Period of Residence*

In determining each personal amount credit for the period of residence, the following personal amounts may only be claimed (if otherwise applicable) to the extent they correspond with the period of residence. As a practical matter, the CRA interprets this to mean they are prorated for the period of residence. The rules for determining the initial applicability of these personal amounts, before applying proration, are found in Chapters 11, 12 and 13. In addition to the amounts listed above at ¶2107.05, these amounts include:

- basic personal amount (line 300 of the T1 return);
- age amount (line 301);
- spouse or common-law partner amount (line 303);
- eligible dependant amount (line 305);
- dependant (infirm) amount (line 306);
- caregiver amount (line 315);
- disability amount (line 316);
- disability amount transferred from dependant (line 318);
- Canada employment amount (line 363);
- Public transit amount (line 364);
- Home buyers' amount (line 369);
- Pension income amount for yourself (line 314);
- unused credits transferred from a spouse (line 326);
- tuition, education and textbook amounts for yourself (line 323); and
- unused tuition/education amounts transferred from child or grandchild (line 324); effective January 1, 2017, the education and textbook tax credits were repealed although credits earned prior to 2017 can be carried forward).

See "Proration for Personal Amounts Listed Above", at ¶2107.12.

All other applicable personal amounts may be claimed in whole, without proration, if they are wholly related to the period of residence.

There might be instances of double counting a particular personal credit after adding together both portions (i.e., for the period of residence and the period of non-residency). An overriding limitation that the total for each specific personal amount may not exceed the amount that would have been available had the taxpayer been resident throughout the year addresses this.

[¶2107.12] *Proration for Personal Amounts Listed Above*

The proration of personal amounts for the residency period is the number of days in the period of residence divided by the number of days in the calendar year.

Where you are claiming personal amounts which include an income threshold (i.e., lines 303, 305, 306, 316, and 318), the following rules apply:

(1) Prorate the maximum claim and the upper and lower income limits for its calculation, based on the number of days you were resident in Canada.

(2) Determine the dependant's income for the part of the year during which you were resident, employed or carrying on business in Canada. Note that this test is based on the period that you were resident in Canada or otherwise taxable in Canada on your worldwide income, not that of the dependant.

(3) Apply the appropriate calculation using the reduced numbers determined in (1) and (2).

[¶2107.14] *Examples Using Basic Personal Credit and Spousal Credit*

Basic Personal Amount Example

You are single, have no dependants, and were resident in Canada until June 30. After that you were non-resident and employed in Canada for an additional three-week period later in the year. During the remainder of the year, you were employed in a foreign country.

For a full year, your basic personal amount would be:

Basic personal amount (2016 figures)	$11,474
Claim: (181/365) × 11,474 =	$5,689

This amount will be converted to a credit against federal tax at the 15% applicable rate, for an effective credit of $853. Proration extends to all amounts, including the income of dependants applied to reduce personal amounts claimed for them.

Generally speaking, the denominator applied to the personal amount proration is 365. However, in a leap year, the denominator applied to personal amounts should be 366.

Credit for Spouse/Common-Law Partner Example

You were a Canadian resident for 181 days in the year. While you were resident, your spouse's worldwide income was $900.

Your credit amount in respect of your spouse is (2016 figures):

$11,474 spousal amount prorated by 181/365	$5,689
Less: Spouse's income while you were resident	900
Exemption	$4,789

The credit would equal 15% of $4,789 = $718.

See the CRA Publications T4055 and T4058 for more examples of the prorated credits.

[¶2107.15] *Transfers from Spouse or Common-Law Partner*

You can claim Schedule 2 transfers from your spouse or common-law partner in calculating your period of residence personal amounts. You must prorate your spouse's basic personal amount, age amount and disability amount (if applicable) for the period of time *your spouse or common-law partner* was resident in Canada during the year. Claims on Schedule 2 for the non-resident portion of the year can only be made where all or substantially all of your world income for that period is included in Canadian taxable income, and subject to the rule that the claims for the two periods cannot exceed the amount available for a full-year resident.

[¶2107.20] *Medical Expenses*

Medical expenses paid while you were resident in Canada (or were otherwise taxable on your worldwide income) are eligible for credit if they meet the requirements described in Chapter 12.

For example, if you emigrated from Canada on June 30 and were not employed in Canada or carrying on business in Canada after that date, the following rules will normally apply:

(1) You may claim medical expenses paid in any 12-month period ending from January 1 to June 30, except you may not claim for expenses already deducted in the previous year;

(2) Your claim cannot include medical expenses paid after June 30, even if they were incurred prior to that date (subject to the "all or substantially all" rule for non-residents); and

(3) The income threshold that applies for the purposes of the credit ($2,237/3% for 2016) would seem to apply to all net income from all sources for the period of residence only (or separately for the period of non-residency where the "all or substantially all" rule is met).

[¶2107.25] *Charitable Donations*

The CRA's view is that charitable donations are subject to the rule that the contributions which may be claimed for the periods of residency vs. non-residency are each limited to 75% of the net income for each respective period (plus whatever additional amounts may be available for capital gifts). For example, if there were charitable donations in each period of $70,000, and income in one period was $120,000 and in the other $80,000, the charitable donation claim in the $80,000 period would be limited to $60,000 (limiting the overall charitable donation claim to $130,000). This applies even though entire year's net income would seem to justify a $140,000 charitable donation claim. Accordingly, the taxpayer who is well prepared will normally ensure that donations are made in the period of residence, which is typically the high net income period for Canadian purposes. Charitable donations in excess of the limitation for the year can be carried forward for five years regardless of residency status. This carryforward is generally cold comfort for the departing Canadian, as it is usually unlikely he or she will have sufficient future tax to absorb the carryforward. Even if it can be used, the reduced Canadian tax will often simply reduce his or her foreign tax credit in the new home country.

Under the treaty rules described at ¶1285, you may be able to deduct donations to U.S. charities made while resident in Canada. You may not, however, deduct from Canadian tax the credit related to donations to U.S. charities made while you were a non-resident, since treaty protection is only offered to residents.

(ITA: 114; 115(1); 118–118.94; IT-262R2 [Archived]; CRA Document No.: Charitable Donations by Part-year Resident, *January 31, 1992*, CRA Document No. 9135052)

[¶2109] TAX AGREEMENTS

The tax position of a part-time resident may be affected by the terms of the tax agreement which Canada has entered into with another country. See ¶2005. See also ¶2181 of this chapter regarding moves between Canada and the United States.

[¶2111] SOCIAL SECURITY AGREEMENTS

Canada has entered into several bilateral social security "totalization" agreements. These agreements reduce the likelihood of being subjected to the social security taxes of two countries, and they coordinate the benefits between the countries. The Services Canada website (http://www.servicecanada.gc.ca/eng/services/pensions/international/index.shtml) has a complete list of Canada's social security agreements with other countries.

Generally, totalization agreements provide that an employee is covered by the system of the country in which he or she is primarily working. However, where the employee is transferred to the foreign country for a "temporary period", the agreement allows the employee to continue making contributions to the home country rather than to the foreign country system.

The temporary transfer rules of a totalization agreement may be significant where the country to which the employee is transferred imposes significantly different social security taxes than Canada. A Canadian employee on temporary transfer to such a country should extend coverage under the Canada Pension Plan. Application forms for Canadian coverage or coverage extension as well as copies of totalization agreements can usually be obtained from the CRA Tax Services Offices (¶287) or the CRA website (www.cra-arc.gc.ca). More detailed information is found under the heading "International Benefits" on the Services Canada website of the Human Resources and Social Development ministry.

The tax treaties discussed at ¶2005 also affect the treatment of pensions paid from one country to another; Information Circular 76-12R6 is a valuable summary of such treaty information up to its date of issue.

See also ¶2127 and ¶922.

[¶2111.10] *Quebec Social Security (Heath Insurance) Agreements*

Quebec has a parallel Social Security system that is separate from CPP (¶915). The Quebec government had entered into reciprocal social security agreements with countries providing for health care coverage. The up-to-date list can be found on the Regie des rentes Quebec website; go to Home/Programs/Quebec Pension Plan/International Agreements.

Under these agreements, temporary workers, students, and "detached workers" (workers carrying out activities in a different country than the one where their employer is located) may be eligible for the Quebec Health Insurance Plan. (The agreement signed with Greece does not apply to students or detached workers.)

The purpose of these social security agreements is to promote mobility between Quebec and the signatory countries by:

- saving persons arriving from outside Canada from having to wait for up to three months before becoming eligible for the Health Insurance Plan; and
- giving students from France access to drugs covered under the Public Prescription Drug Insurance Plan.

The program is administered by the Quebec Régie de l'assurance maladie, and individuals access it by registration with the Régie de l'assurance maladie. At the time of writing, information was available on the health insurance section of the RAMQ. Go to the website and ask the search engine for: social security agreements.

CANADIAN TAXATION OF IMMIGRANTS

[¶2113] INTRODUCTION

(This section discusses the tax implications of an individual moving to Canada. Individuals immigrating to Canada will generally be considered residents for Canadian tax purposes. Under the current tax system in Canada, individuals are taxed on their world wide income if they are considered to be residents of Canada.)

[¶2115] RESIDENCY

The determination of an individual's residency status is a question of fact and is often difficult to resolve with confidence. Several factors are normally taken into account by the CRA. These are discussed in detail in ¶115 and ¶117.

[¶2115.05] *Impact of Tax Treaties on Residence Status*

It is possible for an individual to be considered resident of more than one country under Canada's domestic law; this situation has parallels in many other countries. In such a situation an individual could be subject to double taxation. Relief from this situation is provided by the various income tax conventions which Canada has signed with other countries. These conventions for the most part will provide a determinacy of residency between the two countries that will override domestic law.

Under the *Income Tax Act* (Act), if you are resident in both Canada and a country with which Canada has a tax treaty, Canada will follow the rules in that treaty to determine whether you are resident in Canada. If the treaty rules would make you resident in the other country, Canada deems you to be a non-resident of Canada. This rule is discussed in detail at ¶116. Tax treaties are also discussed at ¶2005 and ¶2007.

A list of the countries with which Canada has treaties can be found on the CRA website at http://www.cra-arc.gc.ca/treaties.

Under the terms of many of Canada's tax agreements, certain residents of Canada may be exempt from Canadian tax. For instance, an individual who is resident in Canada only because he or she is employed by a foreign government in an official or quasi-official capacity may be exempt from taxation in Canada. Employees of foreign embassies are often covered by this rule.

[¶2117] IMPLICATIONS OF ESTABLISHING CANADIAN RESIDENCY

Canada's taxation system is based on residency. Residents of Canada are subject to taxation on their world wide incomes while non-residents are only subject to taxation on certain types of income (essentially, on income considered to be generated in Canada; see Chapter 20). When an individual establishes residency, the provisions of the Act generally attempt to put the individual in a position such that gains or losses accrued prior to establishing residence, which are not taxable to a non-resident, are not taxable in Canada, even if they are realized while resident.

For the year of immigration (i.e., when residency in Canada begins), individuals should use the "General Income Tax and Benefit Guide" for the province or territory where they resided on December 31 of that year.

[¶2117.05] *Deemed Acquisition Rules*

Canadian tax rules deem an individual who establishes Canadian residence to have disposed of and immediately reacquired each property owned (subject to the exceptions listed below) at proceeds equal to fair market value immediately before the time of arrival. Accordingly, gains or losses accrued prior to becoming a Canadian resident are irrelevant to Canadian tax liability when the property is later disposed of. The immigrant will calculate eventual capital gain or loss based on fair market value at the date of immigration.

(1) Exceptions

There is an exception from the deemed disposition and reacquisition rules for certain kinds of property. This exception is provided because, in most cases, future gains or income from this property are taxable to a non-resident of Canada. In these circumstances, the historical adjusted cost base of the non-resident is retained. Common examples include:

- real property situated in Canada;
- real property, eligible capital property, and inventory of business carried on in Canada;

> **Commentary on Bill C-29 Measures (Oct. 25, 2016)**
>
> Note: When Bill C-29, October 25, 2016, achieves Royal Assent, the commentary will be modified to read:
>
> - real property, prior to 2017, eligible capital property and after 2016 property included in Class 14.1, and inventory of business carried on in Canada;

- certain shares of a private corporation which is resident in Canada;
- certain shares of public corporations;
- a Canadian resource property; and
- an "excluded right or interest" (see ¶2153.25), other than an interest in a non-resident testamentary trust that was never acquired for consideration.

Note that where property is moved from a foreign business and put to use in a Canadian business, change of use rules apply giving the property a cost base in Canada equal to its current fair market value at the time, or providing a suitable inventory adjustment.

(ITA: 115; 128.1(4), (10); IT-262R2 [Archived]; IT-451R [Archived])

[¶2119] IMMIGRATION TRUST

Many individuals who immigrate to Canada have significant investment income that would ordinarily be subject to Canada's tax rates after establishing Canadian residency. Historically, investment income could be sheltered from Canadian taxation through the use of a non-resident trust for a period of up to 60 months, provided income earned was not distributed to a Canadian resident who was the settlor.

This mechanism allowed immigrating individuals to set up non-resident trusts for up to 60 months without attracting the trust deemed residency rules. The Department of Finance did away with this exception in its 2014 federal Budget. The exception no longer applies to taxation years ending after February 10, 2014. However, if a non-resident trust was in existence before February 11, 2014 and was subject to the exception immediately before that day, the exception will continue to apply to taxation years ending before 2015, provided that no further contributions were made to the trust after February 10, 2014.

Under the new rules, a trust that is otherwise not resident in Canada will be deemed to be resident in Canada and potentially subject to Canadian income tax on its worldwide income if it has a "resident contributor" or "resident beneficiary". Canada will likely dispute any attempts for relief under a tax treaty under competent authority determinations of trust residency.

Note also the reporting requirements at ¶495 and ¶496.

(ITA: 94; see especially 94(3), (4); Income Tax Folio: S6-F1-C1 Residence of a Trust or Estate; ITTN: 38 No. 38)

[¶2121] EMPLOYMENT INCOME

Generally, Canada taxes employment income upon receipt. If an individual earns employment income abroad while non-resident but is not paid until becoming a Canadian resident, the individual will be taxable in Canada. The individual will likely receive a foreign tax credit; however, there may be a net cost to the individual, given Canada's high tax rates. It is therefore a good tax planning technique to ensure that income related to employment outside of Canada is received by the taxpayer prior to establishing residency.

The courts have not always supported the above position. In one case, the taxpayer was employed by an oil company in Libya for four years and during that time was a non-resident of Canada. While a non-resident employee he put 10% of his salary in a "Thrift Plan" run by his employer. About a month after returning to Canada and becoming (again) a Canadian resident, he received from the plan a refund of his contributions plus approximately $50,000 representing his Libyan employer's contributions with interest. The plan was structured to ensure that the employee could only receive full benefits if he remained with the company for three years. The CRA sought to tax the employer contributions and interest received while in Canada, arguing that income from employment is taxable at the time of receipt. The Tax Court of Canada ruled that the amounts were clearly related to a source outside Canada and were earned while the employee was a non-resident, and were not subject to Canadian tax. The Court said that a different result might occur if the cash payment had been long delayed or paid out as a series of payments. The case perhaps stands as much for a warning to collect such payments while still resident in a low-tax jurisdiction as for the principle that the time of payment is unimportant.

(ITA: 5(1); *Hewitt v. M.N.R.*, 89 DTC 451 (T.C.C.))

[¶2123] STOCK OPTIONS

As discussed at ¶330, Canada taxes the benefit realized on the exercise of a stock option as employment income, either when an option is exercised (non-CCPC) or when the shares are sold (CCPC). Where a non-resident comes to Canada with foreign stock options which are exercised here, there is a significant risk of Canadian taxation and uncertainty over treaty application. Depending on the individual's situation, it may be good tax planning to exercise the options prior to establishing residence or to hold on to them throughout the stay in Canada, if the individual expects to be only a temporary resident. The relative benefit of exercising the stock options will partially depend on the individual's marginal rate in the country of origin.

Further problems can arise related to the timing of income recognition of a stock option and the sourcing of that income. For example, if the country of origin taxes the individual at a time other than that of exercise, double taxation may result. In some cases, the country of origin will delay taxation until the time of disposal of the related shares. If the individual exercises the option in a year but does not dispose of the shares until a later year, the benefit may be taxed in both countries in different years, with a mismatch of foreign income and foreign taxes. The amount of double tax would depend on the rules of the country of origin and on what other taxes are paid to the country of origin. Canada does not allow a carry-over of non-business foreign tax credits.

In terms of allocating employee stock option benefits to Canada or a foreign country, the CRA follows the guidelines set out in paragraphs 12 to 12.15 of the Commentary on Article 15 of the OECD Model Income Tax Convention. Under those guidelines, a stock option benefit is apportioned to each source country based on the number of days of employment exercised in that country over the total number of days in the period during which the employment services from which the stock option is derived are exercised. In making this determination, a stock option benefit is generally presumed to relate to the period of employment that is required as a condition for the employee to acquire the right to exercise the option (i.e., the "vesting period"). Further, a stock option benefit is generally presumed not to relate to past services, unless there is evidence to indicate that past services are relevant in the particular circumstances However, where the terms of the option agreement are such that the grant of the option is treated as a transfer of ownership of the securities (e.g. because the options were in-the-money or not subject to a substantial vesting period), the CRA may attribute the benefit accordingly (CRA document no. 2012-0459411C6).

See also the information under the subheading "Stock Options and Non-Residents" in ¶330 and the discussion of the treatment for employment exercised in Canada and the United States under "U.S. Treaty Changes" in ¶2005.10 and ¶2021.10.

These issues resulting from a timing mismatch may also apply to deferred compensation other than stock options. It is important to have a good understanding of what plans an employee participates in prior to their establishing Canadian residency to be able to advise them on such concerns.

(ITA: 7)

[¶2125] REASONABLE ALLOWANCE FOR BOARD, LODGING, AND TRANSPORTATION FOR EMPLOYMENT AT A SPECIAL WORK SITE OR REMOTE LOCATION

Employees on short-term international transfers are often provided with housing and meals. In general, the value of board and lodging and transportation to and from the job are included in the employee's income (as is an allowance therefor). The same is true for amounts paid to reimburse outlays by the employee for meals, lodging, transportation, or other items which are personal or living expenses.

However, these items are exempt where the employee is at a "special work site" or "remote location".

For further details see ¶360 and ¶361.

(ITA: 6(6); IT-91R4 [Archived])

[¶2127] FOREIGN PENSION PLANS

When an individual immigrates to Canada, the employer may or may not be able to continue contributing to a foreign pension plan on behalf of the employee without triggering Canadian tax consequences. Provided the individual has not been a resident of Canada for greater than 60 months in the preceding 72 months and the individual was a member of the foreign plan prior to establishing Canadian residence, contributions to the plan by an employer are not subject to tax. However, membership in this type of foreign plan will diminish the ability to utilize Canadian tax-deferred savings plans, including RRSPs, RPPs and DPSPs (see ¶2614a for details).

If an individual is a resident of Canada for in excess of 60 of the preceding 72 months, contributions to a foreign pension plan may still be exempt from Canadian taxation. Provided an election is filed by the employer, the individual was a plan member prior to attaining residency and is not a member of an RPP, or DPSP, the plan contributions will remain exempt from Canadian tax.

It should be noted that there is filing requirements for employers related to a foreign pension plan where contributions are made on behalf of an employee resident in Canada.

Distributions received from a foreign pension plan, while an individual is a resident of Canada, are generally taxable in Canada.

For immigrants from the United States, and subject to certain conditions, deductible contributions may be made to the immigrant's 401(k) or similar pension plan for up to 60 months while the emigrant is employed in Canada, if the contributions are attributable to the employment services rendered in Canada (see ¶365a).

(ITA: 6(1)(*a*), (*g*); 56(1); 207.6; 248(1) "retirement compensation arrangement" and "employee benefit plan")

[¶2129] MOVING EXPENSES

Generally, moving expenses are not deductible for moves into and out of Canada. One exception to this general rule is that students leaving Canada to study full-time at a post-secondary educational institution are entitled to deduct moving expenses from scholarships, fellowships, and similar awards, but only to the extent that these amounts are included in income (as discussed at ¶953, most scholarships and fellowships are no longer included in income). In addition, persons who are absent from Canada but are deemed residents or factual residents of Canada can claim moving expenses on a move to or from Canada. In planning a move for employment purposes outside of Canada, it is advisable that an employer reimburse an employee for moving expenses. Moving expense reimbursements are not taxable to an employee on a move within or outside Canada, provided that the expenses reimbursed are reasonable in the circumstances and are necessitated by the move (see ¶2562).

(ITA: 62; 64.1; IT-420R3 [Archived]; Income Tax Folio: S1-F3-C4, "Moving Expenses"; S2-F3-C2 Benefits and Allowances Received from Employment)

[¶2131] RENTAL INCOME

When an individual immigrates to Canada, he or she will often rent out his or her home in his or her home country. Rental income on a foreign property is included in a resident taxpayer's Canadian income. By the same token, a taxpayer may deduct rental losses from ordinary income provided there is a reasonable expectation of profit.

When the individual returns to his or her home country, ceasing Canadian residency, he or she will often re-inhabit that rental property. Where that residence is vacated by the tenant before the taxpayer leaves Canada, there may be a change of use under Canadian rules, resulting in recapture of capital cost allowance (CCA) and a capital gain in Canada. The gain may (or may not) be treaty-protected; the recapture is likely to be taxable. Care should be taken not to trigger a change of use before departure, unless the change confers a benefit (where there is little recapture and an inherent capital loss).

(ITA: 3; 9; 13; 18(1)(a); 45)

[¶2133] EQUALIZATION PAYMENTS

Many international employers that transfer employees in and out of Canada have programs that are intended to "equalize" the employee's standard of living so that he or she can afford approximately the same lifestyle as in the home country. These programs typically use convoluted calculations to arrive at the equalization amount. Transferees to Canada may be equalized for a number of things, Canada's high rates of tax usually chief among them.

These equalization payments, however calculated, usually take the form of additional remuneration to the employee. At one time, it was accepted that such remuneration was itself subject to Canadian tax, and further calculations were done to account for the extra tax on the extra income so that what the employee took home at the end of the day (or month or year) left the employee in the desired "equal" after-tax position (i.e., a gross-up).

In recent years, a number of cases involving the reimbursements of Canadian employees for moving expenses (see ¶1045) suggested to tax advisers and employers that perhaps not all equalization payments were subject to tax after all. Those cases, generally involving a subsidy of higher mortgage rates where an employee moved to another area of Canada where housing was more expensive, seemed to suggest that employer reimbursements intended merely to leave the employee no worse off might not be taxable.

A case on this issue in the context of equalization payments reached the Canadian court system in 1996, and the court gave the taxpayer's argument short shrift. It found the equalization payment to be part of compensation, within the definition of remuneration for employment services, and as such fully subject to tax. See *Gernhart v. The Queen*, 96 DTC 1672 (T.C.C.), tersely affirmed by the Federal Court of Appeal, 98 DTC 6026.

[¶2134] INFORMATION REPORTING RE: FOREIGN ASSETS

Establishing (or re-establishing) Canadian residency causes an individual to become subject to various information reporting requirements with respect to foreign assets (see ¶496). Failure to file the necessary forms in Canada on a timely basis can subject a taxpayer to penalties and interest. Although a first-year exemption exists for individuals that have never been resident in Canada in a previous year, this exemption does not apply to returning Canadians. When advising taxpayers, it is important to have a good understanding of their history and the assets they are retaining in foreign countries to be aware of these potential reporting requirements.

(ITA: 233 to 233.7)

[¶2135] CONCLUSION

The tax consequences of establishing Canadian residency may impose a variety of ordinary and extraordinary tax costs on an individual. These costs may often be reduced with adequate tax planning prior to the move. The planning considerations will differ substantially depending on an individual's circumstances. Any individual planning a move to Canada should seek the advice of a tax professional. See the establishing residence checklist at ¶2195 for a summary of some of the planning considerations discussed in this section.

CANADIAN TAXATION OF EMIGRANTS

[¶2140] INTRODUCTION

(This section discusses the tax implications of an individual moving from Canada. Whether there are any Canadian tax implications when an individual moves from Canada depends primarily on whether the individual is able to cease status as a "factual resident" (¶115) of Canada or is deemed to cease residence (¶116). Under the current tax system in Canada, an individual is taxed on worldwide income if he or she is resident, but only on Canadian-source income (as discussed in Chapter 20) if not resident.

[¶2151] RESIDENCY

See ¶115, ¶116, ¶117, and ¶2125 for a general discussion of this issue.

An individual leaving Canada will often want to be considered a non-resident, although (especially in view of the departure tax (¶2153)) this may not always be true. However, as a practical matter, in disputes with the CRA the issue is usually whether the departing Canadian has truly become non-resident. Under Canadian domestic law, cessation of residency is most often evidenced by:

- renting out or selling Canadian personal-use real estate, so that a residence is not available in Canada.
- spending minimal time in Canada.
- closing Canadian bank and brokerage accounts (other than deferred income plans).
- ensuring that remaining financial institutions are informed of the change in residency.
- advising clubs or professional associations of the change in status from a resident member to a

non-resident member or discontinuing such memberships.

- cancelling provincial health care coverage.

These strategies are not necessary where the taxpayer moves to a treaty country and was already considered a resident there under the rules of that treaty; see ¶116.

(S5-F1-C1, "Determining an Individual's Residence Status")

[¶2153] IMPLICATIONS OF CEASING RESIDENCY

Canada's taxation system is based on residency. Residents of Canada are subject to taxation on their worldwide income while non-residents are only subject to taxation on certain types of Canadian-source income (see Chapter 20).

[¶2153.05] *Filing Requirement*

If you emigrate from Canada owning (at the time of departure) assets with a fair market value of more than $25,000, you are required to file form T1161 by the date you would normally file your tax return for the year of departure. The requirement is independent of the tax return requirement; that is, you must file form T1161 regardless of whether you must otherwise file a return for the year of emigration. For more detail, see the subheading "Special Filing Requirements" below.

[¶2153.10] *Departure Tax*

Where you cease to be a Canadian resident, you are deemed to dispose of and reacquire immediately before ceasing Canadian residence all your property except:

(1) real property situated in Canada, Canadian resource property, and timber resource property;

(2) capital property used in, eligible capital property in respect of, or property described in the inventory of, a business you carried on through a permanent establishment (¶1440) in Canada immediately before departure, and the definition of permanent establishment at ¶1440 will be modified for purposes of this rule to provide:

> **Commentary on Bill C-29 Measures (Oct. 25, 2016)**
>
> Note: When Bill C-29, October 25, 2016, achieves Royal Assent, the commentary will be modified to read:
>
> (2) capital property used in, prior to 2017, eligible capital property and after 2016 property included in Class 14.1 in respect of, or property described in the inventory of, a business you carried on through a permanent establishment (¶1440) in Canada immediately before departure, and the definition of permanent establishment at ¶1440 will be modified for purposes of this rule to provide:

- that where no fixed place of business, there is a permanent establishment at the principal place at which the business is conducted, and
- that if you become resident in a country with which Canada has a tax treaty, the definition of permanent establishment in the treaty will govern.

(3) an "excluded right or interest" (¶2153.12);

(4) if you had not been resident in Canada for more than 60 months (five years) during the 120 months (10 years) ending at the time you again become a non-resident, property you owned at the time you last became a Canadian resident or property left to you by inheritance or bequest after you last became a Canadian resident (see "Departing Short-Term Resident", below); and

(5) taxable Canadian property still held on your return to Canada if, after a period of non-residency, you return to Canada and elect to unwind the deemed departure tax, as discussed under the subheading "Returning Non-Resident" below.

(ITA: 128.1(4)(*a.1*), (*b*))

[¶2153.11] *Election to Deem Disposition of Exempt Property*

You may, within limits, elect to recognize a deemed disposition of properties in (1) or (2) above. You would normally do this to recognize a latent loss in the property on which you elect, and so offset gains which arise under the other rules. Any property on which you make the election is deemed to be disposed of at fair market value, but the losses recognized on such deemed dispositions cannot exceed the increase in your income arising from other deemed dispositions.

This approach may be advantageous, particularly for a principal residence, depending on the anticipated future gains. Since the deemed disposition can also set the U.S. tax basis of the property, it may be worthwhile in this circumstance as well, so that the United States will forgo taxation of gains accrued prior to immigration (¶2190.20).

(ITA: 128.1(4)(*d*))

[¶2153.12] *Excluded Right or Interest*

An "excluded right or interest" of a taxpayer who is an individual means:

(*a*) a right of the individual under, or an interest of the individual in a trust governed by,

(i) a registered retirement savings plan or a plan referred to in subsection 146(12) as an "amended plan",

(ii) a registered retirement income fund,

(iii) a registered education savings plan,

(iii.1) a registered disability savings plan,

(iii.2) a TFSA,

(iv) a deferred profit sharing plan or a plan referred to in subsection 147(15) as a "revoked plan",

(v) an employees profit sharing plan,

(vi) an employee benefit plan (other than a plan described in subparagraph (*b*)(i) or (ii)),

(vi.1) an employee life and health trust,

(vii) a plan or arrangement (other than an employee benefit plan) under which the individual has a right to receive in a year remuneration in respect of services rendered by the individual in the year or a prior year,

(viii) a superannuation or pension fund or plan (other than an employee benefit plan),

(ix) a retirement compensation arrangement,

(x) a foreign retirement arrangement, or

(xi) a registered supplementary unemployment benefit plan;

(*b*) a right of the individual to a benefit under an employee benefit plan that is

(i) a plan or arrangement described in paragraph (*j*) of the definition "salary deferral arrangement" in subsection 248(1) that would, but for paragraphs (*j*) and (*k*) of that definition, be a salary deferral arrangement, or

(ii) a plan or arrangement that would, but for paragraph 6801(*c*) of the *Income Tax Regulations*, be a salary deferral arrangement,

to the extent that the benefit can reasonably be considered to be attributable to services rendered by the individual in Canada;

(*c*) a right of the individual under an agreement referred to in subsection 7(1);

(*d*) a right of the individual to a retiring allowance;

(*e*) a right of the individual under, or an interest of the individual in, a trust that is

(i) an employee trust,

(ii) an amateur athlete trust,

(iii) a cemetery care trust, or

(iv) a trust governed by an eligible funeral arrangement;

(*f*) a right of the individual to receive a payment under

(i) an annuity contract, or

(ii) an income-averaging annuity contract;

(*g*) a right of the individual to a benefit under

(i) the *Canada Pension Plan* or a provincial plan described in section 3 of that Act,

(ii) the *Old Age Security Act*, or

(iv) a plan or arrangement instituted by the social security legislation of a country other than Canada or of a state, province or other political subdivision of such a country;

(*h*) a right of the individual to a benefit described in any of subparagraphs 56(1)(*a*)(iii) to (vi);

(*i*) a right of the individual to a payment out of a NISA Fund No. 2;

(*j*) an interest of the individual in a personal trust resident in Canada if the interest was never acquired for consideration and did not arise as a consequence of a qualifying disposition by the individual (within the meaning that would be assigned by subsection 107.4(1) if that subsection were read without reference to paragraphs 107.4(1)(*h*) and (*i*));

(*k*) an interest of the individual in a non-resident testamentary trust if the interest was never acquired for consideration; or

(*l*) an interest of the individual in a life insurance policy in Canada, except for that part of the policy in respect of which the individual is deemed by paragraph 138.1(1)(*e*) to have an interest in a related segregated fund trust.

(ITA: 128.1(10) "excluded right or interest")

[¶2153.13] *Special Valuation Rules*

Where you own shares of a corporation which owns a life insurance policy under which your life is insured, upon the deemed disposition at departure of your shares in the corporation, a special rule (contained in subsection 70(5.3)) is used in the valuation of the corporation's shares: the cash surrender value of the life insurance policy owned by the corporation is treated as the fair market value of that policy.

[¶2153.14] *Deemed Year End for a Business*

Where you are carrying on a business at the time of emigration (otherwise than through a permanent establishment in Canada), the fiscal period of the business is deemed to have ended immediately before the emigration time and a new fiscal period of the business is deemed to have begun at the emigration time. This ensures the appropriate measurement of your pre-departure income or loss from the business. You are allowed to choose a new fiscal period of the business. The usual rules restricting businesses to a calendar year do not operate for a business that is not carried on in Canada.

[¶2153.20] *Deemed Disposition of Exempt Property*

Where property escaping tax on departure (due to use in a business carried on in Canada) commences to be used in a business carried on outside Canada, there is a deemed disposition of the property at that time for Canadian tax purposes. This may result in capital gain or loss, recapture, or inventory adjustments.

(ITA: 10(12)–(14), 45(1)(*d*))

[¶2153.30] *Instalments*

A specific rule excludes interest on instalment payments for the year of departure to the extent the instalment liability arises from the deemed disposition rules above.

(ITA: 128.1(5))

[¶2153.35] *Security in Lieu of Tax*

You may choose to post security in lieu of paying tax on the departure gain on any particular property. You have until the balance-due date for the year of emigration to either pay the tax or post the security.

The security remains in place until the property is actually disposed of so that there will be proceeds to pay the tax, or until you return to Canada and unwind the tax. The CRA has discretion to extend the deadline for posting security.

The nature of the security posted is negotiated with CRA and can include a variety of assets. The CRA has suggested it will accept private company shares as security for the gain on those shares where "the shares' value can be ensured", presumably against having the underlying value stripped out by the non-resident.

You do not have to post security if the value of the taxable capital gain is less than $50,000.

(ITA: 220(4.51)–(4.54); Other Publications: Department of Finance Technical Notes of June 15, 2000 and March 16, 2001)

[¶2153.40] *Departing Short-Term Resident*

If you have been resident in Canada for 60 months or less during the 10-year period preceding the cessation of Canadian residence, you are not deemed to have disposed of any property you owned on becoming resident in Canada or received by inheritance or bequest while resident. That is, a short-term resident may take out the property he or she came in with or inherited while here, free of departure tax.

This rule operates on a property-by-property basis, discouraging the rearrangement of investment portfolios while resident in Canada.

Short-term residents who own shares on immigration and receive replacement shares under specified tax deferred rollover rules (i.e., under sections 51, 85.1(1), 85.1(8), 86, or 87) are deemed to have the replacement shares considered to be the same shares they arrived with, allowing the replacement shares to qualify for this exemption on emigration within five years.

(ITA: 128.1(4)(*b*)(iv); 128.3; Other Publications: Department of Finance Technical Notes of March 16, 2001)

[¶2153.45] *Returning Non-Resident*

If, having emigrated from Canada after October 1, 1996, you become a Canadian resident again, you can elect to unwind the deemed disposition (and the corresponding deemed reacquisition on becoming a resident of Canada). Anti-avoidance rules attempt to deny losses arising from the extraction of dividends while a non-resident.

There are separate elections for taxable Canadian property and for all other property, and you can make either or both (or none). Once made, an election covers all property of that type.

The elections apply to property you owned at the time of emigration and throughout the period of non-residency. Replacement shares received on a specified Canadian statutory rollover (sections 51, 85.1(1), 85.1(8), 86, and 87 are specified) are in effect deemed to be a continuation of the original property for this purpose.

The following discussion concerns only "other property". For a discussion of the taxable Canadian property rules for returning non-residents, see ¶2153.60, below.

Once you make the election, it applies to all property you owned at the time of emigration and throughout the non-resident period that would normally be subject to a deemed acquisition on immigration (¶2117). For all such property, the election adjusts, on a property-by-property basis, both the proceeds of disposition that were deemed to arise as a consequence of the deemed disposition on your earlier emigration, and the deemed acquisition cost on immigration.

Each of these amounts is adjusted by subtracting the least of:

- the amount that would otherwise be your gain on the property as a result of the deemed disposition on emigration;
- the fair market value of the property immediately before you become resident in Canada; and
- any other amount you specify.

As a result of these adjustments, the returning individual can defer Canadian tax on any gain that had accrued before emigration, while still protecting from Canadian tax gains that accrued during periods of non-residency.

Example (from Department of Finance explanatory notes)

Noah emigrates from Canada in 1999. Noah owns shares of a foreign corporation. When Noah leaves, the shares have a fair market value of $25,000 and an adjusted cost base of $15,000, for an accrued gain of $10,000. In 2012, Noah returns to Canada. At that time the shares have a fair market value of $80,000. Noah chooses to take advantage of the election to control the tax consequences of ceasing to be a Canadian resident. Because he had a capital loss in 1999 of $7,000 from another source, Noah is content to realize a $7,000 capital gain on emigration, but he does not want to realize the other $3,000 accrued gain. Noah therefore chooses an elected amount of $3,000.

Noah's proceeds of disposition on emigration are deemed to be $22,000, being the proceeds of disposition that would otherwise be determined under paragraph 128.1(4)(*b*) ($25,000) minus the least of:

- the amount that would have been Noah's gain on the shares on emigration had this paragraph not applied ($10,000);
- the fair market value of the property at the particular time ($80,000); and
- the elected amount specified ($3,000).

Noah thus reduces his emigration-year gain to $7,000. The same $3,000 that reduces Noah's emigration proceeds is also subtracted from his reacquisition cost on immigration ($80,000), leaving his new adjusted cost base in respect of the property $77,000. The property thus has a latent gain of $3,000 at the time Noah re-establishes Canadian residence.

Noah could have deferred tax on the full $10,000 gain that accrued before emigration, by increasing his elected amount in respect of the shares to $10,000.

Five points should be noted about these rules. First, because there is no certain way of knowing which emigrants will return to Canada, this rule does not directly affect the obligations that arise on emigration. Rather, the rule allows the returning individual retrospectively to modify the obligations. As a practical matter, it is expected that most individuals who plan to return to Canada will use the security provisions discussed above to defer payment of any tax arising as a result of emigration. In that case, the main effect will be to allow the security to be given back intact to the returning emigrant.

Second, these rules do not affect any interest or penalties owing by an individual, including interest and penalties levied on taxes in respect of the individual's emigration, calculated without reference to the rule.

Third, the taxable Canadian property rules (discussed below at ¶2153.60) include features designed to prevent surplus-stripping. Without these features, a resident of Canada could use a temporary period of non-residency to extract, as dividends subject only to low-rate withholding tax, value that represents accrued gains.

Fourth, the rules require separate elections in respect of taxable Canadian property and other property. The effects of the elections differ: an election on taxable Canadian properties removes those properties from the deemed disposition and reacquisition on emigration, subject to dividend stripping rules. An election on other property adjusts the emigration proceeds of disposition and the returning adjusted cost base of the other properties. Each election covers all property of the given sort, but the returning individual may choose to make one election and not the other.

Fifth, failure to make the election will result in a deemed reacquisition of the property at fair market value on immigration, which will itself have tax consequences, such as the potential denial of intervening declines in value.

The unwinding election is subject to the provisions permitting late-filed elections at the discretion of the CRA, discussed in ¶268.

For more on taxable Canadian property election, see ¶2153.60, below.

(ITA: 128.1(6); 128.3; Other Publications: Department of Finance Technical Notes of June 15, 2000 and March 16, 2001)

[¶2153.50] *Returning Trust Beneficiary*

A similar treatment is prescribed for an individual (other than a trust) who:

- emigrates from Canada while being a trust beneficiary;
- receives distributions of trust property as a non-resident; and then
- re-establishes residence in Canada while still owning the property.

This treatment parallels the returning-resident rules described above. In general terms, the rules allow the beneficiary and the trust to jointly elect, upon the beneficiary's return to Canada, to unwind the tax consequences to the trust that occurred when it distributed the property to the non-resident beneficiary.

A number of conditions must be met for the application of these rules:

- the individual must have first been a resident of Canada and subsequently ceased to be resident in Canada after October 1, 1996;
- the individual must have been a beneficiary of the trust at the time he or she ceased to be resident in Canada;
- the distribution must occur after October 1, 1996 and before the individual re-establishes residence in Canada;
- the distribution must be such that subsection 107(2) of the Act would have applied but for subsection 107(5); and
- the individual must re-establish residence in Canada after October 1, 1996 while still owning the property distributed by the trust.

Where these conditions are met, the rules provide an election for taxable Canadian property similar to the election provided above for a returning resident. There are anti-stripping rules similar to those discussed below. There is an election for property other than taxable Canadian property, similar to that above for returning non-residents.

If the trust ceases to exist before the individual's filing-due date for his or her taxation year during which he or she re-establishes residence in Canada, the elections or specifications can be made by the individual alone. However, the individual and the trust will then be jointly and severally liable for any amount payable under the Act by the trust as a result of the election or specification.

Any assessment of tax can be made that is necessary for these elections to be taken into account, but no such assessment shall affect the computation of interest or penalties payable.

(ITA: 128.1(7); Other Publications: Department of Finance Technical Notes of June 15, 2000 and March 16, 2001)

[¶2153.55] *Declines in Value after Emigration*

There is a difficulty with the deemed disposition rules. You may have purchased a property while a resident, and the property may have increased in value by the date you ceased Canadian residency. At that point, you had a deemed disposition on a property, giving rise to tax. Subsequently, while you were a non-resident, the value of the property declined. In this case, you would have been taxed on a gain which you never realized.

To deal with this problem, there is a loss carryback rule. The carryback is available regardless of how many years later the actual disposition occurs. However, these rules apply only to taxable Canadian property (TCP). The definition of TCP was narrowed effective March 4, 2010, so that several types of property no longer qualify. As an example, shares of private corporations generally are not TCP.

Under these rules, you may elect to reduce the proceeds of disposition of a taxable Canadian property that were deemed to arise on deemed dispositions on emigration by the least of:

- an amount you specify;
- the amount that would otherwise be your gain from the deemed disposition of the property at the time of emigration; and
- the amount that would be your loss from the disposition of the property at the time the property is actually disposed of, if the loss were determined with reference to every other provision in the Canadian *Income Tax Act* (including the stop-loss rules in subsection 40(3.7) (discussed below) and section 112 of the Act (¶580d)).

The same amount is added to your proceeds of disposition realized at the time of actual disposition.

Example (from Department of Finance explanatory notes)

Odile emigrated from Canada in 2006, owning a capital interest in a trust resident in Canada that she purchased in 2004. The interest has a fair market value at the emigration time of $150,000 and an adjusted cost base of $40,000, for a latent gain of $110,000 on departure. Odile's tax is assessed on that basis, and she posts security for the tax.

In 2009, Odile sells her trust interest for $60,000. Since Odile has realized a smaller gain than assumed in her tax assessment on emigration, she elects to reduce the gain she was deemed to have realized when she emigrated.

To obtain the maximum benefit from the subsection, Odile specifies an amount of $90,000 in respect of the election. Her proceeds of disposition at the emigration time are deemed to be $60,000, being the proceeds of disposition that would otherwise be determined on emigration ($150,000) minus the least of:

- the amount specified ($90,000);
- the amount that was originally her taxable gain in respect of the trust interest on emigration ($110,000); and
- the amount that would have been her loss on actual disposition of the trust interest had this rule not applied ($150,000 - $60,000 = $90,000).

The same $90,000 amount is added to Odile's proceeds of the actual disposition of the trust interest. The result is that, in respect of the trust interest, Odile is treated as having realized a $20,000 gain in 2006, and no gain or loss on the actual disposition of the property in 2009.

If, while you are abroad, shares you held at departure are replaced by shares received under a specified statutory Canadian rollover (sections 51, 85.1(1), 85.1(8), 86, and 87 are specified), the replacement shares are in effect deemed to be a continuation of the original shares, and this election should apply on disposition of the replacement shares.

This election does not affect any interest or penalties owing by the individual at the time of making the election, including interest and penalties levied on taxes in respect of the property, calculated without reference to the subsection.

A consequential amendment to the statute-barred rules ensures that any necessary assessments of tax will be made in order to take account of this carryback.

The election is to be made in writing in the taxpayer's return of income for the taxation year that includes the time of disposition. Apart from the transitional rule below, there is no provision for late-filing this election. On the other hand, where no timely return is filed for the year of disposition at all, and consequently no assessment or determination of loss is ever issued for the year, it is arguable that there is no machinery to start the statute of limitation running. This rule applies to changes in residence that occur after October 1, 1996.

(ITA: 128.1(8); 128.3; 152(6)(f.1), 248(1) "taxable Canadian property"; Other Publications: Department of Finance Technical Notes of June 15, 2000 and March 16, 2001)

[¶2153.60] *Stop-Loss Rules and Offsetting Credit Where Property Declines in Value after Emigration*

In solving the decline in value problem discussed above, another was created. If the decline in value of shares has been caused by stripping out the assets of the company as dividends at low withholding tax rates, the loss may cause an unfair recovery of tax. The solution to this is a stop-loss rule which reduces the loss recognized on eventual disposition to the extent dividends have been paid during a period of non-residency. The reduction operates regardless of whether the taxpayer has again become resident at the time the loss is recognized.

If you have become a non-resident of Canada and you later re-establish Canadian residence, you can elect, in respect of all the taxable Canadian property you held at the time of departure and throughout the period of non-residency, to unwind the original deemed disposition. The effect of making the election on taxable Canadian property is that the original deemed disposition of this property on last ceasing residence is deemed not to have occurred. (There is a separate election for other property, also discussed under the heading "Returning Non-Resident" at ¶2153.45 above.) Note that failure to make the election will result in a deemed reacquisition of the property at fair market value on immigration, which will itself have tax consequences, such as the potential denial of intervening declines in value. The election is subject to the provisions permitting late-filed elections at the discretion of the CRA, discussed in ¶268.

If, after leaving Canada and realizing a gain on shares, you received dividends on those shares as a non-resident, and you then return to Canada and make an election on taxable Canadian property to unwind the original election, special surplus-stripping rules apply in respect of the property covered by the election. The basic purpose is to ensure that gains that accrued before emigration from Canada, and that have been extracted in the form of dividends during the individual's residence abroad, are subject to Canadian tax as gains.

The surplus stripping rules apply, in respect of taxable Canadian property if you have made the election for such property, where two conditions are met:

- a loss has accrued on the property during your period of non-residency; that is, the property's fair market value immediately before you become resident is less than its fair market value when you left Canada; and
- if you had acquired the property for its fair market value on emigration, and disposed of the property immediately before becoming resident, the stop-loss rule for emigrants would reduce the loss.

Where these conditions are met, the rules create four related effects. First, you are treated as having disposed of the property immediately before emigration, notwithstanding the election.

Second, they establish your proceeds of disposition of the property at that time, as the total of:

(1) the adjusted cost base of the property on emigration; and

(2) the amount, if any, by which the notional loss reduction under stop-loss rules exceeds the lesser of (i) the adjusted cost base on emigration, and (ii) an amount you choose.

Third, the rules treat you as having reacquired the property on emigration, at a cost equal to the excess, if any, of the property's adjusted cost base on emigration (the (1) and (2)(i) amount, above) over the lesser of the notional loss reduction under the stop-loss and the amount you have chosen in (2)(ii), above.

The intended result of the second and third effects is that the income (in this case, dividends) that gives rise to the notional stop-loss reduction is recharacterized as gains. Those gains are, subject to election, distributed between the post-return period and the deemed disposition on emigration.

Fourth, the rules treat you, for the purposes of an offsetting tax credit (see ¶2153.61 and the example below), as having disposed of the property immediately before returning to Canada. This ensures that appropriate credit is given for any withholding tax that triggered the application of the rules.

Example (from Department of Finance explanatory notes)

Marie emigrates from Canada in 1999. Marie is the majority shareholder of a Canadian-controlled private corporation (CCPC) when she leaves Canada. The shares, which are taxable Canadian property to Marie, have a fair market value (FMV) at that time of $50,000 and an adjusted cost base (ACB) of $15,000, for a latent gain of $35,000. Marie receives $35,000 of dividends from the CCPC in 2000. In 2001, Marie returns to Canada. At that time, the shares have a FMV of $15,000. Marie uses the unwinding election to minimize the tax consequences of her earlier emigration from Canada.

If Marie actually disposed of the shares immediately before re-establishing Canadian residence, the stop-loss rule of subsection 40(3.7) would reduce her loss. Therefore, the surplus stripping rules apply in respect of the election.

Marie is treated as having disposed of and reacquired the shares on emigration. Assuming she elects $10,000, Marie's emigration proceeds of disposition are deemed to be $40,000, being the emigration ACB ($15,000) plus the difference between the stop-loss reduction ($35,000) and the ACB/specified amount ($10,000). Marie thus realizes a $25,000 capital gain in the emigration year.

Marie's reacquisition cost is deemed to be $5,000, being the original ACB ($15,000) minus the lesser of the subsection 40(3.7) reduction ($35,000) and the specified amount ($10,000). Since the shares have a FMV of $15,000, Marie will eventually realize a gain of $10,000 (subject to other adjustments to ACB and FMV).

The result is that Marie's $25,000 gain on departure and remaining $10,000 latent gain equal the $35,000 she extracted in the form of dividends. The full $35,000 will thus be realized as capital gains, and the special section 119 tax credit will give Marie credit for any withholding tax she paid on the dividends.

Marie could have altered the timing of her capital gains on the shares. For example, if she had elected an amount of $5,000 under paragraph (a) in respect of the property, Marie's emigration proceeds of disposition would have been $45,000 ($15,000 ACB ($35,000 stop-loss reduction - $5,000 elected amount)), giving an emigration gain of $30,000. This would have been balanced by an increase in Marie's reacquisition cost from $5,000 to $10,000, which in turn would reduce the eventual gain Marie will realize on the shares.

(ITA: 40(3.7); 119; 128.1(6); 152(6)(f.1); Other Publications: Department of Finance Technical Notes of December 17, 1999 and March 16, 2001)

[¶2153.61] *Credit for Former Resident Where Stop-Loss Rule Applies*

The stop-loss rule above applies to a former resident who owned shares of a company at the time of emigration and subsequently disposed of those shares, having received dividends on those shares during the period of non-residency. In general terms, the individual's loss otherwise determined on the subsequent disposition is reduced by the amount of such dividends.

Assuming that the property was taxable Canadian property, section 119 provides a credit that can be claimed for the year in which the individual ceased to be resident (the "emigration year"). The amount of the credit is the lesser of two amounts. The first amount is essentially the proportion of the individual's Part I tax payable in the emigration year that the taxable capital gain arising on the deemed disposition of the property (upon the emigration) is of the individual's total income for the emigration year. The second amount is the proportion of the Part XIII tax paid on the dividends received during the period of non-residency that the amount of the loss reduction under the stop-loss rule above is of the total amount of such dividends. The effect of these rules is to limit the credit to the tax paid on the dividends only to the extent that they were subject to the stop-loss rule, and only to the extent of the individual's tax payable on the gain resulting from the deemed disposition of the property at the time of the individual's emigration from Canada.

These rules apply only to TCP. The definition of TCP was narrowed effective March 4, 2010, so that several types of property no longer qualify. As an example, shares of private corporations generally are not TCP.

The credit is available to emigrant taxpayers without regard to the normal or extended reassessment periods. The rule provides that the CRA shall reassess a taxpayer's tax for the emigration year (and any relevant subsequent year) in order to take into account the credit in respect of a disposition in a subsequent year if the taxpayer has filed a tax return for the emigration year, the credit is claimed, and the taxpayer files a prescribed form with the CRA, on or before the filing-due date of the taxpayer for the subsequent year, amending the return. The rule applies to taxation years that end after October 1, 1996. However, for taxation years that end before June 26, 2013, the filing deadline for the prescribed form amending the emigration year return is deemed to have been filed on a timely basis.

The legislation also provides that the credit is included among those taken into account in computing the alternative minimum tax (discussed in Chapter 24).

(ITA: 119; 152(6.3))

[¶2153.70] *Double Taxation and Special Foreign Tax Credit*

Generally speaking, other countries tax the capital gains of their residents based on the historical cost base of the property, i.e., what you originally paid for it. If you buy property as a Canadian resident for $10, and it is valued at $110 on departure, Canada wants capital gain tax on $100. If you move to Country X and sell the property, X also wants tax on the $100 capital gain. Real estate is commonly the only exception to this rule. Not all of Canada's tax treaties recognize Canada's right to tax the accrued gain on other property, which could lead to double taxation.

The Department of Finance has renegotiated many of its recent treaties (including with the U.S. and U.K.) to prevent the appreciation prior to emigration from being taxed in the foreign jurisdiction. Originally intended as a temporary measure, Finance provided a tax credit intended to be used against the foreign taxes paid in this situation where a treaty did not provide relief against the double taxed capital gain. Although there is no expectation on when these interim provisions will be removed, Finance vowed that it "will monitor the need for a definitive expiry date as additional countries implement protection against double taxation in respect of capital gains in renegotiated treaties".

In general, the credit will be given only for foreign taxes that are paid to countries with which Canada has a tax treaty. However, credit will be given for taxes imposed by any foreign country on gains on real property situated in that country.

The credit provided to an individual under the new rule is computed on a property-by-property basis, as the lesser of the following two amounts:

- The total of those portions of the foreign taxes paid in respect of the disposition of the property that can reasonably be considered to relate to the portion of the gain or profit in question that arose before the individual's emigration from Canada: (A) Where the property in question is real property situated outside Canada, the creditable taxes are those paid to the government of the country where the property is located, or to the government of another country in which the individual is resident and with which Canada has a tax treaty; (B) For other property, creditable taxes are those paid to the government of another country in which the individual is resident and with which Canada has a tax treaty. Note that a tax paid to the government of a political subdivision of another country is included for this purpose in the taxes paid to the government of that country under the definitions generally applicable to Canada's foreign tax credit rules.

- The amount of the individual's ordinary income tax for the year of emigration that is attributable to the deemed disposition of the particular property upon emigration. In determining this amount, previous applications of credit are taken into account.

In computing foreign tax on a disposition, you must reduce it for any credit or tax reduction you may be entitled to under the applicable law or a Canadian tax treaty; Canada wants to ensure that it gets tax first if the foreign jurisdiction gives recognition to Canadian taxes paid either on departure or disposition.

Although the property may not be sold until a year after the year of emigration, the Canadian foreign tax credit mentioned above must be claimed by filing an amended return for the year of deemed disposition on emigration. The amended return must be filed by the due date for a Canadian return for the year in which the foreign taxes are paid, regardless of whether a return for that later year is otherwise required.

Under U.S. domestic law, there is no adjustment to the tax basis of an asset upon immigration. Effective September 19, 2000, a Canadian emigrant to the United States may elect under the treaty, for U.S. tax purposes, to increase the U.S. cost basis of an asset to the fair market value as of the date of emigration. This rule applies to assets where there is a Canadian deemed disposition upon emigration from Canada. This parallels the Canadian ACB adjustment upon migration. Canada already had this rule in place for immigrants, so the new treaty rule really only affected migration to the United States.

A similar rule is found in many other treaties, including those with Australia, Belgium, Germany, Greece, Italy, New Zealand and the United Kingdom.

(ITA: 126(2.21), (2.23); 128.1(4)(*b*); 152(6)(*f*.1); Other Publications: Canada–U.S. Income Tax Treaty, Art. XVIII; Rev. Proc 2010-19; Department of Finance Technical Notes of March 16, 2001; Department of Finance News Releases 2000-045, 2000-068)

[¶2153.75] *Special Filing Requirements*

Where you cease to be a Canadian resident and the fair market value of "reportable properties" at the time of departure is greater than $25,000, details of all such properties must be reported.

The information reporting form (T1161) must be filed on or before the individual's filing-due date for the year of emigration from Canada.

Reportable property means any property of the individual *other than* the following:

(1) money that is legal tender in Canada and deposits of such money;

(2) most excluded personal property (as defined under ¶2153.25, above, but the following items must nevertheless be reported: employee options in shares of corporations or in units of mutual fund trusts; interests in personal trusts resident in Canada; and, interests in a life insurance policy in Canada);

(3) for individuals who were resident in Canada for 60 months or less in the 120-month period that precedes the time of emigration, property, other than taxable Canadian property, that was owned by the individual before the individual became resident in Canada or that was acquired by the individual by inheritance or bequest after becoming resident in Canada; and

(4) any item of personal-use property (¶545) the fair market value of which at the time of emigration is less than $10,000.

(ITA: 128.1(9), (10); Other Publications: Department of Finance Technical Notes of December 17, 1999 as restated June 15, 2000 and March 16, 2001)

[¶2153.80] *Registered Retirement Savings Plans*

The ability to save on a tax-deferred basis is one of the most valuable tax planning strategies available to most Canadians. Fortunately, that advantage does not have to be fully forfeited on leaving the country. A taxpayer can leave accumulated RRSPs, which can continue to grow without current Canadian tax.

If an individual collapses an RRSP in the year of but prior to departure it will be taxable in the year of departure at the individual's marginal tax rate. Where a taxpayer wishes to collapse a plan while he or she is a non-resident of Canada, the withdrawal will attract 25% non-resident withholding tax (subject to any applicable tax treaty provisions).

Under certain circumstances, a "section 217" election can be made to reduce the taxation of amounts paid out of an RRSP by a non-resident. Typically, the benefits of this election will only be realized if an individual has relatively low worldwide income, and will report at least 50% of their worldwide income on the tax return, whereby they can claim personal credits on the tax return. Section 217 elections are discussed in greater detail at ¶2086.

The home-country tax laws and the provisions of any applicable income tax convention must be examined when planning for receiving income from an RRSP as a non-resident. For example, the non-resident withholding tax on RRSP payments received in the form of an annuity by a resident of the United States may, depending on the terms of the annuity, be reduced to 15% by the Canada–U.S. Income Tax Treaty. Alternatively, the new country of residence may consider the RRSP to be ineffective in deferring tax.

(ITA: 56(1)(*h*); 146; 212(1)(*l*); 217; Other Publications: Canada–U.S. Income Tax Treaty, Art. XVIII)

[¶2153.85] *Home Buyers' Plans*

If you have withdrawn funds from an RRSP under the Home Buyers' Plan (¶2625.05) and you cease to be a resident of Canada, you have two choices:

(1) include the remaining balance in your income for the year you cease residency; or

(2) repay the remaining balance to your RRSP before the earlier of 60 days after ceasing residency or the date of filing the tax return for the year.

For option 2, as a practical matter, the CRA will generally allow contributions made up to the normal cut-off date (February 28 or March 1). However, this treatment is not an official administrative concession, so one can use it only at one's peril.

(ITA: 146.01(5))

[¶2153.90] *OAS/CPP/QPP*

Payments of Old Age Security, Canada Pension Plan, and Quebec Pension Plan amounts to non-residents are subject to withholding, unless subject to an overriding tax treaty, as discussed at ¶2076 and ¶2080.04.

[¶2153.95] *Other Income*

Non-residents must pay tax on business and employment income earned in Canada at normal Canadian rates, as discussed in detail in Chapter 20.

Most Canadian-source dividend income paid to non-residents is subject to withholding tax in Canada, and it is essential that a departing emigrant notify each Canadian payer of dividends that he or she has ceased to be a Canadian resident. No further Canadian tax will be imposed on this income. Most interest received from arm's-length parties is exempt from Canadian withholding, as discussed in detail at ¶2080.01. The rate of non-resident withholding tax may be reduced by any applicable income tax convention.

For the treatment of other income earned as a non-resident, such as pensions, alimony, and rental income, see ¶2080.

(ITA: 212(1)(*b*), (2))

[¶2155] IMPLICATIONS OF NOT CEASING RESIDENCY

If an individual does not cease Canadian residency under Canadian law and is not provided relief under an income tax convention, there are other mechanisms to which the individual can turn. Where a resident of Canada earns foreign-source employment income, under certain circumstances, an overseas employment tax credit is available to the individual until 2015 before it was fully phased out in 2016 (¶1458). The foreign tax credit mechanism for foreign business and foreign non-business income is still available to prevent double taxation (¶1450 and ¶1455).

(ITA: 122.3; 126(1); IT-497R4 [Archived])

[¶2157] FOREIGN TAX CREDITS OF PART-YEAR RESIDENTS

For the part of the year when an individual is a resident of Canada, the taxpayer will be subject to Canadian taxes on his or her worldwide income. An individual will often earn foreign-source income prior to ceasing Canadian residency. This income may be subject to foreign tax as well as Canadian tax. A part-year resident may claim a foreign tax credit against Canadian income tax for foreign taxes. A separate calculation must be made for each country for which a foreign tax credit is claimed. In addition, a separate computation is required for business and non-business income tax.

In general, an individual will receive a reduction of Canadian tax equal to the lesser of Canadian taxes payable on the foreign-source income and the foreign taxes paid during the year.

For a part-year resident, the foreign taxes paid include the foreign taxes paid for the entire year. However, the foreign income taxable in Canada includes only the foreign income earned during the period of residence in Canada. Foreign-source income earned in the non-resident period is generally exempt from Canadian tax.

When claiming a foreign tax credit, the CRA usually requires proof that the foreign taxes were paid. Where the foreign tax liability is settled by an amount withheld by the payer, a copy of the foreign tax information slip is usually satisfactory. In other cases, a copy of the tax return filed with the foreign government is required, along with copies of receipts of documents establishing payment. Since October 2015, for any foreign tax credit claim for taxes paid in the United States, the CRA requires not only the U.S., state and local tax returns but a copy of federal account transcript and account statement or similar document from state and/or municipal tax authority as proof of payment.

(ITA: 114; 126(1)(*a*); (2)(*a*); CRA Document No.: 2016-0634941C6, 2016 STEP – Q9- Support for US FTC claims; Income Tax Folio: S5-F2-C1 Foreign Tax Credit)

[¶2157.05] *Calculation of Tax*

The tax of a part-year resident is calculated using the same rules, rates, and tax brackets applicable to full-year residents, except that tax credits will be calculated as discussed above and at ¶2107. If an individual ceases to be resident of Canada during the year, the individual is subject to provincial tax of the province of residence immediately before emigration. A full-year non-resident who is subject to Canadian tax (but not provincial tax) is instead subject to federal surtax in lieu of provincial tax; see ¶1445. For instance, capital gains and rents in respect of real estate are subject to this federal surtax.

[¶2159] EMPLOYMENT INCOME AFTER CEASING CANADIAN RESIDENCY

Employment income is treated as Canadian-source income primarily if it relates to services rendered while physically present in Canada, or while resident in Canada. For instance, after ceasing residency in Canada, one could receive a bonus relating to the resident period or exercise a stock option granted prior to emigration.

Generally, if a part-year resident receives Canadian-source employment income while non-resident, then he or she will be taxed by Canada on that income (unless a treaty prohibits taxation).

Where income is earned by a non-resident for duties performed partly inside and partly outside Canada, a reasonable allocation of income is necessary. The allocation is normally calculated on a *per diem* basis. Employment income earned in Canada by a non-resident is generally subject to provincial tax in the province in which it is earned.

Employment income earned in Canada by a non-resident may be exempt from Canadian income tax under an income tax convention. For example, employment income earned by a U.S. resident is exempt from Canadian tax if:

- the remuneration for employment in Canada for the year does not exceed $10,000 (Canadian); or
- both:
  - the employee is present in Canada less than 183 days in any twelve-month period, and
  - the remuneration is not borne by an employer resident in Canada or by a permanent establishment in Canada of the employer.

(ITA: 2(3); 114; 115; ITR: 2602 Non-Residents; IT-420R3 [Archived]; Other Publications: Canada–U.S. Income Tax Treaty, Art. XV)

[¶2161] SALE OF TAXABLE CANADIAN PROPERTY SUBSEQUENT TO EMIGRATION

An individual will often dispose of his or her Canadian home or other TCP (¶2040) subsequent to emigration from Canada. When this occurs, it is imperative to accommodate the withholding/reporting requirements discussed below at the time of sale.

TCP other than real estate will usually have been subject to deemed disposition and possible tax on departure (¶2153). If its value has declined in the interim, some recovery of departure tax may be possible; where its value has increased, it is subject to additional Canadian tax claims under the rules at ¶2040.

When TCP is sold by a non-resident of Canada, the vendor must, by default, withhold and remit 25% of the gross proceeds.

Alternatively, the vendor may request a clearance certificate from the CRA. In this case, the withholding is reduced to 25% of the estimated gain (selling price in excess of original cost, but not including selling expenses). For depreciable property (such as a building), the rate is 50%. The form can be filed in advance in respect of a proposed sale, but must be filed no later than 10 days after the actual disposition.

On this form, it is possible to request a reduction in withholding in anticipation of the use of the principal residence exemption and the capital gains deduction.

An individual disposing of TCP is required to file a Canadian tax return for the year of the disposal. Gains are subject to the same graduated tax rates as apply to a resident. The tax withheld on sale is credited, and a refund is issued (or in rare cases additional tax is owing).

See also ¶2040.

(ITA: 2(3); 39(1); 110.6; 115(1); 116; 150(1); IC 72-17R6 Procedures concerning the disposition of taxable Canadian property by non-residents of Canada – Section 116; T2062 Request by a Non-Resident of Canada for a Certificate of Compliance Related to the Disposition of Taxable Canadian Property ; T2062A Request by a Non-Resident of Canada for a Certificate of Compliance Related to the Disposition of Canadian Resource or Timber Resource Property, Canadian Real Property (other than capital property) or Depreciable Taxable Canadian Property)

[¶2161.05] *Disposition of Principal Residence*

In Canada, the gain on the sale of a principal residence is normally tax-exempt. If an individual sells a principal residence before leaving Canada, the entire gain realized will be exempt from taxation, provided the house was always qualified as the taxpayer's principal residence (¶553).

If, however, an individual sells his or her home after he or she ceases residency, the proportion of the gain from the sale of his or her principal residence which will be exempt from tax will be prorated based on the following ratio:

- one plus the number of taxation years ending after 1971 during which the property was his or her principal residence and during which he or she was resident in Canada, divided by
- the total number of taxation years ending after 1971 during which the property was owned by him or her

Thus, a portion of the gain from the sale of his or her principal residence will be taxable if the individual is not a resident of Canada for two or more calendar years.

The proportion of gain covered by the principal residence exemption will decrease the longer the individual is a non-resident of Canada. The election to continue to treat a home as a principal residence (¶555) does not alter this result, although it may be useful for other reasons. See ¶2165.

(ITA: 40(2))

[¶2163] MOVING EXPENSES

Generally, moving expenses are not deductible for moves into and out of Canada (see ¶1039).

One exception to this general rule is that students leaving Canada to study full-time at a post-secondary educational institution are entitled to deduct moving expenses from scholarships, fellowships and similar awards.

In addition, persons who are absent from Canada but are deemed residents or remain factual residents of Canada can claim moving expenses on a move to or from Canada. In planning a move for employment purposes outside of Canada, it may be advisable to have an employer reimburse an employee for moving expenses. Moving expense reimbursements are not taxable to an employee, provided that the expenses reimbursed are reasonable in the circumstances and necessitated by the move (see ¶2562).

(ITA: 62; 64.1; IT-178R3 (Consolidated 2001) [Archived]; IT-420R3 [Archived]; IT-470R (Consolidated 1999) [Archived])

[¶2164] AMT ON EMIGRATION

Where you have paid Alternative Minimum Tax (AMT, discussed in Chapter 24), there is a seven-year carryforward which can be used to the extent ordinary income tax liability exceeds AMT liability. If you become a non-resident with no ordinary Canadian tax payable, this carryforward may expire without being used. The credit is not usable against withholding taxes on Canadian-source income paid to you as a non-resident (¶2080). Departure tax may itself create an ordinary liability against which AMT can be claimed.

(ITA: 127.5; 127.55; CRA Document No.: Carryover of minimum tax when non-resident, *January 30, 1996*, CRA Document No. 9510385)

[¶2165] RENTAL INCOME

An individual leaving Canada will often lease out a home or other property. Canadian taxation laws contain special rules for the taxation of rental income earned in Canada by non-residents. A non-resident is, by default, subject to a 25% tax rate on gross rental income (treaty reductions may apply). The tenant or agent must withhold the tax at source and remit it to the CRA.

An individual may file form NR6 with the CRA to request a reduction in this withholding. The CRA usually allows a reduction in the withholding to approximate the tax anticipated on *net* rental income (e.g., gross rental income less expenses relating to the rental of the property, such as maintenance expenses, mortgage interest, but not CCA). The form must be filed prior to the receipt of the first rental payment.

If the NR6 is filed, a Canadian income tax return reporting only net rental income (a "Section 216" return) must be filed within six months of the end of the year (i.e by June 30). If an NR6 is not filed, the individual may elect to file a return up to December 31 of the second year following the end of the current year.

In a departure year, it is possible for the taxpayer to have two tax returns: (a) the part-year tax return per the principles described in ¶2103; and (b) the section 216 return for the non-resident portion of the year.

CCA may be claimed on the section 216 return. The return does not include any other types of income (other than timber royalties), even those from other Canadian sources. Even capital gains on the sale of real estate are excluded from this return.

Tax is applied on net rental income at regular graduated rates, which range from approximately 22% to 49%. No personal credits may be claimed.

In deciding whether to pay tax on a gross or net basis, this return-based net income tax liability should be compared with the 25% gross rate that would otherwise apply. The election to file a tax return is, however, not an irreversible decision. It is made annually.

See also ¶2080(D).

(ITA: 212(1)(*d*); 216; IC 77-16R4 Non-Resident Income Tax; IT-393R2 [Archived]; IT-434R [Archived]; T1159 Income Tax Return for Electing Under Section 216 ; Other Publications: *Income Tax Guide for Electing Under Section 216* (T4144); *Canadian Taxation of Non-residents, 5th ed.*, Michael Atlas)

[¶2165.05] *Rental Property— Change in Use*

If an individual's former home is rented out during his or her stay outside of Canada, then there is a change in use of the property from a principal residence to an income earning property. As a result, the individual is deemed to have disposed of and reacquired his or her home at fair market value at the time of the change in use (¶555). Any gain realized on the deemed disposition of the principal residence will normally be exempt by virtue of the principal residence exemption (¶553).

Should the individual return at a future date and reoccupy the home, there is another change in use of the property from an income earning property to a principal residence. This change in use will again trigger a deemed disposition and reacquisition which may result in a taxable capital gain that may not be sheltered by the principal residence exemption. In addition, the deemed disposition may trigger recapture of any CCA previously claimed. Alternatively, this disposition may result in an allowable capital loss depending on whether the value of the house has decreased from the first to the second deemed disposition. A capital loss can be carried back three years to offset capital gains taxed in Canada and can be carried forward indefinitely to offset capital gains.

This situation can be avoided by filing a subsection 45(2) election in the year of departure when the rental activity begins. This election deems the original change in use from the principal residence to an income producing property not to have occurred. On making this election, the individual may designate the property as his or her principal residence for a period of up to four years (provided no other residence is designated for those years), even though he or she has not actually resided in the home. The four-year period may be extended indefinitely if the following conditions are met:

(1) you live away from your principal residence because your employer, or your spouse's employer, has relocated you;

(2) you and your spouse are not related to the employer;

(3) you return to your original home while you or your spouse are still with the same employer, or before the end of the year following the year in which the employment ends; and

(4) your original home is at least 40 kilometres farther than the temporary residence from your, or your spouse's, new place of employment.

Although this election will prevent the triggering of a capital gain on the change in use of the individual's principal residence, the fact that the individual has been a non-resident will reduce the amount of the principal residence exemption that can be claimed on the actual sale of the principal residence.

An important consequence of filing this election is that the individual will not be able to claim CCA with respect to the property against the income from the property for which the election remains in effect.

The subsection 45(2) election can be made by attaching to the tax return, for the year in which the change in use occurred, a letter signed by the individual describing the property in respect of which the election is being made, and stating that he or she is making the election. However, the CRA has an administrative position which accepts a late-filed subsection 45(2) election, provided that no CCA has been claimed on the property, either since the change in use has occurred or during the period in which the election remains in force.

A subsection 45(2) election may be rescinded within the four-year period. Upon rescission, in a subsequent year, there is a deemed disposition and reacquisition of the property on the first day of the subsequent year. If CCA is claimed, the election is also considered to be rescinded on the first day of the year in which the claim is made, with a deemed disposition occurring at that time.

Alternatively, the individual may allow the subsection 45(2) election to expire. As a consequence, a capital gain would be recognized on the actual disposition of the property. A portion of the capital gain would be exempt under the principal residence exemption.

An alternative to filing the subsection 45(2) election is to make an election under subsection 45(3) in order to prevent the recognition of the capital gain on the change in use from the income earning property to a principal residence. This deems the change in use not to have occurred *provided no CCA has been claimed on the rental property*. As a result, the recognition of the capital gain or loss accruing on the property during its rental producing years can be deferred until the property is actually disposed of. This election is made by filing a statement with the income tax return for the year in which the property is ultimately disposed of, or earlier if a formal demand for the election is issued by the CRA.

Note that the subsection 45(3) election allows the rental property to be considered as the individual's principal residence for up to four years of ownership during the period before he or she ceased to rent it. The fact that an individual has been a non-resident will reduce the amount of the principal residence deduction that can be claimed on the actual sale of the principal residence.

Whether an individual should make a subsection 45(2) election, subsection 45(3) election, or not make any election at all will depend upon a number of factors including the cost of the home, the value of the home, and the anticipated future appreciation.

(ITA: 45(2), (3); 54 "principal residence" (*b*), (*c*); 54.1)

[¶2167] NON-TAX CONSIDERATIONS

In addition to the income tax considerations discussed above there are some other items an individual should be aware of when planning to emigrate from Canada:

[¶2167.05] *Social Security Agreements*

See ¶2111. Canadian residents moving to the United States, see ¶2183.

[¶2167.10] *Provincial Health Care Coverage*

In the discussions above concerning residency, it was noted that the cancellation of provincial health care coverage was one of the recommended steps in establishing non-residency for an individual. Provincial health care coverage in and of itself will not make an individual resident provided the individual has little or no other residential ties. Additionally, an individual may be protected from Canadian residency under an income tax convention. It would therefore be beneficial, and is possible, for some individuals to maintain their provincial health care coverage for a period subsequent to departure.

Each province has its own rules concerning coverage. They do not, generally, match tax residency rules. These rules should be considered if one intends to retain coverage after emigration.

[¶2169] CONCLUSION

As can be appreciated, the tax consequences of ceasing Canadian residence may be very significant. Adverse impacts can often be reduced with adequate tax planning prior to the move. Planning considerations will differ substantially depending on an individual's circumstances. Any individual planning a move from Canada should seek the advice of a tax professional. See also the ceasing residence checklist at ¶2197 for a summary of some of the planning considerations discussed in this section.

UNITED STATES TAXATION OF CANADIANS, IMMIGRANTS, AND EMIGRANTS

[¶2170] INTRODUCTION

The following discussion describes tax issues specific to a Canadian resident with U.S. tax issues, including Canadians with income earned in the United States, U.S. citizens residing in Canada, and individuals moving between these countries. It should be read in conjunction with the previous sections entitled "Canadian Taxation of Immigrants" and "Canadian Taxation of Emigrants". It is also recommended that U.S. citizens planning to move to Canada obtain a copy of IRS Publication 54, "Tax Guide for U.S. Citizens and Resident Aliens Abroad".

[¶2173] U.S. BASIS OF TAXATION

As with most advanced nations, the United States taxes residents on worldwide income, and non-residents only on U.S.-source income. However, unique among advanced nations, it also taxes each citizen on his or her worldwide income, even if he or she is not actually residing in the United States.

Any person who is a citizen or resident of the United States must file an annual U.S. tax return (Form 1040) and remit U.S. taxes regardless of the place he or she actually lives. So residency is generally irrelevant for a citizen (at least in terms of determining whether he or she is subject to worldwide taxation).

An individual who is a non-resident alien (i.e., not a citizen or "resident alien") of the United States is subject to U.S. tax only on U.S.-source income (Form 1040NR).

While it is theoretically possible for an individual to have a non-calendar fiscal year, this choice is exceedingly rare. In practice, virtually all individuals in the United States use a calendar year as the period for taxation.

Unlike Canadian provinces (aside from Quebec), each individual state has its own separate revenue collection mechanism. Some states have no personal income tax, while others have quite substantial taxes.

(Other Publications: IRS Pub. 54; 538)

[¶2174] U.S. RESIDENCY

There are two ways one can be a "resident alien" of the United States:

(1) Lawful Permanent Resident (LPR): An individual admitted as an LPR, often called a "green card" holder, is automatically a resident. In this case, it doesn't matter whether he or she actually lives in the United States.

(2) Substantial Presence Test: This test counts the number of days a person is physically present in the United States. See ¶2174.10 below.

(Other Publications: Treas. Reg. 301.7701(b)-1)

[¶2174.10] *Substantial Presence Test*

An individual who is physically present in the United States for a prescribed amount of time over a period of three years, ending with the current year, is deemed to be resident in the current year. The individual must be present in the United States for at least 30 days in the current year and must equal or exceed 183 days in total, using the following formula:

- Days present in the current year; plus
- Days present in the prior year / 3; plus
- Days present in the second prior year / 6.

[¶2174.13] *Days Not Counted Substantial Presence Test*

Days of U.S. presence in certain circumstances are ignored, among them:

(1) commuters regularly travelling to work from a home in Canada or Mexico;

(2) individuals travelling between two points outside the United States;

(3) students;

(4) teachers;

(5) trainees;

(6) employees of foreign governments;

(7) individuals who cannot leave for medical reasons; and

(8) professional athletes playing in charitable events.

There are limitations on these exemptions, so care is needed in claiming any of them.

(Other Publications: Treas. Reg 301.7701(b)-3)

[¶2174.16] *Closer Connection Exception*

If an individual meets the substantial presence test, but has a closer connection to one or two other countries than to the United States for the full year, then the individual is not considered a resident of the United States.

To claim a closer connection, one must have:

(1) A "tax home" outside the United States. One's tax home is the place one usually works, or if there is no such place, the place one principally resides. It is possible (but rare) to have no tax home;

(2) Personal and economic ties to the foreign country that are more significant than the ones to the United States;

(3) Be present in the United States for under 183 days in the current year; and

(4) File Form 8840 on a timely basis (generally June 15 of the following year).

(Other Publications: Treas. Reg 301.7701(b)-2)

[¶2174.20] *Residency Elections*

Sometimes it is advantageous to be treated as a U.S. resident. For instance, a U.S. resident may file a joint return with a spouse, and this choice can provide benefits such as preferential tax rates.

A non-resident alien may elect to be treated as a U.S. resident in a calendar year if the individual:

(1) Was not a resident in the immediately preceding year;

(2) Meets the substantial presence test for the following calendar year;

(3) Is present in the United States for at least 31 consecutive days in the current year; and

(4) Is present in the United States in the current year for 75% of the days from the first day of the 31-day period to the last day of the year.

A non-resident alien married to a U.S. citizen or resident may also elect to be treated as a resident in order to file jointly.

(Other Publications: IRC 6013(*g*), (h); IRC 7701(*b*)(4))

[¶2174.30] *Residency Commencement and Termination Date*

If an individual was not a resident of the United States during the preceding year, but is a resident during the current year, he or she is subject to tax as a resident (i.e., on worldwide income) beginning with his or her residency starting date, which is the earlier of the following dates:

(1) For an individual who meets the substantial presence test, the first day during the year on which the individual is present in the United States;

(2) For an individual meeting the lawful permanent residence test, the first day in the calendar year on which the person is present in the United States as a lawful permanent resident; or

(3) For a person making the first-year election, the first day the person is treated as a resident.

If an alien is a U.S. resident during the current year and a non-resident during any part of the following year, then this individual ceases to be a resident on the residency termination date. The residency termination date is generally the last day of a calendar year. However, when the individual can demonstrate that a foreign tax home is established, and there is a closer connection to the foreign country, he or she is considered to have ceased U.S. residency on the day on which lawful permanent resident status ceases (in the case of individuals satisfying the lawful permanent resident test) or the last day on which the individual is present in the United States (in the case of individuals satisfying the substantial presence test).

There are certain exceptions under U.S. domestic law and the Canada–U.S. Tax Treaty.

(Other Publications: Treas. Reg 301.7701(b)-4)

[¶2174.60] *Treaty Residency*

Because U.S. and Canadian residency rules (see ¶105) are so different, it is possible for an individual to be considered resident in both Canada and the United States under the domestic law of each country, making him or her a "dual resident". In such a situation, an individual could easily be subject to double taxation. Relief from this situation is provided by the Treaty. The Treaty provides "tie-breaker" rules that cause the individual to be considered a resident of only one country. Under the Treaty, an individual is a resident of the one country:

(1) Where he or she has a permanent home available to him or her (this place need not be owned, or even rented — it simply needs to be permanent and available);

(2) With which his or her personal and economic relations are closer;

(3) Where he or she has an habitual abode (generally, a place where he or she sleeps regularly), or

(4) Of which he or she is a citizen.

These tests are applied in order. If one test indicates the individual is a resident of only one country, the subsequent tests are ignored. For example, if an individual has a permanent home in only one country, that country would be his or her country of residence.

If none of the above tests indicates residency in a single country, then the competent authorities of each country will determine the individual's residency. For the United States, the competent authority is the Assistant Commissioner, International of the IRS. For Canada, the competent authority is the Director of the International Tax Directorate of the CRA.

The United States allows any resident, including a dual resident to file in the same manner as a U.S. resident or citizen (worldwide income on Form 1040).

The treaty can override a domestic law's residency rules, including the starting and termination dates. It is possible for a green card holder to elect to be treated as a U.S. non-resident alien ("NRA") using these rules. In this case, s/he would elect to file as a non-resident alien (U.S. income on form 1040NR). If he or she chooses the latter option, he or she must disclose this choice to the IRS (form 8833), but there may be immigration implications to this choice, and consulting an immigration lawyer is suggested.

In either case, consistency in the filing approach is required.

However, the treaty does not generally override the United States' right to tax a citizen.

(Other Publications: Treas. Reg 301.7701(b)-7; Convention between Canada and the United States of America with Respect to Taxes on Income and on Capital, Art. IV(2), XXIX(2)(a))

[¶2174.80] *Dual-Status Year*

The notion of a dual-status year is analogous to the Canadian concept of a part-year resident. It is generally a year when an individual becomes or ceases to be a U.S. resident. However, it can also apply when an individual who was formerly a citizen renounces citizenship or surrenders his or her green card during the year. An individual must file a tax return for the year with two reporting periods, one reporting period including worldwide income for the period of residency and the other including only U.S.-source income for the period of non-residency. There are limitations on deductions, exemptions and filing status in a dual-status year.

(Other Publications: Treas. Reg 1.871-13)

[¶2174.90] *State Residency*

Each state has its own residency rules. Some are common-law based; some are based on the number of days of physical presence; some are related to domicile; and some are connected to the ownership, rental, or control of a home in the state. Individual states may not necessarily adhere to the federal treaty tie-breaker rules for a dual resident.

[¶2175] U.S. TAXATION OF NON-RESIDENT ALIENS

[¶2176] *Income Subject to Tax*

An NRA is subject to tax only on U.S.-source income. Income is generally considered U.S.-source if it is earned by an activity or from an investment in the United States.

Interest: Interest paid by a U.S. resident or a domestic corporation is generally U.S.-source income. However, there is an exemption for "portfolio interest income" received by an NRA. This includes interest paid by a U.S. bank, savings and loan company, or insurance company. Most commercial debt owned by NRAs will also fall into this category.

Dividends: A dividend paid by a U.S. corporation is, as a general rule, U.S.-source income.

Real property income: Rental income and gains on the sale of real estate located in the United States are U.S.-source income.

Gains on the sale of personal property that forms part of a U.S. trade or business: If a non-resident maintains an office in the United States, this type of gain is U.S.-source income unless the property is sold for use outside the United States and an office outside the United States materially participated in the sale. There are exceptions to the general rule for inventory, depreciable personal property, and intangibles.

Gains on the sale of other personal property: Gains realized by an NRA are foreign-source.

(Other Publications: IRC 862; 871; Treaty Art XIII)

[¶2177] *Types of Income and Tax Applied*

To determine the method of taxation and the applicable rate of tax, income is separated into two categories:

- income not connected with a U.S. business (referred to as fixed, determinable and periodic, or "FDAP"). FDAP generally includes investment income such as interest, dividends, rents, and royalties.
- income effectively connected with a U.S. trade or business (often called effectively connected income, or "ECI"). ECI includes employment income and gains on U.S. real property interests.

From ECI, a taxpayer is allowed limited deductions and exemptions. The remaining taxable income is subject to regular graduated income tax rates — up to 39.6%.

In contrast, only in exceptional circumstances are deductions allowed against FDAP. Tax is applied at a flat rate — the statutory rate is 30%, but it is often reduced by treaty.

(Other Publications: IRC 871(*a*), (*b*))

[¶2178] INCOME NOT CONNECTED WITH A U.S. BUSINESS

There are four types of U.S.-source income that are taxable to an NRA under this category:

(1) fixed or determinable, annual or periodical (FDAP) income such as dividends, interest, pensions, rents, and royalties;

(2) capital gains in limited circumstances;

(3) special statutory gain income, such as lump-sum capital gain distributions from employee trusts, gains on the sale of patents, copyrights and other intangibles, and original issue discount (OID); and

(4) Social Security benefits.

Note: For Canadian residents, many items in this category are exempt from U.S. tax or subject to limited taxation.

As a practical matter, the tax is imposed through withholding on gross income.

(Other Publications: IRC 871(*a*))

[¶2178.20] *Investment Income*

Many types of U.S. FDAP income paid to an NRA are subject to reduced U.S. tax rates under the treaty, including:

- Interest: Exempt
- Dividends: 15%
- Periodic private pension payments and annuities: 15% (lump-sum payments 30%). Individual Retirement Account ("IRA") and 401(k) distributions fall into this category.
- Royalties: 10% or nil
- Trust distributions: 15%

(Other Publications: Canada–U.S. Tax Treaty, Art. X, XI, XII, XXVIII, XXI)

[¶2178.30] *Real Property Rent*

Rent paid in respect of U.S. real property is subject to the normal 30% withholding tax at source. This is true of mineral and petroleum royalties as well.

However, it is possible to elect to file a U.S. return to treat these receipts as ECI. The election allows the taxpayer to deduct related expenses in the normal scheme, just as a U.S.-resident would. These expenses include interest, property taxes, maintenance, management fees, and depreciation, among others.

The net income after expenses is reported along with other ECI, on the same return. Tax is then charged on taxable income, at normal graduated rates.

(Other Publications: IRC 871(*d*); Treas. Reg. 1.871–10)

[¶2178.40] *FDAP Capital Gains*

As a general rule, an NRA is taxed on capital gains where they are realized upon U.S. real property interests or are connected with a U.S. business. This income is considered ECI.

However, under U.S. domestic law, a foreign national who is physically present in the United States for 183 days or more during a tax year is taxed on U.S.-source net capital gains. A

Canadian resident will rarely be caught by this provision, because the Treaty generally exempts such gains from U.S. taxation.

[¶2178.50] *Social Security Benefits*

Under U.S. domestic law, Social Security benefits paid to an NRA are subject to U.S. tax at a flat 30% rate.

However, under the Treaty, the country of residence has exclusive rights to tax social security benefits paid from the other country. Consequently U.S. Social Security received by an individual residing in Canada is exempt from U.S. tax.

Canada taxes this income, but permits a deduction in computing Canadian taxable income for 15% of these benefits (see ¶921).

Additionally, Canadian residents who have been receiving U.S. Social Security payments since before 1996 are entitled to deduct an additional 35% (for a total of 50%) of such benefits. The deduction is also allowed for resident surviving spouses or common-law partners of such persons.

(Other Publications: Canada–U.S. Tax Treaty, Art. XVIII(5))

[¶2179] INCOME EFFECTIVELY CONNECTED WITH A U.S. TRADE OR BUSINESS

A U.S. business is generally defined as the regular and continuous carrying on of commercial or industrial income-producing activities in the United States. Income must arise from assets used or activities located in the United States to be ECI.

The determination of whether income is ECI may overlap tax years. If an NRA receives U.S.-source income in one year, and is not carrying on a U.S. trade or business during that year, but the income is connected to activities that took place during another year when the NRA was carrying on a U.S. trade or business, that income is considered ECI.

One simple example is an employee who works in the United States only in December of Year 1 but does not get paid until January of Year 2. Generally, employees are cash basis taxpayers. Even if the employee had no U.S. activity in Year 2, the U.S. employment income received in Year 2 is considered ECI.

(Other Publications: IRC 871(*b*))

[¶2179.20] *Canadian Residents Working in the United States*

In general, income earned for services is "sourced" to geographic location in which it is earned. Consequently, income earned by an NRA for services physically provided in the United States is taxable in the United States under U.S. domestic law.

Where a person earns income for services in both countries, income is usually allocated to each country based on the number of days that an individual is working in each country. There are exceptions to this guideline, however, particularly where income is more directly traceable to specific activities, and another method is more reflective of the income-earning process. As an example, a commissioned salesperson may allocate income based on the location of sales.

(Other Publications: IRC 861(*a*)(3))

[¶2179.23] *Treaty Exemption for Employees*

The Treaty restricts U.S. taxation of an NRA resident in Canada. An employee is exempt from U.S. tax if either of the following conditions is met:

(1) The remuneration for employment in the United States for the year is US$10,000 or less; or

(2) Both:

(a) The employee is present in the United States for a period or periods not exceeding in the aggregate 183 days in any 12-month period commencing or ending in the year, and

(b) The remuneration is not paid by, or on behalf of, a person who is resident in the United States and is not borne by a permanent establishment in the United States.

(Other Publications: Canada–U.S. Tax Treaty, Art. XV(2))

[¶2179.50] *Treaty Exemption for Self-Employed Individuals*

Under the Treaty, an individual can have an "enterprise". An enterprise providing business services in the United States is exempt from U.S. tax if the enterprise has no permanent establishment (PE) in the United States.

While there are a number of ways that one can have a PE, the most usual one is having control over a piece of real property (whether owned, purchased, or simply made available) that is used for the business.

Under the Treaty, there are two ways an enterprise can be deemed to have a PE when it sends employees to the U.S. to work on a project without having real estate in the U.S.:

(1) A single employee based in the United States for a significant period of time, where:

(a) Services are performed in the United States by an individual who is present in the United States for a period(s) aggregating 183 days or more in a 12-month period beginning or ending during the year; and

(b) During that period(s), the enterprise derives more than 50% of its gross active business revenues from the individual's service in the United States.

(2) Continuous work by one or more employees on a single project, where:

(a) The services are provided in the United States for an aggregate of 183 days or more in any 12-month period;

(b) With respect to the same or connected project for customers;

(c) Who are either residents of the United States or who maintain a permanent establishment in the United States; and

(d) The services are provided in respect of that PE.

For a self-employed individual, Rule 1 is the major exposure. Rule 2 will typically apply to enterprises that have multiple employees (including services partnerships).

(Other Publications: Canada–U.S. Tax Treaty, Art. V; VII)

[¶2179.80] *Tax Limitation for Married NRAs Employed in the United States*

For a married individual, the Treaty provides a limitation on U.S. taxes payable related to employment income earned in the United States, such that the tax is no greater than what would be charged had the individual been a U.S. citizen filing a joint return.

The limitation is provided in a formula whereby the taxpayer calculates U.S. tax payable on worldwide income based on joint rate filing, without a foreign tax credit claim and then prorates the taxes to the portion of his or her U.S. employment income.

The limitation does not impact the tax payable on the other U.S.-source income.

(Other Publications: Canada–U.S. Tax Treaty, Art. XXV(3))

[¶2179.90] *U.S. Retirement Plans*

The United States has several types of retirement plans, collectively known as qualified plans. There are employer-sponsored plans, from traditional pension plans to 401(k)s (essentially, a defined contribution type of plan).

There are a number of plans for individuals, here collectively referred to as IRAs. A Roth IRA is very similar to a Canadian TFSA — contributions are non-deductible, and withdrawals are non-taxable (see ¶478).

(Other Publications: IRC 401 to 408)

[¶2179.92] *U.S. Retirement Plan Contributions*

U.S. retirement plan contributions are generally deductible in both Canada and the United States for the first five years. There are limitations on the amount, but these limitations are usually inconsequential overall.

There is no deduction available in Canada for contributions to either a traditional or a Roth IRA account.

(ITA: 6(1)(*g*); 207.6(5), (5.1); ITR: 8308.1 Foreign Plans; Other Publications: Canada–U.S. Tax Treaty, Art. XVIII (8)–(16); *Window on Canadian Tax* 2954)

[¶2179.94] *U.S. Retirement Plan Earnings*

Investment income earned within a traditional IRA by a resident of Canada is generally not taxable in Canada until amounts are withdrawn. On the other hand, accrued investment income earned within a Roth IRA could become taxable annually in Canada if contributions are made to the account while the contributor is resident in Canada.

(ITA: 94(1)(*b*)(i)(E))

[¶2179.96] *U.S. Retirement Plan Withdrawals*

An individual is only taxable on a withdrawal from an IRA to the extent it is taxable in the United States. Since Roth IRA withdrawals are not taxable in the United States, they are not taxable in Canada, as long as no contribution was made after 2008 while the individual was a resident of Canada. To effect this treatment, an election is required with the first Canadian return affected (usually the year the individual first obtains Canadian residency). There is no prescribed form for the election.

On the other hand, withdrawals from a qualified plan taxable in Canada are generally taxable in the United States. So one must be careful not to make contributions that will create tax on withdrawal without generating a tax benefit upon contribution.

For instance, a Canadian resident could make a traditional IRA contribution while working in the United States. This choice may reduce U.S. tax in the year of contribution, but because the contribution is not deductible for Canadian purposes, the U.S. benefit is absorbed by a reduced Canadian foreign tax credit. The ultimate withdrawal is then still fully taxable in Canada, resulting in double taxation.

It is possible, in certain circumstances, to withdraw a lump sum from a traditional IRA and contribute the funds to an RRSP on a tax-efficient basis. The withdrawal from the IRA is taxable in both the United States and Canada, and the contribution to the RRSP is deductible for Canadian purposes. Canada allows a foreign tax credit for the U.S. tax including 10% additional tax for early withdrawal. Depending on the amounts of the withdrawal and of Canadian tax on other income, the foreign tax credit may equal the U.S. tax.

More detail on the Canadian treatment of IRA withdrawals and transfers is found under the subheadings "Foreign Retirement Arrangements (IRAs)" and "Roth IRAs" at ¶919.

(ITA: 248(1) "foreign retirement arrangement"; ITR: 6803 [Prescribed plan or arrangement – foreign retirement arrangement]; CRA Document No.: 2011-03987417; Other Publications: *International Tax Newsletter* No. 43; Canada–U.S. Tax Treaty, Art. XVIII)

[¶2180] STATE INCOME TAXATION

A large majority of the 50 states impose income taxes, along with the District of Columbia and certain municipalities. Therefore, state and local income tax costs as well as federal tax costs must be considered for tax-planning purposes. State income taxes can be a significant part of an individual's total income tax burden.

State individual income tax is greatly variable. Rates range from zero (Alaska, Florida, Nevada, South Dakota, Texas, Washington, Wyoming) to as high as 13.3% (California). In New York City, the city-included rate is almost 13%. Some states (New Hampshire and Tennessee) tax only dividends and interest. The impact of the state income tax is reduced somewhat by the fact that state taxes are deductible for federal income tax purposes by residents who itemize their deductions in lieu of claiming the standard deduction. Non-residents may deduct state income taxes only if the tax is paid on income connected with a U.S. business.

State rules for residency are as varied as the states themselves. Many use a common-law test, but some count the number of days present. Some use domicile or the ownership/rental of a home in the state as a factor. Some have tests that cover periods greater than one year.

A resident of a state generally is taxed on his or her worldwide income regardless of source. A non-resident is generally only taxed on income from sources within the state. Generally, a part-year resident pays state tax on worldwide income for the period he or she is a resident and on income from within the state for the non-resident period. The source rules are similar to the federal rules but may differ with respect to specific types of income. For example, many states subject personal service income to tax regardless of the time spent in the state or the amount earned. Accordingly, non-residents travelling in a state on business may be subject to state tax because the source of their compensation is considered to be based on working days in the state.

States are not signatories to U.S. tax treaties. As a result, an individual may be exempt from U.S. federal tax, but still subject to state tax. For example, a Canadian-resident citizen employed by a Canadian corporation who works in the United State, but spends 183 days or less there is generally not subject to federal tax on his or her salary, but will often be subject to state income tax.

Fortunately, many states use federal taxable income as the starting point for computing state taxable income, and some states explicitly recognize treaties. Therefore, if federal taxable income is reduced by a treaty, the state may provide treaty benefits.

[¶2181] SOCIAL SECURITY TAXES

The United States is considered by many Canadians to be a low tax country. However, the relatively low income tax rates are partially offset by the high cost of U.S. Social Security taxes relative to Canada's CPP contributions. Benefits are also higher than those provided under the CPP.

Canada and the United States have entered into a Social Security Totalization Agreement ("SSTA") which limits the possibility that an individual will have to pay Social Security taxes in both countries.

[¶2181.05] *Employees — Federal Insurance Contribution Act (FICA)*

In general, an employee and employer are each taxed on the first $118,500 (2016, unchanged from 2015) of gross wages at a rate of 6.2% (the Social Security portion), plus 1.45% (the Medicare portion) on all compensation.

First imposed in 2013, there is an additional tax (imposed only on the employee) equal to 0.9% of wages in excess of

(1) in the case of a joint return, $250,000;

(2) in the case of a married taxpayer filing a separate return, $125,000; and

(3) in any other case, $200,000.

In general, the employee and employer must pay FICA taxes if the employee is principally employed in the United States. It does not matter where the employer is located. The employer does not match the additional tax amount.

An exception to this rule is where an individual is hired initially to work in one country, and is sent on a short-term assignment to work in the other country. Short term has been defined as 60 months or less. When a Canadian resident is on a short-term assignment in the United States, he or she continues paying into the CPP rather than Social Security. An extension of the 60-month time frame may be available in rare circumstances. A return to work in Canada will reset the 60-month clock.

Coverage must be applied for by the individual's employer with the use of form CPT 56, "Certificate of Coverage under the Canada Pension Plan Pursuant to Article V of the Agreement on Social Security between Canada and the United States of America". Once the employer has received the certificate of coverage, it may deduct and remit CPP from the employee rather than FICA. For transfers of less than six months, the form is not required.

(Other Publications: IRC 3101; Canada–U.S. Social Security Totalization Agreement, Art. V)

[¶2181.10] *Self-Employed Individuals — Self-Employment Contribution Act (SECA)*

A self-employed individual is subject to self-employment tax rather than FICA. As with the CPP, the self-employment tax is applied in a manner to make it consistent with FICA.

For 2016, the SECA tax rate is 15.3%, consisting of a 12.4% component for Old-Age, Survivors, and Disability Insurance ("OASDI") and a 2.9% component for Medicare. The 2016 base amount subject to SECA tax is $118,500 for OASDI. There is no upper limit on the amount of earnings subject to the Medicare portion of the tax. The tax is imposed on net income from self-employment, including income from a business and income or loss from a partnership that carries on a business.

The additional 0.9% tax (¶2181.05) applies to this income as well.

A non-resident alien is not subject to SECA.

Under the SSTA, a self-employed individual is subject to the Social Security tax only of the country in which he or she is resident.

(Other Publications: IRC 1401)

[¶2181.15] *Federal Unemployment Tax Act (FUTA)*

Unlike Canada's Employment Insurance, the United States levies a tax to pay for unemployment benefits only on employers, not on employees. For 2016, the rate is 6% on the first $7,000 of wages. Credits are allowed for state employment taxes.

The tax is levied on the employer for services performed within the United States by residents and non-residents. Services rendered outside the United States are exempt from the tax.

Unlike FICA, there is a *de minimis* rule. If a non-resident working in the United States is the only employee employed by a foreign company, he or she spends less than 20 weeks in the United States and his or her quarterly wages are not in excess of $1,500, his or her wages are exempt.

(Other Publications: IRC 3301)

[¶2181.30] *Net Investment Income Tax*

The Net Investment Income Tax (NIIT) is 3.8% of investment income, and is applied only to high-income earners (the same thresholds as the additional Social Security/SECA tax, above). It is not clear whether the NIIT is a Social Security tax, and thus covered by the SSTA (so Americans in Canada would be exempt), or an income tax.

If the NIIT is an income tax, Americans in Canada could be subject to double taxation. Under the enabling legislation, the United States does not offer a foreign tax credit in respect of this tax. It is conceivable that the treaty could offer one, but that is by no means a certainty.

(Other Publications: IRC 1411; Treas. Reg. 1.1411)

[¶2182] SALES OF U.S. REAL PROPERTY

Gain or loss from the sale or exchange of a U.S. real property interest (USRPI) is treated as a U.S.-source income (or loss) effectively connected with a U.S. trade or business (ECI).

USRPI generally includes an interest in real property located in the United States, including personal property associated with the real property. Personal property is a U.S. term, which for most purposes, is similar to the Canadian concept of chattels. It will usually show up as furniture and fixtures.

Stock in a U.S. real property holding corporation (USRPHC) is a USRPI. A USRPHC is a U.S. corporation where 50% or more of the fair market value of its assets consists of USRPIs. A USRPI does not include an interest in a foreign (non-U.S.) corporation, unless an election has been made to treat the foreign corporation as a U.S. corporation.

Assets held by a partnership, trust, or estate are generally treated as held proportionately by its partners or beneficiaries. Thus, if one of these entities disposes of a USRPI, the partners or beneficiaries are also deemed to dispose of the USRPI.

(Other Publications: IRC 897)

[¶2182.50] *Withholding on Sale of a USRPI*

Someone who purchases a USRPI from an NRA is required to withhold and remit to the Internal Revenue Service (IRS) 15% (was 10% for dispositions before February 17, 2016) of the gross purchase price. However for property to be used as a residence, where the price is under $1,000,000, the 10% withholding rate still applies.

The amount realized is the sum of the cash received, the fair market value of other property received, and the amount and any liabilities assumed by the buyer or to which the property is subject (mortgages, liens and such).

There are exceptions to the withholding requirement, most notably where the property is acquired for use as a personal residence and the purchase price is under $300,000.

The purchaser may request that the IRS issue a withholding certificate to reduce or eliminate the withholding tax. This certificate will usually be issued where the anticipated tax is less than the statutory 10%/15% withholding. As a practical matter it is usually the vendor that completes the form, but the responsibility for processing it is with the purchaser. This process is very similar to the Canadian one for sales of taxable Canadian property (¶2042).

(Other Publications: IRC 871(*a*)(2); 897; Canada–U.S. Tax Treaty, Art. XIII; IRS Forms 8288, 8288-A, 8288-B)

[¶2182.60] *Deductions and Personal Exemptions*

After determining adjusted gross income from ECI, an NRA may deduct certain expenses ("itemized deductions"). Some are connected with the conduct of a business in the United States, including, for example, state income taxes, travel and transportation expenses, and professional fees.

Some itemized deductions are eligible without regard to whether the expense is connected with a U.S. business. This category includes U.S. charitable contributions and casualty and theft losses.

Finally, the United States allows "exemptions" in calculating taxable income. An NRA who is a resident of Canada is allowed an exemption for himself, his or her spouse, and each dependant provided that he or she has a valid U.S. taxpayer identification number (either a Social Security Number or "SSN", or Individual Taxpayer Identification Number or "ITIN"). For 2016, the exemption is $4,050.

(Other Publications: IRC 151(*e*); 873)

[¶2182.70] *Tax Calculation*

An NRA pays tax on effectively connected income at graduated tax rates. There are different rate brackets for single and married people, and in the latter category, those filing separately and those filing jointly (¶2183.80).

An NRA may file using only "single" or "married filing separately" rates unless he or she is married to a U.S. citizen or resident, and he or she elects to be treated as a resident (¶2174.20).

(Other Publications: IRC 6013(*g*), (*h*))

[¶2183] U.S. CITIZENS AND RESIDENTS WHO ARE ALSO RESIDENTS OF CANADA

As noted at (¶2173), U.S. citizens and residents are subject to U.S. tax on their worldwide incomes. It is possible to be a U.S. citizen or resident at the same time as being a resident of Canada. The following is a discussion of some of the special reporting issues facing people in this situation.

[¶2183.10] *Income*

The United States measures income in a manner that is similar to Canada's, but there are differences. What follows is a discussion of some of the major ones.

[¶2183.11] *Income Subject to Tax*

For Canada, income is taxable only if it is from enumerated sources. By contrast, for U.S. purposes, all accretions to wealth are taxable except for those that are specifically excluded. This means that some types of income which are non-taxable for Canadian purposes are taxable for U.S. purposes.

[¶2183.12] *Stock Options*

Canada allows a deduction upon the exercise of most stock options, effectively making only half the gain taxable (¶330.25). The United States taxes the actual amount of the receipt. However, provided certain criteria are met regarding the stock and holding period, the gain may be treated as capital in which case the federal tax would be limited to 15%/20% or even a lower rate.

[¶2183.13] *Dividends*

Canada has a gross-up and dividend tax credit system for dividends from Canadian corporations (¶404). The United States taxes the actual amount of the receipt.

There are few instances in the U.S. where a dividend is non-taxable to the recipient. For example, a "capital dividend", while exempt for Canadian tax purposes (¶415.05), is generally taxable in the United States.

"Qualified dividends" are subject to reduced tax rates (the same as long-term capital gains; see ¶2183.14).

- 0% on any amount that otherwise would be taxed at a 10% or 15% rate.
- 15% on any amount that otherwise would be taxed at rates greater than 15% but less than 39.6%.
- 20% on any amount that otherwise would be taxed at a 39.6% rate.

Qualified dividends can include dividends from certain non-U.S. domestic corporations. Most public company dividends are qualified. Most dividends from private Canadian companies are qualified, but one must pay attention to the U.S. Controlled Foreign Corporation and Passive Foreign Investment Company rules.

Ordinary dividends are taxed at regular graduated tax rates.

Depending on the circumstances, a dividend for Canadian purposes may be recharacterized as proceeds of disposition of a share for U.S. purposes. In this case, the "basis" (a concept similar to ACB) may be applied against the gain. Further, a Canadian capital gain distribution may be recharacterized as a dividend for U.S. purposes.

(Other Publications: IRC 1(*h*))

[¶2183.14] *Capital Gains*

Canada taxes only 50% of capital gains. The United States taxes the full amount of the gain.

Long-term capital gains, which are generally capital assets held for more than one year, are subject to reduced tax rates (the same as qualified dividends; see ¶2183.13).

(Other Publications: IRC 1(*h*))

[¶2183.16] *Gambling Winnings*

Gambling winnings are taxable. This includes winnings from games of chance, such as lotteries. In Canada, these winnings are not taxable if the activities do not rise to the level of a business.

Losses are allowed as itemized deductions to the extent of winnings.

(Other Publications: IRC 165(*d*))

[¶2183.18] *U.S. Retirement Plans*

The rules discussed at ¶2179.90 through ¶2179.96 (IRAs, 401(k)s, etc.) apply to U.S. citizens and residents, with a few differences.

Employer contributions to a 401(k) are not taxable in Canada for the first five years of Canadian residence. Subsequent to five years of residency, the employer must make elections to continue tax deferral under the plan. A pension adjustment should be calculated for an employee resident in Canada and participating in a 401(k) plan.

Amounts received by an employee from a 401(k) plan while the individual is a resident of Canada will, in most cases, be subject to Canadian tax on the amounts less the portion that can reasonably be considered a return of the employee's contributions to the plan.

The CRA's view is that contributions made by an employee (as opposed to an employer) are not deductible for Canadian tax computations. Withdrawals of such contributions would be considered non-taxable in Canada.

However, the Canada–U.S. Treaty will generally allow deductions for Canadian tax purposes for the first five years of employment in Canada; see paragraph 8 of Article XIII of the Treaty. Under the treaty, special rules apply for commuters, that is, people who cross the border to work on a regular basis.

Upon withdrawal, a citizen/resident pays tax at graduated rates, up to 39.6%. An "early" withdrawal (before age $59^1/_2$) may attract an additional tax of 10%. Under the treaty, a U.S. citizen resident in Canada should be eligible for a reduction in the tax to 15% for periodic withdrawals (but not lump-sum withdrawals).

All these taxes are creditable in Canada, but in the case of a lump sum, the combined rate may exceed the effective Canadian rate, meaning some U.S. tax may be lost.

(ITA: 56; 60.01; 81(1)(*r*); 248(1) "foreign retirement arrangement"; ITR: 6803 [Prescribed plan or arrangement – foreign retirement arrangement]; CRA Document No.: Foreign Tax Credit on 10% additional US tax, *April 19, 2011*, CRA Document No. 2011-039874117; Other Publications: Canada–U.S. Tax Treaty, Art. XVIII)

[¶2183a] CANADIAN RETIREMENT PLANS

[¶2183a.22] *Canadian Employer-Sponsored Plans*

A U.S. citizen who is a member of a Canadian employer-sponsored plan may deduct contributions to that plan. This includes a group RRSP. The employer contributions are excluded as well.

Withdrawals are fully taxable in both Canada and the United States, so the treatment is parallel on both sides.

There is no requirement to make a formal election in respect of an interest in a Canadian pension plan to defer U.S. tax on the earnings inside the plan.

(CRA Document No.: Foreign Tax Credit on 10% additional US tax, *April 19, 2011*, CRA Document No. 2011-039874117; Other Publications: Canada–U.S. Tax Treaty, Art. XVIII)

[¶2183a.24] *Canadian Individual Retirement Plans*

Under U.S. domestic law, an RRSP/RRIF is a "grantor trust". A U.S. citizen/resident is ordinarily required to account for income, gains and losses inside each plan, ignoring the fact that it is inside a plan. The United States taxes the income on an annual basis, while Canada taxes earnings in the plan only as funds are withdrawn (the United States would not tax the withdrawal).

Because of this timing mismatch, it is possible to have U.S. tax on income earned in the plan, and Canadian tax on that same income later, when it is withdrawn from the plan. This is classic double taxation.

For this reason, under the Treaty, a beneficiary of a Canadian deferred income plan may elect to defer U.S. taxation of income earned inside the plan until a distribution is made from the plan. As income is withdrawn, it is taxed by the United States. This approach helps minimize double taxation, as the Canadian tax on the withdrawal becomes available to claim as a foreign tax credit on the U.S. return.

The IRS will permit the deferral for an RRSP, a RRIF, Registered Pension Plan (RPP), and Deferred Profit Sharing Plan (DPSP). It is unclear at this point whether the Tax-Free Savings Account (TFSA) is covered.

For returns filed prior to December 31, 2014, Form 8891 was used to make the deferral election for RRSPs and RRIFs. However, new guidance was issued on October 7, 2014 where the IRS has indicated that Form 8891 is no longer required for these types of accounts, if the taxpayer had been compliant in filing prior year U.S. tax returns, did not report gross income accrued in the RRSP/RRIF account(s), and accurately reported any distributions received from the plans on his or her U.S. return as if he or she had made the election. Such individuals will be deemed to have made the election in a prior year even if they had not properly done so, and will no longer be required to make an election in future calendar years. Ineligible individuals will remain taxable on the accrued income earned within the accounts, unless they apply for consent from the Commissioner to make an election.

Elections for the other plans may be made without the use of a government form.

(Tax Topics: No. 2116; Other Publications: Canada–U.S. Tax Treaty, Art. XVIII; IRS Rev. Proc. 2014-55; IR-2014-97)

[¶2183a.26] *Withdrawals from Individual Registered Plans Where a U.S. Deferral Election Has Been Made*

If an individual has previously elected to defer U.S. income recognition, withdrawing the funds has two impacts: income inclusion and reporting.

Since previous contributions to the RRSP were generally not deductible, the portion of the withdrawal that represents contributions (or "capital") is not taxable. The remainder ("income") represents accumulated income and is taxable.

To accomplish the necessary calculation, these components need to be tracked on an annual basis, in U.S. dollars.

The IRS is currently treating the income portion as fully taxable at ordinary rates, although this point is not made explicit. This is a point of concern, because following the IRS forms means that the taxpayer loses the benefit of the lower rates applicable to qualified dividends and long-term capital gains. For a resident of Canada, this issue is rarely consequential, because the income is Canadian source, and the foreign tax credit will usually eliminate any U.S. tax. It could be more important for someone who lives outside Canada at the time of withdrawal.

The Canadian tax on the withdrawal is eligible for a foreign tax credit. The United States calculates foreign tax credits using two baskets. It is at this point uncertain whether the withdrawal is treated as entirely "general basket", or partially "passive basket" income for this purpose. Because the withdrawal is being taxed as ordinary retirement income, it would appear that all of the income (and therefore tax) is treated as general basket.

[¶2183a.28] *Whether to Make the Election to Defer*

Typically, moderate to high-income individuals will benefit from the deferral election because it avoids the mismatch in timing of U.S. and Canadian tax.

For lower- to moderate-income individuals, the default (no-deferral) treatment can be advantageous, because the income inclusion may not create U.S. tax. This approach may be beneficial, depending upon their personal circumstances, mostly having to do with the quantum of other income and foreign tax credits. Unfortunately, for these people, properly reporting the income earned inside a plan can be complicated.

[¶2183a.29] *Who Reports an RRSP/RRIF in the United States?*

Because a regular RRSP is a "grantor trust" to the person who contributed the funds, that person is the responsible party while he or she is alive.

The answer is unclear in the case of a spousal RRSP. It could be argued that this plan is not a grantor trust. Similarly, a person (such as a spouse) who inherits an RRSP could argue it's not a grantor trust. As a practical matter, the IRS treats them the same way.

[¶2183a.30] *Social Security Receipts*

Old Age Security (OAS), CPP, and Quebec Pension Plan (QPP) benefits are subject to Canadian tax under normal Canadian rules (¶913 and ¶915).

Above (¶2178.50), it is noted that for a Canadian resident who is a U.S. NRA, U.S. Social Security benefits are exempt from U.S. tax under the Treaty. However, the wording of the Treaty is not as generous in respect of OAS, CPP, and QPP paid to American citizens and residents abroad. From the wording of the Treaty, it would appear that such income paid to Americans residing in Canada are subject to U.S. tax.

However, the IRS administratively treats OAS, CPP, and QPP as Social Security for these purposes, and does not tax these amounts. This income does not need to be reported on the U.S. return.

As a practical matter, in most cases, foreign tax credits would alleviate any double taxation on the U.S. return, so the net tax effect of this uncertainty is rarely meaningful.

(Other Publications: U.S. Treasury Department Technical Explanation of the 3rd Protocol, Art. 9 (1995-13-17))

[¶2183b] OTHER U.S. TAX ISSUES

[¶2183b.40] *Principal Residence*

An individual can exclude from income up to $250,000 ($500,000 if married filing jointly) of the gain from the sale of a principal residence. This is a permanent exclusion, not just a deferral or rollover of gain until a later time.

Generally, to qualify, the individual must have used the property as a principal residence for at least two of the five years preceding the sale. If a taxpayer is unable to fulfill the two-year occupancy requirement because of a transfer by his or her employer, or certain other circumstances, a prorated exclusion may be available based on the ratio of years occupied to two years.

A U.S. citizen resident in Canada who recognizes a large gain on the sale of a home will often be dismayed to see that there is U.S. tax on the gain, when Canada exempts the entire gain.

A former Canadian resident who has moved to the United States can increase the U.S. cost basis in his or her principal residence to its fair market value on the date he or she ceased to be a Canadian resident. For someone who was not a non-U.S. citizen/resident prior to the move, this mechanism excludes from U.S. tax any appreciation during the Canadian residence prior to becoming a U.S. resident.

(Other Publications: IRC 121; Canada–U.S. Tax Treaty, Art. XIII(6))

[¶2183b.50] *Alimony and Child Support*

Alimony/spousal support is taxable only in the country of residence of the recipient.

The Treaty also provides that the recipient is not taxable on such amounts if the amounts are not taxable in the country of residence of the payer. Child support is not taxable or deductible in the United States. It is rarely taxable in Canada (only applying to unmodified support agreements and orders made prior to May 1, 1997).

Thus, where the payer lives in one country, and the recipient in the other, child support will be exempt from tax.

Each country has different rules as to whether a payment is alimony or child support. Where there is doubt as to whether a payment is alimony or child support, the laws of the country of the taxpayer are determinative.

(Other Publications: Canada–U.S. Tax Treaty, Art. XVIII(6))

[¶2183b.60] *Income Exclusion for Citizens or Residents Living Abroad*

A U.S. citizen or resident who has a tax home in Canada may, under certain circumstances, elect to exclude from income taxable in the United States up to US$101,300 (for 2016) of foreign earned income.

An additional amount, known as the housing exclusion or deduction, may also be available for exclusion in respect of certain foreign housing costs. The thresholds for the housing exclusion or deduction are different depending on where the individual lives in Canada.

(Other Publications: IRC 911)

[¶2183b.70] *Itemized Deductions*

An individual is allowed to deduct non-business expenses, referred to as itemized deductions, in computing the amount of income subject to tax. Examples of itemized deductions are:

- medical expenses;
- U.S. state and local income taxes;
- residential property taxes (including those on Canadian real estate);
- home mortgage interest;
- investment interest;
- contributions of cash or property to U.S. and Canadian charities;
- unreimbursed casualty or theft losses in excess of statutory limitations; and
- miscellaneous expenses relating to the production of income, including union dues, safety deposit box fees, and professional fees.

Many of these expenses have floors; that is, amounts below certain thresholds that are not deductible.

Instead of utilizing itemized deductions, an individual may claim a standard deduction. For 2016, the standard deduction for joint returns is $12,600 ($9,300 for head of household; $6,300 for singles and married filing separately).

An additional standard deduction is allowed for individuals who are either blind or 65 years of age or older.

(Other Publications: IRC 63; 151; IR-2013-87)

[¶2183b.75] *Personal Exemption*

Each person may claim a personal exemption for him or herself, a spouse, and each dependant. For 2016, the personal exemption is $4,050.

(Other Publications: IRC 63; IR-2013-87; RP-2013-35)

[¶2183b.80] *U.S. Income Tax Rates*

The United States, like Canada, uses a graduated tax rate system. Unlike Canada, which has only one set of rates which applies to every individual filing a Canadian tax return, the United States has four different sets of tax rates.

An individual can file a U.S. resident tax return as: single, married filing jointly, surviving spouse, married filing separate and head of household. The first two are the most common statutes. These are the rates for 2016:

Single

Taxable income	*Marginal Rate*
$ 0 – $ 9,275	*10%*
9,276 – 37,650	*15%*
37,651 – 91,150	*25%*
91,151 – 190,150	*28%*
190,151 – 413,350	*33%*
413,351 – 415,050	*35%*
415,051 and over	*39.6%*

Married Filing Jointly

Taxable income	*Marginal Rate*
$ 0 – $ 18,550	*10%*
18,551 – 75,300	*15%*
75,301 – 151,900	*25%*
151,901 – 231,450	*28%*
231,451 – 413,350	*33%*
413,351 – 466,950	*35%*
466,951 and over	*39.6%*

Capital gains on assets held for a year and qualified dividends are taxed at lower rates. The rate for individuals with total income in the 10% or 15% tax bracket is 0% for net gains on assets held more than 12 months.

The maximum tax rate on net capital gains remains at 15% for individuals with total income in all but the top bracket. The rate is 20% for individuals in the 39.6% bracket. This rate applies to most assets with the exception of collectibles, certain real property gains, and certain qualified small business stock; different rates apply to these assets.

In addition, there is a Net Investment Income Tax of 3.8%. This tax applies only to investment income (generally, interest, dividends, rents, and royalties), and only to high-income taxpayers (over $250,000 for married filing jointly; $125,000 for married filing separately; $200,000 for others). It is possible that the Canada-US Social Security Totalization Agreement precludes the United States from applying this tax to Canadian residents, but the IRS has not pronounced on this question.

(Tax Topics: No. 2188; Other Publications: IRC 1; 1411; Rev. Proc. 2013-35)

[¶2183b.95] *U.S. Foreign Tax Credits*

For U.S. tax purposes, an individual may choose to claim foreign income tax as a credit or as a deduction against income. It is rarely advantageous to claim the latter.

A taxpayer may elect to claim the credit on either the cash or accrual basis. The accrual basis is most commonly used for Americans in Canada, because it most often best matches the Canadian tax. In this manner, double taxation is easier to avoid. Also, because it uses figures appearing on the tax returns, it is often easiest to administer.

The United States divides foreign income and tax into two primary "baskets"— passive and general. The rules around this division are complex, but essentially passive income includes most interest, dividends, rents, royalties and capital gains. General-basket income includes everything that is not passive.

Under U.S. domestic law, there is no foreign tax credit in respect of the Net Investment Income Tax. It is arguable whether the Canadian treaty would allow for a credit in respect of Canadian-source investment income.

(Tax Topics: No. 2188; Other Publications: IRC 27; 55; 59; 901; 904; Canada–U.S. Tax Treaty, Art. XXIV(4), (5))

[¶2183b.97] *U.S. Alternative Minimum Tax (AMT)*

The United States has an AMT that works in a similar way to Canadian AMT. Certain deductions are added back (e.g., state taxes, miscellaneous deductions) or modified (e.g., depreciation). There is a basic exemption, and the remainder is taxed at a different set of rates than apply to regular tax.

[¶2183b.99] *Options for Delinquent Filers*

Many Canadian-resident individuals are also U.S. citizens or green-card holders. A large number of these are not aware of their U.S. filing obligations, and find themselves not in compliance. In recent years, the IRS has implemented a number of programs with the potential to reduce penalties, to encourage delinquent taxpayers to become compliant:

With the FAST Act becoming law as of December 4, 2015, a U.S. person with a tax debt of $50,000 or more could lose his/her U.S. passport. A tax debt includes penalties. Given the size of penalties for failure to file common international information returns, it is very easy for a U.S. citizen living abroad to reach this threshold.

Offshore Voluntary Disclosure Program (OVDP)

This program requires a taxpayer to file tax returns and reporting forms for the eight most recent tax years for which the filing deadline has already passed. An OVDP filing protects individuals from criminal liabilities. It is primarily intended for people who chose not to disclose offshore assets and/or income. Typically, the penalty under this program is 27.5% of the assets not reported.

Higher 50% penalties may apply if a foreign financial institution at which the taxpayer has an unreported account has been identified as being under investigation.

Streamlined Filing Compliance Procedures

The streamlined procedures are intended for taxpayers whose failure to file income tax returns and report their foreign assets was not due to wilful conduct. This program comes in two types:

(1) Individuals Residing outside the United States (Foreign Offshore Procedures)

Under this program, a taxpayer is generally able to avoid all penalties (failure to file the returns, failure-to-pay, accuracy-related, failure to file a Foreign Bank Account Report (FBAR) and failure to file foreign reporting forms).

To be eligible, the taxpayer's failure to file cannot be wilful and he or she cannot be under IRS investigation or audit. In addition, for at least one of the past three years, the American cannot have an abode in the United States and must have been physically present outside of the United States for at least 330 days per year.

These procedures require the taxpayer to file three years' returns and six years' FBARs (¶2187), pay the outstanding taxes with interest, and certify that his or her failure to file was not wilful. The IRS is also requiring taxpayers with material wealth to describe the way the wealth was accumulated, focusing on whether it was derived from U.S. sources and whether it was legally received.

(2) Individuals Residing in the United States (Domestic Procedures)

To be eligible for this program, an individual must have previously filed U.S. tax returns for the past three years, but failed to report foreign financial assets or income therefrom.

A penalty equal to 5% of the highest aggregate value of the taxpayer's foreign financial assets will be applied, but other penalties, described above, should not be assessed.

To be eligible for the Domestic Procedures, the taxpayer's failure to file cannot be wilful and he or she cannot be under IRS investigation or audit.

These procedures require the taxpayer to file three years' returns and six years' FBARs (¶2187), pay the outstanding taxes with interest, and certify that his or her failure to file was not wilful.

The Streamlined Procedures is not a permanent program. It is not known when the IRS will terminate it, but it has indicated that it will not be available indefinitely.

Delinquent FBAR (see ¶2187 below) Submission Procedures

Provided that the taxpayer is not currently under audit or received a request to file the delinquent forms, Form FinCEN 114 should be filed under regular procedures with a statement explaining the reason for late filing. No penalty should be imposed if all income related to these accounts has been properly reported on a U.S. tax return, and all related U.S. taxes have been paid.

Delinquent International Information Return Submission Procedures

Provided that the taxpayer is not currently under audit or received a request to file the delinquent forms, the taxpayer may file delinquent information returns (Forms 3520/5471/8865, etc.) with a statement establishing reasonable cause for the failure to file and indicating the entity or entities to which the forms related were not engaged in tax evasion.

More information can be found on the IRS website: http://www.irs.gov/Individuals/International-Taxpayers/Delinquent-International-Information-Return-Submission-Procedures.

[¶2184] STATE INCOME TAXATION

See ¶2180.

[¶2186] CANADIAN FOREIGN TAX CREDITS

In general, Canada grants credit for U.S. taxes paid in respect of U.S.-source income.

Credit is allowed only assuming the least possible U.S. tax, whether under domestic law or the treaty rules. Taxes arising in respect of non-U.S.-source income, solely by reason of U.S. citizenship are not eligible for credit. The Net Investment Income Tax (NIIT) applies only to U.S. citizens and residents (and U.S. residents who factually live in Canada are eligible to file as non-resident aliens). Consequently, NIIT is not eligible for a foreign tax credit.

Where U.S. tax is owing solely by virtue of citizenship, the United States will allow an additional foreign tax credit to mitigate the double taxation (NIIT possibly aside).

Where a U.S. citizen resident in Canada earns U.S.-source dividends, complications can arise. Normally, under U.S. domestic law, U.S. tax on qualified dividends is at the preferential long-term capital rate (up to 23.8%,¶2183.80). However, if the dividends are non-qualified, the rate can be higher. In this case, Canada allows a credit for 15% and a deduction for the additional tax. The United States then allows a special foreign tax credit for this same additional tax — a double benefit.

This issue rarely arises with interest or certain royalties, because the U.S. tax on these items are generally limited to zero.

(ITA: 20(11); 126(7) "non-business income tax" (b), (d); CRA Document No.: U.S. citizens resident in Canada, *September 26, 1997,* CRA Document No. 9524810; Foreign tax credit (FTC) in respect of U.S. Alternative Minimum Tax (AMT) and Credit for Prior Year Minimum Tax (MTC), *September 26, 1997,* CRA

Document No. 9717730; U.S. state income taxes, *June 13, 1997,* CRA Document No. 9629001; Taxation of U.S. Citizens Resident in Canada, *October 19, 1998,* CRA Document No. 9826226; Other Publications: Canada–U.S. Tax Treaty, Art. XXIV(4), (5), (7))

[¶2186.10] *Green Card Holders*

As noted above (¶2174), a green card holder by default files a U.S. tax return as a resident, but it is possible for such a person who lives in Canada to elect to file as an NRA.

This choice may adversely impact the individual's immigration status in the United States, or his or her ability to obtain U.S. citizenship in the future. Consequently, some individuals in this situation will choose to file as U.S. residents. A person who does this may pay more U.S. tax as a result. This excess tax is not eligible for credit in Canada.

[¶2187] NON-U.S. FINANCIAL ACCOUNTS

In an effort to ensure that U.S. persons report worldwide income, the United States requires each U.S. persons to report ownership of foreign (non-U.S.) financial accounts and specified financial assets.

There are two separate forms:

- Specified Financial Assets (form 8938) which forms part of the income tax return. For a resident of Canada filing separately in the United States, the threshold for filing is a value of $200,000 per person on December 31, or $300,000 at any time during the year; and

- Foreign Bank Account Report ("FBAR" — form FinCEN 114), which is filed separately. The threshold for filing is $10,000 at any time during the year. This threshold was set in 1970, and is not indexed for inflation. This is filed separately from the U.S. individual income tax return.

Penalties for failure to file are quite significant — beginning at $10,000 per account, per year.

In February 2011, the Financial Crimes Enforcement Network (FinCEN) issued final regulations addressing FBAR filing issues. Changes to both the general filing rules, and specific provisions that address trusts and trust beneficiaries, affect the FBAR rules applicable to trusts and trust beneficiaries. U.S. persons affiliated with trusts holding interests in foreign accounts (including U.S. settlors, trustees, and beneficiaries) and their advisors, will need to review these rules to determine who must report.

Effective September 1, 2012, an individual who has failed to provide such reporting may be able to rectify that failure without penalty.

Effective July 1, 2013, Form FinCEN 114 must be filed electronically. Tax preparers electronically filing forms on a client's behalf should maintain the appropriate authorization form in their records (Form FinCEN 114a).

(Tax Topics: No. 2116; Other Publications: IRC 668; 951-65; 1291-8; 6038-6038D; 6046-6046A; 6048; Forms 8938; FinCEN 114)

[¶2188] NON-U.S. ENTITIES

Many U.S. persons in Canada own interests in Canadian trusts, partnerships, and corporations.

Like many developed countries, including Canada, the United States has complicated regimes surrounding foreign (non-U.S.) entities, including controlled foreign corporations, foreign partnerships, and foreign trusts. Under certain circumstances, an individual may be required to include in U.S. income amounts earned by a corporation or trust, even if undistributed.

Distributions from certain corporations (passive foreign investment companies) or trusts may be subject to additional taxes.

These U.S. taxes can be particularly problematic and ultimately punitive. Canada will not provide a foreign tax credit in respect of them, because (a) the income does not appear on the Canadian return, and (b) the tax arises solely by virtue of the individual's U.S. citizenship. Double taxation often results.

A U.S. person who owns an interest in a foreign entity may be required to include with his or her return a detailed form to report his or her interest in, and the status and activities of that entity. Penalties for failure to file are quite significant.

(Other Publications: IRC 668; 951-65; 1291-8; 6038–6038D; 6046–6046A; 6048; Forms 3520; 3520-A; 5471; 8621; 8858)

[¶2189] FILING DEADLINE

The ordinary U.S. filing deadline is April 15 of the following year.

All taxpayers are entitled to a six-month extension to file a return merely by filing form 4868. This filing does not extend the time to pay the tax, but it means the late-filing penalty will not apply if the return is filed by October 15.

An individual living abroad is entitled to an automatic two-month extension of time (until June 15) to file and pay without filing a form 4868. Interest is charged on unpaid tax from April 15, but there is no late-payment penalty until June 15.

To qualify for this special treatment, on the April 15 due date:

(1) The taxpayer must be living outside the United States and his or her tax home must be outside the United States; or

(2) He or she must be in military service outside the United States.

For these "out of country" taxpayers, filing form 4868 only adds four months (as opposed to six months) to the June 15 filing date otherwise allowed for being outside the United States. The additional four months of time to file is not an extension of time to pay.

A taxpayer who is abroad may request an additional extension of time to file to December 15. This request is made using an ordinary letter. The IRS has discretion to accept or reject this request, but it is ordinarily granted as a matter of course.

When a due date falls on a weekend or U.S. holiday, the due date is extended to the next business day.

(Other Publications: IRC 6072; Treas. Reg. 1.6081-4; 1.6081-5)

[¶2190] MOVING TO OR FROM THE UNITED STATES

[¶2190.20] *Deemed Disposition on Emigration*

Upon cessation of Canadian residency, Canada generally taxes gains arising prior to the date of emigration. This taxation is done by way of a deemed disposition (¶534).

When this happens, the United States allows the individual to elect to treat the asset as having been disposed of at the same time for U.S. tax purposes. For someone who was previously not a U.S. citizen or resident, this election establishes a new tax "basis", to be used in calculating the gain or loss for U.S. tax purposes upon an eventual disposition.

For someone who was a U.S. citizen or resident at the time, this choice may result in immediate U.S. tax, but it will allow the Canadian tax to be used as a foreign tax credit, thus mitigating double taxation.

(ITA: 128.1, (4); Other Publications: Canada–U.S. Tax Treaty, Art. XIII(7); Rev Proc 2010-19; IT-173R2 [Archived])

[¶2190.30] *Moving Expenses*

When an individual immigrates to or emigrates from the United States, there will ordinarily be costs for the move. The following expenses are deductible:

- transportation of household goods and personal effects;
- travel costs; and
- lodging.

The above apply to the individual and his or her family.

The cost of meals, temporary lodging near the new work site, house-hunting trips, and selling or buying a home are not deductible.

Employer-reimbursed moving expenses are excluded from an employee's income, provided that the expenses would be deductible by the employee and they are reimbursed under an accountable plan. Reimbursements in excess of these amounts are taxable.

Reimbursements are sourced to the location to which the employee is moving, except where an employee is moving back to the place where he or she originally came from and the reimbursement is pursuant to an agreement made in advance of the employee's temporary assignment. As a result, an amount paid to an individual in respect of a move to the United States from Canada, regardless of the timing of such a payment, will generally be considered U.S.-source employment income.

(Other Publications: IRC 217)

[¶2191] U.S. ESTATE AND GIFT TAXATION

The United States has a wealth transfer tax system in addition to the various income-type taxes. Canada has not had such a system for some time, so few Canadians are aware of the U.S. system.

The system is not designed to raise meaningful revenue — the base is too narrow, and the rates too high to accomplish that goal. Instead, the main objective is to limit the ability of wealthy individuals to transfer their success to their children. As a result, it is often possible, especially for individuals who live outside the United States, to successfully plan to avoid these taxes, provided proper steps are taken early enough.

The transfer tax system has two main components — estate tax and gift tax, and a secondary one, generation skipping transfer tax (GSTT). These are all unified.

The focal point is estate tax. Most people wait until death to pass on wealth to their heirs. However, an estate tax alone would be easily circumvented by individuals making lifetime gifts, so a gift tax is a necessary tool. Finally, to limit people's ability to avoid the estate tax for one or more generations (for instance, by transferring wealth to grandchildren instead of children), the GSTT provides an added layer of tax.

(Other Publications: IRC 2001 to 2801)

[¶2191.05] *Residency for U.S. Estate and Gift Tax Purposes*

As with income taxes, transfer taxes are applied differently based on U.S. citizenship or residency. A citizen or resident is subject to tax on worldwide transfers. An NRA is subject to tax only on transfers of U.S.-*situs* property.

The term "resident" has a different meaning for transfer tax purposes than for income tax purposes. The green card and substantial presence tests are not determinative. One is a resident only if one is domiciled in the United States. One's domicile is initially established by the location of one's birth or the domicile of one's father (with married parents). It is difficult to change domicile — a change is established when an individual lives in a new jurisdiction with the demonstrated intention of staying indefinitely.

(Other Publications: IRC 20.0-1(*b*)(1))

[¶2191.10] *U.S. Estate Tax*

A decedent's gross estate less allowable deductions leaves the taxable estate. Tax is applied at graduated rates, and then a unified credit is deducted. The remainder is the estate tax. Gift tax previously paid is then deducted from this amount to arrive at the amount payable.

U.S. estate tax is eligible for a Canadian foreign tax credit. The credit is limited to the Canadian tax on gains from U.S.-*situs* property.

(Other Publications: IRC 2001; 2010; 2101; 2102; Canada–U.S. Tax Treaty, Art. XXIX-B(6))

[¶2191.13] *Gross Estate*

The gross estate of a U.S. citizen or domicile includes all tangible and intangible property owned by the resident at the time of death.

For an NRA, only U.S.-*situs* property is included.

For an NRA whose worldwide gross estate is under $1.2 million, the only assets which may be subjected to tax are those upon which U.S. income tax would apply if a capital gain were realized. This rule means that as a practical matter, real estate and business assets are subject to tax. The main effect is to exclude shares of stock of U.S. companies for individuals with modest estates.

It is important to note certain items which may not normally be considered property of the deceased are included in the gross estate, for instance:

- Proceeds of insurance owned by the decedent are included in the gross estate. This fact is important both for NRAs (¶2191.16 treaty unified credit) and U.S. citizens/residents;
- Property previously transferred with rights retained, such as transfers with retained life estates and revocable transfers, are included in the gross estate; and
- The current value of certain types of assets gifted within three years prior to the date of death.

Property is included in the gross estate at fair market value at the date of death or the elective alternate valuation, which is six months after the date of death.

(Other Publications: Canada–U.S. Tax Treaty, Art. XXIX-B(8))

[¶2191.14] *Situs of Property*

The *situs* of property is important for an NRA, because, as noted above, this fact will determine whether it is subject to estate tax. It is also important to a citizen/resident, because it will have an impact on the foreign tax credit (see ¶2191.13).

Situs is determined as follows:

- Real and tangible personal property — physical location.
- Shares of stock of a corporation — where the issuer is organized.
- Debt obligations, including bank deposits — same as shares, except U.S. portfolio debt is treated as foreign.
- Life insurance proceeds on the deceased — the domicile of the decedent.

(Other Publications: IRC 2104-5)

[¶2191.15] *Deductions*

The taxable estate is determined by deducting from the gross estate:

- Transfers for the benefit of a spouse:
  - Property passing to a surviving spouse who is a U.S. citizen. A spouse who is merely a U.S. resident does not qualify.
  - Property passing to a qualified domestic trust (QDoT). A QDoT is a trust set up for a non-citizen spouse. The estate tax becomes payable upon distribution of assets from this trust, or upon the surviving spouse's death. Typically, such a trust requires a U.S. trustee and places restrictions on the spouse's use of the assets.
- Other expenses:
  - Administration expenses;
  - Claims against the estate;
  - Mortgages;
  - Charitable donations to U.S. and Canadian charities; and
  - Losses incurred during the administration of the estate.

An NRA's estate may deduct only a *pro rata* amount of expenses based on the value of U.S. and foreign-*situs* assets. These deductions are allowed only if the executor discloses the entire estate in the estate tax return.

(Other Publications: IRC 2051; 2056)

[¶2191.16] *Rates and Credits for U.S. Citizens and Residents*

The estate tax applies at graduated rates, up to 40% (for 2016). A non-refundable unified credit (UC) is then applied.

The UC is equal to the tax on an estate of $5.45 million for 2016 ($5.43 million for 2015). As a result of this calculation, for a citizen/resident who has made no taxable gifts prior to death, estate tax applies at a flat rate of 40% on the portion of the estate above $5.45 million.

The estate of a decedent who was previously married is entitled to an additional credit. If the first-deceased spouse did not use his or her UC, the second decedent may claim a UC equal to the tax on $10.90 million. This calculation applies only where the first-deceased spouse died after December 31, 2010 and a proper portability election was made.

If the individual paid gift tax in a prior year, that gift tax is credited against the estate tax.

Finally, an individual is entitled to a credit for state and foreign inheritance taxes in respect of foreign-*situs* property. Canadian income tax relating to deemed dispositions on death is deemed to be a foreign inheritance tax.

(ITA: 70(6); Other Publications: IRC 2001-16; Canada–U.S. Tax Treaty, Art. XXIX-B(7))

[¶2191.17] *Rates and Unified Credit for NRAs*

Under U.S. domestic law, the estate of an NRA is entitled to a UC of only $13,000 — equivalent to a mere $60,000 exemption. This is quite small compared to the amount allowed to a U.S. citizen/resident.

However, under the treaty, the estate of a Canadian resident is eligible for the same UC as a U.S. citizen, proportionate to the U.S. *situs* assets. As a mathematical consequence, if the worldwide gross estate is less than $5.45 million (2016), there will be no tax.

To access this credit, all worldwide information necessary for verification and computation must be provided.

(Other Publications: IRC 2101-2; Canada–U.S. Tax Treaty, Art. XXIX-B(6))

[¶2191.18] *Bequest to a Non-Citizen Spouse*

The Treaty provides an additional credit against the U.S. estate tax for qualifying transfers to a non-U.S. citizen spouse if all the following conditions are met:

(1) the individual was, at the time of death, a U.S. citizen or a resident of either the United States or Canada;

(2) the surviving spouse was, at the time of the individual's death, a resident of either the United States or Canada;

(3) if both the individual and the surviving spouse were residents of the United States at the time of death, one or both was a citizen of Canada; and

(4) the executor of the estate elects under these provisions on a timely basis and waives the benefits of any estate tax marital deduction.

The credit is equal to the tax on the U.S.-*situs* assets transferred to the spouse, but the additional credit cannot exceed the original unified credit amount.

(Other Publications: IRC 2001; 2010; 2101; 2102; Canada–U.S. Tax Treaty, Art. XXIX-B)

[¶2191.20] *Filing Requirements*

The personal representative of the estate must file an estate tax return and pay the tax due within nine months after the date of death if the gross estate exceeds the effective exclusion ($5.45 million worldwide for U.S. citizens or domiciled aliens) or $60,000 (U.S.-*situs* for NRAs).

Form 4768, Application for Extension of Time to File a Return and/or Pay U.S. Estate (and Generation-Skipping Transfer) Taxes, may be used to apply for an automatic six-month extension to file.

Generally, a taxpayer has three years from the date the original return was filed, or two years from the date of payment (whichever is later) to file a claim.

[¶2191.30] *State Estate Tax*

Most states have no estate tax. As for the others, exemptions and credits for gifts and estates are often different from those allowable for federal purposes. In addition, not all states recognize the impact of the Canada–U.S. Treaty. Accordingly, it is possible to be liable for state, but not federal, transfer taxes.

[¶2191.40] *Canadian Foreign Tax Credit*

The Treaty allows a credit to a resident of Canada for U.S. estate tax payable in respect of property situated in the United States. This deduction is limited to the Canadian tax on income and gains arising from within the United States (essentially, the assets subjected to U.S. estate tax).

(Other Publications: Canada–U.S. Tax Treaty, Art. XXIX-B(6))

[¶2191.45] *Spousal Rollover: Canadian Rules*

Current Canadian law generally permits capital property of a deceased Canadian resident to be transferred to a Canadian resident spouse (or common-law partner), or to a spousal trust, at cost rather than at fair market value (¶1922). The result is that no taxable gain on the property is realized until the surviving spouse sells the property or dies without passing the property to another spouse under circumstances qualifying for the spousal rollover.

The Treaty provides that an individual who is resident in the United States immediately before death, as well as his or her spouse, will be deemed to be a resident of Canada for purposes of the Canadian spousal rollover provisions. Furthermore, certain U.S. trusts may qualify as a special trust under the rollover provisions, if agreed to, and subject to the conditions set by Canada.

(Other Publications: Canada–U.S. Tax Treaty, Art. XXIX-B(5))

[¶2192] TAXATION OF GIFTS

[¶2192.10] *Gifts Subject to Tax*

A gift tax is levied on the fair market value of property interests transferred without adequate consideration.

U.S. citizens and other individuals domiciled in the United States are subject to the gift tax on transfers of all property regardless of physical location. Because Canada has no gift tax, these transfers are rarely considered from a gift tax perspective. This lack of awareness can create significant exposures to U.S. tax. Here are some common examples of actions by a U.S. citizen than can create gift tax:

- purchasing a home, and registering title in the name of an NRA spouse;
- paying off the mortgage of such a home;
- helping a child purchase a first home by way of a gift, partial ownership, or an interest-free loan; and
- completing an estate freeze of a corporation in favour of a child or an NRA spouse.

NRAs are subject to the tax only on gifts of real property and tangible personal property physically located in the United States (but not intangible property, such as shares of U.S. companies).

The estate and gift taxes are largely designed to be integrated. A notable departure from this approach is that gifts by NRAs of intangible personal property, such as stocks, bonds, notes, bank deposits, and intellectual property, are not subject to tax.

(Other Publications: IRC 2503)

[¶2192.20] *Deductions, Exclusions, and Elections*

Each person can exclude gifts aggregating $14,000 or less per donee (2016).

A person can gift a U.S. citizen spouse an unlimited amount free of gift tax. However, if the spouse is not a U.S. citizen, then the donor is only permitted an annual exclusion of $148,000 for 2016.

U.S. citizens and resident individuals are allowed to exclude gifts to qualifying charitable organizations. NRAs may exclude gifts to qualifying U.S. charitable organizations.

Direct payment of certain medical or educational expenses does not constitute a taxable gift.

A U.S.-citizen couple may elect to "split" gifts, treating them as made one-half by each spouse, resulting in an effective annual exclusion per donee of $28,000 in 2016.

(Other Publications: IRC 2503)

[¶2192.25] *Rates, Credits, and Returns*

Gifts are taxed at marginal rates between 18% and 40% (2016). The tax rate is based on the cumulative amount of lifetime gifts made. Unlike income tax, it doesn't reset to zero each year.

For a U.S. citizen or resident, the UC may be accessed to reduce or eliminate the tax on the first $5.45 million of lifetime gifts. Because the taxes are integrated, the UC utilized on a gift tax return will not be available on the estate tax return.

No UC is allowed to an NRA in respect of a gift. As a result, taxable gifts above the thresholds will create actual tax.

Canada does not allow a foreign tax credit for U.S. gift tax, because it is not a tax levied on income.

Consequently, an NRA should attempt to avoid making gifts of U.S. real and tangible personal property in excess of the annual exclusion amounts.

Taxable gifts must be reported on form 709 by April 15 of the year following the gift. The tax is due at that time.

Form 8892 may be filed to extend the time to file a return, but not to pay the tax. If the taxpayer is required to file an income tax return as well, then any extension of time to file the income tax return automatically extends the time to file the gift tax return. As a result, an NRA will typically have an automatic extension to June 15.

(Other Publications: IRC 2502)

[¶2192.30] *State Gift Taxes*

Many states may also impose gift tax on the worldwide assets of residents and on property within the state owned by non-residents. State exemptions and credits for gifts and estates are often different from those allowable for federal purposes. It is possible to be liable for state, but not federal, gift tax.

[¶2193] PRE-MOVE TAX PLANNING

Moving to the United States offers a number of opportunities and traps. Accordingly, an individual should undertake careful tax planning before moving. Once the move is done, several opportunities are lost, and it may be impossible to avoid some of the traps.

While Canadian and U.S. tax is complicated, planning for moving increases the complexity exponentially. It is highly recommended that professional advice be obtained in advance of the move.

[¶2193.05] *Timing of the Move*

An individual who moves to the United States is frequently treated as a resident for income tax purposes from the first day of arrival. However, there are circumstances where a person may be treated, or elect to be treated as resident January 1 of the year of arrival, January 1 of the following year, or on some other date.

Both Canada and the United States have graduated income tax rates; that is, the higher one's income, the higher the tax rates. In general, to minimize worldwide taxation, a move should take place in the middle of the year to utilize the lower tax rate brackets of both countries.

(Other Publications: Treas. Reg. 301.7701(b)-4; Canada–U.S. Tax Treaty, Art. IV(2))

[¶2193.10] *Carryover of Cost Basis*

In determining the U.S. tax cost "basis", by default, U.S. tax rules apply throughout an asset's life, even when that asset has no U.S. tax effect. In general, an asset brought into the United States by an individual has a basis equal to original cost, adjusted for capital improvements and depreciation.

Therefore, before establishing residence, a migrant may wish to increase the basis in appreciated assets to current value by converting them to cash or otherwise causing the appreciation to be recognized using U.S. income tax concepts. These transactions are called "churning". Income tax implications in Canada should also be considered. It may be possible to design a transaction which has no net effect on Canadian tax, but increases the U.S. tax basis.

This type of planning is not usually necessary, because where Canada treats an individual as having disposed of property immediately before moving to the United States, the individual can elect to be treated as also having disposed of and reacquired the property at its fair market value for U.S. purposes.

There are still situations where churning can be helpful, particularly within RRSPs and corporations.

(Other Publications: Canada–U.S. Tax Treaty, Art. XIII(7); Rev. Proc. 2010-19)

[¶2193.15] *Accelerating or Deferring Income*

There are some circumstances where income may be made to arise before or after the move. In these circumstances, an individual may be able to accelerate and recognize income from sources outside the United States that would otherwise be received after establishing U.S. residence, or doing the opposite — deferring income.

Depending on the circumstances, the Canadian tax on a particular item of income may be larger or smaller than the U.S. and state taxes. An example of income where timing can be adjusted is withdrawals from an RRSP or RRIF. Withdrawal while a resident of Canada makes the income subject to ordinary Canadian tax. Withdrawal while a U.S. resident makes the income subject to Canadian withholding tax, and U.S. tax at ordinary rates.

Stock options are generally taxed more favorably in Canada than in the United States. In order to avoid paying any incremental tax to the United States on the exercise of the stock options, an individual may wish to consider exercising prior to being considered a U.S. resident, particularly if the stock option income will be significant. Non-qualifying stock options are taxed as employment income in the United States at the individual's highest marginal tax rate. Once the stock options have been exercised, the appreciation in the stock from that point forward could be taxed in the United States at the long-term capital gains mentioned in ¶2183.80, providing the stock is held for more than 12 months after the options are exercised. Professional advice should be obtained before exercising stock options.

For most types of income, the timing is not negotiable, or even if it is possible to defer receipt, Canadian tax may have to be paid on the income anyway. One simple example of this is employment income earned for services rendered prior to emigration. If the income is received prior to the move, it is taxable only in Canada. If it is received after the move (i.e., while a U.S. resident), it is taxable in both Canada and the United States (the United States would offer a foreign tax credit to mitigate double tax).

[¶2193.20] *Tax Deferrals and RRSPs*

Many tax deferrals, such as those relating to reserves for sales of capital property, and the Home Buyers' Plan (HBP), are terminated upon emigration. With no planning, the deferral will come into income. It may be helpful to alter the arrangements around the assets that created these deferrals, or to repay items (such as the HBP).

It may be beneficial to make contributions to an RRSP prior to emigration. In years after emigration, the ability to benefit from the contribution room generally disappears.

(ITA: 40(1)(*a*)(iii)(C), 146.01(5))

[¶2193.30] *Gifts and Transfers to Foreign Trusts*

Canadian-situs assets owned by an individual are subject not only to U.S. income tax when residence is established, but may be subject to gift or estate taxes if the assets subsequently are transferred. Individuals should consider making gifts to children or other intended heirs before establishing residence. Gifts of Canadian-situs property to Canadian-situs trusts will avoid not only future estate and gift taxes, but also income tax if the income is not distributed to resident beneficiaries.

However, a Canadian person who plans to establish a residence in the United States cannot avoid U.S. tax by transferring property to another Canadian person who in turn establishes a foreign grantor trust for the first individual. If such a transfer occurs, the individual is considered to be the grantor of the trust and is taxed currently on the trust income.

[¶2193.40] *Canadian Corporations*

A U.S. resident owning an equity interest in a foreign (non-U.S.) corporation may be required to file information returns disclosing corporate financial data. Such a person may also be required to include in income a portion of their share of the foreign corporation's income even if no distribution is received (¶2188).

Other rules may cause adverse U.S. taxation upon the receipt of distributions from foreign corporations or upon the sale of the stock. These rules are extremely complex. Even the mere requirement to report properly is enough to consider selling shares in some foreign corporations before establishing U.S. residence.

[¶2193.50] *Transfer of Assets to Foreign Entities*

Once an individual becomes a U.S. resident, transfers to a foreign corporation, partnership, estate or trust may be taxable, even if the transfer would normally be tax-deferred. Thus, pre-U.S. residency transfers should be considered.

[¶2193.60] *Beneficiaries of Foreign Trusts*

U.S. resident beneficiaries of certain foreign trusts can be subject to adverse U.S. taxation upon receipt of distributions of accumulated income from the trust.

If the trust distributes its income (including gains) annually, and does not accumulate income, this problem is largely avoided. However, many trusts do not have the ability to ensure distribution annually.

TAX PLANNING CHECKLISTS

[¶2195] ENTERING CANADA

(1) If the former (non-Canadian) home is rented, withholding tax may be required by the country you are leaving. The possibility of avoiding or reducing withholding tax should be investigated prior to becoming resident (e.g., electing to pay tax on net income basis).

(2) If the former home is sold, taxes may be required in the foreign jurisdiction.

(3) If a new home is purchased in Canada, investment borrowings should be structured to maximize ability to deduct interest.

(4) Review the stock portfolio with a view to selling stock in a loss position to avoid deeming provisions which may result in a Canadian capital gain and a foreign capital loss.

(5) Consider the use of an immigration trust where investment income is significant.

(6) Ensure all remuneration is received prior to commencement of Canadian residency if the foreign country's tax rate is lower (e.g., bonus, pension plan refunds, etc.).

(7) Consider the Canadian tax effects of employment allowances received while resident in Canada.

(8) Individuals who continue to be taxed in the foreign jurisdictions should ensure that the statutory employment withholding rates are approximately reduced.

(9) Individuals remaining on a foreign payroll may be subject to Canadian withholding tax requirements, or be required to make payments by instalments.

(10) Review consequences of continued participation in foreign benefit plans.

(11) Choose date of change of residence such that the maximum benefit available through lower graduated rates of tax is utilized.

(12) Ensure full advantage is taken of savings available through an RRSP investment.

(13) Obtain provincial medical insurance if it is more comprehensive than that offered in the home country.

(14) Consider the advisability of obtaining an exemption from Canada Pension Plan participation, if covered by the Canada–U.S. Social Security Agreement or any similar agreement.

(15) Consider receiving a moving reimbursement rather than a moving allowance to avoid adverse Canadian income tax effects.

(16) Consider electing to unwind a previous deemed disposition if you are resuming Canadian residency.

[¶2196] MOVING TO CANADA FROM THE UNITED STATES

(1) Consider the additional foreign tax credit available on a U.S. tax return with respect to foreign-source income.

(2) Consider the availability of the foreign earned income and housing exclusions on a U.S. income tax return.

(3) Consider the use of automatic extension of time to file a U.S. income tax return.

(4) Consider the impact of the treaty on IRAs and 401(k) plans.

(5) Consider the impact of the treaty on the taxation of U.S. Social Security income.

[¶2197] LEAVING CANADA: GENERAL CHECKLIST

(1) Ensure date of non-residency is supported by the facts.

(2) When earning Canadian rental income as a non-resident make appropriate elections to reduce withholding tax.

(3) Consider electing no change in use for a former Canadian residence you rent while away to avoid taxation of capital gains when reinhabiting the home upon your return.

(4) When disposing of taxable Canadian property (land, buildings and other certain properties located in Canada), as a non-resident, obtain the necessary clearance certificates.

(5) Avoid selling Canadian home while resident in a foreign country to preclude foreign taxation of the capital gain. (Note that certain tax treaties contain provisions which may override this general rule. Professional advice should be obtained on specific situations.)

(6) Consider deemed disposition rules and elections when ceasing residence, and the possibility of posting security for taxes relating to the deemed disposition of property.

(7) Review investment portfolio prior to leaving with a view to minimizing departure tax.

(8) If departure tax liability is high consider the possibility of moving the date of termination of residence to take advantage of lower graduated rates.

(9) Short-term residents of Canada may be exempt from deemed disposition rules with respect to property they owned prior to attaining residence or inherited during Canadian residence.

(10) Maximize RRSP contributions.

(11) Review the methods of withdrawing funds from an RRSP as a non-resident. Lump-sum withdrawals will be subject to 25% withholding tax. An election to file a Canadian tax return is available and may result in a lower tax liability; however, the ability to reduce taxes using this election has been severely restricted.

(12) Review taxation of Canadian-related employment receipts as all such amounts are taxable in Canada regardless of when or where received.

(13) Plan to give up residence at a date which allows you to split your income between the countries to take advantage of lower marginal tax rates. Remember that personal deductions will be prorated.

(14) Ensure a final Canadian tax return is filed so that any Canadian taxes owing to/from the government can be settled.

(15) Review all health and pension plans, to determine advisability of continued participation.

(16) Review principles of taxation of capital property in the foreign jurisdiction. If tax is assessed on original cost then consideration should be given to realizing accrued gains before departure.

(17) Review shareholdings of any controlled private corporations, as a private corporation which is non-resident-controlled at any time in the year will be taxed at a higher rate than one which is controlled by Canadian residents throughout the year.

(18) Consider impact of any relevant income tax convention.

(19) Canada continues to tax gains on stock options, granted while a resident of Canada, subsequent to ceasing residence.

(20) Consider availability of the overseas employment tax credit and foreign tax credit if Canadian residence will not cease on departure.

(21) Ensure form T1161 has been filed, if required, to report property owned at the date of departure.

[¶2198] MOVING TO THE UNITED STATES: ADDITIONAL CHECKLIST

(1) Foreign business days while a U.S. resident will generate foreign-source income to improve ability to utilize foreign tax credit.

(2) The Canada–U.S. Tax Treaty provides for an exemption from U.S. tax for a Canadian resident in respect of certain employment income earned in the United States.

(3) The Canada–U.S. Tax Treaty permits a U.S. citizen who is subject to the Canadian deemed disposition rules to elect to have such gain recognized for U.S. tax purposes. This election is advantageous in the situation where the Canadian departure taxes arising upon such a deemed disposition would not otherwise be available to reduce U.S. taxes payable on the gain when such property is eventually sold.

(4) The Canada–U.S. Tax Treaty provides for a step-up in the U.S. tax basis of a principal residence located in Canada, when a Canadian resident ceases Canadian residence upon establishing U.S. residency (unless the individual is a U.S. citizen).

(5) Consider the advisability of obtaining an exemption from U.S. Social Security Tax (FICA), if covered by the Canada–U.S. Social Security Agreement.

(6) Consider deferring U.S. income tax on income earned within an RRSP or other eligible Canadian plan. The IRS requires special reporting to deal with RRSPs and certain other plans.

(7) Consider the Canadian taxation of capital gains after ceasing residency under the Canada–U.S. Income Tax Treaty.

(8) Consider planning for U.S. estate and gift taxes, including forming a pre-immigration trust.

(9) Consider election to file a U.S. resident tax return when not deemed a U.S. resident in the first year in the United States.

(10) Consider exercising stock options prior to establishing U.S. residency. Professional advice should be obtained.

(11) Review beneficial ownership or rights in foreign trusts and foreign corporations.

Chapter 22

Oil and Gas and Mining Operations

THESE POINTS ARE COVERED IN THIS CHAPTER

CRA REFERENCES RELATING TO THIS CHAPTER

CRA Forms

AB428, "Alberta Tax and Credits"; **BC428**, "British Columbia Tax"; **T101**, "Statement of Resource Expenses"; **T1086**, "Election by a Partner Waiving Canadian Development Expenses or Oil and Gas Property Expenses"; **T1229**, "Statement of Resource Expenses and Depletion Allowance"; **T5013**, "Statement of Partnership Income"; **T5013-INST**, "Statement of Partnership Income — Instructions for Recipient"

Interpretation Bulletins

IT-438R2, "Crown Charges — Resource Properties in Canada" (Archived)

Income Tax Folios

S3-F8-C1, "Principal-business Corporations in the Resource Industries"

WHAT YOU SHOULD KNOW ABOUT TAXATION OF OIL AND GAS AND MINING OPERATIONS

[¶2200] OIL AND GAS VERSUS MINING OPERATIONS

In oil and gas operations, expenditures are incurred primarily for the acquisition of property (Canadian oil and gas property expenses, ¶2220), for costs attributable to exploration (Canadian exploration expenses, ¶2210), and for costs attributable to development (Canadian development expenses (CDE), ¶2215). Tangible asset costs which are generally included in Class 41 (see Chapter 8) are of less significance.

In mining, expenditures which are tangible in nature are included in Class 41 (see Chapter 8). Costs related to the acquisition of property and certain mine development costs fall under CDE (¶2215). Exploration costs and certain costs of developing a new mine are Canadian exploration expenses (CEE) (¶2210). After 2017, costs of developing a new mine will be treated as CDE.

Certain Canadian development expenses and CEE may flow through to purchasers who acquire shares of principal business corporations that issue flow-through shares.

[¶2201] HOW INCOME FROM OIL AND GAS AND MINING OPERATIONS IS TAXED

Oil and gas and mining income is treated as business income and taxed in the same manner as business income from other sources (see Chapter 7). For individuals, however, resource income as calculated in this chapter is simply included in income subject to normal marginal rates.

Special rules apply in calculating your net income from oil and gas and mining operations including:

- exploration, development and property expenses (see ¶2210 to ¶2227);
- certain investment tax credits; and
- contributions to qualifying environmental trusts (see ¶2232).

You may have participated in oil and gas and mining activities through a partnership or through a co-ownership. Generally, the operator of each of these businesses will supply you with the necessary information to complete your tax return. Also, if you are a member of more than one partnership or co-ownership, the various types of income, deductions, and exploration, development, and property expense pools should be accumulated for all partnerships and co-ownerships.

[¶2202] WHAT IS A CANADIAN RESOURCE PROPERTY?

A Canadian resource property is defined to include interests in oil and gas resource properties and interests in mineral resource properties. The acquisition cost of a Canadian oil and gas resource property is a Canadian oil and gas property expense, and the acquisition cost of a Canadian mineral resource property is a Canadian development expense.

(1) A Canadian oil and gas resource property is any property of a taxpayer that is:

- any right, licence or privilege to explore for, drill for, or take petroleum, natural gas, or related hydrocarbons or store underground petroleum, natural gas, or related hydrocarbons in Canada;
- any oil or gas well in Canada or any real property in Canada, the principal value of which depends on its petroleum or natural gas content (not including any depreciable property); or
- any rental or royalty computed by reference to the amount or value of production from an oil or gas well in Canada or natural accumulation of petroleum or natural gas in Canada, if the payer of the rental or royalty has an interest or right in, the well or accumulation, as the case may be, and 90% or more of the rental or royalty is payable out of, or from proceeds of, the production from the well or accumulation.

(2) A Canadian mineral resource property is any property of a taxpayer that is:

- any right, licence or privilege to prospect, explore, drill or mine for minerals in a mineral resource in Canada other than a bituminous sands deposit or an oil shale deposit;
- any real property in Canada (not including any depreciable property) the principal value of which depends upon its mineral resource content other than where the mineral resource is a bituminous sands deposit or an oil shale deposit; or
- any rental or royalty computed by reference to the amount or value of production from a mineral resource in Canada, other than a bituminous sands deposit or an oil shale deposit, if the payer of the rental or royalty has an interest in or right in, the mineral resource and 90% or more of the rental or royalty is payable out of, or from proceeds of, the production from the mineral resource.

(ITA: 66(15); 248; ITR: 1104(5), (6), (7))

CANADIAN EXPLORATION EXPENSES, CANADIAN DEVELOPMENT EXPENSES, AND CANADIAN OIL AND GAS PROPERTY EXPENSES

[¶2210] WHAT ARE CANADIAN EXPLORATION EXPENSES?

Canadian exploration expenses (CEE) are costs incurred in the year:

- that are for geological, geophysical, or geochemical expenditures incurred for the purpose of determining the existence, location, extent or quality of oil or gas deposits in Canada;
- that are incurred before March 21, 2013 for the purpose of bringing a new mine into production in reasonable commercial quantities and are incurred before the

coming into production of the new mine in such quantities, including:

The definition of CEE was amended to provide that costs associated with undertaking environmental studies and community consultations that are required to obtain an exploration permit are eligible for CEE treatment. The amendment applies in respect of expenses incurred after February 2015.

Although not part of Budget 2016, the Prime Minister's mandate letter to the Minister of Finance in November 2015 included the following mandate which may lead to future amendments: "develop proposals to allow a Canadian Exploration Expenses tax deduction only in cases of unsuccessful exploration and re-direct any savings to investments in new and clean technologies."

Costs incurred after March 20, 2013 have been reclassified as CDE, subject to certain transitional rules that will permit mine development expenses incurred before 2017 to be grandfathered as CEE if they are incurred:

(1) under an agreement entered into before March 21, 2013; or

(2) as part of the development of a new mine.

In order to be considered to be part of the development of a new mine, the following conditions must be satisfied:

(1) the construction of the new mine must have been started by March 21, 2013; or

(2) the engineering and design work for the construction of the new mine must have been started before March 21, 2013.

The explanatory notes to the amendments which came into force in 2013 state that "construction" and "engineering and design work" do not include obtaining permits or regulatory approvals, conducting environmental assessments, community consultations, or impact benefit studies, or similar activities.

The amendments introduced phase-in provisions for the reclassification of mine development expenses from CEE to CDE. These expenses will continue to be CEE if they are incurred prior to 2015. In 2015, 80% of the expenses will be CEE; in 2016, 60% of the expenses will be CEE; and in 2017, 30% of the expenses will be CEE.

- that are for drilling or completing an oil or gas well in Canada, including the costs of site preparation and building temporary access roads:

- that are for the purpose of determining the existence, location, extent or quality of a mineral resource in Canada, including expenses incurred in the course of prospecting, carrying out geological, geophysical or geochemical surveys, drilling by rotary, diamond, percussion, or other methods, or trenching, digging test pits, and preliminary sampling; but do not include any Canadian development expense or expenses related to a mine which has come into production in reasonable commercial quantities;

- that are not expenses of drilling or completing an oil or gas well, but are nonetheless for the purpose of bringing a natural accumulation of petroleum or natural gas in Canada into production, and incurred prior to commencement of production in reasonable commercial quantities from such accumulation. Specifically included are costs of clearing, removing overburden and stripping, and sinking a shaft or constructing an adit or underground entry;

- that were previously Canadian development expenses, but the well has not produced within 24 months from the date of completion of drilling, or is dry or abandoned. The costs will be transferred from the Canadian development expense (¶2215) pool to the Canadian exploration expense pool;

- that are considered Canadian renewable and conservation expenses (as discussed below);

- that are specified oil sands mine development or eligible oil sands mine development expenses incurred by a taxpayer after March 21, 2011 and before 2016;

- your share of any of the above costs incurred by a partnership of which you are a member at the end of the fiscal period, subject to the restrictions imposed by the "at-risk" rules discussed at ¶2229 (the taxpayer should be in receipt of either a T5013 or a statement from the operator of property to determine his or her share of the Canadian exploration expense of the partnership for the year); and

- your share of any of the above costs renounced to you pursuant to a flow-through share agreement. The taxpayer should be in receipt of a T101, which will provide the Canadian exploration expense amounts to be added to the resource pool in the current year.

The cost of depreciable property is not included in a taxpayer's Canadian exploration expense pool.

Any amount paid as rent or for services will only qualify as a Canadian exploration expense to the extent that it relates to the use of property or to services rendered before the end of the year. This specifically disallows any claim for prepaid expenses.

The amount of a Canadian exploration expense that may reasonably be considered to have resulted in revenue is reduced by the amount of the revenue where the expense is a prospecting expense, an expense incurred for the purpose of drilling by rotary, diamond, percussion or other methods or trenching or digging test pits and preliminary sampling or is incurred for the purpose of bringing a new mine into production and the revenue is earned before the mine comes into production, however, only to the extent that the total of all such expenses exceeds the total of those revenues.

A corporation with less than $15 million of taxable capital may renounce to shareholders the first $1 million of Canadian development expenses incurred by it under a special election which will permit these expenses to be treated as Canadian exploration expenses in the hands of the individual investor. These expenses are reported on a T101 as Canadian exploration expenses.

(ITA: 66(12.601); 66.1(6), (9); 66.2(5); 66.8; ITR: 1206 Interpretation)

[¶2210.05] *Canadian Renewable and Conservation Expenses*

Canadian renewable and conservation expenses (CRCE) are a category of expenses eligible for flow-through share treatment. In general, these are intangible development costs associated with projects for which required equipment primarily consists of energy-efficient equipment classified as Class 43.1 or 43.2 assets; see ¶889. CRCE is a subset of Canadian exploration expenses, as defined by regulation. For the purpose of determining whether an outlay or expense in respect of a prescribed energy conservation property is a CRCE, the definition provides that the Technical Guide on this topic, published by the Department of Natural

Resources, is to apply conclusively with respect to engineering and scientific matters.

Classifying CRCE expenses in this manner permits syndication of at least some expenses for the development of renewable resources on a basis comparable to that permitted for resource exploration. See also ¶2521.50.

(ITA: 66.1(6); ITR: 1102(1)(a.1); 1219 Canadian Renewable and Conservation Expense)

[¶2213] DEDUCTION FOR CANADIAN EXPLORATION EXPENSES

The base for the Canadian exploration expense deduction is the cumulative Canadian exploration expense pool. Cumulative Canadian exploration expenses are comprised of:

(1) the prior year cumulative Canadian exploration expenses balance carried forward;

plus

(2) current year Canadian exploration expenses;

(3) bad debts from the sale of or recovery of Canadian exploration expenses; and

(4) any grants or assistance that have been repaid pursuant to a legal obligation;

less

(5) grants or assistance received from any person, including a government, municipality or other public authority on account of expenses incurred (i.e., resource incentives);

(6) any investment tax credit earned in respect of Canadian exploration expenditures and claimed in the preceding taxation year;

(7) proceeds on the sale or recovery of a Canadian exploration expense that is not a resource property, received or receivable in the year (see ¶2202);

(8) where all or substantially all of a person's resource properties are disposed of to a corporation and the taxpayer and corporation have jointly elected to transfer remaining deductions to the corporation (see ¶2228), the balance remaining in the cumulative Canadian exploration expense pool after the current year claim;

(9) amounts recovered on bad debts in respect of a sale or recovery of Canadian exploration expenses; and

(10) current year claim of cumulative Canadian exploration expenses.

The deduction available is 100% of your ending cumulative Canadian exploration expenses before the current year's claim. This deduction is allowed against income from any source.

If there is a negative balance in the cumulative Canadian exploration expense pool at the end of the year, it must be included in your income.

Example:

Mr. Kinson, an individual resident in Canada, incurred geological and geophysical costs of $3,500 and received grants of $500 during the year. His share of Canadian exploration expenses of a partnership is $1,000. His prior year cumulative Canadian exploration expense balance carried forward is $1,000.

The available Canadian exploration expense deduction is calculated as follows:

Cumulative balance carried forward	$1,000
Add: current year Canadian exploration expenses	3,500
Canadian exploration expenses per Box 173 of T5013	1,000
	$5,500
Less: grants received	500
Deduction available	$5,000
Amount claimed in current year	5,000
Available for carryforward	Nil

Where a debt owing by the taxpayer is settled during the year for less than its principal amount, the difference (the amount forgiven) is applied to reduce several tax balances in order. These begin with loss carryforwards and the capital cost of depreciable property. Application of any remaining part of a forgiven amount after the reduction of loss carryforwards becomes optional. Eligible capital amounts, the Canadian exploration expense balance, the Canadian development expense balance, foreign exploration and development expense, and cumulative foreign resource expense balances are on the list of balances which may be reduced. To the extent that the amount forgiven is not applied to tax balances, 50% of it may be included in income. See ¶565.

(ITA: 66.1(1), (3), (6); 66.7)

[¶2215] WHAT ARE CANADIAN DEVELOPMENT EXPENSES?

Canadian development expenses are generally costs incurred by you in the year, to the extent that they do not qualify as Canadian exploration expenses (¶2210), to:

- drill or convert a well in Canada for the disposal of waste liquids from an oil or gas well;
- drill or complete an oil or gas well in Canada, including temporary access roads and site preparation, to the extent that the expense was not a Canadian exploration expense of the taxpayer;
- drill or convert a well in Canada for the injection of water or gas or any other substance to assist in the recovery of petroleum or natural gas from another well;
- drill for water or gas in Canada for injection into a petroleum or natural gas formation;
- drill or convert a well in Canada for the purpose of monitoring fluid levels, pressure changes or other phenomena in an accumulation of petroleum or natural gas;
- drill or recomplete an existing oil or gas well in Canada after commencement of production. Recompletion involves work that is necessary to maintain or extend the life of a production well;
- acquire or preserve any right, licence or privilege to store underground petroleum, natural gas or related hydrocarbons in Canada;

- acquire or preserve any right, licence or privilege to prospect, explore, drill or mine for minerals in a mineral resource in Canada;
- acquire or preserve a Canadian mineral resource property (see ¶2202);
- acquire or preserve a rental or royalty based on production from a mineral resource in Canada; and
- sink, extend, or excavate mine shafts and main haulage ways or similar underground work for a mine in a mineral resource in Canada after the mine came into production.

Also included as Canadian development expenses are:

- your share of any of the above costs incurred by a partnership of which you are a member at the end of the fiscal period, subject to the restrictions imposed by the "at-risk" rules discussed at ¶2229 (the taxpayer should be in receipt of either a form T5013 or a statement from the operator of property to determine his share of the Canadian development expense of the partnership for the year);
- your share of any of the above costs renounced to you pursuant to a flow-through share offering, as described in ¶2521.50; and
- expenses incurred after March 21, 2011 in bringing a new oil sands mine into production and incurred before the new mine comes into production in reasonable commercial quantities, including an expense for clearing the land, removing overburden and stripping, or building an entry ramp. This does not include an expense that is a specified oil sands mine development expense or an eligible oil sands mine development expense because such expenses qualify as Canadian exploration expenses.
- subject to certain transitional rules, expenses incurred after March 20, 2013 for the purpose of bringing a new mine in Canada into production in reasonable commercial quantities. These transitional rules will be phased in with certain pre-production mining expenses being allocated proportionately to CEE and CDE. The phase-in period will apply commencing in 2015 with only a portion of the expenses being classified as CDE. After 2017, all expenses will be treated as CDE.

The cost of depreciable property is not included in a taxpayer's cumulative Canadian development expense pool.

Any amount paid as rent or for services will only qualify as a Canadian development expense to the extent that it relates to the use of property or to services rendered before the end of the year. This specifically disallows any claim for prepaid expenses.

As previously mentioned, the costs you incur to drill wells which have not produced within 24 months from the date of completion of drilling, or are dry holes, or to drill wells which are abandoned will be transferred to the Canadian exploration expense account (¶2213) and will not be included in the Canadian development expense account.

The cost of an interest in or right to a resource property that a taxpayer has acquired indirectly as a beneficiary of a trust or member of a partnership does not qualify as a Canadian development expense.

A taxpayer may elect to have his share of a partnership's Canadian development expenses excluded in determining the taxpayer's own Canadian development expenses. The election may be made (on form T1086) within six months after the end of the taxpayer's taxation year in which the fiscal period of the partnership ends. If the taxpayer makes the election he is not allowed to deduct any amount in computing his income. When the taxpayer subsequently sells his partnership interest his "adjusted cost base" (¶506) is increased by the amount of any elections not to claim Canadian development expenses (see ¶2229).

(ITA: 53(1)(e)(vii.1); 66(12.62), (12.63), (15) "expense"; 66.1(9); 66.2(5))

[¶2217] DEDUCTION FOR CANADIAN DEVELOPMENT EXPENSES

The base for the Canadian development expense deduction is the cumulative Canadian development expense pool. Cumulative Canadian development expenses comprise:

(1) the prior year cumulative Canadian development expense balance carryforward;

plus

(2) current year Canadian development expenses;

(3) bad debts in respect of sales or recoveries of Canadian development expenses; and

(4) any grants or assistance that have been repaid pursuant to a legal obligation;

less

(5) grants or assistance received from any person, including a government, municipality or other public authority, on account of expenses incurred (i.e., resource incentives);

(6) proceeds on the sale or recovery of a Canadian development expense that was not incurred in purchasing a Canadian resource property (i.e., this would include the sale of a development study but not the sale of a mine — see ¶2202 for the definition of a Canadian resource property);

(7) proceeds on the sale of mineral resource property (see ¶2202), or of any right, licence or privilege to store underground petroleum, natural gas or related hydrocarbons in Canada;

(8) negative balances transferred from the cumulative Canadian oil and gas property expense pool (see ¶2223);

(9) where all or substantially all of a person's resource properties are disposed of to a corporation and the taxpayer and corporation have jointly elected to transfer remaining deductions to the corporation (see ¶2228), the balance remaining in the cumulative Canadian development expense pool after the current year claim;

(10) amounts recovered on bad debts in respect of a sale or recovery of Canadian development expenses;

(11) transfer of Canadian development expenses reclassified as Canadian exploration expenses; and

(12) amounts deducted in respect of cumulative Canadian development expenses.

The deduction available is 30% of your ending cumulative Canadian development expenses before the current year's claim. This deduction is allowed against income from any source. The deduction must be prorated on a daily basis for short taxation years (i.e., a taxation year less than 51 weeks).

If there is a negative balance in the cumulative Canadian development expense pool at the end of the year, it must be included in your income.

Example:

Mr. Kinson incurred drilling costs which qualify as Canadian development expenses of $2,600 and received grants of $400 during the year. His share of Canadian development expenses of a partnership is $1,000. His prior year cumulative Canadian development expense balance carryforward is $3,800. The available Canadian development expense deduction is calculated as follows:

Cumulative balance carried forward	$3,800
Add: current year Canadian development expense	2,600
Canadian development expenses per Box 174 of T5013	1,000
	$7,400
Less: grants received	400
Cumulative balance before deduction	$7,000
Current deduction available, 30% of balance before deduction	2,100
Cumulative balance carryforward	$4,900

Where a debt owing by the taxpayer is settled during the year for less than its principal amount, the difference (the amount forgiven) is applied to reduce several tax balances in order. These begin with loss carryforwards and the capital cost of depreciable property. Application of any remaining part of a forgiven amount after the reduction of loss carryforwards becomes optional. Eligible capital amounts, the taxpayer's own cumulative Canadian exploration expense balance, cumulative Canadian development expense balance, cumulative Canadian oil and gas property expense balance, foreign exploration and development expense and cumulative foreign resource expense balances (¶2228) are on the list of balances which may be reduced. To the extent the amount forgiven is not applied to tax balances, 50% of it may be included in income. See ¶565.

(ITA: 66(13.1); 66.2(1), (2), (5); 66.7; 80(2), (8), (13))

[¶2220] WHAT ARE CANADIAN OIL AND GAS PROPERTY EXPENSES?

Canadian oil and gas property expenses are generally costs incurred by you in the year to acquire or preserve a Canadian oil and gas resource property (see ¶2202 for details).

Also included are your share of the above costs incurred by a partnership of which you are a member at the end of the fiscal period, subject to the restrictions imposed by the "at-risk" rules discussed at ¶2229 (the taxpayer should receive either a form T5013 or a statement from the operator of property to determine his share of the Canadian oil and gas property expense of the partnership for the year).

The cost of an interest in or a right to a resource property that a taxpayer has acquired indirectly as a beneficiary of a trust or member of a partnership does not qualify as a Canadian oil and gas property expense.

A taxpayer may elect to have his share of a partnership's Canadian oil and gas property expenses in a fiscal period excluded in determining the taxpayer's own Canadian oil and gas property expenses. The election may be made (on form T1086) within six months after the end of the taxpayer's taxation year in which the fiscal period of the partnership ends. If the taxpayer makes the election, he is not allowed to deduct any amount in computing his income. When the taxpayer sells his partnership interest, his "adjusted cost base" (¶506) is increased by the amount of any elections not to claim Canadian oil and gas property expenses.

(ITA: 53(1)(*e*)(vii.1); 66.4(5))

[¶2223] DEDUCTION FOR CANADIAN OIL AND GAS PROPERTY EXPENSES

The base for the Canadian oil and gas property expense deduction is the cumulative Canadian oil and gas property expense pool. Cumulative Canadian oil and gas property expenses are comprised of:

(1) the prior year cumulative Canadian oil and gas property expense balance carryforward;

plus

(2) current year Canadian oil and gas property expenses;

(3) bad debts in respect of sales or recoveries of Canadian oil and gas property expenses; and

(4) any grants or assistance that have been repaid pursuant to a legal obligation;

less

(5) grants or assistance received from any person, including a government, municipality or other public authority on account of expenses incurred;

(6) proceeds of disposition received or receivable from the sale of Canadian oil and gas resource property (see ¶2202);

(7) where all or substantially all of a person's resource properties are disposed of to a corporation and the taxpayer and the corporation have jointly elected to transfer remaining deductions to the corporation (see ¶2228), the balance remaining in the cumulative Canadian oil and gas property expense pool after the current year claim;

(8) amounts recovered in respect of bad debts from a sale or recovery of Canadian oil and gas property expenses; and

(9) amounts deducted in respect of cumulative Canadian oil and gas property expenses.

The deduction available is 10% of your ending cumulative Canadian oil and gas property expenses before the current year's claim. The deduction must be prorated on a daily basis for short taxation years (i.e., a taxation year less than 51 weeks).

If there is a negative balance in the cumulative Canadian oil and gas property expense pool at the end of the year it should be transferred to the cumulative Canadian development expense pool (see ¶2217).

Example:

Mr. Kinson did not incur any Canadian oil and gas property expenses during the year. However, at the beginning of the year he sold an interest in a resource property for which he received proceeds of $2,000.

Kinson's prior year cumulative Canadian oil and gas property expense balance carryforward is $4,500. The available Canadian oil and gas property expense deduction is calculated as follows:

Cumulative balance carried forward	$4,500
Less: Proceeds of disposition received on the sale of resource property	2,000
Cumulative balance before deduction	$2,500
Current deduction available	250
Cumulative balance carryforward	$2,250

Where a debt owing by the taxpayer is settled during the year for less than its principal amount, the difference (the amount forgiven) is applied to reduce several tax balances in order. These begin with loss carryforwards and the capital cost of depreciable property. Application of any remaining part of a forgiven amount after the reduction of loss carryforwards becomes optional. Eligible capital amounts, the Canadian exploration expense balance, the Canadian development expense balance, the Canadian oil and gas property expense balance, foreign exploration and development expense, and cumulative foreign resource expense balances are on the list of balances which may be reduced. To the extent that the amount forgiven is not applied to available tax balances, 50% of it may be included in income. See ¶565.

(ITA: 66(13.1); 66.2(5); 66.4(2), (5); 66.7; 80(2), (8), (13))

[¶2225] WHAT ARE FOREIGN EXPLORATION AND DEVELOPMENT EXPENSES/FOREIGN RESOURCE EXPENSES?

Foreign exploration and development expenses (FEDE) are costs incurred by you prior to 2000 in respect of both exploring or drilling for petroleum or natural gas and prospecting, exploring, and developing minerals outside of Canada. Expenses that would otherwise be FEDE will be foreign resource expenses (FRE) after 2000. These will generally include all of the types of costs which qualify as Canadian exploration expenses (see ¶2210), Canadian development expenses (see ¶2215) and Canadian oil and gas property expenses (see ¶2220), if incurred in respect of properties outside Canada.

(ITA: 66(15))

[¶2227] DEDUCTION FOR FOREIGN EXPLORATION AND DEVELOPMENT EXPENSES/FOREIGN RESOURCE EXPENSES

There are two groups of FEDE. Those FEDE incurred before 2001 and those incurred after 2000 which are now defined as FRE. FRE is essentially the same as FEDE, except that there are separate FRE accounts in respect of each country to which FRE relates. All pre-2001 FEDE remain in a global pool, while the post-2000 FRE are allocated to separate pools on a country-by-country basis. Foreign resource income is applied to support global FEDE claims (i.e., generated under pre-2001 rules) and any excess is applied to support the post-2000 FRE claim.

You are entitled to claim a deduction of 10% of your pre-2001 FEDE balance against income from any source. If foreign "resource income" exceeds 10% of the pre-2001 balance, a claim against the pre-2001 FEDE balance can be made to the full extent of the foreign resource income.

Foreign resource income includes income from operating an oil or gas well or mine outside Canada, royalties in respect of an oil or gas well or mine outside Canada, your net income from the sale of foreign oil or gas rights or foreign mineral rights, and your share of the income of any partnership, syndicate or association from oil and gas or mineral sources outside Canada.

The deduction is only permitted for taxpayers who are resident in Canada throughout the taxation year. The foreign exploration and development base is further restricted to consider only expenses incurred while the taxpayer was resident in Canada.

A taxpayer is permitted to claim a deduction of an amount of the taxpayer's undeducted foreign exploration and development expenses balance in the year that the taxpayer ceases to be resident in Canada without proration for the number of days the taxpayer is not resident in Canada.

FEDE and FRE must relate to the acquisition of foreign resource property by the taxpayer or be made for the purpose of enhancing the value of foreign resource property owned or to be owned by the taxpayer.

You cannot claim a deduction directly in respect of FRE; instead, you may add the amount of any FRE incurred to your cumulative FRE account (CFRE) on a country-by-country basis. You are entitled to a deduction of up to 10% of your CFRE balance for each country at the end of the year. You are also entitled to deduct the FRE balance against foreign resource income in respect of a country subject to a limitation of 30% of the FRE provided you have not deducted the pre-2001 FEDE against such income. The FRE claim is subject to a limit equal to 30% of the FRE in respect of the country, to support FRE deductions in respect of a country to which the income relates. However, to the extent that the country-by-country limitation would cause a taxpayer's overall maximum FRE deduction for a taxation year to be less than 30% of the total FRE balances, the taxpayer will be permitted to augment the portion of a FRE balance that may be claimed.

Similar to the deduction of FEDE, the deduction of FRE is only permitted for taxpayers who are resident in Canada throughout the taxation year. As well, the taxpayer will be permitted to claim a deduction of an amount of the taxpayer's undeducted FRE balance in the year that the taxpayer ceases to be resident in Canada without proration for the number of days the taxpayer is not resident in Canada.

One element of the CFRE formula requires a taxpayer to add the cost of foreign resource property deemed to have been acquired when the taxpayer last became resident in Canada to the taxpayer's CFRE.

For a foreign levy to qualify for foreign tax credits, it must be computed by reference to net income, after recognition of relevant expenses, and must not be, under a production sharing agreement, either a royalty or any other consideration paid for the exploitation of the resource. Because the rules are intended to accommodate situations where the foreign income tax is calculated pursuant to a production sharing agreement, as opposed to being assessed separately, the rules apply only where the foreign country otherwise imposes what can be regarded as an income tax.

The amount eligible for a foreign tax credit cannot, under these rules, exceed 40% of the taxpayer's income from the business for the year and will be subject to the existing rules governing the claiming of business foreign tax credits and the carryovers of unused credits.

The business foreign tax credit provisions also include specific rules for the recognition of a taxpayer's FEDE and FRE. While there already exists a general requirement in the *Income Tax Act* for taxpayers to recognize FEDE and FRE in computing the amount of the foreign tax credit that can be claimed in respect of foreign source income, these rules specify how FEDE and FRE will be allocated to a particular foreign country for purposes of claiming a foreign tax credit. Due to the complex nature of the FEDE, FRE, and foreign tax credit rules, professional advice is recommended.

Where a debt owing by the taxpayer is settled during the year for less than its principal amount, the difference (the amount forgiven) is applied to reduce several tax balances in order. These begin with loss carryforwards and the capital cost of depreciable property. Application of any remaining part of a forgiven amount after the reduction of loss carryforwards becomes optional. Eligible capital amounts, the taxpayer's own cumulative Canadian exploration expense balance, cumulative Canadian development expense balance, cumulative Canadian oil and gas property expense balance, foreign exploration and development expense and cumulative foreign resource expense balances are on the list of balances which may be reduced. To the extent that the amount forgiven is not applied to available tax balances, 50% of it may be included in income. See ¶565.

(ITA: 66(4); 66.21(1); 80(2), (8), (13); 126(5))

[¶2228] TRANSFERS OF RESOURCE PROPERTIES AND RELATED DEDUCTIONS TO A CORPORATION

The resource deduction pools remaining after the sale of all or substantially all of the resource properties by a taxpayer to a corporation may be transferred to that corporation if a joint election is made by the taxpayer and the corporation. These properties are referred to as "successor properties" and the pool balances associated with them are called "successored pools". The form prescribed for this purpose is T2010, "Election to Deduct Resource Expenses upon Acquisition of Resource Property by a Corporation". The resource pools eligible for transfer include foreign exploration and development expenses (¶2225), cumulative foreign resource expenses, cumulative Canadian exploration expenses (¶2213), cumulative Canadian development expenses (¶2217), and cumulative Canadian oil and gas property expenses (¶2223).

(ITA: 66.7(1)–(8), (12), (13))

[¶2229] LIMITED PARTNERSHIPS

The deductions flowing out from the oil and gas and mining expenditures of limited partnerships are effectively restricted by limiting the resource expenses to the partner's "at-risk" amount. Subject to the "at-risk rules", a taxpayer's Canadian development expenses, Canadian exploration expenses, Canadian oil and gas property expenses and foreign exploration and development expenses include the taxpayer's share of such expenses of a partnership. A partner's "at-risk" amount is generally his investment in the partnership plus his share of earnings less both amounts distributed to the partner and the partnership allocation of resource expenses for previous years (see ¶1818). The partner's share of the resource expenditures exceeding his "at-risk" amount first reduces Canadian oil and gas property expenses to be allocated by the partnership (¶2220), then Canadian development expenses (¶2215), then Canadian exploration expenses (¶2210), then country-specific foreign expenses, and finally, global foreign expenses (¶2227). The partner's share of resource expenses in excess of the "at-risk" amount may be carried forward indefinitely, and will be available for inclusion in the partner's resource pools in a future year, to the extent that such expenses are not limited to the partner's "at-risk" amount in that particular year.

A taxpayer may elect to have his share of a partnership's Canadian development expenses and Canadian oil and gas property expenses in a fiscal period excluded in determining the taxpayer's own Canadian development expenses and Canadian oil and gas property expenses. The election may be made within six months after the end of the taxpayer's taxation years in which the fiscal period of the partnership ends. If the taxpayer makes the election, he is not allowed to deduct any amount in respect of such a share in computing income. Instead, he is entitled to an addition equal to the amount of such a share in computing the adjusted cost base to the taxpayer of his interest in the partnership. This addition will offset the subtraction otherwise required of the same amount in computing the adjusted cost base of the partnership interest.

Example

Individual A is a member of a partnership. His share of Canadian development expenses incurred by the partnership for the fiscal period of the partnership ending January 30, 2014 is $10,000. There is no income or loss at the partnership level in the fiscal period. What are the consequences to individual A if the partnership interest is disposed of for $110,000 on October 1, 2014, assuming individual A makes an election in respect of his share of the expenses and the adjusted cost base to individual A before the end of the fiscal period is $90,000?

Result:

(1) As a consequence of the election, individual A will not be entitled to deduct any portion of the $10,000.

(2) An amount of $10,000 in computing the adjusted cost base of the interest is deducted after the end of the fiscal period under paragraph 53(2)(*c*). However, this amount is offset by the addition of the same amount. The adjusted cost base after the end of the fiscal period to individual A thus remains $90,000.

(3) Individual A, therefore, has a capital gain of $20,000 from the disposition of the partnership interest.

(ITA: 53(1)(e)(vii.1), (2)(c); 66.2(5); 66.4(5); 66.8; 96(2.1), (2.2))

[¶2230] IMPACT ON LIFETIME CAPITAL GAINS EXEMPTION

The lifetime capital gains exemption is available in respect to dispositions of qualified small business corporation shares, qualified farm property, and qualified fishing property (¶502).

The lifetime capital gains exemption of a taxpayer is reduced by his cumulative net investment loss (see ¶502q). The taxpayer's cumulative net investment loss is increased by 50% of a portion of his deductions in respect of:

- foreign exploration and development expenses (¶2227);
- cumulative foreign resource expenses (¶2227);
- Canadian exploration expenses (¶2213);
- Canadian development expenses (¶2217); and
- Canadian oil and gas property expenses (¶2223).

The portion of these expenses that is included in his cumulative net investment loss includes those expenses:

- incurred by a corporation and renounced to him after February 1986, for which the taxpayer has received form T101; and
- incurred by a partnership, of which the taxpayer was a limited or passive partner, after December 15, 1987.

Where a taxpayer has also incurred FEDE, FRE, Canadian exploration expenses, Canadian development expenses, or Canadian oil and gas property expenses that do not meet the criteria above for inclusion in his cumulative net investment loss account, he must allocate his deductions between those expenses that impact his cumulative net investment loss and those that do not. The CRA has not provided any guidelines to assist in this allocation.

(ITA: 66(12.6), (12.62); 66.1(6); 66.2(5); 66.4(5); 110.6(1); 248(1))

[¶2231] CAPITAL COST ALLOWANCE ALSO AVAILABLE

You may deduct capital cost allowance with respect to depreciable assets relating to oil and gas and mining operations in the same way as any business assets. Recent amendments have phased out accelerated capital cost allowance of certain classes of assets for mining. The phase-out is to be completed over the 2017 to 2020 calendar years.

(ITA: 20(1)(*a*); 127(5),(9), (11), (11.1); ITR: 4600 Qualified Property; 4602 Certified Property; 4606 Prescribed Amount; 4607 Prescribed Designated Regions; 4609 Prescribed Offshore Region; 4610 Prescribed Area)

[¶2232] MINING RECLAMATION/QUALIFYING ENVIRONMENTAL TRUSTS

A taxpayer may establish a trust referred to as a "qualifying environmental trust" for the purpose of carrying out later reclamation work resulting from:

- mining operations;
- the extraction of clay, peat, sand, shale, or aggregates, including dimension stone and gravel;
- waste disposal sites; and
- pipeline abandonment.

Amendments effective for 2012 and later years introduced a complete restructuring of the relevant provisions in the *Income Tax Act* relating to qualifying environmental trusts.

In order for a trust to qualify as a "qualifying environmental trust", the maintenance of the trust must be required by a federal, provincial, or territorial law, or under the terms of a contract entered into with the federal or provincial Crown. Contributions to (or the purchase of a beneficial interest in) a qualifying trust will be deductible in the year made (or bought) and taxable in the year withdrawn (or when the beneficial interest is sold).

Investment income earned in the trust on the funds on deposit will be taxable both to the trust and the beneficiary (the contributor or purchaser which buys the beneficial interest). The trust itself will be taxable under Part XII.4 at an amount equal to the general corporate tax rate for the relevant year. Several provinces match these provisions and impose their own tax at the provincial corporate rate. These include British Columbia, Saskatchewan, Ontario, Quebec and the Yukon. The same income taxed in the trust will be considered ordinary taxable income of the beneficiary, but the beneficiary will receive a refundable tax credit on his or her income allocation for the tax paid in the trust equal to the Part XII.4 tax paid by the trust.

[¶2232.05] *General Prohibitions*

Qualifying environmental trusts will be disqualified if they violate a number of detailed prohibitions. For example, they may not borrow money or invest in anything other than qualified investments (such as Canadian cash and deposits; bonds, notes, debentures, mortgages, etc. issued by Canadian federal, provincial, municipal governments, by Crown corporations, or by a hospital or educational institution and guaranteed by a provincial government; and guaranteed investment certificates of a federally or provincially incorporated trust company). Accordingly, a trust that invests in non-qualifying investments (¶2618) will not be a qualifying environmental trust. There are several other restrictions which require specific study. Qualifying environmental trusts will be disqualified if they violate a number of detailed prohibitions. For example, they may not borrow money, nor invest in anything other than: Canadian cash and deposits; bonds, notes, debentures, mortgages, etc. issued by Canadian federal, provincial, municipal governments or Crown corporations or by a hospital or educational institution and guaranteed by a provincial government; and guaranteed investment certificates of a federally or provincially incorporated trust company. There are several other restrictions which require specific study.

(ITA: 12(1)(*z.1*); 20(1)(*ss*), (*tt*); 107.3; 127.41; 204 "qualified investment"; 211.6; 248(1) "qualifying environmental trust")

OIL AND GAS AND MINING REBATES, CREDITS, AND INCENTIVES

[¶2270] REBATES AND CREDITS

This section contains information about the Alberta royalty tax deduction, the Alberta royalty credit, and the provincial forms that must be filed. As a result of the reintroduction of full deductibility of provincial royalties for federal and provincial income tax purposes, Alberta has discontinued the royalty tax deduction and the royalty credit for corporations, individuals, and trusts, effective January 1, 2007. All claims in respect of eligible Alberta crown royalties paid or payable for production before January 1, 2007 must be submitted within three years of the claimant's tax year-end for which the eligible Alberta crown royalties are paid or payable. In the case of individuals, all claims must be submitted within three years from the end of the calendar year for which the eligible Alberta crown royalties are paid or payable.

[¶2273] SASKATCHEWAN

As a consequence of the federal government's initiative to reintroduce full deductibility of provincial resource royalties for federal and provincial income tax purposes, the Saskatchewan Royalty Tax Rebate is no longer necessary and will be wound down. Commencing January 1, 2007, the carryforward period for any outstanding Royalty Tax Rebate balances will be limited to seven years.

HOW TO REPORT EXPENSES FROM OIL AND GAS AND MINING INVESTMENTS

[¶2274] REPORT EXPENSES

Where an individual is an active participant in a petroleum, natural gas, or mining venture, the profit or loss net of applicable deductions for exploration, development and equipping costs is reported as business income on line 135 of the T1 return. An active participant is an individual who owns an interest in a mining or oil and gas property personally or through a partnership in which the individual is a general partner.

Where the individual is a non-active participant in such a venture, the results of the investment and related resource expenses are reported on T1229. A non-active participant is an individual who has an investment in a limited partnership or flow-through shares.

Chapter 23

Divorce and Separation

THESE POINTS ARE COVERED IN THIS CHAPTER

CRA REFERENCES RELATING TO THIS CHAPTER

T1 Lines

- Line 128 — Support payments received — Taxable amount
- Line 156 — Support payments received — Total
- Line 220 — Support payments made — Allowable deduction
- Line 230 — Support payments made — Total
- Line 232 — Other Deductions
- Line 256 — Additional deductions

CRA Guides

5000-G, "General Income Tax and Benefit Guide"; **P102**, "Support Payments — Includes Form T1158"

CRA Forms

T400A, "Objection — *Income Tax Act*"; **T1157**, "Election For Child Support Payments"; **T1158**, "Registration of Family Support Payments"; **T1198**, "Statement of Qualifying Retroactive Lump-Sum Payment"; **T2220**, "Transfer from an RRSP, RRIF, PRPP or SPP to Another RRSP, RRIF, or SPP on Breakdown of Marriage or Common-Law Partnership"

Income Tax Folios

S1-F3-C3, "Support Payments"; **S1-F3-C1**, "Child Care Expense Deduction"

Interpretation Bulletins

IT-99R5 (Consolidated), "Legal and Accounting Fees"; **IT-325R2**, "Property Transfers After Separation, Divorce and Annulment"; **IT-511R**, "Interspousal and Certain Other Transfers and Loans of Property"

WHAT YOU SHOULD KNOW ABOUT SUPPORT PAYMENTS

[¶2300] WHAT ARE SUPPORT AMOUNTS?

[¶2300.05] *Support Amounts*

A support amount is an amount that meets the criteria in ¶2305. As discussed therein, generally speaking, the payment must be payable directly to the recipient spouse or partner on a periodic basis for the maintenance of the recipient, the children of the recipient, or both. Typically, the recipient must have discretion over its use.

However, a payment to a third party may also qualify as a support amount if it meets the criteria described in ¶2315. A payment which is deductible by you under these provisions will be included in the income of your spouse or common-law partner or former spouse or common-law partner whether it is paid to that person directly or paid to a third party on that person's behalf.

[¶2302] FORMS AND GUIDES

The CRA issues a very useful and thorough pamphlet called *Support Payments* (P102), which covers the rules on divorce and separation in considerable detail. As well, Income Tax Folio S1-F3-C3 discusses the deductibility of support payments in somewhat more technical terms.

The CRA issues two forms relevant to this subject. They are:

- T1157, Election for Child Support Payments (election to have the May 1997 rules apply to older agreements so that child support payments are no longer deductible to the payer and taxable to the recipient);
- T1158, Registration of Family Support Payments (required to support deductibility of spousal support payments under orders or agreements made after April 30, 1997).

These forms are discussed at ¶2306.

The Department of Justice publishes federal child support amount guidelines; call 1-888-373-2222 for information.

[¶2305] WHEN ARE SUPPORT PAYMENTS DEDUCTIBLE?

The law lays down very specific rules as to what constitutes support payments (technically called "support amounts") and when they are deductible to the payer (and therefore taxable to the recipient). As a general rule, such payments are deductible only to the extent they are spousal support amounts and not child support payments, and only if they otherwise meet the criteria discussed at ¶2300.05 through ¶2300.30 below.

[¶2305.05] *Where Marriage (or Common-Law Partnership) Breakdown Occurs*

Where marriage breakdown occurs, including the breakdown of a common-law relationship or a common-law partnership (see ¶1113), a payment may constitute a spousal support amount and will therefore be deductible (unless it is a child support payment described in ¶2306) if all the following criteria are met:

(1) the amount is paid under an order of a competent tribunal or under a written agreement; however, a court order or written agreement can validate earlier payments of the year and the preceding year (see ¶2310);

(2) the amount is payable or receivable as an allowance on a periodic basis; however, a court order or written agreement can validate as periodic specified expenses which may in fact be contingent or occasional (see ¶2310 and ¶2315);

(3) the amount is for the maintenance of the recipient, the children of the recipient, or both;

(4) the taxpayer is living apart from the recipient at the time of the payment because of the breakdown of their marriage;

(5) the recipient has discretion as to the use of the amount; the issue is whether payments made to a third party qualify as support amounts; the answer is yes provided the governing order or agreement provides for such third-party payments for the benefit of the recipient or children in the recipient's care; see also ¶2315; and

(6) the amount is not a "child support payment" as discussed at ¶2306.

An order of a competent tribunal is a decree, order or judgment made by a court or other competent tribunal. Nothing less than a concrete pronouncement, decree or direction of a tribunal empowered to make an order will constitute the required order. An agreement deemed by a provincial court to be a court order for purposes of provincial maintenance enforcement legislation, will not, in and of itself, result in the agreement being considered an order made by a competent tribunal for the purposes of the Act.

If the spouses or common-law partners have only a written separation agreement, the support payment will be deductible if the other requirements are met. Generally speaking, a written agreement should be a written document under which a person agrees to make regular payments to maintain his or her current or former spouse or common-law partner, children of his or her current or former spouse or common-law partner, or both. The agreement should normally be duly signed and dated by both parties. The courts have held that cancelled cheques, correspondence and agreements which do not mention an agreement to live separate and apart do not constitute a "written separation agreement".

However, the CRA is prepared to accept that an exchange of written correspondence between the parties or their respective solicitors may be considered to be a written agreement if:

- there was the intention to create a binding and enforceable contractual relation;
- the exchange of written correspondence outlines all of the essential terms and conditions of the agreement in a clear and unambiguous manner; and
- there is a clear and unequivocal acceptance in writing by both parties of all those terms and conditions (paragraph 3.31 of Folio S1-F3-C3).

[¶2305.20] *Where No Marriage or Common-Law Partnership but Court Order for Support*

The situation contemplated here is a relationship which does not constitute a conjugal relationship as in the case of a spouse or common-law spouse or partner, but which produces a child and in due course a court order for support of one parent and/or the child by the other parent.

Where a court order is made providing for maintenance or support, the payments (unless they are child support payments under the rules at ¶2306) will be deductible to the payer taxpayer and taxable to the recipient if all the following conditions are met:

(1) the payer is the legal parent of a child of the recipient;

(2) the amount is received under an order made by a competent tribunal in accordance with the laws of a province (a written agreement is not sufficient nor is a foreign court order); and

(3) conditions (2), (3), (5), and (6) in ¶2305.05 noted above.

It is interesting that the court order in (2) must be made by a tribunal in accordance with provincial law; thus a foreign court order would not suffice in this situation unless it was ratified or upheld by such a tribunal.

[¶2305.30] *General Rules for Deduction (or Inclusion) of Support*

In general, only spousal support payments made under (and therefore on or after) a court order or a written separation agreement are deductible. This requirement is modified for the deduction of payments made prior to the date of a court order or written separation agreement, provided such payments are made in the year of the order or agreement, or in the immediately preceding year. However, the order or agreement must explicitly provide that payments made prior to the date of the order or written separation agreement are to be considered made pursuant to the order or agreement. In addition, the payments must otherwise qualify; that is, they must be periodic allowances meeting all other conditions specified above for the type of payment. This is discussed in greater detail under the subheading "Payments Validated by Agreement or Order" in ¶2310.05.

If you pay additional amounts which are not pursuant to any of the above you will not be allowed a deduction for the additional amount. To render a permanent increase in amounts paid deductible, the separation agreement must be amended or a supplementary court order must be obtained. In addition, the payments must normally be payable on a periodic basis (see ¶2310).

To be allowed a deduction for any support payments made in a year, you must be living apart from the qualified recipient. Whether the couple is considered to be living apart depends on the surrounding circumstances. The couple may be considered to be living apart while residing in the same house if one spouse is considered by law to be in desertion. On the other hand, where a spouse (or common-law partner) visits the other's residence frequently, maintains clothes there and comes and goes freely, the couple may be considered to be not living apart even if they maintain separate residences. A spouse (or common-law partner) who is away at school or in hospital is not considered to be living apart from his or her spouse (or partner).

A payment which is deductible by you will be included in the income of the recipient.

Payments made to non-residents may be deductible to the payer if the conditions are met. However, withholding tax is not required in respect of the payments.

If you deducted amounts on account of support or alimony or maintenance and have received a reimbursement of those amounts pursuant to a decree, order, or judgment of a court or other formal tribunal, you must include the reimbursement in income.

(ITA: 56(1)(*b*), (c.2); 56.1; 60(*b*), (c.2); 60.1; 252; ITR: 6502 [Prescribed class of persons]; Income Tax Folio: S1-F3-C3; *Boos v. M.N.R.*, 61 DTC 520; *Wallace v. M.N.R.*, 63 DTC 128)

[¶2305.35] *Amounts Paid after Death*

In Income Tax Folio S1-F3-C3, the CRA states its views on payments made after death:

> 3.67 If spousal support payments continue to be made after the death of the recipient, they are not deductible by the payer whether they are made to the estate or succession, the children, or anyone else because the payer cannot be the current or former spouse or common-law partner of the new payee. Similarly, payments made by the estate of the payer to a surviving recipient are not deductible because the recipient cannot be the current or former spouse or common-law partner of the estate or succession.
>
> Such payments do not meet the definition of a support amount.

The CRA views appear to be correct and in accordance with the Act.

[¶2306] CHILD SUPPORT PAYMENTS

[¶2306.05] *Introduction*

Effective generally for court orders or agreements made or varied on or after May 1, 1997, a new system was implemented under which separate treatment is prescribed for payments made on account of child support ("child support payments") and payments made on account of support of the recipient (spouse or common-law partner or parent). Child support payments are not taxable to the recipient or deductible to the payer, whereas support payments for the benefit of the recipient are taxable to the recipient and deductible to the payer so long as they meet the criteria at ¶2305. There is a general presumption that payments are child support payments unless otherwise identified (¶2306.10), and new agreements which provide for taxable/deductible (as opposed to child support) payments must be registered with the CRA.

The terms "child" and "children" for these purposes include the broad range of children discussed in the definition of child at ¶1123 (see also subsection 252(1)). Thus, a child of a taxpayer includes

- a person of whom the taxpayer is the legal parent;
- a person who is wholly dependent on the taxpayer for support and of whom the taxpayer has, or immediately before the person attained the age of 19 years had, in law or in fact, the custody and control;
- a child of the taxpayer's spouse or common-law partner; and
- a spouse or common-law partner of a child of the taxpayer.

See also paragraph 3.4 of Folio S1-F3-C3.

[¶2306.10] *What is a Child Support Amount?*

A "child support amount" (subsection 56.1(4)) is any support payment amount which would be deductible under the rules at ¶2305 that is not identified in the agreement or order under which it is made as being solely for the support of a spouse or common-law partner or former spouse or common-law partner or the parent of the taxpayer's child. In short, unless the written agreement or court order which provides for periodic payments specifies that an amount is for the benefit of the recipient and not the child, it is presumed to be child support. Therefore, if a written agreement, for example, provides for a global amount of support to be paid in respect of a spouse and child, the whole amount is considered child support for tax purposes. The same treatment will apply to amounts that are required to be paid directly to third parties but are nevertheless potentially deductible under the rules in ¶2315. Such third-party payments will be treated as child support amounts unless the order or agreement under which they are made clearly identifies the payments as being solely for the support of a spouse or common-law partner, former spouse or common-law partner, or parent of the payer's child, as the case may be.

[¶2306.15] *How are Child Support Payments Determined?*

The amount of a child support payment is determined by agreement of the parties or by a court, as the case may be. Part and parcel of the new child support system, however, are guidelines published under the federal *Divorce Act* as to appropriate amounts of child support in various circumstances. The federal government has no authority to impose these guidelines, since separation and divorce settlements are governed by provincial law as interpreted and applied by provincial courts. However, most provinces either adopt or recommend to their courts either the federal scale or a similar one of their own devising. Even in these circumstances, the guidelines may not be binding, especially where amicable agreements are made outside the ambit of court review. Determination of these amounts is beyond the scope of this book, which is merely concerned with the taxability/deductibility of amounts determined.

The federal Department of Justice publishes the federal child support amount guidelines. Call 1-888-373-2222 for this information. It is also available on the Department of Justice Canada website, www.justice.gc.ca.

[¶2306.20] *To What Agreements or Court Orders Do the Rules Apply?*

The rules regarding the non-deductibility of child support payments apply automatically to payments required under agreements or orders made after April 30, 1997.

The rules may also apply to payments under older orders and agreements in any of the following situations:

- Where an order or agreement made before May 1, 1997 specifies by its terms that the rules will apply on or after May 1, 1997, the rules apply from the date specified; this is to allow agreements made in expectation of the rules to be governed by them. In *Dangerfield v. The Queen*, 2004 DTC 6025 (F.C.A.), the Federal Court of Appeal ruled that a separation agreement concluded in April 1997 which included a specific clause that child support was to commence May 1, 1997 was sufficient to make the payments non-taxable to the recipient parent. The Crown had argued that because the actual order was made earlier and contained other aspects which arguably commenced at an earlier date, it preceded the introduction of the May 1, 1997 child support rules. The Court found that the specified commencement date governed the child support regardless of other elements of the agreement. The Court also rejected out of hand the Crown's contention that the commencement date specified was invalid because the agreement failed to specify that it was intended to be effective for income tax purposes. The commencement day definition in the child support provisions (unlike, say, the periodic payment validation rules in ¶2310 or the third-party payment rules in ¶2315) contains no such requirement.
- Where a previous order or agreement is varied after April 30, 1997 to change the child support amounts payable to the recipient, the rules will apply from the day on which the first payment of the varied amount is required to be made. In *Coombes v. The Queen*, 2005 DTC 5263 (F.C.A.), an agreement made in 1996 under the old rules provided by its original terms that the payments under it would increase in 2000 while the child for whom the support was paid attended university. This did not constitute a variance of the agreement; the payments were made under the original agreement. In *McLaughlan v. The Queen*, 2007 DTC 1151 (T.C.C.), the support amount was varied as of January 1997, but the change was not noted on the agreement until 1999. The Court analyzed the alternatives open to it, and decided that the variance was ineffective in creating a new commencement date, and that it followed that the amount deductible was the amount in the original agreement, not the varied amount.
- Where another order or agreement is made after April 30, 1997, and the effect of the subsequent agreement is to change the total child support amounts orig-

inally payable to the recipient by the payer, the rules will apply from the date of the subsequent order or agreement.

- Where the parties jointly elect (by filing form T1157, *Election for Child Support Payments*, with the CRA) to have the new rules apply, they apply from the date specified in the election (so long as it is after April 30, 1997). This rule permits old agreements and court orders to be governed by the new tax rules where the parties agree. If the entire amount paid under the new agreement is to be non-taxable and non-deductible, the agreement itself need not be filed with form T1157. However, if the agreement specifies separate spousal and child support amounts, and the spousal amounts are to be deductible, the agreement must be filed with form T1157. It would appear that if the old order or agreement merely specifies a global amount, the parties cannot select how much of it is to be governed by the rules. The terms of the order or agreement must specify how much is spousal and how much is child support, or an election will render the whole amount non-taxable and non-deductible.

[¶2306.25] *Registration of Agreements*

Although it is not specified in the legislation, the CRA requires that agreements governed by the new system be registered with the CRA if they provide for any amounts which remain deductible.

You do not have to register an order or agreement made before May 1, 1997, if the new rules relating to the non-taxability of child support do not apply. That is, if all support amounts under an old agreement are deductible and continue to be so, both parties can continue to have the payer deduct the payments and the recipient report them as income, and the agreement need not be registered.

However, whenever the new rules apply (except by election as discussed above) but some amount remains taxable to the recipient and deductible to the payer, the agreement itself must be filed along with form T1158, *Registration of Family Support Payments*. Form T1158 does not specify which party must file it, although it must contain information as to both. It will generally be in the interest of the payer to see that it is filed.

[¶2306.30] *Ordering Rules Where Both Spousal and Child Support Payable*

Given the complex transitional rules that govern implementation of the new system, it is necessary in many situations to have an ordering rule to determine what portion of payments made in a year are taxable to the recipient and deductible to the payer. The formulae for taxability/deductibility are designed to yield the result that, in any year, the amount taxable/deductible will only include amounts paid to the extent that these amounts exceed all child support that became receivable or payable on or after the commencement date on which the new rules apply to a particular order or agreement. The effect should be that there will be no income inclusion to the recipient or deduction to the payer where the total amount of support that has been paid falls short of the amount of child support that is required under the agreement or order. In short, payments are considered in respect of child support first, and only to the extent that those obligations have been fully met can any balance be considered taxable/deductible.

This is achieved by providing that the taxable/deductible amount is:

(1) the total of all amounts paid before the end of the year which qualify as taxable/deductible under the rules at ¶2305

minus the sum of:

(2) all child support that became payable under an order or agreement after it became subject to the new rules and before the end of the year, and

(3) all amounts paid by the payer and deducted from the payer's income for a preceding year (this ensures that amounts previously deducted by the payer cannot be deducted again).

The use of "payable" in (2) means that where there are arrears, for example, payments are deemed to come first on account of non-deductible child support; only when there is none left are payments considered on account of deductible spousal support. In its *Support Payments Guide* P102, the CRA provides the following example of the ordering rule.

Example

Beginning January 2013, Mark had to make monthly support payments of $400 ($150 for his former spouse, and $250 for their children). Mark paid $400 from January to March for a total of $1,200. He made no other payment for the remainder of the year. Mark is in arrears for $1,800 in child support.

When he filed his 2013 income tax and benefit return, Mark could not deduct the spousal support payments because he did not fully pay his child support.

In 2014, Mark must fully pay all child support owing for 2013 and 2014 before he can deduct anything he pays for spousal support.

Payments to more than one recipient

If the payer is making payments to more than one recipient (e.g. two former spouses), the ordering rule applies separately with respect to each recipient. The CRA provides the following example in its Income Tax Folio S1-F3-C3 (paragraph 3.35):

Example - Payments to more than one recipient

Under a court order dated June 15, 2010, Vincent must pay child support to his first wife, Lydia. Under a written separation agreement with his second wife, Judith, he must pay spousal support.

At the end of 2011, he is in arrears in child support payments to Lydia, but has fully paid his spousal support to Judith.

Despite the arrears of child support payable to Lydia, the spousal support payments to Judith may be fully deducted by Vincent because the formula in paragraph 60(b) is applied separately to each recipient.

(ITA: 56(1)(*b*); 56.1; 60(*b*); 60.1; Income Tax Folio: S1-F3-C3)

[¶2307] WHEN ARE SUPPORT PAYMENTS TAXABLE TO RECIPIENT, DEDUCTIBLE TO PAYER?

Generally speaking, any payments deductible to one spouse or common-law partner under the rules at ¶2305 and not denied deduction as child support payments under ¶2306 are taxable in the hands of the recipient spouse or common-law partner. Payments to third parties (¶2315) deductible to one spouse or common-law partner are similarly taxable to the other as if they had been received directly by the spouse or common-law partner for whose benefit they are paid.

The logic of these rules is that a measure of income splitting is permitted as between separated spouses or common-law partners; the higher income spouse or common-law partner is presumably the one making the payments and receiving a deduction against high marginal tax rates; the recipient spouse or common-law partner is presumably taxed at a lower marginal rate. It is expected that tax consequences will be taken into account in working out separation agreements, and this is the basis for requiring written agreements in respect of direct payments (¶2305) and explicit written agreements in respect of third-party payments (¶2315).

If you received and included in income in the taxation year or any previous year amounts on account of support payments, and have been required to repay any part of such amounts pursuant to a decree, order, or judgment of a court or other formal tribunal, you may deduct the repayment in the year it is made or either of the two following years (to the extent it has not been previously deducted).

[¶2307.05] *Payments Received to or from Non-Residents*

Spousal support payments from a non-resident are included in the Canadian-resident recipient's income under subsection 56(1)(*b*) of the Act, assuming they meet the criteria at ¶2305. In some cases, there may be treaty protection from Canadian tax (e.g., under the Australian treaty, where only the source country may tax such payments). If the Canadian resident recipient is subject to withholding tax in the payer's country, a foreign tax credit should be available in Canada.

A taxpayer supporting a spouse in another country will be able to deduct support amounts if the payments are pursuant to the breakdown of a marriage or common-law arrangement and the usual criteria are met; see ¶3.66 of Income Tax Folio S1-F3-C3. There is no withholding tax for spousal support paid or credited to non-residents.

[¶2307.10] *Tax Credits and Deductions Associated with Receipt of Support Payments*

Recipients of support payments, if supporting a child, may be entitled to claim the eligible dependant personal amount credit (¶1120); Schedule 5 is required to support this claim. Claims for child care expenses (¶1049) should also be considered. Where there are minor children, the recipient of support payments typically receives the federal Canada child benefits discussed at ¶1498.

(ITA: 56(1)(*b*), (*c*.2); 56.1; 60(*b*), (*c*.2); 60.1; 252(3))

[¶2307.15] *Receipt of Arrears*

Where periodic payments required by a court order or written agreement have fallen into arrears and one payment is made to bring these requirements up to date, that payment can be considered a support payment (paragraph 3.44 of Folio S1-F3-C3).

If you are receiving taxable support payments and you receive in a particular year one or more lump-sum payments which represent, in whole or in part, payments of prior years, you may be eligible for a form of income averaging. The amount relating to prior years must be $3,000 or more for this provision to apply. (Note that Quebec has a similar provision which applies where the amount related to prior years is $300 or more; see ¶1665.) You are not supposed to do the averaging yourself, but rather bring the matter to the attention of the Canada Revenue Agency, which will subtract the amounts relating to prior years from your income for the year of receipt, thereby lowering tax, and tax them as if each amount had been received in the year to which it properly belonged, thereby increasing tax. If the net adjustment is in your favour, it will appear on your assessment/reassessment as a line 423 tax adjustment. (Older notices of assessments continued for some time to refer to such adjustments as line 423 adjustments, even after the elimination of line 423 on Schedule 1.)

Generally speaking, the CRA expects that the payer will provide you with information detailing the payments and the extent to which they relate to prior years (see ¶1420). In the case of support payments, this may be an unrealistic expectation, but you may be able to document your case to the CRA if you have a complete history of the payments you have received or missed.

Averaging may be of benefit if the lump-sum payments put you in a higher income bracket for the year of receipt, or if they would have been taxed in a lower bracket in the year to which they relate. The technical machinery underlying this provision is discussed at ¶1420. However, as discussed in an article in the 2010 Canadian Tax Journal, No. 1, at 1-24, this state of affairs does not guarantee a benefit, and the averaging may be beneficial only in limited circumstances.

(ITA: 110.2)

[¶2310] WHAT ARE PERIODIC PAYMENTS?

[¶2310.01] *Determining if Payments are Periodic*

If you make a lump-sum payment in settlement of any right the spouse or common-law partner had to a periodic allowance in the future you will normally not be able to deduct the lump-sum payment.

If a lump-sum payment is paid in more than one instalment, it is still considered to be a lump sum and not deductible.

To establish that the payments are "periodic" you should ensure that the order or written agreement requires that the amount be payable at regular intervals. Also for payments to be deductible they must be fixed and predetermined amounts. The courts have previously disallowed payments that were not fixed and predetermined. Consequently, if you agree to pay any amount which is not an allowance or is not to be paid periodically under the terms of the agreement, (i.e., children's medical or education expenses) these should be put in a separate clause in your agreement (see ¶2315). This should prevent any tainting of the tax deductibility of the periodic portion of the payments. Unless these non-periodic amounts can be averaged or estimated and made payable at regular intervals, they may not be deductible for tax purposes (subject to the specific rules in ¶2315).

In Income Tax Folio S1-F3-C3, the CRA suggests the following criteria as important (but perhaps not exclusive) factors in determining whether payments are periodic and therefore deductible, rather than instalments of a lump sum or capital amount which are not deductible:

(1) Length of periods at which payments are made: Weekly or monthly payments suggest maintenance. The matter becomes less clear for longer intervals. If intervals are greater than one year the payments are unlikely to qualify.

(2) Whether payments are for an indefinite period or fixed term: An allowance for maintenance will more commonly provide for its continuance either for an indefinite period or to some event (such as the coming of age of a child) which will cause a material change in the needs of the recipient. Payments for a fixed term are more likely to be capital and not deductible.

(3) Amount of payments is relative to income and living standards of the payer and recipient: Where the payments are in excess of an amount sufficient to maintain the recipient and/or children in the style to which they were accustomed before the breakdown of the relationship, they are not likely to be viewed as an allowance for maintenance. The chance of such amounts qualifying is even less where the payments are made over a short period (presumably because they are seen as a disguised form of capital payment).

(4) Whether the payments purport to release the payer from any future obligation to pay maintenance: If there is such a release, the payments are unlikely to be maintenance (again because they are periodic payments on capital account or for a release of liability).

Where a written agreement requires a lump-sum payment to be made in respect of a period prior to the date of agreement, the payment is not normally deductible (since it was not considered to be payable on a periodic basis).

However, the CRA acknowledges that there may be circumstances where a lump-sum amount paid in a taxation year will be regarded as qualifying as a periodic payment. A lump sum may be accepted as representing periodic payments where (paragraph 3.44 of Folio S1-F3-C3):

- the lump-sum payment represents amounts payable periodically that were due after the date of the order or written agreement that had fallen into arrears;
- the lump-sum amount is paid pursuant to a court order and in conjunction with an existing obligation for periodic maintenance, and the payment represents the acceleration, or advance, of future support payable on a periodic basis, for the sole purpose of securing the funds to the recipient. This point responds to the decision in *Ostrowski v. The Queen*, 2002 DTC 7209 (F.C.A.), in which the Court allowed a taxpayer to deduct some $88,800 which a court had ordered secured from proceeds of the sale of the matrimonial home to cover future maintenance payments. The Court held the payments were deductible in the year of the order in respect of those funds, rather than the future years they were intended to cover; or
- the lump-sum amount is paid pursuant to a court order that establishes a clear obligation to pay retroactive periodic maintenance for a specified period prior to the date of the court order.

The CRA says that in either of the above situations, the lump-sum payment will not, in and of itself, change the nature of the underlying legal obligation of periodic maintenance payments.

On the other hand, a lump-sum payment to obtain a release from a liability imposed by an order or agreement, as mentioned in (4), above, whether such liability is in respect of arrears of maintenance payments, future payments or both, will not qualify as a periodic payment because it was not made in accordance with the agreement. In addition, a lump-sum payment required by a written agreement in respect of a period prior to the date of the agreement is not onsidered a qualifying support amount. Interestingly, in Income Tax Folio S1-F3-C3, the CRA has backed off its former position that a lump-sum payment required by a *court order* in respect of a period prior to the date of the order would not be considered a qualifying support amount (see above).

An amount payable under a court order or written agreement which requires an individual to pay a periodic allowance for only part of the year may still qualify as "periodic". For example, a monthly allowance for the maintenance of a child of the marriage is not disqualified because it is not required to be paid for two months of the year when the child is residing with the paying individual.

In CRA Document No. 2011-0426211E5, February 7, 2012, the CRA confirmed its policy under which a spousal support could be deductible where a separation agreement and/or court order provides for spousal support payments which are tied to bonus and incentive payments. The CRA notes that a specified sum of money which is established by reference to a reasonable formula or index may qualify as an allowance even though the exact future amounts are not specified in the order or agreement. Providing all other requirements of the definition of "support amount" are met, a payment that is calculated with reference to bonuses or incentive payments that are calculated at regular intervals (e.g., annually, quarterly, or monthly), would meet the requirement of being periodic. If the payment is calculated with reference to bonuses or incentive payments that do not occur regularly, then the payment would not meet the requirement of being periodic and presumably would not be deductible. A similar view is expressed in ¶3.39 and ¶3.40 of Income Tax Folio S1-F3-C3.

In the *Berty* court decision (2013 DTC 1171), the taxpayer was required to pay monthly support to his former spouse based on his regular salary. However, he was also required to pay a lump sum equal to 50% of any bonus he would receive from his employment. The Tax Court of Canada disallowed the deduction of the latter amount on the grounds that it was not payable on a periodic basis, in that there was no guarantee that the taxpayer would ever receive the bonus.

(ITA: 56(1)*(b)*, (*c*.2); 60*(b)*, (*c*.2); Window on Canadian Tax: 8358; Income Tax Folio: S1-F3-C3; *Hanlin v. The Queen*, 85 DTC 5052 (F.C.T.D.); *The Queen v. McKimmon*, 90 DTC 6088 (F.C.A.))

[¶2310.05] *Payments Validated by Agreement or Order*

Periodic payments made in the year or the preceding year but before a court order or written separation agreement is made can be validated by the order or agreement. The court order or agreement must provide that the preceding payment is paid and received under the order or agreement. In the absence of this rule the payments would not be "pursuant to" an order or agreement, as is required in situations where they are to be deductible by the payer and taxable to the recipient. The CRA's view is that the prior payments must have met all other requirements at the time. See also ¶2310.01 above relating to lump sum payments.

There is a second method of validation which permits the payer to deduct payments made directly to a spouse or former spouse (including a common-law partner) *for specific expenses* that are required to be paid pursuant to a court order or written separation agreement. In this case, the order or agreement must specify that "subsections 60.1(2) and 56.1(2)" apply to the expenses specified. However, the CRA has indicated that it is willing to accept a clear and unambiguous clause in a court order or written agreement stating the parties understanding that the third-party payments will be taxable to the recipient and deductible to the payer even if it fails to specify the subsection references (paragraph 3.58 of Folio S1-F3-C3). Nevertheless, the better practice is to specify that subsections 60.1(2) and 56.1(2) apply to the expenses specified. Where this alternative is used, there is no requirement that the payments were periodic. Third-party payments may also be validated under this rule, as discussed at ¶2315. Exceptions to this rule provide that it cannot be used to validate payments in respect of a self-contained domestic establishment (¶1122) in which the payer resides, nor payments for tangible property with certain exception. (These exceptions are described in greater detail in ¶2315 with respect to third-party payments, but are identical where the payments are made to a spouse/former spouse for the expenses described at ¶2315.) This rule allows deductible payments to be made, for example, for child care services, medical services, and dental services, even though such payments are not periodic and the recipient may not have discretion over the payments. Payments deductible to a payer spouse/former spouse under these rules will always be taxable to the other spouse/former spouse, whether made directly to the spouse or to a third party (e.g., the dentist). This rule is both prospective and retrospective; that is, it may validate payments made prior to the order or agreement in the current year or the immediately preceding year (but no further back), and may also sanction future payments for specified expenses even though not periodic.

Quebec rules have parallel provisions referring to the corresponding provisions of the Quebec *Taxation Act* (sections 313.0.1 and 336.1). Quebec has legislated a rule that makes it sufficient to cite only the federal sections, although the agreement or order can specify that it is intended to apply those rules only for federal and not Quebec purposes.

(ITA: 56.1; 60.1; Window on Canadian Tax: 2163; Income Tax Folio: S1-F3-C3; Other Publications: Quebec Information Bulletin 2000-4, June 29, 2000, item 1.5.2)

[¶2315] PAYMENTS TO THIRD PARTIES

Where, pursuant to an order, decree, judgment or written separation agreement, a support payment is paid to a third party for the benefit of your spouse, former spouse, former common-law partner, or a child in the custody of such a person, the payment may be deductible in computing your income. Where the new child support rules at ¶2306 apply to the order or agreement, deductibility to the payer and taxability to the spouse only apply to third-party payments which are not child support payments under the rules at ¶2306.

Where certain payments are made to a third party on behalf of a spouse or common-law partner and the payments are pursuant to a court order or written agreement the payments may qualify for deduction to the payer spouse and will be taxable to the other spouse (or common-law spouse) even though they are not periodic and are not at the discretion of the beneficiary spouse. To qualify under the new rule, however, the expenses must be specifically described in the court order or written agreement.

This is the third-party aspect of the rule described at the end of ¶2310 as validating non-periodic payments to a spouse/former spouse or common-law partner for specified expenses under subsections 56.1(2) and 60.1(2). That rule also makes payment of specified expenses deductible to the payer and taxable to the beneficiary spouse/former spouse, etc., even though paid directly to a third party, provided the expenses are for the maintenance of a recipient who is the payer's spouse or former spouse or a defined common-law partner as described at ¶2305, or the recipient's children (provided that they are in the custody of the recipient). In addition, the payments will only be deductible if:

(1) the expense was incurred at a time when the payer and the recipient were separated and living apart; and the court order or written agreement explicitly provides that these provisions (subsections 56.1(2) and 60.1(2) of the *Income Tax Act*) will apply to any payments made pursuant thereto. Quebec rules have parallel provisions referring to the corresponding provisions of the Quebec *Taxation Act* (sections 313.0.1 and 336.1).

This rule essentially waives the periodic requirement as well as the rule that the recipient spouse/partner must have control and discretion over payments made directly to third parties, provided the conditions above are met (and subject to the exclusions described below).

The rule is both prospective and retrospective; that is, it may validate payments made in the year the order or agreement is made or the immediately preceding year (but no further back), even though the payments were made prior to the actual date of the order or agreement, and it may also sanction future payments for specified expenses even though not periodic.

An exception to this rule provides that the following amounts are specifically excluded from its application, i.e., cannot be deducted by the payer *under this special rule*:

(1) amounts paid in respect of a "self-contained domestic establishment" (see ¶1122) in which the payer resides; and

(2) amounts paid on account of an expenditure for the purchase of tangible property unless the expenditure is on account of:

(a) a medical or educational expense or an expense incurred for the maintenance of an owner-occupied home of the spouse, former spouse or common-law partner, or other natural parent holding a maintenance order, as described at ¶2305, or

(b) principal and interest payable on a debt in respect of the purchase or improvement of a self-contained domestic establishment (¶1122) of the spouse, former spouse or common-law partner, or other natural parent holding a maintenance order, as described at ¶2305 to the extent that the aggregate of all such expenditures in the year does not exceed 20% of the original principal amount of the debt.

Alternatively, if the third-party payment otherwise meets the periodic and recipient's discretion requirements, it may be deductible under subsection 60.1(1). The CRA correctly explains the difference between this rule and the rule described above in subsection 60.1(2) as follows (¶3.60 of Folio S1-F3-C3):

> The difference between subsection 60.1(1) and subsection 60.1(2) is that under subsection 60.1(1) the third-party amount is only deemed to have been paid (or payable) to and received (or receivable) by the recipient. The amount must then satisfy the requirements to qualify as a support amount. On the other hand, if all the requirements in subsection 60.1(2) have been satisfied as noted in ¶3.56–¶3.59, the amount is deemed to be an amount payable by the payer to the recipient and receivable by the recipient as an allowance payable on a periodic basis and the recipient is deemed to have discretion as to the use of the amount. Therefore, subsection 60.1(2) provides greater certainty as to the deductibility of the payment of third-party amounts.

(ITA: 56.1; 60.1; ITR: 6502 [Prescribed class of persons]; Other Publications: Quebec Information Bulletin 2000-4, June 29, 2000, item 1.5.2)

[¶2325] TRANSFER OF PROPERTY TO SPOUSE OR FORMER SPOUSE/COMMON-LAW PARTNER

Unless you elect otherwise (see below), there is no immediate tax on transfers of capital property to your spouse, or to your former spouse if the transfer is in settlement of marital property rights. The term "spouse" used in this commentary includes a common-law partner. Both parties must be Canadian residents when the property is transferred.

This rule is an exception to the general rule that when you dispose of capital property to a non-arm's length person the disposition is deemed to occur at fair market value. If you meet the conditions above, you are considered to have disposed of the property at its adjusted cost base (¶505) at the time of the transfer, so that no gain or loss arises. On the other hand, the recipient acquires the property at adjusted cost base, and so will be responsible for tax on the entire capital gain when the property is disposed of. (See ¶510 and ¶531.) Where the property is depreciable property, such as a rental property, the capital cost allowance characteristics also transfer, so there is no recapture to the transferor and no adjustment in available claims or potential recapture to the transferee.

This rule applies to all situations where the spouse or former spouse or common-law partner is deemed or declared to have, is awarded, or has vested in him/her any capital property by virtue of the operation of provincial law or a provincial court order, decree or judgment.

The rule that property may be transferred to a spouse or former spouse at adjusted cost base rather than fair market value also applies to voluntary transfers of capital property between spouses or former spouses; that is, where the transfer is not in settlement of property rights.

Alternatively you may elect in your tax return for the year of transfer not to have the provision which allows the property to be transferred at the adjusted cost base apply. If you make this election, the proceeds of disposition to you and the cost to the transferee are equal to the fair market value of the property at that time. There are various situations under which the election could result in significant tax savings.

For example, it may be beneficial to make this election when you have a non-capital loss carryforward which you do not expect will be otherwise utilized (see ¶576). On the other hand, if your marginal tax rate is significantly higher than that of the transferee and the property in question has a higher fair market value than the adjusted cost base, it may be beneficial not to elect and have the gain on the eventual disposition taxed in the hands of your spouse or common-law partner. However, if the fair market value is less than the adjusted cost base it may be beneficial to elect and recognize the loss accrued to the date of transfer. Note that the loss will be allowed only in the case of transfers to former spouses or common-law partners; if the transfer is to a current spouse or common-law partner, the superficial loss rules will normally apply.

Example

Assume that you have three capital assets.

Asset	*Adjusted cost base*	*Fair market value*	*Potential capital gain or loss*
A	$100	$500	$ 400
B	$200	$250	$ 50
C	$350	$250	$ (100)
			$ 350

If an election is not made the assets transfer without giving rise to income. If you elect on all the assets you will recognize a capital gain of $350. If only A and B are included in the election, you will recognize a capital gain of $450. On the other hand, if you elect on C only, you will recognize a capital loss of $100. If you elect on B and C you will recognize a $50 capital loss.

As each situation is unique you should consider how best to maximize the tax savings through this election prior to signing the separation agreement or obtaining the court order.

Any transfers of property other than an RRSP or RRIF under conditions other than those described above will be considered to have occurred at fair market value. This will result in the realization of a gain or loss to the transferor.

In cases where transactions prior to separation have resulted in the application of the income attribution rules, the rules will cease to apply on separation. See ¶977. In general, attribution rules for capital gains (¶531) do not apply after separation if the spouses or common-law partners jointly elect this result in the year of separation. The election may be made in any year ending after the time of separation, so long as the separation continues.

(ITA: 73; 74.2; 74.5(3)(*b*); IT-325R2 Property transfers after separation, divorce and annulment; IT-511R Interspousal and certain other transfers and loans of property)

[¶2327] PARTITION OF MATRIMONIAL PROPERTY

Partition of property usually refers to a situation in which property subject to joint ownership is divided. When a "matrimonial regime" (marriage) is dissolved, especially under a court order, the court order could have the effect of creating new interests in properties and dissolving old ones in such a way that the usual acquisition, cost base determination, and disposition rules are difficult to apply.

Specific rules in the Act provide that where property is subject to partition on the dissolution of a matrimonial regime, it is deemed to be the property of the partner who brought it into the regime provided it has not been disposed of before the potential partition (usually this would imply a disposition and reacquisition). If the property is not assigned to one spouse or common-law partner under this rule, then it is assigned to the spouse or common-law partner who had the administration of the property immediately before the potential partition (subsection 248(22)).

The rules go on to provide that where after the dissolution of the matrimonial regime the person owning a particular property is not the person who was assigned ownership immediately before the dissolution under the above rules, a transfer of the property from one spouse or common-law partner to the other is deemed to have taken place immediately before the dissolution (subsection 248(23)).

The rules finally contemplate that dissolution may occur by death rather than by divorce; in such a case the same rules apply.

While it is far from clear that the initial assignment of property rules above cover all potential situations, it may give scope for the cost base and disposition rules to operate adequately to permit property to be divided for tax purposes under the rules in ¶2325 or, in the case of death, in Chapter 19.

Special rules also deal with the partition of matrimonial property occurring on the death of a spouse or common-law partner; see ¶1922.

(ITA: 248(22), (23))

[¶2330] TRANSFER OF RRSP AND RRIF

Any funds in your unmatured RRSP may be transferred without tax consequences to an RRSP or RRIF for your spouse or common-law partner or former spouse or common-law partner provided that all the following conditions are met:

(1) you and your spouse/former spouse, etc., are living apart;

(2) the payment is pursuant to either:

- a decree, order or judgment of a competent tribunal, or,
- a written separation agreement relating to a division of property between you and your spouse or common-law partner or former spouse or common-law partner in settlement of rights arising out of your marriage or partnership, on or after the breakdown of your marriage or partnership;

(3) your spouse or common-law partner is not disqualified by reason of age from having an RRSP (¶2616.05); and

(4) the transfer is made directly between plans.

Similarly, you may transfer any funds in a RRIF of which you are the annuitant to a RRIF or RRSP for your spouse or common-law partner or former spouse or common-law partner on the same conditions.

In addition, your spouse or former spouse may withdraw funds from a spousal RRSP (or the RRIF your spouse established therefrom) to which you contributed on your spouse's behalf without triggering the usual inclusion in your income, provided only that at the time your spouse withdraws the funds you and your spouse are living separate and apart by reason of marriage or common-law partnership breakdown. Note that the test in this case is less severe than that above, in that there need not be any formal separation agreement. The test is a factual one of marriage breakdown.

Form T2220 authorizes the transfer of funds among plans on separation or divorce where permitted under the rules above.

(ITA: 60(*l*); 146(1.1), (8.3), (16); 146.3(5.1), (14))

[¶2335] CANADA PENSION PLAN BENEFITS

The *Canada Pension Plan Act* (CPP) allows for the splitting of CPP benefits between a taxpayer and a former spouse.

The CPP permits divorced persons to apply for a share of the CPP credits of the former spouse. This results in equal sharing of pension credits accumulated while the taxpayers were married. The credits earned by both spouses during the marriage will be aggregated and split equally. Generally speaking, there is no time limit on this application, except that where a spouse has died there is a 36-month time limit.

Canada Pension Plan entitlements can be divided on separations of common-law partners if they have lived together for at least one year, and application for division is made within four years of the commencement of separation.

In the case of a legal divorce you do not have to apply for a division of benefits; the Canada Pension Plan simply needs to be notified that the divorce occurred and given certain information with documentation, such as the length of time you lived together. In all other cases, an application is required. There appears to be a distinction without a difference. In either event, you should obtain from Social Development Canada form package ISP 1901, which contain much useful information as well as the requisite forms.

Separated parties can divide CPP "unadjusted pensionable earnings" by agreement or court order, but the order or agreement must specifically refer to "sections 55 or 55.1" of the *Canada Pension Plan Act* to be binding.

(CPP: 2(1); 25; 53.1; 53.2)

[¶2337] OTHER PENSION INCOME

Where pension income (excluding CPP/QPP income which has its own division rules above) is divided between spouses or common-law partners, the tax results may be capricious. For example, in a technical opinion, the CRA gave its view that under Alberta pension standards rules, where a couple agreed voluntarily on a division of pension income rather than obtaining a court order, the division was in effect invalid and all the income would be taxed to the spouse whose pension it technically was.

The same opinion found a different result in British Columbia. At least so long as a pension was divided 50/50, each spouse would report its share of pension income received. It was less clear what would happen if the division was uneven.

On the other hand, the Act allows a taxpayer to split up to 50% of certain types of pension income (e.g., RRSP annuities,

RRIF payments, and RPP benefits) with the taxpayer's spouse or common-law partner. The split is notionaly, in that the spouse is taxed on the split amount even though the taxpayer is the person receiving the amount. This pension income splitting is discussed at ¶1076. It is not allowed for divorced or separated spouses.

(Window on Canadian Tax: 2592)

[¶2340] CHILD CARE EXPENSES

Under certain circumstances a working mother or father who is divorced or separated can claim child care expenses. See ¶1049–¶1061.

[¶2345] DEPENDANT CREDIT IN YEAR OF SEPARATION

If you are required to pay support amounts to a spouse or former spouse (or common-law partner) in a taxation year, and you claim the deduction for such payments in the year or live apart throughout the year, you are not entitled to claim a personal credit under section 118 in respect of the spouse or common-law partner or the child in respect of whom the payments were made. This means that, in the year in which the marriage breakdown occurs, you may be able to claim the personal credits under subsection 118(1) if you do not claim a deduction for your support payments.

See the discussion at ¶1118.

(ITA: 118(1), (5))

[¶2350] DEPENDANT CREDIT IN YEAR SUBSEQUENT TO SEPARATION

If you are required to make support payments described in ¶2305, even if they are not deductible by reason of ¶2306, in years following the year of marriage breakdown, no credits will be available to you in respect of the spouse or common-law partner or children covered by the payments. On the other hand, as the recipient spouse or common-law partner, you will be able to claim the eligible dependant credit for one eligible dependant covered by the payments, provided other criteria at ¶1120 are met.

(ITA: 118(1), (5))

[¶2355] DEDUCTIBILITY OF LEGAL FEES

The CRA is very specific as to when legal fees are considered to be deductible for tax purposes. Income Tax Folio S1-F3-C3 provides the most recent CRA opinions in the context of spousal and child support.

[¶2355.05] *Legal Costs of Obtaining Support*

In the case of *Gallien v. The Queen*, 2000 DTC 2514 (T.C.C.), the Tax Court held that the expenses of obtaining maintenance orders in separation litigation were made to enforce a pre-existing right and consequently deductible. On October 10, 2002, in *Income Tax Technical News* No. 24, the CRA announced that it would accept the logic of the *Gallien* decision, saying:

> As a result, we now consider legal costs to obtain spousal support under the *Divorce Act*, or under applicable provincial legislation in a separation agreement, to have been incurred to enforce a pre-existing right to support. Consequently, these costs are deductible ... We also now accept that the legal costs of seeking to obtain an increase in support or to make child support non-taxable under the [Federal Child Support] Guidelines are also deductible.

In a recent technical interpretation (CRA Document No. 2011-0417661E5), the CRA reiterates that legal costs incurred to establish support payments are deductible, even where the claim for spousal (or child) support is unsuccessful, as long as the claim was a *bona fide* claim with a reasonable chance of success.

Most recently, in Income Tax Folio S1-F3-C3, the CRA outlines its position on the deductibility of legal fees for recipients of support amounts (¶3.81):

> A recipient can deduct legal and accounting fees incurred to:
>
> - establish the amount of support payments from their current or former spouse or common-law partner;
> - establish the amount of support payments from the legal parent of their child (who is not their current or former spouse or common-law partner) where the support is payable under the terms of a court order;
> - seek an increase in support payments;
> - defend against a reduction in support payments;
> - collect late support payments; or
> - request that child support payments be non-taxable.

The CRA also notes that legal and accounting fees are deductible by the recipient even where the claim for support was unsuccessful as long as the claim was *bona fide* and not frivolous, with a reasonable chance of success (consistent with the technical interpretation noted above).

From the payer's perspective, legal costs incurred in negotiating or contesting an application for support payments are not deductible since these costs are personal or living expenses. Similarly, legal costs incurred for the purpose of terminating or reducing the amount of support payments are not deductible since success in such an action does not produce income from a business or property (¶21, Interpretation Bulletin IT-99R5 – now archived). This principle has been upheld in several cases; for a recent decision, see *Landry v. The Queen*, 2014 DTC 1198 (TCC). In Income Tax Folio S1-F3-C3, the CRA further provides (paragraph 3.78):

> Neither the payer nor the recipient may deduct legal and accounting fees incurred to:
>
> - get a separation or divorce;
> - establish custody or visitation rights to a child; or
> - equalize family assets.

[¶2355.15] *Legal Costs of Obtaining Pension Division*

In a technical opinion, CRA Document No. 2002-0177827, dated February 3, 2003, the CRA confirmed its view that the legal costs of obtaining a division of pension rights are not deductible. The opinion goes on to say that where an agreement in respect of a division or settlement of property is negotiated between former spouses, including the division of pension assets, and the terms of the agreement are not satisfied by one of the parties to the agreement, legal fees relating to the enforcement of the pre-existing entitlements may be deductible by the former spouse. The enforcement of a pre-existing entitlement under an existing agreement in respect of a division or settlement of property would be considered to be separate and distinct from the original division or settlement of property arising out of the marriage breakdown.

[¶2360] HISTORICAL NOTE: THE CONSTITUTIONALITY OF TAXING CHILD SUPPORT

In May 1994, the Federal Court of Appeal ruled (in the case of *Thibaudeau v. The Queen*, 94 DTC 6230 (F.C.A.)) that it was unconstitutional to tax a single custodial parent on maintenance payments received for the benefit of children. That is, in the case of separation or divorce, where a single parent who has custody of any of the children receives payments for maintenance of such children from a payer who can deduct them, such payments are not taxable to the recipient, despite the tax law to the contrary.

In May 1995, the Supreme Court of Canada reversed the Federal Court of Appeal (*The Queen v. Thibaudeau*, 95 DTC 5273 (S.C.C.)) and ruled that the then-existing system of deductions to the payer matched by taxability to the recipient was indeed within the rights of Parliament to enact. It found that any flaws in the existing system were not a fundamental fault of the tax system as such. The Court issued two separate majority opinions and two dissenting opinions. Perhaps the most interesting is the dissent of Mme. Justice L'Heureux-Dubé, detailing more clearly than any other opinion at all court levels the inequities of the existing system.

The majority opinion did not so much endorse the then-existing system as find it to be within the bounds of parliamentary authority, and the Department of Finance immediately undertook to review the system as it existed in 1995. The result of that review is the system as it was revised effective May 1, 1997.

Chapter 24

Alternative Minimum Tax

THESE POINTS ARE COVERED IN THIS CHAPTER

CRA REFERENCES RELATING TO THIS CHAPTER

T1 Schedules

- Schedule 1, Line 417 — Federal tax (after certain adjustments)
- Schedule 1, Line 420 — Net federal tax
- Schedule 1, Line 427 — Minimum tax carry-over

CRA Guides

5000-G, "General Income Tax and Benefit Guide"

CRA Forms

T3, "Statement of Trust Income Allocations and Designations"; **T626**, "Overseas Employment Tax Credit"; **T691**, "Alternative Minimum Tax"; **T1206**, "Tax on Split Income"; **T2038(IND)**, "Investment Tax Credit (Individuals)"; **T2203**, "Provincial and Territorial Taxes — Multiple Jurisdictions"; **T2209**, "Federal Foreign Tax Credits"

Income Tax Folios

S5-F2-C1, "Foreign Tax Credit"

WHAT YOU SHOULD KNOW ABOUT ALTERNATIVE MINIMUM TAX

RECENT CHANGES

For taxation years ending prior to 2016, the alternative minimum tax exemption of $40,000 can be claimed by any testamentary trust and by certain pre-1972 trusts. For 2016 and subsequent years, the $40,000 basic exemption is only available to trusts that are "graduated rate estates".

[¶2403] ALTERNATIVE MINIMUM TAX (AMT)

The alternative minimum tax (AMT) was introduced in 1986. It was intended to deal with the perceived problem of individuals (including trusts) with high gross incomes paying little or no income tax in a particular year. There may be any number of reasons for such a situation: loss carryovers, the preferential taxation of capital gains and employee stock options, and tax shelter investments are examples. In many situations, especially those involving tax shelters, the low taxes of a particular year represent timing differences: the tax shelter offers deductions in early years, but in later years will produce taxable income against which related deductions have already been claimed. The AMT itself recognizes this by being essentially a timing difference — AMT paid in a particular year in excess of ordinary tax may be carried forward seven years and can be deducted from your ordinary tax liability that is in excess of AMT liability.

The AMT requires that you perform a revised computation of your income, adding back a number of ordinarily allowed deductions (these addbacks are sometimes called "tax preference items") but deducting the dividend "gross-up" (¶404) to arrive at AMT taxable income. A general exemption of $40,000 is also allowed at this point; it is designed to exclude low to middle income earners generally. The resulting AMT taxable income is subject to federal tax at the lowest federal marginal rate (15%), plus applicable provincial tax expressed as a percentage of the federal AMT. Each province (except Quebec) determines its applicable percentage of federal AMT, and determines whether its rate applies to federal AMT before or after the federal AMT foreign tax credit (¶2475). This provincial surtax varies from province to province. The upshot is that the federal and provincial combined AMT rate varies from about 20% to 25%. For residents of Quebec, the Quebec abatement (¶1435) applies and Quebec imposes its own AMT on its own AMT tax base (see ¶1698). For federal purposes, only the foreign tax credit (see ¶2475), the *refundable* portion of the investment tax credit, the refundable medical expense supplement, and the working income tax benefit (the latter two not likely available if you are subject to AMT) may be claimed against this AMT tax; if the AMT tax is higher than the "ordinarily computed tax" (i.e., tax as calculated in Chapter 14), the higher amount must be paid.

It follows that credits that cannot be claimed against AMT and which are not eligible for carryover, such as political contribution tax credits, will be lost entirely if AMT applies. On the other hand, items such as the investment tax credit have built-in carryover mechanisms which will preserve unused credits denied by AMT.

The balance of this chapter discusses the details of the AMT calculation.

(ITA: 120.2; 127.5 –127.55)

LIABILITY FOR ALTERNATIVE MINIMUM TAX

[¶2405] WHO MUST PAY ALTERNATIVE MINIMUM TAX?

If you earn the types of income (dividends or capital gains), claim the types of deductions (statutory tax shelters, the employee stock option deduction, the employee relocation loan deduction), or claim the types of tax credits (investment, share purchase, scientific research, overseas employment tax) that are subject to the AMT calculation, there is no simple rule of thumb to determine whether or not you will have an AMT liability greater than regular tax liability. However, as a general summary, you *may* be liable to pay AMT if one of the following situations applies.

(1) You reported taxable dividends on line 120.

(2) You claimed any of the following tax credits:

(a) investment tax credit;

(b) federal political contribution tax credit;

(c) overseas employment tax credit (eliminated in 2016); or

(d) labour-sponsored funds tax credit.

(3) You reported a taxable capital gain on line 127. Note that capital gains from foreclosures of mortgages (¶518) or similar amounts from dispositions of eligible capital property (¶768) are not counted.

(4) You claimed one or more of the following:

(a) a loss (including your share of a partnership loss) related to your investment in:

- rental property, including multi-unit residential buildings ("MURBs"),

- certified film property
- leasing property,
- registered tax shelters, and
- any partnership in which you are a limited or passive partner based on any claim for capital cost allowance, interest expense, and financing charges;

(b) a loss resulting from or increased by claiming resource expenses (depletion, exploration, development, Canadian oil and gas property expense, or foreign exploration and development property expense) and interest and/or financing costs in excess of income related to resource properties;

(c) employee stock option plan deduction and other deductions at line 249; and

(d) employee home relocation loan deduction.

If you meet any of the above criteria, you should complete form T691 to determine if AMT will apply to you. In practice, if you add back the deductions referred to in (4), above, and an additional 30% of the capital gains in (3), and if your taxable income is still below $40,000, you are likely not subject to AMT. However, you should still obtain form T691 and fill out the first two pages to determine if you have a potential liability to AMT, in which case you must complete the rest of form T691.

If the preliminary calculation on form T691 indicates that no AMT is payable, you should nevertheless attach a copy of the completed form T691 to your return if you paper-file it. If you do not attach the form (and often even if you do), the CRA's computers may assess AMT if it appears applicable. However, their readings of certain items — especially capital cost allocations on tax shelters may be less precise than your own, and it is in your interest to file form T691 to clarify your position.

If you paid AMT in any of the past seven years but are not liable for AMT this year, you should obtain a form T691, which (in Part 8) will allow you to compute a refund of a previously paid AMT to which you may be entitled in the current year. Generally speaking, you can carry forward the AMT in excess of your regular tax in a year for up to seven years, and can deduct it against your regular tax liability that is in excess of the AMT amount in a future year (see ¶2481).

[¶2407] PARTNERSHIPS

Partnerships as such are not liable to AMT. However, where any partnership income or loss is relevant in computing AMT of a partner, the partner must — in computing taxable income for AMT purposes — make adjustments for deductions allocated from the partnership in the same proportion as "ordinary" income or loss allocation from the partnership. This provision is necessary to ensure that the capital cost allowance and the carrying charge limitations are effective for investments made through a partnership.

(ITA: 127.52(2))

[¶2409] EXCEPTION FOR CERTAIN RETURNS

AMT is not applicable to the special returns of income filed on behalf of a bankrupt taxpayer by the trustee in bankruptcy, or to any year-of-death returns for a deceased taxpayer, including ordinary return of income of an individual who died in the year.

A "spousal trust" (that is, a trust which qualified for spousal rollovers from a deceased taxpayer) is not subject to AMT for the trust's taxation year that includes the time of the beneficiary spouse's death. This exemption extends to a "pre-1972 spousal trust", which is, generally speaking, a tainted spousal trust created before June 18, 1971.

AMT carried forward from prior years may be applied to reduce ordinary tax in excess of AMT on the main year-of-death return only under the general rules at ¶2481. This reduction cannot be applied to any of the special returns described at ¶1941 to ¶1944, nor to the special return filed by a trustee in bankruptcy on behalf of a bankrupt individual.

(ITA: 120.2(4); 127.55)

[¶2410] SPLIT INCOME TAX OVERRIDES AMT

The tax on split income of minors (¶1490) overrides other taxing provisions, so that an individual's tax for the year cannot be less than the amount of split income tax, reduced only by a related dividend tax credit and foreign tax credit (¶1490.25). The AMT liability is explicitly made subject to that rule. Thus where regular tax, including the tax on split income (after those few allowed, related credits), is by itself higher than the AMT, the tax on split income determines the amount payable. On the other hand, where ordinary tax plus split income tax is lower than AMT, AMT will prevail. See ¶2473.

AMT carryovers cannot be used to reduce split income tax; see ¶2481.

(ITA: 120.2(1), (3); 120.4; 127.5)

ADJUSTMENTS TO NET INCOME

[¶2412] DETERMINATION OF "ADJUSTED TAXABLE INCOME"

In computing the "adjusted taxable income" on which AMT is levied, the first step is to revise a number of items that are deducted (and the dividend gross-up that is added) in computing net income and taxable income for ordinary tax purposes. These items are discussed in the following paragraphs.

[¶2420] CARRYING CHARGES AND CAPITAL COST ALLOWANCE ON RENTAL AND LEASING PROPERTY (AND MURBS)

In calculating adjusted taxable income, your deductions for carrying charges and capital cost allowance on rental properties (¶630) or leasing properties (¶873) are restricted. Carrying charges for these purposes include all deductions in respect of the property for interest (¶1063) or for discounted debt, financing expenses incurred in the course of borrowing money or incurring debt (¶764), and premiums on life insurance pledged as collateral (¶764).

The deduction you can claim in calculating adjusted taxable income for capital cost allowance (CCA) and carrying charges is limited to the total of:

(a) the aggregate income for the year from rental or leasing properties computed before deducting the related CCA and carrying charges, plus

(b) taxable capital gains net of allowable capital losses on the dispositions in the year of rental or leasing property, minus

(c) aggregate losses for the year from such properties computed without reference to these items.

Multi-unit rental buildings are considered rental properties for these purposes.

(ITA: 127.52(1)(*b*), (*c*.1))

[¶2422] CARRYING CHARGES AND CAPITAL COST ALLOWANCE ON FILM PROPERTIES

Certified films are eligible for rapid capital cost allowance (CCA) (¶874, ¶2521).

In computing adjusted taxable income, your deductions in respect of CCA and all related carrying costs (i.e., deduction under the rules for interest (¶1063) or for discounted debt, financing expenses incurred in the course of borrowing money or incurring debt (¶764), and premiums on life insurance pledged as collateral (¶764)) are limited to the total of:

(a) the aggregate income for the year from such property before deducting the related CCA and carrying charges plus

(b) taxable capital gains net of allowable capital losses on the dispositions in the year of film properties, minus

(c) aggregate losses for the year from film properties computed without reference to the carrying costs.

(ITA: 20(1)(*a*); 127.52(1)(*c*), (*c*.1)– (*c*.3), (3); ITR: Sch. II, Class 10, 12; 1100; 1104(2))

[¶2423] LOSSES FOR LIMITED PARTNER, SPECIFIED MEMBER OR TAX SHELTER INVESTOR

If you are a limited partner of a partnership, a specified member of a partnership since becoming a partner, or a partner in a partnership for which a tax shelter identification number is required to be obtained or has been obtained, the deductions you claim for your loss from the partnership is restricted in computing your adjusted taxable income.

If you are a limited partner or a specified member of a partnership, your deduction for carrying charges relating to your investment is limited to the income from the investment you report – you cannot claim carrying charges to create or increase a loss.

If you are an investor in a tax shelter, in computing adjusted taxable income, your deduction for the total of your share of:

(a) allowable capital losses,

(b) business losses,

(c) property losses from the partnerships, and

(d) your carrying charges related to your investment,

is limited to the total of:

(e) your share of the partnership's taxable capital gains from dispositions of property in the fiscal period (other than property acquired by the partnership on a rollover basis from a partner), plus

(f) any taxable capital gain for the year from the disposition of your interest in the partnership, if you do not have an interest in the partnership throughout the following taxation year.

[¶2426] RESOURCE INDUSTRY EXPENSES

In computing adjusted taxable income, deductions ordinarily allowed for depletion, exploration, development, Canadian oil and gas property expenses, foreign exploration and development expenses, and foreign resource expenses (see Chapter 22) are allowed only to the extent of resource income (including income from the disposition of resource properties). In computing income from resource properties, your income from an investment in property described in Classes 43.1 or 43.2 is computed without regard to the capital cost allowance you claimed.

As with all other adjustments in computing adjusted taxable income, financing charges for, specifically, flow-through shares (¶2521.50), Canadian resource property (¶2202), foreign resource property (¶2225), and foreign resource expenses are included in the determination of the amount subject to restriction. That is, in determining deductions for carrying charges on resource properties for AMT purposes, the deduction is limited to resource income computed without carrying charges in excess of resource claims for the year.

(ITA: 59; 65; 66; 66.1; 66.2; 66.4; 127.52(1)(*e*), (*e*.1); ITAR: 29(10), (12))

[¶2427] FINANCING (CARRYING) CHARGES OF LIMITED OR SPECIFIED PARTNERS

If you are a limited partner (¶1818.15) or specified partner (¶1842.30), deductions for financing or carrying charges in respect of the acquisition of the partnership interest are limited to income from that partnership. The same restriction applies if you are a member of a partnership that owns a rental or leasing property or a film property (regardless of whether you are a limited or specified member).

The financing or carrying charges referred to are those for interest (¶1063) or for discounted debt, financing expenses incurred in the course of borrowing money or incurring debt (¶764), and premiums on life insurance pledged as collateral (¶764).

Caution must be exercised in determining who is a limited partner, since the definition at ¶1818 is slightly broadened for this purpose (to include exempt interests).

(ITA: 127.52(1)(*c*.2))

[¶2428] REGISTERED TAX SHELTERS

If you invest in a tax shelter registered under the rules at ¶2521, any deductions for property (CCA), outlay or expense are deemed for AMT purposes to be nil in computing AMT. This rule does not apply where the rules in ¶2420, ¶2422, or ¶2423 already apply to the amount, or the per-partnership limitation in ¶2427 already applies.

(ITA: 127.52(1)(*c*.3))

[¶2429] CAPITAL GAINS AND LOSSES

Ordinarily only 1/2 of capital gains net of capital losses for a year are included in income (see ¶500a). This is often referred to as the "taxable portion" of net capital gains.

In computing adjusted taxable income, 80% of capital gains in excess of capital losses for the year are included in income. However, no adjustment is made for capital gains arising from charitable gifts of property to qualified donees (see ¶1265). This is true for all charitable gifts to a qualified donee, regardless of whether the normal capital gains rate applies to the gift, or the nil rate applicable for publicly listed securities and ecologically sensitive property (¶1290d and ¶1268d).

The capital gains adjustment is reflected on form T691 by adding 30% of the capital gains subject to adjustment to income determined under the regular rules. This reflects in adjusted taxable income the 80% AMT inclusion rate.

The capital gains exemption (¶502) is not adjusted in computing adjusted taxable income, to the extent it was claimed for ordinary tax purposes.

[¶2429.05] *Reserves*

Capital gain reserves (¶581) operate for AMT purposes in a manner similar to the capital gains exemption. The reserve reduces the capital gain for both ordinary and adjusted taxable income purposes; however, the inclusion rate portion of the reduced gain is taken into income for ordinary purposes, whereas 80% of the gain remaining after the reserve claim is included in adjusted taxable income.

Example

Victoria had a capital gain of $1,000 in Year 1, and was entitled to a reserve of $800 for the year, leaving an effective Year 1 gain of $200. The taxable capital gain of $100 was included in income and $160 (80% of $200) was included in adjusted taxable income for AMT purposes. If another $300 is recognized in Year 2 (i.e., the remaining $800 is added back and a $500 reserve claimed), the ordinary income inclusion will be $150 (50% of $300), but adjusted taxable income will be $240 (80% of the $300 draw down of the reserve).

[¶2429.10] *Capital Losses*

The capital loss rules are the converse of the capital gain rules. 80% of capital losses in excess of capital gains for the year are available for carryover (back three years and forward indefinitely) against net capital gains of other years in computing adjusted taxable income, provided the taxable portion of the losses has been applied to the taxable portion of capital gains on the ordinary return for that year. As a practical matter, the use of capital loss carryovers on the ordinary return governs their use on form T691 (see ¶2461).

[¶2429.15] *Capital Gains Arising on Foreclosures*

If a mortgage has been foreclosed on you, or property repossessed under a conditional sales contract, you will have a disposition which may result in capital gain or loss, as discussed at ¶518. Where this applies, you need only include the taxable portion (50%) of capital gains arising from the foreclosure or repossession in adjusted taxable income for AMT purposes. Capital loss carryovers are similarly adjusted so that to the extent the loss applied in the year is identified as arising from a foreclosure or repossession, no adjustment is made in computing adjusted taxable income, as discussed at ¶2461. A separate pool should be identified in the year in which such a loss arises. As there is no apparent ordering provision, it should be within your discretion to determine whether or not a particular carryover came first from a net capital loss arising on a foreclosure or from another source.

[¶2429.20] *Capital Gains Arising on Dispositions of Eligible Capital Property*

A disposition of eligible capital property may give rise to a gain and, in certain circumstances, an individual can elect to treat that gain as a capital gain for limited purposes (see ¶766 and ¶768). However, no adjustment is made in computing adjusted taxable income for AMT purposes with respect to a disposition of eligible capital property, whether or not you elect to treat it as a capital gain.

Commentary on Bill C-29 Measures (Oct. 25, 2016)

Note: When Bill C-29, October 25, 2016, achieves Royal Assent, the commentary will be modified to read:

Effective January 1, 2017, the eligible capital property rules have been repealed and replaced by a new Class 14.1 of depreciable property. Property that previously was eligible capital property is now depreciable capital property and expenditures and receipts that previously were accounted for under the eligible capital property rules are now accounted for under the rules for depreciable property and capital property.

[¶2429.25] *Capital Gains Assigned to Individuals from a Trust*

The trust rules provide for various types of income of a personal trust to flow through to beneficiaries with their characteristics intact. Thus, capital gains realized in a trust and paid or made payable to you will be taxed in your hands and not in the trust (see ¶465).

You treat gains from trusts like all other capital gains on Schedule 3 and form T691.

(ITA: 38; 40; 41; 127.52(1)(*d*), (*i*))

[¶2432] DIVIDENDS

[¶2432.05] *Taxable Canadian Dividends*

Dividends from Canadian corporations are subject to a "gross-up" in computing ordinary income (see ¶404). For AMT purposes, only the actual amount of these dividends is included in adjusted taxable income; the dividend gross-up is excluded. However, no dividend tax credit is allowed in the computation of AMT.

[¶2432.10] *Capital Dividends*

Certain dividends from Canadian companies represent underlying capital gains and are not taxed to the shareholders. No adjustment for these dividends is required, as they are non-taxable for both ordinary and AMT purposes. This applies to all the non-taxable dividends described at ¶415.

[¶2432.15] *Foreign Dividends*

There is no adjustment in computing adjusted taxable income for foreign dividend income received during the year.

[¶2432.20] *Capital Gains Dividends*

Dividends which must be reported and treated as capital gains on Schedule 3 fall under the capital gain rules at ¶2429.

[¶2432.25] *Other Dividends*

There are no adjustments required in computing adjusted taxable income for dividends from other sources.

(ITA: 127.52(1)(*f*))

[¶2437] PENSIONS SUBJECT TO SPECIAL AVERAGING

The special averaging rules described from ¶1471 to ¶1480 for pension payments relating to pre-1972 earnings do not apply in computing adjusted taxable income for AMT purposes.

(ITA: 127.52(1)(*j*))

[¶2443] EMPLOYEE STOCK OPTIONS

Only 40% of the amount you deduct in computing your taxable income with respect to stock option benefits is deductible in computing your adjusted taxable income for AMT purposes, not the 50% that you deduct in computing your regular income. The intention is to equate the inclusion of stock option benefits for AMT purposes to the 80% AMT inclusion rate for capital gains. Thus, if the stock option benefit is $100 and the ordinary deduction is $50, the AMT inclusion is $100 and the AMT deduction is 40% of $50 = $20. Therefore, the net stock option benefit for AMT purposes is $100 - $20 = $80.

However, if you make a charitable donation of the optioned shares to a qualified donee that is eligible for the nil taxable capital gain rule (see ¶533) and the additional stock option benefit deduction, no adjustment is made in computing adjusted taxable income for AMT purposes. Thus, if you have no net income inclusion on exercising a stock option and gifting the optioned shares within 30 days, no adjustment is made in computing your adjusted taxable income.

(ITA: 127.52(1)(*h*))

[¶2445] PROSPECTORS' AND GRUBSTAKERS' SHARES

The special deduction claimed for ordinary tax purposes of 40% may be deducted for AMT purposes. The intention is to equate the inclusion rate for this income for AMT purposes to the 80% AMT inclusion rate for capital gains for AMT purposes. Thus, if the prospector's income eligible for the offsetting deduction is $100 and the ordinary deduction is $50, the AMT inclusion is $100 and the AMT deduction is 40% of $50 = $20. Therefore, the income inclusion for AMT purposes is $100– $20 = $80.

(ITA: 127.52(1)(*h*))

[¶2447] DEFERRED PROFIT SHARING PLANS (DPSP)

Where shares are received as part of a lump-sum settlement out of a DPSP on withdrawal from the plan, retirement, or death, elections may allow the recipient to defer tax on the gains in the plan until the shares are disposed of. On disposition, the excess of fair market value at the time of the shares' receipt *over the* shares' cost to the plan will be ordinary income (¶917) with an offsetting deduction at line 249 of the T1 return. This deduction is not allowed for AMT purposes and must be added back in computing adjusted taxable income. Subsequent gains/losses on the shares are *capital* gains/losses. See ¶2429.

(ITA: 127.52(1)(*h*))

[¶2451] HOME RELOCATION LOAN DEDUCTION

The deemed interest benefit on the first $25,000 of a low-interest loan may be deducted in some circumstances (¶409) at line 248 of the T1 return. The deduction may not be claimed for AMT purposes and must be added in computing adjusted taxable income.

(ITA: 127.52(1)(*h*))

[¶2454] NORTHERN RESIDENTS DEDUCTIONS

The northern residents deductions (¶361a) claimed on line 255 of the T1 return are allowable for AMT purposes, and no adjustment should be made to AMT adjusted taxable income.

(ITA: 127.52(1)(*h*))

[¶2457] LIFETIME CAPITAL GAINS EXEMPTION

The lifetime capital gains deduction claimed on line 254 of the T1 return is allowable for AMT purposes and no adjustment is made in computing adjusted taxable income.

(ITA: 127.52(1)(*h*), (*h.1*))

[¶2459] TREATY EXEMPTIONS

Amounts deducted from your taxable income as exempt under a tax treaty between Canada and another country (see ¶990) are allowable deductions for AMT purposes, and no adjustment should be made in calculating adjusted taxable income. Where the treaty exemption includes a capital gain, 100% of the gain is deducted (and not merely the inclusion-rate portion) when computing AMT adjusted taxable income.

(ITA: 127.52(1)(*h*))

[¶2460] ADULT BASIC EDUCATION TUITION DEDUCTION

The amount deducted on line 256 of the T1 return, used to offset basic (primary/secondary) adult education tuition assistance received from the government and included in income (as discussed at ¶971) is allowable for AMT purposes. Hence, no adjustment should be made in computing AMT adjusted taxable income.

[¶2461] LOSSES AND LOSS CARRYOVERS

Losses sustained in the year may be deducted when computing adjusted taxable income, subject to the limitations mentioned below, to the extent they are allowed under ordinary tax rules.

[¶2461.05] *Non-Capital, Farming, and Restricted Farm Loss Carryovers*

These losses, when incurred in other years, may be deducted from AMT adjusted taxable income of the current year to the extent that (1) they are deducted in the current year for ordinary income purposes (see Chapter 13) on line 252 of the T1, and (2) the losses are recomputed for the year they arose in accordance with the restrictions at ¶2420–¶2428. These limitations apply to:

- carrying charges and capital cost allowance deductions claimed for rental, leasing, or film property;
- carrying charges for acquiring an interest in a partnership that owns rental, leasing, or film property;
- carrying charges for acquiring an interest in a partnership in which you are a limited or specified partner;
- losses from partnerships that are tax shelters;
- amounts deductible from having acquired a tax shelter; and
- deductible resource industry expenses.

In other words, in computing CMT adjusted taxable income, only the portion of losses from other years that does not represent a loss created by a tax preference is allowed.

[¶2461.10] *Net Capital Loss Carryovers*

80% of capital losses of other years may be deducted from AMT in the current year to the extent that:

(1) the corresponding taxable portion of the capital loss is deducted in computing ordinary income; that is, the capital loss claim on line 253 of the T1 adjusted as described at ¶2429; and

(2) regardless of the year in which the capital losses arose, 80% of the year's capital losses in excess of capital gains that are used for the computation under the rule in ¶2429. Thus, the portion of the loss that can be applied in computing adjusted taxable income is the portion that would have been allowed if the loss had been incurred in the current year.

As discussed at ¶2429.15, to the extent that a net capital loss from another year arises on a foreclosure or repossession, there is no adjustment in computing adjusted taxable income for AMT purposes.

[¶2461.15] *Limited Partnership Loss Carryovers*

Limited partnership losses are computed in exactly the same way as non-capital losses described above.

See also ¶2423.

[¶2463] BASIC $40,000 EXEMPTION

After making all the adjustments required to arrive at adjusted taxable income for AMT purposes, applicable to 2016 and subsequent taxation years, a deduction of $40,000 is allowed for an individual (other than a trust) or a graduated rate estate before applying the 15% federal tax rate. For taxation years prior to 2016, individuals and certain qualifying trusts (namely testamentary trusts and certain qualified pre-1972 *inter vivos* trusts) could access the $40,000 basic exemption.

(ITA: 127.51; 127.53 (repealed))

[¶2465] SPECIAL RULES FOR TRUSTS

Trusts are generally subject to AMT, though the taxation of trusts is a subject beyond the scope of this book. In applying AMT to trusts, special adjustments are made for capital gains allocated to beneficiaries. As well, prior to 2016 the $40,000 basic exemption is only allowed to testamentary trusts and certain qualified pre-1972 *inter vivos* trusts. After 2015, only a graduated rate estate is allowed to claim the basic exemption.

Prior to 2016, where trusts which qualify for the $40,000 exemption arose from contributions by the same individual, the $40,000 exemption must be allocated between those trusts.

(ITA: 127.52(1)(*g*); 127.51; 127.53 (repealed))

ALTERNATIVE MINIMUM TAX COMPUTATION

[¶2471] DETERMINING IF AMT APPLIES

Once "adjusted taxable income" is calculated, a multi-stage process determines whether AMT is payable, and if so, how much.

Step One

Determine the "gross minimum amount". This is simply the lowest federal marginal tax rate (currently 15%) of adjusted taxable income in excess of the basic $40,000 exemption (¶2463).

Step Two

The gross minimum amount is reduced by all of the personal tax credits you claimed at line 350, except the pension income credit (line 314); the disability credit for a dependant (line 318); the tuition, education, and textbook credit (the education and textbook credits were repealed effective January 1, 2017) transferred from a dependant (line 324); and credits transferred from spouse (line 326) (see ¶2474). The result is the "minimum amount".

Step Three

Subtract from the "minimum amount" the special foreign tax credit, if any (see ¶2475). The result, not technically named, might be called "interim AMT".

Step Four

Step four is to compute ordinary federal tax. Form T691 has its own calculation of this amount. Start with gross federal tax payable, which includes the tax on split income, the surtax on business income earned outside Canada, and any recaptured investment tax credits, and deduct your

(a) non-refundable credits,

(b) family tax cut credit (repealed effective January 1, 2016),

(c) dividend tax credit,

(d) overseas employment tax credit (eliminated in 2016),

(e) foreign tax credit,

(f) logging tax credit,

(g) political contribution tax credit,

(h) investment tax credit, and

(i) labour-sponsored funds tax credit.

No other credits are permitted. The result is that credits denied under this rule are lost altogether unless they contain their own carryover rules, as does, for example, the investment tax credit.

Step Five

Compare your interim AMT from step three with the ordinary tax from step four. If the ordinary tax is higher, no AMT is payable and tax is calculated by completing page 4 of the T1. If AMT is higher, AMT is payable and tax is computed by completing form T691. If the comparison indicates that AMT is payable, it is calculated as described at ¶2473

(ITA: 127.5; 127.51)

[¶2473] AMT CALCULATION

If AMT is determined to be payable as described at ¶2471, your tax payable for the year is your interim AMT as calculated in step three at ¶2471, plus the federal surtax on income not earned in a province (¶1445). This calculation gives federal AMT, which is carried to line 417 of Schedule 1. Note also that this amount cannot be less than the tax on split income, as discussed at ¶2410.

CPP and EI payments, repayments or overpayments are computed and applied independently of AMT.

(ITA: 127.5)

[¶2474] APPLICATION OF PERSONAL AMOUNT CREDITS (BASIC MINIMUM TAX CREDIT)

As noted at ¶2471, most personal amount credits can be applied against AMT; exceptions are itemized at step two of ¶2471.

(ITA: 127.51; 127.531)

[¶2475] SPECIAL FOREIGN TAX CREDIT

The special foreign tax credit allowed for AMT purposes, as referred to at ¶2471, is the lesser of:

(1) the total of the business income tax and $^2/_3$ of the non-business income tax paid to a foreign country, and

(2) the product of the applicable AMT tax rate (currently 15%) and the total of your foreign business income and foreign non-business income.

While the business income tax you pay is taken into account, only $^2/_3$ of your foreign non-business income tax is included in the calculation. This reflects the fact that, while the provinces provide a foreign tax credit in respect of non-business income, they do not provide a credit for foreign tax on business income which is generally not subject to provincial tax.

The special foreign tax credit can be substantially greater than ordinary foreign tax credit, and may in some cases be sufficient to prevent the application of AMT.

(ITA: 127.54)

[¶2477] APPLICATION OF PROVINCIAL TAX

It is intended that provincial tax (except Quebec — see Chapter 16) should be levied on AMT, if AMT applies for federal purposes. By the same token, reductions in federal tax for AMT carryovers (¶2481) will be applicable in determining provincial tax.

[¶2477.10] *Provincial AMT*

Where AMT applies federally, you will also be subject to AMT in your province of residence. Each province applies its own rate in determining the provincial AMT. Where you are entitled to apply an AMT carryover to reduce regular tax, a similar provincial carryover will be allowed. The provincial amount will be based on prior years' provincial AMT calculations.

[¶2481] CARRYOVER OF AMT TO OTHER YEARS

AMT in excess of ordinary tax for a year may be carried forward for seven years to reduce ordinary tax payable in excess of AMT. The AMT carryforward is applied against tax payable before the tax on split income, and the tax on split income (¶1490) is then added to the net amount. The result is that AMT carryforwards do not affect the amount of tax payable on split income.

The amount available from a particular year for carryover, in general terms, is the "minimum amount" for the year from step two of ¶2471 in excess of "ordinary tax liability" for the year (see below) and *minus* "special foreign tax credit in excess of ordinary foreign tax credit" for the year (see ¶2475).

Ordinary Tax Liability

"Ordinary tax liability" is your gross federal tax, including the tax on split income (if any) as reported at line 404 on Schedule 1, less only your non-refundable credits, your family tax cut credit (repealed effective January 1, 2016), your dividend tax credits, and the overseas employment tax credit (eliminated in 2016).

Carryover amounts as determined above may be used in any of the seven succeeding years to the extent in any given year that "ordinary tax payable" as determined above exceeds the "minimum amount" as determined in step two of ¶2471 for that subsequent year.

There is another effective limitation built into the AMT carryforward mechanism. The maximum deduction of AMT carryforward in a given year cannot be more than the amount by which (i) "ordinary tax liability" for the year, not including any tax on split income, exceeds (ii) the amount that would have been an individual's AMT for that year. Thus, as noted earlier, your claim for an AMT amount carried forward will not affect your liability for the tax on split income.

(ITA: 120.2)

[¶2481.05] *Provincial Carryovers of AMT*

See the discussion at ¶2477.

SPECIAL CONSIDERATIONS

[¶2485] AMT ON DEATH

As noted at ¶2409, AMT does not apply to either the ordinary year-of-death return or to any of the special returns which may be filed on death which are described in ¶1901. AMT carried forward may be applied to reduce tax in excess of AMT only on the ordinary year-of-death return, under the general rules at ¶2481. This reduction cannot be applied to any of the special returns referred to above and described at ¶1941 to ¶1944.

A "spousal trust" (that is, a trust which qualified for spousal rollovers from a deceased taxpayer) is not subject to minimum tax for the trust's taxation year that includes the time of the beneficiary spouse's death.

(ITA: 120.2(4); 127.55)

[¶2489] AMT AND OVERSEAS TAX CREDIT

With the introduction of AMT, the foreign tax credit rules (¶1450, ¶1455) were amended to allow an individual the option of claiming a foreign tax credit in respect of foreign taxes on overseas employment income, rather than claiming the overseas employment tax credit (¶1458) in respect of those taxes. If you make any overseas employment tax credit claim, you may nevertheless claim a non-business foreign tax credit on the employment income that is in excess of the income limits eligible for the overseas tax credit. However, you may forego the overseas employment tax credit and claim instead all foreign taxes associated with your overseas employment income.

As discussed at ¶1458, the overseas employment tax credit will be eliminated for the 2016 and subsequent taxation years.

For taxation years prior to 2016 you could elect to claim the foreign tax credit rather than the overseas employment tax credit in circumstances where the overseas employment tax credit would be rendered ineffective by the application of the minimum tax.

Example

Assume that foreign taxes of $500 were paid which would qualify for foreign tax credit if the taxpayer foregoes any claim for overseas employment tax credit.

	Overseas employment tax credit			*Foreign tax credit*		
	Regular tax		*AMT*	*Regular tax*		*AMT*
Tax on taxable income	$900		$800	$900		$800
Less: Overseas employment tax credit	$600		$0	$0		$0
Personal federal tax	$300		$800	$900		$800
Basic federal tax		$800			$900	
Foreign tax credit		$0			$500	
Federal tax payable		$800			$400	
AMT carryover available for subsequent years		$500			$0	

In this example, by claiming the foreign tax credit, the tax is reduced to $400 but the individual forgoes the minimum tax carryover of $500 that could be used to reduce his tax in another taxation year.

(ITA: 122.3 Overseas employment tax credit; 126 Foreign tax deduction)

Chapter 25

Tax Planning

THESE POINTS ARE COVERED IN THIS CHAPTER

CRA REFERENCES RELATING TO THIS CHAPTER

CRA Guides

P102, "Support Payments — Includes Form T1158"; **RC4092**, "Registered Education Savings Plans (RESPs)"; **RC4112**, "Lifelong Learning Plan (LLP) — Includes Form RC96"; **T4001**, "Employers' Guide — Payroll Deductions and Remittances"; **T4037**, "Capital Gains"; **T4044**, "Employment Expenses — Includes Forms GST 370, T777, TL2, and T2200"

CRA Forms

T1A, "Request for Loss Carryback"; **T4**, "Statement of Remuneration Paid"; **T5**, "Statement of Investment Income"; **T657**, "Calculation of Capital Gains Deduction"; **T936**, "Calculation of Cumulative Net Investment Loss (CNIL)"; **T1135**, "Foreign Income Verification Statement"; **T1141**, "Information Return in Respect of Transfers or Loans to a Non-Resident Trust" (For 2006 and prior taxation years); **T1141**, "Information Return in Respect of Contributions to Non-Resident Trusts, Arrangements or entities (For 2007 and later taxation years); **T1142**, "Information Return in Respect of Distributions from and Indebtedness to a Non-Resident Trust"; **T1157**, "Election For Child Support Payments"; **T1158**, "Registration of Family Support Payments"; **T2200**, "Declaration of Conditions of Employment"; **T5001**, "Application for Tax Shelter Identification Number and Undertaking to Keep Books and Records"; **T5003**, "Statement of Tax Shelter Information"; **T5004**, "Claim for Tax Shelter Loss or Deduction"; **T5013**, "Statement of Partnership Income"; **T5013-INST**, "Statement of Partnership Income — Instructions for Recipient"

Income Tax Folios

S1-F1-C1, "Medical Expense Tax Credit"; **S1-F2-C3, "Scholarships, Research Grants and Other Education Assistance"**; **S1-F3-C2**, "Principal Residence"; **S1-F3-C3**, "Support Payments"; **S1-F3-C4**, "Moving Expenses"; **S2-F3-C1**, "Payments from Employer to Employee"; **S2-F3-C2**, "Benefits and Allowances Received from Employment"; **S3-F6-C1**, "Interest Deductibility"; **S3-F10-C1**, "Qualified Investments — RRSPs, RESPs, RRIFs, RDSPs, and TFSAs"; **S3-F10-C2**, "Prohibited Investments — RRSPs, RRIFs, and TFSAs"; **S4-F8-C1**, "Business Investment Losses"

Interpretation Bulletins

IT-87R2, "Policyholders' Income from Life Insurance Policies"; **IT-88R2**, "Stock Dividends"; **IT-109R2**, "Unpaid Amounts"; **IT-128R**, "Capital Cost Allowance — Depreciable Property"; **IT-152R3**, "Special Reserves — Sale of Land"; **IT-167R6**, "Registered Pension Plans — Employee's Contributions"; **IT-337R4 (Consolidated)**, "Retiring Allowances"; **IT-352R2**, "Employee's Expenses, Including Work Space in Home Expenses"; **IT-369R**, "Attribution of Trust Income to Settlor"; **IT-396R**, "Interest Income"; **IT-440R2**, "Transfer of Rights to Income"; **IT-487**, "General Limitation on Deduction of Outlays or Expenses"; **IT-510**, "Transfers and Loans of Property Made After May 22, 1985 to a Related Minor"; **IT-511R**, "Interspousal and Certain Other Transfers and Loans of Property"; **IT-514**, "Work Space in Home Expenses"; **IT-522R**, "Vehicle, Travel and Sales Expenses of Employees"; **IT-531**, "Eligible Funeral Arrangements"

Information Circulars

84-1, "Revision of Capital Cost Allowance Claims and Other Permissive Deductions"; **93-3R1**, "Registered Education Savings Plans"

Income Tax Technical News

No. 34, April 27, 2006, "Third Party Penalties"

[¶2500] INTRODUCTION

A number of tax planning ideas which should provide a useful reference for taxpayers seeking opportunities for tax saving are listed in the following pages. These ideas are presented to stimulate further thought and are not meant to be an exhaustive list of tax planning ideas, but simply a summary of the more significant planning opportunities available today.

If you are a U.S. citizen resident in Canada you should also read Chapter 21, and you should seek professional counsel on any tax planning ideas to ensure both U.S. and Canadian tax law is considered.

Professional advice should be sought to ensure that a particular idea is applicable to your personal situation.

WHAT YOU SHOULD KNOW ABOUT TAX PLANNING

[¶2500a] RECENT CHANGES

2016 Changes

Bill C-15 (Royal Assent June 22, 2016)

The small business deduction rate for Canadian-controlled private corporations is to be maintained at 17.5% for 2016 and subsequent years (the 2015 Budget had proposed the rate be 18% for 2017, 18.5% for 2018, and 19% after 2018). The federal rate for eligible small business income is therefore 10.5% (28% rate minus the 17.5% deduction). See ¶404.22.

Bill C-2 (Introduced December 9, 2015)

The annual contribution limit for contributions to a TFSA was decreased to a $5,500 limit for 2016, to be indexed annually thereafter. See ¶2532c.

Bill C-29 (Introduced October 25, 2016)

There is a new rule applicable to dispositions of interests in life insurance policies after March 21, 2016 to non-arm's length persons. See ¶981.

New rules prevent the multiplication of the small business limit for Canadian-controlled private corporations through the use of partnerships. See ¶2501.02a

A new rule ensures that the interest accrued upon a sale of a "linked note" is included in the vendor's income as interest rather than a capital gain. The rule is discussed at ¶2519.05.

[¶2500b] INTRODUCTION

Effective tax planning is primarily an ingredient of good financial planning. Although there are a few opportunities to save tax when you come to prepare your return (for example, by claiming capital gains exemption or reserves, or choosing carefully the amount of loss carryover to apply or which spouse should claim medical expenses and for what 12-month period), most tax planning requires advance thought.

The completion of your personal tax return may present a good opportunity for that thought. Typically, you will have to gather for your return thorough information on your income and its sources, which is a necessary starting point for financial planning. As well, your return will show you how much you are paying in income tax, and, dividing your total tax payable (line 435) by net income (line 236) will show you how much tax you are paying on every dollar of earnings. If that doesn't motivate you to active tax planning, probably nothing will.

In addition to considering some choices to be made on your tax return itself, this chapter discusses a series of tax planning opportunities available to individuals. Many of these opportunities are formally sanctioned by the CRA authorities; a few arise out of ordinary commercial opportunities which happen to carry appealing tax treatment. Many tax planning opportunities deal with savings, but not necessarily on a grand scale.

Some tax planning opportunities, such as the incorporation of a business or investment in commercial tax shelters, assume you can save significant amounts of income to invest, and generally should not be undertaken without professional advice.

There are, however, also tax planning strategies available to the ordinary taxpayer who is trying to put aside a bit of money to buy a house, provide for a child's education, or provide for eventual retirement or even the proverbial "rainy day". You can accomplish significant financial and tax planning objectives yourself by utilizing government-sanctioned investments such as RRSP contributions, RESP contributions, separate savings accounts for Canada Child Benefits paid by government, and investment in provincial home ownership or stock savings plans.

The ideas in this chapter are organized according to whether you are in business, an employee, have some savings to invest, and so on. You may well be covered by more than one of these sections. Note also Chapter 26, which discusses in greater detail the calculation of RRSP contributions and the special "rollover" contributions which can provide tax saving opportunities in a number of common situations.

BUSINESSES (SELF-EMPLOYMENT)

[¶2501] INCORPORATION VERSUS PROPRIETORSHIP

You may conduct your business as either a corporation or proprietorship. Another alternative, partnership, is discussed in Chapter 18. The following are some of the income tax considerations which may affect your decision as to whether your business should be incorporated:

(1) anticipated earnings;

(2) tax deferrals and savings;

(3) scientific research incentives;

(4) provincial incentives; and

(5) income splitting and estate planning.

[¶2501.01] Anticipated Earnings

A new business often incurs losses in its early years because it has start-up costs and low revenues while it is getting established. Losses for tax purposes may be increased further by deducting maximum capital cost allowances (see Chapter 8), subject to various limitations. If the business is incorporated and you incur losses, the losses will be incurred by the company and not deductible against your other sources of income. Therefore, if you anticipate losses in your start up years *and* you have sufficient income from other sources, you may wish to defer incorporation until your business is profitable. Once the business has attained a certain level of profit, incorporation may offer certain tax savings and deferrals which are discussed below. It should be noted that there may be non-tax reasons why incorporation makes sense for your business, for example, where limited liability protection is an issue.

[¶2501.02] *Tax Deferrals and Savings for Canadian-controlled Private Corporation*

There are potential tax deferral and savings opportunities in earning active business income through a Canadian-controlled private corporation.

Most Canadian-controlled private corporations with net assets of $10 million or less have an effective corporate tax rate on their active business income up to $500,000, whether from services, manufacturing, or other activities other than passive investment, of between 11% and 19%, depending on the province in which the income is earned. Thus, for owners who are in the highest personal marginal tax bracket it is possible to earn up to $500,000 of active business income and have it taxed at a 19% or lower rate in the corporation rather than at a personal rate which will, in most provinces, exceed 40%. The active business income threshold is lower than $500,000 for provincial tax purposes in certain provinces, such as Nova Scotia and Manitoba.

In many provinces, the effective corporate rate on certain kinds of income (manufacturing and processing income) or in certain limited situations (new business) may be considerably lower. Each province has the jurisdiction to set its own corporate tax rates, and in many cases some of these preferences have been phased out or eliminated altogether.

(Note that the income of a personal service business does not qualify for the reduced corporate rates — neither the small business deduction nor the "general corporate rate reduction" applies to personal services business income. Essentially, this represents the incorporation of what would normally be employment income. The rules relating to this type of business are discussed at ¶785. Also, corporations which only earn investment income and have five or fewer employees do not qualify for the above reduced corporate tax rates (see ¶2511).)

The additional cash made available through the lower corporate tax rate can either be reinvested in the corporate business, used for investment purposes in the corporation, or distributed to shareholders, either as a taxable dividend or, in certain cases, as a non-taxable return of capital (or repayment of a loan from the shareholder). To the extent income is distributed to shareholders immediately, no advantage is achieved by incorporation, since the dividend gross-up and credit mechanism (¶2513) will result in approximately the same tax to the individual shareholder as if the income had been earned directly through an unincorporated proprietorship. In this sense, the corporate rate provides a deferral rather than a true tax saving. In general, corporate and personal tax rates are fairly well integrated across all provinces, to prevent absolute tax savings (or cost) through incorporation. In all cases, a careful analysis must be made in each situation to determine the proper structuring of an owner/manager's earnings (dividend and/or salary) for each particular year.

Whether corporate earnings should be reinvested in the business or distributed to the shareholders as a dividend should, of course, be a business decision. The use of a separate personal holding corporation for investment purposes is discussed in ¶2511. Note especially the concerns raised by the attribution rules (¶2529). Further, the timing of the dividend payment to the shareholders should be carefully integrated with the shareholder's personal tax situation to assure the overall tax is minimized.

The tax deferral achieved through incorporation can be rendered a permanent saving via the capital gains exemption if the business is eventually sold at arm's length and it is a "small business corporation". In general, capital gain of up to $824,176 (2016 amount) can be received free of tax by an individual shareholder disposing of shares of a "small business corporation"; this is by itself an additional reason for incorporation. Note, however, that investments made by the corporation other than those directly related to its "active" business can, if they exceed 10% of the assets of the corporation, disqualify the corporation from the capital gains exemption. It is sometimes possible to rearrange the affairs of a potential small business corporation prior to its sale to ensure that only the active business assets remain to be sold; however, this could involve its own tax costs, and it is usually desirable to arrange these matters as early as possible rather than having to attempt them just prior to sale under whatever rules may pertain at that time.

Among the benefits of incorporation is the annual income deferral which may be achieved through the use of bonuses. Remuneration in the form of bonuses accrued in the taxation year of a corporation will normally be deductible to the corporation provided they are *bona fide* obligations and are paid out at some time in the following 180 days. As the individual will be taxed only when he or she receives the bonus, a one-year deferral may be achieved.

(ITA: 78(3); 110.6; 123; 124(1); 125(1), (7); 125.1(1); 181)

Historical Information: Previous System Where Only One Dividend Tax Rate

It had been customary in many cases, prior to 2006, to bonus down income in excess of that eligible for low rates to owner-managers, since it would otherwise be subject to an element of double taxation (counting both corporate and personal tax) when paid as dividend. Under the two-tier dividend tax credit system in effect for 2006 and later years, income taxed at high rates can be paid out subject to the higher dividend tax credit, which should eliminate a double taxation penalty on retaining earnings in the corporation. It follows that, depending on corporate income levels and provincial dividend tax credit rates, it may be beneficial to leave high-rate income in the corporation for dividend treatment rather than bonus it out. No general rule is apparent, but each situation traditionally met with bonuses in the past requires re-examination in the light of the new rules. Papers at the 2006 Ontario and annual conferences of the Canadian Tax Foundation have analyzed the issues. However, the parameters of the issues have changed slightly with the announcement, on October 30, 2007, of an accelerated schedule of general and small business corporate tax rate reductions for 2008 and later years, and by the changes to the "non-eligible" dividend gross-up and tax credit announced in the 2013 and 2015 federal Budgets.

[¶2501.02a *Multiplication of Small Business Limit Using Partnerships*

As noted above, the income threshold for the small business tax rate for Canadian-controlled private corporations ("CCPCs") is $500,000 for federal purposes and most provincial purposes. If various CCPCs are a member of a partnership, they must share the $500,000 limit with respect to the business income earned from the partnership (the "specified partnership limit" for each member), and each CCPC's share of the partnership income then forms part of that CCPC's overall $500,000 limit.

Commentary on Bill C-29 Measures (Oct. 25, 2016)

Note: When Bill C-29, October 25, 2016, achieves Royal Assent, the commentary will be modified to read:

As noted above, the income threshold for the small business tax rate for Canadian-controlled private corporations ("CCPCs") is $500,000 for federal purposes and most provincial purposes. If various CCPCs are a member of a partnership, they must share the $500,000 limit with respect to the business income earned from the partnership (the "specified partnership limit" for each member), and each CCPC's share of the partnership income then forms part of that CCPC's overall $500,000 limit.

In order to avoid this rule and the sharing of the $500,000 limit, in some instances individual partners formed CCPCs that were not partners of their partnership. These CCPCs then entered into contracts with the partnership to provide services to the partnership. Since the CCPCs were not partners, they were not subject to the specified partnership limit and therefore each CCPC could earn up to $500,000 of income from the partnership that could be subject to the small business tax rate. Similar structures had various CCPCs providing services to a corporation in order to get around the specified partnership limit rules.

Changes first announced in the 2016 Federal budget effectively provide that these structures will now be subject to the specified partnership limit rules. In particular, a new definition of "designated member" deems a CCPC to be a member of a partnership that the CCPC is not otherwise at law a member of where certain conditions are met. For example, the income of a CCPC will be specified partnership income (SPI) if: (i) the CCPC provides services or property to the particular partnership at any time in the CCPC's taxation year, (ii) the CCPC is not a member of the particular partnership, and (iii) either: (x) one of the shareholders of the CCPC holds a direct or indirect interest in the partnership, or (y) the CCPC does not deal at arm's length with a person that holds a direct or indirect interest in the partnership, and the CCPC does not derive all or substantially all (generally understood to be 90%) of its income from an active business from providing services or property to arm's length persons or partnerships (excluding any partnership in which a non-arm's length person to the CCPC holds a direct or indirect interest).

New paragraph 125(3.2) allows a CCPC to assign any or all of its business limit to another CCPC where certain conditions are met. To assign the business limit: (a) the assignee CCPC has income from the year that is specified corporate income (SCI), (b) the assignor CCPC's taxation year ends in the assignee CCPC's taxation year, (c) the amount assigned cannot exceed the assignee CCPC's SCI for the year, and (d) each of the CCPCs files a prescribed form with the CRA in its tax return for the particular year. Pursuant to new subsection 125(3.1), the assignee CCPC's business limit is reduced by the amount of such assignment.

These new rules apply to taxation years that begin after March 21, 2016, with some transitional measures. The new rules are also discussed in the companion to this book, "Preparing Your Corporation Income Tax Returns", also published by Wolters Kluwer Canada Limited.

[¶2501.03] *Scientific Research Incentives*

If your business is incorporated and has certain activities that may be considered research and development activities, various tax incentives are available to it which would not be available to an unincorporated business.

For example, the investment tax credit for qualifying Canadian-controlled private corporations incurring scientific research expenditures is 35%, whereas an individual could not claim a credit above 15% for the same expenditure.

In addition to a possible higher rate of credit, scientific research tax credits earned in a corporation may be refunded in cash to the corporation at a higher rate than to individuals. Individuals can obtain a cash refund of 40% of scientific research credits generated in the year in excess of tax (¶1464). A Canadian-controlled private corporation whose income (together with the income of associated corporations) did not exceed $500,000 in the preceding year can claim a 100% cash refund of investment tax credits earned at a rate of 35% in respect of up to $3 million of scientific research expenditures made in the taxation year. (This will not apply to expenditures on depreciable property.) Consequently, annual refunds of up to $1.05 million will be available to small corporations engaging in scientific research. As income exceeds $500,000, the eligible $3 million of eligible expenditure is decreased, ceasing at income of $800,000. Furthermore, the qualifying income limit is reduced if the corporation's taxable capital employed in Canada for its preceding taxation year, along with the taxable capital of its associated corporations for their taxation years ending in the calendar year that ended before the end of the particular taxation year, exceeds $10 million. The 100% refund remains available, however, on whatever amount of R&D expenditure remains eligible for the high rate.

A corporation that is controlled by one or more pension plans, universities, or charitable institutions cannot obtain this refund. For corporate taxation years ending after March 22, 2004, the associated corporation rules are somewhat relaxed to allow access to the full credit for small businesses with common investors, provided certain conditions are met. These are discussed in ¶8701 of the companion Wolters Kluwer volume *Preparing Your Corporate Tax Returns*.

(ITA: 127(5), (9), (11.1)(a), (b), (c); Part VIII)

[¶2501.04] *Provincial Incentives*

Provinces may vary the $500,000 limit below which the federal government offers low corporate rates, although all provinces offer a low provincial corporate tax rate on some amount. In addition to the low rates, provinces may offer additional incentives to corporations. For example, several provinces offer tax credits to corporations investing in new machinery and equipment. Several provinces provide incentives to individuals and corporations willing to invest in incorporated small businesses in the province, thereby making it easier for the incorporated business to raise capital for start-up or expansion. In short, there may be additional tax or tax-driven benefits to incorporation in any particular province.

[¶2501.05] *Income Splitting and Estate Planning*

A reasonable amount of remuneration paid to a spouse or child of the taxpayer for performing employment duties in a proprietorship is deductible for tax purposes to the proprietor. However, incorporation offers other income splitting and estate planning opportunities. For example, if you and your spouse each have wholly-owned corporations, and your corporation has retained earnings from a business which are loaned to your spouse's corporation interest free, investment income on the loaned funds can be paid and taxed to your spouse. Many tax advisers feel that such a loan will not be subject to the "attribution rules" (¶2529), although the matter is perhaps not beyond doubt. Certainly, in the absence of the corporations, attribution rules would apply.

Where a start-up business (one with little current asset or other value) is being incorporated, it is often possible to provide for income splitting by having a spouse purchase shares with the spouse's own money. If the business succeeds, the income can be divided with the spouse through dividends, giving (if the spouse has little other income) a second use of marginal tax rates and personal amount credits. However, dividends allocated to minor children in this fashion will be taxed at top marginal rates under the "split income" rules (the so-called "kiddie tax"), eliminating any income splitting benefits (see ¶2529.03). Additional changes were announced to the kiddie tax rules in the 2014 federal Budget, in order to preclude certain income-splitting structures using trusts that were perceived to be abusive by the Department of Finance.

Nevertheless, having children acquire shares of the incorporated business can permit future growth in the value of the business to be passed on to the next generation in part or in full (depending upon the number and nature of the shares allocated), which can carry the benefits of deferring the costs of taxation on death, spreading the tax costs of any future sale, and perhaps multiplying the capital gains exemption. If savings are intended to fund the higher education of minor children, it may be possible to dam up the savings in the corporation, or in holding corporations for the children, and pay them out as dividends to the child shareholders piecemeal when they reach the age of 18, during the years in which their higher education must be paid for. The availability of tuition tax credits and other related education tax credits (the education and textbook credits are repealed effective January 1, 2017) may ultimately reduce the tax on this income to a negligible amount. As presently structured, the special split income tax on children's dividends will not operate once the child reaches 18. Caution is in order, in that excess funds maintained in the corporation may jeopardize the capital gains exemption, although it is conceivable that proper structuring (such as separate holding companies to hold the children's savings until they are 18) can alleviate this problem. Where the splitting of current income with minor children is not part of the exercise, it may not be necessary to have the child use its own money to acquire the shares; shares acquired with a gift or *bona fide* loan will suffice. Note, however, that the 2011 federal Budget added to the concept of split income by providing that capital gains realized by a minor from a disposition of non-publicly listed shares of a corporation to a non-arm's length person will be treated as taxable dividends that are not eligible dividends, and therefore subject to the tax on split income (see ¶2529). Using the child's own money prevents application of the regular attribution rules; so long as no current property income arises in a year before the child reaches 18, attribution is not a problem (see ¶2529.03).

In these situations, it is common for interests for children, especially minor children, to be held by trusts for the child(ren)'s benefit. For arrangements in place before 2000, this permitted income to be accrued for them at their tax rates while their parents retained control of the funds (so long as they are used for the children's benefit) so they could be used for specific purposes, usually higher education. Where splitting current year income is not the objective, a trust should still facilitate the parents' control of the children's shares (in the event of sale, for example), and incidentally of the underlying business.

If your family is not in place when your business is first incorporated, essentially the same income splitting and growth transfer objectives can be achieved later through an "estate freeze". This is a series of transactions to rearrange your asset holdings so that future increases in their value will accrue to the benefit of your heirs and thus postpone or reduce taxation on your death. This technique can more readily be applied to an incorporated business than to a proprietorship or partnership interest. In addition, it may be possible to establish a trust to hold participating shares where, under the terms of the trust, later-born children can be added to the trust either by the trustees or automatically under the terms of the trust.

You should know that where incorporation is used to achieve income splitting between spouses by putting shares and then dividends into the hands of a spouse, the CRA may examine such transactions closely with a view to finding flaws in the plan and taxing the dividends of a spouse not active in the business to the active shareholder. However, the CRA has had no success in challenging plans which are even moderately well constructed. The CRA has, however, had considerably more success in attacking plans looking to multiply the capital gains exemption through the use of attribution rules in a manner for which they were not designed; see, for example, *Gervais v. The Queen*, 2014 DTC 1119 (T.C.C.).

(ITA: 56(4); 73(5); 74.1–74.5; *Army and Navy Department Stores v. M.N.R.*, 53 DTC 1185 (S.C.C.); *Neuman v. The Queen*, 98 DTC 6297 (S.C.C.))

[¶2501.06] *Summary*

The above tax considerations should be reviewed in light of other valid business and personal factors. You should seek professional tax advice where the incorporation of a business is being considered, or where any of the tax planning steps outlined above are contemplated.

- *Planning Point:*

  If you have or are starting your own unincorporated business and you can make full contributions (a moving target: see ¶2606) to an RRSP and still have income in excess of your current needs, you should seriously consider incorporation. If you require more or less all your income for your personal expenses, it is unlikely incorporation will be beneficial.

- *Planning Point:*

  If you have a business with an inherent value — that is, if you could sell the business as a whole at a profit — you should consider whether the business is or can be made eligible for the capital gains exemption on qualifying small business shares. This determination often requires professional advice, but the potential tax saving should justify the cost. In general, it is more likely that a business will qualify for the exemption if the situation has been analyzed well in advance of a potential sale.

[¶2502] OWNER-MANAGERS AND THE RRSP RULES

The RRSP rules, discussed in Chapter 26, in most cases allow individuals who operate their own businesses (i.e., are self-employed) as proprietors or partners to save substantial amounts through RRSPs. These rules are intended to permit such individuals to save on a tax-deferred basis amounts comparable to those which can be provided to employees on a similar basis through pension plans.

The same tax-deferred RRSP savings are in effect available to most taxpayers who have incorporated small businesses, but they must pay out to themselves sufficient income as salary and bonus to create RRSP contribution room, which is 18% of such earned income up to a maximum limit. Owner-managers of small business corporations commonly provide tax-deferred savings for themselves and/or their spouses and at the same time draw down corporate income which they want to keep below $500,000 per year (to minimize penalties on higher corporate incomes) by paying themselves sufficient salaries and bonuses to make maximum RRSP contributions.

There can be trade-offs involved here, however, since there are also incentives to keep personal net income (after RRSP deductions) at lower levels. For example, individuals who receive Old Age Security benefits will suffer a benefit reduction where net income exceeds $73,756 (2016 figure). The optimal tax calculation in a corporate/personal situation can thus be a matter of complex calculation in specific circumstances, requiring either professional advice, competent computer software, or a mathematical turn of mind. The considerations are now more complex with a higher dividend tax credit on corporate business income in excess of low-rate active business income limits. In some provinces, it may be advantageous to withdraw such income as dividend rather than salary, although the value of withdrawing as salary/bonus sufficient income to make RRSP contributions remains a serious consideration unless the corporation chooses to establish a true pension plan, an alternative which can be relatively complex and costly.

To make a maximum $25,370 deduction on your 2016 return required 2015 earned income of $140,944. The limit is scheduled to rise in annual increments for the foreseeable future, as detailed in a table at ¶2606.

If you choose to incorporate your business, you can more easily establish a registered pension plan (RPP) for the business. Typically, this plan must serve at least a class of employees, such as the executive class, and you may be included in the class. The eventual pension benefits from an RPP may (depending on the kind of plan you establish) be tied to salary and years of service rather than contributions and earnings thereon. Even if you choose an RPP "money purchase" plan where benefits are tied to contributions, an RPP may allow you to save slightly more over a few years than an RRSP in years when contribution limits increase, since RPP limits will rise one year ahead of RRSP limits. Establishing an RPP, however, involves professional advice and possibly professional administration, and will not often be worthwhile for accelerated contributions alone. However, if the RPP serves other business purposes (such as key employee retention, for example), the acceleration may be an additional advantage.

See ¶2608 regarding the possibility of making a once-only double-up of RPP and RRSP contributions — a possibility, however, that has been generally restricted for some time. In addition, specific rules (referred to as the "prohibited investment rules") have greatly curtailed the ability to put private company assets into an RRSP.

- *Planning Point:*

  Be sure that adequate salary and bonus are incurred by year end to support the personal RRSP contribution you want to make in the following year.

(ITA: 146(5); ITR: 8308(2) Prescribed Amount for Connected Persons; 8500(3))

[¶2505] TIMING OF FIXED ASSET ACQUISITIONS

Although only one-half of the normal annual capital cost allowance may be claimed in the year that the asset is acquired, it may nevertheless be advantageous to acquire depreciable assets before the year end rather than in the early months of the next year. Whatever capital cost allowance is available will thereby be accelerated one year. Proration of the allowance is only necessary where the taxation year of the business is less than 12 months. Although, as discussed at ¶804b, "available-for-use" rules require the delay of claims for capital cost allowance in certain cases, it remains true that there will often be a benefit where acquisition can be accelerated to an earlier taxation year. Depreciation for tax purposes cannot be claimed until property is actually put into use to earn income, although there are a number of technical exceptions permitting earlier claims.

These considerations, of course, must be evaluated in the context of the business's overall financial position.

If you have depreciable property acquired in Year 1 which was not eligible for depreciation in Year 1 or Year 2 under the "available-for-use" rule, it should be eligible for depreciation in Year 3 whether or not it has been put in use; moreover, Year 1 acquisitions, which are deemed to be put in use under this "rolling start" rule, are not subject to the half-year rule. Where Year 1 property is both put in use and deemed put in use in Year 3, the deeming rule should prevail; that is, the half-year rule does not apply and full rate CCA can be claimed on that property for the year.

- *Planning Point:*

  Ensure that business assets to be acquired in the near future are acquired and put in use before business year end.

- *Planning Point:*

  When accounting for annual acquisitions for tax purposes, do not forget to include prior year acquisitions which were not counted at the time due to the "available-for-use" rules but are now qualified for tax depreciation. Where these properties have been held at the end of the two prior years without claiming tax depreciation, they may be claimed without regard to the half-year rule. Property put in use in prior years but not claimed for tax depreciation purposes is not now subject to the half-year rule.

[¶2507] LOSS YEAR CONSIDERATIONS

Non-capital losses which arose in taxation years ending before March 23, 2004, can be carried back three years and forward seven years as a deduction to arrive at taxable income. Non-capital losses which arise in taxation years (and so, for individual proprietors or partners, for fiscal periods of the business) ending after March 22, 2004, and before 2006 can be carried back three years and forward 10 years as a deduction to arrive at taxable income. Losses arising in 2006 and later taxation years can be carried back three years and forward 20 years. (Details of the loss carryover rules are found in ¶1087.) If it appears that a loss may not be utilized within the applicable carryforward period, the amount of a business loss may be reduced by deferring certain expenses (discussed below) until subsequent years.

Capital cost allowance (CCA) provides a degree of flexibility in determining the amount of a business loss because it is not a mandatory expense of any given year but can be deferred and claimed in any future year without any time limitation. Thus, if a business loss is suffered in a particular year and there is an income year prior to the expiry of the loss due to the limitation periods discussed above, the taxpayer should consider revising the current year return by reducing the amount of CCA claimed, thus increasing income and the ability to apply loss carryforward. This will absorb loss carryforward for that year and preserve the capital cost allowance until some future year. It is usually preferable to defer CCA on the highest rate classes first, since the depreciation can be used most rapidly when needed.

In addition to CCA, there are numerous expenses which are available as a deduction from income on either a current or deferred basis for tax purposes. Examples of these expenses are:

(1) interest incurred to acquire fixed assets (if certain elections are made, see ¶1073);

(2) cumulative eligible capital deductions (¶766);

(3) reserves for: doubtful debts (¶733), goods and services (¶732), and capital gains (¶581); and

(4) certain scientific research expenditures (¶740).

Note that the CRA will only accept revisions to optional claims after the 90-day period following a notice of assessment if the tax payable for the year in issue does not change. Typically, this presents no problem where there is an overall loss for the year. However, where there is a business loss but a positive total income subject to tax, decisions on the projected rate of loss utilization and the concomitant use of optional claims must be made on a current basis.

- *Planning Point:*

  Keep detailed records of the year of origin of a loss and the subsequent utilization of that loss as carryback or carryforward, so that you can always be certain what carryforward period applies to a particular loss.

- *Planning Point:*

  Do not claim optional deductions in loss years unless the loss can be recovered quickly against other years. Where less than full capital cost allowance is to be claimed, always claim in respect of low rate classes first.

- *Planning Point:*

  Remember that the half-year rule only applies to limit depreciation in the year a property is acquired; if you have deferred a CCA claim in the year of acquisition, you can claim the full CCA amount in any subsequent year.

- *Planning Point:*

  Remember to claim your business loss carryforwards against all sources of income. Do not, however, claim amounts which will eliminate the use of your personal amount credits or other credits, such as political contribution credit, which have no carryover. Depending on your loss situation, you may want to use losses only against income above the 15% federal bracket. See the example at ¶1087. This option is only available for carryovers, not for losses incurred in the current year, which must be fully applied to bring current taxable income to zero.

(ITA: 111; IC 84-1 Revision of capital cost allowance claims and other permissive deductions)

[¶2509] BUSINESS OFFICE AT HOME

Many professional individuals with business income use their homes for activities related to the production of that income. If you use space in your home to earn income, you must meet one of two tests before any deductions may be claimed in respect of the space. Deductions may be claimed if space in your home is either: (a) your principal place of business, or (b) is not your principal place of business but is both used exclusively for earning business income and used on a regular and continuous basis for meeting your clients, customers or patients. Deductible expenses will include a *pro rata* portion of such items as municipal taxes, rent, light, repairs, heat and insurance. See ¶742.

In addition, a claim for capital cost allowance on the portion of a home used for business purposes may be made. However, it may be better not to claim capital cost allowance, because such a claim will usually entail both recapture of the amounts claimed and the loss of a portion of the principal residence exemption upon the eventual sale or disposal of the home (¶553–¶555).

To the extent losses from the particular business against which home office deductions are claimed are created or augmented by those deductions, the losses may not be used to reduce other sources of income, but must be carried forward against the particular business. These rules are discussed at ¶742.

Employees are subject to similar restrictions, and in most cases are limited to a smaller range of potential deductions; see ¶2563. The restrictions do not on their face apply to investors, but this is because an office is generally not considered necessary to earning investment income unless the investment activity is so extensive that it amounts to a business, in which case the limitations above will apply. This level of activity requires extensive trading, and will often open questions as to whether gains or losses are on business rather than capital account. Deduction of the expenses associated with an office in your home used in the course of earning investment income is generally denied as a personal or living expense. See ¶700.

- *Planning Point:*

  If your home office is either (a) your principal place of business, or (b) is not your principal place of business but is both used exclusively for earning business income and used on a regular and continuous basis for meeting your clients, customers or patients, you may deduct home expenses related to that space.

- *Planning Point:*

  Remember to carry forward against current business income any home office expenses deferred in prior years because they exceeded related business income. Keep a running list of such deferrals carried forward from this year with your tax information for next year.

(ITA: 18(1)(*a*), (*h*), (12), (13); IT-487 General limitation on deduction of outlays or expenses; IT-514 Work space in home expenses)

[¶2510] RESERVES

Where the proceeds of disposition from a sale of capital or other property are not all receivable in the year of sale, realization of a portion of the capital gain or income gain may be deferred until the year in which the proceeds become receivable. In general, permitted reserves may be calculated by the formula:

$$\frac{\text{Total gain (in excess of cost)}}{\text{Total proceeds of disposition}} \times \begin{array}{l}\text{Amount not payable}\\ \text{until after Dec. 31}\end{array}$$

However, reserves are permitted only for a limited number of years. The limitations are as follows:

[¶2510.01] *Sale of Capital Assets*

A reserve will be permitted where capital assets are sold and the full proceeds not received by year end. However, the reserve must be the lesser of the amount calculated under the general formula for each asset for a given year and 20% of the capital gain in the year of the disposition, 40% of the gain in the following year, and so on. That is, the gain must be recognized in increments of 20% over five years. Note that there may be a lower than 20% recognition in a particular year if more than 20% of the gain was included in a previous year, such as the year of disposition. In each year both the general calculation and the 20% recognition rule must be compared. See ¶581.

The five-year recognition rule is replaced by an identical 10-year rule where an individual transfers certain farming or fishing property, shares of a family farm or fishing corporation, an interest in a family farm or fishing partnership or qualified small business corporation shares to his or her children. The rule for fishing businesses applies only to transfers after May 1, 2006. Farming or fishing properties are defined by reference eligibility for the rollover to children on death; see ¶1923 and ¶1923d. A small business corporation by contrast is (after May 1, 2006) a Canadian-controlled private corporation eligible for the capital gains exemption at ¶502i.10. This definition was less restrictive for transfers before May 2, 2006.

[¶2510.02] *Transactions Yielding Business Income*

The rules also provide for a (maximum) three-year instalment reserve for dispositions of property that give rise to ordinary income. The reserve will apply to dispositions of land where an amount is due after the end of the year, and to dispositions of other property where an amount is due more than two years after the date of sale. The reserve which may be claimed in each of the three years will be that *pro rata* portion of the profit which relates to the proceeds not due by the year end. See ¶732.

- *Planning Point:*

  In structuring the sale of appreciated assets, be sure you will have sufficient funds to pay the taxes required; if proceeds are deferred over a long period the tax may be due before the proceeds are received.

(ITA: 20(1)(*n*), (8); 40(1), (1.1))

INVESTORS

[¶2511] PERSONAL HOLDING CORPORATION

Personal holding corporations are companies incorporated to hold the investment assets of an individual shareholder. The tax benefits of such a corporation have a checkered history. In theory, the Canadian tax system provides "integration" of personal and corporate tax. This should mean that investment income is taxed when it is received by the corporation at the same rate that an individual would pay directly, so that there is no deferral of tax, and credit for that tax is allowed when the income is passed on to the individual. Through a combination of corporate tax refunds and the individual's dividend tax credit, the tax paid by the individual at the end of the day should be the same regardless of whether the income has passed through a corporation. In practice, however, as corporate and personal tax rates shift at both federal and provincial levels, the system becomes distorted. Its history since 1972, when it was introduced, is a repetitive pattern of near-perfect integration becoming systematically distorted, and eventually rejiggered to restore some measure of equilibrium.

For example, when the system was rejiggered in 1988, there was fairly accurate integration based on an assumed provincial tax rate of 50% of federal tax for individuals and 15% of income for corporations, in addition to federal taxes. In this system there may have been a bias toward personal rather than corporate holdings, due to the $100,000 general capital gains exemption, which was not permitted to corporations.

With the subsequent increases in personal tax rates, especially (but not only) at the provincial level, and the withdrawal of the $100,000 capital gains exemption, integration was once again distorted in favour of corporate holdings. As the top marginal personal rate rose well above 50% for most Canadians, earning income in a corporation typically taxed at about 45% conferred a significant tax deferral until the income had to be distributed to the individual. However, on distribution there was generally an offsetting tax cost (depending on provincial corporate rates). For dividends the rules are slightly different, but the deferral on incorporation had by 1994 reached about 11 points.

In 1995, the system was rejiggered yet again by increasing the rates of refundable corporate taxes. An additional refundable tax was added to the investment income of a Canadian-controlled private corporation. The corporate tax rate on investment income generally will now be about 50% (subject to provincial variation); on dividends it is 33$^{1}/_{3}$%. Depending on provincial tax treatment, there may still be a reduced tax deferral for both investment income and dividends after the change. Additional changes, announced in 2013 and 2015, to the dividend gross-up and tax credit amounts, further tightened the spread between corporate and personal tax rates on investment income, thereby achieving, in many cases, near-perfect integration.

In the circumstances, no general advice is possible. One must weigh in each case (and in each province) the tax deferral on incorporation of investment assets against the eventual tax cost. The disadvantages of incorporation are considerable on a small scale; there is a second set of returns to file, corporate holdings and income must be carefully separated from personal, and there are costs to incorporation itself. For large amounts of investment income used primarily for reinvestment rather than personal use, the tax deferral may from time to time (as the integration system becomes unbalanced) be of sufficient value to justify the offsets. However, you should keep in mind that when this occurs, these distortions render the integration system inherently unstable; sooner or later the government will move to restore stability, as it did in 1995.

A personal holding corporation may perhaps provide a vehicle to split income between family members. One possible method for using a holding company is described at ¶2501.05. You should know, however, that the government has established elaborate rules to prevent income splitting, and while some techniques may nevertheless be effective, you should consider them only with the benefit of professional advice and an awareness that further legislation and litigation may make current plans invalid. See, for example, the limitations on splitting income with children at ¶2501.05 and ¶2529.03 and the discussion of trusts for children at ¶2529a. Prescribed rate loan strategies should also be considered, especially in the current low interest rate environment.

Incorporation of personal assets should always be undertaken with regard to your family situation and the possible distribution of assets on death. Accordingly it virtually always requires sound professional advice from a lawyer, accountant or tax adviser specializing in such matters. Moreover, depending on your province of residence, and the source of income you expect to earn in your personal holding corporation, there can be an advantage or disadvantage to earning income through a corporation. For example, in 2014, in Ontario, retaining income in a corporation provides a 0.5% to 7% deferral advantage depending on the source of income, whereas in Alberta, only foreign dividend income is taxed more favourably in a corporation than in the hands of an individual. In all provinces, foreign dividend income is more advantageously taxed corporately than personally.

[¶2513] DIVIDENDS VERSUS INTEREST

The *Income Tax Act* provides a different set of rules for the taxation of dividends on the one hand and interest or similar investment yields on the other. Thus, before making any investment decisions it is beneficial to consider the tax consequences of such a decision. Dividends received from Canadian corporations are, in most cases, eligible for a dividend tax credit (see ¶1425). A credit is not provided for interest income whether or not it is from a Canadian source.

As discussed in greater detail at ¶1425, to determine the amount of the dividend to be brought into a shareholder's income, a "gross-up amount" is added to the actual dividend received by the shareholder. For eligible dividends received after 2005 and before 2010, the gross-up was 45%, which was reduced to 44% for 2010, 41% for 2011, and is 38% for 2012 and thereafter. An individual is then entitled to claim a credit against federal tax. The dividend tax credit for eligible dividends equals $^{6}/_{11}$ of the gross-up for eligible dividends received after 2011. For 2014 and 2015, the dividend credit for non-eligible dividends equals $^{13}/_{18}$ of the 18% gross-up, the amount has been reduced to 21/29 of the 17% gross-up for 2016 and thereafter. These new figures can be found in ¶404.20.

As a general rule, dividends paid out of income that has been taxed at the general corporate tax rate will be considered eligible dividends and dividends paid out of income that has been eligible for the small business deduction will not be considered eligible dividends. For more details on the definition of "eligible dividend" and the designation to be made by a corporation paying them, see ¶404.10 and ¶404.13.

Dividends which fall under these rules include not only ordinary dividends, but also deemed dividends.

The dividend tax credit is non-refundable and there is no carryover provision, so that if an individual has insufficient income to use the whole amount of the credit in a particular year, the unused part of the dividend tax credit is lost. Under certain circumstances, a taxpayer can elect to have all of the taxable dividends received by his or her spouse/common-law partner from taxable Canadian corporations (including eligible dividends received after 2005) included in the taxpayer's income. This may be done where the amount of a taxpayer's marital tax credit is reduced as a result of the receipt of the dividends by a spouse or common-law partner. Where such an election is made, the taxpayer would include in income the grossed-up amount of the dividends received by the spouse/common-law partner and be eligible for the dividend tax credit on the grossed-up amount.

For actual marginal rates on various types of income by province, see the table at ¶57 preceding Chapter 1.

- *Planning Point:*

  Always compare the after-tax return on investments in your particular situation. Note that dividend tax credit is lost if it cannot be used in the year dividends are received. Try to avoid investing so heavily in dividend yields that dividend tax credit is lost because the credit exceeds your tax. If this should occur, consider giving up optional deductions or items with a carryforward, such as capital cost allowance or charitable donations, so that dividend tax credit is not wasted.

- *Planning Point:*

  When investing in shares for dividend yield, it is important to determine whether a corporation is likely to pay eligible or other dividends. Corporations may disclose corporate policies in this regard, and, in the course of time, history will be an indicator. It will always remain possible that, due to acquisitions of small business corporations, for example, large public corporations which generally distribute eligible dividends may be obliged to distribute other dividends occasionally. However, as a practical matter, such corporations will look for strategies to prevent this outcome, as the public markets generally expect to receive eligible dividends.

- *Planning Point:*

  There are many considerations beyond the annual yield of an investment that should determine your investment decisions. The risk (or lack of risk) associated with a particular investment and the likelihood of increased future value giving rise to capital gain are just a few of the matters to be considered.

(ITA: 82; 121; IT-67R3 Taxable Dividends from Corporations Resident in Canada; IT-295R4 Taxable dividends received after 1987 by a spouse)

[¶2514] STOCK DIVIDENDS

Some corporations allow shareholders to choose either cash or stock dividends. Cash dividends receive the benefit of the tax credit described in ¶2513, and are subject to a lower effective tax than either interest income or capital gains for taxpayers with a low marginal rate and no capital gains exemption.

Stock dividends are treated as ordinary dividends and, as such, are taxed on receipt to the extent of their paid-up capital (typically the stated capital for corporate law purposes). Therefore, there is no deferral of tax. There is a statutory exception for Reed Stenhouse Companies Limited Class I Special Shares issued before January 1, 1986 (see ¶416).

Stock dividends issued by Canadian public corporations prior to May 24, 1985 will give rise to capital gains when the shares are sold. See ¶502, ¶505, ¶512.

(ITA: 53(2); 183.1; 248(1) "stock dividend"; IT-88R2 Stock Dividends)

[¶2517] PERSONAL FINANCING

Interest is deductible for tax purposes only if it is paid on money borrowed to earn business or property income (see ¶1063–¶1073). Interest on loans to finance personal expenditures such as a house, car, boat, vacation, and home improvements is not deductible. A partial exception gives a tax credit at the lowest marginal rate (thus 15%) on the interest portion of student loan repayments (see ¶2529d). As a general rule, where there is a choice, money should be borrowed for business or investment purposes rather than personal purposes.

Interest expense incurred on funds used to finance most investments continues to be fully deductible under most circumstances, regardless of the timing of the related investment income. However, interest expense deductions may be restricted where money has been borrowed under certain tax shelter plans, especially investments in limited partnerships. Essentially, expense deductions may be deferred to match income from the shelter; see ¶1818. Interest and other financing charges incurred outside as well as inside a much broader range of investments than limited partnerships are subject to similar matching limitations where the investment can even remotely be considered a tax shelter; see ¶835 and ¶2521. As well, interest and financing charges on money borrowed to invest in certain tax shelters may be added to the Alternative Minimum Tax base; see Chapter 24.

Interest on money borrowed to make contributions to an RPP, RRSP, or TFSA is not deductible.

The interest on your home mortgage is not normally deductible for tax purposes unless the funds from the mortgage loan were used to finance business or investments rather than the purchase of your home (see ¶1063 and ¶1065). If you have investments that are not financed by loans and you are carrying a non-deductible mortgage on your house you might consider a series of transactions which will allow you to repay your mortgage with your existing investments and then to make new investments with borrowed money. It may be necessary to remortgage your home, but the interest on the mortgage would then be deductible for tax purposes. For example, if you have funds accumulated to buy investments, you could simply pay down the house mortgage with available funds and borrow the funds to be used to finance the investments. The result would be a decrease in non-deductible mortgage interest and an increase in deductible investment interest.

[¶2517.05] *Singleton, Ludco, and Lipson*

The *Singleton* (2001 DTC 5533 (S.C.C.)) and *Ludco* (2001 DTC 5505 (S.C.C.)) cases (released by the Supreme Court of Canada virtually simultaneously on September 28, 2001) support tax planning to maximize interest deductibility. Both cases involve aggressive transactions which were obviously tax-motivated.

The Singleton Case

Singleton involved a so-called "partnership capital rollover". Mr. Singleton basically drew out his partnership capital to buy a home and then borrowed to put capital back into his firm. The transactions were virtually simultaneous. To be deductible under the *Income Tax Act*, interest on borrowed money must be used for the purpose of earning business or investment income. Accordingly, the issue was whether Mr. Singleton used the borrowed money for income-earning purposes — or whether he used the money to buy a home. The majority of the Court held that, since a direct link could be drawn between the borrowed money and an eligible use, Singleton could obtain a deduction since he was refinancing his partnership capital, particularly since this is a strategy similar to that available to corporations — which should analogously be available to individuals. (The majority of the Court rejected the CRA's contention that, because of the "simultaneous nature" of the transactions, the borrowed money was not "used" for the purpose of earning income, i.e., the "indirect" use was to buy a home.)

Simply stated, *Singleton* means that a taxpayer is entitled to restructure his or her financial affairs so that, if a borrowing is "directly linked" to an income-earning asset, an interest deduction can be claimed.

The Ludco Case

Basically, the *Ludco* case involved borrowing a large amount of money to purchase equity in offshore investment corporations. The companies were incorporated in Panama and structured to avoid Canadian taxes except to the extent of some relatively modest dividends paid by the corporations.

In *Ludco*, the underlying concern was that the interest deductions vastly exceeded the dividends paid by the offshore companies. Over the years, about $6,000,000 in interest was deducted by the taxpayers, compared to a "mere" $600,000 received as dividends. Was the purpose of the borrowing to earn dividends from the offshore companies — or was this simply a tax avoidance scheme?

The Supreme Court was unanimous in allowing the interest deduction. In a nutshell, the Court validated interest deductions wherever — considering all the circumstances in an objective manner — there is a "reasonable expectation" of receiving income. The taxpayer's income-earning purpose need not be "dominant" — absent a situation involving a "sham" or "window dressing", an income-earning purpose may be "ancillary". Furthermore, for the purpose of interest deductibility, "income" means gross rather than net income. The significance of *Ludco* is that it is not necessary to establish that a taxpayer will earn a "positive spread" after interest charges, provided that the return is not "window dressing" (in the *Ludco* case itself, the Court indicated that the dividends in question were more than just window dressing).

Taken together, the two (pre-GAAR) cases show, first, that the Supreme Court has opted in favour of certainty rather than expanding anti-avoidance doctrines and, second, that the legalities of a transaction are to be respected, and take precedence over the "economic realities" (e.g., that Mr. Singleton was, in essence, deducting financing costs on his home purchase).

On October 31, 2003, the CRA released Interpretation Bulletin IT-533 indicating the CRA's acceptance of these Supreme Court decisions; this bulletin has since been cancelled and replaced by Income Tax Folio S3-F6-C1.

Also on October 31, 2003, the Department of Finance announced draft legislation to effectively reverse the Supreme Court's decision in *Ludco* (and its decision in *Stewart* at 2002 DTC 6983) and impose a statutory requirement that losses from business or property would only be deductible in a year if it was reasonable to expect in that year that the taxpayer would realize a cumulative profit over the period during which the taxpayer could reasonably be expected to carry on the business or hold the property. Profit for these purposes would not include capital gain or loss. In short, the reasonable expectation of profit test was to be legislated back into existence. The proposals attracted a great deal of criticism, and after several years in draft form they were subsequently withdrawn. (On November 17, 2014, the Government released a new document entitled "List of outstanding specific legislative proposals for listed tax laws announced prior to April 1, 2013" that did not include the October 31, 2003 draft legislation.)

The Lipson Case

It should be noted that the *Singleton* and *Ludco* cases did not involve the general anti-avoidance rule (GAAR). (The CRA could have reassessed *Singleton* under GAAR, but did not do so.)

In *Lipson v. The Queen*, 2009 DTC 5015, the Supreme Court of Canada examined the relationship between interest deductibility manoeuvres and GAAR. While the taxpayer lost the case, the decision appears to support the contention that GAAR should generally not apply when taxpayers arrange their borrowings to minimize their tax liability. However, as will be explained below, *Lipson* may put a number of standard interest deductibility strategies into jeopardy. In order to understand why this is the case, it is important to understand the fact situation in *Lipson*, especially since it is reminiscent of a number of common interest deductibility strategies involving transactions between spouses (some of which are discussed below).

Lipson involved a share swap between spouses (in an attempt to characterize as deductible what would otherwise have been non-deductible mortgage interest) as follows:

(1) The Lipsons entered into an agreement to purchase a residence.

(2) Mrs. Lipson obtained a demand loan and purchased shares of a family company from her husband.

(3) Mr. Lipson used the funds to buy the home.

(4) Mr. and Mrs. Lipson took out permanent financing secured by a mortgage on the new home, and used the proceeds to repay the demand loan.

As the original loan was taken out to buy shares of the family company, the interest was claimed as a deduction. Similarly, since the refinancing was used to retire the loan, the interest thereon was likewise claimed as a deduction pursuant to subsection 20(3), which extends the purpose of the original loan to the refinancing. Because the shares of the family company were transferred on a rollover basis, the "attribution rules" applied to dividends received on the shares and the now associated interest deductions. Accordingly, the attribution rules allowed Mr. Lipson to declare/deduct both on his tax return, rather than Mrs. Lipson, who had actually taken out the loan to buy her husband's shares.

At issue was whether these rules had been "misused and abused" so that GAAR applied. The majority of the Supreme Court of Canada indicated that, insofar as the interest deductibility rules were concerned, the CRA did not establish that these provisions had been misused or abused. In fact, the transactions involving interest deductibility were described as "unimpeachable".

It was the use of the attribution rules to effectively "flip" the interest deduction over to Mr. Lipson that was problematic:

> The problem arose when Mr. Lipson and his wife turned to ss. 73(1) and 74.1(1) in order to obtain the result contemplated in the design of the series of transactions, namely to have Mr. Lipson apply his wife's interest deduction to his own income.

The Supreme Court observed that the purpose of the attribution rules is to prevent spouses from saving taxes by income splitting. As the Court observed in paragraph 42: "It seems strange that the operation of s. 74.1(1) can result in the reduction of the total amount of tax payable by Mr. Lipson on the income from the transferred property." Accordingly, "to allow s. 74.1(1) to be used to reduce Mr. Lipson's income tax from what it would have been without the transfer to his spouse would frustrate the purpose of the attribution rules. Indeed, a specific anti-avoidance rule is being used to facilitate abusive tax avoidance". As a result, the Supreme Court indicated that the interest expense should be available to Mrs. Lipson, not Mr. Lipson. (Since the Supreme Court did not mention the taxation of dividends on the shares of the family corporation, presumably they would continue to be taxable to Mr. Lipson.)

While *Lipson* has been cited as providing support for tax planning to maximize interest deductibility, many strategies involve transfers between spouses on a rollover basis, such that the attribution rules will apply. Disregarding *Lipson* and GAAR, the attribution rules would mean that the transferor may deduct the interest. But the *Lipson* decision relating to the attribution rules may be relevant, and therefore the issue of whether GAAR could apply so as to result in interest deductibility to the transferee-spouse instead.

Furthermore, although the Supreme Court seemed to strongly endorse the portions of the *Lipson* transactions relating to interest deductibility, this may not mean that GAAR can never apply to such transactions. While deductibility can still be claimed under paragraph 20(1)(*c*) based on the direct use of the borrowing, this test is distinct from GAAR, which is focused on whether otherwise valid transactions frustrate the object, spirit, and purpose of the provisions relied on. The Court observed that GAAR is designed "to address the complexity of transactions which fall outside the scope of specific anti-avoidance provisions", relating to the impact of complex series of transactions that often depend on the interplay of discrete income tax provisions — to make sure that the fairness of the tax system is preserved.

The recent case of *Swirsky v. The Queen*, 2013 DTC 1078 (T.C.C.), which was affirmed in 2014 DTC 5037 (F.C.A.), provides a cautionary tale for an interest-deductibility plan gone wrong. In that case, because the taxpayer's spouse testified that she had no expectation of receiving income from the shares, the deduction was denied. The use of the attribution rules to maintain the deduction in the hands of the spouse, denied in *Lipson*, did not appear to trouble the court in *Swirsky*. The CRA announced that *Swirsky* did not change its position on interest deductibility for money borrowed to purchase shares; only where there is a "permanent" corporate policy against paying dividends will the interest deduction be denied.

See also the discussion of interest in excess of related investment income at ¶2524.04, and the discussion of financing your home at ¶2543.

- *Planning Point:*

  In general, where you are going to pay down the amount of a loan, you should pay down non-deductible borrowings first (typically credit card balances and home mortgage).

- *Planning Point:*

  If you purchase Canada Savings Bonds through a payroll deduction plan, the interest which you have paid through the plan is deductible.

- *Planning Point:*

  Where an investment purchased with borrowed money has been disposed of at a loss or become worthless, interest on the borrowing may cease to be deductible. However, interest deductibility can continue on the proportion of borrowed funds considered lost in the reduction of value. This portion of interest will continue to be deductible indefinitely, but will of course be reduced as and when the loan is paid down. Deductibility of interest on the surviving borrowed funds will depend on the use to which they are put. See ¶1063.

- *Planning Point:*

  If you have fully paid-up investment assets on the one hand, and non-deductible interest on the other, it may be useful to review your situation with a professional tax adviser.

- *Planning Point:*

  To ensure interest deductibility when rearranging borrowings, study Income Tax Folio S3-F6-C1.

(ITA: 18(1)(*a*), (*h*), (11)(*b*), (*c*); 20(1)(*c*))

[¶2519] INTEREST INCOME

Interest-bearing investments made in and after 1990 must be reported on an annual accrual basis. That is, you must report the interest annually whether or not you actually receive it. The most common example of deferred interest is compound interest Canada Savings Bonds. When you buy Canada Savings Bonds, you typically have a choice between bonds that pay cash interest annually, and bonds that pay a lump sum when the bond matures (in about 10 years). The lump-sum bonds will pay a higher overall interest rate, since the government has the continuing use of the interest it is not paying you during the life of the bond. However, you must now report interest annually as if you had received it. This rule applies not only to compound interest Canada Savings Bonds, but to most deferred interest debt obligations, which may typically include fixed term deposits (Guaranteed Investment Certificates, also called GICs) with financial institutions, and certain insurance policies and annuity contracts, provided your investment was made in the obligation, or its terms were materially altered, in or after 1990.

For Canada Savings Bonds, your T1 Tax Return Guide will explain in detail the necessary reporting for any particular bond. For Canada Savings Bonds issued in and after 1990 (series 45 and later), T5 slips should be issued for deferred interest as well as for cash interest bonds. Other obligations will usually report accrued interest on a T5 Supplementary.

[¶2519.05] *Sale of Linked Notes and Accrued Interest*

Commentary on Bill C-29 Measures (Oct. 25, 2016)

Note: When Bill C-29, October 25, 2016, achieves Royal Assent, the commentary will be modified to read:

A "linked note" is essentially a debt obligation that pays "interest" based on some reference point such as the future value of a stock market index, commodity index, or similar index or asset. The interest is typically paid upon the maturity of the note. For example, a five-year note may pay the principal and all returns in five years upon maturity, with the "interest" being computed with reference to the value of a stock index at the time of maturity relative to its value at the time of the issuance of the note.

It is often difficult or impossible to apply the regular interest accrual rules to linked notes when they are transferred prior to maturity. As a result, some taxpayers have taken the position that any accrued gain on the transfer should be considered to be a capital gain rather than interest income.

For transfers after 2016 of a linked note (or similar debt obligation described in Regulation 7100(1)(*d*)), subsection 20(14.2) generally provides that the pre-transfer accrued gain on the transfer will be deemed to be interest. The deemed interest will be subject to the accrual rules of subsection 20(14), which add the interest to the transferor's income and provide a deduction in computing the transferee's income. Generally, the deemed interest will equal the transfer price paid for the note minus the original issue price of the note, without regard to portion of the gain, if any, that results from foreign currency fluctuations. Any portion of the accrued gain that is attributable to an increase in the value of fixed-interest payments, if any, because of a decrease in market interest rates, will be excluded from the deemed interest rule under subsection 20(14.2) and will be treated as a capital gain.

[¶2519.20] *Interest on Canada Child Benefits*

Canada Child Benefit amounts may be invested in the name of the child (or children) on behalf of whom they are issued without generating income attribution (¶2529), although technically the income is that of the recipient. Over the years for which family allowance is paid this can amount to a tidy sum, generating reasonable interest taxed to the child and not the parent. It is important to maintain a segregated account for this purpose, to show that the funds are not commingled with funds subject to tax or attribution in the hands of a parent.

Strictly speaking, the attribution rule exception for Canada Child Benefits does not extend to income paid under provincial counterparts to the Canada Child Benefit, such as the B.C. family bonus. As a practical matter, the CRA treats provincial payments under parallel programs in the same manner as federal ones; that is, as not subject to attribution. This informal accommodation is understood to have the blessing of the Department of Finance, and is likely to remain in place until, in the fullness of time, some province comes up with a program sufficiently at variance with federal policy to raise the issue, at which time the CRA will probably punt to Finance.

- *Planning Point:*

If the spouse receiving Canada Child Benefit payments (typically the wife) has other income subject to tax, consider putting the Canada Child Benefit payments in bank accounts held jointly by the spouse and each child. So long as the income on those accounts is treated consistently as that of the child, it will be taxed to the child and not the spouse. See ¶2529.03.

(ITA: 12(4); 74.1(2); IT-396R Interest Income)

[¶2519.25] *Income from Investing Universal Child Care Benefit Amounts*

Prior to July 2016, parents with children under the age of six received the monthly Universal Child Care Benefit, ostensibly for the purpose of paying for child care costs. Income earned by investing the amounts is not subject to the attribution rules, such that they can be invested in the child's name (or for the benefit of the child) without attribution to the parent. The Federal government increased the UCCB for years after 2014. The UCCB was repealed and replaced with a larger Canada Child Benefit, so the final UCCB payment occurred in June 2016. Regardless, the income splitting benefits still apply to past UCCB amounts. See ¶935.

[¶2521] TAX SHELTERS

Tax shelters are investments promoted on the basis that they offer income tax savings. Some of the more popular tax shelters in recent years have been investments in:

(1) Films,

(2) Computer Software,

(3) Resource Investments,

(4) Mutual Fund Fees, and

(5) Acquisitions to be gifted to charities.

Generally, the intended result of a tax shelter is that the purchaser is able to claim a tax deduction equal to a portion or in some cases the entire amount of the investment in a short period of time, creating a current loss from that source which reduces other income subject to current tax. The income from the investment will be taxed upon receipt. Thus, taxes otherwise currently payable are deferred until a later year. Where money is borrowed to make the investment, and especially where it is borrowed from the shelter promoters on the assumption it need not be repaid, the tax savings can be greater than the investment costs.

As discussed below, the government has systematically attacked these tax shelters over several years, and although a few variations may remain, only resource investments remain sanctioned by the government. The faint of heart may want to skip the following recital and read up on resource shelters only under the subheading "Recent Tax Shelters", below. The faint of heart should know, however, that apart from the tax write-off associated with resource investments, which is relatively secure as these things go, the chance of getting an actual return of the investment is always risky.

[¶2521.05] *Tax Shelters*

Previous editions of this publication provided a detailed overview of the long-running effort by the Department of Finance and the CRA to limit the availability of investments, products, or strategies to create losses or other deductions to shelter income from tax. These previous editions can be consulted by those readers with an interest in these historical "Tax Shelter Wars".

As a general summary, the thrust of limitations imposed over the years has been to ensure that tax losses on investments are limited to the income from those specific investments and cannot be used to shelter other income. It is still possible in some cases to invest in a stream of income which is sheltered by the capital cost allowance on the investment, although this will have side effects in terms of the remaining $813,600 capital gains exemption (see ¶2524) should you have another asset eligible for it.

[¶2521.15] *Restricted Tax Shelters Defined*

A tax shelter for purposes of the restrictions discussed above is defined as any property in respect of which it is expected on the basis of representations made with respect to the property that a purchaser will be entitled to deduct losses or other amounts in the four years following the acquisition in excess of the cost of the interest in the property to the purchaser. After February 18, 2003, the definition of "tax shelter" was extended to include the tax benefits which arise from a charitable or political contribution pursuant to a "gifting arrangement" as defined. The four-year rule is still in place, but is extended to include tax credits. Cost is computed each year and is reduced by benefits to be received or enjoyed by the purchaser or non-arm's length persons. Such benefits are prescribed by regulation and include tax credits, revenue guarantees, contingent liabilities, limited recourse debt (as newly redefined) and rights of exchange or conversion. The calculation of losses or other amounts deductible and of the cost to the purchaser is to be made on a prospective basis based upon the statements or representations made or proposed to be made in connection with the property. The definition of tax shelter is sufficiently broad as to encompass private placements as well as public ones. However, the reference to representations made would seem at least to exclude unsyndicated investments, such as your personal acquisition of an individual rental property.

Flow-through shares and certain registered tax deferral plans (e.g., RPPs, RRSPs, DPSPs, RRIFs, RESPs) are explicitly excluded from the definition of tax shelter. On the other hand, certain partnership interests may be tax shelters for purposes of the non-recourse debt limitations even though they escape the registration requirements below.

(ITA: 237.1(1) "tax shelter"; ITR: 231)

[¶2521.20] *Tax Shelter Filing Requirements*

Tax shelter investment deductions must be specifically identified on your income tax returns, and a tax shelter identification number must be provided with respect to each such deduction claimed. Technically, you are not entitled to deduct the shelter benefits without providing the shelter number. The tax shelter promoter obtains an identification number by filing form T5001. The investor must be provided with form T5003 which confirms the identification number.

Amendments first announced in the 2013 federal Budget extend the normal reassessment period if the information return required in respect of a tax shelter investment is not filed on time. The reassessment period in such case is extended to three years after the return is filed, effective for taxation years ending after March 20, 2013. Separate filings are required to be made in respect of Quebec investors.

(ITA: 237.1; 248(30)-(42))

[¶2521.45] *General Comments*

Quebec taxpayers should note that the Quebec government is far more willing than the federal government to use tax incentives to promote investments in Quebec which it regards as important to the Quebec economy. These are discussed at ¶1682.

Finally, you should know that tax shelter investments are often highly speculative and sometimes do not achieve the intended tax or economic results. You should not undertake a commercial tax shelter investment unless you are confident that you understand the economic and tax implications, and that you also know the reputation of the investment syndicators. Some of these projects can readily use your funds to ensure profit for the syndicators but little realistic chance of profit for the investor. While many such projects are valid business opportunities, you should either be able to evaluate the risks and returns yourself or consult professional advisers to review them.

[¶2521.50] *Recent Tax Shelters*

In reviewing any tax shelter, taxpayers should keep the following tax implications in mind:

- Alternative minimum tax (AMT) must be considered, since the amount of tax shelter deduction will be added back for AMT purposes; see Chapter 24.
- The amount of the deductions claimed by the taxpayer will be added to the taxpayer's cumulative net investment loss (CNIL) account (except for flow-through shares, where only 50% of the deduction is added to the CNIL account). As a result, the taxpayer's ability to claim the $824,576 capital gains exemption on qualifying shares and farm and fishing property may be adversely affected (see ¶2524).
- As noted in ¶2521.20 and ¶2521.35, all "tax shelter investments", as defined in the Act, including "gifting arrangements", as defined in the Act, must be registered and have a federal tax shelter identification number. (If the taxpayer resides in Quebec or carries on business in Quebec, a Quebec tax shelter identification number may also be required). Without such identification number, no person may claim any deduction in respect of the tax shelter.

Taxpayers should therefore seek professional tax advice to determine the tax implications on their overall financial position and the registration requirements before purchasing units in any tax shelter.

Past tax shelters included film tax shelters (which generally "died" with the introduction of amended "matchable expenditure" rules in 2001) and computer software tax shelters (which generally "died" when the CCA rules were changed in respect of computer software in 1998). Litigation in respect of certain of these shelters is still continuing.

Resource Investments: Oil and Gas, Mining, and Renewable Energy

Investments in the resource sector appear to retain the blessing of the federal government. The most popular vehicle for syndicating the costs of these investments is the flow-through share, which is expressly excluded from the tax shelter identification and reporting rules.

The main advantage of flow-through shares is that they allow companies in the resource sectors (i.e., mining, oil and gas, and renewable energy) to incur expenditures and renounce them in favour of the investor, who is entitled to claim them. The shares generally (depending on when they were purchased) have a nil adjusted cost base. Therefore, when the shares are sold, a capital gain will result equal to the entire proceeds.

Flow-through shares can be issued in respect of the following types of expenses:

- Canadian exploration expenses (¶2213) 100%
- Canadian development expenses (¶2217) 30%

Certain Canadian development expenses may be renounced as Canadian exploration expenses ("CEE"). The rules facilitate this by allowing a company with taxable capital less than $15 million at the time it receives consideration for the issue of flow-through shares conversion to renounce $1 million of Canadian development expenses as Canadian exploration expenses. This allows costs that could ordinarily be claimed at a rate of only 30% per year by the renouncing company to be claimed at 100% by individual flow-through shareholders, and obviously enhances the shareholder benefits from the underlying investment. Additionally, since a Canadian renewable and conservation expenses ("CRCE") (see ¶2210.05) constitutes CEE, it may also be renounced in accordance with the flow-through share rules.

Although not part of Budget 2016, the Prime Minister's mandate letter to the Minister of Finance in November 2015 included the following mandate which may lead to future amendments: "develop proposals to allow a Canadian Exploration Expenses tax deduction only in cases of unsuccessful exploration and re-direct any savings to investments in new and clean technologies."

Since the government appears to bless these investments, the main risk is the commercial risk, and investors should carefully evaluate the stock of the issuing company. Many investors confuse the concept of income tax deductions with income tax credits. Assuming an investor invests $100 in the purchase of a flow-through share and receives a deduction in the first year of that $100, he or she is out of pocket by approximately $54, since the $100 of deduction will entitle the taxpayer to a tax reduction of approximately $46, assuming a combined federal and provincial tax rate of 46%.

Additionally, a 15% non-refundable investment tax credit is available for individuals (other than trusts) that invest in certain flow-through shares.

The credit in respect of the flow-through shares relates to specified surface "grass-roots" mineral exploration expenses ("eligible expenses") of a corporation that are renounced to the individual shareholders. When the credit was first introduced, it was only available in respect of eligible expenses renounced under a flow-through share agreement made after October 17, 2000 and before 2006. The credit has been extended in most federal budgets since 2006. Presently, eligible expenses may be incurred by a corporation after March 2016 and before 2018 where the expenses are incurred under a flow-through share agreement made after March 2016 and on or before March 31, 2017. Certain provinces also offer provincial incentives in connection with flow-through shares.

Prior to March 22, 2011, donations of publicly listed flow-through shares were regarded as a particularly tax-efficient and acceptable donation arrangement. As noted above, a person who subscribes for flow-through shares has a nil adjusted cost base in respect of such shares. When the rules in the Act were amended in 2006 to eliminate the capital gains tax on donations of all publicly listed securities, promoters saw this as an opportunity to structure donation transactions that would enable holders of publicly traded flow-through shares to avoid realizing any capital gains on the disposition of their flow-through shares.

The CRA previously issued a number of advance tax rulings (see CRA Document Nos. 2007-0242361R3, "Donation of Flow-Through Shares"; 2007-0232271R3, "Donation of Flow-Through Shares"; 2008-0269281R3, "Donation of Flow-Through Shares"; 2008-0281941R3, "Donation of Flow-Through Shares"; 2009-0316961R3, "Donation of Flow-Through Shares"; 2012-0466731R3, "Donation of Flow-Through Shares) to various promoters confirming the tax consequences of making charitable donations of flow-through shares pursuant to a three-stage sequential transaction.

Under these arrangements, first, the investor/donor subscribed for flow-through shares pursuant to a subscription agreement which entitled the investor/permitted the investor/donor to deduct CEE and, in some circumstances, also claim an investment tax credit. Second, the investor/donor immediately donated the flow-through shares to a registered charity or foundation selected by the investor. Third, the charity or foundation immediately sold the flow-through shares to an end purchaser for cash consideration.

The CRA provided, among others, the following rulings in respect of these prior flow-through share donation arrangements:

(1) The arrangement constituted a gifting arrangement pursuant to the definition "gifting arrangement" and a tax shelter pursuant to the definition of "tax shelter";

(2) The donation of the flow-through shares to a charity by an investor/donor would not, in and by itself, preclude the investor/donor from deducting:

(a) Any CEE that the investor/donor would otherwise be entitled to deduct, or

(b) Any investment tax credit that the investor/donor would otherwise be entitled to deduct;

(3) Provided that all of the parties to the arrangement dealt at arm's length, neither the donation of the flow-through shares to the charity by an investor/donor nor the sale of the shares to an end purchaser would, in and by themselves, cause a share to be a "prescribed share" for purposes of the definition of "flow-through share";

(4) An amount equal to the fair market value on the date of the donation of the flow-through shares donated by each investor/donor to the investor/donor's respective charity would qualify as a gift for the purposes of the definition of "total charitable gifts" provided an official receipt containing prescribed information was filed as required;

(5) Provided the flow-through shares were capital property to an investor/donor, no portion of the capital gain arising from the disposition of the flow-through shares, if any, resulting from the making of the gift to the charity would be included in computing the investor/donor's taxable capital gain; and

(6) Participation in the arrangement, in and of itself, would not cause the flow-through shares to not be considered capital property to an investor/donor within the meaning assigned to that term if the

flow-through shares would otherwise be considered to be capital property to the investor/donor.

The CRA opined that any CEE renounced to the investor/donor and any investment tax credit claimed pursuant to the subscription of the flow-through shares would not constitute an "advantage" for the purposes of the split receipting gifting rules.

The CRA also stated in each of the rulings that there were a number of matters upon which the CRA was not expressing an opinion, including, among other things:

(1) The determination of fair market value of the flow-through shares;

(2) The determination of arm's length between any of the parties;

(3) The confirmation that the shares issued would be a flow-through share;

(4) The confirmation that the expenses renounced by the resource company to an investor/donor would qualify as CEE or as a flow-through mining expenditure; and

(5) The confirmation that the property held by the investor/donor was held on income or capital account.

In light of the fact that the CRA issued several favourable rulings, these flow-through share donation arrangements emerged as a popular tax shelter investment since the effect of these transactions was to significantly reduce the after-tax cost of charitable giving by providing the investor/donor with a significant deduction on the purchase of the flow-through share, eliminating any capital gains tax on the donation and entitling the investor/donor to a tax receipt in respect of the donation.

Amendments to the Act that came into force effective March 22, 2011, have reduced the popularity of flow-through share donation arrangements. Under the new rules, any capital gain arising on the donation of a flow-through share will no longer be exempt from tax. As a result, a taxpayer who acquires a flow-through share on or after March 22, 2011 and who subsequently donates the share to a registered charity or foundation, will be deemed to have realized a capital gain on the donation equal to the amount by which the fair market value of the flow-through share exceeds the adjusted cost base of the flow-through share which, as discussed above, is deemed to be nil. It should be noted that the new rules have not completely eliminated these flow-through share donation arrangements, but rather, the after tax cost of these arrangements may not be as attractive as they were prior to March 22, 2011.

While the definition of "tax shelter" expressly excludes a "flow-through share", the CRA has indicated (see CRA Document No. 2008-0289451C6, "Gifting Arrangement of Flow-Through Shares"), that in the case of a gifting arrangement of flow-through shares, where such arrangement constitutes a gifting arrangement, the tax shelter reporting rules apply to such gifting arrangement and no amount may be deducted or claimed unless a tax shelter identification number is obtained; therefore, prior to a donation of flow-through shares to a charity or foundation, investors/donors should ensure that a federal tax shelter identification number has been obtained. For investors/donors who are residents of Quebec, a Quebec tax shelter identification number may also be required.

Although flow-through shares are the most common type of resource investment for individuals, resource expenditures can also be syndicated through limited partnerships and joint ventures. These vehicles also provide for transmission of the expenditures and their tax deduction characteristics to the investors, although limited partnerships are subject to the restrictions discussed at ¶1818, which normally tip the preference for individuals to flow-through shares.

Acquisitions for Charitable Donations

Several tax plans have emerged over the years to try to take advantage of the various rules regarding charitable donations. The perceived benefits of such charitable plans over other historic tax shelters are many. For example, charitable donations do not, in themselves, trigger an alternative minimum tax liability or add to an individual's CNIL account.

Another historical benefit related to the fact that charitable contribution arrangements did not normally fall within the definition of "tax shelter" for the purposes of the tax shelter reporting and identification requirements, since the arrangements involved tax credits rather than reductions in income or taxable income. However, amendments to the *Tax Act* have changed the rules in this regard. Effective after February 18, 2003, most of these arrangements involving charitable donations are subject to the tax shelter reporting and identification rules. Furthermore, the *Tax Act* has been amended so that the amount of any gift or contribution will be reduced by any limited recourse debt associated with the gift. In such case, the gift or contribution will be recognized as the limited recourse debt is repaid. See the commentary under ¶2521.35, above.

The original charitable donation plan was to acquire works of art which would qualify as Canadian cultural property, and donate them at a higher value than the purchase price. Tax credit applies to the donation, and no capital gain is recognized on donations of Canadian cultural property. Assuming a 50% tax rate, the tax savings on the donation would offset the cost of the property so long as the donation valuation was greater than twice the original cost. To the extent valuation exceeded cost by more than this, there was an immediate and permanent cash benefit. The *Tax Act* now requires the fair market value of the donation as well as its cultural status to be certified by Cultural Property Export Review Board. Assuming you have a genuine bargain purchase, however, this plan is still viable. (Once you apply to the Board and it issues a valuation, you are bound by that value if the property is gifted to anyone within two years, whether or not as cultural property.)

Perhaps the most common variety of the art tax shelter was the scheme under which investors would purchase art objects for, say, $100 each, that were valued for donation purposes at $1,000 each. The theory was that these art objects would qualify as personal use properties, and so no capital gain would arise when they are gifted to a charity, since they would each be listed personal property and personal-use property, on which capital gain below $1,000 is not recognized. The government first announced changes on February 28, 2000, that affected these arrangements; these changes provided that personal-use property acquired after February 27, 2000, would not qualify for the $1,000 per item capital gain exemption if the property was acquired in circumstances "in which it is reasonable to conclude that the acquisition of the property relates to an arrangement, plan or scheme that is promoted by another person or partnership and under which it is reasonable to conclude that the property will be the subject of" a charitable donation credit. Even without the benefit of the listed personal property exemption, however, these plans could yield a net tax benefit. This appeared to be true even after gift arrangements were subjected to the tax shelter rules, as discussed above.

This type of plan is not be effective for gifts of property made after 6 p.m. (EST) December 5, 2003, unless the property is certified cultural property, ecological gifts, publicly traded securities, inventory, or real property situated in Canada. Gifts of all other types of properties are subject to special rules found in the *Tax Act*. Under these rules, the value of a gift of property for charitable donation purposes in so-called gifting arrangements is limited to the donor's cost of the property — in particular, it is limited to the lesser of the cost and the fair market value otherwise determined. Furthermore, the rules apply to other gifts of property, and not just those offered under gifting arrangements. The rules also apply to a gift of property (other than on death) if the property was acquired less than three years before the day that the gift was made or if it is acquired less than 10 years before the day the gift was made in circumstances where it is reasonable to conclude that, at the time the taxpayer acquired the property, one of the main reasons for the acquisition was that the taxpayer expected to make a gift of the property. Prior to the December 5, 2003, the CRA's chief recourse in these types of arrangements was to challenge the valuation and/or to impose civil penalties on promoters and valuators who knew or should have known that the valuations were false or misleading. These rules are discussed in greater detail in ¶2521.40, above.

Some of the valuation cases on gifts of art that prompted the December 5, 2003, rules only began to make their way through the courts in 2004. In *Klotz v. The Queen*, 2004 DTC 2236 (T.C.C), the Tax Court ruled that, while the works of art in question were personal-use property even though the taxpayer had never seen them, the fair market value of the gifts was what the purchaser who made the gifts paid for them, and not the higher donation value allegedly established by the promoter of the scheme. However, in three cases, *Nash v. The Queen*, 2004 DTC 3391 (T.C.C.), *Tolley v. The Queen*, 2004 DTC 3360 (T.C.C.), and *Quinn v. The Queen*, 2004 DTC 3328 (T.C.C.), the Tax Court reviewed at length extensive valuation evidence, and valuation principles in arriving at fair market value, and found the spread between acquisition and donation values to be justified. All these cases were appealed. The *Klotz* decision was affirmed by the Federal Court of Appeal (2005 DTC 5279), essentially on the finding that the valuation was a question of fact, and the trial judge had made no palpable error in his finding of fact. In a later decision, the *Nash* cases were reversed by Federal Court of Appeal, 2005 DTC 5696 (F.C.A.). The F.C.A. found that the works of art were purchased in bulk on the wholesale market, whereas the Tax Court had accepted a valuation which ignored the wholesale market and assumed the standard of comparison was the retail market for the works individually. This was, as a matter of law, not the correct comparison in the circumstances. The F.C.A. quoted with approval the Tax Court's decision in *Klotz*, noting that there was "no credible explanation" for the increase in value from the purchase price. The finding with respect to a requirement for a "credible explanation" bodes ill for taxpayers in future cases along these lines, and may cast doubt on future tax schemes depending on sudden increases in value. In what may be *obiter dicta*, given the main holding, the F.C.A. appeared to dismiss out-of-hand the notion that a group of prints purchased wholesale could be personal-use property. Leave to appeal the *Klotz* and *Nash* decisions to the Supreme Court was denied in 2006.

Yet another more recent charitable donation shelter works as follows:

(1) First a taxpayer borrows money to subscribe for units of a limited partnership;

(2) Once the units are acquired, the taxpayer will enter into a second loan and use the limited partnership units as security for the second loan;

(3) The loan proceeds from the second loan are then donated to a charity.

The initial loan for the purchase of the limited partnership units provides the taxpayer with annual deductions in respect of interest costs and financing charges. The taxpayer would not be able to claim any interest deductions on the second loan but the taxpayer will receive a significant donation receipt. The CRA has successfully attacked this type of transaction in *Maréchaux*, 2010 DTC 5174 (F.C.A.), affirming 2009 DTC 1379 (T.C.C.). This case predated the legislative changes which were introduced to attack leveraged donation and held that the leveraged donation (including the cash portion) was not a gift. In *Berg*, 2012 TCC 406, which involved a charitable donation of time-share units which were acquired by a debt, the taxpayer was permitted to claim a donation for the cash portion of his donation but not for the balance of the donation. An upcoming decision of the Tax Court may clarify the rules surrounding the more recent charitable donation shelters involving loans, including the new split receipting rules (see *Cassan et al. v. The Queen*, 2013-355(IT)G).

It should be noted that the CRA announced on October 30, 2012 that it will not process assessments where a tax credit is claimed by a taxpayer in respect of a gifting tax shelter scheme until the scheme is audited. However, based on the Federal Court decision in *Ficek*, it appears that the CRA does not have the authority to delay assessing in this situation.

Accessing RRSP Savings

In a press release first issued November 10, 2005, and a similar release dated November 29, 2007, the CRA warned against schemes which purport to allow taxpayers to access funds in their RRSPs without paying tax on withdrawal. Typically, these schemes involve using a self-directed RRSP to purchase shares of a private company or an interest in mortgages. The funds injected into the company, etc., are loaned back to the RRSP owner. This plan can flounder if the investment is not a qualified investment, or if the RRSP is used as security for a loan. The CRA cited the case of *Dubuc v. The Queen*, 2004 DTC 2811 (T.C.C.), as an example where the RRSP was used as security and the amount of the loan was included in the RRSP holder's income. The CRA is on solid ground in giving this warning. Such schemes should not be undertaken without independent professional tax advice, in the form of a legal opinion by a reputable firm, and probably should not be undertaken at all.

Retirement Compensation Arrangements (RCAs)

In *Income Tax Technical News* No. 34, dated April 27, 2006, the CRA commented on what it considers legitimate RCAs. In particular, it notes that "innovative tax plans purporting to be RCAs are being marketed and promoted to avoid taxes", and comments that "tax avoidance schemes purporting to be RCAs will be targeted for review with the aim of, for example, applying the salary deferral arrangement rules, denying deductibility, applying subsection 15(1) and/or subjecting the arrangements to GAAR". The comments, including examples, are quoted in detail at ¶739.15.

• *Planning Point:*

Prior to making an investment in any of the above shelters, the investor should seek professional advice. Such investments should be made on their economic merits, and not on tax attributes alone.

• *Planning Point:*

In light of the alternative minimum tax it is possible to over shelter income and so lose the tax benefits expected. *Pro forma* tax calculations are necessary where extensive shelter investment is contemplated.

- *Planning Point:*

  Holders of qualified farm property, qualified fishing property, or qualified small business shares may find their capital gain exemption impaired by tax shelter investments.

As noted above, investors should exercise the greatest possible caution when investing in tax shelters and obtain professional tax advice. *Caveat emptor!* — Let the buyer beware!

(ITA: 38.1; 40(12); 65–66.4; 127; 219.1; 248(30)-(42); ITR: 1200 [Deductions allowed]; 1201 Earned Depletion Allowances; 1203 Mining Exploration Depletion)

[¶2522] VENTURE CAPITAL CORPORATIONS AND STOCK SAVINGS PLANS

A number of provinces and territories have established legislation to promote equity funding of developing businesses. Three such plans which are now common are venture capital corporations (VCCs), labour-sponsored venture capital corporations (LSVCCs), and stock savings plans. The LSVCCs have proven so popular that the federal government has its own version, on which provincial and territorial plans can be piggybacked to provide a double benefit. Although the federal government announced previously that it was phasing out its support of LSVCCs by reducing the value of the federal credit ultimately to nil by 2017, it has now enacted measures to apply the phasing out only to shares purchased from federally-registered LSVCCs. For shares purchased from provincially-registered LSVCCs, the credit for 2016 and subsequent taxation years will be calculated at the rate of 15% of the net cost of the shares up to a maximum dollar limit of $750 for a maximum share purchase of $5,000. If a taxpayer purchases shares registered in both federally-registered and provincially-registered LSVCCs in 2016, the dollar limit will be calculated with a formula taking into account both the 5% rate applicable to shares purchased from federally-registered LSVCCs and the 15% rate applicable to shares purchased from provincially-registered LSVCCs. In addition, the federal government no longer registers new federally-registered LSVCCs unless the registration application was received prior to March 21, 2013.

Certain provinces also offer Employee-Sponsored Ownership Plans (ESOPs) and stock savings plans, which provide grants, deductions, or tax credits for employee investment in or buy-out of employers. Unfortunately the terminology used by the provinces/territories in describing the various plans is not consistent, which can lead to confusion as to which type of plans may be available in each province/territory. These plans are discussed in detail by province in Chapter 15 commencing at ¶1510, or in the case of Quebec, in Chapter 16. A brief overview is provided here.

In general, a taxpayer can obtain provincial tax benefits only if the taxpayer is resident in that province on the last day of the year or carries on business in that province.

(1) Venture Capital Corporations

Typically these corporations encourage venture capital formation through specialized corporations that must invest in minority equity positions in specified types of businesses in a province. These corporations allow investors to pool their funds with other investors and rely on the VCC management to invest wisely in developing (and generally high-risk) businesses. Individuals are encouraged to invest in VCCs through the granting of provincial cash grants, tax credits, or deductions in respect of shares purchased in VCCs. The federal government supports these ventures by not taxing the grants, credits, or deductions as a benefit, and not reducing the adjusted cost base of the shares (although capital losses on the shares will be reduced by the provincial grants or tax credits received or receivable).

Some promoters of these plans suggest that shares can be purchased by individuals who can utilize the credits in their own hands and then contribute the shares to their RRSPs, claiming a deduction for the contribution. While this may be true, it does not answer the question of the value of the shares contributed to the RRSP. The CRA appears to take the position that the shares stripped of the credit cannot be worth more than the cost minus the credit, but might well be worth less. It is not clear, however, that the CRA has made any effort to assess on the basis of its published position (found in published CRA administrative practice, including CRA Document Nos. ACC8478 and AC59617), nor to rein in venture capital fund promoters who routinely assert that the original full cost of shares contributed to an RRSP may be deducted. There is certainly an implied contrast, however, with the government's explicit permission for LSVCC shares to be acquired directly by an RRSP with tax benefits directed to the RRSP contributor provided minimal formal rules are followed; see (2), below.

Currently, only British Columbia (see ¶1523) and Quebec (see ¶1642a and ¶1669c) offer credits or deductions in respect of investments in certain venture capital entities. Ontario has a similar program which provides grants rather than tax credits for individual investors (and tax credits for corporate investors).

(2) Labour-Sponsored Venture Capital Corporations

LSVCCs were originally a provincial concept (developed by Quebec and Saskatchewan), which was subsequently adopted by the federal government. Accordingly, there are two types of such plans: those operating under provincial/territorial auspices (provincially/territorially registered), and those operating under federal auspices (federally registered). In principle, both must involve VCCs established by labour unions or employee groups.

In general, LSVCCs have the same investment goals as VCCs and share the objective of allowing investors to pool their resources to invest in smaller businesses in need of funds for growth. To the extent the investments are wisely made, the underlying businesses may generate faster growth and more significant returns than larger existing businesses. On the other hand, they may more readily fail. Given their sponsorship, LSVCCs may have a bias to investing in labour-intensive businesses (which promise jobs) or businesses with a high degree of worker participation in management.

For those taxpayers in provinces that offer an LSVCC tax credit program, it is possible for credits to double up with the federal credit. That is, where the province or territory provides a credit for its fund of, say, 15% of the amount invested up to a maximum of $750, the federal government may provide a matching credit of 15% with a maximum $750 but only for shares purchased from provincially-registered and not federally-registered LSVCCs. The federal government announced previously that the federal credit for the purchase of shares from federally-registered and provincially-registered LSVCCs would be phased out between 2015 and 2017 but subsequently announced that the phasing out would apply only to purchases of shares from federally-registered LSVCCs. For 2015, the maximum federal credit was $500 for the purchase of shares from federally-registered and provincially-registered LSVCCs. For 2016, the dollar limit was calculated with a formula taking into account the 5% rate applicable to shares purchased from federally-registered LSVCCs and the 15% rate applicable to shares purchased from provincially-registered LSVCCs. For 2017 and future years, the federal credit calculated only for shares purchased from provincially-registered LSVCCs will be $750.

One credit is claimed on the federal T1 return (line 414) and the other on the provincial/territorial section of the T1 return (or provincial return in the case of Quebec). The result is a total credit of 30% up to a maximum of $1,500 on a $5,000 investment in an LSVCC. For investments made in certain provinces or territories, a higher total credit may be possible as a result of the availability of additional provincial/territorial credits.

Unfortunately, there is no uniformity concerning the qualification requirements for plans across the provinces/territories or maximum credit limits. For qualifying LSVCC investments, the federal government allows a 15% credit capped at a maximum credit of $750, reached on a $5,000 investment. Most provinces/territories generally provide a higher credit than the federal limit, although the amount of the credit varies from province to province. Other provinces (Alberta and Prince Edward Island, as well as Ontario effective after 2011) simply provide no credits whatsoever.

Where an investor acquires shares in a federally registered plan, the federal credit is generally assured, but provincial/territorial credit is only given if the province/territory recognizes that particular plan as qualified under its rules. Where an investor acquires shares in a provincially/territorially registered plan recognized by federal regulations, the federal government will, for 2003 and later years, provide its credit only if a province/territory grants the investor at least some credit. This may not happen if the investor is beyond an age limit specified by the province/territory or is a non-resident of the relevant province/territory. In addition, the federal government will no longer register new LSVCCs but will continue to recognize provincial LSVCCs.

Note that investments made in the first 60 days of a year are eligible for credit in either the preceding year or the current year. That is, credit on investments made in the first 60 days of 2017 may be claimed on either the 2016 or 2017 returns (although presumably, for shares purchased from federally-registered LSVCCs, it would be more advantageous to claim for 2016 to enjoy the larger credit). For the federal government and most provinces/territories, the credits in excess of tax for the year do not carry over, so there is some advantage to investing in the first 60 days of the year to have the flexibility to apply the credit in either of two years.

Again, in general, most LSVCCs are similar in concept to mutual funds investing in high-risk smaller businesses, and are open to investment by the general public, although you may not be able to cash out of the fund at any time, as you usually can with a mutual fund. To complicate matters further, however, some provincial plans offer credits to more restricted plans designed to allow employees to acquire shares of an employer or members to acquire shares of a co-op. Some of these provincial credits will be matched by the federal government, although most will not. In general, those plans which the federal government will not match are referred to as ESOPs, and are discussed under a separate heading below. Adding to the confusion is the fact that the LSVCC/ESOP nomenclature is not used uniformly by the provinces.

The following is a survey by province or territory of conditions at the time of writing. Readers are cautioned that this information is inherently unstable and is liable to change by federal or provincial authorities at any time. Provincial tax returns often provide telephone numbers of the relevant provincial authorities to make a current determination.

Quebec

Quebec authorizes credits only for its provincial plans, the *Fonds de solidarité des travailleurs du Quebec* ("FTQ") and the *Fonds de développement de la Confédération des syndicats nationaux pour la coopération et l'emploi* ("Fondaction"). For FTQ, the provincial credit rate is 15% of the cost of shares, for a maximum credit of $750. For Fondaction, the provincial credit rate is 25% for shares issued before June 1, 2015 for a maximum credit of $1,250, and 20% for shares issued after May 31, 2015 and before June 1, 2018 for a maximum credit of $1,000. For details see ¶1669.

The federal government will partially match the provincial credits for the Quebec registered labour sponsored plans described above. In 2015, the federal government credit of 10% is added to the Quebec provincial credit. As announced in the 2016 Federal budget and enacted by Bill C-15 (June 22, 2016), for 2016 and subsequent taxation years, the federal government credit that is added to the Quebec provincial credit will be 15%. In all cases, the maximum amount the credit can apply against is a $5,000 investment.

Under the retirement rule, individuals who turn 65 years of age or older in the year, or who turn 45 or older (55 or older for taxation years prior to 2008) and have opted for retirement or early retirement, may request redemption of their shares. Generally, the credit cannot be claimed in these circumstances, but Revenu Québec may permit some exceptions to the retirement rule if you earned business or employment income in the year — see ¶1669 for further information, including details on changes beginning in 2009 with respect to when Revenu Québec considers a shareholder to have opted for retirement or early retirement. Since the federal government will only match the provincial credit, it follows that where Quebec denies the credit the federal government will also deny it.

Quebec permits a temporary redemption of shares to finance a home purchase or educational studies, under rules similar to the RRSP rules. There will be no penalty for redemption of the shares provided the proceeds are used in the context of rules governing the RRSP Home Buyers' Plan (HBP, see ¶2625.05) or RRSP Lifelong Learning Plan (LLP, see ¶2626a). The shares redeemed under these rules must be replaced over the 15-year period applicable to the HBP or the 10-year period applicable to the LLP. Failure to repurchase LSVCC shares on schedule will incur a penalty on the shortfall equal to 15% for shares of the FTQ and 15% or 25% for shares of the Fondaction (depending on when the original shares were acquired). The penalty generally does not apply if the taxpayer could as of right redeem the LSVCC shares before the end of the period on which a particular repayment is due; however, there are specific conditions relating to this exception which must be reviewed in detail when determining the applicability of the penalty tax. The federal government will parallel this treatment for Quebec redemptions; that is, there is no penalty on the redemption so long as there is no Quebec penalty, there is no additional LSVCC credit on replacement share acquisitions, and where Quebec levies the 15% or 25% penalty on replacement shortfalls, the federal government will levy its own 15% penalty in addition. The federal announcement was clear that these special rules would apply only to Quebec LSVCC share redemptions: "Similar changes are not contemplated for federally-registered LSVCCs or LSVCCs registered in other provinces."

Ontario

Before 2012, Ontario recognized federal plans and offered its own credits on investments made in (or within 60 days after) the year end (for reasons of its own, Ontario called its LSVCC funds available to the general public Labour-Sponsored Investment Fund Corporations (LSIFs)).

Effective January 1, 2012, the provincial credit program has been completely phased out in Ontario. For years prior to 2010, Ontario's LSIF credit was 15%. For the 2010 taxation year, the LSIF credit rate was reduced to 10%, with a maximum credit of $750. For the 2011 taxation year, the credit rate was 5%, with a maximum credit of $375. For 2012 and later years, no credit is available. In retrospect, it appears the federal government has modelled its own LSVCC phase-out on what Ontario did between 2010 and 2012.

Ontario also previously offered an extra 5% credit, up to a maximum of $375, on specified research-oriented investment funds (ROIFs), which were LSIFs with a 50% investment in specified research business investments. This additional credit is not matched by the federal government, which offers only the 15%/$750 matching federal credit. The Ontario ROIF credit was eliminated after 2011, in line with the elimination of the Ontario LSIF credit.

For 2007 and later years, the maximum qualifying investment on which Ontario will give credit was increased from $5,000 to $7,500. Accordingly, for investments made in 2007 to 2009 (i.e., years in which the rate of the Ontario LSIF credit was 15%), the maximum Ontario credits were $1,125 on ordinary LSIF investments and $1,500 for ROIF investments. These credits do not double up; that is, you cannot claim both $1,500 on ROIFs and any additional amount on ordinary LSIFs in these years. Rather, you could claim 15% up to $1,125 on ordinary LSIFs plus 5% on any of those investments which are ROIF eligible. Accordingly, for 2007 to 2009, an investment of $5,000 would generate 30% combined federal and Ontario credit ($1,500) plus another 5% from Ontario to the extent the investments are ROIF eligible. An additional $2,500 would generate a 15% Ontario credit only (so, $375), plus 5% to the extent the investments are ROIF eligible.

A list of qualifying LSIFs can be obtained from the Ontario Ministry of Revenue by calling 1-866-668-8297. The list can also be accessed on the Ontario Ministry of Revenue website (www.rev.gov.on.ca). Go to the website, click on "Forms and Publications", "By Client", "Investors", and then "Labour Sponsored Investment Funds List". The list unfortunately does not identify ROIFs, but Ontario Finance will typically provide this information on request.

Prince Edward Island

Prince Edward Island has legislation permitting it to register federal plans but, effective April 9, 1997, withdrew registration of the only plan it had accepted. Accordingly, Prince Edward Island currently does not match federal credits.

Saskatchewan

For 2009 and subsequent taxation years, Saskatchewan offers a 20% credit to a maximum credit of $1,000 on a $5,000 investment. The Saskatchewan credit is available for both federally registered and Saskatchewan-registered funds. Accordingly, a 35% combined federal and Saskatchewan credit can be obtained on a $5,000 investment, subject to the federal credit reductions detailed above. For details, see ¶1586.

Manitoba

For investments in funds registered under Manitoba LSVCC legislation after June 30, 2006, Manitoba offers a 15% credit, to a maximum of $1,800, which is reached on a $12,000 investment. Hence, on a $12,000 investment eligible for both the federal and provincial credits, there would be a Manitoba credit of $1,800 plus a federal credit of $500 ($250 for 2016, $0 for future years), for a total credit of $2,300. For details, see ¶1535.

New Brunswick

New Brunswick offers a provincial LSVCC credit for federally registered funds if prescribed by New Brunswick as eligible. For details, see ¶1543.

The 2009 New Brunswick Budget announced changes to the LSVCC credit. Effective March 17, 2009, the New Brunswick LSVCC credit was enhanced by increasing the tax credit rate to 20% (up from 15%, which had been in effect since 1997) and by doubling the maximum investment that qualifies for the credit from $5,000 (which had been in effect since 1997) to $10,000. Hence, on a $10,000 investment eligible for 2016 for both the federal and provincial credits, there would be a New Brunswick credit of $2,000 plus a federal credit the dollar limit of which would vary with a formula based on both the 5% rate applicable to shares purchased from a federally-registered LSVCC and the 15% rate applicable to shares purchased from a provincially-registered LSVCC. The federal credit limit for 2017 and subsequent taxation years for shares purchased from provincially-registered LSVCCs is $750.

The New Brunswick credit has typically been extended by regulation from year to year. However, recent amendments have extended it indefinitely for 2013 and subsequent years.

Newfoundland and Labrador

Effective April 1, 2009, Newfoundland and Labrador offer a tax credit at the rate of 20% of the amount paid for LSVCC shares (up from the 15% rate in effect from December 2004 to March 2009). Also effective April 1, 2009, the maximum annual eligible investment per investor was increased to $10,000 (up from the $5,000 maximum investment in effect from December 2004 to March 2009). Hence, on a $10,000 investment eligible for 2016 for both the federal and provincial credits, there would be a Newfoundland and Labrador credit of $2,000 plus a federal credit the dollar limit of which would vary with a formula based on both the 5% rate applicable to shares purchased from a federally-registered LSVCC and the 15% rate applicable to shares purchased from a provincially-registered LSVCC. The federal credit limit for 2017 and subsequent taxation years for shares purchased from provincially-registered LSVCCs is $750. There is currently only one fund registered under the Newfoundland and Labrador program. For details, see ¶1547.

Nova Scotia

For qualifying LSVCC investments made in 2007 and later years, Nova Scotia offers a tax credit rate of 20%, to a maximum credit of $2,000, reached on a $10,000 investment. Hence, on a $10,000 investment eligible for 2016 for both the federal and provincial credits, there would be a Newfoundland and Labrador credit of $2,000 plus a federal credit the dollar limit of which would vary with a formula based on both the 5% rate applicable to shares purchased from a federally- registered LSVCC and the 15% rate applicable to shares purchased from a provincially-registered LSVCC. The federal credit limit for 2017 and subsequent taxation years for shares purchased from provincially-registered LSVCCs is $750. For details, see ¶1556.

Northwest Territories

The Northwest Territories has introduced, for 1998 and later years, an investment tax credit (referred to as the "Risk Capital Investment Tax Credit") of 30% on up to $100,000 of eligible investments in territorial businesses or venture capital corporations. Several types of investments could, in theory, be eligible for this credit. One type of permissible investment would be LSVCC-type plans for investment in the Northwest Territories. On these plans, the federal government and the Northwest Territories would each give 15% credit on investments up to $5,000, and the Northwest Territories would give an additional 30% credit against its income tax on the next $95,000 of investment for a maximum credit of $30,000. Qualifying plans must be approved by the N.W.T. government.

The credit only operates if there is regulatory authority for an annual dollar allocation to the program. For 2004, there was no such allocation, and no credits were available. An allocation was restored for 2005, 2006, and 2007, but a decision was taken in 2008 not to extend the program after 2007. The program officially ended February 28, 2008, and therefore the carryforward period for the utilization of the credits ends on February 28, 2015.

Nunavut

Nunavut, having adopted the tax legislation of the Northwest Territories in its entirety, has the authority to approve LSVCC-type investment plans investing in Nunavut. The Nunavut program ended in 2003 and the carryforward period for the utilization of the tax credits ended in 2010.

Yukon

The Yukon has introduced, for 2000 and later years, an LSVCC credit of 25% to a maximum of $1,250, reached on a $5,000 investment. The federal government will match this with their LSVCC credit. In 2015, the maximum Yukon and federal credit is $1,750, reached on a $5,000 investment. The maximum combined credit will be $1,500 in 2016 and $1,250 in 2017 (Yukon credit only). Unused Yukon credits may be carried back three years or forward seven.

British Columbia

British Columbia currently has no LSVCC credit program, although it offers an Employee Venture Capital Plan (EVCC) that provides access to a similar provincial credit, which also qualifies for federal LSVCC credits (see below under the heading "Employee Share Ownership Plans" and ¶1524 for greater detail).

Alberta

Alberta currently has no LSVCC credit program. Alberta taxpayers may invest in federally registered plans and obtain a federal credit only.

Federal

The federal government, in addition to matching provincial credits as discussed above for provincially registered LSVCCs, will provide its full share of tax credit for federally registered "national" LSVCCs regardless of whether the provinces will match this credit. The federal 10% credit (for 2015 — maximum $500) applies to investments in these entities. The federal credit on federally registered LSVCCs is not tied to matching provincial credits. As noted above, the federal program is closed for new federal registrants (but not provincial registrants) as of March 21, 2013. The federal credit for shares purchased from federally-registered LSVCCs will be eliminated in stages starting in 2015 and will be fully eliminated by 2017. For shares purchased from provincially-registered LSVCCs, the rate was reduced from 15% (before 2015) to 10% for 2015 but was reinstated to 15% for 2016 and subsequent taxation years.

In general, both federal and provincial plans provide that investments can be made within 60 days after year end and still qualify for the current year credit.

(3) LSVCCs Held Through RRSPs

For 1992 and later taxation years, the federal government not only explicitly permits an RRSP or a RRIF to hold federal or provincial LSVCC shares (which had been possible before) but also, in the case of an RRSP, permits the individual plan contributor to claim the federal portion of the LSVCC credit. Beginning in 2009, LSVCCs are also allowed to issue Class A shares to an individual's TFSA and legislative amendments also permit LSVCCs to issue certain exchangeable shares.

Under these rules, an investor in an LSVCC is permitted to contribute to a self-administered RRSP of which the investor or the investor's spouse is the annuitant, and cause the RRSP in turn to invest the amount contributed in a federal LSVCC. The federal LSVCC credits go to the investor; they are of course subject to the same rate and amount limitations as for a direct LSVCC investment. For example, for an investment by a taxpayer in the highest marginal federal–provincial tax bracket (at least $200,000 in taxable income for 2016 before RRSP deductions), an investment of $5,000 would yield savings of approximately $2,250 in federal and provincial tax by virtue of the RRSP deduction, and a further $500 in federal LSVCC credit for a purchase of shares in a federally-registered LSVCC and $750 in federal LSVCC credit for a purchase of shares in a provincially-registered LSVCC (in some situations, the tax savings will be significantly higher). Provided the investment is made in a province which matches these rules, there would be yet another credit of at least $750 and the entire $5,000 investment would in fact cost closer to $1,000. It is understood that all provinces which give LSVCC credits conform to this system of permitting the investments through an RRSP, although provincial statutes are not always consistent on the matter.

Investors should be cautioned that things that look too good to be true often are. It may be that the investment value really is $1,000, since these are highly speculative investments. Although the shares can be sold, there is in most plans a five-year or eight-year holding period after share issue (which carries the credit) before the LSVCC is permitted to register the share transfer, so that the transferee cannot redeem the shares until this period is up; not surprisingly, in some LSVCCs there may be no real commercial market for these shares. In some plans, shares cannot be redeemed for value from the LSVCC until you retire, reach age 65, become disabled or terminally ill, or die. Note that Quebec alone will permit you to redeem your Quebec LSVCC shares held in an RRSP if you use the proceeds for either the HBP or the LLP as permitted by RRSP rules; see the discussion of Quebec LSVCCs above. You will have to reacquire Quebec LSVCC shares as you pay your RRSP withdrawal back to the plan.

As the new rules were originally conceived in 1992, it was doubtful that where an RRSP had funds on hand, for example, because a self-administered plan sold a particular investment, or let it mature, it could buy LSVCC shares and obtain credit for the individual plan contributor. This is because the credit flow-through rules require that an individual's contributions "and no other funds" must acquire the LSVCC shares. It now appears that, while this rule still applies, the prevailing interpretation is that since the law provides no date as to when a contribution had been made, it will be possible to use the original contribution portion of an RRSP investment which has been bought and sold to acquire LSVCC shares. It is only the gains and earnings element arising in the RRSP which cannot be invested by the RRSP in LSVCC shares and produce credit for the individual. The trick of properly accounting for this result is the responsibility of the individual.

It has been and remains possible for an individual to buy the shares personally, take the credits, and then contribute the shares to an RRSP; however, this scheme does face the barrier of the CRA's policy that the value of the shares contributed (and corresponding RRSP deduction) cannot exceed the cost of the shares reduced by the credits received, as discussed in the context of VCCs in (1), above. The validity of the CRA policy for LSVCCs in these circumstances is identical to the validity of the policy for VCCs in the same situation. However, the taxpayer will need to determine whether there is any point in taking the risk with the amount of RRSP deduction for an LSVCC share since all credit providers will accept the system of contributing cash (rather than shares) to an RRSP and having the RRSP buy the LSVCC shares with the annuitant taking the LSVCC credit (although in the case of most provinces, the statutory authority for permitting this is unclear).

An individual can contribute the cash to a spousal RRSP and cause the spousal RRSP to buy LSVCC shares. Although the contributor spouse must claim the RRSP credit, it appears that the LSVCC credit which arises in the RRSP trust can be divided between the spouses (or common-law partners) in any proportion they choose. Indeed, it seems that the spousal RRSP could acquire sufficient LSVCC shares to generate full credit to each spouse or common-law partner. Presumably, the provincial credit would follow the same rules.

(4) Employee Share Ownership Plans

These are yet another variation on the VCC/LSVCC concept above, but they tend to be directed to a group of employees investing in or buying out a specific employer. Under these plans an employee group or union, by agreement with the employer, forms a corporation which offers shares to the employees and invests the proceeds in the employer. The employee corporation thus may become a partial or (more rarely) a full owner of the employer business, possibly with rights to be represented by directors and have a say in management decisions. The provincial governments which provide for these plans typically offer a grant or tax credit to the employees who buy shares in the employee corporation under the plan.

Shares issued under these plans may be eligible investments for an RRSP. There is, however, typically no mechanism for an individual's RRSP to acquire the shares directly and transfer the credit to an individual. It is possible to buy the shares, take the credit, and then contribute the shares to an RRSP. This course of action faces the same uncertainties as to the value of the RRSP deduction as with VCC shares discussed in (1), above.

See the discussion in Chapter 15, specifically ¶1524 for British Columbia, ¶1535f for Manitoba and ¶1586 for Saskatchewan.

(5) Stock Savings Plans

These plans allow you to invest directly in qualifying share issues of new or developing corporations. Typically this is done through a plan registered with a provincial stock broker. The province provides tax credits (or, in the case of Quebec, income deductions) in respect of share purchases. Generally, there are holding period requirements, e.g., if shares are not held for two years the provincial benefit may be recaptured by the province. Replacement shares in a plan may be permitted. Your broker, or provincial authorities, should be able to provide details.

As with VCC incentives, the federal government will not treat provincial credits or grants as a taxable benefit but the provincial benefits reduced the adjusted cost base of the shares, providing in effect for recapture of the benefit at capital gains rates on eventual disposition. Losses on eventual disposition will not be recognized to the extent of benefits received (or receivable). These exceptions only apply to benefits related to shares of taxable Canadian companies, and do not apply to resource flow-through shares (¶2624.05).

Currently, only Quebec has a stock savings plan (¶1642). Manitoba had a stock savings plan (which it called an Equity Tax Credit), which was discontinued for shares purchased after June 2008.

(6) Equity Tax Credits

Nova Scotia has an Equity Tax Credit Program. Under this program, designated investments in an eligible company or co-op made after December 31, 2009 qualify for tax credits against Nova Scotia provincial tax equal to 35% of the investment to a maximum of $17,500. Investments made before January 1, 2010 qualify for tax credits against Nova Scotia provincial tax equal to 30% of the investment to a maximum of $15,000. The credits are not refundable but may be carried back three years and applied against earlier taxes and forward seven years. For further details, see ¶1558.

New Brunswick has a Small Business Investor Tax Credit, which offers 50% credit against New Brunswick tax to a maximum of $125,000 credit ($250,000 investment) per year for equity investments made after April 1, 2015 in eligible corporations. The maximum credit was $75,000 (30% on $250,000) from March 16, 2009 to March 30, 2015. For further details, see ¶1543d.

Manitoba provides a Community Enterprise Development Tax Credit for investments in eligible enterprises or investment corporations made before January 1, 2021. Investments made after June 11, 2014 are eligible for a 45% refundable credit to a maximum of $27,000 (on a $60,000 investment). Prior investments were eligible for a 30% non-refundable credit, to a maximum of $9,000 (on a $30,000 investment). For further details, see ¶1535d.

Manitoba also provides a further incentive program, the Small Business Venture Capital Tax Credit Program, which offers a provincial non-refundable income tax credit for individuals and corporations in Manitoba who invest directly in eligible small business corporations that require larger amounts of capital than community ownership can provide. Investments made after June 11, 2014 are eligible for a 45% credit to a maximum for $202,500 (on a $450,000 investment). Prior investments were eligible for a 30% credit to a maximum of $135,000 (on a $450,000 investment). The maximum annual credit that may be claimed in 2014 and subsequent years is $67,500 ($45,000 for prior years), even though the earned credit may be as high as $202,500. Any earned but unused credit amounts may be carried back three years and carried forward 10 years. For further details, see ¶1535e.

Newfoundland and Labrador resident investors who buy qualifying shares of an eligible Newfoundland and Labrador small business can obtain a tax credit under the Direct Equity Tax Credit program of 20% if the investment is made in the Northeast Avalon area of the province, 35% if in the province but outside that area. The maximum credit per investor per year is $50,000. There is a seven-year carryforward/three-year carryback available for unused credits, but credits may not be carried back to taxation years before 2000. For further details, see ¶1547g.

The Northwest Territories and Nunavut have statutory authority for equity tax credit programs but these have ended. The Northwest Territories program technically exists in tax credit carryforward form until February 28, 2015. For further details see ¶1552.

The Yukon Small Business Investment Tax Credit is available to arm's length individuals resident in the Yukon who invest in qualified Yukon companies. Professional corporations do not qualify. The credit is 25% of the cost of eligible shares acquired in the year or within 60 days after the year end, to a maximum annual credit against Yukon tax payable of $25,000. Unused credit is eligible for a three-year carryback and seven-year carryforward. For further details, see ¶1596c.

(7) Other Quebec Programs

Quebec offers special tax savings to its residents on investments in:

- certified Quebec films; and
- Quebec resource exploration expenses.

Where to find books in the library

By subject

Here are some popular subjects with the Dewey numbers, the number that helps you find the book on the shelf.

Fiction and picture books are arranged by the author's last name.

Ancient Civilizations	930
Art	750
Astrology & Supernatural	133
Atlases	912
Birds	598
Bugs	595
Canada	971
Chemistry	540
Cooking & Food	641
Countries	940-990
Crafts	745
Dictionaries & Grammar	400
Dinosaurs	567
Drawing & Cartoons	741
Earthquakes and Volcanoes	551.2
Electricity & Magnets	537
Encyclopedia & World Records	032
Fish & Amphibians	597
Folk and Fairy Tales	398.2
Holidays	394.2
Human Body	612
Inventions	609
Mammals	599
Math	510
Medieval Times	940.1
Music	780
Mythology	290
Native Peoples	970
Pets	636
Plants	580
Poetry and Plays	811-822
Religion	200
Rocks and Minerals	553
Sports	796
Stars and Planets	520
Weather	551.5

TORONTO PUBLIC LIBRARY

›perate in conjunction ›ebec Business Invest- ›perative Investment

4.8; ITR: 6700–6702; 7300)

e of two types. Term ment in the event of stical life expectancy ry. Whole life insur- the savings element the insurance com-

ife insurance did not Premiums are not ket yields on invest- cial and govern- n investments in life ll, the government rual rules to certain the ability to draw ee of current tax.

ance policies with ted income subject borrowings against no tax on death.

insurance policy cific returns on the al after tax, should ments. In the pre- t, the comparison anticipated.

plicable to disposi- after March 21, 1.

r a discussion of

nts involving the with a loan have "leveraged insur- riations of these e most attention t".

sition of a "typ- insurance policy yer acquires the neans of a policy … rate on the borrowing is set at 10% and the rate of return on the saving component within the policy is set at 8%. If structured properly, the 10% interest would be deductible for tax purposes, while the 8% return was not be taxable since it was earned within the policy itself.

The CRA began to attack 10/8 arrangements primarily on the basis that 10% interest was unreasonable and denied the deduction. Rather than allow the 10/8 battle to be played out before the courts, in the 2013 federal Budget, new legislation was proposed (since enacted) to effectively prevent the use of a 10/8 arrangement going forward.

Under these rules, where a "10/8 policy" exists, interest expense related to the borrowing will not be deductible, no part of the insurance premium will be deductible, and the amount to be added to the capital dividend account (in the case of a corporate taxpayer) will be reduced by the amount of the borrowing. A policy will be a 10/8 policy if the rate of return on the policy is determined by reference to the rate of interest on borrowing and would not be available within the policy without the borrowing. A policy will also be a 10/8 policy if the maximum amount of the investment account is determined by reference to the borrowing. These amendments are effective for taxation years that end after March 20, 2013.

A different leveraged insurance arrangement that involves borrowing but includes the purchase of an annuity was also "attacked" in the 2013 federal Budget. If an arrangement exists whereby an insurance policy is acquired and funds are borrowed which are used to acquire an annuity (the payments from which would normally be used to fund the insurance premiums), this will constitute an "LIA policy". If an LIA policy exists, no part of the insurance premium will be deductible, the value of premiums paid under the annuity contract will be included in computing the fair market value of shares deemed to have been disposed on death of the insured and no addition to the capital dividend account will be allowed.

(ITA: 12.2; 56(1)(*d*), (*j*); 148; Part XII.3; IT-87R2 Policyholders' Income from Life Insurance Policies)

[¶2524] CAPITAL GAINS AND CAPITAL LOSSES

[¶2524.01] *Capital Gains Generally*

Investments, such as the purchase of stocks, bonds, real estate, and business interests, typically yield some form of income taxed at general rates. Dividends are something of an exception, being taxed at special rates (¶2513). If the investment itself is sold, it will typically yield a capital gain, and the capital gain will be taxed at somewhat favourable rates in that only 50% of it will be considered income (although 80% will go into the Alternative Minimum Tax base, creating the potential for this to apply; see Chapter 24). In addition, the capital gain may be eligible for the reserves discussed above (¶2510). Capital gains arising from the disposition of qualifying small businesses or farming and fishing businesses may be eligible for an $824,176 (2016 amount and indexed) lifetime capital gains exemption (discussed below). Those arising from the disposition of qualifying farming and fishing businesses after April 20, 2015 may be eligible for a $1 million lifetime capital gains exemption not currently subject to any indexation. These investments are not publicly traded but must be made directly in qualifying businesses.

Note that capital losses have corresponding disadvantages; for example, they are deductible only from capital gains and not from ordinary income.

From a practical point of view, of course, capital gains are inherently speculative. If you buy a bond you know what the return will be. You don't know whether the price of a particular capital property will go up or down in future.

[¶2524.02] *Capital Gains Exemption*

A capital gains exemption remains for gains of up to $824,176 (i.e., $412,088 of taxable capital gains) for dispositions of shares of qualifying small business corporations; family farm businesses, partnerships, and corporations; and family fishing businesses, partnerships, and corporations. This exemption is increased to $1 million for dispositions after April 20, 2015 of family farm or fishing businesses, partnerships, and corporations. The regular $824,176 exemption is a cumulative lifetime total, indexed for years after 2015, and is reduced by any claim previously made under the capital gains exemption rules. The $1 million exemption for the disposition of family farm or fishing businesses, partnerships, or corporations is not currently indexed. The rules governing eligibility for the exemptions are extremely complex (see ¶502f and ¶502i), and generally speaking, professional tax advice is necessary before the disposition to ensure that any particular small business corporation shares or farming or fishing assets qualify.

Note that the capital gains exemption is not available if the gain is knowingly omitted from a return or if a return is filed more than one year late.

Special timing problems can arise where eligible capital gains and other capital losses occur in the same year; see ¶2525.

[¶2524.03] *Investment Expenses and the CNIL Account*

Many investors use the strategy of borrowing money to invest in income-producing assets they could not otherwise obtain (this is called "leveraging"). The interest will be deductible (¶1063) even if it exceeds the income from the asset, and the eventual capital gain will be taxed at reduced rates and, to the extent the $824,176 capital gains exemption applies, be tax-free. The risk, of course, is that the asset will not rise in value, so the taxpayer will ultimately have a net loss augmented by interest costs. To some extent the deductibility of interest is considered to compensate for this risk, or at least force the government to share in it.

By 1988, the government had come to feel that sharing the risk but leaving the taxpayer with a tax-free capital gain by virtue of the capital gains exemption was an excessive contribution to this strategy. The solution was to limit the capital gains exemption to the extent the taxpayer has "cumulative net investment loss" commencing in 1988. This is a lifetime notional account of investment deductions in excess of annual investment income, and it is offset to the extent income exceeds costs. A detailed definition is found in ¶502q.

It follows from this policy that investors, even if they have annual income rather than loss from investments, should keep a running count of their "CNIL" account on form T936 every year (for 1988 it was on Part 7 of form T657), in order to correctly claim the capital gains exemption on the eventual disposition of investments.

The significance of the CNIL account has been much reduced after 1994, affecting only taxpayers who own or may come to own qualified farming or fishing property or small business shares eligible for the $824,176 special exemption. It is understood that the CRA maintains a running account of your CNIL balance as part of its computerized return processing system, and will share their number with you if you ask.

- *Planning Point:*

  Be sure to analyze your capital gains for qualified farm and fishing property and qualified small business shares. You can hardly miss these in any event, since by their nature they are usually significant personal investments. Note that the capital gain exemption on these properties is not available if the gain is knowingly omitted from a return or if a return is filed more than one year late.

- *Planning Point:*

  The CRA keeps a running record of your CNIL account and will tell you the balance according to their records on your request. If the account is likely to be important to you after 1994 (because you have or may acquire qualified small business shares or qualified farm property), you may want to do your own annual accounting on form T936, and verify the CRA's calculations against your own. Although their computer program is very good, it cannot look behind the data entry fields on the return, so if something is reported in the wrong area, for example, the CRA version of the CNIL may be in error.

- *Planning Point:*

  Remember that CNIL account limitations are reversible by generating investment income in excess of investment losses. For example, owners of private corporations in particular may be able to arrange substantial dividend payments in the year a capital gain is realized; in the right circumstances the reduced CNIL account will permit use of the capital gains exemption and result in an overall tax savings, although there will of course be an offsetting tax penalty on the dividends. Still, the cost of action to reduce the CNIL account should be weighed where the existing CNIL would impair the capital gains exemption on a disposition anticipated in the year.

(ITA: 110.6)

[¶2524.04] *Reinvestment of Gains in Small Business Corporations*

Where you realize a capital gain on the disposition of shares in what was an eligible small business corporation when you acquired the shares, tax on the gain can be deferred to the extent the gain is reinvested in qualifying small business corporations. Similarly, only the gain on $2 million of investment will qualify for the rollover. The replacement investment(s) must be purchased in the year of the qualifying disposition or within 60 days after the end of that year, but not later than 120 days after the qualifying disposition. The capital gain deferred will reduce the cost base of the new investment, so that eventually it will be recognized on a final disposition. It is possible, however, to keep deferring gains by continuing rollovers within the parameters of these rules.

Details of this complex but beneficial system are found at ¶572.

- *Planning Point:*

  When disposing of shares in companies which were Canadian-controlled private corporations when acquired and have continued to be active business corporations since, consider in advance potential new opportunities which will qualify for rollover treatment.

- *Planning Point:*

  Remember that, unlike the $824,176 exemption, the reinvestment provisions offer a tax deferral rather than a genuine exemption. On the other hand, gains will qualify for the reinvestment rollover even if the company is no longer a Canadian-controlled private company at the time of disposition.

- *Planning Point:*

  If the company is still a qualifying CCPC for exemption purposes when you dispose of the shares, you may take the exemption up to the $824,176 limit and rollover treatment on the balance of the gain (within the rollover limits).

(ITA: 44.1)

[¶2525] TIMING OF CAPITAL GAINS AND LOSSES

Investments which have declined in value since acquisition or since December 31, 1971 could be sold prior to year end in order to realize the capital loss in the current year and so offset capital gains which are ineligible for or in excess of available capital gains exemption. When disposing of Canadian shares you must remember that the disposition will be deemed to take place at the "settlement date" which is normally three business days after the trading date. Remember that if an identical property is acquired within 30 days before or after the date of sale by yourself, your spouse or an "affiliated person" (such as corporation or partnership controlled by you and/or your spouse), any loss will be considered a superficial loss and not deductible (¶579).

The timing of sales of capital property which will yield capital gains is also very important. A deferral of tax will be achieved for one year if the sale takes place in January rather than in the preceding December. This advantage will be increased if the marginal tax rate in the subsequent year is lower than the current year (and *vice versa*).

Remember that the above tax considerations relating to disposals of capital property should not override sound investment principles.

If allowable capital losses exceed current taxable capital gains, it is possible that the loss may be carried back to any of the preceding three years (see ¶2507).

[¶2525.05] *Capital Loss Timing and the Capital Gains Exemption*

A problem may arise whenever the capital gains exemption for qualifying small business shares (¶502i), farm property (¶502f), or fishing property (¶502f) is claimed in a year where there are offsetting losses. (Effective for the disposition of qualifying farm or fishing property after April 20, 2015, the exemption is increased to $1 million and is not currently indexed.) Where, as is often the case, there is only one such property and the gain is offset by a loss, neither the exemption nor the loss carryover will in practice be available again. A loss carryover from the current to another year is lost because the current year loss is automatically used first against the current year gain. The exemption is lost because there is no other qualified property against which to claim it. Contrast the case in which the gain and loss occur in different years. The gain can then be sheltered by the exemption and the loss carried forward (or back) against other gains, qualifying or otherwise. Of course, it is always open to the taxpayer to build up another business eligible for the exemption. Where this is impractical, however, it is imperative to try to plan for separate years of disposition.

Note that this problem does not arise with loss carryovers, since their application is optional.

- *Planning Point:*

  Consider whether to sell loss assets before year end to offset capital gains in excess of gains eligible for exemption. Remember that reserves of earlier capital gains may count as current year gains.

- *Planning Point:*

  Consider in advance the possible disadvantages of selling property eligible for the $824,176 or $1 million exemption and property with offsetting losses in the same year. These disadvantages arise primarily if there is no other property on hand likely to be eligible for the $824,176 or $1 million exemption.

(ITA: 3(*b*); 40(2)(*g*)(i); 110.6(1), (2); 111(1)(*b*))

[¶2526] USE OF LOSS CARRYOVERS

Capital losses arising in a year must be utilized first against capital gains arising in the year. Any remaining capital loss balance is converted to the 50% which represents the taxable portion of capital gains and allowable portion of capital losses, and this amount becomes a "net capital loss" carryover. Similarly, losses on income account (typically from a business) must be netted first against income for the year (including the taxable portion of capital gains, if any, remaining after the application of capital losses), and any remaining loss becomes an ordinary loss carryover (called a "non-capital loss"). Use the CRA form T1A to do these calculations.

Net capital loss carryovers may be used only against taxable capital gains of other years after the application of capital losses of the year itself. Net capital losses of a year may be carried back three years and forward indefinitely. Non-capital losses may be carried back three years and forward:

- twenty years for losses arising in and after the 2006 taxation year;
- ten years for losses arising in taxation years ending after March 22, 2004, and before 2006; and
- seven years for losses arising in taxation years ending before March 23, 2004.

Where ordinary losses have been applied against capital gains of a year (after 1990) and net capital losses subsequently arise which may be carried to the same year, it is possible to displace the non-capital loss with a net capital loss, and so in effect regenerate the non-capital loss. This will be desirable if the non-capital loss will not otherwise expire, since non-capital losses have more general use than net capital losses.

Generally speaking, you will want to use either capital or non-capital losses for carryback to the three preceding years to the extent of capital gain or income, as the case may be. This will not always be true, however. You may want to preserve your capital losses and use capital gain exemption instead, and you may not want to use losses against income taxed at low rates if you expect to be in a higher tax bracket in the carryforward period. See generally ¶1085–¶1097.

The application of loss carryovers in any particular year is fully optional; that is, the taxpayer can use as much or as little of an available carryover as he or she pleases to reduce income of a particular year.

- *Planning Point:*

  It is up to you to maintain adequate records of your capital and non-capital loss carryforward balances and apply them. While the CRA provides form T1A for loss carrybacks, it has no procedure to ensure the use of loss carryforwards.

- *Planning Point:*

  Remember to claim your business loss carryforwards against all sources of income. Do not, however, claim amounts which will eliminate the use of your personal amount credits or other credits, such as political contribution credit, which have no carryover. Depending on your loss situation, you may want to use losses only against income above the lowest tax bracket level. See the example at ¶1087.

- *Planning Point:*

  If you have a net capital loss arise in the year, be sure to check the three preceding years for any ordinary losses which have been applied to reduce taxable capital gains. It is possible to carry back the net capital loss and regenerate the ordinary loss, but this is only desirable if the ordinary loss can itself be carried back or forward before it expires.

- *Planning Point:*

  It will not be desirable to carry back capital losses to displace capital gains exemption claimed, since the exemption will be lost. You may carry back losses against gains in excess of the exemption for a prior year, but be sure in your calculations you do not impair the prior exemption.

- *Planning Point:*

  Similarly, in applying capital loss carryforwards in the current year, it is essential not to impair the capital gain exemption.

[¶2527] TAX-FREE ZONE VERSUS VALUATION DAY ELECTION

Capital property owned on December 31, 1971, other than depreciable property or an interest in a partnership, may have an adjusted cost base different from its original cost. The general rule is that taxpayers must use the tax-free zone method (¶591) to determine the deemed cost of any such property sold unless they have made the valuation day election in the tax return of the first year subsequent to 1971 that a disposal of pre-1972 capital property was made.

If no disposal of capital property which would require a taxpayer to make a choice between methods has previously occurred, you should consider carefully whether to make the valuation day election. For example, if the majority of your capital assets eligible for the election are worth more at Valuation Day than cost and subsequently decline in value, you might select the valuation day value as a higher base against which to measure any future losses. On the other hand, if most of your capital assets eligible for the election were depressed below cost at Valuation Day and subsequently rise in value, you would probably not make the valuation day election. Rather you would use the tax-free zone method to offset increases in value since Valuation Day with losses in value between acquisition and Valuation Day. The choice of methods, of course, has no effect on capital property acquired after December 31, 1971 (unless you are deemed to have owned it at that date). An informed decision regarding whether to make the valuation day election might save income tax dollars.

(ITAR: 26(3), (7))

[¶2528] GUARANTEED CAPITAL GAINS

Where you so elect in your tax return, all gains and losses for that year and any subsequent year from the disposition of Canadian securities (as long as you are not a trader or dealer in securities at the time of the disposition) will be taxed as capital gains or capital losses. The election is permanent. The election is designed to provide a measure of protection from the risk that what you thought was a capital gain will be taxed fully as ordinary income. See ¶501.

This election is not usually recommended. First, it is usually superfluous, since gains on securities will usually be considered on capital account in any event unless you do a truly enormous volume of trading relative to your other income. If you do have such a large volume, there is always the risk that you will be considered a trader or dealer in any event. The courts have said that an ordinary individual will be considered a "trader or dealer" when "his dealings amount to carrying on a business and can no longer be characterized as an investor's transactions or mere adventures on concerns in the nature of trade". Second, if you do make the election it may bind you on future loss transactions which might be more speculative and arguably on income account.

(ITA: 39(4); *The Queen v. Vancouver Art Metal Works Limited*, 93 DTC 5116 (F.C.A.))

[¶2528c] OFFSHORE INVESTING

[¶2528c.01] *Offshore Investments*

When you invest in a Canadian mutual fund or similar investment fund, the fund must make payable all of its investment income earned to you and the other unitholders or be subject to Canadian tax on that income at the highest rate. The effect of this allocation is that you are generally subject to tax on your share of the trust's income. Offshore funds may not be subject to this rule (although U.S. funds are generally subject to a similar rule). Thus income accumulated in an offshore fund could escape current taxation, and could perhaps be repatriated as a capital gain or tax-free rather than income on the eventual redemption of fund units. This possibility led to tax practitioners designing investments which were not caught by the FAPI rules explained at ¶493.

However, Canada has had rules in place since 1985 to discourage investments in an "offshore investment fund property" if it is reasonable to conclude that "one of the main reasons for acquiring, holding or having an interest in such property" is to defer or reduce the current tax on such property by deeming income to be received by holders of such property. These rules were subject to a modest revision in the technical Bill that was passed into law in June 2013 (a much broader overhaul of these rules — the so-called "foreign investment entity" or "FIE" legislation — was previously proposed by the Department of Finance, but subsequently abandoned; see discussion below). The intention, or motive, test is discussed in *Walton*, 98 DTC 1780 (T.C.C.) and *Gerbro v. The Queen*, 2016 TCC 173.

It is important to note that the definition of "offshore investment fund property" is much broader than mutual funds and investment funds and that the definition of an "offshore investment fund property" includes a share of the capital stock of, an interest in, or a debt of any "non-resident entity", that may reasonably be considered to derive its value, directly or indirectly, primarily from portfolio investments in: (i) virtually any non-resident entity, (ii) commodities, (iii) real estate, (iv) Canadian or foreign resource properties, (v) non-Canadian currency, (vi) rights, or options to acquire or dispose of anything listed in (i)–(vi) above, and (vii) any combination of anything listed in (i)–(vii) above. It should also be noted that the term "portfolio investment" is not defined and would likely be interpreted by its normal commercial meaning. The Tax Court defined the term in the recent decision of *Gerbro v. The Queen*, 2016 TCC 173, as "... the ordinary commercial meaning of portfolio investment in the international investment context is an investment in which the investor ... is not able to exercise significant control or influence over the property invested in ... Portfolio investments are passive investments that do not entail active management of, or control over, the operations of the underlying investment in any manner ..." (at ¶101-¶103). This decision has been appealed.

Specifically excluded from the application of this provision are interests in controlled foreign affiliates, non-commercial "exempt foreign trusts" (as defined in subsection 94(1)), and non-resident entities that are prescribed in the

Income Tax Regulations. The Regulations exclude from this provision any property acquired by way of a bequest or inheritance from a deceased person, who has not been resident in Canada for the five years preceding death, provided that the property had not been acquired from a Canadian resident by the deceased and was not property substituted for property so acquired from a resident of Canada. The excluded exempt foreign trusts are, generally, (a) certain non-resident trusts the income or capital of which is to be used by disabled individuals, (b) certain non-resident trusts which are created as a consequence of a breakdown of marriage to provide support for non-residents, (c) certain enumerated non-resident trusts, including those affiliated with the United Nations and foreign universities, (d) certain non-resident trusts established exclusively for charitable purposes, (e) certain non-resident trusts governed by employee profit sharing plans, retirement compensation arrangements, or foreign retirement arrangement, (f) certain non-resident trusts that provide employee benefit plans, and (g) certain non-resident trusts operated exclusively to provide or administer superannuation or pension benefits for non-residents. In each case, a number of conditions must be met.

Under these rules, a taxpayer is required to include in his or her income the product of the "designated cost" of his or her offshore investment fund property times the prescribed interest rate, plus 2%, less any income otherwise reportable in the year in respect of the property, other than capital gains. The calculation is made monthly based on the designated cost at each month end and amounts included in income are added to the cost of the offshore investment fund property.

Interestingly, in the 1999 federal Budget, the government announced new rules relating to the taxation of offshore investment fund properties known as the foreign investment entity (FIE) proposals. At that time, it was stated by the government that the CRA was having difficulty identifying investments which are caught by the existing rules and proving the taxpayer's intention for the investment. The original FIE proposals did not include an intention test and were very broadly drafted to cover many forms of FIEs. The FIE proposals stated that a holder of a FIE would pay tax annually (i) on a prescribed percentage of the compound cost of the FIE (i.e., cost plus prior income inclusions), or (ii) by adding to (or deducting from) Canadian income the annual increase (or decrease) in the market value of the investor's FIE. Since 1999, the FIE proposals have been presented by the government in several versions but the rules were never enacted. In its 2010 Budget, the government announced that it would not proceed with the FIE proposals and that the existing rules would continue with some minor modifications. These modifications have now been enacted and apply to taxation years ending after March 4, 2010.

It should be noted that if a taxpayer has an investment in an offshore investment fund property, the taxpayer may also have reporting obligations such as reporting ownership of specified foreign property as discussed below in addition to the obligation to report income from such properties in the taxpayer's tax return.

(ITA: 94.1; ITR: 6900 [Prescribed offshore investment fund property])

[¶2528c.02] *Reporting Offshore Trusts, Distributions from Offshore Trusts, Foreign Property, and Foreign Affiliates*

Some taxpayers seek to achieve beneficial tax results by putting funds in offshore trusts (or sometimes corporations or other entities) for the benefit of themselves or their relatives, in low tax rate jurisdictions. Anti-avoidance rules have long been in place to tax current income accumulations in most non-resident trusts where there are Canadian beneficiaries.

Too often, taxpayers did not go to the trouble and expense of attempting to ensure technical compliance with the tax rules, and relied on the lack of Canadian reporting requirements imposed on offshore investments. In 1995, the government announced that it would impose substantial reporting obligations on (1) foreign property holdings of Canadian residents (form T1135), (2) transfers of funds to foreign trusts by Canadian residents (form T1141), (3) Canadian beneficiaries receiving payments from or becoming indebted to non-resident trusts (form T1142), even where such payments are non-taxable, and (4) interests in foreign affiliates (form T1134, now used to report both foreign affiliates other than controlled foreign affiliates and controlled foreign affiliates — prior to 2011 separate forms were used). For more detail, see the forms themselves, which come with extensive explanatory cover sheets. Although the new forms apply to taxation years after 2010, they were not in fact released by the CRA until December 31, 2012 — accordingly, the CRA accepted the old forms until June 30, 2013 in recognition of the fact that many commercial tax software providers would need some time to upgrade their systems. Substantial penalties are provided for late filing and other non-compliance. See the CRA's new "Table of Penalties" at http://www.cra-arc.gc.ca/tx/nnrsdnts/cmmn/frgn/pnlts_grd-eng.html for a breakdown of when penalties can apply in respect of foreign reporting obligations. The upshot of these rules is that taxpayers relying on these offshore plans will have to disclose them and permit the CRA to consider whether they are subject to Canadian tax. In addition, a transitional reporting system applied on an elective basis for 2013 forms.

One important point which should be noted is that the obligation to report foreign property on form T1135 is applicable if the Canadian resident owns "specified foreign property" having an aggregate cost exceeding Canadian $100,000. The government simplified the reporting requirements for taxpayers with foreign property of $250,000 or less. Taxpayers with foreign property of more than $250,000 are required to complete the detailed reporting method on form T1135, while those with foreign property of $250,000 or less will be able to use the simplified reporting method on the same form. The definition of "specified foreign property" is very broad and covers most interests in foreign entities as well as foreign property including foreign bank accounts and most foreign real estate. In this regard, "specified foreign property" includes portfolio interests in non-Canadian resident corporations even if such investments are held through Canadian brokers who provide a T5 to the Canadian investor. For example, if a Canadian investor owns shares of Apple Inc., held through a Canadian broker at a major Canadian financial institution, such shares would be "specified foreign property" even if it is fully reported on the taxpayer's tax return and subject to T5 reporting by the Canadian broker (see *Stemijohn Investments Ltd.*, 2011 DTC 5169 (F.C.A.), affirming 2010 DTC 5156 (T.C.C.)). The new form, discussed below, provides some administrative relief in this situation, indicating that "Where the reporting taxpayer has received a T3 or T5 from a Canadian issuer in respect of a specified foreign property for a taxation year, that specified foreign property is excluded from the T1135 reporting requirement for that taxation year." However, because a box must be checked indicating that this rule applies, it appears the form must still be prepared. In addition, because T3s and T5s are generally not issued by a Canadian issuer unless there is income to be reported, securities held with a Canadian issuer which does not produce income (e.g., shares for a foreign corporation which does not pay a dividend) will still have to be reported.

The current version of the form instructions specifically notes that the physical location of the shares is not relevant; in any event, most public company shares are no longer provided in certificated form. A revised form T1135 was released in June 2013. This form requires substantially more information than the previous version and has led to some outcry regarding the additional expense that taxpayers will incur to meet their filing obligations. For example, the form now requires taxpayer's to disclose: (i) the cost to the taxpayer of the property at year end, (ii) the highest cost amount of the property at any time in the year, and (iii) any income or gains from the foreign property, in each case on a property-by-property basis.

It should also be noted that the Act has specific reporting requirements in respect of foreign affiliates (including controlled foreign affiliates). However, no reporting is required for inactive or dormant foreign affiliates. The term "dormant or inactive foreign affiliates" (for which reporting is not required) is presently set by the CRA as affiliates having less than $25,000 gross receipts in the year and assets the total fair market value of which did not exceed $1 million at any time in the year. It should be noted that this concession is administrative and is not found in the Act and must be applied on an annual basis (see ¶495).

(ITA: 233.2–233.6; Forms T1134; T1135 Foreign Income Verification Statement; T1141 Information Return in Respect of Transfers or Loans to a Non-Resident Trust; T1142 Information Return in Respect of Distributions from and Indebtedness to a Non-Resident Trust)

[¶2528c.03] *Non-Resident Trusts*

In 2013, a long-proposed overhaul of the Canadian non-resident trust rules finally became law, with effect for 2007 and later taxation years. These rules deem a trust that is otherwise not resident in Canada under common law principles to be resident in Canada if the trust (a) has a contributor to the trust who is resident in Canada in the relevant year, or (b) has a Canadian resident beneficially interested (as explained above) in the trust as well as a "connected contributor". A connected contributor is generally defined as a person who contributed to the trust at a time when the contributor was resident in Canada or within five years of ceasing to be resident of Canada or becoming resident of Canada.

The NRT rules also extend the definition of contribution significantly to include numerous transactions such as providing certain services to the trust and certain issuances of shares by a Canadian corporation to a trust. However, certain trusts are excluded from the NRT rules including a trust to which all contributions have been made by persons who have not resided in Canada for 60 months in the relevant year (the so-called "immigration trust"), and certain trusts which are defined as "exempt foreign trusts" including: (a) certain non-resident trusts the income or capital of which is to be used by disabled individuals, (b) certain non-resident trusts which are created as a consequence of a breakdown of marriage to provide support for non-residents, (c) certain enumerated non-resident trusts, including those affiliated with the United Nations and foreign universities, (d) certain non-resident trusts established exclusively for charitable purposes, (e) certain non-resident trusts governed by employee profit-sharing plans, retirement compensation arrangements, or foreign retirement arrangements, (f) certain non-resident trusts that provide employee benefit plans, (g) certain non-resident trusts operated exclusively to provide or administer superannuation or pension benefits for non-residents; (h) certain commercial trusts which meet the statutory requirements, and (i) prescribed trusts (of which currently none are prescribed).

The NRT rules divide the non-resident trust into two notional portions. The "resident portion" generally involves property which has been contributed by a current or former resident of Canada. The "non-resident portion" generally includes all of the other property of the trust. The NRT rules provide generally that a non-resident trust will not be taxed on income derived from its non-resident portion, unless the income is from certain Canadian sources, but only if a timely election is filed to treat the non-resident portion and the resident portion as separate trusts. For more details, see ¶470.

The NRT rules are very complicated and, accordingly, the details are beyond the scope of a general book such as this. However, any contributor (as defined in the extended definition in the NRT rules) and any beneficiary of a non-resident trust should obtain professional advice.

(ITA: 94)

[¶2528c.04] *Going Offshore*

For rules on sending not only your money but yourself offshore, see ¶2547.

[¶2528c.05] *Non-Arm's Length Offshore Transactions*

In 1997, the government announced new rules commencing in 1998 to compel the use of arm's length pricing in dealings with non-arm's length non-residents. Although these rules are clearly aimed at large scale commercial transactions, any quasi-commercial transaction, such as the purchase of a Florida condominium for rental purposes from a U.S. resident brother, could be caught. The rules permit the CRA to restructure the tax consequences of entire transactions according to what it considers arm's length principles. In certain situations, a breach of these principles may also result in significant penalties. For more detail, see ¶796.05.

(ITA: 247)

INDIVIDUALS

[¶2529] INCOME SPLITTING

Income splitting through the use of a personal holding corporation has already been discussed (see ¶2511). Other methods have in the past been used by the taxpayer to split income with a spouse (or common-law partner) and children without being subject to the attribution provisions in the Act (¶977).

Some means of income splitting are:

[¶2529.01] *Loan or Transfer to Spouse or Common-Law Partner*

If you have loaned or transferred any property to or for the benefit of another person who is or has become your spouse or common-law partner, any income or loss derived from the property or from property substituted therefor that relates to a period throughout which you are resident in Canada and that person is your spouse or common-law partner is attributed back to you and taxed in your hands. Certain loans and transfers are, however, exempted from the application of these rules. The most significant exemptions are the exemptions available for loans and transfers which proceed on an arm's length, commercial basis. At a minimum, this usually requires interest at prescribed rates to be charged and paid at least annually.

Note that only income "from property" and taxable capital gains are attributed under these rules. You may still loan money to your spouse or common-law partner to be used in a direct unincorporated business venture; the profits (or losses) will not be attributed to you. This rule may perhaps be stretched to loans to a business partnership in which you and your spouse or common-law partner participate provided your participation is indirect (through a corporation). This may achieve income splitting on future profits from a new business venture.

- *Planning Point:*

  If your spouse or common-law partner needs business capital which you can provide, an interest-free loan remains possible, with business income not attributed to you.

- *Planning Point:*

  If you are contemplating investments which appear to have a yield in excess of prescribed interest rates you can effectively have the excess taxed in the hands of your spouse or common-law partner by loaning the funds to your spouse or common-law partner to make the investment. A table of prescribed interest rates is found at ¶80 preceding Chapter 1; note that the extra 4% included in those rates does not apply for these purposes. It is crucial that your spouse or common-law partner make full, timely annual interest payments to you on the loan at least every January.

(ITA: 74.1; 74.5; IT-511R Interspousal and certain other transfers and loans of property)

[¶2529.02] *Reinvestment of "Attributed" Income*

Any income earned on property you have transferred to someone who is now your spouse or common-law partner (as defined at ¶1113) or your child, niece or nephew who is under 18 years of age (or to any other non-arm's length minor) is generally subject to the income attribution rules and therefore included in your income. However, if your spouse or common-law partner or child reinvests this income, the income earned on the reinvested amount is not attributed back to you.

(ITA: 74.1; IT-510 Transfers and loans of property made after May 22, 1985 to related minor; IT-511R Interspousal and certain other transfers and loans of property)

[¶2529.03] *Income Put in the Hands of a Child*

Loans or transfers to minor children are subject to attribution of income rules similar to those for a spouse. The attribution rules will not function where the child is investing his or her own funds, such as those arising from Canada Child Benefits, or funds gifted by non-residents (e.g., a non-resident grandparent).

However, dividend income from private corporations will be subject to the so-called kiddie tax. In particular, a special tax is imposed on individuals who have not reached 18 years of age at the end of a taxation year. Certain specified income is not subject to ordinary tax rates in the hands of the minor, but rather is taxed at top marginal rates (generally about 50% or more, depending on province of residence). Income subject to this treatment, called "split income" of the minor child, includes:

- taxable dividends received directly or through a trust or partnership in respect of unlisted shares of a corporation (unlisted shares are shares of class not listed on a prescribed Canadian or foreign stock exchange; many of the world's major stock exchanges are prescribed in Regulations 3200 and 3201);
- amounts included in the minor's income as a shareholder benefit in consequence of the ownership by anyone of unlisted shares; and
- income from a partnership or trust derived from the provision of goods or services to a business carried on by (i) a person related to the minor, (ii) a corporation of which a related person is a specified shareholder (generally a 10% shareholder or relative of a 10% shareholder), or (iii) a professional corporation of which a person related to the minor is a shareholder. Amendments changed this type of income to that derived from the provision of property (rather than goods) or services, effective for taxation years ending after December 20, 2002, to ensure that rental income so derived will be caught by the special tax.

The 2011 federal Budget added to the concept of split income by providing that capital gains realized by a minor from a disposition of shares of a corporation to a non-arm's length person will be treated as taxable dividends that are not eligible dividends, if taxable dividends on such shares would have been considered split income (see the first bulleted item above). In other words, these capital gains will be deemed to be dividends and will not benefit from the one-half inclusion rate applicable to capital gains or the lifetime capital gain exemption. The amendments, found in new subsections 120.4(4) and (5), will apply to capital gains realized on or after March 22, 2011.

Effective for 2014 and future taxation years, the tax on split income will apply where: (1) the income is derived from a source that is a business or a rental property; and (2) a person related to the minor is (a) actively engaged on a regular basis in the activity of the trust or partnership to earn income from a business or rental property, or (b) has, in the case of a partnership, an interest in the partnership (whether held directly or through another partnership).

The special tax does not apply to income arising from property inherited from a parent. Where the minor is a full-time student in post-secondary education or is eligible for the disability tax credit, the special tax will not apply to income arising from any inherited property. Finally, the tax does not apply to a minor for a taxation year in which the minor has no parent resident in Canada at any time in the taxation year.

Recognizing that collecting tax from children could prove difficult from a legal, practical, and public relations point of view, a parent active in the business from which the income is derived is jointly and severally liable for any tax liability of the minor child.

It appears that the special tax on minors still leaves several advantages to inclusion of children as shareholders of the family business. Subject to the special corporate taxes on investment income, earnings could be dammed up in the corporation for distribution to children when they reach the age of 18, which coincidentally will typically coincide with their need for funds to finance post-secondary education. Other advantages are discussed at ¶2501.04.

As well, children who can perform legitimate employment activities can be remunerated by the corporation for the value of those services.

See ¶1490 for technical details of this tax.

[¶2529.04] *Loan to a Trust where a Child or Spouse or Common-Law Partner is the Beneficiary*

Loans and transfers to trusts for the benefit of a "designated person", being a spouse or common-law partner (as defined at ¶1113) or related minor child (including a niece and nephew), will result in attribution of the income thereon to the individual lender to the extent that it relates to a period in the year throughout which the individual was resident in Canada and the designated person was the individual's spouse or common-law partner or a child, niece or nephew who did not reach the age of 18 before the end of the year.

The amount determined in respect of a taxation year to be income of the designated person subject to attribution from the loaned or transferred property is the lesser of:

(1) the income of that person from the trust; and

(2) that proportion of the income earned by the trust from the loaned or transferred property or from property substituted therefor that the income of that person from the trust is of the aggregate income from the trust of all persons each of whom is a designated person in respect of the individual to whom the income is attributed.

As with loans to a spouse or common-law partner (see ¶2529.01, above), loans used to produce business income will not result in attribution where made to a child or child trust. Note, however, that minor children who receive dividends or other shareholder benefits from shares not listed on a Canadian or foreign stock exchange will be subject to the tax on split income as discussed under ¶2529.03, above. As well, trust income derived from the business of providing goods or services to a business in which a parent of the child participates may be subject to the tax on split income as discussed in ¶2529.03, above.

Also, although capital gains (or losses) on property loaned or transferred to a spouse or common-law partner will be attributed to the lender or donor, there is no such attribution of capital gains (except on certain farm property) on loans to a child or child trust. Accordingly, investments held for growth potential could be acquired through a trust for minor children to put the eventual gain in their hands (or in their tax brackets). This may also extend the use of the capital gains exemption (¶502) to other family members. See also ¶2529.06, below.

- *Planning Point:*

  "Canada Child Benefits" (¶1498) accumulated directly in segregated bank accounts for the benefit of minor children are considered funds of the child rather than the parent. Accordingly the interest on these funds is not attributed. So long as the funds can be traced to the Canada Child Benefit or family allowance payments, they can be invested in a lucrative investment without attribution. A formal trust is not necessary for the amounts in question; usually a joint bank account for parent and child will suffice. Canada Child Benefits for one child at an estimated $100/month payment set aside in this way and invested at a 5% return compounded monthly would amount to $34,920 by the time the child reaches 18, of which $13,320 would be interest income on which no tax would be required (unless the child has substantial other income). It is not necessary to save the entire amount received, but you should be careful to set aside the amount to be saved in a separate account for the child(ren), and to be able to trace all amounts in that account to Canada Child Benefit cheques. Strictly speaking, this rule does not extend to parallel provincial programs, such as the B.C. family bonus, but so far the CRA has been willing to apply the same policy of non-attribution to provincial as well as federal benefits.

Income earned by investing Universal Child Care Benefit ("UCCB") payments is not subject to the attribution rules, such that they can be invested in the child's name (or for the benefit of the child) without attribution to the parent. Note that the UCCB is cancelled, so its final payment occurred in June 2016. Previous payments remain exempt from attribution regardless.

(ITA: 74.3; 74.5; 75(2); IT-369R Attribution of trust income to settlor; IT-510 Transfers and loans of property made after May 22, 1985 to related minor; IT-511R Interspousal and certain other transfers and loans of property)

[¶2529.05] *Loan or Transfer of Property to a Child or Relative Over 17 Years of Age*

If you loan or transfer property to your child, brother, sister, niece or nephew who is under 18 years of age, the income earned on the transferred property will be deemed to be your income. This rule ceases to operate on income earned on the property after the recipient has reached 18 years of age. It follows that where property is *transferred* to a child, etc., who is over 17 years of age, the income earned is taxed in the child's hands.

Notwithstanding the general rule above, income on loans to non-arm's length persons may be attributed to the lender unless the loan is made at commercial or prescribed rates of interest, or it can be demonstrated that the purpose of the loan was not to shift income. Non-arm's length persons include parents and children, grandparents and grandchildren, etc., adopted children, and brothers and sisters, but not nieces and nephews. This rule extends to loans through a trust for the benefit of non-arm's length persons, and to indebtedness created otherwise than by loan (e.g., by sale of property without actually receiving proceeds). See ¶977.

Note that the rules do, however, allow 15% of tuition fees, together with the per month education credit (the education and textbook credits have been repealed effective January 1, 2017), to be transferred as a tax credit to supporting persons to a maximum of $750 (representing $5,000 of combined tuition and education amounts — see ¶1339).

- *Planning Point:*

  Consider putting property in the hands of children 18 and over to help them finance education or housing costs. Property gifted to adult children will not result in attribution, whereas loans from you to, or indebtedness owing to you from, adult children may result in attribution to you of income earned by the children on the loan or on property acquired through the indebtedness. In gifting property other than money to children, however, the property is deemed disposed of at fair market value and any capital gain inherent in the property will be taxable to you. (Exceptions exist for farm or fishing property.)

(ITA: 56(4.1), (4.2); 74.1; IT-440R2 Transfer of Rights to Income)

[¶2529.06] *Capital Gains Splitting*

As described earlier, funds can be loaned or given to an irrevocable trust for children of any age — typically minors — and invested in assets with good appreciation potential. Although income will attribute back to the lender/donor (assuming it is a resident parent, aunt or uncle), the eventual capital gains can be taxed to the child, who can also utilize its own capital gains exemption (if the property is qualified). There is a specific exclusion from these rules for farm property transferred under a tax-deferred rollover to the child (¶1759(A)); such property will create attribution of capital gain to the transferor. Furthermore, as discussed at ¶2529.03 above, the 2011 federal Budget added to the split income tax by providing that capital gains realized by a minor from a disposition of shares of a non-publicly listed corporation to a non-arm's length person will be treated as taxable dividends that are not eligible dividends. As such, these amounts will not benefit from the one-half inclusion rate for capital gains and will not qualify for the capital gains exemption.. Previously, the CRA unsuccessfully attacked such structures using the GAAR in *Gwartz v. The Queen*, 2013 DTC 1122 (T.C.C.).

It is arguable that something of the same general capital gain transfer result can be achieved with a spouse or common-law partner where the transferee borrows money at arm's length to acquire capital property and the transferor loans or gives money to the transferee to pay off the debt. This is a sophisticated and perhaps speculative argument based on the fact that subsection 74.1(3) is not replicated in section 74.2. It can be justified in policy terms on the basis that only gains arising in future can be split through this mechanism. However, it is not clear that the desired result will in fact be achieved, and accordingly caution should be used and professional advice should be sought in pursuing this strategy. By contrast, it seems clear that capital gains splitting with children is permitted. In both cases, any income earned on the investments will be attributed.

Attribution of both income and gain can always be avoided where loans or dispositions to family members are made on commercial terms or for investment in an active business endeavour of the recipient.

It used to be thought, prior to 1988, that where a capital gain was realized in the hands of a spouse or child on assets acquired with funds subject to income attribution, the income on the gain element would not be subject to attribution. The CRA appears to have changed its position on this with the issuance of Interpretation Bulletin IT-511R. There is some doubt as to whether the old position or the new position is valid. See ¶977.

- *Planning Point:*

  If you can identify investments with low current yield but high capital gain potential, consider giving or loaning money to children (including minor children) for such investments. Even though the income may be attributed to you, the capital gain will be taxed to the children and subject to their tax rates and, for qualified property, capital gain exemptions.

- *Planning Point:*

  Any strategy for multiplying capital gains through the use of attribution rules needs to be carefully considered, especially in light of the Tax Court of Canada's decision in *Gervais v. The Queen*, 2014 DTC 1119 (T.C.C.). In that case, the taxpayers sought to implement a so-called "half loaf" strategy to realize an exempt capital gain in the hands of a shareholder's spouse through the use of gifts and purchases. The Tax Court found that the purchased shares were not held on capital account and, therefore, were not eligible for the capital gains exemption.

(ITA: 74.1; 74.2; 74.5; 75; 75.1)

[¶2529.07] *Canada Pension Plan Splitting*

The *Canada Pension Plan* (CPP) contains rules which allow spouses or common-law partners who are living together (not separated or divorced) to assign retirement pensions to each other. With assignment, each spouse can receive a portion of the other's CPP pension. The amount depends on how long you lived together and on your contributory periods. For example, if you lived together for 20% of both your contributory periods, you keep 80% of your pension and the remaining 20% is divided equally between you and your spouse. It appears that where both spouses are receiving CPP pensions (or one CPP and one QPP pension), the pension sharing must apply to both. Pension sharing commences the month following approval of an application by either spouse to Human Resources Development Canada, and can be terminated by joint application or on certain contingencies such as divorce or death.

The attribution rules specifically provide that an income assigned under these rules (or comparable Quebec Pension Plan rules) is not attributable back to the assignor. It follows that in the right set of circumstances (for example, where one spouse is receiving a pension and the other is not) assignment may result in favourable income splitting.

(*Canada Pension Plan*: 65.1; *Retirement Pension*, website document www.hrdc-drhc.gc.ca/isp/cpp/retire_e.shtml; ITA: 74.1)

[¶2529.08] *Pension Income Splitting*

For 2007 and later years, pension income can be split between spouses or common-law partners. See ¶2533.25.

[¶2529a] TRUSTS FOR CHILDREN; STATUS OF PREFERRED BENEFICIARY ELECTIONS

The preferred beneficiary election allows a trust to accumulate income that is subject to tax in the hands of a beneficiary who is disabled and eligible for the disability tax credit (rather than being subject to tax at the trust level). With other children who are beneficiaries and not disabled, one of the techniques described below may be desirable.

[¶2529a.15] *Dealing with Trust Income without the Election*

A number of techniques have been offered in the tax community to designate funds to a specific beneficiary without current payment, and perhaps to continue the deferral of actual payments to the beneficiary past the age of majority (generally 18). This is usually not so much a matter of tax planning as of the reluctance of parents to cede accumulated income to an 18-year-old rather than controlling it to ensure, say, payment of university tuition. Some of the proposals are as follows.

In new situations, it may be better to have a separate trust for each child which provides for non-discretionary vesting subject to an age condition. These so-called "subsection 104(18) trusts" (described below and in ¶454) would seem to allow funds to accumulate to age 21 of the beneficiary. At age 21, current income must be paid out annually, but it would seem that accumulated income could still be controlled by the trustees.

Ordinary rules, generally speaking, provide that income earned by an *inter vivos* trust in a year is taxed at top personal rates (generally 50% or more) in the trust unless the income is *paid or payable* to beneficiaries in the year, in which case it is taxed to the recipient beneficiaries. Some alleviation is provided by a rule that where trust income has not become payable in the year and was held in the trust for a person under 21 before the end of the year who has a vested right to it otherwise than by the exercise (or non-exercise) of discretion which right is not subject to a future condition (except that the individual survive till an age not exceeding 40), the trust income is deemed payable and taxed to the minor and not the trust (see ¶454 for details).

The remaining alternatives amount to putting current earnings in the hands of minor children directly, either through promissory notes or actual payment to the child, or indirectly through payment to a trust in which the amounts vest immediately and indefeasibly in a particular beneficiary. Where a new trust is set up which meets the vested indefeasibly test, this seems to imply that the beneficiary must be able to access the funds as soon as he or she reaches the age of majority, which typically defeats the purpose of ensuring that the trustees can ensure that the funds are held for post-secondary education. On the other hand, some authorities feel that a vested sub-trust will, as a practical matter, render it more difficult for a child to utilize funds nominally in the hands of trustees, even if the child has a vested right to the funds. On this issue you must obtain legal advice, and decide if the cost of yet another level of trusts is worth the protection provided.

Since income must be paid or payable in the year, it is essential to have a trustee's resolution in the year to pay the income once it is determined (usually income cannot be determined at December 31, any more than you can determine your income before your T4 and T5 slips arrive). This should make the amount payable and avoid taxation in the trust.

Where the trust owns a family business corporation, it has been suggested that the trust can issue non-voting, redeemable, non-retractable preferred shares by way of payment, which would presumably meet the payment criteria but defer the transfer of actual funds until the shares are redeemed by the company. These ideas require caution and professional advice.

[¶2529a.20] *Twenty-One-Year Taxation of Gains in Trust*

In addition to the difficulty of avoiding tax in the trust at top marginal rates, there is another long-run concern with trusts for family members. Canadian tax rules require that the assets of a personal trust are deemed to be disposed of and reacquired every 21 years, thus ensuring periodic taxation of increases in the value of trust assets (such as corporate shares). This rule was introduced in 1972, but its implementation was deferred under complex rules just before it would have taken effect in 1993. However, it has now been reinstituted and was effective for the first time on January 1, 1999.

- *Planning Point:*

  If income is to be made paid or payable to the trust beneficiary to avoid taxation in the trust, there should be a trustees' resolution in place before year end (December 31) each year to say that the trust income is payable as of December 31 and will be paid when the amount can be determined.

- *Planning Point:*

  Plan trust asset acquisitions and dispositions in light of the 21-year deemed disposition rules.

- *Planning Point:*

  Planning for the 21st anniversary of a trust should begin well in advance of that date, for, among other things, a court application regarding a variation of the trust may be necessary.

- *Planning Point:*

  Notwithstanding the many problems associated with the use of trusts for children, they can in many situations remain a valuable tool in providing for your family on a tax-effective basis. Although they may no longer serve a current income splitting purpose, capital gains splitting and potential income splitting when the children reach 18 deserve consideration.

[¶2529d] TAX PLANNING FOR POST-SECONDARY EDUCATION

[¶2529d.05] *Registered Education Savings Plan (RESP)*

These plans originated as a tax splitting device, but have been taken over and regularized by a series of government revisions into an incentive program to encourage individuals to accumulate savings to provide for the post-secondary education of named "beneficiaries", typically children or grandchildren. There are, however, no relationship requirements imposed as between the contributor and beneficiary, so that you may set up an RESP for any relative or deserving beneficiary, including yourself.

An RESP beneficiary must be a Canadian resident who can provide a Canadian Social Insurance Number (SIN).

The benefits of an RESP arise through three mechanisms:

(1) tax deferral, in that income earned on the (non-deductible) contributions you make to the plan is not subject to tax as it is earned; accordingly income accumulates more rapidly in the plan than it would in the hands of the contributor;

(2) income splitting, in that when amounts are paid out of the plan for the post-secondary education of a beneficiary they will be taxed to the beneficiary, whose tax rate is typically lower at that time than the contributor's tax rate; and

(3) incentive grants, in that the government will match contributions with 20% grants paid to the plan on contributions of up to $2,500 per year.

As a contributor (subscriber) to an RESP, you are *not* entitled to a deduction in respect of your contribution; however, the interest income (or other investment income) earned in the plan on your contribution is not taxed in your hands. Rather, the investment income earned in the plan is accumulated free of tax and will be taxed in the student's (child's) hands only when the child receives funds from the plan. See ¶456.

There is no limit to the amount of annual contributions that can be made on behalf of a particular beneficiary.

However, penalty provisions impose an overall "lifetime" per beneficiary limit of:

- for 1997 through 2006 inclusive, $42,000, and
- for 2007 and later years, $50,000.

These contribution limits apply to contributions on behalf of any particular intended beneficiary no matter how many plans are established by how may contributors. A penalty tax of 1% per month of any excess contributions is assigned *pro rata* to each contributor's contributions. The objective, of course, is that the limits cannot be avoided by establishing more than one RESP or by having different subscribers establish RESPs. Excess contributions can be withdrawn.

Contributions can be made until the plan beneficiary is 31 years of age (35 years in the case of a single beneficiary plan for a disabled beneficiary).

In general, the rules ensure that plans must provide that education benefits are only paid to *bona fide* students in attendance in qualifying educational programs at post-secondary educational institutions. As well, the plans must provide for termination after 35 years (40 years for "specified" plans, i.e., single beneficiary plans for a disabled beneficiary). A 1996 amendment eased the rules by permitting an RESP beneficiary to also receive assistance for education from another source. For 1997 and later years, the rules were further eased to permit minor siblings to be substituted for each other as plan beneficiaries.

It is possible under these plans for the original capital contributions to be returned to the contributor, typically in the event that no related beneficiary qualifies by taking post-secondary education within the required time frame.

Consequential amendments effective on Royal Assent December 15, 2004, allow a department, agency or institution that maintains a child or the public trustee or curator of a province to enter into or act in respect of RESPs for that child.

Refunds of RESP earnings may be made to a contributor where none of the intended beneficiaries is pursuing post-secondary education by age 21 and the plan has been in place for at least 10 years. Earnings so returned will be taxable income but not earned income for RRSP purposes. However, returned plan earnings may be contributed to an RRSP of the contributor or the contributor's spouse or common-law partner (as defined at any particular time in ¶1113) to the extent the contributor has adequate RRSP contribution room. (Remember that to the extent RRSP contributions of earlier years fall short of contribution limits, the unused contribution room accumulates and carries forward indefinitely.) Plan earnings received by the contributor which are not contributed to an RRSP (whether because they exceed RRSP contribution room or otherwise) are subject to a special tax of 20% in addition to regular tax payable. See the discussion at ¶2612.65.

RESPs are of two types: group plans and individual plans. In either case the plan is offered under the auspices of a "promoter" who is responsible for the terms, administration and registration of the plan, and for ensuring that the assets are maintained in a trust company. Group plans are typically more rigid, specifying a schedule of payments by the contributor and, generally speaking, controlling the investments made for the plan. Individual plans provide the contributor with greater control over investments made and the timing and amount of educational assistance payments made to beneficiaries. Group plans typically have the virtue of simplicity and more or less compulsory savings. Individual plans are likely to be of greater interest to more sophisticated investors who are accustomed to managing their own investments and are comfortable with seeking tax and investment advice as needed. Plans may be for each child or for all children in a family. Family plans may provide more flexibility to tailor benefits to each child, although individual plans permit transfers of assets to the plans of siblings.

Generally speaking, a transfer of property from one RESP to another RESP can be made without tax consequences (i) where there is a common beneficiary under the transferor plan and the transferee plan; or (ii) between two plans with siblings as beneficiaries, provided that either the transferee plan allows more than one beneficiary under the plan, or the beneficiary of the transferee plan had not attained 21 years of age when the plan was entered into. (For transfers before 2011, the second permitted transfer above was between two sibling plans where the beneficiary under the transferee plan was under 21 years of age.)

Funds accumulated in an RESP and used as intended for full-time education are subject to few restrictions. Generally speaking, an RESP is permitted to make an educational assistance payment (EAP) to an individual only if, at the time of the payment, the individual is enrolled as a student in either a qualifying educational program (which is generally a full-time program) or a specified educational program (which is a part-time program) at a post-secondary educational institution. Individuals enrolled in a qualifying educational program may receive up to $5,000 of EAPs during their first 13-week period of study. Thereafter, there is no dollar limit on the amount of EAPs. Students enrolled in a specified educational program may receive up to $2,500 of EAPs during each 13-week period of study. For 2008 and later taxation years, the requirement that EAPs be made only during periods of enrolment is relaxed by providing a six-month grace period for making EAPs. An RESP may now provide for the payment of an EAP to an individual for up to six months after the individual ceased to be enrolled as a student in a qualifying educational program or a specified educational program, as the case may be. However, this additional flexibility will apply only where the payment would have qualified under the normal rules for EAPs if it had been made immediately before the individual's enrolment ceased. Thus, for example, an individual who had received a $2,000 EAP while enrolled in a ten-week specified educational program would be entitled to receive up to $500 of additional EAPs during the six-month period following the end of the program (that is, without having to enrol in another program). These amendments apply to the 2008 and subsequent taxation years, but they do not apply in respect of cessations of enrolment that occurred before 2008

The benefits of RESPs must be weighed carefully, not simply in tax terms, but with an understanding of plan provisions in the event that beneficiaries do not ultimately attend designated schools within the anticipated time frame.

The CRA puts out a guide called *Registered Education Savings Plans (RESPs)*, (RC4092).

- *Planning Point:*

  Frequent changes to the RESP rules in recent years make these plans attractive as a vehicle for setting aside savings for the higher education of your children, grandchildren, or other young relatives. Permitted plan terms have become far more generous in terms of benefiting your designated beneficiaries and obtaining at least some refund of contributions if those beneficiaries do not in fact go on to higher education as intended. Moreover, federal supplements to your contributions are available, as discussed in the following subsections, and Alberta and Quebec offer enhanced inducements for beneficiaries resident in those provinces. These too are discussed below.

- *Planning Point:*

  If you have invested in a RESP and it begins to appear that no beneficiary will use the plan before its mandatory 35-year expiration (40 years in the case of a single beneficiary plan for a disabled beneficiary), you should consider foregoing RRSP contributions, if necessary, to ensure adequate contribution room to cover a return of plan earnings, as discussed in ¶2612.65. Remember that only earnings give rise to income; contributions can be returned without tax consequences to the extent of contributions made to the plan.

(ITA: 146.1(6), (7); IC 93-3R1; Income Tax Folio: S3-F10-C1 Qualified Investments – RRSPs, RESPs, RRIFs, RDSPs and TFSAs; Other Publications: CRA Information Sheet *Registered Education Savings Plans (RESPs)* (RC4092))

[¶2529d.10] *Canada Education Savings Grants ("CESGs")*

This program is intended to create a further incentive for taxpayers to save through RESPs by providing a direct federal grant to any valid RESP equal to 20% of the first $2,500 per year contributed for each child under 18 years of age. Grants are limited to a specified annual amount. (There is also an overall lifetime maximum of $7,200 of grants for each beneficiary of an RESP.) The grant itself is not included in calculating the lifetime RESP contribution limit, nor in calculating annual contribution limits. Thus, where a $4,000 contribution was made in a year, the grant would provide an additional 20% of $2,500 = $500, so that the total added to the plan would be $4,500 (plus income earned in the plan). Similarly, a contribution or series of contributions which reach the current $50,000 annual limit (for a particular beneficiary) will generate grants in addition to the $50,000, as discussed further below.

The basic annual *grant* limitations (as opposed to contribution limitations) are $500 per year for contributions made in 2007 or later. This basic limit is enhanced, beginning in 2005, by doubling the matching rate to 40% on the first $500 of annual contributions to an RESP for the child of a family with income up to the limit of the lowest marginal rate bracket. Such families may also be entitled to benefit from the Canada Learning Bond program discussed in ¶2529d.15. Families with incomes in the second rate bracket will be entitled to a 30% matching rate on the first $500 of annual contributions to an RESP. Family income will be determined under the Canada Child Benefit rules at ¶1498.

The supplemental grants for lower income families mean that the maximum grant is now $600 per year ($500 for contributions in 2005 or 2006) for a family with income below the lowest marginal rate (40% of the first $500 contributed plus 20% of an additional contribution of up to $2,000) and $550 per year for a family with income below the second rate bracket. However, the lifetime grant limit for each child remains $7,200.

To obtain the grant, the beneficiary must obtain a Canadian Social Insurance Number (SIN), which has to be used when applying for the grant, and must be resident in Canada at the time the grant is made. Obtaining a SIN for a Canadian resident child typically presents no difficulty. With this, you can open an RESP for the child. The RESP provider should provide you with details about the grants available to you, and make the necessary applications on your behalf.

The CESG program is administered by Employment and Social Development Canada (ESDC), which maintains a section of its website devoted to this subject (most recently found at www.esdc.gc.ca/en/student_loans/resp), and a toll-free telephone line capable of providing detailed technical information (1-888-276-3624). If you are merely requesting printed information (pamphlets and the like), there is another toll-free number, 1-800-622-6232. ESDC in turn has devolved much of the administration of this program on the RESP administrators, who actually apply for the grants for specified plan beneficiaries.

As might be expected, the grants are hedged with complex rules to prevent possible misuse. On the positive side of this complexity, the program includes rules to permit shortfalls in contributions in some years to be made up in later years. The machinery is that any child who is a Canadian resident accumulates "grant room" at a rate of, for years before 2007, $400 per year, and for years after 2006, $500 per year, from the later of the child's date of birth or January 1, 1998 until the age of 17 (including the year the child turns 17). Grant room accumulates whether or not a child is an RESP beneficiary. If all RESP contributions made for a beneficiary in one year do not attract the full $500 (or, before 2007, $400) of CESG, the unused part of the CESG will be added to the beneficiary's grant room and will be available for use in another year. In this case, the CESG will be paid on contributions of up to $5,000 a year ($4,000 for contributions made in 2006 and earlier years), with the maximum CESG payable in any particular year being $1,000 ($800 for payments in 2006 and earlier years).

While unused contribution room carries forward, contributions in a year in excess of contribution room do not carry forward to generate grants in later years. Thus, to take the extreme case, a top bracket "subscriber" who contributes (after 2006) for a particular beneficiary, say in the year of birth (2008), the full $50,000 permitted (in total by all subscribers in respect of a particular beneficiary), will generate a grant of $500, but will be able to generate no grants in later years for that beneficiary. Essentially, the parent is wagering that the tax-free compound return on the $50,000 over 18 years (assuming the RESP is created at birth) will exceed the $7,200 available under the grant program. This is discussed further in a planning point below.

On the hedging side, only net new contributions for a beneficiary will receive a grant. Where contributions to RESPs made before the Budget are subsequently withdrawn, contributions for the remainder of the year and for the two subsequent years will not receive the grant. The beneficiary will also lose the grant contribution room that would ordinarily accrue during those two following years. However, these restrictions will not apply to a withdrawal of contributions which earned no grant if the total of such withdrawals in a year is not more than $200.

Contributions for children aged 16 and 17 will receive a grant only if there have been contributions of at least $100 per year in any four years before the year in which the beneficiary turned 16, or if total previous contributions for the children reached $2,000 before the year the beneficiary turned 16. However, as a transitional measure, a child turning 16 or 17 in 1998 was eligible if he or she was a beneficiary of an RESP during any four years before 1998.

If contributions are withdrawn for non-educational purposes from an RESP which has received a CESG, the RESP trustee will be required to make a CESG repayment equal to 20% of the withdrawal. Where a plan contains both contributions which did and contributions which did not earn CESG (because before 1998 or in excess of grant contribution room), the CESG earning contributions will be considered withdrawn first; that is, the 20% repayment will be required on withdrawals until the CESG is in effect exhausted.

Grant repayment will also be required where a payment of RESP income is made for non-educational purposes; where a beneficiary is replaced (except by a sibling or a beneficiary related to the subscriber by blood or adoption); and where a plan is terminated or revoked. Repayments may also be required on transfers between plans.

Grants will not be earned for "family plans" unless the plan provides that no beneficiary 21 or older may be added (as all new plans must provide after 1998). Similarly, grants will not be allowed after 1999 to plans unless they provide that educational assistance payments in respect of courses of less than three months do not exceed the cost of tuition plus $300 per week of study (as all new plans must provide after 1998).

The only useful technical discussion of the details of this program was eventually published by the CRA in Information Circular IC 93-3R2. Any additional information must be obtained from RESP promoters or trustees, or from direct study of the *Department of Human Resources Development Act*, Part III.1, now replaced by the *Canada Education Savings Act*, and the attendant regulations. Fortunately, these are readily accessible from the Department of Justice website at www.laws.justice.gc.ca. Any pending amendments should be available from the Bills section of the parliamentary website.

• *Planning Point:*

If your ability to contribute to RESPs will fluctuate from year to year, you should consider deferring contributions in excess of available grant contribution room in any particular year. Excess contributions do not generate the 20% government contribution, and you might want to put aside an excess contribution in one year and contribute it in a year in which matching is assured. On the other hand, this is only sound so long as you will keep the money on hand to top up a contribution which otherwise would not be matched.

• *Planning Point:*

If, on the other hand, you can afford to fund an RESP to the full extent of the permitted $50,000 per beneficiary, you face a similar but rather different set of considerations. Essentially, you must weigh the fact that the full $50,000 will generate a substantial tax-free return over the years of the plan against the fact that the government contribution will be largely lost. Thus, to take the extreme case, a top bracket "subscriber" who contributes (after 2006) for a particular beneficiary, say in the year of birth, the full $50,000 permitted (in total by all subscribers in respect of a particular beneficiary) will generate a grant of $500, but will be able to generate no grants in later years for that beneficiary. Essentially, the parent is wagering that the tax-free compound return on the $50,000 over 18 years (assuming the RESP is created at birth) will exceed the $7,200 available under the grant program. One alternative, presumably, is to contribute, say, $15,000, in the year of birth, and $2,500 in each of the subsequent 13 years. Over the 14 years the contribution will have totalled $47,500 and the grants will have totalled $7,000. In the final contribution year, the parent can contribute the remaining $2,500 permitted to make up the $50,000 lifetime limit, generate the remaining $200 grant, and have maximized both grants and contributions. The question is whether, over the 15 years, the return on the $35,000 not originally contributed would have substantially exceeded the $6,700 of government money foregone. At, for example, a 5% simple rate of return, the missing $35,000 would generate $1,750 per year as against the maximum $500 (for a top bracket taxpayer) federal CESG grant. Moreover, if $50,000 is merely spare cash to you, and you would otherwise invest it at the same rate of return, the return in the RESP accumulates without tax, which you might otherwise pay at a rate of up to nearly 50%. No general conclusion can be drawn, except that each taxpayer must weigh his or her circumstances carefully. Where large funding amounts can be readily contributed, the advantages may well outweigh the loss of government contributions. This perhaps relegates the CESG to its proper place as an incentive for those who cannot easily invest large amounts.

• *Planning Point:*

If you are planning to contribute to a plan for a child resident in Quebec, and the plan receives federal CESG grants, you should check to see if corresponding Quebec grants are available. If you are contributing to a plan registered outside Quebec, you must ensure that the plan is eligible for the Quebec grants and be familiar with the rules for obtaining them. Quebec grants are discussed at ¶2529d.23, below.

(*Canada Education Savings Act* (Bill C-5, 2004); IC 93-3R1; CRA Information Sheet *Registered Education Savings Plans (RESPs)* (RC4092))

[¶2529d.15] *Canada Learning Bonds*

The Canada Learning Bond is essentially a further inducement (in addition to the CESG program discussed above) for low-income families to set up an RESP for their children.

Essentially, the program provides a $500 Canada Learning Bond (CLB) at birth for children in families that are entitled to the National Child Benefit (NCB) supplement element of the Canada Child Benefit program (see ¶1498). In subsequent years, these children will qualify for $100 CLB instalments until age 15, in each year their family is entitled to the NCB supplement.

Children who are not eligible for the CLB at birth but whose families become entitled to the NCB supplement in a subsequent year will qualify at that time for a $500 CLB. Thereafter, they will qualify for annual $100 CLB instalments, in each year their family is entitled to the NCB supplement.

The CLB will be paid into a registered education savings plan (RESP) established by the family for the child's post-secondary education. Accordingly it will earn income in the plan along with other contributions. An additional $25 will be paid with the initial $500 bond in recognition of the cost of establishing an RESP.

The program is (apparently) synchronized with the Canada Child Benefit program so that families with the requisite income levels who have provided RESP information to the government (and applied for the Canada Child Benefit) will have deposits made automatically. The RESP terms themselves should ensure that the funds are used as intended, and repayment provisions require the trustee to return to the government amounts to which the RESP was not entitled. Adopted children seem to be entitled to the CLB on registration of the RESP and application for the Canada Child Benefit, though of course the total grants will be less to the extent they have fewer years to age 15. Such details as are readily available can be obtained from the Human Resources and Social Development Canada website at www.hrsdc.gc.ca. Look for "Canada Education Savings Program" and then on the next screen "The Canada Learning Bond".

• *Planning Point:*

If you have a child under 17 years of age and your family income is in the lowest income tax bracket, you should seriously consider the merits of enrolling your child in an RESP. Any Canadian bank or other financial institution, scholarship trust or financial planner should be able to advise you on this. Apart from the initial cost of opening the plan, which should be minimal, the mere existence of the plan will ensure annual government contributions until the child reaches the age of 15 so long as your family income is below the income threshold (which increases annually). Enrolling your child in an RESP requires you to obtain a SIN for the child; for this you contact SDC, which maintains local offices across the country (as well as a website). When you apply to an RESP provider to open a plan, ask the provided to ensure that application for the CLB is made.

• *Planning Point:*

If you are an Alberta resident, regardless of income, you may be eligible for the similar Alberta grant discussed below.

- *Planning Point:*

  Once you have obtained a SIN for the child to take advantage of this program, you should consider the advantages of filing a tax return for the child once he or she has even a small amount of earned income. This is discussed in ¶2546.

(*Canada Education Savings Act*; CRA Information Sheet *Registered Education Savings Plans (RESPs)* (RC4092))

[¶2529d.20] *Alberta Centennial Education Savings Plan (ACES)*

Note: This plan was closed by the Alberta government during 2015. The deadline for submitting a completed application to an RESP provider/ACES Plan promoter was July 31st, 2015. See the government website at http://eae.alberta.ca/funding/aces.aspx.

For young children born to a parent resident in Alberta, the province will offer what is in effect a $500 supplement to the federal CLB grant. The Alberta grant will also be available where a child is adopted by an Alberta resident. As with the federal program, someone must open an RESP for the child. The steps to obtain the Alberta grant are: (1) register the birth or adoption of the child; (2) apply for a birth certificate; (3) apply for a SIN for the child; (4) open an RESP account with a financial institution or RESP provider; and (5) apply to Alberta for the Alberta Centennial Education Savings Plan grant. The grant is intended for newborn children, natural or adopted. Applications must be received by the time the child turns two years old (although the Minister of Learning has discretion to extend this period). There is no requirement for the RESP contributor to match the initial grant of $500 but there may be a minimum contribution required to open an RESP account. Unlike the federal program, there appears to be no rule restricting the grant to lower income families.

In addition to the $500 birth grant, grants of $100 will be available to children enrolled in school in Alberta at age 8, 11, and 14 beginning with children born in 2005. A child will not have to receive previous grants in order to qualify for subsequent grants. However, the $100 grants will require a minimum matching deposit by the contributor to the RESP of $100.

The funds will be returned to the provincial government if the beneficiary has not begun post-secondary studies within 26 years of the RESP being opened. The funds will be returned to the government if they were received by a subscriber/beneficiary on the basis of false information.

Alberta contemplates that it will work with the federal government, so that once the federal government receives notification that an individual has opened an RESP account and made a valid application for the Alberta Centennial Education Savings Plan, the grant funds should be deposited into the RESP account.

(CRA Information Sheet *Registered Education Savings Plans (RESPs)* (RC4092) ; Other Publications: Alberta *Centennial Education Savings Plan Act*; Alberta Government website www.learning.gov.ab.ca/aces/caq.asp)

[¶2529d.23] *Quebec CESG Supplements*

Where subscribers to an RESP have made contributions (after February 7, 2007) to the RESP for 2007 or a later year for beneficiaries resident in Quebec at the end of that year, and the contribution has attracted a Canada Education Savings Grant (CESG — ¶2529d.10), Quebec will provide an additional grant of 10% of the contributions per year, to a maximum of $250, with an additional $50 available for low-income families. Note that the RESP subscriber need not be resident in Quebec, since the subscriber is receiving no tax benefit. The benefit is paid to the RESP for the benefit of the designated beneficiary.

Quebec has its own rules on the taxation of amounts when received by beneficiaries, and its own recapture taxes to deal with situations in which funds are withdrawn otherwise than for the intended use by the beneficiary.

In any event, the burden of compliance with the detailed rules for the application of grants will, as with federal rules, fall primarily on the plan provider. In the circumstances, where a subscriber is dealing with a non-Quebec plan provider for a beneficiary resident it Quebec, it would be wise to ensure that the provider is conversant with the Quebec rules, and will indeed obtain the available grants.

(Other Publications: May 24, 2007 Quebec *Additional Information on the Budgetary Measures,* Revenue Measures, item 1.2.1, (page A5–A18), and Section A, Appendix, 1.2.1)

[¶2529d.24] *Other Provincial Supplements*

The provinces of Saskatchewan and British Columbia may add money to an RESP through their provincial grant programs, the Saskatchewan Advantage Grant for Education Savings (SAGES) and B.C. Training and Education Savings Grant, respectively. See the government websites for details, at http://www.saskatchewan.ca/SAGES#utm_campaign=q2_2015&utm_medium=short&utm_source=%2FSAGES (Saskatchewan), and http://www2.gov.bc.ca/gov/content/education-training/k-12/support/bc-training-and-education-savings-grant (British Columbia).

[¶2529d.25] *RRSP Lifelong Learning Plans*

RESPs are essentially designed to assist savings on behalf of children. Recognizing that adult retraining will also be increasingly required, the government permits RRSP withdrawals for the purpose of financing full-time training or education for the plan annuitant or its spouse or common-law partner. Withdrawals may be made over a period of four years, but the total withdrawn may not exceed $20,000 over the four years and may not exceed $10,000 in any particular year.

RRSP funds may be withdrawn under the plan where the recipient (or spouse or common-law partner) is enrolled as a full-time student in a qualifying educational program of at least three months' duration at an eligible educational institution. The full-time requirement will not apply to disabled students. Where funds are withdrawn prior to enrolment, enrolment must occur no later than January of the year following the withdrawal.

Withdrawals from the RRSP must be repaid commencing no later than 60 days after the fifth year following the first withdrawal. Repayments will normally be required in equal annual instalments over a 10-year period. If the student does not complete the educational program, withdrawals may be added back to income unless certain conditions are met; see ¶2626a.

RRSP Learning Plan rules will be similar to Home Buyers' Plan rules in the event of death, emigration, failure of repayment, etc. See ¶2626a. The CRA puts out an excellent summary of these rules, together with the necessary forms, in its *Lifelong Learning Plan (LLP)* Guide (RC4112), available from all Tax Services Offices (¶287) or by download from its website (www.cra.gc.ca).

[¶2529d.30] *Student Loans*

Canada and most provinces have programs to underwrite student loans. Under Canada's program, the government pays interest on the loan while a student is in school and all payments are deferred until the completion of studies. For six months after graduation, interest accrues but payments are not required. Thereafter the loan is to be repaid over 9½ years. In cases of financial hardship (measured by comparing loan payments to income), the federal government may continue to pay interest costs for a period of time.

Individuals repaying student loans are allowed to claim a non-refundable tax credit (calculated at the lowest marginal tax rate) on the interest portion of repayments made in the year or the five preceding years ending after 1997 on account of student loans under the Canada Student Loans Program and provincial post-secondary student loan programs. For details, see ¶1345.

Effective January 2, 2015, the credit may be claimed for interest paid by apprentices on loans made under the *Apprentice Loans Act*.

[¶2529d.35] *Education Tax Credits*

The education and textbook tax credits were repealed effective January 1, 2017 (credits claimed for years prior to 2017 remain available as carryforwards indefinitely). Until then, full-time students are entitled to a personal amount credit (at the lowest marginal rate, federally 15%) of $400 per month for the period of study, plus a "textbook amount" of $65 per month which brings the amount eligible for credit to $465 per month. Part-time students may qualify for a credit of 15% of ($120 + $20 =) $145 per month. However, part-time students who are eligible for the disability tax credit or cannot be enrolled on a full-time basis because of mental or physical impairment qualify for the full-time credit amounts.

As well, a tax credit of 15% of eligible tuition costs may be claimed.

Tuition and education credits which the student pays insufficient tax to utilize can, within certain limits, be transferred to a spouse or common-law partner, parent or grandparent, or carried forward to the day when the student has sufficient tax to absorb them.

Education and tuition tax credit rules are discussed in detail in Chapter 13.

[¶2529d.40] *Child Care Expenses*

Students, including part-time students, may deduct child care expenses, within certain limits, for the period of study. This can include a deduction from the income of a working spouse or common-law partner where the other spouse or common-law partner is a student. See ¶1053.

[¶2529h] REGISTERED DISABILITY SAVINGS PLAN (RDSP)

The RDSP plan permits parents to contribute funds to a plan to provide for the future expenses of disabled children, and allows the older disabled and their families (and others) to contribute to a plan for later years. Contributions to the plan are not deductible, but income earned in the plan is not taxed while in the plan. Plan investments are, in effect, governed by RRSP investment rules, with certain exceptions. Plan contributions are subject to a lifetime limit of $200,000. Plan contributions will to some extent be matched by government contributions, and, in addition, the government will make continuing contributions for low-income families.

Individuals for whom a disability certificate (¶1255) has been accepted for a particular year are, for 2008 and later years, eligible in a year of disability covered by the certificate to establish a Registered Disability Savings Plan (RDSP), of which the individual is the beneficiary. The plan must be established by the disabled person, unless that person is under 18 or is not legally competent, in which case a parent or legal representative may establish the plan. As with an RESP or RRSP, the plan itself is a trust established with an "issuer" authorized to carry on the business of offering trust services in Canada. The person who establishes the plan becomes a "director", and has certain duties and obligations. There can be only one plan per beneficiary. The beneficiary must be resident in Canada when the plan is established.

A "qualifying family member" may establish an RDSP for a beneficiary, generally if the beneficiary has attained the age of majority and, in the issuer's opinion after reasonable inquiry, the beneficiary's contractual competence to enter into a disability savings plan at that time is in doubt. A qualifying family member includes a legal parent or spouse or common-law partner of the beneficiary. This temporary measure is effective as of June 29, 2012 until the end of 2019, by which time it is anticipated that provincial and territorial law will be amended to permit a trusted person to enter into a contract on behalf of an individual who may lack capacity.

Contributions can be made by anyone. Typically, they will be made by parents or other family members, but there is no limitation except that the plan directors must approve the contributions. (This permits them to maximize government contributions.) Contributions to the plan are not deductible, but they will be matched in some degree by government contributions, called Canada Disability Savings Grants (CDSGs). As well, the government will put in certain amounts for low-income families regardless of their contributions (Canada Disability Savings Bonds (CDSBs)). The grants and bonds can continue up to the end of the year in which the disabled person reaches the age of 49.

Private contributions (i.e., excluding government contributions) to a plan cannot exceed $200,000, and cannot be made after the year in which the beneficiary turns 59. Private contributions are not refundable; they must be used for the beneficiary or, on death, go to the beneficiary's estate.

Matching contributions (CDSGs) will be calculated as follows.

For families with net incomes equal to or less than the third marginal tax bracket threshold, the government will provide:

- $3 for every $1 on the first $500 of contributions;
- $2 for every $1 on the next $1,000 of contributions.

Thus, the maximum grant is $3,500, reached on a contribution of $1,500.

For families with net income above the third bracket threshold of $90,563 for 2016, the grant is:

- $1 for every $1 on the first $1,000 of contributions.

Grants are subject to a lifetime limit of $70,000 and will not be paid after the end of the year in which the beneficiary reaches the age of 49.

Government contributions (CDSBs, as opposed to matching grants) of up to $1,000 per year to a cumulative maximum of $20,000 may also be paid into the plan. The annual maximum $1,000 is paid where income of the beneficiary does not exceed the threshold at which the National Child Benefit Supplement begins to phase out. If income exceeds that threshold, the $1,000 is reduced by a formula under which it expires at the lowest marginal rate threshold. Essentially, the $1,000 is reduced by $1,000 minus income over the threshold divided by the difference between the two thresholds. No more than $20,000 may be paid under this program during the lifetime of the beneficiary.

Income is measured under the GST Credit rules (¶1496) for January payments. This means that income determinations look back to the second preceding year, although income thresholds look at the current year. That is, if there were grants or bonds payable in respect of 2009, income would be measured for 2007, although 2009 thresholds would be used. Where the beneficiary is a "qualified dependant" for GST purposes, i.e., has not turned 18 at the end of the year in question, income is the "adjusted net income" of the parent or guardian on whom the child is dependent and the cohabiting spouse or common-law partner of that parent or guardian, as calculated for GST purposes. Essentially, this is income at line 236 of each return, not counting the universal child care benefit (line 117) and the capital gain on property reacquired by the parents on foreclosure (¶518). Where the beneficiary is 18 or older at the end of the year, income is the adjusted net income for GST purposes of the beneficiary and his or her spouse or common-law partner, if any. A child for whom benefits are paid under the *Children's Special Allowances Act* (i.e., a child in foster care) for at least one month in a year is eligible for the high rates of matching grants and the full $1,000 bond amount for that year, regardless of income considerations.

The plans are intended to provide for those with long-term disabilities. Accordingly, there is a provision that government contributions and their associated earnings are subject to a 10-year "holdback", during which they cannot be distributed from the plan and must be paid back to the government if the beneficiary withdraws *any* funds from the plan (including normal annual amounts), loses eligibility for the disability tax credit, or dies. Thus, if money is withdrawn from a RDSP, any bond or grant (and associated investment income) received in the past 10 years must be repaid. However, effective in 2014, the amount of the bonds or grants to be repaid when money is withdrawn from an RDSP will change. The 2012 federal Budget announced a new proportionate repayment rule, under which every $1 withdrawn will require the repayment of $3 of any bonds or grants received in the previous 10 years, up to a maximum of the holdback amount.

Normal payments ("lifetime disability assistance payments") from the plan can commence at any time, but, as discussed above, payments which commence within 10 years of a government contribution will trigger recapture of that contribution. Normal payments, once commenced, must be made at least annually. Payments must commence no later than the year in which the beneficiary turns 60. It appears they can commence at any time, provided plan assets will not fall below the holdback level. Normal payments are closely defined, and generally speaking limited to plan assets divided by life expectancy plus three. Life expectancy is statistically determined unless there is a medical certificate setting out a life expectancy for the particular beneficiary, in which case the certificate governs.

The government contribution elements, and all investment earnings in the plan, are not taxable in the plan. Payments from the plan to the disabled beneficiary are taxable in part. Generally speaking, the non-taxable portion of any payment is the proportion of contributions remaining in the plan divided by total plan assets, not counting the holdback amount. The plan must be terminated if the disability ceases, and the remaining amounts paid to the beneficiary, subject as always to the holdback requirements. The termination payment is, as with ordinary payments, a blended payment, only part of which is taxable. The rules contemplate that the plans will be established by private trust companies, as with RRSPs and RESPs.

Where government contributions prove to have been excessive, because of the holdback rules or otherwise, and have already been paid out to the beneficiary and included in taxable income, they may be recaptured from the beneficiary and deducted from the beneficiary's income when repaid.

Payments from an RDSP will not be counted in means-tested government programs; that is, they will not be included in income reducing GST or Canada Child Benefits. As well, they will not be taken into account to reduce Old Age Security or Employment Insurance benefits.

Amounts in addition to normal payments may be withdrawn from the plan for the beneficiary, subject to two limitations. First, withdrawals will trigger the holdback rule, requiring repayment of government contributions and associated earnings of the past 10 years. Second, where the total of government grants and bonds exceeds private contributions to the plan at the end of a particular year (such plan is referred to as a "primarily government-assisted plan"), only the amount of normal lifetime disability assistance payments (LDAPs) may be withdrawn for the following year. The 2012 federal Budget increased this latter amount that may be withdrawn, effective for 2014. At that time, the amount that can be withdrawn will be the greater of the normal LDAPs for the year, and 10% of the fair market value of the RDSP assets at the beginning of the calendar year (or, if the RDSP owns a locked-in annuity, the sum of 10% of the fair market value of the RDSP assets and the total amount of periodic payments received by the RDSP in the year under the annuity).

Under current rules, beneficiaries of primarily government-assisted plans, once they reach 60 years of age, must withdraw at least the normal LDAP each year. The 2012 federal Budget announced that this minimum withdrawal limit will apply to all RDSPs, beginning in 2014. This legislation has since been enacted.

If the beneficiary ceases in fact to have, throughout a calendar year, any disability for which a disability certificate can properly be issued, the fund must be terminated and the balance paid to the beneficiary by the end of the following calendar year. The payment will be a blended payment; that is, the portion attributable to private contributions will not be taxed. Note that a cancelled disability certificate itself is not sufficient to terminate the plan; there must in fact be no disability condition. However, contributions cannot be made for a year in which there is no valid certificate at any time. The point is that a parent-initiated plan cannot be wound up by the beneficiary cancelling a certificate and taking all the money while the disability condition still exists. On the other hand, cancelling the certificate will prevent further contributions in subsequent years until it is reinstated.

(ITA: 56(1)(q.1); 60(z); 146.4; 160.2; 205; 206; Other Publications: *Canada Disability Savings Act*; *Canada Disability Savings Regulations*)

[¶2529h.01] *Specified Years and Specified Disability Savings Plan*

In a "specified year" of an RDSP of a beneficiary, the withdrawal limits that apply where total government-provided Canada Disability Savings Grants ("CDSG") and Canada Disability Savings Bonds ("CDSB") made into the plan before the year exceed the private contributions into the plan before the year, do not apply in that specified year. Prior to 2011, a "specified year" was the year in which a medical doctor certifies in writing that the beneficiary's state of health was such that, in the professional opinion of the medical doctor, the beneficiary was not likely to survive more than five years, and each of the five calendar years following the particular year. The 2011 federal Budget amended the definition somewhat by extending the amount of specified years, by including, if the plan is a "specified disability savings plan" ("SDSP"), the year of the medical certification plus each subsequent taxation year.

An SDSP is essentially an RDSP under which the beneficiary is certified, as discussed above, as having an expected life of no more than five years, where the plan holder makes an election to have the plan be an SDSP and proper notification is provided to the CRA.

Under another amendment from the 2011 federal Budget, if the plan is an SDSP, the 10-year repayment rule, under which CDSG grants and CDSB bonds paid into the plan within the previous ten years must be repaid if withdrawn, is relaxed. As long as the taxable portions of withdrawals (CCSGs, CDSBs, and income earned in the plan) in a year do not exceed $10,000, the grants and bonds do not have to be repaid. If non-taxable withdrawals are also made, the total withdrawals can exceed $10,000. However, if the $10,000 taxable amount is exceeded in a year, the plan ceases to be an SDSP, meaning that the 10-year repayment rule will be operative with respect to grants and bonds still in the plan.

The 2011 Budget amendments received Royal Assent on June 26, 2011, and apply to the 2011 and subsequent year. However, a transitional rule applies to beneficiaries who obtain the medical certification before 2012, in which case, the 2011 $10,000 taxable withdrawal limit as described above can be utilized in 2012, effectively making it a $20,000 taxable withdrawal limit in 2012.

[¶2529h.05] *Rollover to RDSP upon Death of Parent or Grandparent*

In the March 2010 federal Budget, the government announced a new rollover (inclusion followed by a deduction) similar to the existing deduction provided for financially dependent infirm children and grandchildren of a deceased plan holder of an RRSP, RRIF, or RPP. The existing rules generally allow the deduction where the child uses the proceeds received upon the death to make a contribution to the child's RRSP or to purchase a life annuity or an annuity payable to age 90.

The new rollover rules will allow the child or grandchild to make a similar deduction where the proceeds are contributed to an RDSP of which they are a beneficiary. The rollover will be permitted only to the extent that there is sufficient RDSP contribution room. The contribution must be made in the year of receipt of the proceeds or within 60 days after the end of the year. The new rules generally apply to deaths occurring after March 3, 2010 where the contributions are made after June 2011. However, transitional rules will allow a similar deduction in situations where the death of the RRSP or RRIF annuitant or RPP member occurred in 2008, 2009, or 2010 and the contribution is made after June 2011 and before 2012. See the discussion in Chapter 19 at ¶1914.17.

[¶2529h.10] *Rollover from RESP to RDSP*

Accumulated income earned in an RESP (see ¶1001.05) can be rolled over on a tax-free basis to an RDSP (¶1001.05). The new rules provide that a subscriber of an RESP and a holder of an RDSP may make a joint election in prescribed form to transfer the income of the RESP to the RDSP if, at the time of the election, the RESP beneficiary is the beneficiary under the RDSP and

- the beneficiary has a severe and prolonged mental impairment that prevents him or can reasonably be expected to prevent him from enrolling in post-secondary education; or
- the payment is made in the 35th year after the year in which the RESP began, or it is made in the 10th or subsequent year after the RESP began and each beneficiary under the RESP is at least 21 years old of age and is not eligible to receive educational assistance payments.

The legislation provides that the promoter of the RESP must file the election with the Minister "without delay". If the election is properly made, the income transferred from the RESP to the RDSP is not included in the beneficiary's (or any other person's) income. The amount so transferred on a rollover basis is subject to the lifetime $200,000 contribution limit for RDSPs.

[¶2530] REGISTERED RETIREMENT SAVINGS PLAN (RRSP)

This method of tax deferral is one of the most significant tax planning ideas available to Canadian taxpayers. By making contributions to a plan not later than 60 days after the current year end a deduction from income can be taken in the current year for the amount within certain limitations (see ¶2604). An immediate tax saving results and the tax refund can be reinvested or used currently for personal purposes.

Chapter 26 comprises a detailed RRSP planning guide to assist in calculating RRSP contributions before the annual deadline and to answer common questions on RRSPs. The information that follows here is only a brief summary of RRSP planning opportunities.

The 2011 federal Budget introduced some significant changes regarding penalty taxes applicable to RRSPs. The main objective of these changes is to subject RRSPs (and RRIFs) to certain penalty taxes under Part XI.01 that apply to TFSAs in respect of "advantages", "prohibited investments", and "non-qualified investments". See Chapter 26 at ¶2622.05 for more details.

[¶2530.05] *Contribution Limits*

For 2016, the contribution limit is 18% of 2015 income to a maximum of $25,370 (but possibly reduced by several factors; see ¶2604), plus any unused RRSP room from previous years. Earned income, generally speaking, is income from employment, business and real estate rentals, and certain royalties, but does not include income from investments.

Interest paid on money borrowed to make a contribution to an RRSP is not deductible for income tax purposes. Interest on original loans made for contributions prior to that date is still deductible even if the loan has been refinanced (although the CRA may see an abuse if the refinanced loan makes no provision for repayment of principal).

Amounts paid by you directly for RRSP (or RRIF) administration fees or other services are not deductible.

[¶2530.10] *Spousal Plans*

Deductible contributions may also be made to a registered retirement savings plan for the benefit of a spouse or common-law partner (see ¶2624.05). If the spouse or common-law partner will have lower income at the time the funds are withdrawn and, therefore, be in a lower tax rate bracket, it may be more advantageous to contribute funds to a spousal RRSP. In addition, annuity payments received from a spousal RRSP will be qualifying income for the spouse's (or common-law partner's) $2,000 pension income deduction (¶1311).

If funds are withdrawn from any spousal RRSP you will be required to include in your income an amount equal to your contributions to a spousal plan in the year of withdrawal and the two immediately preceding years. This will apply if the spouse or common-law partner has made his or her own contributions to the plan and the withdrawal could be considered to have been from the spouse's or common-law partner's contributions, and even if your contributions were made to one spousal plan but the withdrawal was from another. If the value of the assets in the spousal RRSP is less than the amount contributed to it (that is, if there is a loss recorded by the plan) only the lesser amount need be included in your income.

However, your beneficiary spouse or common-law partner may make a withdrawal from a spousal RRSP without attracting tax in your (contributing spouse's) hands when at the time of the withdrawal the contributing and beneficiary spouse or common-law partner were living separate and apart by reason of marriage breakdown. An RRSP can also be split on a marriage or relationship breakdown. Funds may be transferred without tax consequences to a spouse's or common-law partner's plan after the breakdown of the marriage if the transfer is made pursuant to a decree, order or judgment of a court or a written separation agreement. See Chapter 23.

Where a spousal RRSP has been converted to retirement income or to a RRIF, the minimum required annual payments can be made to the spouse or common-law partner without attracting tax in the contributor's hands, even if the conversion has occurred within the preceding three years. See ¶2624.05 and ¶2632.05.

[¶2530.15] *Special Contributions to an RRSP*

There are also provisions to make extra contributions to an RRSP based on certain receipts (for example, superannuation or pension benefits, retiring allowances and certain receipts from a deferred profit sharing plan — see ¶2612.05). Extra contributions based on retiring allowances (which include termination payments) are being phased out, insofar as only the portion of a retiring allowance based on years of service prior to 1996 will qualify for this treatment. On the other hand, RRSP contributions representing termination payments could, prior to 1998, trigger or increase Alternative Minimum Tax (AMT) liability. The government announced in 1998 that it would reverse this policy retroactive to 1994, and refund any AMT liabilities for 1994 through 1997 based on such contributions to the extent the AMT has not already been utilized to reduce ordinary tax of other years. Taxpayers who suffered AMT liability in these circumstances should by now have received the promised refund.

Certain lump-sum entitlements from various tax-deferred plans (such as registered pension plans and deferred profit sharing plans) may be transferred directly into an RRSP without tax consequences; note that in these cases the transfers must be authorized directly from one plan to another (¶2612.35).

[¶2530.20] *Undercontributions and Overcontributions*

Where your RRSP contributions deducted for a particular year are less than your annual contribution limits (the maximum you could have contributed based on 18% of prior year earned income up to the dollar maximum) for that year, the difference accumulates and carries forward to provide contribution room in the following years in addition to that arising from immediate prior year's income (and special contributions). See ¶2610.15 for more detail. This accumulated carryforward is reported to you on your annual assessment statement from the CRA.

On the other hand, contributions in excess of your accumulated contribution room are not only not deductible, but to the extent they exceed $2,000 at the end of a month are subject to a monthly penalty tax until they are withdrawn from the RRSP (tax-free, since they were not deducted) or sufficient new contribution room becomes available to shelter them. The $2,000 is cumulative for all years commencing with 1991. The $2,000 buffer before penalty applies is intended to provide a margin of protection against inadvertent overcontributions. However, some taxpayers use it simply to shelter the income on an additional $2,000 from tax.

When the overcontribution limit change was announced on February 26, 1995 to be effective in 1996, provision was made to phase out existing overcontributions without excessive tax resulting from the change (although at the price of excessive complexity and limitations on current contributions until the excess is absorbed). This is discussed at ¶2611.15.

[¶2530.25] *General Plans and Self-Administered Plans*

Most RRSPs are administered by financial institutions and investment managers, who determine the general nature and specific details of the investments to be made with the funds you invest with them. They ensure that the plan investments comply with regulations specifying permissible RRSP investments to avoid penalty taxes. These plans, or their managers, usually explain to you their specific investment philosophy, ranging from guaranteed investment certificates to speculative stocks and bonds. Effective in 1995, there is even a plan which specializes in "C" type (compound interest) Canada Savings Bonds (CSBs). This plan required government cooperation because of the personalized nature of CSBs. Effective in 1997, the government introduced an "RRSP bond" similar to CSBs but available for February RRSP contributions or for substitution for existing investments in an RRSP; see ¶2627.45.

The rules and regulations relating to RRSPs also permit self-administered RRSPs. Self-administered RRSPs are widely available from various financial institutions and allow the individual greater flexibility and control over the assets and performance of their plan. With a self-administered RRSP, it becomes your own responsibility to determine each investment of the plan (although you can invest in other general RRSPs) and ensure compliance with investment limitations.

Self-administered RRSPs can be effective vehicles for tax planning. For example, individuals with a cash balance in their respective RRSPs and fully paid for securities in their investment portfolio could roll their investments into their self-administered RRSP in exchange for the cash value in the plan. This cash could then be used to pay off a mortgage or other loans that may be outstanding upon which the interest expense is non-deductible. The mechanics of the rollover involves a deemed disposition of the securities at fair market value on the day of the transfer with the RRSP immediately repurchasing the shares at fair market value. As a result, capital gains or losses can arise on the transfer. Any capital losses that arise are denied for tax purposes.

Self-administered RRSPs can also be used to defer future gains on portfolio securities presently owned. For example, if the individual expects a large future appreciation in a particular security owned, but the present gain is minimal, he or she could sell the security into an RRSP where the gain would be deferred for tax purposes until the funds were withdrawn from the plan. This deferral could be for many years if the funds are left in the plan to accumulate tax free until retirement. Note, however, that the tax-free 50% of the gain will be lost, since it cannot be removed from the RRSP on a tax-free basis. Also, caution must be exercised because the disposition to the RRSP will be a disposition at fair market value for tax purposes, causing a capital gain on any prior increase in value of the security while held personally, while any capital loss will be denied. Accordingly, the scheme has limited value where there has already been a substantial shift in the value of the asset beyond that covered by the 1994 capital gains election.

It is important to note that all distributions from an RRSP are fully taxable as income in the hands of the recipient. This means the beneficial treatment accorded to capital gains and dividends is, in effect, lost when securities are owned by an RRSP rather than directly. Furthermore, most self-administered RRSPs have an administration cost which, although usually moderate, may exceed similar costs for an ordinary RRSP. (On the other hand, some general RRSPs may impose significant charges against the fund assets for administration and advice.) All these considerations should be taken into account prior to transferring securities into a self-administered RRSP to ensure that the greatest tax advantage to the individual is obtained.

There are various ways in which an RRSP may be of use in financing the acquisition of a home. These are fully discussed in ¶2543 below.

[¶2530.30] *Converting Your RRSP to Retirement Income*

By the end of the calendar year in which you turn 71 years of age, you are obliged to convert your RRSP into either a RRIF (see ¶2532) or an annuity which commences to pay retirement income in the following year. Alternatively, you can simply terminate your RRSP and receive all the funds in a lump sum (although this alternative is not particularly attractive from a tax perspective, as it ends any tax deferral and may subject you to significant tax if the lump sum is sufficiently large).

- *Planning Point:*

Consider contributions to a spousal RRSP. These must be made within your own contribution limits but can result in future income splitting with your spouse or common-law partner.

- *Planning Point:*

If you have received special payments on termination of employment, voluntary or otherwise, a special RRSP deduction may be available if you were employed by your employer in taxation years prior to 1996. It is essential to identify the eligible amount and make an appropriate RRSP contribution within 60 days after the taxation year. Having your employer make a direct contribution of qualifying amounts to your RRSP will avoid having withholding tax levied on the transfer (see ¶2565).

- *Planning Point:*

If you have made contributions to an RRSP which you did not or could not deduct, you must be careful that your undeducted contributions do not exceed your available contribution room by more than $2,000. If your cumulative excess contributions for 1991 through 1995 inclusive were more than $2,000, you must use any new contribution room which becomes available to shelter that excess before any additional contributions can be made. See ¶2611.15.

- *Planning Point:*

If you are over 71 years old, so that your own RRSP has "matured" and been converted into an income plan, but your spouse or common-law partner is not over 71, you can still make spousal RRSP contributions if you have business, employment, or other qualifying "earned income" as discussed in Chapter 26. Your spousal plan contributions will be governed by your own contribution limits. The benefits of RRSP deductions and continued tax-deferred savings are considerable provided you can afford to put the money aside in savings.

- *Planning Point:*

If you have a year in which your income is very low, you might consider withdrawing income from an RRSP in the calendar year in which you have the low earnings. For example, if your earnings were in the lowest tax bracket, you could have withdrawn enough from your RRSP to bring your income up to just below the second tax bracket. It is rarely likely to be beneficial to raise your taxable income above the lowest marginal rate threshold for the current year (shown in a table at ¶64 preceding Chapter 1). If you are interested in this option, you should obtain a table of the actual combined federal and provincial marginal rates for your province for the year of withdrawal (accounting firms and tax and accounting publishers such as Wolters Kluwer usually produce these in early fall, after federal and provincial Budgets have made their changes for the year). This will show you the optimum income level you want to achieve through an RRSP withdrawal.

- *Planning Point:*

Taxpayers in a position to control their "earned income" should note that the contribution deductible in a particular year will be based on income of the *preceding* year. Thus, to make the maximum RRSP contribution of $25,370 in 2016, a 2015 earned income of $140,944 is required. A table of these amounts for the known future is found at ¶2606. Allowable RRSP contributions are reduced for members of pension plans and deferred profit sharing plans. This is further discussed in Chapter 26.

- *Planning Point:*

Unused contribution room (amounts you could have contributed based on ordinary "earned income" but did not) carry forward into the current year. Although the difference between your ordinary earned income contribution limits and your lesser actual contributions for the year will provide additional contribution room in future, special "roll-over" contributions (such as termination payments or RPP payments) must be made in the year the opportunity arises (or within 60 days thereafter) or not at all. Thus if you have both income eligible for "roll-over", such as termination payments or RPP payments, and you cannot afford to contribute both the rollover and earned income amounts, you should always contribute the rollover first and make the special designation on Schedule 7 indicating your choice.

- *Planning Point:*

Since you can build up unused contribution room (see previous point), it may be worth foregoing deductions when income is relatively low to use the deductions against higher marginal rates, especially if some particular event such as a large one-time only capital gain is anticipated. In general, however, it is almost always beneficial to contribute to an RRSP insofar as possible.

- *Planning Point:*

There is probably no rule without its exceptions, and the bias toward making maximum possible contributions to an RRSP may reach its limits as you approach 71 and it appears that your annual retirement income from your RRSP savings will be taxed at top marginal rates.

- *Planning Point:*

Taxpayers saving partially through an RRSP and partially outside an RRSP should consider which savings should be held in which form. In general, it is desirable that investments in property most likely to give rise to the capital gain exemption (for eligible small business shares) or the $1 million capital gains exemption (for eligible farming and fishing property) be held outside the RRSP. This is also a consideration for shares of small businesses where the gains can be deferred by reinvestment. Regardless of the capital gain and reinvestment rollover, remember that capital gains realized personally are taxed on only 50% of their value, and may be offset with capital losses, benefits which are lost if the properties are held in an RRSP. Accordingly, properties held for capital appreciation are not always the best candidates for RRSP as opposed to personal investment. On the other hand, investments such as bonds or guaranteed investment certificates which yield only interest taxed at full rates are always better held in an RRSP (unless there are to be business losses which will offset the income).

(ITA: 18(11)(*b*); 40(2)(*g*)(iv)(B); 60(*j*), (*j.1*); 110.2(1); 146(5), (5.1), (8), (8.1), (8.3), (12); Income Tax Folio: S3-F10-C1 Qualified Investments – RRSPs, RESPs, RRIFs, RDSPs and TFSAs; S3-F10-C2 Prohibited Investments - RRSPs, RRIFs and TFSAs)

[¶2532] REGISTERED RETIREMENT INCOME FUND (RRIF)

A registered retirement income fund (see RRIF, ¶2630) provides a further means of deferring taxes by allowing individuals to roll their RRSPs into another deferred income plan. Typically this provides a continuing deferral when the taxpayer reaches age 71 and must convert an RRSP into some form of income stream (see ¶2630 to ¶2634.10). (Although mandatory in the year you reach 71, this conversion can be made at any earlier time.) A taxpayer may invest in more than one RRIF at a time, may transfer RRSP funds to a RRIF at any age up to 71 and may contribute a refund of premiums from a deceased spouse's or common-law partner's RRSP (or in the case of disabled children, a parent's RRSP) to a RRIF on a tax-free basis. As well, funds can be withdrawn from a RRIF in excess of scheduled retirement payments and either taxed currently or "rolled over" to a life annuity or annuity to age 90 (either of which may provide payments for a surviving spouse or common-law partner) or, age permitting, to an RRSP. See also ¶903.

As with an RRSP, you may open a self-administered RRIF, which allows you to control the plan's assets and performance. The rules and regulations pertaining to these plans are similar to ordinary RRIFs.

The RRIF investment rules are essentially identical to the RRSP investment rules, so that you can usually simply transfer your RRSP assets to a RRIF, and your self-administered RRSP assets to a self-administered RRIF. There is even a Canada Savings Bond RRIF to take transfers from your Canada Savings Bond RRSP.

The RRIF rules permit RRIFs to accept transfers of funds from registered pension plans as well as RRSPs. If you are over age 72, these transfer amounts are limited by a formula based on your age and the amount of pension foregone.

The alternative to a RRIF is to use your RRSP funds to acquire an annuity. Generally speaking, the annuity will not give you the same degree of control over your investments as a RRIF. However, RRIF funds must be withdrawn according to a schedule mandated by the government, whereas an annuity may provide benefits according to a schedule which better suits your needs as you foresee them. You can shop around for annuities, obtaining quotes from several life insurance companies (the usual vendors) through their insurance agents. The investment criteria for RRIFs are typically identical to those for RRSPs.

A more thorough discussion of the merits of RRIFs and annuities is found beginning at ¶2630. As discussed therein, the withdrawal thresholds from RRIFs were relaxed somewhat in the 2015 federal Budget.

The 2011 federal Budget introduced some significant changes regarding penalty taxes applicable to RRIFs. The main objective of these changes is to subject RRIFs (and RRSPs) to certain penalty taxes under Part XI.01 that apply to TFSAs in respect of "advantages", "prohibited investments", and "non-qualified investments". See Chapter 26 at ¶2618 for more details.

- *Planning Point:*

  If you must mature your RRSP because you turn 71 in the year, compare the merits of a RRIF and a life annuity in your particular situation.

(ITA: 146(16)(*c*); Income Tax Folio: S3-F10-C1 Qualified Investments – RRSPs, RESPs, RRIFs, RDSPs and TFSAs; S3-F10-C2 Prohibited Investments - RRSPs, RRIFs and TFSAs)

[¶2532c] TAX-FREE SAVINGS ACCOUNTS (TFSAS)

The Tax-Free Savings Account (TFSA) has been available to individuals since 2009. Financial institutions eligible to issue RRSPs are permitted to issue TFSAs. This includes Canadian trust companies, life insurance companies, banks, and credit unions.

An individual (other than a trust) resident in Canada and 18 years of age or older will be eligible to establish a TFSA. An individual can hold more than one TFSA, but will be subject to overall annual contribution limits. TFSAs can be transferred from one financial institution to another without being considered a withdrawal or contribution; however, transfer fees may apply.

[¶2532c.05] *Contribution Room*

Starting in 2009, individuals 18 years of age and older acquire $5,000 of TFSA contribution room each calendar year in which they are a resident of Canada for at least part of the year. The $5,000 limit was indexed to inflation and the annual additions to contribution room rounded up or down to the nearest $500. It thus remained at $5,000 for 2010, 2011, and 2012, was increased to $5,500 for 2013 and 2014, and was further increased to $10,000 for 2015. The limit was lowered back to $5,500 for 2016 and will be indexed thereafter. Unused contribution room will be carried forward to future years. For example, if an individual contributes $2,000 to a TFSA in 2009, the individual's contribution room for 2010 will be $8,000 ($5,000 for 2010 plus $3,000 carried forward from 2009). There is no limit on the number of years that unused contribution room can be carried forward, nor is there a ceiling on aggregate contributions. However, excess contributions are subject to a tax of 1% per month.

Any amounts withdrawn from an individual's TFSA in a year — which can be used for any purpose — will be added to his or her contribution room for the following year. This gives individuals who access their TFSA savings the ability to recontribute an equivalent amount in the future.

The following example shows that the potential contribution to a TFSA can be significantly more than the regular annual limit $5,000 annually, and thus the individual can earn more tax-free investment income.

Example

Suppose that an individual invests his or her $5,000 TFSA contribution in the stock market, and the investments appreciate rapidly to $15,000. The taxpayer can sell the shares, realize the $15,000 tax-free capital gain in the TFSA, and withdraw the cash proceeds tax free. The $15,000 can be recontributed to the TFSA, in addition to any other unused and current TFSA contribution room, in the following year or later.

There is no restriction on a higher-income taxpayer funding a TFSA for his or her spouse (or adult children). If an individual transfers property to a spouse or common-law partner, the attribution rules generally treat any income earned on that property as income of the individual. However, an exception normally applies to the attribution rules that allows individuals to take advantage of the TFSA contribution room available to them using funds provided by their spouse or common-law partner: the attribution rules will not apply to income earned in a TFSA that is derived from such contributions.

It is possible to make "in-kind" contributions to a TFSA, as long as the property is a qualified investment (see below). The amount of the contribution will be equal to the fair market value of the property. The contributor will be considered to have a deemed sale of the transferred property at its fair market value at the time of the contribution. However, if the cost is more than the fair market value, the resulting capital loss will be denied.

[¶2532c.10] *Tax-Free Amounts*

While contributions to a TFSA are not deductible, income, losses, and gains in respect of investments held within a TFSA, as well as amounts withdrawn, will not be included in computing income for tax purposes or taken into account in determining eligibility for income-tested benefits or credits delivered through the income tax system (for example, the Canada Child Benefit, the Goods and Services Tax Credit, and the Age Credit). Nor will such amounts be taken into account in determining other benefits that are based on the individual's income level, such as Old Age Security benefits, the Guaranteed Income Supplement, or Employment Insurance benefits. Because the investment income within, and withdrawals from, a TFSA are not taxable, interest on money borrowed to invest in a TFSA is not deductible. Like an RRSP, services such as investment counsel or administration fees are not deductible. However, unlike RRSPs, a TFSA may usually be used as security for a loan. In fact, technical amendments introduced in 2009 clarify that none of the rules pertaining to TFSAs apply to prevent the TFSA holder from using his or her interest in the TFSA as security for a loan or other indebtedness. However, to guard against the "sale" or "rental" of TFSA contribution room, this will only be the case if the debt agreement is on arm's length terms and it is reasonable to conclude that none of its main purposes is to enable another person or partnership to benefit from the exemption from tax provided in respect of the TFSA.

[¶2532c.15] *Death, Marriage Breakdown, Non-Residency*

The fair market value of the TFSA on the date of death will be received by the estate tax free. (That is, investment income and gains that accrue in the account after the individual's death will be taxable, while those that accrued before death will remain exempt.) However, an individual will be permitted to name his or her spouse or common-law partner as the successor account holder, in which case the account will maintain its tax-exempt status. Alternatively, the assets of a deceased individual's TFSA may be transferred to a TFSA of the surviving spouse or common-law partner, regardless of whether the survivor has available contribution room and without reducing the survivor's existing room. At time of writing, most provinces have amended their succession legislation to permit the designation of a successor holder or beneficiary on a TFSA, so that the TFSA can pass outside the estate and avoid probate levies, where applicable.

On the breakdown of a marriage or a common-law partnership, an amount may be transferred directly from the TFSA of one party to the relationship to the TFSA of the other. In this circumstance, the transfer will not reinstate contribution room of the transferor, and will not be counted against the contribution room of the transferee.

An individual who becomes non-resident will be allowed to maintain his or her TFSA and continue to benefit from the exemption from tax on investment income and withdrawals. (The "deemed sale" rules do not apply to a TFSA on ceasing to be or becoming a Canadian resident.) No contributions will be permitted while the individual is non-resident (a 1% per month penalty tax applies to non-resident contributions until the contributions are withdrawn or the date when the TFSA holder resumes Canadian residence, if earlier), and no contribution room will accrue for any year throughout which the individual is non-resident. Unlike RRSPs, TFSA withdrawals by non-residents are usually not subject to withholding tax. Withdrawals are added back to contribution room for the following year, but are available only when the individual resumes Canadian residence.

[¶2532c.20] *Reporting*

The CRA will determine TFSA contribution room for each eligible individual who files an annual income tax return (on the individual's Notice of Assessment and through the "My Account" function on the CRA website). Individuals who have not filed returns for prior years (because, for example, there was no tax payable) will be permitted to establish their entitlement to contribution room by filing a return for those years or by other means acceptable to the CRA. To provide the CRA with adequate means to determine contribution room and monitor compliance, TFSA issuers will be required to file annual information returns.

[¶2532c.25] *Qualified Investments*

A TFSA will generally be permitted to hold investments which are quite similar to those allowed for an RRSP. (Qualified investments for RRSPs are discussed at ¶2618.) However, the *Income Tax Act* contains provisions designed to penalize individuals whose TFSA holds a "prohibited investment". Generally, this refers to investments in any entities with which the account holder does not deal at arm's length, a corporation of which the account holder is a "specified shareholder" as defined in the *Income Tax Act*, or another entity in which the account holder has an analogous interest ("specified shareholder" generally refers to a 10% or greater interest in a class of shares of the corporation or a related corporation, counting the holdings of non-arm's length persons).

It is possible for an RRSP to invest in shares of a private corporation. Likewise, it is possible for a TFSA to do so, within the limitations described above. It should be noted that Regulation 4900(12) allows as a qualified investment for an RRSP shares of a "specified small business corporation", provided that the RRSP annuitant is not a "connected shareholder" of the corporation immediately after the acquisition of the share. The connected shareholder definition dovetails with the TFSA requirement because it refers to a person who directly or indirectly holds 10% or more of the shares of any class of the corporation or any corporation related to the corporation. In the case of RRSPs, there is a "safe harbour" rule from the 10% restriction where the person deals at arm's length with the corporation and the cost of the shares in the corporation is less than $25,000, but it does not appear that the safe harbour rules apply to TFSAs. Nevertheless, it may be possible for a TFSA to acquire shares of such a corporation, as long as it retains "specified small business corporation" status.

As is the case with RRSPs, individuals should review administrative and withdrawal fees, transaction charges, and interest (if any) on cash balances.

Note: If property that is considered to be a prohibited investment or a non-qualified investment is acquired, or if property held in the account becomes such, a tax of 50% of the fair market value of the property at the time it was acquired or that it became a non-qualified or prohibited investment is payable. When a TFSA holds a prohibited investment, the holder will also be subject to an additional tax that is based on income earned from the prohibited investment.

[¶2532c.30] *TFSAs versus RRSPs (etc.) — Investment Considerations*

As stated above, individuals and family members will start to accumulate fairly significant TFSA contribution room that, when added to RRSP contribution room, may well be more than accumulating savings. If so, questions will arise as to which vehicle is preferable. In addition, it may be possible to make contributions to an RESP. Of course, there is an additional choice of paying down a mortgage or contributing to an RRSP.

An RRSP is a *tax-deferred* investment vehicle. It offers deductibility for contributions, tax-free accumulation, and withdrawals/retirement benefits which are fully included in income. On the termination of an RRSP, earnings accumulated in the plan are effectively taxable since all amounts received from the RRSP are taxable — this will also recapture the initial deductions for contributions. A TFSA, on the other hand, is a tax-free investment vehicle: contributions are made in after-tax dollars; like an RRSP, earnings accumulate tax-free; but unlike an RRSP, there is no tax on withdrawal. (There are no mechanisms for tax-free transfers to a TFSA from an RRSP or other deferred income plans.)

The financial comparison between these features appears to be similar to the choice between contributing to an RRSP and paying down a mortgage. Provided that a taxpayer remains in the same marginal tax rate before and after retirement, and the interest paid on the mortgage is the same as the return made by the RRSP, the choice between investing in an RRSP and paying down a mortgage appears to be financially neutral. Whereas the interest on the mortgage versus return in the RRSP is a variable in the mortgage versus RRSP decision, this is not the case in the TFSA versus RRSP decision, since similar investments can be made in either vehicle. The remaining variable appears to be tax rates before and after retirement. Assuming these are the same, this results in financial neutrality between the TFSAs and RRSPs (i.e., if the same contribution were made to each plan on an after-tax basis, so that all tax savings from an RRSP were used to enlarge the contribution itself). Although one might expect tax rates to drop because post-retirement income should generally be lower (which would tip the scales in favour of an RRSP), income-based clawbacks (i.e., in respect of OAS, GIS, and the age credit) muddy the waters, as they can effectively propel a taxpayer into a higher effective tax rate. (However, RRIF and RRSP annuity payments are eligible for the pension-splitting rules for couples which came into effect in 2007 and may "even out" post-retirement income, perhaps so as to reduce income-based clawbacks.) An RESP is somewhat similar to a TFSA, except that, while contributions are made on an after-tax basis, earnings are potentially taxable to the student (or may reduce tuition and education transfers; the education and textbook tax credits were repealed effective January 1, 2017); however, this effect may be modest and could be more than offset by the ability to obtain CESGs. Of course, a TFSA cannot be held by a minor.

It should be noted, however, that the financial comparison above between a TFSA and an RRSP assumes that the term of the investment is the same. While an RRSP has mandatory maturity at the end of the year the annuitant turns 71, whereby taxable payouts must commence, there is currently no mandatory maturity for a TFSA, nor is there an age where an individual can no longer contribute. It therefore appears possible for an individual to extend the benefits of tax-free status indefinitely. However, whether this will continue to be the case as the years go by and contributions mount up may be another matter: one cannot eliminate the possibility of future changes to TFSA legislation, for example, to impose mandatory withdrawals by the elderly, or perhaps even income-based restrictions on contributions; but, at the time of writing, this is completely speculative.

As noted previously, the ability to make a tax-free withdrawal from a TFSA which reinstates contribution room presents an advantage over RRSP withdrawals. In the latter case, such withdrawals are taxable, may have an adverse effect on benefits which are based on income, and do not reinstate RRSP contribution room. (An exception is the first-time home buyers' plan (as well as the lifelong learning plan). In this case, however, to avoid tax, the withdrawal must be repaid in equal instalments over 15 years; in addition, the benefits are restricted to "first-time" home buyers (as defined). With a TFSA, there is no required repayment (the withdrawal increases TFSA contribution room so that the TFSA can later be replenished); of course, there is no requirement to be a "first-time" home buyer. The first-time home buyer's plan currently imposes a $25,000-per-individual ceiling on withdrawals.)

It can be seen that seniors, particularly those with low incomes, will benefit from TFSAs because of the lack of impact of withdrawals on income-tested benefits and because there is no age limit for contributions, as well as the fact that, unlike RRSPs, TFSA contributions are not dependent on "earned income". Younger individuals will find tax-free withdrawals and the reinstatement of contribution room to be attractive; however, the lack of tax on withdrawals will remove the psychological barrier — which is present with RRSPs — to retain funds in the plan, for example, for retirement. (For those in temporary low-tax brackets, consideration should be given to contributing to a TFSA and conserving RRSP contribution limits for higher-income years.)

Also, in these vehicles, tax advantages relating to investments, including capital gains status and the dividend tax credit, are lost. (Also lost are the benefits of capital or other tax losses.) As is the case with RRSPs, if the investor has capital outside of his or her plan, it may make sense to make tax-advantaged investments personally and invest high-tax items in either of these plans. As pointed out, if an investor is contemplating a very large shorter-term capital gain (e.g., on an equity investment), the taxable portion of which is likely to be well in excess of returns on fixed-income investments, the equity investment could, in effect, become high-tax, since the tax has to be paid for the year in which the investment is sold. Holding such investment in a TFSA would make even more sense than in an RRSP, since the gain would be entirely tax free, rather than tax-deferred, as is the case with an RRSP.

With rapidly accumulating contribution room in both vehicles, significant non-registered savings may become something of a rarity other than for the wealthy. Generally, passing up contributions to these plans because of the loss of tax advantages is usually not a good idea, unless the taxpayer is in a low bracket.

Finally, for shareholders of closely-held corporations, it should be noted that the ability to earn income on a tax-deferred basis in an RRSP and tax-free basis in a TFSA may put more pressure on making distributions of funds that would otherwise be deployed in corporate-level investments. Although this may result in additional current tax, retaining funds at the corporate level will result in significant tax on investment income. Consideration should therefore be given to ensuring that sufficient funds are distributed to make full contributions to RRSPs and TFSAs.

[¶2532c.35] *Measures against "Aggressive Tax Planning"*

In Department of Finance News Release No. 2009-099, dated October 16, 2009, it was announced that the TFSA provisions would be amended to counter certain avenues for "aggressive tax planning". The amendments were further introduced in draft legislation dated April 30, 2010, and then Bill C-47, which received Royal Assent in December 2010. What Finance sees as the problem areas, and the measures proposed in regard thereto, most of which are to be effective as of October 16, 2009, are outlined below.

Swap Transactions

"Swap transactions", refer to transfers of property (other than cash) for cash or other property between accounts (for example, a registered retirement savings plan (RRSP) and another registered account) that are generally not treated as a withdrawal and re-contribution, but instead as a straightforward purchase and sale. Subject to the application of existing anti-avoidance rules in the *Income Tax Act*, these transfers, when performed on a frequent basis with a view to exploiting small changes in asset value, could potentially be used to shift value from, for example, an RRSP to a TFSA without paying tax, in the absence of any real intention to dispose of the asset.

The amendments effectively prohibit swap transactions between registered or non-registered accounts and TFSAs. The definition of "swap transaction", in relation to a TFSA trust, generally means a transfer of property (other than a transfer or a distribution) occurring between the trust and the holder of the TFSA or a person with whom the holder does not deal at arm's length.

TFSA increases in fair market value that may reasonably be attributed to swap transactions will be subject to the advantage rules in Part XI.01 of the *Income Tax Act*. Where these rules apply, the fair market value of the advantage, including benefits reasonably attributable to swap transactions, will be taxable at 100%.

The CRA may waive or cancel all or part of the liability in respect of an advantage, including a swap transaction, where it considers it just and equitable to do so having regard to all the circumstances. In this regard, the amendments provide that the CRA shall not waive or cancel the liability unless one or more distributions are made without delay under a TFSA of which the individual is the holder, the total amount of which is not less than the amount of the liability waived or cancelled. The distributions will be taxed as regular income (see subsection 207.06(3) and paragraph 207.061(*b*)).

Deliberate Overcontributions

Contributions and associated earnings may accrue tax-free in the TFSA and may be withdrawn at any time without any adverse tax consequences. Contributions in excess of the TFSA contribution limit are subject to a tax of 1% per month on the highest amount of excess contributions for the month. This tax is generally sufficient to neutralize the tax benefit of overcontributions. The Government of Canada became aware that, in certain situations and subject to the existing anti-avoidance rules in the *Income Tax Act*, some TFSA holders were attempting to generate a rate of return on deliberate overcontributions over a short period of time sufficient to outweigh the cost of the 1% tax.

Under the amendments, any income reasonably attributable to deliberate overcontributions will be made subject to the existing advantage rules (as described above) and taxed accordingly. Pursuant to the advantage rules, the tax payable on the income will be 100%.

The CRA will maintain the discretion to waive or cancel all or part of the tax payable and the authority to adjust the taxpayer's TFSA contribution room accordingly in appropriate circumstances, as discussed above.

Prohibited Investments and Non-Qualified Investments

Under the current rules, where a TFSA holds a non-qualified investment or a prohibited investment, the holder of the TFSA is subject to a tax equivalent to 50% of the fair market value of the property. This tax is refundable to the holder if the investment is promptly disposed of from the account (by the end of the year following the year in which the tax arose, or such later time as the Minister of National Revenue considers reasonable), except in circumstances where the holder knew or ought to have known that the investment was non-qualified or prohibited. All or part of the tax may also be waived or cancelled at the discretion of the Minister of National Revenue where the Minister considers it just and equitable to do so having regard to the circumstances.

While the current TFSA regime applicable to prohibited investments and non-qualified investments provides for serious tax consequences for holding such investments, the investment income associated with the investments may remain tax-sheltered in the TFSA, resulting in an unintended permanent increase in TFSA savings and contribution room.

Under the amendments, the existing prohibited investment tax framework will be modified so that any income reasonably attributable to prohibited investments will be considered an "advantage", as described above, and taxed accordingly, i.e., at 100%. The additional taxes on prohibited investment income will be repealed.

In terms of income derived on non-qualified investments, a TFSA is currently subject to tax on such income under Part I of the Act under subsection 146.2(6). Furthermore, the amendments provide that "specified non-qualified investment income" in respect of a TFSA will include income (including capital gains) that is reasonably attributable, directly or indirectly, to the income of the TFSA that is taxable under Part I, i.e., income earned from non-qualified investments or income from a business carried on by the TFSA. Therefore, "specified non-qualified investment income" basically refers to second and subsequent generation income earned on non-qualified investment income or on income from a business carried on by a TFSA. The CRA may notify the holder of the TFSA to remove specified non-qualified investment income from the TFSA within 90 days of the notice pursuant to new subsection 207.06(4). If it is not removed within 90 days of receipt of the notice, it will be considered an "advantage" in respect of the TFSA and subject to the 100% tax on advantages as discussed above. The definition of "specified non-qualified investment income" applies to the 2010 and subsequent taxation years.

Withdrawals

The amendments also include rules to ensure that the withdrawal of amounts that are "specified distributions" do not constitute distributions for TFSA purposes and thus do not create additional TFSA contribution room. A "specified distribution" generally means a distribution made under a TFSA to the extent that it is, or is reasonably attributable to an amount that is, an advantage, specified non-qualified investment income, income that is taxable in a TFSA trust under Part I of the Act (as noted above, income earned from non-qualified investments or from a business carried on by the TFSA), or income earned on excess contributions or non-resident contributions. A specified distribution will not reduce the amount of any "excess TFSA amount", and will not add to the "unused TFSA contribution room".

- *Planning Point:*

  If you are saving at all, you should consider using a TFSA to the extent it is available to you. There is a permanent, government-sanctioned avoidance of tax on all earnings in the plan.

- *Planning Point:*

  If you intend to use a TFSA, especially for short term savings, you should be sure to check on the fees and costs associated with the plan, especially administration fees and withdrawal costs. You must be sure the tax benefits will outweigh the plan costs, however trivial they may seem.

- *Planning Point:*

  In arranging which assets to keep in the plan, probably the most common advice is to put investments with a high rate of interest or similar normally taxable income flow in the plan first. Investments with a high potential for capital gain (or loss) should be carefully evaluated before committing them to the plan, since the gains are taxed at lower rates than income, and capital losses realized in the plan will not offset gains on items held personally outside the plan. There is a contrarian view that it is precisely the high return items that you want to shelter, which may be true if you are confident of your choices.

(ITA: 18(1)(*u*), (11); 40(2)(*c*), (*g*); 69(1)(*b*)(iii); 146.2; 149(1); 207.01–207.07; 248(1) "disposition" (*f*)(vi), "TFSA"; ITR: 5000 Non-prohibited investment; Other Publications: March 13, 2008 Quebec *Additional Information on the Budgetary Measures*, Revenue Measures, 4, pages 127, 129; Department of Finance News Release No. 2009-099, October 16, 2009)

[¶2532c.90] *CRA Publication*

The CRA has released a useful pamphlet, *Tax Free Savings Account (TFSA)*, RC4466, describing the TFSA rules.

[¶2532f] ELIGIBLE FUNERAL ARRANGEMENTS

It is possible to contribute up to $35,000 per person for eligible funeral and cemetery care services. These contributions are in the form of commercial contracts with service providers licensed or authorized under provincial law to provide such services. Since these are commercial contracts, they are subject to the commercial cautions and concerns one must have when advancing funds for the prepayment of services. Providers of these services, although provincially regulated, are not necessarily governed by the regulatory and disclosure rules which govern, for example, trust companies (although they may choose to hold the funds through a trust rather than directly).

Contributions for these services are not deductible, but the funds contributed may (under the terms of a particular contract) earn income which is not subject to tax.

Contributions for any particular individual cannot exceed:

- for an arrangement that covers only funeral services, $15,000;
- for an arrangement that covers only cemetery services, $20,000; and
- for an arrangement that covers both funeral and cemetery services, $35,000.

Contributions need not be made at once, but may be made piecemeal over time so long as the overall limits are not exceeded.

Funeral services include property and services that relate directly to funeral arrangements of the individual in Canada. Funeral services provided outside Canada would not qualify. However, it is understood that preparation and transportation back to Canada of the body of a person who died outside Canada would be included. Funeral notices, transportation of family, and a reception after the funeral are apparently also included.

Cemetery services include property such as interment vaults, markers, flowers, liners, urns, wreaths and shrubs, and services relating to cemetery arrangements in Canada. They include property and services funded out of a cemetery care trust (a trust established under provincial law for the care and maintenance of a cemetery). Funds used to purchase a burial right or an interest in a building or property used for burial purposes are not considered to be paid for cemetery services unless applied as a contribution to a cemetery care trust (sometimes called a perpetual care fund).

In some provinces, funeral and cemetery services cannot be provided by the same operator. The Department of Finance has indicated that, in such cases, an individual can have one "eligible funeral arrangement" for funeral services and one for cemetery services.

Subject to the rules below for transfers after December 20, 2002, direct transfers of funds can be made from one eligible arrangement to another without incurring tax liability; however, funds cannot be withdrawn and recontributed without incurring tax on the withdrawal.

To the extent amounts in the trust are used for the payment of funeral or cemetery services for an individual, they are not taxable. However, funds in excess of contributions which are for any reason returned to anyone or used other than for permissible purposes are subject to taxation in the hands of the recipient as discussed at ¶984. Attribution rules (¶2529) would seem to apply where warranted. The CRA has said that a direct transfer of excess funds to a funeral arrangement for another person would not be subject to tax, although it said further that this is an anomaly not contemplated by the drafters and subject to correction in future technical amendments.

There are rules that apply to transfers from one EFA account to another. In general terms, these rules are:

- A new provision deems the transferred amount to be distributed to the individual from whose EFA account the amount is transferred. However, if that individual is deceased, the amount is deemed to be distributed to the individual to whose EFA account the amount is transferred. This ensures that the transfer is included in income (to the extent that it does not exceed the income accumulated in the transferor account).
- A new provision deems the transferred amount to be a contribution made to the recipient EFA account other than by way of transfer. This ensures that the earnings portion of the transferred amount is not taxed again when it is distributed from the recipient EFA account.
- The provision that requires EFA distributions to be included in income is amended to ensure that the determination of the amount that can subsequently be distributed from the transferor EFA account on a tax-free basis is reduced by the portion of the transferred amount that was not included in income

(i.e., that portion of the transferred amount that represents a return of contributions).

- A new provision provides that these new rules do not apply if the transferor and the recipient EFA accounts are in respect of the same person, the entire balance in the transferor account is transferred to the recipient account and the transferor EFA account is terminated immediately after the transfer.

The upshot of all these rules is that non-deductible contributions can be made for funeral or cemetery purposes and earn income free of tax. To the extent the contributed amounts and the earnings accumulated on them are in fact used for funeral and cemetery services, they remain free of tax when so used. It would seem that contributions can be made not only on behalf of the contributor, but also on behalf of anyone else, such as a parent, spouse or common-law partner, or child. It would also seem that you could pay the funeral or cemetery expenses of someone else out of your own "eligible funeral arrangement" (but not expand the contribution limits thereby). Given the value of tax-free earnings, relatively small contributions at an early age should provide substantial funds when necessary.

- *Planning Point:*

  If you have surplus funds (in excess of those needed to fund your own RRSP contribution), consider funding an eligible funeral arrangement. A small contribution at a young age can build up to a substantial amount which need not be paid out of the tax-paid savings of your estate or family when you die. Funding plans for a spouse or common-law partner or other relatives may be similarly beneficial.

(ITA: 148.1; Tax Topics: No. 1301, February 14, 1997; IT-531)

[¶2533] PENSION INCOME

[¶2533.05] *Pension Income Credit*

You may be entitled to a non-refundable tax credit (at the lowest marginal rate, federally 15%) on up to $2,000 of pension income *per annum*, where pension income is received as part of an annuity for life. OAS/CPP/QPP income is not eligible for the pension income credit. The credit will wholly eliminate tax on $2,000 of pension income if your total income is below the second tax bracket.

If you will be age 65 or older in the year and you do not have sufficient "pension income" to qualify for the full amount of the credit, you can create additional qualifying income by commencing to receive pension income from a life annuity by converting all or part of your RRSP plan into a RRIF or life annuity, or by simply purchasing an ordinary (unregistered) life annuity contract with other available funds.

If you are under age 65 and, because of loss of employment or some other reason, have an opportunity to commence receiving a pension amounts, you should consider whether such amounts will qualify for the credit on $2,000 of such income under the rules at ¶1311, and whether it is advantageous to trigger such income for that reason. If you are the beneficiary of a RRIF by virtue of the death of your spouse, and the RRIF is paying you less than $2,000 a year, and you are not otherwise using the full $2,000 pension amount, you should consider whether it is advantageous to top up your annual RRIF withdrawals to $2,000, which would be tax free (if your income is not taxed above the minimum tax bracket level) but would of course leave less in the RRIF to earn tax-free investment income. Also, surviving spouses or common-law partners should take part of their deceased spouse's or common-law partner's life insurance proceeds as an annuity to create qualified pension income.

- *Planning Point:*

  Consider making contributions to a registered retirement savings plan for the benefit of your spouse or common-law partner. See ¶2624.05. If contributions are made to a plan for each of you, each of you will have qualifying income that is eligible for the pension income deduction at the time you become 65 years of age.

- *Planning Point:*

  If you are 65 years old or older, you should see if you can arrange to have $2,000 of pension income, on which you can receive a tax credit which will reduce the effective tax by about 15 points, i.e., to nil if your total taxable income is below the second tax bracket. One way to accomplish this is, if you are not yet 71, to transfer sufficient RRSP funds to a RRIF to produce a $2,000 annual income.

(ITA: 118(3))

[¶2533.25] *Pension Income Splitting*

RRIF and RRSP annuity payments qualify for the pension splitting rules introduced in 2007. Under these rules, the higher-income spouse can allocate up to 50% of eligible pension income to be taxed in the hands of the lower-income spouse. The allocated amount is deducted from income by the higher-income spouse and included in the income of the lower-income spouse and taxed at his or her lower tax rate.

Besides RRIF and RRSP annuities, income qualifying for the pension tax credit is eligible for pension splitting, such as a pension from a registered pension plan (RPP). Some common types of income that would not qualify are Old Age Security payments, Canada or Québec Pension Plan payments, and payments from certain supplemental retirement compensation arrangements (RCAs).

There is no upper age limit that applies to the transferee. However, the pension income in the transferee's hands retains its character as pension income or qualified pension income, and thus, whether the transferee is eligible for the pension income tax credit will in turn depend on whether he or she is 65 or over, or under, as the case may be (see ¶1311.15).

The optimal amount of split pension income that produces the greatest tax savings varies greatly among couples, depending on each spouse's income. Factors to be considered include the effect of the increase in the lower-income spouse's taxable income on the availability of personal tax credits, as well as OAS and other clawbacks. (Occasionally, more complex factors may come into play, such as loss carry-forwards, capital gains exemptions, alternative minimum tax, multi-jurisdictional income, resource deductions, and foreign tax credits.) Options should be analyzed by the spouses when their tax returns are prepared.

[¶2535] SPOUSAL AND CHILD SUPPORT PAYMENTS

[¶2535.10] *Where Agreement or Court Order After April 30, 1997*

For separation agreements or court orders made after April 30, 1997, payments are divided into child support payments and spousal payments. Spousal payments continue to be taxable to the recipient and deductible to the payer, but child support payments are neither income to the recipient nor a deduction to the payer.

Spousal payments include payments to a common-law spouse or partner as that term is defined (in ¶1113) at the time the court order or agreement is made. It is understood that the

CRA is likely to take the view that an agreement between, for example, same-sex common-law partners who were not considered spousal partners under the law at the time the agreement was made cannot be validated because they would now be considered (retrospectively) to have been common-law partners. However, this could not be confirmed at the time of writing.

Although the new system does not apply to agreements or orders in place before May 1, 1997, payments under these old system agreements or orders can be governed by the new rules in the following circumstances:

- the payer and the payee have filed a joint election with the CRA (on form T1157), agreeing to a non-deduction, non-inclusion system for payments made after April 30, 1997;
- the agreement or order providing child support is changed or varied after April 30, 1997; or
- an agreement reached or court order issued after March 5, 1996 provides by its terms that payments made on or after May 1, 1997 are made on a non-deduction, non-inclusion basis.

Where the tax treatment of child support payments has been changed under any of these circumstances, parties will not be permitted to revert to the old system.

Where a written agreement or a court order does not specify whether an amount is for spousal support or child support, it will be treated, for income tax purposes, as child support (at least where there are children, although the legislation is perhaps a little vague on this point). Similarly, third party payments called for under an agreement or order which are not clearly identified as being exclusively for the benefit of the former spouse will be treated as child support. Arrears are considered paid on account of child support first.

[¶2535.15] *Registration of New-System Agreements If Payments Deductible*

Although it is not provided for in the legislation, the CRA has announced that agreements and court orders made after April 30, 1997, and older agreements/orders which become subject to the new rules under the circumstances set out above, must be registered with the CRA if they provide for any "spousal" payments which are intended to be taxable to the recipient and deductible to the payer. Registration is accomplished by sending a copy of the agreement or court order to the CRA with form T1158 (or T1157 where the parties are jointly electing to have an old agreement/order governed by new rules). See CRA pamphlet P102, "Support Payments", for an explanation of these requirements.

[¶2535.20] *Considerations Where Payments Still Deductible*

Note that the taxability/deductibility rules survive for both old system payments and for payments specifically classified as spouse or common-law partner rather than child support under the new system. The purpose of the taxability/deductibility rule is at least in part to provide a deduction from high rates of tax to the payer spouse or common-law partner and taxability at lower rates to the recipient spouse or common-law partner. This leaves a larger net of tax income to be divided.

One of the drawbacks of the taxability/deductibility system is that no withholding is provided for, so that the recipient spouse or common-law partner may have to turn some of the alimony receipts over to the government on account of the tax liability. Often this is not sufficiently provided for, and is viewed as a hardship. In the circumstances, it may be wise for alimony/maintenance agreements to provide for payments of 20% to 40% of such payments to the government on behalf of the recipient, thus alleviating cash flow problems. Of course, the recipient spouse or common-law partner could instead make these payments as cheques are received. Where the parties are sufficiently wary of each other, the payer could write two cheques, one to the payee and one to the government, but send both to the payee. To assure compliance with the very restrictive rules on third party payments, it would seem that the court order or written agreement governing the payments might have to provide that they are paid at the direction of the recipient spouse, who has the power to direct that they be received personally instead; see the discussion of "Specific Purpose Payments" in the CRA's booklet *Support Payments* (P102).

The results of numerous court cases have emphasized the need for strict adherence to certain conditions in order to obtain a deduction from income (see ¶2305).

At one time, amounts paid by a spouse to a third party for the benefit of the other spouse were generally not considered deductible by the payer spouse or taxable to the recipient. However, for amounts paid after 1983 to third parties, the expenses will be considered taxable/deductible where the court order or written separation agreement under which the amounts were paid so provides for such payments. These expenses would include medical and education expenses, and certain accommodation expenses such as rental or mortgage payments (see ¶2315). Third party payments for the benefit of children are similarly taxable/deductible under pre-April 30, 1997 rules, but will not be under agreements to which the May 1, 1997 rules apply (see ¶2306).

A lump-sum payment for alimony and maintenance is not deductible for tax purposes. Tax planning with respect to the initial division of the family assets can result in tax savings. A common tax planning technique in structuring a separation or divorce agreement is not to pay a substantial lump-sum payment on the initial settlement of the assets which would not be tax deductible. Instead, the periodic monthly payments to the spouse which would be tax deductible are increased. Normally the spouse making the payments is in a higher tax bracket than the person receiving the payment. This spread between the two marginal tax rates will result in a net tax saving. Note that the CRA does say that to be deductible, payments must be reasonably related to the living standards of the payer and payee before the breakdown, presumably to limit excessively blatant property transfers in the guise of maintenance payments.

A lump-sum payment of arrears of alimony or maintenance payments may be considered to be periodic. Periodic payments made prior to a court order or written agreement may be rendered deductible by a subsequent order or agreement made in the year or the subsequent year.

Competent legal and tax advisers should be consulted in structuring such an agreement. As well, you should refer to Chapter 23 for a more detailed discussion.

- *Planning Point:*

  Although separation is not typically a time for careful reflection, consideration of tax implications may provide financial negotiating room for both parties; in any event, defining tax implications where there will be support payments in the separation agreement is an essential protection for the payer, and possibly for the payee as well. This is no less true under the rules applicable to agreements made after April 30, 1997, under which it is possible to have the inclusion/deduction rules apply in part, depending on the extent to which payment will be characterized as for the benefit of the spouse or children. Pressure will thus remain for the parties to negotiate deductibility issues.

- *Planning Point:*

Where agreements were in place prior to May 1996, and so are still governed by the old rules, it may be particularly to the advantage of the payer to ensure strict compliance with the terms. Although default will not necessarily invalidate the old agreement (see *Kennedy v. The Queen*, 2005 DTC 5039 (F.C.A.)), it certainly runs the risk of engendering renegotiation and/or litigation which could result in a new agreement under the new rules.

(ITA: 56(1)(*b*); 56.1; 60(*b*), (*c*); 60.1; *Support Payments* Guide (P102); Income Tax Folio: S1-F3-C3 Support Payments)

[¶2539] MEDICAL EXPENSES

You may claim medical expenses incurred for yourself, your spouse or common-law partner, or any persons you are entitled to claim as dependants on your return. While either spouse or common-law partner may claim the expenses of both, obviously the same expense cannot be claimed twice, once by each spouse or common-law partner.

Medical expenses paid in any 12-month period ending in the year in excess of the lesser of 3% of your net income or $2,237 for 2016 may be claimed. Therefore, it may be to your advantage to group as many medical expenses as possible into one 12-month period and to review carefully the period selected. In filing the return of a deceased taxpayer, the 12-month period is extended to any 24-month period that includes the date of death.

Because the medical expense claim is reduced by 3% of net income of the individual making the claim, in many situations where both spouses or common-law partners pay tax it will be beneficial for the lower-income spouse or common-law partner to make the claim for both. Where the lower income spouse or common-law partner cannot make full use of the medical expense credit, however, the calculation must be made for each spouse or common-law partner to determine the most advantageous use of the credit, remembering that the medical expense level itself can be controlled by use of the 12-month rule. (The addition of a supplemental refundable medical expense credit (see ¶1237) does not alter these considerations. Note that for Quebec provincial tax return purposes this technique no longer works, since income of both spouses must be counted in reducing the medical expense credit; Quebec residents can still benefit from the federal rule on the federal return.)

If a medical expense is paid by your employer and is included in your employment income as a taxable benefit, you are able to treat the amount of the benefit on your return as if the expense had been paid by you personally. See ¶1250. Medical expenses may not be claimed to the extent they have been reimbursed by insurance.

The cost of private (but not government) medical insurance for yourself, your spouse or common-law partner, and members of your household connected by blood, marriage (including common-law partnership), or adoption is itself a qualifying medical expense. This includes premiums for health insurance while outside Canada. Commencing in 1998, self-employed individuals may deduct premiums in certain circumstances. The deduction, if you qualify for it, is usually preferable to the credit, since it is not subject to the 2016 3%/$2,237 threshold; in addition, for taxpayers above the lowest rate bracket a deduction gives a better tax result than the credit. In some circumstances, discussed at ¶741, the health insurance premium deduction is limited to a maximum of $1,500 for each of the taxpayer and spouse and $750 for each child, and if actual premiums are substantially higher, and you are not in the highest tax brackets, the credit may be preferable. You cannot claim the deduction for the up to the limits (if applicable) and the credit on the balance; rather, you must choose between the credit calculated under its rules and the deduction calculated under the deduction rules. The deduction must be converted to tax savings to obtain a fair comparison with the credit.

In addition to the above credit, a taxpayer may claim eligible medical expenses of a dependant relative aged 18 or over that exceed the lesser of 3% of the dependant's net income and the same indexed dollar threshold ($2,237 in 2016). Before 2011, there was a $10,000 cap on these expenses. The 2011 federal Budget removed the cap, so that there is currently no maximum.

An extensive discussion of which medical expenses qualify for credit is found in the first part of Chapter 12.

- *Planning Point:*

In preparing your tax return, choose the most beneficial 12-month period ending in the year for computing medical expenses. It may also be beneficial to have the lower-income spouse claim medical expenses, because of the reduction for 3% of net income.

- *Planning Point:*

Medical expenses include premiums paid to private health insurance plans. This should include premiums for supplementary coverage while outside Canada.

- *Planning Point:*

If you are self-employed and pay private health insurance plan premiums for yourself and your family, you should consider the applicability and value of the rules permitting deduction rather than tax credit for these premiums.

(ITA: 118.2(1), (2)(*a*))

[¶2541] PRINCIPAL RESIDENCE EXEMPTION

Generally when you sell your "owner-occupied" home, the gain on the sale of that home will be exempt from income tax if you elect it to be your principal residence. See ¶554. Problems arise where you or your family have more than one residence which you regularly occupy.

The actual principal residence exemption is determined by prorating the capital gain otherwise determined (selling price minus cost and minus expenses of disposition) by:

$$\frac{\text{One } \textit{plus} \text{ the number of taxation years ending after you last acquired the property (or 1971 if acquired before 1972) for which the property was your principal residence and during which you were resident in Canada}}{\text{The number of taxation years ending after you last acquired the property (or after 1971 if acquired before 1972) during which you owned the property}}$$

Commentary on Legislative Proposals (Oct. 3, 2016)

Note: When the Notice of Ways and Means Motion, October 3, 2016, achieves Royal Assent, the commentary will be modified to read:

The actual principal residence exemption is determined by prorating the capital gain otherwise determined (selling price minus cost and minus expenses of disposition) by:

One plus the number of taxation years ending after you last acquired the property (or 1971 if acquired before 1972) for which the property was your principal residence and during which you were resident in Canada. This one-plus rule may only be used by individuals residing in Canada in the year of acquisition of their residence

---

The number of taxation years ending after you last acquired the property (or after 1971 if acquired before 1972) during which you owned the property

Major renovations or improvements can be added to the cost base of your house to reduce capital gain otherwise determined before applying proration in the formula above. You should keep track of such expenditures for this purpose. See ¶805 for the nature of improvements which constitute a "capital improvement" and may be added to the cost of your house.

You cannot claim principal residence status for more than one principal residence for each year in the numerator above, but you need not put in all the years in which a residence might have qualified. It follows that you can divide a principal residence exemption between homes if you choose to do so, by selecting principal residence status for a particular residence for only certain years in the formula above. You only need to make a decision as to which years will attach to a particular residence in the year you dispose of that residence.

At one time, you and your spouse could each have a separate principal residence (e.g., a house and a cottage) and both of you would be exempt from income tax when the properties were sold. Only one residence of an individual and his spouse may qualify as a principal residence for 1982 and subsequent years. However, if both you and your spouse owned a principal residence prior to 1982, the legislation will disallow the exemption only in respect of any gain accruing after 1981. In order for you to determine the non-exempt portion of any gain accruing after 1981, it may be necessary to obtain a valuation of the property as of the end of 1981. See ¶553.

Common-law spouses (as defined in ¶1113) became subject to the one-exemption-per-family rule in 1993. No special valuation rules are provided, but the rule will only start counting non-exempt years in 1993, so that erosion of the principal residence claim will normally be gradual. Similarly, same-sex common-law partners (as defined in ¶1113) became subject to the one-exemption-per-family rule in 2001 (unless they elected in 1998, 1999, or 2000 to have the rules apply from that time). Again, no special valuation rules are provided, but the rule will only start counting non-exempt years in 2001 (or the year for which an earlier election was made), so that erosion of the principal residence claim will normally be gradual.

If you move from your house and rent it out you may wish to retain its principal residence status. This is possible if you file a special election. See ¶555.

[¶2541.05] *New Spouses and the Principal Residence Rule*

If you marry, or are deemed to acquire a common-law partner under the rules at ¶1113, and you and your spouse or common-law partner each own a principal residence, the principal residence exemption will start to erode from the time of your marriage, etc., by virtue of the rule that only one principal residence is allowed per family. This matters whether the property increases in value before or after the marriage, since the number of years used to prorate any gain will become limited after the marriage by the one-principal-residence-per-family rule.

Note that for 1992 and earlier years, only legal spouses were subject to the rule that only one principal residence exemption could be claimed per family. Two persons living together in a common-law relationship, with each owning a principal residence, perhaps one owning the house and the other the cottage, could effectively claim principal residence exemption on each. Commencing in 1993, common-law spouses as defined at ¶1113 are deemed to be spouses for all tax purposes. It follows that in applying the principal residence exemption formula, the exemption on one residence or the other will begin to erode after 1993.

The same is true for same-sex couples who have common-law relationships which are captured by the extension of common-law partner rules effective in 2001. Where each common-law partner has a principal residence in 2001, the exemption on one or the other will begin to erode after 2001.

These cases are essentially subsets of the general newly married situation just discussed.

If you and/or your new spouse or common-law partner already have children 18 or over (or younger but married), you may consider disposing of one property to them in these situations. Such a transfer must, by law, occur at fair market value; that is, even if you gift the cottage or sell it for less than its value to your children, you will have to report proceeds of disposition equal to the current fair market value of the cottage and report as capital gain the amount of such proceeds in excess of original cost (or 1971 value if you have had the property that long, plus any addition to cost arising from use of the capital gains exemption election in 1994). You can use the principal residence exemption to shelter this gain, which is why you may want to do this before the exemption on one property begins to erode.

The difficulties of a transfer to children are often personal. To which children do you give it; suppose you still want to use it but the children decide to sell it; and so on. Some of these things can be dealt with, for example, by transfer to a trust for children, or by taking back a mortgage on the transfer so that proceeds of sale will come to you and not the children. In any case, you must weigh future tax costs against the possible personal costs of such a step. If this is a major step, professional advice may be warranted to quantify the tax costs and suggest steps to protect your interests.

- *Planning Point:*

  If you and/or your spouse or common-law partner have two houses (e.g., a house and cottage), keep a cost record of major home renovation projects so that the costs can be added to your cost base and reduce the gain on eventual sale. You should do this even if you have only one house (which will be exempt from tax on sale), since you may eventually acquire a second home, even if you don't plan on it now.

- *Planning Point:*

If you have both a house and a cottage in joint ownership with your spouse or common-law partner, and have held both since before 1982, you may be able to rearrange ownership to benefit from the double principal residence exemption that was available for the period before 1982; see the discussion at ¶554a. Note, however, that where property value increases have occurred primarily after 1981, this tactic is of not much use.

- *Planning Point:*

If you have more than one home (typically a house and a cottage) and you sell one of them, you should consider whether claiming the entire principal residence exemption on the property sold will be better than saving some or all of the exemption years for use on the other. This can only be determined on the facts of each case. It is a decision that must be made when you prepare your tax return for the year of the first sale.

- *Planning Point:*

If you acquire a spouse or common-law partner and you each have a property which qualifies as a principal residence, you should note that the full exemption on one property or the other must begin to erode after the year of marriage. You should review whether any change in the status of these properties, such as the transfer of a cottage to adult children, is warranted by the change.

(ITA: 40(2)(*b*), (4), (6), (7); 45(2); IT-128R Capital Cost Allowance — Depreciable Property; Income Tax Folio: S1-F3-C2 Principal Residence)

[¶2543] HOUSING AND HOME MORTGAGES

A common concern for individuals is saving and borrowing to acquire a home. By and large, the tax system is not designed to facilitate this, since home mortgage interest is typically not deductible (but see the comments at ¶2517). As well, if you have a home and are "trading up" to a more expensive one, and you take back a vendor mortgage on your old home, the interest on that will be taxable and not offset by any interest deduction for the interest you pay on your new home. Until recently, the only official federal government concession to encouragement of home ownership was that a modest down-payment can be saved on a tax-assisted basis through an RRSP, as discussed below. The 2009 federal Budget announced two significant initiatives regarding housing: the new Home Renovation Tax Credit (only for 2009) and the new First-Time Home Buyer's Tax Credit (still available; see ¶2543a). The 2015 Federal Budget introduced a Home Accessibility Tax Credit for seniors, persons with disabilities, and other eligible individuals in respect of qualifying expenditures attributable to qualifying renovations made to an eligible dwelling; this credit applies beginning in the 2016 year.

In addition to the three government-sanctioned vehicles, tax advisers have attempted many strategies to achieve some additional tax relief on home purchases. None is entirely satisfactory for most people, but you may want to understand what these strategies are.

[¶2543.01] *The RRSP Home Buyers' Plan (HBP)*

In principle, the Home Buyers' Plan is a special exception to the normal RRSP rules which tax all amounts withdrawn from an RRSP. The Plan allows each taxpayer to borrow up to $25,000 from his or her RRSP to invest in a home which is to be used as a principal place of residence. Couples who have separate RRSPs can make withdrawals up to $25,000 from each individual's RRSP. The rules contemplate that you will identify the residence to be acquired and withdraw funds for that particular purchase, which must be completed within specified time limits. Prior to 1999, it was a rule that an individual could use the Home Buyers' Plan only once in a lifetime. That is, having once used the Plan to acquire a home, you could not use it again in a later year. Revisions in 1999 eliminated this restriction for 1999 and later years, and provides instead that once you have repaid all the funds withdrawn for a prior use you may use the Plan again commencing with the year following the final repayment provided you comply with the five-year rule. The five-year rule provides that you cannot make a qualifying withdrawal under the Home Buyers' Plan if you owned a home at any time in the period commencing January 1 of the fourth year preceding withdrawal of RRSP funds (January 1, 2006 for a 2010 withdrawal) and ending 31 days prior to the withdrawal. Similarly, you cannot use the Home Buyers' Plan if you are currently married (including a common-law relationship as discussed at ¶1113) and your current spouse or common-law partner owned a home that was your principal place of residence during the marriage or common-law relationship within the same time period that applies to you. The five-year rule does not apply to a person with a disability moving to a home more suitable for coping with the disability. The Home Buyers' Plan is discussed in detail at ¶2625.05 *et seq.*

[¶2543.02] *Provincial Assistance for First Time Purchasers*

Most provinces have credits or rebates in respect of land transfer tax payable on the purchase of a first home. Additionally, some provinces have a rebate or refund in respect of the provincial portion of HST payable on newly constructed houses, if any. For example, in Ontario, a refund for first-time buyers of the Ontario land transfer tax is provided up to a maximum of $2,000. Purchasers of newly constructed homes can receive a rebate of the provincial portion of the HST up to $24,000 regardless of the price of the new home. The particulars of each provincial land transfer can be found on the province's revenue ministry website.

[¶2543.03] *Other Tax-Assisted Savings: Using Your RRSP outside the Home Buyers' Plan Limitations*

You can borrow up to $25,000 of funds from your RRSP to purchase a home as discussed in ¶2543.01, just above. This is the simplest and most direct method of using RRSP funds for home purchase. It is discussed in excruciating detail commencing at ¶2625.05. The methods discussed here are supplemental or alternative planning possibilities.

Saving through an RRSP is almost always beneficial as a form of saving for retirement. There are two basic benefits. First, your saving is tax-assisted because your RRSP contributions (within specified limits) are deductible. Thus, in theory, the government is contributing tax dollars to your savings to the extent of your tax savings realized by the deduction. The second benefit is that your earnings in the plan are not currently taxed, so they accumulate much faster than if you earned them directly. Thus, if you invested $4,000 per year for 20 years in an RRSP which earned 10%, your savings would be worth $252,000 after 20 years, compared to $139,000 if you saved $4,000 per year but had to pay tax at 50% on the income earned on the savings. Note that this difference arises wholly from tax on earnings; it does not include additional amounts you may have saved initially because of the tax deduction.

The advantages of RRSP savings raise the question of whether it is beneficial to save this way for home ownership. The answer is mixed.

Your RRSP savings will be taxable when you take them out of a plan at your current tax rate. If your earnings (and tax rates generally) are going up, you may well have to withdraw money from the plan at a higher tax rate than that at which you saved on your original deductions. You will still have had the benefit of compounding in the plan, but compounding takes a long time to show major effects; in the short run this benefit could well be wiped out by higher tax rates if your deductions were made, say, against a 25% tax rate but your withdrawals are taxed at 40% because you are earning more and in a higher tax bracket.

On the other hand, if you are a working spouse or common-law partner and expect to take more than a year off when you have a child, you might reasonably expect that you will be able to withdraw your RRSP funds at that time at the same or a lower rate than your contribution deductions. If you use the funds toward home purchase in a year when you have minimal other income, the RRSP savings will have proved a very effective way to finance your down payment.

Another possibility is using the funds in your RRSP to help mortgage your own home. Generally speaking, this may involve more trouble and cost than it is worth, but it may have advantages in some situations. You may use the funds in your RRSP to mortgage your own home on two conditions: first, the mortgage must be administered by an approved lender. Typically this is the bank or trust company that will finance the rest of your purchase, although it need not be. Second, the mortgage must be insured, usually by either Canada Mortgage and Housing Corporation or Mortgage Insurance Corporation of Canada. Both these conditions add extra cost to the mortgage.

You will have to have a self-directed RRSP in the first place to do this, but if you do not, you can typically transfer your funds to a self-directed plan administered by the primary lender to make all this feasible.

If you are going to use your RRSP in this way, it might work something like this: suppose you have $25,000 in an RRSP and you want to buy a house for $100,000. The bank will lend you $75,000 (typically 75% is the most you can get on a first mortgage). If you want to use RRSP funds as mortgage money, you will probably have to come up with $10,000 cash, since the insurance usually requires you to have 10% equity in your home. You could withdraw this from your RRSP, but remember that you will have to pay tax on the withdrawal at your top marginal rate (and you may be driven into a higher bracket). Assuming you can finance the tax, you could take out the $10,000, and the bank would in effect take over the remaining $15,000 and arrange a joint or second mortgage under its administration. Typically the problem with this scheme is that you must have substantial RRSP amounts to make it feasible; as well, from an economic point of view the best possible use of RRSP funds is simply to make the wisest possible investments. Some trust or mortgage companies may make a point of offering the requisite services when you are financing your purchase through them.

[¶2543.04] *Trading Up: Vendor Take-Back Mortgages*

If you already have a home and are selling to acquire another (or indeed for any reason), you may be asked to take back a mortgage, often to cover the difference between the 75% the bank will finance for the purchaser and his inability to come up with the remaining 25% in cash. You can, if you choose, have your self-directed RRSP advance this money to the purchaser against a second (or later) mortgage. The advantage is twofold: first, you have the money out of your RRSP for your own down payment with no tax. This is because the purchaser has borrowed the money from the RRSP and paid it to you for your old house. It may represent capital gain on the house, but this is typically sheltered by the principal residence rules. Second, the interest on the mortgage payments by the purchaser will accumulate tax free in the RRSP.

This may not be as good as it sounds. It assumes that you do not need the regular cash flow from your sale to make regular payments on your purchase. On the other hand, if the cash you receive from the purchaser allows you to make a much larger down payment, it may reduce your mortgage payments sufficiently to allow for this. Again, the most common problem is insufficient accumulation in the RRSP to make the transaction worthwhile.

Note that if your RRSP is lending money to an arm's length party on the strength of a mortgage, this is a legitimate investment and you do not have to have a mortgage administrator or insurance, although you do have to have a self-administered RRSP. However, if you are not accustomed to mortgage lending, you might well prefer to have a regular mortgage lender such as a trust company administer the mortgage for you.

In this case (and theoretically in case ¶2543.03, above, if you cannot meet your mortgage payments), the real estate could be subject to foreclosure. This can be a problem because while a mortgage is a qualified RRSP investment, real property (i.e., a house) is not. The CRA has indicated that it will solve this problem as an administrative matter by not applying the penalty provisions for non-qualified investments where the property is acquired under a *bona fide* foreclosure and the RRSP holds it for the sole purpose of disposing of it within a reasonable time. The CRA will accept one year as reasonable, longer if the delays can be justified by particular facts. The property so held by an RRSP may be acquired by the RRSP annuitant so long as the sale occurs at fair market value. If it occurs at less than fair market value, the difference is income to the annuitant. More detail can be found at the end of ¶2618.

[¶2543.05] *Mortgage Interest Deductibility*

The deductibility of interest expense depends on the use to which the particular funds are put That is, if you borrow to buy your own home, the interest is not deductible, whereas if you borrow to buy shares, or an income property, the interest expense is deductible. If you buy a mixed property, such as a house of your own which has a rental apartment in it, the interest will be partially deductible. Typically the deductible portion will be allocated on the basis of square footage allocated to rental use over total square footage.

See also the discussion of interest deductibility at ¶2517.

If you have substantial investments outside an RRSP which you can sell with minimal capital gain or with capital gain substantially offset by the lifetime capital gain exemption, you can sell the investments to increase your down payment. If you wish, you can then borrow again (on a mortgage or otherwise) to repurchase your investments. The interest on the money borrowed for this purpose will in general be deductible, assuming the investments have any potential to show long-run income in excess of borrowing costs. (When it comes to more elaborate and very short term rearrangements of borrowings, however, see the cautions expressed in ¶2517.) Remember that capital losses on investments sold will not be recognized if the investments are repurchased within 30 days of sale.

[¶2543.06] *Family Financing*

If your parents have sufficient money to lend you enough to buy a house or make a substantial down payment, this is of course a considerable benefit. You do not have to make interest payments to them. If they require the income flow from the money they lend you, you can make periodic (e.g., monthly) repayments of capital. This will not be deductible to you but will not be taxable to them. Their capital is of course being significantly diminished, although their current income flow may remain the same. In effect, they are living off capital and making you a gift of the interest they are foregoing on their capital. Since they are no longer earning income on that capital, the CRA is not getting a share. Another way of looking at it is that they are providing you with your inheritance piecemeal before they die. If their capital is otherwise substantial enough to provide for their remaining years, this may be a tax beneficial use of funds within the family unit.

[¶2543a] TAX CREDITS RE HOUSING

[¶2543a.10] *First-Time Home Buyer's Tax Credit*

The 2009 federal Budget announced the First-Time Home Buyer's Tax Credit (FTHBTC). The FTHBTC is a new non-refundable tax credit based on an amount of $5,000 and will be available to first-time home buyers who complete a purchase of a home after January 27, 2009. The FTHBTC is calculated by reference to the lowest personal income tax rate for the year and can be claimed for the taxation year in which the home is acquired.

An individual is considered a first-time home buyer if neither the individual nor the individual's spouse or common-law partner owned and lived in another home in the calendar year of the home purchase or in any of the four preceding calendar years. A qualifying home is one that is currently eligible for the Home Buyers' Plan that the individual or individual's spouse or common-law partner intends to occupy as the principal place of residence not later than one year after its acquisition. It is interesting to compare this with the Ontario land transfer tax refund for first-time home buyers, which contains notable differences. For instance, to quality for the Ontario land transfer tax refund for first-time home buyers, the purchaser cannot have previously owned a home or had any ownership interest in a home, anywhere in the world, at any time. Therefore, a person who qualifies for the FTHBTC may not qualify for the Ontario land transfer tax refund for first-time home buyers.

The FTHBTC is available with respect to purchases made for the benefit of individuals entitled to the disability tax credit (a "DTC eligible person") if the purchase was made to enable the DTC eligible person to live in a home better suited to his or her personal needs. In order to claim the FTHBTC, the home must be intended to be the principal residence of the DTC eligible person within one year after acquisition.

The individual acquiring the home or the individual's spouse or common-law partner can claim the FTHBTC. An ownership interest in the particular home for which the FTHBTC is claimed must be registered in the applicable provincial land registration system.

Any unused portion of the FTHBTC relating to an individual can be claimed by such individual's spouse or common-law partner. A home jointly acquired by two individuals will only create one full FTHBTC.

(ITA: 118.05)

[¶2544] FOREIGN VACATION PROPERTIES

From a Canadian point of view, owning a foreign vacation property is no different from owning a vacation home in Canada. If the property is rented for part of the year, there will be rental income. In any event there is capital gain (or loss) on disposition, including deemed disposition at death. By hypothesis, the principal residence rules (¶553 *et seq.*) are unlikely to apply unless there is no primary Canadian residence. However, there is no rule that a foreign property cannot be a principal residence (see S1-F3-C2, paragraph 2.74).

Problems with a foreign vacation property are likely to arise primarily from the potential double taxation of rental income and capital gain in the foreign jurisdiction. If the foreign jurisdiction is a tax haven with low tax rates and perhaps no capital gains tax, the problems may have more to do with the right of a non-resident to rent out property than with the tax system.

On the other hand, where the foreign jurisdiction has a complex tax system, you are likely to expose yourself to the rental/capital gain/death regimes imposed by that system. Foreign tax credits may or may not fully alleviate double taxation, depending on the foreign jurisdiction.

Where you own a vacation property in the U.S., the rules on death may be especially complex. A useful article on the subject is found in the Wolters Kluwer Newsletter *Tax Topics* No. 1898, dated July 24, 2008.

[¶2545] CHARITABLE DONATIONS

The government offers some incentive for charitable donations, notably in the form of a tax credit at top marginal rates on gifts over $200. This means that when you donate money in excess of $200, your tax credit at a minimum fully offsets the tax you paid on the amount donated, and if your taxable income is below the top marginal rate, the credit exceeds the tax you paid to earn the amount donated.

There is a rule that the amount eligible for charitable donation credit in any year cannot exceed 75% of your net income for the year. Donations in excess of this limit will be eligible for credit in any of the five following years, subject again to the 75% of net income limit for the year in which the credit is claimed. Where capital gain or recapture are realized on a gift of capital property, the 75% limit is expanded to accommodate that extra income.

If you make a gift of property rather than cash, the government treats the gift as if you had sold the property and donated the cash received. You are liable for tax on the profit on the notional sale but you have a deduction for the entire value of the gift.

There is a long-standing exception for gifts of certified cultural property. Here, no capital gain will be recognized but the full value of the gift is eligible for credit. At one point the government did find this program subject to abuse, which arose from what it considered excessive valuations placed on the property donated, which could result in a donation credit exceeding the amount paid for the property. This is still true; the only step the government has taken is to provide that the assigned value as well as the cultural significance of the property be reviewed by a government-appointed Cultural Review Board. Quebec has imposed some additional limitations where such gifts are made to organizations whose primary function is not to utilize them.

Normally, where you donate capital property (other than cultural property) you are required to include in income the taxable portion (50% for 2001 and later years) of the capital gain you would have had if you sold the property at its fair market value (FMV). One hundred per cent of this FMV would be eligible for charitable donation credit. However, the capital gains inclusion rate for donations of securities listed on prescribed Canadian and foreign stock exchanges, and of certain other readily valued securities, is lowered to:

- nil, for donations made after May 1, 2006; and
- 25% for donations after 2000 and before May 2, 2006.

Confining the special rate to publicly-traded and similar securities solves any valuation problems the government might otherwise have.

In 2000, the government extended the rule above to donations of shares (and mutual fund units) of publicly traded securities obtained with employee stock options. Essentially, the employee stock option rules (¶2559) substitute an employment benefit for a capital gain on either the exercise of the options or the sale of the shares so obtained. Employees who donate the publicly traded securities so obtained will have a nil benefit for gifts made after May 1, 2006, and half the employment benefit otherwise levied for earlier gifts made before May 2, 2006, but after February 27, 2000, provided the donation is made within 30 days of the exercise of the options (and within the same taxation year). The rules even provide for the employer to expedite the donation as part of the exercise transaction.

The main impact of these changes is to increase the net tax value to you of the charitable donation credit in excess of capital gain liability on gifts of eligible property. It may have an effect on the timing of gifts, and the calculus of offsetting years of anticipated high income with donations.

A charitable gift made by will is deemed made by the deceased immediately before death and therefore gives rise to charitable donation tax credit in the year of death. If an RRSP or RRIF names the estate of the deceased as beneficiary, the value of the RRSP, etc., is included in income of the deceased immediately before death, and if the proceeds are then donated to charity under the will, there is a correct offset of income by charitable donation credit. However, if the RRSP or RRIF names the charity as beneficiary, there is no donation credit for the estate and the estate and charity are jointly liable for the tax liability. The death benefit under a life insurance policy is subject to the same inconsistency where a charity is the named beneficiary. Changes announced in 2000 but retroactive to 1999 permit donation credit to the deceased in the year of death where a charity is named as the beneficiary of an RRSP, RRIF or life insurance policy (provided the policy was issued to a Canadian resident).

Anti-avoidance rules will by contrast deny credit claims on gifts made after July 31, 1997 of certain non-arm's length securities until the charity in turn disposes (within five years of the gift) of the securities at arm's length or the non-arm's length connection with the donor is severed.

Another anti-avoidance rule denies charitable donation credit on gifts after 6:00 p.m. EST December 5, 2003 of property acquired less than three years prior to the gift or of property acquired less than 10 years prior to the gift if a main reason for the acquisition of the property was to make a gift of it. There is an exception for gifts at death. See the discussion at ¶2521.40 and ¶2521.41, above.

The upshot of all this is that the tax consequences of large charitable donations must be anticipated in advance. Where property is to be gifted, special attention is required. Clearly, for example, if you intend to make a donation to charity and must dispose of assets to finance the gift, it is tax beneficial to gift publicly traded shares (assuming they have an inherent capital gain) to the charity rather than to sell the shares and donate the proceeds.

Several tax shelter proposals, some of dubious merit, depend on charitable donation credit. The government has been systematically attacking these, both in the courts and through legislation. See the discussions at ¶2521.35, ¶2521.40, and ¶2521.41, above, and also the discussion at ¶2521.50 under the subheading "(5) Acquisitions for Charitable Donations".

New anti-avoidance rules announced in the 2012 federal Budget and effective as of June 29, 2012 apply to charities in respect of political activities. Generally speaking, a gift made by a charitable organization to a qualified donee will be considered a political activity and not a charitable activity where it can reasonably be considered that a purpose of the gift is to support the political activities of the qualified donee. The CRA may suspend the tax-receipting privileges of the charity if it devotes resources to political activities that are not considered to be devoted to charitable activities.

The 2013 federal Budget introduced the "first time donor super credit", which provides a 40% federal credit for donations of $200 or less, and a 54% federal credit for the portion of donations over $200 but not exceeding $1,000, effectively adding 25% to the credit for eligible donations. The credit can only be claimed once between 2013 and 2017, and only where neither the donor nor his or her spouse has claimed a charitable donation tax credit in the previous five years.

[¶2545.05] *2011 Federal Budget Anti-Avoidance Rules*

The 2011 federal Budget introduced various amendments regarding the charitable tax credit and related matters. Changes include:

- Denying the credit for a grant of an option to a charity or other qualified donee, but allowing a credit at the time that the qualified donee exercises or disposes of the option (see ¶1269.15);
- In respect of gifts of publicly-listed flow-through shares ("FTS"), new rules that effectively provide that the zero inclusion rate for capital gains on such gifts made to qualified donees applies only to the amount by which the capital gain exceeds the actual amount paid for the FTS (see ¶1269.20);
- Rules that tighten up the current anti-avoidance rules that apply to gifts of non-qualified securities (see ¶1290d.15); and
- New rules that deny or restrict the credit where an individual transfers property to a qualified donee and the donated property or another property is subsequently returned by the donee to the donor (see ¶1271).

[¶2546] FILING TAX RETURNS FOR CHILDREN

If you have children with earned income for RRSP purposes, you should consider having them file (or filing for them) a T1 tax return, even if the income is well below taxable levels. Obtaining a Social Insurance Number is a prerequisite, but social insurance numbers can be easily obtained for Canadian children.

Although there may be a natural reluctance to bring children into the labyrinth of government bureaucracy before it is strictly necessary, there are advantages to reporting even relatively small amounts of earned income.

The primary advantage is accumulated RRSP room. Where children are below taxable levels there is no advantage to having them set up an RRSP, but the mere fact of reporting earned income will create RRSP contribution room which can be carried forward forever. This will increase their lifetime RRSP contribution limits. It may also help to solve the problem which arises where someone enters the labour force for the first time and wants to make an RRSP contribution, and there is no contribution room available because current year contribution limits are based on prior years' earnings. (Note that you cannot yourself contribute to an RRSP for your children without running into the overcontribution penalty tax. There is no $2,000 exemption in this situation, so the penalty effectively vitiates any benefit.)

Another advantage can occur if the child has foreign investment income. Say an American aunt buys $1,000 of U.S. mutual fund shares for a Canadian child. The U.S. government will want to impose withholding tax at its general 30% rate on the child's fund income, but this can be reduced to the 15% treaty rate upon proof that the child is a Canadian resident. The most common form of proof is a statement from the tax authorities, and this can readily be obtained from the CRA if the child is a Canadian taxpayer.

[¶2547] TAKE THE MONEY AND RUN?

A certain amount of folklore and some popular books in the 1990s painted a rosy picture of the opportunities for Canadians to move themselves as well as their assets to another country, presumably a tax haven with low or nil personal income tax rates and better weather, and so escape Canadian tax on the income their assets generate, and incidentally the Canadian winter. This is not practical for most Canadians, since the requirements of their business or employment, and often their families and friends, require a Canadian presence which makes non-resident status impossible. Certainly this is true for Canadian politicians and employees of the Department of Finance, who, shivering in the long cold Ottawa nights, seem to have taken exceptional umbrage at the notion that others might not want to shiver with them.

Canada has long had rules (already among the strictest in the world) which require Canadians who become non-residents to continue accounting for the gains realized on Canadian property even after they leave the country. Real estate, investments in Canadian shares (public and private), and so on, remain "taxable Canadian property" which must be accounted for on final disposition or death as they would be for a Canadian resident. Gains on foreign property were to be accounted for on departure, but gains on taxable Canadian property could be deferred for non-residents as for residents. And, of course, most Canadians build most of their wealth in Canadian assets.

On October 2, 1996, the government seems to have decided that if it shivered in the dark much longer, there would be no one left to shiver with it. At any rate, it introduced a punitive new plan under which Canadians ceasing to be resident after October 1, 1996 would be taxable at that time on virtually all gains in their net wealth except those represented by Canadian real estate, Canadian business assets (as opposed to shares), retirement savings invested in approved (and controlled) plans such as registered pension plans and RRSPs, and employee stock options. There are also exceptions for short-term residents, such as frequently transferred employees.

No doubt this seems quite a fair burden to impose on anyone who chooses not to share the Canadian winter, but it is not without its problems. Paying the tax on appreciation in your assets is often impossible without selling the assets to find the money to pay the tax, and not all assets are readily saleable. This is especially true of shares of a private company, which may have value but no ready buyers. Moreover, the government retains the right to impose tax on taxable Canadian property again if its value has increased on the later actual disposition by the now non-resident, but the proposals as originally drafted offered no offset for the emigration tax paid if the value had fallen at the time of eventual disposition. In addition, no provision was originally made to take of account of tax payable in the new jurisdiction on the ultimate disposition of the assets, typically resulting in double taxation on the same gain, first by Canada on emigration, and later by the new jurisdiction on disposition.

Working out solutions to these problems took the government fully five years. On December 23, 1998, the government tabled draft legislation which purports to solve, in inevitably complex and cumbersome fashion and retroactive to October 2, 1996, the problems outlined above, and additional problems which arise in consequence of the solutions. A revised draft was released on December 17, 1999. Further revisions were published June 5, 2000; the final version was published March 16, 2001 and enacted June 14, 2001. The results are discussed in some detail at ¶2153. The final legislation does not, however, solve all problems. In particular, you will still be subject to double taxation if you move to a country with which Canada does not have a tax treaty but which imposes its own income tax on the actual disposition of your property after you leave Canada.

In short, leaving Canada is now, for all but the most indigent, a complex and costly undertaking. Moreover, the government has introduced further rules which may deem you to have left under a tax treaty even if this was not really your intention. In the circumstances, the best remaining offshore tax plan is to leave Canada while you are young and ambitious, and before you make your money. If you are no longer young and ambitious, and have already made your money, the government clearly feels you will welcome the opportunity to repay a fair share, twice if necessary, for the opportunities you have been given.

(Note that ceasing to be a Canadian resident usually implies a full cessation of residential ties, and not merely a "snowbird" sojourn in the south for the winter; see Chapter 1. This is no longer as certain as it was. If you leave Canada after February 23, 1998 for another country with which Canada has a tax treaty, such as the United States, your residence is determined under the treaty rather than traditional Canadian residence rules. The treaty will typically look first to your habitual abode; if you have one in each country, it will look to the country with which your personal and economic relations are closer. If this cannot be determined, citizenship will decide. If, however, you are a citizen of both countries or of neither, the treaty throws up its hands and leaves the matter to a lengthy and complex dispute between the governments. It is thus possible for you to more or less unintentionally become a non-resident and suffer the consequences of the deemed disposition rules. For most snowbirds, this probably is not a practical concern. However, there are bound to be a few cases in which being a snowbird becomes a matter of Canadian tax roulette. This could conceivably work to the snowbird's advantage. Often the snowbird wants to maintain Canadian residence for the sake of Canadian government funded health care. The new deemed non-residence rules presumably apply only for tax and not health care purposes, so if your assets are mainly those not subject to departure tax, such as Canadian pensions and RRSPs, you might conceivable be non-resident for tax purposes, escape departure tax, and still retain Canadian health care, such as it is. While not specifically relevant to most (if any) taxpayers, the recent *Black* case (2014 DTC 1046 (T.C.C.), which was subsequently appealed and dismissed in 2015 DTC 5024) contains an overview of some of these departure tax rules and their interaction with Canada's treaty system.)

EMPLOYEES

[¶2548] TAX PLANNING TECHNIQUES

There are various tax planning techniques available when determining the form and nature of the remuneration your employer could pay to you, including the following:

(1) Incorporating employment income,

(2) Company car,

(3) Company-paid benefits,

(4) Registered deferred compensation plans,

(5) Other deferred compensation plans,

(6) Employee stock options,

(7) Interest-free loans,

(8) Reimbursement of moving expenses, and

(9) Scholarships for employees and their families.

[¶2550] INCORPORATING EMPLOYMENT INCOME

The basic concept of the incorporated employee is that the employee sets up a corporation which offers the employee's services to the employer. If the corporation were taxed as an ordinary business, there would be numerous advantages to this, including an expansion of deductions for earning income, reduced tax on the first $500,000 of corporate income (a benefit generally available to small business corporations), deferral of tax on (especially low rate) income left in the corporation, and, potentially, splitting of employment income with other family members who are shareholders of the corporation.

Not surprisingly, the Department of Finance takes a dim view of the incorporated employee, and has long had in place a series of measures which have effectively discouraged the practice. The definition of "Personal Services Business" (PSB), discussed in ¶305 and ¶785, essentially applies to such a corporation and denies it most deductions as well as the small business tax rate. In the absence of these benefits, the incorporated employee who did not take out the corporation's earnings as salary faced a high degree of double taxation by withdrawing the earnings as dividends. Furthermore, the corporation is not eligible for the general corporate rate deduction, meaning that personal services income is subject to a federal corporate tax rate of 28%. Although some income splitting opportunities could remain, the obstacles have generally been considered too formidable to be worth the cost.

As discussed in ¶404 and ¶2513, for 2006 and later years, the dividend tax credit is enhanced in such a fashion that corporate income not taxed at small business rates may be flowed out as dividends at very little or no extra tax cost as compared with ordinary salary, especially if general corporate tax rates continue to fall as scheduled and provincial enhancements of designated dividend tax credits continue as scheduled.

[¶2551] COMPANY CAR

If you use a company owned or leased car, your employer may be required to include a reasonable standby charge and operating costs (¶326) as a taxable benefit in the taxable income reported on your T4 slip for the year. The cost to you of using the company car will normally be only the income taxes payable on the taxable benefit. However, you should consider the implications described at ¶322–¶327.

If you currently have substantial business use of your employer-provided automobile, your employer may be prepared to give you salary in lieu of a car, plus an allowance or reimbursement of expense. Depending on the arrangement you have with your employer, you may have either a non-taxable per kilometre allowance for business mileage, or you may have a taxable allowance and deduct the expenses of the car yourself, subject to the limitations at ¶370.

The issue of using your own as opposed to a company car has become so complex that some professional tax advisers have attempted to develop computer programs to model an ideal solution for any particular set of facts. It is not clear whether this high-tech solution is especially successful, but it does indicate the difficulty of generalizing. You must look at the options available to you in terms of the value and operating costs of the car you use, the percentage of employment as opposed to personal use, and, of course, the extent to which your employer is prepared to accommodate you.

Similarly, the decision to lease or buy your own automobile to be used in connection with your employment is a function of your particular circumstances. It should be primarily an economic decision. However, the tax system does impact the leasing situation in particular, since the deduction restrictions (¶738) impose a rigid formula which may have bizarre results when applied to some of the many commercial leasing cost variations available.

If you are using an employer's car, your standby charge will be based on actual cost while the employer's deductions will be limited to the prescribed cost or equivalent leasing value. This involves an element of double taxation which may be of concern to you if you are not at arm's length from your employer.

- *Planning Point:*

  If you are in a position to impose upon your company to give you personal and unique treatment on your automobile, and you are prepared to keep meticulous records on its operating cost and business use, you might consider having your company reimburse you for the specific per kilometre expenses you incur in employment. This would involve reimbursement not at a set per-kilometre rate but at the rate that reflects your actual costs. These reimbursements should be fully deductible to the company and tax-free to you. If you have an expensive car and a reasonable degree of business use, this technique could be a substantial benefit. If you lease your car, the lease costs should be includible as an expense, although depreciation on a purchased car would probably not be eligible for reimbursement. Interest expenses associated with a purchased car would seem a reimbursable expense.

(ITA: 6(1)(*e*), (2); 8(1)(*h*), (*j*); IT-522R Vehicle, Travel and Sales Expenses of Employees)

[¶2553] COMPANY-PAID BENEFITS

Certain company-paid benefits effectively stretch the compensation dollars an employer spends on his employees. This occurs when the company has a tax deductible expense and the employee does not have a taxable benefit equal to the expense which the company has incurred. Prior to 1994, group term life insurance (up to a value of $25,000 of term insurance) was an excellent example of this because there was no taxable benefit to the employee but the company incurred a tax deductible expense. However, the premium value of this insurance has become a taxable benefit to the employee as of July 1, 1994. There remain a few scattered employment benefits that "stretch" compensation dollars, such as employer contributions to group sickness or accident insurance plans and supplementary unemployment plans. These group plans have additional benefits since they often provide you and your family additional financial security at a cost not available to individuals on their own. The federal government does not tax the benefit of employer contributions to private health insurance plans, but Quebec treats the employer's contribution as a taxable benefit which may be included as a medical expense of the employee.

Non-taxable benefits include counselling services provided on your retirement (or dismissal), and counselling services provided for the physical and mental health of an employee or relative of an employee. This cannot be stretched to encompass the costs of certain recreational, sporting or similar facilities.

In seeking fringe benefits from your employer, remember that if your taxable benefit equals the company cost you are in the same tax position as if you had received the cash equivalent in salary.

(ITA: 6(1)(*a*)(iv), (4); Income Tax Folio: S2-F3-C2 Benefits and Allowances Received from Employment)

[¶2555] REGISTERED DEFERRED COMPENSATION PLANS

Payments to one or more of the registered pension plans (RPP), registered retirement savings plans (RRSP), and deferred profit sharing plans (DPSP) can be made in certain combinations by you or your employer. You should consider these plans, or combinations thereof, to determine which may be best suited to your personal circumstances.

The registered deferred plan rules (including RPPs and DPSPs) contemplate a "level playing field" in which contributions by an employer and employee together to RPPs and DPSPs cannot exceed 18% of income to a specified annual limit (the money purchase limit), which, for 2016, is $26,010 for RPPs and one-half of that amount for DPSPs, each indexed thereafter by annual wage growth (not the factor used for most tax indexing). RRSP contributions are integrated into this system in that they are based on income of the preceding year and take into account RPP and DPSP contributions and maximum limits of the preceding year. Annual RRSP limits are shown in ¶2606. In general, the integration of these plans is initially the responsibility of the employer, which must limit its contributions appropriately and report the result to you as a Pension Adjustment on your T4 slip, which will limit the amount you can contribute to an RRSP.

[¶2555.01] *Registered Pension Plans*

Registered pension plans (RPPs) are established by an employer, who can make deductible contributions within limits established by regulation. The plans may also require contributions by employees, and these are ordinarily deductible to the employee. The plans may also include "buy-back" options which allow employees in some circumstances to make up for years in which they were not covered by the plan or for years which can now earn more benefits than were provided at the time. While the current deduction rules are relatively simple (you may deduct what the plan requires, and the limitations must be built into the plan itself), the buy-back rules can be quite complex, and will differ depending on whether the past service is for years before 1990 or after 1989. Since the details of plans may vary widely, only the employer or pension plan administrator can usually decipher the correct amounts for a particular plan, and tell you how much is deductible.

It is intended that the funds which can be contributed to an RPP and deducted from income (including the employer's income) should be integrated with the overall amounts which can be put into the tax-deferred savings system for any particular individual. This is achieved by the use of pension adjustments (PAs) and past service pension adjustments (PSPAs), which limit the amount an employee can contribute to an RRSP.

RPPs are of two basic types: defined benefit plans and money purchase plans. Defined benefit plans are more common, at least with large employers, and determine the eventual pension based on a formula which usually involves years of service and annual salary in the last few years of service. The amount contributed to the plan in any particular year is an actuarial calculation related to the benefits eventually expected to be paid. Money purchase plans are more like the familiar RRSP; they are based on amounts contributed to plan on behalf of the employee each year (which are limited by law) and the eventual pension is essentially what the accumulated contributions will fund at retirement. After 2003, retirement income under a money purchase RPP can be taken out under RRIF rules (¶2632.05) as well as in the form of an annuity or by transfer to an RRSP or RRIF.

Where the employer company is essentially a family concern, a money purchase plan RPP and an RRSP should be very comparable. There may be some slight benefit to the money purchase plan in years prior to 2011, as RRSP contribution limits lag behind money purchase contribution limits by $1,000 in each year. The benefit is less after 2010, although there is a slight benefit to RPPs at the RPP limit is adjusted for inflation a year ahead of the RRSP limit.

Where you borrow money to make contributions to a registered pension fund or plan the interest on the loan is not deductible for tax purposes. This applies to contributions made after November 12, 1981. Interest on loans taken out prior to November 13, 1981 to make contributions continues to be deductible even if the loan has been refinanced (although the CRA may see an abuse if the refinanced loan makes no provision for repayment of principal).

If you elect to pay a past service contribution in a year, it is probable that you will be required to pay accrued interest in addition to the basic contribution for the past services. Where a past service contribution, including accrued interest, is to be paid in instalments, it is probable that further interest will have to be paid in respect of each instalment.

In the case of *Walton v. M.N.R,* 89 DTC 423, the Tax Court of Canada overruled the CRA position and held that the interest element of past service contributions is fully deductible where the interest is melded into a periodic payment, even though a different result would be obtained if the taxpayer went to the bank and financed a lump-sum past service contribution. The CRA accepted the Tax Court ruling with unseemly haste (surely not because so many civil servants benefit from the result).

(ITA: 8(1)(*m*), (*m*.1), (11); 20(1)(*s*); 147.2(4); Window on Canadian Tax: 2725; IT-167R6 Registered Pension Plans — Employee's Contributions)

[¶2555.02] *Registered Retirement Savings Plan*

You may consider a registered retirement savings plan (RRSP) in lieu of or in addition to your employer's pension plan. In some cases, small employers will have a program of contributing to an RRSP on your behalf instead of providing a company pension plan. If your employer provides a registered pension plan (see above) or a deferred profit sharing plan (see below), your membership in that plan will generally reduce the amount you can contribute to an RRSP. Where the employer makes contributions to an RRSP on your behalf, the amount contributed reduces the amount of contributions you are allowed to make on your own account: the employer's contributions are counted as amounts paid to you (and so included in income) but deducted again under the RRSP rules. The results are essentially similar to pension plan membership.

You may in principle contribute up to 18% of your prior year's earned income to a maximum contribution of $25,370 in 2016, and $26,010 in 2017. (The dollar maximum is shown in the chart at ¶2606.) However, your 18%/$25,370 or 18%/$26,010 limit will be eroded by your "Pension Adjustment" (PA) for the previous year, calculated by your employer and representing the value of benefits accrued to you under RPPs and DPSPs of the employer. On the other hand, your current year contribution limit can be increased by 1991 or later undercontributions; that is, by contributions you were entitled to make but did not. These additions are referred to as the carryforward of unused contribution room.

For example, if you are calculating the amount you can contribute by March 1, 2017, for deduction on your 2016 tax return to be filed in April 2017, you start with 18% of your 2015 income to a maximum of $24,930 (the maximum for 2015). This is reduced by your 2015 PA. The PA should have been reported to you on your 2015 T4 slip. However, your carryforward amount, 2015 earned income, and 2015 PA should all be included in the Contribution Limit Statement which should be printed as part of the Notice of Assessment for your 2015 return. The Contribution Limit Statement on your Notice of Assessment is merely a statement of information based on your 1992 through 2015 returns and is indicative rather than definitive of your 2016 "RRSP contribution room". For example, there can be a further adjustment to RRSP contribution limits (the Past Service Pension Adjustment) for any pension upgrades not associated with inflationary increases, and this would not be reported on the Contribution Limit Statement. All this is set out in excessive detail in Chapter 26, beginning at ¶2604.

As discussed above, the objective of these rules is to ensure that approximately the same overall limitations on benefits accruing under tax-deferred savings plans will apply to all employees and non-employees. This may not happen where an individual ceases to be a member of a pension or deferred profit sharing plan before rights are fully vested. Such an employee may have had a Pension Adjustment reducing RRSP contribution room on account of pension income which because of the failure to vest will never be received. Commencing in 1999, employees (or former employees) in this situation receive additional RRSP contribution room (to be known as Pension Adjustment Reversal or PAR) to compensate for excessive Pension Adjustments which reduced contribution room in the past. Amounts will be calculated by employers or plan administrators and reported on T4 slips as with Pension Adjustments.

The current $2,000 overcontribution limit, although intended merely to provide scope for error, does provide scope for an ongoing (cumulative $2,000) overcontribution in order to accumulate more tax-deferred earnings in an RRSP. There may be situations, especially close to retirement, where it may be worthwhile to incur penalty tax. See ¶2614c.10.

- *Planning Point:*

If you were employed in a taxation year (and so have "earned income", which is essentially business or employment income) for the first time since 1990 (or for the first time ever if you are just starting out), you will find that you cannot deduct an RRSP contribution for the year. This is because of the time lag rules discussed above; your "contribution room" is measured by the previous year's income plus carryforwards from 1991. Especially if your employer makes RRSP contributions on your behalf, you may find that you have made contributions which you cannot deduct for the year. This occurs once for everyone who joins or rejoins the work force for the first time after 1990. It is usually not a serious problem, in that you will be able to deduct the contributions in the following year. On the other hand, you will not get your anticipated deduction in the first year of work. So long as your total undeductible contributions do not reach $2,000 at any point in a calendar year, there is no penalty to making undeductible contributions on your own account; indeed, there is a benefit in terms of accumulated savings. Where your employer makes RRSP contributions on your behalf under general plan for the benefit of employees, the $2,000 limit may be waived depending on the terms and conditions of the employer's plan. Where undeductible contributions do exceed $2,000 at any point during a calendar year, there may be penalty taxes (although they may not be enough to be serious, they will wipe out the benefits of early contribution). For overcontribution rules and penalties, see ¶2611.15.

- *Planning Point:*

If you have used or propose to use the RRSP Home Buyers' Plan, you cannot make deductible RRSP contributions during a specified period. See ¶2625.10.

- *Planning Point:*

If your employer makes RRSP contributions on your behalf and you propose to use the RRSP Home Buyers' Plan, you may have a particularly intractable problem with the rule just above. The problem is not insoluble; indeed, there are several solutions. Your employer, if you give sufficient notice of your intention, may be able to defer contributions for you, or you may be able to withdraw them under general rules. However, you should discuss the issue with your employer as soon as you decide to use the Home Buyers' Plan.

- *Planning Point:*

Assuming your Pension Adjustment leaves room to make RRSP contributions, all the planning points in ¶2530 and ¶2543 above will apply.

(ITA: 146(5); 204.2)

[¶2555.03] *Deferred Profit Sharing Plans*

Deferred profit sharing plans (DPSPs) can be used to shelter income as an alternative to RPPs. Employers may contribute (per employee) up to $13,005 for 2016. The amount is indexed annually for statistical increases in the average Canadian wage (not the same standard used for other tax indexing). Vesting must occur within two years. Employer contributions to a DPSP in and after 1990 are included in the Pension Adjustment which reduces the amount the employee can contribute to an RRSP in the following year.

Commencing with calendar 1991, employees can no longer contribute to a DPSP at all. However, it will remain possible to deduct the amount of your earlier contributions from the taxable withdrawals that you make from the plan until your contributions have been recovered.

[¶2555.04] *Pooled Registered Pension Plans*

The federal government recently introduced legislation regarding pooled registered pension plans (PRPPs). The *Pooled*

Registered Pension Plans Act received Royal Assent on June 28, 2012, and will take effect on a day to be fixed by order of the Governor in Council. Accompanying amendments to the *Income Tax Act* came into force on December 14, 2012. These plans will allow employers and their employees, or self-employed individuals, to make tax-deductible contributions to the plans similar to those made to money purchase RPPs.

An employer's contribution to a PRPP in a taxation year will not be a taxable benefit to the employee, although it will reduce the employee's RRSP deduction room for the same year (paragraph 146(5)(*b*)). As such, unlike registered pension plans, there will be no pension adjustment (PA) in respect of PRPPs.

The employee's contribution in a year will be treated as a contribution to an RRSP for various purposes, including subsection 146(5) dealing with the amount deductible for an annuitant's contributions to an RRSP (subsection 147.5(11)). As such, the employee's contribution in a year will also reduce the employee's RRSP deduction room for that year. Distributions from the PRPP and paid to the employee will be included in income and can qualify for the pension credit.

Commentary on Legislative Proposals (Sept. 16, 2016)

Note: When Legislative Proposals, September 16, 2016, achieves Royal Assent, the commentary will be modified to read:

Effective December 14, 2012, an amount of PRPP contributions refunded to a member is not included in his/her income if they were made in error or to avoid the revocation of the plan, and if the amount was not deducted as a PRPP contribution in the year of the refund or any preceding year.

Commentary on Legislative Proposals (Sept. 16, 2016)

Note: When Legislative Proposals, September 16, 2016, achieves Royal Assent, the commentary will be modified to read:

Effective December 14, 2012, a PRPP contribution is deemed not to have been made where there is a refund of a contribution made to a PRPP by a taxpayer as a result of a reasonable error or a refund to avoid the revocation of the PRPP, which amount is not deducted as a PRPP contribution for the taxation year in which the refund is made or for any preceding taxation year.

Upon the death of the member of the PRPP, a financially dependent minor child or grandchild of the member who receives a lump-sum payment from the plan will include the amount in income, but will be allowed the offsetting deduction under paragraph 60(*v*) if the amount is used to purchase an annuity payable to age 18 (see ¶1021.10). Similarly, a financially dependent child or grandchild by reason of infirmity will be allowed to rollover a lump sum received upon the member's death to a registered disability savings plan (RDSP) of the child or grandchild under section 60.02 (see ¶1021.10 and ¶1914.17).

Additionally, a tax-free rollover upon the death of the member of the PRPP will apply if a lump sum is transferred to a beneficiary who is either the member's spouse or common-law partner or financially dependent child or grandchild (by reason of infirmity), if the amount is transferred directly to the beneficiary's PRPP, RPP, RRSP, or RRIF, or is used to acquire a qualifying annuity (subsections 147.5(20) and (21)).

(ITA: 147)

[¶2557] OTHER DEFERRED COMPENSATION PLANS

In addition to the above registered plans you may consider negotiating with your employer for other benefits which effectively defer the compensation you receive currently. These other deferred compensation techniques include death benefits, retiring allowances and employee benefit plans.

[¶2557.01] *Death Benefits*

You may wish to negotiate a provision in your employment contract for the payment of a death benefit to your spouse or common-law partner or beneficiaries in the event of your death. (A death benefit is defined as an amount received upon or after the death of an employee in recognition of the employee's service.) The first $10,000 of all death benefits paid by all your employer(s) can be received by your spouse or common-law partner (as defined at ¶1113) or another beneficiary free of tax. If you do not provide for all your death benefits to be left to one spouse or common-law partner, the $10,000 exemption must then be allocated among all recipients *pro rata* to the amounts they receive. If you allocate death benefits to one surviving spouse or common-law partner and other non-spouse beneficiaries, the surviving spouse or common-law partner gets first claim on the $10,000 exemption, with the others sharing the remaining exemption (if any) *pro rata*. If the death benefit must be shared among two or more surviving spouses or common-law partners, whether or not there are also other beneficiaries, everyone takes a *pro rata* share of the $10,000 exemption. See ¶925.

(ITA: 248(1) "death benefit")

[¶2557.02] *Retiring Allowances*

A retiring allowance is an amount payable by your employer to you in recognition of long service or in respect of loss of employment. Retiring allowances are deductible to your company and are taxable to you upon receipt. However, where the retiring allowance relates to employment that commenced before 1996, taxes on the retiring allowance may be partially deferred through contributions to a registered retirement savings plan. The permitted special RRSP contribution (which is over and above normal contributions) will be $2,000 per year of service with the employer before 1996, plus another $1,500 per year of service before 1989 for which there was no pension or DPSP vesting. This benefit is being gradually phased out by denying recognition to years of service after 1995 in the contribution formula. See details at ¶2612.05.

That portion of a retiring allowance eligible for RRSP contribution will, if paid directly by the employer to your RRSP, escape the withholding of tax normally required on compensation paid by the employer. This can prevent financing problems that might otherwise arise on your contribution of the maximum allowance to your RRSP. If the employer transfers more than your contribution limits permit, of course, there can be penalty tax until the excess is withdrawn and becomes subject to tax (¶2611.15).

If you die prior to receiving the retiring allowance, the payment made to your surviving spouse or common-law partner will be considered a death benefit, as described above.

(ITA: 56(1)(*a*)(ii); 248(1) "retiring allowance"; IT-337R4; Other Publications: CRA *Income Tax Technical News* Nos. 19, 20; *Employer's Guide to Payroll Deductions (Basic Information)* (T4001), Chapter 4)

[¶2557.03] *Deferred Compensation Arrangements*

Many deferred compensation plans will now be subject to one set or another of special rules described in Chapter 3. The most commonly applicable rules will be the salary deferral rules discussed at ¶307. It is worth noting that certain bonus plans and sabbatical plans are specifically sanctioned by these rules. As well, certain "phantom" income plans (¶359) may continue to permit deferral opportunities. These plans typically provide for future compensation tied to movements in company stock price.

In some cases, executives (most often owner-managers) will want to stake out entitlements to remuneration when the employer's future cash flow permits. This can normally be accomplished in part. A bonus or contract payment can be awarded to be paid at such future time as the directors consider the company's position to permit it. This is known as a contingency; and so long as the employee has no right to enforce payment at any particular time, and it appears that one of the main purposes for the transaction is not to defer tax, and the company does not endeavour to deduct the compensation on a current basis, there should be no current tax to the employee. Where the agreement creates an enforceable right either now or, less clearly, on the occurrence of some specific future event, problems will arise and professional advice is essential.

(IT-109R2, para. 15(e))

[¶2559] EMPLOYEE STOCK OPTIONS

If you are an employee of a corporation or Canadian mutual fund, and your employer offers a securities option plan, this may prove to be a significant benefit. Employee options permit you to acquire shares or units of the company at a price stated in the option (typically the value of the shares etc. at that time). The economic benefit is that if the value of the company, as reflected in the price of its shares or units, increases, you will be entitled to acquire those securities at the option price, which is less than market price, by exercising the options. You can, for example, acquire shares for $100 which you can sell immediately for $200. The benefit of this plan for the employer is that it costs more or less nothing currently to give you the option, and having the option should encourage you to do your best to raise the value of the company.

The tax consequences vary, but when you exercise the options, the difference between the exercise price and the fair market value on the date of exercise will be considered employment income to you. However, there will be an offsetting deduction from taxable income, so that at the end of the day you will include in income subject to tax only the amount that would be included if the difference were a capital gain rather than employment income. Thus, only half the difference between the exercise price and the fair market value on the date of exercise will be subject to tax.

To qualify for the offsetting deduction, either 1) the option price must equal the fair market value of the shares at the time the option was granted, or 2) the shares must be Canadian controlled private corporation (CCPC) shares that you hold for at least 2 years.

If you are an employee of a CCPC which you do not control, the income inclusion of the stock option benefit is deferred to the year of disposition of the shares.

The government encourages you to make charitable donations of the shares acquired with the qualified options by further reducing the final amount included in income subject to tax to one-half of what it would otherwise be, provided the donation is made within 30 days of exercising the option (and within the same taxation year).

All this is considered in vastly more detail in ¶330.

(ITA: 7(1)(*a*), (1.1); 110(1)(*d*), (*d*.1))

[¶2561] INTEREST-FREE LOANS

If you or a related person are a significant (generally 10% or more) shareholder, the entire value of an employer loan can be included in your income, with specific exceptions permitted. For arm's length employees, an interest-free loan from an employer or related party will create a benefit subject to tax equal to the notional (prescribed) interest rate you otherwise would have had to pay for the loan. The notion is that your benefit is what your employer would have paid you if you borrowed the money commercially and the employer paid you additional salary to offset the interest expense of borrowing the money. Accordingly, such loans entitle you to only minimal tax benefits, if any. However, certain loans can still be structured to provide a benefit. For instance, the loan can be made to the employee to allow him to purchase shares in the corporation or an automobile to be used for company business. This in turn allows the employee to claim the benefit as an interest expense deduction with a proration required for interest related to the automobile loan based on business use. See ¶370 and ¶409.

Employees who relocate on commencing work at a new location can receive a tax-free "home relocation loan" of up to $25,000 for a period of up to five years. The loan will be free of the deemed interest benefit. The home relocation must bring its employee at least 40 kilometres closer to his or her new work location than his or her former home. Although the employee must commence work at a new location, it need not be for a new employer. See ¶353 and ¶409.

- *Planning Point:*

  If you are moving to a new job, consider negotiating a home relocation loan as part of your compensation package. Note also that reimbursements of many moving expenses will be deductible.

(ITA: 6(23); 80.4; 80.5; 248(1) "eligible relocation"; Income Tax Folio: S3-F10-C1 Qualified Investments – RRSPs, RESPs, RRIFs, RDSPs and TFSAs; S3-F10-C2 Prohibited Investments - RRSPs, RRIFs and TFSAs)

[¶2562] MOVING EXPENSES

The deduction for moving expenses is potentially available in most situations where an individual moves to a new work location (even if an employee remains with the same employer) or to attend a post-secondary institution full-time. The deduction can be claimed by both employees and independent businesspeople.

The move must bring the individual at least 40 kilometres closer to his or her new place of work or school. At one time, the distance was measured "as the crow flies". However, *Giannakopoulos v. The Queen*, 95 DTC 5477 (F.C.A.), indicates that the correct approach is to use the shortest normal route open to the public (including ferries and rail lines, where applicable). The minimum distance is not to be measured in a straight line, but by the shortest normal route open to the travelling public.

The proper measurement was recently considered in *Hauser v. The Queen*, 2014 TCC 328. In that case, the Minister asserted that the proper measurement was through the use of a major city road, which resulted in a 25 kilometre journey. The taxpayer argued that the urban road was too congested due to construction and that the preferred route, which bypassed the city, should be used, thereby resulting in a 45 kilometre journey. The Tax Court, applying *Giannakopoulos*, held that while the construction may have made the route more difficult, it did not alter the urban road as the normal route used by the travelling public and, therefore, the appropriate basis for the measurement.

Form T1-M, which should be filed with the taxpayer's moving expense claim, itemizes a number of other important deductions. These include:

- travel costs (including reasonable amounts for meals and lodging) in the course of moving the individual and members of his or her household;
- the cost of transporting or storing household effects in the course of moving — including items such as boats and trailers;
- the cost of meals and lodging near the old or new residence for the taxpayer and members of his or her household, for a period of up to 15 days;
- the cost of cancelling a lease for the old residence;
- selling costs in respect of the sale of the old residence, including real estate commissions (this would also include, for example, mortgage penalties for early discharge, legal fees); and
- where the old residence is being sold by the taxpayer or his or her spouse as a result of the move, the cost of legal services in respect of the purchase of the new residence, as well as any tax, fee, or duty (other than any goods and services tax or value-added tax); this includes transfer or title registration taxes. Other than this, no other costs in respect of the acquisition of the new home are allowable as moving expenses.

More recently, the list of tax-deductible moving expenses has been extended to include certain costs of maintaining a vacant former residence (including mortgage interest and property taxes) to a limit of $5,000. Also deductible are costs of revising legal documents to reflect the address of the taxpayer's new residence, replacing drivers' licenses and non-commercial vehicle permits (excluding any cost for vehicle insurance), and connecting or disconnecting utilities.

With respect to moving expenses, a taxpayer can choose to claim meal and vehicle expenses using one of two methods. First, the taxpayer can claim these expenses in accordance with actual receipts and records of the expenses incurred. Alternatively, meal and/or vehicle expenses can be calculated using a simplified method. In the case of meals, a flat rate per meal is claimed. For vehicle expenses, a record must be kept of the number of kilometres driven in the course of moving. The amount that may be claimed for vehicle expenses is determined by multiplying the number of kilometres travelled in the course of moving by a flat per kilometre rate. Both the meal and travel flat rates are found on the CRA website.

Taxpayers are advised to calculate their expenses using both methods before filing. The differences between the two methods can be dramatic. If an individual has filed using actual receipts, the CRA usually will not permit an amendment to the tax return.

Some restrictions — students may also deduct moving expenses, but in this case, special rules apply. Deductions may be claimed if the student moves to take a job (this includes a summer job). But if a student moves to attend a post-secondary school full- time, deductions can be taken only against taxable scholarships and research grants.

In the year of relocation, expenses can be deducted only against income made in the new location. However, undeducted moving expenses can be applied to next year's tax return against future income in the new job or business. (This would be particularly helpful if the move was late in the year.)

Effective for the 2008 and subsequent taxation years, any amounts received under the *Wage Earner Protection Program Act* (WEPP) in respect of a taxpayer's employment at a new work location are considered to be part of the taxpayer's income when computing the deduction for moving expenses. The WEPP provides a level of compensation for lost employee wages due to employer bankruptcy or insolvency. Amounts received thereunder are intended to place employees in a position similar to the one they would have been in had they been fully compensated by their employer.

Of course, moving expenses that are paid for or reimbursed by the employer are not deductible. However, an employee may, if desired, include partial reimbursements in income, then deduct moving expenses that are eligible for deductions. This will be beneficial if eligible moving expenses exceed the amounts paid by the employer.

See also ¶353, ¶356 and ¶1045.

- *Planning Point:*

If you are moving in the course of employment or to a new employment, consider a reimbursement of expenses from your employer in preference to claiming deductions yourself. There is usually a timing advantage in that you do not have to wait for your tax refund to obtain the benefit, and there may be some items, such as reimbursement if you suffer a loss on your old house, for which you would not be equally compensated by normal deduction/capital loss rules.

(ITA: 6(19)– (21); 248(1) "eligible relocation"; Income Tax Folio: S1-F3-C4 Moving Expenses; *Splane v. The Queen*, 90 DTC 6442 (F.C.T.D.), aff'd 92 DTC 6021 (F.C.A.); *The Queen v. Phillips*, 94 DTC 6177 (F.C.A); *A.G. of Canada v. Hoefele et al.*, 95 DTC 5602 (F.C.A.))

[¶2563] EMPLOYMENT EXPENSES

[¶2563.01] *Overview*

Employees are much more limited than self-employed persons in the deductions they may claim for the expenses of earning income. The limitations are sometimes quite unfair. However, if you do have employment income, are required to incur expenses in the course of earning such income, and you are not reimbursed for these expenses, you should review the possibility of deducting them. See Chapter 3 from ¶362 on, and especially ¶372 and ¶373. For most such claims, you will need a certification from your employer (on form T2200) that the expenses are required to be incurred by you in the course of your employment. The CRA provides a useful review of potential deductions in its T4044) *Employment Expenses* guide, available without charge from its District Offices.

Commission sales employees are allowed a slightly broader range of deductions than employees generally.

Note that deductible expenses generally cannot include personal expenses, such as clothing or transportation to or from work. However, unreimbursed transportation to or from clients might be deductible.

(ITA: 8, especially (2), (10))

[¶2563.02] *Employee's Office in Home*

Maintaining an office in your home in which you conduct employment activities can involve special problems and limitations. Employees seeking to deduct such office-in-home expenses from employment income are limited to a *pro rata* share of rent and supplies costs, and must have the necessity of the home office certified by the employer on form T2200. Supplies will, in general, include a reasonable allocation for heat, light, cleaning and minor repairs, as well as actual office supplies. The employee who rents living accommodation is permitted a *pro rata* share of rent as well as supplies costs, but employees (other than commission sales employees) who own their homes may not deduct any amounts for taxes, insurance, mortgage interest, nor capital cost allowance. Commencing in 1991, employees are also subject to the same restrictions that apply to business offices in the home; that is, the work space must meet one of the two following tests:

(1) the work space must be where the employee principally performs the duties of employment; or

(2) the work space must be both used exclusively to earn employment income and used on a regular and continuous basis for meeting customers or others in the course of employment.

Office-in-home expenses which meet all the tests above cannot be deducted except to the extent of income from the employment to which they relate; any excess can be carried forward indefinitely but only against income from the same employment.

Expenses such as specific long distance phone calls and cellular phone air time, office supplies and similar items are not considered to relate to work space and are not subject to the work space limitations. Typically, if work-related these items can be deducted in full subject to the more general limitations above, such as the form T2200 requirement.

See also ¶373.

(ITA: 8(1)(*f*), (*i*), (10), (13); IT-352R2 Employee's expenses, including work space in home expenses)

[¶2563.03] *Hardship Cases*

Some employees must incur substantial undeductible expenditures in the course of employment. A mechanic who must bring his or her own tools to the job is an example. In this case, it may be possible to generate some taxable business income, and claim expenses or capital cost allowance creating an overall business loss against other (employment) income. This technique must be approached with caution, however. The business must have some profit potential to justify the deductions (see ¶700). As well, you may be inviting inquiry into how extensive your business activities are. Of course, since you should be reporting all your incidental business income, this should not really trouble you.

[¶2563.04] *Automobile Expenses*

The major employee expense deductions often involve use of your personally owned or leased automobile on company business. In general, these expenses are deductible if you have an employer certified form T2200 for them, and if you have reasonable records, usually in the form of mileage logs and expense records, justifying the proportion of expenses allocated to business use. Capital cost allowance may be claimed on owned (as opposed to leased) automobiles under these rules. However, the general limitations on deductions in respect of the cost of the car itself, whether owned or leased, apply to employee claims. These limit the cost eligible for capital cost or leasing cost deductions to the first $30,000 (2001–2015) of the car's cost. See ¶369, ¶370, and ¶2551 concerning these expenses. A further claim for GST rebate may be available if automobile expenses have been deducted; see ¶363.

- *Planning Point:*

  Employees who incur deductible employment expenses which include an element of GST may claim a GST rebate in addition to their employment expense deductions. Employees in New Brunswick, Newfoundland and Labrador and Nova Scotia may also claim a similar HST rebate. In many cases, the rebate will not be worth the trouble of calculating; still, the dedicated tax saver should not overlook this claim. The claim is made on a special form, GST 370 and is described in detail in the CRA's *Employment Expenses* guide (T4044). Claims made in the preceding year under this provision must be accounted for as additions to income or reductions to the capital cost of related assets in the current year. Claims made in the preceding year under this rule must be accounted for in the current year as additions to income or reductions to the capital cost of related assets.

(ITA: 8(1)(*f*), (*h.1*), (*j*), (10); 13(7)(*g*); 67.2; 67.3; ITR: 7307 [Prescribed amount – automobile deduction limits]; IT-522R Vehicle, Travel and Sales Expenses of Employees)

[¶2564] SCHOLARSHIPS FOR EMPLOYEES AND THEIR FAMILIES

Recent amendments have increased the attractiveness of corporate scholarship plans for employees and their families. Scholarships from employers may now be granted for elementary, secondary, and post-secondary education. If properly structured, there is no taxable benefit to the employee, and the scholarship is deductible to the employer and not taxable to the recipient of the scholarship (i.e., the student).

If your employer has paid tuition fees on your behalf, or has reimbursed you for tuition fees paid by you, for a course which is merely of personal interest to you or provides technical skills which are not related to your employer's business, the amount paid should be reported as income by you for the year in which the payment was received.

Courses taken for the maintenance or upgrading of employer-related skills, when it is reasonable to assume that the employee will resume his or her employment for a reasonable period of time after completion of the courses, will generally be considered to primarily benefit the employer and therefore be non-taxable. For example, fees and other associated costs such as meals, travel, and accommodation, which are paid for courses leading to a degree, diploma, or certificate in a field related to the employee's current or potential future responsibilities in the employer's business will not result in a taxable benefit.

Other business-related courses, although not directly related to the employer's business, will generally be considered non-taxable. Examples of non-taxable training include stress management, employment equity, first-aid, and language skills. Normally, in-house training will not be considered a taxable benefit.

If you do include tuition fees in your income, you may be entitled to a tax credit for them; see ¶1319. If your employer has paid your tuition fees, directly or by reimbursing you, and not included the amount in your income, you may not claim either tuition credit or education amount (¶1337; the education credit was repealed effective January 1, 2017). Similarly, if you have been paid by your employer while taking training in connection with duties of employment, you may not claim the education amount for that training. See ¶310 regarding tuition and other financial assistance provided to you by your employer.

In terms of employer-provided financial assistance for dependants of the employee, the CRA's position (since 2007) provides that where a post-secondary educational institution offers free tuition to an employee's dependant or employers offer a scholarship program for employees' dependants the amounts will be reported as scholarships for the dependants and not an employment benefit for the employee. In particular, in its T4130 Employer's Guide on taxable benefits and allowances, the CRA provides the following rules for employers who provide scholarships, bursaries, or tuition to the family members of employees for **post-secondary** education.

- If, as a post-secondary educational institution, you provide free tuition to an employee's family members, do not include the amount in the employee's income. Instead, report the fair market value (FMV) as a scholarship on a T4A slip for the family member.
- If you paid or reimbursed the tuition fees, books, and supplies related to post-secondary education for an employee's family member, do not include the amount in your employee's income. Instead, report the FMV as a scholarship on a T4A slip for the family member.
- If you operate a post-secondary scholarship or bursary program for the family members of your employees, do not include the amount in your employee's income. Instead, report the FMV as a scholarship on a T4A slip for the family member.

A recent legislative amendment which received Royal Assent on June 26, 2013 (subparagraph 6(1)(*a*)(vi)) effectively codifies the non-taxation of such payments received or enjoyed by persons other than the employee, such as the employee's family members, where the employer and employee deal at arm's length and the amount is not a substitute for salary or other remuneration for the employee. The amendment applies after October 30, 2011. Furthermore, in its Tax Folios publication "S1-F2-C3: Scholarships, Research Grants and Other Education Assistance", the CRA explains that the new rule provides that such payments for elementary or secondary education will now be non-taxable to the employee:

> ... these proposals will apply to benefits received or enjoyed by the family member with respect to the family member's attendance at an elementary, secondary or post-secondary school (private or otherwise). It will also apply to tuition discounts provided by such educational institutions to the family members of its employees. The amount of the benefit received or enjoyed by the family member under the program will be included in computing the family member's income under subparagraph 56(1)(*n*)(i). If the family member is eligible to claim the education tax credit under subsection 118.6(2) in connection with his or her enrolment in the educational program, or the benefit is received in connection with the family member's enrolment in an elementary or secondary school educational program, the entire amount may be exempt from tax pursuant to the scholarship exemption.

[¶2565] REDUCTION OF EMPLOYMENT WITHHOLDINGS

In general, your employer is required to withhold from your pay and remit to the government amounts representing the tax you would normally pay for the pay period if you earned income at the same rate throughout the year (see ¶224). These are called "source deductions".

The law permits you to apply directly to the CRA to authorize your employer to reduce your source deductions in cases of "undue hardship". If you are incurring business or investment losses (including tax shelter losses), incurring deductible interest expense, making RRSP contributions or have other deductible expenditures, you may apply to your CRA Tax Services Office in order to have the amount of your withholdings on employment income reduced. This could increase your personal cash flow and allow for investment of the funds that otherwise would not have been received as a tax refund until after filing your personal income tax return.

To obtain a reduction of withholdings, you must request (in writing) a Letter of Authorization from the Client Services Division of your local CRA Tax Services Office (see ¶287). The CRA provides form T1213 for this purpose. Although its use is optional (you may simply send a letter explaining your request), the form does at least indicate the kind of support required in common situations. You should include an explanation of why less tax should be deducted and documentary support, such as a history of monthly RRSP contributions or your deductible support payments and the court order or agreement justifying the deduction. The CRA has a target of four to six weeks for issuing a Letter of Authorization, but will not issue such letters where you owe it money or have a tax return which is overdue for filing. Once the letter is issued to you, you present it to your employer, who should then reduce withholding accordingly.

While the CRA will consider all undue hardship claims on their merits, it has established policies to regularize certain common claims, and will normally grant withholding reductions to recognize the following situations:

- you normally make periodic RRSP contributions;
- you normally make periodic deductible spousal support payments;
- you normally incur deductible child care expenses;
- you have deductible employment expenses;
- your income is normally reduced by interest expense and carrying charges on investment loans; and
- you live in one province but report for work in another.

Your employer does not require a letter of authorization to reduce the amounts withheld for certain compensation which will be non-taxable, typically because an offsetting deduction is permitted. Thus, where the employer pays on your behalf registered pension plan or registered retirement savings plan contributions, union or professional dues, or amounts under a retirement compensation arrangement, or deductible support payments to a former spouse or common-law partner, those amounts (although technically compensation to you) need not be subjected to withholding.

Similarly, transfers of eligible amounts of retiring allowances, including termination payments, directly to your RRSP are not subject to withholding. As well, certain permitted lump-sum transfers to an RPP or RRSP from other deferred income plans should not be subject to withholding.

- *Planning Point:*

  You may be able to more easily afford to save through regular RRSP contributions by obtaining authority for your employer to reduce your withholding tax to reflect the contributions. If your employer contributes to an RRSP directly on your behalf, the letter of authority should not be necessary to obtain the reduction. Similar reductions can be obtained for deductible support payments. Note that reduction of source withholdings is not limited to these cases, and you may apply whenever you can document that your source deductions for a particular year will be excessive.

(ITA: 153(1.1); Other Publications: *Employer's Guide — Payroll Deductions and Remittances* (T4001, Chapter 6))

[¶2565.05] *Withholding Reduction No Longer Allowed for Employee Stock Option Benefits Other Than CCPC Benefits*

The Act always appeared to hold that benefits derived from the exercise of stock options were subject to withholding at source pursuant to the withholding rules of section 153. Historically, the CRA waived the requirement in certain cases where there were insufficient cash funds from which the employer could withhold.

Effective as of 2011 (except for options granted before 2011 if the stock option agreement was entered into before 4:00 p.m. EST on March 4, 2010 and contained a written condition that restricts the employee from disposing of the securities for a period of time after exercise), subsection 153(1.01) of the Act specifically provides that employee stock option benefits will be subject to regular withholding as if the benefit was a bonus payment. The Act also provides that the CRA cannot reduce the withholding at source upon the taxpayer's request (under subsection 153(1.1)) solely because the amount of withholding arose from a non-cash benefit (e.g., the benefit arising on the acquisition of the securities). However, the amount subject to withholding will be reduced by one half if the one-half deduction in computing taxable income under paragraph 110(1)(*d*) is available to the employee (see ¶330.25).

Subsection 153(1.01) does not apply to a benefit in respect of the acquisition of a security of a Canadian-controlled private corporation where the benefit is deferred (¶330.65).

[¶2569] TERMINATION PAYMENTS

If you received any special payments on losing your job, and the job commenced before 1996, some part of the payments may be eligible for contributions to an RRSP provided your offsetting contributions are made in the year of receipt of the termination payments or within 60 days following the year of receipt, subject to the retiring allowance limitations at ¶2557, above. See also ¶923.

(ITA: 60(*j*.1))

Chapter 26

Tax Deferred Plans and Special Income Arrangements

THESE POINTS ARE COVERED IN THIS CHAPTER

CRA REFERENCES RELATING TO THIS CHAPTER

T1 Lines and Schedules

- Line 115 — Other pensions or superannuation
- Line 125 — Registered disability savings plan income
- Line 129 — RRSP income (from all T4RSP slips)
- Line 130 — Other income
- Line 205 — PRPP employer contributions (amount from your PRPP contribution receipts)
- Line 206 — Pension adjustment (box 52 of all T4 slips and box 034 of all T4A slips)
- Line 207 — Registered pension plan deduction (box 20 of all T4 slips and box 032 of all T4A slips)
- Line 208 — RRSP/pooled registered pension plan (PRPP) deduction (see Schedule 7, and attach receipts)
- Line 232 — Other deductions
- Line 437 — Total income tax deducted
- Federal Worksheet, Line 314 — Pension income amount
- Schedule 1, Line 314 — Pension income amount
- Schedule 7, RRSP and PRPP Unused Contributions, Transfers, and HBP or LLP Activities

CRA Guides

5000-G, "General Income Tax and Benefit Guide"; **RC4092**, "Registered Education Savings Plans (RESPs)"; **RC4112**, "Lifelong Learning Plan (LLP) — Includes Form RC96"; **RC4137**, "Pension Adjustment Reversal Guide"; **RC4157**, "Deducting Income Tax on Pension and Other Income, and Filing the T4A Slip and Summary"; **RC4177**, "Death of an RRSP Annuitant"; **RC4178**, "Death of a RRIF Annuitant"; **RC4460**, "Registered Disability Savings Plan"; **RC4466**, "Tax Free Savings Account (TFSA), Guide for Individuals"; **T4040**, "RRSPs and Other Registered Plans for Retirement"; **T4041**, "Retirement Compensation Arrangements Guide"; **T4079**, "T4RSP and T4RIF Guide"; **T4084**, "Pension Adjustment Guide"; **T4099**, "Registered Pension Plan Guide"; **T4104**, "Past Service Pension Adjustment Guide"

CRA Forms

NRTA1, "Authorization for Non-Resident Tax Exemption"; **RC96**, "Lifelong Learning Plan (LLP) Request to Withdraw Funds from an RRSP"; **RC236**, "Application for a TFSA (Tax-Free Savings Account) Identification Number"; **RC240**, "Designation of an Exempt Contribution Tax-Free Savings Account (TFSA)"; **RC243**, "Tax Free Savings Account (TFSA) Return"; **RC243 SCH-A**, "Schedule A — Excess TFSA Amounts"; **RC243 SCH-B**, "Schedule B — Non-Resident Contributions to a Tax-Free Savings Account (TFSA)"; **RC249**, "Post-Death Decline in the Value of a RRIF, an Unmatured RRSP and Post-Death Increase or Decline in the Value of an PRPP — Final Distribution Made in 20__"; **RC298**, "Advantage Tax Return for TFA Issuers"; **RC339**, "Individual Return for Certain Taxes for RRSPs or RRIFs"; **RC341**, "Election on Transitional Prohibited Investment Benefit for RRSPs and RRIFs"; **RC343**, "Worksheet — TFSA Contribution Room"; **RC359**, "Tax on Excess Employee Profit Sharing Plan Amounts"; **RC383**, "Tax Exempt Earned Income and Contributions for a Pooled Registered Pension Plan"; **RC435**, "Rollover from a Registered Education Savings Plan to a Registered Disability Savings Plan"; **RC4532**, "Individual Tax Return for Registered Disability Savings Plan (RDSP)"; **T1-OVP**, "Individual Tax Return for RRSP/PRPP Excess Contributions"; **T1-OVP-S**, "Simplified Individual Tax Return for RRSP, SPP and PRPP Excess Contributions"; **T1E-OVP**, "Individual Tax Return for RESP Excess Contributions"; **T3**, "Statement of Trust Income Allocations and Designations"; **T4**, "Statement of Remuneration Paid"; **T4A**, "Statement of Pension, Retirement, Annuity and Other Income"; **T4PS**, "Statement of Employee Profit Sharing Plan Allocations and Payments"; **T4RIF**, "Statement of Income from a Registered Retirement Income Fund"; **T4A-RCA**, "Statement of Distribution from a Retirement Compensation Arrangement (RCA)"; **T4RSP**, "Statement of RRSP Income"; **T10**, "Pension Adjustment Reversal (PAR)"; **T215**, "Past Service Pension Adjustment (PSPA) Exempt from Certification"; **T746**, "Calculating Your Deduction for Refund of Unused RRSP Contributions"; **T1004**, "Applying for the Certification of a Provisional PSPA"; **T1006**, "Designating an RRSP, an PRPP or an SPP Withdrawal as a Qualifying Withdrawal"; **T1007**, "Connected Person Information Return"; **T1032**, "Joint Election to Split Pension Income"; **T1036**, "Home Buyers' Plan (HBP) Request to Withdraw Funds from an RRSP"; **T1043**, "Deduction for Excess Registered Pension Plan Transfers You Withdrew from an RRSP or RRIF"; **T1090**, "Death of a RRIF Annuitant — Designated Benefit"; **T1171**, "Tax Witholding Waiver on Accumulated Income Payments from RESPs; **T1172**, "Additional Tax on Accumulated Income Payments from RESPs"; **T2011**, "Registered Pension Plan Change of Information Form"; **T2014**, "Request for a Priority Review of a Registered Pension Plan"; **T2019**, "Death of an RRSP Annuitant — Refund of Premiums or Joint Designation on the Death of a PRPP Member"; **T2030**, "Direct Transfer Under Subparagraph 60(l)(v)"; **T2033**, "Direct Transfer Under Subsection 146.3(14.1), 147.5(21) or 146(21), or Paragraph 146(16)(a) or 146.3(2)(e); **T2078**, "Election Under Subsection 147(10.1) for a Single Payment Received from a Deferred Profit Sharing Plan"; **T2142**, "Part XII.3 Tax Return — Tax on Investment income of Life Insurers "; **T2151**, "Direct Transfer of a Single Amount Under Subsection 147(19) or

Section 147.3"; **T2205**, "Amounts from a Spousal or Common-law Partner RRSP, RRIF or SPP to Include in Income"; **T2220**, "Transfer from an RRSP, RRIF, PRPP or SPP to Another RRSP, RRIF or SPP on Breakdown of Marriage or Common-Law Partnership"; **T3012A**, "Tax Deduction Waiver on the Refund of Your Unused RRSP Contributions"

Income Tax Folios

S2-F3-C1, "Payments from Employer to Employee"; **S3-F10-C1**, "Qualified Investments — RRSPs, RESPs, RRIFs, RDSPs, and TFSAs"; **S3-F10-C2**, "Prohibited Investments — RRSPs, RRIFs, and TFSAs"; **S5-F1-C1**, "Determining an Individual's Residence Status"

Interpretation Bulletins

IT-85R2, "Health and Welfare Trusts for Employees"; **IT-87R2**, "Policy Holder's Income from Life Insurance Policies"; **IT-124R6**, "Contributions to Registered Retirement Savings Plans"; **IT-167R6**, "Registered Pension Funds or Plans — Employee's Contributions"; **IT-280RSR**, "Employees Profit Sharing Plans – Payments Computed by Reference to Profits"; **IT-307R4**, "Spousal or Common-Law Partner Registered Retirement Savings Plans"; **IT-309R2**, "Premium on Life Insurance Used as Collateral"; **IT-337R4 (Consolidated)**, "Retiring Allowances"; **IT-379R**, "Employees Profit Sharing Plans — Allocations to Beneficiaries"; **IT-499R**, "Superannuation or Pension Benefits"; **IT-500R**, "Registered Retirement Savings Plans — Death of an Annuitant"; **IT-502**, "Employee Benefit Plans and Employee Trusts"; **IT-502SR**, "Employee Benefit Plans and Employee Trusts"; **IT-508R**, "Death Benefits"; **IT-528**, "Transfers of Funds Between Registered Plans"; **IT-531**, "Eligible Funeral Arrangements"

Information Circulars

07-1, "Taxpayer Relief Provisions"; **72-22R9**, "Registered Retirement Savings Plans"; **77-1R5**, "Deferred Profit Sharing Plans"; **78-18R6**, "Registered Retirement Income Funds"; **93-3R1**, "Registered Education Saving Plans"; **99-1R1**, "Registered Disability Savings Plan"

Income Tax Technical News

No. 39, December 4, 2008, "Settlement of a Shareholder Class Action Suit — Compensation by Way of Cash and Shares"

RECENT CHANGES

2015

Bill C-2 (Introduced December 9, 2015)

This Bill reduces the Tax-Free Savings Account (TFSA) annual dollar limit from $10,000 to $5,500 (with annual indexation when applicable) for 2016 and subsequent taxation years.

REGISTERED RETIREMENT SAVINGS PLANS

GENERAL

[¶2601] ADVANTAGES OF RRSPS

A Registered Retirement Savings Plan (RRSP) is a government sanctioned tax shelter, or tax deferral mechanism. Together with (or as an alternative to) the Registered Pension Plan (RPP) which employers often offer their employees as an employment benefit, the RRSP allows Canadian individual taxpayers to deduct, from income subject to tax, specified amounts contributed to the plan. These amounts are invested, usually (but not always), in publicly traded securities, which may earn interest, dividends, or capital gains, depending on the plan chosen by the taxpayer. These earnings accumulate in the plan free of current tax, so that they grow more rapidly than would the taxable earnings of investments made by the taxpayer directly.

There are thus two separate benefits to an RRSP: first, the current tax savings resulting from the deduction of contributions; and second, the accumulation of tax-free earnings on money while in the plan.

Note that, like most tax shelters, the RRSP merely provides a deferral of tax. When you withdraw money from the plan, either for current needs or for retirement income, that money will be subject to tax (except where it is borrowed from and returned to the RRSP under the Home Buyers' Plan rules discussed at ¶2625.05 *et seq.* or the Lifelong Learning Plan at ¶2626a). However, the tax deductions and tax-free accumulations will have allowed you to save much more than if you had merely saved the same amounts without contributing them to a plan.

Example

Mr. Q saved $4,000 per year and invested it every year in investment certificates which earned 10% per year, year in and year out. He did not contribute to an RRSP, and paid current tax at the top marginal rate (50%) on his annual interest. At the end of 20 years he has almost $139,000, including the $80,000 he saved and his interest earnings. He has no further tax to pay on these amounts.

Ms. S, also subject to a top marginal rate of 50%, contributed $4,000 per year to an RRSP, which also invested in certificates yielding 10% per year. At the end of 20 years, there will be about $252,000 in the RRSP, including contributions and earnings thereon. It is true that if Ms. S now withdrew all the money at once, it would be taxed at 50%, leaving only $126,000. But Ms. S has also saved $40,000 in taxes over the years through deduction of RRSP contributions, compared to Mr. Q who paid that amount in taxes. Counting that additional $40,000 of cash in hand, she has accumulated (or had to spend) $166,000 over the 20 years, compared to Mr. Q's $139,000. Moreover, if she had invested the $2,000 per year tax savings at the same 10% return (but taxable), she would have about $69,500 on hand, as well as the $252,000 in the RRSP.

The real benefit of the RRSP to Ms. S is neither the additional $27,000 in lifetime after-tax position compared to Mr. Q, nor the fact that by using the RRSP deduction to accumulate additional savings she could accumulate an additional $96,500 of after-tax savings for the same out-of-pocket money set aside. Rather, it is that the $252,000 in the RRSP would continue to earn a large tax-free accumulation even after retirement, compared to the earnings on Mr. Q's $139,000. As a practical matter, Ms. S would not withdraw the $252,000 in a lump sum but periodically over the period of her retirement, by converting the RRSP to an annuity or RRIF. While she would pay tax on her retirement income, i.e., her annual withdrawals from the plan, the earnings on the $252,000 capital (compared to Mr. Q's $139,000) would continue to accumulate tax-free in the plan (as illustrated at ¶2631.20). The real goal of RRSP savings is to provide this enhanced capital pool for the retirement period. The enhanced capital pool arises from the tax-free accumulation of earnings in the RRSP.

Put another way, the current deductibility of RRSP contributions allows you to save more than you would otherwise do, since the government is putting up $1 of tax savings for every $4 you save if you are at a 25% marginal rate, $1 for every $2.50 you save if you are at a 40% rate, and $1 for every $2 you save if you are taxed at a 50% marginal rate. Furthermore, your savings grow faster than they otherwise would because you are not paying tax on your earnings in the RRSP.

If your income fluctuates you can achieve tax savings by contributing to an RRSP when your income is high and collapsing the plan when your income is low. There is no limit to the number of RRSPs that you can hold, only on the amount you can contribute. In the extreme case, consider a situation where you have no income at all during the year. You could simply withdraw money from RRSPs equal to the value of your total "personal amounts" (Chapters 11–13) without paying any tax.

[¶2602] REGISTRATION OF AN RRSP

A registered retirement savings plan is a "retirement savings plan" that has been accepted by the Minister of National Revenue for registration as such. It is a contract between an individual and an authorized person under which the individual, or in the case of a "spousal or common-law partner plan", his or her spouse or common-law partner, purchases a retirement income commencing at a so-called "maturity date" or an arrangement by which an individual or his or her spouse or common-law partner makes payments to a corporation in trust to provide for a future purchase of a retirement income.

Generally speaking, a plan will be accepted for registration if it complies with the following conditions:

(1) No benefits may be paid before the maturity date except as:

(a) a refund of premiums on death (see ¶2612.05); and

(b) a payment to the annuitant (which will generally be taxable, whether or not there is an offsetting deduction). Note that this rule allows a partial withdrawal by the annuitant at any time. In fact, this recognized formally what had long been possible by shifting some funds into a new RRSP and collapsing the old one.

(2) No benefits may be paid after the maturity date except as:

(a) retirement income (as defined) paid to the annuitant;

(b) payments to the annuitant in full or partial commutation of retirement income rights; and

(c) payments in commutation of annuity rights where the rights pass to someone other than the annuitant.

(3) The plan must mature before the end of the year in which the annuitant becomes 71 years of age, and no premiums may be contributed after maturity.

(4) After maturity only "retirement income" can be paid (see ¶2616.05). However, retirement income, partial commutation, or rollover to a RRIF may be commenced at any time up to the end of the year you become 71 years old.

(5) Where retirement annuities become payable to someone other than the annuitant, the plan must be commuted.

(6) Retirement income cannot be assigned in whole or in part.

(7) The plan, when it involves a depository, includes provisions stipulating that the depository has no right of offset to the property held under the plan in connection with any debt owing to the depository, nor can the property be pledged, assigned, or alienated as security for a loan or for any purpose other than that of providing for the annuitant a retirement income, commencing at maturity.

(8) All registered plans must contain a requirement that no supplementary advantage that is in any way dependent on the existence of the plan may be conferred on the annuitant under the plan or on a person with whom the annuitant does not deal at arm's length other than:

(a) a right to withdraw plan funds;

(b) the commutation payments described in (2), above;

(c) a payment or allocation to the plan by the issuer;

(d) an advantage arising from the registration as a registered retirement savings plan of the savings component of a life insurance policy;

(e) an advantage from life insurance; or

(f) an advantage derived from the provision of administrative or investment services in respect of the registered retirement savings plan.

The technical rules described above are not necessarily an exhaustive description of registration requirements.

These (and perhaps other) technical rules are generally contained in the legal "boiler plate" that is part of any RRSP. Any registered plan offered to the public as an RRSP is generally in compliance with these rules. It is primarily self-administered plans that run the risk of abusing these rules. Even with these plans, the trust company generally ensures that the plan is in compliance when registered; the risk is that you may inadvertently violate the rules and have the plan become deregistered and the value becomes taxable to you.

Accordingly, self-administered plans must be treated with care and with professional advice where any extraordinary transactions are contemplated.

Retirement income as it is used in the rules above generally means annuity income provided for by the plan itself on maturity, as opposed to RRIF or annuity income acquired by transfer of plan proceeds. Generally speaking, life insurance companies issue RRSPs with built-in annuity options on retirement, whereas plans offered by banks or mutual funds anticipate the transfer of funds to a RRIF or annuity on maturity of the RRSP.

(ITA: 146(1) "refund of premiums", (2)(a), (b), (c.3), (16))

CONTRIBUTIONS

[¶2603] OVERVIEW

To begin, there are three possible sources of RRSP "contribution room" for any particular year. That is, your ability to deduct RRSP contributions from 2016 income (on your 2016 return filed by April 30, 2017) will be based on three factors: (1) your "current limitation", which is based on 18% of 2015 earnings up to a maximum contribution of $25,370 applicable for 2016, subject to variations and limitations discussed in detail in the following paragraphs; (2) your "carryover amount" calculated on the basis of unused contribution room from prior years commencing with 1991, and discussed in detail in ¶2610.05 to ¶2611.15 below; and (3) your "special contribution" limits based on certain relatively unusual types of income you may have received in 2016, as discussed in ¶2612.05 to ¶2614c.10, below.

These three sources of RRSP contribution deductions are all included in the summary calculation at ¶2604.

[¶2603.05] *Overview of Current Contribution Limitation*

Of the three sources of RRSP contribution room discussed above, the most commonly calculated is the "current limitation". There is one basic overall "current limitation" for employees and non-employees alike of *the lesser of* 18% of 2015 earned income *and* (for 2016) $25,370. Earned income is a term specially defined for RRSP purposes; in general it includes net income from employment, business, and rentals, but there are other additions and subtractions and the complete calculation is discussed at ¶2613. There is a one-year time lag in calculating earned income, so that your 2016 contributions will be limited by your 2015 earned income. This time lag allows the RRSP contribution limit for 2016 to mesh with both the earned income calculation and the Pension Adjustment (PA) of the preceding year, as described below.

For employees, the 2016 contribution calculated under the 18%/$25,370 limit will be reduced by your 2015 PA. The PA is calculated by your employer (or in a few cases by your pension plan administrator) and represents the value of pension benefits accruing to you as an employee for the 2015 year. Your PA may also reflect benefits accrued under a registered deferred profit sharing plan (DPSP), if you participate in such a plan.

Your 2015 PA should have been calculated by your employer as part of the February 2016 T4 reporting process and reported to you on your 2015 T4 slip (usually issued in February 2016) in box 52. In a few cases the PA will be reported by your pension plan administrator rather than your employer, and should be reported on a 2015 T4A slip (issued in February 2016) in box 34.

Employees may also suffer a reduction in allowable RRSP contributions deductible in 2016 if their employer or pension plan administrator reported a 2016 Past Service Pension Adjustment (PSPA). The PSPA represents past service benefits (i.e., benefit upgrades not associated with inflationary increases) added to the plan after 1989. These are not reported on the T4 but on a separate PSPA statement, which may be issued at any time during the year. The PSPA will arise only if during 2015 your employer has upgraded your pension plan in respect of service after 1989, if you have purchased past service benefits for service after 1989, or if you have transferred into a new pension plan that provides higher benefits for the same years of service (after 1989) than were already included in your old plan. In short, PSPA adjustments will be relatively rare compared to PA adjustments, which, for employees in pension plans, will be common. For more details on PSPAs see ¶2614c.

There can be a further adjustment, in effect increasing available contribution room where prior year PAs prove to have been excessive because your employment, or your participation in a particular pension plan (or DPSP) provision, has terminated and your entitlement on termination is less than the total PAs and PSPAs related to the plan. See ¶2614b.

The CRA, to its credit, is making a determined effort to keep you informed about the amount you may contribute for the year after all these adjustments. Details of this system are discussed at ¶2609.

Note that the $25,370 current year dollar limitation for 2016 is an amount that is adjusted from year to year; see ¶2606.

[¶2603.10] *CRA Guide*

The CRA publishes a very useful annual guide, *RRSPs and Other Registered Plans for Retirement* (T4040), available without charge as a download from the CRA website.

The CRA also publishes a "T4RSP and T4RIF Guide" (T4079), which instructs RRSP administrators on correct preparation of the forms on which they report to you (and the government) your contributions, withdrawals, and transfers involving the particular plan. It is available too from the CRA website and can be used by taxpayers generally if they are unclear about information presented on the annual reporting slip.

[¶2604] HOW MUCH CAN I CONTRIBUTE?

An individual can make RRSP contributions for deduction on his or her 2016 income tax return at any time between January 1, 2016 and March 1, 2017 up to a limit calculated below. Although the limit will be reported to most taxpayers on Notices of Assessment received in 2016, the following calculation will assist those who have not received such an assessment, or have reason to doubt it (¶2609). This calculation shows your overall contribution limit from all sources, subject to the limitations discussed immediately following it.

Quick RRSP Calculation for Deduction on 2016 Return

2015 earned income (per ¶2613)	$			
	×			
Multiply by 18%	18%			
Equals: limitation (A)		(A)		
Preliminary limit: lesser of (A) and $25,370	$	(B)		
Enter: Pension Adjustment (from all 2015 T4s, box 52, and 2015 T4As, box 34)		(C)		
Subtract: Line (C) from line (B) (if negative enter zero)		(D)		
Enter: Pension Adjustment Reversal if any (from 2016 T10 information slips)		(E)		
Enter: Net Past Service Pension Adjustment if any (from PSPA information on 2016 T215 slip and 2016 T1004 form)		(F)		
2016 current contribution limit: (D) plus (E) minus (F); may (rarely) be negative; see ¶2614c			$	(1)
Enter: Unused contribution room (from 1991–2015 RRSP calculations; may (rarely) be negative; see ¶2610.15)				(2)
2016 contribution limit (including carryovers): (1) plus or minus (2) (if negative enter nil)				(3)
Enter: Special rollover contributions; see ¶2612.05–¶2614c.10				(4)
2016 final contribution limit: (3) plus (4)				

[¶2604.05] *When Can You Not Use the Quick RRSP Calculation?*

Individuals cannot use this calculation if they are persons "connected" to an employer (essentially 10% shareholders or their relatives) who joined the employer's pension plan during the year (2015). These connected persons have special limitations discussed at ¶2608. In effect they have an additional required deduction in arriving at line (1).

If you withdrew money from an RRSP in 2016 under the Home Buyers' Plan (HBP) discussed at ¶2625.05 or the Lifelong Learning Plan (LLP) discussed at ¶2626a, you will not be allowed to deduct any ordinary RRSP contributions made in the 90 days before your HBP or LLP withdrawal to the extent the contributions are necessarily included in the withdrawals. This is discussed in greater detail in ¶2625.10.

Finally, certain Canadian residents who work abroad for foreign employers without a Canadian base (primarily Canadian residents who commute to work in the United States) will have to calculate special limits described at ¶2614a.

[¶2604.10] *Explanation of the Quick Calculation*

In general, you will have a PA on line (C) only if you were an employee in 2015 and had accrued benefits under a deferred income plan of your employer.

You will have a PSPA on line (F) only if your employer has upgraded your pension benefits in respect of 1990 or later years, or if you purchased past service pension benefits in respect of service after 1989. In the former case (general upgrade of pension plan), the PSPA limitation for an upgrade occurring in 2000 or earlier arose in the year of the upgrade, but for 2001 and later, it arises in the year following the upgrade. (It followed that there could be no PSPA of this type in the transitional year of 2001.) In the latter case (buy back), PSPA arises in the year of certification. This can occur in the year of buy back or a later year; thus a PSPA from a buy back in 2016 can affect 2016 contributions without notice from 2015 contribution slips, although the process of buy back and certification thereof (described at ¶2614c(2)) is such that you cannot be without some notice of the issues involved, although you may find them complex.

You will have a PAR on line E only if you left your employment or otherwise terminated participation in a pension plan provision after 1996 and received a pension termination amount in 2016 which was less than the PAs and PSPAs associated with your participation in the plan.

Your RRSP contribution limit information on line (3), above, should match the 2016 contribution limit printed on your Notice of Assessment for your 2015 return. If it does not match, you should try to understand why the difference arises. Several possibilities are discussed at ¶2609. If you think the CRA's information is wrong, you should write to the Taxation Centre where you filed your return or telephone your Tax Services Office to point out the problem. These addresses and phone numbers will be either on the label page in the personalized return package sent to you or in the back of the T1 Guide you picked up from the post office for 2016. Telephone inquiry numbers may also appear on your Notice of Assessment.

In certain circumstances, your final PSPA (at line (F)) could be negative; this would occur where you have made taxable withdrawals from your RRSP to offset excess PSPA. If negative, it would increase rather than decrease your contribution limit; see ¶2614c.

Your unused contribution room at line (2) can in theory be negative, in which case it must be subtracted rather than added to determine your overall contribution (before rollover calculations). Line (2) could be negative only in cases where you have had "PSPA" reported to you in a preceding year (see ¶2614c). Negative unused contribution room can reduce current contribution room to nil but not below nil. It cannot create income nor reduce the special rollover contributions designated on Schedule 7 of the T1 return and described in ¶2612.05 to ¶2612.35. However, negative unused contribution room not fully utilized in the year will carry forward to future years. The calculation of unused contribution room is discussed in detail at ¶2610.15.

The information on line (F) of the Quick Calculation should be reported to you by your employer on form T215 or

T1004, as discussed at ¶2614c. It should also be reported to you late in the year by the CRA on form T1028, "Your RRSP Information for [Year]" as discussed at ¶2609. It will not necessarily be included in the contribution limit stated on your Notice of Assessment.

In making your 2016 contributions, be sure to allow for any 2015 contributions made between January 1 and February 29, 2016, which prove to have been non-deductible for 2015 (see ¶2627.15). You can deduct these amounts on your 2016 return up to the contribution limits for 2016, but of course these catch-up deductions reduce the amount you can otherwise contribute and deduct for 2016. Similarly, you cannot deduct on your 2016 return any contributions made in the first 60 days of 2016 and already properly deducted on your 2015 return.

In making your 2016 RRSP contributions, you must consider not only contributions made in the first 60 days of 2016 which you could not deduct in 2015, but also any contributions made in 1991 through 2014, inclusive, which you could not or did not deduct for those years. Beginning with contributions for 1991, you may carry these undeducted amounts forward indefinitely, so they are available for deduction in 2016. However, to the extent you deduct these carryforwards in 2016, they use up your contribution room for 2016, so that additional contributions will not be fully deductible if they exceed your contribution limit minus previously undeducted contributions carried forward and deducted for 2016. See ¶2611.05. If you made undeductible contributions in excess of $8,000 in the period of January 1, 1991 to the end of any particular month before 1997, you incurred penalties which continue until the overcontribution is either returned to you or absorbed by new contribution room. This overcontribution limit was reduced to $2,000 effective January 1996; however, where overcontributions up to $8,000 arose before February 27, 1995, there will be no penalty due to the lower limit so long as the overcontribution is deducted to the extent possible thereafter; see ¶2611.15.

The "quick calculation" above should remain valid in principle for subsequent years. Note that the maximum of $25,370 at line (B) is valid for 2016 only; values for earlier and later years are set out in ¶2606.

(ITA: 146(1) "net past service pension adjustment", "RRSP deduction limit", "RRSP dollar limit", (5); IT-124R6 Contributions to Registered Retirement Savings Plans)

[¶2605] CONTRIBUTION DEADLINE

A number of deadlines related to RRSP contributions, most notably the deadline for making ordinary contributions which can be deducted in respect of a particular year (e.g., 2015), specify that the deadline is "on or before the day that is 60 days after the end of the year . . .". Generally speaking, this means that the deadline will be March 1 of the following year. However, if a particular year is a leap year, (2016 is a leap year), the 60th day is February 29.

Moreover, where the 60th day after the end of the year falls on a Sunday, defined to be a "holiday" under the Canada *Interpretation Act*, section 26 of that Act appears to require that the deadline be extended to "the day next following that is not a holiday", typically Monday. Generally speaking, the Minister of National Revenue announces this extension some time during the 60-day period.

References to the annual deadline in this book typically use the March 1/February 29 day specified in the *Income Tax Act* and ignore the Sunday/Monday extension permitted under the *Interpretation Act*.

(ITA: 146(5))

[¶2606] DOLLAR CONTRIBUTION LIMITS INCREASE ANNUALLY

The current version of the contribution limits schedule is as follows:

Year	*RRSP dollar limit*	*Income needed in year specified for maximum contribution in the following year*
2011	$22,450	$127,611
2012	$22,970	$132,333
2013	$23,820	$134,833
2014	$24,270	$138,500
2015	$24,930	$140,944
2016	$25,370	$144,500
2017	$26,010	TBD

After 2011, the dollar limits are indexed to increases in the average industrial wage.

Note that since the current year limit will be the stated dollar amount or 18% of prior year earned income, there is for years in which the dollar limit changes a one-year time lag between the earned income limit and the stated dollar limit. That is, the 2016 limit is $25,370 or 18% of 2015 earned income, so that the $25,370 limit is reached at $140,944 of 2015 income.

After 1991, annual contribution maximum dollar amounts are supplemented by unused contribution limits carried forward, as described in ¶2610.05 below.

(ITA: 146(1) "RRSP dollar limit"; 147.1(1) "money purchase limit")

[¶2607] EXAMPLE: CONTRIBUTION LIMIT CHANGES

Example

Maximizing RRSP Contributions for Owner of Incorporated Small Busines

Elise runs her own small business, which is incorporated and typically earns net profit (i.e., profit after expenses) of $140,000 to $160,000 per year. Elise wants to withdraw as salary the amount that will allow her to contribute the maximum possible amount to an RRSP each year.

For 2016, Elise must withdraw from the business $144,500 as salary or bonus received in 2016 in order to make the maximum 2017 contribution of $26,010 (2016 earned income of $144,500 × 18% = $26,010).

Suppose that Elise did withdraw a salary/bonus of $144,500 in 2016; also suppose that at the end of 2016 she discovered that profits had fallen, and while she could take salary of $144,500 out of the company for 2016 (and so maximize 2017 RRSP contribution room), she would have to loan some of it back and could, in fact, only afford to put $10,000 into her RRSP for 2016. (There would be a tax cost to withdrawing the full amount, which might make it undesirable in any event, but that is a separate set of considerations.) The amount she was entitled to contribute but could not afford for 2016 (assume it was $10,000, based on a 2015 draw of $140,944) will create unused contribution room to be carried forward to future years under the rules at ¶2610.15.

Thus, suppose she did take out the $144,500 in 2016 (loaning some of it back). In 2017 she can contribute $15,370 [$25,370 – 10,000] of carryforward "unused contribution room" from 2016 plus $26,010 based on her 2016 earned income ($144,500 × 18% = $26,010, the 2017 maximum).

As well, in 2016 she will have to withdraw $144,500 of salary/bonus to ensure that she can make the maximum possible 2017 contribution (assuming the maximum contribution rises as scheduled), or alternatively have the maximum contribution room available for carryforward.

On the one hand, if Elise does not take funds out currently to create RRSP room, some potential RRSP room is lost forever. On the other hand, funds taken out of a small company will usually be taxed at a much higher rate than funds left in the company, and there is no value in prepaying these taxes unless the RRSP contribution room generated will in fact be used eventually.

[¶2608] WHAT IS A CONNECTED PERSON LIMITATION?

If you join a pension plan, or recommence accruing defined benefits under a pension plan, of an employer with respect to whom you are a "connected person", your RRSP contribution limit for the year may be significantly reduced. A connected person is one with enough influence to affect company policy or a relative of such a person. More precisely, it is a person (i) who owns, directly or indirectly, or through persons related by blood, marriage, or adoption, 10% or more of any class of shares of the employer or a company related to the employer, or (ii) who does not in fact deal with the employer at arm's length.

More specifically, your contribution limits for the year will be reduced if all the following conditions occur in 1991 or a later year:

(1) you have either (i) joined a registered pension plan (RPP) or (ii) commenced to accrue benefits under a defined benefit provision of an RPP following a period in which such benefits did not accrue;

(2) you were connected at the time in (1) or at any time after 1989 with an employer who participates in the RPP in (1);

(3) you did not have a positive pension adjustment (PA) amount for the 1990 year; and

(4) you have not previously been subject to a reduction under this rule.

The problem this rule is supposed to solve essentially arose because RRSP contribution calculations became subject to a time lag in 1991 whereas RPP contributions did not; this permitted 1991 RRSP contributions in effect to be doubled up with registered pension plan contributions without the normal crossover limitations. As this was considered a one-time occurrence, the anti-double-up rules can only operate once in an individual's lifetime, and only on individuals who had no 1990 PA, and the reduction to contribution room which occurs if they do operate is forever limited to the lesser of 18% of 1990 earned income and $11,500 (the 1991 contribution limit).

If you are a connected person who joins an RPP or recommences to accrue benefits, your employer must, within 60 days of your joining the plan or the benefits recommencing to accrue, issue form T1007 notifying you (and the CRA) that you are potentially liable to this rule.

Form T1007 does not calculate the impact on your RRSP contribution limits; the CRA is supposed to do this based on its records of your 1990 PA and 1991 RRSP contribution, and whether you have already been subject to this rule.

Depending on when in the current taxation year (say, 2016) you become subject to T1007 reporting, the consequent adjustment to your RRSP contribution limits may or may not appear on your Contribution Limit Statement on the Notice of Assessment for your (2015) return. It is entirely likely that it will not. If your T1007 is filed quite late in the year, you may not receive notification of the adjustment in time to limit your current year contributions appropriately. This will subject you to the penalty tax and withdrawal of overcontribution rules at ¶2611.15.

(ITA: 146(1) "RRSP deduction limit"; ITR: 8308(2) Prescribed Amount for Connected Persons; IT-124R6 Contributions to Registered Retirement Savings Plans)

[¶2609] CAN I RELY ON MY "CONTRIBUTION LIMIT STATEMENT"?

Every taxpayer who filed a tax return for the preceding year (e.g., 2015) should receive on the Notice of Assessment issued for that return a Contribution Limit Statement of the amount which may be contributed to an RRSP and deducted from income for the current year (2016). Normally, this notice is found in a clearly identified special box printed as part of the Notice of Assessment. This is referred to below as the "Assessment Statement"

The Assessment Statement is valuable if you understand its limitations. Your 2015 Assessment Statement sent to you (usually) in 2016 is based solely on your 2015 return (as initially assessed) and the PA amounts reported on the T4 or T4A slips you submitted with your return. It includes a calculation of 2015 "earned income" (¶2613) based on the return as assessed in that particular notice, and applies the limitation calculation described at ¶2604 (line (1) limit), including limits based on PA on 2015 T4/T4A slips you submitted. It also calculates unused contribution room (¶2610.15) carried forward from 1991–2015 based on contributions deducted (and allowed) on your 1991 and later returns compared to information in its data bank on your 1990–2015 earned income, PA, and RRSP contributions deducted in those years based on earned income. The Assessment Statement may well be in error if any of this information is likely to be wrong; for example, if you submitted late information on any of your 1990–2015 returns which is likely to affect your earned income for any of those years.

The contribution limit statement on your Notice of Assessment obviously cannot include information not available at the time it is processed, which most commonly includes special contribution amounts that arise in the course of the current year. The CRA obviously cannot account for 2016 retiring allowances, RRSP refunds of premiums on death, and similar "rollover" amounts discussed at ¶2612.05 and ¶2612.35 until it has notice of the amounts, which it may not get until the 2016 T4 reporting cycle is complete in February 2017; in some instances, it may not have adequate information until you file your return. Therefore, special contributions are largely outside the contribution limit statement system. Moreover, they provide a unique opportunity to create confusion in the carryforwards based on the year a special contribution is made, so the carryforward based on such a year is particularly apt to warrant your special review. Special contributions themselves are deductible only in the year received and do not create carryforward amounts.

If you withdraw funds from an RRSP during the year under the Home Buyers' Plan or the Lifelong Learning Plan, you cannot rely on your Contribution Limit Statements. If you intend to use either or both of these plans in the near future (especially the next 90 days) you should not make RRSP contributions until you clearly understand the additional contribution limitations described at ¶2625.10, below.

As well, the Assessment Statement may well be unable to include complete information based on PSPAs described in ¶2614c, (2) or (3), or Connected Person Limitations (¶2608). If the CRA receives additional information of this kind by mid-fall of 2016, it will normally send you a form T1028 in late 2016 summarizing the revised limitations. If this new data causes a form T1028 to be issued, it should summarize all information in the hands of the CRA as of its issue date; this would include: (i) 2015 contribution limits based on prior years' earned income/PA based on the latest issued assessment for years beginning with 1990; (ii) unused contribution room carried forward from 1991 and later years; and (iii) 2016 PSPA and Connected Person Limitations reported as of the date of issue. On the other hand, form T1028 will not be issued unless there is PSPA or Connected Person Limitation information to report. The T1028 form is of limited value insofar as it will only report the information received by the CRA up to a particular point in time.

Finally, the Assessment Statement may occasionally be subject to random error, for no apparent reason.

Neither the Assessment Statement nor the T1028 form provides a "safe haven"; that is, if either proves to be wrong and you over- or undercontribute as a result, you have no claim against the CRA for the error. Your protection against error is in the carryforward mechanisms which allow you to carry forward and use in future years unused contribution room arising from undercontributions or unused deductions arising from overcontributions. These mechanisms are described in detail at ¶2610.05 *et seq.*

A format for you to reconcile the CRA's calculation of your contribution limit to your own information is given at ¶2604 above. As well, the CRA usually provides a detailed chart in its guide, *RRSPs and Other Registered Plans for Retirement* (T4040) providing a comprehensive calculation of your current year deduction limit.

Where you make an excess deduction for a year based on a contribution limit statement which is in error, and the error is the CRA's and does not arise from any misreporting on your part, there would seem to be a case for administrative relief from interest on unpaid tax based on the policies in Information Circular 92-2.

The upshot of all this is that the information provided to you by the CRA as to your 2016 Contribution Limit is only a guide. In the common case where you have no PSPA or Connected Person Limitations, the information on your Assessment Statement is likely to be accurate and reliable, subject to any reassessments which may be pending. It conveniently includes your carryforward of unused contribution room from the preceding year.

The CRA includes the reporting of undeducted contributions to you as part of its annual Contribution Limit Statement. This statement is a permanent feature of the T1 tax return, and is the basis for the CRA to report to you the total accumulation of such amounts on the Contribution Limit Statement. Clearly, it is in your interest to report the annual amounts so that they may be deducted without dispute in future years.

Remember that if you permit undeducted amounts to accumulate, they can involve penalty tax where they exceed $2,000. See ¶2611.15.

Finally, you should note that any Contribution Limit Statements described above will not include amounts you can contribute under the rules described at ¶2612.05 *et seq.* The amounts described at ¶2612.05 *et seq.* are in addition to eligible contributions under these rules.

[¶2609.05] *Summary*

There are several limitations to the utility of the Contribution Limit information reported to you on your Notice of Assessment for the 2015 taxation year. First, it may only report 2016 contribution limits based on prior years' earned income and PA plus carryforwards of undercontributions from 1991–2015; it cannot report potential special contributions based on types of income which may arise in 2016 (and are described in ¶2612.05 to ¶2614c.10). Second, it cannot anticipate penalty situations that may arise from withdrawals you make under the Home Buyers' Plan or Lifelong Learning Plan. Third, it may be overtaken by events if you are reassessed, especially for changes in your earned income in earlier years. Fourth, it will not take account of a number of special situations. Essentially these are: if you have in 2016 bought back past service in respect of 1990 or later years and anticipate or have received certification of a form T1004 (¶2614c(2)); if you transferred employment among employers with reciprocal pension plans (¶2614c(3)); if you are a connected person who has joined a pension plan or recommenced accruing benefits in 2015 (and therefore have or expect a form T1007, ¶2608); or if you have or will receive in the year any of the special amounts eligible for rollover as discussed at ¶2612.05.

In PSPA or Connected Person situations only, you should receive a form T1028 from the CRA as well as the reporting slip from your employer or pension plan. The T1028 form will summarize both the Assessment Statement information and the form T215/T1004/ T1007 information received by the CRA. That is, it should be complete except for special contribution amounts described at ¶2612.05 *et seq.* However, the T1028 will be limited to information which is reported to the CRA by a particular point in time, and so it too may be overtaken by subsequent events.

Having noted all the limitations, it must be said that in most common situations the Assessment Statement should be helpful and reliable. It generally provides an accurate statement of the amount you can contribute to an RRSP by March 1, 2017, for deduction on your 2016 income tax return (and, moreover, one that the CRA recognizes as authoritative, subject to subsequent reassessments of prior year income).

[¶2609.10] *Contribution Limit Telephone Inquiries*

The CRA operates a Tax Information Phone Service (T.I.P.S.) with one Canada-wide 800 number (1-800-267-6999). This permits taxpayers with touch-tone push-button phones to directly access certain information, including the latest CRA version of RRSP contribution limits. This service is described in detail in a special section of the T1 Guide which accompanies the T1 tax return.

The feature of the service offering current RRSP deduction limits offers a combined updated contribution limit statement as of the time the inquiry is made. The contribution limit given through this service should include all information available to the CRA at that time: Contribution Room based on earned income/PA from your most recent assessment or reassessment; Unused Contribution Room carried forward; and PSPA or Connected Person Limitations. The service is not equipped to incorporate contribution room based on the special "rollover" contributions described in ¶2612.05 to ¶2612.35, below. Note that this service is only valid insofar as it reports information available to the CRA. Where information has not been reported at the date of your inquiry, whether or not it was due, the CRA will not be responsible for the shortcomings in the information they provide.

Where you want updated information from the CRA and do not have a touch-tone phone, or do not have the number for direct access, you should call your Tax Services Office of the CRA and ask them to access the information for you. To obtain information by phone (direct or through Tax Services Office) you must be prepared to present your Social Insurance Number and month and year of birth, and the amount reported by you on line 150 of your 2014 return (2015 return after April 30, 2016).

[¶2610] CARRYFORWARD OF CONTRIBUTION LIMITS

[¶2610.05] *How Much Can I Deduct in Addition to Current Limits?*

The preceding pages of this chapter were devoted primarily to current limits on RRSP contributions: how much you can deduct for 2016 based on 2015 income and PA and 2016 dollar limits and PSPA. The following paragraphs discuss additional deductions based on undercontributions of earlier years, and the effects of earlier overcontributions. Beginning at ¶2612.05, we discuss additional contributions based on special kinds of income.

The ability to make additional deductible contributions based on unused contribution room (undercontributions) of prior years commenced with deductions on your 1992 return which was to be filed by April 30, 1993. This unused contribution room accumulates from year to year within limits discussed at ¶2610.15, below.

The overall contribution limitation for the year is illustrated at ¶2604. The carryforward of undercontributions (unused contribution room) and overcontributions (undeducted contributions) is discussed in detail below.

[¶2610.10] *Carryforward of Unused Contribution Room and Undeducted Contributions*

RRSPs offer important flexibility in two respects. First, your unused contribution room, being the amount you are entitled to deduct in a particular year less the amount you actually deduct, accumulates year after year and carries forward until you reach the age at which you can no longer contribute to an RRSP (¶2616.05). This is true regardless of whether you make any undeducted contributions for a year. That is, your unused contribution room carries forward and increases permitted deductions in future years; these deductions may be claimed by making new contributions or deducting previously undeducted contributions. Second, if you contribute to an RRSP for a particular year within the current and carryforward (but not rollover) contribution limits available to you for that year, you need not deduct the contribution in respect of the year for which it qualifies. You may if you choose defer the deduction and claim it in any future year, subject to the contribution limits in the later year. You would want to do this if you expected to be in a higher income tax bracket in the next few years. Your money in the RRSP would be set aside as savings and would be earning income on a tax-deferred basis, but the deduction could be claimed in later years against a higher tax rate.

The ability to carry forward undeducted amounts also means that you can make contributions to your own and/or a spousal or common-law partner plan in a year in excess of your total contribution limits for the year (including, after 1991, carryforwards). These overcontributions may be inadvertent (because you miscalculated your limits) or deliberate. In either case, you will not of course be able to deduct the overcontribution in the year it arises, but will be able to deduct it in future years as contribution room becomes available. However, if at the end of any month your cumulative overcontributions exceed your cumulative contribution limit by $2,000, the excess over $2,000 becomes subject to a prohibitive monthly penalty tax levied on you as the contributor (and not on the plan). The overcontribution limit was $8,000 rather than $2,000 for overcontributions made in the period from the beginning of 1991 to the end of 1995. There is still transitional protection for overcontributions between $2,000 and $8,000 where the overcontribution arose before February 27, 1995, and no further contributions are made after February 26, 1995 until new deduction room permits a reduction of the overcontribution below $2,000; see ¶2611.15.

(ITA: 146(5); 204.1–204.3)

[¶2610.15] *Calculation of Unused Contribution Room Carryforward*

You are allowed to deduct RRSP contributions based on the sum of your current year contribution limits under the general formula at ¶2604, line (1), *plus* your carryforward contributions for unused RRSP contribution room for years after 1990. (It is possible, generally where pension upgrades generate PSPA (¶2614c(1)), to have negative carryforward room that reduces current year contribution limits. This is discussed further below.)

Example

George is an employee with a 2015 earned income of $40,000 and a 2015 PA of $3,050. His 2016 contribution limit is 18% × $40,000 = $7,200, minus $3,050, or $4,150. He also has an additional $1,000 of unused contribution room accumulated at the end of 2014, as shown on his Notice of Assessment for the 2014 taxation year (received in 2015), for an overall 2016 contribution limit of $5,150. For 2016, George in fact makes total RRSP contributions of $3,000. He will have a carryforward from 2016 of $2,150, being his 2016 contribution limit ($5,150) minus his actual contribution ($3,000). If he again has $4,150 of 2017 contribution room based on 2016 earnings and PA, his 2016 contribution room will be $4,150 + $2,150 = $6,300. Although this is the practical result, the actual computation of the carryforward is in fact more complex and is set out below.

The carryforward applies to the contribution shortfall for each particular year.

Contributions based on this unused contribution room are in addition to any amounts that can be contributed currently based on prior year earned income, and any contributions based on special receipts (such as retiring allowances) discussed in ¶2612.05.

[¶2610.20] *Keeping Track of Unused Contribution Room*

This is quite simple, because the CRA does it for you and reports it to you each year on your Notice of Assessment. Thus your Notice of Assessment for your 2015 tax return filed in 2016 should report any accumulated contribution room as of the end of 2015. This is particularly handy since it means the CRA automatically tracks and accounts for changes they have made to your earned income in adjusting your return as filed, or on reassessments for prior years issued before the most recent notice.

The CRA's current view of your total current year deduction room, based on prior year earned income, pension adjustment, and unused contribution room is available through its T.I.P.S. telephone service, discussed at ¶2609.

Currently the aggregate unused contribution room is shown separately on your Notice of Assessment. If you want to verify the CRA's numbers, or simply understand where your carryforward is coming from and how it accumulates, and what special uses it might have, the carryforward formula is set out and illustrated below.

[¶2610.25] *Negative Unused Contribution Room*

As the calculation below makes clear, past service pension amounts (PSPA, see ¶2614c) can in a few rare cases result in negative unused contribution room, which will actually reduce your ordinary contribution room based on prior year earned income. See ¶2604.

[¶2610.30] *Carryforward of Unused Contribution Room*

The calculation of unused contribution room, also called "unused RRSP deduction room", is a cumulative amount calculated at the end of each taxation year. For 1990 and earlier years the amount is deemed to be nil at the end of the year, so that it only starts accumulating with your contribution limits for 1991.

Unused contribution room (or unused RRSP deduction room) *at the end of a year* is:

(I) Cumulative unused contribution room (may be positive or negative)

Unused contribution room at the end of the preceding taxation year (nil if prior year is 1990) .... (A)

PLUS

Current year contribution limit (18%/dollar limit minus PA and any connected person limitation but before PSPA) .... (B)

MINUS the sum of:

PSPA for the year .... (i)

Deductions actually taken (and allowed) for contributions to your own or your spousal plan for the current year .... (ii)

Deductions taken (and allowed) for contribution to Saskatchewan Pension Plan for the current year .... (iii)

Total reductions (i + ii + iii) .... (C)

Cumulative unused contribution room (A + B - C) .... (I)[1]

Unused Contribution Room at the end of the year equals (I) .... (UCR)

[1] Note that (I) can be negative if PSPA is greater than the 18% earned income/dollar limit plus preceding year carryforwards. Although PSPA reduces current year limit at ¶2604, it can also create a negative carryforward to the extent it is greater than the current year limit. Although at first glance there may seem to be a double counting of the negative, in fact this does not occur because PSPA here reduces (A) plus (B) before PSPA. Since the lesser of (I) and (II) will be the negative number where (I) is negative, UCR can be negative.

Regrettably, the calculation seems to require considerable explanation.

The unused contribution room at the end of last year is added to (or, if negative, subtracted from) the contribution limit for the current year to obtain the total deductible for the current year. This creates at least initial confusion in timing. In calculating your overall contribution limits in 2016, you would make all the unused contribution room calculations above for the end of the 2015 year (which would accumulate amounts from 1991-2015 inclusive), and then add your 2016 contribution limit as calculated in ¶2604, line 1, to arrive at allowable 2016 deductions permitted (¶2604, line 3) before any special rollover calculations.

Note that the Unused Contribution Room (UCR) calculation is cumulative from year to year. That is, the calculation must be made for every individual year commencing with 1991. Each year's balance is then used in the following year's calculation. For example, if you are calculating allowable 2016 deductions, you must know your 2015 UCR, which in turn can only be calculated when 2014 UCR has been calculated, and so on back to 1991. The CRA does perform these calculations and will normally report them to you on your Notice of Assessment, as discussed at ¶2609. Probably only the most determined (and suspicious) taxpayers will have the fortitude to verify the CRA's calculation each year and question any discrepancies. However, it is suggested that you might want to make a special effort to verify the CRA's calculation following a year in which you have special contributions reported on line 240 of Schedule 7 (¶2612.05–¶2614c.10). Although the CRA's tracking system is very good, this is a point especially susceptible to confusion. In any event, failure to keep your own annual record to verify the CRA calculations will almost certainly leave you at the mercy of those calculations in future years without the ability to verify them later.

If you do decide to keep track of your own unused contribution room from year to year, the CRA publishes a detailed format in its free guide *RRSPs and Other Registered Plans for Retirement* (T4040).

The UCR calculation does a number of things. First, of course, Part (I) keeps a running total of what you might ordinarily consider unused contribution room; that is, it measures for all prior years commencing with 1991 the amount you could have contributed but did not. It takes PAs and PSPAs into account, and it can be a negative amount. It would normally be negative only as a result of "exempt" PSPA, that is, PSPA of a particular year arising as a result of a general pension plan upgrade or, in some cases, as a result of the transfer of a "reciprocal" pension. It is intended that such a negative amount will carry forward to reduce subsequent current contribution room until such time as the negative carryforward at the end of a year is offset by new contribution room of the next year. Negative contribution room carried forward can reduce contribution limits to zero, but it cannot *by itself* create tax liability; liability can arise where contribution limits are reduced to zero *and* contributions are nevertheless made. An illustration of this is found in Example 2 at ¶2611.05, below. The effect of negative carryforward on current year contribution limits is illustrated in the calculation at ¶2604.

(ITA: 146(1) "RRSP deduction limit", "unused RRSP deduction room"; 146(5); 146(5.1); 204.1–204.3)

[¶2611] OVERCONTRIBUTIONS

[¶2611.05] *Carryforward of Undeducted Contributions*

In addition to being able to carry forward contribution room for amounts you were entitled to contribute to an RRSP in a year in excess of your actual deductions for the year (¶2610.15), you can carry forward amounts you contributed on or after January 1, 1991, but did not deduct. Contributions to an RRSP made prior to 1991 had to be deducted in full in the year made or, if made in the first 60 days of a year, deducted in the preceding year; to the extent they were not so deducted, the right to a deduction was lost.

A failure to deduct under the 1991 and later rules may be deliberate, because you want the deduction to be claimed against a higher tax rate in a later year, or accidental, because you miscalculated your contribution limits or had an unexpected PSPA arise after you had made your RRSP contribution for a year.

If you make contributions in excess of your contribution room, you may face penalty taxes (but only if your cumulative overcontributions exceed your cumulative limits by more than $2,000; see ¶2611.15).

In general, people who have taxable incomes below $44,701 in the preceding year (this number is indexed annually for inflation) before deducting RRSP contributions and who can foresee moving into a higher tax bracket should consider forgoing current deductions to take advantage of deductions against a higher rate. Consider, however, the risk that you will not be able to take the deduction at all in future, perhaps because you leave the workforce through job loss or illness. Other factors, such as rejoining a pension plan and buying back past service, could limit anticipated future deductions. However, assuming you can reasonably anticipate continuing income to make the deduction eventually, the risks will often seem minimal compared to the potential savings.

Several other break points in the tax system yield similar results in principle if not in amount. For example, keeping the 2016 adjusted family net income low will maximize Canada Child Benefits for the following year. If the family makes income only in excess of the phase-out limits (see ¶1498) and contributes to RRSPs only occasionally and not annually, spreading deduction of a contribution over several years may be a benefit. For those 65 and older, keeping income below $35,927 will maximize the age credit at line 301 of your return; keeping income below $73,756 eliminates clawback of OAS payments. These 2016 values are indexed annually for inflation.

Individuals might save up unused deductions to reduce tax in a particular year in which they expect to be in an unusually high bracket, perhaps as a result of a foreseeable capital gain. Again, the risk must be considered that PSPA or Alternative Minimum Tax could affect your ability to take the deduction in the particular future year. However, the benefits may well exceed the risks if the future events seem clear. Consider the following example.

Example 1: Deliberate Non-Deduction

Chris was an accounting student. In the fall of 2015 Chris joined an accounting firm at a salary of $28,000 per year, rising to $30,000 on January 1, 2016. For 2015, Chris earned $8,000 for the four months of employment. If all goes well Chris can expect salary increments of about $3,000 per year for the next five years (building up to $45,000 annual salary in 2021). Thereafter there may be promotion and a big jump in salary to $65,000. With further luck, another five years will bring promotion and a $150,000 annual income. Since young accountants are expected to rise to the level of partner, there is no employee pension plan.

For the first five years (from 2016 to 2020), Chris lives at home and can afford to save $1,500 per year, which Chris contributes to an RRSP. None of these contributions are deducted. Note that Chris's unused contribution room is therefore building up without reference to the RRSP contributions, as follows:

	2016	*2017*	*2018*	*2019*	*2020*	*2021*
	$	$	$	$	$	$
Salary	30,000	33,000	36,000	39,000	42,000	45,000
Contribution room:						
End of prior year	nil	1,440	6,840	12,780	19,260	26,280
Plus: Current yr. limit (18% of prior year income to limit):	1,440	5,400	5,940	6,480	7,020	7,560
Minus: deductions taken (none), PSPA (none), SPP (none)	nil	nil	nil	nil	nil	7,500
Equals: unused room	1,440	6,840	12,780	19,260	26,280	26,340

Note that there must be some caution in the start-up year about overcontribution penalties (¶2611.15). In 2015, when he was first employed, his contribution limit would have been nil and his overcontribution limit $2,000. In 2016, his contribution limit would be $1,440 from 2015 ($8,000 × 18%) and his overcontribution limit $3,440 ($1,440 + $2,000). An undeducted contribution of $1,500 is actually eating into his $2,000 of permitted overcontribution room. In 2017, however, his new contribution room is $5,400, his total contribution room (including last year's room) is $6,840, but his total contributions are only $3,000, so he could in fact contribute another $3,840 + $2,000 before incurring penalty. From here on his accumulated contribution room is outstripping his undeducted contributions so there is no danger of overcontribution penalty tax.

At the end of 2020 there will be $26,280 of unused room carried forward, and another $7,560 of current limit will arise in 2021. If Chris gets the raise to $45,000 in 2021, the total $7,500, which he has saved but not contributed, could now be contributed and deducted in 2021 against a tax rate of about 30% (depending on province and assuming more or less constant tax rates), resulting in a tax reduction of $2,250. Taking current deductions from 2016 to 2020 against a tax rate of, say, 22% would have resulted in a tax savings of only $1,600. It is true that Chris will not have had the tax savings to spend or save in earlier years, but it is also true that the contributions made will have been compounding free of tax in the RRSP.

Suppose that Chris now deducts the $7,500, but commences to contribute $5,000 per year without deducting it. After another five years Chris gets promoted into the top tax bracket, and deducts the prior $25,000 against a 46% rate rather than a 30% or 34% rate; the tax savings would be $11,500 rather than, say, $8,250. Note that undeducted contributions suggested here are always below the level at which overcontribution penalties would apply; see ¶2611.15.

Note that Chris could continue to carry forward deductions indefinitely.

Chris should file a 2015 tax return even if his income is below taxable levels to ensure he obtains recognition of his contribution room created by 2015 earned income. Commencing in 2016 he must also report his undeducted contributions on Schedule 7 to ensure that they are recorded and available for future use, as discussed below under the subheading *Reporting Undeducted Contributions: Schedule 7*.

The strategy suggested here may obviously accrue additional marginal benefits if overall tax rates rise year over year, and lose those benefits if rates fall. As well, it must be tailored to personal circumstances and indexed tax brackets. However, so long as the overall rate structure retains its progressive nature, which seems to be a bedrock principle for the foreseeable future, the strategy will continue to be beneficial approximately as outlined.

Although you may choose not to deduct contributions for which you have sufficient contribution room, as in the cases above, you may also find that you are not allowed to make anticipated deductions because your contribution room is insufficient. This can arise unexpectedly in a number of situations, such as unanticipated PSPA (¶2614c) or reassessment of income in the year determining your contribution limits. In these situations, you must beware of the penalty tax where contributions exceed contribution limits by more than $2,000 (see ¶2611.15). Regardless of penalty tax, the amount you contributed in excess of your contribution limit will carry forward for deduction in future years. If you cannot hope to deduct it soon, however, you may withdraw it from the plan without further tax subject to the rules at ¶2611.15. You would prefer to do this if a penalty tax is the alternative. There is still transitional protection for overcontributions between $2,000 and $8,000 if the overcontribution arose before February 27, 1995 and has been deducted to the extent possible thereafter; see ¶2611.15.

Example 2: Inadvertent Non-Deduction

Russ filed a 2015 tax return showing $40,000 of earned income, and so had a 2016 contribution limit of $7,200. Assume he had no carryforward contribution room. In July 2016, he contributed $7,000 to an RRSP. In September, the CRA issued an assessment showing only $30,000 of earned income, the balance having been characterized as investment income. Accordingly, Russ's proper 2016 contribution limit was actually $5,400, and he has made a $1,600 overcontribution. He can either withdraw the $1,600 excess under the rules at ¶2611.15, or leave it in the plan and carry forward the deduction to a future year.

If Russ's contributions had exceeded $7,400 (contribution limit of $5,400 plus $2,000), the excess would be subject to monthly penalty tax until either it was withdrawn or subsequent years' contribution limits became available to shelter the excess. Where overcontributions arose before February 27, 1995, the results would be somewhat different, as discussed in ¶2611.15.

Although you cannot make an RRSP contribution to your own RRSP after the year in which you turn 71 years of age (see ¶2616.05), you can continue to deduct previously undeducted amounts to the extent of contribution room available. It appears that you can continue to generate new contribution room if you have earned income after age 71, and this contribution room can be used to soak up previously undeducted contributions. In some circumstances you may even be willing to endure some amount of penalty tax to maximize contributions (see example at ¶2611.15). Note that if you have a younger spouse or common-law partner, you can continue to make spousal/partner plan contributions until the year your spouse or common-law partner has turned 71 so long as you have contribution room available.

If you die with undeducted contributions on hand, it would appear that deductions can be taken on the year of death return to the extent of prior year unused contribution room (commencing with 1991). However, no additional contributions can be made after death to the RRSP of the deceased, although contributions can still be made to a spousal RRSP as discussed at ¶2624.05.

RRSP deductions claimed for the year can reduce positive income amounts from each employment, business, or property, or any other amount that must be included in income in the year before the deduction of losses from each employment, business, property, or allowable business investment loss. However, RRSP deductions in excess of positive income will not augment loss carryovers to other years. Taxpayers trying to follow this should consult form T1A, "Request for Loss Carryback", following Chapter 10. See also ¶2627.20.

[¶2611.10] *Reporting Undeducted Contributions: Schedule 7*

Schedule 7 permits you both to designate special contribution amounts (¶2612.05–¶2612.35) and to update your undeducted contribution information. Again, it is essential that you file a return including Schedule 7 for any year in which you make additional undeducted contributions.

The use of Schedule 7 is discussed in Example 2 above.

(ITA: 146(5), (5.1))

[¶2611.15] *Penalty Tax on Overcontributions*

For all contributions made on or after January 1, 1991, overcontribution rules apply. In principle, the rules impose a monthly 1% penalty tax on the contributor personally for each month at the end of which cumulative overcontributions made after 1990 exceed a permitted overcontribution tolerance. This tolerance was $8,000 for the period January 1, 1991 to December 31, 1995 inclusive, and is $2,000 commencing January 1, 1996, subject to transitional rules protecting overcontributions arising before February 27, 1995. Note that under these rules overcontributions will accumulate from year to year, offset by new contribution room that accumulates from year to year. It is when the lifetime overcontribution (beginning with 1991) exceeds the tolerance that penalty tax arises.

[¶2611.20] *Calculation of Cumulative Excess Amount*

In principle, the cumulative excess amount at any time before 1996 is the total of 1991 and later contributions you could not or did not deduct in excess of your current contribution room (including carryforward and current year amounts) plus $8,000. The cumulative excess amount at any time after 1995 is the total of 1991 and later contributions you could not or did not deduct in excess of your current contribution room (including carryforward and current year amounts) plus $2,000, subject to the various protection measures discussed above. However, the rules operate in a complex fashion to achieve this and certain other results.

Technically speaking, the rules provide a penalty tax of 1% on the "cumulative excess amount" on hand at the end of any particular month. A cumulative excess amount is any positive balance at the end of any month after 1990 resulting from the following calculation:

(I) *Undeducted contributions*

(1) Prior calendar year undeducted contributions ("Undeducted RRSP premiums")

(a) "Undeducted RRSP premiums" at the end of the preceding year (nil if the preceding year is 1990)[1] .... ______ (a)

(b) RRSP deductions properly claimed for contributions paid to your own or your spousal plan during the preceding calendar year or earlier years (does not include amounts deducted last year for premiums paid in first 60 days of this year, as that shows up in (2), below) .... ______ (b)

Cumulative undeducted contributions to end of prior calendar year ((a) – (b)) .... ______ (1)

(2) Current calendar year contributions

(c) All contributions made in the current calendar year to your own or a spousal plan except: (i) contributions made in first 60 days of the year and properly deducted for the preceding year; (ii) all contributions properly made pursuant to rollovers (see ¶2612.05 *et seq.*) which will be deductible in the current year or the preceding year; and (iii) all contributions properly made by way of direct transfers between tax deferred plans

Current calendar year contributions ______ (c)

(d) Gifts made to a plan of which you are the annuitant, except when the donor is your spouse or common-law partner ...... (d)

Current calendar year contributions ((c) + (d)) .... ______ (2)

(3) Taxable withdrawals from an RRSP, PRPP, or RRIF: All amounts withdrawn from an RRSP, PRPP, or RRIF[2] and taxed to you for the year *except*: (i) amounts withdrawn to reduce pre-1991 penalty tax, and (ii) refunds of premiums (see ¶2612.05) to the extent they will be deducted by you for the current year

Taxed withdrawals .... ______ (3)

Total undeducted contributions ("Undeducted RRSP premiums") at the end of a month ((1) + (2) - (3)) .... ______ (I)

(II) *Unused contribution room*

(4) Your unused contribution room at the end of the preceding year (UCR from ¶2610.15) .... ______ (4)

(5) Your contribution room for the current year per ¶2604 but not including any current year PSPA (18% of prior year income up to dollar limit for current year minus prior year PA and current year connected person amounts); if negative enter nil .... ______ (5)

(6) If the calculation is being made in any year after 1990 but before 1996, net current year PSPA at the time the calculation is being made; after 1995, current PSPA is no longer included, although it will automatically carry forward into future years as a reduction of unused RRSP contribution room at ¶2610.15............ ______ (6)

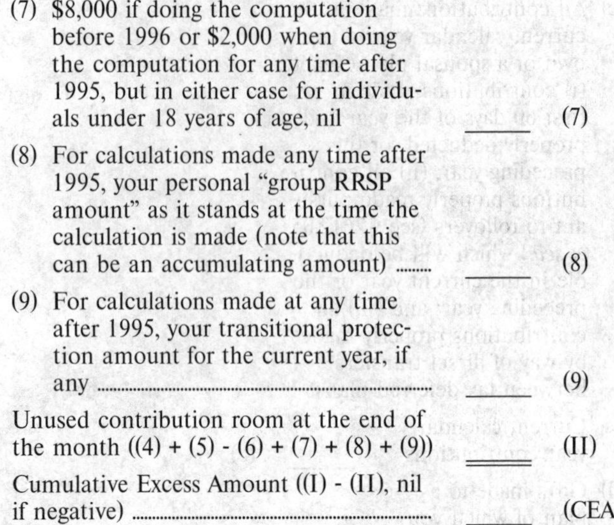

(7) $8,000 if doing the computation before 1996 or $2,000 when doing the computation for any time after 1995, but in either case for individuals under 18 years of age, nil ______ (7)

(8) For calculations made any time after 1995, your personal "group RRSP amount" as it stands at the time the calculation is made (note that this can be an accumulating amount) .... ______ (8)

(9) For calculations made at any time after 1995, your transitional protection amount for the current year, if any .... ______ (9)

Unused contribution room at the end of the month ((4) + (5) - (6) + (7) + (8) + (9)) ______ (II)

Cumulative Excess Amount ((I) - (II), nil if negative) .... ______ (CEA)

---

[1] There is an element of circularity in (1)(*a*), since it must refer to undeducted amounts arrived at under the complete calculation leading to (I) below it. In 1991 only, current year contributions and withdrawals under (2) and (3) can be included in computing undeducted contributions at (I). It must follow that at the end of 1991, the amount included in (a), above, will include 1991 RRSP contributions but not 1991 deductions. Thus cumulative undeducted premiums to the end of the second preceding year plus prior year contributions are included in (1)(*a*), and prior year deductions in (1)(*b*).

[2] When Legislative Proposals, September 16, 2016, achieve Royal Assent, this amount will include specified pension plans.

Although the above computation is complex in detail, it is reasonably clear in concept. Penalty tax will arise if your undeducted contributions (in the ordinary sense) at the end of any particular month after 1990 exceed your contribution carryforwards from prior years plus your current year contribution limits. Since your current year limits are based for the most part on prior year earned income and PA, it will rarely be difficult to make this determination. The situation is more complex where a PSPA arises unexpectedly, and much more complex after 1995 where you had over $2,000 in excess amounts outstanding on February 26, 1995, but the rules seem to deal with these situations in adequate, if convoluted, fashion.

The group RRSP amount in (8), above, is the least of three amounts. Amount one is the lesser of the dollar RRSP limit for the following year (¶2606) and the total of individual's qualifying group RRSP premiums paid to the point at which the calculation is made; as discussed above, the qualifying group premium is by definition the mandatory RRSP premium paid under a group RRSP plan. Amount two is amount one minus the formula "E - F". E is the individual's unused RRSP contribution room at the end of the preceding year plus new RRSP room that becomes available in the year before reduction for PSPAs. F is, for 1996 calculations, the amount by which the individual's undeducted RRSP premiums at the beginning of 1995 exceed its cumulative excess amount at the end of 1995. For 1997 and later years, F is the individual's group RRSP amount at the end of the preceding year. Amount three is the amount that would be the cumulative excess amount at the time of calculation if the value of (8) were nil. Note that group RRSP premiums paid keep adding to the amount of overcontribution tolerated. Although the calculation is excessively complex, it should operate to prevent overcontribution tax from arising where group contributions continue to be made without adequate contribution room arising, so long as no other additional contributions are made. A passable discussion of these amounts, with illustrations, is found in the Department of Finance Technical Notes of July 19, 1995. The calculation itself is incorporated in the CRA's form T1-OVP, which is itself complex but should properly guide you through the results in specific cases. The form is available from the CRA website.

The transitional protection amount in (9), above, is the least of two amounts. The first amount is $6,000, which is of course the reduction in tolerated overcontribution for which protection is provided. The second amount is given by the formula "U - V". U is the balance of the individual's undeducted pre-February 27, 1995 RRSP contributions. That is, it is undeducted contributions outstanding on February 26, 1995, minus ordinary (as opposed to special rollover) deductions taken for 1994 or later years, but in the case of 1994 deductions, not including deductions for contributions paid before February 27, 1995. V is the sum of (i) the individual's RRSP room carried forward from the previous year, (ii) new RRSP room based on earned income and dollar limits and PA for the preceding year but before current year PSPA, and (iii) the $2,000 post-1995 overcontribution tolerance. Whenever U in the formula is nil, the formula result must be read as nil. The transitional protection amount is discussed above, and further details and examples are provided in the Department of Finance Technical Notes of July 19, 1995. Again, use the CRA's form T1-OVP to apply these rules in specific cases.

[¶2611.25] *Paying Penalty Tax to Achieve Final Contribution*

Note that penalty tax arises at the end of a month. In some circumstances, it may be tolerable to accept a certain amount of penalty tax. Consider, for example, Mr. G, who turns 71 in 2016 and must convert his RRSP to retirement income before the end of the year (see ¶2627.30). He continues to be self-employed, has no pension plan, and has a contribution limit for 2016 of $25,370. To maximize his tax-deferred savings, he makes a $51,380 contribution in December 2016. Essentially, this is the $25,370 he can contribute for 2016 plus the $26,010 contribution limit for 2017. At the end of December, therefore, he will have a 26,010 overcontribution and a penalty tax on the amount in excess of $2,000. The penalty will be 1% of ($26,010 – $2,000 =) $24,010, or $240.10. In January 2017, his 2017 contribution room will offset the $26,010 (he knows this because he knows his 2016 income is at least $144,500 [$26,010/18%], which is sufficient to create full 2017 contribution room up to the 2017 dollar limit). Accordingly, for a penalty of $240.10, Mr. G has added $26,010 to his tax-deferred savings accumulation. Remember that Mr. G will have to wind up his RRSP into some form of periodic income before the end of December. It may not be clear beyond all doubt that the cumulative excess amount can apply at the end of the month to an RRSP that is no longer there. However, the rules do seem to suggest that the penalty formula operates on RRSP contributions even if the RRSP itself is no longer there, and this is certainly the position of the CRA.

[¶2611.30] *RRSPs of Children*

The 1991 and later penalty rules catch the situation of RRSPs registered for children. Some parents registered an RRSP in the name of a child and made contributions to the plans up to $5,500 per year. Prior to 1991, no penalty tax would arise in these circumstances. No deduction could be made for the contributions, but money would accumulate tax free for the child and could build to substantial amounts. The

CRA did not like this result and threatened not to register such plans, although there was and is no legal requirement that the plan annuitant cannot be a minor. Under the post-1990 rules, there is no $8,000 (nor $2,000) overcontribution allowance for a person who has not attained the age of 18 in the preceding year. The result is that any amount contributed after 1990 as a gift to a plan of which a minor was the annuitant would create cumulative excess amount for the child (unless the child has earned income and unused deduction room). Technically, this arises from elements (I)(2)(d) and (II)(6) in the calculation formula above. This gives the sensible result that a child with earned income may have an RRSP but a child's RRSP cannot be abused by non-deductible gifts.

[¶2611.35] *Self-Assessment of Penalty Tax*

There may be situations where you will choose to pay penalty tax, as described above, or will notice a penalty tax liability before assessment from the CRA. Penalty tax arising at any time in a year is due and payable 90 days after the end of the year. The CRA provides form T1-OVP to calculate the amount of tax owing, and thereby eliminate the accrual of interest that would otherwise arise.

Form T1-OVP contains a calculation of cumulative excess contributions, as discussed above, and a format for analyzing the penalty tax consequences on a month-by-month basis. The cumulative excess contribution calculation on form T1-OVP may or may not be clearer than the one presented above. The CRA's guide, *RRSP and Other Registered Plans for Retirement* (T4040) contains a useful discussion of the penalty tax and a chart to determine whether, if you have undeducted contributions, you should file form T1-OVP.

Where you inadvertently incur penalty tax, you may want to reduce continuing penalties by withdrawing overcontributions, as discussed below.

[¶2611.40] *Waiver of Penalty Tax*

The CRA does have the authority to waive the penalty tax where the taxpayer can demonstrate that the overcontribution was inadvertent and reasonable steps are being taken to eliminate it.

[¶2611.45] *Withdrawal of Overcontributions*

Under the rules applicable to overcontributions made, any amount contributed and not deducted in a year can be withdrawn in the year it is paid as a contribution or in the following year, or in the year an assessment is issued for the year of payment of the contribution or in the following year. An offsetting deduction will be allowed for this withdrawal unless it seems that the taxpayer did not reasonably expect the premiums to be deductible in the year paid or the following year and intended all along to contribute and withdraw. The intent of these new rules is to allow you to withdraw an overcontribution as soon as you realize that penalty tax may arise (or when it is assessed) with an offsetting deduction for the withdrawal. On the other hand, you are not allowed to make a series of overcontributions and withdrawals to maximize earnings within the plan and to avoid penalty tax.

Remember that under the new rules it is not necessary to withdraw undeductible contributions; you can carry forward amounts until sufficient deduction room opens up for you. You must weigh this against potential penalty tax to the extent your undeducted contributions will exceed the cumulative $2,000 allowance ($8,000 allowance before 1996, subject to transitional rules discussed above).

An anti-avoidance rule denies an offsetting deduction to "prescribed" withdrawals, which include amounts withdrawn in order to create room for past service benefits under a registered pension plan. As well, it is clear that overcontributions which arise out of excess transfers to an RRSP from a registered pension plan (RPP) do give rise to overcontribution tax but may not be deducted under this rule. Rather, they have their own separate deduction rule and form, discussed at ¶2612.35.

You can use form T3012A to obtain a refund of undeducted contributions made after 1990 without the usual withholding tax applied by RRSPs against withdrawals. To obtain a refund without withholding tax, you must fill out Areas I and II on form T3012A and submit it to your CRA Tax Services Office for certification. When it is returned to you, you can use the same form to apply to your RRSP fund for your refund. The correct procedure, if you have withdrawn funds pursuant to form T3012A, is to include the withdrawal in income on line 129 of your T1 return and deduct the T3012A amount on line 232 (in addition to any other amounts which should be shown on that line) and file a copy of the T3012A with your return. The alternative is to withdraw the money subject to withholding and claim the tax withheld as a credit on your T1. If you do not use a T3012A, you must file form T746 with your T1 return.

You can withdraw a refund of undeducted contributions from a successor or matured RRSP or from a RRIF to which the excess RRSP contributions were transferred. Withdrawals from a matured RRSP are typically in the form of partial annuity commutations payments. It appears that these withdrawals must be accounted for on form T746 and not form T3012A.

It has for some time been the CRA's view (in CRA Document No. 9316337) that you cannot withdraw funds from one RRSP to offset overcontributions to an entirely unrelated RRSP, where the only connection between the funds is that you are the annuitant of both. This has been the official position, although it is understood that there was at one time some inconsistency in assessing practice. The law itself seems ambiguous enough to support either position. In *Vale v. The Queen*, 2004 DTC 2362 (T.C.C.), the Tax Court ruled against the CRA, finding that the official interpretation "is not supported by the broad language used" in the *Income Tax Act* and "the Crown was unable to provide any policy reason why the withdrawal should be made from the same RRSP as the one to which the overcontribution was made." Unfortunately this is not necessarily the end of the matter. The *Vale* case was heard under informal procedure rules, and so is technically not binding on the CRA. However, it is certainly a case which the taxpayer can cite in pursuing his or her own argument with the CRA. It is likely that in due course the CRA will have to take a position on *Vale* and, as the Court said, it may be hard pressed to find a reason to dispute it. The 2004 version of form T3012A specifically said that the refund had to be from the same "type of plan" to which the overcontribution was made, which implied, without actually saying, that the CRA had moderated its earlier view. The current version of form T3012A says that the withdrawal must be from "the same type of plan to which I made unused contributions (my own RRSPs or my spouse or common-law partner's RRSPs)". The inference seems to be that the only types of plans recognized are your own plan or your spousal plan, so that as long as you are withdrawing an amount from, say, any plan of which you are the annuitant, you may use it to cover an overcontribution to any plan of which you are the annuitant. Similarly, it seems that you (or your spouse or common-law partner) may receive a refund of an overcontribution to a spousal or common-law partner plan under these rules, whether or not it is the same spousal plan as that to which the actual overcontribution was made, as long as it is a spousal plan. The law seems to presume that the spouse or common-law partner will be the same spouse or common-law partner but does not actually address that issue.

Payments to you out of an RRSP under the Home Buyers' Plan rules are not subject to withholding tax. They may, however, create their own overcontribution problems and where they do, you may withdraw the overcontributions under these rules. See the discussion at ¶2625.05 *et seq.*, below.

(ITA: 146(8.2); 204.1–204.3)

[¶2612] ROLLOVERS, SPECIAL CONTRIBUTIONS AND DIRECT TRANSFERS

[¶2612.05] *Rollovers (Special RRSP Contributions)*

There are a few situations in which you may receive special payments in the year on which you can base RRSP contributions in addition to those calculated above based on earned income. In the situations discussed here, you may actually receive cash payments which, by their nature, qualify for special contribution treatment, and if such payments were received in calendar 2016, you must make the offsetting RRSP contribution by March 1, 2017 to defer tax on the amounts received. These special situations are:

(1) special cash payments you receive on leaving employment, either in recognition of long service or as damages for loss of office, to the extent the employment originally commenced before January 1, 1996;

(2) lump-sum payments received from foreign pension plans for services performed outside Canada (unless the payment is not taxable by virtue of a tax treaty);

(3) lump-sum payments received from a United States IRA and taxable in Canada (unless the payment is not taxable by virtue of its tax-deferred nature in the United States);

(4) amounts you receive (directly or through a trust) from the RRSP or RRIF of a spouse or common-law partner or, in some cases, a parent or grandparent, who has died; and

(5) the "cost amount" of shares you receive, directly or through a trust, in a special lump-sum distribution from a DPSP.

Note that these rules only permit you to make special contributions to your own RRSP, that is, to a plan of which you are the annuitant. They do not increase the amount you can allocate to a spousal RRSP. However, if you make a special contribution under these rules, you may of course decide to allocate a greater portion of your ordinary contribution limits (¶2604) to a spousal or common-law partner RRSP.

Amounts (1) to (5) are cumulative; that is, if you have more than one such type of income, you may deduct a special contribution with respect to each.

Any special contributions that you make under these rules must be "designated" in your income tax return for the year in which the qualifying income arises (i.e., the year in which you receive it or for which it is reported to you as your income). Designation must be accomplished by completing Schedule 7 of the T1 return and filing it with the return.

In addition to amounts you receive under (1) to (5), above, you may in some circumstances have to include in income amounts which you have not received but have transferred directly from one RRSP or RRIF to another. These amounts are eligible for an offsetting deduction to the extent of the direct transfer, but must also be designated on Schedule 7; see ¶2612.35.

Deductions for these special contributions must be claimed in the year the special income arises. No carryforward is provided for undeducted amounts with respect to these items, no unused contribution room available for carryforward is created by them, and overcontributions are liable to penalty tax (as presented in the calculation in ¶2611.20).

(IT-528 Transfers of Funds Between Registered Plans)

[¶2612.10] *Retiring and Termination Payment Rollovers*

If you received in the taxation year amounts in respect of employment commenced before 1996, and these amounts are characterized as a retiring allowance (which includes damages on termination), as defined in the *Income Tax Act*, you may transfer or contribute to an RRSP (or to a Registered Pension Plan, should you still belong to one or have joined a new one) certain specified amounts of the payment in addition to the amounts based on earned income discussed above (¶2604).

A retiring allowance is an amount received upon or after retirement from an office or employment in recognition of long service. It includes a payment in respect of unused sick-leave credits. It also includes amounts received for loss of office or employment (often called termination payments), whether paid by the employer voluntarily (i.e., without a lawsuit being filed or threatened) or received as damages, either in a voluntary settlement of claim by the employer or under an order or judgment of a competent tribunal. The notion of a payment received in respect of loss of employment seems quite broad; see the comments at ¶923. The amount of a retiring allowance you may contribute to an RRSP under these rules is limited by a formula to specified amounts in respect of employment prior to 1996 (as discussed further below).

Not all damages are retiring allowances. If a human rights tribunal awards general damages, the amount is usually not taxable at all. Where a loss of employment involves a human rights violation and is settled out of court, a reasonable amount for general damages can be excluded from income.

Where you do receive damages under a court order or settlement, which fall within the definition of retiring allowance, and the amount includes a provision for prejudgment interest, see the discussion of that subject at ¶923.

There remains some uncertainty as to the scope of termination payments eligible for rollover where departure from employment is "voluntary". The law specifically provides that payments "received in respect of a loss of office or employment ... whether or not received as, on account or in lieu of payment of, damages ..." are qualified. The CRA has attempted to limit the scope of this apparently broad rule by stating that loss of employment usually refers to the abolition of a job or position for economic reasons. That is, where an employee simply leaves a job voluntarily, there should be no scope to categorize payments as termination payments eligible for rollover. Even this limitation may or may not be found justified in law. The CRA does recognize that "Since early retirement incentive plans' are essentially designed to eliminate a number of office or employment positions (albeit on an elective basis), the Department accepts payments made upon such 'retirements' as being in respect of a loss of office or employment". Unfortunately, the line between a voluntary resignation and participation in an "early retirement incentive plan" can be quite uncertain. As a practical matter, much will depend on how the employer reports the amount on a T4 or T4A slip. See also the discussion at ¶923.

In programs designed to encourage voluntary retirement, an employee may have the option of receiving an amount as a lump sum or in instalments over a period of years. The CRA takes the view that if an employee chooses the instalment option "on or before the employment is terminated", the instalments are taxable in the year received. Some or all of each instalment may be transferred to an RRSP in accordance with the normal limits. For example, if four instalments of $15,000 each are to be received, and the employee has an overall limit of $40,000, the employee can transfer $10,000 per year, or up to the $15,000 received in any year, so long as the total transferred does not exceed $40,000. If interest is earned on the outstanding balance, the interest is not considered part of the termination payment.

If you are in doubt about the nature of your payment, consult Interpretation Bulletin IT-337R4 (consolidated), available on request from Tax Services Offices of the CRA (¶287). Some discussion of the comments in that bulletin is found at ¶923.

Your employer is supposed to identify the portion of a retiring allowance paid to you which is eligible for RRSP contribution on your T4 slip (reproduced in Chapter 3) using code 66. As well, your employer is supposed to calculate the ineligible amount of a retiring allowance and report it to you on your T4 using code 67. You should report both amounts as income on line 130 of your T1 return. You should also report RRSP contributions based on the eligible amount on lines 1 and 14 of Schedule 7 and deduct them along with other RRSP contributions on line 208 of your T1 return.

You must make your 2016 RRSP contribution by March 1, 2017, in any case; if you are in doubt about the correct amount and your total RRSP contribution including this rollover will exceed $2,000, you may want to obtain prompt professional advice. If your total contribution will not exceed $2,000, you should probably make the contribution in any event. You are not required to abide by your employer's position represented on a T4 slip; you may make an RRSP contribution and argue directly with the CRA. You will, however, be queried or assessed by the CRA in this case if your employer does not issue a correct T4 form. Remember to file Schedule 7 to make clear your position.

A retiring allowance transfer is usually indirect; that is, the amounts are paid to you and must be contributed to the plan within 60 days following the end of the year of receipt, and designated by you by completing Schedule 7 of the T1 return and filing it with the return. It is possible, however, that your employer will contribute these amounts directly to an RRSP for you. This should eliminate the requirement for the employer to apply the withholding tax that would be required if the payment were made directly to you. You should still receive an RRSP contribution slip, and should report the amounts as income, claim the RRSP deduction, and file Schedule 7 with your return.

The amount of a "retiring allowance" which can be contributed to an RRSP cannot exceed *the lesser of*:

(1) the amount received; and

(2) the sum of:

(a) $3,500 times the number of years before 1989 during which the taxpayer was employed by the employer or a person related to the employer. This $3,500 limit is reduced to $2,000 in respect of the number of years before 1989 during which the taxpayer was employed by the employer or a person related to the employer and for which employer contributions under either a pension fund or plan or a deferred profit sharing plan (DPSP) of the employer or a person related to the employer may reasonably be considered to have vested in the taxpayer at the time of payment of the retiring allowance;

(b) $2,000 per year for each year of service after 1988 and before 1996, regardless of pension or DPSP considerations; and

(c) nil for years of service after 1995.

Note that the retiring allowance/termination payment rollover is effectively phased out by rule (c), above. The rollover is not available for employment commencing after 1995. It will continue to be available for earlier employment to the extent of years of service prior to 1996.

Persons related to the employer include persons whose business was acquired or continued by the employer and any previous employer of the retiree whose service therewith is recognized in determining the retiree's pension benefits.

Note that awards of legal fees may be included in income (but not as a retiring allowance) and actual legal fees may be deducted from awards to the extent the awards have not been contributed to an RRSP.

(ITA: 60(*j*.1); (o.1); 248(1) "retiring allowance"; *Deducting Income Tax on Pension and Other Income, and Filing the T4A Slip and Summary* (RC4157); IT-337R4 (consolidated); *Lorenzen v. The Queen*, 81 DTC 5251 (F.C.T.D.); *Shell v. M.N.R.*, 82 DTC 1369 (T.R.B.); *Berlinski v. M.N.R.*, 89 DTC 433 (T.C.C.))

[¶2612.15] *Rollovers of Unregistered Pension Plan Amounts*

Where you receive a lump-sum payment out of a foreign pension plan for services rendered by you, or where you receive such an amount after June 6, 1990, for services rendered by your spouse or common-law partner, or former spouse or common-law partner, and rendered during a period throughout which the person rendering the services was a non-resident of Canada, the amount can be rolled over to a Canadian RPP or RRSP by making a contribution within 60 days from the end of the year of receipt. To the extent that the receipt is not taxed to you because you invoke the provisions of a tax treaty, it is of course not available for this special contribution. The special contribution must be "designated" by completing Schedule 7 of the T1 return and filing it with the return.

This rule extends to amounts received for non-resident services performed by a common-law partner or former common-law partner, and for amounts received by a common-law partner or former common-law partner (earlier where the common-law partner election at ¶1113 was made). For these purposes a common-law partner at a particular time is defined as discussed at ¶2624.05. Although less than entirely clear, it would appear that the spouse or common-law partner or former spouse or common-law partner test must be met at the time the amount is paid rather than when the services were rendered.

(ITA: 60(*j*); IT-528, para. 26, 27)

[¶2612.20] *Receipts from a United States IRA*

An Individual Retirement Account (IRA) in the United States is similar to a Canadian RRSP. If you have been earning income in the United States, you might have made contributions to an IRA. If you are now a Canadian resident, you might be taxable on any withdrawals you make from an IRA. Canada has adopted specific rules to allow you to escape tax in Canada to the same extent you would escape tax in the United States if you were resident there and received the payments from an IRA. Apparently this is intended to ensure that you may transfer funds between IRAs on a tax-deferred basis if the deferral is available for U.S. purposes. As well, if you receive a lump-sum payment that is taxable in Canada (presumably because it would not be tax-deferred in the U.S. if you were a U.S. resident, as discussed at ¶919)), you may contribute the payment to an RRSP to the extent it derives from contributions to the IRA by you, your spouse or common-law partner or your former spouse or common-law partner. The special contribution must be "designated" by completing Schedule 7 of the T1 return and filing it with the return. See ¶919.

(ITA: 60(*j*); 60.01; 248(1) "common-law partner"; IT-528, para. 26, 27)

[¶2612.25] *Shares of a DPSP*

In some circumstances, if you are the beneficiary of a DPSP, you may receive a lump-sum DPSP payment which may be partially in the form of shares in the employer company. It is possible that these shares themselves may be transferred directly to a registered pension plan or RRSP (¶2612.35) at their fair market value, at your direction. However, you are entitled to receive the shares directly, and to elect (within 60 days after the year of receipt) on form T2078 to treat only the "Cost Amount" of these shares as a taxable benefit to you. If you receive the shares yourself *and* make the cost amount election, you may offset this taxable benefit, to the extent you choose, by making a special contribution to an RRSP. Note that although you receive shares, you may fund the RRSP contribution with cash (see ¶2627.65). The contribution must be made within 60 days of the end of the year for which the shares are reported as a taxable benefit to you, and you must designate the contribution on Schedule 7, to be filed with your T1 return.

(ITA: 60(*j*); 147(19)–(22); IT-528, para. 4)

[¶2612.30] *Amounts Received Through a Trust*

In some circumstances you may receive an amount eligible as a refund of premiums or a special DPSP lump-sum share payment through a trust. Most commonly this will occur where the receipts are on account of death of a plan-holder and go in the first instance to an estate or spousal trust. These payments retain their special contribution characteristics; they should be reported to you on a T3 slip in box 22. Any special contributions under this rule must be "designated" by completing Schedule 7 of the T1 return and filing it with the return.

(ITA: 60(*j*)(ii); IT-528, para. 28)

[¶2612.35] *Direct Transfer Rollovers*

(Direct transfers among various registered deferred income plans — not only RRSPs — are also discussed at ¶1021.)

These are transfers permitted among various registered plans. In principle, when you become entitled to a special lump sum payment from a registered plan, you can choose to keep the payment in some deferred tax plan rather than receive it currently and pay tax on it. However, to accomplish this you must specify to the payer that you want the amount transferred to another deferred plan and have it paid directly between plans. It appears that you may take part of such amounts out in cash (and pay full tax on them) and transfer the balance, but you may not recontribute any amount you take out in cash.

The most common example occurs when you change employment. You may transfer amounts to which you are entitled out of your old pension plan to either your new pension plan with your new employer or to an RRSP (or RRIF). To accomplish this, you will be required to fill out a number of special forms (in particular, form T2151) and present them to your former employer or pension plan administrator to authorize the direct transfer of funds. Any restrictions on these transfers will arise out of the pension rules themselves and pension standards legislation, and not out of tax rules. Where you transfer a lump-sum amount from an RPP or DPSP to another RPP, DPSP, RRSP, PRPP, SPP or RRIF pursuant to form T2151, usually on a change of employment, there is no income inclusion and no designation on Schedule 7.

The December 4, 2008 issue of the *Income Tax Technical News*, No. 39, discusses the settlement of a shareholder class action suit relating to allegations against the corporation of artificially inflated share prices. The bulletin refers to a situation where tax-free direct transfer rollovers may take place. If the settlement payment received by the taxpayer comprises cash and shares, such payments may be made on a tax-free basis to the taxpayer's RRSP or RRIF. This can either be achieved by a direct transfer by the corporation or paid to the taxpayer first with a subsequent transfer to an RRSP or RRIF. The shares given as part of the settlement must be the same class of shares that the taxpayer originally bought in a registered plan such as an RRSP, and the number of shares in the settlement is directly related to the original number of shares bought. If paid to the taxpayer first, the taxpayer may transfer it with no tax consequences to an RRSP or RRIF within a reasonable time (that is, within six months of receipt or by the end of the taxation year of receipt, whichever is later). Otherwise, the cash payment and the fair market value of the shares will be considered income and must be included on the tax return as an RRSP or RRIF benefit received in the year.

Similar rules exist for division of PRPP, RRSP, RRIF, or SPP assets on the breakdown of a marriage or relationship; transfers may be made to registered plans for a spouse or common-law partner pursuant to court order or written separation agreement, but the transfers must be made directly between plans, and not by taking any cash or assets out of a plan altogether, even for a short time. Form T2220 is required for these transfers. No reporting of income or contribution is required on your T1 return. For transfers after March 20, 2003, similar rules apply to DPSP assets.

Transfers from one RRSP or RRIF to another may also be made on this basis. If, for example, you don't like the rate of return (or risk) in a particular plan you have invested in, you may open a new and more favourable plan and direct that the assets be transferred to it. Note that there may be charges associated with these transfers imposed under the terms of the plans themselves. For example, if both are stock mutual funds, it is possible the old fund will impose exit charges and the new fund will impose entrance charges. This will depend on the terms of the plan and has nothing to do with tax law. In most cases, the transferee will provide all the documentation you require. In general, these transfers are made under the authority of form T2033. The form may also be used for certain direct transfers from an SPP or PRPP to an SPP, PRPP, RPP, RRSP, or RRIF. No reporting of income or contribution is required on your T1 return.

Finally, when you decide to convert your RRSP to a RRIF or retirement annuity (¶2616.05), this may be done through a tax-free direct transfer. The issuer of the RRIF or annuity will provide the necessary documentation.

(ITA: 147.3; IT-528 Transfers of Funds Between Registered Plans; ITTN: 39 No. 39)

[¶2612.40] *Special RPP Contributions to RRIF and RRSP*

Lump sum amounts from a defined benefit registered pension plan can be transferred to a registered retirement income fund. The regulations always provided limits on such transfers, calculated by multiplying the amount of annual pension foregone by a prescribed present value factor. Prior to 1996, the multiplier was set at zero for individuals 72 or older. In consequence, these transfers were not permitted. For transfers after 1995, the multipliers are reset and there is no upper age limit at which the transferable amount is nil. However, when making these direct transfers it is essential to consult the limitations table prescribed in Regulation 8517.

The *Income Tax Regulations* allow a larger portion of a commutation payment from an underfunded pension to be transferred to RRIFs and RRSPs in cases of employer insolvency. The conditions for the application of the amended limit are that the transfer occurs on behalf of an employee or former employee of an insolvent employer who has ceased making pension contributions; that the lifetime retirement benefits payable under the defined benefit (DB) portion of the Registered Pension Plan (RPP) have been reduced due to underfunding; that the RPP not be a designated plan as defined by subsection 8515(1) of the *Income Tax Regulations*; and that the application of these rules has been approved by the Minister of National Revenue. This amendment applies to transfers made after 2010.

The rules regarding the deductibility of RRSP contributions create a deduction in certain circumstances where a taxpayer has received an amount in commutation of benefits under a defined benefit (DB) Registered Pension Plan (RPP), after February 2009 and before 2011, where the employer is insolvent. The taxpayer is able to deduct RRSP contributions in respect of DB RPP commutation payments where the taxpayer could have benefited from the revised pension transfer limit in the amended regulations had they been in place before 2011.

(ITA: 146(5.2), 147.3(4); ITR: 8517 Transfer — Defined Benefit to Money Purchase)

[¶2612.45] *Excess Direct Transfers*

Where a lump-sum amount is transferred directly from an RPP to an RRSP or RRIF, usually on death or on termination of an employment, it is possible for the amount to exceed permissible limits. The excess is included in income for the year of transfer. It is considered a "contribution" to an RRSP so that an offsetting deduction may be claimed to the extent of contribution limits available for the year. To the extent the excess cannot be offset in this way, it will be subject to the overcontribution penalty rules at ¶2611.15. However, the usual deduction of overcontribution rules (¶2611.15) will not permit a tax-free withdrawal of these amounts.

There is a special rule, however, which does permit deduction of such excess transfers. The obvious solution, then, would be to withdraw the excess transfer from the RRSP or RRIF and claim this offsetting deduction (on form T1043). This may be complicated by provincial legislation designed to protect pension allocations which may prevent you from withdrawing the excess amount. In this case, the excess amount will be included in your income, and may be subject to overcontribution tax. To the extent that provincial rules do permit you to withdraw the funds over time, the special deduction will carry forward to offset the future income from RRSP/RRIF withdrawals to the extent of the original income inclusion. This prevents double taxation, once at the time of transfer, and again at the withdrawal.

(ITA: 147.3(13.1); IT-528, para. 22, 26)

[¶2612.50] *Direct Transfers Reported as Income*

In certain circumstances you may make a direct transfer between registered plans which is not an excess direct transfer (above) but is nevertheless reported as income to you; in this case you must claim an offsetting deduction and designate the amount on Schedule 7. These transfers occur (1) when you commute all or part of the annuity retirement income under an RRSP and transfer the lump-sum value of that income to another RRSP, RRIF, PRPP, or SPP, or (2) where you transfer from a RRIF an amount (in excess of the amount you must withdraw and include in income) to another RRIF or to an RRSP, SPP, or PRPP. Both these kinds of transfers are made under the authority of form T2030. The amount transferred out of a plan is reported as income on a T4RSP or T4RIF slip, as the case may be, by the administrator of that plan. The amount transferred is reported as a contribution by the administrator of the recipient plan. You must report income and offsetting deduction on your T1 return for the year of transfer, and designate the amount of the transfer by completing Schedule 7 of the T1 return and filing it with the return.

(ITA: 60(*l*)(v); IT-528, para. 22, 26)

[¶2612.55] *Direct Transfers from a Specified Pension Plan (SPP, also known as the Saskatchewan Pension Plan)*

Saskatchewan Pension Plan contributions are limited to RRSP contribution room (excluding special contributions) unused in the year.

SPP death benefit entitlements arising on the death of a spouse or common-law partner or former spouse or common-law partner may be transferred directly to an RRSP, RRIF, or qualified annuity. Death benefits can also be transferred into the surviving spouse's SPP account.

Transfers to an RRSP may also occur upon the death of the SPP plan member, or as a result of the breakdown of marriage where a lump sum is paid from an RRSP to the spouse or common-law partner or former spouse or common-law partner of the plan member.

As with other direct transfers, these permitted direct transfers from the SPP do not become subject to overcontribution calculations. The SPP will provide the necessary transfer forms for all types of direct transfers permitted from the SPP. Several federal forms (as indicated above) may be used to record those direct transfers.

Where there has been a marriage breakdown, The *Saskatchewan Pension Plan Act* (section 19.1) stipulates that, in the case of an unretired member, the receiving spouse or common-law partner must become a member of the Plan. The funds in both accounts remain locked-in until retirement. In the case of a retired member, pension payments are split and then issued to the respective parties. Requests can be addressed to Saskatchewan Pension Plan, Box 5555, Kindersley, SK S0L 1S0; telephone 1-800-667-7153.

(ITA: 146(21), (22); IT-528, para. 33; T4040 RRSPs and Other Registered Plans for Retirement)

[¶2612.60] Rollover to a Registered Disability Savings Plan (RDSP)

A tax-deferred rollover is allowed to a taxpayer's Registered Disability Savings Plan (RDSP) from an RRSP, RRIF, or RPP upon the death of the annuitant or RPP member under certain circumstances. To qualify for the rollover where the deceased has died after March 3, 2010, the following criteria must be met; the individual holding the RDSP would have been entitled to a deduction under paragraph 60(*l*) of the Act if the contribution made to the RDSP had been made to an RRSP; the individual is a child or grandchild of the deceased and was financially dependent on the deceased by reason of physical or mental infirmity; the contribution is made to a plan where the beneficiary is eligible for the disability tax credit, the beneficiary is less than 59 years old in the calendar year the contribution is made, the beneficiary is resident in Canada, the total contributions do not exceed $200,000, and any contributions not made by the holder of the plan are made with the written consent of the holder of the plan; the contribution is made after June 2011; the individual and the holder of the RDSP designate the contribution on Form RC4625 at the time of the contribution; and the contribution is the lesser of the total specified RDSP payments made in the year (or 60 days after the end of the year) or the total amount of eligible proceeds included in the taxpayer's computed income for that year.

When the deceased has died after 2007 and prior to 2011, there are special transitional provisions that apply. To qualify, the deceased must have been an annuitant of an RRSP or RRIF or a member of an RPP and was the parent or grandparent of an eligible individual (child or grandchild of the deceased that was financially dependent on the deceased by reason of physical or mental infirmity). The transitional eligible proceeds must have been received by the eligible individual, the spouse or common-law partner of the deceased, or a beneficiary of the deceased's estate; and the transitional eligible proceeds were included in the computation of that person's income for the year.

Under the transitional provisions, subject to the approval of the Minister of National Revenue, any of the persons mentioned above could deduct contributions made to the RDSP of a child or grandchild of the deceased from the proceeds received from the deceased's RRSP, RRIF, or RPP made before 2013. An election must be made with the prescribed form at the time of the RDSP contribution and filed with both the CRA and Human Resources and Skills Development Canada. The contributions made to the RDSP cannot exceed the proceeds received from the deceased's RRSP, RRIF, or RPP.

For cases where the death occurs before 2011 and after May 3, 2010, taxpayers may use either the general rules or the transitional rules.

Lump-sum death benefits paid out of a "specified pension plan" (i.e., the Saskatchewan Pension Plan) qualify for a rollover to an RDSP in the same manner as rollovers from RPP death benefits. This applies to transfers made after March 3, 2010.

For a more detailed description of RDSPs, see ¶2529h.

(ITA: 60(m); 60.02; RC4460 Registered Disability Savings Plan; RC4625 Rollover to a Registered Disability Savings Plan (RDSP) Under Paragraph 60(m))

[¶2612.65] RESP Income

As discussed at ¶2529d, Registered Education Savings Plans allow a "subscriber" (typically a parent) to make non-deductible contributions to a plan for the future post-secondary education of plan beneficiaries (typically the children). Although contributions are not deductible, earnings in the plan are not currently taxable, but rather are income of the beneficiaries when paid to them for educational purposes. The contributions themselves can return to the subscriber (or beneficiary) without tax. If plan income is not used within 25 years for the education of beneficiaries, it may be returned to the subscriber (previously it was likely to be forfeited). If plan income is returned to a subscriber, it is taxable income when returned, and in addition is subject to a 20% surtax (12% for residents of Quebec, which runs its own 8% recapture tax in this respect) to offset the tax-free accumulation.

The 20% surtax applies to "accumulated income payments". An accumulated income payment is essentially any distribution that is not:

- an education assistance payment (i.e., a payment to a beneficiary to assist in post-secondary education);
- a refund of contributions made to the plan by the subscriber and payable to the subscriber, its heirs or assigns;
- a payment to a designated educational institution; or
- a transfer to another plan.

Accumulated income payments are subject to surtax in a taxation year to the extent they are:

(1) included in the income of the plan subscriber (but this cannot be a subscriber who became a subscriber because of the death of the original subscriber);

(2) where there is no subscriber (presumably because deceased), included in the income of a person who has been a spouse or common-law partner of the subscriber; or

(3) included in income of someone other than those under the rules in (1) and (2), above.

However, there can be reduction in surtax where payments described in (1) and (2), above, are sheltered by offsetting contributions to an RRSP.

Generally speaking, this means that payments in excess of contributions returned from an RESP to anyone who is not a beneficiary, subscriber, or spouse or common-law partner of a deceased subscriber are both included in income and subject to 20% surtax, with no offset permitted for contributions to an RRSP.

To the extent an RESP subscriber who receives a return of plan income has sufficient RRSP contribution room on hand, the income can be sheltered by contributing it to an RRSP. Contributions of returned plan income (based on contribution room otherwise available) will also offset the 20% surtax, but only to the extent of a lifetime limit of $50,000 per plan.

Example

Mr. Ed contributed $42,000 to an RESP for his children. None of the children in fact undertook any post-secondary education in the 25 years before the plan was obliged to wind up. By then its value was $182,000, which was returned to Mr. Ed in year X. In year X, Mr. Ed had RRSP contribution room of $13,500 based on prior year income and $36,500 based on carryforwards of unused contribution room. He in fact contributed $50,000 to an RRSP for himself or his spouse in year X.

Mr. Ed will have to include in his income $140,000 ($182,000 - $42,000 original non-deductible contribution). This will be offset by the $50,000 RRSP contribution (which of course cannot then offset tax from ordinary income in year X).

Mr. Ed will also be subject to 20% special tax on $140,000, but the $140,000 will be reduced by the lesser of:

(1) the lesser of the income inclusion for RESPs and his total RRSP contributions in the year; and

(2) $50,000 minus all amounts previously claimed as reductions of RESP surtax under this rule in prior years.

Accordingly, Mr. Ed's special tax will be 20% of ($140,000 minus the lesser of $50,000 and $50,000), or 20% of $90,000.

If withdrawals commence before the 25th year of the plan and Mr. Ed is not usually in the top marginal rate bracket, he may be able to minimize ordinary tax by withdrawing only enough to use available RRSP room, and making future withdrawals as new room becomes available. He cannot, however, reduce the special 20% tax once the $50,000 lifetime limit is reached. Where it begins to be apparent that plan funds are unlikely to be used for education, withdrawal strategies should be worked out well in advance of the 25-year deadline.

Note that the return of RESP income creates no additional RRSP contribution room. Essentially it provides cash to fund any RRSPs to the extent of any otherwise unused contribution room. RRSP contributions in the year of taxable RESP receipts, whether actually made from the RESP income or otherwise, can reduce the special surtax on such income to the extent of a lifetime aggregate of $50,000.

(ITA: 146.1(1) "accumulated income payment"; "beneficiary"; "contribution"; "educational assistance payment"; "registered education savings plan"; "subscriber"; 204.94; QTA: 1129.63–1129.66; IC 93-3R1; RC4092 Registered Education Savings Plans)

EARNED INCOME CALCULATION

[¶2613] CALCULATION OF EARNED INCOME

The overall earned income limitation calculation is set out below. This calculation applies to determine earned income for all Canadian resident taxpayers, whether employees or others. Most employees will have none of the special receipts or deductions shown in items 2 to 14 below and need only be concerned with the simple calculation in item 1.

The earned income calculation below applies to taxpayers who were resident in Canada throughout the year, and for part-year residents, it applies to the period of Canadian residence. Earned income of non-residents (or for periods of non-residence in a year) is discussed at ¶2613.05 below.

Remember that in calculating your RRSP contribution limit for your 2016 tax return, you are looking at earned income for 2015 as reported on your 2015 income tax return (as revised by assessments, if any), which was due on April 30 (or for the self-employed June 15), 2016.

CALCULATION OF EARNED INCOME

1. Total employment earnings (box 14 of T4, plus other employment income (reported on line 104 of your T1) not on your T4, such as tips) .... $__ (a)

Minus the total of:

- annual union, professional or like dues .... $__
- employment expenses claimed .... __

Subtotal	→ ___	(b)
Amount (a) minus amount (b) (if negative, enter nil)	$ ___	(1)
2. Net income from self-employment or a business in which you were an active partner (a loss is entered at line 11)	___	(2)
3. Royalties for a work or invention of which you were the author or inventor	___	(3)
4. Net rental income from real property (a loss is entered at line 11)	___	(4)
5. Taxable support payments (i.e., alimony or separation allowances) received or reimbursed (line 128 on your return)	___	(5)
6. Net research grants received	___	(6)
7. Amounts received under the *Wage Earner Protection Program Act*	___	(7)
8. Employee profit sharing plan allocations (box 35 of T4PS)	___	(8)
9. Supplementary unemployment benefit plan payments received (do not include EI benefits received)	___	(9)
10. Disability benefits received under Canada Pension Plan or Quebec Pension Plan	___	(10)
11. Subtotal (total of lines 1 to 9)	→ ___	(11)
12. Current-year loss from self-employment or a business in which you were an active partner	___	(12)
13. Current-year rental loss from real property	___	(13)
14. Deductible support payments (alimony or separation allowances) paid	___	(14)
15. Business income from the disposition of eligible capital property in excess of recaptured tax deductions; i.e., the gain element arising from such dispositions	___	(15)
16. Subtotal (total of lines 11 to 14)	→ ___	(16)
Earned Income (line 10 minus line 15)	$ ___	

Note: The following are some types of income that do *not* qualify as earned income when calculating your RRSP contribution limit:

- investment income;
- taxable capital gains;
- pension and DPSP income (but some special contributions may be made; see ¶2624.05; also ¶2612.05 where shares are received from a DPSP);
- RPP, PRPP, RRSP, RRIF, OAS and CPP income (except CPP/QPP disability pension as noted in (10), below);
- retiring allowances (but some special contributions may be made; see ¶2612.05);
- death benefits;
- scholarships and bursaries; and
- business income earned as a limited partner of a limited partnership.

A more detailed explanation of earned income follows.

For the purposes of determining the amount of a registered retirement savings plan contribution that is deductible, earned income is defined to be the total of:

(1) Salary and wages (the earnings from employment in box 14 of your T4, minus any allowable deductions from such income; but see (2), below). Note that salary and wages will technically include such items as employee profit sharing plan allocations (which may be reported on T4PS slips), certain stock option plan benefits, and so on;

(2) Deductions allowable from salary or wages (whether or not claimed) for (i) contributions to a registered pension plan, (ii) deductible contributions to a retirement compensation arrangement, and (iii) deductions for a clergyman's residence; that is, these three items are included in earned income even though they reduce salary and wages;

(3) Tips and gratuities;

(4) Royalties earned as an inventor;

(5) Royalties earned as an author;

(6) Alimony or maintenance payments taxable to you as a spouse, former spouse, or common-law partner (for 1991 and later years these can include amounts previously paid and deducted by you and now refunded to you under a court order);

(7) Research grants included in income, net of related expenses;

(8) Income from a business carried on either alone or as a partner actively engaged in the business;

(9) Rental income from real property; and

(10) Disability benefits *received* in the year (for years after 1990), regardless of whether the benefits relate to another year and are included in income of another year

Minus the total of the following items:

(11) Business losses from a business carried on either alone or as a partner actively engaged in the business;

(12) Rental losses from real property;

(13) Amounts deductible by you as alimony or maintenance payments to or for a spouse or common-law partner (for 1991 and later years, these can include amounts previously received by you and taxable to you and now repaid by you under a court order); and

(14) The portion of business income from a disposition of eligible capital property prior to 2017 (¶768) in excess of recaptured tax deductions, i.e., the gain element on such dispositions. Although this item was added to the list only in 1995, the exclusion was always operative.

Note that amounts received under the *Wage Earner Protection Program Act* (WEPP), reported in box 28 of the T4A slip, are also included in the calculation of earned income.

Note that CPP/QPP disability benefits have been added to earned income at (10), above (for earned income of 1991 and later years). This raises the question of disability payments received under a private disability plan. In general, where the recipient receives the benefits under a plan established by an employer or former employer, the benefits will be included in employment income unless the plan was an employee-pay-all plan (where the employee directly or indirectly paid all the premiums); see ¶328. For purposes of the RRSP earned income determination, if employment disability benefits under an employee plan are reported as taxable income (i.e., the plan was not employee-pay-all), they will be included in salary and wages and thus will be incorporated in RRSP earned income under (1) above. If they are not reported as taxable income (because the plan was an employee-pay-all plan), they are not included in earned income. Probably (although it is not beyond doubt), the same rule applies to benefits under a strictly personal disability insurance policy, such as the policy of a sole proprietor. In general, such insurance premiums would not be deductible from business income and any disability benefits received would not be taxable and would not be earned income. However, if the insurance were charged against the business as business interruption insurance, the proceeds would probably be categorized as taxable business income and therefore earned income.

Earned income calculations can be made on a CRA chart included in its *RRSP and Other Registered Plans for Retirement* tax guide (T4040).

(ITA: 146(1) "earned income"; 56(1)(*r*)(v); *RRSP and Other Registered Plans for Retirement* tax guide (T4040))

[¶2613.05] *Earned Income for Non-Residents*

The rules determining earned income for RRSP purposes for Canadian residents are discussed at ¶2613 above.

Taxpayers who were non-resident (as described in Chapter 1) throughout the year or for a period during the year may include in earned income for the period of non-residence only income from employment performed in Canada and business carried on in Canada (directly or as an active partner), to the extent that such income is not protected from Canadian tax by tax treaties. Business losses from a business carried on in Canada (directly or as an active partner), and property losses from the rental of real property, attributable to a period of non-residence reduce the non-resident's earned income. Alimony or maintenance payments deductible from Canadian tax also reduce earned income generally.

Certain non-residents are taxed in Canada under special rules; these include foreign post-secondary students attending Canadian universities or other post-secondary schools (¶2024), former Canadian residents who have left to continue post-secondary studies or teaching (¶2024), former Canadian resident employees who continue to receive employment income from Canada (¶2022), and non-residents receiving money under contract to perform (or not to perform) services in Canada or as remuneration for employment services to be performed in Canada (¶2022). In general, non-residents subject to Canadian tax under those special rules may include in earned income the amounts subject to Canadian tax, with minor exceptions for scholarships.

PENSION ADJUSTMENTS AND PAST SERVICE PENSION ADJUSTMENTS

[¶2614] WHAT IS A PENSION ADJUSTMENT (PA)?

As discussed at ¶2604, your RRSP contribution deduction for a particular year will be limited to 18% of your earned income for the preceding year (to a dollar maximum) minus your PA for the preceding year. That is, your 2016 RRSP contribution deduction will be limited to 18% of 2015 earned income (but limited to a maximum contribution of $25,370) minus your 2015 PA. Special contributions discussed in the section "Special Contributions" below (¶2612.05) are in addition to this.

Your 2015 PA represents the value of pension benefits accruing to you as an employee for the 2015 year. Your PA may also reflect benefits accrued under a deferred profit sharing plan (DPSP), if you participate in such a plan. Generally speaking, only an employee who is enrolled in a registered pension plan (RPP) or DPSP will have a PA. However, unregistered and foreign pension plans may in certain circumstances give rise to a PA; see ¶2614d. In rare cases involving foreign pension plans, the employee will have to calculate his or her own PA (¶2614a). In a few cases it will be theoretically possible for non-employee members of a pension plan to have a PA; for example, doctors who participated in the retirement savings plan for doctors in British Columbia would have been subject to these rules (¶2614d).

The PA calculation is a wondrous and cumbersome thing; those with sufficient fortitude will find it set out in the CRA's *Pension Adjustment* guide (T4084). In general, PA otherwise calculated for defined benefit (but not money purchase) pension plans is reduced by an arbitrary $600 (prior to 1997, $1,000). The upshot of this is that most PAs automatically increased in 1997, with a corresponding decrease in RRSP contribution room in and after 1998. It might be thought that the $600 reduction would leave all employees with at least $600 of RRSP contribution room, but this is not always the case if pension benefits are high enough. The $600 reduction was eliminated for certain categories of employees (e.g., members of foreign pension plans, ¶2614a) for the period 1997 through 2003.

The PA includes amounts that have accrued to you in your pension plan even if they have not vested, so that you may never actually receive pension benefits for the year in question. Nevertheless, the PA reduces your RRSP contribution room. In theory at least, a PA could be negative or nil; in this case a PA of zero is reported.

The Pension Adjustment Reversal ("PAR"), applies to provide new RRSP contribution room where prior PAs prove to have been excessive because a pension failed to vest due to a termination of employment (or pension participation). See ¶2614b for additional details.

(ITA: 146(1) "RRSP deduction limit"; 248(1) "pension adjustment"; ITR: 8301 Pension Adjustments; 8302 Benefit Entitlement; IT-124R6 Contributions to Registered Retirement Savings Plans)

[¶2614.05] *PA Reporting*

Your 2015 PA should have been calculated by your employer as part of the February 2016 T4 reporting process and reported to you on your 2015 T4 slip (usually issued in February 2016) in box 52. In a few cases the PA will be reported by your pension plan administrator rather than your employer, and should be reported on a 2015 T4A slip (issued in February 2016) in box 34. For 2016, the CRA should have reviewed this PA information on your 2015 T4/ T4A slips and incorporated it into the "contribution limit" reported to you on the Notice of Assessment of your 2015 return (see ¶2609).

[¶2614a] PENSION ADJUSTMENTS OF FOREIGN PENSION PLANS

Where a Canadian resident is a member of a foreign pension plan, special problems can arise. A Canadian resident could be a member of a foreign plan in a number of situations. For example, the Canadian could work for a foreign company operating in Canada, either as a permanent employee in Canada, or as a temporary transfer to Canada. Or, a Canadian resident could commute to work in a foreign jurisdiction (typically the United States) and work for a foreign employer completely beyond Canadian jurisdiction.

In these situations, the Canadian government is concerned that foreign pension plan accruals should be reflected in the limitations on RRSP contributions which the Canadian resident taxpayer can deduct, as is done domestically through the PA system described above at ¶2614. In effect, the government has in most cases accomplished this through a system of forcing the employer to either report PA and PSPA, or register the plan under Retirement Compensation Arrangement rules which in effect prevent the plan from earning tax-free income on pre-tax amounts (see ¶739). Whichever occurs, it is the responsibility of the employer to report any required PA/PSPA adjustments to the employee.

There remain situations in which the Canadian government cannot reach the foreign employer to impose reporting requirements. The most common such situation is that of the Canadian resident who commutes to work in the United States and works for a U.S. employer which has no direct or indirect operations in Canada. The company maintains a U.S. pension plan in which the employee participates. In this and any similar situation, the employee himself or herself must calculate and report PA. In this situation there is to be no requirement forcing the employee to calculate PSPA; any changes made to the foreign pension plan of the commuting Canadian, including upgrades, transfers and buybacks (see ¶2614c) simply will not be reflected in RRSP contribution limits.

The self-reporting rule for PAs applies to an individual who meets all of the following tests:

(1) the individual was at any time in the year a Canadian resident who rendered services primarily outside Canada to an employer, otherwise than in connection with a business carried on in Canada;

(2) the individual became entitled in the year to benefits under a foreign pension plan (essentially a funded pension plan maintained primarily for the benefit of non-residents of Canada) in respect of the services rendered to the non-resident employer while the individual was a Canadian resident; and

(3) the individual continued to be entitled to all or part of the benefits at the end of the year.

An employee who meets the above tests for, say, 2015, *is required to reduce* the portion of *his or her 2016 RRSP contribution limit* based on prior year earned income (18% of prior year income to a maximum for 2016 of $25,370) *by a "prescribed amount" which is the lesser of:*

(1) for 2016 RRSP contributions, $25,370 minus the "PA offset" of $600, so, $24,770. The maximum RRSP contribution permitted under this rule for 2016 is, technically, the money purchase limit for the preceding year ($25,370, which is also the RRSP limit for the current year) reduced by the "PA offset" of the preceding year, which is (after 1996) $600; and

(2) 10% of the employee's resident compensation for the membership year (2015 in this example) from the employer attributable to services rendered by the employee in periods throughout which the employee rendered services described in the first (1), above, i.e., services rendered primarily outside Canada and not in connection with a business carried on in Canada. "Resident compensation" is defined by regulation to include employment income (or income from an "office" such as a directorship) computed under normal Canadian tax rules. It does not, however, include income related to a period of non-residence of the employee nor employment income which is for any reason exempt from Canadian tax under a tax treaty or agreement.

The upshot of all this is that an employee who met the tests for foreign employment in 2015 has a 2016 contribution limit of the lesser of (a) $25,370, and (b) 10% of his or her 2015 employment income earned, while resident in Canada, from the non-resident employer.

Effective for 2009 and later years, amendments to regulation 8308.2 in determining the "prescribed amount" were introduced based on the ratification of the Fifth Protocol to the Canada–United States Tax Convention. Basically, this section has been reorganized. Regulation 8308.2(1), which gives the three tests in order for the self-reporting rule for PAs to apply is essentially the same (as described above). However, the reference to the PA offset is now eliminated such that the ceiling on the prescribed amount for a particular year is the money purchase limit for the preceding year.

Because the prescribed amount is based on benefits provided in the preceding year, the impact of this particular change has been delayed by one year. Thus, for 2009, the impact of the $600 PA offset is still considered by deeming the money purchase limit for the preceding year to be $600 less than it actually is. Under the new rules, the "prescribed amount" is the lesser of:

- the money purchase limit for the service year, and
- the amount determined under the new regulation 8308.2(2).

(Prior to this amendment, regulation 8308.2(2) contained transitional rules for determining prescribed amounts for 1997 to 2003.) The amount determined under the new regulation 8308.2(2) depends on whether the individual is accruing benefits under a money purchase provision, a defined benefit provision, or a combination, as follows:

(1) In general, if the individual is accruing benefits only under the money purchase provision, the amount is the individual's pension credit for the service years as if the plan were a registered pension plan taking into account only the employer's contributions (not the employee contributions).

(2) If the individual is accruing benefits only under a defined benefit provision, the amount is the same as under existing rules (10% of such portion of the individual's resident compensation for the service year from the employer that is attributable to the foreign services).

(3) If the individual is accruing benefits under a combination of the two types of provisions, the amount is the greater of:

- the amount determined under the 10% rule for defined benefit provision, and
- the amount determined in (1), above, if the individual had not accrued benefits under the defined benefit provision.

(ITA: 147.1(1) "money purchase limit"; ITR: 8300(1) "PA offset", "resident compensation"; 8308.2 Prescribed Amount for Member of Foreign Plan; *Pension Adjustment* guide (T4084))

[¶2614b] WHAT IS A PENSION ADJUSTMENT REVERSAL (PAR)?

The Pension Adjustment Reversal (PAR) is an addition to annual contribution limits for 1998 and later years. PAR arises where an employee leaves a pension or deferred profit sharing plan (or provision of a plan) after 1996 and the payments received on termination of the plan or provision are less than accumulated Pension Adjustments (PAs) and Past Service Pension Adjustments (PSPAs) in respect of the plan or provision. Typically PAR will arise where employment is terminated before pension rights are fully vested, but there may be other situations where an employee is terminated from a plan provision without being terminated from employment.

The essence of the PAR concept is that previous PAs and PSPAs (which reduced RRSP contribution limits) prove in retrospect to have been too high because of termination with respect to a plan or plan provision. The PAR is to provide additional compensatory RRSP room on a current basis, which, where not used currently, will be carried forward under the provisions at ¶2611.05.

Typically on termination, whether of employment or participation in a plan provision, there will (eventually) be a payment to the employee (or transfer to the employee's RRSP) of pension plan or DPSP amounts; where these are less than related PA/PSPA, a PAR arises at that time. That is, it is the payment that triggers the timing of the PAR. PARs arising in a calendar quarter must be calculated by employers or plan administrators and reported on a special T10 slip within 60 days after the calendar quarter in which it arises. Thus, the employee having a fourth quarter termination payment (October to December) may not receive notification until the day RRSP contributions are required. It is not clear at the time of writing if any general extension will be granted in these circumstances. RRSP contribution room unused in a particular year will form part of the general carryforward of unused contribution room (¶2611.05) and so may provide the basis for future contributions.

PARs in some situations will interact with PSPAs, presenting a further problem for employers or pension administrators.

(ITA: 146(1) "RRSP deduction limit", "unused RRSP deduction room"; *Pension Adjustment Reversal* guide (RC4137))

[¶2614c] WHAT IS A PAST SERVICE PENSION ADJUSTMENT (PSPA)?

A Past Service Pension Adjustment (PSPA) represents the value of pension plan improvements granted to you in a year in respect of past years, but only past years after 1989. Thus, generally speaking, a PSPA arising in 2016 would only be in respect of pension upgrades for 1990 through 2015, even if the upgrade involved pensionable service for, say, the entire period 1980 to 2015, inclusive. Any current 2016 upgrade should be reflected in PA rather than PSPA.

PSPA is not reported on the T4, but rather is to be reported by your employer or pension plan administrator within 60 days of the decision to improve your pension. A special PSPA reporting slip (Form T215) will be issued for this purpose, with a copy to you and a copy to the CRA, as discussed further below.

In general, PSPA can arise in three distinct situations:

(1) PSPA Arising from Pension Plan Improvements

Your employer can introduce a general improvement of pension plan benefits for virtually all employees. If your revised pension rules would have created a larger PA in 1990 or later years had they been in place, they will create a PSPA when the employer determines to make the improvement. The employer must report PSPA to each employee (and to the CRA) within 60 days of the final decision to make the improvements. PSPA is reported on form T215, "Past Service Pension Adjustment Exempt from Certification". The T215 refers to "exempt PSPA" because PSPA arising from a general plan upgrade is exempt from certification by the CRA (unlike the buy back case below). It is possible in theory for this "exempt PSPA" to create "negative" RRSP room; in this case, where "exempt PSPA" reduces your contribution limit for the year below zero, the negative (below zero) amount carries forward to reduce future RRSP contribution limits until the negative is used up (see ¶2610.15).

For 2000 and earlier years, this exempt PSPA reduced deductible RRSP contribution limits for the year of the decision to upgrade pension benefits, but for 2001 and later years, PSPA reduces contribution limits of the year following the decision. That is, if your employer decided in calendar 2000 to upgrade its general pension plan, its report to you on form T215 reduced 2000 RRSP contribution limits. (If your employer had made this decision at the very end of 2000, you might not have received the T215 until the end of February 2001. Thus, if you had a large PSPA reported to you in the year and you had already made significant RRSP contributions for the same year, you had to deal with any overcontribution under the rules at ¶2611.15.)

For PSPA arising from pension upgrades decided upon in 2001 and later years, revised regulations (announced April 18, 2000 and promulgated January 30, 2001) should solve the timing problems discussed above by creating a time-lag so that exempt PSPAs do not reduce RRSP deduction room until the year following the past service event. The change was intended to ensure that exempt PSPA does not affect the deductibility of RRSP contributions that were made before the occurrence of a past service event on the expectation that the contributions would be deductible. The change is limited to "exempt PSPA" reported on a T215 slip, discussed above; it does not extend to certifiable PSPA discussed below.

As a consequence of the transition from the 2000 to the 2001 rule, no exempt PSPA could reduce your RRSP contribution limits for 2001. 2001 past service events giving rise to exempt PSPA reduced your 2002 contribution limits.

(2) PSPA Arising from Buy backs of Past Service Eligibility

You can "buy back" past service for years after 1989. Usually this will involve a special contribution by you under the rules of a defined benefit registered pension plan (RPP). You may be contributing for years (after 1990) where you did not accrue the maximum benefit for that year, or for years (after 1989) during which you had left the employer but for which you are now able to obtain pension coverage after your return. In all buy back cases, the CRA must certify the PSPA calculated by your employer or pension administrator. A provisional PSPA is the amount that would be created by virtue of the buy back, but it is not final and does not create actual PSPA until certified by the CRA. Your employer or administrator applies for certification (in triplicate) on form T1004, "Application for Certification of a Provisional PSPA". If the CRA certifies the PSPA, it notifies the employer by returning two copies of form T1004 to the employer, etc., who in turn must forward one copy of the certified T1004 to you within 60 days of receiving it. In theory this is your first official notice of the PSPA adjustment, and it reduces your RRSP room for the year as of the date of certification. In practice, the nature of buy backs is such that you should normally be aware that the process is in motion.

If the PSPA creates "negative RRSP room", that is, if it exceeds your contribution limits for the year plus unused RRSP carryforward room, the CRA can compel you to either (i) withdraw amounts from an RRSP and have them subjected to tax, or (ii) fund the buy back in part by a transfer of funds from your RRSP to the pension plan to obtain the certification. That is, you can be compelled to either withdraw or transfer some RRSP funds or reduce your buy back. The CRA has provided a good discussion of the certification process, including possible RRSP withdrawals (which would be "designated" on form T1006 for this purpose), in its guide *RRSPs and Other Registered Plans for Retirement* (T4040), which is available without charge from the CRA website.

Since a PSPA arising from a buy back must be certified by the CRA and does not reduce your contribution limit until the time it is certified, you are likely to know it is coming, if not exactly when. It is important to note that a proposed PSPA will reduce your contribution limit at the point in time at which it is certified; thus if you expect a T1004 in late 2016 but it is not certified and issued to you until 2017, it creates a PSPA in 2017. However, the certification is based on the facts at the time of certification, so that a certification made in January 2017 might be nullified by an RRSP contribution made in February 2017 for 2016 deduction. Or, more precisely, you might have to withdraw some or all of the January 2017 RRSP contribution (using form T1006) to validate the certification. The employer or pension plan administrator in charge of the buy back procedure will be your first source of information on the RRSP consequences of your buy back.

If the amounts you are compelled to withdraw to obtain PSPA certification prove to be excessive, they will result in negative PSPA which will increase your available contribution room. The CRA has included a computation of PSPA allowing for this contingency in the *RRSP deduction limit* chart (step 6) included in its guide *RRSPs and Other Registered Plans for Retirement* (T4040).

(3) PSPA from Employment Transfers

You can move from one employer to another under a "reciprocal arrangement", that is, under an agreement between the employers that service under the old employer will be credited under the new. These plans are most commonly found in the civil service. If the new employer has a richer pension plan than the old, PSPA may arise on the transfer. It appears that the PSPA may or may not require certification, but a transfer of employment should alert you to potential PSPA issues.

[¶2614c.05] *In General*

Details of the calculation of PSPA, which is very complex, can be found in the CRA's *Past Service Pension Adjustment* guide (T4104), available by download from the CRA website. PSPA is also discussed in the book *Canadian Pensions and Retirement Income Planning*, published by CCH Canadian Ltd.

It is unlikely that PSPA will equal the amount you pay for a buy back for a number of reasons. The PSPA is an effort to measure the value of the benefit at the time it might otherwise have arisen, rather than the cost of funding it today.

You may be able to reduce potential PSPA on buy backs to the extent you fund the buy back by the transfer of funds already within the tax-deferred system (your existing pension and RRSP amounts). However, where PSPA will not have a serious effect on your actual RRSP contributions, it may be more desirable to fund the buy backs out of other sources, such as withholding from pay cheques. This will very much depend on the facts of each case and your savings goals.

PSPA can be greater than your contribution limits for the year. This has no immediate effect other than to make current year contributions undeductible. Undeductible contributions may be withdrawn or carried forward under the machinery discussed at ¶2611.05. PSPA which is greater than your current contribution limits (including unused contribution room carried forward) can result in "negative unused contribution room" which would reduce contribution limits in future years as well. See ¶2611.05.

(ITA: 146(1) "net past service pension adjustment", "RRSP deduction limit"; ITR: 8303 Past Service Pension Adjustment; 8402 Past Service Pension Adjustment)

[¶2614c.10] *Recontributions*

Under the rules for PSPA created by buy backs of past service pension room (see ¶2614c), you may be required to withdraw RRSP funds to validate a buy back. If it turns out that you have been required to withdraw more than should have been required, there is a provision for allowing you to recontribute the excess withdrawal and claim a deduction for it.

(ITA: 146(6.1); 147.1(10); ITR: 8307 Certification in Respect of Past Service Events; IT-124R6 Contributions to Registered Retirement Savings Plans)

[¶2614d] PA AND PSPA FOR A NON-PROFIT EMPLOYER OR A GOVERNMENT PLAN

[¶2614d.05] *Specified Retirement Arrangements (SRAs)*

As with foreign pension plans (¶2614a), special problems arise for the government in dealing with unregistered and unfunded pension plans established by non-profit employers, of which there are many, including charities, hospitals, unions, and various levels of government. Since these organizations are indifferent to the deductibility of their pension contributions, they have greater scope than private employers in the construction of unregistered pension plans, where benefits can be set up involving no current tax to employees. In general, where such plans are funded, they will be caught by the Retirement Compensation Arrangement rules (¶359), which provide adequate protection to revenue authorities. Where, however, they are unfunded, it may be possible to escape current tax consequences altogether.

The government is concerned that where such plans exist, the potential benefits should at least erode RRSP contributions, so that employees cannot obtain a double tax deferral. Accordingly, "Specified Retirement Arrangement" (SRA) rules require the employers to report Pension Adjustments (PA) or Past Service Pension Adjustments (PSPA) as appropriate.

Whether a PA must be calculated by an employer under an SRA will depend on several factors in addition to RCA liability. Essentially, where 85% of an employee's resident compensation is subject to PA adjustments under ordinary or foreign pension plans or DPSPs, an SRA need not be calculated. The actual formula is more complex, and is set out in detail in the *Pension Adjustment Guide* (T4084).

(ITR: 8308.3 Specified Retirement Arrangements; *Pension Adjustment Guide* (T4084))

WITHDRAWALS

[¶2615] BASIC RULES

All amounts received as a benefit from an RRSP must be included in income and reported on line 129 of the T1 return. A benefit is any money you withdraw from the plan, either as a lump-sum or periodic payment. It does not include amounts transferred directly from one plan to another held by the same person, or qualifying amounts withdrawn under the Home Buyers' Plan or the Lifelong Learning Plan. Annuity payments received from a registered retirement savings plan may be eligible for the tax credit on the first $2,000 of pension income (see ¶1311).

If you take property, as opposed to money, out of an RRSP, the fair market value of the property will be included in your income (see also ¶905).

A provision exists in subsection 146(15) of the *Income Tax Act* for not taxing a portion of the benefits received from an RRSP if contributions were made to the plan before it was registered and were therefore not deductible. Although regulations have not been issued to make this provision effective, it is understood that the CRA will allow an appropriate reduction of the amount taxable in these circumstances.

This section of the commentary provides an overview of the inclusion of benefits received from an RRSP and related issues.

(ITA: 56(1)(*h*); 146(1) "benefit", (8), (9), (15); 248(1) "amount")

[¶2615.05] *Withholding Tax on Withdrawals*

If you do withdraw funds from your RRSP, the RRSP trustee is obliged to withhold from 10% to 30% of the amount it pays you. The withholding rate depends on the amount of the payment and your province (or country) of residence. Withholding is not required on periodic annuity payments from a matured RRSP, nor on payments which may otherwise be withdrawn and deducted, such as withdrawals of overcontributions (¶2611.45). You get credit for the amount withheld when you file your tax return, as with the withholding taxes on salary or wages.

The CRA has the authority to waive withholding in cases of "undue hardship". See ¶2565.

In a case where the only asset in a self-administered RRSP consisted of shares of a private corporation, the CRA opined that withholding was required notwithstanding the technical difficulties.

(ITA: 146(8); 153(1)(*j*), (1.1); ITR: 103(4), (6)(*c*); Window on Canadian Tax: 8468)

[¶2615.10] *Pension Income Splitting*

You can effectively split your "pension income" if 65 years of age or over, or your "qualified pension income" if under 65, with your spouse or common-law partner. The splitting of such pension income, which includes most forms of income described above (¶2616.05 to ¶2634.10) is discussed at ¶978 and ¶1076.

[¶2615.15] *Can I Use the Money for Emergencies?*

You can withdraw money from a plan (other than a "locked-in RRSP" discussed below) subject to any investment limitations, such as the cancellation penalty on a GIC. Money you withdraw from a plan will be included in your income subject to tax (unless it is withdrawn from a spousal or common-law partner plan in your name and taxed to your spouse or common-law partner, per ¶2624.05). If your income is exceptionally low in a particular year, withdrawal of RRSP funds may be appropriate. See ¶2543.02.

Special provisions allow you to withdraw up to $25,000 from your RRSP for home purchase and up to $20,000 for higher education. Withdrawals must be made in compliance with the rules at ¶2625.05 and/or ¶2626a, and repaid to the RRSP over a period of years.

With these exceptions, it is not intended that you should be able to use your RRSP funds for other than investments by the RRSP without paying tax to withdraw the funds.

In a press release dated November 10, 2005, the CRA reiterated its warning against schemes which purport to allow taxpayers to access funds in their RRSPs without paying tax on withdrawal. In this release, it said that these schemes typically involve using a self-directed RRSP to purchase shares of a private company or an interest in mortgages. The funds injected into the company (etc.) are loaned back to the RRSP owner. This plan can flounder if the investment is not a qualified investment, or if the RRSP is used as security for a loan. The CRA cited the case of *Dubuc v. The Queen*, 2004 DTC 2811 (T.C.C.), as an example where the RRSP was used as security and the amount of the loan was included in the RRSP holder's income. The CRA is on solid ground in giving this warning; such schemes should not be undertaken without independent professional tax advice in the form of a legal opinion by a reputable firm, and probably should not be undertaken at all.

The CRA issues similar Tax Alerts every year on its website during RRSP season.

Note that the CRA does not say such schemes can never work; it is merely informing you of the risks of schemes which are technically inadequate. This is tantamount to saying that the CRA will examine carefully all such schemes which come to its attention and will attack any which seem vulnerable. It is likely that if such transactions can be drafted to withstand attack by the CRA, the Department of Finance will sooner or later step in with remedial legislation.

[¶2615.20] *Locked-In RRSPs*

Where you leave an employer and are allowed to take vested pension benefits out of the employer's pension plan, federal or provincial pension benefits legislation may provide that the funds be rolled over into a "locked-in RRSP". Under the pension legislation, the trustee of the fund may not be entitled to release the money to you except as retirement income. You should investigate these conditions at the time you change employment. Note that these limitations are not imposed by the tax system, but rather by legislation intended to protect your pension income.

Over the years, provincial pension legislation has allowed varying degrees of increased flexibility as to the withdrawal of locked-in funds governed by provincial legislation. In the 2008 federal Budget, the government announced that the rules governing locked-in RRSPs covered by federal pension legislation would also be relaxed.

One of the options available to individuals who work in federally regulated industries and change employment is to take the vested pension benefits they have acquired under a federally regulated registered pension plan in the form of a locked-in RRSP. Typically, this option is chosen by individuals who cannot transfer these vested benefits into the registered pension plan of a subsequent employer, and would prefer not to take them in the form of an annuity or a deferred pension.

To provide an income stream during an individual's retirement years, a locked-in RRSP may be either (i) used to acquire a life annuity (a contract sold by a financial institution which provides fixed payments to the holder at specified intervals), or (ii) converted into a Life Income Fund (LIF), which allows for more flexibility in the amount of income the holder receives in a given year. A LIF is essentially a RRIF created out of income subject to the locked-in RRSP rules, and subject to limitations in addition to the payment requirements which govern all RRIFs (¶2632.05). In the past, the LIF restrictions generally permitted no excess withdrawals over and above mandated minimum RRIF withdrawals (there were minor exceptions).

Amendments to pension regulations permit the following options:

(1) One-Time 50% Unlocking: Individuals 55 or older will be entitled to a one-time conversion of up to 50% of LIF holdings into an unlocked tax-deferred savings vehicle.

(2) Small Balance Unlocking: Individuals 55 or older with small total holdings in federally regulated locked-in funds of up to $27,450 (2016) will be able to wind up their LIFs or convert them to an unlocked tax-deferred savings vehicle.

(3) Financial Hardship Unlocking: Individuals facing financial hardship will be entitled to withdraw up to $27,450 (for 2016) per calendar year. Financial hardship withdrawals are permitted in either of two sets of circumstances: high medical or disability related expenditures, or low income. The medical or disability hardship option is available to individuals who expect to make expenditures of more than 20% of their income in any given calendar year upon medical treatment or upon assistive technology or other expenditures related to a condition or disability that has been attested to by a licensed Canadian physician. These individuals will be allowed to withdraw the total amount of their expected expenditures in any given calendar year, subject to a maximum of 50% of Yearly Maximum Pension Earnings (YMPE) as determined for CPP purposes (as shown in ¶83 at the beginning of this book). The low income withdrawal is permitted for any individual who expects to earn less than the low income limit of 75% of YMPE. Such individuals will be allowed to withdraw an amount based upon their expected income in any given calendar year. This maximum permitted withdrawal is calculated as 50% of YMPE less two-thirds of expected income for the year (less financial hardship withdrawals). Where individuals meet both medical/disability and low income criteria, total permitted withdrawals for any calendar year, regardless of reason, will not be permitted to exceed 50% of YMPE. Income expectations must be supported by notarized "attestations" by the taxpayer, and notarized agreements by the spouse or common-law partner, if any. The format for these attestations is prescribed by pension regulations.

(Other Publications: Department of Finance news release 2008-037, dated March 8, 2008)

[¶2616] RETIREMENT

[¶2616.05] *What Happens When I Retire?*

When you reach the age of 71 in a particular year, you must convert your RRSP into retirement income by the end of that year, and the retirement income payments must commence in the following calendar year.

However, you need not wait to age 71 to commence receiving a retirement income. In theory, you may start at any time, although as a practical matter you should build up your tax-deferred savings while you remain eligible to contribute, and withdraw them only when you (a) absolutely require the money, (b) require retirement income, or (c) reach 71 and must commence to receive retirement income.

When you decide to (or must) begin to receive a retirement income, you can convert your RRSP to either a Registered Retirement Income Fund (RRIF) or an annuity. No tax need be paid on this conversion.

There is a great deal of flexibility on these conversions, so long as the transfer is made directly between plans. That is, you may not withdraw the RRSP funds in cash and later recontribute them to a RRIF or annuity. You can, of course, always withdraw funds you need from your plan at the cost of including them in your income and paying tax on the result, but those funds cannot be returned to the tax-deferred savings system. However, you can use your RRSP funds through direct transfer partly to obtain RRIFs and partly annuities, and you can split one RRSP among several such plans or lump several RRSPs into one such plan.

See also ¶2627.30 for commentary on continuing RRSP contributions for your younger spouse or common-law partner after the year in which you turn 71.

[¶2616.10] *Failure to Convert Plan*

If you fail to convert to retirement income any RRSP of which you are the annuitant by the end of the year in which you reach the mandatory age, the plan is in effect cancelled at the beginning of the following year, and the full fair market value of all the assets are included in your income for that year of cancellation.

[¶2616.15] *Change in Mandatory Retirement Age (2007/2008 Transitional Rules)*

The age at which you must convert your RRSP into retirement income was 71 for many years prior to 1998. For the period 1998 through 2006, the mandatory retirement age was lowered to 69. In the federal Budget of March 19, 2007, it was announced that the 1998 age reduction would be reversed and the age at which your RRSP must be converted to retirement income will again be the year in which you turn 71, if you turn 71 in 2007 or later years.

If you were compelled to convert your plan into retirement income because you turned 69 in 2005 or 2006, transitional rules allow you take advantage of the change in age requirement for 2007 (and 2008 if you turn 70 in 2007), although you cannot make retroactive changes for 2005 or 2006. (If you were already 71 at the beginning of 2007, your position does not change and you simply carry on receiving your retirement income.)

If you have contribution room available, you can make RRSP contributions in 2007 if you turned 71 in 2007, and in 2007 and 2008 if you turned 70 in 2007. You can do this by setting up a new RRSP, or by converting an RRSP that you matured into a RRIF in the year you turned 69 back into an RRSP until the end of the year in which you turn 71.

As well, the requirement that, if you converted your RRSP to a RRIF, you must commence receiving retirement income from the RRIF at the end of the year following the year in which you turned 69 is deferred, so that:

- if you turned 71 in 2007, you are not obliged to take any retirement income from your RRIF for 2007 (although you would have taken such income in 2006, having matured your RRSP in 2005);
- if you turned 70 in 2007, you are not obliged to take any retirement income from your RRIF for 2007 or 2008, even though you matured your RRSP in 2006.

This deferral option remains in place regardless of whether you convert your RRIF back to an RRSP or otherwise make permitted contributions after 2006.

If you converted your RRSP to an annuity rather than a RRIF, the revised rules simply state that, for 2007 and later years, you are not obliged to begin receiving periodic payments until the end of the year in which you turn 72 (rather than 70). It is thus intended that you can defer 2007 and 2008 annuity payments in the same manner as for RRIF payments.

[¶2617] DEATH AND DIVORCE

[¶2617.05] *Rollovers of RRSP or RRIF "Refund of Premiums"*

When a person who has been contributing to an RRSP dies before the plan "matures", that is, before it is converted to a periodic retirement income as described in ¶2631.05 and ¶2634.10, the general rule is that the fair market value of all RRSP assets immediately before death is included in the income of the deceased for the year of death. Values accruing in the plan after death are taxable to the estate of the deceased or to the surviving beneficiaries of the plan. The RRSP itself will become taxable on its earnings beginning with the year following death.

A number of options are available to reduce this income inclusion by shifting taxability to a surviving spouse or common-law partner or to surviving children and/or grandchildren. The recipient spouse or common-law partner, in some cases, child/grandchild may in turn "roll over" these amounts by contributing them to a tax-deferred investment (often an RRSP) of the spouse or common-law partner or child, and deducting the entire contribution to offset the income inclusion.

Sometimes, the fair market value (FMV) of the property of an unmatured RRSP can decrease between the date of death and the date of final distribution to the beneficiary or the estate. If the total of all the amounts paid from an unmatured RRSP is less than the FMV of the RRSP at the time of the annuitant's death, a deduction may be claimed on the final return of the annuitant. The deductible amount will generally be calculated as the difference between the FMV at the time of death that was included in the decedent's income for the year of death and the total of all the amounts paid from the RRSP. This applies where the final payment from the RRSP occurs after 2008. See ¶1914.22 and ¶1916 for further discussion. As a consequence of this, the RRSP issuer is required to issue an information return to report the amount reflecting such RRSP losses.

Where the amount in an RRSP at the death of the "annuitant" is paid to the surviving spouse or common-law partner of the annuitant, this amount is called a "Refund of Premiums", and is taxable to the surviving spouse or common-law partner (and not the deceased). There is an exclusion from the refund of premiums representing the surviving spouse's or common-law partner's share of the increase in value of the plan from January 1 of the year following the year of death. This amount is taxed either in the RRSP trust (since that becomes taxable in the year following death) or in the hands of the recipient beneficiary if paid to the beneficiary in the year; in either case the amount does not qualify for refund of premium treatment.

Where the amount which qualifies as a refund of premiums is paid to a surviving spouse or common-law partner past the age at which contributions to an RRSP can still be made (¶2616.05), the surviving spouse or common-law partner is allowed to transfer all or any part of the "refund of premiums" to a life annuity, a term-to-age-90 annuity, or a RRIF. A surviving spouse or common-law partner under the age of 70 (i.e., still eligible to have an unmatured RRSP) may make any of the above transfers but also has the option to transfer to his or her own RRSP part or all of a refund of premiums not transferred to those other tax-deferred investments. The amount of a refund of premiums contributed by the surviving spouse or common-law partner to any of the above tax-deferred plans in the year received or within 60 days following the year-end may be deducted in full. In the case of an annuity, it must provide for regular payments at least annually, which will be taxed as received. See ¶903.

Where there is no surviving spouse or common-law partner, or, for death's occurring after 1998 (after 1995 under the election described below), regardless of whether there is a surviving spouse or common-law partner, etc., a child or grandchild who receives amounts from the unmatured RRSP of the deceased will receive them as a refund of premiums (subject to the same exclusions for post-death accumulations), provided the child/grandchild was financially dependent on the deceased at the time of death. Accordingly, these distributions will be taxable to the recipient and not the deceased. Where a child/grandchild was financially dependent on the deceased by virtue of physical or mental infirmity, it may also make the full range of transfers to its own tax-deferred plan that would be available to a surviving spouse or common-law partner, as described above, within the same time limits. A minor child or grandchild who was financially dependent on the deceased and receives a refund of premiums can use the refund to provide an annuity to age 18 but not, unless dependent by reason of infirmity, to make any of the other types of transfers. A child of 18 or older who receives a refund of premiums cannot make any transfers to a tax-deferred plan except under the dependent-by-reason-of-infirmity rule. See also ¶903.

Where a taxpayer who is physically or mentally infirm receives a refund of premiums from an RRSP, a designated benefit from a RRIF, or an amount from an RPP of a deceased spouse or common-law partner, or parent or grandparent, on whom the taxpayer was financially dependent, the taxpayer can claim an offsetting deduction for a payment made by or on behalf of the taxpayer to acquire an immediate annuity. There are two types of annuity, one of which is a "life annuity", which is payable for the life of the taxpayer or for a fixed term for 90 years less the age of the taxpayer when the annuity is acquired. The taxpayer must be mentally infirm for a life annuity acquired after 2005 (for a life annuity acquired after 2000 and before 2005, the taxpayer could be physically or mentally infirm). The annuity must be rolled over into a trust where the taxpayer is the sole beneficiary and the trustees must pay the funds in consideration of the needs of the taxpayer. The second type is a "minor term annuity" payable for a fixed term not exceeding 18 years minus the age of the taxpayer when the annuity is acquired. The taxpayer must be the sole beneficiary of the trust that the funds are rolled over into. Finally, if the annuity is acquired after 2005, if the taxpayer dies before the end of the term, then the remaining amounts payable will be commuted into a single payment.

Infirmity for the purposes of these rules is discussed under the subheading "Infirmity Test" toward the end of ¶1209.

It is presumed that a child/grandchild was not financially dependent if its income in the year preceding the death exceeded a specified amount. That presumption can be rebutted by factual evidence. The point is that the specified amount test only comes into play *vis-à-vis* a parent or grandparent on whom the child was in fact dependent. The CRA discusses the criteria it will consider and the circumstances in which financial dependency can be established where the benchmark amounts are exceeded in ruling CRA Document No. 9926947. There it states, among other things, that the CRA "would not normally accept that a grandchild was financially dependent on a grandparent where the grandchild lived with his or her parent(s) and the parent(s) could adequately provide for the grandchild's well being."

For a death in 2001 or after, the specified amount at which the presumption against dependence comes into play is the basic personal amount (¶1106) for the year preceding death, which amount is of course indexed for inflation. Thus where the death occurred in 2016, the 2015 personal amount of $11,327 is used. A table of personal amounts covering recent years is found preceding Chapter 1 at ¶65.

Where the child/grandchild was dependent by reason of mental or physical infirmity on a supporting parent/grandparent who died after 2002, the preceding year basic personal amount used as a benchmark in the presumption of dependency is supplemented by the preceding year disability amount (both as indexed). Thus, where the death occurred in 2016, the infirm child/grandchild looks back to a 2015 amount of $11,327 + $7,899 = $19,226. For a death in 2015, the infirm child/grandchild looks back to a 2014 amount of $11,138 + $7,766 = $18,904. For a death in 2014, the infirm child/grandchild looks back to a 2013 amount of $11,038 + $7,697 = $18,735. For a death in 2013, the infirm child/grandchild looks back to a 2012 amount of $10,822 + $7,546 = $18,368 and so on. A table of personal amounts covering recent years is found preceding Chapter 1 at ¶65.

Here again, infirmity for the purposes of these rules is discussed under the subheading "Infirmity Test" toward the end of ¶1209.

A refund of premium transfer on death of the annuitant need not be a direct transfer from the plan of the annuitant to the plan of the surviving beneficiary (although it can be); it will suffice if contributions are made to the appropriate tax-deferred investment or investments within 60 days of the year-end in which the refund is received. Refund of premium transfers to an RRSP must be designated by completing Schedule 7 of the T1 return and filing it with the return. The amount is deducted on your T1 as an RRSP contribution (on line 208). If the transfer is made to any of the permitted rollover investments other than an RRSP, the issuer should provide an appropriate tax receipt. Claim the deduction on line 232 of the T1 and file the supporting receipt with your T1 return.

Where an RRSP pays the estate rather than a spouse, common-law partner or child, the estate can jointly designate with a qualifying beneficiary the payment to be a refund of premiums. This designation is made on form T2019. Note that form T2019 only transfers the taxability of the refund of premiums; Schedule 7 confirms contributions of amounts as an eligible deduction to an RRSP.

In general, a refund of premiums received directly from an insurance or trust company will be reported on a T4RSP form, although if the payment is made to the estate it may be reported by the estate to you on a T3 slip. In either case if you make a rollover contribution of all or any portion of the refund of premiums to your RRSP you must designate the amount so transferred on Schedule 7.

Amounts which qualify as a refund of premiums paid to a surviving spouse, common-law partner or dependent child are (subject to the limitations below) deducted from the amount included in the year-of-death return of the deceased because they are taxable to the recipient. Representatives of the estate of a deceased can elect to transfer the basic taxability of a refund of premiums back from the recipient to the deceased.

Where the RRSP is divided between a surviving spouse or common-law partner and another beneficiary, the offset of the value included in the deceased's year of death return is fixed as the percentage of total distribution paid out to refund of premium beneficiaries. The refund of premium beneficiary takes all receipts (including post-death growth in the trust) except those arising after January 1 following the year of death as a refund of premiums. Other beneficiaries receive taxable amounts. To the extent the estate elects to be taxable on post-death growth, the recipients will not be taxable.

See also ¶1914.

See ¶2612.60 for rollovers to registered disability savings plans.

(ITA: 56(1)(*d.2*); 60(*l*); 146(1) "refund of premiums"; 146(8.92); 214(6); Death of an RRSP Annuitant (RC4177); IT-500R Registered Retirement Savings Plans — Death of an Annuitant)

[¶2617.10] *Rollover at Death of RRIF or Annuitized RRSP Income*

Where the annuitant of an RRSP has died after the RRSP has matured and been converted to either a RRIF or RRSP annuity (see ¶2616.05, ¶2634.10), the general rule is that the remaining benefits may be assigned by the terms of the plan itself or by will. Where the annuity payments pass to the surviving spouse or common-law partner, the surviving spouse simply takes over the position of annuitant and pays tax on the remaining payments. This transfer usually occurs directly by virtue of the terms of RRIF or annuity, but may occur indirectly where the benefits pass to the estate and the legal representative and surviving spouse or common-law partner agree to the assignment. This will be most common where the surviving spouse or common-law partner under an original RRIF or annuity has subsequently remarried and then died, so the RRIF is being passed on to a new generation of spouse or common-law partner, as it were.

Where a RRIF holder dies and no provision is made in the RRIF contract, will, or by the estate for the surviving spouse or common-law partner to become the new RRIF annuitant, the rules are parallel to those for RRSPs above. That is, the general rule is that the fair market value of RRIF assets at death is included in the year-of-death return of the deceased, subject to a transfer of taxability of amounts which pass to others either directly or by election through the estate.

Where there is a surviving spouse or common-law partner who does not become the successor annuitant, any amount passing to the spouse/partner through the estate automatically becomes a "designated benefit". This designated benefit is taxable to the surviving spouse or common-law partner in the year received and may be contributed by the surviving spouse or common-law partner to an RRSP (age permitting), RRIF or annuity, precisely as if it was an RRSP refund of premiums (see above and ¶903). A transfer to the RRSP, etc. of the surviving spouse or common-law partner must be made within 60 days of the year-end of the year of receipt, and designated on Schedule 7 filed with the tax return of the surviving spouse or common-law partner . Where RRIF amounts pass to the estate of the deceased, the estate and surviving spouse or common-law partner may jointly elect (on form T1090) to have any part of the amount treated as a designated amount of the surviving spouse/partner.

Where there is no spouse or common-law partner, or, for death's occurring after 1998 (after 1995 under the election described below), regardless of whether there is a surviving spouse or common-law partner , and there are surviving children and/or grandchildren who were financially dependent on the deceased at the time of death, the value of property which passes to them will be a "designated benefit" taxable to them.

It is presumed in the first instance that a child/grandchild was not financially dependent if its income in the year preceding the death exceeded a specified amount. That presumption can be rebutted by factual evidence. The point is that the specified amount test only comes into play vis-à-vis a parent or grandparent on whom the child was in fact dependent. The CRA discusses the criteria it will consider and the circumstances in which financial dependency can be established where the benchmark amounts are exceeded in ruling CRA Document No. 9926947. There it states, among other things, that the CRA "would not normally accept that a grandchild was financially dependent on a grandparent where the grandchild lived with his or her parent(s) and the parent(s) could adequately provide for the grandchild's well being."

The specified amount at which the presumption against dependence comes into play is the basic personal amount (¶1106) for the year preceding death, which amount is of course indexed for inflation. For 2016, this basic personal amount for 2015 is $11,327. A table of personal amounts covering recent years is found preceding Chapter 1 at ¶65.

Where the child/grandchild was dependent by reason of mental or physical infirmity on a supporting parent/grandparent who died after 2002, the preceding year basic personal amount used as a benchmark in the presumption of dependency is supplemented by the preceding year disability amount (both as indexed). A table of personal amounts covering recent years is found preceding Chapter 1 at ¶65.

Infirmity for the purposes of these rules is discussed under the subheading "Infirmity Test" toward the end of ¶1209.

Children/grandchildren under 18 years of age or dependent on the deceased by reason of physical or mental infirmity may make the same kind of contributions to an RRSP, RRIF or annuity that would be permitted to them if the designated benefit were an RRSP refund of premiums, as discussed above.

Where property passes to the estate and there is no surviving spouse or common-law partner , or, for death's occurring after 1998, regardless of whether there is a surviving spouse or common-law partner , the estate and financially dependent children/grandchildren (or their representatives) may jointly elect to treat any amount of the RRIF as a designated benefit of the qualifying child.

The rules for exclusion of certain post-death RRIF accumulations from the category of designated benefits, the taxation of designated benefits to the recipient or by election back to the deceased, and the calculation of income in the year-of-death return of the deceased, are all identical to the RRSP refund of premium rules.

See also ¶1916.

See ¶2612.60 for rollovers to registered disability savings plans.

(ITA: 60(*l*); 146.3(1) "annuitant", "designated benefit", (6), (6.1), (6.2); Death of a RRIF Annuitant RC4178)

INVESTMENTS

[¶2618] QUALIFIED INVESTMENTS

Although most RRSPs limit their investments to only a few types of investments, RRSPs can hold any property that is a "qualified investment" under the Act. This is particularly useful for individuals with self-directed RRSPs, who have full control over the type of investments and may wish to hold a diversified portfolio in their RRSPs to maximize their retirement savings.

Determining what types of investments are qualified and non-qualified for an RRSP can be a daunting task, but it is the responsibility of the trustee of the RRSP, not the annuitant. Most types of investments that you would have access to through a full service or discount brokerage will be qualified and the brokerage firm typically will not allow you to invest funds in your RRSP in non-qualified investments. It's even easier if you have a discretionary investment manager for your RRSP, as in that case the picking of individual investments is done by the investment manager, not you.

The CRA has recently published Income Tax Folio S3-F10-C1 on qualified investments for RRSPs and other registered plans.

Here is a list of the most common types of qualified investments:

(1) Money (including cash or coins) denominated in Canadian dollars or foreign currency is a qualified investment provided its fair market value does not exceed its stated value as legal tender.

Rare coins or money held for its numismatic value and digital currencies like Bitcoins are not qualified investments.

(2) Deposits (including guaranteed investment certificates) held with a Canadian branch of a Canadian bank or an authorized foreign bank, or with a Canadian trust company are qualified investments. The terms "bank" and "authorized foreign bank" are defined in section 2 of the *Bank Act*.

Any deposit within the meaning of the *Canada Deposit Insurance Corporation Act* is qualified. Deposits in foreign currency and those with a maturity longer than five years qualify only if they are held with a Canadian branch of a bank or with a Canadian trust company.

(3) Deposits with a credit union are qualified investments, provided the credit union has not granted or extended any benefit or privilege to a connected person under the plan as a result of the plan having invested in a share, obligation or deposit issued by the credit union.

(4) Deposits left with brokers for only a few days in respect of securities transactions are not qualified investments. However, they will not trigger any tax penalties for the plan and planholder.

(5) Securities (excluding futures contracts and other derivative instruments in respect of which the holder's risk of loss may exceed the holder's cost) listed on a designated stock exchange are qualified investments.

This accommodates a wide range of listed securities, including shares of corporations, put and call options, warrants, debt obligations, units of exchange-traded funds, units of real estate investment trusts, units of royalty trusts, and units of limited partnerships.

Here is the list of Canadian and foreign designated stock exchanges:

- Canada: Aequitas NEO Exchange
- Canada: Canadian National Stock Exchange (CNSX)
- Canada: Montréal Exchange
- Canada: Toronto Stock Exchange
- Canada: TSX Venture Exchange (Tiers 1 and 2)
- Australia: Australian Securities Exchange
- Austria: Vienna Stock Exchange
- Belgium: Euronext Brussels
- Bermuda: Bermuda Stock Exchange
- Brazil: BM&F Bovespa Stock Exchange

- Czech Republic: Prague Stock Exchange (Prime Market)
- Denmark: Copenhagen Stock Exchange
- Finland: Helsinki Stock Exchange
- France: Euronext Paris
- Germany: Frankfurt Stock Exchange
- Germany: Boerse Stuttgart AG (Stuttgart Stock Exchange)
- Hong Kong: The Hong Kong Stock Exchange
- Ireland: Irish Stock Exchange
- Israel: Tel Aviv Stock Exchange
- Italy: Milan Stock Exchange
- Jamaica: Jamaica Stock Exchange (Senior Market)
- Japan: Tokyo Stock Exchange
- Luxembourg: Luxembourg Stock Exchange
- Mexico: Mexico City Stock Exchange
- Netherlands: Euronext Amsterdam
- New Zealand: New Zealand Stock Exchange
- Norway: Oslo Stock Exchange
- Poland: The main and parallel markets of the Warsaw Stock Exchange
- Republic of Korea: Korea Exchange (KOSPI and KOSDAQ)
- Singapore: Singapore Stock Exchange
- South Africa: Johannesburg Stock Exchange
- Spain: Madrid Stock Exchange
- Sweden: Stockholm Stock Exchange
- Switzerland: SWX Swiss Exchange
- United Kingdom: London Stock Exchange
- United States: BATS Exchange
- United States: Boston Stock Exchange
- United States: Chicago Board of Options
- United States: Chicago Board of Trade
- United States: Chicago Stock Exchange
- United States: National Association of Securities Dealers Automated Quotation System
- United States: National Stock Exchange
- United States: New York Stock Exchange
- United States: NYSE Arca
- United States: NYSE MKT
- United States: Philadelphia Stock Exchange

Over-the-counter (OTC) quotation systems like the American OTC Bulletin Board and the OTC Link ATS are not designated stock exchanges.

Securities approved for listing or with a conditional approval for listing are not considered to be listed on a designated stock exchange.

The fact that a security is subject to an escrow agreement will not affect its qualified investment status if: (1) the security has been issued; (2) the holder has all the rights of ownership; and (3) identical securities not subject to the escrow agreement are qualified investments.

Securities are qualified investments at a particular time if they are listed on a designated stock exchange at that time. Shares acquired before the listing or before the exchange becomes designated are qualified only at the time of the listing or designation, not retroactively.

Shares that were listed on a designated stock exchange but that were suspended from trading or delisted will generally continue to qualify if the corporation having issued the shares is and remains a public corporation.

(6) Shares or debts including (bonds, debentures, notes, or similar obligations of Canadian public corporations (other than mortgage investment corporations) are qualified investments. However, see item (17) below.

The term "public corporation" is a tax term including corporations with any class of shares listed on a Canadian designated stock exchange and other corporations defined in the *Income Tax Act*. You may contact the company's secretary if you are not sure if an investment in an unlisted corporation will qualify under this rule. A corporation listed on an exchange but that had its trading suspended or was delisted will generally continue to qualify if it remains a public corporation.

(7) Units of a mutual fund trust and shares of most mutual fund corporations are qualified investments.

(8) The following debt obligations are qualified investments if:

- issued or guaranteed by the Government of Canada;
- issued by a province or municipality in Canada or a federal or provincial Crown corporation;
- issued by a corporation, mutual fund trust or limited partnership, the shares or units of which are listed on a designated stock exchange in Canada;
- issued by a corporation, the shares of which are listed on a designated stock exchange outside Canada;
- listed on a designated stock exchange;
- being a bankers' acceptance of a Canadian corporation, if the corporation is not a connected person (essentially the annuitant of the RRSP or a person not dealing at arm's length with the annuitant) under the RRSP;
- issued by an authorized foreign bank and payable at a Canadian branch of that bank;
- having at the time of purchase, an investment grade rating (generally BBB or higher) with a prescribed credit rating agency (or one of its subsidiaries or affiliates) and being issued as part of a single issue or under a continuous issuance program for at least $25 million;
- being a mortgage-backed security (generally an undivided interest or undivided right in a pool of mortgages or hypothecary claims), having an investment grade rating with a prescribed credit rating agency at the time it is acquired by the registered plan, being issued as part of a minimum issuance of $25 million, and deriving all or substantially all of its fair market value from debt obligations that are secured by a mortgage or hypothec on real or immovable property situated in Canada.

Here is a list of the prescribed rating agencies:

- A.M. Best Company, Inc.
- DBRS Limited
- Fitch, Inc.
- Moody's Investors Service Inc.
- Standard & Poor's Financial Services LLC

(9) A share of a specified small business corporation is a qualified investment provided it is not a prohibited investment (essentially one where the annuitant does not deal at arm's length with the corporation or is a specified shareholder of the corporation (generally a shareholder directly or indirectly owning 10% or more of the shares of any class of the corporation)).

A specified small business corporation is basically a Canadian-controlled corporation with all or substantially all of the fair market value of its assets used principally in an active business carried on in Canada, and/or shares or debt of a connected small business corporation. To qualify as a specified small business corporation at a particular time, the corporation must meet the above conditions at that time or at the end of its prior taxation year.

(10) A share of an eligible corporation is a qualified investment if it meets conditions similar to those for specified small business corporations (see item 9 above). One difference is that while the conditions for a specified small business corporation share need only to be met at the time that the share is acquired, a share of an eligible corporation must meet the required conditions throughout the entire period the share is held by the RRSP.

(11) A share of a venture capital corporation or a specified cooperative corporation is a qualified investment if it is not a prohibited investment (see item 9 above) and certain other conditions are met.

(12) Investment-grade gold and silver bullion coins, bars, ingots, wafers, and certificates (including legal tender gold or silver bullion coins produced by the Royal Canadian Mint) are qualified investments.

Investment-grade gold must have a purity of at least 99.5%, while investment-grade silver must have a purity of at least 99.9%. Legal tender bullion coins issued by the Royal Canadian Mint will qualify if they meet the above purity standards and as long as the fair market value of the coin doesn't exceed 110% of the fair market value of its precious metal content. Bullion bars, ingots and wafers will qualify if they are produced by a metal refinery accredited by the London Bullion Market Association, as evidenced by a hallmark identifying the refiner, purity, and weight. Certificates must be issued by the Royal Canadian Mint or a Canadian-resident bank, trust company, credit union, insurance company or registered securities dealer whose business activities are regulated by the Superintendent of Financial Institutions or a similar provincial authority (a "specified corporation") and the bullion represented by the certificate must meet the purity standards noted above.

Coins will only qualify if they are purchased directly from the Royal Canadian Mint or a specified corporation. A bar, ingot or wafer will only qualify if it is purchased directly from the refiner or a specified corporation. A certificate will only qualify if it is purchased directly from the issuer or a specified corporation.

(13) A mortgage fully secured by a Canadian real or immovable property whose mortgagor is not a connected person (essentially the annuitant of the RRSP or a person not dealing at arm's length with the annuitant) is a qualified investment. The mortgage is only fully secured if the value of the property pledged by the borrower covers both the principal and interest of the debt obligation. Any subsequent decline in the value of the property may be ignored for the purpose of determining if the mortgage is a qualified investment.

A taxpayer can use RRSP funds to provide a non-arm's length mortgage on his/her own real estate provided the mortgage is administered by an approved lender under the *National Housing Act*, is insured by the Canada Mortgage and Housing Corporation or by an approved private insurer of mortgages, has normal commercial interest rates and other terms, and in general is administered on an arm's length basis.

A real or immovable property in itself is not a qualified investment but may be acquired by the RRSP plan to protect a mortgage investment in default. The plan and planholder will not be subject to any penalty tax provided the property is sold within a year.

If a mortgage is in default and the plan trustee takes no action to protect its investment or requires authorization from the annuitant of the plan before taking such action, this would be an indication that the borrower may not be dealing at arm's length with the annuitant. If this is determined to be the case after a review of the facts, the mortgage would no longer be, or possibly may never have been, a qualified investment.

(14) An annuity contract issued by a person licensed under Canadian or provincial law to operate an annuities business is a qualified investment if the contract satisfies the following two conditions:

(1) The RRSP trust must be the only person having the right to receive any annuity payments under the contract (disregarding any subsequent transfer of the contract by the plan); and

(2) The annuity contract must give the holder of the contract an ongoing right to surrender the contract for an amount that, ignoring reasonable sales and administrative charges, approximates its fair market value.

This would include a segregated fund annuity,

(15) A retirement income annuity payable to the annuitant at the maturity of the RRSP or one providing that annuity payments may be made to the RRSP before the maturity of the RRSP are qualified investments.

(16) An unlisted option, warrant, or similar right is a qualified investment if it gives to the plan the immediate or future right to acquire a qualified investment that is: (1) a share, unit or debt of the issuer of the right (or of a person or partnership that doesn't deal at arm's length with the issuer), or (2) a warrant issued by the issuer of the right (or a non-arm's length party) to acquire such a share, unit or debt.

The issuer of the right must not be the RRSP annuitant or any person not dealing at arm's length with the annuitant.

(17) A share of a mortgage investment corporation is a qualified investment but only if it does not hold any indebtedness of a connected person (i.e., RRSP annuitant and any person not dealing at arm's length with that annuitant).

(18) A share or unit of a corporation or trust that is a registered investment during the current or immediately preceding taxation year is a qualified investment. If a share or unit is bought by the plan before the corporation or trust becomes a registered investment, they will qualify retroactively to when they were acquired if the registration takes place before the end of the year in which the shares or units are acquired. If they lose their registered investment status in a particular year, the units or shares will still qualify until the end of the cal-

endar year immediately following the year in which the deregistration occurred.

(19) A limited partnership interest in a small business investment limited partnership and an interest in a small business investment trust are qualified investments but an interest in a general partnership is not.

(20) An American Depositary Receipt (ADR) whose underlying security is listed on a designated stock exchange or an ADR that is itself listed on a designated stock exchange are qualified investments.

An ADR represents foreign shares on deposit with an issuing bank or trust company and is a means of trading non-American shares (usually on the New York Stock Exchange).

(21) The interest-paying and principal-paying portions of a strip bond, as well as an undivided interest in a right to receive coupon or residual payments on that bond, are qualified investments, provided the original bond is a qualified investment.

(22) Where an instalment receipt reflects a partial payment on, for example, a share listed on a designated stock exchange, the interest or right in that share is a qualified investment. This would apply to a situation where a corporation has an arrangement to sell its shares on an instalment basis. The purchase and ownership of the shares are evidenced by the instalment receipt.

(23) A foreign exchange contract listed on a designated stock exchange is a qualified investment if the holder's risk of loss does not exceed his or her cost. This would include a foreign currency option contract but would not include: (1) a foreign currency futures contract (since the risk of loss exceeds the cost of the contract); or (2) over-the-counter (OTC) foreign exchange contracts like swaps and forward contracts (since they do not constitute money and the OTC market is not a designated stock exchange).

(ITA: 146(1) "non-qualified investment", "qualified investment"; 204 "qualified investment"; 204.4; 204.5; 207.2; 212(1)(*b*); 262; ITR: 4900 [Prescribed qualified investments]; 5100 [Interpretation]; Income Tax Folio: S3-F10-C1 Qualified Investments – RRSPs, RESPs, RRIFs, RDSPs and TFSAs; S3-F10-C2 Prohibited Investments - RRSPs, RRIFs and TFSAs)

[¶2619] NON-QUALIFIED INVESTMENTS

A non-qualified investment is any investment that is not a qualified investment.

Non-qualified investments will be subject to penalty taxes, may have their income taxed in the RRSP (¶2622.05), and may be included in your income (¶2622.05).

(ITA: 146(1) "non-qualified investment", "qualified investment"; 204 "qualified investment"; 204.4; 204.5; 207.2; 212(1)(*b*); 262; ITR: 4900 [Prescribed qualified investments]; 5100 [Interpretation]; IT-408R (archived); Income Tax Folio: S3-F10-C1 Qualified Investments – RRSPs, RESPs, RRIFs, RDSPs and TFSAs; S3-F10-C2 Prohibited Investments - RRSPs, RRIFs and TFSAs)

[¶2619.05] *Real Estate Acquired on Mortgage Foreclosure*

Note that real estate is generally a non-qualified property while mortgages are qualified (item (13), above). This raises the question as to what happens when an RRSP holding a mortgage is obliged to foreclose on the property to protect its investment. In general, the two penalty provisions which could apply are the inclusion of the value of the property in the annuitant's income, and a 1% per month tax on the trust on the value of the non-qualified investment. The CRA takes the administrative position in paragraph 1.34 of Income Tax Folio S3-F10-C1 that it will not apply these penalty provisions for non-qualified property where (1) the mortgage was a qualified investment, (2) the acquisition through foreclosure or otherwise was necessary to protect the mortgage investment and was the result of actions or default of the mortgagor, and (3) the RRSP holds the property for the sole purpose of disposing of it and in fact does dispose of it within a year.

In fact, the CRA notes in Folio S3-F10-C1 that if the RRSP trustee does not take action to foreclose or otherwise act to protect the investment in the case of default, or requires authorization from the annuitant of the RRSP before so doing, this could be an indication that the borrower may not be dealing with the annuitant at arm's length. If that is found to be the case after a review of the facts, the result would be that the investment would no longer be, and possibly might never have been, a qualified investment.

(ITA: 146(9), (10), (10.1); 207.1; Window on Canadian Tax: 3010; CRA Document No.: 9405965, dated March 23, 1994; Income Tax Folio: S3-F10-C1 Qualified Investments – RRSPs, RESPs, RRIFs, RDSPs and TFSAs; S3-F10-C2 Prohibited Investments - RRSPs, RRIFs and TFSAs)

[¶2621] ANTI-AVOIDANCE RULES FOR RRSPS AND RRIFS

Legislation first introduced in the 2011 federal Budget extended the penalty taxes under Part XI.01 that apply to TFSAs in respect of "advantages", "prohibited investments", and "non-qualified investments" to RRSPs and RRIFs. The new rules generally apply as of March 23, 2011. The Department of Finance subsequently provided some relieving and clarification measures as part of Bill C-4, which are generally applicable as of the same date.

The amendments apply the 100% tax on advantages in respect of TFSAs on the fair market value of a benefit or amount of indebtedness to RRSPs and RRIFs.

In addition, the benefit from "RRSP strips" is added to the list of advantages. An RRSP strip is the amount of a reduction in the fair market value of property of the RRSP or RRIF, where the reduction is part of a transaction or event, or series of transactions or events, one of the main purposes of which is to enable an annuitant of the plan (or a person not dealing at arm's length with the annuitant) to use or obtain property held in connection with the plan. It does not include an amount otherwise included in the annuitant's income. Also, withdrawals under the Home Buyers' Plan and the Lifelong Learning Plan are notable exceptions to the RRSP strip rules and are not considered RRSP strips.

The amendments extend the 50% tax on prohibited investments and non-qualified investments held in a TFSA to RRSPs and RRIFs. Income from prohibited investments in the registered plan is considered an "advantage" and is subject to the 100% tax on advantages. Investment income earned by a TFSA, RRSP, or RRIF on a non-qualified investment is subject to Part I tax. However, any income earned on that non-qualified investment income (second generation income) that remains in the registered plan is considered "specified non-qualified investment income" and is subject to the 100% tax on advantages if it is not removed from the registered plan within 90 days from the receipt of notice from the CRA.

There have been some changes to the definition of "swap transaction" in the new legislation. The basic definition of "swap transaction", in relation to a TFSA trust [which generally means a transfer of property (other than a transfer which is a contribution or a distribution) occurring between the trust and the holder of the TFSA or a person with whom the holder does not deal at arm's length] was kept to apply to RRSPs and RRIFs, but some exceptions were added for RRSPs and RRIFs. Notable exceptions include:

(1) a payment out of or under the registered plan in satisfaction of all or part of the controlling individual's

interest in the plan (this could occur when changing either from one RRSP issuer to another, or from payments that are distributions from the registered plan);

(2) a payment into a registered plan that is a contribution, premium, or property transferred to a RRIF in accordance with paragraph 146.3(2)(*f*) of the *Income Tax Act*;

(3) a transfer of a prohibited investment or a non-qualified investment from the registered plan, in circumstances where the controlling individual is entitled to a refund under subsection 207.04(4) of the *Income Tax Act* (the refund applies where either the registered plan disposes of the prohibited or non-qualified investment within the calendar year where the tax arose as a result of the investment becoming prohibited or non-qualified, or it is not the case that the controlling individual knew or ought to have known that the investment would become prohibited or non-qualified); and

(4) a transfer of property between one registered plan of a controlling individual to another registered plan of the controlling individual if both registered plans are RRSPs or RRIFs (a similar exception is in place for transfers between two TFSAs held by the same individual; however, a transfer between a TFSA and an RRSP or RRIF held by the same individual will be considered a swap transaction and subject to the tax noted above).

The amendments generally apply to transactions occurring, income earned, capital gains accruing, and investments acquired after March 22, 2011.

There is a "transitional prohibited investment benefit" to grant partial relief from the advantage tax on income (including capital gains) on prohibited investments held by an RRSP or RRIF on March 23, 2011, if an election was made in prescribed form before March 2, 2013. The transitional prohibited investment benefit is determined by the formula A — B. For prohibited investments held by an RRSP or RRIF on March 23, 2011, variable A is the total income earned and capital gains realized in a taxation year and earned (or for capital gains, accrued) after March 22, 2011. Variable B is the total of capital losses realized in a taxation year by an RRSP or RRIF that is attributable to a property that is a prohibited investment held by the RRSP or RRIF on March 23, 2011 and accrues after March 22, 2011. The benefit is calculated on a year-by-year basis, and the loss offset does not have a carryback or carryforward mechanism. The relief applies only if the amount is paid out of the RRSP or RRIF to the annuitant within 90 days after the end of the relevant taxation year.

(ITA: 146(5))

[¶2622] PENALTIES

[¶2622.05] *Penalty for Taxpayer Where Non-Qualified Investments Acquired*

If your RRSP acquires a non-qualified investment (¶2619), the fair market value at the time of purchase of such investment will be included in your income in the year of acquisition. However, for investments acquired after March 22, 2011, the foregoing rule does not apply, and instead the 50% penalty tax under Part XI.01 applies. If your RRSP pledges property held in the trust as security for a loan, the fair market value of the property pledged will be included in your income.

If your RRSP disposes of property for an amount less than fair market value or acquires property at an amount greater than fair market value, the difference between the fair market value and the amount of consideration will be included in your income.

The trust company or insurance company that holds your investments is required to notify you of any amount that must be included in your income under these rules.

In addition to the penalties on the annuitant of an RRSP, the plan that holds the non-qualified investments will become subject to ordinary income tax at top marginal rates on the income from such investments, including tax on the full amount (not merely the taxable portion) of capital gains, less any capital losses and the full amount of otherwise exempt capital dividends.

(ITA: 146(9), (10), (10.1); ITR: 214(2))

[¶2622.10] *Disposition of a Non-Qualified Investment and Recovery of Property Used as Security*

Where your registered retirement savings plan has disposed of a property that was a non-qualified investment (¶2618) when it was originally acquired, you may claim a deduction in the year it is sold for the lesser of the amount that was previously included in your income (¶2622.05) or the proceeds received by the registered retirement savings plan on disposition of the non-qualified investment. However, this rule is repealed for investments acquired after March 22, 2011, owing to the application of Part XI.01 tax to such investments.

Where your registered retirement savings plan has pledged assets as security for a loan and these assets are subsequently released, you may claim a deduction in the year the assets are released equal to the amount that was previously included in your income (¶2622.05) minus any net loss sustained by the registered retirement savings plan as a result of using the property as security for the loan.

If the acquisition or pledging takes place in the same year as the disposition or release, it appears that you must add and subtract appropriate amounts in the computation of income, even though the transactions may cancel each other.

SELF-DIRECTED PLANS

[¶2623] SELF-DIRECTED PLANS

[¶2623.05] *Self-Directed RRSPs*

Most RRSPs are "off the shelf" plans which are administered by financial institutions or mutual fund companies, which determine the general nature and specific details of the investments to be made with the funds you invest with them. The investments available in these types of plans are limited to those offered for the type of plan by the company providing them, albeit with "open architecture" investment platforms many companies now sell investments of their competitors in addition to their own products and the range of investments offered can be quite substantial.

An alternative which provides a far greater range of investment options is to open a "self-directed" RRSP. Self-directed RRSPs are widely available from various sources, typically stock brokers and the brokerage arms of financial institutions, and allow the individual greater flexibility and control over the assets and performance of his/her plan. For those wanting the range of investments available in a self-directed RRSP but not wanting to do the day-to-day investment picking themselves, discretionary managed self-directed RRSPs are available, where you delegate your investment decision making to a discretionary investment manager who picks the investments for you based on your investment profile and the general instructions you have given them.

In considering the types of investments to hold in an RRSP, it is important to note that all distributions from an RRSP are fully taxable as income in the hands of the recipient. This means the beneficial treatment accorded to capital gains and dividends is, in effect, lost when securities are owned by an RRSP rather than directly.

Plans that invest in securities other than eligible Canadian stocks and bonds, qualified mortgages, and other explicitly qualified items can subject both the plan and the plan annuitant to severe penalty taxes (see ¶2622.05 *et seq.*). Determining what types of investments are qualified and non-qualified for an RRSP can be a daunting task, but it is the responsibility of the trustee of the RRSP, not the annuitant. Most types of investments that you would have access to through a full service or discount brokerage will be qualified and the brokerage firm typically will not allow you to invest funds in your RRSP in non-qualified investments. It's even easier if you have a discretionary investment manager for your RRSP, as in that case the picking of individual investments is done by the investment manager, not you.

Self-directed RRSPs will also typically have external fees which exceed those associated with a regular RRSP. Note, however, that there are internal charges which may apply and some regular RRSPs may be subject to significant internal charges against the fund assets for administration and investment services. All these considerations should be taken into account in choosing the most appropriate type of RRSP and to ensure that the greatest investment growth and tax advantage is obtained.

[¶2623.10] *Can I Invest in Foreign Assets Through My RRSP?*

Pursuant to the federal Budget of February 2005, restrictions on investments by RRSPs in foreign assets have been eliminated after December 2004 by repealing the penalty tax described below. There is now no limit on the extent to which foreign assets can be held through an RRSP.

As an alternative to direct investment in foreign securities, there are now RRSP qualified Canadian investment funds which contrive to mimic the performance of foreign (typically U.S.) stock markets. See also ¶2530.

[¶2623.15] *Qualified RRSP Investments*

Qualified investments for RRSPs are discussed in general terms in the CRA's *RRSP and Other Registered Plans for Retirement* guide (T4040); in the CRA's Income Tax Folio S3-F10-C1, Qualified Investments–RRSPs, RESPs, RRIFs, RDSPs and TFSAs, and in greater detail at ¶2618.

SPOUSAL OR COMMON-LAW PARTNER PLANS

[¶2624] GENERAL

[¶2624.05] *What is a Spousal or Common-Law Partner RRSP?*

A spousal or common-law partner RRSP is merely an RRSP which names your spouse or common-law partner rather than yourself as "annuitant" but to which you have made a contribution.

In law there is nothing to stop your spouse or common-law partner from setting up a plan to which you contribute; that plan would be a spousal or common-law partner RRSP. It is advisable to keep absolutely separate any plans which you set up as spousal or common-law partner plans and any plans which your spouse or common-law partner sets up on his or her own account. This separation will keep the nature of the plans clear in your mind, and will minimize the chance that you could run afoul of anti-avoidance provisions which could tax you on amounts your spouse or common-law partner withdraws from a spousal or common-law partner plan. There will be no such attribution of amounts so long as your spouse or common-law partner withdraws funds from a plan to which only your spouse or common-law partner has contributed, and which has received no transfers from a spousal or common-law partner plan to which you contributed. These anti-avoidance rules are discussed in greater detail below.

[¶2624.10] *Who is a "Spouse" or "common-law partner"?*

Your spouse is the person to whom you are legally married at a particular point in time, regardless of whether you are living together, or, indeed, regardless of whether either of you are living with someone else. Your common-law partner is your same-sex or opposite sex partner living in a conjugal relationship (whatever that may be) with you. A detailed discussion of this is found at ¶1113.

It seems clear that for RRSP purposes you may have more than one spouse or common-law partner at once under this rule. For example, a taxpayer who leaves a legal spouse and goes to live with the parent of the taxpayer's child seems clearly entitled to treat both the legal spouse and the cohabiting partner as eligible for RRSP spousal or common-law partner plan contributions; although of course the overall contribution limit will not be increased, so that at most the taxpayer can divide contributions between the plans of the two partners. In the case of RRSP spousal or common-law partner contributions, it would seem that the two partners would continue to be eligible for spousal or common-law partner plan contributions until there is either a legal divorce from the legal spouse or a breakdown of the common-law relationship.

You must beware of extending the multiple spouse or common-law partner principle too far, since in each case it will be limited by its technical interplay with the words of another provision. For example, it is clear that you can claim only one personal amount credit for a spouse or common law partner (although it will not always be clear which spouse's or common-law partner's income is used to measure the credit).

However, it does seem that for all RRSP (and RRIF) purposes, your spouse or common-law partner will include both your legal spouse prior to the finalization of divorce and any common-law partners you may have at a particular time under the rules at ¶1113.

The Act defines a "spousal or common-law partner plan" as one of which a spouse or common-law partner is the annuitant.

(ITA: 146(1.1); 248(1) "common-law partner")

[¶2624a] CONTRIBUTIONS

[¶2624a.05] *Amounts Eligible for Spousal or Common-Law Plan Contribution*

The law allows you to contribute any amount which you could have contributed to your own plan under your personal contribution limit as calculated at ¶2604 to a spousal or common-law partner plan instead. Note that this does not permit you to make special "rollover" contributions for such things as termination payments to a spousal or common-law partner plan. However, once you have calculated your ordinary contribution based on earned income (¶2604), you can apportion any amount of that to a spousal or common-law partner plan. Your total contribution to both your own and your spousal or common-law partner plan cannot exceed the contribution limit you calculated for your own plan based on: (i) accumulated unused contribution room carried forward from preceding years, plus (ii) the lesser of (for contributions made for deduction against 2016 income) $25,370 or 18% of the prior year's earned income minus PAs for pension plan employees, plus or minus (iii) the other adjustments discussed at ¶2614b through ¶2614d. In short, the overall 2016 Contribution Limit calculated at line 3 in the Quick Calculation at ¶2604 is the amount that may be allocated between your own and your spousal or common-law partner RRSP.

In future years, your unused contribution room (¶2610.05) will increase your overall contribution limit, which you can apportion between your own and your spousal or common-law partner RRSP.

The deadline for making contributions to a spousal or common-law partner plan eligible for deduction on your 2016 return is the same as for contributions to your own plan (March 1, 2017).

[¶2624a.10] *Contributions by Both Spouses or Common-Law Partners*

Any contributions which you make to a spousal or common-law partner plan will not affect your spouse's or common-law partner's ability to make contributions to his or her own plan based on his or her own earned income.

Example

George is an employee with a 2015 earned income of $40,000 and a 2015 PA of $3,050. His 2016 contribution limit is 18% × $40,000 = $7,200, minus $3,050, or $4,150. Assume he also has an additional $1,000 of unused contribution room from last year, for an overall contribution limit of $5,150. His wife Lynne has a full $25,370 limit for 2016. Lynne decides to contribute $18,270 to her own RRSP and $6,000 to a spousal RRSP for George. George can still contribute up to $5,150 to his own RRSP. Lynne can deduct the $25,370 she has contributed in total, and George can deduct his contributions up to his $5,150 limit.

If Lynne simply made her contribution to George's RRSP, she could still claim the deduction for it, but if George withdrew any money from that RRSP within the calendar year that the premium was paid or either of the two following calendar years, the withdrawal would be taxed to Lynne to the extent of her contribution. If George contributed to his own plan and Lynne to a separate spousal or common-law partner plan for George, George could withdraw the funds from his own plan at any time and the withdrawal would be taxed to him.

[¶2624b] WITHDRAWALS

[¶2624b.05] *Advantages of a Spousal or Common-Law Partner RRSP*

There are two main tax advantages to spousal or common-law partner RRSPs. One is that if you can no longer contribute to an RRSP because of your age (¶2627.30) but still have earned income or contribution room available, and you have a younger spouse or common-law partner who is still eligible to have a plan, you can continue making RRSP contributions. The second advantage of making spousal or common-law partner plan contributions is that you and your spouse or common-law partner will be able to split income at your retirement, and so reduce the overall tax burden based on marginal tax rates.

Example

Mr. and Mrs. Kennedy are now approaching retirement. During most years of their marriage, Mr. Kennedy had a substantial earned income while Mrs. Kennedy had little or no earned income. Mr. Kennedy has always saved through an RRSP, and expects that it will provide $40,000 per year to supplement his OAS/CPP and other income. In addition, Mr. Kennedy will personally have about $10,000 of other income; perhaps OAS/CPP. Total income will therefore be about $50,000 per year.

If Mr. Kennedy has made spousal RRSP contributions throughout the marriage so that each spouse now has equal RRSPs, then he will be taxed on $30,000 per year and Mrs. Kennedy on $20,000. The total tax for the two of them will be about $5,800. If Mr. Kennedy had contributed only to his own plan, he would be taxed on the entire $50,000 and pay about $8,900 in tax. Accordingly, there is an annual tax saving of about $3,100 on retirement income resulting from the use of spousal RRSPs.

(The example above makes several simplifying assumptions, excluding pension credit and old age tax credit, and assuming prior year Ontario tax rates, but it does give a reasonable indication of the level of tax savings.)

Note that a large measure of the tax savings arises because income would be taxed in a higher bracket if it were taxed to one spouse or common-law partner only. If the total income for Mr. and Mrs. Kennedy together after retirement were less than $45,282 for 2016 (as indexed from year to year, i.e., if their combined income for the years after retirement does not exceed the lowest rate bracket in those years), the tax savings arising from a spousal or common-law partner RRSP would be less significant. However, there would still be savings in most cases arising from multiple access to the pension income credit and other basic personal amount credits.

A similar income-splitting benefit can be achieved (even without a spousal or common-law partner RRSP) through the pension-splitting measures in section 60.03, which are described at ¶978 and ¶1076.

[¶2624c] ANTI-AVOIDANCE RULES

There are special anti-avoidance rules applicable to all spousal or common-law partner plans. If your spouse or common-law partner withdraws money from *any* RRSP to which you have ever contributed, or one to which money you contributed can be traced, and if you have contributed to any spousal or common-law partner RRSP in the year of that withdrawal or either of the two preceding years, the lesser of the withdrawal made by your spouse or common-law partner, and the total contributions made by you to *any* spousal or common-law RRSPs in the year of withdrawal or two preceding years will be taxed as if it were your income. That is, if your spouse or common-law partner withdraws money from a spousal or common-law partner RRSP in 2016, and you paid a contribution to a spousal or common-law partner RRSP in calendar 2014, 2015, or 2016, the lesser of the withdrawal or the contribution will be taxed to you rather than your spouse or common-law partner; it will not, however, be taxed to your spouse or common-law partner as well. An exception is permitted where you and your spouse or common-law partner are separated and living apart by reason of marriage breakdown. A spousal or common-law partner RRSP includes any RRSP or RRIF to which any amount from a spousal or common-law partner RRSP has been transferred.

As stated, the general anti-avoidance rules are that any amounts received by your spouse or common-law partner from any registered retirement savings plan to which you have contributed directly or indirectly will have to be included in your income, to the extent that any spousal or common-law partner plan contributions were paid by you in the year of withdrawal or the two immediately preceding years. However, this general rule will not apply in the following cases:

(1) you and your spouse or common-law partner were living separate and apart by reason of marriage breakdown at the time the spousal or common-law partner plan amounts were received by the spouse or common-law partner (see also ¶2330);

(2) your spouse or common-law partner makes a withdrawal in the year of your death (you may find this carries tax planning too far);

(3) either you or your spouse or common-law partner are not resident in Canada at the time the amount would otherwise be included in your income (but see ¶2080.04for withholding tax implications);

(4) transfers are made directly from a spousal or common-law partner plan to another plan (RRSP or RRIF) for your spouse's or common-law partner's benefit; a CRA technical opinion (CRA Document No. 2005-0135951E5) confirms that this would also apply to a transfer to the spouse's/partner's RPP or to a transfer used to fund a legitimate purchase of defined benefit past-service benefits under the spouse's/partner's RPP;

(5) the spousal or common-law partner RRSP has been converted into a retirement income and your spouse or common-law partner received no more than the regular annuity payment provided for (if the RRSP was annuitized per ¶2634.10) or the minimum RRIF payment required by law (if the RRSP was converted to a RRIF), see ¶2632.05; or

(6) where your spouse or common-law partner has died.

Where your spouse or common-law partner has made a direct deductible transfer of spousal or common-law partner RRSP funds to an annuity, another RRSP, or a RRIF, the penalty rules trace the money so that payments out of the new plan will be taxable to the contributor as if the funds had not been transferred.

It appears that if your spouse or common-law partner has, within the time limits described, converted the spousal or common-law partner RRSP to a retirement income that is an annuity, the rules will claw back and tax to you only amounts paid in full or partial commutation of the annuity; the regular annuity payments will not be attributed back. Similarly, if the spousal or common-law partner RRSP has been converted to a RRIF within the time limits, only amounts in excess of the legal minimum withdrawal required from that plan (see ¶2632.05) will be subject to tax in your hands.

Where you are withdrawing an overcontribution from a spousal or common-law partner RRSP pursuant to the rules at ¶2611.15, you will be entitled to an offsetting deduction to the extent you would qualify if the overcontribution had been made to your own plan.

Amounts withdrawn from a spousal or common-law partner RRSP, if they are to be included in the contributor's income under the rules above, are to be calculated on form T2205 and included in income on your T1 return for the year. The T2205 is designed to be used by the plan annuitant, that is, by the spouse or common-law partner whose plan has received money from the other spouse or common-law partner. For example, if the husband has contributed to a spousal or common-law partner plan for his wife or common-law partner, it is the wife or common-law partner who must nominally complete form T2205 The form accounts for withdrawn amounts which may be taxed to either spouse or common-law partner, and comes with three copies; it is intended that each spouse or common-law partner file one copy with its return for the year.

It is important to repeat that, subject to the exceptions above, if your spouse or common-law partner withdraws funds from a spousal or common-law partner RRSP to which you have not made contributions in the current or two preceding years (but to which you have made traceable contributions earlier) but you have paid contributions to another spousal or common-law partner plan within that time, the proceeds of the withdrawn amount will be included in your income as if they were received from the plan to which you contributed more recently. On the other hand, your spouse or common-law partner can withdraw funds from a plan established by the spouse or common-law partner to which you have never contributed (directly or indirectly) without penalty to you.

Note that it is the timing of payment of contributions to a spousal or common-law partner RRSP that governs this recapture rule, not when (or whether) you claimed a deduction.

(ITA: 146(1) "spousal or common-law partner plan", (5.1), (8.3)–(8.7); 146.3(5.1)–(5.3); IT-124R6 Contributions to Registered Retirement Savings Plans; IT-307R4 Spousal or Common-Law Partner Registered Retirement Savings Plans)

[¶2624d] USE OF SPOUSAL RRSP ON DEATH

The CRA policy allows the legal representative of a deceased taxpayer to make contributions to a spousal or common-law partner RRSP for the spouse or common-law partner of the deceased, out of the current (non-RRSP) funds or assets of the deceased, amounts representing any unused contribution room (including current and carryforward amounts) available to the deceased for the year. That is, any amounts which the deceased could have contributed at the time of death to his or her own plan or spousal or common-law partner plan, over and above amounts already contributed at the time of death, can be contributed to a spousal or common-law partner plan. This can be a considerable benefit where the deceased has on the one hand considerable accrued contribution room and on the other a considerable tax liability owing to high taxable earnings in the year or other year-of-death tax consequences such as the recognition of capital gains on assets not transferred to the surviving spouse or common-law partner.

The contributions by the legal representative can be made any time up to 60 days following the end of the calendar year in which the deceased died. All contributions made under this rule are presumably deducted on the year-of-death return of the deceased, reducing tax for that year. The benefits to the surviving spouse or common-law partner of having pre-tax funds added to its RRSP are obvious. Of course, if the surviving spouse or common-law partner is 72 or older in the year, this deferral option is not available, since the surviving spouse's or common-law partner's RRSP must be wound up at the end of the year in which he or she reaches 71 years of age (¶2616.05).

See additional details at ¶1914.30.

HOME BUYERS' PLANS

[¶2625] GENERAL

[¶2625.05] *Using Funds in Your RRSP to Make a Down Payment*

The Home Buyers' Plan allows an individual to "borrow" up to $25,000 for withdrawals made from his or her registered retirement savings plan(s) (RRSP(s)) to use toward the purchase of a home in Canada. There is no immediate tax consequence to withdrawing RRSP funds so long as you use the correct form (CRA form T1036) and comply with the fairly simple rules of the Home Buyers' Plan. In addition, the First-Time Home Buyers' Tax Credit, a non-refundable tax credit, is available to first-time home buyers who acquire a qualifying home. Based on an amount of $5,000, the First-Time Home Buyers' Tax Credit will provide up to $750 in federal tax relief. For more information on this credit, see ¶1359.

The money you borrow from your RRSP must be returned to the RRSP system in annual instalments over a 15-year period, commencing with the second year following the withdrawal. As with ordinary RRSP contributions, you are in fact given 60 days following the year-end to make your RRSP repayment. Thus, if you withdrew funds under the Home Buyers' Plan in 2016, you must commence repayments by March 1, 2019.

When you withdraw RRSP funds under the Home Buyers' Plan, you must identify the home you propose to acquire. However, it is possible that the transaction will not be completed as intended, or not completed at all. In general, you are given until October 1 of the year following the RRSP withdrawal to complete the acquisition of the home you designated or a substitute. This time period may be extended in certain circumstances (see ¶2625a.25, below).

If you fail to acquire a home by the October 1 deadline, you can return the borrowed funds to the RRSP by December 31 of that year without penalty (using Part IV of your original form T1036 to identify the repayment).

If you have funds in several RRSPs, you can withdraw funds from each in the same year up to the overall limitation of $25,000.

The Home Buyers' Plan is essentially intended for first time buyers, but the government has recognized that such a rule would be nearly impossible to track over a lifetime, and would be unfair in a variety of situations. Accordingly, it has instead chosen a five-year period of non-ownership as the test to ensure that current or recent homeowners cannot use the Home Buyers' Plan. You cannot make a qualifying withdrawal under the Home Buyers' Plan if you owned a home at any time in the period commencing January 1 of the fourth year preceding withdrawal of RRSP funds (January 1, 2011 for a 2016 withdrawal) and ending 31 days prior to the withdrawal. Similarly, you cannot use the Home Buyers' Plan if you are currently married (including a common-law relationship as discussed at ¶2624.05) and your current spouse or common-law partner owned a home that was your principal place of residence during the marriage or common-law relationship within the same time period that applies to you.

Where RRSP funds are withdrawn under the Home Buyers' Plan, the rule prohibiting withdrawals by someone who has owned a home in the past five years will not apply to withdrawals by a disabled person or the relative (¶812) of a disabled person where the purpose of the withdrawal is to enable the disabled person to live in a home which is more accessible by the person, on in which the person is more mobile or functional, or which is better suited to the personal care and needs of the person. This exception is discussed in greater detail under the subheading "Specified Disabled Persons" at ¶2625a.05.

Each individual is treated separately with respect to the RRSPs in his or her name, and individuals may use funds withdrawn from an RRSP under the Home Buyers' Plan to purchase a home jointly with others. Most commonly, husband and wife or common-law partner can each withdraw up to $25,000 from his/her own RRSP for the purchase of a jointly owned home. Common-law partners can similarly do this, and indeed any group of related or unrelated individuals, provided they can agree on the intricacies of collective home ownership.

Although there is no withholding tax on the withdrawal of RRSP funds under the Home Buyers' Plan, there may be a commercial penalty depending on the terms of the RRSP and its underlying investments. If your RRSP funds are invested in Guaranteed Income Certificates (GICs), for example, there is often a penalty cost to cashing these in early. Some mutual funds have a "back-end load" which means there is a fee for withdrawing funds. You should understand what these costs are before you withdraw; if you have more than one RRSP you may withdraw funds from each or any up to the overall $25,000 limit for all withdrawals together, and the cost of withdrawal from a particular fund may influence your choice.

All the above rules are discussed in greater detail below.

(ITA: 146(8); 146.01(1); (2); (3); (4))

[¶2625.10] *Limitations on Ordinary RRSP Contributions*

If you withdraw RRSP funds under the Home Buyers' Plan (or the Lifelong Learning Plan discussed at ¶2626a), you will not be allowed to deduct any ordinary RRSP contributions made less than 90 days before the withdrawal to the extent that the contribution is greater than your RRSP balance after the withdrawal.

Example

> Suppose you have $15,000 in your RRSP at the beginning of 2017 and $10,000 in cash. Suppose further that you are entitled to put another $10,000 into your RRSP before March 1, 2017, and in fact you use the cash to pay this amount as an RRSP contribution on February 15, 2017. You now have $25,000 in your RRSP. On March 31, your RRSP is credited with a further $750 earnings in respect of preceding years. On May 1, 2017 (i.e., less than 90 days after the contribution payment on February 15) you withdraw $20,000 under the Home Buyers' Plan, leaving a balance of $5,750. Your RRSP balance immediately after the withdrawal will be $5,750, and your contribution within the 90-day period was $10,000, a difference of $4,250. This amount will be disallowed as an RRSP deduction. In effect, you are allowed to withdraw the $15,000 that was on hand originally, plus all earnings in the plan (whether on old or new money), but you are not allowed to contribute funds within the 90-day period and both deduct them and withdraw them.

You could, in this example, withdraw $15,750 without penalty. You could also, it seems, withdraw the $15,750 on May 1 and, if you have not acquired your home before the 30 days preceding the 90th day after February 15 (i.e., you have not acquired your home before the 30 days preceding May 16) you could now withdraw the remaining $4,250 and use it to further pay down your home cost. The 30-day rule is one of the limitations on Home Buyers' Plan withdrawals, and is discussed at ¶2625a.

The same rules will apply to funds your spouse or common-law partner withdraws from a spousal or common-law partner RRSP. A spousal or common-law partner RRSP is an RRSP where your spouse or common-law partner is the annuitant, i.e., the person entitled to withdraw the funds, but you are the contributor. If you contribute funds to a spousal or common-law partner RRSP and your spouse or common-law partner withdraws the funds under the Home Buyers' Plan within 90 days of your contribution, you will not be allowed to deduct your RRSP contribution to the extent that the contribution is greater than your spouse's or common-law partner's RRSP balance after the withdrawal.

This rule appears to operate on a plan-by-plan basis. That is, if you had $15,000 in RRSP (1) and $5,000 in RRSP (2), and you put an additional $10,000 in either one, you could nevertheless withdraw $15,000 from (1) and $5,000 from (2) within the 90-day period and still deduct the $10,000. However, if you attempted to withdraw the entire $20,000 from either plan, you would find a portion of it disallowed based on the application of the rule to that particular plan.

It would seem that if you have inadvertently made a non-deductible contribution to an RRSP, you cannot hold it over for future deduction. On the other hand, the denial of a deduction under the 90-day rule appears to have no effect on contribution room nor to create an overcontribution penalty (¶2611.15). Given the way the rules work, the penalty only arises to the extent you withdraw funds attributable to the 90-day period, as opposed to funds previously in the plan. The theory seems to be that having withdrawn the funds and spent them on the house, they are gone and the denial of deduction is sufficient penalty. They cannot be withdrawn from the plan under the overcontribution rules because they are no longer there.

The denial of a deduction for an RRSP contribution applies only to "ordinary" contributions. That is, it does not apply to contributions made and deducted under "rollover" rules such as the rules which permit special RRSP contributions for retirement allowances, termination payments, refunds of premiums you received on the death of a spouse or common-law partner or, in some cases, a parent, and direct transfer of funds between RRSPs or from pension plans or the like to RRSPs. In general, these special contributions are recognizable because you must file Schedule 7 to identify them (although other forms may be used for direct transfer payments).

[¶2625.15] *HBP Balance*

Several of the current rules turn on the concept of an HBP balance.

An HBP balance at a particular time is the total of *eligible* withdrawals made before that time less the total of (a) repayments of those amounts designated as repayments (¶2625b.05) for taxation years that ended before that time, and (b) amounts included in income for taxation years that ended before that time either through failure to make adequate repayments (¶2625b.05) or on becoming a non-resident (¶2625b.45).

Example

Ben withdrew $15,000 from an RRSP in Year 1 and acquired a qualifying home in that year. Ben made his first repayment of $1,000 in Year 3. Since he has an HBP balance, he must file a T1 return for Year 3 (and later years for which he has an outstanding HBP balance) even if not otherwise required, and designate the repayment on Schedule 7.

Note that the HBP rules ensure from that Ben cannot make any new HBP withdrawals which might otherwise be permitted, for example to finance a home for a disabled relative, because he had an HBP balance at the beginning of the year (other rules would have prevented this in earlier years).

For Year 4 he failed to make a repayment and had $1,000 included in his income. He must in any event file a T1 return for Year 4, since he has an HBP balance, and should include the $1,000 on line 129.

For Year 5 he has an opening HBP balance (of $13,000). In consequence (1) he must file a Year 5 tax return regardless of whether he has an obligation to file under any other rules, and (2) he cannot make any new HBP withdrawals which might otherwise be permitted, for example to finance a home for a disabled relative. Assume, however, that in February of Year 6 he repaid the remaining $13,000. To qualify the repayment for Year 5, he files a Year 5 T1 return and designates the $13,000. If this is done, he is not obliged, under these rules at least, to file a Year 6 tax return in Year 7, since his HBP balance at January 1 of Year 6 is nil by virtue of the earlier repayments and income inclusions, including the Year 6 repayment attributed to Year 5. For Year 6 he may withdraw funds to finance a home for a disabled relative, although he will still be barred by his current home ownership from making further HBP withdrawals for other purposes.

Note that where a qualified home is not acquired within specified time limits and funds must be returned to an RRSP rather than repaid over time, the original withdrawal was never an eligible amount and there was never an HBP balance, although for a time there appeared to be.

(ITA: 146.01(1) "HBP balance")

[¶2625.20] *Participation Period*

The HBP may be used more than once in limited circumstances (i.e., where there is a specified disabled person or where there is a five-year period of non-ownership). To accommodate the potential repeated use of the plan, the repayment rules apply separately to each "participation period". A participation period is commences with the beginning of the calendar year in which in which you withdraw an eligible amount, and ends immediately before the beginning of the calendar year at the beginning of which your HBP balance is nil.

Again, where funds are withdrawn and returned upon failure to complete a purchase, as in Example 2 above, there would seem in retrospect to have been no participation period at all, since there was never an eligible amount.

If you withdrew funds in 2016, acquired a qualifying home in 2016, and began making repayments for 2018 (i.e., by March 1, 2019), and made the final repayment for 2032 by March 1, 2033, your participation period would begin January 1, 2016 and end December 31, 2032.

(ITA: 146.01(1) "participation period")

[¶2625a] QUALIFYING WITHDRAWALS

Each individual may withdraw funds under the Home Buyers' Plan from one or more RRSPs of which the individual is the annuitant so long as the total of funds withdrawn does not exceed $25,000. The funds need not be withdrawn at precisely the same time, but all withdrawals must be received in the same calendar year, and further limitations will be imposed by the 30-day rule in (3), below.

There is an exception to the rule that all funds must be withdrawn in the same calendar year. A withdrawal of funds requested in Year 1 but not received until January of Year 2 will be considered a Year 1 withdrawal if you have already made a qualifying Year 1 withdrawal. The CRA has the authority to further extend this deadline for actual receipt of funds past January. Clearly the intention is that the Home Buyers' Plan user should not be put offside because of any delay by the RRSP trust in coming up with funds requested.

For 1999 and later withdrawals, the once-in-a-lifetime restriction no longer applies, but the restriction that all funds must be withdrawn in the same calendar year remains, with the same exceptions. The rule now enforces the limitation that qualifying withdrawals can only be made if your "HBP balance" (defined at ¶2625.15) at the beginning of the year of the withdrawal is nil; that is, all prior HBP withdrawals have been repaid or subjected to tax in lieu of repayment.

Since the basic withdrawal rule applies to each individual, spouses or common-law partners, if they have sufficient RRSP funds in the name of each, may collectively withdraw up to $50,000. You may withdraw funds up to $25,000 from RRSPs in your name, and your spouse or common-law partner may withdraw up to $25,000 from RRSP in your spouse's or common-law partner's name, even if your spouse's or common-law partner's RRSPs are spousal or common-law partner RRSPs, that is, RRSPs to which you have contributed. You cannot, however, transfer funds from your RRSP to a spousal or common-law partner RRSP (except in the case of marriage breakdown, which would usually preclude a joint home purchase).

Note that the rules in (5) and (6), below, will normally preclude a spouse or common-law partner from using RRSP funds to purchase a home where either has had a home in the preceding four years. This presents some problems on separation. It would seem that a legal spouse remains a spouse until legal divorce, and therefore the separated spouses remain bound by the four-year rule. However, a common-law partner (¶2624.05) ceases to be one at the commencement of a period of separation due to breakdown of the relationship which proves to have lasted for at least 90 days. Thus the four-year rule *vis-à-vis* a spouse or common-law partner would appear to dissolve with the relationship.

You must comply with all the following rules to make a withdrawal which qualifies under the Home Buyers' Plan:

(1) You must actually receive all funds withdrawn in the same calendar year, subject to the exceptions discussed above.

(2) You must withdraw the funds using form T1036, which requires you to set out the location of a qualifying home which you have begun, or intend no later than one year after acquisition to begin, using as a principal place of residence.

(3) Neither you nor your spouse or common-law partner may have acquired the qualifying home more than 30 days before receiving the RRSP withdrawal amount.

(4) You must have entered into a written agreement for the acquisition of the qualifying home or with respect to its construction before you apply to withdraw the RRSP funds.

(5) You must not have had an owner-occupied home in the period commencing at the beginning of the fourth preceding calendar year which ended before the date of the RRSP withdrawal and ending on the 31st day before the withdrawal (see ¶2625.05 and the text preceding this list for further comments).

(6) Your current spouse or common-law partner may not have had an owner-occupied home during the period in (5), above, that was inhabited by you during the marriage or common-law relationship.

(7) You must be resident in Canada when you receive the funds.

(8) If you have not purchased the home in the 30 days preceding the withdrawal (see (3), above), you must remain resident in Canada from the time you receive the funds out of the RRSP until you actually acquire the qualifying home; [for withdrawals, there is the additional rule that if you have purchased the home before withdrawing the funds, you must have been a resident at the time of purchase as well as the time of withdrawal].

(9) The total of the amount withdrawn plus all funds you have previously withdrawn in the year (subject to the extensions discussed above) under the Home Buyers' Plan must not exceed $25,000.

(10) Your "HBP balance" at the beginning of the year in which you make the withdrawal(s) must be nil. Your HBP balance is the total of qualifying amounts withdrawn on a prior use of the plan minus designated repayments and minus amounts included in your income upon failure to make scheduled repayments and amounts included in your income upon becoming a non-resident of Canada. See ¶2625.15.

(11) You must in fact use the funds within time limits discussed at ¶2625a.25.

If you make a withdrawal from an RRSP which does not comply with all the rules above, the amount withdrawn will be added to your income for the year it was withdrawn, subject to the replacement property rules below and the rules at ¶2625a.35 permitting a return of funds to an RRSP.

[¶2625a.05] *Specified Disabled Persons*

Rules (5) and (6), above, do not apply to withdrawals you make if

(1) the withdrawal request identifies a "specified disabled person";

(2) the residence to be acquired is identified in the withdrawal and is either in use by the disabled person at the time of acquisition (but the acquisition will be subject to the 30-day rule in (3), above) or is intended for use by the disabled person within one year after its acquisition; and

(3) the purpose of the withdrawal is to enable that specified disabled person to live (i) in a dwelling that is more accessible by that person or in which that person is more mobile or functional, or (ii) in an environment better suited to the personal needs and care of that person.

A specified disabled person is an individual or relative of the individual who is entitled to a disability credit (on line 316 of the T1 return), or would so qualify but for the limitations where alternative medical expense credits are claimed for attendant or nursing home care for the person; see ¶1255.

Rules (1) to (11) are further modified so that either the RRSP annuitant or the disabled person (if different) may actually acquire the residence. The annuitant who withdraws the funds must be resident in Canada at the time of withdrawal, but if the home is acquired after the withdrawal rather than before, the annuitant must remain resident in Canada until the annuitant or the disabled person actually acquires a qualifying home. In general, all rules governing the Home Buyers' Plan (e.g., deadlines for acquisition, extension, repayments, etc.) are modified to allow for the fact that the home may be acquired by a related disabled person rather than the annuitant who withdraws the funds.

Individuals are related for purposes of this rule if they meet the definition for related persons in ¶1122.

The upshot of these rules is that a disabled person or the relative of a disabled person may withdraw RRSP funds without regard to the usual five-year limitation since the last time a home was owned. Indeed, a current homeowner may use RRSP funds to acquire a more suitable dwelling for the disabled person. Where the disabled person withdraws his or her own RRSP funds, the home must be acquired (at least in part) by the disabled person, although it may be acquired jointly with others. Where a relative of the disabled person withdraws RRSP funds, the home may in fact be acquired by either the disabled person or the relative who withdrew the funds (or both together), but it must be intended for the use of the disabled person. It would appear, however, that a relative could acquire a suitable home in which the relative (and family) would also live, so long as the purpose is to allow the disabled person to live in a more accessible dwelling or an environment better suited to his or her care as described in (c).

[¶2625a.10] *Replacement Property*

It is clear that you are expected to identify a qualifying home before you make your RRSP withdrawals under the Home Buyers' Plan. However, there is a provision for the substitution of a "replacement property" if your acquisition of the originally designated home falls through. A replacement property is simply another qualifying home you agreed to acquire or began to construct after you requested a withdrawal for the original qualifying home. It cannot, however, be a home you or your spouse or common-law/partner had acquired before your withdrawal request for the original home. This rule applies equally if you are acquiring a home for a related disabled person.

[¶2625a.15] *Qualifying Home*

A qualifying home in these rules merely means a housing unit located in Canada or a share of capital stock of a cooperative housing corporation which entitles you to a housing unit located in Canada. However, you must also "intend" at the time you withdraw the funds from your RRSP(s) to use the home as a "principal place of residence" within one year of its actual acquisition. You fulfill this requirement automatically if you have begun to use it as a principal place of residence before you withdraw the money (but not more than 30 days before under the rules above).

A principal place of residence is not the same thing as a "principal residence" for purposes of the rule which exempts a family's principal residence from capital gains tax (¶553, ¶554). In fact, "principal place of residence" is not a defined term at all. It would appear to be a residence in which you normally spend 184 days or more per year, although if you actually spread your time among three or more residences, it might be the one in which you spend the most time, or which you can demonstrate is your favoured base of operations. In any event, a cottage or other vacation home would not be a principal place of residence unless you intend to move there or spend the majority of your time there within a year of acquisition.

Note that at the time you withdraw the funds you must intend that the qualifying home will become a principal place of residence within one year of acquisition. There seems to be no penalty if this intention is frustrated by events. For example, if you had planned to retire to the new home, or to move to the new home at a new place of employment, and the planned retirement or employment does not occur due to unforeseen events, so that the new home became a vacation home or was sold by you, this would not result in a penalty. However, you might well have to demonstrate to the CRA your original intention and the intervening events that frustrated that intention. If you cannot prove the original intention at the time of the withdrawal of RRSP funds, the withdrawal will be treated as unqualified and added to your income for the year the funds were withdrawn.

Although your intention to occupy the home you acquire as a principal place of residence may change, you must acquire the home for which you withdrew the funds (or a replacement property) within a specified time or return the funds to the RRSP system. This is discussed at ¶2625a.25.

[¶2625a.20] *No Tracing of Funds*

Note that the qualifying withdrawal rules above do not actually require a tracing of funds from your RRSP withdrawal to your home purchase. That is, the rules allow you to make a withdrawal, and treat it as qualifying if you meet the rules above and acquire a qualifying home within the period described in ¶2625a.25. The rules do not specify that you must use the actual money withdrawn to purchase the qualifying home. See also the discussion of qualifying overwithdrawal at ¶2625a.45.

(ITA: 146(8); 146.01(1) "qualifying home", (2)(*d*); Window on Canadian Tax: 2268)

[¶2625a.25] *You Must Acquire a Property Before October 1 of the Following Year*

The HBP rules require you (or a related disabled person) to acquire the qualifying home you specified in a withdrawal of RRSP funds under form T1036, or a replacement property therefor, before (not on) October 1st of the year following the year you first receive funds out of an RRSP under the HBP. This date is called the "completion date". Thus, if you first received funds from an RRSP under the HBP in 2016, you were to acquire your home before the completion date of October 1, 2017.

If the qualifying home you originally specified is not in fact acquired, for example, because an intended transaction failed to close, you can keep the withdrawn funds in hand while you look for a replacement property, but you must acquire the replacement property before the completion date which originally applied. If you fail to do this, you must return the money to an RRSP of which you are the annuitant or have it added to your income, as described in ¶2625a.35, below.

You normally "acquire" a home when the purchase-and-sale transaction closes; that is, when your down payment has been made and accepted and the transfer of title has been registered with the province in which the property is located. You may acquire a property and fulfill this rule without having actually moved into the new home. However, as discussed in ¶2625a.15, you must have an intention to move in within a year of acquisition. For example, if you withdrew funds in 2015, your completion date was October 1, 2016. If you in fact acquired a house on September 30, 2016, you have until September 30, 2017 to actually move in.

Note that acquisition may be made up to 30 days before an actual withdrawal of RRSP funds, as well as after it (¶2625a(3)).

The rules provide that a condominium unit is considered to have been acquired on the day you are entitled to immediate vacant possession of it. This provision is intended to accommodate the case where you are entitled to occupy a condominium unit by the completion date, but you do not become a registered owner of the unit until sometime later. This is sometimes a problem, especially with new condominiums where registered titles may only be issued when an entire project is completed.

You may acquire a property jointly with someone else and the property will qualify under these rules. It is common to acquire property jointly with a spouse or common-law partner, but you can make an acquisition jointly with anyone, related or otherwise, under these rules and the acquisition will not be disqualified because the acquisition is of only an undivided part of the qualified home.

(ITA: 146.01(1) "completion date", "excluded withdrawal")

[¶2625a.30] *Extension of Deadline*

If you fail to acquire a qualifying home (or replacement property) before the completion date, you may still be considered to have met the requirement in either of the two cases set out below. The extension rules apply equally where a related disabled person is acquiring the home for which you made the withdrawal.

EXTENSION I — Written Commitments

You will be considered to have met the original completion date if you meet all the following conditions:

(1) you are obliged, under the terms of a written agreement in effect on the original completion date, to acquire a qualifying home (or replacement property) on or after that day;

(2) you in fact acquire the qualifying home or a replacement property before the day that is one year after the original completion date; and

(3) you were resident in Canada throughout the period commencing on the original completion date, and ending on the earlier of the next October 1 and the day you acquire the property.

EXTENSION II — Withdrawals Paid Out

You will be considered to have met the original completion date if you have made payments totalling all amounts withdrawn by you under the HBP to an arm's length person or company and the payments meet all the following conditions:

(1) they were all made in the period beginning with your first withdrawal under the HBP and ending before your original completion date;

(2) they were all paid to persons (or companies) with whom you deal at arm's length (i.e., are not your relatives or, in the case of companies, controlled by you or your close relatives); and

(3) they were made in respect of the construction of your original qualifying home or a replacement property.

(ITA: 146.01(2))

[¶2625a.35] *If You Fail to Acquire a Qualified Property*

If you or a related disabled person fail to acquire a qualifying home (or replacement property) described in ¶2625a.05 before the applicable completion date, and the extension rules in ¶2625a.25 do not apply to you, you must return the amounts withdrawn to an RRSP with the same issuer(s) from whom you withdrew the funds; however, those amounts need not be returned to the original issuer. This return of withdrawals must be made no later than December 31 following the completion date (i.e., within three months following the completion date). Thus, if you took out funds in 2015 so that your completion date is October 1, 2016, and you fail to acquire a qualifying home before that date, you have until December 31, 2016 to return the funds to your RRSP.

This cancellation of participation in the Plan is made by making a timely repayment contribution to an RRSP and sending copies of the RRSP contribution receipts to the CRA together with the *Home Buyers' Plan (HBP) — Cancellation letter*.

If you fail to acquire the home set out on your original T1036 or a substitute, you are not required to delay the return of funds to the plan. You can return them at any time before December 31 of the year following withdrawal. If you do return the funds under this mechanism, you are considered never to have used the Home Buyers' Plan and you are eligible to use it on another occasion.

If you did not return the funds because you expected to qualify for a written agreement extension described in ¶2625a.25, but you failed to qualify solely because you did not finally acquire your home by the extended deadline allowed under those extension rules, you can return funds to your RRSP(s) before January 1 following the extended date. Thus, if you made a 2015 withdrawal, had an original completion date of October 1, 2016, and qualified for an extended completion date of October 1, 2017, but still failed to complete the transaction by that date, you could return the funds by December 31, 2017.

If you have not acquired your home nor returned the funds within the deadlines described, you will become taxable on the amounts withdrawn in the year you withdrew them, as if they had been ordinary taxable withdrawals from an RRSP.

Where a full refund to the RRSP system is made under these rules, the result is that an eligible withdrawal is deemed never to have been made, but the original withdrawal is not retroactively included in income. In short, it is as if the HBP withdrawal had never been made at all. See also the comments on HBP balance at ¶2625.05.

[¶2625a.40] *A Note on Cancellations of Withdrawal from Spousal or Common-Law Partner RRSPs*

If you fail to acquire a qualifying home on a timely basis you must return the withdrawals made or have them included in income. For returns made before 2000, you had to return the exact amount of funds withdrawn to each issuer from which funds were withdrawn, but you were not required to return them to the same plan. (This of course was essential, since the original plan may have been terminated by the complete withdrawal of assets.) For returns of funds made under these rules before 2000, the definition of issuer seems to imply that a return must be made to a plan for the annuitant who made withdrawal (and only the named annuitant could make a withdrawal), although the matter is perhaps not beyond dispute. Thus amounts contributed to a spousal or common-law partner plan but withdrawn by the spouse or common-law partner annuitant had to be returned to a plan for that spouse or common-law partner annuitant; similarly, amounts withdrawn from the plan of a contributor annuitant could not be returned to the plan of a spouse or common-law partner annuitant. For returns of funds made after 1999, the statute is quite clear that returns of funds must be to the plan of the annuitant.

Where funds are withdrawn from a spousal or common-law partner RRSP by the annuitant spouse or common-law partner and a qualifying home is not acquired within the various applicable deadlines and with withdrawal is not returned to an RRSP of which that spouse or common-law partner was the annuitant, the amount withdrawn would be included in the income of the contributor spouse or common-law partner for the year of withdrawal to the extent required by the attribution rules in ¶2624.05.

It is less clear what happens when funds are withdrawn from a spousal or common-law partner RRSP by the annuitant spouse or common-law partner and later returned to another RRSP for that same annuitant. Does the new RRSP remain a spousal RRSP subject to attribution on later withdrawal? A spousal or common-law partner plan does include a plan which has received "a payment out of or a transfer from" a spousal or common-law partner plan; it is perhaps not entirely certain whether a return of HBP funds constitutes such a transfer. The CRA will surely take the position that it does. In any case, since the cancellation rules seem to require that an anticipated real estate transaction fails to be completed and no substitute property is found, cancellations should be relatively rare. Where the transaction contemplated on form T1036 with which the funds were withdrawn was never intended to be completed, there is an aura of fraud and the CRA would probably have little difficulty in both attributing the withdrawal to the contributing spouse or common-law partner and denying the recontribution deduction to anyone. Clearly, the CRA has not encountered problems with this potential abuse or the rules would have been clarified in the 1999 amendments.

(ITA: 146(1) "issuer", "spousal or common-law partner plan"; 146.01(1) "excluded withdrawal")

[¶2625a.45] *Qualifying Overwithdrawal*

The rules seem to assume that you cannot acquire a home in Canada for less than $25,000 per participant. There is no provision to say that if you withdraw $25,000 but your share of a qualifying home costs less than $25,000 you must return the difference to the plan, except over the 15-year repayment period. Suppose, for example, you and your spouse or common-law partner owned some land in, say, rural Nova Scotia, and you plan to build your retirement home there for use beginning May 1, 2017. You contract with a local contractor in August 2015, to build it for $32,000 during the months of May and June 2016, and you withdraw $25,000 each from your RRSPs in September 2015. Your home will qualify because you will acquire it no later than its completion deadline, which is before October 1, 2016, and you intend to occupy it within one year of its acquisition. It is not wholly clear when you acquire a property under construction; usually it is acquired as you pay for it, but the terms of the contract may affect the result. In fact, there is some variation in construction and you agree to pay $44,000. It appears that you can repay the $50,000 of funds withdrawn over 15 years according to the rules in ¶2625b.05; you cannot simply return the excess $3,000 each to the issuer and treat it as if it had never been withdrawn under the cancellation rules at ¶2625a.35.

Similarly, five brothers and sisters (or five friends) could withdraw $25,000 each and buy a home for, say, $90,000, or $18,000 apiece. They appear to be allowed, indeed required, to return the $7,000 difference over 15 years as described below. Of course, you are forgoing the advantages of tax-deferred earnings on the excess money if you do this, so it doesn't really make a lot of economic sense; still, you can do it if you wish.

If you have funds properly withdrawn from your RRSP but in excess of amounts required to acquire your home, you can treat the funds in any way you want. You can spend the money, or make an advance payment on your HBP repayment schedule, thus lowering the annual repayments in coming years (see ¶2625b.30); or if you have abundant unused RRSP contribution room, you can use the money to fund additional deductible contributions.

(ITA: 146.01(1))

[¶2625b] REPAYMENT

[¶2625b.05] *Repaying Your Withdrawals to an RRSP*

If you do acquire a qualifying home within the required time limits, you must repay the money withdrawn over a 15-year period with the first payment made no later than 60 days after the end of the second year following your first withdrawal. Thus, if you first withdrew funds under the Home Buyers' Plan in 2015 your first year repayments are due for 2017, but you have until March1, 2018 to make the repayment.

The completion date extension rules in ¶2625a.25 do not extend the deadline for commencing periodic repayments. Where the extension rules are met, the original completion date is deemed to have been met rather than extended. Accordingly, the original completion date governs the repayment provisions.

Regardless of whether RRSP withdrawals were made under the old or new rules, repayments may be made in 15 equal annual instalments made no later than 60 days after December 31 of each year commencing as described above. That is, if your first repayment date is March 1, 2016, you must make your repayments in 15 annual instalments commencing no later than that date and continuing each year thereafter. The repayment date will usually be March 1, but in leap years it will be February 29. Where the date falls on a Sunday, it will usually be deferred to the following Monday.

[¶2625b.10] *Designation of Instalment Repayments*

RRSP contributions intended as instalment repayments are not designated when made, but rather designated on Schedule 7 of the T1 tax return package, which must be filed with your T1 tax return for the year to which the repayment relates. Repayments applied to a specific year must be made in that calendar year or within the first 60 days of the following year; that is, within the time frame for normal RRSP contributions for a year. As with ordinary contributions, repayments made in the 60-day period following year-end may be attributable to either the preceding year or the current year, depending on the designations you make on Schedule 7.

You *must* file an income tax return for any year in which you have a positive HBP balance outstanding and repayments to be made. An HBP balance is the total of withdrawals made for a particular purchase less the total of repayments of those amounts designated under these rules and of amounts included in income upon failure to make adequate repayments of a particular set of those withdrawals. In short, where you have not cleared all your remaining repayments in respect of a use of the plan by the first day of a calendar year, either by designated repayments or inclusions in income for earlier taxation years, you must file a return for that year. This is discussed in greater detail, with an example, at ¶2625.15.

Thus, HBP users who must make instalment repayments for 2016 have until March 1, 2017 to actually make the RRSP contributions and until the T1 is normally due to file a return with a designation on Schedule 7. Clearly the intention of the current rules is to permit taxpayers to make RRSP contributions in the usual period and decide after the fact how much is to be treated as repayment and how much under ordinary contribution rules.

In all cases, amounts designated as repayment instalments are not deductible from income, since they represent repayment of money borrowed from the plan (which was entitled to deduction when originally contributed or was earned in the plan free of tax). On the other hand, repayment instalments have no effect on your ordinary RRSP contribution limits, so that if you have sufficient funds on hand you can make both minimum instalment repayments and full RRSP contributions eligible for deduction in any particular year.

At its simplest, your basic repayment instalment represents the total of amounts you withdrew under the Home Buyers' Plan (on form T1036) divided by 15. If you pay this amount each year for 15 years commencing with the due date described above, you have fulfilled your obligation. To the extent you do not make the requisite payment for any particular year, the shortfall for that year will be added to your income. It appears that the spousal or common-law partner plan rules will not attribute income arising under this rule to a contributing spouse or common-law partner.

Complications in the repayment calculations arise only where you choose to make overpayments or underpayments in a particular year, or where there are special circumstances such as spousal or common-law partner plans, age (you cannot have an RRSP to make repayments to after age 71), non-resident status, or death. All these cases will be addressed below.

The CRA has taken the position that a bankruptcy will not extinguish any HBP balance when the taxpayer declares bankruptcy. The CRA does not consider an HBP balance to be a debt under the *Bankruptcy and Insolvency Act* and there is no provision in the *Income Tax Act* to permit a bankrupt individual to reduce his or her HBP balance to zero. Therefore, even if you declare bankruptcy, you must continue to make your annual HBP balance payments until the entire withdrawn amount is repaid.

(CRA Document No.: Home Buyers' Plan and Bankruptcy, *April 8, 2010*, CRA Document No. 2009-0318591E5)

[¶2625b.15] *Which RRSP Contributions May Be Designated*

The Home Buyers' Plan system in theory operates independently of the normal RRSP contribution system. You do not need, and do not use, ordinary contribution limits (¶2604) to make repayments, and the amounts you designate as repayments are not deductible. They simply reduce the automatic tax liability that will result if they are not made.

It follows from this theory that certain RRSP contributions, such as the special rollover contributions discussed at ¶2612.05–¶2614c.10 cannot be designated. In particular, the following RRSP contributions are not eligible for designation:

- contributions you make to the RRSP of your spouse or common-law partner or that your spouse or common-law partner makes to your own RRSP;
- amounts transferred directly to your RRSP (¶2612.35) from an RPP, DPSP, RRIF, SPP, PRPP, or another RRSP;
- amounts you can deduct as a recontribution of an excess qualifying withdrawal that you have designated in order to have a past service pension adjustment approved (¶2614c.10);
- amounts you contribute in the first 60 days of a year that you deducted or designated for the preceding year;
- amounts you received in the year (such as retiring allowances) that you transfer to your RRSP and deduct or will deduct on your return for that year as discussed at ¶2612.05; or
- contributions to an RRSP that is no longer an RRSP at the end of the calendar year in which you actually make the contribution.

A couple of these items require special comment.

If your spouse or common-law partner withdraws funds from a spousal or common-law partner RRSP, the repayment requirement and tax liability for repayment failure stays with your spouse or common-law partner, even if you funded the entire spousal or common-law partner RRSP and your spouse or common-law partner has no tax liability to speak of. This can work to your advantage, as discussed at ¶2625b.35. However, it does mean that if you are funding your spouse's or common-law partner's repayments, you are supposed to do it by handing the funds to your spouse or common-law partner to repay to the spouse's/common-law partner's RRSP. Although in other contexts the CRA accepts that spouses or common-law partners can act as agent for each other, so that it should not matter if you cut the cheque directly to the spousal or common-law partner RRSP, the RRSP trust is likely to issue a receipt to you if you have cut the cheque, which will confuse the issue for the CRA. If a repayment to a spousal or common-law partner plan is funded from a joint bank account, you should clearly document to the trust company that a particular payment to a spousal or common-law partner plan is a HBP repayment paid by your spouse or common-law partner, preferably with a cheque signed by your spouse or common-law partner. What you clearly cannot do, of course, is to deduct and designate the same amount.

The requirement that an RRSP must exist at the end of the calendar year in which a designated repayment is made is an explicit requirement of the statute. It will typically affect those who must convert their RRSP income to retirement income by the end of the year. Thus, if you turn 71 years of age in 2015, you must convert your RRSP by the end of 2015 as discussed in ¶2616.05. There appears to be a technical problem here, especially where the RRSP is converted to a RRIF rather than maturing into an annuity as part of the same plan. The conversion to retirement income must occur by the end of the year you turn 71, but if the plan is not there at the instant of year-end, your HBP repayment contribution for the final year is not valid. The problem also appears to be replicated for RRSPs which convert to annuities. If this were true, you could not, as you can with ordinary contributions, make a final top-up repayment of HBP liability just before the end of 2016 where you turn 71 in 2016; you would have had to do this by the end of 2015. The CRA ignores this in its booklet on HBPs, and quite rightly, since it is clearly intended that the system should allow you to make all final RRSP contributions immediately before wrapping up your RRSP at the end of year in which you reach the mandatory age. Where a repayment liability cannot be completed because of RRSP termination requirements, see ¶2625b.40.

On the other hand, you may designate a contribution to an RRSP so long as it is an RRSP of which you are the annuitant at the end of the year following the year to which the designation relates. This permits you to make a contribution to a new RRSP established in the 60 days following the year for which a repayment is designated and designate that contribution.

If you participate in both the HBP and the Lifelong Learning Plan (LLP — see ¶2626a), which in principle you may do, and you have repayment commitments under both plans in the same year, you cannot (of course) designate the same RRSP contribution as a repayment under both plans. There is nothing in the HBP rules to disallow the designation for HBP purposes, but the LLP rules will disallow designation of a repayment already designated under the HBP rules. In effect this is an ordering rule, allowing a dual designation to operate for HBP purposes only.

(ITA: 146.01(3))

[¶2625b.20] *General (Non-Technical) Calculation of Repayment Instalments*

If you choose to make 15 equal annual repayments commencing for the year they are due as described above, and for each of the succeeding 14 years, you may calculate the repayment amount as follows:

Total of all amounts withdrawn under the Home Buyers' Plan from RRSPs of which you are the annuitant (and not returned on cancellation of the Plan under the rules at ¶2625a.35)	______	(A)
Amount (A) ÷ 15	______	(B)

If you contribute amount B in timely fashion each year for 15 years, properly designated, you have met your repayment obligation. If, however, you made any prepayments in earlier years, overpayments or underpayments for a year, you must look to the technical calculations below.

[¶2625b.25] Technical Calculation of Repayment Instalments

Following are two formulae for calculating the minimum instalment requirements.

The first formula is for the first year for which you are obliged to make a repayment. This was 1995 for all Home Buyers' Plan users under the old rules (withdrawals made or considered made before March 2, 1992) and the second year following your first RRSP withdrawal under the HBP for all later users. Thus for 2013 users, the calculation applies for 2015 to determine the amount which must be repaid by February 29, 2016.

The second formula is for any year following the year for which the first formula must be used. The difference is necessary to take account of any early repayment instalments in the first case and prior year over- and underpayments in the second.

These repayment calculations apply to each individual who has made withdrawals under the HBP which were not returned because of cancellation where no home was acquired. They apply to each such individual who was the annuitant of the RRSP from which the withdrawals were made, regardless of whether the plan was one to which a spouse or common-law partner had contributed (see ¶2624.05). That is, if George withdrew funds from his spousal or common-law partner plan (to which his wife Lynne had contributed) and Lynne withdrew funds from her own plan (to which George had not contributed), each would make the calculation below for his or her own withdrawals, regardless of the fact that one plan was a spousal or common-law partner plan.

Note that these calculations apply only to withdrawals, designations and income inclusions related to the current "participation period" (¶2625.20). Once a participation period is closed out by any combination of income inclusions and designations which amount to full repayment of the amount withdrawn, a new use of the plan (when permitted) starts with a clean slate; old balances from prior participation periods are not referred to.

(1) Calculation of First Repayment Instalment

Total of all amounts withdrawn for the current participation period (¶2625.20) under HBP from RRSPs of which you are the annuitant (and not returned on cancellation of the HBP under ¶2625a.35)	______	(A)
Amount (A) ÷ 15	______	(B)
Total of any repayment instalments for the current participation period (¶2625.20) made in prior years (although not required)	______	(C)
Required first instalment (B - C)	______	(D)

Penalty: Include in income for the year of calculation any portion of amount (D) not paid into an RRSP within 60 days of year-end and properly designated on your return for the year.

Thus, if you withdrew $20,000 in 2015 and repaid $1,000 in 2016 (the year of completion date), your 2016 repayment would be ($20,000 - nil) ÷ 15 = $1,333. The $1,000 previously designated will reduce this amount to a required 2016 designation (or income inclusion) of $333.

Note that any negative income inclusion in (D) is deemed to be nil under section 257 of the Act.

(2) Calculation of Second and Later Repayment Instalments

Total of all amounts withdrawn for the current participation period (¶2625.20) under HBP from RRSPs of which you are the annuitant (and not returned on cancellation of the HBP under ¶2625a.35)	______	(A)
Total of all amounts designated in earlier years of the participation period	______	(B)
Total of all amounts added to income in prior years of the current participation period under these rules (i.e., prior years' underpayments)	______	(C)
Opening balance for the year (A - B - C)	______	(D)
15 minus the number of preceding years in the current participation period for which a repayment was required	______	(E)
Required repayment for the year (D ÷ E)	______	(F)

Penalty: Include in income on your T1 return any portion of amount (F) not paid into an RRSP within 60 days of year-end and designated on your return for the year. This amount for each year will be added to other such amounts and included on line (C) in future years.

Note that prior year repayments, deducted only in (C) after dividing by years in the opening year calculation, are deducted in (B) before the division in later years.

[¶2625b.30] Consequences of Over- and Underpayments

These formulae have several unlikely results. You can make overpayments which will reduce future balances, but only on an averaged basis, so that you cannot make two years' worth of payments in 2015 and none in 2016, for instance. There is a sort of exception for the first year, since unrequired payments made before the first required year will directly reduce payments required in the first year. Since instalment shortfalls are added to income but reduce your future instalment requirements, there may be years in which you have especially low income and choose not to make repayments and include amounts in income at low or nil rates. This is, in fact, similar to making withdrawals of RRSP amounts in years in which you have low income. The formula is what is called a declining balance calculation; that is, as the total opening balance on line (D) is reduced each year by prior year calculations, it is divided by a reduced number on line (E). The result will be that whether you make full payments each year or underpayments, the resulting required payment will be the same each year. It will only be varied if you make overpayments in a particular year.

Underpayments

In June 2014, you withdraw $15,000 from your RRSP under the HBP to finance your home, and the money is properly used.

Your annual repayment for 2016 is $1,000 ($15,000 ÷ 15) and is due by March 1, 2017.

If you decide to repay only $700 for 2016:

- the $300 shortfall from your scheduled annual repayment of $1,000 will be included in your income for 2016;
- your outstanding balance will be reduced by $1,000, being the $700 paid plus the $300 added to your income; and
- your scheduled repayment for 2017 will again be $1,000 (opening balance (D) of $14,000 divided by (15 - 1 = 14)).

The above example remains accurate if you have made precise repayments in preceding years and this is the first year of underpayments.

Overpayments

Assume the facts in the example above, that is, your annual repayment instalments are $1,000, and that you have made those payments (or underpayments) for four years, from 2016 to 2019, inclusive. Your opening unpaid balance for 2020 is $11,000. In 2020, you choose to repay $3,000. The results are:

- your opening balance for 2021 will be $8,000 (instead of $10,000); and
- your scheduled annual repayments for all following years will be $800 ($8,000 ÷ 10 for 2021, $7,200 ÷ 9 for 2022, and so on).

As above, the result is the same for old and new system repayments.

One of the results of the declining balance calculation is overpayments made relatively early in the 15-year repayment period will have a fairly small effect on subsequent required payments. Accordingly, it will in most cases be preferable to apply excess funds on hand to pay down commercial mortgages or to make ordinary deductible RRSP contributions. There will be exceptions, for example, where taxpayers will turn 71 and must mature their RRSPs (¶2627.30) before the repayment period is over, but these require careful examination.

(ITA: 146.01(3), (4))

[¶2625b.35] Spousal or Common-Law Partner Plan Repayment Anomalies

Amounts withdrawn under the Home Buyers' Plan from a plan which is a spousal or common-law partner RRSP, that is, to which the annuitant's spouse or common-law partner has made contributions for the annuitant (¶2624.05), are considered withdrawn by the annuitant. If these withdrawals prove not to have been qualified withdrawals (¶2625a), they will be considered ordinary withdrawals and may be attributed to the contributing spouse or common-law partner under the rules at ¶2624.05. As discussed at ¶2625a.35, if the contemplated home purchase falls through the withdrawals from the plan of a particular annuitant can only be returned to a plan for the same annuitant.

Once qualifying withdrawals have been properly used to acquire a qualifying home, however, the RRSP attribution mechanisms cease to apply. The annuitant spouse or common-law partner who has withdrawn funds from a spousal or common-law partner RRSP has an obligation to repay the funds or face the penalty inclusion in income. The income inclusion to the annuitant spouse or common-law partner cannot be transferred to the contributing spouse or common-law partner. This gives rise to some small scale tax planning opportunities.

Spousal or Common-Law Partner Plan Repayment Anomalies

Jim and Paula Trout, who are husband and wife, made withdrawals under the HBP in 2014 and jointly acquired a qualifying home within the required time limits. Jim withdrew $18,000 from his own RRSP, and Paula withdrew $13,000 from her spousal or common-law partner RRSP. Paula's RRSP was funded by regular annual contributions from Jim.

Commencing in 2016, Jim must make annual repayments of $18,000 ÷ 15 = $1,200 to his plan. Paula must make annual repayments of $13,000 ÷ 15 = $867. In fact, Jim may provide the funds for Paula's repayments, or *vice versa*. Suppose that Jim is working and Paula is not, and they can only afford to make $1,500 of the combined payment of $2,067 ($1,200 + $867) required. If they repay $1,200 to Jim's RRSP and only $300 to Paula's, the shortfall of $867 - $300 = $567 will be added to Paula's income and taxed at her rates. There appears to be no mechanism to transfer this income inclusion to Jim, as would normally happen if Paula had withdrawn funds from an RRSP to which Jim had contributed in the year or the preceding two years.

Note that since there is no crossover between the HBP repayment rules and the ordinary RRSP contribution deductions, Jim could continue to make deductible RRSP contributions to his own or Paula's RRSP even while not making full repayments. This will present some opportunities for tax planning if Jim and Paula are in different tax brackets, in the circumstances indicated above.

It follows that repayment instalments to spousal or common-law partner plan RRSPs should be carefully weighed each year. Where the contributing spouse or common-law partner is taxed at a much higher marginal rate than the annuitant spouse or common-law partner, it will often make more sense to use available funds to make deductible RRSP contributions to the spousal or common-law partner plan than to make repayments to the spousal or common-law partner plan. From the point of view of the family as a whole, it makes sense for a contributing spouse or common-law partner to take a deduction from a 50% marginal tax rate even if there is an addition to the income of the annuitant spouse or common-law partner, taxed at a 20.5–26% marginal rate.

A word of caution, however. The Department of Finance has a record of closing down what it regards as abuses (such as the receipt of social insurance benefits by contributing taxpayers). It is not too much to suppose that sooner or later it will get around to this one.

(ITA: 146.01(1), (3), (4))

[¶2625b.40] *If you Turn 55 or Older in the Year You Use the Home Buyers' Plan*

The repayment period for withdrawals under the HBP extends for 15 years beginning with the second year following your first withdrawal. Thus, if you used the plan in 2016 for the first time, your repayment period would be 2018 to 2032, inclusive. If you first use the plan in 2017, your repayment period will be 2019 to 2033. Since you must convert your RRSP to retirement income at the end of the year you turn 71 (¶2616.05), you may not make any repayments after the year you turn 71. There may actually be a technical glitch here, as discussed at ¶2625b.05. Accordingly, if you will turn 72 before your repayment period is completed, you will be unable to make required repayments to your RRSP on the normal schedule. In this case, you must either make sufficient repayment instalments to your RRSP to repay your withdrawals by the year you turn 71, or you must face the inclusions in income starting in the year you turn 72. The choice will be different for each individual. If you expect to be in a lower tax bracket after you turn 72, the additional tax then may be preferable to making higher instalment repayments now. If you have limited resources and adequate RRSP contribution room now, you might be better off making minimum repayments plus deductible RRSP contributions now and taking deductions against high marginal tax rates, and suffering the income inclusions at lower marginal rates in future. This will depend on your personal financial projections for income at age 72 and older.

(ITA: 146.01(3), (4))

[¶2625b.45] *If You Become a Non-Resident of Canada*

If you leave Canada for an extended period, you must determine whether you are going to become a non-resident for income tax purposes. Generally speaking, the CRA treats an absence of two years or more as a benchmark, but there are many other considerations, such as whether you take your family with you, whether you work for the government of Canada or a Canadian government agency abroad, whether you intend to return to a specific employment, and so on. If you are moving to a country with which Canada has a tax treaty (see list at ¶2005), you may become a non-resident by virtue of treaty provisions. The CRA outlines many of these considerations in its Income Tax Folio S5-F1-C1. An independent discussion of the CRA's policies is found in Chapter 1 of this book.

If you have withdrawn funds from an RRSP under the Home Buyers' Plan and become a non-resident before acquiring your Canadian home, your withdrawals will be disqualified and added to your income in the year of withdrawal; see ¶2625b.45. However, you may cure the disqualification by refunding the withdrawal and cancelling your participation in the plan, using the *Home Buyers' Plan (HBP) — Cancellation* letter, which should be sent together with copies of the RRSP repayment contribution receipts to the CRA address on the form. Your repayment must be made by the earlier of the normal cancellation deadline of December 31 of the year after the year you received the funds, and the time at which you file your income tax return for the year in which you have become a non-resident and so designate the repayment amount.

If you have withdrawn funds from an RRSP under the Home Buyers' Plan and become a non-resident after acquiring your Canadian home, you must repay the entire withdrawal within 60 days of becoming a non-resident. Usually this means within 60 days of leaving Canada to become a non-resident. To the extent you do not make the repayment within 60 days, the unrepaid balance will be included in your income for the period of the year in which you were still a resident of Canada.

If your income for the period preceding your departure from Canada is low enough, the add back may be a reasonable alternative. This must be weighed in advance in each case, given the 60-day limit.

The rules which permit more than one use of the HBP in a lifetime mean that you can suffer the non-resident penalty more than once. However, the penalty does not double up each time this happens. This is not accomplished through the participation period rules, but by permitting a penalty reduction for prior income inclusions under the non-resident rules.

(ITA: 146.01(1), (5))

[¶2625c] DEATH

[¶2625c.05] *Home Acquired before Death Occurs*

If you have withdrawn funds from an RRSP under the HBP and properly *acquired your qualifying home before death*, and you die with an outstanding balance of repayment instalments owing to the RRSP, the outstanding balance is included in your income for the year of your death. The amount is determined by reference to your HBP balance (¶2625.15) immediately before death. If you made ordinary contributions to your RRSP in that year prior to death, your legal representative can designate some or all of such contributions (up to the total recontributions owing) as repayments in the year of death return. Contributions not so designated are deductible on the year of death return subject to normal contribution limits.

However, provided certain conditions are met, your spouse or common-law partner (if resident in Canada immediately before your death) may elect jointly with the legal representative of your estate on your income tax return for the year of your death to treat the outstanding balance as that of the spouse or common-law partner, in addition to any outstanding balance the surviving spouse or common-law partner may have on its own account and regardless of the usual $25,000 per person limit.

The surviving spouse or common-law partner has an unconditional right to make the election, regardless of when or whether the surviving spouse or common-law partner made its own withdrawals under the HBP. If the surviving spouse or common-law partner makes the election, it has the following results:

(1) There is no income inclusion for the deceased in respect of the deceased's HBP withdrawal.

(2) The surviving spouse or common-law partner is deemed to have received the amount that but for the election would have been taxed to the deceased. It seems to follow that if contributions have been made to the RRSP of the deceased in the year but before death, designations can be made in the year of death return to reduce the outstanding repayment balance (the HBP balance) to the extent allowed if the election by the spouse or common-law partner were not made.

(3) If the surviving spouse or common-law partner had made its own eligible withdrawal before the death (other than one in a participation period ending before the year of the death), the completion date of the amount received becomes the same as that of the surviving spouse's or common-law partner's own withdrawal. If the surviving spouse or common-law partner had not made its own withdrawal, the completion date is that of the deceased. The completion date thus assigned serves two functions. First, if a qualified home

has not already been acquired, it fixes the completion date for the acquisition. More commonly, where a home has already been acquired, it fixes the repayment schedule in accordance with the rules at ¶2625b.05. The surviving spouse or common-law partner must repay the transferred amount to its own RRSPs on same schedule used to calculate repayments of its own eligible amounts withdrawn if it made such withdrawals, or on the schedule that applied to the deceased if it did not withdraw its own eligible amounts.

[¶2625c.10] *Home Acquired After Death Occurs*

If you have properly withdrawn funds up to $25,000 from an RRSP under the HBP and you die *before acquiring your qualifying home*, your withdrawals are added to your income in the year of death (and not the year withdrawn, if that was earlier). However, your surviving spouse or common-law partner may elect jointly with the legal representative of your estate on your income tax return for the year of your death to treat the withdrawal as a qualified withdrawal of the spouse or common-law partner, regardless of the $25,000 limit. Technically, in these circumstances there are no further conditions to the election; it may be made by a surviving spouse or common-law partner who has used the Home Buyers' Plan previously as well as one who has not.

Where death occurs before a qualifying home is acquired, there is no option for either the deceased or, if the election is made, the surviving spouse or common-law partner to return the funds of the deceased to an RRSP under the cancellation rules at ¶2625a.35, although if the election is made they may be returned to an RRSP of the surviving spouse or common-law partner under the 15-year repayment rules at ¶2625b.05 at any time.

Amounts properly withdrawn by the deceased and subject to an election are qualified amounts to the surviving spouse or common-law partner and therefore eligible for 15-year repayment regardless of whether the surviving spouse or common-law partner uses those funds to complete a home purchase. Contrast the situation with the surviving spouse's or common-law partner's own withdrawals, if any, which must be used for an acquisition or returned to the RRSP as discussed at ¶2625a.35. However, if the surviving spouse or common-law partner does not complete the home purchase, it would seem that the funds must nevertheless be returned in accordance with the schedule dictated by the completion date prescribed by the election.

LIFELONG LEARNING PLAN

[¶2626] GENERAL — LIFELONG LEARNING PLAN (LLP)

Eligible individuals may make tax-free withdrawals from an RRSP (other than a "locked-in" RRSP discussed at ¶2615.15) of up to $10,000 per year, but not exceeding $20,000 overall, over a period of up to four calendar years. RRSP funds may be withdrawn where the recipient or spouse or common-law partner is enrolled or committed to enrol as a "full-time student" in a "qualifying educational program" of at least three months' duration at an "eligible educational institution". These terms have the same content as for the education credit at ¶1337 (this credit was repealed as of January 1, 2017; the amended definitions remain in effect), except that the reference to "three weeks" as the minimum time for a qualifying educational program is read as "three months" for LLP purposes. The full-time requirement is waived for disabled students.

[¶2626a] QUALIFYING WITHDRAWALS

In general, the designated student (the RRSP annuitant or spouse or common-law partner, as indicated at the time of withdrawal on form RC96) must commence a qualified program at an eligible institution by the end of March following the year of a withdrawal. In addition, the student must meet one of the following tests:

(1) the student must complete the educational program before April of the year following a withdrawal; or

(2) the student must be enrolled in the program at the end of March of the year following a withdrawal; or

(3) less than 75% of the tuition paid after the beginning of the calendar year in which a particular withdrawal was made and before April of the following year in respect of the student and the program is refundable.

Where a withdrawal is made and the conditions above are not met, typically because the student does not commence or withdraws early from the educational program, it is possible to return the funds to an RRSP of the annuitant by the end of the calendar year following the withdrawal and the RRSP annuitant will be treated as if the withdrawals had never been made. This is virtually identical the to the HBP rules at ¶2625a.35; see also ¶2625.15. Where a withdrawal is made and education conditions are not met and amounts are not returned to the plan, or other conditions are not met. the withdrawal will be included in the income of the person who withdrew it.

RRSP withdrawals under this plan must be repaid to an RRSP in equal instalments over a period of 10 years. The repayments must commence for the fifth year following year of the first withdrawal. However, they may have to commence earlier where the eligible student is not entitled to the full-time education credit (the education credit was repealed effective January 1, 2017) at ¶1337 (or to transfer the education credit to a parent or spouse or common-law partner) for a period of at least three months in two consecutive years after the year of the first withdrawal. In this case, the first repayment year will be the second such year in which the three-month test is not met. Where withdrawals are made but the intended education is never pursued, the withdrawals can be returned to the plan Where scheduled repayments are required but not made for a taxation year, the shortfall is included in the income of the RRSP annuitant who made the withdrawals. The fifth year rule generally means that even if withdrawals are spread over a four year period, they are lumped together in calculating the required repayment, which commences for the sixth year. In any event, a required repayment can never include an amount withdrawn in the same year, but all amounts withdrawn in preceding years (in a participation period) are lumped together in calculating repayments. The repayment rules are virtually identical the HBP rules at ¶2625b.05, except for the commencement dates. As with HBP rules, you may make repayments up to 60 days following the year to which they relate, and you designate them on Schedule 7 of your tax return for the year to which they relate.

Where RRSP withdrawals have been made for a student's education, the withdrawer is not permitted to withdraw funds for the education of the student's spouse or common-law partner while the recipient has an outstanding (unrepaid) balance. On the other hand, the student and spouse or common-law partner can each participate in an LLP at the same time; the limitation is that one individual can withdraw amounts for only one student in a participation period (from the beginning of the year of a first withdrawal in respect of a student until the end of the year to which the last required repayment or income inclusion relates).

[¶2626b] REPAYMENT

In general the administrative rules follow those of the Home Buyers' Plan concerning: failure to make timely repayments (¶2625b.05); denial of deduction for RRSP contributions made within 90 days of plan withdrawal (¶2625.10); emigration (¶2625b.45); and death (¶2625c.05).

(ITA: 146.02)

[¶2626b.05] *Form and Guide*

Eligible withdrawals must be made on form RC96.

The CRA has issued a detailed and very useful guide, Lifelong Learning Plan (RC 4112), which should be consulted by everyone who proposes to use the plan. It is available from CRA offices (¶287) and from the CRA website (www.cra-arc.gc.ca).

COMMON RRSP QUESTIONS

[¶2627] COMMON RRSP QUESTIONS

[¶2627.05] *Suppose I Can't Calculate My Contribution by the Deadline*

This problem is no longer common, since most taxpayers can with confidence base their contribution on prior year income and PA, as illustrated at ¶2604 and ¶2607. Moreover, the CRA will in most cases have reported to you your ordinary contribution room (including carryforward room) on your Notice of Assessment for the preceding year, and may report certain additional changes toward the end of the year; this reporting is discussed at ¶2609 above. However, in the following situations you may still find that events not reported until after the end of the year create or limit the contribution room available to you:

(1) you have bought back past service in respect of years after 1989 and anticipate or have received certification of a form T1004 (see ¶2614c);

(2) you have transferred employment and the pension plan of your new employer provides for "reciprocity" with that of the old employer, and the benefits of the new plan are greater than those of the old (see ¶2614c);

(3) you are a "connected person" (essentially a 10% shareholder or related to a 10% shareholder of your employer) who has joined a pension plan of the employer to which you are connected in the year (see ¶2608); or

(4) you have or will receive in the year any of the special amounts eligible for rollover contribution as discussed at ¶2612.05.

In any of the above cases it is possible that the additional limits on your contribution room for the year (in cases (1) to (3)) or additional amounts eligible for special contributions (in case (4)) for the year will not be reported to you until the end of February of the following year or, in a few cases, even later.

In most cases, you will at least have notice of the fact that a special limitation or payment is likely. In the case of special payments, such as termination payments, you should receive the money in the year, although the deductible portion may not be reported to you until the end of February. You may be able to obtain an estimate of the deductible portion from the payer merely by asking.

If information on a special rollover contribution is simply not available to you by the time your contribution must be made, you should try to calculate the amount yourself based on the information that is available to you. In this situation, you may want to err on the side of overcontribution. If you overestimate your 2016 contribution by a fairly small amount, and your contribution is made in the January 1–March 1, 2017 stub period, you will probably be able to deduct the excess on your return for 2017, and you are simply being a wise saver (see "When Should I Contribute?", below). If your overcontribution exceeds both your 2016 and 2017 eligible amounts, you will not be allowed any deduction for it (but you may withdraw it on a timely basis as discussed at ¶2611.15). Remember that overcontributions may carry penalty tax, but only where your cumulative overcontributions exceed $2,000, as discussed at ¶2611.15. Even a small amount of penalty tax for a month or two until definite information is available may be preferable to forgoing a substantial RRSP special contribution.

If your problem is a special limitation (such as PSPA) rather than a special contribution, remember that if you fail to contribute in a year, your unused contribution room (except for rollover contributions) will carry forward, so in this case you may want to err on the side of undercontribution where your overcontributions may exceed $2,000.

In a few cases, your prior year employment income and consequent RRSP contribution room may never have been reported to you to your satisfaction. You should be able to resolve this with your employer, with legal advice and complaints to the CRA if necessary. Where the amount of employment income remains at issue, it is advisable to make a best guess, based on your stated salary (subject to adjustments in the year), or your pay slips. Where pension contributions are unknown, your payroll department may be able to advise you, or you may be able to estimate based on last year's amount, if your employment and pension plan membership has been consistent over the two years. Overcontributions made on an estimated basis will not cause trouble as long as the lifetime total of them does not exceed $2,000. On the other hand, if you do succeed in establishing new contribution room, it will in any event carry forward for future use.

[¶2627.10] *Suppose the CRA Miscalculates My Contribution Room*

As discussed at ¶2609, the CRA may make an error in calculating the contribution room it reports to you on your Notice of Assessment. Where the contribution room misstatement arises because of factors of which the CRA is not aware, as discussed at ¶2627.05, you must assume that they will correct their position eventually and use your best estimate of the true position. See ¶2627.05.

It is possible that the CRA's statements will miscalculate contribution room limits based on the ordinary factors of earned income and contributions. This seems to have become relatively rare; it is perhaps most likely where line 232 of the return is used to report deductions other than special RRSP offsets. Even if errors are rare, they are possible, and you should always attempt to verify your contribution limit statement when you receive your Notice of Assessment. This will leave time to have errors corrected before future contributions are due.

When the CRA agrees to a correction, you should always obtain a statement of their position in writing. Telephone corrections are all very well, but don't always find their way into the computer system in timely fashion.

Where you cannot obtain a correction in time for current contributions you have several choices. If you think the CRA has understated your contribution room, you may contribute and deduct the full amount to which you are entitled. If the deduction is disallowed, you have the normal assessment and objection procedures to invoke, and you can at least obtain a detailed review of your position. So long as the overcontribution does not bring you over the $2,000 penalty tax limit at ¶2611.15, you should be able to take a later deduction for contribution carryforwards (¶2611.05), or to withdraw without penalty any amounts which in fact prove to be overcontributions. The cost of an actual overcontribution therefore will be interest on tax unpaid because of excess RRSP deductions claimed.

Where you think the CRA has overstated your contribution limits, you should of course contribute only the correct amount as a matter of conscience. If your conscience does not prompt you to this course, a contribution which proves to be an overcontribution within the $2,000 limit can have no serious repercussions. It is a nice question whether the CRA would feel obliged to cancel interest charges on deductions improperly claimed because they overstated contribution room through their error.

[¶2627.15] *When Should I Contribute?*

You can make a contribution deductible from your 2016 taxes (i.e., deductible on your return due April 30, 2017) at any time during calendar 2016 and within 60 days thereafter, that is, up to and including March 1, 2017. Similarly, for 2017 you can make deductions at any time in calendar 2017 or within 60 days thereafter (March 1, 2018). Most advisers will tell you to contribute as early in the year as possible, in order to maximize your tax-free earnings in the plan. This is certainly sound advice with respect to ordinary annual contributions. The CRA will in most cases include a statement of your ordinary 2017 contribution room on your Notice of Assessment for your 2016 return (attached to your refund cheque, if any). That statement should be reliable, except in the special cases discussed at ¶2627.05, above. If you did not receive your Notice of Assessment for 2015 (or did not file a 2015 return), you should nevertheless be able to calculate your 2016 contribution limits based on your 2015 tax and income information, following the calculation at ¶2604. Using your tax refund cheque itself to fund RRSP contributions is a wise use of what often feels like found money, and of course the cheque usually comes with a statement of available contribution room.

With respect to special rollover contributions (¶2612.05), it is difficult for many people to calculate the amount eligible for, say, 2016 contribution until the relevant reporting slips are received in 2017. Even here, if you can be sure of a minimum qualifying amount, you may want to make those contributions early. For example, if you were confident in August 2016 that you would be entitled to make a 2016 termination payment rollover contribution of at least $2,000, you could contribute that amount at that time. If in February 2017 you find that the total eligible rollover amount is $2,420, you can contribute the additional $420 by March 1, 2017 and deduct the entire $2,420.

For most individuals, making 2016 contributions in the "stub period" of January 1 to March 1, 2017 has the particular advantage that you have available to you both 2016 and 2017 contribution limits, thus minimizing your exposure to penalty tax. See the example at ¶2611.15.

If you make an ordinary (as opposed to a special or transfer) contribution in the stub period and part of it is to be deducted in 2016 and another part in 2017, remember to record and count the excess in making your 2017 contributions and claiming them on your 2017 return filed in 2018. You must also ensure that the undeducted portion is included on line 3 of your 2016 Schedule 7 (and that the actual deduction is claimed on line 13) and file that Schedule with your 2016 return. It used to be essential to keep extra copies of the RRSP receipt for the split amount and note the part deducted for each year, and submit a copy with your T1 return for each year. However, the use of Schedule 7, which includes information adequate for the CRA to determine undeducted contributions of the year, should make this unnecessary, although you will probably still find it useful as a reminder both to you and the CRA.

[¶2627.20] *Can I Overcontribute to an RRSP?*

You can either overcontribute or overdeduct. You overcontribute if you contribute more than the permitted limits. This may involve penalty tax, as discussed at ¶2611.15.

You overdeduct if you deduct RRSP contributions to such an extent that you are not using personal amount or other non-refundable tax credits available to you. Remember that you are not obliged to deduct all the amounts you contribute in a particular year except where the amounts are based on special contributions discussed in ¶2612.05 to ¶2614c.10. In all other circumstances, so long as the amount you contributed is not subject to penalty taxes, you need not be concerned about not deducting the full amount you did contribute. Both the undeducted contribution and the accompanying limits permitting you to deduct it will carry forward indefinitely, as discussed in ¶2611.05.

Accordingly, if you deduct RRSP contributions (other than special rollover contributions) to such an extent that you are not using personal amount or other non-refundable tax credits available to you, you are in effect overdeducting. You should be careful not to deduct RRSP amounts in excess of the amount that would reduce your tax (not your income) to zero.

Example

Maggie had $30,000 of earned income in 2015 and no PA, entitling her to a 2016 RRSP contribution of $5,400. In fact, she made this contribution. However, her 2016 income was only $12,500. Her only 2016 personal amounts are the basic $11,474 and a CPP amount of $445 (so, $11,919). In effect, she will only pay tax on $12,500 – $11,919 = $581 of income, and should not claim an RRSP deduction in excess of this amount, even if she has contributed more.

On her T1 form, before the RRSP deduction Maggie would show federal tax of 15% on $12,500 of income ($1,875), offset by 15% of $11,919 = $1,788. The resulting tax ($1,875 – $1,788 = $87) would be offset by an RRSP deduction of ($87 ÷ 15% = $580). If Maggie deducts more than this for her RRSP contribution, as the form and the rules allow her to do, she is wasting personal amount credits. On the other hand, she can properly deduct $580 and carry forward her remaining RRSP contribution ($5,400 – $580 = $4,820) for future use.

Note that there is no penalty tax issue here. Maggie had sufficient contribution room to make the full $5,400 contribution. Failure to deduct amounts for which there is sufficient contribution room does not give rise to penalties.

If you do contribute more than is appropriate to deduct, all the money contributed will still earn tax-free income in the RRSP. And eventually you should be able to use your deductions, if only to eliminate tax when you withdraw your contributions.

The average person probably should not make RRSP contributions unless they will reduce tax he or she would otherwise have to pay after claiming deductible losses and tax credits. Remember that unused RRSP contribution room carries forward (¶2610.15). However, if you expect to be in a taxable position soon, it may be beneficial to make contributions now but not deduct them until you can actually reduce tax (see ¶2611.05).

RRSP deductions can be used to reduce positive income amounts for a year down to nil before losses for a year are computed to create net loss carryover. However, RRSP deductions in excess of positive income items for a year cannot be used to augment loss carryovers. RRSP deductions in excess of positive income amounts (adjusted for the value of personal amount credits, if applicable) will be wasted, since they do not find their way into the loss carryforward pool.

[¶2627.25] *Suppose I Had No Income Last Year*

Because RRSP contribution limits are based on the prior year's earned income (see ¶2603), bizarre results occur when you enter or re-enter the work force for the first time. Because you have no earned income for the prior year, you will not be allowed an RRSP deduction for the first year of employment. As the system matures, carryforwards of unused contribution room alleviate this problem to some extent for people who enter, leave, and re-enter the workforce, but it will always remain true that persons who commence to earn income for the first time, or who move from employment in a high-pension job to employment or self-employment in a low-pension situation for the first time, will find that they have no earned income on which to base an RRSP contribution for the first year of substantial earnings.

There is no real solution to this problem; merely a series of more or less unpalatable alternatives. You can make a contribution in the stub period of January/February following the first year of earnings (or indeed at any time thereafter in that second year) up to the contribution limit generated by those first year earnings and deduct this amount in the second year. This of course assumes that income will continue into the second year. If the income does not continue, you may nevertheless make the contribution and deduct it when you have sufficient income. The contribution will be available for deduction forever (¶2611.05). However, if you don't know that you will ever have the income to make the deduction, it makes little sense to make the contribution at all, although it would make a great deal of sense to set aside money up to the contribution limit in a safe investment so that you can make a contribution in future. Remember that your unused contribution limit will carry forward in these circumstances forever (¶2610.15), so that the next time you earn income, you will be able to make a contribution based on the earlier year's income.

Example

Margaret went to work in 2016 for the first time. She earned $40,000. However, her job was terminated at the end of 2016 and she does not expect to work in 2017, nor does she know when she will work again.

Since Margaret did not work before 2016, she will have no carryforward of unused contribution room from earlier years. Since she did not have earned income in the prior year (2015), she has no 2016 contribution limit based on earned income. Accordingly, she cannot deduct from 2016 income any RRSP contributions she might make. The $40,000 she earns in 2016 simply cannot be reduced through an RRSP.

Her 2016 earnings will give rise to a 2017 contribution limit of $7,200 (18% of $40,000, assuming no pension plan and therefore no PA reduction). If her employment were to continue in 2017, she could make this contribution to reduce her 2017 income. However, if she is not employed in 2017 and has no significant taxable income, she can choose not to contribute this amount to an RRSP in 2017. In this case, the unused contribution room of $7,200 will carry forward forever, so that the next time she is employed (or indeed has taxable income from any source, whether earned income, investment income, or otherwise) she will be able to contribute and deduct any amount up to $7,200.

Note that this deferred contribution may or may not confer the same benefit. Suppose, for example, that Margaret works for 6 months in 2016 and earns $25,000. She can contribute and deduct any amount up to $7,200.

Suppose that Margaret expected her employment to continue in 2017 and so did contribute $7,200 early in 2017, then left work in March and had only $10,000 income in 2017 and very little or no tax to pay after personal amount credits. Margaret could simply leave her contribution in the RRSP but not deduct any part of it in 2017. She can withdraw the undeducted funds under the rules at ¶2611.15 without tax. Alternatively, she can leave the funds in the plan; the $7,200 would remain available for deduction in any future year in which there is income, even if the income is only the withdrawal of funds from the RRSP. Earnings on the $7,200 will accumulate free of tax in the RRSP, but if Margaret is below taxable levels anyway there is not much benefit to this. Probably the most sensible option is not to contribute the $7,200 to an RRSP in 2017 if there is little 2017 income, or even to withdraw it under the rules at ¶2611.15, but then to set aside the money in a secure investment or TFSA and make the RRSP contribution in a future year when income is high and the deduction will be clearly beneficial.

Finally, suppose Margaret's employer contributed directly $1,600 to an RRSP for her in 2016 (as an alternative to providing a pension plan). This will of course be taxable income to her, and she will not be allowed any offsetting deduction against 2016 income. In 2017, she could withdraw the funds and, if her income were below taxable levels in any event, pay no tax. Since she never used her RRSP contribution limit to claim a deduction, it would remain available for future use. Of course, if her employment continues, she will simply leave the funds and take the deduction against 2017 income.

Note that if Margaret's employer made contributions to her RRSP in 2016 in excess of $2,000, she would on the face of it have an overcontribution problem with a potential penalty. Where mandatory contributions are made by an employer under a group RRSP plan, the overcontribution limit is supposed to stretch to accommodate them, though not any other contributions that may be made in addition. This is discussed at ¶2611.15.

Essentially, the RRSP system assumes you will continue in the work force at increasing rather than decreasing income levels, in which case the year-of-entry problem, although it exists, is minimal. However, for those incurring earned income not offset by pension adjustments (PA) for the first time this problem will always exist in that first year. Although each case must be decided on its own facts, probably the rule of thumb will be to make RRSP contributions only in the future year in which the deductions are likely to be used.

[¶2627.30] *Can I Contribute if I Am 71 Years Old or Older?*

In the year you become 71 years old, you must mature your RRSP by the end of the year. The age requirement of 71 restores the age requirement of the RRSP system as originally conceived. For 1998 through 2006, you had to mature your RRSP by the end of the year in which you became 69 years old. The lower age limit of course reduced contribution deductions by older individuals and thus increased government revenue. If you matured your RRSP in 2005 or 2006 because of the age 69 requirement, see ¶2627.35 below.

If you fail to mature (or annuitize, which means the same thing) any RRSP of which you are the annuitant by the end of the year in which you reach the mandatory age, the plan is in effect cancelled at the beginning of the following year, and the full fair market value of all the assets are included in your income for that year of cancellation.

To mature or annuitize your RRSP means to "roll over" your RRSP into some form of retirement income. Typically, this will be either an annuity offered by an insurance company or a registered retirement income fund (RRIF). In either case, you must receive periodic payments (at least annually, but you can usually specify monthly payments) from the fund which will be taxable. Depending on the type of retirement plan you choose, you may have a guaranteed income for life for you, or for you and your spouse or common-law partner (whoever you expect to live longer), which income will simply end with your death, or you can provide for a fund with a minimum annual income and with any residual amount remaining in the fund when you and your spouse or common-law partner have both died going to other heirs. See ¶2616.05 *et seq.* below for more detailed commentary on retirement income options.

In any event, in the year you must mature your RRSP you can make a last contribution to it before it is rolled over, but you cannot make a contribution after that time to your own fund.

You may, however, continue to contribute to a spousal or common-law partner RRSP for your spouse or common-law partner up to and including the year in which your spouse or common-law partner reaches the age at which your spouse or common-law partner must mature all RRSPs of which he or she is the annuitant. This assumes that you continue to have qualifying "earned income" or unused contribution room carried forward. Contributions to a spousal or common-law partner RRSP are based solely on your own contribution limits and special pension limitations; they take no account of any earned income of your spouse or common-law partner or any personal RRSP contributions your spouse or common-law partner makes on his or her own behalf. See ¶2624.05.

(ITA: 146(2)(b.4), (5), (5.1))

[¶2627.40] *How Safe Is an RRSP Investment?*

An RRSP investment is as safe as any comparable investment made outside an RRSP. The RRSP itself is merely a trust held by a trust company for your benefit; the money in the trust is invested on your behalf and identified to you. Generally speaking, even if the trust company itself should prove unsound, the assets in the trust should be there and continue to be your property, rather than, say, being accessible to the trust company's creditors.

The investments made by the trust will depend on the kind of plan you choose. At one end of the spectrum, you can invest in a Canada Savings Bond or Canada RRSP bond plan as discussed at ¶2627.45. These bonds are guaranteed by the federal government. Also very secure are the plans offered by a bank or trust company which will invest in savings accounts or guaranteed investment certificates of the bank or trust company. Typically, these are guaranteed by the federal government (you should verify this) up to specified limits. These investments are extremely secure, offering exactly the same guarantees as if you had placed the money directly in a savings account or GIC of the institution.

Moving along the speculative spectrum, as it were, you can invest in mortgage certificates, which may offer higher interest rates but may carry some risk should property values fall rapidly. Or you can invest in mutual funds. These run a large gamut, from funds which invest almost exclusively in government securities to funds which invest almost exclusively in corporate stock, with many degrees of mixture along the way. Bond funds are often more like investing in stock funds than like purchasing bonds you expect to hold to maturity. The price of bonds rises and falls, and the value of the fund to you often depends on this price, rather than being a function of accumulating interest. If you want an investment which cannot fall in value and will return interest only, you should consider a GIC type RRSP such as that offered by banks. Stock mutual funds may outperform interest bearing investments over time, but they are much more dependent on the expertise of investment advisers, and their value may decline, especially in difficult economic times. Some mutual funds will have entrance fees or exit fees, and all will probably have administration fees, and you should be clear as to these costs before you invest. In general, if you invest in mutual funds, you are investing in the expertise of the managers of a particular fund. You should therefore investigate both the track record of the fund and, if possible, the continuity of fund management. Track records are published annually by several sources. Stock brokers or investment advisers may be well informed on the continuity of management of particular funds. Be aware, however, that they often have a vested interest in promoting particular funds, either because it is managed by their own affiliates or because they receive a commission on sales.

Life insurance companies also offer RRSPs. By and large these are mutual funds which cover the same range of risk versus return investments as those discussed for mutual funds. The same considerations as to track record of management and potential bias of the salespeople apply to these as to other mutual funds.

Increasingly, high risk investments (such as LSVCCs) are promoted as suitable for RRSPs. Some of these (along with the risks) are reviewed at ¶2522.

In addition to genuine, if risky, investments that can be made through RRSPs, there have in recent years been promotions of schemes which purport to allow you to access your RRSP savings prematurely without tax penalties. These are very dubious indeed. See ¶2615.15.

[¶2627.45] *Can I Invest in Canada Savings Bonds Through an RRSP?*

As they have evolved, Canada Savings Bonds (CSBs) and Canada Premium Bonds (CPBs) have come to resemble each other. Both are eligible RRSP/RRIF investments, and prior to 2013 an individual could invest in a dedicated plan ("The Canada RSP" and "The Canada RIF") holding only CSB/CPB investments. In both cases, you could also make other investments. That is, you could divide your eligible RRSP contribution room in any given year among several different plans, of which The Canada RSP will be one, and you could divide your RRSP assets among different types of eligible investments at maturity. Investments in The Canada RSP will automatically rollover to The Canada RIF on maturity of the RRSP unless you direct otherwise.

If you currently hold investments in a Canada RSP, you can continue to make contributions. However, since these plans are no longer available to new subscribers, the only way an individual who does not have such a plan can invest in Canada Savings Bonds in an RRSP, is through the transfer of fully paid up bonds into a self-directed RRSP.

Canada Savings Bonds can only be purchased for investment through the Payroll Savings Program and Premium Bonds can be purchased from all normal commercial outlets, such as banks, investment dealers, stock brokers, trust and loan companies, credit unions and caisses populaires. Bond purchases for all the purposes above can also be initiated by telephone. To purchase, call 1-800-575-5151.

Further official information from the Bank of Canada is also available at:

Telephone: 1-800-575-5151
Internet: www.csb.gc.ca

[¶2627.50] *Self-Administered RRSPs*

In addition to investing in an RRSP offered by a Canadian financial institution, life insurance company, mutual fund company, etc., as discussed at ¶2627.40 above, you can establish your own trust with a trust company to invest in whatever eligible Canadian securities appeal to you. This is called a "Self-Administered RRSP". It is generally used by sophisticated investors who are accustomed to making investment decisions, and it requires you to evaluate the eligibility of each acquisition in the plan. Plans that overinvest in securities other than eligible Canadian stocks and bonds, qualified mortgages, and other explicitly qualified items can subject both the plan and the plan annuitant to severe penalty taxes (see ¶2622.05 *et seq.*). For more information on the qualified investments that may be acquired by a self-administered RRSP, see ¶2618.

[¶2627.55] *Can I Invest in Foreign Assets Through My RRSP?*

Pursuant to the federal Budget of February 2005, restrictions on investments by RRSPs in foreign assets have been eliminated after December 2004 by repealing the penalty tax described below. There is now no limit on the extent to which foreign assets can be held through an RRSP, and the discussion below is of historical interest only.

As an alternative to direct investment in foreign securities, there are now RRSP qualified Canadian investment funds which contrive to mimic the performance of foreign (typically U.S.) stock markets. See also ¶2530.

[¶2627.60] *Valid RRSP Investments*

Valid investments are discussed in general terms in the CRA's *RRSP and Other Registered Plans for Retirement* guide (T4040), and in greater detail at ¶2618 above. Taxpayers who propose to operate self-administered (or "self-directed") plans which will hold anything beyond the items clearly sanctioned in the guide should obtain professional advice.

For special high-risk shares with additional tax benefits which may be held by an RRSP, see ¶2522.

[¶2627.65] *Can I Contribute to an RRSP in Kind Rather than in Cash?*

There is nothing in law to prevent you from contributing to an RRSP in kind rather than in cash. There are, however, several practical and tax considerations.

An RRSP administered by a financial institution, etc., described in ¶2627.40, is unlikely in most cases to accept contributions other than in cash. Thus, if you want to make a contribution in kind, you will normally be able to make such a contribution only to a self-administered RRSP.

If you contribute in kind to a self-administered RRSP, you must contribute something that is a valid investment to the RRSP or else face the severe penalty taxes that non-qualified investments will attract; generally this means contributing publicly traded stocks and bonds, although an RRSP may make investments in private Canadian securities provided the investor and related parties do not have an appreciable interest in the issuing companies (see ¶2627.50).

If you contribute securities you own to an RRSP, you are considered to dispose of them when you make the contribution, and any capital gain inherent in the securities will become a taxable capital gain to you. On the other hand, any capital loss you incur on the disposition of securities to an RRSP will not be recognized, but will be deemed to be nil.

Securities you contribute to an RRSP will be considered to be transferred at their fair market value, and to create an RRSP contribution equal to their fair market value. This is not always readily established. For example, you may invest in securities that carry a government incentive such as a provincial grant, take the grant yourself, and contribute the security to an RRSP. The CRA may consider the contributed security to be valued at purchase price less the grant, or even less. In their view, the value of the contribution may be the value of the security in a secondary market, if any, which could be quite low. This issue has yet to be litigated. See also ¶2522.

(ITA: 40(2)(*g*)(iv); 54; IT-124R6 Contributions to Registered Retirement Savings Plans)

[¶2627.70] *Borrowing to Finance an RRSP*

Interest on money borrowed to make RRSP contributions is not a deductible expense for tax purposes. Accordingly, if you have a choice between borrowing to make a general investment and an RRSP investment, you should always borrow to make the general investment. For example, employees are usually offered an opportunity to invest in Canada Savings Bonds through payroll deductions; there are often interest costs associated with these plans, and that interest would be deductible (unless the CSBs are purchased through an RRSP).

If you do not make any deductible borrowings at all, the matter may be somewhat different. Investing in RRSPs to the extent of eligibility always carries the benefits of tax deduction and tax-deferred income accumulation. Accordingly, it may seem preferable to borrow to save in this fashion than not to save at all. If you do this, however, you are, in effect, paying interest (at rates which may easily be higher than the rate of return on your RRSP investment) to force yourself to save. From a strictly economic point of view, you would be much better off to contribute to a savings account RRSP every month some fraction, say 90%, of what you would pay on a loan to make an RRSP contribution.

From a psychological, as opposed to economic, point of view, it may make some practical sense to borrow to make a top-up RRSP contribution. Suppose, for example, you have been saving and made $4,000 of RRSP contributions, and at the end of February you discover you could contribute another $1,200. You estimate that your tax refund will at least cover off the $1,200. It may be sensible to borrow for the few months necessary until your refund comes through, provided you then use it to pay off the loan immediately.

[¶2627.75] *Fees Charged By an RRSP*

Several different kinds of fees may arise in connection with an RRSP, and several questions can arise with each. The basic question is: should the fees be paid by the RRSP, the contributor, or the annuitant? The contributor and annuitant may be different if the plan is a spousal or common-law partner RRSP. Subsidiary questions are, if paid by the contributor or annuitant, are the fees deductible? Do they constitute an additional contribution or gift to the RRSP? If the fees are paid by the plan, do they constitute a taxable benefit to the annuitant?

The most common fee is an annual administration charge imposed by the trust company to compensate it for maintaining the trust. Competition for RRSP business has in most cases reduced these charges to nominal amounts, on the order of $100 per year. This fee can be paid out of the RRSP assets (i.e., by the RRSP), by the annuitant or by the contributor. Prior to March 6, 1996, the preferred method was to have the annuitant pay the fee, since it was deductible to the annuitant (but not to a contributor who was not the annuitant, typically the contributor to a spousal RRSP). Deduction of these fees is no longer permitted. The remaining benefit of having the contributor or annuitant pay the fee is that such external payments will not reduce the amount in the RRSP, out of which the fee would otherwise be paid. Payment of the fee by an annuitant or contributor does not constitute an additional contribution or gift to the RRSP. If the RRSP itself pays the fee, this does not constitute a benefit to the annuitant (this CRA position, stated October 3, 1996, reversed a position of May 24, 1996 that payment by the RRSP constituted a benefit conferred on the annuitant).

A second type of fee which may be incurred in connection with an RRSP (or RRIF) is a fee for investment counselling or management. This typically arises in connection with a self-administered RRSP or RRIF, and is incurred by the contributor for advice and assistance in managing the RRSP investments. The CRA's current position on these fees is that they may be paid either by the annuitant or out of the RRSP assets. If paid by the annuitant they are not deductible (since they benefit the trust and not the annuitant) but neither are they a contribution or gift to the RRSP. Note that this position, given in a CRA opinion dated February 10, 1997, reversed earlier positions that such payments were a gift to the RRSP, and therefore took up contribution room as discussed at ¶2611.15, or a contribution to an RRSP. If the fees are paid by the RRSP, the CRA's current view is that this does not constitute a benefit conferred on the annuitant (this also seems to reverse earlier positions).

Finally, there may be brokerage fees incurred in connection with the purchase and sale of assets held in an RRSP. It is the CRA's view that these can only be expenses of the RRSP and should be paid by the RRSP. If paid by the annuitant (or, presumably, the spouse or common-law partner contributing to a spousal or common-law partner plan), they will be a contribution to the RRSP.

Where investment is made in a mutual fund RRSP, it is now common for the mutual fund to charge a fee based on the entire pool of assets administered; this is typically paid in effect by the RRSP. Some funds may still carry load charges, that is, fees charged either when an investment is made in the mutual fund or when it is sold. These too would be expenses of the RRSP.

If an RRSP (or RRIF) trust pays the cost of preparing the annuitant's income tax return, the CRA sees this as a taxable benefit conferred on the annuitant (CRA Document No. 9720975).

(Window on Canadian Tax: 3444; 3797; 4324; 4592; 5119; IT-124R6, para. 4)

REGISTERED RETIREMENT INCOME FUNDS

[¶2630] GENERAL

A RRIF is essentially a continuation of an RRSP. You may in most cases keep the same investments you had in your RRSP(s), and simply transfer them to the new RRIF plan(s). The difference is that you may not make any new tax-deductible contributions to a RRIF based on your RRSP contribution limits, and that you must receive a specified amount out of the RRIF in each year following the year you establish the RRIF. The "minimum amount" you are required to withdraw each year is, for years prior to the year in which you reach 71 years of age, the opening balance of the RRIF at the beginning of the calendar year, divided by 90 minus your age at the beginning of that year. Once you have reached 71, the minimum amount is determined by a fixed percentage set out in government regulations described below. Effective for 2015, the annual minimum amount that a RRIF planholder must withdraw from his plan from age 71 to 94 is reduced to better reflect long-term historical rates of return and expected inflation. See comparison of old and new rates at ¶2632.20.

If your RRSP is with a bank or trust company, that company will usually offer you a rollover to a RRIF with no change in underlying investments. The same may be true for investments in mutual funds. When investing in mutual funds, however, you may want to change from stock-oriented investments to fixed-income investments to try to limit the risk of falling market values. Some mutual funds provide the option of shifting to such investments. You may also operate a self-administered RRIF, continuing your investments from a self-administered RRSP (¶2623.05).

All amounts earned in a RRIF are tax free (except where a self-administered RRIF fails to maintain qualifying investments; see ¶2623.05). However, all amounts you withdraw from a RRIF, whether because of the minimum amount rule or because you require funds in addition to the minimum amount, are included in your income in the year withdrawn.

Note that as long as RRIF earnings exceed RRIF withdrawals, the money in the RRIF will continue to grow free of tax. On the other hand, whenever withdrawals for a year exceed the earnings in the plan, the overall plan balance will diminish, even though plan earnings continue to be tax free.

In the early years of a RRIF, if you don't need all plan earnings for your retirement income, the value of the plan may increase from year to year. At some point, however, the minimum amount requirements are bound to exceed earnings in the plan, so that the plan will be systematically depleted. The erosion of plan capital will be gradual at first, so that a steady income can be maintained for many years thereafter, but eventually your income from the plan must start to fall. The main variables will be the rate of earnings in the plan and the extent to which you must take out more than the minimum amount to meet your needs. For a RRIF commencing at age 71 earning an 8% annual return and paying only minimum withdrawals, plan depletion would be likely to commence around age 86 and the RRIF would continue to fund minimum withdrawals well past age 100. For a more detailed illustration in which withdrawals above the minimum are made, see ¶2631.20. Where you are concerned that your withdrawal needs will exhaust the RRIF prior to death, you should consider using part or all of your RRSP funds to acquire a lifetime annuity (¶2634.10).

Withdrawals from a RRIF in excess of the required minimum amount are normally subject to withholding at source in somewhat the same way as employment income. The trust or insurance company holding the RRIF is responsible for withholding and reports taxable withdrawals to you annually on a T4RIF slip. You report RRIF income as annuity income on line 115 or 130 of your T1 return, as discussed at ¶480 and claim credit for amounts withheld (if any) on line 437 of your T1 return.

If you are relying on your RRIF income and you are below taxable levels, so that you would benefit from an alleviation of withholding, you might want to ask the Source Deductions Section of your Tax Services Office of the CRA to authorize a reduced withholding, which they will normally do in the circumstances.

[¶2631] CONVERSION OF RRSP TO RRIF

[¶2631.05] *What Happens When I Retire?*

When you reach the age of 71 in a particular year, you must convert your RRSP into retirement income by the end of that year, and the retirement income payments must commence in the following calendar year.

However, you need not wait to age 71 to commence receiving a retirement income. In theory, you may start at any time, although as a practical matter you should build up your tax-deferred savings while you remain eligible to contribute, and withdraw them only when you (a) absolutely require the money, (b) require retirement income, or (c) reach 71 and must commence to receive retirement income.

When you decide to (or must) begin to receive a retirement income, you can convert your RRSP to either a Registered Retirement Income Fund (RRIF) or an annuity. No tax need be paid on this conversion.

There is a great deal of flexibility on these conversions, so long as the transfer is made directly between plans. That is, you may not withdraw the RRSP funds in cash and later recontribute them to a RRIF or annuity. You can, of course, always withdraw funds you need from your plan at the cost of including them in your income and paying tax on the result, but those funds cannot be returned to the tax-deferred savings system. However, you can use your RRSP funds through direct transfer partly to obtain RRIFs and partly annuities, and you can split one RRSP among several such plans or lump several RRSPs into one such plan.

See also ¶2627.30 for commentary on continuing RRSP contributions for your younger spouse or common-law partner after the year in which you turn 71.

[¶2631.10] *Failure to Convert Plan*

If you fail to convert to retirement income any RRSP of which you are the annuitant by the end of the year in which you reach the mandatory age, the plan is in effect cancelled at the beginning of the following year, and the full fair market value of all the assets are included in your income for that year of cancellation.

[¶2631.15] *Change in Mandatory Retirement Age (2007/2008 Transitional Rules)*

The age at which you must convert your RRSP into retirement income was 71 for many years prior to 1998. For the period 1998 through 2006, the mandatory retirement age was lowered to 69. With the 2007 federal Budget, the age at which your RRSP must be converted to retirement income became again the year in which you turn 71, if you turn 71 in 2007 or later years.

If you were compelled to convert your plan into retirement income because you turned 69 in 2005 or 2006, transitional rules allowed you take advantage of the change in age requirement for 2007 (and 2008 if you turn 70 in 2007), although you could not make retroactive changes for 2005 or 2006. If you were already 71 at the beginning of 2007, your position did not change and you simply carry on receiving your retirement income.

If you had contribution room available, you could make RRSP contributions in 2007 if you turned 71 in 2007, and in 2007 and 2008 if you turned 70 in 2007. In addition, if you had converted your RRSP to a RRIF, the requirement that you commence receiving retirement income from the RRIF at the end of the year following the year in which you turned 69 is deferred, so that:

- if you turned 71 in 2007, you were not obliged to take any retirement income from your RRIF for 2007; and
- if you turned 70 in 2007, you were not obliged to take any retirement income from your RRIF for 2007 or 2008, even though you matured your RRSP in 2006.

[¶2631.20] *Example: RRSP Converted to RRIF Retirement Income*

The following example completes the discussion of RRSP benefits at ¶2601 by illustrating the use of an RRSP to create RRIF retirement income.

Example

Let us continue the example of Ms. S at ¶2601. Remember that she had accumulated about $250,000 in an RRSP by contributing $4,000 per year for 20 years. Assume that she has reached age 71 in 2016, and so must by the end of the year convert her RRSP to a retirement income stream (¶2616.05) commencing the following year (2017). Note that she could make this conversion at any earlier age, for example, in the year she retired, if earlier. First, she can make a final contribution to her RRSP *in the calendar year* she reaches the age for mandatory conversion of an RRSP to retirement income, and then transfer the RRSP to a RRIF. Assume that her opening balance in the RRIF at the beginning of the next year (2017) is $280,000 (including her last $4,000 contribution and earnings on her $250,000 balance). Since Ms. S is still 71 at the beginning of 2017, under the rules at ¶2632.20 she must withdraw her opening 2017 balance of $280,000 multiplied by .0528 = $14,784. The $14,784, however, is merely a minimum, and she may withdraw more.

Suppose that she decides she wants to receive $28,000 per year from the plan. The $28,000 will be taxable in her hands, but the balance in the plan will continue to earn tax-deferred income.

If the plan is earning a 10% annual return (which is free of current tax), her $28,000 receipt will exactly match the plan income. Under the minimum amount schedule at ¶2632.05 below, her minimum withdrawal requirements will not exceed the 10% earnings she is withdrawing from the plan. Thus, at the end of 17 years she will still have $280,000 in the plan. Note, however, in the year she turns 89 (is 88 at the beginning of the year), her minimum withdrawal will be $280,000 × .1021 = $28,588. In short, she has reached the point at which she must start to withdraw capital as well as income from the plan. The requirement will increase annually. However, given the 10% rate of return, this erosion will be gradual. Only when she turns 101 (is 100 at the beginning of the year) will her RRIF be depleted to the point that the minimum amount requirement is less than $28,000, and Ms. S can continue to withdraw at $28,000 per year, should she want to return to that amount.

Remember that all income earned in the plan (which will continue even as capital is withdrawn) is tax deferred, but all withdrawals are income to Ms. S.

If Ms. S is married or in common-law relationship, she may elect at the outset (but only before the first RRIF payment is made) to use her spouse's or common-law partner's age rather than her own in computing the annual minimum withdrawal. She would do this if her spouse or common-law partner were younger, thus ensuring that the fund would last as long as possible. If she died before her spouse or common-law partner, payments would, in effect, continue to him on the same basis. If he dies first, it appears that payments to her continue on the same basis, using his age to determine the minimum as if he were alive.

If additional funds are required, the plan holder may at any time make additional taxable withdrawals. The formula provides a minimum annual limit, but there is no maximum limit. Certain investments, such as long-term GICs, may involve penalties where early withdrawals are made. This is a function of the investment, not tax rules.

If Ms. S (and Mr. S, if any) die while there is still a balance in the plan, the balance will be paid to the heirs she designates. In some cases, the heirs may be able to put the balance into a tax-deferred plan, but this will be relatively rare, occurring only in cases of heirs who are dependent by reason of youth or infirmity, or spouse or common-law partner by virtue of remarriage or entering in common-law partnership. The heirs who are able to make these special contributions, incidentally, need not make direct transfers between plans but can actually receive cash out of the plan of the deceased and recontribute, within specified limits, to their own plans. See ¶2617.10, "Rollover at Death of RRIF or Annuitized RRSP Income".

[¶2631.25] *Table of Plan Balances and Withdrawals for Ms. S*

The following table summarizes the plan balances over 30 years for the hypothetical RRIF in the example above. The table makes a few unfortunate assumptions in the interests of simplicity. First, it assumes that plan withdrawals are made in a lump sum at the end of the year required. While this is ideal for maximizing plan earnings, most people will make monthly withdrawals instead. It is this assumption, however, which boosts the opening balance to $308,000, because earnings have accumulated in the plan throughout the first year of withdrawal and only been withdrawn at the end of the year. Second, it uses a 10% return rate, which may not be realistic for investments of the RRIF which must be made or renewed in recent years. Investment returns are now typically rather lower, although it remains to be seen if the lower rates will become firmly established. Third, the table stops at age 100, although it is clear that withdrawals could continue for several more years.

Year	*Age @ Jan. 1*	*Plan balance @ Dec. 31 before w/d*	*Plan balance @ Dec. 31 after w/d*	*Actual withdrawal*	*% of min. withdrawal by age*	*Minimum withdrawal*	*Plan earnings (@ 10%)*	*Capital withdrawal*
2016	71	$308,000	$280,000	$28,000	5.28%	$14,784	$28,000	0
2017	72	308,000	280,000	28,000	5.40%	15,120	28,000	0
2018	73	308,000	280,000	28,000	5.53%	15,484	28,000	0
2019	74	308,000	280,000	28,000	5.67%	15,876	28,000	0
2020	75	308,000	280,000	28,000	5.82%	16,296	28,000	0
2021	76	308,000	280,000	28,000	5.98%	16,744	28,000	0
2022	77	308,000	280,000	28,000	6.17%	17,276	28,000	0
2023	78	308,000	280,000	28,000	6.36%	17,808	28,000	0
2024	79	308,000	280,000	28,000	6.58%	18,424	28,000	0
2025	80	308,000	280,000	28,000	6.82%	19,096	28,000	0
2026	81	308,000	280,000	28,000	7.08%	19,824	28,000	0
2027	82	308,000	280,000	28,000	7.38%	20,664	28,000	0
2028	83	308,000	280,000	28,000	7.71%	21,588	28,000	0
2029	84	308,000	280,000	28,000	8.08%	22,624	28,000	0
2030	85	308,000	280,000	28,000	8.51%	23,828	28,000	0
2031	86	308,000	280,000	28,000	8.99%	25,172	28,000	0
2032	87	308,000	280,000	28,000	9.55%	26,740	28,000	0
2033	88	308,000	279,412	28,588	10.21%	28,588	28,000	588
2034	89	307,353	276,646	30,707	10.99%	30,707	27,941	2,766
2035	90	304,310	271,334	32,976	11.92%	32,976	27,665	5,312
2036	91	298,468	263,031	35,436	13.06%	35,436	27,133	8,303

Year	Age @ Jan. 1	Plan balance @ Dec. 31 before w/d	Plan balance @ Dec. 31 after w/d	Actual withdrawal	% of min. withdrawal by age	Minimum withdrawal	Plan earnings (@ 10%)	Capital withdrawal
2037	92	289,335	251,221	38,113	14.49%	38,113	26,303	11,810
2038	93	276,343	235,294	41,050	16.34%	41,050	25,122	15,927
2039	94	258,823	214,612	44,212	18.79%	44,212	23,529	20,682
2040	95	236,073	193,150	42,922	20.00%	42,922	21,461	21,461
2041	96	212,465	173,835	38,630	20.00%	38,630	19,315	19,315
2042	97	191,219	156,452	34,767	20.00%	34,767	17,384	17,384
2043	98	172,097	140,807	31,290	20.00%	31,290	15,645	15,645
2044	99	154,887	126,726	28,161	20.00%	28,161	14,081	14,081
2045	100	139,399	114,053	25,345	20.00%	25,345	12,673	12,673

[¶2632] MINIMUM ANNUAL WITHDRAWAL

[¶2632.05] Calculating the Minimum Annual RRIF Withdrawal

You must transfer your RRSP into a RRIF or retirement annuity (or some combination of both) by the end of the year you turn 71 years of age, although you may do so earlier. To the extent you choose to use a RRIF, you do not have to withdraw any amount in the year the RRIF is established (although you may). However, commencing in the following year you must withdraw at least a minimum amount.

[¶2632.10] Transitional Rule: If you turn 70 or 71 in 2007, or 71 in 2008

A special transitional rule consequential on the 2007 change in the minimum age for converting an RRSP to retirement income at 71 rather than 69 provides that if you turned 70 or 71 in 2007, your mandatory withdrawal from a RRIF for 2007 is nil (regardless of when the RRIF was entered into). Similarly, if you turn 71 in 2008, your mandatory withdrawal from a RRIF for 2008 is nil (regardless of when the RRIF was entered into). Details of the change are found in ¶2616.15.

[¶2632.15] Calculation of the Minimum Amount: Below Age 71

If you are under 71 when the RRIF is established, *your minimum amount in any year in which you are under 71 at the beginning of the year* is nil in the year the RRIF is established and thereafter is:

$$\frac{\text{the fair market value of the RRIF at the beginning of the year}}{\text{90 - your age at the beginning of the year.}}$$

This rule applied for the period 1997 through 2006 to taxpayers age 70 and 71 (as well as younger taxpayers) notwithstanding that the mandatory age for converting an RRSP to a RRIF was 69 for that period. On the other hand, it does not apply in 2007 to taxpayers who turned 70 or 71 in 2007, or in 2008 to taxpayers who turn 71 in 2008, for whom the mandatory withdrawal in those years is nil, as discussed above.

Example

Sonja turned 65 in February 2015, and decided to transfer her RRSP savings of $100,000 into a RRIF, which she did in 2015. Because of additional earnings in the RRSP and RRIF, which was earning 7% for the year, the RRIF was worth $107,000 at the beginning of 2016. Her minimum amount for 2015 is nil, but in 2016 she must withdraw a "minimum amount" of $107,000 ÷ 25 (being 90 – 65) = $4,280. The age of 65 is used in the calculation of the plan for 2016 because that was Sonja's age at the beginning of the year for which the calculation must be made.

For a qualifying RRIF established in 1992 or earlier, the rule above technically remains in force until the year in which you are age 79 at the beginning of the year (i.e., the year you turn 80). However, for the sake of simplicity and comparison, the formula is converted to a multiplier in the table below.

[¶2632.20] Minimum Withdrawal at Age 71 or Older: RRIFs established in or after 1993

New rules were introduced in 1992 for calculating the minimum annual RRIF withdrawal for RRIFs established in or after 1993. The minimum annual withdrawal is in all cases a percentage of the balance remaining in the RRIF at the beginning of the year. In general the new rules are the same as the old rules for RRIF withdrawals you must make before you reach age 71 (see above). For withdrawals made between ages 71 and 77 inclusive, the new rules require larger annual withdrawals than the old rules. At age 78, the required percentage withdrawal under both rules is the same. After age 78, the annual withdrawal requirement is lower under the new rules than the old.

Your age, for all minimum amount calculation purposes, is your age at the very beginning of January 1 of any particular year.

The introduction of the 1992 rules means that there are now two sets of minimum amount rules in play, and the minimum amount that applies to your RRIF while you are between the ages of 71 and 77 inclusive will be different depending on whether the RRIF was established before 1993 or after 1992. A pre-1993 RRIF will be converted to post-1992 rules if post-1992 contributions are made to it; this is discussed further under the next subheading below. Before age 71 and after age 77 the same withdrawal rules apply regardless of when the RRIF was created.

The overall result of the 1992 changes for all RRIFs is that money can remain in a RRIF over a longer period of time (although for ages 71 through 77, withdrawal rates for post-1992 RRIFs are somewhat higher). Under the old rules, all income had to be withdrawn at age 89. Under the new rules, withdrawals reach a plateau of 20% of the opening RRIF balance at age 94; you are never required to withdraw more than 20% of the RRIF balance.

Since you can always withdraw more than the minimum from a RRIF, it is always the minimum amount that is of concern. For taxpayers who have income in addition to that from the RRIF, there is a preference to keep as much money as possible in the tax-deferred RRIF and live on their other income until RRIF money is absolutely required, as the earnings in a RRIF continue to accumulate tax free.

The 2015 federal Budget reduced the RRIF payment factors, which are set out in the charts below. If you withdrew more than the new minimum, further amendments were made to allow you to recontribute the excess into the plan or an RRSP and deduct the recontribution. The deduction of the recontribution effectively offsets the income inclusion that relates to the withdrawal. These changes also apply to excess withdrawals from money purchase RPPs and PRPPs, which can also be recontributed to an RRSP, a RRIF, or a PRPP.

Your minimum amount for a year in which you are 71 or over at the beginning of the year is nil for the year in which you establish the plan and thereafter is the fair market value of the assets held in the plan on the first day of the calendar year multiplied by the number given below:

Minimum payment factors for RRIFs established after 1992

Age[1]	Pre-2015 Factors (%)	Factors for 2015 and later years (%)
Under 71	1/(90 - age)	1/(90 - age)
71	7.38	5.28
72	7.48	5.40
73	7.59	5.53
74	7.71	5.67
75	7.85	5.82
76	7.99	5.98
77	8.15	6.17
78	8.33	6.36
79	8.53	6.58
80	8.75	6.82
81	8.99	7.08
82	9.27	7.38
83	9.58	7.71
84	9.93	8.08
85	10.33	8.51
86	10.79	8.99
87	11.33	9.55
88	11.96	10.21
89	12.71	10.99
90	13.62	11.92
91	14.73	13.06
92	16.12	14.49
93	17.92	16.34
94	20.00	18.79
95 or older	20.00	20.00

[1] On January 1 of the year for which the minimum amount is being calculated.

Minimum payment factors for qualifying RRIFs established before 1993

Age	Pre-2015 Factors (%)	Factors for 2015 and later years (%)
Under 72	1/(90 - age)	1/(90 - age)
72	1/(90 - age)	5.40
73	1/(90 - age)	5.53
74	1/(90 - age)	5.67
75	1/(90 - age)	5.82
76	1/(90 - age)	5.98
77	1/(90 - age)	6.17
78	1/(90 - age)	6.36
79	8.53	6.58
80	8.75	6.82
81	8.99	7.08
82	9.27	7.38
83	9.58	7.71
84	9.93	8.08
85	10.33	8.51
86	10.79	8.99
87	11.33	9.55
88	11.96	10.21
89	12.71	10.99
90	13.62	11.92
91	14.73	13.06
92	16.12	14.49
93	17.92	16.34
94	20.00	18.79
95 or older	20.00	20.00

(ITR: 7308(3), (4))

[¶2633] ROLLOVERS

[¶2633.05] *Direct Transfer Rollovers*

Direct transfers among various registered deferred income plans — not only RRSPs — are also discussed at ¶1021.

These are transfers permitted among various registered plans. In principle, when you become entitled to a special lump sum payment from a registered plan, you can choose to keep the payment in some deferred tax plan rather than receive it currently and pay tax on it. However, to accomplish this you must specify to the payer that you want the amount transferred to another deferred plan and have it paid directly between plans. It appears that you may take part of such amounts out in cash (and pay full tax on them) and transfer the balance, but you may not recontribute any amount you take out in cash.

The most common example occurs when you change employment. You may transfer amounts to which you are entitled out of your old pension plan to either your new pension plan with your new employer or to an RRSP, RRIF, PRPP, or SPP. To accomplish this, you will be required to fill out a number of special forms (in particular, form T2151) and present them to your former employer or pension plan administrator to authorize the direct transfer of funds. Any restrictions on these transfers will arise out of the pension rules themselves and pension standards legislation, and not out of tax rules. Where you transfer a lump-sum amount from an RPP, DPSP, or SPP to another RPP, DPSP, RRSP, RRIF, PRPP, or SPP pursuant to form T2151, usually on a change of employment, there is no income inclusion and no designation on Schedule 7.

The December 4, 2008 issue of the *Income Tax Technical News*, No. 39, discusses the settlement of a shareholder class action suit relating to allegations against the corporation of artificially inflated share prices. The bulletin refers to a situation where tax-free direct transfer rollovers may take place. If the settlement payment received by the taxpayer comprises cash and shares, such payments may be made on a tax-free basis to the taxpayer's RRSP or RRIF. This can either be achieved by a direct transfer by the corporation or paid to the taxpayer first with a subsequent transfer to an RRSP or RRIF. The shares given as part of the settlement must be the same class of shares that the taxpayer originally bought in a registered plan such as an RRSP, and the number of shares in the settlement is directly related to the original number of shares bought. If paid to the taxpayer first, the taxpayer may transfer it with no tax consequences to an RRSP or RRIF within a reasonable time (that is, within six months of receipt or by the end of the taxation year of receipt, whichever is later). Otherwise, the cash payment and the fair market value of the shares will be considered income and must be included on the tax return as an RRSP or RRIF benefit received in the year.

Similar rules exist for division of RPP, RRSP, RRIF, PRPP, or SPP assets on the breakdown of a marriage or relationship; transfers may be made to registered plans for a spouse or common-law partner pursuant to court order or written separation agreement, but the transfers must be made directly between plans, and not by taking any cash or assets out of a plan altogether, even for a short time. Form T2220 is required for these transfers. No reporting of income or contribution is required on your T1 return. Similar rules apply to DPSP assets.

Transfers from one RRSP or RRIF to another may also be made on this basis. If, for example, you don't like the rate of return (or risk) in a particular plan you have invested in, you may open a new and more favourable plan and direct that the assets be transferred to it. Note that there may be charges associated with these transfers imposed under the terms of the plans themselves. For example, if both are stock mutual funds, it is possible the old fund will impose exit charges and the new fund will impose entrance charges. This will depend on the terms of the plan and has nothing to do with tax law. In most cases, the transferee will provide all the documentation you require. In general, these transfers are made under the authority of form T2033. No reporting of income or contribution is required on your T1 return.

Finally, when you decide to convert your RRSP to a RRIF or retirement annuity (¶2631.05), this may be done through a tax-free direct transfer. The issuer of the RRIF or annuity will provide the necessary documentation.

(ITA: 147.3; IT-528 Transfers of Funds Between Registered Plans; ITTN: 39 No. 39)

[¶2633.10] *Rollover to a Registered Disability Savings Plan (RDSP)*

A tax-deferred rollover is allowed to a taxpayer's Registered Disability Savings Plan (RDSP) from an RRSP, RRIF, RPP, PRPP, or SPP upon the death of the annuitant or RPP member under certain circumstances (see Form RC4625). To qualify for the rollover where the deceased has died after March 3, 2010, the following criteria must be met; the individual holding the RDSP would have been entitled to a deduction under paragraph 60(*l*) of the Act if the contribution made to the RDSP had been made to an RRSP; the individual is a child or grandchild of the deceased and was financially dependent on the deceased by reason of physical or mental infirmity; the contribution is made to a plan where the beneficiary is eligible for the disability tax credit, the beneficiary is less than 59 years old in the calendar year the contribution is made, the beneficiary is resident in Canada, the total contributions do not exceed $200,000, and any contributions not made by the holder of the plan are made with the written consent of the holder of the plan; the contribution is made after June 2011; the individual and the holder of the RDSP designate the contribution in the prescribed form at the time of the contribution (no form prescribed at the time of writing); and the contribution is the lesser of the total specified RDSP payments made in the year (or 60 days after the end of the year) or the total amount of eligible proceeds included in the taxpayer's computed income for that year.

When the deceased has died after 2007 and prior to 2011, there are special transitional provisions that apply. To qualify, the deceased must have been an annuitant of an RRSP or RRIF or a member of an RPP and was the parent or grandparent of an eligible individual (child or grandchild of the deceased that was financially dependent on the deceased by reason of physical or mental infirmity). The transitional eligible proceeds must have been received by the eligible individual, the spouse or common-law partner of the deceased, or a beneficiary of the deceased's estate; and the transitional eligible proceeds were included in the computation of that person's income for the year.

Under the transitional provisions, subject to the approval of the Minister of National Revenue, any of the persons mentioned above could deduct contributions made to the RDSP of a child or grandchild of the deceased from the proceeds received from the deceased's RRSP, RRIF, or RPP made before 2012. An election must be made with the prescribed form at the time of the RDSP contribution and filed with both the CRA and Human Resources and Skills Development Canada. The contributions made to the RDSP cannot exceed the proceeds received from the deceased's RRSP, RRIF, or RPP.

For cases where the death occurs before 2011 and after May 3, 2010, taxpayers may use either the general rules or the transitional rules.

Lump-sum death benefits paid out of a "specified pension plan" (i.e., the Saskatchewan Pension Plan) qualify for a rollover to an RDSP in the same manner as rollovers from RPP death benefits. This applies to transfers made after March 3, 2010.

For a more detailed description of RDSPs, see ¶2529h.

(ITA: 60.02; RC4625 Rollover to a Registered Disability Savings Plan (RDSP) Under Paragraph 60(m))

[¶2633a] DEATH AND DIVORCE

[¶2633a.05] *Rollover at Death of RRIF or Annuitized RRSP Income*

Where the annuitant of an RRSP has died after the RRSP has matured and been converted to either a RRIF or RRSP annuity (see ¶2616.05, ¶2634.10), the general rule is that the remaining benefits may be assigned by the terms of the plan itself or by will. Where the annuity payments pass to the surviving spouse or common-law partner, the surviving spouse or common-law partner simply takes over the position of annuitant and pays tax on the remaining payments. This transfer usually occurs directly by virtue of the terms of RRIF or annuity, but may occur indirectly where the benefits pass to the estate and the legal representative and surviving spouse or common-law partner agree to the assignment. This will be most common where the surviving spouse or common-law partner under an original RRIF or annuity has subsequently remarried and then died, so the RRIF is being passed on to a new generation of spouse or common-law partner, as it were.

Where a RRIF planholder dies and no provision is made in the RRIF contract, will, or by the estate for the surviving spouse or common-law partner to become the new RRIF annuitant, the rules are parallel to those for RRSPs above. That is, the general rule is that the fair market value of RRIF assets at death is included in the year-of-death return of the deceased, subject to a transfer of taxability of amounts which pass to others either directly or by election through the estate.

Where there is a surviving spouse or common-law partner who does not become the successor annuitant, amounts which pass to the spouse or common-law partner through the estate automatically become "designated benefits". These are taxable to the surviving spouse or common-law partner in the year received and may be contributed by the surviving spouse or common-law partner to an RRSP (age permitting), RRIF or annuity, precisely as if they were an RRSP refund of premiums (see above and ¶903). A transfer to the RRSP, etc. of the surviving spouse or common-law partner must be made within 60 days of the year-end of the year of receipt, and designated on Schedule 7 filed with the tax return of the surviving spouse or common-law partner . Where RRIF amounts pass to the estate of the deceased, the estate and surviving spouse or common-law partner may jointly elect (on form T1090) to have any part of the amount treated as a designated benefit of the surviving spouse or common-law partner.

Where there is no surviving spouse or common-law partner and there are surviving children and/or grandchildren who were financially dependent on the deceased at the time of death, the value of property which passes to them will be a "designated benefit" taxable to them.

It is presumed in the first instance that a child/grandchild was not financially dependent if its income in the year preceding the death exceeded a specified amount. That presumption can be rebutted by factual evidence. The point is that the specified amount test only comes into play *vis-à-vis* a parent or grandparent on whom the child was in fact dependent. The CRA discusses the criteria it will consider and the circumstances in which financial dependency can be established where the benchmark amounts are exceeded in ruling CRA Document No. 9926947. There it states, among other things, that the CRA "would not normally accept that a grandchild was financially dependent on a grandparent where the grandchild lived with his or her parent(s) and the parent(s) could adequately provide for the grandchild's well being."

The specified amount at which the presumption against dependence comes into play is the basic personal amount (¶1106) for the year preceding death, which amount is of course indexed for inflation. A table of personal amounts covering recent years is found preceding Chapter 1 at ¶65.

Example

For an individual dying in 2016, the specified amount used to determine if a child or grandchild is financially dependent on him is the 2015 basic personal amount of $11,327.

Where the child/grandchild was dependent by reason of mental or physical infirmity on a supporting parent/grandparent, the preceding year basic personal amount used as a benchmark in the presumption of dependency is supplemented by the preceding year disability amount (both as indexed). A table of personal amounts covering recent years is found preceding Chapter 1 at ¶65.

Infirmity for the purposes of these rules is discussed under the subheading "Infirmity Test" toward the end of ¶1209.

Children/grandchildren under 18 years of age or dependent on the deceased by reason of physical or mental infirmity may make the same kind of contributions to an RRSP, RRIF or annuity that would be permitted to them if the designated benefit were an RRSP refund of premiums, as discussed above.

Where property passes to the estate and there is no surviving spouse or common-law partner, or, for death's occurring after 1998, regardless of whether there is a surviving spouse or common-law partner, the estate and financially dependent children/grandchildren (or their representatives) may jointly elect to treat any amount of the RRIF as a designated benefit of the qualifying child.

The rules for exclusion of certain post-death RRIF accumulations from the category of designated benefits, the taxation of designated benefits to the recipient or by election back to the deceased, and the calculation of income in the year-of-death return of the deceased, are all identical to the RRSP refund of premium rules.

See also ¶1916.

See ¶2612.60 for rollovers to registered disability savings plans.

(ITA: 60(*l*); 146.3(1), (6), (6.1), (6.2))

[¶2633a.10] *Transfer of RRSP and RRIF*

Any funds in your unmatured RRSP may be transferred without tax consequences to an RRSP or RRIF for your spouse or common-law partner or former spouse or common-law partner provided all the following conditions are met:

(1) you and your spouse or common-law partner/former spouse or common-law partner are living apart;

(2) the payment is pursuant to either:

- a decree, order or judgment of a competent tribunal, or,
- a written separation agreement relating to a division of property between you and your spouse or common-law partner or former spouse or common-law partner in settlement of rights arising out of your marriage or partnership, on or after the breakdown of your marriage or partnership;

(3) your spouse or common-law partner is not disqualified by reason of age from having an RRSP (¶2616.05); and

(4) the transfer is made directly between plans.

Similarly, you may transfer any funds in a RRIF of which you are the annuitant to a RRIF or RRSP for your spouse or common-law partner or former spouse or common-law partner on the same conditions.

In addition, your spouse or common-law partner or former spouse or common-law partner may withdraw funds from a spousal or common-law partner RRSP (or the RRIF your spouse or common-law partner established therefrom) to which you contributed on your spouse or common-law partner behalf without triggering the usual inclusion in your income, provided only that at the time your spouse or common-law partner withdraws the funds you and your spouse or common-law partner are living separate and apart by reason of marriage breakdown. Note that the test in this case is less severe than that above, in that there need not be any formal separation agreement. The test is a factual one of marriage breakdown.

Form T2220 authorizes the transfer of funds among plans on separation or divorce where permitted under the rules above.

(ITA: 60(*l*); 146(1.1), (8.3), (16); 146.3(5.1), (14); RC4625)

[¶2634] OTHER OPTIONS

[¶2634.05] *Using Your Spouse's or Common-Law Partner's Age to Calculate the Minimum Amount*

The rules below apply to both spouses and common-law partners.

You are entitled to use your spouse's or common-law partner's age at the beginning of a year rather than your own to calculate the minimum amount. You usually make this choice at the time the RRIF is established; in any event, it can only be made before the first payment is made out of the RRIF. If your spouse or common-law partner is younger than you are, using the spouse's or common-law partner's age will always result in a lower minimum amount and is therefore usually a sensible choice since you can always take out more than the minimum. If you should die first, your spouse or common-law partner can continue to receive RRIF payments under the same minimum amount schedule.

Although you can elect to use your spouse's or common-law partner's age to fix the minimum amount schedule, you must nevertheless convert any RRSP of which you are the annuitant (i.e., you own RRSPs as opposed to your spousal or common-law partner RRSPs) to a retirement income by the end of the year in which you reach age 71. That is, it is only the minimum amount schedule, not the conversion requirement itself, which is subject to the election.

Similarly, if you elect to use your spouse's or common-law partner's age to determine the minimum amount schedule, the income you actually receive from a RRIF created out of your own RRSP will still be your income and not that of your spouse or common-law partner as long as you live.

It appears that once the choice to use your age or your spouse's or common-law partner's age to determine the minimum amount schedule has been made (and any payment has been made out of the RRIF), the schedule so chosen is essentially permanent for that RRIF. Thus, if you have chosen to use the schedule fixed by the age of your younger spouse or common-law partner and your younger spouse or common-law partner dies before you, the minimum amounts remain fixed by the original schedule. The schedule assumes that your spouse or common-law partner continues to age.

It does seem to be technically possible to transfer your RRIF assets directly from one RRIF to another without tax consequences (see ¶2612.35, and you do not have to make the same election in the new RRIF with respect to using your spouse's or common-law partner's age. Accordingly, if your spouse or common-law partner dies and you marry or co-habit with a younger spouse or common-law partner, you could reduce your RRIF minimum amount schedule by transferring your RRIF assets to a nominally new RRIF and electing the new spouse's or common-law partner's age. Indeed, there seems to be nothing to prevent you from changing your mind repeatedly by establishing a new plan, although in general you would always want the lowest required minimum amount. It is conceivable that if you are relying on your RRIF income and you are below taxable levels, so that you would benefit from an alleviation of withholding, you might want to shift to a higher minimum amount to avoid withholding, but normally this could be accomplished more easily simply by asking the Source Deductions Section of your Tax Services Office of the CRA to authorize a reduced withholding, which they will normally do in the circumstances.

Example — Spousal or Common-Law Partner Minimum Age Election

Rudyard turns 71 in 2016; his wife Janet turns 65. Rudyard has an RRSP with a value of $100,000. He must convert his RRSP to a retirement income (RRIF or annuity) by December 31, 2016.

If Rudyard transfers the $100,000 into a RRIF in 2016 he will have a minimum amount of zero for 2016 (always zero for the actual year of conversion) and $100,000 × .0528 = $5,280 in 2017. However, if he elects to use Janet's age to determine minimum amounts, the 2016 minimum amount will still be nil and the 2017 minimum amount will be $100,000 ÷ (90 - 65) = $4,000. The minimum amount will continue to be computed by this formula until Janet turns 71, and then will be computed under the table above with reference to her age. The election should be made when the RRIF is established.

The minimum amount, and any other withdrawals from the RRIF, will be taxable to Rudyard if made during his lifetime regardless of whether or not he elects to use Janet's age to determine his minimum amount.

If Janet should die before Rudyard at any time after the RRIF is established and the election made, the minimum amount schedule will not be affected; it will continue to use her age to determine minimum amount as if she were still alive.

The spousal or common-law partner age option is available under both the new and old minimum amount rules. For a RRIF established in 1992 or earlier, use of the spousal/partner option will not impair the status of the RRIF as a qualifying RRIF. Moreover, it appears that if you transfer the assets of a qualifying RRIF to a new plan but do not contaminate the new plan with any other assets, the new RRIF will also be a qualifying RRIF.

[¶2634.10] *The Annuity Option*

The alternative to a RRIF is an annuity. Generally speaking, an annuity leaves investments in hands of the annuity issuer, although special arrangements may be available. However, the issuer, usually a life insurance company, will guarantee to pay a fixed amount. The annuity may be for your life, or the life of your spouse or common-law partner, or it may match the terms of a RRIF requiring payment of all balances by a particular age for you or your spouse or common-law partner with a guaranteed payment in the event of premature death. Finally, an annuity may be a hybrid of both types.

The advantage of an annuity will usually (depending of course on its terms) be the assurance that income will continue to be paid even if you live well past the age at which you might expect a RRIF might run down. For this, you give up, in effect, in most cases, control over your investments. As well, you may give up the option to take out special lump-sum amounts if you need them, although some annuities may be flexible in this regard. If you think you can get a better rate of return over time than the insurance company, and you want to continue management of your assets, a RRIF will appeal to you. You may want to see if you can provide for the contingency of living to an extremely old age with special insurance or deferred annuities. If management of your assets is not important to you, and security is, you should investigate the payments available under annuitized RRSPs. Your own circumstances, health, etc., must govern your final decision.

TAX FREE SAVINGS ACCOUNTS

[¶2635] GENERAL — TAX-FREE SAVINGS ACCOUNTS (TFSAS)

The Tax-Free Savings Account (TFSA) has been available to individuals since 2009. Financial institutions eligible to issue RRSPs are permitted to issue TFSAs. This includes Canadian trust companies, life insurance companies, banks, and credit unions.

An individual (other than a trust) resident in Canada and 18 years of age or older will be eligible to establish a TFSA. An individual can hold more than one TFSA, but will be subject to overall annual contribution limits. TFSAs can be transferred from one financial institution to another without being considered a withdrawal or contribution; however, transfer fees may apply.

(ITA: 146.2; Tax-Free Savings Account (TFSA) Guide for Individuals (RC4466); Tax-Free Savings Account (TFSA) Return (RC243); Designation of an Exempt Contribution Tax-Free Savings Account (TFSA) (RC240))

[¶2636] CONTRIBUTION LIMITS

The CRA will determine TFSA contribution room for each eligible individual who files an annual income tax return (on the individual's Notice of Assessment and through the "My Account" function on the CRA website). Individuals who have not filed returns for prior years (because, for example, there was no tax payable) will be permitted to establish their entitlement to contribution room by filing a return for those years or by other means acceptable to the CRA. To provide the CRA with adequate means to determine contribution room and monitor compliance, TFSA issuers will be required to file annual information returns.

[¶2636a] OVERCONTRIBUTIONS

[¶2636a.05] *Contribution Room*

Starting in 2009, individuals 18 years of age and older acquire $5,000 of TFSA contribution room each calendar year in which they are a resident of Canada for at least part of the year. The $5,000 limit was indexed to inflation and the annual additions to contribution room were rounded up or down to the nearest $500. It thus remained at $5,000 for 2010, 2011, and 2012, but was increased to $5,500 for 2013 and 2014. Thus, the total contribution room to the end of 2014 was $31,000. The annual dollar limit increased to $10,000 for 2015 before decreasing to $5,500 with indexation after 2015. Unused contribution room will be carried forward to future years. For example, if an individual contributes $2,000 to a TFSA in 2009, the individual's contribution room for 2010 will be $8,000 ($5,000 for 2010 plus $3,000 carried forward from 2009). There is no limit on the number of years that unused contribution room can be carried forward, nor is there a ceiling on aggregate contributions. However, excess contributions are subject to a tax of 1% per month.

Any amounts withdrawn from an individual's TFSA in a year — which can be used for any purpose — will be added to his or her contribution room for the following year. This gives individuals who access their TFSA savings the ability to recontribute an amount equal to the amount withdrawn in the future.

The following example shows that the potential contribution to a TFSA can be significantly more than the regular annual limit and thus the individual can earn more tax-free investment income.

Example

> Suppose that an individual has $25,000 in his or her TFSA invested in the stock market, and the investments appreciate rapidly to $35,000. The taxpayer can sell the shares, realize the $5,000 tax-free capital gain in the TFSA, and withdraw the cash proceeds tax free. The $35,000 can be recontributed to the TFSA, in addition to any other unused and current TFSA contribution room, in the following year or later.

There is no restriction on a higher-income taxpayer funding a TFSA for his or her spouse, common-law partner, or adult children. If an individual transfers property to a spouse or common-law partner, the attribution rules generally treat any income earned on that property as income of the individual. However, an exception normally applies to the attribution rules that allows individuals to take advantage of the TFSA contribution room available to them using funds provided by their spouse or common-law partner: the attribution rules will not apply to income earned in a TFSA that is derived from such contributions.

It is possible to make "in-kind" contributions to a TFSA, as long as the property is a qualified investment (see below). The amount of the contribution will be equal to the fair market value of the property. The contributor will be considered to have a deemed sale of the transferred property at its fair market value at the time of the contribution. However, if the cost is more than the fair market value, the resulting capital loss will be denied.

[¶2636a.10] *Deliberate Overcontributions*

Contributions and associated earnings may accrue tax-free in the TFSA and may be withdrawn at any time without any adverse tax consequences. Contributions in excess of the TFSA contribution limit are subject to a tax of 1% per month on the highest amount of excess contributions for the month. This tax is generally sufficient to neutralize the tax benefit of overcontributions. The Government of Canada became aware that, in certain situations and subject to the existing anti-avoidance rules in the *Income Tax Act*, some TFSA holders were attempting to generate a rate of return on deliberate overcontributions over a short period of time sufficient to outweigh the cost of the 1% tax.

Under the amendments, any income reasonably attributable to deliberate overcontributions will be made subject to the existing advantage rules (see ¶2532c.35) and taxed accordingly. Pursuant to the advantage rules, the tax payable on the income will be 100%.

The CRA will maintain the discretion to waive or cancel all or part of the tax payable and the authority to adjust the taxpayer's TFSA contribution room accordingly in appropriate circumstances, as discussed above.

[¶2637] WITHDRAWALS

While TFSA contributions are not deductible, income, losses, and gains on investments held in a TFSA and amounts withdrawn from a TFSA are not included in computing income for tax purposes or taken into account in determining eligibility for the following income-tested benefits or credits delivered through the income tax system:

- Canada Child Benefit;
- Goods and Services Tax Credit;
- Working Income Tax Benefit; and
- Age Credit

Nor will such amounts be considered in determining the following benefits based on the individual's income level:

- Old Age Security benefits;
- Guaranteed Income Supplement; and
- Employment Insurance benefits.

Because the investment income within, and withdrawals from, a TFSA are not taxable, interest on money borrowed to invest in a TFSA is not deductible. Like an RRSP, deduction for services such as investment counsel or administration fees are not deductible. However, unlike RRSPs, a TFSA may usually be used as security for a loan. In fact, technical amendments introduced in 2009 clarify that none of the rules pertaining to TFSAs apply to prevent the TFSA holder from using his or her interest in the TFSA as security for a loan or other indebtedness. However, to guard against the "sale" or "rental" of TFSA contribution room, this will only be the case if the debt agreement is on arm's length terms and it is reasonable to conclude that none of its main purposes is to enable another person or partnership to benefit from the exemption from tax provided in respect of the TFSA.

See also ¶2532c.35, *Withdrawals*.

[¶2638] DEATH AND DIVORCE

The fair market value of the TFSA on the date of death will be received by the estate tax free. That is, investment income and gains that accrue in the account after the individual's death will be taxable, while those that accrued before death will remain exempt. However, an individual will be permitted to name his or her spouse or common-law partner as the successor account holder, in which case the account will maintain its tax-exempt status. Alternatively, the assets of a deceased individual's TFSA may be transferred to a TFSA of the surviving spouse or common-law partner, regardless of whether the survivor has available contribution room and without reducing the survivor's existing room. At time of writing, most provinces have amended their succession legislation to permit the designation of a successor holder or beneficiary on a TFSA, so that the TFSA can pass outside the estate and avoid probate levies, where applicable.

On the breakdown of a marriage or a common-law partnership, an amount may be transferred directly from the TFSA of one party to the relationship to the TFSA of the other. In this circumstance, the transfer will not reinstate contribution room of the transferor, and will not be counted against the contribution room of the transferee.

An individual who becomes non-resident will be allowed to maintain his or her TFSA and continue to benefit from the exemption from tax on investment income and withdrawals. The "deemed sale" rules do not apply to a TFSA on ceasing to be or becoming a Canadian resident. No contributions will be permitted while the individual is non-resident. A 1% per month penalty tax applies to non-resident contributions until the contributions are withdrawn or the date when the TFSA holder resumes Canadian residence, if earlier, and no contribution room will accrue for any year throughout which the individual is non-resident. Unlike RRSPs, TFSA withdrawals by non-residents are usually not subject to withholding tax. Withdrawals are added back to contribution room for the following year, but are available only when the individual resumes Canadian residence.

[¶2639] QUALIFIED INVESTMENTS

A TFSA will generally be permitted to hold investments which are quite similar to those allowed for an RRSP. (Qualified investments for RRSPs are discussed at ¶2618.) However, the *Income Tax Act* contains provisions designed to penalize individuals whose TFSA holds a "prohibited investment". Generally, this refers to investments in any entities with which the account holder does not deal at arm's length, a corporation of which the account holder is a "specified shareholder" as defined in the *Income Tax Act*, or another entity in which the account holder has an analogous interest ("specified shareholder" generally refers to a 10% or greater interest in a class of shares of the corporation or a related corporation, counting the holdings of non-arm's length persons).

It is possible for an RRSP to invest in shares of a private corporation. Likewise, it is possible for a TFSA to do so, within the limitations described above. It should be noted that Regulation 4900(12) allows as a qualified investment for an RRSP shares of a "specified small business corporation", provided that the RRSP annuitant is not a "connected shareholder" of the corporation immediately after the acquisition of the share. The connected shareholder definition dovetails with the TFSA requirement because it refers to a person who directly or indirectly holds 10% or more of the shares of any class of the corporation or any corporation related to the corporation. In the case of RRSPs, there is a "safe harbour" rule from the 10% restriction where the person deals at arm's length with the corporation and the cost of the shares in the corporation is less than $25,000, but it does not appear that the safe harbour rules apply to TFSAs. Nevertheless, it may be possible for a TFSA to acquire shares of such a corporation, as long as it retains "specified small business corporation" status.

As is the case with RRSPs, individuals should review administrative and withdrawal fees, transaction charges, and interest (if any) on cash balances.

Note: If property that is considered to be a prohibited investment or a non-qualified investment is acquired, or if property held in the account becomes such, a tax of 50% of the fair market value of the property at the time it was acquired or that it became a non-qualified or prohibited investment is payable. When a TFSA holds a prohibited investment, the holder will also be subject to an additional tax that is based on income earned from the prohibited investment.

[¶2639b] NON-QUALIFIED INVESTMENTS

[¶2639b.05] *Measures Against "Aggressive Tax Planning"*

In Department of Finance News Release No. 2009-099, dated October 16, 2009, it was announced that the TFSA provisions would be amended to counter certain avenues for "aggressive tax planning". The amendments were further introduced in draft legislation dated April 30, 2010, and then Bill C-47, which received Royal Assent in December 2010. What Finance sees as the problem areas, and the measures in regard thereto, most of which are effective from October 16, 2009, are outlined below.

The 2011 federal Budget provided that the penalty taxes applicable to TFSAs in respect of "advantages", "prohibited investments", and "non-qualified investments", as described below, would also apply to RRSPs and RRIFs.

[¶2639b.10] *Swap Transactions*

"Swap transactions", refer to transfers of property (other than cash) for cash or other property between accounts (for example, a registered retirement savings plan (RRSP) and another registered account) that are generally not treated as a withdrawal and re-contribution, but instead as a straightforward purchase and sale. Subject to the application of existing anti-avoidance rules in the *Income Tax Act*, these transfers, when performed on a frequent basis with a view to exploiting small changes in asset value, could potentially be used to shift value from, for example, an RRSP to a TFSA without paying tax, in the absence of any real intention to dispose of the asset.

The legislation effectively prohibits swap transactions between registered or non-registered accounts and TFSAs. The definition of "swap transaction", in relation to a TFSA trust, generally means a transfer of property (other than a transfer or a distribution) occurring between the trust and the holder of the TFSA or a person with whom the holder does not deal at arm's length.

TFSA increases in fair market value that may reasonably be attributed to swap transactions are subject to the advantage rules in Part XI.01 of the *Income Tax Act*. Where these rules apply, the fair market value of the advantage, including benefits reasonably attributable to swap transactions, are taxed at 100%.

The CRA may waive or cancel all or part of the liability in respect of an advantage, including a swap transaction, where it considers it just and equitable to do so having regard to all the circumstances. In this regard, the amendments provide that the CRA shall not waive or cancel the liability unless one or more distributions are made without delay under a TFSA of which the individual is the holder, the total amount of which is not less than the amount of the liability waived or cancelled. The distributions are taxed as regular income (see subsection 207.06(3) and paragraph 207.061(*b*)).

[¶2639b.15] *Prohibited Investments and Non-Qualified Investments*

Under the current rules, where a TFSA holds a non-qualified investment or a prohibited investment, the holder of the TFSA is subject to a tax equivalent to 50% of the fair market value of the property. This tax is refundable to the holder if the investment is promptly disposed of from the account (by the end of the year following the year in which the tax arose, or such later time as the Minister of National Revenue considers reasonable), except in circumstances where the holder knew or ought to have known that the investment was non-qualified or prohibited. All or part of the tax may also be waived or cancelled at the discretion of the Minister of National Revenue where the Minister considers it just and equitable to do so having regard to the circumstances.

While the current TFSA regime applicable to prohibited investments and non-qualified investments provides for serious tax consequences for holding such investments, the investment income associated with the investments may remain tax-sheltered in the TFSA, resulting in an unintended permanent increase in TFSA savings and contribution room.

The prohibited investment tax framework was modified so that any income reasonably attributable to prohibited investments is considered an "advantage", as described above, and taxed accordingly, i.e., at 100%.

In terms of income derived on non-qualified investments, a TFSA is currently subject to tax on such income under Part I of the Act under subsection 146.2(6). Furthermore, the amendments provide that "specified non-qualified investment income" in respect of a TFSA will include income (including capital gains) that is reasonably attributable, directly or indirectly, to the income of the TFSA that is taxable under Part I, i.e., income earned from non-qualified investments or income from a business carried on by the TFSA. Therefore, "specified non-qualified investment income" basically refers to second and subsequent generation income earned on non-qualified investment income or on income from a business carried on by a TFSA. The CRA may notify the holder of the TFSA to remove specified non-qualified investment income from the TFSA within 90 days of the notice pursuant to subsection 207.06(4). If it is not removed within 90 days of receipt of the notice, it will be considered an "advantage" in respect of the TFSA and subject to the 100% tax on advantages as discussed above.

[¶2640] COMMON QUESTIONS

[¶2640.05] *TFSAs vs RRSPs or Other Investment Considerations*

As stated above, individuals and family members will start to accumulate fairly significant TFSA contribution room that, when added to RRSP contribution room, may well be more than accumulating savings. If so, questions will arise as to which vehicle is preferable. In addition, it may be possible to make contributions to an RESP. Of course, there is an additional choice of paying down a mortgage or contributing to an RRSP.

An RRSP is a *tax-deferred* investment vehicle. It offers deductibility for contributions, tax-free accumulation, and withdrawals/retirement benefits which are fully included in income. On the termination of an RRSP, earnings accumulated in the plan are effectively taxable since all amounts received from the RRSP are taxable — this will also recapture the initial deductions for contributions. A TFSA, on the other hand, is a tax-free investment vehicle: contributions are made in after-tax dollars; like an RRSP, earnings accumulate tax-free; but unlike an RRSP, there is no tax on withdrawal. There are no mechanisms for tax-free transfers to a TFSA from an RRSP or other deferred income plans.

The financial comparison between these features appears to be similar to the choice between contributing to an RRSP and paying down a mortgage. Provided that a taxpayer remains in the same marginal tax rate before and after retirement, and the interest paid on the mortgage is the same as the return made by the RRSP, the choice between investing in an RRSP and paying down a mortgage appears to be financially neutral. Whereas the interest on the mortgage versus return in the RRSP is a variable in the mortgage versus RRSP decision, this is not the case in the TFSA versus RRSP decision, since similar investments can be made in either vehicle. The remaining variable appears to be tax rates before and after retirement. Assuming these are the same, this results in financial neutrality between the TFSAs and RRSPs (i.e., if the same contribution were made to each plan on an after-tax basis, so that all tax savings from an RRSP were used to enlarge the contribution itself). Although one might expect tax rates to drop because post-retirement income should generally be lower (which would tip the scales in favour of an RRSP), income-based clawbacks (i.e., in respect of OAS, GIS, and the age credit) muddy the waters, as they can effectively propel a taxpayer into a higher effective tax rate. However, RRIF and RRSP annuity payments are eligible for the pension-splitting rules for couples which came into effect in 2007 and may "even out" post-retirement income, perhaps so as to reduce income-based clawbacks. An RESP is somewhat similar to a TFSA, except that, while contributions are made on an after-tax basis, earnings are potentially taxable to the student (or may reduce tuition and education transfers); however, this effect may be modest and could be more than offset by the ability to obtain CESGs. Of course, a TFSA cannot be held by a minor.

It should be noted, however, that the financial comparison above between a TFSA and an RRSP assumes that the term of the investment is the same. While an RRSP has mandatory maturity at the end of the year the annuitant turns 71, whereby taxable payouts must commence, there is currently no mandatory maturity for a TFSA, nor is there an age where an individual can no longer contribute. It therefore appears possible for an individual to extend the benefits of tax-free status indefinitely. However, whether this will continue to be the case as the years go by and contributions mount up may be another matter: one cannot eliminate the possibility of future changes to TFSA legislation, for example, to impose mandatory withdrawals by the elderly, or perhaps even income-based restrictions on contributions; but, at the time of writing, this is completely speculative.

As noted previously, the ability to make a tax-free withdrawal from a TFSA which reinstates contribution room presents an advantage over RRSP withdrawals. In the latter case, such withdrawals are taxable, may have an adverse effect on benefits which are based on income, and do not reinstate RRSP contribution room. An exception is the first-time home buyers' plan (as well as the lifelong learning plan). In this case, however, to avoid tax, the withdrawal must be repaid in equal installments over 15 years; in addition, the benefits are restricted to "first-time" home buyers (as defined). With a TFSA, there is no required repayment (the withdrawal increases TFSA contribution room so that the TFSA can later be replenished); of course, there is no requirement to be a "first-time" home buyer. The first-time home buyer's plan currently imposes a $25,000-per-individual ceiling on withdrawals.

It can be seen that seniors, particularly those with low incomes, will benefit from TFSAs because of the lack of impact of withdrawals on income-tested benefits and because there is no age limit for contributions, as well as the fact that, unlike RRSPs, TFSA contributions are not dependent on "earned income". Younger individuals will find tax-free withdrawals and the reinstatement of contribution room to be attractive; however, the lack of tax on withdrawals will remove the psychological barrier — which is present with RRSPs — to retain funds in the plan, for example, for retirement. For those in temporary low-tax brackets, consideration should be given to contributing to a TFSA and conserving RRSP contribution limits for higher-income years.

Also, in these vehicles, tax advantages relating to investments, including capital gains status and the dividend tax credit, are lost. Also lost are the benefits of capital or other tax losses. As is the case with RRSPs, if the investor has capital outside of his or her plan, it may make sense to make tax-advantaged investments personally and invest high-tax items in either of these plans. As pointed out, if an investor is contemplating a very large shorter-term capital gain (e.g., on an equity investment), the taxable portion of which is likely to be well in excess of returns on fixed-income investments, the equity investment could, in effect, become high-tax, since the tax has to be paid for the year in which the investment is sold. Holding such investment in a TFSA would make even more sense than in an RRSP, since the gain would be entirely tax free, rather than tax-deferred, as is the case with an RRSP.

With rapidly accumulating contribution room in both vehicles, significant non-registered savings may become something of a rarity other than for the wealthy. Generally, passing up contributions to these plans because of the loss of tax advantages is usually not a good idea, unless the taxpayer is in a low bracket.

Finally, for shareholders of closely-held corporations, it should be noted that the ability to earn income on a tax-deferred basis in an RRSP and tax-free basis in a TFSA may put more pressure on making distributions of funds that would otherwise be deployed in corporate-level investments. Although this may result in additional current tax, retaining funds at the corporate level will result in significant tax on investment income. Consideration should therefore be given to ensuring that sufficient funds are distributed to make full contributions to RRSPs and TFSAs.

REGISTERED PENSION PLANS

[¶2645] GENERAL

RPPs are plans established by an employer to provide retirement income. They (and their investments) are usually administered by the employer or by an administrator appointed by the employer.

Defined benefit RPPs typically provide a retirement income by reference to salary in the last years of employment. The employer generally makes the bulk of the contributions necessary to fund these plans, and these contributions are not taxed to the employees; rather, the pension income provided is taxable as received. In some defined benefit RPPs it is possible (or mandatory) for employees to make supplementary contributions, which they may deduct from income. It may also be possible to "buy back" past service where an employee leaves an employer and returns, or transfers between certain plans, or where plan benefits are retroactively upgraded. Where employees make qualifying contributions, they may deduct these amounts from employment income; see ¶365.

Money purchase RPPs provide a retirement income based on the total contributions to the plan in the same manner as Registered Retirement Savings Plans. The employer may contribute according to the terms of the plan as long as the annual contributions do not exceed specified limits. If the plan permits, employees may also make contributions (which will be deductible from employment income) to bring the total contributions up to the legally specified annual limits; see ¶365. The deductible employee contributions are claimed on line 207 of the T1 return. Retirement income is taxable as received.

[¶2646] CONTRIBUTION DEDUCTIONS

Registered pension plans are divided into two kinds: defined benefit plans, where pensions are specified in the plan and unrelated to contributions, and money purchase plans, where pension amounts are a direct function of combined employer–employee contributions.

For defined benefit plans, all required contributions for current or past service in respect of pensionable service after 1989 will be deductible after 1990. For money purchase plans, total allowable employer–employee contributions were limited to $13,500 for 1996 through 2002 inclusive. The limits increase to $15,500 for 2003, $16,500 in 2004, and $18,000 in 2005. Subsequent limits were: $19,000 for 2006, $20,000 for 2007, $21,000 for 2008, and $22,000 for 2009.

Beginning in 2010, the $22,000 number (or the higher indexed amount for 2009) is indexed annually for annual wage growth. As such, the limit is $22,970 in 2011, $23,820 in 2012, $24,270 in 2013, $24,930 in 2014, $25,370 in 2015, and $26,010 in 2016. These values are supposed to buy pensions equal to the value of pensions which will be permitted under defined benefit plans.

Note that the rules in this section deal with contributions made by employees, whether directly or through payroll deduction. For contributions made by employers, see ¶357, ¶359 and ¶735. Current limits are available at ¶82, before Chapter 1.

Under current *Income Tax Regulations*, an Individual Pension Plan (IPP) is defined to be a defined benefit RPP if either (a) the plan has fewer than four members and at least one member is related to a participating employer in the plan, or (b) if it is a designated plan and it is reasonable to conclude that the rights of one or more of the members to receive benefits under the plan exist primarily to avoid the aforementioned definition. One of the amendments states that contributions made to an IPP that relate to past years of employment will be required to be funded first out of either the plan member's existing RRSP assets or the plan member's accumulated RRSP contribution room. The purpose of this amendment is to limit a major tax benefit of an IPP: that is, the ability to defer taxes by contributing a large lump sum into the IPP at the plan's commencement.

(ITR: 8300(1) "individual pension plan"; 8304(10) Individual Pension Plans)

[¶2647] ROLLOVERS FROM OTHER PENSION PLANS

[¶2647.05] *Retiring and Termination Payment Rollovers*

You may transfer or contribute to an RRSP, RPP, PRPP, or SPP, in addition to the amounts based on earned income and rollovers of pension plan or DPSP amounts, specific amounts received as a retiring allowance (which includes damages on termination), as defined at ¶923. The amount of the additional contribution is based on the number of pre-1996 years that you were employed by the employer. The transfer is usually indirect; that is, the amounts are paid to you and must be contributed to the plan within 60 days following the end of the year of receipt, and designated by you on Schedule 7 filed with your tax return. In certain circumstances the amount may be transferred directly between plans, but you must still report the receipt as income and make the designation on Schedule 7.

Details of these rules as well as a detailed example of this rollover are provided at ¶2612.05.

[¶2647.10] *Rollovers of Foreign Pension Plan Amounts*

Where you receive a lump sum payment out of a foreign pension plan for services attributable to a period of non-residence in Canada, the amount can be rolled over to a Canadian RPP, RRSP, PRPP or SPP by making a contribution within 60 days from the end of the year of receipt.

Payments out of certain quasi-pension plans such as U.S. Individual Retirement Accounts may also be eligible for rollover treatment; see ¶919.

(ITA: 60(*j*))

[¶2647.15] *Recontributions of Past Service Event Excess Withdrawals*

Under the complex registered pension plan (RPP) rules, a "past service event" may be permitted to increase the benefits to employees under a *defined benefit RPP*. A retroactive increase in benefits is the most obvious example. For these benefits to be permitted under the plan, the employees affected must have sufficient unused RRSP room (¶2610.15). Where the employee has insufficient room, a special (taxable) RRSP withdrawal may be made. Where the withdrawal proves excessive, for example because the past service event does not in fact qualify, a recontribution of the withdrawal can be made and deducted. See ¶2614c.10.

(ITA: 146(6.1); 147.1(10); ITR: 8307(1), (2), (3))

[¶2647.20] *Rollovers of Unregistered Pension Plan Amounts*

Where you receive a lump-sum payment out of a foreign pension plan for services rendered by you, or where you receive such an amount after June 6, 1990, for services rendered by your spouse or former spouse, and rendered during a period throughout which the person rendering the services was a non-resident of Canada, the amount can be rolled over to a Canadian RPP, RRSP, PRPP or SPP by making a contribution within 60 days from the end of the year of receipt. To the extent that the receipt is not taxed to you because you invoke the provisions of a tax treaty, it is of course not available for this special contribution. The special contribution must be "designated" by completing Schedule 7 of the T1 return and filing it with the return.

This rule extends to amounts received for non-resident services performed by a common-law partner or former common-law partner. For these purposes a common-law partner at a particular time is defined as discussed at ¶2624.05 above. Although less than entirely clear, it would appear that the spouse or common-law partner or former spouse or common-law partner test must be met at the time the amount is paid rather than when the services were rendered.

(ITA: 60(*j*); IT-528, para. 26, 27)

[¶2647.25] *Deferred Profit Sharing Plan Lump-Sum Payment Rollovers*

Lump-sum entitlements from a DPSP may be transferred directly to another DPSP or to an RPP, RRSP, RRIF, PRPP, or SPP on behalf of an employee or on behalf of a person who was the current spouse or common-law partner of an employee in the event of the employee's death. The transfer may also be made for direct transfers to any of these plans on behalf of a former spouse or common-law partner. Amounts may be transferred only to the extent that they would be included in income if paid directly to the individual. Thus, employee contributions made to a DPSP are not transferable. On the other hand, the cost of DPSP shares included in income is transferable (see also ¶917). Direct transfer is not required where the payments pass through a testamentary trust; in this case, a contribution to the surviving spouse's/partner's RPP or DPSP must be made within 60 days of year end and a designation made on Schedule 7 of the T1 return.

Periodic payments from a DPSP are permitted no special transfers to any tax-deferred plan.

(ITA: 60(*j*); 147.1(19)–(22))

[¶2648] EMPLOYER CONTRIBUTIONS

[¶2648.05] *Employer's Contributions to Pension Plans, etc.*

The benefits an employee derives from his/her employer's contributions to or under one of the following plans are not taxable benefits:

- registered pension plan;
- pooled registered pension plan;
- group sickness or accident insurance plan;
- private health services plan;
- supplementary unemployment benefit plan;
- deferred profit sharing plan;
- employee life and health trust; or
- group term life insurance policy.

See the comments at ¶317 with respect to group term life insurance coverage and ¶316 with respect to premiums paid by an employer under provincial hospitalization plans or provincial medical services plans. Employer contributions to an unregistered or non-resident pension plan may create a variety of tax consequences; see ¶307, ¶332 and ¶359.

(ITA: 6(1)(*a*)(i); *Employer's Guide — Taxable Benefits and Allowances* (T4130); IT-502 Employee Benefit Plans and Employee Trusts)

[¶2648.10] *Contributions by Employer*

Both past and current service contributions required under the terms of a registered pension plan to be made by the employer are deductible to the employer if made within 120 days after the end of the taxation year to which they relate. Pension contributions for "defined benefit plans" (where a formula determines the eventual benefit) are now achieved through pension plan limits based on registration restrictions on the plans themselves required by law and regulations.

Employer contributions are in theory now integrated into an overall system of tax-deferred savings which includes registered pension plans (RPPs), registered retirement savings plans (RRSPs), pooled registered pension plans (PRPPs), and deferred profit sharing plans (DPSPs). The maximum contribution (employer and employee) or benefit accrual to all three types of plans for an individual for a particular year should be 18% of earned income subject to a maximum for the year. In order to integrate RRSPs into this system, their contribution limits are based on prior year income, and the annual maximum contribution limit trails one year behind other plans. This permits reporting of prior year RPP/DPSP contributions in assessing eligible RRSP contributions. It also imposes complex new reporting requirements on employers as part of the T4 process.

Employers who have "defined benefit" (as opposed to "money purchase") pension plans may deduct all contributions necessary to fund the defined benefit plan in accordance with its terms for all periods before the end of the taxation year. The employer has 120 days following the end of a taxation year to make any current or past service contributions required for the year by the plan.

"Money purchase plans" are simpler in concept than defined benefit plans. For the employer, the rule for deductions is the same; namely, the employer may deduct amounts in accordance with the terms of the plan in respect of periods before the end of the taxation year. However, the funds which may be contributed to the plan are in effect limited by dollar amounts for each year much like RRSP contributions, rather than by actuarial calculation of the amount needed to support the defined benefits the plan must eventually provide.

Per employee contribution limits on money purchase RPP plans are 18% of pensionable earnings to a maximum of $26,010 for 2016 (for previous years, see the chart at ¶82 at the beginning of this book). Limits are to be reduced by DPSP contributions. Contributions to defined benefit RPPs are in theory equalized to these levels by complex formulae determining the current value of future benefits.

Since the rules attempt to integrate pension plan benefits with employees' RRSP contribution limits, employers face elaborate reporting requirements on their plans. The key limitation under the new rules will be the so-called Pension Adjustment. This is calculated by employers based on the tax-deferred benefits accruing to each employee annually under all of the employer's registered plans — typically pension and deferred profit sharing plans. The employee's contributions to other tax-assisted savings plans (RRSPs) are limited to the lesser of 18% of income and an annual dollar amount, minus the pension adjustment.

Where a plan permits an employee to contribute in respect of past service to acquire money-purchase benefits, such contributions are not deductible. Employee contributions in respect of past services under defined benefit plans may be deducted as discussed at ¶365.

If an employer maintains a funded but unregistered pension plan to supplement registered plan pensions, any contributions (typically made by an employer) made to the plan and any income of the plan will be subject to a special 50% tax to be refundable as pension payments are made. This second rule has been incorporated under the Retirement Compensation Arrangement rules discussed at ¶739.

To the extent that it may be possible for a tax-exempt employer (e.g., a charity, government, or non-resident) to maintain an unregistered retirement plan that is not captured by the RCA rules at ¶739, the Pension Adjustment rules should nevertheless apply to reduce allowable RRSP contributions of employees (see ¶2604).

[¶2649] PAST-SERVICE CONTRIBUTIONS

[¶2649.05] *Registered Pension Plan Contributions*

Registered pension plans are divided into two kinds: defined benefit plans, where pensions are specified in the plan and unrelated to contributions, and money purchase plans, where pension amounts are a direct function of combined employer–employee contributions.

For defined benefit plans, all required contributions for current or past service in respect of pensionable service after 1989 will be deductible after 1990. For money purchase plans, total allowable employer–employee contributions were limited to $13,500 for 1996 through 2002 inclusive. The limits increase to $15,500 for 2003, $16,500 in 2004, and $18,000 in 2005. Subsequent limits were: $19,000 for 2006, $20,000 for 2007, $21,000 for 2008, and $22,000 for 2009.

Beginning in 2010, the $22,000 number (or the higher indexed amount for 2009) is to be indexed annually for annual wage growth. As such, the limit is $22,450 in 2010, $22,970 in 2011, $23,820 in 2012, $24,270 in 2013, $24,930 in 2014, $25,370 for 2015, and $26,010 for 2016. These values are supposed to buy pensions equal to the value of pensions which will be permitted under defined benefit plans.

Under the employee contribution rules for past service contributions in and after 1991 for service prior to 1990, a maximum of $3,500 may be deducted each year in respect of contributions made for years of pre-1990 service while the taxpayer was not a contributor to a pension plan, subject to an overall limit of $3,500 times the number of years of pre-1990 past service. This deduction is in addition to any deduction for current or past service contributions in respect of post-1989 service under the new rules. For years of pre-1990 service during which the employee *was* a contributor, the $3,500 is reduced by *any* contributions deducted in the current year. Contributions which cannot be deducted in a particular year due to this limitation can be carried forward indefinitely until contribution room becomes available under the $3,500 limitation. If this does not occur until the year of death, see ¶1913c.

The ability to deduct contributions to buy past service recognition under defined benefit plans for service after 1989 is limited only by the terms of the plans themselves, but the deduction limits in force for current buy-backs of service before 1990 continue indefinitely.

For past service deductions made after 1990 in respect of past service contributions actually made after March 28, 1988 (unless made after that date pursuant to a written agreement made before that date), you are considered to be a contributor in respect of any past year in which you made any contribution to any registered pension plan, not merely to the plan to which you are making past service contributions. The result of this would appear to be that under the new rules you may buy back years of past service for years in which you made no contributions to any plan at the rate of $3,500 deductible per current year, and years of past service when you were a contributor only to the extent of $3,500 minus your current service contributions this year. Undeducted past service contributions carry forward indefinitely, so that if you are already making $3,500 per year of current service contributions, you will not begin to deduct your past service contributions until you retire, and then you can deduct them at $3,500 per eligible year. This is, in fact, intended to carry forward substantially unchanged the rules previously in place with respect to past service contributions, subject to the March 28, 1988 change.

All additional voluntary contributions (AVCs) to money purchase plans were denied deductibility after October 8, 1986, but the definition of AVCs was limited to contributions made by members which were used to provide benefits under a money purchase provision of the plan and were not required as a general condition of plan membership. Disallowed contributions could be returned to the contributor before 1991 without tax, but will be taxed if returned after that date. Past service contributions for earlier AVCs may survive in limited form; see Interpretation Bulletin IT-167R6, para. 4. For 1991 and later years, deductibility of current service (only) AVCs is restored subject to overall pension plan and pension adjustment limitations. As well, there have been situations in which seemingly past service contributions have been held to survive and permit deductions for contributions for non-existent past service; see the two cases of *Vivian v. The Queen*, 95 DTC 291 (T.C.C.) and 95 DTC 664 (T.C.C.).

Note that the rules in this section deal with contributions made by employees, whether directly or through payroll deduction. For contributions made by employers, see ¶357, ¶359 and ¶735. Current limits are available at ¶82, before Chapter 1.

Under current *Income Tax Regulations*, an IPP is defined to be a defined benefit RPP if either (a) the plan has fewer than four members and at least one member is related to a participating employer in the plan, or (b) if it is a designated plan and it is reasonable to conclude that the rights of one or more of the members to receive benefits under the plan exist primarily to avoid the aforementioned definition. One of the amendments states that contributions made to an IPP that relate to past years of employment will be required to be funded first out of either the plan member's existing RRSP assets or the plan member's accumulated RRSP contribution room. The purpose of this amendment is to limit a major tax benefit of an IPP: that is, the ability to defer taxes by contributing a large lump sum into the IPP at the plan's commencement.

(ITR: 8300(1) "individual pension plan"; 8304(10) Individual Pension Plans)

[¶2649.10] *The Interest Factor in Buying Past Service Pension*

Where you borrow money to make contributions to a registered pension fund or plan, the interest on the loan is not deductible for tax purposes.

If you elect to pay a past service contribution in a year, it is probable that you will be required to pay accrued interest in addition to the basic contribution for the past services. Where a past service contribution, including accrued interest, is to be paid in instalments, it is probable that further interest will have to be paid in respect of each instalment.

The CRA's current position, which depends on which past service years are in issue, is detailed in both IT-167R6, paragraphs 15 and 16, and in Chapter 1 of CRA Guide T4040. The degree of detail presented in those sources is both explicit and more extensive than can be adequately summarized here. The Guide in particular contains useful examples.

[¶2650] WITHDRAWALS

[¶2650.05] *Superannuation and Pension Benefits*

Superannuation or pension benefits received must be included in computing income. This is true for income out of all registered pension plans and most other plans, and includes not only regular pension payments, but also special lump-sum payments, refunds of contributions, etc.

Pension benefits will generally qualify for the pension tax credit providing you meet the other requirements for that credit. See ¶1311.

You may deduct contributions to an RRSP or RPP from certain pension benefits received (see ¶1021). These contributions may be paid in the year that you received the benefits or within 60 days after the end of the year. These special contributions are not affected by the normal deductibility restrictions applicable to RPPs and RRSPs. Also refer to ¶903 which discusses the waiving of withholding taxes on such a transfer.

You may not transfer ordinary periodic pension payments to an RRSP or RPP, although some special lump-sum payments are transferable provided the transfer is made directly between plans. See ¶1021 and ¶2616.05. In the 2014 federal Budget, the lump-sum transfer rule from RPPs to other plans was relaxed somewhat for underfunded defined benefit RPPs; see ¶1021.20.

A number of military pensions, primarily relating to service in the World Wars, are exempt from tax. See ¶991.

If you belong to a funded but unregistered pension plan in Canada, the plan will probably fall within the definition of a Retirement Compensation Arrangement (¶359). You will be taxed on the benefits you receive out of the plan, but if the plan calls for payments to someone else (such as your spouse) in respect of your employment, those payments will be taxed to you rather than to the recipient. If you are a non-resident at the time of the payment, it may instead be taxed to the recipient. It is not clear if double taxation can arise in this situation. If you sell an interest in a retirement compensation arrangement, the proceeds are income to you, except to the extent that money is returned and taxed to your employer in the transaction. If you have made non-deductible contributions to an RCA, payments out of the plan to you are taxable but may be offset by deductions to the extent they constitute a refund of your own non-deductible contribution; see ¶365a.

If you receive an amount that represents several periodic payments lumped together, some of which would ordinarily have been received in *preceding* taxation years, you may be eligible for a form of income averaging to spread the applicable tax calculation over those years. Note that lump-sum payments received as commutations of future payments are not eligible for this treatment. Eligible amounts should be reported to you on form T1198, and the CRA should do the averaging automatically if you deal with form T1198.

The 2015 federal Budget lowered the minimum annual withdrawal amount from a money purchase RPP. See ¶2,632.20.

(ITA: 56(1)(*a*), (*x*), (*y*), (*z*); 57(1), (2), (3); 60(*j*), (*j*.2); 146(5); ITR: 7308(4); IT-397R Amounts Excluded from Income — Statutory Exemptions and Certain Service or RCMP Pensions, Allowances and Compensation; IT-499R Superannuation or pension benefits)

[¶2651] DIRECT TRANSFERS TO OTHER PLANS

[¶2651.05] *Special RPP Contributions to RRIF, RRSP, PRPP, and SPP*

Lump sum amounts from a defined benefit registered pension plan can be transferred to a registered retirement income fund. The regulations always provided limits on such transfers, calculated by multiplying the amount of annual pension foregone by a prescribed present value factor. Prior to 1996, the multiplier was set at zero for individuals 72 or older. In consequence, these transfers were not permitted. For transfers after 1995, the multipliers are reset and there is no upper age limit at which the transferable amount is nil. However, when making these direct transfers it is essential to consult the limitations table prescribed in Regulation 8517.

The *Income Tax Regulations* allow a larger portion of a commutation payment from an underfunded pension to be transferred to RRIFs and RRSPs in cases of employer insolvency. The conditions for the application of the amended limit are that the transfer occurs on behalf of an employee or former employee of an insolvent employer who has ceased making pension contributions; that the lifetime retirement benefits payable under the defined benefit (DB) portion of the Registered Pension Plan (RPP) have been reduced due to underfunding; that the RPP not be a designated plan as defined by subsection 8515(1) of the *Income Tax Regulations*; and that the application of these rules has been approved by the Minister of National Revenue.

The rules regarding the deductibility of RRSP contributions create a deduction in certain circumstances where a taxpayer has received an amount in commutation of benefits under a defined benefit (DB) Registered Pension Plan (RPP), after February 2009 and before 2011, where the employer is insolvent. The taxpayer is able to deduct RRSP contributions in respect of DB RPP commutation payments where the taxpayer could have benefited from the revised pension transfer limit in the amended regulations had they been in place before 2011.

Lump-sum amounts from an RPP may also be transferred directly to a PRPP or SPP.

(ITA: 146(5.2), 147.3(4); ITR: 8517 Transfer — Defined Benefit to Money Purchase)

[¶2651.10] *Excess Direct Transfers*

Where a lump-sum amount is transferred directly from an RPP to an RRSP or RRIF, usually on death or on termination of an employment, it is possible for the amount to exceed permissible limits. The excess is included in income for the year of transfer. It is considered a "contribution" to an RRSP so that an offsetting deduction may be claimed to the extent of contribution limits available for the year. To the extent the excess cannot be offset in this way, it will be subject to the overcontribution penalty rules at ¶2611.15. However, the usual deduction of overcontribution rules (¶2611.15) will not permit a tax-free withdrawal of these amounts.

There is a special rule, however, which does permit deduction of such excess transfers. The obvious solution, then, would be to withdraw the excess transfer from the RRSP or RRIF and claim this offsetting deduction (on form T1043). This may be complicated by provincial legislation designed to protect pension allocations which may prevent you from withdrawing the excess amount. In this case, the excess amount will be included in your income, and may be subject to overcontribution tax. To the extent that provincial rules do permit you to withdraw the funds over time, the special deduction will carry forward to offset the future income from RRSP/RRIF withdrawals to the extent of the original income inclusion. This prevents double taxation, once at the time of transfer, and again at the withdrawal.

This special deduction was introduced for the first time in 1992, although it was retroactive to the extent that income inclusions for 1989–1991 will be included in the carryforward amount for use against 1992 and later RRSP/RRIF income.

(ITA: 147.3(13.1); IT-528, para. 22, 26)

[¶2651.15] *Direct Transfers Reported as Income*

In certain circumstances you may make a direct transfer between registered plans which is not an excess direct transfer (above) but is nevertheless reported as income to you; in this case you must claim an offsetting deduction and designate the amount on Schedule 7. These transfers occur (1) when you commute all or part of the annuity retirement income under an RRSP and transfer the lump-sum value of that income to another RRSP, RRIF, PRPP, or SPP, or (2) where you transfer from a RRIF an amount (in excess of the amount you must withdraw and include in income) to another RRIF or to an RRSP, PRPP, or SPP. Both these kinds of transfers are made under the authority of form T2030. The amount transferred out of a plan is reported as income on a T4RSP or T4RIF slip, as the case may be, by the administrator of that plan. The amount transferred is reported as a contribution by the administrator of the recipient plan. You must report income and offsetting deduction on your T1 return for the year of transfer, and designate the amount of the transfer by completing Schedule 7 of the T1 return and filing it with the return.

(ITA: 60(*l*)(v); IT-528, para. 22, 26)

[¶2651.20] *Refund of Premiums and Similar Amounts Rolled Over to Registered Disability Savings Plan (RDSP)*

In the 2010 federal Budget, the government announced a similar rollover (inclusion followed by off-setting deduction) for RRSP refunds of premiums (and RRIF eligible amounts and lump-sum payments out of an RPP) that are paid to an RDSP under which a child or grandchild was financially dependent upon the deceased by reason of physical or mental infirmity. The deceased does not normally include the amounts in income. The rollover is currently found in section 60.02. The new rule applies to amounts received by the child or grandchild as a refund of premiums out of an RRSP or an eligible amount out of a RRIF or a lump sum from an RPP ("eligible proceeds") as consequence of the death of the annuitant or plan holder after March 3, 2010, where the contribution is made to the RDSP after June 2011. In order to claim the deduction, the contribution must be made in the year in which the amounts are included in the child's or grandchild's income or within 60 days after the year, or any longer period that is acceptable to the Minister. The qualifying amount of the contribution, referred to as the "specified RDSP payment", qualifies for the rollover only to the extent that there is room under the $200,000 limit on contributions to RDSPs under which the eligible individual is a beneficiary.

In technical amendments first published on December 7, 2010, and now passed into law, the rule is amended to allow the same rollover for lump-sum death benefits paid out of the Saskatchewan Pension Plan to the child or grandchild that are transferred to the RDSP. This amendment applies to "specified RDSP payment" (as defined in subsection 60.02(1)) made after June 2011.

Additionally, "transitional eligible proceeds" can be contributed to the RDSP by the infirm child or grandchild, the surviving spouse or common-law partner, or a person who was a beneficiary of the deceased's estate or otherwise received the proceeds as a consequence of the deceased's death, where a person (typically either the recipient or the deceased) is required to include such proceeds in income. Basically, these are amounts received by a person as a consequence of the death of the annuitant after 2007 and before 2011 (before March 4, 2010 in the case of the child or grandchild) out of the deceased annuitant's RRSP (or RRIF or as a lump-sum pension plan payment); or amounts withdrawn from the person's RRSP or RRIF where the person was the deceased's spouse or common-law partner or child or grandchild who rolled such amounts into the RRSP or RRIF under the rules described above at ¶903.15 and ¶1914.15 upon the death of the deceased. In order to qualify for the deduction as a specified RDSP payment, the amount of the transitional eligible proceeds must be contributed to the RDSP of the child or grandchild of the deceased after June 2011 and before 2012.

(ITA: 60(*l*), 60(*m*), 60.02)

[¶2652] DEATH AND DIVORCE

[¶2652.05] *Pension Plan Benefits and Death Benefits*

Pension payments prior to death are included in the deceased taxpayer's return under the rules in ¶1907. Lump-sum payments after death will normally be taxed in the hands of the recipient, who may be either a beneficiary (e.g., spouse, common-law partner, child) or the estate. An individual recipient may in certain circumstances "roll over" these payments into an RRSP to defer current tax (see ¶1021).

Payments to beneficiaries may also qualify as "death benefits" as described at ¶925. These payments would be income of the recipient and not the deceased.

(ITA: 56(1)(*a*); 70(1); 248(1) "death benefit"; IT-212R3 Income of Deceased Persons — Rights or Things)

[¶2652.10] *Receipts from Trusts Representing Pension or DPSP Income*

Where a taxpayer has died and a testamentary trust receives certain pension or DPSP amounts which the trust has allocated as income to a spouse or common-law partner of the deceased, these amounts are eligible for special contribution by the surviving spouse or common-law partner, etc. to the surviving spouse's or common-law partner's RRSP. The trust should identify these amounts on the T3 to the surviving spouse or common-law partner in box 22 of the T3 Supplementary. The surviving spouse or common-law partner , if not disqualified by age from having an RRSP, may deduct as a special contribution any amount up to the amount in box 22 contributed to an RRSP within 60 days of the end of the year to which the T3 relates. The special contribution must be designated on Schedule 7 of the T1 return. See ¶2612.05.

(ITA: 60(*j*); 104(27), (27.1); 147(10.2))

[¶2652.15] *Other Pension Income*

Where pension income (excluding CPP/QPP income which has its own division rules above) is divided between spouses or common-law partners, the tax results may be capricious. For example, in a technical opinion, the CRA gave its view that under Alberta pension standards rules, where a couple agreed voluntarily on a division of pension income rather than obtaining a court order, the division was in effect invalid and all the income would be taxed to the spouse or common-law partner whose pension it technically was.

The same opinion found a different result in British Columbia. At least so long as a pension was divided 50/50, each spouse or common-law partner would report its share of pension income received. It was less clear what would happen if the division was uneven.

The message would seem to be that great care must be taken to comply with provincial formalities on the division of pension income, under both provincial family relations law and provincial pension law. An opinion or advance ruling from the CRA may also be desirable.

(Window on Canadian Tax: 2592)

[¶2653] FOREIGN PENSIONS

Pensions received by Canadian residents from a foreign source are subject to tax in Canada in the same way as private pensions received from a Canadian source, subject to the "foreign retirement arrangement" rules below.

If there is an income tax treaty between Canada and the foreign country, it may alter the taxation of pensions received from that country. See the list of tax treaties at ¶2005 and the discussion of pensions at ¶2080.04. Although the latter is directed at non-residents, the rules are generally reciprocal; that is, similar rules will apply to Canadians receiving foreign pensions.

In general, foreign pension income would seem to qualify for the $2,000 pension income credit (¶1311) to the extent the income is not protected by treaty. Foreign pension income is reported on line 115; the entire amount should be reported there; to the extent foreign pension income is treaty-protected, an offsetting deduction is claimed at line 256. That deduction is also backed out of foreign pension income when claiming pension income credit; the CRA provides a "Line 314 — Pension income amount" chart for this calculation in the worksheets which accompany the T1 package.

Foreign source government pensions similar to OAS may receive special treatment under social security treaties; see ¶2111.

Where you receive a lump-sum payment from a non-registered (typically a foreign) pension plan and the payments are attributable to services rendered outside Canada, the lump-sum payments will be income but you can defer taxation on the receipts to the extent you make offsetting contributions to a registered retirement savings plan (RRSP), pooled registered pension plan (PRPP), specified pension plan (SPP), or registered pension plan (RPP) within 60 days following the end of the year in which you receive the lump-sum payments; see ¶2612.05. However, you cannot deduct such contributions based on foreign pension income to the extent you have claimed treaty-protection on that income.

If you receive an amount that represents several periodic payments lumped together, some of which would ordinarily have been received in *preceding* taxation years, you may be eligible for a form of income averaging to spread the applicable tax calculation over those years. Note that lump-sum payments received as commutations of future payments are not eligible for this treatment. Income is not eligible for this treatment to the extent it is exempt under a tax treaty. Normally, the CRA expects eligible amounts to be reported to you on form T1198, but this may not be practical with foreign plans. The CRA does allow a letter or other explanation from the payer to serve in lieu of form T1198.

For deductibility of contributions to foreign plans, see ¶365a. For foreign social security payments received, see ¶921 (U.S.) and ¶922 (other).

[¶2653.10] *Foreign Retirement Arrangements (FRAs)*

A foreign retirement arrangement is any plan prescribed by regulation to be such. Currently, only Individual Retirement Accounts (IRAs) referred to in subsections 408(a) and (b) of the U.S. *Internal Revenue Code* are prescribed. An IRA is similar in concept to an RRSP.

Payments out of a foreign retirement arrangement established under the laws of a country are not taxable in Canada to the extent they would not be taxable in that country to a resident of that country. That is, payments out of an IRA to a Canadian resident will not be taxed in Canada to the extent they would not be taxed under U.S. law if the Canadian were a U.S. resident. This is intended to allow payments to be transferred from one such foreign plan to another. It may also apply where an individual receives a return of contributions from an IRA in respect of which the individual was not initially entitled to a deduction under U.S. law.

Technical amendments passed into law on June 26, 2013 ensure that for 2002 and later taxation years amounts treated as income distributions from IRAs at any particular time under U.S. rules are similarly treated as income under Canadian rules. This is mainly relevant to conversions of ordinary IRAs to "Roth IRAs", as such is discussed further under the next subheading below. However, the U.S. rules also deem a taxable distribution to occur when money is borrowed from an IRA, or an IRA is used as security for a loan, and such income inclusions would be matched in Canada when they occur under U.S. rules.

This matching rule for deemed distributions is of general application (which is to say it would apply to foreign retirement arrangements other than IRAs if there were any), and treats any amount in respect of a foreign retirement arrangement (FRA) which is, as a result of a transaction, event or circumstance, deemed under the laws of the country in which it is established to be a distribution to an individual, as income in Canada under the FRA rules for the taxation year that includes the transaction, event or circumstance.

A lump-sum payment out of an IRA which is taxable in Canada (because it would be taxable to a U.S. resident) will be eligible for recontribution to a Canadian registered pension plan (RPP), registered retirement savings plan (RRSP), pooled registered pension plan (PRPP), or specified pension plan (SPP) if it derives from contributions made to the IRA by the Canadian taxpayer or the taxpayer's spouse or common-law partner or former spouse or common-law partner; see ¶2612.05.

Transfer to an RPP, RRSP, PRPP, or SPP can be made by contribution within 60 days following the end of the year in which the payment from a foreign retirement arrangement is received (see subheading "Receipts from a United States IRA" in ¶2612.05).

The CRA is of the view that the value of an IRA on death is a "right or thing"; see ¶1908.

For deductibility of contributions to foreign plans, see ¶365a; for rollover of lump sums to RRSP, see ¶2612.05. The CRA takes the view (in the T1 Guide) that IRA payments taxable in Canada are not eligible for the $2,000 pension income credit.

Where amounts are transferred from a U.S. employer's pension plan to an IRA on behalf of a Canadian resident employee, the amount on its face is taxable in Canada. However, where the transfer is exempt under U.S. rules, it would appear that the Canadian resident is entitled to an offsetting deduction for treaty-protected income, pursuant to Article XVIII(1) of the Canada–U.S. Tax Treaty. It may be, however, that the amount is included in net income for the purpose of limiting tax benefits and, perhaps, calculating clawback taxes (see ¶1419).

POOLED REGISTERED PENSION PLANS

[¶2655] GENERAL

The federal government introduced legislation regarding PRPPs on June 28, 2012, and accompanying amendments to the *Income Tax Act* were passed into law on December 14, 2012. These plans allow employers and their employees, or self-employed individuals, to make tax-deductible contributions to the plans similar to those made to money purchase registered pension plans (RPPs) in ¶2614c.10 described above. An employer's contribution to a PRPP in a taxation year or within 120 days after year end are deductible (subsection 147.5(10)). The employer's contribution reduces the employee's RRSP deduction room for the year. The employee's contribution in a year also reduces the employee's RRSP deduction room for the year. Distributions from the PRPP paid to the employee are included in income and can qualify for the pension credit. See also ¶2555.

On October 7, 2014, the Department of Finance and the Minister of State announced that five insurance companies that having federal Pooled Registered Pension Plan (PRPP) licences (Sun Life, Great West Life, Manulife, Standard Life and Industrial-Alliance) had been registered with the Office of the Superintendent of Financial Institutions and the Canada Revenue Agency. This was the final step necessary for the plan administrators to make federal PRPPs available to Canadians.

PRPPs have the following characteristics:

- They establish large-scale, broad-based, voluntary pension arrangements available to employees — with or without a participating employer — as well as the self-employed.
- They are low cost. By pooling pension savings, the cost of administering the pension funds will be spread over a larger group of people, allowing plan members to benefit from lower investment management costs.
- Their administrative and legal burdens are borne by a qualified, licensed, third-party administrator. Under the PRPP program, the onus of this fiduciary duty is transferred to a professional plan administrator.
- They are straightforward in their design, help small businesses and are intended to be largely harmonized across provinces. They will fit seamlessly into the existing system of tax rules and contribution limits for Registered Pension Plans and Registered Retirement Savings.

(ITA: 20(1)(*q*), (*r*); 147.1; 147.2; 149(1)(*u*.3); 248(1) "pooled registered pension plan", 248(1) "registered pension plan"; ITR: 8500–8520)

[¶2655a] CONTRIBUTIONS

An employer's contribution to a PRPP in a taxation year are not a taxable benefit to the employee, although it reduces the employee's RRSP deduction room for the same year (paragraph 146(5)(*b*)). As such, unlike registered pension plans, there is no pension adjustment (PA) in respect of PRPPs.

The employee's contribution in a year is treated as a contribution to an RRSP for various purposes, including subsection 146(5) dealing with the amount deductible for an annuitant's contributions to an RRSP (subsection 147.5(11)). As such, the employee's contribution in a year also reduces the employee's RRSP deduction room for that year.

Any individual who lives or works in a jurisdiction that has enacted PRPP legislation is eligible to join a PRPP. An individual can contribute to a PRPP if the individual's RRSP contribution limit allows it. Contributions to a PRPP directly reduce an individual's RRSP contribution room. Since an individual's RRSP is also reduced directly by the contribution made to the PRPP by the employer, it should always be kept in mind when estimating the amounts that can be contributed.

An individual's participation in a plan is not dependent on an employer being involved. This is one of the differences between PRPPs and other types of pension plans.

Overcontributions to a PRPP are taxed the same as overcontributions to an RRSP.

Commentary on Legislative Proposals (Sept. 16, 2016)

Note: When Legislative Proposals, September 16, 2016, achieves Royal Assent, the commentary will be modified to read:

> Effective December 14, 2012, a PRPP contribution is deemed not to have been made where there is a refund of a contribution made to a PRPP by a taxpayer as a result of a reasonable error or a refund to avoid the revocation of the PRPP, which amount is not deducted as a PRPP contribution for the taxation year in which the refund is made or for any preceding taxation year.

(ITA: 147)

[¶2655b] WITHDRAWALS

Distributions from the PRPP paid to the employee are generally included in income and can qualify for the pension credit. Some provinces have put restrictions on the amount that can be withdrawn in any given period.

> **Commentary on Legislative Proposals (Sept. 16, 2016)**
>
> Note: When Legislative Proposals, September 16, 2016, achieves Royal Assent, the commentary will be modified to read:
>
> Effective December 14, 2012, an amount of PRPP contributions refunded to a member is not included in his/her income if they were made in error or to avoid the revocation of the plan, and if the amount was not deducted as a PRPP contribution in the year of the refund or any preceding year.

Amounts can be transferred from a PRPP to another PRPP, or to an RRSP, RRIF, RPP, SPP, or to a licensed annuities provider to purchase certain annuities on a tax-deferred basis.

PRPP minimum withdrawal amounts are determined using the same factors as applicable to a RRIF. The 2015 federal Budget lowered these annual RRIF and PRPP minimum withdrawals. See ¶2,632.20.

(ITR: 7308(3), (4))

[¶2655c] DEATH

Upon the death of the member of the PRPP, a financially dependent minor child or grandchild of the member who receives a lump-sum payment from the plan must include the amount in income, but is allowed the offsetting deduction under paragraph 60(v) if the amount is used to purchase an annuity payable to age 18 (see ¶1021.10). Similarly, a financially dependent child or grandchild by reason of infirmity will be allowed to rollover a lump sum received upon the member's death to a registered disability savings plan (RDSP) of the child or grandchild under section 60.02 (see ¶1021.10 and ¶1914.17).

Additionally, a tax-free rollover upon the death of the member of the PRPP applies if a lump sum is transferred to a beneficiary who is either the member's spouse or common-law partner or financially dependent child or grandchild (by reason of infirmity), if the amount is transferred directly to the beneficiary's PRPP, SPP, RPP, RRSP, or RRIF, or is used to acquire a qualifying annuity (subsections 147.5(20) and (21)).

(ITA: 147)

EMPLOYEES PROFIT SHARING PLANS

[¶2656] GENERAL

An employees profit sharing plan (EPSP) is an arrangement under which an employer pays a portion of the profits from its business to a trustee to be held and invested for the benefit of its employees who are members of the plan. The principal distinction between an EPSP and a deferred profit sharing plan (DPSP) is that under the former the members pay tax each year on the contributions and trust income allocated to them, whereas in a DPSP they pay tax only as these amounts are actually received from the trust. In either case, the employer's contributions are deductible in the year they are made (subject to upper limits in the case of a DPSP). See ¶332 for a further discussion on EPSPs.

In its 2012 federal Budget, the government announced measures to address its concern that EPSPs have been used by business owners to direct profits to members of their families to reduce or defer payment of income tax on these profits. In particular, the measures include a penalty tax under new Part XI.4 on a specified employee's "excess EPSP amount". See ¶332.20 for a discussion of this penalty tax.

[¶2656a] CONTRIBUTIONS

[¶2656a.05] *Allocation by Trustee to Employees*

Under the terms of an employees' profit sharing plan, an employer may pay amounts to a trustee on behalf of his employees. The trustee is required to allocate the following amounts to the individual employees:

(1) amounts received in the year from the employer or a corporation with which the employer does not deal at arm's length;

(2) income of the trust for the year;

(3) capital gains and capital losses sustained by the trust in the year after 1971; and

(4) amounts originally allocated to other employees who have, after 1971 and in the current year, lost their right thereto.

[¶2656b] INCOME ALLOCATIONS

As a beneficiary of the plan, you are taxed on the basis of allocations made by the trustee and are not subject to tax on payments actually received providing they represent:

(1) payments made by you to the trustee;

(2) net amounts that were previously allocated to you including losses other than capital losses;

(3) capital gains made by the trust for taxation years after 1971 to the extent they have been allocated by

the trust to you (but while you may not pay tax on these, you may want to elect to increase their cost base as described above);

(4) capital gains either realized by the trust prior to 1972 or capital gains representing appreciation in value of trust properties that occurred prior to 1972;

(5) unrealized capital gains, as of December 31, 1971, inherent in the value of property received by you from the trustee;

(6) a dividend received by the trust from a taxable Canadian corporation, to the extent allocated to you. However, certain tax-free dividends received by the trust after May 25, 1976 are excluded from this category and as a result, amounts which a trustee allocates from these dividends will not be included in the sources available for tax-free distribution; or

(7) life insurance proceeds received by the trust upon the death of the life insured, to the extent allocated to you.

Amounts attributable to the above sources will have borne tax at an earlier time or will be of such a nature that no tax is payable at any time.

Contributions to the plan by you as an employee are not allowable as a deduction for income tax purposes.

See also ¶332.20 regarding the new penalty tax on excessive contributions made to certain plans.

If you are a beneficiary under an employees' profit sharing plan and you receive an amount from the trust in a form other than cash, there is a rollover to you. For example, if the trust were to distribute a share on which there was an accrued but unrealized capital gain, the gain would not be taxed on distribution to you, but would be taxed when you dispose of the share.

The cost of the property to you is, in effect, the amount which has been attributed to you and included in your income or is otherwise exempt from inclusion. You should obtain details of your cost of the property from the administrator of the plan.

[¶2656c] FORFEITURE OF PAYMENTS

Where after 1991 you cease to be an EPSP beneficiary during the year (and do not rejoin the plan during the year), you may deduct from employment income the total of all amounts included in computing your income for the year and preceding years *except* that the following adjustments must be made to the current and prior year income inclusions:

(1) where dividends from taxable Canadian corporations have been allocated to the employee, the "gross-up" (¶404) is ignored and only the actual amount of the dividend is included; in addition, an arbitrary 25% of such dividends must also be deducted from current and prior year income allocations; this is a rough justice recognition of the fact that the gross-up and credit mechanism will have resulted in a lower effective tax rate on this income in prior years;

(2) capital gain or loss allocations are not included in the amount deductible, since it is presumed that the net gain will have been tax free by virtue of the capital gains exemption; and

(3) amounts actually received or receivable (as opposed to taxable allocations) are not included in the amount deductible.

It would seem that in some circumstances the deduction of prior income allocations could lead to an employment loss for the year, which would be reported as a negative number on line 101 and deducted from other income reported in the T1 return. In principle, losses from employment income may reduce other sources of net income to zero but not below. Moreover, employment losses do not go into any formal loss carryover pool discussed in Chapter 10. The deduction provision, when references to "a" year and "the" year are properly construed, seems to deal with the issue by providing its own carryforward provision. One result of this is to make any particular amount of the claim optional in the year of forfeiture or any subsequent year. Any amount claimed reduces the amount available for future claim, but unclaimed amounts seem to remain on hand forever. It will be important if there is an income loss not to overclaim the loss so that deductions in the return are not lost.

Where an employee rejoins a plan in the year of forfeiture, no deduction is permitted. Where the employee rejoins a plan in a year subsequent to the year of forfeiture, any carryforward amounts on hand cease to be available for deduction. It would appear, and seems to be the official view, that any carryforwards remaining on hand are simply lost from the year of rejoining forward, even if the employee leaves the plan again. The matter may not be beyond dispute.

The amended rules "clarify" that the forfeiture deduction does not necessarily come into play when an individual dies; rather, it is intended that if forfeiture occurs after death, the estate or heir would be entitled to the deduction.

The amended rules operate for 1993 and later years without a possible alternative.

[¶2656d] PENALTY TAX

In its 2012 federal Budget, the government announced measures to address its concern that employee profit sharing plans (EPSPs) have been used by business owners to direct profits to members of their families to reduce or defer payment of income tax on these profits.

In particular, the measures include a penalty tax under new Part XI.4 on a specified employee's "excess EPSP amount". The latter is defined as the employer's contributions in a year to the EPSP that are allocated in the year to the specified employee in excess of 20% of the employee's gross income from employment for the year (not including regular EPSP allocated amounts included in income or stock option benefits). A "specified employee", defined in subsection 248(1), generally includes an employee who does not deal at arm's length with the employer or who owns at least 10% of the shares of any class of the corporate employer. The penalty tax is payable by the specified employee.

The tax on the excess EPSP amount equals the top federal rate of 33% plus the top provincial rate for the province of the employee's residence (not including Quebec). If the employee is not resident in a province, the second rate is 14%. The CRA may waive or cancel part or all of the tax if it considers it just and equitable to do so.

To prevent double taxation, the excess EPSP amount is deducted in computing the employee's income.

The penalty tax will apply to contributions made after March 28, 2012. However, in the case of contributions to an EPSP pursuant to a legal agreement entered into before March 29, 2012, the tax only applies to contributions made beginning in 2013.

(ITA: 8(1)(*o.1*); 144; IT-280R Employees Profit Sharing Plans — Payments Computed by Reference to Profits; IT-379R Employees Profit Sharing Plans — Allocations to Beneficiaries)

DEFERRED PROFIT SHARING PLANS

[¶2657] GENERAL

A "deferred profit sharing plan" (DPSP) is a plan registered with the CRA under which an employer sets aside an amount calculated with reference to profit for later distribution to employees. The employees are taxed only when they actually receive the funds. Employer contributions to DPSPs are restricted by a number of factors. Among these, per employee contributions are limited to 18% of pensionable earnings (as calculated for registered pension plan purposes) to a maximum of $13,005 for 2016 (for other years, see the table at ¶82). DPSP contributions reduce the contributions that can be made to other plans. Thus, for a DPSP member who also belongs to a money purchase RPP, PRPP, SPP, and who saves through an RRSP, the total contribution to the five plans cannot exceed 18% of earnings to a maximum of $26,010 for 2016.

[¶2657a] CONTRIBUTIONS

The benefits an employee derives from his employer's contributions to or under a registered pension plan, group sickness or accident insurance plan, private health services plan, supplementary unemployment benefit plan, deferred profit sharing plan, employee life and health trust, group term life insurance policy, pooled registered pension plan are not taxable benefits. See the comments at ¶317 with respect to group term life insurance coverage and ¶316 with respect to premiums paid by an employer under provincial hospitalization plans or provincial medical services plans. Employer contributions to an unregistered or non-resident pension plan may create a variety of tax consequences; see ¶307, ¶332 and ¶359.

(ITA: 6(1)(*a*)(i); *Employers' Guide — Taxable Benefits and Allowances* (T4130); IT-502 Employee Benefit Plans and Employee Trusts)

[¶2657b] ROLLOVERS

Lump-sum entitlements from a DPSP may be transferred directly to another DPSP or to an RPP, RRSP, RRIF, PRPP, or SPP on behalf of an employee or on behalf of an employee or on behalf of a person who was the current spouse or common-law partner of an employee in the event of the employee's death. The transfer may also be made for direct transfers to any of these plans on behalf of a former spouse or common-law partner. Amounts may be transferred only to the extent that they would be included in income if paid directly to the individual. Thus, employee contributions made to a DPSP are not transferable. On the other hand, the *cost* of DPSP shares included in income is transferable (see also ¶917). Direct transfer is not required where the payments pass through a testamentary trust; in this case, a contribution to the surviving spouse's or common-law partner's RPP or DPSP must be made within 60 days of year end and a designation made on Schedule 7 of the T1 return.

Periodic payments from a DPSP are permitted no special transfers to any tax-deferred plan.

(ITA: 60(*j*); 147(19)–(22))

[¶2657c] WITHDRAWALS

Payments out of a deferred profit sharing plan are taxable in the recipient's hands when he or she receives them. See ¶917.

[¶2657c.05] *Benefits Received From a Deferred Profit Sharing Plan (DPSP)*

Amounts received by you as a beneficiary under a deferred profit sharing plan (¶736) must be included in your income. If funds of a plan are used to purchase an annuity for you, you will not be taxable on the amount paid for the annuity but you will be taxable on the full amount of each annuity payment you receive. However, annuity payments received from a deferred profit sharing plan may be eligible for the tax credit on the first $2,000 of pension income. See ¶1311.

Under certain circumstances, deductions may be allowed from this income. These are:

(1) If you have made payments into the plan for which you have received no tax deduction, you may deduct the lesser of:

(a) the amount received from the plan during the year minus any amount deductible by virtue of subparagraph (2) below; or

(b) the amount of the above-mentioned payments to the plan to the extent that they have not been deducted in a previous year.

(2) If you were a beneficiary of the plan at a time when it was an employees' profit sharing plan rather than a deferred profit sharing plan, you may deduct the total of:

(a) amounts previously included in your income under the employees' profit sharing plan;

(b) amounts paid into the employees' profit sharing plan by you; and

(c) pre-1972 capital gains allocated to you under the employee's profit sharing plan;

minus the total of:

(d) pre-1972 capital losses allocated to you under the employee's profit sharing plan; and

(e) amounts previously received by you from the plan while it was either an employee's profit sharing plan or a deferred profit sharing plan.

If you receive a lump-sum settlement from a deferred profit sharing plan upon withdrawal from the plan, retirement from employment, or death, and the settlement includes shares or other securities, the income which you will be deemed to have received would normally be equal to the value of the property you received as settlement. Your deemed cost of the securities would also be their value when received. If you are a resident of Canada, you may elect to defer the unrealized gains on the securities accrued since 1971 and reduce the deemed cost of the securities accordingly. The form you must file is T2078, available on the CRA website. When you eventually dispose of the shares on which you have elected, the difference between their tax cost to the plan and their fair market value at the time you received them will be ordinary income to you, but you will be allowed an offsetting deduction of one-fourth of that amount on line 249 of the T1 return on share dispositions occurring in 1990 or later years. This deduction is intended to match capital gain inclusion rates (¶500) but deny the capital gains exemption on the income element. Although the income element is fixed when you receive the shares, the offsetting deduction is fixed according to the year of disposition. As well, any gains or losses on the shares subsequent to your receipt of them will be ordinary capital gains or losses.

If you are related to your employer, and your employer contributes to a DPSP on your behalf or where an amount forfeited under a plan is allocated to you, the amounts contributed or allocated will be included in your income for the year (see ¶736).

DPSP benefits must commence at the same age at which RRSPs must mature and be converted to retirement income (¶2616.05).

[¶2657c.10] *Transfer of Lump-Sum Payments Received*

You may direct that lump-sum amounts you are entitled to receive from a deferred profit sharing plan be transferred directly into another DPSP or into an RPP, RRSP, RRIF, PRPP, or SPP (see ¶1021). The ability to receive periodic payments and transfer them in part or full under the rollover rules at ¶1021 has been removed. See ¶1021.

(ITA: 56(1)(i); 60(*j*); 110(1)(*d*.3); 118(3), (7), (8); 147(10), (10.1), (10.2), (10.3), (11), (12); *RRSPs and Other Registered Plans for Retirement* (T4040), Chapter 5)

[¶2657d] DEATH

If you are the spouse or common-law partner at the time of death of an employee or former employee covered by a DPSP, and accordingly receive a lump-sum payment from a DPSP on the death of the employee or former employee, you can have the plan make a direct transfer of the amount to your own DPSP, or to an RPP, RRSP, RRIF, PRPP, or SPP, thus avoiding immediate tax on the payment to the estate, and deferring tax until such time as you make arrangements for retirement income or other withdrawals from your plan. [Such transfers may also be made where you receive such an amount on the death of a former spouse or common-law partner or must divide your DPSP assets on the breakdown of your marriage or common-law partnership. Since the rules permit direct transfers from DPSPs to RRIFs, this is relevant where the surviving spouse or common-law partner of a deceased employee is over 71 years of age and, therefore, cannot transfer the DPSP assets to an RRSP.]

(ITA: 56(1)(i); 60(*j*); 110(1)(*d*.3); 118(3), (7), (8); 147(10), (10.1), (10.2), (10.3), (11), (12); *RRSPs and Other Registered Plans for Retirement* (T4040), Chapter 5)

RETIREMENT COMPENSATION ARRANGEMENT

[¶2658] GENERAL

Essentially, these are funded unregistered pension plans. More precisely, they are plans under which an employer makes payments to another person in order that benefits may be paid to an employee or any other person on retirement, termination of employment, or a substantial change of employment services. Registered plans and other plans specifically authorized by the *Income Tax Act* are excluded, as are certain non-resident plans (see ¶359) and plans for some athletes and athletic event officials.

Employer contributions to the plans are deductible expense to the employer on a current basis, but the plan itself is subject to a special 50% tax on all contributions and income earned, which is refunded as the pensions are eventually paid out on the basis of $1 refunded for every $2 paid. The intent is to prevent the accumulation of income on pre-tax contributions to the plan.

Contributions to foreign pension plans may or may not fall under the Retirement Compensation Arrangement (RCA) rules. The statutory definition of an RCA excludes foreign pension plans, but there are anti-avoidance rules which can deem foreign pension plan contributions for the account of a Canadian resident to fall under the RCA rules. There is then an alleviating regulation which allows the employer to opt out of these rules by reporting Pension Adjustments and Past Service Pension Adjustments for Canadian employees under the rules for RRSPs discussed in ¶2614a. In effect, this gives the foreign employer a choice between paying 50% refundable tax or reporting a Pension Adjustment or PSPA that will reduce the Canadian employee's contributions to a Canadian RRSP. See also ¶2614a.

In *Income Tax Technical News* No. 34, dated April 27, 2006, the CRA offers the following comments:

> The CRA has recently considered arrangements to fund benefits that are to be provided to employees under the provisions of plans that are identified as unregistered pension or supplementary pension plans. CRA has taken the position that these plans will generally be RCAs if the arrangements are pension plans and the benefits being provided are reasonable. Where a plan provides benefits that are not reasonable, the CRA is of the view that a salary deferral arrangement will exist.
>
> The CRA is taking the view that benefits will not be reasonable if, for example, they are more generous than benefits that would be commensurate with the employee's position, salary and service or they do not take into account benefits that are provided through one or more registered plans.
>
> It has come to the CRA's attention that innovative tax plans purporting to be RCAs are being marketed and promoted to avoid taxes. Here are some examples: corporations that contribute excessive amounts for the benefit of owner/managers who would receive the amounts after moving offshore, corporations that are attempting to use such arrangements to streamline their long-term profits and corporations that are claiming deductions for contributions that are part of a series of contributions/loan-backs. Tax avoidance schemes purporting to be RCAs will be targeted for review with the aim of, for example, applying the salary deferral arrangement rules, denying deductibility, applying subsection 15(1) and/or subjecting the arrangements to GAAR.

The Department of Finance, in its 2012 Budget, indicated that the CRA has uncovered "tax-motivated arrangements" perceived to be an abuse of the RCA rules. Apparently, "some arrangements involve the deduction of large contributions that are indirectly returned to the contributors through a series of steps ending with the purported RCA having little or no assets but still being able to claim the refundable tax using the impaired asset exception (the 207.5(2) election). Other arrangements use insurance products to allocate costs to the arrangement for benefits that arise outside the arrangement."

As a result, there is a new penalty tax (i.e., Part XI.3 Tax) applicable in respect of "prohibited investments", "advantages" and "stripping" rules, very similar to the rules applicable to RRSPs and RRIFs. The new rules do not affect the deduction of employer's contributions to an RCA, but the penalty taxes will obviously be detrimental where they apply.

As well, effective for the 2013 tax year and beyond, distributions from an RCA may be split with a spouse or common-law partner for pension income splitting purposes, provided that the recipient partner is at least 65 years of age and the payment is received in the form of a life annuity supplement to an RPP. Other restrictions may apply.

(ITA: 6(1)(*a*), (*g*), (*h*), (*i*), (10)–(14); 8(1)(*o*); 12(1)(*n.*2); 18(1)(*o*), (*o.*1), (*o.*2), (10); 20(1)(*r*), (*oo*), (*pp*); 32.1; 207.5–207.7; 248(1) "retirement compensation arrangement"; ITR: 6800–6804)

[¶2658a] CONTRIBUTIONS

Contributions are deductible to the employer, but the plan will be limited as to the contributions that it can make. The amount of contributions allowed will be based on what is reasonable under the circumstances and will be an amount that is calculated by an actuary and approved by the CRA.

[¶2658b] INCOME

Income earned in the trust will be subject to a refundable tax of 50%, payable by the plan and refunded when and as payments from the plan are made on the basis of $1 refunded when $2 is paid out.

[¶2658c] WITHDRAWALS

A retirement compensation arrangement (RCA) is essentially an unregistered pension plan, as discussed at ¶359. If you make non-deductible contributions to the plan while resident in Canada, your payments out of the plan (all of which are taxable) will be offset by deductions to the extent they represent a return of non-deductible contributions. These returns are considered to be the first payments out of the plan.

The transfer of amounts from one RCA to another on a tax-free basis has been facilitated, and the deduction for the return of non-deductible contributions will track the funds from plan to plan.

If you have made non-deductible contributions to an RCA, payments out of the plan to you are taxable but may be offset by deductions to the extent they constitute a refund of your own non-deductible contributions; see ¶365a.

(ITA: 60(*t*), (*u*); 207.6(7))

[¶2658d] DEATH

Payments from an RCA could pass outside the estate if there is a named beneficiary, and be taxed in the beneficiary's hands. This has the effect of continuing the tax deferral on that fund as well as it avoids probate in the estate.

SALARY DEFERRAL ARRANGEMENTS

[¶2659] GENERAL

Essentially, a salary deferral arrangement is any funded or unfunded arrangement the principal purpose of which is to defer salary or wages. This is discussed in considerable detail at ¶307. If a plan falls within the definition of a salary deferral arrangement as set out at ¶307, the employer is entitled to a deduction for amounts in respect of services rendered to him in the taxation year the amounts are taxed to the employee, whether or not the amounts have been segregated by a trustee or custodian. An employee may be taxed on amounts subject to a contingency and later forfeited. Where this happens, the employee may take a compensating deduction in the year of forfeiture and the employer must include in income for the year any amount which becomes deductible by the employee in the taxation year. All these rules are effective for 1986 and later taxation years.

(ITA: 6(1)(*i*); 6(11)–6(14); 248(1) "salary deferral arrangement")

[¶2659a] CONTRIBUTIONS

Employees may be taxed on amounts they have earned but not received in the year. Prior to 1986, these "deferred salary amounts" would in all probability have been taxed under employee benefit plan rules (¶359; ¶739) and been taxable to the employee only when received. Now, however, "deferred amounts" under a "salary deferral arrangement" will be taxed in the current year and not the future year of receipt.

The basic taxing provision requires that, where a taxpayer has a right in a year to postpone receipt of his or her salary or wages to a subsequent year under a salary deferral arrangement in respect of the taxpayer, an amount equal to the deferred amount is considered to be an employee benefit received by him or her in the year. As such, this amount must be included in computing the taxpayer's income for the year to the extent it has not already been included in the year or a preceding year.

[¶2659b] INCOME

Related provisions treat as deferred amounts any interest or other amounts in addition to the deferred remuneration that accrue to the taxpayer to the end of a taxation year under his salary deferral arrangement. If, for example, an employer agreed to pay interest on deferred amounts under an unfunded salary deferral arrangement, the interest accrued to the taxpayer to the end of a year will be required to be included as a benefit in computing his income for the year. In order to ensure that these interest or other amounts are not also required to be included in computing the taxpayer's income as accrued interest under the investment income rules described at ¶432, salary deferral arrangements are excluded from the definition of an "investment contract". Interest earned by a trust governed by a salary deferral arrangement is *not* included in employment income presumably because it will not be taxed at personal rates in the trust.

[¶2659c] WITHDRAWALS

The rules require that amounts you received in the year under a salary deferral arrangement be included in your income to the extent they exceed the aggregate of: (1) deferred amounts included in your income in preceding years under the agreement, plus (2) deferred amounts deducted by you in the year or preceding years under the forfeiture rules discussed below. This mopping-up provision does not apply to amounts received out of a trusteed salary deferral arrangement, which are treated as distributions by a trust to which the ordinary rules relating to trusts apply.

[¶2659d] EXCLUSIONS

See ¶307.20, Exclusions — Statutory Plans, and ¶307.25, Exclusions — Regulations.

[¶2659e] DEATH

Upon death, a salary deferral arrangement is deemed to be realized and any amounts previously not taxed will be brought into income under the rules described above under "Withdrawals".

REGISTERED EDUCATION SAVINGS PLANS

[¶2660] GENERAL

(ITA: 146.1(6), (7); IC 93-3R1; *Registered Education Savings Plans (RESPs)* (RC4092); Income Tax Folio: S3-F10-C1 Qualified Investments – RRSPs, RESPs, RRIFs, RDSPs and TFSAs)

RESPs are savings vehicles for higher education. The RESP itself is a trust to which contributions are made (usually but not necessarily by a relative) for the benefit of the potential student. The government will, up to a point, make matching and supplementary contributions. Contributions are not deductible, but income earned in the trust accumulates free of tax, and payments of accumulated income are included in the student's income once the student reaches the post-secondary level of education. Income inclusions are reported as miscellaneous income on line 130 of the T1 Return. Where payments from a plan have been included in income in a year, and the amounts are repaid to the plan in the year or a subsequent year, the repayments are deductible (on line 232). This is only likely to occur when government contributions which have proved excessive have been flowed out to beneficiaries. RESPs are discussed in greater detail in ¶2529d.

These plans originated as a tax splitting device, but have been taken over and regularized by a series of government revisions into an incentive program to encourage individuals to accumulate savings to provide for the post-secondary education of named "beneficiaries", typically children or grandchildren. There are, however, no relationship requirements imposed as between the contributor and beneficiary, so that you may set up an RESP for any relative or deserving beneficiary, including yourself.

An RESP beneficiary must be a Canadian resident who can provide a Canadian Social Insurance Number (SIN). As a practical matter, the CRA began requiring SINs in 1999. Exceptions to the new rule will exist for transfers to new plans from pre-1999 plans or from plans entered into when a current non-resident beneficiary was a resident or was not yet assigned a SIN when the designation was made.

The benefits of an RESP arise through three mechanisms:

(1) tax deferral, in that income earned on the (non-deductible) contributions you make to the plan is not subject to tax as it is earned; accordingly income accumulates more rapidly in the plan than it would in the hands of the contributor;

(2) income splitting, in that when amounts are paid out of the plan for the post-secondary education of a beneficiary they will be taxed to the beneficiary, whose tax rate is typically lower at that time than the contributor's tax rate; and

(3) incentive grants, in that the government will actually match contributions with 20% grants paid to the plan on contributions of up to $2,500 per year for a $500 annual and a $7,200 lifetime limit (see ¶2665.

[¶2661] CONTRIBUTIONS

As a contributor (subscriber) to an RESP, you are *not* entitled to a deduction in respect of your contribution; however, the interest income (or other investment income) earned in the plan on your contribution is not taxed in your hands. Rather, the investment income earned in the plan is accumulated free of tax and will be taxed in the student's (child's) hands only when the child receives funds from the plan. See ¶456.

Since 2007, there has been no limit to the amount of annual contributions that can be made on behalf of a particular beneficiary.

However, penalty provisions impose an overall "lifetime" per beneficiary limit of:

- for 1997 through 2006 inclusive, $42,000, and
- for 2007 and later years, $50,000.

These contribution limits apply to contributions on behalf of any particular intended beneficiary no matter how many plans are established by how may contributors. A penalty tax (Part X.4 Tax) of 1% per month of any excess contributions is assigned *pro rata* to each contributor's contributions. The objective, of course, is that the limits cannot be avoided by establishing more than one RESP or by having different subscribers establish RESPs. Excess contributions can be withdrawn.

Contributions can be made until the plan beneficiary is 31 years of age (35 years in the case of a single beneficiary plan for a disabled beneficiary).

In general, the rules ensure that plans must provide that education benefits are only paid to *bona fide* students in full-time attendance in qualifying educational programs at post-secondary educational institutions. As well, the plans must provide for termination after 35 years (40 years for "specified" plans, i.e., single beneficiary plans for a disabled beneficiary). A 1996 amendment eased the rules by permitting an RESP beneficiary to also receive assistance for education from another source. For 1997 and later years, the rules were further eased to permit minor siblings to be substituted for each other as plan beneficiaries.

It is possible under these plans for the original capital contributions to be returned to the contributor, typically in the event that no related beneficiary qualifies by taking post-secondary education within the required time frame.

As well, a department, agency or institution that maintains a child or the public trustee or curator of a province can enter into or act in respect of RESPs for that child.

Refunds of RESP earnings may be made to a contributor where none of the intended beneficiaries is pursuing post-secondary education by age 21 and the plan has been in place for at least 10 years. Earnings so returned will be taxable income but not earned income for RRSP purposes. However, returned plan earnings may be contributed to an RRSP of the contributor or the contributor's spouse or common-law partner (as defined at any particular time in ¶1113) to the extent the contributor has adequate RRSP contribution room. Remember that to the extent RRSP contributions of earlier years fall short of contribution limits, the unused contribution room accumulates and carries forward indefinitely. Plan earnings received by the contributor which are not contributed to an RRSP (whether because they exceed RRSP contribution room or otherwise) are subject to a special tax of 20% in addition to regular tax payable. See the discussion at ¶2612.65.

RESPs are of two types: group plans and individual plans. In either case the plan is offered under the auspices of a "promoter" who is responsible for the terms, administration and registration of the plan, and for ensuring that the assets are maintained in a trust company. Group plans are typically more rigid, specifying a schedule of payments by the contributor and, generally speaking, controlling the investments made for the plan. Individual plans provide the contributor with greater control over investments made and the timing and amount of educational assistance payments made to beneficiaries. Group plans typically have the virtue of simplicity and more or less compulsory savings. Individual plans are likely to be of greater interest to more sophisticated investors who are accustomed to managing their own investments and are comfortable with seeking tax and investment advice as needed. Plans may be for each child or for all children in a family. Family plans may provide more flexibility to tailor benefits to each child, although individual plans permit transfers of assets to the plans of siblings.

(ITA: 146.1(6), (7); IC 93-3R1; *Registered Education Savings Plans (RESPs)* (RC4092); Income Tax Folio: S3-F10-C1 Qualified Investments – RRSPs, RESPs, RRIFs, RDSPs and TFSAs)

[¶2662] INCOME EARNED

Interest earned on amounts contributed by a subscriber to a registered education savings plan is not income of the subscriber. Benefits received by the student under such a plan must be included in the student's income to the extent of the interest earned on the amounts contributed. See ¶2529d for plan limitations and uses.

Contributions to such plans may not be claimed as charitable donations since the plans do not qualify as registered Canadian charitable organizations.

(ITA: 146.1; IC 93-3R1)

[¶2663] WITHDRAWALS

Funds accumulated in an RESP and used as intended for full-time education are subject to few restrictions. The amount of educational assistance payments withdrawn is limited to $5,000 until the student has completed 13 consecutive weeks in a qualifying educational program. Although normally payments must be in support of qualifying full-time post-secondary education, payments in support of part-time education are permitted for students who cannot enrol full time due to physical or mental impairment.

Generally speaking, an RESP is permitted to make an educational assistance payment (EAP) to an individual only if, at the time of the payment, the individual is enrolled as a student in either a qualifying educational program (which is generally a full-time program) or a specified educational program (which is a part-time program) at a post-secondary educational institution. Individuals enrolled in a qualifying educational program may receive up to $5,000 of EAPs during their first 13-week period of study. Thereafter, there is no dollar limit on the amount of EAPs. Students enrolled in a specified educational program may receive up to $2,500 of EAPs during each 13-week period of study. For 2008 and later taxation years, the requirement that EAPs be made only during periods of enrolment is relaxed by providing a six-month grace period for making EAPs. An RESP may now provide for the payment of an EAP to an individual for up to six months after the individual ceased to be enrolled as a student in a qualifying educational program or a specified educational program, as the case may be. However, this additional flexibility will apply only where the payment would have qualified under the normal rules for EAPs if it had been made immediately before the individual's enrolment ceased. Thus, for example, an individual who had received a $2,000 EAP while enrolled in a ten-week specified educational program would be entitled to receive up to $500 of additional EAPs during the six-month period following the end of the program (that is, without having to enrol in another program). These amendments apply to the 2008 and subsequent taxation years, but they do not apply in respect of cessations of enrolment that occurred before 2008.

(ITA: 146.1(6), (7); IC 93-3R1; *Registered Education Savings Plans (RESPs)* (RC4092); Income Tax Folio: S3-F10-C1 Qualified Investments – RRSPs, RESPs, RRIFs, RDSPs and TFSAs)

[¶2663.10] *Forms and Guide*

The CRA publishes a pamphlet, *Registered Education Savings Plans (RESPs)*, RC4092, which describes the details of the plans and the taxation of accumulated income payments. The CRA also publishes form T1172, *Additional Tax on Accumulated Income Payments from RESPs*, which is required to calculate the additional tax, net of RRSP offset, on these payments.

[¶2664] ROLLOVERS

Generally speaking, a transfer of property from one RESP to another RESP can be made without tax consequences (i) where there is a common beneficiary under the transferor plan and the transferee plan; or (ii) pursuant to changes announced in the 2011 federal Budget, between two plans with siblings as beneficiaries, provided that either the transferee plan allows more than one beneficiary under the plan, or the beneficiary of the transferee plan had not attained 21 years of age when the plan was entered into. For transfers before 2011, the second permitted transfer above was between two sibling plans where the beneficiary under the transferee plan was under 21 years of age.

[¶2665] CANADA EDUCATION SAVINGS GRANTS AND CANADA LEARNING BONDS

[¶2665.05] *Canada Education Savings Grants ("CESGs")*

The Canada Education Savings Grant program creates a further incentive for taxpayers to save through RESPs by providing a direct federal grant to any valid RESP equal to 20% of the first $2,500 per year contributed for each child under 18 years of age. Grants are limited to a specified annual amount. There is also an overall lifetime maximum of $7,200 of grants for each beneficiary of an RESP. The grant itself is not included in calculating the lifetime RESP contribution limit. Thus, a contribution or series of contributions which reach the current $50,000 lifetime limit (for a particular beneficiary) will generate grants in addition to the $50,000, as discussed further below.

The basic annual *grant* limitations are $500 per year. This basic limit is enhanced, beginning in 2005, by doubling the matching rate to 40% on the first $500 of annual contributions to an RESP for the child of a family with income up to the limit of the lowest marginal rate bracket. Such families may also be entitled to benefit from the Canada Learning Bond program discussed in ¶2529d.15. Families with incomes in the second rate bracket will be entitled to a 30% matching rate on the first $500 of annual contributions to an RESP. Family income will be determined under the Canada Child Benefit rules at ¶1498.

The supplemental grants for lower income families mean that the maximum grant is now $600 per year for a family with income below the lowest marginal rate (40% of the first $500 contributed plus 20% of an additional contribution of up to $2,000) and $450 per year for a family with income below the second rate bracket. However, the lifetime grant limit for each child remains $7,200.

For more information on CESGs, see ¶2529d.10.

(*Canada Education Savings Act; IC 93-3R1; Registered Education Savings Plans (RESPs)* (RC4092))

[¶2665.10] *Canada Learning Bonds ("CLBs")*

The Canada Learning Bonds program creates a further inducement (in addition to the CESG program discussed above) for low-income families to set up an RESP for their children.

Essentially, the program provides a $500 Canada Learning Bond (CLB) at birth for children in families that are entitled to the National Child Benefit (NCB) supplement element of the Canada Child Benefit program (see ¶1498). In subsequent years, these children will qualify for $100 CLB instalments until age 15, in each year their family is entitled to the NCB supplement.

Children born after 2003 who are not eligible for the CLB at birth but whose families become entitled to the NCB supplement in a subsequent year will qualify at that time for a $500 CLB. Thereafter, they will qualify for annual $100 CLB instalments, in each year their family is entitled to the NCB supplement.

The CLB will be paid into a registered education savings plan (RESP) established by the family for the child's post-secondary education. Accordingly it will earn income in the plan along with other contributions. An additional $25 will be paid with the initial $500 bond in recognition of the cost of establishing an RESP.

The program is (apparently) synchronized with the Canada Child Benefit program so that families with the requisite income levels who have provided RESP information to the government (and applied for the Canada Child Benefit) will have deposits made automatically. The RESP terms themselves should ensure that the funds are used as intended, and repayment provisions require the trustee to return to the government amounts to which the RESP was not entitled. Adopted children seem to be entitled to the CLB on registration of the RESP and application for the Canada Child Benefit, though of course the total grants will be less to the extent they have fewer years to age 15. Such details as are readily available can be obtained from the Human Resources and Social Development Canada website at www.hrsdc.gc.ca. Look for "Canada Education Savings Program" and then on the next screen "The Canada Learning Bond".

For more information on CESGs, see ¶2529d.15.

(*Canada Education Savings Act; Registered Education Savings Plans (RESPs)* (RC4092); IC 93-3R1)

[¶2666] TRANSFER TO RRSP

As discussed at ¶2529d, Registered Education Savings Plans allow a "subscriber" (typically a parent) to make non-deductible contributions to a plan for the future post-secondary education of plan beneficiaries (typically the children). Although contributions are not deductible, earnings in the plan are not currently taxable, but rather are income of the beneficiaries when paid to them for educational purposes. The contributions themselves can return to the subscriber (or beneficiary) without tax. If plan income is not used within 25 years for the education of beneficiaries, it may be returned to the subscriber (previously it was likely to be forfeited). If plan income is returned to a subscriber, it is taxable income when returned, and in addition is subject to a 20% surtax (12% for residents of Quebec, which runs its own 8% recapture tax in this respect) to offset the tax-free accumulation.

The 20% surtax applies to "accumulated income payments". An accumulated income payment is essentially any distribution that is not:

- an education assistance payment (i.e., a payment to a beneficiary to assist in post-secondary education);
- a refund of contributions made to the plan by the subscriber and payable to the subscriber, its heirs or assigns;
- a payment to a designated educational institution; or
- a transfer to another plan.

Accumulated income payments are subject to surtax in a taxation year to the extent they are:

(1) included in the income of the plan subscriber (but this cannot be a subscriber who became a subscriber because of the death of the original subscriber);

(2) where there is no subscriber (presumably because deceased), included in the income of a person who has been a spouse or common-law partner of the subscriber; or

(3) included in income of someone other than those under the rules in (1) and (2), above.

However, there can be reduction in surtax where payments described in (1) and (2), above, are sheltered by offsetting contributions to an RRSP.

Generally speaking, this means that payments in excess of contributions returned from an RESP to anyone who is not a beneficiary, subscriber, or spouse or common-law partner of a deceased subscriber are both included in income and subject to 20% surtax, with no offset permitted for contributions to an RRSP.

To the extent an RESP subscriber who receives a return of plan income has sufficient RRSP contribution room on hand, the income can be sheltered by contributing it to an RRSP. Contributions of returned plan income (based on contribution room otherwise available) will also offset the 20% surtax, but only to the extent of a lifetime limit of $50,000 per plan.

(ITA: 146.1(1); 204.94; QTA: 1129.63–1129.66; IC 93-3R1; *Registered Education Savings Plans (RESPs)* (RC4092))

[¶2667] PROVINCIAL PLANS

See [¶2529d.20] and [¶2529d.23]

REGISTERED DISABILITY SAVINGS PLANS

[¶2670] GENERAL

The Registered Disability Savings Plan permits parents to contribute funds to a plan to provide for the future expenses of disabled children, and allows the older disabled and their families (and others) to contribute to a plan for later years. Contributions to the plan are not deductible, but income earned in the plan is not taxed while in the plan. Plan investments are, in effect, governed by RRSP investment rules, with certain exceptions. Plan contributions are subject to a lifetime limit of $200,000. Plan contributions will to some extent be matched by government contributions, and, in addition, the government will make continuing contributions for low-income families.

Income is measured under the GST Credit rules (¶1496) for January payments. This means that income determinations look back to the second preceding year, although income thresholds look at the current year. That is, if there were grants or bonds payable in respect of 2016, income would be measured for 2014, although 2016 thresholds would be used. Where the beneficiary is a "qualified dependant" for GST purposes, i.e., has not turned 18 at the end of the year in question, income is the "adjusted net income" of the parent or guardian on whom the child is dependent and the cohabiting spouse or common-law partner of that parent or guardian, as calculated for GST purposes. Essentially, this is income at line 236 of each return, not counting the universal child care benefit (line 117) and the capital gain on property reacquired by the parents on foreclosure (¶518). Where the beneficiary is 18 or older at the end of the year, income is the adjusted net income for GST purposes of the beneficiary and his or her spouse or common-law partner, if any. A child for whom benefits are paid under the *Children's Special Allowances Act* (i.e., a child in foster care) for at least one month in a year is eligible for the high rates of matching grants and the full $1,000 bond amount for that year, regardless of income considerations.

The plans are intended to provide for those with long-term disabilities. Accordingly, there is a provision that government contributions and their associated earnings are subject to a 10-year "holdback", during which they cannot be distributed from the plan and must be paid back to the government if the beneficiary withdraws *any* funds from the plan (including normal annual amounts), loses eligibility for the disability tax credit, or dies. Thus, if money is withdrawn from a RDSP, any bond or grant (and associated investment income) received in the past 10 years must be repaid. However, effective in 2014, the amount of the bonds or grants to be repaid when money is withdrawn from an RDSP will change. The 2012 federal Budget announced a new proportionate repayment rule, under which every $1 withdrawn will require the repayment of $3 of any bonds or grants received in the previous 10 years, up to a maximum of the holdback amount.

(*Canada Disability Savings Act; Canada Disability Savings Regulations;* ITA: 56(1)(*q.1*); 60(*z*); 146.4; 160.2; 205; 206; RC4460 Registered Disability Savings Plan; RC4532 Individual Tax Return for Registered Disability Savings Plan (RDSP); RC4625 Rollover to a Registered Disability Savings Plan (RDSP) Under Paragraph 60(m))

[¶2671] REGISTRATION

Individuals for whom a disability certificate (¶1255) has been accepted for a particular year are eligible in a year of disability covered by the certificate to establish a Registered Disability Savings Plan (RDSP), of which the individual is the beneficiary. The plan must be established by the disabled person, unless that person is under 18 or is not legally competent, in which case a parent or legal representative may establish the plan. As with an RESP or RRSP, the plan itself is a trust established with an "issuer" authorized to carry on the business of offering trust services in Canada. The person who establishes the plan becomes a "director", and has certain duties and obligations. There can be only one plan per beneficiary. The beneficiary must be resident in Canada when the plan is established.

A "qualifying family member" may establish an RDSP for a beneficiary, generally if the beneficiary has attained the age of majority and, in the issuer's opinion after reasonable inquiry, the beneficiary's contractual competence to enter into a disability savings plan at that time is in doubt. A qualifying family member includes a legal parent or spouse or common-law partner of the beneficiary. This temporary measure is effective as of June 29, 2012 until the end of 2018 by which time it is anticipated that provincial and territorial law will be amended to permit a trusted person to enter into a contract on behalf of an individual who may lack capacity.

[¶2672] CONTRIBUTIONS

Contributions can be made by anyone. Typically, they will be made by parents or other family members, but there is no limitation except that the plan directors must approve the contributions. (This permits them to maximize government contributions.) Contributions to the plan are not deductible, but they will be matched in some degree by government contributions, called Canada Disability Savings Grants (CDSGs). As well, the government will put in certain amounts for low-income families regardless of their contributions (Canada Disability Savings Bonds (CDSBs)). The grants and bonds can continue up to the end of the year in which the disabled person reaches the age of 49.

Private contributions (i.e., excluding government contributions) to a plan cannot exceed $200,000, and cannot be made after the year in which the beneficiary turns 59. Private contributions are not refundable; they must be used for the beneficiary or, on death, go to the beneficiary's estate.

[¶2673] CANADA DISABILITY SAVINGS GRANTS AND CANADA DISABILITY SAVINGS BONDS

Matching contributions in the form of Canada disability savings grants (CDSGs) will be calculated as follows.

For families with net incomes equal to or less than the third marginal tax bracket threshold, the government will provide:

- $3 for every $1 on the first $500 of contributions;
- $2 for every $1 on the next $1,000 of contributions.

Thus, the maximum grant is $3,500, reached on a contribution of $1,500.

For families with net income above the third bracket threshold of $90,563 for 2016, the grant is:

- $1 for every $1 on the first $1,000 of contributions.

Grants are subject to a lifetime limit of $70,000 and will not be paid after the end of the year in which the beneficiary reaches the age of 49.

Government contributions in the form of Canada disability savings bonds (CDSBs, as opposed to matching grants) of up to $1,000 per year to a cumulative maximum of $20,000 may also be paid into the plan. The annual maximum $1,000 is paid where income of the beneficiary does not exceed the threshold at which the National Child Benefit Supplement begins to phase out. If income exceeds that threshold, the $1,000 is reduced by a formula under which it expires at the lowest marginal rate threshold. Essentially, the $1,000 is reduced by $1,000 minus income over the threshold divided by the difference between the two thresholds. No more than $20,000 may be paid under this program during the lifetime of the beneficiary.

[¶2674] TAXATION OF DISTRIBUTIONS

Normal payments ("lifetime disability assistance payments") from the plan can commence at any time, but, as discussed above, payments which commence within 10 years of a government contribution will trigger recapture of that contribution. Normal payments, once commenced, must be made at least annually. Payments must commence no later than the year in which the beneficiary turns 60. It appears they can commence at any time, provided plan assets will not fall below the holdback level. Normal payments are closely defined, and generally speaking limited to plan assets divided by life expectancy plus three. Life expectancy is statistically determined unless there is a medical certificate setting out a life expectancy for the particular beneficiary, in which case the certificate governs.

The government contribution elements, and all investment earnings in the plan, are not taxable in the plan. Payments from the plan to the disabled beneficiary are taxable in part. Generally speaking, the non-taxable portion of any payment is the proportion of contributions remaining in the plan divided by total plan assets, not counting the holdback amount. The plan must be terminated if the disability ceases, and the remaining amounts paid to the beneficiary, subject as always to the holdback requirements. The termination payment is, as with ordinary payments, a blended payment, only part of which is taxable. The rules contemplate that the plans will be established by private trust companies, as with RRSPs and RESPs.

Where government contributions prove to have been excessive, because of the holdback rules or otherwise, and have already been paid out to the beneficiary and included in taxable income, they may be recaptured from the beneficiary and deducted from the beneficiary's income when repaid.

Payments from an RDSP will not be counted in means-tested government programs; that is, they will not be included in income reducing GST or Canada Child Benefits. As well, they will not be taken into account to reduce Old Age Security or Employment Insurance benefits.

Amounts in addition to normal payments may be withdrawn from the plan for the beneficiary, subject to two limitations. First, withdrawals will trigger the holdback rule, requiring repayment of government contributions and associated earnings of the past 10 years. Second, where the total of government grants and bonds exceeds private contributions to the plan at the end of a particular year (such plan is referred to as a "primarily government-assisted plan"), only the amount of normal lifetime disability assistance payments (LDAPs) may be withdrawn for the following year. The 2012 federal Budget increased this latter amount that may be withdrawn, effective for 2014. At that time, the amount that can be withdrawn will be the greater of the normal LDAPs for the year, and 10% of the fair market value of the RDSP assets at the beginning of the calendar year (or, if the RDSP owns a locked-in annuity, the sum of 10% of the fair market value of the RDSP assets and the total amount of periodic payments received by the RDSP in the year under the annuity).

Under current rules, beneficiaries of primarily government-assisted plans, once they reach 60 years of age, must withdraw at least the normal LDAP each year. The 2012 federal Budget announced that this minimum withdrawal limit will apply to all RDSPs, beginning in 2014.

If the beneficiary ceases in fact to have, throughout a calendar year, any disability for which a disability certificate can properly be issued, the fund must be terminated and the balance paid to the beneficiary by the end of the following calendar year. The payment will be a blended payment; that is, the portion attributable to private contributions will not be taxed. Note that a cancelled disability certificate itself is not sufficient to terminate the plan; there must in fact be no disability condition. However, contributions cannot be made for a year in which there is no valid certificate at any time. The point is that a parent-initiated plan cannot be wound up by the beneficiary cancelling a certificate and taking all the money while the disability condition still exists. On the other hand, cancelling the certificate will prevent further contributions in subsequent years until it is reinstated.

[¶2675] ROLLOVERS

A tax-deferred rollover is allowed to a taxpayer's Registered Disability Savings Plan (RDSP) from an RRSP, RRIF, RPP, or PRPP upon the death of the annuitant or member under certain circumstances. To qualify for the rollover where the deceased has died after March 3, 2010, the following criteria must be met; the individual holding the RDSP would have been entitled to a deduction under paragraph 60(*l*) of the Act if the contribution made to the RDSP had been made to an RRSP; the individual is a child or grandchild of the deceased and was financially dependent on the deceased by reason of physical or mental infirmity; the contribution is made to a plan where the beneficiary is eligible for the disability tax credit, the beneficiary is less than 59 years old in the calendar year the contribution is made, the beneficiary is resident in Canada, the total contributions do not exceed $200,000, and any contributions not made by the holder of the plan are made with the written consent of the holder of the plan; the contribution is made after June 2011; the individual and the holder of the RDSP designate the contribution in the prescribed form at the time of the contribution (no form prescribed at the time of writing); and the contribution is the lesser of the total specified RDSP payments made in the year (or 60 days after the end of the year) or the total amount of eligible proceeds included in the taxpayer's computed income for that year.

Lump-sum death benefits paid out of a "specified pension plan" (i.e., the Saskatchewan Pension Plan) qualify for a rollover to an RDSP in the same manner as rollovers from RPP death benefits. This applies to transfers made after March 3, 2010.

For a more detailed description of RDSPs, see ¶2529h.

(ITA: 60.02; RC4460 Registered Disability Savings Plan; RC4625 Rollover to a Registered Disability Savings Plan (RDSP) Under Paragraph 60(m))

[¶2675.10] *Rollover from RESP to RDSP*

New rules first announced in the 2012 federal Budget provide that accumulated income earned in an RESP (see ¶1001.05) can be rolled over on a tax-free basis to an RDSP

(¶1001.05). The new rules provide that a subscriber of an RESP and a holder of an RDSP may make a joint election in prescribed form to transfer the income of the RESP to the RDSP if, at the time of the election, the RESP beneficiary is the beneficiary under the RDSP and

- the beneficiary has a severe and prolonged mental impairment that prevents him or her or can reasonably be expected to prevent him or her from enrolling in post-secondary education; or

- the payment is made in the 35th year after the year in which the RESP began, or it is made in the 10th or subsequent year after the RESP began and each beneficiary under the RESP is at least 21 years old of age and is not eligible to receive educational assistance payments.

The promoter of the RESP must file the election with the Minister "without delay". If the election is properly made, the income transferred from the RESP to the RDSP will not be included in the beneficiary's (or any other person's) income. The amount so transferred on a rollover basis is subject to the lifetime $200,000 contribution limit for RDSPs.

The rollover applies beginning in 2014.

[¶2676] DEATH

If the deceased was a beneficiary under a registered disability savings plan ("RDSP"), all amounts remaining in the plan after any required repayment of government grants and bonds must be paid to the beneficiary's estate by December 31 following the calendar year in which the beneficiary dies. The taxable portion of the payments must be included in the income of the beneficiary's estate's taxation year in which the payment is made, and, therefore, is not reported on the deceased's terminal return. Payments made to the deceased while the person was alive are included in the deceased's income. The taxable portion is the amount of the payment in excess of the "non-taxable portion", the latter of which is essentially a fraction of the payment equalling the amounts of contributions formerly made to the plan or other plans of the beneficiary (net of non-taxable portions paid out previously) divided by the fair market value of the property held by the plan immediately before the payments.

(ITA: 146.4(6); 146.4(7))

[¶2676.10] *Rollover to RDSP Upon Death of Parent or Grandparent*

In the March 2010 federal Budget, the government announced a new rollover (inclusion followed by a deduction) similar to the existing deduction provided for financially dependent infirm children and grandchildren of a deceased plan holder of an RRSP, RRIF, or RPP. The existing rules generally allow the deduction where the child uses the proceeds received upon the death to make a contribution to the child's RRSP or to purchase a life annuity or an annuity payable to age 90.

These rollover rules will allow the child or grandchild to make a similar deduction where the proceeds are contributed to an RDSP of which they are a beneficiary. The rollover will be permitted only to the extent that there is sufficient RDSP contribution room. The contribution must be made in the year of receipt of the proceeds or within 60 days after the end of the year. The new rules generally apply to deaths occurring after March 3, 2010 where the contributions are made after June 2011. However, transitional rules will allow a similar deduction in situations where the death of the RRSP or RRIF annuitant or RPP member occurred in 2008, 2009, or 2010 and the contribution is made after June 2011 and before 2012. See the discussion in Chapter 19 at ¶1914.17.

[¶2677] SPECIFIED DISABILITY SAVINGS PLANS

In a "specified year" of an RDSP of a beneficiary, the withdrawal limits that apply where total government-provided Canada Disability Savings Grants ("CDSG") and Canada Disability Savings Bonds ("CDSB") made into the plan before the year exceed the private contributions into the plan before the year, do not apply in that specified year. Prior to 2011, a "specified year" was the year in which a medical doctor certifies in writing that the beneficiary's state of health was such that, in the professional opinion of the medical doctor, the beneficiary was not likely to survive more than five years, and each of the five calendar years following the particular year. The 2011 federal Budget amended the definition somewhat by extending the amount of specified years, by including, if the plan is a "specified disability savings plan" ("SDSP"), the year of the medical certification plus each subsequent taxation year.

An SDSP is essentially an RDSP under which the beneficiary is certified, as discussed above, as having an expected life of no more than five years, where the plan holder makes an election to have the plan be an SDSP and proper notification is provided to the CRA.

Under another amendment from the 2011 federal Budget, if the plan is an SDSP, the 10-year repayment rule, under which CDSG grants and CDSB bonds paid into the plan within the previous ten years must be repaid if withdrawn, is relaxed. As long as the taxable portions of withdrawals (CCSGs, CDSBs, and income earned in the plan) in a year do not exceed $10,000, the grants and bonds do not have to be repaid. If non-taxable withdrawals are also made, the total withdrawals can exceed $10,000. However, if the $10,000 taxable amount is exceeded in a year, the plan ceases to be an SDSP, meaning that the 10-year repayment rule will be operative with respect to grants and bonds still in the plan.

The 2011 Budget amendments received Royal Assent on June 26, 2011, and apply to the 2011 and subsequent year. However, a transitional rule applies to beneficiaries who obtain the medical certification before 2012, in which case, the 2011 $10,000 taxable withdrawal limit as described above can be utilized in 2012, effectively making it a $20,000 taxable withdrawal limit in 2012.

REGISTERED SUPPLEMENTARY UNEMPLOYMENT BENEFIT PLANS

[¶2681] GENERAL

A Supplementary Unemployment Benefit Plan is a plan established by an employer or group of employers to top up employees' employment insurance (EI) benefits during a period of unemployment because of training, sickness, accident or disability, maternal or parental leave, or a temporary stoppage of work (i.e., temporary lay-off).

Where you, as an employer, make payments to a trustee in trust, exclusively for the payment of periodic amounts to employees or former employees who are or may be laid off for any temporary or indefinite period, such payments are deductible in computing your business income if they were made in the year or within 30 days after the end of the year providing the plan has been registered with the Minister of National Revenue.

Any amount you receive as an employer from a trustee under a registered supplementary unemployment benefit plan to which you have made payments, resulting from an amendment, modification or termination of the plan, is to be included in your income.

The trust itself is not taxable on its income as the employee or former employee who receives the periodic payments is taxable on such amounts when received by him.

If you wish to establish such a plan, you should obtain a copy of Information Circular IC 72-5R2 from your Tax Services Office. As is recommended for new pension and deferred profit sharing plans, professional advice should be obtained before attempting to establish this type of plan.

(ITA: 145; IC 72-5R2 Registered Supplementary Unemployment Benefit Plans)

[¶2681a] CONTRIBUTIONS

Where an employer makes a payment to a trustee in trust under a supplementary employment benefit plan, exclusively for the payment of periodic amounts to employees or former employees who are or may be laid off for any temporary or indefinite period, such payments are deductible in computing your business income if they were made in the year or within 30 days after the end of the year providing the plan has been registered with the Minister of National Revenue.

(ITA: 145(5))

[¶2681b] WITHDRAWALS

Any amount received by an employee from a trustee under a registered supplementary unemployment benefit plan (sometimes referred to as a guaranteed annual wage plan), must be included in income.

Any amount received by an employer on the amendment or wind-up of a supplementary employment benefit plan must be included in the income of the employer in the year received.

(ITA: 56(1)(g); 145(3); 145(4))

EMPLOYEE LIFE AND HEALTH TRUSTS

[¶2682] GENERAL

In general terms, an employee life and health trust (an "ELHT") is a trust under which employer contributions to the trust are used to fund "designated employee benefits" for the employer's employees, their spouse or common-law partners, and related members of their households. The "designated employee benefits" are defined to mean benefits from a group sickness or accident insurance plan, a group term life insurance policy, or a private health services plan.

The ELHT rules allow employer's contributions to the plan to be deductible in the year of contribution to the extent of benefits provided in those years. Basically, an employer's deduction in the year is limited to the amount of the contribution that enable the ELHT to pay premiums to a private insurance company for insurance coverage for the year or a prior year in respect of the beneficiaries, or otherwise provide group life term insurance, or designated employee benefits that are payable in the year or a prior year to the beneficiaries. Excess contributions in the year that enable the trust to provide or pay these types of benefits in a subsequent year are generally deductible in that subsequent year. Special rules apply to multi-employer ELHTs who, among other things, are required to contribute pursuant to a collective agreement and whose contributions are based on the number of hours worked by an employee or some other measure that is specific to the employee (subsection 144.1(6)).

There are various conditions required of an ELHT in order for these measures to apply. For example, the ELHT must have at least one class of beneficiaries that contains at least 25% of all of the beneficiaries of the trust who are employees of the employer, and at least 75% of the members of the class must be employees who are not "key employees". The rights under the ELHT of each key employee cannot be more advantageous than the rights of this one class of beneficiaries. In general terms, a "key employee" in a taxation year means (1) an employee who was at any time in the taxation year or in a preceding taxation year a "specified employee" of the employer (generally, an employee owning 10% or more of any class of shares in the employer, or who does not deal at arm's length with the employer), or (2) an employee whose employment income in any two of the five taxation years preceding the year exceeded five times the Year's Maximum Pensionable Earnings used for CPP purposes.

(ITA: 6(1)(a)(i); 18(1)(o.3); 20(1)(s); 56(1)(z.2); 144.1)

[¶2682a] CONTRIBUTIONS

Employer contributions to the ELHT are not themselves taxable benefits for the employees. The new rules will generally preserve the same tax treatment for designated employee benefits from the trust as if they had been received directly without the trust.

Employee contributions to the ELHT are allowed, and the trust can identify the designated employee benefits to which they relate such that the contributions will retain their character for certain provisions of the Act. The trust must identify the contributions as such at the time of the contribution. For example, if properly "identified" by the trust, employee contributions made to a group sickness or accident benefits plan will generally be deductible for the employee against future payments out of the plan (see above). Employee contributions that relate to premiums under a private health services plan will qualify for the medical tax credit. The explanatory notes to the provision indicate that the trust should notify the employer of the type of contribution, who should then report the contribution on the employee's pay stub.

[¶2682b] WITHDRAWALS

Private health services benefits received by an employee through a private health services plan in the trust (e.g., health or dental services) are generally tax-free. Payments out of a group sickness or accident insurance plan will be included in the income of the recipient employee if any employer contributions have been made to the plan, with a corresponding deduction for previous employee contributions; see ¶328. If no employer contributions had been made to the group sickness or accident plan, the payment will be non-taxable. If employer contributions to the ELHT are used to purchase group term life insurance, the prescribed value of the group term life insurance coverage will be a taxable employment benefit during each year of coverage under the plan; see ¶317.

Other payments out of the ELHT to an employee will generally be taxable.

LIFE INSURANCE POLICIES

[¶2683] GENERAL

In general, life insurance policies are of two types, namely term insurance and whole life. Term insurance simply provides a specified payment in the event of untimely death. The cost is based on statistical life expectancy in the context of personal medical history. Whole life insurance includes a savings component. The savings element can sometimes be drawn out (as "policy loans") from the insurance policy.

Premiums are not deductible. In an environment of high market yields on investments and a plethora of commercial and government-sanctioned tax shelters, the returns on investments in life insurance were considered scant. As well, the government applied its three-year (and now annual) accrual rules to certain policies, and provided some limitations on the ability to draw out accumulated income as policy loans free of current tax.

Nevertheless, there remain life insurance policies with savings features which can offer accumulated income subject to only 15% tax and potentially useful borrowings against policy value. As well, typically there will be no tax on death.

Investment in a savings feature life insurance policy should be treated as an investment; the specific returns on the policy after tax, and the accessibility of capital after tax, should be compared to other contemplated investments. In the present investment and tax shelter environment, the comparison may be more favourable to insurance than anticipated.

[¶2683.05] *Leveraged Life Insurance Arrangements*

Arrangements involving the acquisition of an insurance policy combined with a loan are commonly called "leveraged insurance arrangements (LIA)" and were very popular. There are several variations of these structures but the one that has attracted the most attention recently is referred to as a "10/8 arrangement".

A 10/8 arrangement involves the acquisition of a "typical" universal life insurance policy, i.e., a life insurance policy which has a savings component. The taxpayer acquires the policy and then borrows against it either by means of a policy loan or separate credit facility. The interest rate on the borrowing is set at 10% and the rate of return on the saving component within the policy is set at 8%. If structured properly, the 10% interest would be deductible for tax purposes, while the 8% return was not be taxable since it was earned within the policy itself.

The CRA attacked 10/8 arrangements primarily on the basis that 10% interest was unreasonable and denied the deduction. As a result, in the 2013 federal Budget, new legislation was introduced to effectively prevent the use of a 10/8 arrangement going forward.

Legislation now provides that if a policy is defined as a "10/8 policy", interest expense related to the borrowing will not be deductible, no part of the insurance premium will be deductible and the amount to be added to the capital dividend account (in the case of a corporate taxpayer) will be reduced by the amount of the borrowing. A policy will be a 10/8 policy if the rate of return on the policy is determined by reference to the rate of interest on borrowing and would not be available within the policy without the borrowing. A policy will also be a 10/8 policy if the maximum amount of the investment account is determined by reference to the borrowing. These amendments are effective for taxation years that end after March 20, 2013.

A different LIA that involves borrowing but includes the purchase of an annuity was also "attacked" in the 2013 federal Budget. If an arrangement exists whereby an insurance policy is acquired and funds are borrowed which are used to acquire an annuity (the payments from which would normally be used to fund the insurance premiums), this will constitute an "LIA policy". If an LIA policy exists, no part of the insurance premium will be deductible, the value of premiums paid under the annuity contract will be included in computing the fair market value of shares deemed to have been disposed on death of the insured and no addition to the capital dividend account will be allowed.

[¶2684] PREMIUMS

The cost of premiums paid under life insurance policies is not generally deductible (except where the insurance is an employee benefit; see ¶741). However, a deduction is permitted under paragraph 20(1)(*e*.2) of the Act in respect of life insurance premiums under a policy that is assigned as collateral for a loan, provided (1) the assignment is required by the lender; (2) the lender is a Canadian (or Quebec) licensed bank, trust company, credit union, insurance company, or any other corporation whose principal business is lending money to or purchasing debt obligations from arm's length persons; and (3) the interest payable on the loan is either deductible or would be deductible but for the limitations on interest and property on vacant land (¶665), the soft cost limitations (¶771), or the capitalized interest election (¶1073).

Pursuant to amendments first announced in the 2013 federal Budget, the deduction is not allowed for premiums paid in respect of an "LIA policy" or a "10/8 policy".

Under the rules permitting deduction of premiums, a whole life policy could be assigned as collateral, but only the "net cost of pure insurance" for the period would be deductible. However, an alternative limitation provides that the full premiums paid will only be deductible to the extent they may reasonably be considered to relate to the amount owing under the loan for which the policy is collateral. Thus if the policy is for $500,000, but the average loan balance during the taxation year is $200,000, the deduction for premiums will be limited to the lesser of (a) $^2/_5$ (40%) of the premiums payable and (b) the net cost of pure insurance for the policy in respect of the year. The net cost of pure insurance is determined by the insurer in accordance with regulations. Typically the insurer will provide this information on request.

Although a self-employed person cannot usually deduct the cost of life insurance on his or her own life (subject to the rules above), it is possible to deduct premiums paid for an employee's life insurance policy under ordinary rules concerning the payment of remuneration. Typically, this occurs where the employee or employee's family is a beneficiary, and the premiums paid by the employer are a taxable fringe benefit to the employee. By far the most common example of this is group term life insurance provided by employers for employees. In all cases where an employer may deduct insurance payments, whether for employees' life insurance or otherwise, there may be restrictions to the company on the timing of the deductions; see ¶741 and ¶753.

(ITA: 20(1)(e), (e.1), (e.2); Window on Canadian Tax: 8228; IT-309R2 Premiums on life insurance used as collateral)

[¶2685] WITHDRAWALS

[¶2685.05] *Insurance Advances to the Terminally Ill*

In a Technical Opinion (found in CRA Document No. 2002-0138895), the CRA said:

> We understand that the Financial Services Commission of Ontario has adopted a recommendation that life insurance companies should provide funds to terminally ill policyholders who have a life expectancy of less than 24 months. While not legally obligated to provide funding to these policyholders, many life insurers are considering implementing the recommendation by providing loans to the policyholders out of the insurer's general funds. As security for the loan payment received from the life insurer, the policyholder assigns the life insurance policy to the life insurer. Provided there is no amendment made to the life insurance policy, it is our general view that the payment of the loan proceeds by the life insurer would not cause the CRA to view the life insurance policy to have been disposed of by the individual for purposes of section 148 of the Act and a new life insurance policy to have been issued. However, where such a loan is provided for under the terms and conditions of the life insurance policy, the loan would be a "policy loan" as defined in subsection 148(9) of the Act, and would result in a disposition of an interest in the policy pursuant to paragraph (*b*) of the definition of "disposition" in subsection 148(9) of the Act.

[¶2686] CAPITAL GAINS — PROCEEDS OF LIFE INSURANCE POLICIES

In 1983, amendments to the *Income Tax Act* were introduced which altered the taxation of life insurance policies and annuities. These amendments are generally designed to include in income the actual or accruing income on the savings element of life insurance policies and annuities (see ¶432). However, the mortality gain arising on the death of the insured remains exempt.

If you have an interest in a life insurance policy and become entitled to receive proceeds in respect of a disposition of your interest in the policy during the lifetime of the insured, a portion of the amounts received may be subject to tax. The taxable portion will be the excess of the "proceeds of disposition" over the "adjusted cost basis" of your interest in the insurance policy. Your insurance company will advise you annually of the amount of any "proceeds" you have become entitled to receive under the income tax rules. Technically, you are required to make your own calculation of "adjusted cost basis" to determine the portion of the proceeds, if any, which must be included in income, but most insurance companies will assist their policyholders in making this calculation.

There is no income inclusion in respect of a disposition of the following life insurance policies:

(1) a policy that is issued pursuant to: (i) a registered pension fund or plan; (ii) a registered retirement savings plan; (iii), a registered retirement income fund; (iv) an income averaging annuity contract; (v) a deferred profit sharing plan; (vi) a tax-free savings account or a pooled registered pension plan and

(2) an annuity contract that is purchased with the proceeds of a registered retirement savings plan received as a refund of premiums by a surviving spouse or common-law partner over 71 years of age, or by a child that was dependent by virtue of physical or mental infirmity.

A disposition of a term certain annuity contract after November 12, 1981 will be subject to tax as set out above.

"Proceeds of disposition" of an interest in an insurance policy will include all amounts which you become entitled to receive as a result of surrender, disposition by operation of law, the maturity of the policy, policy dividends except policy dividends after December 20, 1991 automatically applied to pay a premium or pay down a policy loan, or certain amounts received in respect of policy loans after March 31, 1978. "Proceeds of disposition" with respect to a policy loan after March 31, 1978 will be equal to the lesser of the amount of the loan and the excess of the cash surrender value of the policy immediately before the loan was made over the policy loans outstanding at that time. However, an assignment of the policy for the purpose of securing a loan will not, in itself, be considered as the disposition of an interest in the policy, nor will a lapse of the policy as a result of unpaid premiums if the policy is reinstated within 60 days after the end of the calendar year in which the lapse occurred. Nor will payments under a policy received as a disability benefit or an accidental death benefit, annuity payments and payments on death for policies, other than annuity contracts, acquired prior to December 2, 1982 or for exempt policies or prescribed annuities issued after December 1, 1982. (Exempt policy is a complex technical term prescribed by regulations. Your insurance company will inform you as to whether or not your policy is exempt.)

There are certain additional circumstances in which a life insurance policy or annuity contract is deemed to have been disposed of. These are as follows:

(1) On the death of a holder of a life insurance policy, or of the insured or the annuitant under a life insurance policy (other than an exempt policy) issued after December 1, 1982 or an annuity contract (other than a life annuity contract issued prior to November 13, 1981 or a prescribed annuity contract) the policyholder is deemed to have disposed of the interest in the policy or the annuity immediately before his or her death for proceeds equal to the accumulating fund. The policyholder acquires the policy at a cost equal to the accumulating fund after death.

(2) When a life insurance policy acquired after December 1, 1982 or a life insurance policy acquired before December 2, 1982 which becomes subject to the income accrual rules, as a result of a premium payment and increase in the death benefit on death after that date, ceases to be an exempt policy, the policyholder is deemed to dispose of it for proceeds equal to the accumulating fund and to reacquire it at a cost equal to the proceeds at that time. Exceptions to this deemed disposition rule apply where the policy ceases to be an exempt policy as a consequence of the death of the insured or at a time when the insured is totally and permanently disabled.

If you dispose of a part of a policy or annuity contract acquired after December 1, 1982, only the proportion of the adjusted cost basis attributable to the part disposed of will be deductible in determining the income resulting from the disposition. This rule does not apply to a deemed disposition arising as a result of an entitlement to a policy dividend or to a policy loan. The proportion of the adjusted cost basis of a policy that may be deducted on a partial disposition is the ratio of the proceeds to its accumulating fund.

A payment out of a life annuity contract entered into after November 16, 1978 and before November 13, 1981 that is not an annuity payment, loan or a dividend will be treated as a disposition of an interest in a life insurance policy. If you are in receipt of such payment from a life annuity contract, you will be taxed to the extent the payment exceeds the adjusted cost basis of the policy.

"Adjusted cost basis" of your interest in an insurance policy means:

(1) Cost of acquiring your interest in the policy (including amounts paid to another person from whom the policy was purchased); plus

(2) All amounts paid by you or on your behalf as premiums under the policy and any non-refundable prepaid premium paid after November 12, 1981. Excluded are costs incurred after May 31, 1985 that relate to accidental death and disability benefits and to certain additional risks for policies acquired after December 1, 1982; plus

(3) Interest paid after 1977 on a policy loan, if the interest was not deductible in computing income (see ¶1063); plus

(4) All portions of annuity payments made to a non-resident that were subject to withholding tax; plus

(5) Amounts previously taxed on a partial disposition of the policy; plus

(6) Amounts included in income from a policy subject to the income accrual rules; plus

(7) Repayments after March 31, 1978 of policy loans outstanding at that time or received after that time to the extent they constituted proceeds of disposition, except for the portion of such repayments which is deductible; plus

(8) The mortality gain with respect to life annuity contracts that are subject to the income accrual; plus

(9) The excess of the cash surrender value on the first anniversary date after March 31, 1977 over the adjusted cost basis on that date, using the prior definition (your insurance company should be able to supply you with this information),

MINUS the aggregate of:

(10) Prior proceeds of disposition;

(11) Policy loans owing on March 31, 1978 including interest owing;

(12) The capital element of an annuity payment previously deducted;

(13) The net cost of pure insurance, as determined by prescribed regulations at the end of each calendar year for taxation years that commence after May 31, 1985 of a life insurance policy acquired after December 1, 1982 that is not an annuity contract (this will be supplied by your insurance company);

(14) Annuity payments made after 1982 in respect of annuity contracts which are subject to the income accrual rules; and

(15) The mortality loss in respect of a life annuity contract.

Where under the terms of a life insurance policy last acquired before December 2, 1982, you become entitled before the death of the insured to receive an annuity in respect of all of your interest in the policy (except policy dividends), then you will determine the amount to be included in income under the rules for annuities (see ¶480) and the cost of the annuity contract will be deemed to be your "adjusted cost basis" in the insurance policy immediately before the first annuity payment. Where an insurance policy is acquired after December 1, 1982, its conversion into an annuity triggers a disposition with proceeds equivalent to cash surrender value.

Where you have an interest in a life insurance policy and you sell your interest or transfer it in any manner to a person with whom you do not deal at arm's length, you will be deemed to have received proceeds of disposition equal to the cash surrender value of your interest in the policy at the time of transfer, and the transferee will be deemed to have acquired the policy at its cash surrender value. The same rule will apply if you dispose of the policy by gift, bequest, distribution from a corporation, or by operation of law to any person, including persons with whom you deal at arm's length. These rules do not apply to a deemed disposition that arises on death in respect of life insurance policies acquired after December 1, 1982 other than exempt policies and in respect of annuities (other than life annuity contracts acquired prior to November 13, 1981).

There are provisions to transfer a policy to an insured spouse, common-law partner, or child on a rollover basis. Where a spouse or common-law partner is not also insured under a life insurance policy or annuity, provision is made for transfers to a spouse or common-law partner or former spouse or common-law partner on the same tax basis as the transfer of other capital property (¶531), except that the provisions for transfer at cost are mandatory rather than elective. Special cost base adjustments to the policy may apply on the spousal/partner rollover.

(ITA: 148(1), (2), (4), (6), (7), (9); ITR: Part III Annuities and Life Insurance Policies)

[¶2687] DEATH BENEFITS

Death benefits received under life insurance policies are not taxable, since they are specifically exempted under the law.

However, gains arising at the time of maturity of a life insurance policy, or upon cancellation or transfer of the policy before maturity, are taxable as discussed at ¶981.

[¶2688] SEGREGATED FUNDS

A segregated fund life insurance policy is a policy which fluctuates in value depending upon the fair market value of investments held by the insurance company in a "segregated fund" for the benefit of the policyholders. It is similar in concept to a combination of an insurance policy plus an interest in a mutual fund. For tax purposes the fund is treated as a trust.

If you have an interest in a segregated fund life insurance policy, you will be taxable each year on amounts allocated to you by the insurance company in respect of the income from the investments in the segregated fund. This allocation may include an allocation of capital gains, capital losses, dividends from taxable Canadian corporations, or income from foreign sources and foreign income tax thereon, in which case you will be entitled to claim a dividend tax credit (¶1425) or foreign tax credit (¶1450) respectively. The amounts allocated to you which must be included in your income will not necessarily be paid to you by the insurance company.

Your insurance company will advise you by form T3 of all amounts allocated to you from income of the segregated fund, and the amount of dividends from taxable Canadian corporations, foreign source income, and foreign tax paid included thereon. Taxation and reporting of these items are discussed in Chapter 4.

When you dispose of your segregated fund policy, you may have a capital gain or a capital loss. This will be determined by subtracting your adjusted cost base from your proceeds of disposition. The rules in Chapter 5 will be applicable.

AMATEUR ATHLETES' RESERVE FUNDS

[¶2691] GENERAL

The regime described below deals specifically with tax payable on amounts received by or on behalf of individuals who are amateur athletes. An amateur athlete is defined as an individual (other than a trust) who is a member of a registered Canadian amateur athletic association, who is eligible to compete as a Canadian national team member in an international sporting event sanctioned by an international sports federation, and who is not a professional athlete who receives compensation for, or income attributable to, activities as a player or athlete in a professional sport.

Where an individual who is an amateur athlete enters into an arrangement to deposit specific types of income into a qualifying account administered by either an eligible national sports organization or another third-party issuer, a trust ("amateur athlete trust") is deemed to be created for the benefit of that individual. Property held under the arrangement is considered to be property of the trust, with the Canadian sports organization or other third-party issuer as trustee and the athlete as beneficiary. The trust would be exempt from income tax. However, any amounts distributed by the organization under the arrangement, or for the benefit of the athlete, are deemed to be payments from the trust received by the athlete and subject to tax as income from business or property. Accordingly, associated expenses incurred by the athlete can be deducted in computing income.

Under the eligibility standards of certain international sport federations, in order to preserve the eligibility status of an athlete for international competition, certain types of income earned by the athlete must be deposited with, controlled and administered by the applicable national sport organization. In Canada, such national sport organizations are typically registered charities for income tax purposes (see Chapter 12). Under these rules, to preserve international competition eligibility, any arrangement under which amounts earned by an athlete are required by international sport rules to be held by a tax-registered Canadian national sport organization will result in the creation of a trust for tax purposes with the national sport organization as trustee. The trust is deemed to be created on the later of the day the first payment is received and January 1, 1992. Although not effective until 1992, a taxpayer may elect to have the provisions apply to any earlier year ending after 1987, provided the taxpayer was resident in Canada throughout the year.

A trust can also be created where an athlete enters into a "qualifying arrangement" with a third-party issuer to deposit qualifying performance income, interest, or other income attributable to property of the trust into an eligible account controlled and administered by the issuer for the benefit of the individual. The third-party issuer is deemed to be the trustee of the trust and must be a mandatory signatory on any payment from the account. A "qualifying arrangement" generally includes an account offered by a financial institution, credit union, or insurance company that is maintained for the exclusive benefit of an individual, but does not include an RRSP or TFSA.

Where the athlete is a non-resident at the time of deemed wind-up of the trust, the amount of the deemed distribution is reduced to 60% of the value of the trust. This is intended to provide the trustee with the tax payable at a 40% rate (36% in 2015 and prior years), and this tax will be required of the trustee organization at that time.

The February 11, 2014 Budget proposed to allow the income placed in such a trust to qualify as "earned income" for RRSP purposes. The measure was enacted, applicable to 2011 and subsequent taxation years.

(ITA: 12(1)(*z*); 143.1; 149(1)(*l*); 149(1)(*v*); 212(1)(*u*); 214(3))

[¶2691a] CONTRIBUTIONS

"Qualifying performance income" is defined as endorsement income, prize money, or income from public appearances or speeches received by an individual who was, at any time in the year, an amateur athlete and was not at any time a professional athlete, and which may reasonably be considered to be in connection with the individual's participation as an amateur athlete in one or more international sporting events. Where an individual contributes eligible income earned in the 2008 taxation year to a qualifying arrangement with a third-party issuer before March 3, 2009, that income will be deemed to be income of the trust for the 2009 taxation year and not income of the individual for the 2008 taxation year, where the individual so elects by the filing due-date of their 2008 return.

[¶2691b] WITHDRAWALS

Revenues placed in a qualifying trust are taxed on the earlier of two dates:

(1) the date the funds are distributed to the athlete or

(2) eight years after the creation of the trust or the last year in which the athlete was eligible to compete as a Canadian national team member in an international sporting event, whichever comes first.

Where an individual has not competed in an international sporting event as a Canadian national team member for eight years, the trust will be deemed to be wound up and the amounts held by the trust at the end of the year are deemed to be distributed to the athlete at that time, and are therefore subject to tax. The eight-year period commences with the later of the last year in which the athlete so competed and the year in which the trust was created. For an arrangement entered into prior to 1992, the trust is nevertheless deemed to be created on January 1, 1992.

[¶2691c] DEATH

Where the athlete dies, the trust is effectively considered wound up immediately before death, with its value included in income for the year of death or, if the athlete is non-resident at the time of death, deemed distribution of 64% with the balance assessed as a special tax payable by the trustee.

ELIGIBLE FUNERAL ARRANGEMENTS

[¶2692] GENERAL

The CRA defines an Eligible Funeral Arrangement (EFA) as an arrangement established and maintained by a qualifying person (e.g., a funeral director or cemetery operator) for the sole purpose of funding funeral or cemetery services for one or more individuals. An EFA must have one or more custodians, each of whom was resident in Canada when the arrangement was established. A custodian could be either a trustee of a trust governed by the arrangement or, if no trust is involved, a qualifying person.

Contributions made to an EFA are not deductible in computing taxable income, however it is possible to contribute up to $35,000 per person for eligible funeral and cemetery care services. These contributions are in the form of commercial contracts with service providers licensed or authorized under provincial law to provide such services. Since these are commercial contracts, they are subject to the commercial cautions and concerns one must have when advancing funds for the prepayment of services. Providers of these services, although provincially regulated, are not necessarily governed by the regulatory and disclosure rules which govern, for example, trust companies (although they may choose to hold the funds through a trust rather than directly).

Funeral services include property and services that relate directly to funeral arrangements of the individual in Canada. Funeral services provided outside Canada would not qualify. However, it is understood that preparation and transportation back to Canada of the body of a person who died outside Canada would be included. Funeral notices, transportation of family, and a reception after the funeral are apparently also included.

Cemetery services include property such as interment vaults, markers, flowers, liners, urns, wreaths and shrubs, and services relating to cemetery arrangements in Canada. They include property and services funded out of a cemetery care trust (a trust established under provincial law for the care and maintenance of a cemetery). Funds used to purchase a burial right or an interest in a building or property used for burial purposes are not considered to be paid for cemetery services unless applied as a contribution to a cemetery care trust (sometimes called a perpetual care fund).

In some provinces, funeral and cemetery services cannot be provided by the same operator. The Department of Finance has indicated that, in such cases, an individual can have one "eligible funeral arrangement" for funeral services and one for cemetery services.

Subject to the rules below for transfers after December 20, 2002, direct transfers of funds can be made from one eligible arrangement to another without incurring tax liability; however, funds cannot be withdrawn and recontributed without incurring tax on the withdrawal.

The upshot of all these rules is that non-deductible contributions can be made for funeral or cemetery purposes and earn income free of tax. To the extent the contributed amounts and the earnings accumulated on them are in fact used for funeral and cemetery services, they remain free of tax when so used. It would seem that contributions can be made not only on behalf of the contributor, but also on behalf of anyone else, such as a parent, spouse or common-law partner, or child. It would also seem that you could pay the funeral or cemetery expenses of someone else out of your own "eligible funeral arrangement" (but not expand the contribution limits thereby). Given the value of tax-free earnings, relatively small contributions at an early age should provide substantial funds when necessary.

- *Planning Point:*

  If you have surplus funds (in excess of those needed to fund your own RRSP contribution), consider funding an eligible funeral arrangement. A small contribution at a young age can build up to a substantial amount which need not be paid out of the tax-paid savings of your estate or family when you die. Funding plans for a spouse or common-law partner or other relatives may be similarly beneficial.

(ITA: 148.1; Tax Topics: No. 1301, February 14, 1997; IT-531)

[¶2692a] CONTRIBUTIONS

It is possible to contribute up to $35,000 per person for eligible funeral and cemetery care services. These contributions are in the form of commercial contracts with service providers licensed or authorized under provincial law to provide such services. Since these are commercial contracts, they are subject to the commercial cautions and concerns one must have when advancing funds for the prepayment of services. Providers of these services, although provincially regulated, are not necessarily governed by the regulatory and disclosure rules which govern, for example, trust companies (although they may choose to hold the funds through a trust rather than directly).

Contributions for these services are not deductible, but the funds contributed may (under the terms of a particular contract) earn income which is not subject to tax.

Contributions for any particular individual cannot exceed:

- for an arrangement that covers only funeral services, $15,000;
- for an arrangement that covers only cemetery services, $20,000; and
- for an arrangement that covers both funeral and cemetery services, $35,000.

Contributions need not be made at once, but may be made piecemeal over time so long as the overall limits are not exceeded.

[¶2692b] WITHDRAWALS

To the extent amounts in the trust are used for the payment of funeral or cemetery services for an individual, they are not taxable. However, funds in excess of contributions which are for any reason returned to anyone or used other than for permissible purposes are subject to taxation in the hands of the recipient as discussed at ¶984. Attribution rules (¶2529) would seem to apply where warranted. The CRA has said that a direct transfer of excess funds to a funeral arrangement for another person would not be subject to tax, although it said further that this is an anomaly not contemplated by the drafters and subject to correction in future technical amendments.

[¶2692c] TRANSFERS

Technical amendments first published December 20, 2002, effective for transfers made after that date, provide specific rules for transfers from one EFA account to another. In general terms, these rules are:

- A new provision deems the transferred amount to be distributed to the individual from whose EFA account the amount is transferred. However, if that individual is deceased, the amount is deemed to be distributed to the individual to whose EFA account the amount is transferred. This ensures that the transfer is included in income (to the extent that it does not exceed the income accumulated in the transferor account).

- A new provision deems the transferred amount to be a contribution made to the recipient EFA account other than by way of transfer. This ensures that the earnings portion of the transferred amount is not taxed again when it is distributed from the recipient EFA account.

- The provision that requires EFA distributions to be included in income is amended to ensure that the determination of the amount that can subsequently be distributed from the transferor EFA account on a tax-free basis is reduced by the portion of the transferred amount that was not included in income (i.e., that portion of the transferred amount that represents a return of contributions).

- A new provision provides that these new rules do not apply if the transferor and the recipient EFA accounts are in respect of the same person, the entire balance in the transferor account is transferred to the recipient account and the transferor EFA account is terminated immediately after the transfer.

[¶2692d] DEATH

Normally, on death the plan will pay the funeral and/or cemetery expenses of the beneficiary, and the service provider will recognize the income as business income at that time. If there is any payment out of the plan for anything other than the provision of funeral or cemetery services as defined, there will be an income inclusion to the recipient. This rule contemplates (but does not specify) either (i) cancellation of the plan by the contributor, or (ii) a refund owing the estate, presumably because the funeral cost less than the funds in the plan. Essentially, the rule assumes that any such non-funeral payments out of the plan represent taxable income to the extent of earnings in the plan, and then a refund of contributions. That is, where there is a payment otherwise than for funeral services, the recipient must include in income the lesser of the amount received and:

(1) the remaining balance in the plan immediately before payment

PLUS

(2) all payments made from the EFA for the provision of funeral or cemetery services for the individual (beneficiary) covered by the plan before the payment

MINUS

(3) contributions made to the plan for the purpose of funding funeral arrangements for the beneficiary, or the contribution portion of transfers from other eligible plans for the beneficiary, [reduced, for transfers, credits or additions occurring after December 20, 2002, by the portion of the transferred amount that was not previously included in income, i.e., the portion that represents a return of contributions.]

Example 1

Mr. Gilbert contributed $8,000 to a prepaid funeral arrangement. The balance grew to $10,000 before his death. The plan paid $9,500 for funeral services. The $500 balance was refunded to the estate. The EFA should report $500 on a T5 issued the estate. This is the lesser of (i) $500 (the amount of the refund), and (ii) $2,000 ($500 + $9,500 - $8,000).

Property in a cemetery care trust in not included in the computation.

Income received under these rules is considered to be income from property (see Chapter 4).

Topical Index

Please note that the numerical references following index entries are to paragraph numbers (¶) used in the text, not page numbers of the book.

S